THE WORKS OF
PHILO

Complete and Unabridged

NEW UPDATED EDITION

THE WORKS OF
PHILO

Complete and Unabridged

NEW UPDATED EDITION

Translated by
C. D. Yonge

THE WORKS OF PHILO: NEW UPDATED EDITION
Complete and Unabridged in One Volume

Copyright © 1993 by Hendrickson Publishers Marketing, LLC
ISBN: 978-1-56563-809-9

Eleventh printing — May 2013

Printed in the United States of America

About the cover:
The cover illustration depicts a piece of "gold glass" found near Rome.
The menorah, or seven-branched lamp stand, was a popular symbol of Judaism
and can be found on such famous architectural monuments as the Arch of Titus.
The scene on this "gold glass" also shows other items of Jewish ritual significance,
including the Ark of the Covenant flanked by two Lions, a "shofar" or trumpet,
a palm branch, and an oil jar. Many of these items held strong messianic
signficance and figured prominently in the life of Israel, such as in the
Feast of Tabernacles (or Booths). The photo appears courtesy of the
Vatican library and is used with permission.

TABLE OF CONTENTS

PUBLISHER'S PREFACE

Publishing this new edition of C. D. Yonge's translation of the works of Philo has been rewarding indeed, but throughout the process of retypesetting, reorganizing, verifying, and redesigning, we've been asked why we undertook such a daunting project. A major reason stems from the relative lack of availability of Philo's works. The only other English text of Philo exists in ten volumes plus two supplementary volumes in the prestigious (and expensive) Loeb Classical Library published by Harvard University Press. The Loeb edition includes the Greek text of Philo and is particularly prized by the scholarly community. Unfortunately, however, this series has been largely out of the reach of most students of Jewish and Christian antiquity.

Further motivation for producing this edition concerns Philo's significance for studying the worlds of first-century Hellenistic Judaism and the New Testament. As C. H. Dodd put it in his classic, *Interpretation of the Fourth Gospel,* Philo is "the best known and most representative figure of Hellenistic Judaism"—the "world" of Paul and many of the earliest believers. Although Philo does not speak explicitly about his contemporaries Jesus and Paul, it is from Philo that we learn of the religious and philosophical thought world of first-century Alexandrian Judaism. It simply cannot be overemphasized that Philo affords unique perspectives that not even Josephus permits and that his writings contain a treasury of insights into aspects of the New Testament world—such as the nature of Roman political structures and civic attitudes, or the character of Jewish sects and philosophy. Philo also wrote extensively on the Old Testament Scripture, including allegorical interpretations of Genesis and studies on the lives of Moses, Abraham, and Joseph.

Nonetheless, this undertaking was not without its challenges. Yonge's 1854 translation relied upon the best text of Philo available at that time—Mangey's text. Approximately forty years after its publication, however, the superior Cohn-Wendland critical text began making its appearance (1896–1914). Compared to the Cohn-Wendland text, Yonge's translation differs in sequence at several points, lacks some passages, and uses or includes titles of works different from the standard ones of present scholarship. Yonge also relies on a Latin translation of the Armenian versions of *Questions and Answers on Genesis* and apparently lacked access to *Questions and Answers on Genesis, IV* and *Questions and Answers on Exodus* in either Latin or Armenian, but instead included only Greek fragments of *Questions and Answers on Genesis and Exodus* found in ancient authors like Eusebius and John of Damascus along with other fragments of Philo which are not included in the Cohn-Wendland text.

To address these differences, we have rearranged parts of Yonge's translation to conform to the sequence of the Cohn-Wendland text, have included newly translated passages where necessary, and have used the currently standard titles for the works. We chose to retain what Yonge used without trying to complete the missing passages from the Armenian versions of *Questions and Answers on Genesis, IV* and *Questions and Answers on Exodus* and have placed the material not found in the Cohn-Wendland text in an appendix.

We are indebted to Dr. David M. Scholer for graciously agreeing to make time in his busy schedule to supervise the work of keying Yonge's translation to the numbering system used in the Loeb Classical Library edition, to sort out the differences between Yonge's text and the Cohn-Wendland text, and to prepare a foreword for this edition. It is especially fitting that he would have consented to help since the ideas for producing both this edition of Philo's works and our previously published edition of *The Works of Josephus* really grow out of his classroom—having been inspired by his often expressed regret about the lack of an affordable and accessible edition of these important works.

Understandably, sorting out the various versions, fragments, and divisions in Philo, and then conforming them to an acceptable scholarly format, was a formidable task. While we have attempted to correct errors in Yonge's original edition along the way, it is inevitable that some have eluded our attention. It is hoped that this present edition, despite any minor shortcomings, will nonetheless prove indispensable and will provide a new window into the world of the first century.

FOREWORD
AN INTRODUCTION TO PHILO JUDAEUS OF ALEXANDRIA
by David M. Scholer

Philo, usually known as Philo the Jew (Philo Judaeus) or Philo of Alexandria (a city in Egypt with a large Jewish Diaspora population in Greco-Roman times), lived from about 20 B.C. to about A.D. 50. He is one of the most important Jewish authors of the Second Temple period of Judaism and was a contemporary of both Jesus and Paul. Yet, Philo is not nearly as well known or as frequently read as the first century A.D. Jewish historian Josephus.

Part of the reason for the relative neglect of Philo has had to do with the general unavailability of a convenient English translation of Philo, such as exists for Josephus in the frequently reprinted one-volume translation of William Whiston (originally 1736; for an excellent modern printing of this translation which utilizes the current scholarly numbering system for Josephus' writings, see *The Works of Josephus: Complete and Unabridged* [trans. William Whiston; new updated edition; Peabody, Mass.: Hendrickson, 1987]).

Philo wrote in Greek, and most of his writings survive in Greek, but a few have survived only in ancient Armenian translations. Only two complete English translations of Philo have ever been published. The most authoritative one, which is still in print, is the twelve-volume edition in the Loeb Classical Library (Cambridge, Mass.: Harvard University Press/London: William Heinemann, 1929–1953). The Loeb edition includes the Greek text of Philo (except for the few writings for which there is no extant Greek text) along with an English translation, as well as introductions, notes, and indexes (the Loeb text is based on the standard major edition of the Greek text of Philo by L. Cohn and P. Wendland, *Philonis Alexandrini opera quae supersunt* [7 vols. in 8; Berlin, 1896–1930; reprinted Berlin, 1962]). The edition was the work of F. H. Colson and G. H. Whitaker for the first ten volumes; the two additional volumes containing works of Philo available only in an Armenian version were prepared by Ralph Marcus. Because of its size, the presence of the Greek text, and its relatively high cost, this edition has not usually been purchased and used by the "average" Jewish or Christian student or rabbi and pastor and not even by many scholars and professors who might well make more use of Philo.

The only other English translation of Philo was the work of Charles Duke Yonge (1812–1891), which appeared in 1854–1855 in four volumes in Bohn's Ecclesiastical Library (*The Works of Philo Judaeus, the Contemporary of Josephus, Translated from the Greek* [London: Henry G. Bohn]). Yonge was educated in classics at St. Mary Hall, Oxford. From 1866 until his death he was professor of modern history and English literature at Queen's College, Belfast. He published over thirty-five works of his own on a wide range of subjects and also translated numerous writings from antiquity for the various Bohn publications, including this translation of Philo. Yonge's translation has long been out of print and is quite scarce. It is this translation that is published here. It is, however, now in one volume, completely reset in modern easy to read type, keyed to the standard numbering system used in the Loeb Classical Library edition, and supplemented with adequate notes and with new translations of sections not included in Yonge's original edition now inserted at the appropriate places. It is hoped that this presentation of Philo will encourage much greater and more broadly based reading, study, and use of Philo. This introduction offers suggestions for going beyond this volume to learn more about Philo and his significance for ancient Judaism, early Christianity, and Greek philosophy.

Relatively little is known about Philo's life. He lived his entire life in Alexandria, Egypt, location of the single largest Jewish community outside of Palestine in this period (the Jewish population of Alexandria was perhaps one million people). Philo came from a prominent and wealthy family, was well educated, and was a leader within the Alexandrian Jewish community. So far as is known, Philo visited the temple in Jerusalem only once in his lifetime (*On Providence* 2.64).

Philo was involved in the crisis in his community related to the pogrom initiated in A.D. 38 by the prefect Flaccus, during the reign of the Roman emperor, Gaius Caligula. Philo was selected to head the Jewish delegation that went to Rome to see Gaius Caligula. Philo's account of these events is found in his two writings *Flaccus* (*In Flaccum*) and *The Embassy to Gaius* (*De Legatione ad Gaium*—for details on these events and writings, as well as all other facets of Philo's life and literary production, see the books and articles recommended near the conclusion of this introduction).

Philo's brother, Alexander, held various offices for Rome in Egypt and used his money to plate the gates of the temple in Jerusalem with silver and gold and to make a loan to Herod Agrippa I (see Josephus, *Jewish Antiquities* 18.159–160; *Jewish War* 5.205). Alexander's two sons, Marcus and Tiberius Iuius Alexander, Philo's nephews, were also involved in Roman affairs. Marcus married Bernice, the daughter of Herod Agrippa I (Josephus, *Jewish Antiquities* 19.276–277; this is the Bernice mentioned in Acts 25:13, 23; 26:30). Tiberius Alexander became an apostate from Judaism, held the office of procurator of Judaea (A.D. 46–48), and was a prefect in Egypt (A.D. 66–70).

In at least one important passage Philo reveals something of his perspective on his life and work (*On the Special Laws* 3.1–6). Here Philo remembers that " There was once a time when, devoting my leisure to philosophy and to the contemplation of the world and the things in it, I reaped the fruit of excellent, and desirable, and blessed intellectual feelings. ... I appeared to be raised on high and borne aloft by a certain inspiration of the soul. ..." But this life was interrupted with "... the vast sea of the cares of public politics, in which I was and still am tossed about without being able to keep myself swimming at the top." But all was not lost, for "... even in these circumstances I ought to give thanks to God, that though I am so overwhelmed by this flood, I am not wholly sunk and swallowed up in the depths. But I open the eyes of my soul ... and I am irradiated with the light of wisdom. ... Behold, therefore, I venture not only to study the sacred commands of Moses, but also with an ardent love of knowledge to investigate each separate one of them, and to endeavour to reveal and to explain to those who wish to understand them, things concerning them which are not known to the multitude."

It is this concern to reveal what is not generally known about the writings of Moses that permeates most of Philo's literary output (see the table below for full titles and abbreviations). Many of Philo's writings paraphrase the biblical texts of Moses; in these Philo expands the text, giving his own views on various matters. These writings include: *On Abraham, On the Decalogue, On Joseph, On the Life of Moses, On the Creation, On Rewards and Punishments, On the Special Laws* and *On the Virtues*. Most of his other writings are allegorical commentaries on Genesis 2–41: *On Husbandry, On the Cherubim, On the Confusion of Tongues, On the Preliminary Studies, The Worse Attacks the Better, On Drunkenness, On Flight and Finding, On the Giants, Allegorical Interpretation, On the Migration of Abraham, On the Change of Names, On Noah's Work as a Planter, On the Posterity and Exile of Cain, Who is the Heir, On the Unchangeableness of God, On the Sacrifices of Abel and Cain, On Sobriety* and *On Dreams*. Also in this general category are his exegetical *Questions and Answers on Genesis* and *Questions and Answers on Exodus*.

Philo's remaining writings are usually placed into two categories. The philosophical writings include: *On the Eternity of the World, On the Animals* (see p. xvi below), *On Providence* and *Every Good Man Is Free*. The historical-apologetic writings include: *Flaccus, Hypothetica, On the Embassy to Gaius,* and *On the Contemplative Life*. Even these writings, however, relate to Philo's concerns as an exegete of the Pentateuch of Moses.

Philo's concern to interpret Moses shows constantly both his deep devotion and commitment to his Jewish heritage, beliefs, and community, and also reflects his unabashed use of philosophical categories and traditions "... to investigate each separate one of them [Moses' commands], and to endeavour to reveal and to explain to those who wish to understand them, things concerning them which are not known to the multitude" (*On the Special Laws* 3.6). The scholarly discussion over whether Philo is primarily Jewish or Greek is actually misguided. In Philo's time much of Judaism was significantly Hellenized. Philo's commitment to and passion for the law of Moses was genuine and controlling. Philo, too, drank deeply at the philosophical well of the Platonic tradition and saw it as strengthening and deepening his understanding of the God of Moses. Philo probably represents Middle Platonism (the Platonic tradition between Plato's immediate successors and the rise of third century A.D. Neoplatonism), although some scholars debate this classification.

Because of Philo's participation in Middle Platonism and Hellenistic philosophical traditions, he is important for the study of Hellenistic philosophy. Philo also participated in the allegorical interpretive traditions, developed and used in Alexandria for understanding Homer and other Greek traditions, characteristic of his Hellenistic culture. Allegorical interpretation became a deep part of Philo's exegetical and hermeneutical understanding of the law of Moses. Philo has sometimes been labeled a gnostic or participant in gnosticism, but this is a misunderstanding of his Platonism in service to his interpretation of the Mosaic law (see especially Birger A. Pearson, "Philo and Gnosticism," *Aufstieg und Niedergang in der römischen Welt* 2 21,1 [ed. W. Haase; Berlin/New York: de Gruyter], pp. 295–342).

Philo is significant for the understanding of first century A.D. Hellenistic Judaism. He is the main surviving literary figure of the Hellenized Judaism of the Second Temple period of ancient Judaism. Philo is critical for understanding many of the currents, themes, and interpretive traditions which existed in Diaspora and Hellenistic Judaism. Philo confirms the multifaceted character of Second Temple Judaism; it was certainly not a monolithic phenomenon. Judaism, in spite of its concerns for purity and ethnic identity with reference to the law of Moses, also found considerable freedom to participate in many aspects of Hellenistic culture, as Philo so clearly evidences.

Philo is also noteworthy for understanding the early church and the writings of the New Testament, especially those of Paul, John, and Hebrews. It is sometimes forgotten that the New Testament documents were written in Greek by authors who were Jews (of course now committed to understanding Jesus as Christ and Lord) who were part of the Hellenistic culture of the Greco-Roman world. Most of the early churches reflected and described in the New Testament were part of the social fabric of the Hellenistic Greco-Roman world. Precisely because Philo is a Hellenistic Jew, he is essential for New Testament studies. The Christian church has been the primary preserver of the writings of Philo, who was virtually unknown in the Jewish tradition after his own time until the sixteenth century A.D. (presumably the Christian attachment to Philo grew out of, at least in part, Eusebius' [ca. A.D. 260–339] belief that the Jewish group described in the *Contemplative Life*, the Therapeutae, was a Christian group).

Philo's discussions of circumcision, clearly perceived within Judaism at this time as a critical identity factor, may serve both to illustrate the tensions with Philo's Jewish and Greek contexts and also to provide background to the debate about circumcision in the early church (e.g., Acts 15:1–2; Galatians). In *On the Special Laws* 1.1–11 Philo acknowledges that circumcision is ridiculed among many people. He then gives six reasons (four from the traditions and two he wishes to add) in strong support of the practice of circumcision. The reasons given relate primarily to what may be called health concerns, but Philo does say that circumcision is a symbol of "... the excision of the pleasures which delude the mind" (1.9).

Philo's other notable discussion about circumcision occurs in *On the Migration of Abraham* 89–93. Here Philo is worried about those who would emphasize the symbolic meaning of circumcision to the neglect of literal circumcision: "For there are some men, who, looking upon written laws as symbols of things appreciable by the intellect, have studied some things with superfluous accuracy, and have treated others with neglectful indifference ..." (89). He argues that sabbath observance has a clear symbolic meaning, but then he states that: "... it does not follow that on that account we may abrogate the laws which are established respecting it ..." (91). He argues similarly for the understanding of Jewish festivals. Thus, he reasons: "... because the rite of circumcision is an emblem of the excision of pleasures and of all the passions, ... does it follow that we are to annul the law which has been enacted about circumcision?" (92). He concludes by urging reflection on symbolic meanings, but also stating that "... so also must we take care of the laws that are enacted in plain terms: for while they are regarded, those other things also will be more clearly understood ..." (93).

It may be assumed from Philo's discussion that there was probably internal debate within Judaism over the necessity of literal circumcision (see also, e.g., Josephus, *Jewish Antiquities* 20.38–45). One is tempted to speculate as well whether Philo's nephew Tiberius Alexander's apostasy from Jewish practices, noted earlier, had any specific impact on his thinking at this point. Certainly Philo's perspective helps in understanding the deep commitment of the so-called Judaizers in the early church to circumcision and the "radical" nature of Paul's strong rejection of circumcision for gentile believers in Jesus as Christ and Lord.

Another area of importance in the study of Philo is his use of Logos (Word) and Wisdom concepts and beliefs. These issues pervade Philo's writings and illustrate the depth of Philo's utilization of Hellenistic philosophical traditions in his understanding of God and the created universe. Philo's discussions here are vital for understanding the nature of Middle Platonism, of Hellenistic Judaism, and probably part of the pre-history of gnosticism and its views of God and the cosmology. Philo's ideas about Logos/Wisdom are also indispensable for New Testament studies, probably most directly and dramatically in the interpretation of the Gospel of John, especially the Prologue (1:1–14). C. H. Dodd's famous discussion of these issues bears careful reading, even though the debate over his judgments continue to this day. Dodd argues that in addition to the Prologue's indebtedness to Old Testament concepts, it cannot be fully understood apart from the ideas of Hellenistic Judaism, especially Philo (see C. H. Dodd, *The Interpretation of the Fourth Gospel* [Cambridge: Cambridge University Press, 1953; repr. 1968], Part I, A73 "Hellenistic Judaism: Philo of Alexandria," pp. 54–73; Part II, A712 "Logos," pp. 263–85).

Philo has also often been considered especially significant for the conceptual background of the Epistle to the Hebrews (beginning with the work of Johannes B. Carpzov in 1750). It seems clear that there is no evidence that the author of Hebrews had read Philo and that the author utilizes a whole range of Jewish traditions, some of which have remarkable similarities to the writings of Qumran and the writings of Philo. One of the major assessments of the possible relationship between Hebrews and Philo is that of Ronald Williamson (*Philo and the Epistle to the Hebrews* [Arbeiten zur Literatur und Geschichte des hellenistischen Judentums 4]; Leiden: E. J. Brill, 1970; see also his anthology of Philo cited below). As the recent commentator on Hebrews Harold W. Attridge, observes: "... there are undeniable parallels that suggest that Philo and our author [of Hebrews] are indebted to similar traditions of Greek-speaking and-thinking Judaism" (*The Epistle to the Hebrews: A Commentary on the Epistle to the Hebrews* [Hermeneia; Philadelphia: Fortress, 1989], p. 29).

One passage in Hebrews illustrates the possible connections between the thought worlds of Philo and the author of Hebrews. In Hebrews 8:5 the author argues: "They offer worship in a sanctuary that is a sketch and shadow of the heavenly one" (NRSV). The distinction between a "heavenly reality" and the observable, phenomenal world as "sketch and shadow" is a (Middle) Platonic idea, but bears much in common with Philo's expressions of these ideas (see Attridge, p. 219).

Philo has considerable relevance for understanding the position of women and attitudes towards them by literate men at the time of Second Temple Judaism and the early church.

Philo makes numerous comments on women and on issues of the "feminine." At least two books in English have been devoted to these matters:

Baer, Richard A. *Philo's Use of the Categories Male and Female.* Arbeiten zur Literatur und Geschichte des hellenistischen Judentums 3. Leiden: E. J. Brill, 1970; and

Sly, Dorothy. *Philo's Perception of Women.* Brown Judaic Studies 209. Atlanta: Scholars Press, 1990.

One might also want to consult the numerous references to Philo (see index) in Leonard Swidler, *Women in Judaism: The Status of Women in Formative Judaism* (Metuchen, N.J.: Scarecrow, 1976).

There are numerous passages in Philo that one might consult as an introduction to the issues of Philo's perception of women. Perhaps the most important are: *Flaccus* 89; *On the Special Laws* 1.200; 2.124; 3.169–177; *On the Creation* 151–152; *Questions and Answers on Genesis* 1.33; and *Contemplative Life* (throughout; on this see Ross Shepard Kraemer, *Her Share of the Blessings: Women's Religions Among Pagans, Jews, and Christians in the Greco-Roman World* [New York/Oxford: Oxford University Press, 1992], pp. 106–27). These texts and their perceptions are part of a significant cultural perspective for the interpretation and assessment of the texts about women and their roles in the New Testament.

Philo is significant for lexical and conceptual terms and ideas that are reflected in the language of the New Testament. Most of the articles in the well-known *Theological Dictionary of the New Testament* (ed. Gerhard Kittel and Gerhard Friedrich; trans. Geoffrey W. Bromiley; 10 volumes [vol. 10 is the index by Ronald E. Pitkin]; Grand Rapids: William B. Eerdmans, 1964–1976) include discussions, often lengthy, of Philo's use of a particular term and concept. The index to *The New International Dictionary of New Testament Theology* (ed. Colin Brown; 3 volumes; Grand Rapids: Zondervan, 1975–1978) prepared by David Townsley and Russell Bjork (Grand Rapids: Zondervan, 1985; now bound with the *Dictionary* in four volumes) actually includes Philo and has about 500 references to specific citations of Philo in the *NIDNTT.*

One of the primary goals of this one-volume, accessible translation of Philo is to enable any person to look up easily the full context of passages cited from Philo in Kittel-Friedrich's *TDNT,* C. Brown's *NIDNTT,* critical commentaries, and scholarly articles. It is also hoped that persons will read whole works of Philo in order to get a genuine feeling for this type of Hellenistic Jewish exegetical tradition. The few suggestions offered in this introduction are meant both to whet the appetite for such study and to serve as examples of the richness of Philo as a resource for the study of Second Temple Judaism and the early church, especially the New Testament. It should be noted, however, that Philo is also helpful for the study of some of the early church fathers, especially perhaps Clement of Alexandria (ca. A.D. 160–215) and Origen (ca. A.D. 185–251).

The standard titles given to the writings of Philo are in Latin, as are the common abbreviations. The following table gives the "official" list of Philo's main writings along with the standard English title as represented in the Loeb Classical Library edition of Philo.

Abr.	*De Abrahamo*	*On Abraham*
Aet.	*De Aeternitate Mundi*	On the Eternity of the World
Agr.	*De Agricultura*	On Husbandry
Cher.	*De Cherubim*	On the Cherubim
Conf.	*De Confusione Linguarum*	On the Confusion of Tongues
Congr.	*De Congressu Eruditionis gratia*	On the Preliminary Studies
Decal.	*De Decalogo*	On the Decalogue

Det.	*Quod Deterius Potiori insidiari solet*	The Worse attacks the Better
Ebr.	*De Ebrietate*	On Drunkenness
Flacc.	*In Flaccum*	Flaccus
Fug.	*De Fuga et Inventione*	On Flight and Finding
Gig.	*De Gigantibus*	On the Giants
Hyp.	*Hypothetica/Apologia pro Iudaeis*	Apology for the Jews
Jos.	*De Josepho*	On Joseph
Leg.	*De Legatione ad Gaium*	On the Embassy to Gaius
Leg. All.	*Legum Allegoriarum*	Allegorical Interpretation
Mig.	*De Migratione Abrahami*	On the Migration of Abraham
Mos.	*De Vita Mosis*	Moses
Mut.	*De Mutatione Nominum*	On the Change of Names
Op.	*De Opificio Mundi*	On the Creation
Plant.	*De Plantatione*	On Noah's Work as a Planter
Post.	*De Posteritate Caini*	On the Posterity and Exile of Cain
Praem.	*De Praemiis et Poenis*	On Rewards and Punishments
Prov.	*De Providentia*	On Providence
Quaest. in Gn.	*Questiones et Solutiones in Genesin*	Questions and Answers on Genesis
Quaest. in Ex.	*Questiones et Solutiones in Exodum*	Questions and Answers on Exodus
Quis Her.	*Quis rerum divinarum Heres sit*	Who is the Heir
Quod Deus	*Quod Deus sit Immutabilis*	On the Unchangeableness of God
Quod Omn. Prob.	*Quod omnis Probus Liber sit*	Every Good Man is Free
Sac.	*De Sacrificiis Abelis et Caini*	On the Sacrifices of Abel and Cain
Sob.	*De Sobrietate*	On Sobriety
Som.	*De Somniis*	On Dreams
Spec. Leg.	*De Specialibus Legibus*	On the Special Laws
Virt.	*De Virtutibus*	On the Virtues
Vit. Cont.	*De Vita Contemplativa*	On the Contemplative Life

For many of Philo's works, either the manuscripts and/or Cohn, in his classic edition of Philo, give (sub-)titles for sections within a particular work of Philo (e.g., for *De Virtutibus* the sections are named *De Fortitudine* [Chapters I–VIII]; *De Humanitate* [Chapters IX–XXXII]; *De Poenitentia* [Chapters XXXIII–XXXIV]; and *De Nobilitate* [Chapters XXXV–XLI]). For details on all of this data, one should consult the detailed information in the General Introduction to each of the Philo volumes in the Loeb Classical Library edition.

Questions and Answers on Genesis and *Questions and Answers on Exodus* have survived only in an Armenian version. *Apology for the Jews* and *On Providence* are fragmentary works which survive as quoted by the ancient church historian Eusebius.

Another one of Philo's writings, extant only in Armenian (apart from four very brief Greek fragments), has recently been translated into English for the first time (and for the first time into any modern language). This is *On Animals (Anim.; De Animalibus):*

Terian, A. *Philonis Alexandrini De Animalibus: The Armenian Text with an Introduction, Translation, and Commentary.* Studies in Hellenistic Judaism, Supplements to *Studia Philonica* 1. Chico, Calif.: Scholars Press, 1981.

There are many texts which have been incorrectly attributed to Philo. For a study of these matters one should consult:

Royse, J. R. *The Spurious Texts of Philo of Alexandria: A Study of the Textual Transmission and Corruption with Indexes to the Major Collections of Greek Fragments.* Arbeiten zur Literatur und Geschichte des hellenistischen Judentums 22. Leiden: E. J. Brill, 1991.

For an index to the Greek texts of Philo, one should consult the following (which now supersedes the indexes of H. Leisegang in the L. Cohn–P. Wendland edition and of G. Mayer):

Borgen, P., Fuglseth, K., and Skarsten, R. *The Philo Index: A Complete Greek Word Index to the Writings of Philo of Alexandria.* Grand Rapids/Cambridge: William B. Eerdmans/ Leiden: E. J. Brill, 2000.

For English readers, in addition to the indexes in the present volume, volume 10 of the Loeb Classical Library edition of Philo provides various indexes prepared by J. W. Earp: Scripture Index (pp. 189–268); Index of Names (pp. 269–433); Index to Translators' Notes (pp. 434–86); and Index to Greek Words in the Translators' Notes (pp. 487–520). For additional help in lexical searches in Philo's Greek text, one should consult D. T. Runia, "How To Search Philo," *The Studia Philonica Annual: Studies in Hellenistic Judaism,* vol. 2, 1990 (ed. D. T. Runia; Brown Judaic Studies 226; Atlanta: Scholars Press, 1990), pp. 106–39.

Three anthologies of selections of Philo in English have appeared in the last four decades. These volumes are useful collections; the two by Winston and Williamson contain helpful, up-to-date introductions to Philo. These collections are:

Glatzer, N. N. *Philo Judaeus: The Essential Philo.* New York: Schocken, 1971 [this anthology uses the translation of C. D. Yonge, reproduced in this volume].
Winston, D. *Philo of Alexandria: The Contemplative Life, The Giants, and Selections: Translation and Introduction.* Preface by J. Dillon. Classics of Western Spirituality. New York/ Ramsey/Toronto: Paulist, 1981.
Williamson, R. *Jews in the Hellenistic World: Philo.* Cambridge Commentaries on Writings on the Jewish and Christian World 200 BC to AD 200 I.ii. Cambridge: Cambridge University Press, 1989.

An older and fascinating short anthology of selections from Philo is the following:

Lewy, H. *Philo.* Philosophia Judaica. Oxford: East and West Library, 1946.

Four major books in English for a sound understanding of Philo are:

Borgen, P. *Philo of Alexandria: An Exegete for His Time.* (Supplements to Novum Testamentum 86.) Leiden: E. J. Brill, 1997.
Goodenough, E. R. *An Introduction to Philo Judaeus.* New Haven: Yale University Press, 1940. 2d ed. Oxford: Basil Blackwell, 1962.
Sandmel, S. *Philo of Alexandria: An Introduction.* New York/Oxford: Oxford University Press, 1979.
Schenck, K. *A Brief Guide to Philo.* Louisville: Westminster John Knox, 2005.

Some of the most noteworthy, recent survey articles on Philo include:

Borgen, P. "Philo of Alexandria." *Anchor Bible Dictionary.* 6 vols. Edited by D. N. Freedman; New York: Doubleday, 1992, 5.333–42.
Borgen, P. "Philo of Alexandria." Pages 233–82 in *Jewish Writings of the Second Temple Period: Apocrypha, Pseudepigrapha, Qumran Sectarian Writings, Philo, Josephus.* Edited by M. E. Stone; Compendia Rerum Iudaicarum ad Novum Testamentum 2. Assen/ Maastricht: Van Gorcum/Philadelphia: Fortress, 1984.
Borgen, P. "Philo of Alexandria: A Critical and Synthetical Survey of Research since World War II." Pages 98–154 in *Aufstieg und Niedergang der römischen Welt* 2 21,1. Edited by W. Haase; Berlin and New York: de Gruyter, 1984.

Morris, J. "The Jewish Philosopher Philo." A734 in *The History of the Jewish People in the Age of Jesus Christ (175 B.C.–A.D. 135)*. E. Schürer; new English version revised and edited by G. Vermes, F. Millar, and M. Goodman. Edinburgh: T&T Clark, 1987, vol. 3, pt. 2, 809–89.
Runia, D. T. "How to Read Philo." *Nederlands Theologisch Tijdschrift* 40 (1986): 185–98.
Sterling, G. E. "Philo," Pages 789–93 in *Dictionary of New Testament Background*. Edited by C. A. Evans and S. E. Porter; Downers Grove/Leicester: InterVarsity, 2000.

Another important research tool for the study of Philo and his influence is:

Runia, D. T. *Philo in Early Christian Literature: A Survey*. Compendia Rerum Iudaicarum ad Novum Testamentum III/3. Assen: Van Gorcum/Minneapolis: Fortress, 1993.

A very important series for the study of Philo has been initiated under the general editorship of G. E. Sterling, the *Philo of Alexandria Commentary Series* (Leiden: E. J. Brill, 2001–; PACS). The series will ultimately consist of approximately twenty volumes. The volumes will contain an introduction, a fresh translation, and a commentary. The volumes published to date:

Runia, D. T. *On the Creation of the Cosmos according to Moses: Introduction, Translation and Commentary*. PACS 1. Leiden: E. J. Brill, 2001.
Horst, P. van der. *Philo's Flaccus: The First Pogrom: Introduction, Translation, and Commentary*. PACS 2. Leiden: E. J. Brill, 2003.

There are excellent bibliographic resources for identifying and locating scholarly publications on Philo. The major ones, in order of publication, are:

Goodenough, E. R., and Goodhart, H. L. "A General Bibliography of Philo." Pages 128–348 in E. R. Goodenough, *The Politics of Philo Judaeus*. New Haven: Yale University Press, 1938. Repr., Hildesheim, 1967.
Feldman, Louis. *Studies in Judaica: Scholarship on Philo and Josephus (1937–1962)*. New York: Yeshiva University, n.d. [1963].
Hilgert, E. "Bibliographia Philoniana 1935–1981." Pages 47–97 in *Aufstieg und Niedergang der römischen Welt* 2 21,1. Edited by W. Haase. Berlin and New York: de Gruyter, 1984 [this combines the bibliographies of E. Hilgert which appeared in each of the six issues of *Studia Philonica* between 1972 and 1980].
Radice, R., and D. T. Runia, with R. Bitter and D. Satran. *Philo of Alexandria: An Annotated Bibliography 1937–1986*. 2d ed. Supplements to Vigiliae Christianae 8. Leiden: E. J. Brill, 1992.
Runia, D. T. et al. *Philo of Alexandria: An Annotated Bibliography, 1987–1996: With Addenda for 1937–1986*. Supplements to Vigiliae Christianae 57. Leiden: E. J. Brill, 2000.

Continuing bibliography after 1996 on Philo is provided annually in *The Studia Philonica Annual*. Volumes 12–19 published 2000–2007 (12–17 Providence: Brown Judaic Studies; 18–19 Atlanta: Society of Biblical Literature) cover 1997–2004, with a provisional bibliography for 2005–2007.

I want to express my appreciation to Gregory Sterling, on the faculty at the University of Notre Dame, for translating most of the Philo texts added to the work of C. D. Yonge, and to James Ernest, doctoral student at Boston College, for translating one Philo text. I am grateful to two of my student assistants at North Park Theological Seminary, Donald

Nelson and Jeffrey Koenig, for their significant help in keying Yonge's translation to the numbering system used in the Loeb Classical Library. I am indebted to the patience, help, and friendship of David Townsley and Patrick Alexander of Hendrickson Publishers. They kindly invited me to produce an introduction to this edition of Philo and worked with diligence and grace in bringing the project to completion. Another kind of gratitude, for which I cannot now find the appropriate words, goes to my wife Jeannette and our daughters Emily and Abigail for their encouragement; they will always know what I mean.

I want to thank Shirley Decker-Lucke of Hendrickson Publishers for her support and help in working on revisions for the sixth and now ninth printings of this volume and for the opportunity given to me to make some important revisions and additions to this foreword. I wish to thank, too, James N. Rhodes for his important assistance in identifying corrections that needed to be made within the text of Philo's work.

David M. Scholer
Fuller Theological Seminary
May 2008

PREFACE
TO THE ORIGINAL EDITION

The author of the following Treatises was, as the title by which he is generally known imports, of Jewish extraction, and a descendant of the sacerdotal tribe of Levi. He is spoken of by Josephus as one of the most eminent of his contemporary countrymen, and as the principal of the embassy which was sent to Caligula to solicit him to recall the command which he had issued for the erection of his statue in the temple at Jerusalem. The embassy was unsuccessful, though the death of the emperor saved the sacred edifice from the meditated profanation; but we see that Philo suffered no diminution of his credit from its unsuccessful result, since, at a subsequent period, his nephew, Tiberius Alexander, married Berenice, the daughter of King Agrippa.

The date of his birth and that of his death are alike uncertain; he speaks of himself as an old man when the embassy to Rome took place; and the treatise in which he gives an account of it was apparently written in the reign of Claudius, who succeeded Caligula A.D. 41, and reigned nearly fourteen years. His chief residence was at Alexandria, which at that period was, next to Athens, the most celebrated seat of philosophy in the world, and which had long been a favourite abode of the learned Jews. On one occasion he mentions having visited Jerusalem; and this is all we know of his personal history.

In his religious opinions he appears to have been a Pharisee, to the principles of which sect some portion of his fondness for allegorical interpretation may perhaps be owing.

It was, however, rather to his philosophical labours that his celebrity among his contemporaries and his notoriety at the present day are mainly owing. He was so devoted a follower of the great founder of the Academic school, that it appears to have been a saying among the ancients that, "either Plato Philonises, or Philo Platonises." And there are many doctrines asserted in the following treatises which can be clearly traced to the principles and even to the extant works of the son of Ariston; and it is in consequence of this tendency that he is spoken of as the first of the Neo-Platonists, that is to say, of that school which attempted to reconcile the doctrines of the Greek, and more especially of the Academic, philosophy with the revelations contained in the sacred scriptures, while, at the same time, he transferred into the Platonic system many of the opinions which he borrowed from the East.

According to the manner of the Eclectics, however, he mingled with his Platonism many doctrines derived from other schools, and those of Pythagoras in particular, to such an extent, that Clemens, of Alexandria, calls him a Pythagorean not recollecting that Aristotle tells us, that the Academy harmonized in very many points with the philosophy of Cortona. In many points, again, especially in the supremacy which he assigns to virtue, he betrays an inclination to the principles of the Stoics.

The attempt to reconcile the heathen philosophy with the Bible was not altogether new. As early as the time of Ptolemy Lagus, many Jews had been settled in Alexandria; and, at the period when Philo flourished, they are supposed to have formed half the population of that city—the splendid library of which opened to the learned men of their nation those stores of Greek wisdom and eloquence with which they were previously unacquainted; and as they could not fail to be struck with the truth of many of the principles which they found laid down in those works, it was not unnatural that, being also formerly convinced of the divine origin of their own scriptures, they should endeavour to reconcile two systems, both of which appeared in so great a degree to rest on the same foundation. The truth of their own books they knew to proceed from divine revelation; that of the Greek philosophers they looked upon as an efflux more or less remote from that revelation, and the pride of human intellect led them to endeavour to display their superior penetration by discerning a hidden sense in their own scriptures, which should contain the germ of the Greek philosophy.

Of all the writers of this school the most eminent was Philo, and his works are highly interesting as showing us the manner in which the Sophists of his age and national sought to appropriate the Greek philosophy by an allegorical interpretation of the works of Moses, which they thus represented as containing all the principles which the Greeks subsequently expanded into the precise doctrines of their several sects. Accordingly, he represents Jehovah as a single uncompounded Being; unchangeable, eternal, incomprehensible, the knowledge of whom is to be looked upon as the ultimate object of all human efforts. He teaches that visible phaenomena are to lead men over to the invisible world, and that the contemplation of the world so wonderfully and beautifully made proves a wise and intelligent Cause and creator of it. Having adopted, however, the Epicurean doctrine, that nothing can be produced out of nothing, he also assumed the existence of a mass of lifeless matter, passive and primeval, destitute of quality and form, but containing within itself the four primary elements; and of this mass, he looked upon the Spirit of God as the divider and fashioner into distinct shape.

Matter again he conceived as something subordinate to, and at the same time resisting, the divine arrangement, and in this latter character as the source of all imperfection and evil. Moreover, not having arrived at any just notion of the Deity as the immediate cause of the existence of the world, he assumed the existence of an intermediate cause which he called the Logos; and he also imagined an invisible world, appreciable only by the intellect, as the pattern of the visible world in which we live; carrying out his theory so as to give an outline of that doctrine of emanations, which at a later period was elaborated and fully developed by the Gnostics.

The treatises contained in the present volume refer to the books of Moses. At the beginning of the first, that on the Creation of the World, he intimates that his object is to show how the law and the world accord with one another, and how the man who lives according to the law is as such a citizen of the world. For Moses, as he remarks in his treatise on the the life of that prophet, demonstrates in his history that the same Being is the Father and Creator of the universe, and the true lawgiver of the world; and accordingly, that whoever follows his laws is adapting himself to the course of nature and living in harmony with the general laws of the universe; while again, the man who transgresses those laws is punished by the operations of nature, such as floods, fire from heaven, and such means.

In his treatise on the Laws, he divides them into what he looks upon as unwritten laws, that is to say, the living patterns of a blameless life which the scripture sets before us in Enoch, Noah, Abraham, etc., and particular laws in the narrower technical common acceptation of the word.

In the other treatises, he deduces an allegorical meaning from the plain historical account of Moses, which serves him as the foundation for his philosophical system.

In all these works he exhibits profound and varied learning, showing himself deeply versed in Greek literature of every age and description, and of considerable skill in the sciences of music, geometry, and astronomy. His style is clear, and even though he may at times be open to the charge of an over-refined subtilty, it is impossible to deny him the praise of acuteness and ingenuity, set off to their best advantage by neatness of language and felicity of expression.

For the Christian reader these treatises have a peculiar interest from the ample materials which many of them furnish for the illustration of St. Paul's Epistles; materials so copious and so valuable that an eminent divine of the present day has pronounced an opinion (referring probably more especially to the treatises on the Sacrifices of Abel and of Cain—on the Different Incidents in the Life of Noah—on Abraham—on the Life of Moses—on the Ten Commandments—and on Providence) that all the other ancient commentators on the Scriptures put together have not left works of greater value for that most important object. It is even asserted by Eusebius that he formed an acquaintance with St. Peter while at Rome, but that statement is generally looked upon as wanting confirmation. From his treatise against Flaccus, and in that which refers to his embassy to Rome, we likewise derive information with respect to the condition of the Jews in the time of our Saviour, and to the manner in which they were treated by the Roman governors, which supplies much incidental corroboration of some of the historical allusions contained in different parts of the New Testament.

The text which has been used in this translation has been generally that of Mangey.

THE WORKS OF
PHILO

ON THE CREATION†

(De Opificio Mundi)

I. (1) Of other lawgivers, some have set forth what they considered to be just and reasonable, in a naked and unadorned manner, while others, investing their ideas with an abundance of amplification, have sought to bewilder the people, by burying the truth under a heap of fabulous inventions. (2) But Moses, rejecting both of these methods, the one as inconsiderate, careless, and unphilosophical, and the other as mendacious and full of trickery, made the beginning of his laws entirely beautiful, and in all respects admirable, neither at once declaring what ought to be done or the contrary, nor (since it was necessary to mould beforehand the dispositions of those who were to use his laws) inventing fables himself or adopting those which had been invented by others.

(3) And his exordium, as I have already said, is most admirable; embracing the creation of the world, under the idea that the law corresponds to the world and the world to the law, and that a man who is obedient to the law, being, by so doing, a citizen of the world, arranges his actions with reference to the intention of nature, in harmony with which the whole universal world is regulated. (4) Accordingly no one, whether poet or historian, could ever give expression in an adequate manner to the beauty of his ideas respecting the creation of the world; for they surpass all the power of language, and amaze our hearing, being too great and venerable to be adapted to the sense of any created being. (5) That, however, is not a reason for our yielding to indolence on the subject, but rather from our affection for the Deity we ought to endeavour to exert ourselves even beyond our powers in describing them: not as having much, or indeed anything to say of our own, but instead of much, just a little, such as it may be probable that human intellect may attain to, when wholly occupied with a love of and desire for wisdom.

(6) For as the smallest seal receives imitations of things of colossal magnitude when engraved upon it, so perchance in some instances the exceeding beauty of the description of the creation of the world as recorded in the Law, overshadowing with its brilliancy the souls of those who happen to meet with it, will be delivered to a more concise record after these facts have been first premised which it would be improper to pass over in silence.

II. (7) For some men, admiring the world itself rather than the Creator of the world, have represented it as existing without any maker, and eternal; and as impiously as falsely have represented God as existing in a state of complete inactivity, while it would have been right on the other hand to marvel at the might of God as the creator and father of all, and to admire the world in a degree not exceeding the bounds of moderation.

(8) But Moses, who had early reached the very summits of philosophy,[1] and who had learnt from the oracles of God the most numerous and important of the principles of nature, was well aware that it is indispensable that in all existing things there must be an active cause, and a passive subject; and that the active cause is the intellect of the universe, thoroughly unadulterated and thoroughly unmixed, superior to virtue and superior to science, superior even to abstract good or abstract beauty; (9) while the passive subject is something inanimate and incapable of motion by any intrinsic power of its own, but having been set in motion, and fashioned, and endowed with life by the intellect, became transformed into that most perfect work, this world. And those who describe it as being uncreated, do, without being aware of it, cut off the most useful and necessary of all the qualities which tend to produce piety, namely, providence: (10) for reason proves that the father and creator has a care for that which has been created; for a father is anxious for the life of his children, and a workman aims at the duration of his works, and employs every device imaginable to ward off everything that is pernicious or injurious, and is desirous by every means in his power to provide everything which is useful or profitable for them. But with regard to that which has not been created, there is no feeling of interest as if it were his own in the breast of him who has not created it.

(11) It is then a pernicious doctrine, and one for which no one should contend, to establish a system in this world, such as anarchy is in a city, so that it should have no superintendant, or reg-

---

† Yonge's title, *A Treatise on the Account of the Creation of the World, as Given by Moses.*

[1] This is in accordance with the description of him in the Bible, where he is represented as being learned in all the wisdom of the Egyptians.

ulator, or judge, by whom everything must be managed and governed.

(12) But the great Moses, thinking that a thing which has not been uncreated is as alien as possible from that which is visible before our eyes (for everything which is the subject of our senses exists in birth and in changes, and is not always in the same condition), has attributed eternity to that which is invisible and discerned only by our intellect as a kinsman and a brother, while of that which is the object of our external senses he had predicated generation as an appropriate description. Since, then, this world is visible and the object of our external senses, it follows of necessity that it must have been created; on which account it was not without a wise purpose that he recorded its creation, giving a very venerable account of God.

III. (13) And he says that the world was made in six days, not because the Creator stood in need of a length of time (for it is natural that God should do everything at once, not merely by uttering a command, but by even thinking of it); but because the things created required arrangement; and number is akin to arrangement; and, of all numbers, six is, by the laws of nature, the most productive: for of all the numbers, from the unit upwards, it is the first perfect one, being made equal to its parts, and being made complete by them; the number three being half of it, and the number two a third of it, and the unit a sixth of it, and, so to say, it is formed so as to be both male and female, and is made up of the power of both natures; for in existing things the odd number is the male, and the even number is the female; accordingly, of odd numbers the first is the number three, and of even numbers the first is two, and the two numbers multiplied together make six. (14) It was fitting therefore, that the world, being the most perfect of created things, should be made according to the perfect number, namely, six: and, as it was to have in it the causes of both, which arise from combination, that it should be formed according to a mixed number, the first combination of odd and even numbers, since it was to embrace the character both of the male who sows the seed, and of the female who receives it. (15) And he allotted each of the six days to one of the portions of the whole, taking out the first day, which he does not even call the first day, that it may not be numbered with the others, but entitling it one, he names it rightly, perceiving in it, and ascribing to it the nature and appellation of the limit.

IV. We must mention as much as we can of the matters contained in his account, since to enumerate them all is impossible; for he embraces that beautiful world which is perceptible only by the intellect, as the account of the first day will show: (16) for God, as apprehending beforehand, as a God must do, that there could not exist a good imitation without a good model, and that of the things perceptible to the external senses nothing could be faultless which was not fashioned with reference to some archetypal idea conceived by the intellect, when he had determined to create this visible world, previously formed that one which is perceptible only by the intellect, in order that so using an incorporeal model formed as far as possible on the image of God, he might then make this corporeal world, a younger likeness of the elder creation, which should embrace as many different genera perceptible to the external senses, as the other world contains of those which are visible only to the intellect.

(17) But that world which consists of ideas, it were impious in any degree to attempt to describe or even to imagine: but how it was created, we shall know if we take for our guide a certain image of the things which exist among us.

When any city is founded through the exceeding ambition of some king or leader who lays claim to absolute authority, and is at the same time a man of brilliant imagination, eager to display his good fortune, then it happens at times that some man coming up who, from his education, is skilful in architecture, and he, seeing the advantageous character and beauty of the situation, first of all sketches out in his own mind nearly all the parts of the city which is about to be completed-the temples, the gymnasia, the prytanea, and markets, the harbour, the docks, the streets, the arrangement of the walls, the situations of the dwelling houses, and of the public and other buildings. (18) Then, having received in his own mind, as on a waxen tablet, the form of each building, he carries in his heart the image of a city, perceptible as yet only by the intellect, the images of which he stirs up in memory which is innate in him, and, still further, engraving them in his mind like a good workman, keeping his eyes fixed on his model, he begins to raise the city of stones and wood, making the corporeal substances to resemble each of the incorporeal ideas. (19) Now we must form a somewhat similar opinion of God, who, having determined to found a mighty state, first of all conceived its form in his mind, according to which form he made a world perceptible only by the intellect, and then completed one visible to the external senses, using the first one as a model.

V. (20) As therefore the city, when previously shadowed out in the mind of the man of architectural skill had no external place, but was stamped solely in the mind of the workman, so in the same manner neither can the world which existed in ideas have had any other local position except the divine reason which made them; for what other place could there be for his powers which should be able to receive and contain, I do not say all, but even any single one of them whatever, in its simple form? (21) And the power and faculty which could be capable of creating the world, has for its origin that good which is founded on truth; for if any one were desirous to investigate the cause on account of which this universe was created, I think that he would come to no erroneous conclusion if he were to say as one of the ancients did say: "That the Father and Creator was good; on which account he did not grudge the substance a share of his own excellent nature, since it had nothing good of itself, but was able to become everything." (22) For the substance was of itself destitute of arrangement, of quality, of animation, of distinctive character, and full of all disorder and confusion; and it received a change and transformation to what is opposite to this condition, and most excellent, being invested with order, quality, animation, resemblance, identity, arrangement, harmony, and everything which belongs to the more excellent idea.

VI. (23) And God, not being urged on by any prompter (for who else could there have been to prompt him?) but guided by his own sole will, decided that it was fitting to benefit with unlimited and abundant favours a nature which, without the divine gift, was unable to itself to partake of any good thing; but he benefits it, not according to the greatness of his own graces, for they are illimitable and eternal, but according to the power of that which is benefited to receive his graces. For the capacity of that which is created to receive benefits does not correspond to the natural power of God to confer them; since his powers are infinitely greater, and the thing created being not sufficiently powerful to receive all their greatness would have sunk under it, if he had not measured his bounty, allotting to each, in due proportion, that which was poured upon it. (24) And if any one were to desire to use more undisguised terms, he would not call the world, which is perceptible only to the intellect, any thing else but the reason of God, already occupied in the creation of the world; for neither is a city, while only perceptible to the intellect, anything else but the reason of the architect, who is already designing to build one perceptible to the external senses, on the model of that which is so only to the intellect—(25) this is the doctrine of Moses, not mine. Accordingly he, when recording the creation of man, in words which follow, asserts expressly, that he was made in the image of God—and if the image be a part of the image, then manifestly so is the entire form, namely, the whole of this world perceptible by the external senses, which is a greater imitation of the divine image than the human form is. It is manifest also, that the archetypal seal, which we call that world which is perceptible only to the intellect, must itself be the archetypal model, the idea of ideas, the Reason of God.

VII. (26) Moses says also; "In the beginning God created the heaven and the earth:" taking the beginning to be, not as some men think, that which is according to time; for before the world time had no existence, but was created either simultaneously with it, or after it; for since time is the interval of the motion of the heavens, there could not have been any such thing as motion before there was anything which could be moved; but it follows of necessity that it received existence subsequently or simultaneously. It therefore follows also of necessity, that time was created either at the same moment with the world, or later than it—and to venture to assert that it is older than the world is absolutely inconsistent with philosophy. (27) But if the beginning spoken of by Moses is not to be looked upon as spoken of according to time, then it may be natural to suppose that it is the beginning according to number that is indicated; so that, "In the beginning he created," is equivalent to "first of all he created the heaven;" for it is natural in reality that that should have been the first object created, being both the best of all created things, and being also made of the purest substance, because it was destined to be the most holy abode of the visible Gods who are perceptible by the external senses; (28) for if the Creator had made everything at the same moment, still those things which were created in beauty would no less have had a regular arrangement, for there is no such thing as beauty in disorder. But order is a due consequence and connection of things precedent and subsequent, if not in the completion of a work, at all events in the intention of the maker; for it is owing to order that they become accurately defined and stationary, and free from confusion.

(29) In the first place therefore, from the model of the world, perceptible only by intellect, the Creator made an incorporeal heaven, and an invisible earth, and the form of air and of empty space: the former of which he called darkness, because the air is black by nature; and the other he called the abyss, for empty space is very deep and yawning with immense width. Then he created the incorporeal substance of water and of air, and above all he spread light, being the seventh thing made; and this again was incorporeal, and a model of the sun, perceptible only to intellect, and of all the light-giving stars, which are destined to stand together in heaven.

VIII. (30) And air and light he considered worthy of the pre-eminence. For the one he called the breath of God, because it is air, which is the most life-giving of things, and of life the causer is God; and the other he called light, because it is surpassingly beautiful: for that which is perceptible only by intellect is as far more brilliant and splendid than that which is seen, as I conceive, the sun is than darkness, or day than night, or the intellect than any other of the outward senses by which men judge (inasmuch as it is the guide of the entire soul), or the eyes than any other part of the body. (31) And the invisible divine reason, perceptible only by intellect, he calls the image of God. And the image of this image is that light, perceptible only by the intellect, which is the image of the divine reason, which has explained its generation. And it is a star above the heavens, the source of those stars which are perceptible by the external senses, and if any one were to call it universal light he would not be very wrong; since it is from that the sun and the moon, and all the other planets and fixed stars derive their due light, in proportion as each has power given to it; that unmingled and pure light being obscured when it begins to change, according to the change from that which is perceptible only by the intellect, to that which is perceptible by the external senses; for none of those things which are perceptible to the external senses is pure.

IX. (32) Moses is right also when he says, that "darkness was over the face of the abyss." For the air is in a manner spread above the empty space, since having mounted up it entirely fills all that open, and desolate, and empty place, which reaches down to us from the regions below the moon. (33) And after the shining forth of that light, perceptible only to the intellect, which existed before the sun, then its adversary darkness yielded, as God put a wall between them and separated them, well knowing their opposite characters, and the enmity existing between their natures. In order, therefore, that they might not war against one another from being continually brought in contact, so that war would prevail instead of peace, God, bringing want of order into order, did not only separate light and darkness, but did also place boundaries in the middle of the space between the two, by which he separated the extremities of each. For if they had approximated they must have produced confusion, preparing for the contest, for the supremacy, with great and unextinguishable rivalry, if boundaries established between them had not separated them and prevented them from clashing together, (34) and these boundaries are evening and morning; the one of which heralds in the good tidings that the sun is about to rise, gently dissipating the darkness: and evening comes on as the sun sets, receiving gently the collective approach of darkness. And these, I mean morning and evening, must be placed in the class of incorporeal things, perceptible only by the intellect; for there is absolutely nothing in them which is perceptible by the external senses, but they are entirely ideas, and measures, and forms, and seals, incorporeal as far as regards the generation of other bodies. (35) But when light came, and darkness retreated and yielded to it, and boundaries were set in the space between the two, namely, evening and morning, then of necessity the measure of time was immediately perfected, which also the Creator called "day." and

He called it not "the first day," but "one day;" and it is spoken of thus, on account of the single nature of the world perceptible only by the intellect, which has a single nature.

X. (36) The incorporeal world then was already completed, having its seat in the Divine Reason; and the world, perceptible by the external senses, was made on the model of it; and the first portion of it, being also the most excellent of all made by the Creator, was the heaven, which he truly called the firmament, as being corporeal; for the body is by nature firm, inasmuch as it is divisible into three parts; and what other idea of solidity and of body can there be, except that it is something which may be measured in every direction? therefore he, very naturally contrasting that which was perceptible to the external senses, and corporeal with that which was perceptible only by the intellect and incorporeal, called this the firmament. (37) Immediately afterwards he, with great propriety and entire correctness, called it the heaven, either because it was already the boundary[2] of everything, or because it was the first of all visible things which was created; and after its second rising he called the time day, referring the entire space and measure of a day to the heaven, on account of its dignity and honour among the things perceptible to the external senses.

XI. (38) And after this, as the whole body of water in existence was spread over all the earth, and had penetrated through all its parts, as if it were a sponge which had imbibed moisture, so that the earth was only swampy land and deep mud, both the elements of earth and water being mixed up and combined together, like one confused mass into one undistinguishable and shapeless nature, God ordained that all the water which was salt, and destined to be a cause of barrenness to seeds and trees should be gathered together, flowing forth out of all the holes of the entire earth; and he commanded dry land to appear, that liquid which had any sweetness in it being left in it to secure its durability. For this sweet liquid, in due proportions, is as a sort of glue for the different substances, preventing the earth from being utterly dried up, and so becoming unproductive and barren, and causing it, like a mother, to furnish not only one kind of nourishment, namely meat, but both sorts at once, so as to supply its offspring with both meat and drink; wherefore he filled it with veins, resembling breasts, which, being provided with openings, were destined to pour forth springs and rivers. (39) And in the same way he extended the invisible irrigations of dew pervading every portion of arable and deep-soiled land, to contribute to the most liberal and plenteous sup-

---

[2] Philo means that *ouranos* was derived either from *horos*, a boundary, or from *horao*, to see, *horatos*, visible.

ply of fruits. Having arranged these things, he gave them names, calling the day, "land," and the water which was separated from it he called "sea."

XII. (40) After this he began to adorn the land, for he bade it bring forth grass, and bear corn, producing every kind of herb, and plains clothed with verdure, and everything which was calculated to be fodder for cattle, or food for men. Moreover he commanded every kind of tree to spring up, omitting no kind, either of those which are wild or of those which are called cultivated. And simultaneously with their first production he loaded them all with fruit, in a manner different from that which exists at present; (41) for now the different fruits are produced in turn, at different seasons, and not all together at one time; for who is there who does not know that first of all comes the sowing and the planting; and, in the second place, the growth of what has been sown and planted, in some cases the plants extending their roots downwards like foundations, and in others raising themselves upwards to a height and displaying long stalks? After that come the buds, and the putting forth of leaves, and then after everything else comes the production of fruit. And again, the fruit when first produced is not perfect, but it contains in itself all kinds of change, with reference both to its quantity in regard of magnitude, and to its qualities in its multiform appearance: for the fruit is produced at first like indivisible grains, which are hardly visible from their diminutive size, and which one might correctly enough pronounce to be the first things perceptible by the external senses; and afterwards by little and little, from the nourishment conveyed in channels, which waters the tree, and from the wholesome effect of the breezes, which blow air at the same time cold and gentle, the fruit is gradually vivified, and nursed up, and increased, advancing onward to its perfect size; and with its change of magnitude it changes also its qualities, as if it were diversified with varying colours by pictorial science.

XIII. (42) But in the first creation of the universe, as I have said already, God produced the whole race of trees out of the earth in full perfection, having their fruit not incomplete but in a state of entire ripeness, to be ready for the immediate and undelayed use and enjoyment of the animals which were about immediately to be born. (43) Accordingly he commanded the earth to produce these things. And the earth, as though it had for a long time been pregnant and travailing, produced every sort of seed, and every sort of tree, and also of fruit, in unspeakable abundance; and not only were these produced fruits to be food for living animals, but enough also to serve as a preparation for the continuous production of similar fruits hereafter; covering substances consisting of seed, in which are the principles of all plants undistinguishable and invisible, but destined hereafter

to become manifest and visible in the periodical maturity of the fruit. (44) For God thought fit to endue nature with a long duration, making the races that he was creating immortal, and giving them a participation in eternity. On which account he led on and hastened the beginning towards the end, and caused the end to turn backwards to the beginning: for from plants comes fruit, as the end might come from the beginning; and from the fruit comes the seed, which again contains the plant within itself, so that a fresh beginning may come from the end.

XIV. (45) And on the fourth day, after he had embellished the earth, he diversified and adorned the heaven: not giving the precedence to the inferior nature by arranging the heaven subsequently to the earth, or thinking that which was the more excellent and the more divine worthy only of the second place, but acting thus for the more manifest demonstration of the power of his dominion. For he foreknew with respect to men who were not yet born, what sort of beings they would be as to their opinions, forming conjectures on what was likely and probable, of which the greater part would be reasonable, though falling short of the character of unadulterated truth; and trusting rather to visible phenomena than to God, and admiring sophistry rather than wisdom. And again he knew that surveying the periods of the sun and moon, to which are owing the summers and winters, and the alternations of spring and autumn, they would conceive the revolutions of the stars in heaven to be the causes of all the things which every year should be produced and generated on the earth, accordingly that no one might venture either through shameless impudence or inordinate ignorance to attribute to any created thing the primary causes of things, he said: (46) "Let them run over in their minds the first creation of the universe, when, before the sun or the moon existed, the earth brought forth all kinds of plants and all kinds of fruits: and seeing this in their minds let them hope that it will again also bring forth such, according to the appointment of the Father, when it shall seem good to him, without his having need of the aid of any of the sons of men beneath the heavens, to whom he has given powers, though not absolute ones." For as a charioteer holding the reigns or a helmsman with his hand upon the rudder, he guides everything as he pleases, in accordance with law and justice, needing no one else as his assistant; for all things are possible to God.

XV. (47) This is the cause why the earth bore fruit and herbs before God proceeded to adorn the heaven. And next the heaven was embellished in the perfect number four, and if any one were to pronounce this number the origin and source of the all-perfect decade he would not err. For what the decade is in actuality, that the number four, as it seems, is in potentiality, at all events if the numerals from the unit to four[3] are placed together in order, they will make ten, which is the limit of the number of immensity, around which the numbers wheel and turn as around a goal.

(48) Moreover the number four also comprehends the principles of the harmonious concords in music, that in fours, and in fifths, and the diapason, and besides this the double diapason from which sounds the most perfect system of harmony is produced. For the ratio of the sounds in fourths is as four to three; and in fifths as three to two; and in the diapason that ratio is doubled: and in the double diapason it is increased fourfold, all which ratios the number four comprehends. At all events the first, or the epistritus, is the ratio of four to three; the second, or the hemiolius, is that of three to two: the twofold ratio is that of two to one, or four to two: and the fourfold ratio is that of four to one.

XVI. (49) There is also another power of the number four which is a most wonderful one to speak of and to contemplate. For it was this number that first displayed the nature of the solid cube, the numbers before four being assigned only to incorporeal things. For it is according to the unit that that thing is reckoned which is spoken of in geometry as a point: and a line is spoken of according to the number two, because it is arranged by nature from a point; and a line is length without breadth. But when breadth is added to it, it becomes a superficies, which is arranged according to the number three. And a superficies, when compared with the nature of a solid cube, wants one thing, namely depth, and when this one thing is added to the three, it becomes four. On which account it has happened that this number is a thing of great importance, inasmuch as from an incorporeal substance perceptible only by intellect, it has led us on to a comprehension of a body divisible in a threefold manner, and which by its own nature is first perceived by the external senses. (50) And he who does not comprehend what is here said may learn to understand it from a game which is very common. Those who play with nuts are accustomed when they have placed three nuts on the floor, to place one more on the top of them producing a figure like a pyramid. Accordingly the triangle stands on the floor, arranged up to the number three, and the nut which is placed upon it makes up four in number, and in figure it produces a pyramid, being now a solid body.

(51) And in addition to this there is this point also of which we should not be ignorant, the number four is the first number which is a square, being equal on all sides, the measure of justice and equality. And that it is the only number the nature of which is such that it is produced by the same numbers whether in combination, or in power. In combination when two and two are added together; and again in power when we speak of twice two;[4] and in this is displays an exceedingly beautiful kind of harmony, which is not the lot of any other number.

If we examine the number six which is composed of two threes, if these two numbers are multiplied it is not the number six that is produced, but a different one, the number nine. (52) And the number four has many other powers also, which we must subsequently show more accurately in a separate essay appropriated to it. At present it is sufficient to add this that it was the foundation of the creation of the whole heaven and the whole world. For the four elements, out of which this universe was made, flowed from the number four as from a fountain. And in addition to the four elements the seasons of the year are also four, which are the causes of the generation of animals and plants, the year being divided into the quadruple division of winter, and spring, and summer, and autumn.

XVII. (53) The aforesaid number therefore being accounted worthy of such pre-eminence in nature, the Creator of necessity adorned the heaven by the number four, namely by that most beautiful and most godlike ornament the light-giving stars. And knowing that of all existing things light is the most excellent, he made it the instrument of the best of all the senses, sight. For what the mind is in the soul, that the eye is in the body. For each of them sees, the one beholding those existing things which are perceptible only to the intellect, and the other those which are perceptible to the external senses.

But the mind is in need of knowledge in order to distinguish incorporeal things, and the eyes have need of light in order to be able to perceive bodies, and light is also the cause of many other good things to men, and particularly of the greatest, namely philosophy. (54) For the sight being sent upwards by light and beholding the nature of the stars and their harmonious movement, and the well-ordered revolutions of the fixed stars, and of the planets, some always revolving in the same manner and coming to the same places, and others having double periods in an anomalous and somewhat contrary manner, beholding also, the harmonious dances of all these bodies arranged according to the laws of perfect music, causes an ineffable joy and delight to the soul. And the soul, feasting on a continuous series of spectacles, for one succeeds another, has an insatiable love for beholding such. Then, as is usually the case, it examines with increased curiosity what is the substance of these things which are visible; and whether they have

---

[3]By addition, that is $1 + 2 + 3 + 4 = 10$.

[4]Thus $2 + 2 = 4$, or $2 \times 2 = 4$

an existence without having been created, or whether they received their origin by creation, and what is the character of their movement, and what the causes are by which everything is regulated. And it is from inquiries into these things that philosophy has arisen, than which no more perfect good has entered into human life.

XVIII. (55) But the Creator having a regard to that idea of light perceptible only by the intellect, which has been spoken of in the mention made of the incorporeal world, created those stars which are perceptible by the external senses, those divine and superlatively beautiful images, which on many accounts he placed in the purest temple of corporeal substance, namely in heaven. One of the reasons for his so doing was that they might give light; another was that they might be signs; another had reference to their dividing the times of the seasons of the year, and above all dividing days and nights, of months and years, which are the measures of time; and which have given rise to the nature of number. (56) And how great is the use and how great the advantage derivable from each of the aforesaid things, is plain from their effect. But with a view to a more accurate comprehension of them, it may perhaps not be out of place to trace out the truth in a regular discussion.

Now the whole of time being divided into two portions day and night, the sovereignty of the day the Father has assigned to the Sun, as a mighty monarch: and that of the night he has given to the moon and to the multitude of the other stars. (57) And the greatness of the power and sovereignty of the sun has its most conspicuous proof in what has been already said: for he, being one and single has been allotted for his own share and by himself one half portion of all time, namely day; and all the other lights in conjunction with the moon have the other portion, which is called night. And when the sun rises all the appearances of such numbers of stars are not only obscured but absolutely disappear from the effusion of his beams; and when he sets then they all assembled together, begin to display their own peculiar brilliancy and their separate qualities.

XIX. (58) And they have been created, as Moses tells us, not only that they might send light upon the earth, but also that they might display signs of future events. For either by their risings, or their settings, or their eclipses, or again by their appearances and occultations, or by the other variations observable in their motions, men oftentimes conjecture what is about to happen, the productiveness or unproductiveness of the crops, the birth or loss of their cattle, fine weather or cloudy weather, calm and violent storms of wind, floods in the rivers or droughts, a tranquil state of the sea and heavy waves, unusual changes in the seasons of the year when either the summer is cold like winter, or the winter warm, or when the spring

assumes the temperature of autumn or the autumn that of spring. (59) And before now some men have conjecturally predicted disturbances and commotions of the earth from the revolutions of the heavenly bodies, and innumerable other events which have turned out most exactly true: so that it is a most veracious saying that "the stars were created to act as signs, and moreover to mark the seasons." And by the word seasons the divisions of the year are here intended. And why may not this be reasonably affirmed? For what other idea of opportunity can there be except that it is the time for success? And the seasons bring everything to perfection and set everything right; giving perfection to the sowing and planting of fruits, and to the birth and growth of animals.

(60) They were also created to serve as measure of time; for it is by the appointed periodical revolutions of the sun and moon and other stars, that days and months and years are determined. And moreover it is owing to them that the most useful of all things, the nature of number exists, time having displayed it; for from one day comes the limit, and from two the number two, and from three, three, and from the notion of a month is derived the number thirty, and from a year that number which is equal to the days of the twelve months, and from infinite time comes the notion of infinite number.

(61) To such great and indispensable advantages do the natures of the heavenly bodies and the motions of the stars tend. And to how many other things might I also affirm that they contribute which are as yet unknown to us? for all things are not known to the will of man; but of the things which contribute towards the durability of the universe, those which are established by laws and ordinances which God has appointed to be unalterable for ever, are accomplished in every instance and in every country.

XX. (62) Then when earth and heaven had been adorned with their befitting ornaments, one with a triad, and the other, as has been already said, with a quaternion, God proceeded to create the races of mortal creatures, making the beginning with the aquatic animals on the fifth day, thinking that there was no one thing so akin to another as the number five as to animals; for animate things differ from inanimate in nothing more than in sensation, and sensation is divided according to a fivefold division, into sight, hearing, taste, smell, and touch. Accordingly, the Creator allotted to each of the senses its appropriate matter, and also its peculiar faculty of judgment, by which it should decide on what came before it. So sight judges of colours, and hearing of sounds, and taste of juices, and smell of vapours, and touch of softness and hardness, and of heat and cold, and of smoothness and roughness: (63) therefore He commanded all the races of fish and sea-monsters to stand together in their places, animals differing both in their sizes and in their qualities; for they vary in different seas, though in some cases they are the same, and every animal was not formed to live every where. And was not this reasonable? For some of them delight in marshy places, and in water which is very deep; and some in sewers and harbours, being neither able to crawl up upon the land, nor to swim off far from the land. Some, again, dwell in the middle and in the deep sea, and avoid all the projecting promontories and islands and rocks: some also exult in fine weather and in calm, and some in storms and heavy surf. For being exercised by continual buffetings, and being in the habit of withstanding the current by force, they are very vigorous and become stout.

After that he created the races of birds as akin to the races of aquatic animals (for they are each of them swimmers), leaving no species of creatures which traverse the air unfinished.

XXI. (64) So now when the air and the water had received their appropriate races of animals as an allotment that was their due, God again summoned the earth for the creation of that share which still remained: and after the production of plants, the terrestrial animals still remained. And God said, "Let the earth bring forth cattle and beasts, and creeping things of each kind." And the earth did as it was commanded, and immediately sent forth animals differing in their formation and in their strength, and in the injurious or beneficial powers that were implanted in them.

(65) And after all He made man. But how he made him I will mention presently, after I have first explained that he adopted the most beautiful connection and train of consequences according to the system of the creation of animals which he had sketched out to himself; for of souls the most sluggish and the most weakly formed has been allotted to the race of fishes; and the most exquisitely endowed soul, that which is in all respects most excellent, has been given to the race of mankind, and one something between the two to the races of terrestrial animals and those which traverse the air; for the soul of such creatures is endowed with more acute sensations than the soul of fishes, but is more dull than that of mankind. (66) And it was on this account that of all living creatures God created fishes first, inasmuch as they partake of corporeal substance in a greater degree than they partake of soul, being in a manner animals and not animals, moving soulless things, having a sort of semblance of soul diffused through them for no object beyond that of keeping their bodies live (just as they say that salt preserves meat), in order that they may not easily be destroyed. And after the fishes, he created winged and terrestrial animals: for these are endowed with a higher degree of sensation, and from their formation show that the properties of their animating principle are of a

higher order. But after all the rest, then, as has been said before, he created man, to whom he gave that admirable endowment of mind—the soul, if I may so call it, of the soul, as being like the pupil to the eye; for those who most accurately investigate the natures of things affirm, that it is the pupil which is the eye of the eye.

XXII. (67) So at last all things were created and existing together. But when they all were collected in one place, then some sort of order was necessarily laid down for them for the sake of the production of them from one another which was hereafter to take place. Now in things which exist in part, the principle of order is this, to begin with that which is most inferior in its nature, and to end with that which is the most excellent of all; and what that is we will explain. It has been arranged that seed should be the principle of the generation of animals. It is plainly seen that this is a thing of no importance, being like foam; but when it has descended into the womb and remained there, then immediately it receives motion and is changed into nature; and nature is more excellent than seed, as also motion is better than quiet in created things; and nature, like a workman, or, to speak more correctly, like a faultless art, endows the moist substance with life, and fashions it, distributing it among the limbs and parts of the body, allotting that portion which can produce breath, and nourishment, and sensation to the powers of the soul: for as to the reasoning powers, we may pass over them for the present, on account of those who say, that the mind enters into the body from without, being something divine and eternal.

(68) Nature therefore began from an insignificant seed, and ended in the most honourable of things, namely, in the formation of animals and men. And the very same thing took place in the creation of every thing: for when the Creator determined to make animals the first created in his arrangement were in some degree inferior, such as the fishes, and the last were the best, namely, man. And the others the terrestrial and winged creatures were between these extremes, being better than the first created, and inferior to the last.

XXIII. (69) So then after all the other things, as has been said before, Moses says that man was made in the image and likeness of God. And he says well; for nothing that is born on the earth is more resembling God than man. And let no one think that he is able to judge of this likeness from the characters of the body: for neither is God a being with the form of a man, nor is the human body like the form of God; but the resemblance is spoken of with reference to the most important part of the soul, namely, the mind: for the mind which exists in each individual has been created after the likeness of that one mind which is in the universe as its primitive model, being in some sort the God of that body which carries it about and bears its image within it. In the same rank that the great Governor occupies in the universal world, that same as it seems does the mind of man occupy in man; for it is invisible, though it sees everything itself; and it has an essence which is undiscernible, though it can discern the essences of all other things, and making for itself by art and science all sorts of roads leading in divers directions, and all plain; it traverses land and sea, investigating everything which is contained in either element. (70) And again, being raised up on wings, and so surveying and contemplating the air, and all the commotions to which it is subject, it is borne upwards to the higher firmament, and to the revolutions of the heavenly bodies. And also being itself involved in the revolutions of the planets and fixed stars according to the perfect laws of music, and being led on by love, which is the guide of wisdom, it proceeds onwards till, having surmounted all essence intelligible by the external senses, it comes to aspire to such as is perceptible only by the intellect: (71) and perceiving in that, the original models and ideas of those things intelligible by the external senses which it saw here full of surpassing beauty, it becomes seized with a sort of sober intoxication like the zealots engaged in the Corybantian festivals, and yields to enthusiasm, becoming filled with another desire, and a more excellent longing, by which it is conducted onwards to the very summit of such things as are perceptible only to the intellect, till it appears to be reaching the great King himself. And while it is eagerly longing to behold him pure and unmingled, rays of divine light are poured forth upon it like a torrent, so as to bewilder the eyes of its intelligence by their splendour.

But as it is not every image that resembles its archetypal model, since many are unlike, Moses has shown this by adding to the words "after his image," the expression, "in his likeness," to prove that it means an accurate impression, having a clear and evident resemblance in form.

XXIV. (72) And he would not err who should raise the question why Moses attributed the creation of man alone not to one creator, as he did that of other animals, but to several. For he introduces the Father of the universe using this language: "Let *us* make man after our image, and in our likeness." Had he then, shall I say, need of any one whatever to help him, He to whom all things are subject? Or, when he was making the heaven and the earth and the sea, was he in need of no one to co-operate with him; and yet was he unable himself by his own power to make man an animal so short-lived and so exposed to the assaults of fate without the assistance of others? It is plain that the real cause of his so acting is known to God alone, but one which to a reasonable conjecture appears probable and credible, I think I should not conceal; and it is this.

(73) Of existing things, there are some which partake neither of virtue nor of vice; as for instance, plants and irrational animals; the one, because they are destitute of soul, and are regulated by a nature void of sense; and the other, because they are not endowed with mind of reason. But mind and reason may be looked upon as the abode of virtue and vice; as it is in them that they seem to dwell. Some things again partake of virtue alone, being without any participation in any kind of vice; as for instance, the stars, for they are said to be animals, and animals endowed with intelligence; or I might rather say, the mind of each of them is wholly and entirely virtuous, and unsusceptible of every kind of evil. Some things again are of a mixed nature, like man, who is capable of opposite qualities, of wisdom and folly, of temperance and dissoluteness, of courage and cowardice, of justice and injustice, in short of good and evil, of what is honourable and what is disgraceful, of virtue and vice. (74) Now it was a very appropriate task for God the Father of all to create by himself alone, those things which were wholly good, on account of their kindred with himself. And it was not inconsistent with his dignity to create those which were indifferent since they too are devoid of evil, which is hateful to him. To create the beings of a mixed nature, was partly consistent and partly inconsistent with his dignity; consistent by reason of the more excellent idea which is mingled in them; inconsistent because of the opposite and worse one.

(75) It is on this account that Moses says, at the creation of man alone that God said, "Let *us* make man," which expression shows an assumption of other beings to himself as assistants, in order that God, the governor of all things, might have all the blameless intentions and actions of man, when he does right attributed to him; and that his other assistants might bear the imputation of his contrary actions. For it was fitting that the Father should in the eyes of his children be free from all imputation of evil; and vice and energy in accordance with vice are evil. (76) And very beautifully after he had called the whole race "man," did he distinguish between the sexes, saying, that "they were created male and female;" although all the individuals of the race had not yet assumed their distinctive form; since the extreme species are contained in the genus, and are beheld, as in a mirror, by those who are able to discern acutely.

XXV. (77) And some one may inquire the cause why it was that man was the last work in the creation of the world. For the Creator and Father created him after every thing else as the sacred scriptures inform us. Accordingly, they who have gone most deeply into the laws, and who to the best of their power have investigated everything that is contained in them with all diligence, say that God, when he had given to man to partake of kindred with himself, grudged him neither reason, which is the most excellent of all gifts, nor anything else that is good; but before his creation, provided for him every thing in the world, as for the animal most resembling himself, and dearest to him, being desirous that when he was born, he should be in want of nothing requisite for living, and for living well; the first of which objects is provided for by the abundance of supplies which are furnished to him for his enjoyment, and the other by his power of contemplation of the heavenly bodies, by which the mind is smitten so as to conceive a love and desire for knowledge on those subjects; owing to which desire, philosophy has sprung up, by which, man, though mortal, is made immortal. (78) As then, those who make a feast do not invite their guests to the entertainment before they have provided everything for festivity, and as those who celebrate gymnastic or dramatic contests, before they assemble the spectators, provide themselves with an abundance of competitors and spectacles, and sweet sounds, with which to fill the theatres and the stadia; so in the same manner did the Ruler of all, as a man proposing games, or giving a banquet and being about to invite others to feast and to behold the spectacle, first provide everything for every kind of entertainment, in order that when man came into the world he might at once find a feast ready for him, and a most holy theatre; the one abounding with everything which the earth, or the rivers, or the sea, or air, brings forth for use and enjoyment, and the other being full of every description of light, which has either its essence or its qualities admirable, and its motions and revolutions worthy of notice, being arranged in perfect order, both as to the proportions of its numbers, and the harmony of its periods. And a man would not be far wrong who should say that in all these things there might be discovered that archetypal and real model music, the images of which the subsequent generations of mankind engraved in their own souls, and in this way handed down the art which is the most necessary and the most advantageous to human life.

XXVI. (79) This is the first reason on account of which it seems that man was created after all other animals. And there is another not altogether unreasonable, which I must mention. At the moment of his first birth, man found all the requisites for life ready prepared for him that he might teach them to those who should come afterwards. Nature all but crying out with a distinct voice, that men, imitating the Author of their being, should pass their lives without labour and without trouble, living in the most ungrudging abundance and plenty. And this would be the case if there were neither irrational pleasures to obtain mastery over the soul raising up a wall of gluttony and lasciviousness, nor desires of glory, or power, or riches, to assume dominion over life, nor pains to contract and warp the intellect, nor that evil councillor—fear, to restrain the natural inclinations towards virtuous actions, nor folly and cowardice, and injustice, and the incalculable multitude of other evils to attack them. (80) But now that all the evils which I have now been mentioning are vigorous, and that men abandon themselves without restraint to their passions, and to those unbridled and guilty inclinations, which it is impious even to mention, justice encounters them as a suitable chastiser of wicked habits; and therefore, as a punishment for wrong doers, the necessaries of life have been made difficult of acquisition. For men ploughing up the plains with difficulty, and bringing streams from rivers, and fountains by channels, and sowing and planting, and submitting indefatigably day and night to the labour of cultivating the ground, provide themselves every year with what is necessary, even that at times being attended with pain; and not very sufficient in quantity, from being injured by many causes. For either a fall of incessant rain has carried away the crops, or the weight of hail which has fallen upon them has crushed them altogether, or snow has chilled them, or the violence of the winds has torn them up by the roots; for water and air cause many alterations, tending to destroy and productiveness of the crops. (81) But if the immoderate violence of the passions were appeased by temperance, and the inclination to do wrong and depraved ambition were corrected by justice, and in short if the vices and unhallowed actions done in accordance with them, were corrected by the virtues, and the energies in accordance with them, the war of the soul being terminated, which is in good truth the most grievous and heavy of all wars, and peace being established, and founding amid all our faculties, a due regard for law, with all tranquillity and mildness, then there would be hope that God, as being a friend to virtue, and a friend to honour, and above all a friend to man, would bestow upon the race of man, all kinds of spontaneous blessings from his ready store. For it is evident that it is easier to supply most abundantly the requisite supplies without having recourse to agricultural means, from treasures which already exist, than to bring forth what as yet has no existence.

XXVII. (82) I have now mentioned the second reason. There is also a third, which is as follows:—God, intending to adapt the beginning and the end of all created things together, as being all necessary and dear to one another, made heaven the beginning, and man the end: the one being the most perfect of incorruptible things, among those things which are perceptible by the external senses; and the other, the best of all earthborn and perishable productions—a short-lived heaven if one were to speak the truth, bearing within himself many starlike natures, by means of certain arts and sciences, and illustrious speculations, according to every kind of virtue. For since the corruptible and the incorruptible, are by nature opposite, he has allotted the best thing of each species to the beginning and to the end. Heaven, as I before said, to the beginning, and man to the end.

XXVIII. (83) And besides all this, another is also mentioned among the necessary causes. It was necessary that man should be the last of all created beings; in order that being so, and appearing suddenly, he might strike terror into the other animals. For it was fitting that they, as soon as they first saw him should admire and worship him, as their natural ruler and master; on which account, they all, as soon as they saw him, became tame before him; even those, who by nature were most savage, becoming at once most manageable at the first sight of him; displaying their unbridled ferocity to one another, and being tame to man alone. (84) For which reason the Father who made him to be a being dominant over them by nature not merely in fact, but also by express verbal appointment, established him as the king of all the animals, beneath the moon, whether terrestrial or aquatic, or such as traverse the air. For every mortal thing which lives in the three elements, land, water or air, did he put in subjection to him, excepting only the beings that are in heaven, as creatures who have a more divine portion. And what is apparent to our eyes it the most evident proof of this. For at times, innumerable herds of beasts are led about by one man, not armed, nor wearing iron, nor any defensive weapon, but clad only in a skin for a garment, and carrying a staff, for the purpose of making signs, and to lean upon also in his journeys if he become weary. (85) And so the shepherd, and the goatherd, and the cowherd, lead numerous flocks of sheep, and goats, and herds of oxen; men neither vigorous, nor active in their bodies, so as to strike those who behold them with admiration because of their fine appearance; and all the might and power of such numerous and well-armed beasts (for they have means of self-defence given them by nature), yet dread them as slaves do their master, and do all that is commanded them. Bulls are yoked to the plough to till the ground, and cutting deep furrows all day, sometimes even for a long space of time together, while some farmer is managing them. And rams being weighed down with heavy fleeces of wool, in the spring season, at the command of the shepherd, stand quietly, and lying down, without resistance, permit their wool to be shorn off, being accustomed naturally, like cities, to yield a yearly tribute to their sovereign. (86) And moreover, that most spirited of animals, the horse, is easily guided after he has been bridled; in order that he may not become frisky, and shake off the rein; and he hollows his back in an admirable manner to receive his rider and to afford him a good seat, and then bearing

him aloft, he gallops at a rapid pace, being eager to arrive at and carry him to the place to which he is urging him. And the rider without any toil, but in the most perfect quiet, makes a rapid journey, by using the body and feet of another animal.

XXIX. (87) And any one who was inclined to dwell upon this subject might bring forward a great many other instances, to prove that there is no animal in the enjoyment of perfect liberty, and exempt from the dominion of man; but what has been already said is sufficient by way of example. We ought, however, not to be ignorant of this also, that it is no proof because man was the last created animal that he is the lowest in rank, and charioteers and pilots are witnesses of this; (88) for the charioteers sit behind their beasts of burden, and are placed at, their backs, and yet when they have the reins in their hands, they guide them wherever they choose, and at one time they urge them on to a swift pace, and at another time they hold them back, if they are going on at a speed greater than is desirable. And pilots again, sitting in the hindmost part of the ship, that is the stern are, as one may say, the most important of all the people in the ship, inasmuch as they have the safety of the ship and of all those who are in it, in their hands. And so the Creator has made man to be as it were a charioteer and pilot over all other animals, in order that he may hold the reins and direct the course of every thing upon earth, having the superintendence of all animals and plants, as a sort of viceroy of the principal and mighty King.

XXX. (89) But after the whole world had been completed according to the perfect nature of the number six, the Father hallowed the day following, the seventh, praising it, and calling it holy. For that day is the festival, not of one city or one country, but of all the earth; a day which alone it is right to call the day of festival for all people, and the birthday of the world. (90) And I know not if any one would be able to celebrate the nature of the number seven in adequate terms, since it is superior to every form of expression. But it does not follow that because it is more admirable than anything that can be said of it, that on that account one ought to keep silence; but rather we ought to try, even if one cannot say everything which is proper, or even that which is most proper, at all events to utter such things as may be attainable by our capacities.

(91) The number seven is spoken of in two ways; the one within the number ten which is measured by repeating the unit alone seven times, and which consists of seven units; the other is the number outside ten, the beginning of which is altogether the unit increasing according to a twofold or threefold, or any other proportion whatever; as are the numbers sixty-four, and seven hundred and twenty-nine; the one number of which

is increased by doubling on from the unit, and the other by trebling. And it is not well to examine either species superficially, but the second has a most manifest pre-eminence. (92) For in every case the number which is combined from the unit in double or treble ratio, or any other ratio, whatsoever, is the seventh number, a cube and a square, embracing both species, both that of the incorporeal and that of the corporeal essence. That of the incorporeal essence according to the superficies which quadrangular figures present, and that of the corporeal essence according to the other figure which cubes make; (93) and the clearest proof of this is afforded by the numbers already spoken of. In the seventh number increasing immediately from the unit in a twofold ratio, namely, the number sixty-four, is a square formed by the multiplication of eight by eight, and it is also a cube by the multiplication of four and four, four times. And again, the seventh number from the unit being increased in a threefold ratio, that is to say, the number seven hundred and twenty-nine, is a square, the number seven and twenty being multiplied by itself; and it is also a cube, by nine being multiplied by itself nine times. (94) And in every case a man making his beginning from the unit, and proceeding on to the seventh number, and increasing in the same ratio till he comes to the number seven, will at all times find the number, when increased, both a cube and a square. At all events, he who begins with the number sixty-four, and combines them in a doubling ratio, will make the seventh number four thousand and ninety-six, which is both a square and a cube, having sixty-four as its square root, and sixteen as its cube root.

XXXI. (95) And we must also pass on to the other species of the number seven, which is contained in the number ten, and which displays an admirable nature, and one not inferior to the previously mentioned species. The number seven consists of one, and two and four, numbers which have two most harmonious ratios, the twofold and the fourfold ratio; the former of which affects the diapason harmony, while the fourfold ratio causes that of the double diapason. It also comprehends other divisions, existing in some kind of yoke-like combination. For it is divided first of all into the number one, and the number six; then into the two and the five; and last of all, into the three and the four. (96) And the proportion of these numbers is a most musical one; for the number six bears to the number one a sixfold ratio, and the sixfold ratio causes the greatest possible difference between existing tones; the distance namely, by which the sharpest tone is separated from the flattest, as we shall show when we pass on from numbers to the discussion of harmony. Again, the ratio of four to two displays the greatest power in harmony, almost equal to that of the diapason, as is most evidently shown in the rules of that art.

And the ratio of four to three effects the first harmony, that in the thirds, which is the diatessaron.

XXXII. (97) The number seven displays also another beauty which it possesses, and one which is most sacred to think of. For as it consists of three and four, it displays in existing things a line which is free from all deviation and upright by nature. And in what way it does so I must show.

The rectangular triangle, which is the beginning of all qualities, consists of the numbers[5] and four, and five; and the three and the four, which are the essence of the seven, contain the right angle; for the obtuse angle and the acute angle show irregularity, and disorder, and inequality; for one may be more acute or more obtuse than another. But a right angle does not admit of comparison, nor is one right angle more a right angle than another: but one remains similar to another, never changing its peculiar nature. But if the right-angled triangle is the beginning of all figures and of all qualities, and if the essence of the number seven, that is to say, the numbers three and four together, supply the most necessary part of this, namely, the right angle, then seven may be rightly thought to be the fountain of every figure and of every quality. (98) And besides what has been already advanced, this also may be asserted that three is the number of a plane figure, since a point has been laid down to be, according to a unit, and a line according to the number two, and a plane superficies according to the number three. Also, four is the number of a cube, by the addition of one to the number of a plane superficies, depth being added to the superficies. From which it is plain that the essence of the number seven is the foundation of geometry and trigonometry; and in a word, of all incorporeal and corporeal substances.

XXXIII. (99) And such great sanctity is there in the number seven, that it has a pre-eminent rank beyond all the other numbers in the first decade. For of the other numbers, some produce without being produced, others are produced but have no productive power themselves; others again both produce and are produced. But the number seven alone is contemplated in no part. And this proposition we must confirm by demonstration. Now the number one produces all the other numbers in order, being itself produced absolutely by no other; and the number eight is produced by twice four, but itself produces no other number in the decade. Again, four has the rank of both, that is, of parents and of offspring; for it produces eight when doubled, and it is produced by twice two.

---

[5] This discussion about numbers is not very intelligible; but here Philo is probably referring to the problem of Euclid on the subject of the square of the hypothenuse. Thus, if 3 and 4 represent the sides containing the angle, and 5 the side subtending it, we get $(3 \times 3) + (4 \times 4) = 9 + 16 = 25; 5 \times 5 = 25$.

(100) But seven alone, as I said before, neither produces nor is produced, on which account other philosophers liken this number to Victory, who had no mother, and to the virgin goddess, whom the fable asserts to have sprung from the head of Jupiter: and the Pythagoreans compare it to the Ruler of all things. For that which neither produces, nor is produced, remains immovable. For generation consists in motion, since that which is generated, cannot be so without motion, both to cause production, and to be produced. And the only thing which neither moves nor is moved, is the Elder, Ruler, and Lord of the universe, of whom the number seven may reasonably be called a likeness. And Philolaus gives his testimony to this doctrine of mine in the following words:—"For God," says he "is the ruler and Lord of all things, being one, eternal, lasting, immovable, himself like to himself, and different from all other beings."

XXXIV. (101) Among the things then which are perceptible only by intellect, the number seven is proved to be the only thing free from motion and accident; but among things perceptible by the external senses, it displays a great and comprehensive power, contributing to the improvement of all terrestrial things, and affecting even the periodical changes of the moon. And in what manner it does this, we must consider. The number seven when compounded of numbers beginning with the unit, makes eight-and-twenty, a perfect number, and one equalised in its parts. And the number so produced, is calculated to reproduce the revolutions of the moon, bringing her back to the point from which she first began to increase in a manner perceptible by the external senses, and to which she returns by waning. For she increases from her first crescent-shaped figure, to that of a half circle in seven days; and in seven more, she becomes a full orb; and then again she turns back, retracing the same path, like a runner of the diaulos,[6] receding from an orb full of light, to a half circle again in seven days, and lastly, in an equal number she diminishes from a half circle to the form of a crescent; and thus the number before mentioned is completed. (102) And the number seven by those persons who are in the habit of employing names with strict propriety is called the perfecting number; because by it, everything is perfected. And any one may receive a confirmation of this from the fact, that every organic body has three dimensions, length, depth, and breadth; and four boundaries, the point, the line, the superficies, and the solid; and by theses, when combined, the number seven is made up.

But it would be impossible for bodies to be measured by the number seven, according to the combination of the three dimensions, and the four boundaries, if it did not happen that the ideas of the first numbers, one, two, three and four, in which the number ten is founded, comprised the nature of the number seven. For the aforesaid numbers have four boundaries, the first, the second, the third, the fourth, and three intervals. The first interval being that between one and two; the second, that between two and three; the third, that between three and four.

XXXV. (103) And besides what has been already said, the growth of men from infancy to old age, when measured by the number seven, displays in a most evident manner its perfecting power; for in the first period of seven years, the putting forth of the teeth takes place. And at the end of the second period of the same length, he arrives at the age of puberty: at the end of the third period, the growth of the beard takes place. The fourth period sees him arrive at the fulness of his manly strength. The fifth seven years is the season for marriage. In the sixth period he arrives at the maturity of his understanding. The seventh period is that of the most rapid improvement and growth of both his intellectual and reasoning powers. The eighth is the sum of the perfection of both. In the ninth, his passions assume a mildness and gentleness, from being to a great degree tamed. In the tenth, the desirable end of life comes upon him, while his limbs and organic senses are still unimpaired: for excessive old age is apt to weaken and enfeeble them all.

(104) And Solon, the Athenian lawgiver, described these different ages in the following elegiac verses:—

In seven years from th'earliest breath,
The child puts forth his hedge of teeth;
When strengthened by a similar span,
He first displays some signs of man.
As in a third, his limbs increase,
A beard buds o'er his changing face.
When he has passed a fourth such time,
His strength and vigour's in its prime.
When five times seven years o'er his head
Have passed, the man should think to wed;
At forty two, the wisdom's clear
To shun vile deed of folly or fear:
While seven times seven years to sense
Add ready wit and eloquence.
And seven years further skill admit
To raise them to their perfect height.
When nine such periods have passed,
His powers, though milder grown, still last;
When God has granted ten times seven,
The aged man prepares for heaven.

XXXVI. (105) Solon therefore thus computes

---

[6] This refers to the Greek games. "The straight race was called *stadion* or *dromos*. In the *diaulos dromos* the runners turned round the goal, and came back to the starting place."—*Smith in v. Stadium.*

the life of man by the aforesaid ten periods of seven years. But Hippocrates the physician says that there are seven[7] ages of man, infancy, childhood, boyhood, youth, manhood, middle age, old age; and that these too, are measured by periods of seven, though not in the same order. And he speaks thus; "In the nature of man there are seven seasons, which men call ages; infancy, childhood, boyhood, and the rest. He is an infant till he reaches his seventh year, the age of the shedding of his teeth. He is a child till he arrives at the age of puberty, which takes place in fourteen years. He is a boy till his beard begins to grow, and that time is the end of a third period of seven years. He is a youth till the completion of the growth of his whole body, which coincides with the fourth seven years. Then he is a man till he reaches his forty-ninth year, or seven times seven periods. He is a middle aged man till he is fifty-six, or eight times seven years old; and after that he is an old man."

(106) And it is also affirmed for the particular praise of the number seven, that it has a very admirable rank in nature, because it is composed of three and four. And if any one doubles the third number after the unit, he will find a square; and if he doubles the fourth number, he will find a cube. And if he doubles the seventh from both, he will both a cube and a square; therefore, the third number from the unit is a square in a double ratio. And the fourth number, eight, is a cube. And the seventh number, being sixty-four, is both a cube and a square at the same time; so that the seventh number is really a perfecting one, signifying both equalities,—the plane superficies by the square, according to the connection with the number three, and the solid by the cube according to its relationship to the number four; and of the numbers three and four, are composed the number seven.

XXXVII. (107) But this number is not only a perfecter of things, but it is also, so to say, the most harmonious of numbers; and in a manner the source of that most beautiful diagram which describes all the harmonies, that of fourths, and that of fifths, and the diapason. It also comprises all the proportions, the arithmetical, the geometrical, and moreover the harmonic proportion. And the square consists of these numbers, six, eight, nine, and twelve; and eight bears to six the ratio of being one third greater, which is the diatessaron of harmony. And nine bears to six the ratio of being half as great again, which is the ratio of fifths. And twelve is to six, in a twofold proportion; and this is the same as the diapason. (108) The number seven comprises also, as I have said, all the proportions of arithmetical proportion, from

the numbers six, and nine, and twelve; for as the number in the middle exceeds the first number by three, it is also exceeded by three by the last number. And geometrical proportion is according to these four numbers. For the same ratio that eight bears to six, that also does twelve bear to nine. And this is the ratio of thirds. Harmonic ratio consists of three numbers, six, and eight, and twelve. (109) But there are two ways of judging of harmonic proportion. One when, whatever ratio the last number bears to the first, the excess by which the last number exceeds the middle one is the same as the excess by which the middle number exceeds the first. And any one may derive a most evident proof of this from the numbers before mentioned, six, and eight, and twelve: for the last number is double the first. And again, the excess of twelve over eight is double the excess of eight over six. For the number twelve exceeds eight by four, and eight exceeds six by two; and four is the double of two. (110) And another test of harmonic proportion is, when the middle term exceeds and is exceeded by those on each side of it, by an equal portion; for eight being the middle term, exceeds the first term by a third part; for if six be subtracted from it, the remainder two is one third of the original number six: and it is exceeded by the last term in an equal proportion; for if eight be taken from twelve, the remainder four is one third of the whole number twelve.

XXXVIII. (111) Let this then be premised, as of necessity it must, respecting the honourable qualities which this diagram or square has, and the name to which it is entitled, and the number seven unfolds an equal number of ideas, and even more in the case of incorporeal things, which are perceptible only by the intellect; and its nature extends also over every visible essence, reaching to both heaven and earth, which are the boundaries of every thing. For what portion of all the things on earth is there which is not fond of seven; being subdued by an affection and longing for the seventh. (112) Accordingly men say, that the heaven is girdled with seven circles, the names of which are as follows; the arctic, the antarctic, the summer tropic, the winter tropic, the equinoctial, the zodiac, and last of all the galaxy. For the horizon is something which affects ourselves, in proportion as any one has acute vision, or the contrary; our sensation cutting off at one time a lesser, and at another time a greater circumference. (113) The planets too, and the corresponding host of fixed stars, are arrayed in seven divisions, displaying a very great sympathy with the air and the earth. For they turn the air towards the times, that are called the seasons of the year, causing in each of them innumerable changes by calm weather, and pleasant breezes, and clouds, and irresistible blasts of wind. And again, they make rivers to overflow and to subside, and turn plains into lakes; and again,

---

[7] It is hardly necessary to remind the reader of the description of the seven ages of man in Shakespeare. As You Like It, Act II. sc. 7.

on the contrary, they dry up the waters: they also cause the alterations of the seas, when they recede, and return with a reflux. For at times, when the tide recedes on a sudden, an extensive line of shore occupies what is usually a wide gulf of sea; and in a short time afterwards, the waters are brought back, and there appears a sea, sailed over, not by shallow boats, but by ships of exceeding great burden.

And they also give increase and perfection to all the terrestrial animals and plants which produce fruit, endowing each with a nature to last a long time, so that new plants may flourish and come to maturity;—the old ones having passed away, in order to provide an abundant supply of necessary things.

XXXIX. (114) Moreover, the constellation Ursa Major, which men call the guide of mariners, consists of seven stars, which the pilots keeping in view, steer in innumerable paths across the sea, directing their endeavours towards an incredible task, beyond the capacity of human intellect. For it is through conjectures, directed by the aforementioned stars, that they have discovered countries which were previously unknown; those who dwell on the continent having discovered islands, and islanders having found out continents. For it was fitting that the recesses both of earth and sea should be revealed to that God-loving animal, the race of mankind, by the purest of essences, namely heaven.

(115) And besides the stars above mentioned the band of the Pleiades is also made up of seven stars, the rising and occultation of which are the causes of great benefits to all men. For when they set, the furrows are ploughed up for the purpose of sowing; and when they are about to rise, they bring glad tidings of harvest; and after they have arisen, they awaken the rejoicing husbandman to the collection of their necessary food. And they with joy store up their food for their daily use. (116) And the sun, the ruler of the day, making two equinoxes every year, both in spring and autumn, the spring equinox in the constellation of Aries, and the autumnal one in Libra, gives the most evident demonstration possible of the divine dignity of the number seven. For each of the equinoxes takes place in the seventh month, at which time men are expressly commanded by law to celebrate the greatest and most popular and comprehensive festivals; since it is owing to both these seasons, that all the fruits of the earth are engendered and brought to perfection; the fruit of corn, and all other things which are sown, being owing to the vernal equinox; and that of the vine, and of all the other plants which bear hard berries, of which there are great numbers, to the autumnal one.

XL. (117) And since all the things on the earth depend upon the heavenly bodies according to a certain natural sympathy, it is in heaven too that the ratio of the number seven began, and from thence it descended to us also, coming down to visit the race of mortal men. And so again, besides the dominant part of our mind, our soul is divided into seven divisions; there being five senses, and besides them the vocal organ, and after that the generative power. All which things, like the puppets in a raree show, which are moved by strings by the manager, are at one time quiet, and at another time in motion, each according to its suitable habits and capacities of motion.

(118) And in the same way, if any one were to set about investigating the different parts of the body, in both their interior and the exterior arrangement, he will in each case find seven divisions. Those which are visible are as follow;—the head, the chest, the belly, two arms, and two legs; the internal parts, or the entrails, as they are called, are the stomach, the heart, the lungs, the spleen, the liver, and the two kidneys. (119) Again, the principal and dominant part in an animal is the head, and that has seven most necessary divisions: two eyes, an equal number of ears, two channels for the nostrils, and the mouth to make up seven, through which as Plato says, mortal things find their entrance, and immortal things their exit. For into the mouth do enter meat and drink, perishable food of a perishable body; but from out of it proceed words—the immortal laws of an immortal soul, by means of which rational life is regulated.

XLI. (120) Again, the things which are judged of by the best of the senses, sight, partake of number according to their kind. For the things which are seen are seven; body, distance, shape, magnitude, colour, motion, tranquillity, and besides these there is nothing. (121) It also happens that all the changes of the voice amount to seven; the acute, the grave, the contracted, in the fourth place the aspirated sound, the fifth is the tone, the sixth the long, the seventh the short sound.

(122) There are also seven motions; the motion upwards, the motion downwards, that to the right, that to the left, the forward motion, the backward motion, and the rotatory motion, as is most especially shown by those who exhibit dances. (123) It is affirmed also that the secretions of the body are performed in the aforesaid number of seven. For tears are poured out through the eyes, and the purifications of the head through the nostrils, and through the mouth the saliva which is spit out; there are, besides two other channels for the evacuation of the superfluities of the body, the one being placed in front and the other behind; the sixth mode of evacuation is the effusion of perspiration over the whole body, and the seventh that most natural exercise of the generative powers. (124) Again, in the case of women, the flux called the catamenia, is usually carried on for seven days. Also, children in the womb receive life at the end of seven months, so that a very

extraordinary thing happens: for children who are born at the end of the seventh month live, while those who are born at the expiration of the eighth month are altogether incapable of surviving.

(125) Again, the dangerous diseases of the body, especially when lasting fevers, arising from the distemperature of the powers within us, attack us, are usually decided about the seventh day. For that day determines the contest for life, allotting safety to some men, and death to others.

XLII. (126) And the power of this number does not exist only in the instances already mentioned, but it also pervades the most excellent of the sciences, the knowledge of grammar and music. For the lyre with seven strings, bearing a proportion to the assemblage of the seven planets, perfects its admirable harmonies, being almost the chief of all instruments which are conversant about music. And of the elements of grammar, those which are properly called vowels are, correctly speaking, seven in number, since they can be sounded by themselves, and when they are combined with other letters, they make complete sounds; for they fill up the deficiency existing in semi-vowels, making the sounds whole; and they change and alter the natures of the mutes inspiring them with their own power, in order that what has no sound may become endowed with sound. (127) On which account it appears to me that they also originally gave letters their names, and acting as became wise men, did give the name to the number seven from the respect[8] they had for it, and from regard to the dignity inherent in it. But the Romans, adding the letter S, which had been omitted by the Greeks, show still more conspicuously the correct etymological meaning of the word, calling it *septem,* as derived from *semnos,* venerable, as has been said before, and from *sebasmos,* veneration.

XLIII. (128) These things, and more still are said in a philosophical spirit about the number seven, on account of which it has received the highest honours, in the highest nature. And it is honoured by those of the highest reputation among both Greeks and barbarians, who devote themselves to mathematical sciences. It was also greatly honoured by Moses, a man much attached to excellence of all sorts, who described its beauty on the most holy pillars of the law, and wrote it in the hearts of all those who were subject to him, commanding them at the end of each period of six days to keep the seventh holy; abstaining from all other works which are done in the seeking after and providing the means of life, devoting that day to the single object of philosophizing with a view to the improvement of their morals, and the examination

of their consciences: for conscience being seated in the soul as a judge, is not afraid to reprove men, sometimes employing pretty vehement threats; at other times by milder admonitions, using threats in regard to matters where men appear to be disobedient, of deliberate purpose, and admonitions when their offences seem involuntary, through want of foresight, in order to prevent their hereafter offending in a similar manner.

XLIV. (129) So Moses, summing up his account of the creation of the world, says in a brief style, "This is the book of the creation of the heaven and of the earth, when it took place, in the day on which God made the heaven and the earth, and every green herb before it appeared upon the earth, and all the grass of the field before it sprang up." Does he not here manifestly set before us incorporeal ideas perceptible only by the intellect, which have been appointed to be as seals of the perfected works, perceptible by the outward senses. For before the earth was green, he says that this same thing, verdure, existed in the nature of things, and before the grass sprang up in the field, there was grass though it was not visible. (130) And we must understand in the case of every thing else which is decided on by the external senses, there were elder forms and motions previously existing, according to which the things which were created were fashioned and measured out. For although Moses did not describe everything collectively, but only a part of what existed, as he was desirous of brevity, beyond all men that ever wrote, still the few things which he has mentioned are examples of the nature of all, for nature perfects none of those which are perceptible to the outward senses without an incorporeal model.

XLV. (131) Then, preserving the natural order of things, and having a regard to the connection between what comes afterwards and what has gone before, he says next, "And a fountain went up from the earth and watered the whole face of the earth." For other philosophers affirm that all water is one of the four elements of which the world was composed. But Moses, who was accustomed to contemplate and comprehend matters with a more acute and far-sighted vision, considers thus: the vast sea is an element, being a fourth part of the entire universe, which the men after him denominated the ocean, while they look upon the smaller seas which we sail over in the light of harbours. And he drew a distinction between the sweet and drinkable water and that of the sea, attributing the former to the earth, and considering it a portion of the earth, rather than of the ocean, on account of the reason which I have already mentioned, that is to say, that the earth may be held together by the sweet qualities of the water as by a chain; the water acting in the manner of glue. For if the earth were left entirely dry, so that no moisture arose

---

[8] The word used is *sebasmos,* as if *hebdomas* were derived from that; and the Romans formed *septem* from *hepta,* by the addition of *s.*

and penetrated through its holes rising to the surface in various directions, it would split. But now it is held together, and remains lasting, partly by the force of the wind which unites it, and partly because the moisture does not allow it to become dry, and so to be broken up into larger and smaller fragments.

(132) This is one reason; and we must also mention another, which is aimed at the truth like an arrow at a mark. It is not the nature of anything upon the earth to exist without a moist essence. And this is indicated by the throwing of seed, which is either moist, as the seed of animals, or else does not shoot up without moisture, such as the seeds of plants; from which it is evident that it follows that the aforesaid moist essence must be a portion of the earth which produces everything, just as the flux of the catamenia is a part of women. For by men who are learned in natural philosophy, this also is said to be the corporeal essence of children. (133) Nor is what we are about to say inconsistent with what has been said; for nature has bestowed upon every mother, as a most indispensable part of her conformation, breasts gushing forth like fountains, having in this manner provided abundant food for the child that is to be born. And the earth also, as it seems, is a mother, from which consideration it occurred to the early ages to call her Demetra, combining the names of mother (*mētēr*), and earth (*gē* or *dē*). For it is not the earth which imitates the woman, as Plato has said, but the woman who has imitated the earth which the race of poets has been accustomed with truth to call the mother of all things, and the fruit-bearer, and the giver of all things, since she is at the same time the cause of the generation and durability of all things, to the animals and plants. Rightly, therefore, did nature bestow on the earth as the eldest and most fertile of mothers, streams of rivers, and fountains like breasts, in order that the plants might be watered, and that all living things might have abundant supplies of drink.

XLVI. (134) After this, Moses says that "God made man, having taken clay from the earth, and he breathed into his face the breath of life." And by this expression he shows most clearly that there is a vast difference between man as generated now, and the first man who was made according to the image of God. For man as formed now is perceptible to the external senses, partaking of qualities, consisting of body and soul, man or woman, by nature mortal. But man, made according to the image of God, was an idea, or a genus, or a seal, perceptible only by the intellect, incorporeal, neither male nor female, imperishable by nature. (135) But he asserts that the formation of the individual man, perceptible by the external senses is a composition of earthy substance, and divine spirit. For that the body was created by the Creator taking a lump of clay, and fashioning the human form out of it; but that the soul proceeds from no created thing at all, but from the Father and Ruler of all things. For when he uses the expression, "he breathed into," etc., he means nothing else than the divine spirit proceeding from that happy and blessed nature, sent to take up its habitation here on earth, for the advantage of our race, in order that, even if man is mortal according to that portion of him which is visible, he may at all events be immortal according to that portion which is invisible; and for this reason, one may properly say that man is on the boundaries of a better and an immortal nature, partaking of each as far as it is necessary for him; and that he was born at the same time, both mortal and the immortal. Mortal as to his body, but immortal as to his intellect.

XLVII. (136) But the original man, he who was created out of the clay, the primeval founder of all our race, appears to me to have been most excellent in both particulars, in both soul and body, and to have been very far superior to all the men of subsequent ages from his pre-eminent excellence in both parts. For he in truth was really good and perfect. And one may form a conjecture of the perfection of his bodily beauty from three considerations, the first of which is this: when the earth was now but lately formed by its separation from that abundant quantity of water which was called the sea, it happened that the materials out of which the things just created were formed were unmixed, uncorrupted, and pure; and the things made from this material were naturally free from all imperfection. (137) The second consideration is that it is not likely that God made this figure in the present form of a man, working with the most sublime care, after he had taken the clay from any chance portion of earth, but that he selected carefully the most excellent clay of all the earth, of the pure material choosing the finest and most carefully sifted portion, such as was especially fit for the formation of the work which he had in hand. For it was an abode or sacred temple for a reasonable soul which was being made, the image of which he was about to carry in his heart, being the most God-like looking of images. (138) The third consideration is one which admits of no comparison with those which have been already mentioned, namely, this: the Creator was good both in other respects, and also in knowledge, so that every one of the parts of the body had separately the numbers which were suited to it, and was also accurately completed in the admirable adaptation to the share in the universe of which it was to partake. And after he had endowed it with fair proportions, he clothed it with beauty of flesh, and embellished it with an exquisite complexion, wishing, as far as was possible, that man should appear the most beautiful of beings.

XLVIII. (139) And that he is superior to all

these animals in regard of his soul, is plain. For God does not seem to have availed himself of any other animal existing in creation as his model in the formation of man; but to have been guided, as I have said before, by his own reason alone. On which account, Moses affirms that this man was an image and imitation of God, being breathed into in his face in which is the place of the sensations, by which the Creator endowed the body with a soul. Then, having placed the mind in the dominant part as king, he gave him as a body of satellites, the different powers calculated to perceive colours and sounds, and flavours and odours, and other things of similar kinds, which man could never have distinguished by his own resources without the sensations. And it follows of necessity that an imitation of a perfectly beautiful model must itself be perfectly beautiful, for the word of God surpasses even that beauty which exists in the nature which is perceptible only by the external senses, not being embellished by any adventitious beauty, but being itself, if one must speak the truth, its most exquisite embellishment.

XLIX. (140) The first man, therefore, appears to me to have been such both in his body and in his soul, being very far superior to all those who live in the present day, and to all those who have gone before us. For our generation has been from men: but he was created by God. And in the same proportion as the one Author of being is superior to the other, so too is the being that is produced. For as that which is in its prime is superior to that the beauty of which is gone by, whether it be an animal, or a plant, or fruit, or anything else whatever of the productions of nature; so also the first man who was ever formed appears to have been the height of perfection of our entire race, and subsequent generations appear never to have reached an equal state of perfection, but to have at all times been inferior both in their appearance and in their power, and to have been constantly degenerating, (141) which same thing I have also seen to be the case in the instance of the sculptors' and painters' art. For the imitations always fall short of the original models. And those works which are painted or fashioned from models must be much more inferior, as being still further removed from the original. And the stone which is called the magnet is subject to a similar deterioration. For any iron ring which touches it is held by it as firmly as possible, but another which only touches that ring is held less firmly. And the third ring hangs from the second, and the fourth from the third, and the fifth from the fourth, and so on one from another in a long chain, being all held together by one attractive power, but still they are not all supported in the same degree. For those which are suspended at a distance from the original attraction, are held more loosely, because the attractive power is weakened, and is no longer able to bind them in an equal degree.

And the race of mankind appears to be subject to an influence of the same kind, since in men the faculties and distinctive qualities of both body and soul are less vivid and strongly marked in each succeeding generation. (142) And we shall be only saying what is the plain truth, if we call the original founder of our race not only the first man, but also the first citizen of the world. For the world was his house and his city, while he had as yet no structure made by hands and wrought out of the materials of wood and stone. And in this world he lived as in his own country, in all safety, removed from any fear, inasmuch as he had been thought worthy of the dominion over all earthly things; and had everything that was mortal crouching before him, and taught to obey him as their master, or else constrained to do so by superior force, and living himself surrounded by all the joys which peace can bestow without a struggle and without reproach.

L. (143) But since every city in which laws are properly established, has a regular constitution, it became necessary for this citizen of the world to adopt the same constitution as that which prevailed in the universal world. And this constitution is the right reason of nature, which in more appropriate language is denominated law, being a divine arrangement in accordance with which everything suitable and appropriate is assigned to every individual. But of this city and constitution there must have been some citizens before man, who might be justly called citizens of a mighty city, having received the greatest imaginable circumference to dwell in; and having been enrolled in the largest and most perfect commonwealth. (144) And who could these have been but rational divine natures, some of them incorporeal and perceptible only by intellect, and others not destitute of bodily substance, such in fact as the stars? And he who associated with and lived among them was naturally living in a state of unmixed happiness. And being akin and nearly related to the ruler of all, inasmuch as a great deal of the divine spirit had flowed into him, he was eager both to say and to do everything which might please his father and his king, following him step by step in the paths which the virtues prepare and make plain, as those in which those souls alone are permitted to proceed who consider the attaining a likeness to God who made them as the proper end of their existence.

LI. (145) We have now then set forth the beauty of the first created man in both respects, in body and soul, if in a way much inferior to the reality, still to the extent of our power, and the best of our ability. And it cannot be but that his descendants, who all partake of his original character, must preserve some traces of their relationship to their father, though they may be but faint. And what is this relationship? (146) Every man in regard of his intellect is connected with divine reason, being an impression of, or a fragment or a ray of that blessed nature; but in regard of the structure of his body he is connected with the universal world. For he is composed of the same materials as the world, that is of earth, and water, and air and fire, each of the elements having contributed its appropriate part towards the completion of most sufficient materials, which the Creator was to take in order to fashion this visible image. (147) And, moreover, man dwells among all the things that have been just enumerated, as most appropriate places having the closest connection with himself, changing his abode, and going at different times to different places. So that one may say with the most perfect propriety that man is every kind of animal, terrestrial, aquatic, flying, and celestial. For inasmuch as he dwells and walks upon the earth he is a terrestrial animal; but inasmuch as he often dives and swims, and sails, he is an aquatic creature. And merchants and captains of ships and purple dyers, and all those who let down their nets for oysters and fish, are a very clear proof of what is here said. Again, inasmuch as his body is raised at times above the earth and uses high paths, he may with justice be pronounced a creature who traverses the air; and, moreover, he is a celestial animal, by reason of that most important of the senses, sight; being by it brought near the sun and moon, and each of the stars, whether planets or fixed stars.

LII. (148) And with great beauty Moses has attributed the giving of names to the different animals to the first created man, for it is a work of wisdom and indicative of royal authority, and man was full of intuitive wisdom and self-taught, having been created by the grace of God, and, moreover, was a king. And it is proper for a ruler to give names to each of his subjects. And, as was very natural, the power of domination was excessive in that first-created man, whom God formed with great care and thought worthy of the second rank in the creation, making him his own viceroy and the ruler of all other creatures. Since even those who have been born so many generations afterwards, when the race is becoming weakened by reason of the long intervals of time that have elapsed since the beginning of the world, do still exert the same power over the irrational beasts, preserving as it were a spark of the dominion and power which has been handed down to them by succession from their first ancestor.

(149) Accordingly, Moses says, that "God brought all the animals to man, wishing to see what names he would give to each." Not because he knew that he had formed in mortal man a rational nature capable of moving of its own accord, in order

that he might be free from all participation in vice. But he was now trying him as a master might try his pupil, stirring up the disposition which he had implanted in him; and moreover exciting him to a contemplation of his own works, that he might extemporise them names which should not be inappropriate nor unbecoming, but which should well and clearly display the peculiar qualities of the different subjects. (150) For as the rational nature was as yet uncorrupted in the soul, and as no weakness, or disease, or affliction had as yet come upon it, man having most pure and perfect perceptions of bodies and of things, devised names for them with great felicity and correctness of judgment, forming very admirable opinions as to the qualities which they displayed, so that their natures were at once perceived and correctly described by him. And he was so excellent in all good things that he speedily arrived at the very perfection of human happiness.

LIII. (151) But since nothing in creation lasts for ever, but all mortal things are liable to inevitable changes and alterations, it was unavoidable that the first man should also undergo some disaster. And the beginning of his life being liable to reproach, was his wife. For, as long as he was single, he resembled, as to his creation, both the world and God; and he represented in his soul the characteristics of the nature of each, I do not mean all of them, but such as a mortal constitution was capable of admitting. But when woman also was created, man perceiving a closely connected figure and a kindred formation to his own, rejoiced at the sight, and approached her and embraced her. (152) And she, in like manner, beholding a creature greatly resembling herself, rejoiced also, and addressed him in reply with due modesty. And love being engendered, and, as it were, uniting two separate portions of one animal into one body, adapted them to each other, implanting in each of them a desire of connection with the other with a view to the generation of a being similar to themselves. And this desire caused likewise pleasure to their bodies, which is the beginning of iniquities and transgressions, and it is owing to this that men have exchanged their previously immortal and happy existence for one which is mortal and full of misfortune.

LVI. (153) But while man was still living a solitary life, and before woman was created, the history relates that a paradise was planted by God in no respect resembling the parks which are seen among men now. For parks of our day are only lifeless woods, full of all kinds of trees, some evergreen with a view to the undisturbed delectation of the sight; others budding and germinating in the spring season, and producing fruit, some eatable by men, and sufficient, not only for the necessary support of nature as food, but also for the superfluous enjoyment of luxurious life; and some not eatable by men, but of necessity bestowed upon the beasts. But in the paradise, made by God, all the plants were endowed in the souls and reason, producing for their fruit the different virtues, and, moreover, imperishable wisdom and prudence, by which honourable and dishonourable things are distinguished from one another, and also a life free from disease, and exempt from corruption, and all other qualities corresponding to these already mentioned. (154) And these statements appear to me to be dictated by a philosophy which is symbolical rather than strictly accurate. For no trees of life or of knowledge have ever at any previous time appeared upon the earth, nor is it likely that any will appear hereafter. But I rather conceive that Moses was speaking in an allegorical spirit, intending by his paradise to intimate the dominant character of the soul, which is full of innumerable opinions as this figurative paradise was of trees. And by the tree of life he was shadowing out the greatest of the virtues—namely, piety towards the gods, by means of which the soul is made immortal; and by the tree which had the knowledge of good and evil, he was intimating that wisdom and moderation, by means of which things, contrary in their nature to one another, are distinguished.

LV. (155) Therefore, having laid down these to be boundaries as it were in the soul, God then, like a judge, began to consider to which side men would be most inclined by nature. And when he saw that the disposition of man had a tendency to wickedness, and was but little inclined to holiness or piety, by which qualities an immortal life is secured, he drove them forth as was very natural, and banished him from paradise; giving no hope of any subsequent restoration to his soul which had sinned in such a desperate and irremediable manner. Since even the opportunity of deceit was blameable in no slight degree, which I must not pass over in this place.

(156) It is said that the old poisonous and earthborn reptile, the serpent, uttered the voice of a man. And he on one occasion coming to the wife of the first created man, reproached her with her slowness and her excessive prudence, because she delayed and hesitated to gather the fruit which was completely beautiful to look at, and exceedingly sweet to enjoy, and was, moreover, most useful as being a means by which men might be able to distinguish between good and evil. And she, without any inquiry, prompted by an unstable and rash mind, acquiesced in his advice, and ate of the fruit, and gave a portion of it to her husband. And this conduct suddenly changed both of them from innocence and simplicity of character to all kinds of wickedness; at which the Father of all was indignant. For their actions deserved his anger, inasmuch as they, passing by the tree of eternal life, the tree which might have endowed them with perfection of virtue, and by means of which they might

have enjoyed a long and happy life, preferred a brief and mortal (I will not call it life, but) time full of unhappiness; and, accordingly, he appointed them such punishment as was befitting.

LVI. (157) And these things are not mere fabulous inventions, in which the race of poets and sophists delights, but are rather types shadowing forth some allegorical truth, according to some mystical explanation. And any one who follows a reasonable train of conjecture, will say with great propriety, that the aforesaid serpent is the symbol of pleasure, because in the first place he is destitute of feet, and crawls on his belly with his face downwards. In the second place, because he uses lumps of clay for food. Thirdly, because he bears poison in his teeth, by which it is his nature to kill those who are bitten by him. (158) And the man devoted to pleasure is free from none of the aforementioned evils; for it is with difficulty that he can raise his head, being weighed down and dragged down, since intemperance trips him up and keeps him down. And he feeds, not on heavenly food, which wisdom offers to contemplative men by means of discourses and opinions; but on that which is put forth by the earth in the varying seasons of the year, from which arise drunkenness and voracity, and licentiousness, breaking through and inflaming the appetites of the belly, and enslaving them in subjection to gluttony, by which they strengthen the impetuous passions, the seat of which is beneath the belly; and make them break forth. And they lick up the result of the labours of cooks and tavern-keepers; and at times some of them in ecstasy with the flavour of the delicious food, move about his head and reach forward, being desirous to participate in the sight. And when he sees an expensively furnished table, he throws himself bodily upon the delicacies which are abundantly prepared, and devotes himself to them, wishing to be filled with them all together, and so to depart, having no other end in view than that he should allow nothing of such a sumptuous preparation to be wasted. Owing to which conduct, he too, carries about poison in his teeth, no less than the serpent does; (159) for his teeth are the ministers and servants of his insatiability, cutting up and smoothing everything which has a reference to eating, and committing them, in the first place to the tongue, which decides upon, and distinguishes between the various flavours, and, subsequently, to the larynx. But immoderate indulgence in eating is naturally a poisonous and deadly habit, inasmuch as what is so devoured is not capable of digestion, in consequence of the quantity of additional food which is heaped in on the top of it, and arrives before what was previously eaten is converted into juice.

(160) And the serpent is said to have uttered a human voice, because pleasure employs innumerable champions and defenders who take care

to advocate its interests, and who dare to assert that the power over everything, both small and great, does of right belong to it without any exception whatever.

LVII. (161) Now, the first approaches of the male to the female have a pleasure in them which brings on other pleasures also, and it is through this pleasure that the formation and generation of children is carried on. And what is generated by it appears to be attached to nothing rather than to it, since they rejoice in pleasure, and are impatient at pain, which is its contrary. On which account even the infant when first brought forth cries, being as it seems in pain at the cold. For coming forth on a sudden into the air from a very warm, and indeed, hot region—namely, the womb, in which it has been abiding a considerable time, the air being a cold place and one to which it is wholly unaccustomed, it is alarmed, and pours forth tears as the most evident proof of its grief and of its impatience at pain. (162) For every animal, it is said, hastens to pleasure as to the cud which is most indispensable and necessary to its very existence; and, above all other animals, this is the case with man. For other animals pursue pleasure only in taste and in the acts of generation; but man aims at it by means of his other senses also, devoting himself to whatever sights or sounds can impart pleasure to his eyes or ears. (163) And many other things are said in the way of praise of this inclination, especially that it is one most peculiar and kindred to all animals.

LVIII. But what has been already said is sufficient to show what the reasons were on account of which the serpent appears to have uttered a human voice. And it is on this account that Moses appears to me in the particular laws also which he issued in the respect to animals, deciding what were proper to be eaten, and what were not, to have given especial praise to the animal called the serpent fighter. This is a reptile with jointed legs above its feet, by which it is able to leap and to raise itself on high, in the same manner as the tribe of locusts. (164) For the serpent fighter appears to me to be no other than temperance expressed under a symbolical figure, waging an interminable and unrelenting warfare against intemperance and pleasure. For temperance especially embraces economy and frugality, and pares down the necessities to a small number, preferring a life of austerity and dignity. But intemperance is devoted to extravagance and superfluity, which are the causes of luxury and effeminacy to both soul and body, and to which it is owing that in the opinion of wise men life is but a faulty thing, and more miserable than death.

LIX. (165) But its juggleries and deceits pleasure does not venture to bring directly to the man, but first offers them to the woman, and by her means to the man; acting in a very natural and saga-cious manner. For in human beings the mind occupies the rank of the man, and the sensations that of the woman. And pleasure joins itself to and associates itself with the sensations first of all, and then by their means cajoles also the mind, which is the dominant part. For, after each of the senses have been subjected to the charms of pleasure, and has learnt to delight in what is offered to it, the sight being fascinated by varieties of colours and shapes, the hearing by harmonious sounds, the taste by the sweetness of flowers, and the smell by the delicious fragrance of the odours which are brought before it, these all having received these offerings, like handmaids, bring them to the mind as their master, leading with them persuasion as an advocate, to warn it against rejecting any of them whatever. And the mind being immediately caught by the bait, becomes a subject instead of a ruler, and a slave instead of a master, and an exile instead of a citizen, and a mortal instead of an immortal. (166) For we must altogether not be ignorant that pleasure, being like a courtesan or mistress, is eager to meet with a lover, and seeks for panders in order by their means to catch a lover. And the sensations are her panders, and conciliate love to her, and she employing them as baits, easily brings the mind into subjection to her. And the sensations conveying within the mind the things which have been seen externally, explain and display the forms of each of them, setting their seal upon a similar affection. For the mind is like wax, and receives the impressions of appearances through the sensations, by means of which it makes itself master of the body, which of itself it would not be able to do, as I have already said.

LX. (167) And those who have previously become the slaves of pleasure immediately receive the wages of this miserable and incurable passion. For the woman having received vehement pains, partly in her travail, and partly such as are a rapid succession of agonies during the other portions of her life, and especially with reference to the bringing forth and bringing up of her children, to their diseases and their health, to their good or evil fortune, to an extent that utterly deprives her of her freedom and subjects her to the dominion of the man who is her companion, finds it unavoidable to obey all his commands. And the man in his turn endures toils and labours, and continual sweats, in order to the providing of himself with necessaries, and he also bears the deprivation of all those spontaneous good things which the earth was originally taught to produce without requiring the skill of the farmer, and he is subjected to a state in which he lives in incessant labour, for the purpose of seeking for food and means of subsistence, in order to avoid perishing by hunger.

(168) For I think that as the sun and the moon do continually give light, ever since they were originally commanded to do so at the time of the orig-

inal creation of the universe, and as they constantly obey the divine injunction, for the sake of no other reason but because evil and disobedience are banished to a distance far from the boundaries of heaven: so in the same way would the fertile and productive regions of the earth yield an immense abundance in the various seasons of the year, without any skill or co-operation on the part of the husbandman. But at present the ever-flowing fountains of the graces of God have been checked, from the time when wickedness began to increase faster than the virtues, in order that they might not be supplying men who were unworthy to be benefited by them. (169) Therefore, the race of mankind, if it had met with strict and befitting justice, must have been utterly destroyed, because of its ingratitude to God its benefactor and its Saviour. But God, being merciful by nature, took pity upon them, and moderated their punishment. And he permitted the race to continue to exist, but he no longer gave them food as he had done before from ready prepared stores, lest if they were under the dominion of his evils, satiety and idleness, they should become unruly and insolent.

LXI. (170) Such is the life of those who originally were men of innocence and simplicity, and also of those who have come to prefer vice to virtue, from whom one ought to keep aloof. And in his beforementioned account of the creation of the world, Moses teaches us also many other things, and especially five most beautiful lessons which are superior to all others. In the first place, for the sake of convicting the atheists, he teaches us that the Deity has a real being and existence. Now, of the atheists, some have only doubted of the existence of God, stating it to be an uncertain thing; but others, who are more audacious, have taken courage, and asserted positively that there is no such thing; but this is affirmed only by men who have darkened the truth with fabulous inventions.

(171) In the second place he teaches us that God is one; having reference here to the assertors of the polytheistic doctrine; men who do not blush to transfer that worst of evil constitutions, ochlocracy, from earth to heaven.

Thirdly, he teaches, as has been already related, that the world was created; by this lesson refuting those who think that it is uncreated and eternal, and who thus attribute no glory to God.

In the fourth place we learn that the world also which was thus created is one, since also the Creator is one, and he, making his creation to resemble himself in its singleness, employed all existing essence in the creation of the universe. For it would not have been complete if it had not been made and composed of all parts which were likewise whole and complete. For there are some persons who believe that there are many worlds, and some who even fancy that they are boundless in extent, being themselves inexperienced and ignorant of the truth of those things of which it is desirable to have a correct knowledge.

The fifth lesson that Moses teaches us is, that God exerts his providence for the benefit of the world. (172) For it follows of necessity that the Creator must always care for that which he has created, just as parents do also care for their children. And he who has learnt this not more by hearing it than by his own understanding, and has impressed on his own soul these marvellous facts which are the subject of so much contention—namely, that God has a being and existence, and that he who so exists is really one, and that he has created the world, and that he has created it one as has been stated, having made it like to himself in singleness; and that he exercises a continual care for that which he has created will live a happy and blessed life, stamped with the doctrines of piety and holiness.

ALLEGORICAL INTERPRETATION, I†

(Legum Allegoriae, I)

I. (1) "And the heaven and the earth and all their world was completed."[1] Having previously related the creation of the mind and of sense, Moses now proceeds to describe the perfection which was brought about by them both. And he says that neither the indivisible mind nor the particular sensations received perfection, but only ideas, one the idea of the mind, the other of sensation. And, speaking symbolically, he calls the mind heaven, since the natures which can only be comprehended by the intellect are in heaven. And sensation he calls earth, because it is sensation which has obtained a corporeal and somewhat earthy constitution. The ornaments of the mind are all the incorporeal things, which are perceptible only by the intellect. Those of sensation are the corporeal things, and everything in short which is perceptible by the external senses.

II. (2) "And on the sixth day God finished his work which he had made." It would be a sign of great simplicity to think that the world was created in six days, or indeed at all in time; because all time is only the space of days and nights, and these things the motion of the sun as he passes over the earth and under the earth does necessarily make. But the sun is a portion of heaven, so that one must confess that time is a thing posterior to the world. Therefore it would be correctly said that the world was not created in time, but that time had its existence in consequence of the world. For it is the motion of the heaven that has displayed the nature of time.

(3) When, therefore, Moses says, "God completed his works on the sixth day," we must understand that he is speaking not of a number of days, but that he takes six as a perfect number. Since it is the first number which is equal in its parts, in the half, and the third and sixth parts, and since it is produced by the multiplication of two unequal factors, two and three. And the numbers two and three exceed the incorporeality which exists in the unit; because the number two is an image of matter being divided into two parts and dissected like matter. And the number three is an image of a solid body, because a solid can be divided according to

a threefold division. (4) Not but what it is also akin to the motions of organic animals. For an organic body is naturally capable of motion in six directions, forward, backwards, upwards, downwards, to the right, and to the left. And at all events he desires to show that the races of mortal, and also of all the immortal beings, exist according to their appropriate numbers; measuring mortal beings, as I have said, by the number six, and the blessed and immortal beings by the number seven. (5) First, therefore, having desisted from the creation of mortal creatures on the seventh day, he began the formation of other and more divine beings.

III. For God never ceases from making something or other; but, as it is the property of fire to burn, and of snow to chill, so also it is the property of God to be creating. And much more so, in proportion as he himself is to all other beings the author of their working. (6) Therefore the expression, "he caused to rest," is very appropriately employed here, not "he rested." For he makes things to rest which appear to be producing others, but which in reality do not effect anything; but he himself never ceases from creating. On which account Moses says, "He caused to rest the things which he had begun." For all the things that are made by our arts when completed stand still and remain; but all those which are accomplished by the knowledge of God are moved at subsequent times. For their ends are the beginnings of other things; as, for instance, the end of day is the beginning of night. And in the same way we must look upon months and years when they come to an end as the beginning of those which are just about to follow them. (7) And so the generation of other things which are destroyed, and the destruction of others which are generated is completed, so that that is true which is said that—

And nought that is created wholly dies;
But one thing parted and combined with others
Produces a fresh form.

IV. (8) But nature delights in the number seven. For there are seven planets, going in continual opposition to the daily course of the heaven which always proceeds in the same direction. And likewise the constellation of the Bear is made up of seven stars, which constellation is the cause of communication and unity among men, and not merely of traffic. Again, the periodical changes of

---

†Yonge's title, *The First Book of the Treatise on The Allegories of the Sacred Laws, after the Work of the Six Days of Creation.*
[1]Genesis 2:1.

the moon, take place according to the number seven, that star having the greatest sympathy with the things on earth. And the changes which the moon works in the air, it perfects chiefly in accordance with its own configurations on each seventh day. (9) At all events, all mortal things, as I have said before, drawing their more divine nature from the heaven, are moved in a manner which tends to their preservation in accordance with this number seven. For who is there who does not know that those infants who are born at the end of the seventh month are likely to live, but those who have taken a longer time, so as to have abided eight months in the womb, are for the most part abortive births? (10) And they say that man is a reasoning being in his first seven years, by which time he is a competent interpreter of ordinary nouns and verbs, making himself master of the faculty of speaking. And in his second period of seven years, he arrives at the perfection of his nature; and this perfection is the power of generating a being like himself; for at about the age of fourteen we are able to beget a creature resembling ourselves. Again, the third period of seven years is the termination of his growth; for up to the age of one and twenty years man keeps on increasing in size, and this time is called by many maturity.

(11) Again, the irrational portion of the soul is divisible into seven portions; the five senses, and the organ of speech, and the power of generation. (12) Again, the motions of the body are seven; the six organic motions, and the rotatory motion.

Also the entrails are seven—the stomach, the heart, the spleen, the liver, the lungs, and the two kidneys.

In like manner the limbs of the body amount to an equal number—the head, the neck, the chest, the two hands, the belly, the two feet. Also the most important part of the animal, the face, is divisible according to a sevenfold division—the two eyes, and the two ears, and as many nostrils, and in the seventh place, the mouth.

(13) Again, the secretions are seven—tears, mucus from the nose, saliva, the generative fluid, the two excremental discharges, and the sweat that proceeds from every part of the body.

Moreover, in diseases the seventh day is the most critical period—and in women the catamenial purifications extend to the seventh day.

V. (14) And the power of this number has extended also to the most useful of the arts—namely, to grammar. At all events, in grammar, the most excellent of the elements, and those which have the most powers, are the seven vowels. And likewise in music, the lyre with seven strings is nearly the best of all instruments; because the euharmonic principle which is the most dignified of all the principles of melody, is especially perceived in connection with it.

Again, it happens that the tones of the voice are seven—the acute, the grave, the contracted, the aspirate, the lene, the long and the short sound. (15) The number seven is also the first number which is compounded of the perfect number, that is to say of six, and of the unit. And in some sense the numbers which are below ten are either generated by, or do themselves generate those numbers which are below ten, and the number ten itself. But the number seven neither generates any of the numbers below ten, nor is it generated by any of them. On which account the Pythagoreans compare this number to the Goddess always a virgin who was born without a mother,[2] because it was not generated by any other, and will not generate any other.

VI. (16) "Accordingly, on the seventh day, God caused to rest from all his works which he had made."[3] Now, the meaning of this sentence is something of this kind. God ceases from forming the races of mortal creatures when he begins to create the divine races, which are akin to the nature of the number seven. And the reference which is here contained to their moral character is of the following nature. When that reason which is holy in accordance with the number seven has entered into the soul the number six is then arrested, and all the mortal things which this number appears to make.

VII. (17) "And God blessed the seventh day, and hallowed it." God blesses the manners which are formed in accordance with the seventh and divine light, as being truly light, and immediately declares them holy. For that which is blessed, and that which is holy, are closely connected with one another. On this account he says, concerning him who has vowed a great vow, that "If a sudden change comes over him, and pollutes his mind, he shall no longer be holy."[4]

But the previous days were not taken into the calculation, as was natural. For those manners which are not holy are not counted, so that which is blessed is alone holy. (18) Correctly therefore, did Moses say that "God blessed the seventh day and hallowed it," because on it he "caused to rest from all his works which he had begun to make." And this is the reason why he who lives and conducts himself in accordance with the seventh and perfect light is blessed and holy, since it is in accordance with his nature, that the creation of mortal beings was terminated. For the case is thus: when

---

[2]*i.e.,* Minerva.
[3]Genesis 2:2.
[4]Numbers 6:9.

the light of virtue, which is brilliant and really divine, rises up, then the generation of the contrary nature is checked. And we have shown that God never desists from creating something, but that when he appears to do so he is only beginning the creation of something else; as being not only, the Creator, but also the Father of everything which exists.

VIII. (19) "This is the book of the generation of heaven and earth, when they were created."[5] This is perfect reason, which is put in motion in accordance with the number seven, being the beginning of the creation of that mind which was arranged according to the ideas, and also of the sensation arranged according to the ideas, and perceptible only by the intellect, if one can speak in such a manner. And Moses calls the word of God a book, in which it is come to pass that the formations of other things are written down and engraved. (20) But, lest you should imagine that the Deity does anything according to definite periods of time, while you should rather think that everything done by him is inscrutable in its nature, uncertain, unknown to, and incomprehensible by the race of mortal men. Moses adds the words, "when they were created," not defining the time when by any exact limitation, for what has been made by the Author of all things has no limitation. And in this way the idea is excluded, that the universe was created in six days.

IX. (21) "On which day God created the heaven and the earth, and every green herb of the field, before it appeared upon the earth, and all the grass of the field before it sprang up. For God did not rain upon the earth, and man did not exist to cultivate the earth." This day Moses has previously called a book, since at least he describes the generation of both heaven and earth in each place. For by his most conspicuous and brilliant word, by one command, God makes both things: the idea of mind, which, speaking symbolically, he calls heaven, and the idea of sensation, which by a sign he named earth. (22) And he likens the idea of mind, and the idea of sensation to two fields; for the mind brings forth fruit, which consists in having intellectual perception; and sensation brings forth other fruits which consist in perceiving by the agency of the external senses. And what he says has the following meaning;—as there was a previously existing idea of the particular mind, and also of the indivisible minds to serve as an archetype and model for either; and also a pre-existent idea of particular sensation, being, so to say, a sort of seal which gave impressions of forms, so before particular things perceptible only by the intellect had any existence, there was a pre-existent abstract

idea of what was perceptible only by intellect, by participation in which the other things also received their names; and before particular objects perceptible by the external senses, existed, there was also a generic something perceptible by the external senses, in accordance with a participation in which, the other things perceptible by the external senses were created.

(23) By "the green herb of the field," Moses means that portion of the mind which is perceptible only by intellect. For as in the field green things spring up and flourish, so also that which is perceptible only by the intellect is the fruit of the mind. Therefore, before the particular something perceptible only by intellect existed, God created the general something perceptible only by intellect, which also he correctly denominated the universe. For since the particular something perceptible only by intellect is incomplete, that is not the universe; but that which is generic is the universe, as being complete.

X. (24) "And all the grass of the field," he proceeds, "before it sprang up." That is to say, before the particular things perceptible by the external senses sprang up, there existed the generic something perceptible by the external senses through the fore-knowledge of the Creator, which he again called "the universe." And very naturally he likened the things perceptible by the external senses to grass. For as grass is the food of irrational animals, so also that which is perceptible by the external senses is assigned to the irrational portion of the soul. For why, when he has previously mentioned "the green herb of the field," does he add also "and all the grass," as if grass were not green at all? But the truth is, that by the green herb of the field, he means that which is perceptible by the intellect only, the budding forth of the mind. But grass means that which is perceptible by the external senses, that being likewise the produce of the irrational part of the soul.

(25) "For God did not rain upon the earth, and man did not exist to cultivate the earth," speaking in the strictest accordance with natural philosophy. For if God did not shed the perceptions of things subject to them, like rain upon the senses, in that case the mind too would not labour nor employ itself about sensation. For he himself would be unable to effect anything by himself, unless he were to pour forth, like rain or dew, colours upon the sight, and sounds upon the hearing, and flavour on the tastes, and on all the other senses, the things proper to produce the requisite effects. (26) But when God begins to rain sensation on the things perceptible by the external senses, then also the mind is perceived to act like the cultivator of fertile soil. But the idea of sensation, which he, speaking figuratively, has called the earth, is in no need of nourishment. But the nourishment of the

---

senses, are the particular objects perceptible by the external senses; and these objects are bodies. But an idea is a thing different from bodies.

Before, therefore, there existed any individual compound substances, God did not rain upon that idea of sensation to which he gave the name of the earth. And that means that he did not furnish it with any nourishment; for, indeed, it had altogether no need of any object perceptible by the external senses.

(27) But when Moses says, "And man did not exist to cultivate the earth," that means that the idea of intellect did not labour upon the idea of the sensations. For my intellect and yours work up the sensations by means of things perceptible by the external senses: but the idea of mind as must be the case while there is no individual body connected with it does not work upon the idea of sensation. For if it did so work, it would of course work by means of objects, perceptible by the external senses. But there is no such object in ideas.

XI. (28) "But a fountain went up upon the earth, and watered all the face of the earth." He here calls the mind the fountain of the earth, and the sensations he calls the face of the earth, because there is the most suitable place in the whole body for them, with reference to their appropriate energies, a place that nature which foreknows everything, has assigned to them. And the mind waters the sensations like a fountain, sending appropriate streams over each.

See now how all the powers of a living animal depend upon one another like a chain. For as the mind, and sensations, and the object perceptible by the external sense are three different things, the middle term is sensation; and the mind, and the object perceptible by the external sense, are the two extremes. (29) But the mind is unable to work; that is to say, to energize according to sensation, unless God rains upon and irrigates the object perceptible by the external senses, nor is there any advantage from the object perceptible to the external sense when watered, unless the mind, like a fountain, extending itself as far as the sensation, puts it in motion when it is quiet, and leads it on to a comprehension of the subject. So that the mind, and the object perceptible by the external senses, are always endeavouring to reciprocate with one another, the one the being subject to the sensations as a kind of material would be, and the mind stirring up the sensations toward the external object, as a workman would do, in order to create an appetite. (30) For a living animal is superior to that which is not a living animal in two points, imagination and appetite. Accordingly, imagination consists in the approach of the external object striking the mind by means of the sensations. And appetite is the brother of imagination, according to the intensive power of the mind,

which the mind keeps on the stretch, by means of the sensation, and so touches the subject matter, and comes over to it, being eager to arrive at and comprehend it.

XII. (31) "And God created man, taking a lump of clay from the earth, and breathed into his face the breath of life: and man became a living soul." The races of men are twofold; for one is the heavenly man, and the other the earthly man. Now the heavenly man, as being born in the image of God, has no participation in any corruptible or earth-like essence. But the earthly man is made of loose material, which he calls a lump of clay. On which account he says, not that the heavenly man was made, but that he was fashioned according to the image of God; but the earthly man he calls a thing made, and not begotten by the maker. (32) And we must consider that the man who was formed of earth, means the mind which is to be infused into the body, but which has not yet been so infused. And this mind would be really earthly and corruptible, if it were not that God had breathed into it the spirit of genuine life; for then it "exists," and is no longer made into a soul; and its soul is not inactive, and incapable of proper formation, but a really intellectual and living one. "For man," says Moses, "became a living soul."

XIII. (33) But some one may ask, why God thought an earth-born mind, which was wholly devoted to the body, worthy of divine inspiration, and yet did not treat the one made after his own idea and image in the same manner. In the second place he may ask, what is the meaning of the expression "breathed into." And thirdly, why he breathed into his face: fourthly also, why, since he knew the name of the Spirit when he says, "And the Spirit of God moved upon the face of the waters,"[6] he now speaks of breath, and not of the Spirit. (34) Now in reply to the first question we must say this one thing; God being very munificent gives his good things to all men, even to those who are not perfect; inviting them to a participation and rivalry in virtue, and at the same time displaying his abundant riches, and showing that it is sufficient for those also who will not be greatly benefited by it; and he also shows this in the most evident manner possible in other cases; for when he rains on the sea, and when he raises up fountains in desert places, and waters shallow and rough and unproductive land, making the rivers to overflow with floods, what else is he doing but displaying the great abundance of his riches and of his goodness? This is the cause why he has created no soul in such a condition as to be wholly barren of good, even if the employment of that good be beyond the reach of some people. (35) We must

---

[6]Genesis 1:2.

also give a second reason, which is this: Moses wished to represent all the actions of the Deity as just—therefore a man who had not had a real life breathed into him, but who was ignorant of virtue, when he was chastised for the sins which he had committed would say that he was punished unjustly, in that it was only through ignorance of what was good that he had erred respecting it; and that he was to blame who had not breathed any proper wisdom into him; and perhaps he will even say, that he has absolutely committed no offence whatever; since some people affirm that actions done involuntarily and in ignorance have not the nature of offences.

(36) Now the expression "breathed into" is equivalent to "inspired," or "gave life to" things inanimate: for let us take care that we are never filled with such absurdity as to think that God employs the organs of the mouth or nostrils for the purpose of breathing into anything; for God is not only devoid of peculiar qualities, but he is likewise not of the form of man, and the use of these words shows some more secret mystery of nature; (37) for there must be three things, that which breathes in, that which receives what is breathed in, and that which is breathed in. Now that which breathes in is God, that which receives what is breathed in is the mind, and that which is breathed in is the spirit. What then is collected from these three things? A union of the three takes place, through God extending the power, which proceeds from himself through the spirit, which is the middle term, as far as the subject. Why does he do this, except that we may thus derive a proper notion of him? (38) Since how could the soul have perceived God if he had not inspired it, and touched it according to his power? For human intellect would not have dared to mount up to such a height as to lay claim to the nature of God, if God himself had not drawn it up to himself, as far as it was possible for the mind of man to be drawn up, and if he had not formed it according to those powers which can be comprehended.

(39) And God breathed into man's face both physically and morally. Physically, when he placed the senses in the face: and this portion of the body above all others is vivified and inspired; and morally, in this manner, as the face is the dominant portion of the body, so also is the mind the dominant portion of the soul. It is into this alone that God breathes; but the other parts, the sensations, the power of speech, and the power of generation, he does not think worthy of his breath, for they are inferior in power. (40) By what then were these subordinate parts inspired? beyond all question by the mind; for of the qualities which the mind has received form God, it gives a share to the irrational portion of the soul, so that the mind is vivified by God, and the irrational part of

the soul by the mind; for the mind is as it were a god to the irrational part of the soul, for which reason Moses did not hesitate to call it "the god of Pharaoh."[7]

(41) For of all created things some are created by God, and through him: some not indeed by God, but yet through him: and the rest have their existence both by him and through him.

At all events Moses as he proceeds says, that God planted a paradise, and among the best things as made both by God and through God, is the mind. But the irrational part of the soul was made indeed by God but not through God, but through the reasoning power which bears rule and sovereignty in the soul; (42) and Moses has used the word "breath," not "spirit," as there is a difference between the two words; for spirit is conceived of according to strength, and intensity, and power; but breath is a gentle and moderate kind of breeze and exhalation; therefore the mind, which was created in accordance with the image and idea of God, may be justly said to partake in his spirit, for its reasoning has strength: but that which is derived from matter is only a partaker in a thin and very light air, being as it were a sort of exhalation, such as arises from spices; for they, although they be preserved intact, and are not exposed to fire or fumigation, do nevertheless emit a certain fragrance.

XIV. (43) "And God planted a paradise in Eden, in the east: and there he placed the man whom he had formed:"[8] for he called that divine and heavenly wisdom by many names; and he made it manifest that it had many appellations; for he called it the beginning, and the image, and the sight of God. And now he exhibits the wisdom which is conversant about the things of the earth (as being an imitation of this archetypal wisdom), in the plantation of this Paradise. For let not such impiety ever occupy our thoughts as for us to suppose that God cultivates the land and plants paradises, since if we were to do so, we should be presently raising the question of why he does so: for it could not be that he might provide himself with pleasant places of recreation and pastime, or with amusement. (44) Let not such fabulous nonsense ever enter our minds; for even the whole world would not be a worthy place or habitation for God, since he is a place to himself, and he himself is full of himself, and he himself is sufficient for himself, filling up and surrounding everything else which is deficient in any respect, or deserted, or empty; but he himself is surrounded by nothing else, as being himself one and the universe.

(45) God therefore sows and implants ter-

---

[7] Exodus 7:1.
[8] Genesis 2:8.

restrial virtue in the human race, being an imitation and representation of the heavenly virtue. For, pitying our race, and seeing that it is exposed to abundant and innumerable evils, he firmly planted terrestrial virtue as an assistant against and warder-off of the diseases of the soul; being, as I have said before, an imitation of the heavenly and archetypal wisdom which he calls by various names.

Now virtue is called a paradise metaphorically, and the appropriate place for the paradise is Eden; and this means luxury: and the most appropriate field for virtue is peace, and ease, and joy; in which real luxury especially consists. (46) Moreover, the plantation of this paradise is represented in the east; for right reason never sets, and is never extinguished, but it is its nature to be always rising. And as I imagine, the rising sun fills the darkness of the air with light, so also does virtue when it has arisen in the soul, irradiate its mist and dissipate the dense darkness. (47) "And there," says Moses, "he placed the man whom he had formed:" for God being good, and having formed our race for virtue, as his work which was most akin to himself, places the mind in virtue, evidently in order that it, like a good husband, may cultivate and attend to nothing else except virtue.

XV. (48) And some one may ask here, why, since it is a pious action to imitate the works of God, it is forbidden to me to plant a grove near the altar, and yet God plants a paradise? For Moses says, "You shall not plant a grove for yourself; you shall not make for yourself any tree which is near the altar of the Lord your God."[9] What then are we to say? That it is right for God to plant and to build up the virtues in the soul. (49) But the selfish and atheistical mind, thinking itself equal with God while it appears to be doing something, is found in reality to be rather suffering. And though God sows and plants good things in the soul, the mind which says, "I plant," is acting impiously. You shall not plant therefore where God is planting: but if, O mind, you fix plants in the soul, take care to plant only such trees as bear fruit, and not a grove; for in a grove there are trees of a character to bear cultivation, and also wild trees. But to plant vice, which is unproductive in the soul, along with cultivated and fertile virtue, is the act of a double-natured and confused leprosy. (50) If, however, you bring into the same place things which ought not to be mingled together, you must separate and disjoin them from the pure and incorrupt nature which is accustomed to make blameless offerings to God; and this is his altar; for it is inconsistent with this to say that there is any such thing as a work of the soul, when all things are referred to God, and to mingle barren things with those which

are productive; for this would be faulty: but they are blameless things which are offered to God. (51) If therefore you transgress any one of these laws, O soul! you will be injuring yourself, not God. On this account God says, "You shall not plant for yourself:" for no one works for God, and especially what is evil does not. And again, Moses adds: "You shall not make for yourself." And in another place he says, "You shall not make gods of silver with me, and you shall not make gods of gold for yourselves." For he who conceives either that God has any distinctive quality, or that he is not one, or that he is not uncreated and imperishable, or that he is not unchangeable, injures himself and not God. "For you shall not make them for yourselves," is what he says. For we must conceive that God is free from distinctive qualities, and imperishable, and unchangeable; and he who does not conceive thus of him is filling his own soul with false and atheistical opinions. (52) Do you not see that—even though God were to conduct us to virtue, and though when we had been thus conducted we were to plant no tree which was barren, but only such as produce fruit, he would still command us to purify its impurity, that is to say, the appearing to plant. For he here orders us to cut away vain opinions; and vain opinions are a thing impure by nature.

XVI. (53) "And the man whom he had formed," Moses says, "God placed in the Paradise,"[10] for the present only. Who, then, is he in reference to whom he subsequently says that "The Lord God took the man whom he had formed, and placed him in the Paradise to cultivate it and to guard it."[11] Must not this man who was created according to the image and idea of God have been a different man from the other, so that two men must have been introduced into the Paradise together, the one a fictitious man, and the other modelled after the image of God? (54) Therefore, the man modelled after the idea of God, is perceived not only amid the planting of the virtues, but, besides this, he is their cultivator and guardian; that is to say, he is mindful of the things which he has heard and practised. But the man who is factitious, neither cultivates the virtues, nor guards them, but is only introduced into opinions by the abundant liberality of God, being on the point of immediately becoming an exile from virtue. (55) Therefore, he calls that man whom he only places in Paradise, factitious; but him whom he appoints to be its cultivator and guardian he calls not factitious, but "the man whom he had made." And him he takes, but the other he casts out. And him whom he takes he thinks worthy of three things, of which

---

[9] Deuteronomy 16:21.

[10] Genesis 2:8.
[11] Genesis 2:15.

goodness of nature especially consists: namely, expertness, perseverance, and memory. Now, expertness is his position in Paradise; memory is the guarding and preservation of holy opinions; perseverance is the effecting of what is good, the performance of virtuous actions. But the factitious mind neither remembers what is good, nor does it, but is only expert, and nothing more; on which account, after it has been placed in Paradise, in a short time afterwards it runs away, and is cast out.

XVII. (56) "And God caused to rise out of the earth every tree which is pleasant to the sight and good for food, and the tree of life he raised in the middle of the Paradise, and also the tree of the knowledge of good and evil." He here gives a sketch of the trees of virtue which he plants in the soul. And these are the particular virtues, and the energies in accordance with them, and the good and successful actions, and the things which by the philosophers are called fitting; (57) these are the plants of the Paradise. Nevertheless, he describes the characteristics of these same trees, showing that that which is desirable to be beheld is likewise most excellent to be enjoyed. For of the arts some are theoretical and not practical, such as geometry and astronomy. Some, again, are practical and not theoretical, such as the art of the architect, of the smith, and all those which are called mechanical arts. But virtue is both theoretical and practical; for it takes in theory, since the road which leads to it is philosophy in three of its parts—the reasoning, and the moral, and the physical part. It also includes action; for virtue is art conversant about the whole of life; and in life all actions are exhibited. (58) Still, although it takes in both theory and practice, nevertheless it is most excellent in each particular. For the theory of virtue is thoroughly excellent, and its practice and observation is a worthy object to contend for. On which account Moses says that the tree was pleasant to the sight, which is a symbol of theoretical excellence; and likewise good for food, which is a token of useful and practical good.

XVIII. (59) But the tree of life is that most general virtue which some people call goodness; from which the particular virtues are derived, and of which they are composed. And it is on this account that it is placed in the centre of the Paradise; having the most comprehensive place of all, in order that, like a king, it may be guarded by the trees on each side of it. But some say that it is the heart that is meant by the tree of life; since that is the cause of life, and since that has its position in the middle of the body, as being, according to them, the dominant part of the body. But these men ought to be made aware that they are expounding a doctrine which has more reference to medical than to natural science. But we, as has been said before, affirm that by the tree of life is

meant the most general virtue. (60) And of this tree Moses expressly says, that it is placed in the middle of the paradise; but as to the other tree, that namely of the knowledge of good and evil, he has not specified whether it is within or outside of the Paradise; but after he has used the following expression, "and the tree of the knowledge of good and evil," he says no more, not mentioning where it is placed, in order that any one who is uninitiated in the principles of natural philosophy, may not be made to marvel at his knowledge.

(61) What then must we say? That this tree is both in the Paradise and also out of it. As to its essence, indeed, in it; but as to its power, out of it. How so? The dominant portion of us is capable of receiving everything, and resembles wax, which is capable of receiving every impression, whether good or bad. In reference to which fact, that supplanter Jacob makes a confession where he says, "all these things were made for me."[12] For the unspeakable formations and impression of all the things in the universe, are all borne forward into, and comprehended by the soul, which is only one. When, therefore that receives the impression of perfect virtue, it has become the tree of life; but when it has received the impression of vice, it has then become the tree of the knowledge of good and evil, and vice and all evil have been banished from the divine company. Therefore the dominant power which has received it is in the Paradise according to its essence; for there is in it that characteristic of virtue, which is akin to the Paradise. But again, according to its power it is not in it, because the form of virtue is inconsistent with the divine operations; (62) and what I here say, any one may understand in this manner. At this moment, the dominant part is in my body, according to its essence, but according to its power it is in Italy, or Sicily, when it applies its consideration to those countries, and in heaven when it is contemplating the heaven. On which principle it often happens that some persons who are in profane places, according to their essence, are in the most sacred places, thinking of those things which relate to virtue. And again, others who are in the temples of the gods, and profane in their minds, from the fact of their minds receiving a change for the worse, and evil impressions; so that vice is neither in the Paradise, nor not in it. For it is possible that it may be in it according to its essence, but it is not possible that it should be according to its power.

XIX. (63) "And a river goes forth out of Eden to water the Paradise. From thence it is separated into four heads: the name of the one is Pheison. That is the one which encircles the whole land of

---

[12]Genesis 42:36.

Evilat. There is the country where there is gold, and the gold of that land is good. There also are the carbuncle and the sapphire stone. And the name of the second river is Gihon; this is that which encircles the whole land of Ethiopia. And the third river is the Tigris. This is the river which flows in front of the Assyrians. And the fourth river is the Euphrates."[13] In these words Moses intends to sketch out the particular virtues. And they also are four in number, prudence, temperance, courage, and justice. Now the greatest river from which the four branches flow off, is generic virtue, which we have already called goodness; and the four branches are the same number of virtues. (64) Generic virtue, therefore, derives its beginning from Eden, which is the wisdom of God; which rejoices and exults, and triumphs, being delighted at and honoured on account of nothing else, except its Father, God, and the four particular virtues, are branches from the generic virtue, which like a river waters all the good actions of each, with an abundant stream of benefits.

(65) Let us examine the expressions of the writer: "A river," says he, "goes forth out of Eden, to water the Paradise." This river is generic goodness; and this issues forth out of the Eden of the wisdom of God, and that is the word of God. For it is according to the word of God, that generic virtue was created. And generic virtue waters the Paradise: that is to say, it waters the particular virtues. But it does not derive its beginnings from any principle of locality, but from a principle of pre-eminence. For each of the virtues is really and truly a ruler and a queen. And the expression, "is separated," is equivalent to "is marked off by fixed boundaries;" since wisdom appoints them settled limits with reference to what is to be done. Courage with respect to what is to be endured; temperance with reference to what is to be chosen; and justice in respect of what is to be distributed.

XX. (66) "The name of one river is Pheison. This is that river which encircles all the land of Evilat; there is the country where there is gold. And the gold of that land is good; there also are the carbuncle and the sapphire stone." One of the four virtues is prudence, which Moses here calls Pheison: because the soul abstains,[14] from, and guards against, acts of iniquity. And it meanders in a circle, and flows all round the land of Evilat; that is to say, it preserves a mild, and gentle, and favourable constitution. And as of all fusible essences, the most excellent and the most illustrious is gold, so also the virtue of the soul which enjoys the highest reputation, is prudence. (67) And when he uses the expression, "that is the

country where there is gold," he is not speaking geographically, that is, where gold exists, but that is the country in which that valuable possession exists, brilliant as gold, tried in the fire, and valuable, namely, prudence. And this is confessed to be the most valuable possession of God.

But with reference to the geographical position of virtue, there are two personages, each invested with distinctive qualities. One, the being who has prudence, the other, the being who exerts it; and these he likens to the carbuncle and the emerald.

XXI. (68) "And the name of the second river is Gihon. This is that which encircles all the land of Ethiopia." Under the symbol of this river courage is intended. For the name of Gihon being interpreted means chest, or an animal which attacks with its horns; each of which interpretations is emblematical of courage. For courage has its abode about the chest, where also is the seat of the heart, and where man is prepared to defend himself. For courage is the knowledge of what is to be withstood, and of what is not to be withstood, and of what is indifferent. And it encircles and surrounds Ethiopia, making demonstrations of war against it; and the name of Ethiopia, being interpreted, means humiliation. And cowardice is a humiliating thing; but courage is adverse to humiliation and to cowardice.

(69) "And the third river is the Tigris; this is that which flows in front of Assyria." The third virtue is temperance, which resolutely opposes that kind of pleasure which appears to be the directress of human infirmity. For the translation of the name Assyrians in the Greek tongue is *euthynontes*, (directors). And he has likened desire to a tiger, which is the most untameable of beasts; it being desire about which temperance is conversant.

XXII. (70) It is worth while therefore to raise the question why courage has been spoken of as the second virtue, and temperance as the third, and prudence as the first; and why Moses has not also explained the course of action of the other virtues. Now we must understand that our soul is divided into three parts, and that it has one portion which is conversant about reason; another which is subject to passion; and another which is that in which the desires are conceived. And we find that the proper place and abode of the reasoning part of the soul, is the head; of the passionate part, the chest; and of the part in which the desires are conceived, the stomach. And we find that appropriate virtues are adapted to each of these parts. To the rational part, prudence; in it is the office of reason, to have a knowledge of what one might, and of what one ought not to do. And the virtue of the passionate part of the soul is courage: and of the appetitive part, temperance.

---

[13] Genesis 2:13.
[14] *Pheisōn* from *pheidomai*, to spare, or abstain from.

For it is through temperance that we remedy and cure the appetites. (71) For as the head is the principle and uppermost part of the animal, and the chest the next highest, and the liver the third, in point both of importance and of position; so in the soul again, the first is the rational part, the second the passionate part, and the third the appetitive part. In the same way again of the virtues; the first is that which is conversant about the first portion of the soul, which is the reasoning portion, and which at the same time has its abode in the head of the body; in short it is prudence. And the second of the virtues is courage, because it is conversant about the second portion of the soul, namely, about passion, and has its abode in the second portion of the body, namely, in the chest. And the third virtue is temperance, which is placed in the stomach which is the third portion of the body, and it is conversant about the appetitive part, which has been allotted the third part of the soul, as being its subject matter.

XXIII. (72) "And the fourth river," continues Moses, "is the river Euphrates." And this name Euphrates means fertility; and symbolically taken, it is the fourth virtue, namely, justice, which is most truly a productive virtue, and one which gladdens the intellect. When therefore does this happen? When the three parts of the soul are all in harmony with one another; and harmony among them is in reality the predominance of the most important; as for instance, when the two inferior parts, the passionate and the appetitive part, are disposed to yield to the superior part, then justice exists. For it is just that the better portion should rule at all times, and in all places, and that the inferior part should be ruled. Now the rational part is the better part, and the appetitive and the passionate parts are the inferior ones. (73) But when, on the contrary, passion and appetite get riotous and disobey the reins, and by the violence of their impetuosity throw off and disregard the charioteer, that is to say reason, and when each of these passions get hold of the reins themselves, then there is injustice. For it is inevitable, that through any ignorance or vice of the charioteer, the chariot must be borne down over precipices, and must fall into the abyss; just as it must be saved when the charioteer is endowed with skill and virtue.

XXIV. (74) Again, let us look at the subject in this way also. Pheison, being interpreted, is the change of the mouth; and Evilat means bringing forth, and by these two names prudence is signified. For people in general think a man prudent who is an inventor of sophistical expressions, and clever at explaining that which he has conceived in the mind. But Moses considered such an one a man fond of words, but by no means a prudent man. For in the changing of the mouth, that is to say of the power of speaking and explaining one's

ideas, prudence is seen. And prudence is not a certain degree of acuteness in speech, but ability which is beheld in deeds and in serious actions. (75) And prudence surrounds Evilat, which is in travail, as it were with a wall, in order to besiege it and destroy it. And "bringing forth," is an especially appropriate name for folly, because the foolish mind, being always desirous of what is unattainable, is at all times in travail. When it is desirous of money it is in labour, also when it thirsts for glory, or when it is covetous of pleasure, or of any thing else. (76) But, though always in labour, it never brings forth. For the soul of the worthless man is not calculated by nature to bring any thing to perfection which is likely to live. But every thing which it appears to bring forth is found to be abortive and immature. "Eating up the half of its flesh, and being like a death of the soul."[15] On which account that holy word Aaron entreats the pious Moses, who was beloved by God, to heal the leprosy of Miriam, in order that her soul might not be occupied in the labour of bringing forth evil things. And in consequence he says: "Let her not become like unto death, as an abortion proceeding out of the womb of her mother, and let her not devour the half of her own flesh."[16]

XXV. (77) "That," says Moses, "is the country, where there is gold." He does not say that that is the only place where there is gold, but simply that is the country where there is gold. For prudence which he likened to gold, being of a nature free from deceit, and pure, and tried in the fire, and thoroughly tested, and honourable, exists there in the wisdom of God. And being there, it is not a possession of wisdom, but something belonging to the God who is its creator and owner, whose work and possession this wisdom likewise is. (78) "And the gold of that land is good." Is there, then, any other gold which is not good? Beyond all doubt; for the nature of prudence is twofold, there being one prudence general, and another particular. Therefore, the prudence that is in me, being particular prudence, is not good; for when I perish that also will perish together with me; but general or universal prudence, the abode of which is the wisdom of God and the house of God, is good; for it is imperishable itself, and dwells in an imperishable habitation.

XXVI. (79) "There also is the carbuncle and the emerald." The two beings endowed with distinctive qualities, the prudent man and the man who acts prudently, differ from one another; one of them existing according to prudence, and the other acting wisely according to the rules of wisdom. For it is on account of these two beings thus

---

[15] Numbers 12:12.
[16] Numbers 12:13.

endowed with distinctive qualities God implanted prudence and virtue in the earth-born man. For what would have been the use of it, if there had been no reasoning powers in existence to receive it, and to give impressions of its form? So that virtue is very properly conjoined with prudence, and the prudent man is rightly joined with him who displays prudence in his actions; the two being like two precious stones. (80) And may not they be Judah and Issachar? For the man who puts in practice the prudence of God confesses himself to be bound to feel gratitude, and to feel it towards him who has given him what is good without grudging; and he also does honourable and virtuous actions. Accordingly Judah is the symbol of a man who makes this confession "in respect of whom Leah ceased from child-bearing."[17] But Issachar is the symbol of the man who does good actions, "For he put forth[18] his shoulder to labour and became a man tilling the earth." With respect to whom Moses says, hire is in his soul after he has been sown and planted, so that his labour is not imperfect, but is rather crowned and honoured with a reward by God.

(81) And that he is making mention of these things, he shows when speaking on other subjects; when describing the garment, which reached to the feet he says, "And thou shalt weave in it sets of stones in four rows. The row of stones shall be the sardine stone, the topaz, and the emerald are the first row." Reuben, Simeon, and Levi are here meant. "And the second row," he says, "are the carbuncle and the sapphire."[19] And the sapphire is the same as the green stone. And in the carbuncle was inscribed the name of Judah, for he was the fourth son: and in the sapphire the name of Issachar. (82) Why then as he had called the sapphire the green stone, did he not also speak of the red stone? Because Judah, as the type of a disposition inclined to confession, is a being immaterial and incorporeal. For the very name of confession (*exomologēseōs*) shows that it is a thing external to (*ektos*) himself. For when the mind is beside itself, and bears itself upward to God, as the laughter of Isaac did, then it makes a confession to him who alone has a real being. But as long as it considers itself as the cause of something, it is a long way from yielding to God, and confession to him. For this very act of confessing ought to be considered as being the work not of the soul, but of God who teaches it this feeling of gratitude. Accordingly Judah, who practises confession, is an immaterial being.

(83) But Issachar who came forth out of labour

is in need of corporeal matter; since if it were otherwise how could a studious man read without his eyes? And how could any one hear words exhorting him to any cause, if he were not endowed with hearing? And how could he obtain meat and drink without a belly, and without a wonder working art exercised towards it? And it is on this account that he was likened to a precious stone.

(84) Moreover the colours of the two are different. For the colour of a coal when on fire is akin to that of the man who is inclined to confession: for he is inflamed by gratitude to God, and he is intoxicated with a certain sober intoxication: but the colour of the green stone is more appropriate to the man who is still labouring: for those who are devoted to constant labour are pale on account of the wearing nature of toil, and also by reason of their fear that perhaps they may not attain to such an end of their wish as is desired in their prayers.

XXVII. (85) And it is worth while to raise the question why the two rivers the Pheison and the Gihon encircle certain countries, the one surrounding Evilat, and the other Ethiopia, while neither of the other rivers is represented as encompassing any country. The Tigris is indeed said to flow in front of the land of the Assyrians, but the Euphrates is not mentioned in connection with any country whatever. And yet in real truth the Euphrates does both encircle some countries, and has several also in front of it. But the truth is that the sacred writer is here speaking not of the river, but of the correction of manners. (86) It is necessary therefore to say that prudence and courage are able to raise a wall and a circle of fortification against the opposite evils, folly, and cowardice; and to take them captives: for both of them are powerless and easy to be taken. For the foolish man is easily to be defeated by the prudent one; and the coward falls before the valiant man. But temperance is unable to surround appetite and pleasure; for they are formidable adversaries and hard to be subdued. Do you not see that even the most temperate men are compelled by the necessities of their mortal body to seek meat and drink; and it is in those things that the pleasures of the belly have their existence. We must be content therefore to oppose and contend with the genus appetite. (87) And it is on this account that the river Tigris is represented as flowing in front of the Assyrians, that is to say temperance is in front of or arrayed against pleasure.

But justice, according to which the river Euphrates is represented, neither besieges any one, nor draws lines of circumvallation round any one, nor opposes any one;—why so? Because justice is conversant about the distribution of things according to merit, and does not take the part either of accuser or of defendant, but acts as a judge. As

---

[17] Genesis 29:35.
[18] Genesis 49:15.
[19] Exodus 28:17.

therefore a judge does not desire beforehand to defeat any one, nor to oppose and make war upon any one; but delivers his own opinion and judges, deciding for the right, so also justice, not being the adversary of any one, distributes its due to every thing.

XXVIII. (88) "And the Lord God took the man whom he had made and placed him in the Paradise, to cultivate and to guard it." The man whom God made differs from the factitious man, as I have said before. For the factitious mind is somewhat earthly; but the created mind is purer and more immaterial, having no participation in any perishable matter, but having received a purer and more simple constitution. (89) Accordingly God takes this pure mind, not permitting it to proceed out of itself, and after he has taken it, he places it among the virtues which are firmly rooted and budding well, that it may cultivate and guard them. For many men who were originally pratisers of virtue, when they come to the end fall off; but he to whom God gives lasting knowledge is also endowed by him with both qualities, namely with the disposition to cultivate the virtues, and the resolution never to desert them, but always to minister to and guard every one of them. So Moses here uses the expression "cultivate" as equivalent to "act," and the word "guard" instead of "remember."

XXIX. (90) "And the Lord God commanded Adam, saying, Of every tree that is in the Paradise thou mayest freely eat; but of the tree of the knowledge of good and evil ye shall not eat; but in the day on which ye eat of it ye shall die the death."

A question may arise here to what kind of Adam he gave this command and who, this Adam was. For Moses has not made any mention of him before; but now is the first time that he has named him.

Are we then to think that he is desirous to supply you with the name of the factitious man? "And he calls him," continues Moses, "Earth." For this is the interpretation of the name of Adam. Accordingly, when you hear the name Adam, you must think that he is an earthly and perishable being; for he is made according to an image, being not earthly but heavenly. (91) But we must inquire how it was that after he had given names to all the other animals, he did not give one also to himself. What then are we to say about this? The mind which is in each of us is able to comprehend all other things, but has not the capability of understanding itself. For as the eye sees all other things, but cannot see itself, so also the mind perceives the nature of other things but cannot understand itself. For if it does, let it tell us what it is, or what kind of thing it is, whether it is a spirit, or blood, or fire, or air, or any other substance: or even only

so much whether it is a substance at all, or something incorporeal. Are not those men then simple who speculate on the essence of God? For how can they who are ignorant of the nature of the essence of their own soul, have any accurate knowledge of the soul of the universe? For the soul of the universe is according to our definition,—God.

XXX. (92) It is therefore very natural that Adam, that is to say the mind, when he was giving names to and displaying his comprehension of the other animals, did not give a name to himself, because he was ignorant of himself and of his own nature. A command indeed is given to man, but not to the man created according to the image and idea of God; for that being is possessed of virtue without any need of exhortation, by his own instinctive nature, but this other would not have wisdom if it had not been taught to him: (93) and these three things are different, command, prohibition, and recommendation. For prohibition is conversant about errors, and is directed to bad men, but command is conversant about things rightly done; recommendation again is addressed to men of intermediate character, neither bad nor good. For such a one does not sin so that any one has any need to direct prohibition to him, nor does he do right in every case in accordance with the injunction of right reason. But he is in need of recommendation, which teaches him to abstain from what is evil, and exhorts him to aim at what is good. (94) Therefore there is no need of addressing either command, or prohibition, or recommendation to the man who is perfect, and made according to the image of God; For the perfect man requires none of these things; but there is a necessity of addressing both command and prohibition to the wicked man, and recommendation and instruction to the ignorant man. Just as the perfect grammarian or perfect musician has need of no instruction in the matters which belong to his art, but the man whose theories on such subjects are imperfect stands in need of certain rules, as it were, which contain in themselves commands and prohibitions, and he who is only learning the art requires instruction.

(95) Very naturally, therefore, does God at present address commands and recommendations to the earthly mind, which is neither bad nor good, but of an intermediate character. And recommendation is employed in the two names, in that of the Lord and of God. For the Lord God commanded that if man obeyed his recommendations, he should be thought worthy of receiving benefits from God; but if he rejected his warnings, he should then be cast out to destruction by the Lord, as his Master and one who had authority over him. (96) On which account, when he is driven out of Paradise, Moses repeats the same names; for he says, "And the Lord God sent him forth out of the Paradise

of happiness, to till the ground from which he had been taken."[20] That, since the Lord had laid his commands on him as his Master, and God as his Benefactor, he might now, in both these characters, chastise him for having disobeyed them; for thus, by the same power by which he had exhorted him does he also banish him, now that he is disobedient.

XXXI. (97) And the recommendations that he addresses to him are as follows: "Of every tree that is in the Paradise thou mayest freely eat."[21] He exhorts the soul of man to derive advantage not from one tree alone nor from one single virtue, but from all the virtues; for eating is a symbol of the nourishment of the soul, and the soul is nourished by the reception of good things, and by the doing of praiseworthy actions. (98) And Moses not only says, "thou mayest eat," but he adds "freely," also; that is to say, having ground and prepared your food, not like an ordinary individual, but like a wrestler, you shall thus acquire strength and vigour. For the trainers recommend the wrestlers not to cut up their food by biting large pieces off, but to masticate it slowly, in order that it may contribute to their strength; for I and an athlete are fed in different manners. For I feed merely for the purpose of living, but the wrestler feeds for the purpose of acquiring flesh and deriving strength from it; on which account one of his rules of training and exercise is to masticate his food. This is the meaning of the expression, "Thou mayest freely eat."

(99) Again let us endeavour to give a still more accurate explanation of it. To honour one's parents is a nourishing and cherishing thing. But the good and the wicked honour them in different manners. For the one does it out of habit, as men eat who do not eat freely, but who merely eat. When, then, do they also eat freely? When having investigated and developed the causes of things they form a voluntary judgment that this is good, and the causes of their eating freely, that is to say, of their honouring their parents in a proper spirit, is—they became our parents; they nourished us; they instructed us; they have been the causes of all good things to us. Again, to honour the living God is spoken of symbolically as to eat. But to eat "freely," is when it is done with a proper explanation of the whole matter, and a correct assignment of the causes of it.

XXXII. (100) "But of the tree of the knowledge of good and evil he shall not eat." Therefore this tree is not in the Paradise. For God encourages them to eat of every tree that is in the Paradise. But when he forbids them to eat of this tree, it is plain that it is not in the Paradise; and this is in accordance with natural philosophy. For it is there in its essence, as I have said before, and it is not there in its power. For as in wax there are potentially many seals, but in actual fact only one which has been carved on it, so also in the soul, which resembles wax, all impressions whatever are contained potentially; but in really one single characteristic which is stamped upon it has possession of it; until it is effaced by some other which makes a deeper and more conspicuous impression.

(101) Again, this, also, may be made the subject of a question. When God recommends men to eat of every tree in the Paradise, he is addressing his exhortation to one individual: but when he forbids him to eat of the tree of the knowledge of good and evil he is speaking to him as to many. For in the one case he says, "Thou mayest freely eat of all;" but in the second instance, "Ye shall not eat;" and "In the day in which ye shall eat," not "thou shalt eat;" and "Ye shall die," not "Thou shalt die." (102) We must, therefore, say this,—that the first good is rare, imparted to but few; but the evil is comprehensive. On this account it is a hard matter to find one single man wise and faithful, but the number of bad men is beyond all computation. Very appropriately, therefore, God does not address his exhortation to nourish one's self amid the virtues, to one individual, but he encourages many to abstain from extravagant wickedness; for innumerable men are addicted to it.

(103) In the second place, for the due comprehension and adoption of virtue man requires one thing alone, namely reason. But the body not only does not co-operate in it at all, but rather impedes the progress of the reason towards it. For it may be almost called the peculiar task of wisdom to alienate itself from the body and form the corporeal appetites. But for the enjoyment of evil it is not only necessary for a man to have mind in some degree, but also senses, and reason, and a body. (104) For the bad man has need of all these things for the completion of his own wickedness. Since how will he be able to divulge the sacred mysteries unless he has the organ of voice? And how will he be able to indulge in pleasures if he be deprived of the belly and the organs of sensation? Very properly, therefore, does Moses address reason alone on the subject of the acquisition of virtue, for reason is, as I have said before, the only thing of which there is need for the establishment of virtue. But for indulgence in vice a man requires many things—soul, and reason, and the external senses of the body; for it is through all these organs that vice is exhibited.

XXXIII. (105) Accordingly God says, "In the day in which ye eat of it ye shall die the death." And yet, though they have eaten of it, they not only do not die, but they even beget children, and

---

[20] Genesis 3:23.
[21] Genesis 2:16.

are the causes of life to other beings besides themselves. What, then, are we to say? Surely that death is of two kinds; the one being the death of the man, the other the peculiar death of the soul—now the death of the man is the separation of his soul from his body, but the death of the soul is the destruction of virtue and the admission of vice; (106) and consequently God calls that not merely "to die," but "to die the death;" showing that he is speaking not of common death, but of that peculiar and especial death which is the death of the soul, buried in its passions and in all kinds of evil. And we may almost say that one kind of death is opposed to the other kind. For the one is the separation of what was previously existing in combination, namely, of body and soul. But this other death, on the contrary, is a combination of them both, the inferior one, the body, having the predominance, and the superior one, the soul, being

made subject to it. (107) When, therefore, God says, "to die the death," you must remark that he is speaking of that death which is inflicted as punishment, and not of that which exists by the original ordinance of nature. The natural death is that one by which the soul is separated from the body. But the one which is inflicted as a punishment, is when the soul dies according to the life of virtue, and lives only according to the life of vice.

(108) Well, therefore, did Heraclitus say this, following the doctrine of Moses; for he says, "We are living according to the death of those men; and we have died according to their life." As if he had said, Now, when we are alive, we are so though our soul is dead and buried in our body, as if in a tomb. But if it were to die, then our soul would live according to its proper life, being released from the evil and dead body to which it is bound.

ALLEGORICAL INTERPRETATION, II[†]

(Legum Allegoriae, II)

I. (1) "And the Lord God said, It is not good for man to be alone: let us make him a help meet for him." Why, O prophet, is it not good for man to be alone? Because, says he, it is good, that he who is alone should be alone. But God is alone, and by himself, being one; and there is nothing like unto God. So that, since it is good that he who only has a real existence should be alone (for that which is about itself alone is good), it cannot be good for man to be alone. (2) But the fact of God being alone one may receive in this sense; that neither before the creation was there anything with God, nor, since the world has been created, is anything placed in the same rank with him; for he is in need of absolutely nothing whatever.

But the better way of understanding this passage is the following: God is alone: a single being: not a combination: a single nature: but each of us, and every other animal in the world, are compound beings: for instance, I myself am made up of many things, of soul and body. Again, the soul is made up of a rational part and an irrational part: also of the body, there is one part hot, another cold; one heavy, another light; one dry, another moist. But God is not a compound being, nor one which is made up of many parts, but one which has no mixture with anything else; (3) for whatever could be combined with God must be either superior to him, or inferior to him, or equal to him. But there is nothing equal to God, and nothing superior to him, and nothing is combined with him which is worse than himself; for if it were, he himself would be deteriorated; and if he were to suffer deterioration, he would also become perishable, which it is impious even to imagine. Therefore God exists according to oneness and unity; or we should rather say, that oneness exists according to the one God, for all number is more recent than the world, as is also time. But God is older than the world, and is its Creator.

II. (4) But it is not good for any man to be alone. For there are two kinds of men, the one made according to the image of God, and the other fashioned out of the earth; for it longs for its own likeness. For the image of God is the antitype of all other things, and every imitation aims at this of which it is the imitation, and is placed in the

same class with it. And it is not good for either the man, who was made according to the image of God, to be alone: nor is it any more desirable for the factitious man to be alone, and indeed it is impossible. For the external senses, and the passions, and the vices, and innumerable other things, are combined with and adapted to the mind of this man. (5) But the second kind of man has a help-meet for him, who, in the first place, is created; "For I will make him," says God, "a help-meet for him." And, in the second place, is younger than the object to be helped; for, first of all, God created the mind, and subsequently he prepares to make its helper. But all this is spoken allegorically, in accordance with the principles of natural philosophy; for external sensation and the passions of the soul are all younger than the soul, and how they help it we shall see hereafter, but at present we will consider the fact of their being helpers younger than the object helped.

III. (6) As, according to the most skilful physicians and natural philosophers, the heart appears to be formed before the rest of the body, after the manner of the foundation of a house or the keel of a ship, and then the rest of the body is built upon it; on which account, even after death, the physicians say, that the heart still quivers, as having been created before the rest of the body, and being destroyed after it; so also does the dominant portion of the soul appear to be older than the whole of the soul, and the irrational part to be younger; the formation of which Moses has not yet mentioned, but he is about to give a sketch of it, how the irrational part of the soul is the external sensation, and the passions which spring from it, especially if the judgments are our own. And this assistant of God is younger, and created, being thus described with perfect propriety.

(7) But now let us see how that part, which was postponed before, acts as an assistant: how does our mind comprehend that such and such a thing is black or white, unless it employs sight as its assistant? and how does it know that the voice of the man who is singing to his harp is sweet, or, on the contrary, out of tune, if it has not the assistance of the faculty of hearing to guide it? And how can it tell that exhalations are fragrant or foul-smelling, unless it makes use of the sense of smell as its ally? How again does it judge of the different flavours, except through the instrumentality of its assistant, taste? (8) How can it distinguish between what is rough and what is smooth, except by touch?

[†] Yonge's title, *The Second Book of the Treatise on The Allegories of the Sacred Laws, after the Work of the Six Days of Creation.*

There is also another class of assistants, as I have already said, namely, the passions: for pleasure also is an assistant, co-operating towards the durability of our race, and in like manner concupiscence, and pain, and fear, biting the soul, lead it to treat nothing with indifference. Anger, again, is a defensive weapon, which has been of great service to many people, and so too have the other passions in the same manner. On which account Moses has said, with great felicity, "that he was an assistant to himself:" for he is in reality an assistant to the mind, as if he were its brother and near kinsman: for the external sensations and the passions are parts of one soul, and are its offspring.

IV. (9) Now of assistants there are two kinds, the one consisting in the passions and the other in the sensations. [...][1] But the prior kind is that of generation, for Moses says, "And God proceeded and made all the beasts of the field out of the earth, and all the birds of heaven; and he brought them to Adam to see what he would call them, and whatever Adam called any living soul that became its name." You see here who are our assistants, the beasts of the soul, the passions. For after God had said, "I will make him a helpmeet for him," Moses adds subsequently, "He made the beasts," as if the beasts also were assistants to us. (10) But these are not, properly speaking, assistants, but are called so only in a catachrestic manner, by a kind of abuse of language, for they are found in reality to be enemies to man. As also in the case of cities, the allies turn out at times to be traitors and deserters; and in the case of friendship, flatterers are found to be enemies instead of companions; and Moses here speaks of the heaven and the field synonymously, describing the mind in this allegorical manner; for the mind, like the field, has innumerable periods of rising and budding forth; and, like the heaven, has brilliant, and divine, and happy characteristics of nature.

(11) But the passions he compares to beasts and birds, because they injure the mind, being untamed and wild, and because, after the manner of birds, they descend upon the intellect; for their onset is swift and difficult to withstand; and the word "besides," as attached to "he made," is not superfluous. Why so? because he has previously said, that the beasts were formed before the creation of man, and he shows it in the following words, which are an account of what was done on the sixth day.

"And God said, Let the earth bring forth living creatures after their kind, four-footed animals, and creeping things, and wild beasts." (12) Why, then, is it that he makes other animals now, not being content with those already existing? now this must be stated according to the principles of moral philosophy. The species of evil are abundant in created man, so that the most evil things are continually produced in him; and this other thing must be affirmed on principles of natural philosophy. First of all, in the six days he created the different kinds of passions, and the ideas, but now, in addition to them, he is creating the species. (13) On which account Moses says, "And besides he made..." and that what had been previously created were genera is plain from what he says, "Let the earth bring forth living souls," not according to species but according to genus. And this is found to be the course taken by God in all cases; for before making the species he completes the genera, as he did in the case of man: for having first modelled the generic man, in whom they say that the male and female sexes are contained, he afterwards created the specific man Adam.

V. (14) This therefore he denominated the species of assistants, but the other part of the creation, the description, that is, of the formation of the external sensations, was postponed till he began to form the woman; and having put off this he then gives an account of the distribution of names; and this is an explanation, partly figurative and partly literal, which is worthy of our admiration. It is literal, inasmuch as the Lawgiver has attributed the imposition of names to the firstborn man; (15) for those also among the Greeks, who study philosophy, say that they were wise men who first gave names to things: but Moses speaks more correctly in the first place, because he attributes this giving of names, not to some of those men who lived in early times, but to the first man who was created upon the earth; so that, just as he himself was created to be the beginning of creation to all other animals, he might also be considered the beginning of conversation and language: for if there were no such things as names there could be no such thing as language: and, secondly, because, if many different persons gave names, they must have been different and devoid of all connexion, since different persons would have given different names: but if only one person did so, the name given by one was sure to be adapted to the thing: and the same name was likely to be a token to every one of the existing things signified by it.

VI. (16) But the moral meaning of this passage is as follows:—We often use the expression *ti* instead of *dia ti*; (why?) as when we say, why *(ti)* have you washed yourself? why *(ti)* are you walking? why *(ti)* are you conversing? for in all these cases *ti* is used instead of *dia ti*; when therefore Moses says, "to see what he would call them," you must understand him as if he had said *dia ti* (why), instead of *ti* (what): and the mind will invite

---

[1] A word or two are lost here. Pfeiffer thinks that several sentences are wanting; and there is a great want of connection between what follows and what has gone before.

and embrace each of these meanings. Is it then only for the sake of what is necessary that the mortal race is of necessity implicated in passions and vices? or is it also on account of that which is immoderate and superfluous? And again, is it because of the requirements of the earth-born man, or because the mind judges them to be most excellent and admirable things; (17) as for instance, is it necessary for every created thing to enjoy pleasure? But the bad man flies to pleasure as to a perfect good, but the good man seeks it only as a necessary; for without pleasure nothing whatever is done among the human race.

Again, the bad man considers the acquisition of riches as the most perfect good possible; but the good man looks upon riches only as a necessary and useful thing. (18) Very naturally, therefore, God desires to see and to learn how the mind denominates and appreciates each of these things, whether it looks upon them as good, or as things indifferent, or as evil in themselves, but nevertheless in some respects necessary. On which account, thinking that everything which he invited towards himself, and embraced as a living soul, was of equal value and importance with the soul, this became the name, not only of the thing which was thus invited, but also of him who invited it: as for instance, if the man embraced pleasure, he was called a man devoted to pleasure; if he embraced appetite, he was called a man of appetite; if he invited intemperance, he himself also acquired the name of intemperate; if he admitted cowardice, he was called cowardly; and so on in the case of the other passions. For as he who has any distinctive qualities according to the virtues, is called from that virtue with which he is especially endowed, prudent, or temperate, or just, or courageous, as the case may be; so too in respect of the vices, a man is called unjust, or foolish, or unmanly, when he has invited and embraced these habits of mind and conduct.

VII. (19) "And God cast a deep trance upon Adam, and sent him to sleep; and he took one of his ribs," and so on. The literal statement conveyed in these words is a fabulous one; for how can any one believe that a woman was made of a rib of a man, or, in short, that any human being was made out of another? And what hindered God, as he had made man out of the earth, from making woman in the same manner? For the Creator was the same, and the material was almost interminable, from which every distinctive quality whatever was made. And why, when there were so many parts of a man, did not God make the woman out of some other part rather than out of one of his ribs? Again, of which rib did he make her? And this question would hold even if we were to say, that he had only spoken of two ribs; but in truth he has not specified their number. Was it then the right rib, or the left rib? (20) Again, if he filled up the place

of the other with flesh, was not the one which he left also made of flesh? and indeed our ribs are like sisters, and akin in all their parts, and they consist of flesh. What then are we to say? (21) ordinary custom calls the ribs the strength of a man; for we say that a man has ribs, which is equivalent to saying that he has vigour; and we say that a wrestler is a man with strong ribs, when we mean to express that he is strong: and we say that a harp-player has ribs, instead of saying that he has energy and power in his singing.

(22) Now that this has been premised we must also say, that the mind, while naked and free from the entanglement of the body (for our present discussion is about the mind, while it is as yet entangled in nothing) has many powers, namely, the possessive power, the progenitive power, the power of the soul, the power of reason, the power of comprehension, and part of others innumerable both in their genus and species. Now the possessive power is common to it with other inanimate things, with stocks and stones, and it is shared by the things in us, which are like stones, namely, by our bones. And natural power extends also over plants: and there are parts in us which have some resemblance to plants, namely, our nails and our hair: (23) and nature is a habit already put in motion, but the soul is a habit which has taken to itself, in addition, imagination and impetuosity; and this power also is possessed by man in common with the irrational animals; and our mind has something analogous to the soul of an irrational animal.

Again, the power of comprehension is a peculiar property of the mind; and the reasoning power is perhaps common to the more divine natures, but is especially the property of the mortal nature of man: and this is a twofold power, one kind being that in accordance with which we are rational creatures, partaking of mind; and the other kind being that faculty by which we converse.

(24) There is also another power in the soul akin to these, the power of sensation, of which we are now speaking; for Moses is describing nothing else on this occasion except the formation of the external sense, according to energy and according to reason.

VIII. For immediately after the creation of the mind it was necessary that the external sense should be created, as an assistant and ally of the mind; therefore God having entirely perfected the first, proceeded to make the second, both in rank and power, being a certain created form, an external sense according to energy, created for the perfection and completion of the whole soul, and for the proper comprehension of such subject matter as might be brought before it. (25) How then was this second thing created? As Moses himself says in a subsequent passage, when the mind was gone to sleep: for, in real fact, the external sense then comes forward when the mind is asleep. And again, when the mind is awake the outward sense is extinguished; and the proof of this is, that when we desire to form an accurate conception of anything, we retreat to a desert place, we shut our eyes, we stop up our ears, we discard the exercise of our senses; and so, when the mind rises up again and awakens, the outward sense is put an end to.

(26) Let us now consider another point, namely, how the mind goes to sleep: for when the outward sense is awakened and has become excited, when the sight beholds any works of painting or of sculpture beautifully wrought, is not the mind then without anything on which to exercise its functions, contemplating nothing which is a proper subject for the intellect? What more? When the faculty of hearing is attending to some melodious combination of sound, can the mind turn itself to the contemplation of its proper objects? by no means. And it is much more destitute of occupation, when taste rises up and eagerly devotes itself to the pleasures of the belly; (27) on which account Moses, being alarmed lest some day or other the mind might not merely go to sleep, but might become absolutely dead, says in another place, "And it shall be to you a peg in your girdle; and it shall be, that when you sit down you shall dig in it, and, heaping up earth, shall cover your shame."[2] Speaking symbolically, and giving the name of peg to reason which digs up secret affairs; (28) and he bids him to bear it upon the affection with which he ought to be girded, and not to allow it to slacken and become loosened; and this must be done when the mind, departing from the intense consideration of objects perceptible by the intellect, is brought down to the passions, and sits down, yielding to, and being guided by, the necessities of the body: (29) and this is the case when the mind, being absorbed in luxurious associations, forgets itself, being subdued by the things which conduct it to pleasure, and so we become enslaved, and yield ourselves up to unconcealed impurity.

But if reason be able to purify the passion, then neither when we drink do we become intoxicated, nor when we eat do we become indolent through satiety, but we feast soberly without indulging in folly. (30) Therefore, the awakening of the outward senses is the sleep of the mind; and the awakening of the mind is the discharge of the outward senses from all occupation. Just as when the sun arises the brightness of all the rest of the stars becomes invisible; but when the sun sets, they are seen. And so, like the sun, the mind, when it is awakened, overshadows the outward senses, but when it goes to sleep it permits them to shine.

IX. (31) After this preface we must now proceed to explain the words: "The Lord God," says Moses, "cast a deep trance upon Adam, and sent

him to sleep." He speaks here with great correctness, for a trance and perversion of the mind is its sleep. And the mind is rendered beside itself when it ceases to be occupied about the things perceptible only by the intellect which present themselves to it. And when it is not energizing with respect to them it is asleep. And the expression, "it is in a trance," is very well employed, as it means that it is perverted and changed, not by itself, but by God, who presents to it, and brings before it, and sends upon it the change which occurs to it. (32) For the case is this:—if it were in my own power to be changed, then whenever I chose I should exercise this power, and whenever I did not choose I should continue as I am, without any change. But now change attacks me from an opposite direction, and very often when I am desirous to turn my intellect to some fitting subject, I am swallowed up by an influx contrary to what is fitting: and on the other hand, when I conceive an idea respecting something unseemly, I discard it by means of pleasant notions while God by his own grace pours into my soul a sweet stream instead of the salt flood. (33) It is necessary therefore, that every created thing should at times be changed. For this is a property of every created thing, just as it is an attribute of God to be unchangeable. But of these beings who have been changed, some remain in their altered state till their final and complete destruction, though others are only exposed to the ordinary vicissitudes of human nature; and they are immediately preserved.

(34) On which account Moses says that "God will not suffer the destroyer to enter into your houses to smite them."[3] For he does permit the destroyer (and change is the destruction of the soul) to enter into the soul, in order to exhibit the peculiar characteristic of the created being. But God will not permit the offspring of the seeing Israel to be changed in such a manner as to be stricken down by the change; but he will compel it to emerge and rise up again like one who rises up from the deep, and so he will cause it to be saved.

X. (35) "He took one of his ribs." He took one of the many powers of the mind, namely, that power which dwells in the outward senses. And when he uses the expression, "He took," we are not to understand it as if he had said, "He took away," but rather as equivalent to "He counted, He examined;" as he says in another place, "Take the chief of the spoils of the captivity."[4] What, then, is it which he wishes to show? (36) Sensation is spoken of in a twofold manner;—the one kind being according to habit, which exists even when we are asleep, and the other being according to energy.

[2] Deuteronomy 23:13.

[3] Exodus 12:23.
[4] Numbers 31:26.

Now, in the former kind, the one according to habit, there is no use: for we do not comprehend any one of the objects presented to our view by its means. But there is use in the second, in that which exists according to energy; for it is by means of this that we arrive at a comprehension of the objects perceptible by the outward senses.

(37) Accordingly, God, having created the former kind of sensation, that existing according to habit, when he was creating the mind (for he was furnishing that with many faculties in a state of rest), desires now to complete the other kind which exists according to energy. And this one according to energy is perfected when the one which exists according to habit is put in motion, and extended as far as the flesh and the organs of sense. For as nature is perfected when the seed is put in motion, so, also, energy is perfected when the habit is put in motion.

XI. (38) "And he filled the space with flesh instead of it." That is to say, he filled up that external sense which exists according to habit, leading it on to energy and extending it as far as the flesh and the whole outward and visible surface of the body. In reference to which Moses adds that "he built it up into a woman:" showing by this expression that woman is the most natural and felicitously-given name for the external sense. For as the man is seen in action, and the woman in being the subject of action, so also is the mind seen in action, and the external sense, like the woman, is discerned by suffering or being the subject of action. (39) And it is easy to learn this from the way in which it is affected in practice. Thus the sight is affected by these objects of sight which put it in motion, such as white and black, and the other colours. Again, hearing is affected by sounds, and taste is disposed in such or such a way by flavours; the sense of smell by scents; and that of touch by hardness or softness. And, on the other hand all the outward senses are in a state of tranquillity until each is approached from without by that which is to put it in motion.

XII. (40) "And he brought her to Adam. And Adam said, This is now bone of my bone, and flesh of my flesh." God leads the external sense, existing according to energy, to the mind; knowing that its motion and apprehension must turn back to the mind. But the mind, perceiving the power which it previously had (and which, while it was existing according to habit was in a state of tranquillity), now have to become a complete operation and energy, and to be in a state of motion, marvels at it, and utters an exclamation, saying that it is not unconnected with it, but very closely akin to it. (41) For Adam says, "This now is bone of my bone;" that is to say, This is power of my power; for bone is here to be understood as a symbol of strength and power. And it is, he adds, suffering of my sufferings; that is, it is flesh of my flesh.

For every thing which the external sense suffers, it endures not without the support of the mind; for the mind is its fountain, and the foundation on which it is supported.

(42) It is also worth while to consider why Adam added the word "now," for he says, "This now is bone of my bone." The explanation is, external sensation exists now, having its existence solely with reference to the present moment. For the mind touches three separate points of time; for it perceives present circumstances, and it remembers past events, and it anticipates the future. (43) But the external sensations have neither any anticipation of future events, nor are they subject to any feeling resembling expectation or hope, nor have they any recollection of past circumstances; but are by nature capable only of being affected by that which moves them at the moment, and is actually present. As, for example, the eye is made white by a white appearance presented to it at the moment, but it is not affected in any manner by that which is not present to it. But the mind is agitated also by that which is not actually present, but which may be past; in which cast it is affected by its recollection of it; or it may be future, in which case it is, indeed, the influence of hope and expectation.

XIII. (44) "And she shall be called woman." This is equivalent to saying, On this account the outward sensation shall be called woman, because it is derived from man who sets it in motion. He says "she;" why, then, is the expression "she" used? Why, because there is also another kind of outward sensation, not derived from the mind, but having been created, at the same moment with it. For there are, as I have said before, two different kinds of outward sensation; the one kind existing according to habit, and the other according to energy. (45) Now, the kind existing according to habit is not derived from the man, that is to say from the mind, but is created at the same time with him. For the mind, as I have already shown, when it was created was created with many faculties and habits; namely, with the faculty and habit of reasoning, and of existing, and of promoting what is like itself, as also with that of receiving impressions from the outward senses. But the outward sensation, which exists according to energy, is derived from the mind. For it is extended from the outward sensation which exists in it according to habit, so as to become the same outward sense according to energy. So that this second kind of outward sense is derived from the mind, and exists according to motion. (46) And he is but a foolish person who thinks that any thing is in true reality made out of the mind, or out of itself. Do you not see that even in the case of Rachel (that is to say of outward sensation) sitting upon the images, while she thought that her motions came from the mind, he who saw her reproved her. For she says, "Give me my children, and if you give them not to me I shall die."[5] And he replied: "Because, O mistaken woman, the mind is not the cause of any thing, but he which existed before the mind; namely God." On which account he adds: "Am I equal to God who has deprived you of the fruit of your womb?" (47) But that it is God who creates men, he will testify in the case of Leah, when he says, "But the Lord, when he saw that Leah was hated, opened her womb. But Rachel was barren."[6] But it is the especial property of man to open the womb.

Now naturally virtue is hated by men. On which account God has honoured it, and gives the honour of bearing the first child to her who is hated. (48) And in another passage he says: "But if a man has two wives, one of them being loved and one of them being hated, and if they bear him children, and if the first-born son be the child of her who is hated; he will not be able to give the honours of the birthright to the child of the wife whom he loves, overlooking the first-born son the child of her who is hated."[7] For the productions of virtue which is hated, are the first and the most perfect, but those of pleasure, which is loved, are the last.

XIV. (49) "On this account a man will leave his father and his mother and will cleave to his wife; and they two shall become one flesh." On account of the external sensation, the mind, when it has become enslaved to it, shall leave both its father, the God of the universe, and the mother of all things, namely, the virtue and wisdom of God, and cleaves to and becomes united to the external sensations, and is dissolved into external sensation, so that the two become one flesh and one passion. (50) And here you must observe that it is not the woman who cleaves to the man, but on the contrary, the man who cleaves to the woman; that is to say, the mind cleaves to the external sensations. For when that which is the better, namely, the mind, is united to that which is the rose, namely, the external sensation, it is then dissolved into the nature of flesh, which is worse, and into outward sensation, which is the cause of the passions.

But when that which is the inferior, namely, the outward sensation, follows the better part, that is the mind, then there will no longer be flesh, but both will become one, namely, mind. And this is a thing of such a nature that it prefers the affections to piety. (51) There is also another being called by an opposite name, Levi; he who says to his father and mother: "He saw you not, and he did not recognize his brethren, and repudiated his

children."[8] This man leaves his father and mother; that is to say, his mind and the material of his body, in order to have as his inheritance the one God; "For the Lord himself is his inheritance."[9] (52) And, indeed, suffering is the inheritance of him who is fond of suffering; but the inheritance of Levi is God. Do you not see that "he bids him on the tenth day of the months bring two goats as his share, one lot for the Lord and one lot for the scape-goat."[10] For the sufferings inflicted on the scape goat are in real truth the lot of him who is fond of suffering.

XV. (53) "And they were both naked, both Adam and his wife, and they were not ashamed; but the serpent was the most subtle of all the beasts that were upon the earth, which the Lord God had made:"[11]—the mind is naked, which is clothed neither with vice nor with virtue, but which is really stripped of both: just as the soul of an infant child, which has no share in either virtue or vice, is stripped of all coverings, and is completely naked: for these things are the coverings of the soul, by which it is enveloped and concealed, good being the garment of the virtuous soul, and evil the robe of the wicked soul. (54) And the soul is made naked in these ways. Once, when it is in an unchangeable state, and is entirely free from all vices, and has discarded and laid aside the covering of all the passions. With reference to this Moses also pitches his tabernacle outside of the camp, a long way from the camp, and it was called the tabernacle of testimony.[12] (55) And this has some such meaning as this: the soul which loves God, having put off the body and the affections which are dear to it, and having fled a long way from them, chooses a foundation and a sure ground for its abode, and a lasting settlement in the perfect doctrines of virtue; on which account testimony is borne to it by God, that it loves what is good, "for it was called the tabernacle of testimony," says Moses, and he has passed over in silence the giver of the name, in order that the soul, being excited, might consider who it is who thus beareth witness to the dispositions which love virtue. (56) On this account the high priest "will not come into the holy of holies clad in a garment reaching to the feet;[13] but having put off the robe of opinion and vain fancy of the soul, and having left that for those who love the things which are without, and who honour opinion in preference to truth, will come forward naked, without colours or any sounds, to make an offering of the blood of the soul, and to sacrifice the whole mind to God

---

[5]Genesis 30:1.
[6]Genesis 29:31.
[7]Deuteronomy 21:15.

[8]Deuteronomy 33:9.
[9]Deuteronomy 10:9.
[10]Leviticus 16:7.
[11]Genesis 2:25; 3:1.
[12]Exodus 33:7.
[13]Leviticus 16:1.

the Saviour and Benefactor; (57) and certainly Nadab and Abihu,[14] who came near to God, and left this mortal life and received a share of immortal life, are seen to be naked, that is, free from all new and mortal opinion; for they would not have carried it in their garments and borne it about, if they had not been naked, having broken to pieces every bond of passion and of corporeal necessity, in order that their nakedness and absence of corporeality might not be adulterated by the accession of atheistical reasonings; for it may not be permitted to all men to behold the secret mysteries of God, but only to those who are able to cover them up and guard them; (58) on which account Mishael and his partisans concealed them not in their own garments, but in those of Nadab and Abihu, who had been burnt with fire and taken upwards; for having stripped off all the garments that covered them, they brought their nakedness before God, and left their tunics about Mishael. But clothes belong to the irrational part of the animal, which overshadow the rational part.

Abraham also was naked when he heard, (59) "Come forth out of thy land and from thy kindred;"[15] and as for Isaac, he indeed was not stripped, but was at all times naked and incorporeal; for a commandment was given to him not to go down into Egypt,[16] that is to say, into the body.

Jacob also was fond of the nakedness of the soul, for his smoothness is nakedness, "for Esau was a hairy man, but Jacob," says Moses, "was a smooth man,"[17] on which account he was also the husband of Leah.

XVI. (60) This is the most excellent nakedness, but the other nakedness is of a contrary nature, being a change which involves a deprivation of virtue, when the soul becomes foolish and goes astray. Such was the folly of Noah when he was naked, when he drank wine.[18] But thanks be to God, that this change and this tripping naked of the mind according to the deprivation of virtue, did not extend as far as external things, but remained in the house; for Moses says, that "he was stripped naked in his house:" for even if a wise man does commit folly, he still does not run to ruin like a bad man; for the evil of the one is spread abroad, but that of the other is kept within bounds, and therefore he becomes sober again, that is to say, he repents, and as it were recovers from his disease.

(61) But let us now more accurately examine the statement, "that the stripping of him naked took place in his house." When the soul, being

changed, only conceives some evil thing and does not put it in execution, so as to accomplish it in deed, then the sin is only in the private domain and abode of the soul. But if, in addition to thinking some wickedness it proceeds also to accomplish it and carry it into execution, then the wickedness is diffused over the parts beyond his house: (62) and on this account he curses Canaan also, because he related the change of his soul abroad, that is to say, he extended it into the parts out of doors, and gave it notoriety, adding to his evil intention an evil consummation by means of his actions: but Shem and Japhet are praised, because they did not attack his soul, but rather concealed its deterioration.

(63) On this account also the prayers and vows of the soul are invalidated when "they are made in the house of one's father or one's husband,[19] while the reasoning powers are in a state of quiescence, and do not attack the alteration which has taken place in the soul, but conceal the delinquency; for then also "the master of all things" will purify it: but he hears the prayer of the widow and of her who is divorced without revoking it; for "whatever," says he, "she has vowed against her own soul shall abide to her," and very reasonably; for, if, after she has been put away, she has advanced as far as the parts out of the house, so that not only is her place changed, but that she also sins in respect of deeds that she has perfected, she remains incurable, having no communion of conversation with her husband, and being deprived also of the advocacy and consolation of her father.

(64) The third description of stripping naked is the middle one, according to which the mind is destitute of reason, having no share in either virtue or vice; and it is with reference to this kind of nakedness which an infant also is partaker of, that the expression is used which says, "And the two were naked, both Adam and his wife;" and the meaning of it is this, neither did their intellect understand, nor did their outward senses perceive this nakedness; but the former was devoid of all power of understanding, and naked; and the latter was destitute of all perception.

XVII. (65) And the expression, "they were not ashamed," we will examine hereafter: for there are three ideas brought forward in this passage. Shamelessness, modesty, and a state of indifference, in which one is neither shameless nor modest. Now shamelessness is the property of a worthless person, and modesty the characteristic of a virtuous one; but the state of being neither modest nor shameless, is a sign of a person who is void of comprehension, and who does not act from any settled opinion; and it is of such a one that we are now speaking: for he who has not yet

---

[14]Leviticus 10:1.
[15]Genesis 13:1.
[16]Genesis 26:2.
[17]Genesis 25:25.
[18]Genesis 9:21.

[19]Genesis 25:25.

acquired any comprehension of good or evil, is not able to be either shameless or modest, (66) therefore the examples of shamelessness are all the unseemly pieces of conduct, when the mind reveals disgraceful things, while it ought rather to cover them in the shade, instead of which it boasts of and glories in them. It is said also in the case of Miriam, when she was speaking against Moses, "If her father had spit in her face, ought she not to keep herself retired for seven days?"[20]

(67) For the external sense, being really shameless and impudent, though considered as nothing by God the father, in comparison of him who was faithful in all his house, to whom God himself united the Ethiopian woman, that is to say, unchangeable and well-satisfied opinion, dared to speak against Moses and to accuse him, for the very actions for which he deserved to be praised; for this is his greatest praise, that he received the Ethiopian woman, the unchangeable nature, tried in the fire and found honest; for as in the eye, the part which sees is black, so also the part of the soul which sees is what is meant by the Ethiopian woman. (68) Why when, as there are many works of wickedness, does he mention one only, namely, that which is conversant about what is shameful, saying, "they were not ashamed:" but were they not doing wrong, or were they not sinning, or were they not acting indecorously? But the cause is at hand. No, by the only true God, I think nothing so shameful as to suppose that I comprehend with my intellect, or perceive by my outward sense. (69) Is my mind the cause of my comprehending? How so? for does it even comprehend itself, and know what it is, or how it came to exist? And are the outward senses the cause of man's perceiving anything? How can it be said to be so, when it is neither understood by itself nor by the mind? Do you not see, that he who fancies that he comprehends is often found to be foolish in his acts of covetousness, in his drunkenness, in his deeds of folly? Where then is his intellectual capacity shown in these actions?

Again, is not the outward sensation often deprived of the power of exercising itself? Are there not times when seeing we do not see, and hearing we do not hear, when the mind has its attention ever so little drawn off to some other object of the intellect, and is applied to the consideration of that? (70) As long as they are both naked, the mind naked of its power of exciting the intellect, and the outward sense of its power of sensation, they have nothing disgraceful in them; but the moment that they begin to display any comprehension, they become masked in shame and insolence: for they will often be found behaving with simplicity and folly rather than with any sound

knowledge, and this not only in particular acts of covetousness, or spleen, or folly, but also in the general conduct of life: for when the outward sense has the dominion the mind is enslaved, giving its attention to no one proper object of its intellect, and when the mind is predominant, the untoward sense is seen to be without employment, having no comprehension of any proper object of its own exercise.

XVIII. (71) "Now the serpent was the most subtle of all the beasts which are upon the earth, which the Lord God made."[21] Two things having been previously created, that is, mind and outward sense, and these also having been stripped naked in the manner which has already been shown, it follows of necessity that pleasure, which brings these two together, must be the third, for the purpose of facilitating the comprehension of the objects of intellect and of outward sense: for neither could the mind, without the outward sense, be able to comprehend the nature of any animal or of any plant, or of a stone or of a piece of wood, or, in short, of any substance whatever; nor could the outward sense exercise its proper faculties without the mind. (72) Since, therefore, it was necessary for both these things to come together for the due comprehension of these objects, what was it which brought them together except a third something which acted as a bond between them, the two first representing love and desire, and pleasure not obtaining the dominion and mastery, which pleasure Moses here speaks of symbolically, under the emblem of the serpent. (73) God, who created all the animals on the earth, arranged this order very admirably, for he placed the mind first, that is to say, man, for the mind is the most important part in man; then outward sense, that is the woman; and then proceeding in regular order he came to the third, pleasure. But the powers of these three, and their ages, are different only in the night, for in point of time they are equal; for the soul brings forward everything at the same moment with itself: but some things it brings forward in their actuality, and others in their power of existing, even if they have not yet arrived at the end.

(74) And pleasure has been represented under the form of the serpent, for this reason, as the motion of the serpent is full of many windings and varied, so also is the motion of pleasure. At first it folds itself round a man in five ways, for the pleasures consist both in seeing, and in hearing, and in taste, and in smell, and in touch. But the most vehement and intense are those which arise from connection with woman, through which the generation of similar beings is appointed by nature to be effected. (75) And yet this is not the only rea-

---

son why we say that pleasure is various in appearance, namely, because it folds itself around all the divisions of the irrational part of the soul, but because it also folds itself with many windings around each separate part. For instance, the pleasures derived from sight are various, there is all the pleasure which arises from the contemplation of pictures or statues; and all other works which are made by art delight the sight. So also do the different stages through which plants go while budding and flowering and bearing fruit; and likewise the diversified beauty of the different animals. In the same manner the flute gives pleasure to the sense of hearing, as does the harp, and every kind of instrument, and the harmonious voices of the irrational animals, of swallows, of nightingales; and likewise the melody of such rational beings as nature has made musical, the tuneful voice of the harp-players, and of those who represent comedy, or tragedy, or any other histrionic performance.

XIX. (76) Why need we enlarge on the pleasures of the belly? For we may almost say that there are as may varieties of pleasure as there are of gentle flavours which are presented to the belly, and which excite the outward sense. Was it not then, with great propriety that pleasure, which is derived form many varied sources, was presented to an animal endowed with varied faculties? (77) On this account, too, that part in us which is analogous to the people, and which acts the part of a multitude, when it seeks "the houses in Egypt,"[22] that is to say, in its corporeal habitation, becomes entangled in pleasures which bring on death; not that death which is a separation of soul and body, but that which is the destruction of the soul by vice. For Moses says, "And the Lord God sent among the people deadly serpents, and they bit the people, and a great multitude of the children of Israel died."[23] For in real truth there is nothing which so much bringeth death upon the soul as an immoderate indulgence in pleasures. (78) And that which perishes is not the dominant portion in us but the subject one, that which acts the part of the multitude; and it receives death up to this point, namely, until it turns to repentance, and confesses its sin, for the Israelites, coming to Moses, say, "We have sinned in that we have spoken against the Lord and against you; pray, therefore, for us to the Lord, and let him take away the serpents from us." It is well put here, not we have sinned because we have spoken against the Lord, but because we were inclined to sin we have spoken against the Lord, for when the mind sins and departs from virtue, it blames divine things, imputing its own sins to God.

XX. (79) How, then, can there be any remedy for this evil? When another serpent is created, the enemy of the serpent which came to Eve, namely, the word of temperance: for temperance is opposite to pleasure, which is a varied evil, being a varied virtue, and one ready to repel its enemy pleasure. Accordingly, God commands Moses to make the serpent according to temperance; and he says, "Make thyself a serpent, and set it up for a sign." Do you see that Moses makes this serpent for no one else but for himself? for God commands him, "Make it for thyself," in order that you may know that temperance is not the gift of every one, but only of that man who loves God. (80) And we must consider why Moses makes a brazen serpent, when no command was given to him respecting the material of which it was to be formed. May it not have been for this reason? In the first place, the graces of God are immaterial, being themselves only ideas, and destitute of any distinctive quality; but the graces of mortal men are only beheld in connection with matter. In the second place, not only does Moses love the incorporeal virtues, but our own souls, not being able to put off their bodies, do likewise aim at corporeal virtue, (81) and reason, in accordance with temperance, is likened to the strong and solid substance of brass, inasmuch as it is form and not easily cut through. And perhaps brass may also have been selected inasmuch as temperance in the man who loves God is a most honourable thing, and like gold; though it has only a secondary place in a man who has received wisdom and improved in it. "And whomsoever the one serpent bites, if he looks upon the brazen serpent shall live:" in which Moses speaks truly, for if the mind that has been bitten by pleasure, that is by the serpent which was sent to Eve, shall have strength to behold the beauty of temperance, that is to say, the serpent made by Moses in a manner affecting the soul, and to behold God himself through the medium of the serpent, it shall live. Only let it see and contemplate it intellectually.

XXI. (82) Do you not see that wisdom when dominant, which is Sarah, says, "For whosoever shall hear it shall rejoice with me."[24] But suppose that any were able to hear that virtue has brought forth happiness, namely, Isaac, immediately he will sing a congratulatory hymn. As, therefore, it can only be one who has heard the news that can sympathise in one's joy, so also it can only be he who has clearly seen temperance and God, who is safe from death. (83) But many souls that have been in love with perseverance and temperance, when removed to a distance from the passions, have nevertheless withstood the power of God, and have undergone a change for the worse, while their Master has made a display of himself and of the work of creation; of himself, that he is always immov-

---

[22]Numbers 21:5.
[23]Numbers 21:6.

[24]Genesis 21:6.

able, and of the work of creation, that it vibrates as if in a scale, and inclines opposite ways at different times. (84) For Moses speaks to the Israelites of God, "Who led ye then through that great and terrible wilderness, where there were biting serpents, and scorpions, and thirst; where there was no water? who brought forth for thee out of the hard rock a fountain of water? who fed thee with manna in the desert, which thy fathers knew not?"[25]

Do you not see that not only did the soul, while longing for the passions which prevailed in Egypt, fall under the power of the serpents, but that, also, while it was in the wilderness, it was bitten by pleasure, that affection of varied and serpent-like appearance? And the work of pleasure has received a most appropriate name, for it is called a biting. (85) Moreover, not only they who were in the desert were bitten by serpents, but also they who were scattered abroad, for I, also, often having left the men who were my kinsmen and my friends, and my country, and having gone into the desert in order that I might perceive some of those things which are worthy of being beheld, have profited nothing. But my mind, being separated from me, or being bitten by passion, has withdrawn towards the things opposite to them. And there are times when in the midst of a multitude composed of infinite numbers of men, I can bring my mind into solitude, God having scattered for me the crowd which perplexes my soul, and having taught me that it is not the difference of place that is the cause of good and evil, but rather God, who moves and drives this vehicle of the soul wherever he pleases.

(86) Moreover, the soul falls in with a scorpion, that is to say, with dispersion in the wilderness; and the thirst, which is that of the passions, seizes on it until God sends forth upon it the stream of his own accurate wisdom, and causes the changed soul to drink of unchangeable health; for the abrupt rock is the wisdom of God, which being both sublime and the first of things he quarried out of his own powers, and of it he gives drink to the souls that love God; and they, when they have drunk, are also filled with the most universal manna; for manna is called something which is the primary genus of every thing. But the most universal of all things is God; and in the second place the word of God. But other things have an existence only in word, but in deed they are at times equivalent to that which has no existence.

XXII. (87) See now the difference between him who turns to sin in the desert and him who sins in Egypt. For the one is bitten by serpents which cause death, that is to say by insatiable pleasures

which inflict death; but the other, he who meditates in the wilderness, is only bitten by pleasure and driven astray, but is not killed. And the one, indeed, is healed by temperance, which is the brazen serpent which was made by the wise Moses; but the other is supplied by God with a most beautiful draught to drink, namely, wisdom, from the fountain which He himself has brought forth out of his own wisdom. (88) Nor, indeed, does the pleasure which is in the form of a serpent, abstain from attacking that most sincere lover of God, Moses, for we read as follows; "If, therefore, they will not obey me, nor listen to my voice— for they will say, God has not been seen by you— what shall I say to them? And the Lord said unto Moses, What is that which is in thy hand? And he said, A rod. And God said, Cast it on the ground. And he cast it on the ground, and it became a serpent, and Moses fled from it. And the Lord said unto Moses, Stretch forth thy hand, and take hold of it by the tail. And having stretched forth his hand, he took hold of it by the tail, and it became a rod in his hand. And the Lord said unto him, That they may believe thee."[26]

(89) How can any one believe God? If he has learnt that all other things are changed, but that he alone is unchangeable. Therefore, God asks of the wise Moses what there is in the practical life of his soul; for the hand is the symbol of action. And he answers, Instruction, which he calls a rod. On which account Jacob the supplanter of the passions, says, "For in my staff did I pass over this Jordan."[27] But Jordan being interpreted means descent. And of the lower, and earthly, and perishable nature, vice and passion are component parts; and the mind of the ascetic passes over them in the course of its education. For it is too low a notion to explain his saying literally; as if it meant that he crossed the river, holding his staff in his hand.

XXIII. (90) Well, therefore, does the God-loving Moses answer. For truly the actions of the virtuous man are supported by education as by a rod, tranquillizing the disturbances and agitations of the mind. This rod, when cast away, becomes a serpent. Very appropriately. For if the soul casts away instruction, it becomes fond of pleasure instead of being fond of virtue. On which account Moses fled from it, for the man who is fond of virtue does flee from passion and from pleasure. (91) But God did not praise his flight. For it is fitting, indeed, for your mind, before you are made perfect, to meditate flight and escape from the passions; but Moses, that perfect man, ought rather to persevere in his war against them, and to resist them, and to strive against them, otherwise they, relying on their freedom from danger and on their power, will ascend up to the citadel of the soul, and take it by storm, and will plunder it entirely, like a tyrant. (92) On which account God commanded Moses "to take hold of it by the tail," that is to say, let not the hostile and untameable spirit of pleasure terrify you, but with all your power take hold of it, and seize it firmly, and master it. For it will again become a rod instead of a serpent, that is to say, instead of pleasure it will become instruction in your hand; (93) but it will be in your hand, that is in the action of a wise man, which, indeed, is true.

But it is impossible to take hold of and to master pleasure, unless the hand be first stretched out, that is to say, unless the soul confesses that all actions and all progress is derived from God; and attributes nothing to himself. Accordingly he, when he saw this serpent, decided to flee from it? But he prepared another principle, that of temperance, which is the brazen serpent: that whosoever was bitten by pleasure, when he looked on temperance, might live a real life.

XXIV. (94) Such a serpent Jacob boasts that Dan is, and he speaks thus: "Dan will judge his people, as one of the tribes of Israel:"[28] and again, "Let Dan be a serpent in the path, sitting upon the road, biting the heel of the horse, and the rider shall fall backwards, waiting the salvation of the Lord."[29] The fifth son of Leah is Issachar, the legitimate son of Jacob; but if the two sons of Zilpah are counted he is the seventh; but the fifth son of Jacob is Dan, the son of Billah, the handmaid of Rachel; and the cause of this we will investigate in the proper place, but concerning Dan we must examine further now. (95) The soul produces two kinds, the one divine and the other perishable; that which is the better kind it has already conceived, and ends in it; for when the soul was able to confess to God and to yield everything to him, it was not after that capable of receiving any more valuable possession; on this account she ceased to bring forth, after she had borne Judah, the emblem of the disposition of confessing— (96) and now she begins to form the mortal race—now the mortal race subsists by imbibing; for, like a foundation, the sense of taste is the cause of the duration of animals; but the name Billah, being interpreted, means imbibing. From her was born Dan, which name being interpreted means judgment, for this kind distinguishes between the separates immortal from mortal things, therefore he prays that he may become a workman of temperance. But he will not pray for Judah, for Judah already has the capacity of praying to and pleasing God: (97)

"Therefore let Dan," says he, "be a serpent in the path."—One path is the soul.

For as in the roads one may behold a great variety of living beings, inanimate and animate, irrational and rational, good and bad, slaves and free, young and old, male and female, strangers and natural citizens, sick and healthy, mutilated and perfect; so also in the soul there are motions inanimate, and imperfect, and diseased, and slavish, and female, and innumerable others of the class of evils; and on the other hand, there are motions which are living, and perfect, and masculine, and free, and healthy, and ripe, and virtuous, and genuine, and really legitimate. (98) Let then the principle of temperance be a serpent in the soul, which makes its advance through all the circumstances of life, and let it sit in the path. But what is the meaning of this expression?—The field of virtue is not trodden down; for they are few who walk along it, but that of vice is trodden and worn? And he recommends him here to occupy and to fill, with ambush and stratagem, the well-trodden path of passion and vice, in which the thoughts which are deserters from virtue pass their life.

XXV. (99) "Biting the heel of the horse,"— Very consistently the disposition which shakes the stability of the created and perishable being is called the supplanter, and the passions are compared to a horse; for passion has four legs as a horse has, and is an impetuous beast, and full of insolence, and by nature a most restive animal. But the reasoning of temperance is wont to bite, and to wound, and to destroy passion. Therefore passion having been tripped up, and having fallen, "the horseman will fall backwards." We must comprehend that the horseman who has mounted upon the passions is the mind, who falls from the passions when they are reasoned upon closely, and so are supplanted; (100) and it is well figured, that the soul does not fall forward, for it must not go before the passions, but rather advance behind them, and behave with moderation.

And there is sound learning in what he says here. If the mind, though desirous to act unjustly, comes too late and falls backward, it will not act unjustly; but if, when it is moved onwards to some irrational passion it does not run forward but remains behind, it will then receive freedom from the dominion of the passions, which is a most excellent thing. (101) On which account Moses, approving of this backward fall from off the vices, adds further, "waiting for the salvation of the Lord," for, in good truth, he who falls from the passions is saved by God, and remains safe after their operation. May my soul meet with such a fall as this, and may it never afterwards remount upon that horselike and restive passion, in order that it may await the salvation of God, and attain to happiness! (102) On this account also it was that Moses praised God in his hymn, because "the horse and

[28]Genesis 49:16.
[29]Genesis 49:17.

his rider has he thrown into the sea,"[30] meaning that he has thrown the four passions, and the miserable mind which is mounted on them, down into ruin as to its affairs, and into the bottomless pit, and this is almost the burden of the whole hymn, to which every other part of it is referred, and indeed that is the truth; for if once a freedom from the passions occupies the soul, it will become perfectly happy.

XXVI. (103) And we must also inquire, what is the reason why Jacob says, that "the rider will fall backward,"[31] and Moses says, that "the horse and his rider have been thrown into the sea." We must say, therefore, that that which is thrown into the sea is the Egyptian disposition, which indeed flies and escapes under the water, that is to say, under the advance of the passions. But the rider who falls backwards is not one of the persons who loves to yield to the passions; and the proof is, that Moses calls the one the horseman (*hippeus*), and the other the rider (*anabatēs*). (104) Now it is the business of the horseman to subdue the horse, and when he resists the rein to make him tractable; but it is the part of the rider to be conveyed wherever the animal carries him, and in the sea it is the office of the pilot to guide the ship, and to keep it straight, and to preserve it in the right course; but it is the part of the sailor to endure all that happens to the ship.

And in reference to this the horseman who subdues the passions is not drowned in the sea, but dismounting from them awaits the salvation of the master. (105) Accordingly, the word of God in Leviticus recommends men "to feed on those creeping things which go on four feet, and which have legs above their feet, so that they are able to leap with them;"[32] among which are the locust, and the attacus, and the acris,[33] and in the fourth place the serpent-fighter; and very properly; for if pleasure, like a serpent, is an unprofitable and pernicious thing, then the nature which contends against pleasure must be a most profitable and saving thing, and this is temperance.

(106) Fight thou then, O my mind, against every passion, and especially against pleasure, for "the serpent is the most subtle of all the beasts that are upon the earth, which the Lord God has made." (107) And of all the passions the most mischievous is pleasure. Why so? Because all things are the slaves of pleasure; and because the life of the wicked is governed by pleasure as by a master. Accordingly, the things which are the efficient causes of pleasure are found to be full of all wickedness: gold and silver, and glory and honours, and powers and the objects of the outward senses, and the mechanical arts, and all other things which cause pleasure, being very various, and all injurious to the soul; and there are no sins without extreme wickedness; (108) therefore do thou array against it the wisdom which contends with serpents; and struggle in this most glorious struggle, and labour to win the crown in the contest against pleasure, which subdues every one else; winning a noble and glorious crown, such as no assembly of men can confer.

---

[30]Exodus 15:1.
[31]Genesis 49:17.

[32]Leviticus 11:22.
[33]These are different kinds of locusts

ALLEGORICAL INTERPRETATION, III[†]

(Legum Allegoriae, III)

I. (1) "And Adam and his wife hid themselves from the face of the Lord God in the midst of the trees of the Paradise."[1] A doctrine is introduced here which teaches us that the wicked man is inclined to run away. For the proper city of wise men is virtue, and he who is incapable of becoming a partaker in that is driven from his city; and no bad man is capable of becoming a partaker of it; therefore the bad man alone is driven away and becomes a banished man. But he who is banished from virtue is at once concealed from the face of God, for if the wise men are visible to God, inasmuch as they are dear to him, it follows plainly that the wicked are all concealed from him, and enveloped in darkness, as being enemies and adversaries to right reason. (2) Now that the wicked man is destitute of a city and destitute of a home, Moses testifies in speaking of that hairy man who was also a man of varied wickedness, Esau, when he says, "But Esau was skilful in hunting, and a rude man."[2] For it is not natural for vice which is inclined to be subservient to the passions to inhabit the city of virtue, inasmuch as it is devoted to the pursuit of rudeness and ignorance, with great folly. But Jacob, who is full of wisdom, is both a citizen and one who dwells in a house, that is to say, in virtue. Accordingly Moses says of him, "But Jacob is a man without guile, dwelling in a house;" (3) On which account also "the midwives, since they feared God made themselves houses."[3]

For they, being inclined to seek out the secret mysteries of God, one of which was that the male children should be preserved alive, build up the actions of virtue, in which they had previously determined to dwell. Accordingly, in this account it is shown how the wicked man is destitute of a city and destitute of a home: inasmuch as he is an exile from virtue, but that the virtuous man has a city and is allotted a home, namely wisdom.

II. (4) And let us in the next place consider how any one is said to be concealed from God; but unless any one receives this as an allegorical saying it would be impossible to comprehend what is here stated. For God has completed everything and has penetrated every thing, and has left no one of all his works empty or deserted. What kind of place then can any one occupy in which God is not? And Moses testifies to this in other passages, when he says, "God is in the heaven above, and in the earth beneath; and there is nothing anywhere but he."[4] And in another place he speaks in this manner, "I stood here before you did."[5] For God is of older date than any created being, and he will be everywhere, so that it cannot be possible for any one to be concealed from him: and what need we wonder at? (5) For even if any thing were to happen to us we should not be able to escape the notice of, and to conceal ourselves from the most elementary of created things; for instance, let any one try to flee from the earth, or the water, or the air, or the heaven, or the entire universe, and he will fail; for it is impossible but what he must be contained in these things, for no one will be able to flee out of the world.

(6) Again how could any man who is unable to conceal himself from the parts of the world, and from the whole world itself, be able to escape the notice of God? He never could do so. What then is the meaning of the expression, "they hid themselves?" The bad man thinks that God is in a certain place, not surrounding it, but being surrounded by it. On which account also he thinks that he can conceal himself from him, as if God were without any prevailing reason at a distance form that part of the world in which he has determined to lurk.

III. (7) And we must understand this in the following manner. In the wicked man the true opinion concerning God is overshadowed and kept out of sight, for he is full of darkness, having no divine irradiation, by means of which he may be able to contemplate things as they are. And such a man is a fugitive from the divine company just as a leper is or a man with any other impure disease, the one bringing together into the same place God and Creation, two opposite natures of two different complexions, as the causes of things, when there is really but one cause, the great Creator; and the other, a man afflicted with a foul disease, believing that everything is created from the world, and again is dissolved into the world, but thinking that nothing has been created by God, being a follower of the doctrine of Heraclitus introduces covetous-

---

[†] Yonge's title, *The Third Book of the Treatise on The Allegories of the Sacred Laws, after the Work of the Six Days of Creation.*
[1] Genesis 8:8.
[2] Genesis 25:27.
[3] Exodus 1:21.

[4] Deuteronomy 4:39.
[5] Exodus 17:6.

ness and indigence, and one universe, and all kinds of things alternately. (8) In reference to which the Holy Scripture says "Let them send forth from the holy soul every leper, and every one afflicted with foul disease, and every one who is impure in his soul, both male and female, and all mutilated persons, and all these who are emasculated, and all whoremongers,"[6] men who flee from the authority of one God, and who are expressly forbidden "to come into the assembly of God;"[7] (9) but wise reasons are not only not concealed, but are even eager to manifest themselves. Do you not see that Abraham was still standing in the place of the Lord, and coming near to him said "do not then destroy the righteous with impious,"[8] him who is manifest to you and well known by you, with him who flees from you and seeks to escape your notice, for he indeed is impious, but the righteous man is one who stands before you and does not flee. For it is right indeed master that you alone should be honoured, (10) but it does not follow that as an impious man is discovered so also is a pious man; but it is sufficient if he is just. On which account he says "do not then destroy the righteous with the wicked." For not even one single man on earth honours God in a worthy manner, but only according to righteousness. For when it is not possible for a man to exhibit due gratitude even to his parents, for it is impossible for him to become their parents in his turn; how can it be anything but absolutely impossible adequately to requite God, or worthily to praise him who created the whole universe out of things that had no previous existence. "For God made all virtue."

IV. (11) Be thou therefore O my soul in all your entirety always visible to God, for three separate times, that is to say for time divided according to a threefold division; not drawing after you the female passion arising from external sensation, but offering up to him manly thought, the encourager to and practiser of persevering courage. "For at three seasons of the year every male must appear before the Lord the God of Israel"[9] this is the injunction of the holy scriptures. (12) On this account Moses when he appears to God in visible form, flees from the dispersing disposition, that is from Pharaoh, who boasts, saying, that he does not know the Lord, "for Moses," says he, "retreated from the presence of Pharaoh, and dwelt in the land of Midian"[10] that is to say, being interpreted, in the judgment of the nature of things; and sat down upon a well, waiting to see what good which might be drank in God would rain upon his thirsting and eager soul. (13) Accordingly he retreats

from the impious opinion which is the mistress of the passions, namely from Pharaoh; and he retreats into Midian, that is to say into judgment, considering anxiously whether he ought to live in tranquil inactivity or whether he ought again to contend with that wicked man to his own destruction. And he considers whether if he attacks him he shall be able to gain the victory, from which consideration he restrains himself waiting, as I have already said, to see if God will give to his deep and not frivolous consideration, a fountain sufficient to wash away the impetuosity of the king of Egypt, that is to say of his own passions. (14) And he is thought worthy of grace, for having fought the good fight in behalf of virtue he never ceases from warring till he sees the pleasures overthrown and baulked of their object.

And with this view Moses does not flee from Pharaoh, for if he had done so he would have fled without returning; but withdraws for a time, that is to say he makes a truce from the war, after the fashion of a wrestler who seeks a respite and collects his breath again, until, having aroused the alliance of prudence and the other virtues he attacks his enemy once more, by divine reason, with the most vigorous power. (15) But Jacob, for he is a supplanter, having acquired virtue by regular system and discipline, not without hard labour, for his name had not as yet been changed to Israel, "fled from the affairs of labour"[11] that is to say from colours and figures, and in short from bodies the nature of which is to wound the soul through the objects of outward sense; for since, when he was present, he could not entirely and utterly subdue them, he fled, fearing to be subdued by them. And he is very worthy of praise for so doing; for "says Moses you will make the children of Israel cautious,"[12] but not bold, or covetous of those things, which do not belong to them.

V. (16) "And Jacob concealed himself from Laban the Syrian, in that he told him not that he was about to flee from him, and he fled from him, taking with him all that he had, and he crossed the river, and proceeded towards the Mount Gilead." It was most natural for him to conceal that he was about to flee, and not to inform Laban, who was a man depending wholly on thoughts such as arise from the outward senses, just as if you have seen some excellent beauty and are charmed with it, and are likely to be led into error in respect of it, you should privily flee from the imagination of it, and never tell it to your mind, that is to say, never think of it again nor give it any consideration, for continued recollections of anything are not without making some distinct impression, and injure the intellect and turn it out of the right way,

---

[6]Numbers 5:2.
[7]Deuteronomy 23:2.
[8]Genesis 18:23.
[9]Deuteronomy 15:16.
[10]Exodus 2:15.

[11]Genesis 31:20.
[12]Leviticus 15:31.

even against its will. (17) And the same reasoning applies to all temptations which arise in respect of any one of the external senses, for in all such cases secret flight is the preserver from danger. But to keep recalling the temptation to one's mind, and to talk of it and dwell upon it subdues and enslaves the reason by force. Do not these then ever, O my mind, report to yourself any object of outward sense that has been seen by you, if you are likely to be led away captive by it, and do not dwell on it, in order that you may not become miserable by being subdued by it, but rather, while you are still free, rise up and flee, preferring untamed liberty to slavery and subjection to a master.

VI. (18) But why now, as if Jacob had been ignorant that Laban was a Syrian, does Moses say, "And Jacob concealed himself from Laban the Syrian." This expression, however, has a reason in it which is not superfluous; for the name Syria, being interpreted, means high. Jacob, therefore, being an experienced man, that is to say, being mind, when he sees passion low and powerless, abides it, thinking that he shall be able to subdue it by force: but when he beholds it high, and bearing its neck haughtily, and full of arrogance, then experienced mind flees first, and afterwards the other parts of his experience do also flee, namely reading, meditation, care, the recollection of what is honourable, temperance, the energy in pursuit of what is becoming; and so he crosses over the river of the objects affecting the outward senses, which wash over and threaten to submerge the soul by the impetuosity of the passions, and having crossed over he proceed towards the high and lofty reason of perfect virtue; (19) for "he proceeded towards the Mount of Gilead;" and Gilead being interpreted means the migration of testimony, since God caused the soul to migrate from the passions which surrounded Laban, and bore witness to it, that it should migrate and receive another settlement, because it was profitable and expedient, and conducted it onwards from the evils calculated to render the soul base, and seeking the things that are on the earth, to the height and magnitude of virtue.

(20) On this account Laban, the friend of the outward senses, and one who energised according to them and not according to his mind, is indignant, and pursues after him and says, "why did you flee from me secretly, and not remain for the enjoyment of your soul, and for the opinions which judge concerning the body and the external good things of the world?" But in fleeing from this opinion you have despoiled me also of my prudence, Leah and Rachel; for they, when they remained in the soul created, prudence in it, but now that they have departed they have left it ignorance and inexperience." On which account he adds, "You

have stripped me," that is to say, you have robbed me of my prudence.

VII. (21) And what that prudence was he will proceed to tell us, for he adds, "And you have led away my daughters as captives; and if you had told me, I would myself have sent you away."[13] You would not have sent away things which were at variance with one another, for if you had sent them away really, and had emancipated the soul, you would have removed from it all bodily sounds, and such as affect the outward senses; for in this way the intellect is emancipated from evils and passions. But now you say that you send it away free, but by your actions you confess that you would have retained it in a prison; for if you had sent it on its way with musical instruments, and drums and harps, and all the pleasures which affect the outward senses, you would not in reality have released it at all; (22) for it is not you then only from whom we are fleeing, O Laban, thou companion of bodies and colours, but we are also escaping from everything that is thine, in which the voices of the outward senses sound in harmony with the energies of the passions. For we, if at least we are practisers of virtue, have meditated a very necessary meditation, which Jacob also meditated, namely, to overthrow and destroy those gods who are hostile to the soul, gods made by hands, gods whom Moses forbade the people to make;[14] and these gods are the destruction of virtue and of a good state of the passions, but the consolation and confirmation of vice and the appetites; for that metal which is cast, after it has been fused, is soon consolidated again.

VIII. (23) But Moses speaks thus, "And they gave to Jacob the foreign gods which were in their hands, and the earrings which were in their ears; and Jacob hid them under the turpentine tree which was in Shechem."[15] These are the gods of the wicked, but Jacob is not said to have taken them, but to have concealed and destroyed them, for every case being most accurately described, for the virtuous man will take nothing from wickedness for his own advantage, but will conceal all such things and destroy them secretly. (24) Just as Abraham tells the king of Sodom, when he was proposing to give him things of irrational nature in exchange for rational animals, namely, horses in exchange for men, "that he would take nothing that belonged to him, but that he would stretch out "the action of his soul," which, speaking symbolically, he called "his hand," to the most high God;[16] "for that he had not taken from a thread

---

[13] Genesis 31:27.
[14] Leviticus 19:4.
[15] Genesis 35:4.
[16] Genesis 14:21.

even to a shoe-latchet of all that was his (the king of Sodom's), in order that the king might never say that he had made the discerning man," namely Abraham, "rich," exchanging poverty for wealthy virtue.

(25) The passions are always concealed and guarded in Shechem; and the name Shechem being interpreted means "the shoulder;" for he who labours concerning pleasures is inclined to preserve them. But the passions are concealed and destroyed by the wise man, and that too not for a brief space of time, but up to this present day, that is to say, for ever, for all time is measured by the present day, for the cycle of one day is the measure of all time. (26) On which account Jacob gives Joseph Shechem, [17] as an especial portion beyond the rest of his brethren, meaning thereby the bodily things which are the objects of the outward senses, since he had gone through labour in respect of them; but to Judah the confessor he gave not presents but praise, and hymns and divine songs, in which he should be celebrated by his brethren. And Jacob did not receive Shechem as a gift from God, but he took it with his sword and with his bow, that is to say, by words, which had the power of cutting and repelling; for the wise man subjects all secondary things to himself, and when he has so subjected them he does not retain them, but makes a present of them to him who is by nature adapted to them. (27) Do you not see that also, when he appeared to take the gods, he did not take them but concealed them and put them out of the way, and destroyed them out of his sight for ever. Now to what soul could it have happened to conceal vice and to put it out of the way, except to that soul to which God was revealed, and which he considered worthy to receive the revelation of his unspeakable mysteries? For he says, "shall I hide from Abraham my son that thing which I am doing?" [18] Well done, O Saviour, in that thou showest thy works to the soul which desires good things, and has concealed from it no one of thy works: and by reason of this conduct of thine he is able to avoid evil, and to conceal it and keep it out of sight, and to destroy for ever the passions which are injurious.

IX. (28) We have shown, therefore, in what manner the wicked man is a fugitive, and how he conceals himself from God; but now let us consider where he conceals himself. "In the middle," says Moses, "of the trees of the garden;" [19] that is to say, in the middle of the mind, which again is itself the centre of the whole soul, as the trees are of the garden. For the man who escapes from God flees to himself, (29) for, since there are two

things, the mind of the universe, which is God, and also the separate mind of each individual, he who escapes from the mind which is in himself flees to the mind of the universe; and conversely, he who forsakes his own individual mind, confesses that all the things of the human mind are of no value, and attributes everything to God; again, he who seeks to escape from God asserts, by so doing, that God is not the cause of anything, but looks upon himself as the cause of everything that exists.

(30) At all events it is affirmed by many people, that everything in the world is borne on spontaneously without any guide or governor, and that the human mind, by its own single power, has invented arts and pursuits, and laws and customs, and all the principles of political and individual, and common justice, with reference both to men and to irrational animals. (31) But dost thou not see, O soul, the unreasonable character of these opinions? For one of them having the particular mind, which was created and which is mortal, does in reality ascribe it to the mind of the universe, which is uncreated and immortal: and the other again, repudiating God, most inconsistently drags forward, as an ally, that mind which is unable even to assist itself.

X. (32) On this account also Moses says, that "If a thief be detected in the act of breaking into a house, and be smitten so that he die, that shall not be imputed as murder to him who has smitten him; but if the sun be risen upon him, then he is liable, and shall die in retaliation." [20] For if any one cuts down and destroys that reason which stands upright and is sound and correct, which testifies to God that he alone is able to do everything, and is found in the act of breaking in upon it, that is to say, standing over this reason thus wounded and destroyed, and who recognises his own mind as energising, and not God, is a thief, taking away what belongs to others, (33) for all things belong to God; so he who attributes anything to himself is taking away what belongs to another, and receives a very severe blow and one difficult to heal, namely, arrogance, a thing nearly akin to imprudence and ignorance. But he says nothing as to the name of him who has smitten him, for the smiter is not a different person from him who is smitten.

But as a man who rubs himself is likewise a person who is rubbed, and as he who stretches himself out is also the person who is stretched out, for he himself both exerts the power of the agent, and also fills the part of the patient. In like manner is he, who steals the things which belong to God, and attributes them to himself, subjected to the tortures of his own impiety and arrogance. (34) Would that the man so stricken might die, that is

[17] Genesis 48:22.
[18] Genesis 18:17.
[19] Genesis 3:8.

[20] Exodus 22:1.

to say might perish before he had succeeded in his objects, for then he will appear to be less sinful, for of vice one kind is discerned in habit, and another kind in motion; but the one which is discerned in motion has an inclination towards the perfecting of its operation, on which account it is more mischievous than the one which is discerned only in habit. (35) If therefore the mind, which imagines itself and not God to be the cause of things, dies, that is to say, becomes inactive and contracts itself, then there is no cause of death in it; it has not absolutely destroyed the living opinion, which attributes all power, and all exertion of power to God, but if the Sun rises, that is to say the mind which appears brilliant in us, and if it appears to see through everything and to judge everything, and not to flee from itself, it then becomes liable to death, and shall die in retaliation for the living doctrine which it has destroyed; according to which God alone is the cause of everything, being found to be wholly unable to effect any good purpose, and to be truly dead in as much as it has shown itself the interpreter of a lifeless and dead and departed doctrine.

XI. (36) And it is in reference to this that the Holy Scripture curses "any one who has placed in any secret place any carved thing, or any thing made of cast metal, the work of the hands of an artist."[21] For why, O mind, do you store and treasure up within yourself depraved opinions, that God is a being of such and such qualities, (he who has no distinctive qualities) like a carved work; or that he who is imperishable is perishable like images that are cast in the foundry; and why do you not rather bring them forward openly that you may learn what is right from men who practise the truth? For you think that you are endowed with some great skill because you have devised absurd opinions imposing upon you by an appearance of probability, in opposition to the truth: but in reality you are proved to be destitute of skill, in as much as you are unwilling to be healed of that terrible disease of the soul, ignorance.

XII. (37) But that the wicked man skins into and is concealed within his own scattered mind, fleeing from the real mind or truth, is testified by Moses "who smote the Egyptian and buried him in the sand,"[22] the meaning of which is that he by his arguments convinced him who asserted that the good things of the body were the most excellent, and who thought that the good things of the soul were of no value, and who likewise esteemed the pleasures as the end of life. (38) For when he had comprehended the labour of him who beholds God, which the king of Egypt had imposed on him, (and by the king of Egypt is meant vice,

which is the guide of the passions) he sees an Egyptian man, that is to say human passions operating at a seasonable moment, beating and insulting the man who behold God, and looking round upon the whole soul on this side and on that side, and seeing no one standing by except the true God, and everything else in a state of confusion and disorder, having stricken down and convicted the lover of pleasure, he hides him in the dispersed and agitated mind, which is deprived of all kindred with and comprehension of what is good.

(39) This man then is hidden in himself, but the man who is opposite to him escapes from himself, and flees to the God of all existing things.

XIII. On which account Moses says moreover, "He led him forth out of doors and said to him, look up to heaven, and count the stars,"[23] which we should be glad indeed to see thoroughly and to comprehend; since we are insatiable in our love for notice, but nevertheless we are unable to measure the riches of God. (40) Nevertheless thanks be to that magnificent and bounteous God because he says that he has implanted in the soul seeds as brilliant, as visible at a distance, and as eternally new as the stars in heaven. And it is not a superfluous addition when after having said "he led him forth," he subjoins "out of doors," for who is ever led forth in doors? But perhaps what he says here has some such meaning as this; he led him forth into the outermost place, not into some place or other out of doors, which might be surrounded by other places.

For as in dwelling houses the man's chamber is outside the woman's chamber, and the inner chamber is within, and the vestibule is outside of the hall but within the doorway, so also in the case of the soul that which is within one thing may be outside of some other thing. (41) This then is the sense in which we must understand this passage; he led the mind forth into the outermost place, for what was the use of his leaving the body and fleeing to the outward senses; and what would have been the use of his discarding the outward senses, and subjecting that which exists to the voice? For it is fitting that the mind which is about to be led forth, and to be dismissed in freedom should be emancipated from all corporeal necessities, from all the organs of the outward senses, from all sophistical ratiocinations, and plausible persuasions, and last of all from itself.

XIV. (42) On which account in another passage also he boasts, saying "the Lord the God of Heaven, and the God of earth who took me out of the house of my father."[24] For it is not possible for one who dwells in the body and belongs to the race of mortals to be united with God, but he alone

---

[21]Deuteronomy 27:15.
[22]Exodus 2:12.

[23]Genesis 15:5.
[24]Genesis 24:7.

can be so whom God delivers from that prison house of the body. (43) On which account also, that joy of the soul, Isaac, when he is conversing and discoursing privately with God, comes forth forsaking himself and his own mind, for he says, "Come forth, O Isaac, to converse in the plain towards evening,"[25] and Moses, that word of prophecy, says, "When I go forth from the city," that is from my soul, (for the soul is the city of the living creature, in as much as it is the soul which gives it its laws and customs), "I will stretch forth my hands,"[26] and I will reveal and unfold all my actions to God, invoking him as a witness and inspector of every one of them, from whom it is impossible by its own nature that vice should be hidden, but to whom it must be unfolded and by whom it must be clearly discerned.

(44) When therefore the soul is made manifest in all its sayings and doings, and is made a partaker of the divine nature, the voices of the external senses are reduced to silence, and so likewise are all troublesome and ill-omened sounds, for the objects of sight often speak loudly and invite the sense of sight to themselves; and so do voices invite the sense of hearing; scents invite the smell, and altogether each varied object of sense invites its appropriate sense. But all these things are put at rest when the mind going forth out of the city of the soul, attributes all its own actions and conceptions to God.

XV. (45) "For the hands of Moses are heavy."[27] For since the actions of the wicked man are like the wind and light, those of the wise man on the other hand are heavy and immovable, and not easily shaken; in reference to which his hands are held up by Aaron, who is reason, or by Ur, who is light. Now of all existing things there is nothing clearer than the truth; therefore Moses intends here to signify by a symbolical form of expression, that the actions of the wise man are supported by the most necessary of all qualities, reason and truth. On this account also, when Aaron dies, that is to say, when the truth is completely asserted, he ascends up to Ur,[28] that is to say, to Light; for the proper end of reason is truth, which is more visible than any light, and to it reason is always striving to come.

(46) Do you not see that also when he received the tabernacle from God, and this tabernacle is wisdom, in which the wise man tabernacles and, dwells, he fixed it firmly and founded and built it up strongly, not in the body but out of it; for he likens this to an encampment, to a camp I say full of wars and of all the evils which war causes, and which has not portion with peace.

"And it was called the tabernacle of testimony;"[29] that is to say wisdom was borne witness to by God. For every one who seeks the Lord went forth out of his house. And this is well said. (47) For if you seek God, O my mind, go forth out of yourself, and so seek for him; but if you remain in the substance of the body, or in the vain opinions of the mind, you are then without any real wish to search into divine things, even if you do put on the appearance and pretence of seeking them. If when you search you will find God, is uncertain; for there have been many persons to whom he has not revealed himself, but they have expended a vain labour all their time. But the mere act of seeking for him is sufficient to entitle you to a participation in good things, for the desire for what is good, even if it fails in attaining the end which it seeks, does at all events always gladden the heart of those who cherish it.

(48) Thus the wicked man who flees from virtue, and who seeks to conceal himself from God, flees to a powerless ally, that is his own mind, but the good man on the contrary seeking to escape from himself turns to the knowledge of the one God, and is victorious in the honourable race, and in that contest which is of all the most excellent.

XVI. (49) "And the Lord God called Adam, and said unto him, where art thou?"[30] Why now is Adam, alone called, when his wife also was concealed together with him? In the first place we must say that the mind is summoned, and asked where it is. When it is converted, and reproved for its offence, not only is it summoned itself but all its faculties are also summoned, for without its faculties the mind by itself is found to be naked, and to be absolutely nothing, and one of its faculties is also the outward sense, that is to say the woman. (50) The woman therefore, that is the outward sense is also summoned together with Adam, that is the mind, but separately God does not summon her. Why not? Because being destitute of reason she is incapable of being convicted by herself. For neither can sight, nor hearing, nor any one of the other external senses be taught, and moreover none of them are capable of receiving the comprehension of things; for the Creator has not made them capable of distinguishing anything but bodies only. But the mind is able to receive teaching: on account of which fact God calls that, but not the external senses.

XVII. (51) And the expression "Where art thou?" admits of being interpreted in many ways. In the first place it may be taken not as an interrogation, but as an affirmation, equivalent to the words "You are somewhere," if you alter the accent on the particle *pou* "where." For, since you have

---

[25] Genesis 24:62.
[26] Exodus 9:29.
[27] Exodus 17:12.
[28] Numbers 20:25.

[29] Exodus 33:7.
[30] Genesis 3:9.

thought that God was walking in the garden, and was surrounded by it, learn now that in this you were mistaken, and hear from God who knows all things that most true statement that God is not in any one place. For he is not surrounded by anything, but he does himself surround everything. For that which is created is in place; for it is inevitable that it must be surrounded, and not be the thing which surrounds.

(52) In the second placed, that which is said is equivalent to this, Where hast thou been, O soul? What evils hast thou chosen instead of what good things? When God invited you to a participation in virtue, have you pursued vice? And when he offered to you for your enjoyment the tree of life, that is to say the tree of wisdom by which you might live, have you hastened into ignorance and to destruction, preferring misery, the death of the soul to the happiness of eternal life?

(53) The third interpretation is the interrogative one; to which there may be two answers given. The one, if the answer be given to the inquirer, "Where art thou?" is, "Nowhere." For the soul of the wicked man has no place to which it can go, or in which it can be situated. In respect of which fact the wicked man is said to be destitute of place; but an evil destitute of place is one which is difficult to manage. And such is the man who is void of good qualities, being always agitated and in a state of confusion, and wavering about after the fashion of an unsteady breeze being altogether the companion of no single steady opinion.

(54) The other answer may be of this kind; that which Adam himself uses. "Hear where I am," where those are who are unable to see God; where those are who do not listen to God; where those are who endeavour to conceal themselves from him who is the author of all things: where those are who flee from virtue, where those are who are destitute of wisdom, where those are who are alarmed and tremble because of the unmanliness and cowardice of their souls. For when Adam says, "I heard thy voice in the paradise and I was afraid because I was naked and I hid myself," he exhibits all the qualities enumerated above, as I have shown, more at length, in the former books of this treatise.

XVIII. (55) And yet Adam is not now naked. It has been said a little before that "they made themselves girdles," but by this expression Moses intends to teach you that he is not meaning here to speak of the nakedness of the body, but of that in respect of which the mind is found to be wholly deficient in and destitute of virtue. (56) "The woman," says Adam, "whom you gave to be with me, she gave me of the tree and I did eat." The expression here is very accurate, inasmuch as he does not say, "The woman whom you gave to me," but "The woman whom you gave to be with me." For you did not give me the outward senses as a possession, but you left them free and unim-

peded, and in some sort not at all yielding to the injunctions of my intellect. If therefore the mind were to be inclined to command the sight not to see, it nevertheless would see any subject which came before it. And the hearing also will in every case apprehend any sound which falls upon it, even if the mind in its jealousy were to command it not to hear. And again the smell will smell every scent which reaches it, even if the mind were to forbid it to apprehend it.

(57) On this account it is that God did not give the outward sense to the creature, but to be with the creature. And the meaning of this is, the inward sense in conjunction with our mind knows every thing, and does so too at the same moments with the mind. As for instance the sense of sight in conjunction and simultaneously with the mind strikes upon the subject of sight; for the eye sees the substance, and immediately the mind comprehends the thing seen, that is black or white, or pale, or red, or triangular, or quadrangular, or round, or that is of any other colour or shape as the case may be. And so again the sense of hearing is affected by a sound, and with the sense of hearing the mind is also affected; and the proof of it is this; the mind immediately distinguishes the character of the voice, that it is thin, or that it has substance, or that it is melodious and tuneful; or, on the other hand, that it is out of tune and inharmonious. And the same is found to be the case in respect of the rest of the inward senses.

(58) And very appropriately do we see that Adam adds this assertion, "She gave me of the tree;" but he gives an habitation made of wood and perceptible by the outward senses to the mind except that outward sense itself. For what gave to the mind to be able to distinguish body, or whiteness? Was it not the sight? And what enabled it to distinguish sounds? Was it not the hearing? What, again, endowed it with the faculty of judging of smells? Was it not the sense of smell? What enabled it to decide upon flavours? Was it not the taste? What invested it with the power of distinguishing between rough and smooth? Was it not the touch? Correctly, therefore, and with complete truth was it said by the mind, that it was the outward sense alone which gave me the power to comprehend the corporeal substance.

XIX. (59) And God said to the woman, "What is this that thou hast done?" And she said, "The serpent beguiled me and I did eat." God asks one question of the outward sense, and she replies to a different one. For he is putting a question which has reference to the man; but she in her reply speaks not of the man but of herself, saying, "I ate," not I gave. (60) May we then by the use of allegory solve the question which was here put, and show that the woman gave a felicitous and correct answer to the question? For it follows of necessity that when she had eaten, her husband did also eat, for when the outward sense striking upon its object is filled with its appearance, then immediately the mind joins it and takes its share of it, and is in a manner made perfect by the nourishment which it receives form it. This therefore is what she says, I unintentionally gave it to my husband, for while I was applying myself to what was presented to me, he, being very easily and quickly moved, impressed its appearance and image upon himself.

XX. (61) But take notice that the man says that the woman gave it to him; but that the woman does not say that the serpent gave it to her, but that he beguiled her; for it is the especial property of the outward sense to give, but it is the attribute of pleasure which is of a diversified and serpent-like nature to deceive and to beguile. For instance, the outward sense presents to the mind the image of what is white by nature, or black, or hot, or cold, not deceiving it, but acting truly; for the subjects of the outward sense are of such a character, as also is the imagination which presents itself to man from them, in the case of the great majority of men who do not carry their knowledge of natural philosophy to any accurate extent. But pleasure does not present to the mind that the subject is such as it is in reality, but deceives it by its artifice, thrusting that, in which there is no advantage, into the class of things profitable.

(62) For as we may at times see ill-looking courtezans dyeing and painting their faces in order to conceal the plainness of their countenances, so also may we see the intemperate man acting who is inclined to the pleasures of the belly. He looks upon great abundance of wine and a luxurious store of food as a good thing, though he is injured by them both in his body and in his soul. (63) Again, we may often see lovers madly eager to be loved by the ugliest of women, because pleasure deceives them and all but affirms positively to them that beauty of form, and delicacy of complexion, and healthiness of flesh, and symmetry of limb, exists in those who have the exact contraries to all these qualifications. Accordingly, they overlook those who are truly possessed of perfectly irreproachable beauty, and waste away with love for such creatures as I have mentioned. (64) Every kind of deceit therefore is closely connected with pleasure; and every kind of gift with the outward sense: for the one bewilders the mind with sophistry and misleads it, representing to it anything that comes before it, not in the character which really belongs to it, but in one that does not. But the outward sense presents bodies, plainly as they are according to their real nature, without any device or artifice.

XXI. (65) "And the Lord God said to the serpent, Because thou hast done this thing, thou art cursed above all cattle and every beats of the field; upon thy breast and upon thy belly shalt thou go,

and dust shalt thou eat all the days of thy life. And I will put enmity in the midst between thee and between the woman, and in the midst between thy seed and between her seed, He shall bruise thy head, and thou shalt bruise his heel."[31] What is the reason why he curses the serpent without allowing him to make any defence, when in another place he commands that "both the parties between whom there is any dispute shall be heard,"[32] and that one shall not be believed till the other has been heard? (66) And indeed in this case you see that he did not give a prejudged belief to Adam's statement against his wife; but he gave her also an opportunity of defending herself, when he asked her, "Why hast thou done this?" But she confessed that she had erred through the deceitfulness of serpent-like and diversified pleasure. Why, therefore, when the woman had said, "The serpent deceived me,"[33] did he forbid the putting of the question to the serpent whether it was he who had thus deceived her; and why did he thus appoint him to be condemned without trial and without defence?

(67) We must say, therefore, that the external senses are not a peculiar property of either bad or good men, but that they are of an intermediate nature, and common to both the wise man and the fool, and when they are found in the fool, they are bad; but when they are found in the wise man, they are good. Very naturally therefore, since it has a nature which is not necessarily and intrinsically evil, but one which being capable of either character, inclines at different times and under different circumstances towards either extremity, it is not condemned till it has itself confessed that it followed the worse inclination. (68) But the serpent, that is pleasure, is of itself evil. On this account it is absolutely not found at all in the virtuous man; but the wicked man alone enjoys it. Very properly therefore does God curse it before it has time to make any defence, inasmuch as it has no seed of virtue within it, but is at all times and in all places blameable and polluting.

XXII. (69) On this account also, God "saw that Er was wicked,"[34] without any apparent cause for this judgment of his character, and he slew him. For God is not unaware that that leathern mass which covers us, namely, the body; for Er being interpreted means leather, is an evil thing, and one which plots against the soul, and which is at all times lifeless and dead. For what else does he compel any one of us to do but to carry about a dead body, our soul raising up the body which as far as its own nature goes is dead, and bearing it

[31]Genesis 3:14.
[32]Deuteronomy 19:17.
[33]Genesis 3:13.
[34]Genesis 38:7.

almost without difficulty? And just consider, if you will, the great energy of the soul, (70) for the most vigorous athlete would not be able to carry about a statue of himself for even a short time; but the soul, without any exertion and without any fatigue, carries about the statue of a man occasionally even for as long a time as a hundred years; for even at the end of that period it does not kill it, but only gets rid of a body which was dead from the beginning. (71) And it is evil by nature, as I have said before, and a thing which plots against the soul, but which is not visible to all men, but only to God, and to such men as are friends to God. "For the wicked Er," says Moses, "was an enemy of the Lord."

For when the mind busies itself with sublime contemplations, and becomes initiated into the mysteries of the Lord, it judges the body to be a wicked and hostile thing; but when it abandons its investigations of divine things, it then looks upon the body as something friendly, and belonging to and nearly akin to itself; and accordingly it flies to the things which are dear to it. (72) On this account the soul of the athlete and the soul of the philosopher differ; for the athlete attributes all his importance to the good condition of his body, and would throw away his soul itself in the cause of his body, as being a man devoted to his body; but the philosopher, being a lover of what is virtuous, cares for that which is alive within him, namely his soul, and disregards his body which is dead, having no other object but to prevent the most excellent portion of him, namely his soul, from being injured by the evil and dead thing which is connected with it.

XXIII. (73) You see that it is not the Lord who is here spoken of as slaying Er, but God. For he does not kill the body in respect of the absolute and irresponsible power which he possesses, and by which he rules and governs the universe, but in respect of that authority which he possesses in consequence of his goodness and excellence, for God is the name of goodness, the cause of all things; that you may understand that he also created all inanimate things, not by his authority, but by his goodness, by which also he created all living things; for it was requisite for the manifestation of the better things, that there should also be a subordinate creation of the inferior things, through the power of the same goodness which was the cause of all, which is God. (74) When, then, O Soul! shall you most especially consider that you have gained a victory? Will it not be when you are made perfect, and when you have been thought worthy of decisions in your favour and of crowns? For then you will be a lover of God, not of the body, and you will receive prizes, inasmuch as your wife shall be Thamar the bride of Judah, and Thamar being interpreted means the palm-tree, the symbol of victory. And a proof of this is,

that when Er married her, he was at once discovered to be a wicked man, and was slain; for Moses says, "And Judah took a wife for Er, his first-born son, whose name was Thamar;" and immediately afterwards he adds, "And Er was a wicked man before the Lord, and God slew him;" for when the mind has carried off the prize of virtue, it condemns the dead body to death.

(75) You see that God also curses the serpent without allowing it to make any defence, for it is pleasure: and so also he slays Er without any visible cause being alleged, for Er is the body. And if you consider, O good friend, you will find that God has created in the soul some natural qualities which are in themselves faulty and blameless, and also in every soul some which are virtuous and praiseworthy, as is the case likewise with plants and animals. (76) Do you not see that the Creator has made some plants capable of cultivation and useful and salutary, and others incapable of cultivation, wild, pernicious, the causes of diseases and destruction; and animals too of similar variety of character, as beyond all question is the serpent, of which we are now speaking; for he is a destructive and deadly animal by his intrinsic nature. And as the serpent affects man, so does pleasure too affect the soul; in reference to which fact the serpent has been compared to pleasure.

XXIV. (77) As, therefore, God hates pleasure and the body without any especial cause, so also does he give pre-eminent honour to virtuous natures without any visible cause; not alleging any action of theirs before the praises of them which he utters. For if any one were to ask why Moses says that "Noah found grace before the Lord God,"[35] without having previously done any good thing, as far at least as we know, we shall be very properly answered, that he was proved to be a praiseworthy character and order of creation; for the name Noah, being interpreted, means rest, or just: and it follows of necessity that one who is resting from acts of injustice and from sins, and who, so resting, lives with virtue and justice, must find grace before God; (78) and to find grace, is not only, as some call it, equivalent to the expression "pleasing God," but it has some such meaning as this.

The just man seeking to understand the nature of all existing things, makes this one most excellent discovery, that everything which exists, does so according to the grace of God, and that there is nothing ever given by, just as there is nothing possessed by, the things of creation. On which account also it is proper to acknowledge gratitude to the Creator alone. Accordingly, to those persons who seek to investigate what is the origin of creation, we may most correctly make answer, that

---

[35] Genesis 6:8.

it is the goodness and the grace of God, which he has bestowed on the human race; for all the things which are in the world, and the world itself, are the gift and benefaction and free grace of God.

XXV. (79) Moreover, God made Melchisedek, the king of peace, that is of Salem, for that is the interpretation of this name, "his own high priest,"[36] without having previously mentioned any particular action of his, but merely because he had made him a king, and a lover of peace, and especially worthy of his priesthood. For he is called a just king, and a king is the opposite of a tyrant, because the one is the interpreter of law, and the other of lawlessness. (80) Therefore the tyrannical mind imposes violent and mischievous commands on both soul and body, and such as have a tendency to cause violent suffering, being commands to act according to vice, and to indulge the passions with enjoyment. But the other, the kingly mind, in the first place, does not command, but rather persuades, since it gives recommendations of such a character, that if guided by them, life, like a vessel, will enjoy a fair voyage through life, being directed in its course by a good governor and pilot; and this good pilot is right reason. (81) We may therefore call the tyrannical mind the ruler of war, and the kingly mind the guide to peace, that is Salem.

And this kingly mind shall bring forth food full of cheerfulness and joy; for "he brought forth bread and wine," which the Ammonites and Moabites were not willing to give to the beholder, that is Israel; by reason of such unwillingness they are shut out from the companionship and assembly of God. For the Ammonites being they who are sprung from the outward sense of the mother, and the Moabites, who originate in the mind of the father, are two different dispositions, which look upon the mind and the outward sense as the efficient causes of all existing things, but take no notice of God. Therefore "they shall not come," says Moses, "into the assembly of the Lord, because they did not come to meet you with bread and water when you came out of Egypt,"[37] that is, out of the passions.

XXVI. (82) But Melchisedek shall bring forward wine instead of water, and shall give your souls to drink, and shall cheer them with unmixed wine, in order that they may be wholly occupied with a divine intoxication, more sober than sobriety itself. For reason is a priest, having, as its inheritance the true God, and entertaining lofty and sublime and magnificent ideas about him, "for he is the priest of the most high God."[38] Not that there is any other God who is not the most high; for

God being one, is in the heaven above, and in the earth beneath, and there is no other besides him."[39] But he sets in motion the notion of the Most High, from his conceiving of God not in a low and grovelling spirit, but in one of exceeding greatness, and exceeding sublimity, apart from any conceptions of matter.

XXVII. (83) And what good thing had Abraham done as yet when God called him and bade him become a stranger to his country and to this "generation," and to dwell in the land which the Lord should give him?[40] And that is a good and populous city, and one of great happiness. For the gifts of God are great and honourable. But he made this position of Abraham also to be typical, containing an emblem worthy of attentive consideration. For Abraham, being interpreted, means "Lofty Father;"[41] a title of admiration in both its divisions. (84) For when the mind does not, like a master, threaten the soul, but rather guides it, like a father, not indulging it in the pleasant things, but giving it what is expedient for it, even against its will, and also turning it away from all lowly things and such as lead it to mortal paths, it leads it to sublime contemplations and makes it dwell amid speculations on the world and its constituent parts. And, moreover, mounting up higher, it investigates the Deity itself, and his nature, through an unspeakable lore of knowledge, in consequence of which it cannot be content to abide in the original decrees, but, being improved itself, becomes also desirous of removing to a better habitation.

XXVIII. (85) But there are some persons whom, even before their creation, God creates and disposes excellently; respecting whom he determines beforehand that they shall have a most excellent inheritance. Do you not see what he says about Isaac to Abraham, when he had no hope of any such thing, namely, that he should become the father of such an offspring, but did rather laugh at the promise, and asked, "Shall a son be born to me, who am a hundred years old; and shall Sarah, who is ninety years old, bring forth a child?"[42] But God asserts it positively, and ratifies his promise saying, "Yea, behold Sarah, thy wife, shall bear thee a son, and thou shalt call his name Isaac, and I will establish my covenant towards him for an everlasting covenant."

(86) What then is the reason which caused this man, also, to be praised before his birth? There are some good things which are an advantage to a man both when they are past, and when they are present, such as good health, a sound condition of the outwards senses, riches, if he be

---

[36] Genesis 14:18.
[37] Deuteronomy 23:4.
[38] Genesis 14:18.

[39] Deuteronomy 4:39.
[40] Genesis 12:1.
[41] Or, "Father of a great multitude," according to the marginal translation in the Bible.
[42] Genesis 17:17.

endowed with them, a good reputation; for all these things may, by a slight perversion of words, be called good things. But some are so not merely when they have been given to us, but even when it is predicted that they shall be so given, as joy as a good affection of the soul; for this does not cheer a man only when it is present and energises actively in him, but it delights him also by anticipations when it is hoped for—for it has this especial quality; all other good qualities have their own separate operation and effect, but joy is both a separate good and a common good, for it comes as a crowning one after all the rest—for we feel joy at good health, and we feel joy at liberty and at honour, and at all other such things, so that one may say with propriety that there is not one single good thing which has not the additional good of joy. (87) But not only do we rejoice at other good things which are already previously past and also at those which are present, but we rejoice also at good things when about to happen to us and expected; as for instance, when we hope that we shall become rich, or that we shall obtain power, or that we shall receive praise, or that we shall find a means to get rid of an illness, or that we shall acquire vigour and strength, or that we shall become learned instead of ignorant, in all these cases we are rejoiced in no slight degree.

Since, then, joy diffuses itself over and cheers the soul, not only while it is present but also even when it is expected, it was very consistent and natural for God to think Isaac worthy of a good name and of a great gift before he was born, for the name of Isaac, being interpreted, means laughter of soul, and delight, and joy.

XXIX. (88) Again, they say that Jacob and Esau, the former being the ruler, and governor, and master, and Esau being the subject and the slave, had their several estates appointed to them while they were still in the womb. For God, the creator of all living things, is thoroughly acquainted with all his works, and before he has completely finished them he comprehends the faculties with which they will hereafter be endowed, and altogether he foreknows all their actions and passions. For when Rebecca, that is the patient soul, proceeds to ask an oracle from God, the answers are, "Two nations are in thy womb, and two people shall come forth from thy bowels, and one people shall be stronger than the other people, and the elder shall serve the younger."[43] (89) For that which is wicked and void of reason is, by its own nature, a slave in the eye of God; but that which is good and endowed with reason and better, is looked upon as powerful and free by him. And this is the case not only when each of these two different characters is perfect in the soul, but when there

is a doubt on the subject; for, altogether, a slight breeze of virtue shows power and supremacy, and not freedom only, and on the other hand, the existence of even an ordinary degree of vice enslaves the reason, even though not by any means as yet come to maturity.

XXX. (90) Again, why did the same Jacob when Joseph brought him his two sons, the elder being Manasses and the younger Ephraim, change his hands, and put his right hand upon the younger brother Ephraim, and his left hand upon the elder brother Manasses? And when Joseph thought this a grievous thing, and thought that his father had unintentionally made a mistake in the matter of the imposition of hands, Jacob said, "I did not make a mistake, but I knew, my son, I knew that this one should be a father of a nation, and should be exalted; but, nevertheless, his younger brother shall be greater than he."[44] (91) What, then, must we say but this? That two natures, both utterly necessary, were created in the soul by God, one memory and the other recollection, of which memory is the best and recollection the worst. For the one has its perceptions fresh and harmonious and clear, so that it never errs through ignorance. But forgetfulness does, in every case, precede recollection, which is but a mutilated and blind thing. (92) And, although recollection is worse, it is nevertheless older than memory, which is better than it, and is also conjoined with and inseparable from it; for when we are first introduced to any art we are unable at once to make ourselves masters of all the speculations which bear upon it. Being, therefore, affected with forgetfulness at first, we subsequently recollect, until from a frequent recurrence of forgetfulness and a frequent recurrence of recollection, memory at last prevails in us in a lasting manner. On which account it is younger than recollection, for it is later in its existence.

(93) And Ephraim is a symbolical name, being, to be interpreted, memory. For, being interpreted, it means the fertility of the soul of the man fond of learning, which brings forth its appropriate fruit when it has confirmed its speculations, and preserves them in its memory. But Manasses, being interpreted, means recollection, for he is spoken of as one who has been translated from forgetfulness, and he who escapes from forgetfulness does unquestionably recollect. Most correctly, therefore, does that supplanter of the passions and practiser of virtue, Jacob, give his right hand to that prolific memory, Ephraim, while he places Manasses, or recollection, in the second rank. (94) And, Moses, also, of all those who sacrificed the passover, praised those who sacrificed first most, because they having crossed over from the pas-

---

sions, that is to say, from Egypt, remained by the passage, and did not hasten any more to the passions which they had quitted; and the others he also thinks worthy to be placed in the second rank, for, having turned back, they retraced their steps, and, as if they had forgotten what it became them to do, they again hastened to do the same things; but the former men continued in their course without turning back. Therefore, Manasses, who is born of forgetfulness, resembles those who were the second party to sacrifice the passover; but the fertile Ephraim is like those who had sacrificed previously.

XXXI. (95) On which account God also calls Bezaleel by name, and says that "He will give him wisdom and knowledge, and that He will make him the builder and the architect of all the things which are in his tabernacle;"[45] that is to say, of all the works of the soul, when he had up to this time done no work which any one could praise—we must say, therefore, that God impressed this figure also on the soul, after the fashion of an approved coin. And we shall know what the impression is if we previously examine the interpretation of the name. (96) Now, Bezaleel, being interpreted, means God in his shadow. But the shadow of God is his word, which he used like an instrument when he was making the world. And this shadow, and, as it were, model, is the archetype of other things. For, as God is himself the model of that image which he has now called a shadow, so also that image is the model of other things, as he showed when he commenced giving the law to the Israelites, and said, "And God made man according to the image of God."[46] as the image was modelled according to God, and as man was modelled according to the image, which thus received the power and character of the model.

XXXII. (97) Let us now, then, examine what the character which is impressed upon man is. The ancient philosophers used to inquire how we obtained our conceptions of the Deity? Men who, those who seemed to philosophise in the most excellent manner, said that from the world and from its several parts, and from the powers which existed in those parts, we formed our notions of the Creator and cause of the world. (98) For as, if a man were to see a house carefully built and well provided with outer courts and porticoes, and men's chambers and women's chambers, and all other necessary apartments, he would form a notion of the architect; for he would never suppose that the house had been completed without skill and without a builder; (99) and, as he would argue in the same manner respecting any city, or any ship, or anything whatever that is made, whether it be great or small, so likewise any one entering this world, as an exceedingly large house or large city, and seeing the heaven revolving round it in a circle and comprehending everything within it, and all the planets and fixed stars moving onwards in the same manner and on the same principles, all in regular order and in due harmony and in such a manner as is most advantageous for the whole created universe, and the earth stationed in the central situation, and the effusions of air and water affixed on the boundaries, and, moreover, all the animals, both mortal and immortal, and the different kinds of plants and fruits, he will surely consider that undoubtedly all these things were not made without skill, but that God both was and is the creator of this whole universe. They, then, who draw their conclusions in this manner perceive God in his shadow, arriving at a due comprehension of the artist through his works.

XXXIII. (100) There is also a more perfect and more highly purified kind which has been initiated into the great mysteries, and which does not distinguish the cause from the things created as it would distinguish an abiding body from a shadow; but which, having emerged from all created objects, receives a clear and manifest notion of the great uncreated, so that it comprehends him through himself, and comprehends his shadow, too, so as to understand what it is, and his reason, too, and this universal world. (101) This kind is that Moses, who speaks thus, "Show thyself to me; let me see thee so as to know thee."[47] for do not thou be manifested to me through the medium of the heaven, or of the earth, or of water, or of air, or, in short, of anything whatever of created things, and let me not see thy appearance in any other thing, as in a looking-glass, except in thee thyself, the true God. For the images which are presented to the sight in executed things are subject to dissolution; but those which are presented in the One uncreate may last for ever, being durable, eternal, and unchangeable.

On this account "God called Moses to him and conversed with him,"[48] (102) and he also called Bezaleel to him, though not in the same way as he had called Moses, but he called the one so that he might receive an idea of the appearance of God from the Creator himself, but the other so that he might by calculation form an idea of the Creator as if from the shadow of the things created. On this account you will find the tabernacle and all its furniture to have been made in the first instance by Moses, and again subsequently by Bezaleel. For Moses fashioned the archetypal forms, and Bezaleel made the imitations of them. For Moses had God himself for an instructor, as he

---

[45] Exodus 31:2.
[46] Genesis 1:26.

[47] Exodus 33:13.
[48] Exodus 35:30.

tells us, when he represents God as saying to him, "Thou shall make every thing according to the example which was shown thee in the Mount"[49] (103) And Bezaleel had Moses for his instructor; and this was very natural. For Aaron the word, and Miriam the outward sense, when they rose up against Moses were expressly told that "If there shall arise a prophet to the Lord, God shall be made known to him in a vision, and in a shadow, but not clearly.[50] But with Moses, who is faithful in all his house, God will speak mouth to mouth in his own form, and not by riddles."

XXXIV. (104) Since therefore we find that there are two natures which have been created and fashioned and accurately and skilfully framed by God; the one being in its own intrinsic nature pernicious and open to reproach, and accursed, and the other beneficial and praiseworthy, the one too having a spurious stamp upon it, but the other having undergone a strict test; we will utter a beautiful and suitable prayer which Moses also addressed to God, praying that God may open his treasurehouse, and may lay before us his sublime word pregnant with divine lights, which he calls the heaven, and may bind fast the storehouses of evil. (105) For, just as there are storehouses of good things so are there also storehouses of evil things with God; as he says in his great song, "Behold are not these things collected with me, and sealed up in my treasurehouses, against the day of vengeance when their foot shall be tripped up?"[51]

You see then that there are several storehouses of evil things, and only one of good things. For since God is One, so also is his storehouse of good things one likewise. But there are many storehouses of evil things because the wicked are infinite in number. And in this observe the goodness of the true God, He opens the treasurehouse of his good things freely, but he binds fast that which contains the evil things. For it is an especial property of God to offer his good things freely and to be beforehand with men in bestowing gifts upon them, but to be slow in bringing evil on them, (106) and Moses dwelling at length upon the munificent and gracious nature of God, says that not only have his storehouses of evil things been sealed up in all other times, but also when the soul is tripped up in the path of right reason, when it is especially fair that it should be considered worthy of punishment; for he says that, "In the day of vengeance the storehouses of evil things have been sealed up," the sacred word of scripture showing that God does not visit with his vengeance even those who sin against him, immediately, but that

he gives them time for repentance, and to remedy and correct their evil conduct.

XXXV. (107) And the Lord God said to the serpent, "Thou art cursed over every creature and over all the beasts of the field." As joy being a good state of the passions is worthy to be prayed for; so also pleasure is worthy to be cursed being a passion, which has altered the boundaries of the soul, and has rendered it a lover of the passions instead of a lover of virtue. And Moses says in his curses, that "He is cursed who removes his neighbour's land mark,"[52] for God placed virtue, that is to say, the tree of life, to be a land mark, and a law unto the soul. But pleasure has removed this, placing in its stead the land mark of vice, the tree of death, (108) "Cursed indeed is he who causeth the blind man to wander in the road." This also is done by that most impious thing pleasure, for the outward sense, inasmuch as it is destitute of reason, is a thing blinded by nature, since the eyes of its reason are put out. In reference to which we may say that it is by reason alone that we attain to a comprehension of things, and no longer by the outward sense; for they are bodies alone that we acquire a conception of by means of the outward senses.

(109) Pleasure therefore has deceived the outward sense which is destitute of any proper comprehension of things, inasmuch as though it might have been turned to the mind, and have been guided by it, it has hindered it from being so, leading it to the external objects of outward sense, and making it desirous of every thing which can call it into operation, in order that the outward sense being defective may follow a blind guide, namely the object of the outward sense, and then the mind being guided by the two things, which are themselves both blind, may plunge headlong to destruction and become utterly unable to restrain itself. (110) For if it were to follow its natural guide then it would be proper for defective things to follow reason which sees clearly, for in that way mischievous things would be less formidable in their attacks. But now, pleasure has put such great artifices in operation to injure the soul, that it has compelled it to use them as guides, cheating it, and persuading it to exchange virtue for evil habits, and to give good habit sin exchange for vice.

XXXVI. But the holy scripture has prohibited such an exchange as this when it says, "Thou shalt not exchange good for evil"[53] (111) On this account therefore pleasure is accursed, and let us now see how well adapted to it are the curses which the scripture denounces against it, "Thou shalt be cursed" says God, "above all creatures." Therefore, the whole race of animals is irrational and

[49]Exodus 25:40.
[50]Numbers 12:6.
[51]Deuteronomy 32:34.

[52]Deuteronomy 27:17.
[53]Leviticus 27:33.

under the guidance only of the external senses; but every one of the outward senses curses pleasure as a most inimical and hostile thing to it; for it is in reality hostile to the outward senses. And the proof of this is that, when we are sated with an immoderate indulgence in pleasure, we are not able either to see, or to hear, or to smell, or to taste, or to touch with any clearness of our faculties, but we make all our essays and approaches in an obscure and imbecile manner. (112) And this happens to us when we are for a moment at a distance from its infection; but at the exact moment of the enjoyment of pleasure we are completely deprived of all such perception as can arise from the operation of the outward senses, so that we seem to be mutilated. How then can it be anything but natural for the outward sense to denounce curses upon pleasure which thus deprives it of its faculties?

XXXVII. (113) "And he is accursed beyond all the beasts of the field." And I mean by this, beyond all the passions of the soul, for it is only there that the mind is wounded and destroyed. Why then does this one appear to be worse than all the other passions? Because it is almost at the bottom of them all, as a sort of base or foundation for them, for desire originates in the love of pleasure, and pain consists in the removal of pleasure; and fear again is caused by a desire to guard against its absence. So it is plain that all the passions are anchored on pleasure; and perhaps one might say that they would absolutely have had no existence at all if pleasure had not been previously laid down as a foundation to support them.

XXXVIII. (114) "Upon thy breast and upon thy belly shalt thou go."[54] For passion works around these parts, the breast and the belly, like a serpent in his hole; when pleasure has its efficient causes and its subject-matter, then it is in operation around the belly and the parts adjacent to the belly; and when it has not these efficient causes and this subject-matter, then it is occupied about the breast which is the seat of anger, for lovers of pleasure when deprived of their pleasures become embittered by their anger. (115) But let us see what is shown by this sentence with greater accuracy. It so happens that our soul is divisible into three parts, and that one of its parts is the seat of reason, the second, the seat of courage, the third, the seat of the appetites. Some therefore of the philosophers have separated these parts from one another only in respect of their operations, and some have distinguished them also by their places. And then they have assigned the parts about the head to the residing part, saying where the king is, there also are his guards, and the guards of the mind are the external senses, which

are seated about the head, so that the king may very naturally have his abode there too, as if he had been assigned the highest part of the city to dwell in. The chest is assigned to the courageous part, and they say, it is on this account, that nature has fortified that part with a dense and strong defence of closely conjoined bones, as though she had been arming a valiant soldier with a breastplate and shield to defend himself against his enemies. To the appetitive part they have assigned a situation about the liver and the belly, for there it is that appetite dwells, being an irrational desire.

XXXIX. (116) If therefore you shall ever inquire, O my mind, what situation has been assigned to pleasure, do not take into your consideration the parts about the head, where the reasoning faculties of man have their abode, for you will not find it there; since reason is at war with passion, and cannot possibly remain in the same place with it. For the moment that reason gets the upper hand pleasure is discarded; but as soon as ever pleasure prevails, reason is put to flight. But seek first rather in the breast and in the belly, where courage and anger, and appetite abide, all which are parts of the irrational faculties. For it is there that our judgment is discovered, and also our passions. (117) Therefore, the mind is not hindered by any external force from abandoning the legitimate objects of its attention, which can only be perceived by the intellect, and surrendering itself to those which are worse; but still this never happens except when there is a war in the soul, for then indeed it follows of necessity that reason must fall under the power of the inferior part of man, inasmuch as it is not of a warlike character, but is fond of peace.

XL. (118) At all events the holy scripture being well aware how great is the power of the impetuosity of each passion, anger and appetite, puts a bridle in the mouth of each, having appointed reason as their charioteer and pilot. And first of all it speaks thus of anger, in the hope of pacifying and curing it: (119) "And you shall put manifestation and truth (the Urim and the Thummim), in the oracle of judgment, and it shall be on the breast of Aaron when he comes into the holy place before the Lord."[55] Now by the oracle is here meant the organs of speech which exist in us, which is in fact the power of language. Now language is either inconsiderate, and such as will not stand examination, or else it is judicious and well approved, and it brings us to form a notion of discreet speech. For Moses here speaks not of a random spurious oracle, but of the oracle of the judgment, which is equivalent to saying, a well-judged and carefully examined oracle; (120) and of this well approved kind of language he says that there

---

[54]Genesis 3:14.

[55]Exodus 28:30.

are two supreme virtues, namely, distinctness and truth, and he says well. For it is language which has in the first place enabled one man to make affairs plain and evident to his neighbour, when without it we should not be able to give any intimation of the impression produced on our soul by outward circumstances, nor to show of what kind they are.

XVI. On which account we have been compelled to have recourse to such signs as are given by the voices, that is nouns and verbs, which ought by all means to be universally known, in order that our neighbours might clearly and evidently comprehend our meaning; and, in the next place, to utter them at all times with truth. (121) For of what advantage would it be to make our assertions clear and distinct, but nevertheless false? For it follows inevitably that if this were allowed the hearer would be deceived, and would reap the greatest possible injury with ignorance and delusion. For what would be the advantage of my speaking to a boy distinctly and clearly, and telling him, when I show him the letter A, that it is G, or that the letter E is O? Or what would be the good of a musician pointing out to a pupil whom comes to him to learn the rudiments of his art that the harmonic scale was the chromatic; or the chromatic, the diatonic; or that the highest string was the middle one; or that conjoined sounds were separated; or that the highest tone in the tetrachord scale was a supernumerary note? (122) No doubt, a man who said this might speak clearly and distinctly, but he would not be speaking truly, but by such assertions he would be implanting wickedness in language. But when he joins both distinctness and truth, then he makes his language profitable to him who is seeking information, employing both its virtues, which in fact are nearly the only ones of which language is capable.

XLII. (123) Moses, therefore, says that discreet discourse, having its own peculiar virtues, is placed on the breast of Aaron, that is to say, of anger, in order that it may in the first instance be guided by reason, and may not be injured by its own deficiency in reason, and, in the second place, by distinctness, for there is no natural influence which makes anger a friend to distinctness. At all events, not only are the ideas of angry men, but all their expressions also, full of disorder and confusion, and therefore it is very natural for the want of clearness on the part of anger to be rectified by clearness, (124) and, in addition, by truth; for, among other things, anger has also this particular property of being inclined to misrepresent the truth. At all events, of all those who give way to this disposition scarcely any one speaks the strict truth, as if it were his soul and not his body that is under the influence of its intoxication. These, then, are the chief remedies suitable for that part of the soul which is influenced by anger,

namely, reason, disinterestedness of language, and truth of language, for the three things are in power only one, namely, reason, curing anger, which is a pernicious disease of the soul, by means of the virtues truth and perspicuity.

XLIII. (125) To whom, or to what, then, does it belong to bear these things? Not to my mind, or to that of any chance person, but to the consecrated and purely sacrificial intellect, that, namely, of Aaron. And not even to this at all times, for it is frequently subject to change, but only when it is going on unchangeably, when it is entering into the holy place, when reason is entering in together with holy opinions, and is not abandoning them. (126) But it often happens that the mind is at the same time entering into sacred and holy and purified opinions, but still such as are only human; such, for instance, as opinions on what is expedient; opinions on successful actions; opinions on what is in accordance with established law; opinions concerning virtue as it exists among men. Nor is the mind, when disposed in this way, competent to bear the oracle on its breast together with he virtues, but only that one which is going in before the Lord, that is to say, that one which doeth everything for the sake of God, and which estimates nothing as superior to the things of God; but attributes to them also their due rank, not indeed dwelling on them, but ascending upwards to the knowledge and understanding of an appreciation of the honour due to the one God. (127) For, in a mind which is thus disposed, anger will be directed by purified reason, which takes away its irrational part, and remedies what there is confused and disorderly in it by the application of distinctness, and eradicates its falsehood by truth.

XLIV. (128) Aaron, therefore, for he is a second Moses, restraining the breast, that is to say, the angry passions, does not allow them to be carried away by undistinguishing impulse, fearing lest, if they obtain complete liberty, they may become restiff, like a horse, and so trample down the whole soul. But he attends to and cures it, and bridles it in the first instance by reason, that so, being under the guidance of the best of charioteers, it may not become exceedingly unmanageable, and in the second place, by the virtues of language, distinctness, and truth. For, if the angry passions were educated in such a way as to yield to reason and distinctness, and to cultivate the virtue of truthfulness, they would deliver themselves from great irritation and make the whole soul propitious.

XLV. (129) But he, as I have already said, having this passion, endeavours to cure it by the saving remedies already enumerated. But Moses thinks that it is necessary completely to extirpate and eradicate anger from the soul, being desirous to attain not to a state of moderation in the indulgence of the passions, but to a state in which they shall have absolutely no existence whatever, and the most Holy Scriptures bear witness to what I am here saying; for it says, "Moses having taken the breast took it that it might be an offering before the Lord, from the ram of consecration, and this was Moses's part."[56] (130) Speaking very accurately, for it was the conduct of one who was both a lover of virtue and a lover of God, after having contemplated the whole soul, to take hold of the breast, which is the seat of the angry passions, and to take it away and eradicate it, that so when the warlike part had been wholly removed, the remainder might enjoy peace. And he removes this part not from any chance animal, but from the ram of consecration, although, indeed, a young heifer had been sacrificed; but, passing by the heifer, he came to the ram, because that is by nature an animal inclined to pushing and full of anger and impetuosity, in reference to which fact the makers of military engines call many of their warlike machines rams. (131) This ramlike and impetuous and undistinguishing character in us, therefore, is something fond of contention, and contention is the mother of anger. In reference to which fact, they who are somewhat quarrelsome are very easily made angry in investigations and other discussions.

Moses, therefore, does very properly endeavour to eradicate anger, that pernicious offspring of a contentious and quarrelsome soul, in order that the soul may become barren of such offspring and may cease from bringing forth mischievous things, and may become a portion consistent with the character of a lover of virtue, not being identical with either the breast or with anger, but with the absence of those qualities, for God has endowed the wise man with the best of all qualities, the power, namely, of eradicating his passions.

You see, then, how the perfect man is always endeavouring to attain to a complete emancipation from the power of the passions. But he who eradicates them being next to him, that is Aaron, labours to arrive at a state in which the passions have only a moderate power, as I have said before; (132) for he is unable to eradicate the breast and the angry passions. But he bears the oracle, on which is distinctness and truth even beyond the guide himself, together with the appropriate and kindred virtues of language.

XLVI. (133) And he will, moreover, make the difference more evident to us by the following expression:—"For the wave-breast and the heave-shoulder have I taken of the children of Israel from off the sacrifices of their peace offerings, and have given them to Aaron the priest, and unto his sons, for ever."[57] (134) You see here that they are not able to take the breast alone, but they must take

it with the shoulder; but Moses can take it without the shoulder. Why is this? Because he, being perfect, has no inadequate or lowly ideas, nor is he willing to remain in a state in which the passions have even a moderate influence; but he, by his exceeding power, does utterly extirpate the whole of the passions, root and branch. But the others, who go with faint endeavours and with but slight strength to war against the passions, are inclined to a reconciliation with them, and make terms with them, proposing terms of accommodation, thinking that thus, like a charioteer, they may be able to bridle their extravagant impetuosity.

(135) And the shoulder is a symbol of labour and of the endurance of hardship; and such a person is he who has the charge of and the care of administering the holy things, being occupied with constant exercise and labour. But he has no labour to whom God has given his perfect good things in great abundance, and he who attains to virtue by labour will be found to be less vigorous and less perfect than Moses, who received it as a gift from God without any labour or difficulty. For the mere fact of labouring is of itself inferior to and worse than the condition of being exempt from labour, so, also, what is imperfect is inferior to that which is perfect, and that which learns anything to that which has knowledge spontaneously and naturally.

On this account it is that Aaron can only take the breast with the shoulder, but Moses can take it without the shoulder. (136) And he calls it the heave-shoulder for this reason, because reason ought to be set over and to be predominant above the violence of anger, as a charioteer who is driving a hard-mouthed and restiff horse. And then the shoulder is no longer called the heave-shoulder, but the shoulder of removal, on this account, because it is fitting that the soul should not attribute to itself labour in the cause of virtue, but should remove it from itself and attribute it to God, confessing that it is not its own strength or its own power which has thus acquired what is good, but He who gave it a love for goodness. (137) And so neither the breast nor the shoulder is taken, except from the virtue which bringeth salvation, as is natural, for then the soul is sacred when the angry passions are under the guidance of reason, and when labour does not bring conceit to the labourer, but when he owns his inferiority to God, his benefactor.

XLVII. (138) Now that pleasure dwells not only in the breast but also in the belly, we have already stated, showing that the belly is the most appropriate situation for pleasure; for we may almost call the belly the vessel which contains all the pleasures; for when the belly is filled, then the desires for all other pleasures are intense and vigorous, but when it is empty, they they are tranquil and steady. (139) On which account Moses says, in another place, "Every animal that goeth upon its

[56]Leviticus 8:29.
[57]Leviticus 7:34.

belly, every animal which goeth on four legs at all times, and that has a multitude of feet, is unclean."[58] And such a creature is the lover of pleasure, inasmuch as he is always going upon his belly and pursuing the pleasures which relate to it. And God unites the animal which goes on four legs with him that crawls upon his belly, naturally; for the passions of those who are absorbed in pleasure are four, as one most egregious account teaches. Therefore he who devotes himself as a slave to one of them, namely, to pleasure, is impure as much as he who lives in the indulgence of the whole four.

(140) This much having been premised, behold again the difference between the perfect man and him who is still advancing towards perfection. As, therefore, the perfect man was, just now, found to be competent to eradicate the whole of the angry feelings from the contentious soul and to make it submissive and manageable, and peaceable and gentle to every one, both in word and deed; and as he who is still advancing towards perfection is not able wholly to eradicate passion, for he bears the breast about with him, though he does educate it by the aid of judicious language, which is invested with two virtues perspicuity and truth.

XLVIII. So, also, now he who is perfectly wise, that is, Moses, will be found to have utterly shaken off and discarded the pleasures. But he who is only advancing towards perfection will be found to have escaped not from every pleasure, but to cling still to such as are desirable and simple, and to deprecate those which are superfluous and extravagant as unnecessary additions, (141) for, in the case of Moses, God speaks thus: "And he washed his belly and his feet, with the blood of the entire burnt offering."[59] Speaking very truly, for the wise man consecrates his entire soul as what is worthy to be offered to God, because it is free from all reproach, whether wilfully or unintentionally incorrect, and being thus disposed, he washes his whole belly and all the pleasures which it knows, and all which pursue it, and cleanses them and purifies them from all uncleanliness, not being content with any partial cleansing. But he is disposed to regard pleasures so contemptuously that he has no desire for even the necessary meat or drink, but nourishes himself wholly on the contemplation of divine things. (142) On which account in another passage, he bears witness to himself, "For forty-eight years he did not eat bread, and he did not drink water,"[60] because he was in the holy mouth listening to the oracular voice of God, who was giving him the law.

But not only does he repudiate the whole belly, but he also at the same time washes off all the dirt from his feet, that is to say, to the supports in which pleasure proceeds. And the supports of pleasure are the efficient causes of it. (143) For he who is advancing onwards to perfection is said "to wash his bowels and his feet,"[61] and not his whole belly. For he is not capable of rejecting the whole of pleasure, but he is content if he can purify his bowels, that is to say, his inmost parts from it, which the lovers of pleasure say are certain additions to preceding pleasures, and which originate in the superfluous ingenuity of cooks and makers of delicacies and laborious gourmands.

XLIX. (144) And he also displays, in a further degree, the moderation of the passions of the man who is advancing towards perfection, by the fact that the perfect man discards all the pleasures of the belly without being prompted by any command to do so, but that he who is only advancing onwards towards perfection only does so in consequence of being commanded. For, in the case of the wise man, we find the following expression used:—"He washes his belly and his feet with water,"[62] without any command, in accordance with his own unbidden inclination. But, in the case of the priests, he spoke thus: "But their bowels and their feet," not they have washed, but "they do wash;"[63] speaking with very cautious exactness, for the perfect man must be moved in his own inclination towards the energies in accordance with virtue. But he who is only practising virtue must be instigated by reason, which points out to him what he ought to do, and it is an honourable thing to obey the injunctions of reason.

(145) But we ought not to be ignorant that Moses repudiates the whole of the belly, that is to say, the filling and indulging the belly, and almost renounces all the other passions likewise; the lawgiver giving a lively representation of the whole from one part, starting from a universal example, and discussing, potentially at least, the other points as to which he was silent.

L. The filling of the belly is a most enduring and universal thing; and, as it were, a kind of foundation of the other passions. At all events, there is not one of them which can find any existence if it is not supported by the belly, on which nature has made everything to depend. (146) On this account, when the goods of the soul had previously been born of Leah, and had ended in Judah,[64] that is to say, in confession, God being about to create also the improvements of the body, prepared Bilhah, the hand-maid of Rachel, to bear children on behalf of and before her mistress. And the

---

[58]Leviticus 11:42.
[59]Leviticus 9:14.
[60]Exodus 34:28.

[61]Leviticus 1:9.
[62]Leviticus 9:14.
[63]Leviticus 1:13.
[64]Genesis 29:35.

name Bilhah, being interpreted, means deglutition. For he knew that not one of the corporeal faculties can exist without imbibing moisture and without the belly; but the belly is predominant over and the ruler of the whole body, and the preserver of this corporeal mass in a state of existence.

(147) And observe the subtle way in which all this is expressed; for you will not find a single word used superfluously. Moses indeed "takes away the breast," but as for the belly he does not take that away, but he washes it.[65] Why so? Because the perfectly wise man is able to repudiate and to eradicate all the angry passions, making them rise up and abandon anger; but he is unable to cut out and discard the belly, for nature is compelled to use the necessary meats and drinks, even if a man, being content with the scantiest possible supply of necessaries should despise it, and purpose to himself to abjure eating. Let him therefore wash and purify it from all superfluous and unclean preparations; for to be able to do even this is a very sufficient gift from God to the lover of virtue.

LI. (148) On this account Moses says, with respect to the soul which is suspected of having committed adultery,[66] that, if having abandoned right reason, which is man living according to the law, it shall be found to have gone over to passion, which pollutes the soul, "it shall become swollen in the belly," which means it shall have all the pleasures and appetites of the belly unsatisfied and insatiable, and it shall never cease to be greedy through ignorance, but pleasures in boundless number shall flow into it, and thus its passions shall be interminable. (149) Now I know many people who have fallen into error in respect of the appetites of the belly, that while still devoting themselves to their gratifications, they have again rushed with eagerness to wine and other luxuries; for the appetites of the intemperate soul bear no analogy to the mass of the body. But some men, like vessels made to hold a certain measure, desire nothing extravagant, but discard everything that is superfluous; but appetite on the other hand is never satisfied, but remains always in want and thirsty. (150) In reference to which the expression, that "the thigh shall fall away," is added in immediate connexion with the denunciation that "her belly shall swell;" for then right reason, which has the seeds and originating principles of good, falls from the soul.

"If therefore," says Moses, "she has not been corrupted, then she shall be pure, and free from all infliction from generation to generation;" that is to say, if she has not been polluted by passion, but has kept herself pure in respect of her legitimate husband, sound reason, her proper guide,

she shall have a productive and fertile soul, bearing the offspring of prudence and justice and all virtue.

LII. (151) Is it then possible for us, who are bound up in our bodies, to avoid complying with the necessities of the body? And if it is possible, how is it possible? But consider, the priest recommends him who is led away by his bodily necessities to indulge in nothing beyond what is strictly necessary. In the first place, says he, "Let there be a place for thee outside of the camp;"[67] meaning by the camp virtue, in which the soul is encamped and fortified; for prudence and a free indulgence in the necessities of the body cannot abide in the same place. (152) After that he says, "And you shall go out there." Why so? Because the soul, which is abiding in companionship with prudence and dwelling in the house of wisdom, cannot indulge in any of the delights of the body, for it is at that time nourished on a diviner food in the sciences, in consequence of which it neglects the flesh, for when it has gone forth beyond the sacred thresholds of virtue, then it turns to the material substances, which disarrange and oppress the soul. How then am I to deal with them? (153) "It shall be a peg," says Moses, "upon thy girdle, and thou shalt dig with it;"[68] that is to say, reason shall be close to you in the case of the passion, which digs out and equips and clothes it properly; for he desires that we should be girded up in respect of the passions, and not to have them about us in a loose and dissolute state. (154) On which account, at the time of the passage through them, which is called the passover, he enjoins us all "to have our loins girded,"[69] that is to say, to have our appetites under restraint. Let the peg, therefore, that is to say reason, follow the passion, preventing it from becoming dissolute; for in this way we shall be able to content ourselves with only so much as is necessary, and to abstain from what is superfluous.

LIII. (155) And in this way when we are at entertainments, and when we are about to come to the enjoyment and use of luxuries that have been prepared for us, let us approach them taking reason with us as a defensive armour, and let us not fill ourselves with food beyond all moderation like cormorants, nor let us satiate ourselves with immoderate draughts of strong wine, and so give way to intoxication which compels men to act like fools. For reason will bridle and curb the violence and impetuosity of such a passion. (156) I myself, at all events, know that it has done so with regard to many of the passions, for when I have gone to entertainments where no respect was paid to dis-

---

[65] Leviticus 8:29–9:14.
[66] Numbers 5:27.

[67] Deuteronomy 23:12.
[68] Deuteronomy 23:13.
[69] Exodus 12:11.

cipline, and to sumptuous banquets, whenever I went without taking Reason with me as a guide, I became a slave to the luxuries that lay before me, being under the guidance of masters who could not be tamed, with sights and sounds of temptation, and all other such things also as work pleasure in a man by the agency of his senses of smell and taste. But when I approach such scenes in the company of reason, I then become a master instead of a slave: and without being subdued myself win a glorious victory of self-denial and temperance; opposing and contending against all the appetites which subdue the intemperate. (157) "Thou shalt be armed," Moses therefore says, "with a peg."[70] That is to say, you, by the aid of reason, shall lay bare the nature which each of the separate passions has, eating, and drinking, and indulging in the pleasures of the belly, and you shall distinguish between them, that when you have so distinguished you may know the truth. For then you shall know that there is no good in any of these things, but only what is necessary and useful. (158) "And bringing it over, you shall cover what is indecorous,"[71] speaking very appropriately. For come to me, O my soul, bring reason to everything by which all unseemliness of flesh and of passion is concealed, and overshadowed and hidden. For all the things which are not in combination with reason are disgraceful, just as those which are done in union with reason are seemly. (159) Therefore the man who is devoted to pleasure goes on his belly, but the perfect man washes his whole belly, and he who is only advancing towards perfection washes the things in his belly. But he who is now beginning to be instructed proceeds out of doors when he is intent upon curbing the passions of the belly by bringing reason to work upon the necessities of the belly, and reason is called symbolically a peg.

LIV. (160) Moses therefore does well when he adds, "Thou shalt go upon thy breast and upon thy belly."[72] For pleasure is not one of the things which is tranquil and steady, but is rather a thing which is in constant motion and full of confusion, for as flame is excited by being moved, so passion when it is put in motion in the soul, being in some respects like a flame, does not suffer it to rest. On which account he does not agree with those who pronounce pleasure a stable feeling, for tranquillity is connected with stones and trees, and all kinds of inanimate things, but is quite inconsistent with pleasure; for it is fond of tickling and convulsive agitation, and with regard to some of its indulgences it has not need of tranquillity but of an intense and violent unseemliness of commotion.

LV. (161) But the expression, "And dust shalt thou eat all the days of thy life," is also used with great propriety. For the pleasures which are derived from the food of the body are all earthly. And may we not reasonably speak thus? There are two several parts of which we consist, the soul and the body; now the body is made of earth, but the soul consists of air, being a fragment of the Divinity, for "God breathed into man's face the breath of life, and man became a living soul."[73] It is therefore quite consistent with reason to say that the body which was fashioned out of the earth has nourishment which the earth gives forth akin to the matter of which it is composed; but the soul, inasmuch as it is a portion of the ethereal nature, is supported by nourishment which is ethereal and divine, for it is nourished on knowledge, and not on meat or drink, which the body requires.

LVI. (162) But that the food of the soul is not earthly but heavenly the Holy Scriptures will testify in many passages, "Behold I will rain upon you bread from heaven, and the people shall come forth, and shall collect from day to day, when I will try them, whether they will walk according to my law or not."[74] You see that the soul is nourished not on earthly and corruptible food, but on the reasons which God rains down out of his sublime and pure nature, which he calls heaven. (163) "Let the people indeed go forth and the whole system of the soul likewise, and let it collect science and begin knowledge, not in large quantities but from day to day." For, in the first place, in that way it will not exhaust all at once the abundant riches of the grace of God: but it will overflow like a torrent with their superfluity. Secondly, it will happen that when they have taken such good things as are sufficient for them and duly measured, they will think God the dispenser of the rest. (164) But he who endeavours to collect everything at once is only acquiring for himself despair with great sorrow,[75] for he becomes full of despair if he expects that God will only rain good things upon him at the present moment, and that he will not do so hereafter. And he becomes inclined to infidelity if he does not believe that the graces of God will be both at present and in all time abundantly poured upon those who are worthy of them. And he is foolish, moreover, if he thinks that he shall be a competent guardian of what he has collected contrary to God's will. For a very slight inclination is sufficient to make the mind, which in its boastfulness attri-

---

[70]Deuteronomy 23:12.
[71]Deuteronomy 23:14.
[72]Genesis 3:14.

[73]Genesis 2:7.
[74]Exodus 16:4.
[75]It seems that for *anias*, sorrow, we ought rather to read *apistias*, infidelity, as it is *apistos* which is afterwards joined with *dyselpis*.

butes safety and stability to itself, an impotent and unsure keeper of those things of which it fancied itself a safe guardian.

LVII. (165) Collect therefore, O my soul, what is sufficient and proper, and in such a quantity as shall neither exceed by being more than is sufficient, nor fall short by being less than what is requisite: that so, using just measures you may not be led into the commission of injustice.

For while meditating on the migration from the passions and sacrificing the passover you ought to take the advance towards perfection, that is to say the sheep, in a moderate spirit. "For each person of you," says Moses, "shall take a sheep, such as shall be sufficient for him according to the number of his house."[76]

(166) And in the case of the manna therefore, and of every gift which God gives to the race of mankind, the principle being guided by numbering and by measure, and of not taking what is more than is necessary for us, is good; for the opposite conduct is covetousness. Let therefore one soul collect what is sufficient for it from day to day,[77] that it may show that it is not itself which is the guardian of good things, but the bounteous giver, God.

LVIII. (167) And this appears to me to be the reason why the sentence which I have cited above was uttered. Day is an emblem of light, and the light of the soul is instruction. Many persons therefore have provided for themselves the lights that can exist in the soul against night and darkness, but not against day-time and light; such lights for instance, as are derived from rudimental instruction, and those branches of education which are called encyclical, and philosophy itself, which is sought after for the sake both of the pleasure which is derived from it, and also of the influence which it gives among rulers. But the good man seeks the day for the sake of the day, and the light for the light's sake; and he labours to acquire what is good for the sake of the good itself, and not of anything else, on which account Moses adds, "In order that I may tempt them and see whether they will walk according to my law or not,"[78] for the divine law enjoins us to honour virtue for its own sake. (168) Accordingly, right reason tests those who practise virtue as one might test a coin, to see whether they have contracted any stain, referring the good things of the soul to any of the external things; or whether they decide upon it as good money, preserving it in the intellect alone. These men are nourished not on earthly things, but on heavenly knowledge.

LIX. (169) And Moses shows this in other pas-

sages also, when he says, "And in the morning the dew lay round about the hosts; and when the dew that lay in the morning was gone up, behold! upon the face of the wilderness there lay a small round thing, small as coriander seed,[79] and white like the hoar-frost upon the earth. And when they saw it, they said one to another, what is this? for they knew not what it was, and Moses said to them, This is the bread which the Lord hath given you to eat, this is the thing which the Lord hath commanded you."[80]

You see now what kind of thing the food of the Lord is, it is the continued word of the Lord, like dew, surrounding the whole soul in a circle, and allowing no portion of it to be without its share of itself. (170) And this word is not apparent in every place, but wherever there is a vacant space, void of passions and vice; and it is subtle both to understand and to be understood, and it is exceedingly transparent and clear to be distinguished, and it is like coriander seed. And agriculturists say that the seed of the coriander is capable of being cut up and divided into innumerable pieces, and if sown in each separate piece and fragment, it shoots up just as much as the whole seed could do. Such also is the word of God, being profitable both in its entirety and also in every part, even if it be ever so small.

(171) May it not be also likened to the pupil of the eye? For as that, being the smallest portion of the eye, does nevertheless behold the entire orbs of existing things and the boundless sea, and the vastness of the air, and the whole immeasurable space of heaven, which the sun, whether rising in the east or setting in the west, can bound; so also is the word of God, very sharp-sighted, so as to be capable of beholding every thing, and by which all things that are worth seeing can be beheld, in reference to which fact it is white. For what can be more brilliant or visible at a greater distance than the divine word, by participation in which all other things can repel mists and darkness, being eager to share in the light of the soul?

LX. (172) There is a certain peculiarity which is attached to this word. For when it calls the soul to itself, it excites a congealing power in everything which is earthly, or corporeal, or under the influence of the external senses. On which account it is said to be "like the hoar-frost on the earth."[81] For when the man who beholds God, meditates a flight from the passions, "the waves are frozen," that is to say, the impetuous rush, and the increase, and the haughty pride of the waves are arrested, in order that he who might behold the living God

[76]Exodus 12:4.
[77]Exodus 12:4.
[78]Exodus 16:4.

[79]Numbers 11:7.
[80]Exodus 16:13.
[81]Exodus 6:16.

might then pass over the passion.[82] (173) Therefore the souls inquire of one another, those, that is, that have clearly felt the influence of the word, but which are not able to say what it is. For very often, when sensible of a sweet taste, we are nevertheless ignorant of the flavour which has caused it, and when we smell sweet scents, we still do not know what they are. And in the same manner also the soul very often, when it is delighted, is yet unable to explain what it is that has delighted it; but it is taught by the hierophant and prophet Moses, who tells it, "This is the bread, the food which God has given for the soul,"[83] explaining that God has brought it, his own word and his own reason; for this bread which he has given us to eat is this word of his.

LXI. (174) He says also in Deuteronomy, "And he has humbled thee, and suffered thee to hunger, and fed thee with manna, which thou knowest not, neither did thy fathers know, that he might make thee know that man shall not live by bread alone, but by every word which proceedeth out of the mouth of the Lord doth man live."[84] Now this ill-treating and humbling of them is a sign of his being propitiated by them, for he is propitiated as to the souls of us who are wicked on the tenth day. For when he strips us of all our pleasant things, we appear to ourselves to be ill-treated, that is in truth to have God propitious to us.

(175) And God also causes us hunger, not that which proceeds from virtue, but that which is engendered by passion and vice. And the proof of this is, that he nourishes us with his own word, which is the most universal of all things, for manna being interpreted, means "what?" and "what" is the most universal of all things; for the word of God is over all the world, and is the most ancient, and the most universal of all the things that are created. This word our fathers knew not; I speak not of those who are so in truth, but of those who are grey with age, who say, "Let us give them a guide, and let us turn back"[85] unto passion, that is to say, to Egypt. (176) Therefore, let God enjoin the soul, saying to it that, "Man shall not live by bread alone," speaking in a figure, "but by every word that proceedeth out of the mouth of God," that is to say, he shall be nourished by the whole word of God, and by every portion of it. For the mouth is the symbol of the language, and a word is a portion of it. Accordingly the soul of the more perfect man is nourished by the whole word; but we must be contented if we are nourished by a portion of it.

LXII. (177) But these men pray to be nourished by the word of God: but Jacob, raising his head above the word, says that he is nourished by God himself, and his words are as follows; "The God in whom my father Abraham and Isaac were well-pleased; the God who has nourished me from my youth upwards to this day; the angel who has delivered me from all my evils, bless these children."[86] This now being a symbol of a perfect disposition, thinks God himself his nourisher, and not the word: and he speaks of the angel, which is the word, as the physician of his evils, in this speaking most naturally. For the good things which he has previously mentioned are pleasing to him, inasmuch as the living and true God has given them to him face to face, but the secondary good things have been given to him by the angels and by the word of God. (178) On this account I think it is that God gives men pure good health, which is not preceded by any disease in the body, by himself alone, but that health which is an escape from disease he gives through the medium of skill and medical science, attributing it to science, and to him who can apply it skilfully, though in truth, it is God himself who heals both by these means, and without these means. And the same is the case with regard to the soul, the good things, namely food, he gives to men by his power alone; but those which contain in them a deliverance from evil, he gives by means of his angels and his word.

LXIII. (179) And he uttered this prayer, blaming Joseph the statesman and governor, because he had ventured to say, "I will feed them in that land,"[87] for, "hasten ye," said Joseph, "and go up to my father, and say unto him, Thus says Joseph," and so on, and presently he adds, "Come down unto me, and do not tarry, come with all thou hast, and I will feed thee in that land; for still the famine lasts for five years." Jacob, therefore, speaks as he does reproving and at the same time instructing this imaginary wise man, and he says to him, "O my friend, know thou that the food of the soul is knowledge, which it is not the word which is intelligible by the external senses that can bestow, but God only who has nourished me from youth, and from my earliest age till the time of perfect manhood, he shall fill me with it. (180) Joseph therefore was treated in the same way with his mother Rachel, for she also thought that the creature had some power; on which account she used the expression, "Give me children," but the supplanter, adhering to his proper character, says to her, "You have used a great error; for I am not in the place of God, who alone is able to open the womb of the soul,[88] and to implant virtues in it, and to cause it to be pregnant, and to bring forth

[82] Exodus 16:15.
[83] Exodus 16:15.
[84] Deuteronomy 8:3.
[85] Numbers 14:1.

[86] Genesis 48:15.
[87] Genesis 45:11.
[88] Genesis 30:1.

what is good. Consider also the history of thy sister Leah, and you will find that she did not receive seed or fertility from any creature—but from God himself."

"For the Lord, seeing that Leah was hated, opened her womb, but Rachel was barren."[89] (181) And consider, now, in this sentence, again, the subtlety of the writer spoken of. God opens the wombs, implanting good actions in them, and the womb, when it has received virtue from God, does not bring forth to God, for the living and true God is not in need of any thing, but she brings forth sons to me, Jacob, for it was for my sake, probably, that God sowed seed in virtue, and not for his own. Therefore, another husband of Leah is found to be passed over in silence, and another father of Leah's children, for he is the husband who openeth the womb, and he is the father of the children to whom the mother is said to bear them.

LXIV. (182) "And I will place enmity between thee and between the woman."[90] In reality, pleasure is hostile to the external sense, although, to some persons, it appears to be especially friendly to it. But as one would not call a flatterer a companion (for flattery is a disease of friendship), nor would one call a courtezan friendly to her lover, for she adheres only to those who give her presents, and not to those who love her; so, also, if you investigate the nature of pleasure, you will find that she has but a spurious connection with the external senses. (183) When we are sated with pleasure, then we find that the organs of the external senses in us lose their tone. Or do not you perceive the state of those men who from love of wine get drunk?—that seeing they do not see, and hearing they do not hear; and, in the same way, they are deprived of the accurate energies of the other external senses? And, at times, through immoderate indulgence in food, all the vigour of the external senses is relaxed when sleep overtakes them, which has derived its name from the relaxation of them. For, at that time, the organs of the external senses are relaxed, just as they are on the stretch in our waking hours, when they no longer receive unintelligible blows from external things, but such as speak loudly and are evident, and which transmit their impressions to the mind. For the mind, when stricken, must recognize the external thing, and receive a visible impression from it.

LXV. (184) And take notice here, that Moses does not say, "I will cause enmity to thee and the woman," but, "I will place enmity between thee and between the woman:"—why so? because the war between these two is concerning what is in the middle, and what lies, as it were, on the borders of pleasure and of the outward sense. And that which lies between them is what is drinkable, and what is eatable, and what is inclined to all such things, every one of which is an object to be appreciated by the outward sense, and an efficient cause of pleasure. When, therefore, pleasure wallows immoderately in these things, it at once by so doing inflicts injury on the outward sense. (185) And again, the expression, "between thy seed and between her seed," is uttered with strict natural propriety, for all seed is the beginning of generation. But the beginning of pleasure is not passion, but an emotional impulse of the outward sense, set in motion by the mind. For from this, as from a fountain, the faculties of the outward senses are derived, especially, according to the most sacred Moses, who says that the woman was formed out of Adam, that is to say, the outward sense was formed out of the mind. The part, therefore, that pleasure acts towards the outward sense, passion also acts towards the mind. So that, since the two former are at enmity with one another, the two latter must likewise be in a state of hostility.

LXVI. (186) And the war between these things in manifest. At all events, according to the superiority of the mind when it applies itself to incorporeal objects, which are perceptible only to the intellect, passion is put to flight. And, on the other hand, when this latter gains a shameful victory, the mind yields, being hindered from giving its attention to itself and to all its actions. At all events, he says in another place, "When Moses lifted up his hands Israel prevailed, and when he let them down Amalek prevailed."[91] And this statement implies, that when the mind raises itself up from mortal affairs and is elevated on high, it is very vigorous because it beholds God; and the mind here means Israel. But when it relaxes its vigour and becomes powerless, then immediately the passions will prevail, that is to say, Amalek; which name, being interpreted, means, the people licking. For he does, of a verity, devour the whole soul, and licks it up, leaving no seed behind, nor anything which can excite virtue; (187) in reference to which it is said, "Amalek is the beginning of nations;"[92] because passion governs, and is the absolute lord of nations, all mingled and confused and jumbled in disorder, without any settled plan; and, through passion, all the war of the soul is fanned and kept alive. For God makes a promise to the same minds to which he grants peace, that he will efface the memorial of Amalek from all the lands beneath the heaven.

LXVII. (188) And the expression, "He shall watch thy head, and thou shalt watch his heel,"[93]

[89]Genesis 29:31.
[90]Genesis 3:15.
[91]Exodus 17:11.
[92]Numbers 24:20.
[93]Genesis 3:15.

is, as to its language, a barbarism, but, as to the meaning which is conveyed by it, a correct expression. Why so? It ought to be expressed with respect to the woman: but the woman is not he, but she. What, then, are we to say? From his discourse about the woman he has digressed to her seed and her beginning. Now the beginning of the outward sense is the mind. But the mind is masculine, in respect of which one may say, he, his, and so on. Very correctly, therefore, does God here say to pleasure, that the mind shall watch your principal and predominant doctrine, and you shall watch the traces of the mind itself, and the foundations of the things which are pleasing to it, to which the heel has very naturally been likened.

LXVIII. (189) But the words, "shall watch," intimate two things: in the first place it means as it were "shall keep," and "shall preserve." And, in the second place, it is equivalent to "shall watch for the purpose of destroying." Now it is inevitable that the mind must be either bad or good. Now, if it be bad, it would be but a foolish guardian and dispenser of pleasure, for it rejoices in it. But the good man is an enemy to it, expecting that, when he once attacks it, he will be able utterly to destroy it. And, indeed, on the other hand, pleasure watches the footsteps of the foolish man, but endeavours to trip up and undermine the standing ground of the wise man, thinking that he is always meditating its destruction; but that the fool is always considering the means by which its safety may be best secured. (190) But, nevertheless, though pleasure appears to trip up and to deceive the good man, it will in reality be tripped up itself by that experienced wrestler, Jacob; and that, too, not in the wrestling of the body, but in that struggle which the soul carries on against the dispositions which are antagonistic to it, and which attack it through the agency of the passions and vices; and it will not let go the heel of its antagonist, passion, before it surrenders, and confesses that it has been twice tripped up and defeated, both in the matter of the birthright, and also in that of the blessing. (191) For "rightly," says Esau, "is his name called Jacob, for now has he supplanted me for the second time; the first time he took away my birthright, and now he has taken away my blessing."[94]

But the bad man thinks the things of the body the more important, while the good man assigns the preference to the things of the soul, which are in truth and reality the more important and the first, not, indeed, in point of time, but in power and dignity, as is a ruler in a city. But the mistress of the concrete being is the soul.

LXIX. (192) Therefore the one who as superior in virtue received the first place, which, indeed,

fell to him as his due. For he also obtained the blessing in connection with the perfection of prayer. But he is a vain and conceited pretender to wisdom who said, "He took away my blessing and also my birthright." For what he took, O foolish man, was not yours, but was rather the opposite to what was yours. For your deeds are thought worthy of slavery, but his are thought worthy of supremacy. (193) And if you are content to become the slave of the wise man, you shall receive your share of reproof and of correction, and so you shall discard ignorance and folly which are the destruction of the soul. For thy father, when praying, says to you, "You shall serve your brother,"[95] but not now; for he will not be able to endure your endeavouring to throw off the yoke. But when you have loosed his yoke from off your neck, that is to say, when you have cast off the boastfulness and arrogance which you had, after you had yoked yourself to the chariot of the passions, under the guidance of the charioteer, Folly. (194) Now, indeed, you are the slave of cruel and intolerable masters, who are within yourself, and who look upon it as a law never to set any one free; but if you run away and escape from them, then the master who loves slaves will receive you in a good hope of freedom, and will not surrender you any more to your former companions, having learnt from Moses that necessary doctrine and lesson, "Not to give up a servant to his master who has escaped from his master unto him; for he shall dwell with him in any place which shall please him."[96]

LXX. (195) But as long as you did not escape, and while you were still bridled with the bridle of those masters, you were unworthy to be the servant of a worse master. Giving thus the greatest proof of a mean, and lowly, and servile disposition, when you said, "My birthright and my blessing."[97] For these are the words of men who have fallen into immoderate ignorance, since it belongs to God alone to say, "Mine;" for to him alone do all things properly belong. (196) And to this he will himself bear witness when he says, "My gifts, my offerings, my first fruits."[98]

You must take notice here that gifts are spoken of in contradistinction to offerings. For the former display the manifestation of the vastness of the perfect good things which God gives to those men who are perfect, but the latter are only prepared to last a very short time, and are partaken of by well-disposed practisers of virtue who are making progress towards perfection. (197) On which account Abraham also, when following the will of God, retained those things which had been given

---

94 Genesis 27:36.

95 Genesis 27:40.
96 Deuteronomy 23:16.
97 Genesis 27:36.
98 Numbers 28:2.

to him by God: "but sends back the horses of the king of Sodom"[99] as the wages of harlots. And Moses also condescends to administer justice in most important points, and with reference to things of the greatest value. But the more unimportant causes and trials he commits to judges of inferior rank to investigate. (198) And whoever ventures to assert that any thing is his own shall be set down as a slave for ever and ever; as he who says, "I have loved my master, and my wife, and my children; I will not depart and be free."[100] He does well on confessing that slavery is proper for him; for can he be any thing but a slave who says, "Mine is mind, which is the master, being its own master, and possessed of absolute power; mine, also are the outward senses, the sufficient judges of corporeal substances; mine, also are the offspring of these objects of intellect which are the offspring of the mind, and the objects of the outward senses, which are the offspring of those same outward senses; for it is in my power to exert both the mind and the outward senses?" (199) But it is not sufficient for such a man only to bear witness against himself, but, being also condemned by God, who sentences him to most durable and everlasting slavery, he shall undergo his sentence: and be bored in the ear, that he may not receive the language of virtue, but that he may be a slave for ever, both in his mind and in his outward senses, which are bad and pitiless masters.

LXXI. (200) "And to the woman he said, I will greatly multiply thy sorrow and thy groaning."[101] The affection which is called pain is a suffering peculiar to woman, who is a symbol of the outward sense. For to suffer pain belongs to the same subject to which to experience pleasure does also belong. But we experience pleasure through the medium of our outward senses, as of necessity we also suffer pain through the same medium. But the virtuous and purified mind suffers pain in the least degree; for the outward senses have the least degree of power over him. But passion is exceedingly powerful in the case of the foolish man, inasmuch as he has no antidote in his soul by which he can ward off the evils which proceed from the outward senses and from those objects which can only be perceived by them. (201) For as an athlete and a slave are beaten in two different manners, the one in an abject manner, giving himself up to the ill-treatment, and yielding to it submissively; but the athlete opposing, and resisting, and parrying the blows which are aimed at him. And as you shave a man in one way, and a pillow in another; for the one is seen only in its suffering the shaving, but the man does himself do some-

thing likewise, and as one may say, aids the infliction, placing himself in a posture to be shaved; (202) so the irrational man, like a slave, submits himself to another, and surrenders himself to the endurance of pains as to intolerable mistresses, being unable to look them in the face, and wholly incapable of conceiving any masculine or free thoughts. On which account a countless number of painful things are endured by him through the medium of the outward senses. But the man of experience, valiantly resisting like a brave athlete with strength and vigour, opposes himself resolutely to all painful things, so as not to be wounded by them; but so as to keep all their blows at a distance. And it seems to me that he might with great spirit utter the verses of the tragedian against pain in this manner:—

"Now scorch and burn my flesh, and fill yourself
With ample draughts of my life's purpled blood;
For sooner shall the stars' bright orbs descend
Beneath the darkened earth, the earth uprise
Above the sky, and all things be confounded,
Than you shall wrench one flattering word from me."[102]

LXXII. (203) But as God has allotted all painful things to the outward sense in great abundance and intensity, so also has he bestowed on the virtuous soul a boundless store of good things. Accordingly he speaks with reference to the perfect man Abraham in the following manner: "By myself have I sworn, saith the Lord, that because thou hast done this thing and hast not withheld thy son, thy beloved son from me, that in blessing I will bless thee, and in multiplying I will multiply thy seed as the stars of heaven, and as the sand which is on the shore of the sea."[103] He says this, and having confirmed his promise solemnly and by an oath, and by an oath, too, such as could alone become God. For you see that God does not swear by any other being than himself, for there is nothing more powerful than he is; but he swears by himself, because he is the greatest of all things.

(204) But some men have said that it is inconsistent with the character of God to swear at all; for that an oath is received for the sake of the confirmation which it supplies; but God is the only faithful being, and if any one else who is dear to God; as Moses is said to have been faithful in all his house.[104] And besides, the mere words of God are the most sacred and holy of oaths, and laws, and institutions. And it is a proof of his exceeding power, that whatever he says is sure to take place; and this is the most especial characteristic of an

---

[99]Genesis 14:21.
[100]Genesis 21:5.
[101]Genesis 3:16.

[102]This is a fragment of the Syleus of Euripides. The lines are put in the mouth of Hercules.
[103]Genesis 22:16.
[104]Numbers 12:7.

oath. So that it would be quite natural to say that all the words of God are oaths confirmed by the accomplishment of the acts to which they relate.[105]

LXXIII. (205) They say, indeed, that an oath is a testimony borne by God concerning a matter which is the subject of doubt. But if God swears he is bearing testimony to himself, which is an absurdity. For the person who bears the testimony, and he on whose behalf it is borne, ought to be two different persons. What, then, are we to say? In the first place, that it is not a matter of blame for God to bear testimony to himself. For what other being could be competent to bear testimony to him? In the second place, He himself is to himself every thing that is most honourable—relative, kinsman, friend, virtue, prosperity, happiness, knowledge, understanding, beginning, end, entirety, universality, judge, opinion, intention, law, action, supremacy.

(206) Besides, if we only receive the expression, "By myself have I sworn," in the manner in which we ought, we shall be in no danger from sophistry. May we not, then, say, that the truth is something of this sort? None of those beings which are capable of entertaining belief, can entertain a firm belief respecting God. For he has not displayed his nature to any one; but keeps it invisible to every kind of creature. Who can venture to affirm of him who is the cause of all things either that he is a body, or that he is incorporeal, or that he has such and such distinctive qualities, or that he has no such qualities? or who, in short, can venture to affirm any thing positively about his essence, or his character, or his constitution, or his movements? But He alone can utter a positive assertion respecting himself, since he alone has an accurate knowledge of his own nature, without the possibility of mistake. (207) His positive assertion, therefore, is one which may be thoroughly trusted in the first place, since he alone has any knowledge respecting his actions; so that he very appropriately swore by himself, adding himself confirmation to his assertion, which it was not possible for any one else to do. On which account men who say that they swear by God may well be considered impious. For no man can rightly swear by himself, because he is not able to have any certain knowledge respecting his own nature, but we must be content if we are able to understand even his name, that is to say, his word, which is the inter-

preter of his will. For that must be God to us imperfect beings, but the first mentioned, or true God, is so only to wise and perfect men.

(208) And Moses, too, admiring the exceeding excellency of the great uncreated God, says, "And thou shalt swear by his name,"[106] not by himself. For it is sufficient for the creature to receive confirmation and testimony from the word of God. But God is his own confirmation and most unerring testimony.

LXXIV. (209) But the expression, "Because thou hast done this thing,"[107] is a symbol of piety. For to do everything for the sake of God alone is pious. In consequence of which we do not spare even that beloved child of virtue, prosperity, surrendering it to the Creator, and thinking it right that our offspring should become the possession of God, but not of any created being. And that expression, also, is a good one, "In blessing I will bless thee." (210) For some persons do many acts worthy of a blessing, but yet not in such a way as to obtain a blessing. Since even a wicked man does some actions that are proper, but he does not do them from being of a proper disposition. And sometimes a drunken man or a mad man speaks and acts in a sober manner, but still he is not speaking or acting from a sober mind. And children, who are actually infants, both do and say many things which reasonable men do also do and say; but they, of course, do it not in consequence of any rational disposition, for nature has not yet endowed them with a capacity of reasoning. But the lawgiver wishes the wise man to appear deserving of blessing not occasionally, accidentally, and, as it were, by chance, but in consequence of habits and a disposition deserving of blessing.

LXXV. (211) Therefore it is not sufficient for the unfortunate external sense to be abundantly occupied with pains, but it must also be full of groaning. Now groaning is a violent and intense pain. For we are very often in pain without groaning. But, when we groan, we are under the influence of most grievous and thickly pressing pain. Now, groaning is of a twofold nature. One kind is that which arises in those who desire and are very eager for august objects and who do not succeed in them, which is wicked; the other kind is that which proceeds from persons who repent and are distressed for previous sins, and who say, "Miserable are we, how long a time have we passed infected with the disease of foolishness, and in the practice of all kinds of folly and iniquity." (212) But this kind of groaning does not exist unless the king of Egypt, that is to say, the impious disposition wholly devoted to pleasure, has perished and

---

[105]There is a remarkable coincidence between Philo's argument here, and that employed by St. Paul in reference to the same event. St. Paul, Hebrews 6:13, says, "For when God made promise to Abraham, because he could swear by no greater, he swore by himself, saying. ...For man verily swears by the greater; and an oath for confirmation is to them the end of strife."

[106]Deuteronomy 6:13.
[107]Genesis 22:16.

departed from our soul, "For, after many days, the king of Egypt died." [108]

Then immediately, as soon as vice is dead, the man who has become alive to the perception of God and of his own sin, groans, "For the children of Israel groaned at the corporeal and Egyptian works;" since the reigning disposition devoted to pleasure, while it is alive within us, persuades the soul to rejoice at the sins which it commits; but, when that disposition is dead, it groans over them; (213) on which account it cries out to its master, beseeching him that it may not again be perverted, and that it may not arrive at only an imperfect sort of perfection. For many souls who have wished to turn to repentance have not been allowed to do so by God, but, been dragged back, as it were by the ebbing tide, having returned to their original courses; in the manner in which Lot's wife did, who was turned into stone because she loved Sodom, and who reverted to the disposition and habits which had been condemned by God.

LXXVI. (214) But now Moses says that "Their cry has gone up to God, bearing witness to the grace of the living God." For if he had not powerfully summoned up to himself the supplicatory language of that people it would not have gone up; that is to say, it would never have gained power and increase, would never have begun to soar so high, flying from the lowness of earthly things. On which account, in the next passage, God is represented as saying, "Behold the cry of the children of Israel has come up to me." [109] (215) Very beautifully here does Moses represent that their supplications have reached God, but they would not have reached him if he who was working him had not been a good man.

But there are some souls which God even goes forward to meet: "I will come to you and bless you." You see here how great is the kindness of the Creator of all things, when he even anticipates our delay and our intentions, and comes forward to meet us to the perfect benefiting of our souls. And the expression and used here is an oracle full of instruction. For, if a thought of God enters the mind, it immediately blesses it and heals all its diseases. (216) But the outward sense is always grieved and groans, and brings forth the perception of its objects with pain and intolerable anguish. As also God himself says, "In sorrow thou shalt bring forth children."

Now, the sense of sight brings forth the operation of seeing, the sense of hearing is the parent of the operation of hearing, so is the sense of taste of tasting; and, in short, each outward sense is respectively the parent of its corresponding operation; but still it does not produce all these effects in the foolish man without severe pain. For such a man is affected by pain when he sees, and when he hears, and when he tastes, and when he smells, and, in fact, when he exerts any one of these outward senses.

LXXVII. (217) On the other hand, you will find virtue not only conceiving with extraordinary joy, but also bringing forth her good offspring with laughter and cheerfulness; and you will also find the offspring of the two parents to be actually cheerfulness itself. Now that the wise man becomes a parent with joy, and not with sorrow, the word of God itself will testify to us when it speaks thus: "And God said unto Abraham, Sarai, thy wife, shall no longer be called Sarai, but her name shall be Sarah; I will bless her, and give thee a son from her." [110] And, afterwards, Moses proceeds to say, "And Abraham fell upon his face and laughed, and said, 'Shall a son be born to him who is a hundred years old; and shall Sarah, who is ninety years old, have a son?' " (218) Abraham, therefore, appears here to be in a state of joy, and to be laughing because he is about to become the father of happiness, that is to say, of Isaac; and virtue, that is to say, Sarah, laughs also. And the same prophet will further bear witness, speaking thus, "And it had ceased to be with Sarah after the manner of women, and she laughed in her mind and said, such happiness has never yet happened to me to this time, and my lord," that is to say, the divine Lord, "is older than I;" in whose power, however, this thing must inevitably be, and in whose power it is becoming to place confidence. For the offspring is laughter and joy. For this is the meaning and interpretation of the name of Isaac. Therefore, let the outward sense be grieved, but let virtue be always rejoicing.

(219) For, also, when happiness, that is Isaac, was born, she says, in the pious exaltation, "The Lord has caused me laughter, and whoever shall hear of it shall rejoice with me." [111] Open your ears, therefore, O ye initiated, and receive the most sacred mysteries. Laughter is joy; and the expression, "has caused," is equivalent to "has begotten." So that what is here said has some such meaning as this, "The Lord has begotten Isaac." For he is the father of perfect nature, sowing and begetting happiness in the soul.

LXXVIII. (220) "And thy desire," says God, "shall be to thy husband." [112] There are two husbands of the outward senses. The one a legal one, the other a destroyer. For the object of sight, acting upon it like a husband, puts the sense of sight in motion; and so does sound affect the sense of

---

[108] Exodus 2:23.
[109] Exodus 3:9.

[110] Genesis 17:15. Sarah is interpreted Princess in the margin of the Bible.
[111] Genesis 21:7.
[112] Genesis 3:16.

hearing, flavour the sense of taste, and so on with each of the outward senses respectively. And these things attract the attention of and call the irrational outward sense to itself, and become the master of it and govern it. For beauty enslaves the sight, and sweet flowers enslave the sense of taste, and each of the other objects of outward sense enslaves that sense which corresponds to them. (221) See the glutton, what a slave he is to all the preparations which cooks and confectioners devise. Behold the man who is devoted to the study of music, how he is governed by the harp, or the flute, or by any one who is able to sing. But the sense which turns itself to its legitimate husband, that is to say, to the mind, derives the greatest possible advantage from that object.

LXXIX. (222) Let us now see what account Moses gives of the mind itself, when it is set in motion in a way contrary to right reason. And God said unto Adam, "Because thou hast listened to the voice of thy wife, and hast eaten of the tree of which I commanded thee not to eat, because thou hast eaten of it, cursed is the earth in thy actions." [113] It is a most mischievous thing, therefore, for the mind to be swayed by the outward senses, but not for the outward senses to be guided by the mind. For it is at all times proper that that which is better should rule, and that that which is worse should be ruled. (223) And the mind is better than the outward senses. As, therefore, when the charioteer has his horses under command and guides the animals with the rein, the chariot is guided wherever he pleases; but if they become restiff, and get the better of the charioteer, he is often dragged out of his road, and sometimes it even happens that the beasts themselves are borne by the impetuosity of their course into a pit, and everything is carried away in a ruinous manner. And, as a ship holds on her right course when the pilot has the helm in his hand and steers her, and she is obedient to her rudder, but the vessel is upset when some contrary wind descends upon the waves and the whole sea is occupied by billows; (224) so when the mind, which is the charioteer or pilot of the soul, retains the mastery over the entire animal, as a ruler does over a city, the life of the man proceeds rightly. But when the outward sense, which is devoid of reason, obtains the supremacy, then a terrible confusion overtakes the man, as might happen if a household of slaves were to conspire and to set upon their master. For then, if one must tell the truth, the mind is set fire to and burnt, the outward senses handling the flame and placing the objects of their operation beneath, as fuel.

LXXX. And Moses, indeed, speaks of and describes such a conflagration of the mind as this

which arises in consequence of the operation of the outward senses, when he says, (225) "And the women still burnt additional fires in Moab." [114] For this expression being interpreted means, from the father, because the mind is our father. "For then," says Moses, "the expounders of riddles will say, Come to Heshbon, that the city of Sihon may be built and furnished. Because fire has gone forth out of Heshbon, and a flame out of the city of Sihon, and has devoured as far as Moab, and has consumed the high places of Arnon. Woe unto thee, Moab, Chemosh is destroyed: their sons who had sought to escape have been given up, and their daughters have become captive to Sihon, king of the Amorites. And the seed of them shall perish, from Heshbon even to Dibon. Moreover, the women still burnt additional fire in Moab." (226) Heshbon being interpreted means reasonings; and these must here mean enigmas, full of indistinctness. Behold the reasoning of the physician:—"I will purge the sick man, I will nourish him, I will heal him with medicines and with diet, I will extirpate his diseased parts, I will cauterise him." But very often nature has healed the man without these remedies; and very often too has suffered him to die though they were applied: so that the reasonings of the physician have been utterly found out to be dreams, full of all indistinctness and of riddles.

Again, the husbandman says, (227) I will scatter seed, I will plant; the plants shall grow, they shall bear fruit, which shall not only be useful for necessary enjoyment, but which shall also be abundant for superfluity; and then, on a sudden, fire, or a storm, or continued rains, have destroyed everything. But at times man has brought his labours to their due accomplishment, and yet he who formed all these plans has derived no advantage from their being accomplished, but has died before they were accomplished, and has in vain promised himself the enjoyment of the fruits of his labours.

LXXXI. (228) It is best, therefore, to trust in God, and not in uncertain reasonings, or unsure conjectures. "Abraham trusted in the Lord, and it was counted to him for righteousness." [115] And Moses governed the people, being testified to that he was faithful with his whole house. But if we distrust our own reason, we shall prepare and build ourselves a city of the mind which will destroy the truth. For Sihon, being interpreted means destroying. (229) In reference to which he who had dreamed, waking up, found that all the motions and all the advances of the foolish man are merely dreams that have no portion of truth in them, for the very mind is found to be a dream; and the only true doctrine is to believe in God, and to trust to

[113] Genesis 3:17.

[114] Numbers 21:27.
[115] Genesis 15:6.

vain reasonings is a mere delusion. But irrational impulse goes forth and proceeds to each extremity, while both the reasonings and the mind corrupt the truth. On which account, Moses says that "fire went out of Heshbon, and flame out of the city of Sihon." So absurd is it to trust either to plausible reasonings, or to the mind which corrupts the truth.

LXXXII. (230) "And it devours even as far as Moab;" that is to say, as far as the mind. For what other creature, except the miserable mind, can a false opinion deceive? It devours and consumes, and, in truth, it swallows up the pillars in it; that is to say, all the particular notions which are engraved and impressed upon it, as upon a pillar. But the pillars are Arnon, which, being interpreted, means the light of Arnon, since every one of these facts is made clear by reasoning. (231) Accordingly, Moses beings presently to lament over the self-satisfied and arrogant mind in this manner: "Woe unto thee, O city of Moab!" For, if you give attention to the riddles which arise out of the perception of what is probable, you have destroyed the truth by so doing.

"The people of Chemosh," that is to say, thy people and thy power, have been found to be mutilated and blinded. For Chemosh, being interpreted, means feeling with the hand. And this action is the especial characteristic of one who does not see. (232) Now, their sons are particular reasonings—exiles; and their opinions are in the place of daughters, being captives to the king of the Amorites, that is to say, of those who converse with the sophist. For the name Amorites, being interpreted, means talkers, being a symbol of the people who talk much; and their guide and leader is the sophist, and he who is skilful in reasoning and clever in investigating arts; a man by whom all those are deceived who once overpass the boundary of truth.

LXXXIII. (233) Sihon, then, who destroys the sound rule of truth, and his seed also, shall both perish; and so shall Heshbon, namely, the sophistical riddles, as far as Debon; which, being interpreted, means adjudication. And very consistently with nature shall this be. For what is probable and plausible has not a positive knowledge respecting truth, but only a trial and controversy and a litigious contest and strife, and all such things as these. (234) But it was not sufficient for the mind to have its own peculiar evils, which were perceptible only to the intellect; but still the women burnt additional fire, that is to say, the outward senses excited a great conflagration to have an effect upon it.

See, now, what the meaning is of what is here said. We who very often by night desist from energizing according to any one of the outward senses, receive absurd impressions respecting many different things, since our souls exist in a state of perpetual motion and are capable of an infinite variety of changes. There were, therefore, things quite sufficient for its destruction which it brought forth out of itself. (235) But now, as it is, the multitude of the outward senses has brought against it a most incalculable multitude of evils, partly from objects of sight and partly from sounds; and besides that, from flavours and from such essences as affect the sense of smell. And one may almost say that the flavour which arises from them has a more pernicious influence on the disposition of the soul than that which is engendered in the soul itself, without any co-operation or agency of the organs of sense.

LXXXIV. (236) One of these women is Pentephoë, the wife of Pharaoh's chief cook.[116] We must now consider how a man who was a eunuch can be represented as having a wife. For there will here be something which will seem to offer a reasonable ground for perplexity to those who do not take the expressions of the law in an allegorical sense. For the mind is really a eunuch, and really the chief of cooks, using not merely such pleasures as are simple, but those also which are superfluous, and is therefore called a eunuch and barren of all wisdom, being the eunuch and slave of no other master than of that squanderer of all good things, Pharaoh. On another principle, therefore, it might appear a most desirable thing to be a eunuch, if our soul, by that means escaping vice, might be able also to avoid all knowledge of passion. (237) On which account Joseph, that is to say, the disposition of continence, says to Pleasure, who accosts him with, "Lie with me, and being a man behave as a man, and enjoy the pleasant things which life can afford." He, I say, refuses her, saying, "I shall be sinning against God, who loves virtue, if I become a votary of pleasure; for this is a wicked action."

LXXXV. (238) And, at first, he only skirmishes, but presently he fights and resists valiantly, when the soul enters into her own dwelling, and, having recourse to her own strength and energy, renounces the temptations of the body, and performs her own appropriate actions as those which are the proper occupation of the soul; not appearing in the house of Joseph, nor of Pentephoë, but in the house. Nor does Moses add a word to describe whose house he means, in order to give you opportunity to interpret allegorically, in an inquisitive spirit, the meaning of the expression, "to do his business." (239) The house, therefore, is the soul, to which he runs, leaving all external affairs, in order that what is spoken of may there be done.

But may we not say that the conduct of the temperate man is what it is, and is directed by the

---

[116] Genesis 39:1.

will of God? For there was not present any inconsistent idea of all those which are accustomed to
find their place within the soul. Moreover, pleasure never ceases from struggling against the yoke,
but, seizing hold of his clothes, she cries, "Lie with
me." Now, clothes are, as it were, the covering of
the body, just as life is protected by meat and drink.
And she says here, "Why do you renounce pleasure, without which you cannot live? (240) Behold,
I take hold of the things which cause it; and I say
that you could not possibly exist unless you also
made use of some of the things which cause it."

What, then, says the temperate man? "Shall
I," says he, "become a slave to passion, on account
of the material which causes passion? Nay, I will
depart out of reach of the passion." For, leaving
his garment in her hand, he fled, and escaped out
of doors.

LXXXVI. (241) And who, some one perhaps,
may say, ever escapes in-doors? Do not many do
so? Or have not some people, avoiding the guilt
of sacrilege, committed robberies in private
houses, or though not beating their own fathers,
have not they insulted the fathers of others? Now
these men do escape from one class of offences,
but they run into others. But a man who is perfectly temperate, ought to avoid every description
of offence, whether greater or less, and never to
be detected in any sin whatever. (242) But Joseph,
for he is a young man, and because as such he
was unable to struggle with the Egyptian body and
to subdue pleasure, runs away. But Phineas the
priest, who was zealous with a great zeal for God's
service, did not provide for his own safety by flight;
but having taken to himself a yoke horse, that is
to say, zeal combined with reason, would never
desist till he had wounded the Midianitish woman
(that is to say the nature which was concealed in
the divine company), through her belly, [117] in order
that no plant or seed of wickedness might ever
be able to shoot out from it.

LXXXVII. On which account after folly has
been utterly eradicated, the soul receives a twofold prize, and a double inheritance, peace and holiness, two kindred and sister-like virtues. (243)
We must therefore refuse to listen to such a
woman, that is to say to a wicked temptation of
the outward senses, since "God gave a good reward
to the midwives," [118] because they disregarded the
commands of the wasteful Pharaoh, "saving the
male children of the soul alive," which he wished
to destroy, being a lover of the female offspring
alone, and rejecting all knowledge of the Cause
of all things, and saying, "I know him not." [119] (244)
But we must give our belief to another woman,

such as it was ordained that Sarah should be, Sarah
being in a figure the governing virtue; and the wise
Abraham was guided by her, when she recommended him such actions as were good. [120] For
before this time, when he was not yet perfect, but
even before his name was changed, he gave his
attention to subjects of lofty philosophical speculation; and she, knowing that he could not produce anything out of perfect virtue, counselled him
to raise children out of her handmaid, that is to
say out of encyclical instruction, out of Agar, [121]
which name being interpreted means a dwelling
near; for he who meditates dwelling in perfect virtue, before his name is enrolled among the citizens of that state, dwells among the encyclical studies, in order that through their instrumentality he
may make his approaches at liberty towards perfect virtue.

(245) After that, when he saw that he was now
become perfect, and was now able to become a
father, although he himself was full of gratitude
towards those studies, by means of which he had
been recommended to virtue, and thought it hard
to renounce them; he was well inclined to be
appeased by an oracle from God which laid this
command on him. "In everything which Sarah says,
do thou obey her voice." [122] Let that be a law to
every one of us to do whatever seems good to virtue; for if we are willing to submit to everything
which virtue recommends we shall be happy.

LXXXVIII. (246) And the expression, "And
thou eatest of the tree of which alone I commanded
thee that thou shouldst not eat," [123] is equivalent
to saying, You made a covenant with wickedness,
which you ought to have repelled with all your
strength. On this account, "Cursed art thou;" not,
cursed is the earth for thy works. What, now, is
the reason of this? That serpent, pleasure, which
is an irrational elevation of the soul, this is intrinsically accursed in its own nature; and being such,
attaches itself only to the wicked man, and to no
good man. But Adam is the intermediate sort of
mind which at one time if investigated is found to
be good, and at another time bad; for inasmuch
as it is mind, it is not by nature either good or
bad, but from contact with virtue or with vice, it
frequently changes for the better or for the worse;
(247) therefore it very naturally is not accursed
of its own nature, as neither being itself wickedness nor acting according to wickedness, but the
earth is accursed in its works: for the actions which
proceed from the entire soul, which he calls the
earth, are open to blame and devoid of innocence,
inasmuch as he does everything in accordance with

---

[117]Numbers 25:7.
[118]Exodus 1:20.
[119]Exodus 3:17.

[120]Genesis 21:12.
[121]Genesis 16:2.
[122]Genesis 21:11.
[123]Genesis 3:17.

vice. In reference to which fact God adds, that "In sorrow thou shalt eat of it." Which is equivalent to saying, you shall enjoy your soul in sorrow; for the wicked man does enjoy his own soul with great pain the whole of his life, having no legitimate cause for joy; for such cause is only produced by justice and prudence, and by the virtues which are enthroned as companions with them.

LXXXIX. (248) "Thorns, therefore, and thistles shall it bring forth to you." But what is it which is produced and which shoots up in the soul of the foolish man except the passions which goad and sting and wound it? Which Moses here, speaking symbolically, calls thorns, and which irrational appetite rushes upon at first like fire, and so hastens to meet, and afterwards uniting itself to them, it consumes and destroys all its own nature and actions. For Moses speaks thus:—"But if fire when it has gone forth finds thorns, and shall also burn a threshing-floor, or a crop of wheat, or a field of corn, then he who kindled the fire shall pay the damage."[124] (249) You see therefore when it has gone forth, that is to say, irrational impetuosity, it does not only burn the thorns, but finds them: for being inclined to seek out the passions, it attains to what it has been desiring to find; but when it has found it, it consumes these three things,—perfect virtue, improvement, and goodness of disposition. Moses therefore here compares virtue to a threshing-floor; for as the crops when collected are brought to the threshing-floor, so also are the good things which exist in the soul of the wise man brought to virtue; and improvement he likens to the crop of wheat, inasmuch as both the one and the other are imperfect, aiming at the end; and goodness of disposition he compares to a field of corn, because it is well adapted to receive the seeds of virtue; (250) and each of the passions he calls thistles *(tribolia)*, because they are divisible into three parts: the passion itself, the efficient cause, and the effect which arises from the combined operation of the two. As for instance pleasure, what is pleasant, and the being pleased; appetite, the object of appetite, and the indulgence

of appetite; pain, what is painful, and the suffering pain; fear, what is fearful, and the being in a state of fear.

XC. (251) "And thou shalt eat the herb of the field; in the sweat of thy brow shalt thou eat thy bread." He here speaks of the herb of the field and of bread, as if they were synonymous, or identical with one another. The herb of the field is the food of the irrational animal; but the irrational animal is a worthless creature, which has been deprived of right reason. The outward senses are also irrational, though they are part of the soul. But the mind, which is eager for the attainment of those things which are the objects of the outward sense by means of the irrational outward senses, does not attain its desires without labour and sweat; for the life of the foolish man is very full of distress and very burdensome, since he is always aiming at and greedily coveting the things which give pleasure, and all such things as wickedness is wont to do.

(252) And how long shall this last? "Until," says God, "you return to the dust form which you were taken." For is he not now ranked among the things of the earth, and among things which have no consistency, ever since he deserted the wisdom which is from heaven? We must consider therefore to what point he is coming back; but may we not consider whether what he says has not some such meaning as this, that the foolish mind is at all times averted from right reason, and that it has been originally taken not from any sublime nature, but from some more earthly material, and whether it is stationary, or whether it is in motion, it is always the same, and desirous of the same objects. (253) On which account, God adds that, "Dust thou art, and unto dust shalt thou return." And this is equivalent to what has been said before.

Moreover this sentence also signifies, the beginning and the end are one and the same thing. For there hadst thou beginning in the perishable bodies of the earth; and again, thou shalt end in them, during the interval of your life, between its beginning and its end, passing along a road which is not plain and easy, but rough, full of briars and thorns, the nature of which is to tear and wound thee.

---

[124] Exodus 22:6.

ON THE CHERUBIM†

(De Cherubim)

PART 1

I. (1) "And God cast out Adam, and placed him opposite the paradise of happiness; and he placed there the cherubim and a flaming sword, which turned every way, to keep the way of the tree of life.[1]

In this place Moses uses the expression, "He cast out," but previously he said, "He sent out," not using the various expressions at random, but being well aware with reference to what parts he was employing them with propriety and felicity. (2) Now a man who is sent out is not hindered from returning at some subsequent time; but he who is cast out by God must endure an eternal banishment, for it is granted to him who has not yet been completely and violently taken prisoner by wickedness, to repent, and so to return back to virtue, from which he has been driven, as to his great country; but he who is weighed down by, and wholly subjected to, a violent and incurable disease, must bear his misfortunes for ever, being for all times unalterably cast out into the place of the wicked, that there he may endure unmitigated and everlasting misery.[2] (3) Since we see Agar,[3] by whom we understand the middle kind of instruction which is confined to the encyclical system, twice going forth from Sarah, who is the symbol of predominant virtue, and once returning back by the same road, inasmuch as after she had fled the first time, without being banished by her mistress, she returned to see her master's house, having been met by an angel, as the holy scriptures read: but the second time, she is utterly cast out, and is never to be brought back again.

II. (4) And we must speak of the causes of her first flight, and then again of her second perpetual banishment.

Before the names of the two were changed, that is to say, before they had been altered for the better as to the characteristics of their souls, and had been endowed with better dispositions, but while the name of the man was still Abram, or the sublime father, who delighted in the lofty philosophy which investigates the events which take place in the air, and the sublime nature of the beings which exist in heaven, which mathematical science claims for itself as the most excellent part of natural philosophy, (5) and the name of the woman was still Sarai; the symbol of my authority, for she is called my authority, and she had not yet changed her nature so as to become generic virtue, and all genus is imperishable, but was as yet classed among things particular and things in species; that is to say, such as the prudence which is in me, the temperance which is in me, the courage, the justice, and so on in the same manner; and these particular virtues are perishable, because the place which receives them, that is to say I, am also perishable. (6) Then Agar, who is the middle kind of encyclical instruction, even if she should endeavour to escape from the austere and stern life of the lovers of virtue, will again return to it, since it is not, as yet, able to receive the generic and imperishable excellencies of virtue, but can only touch the particular virtues, and such as are spoken of in species, in which it is sufficient to attain to mediocrity instead of extreme perfection.

(7) But when Abram, instead of an inquirer into natural philosophy, became a wise man and a lover of God, having his name changed to Abraham, which being interpreted means the great father of sounds; for language when uttered sounds, and the father of language is the mind, which has attained to what is virtuous. And when Sarai instead of being my authority, had her name also changed to Sarah, the meaning of which is princess, and this change is equivalent to becoming generic and imperishable virtue, instead of virtue special and perishable: (8) then will arise the genus of happiness that is to say, Isaac; and he, when all the feminine affections[4] have ceased, and when the passion of joy and cheerfulness are dead, will eagerly pursue, not childish amusements, but divine objects; then too those elementary branches of instruction which bear the name of Agar, will be cast out, and their sophistical child will also be cast out, who is named Ishmael.

III. (9) And they shall undergo eternal banishment, God himself confirming their expulsion, when he bids the wise man obey the word spoken by Sarah, and she urges him expressly to cast out the serving woman and her son; and it is good to be guided by virtue, and especially so when it

---

† Yonge's title, *A Treatise on the Cherubim; and On the Flaming Sword; and On the First-Born Child of Man, Cain.*

[1] Genesis 3:24.
[2] Genesis 16:9.
[3] Genesis 21:14.

[4] The Greek text here is corrupt and unintelligible. I have followed the Latin translation of Mangey.

teaches such lessons as this, that the most perfect natures are very greatly different from the mediocre habits, and that wisdom is a wholly different thing from sophistry; for the one labours to devise what is persuasive for the establishment of a false opinion, which is pernicious to the soul, but wisdom, with long meditation on the truth by the knowledge of right reason, bring real advantage to the intellect. (10) Why then do we wonder if God once for all banished Adam, that is to say, the mind out of the district of the virtues, after he had once contracted folly, that incurable disease, and if he never permitted him again to return, when he also drives out and banishes from wisdom and from the wise man every sophist, and the mother of sophists, the teaching that is of elementary instruction, while he calls the names of wisdom and of the wise man Abraham, and Sarah.

IV. (11) Then also, "The flaming sword and the cherubim have an abode allotted to them exactly in front of paradise." The expression, "in front," is used partly to convey the idea of a resisting enemy, and partly as suitable to the notion of judgment, as a person whose cause is being decided appears in front of his judge: partly also in a friendly sense, in order that they may be perceived, and may be considered in closer connection by reason of the more accurate view of them that is thus obtained, just as archetypal pictures and statues are placed in front of painters and statuaries.

(12) Now the first example of an enemy placed directly in front of one is derived from what is said in the case of Cain, that "he went out from the face of God, and dwelt in the land of Nod, in the front of Eden." [5] Now Nod being interpreted means commotion, and Eden means delight. The one therefore is a symbol of wickedness agitating the soul, and the other of virtue which creates for the soul a state of tranquillity and happiness, not meaning by happiness that effeminate luxury which is derived from the indulgence of the irrational passion of pleasure, but a joy free from toil and free from hardship, which is enjoyed with great tranquillity. (13) And it follows of necessity that when the mind goes forth from any imagination of God, by which it would be good and expedient for it to be supported, then immediately, after the fashion of a ship, which is tossed in the sea, when the winds oppose it with great violence, it is tossed about in every direction, having disturbance as it were for its country and its home, a thing which is the most contrary of all things to steadiness of soul, which is engendered by joy, which is a term synonymous with Eden.

V. (14) Now of the kind of opposition of place which is connected with standing in front of a judge for judgment, we have an example in the case of the woman who has been suspected of having committed adultery. For, says Moses, "the priest shall cause the woman to stand in front of her lord, and she shall uncover her head." [6] Let us now examine what he intends to show by this direction.

It often happens that what ought to be done is not done, in the manner in which it ought to be done, and sometimes too that which is not proper is nevertheless done in a proper manner. For instance, when the return of a deposit is not made in an honest spirit, but is intended either to work the injury of him who receives it back again, or by way of a snare to bear out a denial in the case of another deposit of greater value, in that case a proper action is done in an improper manner. (15) On the other hand, for a physician not to tell the exact truth to a sick patient, when he has decided on purging him, or performing some operation with the knife or with the cautery for the benefit of the patient, lest if the sick man were to be moved too strongly by the anticipation of the suffering, he might refuse to submit to the cure, or through weakness of mind might despair of its succeeding; or in the case of a wise man giving false information to the enemy to secure the safety of his country, fearing lest through his speaking the truth the affairs of the adversaries should succeed, in this case an action which is not intrinsically right is done in a proper manner.

In reference to which distinction Moses says, "to pursue what is just justly," [7] as if it were possible also to pursue it unjustly, if at any time the judge who gives sentence does not decide in an honest spirit. (16) Since therefore what is said or done is openly notorious to all men, but since the intention, the consequence of which what is said is said, and what is done is done, is not notorious, but it is uncertain whether it be a sound and healthy motive, or an unhealthy design, stained with numerous pollutions; and since no created being is capable of discerning the secret intention of an invisible mind, but God alone; in reference to this Moses says that "all secret things are known to the Lord God, but only such as are manifest are known to the creature." (17) And therefore it is enjoined to the priest and prophet, that is to say to reason, "to place the soul in front of God, with the head uncovered," [8] that is to say the soul must be laid bare as to its principal design, and the sentiments which it nourished must be revealed, in order that being brought before the judgment seat of the most accurate vision of the incorruptible God, it may be thoroughly examined as to all its concealed disguises, like a base coin, or, on the

---

[5] Genesis 4:16.

[6] Numbers 5:18.
[7] Deuteronomy 16:20.
[8] Numbers 5:14.

other hand, if it be found to be free from all participation in any kind of wickedness, it may wash away all the calumnies that have been uttered against its bringing him for a testimony to its purity, who is alone able to behold the soul naked.

VI. (18) This, then, is the meaning of coming in front of one's judge, when brought up for judgment. But the case of coming in front of any one which has a bearing upon connection or familiarity, may be illustrated by the example of the all-wise Abraham. "For," says Moses, "he was still standing in front of God."[9] And a proof of his familiarity is contained in the expression that "he came near to God, and spoke." For it is fitting for one who has no connection with another to stand at a distance, and to be separated from him, but he who is connected with him should stand near to him. (19) And to stand, and to have an unchangeable mind comes very near to the power of God, since the Divinity is unchangeable, but that which is created is intrinsically and essentially changeable. Therefore, if any one, restraining the changeableness natural to all created things by his love of knowledge, has been able to put such violence on any thing as to cause it to stand firm, let him be sure that he has come near to the happiness of the Deity.

(20) But God very appropriately assigns to the cherubim and to the flaming sword a city or abode in front of Paradise, not as to enemies about to oppose and to fight him, but rather as to near connections and friends, in order that in consequence of a continued sight and contemplation of one another, the two powers might conceive an affection for one another, the all-bounteous God inspiring them with a winged and heavenly love.

VII. (21) But we must now consider what the figurative allusions are which are enigmatically expressed in the mention of the cherubim and of the flaming sword which turned every way. May we not say that Moses here introduces under a figure an intimation of the revolutions of the whole heaven? For the spheres in heaven received a motion in opposite directions to one another, the one sphere receiving a fixed motion towards the right hand, but the sphere of the other side receiving a wandering motion towards the left. (22) But that outermost circle of what are called the fixed stars is one sphere, which also proceeds in a fixed periodical revolution from east to west. But the interior circle of the seven planets, whose course is at the same time compulsory and voluntary, has two motions, which are to a certain degree contrary to one another. And one of these motions is involuntary, like that of the planets. For they appear every day proceeding onwards from the east to the west. But their peculiar and voluntary motion

is from west to east, according to which last motion we find that the periods of the seven planets have received their exact measure of time, moving on in an equal course, as the Sun, and Lucifer, and what is called Stilbon. For these three planets are of equal speed; but some of the others are unequal in point of time, but preserve a certain sort of relative proportion to one another and to the other three which have been mentioned.

(23) Accordingly, by one of the cherubim is understood the extreme outermost circumference of the entire heaven, in which the fixed stars celebrate their truly divine dance, which always proceeds on similar principles and is always the same, without ever leaving the order which the Father, who created them, appointed for them in the world.

But the other of the cherubim is the inner sphere which is contained within that previously mentioned, which God originally divided in two parts, and created seven orbits, bearing a certain definite proportion to one another, and he adapted each of the planets to one of these; (24) and then, having placed each of these stars in its proper orbit, like a driver in a chariot, he did not entrust the reins to any one of them, fearing that some inharmonious sort of management might be the result, but he made them all to depend upon himself, thinking that, by that arrangement, the character of their motion would be rendered most harmonious. For every thing which exists in combination with God is deserving of praise; but every thing which exists without him is faulty.

VIII. (25) This, then, is one of the systems, according to which what is said of the cherubim may be understood allegorically. But we must suppose that the sword, consisting of flame and always turning in every direction, intimates their motion and the everlasting agitation of the entire heaven. And may we not say, according to another way of understanding this allegory, that the two cherubim are meant as symbols of each of the hemispheres? For they say that they stand face to face, inclining towards the mercy-seat; since the two hemispheres are also exactly opposite to one another, and incline towards the earth which is the centre of the whole universe, by which, also, they are kept apart from one another.

(26) But the only one of all the parts of the world that stands firmly was most appropriately named Vesta[10] by the ancients, in order that there might be an excellently arranged revolution of the two hemispheres around some object firmly fixed in the middle. And the flaming sword is a symbol of the sun; for as he is a collection of an immense body of flame, he is the swiftest of all existing things, to such a degree that in one day he revolves round the whole world.

IX. (27) I have also, on one occasion, heard a more ingenious train of reasoning from my own soul, which was accustomed frequently to be seized with a certain divine inspiration, even concerning matters which it could not explain even to itself; which now, if I am able to remember it accurately, I will relate. It told me that in the one living and true God there were two supreme and primary powers—goodness and authority; and that by his goodness he had created every thing, and by his authority he governed all that he had created; (28) and that the third thing which was between the two, and had the effect of bringing them together was reason, for that it was owing to reason that God was both a ruler and good.

Now, of this ruling authority and of this goodness, being two distinct powers, the cherubim were the symbols, but of reason the flaming sword was the symbol. For reason is a thing capable of rapid motion and impetuous, and especially the reason of the Creator of all things is so, inasmuch as it was before everything and passed by everything, and was conceived before everything, and appears in everything. (29) And do thou, O my mind, receive the impression of each of these cherubims unadulterated, that thus becoming thoroughly instructed about the ruling authority of the Creator of all things and about his goodness, thou mayest receive a happy inheritance; for immediately thou shalt understand the conjunction and combination of these imperishable powers, and learn in what respects God is good, his majesty arising from his sovereign power being all the time conspicuous; and in what he is powerful, his goodness, being equally the object of attention, that is this way thou mayest attain to the virtues which are engendered by these conceptions, namely, a love and a reverential awe of God, neither being uplifted to arrogance by any prosperity which may befall thee, having regard always to the greatness of the sovereignty of thy King; nor abjectly giving up hope of better things in the hour of unexpected misfortune, having regard, then, to the mercifulness of thy great and bounteous God. (30) And let the flaming sword teach thee that these things might be followed by a prompt and fiery reason combined with action, which never ceases being in motion with rapidity and energy to the selection of good objects, and the avoidance of all such as are evil.

X. (31) Do you not see that even the wise Abraham, when he began to measure everything with a reference to God, and to leave nothing to the creature, took an imitation of the flaming sword, namely, "fire and a sword,"[11] being eager to slay and to burn that mortal creature which was born of him, that so being raised on high it might soar up to God, the intellect being thus disentangled from the body.

(32) Moses also represents Balaam, who is the symbol of a vain people, stripped of his arms, as a runaway and deserter, well knowing the war which it becomes the soul to carry on for the sake of knowledge; for he says to his ass, who is here a symbol of the irrational designs of life which every foolish man entertains, that "If I had had a sword, I should ere now have slain thee."[12] And great thanks are due to the Maker of all things, because he, knowing the struggles and resistance of folly, did not give to it the power of language, which would have been like giving a sword to a madman, in order that it might have no power to work great and iniquitous destruction among all whom it should meet with. (33) But the reproaches which Balaam utters are in some degree expressed by all those who are not purified, but are always talking foolishly, devoting themselves to the life of a merchant, or of a farmer, or to some other business, the object of which is to provide the things necessary for life. As long, indeed, as everything goes on prosperously with respect to each individual, he mounts his animal joyfully and rides on cheerfully, and holding the reins firmly he will by no means consent to let them go. And if any one advises him to dismount and to set bounds to his appetites, because of his inability to know what will befall him hereafter, he reproaches him with jealousy and envy, saying that he does not address him in this way out of good will. (34) But when any unexpected misfortune overtakes him, he then looks upon those who have given him warnings as good prophets and men able, above all others, to foresee the future, and lays the blame of his distress on what is absolutely the cause of no evil whatever, on agriculture, on commerce, or on any other pursuit which he may have thought fit to select for the purpose of making money.

XI. (35) But these pursuits, although they are destitute of the organs of speech, will, nevertheless, through the medium of actions, utter a language clearer than any speech which proceeds from the tongue, and will say, "O you sycophant and false accuser, are not we the pursuits which you mounted upon holding your head high, as you might have mounted upon a beast of burden? And have we, by any insolence or obstinacy of ours, caused you any suffering? Behold reason armed and standing in opposition to God, by whom all good and all bad fortune is brought to its accomplishment. Do you not see it? (36) Why, then, do you reproach us now, when you formerly had no fault to find with us, while your affairs were proceeding prosperously? For we are the same as we were before, having changed nothing of our nature,

---

[11]Genesis 22:6.

[12]Numbers 22:29.

not the slightest jot. But you are now applying tests which have no soundness in them, and in consequence are unreasonably violent against us; for if you had understood from the beginning that it is not the pursuits which you follow that are the causes of your participation in good or in evil, but rather the divine reason, which is the helmsman and governor of the universe, then you would more easily have borne the events which have befallen you, ceasing to bring false accusations against us, and to attribute to us effects which we are unable to produce.

(37) "If therefore this reason now again, putting an end to that strife, and dispersing the sad and desponding ideas which arise from it, should promise you tranquillity of life, you will then again, with cheerfulness and joy, give us your right hand though we shall be like what we are now. But we are neither puffed up by your friendly favour, nor do we think it of great importance if you are angry with us; for we know that we are not the causes of either good or evil fortune, not even if you believe that we are, unless indeed you attribute to the sea the cause of sailors making favourable voyages, or of the shipwrecks which at times befall them, and not rather to the variations of the winds, which blow at one time gently, and at another with the most violent impetuosity; for as all water is by its own nature tranquil, (38) accordingly, when a favourable gale blows upon the stern of a ship, every rope is bent, and the ship is in full sail, conveying the mariners to the harbour; but when on a sudden the wind changes to the opposite direction, and blows against the head of the vessel, it then raises a heavy swell and great disturbance in the water, and upsets the ship and the sea, which was in no respect the cause of what has happened is blamed for it, though it notoriously is either calm or stormy according to the gentleness or violence of the winds."

(39) By all these considerations I think it has been abundantly shown, that nature has made reason the most powerful coadjutor of man, and has made him, how is able to make a proper use of it, happy and truly rational; but him who has not this faculty, she has rendered irrational and unhappy.

PART 2
OF CAIN AND HIS BIRTH

XII. (40) "And Adam knew his wife, and she conceived and brought forth Cain; and she said I have gotten a man by means of the Lord; and he caused her also to bring forth Abel his brother." [13] These men, to whose virtue the Jewish legislation bears testimony, he does not represent as knowing their wives, such as Abraham, Isaac, Jacob, Moses, and if there are any others of like zeal with them; (41) for since we say, that woman is to be understood symbolically as the outward sense, and since knowledge consists in alienation from the outward sense and from the body, it is plain that the lovers of wisdom must repudiate the outward sense rather than choose it, and is not this quite natural? for they who live with these men are in name indeed wives, but in fact virtues. Sarah is princess and guide, Rebecca is perseverance in what is good; Leah again is virtue, fainting and weary at the long continuance of exertion, which every foolish man declines, and avoids, and repudiates; and Zipporah, the wife of Moses, is virtue, mounting up from earth to heaven, and arriving at a just comprehension of the divine and blessed virtues which exist there, and she is called a bird.

(42) But that we may describe the conception and the parturition of virtues, let the superstitious either stop their ears, or else let them depart; for we are about to teach those initiated persons who are worthy of the knowledge of the most sacred mysteries, the whole nature of such divine and secret ordinances. And those who are thus worthy are they who, with all modesty, practise genuine piety, of that sort which scorns to disguise itself under any false colours. But we will not act the part of hierophant or expounder of sacred mysteries to those who are afflicted with the incurable disease of pride of language and quibbling expressions, and juggling tricks of manners, and who measure sanctity and holiness by no other standard.

XIII. (43) But we must begin our explanation of these mysteries in this way. A husband unites with his wife, and the male human being with the female human being in a union which tends to the generation of children, in strict accordance with and obedience to nature. But it is not lawful for virtues, which are the parents of many perfect things, to associate with a mortal husband. But they, without having received the power of generation from any other being, will never be able by themselves alone to conceive any thing. (44) Who, then, is it who sows good seed in them, except the Father of the universe, the uncreated God, he who is the parent of all things? This, therefore, is the being who sows, and presently he bestows his own offspring, which he himself did sow; for God creates nothing for himself, inasmuch as he is in need of nothing, but he creates every thing for him who is able to take it.

(45) And I will bring forward as a competent witness in proof of what I have said, the most holy Moses. [14] For he introduces Sarah as conceiving a son when God beheld her by himself; but he represents her as bringing forth her son, not to him

---

[13] Genesis 4:1.

[14] Genesis 21:1.

who beheld her then, but to him who was eager to attain to wisdom, and his name is called Abraham. (46) And he teaches the same lesson more plainly in the case of Leah, where he says that "God opened her womb."[15] But to open the womb is the especial business of the husband. And she having conceived, brought forth, not to God, for he alone is sufficient and all-abundant for himself, but to him who underwent labour for the sake of that which is good, namely, for Jacob; so that in this instance virtue received the divine seed from the great Cause of all things, but brought forth her offspring to one of her lovers, who deserved to be preferred to all her other suitors.[16]

(47) Again, when the all-wise Isaac addressed his supplications to God, Rebecca, who is perseverance, became pregnant by the agency of him who received the supplication; but Moses, who received Zipporah,[17] that is to say, winged and sublime virtue, without any supplication or entreaty on his part, found that she conceived by no mortal man.

XIV. (48) Now I bid ye, initiated men, who are purified, as to your ears, to receive these things, as mysteries which are really sacred, in your inmost souls; and reveal them not to any one who is of the number of the uninitiated, but guard them as a sacred treasure, laying them up in your own hearts, not in a storehouse in which are gold and silver, perishable substances, but in that treasurehouse in which the most excellent of all the possessions in the world does lie, the knowledge namely of the great first Cause, and of virtue, and in the third place, of the generation of them both. And if ever you meet with any one who has been properly initiated, cling to that man affectionately and adhere to him, that if he has learnt any more recent mystery he may not conceal it from you before you have learnt to comprehend it thoroughly. (49) For I myself, having been initiated in the great mysteries by Moses, the friend of God, nevertheless, when subsequently I beheld Jeremiah the prophet, and learnt that he was not only initiated into the sacred mysteries, but was also a competent hierophant or expounder of them, did not hesitate to become his pupil. And he, like a man very much under the influence of inspiration, uttered an oracle in the character of God, speaking in this manner to most peaceful virtue: "Hast thou not called me as thy house, and thy father, and the husband of thy virginity?"[18] showing by this expression most manifestly that God is both a house, the incorporeal abode of incorporeal ideas, and the Father of all things, inasmuch as it is he who has

created them; and the husband of wisdom, sowing for the race of mankind the seed of happiness in good and virgin soil. For it is fitting for God to converse with an unpolluted and untouched and pure nature, in truth and reality virgin, in a different manner from that in which we converse with such. (50) For the association of men, with a view to the procreation of children, makes virgins women. But when God begins to associate with the soul, he makes that which was previously woman now again virgin. Since banishing and destroying all the degenerate appetites unbecoming a human being, by which it had been made effeminate, he introduces in their stead genuine, and perfect, and unadulterated virtues; therefore, he will not converse with Sarah before all the habits, such as other women have, have left her,[19] and till she has returned into the class of pure virgins.

XV. (51) But it is, perhaps, possible that in some cases a virgin soul may be polluted by intemperate passions, and so become impure. On which account the sacred oracle has been cautious, calling God the husband, not of a virgin, for a virgin is subject to change and to mortality, but of virginity; of an idea, that is to say, which is always existing in the same principles and in the same manner. For as all things endowed with distinctive qualities are by nature liable to origination and to destruction, so those archetypal powers, which are the makers of those particular things, have received an imperishable inheritance in their turn. (52) Therefore is it seemly that the uncreated and unchangeable God should ever sow the ideas of immortal and virgin virtues in a woman who is transformed into the appearance of virginity? Why, then, O soul, since it is right for you to dwell as a virgin in the house of God, and to cleave to wisdom, do you stand aloof from these things, and rather embrace the outward sense, which makes you effeminate and pollutes you? Therefore, you shall bring forth an offspring altogether polluted and altogether destructive, the fratricidal and accursed Cain, a possession not to be sought after; for the name Cain being interpreted means possession.

XVI. (53) And one may wonder at the kind of narration which the Jewish lawgiver frequently employs in many instances, where he departs from the usual style. For after giving the history of those parents of the human race who were created out of the earth, he begins to relate the story of the first-born of human parents, concerning whom he says absolutely nothing, as if he had already frequently mentioned his name, and were not now bringing it forward for the first time. Accordingly, he simply says that "she brought forth Cain." What sort of being was he, O writer; and what have you

---

[15] Genesis 29:13.
[16] Genesis 25:21.
[17] Exodus 2:21.
[18] Jeremiah 3:4.

[19] Genesis 18:11.

ever said about him before of either great of small importance? (54) And yet you are not ignorant of the importance of a proper application of names. For before this time, as you proceed in your history, you show this, when speaking in reference to the same person you say, "And Adam knew Eve his wife, and she conceived and brought forth a son, and she called his name Seth."[20] Therefore it was much more necessary in the case of the first-born, who was the beginning of the generation of men from one another, to display the nature of him who was thus conceived and born, in the first place showing that he was a male child, and secondly mentioning his peculiar name, Cain. (55) Since, therefore, it was not owing to inexperience or to ignorance of according to what persons he ought to give names, that he appears to have discarded his usual practice in the case of Cain, we must now consider on what account he thus named those who were born of our first parents, rather mentioning the name in an incidental way than actually giving it. And the cause, as it appears to me, according to the best conjecture that I can form, is this.

XVII. (56) All the rest of the human race gives names to things which are different from the things themselves, so that the thing which we see is one thing, but the name which we give it is another; but in the history of Moses the names which he affixes to things are the most conspicuous energies of the things themselves, so that the thing itself is at once of necessity its name, and is in no respect different from the name which is imposed on it. And you may learn this more clearly from the previous example which I have mentioned. (57) When the mind which is in us, and let it be called Adam, meeting with the outward sense, according to which all living creatures appear to exist (and that is called Eve), having conceived a desire for connection, is associated with this outward sense, that one conceives as in a net, and hunts after the external object of outward sense naturally. For by means of the eyes it arrives at a conception of colour, by the ears it conceives sound, by the nostrils it arrives at a conception of smells, of flavours by the organs of taste, and of all substance by those of touch; and having thus conceived it becomes pregnant, and immediately it is in labour, and brings forth the greatest of all the evils of the soul, namely, vain opinion, for it conceives an opinion that everything that it has seen, that it has heard, that it has tasted, that it has smelled, or that it has touched, belongs to itself, and to looks upon itself as the inventor and creator of them all.

XVIII. (58) And there is nothing unnatural in its receiving this impression, for there was a time once when the mind had no conversation with the outward sense, and had no outward sense, being very far removed from all things which were gregarious and in the habit of associating together, and itself resembling those solitary animals which feed by themselves. Accordingly as at that time it was classed by itself it did not touch any body, inasmuch as it had no organ in itself by which to take hold of external objects, but it was blind, and devoid of power, not being such a being as most people call a person when they see any one deprived of his eyes, for such a person is destitute of only one external sense, and has great and abundant vigour in the others. (59) But this mind, being curtailed of all the faculties which are derived from the outward senses, and being really powerless, being but the half of a perfect soul, destitute of the faculty by which it might naturally be able to conceive bodies, being but a garment of itself, deprived of its kindred organs, and as such unfortunately is wholly deprived of these organs of the external senses on which it might rely as on a staff, and by which it might have been able to support itself when tottering. From which cause a great darkness is spread over all bodies, so that nothing can be visible through it; for there was no outward sense by which things could be distinguished.

(60) God therefore, wishing to give it the faculty of comprehending not only incorporeal but also solid bodies, filled up the entire soul, attaching a second portion to that which he had already created, which he called appellatively woman, and by an especial name Eve, intimating the outward sense by a metaphorical expression.

XIX. (61) And she, the first moment that she was born, pours forth abundant light in a flood into the mind through each of her subordinate parts, as through so many holes, and having dissipated the previously existing mist, enabled it like a master to discern the natures of bodies at a distance and with perfect clearness; (62) and the mind being now irradiated with light, as if the beams of the sun had suddenly shone upon it after night, or as if it had just arisen from a deep sleep, or as if it had been to see a blind man suddenly restored to sight, came at once upon all the things with which creation was concerned, heaven, and earth, and water, and air, and plants, and animals, and their habits, and distinctive qualities, and faculties, and dispositions, and movements, and energies, and actions, and changes, and ends; and some things he saw, and some thing he heard, and some he tasted, and some he smelled, and some he touched; and towards some he felt an inclination as they were productive of pleasure, and to some he felt aversion inasmuch as they caused pain.

(63) Having therefore looked around it on all sides, and having contemplated itself and its own faculties, it ventured to utter the same boast that

---

Alexander the king of the Macedonians did, for they say that he, when he determined to lay claim to the supreme dominion over Europe and Asia, stood in a suitable place, and looking around him upon every thing, said, "All things on this side and all things on that side are mine," displaying thus the emptiness of soul truly childish and infantine and foolish, and not at all royal. (64) But the mind, having first laid a claim to the faculties of the outward sense, and by means of them having conceived every idea of bodily substance, became filled with unreasonable pride and was puffed up, so as to think everything in the world its own property, and that nothing at all belonged to any one else.

XX. (65) This is that disposition in us which Moses characterised when he gave Cain his name, a name which being interpreted means possession, Cain himself being full of all folly or rather of all impiety; for instead of thinking that all possession belonged to God, he conceived that they all belonged to himself, though he was not only not able to possess even himself steadily, but he did not even know of what essence he consisted; but nevertheless he placed confidence in the outward senses, as being competent to attain the objects perceivable only by them.

Let him tell us therefore how he will be able to avoid seeing wrongly, or being mistaken as to his hearing, or to escape even in any other of these outward senses. (66) And in truth it is inevitable that these errors should continually befall every one of us, even if we should happen to be endowed with the most accurately constructed organs possible; for it is difficult, or I might rather say impossible, for any one completely to avoid the natural blemishes and involuntary errors which arise, since the efficient causes of erroneous opinions are innumerable, both within us and around us, and outside of us, and since they are to be found in every mortal creature, man, therefore, very improperly conceives every thing to belong to himself, however proud he may be, and however high he may carry his head.

XXI. (67) And Laban, who relied greatly on his distinctive qualities, appears to me to have afforded great amusement to Jacob, who was beyond all other men, a clear-sighted contemplator of the nature, which was free from any such qualities, when he ventured to say to him that, "My daughter, and my sons, and my cattle, and all that you see, belong to me and to my daughters."[21] For adding the word "my" to each of these articles, he never ceases from speaking and boasting about himself. (68) Your daughters now, tell me—and they are the arts and sciences of the soul—do you say that your daughters are your own property?

How so? In the first place did you not receive them from the mind which taught them? in the second place it is naturally possible for you to lose these also, as you might lose anything else, either forgetting them through the greatness of your other cares, or through severe and lasting sicknesses of body, or because of the incurable disease which is at all events destined for those who grow old, namely old age, or through ten thousand other accidents, the number of which it is impossible to calculate.

(69) And what will you say about the sons?—and the sons are the reasonings which take place in portions of the soul,—if you pronounce that the sons belong to you, are you speaking reasonably, or are you downright mad for thinking so? For melancholic thoughts, and follies, and frenzies of the mind, and untrustworthy conjectures, and false ideas about things, and empty attractions of the mind, resembling dreams, and bringing with them convulsive agitation, and the disease which is innate in the soul, namely forgetfulness, and many other things beyond those that I have mentioned, take away the stability of your master-like authority, and show that these are the possession of some one else and not of you. (70) Again, what will you say about the cattle? Now the cattle are the outward senses, for the outward sense is something unreasonable and brutish, like cattle, will you dare to call the cattle your property? Tell me when you see erroneously, when you constantly hear erroneously, when you at one time think sweet flavours brackish, and at others look upon bitter flavours as sweet, when you in fact, in respect of every single one of these outward senses, are in the habit of being mistaken more frequently than you come to a correct decision, do you not blush? and if so, will you give yourself airs, and boast yourself as if you employed all the faculties and energies of the soul in such a way as never to err or to be mistaken.

XXII. (71) But if you were to become changed, and to become possessed of the senses which you ought to have, you would then affirm that everything was the property of God, not of yourself, all conceptions, all knowledge, all art, all speculation, all particular reasonings, all the outward senses, and all the energies of the soul, whether exerted by them or without them; and if you leave yourself throughout the whole of your life without any instructor, and without any teaching, you will be a slave for ever to harsh mistresses, such as vain opinions, appetites, pleasures, acts of injustice, follies, and erroneous conceptions; (72) "For if," says Moses, "the servant shall answer and say, I am content with my master, and with my wife, and with my children, I will not depart and be free, then, being brought before the judgment-seat of God," and, having him for his judge, he shall securely have what he asked, "having first had his

---

[21] Genesis 31:43.

ear bored through,"[22] that he may not hear the words of God about freedom of soul. (73) For it is a sign of a mind which is as it were rejected from the sacred contest and wholly discarded, and of reasoning faculties wholly childish and deficient, to make a boast of the mind being contented, and of thinking one's mind one's own lord and benefactor, and to boast of being very sufficiently pleased with the outward senses, and of thinking them one's own property, and the greatest of all good things, and their offspring with them; the offspring of the mind being to comprehend, to reason, to discriminate, to will, to conjecture; and the offspring of the outward sense being to see, to hear, to taste, to smell, to touch, in short to feel.

XXIII. (74) It follows inevitably that he who is held in bondage by these two masters can never enjoy even a dream of freedom; for it is only by a flight and complete escape from them that we arrive at a state of freedom from fear. But there is another man besides him, who is so taken up with himself, who makes an exhibition of insanity, and says that even if any one were to take his possessions away from him he would gain a victory over him, like a man contending for his own property. "For," says he, "I will pursue and will take captive; I will divide the spoil; I will satisfy my soul, and I will slay with my sword; my right hand shall obtain the mastery."[23]

(75) To whom I would say, Thou hast forgotten, fool, that every one who thinks himself at his birth born to be a persecutor, is persecuted; for diseases, and old age, and death, with all the rest of the multitude of calamities incurred, voluntarily and involuntarily, agitate and harass and persecute every one of us; and he who thinks to take captive or to subdue is himself taken captive and subdued; and he who expects to carry off the spoil, and who arranges a distribution of the booty, is defeated, and becomes subject to the enemies who have defeated him, receiving emptiness instead of abundance, and slavery for his soul instead of mastership, and being slain instead of slaying, and forcibly suffering himself all that he had designed to do to others. (76) For such a man was truly the enemy of reason which establishes the truth, and of nature herself, setting up a claim to everything which was done as his own, and remembering not one of the things which happened to him while he was suffering, as if he had escaped all the evils which could arise from any source whatever.

XXIV. (77) For, says he, the enemy has said, "I will pursue and take captive." Who, then, could be a more determined enemy to the soul than he who out of arrogance appropriates the especial attributes of the Deity to himself? Now it is an espe-cial attribute of God to create, and this faculty it is impious to ascribe to any created being. (78) But the special property of the created being is to suffer; and he who has previously considered how akin to and inevitable for man this is, will easily endure everything that befalls him, however grievous it may be. But if he thinks that it is inconsistent with his destiny ,then, if he be oppressed with any very terrible calamity, he will suffer the punishment of Sisyphus, not being able to raise his head, not even ever so little, but being exposed to all sorts of evils coming upon him and overwhelming him, and meeting them all with submission and non-resistance, the passions of a degenerate and unmanly soul; for he ought rather to have endured with patience; still, however, resisting and striving against calamity, strengthening his mind, and raising a bulwark against sorrow by his own patience and fortitude, which are the most powerful of virtues.

(79) For as to be shaved is an operation of a twofold nature, as in the one case the creature shaved is either the active agent and the passive subject; and in the other case, he does nothing but yield and submit to the barber: for a sheep is shorn either of his whole hide, or of that which is called the pillow; doing nothing of itself, but only suffering at the hands of another. But man cooperates with the barber, and puts himself in the proper attitude, and makes himself convenient, mingling the characters of the subject and the agent. (80) So also in the case of beating, that may happen either to a servant who has committed offences worthy of stripes, or to a freeman who is stretched on the wheel as a punishment for wickedness, or to some inanimate thing; for stones and trees are beaten, and gold and silver, and whatever material is wrought in a forge, or is cut in two. (81) And to be beaten, also happens to athletes who contend in boxing, or in the pancratium for victory and crowns. The boxer parries blows which are aimed at him with one of his hands, and stooping his neck on this side and on that side, guards against being struck; and very often he stands on tiptoe, and raises himself as high as he can, or else he stoops and contracts himself on the other hand, and compels his antagonist to waste his blows on the empty air, very nearly as if he were fighting with a shadow.

But the servant or the brass, doing nothing in return, is subjected to the will of the other party, suffering at his hands whatever he pleases: (82) let us therefore never admit the influence of this passion, neither in our body, nor, what is of much greater importance, in our soul; but let us rather admit that feeling which suffers in return, since it is inevitable that that which is mortal must suffer; so that we may not, like effeminate persons, broken in spirit, dissolute, and falling to pieces before our time, be weak through the utter pros-

---

[22]Exodus 21:6.
[23]Exodus 15:9.

tration and relaxation of the powers of the soul, but rather that, being invigorated in the nerves and tone of our minds, we may be able to bear cheerfully and easily the rush of such calamities as may be impending over us.

(83) Since therefore it has been proved, that no mortal is positively and assuredly the master of anything whatever (and they who are called masters are so in appearance only, and are not called so in truth), it follows of necessity, that as there is a subject and a slave, so there must also be a ruler and lord in the universe, and he must be the true real ruler and lord, the one God, to whom it was becoming to say, that "All things belong to him."

XXV. (84) And let us now consider with what magnificent fitness and with what divine majesty he speaks of these things. Let us consider the expression, "All things are mine," and "all things" mean as he says, "gifts, and offerings, and fruits of labour, which, on watching carefully, he will bring to me on the days of my festivals."[24] Showing, very manifestly, that of all existing things some are thought worthy of moderate grace which is called an offering, and some of that higher grace which is called by the appropriate name of a free gift. And these things again are of such a nature that they are able, not only to bring forth virtues as their fruit, but that good fruit and eatable does actually pervade the whole of them, by which alone the soul of him who loves contemplation is supported; (85) and he who has learnt this lesson, and who is able to keep and preserve these things in his mind, will bring to God a faultless and most excellent offering, namely faith, on the festivals, which are not feasts of mortal things; for he has assigned feasts also to himself, laying down this as the most inevitable doctrine to those who are revellers in philosophy.

(86) And the doctrine is this: God alone keeps festival in reality, for he alone rejoices, he alone is delighted, he alone feels cheerfulness, and to him alone is it given, to pass an existence of perfect peace unmixed with war. He is free from all pain, and free from all fear; he has no participation in any evils, he yields to no one, he suffers no sorrow, he knows no fatigue, he is full of unalloyed happiness; his nature is entirely perfect, or rather God is himself the perfection, and completion, and boundary of happiness, partaking of nothing else by which he can be rendered better, but giving to every individual thing a portion of what is suited to it, from the fountain of good, namely, from himself; for the beautiful things in the world would never have been such as they are, if they had not been made after an archetypal pattern,

which was really beautiful, the uncreate, and blessed, and imperishable model of all things.

XXVI. (87) And on this account too Moses calls the sabbath, which name being interpreted means "rest," "the sabbath of God."[25] Touching upon the necessary principles of natural philosophy, not of the philosophy of men, in many parts of his law, for that among existing things which rests, if one must tell the truth, is one thing only, God. And by "rest" I do not mean "inaction" (since that which is by its nature energetic, that which is the cause of all things, can never desist from doing what is most excellent), but I mean an energy completely free from labour, without any feeling of suffering, and with the most perfect ease; (88) for one may say, without impropriety, that the sun and the moon, and the entire heaven, and the whole world labour, inasmuch as they are not endowed with independent power, and are continually in a state of motion and agitation, and the most undeniable proofs of their labour are the yearly seasons; for these things, which have the greatest tendency in the whole heaven to keep things together, vary their motions, making their revolutions at one time northern, at another time southern, and at other times different from both.

(89) The air, again, being sometimes warmed and sometimes cooled, and being capable of every sort of change, is easily proved to labour by the variations to which we feel that it is subject, since the most general cause of change is fatigue, and it would be folly to enter into any long detail about terrestrial or aquatic animals, dwelling at any length upon their general or particular changes; for these animals very naturally are liable to weakness in a much greater degree than those sublime objects, inasmuch as they partake to the greatest extent of the lowest, that is of earthly essence.

(90) Since therefore it is naturally the case that things, which are changed, are changed in consequence of fatigue, and since God is subject to no variation and to no change, he must also by nature be free from fatigue, and that, which has no participation in weakness, even though it moves everything, cannot possibly cease to enjoy rest for ever. So that rest is the appropriate attribute of God alone.

XXVII. And it has been shown that it is suitable to his character to keep festival; sabbaths therefore and festivals belong to the great Cause of all things alone, and absolutely to no man whatever. (91) For come, if you please, and contemplate with me the much celebrated festive assemblies of men. As for those which among the barbarian and Grecian nations have been established in compliance with fabulous fictions, all tend-

---

[24] Numbers 28:2.   [25] Leviticus 23:2.

ing to no other object than to excite vain pride in various nations, they may be all passed over, for the entire life of a man would not be long enough to make an accurate and thorough investigation of all the absurdities which existed in each of those festivals. But with a due regard to our time, we will mention a few points in the most important of them, as a specimen of the whole. (92) In every festival then and assembly among men, the following are the most remarkable and celebrated points, security, relaxation, truce, drunkenness, deep drinking, revelling, luxury, amusement, music at the doors, banquets lasting through the night, unseemly pleasures, wedding feasts during the day, violent acts of insolence, practices of intemperance, indulgence of folly, pursuits of shameful things, an utter destruction and renunciation of what is good, wakefulness during the night for the indulgence of immoderate appetites, sleep by day when it is the proper time to be awake, a turning upside down of the laws of nature. (93) At such a time virtue is ridiculed as a mischievous thing, and vice is caught at as something advantageous.

Then actions that ought to be done are held in no honour, and such as ought not to be done are esteemed. Then music and philosophy and all education, the really divine images of the divine soul, are reduced to silence, and such practices as are panders and pimps of pleasure to the belly, and the parts adjacent to the belly, are alone allowed to raise their voice.

XXVIII. (94) Such are the festivals of those who call themselves happy men, and even while they confine their unseemly conduct within their houses and unconsecrated places, they appear to me to be less guilty. But when, like the rush of a torrent carrying everything away with it, their indecency approaches and insults the most holy temples, it immediately overtaxes all that there is sacred in them, performing unhallowed sacrifices, offering victims which ought not to be sacrificed, and prayers such as should never be accomplished; celebrating impious mysteries, and profane rites, displaying a bastard piety, an adulterated holiness, an impure purity, a falsified truth, a debauched service of God. (95) And besides all this, they wash their bodies with baths and purifications, but they neither desire nor endeavour to wash off the passions of their souls, by which their whole life is polluted; and they are eager to flock to the temples in white garments, clothed in robes without spot or stain, but they feel no shame at bringing a polluted mind up to the very inmost shrine. (96) And if any one of the beasts, to be sacrificed, is found to be not perfect and entire, it is driven out of the sacred precincts, and is not allowed to be brought to the altar, even though all these corporeal imperfections are quite involuntary on its part; but though they may themselves be wounded in their souls by sensible diseases, which the

invincible power of wickedness has inflicted on them, or though, I might rather say, they are mutilated and curtailed of their fairest proportions, of prudence, and courage, and justice, piety, and of all the other virtues which the human race is naturally formed to possess, and although too they have contracted all this pollution and mutilation of their own free will, they nevertheless dare to perform sacrifices, thinking that the eye of God sees external objects alone, when the sun co-operates and throws light upon them, and that it cannot discern what is invisible in preference to what is visible, using itself as its own light.

(97) For the eye of the living God does not need any other light to enable him to perceive things, but being himself archetypal light he pours forth innumerable rays, not one of which is capable of being comprehended by the outward sense, but they are all only intelligible to the intellect; in consequence of which God alone uses them who is only comprehensible to the intellect, and nothing that has any portion in creation uses them at all; for that which has been created is perceptible to the outward senses, but that nature which is only perceptible to the intellect cannot be comprehended by the outward sense.

XXIX. (98) Since, therefore, he thus invisibly enters into this region of the soul, let us prepare that place in the best way the case admits of, to be an abode worthy of God; for if we do not, he, without our being aware of it, will quit us and migrate to some other habitation, which shall appear to him to be more excellently provided. (99) For if when we are about to receive kings, we prepare our houses to wear a more magnificent appearance, neglecting nothing which may give them ornament, but using every thing in a liberal and unsparing manner, having for our object that they shall have an abode pleasant to them, and in all respects suitable to their majesty; what sort of habitation ought we to prepare for the King of kings, for God the ruler of the whole universe, condescending in his mercy and lovingkindness for man to visit the beings whom he has created, and to come down from the borders of heaven to the lowest regions of the earth, for the purpose of benefiting our race? (100) Shall we prepare him a house of stone or of wooden materials? Away! such an idea is not holy even to utter; for not even if the whole earth were to change its nature and to become on a sudden gold, or something more valuable than gold, and if it were then to be wholly consumed by the skill of workmen, who should make it into porticoes and vestibules, and chambers, and precincts, and temples—not even then could it be a place worthy for his feet to tread upon, but a pious soul is his fitting abode.

XXX. (101) If therefore we call the invisible soul the terrestrial habitation of the invisible God, we shall be speaking justly and according to reason; but that the house may be firm and beautiful, let a good disposition and knowledge be laid as its foundations, and on these foundations let the virtues be built up in union with good actions, and let the ornaments of the front be the due comprehension of the encyclical branches of elementary instruction; (102) for from goodness of disposition arise skill, perseverance, memory; and from knowledge arise learning and attention, as the roots of a tree which is about to bring forth eatable fruit, and without which it is impossible to bring the intellect to perfection.

(103) But by the virtues, and by actions in accordance with them, a firm and strong foundation for a lasting building is secured, in order that anything which may endeavour to separate and alienate the soul from honesty and make it such another haunt, may be powerless against so strong a defence, (104) and by means of the study of the encyclical branches of elementary education, the things requisite for the ornament of the soul are provided; for as whitewashing, and paintings, and tablets, and the arrangement of costly stones, by which men decorate not merely the walls, but even the lower parts of their houses, and all other such things as these do not contribute to strength, but only give pleasure to those who live in the house; (105) so the knowledge of the encyclical accomplishments decorates the whole habitation of the soul, while grammar investigates the principles of poetry and follows up the history of ancient events, and geometry labours at equalities according to analogy, and endeavours to remedy whatever in us is deficient in rhythm or in moderation, or in harmony, by giving us rhythm, and moderation, and harmony, by means of a polished system of music; and rhetoric aims at giving us acuteness in everything, and at properly adapting all proper interpretations to everything, claiming for itself the control of all intenseness and all the vehement affections, and again of all relaxations and pleasures, with great freedom of speech, and a successful application of the organs of language and voice.

XXXI. (106) Such a house then being prepared in the race of mankind, all things on earth will be filled with good hopes, expecting the return of the powers of God; and they will come, bringing laws from heaven, and bonds, for the purpose of sanctifying the hallowing it, according to the command of their Father; then becoming the associates and constant companions of these souls which love virtue, they sow in them the genus of happiness: as they gave to the wise Abraham his son Isaac as the most perfect proof of their gratitude for the hospitality which they experienced from him.

(107) And the purified intellect rejoices in nothing more than in confessing that it has for its master him who is the Lord of all; for to be the servant of God is the greatest boast, and is more honourable, not only than freedom, but even than

riches or dominion, or than anything which the race of mankind is eager for. (108) And of the supreme authority of the living God, the sacred scripture is a true witness, which speaks thus: "And the land shall not be sold for ever; for all the earth is mine, because ye are all strangers and sojourners in my sight."[26] Does not the scripture here most manifestly show that all things belong to God by virtue of possession, (109) but to created things only inasmuch as they have the use of them? For, says God, nothing shall be permanently sold to any one of all created beings, since there is one being to whom the possession of the universe does permanently and surely belong; for God has given the use of all created things to all men, not having made any one of those things which are only in part perfect, so as to have absolutely no need of anything else, (110) in order that, being desirous to obtain that of which it has need, it may of necessity unite itself to that which is able to supply it, and that other may in its turn unite with it, and both may thus combine with one another; for thus, the two combining and mingling together, and like a lyre which is composed of dissimilar sounds, coming into one combination and symphony, must of necessity sound together, while all things giving and receiving in turn contribute to the completion and perfection of the universal world.

(111) In this way inanimate things combine with those which have life, irrational things with those endowed with reason, trees with men, and men with plants, things untameable with those which are tame, and domestic animals with savage ones, the male with the female, and the female with the male; in short, terrestrial animals with such as live in the water, aquatic creatures with those whose home is in the air, and flying animals with any of these described above. And besides all those things, earth with heaven, and heaven with earth, air with water, and water with air. And again the intermediate natures with one another, and with these at their extremities, and the extremities too form an attachment to the intermediate natures and to one another. (112) So again winter feels a need of summer, and summer of winter, spring of both, and autumn of spring, and each of these seasons of each other season; and, so to say, everything has a need and want of everything else. So that the whole universe of which all these are parts, namely the world, is clearly a complete work, worthy of its Maker.

XXXII. (113) Thus, therefore, putting all these things together, God appropriated the dominion over them all to himself, but the use and enjoyment of themselves and of each other he allowed to those who are subject to him; for we have the complete use of our own faculties and of every-

---

[26] Leviticus 25:23.

thing which affects us: I therefore, consisting of soul and body, and appearing to have a mind, and reason, and outward sense, find that not one of all these things is my own property. (114) For where was my body before my birth? and where will it go when I am departed? And what becomes of the differences of age of that being which at present appears to exist? Where is now the infant?—where the child?—where the boy?—where the youth just arriving at the age of puberty?— where the young man?—where is he now whose beard is just budding, the vigorous and perfect man? Whence came the soul, and whither will it go? and how long will it remain with us? and what is its essence, or what may we speak of as such? Moreover, when did we acquire it? Was it before our birth?—But then we ourselves did not exist. Shall we have it after our death?—But then we shall not exist, we who are now a combination of distinctive qualities in combination with our bodies; but rather we shall then be hastening to a regeneration, becoming in combination with incorporeal beings: (115) and now, when we are alive we are governed rather than governing, and we are understood ourselves rather than understanding anything else; for our soul understands us without being understood by us, and it imposes commands upon us which we are necessitated to obey, as servants are compelled to obey a mistress; and whenever it chooses to abandon us and to depart to the Ruler of all things, it will depart, leaving our house destitute of life. And even if we attempt to compel it to remain, it will disappear; for its nature is composed of unsubstantial parts, such as afford no handle to the body.

XXXIII. (116) But the mind is my peculiar place of abode. Is this the language of the mistaken conjecturer, of the former of erroneous opinions, of the man out of his mind, of the fool, of him who is found to be destitute of his senses through a trance, or through melancholy, or from old age? Will any one then say, reason is my possession, or the organs of voice are my possession? Has not a very slight pretext of disease disabled the voice? has it now sewn up the mouths of even very eloquent men? Has not an expectation of danger, when it has come upon men, rendered myriads speechless?

(117) And in truth I am not found to be the governor of the outward senses, or perhaps I may even turn out to be their slave, following where they lead me, to colours, to shapes, to sounds, to smells, to flavours, or to other kinds of substances. By all which I think it is shown that we have the use of possessions which in reality belong to others, and that neither glory, nor riches, nor honours, nor authority, nor anything else which concerns our bodies or souls is really our own, nor indeed even life itself.

(118) But having the use of these things, if we are judicious and prudent, we shall take care of them as possessions of God, being well aware beforehand that it is the law, that the master, whenever he pleases, may reclaim his own property. For by these considerations we shall diminish our grief for the deprivation of such things. But now, men in general, thinking that every thing is really their own property, are in a moment afflicted with extraordinary grief at the absence or loss of any thing. (119) It is, therefore, not only true, but a thing also which most especially tends to consolation, to consider that the world and all the things in the world are the works and the property of him who created them. And his own work, he who is its real possessor, gives to others, because he has no need of it himself. But he who uses it has no property in it, because there is one Lord and master of all things, who says most truly, "All the earth is mine," a saying which is equivalent to—every created thing is mine; and "ye are all strangers and sojourners in my sight."

XXXIV. (120) For all mortals, being compared with one another, are looked upon as natives of the soil, and nobly born persons, all enjoying equal honours, and equal rank; but by God they are looked upon as strangers and sojourners; for each of us has come into this world as to a new city, in which he had no share before his birth, and having come into it he dwells here, until he has completed the period of life allotted to him. (121) At the same time, also, this doctrine of exceeding wisdom is introduced, that the Lord God is the only real citizen, and that every created being is but a stranger and a sojourner. But those who are called citizens are called so rather in consequence of a slight misapplication of the name than in strict truth. And it is a sufficient gift to wise men—if considered comparatively with the only true citizen, God—for them to have the rank of strangers and sojourners. With respect to foolish men, of them there is absolutely no one who is a stranger or sojourner in the city of God, but such an one is found to be utterly an exile. And this is implied in what he said besides as a most authoritative doctrine, "The land shall not be utterly sold away." Nor did God add "by whom," in order that from that point being passed over in silence, he who was not wholly uninitiated in natural philosophy, might be benefited in respect of knowledge.

(122) Therefore, if you consider the matter, you will find that all men, and especially those who have been alluded to as giving gratuitously, sell rather than give; and that they, who we fancy are receiving favours, are, in reality, purchasing the benefits which they derive; for they who give, hoping to receive a requital, such as praise or honour, and seeking for a return of the favour which they are conferring, under the specious name of a gift, are, in reality, making a bargain. Since it is usual, for those who sell, to receive a price in return for

what they part with; but they who, receiving presents, feel anxiety to make a return for them, and make such a return in due season, they in reality perform the part of purchasers; for as they know how to receive, so also do they know how to requite. (123) But God distributes his good things, not like a seller vending his wares at a high price, but he is inclined to make presents of everything, pouring forth the inexhaustible fountains of his graces, and never desiring any return; for he has no need of anything, nor is there any created being competent to give him a suitable gift in return.

XXXV. (124) As all things then are confessed to be the possessions of God, and proved to be so by sound reasonings and testimonies, which cannot possibly be convicted of bearing false witness, for they are the sacred oracles which Moses has recorded in the Holy Scriptures that bear witness; we must deprecate that mind which fancied that that which originated in a meeting with the outward sense was his own property, and which called it Cain, and said, "I have gotten a man by means of God," in this also greatly erring. But in what did he err? (125) Because God was the cause, not the instrument; and what was born was created indeed through the agency of some instrument, but was by all means called into existence by the great first cause; for many things must co-operate in the origination of anything; by whom, from what, by means of what, and why? Now he by whom a thing originates is the cause; that from which a thing is made is the material; that by means of which it was made is the instrument; and why, is the object.

(126) For come now, suppose any one should say, what things must meet together, that any house or city may be made? Must there not be a builder, and stones, and timber, and tools? What then is the builder, but the cause by whom the house or city is built? And what are the stones and timber, but the materials of which the buildings is made? And what are the tools, but the things by means of which it is made? (127) And for what reason is it built, except to serve as a shelter and protection? This is the object. Now passing on from these particular buildings, consider the greatest house or city, namely, this world, for you will find that God is the cause of it, by whom it was made. That the materials are the four elements, of which it is composed; that the instrument is the word of God, by means of which it was made; and the object of the building you will find to be the display of the goodness of the Creator.

This is the discriminating opinion of men fond of truth, who desire to attain to true and sound knowledge; but they who say that they have gotten anything by means of God, conceive that the cause is the instrument, the Creator namely, and the instrument the cause, namely, the human mind. (128) And all sound reason would reproach Joseph for saying, "That the true interpretation of the dreams would be found out by means of God;"[27] for he should have said, that owing to him, as the cause indeed, would be the unfolding and accurate understanding of those things which were obscure; for we are the instruments by whom the particular energies are developed, both in our states of tension and of relaxation; but the Creator is "he who gives the blow which sets in motion" the faculties of body and soul, by whom all things are moved.

(129) Those then who are unable to distinguish between the differences of things must be instructed as ignorant; but those who, from a contentious spirit, invert the orders of the things signified, must be avoided as disputatious; but those who, after an accurate investigation into the phaenomena which present themselves to them, assign its proper place to each of the objects discovered, must be praised as men who have attained to a true philosophy, and are void of error. (130) For Moses says to those who fear lest they should be destroyed by the wicked man, who is pursuing them with all his host, "Stand still, and see the salvation which is from the Lord, and which he will work for you;"[28] teaching them that salvation is effected, not by means of God, but by him as the direct cause.

---

[27] Genesis 40:8.
[28] Exodus 14:13.

ON THE BIRTH OF ABEL AND THE SACRIFICES OFFERED BY HIM AND BY HIS BROTHER CAIN†

(De Sacrificiis Abelis et Cain)

I. (1) "And he also added, that she should bring forth his brother."[1] The addition of one thing is a taking away of some other; as for instance, of particles in arithmetic, and of reasons in the soul. If then we must say that Abel is added, we must also think that Cain is taken away. But that the unusual character of expression may not cause perplexity to many we will endeavour to explain accurately the philosophy which is apparent beneath them, as clearly as may be in our power.

(2) It happens then, that there are two opinions contrary to and at variance with one another; the one of which commits everything to the mind as the leader of all reasoning, or feeling, or moving, or being stationary; and the other, attributing to God all the consequent work of creation as his own. Now the symbol of the former of these is Cain, which name, being interpreted means, "possession," from his appearing to possess all things; and the symbol of the other is Abel; for this name, being interpreted, means "referring to God." (3) Now both these opinions were brought forth by one soul. But it follows of necessity that as soon as they were born they must have been separated; for it was impossible for enemies to dwell together for ever. Until then the soul brought forth the God-loving doctrine Abel, the self-loving Cain dwelt with her. But when she brought forth Abel, or unanimity with God, she abandoned unanimity with that mind which was wise in its own conceit.

II. (4) And this will be more evidently shown by the oracle which was given to Perseverance, that is to Rebecca;[2] for she also, having conceived the two inconsistent natures of good and evil, and having considered each of them very deeply according to the injunctions of prudence, beholding them both exulting, and making a sort of skirmish as a prelude to the war which was to exist between them; she, I say, besought God to explain to her what this calamity meant, and what was the remedy for it. And he answered her inquiry, and told her, "Two nations are in thy womb." This calamity is the birth of good and evil. "But two peoples shall be divided in thy bowels." And the remedy is, for these two to be parted and separated from one another, and no longer to abide in the same place.

(5) God therefore having added the good doctrine, that is Abel, to the soul, took away from it evil doctrine, that is Cain: for Abraham also, leaving mortal things, "is added to the people of God,"[3] having received immortality, and having become equal to the angels; for the angels are the host of God, being incorporeal and happy souls. And in the same manner Jacob, the practiser of virtue, is added to the better one,[4] because he had quitted the worse. (6) And Isaac, who was thought worthy of self-taught knowledge, of his own accord also leaves all the corporeal essence which was attached to his soul, and is added to and made an inheritor with (not the people, as the others whom I have mentioned were), but with the "race,"[5] as Moses says; for "race" is one, and the highest of all: but "people," is the name of many. (7) As many, therefore, as through instruction and learning have improved and at last arrived at perfection, are classed among the larger number. Nor is number insignificant of those who have learnt from oral instruction and demonstration, and whom Moses calls the people. But those men who have forsaken human instruction, and having become well-disposed disciples of God, and having arrived at a comprehension of knowledge acquired without labour, have passed over to the immortal and most perfect race of beings, and have so received an inheritance better than the former generations of created men; and of these men Isaac is reckoned as a companion.

III. (8) There is also another proof that the mind is immortal, which is of this nature:—There are some persons whom God, advancing to higher degrees of improvement, has enabled to soar above all species and genera, having placed them near himself; as he says to Moses, "But stand thou here with me."[6] When, therefore, Moses is about to die, he is not added to one class, nor does he

---

†Yonge's title, *A Treatise on the Sacrifices of Abel and Cain.*
  [1]Genesis 4:2.
  [2]Genesis 25:24.

[3]Genesis 25:8.
[4]Genesis 49:33.
[5]Genesis 35:25.
[6]Deuteronomy 5:31.

forsake another, as the men before him had done; nor is he connected with "addition" or "subtraction," but "by means of the word of the Cause of all things, by whom the whole world was made."[7] He departs to another abode, that you may understand from this that God accounts a wise man as entitled to equal honour with the world itself, having both created the universe, and raised the perfect man from the things of earth up to himself by the same word.

(9) Not but what, when he gave him the use of all earthly things and suffered him to dwell among them, he assigned to him not such a power as he might exercise in common with an earthly governor or monarch, by which he should forcibly rule over the passions of the soul, but he appointed him to be a sort of god, making the whole of the body, and the mind, which is the ruler of the body, subjects and slaves to him; "For I give thee," says he, "as a god to Pharaoh."[8] But God is not susceptible of any subtraction or addition, inasmuch as he is complete and entirely equal to himself. (10) In reference to which it is said of Moses, "That no one is said to know of his tomb;"[9] for who could be competent to perceive the migration of a perfect soul to the living God? Nor do I even believe that the soul itself while awaiting this event was conscious of its own improvement, inasmuch as it was at that time becoming gradually divine; for God, in the case of those persons whom he is about to benefit, does not take him who is to receive the advantage into his counsels, but is accustomed rather to pour his benefits ungrudgingly upon him without his having any previous anticipation of them.

This is something like the meaning of God's adding the creation of what is good to the perfect mind. But the good is holiness, the name of which is Abel.

IV. (11) "And Abel became a shepherd of sheep; but Cain was a tiller of the ground." Why now has Moses, who represents Cain as older than Abel, now transposed them in the order in which he here mentions them, so as to name the younger first when relating their choice of a way of life? For it was natural that the elder should lead the way and adopt the cultivation of the land, and that the younger should subsequently come to the care of sheep. (12) But Moses is not influenced by what is likely and probable, but pursues the plain unadulterated truth. And when he alone comes to God by himself, he tells him with all freedom that "he is not eloquent," which statement is equivalent to saying that he does not aim at specious and plausible reasonings, and that this has happened to him "now yesterday, or the day before yesterday, but ever since God began to converse with him as his servant."[10] (13) For they who have come into the billows and heavy waves of life must be borne on by swimming, not being able to take hold of any firm point of the matters which lie within the province of knowledge, but depending on what is only likely and probable. But it becomes a servant of God to lay hold of the truth, disregarding and rejecting all the uncertain and fabulous statements which rest on the conjectures of plausible men.

(14) What, then, is the truth in these matters which we are considering? Why, that wickedness is older than virtue in point of time, but younger in power and rank. Therefore, when the birth of the two is narrated, let Cain have the precedence; but when a comparison of their pursuits is instituted, then let Abel be the first; (15) for it happens to the being that is born, from his very swaddling clothes till the time when the innovating vigour of his ripe age extinguishes the fiery heat of his passions, to have for his foster brethren, folly, intemperance, injustice, fear, cowardice, and the other evil things which are born with him, every one of which his nurses and tutors foster and cause to grow up within him; by their habits and practices banishing piety, and by their uniform instructions introducing superstition, which is a thing nearly akin to impiety. (16) But when the child has now passed the age of youth, and when the impetuous disease of the passions has become mollified, as if a calm had come over them, then the man begins to enjoy tranquillity, having been at length and not without difficulty strengthened in the foundation of virtue, which has allayed that continued and incessant agitation which is the greatest evil of the soul.

Thus wickedness has the superiority in point of time; but virtue in point of rank, and honour and real glory. And this same lawgiver is a trustworthy evidence of this fact; (17) for having introduced Esau, who bears the name of folly, as the elder in point of time, he gives the birthright and chief honour to the younger, who, from his practice of virtue, was called Jacob. And he is not seen to obtain this pre-eminence before (as is the case in athletic contests) his adversary renounces the combat, putting down his hands from weakness, and yielding up the decision and the crown to him who has carried on a truceless and irreconcilable war against the passions; for, says Moses, "He sold his birthright to Jacob,"[11] (18) avowing, in plain

---

[7]Deuteronomy 34:5.
[8]Exodus 7:1.
[9]Deuteronomy 34:6.

[10]Exodus 4:10.
[11]Genesis 25:33.

terms that the pre-eminence in power and the honours of virtue belong to no wicked man, but only to him who is a lover of wisdom, just as the flute and the lyre and the other instruments of music belong to the musician alone.

V. (19) And concerning this doctrine Moses also records a law, which he makes with great beauty and suitableness. And it runs thus, "If a man have two wives, the one of them beloved and the other hated; and if both the one who is beloved and the one who is hated have borne him children, and if the child of her who is hated is the first-born, then it shall be in the day in which he divides the inheritance of his possessions among his sons that he shall not be able to give the inheritance of the first-born to the son of the wife that is beloved, overlooking his first-born son, the son of her who is hated; but he shall recognise the son of her who is hated as his first-born, to give him a double share of all the property that he has acquired; because he is the beginning of his children, and the right of the first-born is his."[12]

(20) Consider, O my soul, and know who it is who is hated, and who is the son of her who is hated, and immediately you shall perceive that the chief rights and chief honours belong to no one else but to him alone; for there are two wives cohabiting with each individual of us, hostile and inimical to one another, filling the abode of the soul with the contentions which arise from jealousy. Of these we love one, which is gentle and tractable, and which we think very affectionate and akin to ourselves, and its name is pleasure; but the other we hate, looking upon it as untameable, ungentle, fierce, and very hostile to us, and the name of this one is virtue.[13] (21) Accordingly, the one comes to us luxuriously dressed in the guise of a harlot and prostitute, with mincing steps, rolling her eyes about with excessive licentiousness and desire, by which baits she entraps the souls of the young, looking about with a mixture of boldness and impudence, holding up her head, and raising herself above her natural height, fawning and giggling, having the hair of her head dressed with most superfluous elaborateness, having her eyes pencilled, her eyebrows covered over, using incessant warm baths, painted with a fictitious colour, exquisitely dressed with costly garments, richly embroidered,

adorned with armlets, and bracelets, and necklaces, and all other ornaments which can be made of gold, and precious stones, and all kinds of female decorations; loosely girdled, breathing of most fragrant perfumes, thinking the whole market her home; a marvel to be seen in the public roads, out of the scarcity of any genuine beauty, pursuing a bastard elegance.

(22) And with her there walk as her most intimate friends, bold cunning, and rashness, and flattery, and trick, and deceit, and false speaking, and false opinion, and impiety, and injustice, and intemperance, in the middle of which she advances like the leader of the company, and marshalling her band, speaks thus to her mind, "My good friend, the treasuries of all human blessings and stores of happiness are in my power (for as for divine blessings they are all in heaven), and besides them you will find nothing.

(23) "If you will dwell with me I will open to you all these treasures, and will bestow on you for ever the most unsparing use and enjoyment of them. And I desire to inform you beforehand of the multitude of good things which I have stored up there, that if you are so inclined you may of your own accord live happily, and that if you refuse you may not decline them out of ignorance.

"There is in my power perfect relaxation, and exemption from all fear, and tranquillity, and a complete absence of all care and labour, and an abundant variety of colours, and most melodious intonations of the voice, and all kinds of costly viands and drinks, and plentiful varieties of the sweetest scents, and continual loves, and sports such as require no teacher, and connections which will never be inquired into, and speeches which will have no shade of reproof in them, and actions free from all necessity of being accounted for, and a life free from anxiety, and soft sleep, and abundance without any feeling of satiety. (24) If therefore you are inclined to take up your abode with me, I will give you what is suitable for you of all the things which I have prepared, considering carefully by eating or drinking what you may be most thoroughly cheered, or by what sights addressed to your eyes, or by what sounds visiting your ears, or by the small of what fragrant odours you may be most delighted.

"And nothing which you can desire shall be wanting to you; for you shall find what is produced anew more abundant than what is expended and consumed; (25) for in the treasuries which I have mentioned there are ever-flourishing plants, blossoming and producing an incessant series of fruits, so that the beauty of those in their prime and fresh appearing overtakes and overshadows those which are already fully ripe; and no war, either domestic or foreign, has ever cut down these plants, but from the very day that the earth first received them

---

[12]Deuteronomy 21:15.

[13]Sections 21–33a were misplaced in Yonge's translation because the edition on which Yonge based his translation, Thomas Mangey, *Philonis Iudaei opera omnia graece et latine ad editionem Thomae Mangey collatis aliquot mss. edenda curavit Augustus Fridericus Pfeiffer* (Erlangae: In Libraria Heyderiana, 1820), lacked this material. The lines in Yonge's edition were originally located in *On the Special Laws* 2.284ff.

it has cherished them like a faithful nurse, sending down into its lowest depths the roots to act like the strongest branches, and above ground extending its trunk as high as heaven, and putting forth branches which are by analogy imitations of the hand and feet which we see in animals, and leaves which correspond to the hair. I have prepared and caused that to blossom which shall be at the same time a covering and an ornament to you; and besides all this, I have provided fruit for the sake of which the branches and leaves are originally produced."

(26) When the other woman heard these words (for she was standing in a place where she was out of sight but still within hearing), fearing lest the mind, without being aware of it, might be led captive and be enslaved, and so be carried away by so many gifts and promises, yielding also to the tempter in that she was arrayed so as to win over the sight, and was equipped with great variety of ingenuity for the purposes of deceit; for by all her necklaces and other appendages, and by her different allurements, she spurred on and charmed her beholders, and excited a wonderful desire within them; she in her turn came forward, and appeared on a sudden, displaying all the qualities of a native, free-born, and lady-like woman, such as a firm step, a very gentle look, the native colour of modesty and nature without any alloy or disguise, an honest disposition, a genuine and sincere way of life, a plain, honest opinion, an language removed from all insincerity, the truest possible image of a sound and honest heart, a disposition averse to pretence, a quiet unobtrusive gait, a moderate style of dress, and the ornaments of prudence and virtue, more precious than any gold.

(27) And she was attended by piety, and holiness, and truth, and right, and purity, and an honest regard for an oath, and justice, and equality, and adherence to one's engagements and communion, and prudent silence, and temperance, and orderliness, and meekness, and abstemiousness, and contentment, and good-temper, and modesty, and an absence of curiosity about the concerns of others, and manly courage, and a noble disposition and wisdom in counsel, and prudence, and forethought, and attention, and correctness, and cheerfulness, and humanity, and gentleness, and courtesy, and love of one's kind, and magnanimity, and happiness, and goodness. One day would fail me if I were to enumerate all the names of the particular virtues. (28) And these all standing on each side of her, were her bodyguards, while she was in the middle of them.

And she, having assumed an appearance familiar to her, began to speak as follows: "I have seen pleasure, that worker of wonderous tricks, that conjuror and teller of fables, dressed in a some-what tragic style, and constantly approaching you in a delicate manner; so that (for I myself do by nature detest everything that is evil) I feared lest, without being aware of it, you might be deceived, and might consent to the very greatest of evils as if they were exceeding good; and therefore I have thought fit to declare to you with all sincerity what really belongs to that woman, in order that you might not reject anything advantageous to you out of ignorance, and so proceed unintentionally on the road of transgression and unhappiness.

(29) "Know, then, that the very dress in which she appears to you wholly belongs to some one else; for of ten things which contribute to genuine beauty, not one is ever brought forward as being derived from or as belonging to her. But she is hung round with nets and snares with which to catch you with a bastard and adulterated beauty, which you, beholding beforehand, will, if you are wise, take care that her pursuit shall be unprofitable to her; for when she appears she conciliates your eyes, and when she speaks she wins over your ears; and by these, and by all other parts of her conduct, she is well calculated by nature to injure your soul, which is the most valuable of all your possessions; and all the different circumstances belonging to her, which were likely to be attractive to you if you heard of them, she enumerated; but all those which would not have been alluring she suppressed and made no mention of, but, meaning mischief to you, concealed utterly, as she very naturally expected that no one would readily agree with them."

(30) But I, stripping off all her disguises, will reveal her to you; and I will not myself imitate the ways of pleasure, so as to show you nothing in me but what is alluring, and to conceal and to keep out of sight everything that has any unpleasantness or harshness in it; but, on the contrary, I will say nothing about those matters which do of themselves give delight and pleasure, well knowing that such things will of themselves find a voice by their effects; but I will fully detail to you all that is painful and difficult to be borne about me, putting them plainly forward with their naked appellation, so that their nature may be visible and plain even to those whose sight is somewhat dim. For the things which, when offered by me, appear to be the greatest of my evils, will in effect be found to be more honourable and more beneficial to the users than the greatest blessings bestowed by pleasure. But, before I begin to speak of what I myself have to give, I will mention all that may be mentioned of those things which are kept in the back ground by her.

(31) For she, when she spoke of what she had stored up in her magazines, such as colours, sounds, flavours, smells, distinctive qualities, powers relating to touch and to every one of the out-

ward senses, and having softened them all by the allurements which she offered to the hearing, made no mention at all of those other qualities which are her misfortunes and diseases; which, however, you will of necessity experience if you choose those pleasures which she offers; that so, being borne aloft by the breeze of some advantage, you may be taken in her toils.

(32) Know, then, my good friend, that if you become a votary of pleasure you will be all these things: a bold, cunning, audacious, unsociable, uncourteous, inhuman, lawless, savage, ill-tempered, unrestrainable, worthless man; deaf to advice, foolish, full of evil acts, unteachable, unjust, unfair, one who has no participation with others, one who cannot be trusted in his agreements, one with whom there is no peace, covetous, most lawless, unfriendly, homeless, cityless, seditious, faithless, disorderly, impious, unholy, unsettled, unstable, uninitiated, profane, polluted, indecent, destructive, murderous, illiberal, abrupt, brutal, slavish, cowardly, intemperate, irregular, disgraceful, shameful, doing and suffering all infamy, colourless, immoderate, unsatiable, insolent, conceited, self-willed, mean, envious, calumnious, quarrelsome, slanderous, greedy, deceitful, cheating, rash, ignorant, stupid, inharmonious, dishonest, disobedient, obstinate, tricky, swindling, insincere, suspicious, hated, absurd, difficult to detect, difficult to avoid, destructive, evil-minded, disproportionate, an unreasonable chatterer, a proser, a gossip, a vain babbler, a flatterer, a fool, full of heavy sorrow, weak in bearing grief, trembling at every sound, inclined to delay, inconsiderate, improvident, impudent, neglectful of good, unprepared, ignorant of virtue, always in the wrong, erring, stumbling, ill-managed, ill-governed, a glutton, a captive, a spendthrift, easily yielding, most crafty, double-minded, double-tongued, perfidious, treacherous, unscrupulous, always unsuccessful, always in want, infirm of purpose, fickle, a wanderer, a follower of others, yielding to impulses, open to the attacks of enemies, mad, easily satisfied, fond of life, fond of vain glory, passionate, ill-tempered, lazy, a procrastinator, suspected, incurable, full of evil jealousies, despairing, full of tears, rejoicing in evil, frantic, beside yourself, without any steady character, contriving evil, eager for disgraceful gain, selfish, a willing slave, an eager enemy, a demagogue, a bad steward, stiffnecked, effeminate, outcast, confused, discarded, mocking, injurious, vain, full of unmitigated unalloyed misery.

(33) These are the great mysteries of that very beautiful and much to be sought for pleasure, which she designedly concealed and kept out of sight, from a fear that if you knew of them you would turn away from any meeting with her. But who is there who could worthily describe either the multitude or the magnitude of the good things which are stored up in my treasure houses?

They who have partaken of them already know it, and those whose nature is mild will hereafter know, when they have been invited to a participation in the banquet, not the banquet at which the pleasures of the satiated belly make the body fat, but that at which the mind is nourished and at which it revels among the virtues, and exults and revels in their company.

VI. (34) Now, on account of these things, and because of what was said before, namely, that the things which are really pious, holy, and good do naturally utter a voice from themselves, even while they keep silence, I will desist from saying any more about them; for neither does the sun nor the moon require an interpreter, because they, being on high, fill the whole world with light, the one shining by day and the other by night. But their own brilliancy is an evidence in their case which stands in no need of witnesses, but which is confirmed by the eyes, which are more undeniable judges than the ears. (35) But I will speak with all freedom of that point in virtue which appears to have the greatest amount of difficulty and perplexity, for this, too, does appear to the imagination, at their first meeting, to be troublesome; but, on consideration, it is found to be very pleasant and, as arising from reason, to be suitable. But labour is the enemy of laziness, as it is in reality the first and greatest of good things, and wages an irreconcilable war against pleasure; for, if we must declare the truth, God has made labour the foundation of all good and of all virtue to man, and without labour you will not find a single good thing in existence among the race of men. (36) For, as it is impossible to see without light, since neither colours nor eyes are sufficient for the comprehension of things which we arrive at by means of sight (for nature has made light beforehand to serve as a link to connect the two, by which the eye is brought near and adapted to colour, for the powers of both eye and of colour are equally useless in darkness), so in the same manner is the eye of the soul unable to comprehend anything whatever of the actions in accordance with virtue, unless it takes to itself labour as a coadjutor, as the eye borrows the assistance of light; for this, being placed in the middle, between the intellect and the good object which the intellect desires, and understanding the whole nature of both the one and the other, does itself bring about friendship and harmony, two perfect goods between the two things on either hand of it.

VII. (37) For, choose whatever good thing you please, and you will find that it owes its existence and all its strength and solidity to labour. Now, piety and holiness are good things, but still we are not able to attain to them without the worship of the gods, and the worship of them is combined with perseverance in labours. Again, prudence and courage and justice are all beautiful things and perfect goods, but still they are not to be acquired by laziness, and we must be content if they can be attained to by continued diligence.

Now, since the organs of every soul are not able to support a familiarity with God and with virtue, as being a very intense and mighty harmony, they very often get lax and become remiss so as to descend from the highest unto those of more moderate character; (38) but, nevertheless, even in these moderate ones there is great labour requisite. Look at all those who practise the encyclical branches of what is called elementary instruction; look at those who cultivate the land, and at all who provide the means of subsistence by any regular business. These men are never free from care night or day, but always and continually, as it is said, they labour with hand and foot and with all their power, and never cease from suffering hardship, so as often to encounter even death from it.

VIII. (39) But as those who are thus anxious to render their souls propitious must of necessity cultivate the virtues of the soul, so also they who purpose to render their bodies favourable to their objects, must cultivate health and those powers which are akin to health, and these too they cultivate with unremitting and ceaseless labours, being overwhelmed with care, arising from the faculties in them of which they are compounded.

(40) You see, therefore, that all good things spring up and shoot out from labour as from one general root, and this you must never allow yourself to neglect; for if you do, you will without being aware of it, be also letting slip the collected heap of goods which it brings with it; for the Ruler of the universe, of heaven, and of the world, both himself possesses and bestows on whomsoever he pleases, his good things, with all ease and abundance. Since formerly he created this world, vast as you see it is, without any labour, and how too he never ceases holding it together, so that it may last for ever. And absence from all labour and fatigue is the most appropriate attribute of God; but nature has not given the acquisition of good things to any mortal without labour,[14] in order that in consequence of this arrangement, God alone of existing beings may be called happy and enjoy felicity.

IX. (41) For labour appears to me to have nearly the same properties as food. As therefore this latter makes life to depend upon itself, having combined all the actions and all the passions in living, so also has labour caused all good things to depend upon itself. For as those persons who are desirous to live must not neglect food, so too they who are anxious to attain to good things must pay due attention to labour, for what food is to life that labour is to virtue. Do not you then ever slight that, though it is but a single thing, that by its means you may enjoy the collective blessings of all good things. (42) For thus, though you may be younger by birth you shall be called the elder, and you shall be thought worthy of the pre-eminence in honour. But if, having gone through a constant course of improvement you shall at last arrive at the end, then not only shall the Father give thee the pre-eminence, but he shall also bestow on thee all the inheritance of the Father, as he did to Jacob, who overthrew all the foundations and seats of passion, and who confessed what he suffered, saying that "God has pitied me, and all things belong to me,"[15] uttering a doctrine full of instruction, for he makes everything to anchor in the mercy of God.

X. (43) And he learnt all these things from Abraham his grandfather, who was the author of his own education, who gave to the all-wise Isaac all that he had,[16] leaving none of his substance to bastards, or to the spurious reasonings of concubines, but he gives them small gifts, as being inconsiderable persons. For the possessions of which he is possessed, namely, the perfect virtues, belong only to the perfect and legitimate son; but those which are of an intermediate character, are suitable to and fall to the share of those who are not perfect, but who have advanced as far as the encyclical branches of elementary education, of which Agar and Cheturah partake, Agar meaning "a dwelling near," and Cheturah meaning "sacrificing."

(44) For he who attends only to the encyclical instruction abides near wisdom but does not dwell with it, as sending a certain sweet fragrance from the elegance of contemplation to his own soul. But such a man requires food, and not sweet scents to bless him with good health. But nature is said to have made, with great skill and propriety, smell to serve as a handmaid to taste, as a sort of subject and taster to the other, or her queen; and we must always attend to the sovereign powers before those who are ruled over by them, and to the indigenous and native sciences before those which are strangers. (45) The mind bearing this rejects pleasure, and attaches itself to virtue, perceiving its genuine, and unalloyed, and very divine beauty. Then it becomes the shepherd of sheep, being the charioteer and pilot of the irrational faculties which exist in the soul, "not permitting them to be borne

---

[14]This is not only the same idea, but almost the very language of Horace in Sat. I. 9.60.

[15]Genesis 33:11.
[16]Genesis 25:5.

about at random and in an inconsistent manner, without any superintendant or guide;[17] that they may not fall into a sort of orphan state, destitute of guardians and protectors, owing to their want of any allies, in which case they would perish without any saving hand to restrain them.

XI. (46) Accordingly, Jacob, the practiser of contemplation, conceiving this to be an employment most closely akin to virtue, endured "to be the shepherd of the flocks of Laban,"[18] a man wholly devoted to colours and to forms, and, in sort, to lifeless substances; and he tended not all of them, but the residue only. Now, what is the interpretation of this?

The irrational animal is of a twofold character; one consisting in a misuse of that reason which should direct the choice, and such we call people out of their mind: the other consisting in an absolute privation of reason, which we see to exist in these animals which we call brutes. (47) Now, the irrational impulses of the mind, I mean those faculties which are developed in a misuse of that reason which should direct the choice, the sons of Laban, "when they had departed three days' journey,"[19] paid great regard to; being thus under a symbol cut off from virtue for the whole period of their life; for time is capable of being divided into three parts, consisting of the past, and the present, and the future. But these animals which are irrational in the second sense, and which are destitute not only of right reason but of all reason whatever, under which class the brute beasts are reckoned, the practiser of contemplation will think worthy of all his care, considering that their errors have proceeded, not so much from deliberate wickedness as from ignorance, which was devoid of a guide.

(48) Ignorance, therefore, being but a slight and also an involuntary calamity, admits of a cure which is neither difficult nor troublesome, namely instruction. But, wickedness being a voluntary disease of the soul, admits of no remedy but such as if difficult, and almost impossible. Therefore his sons, as men who have been instructed by a father of exceeding wisdom, even if they do go down to Egypt, that is to say, to the body which is inclined to be a slave to the passions, and even if they meet with Pharaoh, that squanderer of all good things, who appears to be the sovereign of the composite animals, being not at all bewildered with the abundance of the preparations which they behold, confess that they are shepherds of sheep, and not only they but their fathers also.[20]

XII. (49) And yet no one would ever utter so great a boast in consequence of any power and sovereignty as these men do in respect of their being shepherds; to those indeed who are able to reason correctly, it is a more noble employment than that of a king, to be able to govern the body and the outward senses, and the belly, as one might govern a city or a country, and to restrain the pleasures which have their seat around the belly, and the other passions, and one's tongue, and, in short, all the different parts of one's composite nature, with vigour and exceeding power, and again to guide them in the right way with due gentleness; for it is necessary at one time to act like a charioteer who slackens the reins with which he holds the horses which are yoked to his chariot, and at other times one must draw them tight, and resist the haste of the steeds, that no precipitation and impetuous pursuit of outward objects may take place, and lead them into rebellion. (50) And I admire that guardian of the laws, Moses, who, thinking it a great and noble task to be a shepherd, has attributed that employment to himself; for he manages and conducts the doctrines of Jethro, leading them from the tumultuous vexations of political affairs into the desert, for the purpose of avoiding all temptation to injustice.

"For he led the sheep into the wilderness."[21] (51) The consequence of which conduct of his was that "Every shepherd of sheep is an abomination to the Egyptians."[22] For every man who loves his passions hates right reason as the governor and guide to good things; just as foolish children hate their tutors and teachers, and every one who reproves them or corrects them, or would lead them to virtue. But Moses says that he "will sacrifice the abominations of the Egyptians to God."[23] namely the virtues which are faultless and most becoming victims, which every foolish man abominates. So that very appropriately, Abel, who brought the best offerings to God, is called a shepherd; but he, who offered every thing to himself and to his own mind, is called a tiller of the earth, namely Cain. And what is meant by tilling the earth[24] we have shown in our previous treatises.

XIII. (52) And it came to pass after some days that Cain brought of the fruits of the earth as an offering to the Lord. Here are two accusations against the self-loving man; one that he showed his gratitude to God after some days, and not at once, the other that he made his offering from the fruits, and not from the first fruits, which have a name in one word, the first fruits. Let us now examine into each of these subjects of reproach, and first into that which is first in order, (53) we must

---

[17] Numbers 27:17.
[18] Genesis 30:36.
[19] Ibid.
[20] Genesis 47:3.

[21] Exodus 3:1.
[22] Genesis 46:34.
[23] Exodus 8:26.
[24] Genesis 4:2.

do good works, hastening with all speed, and labouring to outstrip others, casting away all slowness and delay. And the best of all good works is the pleasing the first good without any postponement of energy, on which account it is also enjoined, "If thou vowest a vow, thou shalt not delay to perform it." [25] A vow now is a request for good things addressed to God, and the injunction is, that when one has attained the object of one's hopes, one must offer offerings of gratitude to God, and not to one's self, and to offer them if possible without any loss of time, and without any delay; (54) and of those who do not act rightly in this particular, some through forgetfulness of the benefits which they have received, have failed in that great and beautiful virtue of thankfulness, and others form an excessive conceit, have looked upon themselves as the authors of the good things which have befallen them, and have not attributed them to him, who is really the cause of them.

A third class are they who commit an offence slighter indeed than the fault of these latter, but more serious than that of the first mentioned, for though they confess that the supreme Ruler is the cause of the good that has befallen them, they still say that they deserved to receive it, for that they are prudent, and courageous, and temperate, and just, so that they may well on these accounts be esteemed by God to be worthy of his favours.

XIV. (55) Now the holy scriptures are opposed to all these classes, and reply to each of them, saying to the first class which has discarded recollection, and humbled forgetfulness, "Take care, my good man, lest when you have eaten and are filled, and when you have built fine houses and inhabited them, and when your flocks and your herds have increased, and when your silver and gold, and all that you possess is multiplied, you be lifted up in your heart, and forget the Lord your God." [26] When is it then that you do not forget God? when you do not forget yourself; for if you remember your own nothingness in every particular, you will also be sure to remember the exceeding greatness of God in everything.

(56) And Moses reproves the man who looks upon himself as the cause of the good things that have befallen him in this manner, "Say not," says he, "my own might, or the strength of my right hand has acquired me all this power, but remember always the Lord thy God, who giveth thee the might to acquire power." [27]

(57) And he who conceives that he was deserving to receive the possession and enjoyment of good things, may be taught to change his opinion by the oracle which says, "You do not enter into this land to possess it because of thy righteousness, or because of the holiness of thy heart; but, in the first place, because of the iniquity of these nations, since God has brought on them the destruction of wickedness; and in the second place that he may establish the covenant which he swore to our fathers." [28]

Now by the covenant of God his graces are figuratively meant (nor is it right to offer to him anything that is imperfect), as all the gifts of the uncreated God are complete and entirely perfect, and virtue is a thing complete among existing things, and so is the course of action in accordance with it. (58) If therefore we discard forgetfulness and ingratitude, and self-love, and the present wickedness of all these things, namely, self-opinion, we shall not longer through our delay miss attaining the genuine worship of God, but outrunning and bounding on beyond all created beings, before we embrace any mortal thing we shall meet our master himself, having prepared ourselves to do the things which he commands us.

XV. (59) For Abraham also, having come with all haste and speech and eagerness, exhorts virtue, that is to say, Sarah, "to hasten and knead three measures of fine meal, and to make cakes upon the hearth." [29] When God, being attended by two of the heavenly powers as guards, to wit, by authority and goodness, he himself, the one God being between them, presented an appearance of the figures to the visual soul; each of which figures was not measured in any respect; for God cannot be circumscribed, nor are his powers capable of being defined by lines, but he himself measures everything. His goodness therefore is the measure of all good things, and his authority is the measures of things in subjection, and the Governor of the universe himself, is the measure of all things to the corporeal and incorporeal. On which account, his powers also having been looked upon in the light of rules and models, have weighed and measured other things with reference to them. (60) Now it is very good that these three measures should, as it were, be kneaded together in the soul, and mixed up together, in order that so the soul, being persuaded that the supreme being is God, who has raised his head above all his powers, and who is beheld independently of them, and who makes himself visible in them, may receive the characters of his power and beneficence, and becoming initiated into the perfect mysteries, may not be too ready to divulge the divine secrets to any one, but may treasure them up in herself, and keeping a check over her speech, may conceal them in silence; for the words of the scripture are, "To make secret cakes;" because the sacred and

[25] Deuteronomy 23:21.
[26] Deuteronomy 8:12.
[27] Deuteronomy 8:17.

[28] Deuteronomy 9:5.
[29] Genesis 18:6.

mystic statements about the one uncreated Being, and about his powers, ought to be kept secret; since it does not belong to every one to keep the deposit of divine mysteries properly.

XVI. (61) For the stream of the intemperate soul, flowing outwards through the mouth and tongue, is pumped up and poured into all ears. Some of which having wide channels, keeps that which is poured into them with all cheerfulness; but others, through the narrowness of the passages, are unable to be bedewed by it. But that which overflows being poured forth in an unrestrained manner, is scattered in every direction: so that what has been concealed escapes and floats on the top of it, and, like a random torrent of mud, bears along with it in its flood, things worthy of being tended with all care. (62) In reference to which, those persons appear to me to have come to a right decision who have been initiated in the lesser mysteries before learning anything of these greater ones. "For they baked their flour which they brought out of Egypt, baking secret cakes of unleavened bread."[30] That is to say, they dealt with the untameable and savage passions, softening them with reason as they would knead bread; fore they did not divulge the manner of their kneading and improving it, as it was derived from some divine system of preparation; but they treasured it up in their secret stores, not being elated at the knowledge of the mystery, but yielding and being lowly as to their boasting.

XVII. (63) Let us then, with reference to our gratitude to and honouring of the omnipotent God, be active and ready, deprecating all sluggishness and delay; for those who are passing over from obedience to the passions to the contemplation of virtue, are enjoined to keep the passover with their loins girded up, being ready to do service, and binding up the burden of the flesh, or, as it is expressed, their shoes, "standing upright, and firmly on their feet, and having in their hands a staff,"[31] that is to say education, with the object of succeeding without any failure in all the affairs of life; and lastly, "to eat the passover in haste." For, by the passover, is signified the crossing over of the created and perishable being to God:—and very appropriately; for there is no single good thing which does not belong to God, and which is not divine.

(64) Seek it therefore, quickly, O my soul! as did that practiser of contemplation, Jacob, who, when his father asked him, "How found you this so quickly, I my son?"[32] answered, with a doctrine concealed underneath his words, "The Lord God brought it before me." For he, being well skilled in many matters, knew that whatever creation be-

stows on the soul is confirmed by long time, as those men know who give to their pupils arts, and lessons in arts: for their case is not like that of men who pour water into a vessel, they are not in a moment able to fill their minds with the lessons which have been brought before them. But when the fountain of wisdom, that is to say, God, gives knowledge of the sciences to the race of mankind, he gives it to them without any limitation of time. But they, as being disciples of the only wise Being, and being competent by nature, quickly accomplish the discovery of the things which they seek to understand.

XVIII. (65) But the principal virtue of pupils is to endeavour to imitate their perfect master, as far as those who are imperfect can imitate a perfect man. But the master is more rapid than any time, which did not even co-operate with him when he was creating the universe, since it is plain that time itself was created at the same moment that the world was made. For God, while he spake the word, did at the same moment create; nor did he allow anything to come between the word and the deed; and if one may advance a doctrine which is pretty nearly true, His word is his deed. But among the race of mankind nothing is more easily moved than the word; for by its rapidity and by the volubility of its nouns and verbs, it outstrips even the comprehension which hastens to overtake them. (66) As, therefore, everlasting springs, which are poured down in rivers, have a course which never ceases, the stream as it comes on continually taking up the cessation of the waves which have preceded, so too the abundant flow of words, when they begin to be poured forth, keep pace with the most swiftly-moving of all the qualities which are in us, namely, the mind, which can itself outstrip even flying natures.

As therefore the uncreated God outstrips all creation, so also does the word of the uncreated God outrun the word of creation, and is borne on with exceeding swiftness in the clouds. On which account God speaks freely, saying, "Now you shall see, because my word shall overtake you."[33] As the divine word can outstrip and overtake everything, (67) but if his word can thus outstrip everything, much more can he who utters it, as he testifies in another place, where he says, "Here am I, I stood here before you."[34] For he declares here that he stood before any created being: and he who is here is also there, and in other places, and every where, having filled every place in every direction, and having left nothing whatever destitute of himself: (68) for he does not say, "Here I stand and there, but now also when I am present do I stand there also at the same moment;" not being moved

[30]Exodus 12:34.
[31]Exodus 12:11.
[32]Genesis 27:20.

[33]Numbers 11:23.
[34]Exodus 16:6.

or changing his place so as to occupy one place and to quit another, but using one intense motion.

Very properly therefore do his subject children, imitating the nature of their father, do all that is right without any delay, and with all diligence, their most excellent employment being the paying prompt and unremitting honour to God.

XIX. (69) But Pharaoh, the squanderer of all things, not being able himself to receive the conception of virtues unconnected with time, inasmuch as he was mutilated as to the eyes of his soul, by which alone incorporeal natures are comprehended, would not endure to be benefited by virtues unconnected with time; but being weighed down by soulless opinions, I mean here by the frogs, animals which utter a sound and noise wholly void and destitute of reality, when Moses says, "appoint a time to me when I may pray for you and for your servants that God will make the frogs to disappear,"[35] though he ought, as he was in very imminent necessity, to have said, Pray this moment, nevertheless postponed it, saying, "Pray to-morrow," in order that he might in every case preserve the folly of his impiety. (70) And this happens to nearly all those men who hesitate and vacillate between two opinions, even if they do not confess it in express words. For when any thing unexpected befalls them, inasmuch as they did not previously believe firmly in God the Saviour, they take refuge in the assistance of created things, of physicians, of herbs, of the composition of drugs, in a carefully considered plan of life, and in any other aid which may be derived from mortal man. And if any one were to say to them, "Flee, O ye wretched men, to Him who is the only physician for the diseases of the soul, and discard all this falsely called assistance which ye are seeking to find in the creature who is subject to the same sufferings as yourselves," they would laugh at and ridicule him; saying, "Tell us this to-morrow." Since, even if any thing were to happen to them they would not supplicate the Deity to avert the present evils from them.

(71) But when it is found that there is no relief from man, and when even all the remedies are proved to be injurious, then in great perplexity they renounce all ideas of assistance from other quarters, and, like wretched men as they are and sorely against their will, they reluctantly and tardily flee to the only Saviour, God. But he, as well knowing that there is no dependence to be placed on reformation extorted by necessity, does not apply his law to every one of them, but only to those in whose case it appears good and suitable.

Let every reasoning therefore that thinks that all possessions belong to itself, and that honours itself before God, for the expression, "sacrificing

after a few days," involves such a notion as this, know that it is liable to the accusation of impiety.

XX. (72) We have now adequately gone through the first article of our accusation against Cain. And the second is of this nature, Why does he bring the first fruits of the fruits of the earth, but not of the first produce? May it not be for the same reason, that he may give the pre-eminence in honour to creation, and may requite God himself with what is the second best? For as there are some persons who place the body before the soul, the slave before the mistress, so also there are persons who honour the creation more than God, though the lawgiver delivered this injunction, that "we should bring the first fruits of the first produce of the earth into the house of God,"[36] and not assign them to ourselves. For it is just to refer all the first motions of the soul, whether in point of order or of power, to God. (73) Now the first things in point of order are such as these, in which we participated from the first moment of our original birth: nourishment, growth, sight, hearing, taste, smell, touch, speech, the mind, the parts of the soul, the parts of the body, the energies of these parts, and in short all the motions and conditions which are in accordance with nature.

But those things which are first in consideration and in power are good actions, the virtues, and conduct in accordance with the virtues. (74) It is right therefore to offer the first fruits of these things: and the first fruits are the language of gratitude sent up from sincere truth of mind. And this language divides itself according to appropriate divisions in the same manner as the lyre and the other musical instruments are divided. For in each of those instruments each sound is by itself harmonious, and also exceedingly adapted to making a symphony with the rest. As in grammar also those of the elements which are called vowels are both capable of being uttered by themselves, and they also make a complete sound in conjunction with other letters. (75) But nature which has created many powers in ourselves, some consisting of the outward senses, some reasoning and intellectual and which has directed each to some appropriate work, and which again has adapted all in due proportion by a union and harmony with one another, may be most properly pronounced happy both in each particular and in all of them.

XXI. (76) On which account if you bring a sacrifice of the first fruits, you must divide it as the sacred scripture teaches, first of all offering those fruits which are green, then those which are toasted, then those which are cut up, and after all the others those which are ground. Those which are green, on this account, because he teaches those who are lovers of the old, and obsolete, and

---

fabulous times, and who do not comprehend the rapid power of God, illimitable by time, warning them to adopt new, and flourishing, and vigorous thoughts, in order that they may not embrace false opinions from being nourished among the old fabulous systems which a long lapse of ages has handed down to the deceiving of mortals; but that, receiving new and fresh good things in all abundance from God, who never grows old, but who is always young and vigorous, they may be taught to think nothing old that is with him, and nothing passed away or obsolete, but to look upon everything as created and existing without any limitation as to time.

XXII. (77) On which account he says in another place, "Thou shalt rise up from before a hoary head, and thou shalt honour the face of an elder."[37] As if the difference were very great. For what is hoary is that time which energizes not at all, from which one ought to rise up, and depart, and flee, avoiding that idea which deceives tens of thousands, that time has a natural capacity of doing something. But by an elder is meant one who is worthy of honour, and respect, and of pre-eminence, and examination of whom is committed to Moses, the friend of God. "For those whom thou knowest," says God to Moses, "they are the elders."[38] As he was a man who admitted no innovations of any kind, but was by custom attached to his elders, and to those who were worthy of the highest honours.

(78) It is advantageous, therefore, if not with reference to the acquisition of perfect virtue, still at all events with reference to political considerations, both to be nourished in ancient and primeval opinions, and also to be acquainted with the ancient records of glorious actions, which historians and the whole race of poets have delivered to their contemporaries and to subsequent ages, to be preserved in their recollection. But when the sudden light of self-taught wisdom has shone upon those who had no foreknowledge or expectation of it, and opening the previously closed eyes of the soul, makes men spectators of knowledge instead of being merely hearers of it, implanting in the mind the swiftest of the outward senses, sight, instead of hearing, which is slower; it is then in vain to exercise the ears with speeches.

XXIII. (79) On which account it is said also: "And ye shall eat old store, and old food from the old store, and you shall also bring forward the old out of the sight of the new."[39] As it is fitting to repudiate no ancient piece of learning from considerations of time, while we endeavour to meet with the writings of wise men, and to be present as it were with the opinions and expositions of those who relate ancient matters, and to be always fond of inquiring about the former ages of men, and ancient events, since it is the pleasantest of all things to be ignorant of nothing. But when God causes new shoots of self-taught wisdom to spring up in the soul, then it behoves us immediately to circumscribe and to contract the things which we have acquired from instruction, which of their own accord do return and flow back to their source. For it is impossible that one who is a follower, or a friend, or a disciple of God, or any other name which one may think fit to call him, should tolerate mortal lessons.

XXIV. (80) And let the ripeness of the new soul be toasted. That is to say, as gold is tried in the fire, let this also be tested by powerful reason. And the being consolidated is a sign of having been tried, and tested, and approved. For as the fruit of flourishing stalks of corn is toasted, that it may no longer be damp, and as this cannot in the nature of things take place without fire, so also is it necessary that the young and fresh ripeness, advancing by means of powerful and unalterable reason to the perfection of virtue, must be made solid and stable. But it is the natural characteristic of reason not only to ripen speculations in the soul, preventing them from dissolving, but also vigorously to put an end to the impetuosity of irrational passion.

(81) Behold the practiser of contemplations, Joseph, cooking it, when, "Esau is in a moment discovered to be fainting."[40] For wickedness and passion are the foundations of those who love themselves, supported on which the man, when he sees them defeated and extinguished by reason which has refuted them, does not unnaturally relax his exertions and his strength. (82) But suppose the language is not confused, but divided into appropriate divisions, the meaning of the expression, "those that are cut up," is something of this kind. For in everything order is better than disorder, and most especially is it so in the most swiftly flowing nature—speech.

XXV. We must therefore divide it into the principal heads, which are called incidents, and we must assign to each its appropriate preparation, imitating in this point skilful archers, who, when they have chosen a mark, endeavour to shoot every one of their arrows straight at it. For the head resembles the mark, and the preparation is similar to the arrows. (83) And thus the most excellent of all branches of learning, speech, is harmoniously connected together. For the lawgiver cuts leaves of gold into thin hairs, so as to plait appropriate works of that material in a durable manner. And in like manner, speech, which is more precious

---

[37] Leviticus 19:32.
[38] Numbers 11:16.
[39] Leviticus 26:10.

[40] Genesis 25:29.

than gold, is completed in a praiseworthy manner of innumerable varieties of ideas, then, being divided into the thinnest possible heads, after the fashion of a woven web, it receives an harmonious demonstration, like a work of the distaff.

(84) It is enjoined therefore that sacrificers, when they have flayed the burnt offering, shall cut it up joint by joint, in order in the first place that the soul may appear naked without any coverings, such as are made by empty and false opinions; and in the second place that it may be able to receive suitable divisions, for virtue is a whole and one, which is divided into corresponding species, such as prudence and temperance, justice and courage, that we, knowing the differences of each of these qualities, may submit to a voluntary service of them both in their entirety and in particulars.

(85) And let us consider how we may train the soul so that it may not, from being thrown into a state of confusion, be deceived by general and unintelligible appearances, but that by making proper divisions of things it may be able to inspect and examine each separate thing with all accuracy, adopting language which will not, through being borne forward by disorderly impetuosity, cause any indistinctness, but being divided into its appropriate headings and into the demonstrations suitable to each, will be compounded like some living animal of perfect parts, properly put together. And we ought to apply ourselves to a continual meditation on and practice of these things, if we wish the use of them to be confirmed in us, as after having touched knowledge, not to abide in it is like tasting meat and drink, but being prevented from feeding on them in sufficient quantities.

XXVI. (86) After those that are cut up, it was very natural to make an offering of such as are ground; that is to say, it is natural after the division to dwell among and pass one's leisure among what had been thus discovered, for continued practice produces firm and stable knowledge, just as continued indifference produces ignorance. Therefore numbers of men from fear of the labour of practice, have lost the strength with which they were endowed by nature, whom those men have not imitated who nourished their souls on prophecy, which is signified under the name of manna, "for they ground it in mills or beat it in a mortar, and baked it in pans, and made cakes of it."[41] every one of them knowing well how to knead and soften the heavenly language of virtue for the sake of making the intellect firmer.

(87) When therefore you confess that the young and fresh corn, that is to say vigour, and the toasted corn, that is to say speech tried in the fire and invincible, and the corn cut up, which signifies the cutting up and division of things, and the

corn ground, that is to say anxious care about the examination into what has been found out, do all proceed from God, you will then be offering a sacrifice of the first fruits of the first produce, of the first and best things which the soul has brought forth; and even if we are slow, nevertheless he does not delay to take to himself those who are fit to worship him. For "I will take," says he, "you to be a people for myself, and I will be your God, and you shall be my people: I am the Lord."

XXVII. (88) These now, and such as these, are the accusations brought against Cain, who after some days offered sacrifice; but Abel did not bring the same offerings, nor did he bring his offerings in the same manner; but instead of inanimate things he brought living sacrifices, and instead of younger things, worthy only of the second place, he offered what was older and of the first consideration, and instead of what was weak he offered what was strong and fat, for he says that "he made his sacrifice of the first-born of his flocks, and of their fat,"[42] according to the most holy commandment.

(89) Now the commandment is as follows: "And it shall be," say the scriptures, "when God shall bring thee forth into the land of the Canaanites, in the manner which he swore to thy fathers, and shall give it to thee, that thou shalt set apart unto the Lord all that openeth the womb of all thy flocks, and of all the beasts which thou hast, and shalt set apart all the males for the Lord. Every offspring of an ass that openeth the womb shalt thou exchange for a sheep; and if thou dost not exchange it thou shall redeem it with money."[43] For that which openeth the womb is Abel, that is to say, a gift, the first-born, and you must examine how and when it is to be offered up; (90) now the most suitable time is when God shall lead thee into fluctuating reason, that is to say, into the land of the Canaanites, not in any chance manner, but in the manner in which he himself swore that he would; not in order that being tossed about hither and thither in the surf and tempest and heavy waves, you may be deprived of all rest or stability, but that having escaped from such agitation you may enjoy fine weather and a calm, and reaching virtue as a place of refuge, or port, or harbour of safety for ships, may lie in safety and steadiness.

XXVIII. (91) But when Moses says that God swears, we must consider whether he really asserts this as a thing appropriate for him to do; since to very many people it appears inconsistent with the character of God; for the meaning implied in an oath is, that it is the testimony of God in a matter which is doubtful. But to God there is nothing uncertain and nothing in doubt; (92) as it is he

---

[41]Numbers 11:8.

[42]Genesis 4:3.
[43]Exodus 13:11.

who demonstrates clearly to others all the clear indications of truth. And accordingly he is in need of no witness; for neither is there any other god of equal honour with him. I omit to mention that he who bears witness, inasmuch as he bears witness, is better than he to whom he bears witness; for the one stands in need of something, and the other serves him: and he who serves is more worthy of credit than he who requires to be served. But it impious to conceive that any thing can be better than the Cause of all things, since there is nothing equal to him, nothing that is even a little inferior to him;[44] but every thing which exists in the world is found to be in its whole genus inferior to God.

(93) Now it is for the sake of obtaining credence that those men who are disbelieved have recourse to an oath. But God is to be believed when simply he says any thing; so that, as far as certainty goes, his words do in no respect differ from oaths. And it happens, indeed, that our opinions are confirmed by an oath; but that an oath itself is confirmed by the addition of the name of God. God, therefore, does not become credible because of an oath, but even an oath is confirmed by God.

XXIX. (94) Why, then, has this hierophant thought fit to introduce him as swearing? That he might demonstrate the weakness of the created being, and after he had demonstrated it, might comfort him: for we are not able at all times to have ready in our soul that principal fact which ought to be remembered concerning God, namely, that "God is not as a man,"[45] So that we may rise above those assertions which are advanced concerning man; (95) but we, since we have the greatest share in what is mortal, and since we are not able to conceive any thing apart from ourselves, and have no power to go beyond or to escape our own calamities, but since we have got into mortality as snails have into their shells, and since we are revolved round and round ourselves in a ball, like so many hedgehogs, and have only the same opinions about the blessed and immortal God which we have about ourselves, avoiding all absurdity of assertion, such for instance as that God has the same form as man, but in reality being guilty of the impiety of attributing to him that he has the same passions as man; (96) we do on this account fashion for him in our minds hands and feet, a coming in and a going out, hatred, aversion, alienation, and anger; parts and passions very inconsistent with the character of the Cause of all things, an oath by which is often an assistant of our weakness. (97) "If God shall give thee the things which thou desirest," says Moses, speaking very eloquently and accurately; for if he does not give them thou wilt not have them, since every thing belongs to him, both things external, and the body, and the outward sense, and the power of speech, and the mind, and the energies and essences of all the faculties. And not you, but all this world also, and whatever you cut off and divide from it, you will find does not belong to you; for you do not possess the earth, or the water, or the air, or the heaven, or the stars, or any of the kinds of animals or plants, whether perishable or immortal, as your own; so that, whatever from them you bring to offer to him as a sacrifice, you are bringing as the possession of God, and not as your own.

XXX. (98) And take notice how very clearly it is enjoined, that he who is sacrificing may take a part of what is offered, and that he is not bound to offer the whole of what has been given him. For nature has given us a countless number of things, suitable to the human race, of all of which it receives no share itself: for instance, she has given us creation, though she is herself uncreate; and food, though she has no need of food; and growth, though she always remains in the same condition; and age, with reference to time, though she herself admits neither of addition nor of subtraction; an organic body, which she is incompetent to receive: also the powers of coming forward, of seeing, of applying food, and of disposing of it again when digested; of judging between the differences of scents, of using speech, of giving vent of laughter. (99) There are also many other things in us which have reference to our necessary and beneficial uses: but one may pronounce these things indifferent, but those which are confessedly good ought to be attributed to and comprehended in nature.

Come, therefore, let us investigate those things which are especially admired among us, of the things which are really goods, every one of which we pray to attain to at suitable seasons, and if we do attain to them, we are called the happiest of men. (100) Now who is there who is ignorant, that a happy old age and a happy death are the greatest of human goods? neither of which can nature partake of, inasmuch as nature can neither grow old nor die. And what is there extraordinary in the fact, if that which is uncreated does not condescend to use the good things of created beings, when even that which has been created desires different virtues, according to the differences of ideas into which it is divided. At all events men would not be rivals to women, nor would women be rivals to men, in these matters with which the opposite sex alone ought to have any concern. But if the women were to emulate the pursuits of men they would be looked upon as half men, and if the men were to apply themselves to the pursuits of

---

[44]The similarity to Horace is here again very remarkable. Horace, speaks of the Parent and Governor of the universe in Od. I. 12.17.

[45]Numbers 23:19.

women they would acquire an evil reputation as man-women.

(101) But are there not some virtues between which nature herself has made such distinction, that by no practice can they be brought into the common use of both sexes? At all events, to sow and to beget children is the especial property of man, according to his peculiar capacity, and no woman could manage to do this. And again, the nature of man does not make him capable of bearing children, which is the good deed of women; therefore these things, which are innate in the nature of man, cannot be predicated with propriety of God, but it is done only through some catachrestical misapplication of terms, by which we make amends for our weakness. You will take away therefore, O my mind, whatever is created or mortal, or changeable or unconsecrated, from your conceptions, regarding the uncreate God, immortal, unchangeable, and holy, the only God, blessed for ever.

XXXI. (102) But it is most entirely in accordance with nature "to sacrifice the males of every creature that openeth the womb, to God."[46] For as nature has given to women the womb, as the part most excellently adapted for the generation of animals, so also for the production of things she has placed a power in the soul, by means of which the mind conceives and is in travail, and brings forth many things. (103) But of the ideas which are brought forth by the mind, some are male and some female, as in the case of animals. Now the female offspring of the soul are wickedness and passion, by which we are made effeminate in every one of our pursuits; but a healthy state of the passions and virtue is male, by which we are excited and invigorated. Now of these, whatever belongs to the fellowship of men must be attributed to God, and everything that relates to the similarity to women must be imputed to one's self, on which account the command was delivered, "Of everything which openeth the womb the males belong to the Lord."

XXXII. (104) But also he says, "The males belong to the Lord of everything which openeth the womb, of thy flocks and of thy cattle, and of all that belongs to thee." Having spoken of the offspring of the principal part of the soul, he begins to give us information about the produce of the irrational part, which the outward senses have obtained for their inheritance, which he likens to cattle, and to the young which are bred up in the herds, being tame and tractable, inasmuch as they are guided by the care of their overseer, that is to say, of the shepherd; for those which are let run loose and are indulged with freedom, are made wild from want of any one to make them gentle. But those which have guides, such as goatherds,

cowherds, and shepherds, who are the managers of every species of cattle, they I say are of necessity made tame. (105) Moreover the genus of the outward senses is formed by nature, so as to be in one instance wild and in another tractable; it is wild, when having shaken off the rein of the mind as of its herdsman, it is borne on irrationally towards the external objects of the outward senses; but it is tame when having yielded in an obedient manner to reason, which is the guide of the discernment, it is regulated and directed in its course by it.

Whatever therefore it sees or hears, or, in short, whatever it feels with any one of its inward senses according to the injunction of the mind, all these things are male and perfect, for goodness is added to each; (106) but whatever is done without any guide, in a state of anarchy, in such case the body ruins us as anarchy ruins a city. Again, we must consider that those motions of the outward senses which proceed in obedience to the mind, and which of necessity are the better, do take place according to the dispensation of God; but these which are obstinate and disobedient, we must impute to ourselves, when we are carried away irrationally by the impetuosity of the outward senses.

XXXIII. (107) And he has commanded us to take a portion not only from the things which have just been mentioned, but also from the entire mass in combination. And the command is couched in the following words: "And it shall be, when ye eat of the fruit of the land, that ye shall take a part to offer up has a heave-offering unto the Lord: ye shall offer up a cake of the first of your dough for a heave-offering as ye do the heave-offering of the threshing-floor, so shall ye offer it."[47] (108) Now speaking properly, if we must avow the exact truth, it is we ourselves who are this dough; since many essences are kneaded and combined together that we may be made perfect: for the great Creator having mingled and kneaded together the cold and hot, dry and moist, opposite properties, has made out of them all one distinct combination, ourselves, from which the expression dough is applied to us. Now, of this combination in which body and soul, two most important divisions, are united, the first fruits are to be consecrated. (109) But the first fruits are the holy motions of each in accordance with virtue; on which account they have been compared to a threshing-floor. As, therefore, on a threshing-floor there is wheat and barley, and as many more of such things as are capable of being separated by themselves, and husks and chaff, and whatever other refuse is dissipated and scattered in different directions, so too, with us, there are some things which are excellent and useful, and

---

[46]Exodus 13:12.

[47]Numbers 15:19.

which afford real nourishment, by means of which a good life is brought to perfection; all which things we should attribute to God. But there are other things which are not divine, which we must leave like refuse to the race of mankind; but from these some portions must be taken away, (110) and there are some entire virtues, free from all wickedness, which it would be impious to mutilate by dividing them, and which resemble those indivisible sacrifices, the whole burnt-offerings, of which Isaac is a manifest pattern, whom his father was commanded to offer up like a victim, sharing in no destructive passion.

(111) And in another passage it is said, "My gifts, and my offerings, and my sacrifices, ye will take care to offer to me at my festivals:" not taking away from them, nor dividing them, but bringing them forward full, and entire, and perfect; for the feast of the soul is cheerfulness in perfect virtues; and the perfect virtues are all those which the human race exhibits, free from all stain or spot. But the wise man alone can keep such a festival as this, and no other human being; for it is a most rare thing to find a soul which has never tasted of wickedness of passions.

XXXIV. (112) Having therefore given an account of the dominant and subject divisions of the soul, and having shown what portion in each is male and female, Moses proceeds after this very consistently to explain the divisions of the body. For being well aware that without labour and care it is not possible to obtain a masculine offspring, he proceeds to say, "Every foal of an ass that openeth the womb, thou shalt exchange for the young of a sheep."[48] Which expression is equivalent to, "Exchange all labour for improvement." For an ass is the symbol of labour, being a much enduring animal, and a sheep is the emblem of improvement, as its very name shows,[49] (113) being a symbol of the care which is required to be expended in arts and professions, and all other things which are matters of instruction, and that with no negligence or indifference, but it is necessary with all anxiety to have prepared one's mind to encounter vigorously every amount of labour, and to strive not to be held in bondage by ill-considered toil, but to find advance and improvement by pushing on to the most glorious end; for labour is to be endured for the sake of improvement. (114) But if you indeed receive fatigue from labour, and still your nature does not advance at all on the road to improvement, but is rather opposed to your becoming better by progress, then abandon the pursuit and be quiet, for it is a difficult task to go against nature. On which account the scripture

adds: "And if you do not exchange it, you shall ransom it for money;" which means, but if you are not able to exchange labour for improvement, then give up your labour; for the idea of ransoming carries with it the notion of emancipating the mind from vain and unproductive care.

XXXV. (115) But I am speaking here, not of the virtues but of the arts of intermediate character, and of other necessary studies which are conversant about the attention due to the body, and about the abundance of external goods. But since the labour which is applied to what is perfectly good and excellent, even if it fall short of attaining its object, is nevertheless of such a character that it by itself does good to those who exert it, while the things which are unconnected with virtue unless their aim is attained, are entirely unprofitable. For as in the case of animals, if you take away the head there is an end of the whole animal, but the head of actions is their end, as they in a manner live if the end is arrived at, but if you cut off their end and mutilate them they die. (116) So too let those athletes who are not able to gain the victory but who are invariably defeated, condemn their trade; and if any merchant or captain of a ship in all his voyages meets with incessant disasters, let him turn away from the business and rest. And those men who, having devoted themselves to the intermediate arts, have nevertheless through the ruggedness of their nature been unable to acquire any learning, are to be praised for abandoning them: for such studies are not practised for the sake of the practice, but for the sake of the object towards which the labourer is borne. (117) If therefore nature hinders one's improvement for the better, let us not strive against her in an unprofitable way, but if she co-operates with us then let us honour the Deity with the first fruits and honours, which are the ransom of our soul, emancipating it from subjection to cruel masters, and elevating it to freedom.

XXXVI. (118) For Moses confesses that the Levites who being taken in exchange for the first-born, were appointed ministers of him who alone is worthy to be ministered unto, were the ransom of all the rest of the Israelites. "For I," says God, "behold, I have chosen the Levites out of the midst of the children of Israel, instead of every first-born that openeth the womb from among the children of Israel; they shall be their ransom and the Levites shall belong to me: for every first-born is mine; from that day in which I smote all the first-born in the land of Egypt, I dedicated to myself all the first-born of Israel."[50]

(119) Reason which fled to God and became his suppliant, is what is here called the Levite; God having taken this from the most central and

---

[48]Exodus 13:13.

[49]*Probaton*, derived from *probainō*, to advance forward.

[50]Leviticus 3:12.

dominant part of the soul, that is to say, having taken it to himself and appropriated it as his own share, thought it worthy of the honour due to the first-born. So that from these it is plain that Reuben is the first-born of Jacob, but Levi the first born of Israel, the one having the honours of seniority according to time, but the other according to dignity and power. (120) For Jacob being the symbol of labour and improvement, is also the beginning of goodness of disposition, which is signified in Reuben: but the fountain of contemplation of the only wise being, according to which the name of Israel is given, is the principle of being inclined to minister to him; and of such ministry the Levite is the symbol.

As therefore Jacob is found to be the inheritor of the birth-right of Esau, eagerness in wickedness having been defeated by virtuous labour, so also Levi, as one who devotes himself to perfect virtue, will carry off the honours of seniority from Reuben, the man of a good disposition. But the most undeniable proof of perfection is for a man to be a fugitive to God, having abandoned all concern for the things of creation.

XXXVII. (121) These then, to speak with strict propriety are the prices to be paid for the preserving and ransoming of the soul which is desirous of freedom. And may we not say that in this way a very necessary doctrine is brought forward? Namely that every wise man is a ransom for a worthless one, who would not be able to last for even a short time, if the wise man by the exertion of mercy and prudence did not take thought for his lasting; as a physician opposing himself to the infirmities of an invalid, and either rendering them slighter, or altogether removing them unless the disease comes on with irresistible violence, and surmounts all the ingenuity of medical skill. (122) And in this way Sodom was destroyed, since there was, as it were, no good which could be put in the scale sufficient to outweigh the unspeakable multitude of its wickednesses. So that if the fiftieth number could have been found, according to which an emancipation for the slavery of the soul and complete freedom is proclaimed, or if any one of the numbers below fifty which the wise Abraham enumerated descending at last down to ten, the number peculiar to instruction, the mind would not have been destroyed in so inglorious a manner. (123) We ought at times to endeavour as far as possible to preserve those who are not on the point of being utterly destroyed by the wickedness that is in them; imitating good physicians who, even if they see that it is impossible for those who are sick to recover, nevertheless apply their remedies with cheerfulness, lest it should appear that it was owing to their neglect that the affair did not turn out as it was desired. And if ever so slight a seed of good health is seen, this is to be cherished as a spark of fire with all imaginable care;

for there is hope that if it can have its duration protracted and its strength increased the man may for the future have a better life and one more free from danger.

(124) Therefore when I see any good man dwelling in any house or city, I pronounce that house or that city happy, and I think that its enjoyment of its present good things is sure, and that its expectation of future happiness will be accomplished, inasmuch as, for the sake of those who are worthy, God will bestow his boundless and illimitable riches even on the unworthy. And I pray that they may live to as great an age as possible, since it is not possible that they should ever grow old, as I expect that good fortune will remain to men as long as these men are able to live in the practice of virtue. (125) When, therefore, I see or hear that any one of these men is dead, I am exceedingly downcast and grieved, and I lament those who are left behind alive as much as I lament them; for to the one I see, that the necessary end has arrived in consistency with the ordinances of nature, and that they have exhibited a happy life and a glorious death. But I look upon the others as now deprived of the great and mighty hand by which they were saved, and as likely, now that they are bereft of it, soon to feel the evils which are due to them, unless, indeed, instead of the former men, who are gone, nature should be preparing to make other young men shoot up, as in the case of a tree which has already shed its ripe fruit for the nourishment and enjoyment of those who are able to make use of it. (126) As, therefore, good men are the strongest part of cities, with a view to their duration, so also in that state of each individual of us, which consists of soul and body, the reasoning powers which are attached to prudence and knowledge, are the firmest part of its foundation; which the legislator, using metaphorical language, calls the ransom and the first-born, on account of those reasons which I have already mentioned.

(127) In this way he also says, "The cities of the Levites are ransomed for ever, because the minister of God enjoys eternal freedom, according to the continuous revolutions of the ever-moving soul," and he admits incessant healing applications; for when he calls them ransomed, not once, but for ever, as he says, he means to convey such a meaning as this, that they are always in a state of revolution, and always in a state of freedom, the state of revolution being implanted in them because of their natural mortality, but their freedom coming to them because of their ministration to God.

XXXVIII. (128) But it is worth while to consider, in no passing manner, why he granted the cities of the Levites to fugitives, thinking it right that even these, who appear entirely impious, should dwell with the most holy of men. Now these fugitives are they who have committed, unintentionally, homicide. First of all, therefore, we must repeat what is consistent with what has been already said, that the good man is the ransom of the worthless one, so that they who have sinned will naturally come to those who have been hallowed, for the sake of being purified; and, in the second place, we must consider that the Levites admit the fugitives because they themselves are potentially fugitives; (129) for as they are driven away from their country, so these others also have left their children, their parents, their brethren, their nearest and dearest things, in order that they may receive an immortal inheritance instead of a mortal one. But they differ, because the flight of the one is involuntary, being caused by an unintentional action, but the flight of the others is voluntary, from a love of what is most excellent; and because the one have the Levites for a refuge; but the Levites have the Lord of all for their refuge, in order that those who are imperfect may have the sacred scriptures for their law; but that the others may have God for theirs, by whom they are hallowed. (130) Moreover, those who have committed unintentional homicide, have been allotted the same cities as the Levites to dwell in, because they also were thought worthy of a privilege because of a holy slaughter.

When therefore the soul being changed, came to honour the Egyptian God, the body, as fine gold, then all the sacred writings rushing forth of their own accord with defensive weapons, namely demonstrations according to knowledge, putting forward as their leader and general the chief priest, and prophet, and friend of God, Moses, proclaimed an unceasing war in the cause of piety, and would not hear of peace till they had put down all the doctrines of those who opposed them, so that they naturally came to inhabit the same dwellings, inasmuch as they had done similar actions, though not the same.

XXXIX. (131) There is also another opinion bruited about, as something of a secret, which it is right to lay up in the ears of the elders, not divulging it to the younger men; for of all the most excellent powers which exist in God, there is one equal to the others in honour, that is the legislative one (for he himself is a lawgiver and the fountain of all laws, and all particular lawgivers are subordinate to him), and this legislative power is divided in a twofold division, the one having reference to the rewarding of those who do well, and the other to the punishment of those who have sinned; (132) accordingly the Levite is the minister of the former division, for he performs all the ministrations which have a reference to perfect holiness, according to which the human race is raised up to and brought to the notice of God, either by whole burnt offerings, or else by saving sacrifices, or else by repentance for one's sins.

But of the other and punishing division of the legislative power, those who have committed unintentional homicide are the ministers. (133) And Moses bears witness to this saying, "He was not willing, but God gave him into his hands,"[51] so that his hands are here taken as instruments; but he who energizes by their means in an invisible manner, must be the other being, the invisible. Let therefore the two servants dwell together, being the ministers of the two species of the legislative power; the Levite being the minister of the division which has reference to the reward of them that do well, and the unintentional homicide of the division which is conversant about punishment.

(134) "But in the day," says God, "on which I smote the first-born in the land of Egypt, I consecrated to myself all the first-born of Israel."[52] And he says this not to lead us to suppose that at the time when Egypt was stricken with this mighty blow by the destruction of all its first-born, the first-born of Israel all became holy, but because both in former times, and now, and hereafter, and for ever, this naturally happens in the case of the soul, that when the most dominant parts of blind passion are destroyed, then the elder and most honourable offspring of God, who sees everything with a piercing sight, becomes holy; (135) for the departure of wickedness brings about the entrance of virtue, as, on the other hand, when what is good is driven away, then what was bad, having been lying in ambush, comes in to supply the void. Jacob then had scarcely at all gone out,[53] when Esau entered, not the mind which receives everything, being stamped with the impression of wickedness instead of the figures of virtue, if that is possible; but he would not have been able to effect this, for he will be supplanted and overthrown by the wise man before he knows it, the wise man being prompt to repel the impending injury before it can affect him.

XL. (136) And he brings not only the first fruits from the firstborn, but also from the fat; showing by this that whatever there is in the soul that is cheerful, or fat, or preservative and pleasant, might all be surrendered to God. And I see also in the arrangements established about sacrifices, that three things are enjoined to be offered from the victims; in the first place the fat, and the kidneys, and the lobe of the liver, about which we will speak separately; but not the brain or the heart which it seemed natural should be dedicated before the other parts, since, according to the language of the lawgiver, the dominant power is recognised as existing in one of them.

(137) But may it not be owing to an exceeding holiness and to very accurate consideration of the

---

[51]Exodus 21:13.
[52]Exodus 13:15.
[53]Genesis 27:1.

matter that he did not bear these things to the faithful altar of God? because that dominant part being subject to changes in either direction, either for bad or good, in an indivisible moment of time receives impressions which are continually changing, at one time impressions of what is pure and approved, and at others of an adulterated and base coinage.

(138) Therefore the lawgiver judging a place which was capable of receiving both these opposite qualities, namely, what is honourable, and what is disgraceful, and which was adapted to each, and distributed equal honour to both, to be quite as much impure as holy, removed it from the altar of God. For what is disgraceful is profane, and what is profane is by all means unholy; (139) and this is why the dominant part is kept away from sacrifices, but if it is subjected to examination, then, when all its parts have been purified, it will be consecrated as a burnt offering, free from all stain, and from all pollution. For this is the law respecting whole burnt offerings, that with the exception of the refuse of the food, and of the skin which are tokens of the weakness of the body and not of wickedness, nothing else should be left to the creature, but that all the other parts which exhibit the soul perfect in all its parts, should be presented as a whole burnt offering to God.

THAT THE WORSE IS WONT TO ATTACK THE BETTER†

(Quod Deterius Potiori Insidiari Soleat)

I. (1) And Cain said to Abel his brother, "Let us go to the field. And it came to pass, that while they were in the field, Cain rose up against Abel his brother, and slew him."[1] What Cain proposes to do is this: having by invitation led Abel on to a dispute, to convince him by main force, using plausible and probable sophisms; for the field to which he invites him to come, we may call a symbol of rivalry and contention, forming our conjectures of things that are uncertain from our perception of those which are manifest. (2) For we see that most contests, both in peace and in war, take place in the open fields. In peace, therefore, all those who practise gymnastic contests, seek for level race-courses and plain fields: and, in a war, it is not usual to have battles, of either infantry or cavalry, on hills; for many more disasters arise from the unfavourable character of the ground, than from anything that the enemies do to one another.

II. (3) And a very great proof of this is the conduct of the practiser of knowledge, Jacob, when warring against the opposite disposition, ignorance; when it is beheld in the field how he regulates the irrational faculties in the soul after a fashion, reproving and correcting them. "For Jacob having sent, called Leah and Rachel into the plain where the flocks were;"[2] (4) showing here clearly, that the plain is the symbol of revolt and contention. And he calls them and says, "I see the face of your father, that it is not to me as it was yesterday and the day before yesterday,[3] but the God of my father was with me." And on this account I should be inclined to say, Laban is not favourable to you because God is on your side; for in the soul, by which the external object of the outward senses is honoured as the greatest good, perfect reason is not found to exist; but in the soul, in which God walks, the external object of the outward senses is not looked upon as the greatest good, according to which object the name of Laban is given and understood. (5) And all those who, through the improvement of their reason, are adorned in the similitude of the Father, in consequence of education, unlearn all subserviency to the irrational impulses of the soul, selecting the plain as a suit-

able place, for it is said to Joseph, "Are not thy brethren keeping sheep in Sichem? Come, I will send thee to them. And he said, Behold, here am I. And Jacob said unto him, Go and see if thy brethren and the flocks are well, and come and tell me. And he sent him from the valley of Chebron, and he came to Sichem, and a man found him wandering in the plain: and the man asked him, What seekest thou? And he said, I am seeking my brethren, tell me where they are feeding their sheep. And the man said unto him they have departed from hence, for I heard them saying, Let us go to Dotham."[4]

III. (6) Therefore, from what has here been said it is plain, that they make the halting-place of the irrational faculties, which are in them, in the plain. But Joseph is sent unto them because he is unable to bear the somewhat austere knowledge of his father; that he may learn, under gentler instructors, what is to be done and what will be advantageous; for he uses a doctrine woven together from divers foundations, very variegated and very artfully made, in reference to which the law-giver says, that he had "a robe of many colours made for him;"[5] signifying by this that he is an interpreter of labyrinth-like learning, such as is hard to be explained; (7) for as he philosophises more with a regard to political wisdom than to truth, he brings into one place and connects together the three kinds of good things, namely, external things, the things concerning the body, and those concerning the soul, things utterly different from one another in their whole natures; wishing to show that each has need of each, and that everything has need of everything; and that that which is really the complete and perfect good, is composed of all these things together, and that the parts of which this perfect good is compounded are parts or elements of good, but are not themselves perfect goods. (8) In the same way, as neither fire, nor earth, nor any one of the four elements, out of which the universe was created, are the world, but the meeting and mixture of all the elements together; in the same way also happiness ought not peculiarly to be sought for either in the external things, or in the things of the body, or in the things of the soul, taken by themselves; for each of the aforementioned things has only the

---

† Yonge's title, *A Treatise on the Principle that the Worse is Accustomed to be Always Plotting Against the Better.*
[1] Genesis 4:8.
[2] Genesis 31:4.
[3] Genesis 31:5.
[4] Genesis 37:12.
[5] Genesis 37:3.

rank of parts and elements, but it must be looked for in the combination of them all together.

IV. (9) He therefore is sent, to be untaught this doctrine, to men who think nothing honourable but what is good, which is the peculiar attribute of the soul as the soul; but all external goods, which are called the good things of the body, they believe to be only superfluities, and not true and real goods: "For behold," says he, "thy brethren are tending their sheep," that is to say, they are governing all the irrational part that is in them, "in Sichem;"[6] and the name Sichem, being interpreted, means a shoulder, the symbol of enduring labour. For the men who are lovers of virtue endure a great burden, the opposition to the body and the pleasure of the body, and also the opposition to external things and to the delights which arise from them. (10) "Come, therefore, let me send them to them,"[7] that is to say, listen to my bidding and come over, receiving in your mind a voluntary impulse to learn better things. But up to the present time you are full of self-complacency, as one who has received true instruction; for although you have not as yet plainly asserted this, you still say that you are ready to be taught again, when you say, "Behold, here am I," by which expression you appear to me to exhibit your own rashness and easiness to be persuaded more than your readiness to learn; and a proof of what I say is this, "And a little afterwards the true man will find you wandering in the way,"[8] while you would not have been led astray, if you had come to the practice of virtue with a sound intention.

(11) And yet the adhortatory speech of your father's imposes no irresistible necessity upon you, to turn of your own accord and at the instigation of your own mind to better things; for he says, "Go and see," behold, consider, and meditate in the matter with entire accuracy. For you ought first to know the affair concerning which you are going to labour, and then after that to proceed to a care how to accomplish it. (12) But after you have examined into it, and after you have inspected it carefully, casting your eyes over the whole of the business, then examine, besides, those who have already given their attention to the matter, and who have become practisers of it, whether now that they do this they are in a sound state, and not mad, as the lovers of pleasure think who calumniate them and cover them with ridicule. And do not form a positive judgment in your own mind either as to the appearance of the matter, or as to the soundness of condition enjoyed by those who practise these things, before you have reported the matter to and laid it before the father; for the opinions of those who have only lately begun to learn are unstable and without any firm foundation; but the sentiment of those who have made some advance are solid, and from their opinions they must of necessity derive firmness and steadiness.

V. (13) Therefore, O my mind, if you in this manner investigate the holy thoughts of God with which man is inspired by divine agency and the laws of such men as love God, you will not be compelled to admit any thing lowly, anything unworthy, of their greatness. For how could any man who is endowed with sound sense and wisdom, receive this very thing concerning which our present discussion now is? Can any one believe that there was such a great want of servants and attendants in the household of Jacob who was possessed of treasures equal to those of a king, that it was necessary for him to send his son away to a distant country to bring him word of the health of his other children and of his flocks? (14) His grandfather, besides the multitude of captives whom he had carried off when he defeated the nine kings, had more than three hundred domestic servants, and all this household had suffered no diminution, but rather, as time advanced, all his wealth had received great increase in all its parts.

Would he not then, when he had an abundance of servants of all kinds ready to his hand, have preferred sending one of them, to sending his son, whom he loved above all things, on a business which any one of the lowest of his servants could easily have brought to a successful issue?

VI. (15) But you see that he here gives a superfluously minute description of the country from which he sends him forth, in a way which all but commands us to forsake the strict letter of what is written. "For out of the valley of Chebron," now the name Chebron, when interpreted, means conjoined and associated, being a figurative way of intimating our body which is conjoined and which is associated in a sort of companionship and friendship with the soul. Moreover, the organs of the outward senses have valleys, great ducts to receive everything external which is an object of the outward senses, which collect together an infinite number of distinctive qualities, and by means of those ducts pour them in upon the mind, and wash it out, and bring it in the depths. (16) On this account, in the law concerning leprosy, it is expressly ordered, "when in any house hollows appear of a pale or fiery red colour, that the inhabitants shall take out the stones in which such hollows appear, and put in other stones in their places;"[9] "that is to say, when different destructive qualities which the pleasures and the appetites, and the passions akin to them, have wrought in men, weighing down and oppressing the whole

[6]Genesis 37:12.
[7]Genesis 37:13.
[8]Genesis 37:15.

[9]Leviticus 14:36.

soul, have made it more hollow and more lowly than its natural condition would be, it is well to remove the reasons which are the cause of this weakness, and to bring in such in their stead as are sound by a legitimate style of education and a healthy kind of discipline.

VII. (17) Seeing therefore that Joseph has wholly entered into the hollow valleys of the body and of the outward senses, he invites him to come forth out of his holes, and to bring forward the free air of perseverance, going as a pupil to those who were formerly practisers of it themselves, and who are now become teachers of it; but he who appears to himself to have made progress in this, is found to be in error; "For a man," says the holy scripture, "found him wandering in the plain,"[10] showing that it is not labour by itself, intrinsically considered, but labour with skill, that is good. (18) For as it is of no use to study music in an unmusical manner, nor grammar without any attention to its true principles, nor, in short, any art whatever in a manner either devoid of art or proceeding on false rules of art, but each art must be cultivated on a strict obedience to its rules; so also it is of no avail to apply one's self to the study of wisdom in a crafty spirit, or to the study of temperance in a nigardly and illiberal frame of mind, nor to courage rashly, nor to piety superstitiously, nor, in fact, to any other science which is in accordance with virtue in an unscientific manner. For all these steps are confessedly erroneous. In reference to which, a law has been delivered to us "to pursue what is just in a just manner,"[11] that we may cultivate justice and every other virtue by those works which are akin to it, and not by those which are contrary to it.

(19) If, therefore, you see any one desiring meat or drink at an unseasonable time, or repudiating baths or ointments at the proper season, or neglecting the proper clothing for his body, or lying on the ground and sleeping in the open air, and by such conduct as this, pretending to a character for temperance and self-denial, you, pitying his self-deception, should show him the true path of temperance, for all the practices in which he has been indulging are useless and profitless labours, oppressing both his soul and body with hunger and all sorts of other hardships.

(20) Nor if anyone, using washings and purifications soils his mind, but makes his bodily appearance brilliant; nor if again out of his abundant wealth he builds a temple with brilliant artments of all kinds, at a vast expense; nor if he offers up catombs and never ceases sacrificing oxen; nor if he adorns temples with costly offerings, bringing timber in abundance, and skilful orna-ments, more valuable than nay of gold or silver, (21) still let him not be classed among pious men, for he also has wandered out of the way to piety, looking upon ceremonious worship as equivalent to sanctity, and giving gifts to the incorruptible being who will never receive such offerings, and flattering him who can never listen to flattery, who loves genuine worship (and genuine worship is that of the soul which offers the only sacrifice, plain truth), and rejects all spurious ministrations, and those are spurious which are only displays of external riches and extravagance.

VIII. (22) But some say that the proper name of the man who found him wandering in the plain is not mentioned, and they themselves are in some degree mistaken here, because they are unable clearly to discover the true way of this business, for if they had not been mutilated as to the eye of the soul, they would have known that of one who is truly a man, the most proper, and appropriate, and felicitous name is this very name of man, being the most appropriate appelation of a well regulated and rational mind. (23) This man, dwelling in the soul of each individual, is found at one time to be a ruler and monarch, and at another time to be a judge and umpire of the contest which take place in life. At times also he takes the place of a witness and accuser, and without being seen he corrects us from within, not suffering us to open our mouths, but taking up, and restraining, and bridling, with the reins of conscience the self-satisfied and restive course of the tongue.

(24) This convicting feeling it is which inquires of the soul when it sees it wandering about, What seekest thou? Is it wisdom? why then do you go after wickedness? Or is it temperance? but this path of yours leads to niggardliness. Or is courage? by this path you will only arrive at rashness. Or are you in pursuit of piety? this is the road to superstition. (25) But if it should say that it is seeking words of wisdom, and that it is longing for them, as for what is nearest akin to its own race, we must not give implicit belief to this, for the question was not, Where are they feeding their flocks? but Where are they tending them? for they who feed their flocks supply nourishment, and all the objects of the outward senses to the animal of the outward senses devoid of reason and insatiable; by means of which outward senses and their indulgence, we become unable to govern ourselves and fall into misfortune; but they who tend their flocks, having the power of rulers and governors, make those gentle which were fierce before, checking the mighty power of the appetites. (26) If, therefore, he was in all sincerity seeking the practices of virtue, he would have sought for them among kings, and not among cup-bearers, or cooks, or confectioners, for these last prepare things which have reference to pleasure, but the former are masters of pleasure.

[10]Genesis 37:15.
[11]Deuteronomy 16:20.

IX. Therefore the man, who saw the deceit, answered rightly, "They are departed hence." (27) And he shows here the mass of the body; clearly proving that all those by whom labour is practised for the sake of the acquisition of virtue, having left the regions of earth, have determined on contemplating only what is sublime, dragging with them no stain of the body. For he says, too, that he had heard them say, (28) "Let us go to Dotham:" and the name Dotham, being interpreted, means "a sufficient leaving;" showing that it was with no moderate resolution, but with extreme determination that they had decided on leaving and abandoning all those things which do not co-operate towards virtue, just as the customs of women had ceased any longer to affect Sarah. But the passions are female by nature, and we must study to quit them, showing our preference for the masculine characters of the good dispositions.

Therefore the interpreter of divers opinions, the wandering Joseph, is found in the plain, that is to say, in a contention of words, having reference to political considerations rather than to useful truth; (29) but there are some adversaries who, by reason of their vigorous body, their antagonists having succumbed, have gained the prize of victory without a struggle, not having even had, to descend into the arena to contend for it, but obtaining the chief honours on account of their incomparable strength. Using such a power as this with reference to the most divine thing that is in us, namely, our mind, "Isaac goes forth into the plain;"[12] not for the purpose of contending with any body, since all those who might have been his antagonists, are terrified at the greatness and exceeding excellence of his nature in all things; but only wishing to meet in private, and to converse in private with the fellow traveller and guide of his path and of his soul, namely God. (30) And the clearest possible proof of this is, that no one who conversed with Isaac was a mere mortal. Rebecca, that is perseverance, asks her servant, seeing but one person, and having no conception but of one only, "Who is this man who is coming to meet us?" For the soul which perseveres in what is good, is able to comprehend all self-taught wisdom, which is named Isaac, but is not yet able to see God, who is the guide of wisdom. (31) Therefore, also, the servant confirming the fact that he cannot be comprehended who is invisible, and who converses with man invisibly, says, "He is my lord," pointing to Isaac alone. For it is not natural that, if two persons were in sight, he should point to one alone; but the person whom he did not point to, he did not see, inasmuch as he was invisible to all persons of intermediate character.

X. (32) Now I think that it has already been sufficiently shown, that the field to which Cain invites Abel to come, is a symbol of strife and contention. And we must now proceed to raise the question what the matters are concerning which, when they have arrived in the plain, they are about to institute an investigation. It is surely plain that they are opposite and rival opinions: for Abel, who refers everything to God, is the God-loving opinion; and Cain, who refers everything to himself (for his name, being interpreted, means acquisition), is the self-loving opinion. And men are self-loving when, having stripped and gone into the arena with those who honour virtue, they never cease struggling against them with every kind of weapon, till they compel them to succumb, or else utterly destroy them; (33) for, as the proverb is, they leave no stone unturned, saying, Is not the body the house of the soul? Why, then, should we not take care of the house that it may not become ruinous? Are not the eyes and the ears, and all the company of the other outward senses, guards, as it were, and friends of the soul? Ought we not, then, to honour men's friends and allies equally with themselves? And has nature made pleasures and enjoyments, and all the delights which are spread over the whole of life for the dead, or for those who have never even had any existence at all, and not rather for those who are alive? And what ought we not to do to procure for ourselves riches, and glory, and honours, and authority, and all other things of that sort, which are the only means of living not only safely, but happily? (34) And the life of these men is a proof of this. For they who are called lovers of virtue are nearly all of them men inglorious, easily to be despised, lowly, in need of necessary things, more dishonourable than subjects, or even than slaves, sordid, pale, cadaverous-looking, bearing want and hunger in their countenances, full of diseases, men who would be glad to die. But those who take care of themselves are men of reputation, rich, leaders, men in the enjoyment of praise and honour; moreover, they are healthy, stout, and vigorous; living delicately, nursed in luxury, strangers to labour, living in the constant company of pleasure, and using all their outward senses to bring delights to the soul, which is capable of receiving them all.

XI. (35) Arguing therefore in this prolix train of reasoning, they thought that they got the better of those who were not accustomed to deal in sophistry. But the cause of their victory was not the strength of those who got the better, but the weakness of their adversaries in these matters. For of those who practise virtue, some treasured up what is good in their soul alone, becoming practisers of praiseworthy actions, and having no knowledge whatever of sophistries of words. But they who were armed in both ways, having their minds furnished with wise counsel and with good deeds, and having also good store of reasons to bring for-

---

[12] Genesis 24:63.

ward according to the arts of the sophists, (36) they had a good right to oppose the contentious behaviour of some others, having means at hand by which to repel their enemies. But the former sort had no safety whatever. For what men could fight naked against armed enemies on equal terms, when, even if they had been both equally armed, the contest would still have been unequal?

(37) Abel therefore had not learnt any of the arts of reasoning, but he knew what was good by his intellectual disposition alone; on account of which he ought to have refused to go down to the plain, and to have disregarded the invitation of his enemy. For any display of fear is better than being defeated; but such fear a man's enemies call cowardice, but his friends entitle it safe prudence, and we must believe friends in preference to enemies, inasmuch as they tell us the truth.

XII. (38) And it is on this account, as you see, that Moses rejected the sophists in Egypt, that is to say, in the body whom he calls magicians (for it is owing to the tricks and deceits of their sophistical tricks that good dispositions and good habits are infected and corrupted), saying that he was "not an eloquent man,"[13] which is equivalent to saying that he was not formed by nature for the conjectural rhetoric of plausible and specious reasons. And immediately afterwards he confirms the assertion by adding, that he is not only not eloquent, but altogether "void of words,"[14] meaning this, not in the sense in which we do when we call animals void of words, but speaking of himself as one who did not choose to employ words by means of his organs of speech, but who impresses and stamps the principles of true wisdom upon his mind alone, which is the most perfect opposite to false sophistry. (39) And he will not go to Egypt, nor will he descend into the arena to strive against the sophists who contend in it, till he has thoroughly studied and practised the art of argumentative reasoning; God himself showing to him all the ideas which belong to such elocution, and making him perfect in them by the election of Aaron who was the brother of Moses, and whom he was accustomed to call his mouth-piece, and interpreter, and prophet.[15] (40) For all these attributes belong to speech, which is the brother of the intellect; for the intellect is the fountain of words, and speech is its mouth-piece, because all the conceptions which are entertained in the mind are poured forth by means of speech, like streams of water which

flow out of the earth, and come into sight. And speech is an interpreter of the things which the mind has decided upon in its tribunal. Moreover, it is a prophet and a soothsayer of those things which the mind unceasingly pours forth as oracles from its inaccessible and invisible retreats.

XIII. (41) In this manner, then, it is useful to oppose those who are ostentatious about doctrines. For if we have been well exercised in various species of discourses, we shall no longer stumble through inexperience and want of acquaintance with the manoeuvres of sophists. But rising up and making a firm and resolute stand against them, we shall with ease escape from their artificial entanglements. But they, when their tricks have once been found out, will appear to be exhibiting the conduct of sparrers rather than of regular combatants. For they too, in their own opinion, get great credit by their style of beating the air; but when they come to a real contest they meet with no moderate disgrace. (42) And if any one is adorned as to his soul with all imaginable virtues, and yet has paid no attention to the art of speaking and arguing, if he only preserves silence he will obtain safety, a prize won without danger. But if he comes forth like Abel into a contest with sophists, he will be thrown down before he has obtained a firm footing.

(43) For, as in medical science, some practitioners who know how to cure almost every complaint, and disease, and infirmity, can nevertheless give no true or even probable account of any one of them; and on the other hand, others are very clever, as far as giving an account of the diseases goes, and in explaining their symptoms and causes, and the modes of cure, and are the most excellent interpreters possible of the principles of which their art is made up, but are utterly useless in the matter of attending the bodies of the sick, to the cure of which they are not able to contribute even the slightest assistance. In the same way, those who have devoted themselves to practical wisdom have often neglected to pay attention to their language; and those who have learnt their professions thoroughly as far as words go, have yet treasured up no good instruction in their soul. (44) It is therefore nothing extraordinary, that these men being in the habit of indulging an unbridled tongue, should be full of self-sufficiency and boldness, displaying all the folly which they have from the first beginning cherished. But it is better to trust to those who, like skilful physicians, have a knowledge of the means of healing the diseases and evil affections of the soul, until God provides an excellent interpreter, and displays to and pours upon him the fountains of his eloquence.

XIV. (45) It would therefore have been consistent for Abel to practise prudence, a very saving virtue, and to have remained at home, disregarding the invitation to the arena of discussion

---

[13]Exodus 4:10.

[14]It is not possible to give the exact force of the original here. The Greek word is *alogos*, which usually means "irrational," as derived from *logos*, "reason," which word has also the sense of "a word," "speech." The Bible translation in the passage alluded to, Exodus 6:12, is "who am of uncircumcised lips."

[15]Exodus 7:1.

and contest, which was given to him, imitating Rebecca, that is perseverance, who, when Esau, the companion of wickedness, was pouring forth threats, advised the practiser of wisdom, Jacob, to retreat before him who was about to plot against him, until he should have relaxed in his fierce hostility to him, (46) for Esau had been holding out an intolerable threat over Jacob, saying, "The days of mourning for my Father are at hand, that then I may slay my brother Jacob;"[16] for he is wishing only that that species in the nature of things which is void of passions, namely, Isaac (to whom the oracle had been given, that he should not descend into Egypt),[17] may be the victim of an irrational affection, in order I suppose that he may be wounded by the stings of pleasure or pain, or of any other passion, showing that the man who is not wholly perfect and who makes laborious improvements, will receive not merely a wound, but utter destruction. However, the good God will neither allow that invulnerable species among created things to be subdued by passion, nor will he surrender the practice of virtue to bloody and raging destruction.

(47) On which account we read in a subsequent passage, "Cain rose up against Abel, his brother, and slew him."[18] For according to the first imagination, he suggests the idea that Abel has been killed. But if you look at it according to the most accurate investigation, you will see that he intimates that Cain himself was slain by himself, so that we ought to read it thus: "Cain rose up and killed himself," and not the other. (48) And very reasonably may we attribute this to him. For the soul, which destroys out of itself the virtue-loving and God-loving principle, has died as to the life of virtue, so that Abel (which appears a most paradoxical assertion) both is dead and alive. He is dead, indeed, having been slain by the foolish mind, but he lives according to the happy life which is in God. And the holy oracle which has been given will bear witness, which expressly says, that he cried out loudly, and betrayed clearly by his cries[19] what he had suffered from the concrete evil, that is from the body. For how could one who no longer existed have conversed?

XV. (49) The wise man, therefore, who appears to have departed from this mortal life, lives according to the immortal life; but the wicked man who lives in wickedness has died according to the happy life. For in the various animals of different kinds, and in general in all bodies, it is both possible and easy to conceive, that the agents are of one kind, and the patients of another. For when a father beats his son, correcting him, or when a teacher beats his pupil, he who beats is one, and he who is beaten is another. But in the case of these beings, which are united and made one, only in the part as to which both acting and suffering are found to exist; these two things are there, neither at different times, nor do they affect different people, but they affect the same person in the same manner at the same time.

At all events, when an athlete rubs himself for the sake of taking exercise, he is by all means rubbed also; and, if any one strikes himself, he himself is struck and wounded; and so also he who mutilates or kills himself as the agent, is mutilated or killed as the patient. (50) Why, then, do I say this? Because it appears inevitable that the soul, inasmuch as it consists not of particles which are separated but of those which are united, should suffer what it appears to do, as in real truth it did in this instance; for, when it appeared to be destroying the God-loving doctrine, it destroyed itself. And Lamech is a witness to this, the descendant of the impiety of Cain, who says to his wives, who are the representatives of two inconsiderate opinions, "I have slain a man to my hurt, and a young man to be a scar to me."[20] (51) For it is evident that if any one slays the principle of courage, he wounds himself with the opposite disease of cowardice; and if any one in the practice of honourable studies slays his vigorous strength, he is inflicting on himself wounds and great injuries with no moderate degree of disgrace. Therefore, indeed, perseverance says that if practice and improvement be destroyed she will lose not only one child but also her others also, and be an instance of complete childlessness.

XVI. (52) But as he who injures a good man is proved to be doing injury to himself, so also does he who thinks his betters worthy of privileges, in word indeed claim advantage for them, but in fact he is procuring it for himself. And nature here bears testimony in support of my argument, and so do all the laws which have been established in consistency with her; for there is a positive and express and intelligible command laid down in these words: "Honour thy father and thy mother, that it may be well with thee;"[21] not well with those who receive the honour, says the Scripture, but with thee; for if we look upon the intellect as the father of this concrete animal, and if we honour the outward senses as its mother, we ourselves shall be well treated by them. (53) But the proper honour to be paid to the mind is first to be honoured on account of what us useful, and not on account of what is pleasant; but all things proceeding from virtue are useful. And the honour

---

[16] Genesis 27:41.
[17] Genesis 26:2.
[18] Genesis 4:8.
[19] Genesis 4:10.

[20] Genesis 4:23.
[21] Genesis 27:45.

proper to be paid to the outward sense is when we do not allow ourselves to be carried away by its impetuosity towards the external objects of the outward senses, but compel it to be curved by the mind, which knows how to govern and guide the irrational powers in us. (54) If, therefore, each of these things, the outward sense and the mind, receive the honour which I have been describing, then it follows of necessity that I, who use them both, must derive advantage from them. But if, carrying your language away a long distance from the mind and from the outward sense, you think your father, that is to say, the world which produced you, and your mother, wisdom, by means of which the universe was completed, worthy of honour, you yourself shall be well treated; for neither does God, who is full of everything, nor sublime and perfect knowledge, want anything. So that he who is inclined to pay proper attention to them, benefits not those who receive his attentions and who are in no need of anything, but himself most exceedingly. (55) For skill in horsemanship and in judging of dogs, being in reality a ministering to horses and dogs, supplies those animals with the useful things of which each species is in need; and if it were not so to supply them it would seem to neglect them. But it is not proper to call piety, which consists in ministering to God, a virtue which is conversant about supplying the things which will be of use to the Deity; for the Deity is not benefited by any one, inasmuch as he is not in need of anything, nor is it in the power of any one to benefit a being who is in every particular superior to himself. But, on the contrary, God himself is continually and unceasingly benefiting all things.

(56) So, when we say that piety is a ministering to God, we say that it is in some such a service as slaves discharge to their masters, who are taught to do without hesitation that which is commanded them; but, again, there will be a difference, because the masters are in need of service, but God has no such want. So that, in the case of the masters, the servants do supply that which will be of use to them, but to God they supply nothing beyond a mind imbued with a spirit of willing obedience; for they will not find anything which they can improve, since all things belonging to masters are, from the very beginning, most excellent; but they will benefit themselves very greatly by determining to become friends to God.

XVII. (57) I think, therefore, that enough has been now said with respect to those who appear to think that they do others good or harm. For it has been shown, that that which they think that they are doing to others, they in either case do to themselves. We will now examine the remainder of this event; the question is as follows:—"Where is Abel, thy brother?"[22] To which answer is made,

"I do not know; am I my brother's keeper?" It is therefore worth while to consider the question whether it can be appropriately said of God that he asks a question. For he who asks a question or puts an inquiry is asking or inquiring about something of which he is ignorant; seeking an answer through which he will know what he as yet does not know. But everything is known to God, not only all that is present, and all that is past, but also all that is to come. (58) What need, then, has he of an answer which cannot give any additional knowledge to the questioner? But we must say that such things cannot properly be uttered by the Cause of all things, but that, as it is possible to say what is not true without lying, so it is possible for one to put question or an interrogatory without either making inquiry or seeking for information. "Why, then," some one will say, "are such words spoken?" In order that the soul which is about to give the answer may prove by itself what it answers correctly or incorrectly, having no one else either as an accuser or an adversary.

(59) Since, when he asks the wise man, Where is virtue?[23] that is to say, when he asks Abraham about Sarah, he asks, not because he is ignorant, but because he thinks that he ought to answer for the sake of eliciting praise from the answer of him who speaks. Accordingly, Moses tells us that Abraham answered, "Behold, she is in the tent;" that is to say, in the soul. What then is there in this answer that contains praise? Behold, says he, I keep virtue in my house as a treasure carefully stored up, and on account of this I am immediately happy. (60) For it is the use and enjoyment of virtue that is happiness, and not the bare possession of it. But I should not be able to use it unless you, by letting down the seeds from heaven, had yourself made virtue pregnant; and unless she had brought forth the germs of happiness, namely, Isaac. And I consider that happiness is the employment of perfect virtue in a perfect life. In reference to which he, approving of his own determination, promises that he will complete perfectly all that he asked.

XVIII. (61) To him therefore the answer brought praise, as he confessed that virtue without the divine favour was not sufficient of itself to help any one; and, in consequence, it also brings blame to Cain, who says that he does not know where he is who has been treacherously slain by him. For he appears by this answer to be wishing to receive his hearer, as one who does not see everything, and who has no previous suspicion of the deceit which he is about to use. But every one

---

[22] Genesis 4:9.
[23] Genesis 18:9.

is wicked and worthy of proscription who thinks that the eye of God can ever fail to see anything. (62) But Cain here speaks arrogantly, "Am I my brother's keeper?" For we might altogether say he was sure hereafter to lead a miserable life, if nature made you the guardian and keeper of so good a man. Do you not see that the lawgiver entrusts the keeping and preservation of the holy things not to any chance person, but to the Levites, who were the most holy persons in their opinions? for whom the earth and the air and the water were considered an unworthy inheritance, but the heaven and the whole world were looked upon as their due. And the Creator alone is worthy of these things, to whom they have fled for refuge, becoming his sincere suppliants and servants, showing their love for their master in their continued service, and in the unhesitating observance of all the commands which are laid upon them, and in the preservation of the things entrusted to them.

XIX. (63) And it has not fallen to the lot of all the suppliants to become guardians of the holy things, but to those only who have arrived at the number fifty, which proclaims remission of offences and perfect liberty and a return to their ancient possessions. "For this," says the Scripture, "is the law concerning the Levites: from twenty-five years old and upwards, they shall go in to wait upon the service of the tabernacle of the congregation: and from the age of fifty years they shall cease waiting upon the service thereof, and shall serve no more; but shall minister with their brethren in the tabernacle of the congregation, and they shall keep what is to be kept, and shall do no service." [24] (64) Therefore, the Scripture charges him who has half perfection (for the number fifty is perfect, and the number twenty-five is the half of fifty), to work and to do what is holy, approving his ministration by his works. And the beginning, as an old writer has said, is half of the whole. But the perfect man it does not enjoin to labour any longer, but only to preserve what he has acquired by labour and diligence. For may I never become a practiser of what I ought not to be a preserve; (65) subsequently practice therefore is mediocrity not perfection, for it takes place not in perfect souls, but in such as are seeking after perfection. But it is the perfect duty of guardianship to deliver to memory the well-practised contemplations of holy things, the excellent deposit of knowledge to a faithful guardian, who is the only one who disregards the ingenious and manifold nets of forgetfulness; so that the Scripture, with great propriety and felicity, calls him who is mindful of what he has learnt, the guardian of it. (66) And such an one before he practised was a pupil, having another to teach him; but when he became competent himself to

guard what he had learnt, he then received the power and rank of a teacher, having appointed his brother, his own uttered discourse, to the ministration of teaching.

For it is said that, "His brother shall minister;" [25] so that the mind of the good man is the guardian and steward of the doctrines of virtue. But his brother, that is to say, uttered discourse, shall minister instead of him, going through all the doctrines and speculations of wisdom to those who are desirous of instruction. (67) On which account Moses, also, in his praises of Levi, having previously said many admirable things, adds subsequently, "He has guarded thy oracles and kept thy covenant." [26] And presently he continues, "They shall show thy justification to Jacob, and thy law to Israel. (68) Therefore, he here clearly asserts that the good man is the guardian of the words and of the covenant of God. And, indeed, in another place he has shown that he is the best interpreter and declarer of his justifications and laws; the faculty of interpretation being displayed through its kindred organ—the voice, and guardianship being exerted through the mind, which having been made by nature as a great storehouse, easily contains the conceptions of all things, whether bodies or things. It would therefore have been worth the while of this self-loving Cain to have been the keeper of Abel; for if he had kept him he would have attained to a compounded and moderate kind of life, and would not have been filled with unmodified and absolute wickedness.

XX. (69) And God said, "What has thou done? The voice of the blood of thy brother cries out to me from out of the ground." [27] The expression, "What hast thou done," shows indignation at an unhallowed action, and also ridicules the man who thought he had committed the murder secretly. The indignation now arises at the intention of the man who has done the deed, because he designed to destroy what was good; but the ridicule is excited by his thinking that he has plotted against one who is better than himself, and at his having plotted not so much against him as against himself. (70) For, as I have said before, he who appears to be dead is alive, inasmuch as he is found to be a suppliant of God and to utter a voice; and he who believes that he is still alive is dead, as to the death of the soul, inasmuch as he is excluded from virtue, according to which alone he is worthy to live. So that the expression, "What hast thou done?" is equivalent to, "Thou hast done nothing; thou hast done no good for thyself."

---

[24] Numbers 8:24.

[25] In quoting this passage above, I used the translation as given in the Bible, they "shall minister with their brethren in the tabernacle;" but the Greek of the text was the same in that passage as it is here.

[26] Deuteronomy 33:9.

[27] Numbers 23:8.

(71) For neither was the sophist, Balaam, who was an empty multitude of contrary and contending doctrines, when he was desirous to imprecate curses upon and to injure the good man, able to do so; since God turned his curses into a blessing, in order to correct the unjust man of wickedness and to display his own love of virtue.

XXI. (72) But it is the nature of sophists to have for enemies the faculties which are in them, while their language is at variance with their thoughts and their thoughts with their language, and while neither is in the least degree consistent with the other. At all events, they wear out our ears, arguing that justice is a great bond of society, that temperance is a profitable thing, that continence is a virtuous thing, that piety is a most useful thing, and, of each other virtue, that it is a most wholesome and saving quality. And, on the other hand, that injustice is a quality with which we ought to have no truce, that intemperance is a diseased habit, that impiety is scandalous, and so going through every kind of wickedness, that each sort is most pernicious. (73) And, nevertheless, they never cease showing by their conduct that their real opinion is the reverse of their language. But, when they extol prudence and temperance and justice and piety, they then show that they are, above all measure, foolish, and intemperate, and unjust, and impious; in short, that they are throwing into confusion and overturning all divine and human regulations and principles. (74) And to them, therefore, one may very properly say what the divine oracle said to Cain, "What is this that thou hast done?" What good have ye done yourselves? What have all these discourses about virtue profited your souls? In what particular of life, whether small or great, have ye done well? What? Have you not, on the contrary, contributed to advancing true charges against yourselves? because, by expressing your approval of what is good, and philosophising as far as words go, you have been excellent interpreters, but are nevertheless discovered to be men who both think and practise shameful things. In fact, all good things are dead in your souls, these evils having been there kindled; and, on this account there is no one of you who is really alive.

(75) For as, when some musician or grammarian is dead, the music and grammar which existed in them dies with them, but their ideas survive, and in a manner live as long as the world itself endures; according to which the existing race of men, and those who are to exist hereafter in continual succession, will, to the end of time, become skilful in music and grammar. Thus, also, if the prudence, or the temperance, or the courage, or the justice, or, in short, if the wisdom of any kind existing in any individual be destroyed,

nevertheless the prudence existing in the nature of the immortal universe will still be immortal; and every virtue is erected like a pillar in imperishable solidity, in accordance with which there are some good people now, and there will be some hereafter. (76) Unless, indeed, we should say that the death of any individual man is the destruction of humanity and of the human race, which, whether we ought to call it a genus, or a species, or a conception, or whatever else you please, those who are anxious about the investigation of proper names may determine. One seal has often stamped thousands upon thousands of impressions in infinite number, and though at times all those impressions have been effaced with the substances on which they were stamped, still the seal itself has remained in its pristine condition without being at all injured in its nature. (77) Again, do we not think that the virtues, even if all the characters which they have impressed upon the souls of those who have sought them should become effaced by wicked living, or by any other cause, would nevertheless preserve their own unadulterated and imperishable nature? Therefore, they who have not been duly initiated in instruction, not knowing anything about the differences between wholes and parts, or between genera and species, or about the homonymies which are incidental to these things, mix up all things together in a confused mass. (78) On which account every one who is a lover of self, by surname Cain, should learn that he has destroyed the namesake of Abel, that is to say species, individuality, the image made according to the model; not the archetypal pattern, nor the genus, nor the idea, which he thinks are destroyed together with animals, though, in fact, they are indestructible.

Let any one then say to him, reproving and ridiculing him, What is this that thou hast done, O wretched man? Does not the God-loving opinion which you flatter yourself that you have destroyed, live in the presence of God? But it is of yourself that you have become the murderer, by destroying from out of its seat the only quality by which you could live in a blameless manner.

XXII. (79) And what was said afterwards is uttered very beautifully, with reference either to the beauty of the interpretation of which it is susceptible, or to the conception which may be discovered in it. "The voice of the blood of thy brother calls to me from out of the earth." This now, which is a very sublime expression if we regard the language in which it is couched, is intelligible to all those who are not utterly uninitiated in eloquence. But let us consider the ideas which are apparent in it as well as we are able.

And first of all, let us consider what is said about the blood; (80) for in many places of the law as given by Moses, he pronounces the blood to be the essence of the soul or of life, saying distinctly,

"For the life of all flesh is the blood thereof."[28] And when the Creator of all living things first began to make man, after the creation of the heaven and the earth, and all the things which are between the two, Moses says, "And he breathed into his face the breath of life, and man became a living soul," showing again by this expression that it is the breath which is the essence of the life. (81) And, indeed, he is accustomed diligently to record all the suggestions and purposes of God from the beginning, thinking it right to adopt his subsequent statements to aid to make them consistent with his first accounts. Therefore, after he had previously stated the breath to be the essence of the life, he would not subsequently have spoken of the blood as occupying the most important place in the body, unless he had been making a reference to some very necessary and comprehensive principle. (82) What then are we to say? The truth is, that every one of us according to the nearest estimation of numbers, is two persons, the animal and the man. And each of these two has a cognate power in the faculties, the seat of which is the soul assigned to it. To the one portion is assigned the vivifying faculty according to which we live; and to the other, the reasoning faculty in accordance with which we are capable of reasoning. Therefore, even the irrational animals partake of the vivifying power; but of the rational faculty, God—I will not say partakes, but—is the ruler, and that is the fountain of the most ancient Word.

XXIII. (83) Therefore, the faculty which is common to us with the irrational animals, has blood for its essence. And it, having flowed form the rational fountain, is spirit, not air in motion, but rather a certain representation and character of the divine faculty which Moses calls by its proper name an image, showing by his language that God is the archetypal pattern of rational nature, and that man is the imitation of him, and the image formed after his model; not meaning by man that animal of a double nature, but the most excellent species of the soul which is called mind and reason.

(84) On this account, Moses represents God as calling the blood the life of the flesh, though he is aware that the nature of the flesh has no participation in intellect, but that it does partake of life, as also does our whole body. And the soul of man he names the spirit, meaning by the term man, not the compound being, as I said before, but that Godlike creation by which we reason, the roots of which he stretched to heaven, and fastened it to the outermost rim of the circle of those bodies which we call the fixed stars. (85) For God made man, the only heavenly plant of those which he placed upon the earth, fastening the heads of the others in the mainland, for all of them bend

their heads downwards;"[29] but the face of man he has exalted and directed upwards, that it might have its food of a heavenly and incorruptible nature, and not earthly and perishable. With a view to which, he also rooted in the earth the foundations of our body, removing the most insensible part of it as far as possible from reason; and the outward senses, which are as it were the body-guards of the mind, and the mind itself, he established at a great distance from the earth, and from all things connected with it, and bound it with the periodical revolutions of the air and of the heavens, which are imperishable.

XXIV. (86) Let us then no longer doubt, we who are the disciples of Moses, how man conceived an idea of God who is destitute of all figure, for he was taught the reason of this by the divine oracle, and afterwards he explained it to us. And he spoke as follows:—"He said that the Creator made no soul in any body capable of seeing its Creator by its own intrinsic powers. But having considered that the knowledge of the Creator and the proper understanding of the work of Creation, would be of great advantage to the creature (for such knowledge is the boundary of happiness and blessedness), he breathed into him from above something of his own divine nature. And his divine nature stamped her own impression in an invisible manner on the invisible soul, in order that even the earth might not be destitute of the image of God. (87) But the archetypal pattern was so devoid of all figure, that its very image was not visible, being indeed fabricated in accordance with the model, and accordingly it received not mortal but immortal conceptions. For how could a mortal nature at the same time remain where it was and also emigrate? or how could it see what was here and what was on the other side? or how could it sail round the white sea, and at the same time traverse the whole earth to its furthest boundaries, and inspect the customs and laws of the nations on all the affairs and bodies which are in existence?

On separating them from the things of the earth, how could it arrive at a contemplation of the sublimer things of the air and its revolutions, and the peculiar character of its seasons, and all the things which at the periodical changes of the year are made anew, and, according to their usual habit, brought to perfection? (88) Or again, how could it fly through the air from earth to heaven, and investigate the natures which exist in heaven, and see of what nature they are, how they are moved, what are the limits of their movements, of their

---

[28]Leviticus 17:11.

[29]This idea is the same as that which Ovid has expressed in the beginning of the Metamorphoses, which may perhaps be translated—"And while all other creatures from their birth / With downcast eyes gaze on their kindred earth, / He bids man walk erect, and scan the heaven / From which he springs, to which his hopes are given."

beginning and of their end; how they are adapted to one another and to the universe according to the just principles of kindred? Is it easy to have an accurate comprehension of the different arts and of the different branches of knowledge which bring external things into shape, and which are concerned with the affairs of the body and of the soul, with a view to the improvement of the two, and to understand ten thousand other things, of which it is not easy to describe either the number or the nature in language? (89) For of all the faculties which exist in us, the mind alone, as being the most rapid in its motions of all, appears to be able to outrun and to pass by the time in which it originates, according to the invisible powers of the universe and of its parts existing without any reference to time, and touching the universe and its parts, and the causes of them.

And now, having gone not only to the very boundaries of earth and sea, but also to those of air and heaven, it has not stopped even there, thinking that the world itself is but a brief limit for its continued and unremitting course. And it is eager to advance further; and, if it can possibly do so, to comprehend the incomprehensible nature of God, even if only as to its existence. (90) How, then, is it natural that the human intellect, being as scanty as it is, and enclosed in no very ample space, in some membrane, or in the heart (truly very narrow bounds), should be able to embrace the vastness of the heaven and of the world, great as it is, if there were not in it some portion of a divine and happy soul, which cannot be separated from it? For nothing which belongs to the divinity can be cut off from it so as to be separated from it, but it is only extended. On which account the being which has had imparted to it a share of the perfection which is in the universe, when it arrives at a proper comprehension of the world, is extended in width simultaneously with the boundaries of the universe, and is incapable of being broken or divided; for its power is ductile and capable of extension.

XXV. (91) Let this then be enough to say concisely about the essence of the soul. And now proceeding in regular order, we will explain the expression, that "the voice of his blood cries out," in this manner,—of our soul, one part is dumb, and one part is endowed with utterance. All that part which is devoid of reason is likewise destitute of voice, but all that part which is rational is capable of speech, and that part alone has formed any conception of God; for, by the other parts of us, we are not able to comprehend God, or any other object of the intellect. (92) Of our vivifying power, therefore, of which the blood is, as it were, the essence, one portion has particular honour, namely, that of speech and reason; I do not mean the stream which flows through the mouth and tongue, but I speak of the fountain itself, from which the channels of utterance are, in the course of nature, filled. And this fountain is the mind; by means of which, all our conversations with and cries to the living God take place, at one time being voluntary, and at another involuntary. (93) But he, as a good and merciful God, does not reject his suppliants, and most especially he does not, when they, groaning at the Egyptian deeds and passions, cry to him in sincerity and truth. For at such a time Moses says that, "their words go up to God,"[30] and that he listens to them, and delivers them from the evils that surround them. (94) But that all these things should happen when the king of Egypt dies, should be a most strange thing; for it would be natural that when the tyrant died, all those who have been tyrannised over by him should rejoice and exult; but at that time they are said to groan. "For after many days the king of Egypt died, and the children of Israel groaned."[31]

(95) Now here, if we look merely at the words, the expression does not appear to be reasonable; but if we have regard to the faculties in the soul, then its consistency is discovered. For as long as he who scatters abroad and dissipates the opinions about good things, namely, Pharaoh, is vigorous in us, and appears in a sound and healthy state, if indeed we can say that any wicked man is in such a condition, we receive pleasure, driving temperance away from our borders. But when he loses his strength, and in a manner dies, he who has been the cause of men's living in a filthy and lascivious manner, then we, fixing our eyes on modesty of life, bewail and groan over ourselves on account of our former way of living; because honouring pleasure before virtue, we joined a mortal life to an immortal one; and the law taking pity on our continued lamentation, gently receives our suppliant souls, and easily drives away the Egyptian calamities which are brought upon them by the passions.

XXVI. (96) But on him who is incapable of receiving repentance on account of the enormity of the pollution which he has incurred by the murder of his brother, namely, on Cain, he lays well-deserved and fitting curses; for in the first place he says to him, "And now, cursed art thou upon the earth:"[32] showing first of all that he is polluted and accursed, not now for the first time when he has committed the murder, but that he was so before, the moment that he conceived the idea of it, the intention being of equal importance with the perfected action; (97) for as long as we only conceive wicked things in the bad imagination of our minds, still, during that time, we are guilty of thoughts only, for the mind is capable of

---

[30] Exodus 2:21.
[31] Exodus 2:25.
[32] Genesis 4:11.

being changed even against its will; but when performance is added to the intention that has been conceived, then our deliberate purpose becomes also guilty; for this is the chief distinction between voluntary and involuntary sin. (98) But the scripture here pronounces that the mind shall be accursed, not from anything else, but from the earth; for of all the most grievous calamities which can happen to it, the earthly portion which exists in each of us is found to be the cause. At all events, when the body is afflicted with disease, it adds the miseries which are derived from itself, and so fills the mind with grief and despondency; or, on the other hand, if it has grown fat immoderately through enjoyment of pleasures, it makes all the faculties of the mind duller for the comprehension of nobler objects.

(99) For, indeed, each of the outward senses is capable of receiving injury; for either a man beholding beauty is wounded by the darts of love, which is a terrible passion; or else, perhaps, if he hears of the death of any one related to him by birth, he is bowed down by sorrow: very often, too, taste gets the mastery of a man, when it is either tortured by disagreeable flavours, or weighed down by the multitude of delicacies. And why need I speak of the impetuous passions, which tend to the connexion of the two sexes? These have destroyed whole cities, and countries, and mighty nations of the earth; to which fact nearly the whole multitude, both of poets and of historians, bears abundant testimony.

XXVII. (100) And as to the manner in which the mind becomes accursed upon the earth, he adds further information immediately afterwards, saying: "The earth which opened her mouth to receive the blood of thy brother." For it is very difficult for the mouths of the outward senses to be opened and widened, as even when they are not open the flood of the objects appreciable only by them rushes in like an overflowing river, nothing being capable of resisting their evident impetuosity; for then the mind is found to be overwhelmed, being wholly absorbed by so vast a wave, and being utterly unable to swim against it, or even to raise its head above it; (101) but it is necessary to employ all these things not so much for whatever objects can possibly be effected, but for those that are best; for the sight can perceive all colours and all shapes; but still it ought to behold only things worthy of light, and not of darkness. Again, the ear can receive all kinds of sounds; but some it ought to disregard; for myriads of the things that are said are disgraceful. Nor, O foolish and arrogant man, because nature has given you the faculty of taste, ought you to fill yourself insatiably with everything, like a cormorant; for there are many things not merely among such as are nutritious, but of those which are exceedingly so, which have,

nevertheless, produced diseases accompanied with great suffering.

(102) Nor does it follow that, because for the sake of the perpetuation of your race you have been endowed with the powers of generation, you ought to pursue pollutions and adulteries and other impure connections; but only such as, in a legitimate manner, engender and propagate the race of mankind. Nor, because you have been made endowed with a mouth and a tongue and the organs of speech, ought you to say everything and to reveal what ought not to be spoken, for there are times when to hold one's peace is useful. And, in my opinion, those who have learnt to speak have also learnt to be silent, the same capacity teaching a man both lines of conduct. But those men who relate what they ought not, do not display the faculty of eloquence, but the weakness of their faculty of silence. (103) On which account we labour to bind each of the mouthpieces of the senses beforementioned with the imperishable bonds of temperance. "For whatever is not bound with a bond," says Moses, in another passage, "is impure,"[33] as if the cause of its unhappiness was the fact of the parts of the soul being relaxed and open and dissolved; but that the fact of their being compacted and tightly bound together contributed to goodness and soundness of life and reason.

He, therefore, curses the godless and impious Cain with deserved curses; because, having opened the caverns of this concrete creature, he opened his mouth for all external things, praying to receive them in an insatiable manner and to contain them, to the utter destruction of the God-loving doctrine, Abel.

XXVIII. (104) "On this account shall he cultivate the earth;"[34] he does not say, "He shall become a farmer." For every farmer is an artist, because farming is an art. But any of the common people are cultivators of the earth, giving their service to provide themselves with necessaries, without any skill. These men, then, as they have no superintendent in all that they do, do much harm; and whatever they do well they do by chance, and not in accordance with reason. But the works of farmers, which are performed according to knowledge, are all of them, of necessity, useful.

(105) On this account it is that the law-giver has attributed to the just Noah the employment of a farmer;[35] showing by this that, like a good farmer, the virtuous man eradicates in the wild wood all the mischievous young saplings which have been planted by the passions or by the vices, but

---

[33] Numbers 19:15.
[34] Genesis 4:12.
[35] Genesis 9:20.

leaves untouched all those which bear fruit, and which may act instead of a wall and prove a firm defence for the soul. And, again, among the trees capable of cultivation he manages them in different ways, and not all in the same way: pruning some and adding props to others, training some so as to increase their size, and cutting down others so as to keep them dwarf. (106) Again, when he sees a vine flourishing and luxuriant he bends down its young shoots to the ground, digging trenches to receive them, and again heaping up the ground on the top of them; and they at no distant period, instead of parts, become whole trees, and instead of daughters they become mothers, having moreover put off the old age which is the usual companion of maternity. For, having desisted from distributing and apportioning its nourishment amongst numerous offspring, inasmuch as they are able to support themselves, that which was previously weak from being drained by this cause becomes so fully satiated as to grow fat and young again.

(107) And I have seen another man who cut away the less desirable shoots of trees which admitted of cultivation, as soon as they appeared above the ground, and left only a small piece adhering to the root itself. And then taking a branch in good condition from another tree of a good sort, he scraped away the one shoot down till he came to the pith, and the shoot which was attached to the root he cut at no great depth, but opening it just sufficiently to make the union perfect, and then putting into the cleft the shoot which he had pared away he fitted it in; (108) and from these two shoots one single tree of one united nature sprang up, each portion giving to the other that which was useful to it; for the roots support the shoot which has been fitted into them, and prevent it from drying up and withering, and the shoot which has been inserted as a reward for its nourishment supplies the root with good fruit in requital. There are also an innumerable host of other operations in farming which proceed on rules of art, which it would be superfluous to enumerate on the present occasion, for we have only dwelt on this point at such length for the purpose of showing the difference between the man who is only a cultivator of the earth, and one who is a farmer.

XXIX. (109) Accordingly the bad man never ceases from employing, without any of the principles of art, his earth-like body, and the outward senses which are akin to it, and all the external objects of these outward senses, and he injures his miserable soul, and he also injures what he fancies he is benefiting exceedingly, his own body.

But the good man, for he has skill in the art of a farmer, manages the whole of his materials in accordance with the principles of art and reason; for when the outward senses behave insolently, being borne forward with irresistible impetuosity towards the external objects of the outward senses, they are easily restrained by some contrivance among those which art has devised; (110) but when an impetuous passion in the soul becomes violent, bringing forth voluptuous itchings and ticklings arising from pleasure or from appetite, or on the other hand, stings and agitation, caused by fear or grief, it is softened by the previously prepared saving medicine; and if any evil devouring as it goes, proceeds further, like a sister of the cancerous disease, which creeps over the body, it is cut out by reason which proceeds in its operations in accordance with knowledge.

(111) In this manner then the trees of the wild wood are brought into a state of tameness, but all the plants of the cultivated and fruit-bearing virtues have for their shoots studies, and for their fruits virtuous actions, of each of which the farming skill of the soul promotes the growth, and as far as depends upon it, it makes them immortal by its industry.

XXX. (112) Very clearly therefore is the good man thus shown to be a farmer, and the bad man to be only a cultivator of the land; and I wish that while he is thus cultivating the land, the earthly nature which environs him, had imparted some vigour to him, and had not, as it has, taken away something of the power which he had before, for we read in the scripture, "It shall not add its strength to thee to give it to thee," (113) and such would be the character of a man who was always eating or drinking and never satisfied, or who was incessantly indulging in the pleasures of the belly, and devoting his energies to the gratifying of his carnal appetites, for deficiency produces weakness, but fulness produces strength; but when, amid abundance of things an insatiability is united with excessive intemperance, that is hunger; and they are truly wretched whose bodies are filled, while their passions are empty and still thirsting; (114) but of the lovers of knowledge the prophet speaks in a great song, and says, "That she has made them to ascend upon the strength of the earth, and has fed them upon the produce of the fields,"[36] showing plainly that the godless man fails in attaining his object, in order that he may grieve the more while strength is not added to these operations in which he expends his energies, but while on the other hand it is taken from them; but they who follow after virtue, placing it above all these things which are earthly and mortal, disregard their strength in their exceeding abundance, using God as the guide to conduct them in their ascent, who proffers to them the produce of the earth for their enjoyment and most profitable use, likening the virtues to fields, and the fruits of the virtues to the produce of the fields, according to the principles of their generation; for from prudence is

---

[36]Deuteronomy 32:13.

derived prudent action, and from temperance temperate action, and from piety pious conduct, and from each of the other virtues is derived the energy in accordance with it.

XXXI. (115) Now these energies are especially the food of the soul, which is competent to give suck, as the lawgiver says, "Honey out of the rock, and oil out of the solid rock,"[37] meaning by the solid rock which cannot be cut through, the wisdom of God, which is the nurse and foster-mother and educator of those who desire incorruptible food; (116) for it, as the mother of those things which exist in the world, immediately supplies food to those beings which are brought forth by her; but they are not all thought worthy of divine food, but only such as do not show any degeneracy from their parent; for there are many which a scarcity of virtue, which is more terrible than a scarcity of meat and drink, has destroyed; (117) but the fountain of divine wisdom is borne along, at one time in a more gentle and moderate stream, and at another with greater rapidity and a more exceeding violence and impetuosity. When, therefore, it descends gently it sweetens after the manner of honey, but when it comes on swiftly the whole material enters like oil into the light of the soul.

(118) This rock, Moses, in another place, using a synonymous expression, calls manna the most ancient word of God, by which appellation is understood, something of the most general possible nature, from which two cakes are made, one of honey and the other of oil, that is to say, two different systems of life, exceedingly difficult to distinguish from one another, both worthy of attention, at the very beginning instilling the sweetness of these contemplations which exist in the sciences, and again emitting the most brilliant light to those who take hold of the things which are the objects of their desire, not fastidiously, but firmly, and scarcely by means of unremitting and incessant perseverance. These then, as I have said before, are they who ascend up upon the strength of the earth.

XXXII. (119) But to the impious Cain, neither does the earth contribute anything to give him vigour, even though he never concerns himself about anything which is exterior to it; on which account, in the next sentence, he is found "groaning and trembling upon the earth,"[38] that is to say, under the influence of grief and terror; and such also is the miserable life of a wicked man, who has received for his inheritance the most painful of the four passions, pain and terror; the one being equivalent to groaning, and the other to trembling; for it is inevitable, that some evil should either be present to or impending over such a man. Now the expectation of impending evil causes fear, but the suffering of present evil causes pain.

(120) On the other hand, he who pursues virtue is found to be in the enjoyment of corresponding blessings; for either he has acquired what is good or he will attain to it. Now the present possession perfects joy, which is the best of all possessions; but the expectation of possessing it brings hope, the food of those souls which love virtue; on account of which, putting away sluggishness, we, with spontaneous readiness, hasten onwards to good actions. (121) From that soul therefore, in which justice has brought forth a male offspring, that is to say just thoughts, it has also at the same time removed all painful things, and the birth of Noah will bear testimony in confirmation of this, and the interpretation of the name of Noah is just; and of him it is said, "he will make us to rest from our works, and from the labours of our hands, and from the earth, which the Lord God has cursed;"[39] (122) for it is the nature of justice in the first place to cause rest instead of labour, being utterly indifferent to the things that are in the confines between wickedness and virtue, riches and glory, and power and honour, and all other things which are akin to these, which are the chief objects of the energies of the human race. And, in the second place, to destroy those pains which exist in accordance with our own energies; for Moses does not (as some wicked men do) say, that God is the cause of evils, but our own hands; indicating, by a figurative expression, the works of our hand, and the voluntary inclinations of our mind to the worser part.

XXXIII. Last of all, Noah is said "to comfort us concerning our work, because of the ground which the Lord God hath cursed."[40] (123) But by this is meant wickedness, which is established in the souls of foolish men; the remedy for which (as one seeks for remedies for a severe disease) is found to be the just man, who is in possession of the panacea, justice. When, therefore, he has repelled these evils he is filled with joy, as also is Sarah; for she says, "The Lord hath caused me laughter;" and she adds further, "so that whosoever hears it shall rejoice with me."[41] (124) For God is the author of virtuous laughter and joy; so that we must look upon Isaac not as the offspring of creation, but as the work of the uncreate God. For if Isaac, being interpreted, means laughter, and if it be God who is the cause of laughter according to the true testimony of Sarah, then he may be most properly said to be the father of Isaac. And he also gives a share to Abraham of his own proper

---

[37] Deuteronomy 23:13.
[38] Genesis 4:12.
[39] Genesis 5:29.
[40] Genesis 5:29.
[41] Genesis 21:6.

appellation, to whom, when he eradicated pain from wisdom, he gave rejoicing as an offspring. (125) If, therefore, any one is worthy to listen to the account of the creative power of God he is of necessity joyful, and rejoices in company with those who have had a longing to hear the same. And in the account of the creative power of God you will find no cunningly devised fable, but only unalloyed laws of truth firmly established. Moreover, you will find no vocal measures or rhythm, no melodies alluring the hearing with musical art; but only most perfect works of virtue, which have all of them a peculiar harmony and fitness. And as the mind rejoices which is eager to hear of the works of God, so also does language, which is in harmony with the conceptions of the mind, and which in a manner is compelled to attend to them, feel exultation.

XXXIV. (126) And this will also be proved by the oracle which was given to the all-wise Moses, in which these words are contained: "Behold, is there not Aaron thy brother, the Levite? I know that he will speak for thee; and behold he will be coming forth to meet thee, and he will rejoice in himself when he seeth thee."[42] For here the Creator says, that he knows that uttered speech is a burden to the mind, because it speaks; for he represents it, that is to say, articulate sound, as the organ, as it were, of all this concrete being of ours. (127) This speech speaks, and discourses, and interprets both in your case and mine, and in that of all mankind, the things conceived in the mind, and it moreover comes forward to meet the things which the mind conceives; for when the mind being excited towards any object connected with it receives an impetus, either because it has been moved internally by itself, or because it has received some remarkable impressions from external circumstances, it then becomes pregnant and labours to bring forth its conceptions. And, though it tries to deliver itself of them, it is unable to do so till sound, like a midwife, acting either through the medium of the tongue or of some other of the organs of speech, receives those conceptions and brings them to light. (128) And this voice is itself the most manifest of all the conceptions. For, as what is laid up is hidden in darkness until light shines upon it and exhibits it, in the same manner the conceptions are stored away in an invisible place, namely, the mind, until the voice, like light, sheds its beams upon them and reveals everything.

XXXV. (129) Very beautifully, therefore, was it said that speech goes forth to meet the conceptions, and that it runs on endeavouring to overtake them, from its desire of giving information respecting them, for everything has the greatest affection for its own proper employment; and the proper employment of speech is to speak, to which employment therefore it hastens by a kind of natural kindred and propriety. And it rejoices and exults when, shedding its rays upon it as it were, it accurately sees and overtakes the sense of the matter exhibited; for then, seizing it in its embrace, it becomes its most excellent interpreter. (130) At all events, we repudiate those chatterers and interminable talkers, who, in the long passages of their conversations, do not properly keep to their conceptions, but merely connect long and empty and, to say the truth, lifeless sentences.

Therefore the conversation of such men as these is indecorous, and is justly condemned to groan; as, on the other hand, it is inevitable that that conversation which proceeds from a proper consideration of the objects of its consideration must rejoice, since it comes in an adequate manner to the interpretation of the things which it saw and comprehended vigorously; (131) and this is a matter within the knowledge of almost every one from his daily experience. For, when we thoroughly understand what we are saying, then our speech rejoices and exults, and is rich in most emphatic and appropriate expressions, with which, using great copiousness and fluency of unhesitating diction, it sets before the hearer what it desires to exhibit to him in a most evident and efficient manner. But when the comprehension of the conceptions is doubtful, then the speech stumbles and exhibits a great deficiency of suitable and felicitous expressions, and speaks very inappropriately; on which account it is tedious and wearisome and wanders about, and instead of persuading its hearers it pains their ears.

XXXVI. (132) Again, it is not every speech which should come forward to meet the conceptions; nor is it every kind of conception that it should come to meet; but only the perfect Aaron who should come forward to meet the conceptions of the most perfect Moses. Since else why, when God had said, "Behold, is not Aaron thy brother?" did he add, "the Levite," if it were not for the sake of teaching that it belongs to the Levite and priest, and to virtuous speech alone, to give information respecting the conceptions of the mind, which are shoots of the perfect soul. (133) For never may the speech of a wicked man be interpreter of divine doctrines, for such an one would deform their beauty by his own pollutions; and, on the other hand, may what is intemperate and disgraceful never be related by the utterance of a virtuous man, but may sacred and holy conversations always deliver the relation of holy things.

(134) In some of the best governed cities of the world they say that such a custom as this prevails. When any man who has not lived well attempts to deliver his opinion, either in the council or in the assembly of the people, he is not permitted to do so by his own mouth, but is com-

---

[42] Exodus 4:14.

pelled by the magistrates to deliver his opinion to some virtuous and honourable man to explain in his behalf; and then he, when he has heard what he wishes said, rises up and unfolds the meaning of the sewn up mouth of his instructor, becoming his extempore pupil; and he displays the imaginations of another, scarcely considering the original concern for them even in the rank of a hearer or spectator. So some people do not choose to receive even benefits from unworthy persons, but look upon the injury accruing from the shame of taking their advice as greater than the advantage which can be derived from it.

XXXVII. (135) This lesson the most holy Moses appears to teach; for such is the object of the statement that Aaron the Levite is coming forward to meet his brother Moses, and that when he sees him he rejoices in himself; and the statement that he rejoices in himself shows also, besides the doctrine which has already been mentioned, another more connected with politics, since the lawgiver is here exhibiting that genuine joy which is most especially akin to the human race; (136) for to speak strictly, the feeling of joy does not belong to abundance of money, or of possessions, or to brilliancy of renown, nor, in short, to any one of those external circumstances which are lifeless and unstable, and which contain the seeds of their decay in themselves: nor yet does it belong to personal strength and vigour, and to the other advantages of the body, which are common to even the most worthless men, and which have often brought inevitable destruction on those who possessed them.

(137) Since then it is only in the virtues of the soul that genuine and unadulterated joy is found, and since every wise man rejoices, he rejoices in himself, and not in his surrounding circumstances; for the things that are in himself are the virtues of the mind on which it is worthy for a man to provide himself; but the circumstances which surround him are either a good condition of body or an abundance of external wealth, which are not proper objects for a man to pride himself on.

XXXVIII. (138) Having shown, therefore, as far as we could by the most unmistakeable testimony of Moses that, to rejoice is the peculiar property of the wise man, we will now also show that to hope also belongs to him alone; and here again we shall have no need of any other witness than Moses; for he tells us that the name of the son of Seth was Enos: and Enos, being interpreted, means hope. "He hoped first," says Moses, "to call upon the name of the Lord his God." [43] Speaking wisely: for to a man inspired with the principles of truth what can be more akin and appropriate than a hope and expectation of the

acquisition of good things from the one bounteous God? This, if one must speak the plain truth, is, properly speaking, the only real birth of men, as those who do not hope in God have no share in rational nature. (139) On which account Moses, after he had previously mentioned with respect to Enos that "he hoped to call upon the name of the Lord his God," adds in express words, "This is the book of the generation of men;" [44] speaking with perfect correctness: for it is written in the book of God that man is the only creature with a good hope. So that arguing by contraries, he who has no good hope is not a man. The definition, therefore, of our concrete being is that it is a living rational mortal being; but the definition of man, according to Moses, is a disposition of the soul hoping in the truly living God.

(140) Let good men, then, by all means having received joy and hope for their blessed inheritance, either possess or expect good things: but let bad men, of whom Cain is a companion, living in fear and pain, reap a harvest of a most bitter portion, namely, either the presence or the expectation of evils, groaning over the miseries which are actually oppressing them, and trembling and shuddering at the expected fearful dangers.

XXXIX. (141) However, we have now said enough on this subject, and let us proceed to investigate what comes afterwards.

He continues thus: "And Cain said unto the Lord, My crime is too great to be forgiven." [45] Now what is meant by this will be shown by a consideration of simple passages. If a pilot were to desert his ship when tossed about by the sea, would it not follow of necessity that the ship would wander out of her course in the voyage? Shall I say more? If a charioteer in the contest of the horse-race were to quit his chariot, is it not inevitable that the course of the free horses would be disorderly and irregular? Again, when a city is left destitute of rulers or of laws, and laws, undoubtedly, are entitled to be classed on an equality with magistrates, must not that city be destroyed by those greatest of evils, anarchy and lawlessness? (142) And in the same manner, by the ordinances of nature, the body must perish if the soul be absent; and the soul, if reason be absent. Reason, too, must be destroyed by the absence of virtue. But if each of these things is such an injury to the things that are abandoned by them, then how great must we consider is the misfortune of those persons who are abandoned by God? Whom he has rejected as deserters from his band: and put out of the pale of his sacred laws, considering them unworthy of his superintendence and government. For we must absolutely be certain that a person who is deserted by his superior

---

[43] Genesis 4:26.

[44] Genesis 5:1.
[45] Genesis 4:14.

and benefactor is guilty of great crimes and liable to severe accusations. For when would you say that a man destitute of skill is most greatly injured? Would it not be when he is utterly abandoned by knowledge? (143) And when would you say that the ignorant and wholly uninstructed man is most injured? Must it not be when instruction and education complete their desertion of him? When again do we most deplore the condition of the foolish? Is it not when prudence has utterly rejected them? And when do we pronounce intemperate or unjust men, miserable? Is it not when temperance and justice have condemned them to an eternal banishment from their dominion? When do we pronounce the impious, wretched? Is it not when piety has cut them off from her peculiar rites? (144) So that it seems to me that those who are not utterly impure should pray to be chastised and rejected rather than deserted; for desertion will most easily ruin them, as vessels without ballast and without a pilot; but correction will set them right again. (145) Are not those boys who are beaten by their preceptors, for whatever errors they commit, better than those who have no schoolmaster? And are not those who are reproved by their teachers, for all the errors they commit in the arts which they are studying, better than those who receive no such reproof? And are not those young men who have been accounted especially worthy of that natural superintendence and government, which those who are parents exercise over their children, more fortunate and better than those who have had no such protectors? And if they have not such natural protectors, do they not receive guardians as governors in a secondary rank, who are accustomed to be appointed over them out of pity for their orphan state; to fill the place of parents to them in all things that are expedient?

XL. (146) Let us, therefore, address our supplications to God, we who are self-convicted by our consciousness of our own sins, to chastise us rather than to abandon us; for if he abandons us, he will no longer make us his servants, who is a merciful master, but slaves of a pitiless generation: but if he chastises us in a gentle and merciful manner, as a kind ruler, he will correct our offences, sending that correcting conviction, his own word, into our hearts, by means of which he will heal them; reproving us and making us ashamed of the wickednesses which we have committed. (147) On this account the law-giver says, "Every word which a widow or a woman who is divorced vows against her own soul shall remain against it."[46] For if we call God the husband and father of the universe, supplying the origin and generation of all things, we shall be speaking rightly: as we shall if we call that heart widowed and divorced from God which

either has not received divine seed, or, after having received it, has again voluntarily made it abortive. (148) Therefore every thing which it decides it shall decide against itself: and these things shall remain utterly incurable.

For how can it be anything but a most intolerable evil, for a creature which is inconstant and easily moved in every direction, to lay down any positive decision and determination about itself, attributing to itself the virtues of the Creator? One of which is that, according to which, it defines in an unhesitating and unalterable manner. (149) Therefore, not only shall it be widowed of knowledge, but it shall likewise be divorced from it. And the meaning of this expression is as follows:—For the soul which is widowed of, but is not yet divorced from, what is good, is able, in a manner, after long perseverance, to come to a reconciliation and agreement with her lawful husband, right-reason. But the soul which has once been utterly separated from it, and which has been utterly separated from it, and which has been removed to a different abode, has been cast out for ever and ever, as utterly incapable of reconciliation or peace, and is entirely unable to return to its previous habitation.

XLI. (150) This, then, may be enough to say about the expression, "My crime is too great to be forgiven."[47]

Let us now consider what follows that verse— Cain says, "But if thou castest me out this day from off the face of the earth, and from thy face I shall be hidden."[48] What sayest thou, my good man? If thou art utterly cast out from the whole earth, shall you still be hidden? In what manner? (151) For shall you be able to live? or are you ignorant of this, that nature has given animals different places to live in, and has not assigned the same place to them all? She has allotted the sea to the fishes, and to the whole race of aquatic animals, and the land to all the terrestrial animals. And man too, according, at least, to the composite nature of his body, is a terrestrial animal. And it is owing to this that all animals easily die when they have quitted the place which properly belongs to them, and have gone, as it were, into a foreign country; as, for instance, when terrestrial animals go under the water, or when aquatic animals have sailed out upon the land.

(152) If, therefore you, being a man, should be cast out from the land, whither will you turn? Will you dive under water, imitating the nature of aquatic animals? But you will die the moment that you are underneath the water. Or will you take

---

47This is not the translation given in the text of the Bible, though it is inserted in the margin. In the text of the Bible we read, "And Cain said unto the Lord, my punishment is greater than I can bear."—Genesis 4:13.
48Genesis 4:14.

wings and raise yourself aloft, and so attempt to traverse the regions of the air, changing your character of a terrestrial, for that of a flying animal? But, if it is in your power, change and re-fashion the divine impress that you bear. You cannot do so. For in proportion as you raise yourself to a greater height, so much the more rapidly will you descend from that higher region and with the greater impetuosity to the earth, which is your appropriate place.

XLII. (153) Can a man, then, or any other created animal, hide himself from God? Where can he do so? Where can he hide himself from that being who pervades all places, whose look reaches to the very boundaries of the world, who fills the whole universe, of whom not even the smallest portion of existing things is deficient? And what is there extraordinary in the fact, that it is not practicable for any created being to conceal himself from the living God, when it is not even in his power to escape from all the material elements by which he is surrounded, but he must, if he abandon me, by that very act enter into another? (154) At all events, if the Creator, employing that act by which he created amphibious animals, had chosen also by the same act to create a new animal, one capable of living in any element, then, this animal, if it forsook the weighty elements of earth and water, would necessarily have gone to those which are naturally light, namely, air and fire. And, on the other hand, supposing that it had originally dwelt among those elements whose place is on high, if it had sought to effect a migration from them, it would have changed to the opposite region; for it was at all events necessary for it to appear steadily in one portion of the world, since it was not possible for it to run away out of every element: since, in order that nothing external might be omitted, the Creator scattered the whole of the four principles of everything over the universe, in order to create the existing condition of the world, in order to make a most perfect universe of perfect parts.

(155) As therefore it is impossible for any one to escape from the whole of the creation of God, how can it be anything but still more impossible to escape from the Creator and Ruler himself? Let no one therefore too easily receiving these words in their obvious and literal acceptation without examination, affix his own simplicity and folly to the law; but let him rather consider what is here enigmatically intimated by figurative expressions, and so understand the truth.

XLIII. (156) Perhaps now that which is intimated by the expression, "If thou castest me out this day from off the face of the earth, from thy face I shall be hidden," may be this, if thou dost not bestow on me the good things of the earth, I will not receive those of Heaven; and if no use

and enjoyment of pleasure is afforded me, I have no desire for virtue, and if thou dost not allow me to participate in human advantages, thou mayest retain the divine ones to thyself. (157) Now the things which among us are accounted necessary and valuable and genuine real goods are these; to eat, to drink, to be clothed in favourite colours and fashions; by means of the faculty of sight, to be delighted with pleasant sights; by means of one's faculty of hearing to be delighted with melodies of all sorts of sounds; to be gratified through our nostrils with fragrant exhalations of odours; to indulge in all the pleasures of the belly and of the parts adjacent to the belly to satiety; not to be indifferent to the acquisition of silver and gold; to be invested with honours and post of authority, and all other things which may tend to man's reputation; but as for prudence, or fortitude, or justice, austere dispositions which only make life laborious, those we pass by, and if we are forced to admit them into one calculation we must do so, not as perfect goods in themselves, but only as efficients of good.

(158) Do you therefore, O ridiculous man, affirm that if you are deprived of a superfluity of bodily advantages and external good things, you will not come into the sight of God? But I tell you that even if you are so deprived of them, you will by all means come into his sight; for when you have been released from the unspeakable bonds of the body and around the body, you will attain to an imagination of the uncreated God.

XLIV. (159) Do you not see in the case of Abraham that, "when he had left his country, and his kindred, and his father's house," [49] that is to say, the body, the outward senses, and reason, he then began to become acquainted with the powers of the living God? for when he had secretly departed from all his house, the law says that, "God appeared unto him," [50] showing that he is seen clearly by him who has put off mortal things, and who has taken refuge from this body in the incorporeal soul; (160) on which account Moses taking his tent "pitches it without the tabernacle," [51] and settles to dwell at a distance from the bodily camp, for in that way alone could he hope to become a worthy suppliant and a perfect minister before God. And he says that this tent was called the tent of testimony, taking exceeding care that it may really be the tabernacle of the living God, and may not be called so only.

For of virtues, the virtues of God are founded in truth, existing according to his essence: since God alone exists in essence, on account of which

---

[49] Genesis 12:1.
[50] Genesis 12:7.
[51] Exodus 33:7.

fact, he speaks of necessity about himself, saying, "I am that I am,"[52] as if those who were with him did not exist according to essence, but only appeared to exist in opinion.

But the tent of Moses being symbolically considered, the virtue of man shall be thought worthy of appellation, not of real existence, being only an imitation, a copy made after the model of that divine tabernacle, and consistent with these facts is the circumstance that Moses when he is appointed to be the God of Pharaoh, was not so in reality, but was only conceived of as such in opinion, "for I know that it is God who gives and bestows favours, (161) but I am not able to perceive that he is given, and it is said in the sacred scriptures, "I give thee as a God to Pharaoh," and yet what is given is the patient, not the agent; but he that is truly living must be the agent, and beyond all question cannot be the patient.

(162) What then is inferred from these facts? Why, that the wise man is called the God of the foolish man, but he is not God in reality, just as a base coin of the apparent value of four drachmas is not a four drachma piece. But when he is compared with the living God, then he will be found to be a man of God; but when he is compared with a foolish man, he is accounted a God to the imagination and in appearance, but he is not so in truth and essence.

XLV. (163) Why then do you talk nonsense, saying, "If thou castest me forth from off the earth, and from thee I shall be hidden." For one might say on the contrary, if I remove thee from the earth by part of thee, then I will manifestly show thee my own image. And a proof of this is, thou wilt depart from before the face of God, but when thou hast departed thou wilt not the less inhabit thy earthly body. For Moses says, afterwards, "And Cain went forth from before the face of God and dwelt in the earth,"[53] so that when thou art cast out from the earth, thou art not hidden from the living God; but when thou desertest him thou takest refuge on earth in a mortal country. (164) And indeed it will not be the case, that every one who findeth thee will hide thee, as thou sayest, speaking sophistically. For that which is found, is found in every case by two people, by one who resembles itself, or by one who is dissimilar. By one who resembles itself according to the kindred and relationship which exists in all things, and by him who is not like, according to the contrary unlikeness.

The one, therefore, that is like, endeavours to preserve that which resembles itself, and that which is dissimilar endeavours to destroy that which differs from it. (165) And let them know that Cain, and all other wicked men will not be slain by any one who meets them, but that evil doers imitating their kindred and connected wickednesses, will become guardians and preservers of them; but all those who have cultivated prudence or any other virtue, will destroy them if they can, as irreconcileable enemies. For, in short, all bodies and all things are preserved by the things which are akin to and attached to them, but are destroyed by those that are alien and hostile to them. (166) On this account, also, the oracle which bears testimony against this pretended simplicity of Cain, says, "You do not think as you say." For you say, indeed, that whosoever finds out the devices of your act will slay you. But you know that it is not every one who will do so, as there are millions of men enrolled in your alliance; but he only who is a friend to virtue and an irreconcileable enemy to you. And God says, he "who slays Cain shall suffer sevenfold." But I do not know what analogy this real meaning of this expression bears to the literal interpretation of it, "He shall suffer sevenfold. For he has not said what is to be sevenfold, nor has he described the sort of penalty, nor by what means such penalty is excused or paid.

XLVI. (167) Therefore, one must suppose that all these things are said figuratively and allegorically; and perhaps what God means to set before us here is something of this sort. (168) The irrational part of the soul is divided into seven parts, the senses of seeing, of smelling, of hearing, of tasting, and of touch, the organs of speech, and the organs of generation. If, therefore, any one were to slay the eighth, that is to say, Cain, the ruler of them all, he would also paralyse all the seven. For they are all confirmed by the vigorous strength of the mind, and they all feel weak simultaneously with any weakness exhibited by the mind, and they all endure relaxation and complete dissolution in consequence of the destruction which complete wickedness brings upon them.

(169) Now these seven senses are unpolluted and pure in the soul of the wise man, and here also they are found worthy of honour. But in that of the foolish man they are impure and polluted, and as I said before, punished, that is, they are worthy of punishment and chastisement. (170) At all events, when the Creator determined to purify the earth by means of water, and that the soul should receive purification of all its unspeakable offences, having washed off and effaced its pollutions after the fashion of a holy purification, he recommended him who was found to be a just man, who was not borne away by the violence of the deluge, to enter into the ark, that is to say, into the vessel containing the soul, namely, the body, and to lead into it "seven of all clean beasts, male and female,"[54] thinking it proper that virtuous reason

[52] Exodus 3:14.
[53] Genesis 4:16.
[54] Genesis 7:2.

should employ all the pure parts of the irrational portion of man.

XLVII. (171) And this injunction which the law-giver laid down, is of necessity applicable to all wise men; for they have their sense of sight purified, their sense of hearing thoroughly examined, and so on with all the rest of their outward senses. Accordingly, they have the faculty of speech free from all spot or stain, and their appetites which prompt them to indulge the passions in a state of due subjection to the law. (172) And every one of the seven outward senses is in one respect male, and in another, female. For when they are station-ary, or when it is in motion, they are stationary while quiescent in sleep, and they are in motion while they are energising in their waking state; and the one in accordance with habit and tranquillity, as being subject to passion, is called the female; and the one which exists according to motion and energy, as one that is only conceived in action, is called the male.

(173) Thus, in the wise man, the seven senses appear to be pure; and on the contrary in the wicked man, they appear to be all liable to punish-ment. For how great a multitude of things do we imagine to be each day wrongly represented by our eyes, which go over to colours and shapes, and to things which it is not lawful to see? And how so great a multitude of things suffer similar treatment from the ears which follow all kinds of sounds? How many too are misrepresented by the organs of smelling and of taste, and by flavours and vapours, and other things led on according to innu-merable variations? (174) I say nothing of that multi-tude of persons whom the unrestrainable impetu-osity of an unbridled tongue has destroyed, or the incurable violence which leads man on to carnal connections with intemperate appetite. Cities are full, and all the earth from one side to the other, is full of these evils, in consequence of which, con-tinual and unceasing and terrible wars are set on foot among men, even in times of peace, both pub-licly and privately.

XLVIII. (175) On which account it appears to me that all men who are not utterly uneducated would choose to be mutilated and to be come blind, rather than to see what is not fitting to be seen, to become deaf rather than to hear pernicious dis-courses, and to have their tongues cut out if that were the only way to prevent their speaking things, which ought not to be spoken. (176) At all events, they say that some wise men, when they have been tortured on the wheel to make them betray secrets which are not worthy to be divulged, have bitten out their tongues, and so have inflicted on their torturers a more grievous torture than they them-selves were suffering, as they could not learn from them what they desired; and it is better to be made an eunuch than to be hurried into wickedness by the fury of the illicit passions: for all these things, as they overwhelm the soul in pernicious calamities, are deservedly followed by extreme punishments.

(177) Moses says in the next passage that the Lord God set a mark upon Cain in order to pre-vent any one who found him from slaying him; but what this mark is, he has not shown, although he is in the habit of explaining the nature of every-thing by a sign, as he does in the affairs of Egypt, where God changed his rod into a serpent, and withered the hand of Moses till it became like snow, and turned the river into blood. (178) Or may we not suppose that this mark was set upon Cain to prevent his being slain, as a token that he would never be destroyed? For he has never once men-tioned his death in the whole of the law, showing enigmatically that, like that fabulous monster Scylla, so also folly is an undying evil, which never entirely perishes, and yet which as to its capa-bility of dying receives all time, and is never wholly free from death.

And I would that the opposite event might hap-pen, that all evils might be utterly eradicated, and might endure total destruction; but as it is they are constantly budding forth, and inflict an incur-able disease on all who are once infected by them.

ON THE POSTERITY OF CAIN AND HIS EXILE†

(De Posteritate Caini)

I. (1) "And Cain went out from before the face of God, and dwelt in the land of Nod, opposite to Eden."[1] Now we may raise the question whether we are to take the expressions which occur in the books that have been handed down to us by Moses and to interpret them in a somewhat metaphorical sense, while the ideas which readily present themselves as derived from the names are very deficient in truth. (2) For if the living God has a face, and if he who desires to leave it can with perfect ease rise up and depart to another place, why do we repudiate the impiety of the Epicureans, or the godlessness of the Egyptians, or the mythical suggestions of which life is full? (3) For the face is a portion of an animal; but God is a whole, not a part: so that it becomes necessary to invent for him other parts also, a neck, and a chest, and hands, and moreover a belly, feet, and generative organs, and all the rest of the countless number of internal and external faculties. (4) And the fact of God's having passions like unto those of man follows of necessity from the fact of his having a form like that of man: since all those limbs are not superfluous and mere exuberances, but have been made by nature as assistants of the weakness of those who possess them, and she has adapted them in a manner suitable to and consistent with their natural necessities and offices. But the living God has need of nothing; so that as he does not at all require the assistance to be derived from the parts of the body, he cannot possibly have such parts at all.

II. (5) And from whence does Cain go forth? is it from the palace of the ruler of the world? But what house of God can exist perceptible by the outward senses except this world which it is impossible and impracticable to quit? For the great circle of the heaven binds round and contains within itself everything which has ever been created; and of those things which have already perished, the component parts are resolved into their original elements, and are again portioned off among those powers of the universe of which they consist, the loan which, as it were, was advanced to each, being restored back at unequal periods of time, in accor-

dance with laws previously laid down, to the nature which originally made it, whenever that nature chooses to call in its debts.

(6) Again, if any person goes out from any place, that which he leaves behind him is in a different place from that in which he now is, but if this be true it must follow that there are some portions of the universe deprived of the presence of God, who never leaves any place empty or destitute of himself, but who fills up all things for all time; (7) and if God has not a face (inasmuch as he is not bound by what may seem appropriate for created things), and if he does not exist in parts inasmuch as he surrounds all things and is not surrounded by any, it is impossible for anything to remove and depart from this world as from a city, as there is no portion of it left without.

It now remains for us, considering that none of these things are spoken of in terms of strict propriety, to turn to the allegorical system, which is dear to men versed in natural philosophy, taking the first principles of our argument from this source.

(8) If it is hard to depart from before the face and out of the sight of a mortal king, how can it be anything but extremely difficult to depart and quit the appearance of God, and to determine no longer to come into his sight. This indeed is to be left without any idea of him, and to be mutilated as to the eyes of the soul, (9) and all those who of necessity have endured this fate, being weighed down by the might of irresistible and implacable power, are objects rather for pity than for hatred; but all those who voluntarily and of deliberated purposes have rejected the living God, exceeding even the bounds of wickedness itself, for what other evil of equal weight can possibly be found? Such men should suffer not the usual punishments of evil doers, but something new and extraordinary. And surely no one could invent a more novel or more terrible penalty than a departure and flight from the presence of the Ruler of the universe.

III. (10) Accordingly God banished Adam; but Cain went forth from his presence of his own accord; Moses here showing to us the manner of each sort of absence from God, both the voluntary and the involuntary sort; but the involuntary sort as not existing in consequence of any intention on our part, will subsequently have such a remedy applied to it as the case admits of; for God

---

†Yonge's title, *A Treatise on the Posterity of Cain, the Man Wise in His own Conceit; and on the Way in Which Cain Became an Exile.*
[1]Genesis 4:16.

will raise up another offspring in the place of Abel, whom Cain slew, a male offspring for the soul which has not turned by its own intention, by name Seth, which name being interpreted means irrigation; (11) but the voluntary flight from God, as one that has taken place by deliberate purpose and intention, will await on irremediable punishment in all eternity, for as good deeds that are done in consequence of forethought and design, are better than unintentional ones, so also among offences those that are undesigned are of less heinousness than those that are premeditated.

IV. (12) Therefore punishment which is the chastiser of impious men, will await Cain who has now departed from before the face of God, but Moses will suggest to those who know God, a most excellent suggestion, to love God and to obey him, and cleave to him, for he tells men that this is the life which in truth is tranquil and lasting,[2] and he very emphatically invites us to the honour of the one being who is above all others to be beloved and honoured, bidding us cleave to him, recommending to us a continual and constant and inseparable harmony and union of friendship with him. (13) These suggestions and such as these are what he gives to the rest of the world, but he himself so insatiably desires to behold him, and to be beheld by him, that he supplicates him to display to his eye his nature of which it is impossible to form a conjecture, so that he may become acquainted with it,[3] that thus he might receive a most well-grounded certainty of knowledge that could not be mistaken, in exchange for uncertain doubts; and he will never cease from urging his desire, but even, though he is aware that he desires a matter which is difficult of attainment, or rather which is wholly unattainable, he still strives on, in no way remitting his intense anxiety, but without admitting any excuse, or any hesitation, or vacillation; using all the means in his power to gain his object.

V. (14) At all events, he will now penetrate into "the darkness where God was."[4] That is to say, into those unapproachable and invisible conceptions which are formed of the living Do. For the great Cause of all things does not exist in time, nor at all in place, but he is superior to both time and place; for, having made all created things in subjection to himself, he is surrounded by nothing, but he is superior to everything. And being superior to, and being also external to the world that he has made, he nevertheless fills the whole world with himself; for, having by his own power extended it to its utmost limits, he has connected every por-

tion with another portion according to the principles of harmony.

(15) When, therefore, the soul that loves God seeks to know what the one living God is according to his essence, it is entertaining upon an obscure and dark subject of investigation, from which the greatest benefit that arises to it is to comprehend that God, as to his essence, is utterly incomprehensible to any being, and also to be aware that he is invisible. (16) And it appears to me that the great hierophant had attained to the comprehension of the most important point in this investigation before he commenced it, when he entreated God to become the exhibitor and expounder of his own nature to him,[5] for he says, "Show me thyself;" showing very plainly by this expression that no created being is competent by himself to learn the nature of God in his essence.

VI. (17) On this account too, Abraham, when he had come unto the place which God had told him of, "On the third day, looking up, saw the place afar off."[6] What kind of place? Was it the place to which he came? And how was it still afar off, if he had already come to it? (18) But perhaps the meaning which is intended under this expression may be something like this:—The wise man, being always desirous to comprehend the nature of the Ruler of the universe, when he is proceeding along the road which leads by knowledge and wisdom, previously meets with words of God, among which he rests for a while; and though he had previously determined to proceed by some other road, he now stops and hesitates; for the eyes of his mind being opened, he sees more clearly that he had entered upon a chase after a thing which was difficult to overtake, which constantly retreated before him, and was always at a distance, and which outstripped its pursuers by placing an immeasurable distance between them. (19) You think, therefore, rightly that all the speediest things which are under heaven would appear to be standing still if compared with the rapidity of the sun, and moon, and other stars. And yet the whole heaven was made by God; and the maker always goes before that which is made. So that, of necessity, not only the other things which exist among us, but also that which has the most rapid motion of all, namely, the mind, may fall short of a proper comprehension of the great cause of all things by an undescribable distance.

But the stars, as they are themselves in motion, pass by all things that move; but, though it seems incredible, God, while standing still, outstrips everything. (20) And it is said that he, at the same moment, is close to us and at a great distance, touching us with his creative or his punishing pow-

---

[2]Deuteronomy 30:20.
[3]Exodus 33:18.
[4]Exodus 20:13.

[5]Exodus 33:12.
[6]Genesis 22:4.

ers, which are close to each individual, and yet at the same time driving away the creature to an excessive distance from his nature as existing according to its essence, so that it cannot touch him without even the unalloyed and incorporeal efforts of the intellect. (21) Therefore we sympathise in joy with those who love God and seek to understand the nature of the living, do, even if they fail to discover it; for the vague investigation of what is good is sufficient by itself to cheer the heart, even if it fail to attain the end that it desires. But we participate in indignation against that lover of himself, Cain; because he has left his soul without any conception whatever of the living God, having of deliberate purpose mutilated himself of that faculty by which alone he might have been able to see him.

VII. (22) It is worth while also to consider the wickedness into which a man who flies from the face of God is driven, since it is called a tempest. The law-giver showing, by this expression, that he who gives way to inconsiderate impulses without any stability or firmness exposes himself to surf and violent tossing, like those of the sea, when it is agitated in the winter season by contrary winds, and has never even a single glimpse of calm or tranquillity. But as when a ship having been tossed in the sea is agitated, it is then no longer fit to take a voyage or to anchor in harbour, but being tossed about hither and thither it leans first to one side and then to the other, and struggles in vain against the waves; so the wicked man, yielding to a perverse and insane disposition, and being unable to regulate his voyage through life without disaster, is constantly tossed about in perpetual expectation of an overturning of his life.

(23) But the connection of the consequence affects me in no moderate degree; for it happens that that which comes near to him who is standing still longs for tranquillity, as being something which resembles itself. Now that which stands still without any deviation is God, and that which is moved is the creature, so that he who comes near to God desires stability; but he who departs from him, as by so doing he is approaching a creature easily overturned, is borne towards that which resembles it.

VIII. (24) On this account it is written in the curses contained in scripture, "Thou shalt never rest; nor shall there be any rest for the sole of thy foot."[7] And, a little afterwards, we read that, "Thy life shall hang in doubt before them."[8] For it is the nature of the foolish man, who is always being tossed about in a manner contrary to right reason, to be hostile to tranquillity and rest, and

not to stand firmly or with a sure foundation on any doctrine whatever. (25) Accordingly he is full of different opinions at different times, and sometimes, even in the same circumstances, without any new occurrence having arisen to affect them, he will be perfectly contrary to himself,—now great, now little, now hostile, now friendly; and, in short, he will, so to say, be everything that is most inconsistent in a moment of time. And, as the law-giver says, "All his life shall hang in doubt before him;" having no firm footing, but being constantly tossed about by opposing circumstances, which drag it different ways. (26) On which account Moses says, in another place, "Cursed of God is he that hangeth on a tree;"[9] because what he ought to hang upon is God.

But such a man has, of his own accord, bound himself to the body, which is a wooden burden upon us, exchanging hope for desire and a perfect hope for the greatest of evils; for hope, being the expectation of good things, causes the mind to depend upon the bounteous God; but appetite, creating only unreasonable desires, depends on the body, which nature has made to be a sort of receptacle and abode for the soul.

IX. (27) Let these men, then, hang by their appetites as by a halter; but the wise Abraham, where he stands, comes near to God, who is also standing. For Moses says that "Abraham was standing near to God; and coming nigh unto him, he said,"[10] ... For in good truth the unalterable soul is the only thing that has access to the unalterable God; and being of such a disposition, it does really stand very near to the Divine power. (28) Therefore the oracle which was given to the allwise Moses most manifestly shows the lasting good condition and stability of the virtuous man. Now, the oracle is as follows: "And do thou thyself stand with me."[11] By which expression, two things are made clear. One, that it is the living God, who moves and turns about all other beings, being himself unchangeable and immoveable. The second is, that he makes the virtuous man a participator in his own tranquil nature. For, as I suppose, the crooked things are made straight by his straight rule; so, likewise, are the things that are in motion restrained and made stationary by the power of him who always stands still and firm.

(29) In this passage, therefore, he commands another being to stand with him: but in another place he says, "I will go down with thee to Egypt, and I will conduct thee to the end."[12] He does not say, Thou shalt go down with me. Why not?

[7]Deuteronomy 28:65.
[8]Deuteronomy 28:66.

[9]Deuteronomy 21:23.
[10]Genesis 18:22, 23.
[11]Deuteronomy 5:31.
[12]Genesis 46:4.

Because calmness and stability are the especial attributes of God; but a liability to change one's place, and every kind of motion which has a tendency to change the place, is incident to a created being. When, therefore, he invites the man to his own peculiar good, he says, "Stand thou with me:" not "I will stand with thee." For "will stand," cannot be said of God, who always stands still.

(30) But when he comes to that which is the peculiar attribute of the creature, he says, with the most perfect correctness, "I will go down with you;" for change of place is adapted to you: so that no one shall go down with me, for in me there is no changing; but whatever is consistent with me, that is to say, with rest, shall stand. And with those who go down in such a manner as to change their place (for change of place is akin to and closely connected with them), I will go down also, not indeed changing my situation as to its actual place, inasmuch as I fill every place with myself. (31) And this, too, I do through the pity which exists in rational nature, in order that it may be raised from the hell of the passions to the heavenly region of virtue; I being the guide, who also have made the road which leads to heaven, so that it may be a plain road for suppliant souls, and have shown it to them all, in order that they may not foolishly wander out of the way.

X. (32) Having, therefore, now pointed out each variety, the tranquillity of the good man, and the state of agitation in which the bad man lives, let us now consider what follows the statement which we have hitherto been examining. For Moses says that Nod, which name, being interpreted, means the tumult into which the soul has migrated, is opposite to Eden. Now Eden is a symbolical expression for correct and divine reason, on which account its interpretation is luxury; because divine reason is, above all other things, delighted with and exults among unmingled and pure, and also well filled up and complete pleasure, God, the giver of all good things, raising his virgin and undying graces upon it. But by its own intrinsic nature, the bad is always striving with the good, the unjust with the just, the wise with the foolish, and all the different species of virtue with all the different species of vice. Something like this is the meaning of the statement that Nod is opposite to Eden.

XI. (33) After he had said this he proceeds to say, "And Cain knew his wife, and she conceived and bare Enoch; and he built a city, and called the name of the city after the name of his son Enoch."[13] Is it not here reasonable to raise the question, why Cain knew his wife? for there had been no birth of any one other woman since that of Eve who was formed out of the side of the man, until the woman who is here mentioned; (34) and if any one says that Cain took his sister to wife, putting the impiety of such a connection out of the question, he will speak falsely; for Moses represents the daughters of Adam as born late. What then are we to say? As I imagine, Moses here calls his wife opinion of impious reason which it forms about things, as crowds of those who have studied philosophy do: some of them introducing the same opinions into human life, and others introducing such as are wholly at variance with one another.

(35) What then is the position of the impious man? Why, that the human mind is the measure of all things; which also they say that one of the ancient philosophers, Protagoras, used to employ, being a descendant of the folly of Cain. And from thence I conjecture that his wife, being known to him, brought forth Enoch; and the name Enoch being interpreted means, thy grace. (36) For if man is the measure of all things, then, also, all things are a grace and a free gift of the mind; so that we refer to the eye the grace of sight, to the ears that of hearing, and to each of the other external senses their appropriate object, and also to the speech and utterance do we attribute the power of speaking.

And if we judge in this manner of these things, so also do we with respect to intelligence, in which ten thousand things are comprised, such as thoughts, perceptions, designs, meditations, conceptions, sciences, arts, dispositions, and a number of other faculties almost incalculable. (37) What is it then that the gravest philosophers, who have talked in the most grandiloquent manner about divine law and the honour due to God, have determined both to say and to allow to be said, If ye have in ye a mind which is equal to God, which regulating by its own power all the good and bad things which exist among men, occasionally mingles both in certain persons, and sometimes distributes both good and bad to some in an unalloyed state; (38) and if any one accuses you of impiety, make your defence with a good courage, saying that you have been brought up very admirably by your guide and teacher, Cain, who recommended you to honour the powers that are nearest in preference to that cause which was afar off, to whom you ought to attend for many other reasons, and most especially because he showed the power of his doctrine by very evident works, having conquered Abel the expounder of the opposite doctrine, and having removed and destroyed his doctrine as well as himself. (39) But in my opinion and in that of my friends, death in the company of the pious would be preferable to life with the impious; for those who die in the company of the pious everlasting life will receive, but everlasting death will be the portion of those who live in the other way.

---

[13] Genesis 4:17.

XII. (40) But as after Cain had begotten Enoch, one of the posterity of Seth is also subsequently called Enoch, it may be well to consider, whether the two namesakes were men of different or of similar dispositions and characters. And at the same time that we examine this question let us also investigate the differences between other persons bearing the same name. For as Enoch was, so also Methusaleh and Lamech were both descendants of Cain, and they were no less the descendants of Seth also. (41) We must therefore be aware that each of the aforesaid names, being interpreted, has a double signification; for Enoch, being interpreted, means, as I have already said, "thy grace," and Methusaleh means, the sending forth of death. Lamech, again means, humiliation. Now the expression, "Thy grace," is by some persons referred to the mind that is in us; and by more learned and sounder interpreters it is referred to the mind of other persons. (42) They therefore who say that all thinking, and feeling, and speaking, are the free gifts of their own soul, utter an impious and ungodly opinion, and deserve to be classed among the race of Cain, who, though he was not able to master himself, yet dared to assert that he had absolute possession of all other things; but as for those persons who do not claim all the things in creation as their own, but who ascribe them to the divine grace, being men really noble and sprung out of those who were rich long ago, but of those who love virtue and piety, they may be classed under Seth as the author of their race. (43) The race of these men is difficult to trace, since they show a life of plotting, and cunning, and wickedness, and dissoluteness, full of passion and wickednesses, as such a life must be. For all those whom God, since they pleased him well, has caused to quit their original abode, and has transformed from the race of perishable beings to that of immortals, are no longer found among the common multitude.

XIII. (44) Having, therefore, thus distinguished the indications intended to be afforded by the name of Enoch, let us now proceed in regular order to the name of Methuselah; and this name is interpreted, a sending forth of death. Now there are two meanings contained in this word; one, that according to which death is sent to any one, and the other, that according to which it is sent away from any one. He, therefore, to whom it is sent, immediately dies, but he, from whom it is sent, lives and survives. (45) Accordingly, he who receives death is akin to Cain, who is dying as to the life in accordance with virtue; but he from whom death is sent away and kept at a distance, is most nearly related to Seth, for the good man enjoys real life. (46) And again, the name Lamech, which means humiliation, is a name of ambiguous meaning; for we are humiliated either when the

vigour of our soul is relaxed, according to the diseases and infirmities which arise from the irrational passions, or in respect of our love for virtue, when we seek to restrain ourselves from swelling self-opinions.

(47) Now the former kind of humiliation arises out of weakness, being a species of that multiform disease of many changes, leprosy. "For when his appearance seems more humble,"[14] being broken as to its level and fresh face, than the lawgiver says that that humble disease leprosy exists. (48) But the second kind of humiliation arises from the strength of perseverance, which is followed by propitiation, according to the perfect number of the decade; for the people are enjoined to humble their souls on the tenth day of the month, and this means to put away all high boasting, the putting away of which works the rejection of all offences, both voluntary and involuntary. Accordingly, the Lamech who is humbled in this sense, is the descendant of Seth, and the father of the just Noah; but he who is humbled in the former manner is the descendant of Cain.

XIV. (49) And it may become us next to consider on what account this same man is represented as founding and building a city, for it is only a multitude of men who have need of a city to dwell in; but the three who were the only human beings in existence at that time might have thought the foot of a mountain, or a small cave, a most sufficient abode. And I said, indeed, the three; but in all probability I might have spoken of him by himself; for the parents of Abel, who had been so treacherously slain, would never have endured to inhabit the same city with his murderer—a man who had committed fratricide, which is a greater pollution than even homicide.

(50) For it is plain that it is not only extraordinary, but utterly contrary to all reason, that one man should build a city. In what manner could he do it? He could not build even the most trifling portion of a house, unless he employed other men as his assistants. Would the same man be able at the same time to cut stones, to cut wood, to work in iron and in brass, and to throw the vast circumference of walls round the city? to build up propylaea, and inter-walls, and temples, and sacred precincts, and porticoes, and docks, and houses, and all the other public and private buildings which one is accustomed to find in a city? And moreover, besides all these things, would he be able to carry burdens, to move away masses of earth, to widen narrow passages, to make fountains and water-courses, and all the other things with which a city ought to be provided? (51) Perhaps, therefore, since all these ideas are inconsistent with

---

[14]Leviticus 13:3.

truth, it would be better to look upon the statement as an allegory, and to say that Cain determined to build up his own doctrine like a city.

XV. (52) Since, therefore, every city consists of houses and inhabitants, and laws, the houses, in Cain's case, are the reasons which he alleges to prove his point; by which, as from a wall, he fights against the persuasive attacks of his enemies; inventing fabulous devices against the truth. The inhabitants are the companions of impiety, ungodliness, self-love, haughtiness, falsehood, vain opinions; the men wise in their own conceit, the men who know not wisdom as relating to truth, the men who are full of ignorance, and stupidity, and folly; and all the other similar and kindred evils. The laws are, lawlessness, injustice, inequality, intemperance, boldness, folly, insolence, immoderate indulgence in pleasure, and innumerable appetites in despite of nature.

(53) Now of such a city as this, every impious man is found to be a builder in his own miserable soul, until God deliberately causes complete and great confusion to their sophistical arts. [15] And this will be, when not only "they build a city and tower, the head of which will reach to heaven," that is to say, [...] [16] the mind or the reason of each individual as conversant about making great works, which they represent as having for its head a conception peculiar to itself, which is called in symbolical language heaven. For it is plain that the head and object of every reasoning must be the aforesaid mind; for the sake of which, long digressions and sentences are in the habit of being used by men who write histories.

XVI. (54) And to such a pitch of accursed impiety have they gone, that not only do they attempt to raise up such cities by themselves, but they even compel the virtue-loving multitude of Israel to join them, appointing superintendents and teachers of evil actions to govern them. For it is said that, when they were ill-treated by the superintendents, they built three cities for the prince of the country, Peithom, Rameses, [17] and On, which is Heliopolis. (55) And these cities, if taken symbolically, mean mind, the outward sense, and the faculty of speech, which are the three principal things in us; for Peithom means speech, because persuasion *(to peithein)* arises from speech; and the interpretation of Peithom is, a mouth-uttering, since the reasoning of the wicked man comes from without, and occupies itself with endeavouring to overturn all that is good: and Rameses is the inward sense; (56) for the mind

is eaten out and destroyed by each separate one of the outward senses as by a moth, being shaken to pieces and lacerated; for the imaginations which enter it, not according to pleasure, make life itself mutilated and laborious. (57) But On is said to be a hill, and it means, symbolically, the mind; for all reasonings are stored up in the mind: and the lawgiver himself is a witness of this, calling On, Heliopolis, the city of the sun. For as the sun, when he rises, shows visibly the things which have been hidden by night, so also the mind, sending forth its own proper light, causes all bodies and all things to be seen visibly at a distance. (58) On which account, a man would not be wrong who called our minds the sun of our composition; as the mind, if it does not rise and shed its own light in man, who may be looked upon as a small world, leaves a great darkness diffused over all existing things, and suffers nothing to be brought to light.

XVII. (59) This hill Jacob, the wrestler with God, in his agreements with Laban, calls a witness, showing in a most express manner, and in the form of a precept, that the mind is a witness to each individual of the determinations which he comes to in secret; and conscience, which is the most incorruptible and truth-telling witness of all, was built before these cities; (60) for Moses says that the spies came to Chebron, and these three are Acheman, and Jesein, and Thalamein, of the sons of Enoch: and this he adds, "and Chebron was built seven years before Janis, in Egypt," [18] and these synonymous appellations are distinguished according to their species in a most natural manner.

Chebron, being interpreted, means compunction, and this is of two kinds; one with reference to the soul being joined to the body, the other with reference to its being adapted to virtue. (61) Now the soul that subjects itself to bodily compunctions has the beforementioned inhabitants. Acheman, being interpreted, means, my brother, and Jesein means "outside of me," and Thalmein means, some one in suspense; for it follows of necessity, that the body must be thought akin to the souls that love the body, and that external good things must be exceedingly admired by them, and all the souls which have this kind of disposition depend on dead things, and, like persons who are crucified, are attached to corruptible matter till the day of their death.

(62) But the soul that is united to virtue has for its inhabitants those persons who are preeminent for virtue, persons whom the double cavern has received in pairs, Abraham and Sarah, Isaac and Rebeckah, Leah and Jacob, virtues and those who possess them; Chebron itself keeping the treasure-house of the memorials of knowledge

---

[15]Genesis 11:4.

[16]There is a hiatus in the text here: Mangey translates it as if the deficiency were to be supplied by *ton noun*, "the mind."

[17]Exodus 1:11.

[18]Numbers 13:23.

and wisdom, which is more ancient than Janis and the whole land of Egypt, for nature has made the soul more ancient than the body, that is than Egypt, and virtue more ancient than vice, that is than Janis (and the name Janis, being interpreted, means the command of answer), estimating seniority rather by dignity than by length of time.

XVIII. (63) On which principle also it is that he also calls Israel, who was the younger brother in point of time, "the first born son,"[19] judging of him by his merit, signifying thereby that, since to see God is the most clear proof of primogeniture, he is in consequence pardoned as the eldest offspring of the uncreate incomprehensible God, conceived by that virtue which is hated among men, and to whom the law enjoins that "the honours due to seniority shall be paid, as being the eldest."[20]

(64) On this account also the number seven is produced in its order, subsequently to the number six, but in power it is superior to every other number, and differs not from the unit, and Moses also shows us this in the conclusion of his account of the creation, where he says, "And God ceased on the seventh day from all the works that he had made; and God blessed the seventh day, and hallowed it," because on it he ceased from all his works which God had begun to make,[21] (65) and after that he concludes his account in these words, "This is the book of the generation of heaven and of earth when they were made, on the day in which God made the heaven and the earth; and these things were done in the first day, so that the seventh day is referred to the unit which is the first day and the beginning of the whole.

I have dwelt at length on this topic, with the object of showing more plainly the opinion which Cain thought it right to build up like a city.

XIX. (66) Now the son of Enoch is called Gaidad,[22] which, being interpreted, means a flock of sheep, very consistently with what has gone before; for he who attributes everything to the mind, which is not able to comprehend even its own nature, so as to pronounce what kind of thing it is, would be very likely to beget a number of irrational powers collected into one flock; for such is not the opinion of men who are able to reason. (67) But every flock which has not a shepherd to govern it does of necessity meet with great disasters, inasmuch as it is not able, of its own power, to repel what is injurious to it, and to choose what will be advantageous; in respect of which Moses says in his prayer, "Let the Lord, the God of spir-

its and of all flesh, look out a man who shall be over this assembly, who shall go out before their faces, and who shall come in, and who shall bring them out, and who shall bring them in, and so the synagogue of the Lord shall not be like unto sheep which have no shepherd."[23] (68) For when the president, or superintendent, or father, or whatever we like to call him, of our composite body, right reason, is departed, having left the flock that is in us, it being neglected and suffered to go its own way, perishes and the loss to its master is great. But the irrational and wandering flock, being deprived of its shepherd, who ought to admonish and instruct it, strays away to a great distance from rational and immortal life.

XX. (69) On which account the son of Gaided is called Mehel, the name which, being interpreted, means, "from the life of God." For since the flock is devoid of reason, and God is the fountain of reason, it follows of necessity, that a man who lives in an irrational manner is separated from the life of God; for to live according to God is defined by Moses to consist in loving him; for Moses says to the children of Israel, "Your life is to love the living God."[24] (70) And he gives as an example of the opposite lot the goat, on which the lot falls to be the scape-goat, for he says, "He shall place it living before the Lord, that he may offer prayers over it, and send it out into the wilderness,"[25] giving these directions with great exactness. (71) For as no one in his senses would greatly extol old men for abstaining from pleasure, because old age, which is a long and incurable disease, has relaxed and enfeebled the nerves of their appetites; but one would praise young men, because, while their appetites are influenced by the vigour of youth, nevertheless they, being well supplied with instruments to check them, namely, with reasons derived from good instruction, have allayed the great conflagration and boiling over of the passions: so, in the case of these men, whom no disease is accustomed to detach from any evil way of life, less praise is due to them, because they are fortunate without any express intention of their own, according to the good fortune of their nature: but those whom such a disease does rise up against and attack, receive greater praise; if they, making a fair stand, are willing and prove able to destroy it; (72) for to be able, by a vigorous exertion, to destroy the baits of attractive pleasure, properly receives that praise which belongs to good actions, done with a deliberate purpose.

Since, therefore, [...][26] but diseases and infir-

---

[19] Exodus 4:22.
[20] Deuteronomy 21:17.
[21] Genesis 2:2.
[22] Genesis 4:18.

[23] Numbers 26:16.
[24] Deuteronomy 30:20.
[25] Leviticus 16:10.
[26] There is something lost from the text here, and Mangey professes himself unable to supply it without the

mities which have been sent against us flourish; let us endeavour to overturn and destroy them. For to offer prayers over them has nearly such an effect as this: it is confessing that, though we have them in our soul living and flourishing, we nevertheless do not yield, but make a stand against them all, and resist them vigorously, until we have entirely sent away the scape-goat and made atonement.

XXI. (73) What, then, follows a man who lives not in accordance with the will of God but the death of the soul? And this is named Methuselah, the interpretation of which name is, "the sending out of death," on which account he is the son of Mehel, who has quilted his own life, to which death is sent, that is to say the death of the soul, which is nothing else than a conversion of it by irrational passion. (74) This passion, therefore, when it has conceived, brings forth incurable diseases and infirmities with great pains, by which it is thrown down and convulsed, and humbled and tortured. For each of the diseases oppresses it, bringing upon it an unspeakable burden, such that no one is able even to raise his head beneath it. And this is named Lamech; the interpretation of which name is, "humiliation;" so that Lamech is properly represented as the son of Methuselah, being the passion of the death of the soul, humble, yielding, an infirmity which is the offspring of irrational desire.

XXII. (75) "And Lamech took to himself two wives; the name of the one was Adah, and the name of the other was Zillah."[27] Everything which a wicked man taketh himself is altogether blameable, as being polluted by his impure mind; and so, on the contrary, all deliberate actions of virtuous men are praise-worthy; on which account now, Lamech, who is taking wives unto himself, is choosing the greatest possible evils. Again, when Abraham, Jacob, and Aaron take to themselves wives, they choose appropriate good things to dwell with. (76) Now Moses speaks thus in the case of Abraham: "And Abraham and Nachor took unto themselves wives; the name of Abraham's wife was Sarai."[28] And in the case of Jacob he says, "Rise up and go into Mesopotamia, to the house of Bethuel, thy mother's father, and take unto thyself a wife from thence of the daughters of Laban thy mother's brother."[29] In the case of Aaron he says, and Aaron took Elizabeth, the daughter of Aminadab, the sister of Naassom, unto him to be his wife."[30] (77) Isaac too and Moses take unto themselves wives, but they do not take them of

their own act entirely; but Isaac, "When he went into the house of his mother,"[31] is said to have taken a wife; and to Moses, "The man with whom he lodged gave his daughter Zipporah to be his wife."[32]

XXIII. (78) Now it is not without a purpose that the differences between these persons are recorded by the lawgiver. For in the case of those who practise virtue and improve, and become better, their deliberate choice of the good bears testimony that their labour shall not be dismissed without its reward; but in the case of those who are endued with self-taught and naturally implanted wisdom, it follows that reason is betrothed to them not by their own act, but by God, and that they take unto themselves knowledge, the fitting companion through life of the wise. (79) But he who is wholly devoted to the things of ordinary men, the lowly and grovelling-minded Lamech, first of all takes for his wife Adah, which name being interpreted, means "witness," having been his own manager of this marriage. For he thinks that Leah, which means the motion and passage out of the mind according to easy perceptions, without anything interfering to hinder its easy comprehension of all things, is the first good for man. (80) "For what," says he, "could be better than that one's thoughts, one's contemplations, one's conjectures, one's suspicions, in a word, all one's ideas, should, as I may say, proceed on well-set feet, so as to arrive at their desired goal without stumbling, the mind being borne witness to in everything that is uttered." But I, if any man employs a felicitous and well directed mind to good objects only, account that man happy taking the law for my teacher in this view. For the law called Joseph "a prosperous man,"[33] not in all things, but "in those matters in which God gave him prosperity." And all the gifts of God are good. (81) But if any one uses the acuteness and readiness of his nature, not solely for virtuous objects, but also for opposite purposes, being himself indifferent in a matter which is not indifferent, he should be accounted unhappy. At all events, it is said, in the manner of a curse, in the place where mention is made of the confusion of tongues, "And now nothing will be restrained from them of all the things which they have imagined to do."[34]

For in truth it is an irremediable calamity for the soul to be prosperous in whatever it undertakes, when its undertakings are disgraceful. (82) But I should pray, if ever I had a design to commit injustice, that I might fail in my iniquity; and if I had a wish to live in a manner unbecoming a man,

---

assistance of some MS. which may be hereafter discovered.

[27] Genesis 4:19.
[28] Genesis 11:29.
[29] Genesis 28:2.
[30] Exodus 6:23.

[31] Genesis 24:67.
[32] Exodus 2:21.
[33] Genesis 39:3.
[34] Genesis 11:6.

that I might fail in my intemperance; and if I wished to conduct myself with boldness and unscrupulous wickedness, that my failure in such boldness and unscrupulous wickedness might be complete: unless in the case of those who have determined to steal, or to commit adultery, or to murder, it is not an advantage to find their purposes in all these matters fail and become abortive.

XXIV. (83) Do thou, therefore, O my mind, avoid Adah, who bears witness to evil things, and who is borne witness to on each of its attempts at such things. And if you think fit to take her as a partner, she will bring forth to you the greatest possible evil, namely, Jubal,[35] the interpretation of which name is "changing;" for if you are delighted with any chance testimony, you will become desirous to upset and overturn every thing, changing the limits which have been affixed by nature to every thing. (84) And Moses is very indignant with such people as these, and curses them, saying, "Cursed is he that removeth his neighbour's landmark."[36] And what he means by one's neighbours, and that which is near to a man, is the good. "For it is not good," says he, "to depart to the heave, nor to go beyond the sea,"[37] in the search after what is good; for that stand near to, and close by, each individual.

(85) And he divides the good by a threefold division, speaking most strictly in accordance with natural philosophy. "For it is," says he, "in thy mouth, and in thy heart, and in they hands;" that is to say, in thy words, and in thy intentions, and in thy actions; for these are the component parts of the good, of which it is naturally compounded. So that the want of one portion does not only make the whole incomplete, but does entirely destroy it; (86) for of what use is it to say what is excellent, but to think and to do what is most shameful? This is the way of the sophists. For those who make long speeches about prudence and perseverance, annoy the ears even of those who are very fond of hearing good conversation; and yet, in their designs and in the actions of their lives they are found to err. (87) And what is the use of entertaining such sentiments as are proper, but acting and speaking most improperly, and injuring by your actions all who are exposed to the effect of them? Again, it is blameworthy even to do what is right, without any intention or reason; (88) for what is done without these is a portion of involuntary conduct, and is on no account, and under no circumstances to be praised; but if it were to happen that, as in the case of a lyre, so all the sounds of the good could be adapted to any man, and that we

could make the conversation agree with the intention, and the intention with the action; then such a man would be considered perfect and really well constituted. So that he who removes the landmarks of the good is justly accursed, and is justly spoken of as such.

XXV. (89) But it is not our creation that has established these boundaries, but reasons, which are older than we, or than any thing upon the earth; and which, moreover, are divine. In accordance with which the law also has declared the same thing, charging every one of us not to adulterate the coinage of virtue, in these words, "Thou shalt not remove thy neighbour's landmark which thy fathers established."[38] And in another passage he says, "Ask thy father, and he will tell thee; ask thy elders, and they will make it known to thee, how the Most High, when he divided the nations, dispersed the sons of Adam, and fixed the boundaries of the nations according to the number of the angels of God. And the portion of the Lord was his people Jacob, the limitation of the inheritance of Israel."[39]

(90) Shall I then inquire of the father who begat me and brought me up, or of those who are his contemporaries, but older than I am? or has God divided the nations, or sown them, or settled them in the land? and will they answer me accurately how this was done, as if they had been present at every division? Surely not. For they will say, We also in our youth were fond of inquiring of our parents and of those who were older than we, and learnt nothing certain; for they had nothing to tell us, and they again professed themselves pupils of those who knew, since they themselves were ignorant.

XXVI. (91) Perhaps, therefore, it is the right reason of our souls that he calls their father, and its companions and friends that he calls elders. These are they who first established the boundaries of virtue, to whom it is worth while to become pupils for the sake of learning and instruction in necessary things. And what is necessary is as follows. When God was dividing and drawing a wall between the nations of the soul, separating those who spoke different languages; and when establishing the sons of the earth in their abodes, he dispersed them and removed to a distance from himself those whom he called the sons of Adam; then he fixed the boundaries of the offspring of virtue, making them equal in number to the angels; for as many angels of God as there are, so many nations and species of virtue are there.

(92) What, then, are the portions of his angels, and what is that share which is the inheritance of

---

[35] Genesis 4:20.
[36] Deuteronomy 27:17.
[37] Deuteronomy 30:12.

[38] Deuteronomy 19:14.
[39] Deuteronomy 32:7.

the ruler and governor of all? The portion of those ministers are the specific virtues; but the portion of the ruler of all its his chosen people Israel. For he who sees God, being led on by his most surpassing beauty, has his inheritance and portion assigned to him in that which he sees. (93) How, then, can we do any thing but blame Jubal, whose name being interpreted into the Greek language, means one who (*metalloiōn ē metapoiōn*) changes or alters the natures of things? For those most divine beauties of prudence, and fortitude, and justice, and other virtues, he did change for the opposite impressions of folly, and intemperance, and injustice, and all wickedness, effacing all the impressions which had previously been stamped upon the natures of things.

XXVII. (94) For it is always the case that if a second impression is stamped upon any thing, the mark of any previous one is effaced. But the impression which is thus made is so far from permitting evil things to be taken in exchange for what is good, that it does not allow even what is beautiful to be taken in exchange for what is laborious; but looking upon what is laborious (*ponēron*) as evil, since it would be downright folly not to discard what is bad for the sake of the acquisition of what is better, but only taking (*ponēros*) to be equivalent to *epiponos* or *kamatēros*, in which sense, indeed, the Attic writers use the word when they mark the first syllable with an acute, thus, *ponēros*.

(95) Now the precept is of this kind, "Of every thing which passeth under the rod, the tenth is sacred to the Lord; thou shalt not exchange good for bad, and if thou dost exchange, both the thing itself and that for which it is exchanged shall be sacred,"[40] and yet how can that which is evil possibly be sacred? The truth is that, as I said, he means here what is laborious, not what is bad; so that what is really intended is something of this kind:—The honourable is a perfect good, but labour is an imperfect advantage. If therefore you acquire what is perfect, you need no longer seek what is deficient; but if with an excessive superfluity you choose still to continue labouring, then know that you will appear to be exchanging one thing for another, but in reality you will be acquiring both, for even if both are of equal value they nevertheless are not completely whole.

XXVIII. (96) But a thing which is sacred is proved to be so by three witnesses, the middle number, education, and perfect number. On which account it is said, "Of everything which cometh in the number under the rod, the tenth is sacred," for that which is not accounted worthy of being comprehended under number is profane, not sacred; but that which is according to number is approved, as having been already tested. Accordingly the law says, that the corn which was collected in Egypt by Joseph could not be counted,"[41] and adds, "for it was without number," since the things which nourish the body and the Egyptian passions, are utterly unworthy to be included in any calculation.

(97) But the rod is the symbol of education, for without being looked at sternly, and chastised for some causes, it is impossible for any one to be admonished and corrected to any good purpose; but the number ten is a confirmation of that perfection which takes place in accordance with improvement, with which he must begin who having brought forth an offspring educated it, and brought forth the wished-for fruit to maturity.

XXIX. (98) Thus much it may be sufficient to say concerning him who changes and adulterates the ancient coinage, whom Moses also calls the father "of those that dwell in the tents of those who fed cattle." Now by cattle here he means the irrational and outward senses, and by those who feed cattle he means the worshippers of pleasure and indulgences of the passions, who supply these senses with their external objects by way of food, and are a long way removed from shepherds. For some, like rulers, chastise those of their flocks who are unruly; but others, like entertainers or masters of a feast, supply them with unlimited food, and give them fearlessness as to the consequences of their sins; for it follows of necessity that such men are at once victims of insatiable appetite, and of insolence, the daughter of satiety; (99) accordingly, he who re-fashions and changes all honourable things in a seemly and natural manner, is the father of those who pursue every object of the outward sense, and all other inanimate objects; for if he had pursued the incorporeal natures which are accessible only to the intellect, he would have preserved those boundaries marked out by his elders, which they established as a defence to virtue, stamping each appearance of virtue with its own appropriate image.[42]

XXX. (100) And Jabal's brother, he says, was Jubal,[43] and the interpretation of this latter name is "inclining," being symbolically speech according to utterance; for this is naturally the brother of intellect; and it is with extraordinary propriety that he called the conversation of that intellect which changes affairs, "inclining," for it agrees after a fashion and harmonizes with both, as the equivalent weight does in a scale, or as a vessel which is tossed by the sea inclines first to one side and

---

[40]Leviticus 27:32.

[41]Genesis 41:49.
[42]Deuteronomy 27:2.
[43]Genesis 4:21.

then to the other, from the violence of the waves; for the foolish man has not learnt how to say anything firm or stable.

(101) But Moses does not think it right to incline either to the right or to the left, or in short to any part of the earthly Edom; but rather to proceed along the middle way, which he with great propriety calls the royal road,[44] for since God is the first and only God of the universe, so also the road to him, as being the king's road, is very properly denominated royal; and this royal road you must consider to be philosophy, not that philosophy which the existing sophistical crowd of men pursues (for they, studying the art of words in opposition to truth, have called crafty wickedness, wisdom, assigning a divine name to wicked action), but that which the ancient company of those men who practised virtue studied, rejecting the persuasive juggleries of pleasure, and adopting a virtuous and austere study of the honourable—(102) this royal road, which we have stated to be true and genuine philosophy, the law calls the word and reason of God; for it is written, "Thou shalt not turn aside from the word which I command thee this day, to the right hand nor to the left," So that it is shown most manifestly that the word of God is identical with the royal road, since Moses' words are not to depart either from the royal road, or from this word, as if the two were synonymous, but to proceed with an upright mind along the middle and level road, which leads one aright.

XXXI. (103) "Now this Jubal," says Moses, "is the father who showed men the use of the psaltery and of the harp."[45] He in the strictest consistency with nature calls distinctly uttered language the father of music and of all the instruments used in music; for nature, having given the organ of voice to animals as the first and most perfect of organs, afterwards gave to this organ all the harmonies, and all the different kinds of melodies, in order that it might be a previously made model for those organs which are hereafter to be made by art. (104) And as he made an ear spherical, fashioning lesser circles in their greater ones and framing it as in a lathe, with the object of preventing the sounds of the voice which come from without from being wasted and dissipated, so that the voice when collected together and closely packed within the circle might, by a sort of diffusion of the power of hearing, be poured over the different channels of the principal part. And this immediately served as a model for those theatres which are found in handsome cities; so that the shape of a theatre is skilfully dictated by the mechanism of the ear.

So also, nature, which formed animals, stretching the rough artery like a musical canon, and wearing beneath the harmonic and chromatic and diatonic kinds of sounds, according to the innumerable variations of combined and separated melodies, made a model in accordance with which every musical instrument might be made.

XXXII. (105) Perhaps, at all events, flutes and lyres, and similar instruments which utter melodies, are as far inferior to the music of nightingales or swans as a thing made after a model, and an imitation must be from the archetypal model, or a perishable species from an imperishable genus; for it is not fitting to compare the music of man with that of any other animal, since it has an especial privilege with which it is honoured, namely, articulate distinctness of speaking; (106) for all other animals, having a broken utterance in their voice, by this and by an incessant change of tones alone give pleasure to our ears. But man, being furnished by nature with the means not only of speaking but also of singing articulately, charms both the sense of hearing and the mind, soothing the one with his song and influencing the other with ideas; (107) for, as an instrument, if it be given into the hands of a man who has no skill as a musician, is inharmonious, but if given to a musician it becomes harmonious according to the skill that is in him. So in the same manner speech, when put in motion by a worthless mind, is inharmonious; but, when it is put in motion by a virtuous mind, it is found to be very melodious. (108) A lyre, indeed, or any similar instrument, if it be not struck by some one, is silent; and speech, too, if it be not struck by the principal part, that is to say, the mind, is of necessity tranquil. And, again, as musical instruments are transposed and adapted to an infinite number of mixtures of airs, so also speech corresponds to them, becoming an interpreter of things; (109) for who would converse in a similar manner with parents and children, being by nature the slave of the one, and by birth the master of the others? And who, again, would talk in the same manner to brothers or cousins; or, in short, to near and to distant relations? Who, again, could do so to friends and to strangers, to fellow citizens and to foreigners, though there may be no great difference in point of fortune, or nature, or age between them? For one must behave differently while associating with an old man and with a young one; and, again, with a man of high reputation and a humble man, with a servant and a master; and, again, with a woman and a man, and with an illiterate and a clever man. (110) And why need one cite an incredible variety of persons to whom speech varies itself, so as at one time to assume one character and at another time another? For it would not interpret great things and small, numerous things and rare, private and public mat-

---

[44] Numbers 20:17.
[45] Genesis 4:21.

ters, sacred and profane affairs, or old and new events in the same manner; but would use, in each case, language appropriate to the number, or importance, or magnitude of the affairs under discussion; at one time elevating itself to a lofty style, and at another time, on the contrary, confining and humbling itself.

(111) But as circumstances and persons give varieties to speech, so also do the causes of things and the manner in which they are done; and, moreover, those points especially with which everything is concerned, namely, time and place. Very beautifully, therefore, is he who inclines voices, namely Jubal, called "the father of the psaltery and of the harp," from a portion of the whole science of music, as has been shown already.

XXXIII. (112) The descendants, therefore, of Adah, and what she herself is, have now been explained. Let us consider next the other wife of Lamech, Zillah, and what she brings forth. Zillah, then, being interpreted, means "shadow," a symbol of the equalities of the body and of the external good things, which, in their real essence, are in no way better than a shadow. Is not beauty a shadow, which, after it has flourished for a brief time, withers away? And are not strength and activity of body shadows, which any chance disease can destroy? And the organs of the external senses, and the accuracy of their use, which any sudden cold may obstruct, or old age, that inevitable and common disease of all men, may impair, are not they shadows? And, again, are not riches and glory, and authority and honours, and all the external circumstances which are accounted goods, are not they, I say, all shadows? (113) But one ought to lead the mind, as if by the steps of a flight of stairs, up to the origin of everything.

Men in the rank of those who are considered illustrious have gone to Delphi, who have consecrated their happy lives to the service of that place, and like writings which have become effaced, not only in consequence of the lapse of ages but also by the vicissitudes which time brings bout, they have then expired [...] [46] There are some again whom the impetuosity of an overflowing torrent, as it were, has suddenly extinguished and carried away. (114) From all these shadows, then, and all these unsubstantial dreams a son is born, whom his parents called Tubal (this name being interpreted means "all"). For they with great wisdom laying it down (instead of those things which are accounted good things by the multitude) that competency combined with good health is happiness, consider that in that is united everything great or small, in short everything. (115) But if there were

any such thing as an absolutely independent authority added, then becoming full of arrogant domination, and elated with vanity and false opinions, forgetting themselves and the contemptible material of which they are composed, they look upon themselves as composed of a more valuable material than the composition of man admits of; and becoming swollen with pride, they think themselves worthy of even divine honours. At all events, before now some persons have ventured to say, that they "do not know the true God," [47] forgetting their own human nature, by reason of the immoderate excess of corporeal and external things [...] and each imagining [...] [48]

XXXIV. (116) Then Moses says, "He was a hammer-beater and forger of brass and iron:" [49] for the soul of that man who is intent on corporeal pleasures or external things is beaten by a hammer, like a piece of iron on an anvil, being drawn out according to the long and thin-drawn extensions of the appetites. Accordingly, you may see men fond of their bodies at every time, and in every place laying lines and nets to catch those objects that they desire; and others, who are lovers of money or covetous of glory, letting loose their desire and eagerness for those things to the furthest boundaries of earth and sea, and dragging in from all quarters by their unlimited desires, as if by so many nets, whatever can gratify them, till the excessive tension, being broken by its great violence, drags back those who are dragging at it, and throws them down headlong. (117) All these men are causes of war, on account of which they are said to be workers in brass and iron, by means of which metals wars are carried on. For if any one contemplates the history of the greatest public or private quarrels that have arisen among men and among cities, he will not be wrong if [...] [50] he looks upon all of them, whether upon those which took place long ago, or upon those which are now raging, or on all that will ever arise hereafter, as being caused either by the beauty of a woman, or by a love of money, or, in short, by some desire for the excessive indulgence of the body, and for some superfluity of external things: (118) but no foreign war and no civil war has ever existed for the sake of instruction or virtue, which are the good things of the mind, which is the best part of us; for these things are in their nature peaceful, and by them good laws and tranquil stability, and whatever else is most beautiful to the sharp-seeing eyes of the soul, not to the dim perceptions of the body, are seen to be established.

---

[46]There is an hiatus in the text in this sentence. I have followed Mangey's Latin translation.

[47]Exodus 5:2.
[48]Another hiatus occurs here.
[49]Genesis 4:22, where he is called Tubalcain.
[50]Here again there is an hiatus in the text.

For the perceptive powers of the body look only upon the external surface, but the eye of the mind penetrates within, and going deep down surveys all the interior and hidden things which are removed out of the reach of bodily sight. (119) And nearly all the troubles, and confusions, and enmities which arise among men, are about absolutely nothing, but about what is really a shadow: for Moses called Tubal the son of Zillah, that is to say of shadow, the maker of the warlike instruments of brass and iron, speaking philosophically, and being guided not by verbal technicalities, but by the exceeding propriety of the names; for he knew that every naval and every land expedition chooses to encounter the greatest dangers for the sake of bodily pleasures, or with a view to obtain a superfluity of external good things, of which nothing is firm or solid, as is testified by the history of time, which brings all things to proof: for they are like superficial sketches, being in themselves perishable and of no duration.

XXXV. (120) Moses proceeds to say, that Tubal's sister was Noeman, the interpretation of which name is "fatness." For it follows that those who pursue a luxurious condition of the body, and the other objects which I have mentioned, do get fat when they obtain any of the things that they desire: but such fatness as this I lay down as not strength but weakness; for it teaches a man to depart from the honour due to God, which is the first and most excellent power of the soul: (121) and the law is a witness to this which in the great hymn speaks thus—"He was fat, he was rich, he was exceeding broad, and he forsook God who had made him, and he forgot God his Saviour."[51] For in truth those men whose lives have been exceedingly fortunate and are so at the time, do not remember the eternal God, but they think time their god; (122) on which account Moses bears witness, exhorting us to war against the contrary opinions, for he says, "The time has departed from them, and the Lord is among us."[52]

So that those men by whom the life of the soul is honoured, have divine reason dwelling among them, and walking with them; but those who pursue a life of pleasure have only a brief and fictitious want of opportunities: these men, therefore, having swollen extravagantly, and become enormously distended by their profuse fatness and luxury, have burst asunder. But the others, being made fat by that wisdom which nourishes the souls that love virtue, have a firm and unshaken power, a specimen of which is the fat which is sacrificed as a whole burnt-offering from every victim: (123) for Moses says, "All the fat shall belong to the Lord

by the everlasting law;"[53] so that the fat of the mind is offered up to God and is appropriated to him, owing to which it is made immortal; but the fat which clings to the body and belongs to external things is referred to time, which is contrary to God, through which it very rapidly wastes away.

XXXVI. (124) Therefore, concerning the wives of Lamech and his children, I think that enough has been said. Let us now consider what we may look upon as the resurrection of Abel, who was treacherously slain.

Moses tells us, "And Adam knew his wife Eve, and she conceived and brought forth a son, and he called his name Seth; for, said he, "God has raised me up another seed instead of Abel, whom Cain slew."[54] The interpretation of the name Seth, is "irrigation." (125) As, therefore, the seeds and plants which are put into the ground grow and blossom through being irrigated, and are thus made fertile for the production of fruits, but if they are deprived of moisture they wither away, so likewise the soul, as it appears when it is watered with the wholesome stream of wisdom, shoots forth, and brings fruit to perfection. (126) Now, irrigation may be looked upon in a two-fold light: with regard to that which irrigates, and with regard to that which is irrigated. And might one not say that each of the outward senses is irrigated by the mind as by a fountain, which widens and extends all their faculties, as if they were so many channels for water? No one, therefore, in his senses would say, that the eyes see, but that the mind sees by means of the eyes; or that the ears hear, but that the mind hears by the instrumentality of the ears; or that the nostrils smell, but that the predominant part of man smells through the medium of the nostrils.

XXXVII. (127) On which account it is said in Genesis, "And a fountain went up from the earth, and watered all the face of the earth."[55] For since nature has allotted the most excellent portion of the whole body, namely the face, to the outward senses, therefore the fountain which goes up from the superior part, being diffused over various parts, and sending up its streams like so many watercourses as high as the face, by their means conducts the faculties to each of the organs of the outwards senses. In this way in truth, it is that the word of God irrigates the virtues; for that is the beginning and the fountain of all good actions. (128) And the lawgiver shows this, when he says, "And a river went out of Eden to water the Paradise; and from thence it is divided into four heads."[56]

For there are four generic virtues: prudence,

---

[51]Deuteronomy 32:15.
[52]Numbers 14:9.

[53]Leviticus 3:16.
[54]Genesis 4:25.
[55]Genesis 2:6.
[56]Genesis 2:10.

courage, temperance, and justice. And of these, every single one is a princess and a ruler; and he who has acquired them is, from the moment of the acquisition, a ruler and a king, even if he has no abundance of any kind of treasure; (129) for the meaning of the expression, "it is divided into four heads," is [...][57] nor distance; but virtue exhibits the pre-eminence and the power. And these spring from the word of God as from one root, which he compares to a river, on account of the unceasing and everlasting flow of salutary words and doctrines, by which it increases and nourishes the souls that love God.

XXXVIII. (130) And of what kind they are, he proceeds to show in a few words, deriving his explanation from the natural things of art; for he introduces Agar as filling a leathern bag with water, and giving her child drink.[58] Now Agar is the handmaid of Sarah, the new dispensation of perfect virtue; and she is correctly represented so. Since, therefore, having come to the depth of knowledge, which Moses here calls a well, she draws up (filling the soul as if it were a vessel) the doctrines and speculations which she is in pursuit of, wishing to feed her child on the things on which she herself is fed. (131) And Moses, by her child, means, a soul which has lately learnt to desire instruction, and which has, in a manner, just been born to learn. In reference to which, the boy, when he has grown up to man's estate, becomes a sophist, whom Moses calls an archer;[59] for whatever argument he applies his mind to, at that, as at a target, he shoots all his reasons, as an archer shoots his arrows.

XXXIX. (132) But Rebekkah is found to give her pupil drink no longer by improvement, but by perfection. How so the law will tell us: "For the damsel," says Moses, "was very beautiful to the sight, and was a maiden; no man had known her. And when he had gone down to the fountain, she filled her pitcher, and came up again; and the servant ran forward to meet her, and said, Give me now to drink a little water from thy pitcher. And she said, Drink, my lord. And she made haste, and took down the pitcher on her arm, and gave to him to drink until he ceased drinking, And said, and I will also give to thy camels to drink, until they have all drunk; and she made haste, and emptied her pitcher into the trough, and running to the well, she drew water for the camels."[60]

(133) Here who can help wondering at the minute accuracy of the lawgiver as to every particular? He calls Rebekkah a maiden, and a very beautiful maiden, because the nature of virtue is unmixed and free from guile, and unpolluted, and the only thing in all creation which is both beautiful and good; from which arose the Stoic doctrine, that the only thing that was beautiful was the good.

XL. (134) Now of the four virtues, some are always virgins, and some from having been women become changed into virgins, as Sarah did; "For it had ceased to be with her after the manner of women,"[61] when she began to conceive her happy offspring Isaac. But that which is always a virgin, is that of which Moses says, "And no man whatever knows her." For in truth, it is not permitted to any mortal to pollute incorruptible nature, nor even clearly to comprehend what it is. If indeed he were able by any means to become acquainted with it, he would not cease to hate and regret it; (135) on which account Moses, in strict accordance with the principles of natural philosophy, represents Leah as hated.[62] For those who are charmed by pleasures, which are with Rachel, that is to say, with the outward sense, cannot be endured by Leah, who is situated out of the reach of the passions; on which account they repudiate and detest her. But as far as she herself is concerned, her alienation from the creature produces her a close connection with God, from whom she receives the seeds of wisdom, and conceives, and travails, and brings forth virtuous ideas, worthy of the father who begot them. If therefore, you, O my soul, imitating Leah, reject mortal things, you will of necessity turn to the incorruptible God, who will shed over you all the fountains of his good.

XLI. (136) "But Rebekkah," says Moses, "went down to the fountain to fill her pitcher, and came up again." For from what source is it natural for the mind that thirsts after wisdom to be filled, except from the wisdom of God, that fountain which never fails, and to which the soul that descends comes up again like a virtuous disciple? For those who descend out of a vain pride, the reason of virtue receives, and taking them up by means of fame raises them to a height. On which account it is that Moses seems to me to use the expression, "Go, descend, and come up,"[63] as if every one who measures his own lowliness comes forth more gloriously in the eyes of the judges of truth. And he speaks of these matters with great caution. (137) For Agar bears a leathern bag to the well, but Rebekkah carries a pitcher. For the one who devotes himself to instruction and to the encyclical branches of learning has need of some incorporeal things as it were of the outward senses,

---

[57]Here again is an hiatus, which Mangey does not attempt to supply.
[58]Genesis 21:19.
[59]Genesis 21:20.
[60]Genesis 24:16.

[61]Genesis 18:11.
[62]Genesis 29:31.
[63]Exodus 32:7.

of vessels, and eyes, and ears, for a proper contemplation of the objects of her speculation. For from seeing many things and hearing many things, there is derived, in the case of those who are fond of learning the advantage which proceeds from knowledge. But the one who is filled with unalloyed wisdom has need only of a leathern habitation, which is no better than none at all. For the soul which loves unsubstantial things has learnt to put off the whole leathern bag of reasons, that is to say the body, and brings only a pitcher which is the symbol of a vessel, which contains the principal portion in great size and abundance, like water; as to which, those who are clever in such matters may make it a subject of philosophical speculation, whether it is a membrane or a heart. (138) Therefore, the man who is fond of learning, seeing men imbibing the sciences like water, from wisdom that divine fountain, runs up, and meeting them becomes a suppliant to them to know how he may allay his thirst for learning. And the soul which has received the best possible education, namely, the lesson not to envy, and to be liberal, immediately proffers to him the stream of wisdom, and invites him to drink abundantly, adding also this that she calls him who is only a servant her lord. This is the meaning of that most dogmatic assertion, that the wise man alone is free, and a king, even if he have ten thousand masters over his body.

XLII. (139) Most correctly, therefore, after the servant has said, "Give me a little water to drink," does she make answer, not in the manner corresponding to his request: "I will give you to drink," but "Drink." For the one expression would have been suited to one who was displaying the riches of God, which are poured forth for all who are worthy of them and who are able to think of them; but the other expression is appropriate to one who professes that she will teach. But nothing which is connected with mere professions is akin to virtue. (140) But he describes in a most skilful manner the language used by her who teaches and benefits her pupils. For "she made haste," he says, "and took down the pitcher on her arm." Her alacrity to serve the man was displayed by her making haste, and such alacrity is seated in the mind, beyond which envy is cast away. But by the expression, "taking down the pitcher on her arm," we see intimated the prompt and eager attention of the teacher to the pupil; (141) for those teachers are foolish who attempt to regulate their explanations not by a reference to the capacity of their pupils, but to their own superior ability, not being aware that there is a vast difference between making a display and giving a lesson.

For he who is making a display, relying on the good fortune of his present way of proceeding, brings into sight, without any trouble, the works at which he has for a long while been labouring at home, like the works of painters or sculptors, seeking for praise from the multitude. But he who is endeavouring to teach others, like a good physician, has a regard not to the greatness of his own skill, but to the capacity of his patient who is to be healed; not thinking how much he can do by his art, for it is unspeakable how much this may be; but what the patient requires, aiming at moderation, and bringing forward what may improve him.

XLIII. (142) On which account Moses says in another passage, "Thou shalt lend a loan to him who asks you for one, as much as he requires, having regard to what he requires."[64] By the second phrase showing that it is not everything which is to be given, but only such things as are suitable to the requirements of those who are asking for them. For to give an anchor, or an oar, or a rudder to a husbandman, or ploughs or a spade to a captain of a ship, or a lyre to a physician, or instruments suited to manual labour to a musician, would be ridiculous, unless indeed one ought to offer a thirsty man costly viands, or a hungry man unmixed wine in abundance, so as to show at once one's own riches and one's want of humanity, by turning the souls of one's companions into ridicule.

The quantity to be given in an act of beneficence is defined according to due proportion, which is a most useful thing. For, says Moses, do not give all that right reason is able to give, but as much as he who is asking the loan is worthy to receive. (143) Do you not see that even God does not utter his oracles, having a regard to their being in proportion to the magnitude of his own oracular power, but always having respect to the capacity of those who are to be benefited by them? Since who could receive the whole power of the words of God, which are too mighty for any one to listen to? On which account those persons appear to speak with great truth, who say to Moses, "Do thou speak to us, and let not God speak to us, lest we die."[65] For they know that they have not in themselves any organ which can be worthy of God who is giving laws to his church; (144) nor, indeed, could even the whole world, both land and sea, contain his riches if he were inclined to display them, unless we think that the descent of the rains and of the other things that happen in the world are appointed to take place according to the pre-arranged periods of the seasons, and not all at once, because of the scarcity and rarity of the things themselves, and not from any regard to the advantage of those who are benefited by them; who would be injured rather than be benefited by a continual enjoyment of such gifts.

---

[64]Deuteronomy 15:8.
[65]Exodus 20:19.

(145) On this account it is, that God always judiciously limits and brings out with wise moderation his first benefits, stopping them before those who partake of them become wanton through satiety; and then he bestows others in their stead; and again a third class of advantages instead of the second set, and so on, continually substituting new blessings for those of older date, at one time giving such as are different from those which went before, and at another time such as are almost identical with them; for the creature is never wholly destitute of the blessings bestowed by God, since if he were he would be utterly destroyed; but he is unable to endure an unlimited and measureless abundance of them. On which account, as he is desirous that we should derive advantage from the benefits which he bestows upon us, he weighs out what he gives so as to proportion it to the strength of those who receive it.

XLIV. (146) Rebekkah, therefore, must be praised, who, in obedience to the injunctions of her father, having taken down the vessel of wisdom on her arm from a higher place, proffered her pitcher to the disciple; by the pitcher being understood that teaching which he is competent to receive. (147) And beyond all other things, I especially admire her exceeding liberality; for though she had only been asked for a small draught, she gave a large one, until she had filled the whole soul of the learner with wholesome speculations. For Moses says, "She gave him to drink till he ceased from drinking," a most marvellous example to teach us humanity. For if any one should not happen to be in want of many things, but should come forward, and out of shame ask only for a very little, let us not give him only what he mentions, but also those things of which he makes no mention, but of which he is nevertheless in reality in need. (148) But it is not sufficient for the complete enjoyment of his teacher's lessons, that the disciple should merely comprehend what the master has taught him, unless he has also got memory. On which account, making a display of her bounteous disposition, when he has satisfied himself with the water, she offers to give his camels water also, which we have already said are here put symbolically for memory. For the animal while eating its food ruminates, and when, having stooped down it has received a heavy burden, with exceedingly great vigour of muscle it rises up lightly; (149) and in the same manner also, the soul of the man who is devoted to learning, when the burden of its speculations is placed upon it, becomes more lowly, and when it has risen up it rejoices; and from that mastication, and as it were the softening, of the first food that is placed down before it, arises its memory of those speculations.

(150) But she, beholding the nature of the servant to be well calculated for the reception of virtue, emptied her whole pitcher into the cistern, that is to say, she emptied the whole knowledge of the teacher into the soul of the learner. For the sophists, from a desire of gain and also from envy, repressing the natural characters of their pupils, keep silence about many things which ought to be mentioned, laying up for themselves a source of gain for future times. (151) But virtue is an ungrudging and most liberal feeling, so that it does not hesitate to assist another with hand and foot, as the proverb goes, and with all its power. Therefore, pouring all that she knew into the mind of the pupil as into a cistern, she went again to the well to draw water, that is to say, she went to the ever-flowing wisdom of God, that what had been already imparted might be firmly fixed in by memory, and that he might also be irrigated with the knowledge of other and newer things. For the wealth of the wisdom of God is illimitable, and as a tree which is continually putting forth new shoots after the old ones, so that it never ceases growing young again, and being in the flower of its strength. (152) So that they are marvellously simple people who have ever had an idea of coming to the end of any branch of knowledge whatever. For that which has seemed to be near and within reach is nevertheless a long way distant from the end; since no created being is perfect in any department of learning, but falls as far short of it as a thoroughly infant child just beginning to learn does, in comparison of a man who both by age and skill is qualified to be a master.

XLV. (153) And we must inquire the cause why the handmaid gave the servant drink from the fountain, but gave the camels water from the well. May it not perhaps be that the stream here signifies the sacred scripture itself, which irrigates the sciences, and that the well is rather akin to memory? For the depths which he has already mentioned, he produces by means of memory as it were out of a well; (154) and such persons as these one ought to admit because of the goodness of their natural disposition. But there are some men among those who practise virtue to whom the all-beneficent God has shown the way that leads to virtue, such that at first it is accounted rough, and steep, and difficult, but subsequently level and easy, having changed the bitterness of the wayfarer's labour to sweetness. And how he has wrought this change we will now tell. (155) When he led us forth out of Egypt, that is to say, out of the passions which excite the body, we, travelling in the desert, that is to say, in the path of pleasure, encamped in the place called Marah, a place which had no drinkable water, but where all the water was bitter. [66] For still the pleasures which

---

[66] Exodus 15:23.

are brought into action by means of the eyes, and ears, and belly, and the parts adjacent to the belly, were tempting to us, and charmed us exceedingly, sounding close to us. (156) When, therefore, we desired to be entirely separated from them, they dragged us back, exerting themselves in opposition to us, and entwining themselves round us, and soothing us with all kinds of juggling tricks and assiduous blandishments; so that we, yielding to their unremitting caresses, became alienated from and disinclined to labour, as something very bitter and intolerable, and designed to run back again to Egypt, that is to say, to the condition of an intemperate and lascivious life, if the Saviour had not speedily taken pity on us, and thrown a sweetening branch like a medicine upon our soul, causing it to love labour instead of hating it. (157) For he knew, inasmuch as he was our Creator, that we could not possibly survive any existing thing unless there were in us an intense love of doing so. Therefore, men never succeed in attaining any object that they desire if they pursue it without any connection with or consideration of fitness. But when friendship is added, and also a familiarity with the loved object, their endeavours then succeed rightly.

XLVI. (158) This is the food of a soul which is inclined to the practice of virtue, to consider labour a very sweet thing instead of a bitter one, which, however, it is not allowed to all persons to participate in; but to those only by whom the golden calf, the animal made by the Egyptians, the body, is sprinkled over with water after having been burnt with fire, and broken to pieces. For it is said in the sacred scriptures, that "Moses having taken the calf burnt it with fire, and broke it up into small pieces, and threw the pieces into the water and caused the children of Israel to drink thereof."[67] (159) For the love of virtue being inflamed and excited by the brilliant appearance of virtue, burns to ashes the pleasures of the body, and then cuts them to pieces and pounds them to nothing, using the divine word which can at all times divide everything. And in this manner he teaches us that among the bodily advantages are health, and beauty, and the accuracy of the outward senses, and the perfection of bodily vigour with strength and mighty energy; but still that all these things are common to accursed and wicked persons, while if they were really good no wicked person would be allowed to partake of them. (160) But these men, even if they are utterly wicked, still, inasmuch as they are men, and so far partake of the same human nature as virtuous men, do also partake of these advantages of the body.

And, in fact, at present those wild beasts which are the most untameable, enjoy these good things, if indeed they are in reality good things, in a greater degree than rational beings; (161) for what wrestler could be compared in might with the strength of a bull or of an elephant? And what runner could put himself on a level with the speed of a hound or of a hare? And the most sharp-sighted of men is absolutely blind if his sight is compared with that of antelopes or eagles. Again, in hearing and in smell, often other animals are very far beyond man; as, for instance, the ass, which appears to be the stupidest of all animals, would show that our sense of hearing is very obtuse if he were brought into comparison with us. The dog, too, would make the nostrils in man appear a perfectly useless part from the exceeding superiority of the quickness of his own sense of smell; for, in him, that sense is pushed to such a degree that it almost equals the rapidity of the eye-sight.

XLVII. (162) And why need I dwell on the subject more, going through each of the senses and animals separately? For this point has been long agreed upon among all the most eminent historians and philosophers, who have all said that nature is the mother of the irrational animals, and the stepmother of men, perceiving the bodily weakness of men, and the surpassing strength of brute animals in everything. With great propriety, therefore, the artist pounded the calf to pieces; that is to say, dividing it into parts, he showed that all the things which the body has in abundance are very far removed from real good, and are in no respect different from those things which are scattered on the water. (163) On which account the scripture tells us that the calf, after having been pounded to pieces, was scattered on the water, to signify that no genuine plant of good can ever flourish in corruptible matter; for as a seed, when thrown into the stream of a river or into the sea, cannot display its proper powers; for it is impossible, unless it has once taken hold with its roots, as with anchors, of some firm portion of earth, that any branch should be firmly fixed or should shoot up, I do not say to any height, but even as a creeper along the ground, or that it should ever bring forth fruit at the periodical seasons of the year, for any great and violent rush of water coming on washes away all the germinating vigour of the seed. In the same manner all the superfluities contained in the vessel of the soul which are ever spoken of or celebrated are destroyed before they can have any existence, the corporeal substance continually flowing off from them. (164) For how can there be such things as disease and old age and all kinds of corruptions, if there were not a continual drawing off of words, which are theoretical streams; the hierophant, therefore, thinks

---

[67] Exodus 32:20.

it right[68] to irrigate our minds with these words, for the sake of burning up the pleasures, of pounding to pieces and reducing to a thin and impalpable dust, and utterly destroying the system of the corporeal goods; and of making us recollect that the true good has never at any time germinated or blossomed from any one of them, just as nothing flourishes from seeds which are sown in water.

XLVIII. (165) But bulls, and rams, and goats, which Egypt holds in honour, and all other images of corruptible matter which, in report alone, are accounted God's, have no real existence, but are all fictitious and false; for those who look upon life as only a tragedy full of acts of arrogance and stories of love, impressing false ideas on the tender minds of young men, and using the ears as their ministers, into which they pour fabulous trifles, waste away and corrupt their minds, compelling them to look upon persons who were never even men in their minds, but always effeminate creatures as God's; (166) for the calf was not made of every description of female ornament, but only of the earrings of the women. The lawgiver showing us by this that nothing wrought with hands is a visible and true God, but only so by report, and as far as he is thought so, and that, too, the report of a woman and not of a man; for it is the conduct of a soul utterly enervated and rendered completely effeminate to receive such nonsense.

(167) But he who is truly God is perceived, and felt, and recognised, not only by means of one's ears, but also by the eyes of our mind, through his mighty works which are done in the world, and through the rapidity of his operations; on which account in the great song it is said (the speaker assuming the character of God), "Behold! behold! it is I!"[69] as if that real existing God could be more easily conceived by the mind than proved by verbal demonstration; (168) but it is not correct to say that the living God is visible, that is rather an abuse of language, arising from referring God himself to his separate acts of power; for even in the passage cited above, he does not say, "Behold me," for it is wholly impossible that God according to his essence should be perceived or beheld by any creature, but he says, "Behold! it is I," that is to say, behold my existence; for it is sufficient for the reasoning powers of man to advance so far as to learn that there is and actually exists the great cause of all things, and to attempt to proceed further, so as to pursue investigations into the essence or distinctive qualities of God, is an absolute piece of folly; (169) for God did not grant this

even to the all-wise Moses; not though he addressed innumerable requests to him, all having this object; but an oracle was delivered to him, telling him, "Thou shalt see my back parts, but my face thou shalt not see;"[70] and the meaning of this is, that all the things which are behind God are within the comprehension of a virtuous man, but he himself alone is incomprehensible; and he is incomprehensible by any direct and immediate access (for by such means it is only explained what kind of being he is), but he may be understood in his subsequent and consistent faculties; for they, by means of the works accomplished by them, declare not his essence, but his existence.

XLIX. (170) Therefore the mind having generated the foundation of good [...][71] and the primary principle of virtue, namely Seth, or irrigation, boasts with an honourable and holy boast; for she says, "God has raised up to me another seed, instead of Abel whom Cain slew,"[72] for it has been said with great exactness and neatness, that no single divine seed ever falls to the ground, but that they all rise up from the things of earth, and leave them, and are borne upwards to heaven; (171) but the seeds which are sown by mortals, whether for the generation of animals or of plants, do not all come to perfection; but we must be content if more are not wasted than those which remain above; and God sows nothing in our souls which is incomplete; but his seed is all so seasonable and so perfect that every one of them is at once borne forward to produce abundance of its appropriate fruit.

L. (172) But when Moses says here that Seth sprung up as another or different seed, he does not say from which it was different; was it different from Abel who was treacherously slain, or from Cain who slew him? But may we not say perhaps that the original seed from which each of these sprung was different? That from which Cain sprung, inasmuch as it was hostile; for a thirst for virtue is the most hostile thing possible to that deserter, wickedness; that from which Abel sprung, as friendly and kindred; for that which is beginning to exist is a different thing from, but not a contrary thing to, that which is perfected; and so that which pertains to creation is different from that which pertains to the uncreate.

(173) On this account Abel, after having quitted the mortal body, departed to the better nature, and took up his abode with that. But Seth, as being the seed of human virtue, will never quit the race of mankind. But first of all he will receive his growth

---

[68] I have followed Mangey here in reading *axioi*, instead of *apaxioi*, though he prints the latter in the text as the reading of all the MSS.
[69] Deuteronomy 32:39.

[70] Exodus 33:23.
[71] There is again an hiatus in the text here. Mangey conjectures *diagōgēs*, "way of life," to be the word which has fallen out.
[72] Genesis 4:25.

up to the number ten, that perfect number, according to which the just Noah exists; and then he will receive a second and a better growth from his son Shem, ending in a second ten, from which the faithful Abraham is named. And he will also have a third growth, and one more perfect than the number ten, extending from him to Moses, that man who is wise in all things, for he is the seventh from Abraham, not revolving, like an initiated worshipper, in the circle which is exterior to holy things, but like a hierophant, making his abode in the inmost shrines.

LI. (174) And consider the advances towards improvement made by the soul of the man who is eager for, and insatiable in, his craving after good things; and the illimitable riches of God, who gives the end of some things to be the beginnings of others; for the end of the knowledge which is according to Seth is the beginning of the just Noah; and his perfection again is the beginning of the education of Abraham; and the most perfect wisdom of Abraham is the first instruction of Moses; (175) and the two daughters of Lot, the man who was subdued and overthrown by the weakness of the soul, namely, intention and agreement, desire to become pregnant by the mind, that is to say, by their father, acting in opposition to him who said, "God has raised up for me ..."[73] For that which the living God did for him, this they affirm that the mind is able to do for them, introducing the doctrine of an intoxicated and frenzied soul.

It is indeed the act of sober reason, both to confess that God is the Creator and the Father of the universe; and the conduct of one utterly fallen in intoxication and drunkenness, to fancy that he himself is the bringer about of each of human affairs. (176) Evil opinions therefore will not come into association with their father, before a great quantity of the unmixed wine of folly has been found upon him, and destroyed any sense that may have previously been in him; for it is written, "They made their father drink wine." So that if they do not give him drink, they will never receive legitimate seed from him while he is sober; but when he has been soaked in wine, and has become utterly intoxicated and senseless, then they will become pregnant, and have a culpable labour and offspring, which will be truly accursed.

LII. (177) On which account Moses has separated his impious and obscure progeny from the whole of the divine company; for he says, "The Ammonites and the Moabites shall not come into the assembly of the Lord:"[74] and these are the descendants of the daughters of Lot, supposing that everything is generated of the outward sense

and of mind, being male and female like a father and mother, and looking upon this as in real truth the cause of all generation: (178) but as, even if we were to commit such an error as this, still emerging as it were out of that troubled sea, we may lay hold on repentance, which is a firm and saving thing, and must never let it go till we have completely escaped from the billowy sea, the headlong violence of sin: (179) as Rachel, when formerly praying for mind, as if that were able to raise up children, and when she received the answer, "Am I equal to God?"[75] attended to what was said to her, and when she understood it, made a most pious recantation; for the recantation of Rachel is recorded in scripture, a most God-loving prayer, "May God grant to me another son,"[76] such a prayer as no foolish person is permitted to make, who pursues no object but his own pleasure, and who thinks everything else mere folly and ridiculousness.

LIII. (180) And the leader of this opinion is Onan the brother of the skin-wearing Er. "For he," says the scripture, "knowing that the seed would not be his, when he went in unto his brother's wife, spilled his seed upon the ground:"[77] he transgressed all the boundaries of self-love and of fondness for pleasure. (181) Should I not say to this man, If you have a regard to your own advantage you will destroy everything that is excellent, and that too without deriving any advantage therefrom? You will put an end to the honour due to parents, the attention of a wife, the education of children, the blameless services of servants, the management of a house, the government of a city, the firm establishment of laws, the guardianship of morals, reverence to one's elders, the habit of speaking well of the dead, good fellowship with the living, piety towards God as shown both in words and in deeds: for you are overturning and throwing into confusion all these things, sowing seed for yourself alone, and nursing up pleasure, that gluttonous intemperate origin of all evil.

LIV. (182) From which that priest and servant of the only good God, Phineas, rising up[78]—that wise regulator of all the corporeal words and expressions, so as never to behave erroneously or insolently through the medium of them; for the interpretation of the name Phineas is "the bridle of the mouth"—having taken a coadjutor, that is to say, having inquired into and examined the nature of things, and having found that nothing is more honourable than virtue, stabbed and slew with a sword the creature devoted to pleasure, and hos-

---

[73]Genesis 19:32.
[74]Deuteronomy 23:3.

[75]Genesis 30:2.
[76]Genesis 30:24.
[77]Genesis 38:9.
[78]Numbers 25:11.

tile to virtue, and all the places from which all false and illegitimate delights and enjoyments spring: (183) for the law says that, "He thrust the woman through her belly."

Thus, therefore, having caused the difference that existed in him to cease, and having discarded his own pleasure, and burning with zeal for God, the First Cause and holy God, he was honoured and crowned with the two most valuable of all prizes, peace and the priesthood; with the one because both his name and his conduct are akin to peace: (184) for it follows of necessity that a consecrated mind, being its minister and servant, must do everything in which its master delights; and he delights in the firm establishment of good law, and tranquillity, and stability, and in the discarding of wars and [...] [79] meaning not only such as cities make upon one another, but also those which take place in the soul; and these are more important and more injurious, inasmuch as they injure the more divine portion of us, namely, our reason, while arms and weapons can only reach to the injury of our bodies or possessions, but have never any power to injure a healthy soul.

(185) Rightly therefore have cities established a custom, that before they turn arms and engines of destruction against one another to lead to slavery and utter destruction, they should seek to persuade all the citizens to put an [80] end to the great and formidable and unceasing factions which exist in themselves, for faction and sedition, if we must speak the truth, is the archetypal model of wars, and if that be destroyed, there will no longer be any wars which are made in imitation of it; but the race of mankind will attain to the blessing and enjoyment of profound peace, being taught by the law of nature, that is, by virtue, to honour God, and to cleave to the employment of serving him, for this is the source of happiness and length of life.

---

[79]There is another hiatus here, which Mangey proposes to fill up with the words *kai staseōn, "and seditions."*

[80]The text is corrupt here. The text has *katagēs*, a word manifestly mutilated. Mangey proposes *katargēsasthai*, and translates it "ut tollerent."

ON THE GIANTS

(De Gigantibus)

I. (1) "And it came to pass when there began to be many men upon the earth, that daughters also were born to them."[1] I think it here worth while to raise the question why, after the birth of Noah and his sons, our race increased to a degree of great populousness. But, perhaps, it is not difficult to explain the cause of this; for it always happens if anything appears to be rare that its contrary is found exceedingly numerous. (2) Therefore, the good disposition of one displays the evil disposition of myriads, and the fact of those things which are done in accordance with art, and science, and virtue, and beauty, being few, shows how incalculable a number of things devoid of art, and of science, and of justice, and, in short, utterly worthless, lie concealed beneath. (3) Do you not see that in the universe, also, the sun, being one body, by his shining forth dissipates the thick and dense darkness which is shed over earth and sea? With great propriety, therefore, the generation of the just Noah and his sons is represented as bringing into existence a great number of unjust persons; for it is by the contrary that it is especially the nature of contraries to be known. (4) And no unjust man at any time implants a masculine generation in the soul, but such, being unmanly, and broken, and effeminate in their minds, do naturally become the parents of female children; having planted no tree of virtue, the fruit of which must of necessity have been beautiful and salutary, but only trees of wickedness and of the passions, the shoots of which are womanlike.

(5) On account of which fact these men are said to have become the fathers of daughters, and that no one of them is said to have begotten a son; for since the just Noah had male children, as being a man who followed reason, perfect, and upright, and masculine, so by this very fact the injustice of the multitude is proved to be altogether the parent of female children. For it is impossible that the same things should be born of opposite parents; but they must necessarily have an opposite offspring.

II. (6) "And when the angels of God saw the daughters of men that they were beautiful, they took unto themselves wives of all of them whom they chose."[2] Those beings, whom other philosophers call demons, Moses usually calls angels; and they are souls hovering in the air. (7) And let no one suppose, that what is here stated is a fable, for it is necessarily true that the universe must be filled with living things in all its parts, since every one of its primary and elementary portions contains its appropriate animals and such as are consistent with its nature;—the earth containing terrestrial animals, the sea and the rivers containing aquatic animals, and the fire such as are born in the fire (but it is said, that such as these last are found chiefly in Macedonia), and the heaven containing the stars: (8) for these also are entire souls pervading the universe, being unadulterated and divine, inasmuch as they move in a circle, which is the kind of motion most akin to the mind, for every one of them is the parent mind.

It is therefore necessary that the air also should be full of living beings. And these beings are invisible to us, inasmuch as the air itself is not visible to mortal sight. (9) But it does not follow, because our sight is incapable of perceiving the forms of souls, that for that reason there are no souls in the air; but it follows of necessity that they must be comprehended by the mind, in order that like may be contemplated by like. (10) Since what shall we say? Must we not say that these animals which are terrestrial or aquatic live in air and spirit? What? Are not pestilential afflictions accustomed to exist when the air is tainted or corrupted, as if that were the cause of all such assuming vitality? Again, when the air is free from all taint and innocent, such as it is especially wont to be when the north wind prevails, does not the imbibing of a purer air tend to a more vigorous and more lasting duration of life? (11) It is then natural that that medium by which all other animals, whether aquatic of terrestrial, are vivified should itself be empty and destitute of souls? On the contrary, even if all other animals were barren, the air by itself would be bound to be productive of life, having received from the great Creator the seeds of vitality by his especial favour.

III. (12) Some souls, therefore, have descended into bodies, and others have not thought worthy to approach any one of the portions of the earth; and these, when hallowed and surrounded by the ministrations of the father, the Creator has been accustomed to employ, as hand-maidens and servants in the administration of mortal affairs. (13) And they having descended into the body as into a river, at one time are carried away and swallowed up by the voracity of a most violent whirlpool; and,

---

[1]Genesis 6:1.
[2]Genesis 6:2.

at another time, striving with all their power to resist its impetuosity, they at first swim on the top of it, and afterwards fly back to the place from which they started.

(14) These, then, are the souls of those who have been taught some kind of sublime philosophy, meditating, from beginning to end, on dying as to the life of the body, in order to obtain an inheritance of the incorporeal and imperishable life, which is to be enjoyed in the presence of the uncreate and everlasting God. (15) But those, which are swallowed up in the whirlpool, are the souls of those other men who have disregarded wisdom, giving themselves up to the pursuit of unstable things regulated by fortune alone, not one of which is referred to the most excellent portion of us, the soul or the mind; but all rather to the dead corpse connected with us, that is to the body, or to things which are even more lifeless than that, such as glory, and money, and offices, and honours, and all other things which, by those who do not keep their eyes fixed on what is really beautiful, are fashioned and endowed with apparent vitality by the deceit of vain opinion.

IV. (16) If, therefore, you consider that souls, and demons, and angels are things differing indeed in name, but not identical in reality, you will then be able to discard that most heavy burden, superstition. But as men in general speak of good and evil demons, and in like manner of good and evil souls, so also do they speak of angels, looking upon some as worthy of a good appellation, and calling them ambassadors of man to God, and of God to man, and sacred and holy on account of this blameless and most excellent office; others, again, you will not err if you look upon as unholy and unworthy of any address. (17) And the expression used by the writer of the psalm, in the following verse, testifies to the truth of my assertion, for he says, "He sent upon them the fury of His wrath, anger, and rage, and affliction, and he sent evil angels among them."[3] These are the wicked who, assuming the name of angels, not being acquainted with the daughters of right reason, that is with the sciences and the virtues, but which pursue the mortal descendants of mortal men, that is the pleasures, which can confer no genuine beauty, which is perceived by the intellect alone, but only a bastard sort of elegance of form, by means of which the outward sense is beguiled; (18) and they do not all take all the daughters in marriage, but some of them have selected some of that innumerable company to be their wives; some choosing them by the sight, and others by the ear, others again being influenced by the sense of taste, or by the belly, and some even by the pleasures below the belly; many also

have laid hold of those the abode of which is fixed at a great distance, putting in action various desires among one another. For, of necessity, the choices of all the various pleasures are various, since different pleasures are established in different places.

V. (19) And, in all such matters, it is impossible for the spirit of God to remain and to pass all its time, as the law-giver himself shows. "For," says Moses, "the Lord said, My spirit shall not remain among men for ever, because they are flesh."[4] (20) For, at times, it does remain; but it does not remain for ever and ever among the greater part of us; for who is so destitute of reason or so lifeless as never, either voluntarily or involuntarily, to conceive a notion of the all good God. For, very often, even over the most polluted and accursed beings, there hovers a sudden appearance of the good, but they are unable to take firm hold of it and to keep it among them; (21) for, almost immediately, it quits its former place and departs, rejecting those inhabitants who come over to it, and who live in defiance of law and justice, to whom it never would have come if it had not been for the sake of convicting those who choose what is disgraceful instead of what is good.

(22) But the spirit of God is spoken of in one manner as being air flowing upon the earth, bringing a third element in addition to water. In reference to which, Moses says, in his account of the creation of the world, "The spirit of God moved upon the face of the waters."[5] Since the air, as it is very light, is raised and borne aloft, having water, as it were, for its foundation; and, in another manner, unalloyed knowledge is said to be so, which every wise man naturally partakes of. (23) And Moses shows us this, when speaking of the creator and maker of the holy work of the creation, in these words: "And God summoned Bezaleel, and filled him with his Holy Spirit, and with wisdom, and understanding, and knowledge, to be able to devise every work."[6] So that, what the spirit of God is, is very definitively described in these words.

VI. (24) Such also is the spirit of Moses, which came upon the seventy elders, for the sake of making them differ from, and be superior to the rest of the Israelites, who could not possibly be elders in real truth, unless they had partaken of that all-wise spirit. For it is said, "I will take of my spirit which is upon thee, and I will pour it upon the seventy elders."[7] (25) But think not that thus this taking away, could be by means of cutting off or separation; but it is here, as is the case in an op-

---

[3]Psalm 77:49.

[4]Genesis 6:3.
[5]Genesis 1:2.
[6]Exodus 31:1.
[7]Numbers 11:17.

eration effected by fire, which can light ten thousand torches, without itself being diminished the least atom, or ceasing to remain as it was before. Something like this also is the nature of knowledge. For though it has made all its pupils, and all who have become acquainted with it, learned, still it is in no degree diminished itself, but very often it even becomes improved, just as, they say, that fountains sometimes are by being drained dry; for, it is said, that they sometimes become sweeter by such a process.

(26) For continual association with others, engendering diligence and practice, gradually works out entire perfection. If, then, the individual spirit of Moses, or of any other creature, was about to be distributed to so great a multitude of pupils, then, if it were divided into such a number of small portions, it would be diminished. (27) But now, the spirit which is upon him is the wise, the divine, the indivisible, the undistributable, the good spirit, the spirit which is everywhere diffused, so as to fill the universe, which, while it benefits others, is not injured by having a participation in it given to another, and if added to something else, either as to its understanding, or its knowledge, or its wisdom.

VII. (28) On which account, it is possible that the spirit of God may remain in the soul, but that it should remain for ever is impossible, as we have said. And why need we wonder? since there is no other thing whatever, the possession of which, is stable and lasting; but mortal affairs are continually wavering in the scale, and inclining first to one side, and then to the other, and liable at different times to different changes. (29) And the greatest cause of our ignorance is the flesh, and our inseparable connection with the flesh. And this, Moses represents God as admitting, where he says that, "Because they are flesh," the spirit of God cannot abide in them. And yet marriage and the rearing of children, and the furnishing of necessary things, and ingloriousness conjoined with a want of money and business, both private and public, and a countless number of other things cause wisdom to waste away, before it begins to flourish vigorously. (30) But there is nothing which is so great a hindrance to its growth as the fleshly nature. For that, as if it were the principal and most solid foundation of folly and ignorance, is laid down firmly, and then each of the aforenamed evils is built up upon it.

(31) For those souls which are devoid of flesh and of the body, remaining undisturbed in the theatre of the universe, occupied in seeing and hearing divine things, of which an insatiable desire has seized them, enjoy a pleasure to which no one offers any interruption. But those which bear the heavy burden of the flesh, being weighed down and oppressed by it, are unable to look upwards to the revolutions of the heaven, but being dragged downwards, have their necks forcibly pressed to the ground like so many quadrupeds.

VIII. (32) In reference to which fact, the lawgiver having determined to put an end to all illegal and illegitimate associations and unions, begins his denunciations in the following manner: "Man shall not come near to any one who is akin to his own flesh, to uncover his nakedness: I am the Lord."[8] How could any one more forcibly exhort man to despise the flesh and what is akin to the flesh than in this way? (33) And indeed he does not only exhort us to abandon such things, but he shows positively that he who is really a man will never come of his own accord to those pleasures which are dear to and connected with the body, but will always be meditating to alienate himself from them entirely. (34) For the saying, "Man, man," not once but twice, is a sign that what is here meant is not the man composed of body and soul, but him only who is possessed of virtue. For such an one is really a true man, whom some one of the ancient philosophers having lighted a lantern at midday, went in search of, and told those who asked him that he was seeking a man. And as for the prohibition against every man coming near to any one who is akin to his own flesh, this is induced by necessary reasons. For there are some things which we should admit, such for instance as those useful things, by the employment of which we may be able to live in freedom from disease and in good health; and there are other things which should be rejected, by which, when the appetites become inflamed, they burn up all goodness in one vast conflagration.

(35) Let not then our appetites rush eagerly in pursuit of all the things that are pleasant to the flesh, for the pleasures are often untameable, when like dogs they fawn upon us, and all of a sudden, change and bite us, inflicting incurable sounds. So that by cleaving to frugality, which is a friend to virtue, in preference to the pleasures akin to the body, we shall defeat the numerous and infinite multitude of irreconcilable enemies. And if any occasion should seek to compel us to take more than what is moderate or sufficient, let us not yield; for the scripture saith, "He shall come near to him to uncover his nakedness."

IX. (36) And what is meant by this, it is worth while to explain. It has often happened, that some who have not been themselves providers of wealth, have nevertheless had unlimited abundance. And others, who have not been eager in the pursuit of glory have been thought worthy of public praises and honours. Others again, who have not expected to acquire even a little strength, have arrived at the greatest vigour and activity. (37) Now, let all these men learn not to cleave in their minds to

---

[8]Leviticus 18:6.

any one of these qualities; that is to say, not to admire them and grasp at them in an immoderate degree, looking upon them all, that is to say on riches, on glory, and on bodily strength, not only not as intrinsically good, but as the greatest of evils. For to misers, the pursuit of money is appropriate, and the pursuit of glory is so to ambitious men, and the acquisition of bodily strength is so to men fond of athletic and of gymnastic exercises. For that which is the better part of them, namely, the soul, they have abandoned as a slave to those things which are inferior to themselves, namely, to inanimate things.

(38) But as many as are masters of themselves show that all that brilliant prosperity, which is an object of so much contention, is in subordination to the mind, which is the principal part of them, receiving it when it comes, so as to make a good use of it, but not pursuing it if it keeps aloof, as being able to be happy even without it. (39) But he who pursues it eagerly and follows upon its track, fills philosophy with base opinions; on which account he is said to uncover its nakedness, for how can there be any concealment or ignorance of the reproaches to which those men are justly exposed, who profess indeed to be wise men, but who make a traffic of wisdom, and bargain for the sale of it, as they say men do in the market, who put up their wares for sale, sometimes for a slight gain, sometimes for sweet and caressing speeches, and sometimes for insecure hopes, founded on no sure ground, and sometimes even for promises which are in no respect better than dreams.

X. (40) And the sentence which follows, "I am the Lord," is uttered with great beauty and with most excessive propriety, "for," says the Lord, "oppose, my good man, the good of the flesh to that of the soul, and of the whole man;" therefore the pleasure of the flesh is irrational, but the pleasure of the soul and of the whole man is the mind of the universe, namely God; (41) and the comparison is an admirable one, and one difficult to be instituted, so as for any one to be deceived by the close similitude, unless any one will say that living things are in reality the same as lifeless things, rational things the same as irrational things; well adapted the same as those ill adapted; odd numbers identical with even ones; light with darkness, and day with night; and in short every thing that is contrary the same as its contrary.

(42) And yet even although these things have some kind of union and connection together by reason of their being created, still God is not in any respect like the very best of created beings, inasmuch as these have been born, and are liable to suffering; but he is uncreated, and always acting not suffering. (43) Now it is well not to desert the ranks of God, in which it follows inevitably that all who are arrayed must be most excellent, and it would be shameful to quit those ranks, to fly to

unmanly and effeminate pleasure, which injures its friends and benefits its enemies, for its nature is a very singular one; for all those to whom it chooses to give a share of its special advantages, it at once chastises and injures; and those whom it thinks fit to deprive of its good things, it benefits in the greatest possible degree, for it injures them when it gives, but it benefits them when it takes away.

(44) If therefore, O my soul, any one of the temptations of pleasure invites you, turn yourself away, and directing your views towards another point, look at the genuine beauty of virtue, and having surveyed it, remain, until a desire for it has sunk into you, and draws you to it, like a magnet, and immediately leads you and attaches you to that which has become the object of your desire.

XI. (45) And the expression, "I am the Lord," must be listened to, not only as if it were equivalent to, "I am the perfect, and incorruptible, and true good," with which if any one is surrounded he will reject all that is imperfect, and corruptible, and attached to the flesh; but also as equivalent to, "I am the ruler, and the king, and the master." (46) And it is not safe for subjects to do wrong in the presence of their rulers, nor for slaves to err before their masters; for when the punishers are near, those whose nature is not quick at submitting to admonitions are held in restraint and order by fear; (47) for God, having filled everything with himself, is near at hand, so that he is looking over everything and standing by, we being filled with a great and holy reverence, or if not with that, at all events, having a prudent fear of the might of his authority, and of the fearful nature of his punishment, which cannot be avoided, whenever he determines to exert his punishing power, shall desist from doing wrong. In order that the divine spirit of wisdom may not be inclined to quit our neighbourhood and depart, but that it may remain a very long time with us, as it did also with the wise Moses; (48) for Moses is a being of the most tranquil habits, either standing still or sitting still, and not at all disposed by nature to subject himself to turns and changes; for the scripture says, "Moses and the ark did not move,"[9] inasmuch as the wise man cannot depart from virtue, or inasmuch as virtue is not liable to move, nor is the virtuous man inclined to changes, but each of these things is established on the sure foundation of right reason.

(49) And again, the scripture saith in another passage, "But stand thou here with me."[10] For this is an oracle of God, which was given to the prophet, and his station was to be one of unmoved tranquillity by God, who always stands immovably; for

---

[9]Numbers 14:44.
[10]Deuteronomy 5:31.

it is indispensable, that all things which are placed by the side of him must be kept straight by such an undeviating rule. (50) On this account it is, as it seems to me, that excessive pride, named Jethro, marvelling at his unvarying and always equal choice of what was wise, a choice which always looked at the same things in the same way, was perplexed, and put a question to him in this form, "Why dost thou sit by thyself?"[11] (51) For any one who considers the continual war raging among men in the middle of peace, and existing, not merely among nations, and countries, and cities, but also among private houses, or I might rather say, between every individual man and the inexpressible and heavy storms which agitate the souls of men, which, by their evident impetuosity, throw into confusion all the affairs of life, may very naturally wonder, if in such a storm, any one can enjoy tranquillity, and can feel a calm in such a billowy state of the stormy sea.

(52) You see that even the high priest, that is to say, reason, who might at all times remain and reside in the holy dwelling of God, has not free permission to approach them at all times, but only once in each year; for whatever is associated with reason by utterance is not firm, because it is of a twofold nature. But the safest conduct is to contemplate the living God by the soul alone, without utterance of any voice, because he exists according to the indivisible unit.

XII. (53) As, therefore, among men in general, that is to say, among those who propose to themselves many objects in life, the divine spirit does not remain, even though it may abide among them for a very short time, but it remains among one species of men alone, namely, among those who, having put off all the things of creation, and the inmost veil and covering of false opinion, come to God in their unconcealed and naked minds. (54) Thus also Moses, having fixed his tent outside of the tabernacle and outside of all the corporeal army,[12] that is to say, having established his mind so that it should not move, begins to worship God, and having entered into the darkness, that invisible country, remains there, performing the most sacred mysteries; and he becomes, not merely an initiated man, but also an hierophant of mysteries and a teacher of divine things, which he will explain to those whose ears are purified; (55) therefore the divine spirit is always standing by him, conducting him in every right way: but from other men, as I have said before, it very soon separates itself, and completes their life in the number of a hundred and twenty years.

For God says, "their days shall be an hundred and twenty years;"[13] (56) but Moses, when he had arrived at that number of years, departed from mortal life to another. How, then, can it be natural for men who are guilty to live an equal length of time with the all-wise prophet? for the present, it will be sufficient to say this, that things which bear the same name are not in all cases alike, but very often they are distinct in their whole genus; and also that which is bad may have equal numbers and times with what is good, since they are represented as twofold, but still they have their respective powers, distinct from one another, and as remote and different as possible.

(57) And we shall hereafter institute a more exact discussion of this period of a hundred and twenty years, which we will however postpone, till we come to an examination of the whole life of the prophet, when we have become fit to be initiated in it, but at present we will discuss what comes next in order.

XIII. (58) "And there were giants on the earth in those days."[14] Perhaps some one may here think, that the lawgiver is speaking enigmatically and alluding to the fables handed down by the poets about giants, though he is a man as far removed as possible from any invention of fables, and one who thinks fit only to walk in the paths of truth itself; (59) in consequence of which principle, he has banished from the constitution, which he has established, those celebrated and beautiful arts of statuary and painting, because they, falsely imitating the nature of the truth, contrive deceits and snares, in order, through the medium of the eyes, to beguile the souls which are liable to be easily won over. (60) Therefore he utters no fable whatever respecting the giants; but he wishes to set this fact before your eyes, that some men are born of the earth, and some are born of heaven, and some are born of God: those are born of the earth, who are hunters after the pleasures of the body, devoting themselves to the enjoyment and fruition of them, and being eager to provide themselves with all things that tend to each of them. Those again are born of heaven who are men of skill and science and devoted to learning; for the heavenly portion of us is our mind, and the mind of every one of those persons who are born of heaven studies the encyclical branches of education and every other art of every description, sharpening, and exercising, and practising itself, and rendering itself acute in all those matters which are the objects of intellect.

(61) Lastly, those who are born of God are priests and prophets, who have not thought fit to mix themselves up in the constitutions of this

---

[11] Exodus 18:14.
[12] Exodus 33:7.

[13] Deuteronomy 24:7.
[14] Genesis 6:4.

world, and to become cosmopolites, but who having raised themselves above all the objects of the mere outward senses, have departed and fixed their views on that world which is perceptible only by the intellect, and have settled there, being inscribed in the state of incorruptible incorporeal ideas.

XIV. (62) Accordingly, Abraham, as long as he was abiding in the land of the Chaldaeans, that is to say, in opinion, before he received his new name, and while he was still called Abram, was a man born of heaven, investigating the sublime nature of things on high, and all that took place in these regions, and the causes of them, and studying everything of that kind in the true spirit of philosophy; on which account he received an appellation corresponding to the pursuits to which he devoted himself: for the name Abram, being interpreted, signifies the sublime father, and is a name very fitting for the paternal mind, which in every direction contemplates sublime and heavenly things: for the mind is the father of our composite being, reaching as high as the sky and even farther.

(63) But when he became improved, and was about to have his name changed, he then became a man born of God, according to the oracle which was delivered to him, "I am thy God, take care that thou art approved before me, and be thou blameless."[15] (64) But if the God of the world, being the only God, is also by especial favour the peculiar God of this individual man, then of necessity the man must also be a man of God; for the name Abraham, being interpreted, signifies, "the elect father of sound," the reason of the good man: for he is chosen out of all, and purified, and the father of the voice by which we speak; and being such a character as this, he is assigned to the one only God, whose minister he becomes, and so makes the path of his whole life straight, using in real truth the royal road, the road of the only king who governs all things, turning aside and deviating neither to the left hand nor to the right.

XV. (65) But the sons of earth removing their minds from contemplation, and becoming deserters so as to fly to the lifeless and immovable nature of the flesh, "for they two became one flesh,"[16] as the lawgiver says, adulterated the excellent coinage, and abandoned the better rank which had been allotted to them as their own, and deserted to the worse rank, which was contrary to their original nature, Nimrod being the first to set the example of this desertion; (66) for the lawgiver says, "that this man began to be a giant upon the earth:"[17] and the name Nimrod, being interpreted, means, desertion; for it was not enough for the thoroughly miserable soul to stand on neither side, but having gone over to its enemies, it took up arms against its friends, and resisted them, and made open war upon them; in reference to which fact it is that, Moses calls the seat of Nimrod's kingdom Babylon, and the interpretation of the word Babylon is "change;" a thing nearly akin to desertion, the name, too, being akin to the name, and the one action to the other; for the first step of every deserter is a change and alteration of mind, (67) and it would be consistent in the truth to say that, according to the most holy Moses, the bad man, as being one destitute of a home and of a city, without any settled habitation, and a fugitive, is naturally a deserter also; but the good man is the firmest of allies.

Having said thus much at present, and dwelt sufficiently on the subject of the giants, we will now proceed to what comes next in our subject, which is this.

---

[15] Genesis 17:1.

[16] Genesis 2:24.

[17] Genesis 10:29 is the passage supposed to be alluded to; but as translated in the Bible it only says "He was a mighty hunter before the Lord."

ON THE UNCHANGEABLENESS OF GOD

(Quod Deus Immutabilis Sit)

I. (1) "And after this," says Moses, "it came to pass that the angels of God went in unto the daughters of men, and they bore children unto them."[1] It is worth while, therefore, to consider what is meant by the expression, "And after this." It is therefore a reference to something that has been said before, for the purpose of explaining it more clearly; (2) and a mention of the divine spirit has already been made, as he has already stated, that it is very difficult for it to remain throughout all ages in the soul, which is divisible into many parts, and which assumes many forms, and is clothed with a most heavy burden, namely its bulk of flesh; after this spirit, therefore, the angels of God go in unto the daughters of men. (3) For as long as the pure rays of wisdom shine forth in the soul, by means of which the wise man sees God and his powers, no one of those who bring false news ever enters into the reason, but all such are kept at a distance outside of the sacred threshhold.

But when the light of the intellect is dimmed and overshadowed, then the companions of darkness having become victorious, associate themselves with the dissolute and effeminate passions which the prophet calls the daughters of men, and they bear children to them and not to God. (4) For the appropriate progeny of God are the perfect virtues, but that offspring which is akin to the wicked, is unregulated wickedness. But learn thou, if thou wilt, O my mind, not to bear children to thyself, after the example of that perfect man Abraham, who offered up to God "The beloved and only legitimate offspring of his soul,"[2] the most conspicuous image of self-taught wisdom, by name Isaac; and who gave him up with all cheerfulness to be a necessary and fitting offering to God. "Having bound,"[3] as the scripture says, this new kind of victim, either because he, having once tasted of the divine inspiration, did not condescend any longer to tread on any mortal truth, or because he saw that the creature was unstable and moveable, while he recognised the unhesitating firmness existing in the living God, on whom he is said to have believed.[4]

II. (5) His disciple and successor was Hannah, the gift of the wisdom of God, for the interpretation of the name is her grace. For when she had become pregnant, having received the divine seed, and after she had completed the time of her labour, she brought forth, in the manner appointed by the arrangement of God, a son, whom she called Samuel; and the name Samuel being interpreted, means "appointed by God." She therefore having received him restores him to the giver; not looking upon anything as a good belonging to herself which is not divine grace. (6) For in the first book of Kings,[5] she speaks in this manner: "I give him unto thee freely," the expression here used being equivalent to, "I give him unto thee whom thou hast given to me." According to that most sacred scripture of Moses, "My gifts and my offerings, and my first fruits, ye shall observe to offer unto me."[6] (7) For to what other being should one bring gifts of gratitude except to God? and what offerings can one bring unto him except of those things which have been given to us by him? For it is not possible for us to have an abundance of anything else.

And he has no need of any of those things which he enjoins men to offer unto him, but he bids us bring unto him the things which are his own, through the excess of his beneficence to our race. For we, studying to conduct ourselves with gratitude to him, and to show him all honours, should purify ourselves from sin, washing off all things that can stain our life in words, or appearance, or actions. (8) For it is foolishness to imagine, that it is unlawful to enter into temples, unless a man has first washed his body and made that look bright, but that one may attempt to sacrifice and to pray with a mind still polluted and disordered. And yet temples are made of stones and timber, mere lifeless materials, and it is not possible for the body, if it is devoid of life by its own nature, to touch things devoid of life, without using ablutions and purifying ceremonies of holiness; and shall any one endure to approach God without being purified as to his soul, shall any one while impure come near to the purest of all beings, and this too without having any intention of repenting? (9) Let him, indeed who, in addition to having committed no new crimes, has also endeavoured to wash off his old misdeeds, come cheerfully before him; but let the man who is without any such preparation,

---

[1]Genesis 6:2.
[2]Genesis 22:2.
[3]Genesis 22:9.
[4]Genesis 15:6.

[5]1 Samuel 1:28.
[6]Numbers 28:2.

and who is impure, keep aloof. For he will never escape the notice of him who can look into the recesses of the heart, and who walketh in its most secret places.

III. (10) Now the most evident sign of a soul devoted to God is that song in which that expression occurs, "She that was barren has borne seven children, and she that had many children has become weak."[7] (11) And yet she who is speaking is in reality only the mother of one son, namely, of Samuel. How then does she say that she has borne seven children, unless indeed any one thinks that the unit is in its strictest nature identical with the number seven, not only in number, but also in the harmony of the universe, and in the reasonings of the soul which is devoted to virtue? For he who was devoted to the one God, that is Samuel, and who had no connection whatever with any other being, is adorned according to that essence which is single and the real unit; (12) and this is the constitution of the number seven, that is to say, of the soul that rests in God, and which no longer concerns itself about any mortal employment, when it has quitted the number six which it allotted to those who were not able to attain to the first rank, but who of necessity contented themselves with arriving at the second.

(13) It is therefore not incredible that the barren woman, not being one who is incapable of becoming fruitful, but one who is still vigorous and fresh, striving for the chief reward in the arena of fortitude, patience, and perseverance, may bring forth a seven, equal in honour to the unit, of which numbers, nature is very productive and prolific. (14) And she says, that "she that had many children has become weak," speaking accurately and very plainly. For when the soul, although only one, brings forth many children when separated from the one, it then naturally becomes infinite in number; and then being weighed down and overwhelmed by the multitude of children who depend upon it, (and the greatest part of them are premature and abortive), it becomes weak. (15) For it brings forth the desire of forms and colours, as gratified by the eyes, and the pleasures arising from sound, as gratified by the ears. It is pregnant also of the pleasures of the belly and of the parts beneath the belly, so that, as many children are attached to it, it becomes exhausted by bearing this heavy burden, and drops its hands from weakness, and faints away. And in this way it comes to pass that all those things are subdued which bring forth perishable children to themselves, who are likewise perishable.

IV. (16) But some persons, through their self-love, have incurred not only defeat but even death also. At all events Onan, "knowing that the seed should not be his,"[8] did not desist from injuring the rational principle, which is the best thing in kind of all existing things, until he himself met with utter destruction. And this, too, very properly and deservedly; (17) for if some men do all things for the sake of themselves alone, not with a view to the honour of their parents, or the proper regulation of their children, or the salvation of their country, or the guardianship of the laws, or the preservation of good morals, or with a view to the due performance of any public or private duty, or of a proper celebration of sacred rites, or the pious worship due to the gods, they will be deservedly miserable. (18) For the sake of one of the objects which I have mentioned, it is glorious even to quit life itself. But these men say that, unless they are likely to gain some pleasure by the pursuit of them, they would disregard the whole lot of them—glorious objects as they are.

Therefore, the incorruptible God banishes the wicked exposition of unnatural opinion, which is named Onan. (19) And altogether these persons are to be detested who beget children for themselves, that is to say, who, pursuing their own private advantage alone, disregard all other objects, as if they had been born for themselves alone, and not for ten thousand other persons also, for their fathers, and their mothers, and their wives, and their children, and their country, and for all mankind. And if we must go further and add any thing to this enumeration, we may say for heaven, and earth, and the whole universe, and for the sciences, and for the virtues, and for the Father and Ruler of all; to every one of which a man ought to pay what is due to the best of his power, not looking upon all the world as an addition to himself, but on himself as an addition to the rest of the world.

V. (20) However, we have said enough on this head; let us now connect what follows with it:—

"The Lord God, therefore," says Moses, "seeing that the wickedness of man was multiplied upon the earth, and that every one of them was carefully studying wickedness in his heart all his days; God considered in his mind that he had made man upon the earth, and he thought upon it; and God said, I will destroy man whom I have made from off the face of the earth."[9] (21) Perhaps some very wicked persons will suspect that the lawgiver is here speaking enigmatically, when he says that the Creator repented of having created man, when he beheld their wickedness; on which account he determined to destroy the whole race. But let those who adopt such opinions as these know, that they are making light of and extenuating the offences of these men of old time, by rea-

---

[7] 1 Samuel 2:5.

[8] Genesis 38:9.
[9] Genesis 6:5.

son of their own excessive impiety; (22) for what can be a greater act of wickedness than to think that the unchangeable God can be changed? And this, too, while some persons think that even those who are really men do never hesitate in their opinions, for that those, who have studied philosophy in a sincere and pure spirit, have derived as the greatest good arising from their knowledge, the absence of any inclination to change with the changes of affairs, and the disposition, with all immovable firmness and sure stability, to labour at every thing that it becomes them to pursue.

VI. (23) And it seems good to the lawgiver that the perfect man should desire tranquillity; for it was said to the wise man in the character of God, "But stand thou here with me,"[10] this expression showing the unchangeable and unalterable nature of the mind which is firmly established in the right way; (24) for it is really marvellous when any one touches the soul, like a lyre tuned in musical principles, not with sharp and flat sounds, but with an accurate knowledge of contrary tones, and employing only the best, not sounding any too loudly, nor on the other hand letting any be too weak, so as to impair the harmony of the virtues and of those things which are good by nature, and when he, preserving it in an equal condition plays and sings melodiously; (25) for this instrument nature has made to be the most perfect of all, and to be the model of all instruments made by the hand. And if this be properly tuned, it will utter the most exquisite of all symphonies, which consists not in the combination and tones of a melodious voice, but in a harmonious agreement of all the actions in life; (26) therefore, as the soul of man can allay the excessive storm and swell of the sea, which the violent and irresistible gale of wickedness has suddenly raised, by the gentle breezes of knowledge and wisdom, and having mitigated its swelling and boisterous fury, enjoys tranquillity resting in an unruffled calm. Do you doubt whether the imperishable, and everlasting, and blessed God, the Being endowed with all the virtues, and with all perfection, and with all happiness is unchangeable in his counsels, and whether he abides by the designs which he originally formed, without changing any of them. (27) Facility of change is indeed an attribute of man, which is of necessity incidental to their nature by reason of its external want of firmness; as in this way, for instance:—often when we have chosen friends, and have lived some short time with them, without having any thing to accuse them of, we then turn away from them, so as to place ourselves in the rank of enemies, or at least of strangers to them; (28) now this conduct shows the facility and levity of ourselves, who are unable steadily to adhere to the professions which we originally made; but God is not so easily sated or wearied.

Again there are times when we determine to abide by the same judgment that we have formed; but those who join us do not equally abide by theirs, so that our opinions of necessity change as well as theirs; (29) for it is impossible for us, who are but men, to foresee all the contingencies of future events, or to anticipate the opinions of others; but to God, as dwelling in pure light, all things are visible; for he penetrating into the very recesses of the soul, is able to see, with the most perfect certainty, what is invisible to others, and being possessed of prescience and of providence, his own peculiar attributes, he allows nothing to abuse its liberty, and to stray out of the reach of his comprehension, since with him, there is no uncertainty even in the future, for there is nothing uncertain nor even future to God.

(30) It is plain therefore that the creator of all created things, and the maker of all the things that have ever been made, and the governor of all the things which are subject to government, must of necessity be a being of universal knowledge; and he is in truth the father, and creator, and governor of all things in heaven and in the whole world; and indeed future events are overshadowed by the distance of future time, which is sometimes a short and sometimes a long interval. (31) But God is the creator of time also; for he is the father of its father, and the father of time is the world, which made its own mother the creation of time, so that time stands towards God in the relation of a grandson; for this world is a younger son of God, inasmuch as it is perceptible by the outward sense; for the only son he speaks of as older than the world, is idea,[11] and this is not perceptible by the intellect; but having thought the other worthy of the rights of primogeniture, he has decided that it shall remain with him; (32) therefore, this younger son, perceptible by the external senses being set in motion, has caused the nature of time to shine forth, and to become conspicuous, so that there is nothing future to God, who has the very boundaries of time subject to him; for their life is not time, but the beautiful model of time, eternity; and in eternity nothing is past and nothing is future, but everything is present only.

VII. (33) Having therefore now sufficiently discussed the question of the living God never knowing repentance, it comes next in order for us to explain what is the meaning of the expression, "God considered that he had made man upon the earth, and he thought within himself." (34) Then the creator of the world, having attached to himself the two most lasting powers of cogitation and

---

[10]Deuteronomy 5:31.

[11]I have followed Mangey, who proposes to read *idean* here but the reading in the text is *sydena*.

deliberation—the one being a conception conceived within his own breast, and the other the discussion of such conception—and since he continually employs them for the contemplation of his own works, those things which do not leave their appointed station he praises for their obedience, but those which change their place he pursues with the punishment appointed for deserters; (35) for some bodies he has endowed with habit, others with nature, others with soul, and some with rational soul; for instance, he has bound stones and beams, which are torn from their kindred materials, with the most powerful bond of habit; and this habit is the inclination of the spirit to return to itself; for it begins at the middle and proceeds onwards towards the extremities, and then when it has touched the extreme boundary, it turns back again, until it has again arrived at the same place from which it originally started. (36) This is the continued unalterable course, up and down, of habit, which runners, imitating in their triennial festivals, in those great common spectacles of all men, display as a brilliant achievement, and a worthy subject of rivalry and contention.

VIII. (37) And he has given to plants a nature which he has combined of as many powers as possible, that is of the nutritive, and the changeable, and the forming power; for they are nourished when they have need of nourishment; and a proof of this is that those plants which are not irrigated waste away and are dried up, as on the other hand those which have water supplied to them do visibly grow, for those which for a time were mere creepers on the ground, by reason of their shortness, suddenly spring up and become very long branches. And why need I speak of the changes which they undergo? (38) for at the time of the winter solstice their leaves wither and fall to the ground; and the eyes, as they are called by the agricultural labourers, which appear on the young shoots, close up like the eyes of animals, and all the mouths which are calculated to send forth young buds, are bound up; their internal nature being at that time confined and quiet, in order that, when it has taken breath, like a wrestler who has gone through a little preliminary exercise, and having again collected its appropriate strength, it may return again to its customary operations.

And this happens at the seasons of both spring and summer, (39) for then their nature, waking as it were out of a deep sleep, opens its eyes, and expands and widens its previously closed mouth; and then it brings forth all those things of which it was pregnant, leaves, and young shoots, and tendrils, and feelers, and fruit on all its branches; and then when these things have come to perfection it affords nourishment and food to them, as a mother does to her child by some invisible passages which are similar in principle to the breasts in women, and it never ceases to nourish them

until the fruit be come to complete ripeness; (40) and that which is thoroughly ripe is then perfected, when, even if no one gathers it, it of its own accord hastens to separate itself from its kindred branch, inasmuch as it no longer stands in need of nourishment from its parent, being able, if it should meet with a fitting soil, itself to sow and beget offspring resembling its own parents.

IX. (41) And the Creator has made the soul to differ from nature in these things—in the outwards sense, and imagination, and impetuosity; for plants are destitute of impetuosity and devoid of imagination, and without any participation in the outward sense. But every animal partakes of all these qualities above-mentioned, all together. (42) Now the outward sense, as indeed its name shows, in some degree is a kind of insertion, placing the things that are made apparent to it in the mind; for in the mind, since that is the greatest storehouse and receptacle for all things, is everything placed and treasured up which comes under the operation of the sense of seeing or hearing, or the other organs of the outward senses. (43) And imagination is an impression of figures in the soul; for the things which each of the outward senses has brought in, like a ring or a seal, on them it imprints its own character. And the mind, being like wax, having received the impression, keeps it carefully in itself until forgetfulness, the enemy of memory, has smoothed off the edges of the impression, or else has rendered it dim, or perhaps has completely effaced it.

(44) And that which has been visible and has been impressed upon the soul at times affects the soul in a way consistent with itself, and at other times in a different way; and this passion to which it is subject is called appetite, which philosophers who define such things say is the first motion of the soul. (45) In such important points are animals superior to plants.

Let us now see in what man is superior to the rest of the animal creation.

X. Man, then, has received this one extraordinary gift, intellect, which is accustomed to comprehend the nature of all bodies and of all things at the same time; for, as in the body, the sight is the most important faculty, and since in the universe the nature of light is the most pre-eminent thing, in the same manner that part of us which is entitled to the highest rank is the mind. (46) For the mind is the sight of the soul, shining transcendently with its own rays, by which the great and dense darkness which ignorance of things sheds around is dissipated. This species of soul is not composed of the same elements as those of which the other kinds were made, but it has received a purer and more excellent essence of which the divine natures were formed; on which account the intellect naturally appears to be the only thing in us which is imperishable, (47) for that is the only quality in us which the Father, who created us, thought deserving of freedom; and, unloosing the bonds of necessity, he let it go unrestrained, bestowing on it that most admirable gift and most connected with himself, the power, namely, of spontaneous will, as far as he was able to receive it; for the irrational animals, in whose soul there is not that especial gift tending to freedom, namely, mind, are put under the yoke and have bridles put in their mouths, and so are given unto men to be their slaves, as servants are given to their masters. But man, who has had bestowed on him a voluntary and self-impelling intellect, and who for the most part puts forth his energies in accordance with deliberate purpose, very properly receives blame for the offences which he designedly commits, and praise for the good actions which he intentionally performs. (48) For, in the case of other plants and other animals, we cannot call either the good that is caused by them deserving of praise, nor the evil that they do deserving of blame; for all their motions in either direction, and, all their changes, have no design about them, but are involuntary. But the soul of man, being the only one which has received from God the power of voluntary motion, and which in this respect has been made to resemble God, and being as far as possible emancipated from the authority of that grievous and severe mistress, necessity, may rightly be visited with reproach if she does not pay due honour to the being who has emancipated her. And therefore, in such a case, she will most deservedly suffer the implacable punishment denounced against slavish and ungrateful minds.

(49) So that God "considered" and though within himself, not now for the first time, but long ago, and with great steadiness and resolution, "that he had made man;" that is to say, he considered within himself what kind of being he had made him. For he had made him free from all bondage or restraint, able to exert his energies in accordance with his own will and deliberate purpose, on this account: that so knowing what things were good and what, on the contrary, were evil, and having arrived at a proper comprehension of what is honourable and what is disgraceful, and apprehending what things are just and what unjust, and, in short, what things flow from virtue and what from wickedness, he might exercise a choice of the better objects and an avoidance of their opposites; (50) and this is the meaning of the oracle recorded in Deuteronomy, "Behold, I have put before thy face life and death; good and evil. Do thou choose life."[12] Therefore he teaches us by this sentence both that men have a knowledge of good and of the contrary, evil, and that it is their duty to choose the better in preference to the worse, preserving

reason within themselves as an incorruptible judge, to be guided by the arguments which sound sense suggests, and to reject those which are brought forward by the contrary power.

XI. (51) Having now therefore explained these matters sufficiently, let us pass on to what comes next.

And this is what follows: "I will destroy," says God, "the man whom I have made from off the face of the earth, from man to beast, from creeping things to the fowls of the air, because I have considered and repent that I have made them."[13] (52) Now, some persons, when they hear the expressions which I have just cited, imagine that the living God is here giving away to anger and passion; but God is utterly inaccessible to any passion whatever. For it is the peculiar property of human weakness to be disquieted by any such feelings, but God has neither the irrational passions of the soul, nor are the parts and limits of the body in the least belonging to him. But, nevertheless, such things are spoken of with reference to God by the great lawgiver in an introductory sort of way, for the sake of admonishing those persons who could not be corrected otherwise. (53) For of all the laws which are couched in the form of injunction or prohibition, and such alone are properly speaking laws; there are two principal positions laid down with respect to the great cause of all things: one, that God is not as a man; the other, that God is as a man.[14] (54) But the first of these assertions is confirmed by the most certain truth, while the latter is introduced for the instruction of the many. In reference to which, it is said concerning them, "as a man would instruct his son."[15] And this is said for the sake of instruction and admonition, and not because he is really such by nature. (55) For of men some are attached to the service of the soul, and others to that of the body; now the companions of the soul, being able to associate with incorporeal natures, appreciable only by the intellect, do not compare the living God to any species of created beings; but, dissociating it with any idea of distinctive qualities (for this is what most especially contributes to his happiness and to his consummate felicity, to comprehend his naked existence without any connection with figure or character), they, I say, are content with the bare conception of his existence, and do not attempt to invest him with any form.

(56) But those who enter into agreements and alliances with the body, being unable to throw off the robes of the flesh, and to behold that nature, which alone of all natures has no need of anything, but is sufficient for itself, and simple, and unalloyed,

---

[12]Deuteronomy 30:15.

[13]Genesis 6:7.
[14]Numbers 23:19.
[15]Deuteronomy 1:31.

and incapable of being compared with anything else, from the same notions of the cause of all things that they do of themselves; not considering that in the case of a being who exists through a concurrence of many faculties, he has need of many parts in order to supply the necessities of each of those faculties.

XII. But God, inasmuch as he is uncreated, and the Being who has brought all other things to creation, stood in need of none of those things which are usually added to creatures. (57) For what are we to say? Shall we say, if he is possessed of the different organic parts, that he has feet for the sake of walking? But where is he to walk who fills all places at once with his presence? And to whom is he to go, when there is no one of equal honour with himself? And why is he to walk? It cannot be out of any regard for his health as we do. Again, are we to say that he has hands for the purpose of giving and taking? he never receives anything from any one. For in addition to the fact of his wanting nothing he actually has everything; and when he gives, he employs reason as the minister of his gifts, by whose agency also he created the world.

(58) Once more, he had no need of eyes, the organs without which there can be no comprehension of the light perceptible by the outward senses; but the light perceptible by the outward senses is a created light; and even before the creation God saw, using himself as light. (59) And why need we mention the organs of luxury? For if he has these organs, then he is fed, and when he has satisfied himself he leaves off eating, and after he has left eating he wants food again; and I need not enumerate other particulars which are the necessary consequences of this; for these are the fabulous inventions of impious men, who represent God, in word indeed only as endued with human form, but in fact as influenced by human passions.

XIII. (60) Why, then, does Moses speak of the Uncreate as having feet and hands, and as coming in and as going out? And why does he speak of him as clothed in armour for the purpose of repelling his enemies? For he does speak of him as girding himself with a sword, and as using arrows, and winds, and destructive fire. And the poets say that the whirlwind and the thunderbolt, mentioning them under other names, are the weapons of the Cause of all things. Moreover, speaking of him as they would of men, they add jealousy, anger, passion, and other feelings like these. But to those who ask questions on these subjects, one may answer, (61) "My good men! A man who would establish the most excellent system of laws, ought to keep one end constantly in view, namely, to do good to all who come within his reach." Those, therefore, who have received a fortunate disposition, and an education in all respects blameless, finding the path of life which proceeds in this direction plain and straight, take truth with them as the companion of their journey; by which they are initiated in the true mysteries relating to the living God, and therefore they never attribute any of the properties of created beings to him.

(62) Now to these disciples, that principal assertion in the sacred oracles is especially well adapted, that "God is not as man," but neither is he as heaven, nor as the world; for these species are endued with distinctive qualities, and they come under the perception of the outward senses. But he is not even comprehensible by the intellect, except merely as to his essence; for his existence, indeed, is a fact which we do comprehend concerning him, but beyond the fact of his existence, we can understand nothing.

XIV. (63) But those who have received a duller and more sluggish nature, and who have been wrongly brought up as children, and who are unable to see acutely, stand in need of physicians for lawgivers, who may be able to devise an appropriate remedy for the existing complaint, (64) since a severe master is a beneficial thing for untractable and foolish servants; for they, fearing his inflictions and his threats, are chastened by fear, in spite of themselves. Let, therefore, all such men learn false terrors, by which they may be benefited if they cannot be led into the right way by truth. (65) For in the case of men who are afflicted with dangerous illnesses, the most legitimate physicians do not venture to tell them the truth, knowing that by such conduct they will be rendered more desponding, and so that the disease will not be cured; but that by contrary language and comfort, they will bear the disease which presses upon them more easily, and the illness will be more likely to be allayed. (66) For what man is his senses would say to a patient under his care, "My good man, you shall have the knife applied to you, and cautery, and your limbs shall be amputated," even if such things were absolutely necessary to be endured? No man on earth would say so. For if he did, his patient would sink in his heart before the operations could be performed, and so receiving another disease in his soul, more grievous than that already existing in his body, he would resolutely renounce the cure; but if, on the other hand, through the deceit of the physician he is led to form a contrary expectation, he will submit to everything with a patient spirit, even though the means of his salvation may be most painful.

(67) Therefore the lawgiver, being a most admirable physician of the passions and diseases of the soul, has proposed to himself one task and one end, namely, to eradicate the diseases of the mind by the roots, so that there may not be a single one left behind to put forth any shoot of incurable distemper. (68) In this way, then, he hoped to be able to eradicate it, if he were to represent the Cause of all things as indulging in threats and

indignation, and implacable anger, and, moreover, as employing defensive arms to ward off attacks, and to chastise the wicked; for the fool alone is corrected by such means: (69) and therefore it is that it appears to me that with these two principal assertions above mentioned, namely, that God is as a man and that God is not as a man, are connected two other principles consequent upon and connected with them, namely, that of fear and that of love; for I see that all the exhortations of the laws to piety, are referred either to the love or to the fear of the living God. To those, therefore, who do not attribute either the parts or the passions of men to the living God, but who, as becomes the majesty of God, honour him in himself, and by himself alone, to love him is most natural; but to the others, it is most appropriate to fear him.

XV. (70) Such, then, are the things which it was proper to premise before we entered upon the following investigation:—

But we must now go back again to the original consideration, according to which we were in doubt what the meaning is which is concealed under the expression, "I was indignant that I had made them." Perhaps Moses here means to show, that bad men are made so by the anger of God, but good men by his grace; for immediately afterwards he proceeds to add, but "Noah found grace in the eyes of the Lord." (71) But anger, which is a passion peculiar to man, is here spoken of with especial felicity, but still more metaphorically than the real truth, in order to the explanation of a matter which is extremely necessary, namely, to show that everything that we do through anger, or fear, or pain, or grief, or any other passion, is confessedly faulty and open to reproach; but all that we do in accordance with right reason and knowledge is praiseworthy.

(72) You see now what great caution he uses in speaking here, when he says, "I was indignant that I had made them," not reversing the order of the words so as to say, "Because I had made them I was indignant;" for the latter expression would have become a person who repented of what he had done, an idea which is inconsistent with the nature of God, which foresees everything. But the other doctrine is a general one, being the expression of a man who means to explain by it that anger is the fountain of all sins, and reason the source of all good actions. (73) But God, remembering his own perfect goodness in every particular, even if the whole or the greater part of mankind fall off from him by reason of the abundance and extravagance of their sins, stretching forth his right hand, his hand of salvation, supports man and raises him up, not permitting the whole race to be utterly destroyed and to perish everlastingly.

XVI. (74) On which account God now says, that Noah found grace in his sight, when all the rest of mankind appearing ungrateful were about to receive punishment, in order that he might mingle saving mercy with judgment against sinners. As the psalmist has said somewhere, "My song shall be of mercy and judgment." [16] (75) For if God were to choose to judge the race of mankind without mercy, he would pass on them a sentence of condemnation; since there has never been a single man who, by his own unassisted power, has run the whole course of his life, from the beginning to the end, without stumbling; but since some men have fallen into voluntary, and some into involuntary sins, (76) that therefore the human race might still subsist, even though many of the subordinate members of it go to destruction. God mingles mercy with his justice, which he exercises towards the good actions of even the unworthy; and he not only pities them while judging, but judges them while pitying them, for mercy is older than justice in his sight, inasmuch as he knew the man who deserved punishment, not after he had passed sentence on him, but also before sentence.

XVII. (77) On which account he says in another passage, "The cup is in the hand of the Lord; full of the mixture of unmixed wine;" [17] and yet that which is mixed is not unmixed; but these words are spoken in a sense in the strictest accordance with natural philosophy and in one perfectly consistent with what has been said before; for God exerts his power in an untempered degree towards himself, but in a mixed character towards his creatures; for it is impossible for a mortal nature to endure his power unmitigated. (78) Do you think that you would be unable to look at the unmodified light of the sun? If you were to try to do so, your sight would be extinguished by the brilliancy of his rays, and be wholly blinded by a close approach to that luminary, before it could perceive anything, and yet the sun is only one of the works of God, a portion of the heaven, a fragment of compressed aether, but you are nevertheless able to gaze upon those uncreated powers which exist around him, and emit the most dazzling light, without any veil or modification.

(79) As, therefore, the sun extends his rays from heaven to the boundaries of the earth, tempering and dissolving the exceeding violence of the heat that is in them by cool air, for he mixes his rays with that, in order that that portion of them which gives light being separated from that portion which gives heat, he may remit somewhat of his power of burning, but retain the power by which he gives light, and so be received with welcome, when meeting that kindred and friendly light which is situated in the eyes of man; for the meeting of these two lights in the same place, coming from an opposite direction, and the reception of the one

---

[16] Psalm 100:1.
[17] Psalm 75:9.

by the other, is what causes that comprehension which we arrive at by our faculty of sight: but what mortal could possibly receive in this manner the knowledge, and wisdom, and prudence, and justice, and all the other virtues of God, in an unalloyed state? The whole heaven, the whole world, could not do so.

(80) Therefore the Creator, knowing the way in which he exceeded in all things that were most excellent, and the inherent natural weakness of created beings, even though they boast loudly, does not think either to benefit them or to chastise them to the extremity of his power, but only as far as he sees that those who are to be the objects of his benefits or of his chastisements have power to receive either. (81) If, then, we are able to drink of and to enjoy a gentle and moderate mixture of his powers, we might receive sufficient happiness therefrom, than which the race of man ought not to seek to receive any more complete enjoyment.

We have now explained what the mixed and unmixed powers and what those really supreme faculties are which exist in the living God alone.

XVIII. (82) And similar to what has been previously said, is that passage which occurs in another place, "God spake once, and twice I have also heard the same."[18] The expression "once" resembles the unmixed power, for the unmixed power is the unit, and the unit is the unmixed power; but the "twice" resembles the mixed power, for neither one nor the other is a simple thing, inasmuch as it admits of combination or of division. (83) God, therefore, utters unmixed units: for the word which he utters is not a beating of the air, being absolutely mingled with nothing else whatever, but it is incorporeal and naked, in no respect different from the unit. But we hear by the number two; (84) for the breath being sent from the dominant part of us through the artery called the trachea, is formed in the mouth by the tongue, as by a kind of workman, and being borne outward, and mingled with its kindred air, and having struck it thus harmoniously, completes the mixture of the two powers; for that which sounds together by a combination of different noises is at first adapted to a divisible dyad, having one sharp and one flat tone: (85) very beautifully, therefore, did he oppose one just reason to the multitude of unjust reasons, less indeed in number, but superior in power, in order that the worse of the two might not, like a weight put in a scale, weigh down the other; but that, by the power of the weight of the better one in the opposite scale it might have its lightness detected, and so be weakened.

XIX. (86) But what is the meaning of the sentence, "Noah found grace in the sight of the Lord God?" Let us now consider this: for those who find anything, some are finding what they formerly had and have lost; and some are discovering what they never had before, and now possess for the first time. Accordingly, those men who occupy themselves with the investigation of appropriate names, are accustomed to call the latter kind finding (heuresis), and the former kind re-finding (aneuresis). (87) Of the former species we have a conspicuous example afforded us in the injunctions given about the great vow.[19] Now a vow is a request for good things from God; and the spirit of the great vow is to believe that God himself is the cause of good things from himself, without anyone else ever co-operating with him, of the things which may appear to be beneficial, neither the earth as fruitful, nor the rain as helping to promote the growth of seeds and plants, nor the air as calculated to nourish man, nor agriculture as the cause of production, nor the skill of the physician as the cause of health, nor marriage as the cause of the procreation of children: (88) for all these things receive changes and alterations through the power of God, to such a degree and in such a way as often to have effects contrary to their usual ones. Moses, therefore says, that this man is "holy who nourishes the hair of his head;" the meaning of which is, that he is holy who promotes the growth in the principal portion of himself of the principal shoots of the doctrines of virtue, and who in a manner prides himself and takes delight in these doctrines: (89) but sometimes he loses them, a sort of whirlwind, as it were, suddenly darting down upon the soul, and carrying off everything that was good out of it; and this whirlwind is an involuntary change, which pollutes the mind in a moment, which Moses calls death.[20] (90) But nevertheless, when he has afterwards got rid of this and become purified, he recovers and recollects again, what for a time, he had forgotten, and finds what he had lost, so that the days of his former change are not included in the computation, either because such change is a matter which cannot be reduced to calculation, inasmuch as it is inconsistent with right reason and has no partnership with prudence, or because it does not deserve to be taken into calculation; "for of such things," some ancient writer says, "there is no account nor calculation taken."[21]

XX. (91) And we have often met with such things as previously we had never seen even in a dream; like a husbandman whom some persons say while digging a hole for the purpose of planting some fruit-bearing tree, found a treasure, meeting with good fortune which he had never hoped for. (92) Therefore Jacob, the wrestler with God,

---

[18]Psalm 61:12.

[19]Numbers 6:2.
[20]Numbers 6:9.
[21]Alluding probably to Theocritus—14.17.

when his father asked him the manner in which he had acquired this knowledge, saying, "How didst thou find this so quickly, my son?" answered and said, "Because the Lord my God brought it before me."[22] For when God bestows on any one the treasures of his own wisdom without any toil or labour, then we, without having expected such things, suddenly perceive that we have found a treasure of perfect happiness.

(93) And it often happens to those who seek with great labour, that they miss that for which they are seeking; while others, who are seeking without any diligence, find with great ease even things that they never thought of finding. For those who are dull and slow in their souls, like men bereft of their eyesight, find the labour which they devote to the contemplation of objects of science useless and wasted; while others, through the richness of their natural endowments, find out immeasurable things without any investigation at all, by the help of felicitous and well directed conjectures; so that it would seem that they attain their objects not in consequence of any labour of their own, but because the things themselves do of their own accord come to meet them and hasten to present themselves to their view, and so give them the most accurate comprehension of them.

XXI. (94) To these men the lawgiver says were given, "Great and beautiful cities, which they had not built; houses full of good things, which they had not filled; cisterns cut out of the solid rock, which they had not hewn; vineyards and olive gardens, which they had not planted."[23] (95) Now, by cities and houses, he here symbolically sketches out the generic and specific virtues; for genus resembles a city, because it is marked out in larger circumferences, and because it is common to many individuals; and species resembles a house, because it is more contracted and avoids community; (96) and cisterns prepared before-hand intimate the rewards which fall to the lot of some for their labour, while they are given spontaneously to others, being channels of heavenly and wholesome waters and well prepared treasures for the preservation of the virtues before mentioned, by means of which joy is shed over the perfect heart, irradiating it all over with the light of truth. Again, when Moses speaks of the vineyards, he means them as an emblem of cheerfulness, and the olive gardens as a symbol of light.

(97) Happy, therefore, are they who, suffering something like those persons who awoke up out of deep sleep, on a sudden, without any labour or exertion on their part, behold the world before them; and miserable are they to whom it happens to be eagerly contentious for objects to which they are not fitted by nature, being full of a contentious spirit, which is the most grievous of diseases. (98) For, in addition to failing in the object which they are desirous of attaining, they do further incur great disgrace with no slight injury, like ships which are attempting to make their way by sea against opposing winds; for they, in addition to being unable to proceed in their course towards the point to which they are hastening, are very often upset with their crews and their cargoes, and so cause pain to their friends and pleasure to their enemies.

XXII. (99) Therefore the law says that some persons, having made a violent effort, went up to the mountain, "And the Amorites came forth who dwell on that mountain, and wounded them, as bees might have done, and pursued them from Seir even to Hormah."[24] (100) For it follows of necessity that those persons who, being by nature unfitted for the comprehension of arts, if by making violent efforts they do something in them, not only fail of attaining their end, but also incur disgrace; and those who voluntarily, but still without any deliberate consent of their mind, do something that they ought to do, putting a sort of constraint on their own voluntary principle, do not succeed, but are wounded and harassed by their own consciences.

(101) So also those who restore deposits of small value in the hope of having larger deposits entrusted to them, which they may be able to appropriate, you would call men of good faith; and yet even when they are restoring the deposits, they put a great constraint on their natural faithlessness, by which it is to be hoped, they will be unceasingly tormented.

(102) And do not all those who offer but a spurious kind of worship to the only wise God, putting on a profession of a rigid life like a dress on a magnificent stage, merely with the object of making a display before the assembled spectators, having imposture rather than piety in their souls, do not they, I say, stretch themselves on the rack as it were, and torment themselves, compelling even the truth itself to assume a false appearance. (103) Therefore, they being for a brief period overshadowed with the emblems of superstition, which is the great hindrance to holiness, and a great injury to those who have it and to those who associate with it; after that again stripping off their disguise, display their naked hypocrisy. And then like men, convicted of being aliens, they are looked upon as enemies, having entered themselves as citizens of that noblest of cities—virtue, while they have really no connection with it. For whatever is violent (*biaion*) is also of short duration, as its very name imports, since it closely resembles short (*baion*). And the ancients used the two words

---

[22] Genesis 27:20.
[23] Deuteronomy 6:11.
[24] Deuteronomy 1:43.

(baion) and *(oligochronion)* of short duration as synonymous.

XXIII. (104) We must now consider the question which is meant by "Noah found grace in the sight of the Lord God."[25] Is the meaning of what is here expressed this, that he received grace, or that he was accounted worthy of grace? The former idea it is not natural for us to entertain; for what was given to him beyond what was given to all, as one may say, not only to all concrete natures only, but to all elementary and simple natures which have been accounted worthy of divine grace? (105) But the second interpretation has a reason in it which is not altogether inconsistent, that the cause of all things, judges those persons worthy of his gifts, who do not corrupt the divine impression which has been stamped upon them, namely, the most sacred mind, with disgraceful practices; still perhaps even this is not the true meaning of the words. (106) For what kind of person must he be who would be accounted before God to be worthy of his grace? I indeed think that the whole world put together could scarcely attain to such a pitch, and yet the world is the first, and greatest, and most perfect of all the works of God. (107) May it not then perhaps be better to understand this expression as meaning that the virtuous man being fond of investigating things, and eager for learning, amid all the different things that he has investigated, has found this one most certain fact, that all things that exist, the earth, the water, the air, the fire, the sun, the stars, the heaven, all animals and plants whatever, are the grace of God.

(108) But God has given nothing to himself, for he has no need of anything; but he has given the world to the world, and its parts he has bestowed on themselves and on one another, and also on the universe, and without having judged anything to be worthy of grace, (for he gives all his good things without grudging to the universe and to its parts), he merely has regard to his own everlasting goodness, thinking the doing good to be a line of conduct suitable to his own happy and blessed nature; so that if any one were to ask me, what was the cause of the creation of the world, having learnt from Moses, I should answer, that the goodness of the living God, being the most important of his graces, is in itself the cause.

XXIV. (109) But here we must observe that Moses says, that "Noah pleased" the powers of the living God, "the Lord and God," but that he tells us that Moses himself pleased the Being who is attended by those powers as his body guard, and who, without them, is conceived only according to his essence. For it is said, here, speaking in the person of God, "Because thou hast found grace in my sight,"[26] pointing out himself instead of any one else whatever. (110) Thus, therefore, he who exists himself by himself alone, thinks the exceeding wisdom which is found in Moses worthy of grace, and that other wisdom which was formed on the model of his, he considers of an inferior class, and more a wisdom of species, as consisting of subordinate powers, according to which he is both Lord and God, and ruler and benefactor.

(111) But another mind attached to the body and the slave of the passions, having been sold as slave to the chief cook,[27] that is to say to the pleasure of our compound being, and being castrated and mutilated of all the masculine and generative parts of the soul, being afflicted with a want of all good practices, and being incapable of receiving the divine voice, being also separated and cut off from the sacred assembly, in which conferences and discussions about virtue are continually being brought up, is conducted into the prison of the passions, and finds grace, (a grace more inglorious than dishonour), with the keeper of the prison.[28]

(112) For these men are properly called prisoners, not those who after they have been condemned at the judgment seat by the legitimate magistrates, or by judges formally appointed, are led away by the officers into the place appointed for malefactors; but those in whom nature has condemned the disposition of their souls, men who are full of intemperance, and cowardice, and injustice, and impiety, and innumerable other evils; (113) but the steward, and keeper, and guardian of these men, is the keeper of the prison, a composition and combination of all kinds of various wickednesses, united together into one mass, to please whom is the greatest of punishments.

But some people who do not perceive this, being deceived with respect to what is injurious to such a degree, as to look upon it as advantageous, come to him with great joy, and offer themselves as his body-guards, that being accounted faithful by him, they may become his lieutenants and successors in the guardianship of involuntary and voluntary offences; (114) but do thou, O my soul, thinking such an office and magistracy as that, more grievous than the most laborious slavery, adopt, as far as you can, an unrestrained, and unconfined, and free system of life, (115) and if you are caught by the baits of passion, endure rather to be a prisoner yourself, than the keeper of a prison; for then if you suffer distress, and groan aloud, you will obtain pity; but if you give yourself up to ambition of great posts, and to a covetousness of honour, you will receive that pleasant and

---

[25]Genesis 6:8.

[26]Exodus 33:17.
[27]Genesis 39:1.
[28]Genesis 39:21.

greatest evil of being keeper of the prison, by which you will be influenced the whole of your life.

XXV. (116) Reject therefore with all your might all idea of pleasing the keepers of the prison; but on the contrary, with all your ability and all your earnestness, labour to please him who is the cause of all things; and if you are unable to do so, (for the greatness of his dignity is exceeding high), at all events advance, without ever turning back, towards his powers, and present yourself to them as their suppliant, until they admitting the continual assiduity and sincerity of your service, place you in the ranks of those who have pleased them, as they did Noah, of whose descendants Moses has made a most admirable and novel catalogue; (117) for he says, "These are the generations of Noah: Noah was a just man, being perfect in his generation, and Noah pleased God;"[29] for the descendants of the compound being were naturally compound beings also themselves; for horses do of necessity beget horses, and lions beget lions, bulls become the parents of bulls, and so too men beget men; (118) but such things are not the appropriate offspring of a good mind; the progeny of that are the virtues before mentioned, namely the being a man, the being just, the being perfect, the pleasing God, which last particular, inasmuch as it is the crowning one, and as it were the boundary of perfect happiness, is enumerated last of all.

(119) But there is one kind of creation, which is a sort of conducting and travelling from that which does not exist to existence. This is the one which plants, and animals do of necessity use; and there is another kind, which is a transition and change from a better genus to a rose species, which Moses mentions when he says, "These are the generations of Jacob; Joseph when he was seventeen years of age, was keeping the sheep with his brethren, being a youth with the sons of Billah, and with the sons of Zilpah, his father's wives."[30] (120) For when this reason inclined to meditation and devoted to learning, was driven down from its more divine speculations, human and mortal opinions, then Joseph, the companion of the body, and of all the things which pertain to the body was born, being still but a youth, even though in the lapse of time he may become greyheaded, as being one who never listened to any older discourse or opinions, which the companions of Moses acquired as the most useful possessions for themselves and their disciples. (121) On this account it seems to me that Moses wishing to describe his figure and to give a more accurate idea of his appearance, so as to make it known, introduced him as tending his father's sheep, not in the company of any one

of his father's legitimate sons, but with his illegitimate brethren, who, being the sons of concubines, derive their name from the inferior sex, that of the women, and not from the superior sex, that, namely of the man; for they here are called the sons of Jacob's wives, Billah and Zilpah, and not the sons of their father Israel.

XXVI. (122) And one may here very fitly raise the question for what reason it was that after mentioning the perfection of Noah in virtue, he then immediately adds that "the earth was become corrupt in the sight of God, and was filled with wickedness."[31] But perhaps it is not difficult to arrive at a solution of this doubt, for any one who is not exceedingly ignorant of all instruction. (123) We must say therefore, that when an incorruptible species arises in the soul, the mortal part is immediately destroyed; for the birth of virtuous studies is the death of disgraceful ones, since also when light shines forth darkness disappears. On this account, in the law of leprosy, it is most expressly enjoined that "If the living skin arise in the leper, he shall be polluted;"[32] (124) and further ratifying this same injunction, and as it were setting a seal to it, he adds, "and the flesh which is sound shall pollute him," delivering this injunction in opposition to what is natural or usual: for all men think the things that are sick the pollution of those that are in health, and those that are dead the pollution of the living, and not, on the contrary, that the healthy and the living are the pollution of the wick and of the dead, but rather, they account them their salvation. (125) But the lawgiver being full of the most modern wisdom in everything, has this peculiarity in his expositions, that he teaches that the healthy and the living are the causes of our not being pure from pollution; for the healthy and living complexion in the soul is truly conviction which rises up against it: (126) when this conviction rises up, it makes a catalogue of all the offences of the soul, and reproaching it with them, and looking sternly at it, it is scarcely able to be stopped in its attacks upon it; and the soul being convicted recognises all its actions by which it has offended against right reason, and perceives that it is foolish, and intemperate, and unjust, and full of pollutions.

XXVII. (127) On which account Moses also establishes a most extraordinary law, in which he enjoins that "the man who is in part leprous shall be accounted impure, but that he who is wholly, from the sole of his foot to the crown of his head overwhelmed with leprosy, shall be considered pure;"[33] for any one else, I apprehend, reasoning from probability, would say the exact contrary, and

---

[29] Genesis 6:9.
[30] Genesis 37:2.

[31] Genesis 6:11.
[32] Leviticus 13:14.
[33] Leviticus 13:11.

would think that the leprosy which was contracted, and which extended over only a small portion of the body, was less impure, but that the leprosy which was diffused, so as to spread over the whole body was more impure: (128) but Moses here, as it appears to me, uses this symbolical expression to intimate this most undeniable truth, that unintentional misdeeds, even if they be of the greatest enormity, are not deserving of blame, and are pure, inasmuch as they have not conscience, that terrible accuser, to testify against them: but that intentional offences, even if they do not extend over a wide surface, being convicted by the judge who passes sentence against the soul, are rightly accounted unholy, and polluted, and impure.

(129) This leprosy, therefore, being of a twofold character, and putting forth two complexions, signifies voluntary depravity; for the soul, though it has healthy, and vivifying, and right reason in itself, does not use it for the preservation of its good things, but surrendering itself to persons unskilled in navigation, it overturns the whole bark of life, which might have been saved in calm fine weather; (130) but when it changes so as to assume one uniform white appearance, it displays an involuntary change; since the mind, entirely deprived of the power of reasoning, not having left in it one single seed to beget understanding, like a man in a mist or in deep darkness, sees nothing that ought to be done; but, like a blind man, falling without seeing his way before him into all kinds of error, endures continual falls and disasters one after another, in spite of all its efforts.

XXVIII. (131) And like this is the injunction given respecting the house in which it happens that leprosy often arises; for Moses says that, "If there be a taint of leprosy in the house, the owner shall come, and shall tell it to the priest, saying there is something like a taint of leprosy has been seen by me in my house,"[34] and presently he adds, "And the priest shall command him to dismantle his house, before the priest enters into the house to see it, and all the things that are in the house shall not be impure; and after that the priest shall enter the house to examine it." (132) Therefore, before the priest enters in, the things in the house are pure; but after he has entered in, from that time forth they are all impure. And yet the contrary would have been natural, that when a man thoroughly purified and perfect, who is in the habit of offering up prayers and purifications, and sacrifices for all the people come into a house, all that is therein would be improved by his presence, and would become pure from having been impure; but now they do not even remain in the same condition as before, but they are brought into a worse state by the arrival of the priest.

(133) But whether this is consistent with the literal and obvious order of the words, those men may inquire who are in the habit of, and fond of pursuing such investigations; but we must affirm distinctly, that no one thing can be more consistent with another than the fact, that when the priest enters in, all the things in the house should be polluted; (134) for as long as the divine word has not come to our souls as to a hearth of hospitality, all its actions are blameless; for the overseer, or the father, or the teacher, or whatever else it may be fit to entitle the priest, by whom alone it is possible for it to be admonished and chastened, is at a distance: and those persons are to be pardoned who do wrong from inexperience, out of ignorance what they ought to do: for they do not look upon their deeds in the light of sins, but even sometimes they believe that they are doing right in cases in which they are erring greatly; (135) but when the real priest, conviction, enters our hearts, like a most pure ray of light, then we think that the designs which we have cherished within our souls are not pure, and we see that our actions are liable to blame, and deserving of reproach, though we did them through ignorance of what was right. All these things, therefore, the priest, that is to say, conviction, pollutes, and orders that they should be taken away and stripped off, in order that he may see the abode of the soul pure,[35] and, if there are any diseases in it, that he may heal them.

XXIX. (136) And the woman who met the prophet,[36] in the book of Kings, resembles this fact: "And she is a widow;" not meaning by that, as we generally use the word, a woman when she is bereft of her husband, but that she is so, from being free from those passions which corrupt and destroy the soul, as Thamar is represented by Moses. (137) For she also being a widow, was commanded to sit down in the house of the father, the only Saviour;[37] on whose account, having forsaken for ever the company and society of men, she is at a distance from and widowed of all human pleasures, and receives a divine seed; and being filled with the seeds of virtue, she conceives, and is in travail of virtuous actions. And when she has brought them forth, she carries off the prize against her adversaries, and is enrolled as victorious, bearing the palm as the emblem of her victory.

For the name Thamar, being interpreted, means the palm-tree. (138) And every soul that is beginning to be widowed and devoid of evils, says to the prophet, "O, man of God! hast thou come to me to remind me of my iniquity and of my sin?"[38]

---

[34]Leviticus 14:35.

[35]Ibid.
[36]1 Kings 17:10.
[37]Genesis 38:11.
[38]1 Kings 17:18.

For he being inspired, and entering into the soul, and being filled with heavenly love, and being amazingly excited by the intolerable stimulus of heaven-inflicted frenzy, works in the soul a recollection of its ancient iniquities and offences: not in order that it may commit such again,—but that, greatly lamenting and bitterly bewailing its former error, it may hate its own offspring, and reject them with aversion, and may follow the admonitions of the word of God, the interpreter and prophet of his will. (139) For the men of old used to call the prophets sometimes men of God, and sometimes seers,[39] affixing appropriate and becoming names to their enthusiasm, and inspiration, and to the foreknowledge of affairs which they enjoyed.

XXX. (140) Very properly, therefore, the most sacred Moses says that, the earth was corrupted at that time when the virtues of the just Noah were made manifest: "And the whole earth," says he, "was corrupted, because all flesh had corrupted his (*autou*) way upon the earth."[40] (141) Now to some persons this expression will seem to have been incorrectly used, and that the consistency with the context, and the truth of the fact will require that we should read rather that, "All flesh had corrupted its (*autēs*) way upon the earth." For it does not agree with the feminine noun "flesh" (*tē sarki*), if we subjoin a masculine case, the word *autou* in connection with it. (142) But perhaps, Moses does not mean here to speak of the flesh alone as corrupting his way upon the earth, so that he deserves to be considered to have erred in the expression which he has used, but rather to speak of the things of the flesh, which is corrupted, and of that other being whose way the flesh endeavours to injure and to corrupt.

So that we should explain this expression thus:—All flesh corrupted the perfect way of the everlasting and incorruptible being which conducts to God. (143) And know that this way is wisdom. For the mind being guided by wisdom, while the road is straight and level and easy, proceeds along it to the end; and the end of this road is the knowledge and understanding of God. But every companion of the flesh hates and repudiates, and endeavours to corrupt this way; for there is no one thing so much at variance with another, as knowledge is at variance with the pleasure of the flesh. Accordingly, the earthly Edom is always fighting with those who wish to proceed by this road, (144) which is the royal road for those who partake of the faculty of seeing who are called Israel; for the interpretation of the name Edom, is "earthly," and he labours with all earnestness, and by every means in his power, and by threats, to hinder them

from this road, and to make it pathless and impracticable for ever.

XXXI. (145) Therefore the ambassadors who are sent speak as follows:—"We will pass on through thy land; we will not pass through thy fields nor through thy vineyards; we will not drink water from thy cistern; we will proceed by the royal road; we will not turn aside out of the way, to the right hand, nor to the left, until we have passed over thy borders. But Edom answered and said, Thou shalt not pass through my land: and if thou dost, I will come against thee in battle to meet thee. And the children of Israel said unto him. We will pass by thy mountain; but if I or my cattle drink of thy water, I will pay thee the price thereof. But it is of no consequence, we will pass by thy mountain. And he said, 'Thou shalt not pass through my land.'"[41]

(146) It is said of some man of old time, that when he saw a sumptuous procession properly equipped passing by, he looked towards one of his acquaintances and said, "My friends, see how many things there are of which I have no need," in a very few words uttering what was truly a great and heavenly boast. What dost thou say? (147) Were you crowned as conqueror in the Olympic games in opposition to all the wealth arrayed against you; and were you so to that degree there that you took nothing from thence for your enjoyment or for your use? It is a marvellous statement, but the sentiment is more admirable still, which advanced to such a degree of strength, as to be able without any extraordinary exertion, nevertheless to carry off the victory by force.

XXXII. (148) But it is not allowed to one man alone to boast before Moses who has been instructed in the highest perfection of wisdom, but it belongs to the whole of a most populous nation. And this is the proof of that fact. The soul of every one of his friends felt confidence and was bold towards the king of all the apparent good things, the earthly Edom; for in fact all earthly good things are good only in appearance; they then I say were bold, so as to say, "I will now pass by thy land." (149) Oh, the magnanimous and sublime promise! Tell me, will ye be able to surmount, to pass by, to run past all these things which on earth appear to be and are believed to be good? And is there nothing which will be able to check and restrain your forward advance by the power with which it resists you? (150) And when you have beheld all the treasures of riches one after another, and all full, will ye turn from them with aversion, and avert your eyes from them? And will ye look down upon the dignities of your ancestors, and on those which come to yourselves from your father and your

[39] 1 Samuel 9:9.
[40] Genesis 6:12.

[41] Numbers 20:17.

mother, and on their nobility which is so celebrated in the mouths of the multitude? And will ye forsake the glory for which men are ready to barter everything, leaving it behind as if it were something most utterly valueless? What more shall I say? Will ye disregard the health of the body, and the accurate perfection of the outward senses, and beauty, which is an object of contention to many, and strength such as no one can oppose, and all those other things by which the house or the tomb of the soul, or whatever else one ought to call it is adorned, will ye, I say, disregard all these things, so far as not to class any one of them among good things? (151) These are mighty deeds of boldness for a heavenly and celestial soul, which has utterly forsaken the regions of earth, and which has been drawn up on high, and has its abode among the divine natures. For being filled with the sight of the genuine and incorruptible good things, it very naturally repudiates those which only last a day and are spurious.

XXXIII. (152) What is the advantage then of passing over all the mortal advantages of mortal man, and passing them by too, not in accordance with right reason, but as some do through their hesitation, or sluggishness, or inexperience; for everything is not honoured everywhere, but different things are esteemed by different persons. (153) On this account, Moses wishing to teach further, that they had become by correctness of reason inclined to despise what was said, adds to the words, "I will pass by," the further description, "through your land." For this is exceedingly necessary, that when surrounded by an abundance of those things which are usually accounted advantages, we should avoid being taken prisoners by any of the toils which are spread by each separate pleasure; and that like fire, we should be able at one onset to break through their attacks which are so continually armed against us.

(154) The Israelites say then that they will pass by this way, but that they will not pass any longer through the fields and vineyards; for it would be doting simplicity to pass by all the plants in the soul worthy of cultivation and producing eatable fruit, that is to say virtuous discourses and praiseworthy actions. For it would be proper rather to remain, and to gather the fruit, and to feed on it to satiety. For nothing is more beautiful than an insatiable cheerfulness and amid perfect virtues, of which cheerfulness, the aforesaid vineyards are the symbol. (155) But we, on whom God pours and showers his fountains of good things from above, we drank from that cistern, and we were seeking scanty moisture beneath the earth, while the heaven was raining upon us, from above without ceasing, the more excellent food of nectar and ambrosia, far better than that celebrated in the fables of the poets.

XXXIV. (156) Moreover, should we while draining draughts stored up by the contrivance of men through distrust, seek a refuge and place of escape where the Saviour of the universe has opened to us his heavenly treasury for our use and enjoyment? For Moses, the hierophant, prays that "the Lord may open to us his good treasure, his heavenly one, to give us his rain,"[42] and the prayers of the man who loves God are sure to obtain a hearing. (157) And what does he say who neither thinks the heaven, or the rain, or a cistern, or in fact anything whatever in all creation sufficient to nourish him, but who goes beyond all these things, and relating what he has suffered, says, "The God who has nourished me from my youth up."[43] Does not this man appear to you not to think all the collections of water under the earth put together worthy even of looking at? (158) Nor therefore would he drink out of a cistern to whom God gives draughts of unmixed wine; at one time, by the ministrations of some angel whom he has thought worthy to act as cupbearer, and at another time by his own means, placing no one between the giver and the receiver.

(159) Let us then, without any delay, attempt to proceed by the royal road, since we think fit to pass by all earthly things; and the royal road is that of which there is not private individual in the world who is master, but he alone who is also the only true king. (160) And this is, as I said a little while ago, wisdom, by which alone suppliant souls can find a way of escaping to the uncreate God; for it is natural that one who goes without any hindrance along the royal road, will never feel weariness before he meets with the king.

(161) But, then, those who have come near to him recognise his blessedness and their own deficiency; for Abraham, when he had placed himself very near to God, immediately perceived that he was but dust and ashes.[44] (162) And let them turn away out of the royal road, neither to the right hand nor to the left, but let them advance along the middle of it; for any deviation in either direction is blameable, as that on the one side has a tendency to excess and that on the other side to deficiency; for the right hand is, in this instance, no less blameable than the left hand. (163) In the case of those who live according to impulse, the right hand is temerity and the left hand cowardice. As regards those who are illiberal in the management of money, on the right hand stands stinginess, and on the left hand extravagant prodigality; and those men, who are very subtle in calculating, judge craftiness to be desirable and simplicity to be a thing to be shunned. Again, some persons incline towards superstition as being placed on the

---

[42] Deuteronomy 28:12.
[43] Genesis 48:15.
[44] Genesis 18:27.

right hand, and flee from impiety as a thing to be avoided on the left.

XXXV. (164) But that we may not, through deviating from the right road, be compelled to yield to one of two rival faults, let us desire and pray to be able to proceed straight along the middle of the road. Now, the middle between temerity and cowardice, is courage; the mean between profuse extravagance and illiberal stinginess, is temperance; that between crafty unscrupulousness and folly, is prudence; and the proper path between superstition and impiety, is piety. (165) These lie in the middle between the deviations on either side, and are all roads easily travelled, and level, and plain, which we must walk upon not with our bodily organs, but with the motions of a soul continually desiring what is best.

(166) At this, the earthly Edom, being excessively indignant (for he is afraid of the overthrow and confusion of his own doctrines), will threaten us with irreconcilable wars, if we attempt to force our way along it, cutting down and clearing away continually as we advance the fruitful trees of his soul, which he planted for the destruction of wisdom, but has not gathered the fruit thereof; for he says, "Thou shalt not pass by me; and if thou dost, I will come forth in battle against thee to meet thee." (167) But let us regard none of his threats, but make answer that we will pass by his mountain; that is to say, we being accustomed to associate with high and sublime powers and to investigate everything according to its true definition, and being used to inquire into the reason of everything whatever, of every kind, by means of which the knowledge is attained of what anything is, hold in utter contempt everything which is external and which affects the body alone; for such things are lowly and grovelling in the ground, dear indeed to you, but hated by us, for which reason we will not have anything to do with any one of them. (168) For if, as the proverb says, we only touch this with the tip of our finger, we shall be giving honour and dignity to you; for then you will give yourself airs and will boast, as if we who are lovers of virtue had been brought over to you by the allurements of pleasure.

XXXVI. (169) "For if," says Israel, "I and my cattle drink of thy water, I will pay you a price for it." Not meaning by that such price as is spoken of by the poets, money of silver or gold, or anything else; such among dealers is accustomed to be given to those who sell wares in exchanges for their wares, but the price will be the honour which he now claims; (170) for, in reality, every intemperate, or unjust, or cowardly man, when he sees any one who is more austere either avoiding labour, or subdued by gain, or yielding to any one of the allurements of pleasure, rejoices and exults, and thinks that he himself has received honour. And, moreover, going on in his rejoicing and displaying

his exultation to the multitude, he begins to philosophise about his own errors as very unavoidable and not useless, saying that if they were not of such a character, that respectable man, so and so, would never have indulged in them.

(171) Let us, then, say to every wicked man, if we drink of thy water, if we touch anything, whatever that is yours, owing to an indiscreet impetuosity, we shall be giving you honour, and acceptance, instead of dishonour and rejection (for these are what you deserve to receive); (172) and, in truth, the matters about which you are anxious are absolutely nothing. Do you think that anything mortal has any real being and existence, and that it is not rather something borne up and suspended by the rope of some false and untrustworthy opinion, resting on empty air, and in no respect differing from deceitful dreams? (173) And if you are unwilling to contemplate the fortunes of particular men, think upon the changes, whether for the better or for the worse, of whole countries and nations.

At one time Greece was flourishing, but the Macedonians took away the power of that land; then, in turn, Macedonia became mighty, but that, being divided into small portions became weak, until at last it was entirely extinguished. (174) Before the time of the Macedonians the Persians prospered, but one day overthrew their exceeding and extensive prosperity. And now the Parthians are more powerful than the Persians, who a little while ago were their masters, ever were; and those who were their subjects are now masters. Once, and for a very long time, Egypt was a mighty empire, but its great dominion and glory have passed away like a cloud. What has become of the Ethiopians, and of Carthage, and of the kingdoms of Libya? Where now are the kings of Pontus? (175) What has become of Europe and Asia, and, in short, of the whole of the inhabited world? Is it not tossed up and down the agitated like a ship that is tossed by the sea, at one time enjoying a fair wind and at another time being forced to battle against contrary gales? (176) For the divine Word brings round its operations in a circle, which the common multitude of men call fortune. And then, as it continually flows on among cities, and nations, and countries, it overturns existing arrangements and gives to one person what has previously belonged to another, changing the affairs of individuals only in point of time, in order that the whole world may become, as it were, one city, and enjoy the most excellent of constitutions, a democracy.

XXXVII. (177) No one, therefore, of all the objects of human anxiety or of human labour, is of any importance or value; but every such thing is a mere shadow or breath, disappearing before it can get any firm footing; for it comes and then again it departs, like the ebbing tide. For the sea, in its ebb and flow, is at one time borne forwards with great violence, and roaring, and noise, and overflowing its bounds makes a lake of what has previously been dry land; and, at another time, it recedes and makes a large portion of what has been sea, dry land. (178) In the same manner, at times, prosperity overflows a mighty and populous nation, but afterwards turns the impetuosity of its stream in the opposite direction, and does not leave even the slightest drop, so as to suffer no trace whatever to remain of its former richness. (179) But it is not everybody who receives the complete and full meaning of these events, but only those receive it who are accustomed always to proceed in accordance with true and solid reason and limitation; for we find the same men saying both these things, "All the affairs of the created world are absolutely nothing;" and, "We will go by thy mountain." (180) For it is impossible for one who is not in the habit of using high and mountainous roads to repudiate all mortal affairs, and to turn aside and change his paths for what is immortal.

Therefore the earthly Edom thinks it right to blockade the heavenly and royal road of virtue, and the divine reason blockades his road, and that of all who follow his opinions; (181) among whom we must enroll Balaam, for he also is a child of the earth, and not a shoot of heaven, and a proof of this is, that he, being influenced by omens and false prophecies, not even when the eye of his soul,

which had been closed, recovered its sight, and "saw the angel of God standing against him in the way;"[45] not even then did he turn back and desist from doing wrong, but giving way to a mighty torrent of folly, he was washed away and swallowed up by it.

(182) For then the diseases of the soul are truly not only difficult of cure, but even utterly incurable, when, though conviction is present to us (and this is the word of God, coming as his angel and as our guide, and removing the obstacles before our feet, so that we may travel without stumbling along the level road), we nevertheless prefer our own indiscreet opinions, to the explanations and injunctions which he is accustomed to address to us for our admonition, and for the chastening and regulating of our whole life. (183) On this account he who is not persuaded by, and who shows no respect to, conviction, when it thus opposes him, will, in his turn, incur destruction with the wounded,[46] whom the passions have wounded and overthrown; and his calamity will be a most sufficient lesson for all those who are not utterly impure, to endeavour to keep the judge, that is within them, favourable to them, and he will be so if they do not reverse what has been rightly decided by him.

---

[45] Numbers 22:31.
[46] Numbers 31:8.

ON HUSBANDRY†

(De Agricultura)

I. (1) "And Noah began to be a husbandman; and he planted a vineyard, and he drank of the wine, and he was drunk in his house."[1] The generality of men not understanding the nature of things, do also of necessity err with respect to the composition of names; for those who consider affairs anatomically, as it were, are easily able to affix appropriate names to things, but those who look at them in a confused and irregular way are incapable of such accuracy. (2) But Moses, through the exceeding abundance of his knowledge of all things, was accustomed to affix the most felicitous and expressive appellations to them. Accordingly, in many passages of the law, we shall find this opinion, which we have expressed, confirmed by the fact, and not least in the passage which we have cited at the beginning of this treatise, in which the just Noah is represented as a husbandman. (3) For what man is there who is at all hasty in forming an opinion, who would not think that the being a husbandman *(geōrgia)*, and the occupying one's self in cultivating the ground *(hē gēsergasia)*, were the same thing? And yet in real truth, not only are these things not the same, but they are even very much separated from one another, so as to be opposed to, and at variance with one another.

(4) For a man without any skill may labour at taking care of the land; but if a man is called a husbandman, he, from his mere name, is believed to be no unskilful man, but a farmer of experience, inasmuch as his name *(geōrgos)* has been derived from agricultural skill *(geōrgikē technē)*, of which he is the namesake. (5) And besides all this, we must likewise consider this other point, that the tiller of the ground *(ho gēs ergatēs)* looks only to one end, namely, to his wages; for he is altogether a hireling, and has no care whatever to till the land well. But the husbandman *(ho geōrgos)* would be glad also to contribute something of his own, and to spend in addition some of his private resources for the sake of improving the soil, and of avoiding blame from those who understand the business; for his desire is to derive his revenues every year not from any other source, but from his agricultural labours, when they have been brought into a productive state. (6) He therefore

occupies himself with improving the character of wild trees, and making them fruitful, and with further improving the character of fruitful trees by his care, and with reducing by pruning those branches which through superfluity of nourishment are too luxuriant, and with inducing those which are contracted and crowded to grow by the extension of their young shoots. Moreover, those trees which are of good sorts, and which make many shoots, he propagates by extending them under the earth in ditches of no very great depth, and those which do not produce good fruit he endeavours to improve by the insertion of other kinds into their roots, connecting them by the most natural union.

For the same thing happens likewise in the case of men, that they firmly unite into their own family adopted sons, who are unconnected with them in blood, but whom they make their own on account of their virtues. (7) The husbandman, therefore, takes up innumerable shoots, with their roots entire, which have by natural process become barren, as far as bearing fruit is concerned, and which even do great injury to those plants which do bear by reason of their being planted near them. Such, then, is the art which is applied to those plants which grow out of the ground. And now let us turn our consideration to the husbandry of the soul in its turn.

II. (8) First of all, therefore, the husbandman is not anxious to plant or to sow anything that is unproductive, but only all such things as are worth cultivation, and as bear fruit, which will bring a yearly produce to their master man. For nature has pointed him out as the master of all trees and animals, and all other things whatever which are perishable; (9) and what can man be but the kind that is in every one of us, which is accustomed to reap the advantage from all that is sown or planted? But since milk is the food of infants, but cakes made of wheat are the food of fullgrown men, so also the soul must have a milk-like nourishment in its age of childhood, namely, the elementary instruction of encyclical science. But the perfect food which is fit for men consists of explanations dictated by prudence, and temperance, and every virtue.

For these things being sown and implanted in the mind will bring forth most advantageous fruit, namely, good and praiseworthy actions. (10) By means of this husbandry, all the trees of the pas-

---

†Yonge's title, *A Treatise on the Tilling of the Earth by Noah.*
[1]Genesis 9:20.

sions and vices, which soot forth and grow up to a height, bringing forth pernicious fruits, are rooted up, and cut down, and cleared away, so that not even the smallest fragment of them is left, from which any new shoots of evil actions can subsequently spring up. (11) And if, besides, there are any trees which produce no fruit at all, neither good nor bad, the husbandman will cut them down too, but still he will not suffer them to be completely destroyed, but he will apply them to some appropriate use, making them into stakes and fixing them as pales all round his homestead, or using them as a fence for a city to serve instead of a wall.

III. (12) For Moses says, "Every tree which bringeth not forth fruit good to eat thou shalt cut down; and thou shalt make it into stakes against the city which shall make war upon them."[2] And these trees are likened to those powers developed in words alone, which have nothing in them but mere speculation, (13) among which we must class medical science, when unconnected with practice, by which it is natural that such persons may be cured, and also the oratorical and hireling species of rhetoric, which is conversant not about the discovery of the truth, but solely about the means of deceiving the hearers by plausible persuasion; and in the same class we must place all those parts of dialectics and geometry which have no connection with a proper regulation of the character or morals, but which only sharpen the mind, not suffering it to exercise a dull apprehension towards each question which is raised and submitted to it, but always to dissect the question and divide it, so as to distinguish the peculiar character of each thing from the common qualities of the whole genus.

(14) At all events, men say, that the ancients compared the principles of philosophy, as being threefold, to a field; likening natural philosophy to trees and plants, and moral philosophy to fruits, for the sake of which the plants are planted; and logical philosophy to the hedge or fence: (15) for as the wall, which is erected around, is the guardian of the plants and of the fruit which are in the field, keeping off all those who wish to do them injury and to destroy them, in the same manner, the logical part of philosophy is the strongest possible sort of protection to the other two parts, the moral and the natural philosophy; (16) for when it simplifies twofold and ambiguous expressions, and when it solves specious plausibilities entangled in sophisms, and utterly destroys seductive deceits, the greatest allurement and ruin to the soul, by means of its own expressive and clear language, and its unambiguous demonstrations, it makes the whole mind smooth like wax, and ready

to receive all the innocent and very praiseworthy impressions of sound natural and moral philosophy.

IV. (17) These then are the professions and promises made by the husbandry of the soul, "I will cut down all the trees of folly, and intemperance, and injustice, and cowardice; and I will eradicate all the plants of pleasure, and appetite, and anger, and passion, and of all similar affections, even if they have raised their heads as high as heaven. And I will burn out their roots, darting down the attack of flame to the very foundations of the earth, so that no portion, nay, no trace, or shadow whatever, of such things shall be left; (18) and I will destroy these things, and I will implant in those souls which are of a childlike age, young shoots, whose fruit shall nourish them. And those shoots are as follows: the practice of writing and reading with facility; an accurate study and investigation of the works of wise poets; geometry, and a careful study of rhetorical speeches, and the whole course of encyclical education. And in those souls which have arrived at the age of puberty or of manhood, I will implant things which are even better and more perfect, namely, the tree of prudence, the tree of courage, the tree of temperance, the tree of justice, the tree of every respective virtue. (19) And if there be any tree belonging to what is called the wild class, which does not bear eatable fruit, but which is able to be a fence to and a protector of that which is eatable, that also I will manage, not for its own sake, but because it is calculated by nature to be of use to what is necessary and very useful.

V. (20) Therefore, the allwise Moses attributes to the just man a knowledge of the husbandry of the soul, as an act consistent with his character, and thoroughly suited to him, saying, "Noah began to be a husbandman." But to the unjust man he attributes the task of tilling the ground, which is an employment bearing the heaviest burdens without any knowledge. (21) For "Cain," says he, "was a tiller of the ground;" and a little afterwards, when he is detected in having contracted the pollution of fratricide, it is said, "Cursed art thou by the earth, which opened her mouth to receive the blood of thy brother from thy hand, with which thou tillest the earth, and it shall not put forth its strength to give unto thee." (22) How then could any one show more manifestly, that the lawgiver looks upon the wicked man as a tiller of the earth, and not as a husbandman, than by such language as we here see used? We must not indeed suppose that what is here said, is said of a man who is able to work by his hands or by his feet, or by any other of the powers of his body, or of any mountain land, or of any champaign country, but that is applicable to the powers existing in every one of us; for it happens that the soul of the wicked man is not concerned about any thing else except about his

[2]Deuteronomy 20:20.

earthly body, and about all the pleasures of that body.

(23) Moreover, the general crowd of men, travelling over the different climates of the earth and penetrating to its furthest boundaries, and traversing the seas, and investigating the things that lie hid in the recesses of the ocean, and leaving no single part of the whole universe unexplored, is continually providing from every quarter the means by which it can increase pleasure. (24) For as fishermen let down their nets at times to the most extraordinary depths, comprehending a vast surface of the sea in their circle, in order to catch the greatest possible number of fish enclosed within their nets, like people shut up within the walls of a besieged city; so in the same manner the greatest part of men having extended their universal nets to take everything, as the poets somewhere say, not only over the parts of the sea, but also over the whole nature of earth, and air, and water, seek to catch everything from every quarter for the enjoyment and attainment of pleasure. (25) For they dig mines in the earth, and they sail across the seas, and they achieve every other work both of peace and war, providing unbounded materials for pleasure, as for their queen, being utterly uninitiated in that husbandry of the soul which sows and plants the virtues and reaps their fruit, which is a happy life.

But they labouring to procure, and reducing to a system those things which are pleasant to the flesh, cultivate with all imaginable care that composite mass, that carefully fashioned statue, the narrow house of the soul, which, from its birth to its death it can never lay aside, but which it is compelled to bear till the day of its death, burdensome as it is.

VI. (26) We have now therefore explained, in what respect, the occupation of tilling the ground differs from husbandry, and a tiller of the ground from a husbandman. And we must now consider whether there are not some other species akin to these already mentioned, but which, through the common names borne by them and others, conceal the real difference which exists between them. At least there are two which we have discovered by investigation, concerning which we will say what is fitting, if it is in our power.

(27) Therefore, as we found a tiller of the earth and a husbandman, though there did not appear to be any difference between them (till we came to investigate the allegorical meaning concealed under each name), nevertheless very far removed from one another in fact, such also shall we find to be the case with a shepherd and a keeper of sheep. For the lawgiver sometimes speaks of the occupation of a shepherd, and sometimes of that of a keeper of sheep. (28) And those who do not examine expressions with any excessive accuracy,

will perhaps fancy that these two appellations are synonymous terms for the same employment. They are, however, in reality the names of things which are widely different in the meaning affixed to their concealed ideas. (29) For if it is customary to give both the names of shepherd and keeper of sheep to those who have the management of flocks, still they do not give these names to that reason which is the superintendant of the flock of the soul; for a man who is but an indifferent manager of a flock is called a keeper of sheep, but a good and faithful one is called a shepherd, and in what way we will proceed to show immediately.

VII. (30) Nature has made cattle akin to every individual among us, the soul putting forth two young branches as from one root; one of which being entire and undivided, and being left in its integrity is called the mind; but the other part is separated by six divisions into seven natures, five outward senses, and two other organs, the organs of speech, and that of generation. (31) But all this multitude of external senses and organs being destitute of reason is compared to a sheep, but since it is composed of many parts, it of necessity stands in need of a governor by the unvarying law of nature. Whenever therefore a man who is ignorant how to govern, and at the same time wealthy, rises up and appoints himself governor, he becomes the cause of innumerable evils to the flocks, (32) for he supplies all necessary things in superabundance, and the flock being immoderately glutted with them becomes insolent through the superfluity of food; for insolence is the genuine offspring of satiety. Accordingly, they become insolent and exult, and shake off all restraint, and being scattered in small divisions they break the appointed order of the Lord. (33) But he who, for a while, was then governor, being deserted by the flock under his orders, appears stripped of his authority, and runs about earnestly endeavouring, if possible, to collect the scattered flock together and to unite it again; but when he finds that he is unable to do this he groans and weeps, blaming his own remissness, and reproaching himself as the cause of all that has happened.

(34) In this manner, also, the offspring of the outward senses, when the mind is supine and indolent, being satiated in the most unbounded degree with a superfluity of the pleasures of the outward senses, toss their heads, and frisk about, and rove about, at random, wherever they please; the eyes being opened wide to embrace every object of sight, and hastening even to feast themselves on objects which ought not to be looked at; and the ears eagerly receiving every kind of voice, and never being satisfied, but always thirsting for superfluity and the indulgence of vain curiosity and sometimes even for such delights as are but little suited to a free man.

VIII. (35) Since on what other account can we imagine, that in every quarter of the habitable globe, the theatres are every day filled with incalculable myriads of spectators? For they, being wholly under the dominion of sounds and sights, and allowing their ears and their eyes to be carried away without any restraint, go in pursuit of harp-players and singers to the harp, and every description of effeminate and unmanly music; and, moreover, eagerly receiving dancers and every other kind of actors, because they place themselves and move in all kinds of effeminate positions and motions, they are continually by their applause exciting the factions of the theatre, never thinking either of the propriety of their own conduct or of that of the general body of the citizens; but, miserable as they are, upsetting all their own plan of life for the sake of their eyes and ears.

(36) And there are others who are still more unfortunate and miserable than these men, who have released their sense of taste out of prison as it were; and that sense, immediately rushing, in an unrestrained manner, to every kind of meat and drink, selects from the things that are already prepared, and also cherishes an indiscriminate and insatiable hunger for what is not present. So that, even if the channels of the belly are filled, its ever unsatisfied appetites, raging and ravening around, continue to look and stalk about in every direction, lest there should any where be any fragment which has been overlooked, that it may swallow that up also like a devouring fire. (37) And this gluttony is followed by its usual natural attendant, an eagerness for the connections of the sexes, which brings in its train a strange frenzy, an unrestrainable madness and a most grievous fury; for, when men are oppressed by the indulgence of gluttony and delicate food, and by much unmixed wine and drunkenness, they are no longer able to restrain themselves, but hastening to amorous gratifications they revel and disturb the doors, until they are at last able to rest when they have drawn off the great violence of their passion. (38) On which account nature, as it would seem, has placed the organs of such connection beneath the belly, being previously aware that they do not delight in hunger, but that they follow upon satiety and then rise up to fulfil their peculiar operations.

IX. (39) Those, then, who permit the flock committed to their charge to satiate themselves all at once with all the things that they desire, we must call keepers of sheep; but those, on the contrary, we should entitle shepherds, who supply their flocks with only so much as is necessary and proper for them; cutting off and utterly rejecting all superfluous and useless extravagance and abundance, which is not less injurious than want and deficiency, and who guard with great prudence against the possibility of the flock becoming dis-

eased through their want of care and indolence, praying that those diseases, which at times are liable to attack flocks from external causes, may not visit theirs. (40) And they take equal care that it may not straggle about at random and get scattered, holding out to them as an object of fear one who will chastise those who never obey reason, and inflicting continual punishment, moderate when applied to those who err only in such a degree as admits of a remedy, but very severe when laid upon those whose wickedness is uncurable; for though in its essence it may appear an abominable thing, nevertheless punishment is the greatest good to foolish persons, great as the remedies of the physician are to those who are ill in the body.

X. (41) These, then, are the occupations of shepherds who prefer those things which are useful, though mixed with unpleasantness, to those which are pleasant but pernicious. Thus, at all events, the occupation of a shepherd has come to be considered a respectable and profitable employment, so that the race of poets has been accustomed to call kings the shepherds of the people; but the law giver gives this title to the wise, who are the only real kings, for he represents them as rulers of all men of irrational passions, as of a flock of sheep. (42) On this account he has attributed to Jacob, the man who was made perfect by practice, a skill in the science of a shepherd, saying: "For he is the shepherd of Laban's sheep."[3] That is, of the sheep of the foolish soul, which thinks only those things good which are the objects of the outward senses and apparent to them, being deceived and enslaved by colours and shadows; for the name, Laban, being interpreted, means "whitening."

(43) He also attributes the same skill to the all-wise Moses,[4] for he also is represented as the shepherd of the mind which embraces pride in preference to truth, and which receives appearance rather than reality; for the interpretation of the name Jethro is "superfluous," and superfluity is pride adopted for the purpose of introducing error into correct life; which is the cause why different things are looked upon as right in different cities, and not those principles which ought to be looked upon as just everywhere, inasmuch as it never sees, not even in a dream, the common and immovable principles of the justice of nature. For, it is said, that "Moses was the shepherd of the sheep of Jethro, the priest of Midian." (44) And this man himself prays that the flock may not be left without a shepherd, meaning by the flock the whole multitude of the parts of the soul; but that they

---

[3] Genesis 30:36.
[4] Exodus 3:1.

may meet with a good shepherd, who will lead them away from the nets of folly, and injustice, and all wickedness, and conduct them to the doctrines of learning and all other virtue; for, says Moses, "Let the Lord the God of spirits and of all flesh look down upon man and upon this assembly."[5] And then, a little further on, he adds, "And the assembly of the Lord shall not be like sheep who have no shepherd."

XI. (45) But is it not well worth praying for, that the flock which is akin to each individual of us, and of so much value, may not be left without any superintendent or governor, so that we may not, through being filled with a love of the worst of all constitutions, an ochlocracy, which is a base copy of the best form, democracy, pass our lives for ever and amid tumults, and disorders, and intestine seditions? (46) Certainly it is not anarchy alone that is an evil, through being the parent of ochlocracy, but also the insurrection of any lawless and violent force against authority; for the tyrant who, by his own nature is hostile, is, in the case of cities, a man, but in the case of the body and the soul, and all transactions having reference to either, he is a mind resembling the brute beasts, besieging the citadel of each individual; (47) but not only are these dominations unprofitable, but so also are the governments and authority of other persons, who are very gentle, for gentleness is a line of conduct very likely to be despised, and injurious to both parties, both to the rulers and the subjects. To the one from the disregard with which their subjects treat them, so that they are unable to manage any matter, whether of public or of their own private business successfully, are sometimes even compelled to abdicate their authority; and to the others, because of their continual disrespect to their governors, disregarding all persuasion, so that they contract a habit of self-willed insolence, a possession of great evil. (48) We must then think that one of these classes of governors differs in no respect from keepers of sheep, while the others resemble the sheep themselves, for the governors persuade the governed to be luxurious, through the extravagance of the supplies with which they provide them; and the governed being unable to bear their satiety become insolent; but what is really desirable is, that our mind should govern all our conduct, like a goatherd, or a cowherd, or a shepherd, or, in short, like any herdsman of any kind; choosing in preference to what is pleasant that which is for the advantage both of himself and of his flock.

XII. (49) But the providence of God is the principal and almost the only cause that the divisions of the soul are not left entirely without any gov-

ernor, and that they have met with a blameless and in all respects good shepherd. In consequence of whose appointment it is impossible that the company of the mind should become scattered; for it will of necessity appear in one and the same order, looking to the authority of its one governor, since the heaviest burden of all is to be compelled to obey a variety of rulers. (50) Thus, indeed, being a shepherd is a good thing, so that it is justly attributed, not only to kings, and to wise men, and to souls who are perfectly purified, but also to God, the ruler of all things; and he who confirms this is not any ordinary person, but a prophet, whom it is good to believe, he namely who wrote the psalms; for he speaks thus, "The Lord is my shepherd, and he shall cause me to lack nothing;"[6] (51) and let every one in his turn say the same thing, for it is very becoming to every man who loves God to study such a song as this, but above all this world should sing it.

For God, like a shepherd and a king, governs (as if they were a flock of sheep) the earth, and the water, and the air, and the fire, and all the plants, and living creatures that are in them, whether mortal or divine; and he regulates the nature of the heaven, and the periodical revolutions of the sun and moon, and the variations and harmonious movements of the other stars, ruling them according to law and justice; appointing, as their immediate superintendent, his own right reason, his first-born son, who is to receive the charge of this sacred company, as the lieutenant of the great king; for it is said somewhere, "Behold, I am he! I will send my messenger before thy face, who shall keep thee in the road."[7] (52) Let therefore all the world, the greatest and most perfect flock of the living God, say "The Lord is my shepherd, and he shall cause me to lack nothing," (53) and let every separate individual say the same thing; not with the voice which proceeds from his tongue and his mouth, extending only through a scanty portion of the air, but with the wide spreading voice of the mind, which reaches to the very extremities of this universe; for it is impossible that there should be a deficiency of anything that is necessary, where God presides, who is in the habit of bestowing good things in all fulness and completeness in all living beings.

XIII. (54) But there is a very beautiful encouragement to equality contained in the song before mentioned; for in real truth, the man who appears to have everything else, and yet who is impatient under the authority of one master, is incomplete in his happiness, and is poor; but if a soul is governed by God, having that one and only thing on

---

5Numbers 27:16.

6Psalm 23:1.
7Exodus 23:20.

which all other things depend, it is very naturally in no need of other things, regarding not blind riches, but only such as are endowed with real and acute sight.[8] (55) All true disciples have come to conceive an earnest and unalterable love for that; and therefore laughing at the mere keeping of sheep, they have directed their attention to the attainment of a shepherd's knowledge; and a proof of this is to be found in the case of Joseph, (56) who was always studying that knowledge which is conversant about the body and vain opinions, not being able to rule and govern irrational nature (for it is customary for old men to be appointed to offices of irresponsible authority; but this man is always young, even if after a lapse of time he may come to support old age, which has at last reached him); and being accustomed to nourish this and to lead it on to growth, he expects to be able to persuade the lovers of virtue to change and come over to him, in order that in so changing to irrational and inanimate objects, they may have no leisure for applying themselves to the studies of a rational soul.

(57) For Moses represents Joseph as saying, "If the king," that is to say, the mind, the king of the body, "shall ask you, What is your occupation? answer, We are men, the keepers of cattle."[9] When they hear this they are naturally impatient, not liking the idea, while they are rulers, of confessing that they hold the rank of subordinates; (58) for those who supply food to the outward senses, through the abundance of the objects perceptible only by them, become the slaves of those who are nourished, like servants who pay to their mistresses a compulsory reverence every day; but those who preside over them are rulers, and they bridle the vehement impetuosity with which they are hurried on to luxury.

(59) At first therefore, although they do not hear what is said with any pleasure, they will still keep silence, thinking it unseemly to discuss the difference between the employment of a keeper of cattle and a shepherd, before those who do not understand it; but subsequently, when a contest about these things arises, they will contend with all their power, and will never desist till they have carried their point by main force, having exhibited the liberality, and nobleness, and royal character of their nature to the living God. Accordingly when the king asks, "What is your occupation?" they will answer "We are shepherds, we and our fathers."

XIV. (60) Would they not then appear to boast as much of their occupation as shepherds, as the king himself, who is conversing with them, does of his mighty power and dominion? At least they are testifying their high opinion of the profession of life which they have adopted, not in honour of themselves alone, but of their father also, as being worthy of all possible care and diligence; (61) and yet, if the discussion had been merely about the care of goats or sheep, perhaps they would have been ashamed to make such an admission through desire to avoid dishonour; for such occupations are accounted inglorious and mean among those who are loaded with great prosperity, without being at the same time endowed with prudence, and especially among kings. (62) And the Egyptian character is by nature most especially haughty and boastful whenever so slight a breeze of prosperity does merely blow upon it, so that men of that nation look upon the pursuits of life and objects of ambition of ordinary men, as subjects for laughter and downright ridicule.

(63) But since the matter before us, at present, is to consider the rational and irrational powers in the soul, those persons will naturally boast, who are persuaded that they are able to master the irrational faculties, by taking the rational ones for their allies. (64) If therefore any envious or captious person should blame us, and say, "How then have ye, who are devoted to the employment of shepherds, and who profess to be occupied in the care and management of the flocks which belong to you, ever thought of approaching the country of the body and the passions, namely Egypt? and why have ye not turned your voyage in another direction? You must say to him in reply, with all freedom of speech, We have come hither as sojourners, not as inhabitants." (65) For in reality every soul of a wise man has heaven for its country, and looks upon earth as a strange land, and considers the house of wisdom his own home; but the house of the body, a lodging-house, on which it proposes to sojourn for a while. (66) Therefore since the mind, the ruler of the flock, having taken the flock of the soul, using the law of nature as its teacher, governs it consistently and vigorously, rendering it worthy of approbation and great praise; but when it manages it sluggishly and indulgently, with a disregard of law, then it renders it blameable. Very naturally, therefore, the one will assume the name of a king, being addressed as a shepherd, but the other will only have the title of a confectioner, or of a baker, being called a keeper of sheep, supplying the means of feasting and gluttonous eating to cattle accustomed to gorge themselves to satiety.

XV. (67) I have now therefore explained, in no superficial manner, in what way a husbandman differs from a tiller of the ground, and a shepherd from a keeper of sheep. There is also a third point, having some connection with what has already

---

[8]I have again followed Mangey's proposed translation for this text which he pronounces corrupt and unintelligible.
[9]Genesis 46:33.

been said, which we will now proceed to speak of. For I consider that a horseman and a rider differ; meaning by this statement, not merely that one man who is carried on a neighing animal differs from another man who is carried on a similar beast, but the motion of the one is different from the motion of the other; therefore the man who gets on a horse without any skill in horsemanship, is correctly called a rider, (68) and he has given himself up to an irrational and restive animal, to such a degree that it is absolutely inevitable that he must be carried wherever the animal chooses to go, and if he fails to see beforehand a chasm in the earth, or a deep pit, it has happened before now that such a man, in consequence of the impetuosity of his course, has been thrown headlong down a precipice and dashed to pieces. (69) But a horseman, on the other hand, when he is about to mount, takes the bridle in his hand, and then taking hold of the mane on the horse's neck, he leaps on; and though he appears to be carried by the horse, yet, if one must tell the truth, he in reality guides the animal that carries him, as a pilot guides a ship. For the pilot too, appearing to be carried by the ship which he is managing, does in real truth guide it, and conducts it to whatever harbour he is himself desirous to hasten. (70) While, therefore, the horse goes on in obedience to the rein, the horseman pats the horse, as if praising it; but when it goes on with too great impetuosity, and is carried away beyond moderation, then he pulls it back with force and vigour, so as to restrain its speed. But if the horse continue to be disobedient, then he takes the whole bridle, and pulls him back, and drags back his neck, so that he is compelled to stop. (71) And for all his restiveness and his continued disregard of the rein, there are whips and spurs prepared, and all other instruments of punishment which have been invented by horse-breakers. And it is not wonderful: for when the horseman mounts, the art of horsemanship mounts too; so that there then being two parties borne by the horse, and skilful in horsemanship, they will very naturally get the better of one animal who is subjected to them, and who is incapable of acquiring skill.

XVI. (72) Therefore now, leaving the consideration of these neighing animals, and of the parties carried by them, investigate, if you will, the condition of your own soul. For in its several parts you will find both horses and a rider in the fashion of a charioteer, just as you do in external things. (73) Now, the horses are appetite and passion, the one being male and the other female. On this account, the one giving itself airs, wishes to be unrestrained and free, and holds its head erect, as a male animal naturally does; and the other, not being free, but of a slavish disposition, and rejoicing in all kinds of crafty wickedness, devours the

house, and destroys the house, for she is female. And the rider and charioteer is one, namely the mind. When, indeed, he mounts with prudence, he is a charioteer; but when he does so with folly, then he is but a rider. (74) For a fool, through ignorance, is unable to keep hold of the reins; but they, falling from his hands, drop on the ground. And the animals, immediately that they have got the better of the reins, run on in an ill-regulated and unrestrained course. (75) But the man who has mounted behind them, not being able to take hold of anything by which he may steady himself, falls, and lacerating his knees and his hands and his face, like a miserable man as he is, he bitterly weeps over his disaster; and after hanging by his feet to the chariot after he has been overturned, he is suspended, with his face upwards, lying on his back; and as the chariot proceeds, he is dragged along, and injured in his head, and neck, and both his shoulders; and then, being hurried on in this direction and in that, and being dashed against everything which lies in the way, he endures a most pitiable death.

(76) He then meets with an end, such as I have been describing; and the chariot, being lightened by his fall and bounding along violently, when, at last, it is dashed to the ground in the rebound, is easily broken to pieces, so that it can never again be joined or fastened together. And the animals, being now released from everything which could restrain them, proceed at random, and are frantic, and do not cease galloping on, till they are tripped up and fall, or till they are hurried over some high precipice, and so are dashed to pieces and destroyed.

XVII. (77) In this manner, then, it seems that the whole chariot of the soul is destroyed, with its passengers; and all through the carelessness or unskilfulness of the driver. But it is desirable for them that such horses, and such drivers, and riders, so wholly without skill, should be destroyed, in order that the faculties of virtue may be roused; for when folly has fallen, it follows of necessity that wisdom must rise up. (78) On this account Moses, in his passages of exhortation, says, "If thou goest forth to battle against thy enemies, and if thou seest numbers of horses, and riders, and people, be not afraid, because the Lord thy God is with thee."[10] For we must neglect anger and desire, and, in short, all the passions, and indeed the whole company of reasonings, which are mounted upon each of the passions as upon horses, even if they believe that they can exert irresistible strength; at least, all those must do so who have the power of the great King holding a shield over them, and in every place, and at every time, fighting in their defence.

---

[10]Deuteronomy 20:1.

(79) But the divine army is the body of virtues, the champions of the souls that love God, whom it becomes, when they see the adversary defeated, to sing a most beautiful and becoming hymn to the God who giveth the victory and the glorious triumph; and two choruses, the one proceeding from the conclave of the men, and the other from the company of the women, will stand up and sing in alternate songs a melody responsive to one another's voices.

(80) And the chorus of men will have Moses for their leader; and that of the women will be under the guidance of Miriam, "the purified outward sense."[11] For it is just that hymns and praises should be uttered in honour of God without any delay, both in accordance with the suggestions of the intellect and the perceptions of the outward senses, and that each instrument should be struck in harmony, I mean those both of the mind and of the outward sense, in gratitude and honour to the holy Saviour. (81) Accordingly, all the men sing the song on the sea-shore, not indeed with a blind mind, but seeing sharply, Moses being the leader of the song; and women sing, who are in good truth the most excellent of their sex, having been enrolled in the lists of the republic of virtue, Miriam being their leader.

XVIII. (82) And the same hymn is sung by both the choruses, having a most admirable burden of the song which is beautiful to be sung. And it is as follows: "Let us sing unto the Lord, for he has been glorified gloriously; the horse and his rider hath he thrown into the sea."[12] (83) For no one, if he searches ever so eagerly, can ever discover a more excellent victory than that by which the most mighty army, four-footed, restive, and proud as it was, of the passions and vices was overthrown. For the vices are four in genus, and the passions likewise are equal in number. Moreover, the mind, which is the character of them all, the one which hates virtue and loves the passions, has fallen and perished—the mind, which delighted in pleasures and appetites, and deeds of injustice and wickedness, and likewise in acts of rapine and of covetousness.

(84) Very beautifully, therefore, does the lawgiver in his recommendations, teach us not to elect as a chief, a man who is a breeder of horses, thinking that such a one is altogether unsuited to exercise authority, inasmuch as he is in a frenzy about pleasures and appetites, and intolerable loves, and rages about like an unbridled and unmanageable horse. For he speaks thus, "Thou shalt not be able to set over thyself a man that is a stranger, because he is not thy brother; because he will not multiply

for himself his horses, and will not turn his people towards Egypt."[13] (85) Therefore, according to the most holy Moses, no man that was a breeder of horses was ever born fit for dominion; and yet some one perhaps may say that power in cavalry is a great strength to the king, not inferior either to infantry or to a naval force, but in many places far more advantageous than either, and especially in those cases in which one has need of swiftness of motion without delay, but prompt and energetic, when the times do not admit of delay, but are at the very crisis of action, so that those who arrive too late are very naturally not considered to have been sluggish so much as to have been wholly useless, the opportunity for action having passed by like a cloud.

XIX. (86) And we would say to these people: My good men, the lawgiver is removing no protection whatever from the ruler, nor is he in any respect mutilating the army of his power which he has collected, by cutting off the force of cavalry which is the most efficient part of his army; but he is endeavouring to the best of his power to increase and strengthen it, in order that his allies, contributing to its strength and number, may most easily destroy their enemies. (87) For who else is equally skilful in marshalling and arraying armies, and in distributing them in squadrons, and in appointing captains of regiments and leaders of squadrons, and other commanders of large and small bodies, and in displaying a knowledge of all the other suggestions of tactics and strategy, and in explaining the principles of the military art to those who will avail themselves of them skilfully, through the great superabundance of his knowledge of such matters? (88) But the question is not now about his force of cavalry, which it is necessary to collect around the rulers for the destruction of their enemies and the protection of their friends; but concerning the irrational, and immoderate, and unmanageable impetuosity of the soul, which it is desirable to check, lest it should turn all its people towards Egypt, the country of the body, and labour with all its might to render it devoted to pleasures and to the passions, rather than to the service of virtue and of God; since it follows inevitably that he who has acquired a body of cavalry for himself, must, as he said himself, proceed on the road which leads to Egypt.

(89) For when the wave rises high and dashes over each side of the soul (looking upon it as a ship), that is to say, over the mind and the outward sense, being lifted up by evident passions and iniquities which blow fiercely upon it, so that the soul leans on one side and is nearly overbalanced; then, as is natural, the mind becoming

---

[11] Exodus 15:20.
[12] Exodus 15:1.

[13] Deuteronomy 17:15.

water-logged, goes down, and the deep in which it is sunk and overwhelmed is the body, which is compared to Egypt.

XX. (90) Beware, therefore, never to occupy yourself in this kind of horse-breeding, for they who pursue the other kind are themselves also blameable, for how can they not be? inasmuch as by them irrational animals are exceedingly humoured, and from their houses troops of well-fed horses continually go forth; while to the men who conduct them, not a person is found who ever gives the slightest contribution to relieve their wants, nor any present to increase their superfluities. (91) But, nevertheless, they err in a lighter degree; for these men who breed horses to contend for the prize, assert that by so doing they are adorning the sacred games and the assemblies, which are held in honour everywhere, and they affirm that they are the causes not only of pleasure to the spectators, and of that kind of delight which arises from beholding the spectacle, but that they also give them an inducement to study and practise praiseworthy pursuits. For they who attribute to animals a desire for victory, using, out of their love of honour and rivalry in excellence, a certain unceasing exhortation, and encouragement, and eagerness, enduring pleasant labours, will never desist from what is suitable and becoming to them, till they attain the end that they desire.

(92) But these men seek pretexts to excuse themselves, while doing wrong, but those who do wrong without excuse are they, who would make the mind a rider, and mount him upon his horse, though ignorant of the science of horsemanship, his horse being that four-footed vice and passion; (93) but if after having been taught the art of managing a chariot, you devote greater pains and study to it, and think yourself at last competent and able to manage horses, mount, and take hold of the reins. For thus, even if they are restive, you will not, by being thrown out of the chariot, receive wounds difficult to be cured, and also afford a subject of ridicule to all the spectators who delight in mischief; nor, on the other hand, will you be overwhelmed by your enemies coming against you or running over you from behind, since by your own speed you will outstrip and leave behind those who are coming after you, and you will be able to afford to disregard those who are coming towards you, because of your skill in getting safely out of the way.

XXI. (94) It is not unnaturally, therefore, that Moses, singing his song of triumph on the destruction of the riders, nevertheless prays for complete safety for the horsemen; for these are able, putting their bridles into the mouths of the irrational powers, to check the impetuosity of their superabundant violence. What then his prayer is must be told: he says, "Let Dan be a serpent in the way, sitting in the path, biting the heel of the horse; and the horseman shall fall backwards, awaiting the salvation of the Lord."[14] (95) But we must explain what is the enigmatical meaning which he conceals under this prayer, the name of Dan, being interpreted, means "judgment;" therefore he here likens that power of the soul which investigates, and accurately examines, and distinguishes between, and, in some degree, decides on each part of the soul, to a dragon (and the dragon is an animal various in its movements, and exceedingly cunning, and ready to display its courage, and very powerful to repel those who begin acts of violence), but not to that friendly serpent, the counsellor of life, which is wont to be called Eve in his national language, but to the one made by Moses, of the material of brass, which, when those who had been bitten by the poisonous serpents, and who were at the point of death beheld, they are said to have lived and not to have died.

XXII. (96) And these things thus expressed resemble visions and prodigies; I mean the account of one dragon uttering the voice of a man and pouring his sophistries into most innocent dispositions, and deceiving the woman with plausible arguments of persuasion; and of another becoming a cause of complete safety to those who looked upon it. (97) But, in the allegorical explanations of these statements, all that bears a fabulous appearance is got rid of in a moment, and the truth is discovered in a most evident manner.

The serpent, then, which appeared to the woman, that is to life depending on the outward senses and on the flesh, we pronounce to have been pleasure, crawling forward with an indirect motion, full of innumerable wiles, unable to raise itself up, ever cast down on the ground, creeping only upon the good things of the earth, seeking lurking places in the body, burying itself in each of the outward senses as in pits or caverns, a plotter against man, designing destruction to a being better than itself, eager to kill with its poisonous but painless bite. But the brazen serpent, made by Moses, we explain as being the disposition opposite to pleasure, namely, patient endurance, on which account it is that he is represented as having made it of brass, which is a very strong material. (98) He, then, who with sound judgment contemplates the appearance of patient endurance, even if he has been previously bitten by the allurements of pleasures, must inevitably live; for the one holds over his soul a death to be averted by no prayers, but self-restraint proffers him health and preservation of life; and temperance, which repels evils, is a remedy and perfect antidote for intemperance. (99) And every wise

---

[14]Genesis 49:17.

man looks upon what is good as dear to him, which is also altogether calculated to ensure his preservation.

So that when Moses prays that it may happen to Dan, either himself, to be that serpent (for the words may be understood in either sense), he means a serpent closely resembling the one which has been made by himself, but not like the one which appeared to Eve, for then the prayer is an entreaty for good things; (100) therefore the character of patient endurance is good, and capable of receiving immortality, which is the perfect good. But the character of pleasure is evil, bringing in its train the greatest of all punishments, death. On which account Moses says, "Let Dan become a serpent," and that not in any other place rather than in the road. (101) For the indulgences of intemperance and gluttony, and whatever other vices the immoderate and insatiable pleasures, when completely filled with an abundance of all external things, produce and bring forth, do not allow the soul to proceed onwards by the plain and straight road, but compel it to fall into ravines and gulfs, until they utterly destroy it; but those practices which adhere to patience, and endurance, and moderation, and all other virtues, keep the soul in the straight road, leaving no stumbling block in the way, against which it can stumble and fall. Very naturally, therefore, has Moses declared that temperance clings to the right way, because it is plain that the contrary habit, intemperance, is always straying from the road.

XXIII. (102) And the expression, "Sitting in the path," suggests some such meaning as this, as I persuade myself: a path is a road calculated for riding horses and driving carriages on, well beaten by men and beasts. (103) This road they say is very like pleasures, for almost from their earliest birth to extreme old age men proceed and walk along it, and with great indolence and easiness of temper spend all their lives in it, and not men only, but every species of animal whatever; for there is no single thing which is not attracted by the allurements of pleasure, and which is not, at times, entangled in its multifarious nets, and from which it is very difficult to escape. (104) But the paths of prudence, and temperance, and the other virtues, even though they may not be utterly untravelled, are, at all events, not beaten much; for the number of those who proceed by those roads, and who philosophise in a genuine spirit, and who form associations with virtue alone, disregarding, once for all, all other allurements, is very small. (105) Therefore he sits constantly in the road, and not once only, who has an eagerness for, and a care for, patient endurances, in order to watch from his ambush and attack pleasure, to which men in general are accustomed, that fountain of everlasting evils, and so to keep it off, and to eradicate

it from the whole district of the soul. (106) Then, as Moses says, proceeding to the natural consequence of his position, he will of necessity bite the heel of the horse; for it is the especial attribute of patient endurance and temperance to shake and overturn the foundations of vice, which lifts its head on high, and of exerted, and quickly-moved, and unmanageable passion.

XXIV. (107) Moses, therefore, represents the serpent that appeared to Eve as planning the death of man, for he records, that God says in his curses, "He shall bruise thy head, and thou shalt bruise his heel." But he represents the serpent of Dan, which is the one which we are now discussing, as biting the heel of the horse and not of the man, (108) for the serpent of Eve, being the symbol of pleasure, as has been already shown, attacks man, that is to say, the reasoning power which is in every one of us; for the enjoyment and free use of excessive pleasure is the destruction of the mind; (109) and the serpent of Dan being a sort of image of vigorous virtue and of patient endurance, will bite the horse, who is the emblem of passion and wickedness, because temperance is occupied about the over throw and destruction of these things. Accordingly, when they are bitten and when they have fallen, "the horseman also," says Moses, "will fall;" (110) and the meaning which he conceals under this enigmatical expression is such as this, that we must think it an excellent thing and an object worthy of all labour, that our mind shall not be mounted upon any one of the passions or vices, but that whenever an attempt is made by force to put it upon one of them, we must endeavour to leap off and fall, for such falls produce the most glorious victories. On which account one of the ancients, when challenged to a contest of abuse, said, "I will never engage in such a contest as that in which he who wins is more dishonoured than he who is defeated."

XXV. (111) Do you, therefore, my friend, never enter into a contest of evil, and never contend for the pre-eminence in such practices, but rather exert yourself with all your might to escape from them. And if ever, being under the compulsion of some power which is mightier than yourself, you are compelled to engage in such a strife, take care to be without delay defeated; (112) for then you, being defeated, will be a glorious conqueror, and those who have gained the victory will have got the worst. And do not ever entrust it to a herald to proclaim the victory of your rival or to the judge to crown; but do you go yourself and offer to him the acknowledgment of victory and the palm, and crown him, if he will, and bind him with wreaths of triumph, and proclaim him as conqueror yourself, pronouncing with a loud and piercing voice such a proclamation as this: "O ye spectators, and ye who have offered prizes at these games! In this contest which you have proposed to us of appetite, and passion, and intemperance, and folly, and injustice, I have been defeated, and this man whom ye behold has gained the victory. And he has gained it by such a superabundance of excellence, that even we, who might very naturally have envied our conquerors, do not grudge him the triumph."

(113) Therefore, in all these unholy contests, surrender the prizes to others; but, as for those which are really holy, study yourself to gain the crown in them. And think not those contests holy which the different cities propose in their triennial festivals, when they build theatres and receive many myriads of people; for in those he who has overthrown any one in wrestling, or who has cast him on his back or on his face upon the ground, or he who is very skilful in wrestling or in the pancratium, carries off the first prize, though he may be a man who has never abstained from any act of violence or of injustice.

XXVI. (114) There are some men, again, who, having armed and strongly fortified both their hands in a most hard and terrible manner, like iron, attack their adversaries, and batter their heads and faces, and the other parts of their bodies, and whenever they are able to plant a blow, they inflict great fractures, and then claim the decision in their favour, and the crown of victory, by means of their merciless cruelty. (115) But what man in his senses would not laugh at the other competitions of runners, and candidates for the prize in the pentathlum, to see men studying with all their energies to leap the longest distance, and measuring spaces and distances, and contending with one another in swiftness of foot? men whom, not only those more active animals, an antelope, or a deer, but even the very smallest beasts, such as a dog, or a hare, without making any extraordinary haste, would outrun, though they were to exert themselves with all their speed, and to put themselves out of breath.

(116) Of all these contests, then, there is not one which is truly sacred; no, not though all the men in the world should combine to bear witness in their favour, but they must be convicted by themselves of bearing false witness if they do so: for they who admire these things have established laws against men who behave with insolent violence, and have affixed punishments to assaults, and have appointed judges to decide on every action of that kind. (117) How, then, is it natural for the same persons to be indignant at those who insult and assault others privately, and to establish in their cases punishments which cannot be avoided, but yet, in the case of those who commit these assaults publicly, and in assemblies of the people, and in theatres, to establish by law that they shall receive crowns, and that proclamations shall be made in their honour, and all sorts of other glorious circumstances? (118) For when two opposite opinions are established concerning any one thing, whether it be person or action, it follows of necessity that one or other of them must be wrong, and the other right, for it is impossible for them both to be right: which is the two, then, will you praise deservedly? Will you not say that that sentence is right which orders those who begin acts of violence to be punished? You would justly blame the contrary law, which commands such persons to be honoured; that nothing sacred may be blamed, every such thing must be altogether glorious.

XXVII. (119) Therefore the Olympian contest is the only one that justly deserves to be called sacred; meaning by this, not that which the inhabitants of Elis celebrate, but that which is instituted for the acquisition of the divine, and Olympian, and genuine virtues. Now, as competitors in this contest, all those have their names inscribed who are very weak in their bodies, but very vigorous in their souls; and then, having stripped off their clothes, and smeared themselves in the dust, they do all those actions which belong to skill and to power, omitting nothing which may conduce to their gaining the victory. (120) These men, therefore, get the better of their adversaries: and then, again, they have a competition with one another for the prize of pre-eminence, for they are not all victorious in the same manner, but all are worthy of honour, having routed and overthrown most grievous and formidable enemies; (121) and he who shows himself superior to all the rest of these is most admirable, and we must not envy him, when he gets the first prize of all the wrestlers. And those who are thought worthy of the second or of the third place, must not be cast down; for these prizes are proposed for the acquisition of virtue. But to those who are unable to attain to the very highest eminence, even the acquisition of a moderate prize is serviceable. And it is even said that such is more stable, since it avoids the envy which always sticks to those who are excessively eminent.

(122) Therefore it is said in a way to convey much instruction, "The horseman will fall," that if any one falls from vice, he may be raised up by leaning on good things, and so may stand upright again. And in a still more instructive manner is that other expression used, which bids one not leap off in front, but "fall backwards," since it is always advantageous to be behind-hand in vice and passion; (123) for it is always good to be beforehand in doing what is good, but to be slack in doing what is disgraceful: and, on the other hand, it is good to come close to the one, but to stand aloof from and to be as far as possible removed from the other. And that man is free from all disorder, to whom it happens to be removed at a distance from the errors of passion. Accordingly, Moses says that

he is "awaiting the salvation which comes from God," [15] in order that, as far as he is removed from committing iniquity, so far he may also advance in well-doing.

XXVIII. (124) Everything, then, that is requisite has now been said on the subject of a horseman and a rider, and a keeper of sheep and a shepherd, and a tiller of the ground and a husbandman; and all the difference existing between each of these pairs has been very accurately defined, as far as it was in our power. It is time now to turn to what follows.

(125) Moses, then, introduces the man who is desirous of virtue as not possessing a complete knowledge of the whole business of a husbandman, but only as labouring with diligence at its principles and rudiments; for he says, "Noah began to be a husbandman." [16] And the beginning, as the proverb of the old writers has it, is half of the whole; as yet, therefore, he is half of the distance removed from the end, and where the end is not attained, it has been often injurious to many persons, to have begun great enterprises. (126) At all events, before now, some persons whose minds were not right, through their thoughts revolving in continued changes, have conceived a notion of some good things, but have derived no advantage from it; for it has happened that, as they did not attain the end which they desired, they have been overwhelmed by the impetuosity of a number of adverse circumstances coming against them, and so that good conception has been destroyed.

XXIX. (127) Was it not on this account that when Cain fancied that he had offered up a blameless sacrifice, an oracle came to him bidding him not to feel confidence as a man who had presented a well approved offering? for that he had not sacrificed with holy and perfect victims.

And the oracle is as follows: "If thou dost not bring thy offering properly, and if thou dost not distribute it rightly." [17] (128) What is right, then, here is the honour of God, and that which is not properly distributed is not right. But let us now examine what meaning is contained under this expression.

There are some persons who look upon piety as consisting in the affirmation that all things have been made by God, both what is good and the contrary; (129) to whom we would say that one portion of your opinion is praiseworthy, but the other portion blameable. One portion is praiseworthy, because it properly honours that which alone is worthy to receive honour; but that portion is blameable, which does so without any discrimination or

division. For it was not proper to confuse and mingle everything together, nor to declare God the cause of everything without distinction, but to make a difference, and to pronounce him the cause only of those things which are good; (130) for it is an absurdity to be anxious about priests, taking care that they shall be perfect in their bodies and free from all defect and mutilation, and to be very particular about the animals which are offered in sacrifice, to be sure that they have no defect of any kind whatever, not even the most insignificant possible; and to appoint men, and to say whom and how many ought to be appointed for this business, whom some call inspectors of blemishes, to take care that the victims may be brought to the altar without any blemish or imperfection, and yet to allow the opinions which are held concerning God to be in confusion in the soul of each individual, and not to take care that they are discriminated by the rule of right reason.

XXX. (131) Do you not see that the law pronounces the camel to be an unclean beast, because it chews the cud and does not part the hoof. [18] And yet, if we considered this sentence as it is expressed in its literal sense, I do not see what reason there is in it when it is interpreted; but if we look at it in its allegorical meaning, it is very clear and inevitable. (132) For as the animal which chews the cud, again masticates the food which is put before it and devoured by it, when it again rises up to its teeth, so also the soul of the man who is fond of learning, when it has received any speculative opinions by hearing them, does not abandon them to forgetfulness, but quietly by itself revolves over every one of them again in its mind in all tranquillity, and so comes to the recollection of them all. (133) But it is not every memory which is good, but only that which is exerted on good subjects, since it is a most pernicious thing that what is bad should not be forgotten; on which account, with a view to perfection, it is necessary that the hoofs should be parted, in order that so the faculty of memory, being divided into two sections, the word which flows through the mouth may divide the lips, as being things which nature has made of a two-fold character, and may also separate the advantageous species of memory from that which is mischievous.

(134) Again, the dividing the hoof without chewing the cud does not by itself appear to bring any advantage with it. For what advantage is there in distinguishing the natures of things beginning at the top, and going down to the most unimportant points, and yet not to be able to do so in one's self, not to have one's own divisions clearly distinguished, which by some persons are with great

---

[15] Genesis 49:18.
[16] Genesis 9:20.
[17] Genesis 4:7.

[18] Leviticus 11:4.

felicity named atoms and indivisible portions? (135) for all these things are manifest displays of intelligence and excessive accuracy, sharpened to a degree of the most acute comprehension. But they have no influence in causing virtue, or in making men live a life free from reproach.

XXXI. (136) Accordingly, in their daily discussions, the company of sophists all over the world annoys the ears of those whom they meet, by discussing with minute accuracy, and expounding precisely, all expressions of a double and ambiguous character, and distinguishing everything which appears to occur to the recollection (and a great many things are fixed deeply in it). Do not these men divide the elements of grammatical speech into consonants and vowels? And do not some men divide speech into their first principles, noun, verb, and conjunction? (137) Do not musicians again divide their own science into rhythm, and part, and melody? and subdivide melody into the chromatic, the enharmonic, and the diatonic species, into the divisions of fourths, and fifths, and the diapason, and into combined and distinct melodies? (138) Do not geometricians divide their science into two generic lines, the straight line, and the circumference? And do not other professors of other arts draw careful distinctions between the species which exist in each of their arts, going accurately through them all from beginning to end? (139) And the whole company of students of philosophy may argue with them on their line of conduct, each going through the studies to which he is accustomed; because, of all existing things some are corporeal, and some incorporeal; some again are inanimate, and some have vitality; some are endowed with, others destitute of reason; some are mortal, others divine; and of mortals some are male, and some female, these being the two divisions of the human race. (140) Again, of incorporeal things, some are perfect and others imperfect; and of perfect things, some are questions and interrogations, others are imprecatory or adjurative; and there are other kinds which have special differences in the elementary principles of such things.

Again, there are some things which the dialecticians are accustomed to call actions; (141) and of these some are simple, and others are not simple; and of those which are not simple some are conjunctive, and others are adjunctive in a greater or lesser degree; moreover some are disjunctive, and there are others which come under a similar description. Again, some are true, some are false, some are doubtful; some possible and some impossible; some are corruptible, others incorruptible; some necessary, and others not necessary; some are easy of solution, others difficult to understand; and there are other classifications akin to these. Again, of those which are imperfect there are proximate divisions into what are called categorems and accidents, and other classifications which are subordinate to these.

XXXII. (142) And although the intellect, when it has sharpened itself so as to render itself more acute than before (as a physician gives strength to bodies), dissects the natures of things, but yet derives no advantage with respect to the acquisition of virtue; it will divide the hoof, being able to divide, and to distinguish, and to discriminate between each separate thing; but it will not chew the cud so as to avail itself of any useful food which may be able, by means of its recollections, to soften the asperity of the soul which has been engendered by sins, and to produce a really gentle and pleasant motion. (143) Therefore a vast number of those who are called sophists, being admired in their respective cities, and having attracted almost all the world to look upon them with honour, on account of the accuracy of their definitions and their excessive cleverness in inventions, have grown old while vehemently bound by the passions, and have passed their whole life in them, in no respect differing from private individuals who are of no account and are held in no consideration. (144) For which reason the lawgiver very admirably compares those of the sophists who live in this manner to the race of swine, who live a life in no respect pure or brilliant, but confused and disorderly, and who are devoted to the basest habits.

(145) For he says that the swine is an unclean animal, because it divides the hoof and does not chew the cud, just as he has pronounced the camel unclean for the contrary reason because it chews the cud and does not divide the hoof. But as many animals as partake of both these qualities are very appropriately described as clean, because they have avoided impropriety in both the aforementioned particulars. For division without memory, and care, and a diligent examination of what is best, is but an imperfect good; but the combination and union of the two in the same animal is a most perfect good.

XXXIII. (146) And even the enemies of the soul are afraid of this perfection, whom, as they are no longer able to stand up against it, a genuine peace gets the mastery over. And all those who have attained to a half-perfect or half-established wisdom, are too weak to be able to make any effectual opposition to the brood of sins, which have become confined by long usage, and which have gained strength by time. (147) On this account, when in the time of war the general makes a levy of his army, he does not summon all the youth, not even, though it displays all imaginable willingness and spontaneous readiness to come forward to repel the enemy. But he commands some to depart and to remain at home, in order that by continued exercise they may acquire such an amount of military power and skill as may afterwards be sufficient to secure the victory.

(148) And the order of this levy is made through the medium of the heralds of the army when the war is at hand, and already at the very gates. And the heralds will make this announcement: "What man is there who has built a new house, and has not handselled it? Let him go and return to his house, that he may not die in the war, and another man handsel it instead of him. And what man is there who has planted a vineyard and has not received any joy from the fruit thereof? Let him go and turn away back to his house, that he may not die in the war, and another man be delighted with the fruit of his vineyard. And what man has espoused a wife, and has not received her? Let him go and return back to his house, that he may not die in the war, and another man take his wife.[19]

XXXIV. (149) For why, I should say, O most excellent man, do you not think it more proper to summon these men to follow you to the contest of war rather than the others, men who have acquired marriages, and houses, and vineyards, and all other kinds of possessions in abundance? For they will most cheerfully undergo dangers, even if they be altogether most formidable, for the sake of the safety of all these things. Since those men who have none of these things which have been enumerated will be very likely to exhibit indifference and inactivity in the war, as having no very important pledges at stake. (150) Or do you think that, just in proportion to the absence of any enjoyment from the possession of such things that they have hitherto felt, will be their apprehension lest they never be able to enjoy such things, and that this will give them energy? For what advantage from all the possessions that they may have acquired is left to those who have been subdued in war? But will they not be taken prisoners? Then they will immediately suffer for their absence from the field of battle; for while they are sitting at home and wallowing in luxury, it is evidently inevitable that their enemies, who are conducting all the operations of the war with energy, will ,not merely without any loss, but even without the slightest exertion, make themselves masters of all that they possess. (151) But the multitude of their other allies will cheerfully encounter the contest on behalf of these things. At first sight, indeed, it seems absurd to rely upon the energies or fortune of others; and especially when it is both an individual and a common danger, involving defeat, and slavery, and utter destruction, which hangs over men's heads, who are able of themselves to encounter the toils and perils of war, and who are

not hindered by any disease, or by old age, or by any other disaster. It is rather fitting that those, whom the danger chiefly concerns, should seize their arms and stand in the front battalions and hold their shields over their allies, fighting cheerfully and with a spirit which even courts dangers.

XXXV. (152) In the next place, will they not have displayed examples, not of treachery only, but of the greatest insensibility, if they allow others to fight in their cause, while they themselves are occupied about their domestic affairs? And shall others be willing to incur contests and dangers in the cause of their safety, which they are afraid to encounter for their own? And shall others cheerfully endure scarcity of provisions, and sleeping on the ground, and other hardships of body and soul, from their desire for victory, while they, covering their houses with stucco and nonsense, so much lifeless ornament, or gathering in their harvests from their fields, and celebrating the festival of the vintage, or coming into connection, now for the first time, with virgins who have long since been betrothed to them, and sleeping with them, as if it were the most opportune reason for marriage, pass their time in such vanities? (153) It is a good thing, no doubt, to take care of one's walls, to collect one's revenues, to feast, to revel in wine, to contract marriages, to go courting the old and withered dames (as the proverb calls them); but these are the employments of peace, and to do all these things in the crisis of a war raging in all its freshness and vigour, (154) while neither father, nor brother, nor any relation or connection whatever shares the fatigues of the war; when this, I say, is the case, must we not say that universal cowardice has occupied the whole house? Oh, but you will say there are at all events myriads of relations who are fighting in their cause. Then, while they are encountering danger to their lives, must not those who are spending their time in luxury and delicate living appear to surpass even the worst of wild beasts in the excess of their inhumanity? (155) Again, they will say, but it is hard that others, without enduring any labour themselves, should reap the fruits of our labours. Which, then, is worst, that enemies should come into one's inheritance while one is still alive, or that friends and relations should do so after one is dead? It is absurdity even to compare things which are so widely different; (156) and yet it is not inconsistent with reason, not only that all the property which belongs to these men who shun military service, but that even they themselves, too, may become the property of their enemies when they have obtained the mastery. So those, indeed, who die in defence of the general safety, even if they have not enjoyed as yet any advantage from those possessions which they previously had, meet with death in its most pleasant form, considering that,

---

[19]Deuteronomy 20:5.

by their saving the others, their property goes to those whom they desired to have for their successors.

XXXVI. (157) Therefore the words of the law here admit, perhaps, of all these and even of still more excuses; but that no one of those who study evil cunning, through his ingenuity in devising excuses, may feel any confidence in their validity, we will proceed with the allegory, and say that, in the first place, the law does not only think it right for men to labour for the acquisition of good things, but also for the enjoyment of those which they have already acquired; and that it looks upon happiness as consisting in the exercise of perfect virtue, which makes life safe and complete. In the second place, that the question here is not about a house, or a vineyard, or a betrothed and espoused wife, in order that he may marry her as an accepted suitor, and that he who planted the vineyard may gather the fruit thereof and press it out, and then, drinking the unmixed wine, may be gladdened in his heart, and that the man who has built a house may dwell in it; but the question is rather about the faculties of the soul, to which the beginnings, and progress, and perfection of all praiseworthy actions are owing. (158) Now, the beginnings have usually especial connection with a suitor; for as he who courts a wife is about to become her husband, since he is not so already, so in the same manner whoever, endued with a good disposition, hopes to marry that well-born and pure maiden, education, courts her immediately. Progress has especial reference to the husbandman; for as it is an object of particular care to the planter to make his trees grow, so also is it to him, who is devoted to learning, that the speculations of wisdom should receive the greatest possible improvement. And perfection especially belongs to the building of a house when it is finished, but has not yet settled and become firm.

XXXVII. (159) But in all these different circumstances, at the beginning, or in the progress, or at the end of any undertaking, it is alike becoming to men to live without contention, and not engage in the war of the sophists, which is always stirring up a quarrelsome confusion, which tends to the adulteration of the truth; since the truth is dear to peace, which is at variance with their interests. (160) For if they come to this contest, being private individuals engaging in a struggle against men experienced in warfare, they will by all means be defeated; and one who is only beginning, because he is destitute of experience; the one who is in a state of progress, because he is still imperfect; and the one who is perfect, because he is not yet thoroughly practised in virtue. But just as it is necessary that plaster, after it has been applied to a wall, must become solid and acquire firmness, so also it is indispensable that the souls of those

who have attained to perfection, must become strengthened, and be established on firmer foundations by continual study and incessant practice. (161) And those who do not arrive at this point are by philosophers indeed called wise men, but it is without their own knowledge: for they say that it is impossible for them who have advanced as far as the perfection of wisdom, and who have now for the first time reached its summit to be aware of their own perfection; for they affirm that it is impossible for both these things to happen at the same time, namely the arrival at the desired goal, and the apprehension that one has arrived there; but they affirm that on the border between the two, there is ignorance, of such a sort, that it is not far removed from knowledge, but that it is very near to it, and close to its doors.

(162) When a man has acquired this, and thoroughly comprehends it, and is entirely acquainted with the powers of his adversaries, it will be his task to war against the company of contentious sophists, for there is good hope that such a man may conquer; but he who is still impeded by the cloud of ignorance in front of him, and who is not yet able to pour forth the light of knowledge, may safely remain at home; that is to say, it is well for him not to enter into a contest with respect to those matters with which he is not thoroughly acquainted, but he had better rest and keep quiet.

(163) But the man who is elevated by self-sufficiency, not being acquainted with the skill or power of his adversaries, will undoubtedly meet with disaster before he can do anything, and will endure the death of knowledge, which is a more grievous death than that which separates the soul from the body. (164) And this ought to happen to those who allow themselves to be deceived by the sophists; for when they are not able to find a solution for their sophisms, believing their fallacies as if they were true statements, they die as to the life of knowledge, suffering the same thing that they do who are cajoled by flatterers; for in the case of those men too, their soul, while in a healthy and genuine state, is driven off and overthrown by a friendship which is diseased in its very nature.

XXXVIII. (165) We must therefore advise those who are beginning to learn not to go forth into such contests, for they have not sufficient knowledge; and we must counsel those who are making some progress to abstain from them, because they are not perfect; and those who have now for the first time just attained to perfection, we must urge to forbear, because in some degree their perfection has escaped their own notice. (166) But of those who disregard our warnings, Moses says, "One man will inhabit his house, and another will obtain his vineyard, and another will marry a wife." And the meaning of this is something of this kind: the powers which have been enumerated, of careful beginning, and improvement, and perfection, will never fail altogether, but will at different times approach and unite themselves with different persons, and will not be always forming the same souls, but will change about, resembling seals; (167) for seals, when they have stamped an impression on one piece of wax, without suffering any alteration themselves, though they impress on it a form which is derived from themselves, remain in the same condition as before; and if the piece of wax which has been stamped, be melted, and the impression effaced, then another piece may be substituted in its place.

So that, my good friends, do not think, that when you yourselves perish, your powers perish with you; for they, being immortal, have, on account of their own glory, embraced ten thousand other persons before they came to you, who, they perceived, did not behave like you, out of an aversion to danger, shunning their society, but who rather came forward to meet them, and showed an eagerness to consult their safety. (168) And if any one is a friend of virtue, let him pray that all good things may be implanted in him, and may appear in his soul, like some symmetrical proportion conducing to beauty in a statue or a picture, considering that there are innumerable persons watching at hand, to whom nature will give all these things instead of giving them to him, namely, facility of learning, improvement, and perfection; but it is better that he should shine out rather than they, guarding safely the graces which have been bestowed on him by God; and that he himself should not, by carrying forward destruction, afford an easy prey to his unsparing enemies.

XXXIX. (169) Are we then to say that there is but little use in a beginning to which a fortunate end does not set its seal? It has often indeed happened that even some who have attained to perfection have still been thought imperfect, from appearing to have improved through their own earnestness alone, and not according to the will of God. And on this account, being exceedingly elated by their vain opinion, and elevated to a great height, they have fallen from a high position to the lowest depths, and so been destroyed. (170) "For if," says Moses, "you have built a new house, you shall also erect a battlement on the house, and then shall commit no murder in your house if any one falls from it."[20] (171) For the most grievous of all falls is for a man to stumble and fall from the honour due to God; crowning himself rather than God, and committing domestic murder. For he who does not duly honour the living God kills his own soul: so that the building of education which he has erected

is of no advantage to him. But instruction has a nature which never grows old; on which account Moses calls its house a new house, for all other things are gradually destroyed by time. But instruction, in proportion as it advances towards perfection, is fresh and vigorous, looking blooming with an ever-flourishing appearance, and putting itself in motion with continual studies.

(172) And in his hortatory admonitions Moses recommends that those who have received the most abundant possession of good things should not look upon themselves as the causes of their acquisition, but should "remember God who gave them strength to acquire the power."[21] (173) This then is the utmost limit of good fortune, and the other things are its beginnings, so that those who forget the end cannot possibly derive any advantage from the acquisitions which they have made. And so the falls which these men endure are self-incurred, through their own self-sufficiency, because they could not endure to call the loving and all-accomplishing God the cause of their good things.

XL. (174) There are also some people who, letting loose every cable of piety, hasten to make a speedy voyage, in the hope of anchoring in its harbours. And afterwards, when they are at no great distance off, but are just on the point of reaching the haven, on a sudden there comes a violent wind, blowing in their teeth and coming upon them closely, which drives back the vessel which was proceeding onwards in its straight course, in such a manner as to destroy a great many of the things which were of use to contribute to a fair voyage; (175) no one then could blame those people for being still tossed about by the sea, for the slowness, which they have displayed in completing their voyage, has been unintentional on their part. Who then can be likened to them rather than he who prayed what is called the great prayer? "For if," says Moses, "any one dies in his presence suddenly, then immediately the head of his vow shall be polluted and he shall be shaved;"[22] and then after saying a few more sentences he thus proceeds, "And the former days shall not be taken into the computation, because the head of his vow was polluted." (176) Now by the two expressions suddenly and immediately, the involuntary character of the deviation of the soul is manifested.

For with reference to intentional sins there is need of time to consider where, and when, and how a thing is to be done. But unintentional sins are committed suddenly, without any consideration, and, if it be possible to say such a thing they strike upon the man without any time at all. (177)

---

[20]Deuteronomy 22:8.

[21]Deuteronomy 8:18.
[22]Numbers 6:9.

For it is very difficult, as in the case of runners, for men, when they first begin to travel by the road which leads to piety, to keep their course straight onward without stumbling and without being out of breath; since there are innumerable hindrances to every human being, (178) but above all things, that which is the one and only thing in the way of doing good, namely the abstaining from any intentional misdeeds, is of service also to keep off the incalculable number of voluntary sins; and, in the second place, even of those which are involuntary, they are but few which are committed, and they do not cling to a person for any very long time.

(179) Very beautifully, therefore, has Moses said that the days of unintentional error do not come into the computation *(alogos)*; not only because the error was one without calculation, but also because it is not possible to give an account *(logos)* of involuntary offences. Therefore, it often happens, when we are asked the reason of such and such a thing, that we say that we do not know, and that we cannot tell, in that we were not present when they were done, and also that we were ignorant of their being done. (180) It is, therefore, a very rare thing when God gives to any one to keep his life in a steady course from the beginning to the end, without either stumbling or falling; but escaping both kinds of offences, unintentional as well as intentional, with great speed and owing to the celerity and impetuosity of one's motions.

(181) These things then are here said about beginning and end, because of the instance of the just Noah, who, after he had acquired the first and elementary principles of the knowledge of husbandry, was unable to reach its furthest limits. For it is said that "he began to be a husbandman," not that he arrived at the extreme end of complete knowledge: but what is said about his planting we will discuss subsequently.

CONCERNING NOAH'S WORK AS A PLANTER†

(De Plantatione)

I. (1) In the former part of this treatise we have spoken of the art of husbandry as to its genus, dwelling on it at as great a length as the time admitted of; but in this book we will discuss the question of his cultivation of his vineyard with regard to the species as far as it is in our power. For Moses represents the just Noah not only as a husbandman, but also especially as occupied with the cultivation of vines, saying, "Noah began to be a husbandman of the earth; and he planted a vineyard."[1] (2) And it is fitting that a man who was about to discuss the whole question of separate plants and manners of cultivation, should first of all acquire an accurate comprehension of the most perfect plants in the universe, and of the great planter and superintendent of them.

He then who is the greatest of all planters and the most perfect in art, is the Ruler of the universe; and his plant is not one which comprises within itself only individual plants, but rather infinite numbers of them springing up like suckers from one root, namely, this world. (3) For after the Creator of the world, reducing that substance, which was in its own nature destitute of order and regularity, into a state of order, and bringing it from a condition of confusion into a distinct system, began to fashion and shape it, he placed the earth and the water in the middle, and the plants of air and fire he drew up from their previously central position to a lofty eminence; and the aether he arranged all round, placing it as a boundary to and preservation of the things within, from which also it seems that the heaven[2] derives its name, causing the earth to be borne upon the water in such a way that it continues dry, which, however, there was reason to fear might be dissolved by water; and this great worker of marvels, moreover, united the air, which was exceedingly cold by its own nature, to fire which is very hot; a most surprising miracle. (4) For how can it be looked upon as anything but a prodigy, for that which would dissolve another thing, to be held together by that which it would dissolve: that is to say, for water

to be held together by earth; and again, for that which is the hottest of all things to be placed upon that which is the coldest without its nature being destroyed, that is to say, for fire to be placed upon air? And these are the elements of this most perfect plant; but the very great and all productive plant is this world, of which the aforesaid branches are the main shoots.

II. (5) We must now therefore consider where God placed its foundations, and in fact, what foundation it has on which it is supported, as a statue is on a pedestal; certainly we cannot imagine that any body is left outside and wandering about, since God has worked up and arranged every imaginable material throughout the whole universe. (6) For it was fitting that the most perfect and greatest of all works should be made by the greatest of all makers; and it would not have been the most perfect of works if it had not been filled up by perfect parts, so that this world consists of all earth, and all water, and all air, and all fire, not a single particle, no not the smallest imaginable atom, being omitted.

(7) It follows therefore of necessity, that what is outside must either be a vacuum or nothing at all. If now it is a vacuum, than how can that which is full and solid, and the heaviest of all things, avoid being pressed down by its own weight, since there is no solid thing to hold it up? from which consideration it would appear to be something like a vision, since the mind is always seeking for some corporeal foundation, such as everything which is moved, must of necessity have: and especially the world, inasmuch as it is the greatest of all bodies, and embraces a multitude of other bodies as it sown appropriate parts.

(8) If therefore any one wishes to escape from the difficulties of this question which present themselves in the different doubts thus raised, let him speak freely and say that there is nothing in any material of such power as to be able to support this weight of the world. But it is the eternal law of the everlasting God which is the most supporting and firm foundation of the universe. (9) This it is which, being extended from the centre of the borders, and again from the extremities to the centre, runs through the whole unsubdued course of nature, collecting all the parts and binding them firmly together; for the father who created them has made it the indissoluble bond of the universe. (10) Very naturally and appropriately therefore, all earth will not be dissolved by all water, which the

---

†Yonge's title, *The Second Part of the Treatise about the Planting of Noah;* the mention of *"The Second Part"* shows that Yonge regarded *On Husbandry (De Agricultura)* to be closely tied to *Concerning Noah's Work as a Planter (De Plantatione)*.

[1] Genesis 9:20.

[2] *Ouranos,* "heaven;" as if derived from *horos* or *houros,* "a boundary."

bosom of the earth contains, nor will fire be extinguished by air, nor again will air be burnt up by fire, since the divine law establishes itself as a boundary to all these elements, like a vowel among consonants, so that the universe may, as it were, be harmonious in concert with the music expressed by letters; persuasion, by its own authority, putting an end to the threatening conflicts of contrary natures.

III. (11) Thus then the plant which bears all things was rooted, and when it was rooted was made strong. But of the particular plants, and those of smaller growth, some were moveable, so as to have their places changed; and some were made so as, without any such change, to stand steadily in the same place. (12) Those then that are affected by motion, inducing change of place, which we call animals, are attached to the most important portions of the universe; the terrestrial animals to the earth, the animals which swim to the water, the winged animals to the air and those which can live in the flame to the fire (which last are said to be most evidently produced in Macedonia), and the stars are attached to the heaven. For those who have studied philosophy pronounce the stars also to be animals, being endowed with intellect and pervading the whole universe; some being planets, and moving by their own intrinsic nature; and others, that is the fixed stars, being borne along with the revolutions of the universe; so that they likewise appear to change their places. (13) But those which are regulated according to a nature devoid of all sensation, which are peculiarly called plants, have no participation in that motion which involves a change of place.

IV. (14) But the Creator made two different races on the earth and in the air. In the air, he made the winged animals capable of being perceived by the external senses, and other powers which can by no means be comprehended in any place by the external senses; and this is the company of incorporeal souls arranged in order, but not in the same classifications. For it is said that some are assigned to mortal bodies, and are again subjected to a change of place according to certain defined periodical revolutions; but that others which have received a more divinely prepared habitation, look down upon the region of the earth, and that in the highest place, near the ether itself, the purest souls are placed, which those who have studied philosophy among the Greeks call heroes, but which Moses, by a felicitous appellation, entitles angels; souls which go as ambassadors and messengers of good from the ruler of all things to his subjects, and messengers also to the king respecting those things of which his subjects have heard. To the earth again he assigned two classes, terrestrial animals and plants, wishing that she should be at the same time their mother and their nurse. (15) For, as in the case of woman and every

animal of the female sex, fountains of milk spring up in them when they are about to bring forth, in order that they may supply the offspring that is born of them with necessary and suitable food; so in a similar manner God has assigned to the earth, which is the mother of all terrestrial animals, all the different species of plants, in order that the animals produced by the earth may have such food as is akin to them, and not alien from their natures.

(16) And, indeed, God has caused plants to grow with their heads downwards, having fixed their heads in the deepest parts of the earth; and having drawn up the heads of the irrational animals from the earth, he has set them up high on long necks, putting their fore feet under their necks as a kind of foundation. (17) But man has received a pre-eminently superior formation. For of all other animals God has bent the eyes downwards, so that they look upon the ground; but on the other hand, he has raised the eyes of man so that he may behold the heaven, being not a terrestrial but a celestial plant as the old proverb is.[3]

V. (18) But the others who say that our mind is a portion of the ethereal nature, have by this assertion attributed to man a kindred with the air; but the great Moses has not named the species of the rational soul by a title resembling that of any created being, but has pronounced it an image of the divine and invisible being, making it a coin as it were of sterling metal, stamped and impressed with the seal of God, the impression of which is the eternal word. (19) For, says Moses, "God breathed into man's face the breath of life,"[4] so that it follows of necessity, that he that received the breath must be fashioned after the model of him who sent it forth. On which account it is said too, that "Man was made after the image of God,"[5] and not after the image of any created being. (20) It follows, therefore, since the soul of man has been fashioned in accordance with the archetypal word of the great cause of all things, that his body also, having been raised up to the purest portion of the universe—the heaven, must extend its vision, in order that, by a comparison with what is visible, it may attain to an accurate comprehension of what is invisible.

(21) Since, therefore, it was impossible for any one to perceive the attraction of the mind to the living God, except for those persons alone who were drawn towards him (for that which each person suffers, he alone particularly knows), God has

---

[3]This is similar to what Ovid says, which may be translated—And while all other creatures from their birth / With downcast eyes gaze on their kindred earth, / He bids man walk erect, and scan the heaven, / From whence he sprung, to which his hopes are given.
[4]Genesis 2:7.
[5]Genesis 1:27.

given us the eyes of the body (as an evident and visible image of the invisible eye), which are able to look up to the heaven; (22) for when the eyes, composed of perishable material, have raised themselves to such a height, as to be able from the region of the earth to mount up to heaven which is removed at so great a distance from the earth, and to reach its utmost heights, how great a course in every direction must we suppose to be within the power of the eyes of the soul? which, being endowed with wings from their excessive desire to see the living God clearly, reach up not only to the highest regions of the air, but even pass over the boundaries of the whole world, and hasten towards the Uncreated.

VI. (23) On this account, those persons who are insatiable in their desire for wisdom and knowledge are said in the sacred oracles to be "called up."[6] (24) For it is legitimate that those persons should be called up to the Deity who have been inspired by him. For it would be a terrible thing if whirlwinds and hurricanes have power to tear trees up by their roots, and to toss them in the air, and to carry off vessels of many tons' burden, though loaded with cargoes, as if they were the lightest things imaginable, out of the middle of the sea; and if even lakes and rivers are raised on high, when their streams actually leave the bosom of the earth, having been drawn up by the ardent and diversified eddies of the winds: and yet, if the mind, which is intrinsically light, cannot be raised up by the nature of the Divine Spirit, which is able to do everything and to subdue all things below, and cannot be elevated to an exceeding height; and especially the mind of the man who studies philosophy in a genuine manner. (25) For he does not incline downwards to the things dear to the body and to the earth, from which he separates himself, and studies to alienate himself as far as possible but he is borne upwards, being insatiably devoted to sublime, holy, magnificent, and happy natures.

(26) Therefore, also, Moses will be summoned upwards, the steward and guardian of the sacred mysteries of the living God. For we read in the book of Leviticus, "He called Moses up to him."[7] Bezeleel also will be summoned up, being thought worthy of the same honours. For him, also, God calls up for the preparation of the sacred furniture and for the care of the sacred works. (27) But he receives only the second honour of this summons, and the all-wise Moses shall have the first place assigned to him. For the former fashions shadows only, like painters do, in which it is not right to form any living thing. For the very name Bezeleel

is interpreted to mean, "working in shadows." But Moses does not make shadows, but the task is assigned to him of forming the archetypal natures of things themselves. And in other places, also, the great Cause of all things is accustomed to reveal his secrets to some in a more conspicuous and visible manner, as if in the pure light of the sun, and to others more sparely, as though in the shade.

VII. (28) Having therefore gone through all the larger plants in the universe, let us see in what manner the all-wise God made the trees which exist in the smaller world, that is to say, in man. In the first place, then, taking our body as if it were a field of deep soil, he created the external senses to be in it as so many channels. (29) And after that, he arranged the place of each separate one of them, as if it had been a fruit-bearing and most useful tree, assigning the sense of hearing to the ear, that of sight to the eyes, that of smell to the nostrils, and each of the other senses and faculties to their kindred and appropriate organs. And the divine man bears his testimony to this account of mine, speaking thus in his Psalms, "He that planted the ear, doth he not hear? and he that made the eyes, shall he not see?"[8] (30) Moreover, all the different powers which run down as far as the legs and hands, and all the other parts of the body, whether internal or external, are all those of an unimportant kind. (31) But those which are better and more perfect he has rooted in the more central portion; that which is pre-eminently able to bring forth fruit, the dominant portion of the man. These faculties are perception, comprehension, felicity of conjecture, study, memory, habit, disposition, the various species of art, the firmness of knowledge of different things, the apprehension of the speculations of universal virtue in such a way as is never forgotten. Now, no mortal is competent to plant any one of these things himself. But of all of them together there is one architect, the uncreated God, who has not only made them originally, but who also makes them for and implants them in every individual man that is born.

VIII. (32) Now the account of the planting of Paradise is consistent with what has been already said. For it is stated, "God planted a Paradise in Eden, towards the east; and there is placed the man whom he has made."[9] Now, to think that it is here meant that God planted vines, or olive trees, or apple trees, or pomegranates, or any trees of such kinds, is mere incurable folly. (33) For why should he have done so? any one may ask. Was it that he might have a pleasant abode to spend his time in? Even the whole world could not be considered a dwelling sufficient for God, the governor of the universe. Would it not appear to be

[6]Exodus 19:20.
[7]Exodus 31:2 is the passage alluded to, and not any verse in Leviticus.

[8]Psalm 94:9.
[9]Genesis 2:8.

deficient in innumerable other things, so that it could never be looked upon as a place worthily suited to the reception of the great King? True, indeed, it is impiety to think that the Cause of all things can be contained in that which he has caused, especially as even those trees do not invariably bear their annual fruit.

(34) For whose enjoyment and use, then, is it that the Paradise is to produce fruit? For that of no man. For there is absolutely no one at all who is represented as inhabiting the Paradise, since Moses says that God removed the first man who was created out of the earth, by name Adam, from his original place, and placed him here. (35) And, moreover, God has no need of food any more than he has of anything else; for it follows necessarily that he who uses food must first of all stand in need of it. And in the second place, that he must have organs adapted for the reception of it, by means of which he can receive it when it enters him; and then dismiss it from him when he has digested it. But all these things, which are parts of the happiness and blessedness which surround the Great Cause of all things, are inconsistent with the doctrine of those men who represent him as clothed with human form, and influenced by human passions to the utter destruction of all piety and religious feeling—both great virtues; such notions being contrary to all law and right.

IX. (36) We must therefore have recourse to allegory, which is a favourite with men capable of seeing through it; for the sacred oracles most evidently conduct us towards and instigate us to the pursuit of it. For they say that in the Paradise there were plants in no respect similar to those which exist among us; but they speak of trees of life, trees of immortality, trees of knowledge, of comprehension, of understanding; trees of the knowledge of good and evil. (37) Now these cannot have been trees of the land, but must indisputably have been plants of a rational soil, which was a road to travel along, leading to virtue, and having for its end life and immortality; and another road leading to vice, having for its end the loss of life and immortality, that is to say, death.

Therefore, we must suppose that the bounteous God plants in the soul, as it were, a paradise of virtues and of the actions in accordance with them, which lead it to perfect happiness. (38) On this account, also, he has assigned a most appropriate place to the Paradise, called Eden (and the name Eden, being interpreted, means "delight"), an emblem of the soul, which sees right things, and revels amid the virtues, and exults by reason of the abundance and magnitude of its joy; proposing to itself one source of enjoyment in the place of the innumerable things which are accounted pleasant among men, namely the service of the one wise God. (39) He, then, who had drunk of this unmixed source of joy, and was a follower of

and fellow rejoicer with Moses, and not one of the least valued of that body, in his Psalms addressed his own mind, saying, "Delight thou in the Lord."[10] Exciting himself and his mind towards heavenly and divine love by these words, and indignantly turning away from the luxury and effeminacy existing among what are called and believed to be human goods; and being hurried away in his whole heart by divine inspiration and fervour, and finding his joy in God alone.

X. (40) And the statement that "the Paradise was in the east," is a proof of what has been here said. For folly is a thing of darkness and setting, and which brings on the night; but wisdom is a most brilliant thing, radiant all around, and in the truest sense of the word, rising. And, as the sun, when it arises, fills the whole circle of the heaven with its light, so in the same manner, when the beams of virtue shine forth, they made the whole place occupied by the mind full of pure light. (41) Therefore the possessions of man have guards and keepers, very fierce beasts, for the repulse of invading and attacking enemies. But the possessions of God have rational natures for their guards. For "there," says Moses, "God placed the man whom he had made;" that is to say, he placed him among the rational virtues alone; (42) therefore the practices and uses of the virtues have received from God this especial honour beyond the souls of other animals. And therefore, also, it is most expressly and plainly declared that God placed that man which is really man in us, namely, the mind, among the most sacred shoots and plants of excellence and virtue. But among those animals which have no share in mind, no one has ever cultivated any plant worth speaking of, since there is not one of them capable by nature of receiving comprehension.

XI. (43) We cannot therefore raise any question as to why it was ordained that all the different species of animals should be collected in the ark which was made at the time of the great deluge, while more were brought into the Paradise. For the ark was an emblem of the body, which of necessity therefore contained all the most tameable and ferocious evils of the passions and vices; but the Paradise contained only the virtues: and the virtues do not receive anything savage or in short anything destitute of reason. (44) And Moses also speaks very carefully, not representing the man who was made after God's own image, but the man who was formed of clay, as the one who was placed in the paradise. For the one who was made after the image of God, and stamped with the truth of God, does, as it appears to me, in no respect differ from the tree which bore as its fruit everlasting life. For they are both imperishable, and have

---

[10] Psalm 37:4.

both been thought worthy of the most central position in the dominant part of man. For it is said that "the tree of life is in the midst of the Paradise."

But the other man, he of the composite and more earthly body, who has no justification in uncreated and simple nature, the cultivator of which is the only person who knows how to dwell in the house and in the courts of the Lord. For Jacob is represented "as a plain man dwelling in a house,"[11] having a disposition full of ingenuity, and compounded and made up of all kinds of materials. (45) It was natural therefore to place and firmly root the mind in the middle of the paradise, that is, of the universal world, having in itself faculties which draw it in contrary directions, so that it should be kept in a state of doubt when called upon to discriminate as to what it should choose and what it should avoid, since if it chose the better part it would reap immortality and glory; and if it chose the worse it would meet with reproach and death.

XII. (46) Such then are the trees which the only wise God has planted in rational souls. But Moses, pitying those who were exiled and compelled to quit the paradise of the virtues, addresses a prayer to the absolute authority of God and to his merciful and propitious powers, entreating that in the place from which the earthly mind, Adam, was banished, there a people capable of seeing the truth might be planted. (47) For he says, "Bring them in and plant them in the mountain of thy inheritance which thou dost give them; thou hast made them to sit in thy seat, O Lord; in the sanctuary, O Lord, which thy hands have made. The Lord shall be king of ages, for ever and ever."[12]

(48) Therefore he had learnt, as plainly as any man that ever lived, that God, having fixed the roots and seeds of everything down in the earth, is the cause also of the greatest of all plants, namely this world, shooting up; which world he here seems to speak of enigmatically in the song which I have just quoted, where he calls it the mountain of his inheritance; since that which is made is the most appropriate possession and inheritance, of him who has made it. (49) Therefore he prays that we may be planted in it, not in order that we may become irrational and unmanageable in our natures; but that, in due obedience to the arrangement of the all-perfect governor, imitating his perpetual and undeviating consistency, we may live a temperate and innocent life. For to be able to live in a strict uniformity with nature, is what the men of old have defined as the end of happiness.

(50) And accordingly what is said afterwards is in strict agreement with what is said before, namely, that the world is the beautiful and properly prepared house of God, appreciable by the external senses; and that he himself made it and that it is not uncreated, as some persons have thought. And he uses the word "sanctuary," as meaning a splendour emitted from holy objects, an imitation of the archetypal model; since those things which are beautiful to the external senses are to the intellectual senses models of what is beautiful.

The expression that "it was prepared by the hands of God," means that it was made by his world-creating powers. (51) But in order that no one may suppose that the Creator had need of any one of the things which he created, he adds the most necessary assertion, "Being King of ages for ever and ever." But a king is in need of nothing, but everything which is subject to him is inevitably in need of the king. (52) And some persons have said that God is and is properly called the inheritance of God, the use and enjoyment of which Moses has now prayed may be afforded to us. For, says he, representing us as children just beginning to learn by means of the doctrines and speculations of wisdom, and not leaving us destitute of the elements of knowledge, plant them in sublime and heavenly reason. (53) For this is the most thoroughly prepared inheritance; the house most completely ready, the abode most entirely suitable, which "thou hast made holy." For, O master, thou art the maker of all good and holy things, as, on the other hand, corruptible creation is of what is evil and profane. Reign thou throughout infinite eternity over the suppliant soul; not leaving it for a single moment without a governor. For an uninterrupted service under them is not only better than freedom, but even than the most extensive dominion.

XIII. (54) In many people perhaps an inquiry may suggest itself as to what is the meaning of the expression, "In the mountain of thy inheritance." It is plain that God bestows inheritance, but perhaps it is not reasonable to think that he receives inheritances, since everything in the world belongs to him. (55) But perhaps this is said of those who are subject to him as their master, according to some special computation of connection; just as kings govern indeed all their subjects, but rule their own servants in a different and peculiar manner, whom they are accustomed to employ as ministers for the care of their bodies and the rest of their manner of life. (56) And again, though they are lords of all the possessions in their whole country, even of those which appear to belong to private individuals, they nevertheless are accounted owners only of those portions which they can entrust to superintendents and overseers, from whom they receive yearly revenues, which properties they often visit for the sake of relaxation and amusement, when they lay aside for a while the heaviest portion of the burden of the cares which arise to them in the administration of

---

[11] Genesis 25:27, where the expression, however, is "dwelling in *tents.*".
[12] Exodus 15:17.

public affairs and in the government of their kingdoms; and these possessions are called especially the royal properties.

(57) Moreover all the silver and gold, and other treasures which are stored up in the coffers of their subjects, do all in reality belong more to the rulers than to those who possess them. But nevertheless there are some which are peculiarly called the royal treasures, in which those who are appointed collectors of the produce lay up the revenues which are derived from the country. (58) Do not wonder, therefore, if the company of wise souls is pronounced to be the especial inheritance of the all-powerful God who has authority and dominion over everything, since he sees most acutely of all beings, exercising the irreproachable and unadulterated eye of the mind, which is never shut, but is always wide open and looking intensely into every thing.

XIV. (59) And on this account, indeed, it is said in the greater prayer, "Inquire of thy father, and he will tell thee; of thy elders, and they will reply to thee, when the Most High divided the nations, when he separated the sons of Adam, he fixed the boundaries of the nations, according to the number of the angels of God, and the portion of the Lord himself was his people Israel."[13] (60) For, behold, here again, he uses the expression, "the portion and inheritance of God," meaning that disposition which is capable of seeing him, and which sincerely worships him; and he says that the children of the earth, whom he calls the sons of Adam, were scattered and dispersed, and brought together again, and that a company was formed of them, since they were unable to use right reason as their guide. For, in real truth, virtue is the cause of harmony and unity, and the opposite disposition is the cause of dissolution and disagreement. (61) Indeed, it is a proof of what has been said, what happens every year on the day called the day of atonement; for on that day the people are enjoined "to take by lot two goats, one for the Lord, and one to be the scapegoat;"[14] that is to say, two reasons, the one in accordance with God, the other consistent with creation. He, therefore, who wishes to exalt the Cause of all things will acquire honour to himself; but he who attributes honour to creation will be banished, being driven from the most sacred places, and compelled to fall into inaccessible and wicked gulfs.

XV. (62) Moses, therefore, has such intimate connection with God, that, relying upon this in a very great degree, he is in the habit of using more fervent and energetic expressions and doctrines than are calculated for the ears of us inferior persons; for he not only thinks it fit to speak of God

as an inheritor, but even, which is a more startling thing to the comprehension, he calls him the inheritance of others; (63) for to the entire tribe which came to him as a fugitive and a suppliant, he did not think fit to allot only a portion of land, as he did to the other eleven tribes, but he chose that they should receive an especial honour, namely, the priesthood, a possession not of earth, but of heaven. "For there shall not be," says God, as Moses represents, "a portion to the tribe of Levi, nor any inheritance among the children of Israel, because the Lord himself is their inheritance."[15] And again he speaks in the person of God, in his holy oracles, in this manner: "I am thy portion and inheritance."[16] (64) For, in real truth, the mind which is perfectly purified, and which knows all the things of creation, knows and recognizes one only God, the Uncreate, whom it approaches, and by whom it is received. For to whom is it permitted to say, "He alone is my God," except to the man who is attached to none of the objects which are inferior to him? And this is the custom of the Levites; for the name of Levi, being interpreted, means, "He is to me," because different things are honoured by different people, but by him only that which is highest and most excellent, the Cause of all things.

XVI. (65) They tell an old story, that some man in ancient times, who had fallen madly in love with the beauty of wisdom, as if it had been the beauty of a most lovely woman, once, when he saw a most sumptuous preparation of unbounded and costly magnificence, looked towards some of his friends, and said, "Behold, O companions, how many things there are of which I have no need!" And yet he had nothing whatever of even necessary things beyond his mere clothes, so that he was not puffed up with the magnitude of his riches, which has been the case with numbers of people; so that, on this account, he spoke arrogantly against pomp and show.

(66) The lawgiver teaches us that we should account those people wise who are not eager to be rich in created things, but who despise all created things in comparison of the friendship of the uncreated God, whom they look upon as the only true wealth, and the boundary of most perfect happiness. (67) Never, then, let those men boast, who have acquired power and sovereignty, as some do, because they have subdued one city, or country, or nation; and others, because they have acquired the dominion over all the countries of the earth, to its furthest borders, and over all Grecian and barbarous nations, and over all the rivers and seas, infinite both in number and magnitude. (68) For if, besides these things, they had

---

[13]Deuteronomy 32:7.
[14]Deuteronomy 15:6.

[15]Deuteronomy 10:9.
[16]Numbers 18:20.

made themselves masters (which it is impious even to mention) of that sublime nature which was the only thing that the Creator made free from the bond of slavery and servitude, they would still be looked upon but as private individuals in comparison with the great kings who have received God for their inheritance; for in proportion as that nature which has acquired a possession is better than the possession itself, and the Creator than the thing created, by so much also are they more royal.

XVII. (69) Therefore, some people considered, that they who said that everything was the property of the one good Being, were speaking in an unreasonable manner, looking at the deficiencies and abundance which existed externally, and thinking no one rich who was in want of either money or possessions. But Moses thinks wisdom a thing of such pre-eminent value, and deserving to be so eagerly sought after, that not only the whole world deserves to be his inheritance, but that he even looks upon the Governor of the universe in that light; (70) and these are the doctrines, not of men who are halting between two opinions, but of those who are occupied in a firm and sure faith; since, even now, there are some persons among those who make a show and pretence of piety, who calumniate the literal meaning of this saying, saying that it is neither pious nor safe to speak of God as the inheritance of a man. (71) You say this—I should say to them—because ye have come not from genuine passion, but from a supposititious and illegitimate one, to the investigation of things. For you thought it a matter of equal consequence for God to be called the inheritance of possessions, of vineyards, and olive-yards, and such matters, and of wise men; and ye did not perceive that paintings are said to be the inheritance of painters, and, in short, that any art is said to be the inheritance of the artist, not looked at as an earthly possession, but as a heavenly prize; for none of such things are the property of any master, (72) but still they are an advantage to those who possess them: so that you, O sycophants, hear of the living God as an inheritance, not in the sense of being a possession, like those which I have enumerated, but as being the most beneficial and greatest of goods to those who think fit to worship the Cause of all good.

XVIII. (73) Having, therefore, now said what is proper concerning the original planter and the original plant, let us next proceed, in due order, to the consideration of matters of instruction and imitation.

In the first place, then, the wise Abraham is said "to have planted a field at the well of the oath, and to have called upon the name of the everlasting Lord God." [17] And here there is no peculiar property of the plants mentioned, but only the magnitude of the place. (74) And they who are in the habit of investigating these matters say, that everything which belongs to God has been very carefully and accurately described, both tree and place, and the fruit of the tree. Accordingly, they say that the tree was the field itself, not like those trees which sprung up out of the ground, but rather to those which grow according to the firmly-rooted mind of the man who loves God: and the place, they say, is the well of the oath, and the fruit, the change of the name of the Lord into that of "The Eternal God."

(75) And it is necessary further to give the probable explanation of each point of the things here mentioned. The field, then, being in length a hundred cubits, and as many in breadth, multiplied together according to the nature and character of a square, is composed of ten thousand superficial cubits; (76) and this is the greatest limit of those numbers which increase from the unit, and also the most perfect: so that the limit is the beginning of numbers, and the end, in those calculations, according to the first combination, is the number ten thousand; in reference to which fact, some persons have not erred greatly, who have compared the limit to the starting-place, and the number ten thousand to the goal, and all the numbers between these two to those who contend in a race; for they, beginning to start from the unit, as from the starting place, come to the number ten thousand as to the goal. (77) Therefore, some persons, departing from these numbers, as from signals, have said that God is the beginning and end of everything, which is a doctrine admirably calculated to engender piety. This doctrine, being implanted in the soul, produces a most beautiful and nutritious fruit, holiness; and the place most suitable for this fruit, (78) is the well which is called the oath, in which there is a report that no water could be found. For, says Moses, "the children of Israel, coming thither, reported to him concerning the well which they had digged: and they said, We found no water; and he called that place, 'The Oath.'" [18] Let us now consider what is the meaning of this statement.

XIX. (79) Those who investigate the nature of things as they actually exist, and who conduct their examinations of each individual matter in no negligent manner, behave very like those men who dig wells; for they also are seeking springs in an obscure place. And all men have one common desire, to find something to drink. But some men's nature is to be nourished by the food of the soul, and that of others by the food of the body. (80)

----

[17] Genesis 21:33.
[18] Genesis 26:32.

As, therefore, some of those who have dug wells have often done so without finding water; so likewise those who advance far in knowledge, and who have made great progress in it, are still often unable to attain to the end which they desire. At all events, they say that men of extensive learning often find fault with their terrible ignorance, for they only just know how far they are removed from the truth. And there is a story that some man of old time, when he was admired for his wisdom, said, that it was a fine thing that he should be admired, who only just knew that he knows nothing.

(81) And choose, if you like, any art you please, whether trifling or important, and the man, too, who is most excellent, and most highly thought of in regard to his skill in it, and then consider if the professions held out by the art are equal to the performances of the artist; for if you duly examine the matter, you will find that the performance falls short of the profession, not by a small, but by a vast distance, it being almost impossible for a man to be perfect in any art whatever, which is in continual motion like a fountain, and is constantly pouring forth various species of all kinds of speculations. (82) On this account, it is most appropriately denominated an oath, being the most certain sign of faith, comprehending also the testimony of God: for as he who swears, calls God to be a witness to a matter concerning which a question is raised, so it is not possible to swear so truly about any matter, as to the fact that the perfection of no art whatever can be found in the artist who professes it.

(83) And the same assertion holds good also with respect to all the other powers which exist in us, or very nearly so; for, as they say, that no water was found in the well which had been mentioned, so also neither was there the faculty of seeing in the eyes, or that of hearing in the ears, or that of smelling in the nostrils, or, in short, any one of the senses in its corresponding organ; and similarly in the mind, there was not the faculty of comprehension. (84) For how could it have happened that any one should have made a mistake in what he saw, or in what he heard, or in what he understood, if the comprehensions of each of these faculties had been well established, and if they had had a trustworthy nature of themselves without God implanting accuracy in them?

XX. (85) Having now, therefore, discussed the place sufficiently in which the tree flourishes, let us now, in conclusion, examine also the subject of the fruit:—

Now, what the fruit is, Moses will tell us himself: "For the Lord God everlasting," says he, "called it by its name." [19] (86) Therefore the appellations already mentioned reveal the powers existing in the living God; for one title is that of Lord, according to which he governs; and the other is God, according to which he is beneficent. For which reason also, in the account of the creation of the world, according to the most holy Moses, the name of God is always assumed by him: for it was fitting that the power according to which the Creator, when he was bringing his creatures into the world, arranged and adorned them, should be invoked also by that creation. (87) Inasmuch, therefore, as he is a ruler, he has both powers, that, namely, of doing good, and that of doing harm; regulating his conduct on the principle of requiting him who has done anything. But inasmuch as he is a benefactor, he is inclined only to one of these two courses, namely, to do good. (88) And it would be the greatest possible advantage to the soul no longer to feel any doubt about the power of the King for both purposes, but steadily to emancipate itself from the fear, which is suspended over it, on account of the vastness of his authority, and to kindle and keep alive a most firm hope of the acquisition and enjoyment of blessings arising from his being beneficent by deliberate intention.

(89) Now the expression, "everlasting God," is equivalent to, God who bestows gifts, not sometimes giving and sometimes not, but always and incessantly; it is equivalent to, God who does good uninterruptedly; to God who, without intermission, is connecting a flow of benefits, coming one after the other; God, who pours forth blessings upon blessings, who is made up of mercies connected and united; God, who never omits any single opportunity of doing good; God, who is also the Lord, so that he is able to injure.

XXI. (90) This also Jacob, the practiser of virtue, asked at the end of his most holy prayers. For he said, "And the Lord shall be to me as God." Which is equivalent to: He will no longer display towards me the despotic power of his absolute authority, but rather the beneficent influence of his universally propitious and saving power, utterly removing the fear with which he is regarded as a master, and filling the soul with affection and benevolence as felt towards a benefactor. (91) What soul could ever conceive thus that the master and ruler of the universe, without changing anything of his own nature, but remaining in the condition in which he always was, is continually kind and uninterruptedly bounteous? (92) owing to which he is, to those who are happy, the most perfect cause of unlimited and overflowing blessings. And to trust in a king who is not by reason of the magnitude of his authority elated so as to do injury to his subjects, but who, through his love to mankind, prefers that every one should enjoy happiness without fear, is the greatest possible bulwark of prosperity and security.

XXII. (93) What, therefore, we originally undertook we have now nearly fulfilled, namely,

---

[19] Genesis 21:33.

to demonstrate that the fact spoken of must be taken to mean the principle which declares God to be the most glorious of all things. The portion of the subject which follows next, is the demonstration that perfection is found in no created thing, but that it does appear in them at times owing to the grace of the great Cause of all things. And the fruit of the tree is, that the graces of God endure for ever and ever, and that they are shed incessantly upon mankind, and never cease. (94) Thus, in truth, the wise man, following the practice of the first and greatest planter, displays his knowledge of husbandry; and the sacred scripture wishes the labours of husbandry to be performed, even by those of us who are not yet perfect, but who are still reckoned among the middle numbers of those things which are accounted duties; for it says, (95) "When you go forth into the land which the Lord your God giveth to you, and when you plant every tree which is good for food, you shall completely purify its uncleanness. For three years it shall be unclean as to its fruit, it shall not be eaten; but in the fourth year, all its fruit shall be holy, being praised by the Lord. And in the fifth year you shall eat the fruit thereof; and everything that it bears shall be useful to you: I am the Lord your God."[20] Therefore it was impossible for the children of Israel, to plant those trees which are eatable, before they arrived in the country which had been given them by God; for he says, "When you go forth into the land, ... and when you plant every tree which is good for food." (96) So that while we are outside of the promised land, we should not be able to cultivate such trees; and this is very natural; (97) for as long as the mind has not entered upon the path of wisdom, but turns aside and wanders out of the road, it cares only for the trees which do not admit of being cultivated or used for food of men,—trees which are barren and useless, and which, though they bear, bear no fruit which is eatable. (98) But when the mind, having entered upon the path of wisdom, marches along with its doctrines, and begins to keep pace with them all, it then cultivates the useful trees, which are capable of bearing eatable fruit, instead of caring for those useless kinds; it cultivates a mastery over, instead of the indulgence of the passions, and knowledge instead of ignorance, and good instead of evil.

(99) Since therefore he who is led into the path of virtue is still at a long distance from the end, it is very naturally laid as an injunction upon the man who plants, to remove the uncleanness of that which is planted. And what this is, we will now consider.

XXIII. (100) These duties which are as it were in the middle, appear to me to be properly looked upon in the same light as those trees, which admit of being cultivated and used for food; for each of them bears most useful fruits, the one for the body, and the other for the soul. But in the middle there must necessarily be many injurious plants springing up with and growing along-side of them, which must be removed in order that the better sorts may not be injured. (101) May I not call the restoration of a deposit a useful plant of the soul? But still this plant requires purification and exceeding attention. What then is the purification? This. Having taken a deposit from a man while he is sober, you must not restore it to him while he is drunk, or intemperate, or mad; for in such a case though he may have received the advantage of having his own back again, he will have no opportunity of being benefited by it. Again. You must not restore a deposit to debtors or to slaves while their creditors or their masters are present; for that is betraying, and not a restoration of a deposit. Nor must you keep faith in small things in the hope merely of gaining confidence, so as to have greater things entrusted to you. (102) For those who fish, and who let down small baits into the sea, with the view of catching larger fish, are not very much to be blamed, as they say that they are providing for the good supply of the market, and in order that they may supply men with unlimited food for every day. (103) But no one should use as a bait, the restoration of a deposit of small value by way of obtaining a larger one, holding forth in his hands, and displaying the deposit of one individual, and that a trifling one, and in his intention appropriating the deposits of every body, and those too of unspeakable value. If, therefore, you remove the uncleanness of your deposit, as of these trees, namely, the inquiries threatened by plotters, the evils arising from want of opportunity and treachery, and all things of similar kinds; you will bring into a state of cultivation and usefulness, that which was on the point of becoming wild.

XXIV. (104) And in the case of the tree of friendship, it is necessary to cut down and eradicate these things which shoot up by the side of it for the sake of preserving the more valuable plant. And the evil plants which spring up alongside are these: the tricky blandishments of courtesans towards their lovers, and the deceitfulness of parasites to those whom they flatter. (105) For one may see those who make a traffic of their personal beauty, clinging to their lovers as if they were excessively fond of them; but they love not them but themselves, and they are eager only for their daily gains. And as for flatterers, sometimes they conceal unspeakable hatred towards those whom they flatter; but still, being slaves to gluttony and intemperance, they are on that account induced to pay court to those who can supply their immoderate appetites. (106) But the tree of science and unadulterated friendship having rejected and dis-

---

carded these things, will bear fruit of the greatest possible service to those who use it, namely, incorruptible good faith. For good-will is a desire that one's neighbour should enjoy good things for his own sake. But courtesans and flatterers are anxious solely for their own advantage, which is the only motive why they should confer pleasure, the first on their lovers, and the latter on the objects of their flatteries. We must therefore cut down all trickeries and flatteries as evil plants growing up near the tree of friendship.

XXV. (107) The due attention to sacred rites, and good faith in the matter of sacrifices, are the most excellent of trees; but along-side of them an evil grows up, namely, superstition, which it is desirable to eradicate before it has time to blossom. For some persons have fancied the sacrificing of oxen to be piety, and they assign a portion of all that they steal or obtain by denials, or by cheating their creditors, or by plundering, to the altars. Impious wretches that they are, thinking that thus they are paying a price to buy themselves off from suffering punishment for their offences. (108) But to such persons I would say, O ye men, the tribunal of God is not to be corrupted by bribes; so that those who have guilty minds will be rejected, even if they sacrifice a hundred oxen every day; and those who are innocent will be received, even if they never sacrifice at all. For God delights in altars on which no fire is burned, but which are frequented by virtues, and which do not blaze with great flame, such as those sacrifices do kindle which are offered by impious men, and which are no sacrifices at all, and which serve to remind one of the ignorances and wickedness of each of the sacrificers; for Moses has somewhere spoken of a sacrifice "reminding one of sin."[21]

(109) All such things therefore, being the causes of great injury, it is necessary to cut off and eradicate, in obedience to the oracle in which it is enjoined "to remove the uncleanness of the tree which has been planted, bearing eatable fruit."[22]

XXVI. (110) But we, even after we have been instructed, make no progress in learning; but some persons, having a self-taught natural instinct, purify what is good from the evils which surround it, as Jacob did, he who was surnamed the practicer of virtue; for he "peeled the rods, leaving on the white bark, having stripped off all the green;"[23] in order that the dark and dusky vanity in the middle being taken away in every case, a white appearance might be displayed, which should be produced so as to be akin to it, not by diversified art but

by nature; (111) in reference to which it is also commanded in the law which was established in cases of leprosy, that "the man who was not infected with any variation of colour, but who was white all over from the head to the extremity of his feet, should be pure."[24] In order that, according to the similitude of the body, those who have discarded the crafty, and unscrupulous, and ambiguous, and uncertain disposition of mind, may embrace the simple, uncoloured, unambiguous, plain complexion of truth; (112) therefore, to say that the tree is purified, contains a principle, the assertion of which is founded surely in truth, but to make the same statement with respect to the fruit is saying what is not equally clear or credible; for no cultivator of figs or grapes, or, in sort, of any fruit whatever, purifies them.

XXVII. (113) And again Moses says, "Its fruit shall be impure for three years, it shall not be eaten;"[25] as if in fact it were customary for it to be purified for ever. We must, therefore, say that this is one of those expressions which have a concealed meaning, since the words themselves are not quite consistent with it; for the expression is an ambiguous one; for it bears one sense of this kind, the fruit shall remain for three years; and then there is a distinct injunction, "it shall not be eaten before it is purified." But there is also another meaning, "the fruit of the tree shall for three years be unpurified, and while in that state it shall not be eaten." (114) According, then, to the former statement one may understand it in this manner: the three years being taken from time which is divided into three portions; for it is the nature of time to be divided into the past, the present, and the future; therefore the fruit of education will exist, and will endure, and will last unimpaired through all the divisions of time, a statement equivalent to—it will never receive any corruption, for the nature of good is imperishable.

But the fruit which is not purified shall not be eaten; inasmuch as virtuous reasons, duly purified and rendered sound, nourish the soul, and give vigour to the mind; but the opposite kinds are not nutritious, but bring disease and destruction on the soul.

(115) According to the other meaning, as in the disputes of dialecticians, the word "undemonstrated" is used in a double sense, either of a proposition which is hard to demonstrate by reason of its difficulty, or of one which is intrinsically so plain as to require no demonstration, and the truth of which is established not by the testimony of any one else, but by its own internal evidence. So also fruit may be understood as not being purified, either when it is so impure as to be dif-

---

21 Numbers 5:15.
22 Leviticus 19:23.
23 Genesis 30:37.

24 Leviticus 13:12.
25 Leviticus 19:23.

ficulty to purify, or when it requires no purification, but is bright, and clear, and pure of itself.

(116) Such now is the fruit of education; being for three years, that is to say for all time, divided as it is into three portions, most completely pure and brilliant, being overshadowed by no injurious thing, and having no need whatever of any washings or purifications, or any thing else whatever which tends to cleansing.

XXVIII. (117) "But in the fourth year," says the scripture, "all the fruit of the tree shall be sacred, being praised by the Lord."[26] The prophetic books appear often to dignify the number four in many places of the exposition of the law, and most especially in the account of the creation of the universe; (118) for the light which is perceptible by the outward senses, and held in honour, being that which throws the most brilliant light both upon itself and upon other things, and upon its own parents the sun and the moon, and upon the most sacred company of the stars, which by their rising and setting fix the boundaries of night and day, and moreover, of months and years, and which have shown the nature of number, to which, also, the greatest good of the soul is attributed, Moses says was created on the fourth day. (119) And now he honours this day in a remarkable degree, assigning the fruit of the trees to God, in accordance with no other time than with the fourth year after they are planted; (120) for this has a principle in it very consistent with nature and with good morals.

At all events it so happens that the roots of the universe, the elements of which the world is composed, are four—earth, water, air, and fire. Also, that the seasons of the year are equal in number, namely, winter and summer, and those others which are between these two, spring and autumn. (121) And as this is the most ancient of all square numbers, it is found to exist in right angles, as the figure of a square in geometry shows. And right angles are manifest examples of correctness of reason. And right reason is an everlasting fountain of virtues. (122) It follows, therefore, of necessity that the sides of a square must be all equal to one another. And equality is the parent of justice, which is the mistress and ruler of all the virtues, so that it is proved that this number four is the symbol of equality, and justice, and of all virtue, beyond any other number. (123) And the number four is likewise called "all," because it comprehends in its power the numbers up to ten, and the number ten itself.

XXIX. That it comprehends all the numbers up to itself is manifest to every one; but that it also comprehends the numbers which come after it, is very easily seen by a calculation of numbers, (124) when we have put them together, one, two,

three, four, we shall find what we were doubting about; for of one and four, the number five will be found to be composed, and of two and four six are made up; the number seven, again, consists of three and four; again, according to a triple combination of one, and three, and four, the number eight is composed; also of two, and three, and four, the number nine; and the number ten is made of all the numbers together, for one, and two, and three, and four make ten. (125) On this account also, Moses said that in the fourth year all the fruit of the tree shall be holy; for this number has an even, and an entire, and a full, and (as one may almost say) every possible reason in it, because the number ten, of which four is the parent, is the first starting place of all the numbers when put together after the unit; and the number four and the number ten are both also called "all," but the number ten is so called by reason of its operation, this number four with reference to its potentiality.

XXX. (126) And Moses very appropriately says that the fruit of education is not only holy but also praised; for every one of the virtues is a holy thing, but most especially is gratitude holy; but it is impossible to show gratitude to God in a genuine manner, by those means which people in general think the only ones, namely offerings and sacrifices; for the whole world could not be a temple worthy to be raised to his honour, except by means of praises and hymns, and those too must be such as are sung, not by loud voices, but by the invisible and pure mind, which shall raise the shout and song to him. (127) At all events there is an old saying often quoted, originally invented by wise men, but, as is often the case, handed down in succession to future ages, and one which has not escaped our ears, which are always greedy of instruction, and it is to this effect, "When," say they, "the Creator had finished the whole world, he asked of one of his ministers, whether he felt that any thing that was wanting which had not been created of all the things that are in the earth, or in the water, or of all that have received the sublime nature of the air, or the loftiest nature of all the universe, namely, that of the heaven; (128) and he replied, that every thing every where was perfect and complete; but that he wished for one thing only, namely for reason, which should be able duly to praise it all, and which should not so much praise as give an accurate account of the exceeding excellence existing throughout, even in these things which appeared the most unimportant and the most obscure; for he said that an exact account of the works of God was their most complete and adequate panegyric, since they required no addition of external things to set them forth, but were of such a character that the bare plain truth was their most perfect encomium." (129) And when the Father had heard what he said he praised it all, and at no distant time produced a race, which

---

[26]Leviticus 19:25.

should be capable of receiving all learning, and of composing hymns of praise, producing them from one of the faculties existing around him, the virgin memory, whose name men in general distort and call her Mnemosyne.

XXXI. (130) This is then the purport of that legend of the ancients, and we in accordance with that story say, that it is the most appropriate work of God to confer benefits, and of created beings to show gratitude, since they are unable to give any requital of those benefits beyond gratitude; for whatever he might be inclined to give as a requital for the other things which he has received, will be found to be the private property of him who is the Creator of all things, and not of the nature which offers it. (131) Having learnt therefore that there is only one employment possible for us of all the things that seem to contribute to the honour of God, namely the display of gratitude, let us at all times and in all places study this, with our voice, and with useful writings, and let us never desist composing encomiastic orations and poems, in order that both the Creator and the world may be honoured by every description of utterance which can be exhibited in either speaking or singing; the one being, as some has said, the best of all causes, and the other the most perfect of all created things.

XXXII. (132) Since therefore all the fruit of the soul is consecrated in the fourth year and the fourth number; in the fifth year we ourselves shall be allowed the use and enjoyment of it for ourselves; for the scripture says, "In the fifth year ye shall eat the fruit thereof;" since it has been established by a perpetual law of nature, that account shall be taken of the creation after the Creator in every thing; so that even if we are thought worthy of the second place, it must be considered a marvellous thing; (133) and on this account it assigns to us the fruit of the fifth year, because the number five is the number appropriate to the outward sense; and if one must tell the truth, that which nourishes our minds is the outward sense, which by means of our eyes sets before us the distinctive qualities of colours and forms, and by means of our ears presents us with all the various peculiarities of sounds, and with smells by means of the nose, and with tastes through the medium of the mouth, and which enables us to judge of the yielding softness and resisting hardness, or of softness and roughness, or again of heat and cold, by means of the faculty which is dispersed over the whole body, which we usually denominate touch.

XXXIII. (134) But the most correct example of what has been said, is afforded by the sons of Leah, that is of virtue, not all her sons, but the fourth and fifth; for with respect to the fourth, Moses says that, then she ceased to bring forth,[27]

and his name was called Judah, which, being interpreted, is "confession to the Lord," and the fifth she called Issachar, and the name being interpreted, means "reward;" and after she had brought forth in this manner, the soul immediately spoke and related what it had suffered; for says Moses, "She called his name Issachar, which means reward."[28] (135) Therefore Judas, the mind which blesses God, and which is without ceasing, devoted to pouring forth hymns of praise and gratitude to him, is himself in truth "the holy and praiseworthy fruit,"[29] being produced not by the trees of the earth but by a rational and virtuous nature. In reference to which, the nature which brought him forth is said to have desisted from bringing forth, since she knew not which way to turn, when she had come to the limit of perfection; for of all successful actions which are brought forth, the best and most perfect production is a hymn to the Father of the universe; (136) and the fifth son is in no respect different from the enjoyment of the trees planted in the fifth year; for the tiller of the earth after a fashion takes his reward from the trees in the fifth year, and he takes the offspring of the soul, Issachar, who was called the "reward," and very naturally, being brought forth after the grateful Judah; for to a grateful person gratitude is a most sufficient reward. (137) Therefore, the fruits of the trees are called the produce of the owners of the trees; but the fruit of instruction and wisdom is no longer the produce of man, but as Moses says, "of the universal Governor alone;" for after he has spoken of his produce, he adds, "I am the Lord your God," asserting most distinctly that there is one God, whose fruit is the produce of the soul.

(138) And with this assertion, this oracle delivered by one of the prophets is consistent, "Fruit from me has been found by you. What wise man will understand this? Will any intelligent person comprehend it?"[30] For it does not belong to every one, but only to the wise man, to understand whose the fruit of the mind is.

XXXIV. (139) Therefore, concerning that most ancient and sacred husbandry, which the Cause of all things uses with reference to the world, that most productive of trees, and concerning that other kind in imitation of it which the virtuous man studies, and concerning the ordinary quaternion of prizes, and the laws and precepts which all tend to the same point, we have now spoken to the best of our power.

(140) Let us now consider the vine-planting of the just Noah which is a species of husbandry.

---

[27] Genesis 29:35.
[28] Genesis 30:18.
[29] Leviticus 19:24.
[30] Hosea 14:9.

For it is said that "Noah began to be a husbandman of the earth, and he planted a vineyard, and drank of the wine, and got drunk."[31] Therefore, the wise man here cultivates with skill and science the tree of drunkenness, though fools enter upon its management in an unartistic and negligent manner, (141) so that it is necessary for us now to speak in a fitting manner about drunkenness; for we shall presently know the power also of that tree which gives rise to it. Afterwards, we will examine with accuracy what has been said by the lawgiver concerning drunkenness, but at present we will examine what determination others have come to on this subject.

XXXV. (142) Now, among many philosophers, this question has been investigated with no slight degree of pains, and the question is proposed in this manner, whether the wise man will get drunk? Therefore, to get drunk is a matter of a twofold nature, one part of it being equivalent to being overcome with wine; the other, to behaving foolishly in one's cups. (143) But of those who have dealt with this proposition, some have said that the wise man never takes too much unmixed wine, and never behaves foolishly; for that the one is an error, and that the other is an efficient cause of error, and that both the one and the other is inconsistent with good conduct. (144) Others again have asserted, that to be overcome with wine is appropriate even to a virtuous man, but that to behave foolishly is inconsistent with his character. For that the wisdom which is in him is sufficient to resist those things which attempt to do him injury, and to destroy the innovations which they seek to produce in the soul, and that wisdom is endued with a power capable of extinguishing the passions, whether they be fanned by the impetuous gale of furious love, or kindled by abundant and heating wine, and that owing to this power it will always be superior to them.

Since also of those who dive beneath a deep river or under the sea, some are destroyed from being ignorant of the art of swimming, but others who are possessed of this knowledge are very speedily saved; and, indeed, a great quantity of wine, inundating the soul like a torrent, sometimes weighs it down and precipitates it to the lowest depth of ignorance, but at other times is unable to part it, because it is supported and borne aloft by saving instruction.

(145) Those again who have not sufficiently observed the greatness of this excess with respect to passion in the wise man, have pressed him down, when he was applying himself to the study of sublime things, from heaven to earth, as those men do who are seeking to catch birds, in order to involve him in disasters similar to their own; but

others, seeing the great height of his virtue, have said that a wise man, if he indulges in wine beyond the bounds of moderation, will by all means cease to be master of himself, and will go astray, and will not only let his hands droop out of weakness, like those athletes do who are defeated, but will also droop his neck and his head, and stumble, and fall down, coming to the ground with his whole body.

XXXVI. (146) Having then learnt this beforehand, the wise man will never of his own accord think fit to enter upon a contest of hard drinking, unless there were great things at stake, such as the safety of his country, or the honour of his parents, or the preservation of his children, or of his nearest relations, or in short, the success and prosperity of some important public or private interest. (147) For he would not take a deadly poison unless the occasion compelled him very strongly to depart from life, as it might urge him to depart from his country. And at all events it is plain, that unmixed wine is a poison, which is the cause, if not of death, at least of madness, and why may we not pronounce madness to be death, since by it the most important thing in us dies, namely, the mind? But it appears to me that a man would without the slightest hesitation choose (if a choice was permitted him), that death which separates and disunites the soul and the body as a lesser evil in preference to that greater one—the alienation of the mind.

(148) On this account, forsooth, men of old time called skill in the art of making wine madness *(mainomenē)*, and called the Bacchae who were carried away under the influence of wine, mad women *(Mainades)*, since wine is the cause of madness and folly to those who indulge in it insatiably.

XXXVII. (149) Such then are, as it were, the prefaces of this discussion or investigation. Let us now go on to the other parts of this question which is divided into two heads as is natural; the one view affirming that the wise man will occasionally be drunk, and the other, on the contrary, insisting that he will not get drunk. (150) Now it is well to ruminate the arguments which are adduced in support of the former view, having first of all take our beginning from this point, that of things some are homonymous, and others are only synonymous. And it is admitted that the being homonymous and the being synonymous are two opposite things, because homonymy is predicated of many subjects which have one common name; and synonymy is the application of many different names to one subject. (151) For instance, the name of dog is beyond all question a homonymy, inasmuch as it comprehends many dissimilar things which are signified by that appellation. For there is a terrestrial barking animal called a dog; there is also a marine monster with the same name: there is also the star

---

[31] Genesis 9:20.

in heaven, which the poets calls the autumnal star, because it rises at the beginning of autumn, for the sake of ripening the fruits and bringing them to perfection. Moreover, there were the philosophers who came from the cynic school. Aristippus and Diogenes; and others too who chose to practise the same mode of life, an incalculable number of men.

(152) Again there are other appellations which differ from one another, but still signify but one thing, as a shaft, a bolt, and arrow; for all these terms are applied to the weapon which is sent from the string of the bow against the mark; and again there are the words, oar, scull, and blade, to express the instrument used for propelling a vessel, of equal power with sails; for whenever a ship, by reason of a calm or of unfavourable winds cannot use its sails, then, those, whose business it is, sitting down as rowers, and stretching out their oars on each side like wings, compel to it proceed onwards as if borne on wings; and so the vessel being borne on the top of the waves, and rather running over them than cutting through them, hastens along with a speedy voyage, and speedily anchors in a safe harbour. (153) And again, a staff, and a stick, and a cane, are all different appellations of one subject with which we can strike, or support one's self steadily, and on which one can lean, and do many other things besides. And we have enumerated these instances not for the purpose of making a long story, but in order that the matter under investigation may be more clearly understood.

XXXVIII. (154) The ancients called unmixed wine *oinos*, and also *methy*. At all events, this latter name is used in very many passages of poetry, so that if those names are accounted synonymous which are applied to one subject, then *oinos* and *methysma*, and other words derived from them will differ in nothing but sound, and the being overcome with wine (*oinousthai*), and the being drunk (*methyein*), are one and the same thing. (155) And both these words intimate a taking of too much wine, which nevertheless there may be many reasons for a good man not turning away from; and if he be overcome with wine he will also be drunk, being nevertheless not made in any respect the worse by his drunkenness, but remaining the same as if he had simply been well filled with wine.

(156) We have now detailed one of the opinions concerning a wise man getting drunk: and the second is as follows:—

The men of the present day, with the exception of a small portion of them, do not choose in any way to resemble the men of old times; but both in mind and action they show that they are in no respect agreed with them, but that they differ from them widely. (157) For they have made such a revolution as to bring reasons which were sound and healthy into incurable decay and destruction. And

in the place of a vigorous and athletic habit, they have brought almost every thing into a state of disease; and in the place of a full, and strong, and sinewy body, they have rendered it weak, inducing an unnatural, and swollen, and sickly habit, filling it up with empty wind alone, which soon bursts by reason of the want of any power to keep it together, when it is extended in the greatest degree. (158) And the actions of created beings, which are most worthy of attention, and which were, as one may say, masculine actions, those also they have made disgraceful feminine instead, and discreditable instead of honourable, so that there are very few persons found, either in deed or in words, inclined to an imitation of the ancient manners.

(159) Therefore, the poets and historians who lived in their time, and all other men who devoted themselves to literary studies, did not confine themselves to soothing and tickling the ears with rhythmical sounds, but, if there was anything broken, so to say, and relaxed in the mind, they roused it up, and whatever there was in it suited to their purpose they improved by initiation into natural philosophy and virtue. But the cooks and confectioners of our time, and those persons who are only artists of superfluous luxury, in the arts of dyeing and making perfumes, are always building up the outward senses with some new colour, or shape, or scent, or flavour, so as utterly to destroy the most important part of us, the mind.

XXXIX. (160) And why do I mention these things? In order to show that the men of the present day do not use wine now as the ancients did. For now they drink eagerly without once taking breath, till the body and soul are both wholly relaxed, and they keep on bidding their cup-bearers to bring more wine, and are angry with them if they delay while they are cooling what is called by them the hot drink; and in a vile imitation of the gymnastic contests, they institute a contest among their fellow revellers as to who can drink most wine, in which they do many glorious things to one another, biting one another's ears and noses, and the tips of the fingers of their hands, and any other parts of the body they can get at. (161) Now, these are the contests of revelry while in youth and vigour, and, as one may say, in its prime; but the others are the deeds of that ancient and more old-fashioned sort. For the men of old time began every good action with perfect sacrifices, thinking that in that way the result would be most favourable to them; and even if the occasion required especial promptitude in action, still they did not begin till they had offered prayers and sacrifices. But in all cases waited, thinking that haste was not in every case better than slowness. For speed, which is not accompanied with forethought, is injurious, but slowness, when founded on good hope, is advantageous.

(162) Knowing, therefore, that the use and

enjoyment of wine require much care, they did not drink unmixed wine either in great quantities or at all times, but only in moderation and on fitting occasions. For first, of all, they offered up prayers and instituted sacrifices, and then, having propitiated the deity, and having purified their bodies and souls, the former with baths, and the latter with the waters of laws and of right instruction, they then turned their cheerful and rejoicing countenances to more luxurious food, very often not returning home but, walking about in the temples in which they sacrificed, in order that, by keeping in mind their sacrifices, and having a due respect for the place, they might enjoy what should be really a most sacred feast, doing no wrong either in word or deed. (163) And this, indeed, is what they say the word *methyein*, to be drunk, derives its name from; because, *meta to thyein* (after sacrificing) it was the custom of the men of old to drink great quantities of wine.

And to whom could the manner of using unmixed wine described above be more appropriate than to wise men to whom the work to be done before drinking, namely, sacrificing, is so appropriate? (164) For one may almost say that no bad man can really perform sacrifices, not even if he were to bring the altar ten thousand oxen every day without intermission; for his most important and indispensable offering, namely his mind, is polluted. And it is impious for polluted things to come near to the altar. (165) This, now, is the second point of view in which this question may be regarded, by which we have shown that it is not inconsistent with the character of the wise man to get drunk.

XL. There is a third way of looking at this subject, which depends chiefly on the exceeding plausibility of an argument derived from etymology. For some persons think that drunkenness *(methē)* derives its name not merely from the fact of its being admitted after sacrifice, but also because it is the cause of relaxation *(methesis)* to the soul. (166) But the reason of foolish men is relaxed so as to get strength for many sins; while that of those inclined to be sensible is relaxed, so as to enjoy freedom from care, and cheerfulness, and lightness of heart. For the wise man, when he is intoxicated, becomes more good-humoured than when he is sober; so that in this respect we should not be at all wrong in saying that he may get drunk. (167) And besides all this, we must likewise add, that we are not speaking of a stern-looking and sordid kind of wisdom, contracted by profound thought and ill-humour; but, on the other hand, of that wisdom which wears on tranquil and cheerful appearance, being full of joy and happiness, by which men have often been led on to sport and divert themselves in no inelegant manner, indulging in amusements suitable to their dignified and earnest character, just as in a well-tuned lyre one

may have a combination uniting, by means of opposite sounds, in one melodious harmony.

(168) At all events, according to the most holy Moses, the end of all wisdom is amusement and mirth, not such mirth as is pursued by foolish people, uncombined with any prudence, but such as is admitted even by those who are already grey, not only through old age alone, but also through deep thinking. Do you not see that he speaks of the man who has drunk deeply of that wisdom which is to be derived from a man's own hearing and learning, and study; not as one who partakes of mirth, but who is actually mirth in itself? (169) This is Isaac, for the name Isaac being interpreted means "laughter," with whose character it is very consistent that he should have been sporting with "perseverance," which the Hebrews call Rebekkah.

XLI. But it is not lawful for a private individual to behold the divine instruction of the soul, but the king may behold it, as one with whom wisdom has dwelt for a very long time, if we may not rather say that it dwells with him all his life. His name is Abimelech, who, looking out through the window with the well-opened and radiant eye of the mind, saw Isaac sporting with Rebekkah his wife. (170) For what employment is more suitable for a wise man than to be sporting, and rejoicing, and diverting himself with perseverance in good things? From which it is plain that he will become intoxicated, since intoxication contributes to good morals, and also produces relaxation and advantage; (171) for unmixed wine seems to increase and render more intense all the natural qualities, whether they be good or the contrary, as many other things do too. For money is to a good man a cause of good things, and to a bad man, as some one has said, it is a cause of bad things. And again, high rank makes the wickedness of a fool more conspicuous, but it renders the virtue of the just man more glorious.

So also unmixed wine, being poured forth in abundance, makes the man who is the slave of his passions, still more subservient to them, but it renders him who has them under control more manageable and amiable. (172) Who, indeed, is there who does not know that of two opposite things, when one kind is suitable to most people, the other kind must of necessity be suited to some? As, for instance, white and black are two opposite colours: if white is suitable both to good and to bad things, then black must also be necessarily equally suitable to both, and not to one of the two alone. And, again, to be sober and to be drunk are two opposite things; accordingly, both bad men and good, as the ancient proverb says, partake of sobriety; therefore, also, drunkenness is suitable to both classes. Therefore the virtuous man will get drunk without losing any of his virtue by it.

XLII. (173) But if, like persons before a court

of justice, one must bring forward not only such proofs as are in accordance with the rules of art, but those too which have no connection with art, one of which is proof by testimony, we will then produce many sons of physicians and philosophers of high repute to give evidence, not by words alone, but also by writings. (174) For they have left behind ten thousand commentaries entitled treatises on drunkenness; in which they consider nothing beyond the bare use of wine, without pursuing any investigation with respect to those who are accustomed to behave foolishly in their cups, and in fact omitting every thing which has reference to conduct under the influence of wine; so that it is very plainly confessed in their writings that drunkenness is the same as drinking wine freely. And to drink a superabundant quantity of wine on proper occasions is not unsuitable to a wise man; therefore we shall not be wrong if we say that a wise man may get drunk.

(175) But since no one is ever inscribed on the rolls as a conqueror if he has contended by himself alone, for if he does this he appears only to be fighting with a shadow, and very naturally too; it follows that we must also produce the arguments of those who contend for the opposite side of the question, that by this means a most just judgment may be formed, and that the other side of the question may not be decided against through default. (176) And the first and the most powerful argument is this: if no one in his senses would entrust a secret which he wished to be kept to a drunken man, then a good and wise man will not get drunk. But before we collect all the other arguments in their order, it may be better to reply to each objection separately, in order that we may not appear to be too prolix, and consequently to be troublesome.

(177) Some one then will say in opposition that, according to the argument that has been advanced, the wise man must never have a bilious attack, and never go to sleep, and above all must never die. But he to whom some of these things happens is either an inanimate being or a divine one; but beyond all question he is not a man at all. Imitating this perversion of the arguments, one may apply it equally to a bilious man, or to a sleeping man, or to a dying man; for no one in his senses would tell a secret to a man in any of these conditions, but it would be reasonable for him to tell it to a wise man, for the wise man is never bilious, never goes to sleep, and never dies.

ON DRUNKENNESS
(De Ebrietate)

I. (1) What has been said by other philosophers about drunkenness we have to the best of our ability recorded in the treatise before this present one. But now let us consider what is the opinion of the lawgiver, who was in all respects great and wise, on this subject; (2) for in many places of his history of the giving of the law he mentions wine, and the plant which produces wine, namely the vine; and he commands some persons to drink it, but some he does not permit to do so; and at time he gives contrary directions to the same people, ordering them sometimes to drink and some times to abstain. These therefore are the persons who have taken the great vow, to whom it is expressly forbidden to drink unmixed wine, being the priests who are engaged in offering sacrifices. But those who drink wine are numerous beyond all calculation, and among them are all those who are especially praised by the lawgiver for their virtue. (3) But before we begin to talk of these subjects we will examine with accuracy some points that concern this argument, and, as I at least imagine they are these.

II. (4) Moses looks upon an unmixed wine as a symbol not of one thing only but of many, namely of trifling, and playing the fool, and of all kinds of insensibility and of insatiable greediness, and of a covetousness which is hard to be pleased, and of a cheerfulness which comprehends many other objects, and of a nakedness which is apparent in all the things now mentioned, such as that which he says Noah, when drunk, displayed himself in. Wine, then, is said to produce all these effects. (5) But great numbers of persons who, because they never touch unmixed wine, look upon themselves as sober, are involved in the same accusation. And one may see some of them acting in a foolish and senseless manner, and others possessed by complete insensibility; and others again who are never satisfied, but are always thirsting for what cannot be obtained, because of their want of knowledge; others, on the other hand rejoicing and exulting; and others in good truth naked. (6) The cause now of behaving foolishly is a mischievous ignorance; I mean by this expression, not an ignorance of such things as are matters of instruction but an alienation from, and dislike of knowledge.

The cause again of insensibility is a treacherous and mutilated ignorance. The cause of insatiability is a most grievous appetite for the indulgence of the passions of the soul. The cause of cheerfulness is at once the acquisition and the employment of virtue. Of nakedness there are many causes—an ignorance of such things as are opposite to one another; complete innocence and simplicity of manners; truth, which strips off all the coverings of such things as are concealed, on the one side revealing virtue to our eyes, and on the other side, in its turn, uncovering vice; (7) for no one can possibly put off both these things at one time, nor can he either strip them both off together. But when any one discards the one, he must of necessity take up and clothe himself with the other. (8) For as the old story tells us, God, when he had combined pleasure and pain, two things naturally at variance, under one head, gave to us an outward sense capable of appreciating them both, not at the same moment, but at different times, fixing the period of the return of one to be simultaneous with the moment of the flight of the other. Thus from one root of the dominant principle, the two shoots of virtue and vice sprang up, neither blossoming nor bearing fruit at the same time; (9) for when the one loses its leaves and fades away, then the other begins to shoot, and blossom, and look green, so that one might fancy that the one withered through dissatisfaction at the blooming appearance of the other.

It is with reference to this that Moses represents in a most natural manner the departure of Jacob to be contemporaneous with the arrival of Esau; "For it came to pass," says he, "that as Jacob went out his brother Esau came in."[1] (10) As long, indeed, as prudence dwells in and makes his abode in the soul, so long every companion of folly is discarded and banished to a distance; but when prudence departs then folly rejoices and enters, since its enemy and adversary, for whose sake it was driven away and banished, is no longer inhabiting the same place as before.

III. (11) We have now then said enough by way of preface to this treatise. We will proceed to adduce the proofs of all that we have said, beginning first of all to establish the first point.

We said, then, that ignorance was the cause of man's behaving foolishly and misconducting himself, just as a great quantity of unmixed wine is to great numbers of foolish persons; (12) for ignorance is the primary evil of all the errors of the soul, if we must tell the truth, from which, as from

---

[1] Genesis 27:30.

a spring, all the actions of life do flow, never producing to any one, one single stream of wholesome or drinkable water, but only brackish water, the cause of disease and destruction to all who use it. (13) Thus, at all events, the lawgiver is very indignant with all uninstructed and unmanageable persons, more than he is with any other description of people whatever. And a proof of this is this: who are they who are united in alliance not so much by study as by nature, whether among men or among the other kinds of animals? No one; not even a madman would say that any beings were so closely united as parents and children; for even by the mere untaught instinct of nature the parent always cares for his offspring, and in every case endeavours to provide for its safety and durability.

IV. (14) Those, then, who are the natural protectors of others, Moses represents as having crossed over to the ranks of enemies, making those accusers who would naturally have been advocates, I mean the father and mother, in order that the children may be destroyed by those by whom above all others it was natural they should be saved; "For if," says he, "any man's son be disobedient, or contentious, not obeying the voice of his father and of his mother, and if they reprove him and he does not listen to them, then his father and his mother shall take him, and shall bring him before the elders of the city, and shall bring him to the gate of that place, and shall say to the men of their city, This our son is disobedient and contentious, and does not obey our voice, but spends his time in revelling and drunkenness. And the men of that city shall stone him, and you shall destroy that wicked one from among you."[2] (15) Therefore, here the accusations are four in number—disobedience, and contentiousness, and love of revelling, and drunkenness; and the last of these is the greatest, deriving its growth from the first, namely, from disobedience; for when the soul begins to be restive it advances onward through contention and quarrelsomeness, and arrives at last at the furthest boundary, drunkenness, the cause of alienation of mind and folly. But it is requisite to see the force of each of all these accusations, beginning with the first in order.

V. (16) It is then confessed by all most undeniably, that it is both honourable and advantageous to yield and to become obedient to virtue, so that on the other hand to be disobedient to it must be disgraceful and in no moderate degree disadvantageous. And to be contentious and obstinate is a quality which comprehends every extravagance of evil; for the man who is disobedient is less wicked than he who is contentious, since the one only disregards what he is commanded to do, but the other also exerts himself to do the

contrary. (17) Come, now, let us investigate the true nature of these things.

Since the law commands, for instance, that men should honour their parents, he who does not honour them is disobedient; but he who dishonours them is contentious. And again, since it is a righteous action to preserve one's country, we must call the man who admits of hesitation in the pursuit of the object disobedient, but the man who is prepared moreover to betray it we must pronounce perverse and contentious. (18) Again, he who, when requested to requite a favour, contradicts the man who says that he ought to consider himself a debtor, is disobedient; but he who, in addition to making no return, is so carried away by contentiousness that he endeavours to do the person what harm he can, commits unredeemable wickedness. And further, he who never approaches, nor practises sacrifices, or any of the other observances required by piety, disobeys the commandments which the law usually ordains in such matters; but he who resists and turns aside to the opposite disposition, impiety, is a wicked man and a minister of impiety.

VI. (19) Such a man as this was he who said, "Who is there whom I am to obey?" and again, "I do not know the Lord."[3] For by his first expression he states that there is no such thing as a Deity; and by the second question he means, that even if there is such a being, still he will not recognize him, which arises from a deficiency in his providence; for if he were possessed of providence he would be recognized.

(20) Now to bring contributions and supplies in aid of an entertainment with a view to a participation in that best of all possessions, prudence, is praiseworthy and advantageous. But to do so with a view to the worst of all objects, folly, is disadvantageous and blameable; (21) therefore, the contributions for the most excellent object are the desire of virtue, the imitation of good men, continued care, laborious practice, incessant and unwearied labours; the contributions for the opposite object are relaxation, indifference, luxury, effeminacy, and a complete desertion of what is right. (22) And we may see those who every day descend into the arena to contend in drinking much wine, and practising this quality every day, and striving to gain the victory in greediness and voracity, bringing their contributions as though they had some desirable object in view, and injuring themselves in every thing, in their property, and their bodies, and their souls; for by contributing their property they diminish their substance; and they break down and enervate the powers of their bodies by their luxurious way of life, and as for their souls, inundating them with immoderate food like a swol-

---

[2]Deuteronomy 21:18.

[3]Exodus 5:2.

len torrent, they compel that to sink down to the lowest depth.

(23) For the same manner all those, who bring contributions for the destruction of learning, injure the most important thing in them, namely, their mind, cutting off every thing that might save it—prudence, and temperance, and courage, and justice; on which account he seems to me himself to use a compound word, *symbolokopōn*, for the more manifest manifestation of his meaning, because they who bring forward attempts at virtue as their offering and contribution, wound and lacerate, and cut to pieces, obedient and learning-loving souls to the extent of their utter destruction.

VII. (24) Therefore the wise Abraham is said to have returned again from the slaughter of Chedorlaomer, and of the kings who were with him.[4] And on the other hand, Amalek is said to have cut to pieces the rear of the company of the mediator of virtue,[5] in strict accordance with the truth of nature; for what is contrary to one is also hostile to the other, and such things are always meditating the destruction of one another. (25) But one may especially blame a man who contributes offerings on this account, because such an one has not only determined to do wrong, but also to cooperate with others in doing wrong, thinking fit in some things to be the leader himself, and in others to follow the leadership of others; so that, erring both by nature and through what he has learnt, he leaves himself no good hope of safety, and this, too, though the law has expressly said that one must "not follow a multitude to do evil;"[6] (26) for, in truth, evil is a very manifold and very fertile thing in the souls of men, but good is but a contracted and rare thing. Again it is a most useful recommendation, not to join with many persons to do evil, but to unite with a few whose chief practice is to do justly.

VIII. (27) The fourth and greatest of the accusations, is that of drunkenness, not slight but excessive drunkenness. For devotion to crime is equivalent to devotion to swelling up, and kindling, and inflaming the poison which is the great cause of folly, namely ignorance, a thing which can never be extinguished, but which is at all times and in every case raising a conflagration and fury in the soul. (28) Very naturally, therefore, justice will follow which purifies every evil disposition of the mind, for it is said, "Thou shalt utterly get rid of the wicked man," not out of the city, or out of the country, or out of the nation, but "out of yourselves."[7] For there are many faulty and blameable thoughts lurking in us, and taking up their abode

in the recesses of our hearts, which, since they are incurable, it is necessary to eradicate and destroy.

(29) Therefore it is just that this disobedient and contentious man, who is always advancing plausible reasons as a sort of offering and contribution on his part towards the destruction of what is good, and who is inflamed with strong wine, and raging in a drunken manner against virtue, and being absurdly excited to his own injury by wine, should have his allies for his accusers, his own father and mother, since he ought to receive every possible reproof and chastisement from those who can be saved; (30) but of the father and mother the appellations are common, but their powers are different. At all events we shall speak with justice, if we say that the Creator of the universe is also the father of his creation; and that the mother was the knowledge of the Creator with whom God uniting, not as a man unites, became the father of creation. And this knowledge having received the seed of God, when the day of her travail arrived, brought forth her only and well-beloved son, perceptible by the external senses, namely this world. (31) Accordingly wisdom is represented by some one of the beings of the divine company as speaking of herself in this manner: "God created me as the first of his works, and before the beginning of time did he establish me." For it was necessary that all the things which came under the head of the creation must be younger than the mother and nurse of the whole universe.

IX. (32) Who then is able to encounter the accusation of these parents? No one can withstand even their moderate threats, or their very slightest reproach; for neither is any one able to contain the immeasurable multitude of their gifts, perhaps even the whole world is not; but like a shallow channel, when the great fountain of the bounties of God flows into it, it will be very speedily filled so as to overtop its bounds and overflow; but if we are unable to receive his benefits, how shall we endure his chastising powers when they come upon us?

(33) But these parents of the universe must be taken out of the present discussion; and for the present let us consider their pupils and acquaintances who have had assigned to them the care and superintendence of such souls as are not unwilling to learn and illiterate. Therefore we say that the father is masculine and perfect right reason, and that the mother is that middle and encyclical course of study, and instruction, and learning, which it is honourable and advantageous to obey as a child obeys his parents. (34) The recommendation then of the father, that is of right reason, is to follow and obey reason, pursuing naked and undisguised truth; and the injunction of learning, the mother that is, is to obey the just customs, which ancient men who embraced opinion,

---

[4]Genesis 14:17.
[5]Deuteronomy 25:18.
[6]Exodus 23:2.
[7]Deuteronomy 21:21.

as if it were truth, have established in cities, and nations, and countries.

(35) Now these parents have four classes of children. First of all comes that class which is obedient to them both, the second is that which attends to neither, being the opposite of the former one. Of the others, each is half perfect. For the one is exceedingly attached to its father, and attends to him, but disregards its mother and her injunctions. The other again appears to be attached to its mother, and obeys her in everything, but pays but little attention to its father. The first class, therefore, will carry off the prize of victory as superior to all the others; the second, which is the contrary of it, will meet with defeat and destruction at the same time; and as to each of the others they will claim, one the second prize, and the other the third. The one which is obedient to its father being the second in honour, and the one which obeys its mother being the third.

X. (36) Now of the soul attached to its mother, yielding to the opinions of the many and constantly changing its appearance in accordance with the various forms arising from the manifold and different ways of life, after the manner of the Egyptian Proteus, who was able to assume the likeness of anything in the whole world, and to conceal his real form so as to render it entirely invisible, the most visible image is Jothor, a compound of pride, who evidently represents a city and constitution of men from all quarters, and of all nations, carried away by vain opinions. (37) For after the wise Moses had invited the whole people of the soul to observe piety and to pay the honour due to God, and had taught them the commandments and the most sacred laws, (for he says, "When there is a controversy among them and they come to me, I will decide between them all, and I will bring together to them the commandments of God and his law.") [8] then Jothor, wise in his own conceit, uninitiated in the divine blessings, but having principally lived among human and corruptible things, harangues the people, and proposes laws contrary to those of nature, having regard only to opinion, while those other laws are all referrible to the standard of reality and truth.

(38) And indeed the prophet, pitying this man and commiserating his exceeding error, thinks it fitting to endeavour to teach him better things, and to persuade him to change his ways, and to forsake vain opinions and steadily to follow the truth. (39) For says he, "We after having cut up and eradicated the vain pride of the mind, will leave our abodes and depart to the place of knowledge, which we shall gain possession of by the divine oracles and their agreement of the result with them. Come now with us, and we will do thee good." [9] For so doing you will get rid of that most pernicious thing, false opinion, and you will acquire that most advantageous thing, truth. (40) But he, being as it were subdued by enchantment in this way, will neglect what is said, and will by no means follow any kind of knowledge whatever, but will retire and will run off to his own individual and empty pride. For it is said in the scripture that he replied to him, "I will not go, except to my own country and to my own race;" that is to say, to his kindred infidelity imbued with false opinions, since he had not learnt that true faith which is dear to men.

XI. (41) For, when desiring to make a display of his piety, he says, "Now I know that God is a great Lord in comparison of all gods," [10] he accuses himself of impiety in the eyes of all men who are competent to form a judgment; for they will say to him, (42) "Dost thou now know, O impious man, the power of the Ruler of the universe? but before this thou didst not know it. For was there anything which thou hast ever fallen in with of more antiquity or power than God? And are not the virtues of their parents known to the children before anything else in the world? And was not the Ruler of the universe the creator and the father of it? So that if you now say that you know it, you do not know it now, because you did not know it from the beginning of the creation." (43) And you are not the less convicted of false pretences, when you profess to compare things that cannot be compared, and say that you now recognise the greatness and pre-eminence of God in comparison of all other gods.

For if thou hadst in real truth known the living God, you would never have supposed that there was any other god endued with independent authority; (44) for as the sun, when he has arisen, hides the stars, pouring forth his own light altogether over our sight, so also when the beams of the light-giving God, unmingled as they are, and entirely pure, and visible at the greatest distance, shone upon the eye of the soul, being comprehensible only by the intellect, then the eye of the soul can see nothing else; for the knowledge of the living God having beamed upon it, out-dazzles everything else, so that even those things which are most brilliant by their own intrinsic light appear to be dark in comparison.

(45) Therefore he would never have ventured to compare the true and faithful God to those falsely named gods, if he had really known him; but ignorance of the one God has caused him to entertain a belief of many as gods, who have in reality no existence at all.

XII. (46) Now this same opinion is entertained

---

[8]Exodus 18:16.

[9]Numbers 10:29.
[10]Exodus 18:11.

by every one who, having thoroughly comprehended the affairs of the soul, looks with astonishment on the affairs of the body and on the things external to the body, diversified as they are with different colours and forms, in order to deceive the outward sense, which is easily worked upon. (47) Such a man as this the lawgiver calls labour, who, not perceiving the true laws of nature, falsely assents to those which are in force among men, saying, "It is not the custom in our country to give the younger daughter in marriage before the elder."[11] (48) For he thinks that it behoves him to adhere to the classification arising from the consideration of time, according to which, that which is oldest is entitled to priority, and after that, that which is the younger is admitted to a participation in their joint rights. But the practiser in wisdom, knowing that natures are not subject to time, desires what is younger first, and what is older afterwards.

And moral reason agrees with him in this matter, for it is necessary for those who practise anything, first of all to come to the more recent learning, in order that after that, they may be able to derive advantage from that which is more perfect. (49) And, on this account, the lovers of virtue and excellence do not approach the doors of the older philosophy before they have become familiar with these younger parts of it, grammar, and geometry, and the whole range of encyclical learning; for these subordinate branches do always attend upon those, who with sincerity and purity of purpose court wisdom. (50) But he acts cunningly in opposition to these principles, wishing us to take to ourselves the elder sister first, not in order that we may have her in a lasting manner, but that being attracted by the allurements of the younger, we may hereafter relax in our desire for the elder one.

XIII. (51) And we may almost say that this has happened to many of those who have used out of the way roads to learning; for still, as one may say, men coming from their very swaddling clothes to the most perfect study and way of life, philosophy, not thinking it fit to be utterly ignorant of encyclical learning, have still determined to apply themselves to them late and unwillingly. And then, descending from the older and more important kinds of learning to the contemplation of the inferior and younger branches, they have grown old among them so as no longer to be able to return to those pursuits with which they began. (52) It is on this account, I imagine, that he says, "Accomplish her seven years," which is equivalent to: let not the good of the soul be unaccomplished by you; but let it have an end and a due completion, in order that you may meet with the younger classification of good things, of which

personal beauty, and glory, and riches, and such things as these make up the sum. (53) But he does not promise to accomplish them, but only agrees to fulfil them; that is to say, studying never to omit anything which may conduce to its growth and fulness, but in every instance labouring to get the better of all his difficulties, even though there may be innumerable impediments hindering and drawing him in the opposite direction.

(54) And the scripture here appears to me to show very plainly, that customs are regarded by men more than by women, as is clear by the words of Rachel, who admires only those things which are perceptible by the outward senses; for she says to her father, "Be not angry, my lord, that I am unable to rise up before thee in thy presence, because the custom of women is upon me."[12] (55) Therefore it is especially the conduct of women to pay regard to customs; for, indeed, that is the habit of the weaker and more feminine soul; while the nature of men, and of that reason which is really vigorous and masculine, is to be guided by nature.

XIV. (56) But I marvel at the sincerity and truth of the soul which, in its conversation, confesses that it is unable to rise up against apparent good things, and nevertheless admires and honours every one of them, and all but prefers them to itself. (57) Since who of us does resist wealth, and who of us enters the lists against glory? And who despises honour or authority, who, I may say, of almost all those who are still stained by vain opinions? No one whatever. (58) But as long as we have none of these things we talk loudly and proudly, as if we were men of small wants, and companions of frugality, which renders life all-sufficient for itself, and just, and suitable for free and nobly born men. But when there is hope of any of the things which I have enumerated, or when only the slightest breeze of such hope blows upon us, then we are found out, for we at once yield, and submit, and are unable to hold out or resist; and being betrayed by the outward senses, which are so dear to us, we abandon the whole alliance of the soul, and we desert not in a concealed manner, but openly and undisguisedly. And perhaps this is not more than is reasonable to expect.

(59) For the customs of women are still predominant in us, while we are not as yet able to wash them off, or to rise and cross over to the hearth of the men's chamber, as is related of the mind which loved virtue, by name Sarah; (60) for she is represented in the sacred oracles as having ceased to be influenced by the customs of women,[13] when she was about to be in travail and to bring forth the self-taught offspring, being by name Isaac. (61) And she is said not to have had

---

[11]Genesis 29:26.

[12]Genesis 31:35.
[13]Genesis 18:11.

a mother, having received the inheritance of relationship from her father only, and not from her mother, having no share in the female race; for some one has said somewhere, "And yet, in truth, she is my sister, the daughter of my father, but not the daughter of my mother."[14] For she is not formed of the material perceptible by the outward senses, which is always in a state of formation or of dissolution, which is called the mother, and nurse and bringer up of created things; among which, first of all, the tree of wisdom sprang up, but rather of the cause and father of all. (62) She, therefore, having emerged out of the whole corporeal world, and exulting from the joy which is in God, laughs at the pursuits of men, which are conversant about either war or peace.

XV. (63) We, then, being overcome by the unmanly and women-like association with the outward senses, and the passions, and the objects of the outward senses, are not able to stand up in opposition to anything that is apparent. But are dragged on, some of us, in spite of ourselves, and others of us willingly, by everything which comes across us; (64) and if our army, not being able to execute the commands of the father, were to yield, it would nevertheless have for an ally its mother, moderate learning, which enacts in different cities such laws as are in common use, and appear to be just, and establishes different institutions in different countries.

(65) But there are some persons who, neglecting the precepts of their mothers, adhere with all their might to the injunctions of their fathers, whom right reason has thought worthy of the greatest honour, namely, of the priesthood; and if we go through their actions, by which they have obtained this honour, we shall perhaps incur the ridicule of many, who are deceived by the first appearances which present themselves to them, and who do not perceive those powers which are invisible and kept in the shade. (66) For those who have applied themselves to prayers and sacrifices, and the whole body of ceremonies connected with the temple, are, what seems a most paradoxical thing, homicides, fratricides, murderers of those persons who are nearest and dearest to them, though they ought to be pure, and sprung from the pure, having no connection with any pollution, intentionally incurred, nay, not even unintentionally. (67) For it is said, "Each of you slay his brother, and each of you slay his neighbour, and each of you slay his nearest relations. And the sons of Levi did as Moses had spoken; and there fell of the people in that day about three thousand men."[15] And those who had slain such a vast multitude he praises, saying, "Ye have this day, each of you, filled your hands to the Lord in your son, or your brother, so that blessing shall be given to you."

XVI. (68) What, then, are we to say, but that such men are caught by the common customs of men, having, as their accuser, their mother, who lives according to the laws of the state, and acts like a demagogue, namely, custom: but that the others preserve the laws of nature, having, for their ally, their father, namely, right reason; (69) for it is not the case, as some persons think, that the priests slay men, rational animals, compounded of soul and body, but they only eradicate from their minds all those things which are akin to and dear to the flesh, thinking it seemly for those who have become ministers of the only wise God, to alienate themselves from all the things of creation, and to look upon all such things as enemies and thoroughly hostile.

(70) On this account it is, that we shall slay a brother, not a man, but the body, which is brother to the soul; that is to say, we shall separate that which is devoted to the passions and mortal, from that which is devoted to virtue and divine. And, again, we shall slay a neighbour, not a man, but a company and a band; for such a company is, at the same time, akin to, and hostile to, the soul, laying baits and spreading snares for it, in order that being inundated by the objects of the outward senses, which overflow it, it may never emerge and look up to heaven, so as to embrace the beautiful and God-like natures. And we shall also slay those nearest to us: but that which is nearest to the mind is uttered speech, inserting false opinions among reasonable and natural plausibilities and probabilities, to the destruction of that best of all possessions, truth.

XVII. (71) Why, then, are we not also to repel this being, too, who is a sophist and a polluted person, condemning him to the death which is suited to him, namely, silence (for silence is the death of speech), in order that the mind may be no longer led away by its sophisms, but being completely emancipated from all the pleasures which are according to the body, "the brother," and being alienated from, and having shaken off the yoke of, all the trickeries according to "the neighbour," and the neighbouring outward senses, and from the sophistries in accordance with the "nearest" speech, may be able, in all purity, to apply itself to all the proper objects of the intellect.

(72) This is he "who says to his father and to his mother," his mortal parents, "I have not seen you," ever since I have beheld the things of God, who "does not recognize his sons," ever since he has become an acquaintance of wisdom, who "disowns his brethren,"[16] ever since he has ceased to be disowned by God, and has been thought

---

[14]Genesis 20:12.
[15]Exodus 32:27.
[16]Deuteronomy 33:9.

worthy of perfect salvation. (73) This is he who "took as coadjutor," that is to say, who searched for and sought out the things of corruptible creation, of which the chief happiness is laid up in eating and drinking, and who went, Moses says, "to the chimney," which was burning and flaming with the excesses of wickedness, and which could never be extinguished, namely, the life of man, and who, after that, was able even to pierce the woman through her belly,[17] because she appeared to be the cause of bringing forth, being, in real truth, rather the patient than the agent, and even every "man," and every reasoning which follows the opinion which attributes passions to the essence of God, who is the cause of all things.

XVIII. (74) Will not this person be justly looked upon as a murderer, by many who are influenced by the customs which have so much weight among women? But with God, the ruler and father of the universe, he will be thought worthy of infinite praises and panegyrics, and of rewards which can never be taken away; and the rewards are great, and akin to one another, being peace and the priesthood: (75) for it was an illustrious achievement, after having put to flight the almost invincible troops of men who live according to the common fashion, and having put down the civil war of the appetites in the soul, to establish a peace firmly; and for this great exploit to receive nothing else, not riches, not glory, not honour, not authority, not beauty, not strength, not any of the advantages of the body, nor, on the other hand, earth or heaven, or all the world, but that most important and valuable of all things, the rank of the priesthood, the office of serving and paying honour to Him who is in truth the only being worthy of honour and service; this is an admirable thing, an object worthy of contention.

(76) And I was not wrong when I called those rewards, brothers to one another, but I said so, knowing that he cannot be made a true priest who is still serving in human and mortal warfare, in which vain opinions are the officers of the companies; and that he cannot be a peaceful man, who does not in sincerity cultivate and serve, with all simplicity, the only Being who has no share in warfare, and everlasting peace.

XIX. (77) Such are the persons who honour their father, and the things belonging to their father, but who pay but little regard to their mother and to things that belong to her. But Moses represents the man who is at variance with both his father and his mother, and brings them forward as saying, "I know not the Lord; and I will not let Israel go."[18] For he appears to put himself in opposition to those divine things, which are established in accordance with divine reason, and also to those which are established with reference to created beings, by means of education, and to be throwing everything into confusion in every direction. (78) And there are even now—for the human race has not as yet entirely purified itself from unmixed wickedness—there are still persons who have absolutely determined to do nothing which has any bearing on piety or on human society, but who, on the contrary, are the companions of impiety and atheism, and treacherous towards their equals.

(79) And these men go about, being the greatest imaginable pests of their cities, out of curiosity and a love of interfering, mixing themselves up with, or rather, if one must tell the truth, throwing into confusion all kinds of affairs, both public and private, men who ought to have put up prayers and offered sacrifices to avert (as if it had been a great disease) famine, or pestilence, or any other evil inflicted by God; for these calamities are great evils to those on whom they fall; in reference to which Moses sings their destruction, when they have been destroyed by their own allies, and swallowed up by their own opinions, as if by the waves of a stormy sea.

XX. (80) Let us now, therefore, proceeding in regular order, speak of the enemies of these persons, men who honour instruction and right reason, among whom are those who are attached to the virtue of one of their parents, being half-perfect companions; these men are the most excellent guardians of the laws which the father, that is to say, right reason, established, and faithful stewards of the customs which education, their mother, instituted; (81) and they were instructed by right reason, their father, to honour the Father of the universe, and not to neglect the customs and laws established by education, their mother, and considered by all men to be founded in justice.

(82) When, therefore, Jacob, the practiser of virtue, and the man who entered into the lists of, and was a candidate for, the prizes of virtue, was inclined to give his ears in exchange for his eyes, and words for actions, and improvements for perfection, as the bounteous God was willing to give eyes to his mind, in order that he might for the future clearly see what hitherto he had only comprehended by hearing (for the eyes are more trustworthy than the ears), the oracle sounded in his ears, "Thy name shall not be called Jacob; but Israel shall thy name be, because thou hast prevailed with God and with men, with power."[19] Jacob then is the name of learning and or improvement, that is to say of those powers which depend upon learning, and Israel is the name of perfection, for the name being interpreted means "the sight of God;" (83) and what can be more perfect among all the

---

[17] Numbers 25:8.
[18] Exodus 5:2.

[19] Genesis 32:28.

virtues than the sight of the only living God? Accordingly he who hath seen this good thing is confessed to be good by both his parents, having attained to strength in God and power both before the Lord and before men.

(84) And it appears to me to be very well said in the book of Proverbs, "Men who see what is right before God and before men."[20] Since it is by the aid of both these that men attain to the complete possession of good. For when you have been taught to observe the laws of your Father,[21] and not to disregard the injunctions of your mother, you will be able to say with confidence and pride, "For I also was born a son, subject to my father, and beloved before the face of my "mother."

XXI. But, I should say to this man, were you not fated to be loved, if you kept the laws established among mortals out of a desire for fellowship, and if you paid due respect to the ordinances of the uncreate God out of a love for, and a desire to exhibit piety? (85) Therefore Moses, the divine prophet of God, in his description of the building of the temple, shows the perfection of the temple in both points; for it is not without due consideration for us that he covers the ark both within and without with gold, or that he gives two robes to the chief priest, or that he builds two altars, one outside the tabernacle for the victims, and the other inside for the burning incense; but he does this, wishing by these emblems to exhibit the virtues of each species; (86) for it is fitting that the wise man should be adorned both with the invisible excellences existing within in the soul, and also with those external ones which are outwardly visible, and with prudence which is more valuable than gold.

And whenever it departs from human studies, worshipping the living God alone, it puts on the simple unvaried robe of truth, which no mortal thing can ever touch, for it is made of linen material, a material not produced from any being whose nature it is to die. But whenever it passes over to mix in political affairs, then it lays aside the man's robe and assumes the other embroidered one of a most admirable beauty to look at; for life being a thing of great variety and of great changes, requires the diversified wisdom of the pilot who is to hold the helm; (87) and he will appear in the outer conspicuous altar of life to exercise abundant prudence with respect to the skin, and flesh, and blood, and everything relating to the body, in order not to offend the common multitude which gives the second place in honour to the good things of the body in close proximity to the good things of the soul; and at the inner altar he will use bloodless, fleshless, incorporeal things, things proceeding from reasoning alone, which are compared to frankincense and other burnt spices; for as these fill the nostrils, so do those fill the whole region of the soul with fragrance.

XXII. (88) We must also not be ignorant that wisdom, being the art of arts, appears to vary according to its different materials, but it shows its true species without alteration to those who have acute sight, and who are not carried away by the burden of the body with which they are surrounded: but who see the impression which is stamped upon it by art itself. (89) They say that Phidias, the celebrated statuary, made statues of brass, and of ivory, and of gold, and of other different materials, and that in all these works he displayed one and the same art, so that not only good judges, but even those who had no pretensions to the title, recognized the artist from his works. (90) For, as in the case of twins, nature having often employed the same character, has produced similitudes very slightly indeed differing from one another; in the same manner perfect art, being the imitation and copy of nature, when it has taken different materials, fashions and stamps the same appearance on all, so that the works produced by her are in the highest possible degree kindred, and brother-like, and twins.

(91) And the power which exists in the wise man will show the same result: for when it is occupied with the affairs of the living God it is called piety and holiness: but when it employs itself upon the heaven, and the things in heaven, it is natural philosophy; and when it devotes itself to the investigation of the air, and of the different circumstances attending its variations and changes, whether taking place in the uniform yearly revolutions of the seasons, or in the partial periods of months and days, it is then called meteorology. It is called moral philosophy when it busies itself about the rectification of human morals; and this moral philosophy is divided into several subordinate species; that namely of politics, when occupied about state affairs; economy, when applied to the management of a household; when it is devoted to the subject of banquets and entertainments, it is then convivial philosophy.

Again, that power which concerns itself about the government of men, is royal; that which is conversant with commands and prohibitions, is legislative. (92) For all these different powers the wise man of many names and many celebrities does truly contain within himself, namely, piety, holiness, natural philosophy, meteorology, moral philosophy, political knowledge, economy, royal power, legislative wisdom, and innumerable other faculties; and in every one of them he will be seen to wear one and the same appearance.

XXIII. (93) But now that we have discussed the four different classes of children, we must beware not to overlook this, which may be the most

---

[20] Proverbs 3:4.
[21] Proverbs 4:3.

excellent proof of this partition and division of the chapter; for when a child is elated and puffed up by folly, his parents accuse him in this manner, saying, "This is our son,"[22] pointing to the disobedient and stiff-necked youth; (94) for by the demonstration "this," they show that they have other sons likewise, some of whom obey one of them, and others of whom obey them both, being well-disposed reasonings, of whom Reuben is an example; others again, who are fond of hearing and learning, of whom Simeon is a specimen, for his name, being interpreted, means "hearing;" others, people who fly to and become suppliants of God, this is the company of the Levites; others singing a song of gratitude, not so much with a loud voice as with the mind, of whom Judah is the leaders; others, who have been thought worthy of rewards and presents, on account of their voluntary acquisition of virtue through labour, like Issachar; others, persons who have abandoned the Chaldaean meteorological speculations, and passed over to the contemplation of the uncreate God, like Abraham; some, who have attained to self-taught and spontaneous virtue, like Isaac; some, full of wisdom and strength, and beloved by God, like the most perfect Moses.

XXIV. (95) Very naturally, therefore, the sacred law commands the disobedient and contentious man—who brings contributions of evil, that is to say, who joins together and heaps up sin upon sin, great crimes on little ones, fresh guilt upon ancient, intentional upon involuntary misdeeds; and who, like a person inflamed by wine, is always intoxicated and drunk, and raging with ceaseless and unrestrained drunkenness, during the whole of his life—to be stoned; because he has drunk of the unmixed and abundant cup of folly, and because he has destroyed the injunctions of right reason, his father, and the legitimate expositions of his mother's instruction. And though he had an example of excellence and virtue in his brothers, who were approved of by his parents, he did not imitate their virtue, but, on the contrary, he thought fit to go to an additional length in his transgressions, so as to make a god of the body, and to make a god of Typhus, who is especially honoured among the Egyptians, the emblem of whom was the figure of a golden bull; around which his mad worshippers establish dances, and sing, and prelude, not with such melodies as are redolent of wine and revelry, like the sweet songs sung at feasts and entertainments, but a really melancholy and mournful lamentation, like men intoxicated, who have relaxed and quite destroyed the tone and energy of the soul.

(96) For it is said, that when Joshua heard the people crying out he said to Moses, "There is the sound of war in the camp. And he said, It is not the voice of man beginning to exert themselves in battle, nor is it the voice of men betaking themselves to flight, but it is the voice of men beginning revelry and drunkenness that I hear: and when he came near to the camp he saw the calf and the dances."[23] And the enigmatical meaning, which is concealed under these figurative expressions, we will explain to the best of our ability.

XXV. (97) Our own affairs are at one time in a state of tranquillity, and at another they behave as it were with unseasonable impetuosity and loud cries; and their tranquillity is profound peace, and their condition, when in an opposite state, is interminable war; (98) and the witness to this fact is one who has experienced its truth, and who cannot lie; for having heard the voice of the people crying out, he says to the manager and superintendent of the affairs, "There is a sound of war in the tent;" for as long as the irrational impulses were not stirred up, and had not raised any outcry in us, our minds were established with some firmness; but when they began to fill the place of the soul with all sorts of voices and sounds, calling together and awakening the passions, they created a civil sedition and war in the camp. (99) Very naturally, for where else should there be strife, and battle, and contention, and all the other deeds of interminable war, except in the life according to the body, which he, speaking allegorically, calls the camp? This life the mind is accustomed to leave, when under the influence of God it approaches the living God, contemplating the incorporeal appearances; (100) "for Moses," says the scripture, "having taken his own tent, fixed it outside the camp," and that too not near it, but a long way off, and at a great distance from the camp. And by these statements he tells us, figuratively, that the wise man is but a sojourner, and a person who leaves war and goes over to peace, and who passes from the mortal and disturbed camp to the undisturbed and peaceful and divine life of rational and happy souls.

XXVI. (101) And he says in another passage that, "When I have gone out of the city I will stretch forth my hands unto the Lord, and the voices shall cease."[24] Think not here that he who is speaking is a man, a contexture, or composition, or combination of soul and body, or whatever else you may choose to call this concrete animal; but rather the purest and most unalloyed mind, which, while contained in the city of the body and of mortal life is cramped and confined, and like a man who is bound in prison confesses plainly that he is unable to relish the free air. But as soon as it has escaped from this city, then being released, as to its

---

[22]Deuteronomy 21:19.

[23]Exodus 32:17.
[24]Exodus 9:29.

thoughts and imaginations, as prisoners are loosened as to their hands and feet, it will put forth its energies in their free, and emancipated, and unrestrained strength, so that the commands of the passions will be at once put an end to.

(102) Are not the outcries of pleasure very loud with which she is accustomed to deliver such commands as please her? And is not the voice of appetite unwearied when she pours forth her bitter threats against those who do not serve her? And so again all the other passions have a voice of loud and varied sound. (103) But even, if each one of the passions were to exert the ten thousand mouths and voices, and all the power of making an uproar spoken of by poets, it would not be able to perplex the ears of the perfect man, after he has already passed from them, and determined no longer to dwell in the same city with them.

XXVII. (104) But the sacred Scriptures agree with the man who can speak from experience, when he says that in the camp of the body all the sounds of war were heard, the tranquillity dear to peace having been driven to a distance. For he does not say that it is not such a shout of war, but that it is not such a shout as some persons think the cry of men who have conquered or who have been conquered to be, but rather such an one as would proceed from men heavy and overwhelmed with wine. (105) For the expression, "It is not the voice of men beginning to exert themselves in battle," is equivalent to the words, "of men who have got the better in war," for exertion in battle is the cause of victory.

Thus he represents the wise Abraham, after the destruction of the nine kings, that is, of the four passions and the five powers of the outward senses, which were all set in motion in a manner contrary to nature, preluding with a hymn of gratitude, and saying, "I will stretch forth my hand to the most high God, who made heaven and earth; that I will not take from a thread even to a shoe-latchet of any thing that is thine,"[25] (106) And he means, as it appears to me, by this expression, everything in the world, the heaven, the earth, the water, the air, and all animals, and all plants.

For to every one of them, he who directs all the energies of his soul towards God, and who looks to him alone as the only source form which he can hope for advantage, may fitly say—I will take nothing that is yours; I will not receive from the sun the light of day, nor by night will I receive light from the moon or from the other stars, nor rain from the air and from the clouds, nor meat and drink from the earth and from the water, nor the power of sight from the eyes, nor the faculty of hearing from the ears, nor that of smelling from the nostrils, nor from the palate in the mouth the sense of taste, nor the faculty of speaking from the tongue, nor the power of giving and taking from the hands, nor that of approaching and of retreating from the feet, nor that of breathing from the lungs, nor that of digesting from the liver, nor from the other internal organs of the body the power of exciting the energies which belong to them, nor the yearly produce from trees and seeds; but I will look upon every thing as proceeding from the only wise God, who extends his own beneficial powers in every direction, and who by their agency benefits me.

XXVIII. (107) He then who can thus look upon the living God, and who thus comprehends the nature of the cause of all things, honours the things of which he is the cause in a secondary degree to himself; while at the same time he confesses their importance though without flattering them. And this confession is most just: I will receive nothing from you, but everything from God, to whom all things belong, though perhaps the benefits may be bestowed through the medium of you; for ye are instruments to minister to his everlasting graces. (108) But man, who is devoid of any consideration, who is blinded as to his mind, by which alone the living God is comprehensible, does, by means of that mind, never see anything anywhere, but sees all the bodies which are in the world by his own outward senses, which he looks upon as the causes of all things which exist.

(109) On which account, beginning to make gods for himself, he has filled the world with images and statues, and innumerable other representations, made out of all kinds of different materials, fashioned by painters and statuaries, whom the lawgiver banished to a distance form his state, proposing both publicly and privately great rewards and surpassing honours to them, by which conduct he has brought about a contrary result to that which he intended, namely, impiety instead of religion. (110) For the worship of many gods in the souls of ignorant people is mere impiety; and they who deify mortal things neglect the honour due to God; who are not content with making images of the sun and of the moon to the extent of their inclination, and of all the earth, and of all the water, but they even gave beasts and plants devoid of reason a share in those honours, which belonged of right only to immortal beings. And he, reproving them, began a song of victory as has here been shown.

XXIX. (111) And Moses indeed, in the same manner, when he saw the king of Egypt,[26] that arrogant man with his six hundred chariots, that is to say, with the six carefully arranged motions of the organic body, and with the governors who were appointed to manage them, who, while none

---

[25]Genesis 14:22.

[26]Exodus 14:7.

of all created things are by nature calculated to stand still, think nevertheless that they may look upon everything as solidly settled and admitting of no alteration; when he, I say, saw that this king had met with the punishment due to his impiety, and that the people, who were practisers of virtue, had escaped from the attacks of their enemies, and had been saved by mighty power beyond their expectation, he then sang a hymn to God as a just and true judge, beginning a hymn in a manner most becoming and most exactly suited to the events that had happened, because the horse and his rider he had thrown into the sea;"[27] having utterly destroyed that mind which rode upon the irrational impulses of that four-footed and restive animal, passion, and had become an ally, and defender, and protector of the seeing soul, so as to bestow upon it complete safety.

(112) And the same prophet begins a song to the well, not only for the destruction of the passions, but also because he has had strength given to him to acquire the most valuable of all possessions, namely incomparable wisdom, which he compares to a well; for it is deep, and not superficial, giving forth a sweet stream to souls who thirst for goodness and virtue, a drink at once most necessary and most sweet.

(113) But it is not entrusted to any person who is not initiated in wisdom to dig this well, but only to kings, on which account it is said, "Kings hewed it out of stone."[28] For it is the office of mighty rulers to investigate and to establish wisdom, not meaning those who with their arms have subdued sea and land, but those who with the powers of the soul have fought against and subdued its diversified, and mingled, and confused multitude.

XXX. (114) Now the pupils and followers of these persons are those who say, "Thy sons have taken the sum of the men of war who are under our charge, and there is not one of them who has refused, but each man has brought his gift to the Lord of that which he has found."[29] (115) For these men are likely again to prelude with a song of triumph, being eager to attain to perfect and dominant powers. For they say that the man who has taken the sum of the whole, has also taken the greatest number of the reasons of courage, which are by nature inclined to war, being arrayed in opposition to two squadrons, one of which is led by cowardice, which is difficult to overtake, and the other by frantic temerity and rashness; and neither of them has any share in sound wisdom.

(116) And it is very admirably said that no one refused, by way of intimating a participation in perfect and complete courage; just as the lyre and any other musical instrument is out of tune, if there is one single discordant note in it; but is in tune when the strings are all harmonious and pour forth the same symphony at one touch. In the same manner also, the instrument of the soul is out of tune when it is either strained by rashness and urged on to a degree of exceeding sharpness, or relaxed by cowardice in an immoderate degree, so as to be let down and become very flat. But it is in tune when all the tones of courage and of every virtue are well united and combined together, and so produce one well-arranged melody. (117) And it is a great proof of good tune and of skilful management to bring his due gift to God; and this is to honour the living God in a becoming manner, by means of confessing most distinctly that this whole universe is his gift to us; (118) for he says in, strictest accordance with natural truth, "the man has brought the gift which he found." But every one of us, the moment that he is born, finds the great gift of God, namely the universal world, which he has given to him, and to the most excellent parts of him.[30]

XXXI. (119) There are also particular gifts which it is suitable both to God to give, and to men to receive. And these must be the virtues and the energies in accordance with them, at the discovery of which, being almost without any connexion with time, by reason of the surpassing rapidity of the giver which he is accustomed to exhibit in his gifts, every one is full of admiration, even those to whom nothing else in the world appears great. (120) On which account also, the question is put, "How didst thou find it so quickly, O my son?"[31] the questioner marvelling at the promptness of the virtuous disposition; and he who has received the benefit answers felicitously, "Because the Lord God gave it to me." For the gifts and explanations of men are slow, but those of God are most rapid, outstripping the motion of even the most speedy time.

(121) Therefore those who by their strength and courage have become chiefs and leaders of the chorus which raises the song of triumph and of gratitude, are those who have been already mentioned; but those who, by reason of having been put to flight, and of their weakness, are companions of the song of lamentation which is raised on occasion of defeat, are men whom one ought to look upon as cowards, rather than to pity; like those who have a body labouring under some natural defect, to whom any ordinary occasion of sickness is a great hindrance to their cure. (122) But some persons have succumbed contrary to their inclinations, not because the energies of their souls

---

[27] Exodus 15:4.
[28] Numbers 21:18.
[29] Numbers 31:49.

[30] This passage is certainly corrupt. Markland thinks that some words at least have been lost.
[31] Genesis 27:20.

are more effeminate, but because they have been overwhelmed by the more vigorous strength of their adversaries; and imitating those who are willing slaves, they have voluntarily cast themselves down before their masters, though they were freemen by birth; on which account being unable to be sold they have, which is the most incredible of all things, bought masters for themselves and so become slaves, doing the very same thing with those who are insatiably eager for drunkenness with wine; (123) for they also of their own free will and without any compulsion, drink unmixed wine, so that of their own accord they eradicate sobriety from their souls, and choose folly; for, says the scripture, "I hear the voice of those who are beginning revelry and drunkenness;" that is to say, of men who are exhibiting a madness which is not involuntary, but who injure themselves with a voluntary and deliberate frenzy.

XXXII. (124) And every one who comes near the camp sees the calf and the dances, and he himself also is soon infected. For we fall in with Typhus and the revellers of Typhus, whenever we deliberately purpose to come near to the camp of the body; since those who are fond of contemplation and are eager to see incorporeal objects, as being persons who practise obstinacy from pride, are accustomed to dwell at a distance from the body.

(125) Do then therefore pray to God never to begin revelry or drunkenness, that is to say, never intentionally to set forth in the road which leads to ignorance and folly; for unintentional errors are as light again as deliberate sins, inasmuch as they are not weighed down by the irresistible conviction of conscience.

(126) And when your prayers have been accomplished, you will no longer be able to remain in ignorance or out of office, but you will acquire the most important of all offices, namely, the priesthood. For it is almost the only occupation of the priests and ministers of God to offer abstemious sacrifices, abstaining in the firmness of their minds from wine and from every other cause of folly. (127) For, says the scripture, "The Lord spoke unto Aaron, saying, Wine and strong drink shalt thou not drink, neither thou nor thy sons after thee, when ye come into the tabernacle of the testimony, or when ye approach the altar of sacrifice, so that ye may not die. This shall be an everlasting law for all your generations to distinguish between what is sacred and what is profane, and between what is pure and what is impure."[32] (128) But Aaron is the priest, and the interpretation of his name is "mountainous;" reasoning occupying itself with sublime and lofty objects, not on account of the superabundant excess of the arrogance of empty pride, but by reason of the magnitude of

its virtue, which, elevating the thoughts beyond even heaven, suffers it not to contemplate anything that is lowly.

And no one who is disposed in this manner will ever voluntarily touch unmixed wine or any other medicine of folly, (129) for it is inevitable that he must either make one in the solemn procession and enter the tabernacle, being about to perform[33] the rites which may not be seen, or else, that approaching the altar he must offer sacrifices of gratitude for all the public and private blessings which have been showered upon him; and these things require sobriety and great presence of mind.

XXXIII. (130) Therefore, any one may here rightly admire the expressions in which the command is conveyed. For how can it be anything but admirable for people, while sober and masters of themselves, to apply themselves to prayers and to the offering of sacrifices? just as on the other hand it is ridiculous for men to do so when relaxed both in body and soul by wine; (131) unless indeed as often as servants, and sons, and subjects, are about to approach masters, and parents, and sovereigns, they take care to be sober in order not to offend in either word or deed, lest if they in any respect act as if contemptuous of their rank, they should be punished, or to speak in the most moderate manner, should at least suffer ridicule; and yet any one when about to become the minister of the Ruler and father of the universe, is not then to show himself superior to meat, and drink, and sleep, and all the vulgar necessities of nature, but is to turn aside to luxury and effeminacy, and imitate the life of the intemperate, had having his eyes weighed down with wine, and his head shaking, and bending his neck to one side, and belching from intemperance, and being weak and tottering in his whole body, is in that condition to approach the sacred purifications, and altars, and sacrifices. No: such a man may not without impiety even behold the sacred flame at a distance.

(132) But, if indeed one is to understand these things as said not of the tabernacle or altar of sacrifice which are visible, and which are made of inanimate and perishable materials, but of those objects of speculation which are invisible and perceptible only by the intellect, of which these other things are only the images perceptible by the outwards senses; he will all the more marvel at the explanation. (133) For since the Creator has in every instance made one thing a model and another a copy of that model, he has made the archetypal pattern of virtue for the seal, and then he has on this stamped an impression from it very closely resembling the stamp. Therefore, the archetypal seal is the incorporeal idea being a thing as to its intrinsic nature an object of the outward senses,

---

[32] Leviticus 10:8.

[33] There is some corruption in the Greek text here.

but yet not actually coming within the sphere of their operations. Just as if there is a piece of wood floating in the deepest part of the Atlantic sea, a person may say that the nature of wood is to be burned, but that that particular piece never will be burnt because of the way in which it is saturated with salt water.

XXXIV. (134) Let us then look upon the tabernacle and the altar as ideas, the one being the idea of incorporeal virtue, and the other as the emblem of an image of it, which is perceptible by the outward senses. Now it is easy to see the altar and the things which are on it, for they have all their preparations out of doors, and are consumed by unquenchable fire, so as to shine not by day alone, but also by night; (135) but the tabernacle and all things that are therein are invisible, not only because these are placed in the innermost recesses and in the most holy shrines, but also because God has affixed according to the injunctions of the law, the inevitable punishment of death, not only to any one who touches them, but to any one who through the superfluous curiosity of his eyes beholds them. The only exception is, if any one is perfect and faultless, unpolluted by any error whether it be great or small, having a nature entirely even and full, and in all respects most perfect; (136) for to such a man it is permitted once in each year to enter in and behold what is invisible to others, since in him alone of all men the winged and heavenly love of incorruptible and incorporeal good things abides.

(137) When, therefore, any one being smitten by the idea is influenced by the seal which gives an impression of the particular virtues, perceiving, and comprehending, and admiring the most God-like beauty of that idea which he is approaching, as having received the impression of that seal, then a forgetfulness of ignorance and folly is at once engendered in him, accompanied by a simultaneous recollection of instruction and learning. (138) On which account the scripture says, "Wine and strong drink thou shalt not drink, neither thou nor thy sons after thee," when ye enter into the tabernacle of the testimony or approach the altar of sacrifice; and he goes through all these details not more by way of prohibition than of explaining his intention.

In truth, for one who was issuing prohibitions, it was appropriate to say, Drink not wine when you are performing sacrifice; but for one who is declaring his opinion, it is more suitable to say, Ye shall not drink. For it is impossible for a man to admit ignorance, which is the cause of intoxication and of ignorance of the soul, if he be one who studies the generic and specific virtues and devotes himself to the pursuit of them. (139) And he very often speaks of the tabernacle of testimony, in truth, inasmuch as God is the witness of virtue, to whom it is honourable and expedient to attend, or inas-

much as it is virtue which implants steadiness in our souls, eradicating ambiguous, and doubtful, and hesitating, and vacillating reasonings out of them by force, and revealing truth in life as in a court of justice.

XXXV. (140) And the scripture says that, "he shall not die who offers abstemious sacrifices;" since ignorance brings death, and education and instruction bring immortality. For as in our own bodies disease is the cause of dissolution, and health of preservation; so in the same manner in our souls also, that which saves is prudence, for this is a kind of good health of the mind; and that which destroys is folly, which inflicts an incurable disease. (141) And he expressly declares his opinion, and pronounces this last to be an everlasting evil.[34] For he considers that there is an undying law set up and established in the nature of the universe embracing these principles, that instruction is a salutary and saving thing, but that ignorance is the cause of disease and destruction.

(142) He also besides delivers this further statement, that the laws which are established in accordance with truth are at once everlasting; since right reason, which is law, is not perishable. For also, on the other hand, the contrary thing, namely lawlessness, is a thing of brief existence, and by its own intrinsic nature easily destructible, as it is confessed to be by all persons of sound sense. (143) And it is an especial property of law and of instruction to distinguish what is profane from what is holy, and what is unclean from what is clean; as, on the other hand, it is the effect of lawlessness and ignorance to combine things that are at variance with one another by force, and to throw everything into disorder and confusion.

XXXVI. On this account the greatest of the kings and prophets, Samuel, as the sacred scriptures tell us, drank no wine or intoxicating liquors to the day of his death;[35] for he is enrolled among the ranks of the divine army which he will never leave in consequence of the prudence of the wise captain. (144) But Samuel was perhaps in reality a man, but he is looked upon not as a compound animal, but as mind rejoicing only in the service and ministrations of God. For the name Samuel, being interpreted, means "appointed to God;" because he looked upon all such actions as are done in accordance with vain and empty opinions to be shameful irregularity. (145) He was born of a human mother, whose name when interpreted means "grace." For without divine grace it is impossible either to abandon the ranks of mortal things, or to remain steadily and constantly with those which are imperishable. (146) But whatever soul is filled with grace is at once in a state of exul-

---

[34] Leviticus 10:9.
[35] 1 Samuel 1:14.

tation, and delight, and dancing; for it becomes full of triumph, so that it would appear to many of the uninitiated to be intoxicated, and agitated, and to be beside itself. On which account it was said to it by a young boy, and that not by one only but by every one who was old enough for juvenile sauciness and for a readiness to mock at what is good, "How long will you be drunk? Put an end to your wine-bibbing."

(147) For in the case of those who are under the influence of divine inspiration, not only is the soul accustomed to be excited, and as it were to become frenzied, but also the body is accustomed to become reddish and of a fiery complexion, the joy which is internally diffused and which is exulting, secretly spreading its affections even to the exterior parts, by which many foolish people are deceived, and have fancied that sober persons were intoxicated. (148) And yet indeed those sober people are in a manner intoxicated, having drunk deep of all good things, and having received pledges from perfect virtue. But those are intoxicated with that drunkenness which proceeds from wine, who pass their whole lives without ever having tasted wisdom, though they have a continued hunger and desire for it. (149) Very naturally therefore is answer made to the man who acts with the impetuosity of youth, and thinks to produce laughter at the venerable and austere mode of life of prudence, "My good man I am a hard woman, a severe day, and I drink no wine or strong drink, and I pour out my soul before the Lord."

Very great is the freedom of speech of that soul which is filled with the graces of God. (150) In the first place it calls itself a severe day, having regard to the boy who is mocking it; for by him and by every fool the road which leads to virtue is looked upon as rough and difficult to travel and most painful, as one of the old poets testifies, saying:—

Vice one may take in troops with ease,
But in fair virtue's front
Immortal God has stationed toil,
And care, and sweat, to bar the road.
Long is the road and steep,
And rough at first, which leads the steps
Or mortal men thereto;
But when you reach the height, the path
Is easy which before was hard,
And swift the onward course.

XXXVII. (151) After this the soul goes on to deny that it drinks wine or strong drink, boasting in its being continually sober throughout the whole of its life. For to have the reasoning powers really free, and unfettered, and pure, and intoxicated by no passion, was really a very important and admirable thing. (152) And from this it results that the mind which is filled with unmixed sobriety is of

itself a complete and entire libation, and is offered as such to and consecrated to God. For what is the meaning of the expression, "I will pour out my soul before the Lord," but "I will consecrate it entirely to him?" Having broken all the chains by which it was formerly bound, which all the empty anxieties of mortal life fastened around it, and having led it forth and emancipated it from them, he has stretched, and extended, and diffused it to such a degree that it reaches even the extreme boundaries of the universe, and is borne onwards to the beautiful and glorious sight of the uncreate God. (153) Therefore this company is one of sober persons who have made instruction their guide; but the former one is a company of drunkards, whose leader is ignorance.

XXXVIII. (154) But since intoxication does not only display folly, which is the child of ignorance, but also utter insensibility; and since, again, wine is the cause of that insensibility which affects the body, while the cause of the insensibility of the soul is the ignorance of those things with which it is proper and natural to be acquainted; we must now say a few words about ignorance, reminding the reader of only the most important particulars relating to it.

(155) To which, then, of the passions which affect the body shall we compare that passion in the soul which is called ignorance? To the deprivation of the organs of the external senses? Therefore all those, who have been injured in their eyes or ears, are no longer able to see or hear at all, but have no acquaintance with day or light, which are the only objects for the sake of which, if we are to tell the plain truth, life is really desirable, but dwell in lasting darkness and everlasting night, being made insensible to everything whether of small or great importance; men whom ordinary conversation naturally is accustomed to call infirm.

(156) For even if all the other faculties of the rest of the body, should attain to the very extreme limit of strength and vigour, still, if they are tripped up, as it were, and deprived of their foundation by the deprivation of the eyes and ears, they will meet with a great fall, so as never again to be able to rise; for the things which support man and keep him erect are in name, indeed, the feet, but in reality the powers of hearing and seeing; and the man who possesses them in their complete integrity is awake and stands upright, but he who is deprived of them falls and will be utterly destroyed. (157) And ignorance does produce completely similar effects on the soul, depriving it of its faculties of seeing and of hearing, and allowing neither light nor reason to enter into it, lest the one should instruct it and the other should exhibit the truth to it. But shedding upon it dense darkness and abundant folly, it renders the most beautiful soul a deaf, and dumb, and lifeless stone.

XXXIX. (158) For knowledge, which is the

opposite of ignorance, may be called, in a manner, the eyes and ears of the soul; for it applies the mind to what is said, and fixes its eyes upon things as they exist, and cannot endure to form a false judgment of anything which it either sees or hears. But it examines and carefully surveys every object which is worthy of being seen or heard, and even if it be necessary to sail or to travel over sea and land, it will traverse them to its furthest boundaries that it may see anything more important, or hear anything more modern; (159) for the love of knowledge admits of no hesitation or delay, it is an enemy to sleep and a friend to waking. Therefore, continually rousing up, and awakening, and sharpening the intellect, it compels it to roam about in every direction, where instruction is to be obtained, inspiring it with an avidity for hearing, and infusing into it an insatiable thirst for learning. (160) Therefore knowledge causes hearing and seeing, by means of which faculties success and rectitude of conduct are arrived at; for he who sees and hears, knowing what is expedient, chooses that, and rejecting the contrary is benefited by his knowledge. But ignorance causes to the soul a mutilation more grievous than the mutilation of the body, and is the cause of many errors, since it is unable to derive any assistance from without, either by foreseeing anything, or by any acuteness of hearing. Therefore, owing to its exceeding desolateness of condition, it is left utterly undefended and unprotected, and is exposed to the plots of all kinds of men and to dangers from all kinds of events. (161) Let us, then, never drink unmixed wine in such quantities as to cause insensibility to our outward senses, nor let us alienate ourselves to such a degree from knowledge as to diffuse ignorance, that vast and dense darkness, over our souls.

XL. (162) But there are two kinds of ignorance, one simple, being complete insensibility; and the other of a twofold nature, when a man is not only enveloped in ignorance, but also thinks that he knows what he never has known, being elated with an ungrounded opinion of his knowledge. (163) The former evil is the lighter one, for it is the cause of lighter offences, and of what we may perhaps call involuntary errors; but the second is of more importance, for it is the parent of great evils, and not only of unintentional but also of deliberate offences. (164) These are the offences of which Lot, the father of daughters, appears to me to be especially guilty, not being able to nourish a masculine and perfect plant in his soul; for he had two daughters by his wife, who was afterwards turned to stone, whom, using an appropriate appellation, one may call habit, a nature at variance with truth, and always, whenever any one tries to lead it on, lagging behind and looking round upon its ancient and customary ways, and remaining in the midst of them like a lifeless pillar.

(165) Of these daughters of his the elder may be called Counsel, and the younger may be named Assent, for assent follows upon taking counsel; but no one after he has assented still takes counsel. Accordingly the mind, when it has taken its seat in its council chamber, begins to put its daughters in motion; and with the elder one, namely, Counsel, it begins to consider and investigate everything; and with the younger one, Assent, it begins easily to assent to the circumstances that arise, and to embrace what is hostile as though it were friendly, if they only present ever so slight an attraction of pleasure from this source. (166) But sober reasoning does not admit these things, but only that reasoning does so which is overcome with wine, and, as it were, drunk.

XLI. On which account it is said, "They made their father drink wine,"[36] That is to say, they brought complete insensibility on the mind, so that it fancied itself competent by its own abilities to judge what was expedient, and to assent to all sorts of apparent facts, as if they really had solid truth in them; human nature being by no means and under no circumstances competent either to ascertain the truth by consideration, or to choose real truth and advantage, or to reject what is false and the cause of injury; (167) for the great darkness which is spread over all existing bodies and things does not permit one to see the real nature of each thing, but even if any one, under the influence of immoderate curiosity or of real love of learning, wishes to emerge from ignorance and to obtain a closer view, he, like people wholly deprived of sight, stumbling over what is before his feet, will fall, and so get behind hand before he can lay hold of anything; or else, snatching at something with his hands, he will make uncertain guesses, having only conjecture in the place of truth.

(168) For even if education, holding a torch to the mind, conducts it on his way, kindling its own peculiar light, it would still, with reference to the perception of existing things, do harm rather than good; for a slight light is naturally liable to be extinguished by dense darkness, and when the light is extinguished all power of seeing is useless. (169) Accordingly we must, on these accounts, remind the man who gives himself airs by reason of his power of deliberating, or of wisely choosing one kind of objects and avoiding others, that if the same unalterable perceptions of the same things always occurred to us, it might perhaps be requisite to admire the two faculties of judging which are implanted in us by nature, namely, the outward senses and the intellect, as unerring and incorruptible, and never to doubt or hesitate about anything, but trusting in every first appearance to choose one kind of thing and to reject the contrary kind.

---

[36] Genesis 19:33.

(170) But since we are found to be influenced in different manners by the same things at different times, we should have nothing positive to assert about anything, inasmuch as what appears has no settled or stationary existence, but is subject to various, and multiform, and ever-recurring changes.

XLII. For it follows of necessity, since the imagination is unstable, that the judgment formed by it must be unstable likewise; (171) and there are many reasons for this. In the first place, the differences which exist in animals are not in one particular only, but are unspeakable in point of number, extending through every part, having reference both to their creation and to the way in which they are furnished with their different faculties, and to their way of being supported and their habits, and to the manner in which they choose and avoid different things, and to the energies and motions of the outward senses, and to the peculiar properties of the endless passions affecting both the soul and body. (172) For without mentioning those animals which have the faculty of judgment, consider also some of those which are the objects of judgment, such as the chameleon and the polypus; for they say that the former of these animals changes his complexion so as to resemble the soils over which he is accustomed to creep, and that the other is like the rocks of the sea-shore to which it clings, nature herself, perhaps, being their saviour, and endowing them with a quality to protect them from being caught, namely, with that of changing to all kinds of complexions, as a defence against evil.

(173) Again, have you never perceived the neck of the dove changing colour so as to assume a countless variety of hues in the rays of the sun? is it not by turns red, and purple and fiery coloured, and cinereous, and again pale, and ruddy, and every other variety of colour, the very names of which it is not easy to enumerate? (174) They say indeed that among the Scythians, among that tribe which is called the Geloni, most marvellous things happen, rarely indeed, but nevertheless it does happen; namely that there is a beast seen which is called the tarandus, not much less than an ox in size, and exceedingly like a stag in the character of his face. The story goes that this animal continually changes his coat according to the place in which he is, or the trees which he is near, and that in short he always resembles whatever he is near, so that through the similarity of his colour he escapes the notice of those who fall in with him, and that it is owing to this, rather than to any vigour of body, that he is hard to catch. (175) Now these facts and others which resemble them are visible proofs of our inability to comprehend everything.

XLIII. In the next place, not only are there all these variations with respect to animals, but there are also innumerable changes and varieties in men, and great differences between one man and

another. (176) For not only do they form different opinions respecting the same things at different times, but different men also judge in different manners, some looking on things as pleasures, which others on the contrary regard as annoyances. For the things with which some persons are sometimes vexed, others delight in, and on the contrary the things, which some persons are eager to acquire and look upon as pleasant and suitable, those very same things others reject and drive to a distance as unsuitable and ill-omened. (177) At all events I have before now often seen in the theatre, when I have been there, some persons influenced by a melody of those who were exhibiting on the stage, whether dramatists or musicians, as to be excited and to join in the music, uttering encomiums without intending it; and I have seen others at the same time so unmoved that you would think there was not the least difference between them and the inanimate seats on which they were sitting; and others again so disgusted that they have even gone away and quitted the spectacle, stopping their ears with their hands, lest some atom of a sound being left behind and still sounding in them should inflict annoyance on their morose and unpleasable souls.

(178) And yet why do I say this? Every single individual among us (which is the most surprising thing of all) is subject to infinite changes and variations both in body and soul, and sometimes chooses and sometimes rejects things which are subject to no changes themselves, but which by their intrinsic nature do always remain in the same condition. (179) For the same fancies do not strike the same men when they are well and when they are ill, nor when they are awake and when they are asleep, nor when they are young and when they are old. And a man who is standing still often conceives different ideas from those which he entertains when he is in motion; and also when he is courageous, or when he is alarmed; again when he is grieved, or when he is delighted, and when he is in love, he feels differently from what he does when he is full of hatred. (180) And why need I be prolix and deep dwelling on these points? For in short every motion of both body and soul, whether in accordance with nature or in opposition to nature, is the cause of a great variation and change respecting the appearances which present themselves to us; from which all sorts of inconsistent and opposite dreams arise to occupy our minds.

XLIV. (181) And that is not the least influential cause of the instability of one's perceptions which arises from the position of the objects, from their distance, and from the places by which they are each of them surrounded. (182) Do we not see that the fishes in the sea, when they stretch out their fins and swim about, do always appear larger than their real natural size? And oars too, even though they are very straight, look as if they were broken when they are under water; and things at a great distance display false appearances to our eyes, and in this way do frequently deceive the mind. (183) For at times inanimate objects have been imagined to be alive, and on the contrary living animals have been considered to be lifeless; sometimes again stationary things appear to be in motion, and things in motion appear to be standing still: even things which are approaching towards us do sometimes appear to be retreating from us, and things which are going away do on the other hand appear to be approaching. At times very short things seem to be exceedingly long, and things which have many angles appear to be circular. There is also an infinite number of other things of which a false impression is given though they are open to the sight, which however no man in his senses would subscribe to as certain.

XLV. (184) What again are we to say of the quantities occurring in things compounded? For it is through the admixture of a greater or a lesser quantity that great injury or good is often done, as in many other instances, so most especially in the case of medicines compounded by medical science. (185) For quantity in such compounds is measured by fixed limits and rules, and it is not safe either to stop short before one has reached them, nor to advance beyond them. For if too little be applied, it relaxes, and if too much, it strains the natural powers; and each extremity is mischievous, the one from its impotence being capable of producing any effect at all, and the other by reason of its exceeding strength being necessarily hurtful.

Again it is very plain with reference to smoothness, and roughness, and thickness, and close compression, or on the other hand leanness and slackness, how very much influence all these differences have in respect of doing good or harm. (186) Nor indeed is any one ignorant that scarcely anything whatever of existing things, if you consider it in itself and by itself, is accurately understood; but by comparing it with its opposite, then we arrive at a knowledge of its true nature. As for instance, we comprehend what is meant by little by placing it in juxta-position with what is great; we understand what dry is by comparing it with wet, cold by comparing it with heat, light by comparing it with heavy, black by contrasting it with white, weak by contrasting it with strong, and few by comparing it with many.

In the same way also, in whatever is referred to virtue or to vice, (187) what is advantageous is recognised by a comparison with what is injurious, what is beautiful by a comparison with what is unseemly, what is just and generally good, by placing it in juxta-position with what is unjust and bad. And, indeed, if any one considers everything that there is in the world, he will be able to arrive at a proper estimate of its character, by taking it

in the same manner; for each separate thing is by itself incomprehensible, but by a comparison with another thing, is easy to understand it. (188) Now, that which is unable to bear witness to itself, but which stands in need of the advocacy of something else, is not to be trusted or thought steady. So that in this way those men are convicted who say that they have no difficulty in assenting to or denying propositions about anything. (189) And why need we wonder? For any one who advances far into matters, and who contemplates them in an unmixed state will know this, that nothing is ever presented to our view according to its real plain nature, but that everything has the most various possible mixtures and combinations.

XLVI. (190) Some one will say, We at once comprehend colours. How so? Do we not do so by means of the external things, air and light, and also by the moisture which exists in our eyes themselves? And in what way are sweet and bitter comprehended? Is it apart from the moisture in our mouths? And as to all the flavours which are in accordance with, or at variance with nature, are not they in the same case? What, again, are we to say of the smells arising from perfumes which are burnt? Do they exhibit plain unmixed simple natures, or rather qualities compounded of themselves and of the air, and sometimes also of the fire which consumes their bodies, and also of the faculty existing in our own nostrils?

(191) From all this we collect the inference that we have neither any proper comprehension of colours, not only of the combination which consists of the objects submitted to our view and of light; nor of smells, but only of the mixture which consists of that which flows from substances and the all-receiving air; nor of tastes, but only of the union which arises from the tasteable object presented to us, and the moist substance in our mouths.

XLVII. (192) Since, then, this is the state of affairs with respect to these matters, it is worth while to appreciate correctly the simplicity, or rashness, or impudence of those who pretend to be able with ease to form an opinion, so as to assent to or deny what is stated with respect to anything whatever. For if the simple faculties are wanting, but the mingled powers and those which are formed by contributions from many sources are within sight, and if it is impossible for those which are invisible to be seen, and if we are unable to comprehend separately the character of all the component parts which are united to make up each faculty, then what remains except that we must think it necessary to suspend our judgment? (193) And then, too, do not those facts which are diffused over nearly the whole world, and which have caused both to Greeks and barbarians such erroneous judgments, exhort us not to be too ready in giving our credence to what is not seen? And what are these facts? Surely they are the instructions which we have received from our childhood, and our national customs and ancient laws, of which it is admitted that there is not a single one which is of equal force among all people; but it is notorious that they vary according to the different countries, and nations, and cities, aye, and even still more, in every village and private house, and even with respect to men, and women, and infant children, in almost every point. (194) At all events, what are accounted disgraceful actions among us, are by others looked upon as honourable; what we think becoming, others call unseemly; what we pronounce just, others renounce as iniquitous; others think our holy actions impious, our lawful deeds lawless: and further, what we think praiseworthy, they find fault with; what we think worthy of all honour, is, in the eyes of others, deserving of punishment; and, in fact, they think most things to be of a contrary character to what we think.

(195) And why need I be prolix and dwell further on this subject, when I am called off by other more important points? If then, any one, leaving out of the question all other more remarkable subjects of speculation, were to choose to devote his time to an investigation of the subject here proposed, namely, to examine the education, and customs, and laws of every different nation, and country, and place, and city; of all subjects and rulers; of all men, whether renowned or inglorious, whether free or slaves, whether ignorant or endowed with knowledge, he would spend not one day or two, nor a month, nor even a year, but his whole life, even though he were to reach a great age, in the investigation; and he would nevertheless still leave a vast number of subjects unexamined, uninvestigated, and unmentioned, without perceiving it. (196) Therefore, since there are some persons and things removed from other persons and things, not by a short distance only, but since they are utterly different, it then follows of necessity that the perceptions which occur to men of different things must also differ, and that their opinions must be at variance with one another.

XLVIII. (197) And since this is the case, who is so foolish and ridiculous as to affirm positively that such and such a thing is just, or wise, or honourable, or expedient? For whatever this man defines as such, some one else, who from his childhood, has learnt a contrary lesson, will be sure to deny. (198) But I am not surprised if a confused and mixed multitude, being the inglorious slave of customs and laws, however introduced and established, accustomed from its very cradle to obey them as if they were masters and tyrants, having their souls beaten and buffeted, as it were, and utterly unable to conceive any lofty or magnanimous thoughts, believes at once every tradition which is represented to it, and leaving its mind without any proper training, assents to and denies propositions without examination and without deliberation. But even the multitude of those who are called philosophers, pretending that they are really seeking for certainty and accuracy in things, are divided into ranks and companies, coming to discordant, and often even to diametrically opposite decisions, and that too, not about some one accidental matter, but about almost everything, whether great or small, with respect to which any discussion can arise.

(199) For when some persons affirm that the world is infinite, while others pronounce it to be confined within limits; or while some look upon the world as uncreated, and others assert that it is created; or when some persons look upon it as destitute of any ruler and superintendent, attributing to it a motion, deprived of reason, and proceeding on some independent internal impulse, while others think that there is a care of and providence, which looks over the whole and its parts of marvellous power and wisdom, God ruling and governing the whole, in a manner free from all stumbling, and full of protection.

How is it possible for any one to affirm that the comprehension of such objects as are brought before them, is the same in all men?

(200) And again, the imaginations which are occupied with the consideration of what is good, are not they compelled to suspend their judgment rather than to agree? While some think that it is only what is good that is beautiful, and treasure that up in the soul, and others divide it into numbers of minute particles, and extend it as far as the body and external circumstances. (201) These men affirm that such pieces of prosperity as are granted by fortune, are the body-guards of the body, namely strength and good health, and that the integrity and sound condition of the organs of the external senses, and all things of that kind, are the guards of that princess, the soul; for since the nature of good is divided according to three divisions, the third and outermost is the champion and defender of the second and yielding one, and the second in its turn is a great bulwark and protection to the first; (202) and about these very things, and about the different ways of life, and about the ends to which all actions ought to be referred, and about ten thousand other things which logical, and moral, and natural philosophy comprehends, there have been an unspeakable number of discussions, as to which, up to the present time, there is no agreement whatever among all these philosophers who have examined into such subject.

XLIX. (203) Is it not then strictly in accordance with nature that while its two daughters, Counsel and Assent, were agreed together, and sleeping together, the mind is introduced as embarrassed by an ignorance of all knowledge? for we read in the scripture, "He knew not when they lay down, or when they rose up."[37] (204) For it was not likely that in his state he could clearly and distinctly comprehend either sleep or waking, or a stationary position or motion; but when he appears to have come to an opinion in the best manner, then above all other times is he found to be most foolish, since his affairs then come to an end, by no means resembling that which was expected; (205) and whenever he has decided on assenting to some things as true, then he incurs a reproach and condemnation for his facility in adopting opinions, those things which he previously believed as most certain now appearing untrustworthy and uncertain; so that, as matters are in the habit of turning out contrary to what was expected, the safest course appears to be to suspend one's judgment.

L. (206) Having now discussed these matters sufficiently, let us turn to what follows the points already examined. We said, then, that under the name of drunkenness was signified that covetousness and greediness, which has often greatly injured many persons, and the votaries of which one may see, even though they may be amply filled in all the channels of their bodies, still unsatisfied and empty as to their desires. (207) These men, if, being distended by the abundance of the things which they have devoured, they nevertheless get breath again for a short time, like wrestlers who are tired, soon descend again to the same contest.

(208) Moreover, the king of the Egyptian country, that is of the body, appearing to the minister of drunkenness, his cupbearer, to be angry with him; again at no great distance of time is represented in the sacred scriptures as reconciled to him remembering that passion which breaks down the appetites in the day of his perishable creation, not in the imperishable light of the uncreated luminary; for it is said that it was Pharaoh's birthday,[38] when he sent for the chief butler out of his prison, that he might appear at his banquet; (209) for it is a peculiar characteristic of the man who is devoted to the passions, to think created and perishable things beautiful, because he is enveloped in night and dense darkness, as to the knowledge of imperishable things. On which account he embraces drunkenness as the beginning of all pleasures, and its minister the cupbearer.

LI. (210) Now there are three companions of and servants of the intemperate and incontinent soul, the chief baker, the chief cook, and the chief butler, whom the admirable Moses mentions in these words, "And Pharaoh was angry with the two eunuchs, with the chief butler, and with the chief baker, and he put them in prison with the chief cook;" and the chief cook is eunuch; for he says in another place, "And Joseph was brought down to Egypt, and a eunuch became his master, Pharaoh's chief cook,"[39] (211) and again, they sold Joseph to Pharaoh's eunuch, the chief cook;[40] and why is it that the aforesaid offices are absolutely committed to one who is neither man nor woman? Is it because men are by nature calculated to sow seed, and woman to receive it, and that the meeting of the two together is the cause of the generation, and also of the duration of all animals? But it belongs to an unproductive and barren soil, or one may rather say to one which has been made a eunuch, to delight in costly meats and drinks, and in superfluous extravagant preparations of delicacies, since it is unable in reality either to scatter the masculine seeds of virtue, or to receive and nourish them after they have been shed upon it; but, like a rough and stony field, only to destroy those things which ought to have lived for ever.

(212) And it is laid down as a doctrine of the most general applicability and usefulness, that every author of pleasure is unproductive of wisdom, being neither male nor female, because it is incompetent either to give or to receive the seeds which have a tendency to incorruptibility, but is able only to study the most disgraceful habits of life, to destroy what ought to be indestructible, and to extinguish the torches of wisdom, which ought to be enduring and inextinguishable. (213) None of such persons does Moses permit to come into the assembly of God; for he says that, "A man who is bruised or castrated shall not enter into the assembly of the Lord."[41]

LII. For what advantage is there, from the hearing of the sacred scriptures, to a man who is destitute of wisdom, whose faith has been eradicated, and who is unable to preserve that deposit of doctrines most advantageous to all human life? (214) Now, there are three persons who contribute to the conviviality of the human race,—the chief baker, the cup-bearer, and the maker of delicacies: very naturally, since we desire the use and enjoyment of three things—meat, confections, and drink. But some men only desire that indispensable food which we use of necessity for the sake of our health, and in order to avoid living in an illiberal manner. Others again desire immoderate and exceedingly extravagant luxuries, which, breaking through the appetites, and weighing down, and overwhelming the channels of the body by their number, usually become the parents of all sorts of terrible diseases.

(215) Those, therefore, who are inexperienced in pleasure and the indulgence of the appetites and

---

[37] Genesis 19:35.
[38] Genesis 40:20.

[39] Genesis 39:1.
[40] Genesis 37:36.
[41] Deuteronomy 23:1.

diseases, like the common people in cities, living a life free alike from hatred and from annoyances, as frugal people, have no need of all kinds of various ministers of refined skill, being contented with ordinary cooks, and cup-bearers, and confectioners.

(216) But they who think that the most important and royal object of life is to live pleasantly, and who refer everything, whether of great or small importance, to this object, desire to avail themselves of the services of chief cooks and chief cup-bearers, and chief confectioners, that is to say, of men possessed of the highest degree of skill in the arts which they profess. (217) For those who are skilful in the making of confections and luxuries invent the most various possible kinds of cheese-cakes, and honey cakes, and of innumerable other sweetmeats, varying from one another, not merely in the difference of their material, but also in the manner in which they are made, and in their shape, in such a way as not only to please the taste, but also to beguile the eye. (218) And again, the contrivances displayed in the examination of different kinds of wine to produce some, the effect of which shall speedily go off, and which shall not produce headache, but, on the contrary, shall be devoid of any tendency to heat the blood, and shall be very fragrant, admitting either a copious or a scanty admixture with water, according as the object is to have a strong and powerful draught, or a gentle and imperceptible one. And all the other devices and inventions of cup-bearers all come to the same end of art. (219) And to cook up and prepare fish, and birds, and similar viands, in every variety of manner, and to make all other kinds of sweetmeats and delicacies, we have plausible confectioners of exceeding skill; and there are thousands of other luxuries which they are clever at contriving, besides those which they have heard of or seen made by others, having devised them themselves out of their continued care and attention to be the object of making life luxurious, and effeminate, and not worth living.

LIII. (220) But all these men have been now spoken of as eunuchs, being utterly barren of wisdom. But the mind, with which the king of the belly makes a treaty and agreement, was the cupbearer; for by its own nature, the human race is very fond of wine, and this is the sole thing of which it is immeasurably insatiable, since there is no one who is impossible to be satisfied with sleep, and eating, and carnal enjoyments, and things like these; but nearly every one is insatiably fond of wine, and especially those who are occupied with serious business; (221) for after they have drunk they are still thirsty, and they begin drinking at first out of small cups, then, as they proceed, they tell their servants to bring them wine in larger goblets,

and when they are pretty full and getting riotous, being no longer able to restrain themselves, they take bowls and goblets of all the largest sizes that they can get, and drink the wine unmixed in huge draughts, until they are either overcome by deep sleep, being no longer able to govern themselves, or till what they have poured into themselves is vomited out again through repletion. (222) But even then, nevertheless, the insatiable desire which exists within them continues to rage as though it were still under the influence of hunger. "For their wine is of the vine of Sodom," as Moses says, "and their tenderils are from Gomorrah; their grapes are grapes of gall, and their branches are bitter branches. The rage of dragons is their wine, and the incurable fury of serpents." [42]

The interpretation of the name Sodom is "barrenness and blindness." But Moses here compares those who are the slaves of greediness for wine and general gluttony, and of other most disgraceful pleasures to a vine, and to the different products of the vine; (223) and the enigmatical meaning which he conceals under this allegory is this:—There is no plant of true joy naturally implanted in the soul of the bad man; inasmuch as it has no healthy roots, but only such as are burnt and reduced to ashes, since, instead of water, Heaven has poured upon it the fire of lightning which cannot be quenched, God having adjudged that as fitting punishment for the impious. But there is implanted in it the plant of excessive desire, barren of all good things, and destitute of anything deserving of regard or contemplation, which he here compares to a vine. Not meaning that one which is the parent of eatable fruit, but that one which produces bitterness, and wickedness, and ungodly cunning; and which is most fertile in anger, and fury, and the most savage dispositions; biting the soul like an asp or a viper, inflicting envenomed wounds, utterly incurable.

(224) For which wounds, however, we pray that a relief may be found by propitiating the all-merciful God, in order that he may destroy this wild vine, and may condemn the eunuchs and all persons who are barren of virtue to everlasting punishment; and that, instead of them he may implant in our souls the valuable trees of right instruction, and may bestow upon us noble and masculine reason as its fruit, such as is able to bear within it good actions by way of seed, and is able to increase the virtues, and is calculated to maintain and preserve for ever the entire connection and system of happiness.

---

[42]Deuteronomy 32:32.

ON THE PRAYERS AND CURSES UTTERED BY NOAH WHEN HE BECAME SOBER†

(De Sobrietate)

I. (1) Having examined in the preceding treatise what has been said by the lawgiver about wine and the nakedness which attends upon it, we will now begin to connect the following essay with the statements advanced in that work.

Now in the sacred scriptures we come to the following words immediately after the account we have just been examining, "And Noah awoke from his wine, and knew all that his younger son had done to him."[1] (2) Sobriety is confessed to be a most advantageous thing, not only for souls but also for bodies, for it drives away the diseases which arise from immoderate repletion, and it sharpens the outward senses to an exceeding degree of acuteness, and it altogether prevents bodies from being weighed down so as to fall, but keeps them light, and raises them up, and incites them to the exercise of their appropriate energies, implanting in every part a promptness and vigour; and in short, sobriety is the cause of exactly as many good things, as drunkenness, on the contrary, is of evils.

(3) Since then sobriety is most advantageous to those bodies to which the drinking of wine is naturally suitable, is it not much more so to souls, with which all perishable food is inconsistent; for what thing in human nature can be more noble than a sober mind? what glory can be more glorious? what wealth can be more rich? what authority more powerful? what strength more vigorous? of all admirable things what can be more admirable? Let there only be the eye of the soul fit to act, which is able to penetrate every where and to open every thing, being in no part hindered or dimmed by the suffusion of its own moisture; for being then most exceedingly sharpsighted as to its comprehension, and looking into wisdom itself, it will meet with images such as are intelligible only by the intellect, the contemplation of which attracts the soul and will not suffer it any longer to turn aside to the objects which belong to the outward senses.

(4) And why should we wonder if there is no created thing equal in honour to a man who is sober in his soul, and gifted with acute vision? for the eyes of the body and the light which is appreciable by the outward senses are honoured in an excessive degree by all of us. Accordingly, many who have lost their sight, have voluntarily also thrown away life, thinking as far as they were concerned, that death itself was a lighter evil than such deprivation. (5) In proportion then as the soul is superior to the body, in the same proportion also is the mind better than the eyes; and the mind while it is free from injury and imperfection, not being oppressed by any of the iniquities or passions which are produced by insane drunkenness, renounces sleep as a thing which causes forgetfulness and hesitation in what is to be done; but it embraces wakefulness, and uses acuteness of vision, with respect to every object worthy of being beheld, being kept awake by exceedingly perfect memory, and committing actions which are in accordance with the knowledge that it acquires.

II. (6) Such then is the condition of the sober man; but when Moses speaks of Noah's "younger son," he is not so much meaning to make a statement respecting his age, as to show the disposition with which those persons are endued who are inclined to innovation; since how could he have forced himself to see, what ought not to be seen, in defiance of all law and justice, or to divulge what ought to have been concealed in silence, or to bring to light what might have been kept in the shade at home, and to transgress all the boundaries which should confine the soul, if he had not been eager for change and innovation, laughing at what happens to others when he ought rather to lament over such accidents, and not to ridicule things which it was more natural and decent and proper to grieve for. (7) In many places indeed of the exposition of the law, Moses speaks of those who are somewhat advanced in age as young men, and on the other hand those who are not yet arrived at old age he entitles elders; not having regard to the number of their years, whether it be a short or a very long time that they have lived, but to the faculties of their soul, according to the way in which it is influenced, whether it be for good or for evil. (8) Accordingly he calls Ishmael when he has now lived a space of nearly twenty years a child, speaking by a comparison with Isaac who is perfect in virtue; for, says he, "he took bread, and a skin of water, and gave it to Agar, and put it upon her shoulder, and the child also, when Abra-

---

†Yonge's title, *A Treatise on the Words that Noah Uttered When He Awoke from His Wine, or On Sobriety.*
[1]Genesis 9:23.

ham sent them forth from his house."[2] And again he says, "She put the child down under a pine tree;" and further on he says, "that I may not see the death of the child."

And yet before Ishmael was born and circumcised, thirteen years before the birth of Isaac, and having been now weaned for more than seven years, he was banished with his mother, because he being illegitimate was mocking the legitimate son, as though he were on terms of equality with him. (9) But nevertheless, though in reality a young man, he is still called a child, being as it were a sophist put in comparison with a wise man; for Isaac received wisdom for his inheritance, and Ishmael sophistry, as when we define the characters of each we purpose to show in certain dialogues. For the same relation which a completely infant child bears to a full-grown man, the same does a sophist bear to a wise man, and the encyclical branches of education to real knowledge in virtue.

III. (10) And again in his great song he calls the whole people, when it is smitten with a desire of innovation by the name suited to foolish and infant age, entitling them "children." "For," says he, "the Lord is just and holy; have they not sinned against him, blameworthy children that they are? O crooked and perverse generation, is this the requital that ye offer to the Lord? is the people so foolish and not wise?"[3] (11) Therefore, he here distinctly calls those men children who deserve blame and have guilt in their souls, and who through folly and senselessness commit many errors in their actions which are not according to uprightness of life; not having regard to the bodily age of the children, but to the irrational and really childish condition of their minds.

(12) Thus indeed, Rachel also, that is beauty of body, is represented as younger than Leah, who is beauty of soul. For the beauty of the body is mortal, but that of the soul is immortal; and all the things which are accounted honourable when judged of with reference to the outward senses, are all taken together inferior to the one single thing, the beauty of the soul. And it is in accordance with this principle that Joseph is always spoken of as young and as "the youngest."[4] For when he manages the flock "with his illegitimate brethren,"[5] he is called young; and when his father prays for him, he says, "My youngest son whom I have prayed for, return to me." (13) This is the champion of all the power of the body and the unflattering companion of the abundant supply of external things, who has not yet found out any perfect good more valuable and honourable than that

of the elder soul; for if he had found it, he would have departed and abandoned the whole of Egypt without ever turning back.

But now he chiefly prides himself on his nourishing it and supporting it as a nurse; and when he who sees beholds the warlike and authoritative part of it overwhelmed in the sea and destroyed, he sings a hymn to God.

(14) It is therefore a juvenile disposition, which is not yet able to tend the sheep with the legitimate genuine virtues, that is to say, to govern and superintend the irrational nature existing in accordance with the soul, but which still with its illegitimate brethren, honours the things which appear good, in preference to joining his legitimate brothers and to those things which really are good. (15) But he is spoken of as "youngest," even although he keeps on increasing and improving for the better, in comparison with the perfect man, who thinks nothing honourable but what is good. On which account he says in an encouraging manner, by way of exhortation, "Return to me," a phrase equivalent to, "Desire the elder opinion." Do not be in everything aiming at innovation, do now love virtue for herself alone; do not, like a foolish child dazzled by the splendour of the events of fortune, allow yourself to be filled entirely by deceit and erroneous opinions.

IV. (16) It has therefore been proved, that in many passages Moses is in the habit of calling a person young, having regard not to the age of the body, but to the desire of the soul for innovation; and also we will now proceed to show that he calls some persons elders, not because they are oppressed by old age, but as being worthy of honour and respect. (17) Who then of those persons, who are acquainted with the sacred scriptures, is ignorant that the wise Abraham is represented as less long lived than almost any one of his ancestors? And yet of all those who lived to the most extreme old age there is not one, as I think, who is called an elder, but he alone has this title given to him. Therefore, the sacred scriptures say, that "Abraham was now old and advanced in years," and, "The Lord blessed Abraham in all things."[6] (18) This appears to me to be added as a sort of explanatory cause for what has been said before, namely, why the wise man is called the elder. For when the rational part of the soul is made of a good disposition by the kind providence of God, and when it reasons not only about one species, but about everything which is presented to it, using older opinion, it then becomes blessed, and is itself the older part of the people.

(19) Thus also he is accustomed to call the members of the assembly of the God-loving people which consists of the number of ten sevens,

[2] Genesis 21:14.
[3] Deuteronomy 32:5.
[4] Genesis 49:22.
[5] Genesis 39:1.

[6] Genesis 24:1.

elders. For we read in the scripture the direction given to Moses, "Assemble for me seventy men of the elders of Israel, whom you yourself know that they are elders."[7] (20) Therefore, it is not only those persons who are looked upon by ordinary people as old men, inasmuch as they are hierophants, but those whom the wise man alone knows, whom he thinks worthy of the appellation of elders. For those whom he rejects, like a skilful money-changer, from the coinage of virtue, being alloyed, are all in their souls inclined to innovation; but those whom he wishes to make friends to himself, are of necessity well tested and approved, and elders as to their minds.

V. (21) Therefore, the scripture is seen to prove each particular of what I have said more plainly to those who have taught themselves to obey one injunction of the law. "For if," says the scripture, "a man has two wives, the one beloved and the other hated, and if she who is beloved bears him a child, and also she who is hated, and if the child of the wife who is hated be the first born, then, on the day on which he bestows on his sons the inheritance of his substance, he shall not be able to give the share of the first born to the son of her who is beloved, overlooking his real first born son, the child of her who is hated; but he must recognize the son of her who is hated as his first born, to give him a double share of all the possessions that belong to him, because he is the beginning of his children, and the rights of the first born belong to him."[8] (22) You observe here now that he never calls the son of the wife that is beloved the first born or the elder, but he often gives this title to the son of her who is hated; and yet he has already pointed out that the son of her who is beloved was in point of time the first, and the son of her who is hated the last, at the very beginning of this injunction; for he says, "If the beloved wife and she who is hated both bear children." But nevertheless the offspring of the first mentioned, even though it may be considerably earlier in point of time is looked upon as younger by right reason when it comes to decide between them. But the offspring of her who is spoken of in the second place, even though it may come after as to the time of its birth, is thought worthy of the more important and elder share. (23) Why so? because we say that she who is beloved is the symbol of pleasure, and she who is hated is the emblem of prudence.

For the chief multitude of men love the company of the one to excess, inasmuch as she, from her own treasures, profers them most seductive charms and allurements, from the very first moment of their birth to the extremity of old age;

but of the other they detest excessively the austere and very dignified look, just as silly children dislike the profitable but unpleasant reproofs of their parents and guardians. (24) And both the wives become mothers: the one bringing forth that disposition in the soul which loves pleasures, and the other that which loves virtue; but the lover of pleasure is imperfect, and in reality is always a child, even if he reaches a vast age of many years. But, on the other hand, the lover of virtue, though he is in old age as to his wisdom, while still in his swaddling clothes, as the proverb has it, will never grow old. (25) In reference to which Moses says very emphatically with respect to the son of virtue, which is hated by the generality of men, that "he is the beginning of his children," being, forsooth, the first both in order and precedency. And to him belong the rights of the first-born by the law of nature, and not by the lawless principle existing among men.

VI. (26) The prophet, then, in accordance with this law, and as it were shooting his arrows with happy aim at the appointed mark, in strict agreement with what has gone before, represents Jacob as younger in point of age than Esau (because from our very earliest birth folly is bred up with us, and the desire of what is honourable is engendered subsequently), but as older in point of power. In consequence of which Esau id deprived of his birthright as the elder son, but Jacob is very naturally invested with it; (27) and the arrangements made with respect to the sons of Joseph are consistent, if we examine them carefully and with much consideration; when the wise man, under the influence of immediate inspiration, having them both standing before him, does not put his hands on their heads, directing them as the youths are straight before him and immediately, but crossing his hands, so as to touch with his left the head of the one who appears to be the elder, and with his right that of him who seems the younger; and the elder one in point of age is called Manasseh, and the younger is called Ephraim.[9] (28) And these names, if they are translated into the Greek language will be found to be symbols of memory and recollection; for the name Manasseh, being interpreted, means "from forgetfulness," and which by another name is called "recollection;" for he who comes to a recollection of what he has forgotten is advancing out of forgetfulness.

But Ephraim being interpreted means "fruitbearing," a most appropriate appellation for memory; because the fruit which is the most useful and truly eatable for souls is lasting memory, which never forgets. (29) Memory, therefore, exists best when meeting with manly and solid natures, in respect of which it is looked upon as

[7]Numbers 11:16.
[8]Deuteronomy 21:15.

[9]Genesis 48:13.

younger, having been brought forth late; but forgetfulness and recollection, almost from the earliest birth of a man, dwell alternately with every one, on which account recollection has the precedence in point of time, and is placed on the left hand by the wise man when he is arranging the two in order; but memory will share the chief honours of virtue, which the lover of God, receiving eagerly, will think worthy of a better portion by himself.

(30) Therefore, the first man, being become sober, and knowing what his younger son had done to him, imprecates very terrible curses on him; for, in truth, when the mind recovers its sobriety, it does in consequence immediately perceive all that innovating wickedness has previously done to it, which, while it was intoxicated, it was unable to comprehend.

VII. (31) We must now then consider whom the wise man here curses; for this is one of the matters especially deserving of investigation, since he curses not the son who appears to have done the wrong, but his son, and his own grandson, of whom he has not mentioned any apparent sin at present, either small or great; (32) for he who from superfluous curiosity wished to see his father naked, and who laughed at what he saw, and who divulged what ought properly to have been concealed in silence, was Ham, the son of Noah; but he who bears the blame for the offences committed by the other, and who reaped the fruit of them in curses is Canaan; for it is said, "Cursed is Canaan the son, the servant, the servant of servants, shall he be to his brethren."[10] (33) And yet, as I said before, what sin had he committed? But they, who are accustomed to explain the formal, and literal, and obvious interpretations of the laws have perhaps considered this by themselves; but we, being guided by right reason, as it suggest itself to us, will interpret it according to the explanation which is ready to hand, having just made this necessary preface.

VIII. (34) A stationary position and motion differ from one another; for the one is a state of tranquillity, but motion is impetuosity, of which last there are two species—the one that which changes its place, the other that which is constantly revolving about the same place. Now habit is closely akin to the stationary position, and energy to motion; (35) and what we have here said may be more easily understood by an appropriate example.

It is customary to call an architect, or a painter, or a farmer, or a musician (and so on with other artists), by the aforesaid name of their profession, even if they remain inactive, doing nothing in the way of working at their respective arts, with reference to the skill and knowledge which they have

each of them acquired in their respective professions; (36) but when the architect has taken a material of wood and is working it up, and when the painter having mixed his proper colours on his pallet, paints the figures which he has in his head; and when, again, the former cutting furrows in the earth, throws in the seed, and plants, cuttings, and shoots of tree; and when, also, by way of supplying what he has planted with nourishment, he waters them and draws up channels of water to their roots, and does every thing else which a farmer may be expected to do; and also, when the musician adapts metres, and rhythm, and all kinds of melody to his flutes, and harps, and other instruments, and is able even without any manufacturers' instruments to use the organ with which he is furnished by nature by means of his voice which is furnished with all the tones; and so on with all the other artists, if it were worth while to mention them separately. In all these cases, besides the aforei said names derived from their profession, other names akin to the former ones are added with reference to their work; so that we predicate of the architect that he builds, of the painter that he portrays, of the farmer that he cultivates the land, of the musician that he plays the flute or the harp, or that he sings, or does something similar.

(37) Now, what men are followed by praise and blame? Is it not those men who energise and do something? For when they succeed they meet with praise; and when, on the other hand, they fail they incur blame; but those who are scientific, without proceeding to action, remain in tranquillity having attained this one honour unattended with danger, namely, peace.

IX. (38) Therefore, the same assertion applies to those who live according to folly, and also to all those who live in accordance with virtue or vice. Those who are prudent, and temperate, and manly, and just men in their dispositions are infinite in number, having a happy portion in nature, and institutions in accordance with the law, and exerting themselves in invincible and unhesitating labours; but the beauty which exists in the ideas in their minds they are not able to display by reason of their poverty, or of their want of rank, or of some disease of the body, or of some one of the other disasters which surround human life; (39) therefore, they being good have got their good things as it were in bondage and prison.

But there are others who have them in an unconfined, and emancipated, and wholly free condition, having unlimited materials and opportunities for their exhibition. (40) The wise man having an abundance of private and public assisting circumstances by which he can display his acuteness and his wisdom; the temperate man will make riches which are usually blind and accustomed to excite and tempt men to luxury, farsighted for the future: the just man will exercise authority by which

---

[10]Genesis 9:25.

he will for the future be able to assign to each individual without any hindrance, such a share of existing things as agrees with his deserts. The practiser of virtue will display piety, holiness, and a proper care of the sacred places and of the sacred rites performed in them.

(41) But without proper opportunities virtues indeed exist, but they are immoveable and like silver and gold, which is of no use in the world, because it is treasured up in the secret recesses of the earth. (42) On the other hand again, one can see innumerable persons, unmanly, intemperate, foolish, unjust, impious in their minds, but unable fully to display the disgraceful character of all their vices by reason of the want of opportunity to sin; but if any important or frequent opportunities present themselves, then filling earth and sea to its extremest boundaries with unspeakable wickedness, and leaving nothing whether great or small uninjured, they overturn and destroy everything at one blow. (43) For as the power of fire is quiet when it has no fuel, but when there are proper materials it blazes up so also all the powers which have reference to the virtue or vice of the soul are extinguished by want of opportunity, as I have said before, but are kindled by a favourable occasion and a happy concurrence of circumstances.

X. (44) Why then have I said these things, except with the object of teaching that Ham the son of Noah, is the name of wickedness in a state of inactivity, but his grandson, Canaan, is the name of wickedness in a state of motion? For Ham being interpreted, means "warm," but Canaan means "commotion;" (45) and warm in a body implies fever, but in the soul it implies wickedness. For as I suppose disease is the foundation of fever, not only of a part but of the whole body; so also wickedness is a disease of the whole soul. But at one time it is in a state of tranquillity, and at another in motion; now he calls its motion commotion *(salos)*, which in the Hebrew language is called Canaan. (46) But no lawgiver ever affixes a punishment to wicked men while in a state of inaction, but only when they are in a state of motion and practise actions in accordance with injustice, just as a moderate man would not care about killing a snake if it were not about to bite him. For we must leave out of the question, that natural cruelty of soul which in the case of some persons delights to deal destruction upon everything.

(47) Very appropriately, therefore, the just man will appear to have launched his curses against his grandson, Canaan. But I have used the expression "will appear," because in effect he is cursing his son Ham through the medium of Canaan; for Ham being moved to commit sin does himself become Canaan. For there is one subject, namely wickedness, of which one kind is contemplated in a stationary condition, and the other in motion.

But a stationary condition is antecedent to motion, so that that which is moved appears to have the relation of offspring to that which is stationary. (48) In reference to which fact Canaan is, according to the order of nature, described as the son of Ham; commotion as the offspring of tranquillity, in order that the statement made in another passage may be true, namely, "visiting the iniquities of the fathers upon the sons to the third and fourth generations." [11] For against these accomplishments of, and as it were, children of thoughts, punishments advance which await them, but which will hardly seize upon these thoughts which are not carried out by any action, and which consequently escape accusation.

(49) On this account, therefore, in the law concerning leprosy the great and wise Moses speaks of motion and its further progress and diffusion as unclean, but of tranquillity as pure. For he says, "If it be diffused over the skin the priest shall pronounce him polluted. But if the bright colour remain in its place and be not diffused, he shall pronounce him clean." [12] So that, as tranquillity is an abiding of evils and of the passions within the soul (for that is what is intimated by leprosy), it is not liable to reproach; but its motion and progress are of necessity open to accusation. (50) There is also something like this in the sacred scriptures, where the account of the creation of the universe is given and it is expressed more distinctly. For it is said to the wicked man, "O thou man, thou hast sinned. Cease to sin:" [13] because sin is condemned with reference to its being in motion and energising according to wickedness: but tranquillity is free from blame, and is even preservative because of its remaining stationary and inactive.

XI. (51) These things then, I imagine, have now been sufficiently discussed. Let us now examine the affair of the curses, and see what the case is with respect to them: "Cursed," says the scripture, "is Canaan the child; he shall be a servant to his brethren. Blessed be the Lord God of Shem; and Canaan shall be a servant unto them." (52) We said some time ago that Shem bears the same name as good, being called not by a special name, but the whole genus of good is his name; in reference to which, the good is the only thing to be named, the only thing worthy of a good report and of glory; as, on the other hand, evil is the thing with no good report and with an evil fame.

(53) Of what prayer then does he think the man worthy who has received a share of the nature of good? Surely of some new and extraordinary benediction, which no mortal is able to act up to, and from which, almost as from the ocean itself,

[11] Exodus 20:5.
[12] Leviticus 13:12.
[13] Genesis 4:7.

abundant and unceasing springs of good things do gush out ever rising high and overflowing; for he calls the Lord and God of the world and of all the things in it, by a particular grace, the private especial God of Shem. (54) And see now how this exceeds all imaginable excess; for the man of whom such a thing is said, almost receives equal honour with the world; for when the same being cares for and superintends them both, it follows of necessity that the two things so superintended must be of equal honour and importance; (55) may we not even say that these gifts are poured out upon him abundantly? For the master and benefactor of the world, perceptible by the external senses, is called by these appellations, Lord and God; but of the Good which is appreciable by the intellect, he is merely called the saviour and benefactor, not the master or lord; for what is wise is dearer to God than what is slavish. In reference to which principle he speaks clearly in the case of Abraham, saying, "I will not hide from Abraham who is dear to me."[14] (56) But the man who has this inheritance has advanced beyond the bounds of human happiness; for he alone is nobly born, inasmuch as he has God attributed to him as his father, and being his adopted only son, he is not rich, but all-wealthy, dwelling luxuriously in abundance and among genuine good things, not worn out by age, but in a state of vigour and continual renewal, such that besides them there is no good; (57) being a man not of fair reputation, but of exceeding glory and receiving praise, not of that bastard sort which proceeds from flattery, but that which is founded on truth.

He is the only king, having received from the Ruler of all things an irresistible power, without a rival, and authority over all things. He is the only free man, being emancipated from that most grievous mistress, vain opinion, whom God who makes free has torn down, since she was very proud, from her citadel on high, and has utterly destroyed.

(58) What then ought a man to do who has been thought worthy of such great and such exceeding blessings, all united in his case? What ought he to do, except requite his benefactor with words, and hymns, and songs of praise? This is as it seems what is obscurely intimated to him in the words, "Blessed is the Lord God of Shem;"[15] since it becomes him who has received the inheritance of God to bless and praise him, since this is the only requital that it is in his power to offer, and since he is utterly unable by any means whatever to do anything further.

XIII. (59) This, then, is the prayer which Noah offers for Shem; let us now see what kind of prayer

it is that he puts forth for Japhet. He says, "May God make Japhet broad, and let him dwell in the tents of Shem, and Canaan shall be their servant." (60) The object of a man who thinks nothing beautiful but what is good is limited and contracted, for of all the innumerable guides which influence different men he is confined to one alone, namely, to the mind. But the object of a man who attributes good to three different kinds of things, dividing it as it has reference to the soul, and to the body, and to external things, is more extended, inasmuch as he cuts up the good into a number of small and dissimilar fragments; (61) on which account Noah very appropriately prays that breadth may be added to him, in order that he may be able to exercise the virtues of the soul, prudence, and temperance, and all the others, and likewise the vigorous health and acute perceptions of the body, strength and vigour, and the other qualities akin to them; and also the external advantages which contribute to wealth and glory, and to the enjoyment and use of necessary pleasures.

XIII. (62) Thus much we may say concerning breadth. We must now consider who it is who Noah prays may dwell in the tents of Shem, for he does not say very clearly. One may affirm that he means the Lord of the universe; for what more suitable and beautiful abode in all creation could be found for God beyond a soul completely purified, and thinking nothing beautiful but what is good, and looking upon all things, which are usually held in estimation among men, in the light of subjects and body-guards of that one thing, good? (63) But God is said to dwell in a house, not as in respect of place (for he contains everything and is contained by nothing), but as in a most especial degree exerting his providence and care in favour of that place; for it follows inevitably in the case of every one who is master of a house that he has a particular care for that house.

(64) But let every one, on whom the love of God has showered good things, pray to God that he may have as a dweller within him the Ruler of all things, who will raise this small house, the mind, to a great height above the earth, and will connect it with the bounds of heaven. (65) And what is said in the scriptures appears to coincide with this, for Shem is planted as a root of excellence and virtue; and from this root there sprang up a tree bringing forth good fruit, namely, Abraham, of whom the self-instructed and self-teaching offspring, Isaac, was the fruit, by whom again the virtues which are displayed in labour are sown, the practiser of which is Jacob, the man trained and exercised in wrestling with the passions, having the admonitions of angels for his gymnastic trainers. (66) He is the prince of the twelve tribes, which the scriptures call the "kingdom and priesthood

of God." [16] in reference to their agreement with the original author of their race, Shem, in whose house it was prayed that God might dwell; for a kingdom is the house of a king, being truly sacred, and the only house free from danger of being plundered. (67) Perhaps, indeed, the prayer has reference also to Japhet, that he also may make his abode in the dwellings of Shem, for it is well to pray for one who thinks the good things of the body and external advantages the only goods, that he may come over to the only true good, that of the soul, and may not wander from true opinions all his life, thinking advantages which are common to the most accursed and worst of men, such as health, and riches, and all such things as those, goods, when nature has not given any portion of what is really good to any wicked man; for, by its own nature, what is good can have no participation in what is bad.

(68) On this account good is treasured up in the soul alone, in the beauty of which no foolish man has any share. Now, the original progenitor of a virtuous posterity has written that he prayed for this for some of his friends, saying, "Return unto me," [17] in order that, returning to adopt his opinions, and looking upon good alone as beautiful, he might pass by the reports of mistaken men as to the nature of good.

Let him, then, dwell in the house of him who says that the good of the soul is the only beautiful thing; passing by and repudiating the abodes of others, by whom corporeal and external advantages are held in honour. (69) And very appropriately has he assigned the fool to be a slave to those who cultivate virtue, that, either by passing under a better government he may live a better life, or if he continue in evil doing he may easily be punished by the independent authority of his masters.

---

[16]Exodus 19:6.

[17]Genesis 49:22.

ON THE CONFUSION OF TONGUES†

(De Confusione Linguarum)

I. (1) As to the preceding topics, what has been already said will be sufficient. We might next proceed to consider, and that in no slight or cursory manner, the philosophical account which Moses gives us of the confusion of languages; for he speaks in the following manner: "And all the earth had one pronunciation, and there was one language among all men. And it came to pass, as they were moving from the east, that they found a plain in the land of Shinar, and dwelt there. And one man said to his neighbour, Come, let us make bricks, and let us burn them with fire; and they had bricks for stone, and asphalt for mortar. And they said, Come, let us build ourselves a city, and a tower whose head shall reach to heaven; and let us make for ourselves a name, before we are scattered over the face of all the earth. And the Lord came down to see the city, and the tower, which the sons of men had builded. And the Lord said, Behold, all mankind is one race, and there is but one language among them all; and they have begun to do this thing, and now there will not fail unto them anything of all the things which they desire to do. Come, let us go down and confuse their language there, so that each may not understand the voice of his neighbour. And the Lord scattered them from thence over the face of all the earth, and they desisted from building the city, and the tower. On this account, the name of it was called Confusion, because there the Lord confused the languages of all the earth, and from thence the Lord scattered them over the face of all the earth."[1]

II. (2) Those who are discontented at the constitution under which their fathers have lived, being always eager to blame and to accuse the laws, being impious men, use these and similar instances as foundations for their impiety, saying, "Are ye even now speaking boastfully concerning your precepts, as if they contained the rules of truth itself? For, behold, the books which you call the sacred scriptures do also contain fables, at which you are accustomed to laugh, when you hear others relating to them." (3) And what is the use of devoting our leisure to collecting the fables interspersed in so many places throughout the history of the giving of the law, as if we had especial leisure for the consideration of calumnies, and as if it were not better to attend merely to what is under our hands and before us? (4) Certainly, this one fable resembles that which is composed about the Aloadae, who the greatest and most glorious of all poets, Homer, says, had in contemplation to heap the three loftiest mountains on one another, and to build them into one mass, hoping that by this means there would be a road for them, as they were desirous to mount up to heaven, and that by these mountains it would be easy for them to be raised to the height of the sky. And the verses of Homer on this subject are these:—

> High on Olympus' top they strove to raise
> Gigantic Ossa; and on Ossa's heights
> To place the leafy Pelion, that heaven
> Might thus become accessible.

But Olympus and Ossa and Pelion are the names of mountains. (5) But instead of these mountains the lawgiver represents a tower as having been built by these men, who, out of ignorance and wicked ambition, were desirous to reach the heaven. Every alienation of mind, then, is grievous; for even if every portion of the whole earth could be built over, a slight foundation is being first laid, and then if a superstructure could be raised in the fashion of a single pillar, it would still be an enormous distance removed from the heavenly sphere, and above all would it be so according to the tenets of those curious philosophers who have affirmed that the earth is the centre of the universe.

III. (6) And there is also another story akin to this, related by the deviser of fables, concerning the sameness of language existing among animals: for they say that formerly, all the animals in the world, whether land animals, or aquatic ones, or winged ones, had but one language, and that, just as among men Greeks speak the same language as Greeks, and the present race of barbarians speaks the same language as barbarians, exactly in the same manner every animal was able to converse with every other animal with which it might meet, and with which it did anything, or from which it suffered anything, so that they sympathised with one another at their mutual misfortunes, and rejoiced whenever any of them met with any good fortune; (7) for they could impart their pleasures and their annoyances to one another by their sameness of language, so that they felt pleasure together and pain together; and this similarity of manners and union of feelings lasted, until being

---

† Yonge's title, *A Treatise on the Confusion of Languages*.
[1] Genesis 11:1.

sated with the great abundance of good things which they enjoyed, as often happens, they were at last drawn on to a desire of what was unattainable, and even sent an embassy to treat for immortality, requesting to be released from old age, and to be always endowed with the vigour of youth, saying, that already one animal of their body, and that a reptile, the serpent, had received this gift; for he, having put off old age, was allowed again to grow young; and that it was absurd for the more important animals to be left behind by an inferior one, or for their whole body to be distanced by one. (8) However, they suffered the punishment suitable to their audacity, for they immediately were separated in their language, so that, from that time forth, they have not been able to understand one another, by reason of the difference in the dialects into which the one common language of them all had been divided.

IV. (9) But he who brings his account nearer the truth, has distinguished between the rational and irrational animals, so that he testifies that identity of language belongs to men alone: and this also, as they say, is a fabulous story. And indeed they affirm, that the separation of language into an infinite variety of dialects, which Moses calls the confusion of tongues, was effected as a remedy for sins, in order that men might not be able to cooperate in common for deeds of wickedness through understanding one another; and that they might not, when they were in a manner deprived of all means of communication with one another, be able with united energies to apply themselves to the same actions. (10) But this precaution does not appear to have turned out of any use; for since that time, though men have been separated into different nations, and have no longer used one language, nevertheless, land and sea have been repeatedly filled with unspeakable evils.

For it was not the languages which were the causes of men's uniting for evil objects, but the emulation and rivalry of their souls in wrong-doing. (11) For even those who have had their tongues cut out can intimate what they wish by nods and looks, and other positions and motions of the body, not less than by a distinct utterance of words. And besides this consideration, there is the fact that, very often, one nation by itself, having not merely one language, but one code of laws, and one system of manners, has arrived at such a pitch of iniquity that, as to a superfluity of wickedness, it may counterbalance the sins of all the men in the world put together. (12) And again, through ignorance of foreign languages, many persons, having no foreknowledge of the future, have been anticipated and overwhelmed by those who were plotting against them; as, on the other hand, by knowledge of foreign languages, men have been able to repel fears and dangers with which they have been threatened; so that a community of language is an advan-

tageous thing rather than an injurious one: since, even at the present day, nothing contributes so greatly to the safety and protection of the people of each country, and particularly of the natives, as their being of one language. (13) For if a man has learnt many dialects, he immediately is looked upon with consideration and respect by those who are also acquainted with them, as being already a friendly person, and contributing no small introduction and means of friendship by reason of his familiarity with words which they too understand; which familiarity very commonly imparts a feeling of security, that one is not likely to suffer any great evil at the hands of such a man. Why, then, did God remove sameness of language from among men as a cause of evils, when it seems it should rather have been established as a most useful thing?

V. (14) Those, then, who put these things together, and cavil at them, and raise malicious objections, will be easily refuted separately by those who can produce ready solutions of all such questions as arise from the plain words of the law, arguing in a spirit far from contentious, and not encountering them by sophisms drawn from any other source, but following the connection of natural consequences, which does not permit them to stumble, but which easily puts aside any impediments that arise, so that the course of their arguments proceeds without any interruption or mishap.

(15) We say then that by the expression, that "all the earth had but one pronunciation and one language," is intimated a symphony of great and unspeakable evils, which cities have inflicted upon cities, nations upon nations, and countries upon countries, and through which men not only wrong one another, but also behave with impiety towards God, and yet these things are the iniquities if many; but let us consider the ineffable multitude of evils which proceed from each individual man, and especially when he is under the influence of that ill-timed, and inharmonious, and unmusical agreement.

VI. (16) Now who is there who does not know the great influence of fortune, when men, in addition to the diseases or mutilations of the body, are attacked also by poverty and want of reputation? And again, when these things are further united to diseases of the soul, in consequence of moody melancholy, driving men beside themselves, or of extreme old age, or of any other severe calamity which presses upon them? (17) For even one of these evils here mentioned by itself, when it opposes a man with violence, is sufficient to overthrow and to crush even one who is very proud and haughty; but when all these evils, to wit, the evils of the body, and the evils of the soul, and external misfortunes, all come together as one if in one regular battalion, moving by previous arrangement at the same time, so as to attack him in the body, what resolution is there which they will not overpower? For when the guards are slain, it follows of necessity that he who relies on his guards must fall. (18) Now the guards of his body are wealth, glory, and honours, which set it up and raise it on high, and make it proud, just as the contrary things, dishonour, want of reputation, and poverty, throw it down like so many enemies.

(19) Again, the body-guards of the soul are hearing, and seeing, and smelling, and taste, and the whole band of the outward senses, and also health, and strength, and vigour, and energy. For the mind, when walking among the living and in the company of these things, as between well-fortified boundaries firmly standing and solidly established, triumphs and rejoices, meeting with no hindrance on any side to prevent it from exerting its own impulses, but having its road in every direction easy, and level, and open, and easy to be travelled. (20) But the things which are set in opposition and hostility to these guards are mutilation of the organs of the outward senses, and disease, as I have said before, by which the mind is often precipitated into disaster; and these things are all the results of fortune, very grievous and intrinsically miserable, but still, if compared with those which are brought on ourselves by our own deliberate will, they are far lighter.

VII. (21) Let us now again in its turn consider what is the united body of evils voluntarily incurred. Our souls being capable of being divided into three divisions, one division is said to have fallen to the lot of the mind and of reason, the second to passion, and the third to appetite; and each separate one of these has its own peculiar evils, and also they have all common and mutual diseases. Since the mind reaps the harvest which folly, and cowardice, and intemperance, and injustice sow; and passion brings forth frantic and insane strife and conflict, and all the other numerous evils with which it is pregnant; and appetite disseminates in every direction the impetuous and fickle loves of youth which descend upon every object, animate or inanimate, which it chances to meet with. (22) For then, as if in any vessel, the sailors, and the passengers, and the pilots, had all, under the influence of insanity, agreed to destroy it, those who have joined in the plot against it are none the less involved in the same destruction.

For the heaviest of all evils, and almost the only one that is incurable, is the unanimous energy of all the parts of the soul agreeing to commit sin, not one of the parts being able to act with soundness (just as is the case in an evil affecting the whole people), so as to heal those that are sick; but even the physicians being diseased as well as their patients, whom the pestilential disease has overwhelmed and weighs down under a confessed calamity.

(23) Of this great evil, that great deluge described by the lawgiver is an image; for the torrents from heaven continually pouring down cataracts of wickedness itself with impetuous violence, and springs from the ground (by which I mean the body) continually bursting up and pouring forth streams of every passion in great numbers and vast size, which, uniting and being mingled in the same stream with the other waters, are thrown into confusion, and overthrow the whole region of the soul which has received them with incessant eddies and whirlpools. (24) "For," says Moses, "the Lord God, seeing that the wickedness of men was multiplied upon the earth, and that every one did think continually in his heart nothing but evil all his days, determined to punish man" (and here by man I understand the mind, together with all the reptiles and the winged creatures, and all the rest of the multitude of wild animals which surround him), by reason of his incurable wickedness; and the punishment which God decided upon was the deluge. (25) For there was unbounded freedom in sinning, and unlimited licence in doing wrong, no one hindering it, but all restraints being shamelessly broken down in such a way that there was no fear left behind to restrain those who were thoroughly ready to snatch at abundant supplies for enjoyment of every kind. And may we not say that this was natural? For it was not only one portion of the soul which was corrupted in such a way that it could still be preserved by the sound condition of the other parts; but there was no part whatever of it which was left free from disease or from corruption. For the incorruptible Judge, says Moses, seeing that every thought of man's heart (not one single idea by itself) was evil continually, inflicted upon him a deserved punishment.

VIII. (26) These are they who "made a treaty with one another in the valley of Salt."[2] For the region of the vices and of the passions is a hollow valley, rough, and full of ravines; truly salt, and producing bitter pains; and their treaty, as one that was not worthy of being confirmed by any oath or by any libation, the wise Abraham, who knew the character of it, annulled. For it is said in the scripture that, "All these men made a treaty at the valley of Salt, that is the sea of Salt." (27) Do you not perceive that they who are barren of wisdom and blinded as to the intellect which it would be natural to expect should be sharp-sighted, having the name of Sodomites from their real character," did, with all their people united together, from young to old, surround the house in a circle"[3] (that is to say, the house of the soul), in order to pollute and contaminate those strangers from a foreign land, who had been received in hospitality,

---

[2] Genesis 14:3.
[3] Genesis 19:4.

namely, sacred and holy reasons, the guards and defenders of the soul; no one whatever attempting either to resist those wrong doers, or to avoid doing wrong himself? (28) For Moses does not speak of some as having consented and of others having stood aloof; but, as he says, "The whole people surrounded the house all together, both old and young," having entered into a conspiracy against all those holy actions and words which it is customary to call angels.

IX. (29) But Moses, the prophet of God, will meet them and check them, though they come on with exceeding boldness; even though, placing in the front him who is the boldest and the most forward and able speaker among them as their king, namely speech, they rush on with one impulse, hoping to increase their strength as they go on, and overflowing like a river; "For behold," says Moses, "the king of Egypt is coming to the water; but do thou go to meet him, and stand on the bank of the river."[4] (30) Therefore the wicked man goes forth to the stream of iniquities and passions, and all collected evils, which are here likened to water; but the wise man first obtains from God, who always stands firm, an honour akin to his undeviating, and in all respects and under all circumstances, unchangeable power; for we read in the scripture, (31) "But do thou stand here with me,[5] that having laid aside doubt and vacillation, the dispositions of an infirm soul, he may put on that most steadfast and trustworthy disposition, faith. In the next place, even while standing still, he (which seems a most extraordinary thing) goes forward to meet him; for it is said to him, "Thou shalt stand meeting him," and yet to go to meet is a part of motion, while to stand still is regarded as characteristic of tranquillity.

(32) But the prophet does not here say things which are inconsistent, but rather such as are exceedingly in accordance with nature; for the man whose mind is naturally disposed to be tranquil, and is established undeviatingly, must necessarily be at variance with all those who delight in disorder and confusion, and who by artificial storms seek to disturb him who is capable of enjoying tranquillity.

X. (33) It is very appropriately said that the meeting took place on the bank of the river; but the banks are also called the lips, and the lips are the boundaries of the mouth, and are a sort of fence to the tongue, through which the stream of discourse is borne, when it begins to be uttered; (34) but those who hate virtue and who love learning, use speech as their ally for the exposition of doctrines which are disapproved; and again, on the other hand, virtuous men employ it for the refuta-

tion of such doctrines, and for establishing the irresistible strength of the better and true wisdom. (35) When then, after having had recourse to every expedient of contentious doctrines, men are destroyed, being overwhelmed by the opposing violence of contrary arguments, then the wise man will very justly and suitably establish a most sacred chorus, and melodiously sing a triumphal song; (36) "For," says Moses, "Israel saw the Egyptians," not dead in any other place, but "on the bank (cheilos) of the river;"[6] meaning here by death, not the separation of the soul from the body, but the impetuous onset of unholy doctrines and assertions, which men utter by the mouth, and tongue, and the other organs of speech.

(37) But the death of speech is silence, not that silence which well-bred people cultivate, making it a symbol of modesty—for this silence is itself a faculty and a sister of that one which is developed in speech, arranging what is to be said with reference to time—but that silence which the sick and the weary against their will endure, on account of the strength of their antagonists, because they cannot find any handle to answer them; (38) for whatever they touch slips away from them, and whatever thing they seek to take their stand on does not remain, so that they of necessity fall before they stand, like that hydrostatic machine called the helix; for in the middle of that engine there are some steps, which the husbandman when he desires to water his fields mounts up upon, but is rolled round of necessity; and in order to avoid falling he is continually catching at the nearest firm thing that he can lay his hands on, which he takes hold of and so supports his whole body; for instead of his hands he uses his feet, and instead of his feet he uses his hands; for he stands on his hands, by means of which, actions are usually done, and he acts with his feet on which it is natural to stand.

XI. (39) But many, who are not able vigorously to refute the plausible inventions of the sophists, because they have not very much practised discussion by reason of their continued application to action, having taken refuge in the alliance of the only wise Being, and have besought him to become their defender. As one of the friends of Moses, when praying, says in his hymns, "Let the treacherous lips become mute;"[7] and how can they become mute if they are not curbed by the only being who has speech itself as his subject? (40) We must therefore flee, without ever turning back, from all associations entered into for the purposes of sin; but the alliance made with the companions of wisdom and knowledge must be confirmed. (41) In reference to which I admire those who say, "We are all one man's sons, we are

---

[4]Exodus 7:15.
[5]Deuteronomy 5:31.

[6]Exodus 14:30.
[7]Psalm 30:19.

men of peace,"[8] because of their well-adapted agreement; since how, I should say, could you, O excellent men, avoid being grieved at war, and delighted in peace, being the sons of one and the same father, and he not mortal but immortal, the man of God, who being the reason of the everlasting God, is of necessity himself also immortal?

(42) For they who make out many beginnings of the origin of the soul, being devoted to the evil which is called polytheism, and turning each individual of them, to the honour of different beings, having caused great confusion and dissension both at home and abroad, from the beginning of their birth to the end of their life, filling life with irreconcilable quarrels; (43) but they who rejoice in one kind alone, and who honour one as their father, namely right reason, admiring the well-arranged and all-musical harmony of the virtues, live a tranquil and peaceful life, not an inactive and ignoble one, as some persons think, but one of great manliness, and sharpened, and vigorous against those who endeavour to break the confederacy which they have formed, and who are always studying to bring about a violation of the oaths which have been taken; for it has come to pass that the men of peace have become men of war, sitting down to attack and to oppose them who seek to overturn the firmness of the soul.

XII. (44) And there is testimony in support of this assertion of mine; first of all, in the disposition of every lover of virtue which acknowledges these inclinations; and secondly, in that comrade of the band of the prophets, who being inspired with a sacred frenzy, spoke thus, "O my mother, how hast thou brought me forth, a man of war, and a man of disquietude to all the earth! I have not benefited them, and they have not benefited me; nor is my strength free from their curses."[9] (45) But is not every wise man of necessity an irreconcilable enemy to all wicked men, not indeed using the apparatus of triremes or warlike engines, or arms, or soldiers, for his defence, but reasons? (46) For when he sees war stirred up in the midst of tranquil peace, so as to be continued and incessant among all men, both public and private, not existing only among nations and countries, and cities and villages, but also in every house, and between each particular individual; who is there who does not reproach and admonish and seek to correct the foolish men whom he sees, and not by day only, but also by night, his soul being unable to remain tranquil by reason of the hatred of wickedness implanted in his nature?

(47) For they do in peace every thing that is done in war; they plunder, they ravage, they drag

into slavery, they carry off booty, they lay waste, they behave insolently, they assault, they destroy, they pollute, they murder treacherously, they murder openly if they are the more powerful; (48) for every one of them, proposing to himself riches or glory as his object, aims all the actions of his life as so many arrows at it, and neglects equality, and pursues inequality, and repudiates associations, and labours to acquire to himself all the possessions together properly belonging to every one; he is a misanthrope and a hater of all his fellows, making a hypocritical pretence of benevolence, being a companion of a bastard kind of flattery, an enemy of genuine friendship, a foe to truth, a champion of falsehood, slow to do good, swift to do injury, very ready to calumniate, very slow to defend, clever at deceiving, most perjured, most faithless, a slave of anger, yielding to pleasure, a guardian of all that is evil, a destroyer of all that is good.

XIII. (49) These and other similar gifts are the most desirable treasures of peace, that blessing so celebrated and so admired, which the mind of each individual among the foolish men sets up for itself as an image, and admires and worships; at whom, very naturally, every wise man is grieved, and is accustomed to say to his mother and nurse, wisdom, "O mother, what a person hast thou brought me forth!" not in strength of body but in energy and courage, a determined hater of wickedness, a man of disquietude and battle, by nature peaceful, and, on this very account, an enemy to those who pollute the desirable beauty of peace. (50) "I have done no good to them, nor have they done any good to me;" nor have they even derived any advantage from my good things, nor have I from their evil things; but according to the word of Moses, "I have received no desirable thing from any of them,"[10] inasmuch as I look upon as exceedingly pernicious every object of their desire, which they treasure up in their hearts as the greatest possible advantage; (51) "Nor has my strength failed by reason of the curses which they laid upon me;"[11] but embracing the divine doctrines with my most earnest power, I was not wearied so as to give up, but rather I vigorously reproached those who cursed me from their hearts.

(52) For God made us to be a contradiction to our neighbours, as is said in my hymns, meaning all of us who aim at right reason: but are not all those people naturally found of contradiction who have a zeal for knowledge and virtue, being always at variance with the neighbours of their soul, reproving the pleasures which live in union with them, and reproving the appetites which have the same abode, and looking morosely at acts of cow-

---

[8]Genesis 42:11.
[9]Jeremiah 15:10.

[10]Numbers 16:15.
[11]Psalm 79:7.

ardice and fear, and the whole body of passions and vices?

Reproving then every outward sense, the eyes for what they saw, and the ears for what they heard, and the sense of smell for the smells that presented themselves to it, the taste for the flavours which were subjected to it, and moreover the touch for its various powers developed in the body, with reference to the peculiarities which come under its notice; and even uttered speech for the matters which it may have chosen to discuss; (53) for what the outward sense has perceived, or how it has done so, or why, or what speech has uttered, or how or why, or in what manner, and how and why passion has disposed men, it is worth while to investigate in no superficial manner, and to examine each of the errors into which they fall; (54) but he who contradicts none of these things, but who assents to every one of them in succession, without being aware of it, is deceiving himself, and building up troublesome neighbours for his soul, which he had better have as subjects than as rulers; for as rulers they will do him manifold and great injury, since folly reigns among them; but as subjects they will serve him obediently in suitable matters, and will not at all raise their heads in arrogance, as they will if they are rulers.

(55) Thus, indeed, while some are learning to be subjects, and others are obtaining authority, not by knowledge only but also by power, all the body-guards and champions of the soul, that is to say, its reasonings will keep them in order, and coming to that which is most important among them will say, "Thy children have taken the sum of the men that are warriors among us, and there is not one of them who has disagreed;"[12] but like musical instruments, skilfully tuned in all their tones, so we sound in harmony in all our explanations, neither uttering any word nor doing any action which shall be unmelodious or discordant, that we may by the contrast show, that the other company of unlettered men is, in all respects, voiceless and dead, and an object of deserved ridicule, namely, that nourishment of the corporeal parts, Midian, and that his offspring too, that mass of skins, whose name is Belphegor, is asleep; (56) "for we are of the race of picked men of Israel, that sees God, of whom not one has disagreed;"[13] that the instrument of the universe, the whole world, may be melodiously sounded in musical harmony.

(57) On this account Moses says that the "reward of peace"[14] was given to the very warlike reason, which is called Phinehas; because, hav-

ing received a zeal for virtue, and having taken up war against vice, he cut up the whole of generation; and in the second place, to all those who are willing, after a careful examination and investigation, using their eyes in preference to their ears as a trustworthy witness, to believe that the human race is full of infidelity, depending solely on opinion. (58) Therefore, the afore-mentioned agreement is admirable; and most admirable of all is that common one which exceeds all the harmonies of all the others, according to which the whole people is represented as saying with one accord, "All the things which God has spoken, we will obey and do."[15] (59) For these men no longer obey reason as their ruler, but God, the governor of the universe, by whom they are assisted so as to display their energies in actions rather than in words. For when they hear of others doing such and such things, these men, which is a thing most contrary to what one would expect, say that, from some inspiration of God, they will act first and obey afterwards; in order that they may seem to have advanced to good actions, not in consequence of instruction and admonition, but by their own spontaneous and self-taught mind. And then, when they have accomplished these actions, they say that they will obey in order that they may form an opinion of what they have done, as to whether their actions are consistent with the divine injunctions and the sacred admonitions of scripture.

XIV. (60) But those who conspired to commit injustice, he says, "having come from the east, found a plain in the land of Shinar, and dwelt there;"[16] speaking most strictly in accordance with nature. For there is a twofold kind of dawning in the soul, the one of a better sort, the other of a worse. That is the better sort, when the light of the virtues shines forth like the beams of the sun; and that is the worse kind, when they are overshadowed, and the vices show forth. (61) Now, the following is an example of the former kind: "And God planted a paradise in Eden, toward the east,"[17] not of terrestrial but of celestial plants, which the planter caused to spring up from the incorporeal light which exists around him, in such a way as to be for ever inextinguishable.

(62) I have also heard of one of the companions of Moses having uttered such a speech as this: "Behold, a man whose name is the East!"[18] A very novel appellation indeed, if you consider it as spoken of a man who is compounded of body and soul; but if you look upon it as applied to that incorporeal being who in no respect differs from the divine image, you will then agree that the name

---

[12]Numbers 31:49.
[13]Exodus 24:11.
[14]Numbers 25:12.

[15]Deuteronomy 5:27.
[16]Genesis 11:2.
[17]Genesis 2:8.
[18]Zechariah 6:12.

of the east has been given to him with great felicity. (63) For the Father of the universe has
caused him to spring up as the eldest son, whom,
in another passage, he calls the firstborn; and he
who is thus born, imitating the ways of his father,
has formed such and such species, looking to his
archetypal patterns.

XV. (64) But an example of the worse kind of
dawning is afforded by the words used by the man
who was willing "to curse the people who were
blessed by God."[19] For he also is represented as
dwelling in the east. And this dawning, having the
same name as the former one, has nevertheless
an opposite nature to it, and is continually at war
with it. (65) For Balaam says, "Balak sent for me
out of Mesopotamia, from the mountains of the
east, saying, Come, curse me the people whom
God doth not curse." But the name of Balak, being
interpreted means, "void of sense;" a very felicitous name. For how can it be otherwise than
shocking to hope to deceive the living God, and
to turn aside his most enduring and firmly established counsels by the sophistical devices of men?
(66) On this account he is represented as living
in Mesopotamia, for his mind is overwhelmed as
in the middle of the depth of the river, and is not
able to emerge and to swim away. And this condition is the dawning of folly and the setting of
sound reason.

(67) They, then, who are tuned in an inharmonious symphony are said to be moved from the
east. Is this, then, the east according to wickedness? But the dawning in accordance with virtue
is described as a complete separation, and the
motion from the dawning according to vice is a
united one, as when the hands are moved, not separately and disjunctively, but in a certain harmony
and connection with the whole body. (68) For folly
is to the wicked man the beginning of his energy
in the works which are contrary to nature, that
is, of his approach to the region of wickedness.
But all those who have quitted the region of virtue, and have set forth to go over to folly, have
found a most appropriate place in which they dwell,
which is called in the Hebrew language Shinar. And
Shinar in Greek, is called "shaking;" (69) for the
whole life of the wicked is shaken, and agitated,
and torn to pieces, being always kept in a state
of commotion and confusion, and having no trace
of any genuine good laid up in itself. For as everything which is not held together by close union,
falls out of what is violently shaken, in the very
same manner, it seems to me, that the soul is
shaken of every man who associates with others
for the purpose of doing wrong; for he casts away
every appearance of good, so that no shadow or
image of it ever appears.

XVI. (70) Accordingly, the body-loving race of
the Egyptians is represented as fleeing, not from
the water, but "under the water," that is to say,
beneath the impetuous speed of the passions. And
when it has once placed itself under the power of
the passions, it is shaken and agitated; it casts away
the stable and peaceable qualities of virtue, and
takes up in their stead the turbulent and confused
character of wickedness; for it is said that "God
shook the Egyptians in the middle of the sea, fleeing under the water."[20] (71) These are they who
neither knew Joseph—the diversified pride of life—
but who, having their sins revealed, have not
received any trace, or shade, or image of goodness and excellence. (72) For, says Moses,
"Another king arose over the Egyptians who knew
not Joseph,"[21] the latest and most modern good
perceptible by the outward senses, who utterly
destroyed not only the perfections but even all
improvements, and all the energy which can be
exerted by the sight, and all the teaching which
can be implanted by means of the hearing, saying,
"Come, curse me Jacob; and come, defy Israel for
me;"[22] an expression which is equivalent to,
Destroy both these things, the sight and the hearing of the soul, that it may neither see nor hear
any true and genuine good thing; for Israel is the
emblem of seeing and Jacob of hearing. (73) Accordingly the mind of such persons rejects the
nature of good, being in some degree shaken; and,
on the other hand, the mind of good persons, setting up a claim to the unmingled and unalloyed ideas
of good things, shakes off and discards all that
is evil.

(74) Consider, therefore, what the practiser
of virtue says: "Take up the foreign gods that are
among you from out of the midst of you, and purify yourselves, and change your garments, and
rise up and let us go to Bethel;"[23] in order that,
even if Laban should demand a power of examining, the images might not be found in his whole
house, but only such things as have a real subsistence and essence, being fixed like pillars in
the mind of the wise man, which the self-taught offspring Isaac has received as his inheritance; for he
alone receives his father's substance as his
inheritance."[24]

XVII. (75) And take notice that Moses does
not say that they came unto a plain in which they
remain, but that they "found' one, having searched
around in every direction, and having considered
what might be the most suitable region for folly;
for in reality every foolish man does not take from
another for himself, but he seeks for and finds evils,

[19]Numbers 23:7.

[20]Exodus 14:27.
[21]Exodus 1:8.
[22]Numbers 23:7.
[23]Genesis 35:2.
[24]Genesis 25:5.

not being content only with those which wicked nature proceeds towards of its own accord, but also adding thereto such perfect skill in evil as arises from constant practice in contriving wrong. (76) And I wish indeed that after he had remained there a brief time he had changed his abode; but even now he thinks fit to remain, for it is said that having found the plain they dwelt there; having settled there as if in their own country and not as if in a foreign land; for it would have been less trouble for men who had fallen in with wicked actions to look upon them as strange and foreign to them, and not to consider that they had any kindred or connection with them. For if they had looked upon themselves as sojourners among them, they would have changed their abode at a subsequent time, but now having settled fixedly among them they were likely to dwell there for ever.

(77) For this reason all the wise men mentioned in the books of Moses are represented as sojourners, for their souls are sent down from heaven upon earth as to a colony; and on account of their fondness for contemplation, and their love of learning, they are accustomed to migrate to the terrestrial nature. (78) Since therefore having taken up their abode among bodies, they behold all the mortal objects of the outward senses by their means, they then subsequently return back from thence to the place from which they set out at first, looking upon the heavenly country in which they have the rights of citizens as their native land, and as the earthly abode in which they dwell for a while as in a foreign land.

For to those who are sent to be the inhabitants of a colony, the country which has received them is in place of their original mother country; but still the land which has sent them forth remains to them as the house to which they desire to return. (79) Therefore, very naturally, Abraham says to the guardians of the dead and to the arrangers of mortal affairs, after he has forsaken that life which is only dead and the tomb, "I am a stranger and a sojourner among you,"[25] but ye are natives of the country, honouring the dust and earth more than the soul, thinking the name Ephron worthy of precedence, for Ephron, (80) being interpreted, means "a mound" and naturally, Jacob, the practiser of virtue, bewails his being a sojourner in the body, saying, "The days of the years of my life which I spend here as a sojourner have been few and evil; they have not come up to the days of my fathers which they spent as sojourners."[26] (81) But to him who was self-taught the following injunction of scripture was given, "Do not go down," says the scripture, "to Egypt," that is to say to passion; "but dwell in this land, land

which I will tell thee of,"[27] namely, in the incorporeal wisdom which cannot be pointed out to the eye; and be a sojourner in this land, the substance which can be pointed out and appreciated by the external sense. And this is said with a view to show, that the wise man is a sojourner in a foreign land, that is to say in the body perceptible by the outward senses, who dwells among the virtues appreciable by the intellect as in his native land, which virtues God utters as in no way differing from the divine word. (82) But Moses says, "I am a sojourner in a foreign land;" speaking with peculiar fitness, looking upon his abode in the body not only as foreign land, as sojourners do, but also as a land from which one ought to feel alienated, and never look upon it as one's home.

XVIII. (83) But the wicked man, desiring to exhibit the fact that identity of language, and the sameness of dialect does not consist more in names and common words than in his participation in iniquitous actions, begins to build a city and a tower as a citadel for sovereign wickedness; and he invites all his fellow revellers to partake in his enterprise, preparing beforehand abundance of suitable materials. (84) For, "Come," says he, "let us make bricks, and let us bake them in the fire," an expression equivalent to, Now we have all the parts of the soul mingled together and in a state of confusion, so that there is no species whatever the form of which is evident to be seen. (85) Therefore it will be consistent with these beginnings that, as we have assumed a certain essence destitute of all particular species; and of all distinctive qualities, and have also taken up with passion and vice, we should also divide it into suitable qualities, and keep on reducing the proximate to the ultimate species; and with a view to the more distinct comprehension of them, and also to this employment and enjoyment of them combined with experience, which appears to produce many pleasures and delights.

(86) Come, therefore, all ye reasonings of counsellors, in some way or the other to the assembly of the soul; come, all ye who meditate the destruction of justice and of all virtue, and let us consider carefully how we may attain to the end which we desire. (87) Now of success in this matter these will be the most established foundations: to give to things without form shape and character, and to distinguish each thing separately with distinct outlines, lest, if they become shaken and lame (though fixed on firm foundations,) and if they have assumed a connection with the nature of a quadrangular shape, (for this is a nature always unshaken), they may then, being established steadily like a building of bricks, support even those things which are built upon them.

[25] Genesis 23:4.
[26] Genesis 47:9.

[27] Genesis 26:9.

XIX. (88) Of such a structure as this every mind adverse to God, which we call the king of Egypt (that is to say of the body), is found to be the maker. For Moses represents the mind as rejoicing in the buildings made of brick; (89) for after some being or other made the two substances of water and earth to be the one dry and the other solid, and mingling the two together, for they were easily dissoluble and corruptible, made a third substance to be on the confines of the two, which is called clay, he has never ceased from dissecting this into small portions, giving its own appropriate figure to each of the fragments, in order that they might be very well compacted together, and very suitable to the objects for which they were intended. For in this way what was being made was sure to be very easily perfected.

(90) Imitating this work, those men who are wicked in their natures, when they mingle the irrational and extravagant impulses of the passions with the most grievous vices, are, in reality, dissecting that which has been combined into various species, and unhappy that they are fashioning them again and reducing them into shape, by means of which the blockade of the soul will be raised on high; these being, in fact, the divisions of the outward sense into seeing, and hearing, and taste, and smell, and touch. Passion again, is divided into pleasure, and appetite, and fear, and grief; and the universal genus of vices is divided into folly, and intemperance, and cowardice, and injustice, and all the other vices which are akin to or closely connected with them.

XX. (91) And before now some persons, even more excessively extravagant in wickedness than these, have not only prepared their own souls for such actions, but have also put a force upon those of a superior class and of the genus which is endowed with acuteness of vision, and have "compelled them to make bricks and to build strong cities"[28] for the mind, which has appeared to occupy the place of king, wishing to point out this fact, that what is good is the slave of what is evil, and that subjection to the passions is more powerful than tranquillity of soul, and prudence, and all virtue is, but, as it were, a subject of folly and all wickedness, so as of necessity to minister in all the matters which the master power enjoins; (92) for behold, says Moses, the most pure, and brilliant, and far-sighted eye of the soul, to which alone is permitted to behold God, by name Israel, being formerly bound in the corporeal nets of Egypt, endures severe commands, so as to be compelled to make bricks and all sorts of things of clay with the most grievous and intolerable labours, at which it is very naturally pained, and at which it groans, having laid up this, as it were,

to be its only treasure amid its evils, the power of bewailing its present distresses.

(93) For it is said, very correctly, that "the children of Israel groaned by reason of their tasks."[29] And what man in his senses is there who, if he saw the tasks of the generality of men, and the exceeding earnestness with which they labour at the pursuits to which they are accustomed to devote themselves, whether it be the acquisition of money, or glory, or the enjoyment of pleasure, would not be greatly concerned and cry out to God, the only Saviour, that he would lighten their labours, and pay a ransom and price for the salvation of the soul, so as to emancipate and deliver it?

(94) What, then, is the surest freedom? The service of the only wise God, as the scriptures testify, in which it is said, "Send forth the people, that they may serve me."[30] (95) But it is a peculiar property of those who serve the living God neither to regard the work of cup-bearers, or bakers, or cooks, or any other earthly employments, nor to trouble themselves about arranging or adorning their bodies like bricks, but to mount up with their reason to the height of heaven, having elected Moses, the type of the race which loves God, to be the guide of their path; (96) for then "they will see the place which is visible,"[31] on which the unchangeable and unalterable God stands; and the footstool beneath his feet, which is, as it were, a work of sapphire stone, and, as it were, a resemblance to the firmament of heaven, namely, the world perceptible by the outward senses, which he describes allegorically by these figures. (97) For it is very suitable for those who have made an association for the purpose of learning to desire to see him; and, if they are unable to do that, at least to see his image, the most sacred word, and, next to that, the most perfect work of all the things perceptible by the outward senses, namely, the world? For to philosophise is nothing else but to desire to see things accurately.

XXI. (98) But he says that the world perceptible to the outward senses is, as it were, the footstool of God on this account: first of all, that he may show that there is no efficient cause in the creatures; secondly, for the purpose of displaying that even the whole world has not a free and unrestrained spontaneous motion of its own, but God, the ruler of the universe, takes his stand upon it, regulating it and directing everything in a saving manner by the helm of his wisdom, using, in truth, neither hands nor feet, nor any other part whatever such as belongs to created objects; for God is not as man, but the reason why we at times rep-

---

[28] Exodus 1:11.

[29] Exodus 2:23.
[30] Exodus 8:1.
[31] Exodus 24:10.

resent him as such, for the sake of instruction, is because we are unable to advance out of ourselves, but derive our apprehension of the uncreate God from the circumstances with which we ourselves are surrounded.

(99) And it is very beautifully said by Moses, in the form of a parable, when he speaks of the world as if it resembled a brick; for the world appears to stand and to be firmly fixed like a brick in a house, as far as the vision of the sight of the outward senses can inform us, but it has a very swift motion, and one which is able to outstrip all particular motions. (100) For the eyes of our body look upon the appearance of the sun by day and of the moon by night as standing still, and yet who is there who does not know that the rapidity of movements of these two bodies is incomparable, since they go round the whole heaven in one day? Thus, indeed, the universal heaven itself also, while appearing to stand still, revolves in a circle; its movements being detected and comprehended by the invisible and more divine eye which is placed in our mind.

XXII. (101) And they are represented as baking the bricks in the fire, for the purpose of intimating by this symbolical expression that they are strengthened and hardened as to their vices and their passions by warm and most energetic reason, so that they can never be overthrown by the body-guards of wisdom, by whom engines for their defeat are being continually put in operation. (102) On which account we have this further statement also made, "Their brick was to them for stone;" for the weak and lax character of that impetuosity which is not in company with reason, when it is closely pressed and condensed so as to assume a nature capable of solidity and resistance, owes this change to powerful reasons and most convincing demonstrations; the comprehension of such speculations being, in a manner, endowed with manliness and vigour, which comprehensions, while in a tender age, melt away by reason of the mixture of the soul, which is not as yet able to consolidate and preserve the character impressed upon it.

(103) "And they had slime for mortar;" not, on the contrary, mortar for slime. For the wicked appear to strengthen and fortify what is weak against what is most powerful, and from their own resources to consolidate and preserve what melts and flows away from such things, in order that they may aim and shoot at virtue from a safe place. But the merciful God and father of the good will not permit their buildings to be established in indissoluble safety, their work of melting zeal not being able to withstand, but becoming like soft mud.

(104) For, if their clay had become mortar, then perchance that earthy thing perceptible by the outward senses, which is for ever and ever in a continued state of flux, would have been able to arrive at a safe and unalterable power; but since, on the contrary, their mortar became mere slime, we must not despair, for there is in this, certain hope that the strong fortifications of vice may be overthrown by the might of God. (105) Therefore the just man, even in the great and incessant deluge of life, while he is not as yet able to see things really as they are by the energy of his soul alone without the assistance of the outward sense, will anoint "the ark," by which I understand the body, "both within and without the pitch,"[32] strengthening his imaginations and energies by his own resources; but when the danger has ceased and the violence of the flood abated, then he will come forth, availing himself of his incorporeal mind for the comprehension of truth.

(106) For the good disposition being from the very birth of the man planted in virtue, and being spoken of as of such, its name being Moses, dwelling in the whole world as his native city and country, becoming, as it were, a cosmopolite, being bound up in the body, smeared over as with "bitumen and pitch,"[33] and appearing to be able to receive and to contain in security all the imaginations of all things which might be subjected to the outward senses, weeps[34] at being so bound up, being overwhelmed with a desire for an incorporeal nature. And he weeps over the miserable mind of men in general as being wandering and puffed up with pride, inasmuch as, being elated with false opinion, it thinks that it has in itself something firm and safe, and, as a general fact, that there something immutable in some creature or other, though the example of perpetual stability, which is at all times the same, is set up in God alone.

XXIII. (107) And the expression, "Come, let us build ourselves a city and a tower, the top of which shall reach to heaven," has such a meaning as this concealed beneath it; the lawgiver does not conceive that those only are cities which are built upon the earth, the materials of which are wood and stone, but he thinks that there are other cities also which men bear about with them, being built in their souls; (108) and these are, as is natural, the archetypes and models of the others, inasmuch as they have received a more divine building, and the others are but imitations of them, as consisting of perishable substances.

But there are two species of cities, the one better, the other worse. That is the better which enjoys a democratic government, a constitution which honours equality, the rulers of which are law and justice; and such a constitution as this is a hymn to God. But that is the worse kind which adulterates this constitution, just as base and clipped

---

[32]Genesis 6:14.
[33]Exodus 2:3.
[34]Exodus 2:6.

money is adulterated in the coinage, being, in fact, ochlocracy, which admires inequality, in which injustice and lawlessness bear sway. (109) Now good men are enrolled as citizens in the constitution of the first-mentioned kind of city; but the multitude of the wicked clings to the other and worst sort, loving disorder more than orderliness, and confusion rather than well-established steadiness.

(110) And the wicked man seeks for coadjutors in his practice of wickedness, not looking upon himself as sufficient by himself. And he exhorts the sight, and he exhorts the hearing, and he exhorts every outward sense in succession, to range itself on his side without delay, and every one of them to bring to him all things necessary for his service. And he raises up and sharpens all the rest of the company of the passions, which are by their own nature unmanageable, in order that by the addition of practice and care they may become irresistible. (111) The mind, therefore, having called in these allies, says, "Let us build ourselves a city;" an expression equivalent to, Let us fortify our own things; let us fence them around to the best of our power, so that we may not be easily taken by those who attack us; let us divide and distribute, as into tribes and boroughs, each of the powers existing in the soul, allotting some to the rational part, and some to the irrational part; (112) let us choose competent rulers, wealth, glory, honour, pleasure, by means of which we may be able to become masters of everything; banishing to a distance justice, the invariable cause of poverty and ingloriousness; and let us enact laws, which shall confirm the chief power and advantage to those who are always able to get the better of others.

(113) And let a tower be built in this city as a citadel, to be a strong palace for the tyrant vice, whose feet shall walk upon the earth, and its head shall, through pride, be raised to such a height as to reach even to heaven; (114) for, in good truth, it rests not only upon human sins, but it also hastens forward as far as heaven, pushing up its words of impiety and ungodliness, since it either speaks of God so as to assert that he has no existence, or that, though he exists, he has no providence, or to affirm that the world had no beginning of creation, or that, admitting that it has been created, it is borne on by unsteady causes, just as chance may direct, at one time wrongly, at another time in an irreproachable manner, just as often happens in the case of chariots or ships. (115) For sometimes the voyage of a ship, or the course of a chariot, goes on properly even without charioteers or pilots; but success is not only now and then owing to providences, but very often to human prudence and invariably to divine, since error is admitted to be altogether incompatible with divine power. Now what object can the foolish man have who, speaking figuratively, build up the reasonings of wickedness like a tower, except the desire of leaving behind them a name which shall be far from a good name?

XXIV. (116) For they say, "Let us make for ourselves a name." O, the excessive and profligate impudence of such a saying! What say ye? When ye ought to seek to bury your iniquities under night and profound darkness, and to assume as a veil for them, shame, if not genuine, at all events pretending shame, whether for the sake of gaining favour in the eyes of the moderate and virtuous, or for that of avoiding punishment for admitted wickedness; do ye, nevertheless, proceed to such a pitch of audacity, as all but to come forth and display yourselves in the light and in the most brilliant beams of the sun, and to fear neither the threats of better men, nor the implacable justice of God, which impends over such ungodly and desperate men? But ye think fit even to send around in every direction reports, to carry intelligence of your domestic iniquities, in order that no one may be uninformed of or unacquainted with your deeds of daring wickedness, wretched and infamous men that ye are.

(117) What name, therefore, do ye wish to assume? Is it the one which is most suitable to your actions? But is there not one name only which is suited to them? It may, perhaps, be one in genus; but there are ten thousand such names in species, which you will hear from others, even if ye keep silence yourselves. The names adapted to your conduct are, rashness united with shamelessness, insolence combined with violence, violence in union with homicide, corruption in combination with adultery, undefined appetite accompanied by unmeasured indulgence in pleasures, folly joined with impudence, injustice united to crafty wickedness, theft combined with rapine, perjury united with lying, impiety combined with utter lawlessness. Such, and similar to these, are the names of such actions. (118) And it is well for them to boast over and pride themselves, upon seeking for reputation from actions which it would be more seemly to hide and to be ashamed of.

And, indeed, some persons do pride themselves on these things, thinking that in consequence of them they do derive a certain irresistible degree of power among men from this idea being entertained respecting them; but they will not escape the divine vengeance for their enormous audacity, and very soon they will have occasion not only to anticipate at a distance, but even to see immediately impending their own death. For they say, "Before we are dispersed, let us have a care for our name and our glory." (119) Should I not then say to them, Ye know that ye will be dispersed? Why, then, do ye commit iniquity?

But perhaps he is here placing before us the manner of foolish men who, even when the very greatest punishments are not obscurely impending over them, but are often visibly threatening them, nevertheless do not hesitate to commit iniquity. And the punishments, however they may seem to be concealed, are in reality most notorious, which are inflicted by God. (120) For all the most wicked of men adopt ideas that they can never escape the knowledge of the deity when doing wrong, and that they shall never be able to ward off altogether the day of retribution. (121) Since otherwise, how do they know that they will be dispersed? And yet they say, "Before we are dispersed." But their conscience, which is within, convicts them, and pricks them vehemently, when devoting themselves to ungodliness, so as to draw them against their will to a confession that all the circumstances affecting men are overlooked by a superior nature, and that justice is watching above, as an incorruptible chastiser, hating the unjust actions of the impious, and the reasonings and speeches which undertake their defence.

XXV. (122) But all these men are the offspring of that wickedness which is always dying but which never dies, the name of which is Cain. Is not Cain represented as having begotten a son whom he called Enoch,[35] and as building a city to which he gave the same name, and as after a fashion building up created and mortal things to the destruction of those things which have received a more divine formation? (123) For the name Enoch, being interpreted, means "thy grace." But every impious man supposes that what he thinks and understands is owing to the bounty of his intellect towards him; that what he sees is the gift of his eyes to him, what he hears of his ears, what he smells of his nostrils, and so that each of his outward senses bestows on him those perceptions which are in accordance with them. Again, that it is the organs of the voice which endow him with the capacity of speaking, and that there is actually no such thing as a God at all, or at all events that he is not the primary cause of things.

(124) Because of these views he assigns to himself the first fruits of the fruits which he extracts from the earth by his husbandry, being contented afterwards to offer to God some of the fruit, and that too though he has a sound example at hand; for his brother offers a sacrifice of the offspring of the flock, offering the firstborn, and not those which are of secondary value; confessing that the eldest causes of all existing things are suited to the eldest and first cause. (125) But the impious man thinks exactly the contrary, namely, that the mind is endowed with absolute power to do whatever it desires, and that the outward senses have absolute power as to all that they feel, for that both the mind and the outward senses decide in an irreproachable and unerring manner, the one on bodies, and the other on everything. (126) Now what can be more open to blame, or more capable of conviction by truth, than such ideas as these? Has not the mind been repeatedly convicted of innumerable acts of folly? And have not all the outward senses been convicted of bearing false witness, and that too not by irrational judges who, it is natural to suppose, may be deceived, but before the tribunal of nature herself, which it is impossible to corrupt or to pervert?

(127) And indeed as the criteria both of our mind and of our outward senses are liable to error respecting even ourselves, it follows of necessity that we must make the corresponding confession that God sheds upon the mind the power of intellect, and on the outward senses the faculty of apprehension, and that these benefits are conferred upon us not by our own members but by him to whom also we owe our existence.

XXVI. (128) The children who have received from their father the inheritance of self-love are eager to go on increasing up to heaven, until justice, which loves virtue and hates iniquity, coming destroys their cities which they have built up by the side of their miserable souls, and the tower the name which is displayed in the book which is entitled the Book of Judgment. (129) And the name is, as the Hebrews say, Phanuel, which translated into our language means, "turning away from God." For any strong building which is erected by means of plausible arguments is not built for the sake of any other object except that of averting and alienating the mind from the honour due to God, than which object what can be more iniquitous? (130) But for the destruction of this strong fortification a ravager and an enemy of iniquity is prepared who is always full of hostility towards it; whom the Hebrews call Gideon: which name being interpreted means, "a retreat for robbers." "For," says Moses, "Gideon swore to the men of Phanuel, saying, On the day when I return victorious in peace, I will overthrow this tower."[36] (131) A very beautiful and most becoming boast for the soul which hates wickedness and is sharpened against the impious, namely, that it is resolved to overthrow every reasoning which by its persuasions seeks to turn the mind away from holiness, and this indeed is the natural result. For when the mind turns round, then that which turns away from it, and rejects it is again dissolved, (132) and this is the opportunity for destroying it which (a most wonderful thing) he calls not war but peace. For, owing to the stability and firmness of the mind which piety is accustomed to produce, every reasoning which impiety has formed is overturned.

(133) Many also have erected the outward

[35] Genesis 4:17.

[36] Judges 8:9.

senses after the fashion of a tower, raising them to such a height as to be able to reach the very borders of heaven. But the term heaven is here used symbolically to signify our mind, according to which the best and most divine natures revolve. But they who dare such deeds prefer the outward senses to the intellect, and desire by means of the outward senses forcibly to destroy all the objects of intellect, compelling those things which are, at present masters to descend into the rank of servants, and raising those things which are by nature slaves to the rank of masters.

XXVII. (134) And the statement, "The Lord went down to see that city and that tower" must be listened to altogether as if spoken in a figurative sense. For to think that the divinity can go towards, or go from, or go down, or go to meet, or, in short, that it has the same positions and motions as particular animals, and that it is susceptible of real motion at all, is, to use a common proverb, an impiety deserving of being banished beyond the sea and beyond the world. (135) But these things are spoken, as if of man, by the lawgiver, of God who is not invested with human form, for the sake of advantage to us who are to be instructed, as I have often said before with reference to other passages. Since who is there who does not know that it is indispensable for a person who goes down, to leave one place and to occupy another? (136) But all places are filled at once by God, who surrounds them all and is not surrounded by any of them, to whom alone it is possible to be everywhere and also nowhere. Nowhere, because he himself created place and space at the same time that he created bodies, and it is impious to say that the Creator is contained in anything that he has created.

Again, he is everywhere, because, having extended his powers so as to make them pervade earth, and water, and air, and heaven, he has left no portion of the world desolate, but, having collected everything together, he has bound them with chains which cannot be burst,[37] so that they are never emancipated, on which account he is especially to be praised with hymns.

(137) For that which is higher than all powers is understood to exceed them, not merely in the fact of its existence. But the power of this being which made and arranged everything is with perfect truth called God, and it contains everything in its bosom, and pervades every portion of the universe. (138) But the divine being, both invisible and incomprehensible, is indeed everywhere, but still, in truth, he is nowhere visible or comprehensible. But when he says, "I am he who

stands before thee"[38] he appears indeed to be displayed and to be comprehended, though before any exhibition or conception he was superior to all created things. (139) Therefore, no one of the word which implies a motion from place to place is appropriate to that god who exists only in essence; such expressions, I mean, as going upwards or downwards, to the right or to the left, forwards or backwards. For he is not conceived of in any one of the above mentioned ideas, inasmuch as he never turns around or changes his place.

(140) But, nevertheless, he is said to have come down and to have seen, he who by his foreknowledge comprehends everything, not only that has happened, but even before it happens; and this expression is used for the same of exhortation and instruction, in order that no man, indulging in uncertain conjectures about matters which he is not present to behold may, while standing afar off, be too prompt to believe idle fancies, but that every one may come close to the facts, and examining each one separately, may carefully and thoroughly consider them. For certain sight is more deserving to be looked upon as a trustworthy witness than fallacious hearing. (141) On which account a law has been enacted among these nations which have the most excellent constitution, that one must not give evidence on hearsay, because by its own nature the tribunal of the sense of hearing is liable to be corrupted. And Moses indeed says in the prohibitory part of his law, "Thou shalt not receive vain hearing."[39] Meaning not only this, that one ought not to receive false or silly reports by hearsay, but that, as far as the clear comprehension of the truth is concerned, the hearing is a long way behind the sight, being full of vanity.

XXVIII. (142) We say that this is the reason why it is said that God went down to see the city and the tower; and the addition, "Which the sons of men had built," is not a mere superfluity. For perhaps some profanely disposed person may mock and say, "The lawgiver is here teaching us a very novel kind of lesson, when he says that no one else but the sons of men build cities and towers; for who, even of the most crazy people is ignorant of what is so evident and notorious as that?" (143) But we must not suppose that such a plain and unquestionable fact as that, is what is intended to be conveyed by the mention of it in the holy scriptures, but rather there is some hidden meaning concealed under these apparently plain words which we must trace out. (144) What then is this hidden meaning?

Those who, as it were, attribute many fathers to existing things, and who represent the company of the gods as numerous, displaying great

---

[37]The text has *aoratois*, "invisible," but I have followed Mangey's translation, who reads *arrhēktois*. The remainder of the sentence is exceedingly corrupt.

[38]Exodus 17:6.
[39]Exodus 23:1.

ignorance of the nature of things and causing great confusion, and making pleasure the proper object of the soul, are those who are, if we must tell the plain truth, spoken of as the builders of the aforesaid city, and of the citadel in it; having increased the efficient causes of the desired end, building them up like houses, being, as I imagine, in no respect different from the children of the harlot whom the law expels from the assembly of God, where it says, "The offspring of a harlot shall not come into the assembly of the Lord."[40]

Because, like archers shooting at random at many objects, and not aiming skilfully or successfully at any one mark, so these men, putting forward ten thousand principles and causes for the creation of the universe, every one of which is false, display a perfect ignorance of the one Creator and Father of all things; (145) but they who have real knowledge, are properly addressed as the sons of the one God, as Moses also entitles them, where he says, "Ye are the sons of the Lord God."[41] And again, "God who begot thee;"[42] and in another place, "Is not he thy father?"

Accordingly, it is natural for those who have this disposition of soul to look upon nothing as beautiful except what is good, which is the citadel erected by those who are experienced in this kind of warfare as a defence against the end of pleasure, and as a means of defeating and destroying it. (146) And even if there be not as yet any one who is worthy to be called a son of God, nevertheless let him labour earnestly to be adorned according to his first-born word, the eldest of his angels, as the great archangel of many names; for he is called, the authority, and the name of God, and the Word, and man according to God's image, and he who sees Israel. (147) For which reason I was induced a little while ago to praise the principles of those who said, "We are all one man's sons."[43] For even if we are not yet suitable to be called the sons of God, still we may deserve to be called the children of his eternal image, of his most sacred word; for the image of God is his most ancient word.

(148) And, indeed, in many passages of the law, the children of Israel are called hearers of him that seeth, since hearing is honoured with the second rank next after the sense of sight, and since that which is in need of instruction is at all times second to that which can receive clear impressions of the subjects submitted to it without any such information. (149) And I also admire the things which are spoken under divine inspiration in the books of Kings, according to which those who

flourished many generations afterwards and lived in a blameless manner, are spoken of as the sons of David who wrote hymns to God;[44] though, during his lifetime, even their great grandfathers had not yet been born. The truth is, that the birth here spoken of is that of souls made immortal by their virtues, not of perishable bodies, and this birth is naturally referred to the leaders of virtue, as its parents and progenitors.

XXIX. (150) But against those who praise themselves on justice, the Lord said, "Behold, there is one race and one language among them all," an expression equivalent to, Behold, there is one family and one bond of relationship, and also, one harmony and agreement among them all together, no one being in his mind at all alienated from or disconnected with his neighbour, as is the case with illiterate men. For at times, the organ of speech among them is, in all its tones, out of tune and inharmonious in no slight degree, being in fact carefully arranged so as to produce inharmoniousness, and having only such a concert as will cause a want of melody.

(151) And in the case of fevers,[45] one may see very similar effects; for there are periodical changes, in some recurring every day, in others every third or every fourth day, as the sons of the physicians say; and they have also stated hours, both by day and night, at which important crises may be expected, and they at all times keep nearly the same order.

(152) And the expression, "And they began to do this," is said with no moderate indignation, because it has not been sufficient for wicked men to confuse all the principles of justice which affect those of the same country as themselves, but they have ventured to transgress even the laws of Heaven, sowing injustice and reaping impiety. But these wretched men derive no advantage, (153) for though those who seek to inflict mutual injuries on one another, succeed in many of the objects which they have at heart, bringing to their accomplishment in action what they have decided on in their unwise minds, yet the case is not the same with the impious. For all things belonging to the Deity are incapable of receiving either damage or injury, and the unclean can only find out the beginnings of sinning in respect of them, but can never arrive at the end which they propose to themselves; (154) on which account this expression also occurs, "They *began* to do."

Men full of an insatiable desire of doing wrong, not being content with the crimes which they can perpetuate on earth, by sea, and in the air, inas-

---

[40] Deuteronomy 23:2.
[41] Deuteronomy 14:1.
[42] Deuteronomy 32:18.
[43] Genesis 42:11.
[44] 2 Ezr. 8:2.
[45] I have translated Mangey's Latin translation. He pronounces the whole passage in the original text corrupt and unintelligible. The word translated fever is *politidos*, a word manifestly corrupt.

much as they are of a perishable nature, have determined to array themselves against the divine natures existing in heaven; which, as they are not reckoned among existing creatures are also out of all reach of injury.[46] Even calumny itself can inflict no injury on those things if it ventures to speak ill of them, inasmuch as they are never moved from their everlasting and eternal natures, but it inflicts incurable calamity on those who accuse it.

(155) Are they not to be blamed, since indeed they have only begun, being unable to arrive at the end of the impiety they propose to themselves, are they not, I say, to be blamed just as much as if they had accomplished all the objects that they had in view? On this account also, Moses speaks of them as having finished the tower, though in fact they had not yet completed it, where he says, "The Lord went down to see the city and the tower," not which the sons of men were going to build, but which they had built.

XXX. (156) What, then, is the proof that they had not entirely completed this building? First of all, the manifest notoriety of the fact. For it is impossible for even so slight a portion of the earth to touch the heaven, by reason of the cause beforementioned, that no centre can ever touch the circumference; in the second place, because the aether *aithēr* is sacred fire and an unquenchable flame, as its very name shows, being derived from *aithō*, to burn, which is a synonymous word with *kaiō*. (157) And we have a witness in our favour in one portion of the heavenly system of fire, that is in the sun, who, though he is at such a distance from the earth, sends his beams down into his inmost recesses, and sometimes warms and at times even scorches the earth itself, and the air which reaches from earth up to the heavenly sphere, though it is by nature cold; for, all those things which are removed to a distance from his rapid course, or which are in an oblique direction, one side of it only warms; but those which are near to him, or which are in a direct line from him, are violently burnt up.

If, then, these things are so, was it not necessary that those men who were endeavouring to mount up to heaven must have been stricken with thunderbolts and burnt up, their high-minded and proud designs being unaccomplished by them? (158) This is the meaning which Moses appears to intend to convey, figuratively, by the expressions which follow: "For they ceased," says, he, "to build the city and the tower."[47] Not, indeed, because they had finished their work, but because

they were prevented from accomplishing it by the confusion which supervened. Nevertheless, they have not escaped blame for their actions, inasmuch as they had decided on them and attempted to carry them out.

XXXI. (159) At all events, the law says that that soothsayer and diviner who was led into folly in respect of his unstable conjectures (for the name, Balaam, being interpreted, means unstable), "cursed the people that saw;"[48] and that, too, though as far as his words go he uttered only words of good omen and prayers. The law here looking not at the words he uttered, which, through the providence of God, did change their character, becoming good money instead of base coinage, but having regard to the intention in which injurious things were resolved in preference to beneficial ones. But these things are, by nature inimical to one another, conjectures being at variance with truth, and vain opinion with knowledge, and prophecy, which is not dictated by divine inspiration, being directly opposed to sober wisdom.

(160) And even if any one, rising up as it were from his ambush, were to try, but to be unable, to slay a man, still he is none the less liable to the punishment due to homicides, as the law which is enacted about such persons shows. "For if," says the law, "any one attacks his neighbour, wishing to slay him by treachery, and escapes, thou shalt apprehend him, even at the altar, to put him to death."[49] And yet the thing condemned is the attacking with intent to kill, not the actual killing, but the law looks upon the intention to slay as equal in guilt to the actual slaying; on which account it does not grant pardon to such a man even if he supplicates for it, but bids one drag the man who has cherished so unholy a design even from the temple itself.

(161) And such a man is unholy, not merely because he has plotted slaughter against a soul which might have lived for ever through its acquisition and use of virtue, making an attack on it through the agency of wickedness, but also because he blames God as the cause of his ungodly audacity; for the word, "escapes," has such a meaning as this concealed under it. Because many men wish to escape from accusations which are brought against themselves, and think it fitting that they should be delivered from the punishments due to the offences which they have committed, and so they attribute their own iniquity to him who is the cause of no evil, but of all kinds of good, namely, to God; for which reason it was accounted as no violation of divine law to drag such men even from the altars themselves.

(162) And it was an excessive punishment

---

[46]This passage again in the text is unintelligible, and pronounced by Mangey to be in a state of hopeless corruption.
[47]Genesis 11:8.

[48]Deuteronomy 23:4.
[49]Exodus 21:14.

which was then denounced against the reasons which were thus built up and put together for purposes of impiety; which, however, perhaps some foolish persons will look upon not as injury, but as a benefit. "For," says Moses, "there shalt not fail to them any one of the things which they have endeavoured to do."[50] Alas for their unlimited and interminable misery! All the objects which the most insane intention fixes its desires upon shall be successfully carried out, and shall obey its will, so that nothing whatever shall fail, either small or great, but everything shall, as it were, make haste to meet and to anticipate their requirements.

XXXII. (163) These things are an exhibition of a soul destitute of prudence, and which meets with no impediment to its indulging in sin; for whoever is not utterly incurable would rather pray that all the purposes of his mind might fail, so that if he had formed a resolution to steal, or to commit adultery, or to murder a man, or to commit sacrilege, or to perpetrate any similar crime, he might not succeed, but might find innumerable obstacles. For such hindrance would get rid of the greatest of all diseases, injustice; but any one who is free from all fear is sure to admit this malady.

(164) Why, then, my friends, do you any longer praise or admire the fortune of tyrants, owing to which they succeed with ease in everything which they undertake, and which a frenzied and unrestrained mind prompts them to do? And yet one ought rather to lament over them, since inability and powerlessness to succeed in their objects is advantageous to the wicked, just as abundant opportunity and power is the most beneficial thing for the good. (165) But one of the crowd of foolish men, perceiving to what an abundant superfluity of misery indulgence in sinning leads, said, speaking with perfect freedom, "My wickedness is too great for me to be forgiven."[51]

It is, therefore, very melancholy indeed for the soul, which is by its own nature unmanageable, to be left without any restraint; while it is scarcely possible for any one to hold it in with reins, and by that means, in conjunction with the infliction of stripes, to reduce it to reason. (166) On which account an oracle of the all-merciful God has been given, full of gentleness, which shadows forth good hopes to those who love instruction, in these terms: "I will never leave thee, nor forsake thee."[52] For when the chains of the soul, by which it has been used to be held in bondage, are loosened, then the greatest of all calamities follows, namely, the being deserted by God, who has fastened chains which can never be broken round the universe, namely, his own powers, with which he binds everything, willing that it shall never more be released. (167) Accordingly, he says, in another passage, that "all things which are bound with a chain are pure;"[53] since unbinding is the cause of the destruction of that which is impure.

Beware, then, lest when you see a man accomplishing without difficulty all the objects which he endeavors to effect, you admire him as a prosperous man; take care rather to pity him as a very unfortunate one, because he passes his whole life in a perfect destitution of virtue and a great abundance of vice.

XXXIII. (168) And it is worth while to consider in no superficial manner what the meaning of that expression which is put by Moses into the mouth of God: "Come, let us go down and confuse their language there."[54] For here God is represented as if he were speaking to some beings who were his coadjutors. And the very same idea may be excited by what is said in the account of the creation of the world, (169) for there, too, Moses records that "the Lord God said, Come, let us now make man in our image; man in our similitude.[55] The expression, "Let us make," implying a number of creators. And, in another place, we are told that God said, "Behold, the man, Adam, has become as one of us, in respect of his knowing good and evil;"[56] for the expression, "as one of us," is not applicable to one person, but to many.

(170) In the first place, then, we must say this, that there is no existing being equal in honor to God, but there is one only ruler and governor and king, to whom alone it is granted to govern and to arrange the universe. For the verse—

A multitude of kings is never good,
Let there one sovereign, one sole monarch be,[57]

is not more justly said with respect to cities and men than with respect to the world and to God; for it is clear from the necessity of things that there must be one creator, and one father, and one master of the one universe.

XXXIV. (171) This point then being thus granted, it is necessary to convert with it also what follows, so as to adapt it properly. Let us then consider what this is: God, being one, has about him an unspeakable number of powers, all of which are defenders and preservers of every thing that is created; and among these powers those also which are conversant with punishment are involved. But even punishment is not a disadvantageous thing,

---

[50]Genesis 11:6.
[51]Genesis 4:13.
[52]Joshua 1:5.
[53]Numbers 19:15.
[54]Genesis 11:7.
[55]Genesis 1:26.
[56]Genesis 3:22.
[57]Iliad 2.204.

inasmuch as it is both a hindrance to and a correction of doing wrong.

(172) Again, it is by means of these powers that the incorporeal world, perceptible by the intellect, has been put together, which is the archetypal model of this invisible world, being compounded by invisible species, just as this world is of invisible bodies. (173) Some persons therefore, admiring exceedingly the nature of both these worlds, have not only deified them in their wholes, but have also deified the most beautiful parts of them, such as the sun and the moon, and the entire heaven, which, having no reverence for anything, they have called gods. But Moses, perceiving their design, says, "O Lord, Lord, King of the gods,"[58] in order to show the difference between the ruler and those subject to him, (174) "And there is also in the air a most sacred company of incorporeal souls as an attendant upon the heavenly souls; for the word of prophecy is accustomed to call these souls angels.

It happens therefore that the whole army of each of these worlds, being marshalled in their suitable ranks, are servants and ministers of the ruler who has marshalled them, whom they follow as their leader, in obedience to the principles of law and justice; for it is impossible to suppose that the divine army can even be detected in desertion. (175) But it is suitable to the character of the king to associate with his own powers, and to avail himself of them, with a view to their ministrations in such matters as it is not fitting should be settled by God alone, for the Father of the universe has no need of anything, so as to require assistance from any other quarter if he wishes to make any thing.

But seeing at once what is becoming, both for himself and for his works of creation, there are some things which he has entrusted to his subordinate powers to fashion; and yet he has not at once given even to them completely independent knowledge to enable it to accomplish their objects, in order that no one of those things which come to be created may be found to be erroneously made.

XXXV. (176) These things, then, it was necessary to give an idea of beforehand; but for what reason this was necessary we must now say. The nature of animals was originally divided into the portion endowed with and into that devoid of reason, the two being at variance with one another. Again the rational division was subdivided into the perishable and imperishable species, the perishable species being the race of mankind, and the imperishable species being the company of incorporeal souls which revolve about the air and heaven.

(177) But these have no participation in wickedness, having received from the very beginning an inheritance without stain and full of happiness; and not being bound up in the region of interminable calamities, that is to say, in the body. The divisions also of the irrational part are free from any participation in wickedness, inasmuch as, having no endowment of intellect, they are never convicted of those deliberate acts of wickedness which proceed upon consideration.

(178) But man is almost the only one of all living things which, having a thorough knowledge of good and evil, often chooses that which is worst, and rejects those things which are worthy of earnest pursuit, so that he is often most justly condemned as being guilty of deliberate and studied crime.

(179) Very appropriately therefore has God attributed the creation of this being, man, to his lieutenants, saying, "Let us make man," in order that the successes of the intellect may be attributed to him alone, but the errors of the being thus created, to his subordinate power: for it did not appear to be suitable to the dignity of God, the ruler of the universe, to make the road to wickedness in a rational soul by his own agency; for which reason he has committed to those about him the creation of this portion of the universe; for it was necessary that the voluntary principle, as the counterpoise to the involuntary principle, should be established and made known, with a view to the completion and perfection of the universe.

XXXVI. (180) And this may be enough to say in this manner; and it is right that this point also should be considered, namely that God is the cause only of what is good but is absolutely the cause of no evil whatever, since he himself is the most ancient of all existing things, and the most perfect of all goods; and it is most natural and becoming that he should do what is most akin to his own nature, that is to say, that the best of all beings should be the cause of all the best things, but that the punishments appointed for the wicked are inflicted by the means of his subordinate ministers. (181) And there is an evidence in favour of this assertion of mine in this expression, which was uttered by the man who was made perfect by practice; "The God who nourished me from my youth up, the angel who defended me from all evils;"[59] for by this word he already confesses that those genuine good things which nourish the souls which love virtue, are referred to God as their sole cause; but the fate of the wicked is, on the other hand, referred to the angels, and even they have not independent and absolute power of inflicting punishment, that this salutary nature may not afford an

---

[58]Deuteronomy 10:17.

[59]Genesis 48:16.

opportunity to any one of the things which tend to destruction.

(182) For this reason God says, "Come, let us go down and confuse;" for the wicked, deserving to meet with such punishment as this, that the merciful, and beneficent, and bounteous, powers of God should become known to them chiefly by its inflictions. Knowing therefore that these powers are beneficial to the race of man, he has appointed the punishments to be inflicted by other beings; for it was expedient that he himself should be looked upon as the cause of well-doing, but in such a way that the fountains of his everlasting graces should be kept unmingled with any evils, not merely with those that are really evils, but even with those which are accounted such.

XXXVII. (183) We must now examine what this confusion is. How then shall we enter on this examination? In this manner, in my opinion. We have very often known those whom we had knowledge of before, from certain similarities and a comparison of circumstances which have some connection with them. Therefore we also become acquainted with things in the same manner, which it is not easy to form a conception of from their own nature, from some similarity of other things connected with them. (184) What things then resemble confusion? Mixture, as the ancient report has it, and combination; but mixture takes place in dry things, and combination is looked upon as belonging to wet substances. (185) Mixture then is a placing side by side of different bodies in no regular order, as if any one were to make a heap, bringing barley, and wheat, and pease, and all sorts of other seeds, all into one mass; but combination is not a placing side by side, but rather a mutual penetration of dissimilar parts entering into one another at all points, so that the distinctive qualities are still able to be distinguished by some artificial skill, as they say is the case with respect to wine and water; (186) for these substances coming together form a combination, but that which is combined is not the less capable of being resolved again into the distinctive qualities from which it was originally formed.

For with a sponge saturated with oil it is possible for the water to be taken up and for the wine to be left behind, which may perhaps be because the origin of sponge is derived from water, and therefore it is natural that water being a kindred substance is calculated by nature to be taken up by the sponge out of the combination, but that that substance which is of a different nature, namely the wine, is naturally left behind.

(187) But confusion is the destruction of all the original distinctive qualities, owing to their component parts penetrating one another at every point, so as to generate one thing wholly different, as is the case in that composition of the physicians which they call the tetrapharmacon. For that, I imagine, is made up of wax, and fat, and pitch, and resin, all compounded together, but when the medicine has once been compounded, then it is impossible for it again to be resolved into the powers of which it was originally composed, but every one of them is destroyed separately, and the destruction of them all has produced one other power of exceeding excellence. (188) But when God threatens impious reasonings with confusion, he is in fact not only commanding the whole species and power of each separate wickedness to be destroyed, but also that thing which has been made up of all their joint contributions; so that neither the parts by themselves, nor the union and harmony of the whole, can contribute any strength hereafter towards the destruction of the better part; (189) on which account, he says, "Let us then confuse their language, so that each of them may not understand the voice of his neighbour;" which is equivalent to, let us make each separate one of the parts of wickedness deaf and dumb, so that it shall neither utter a voice of its own, nor be able to sound in unison with any other part, so as to be a cause of mischief.

XXXVIII. (190) This, now, is our opinion upon and interpretation of this passage. But they who follow only what is plain and easy, think that what is here intended to be recorded, is the origin of the languages of the Greeks and barbarians, whom, without blaming them (for, perhaps, they also put a correct interpretation on the transaction), I would exhort not to be content with stopping at this point, but to proceed onward to look at the passage in a figurative way, considering that the mere words of the scriptures are, as it were, but shadows of bodies, and that the meanings which are apparent to investigation beneath them, are the real things to be pondered upon. (191) Accordingly, this lawgiver usually gives a handle for this doctrine to those who are not utterly blind in their intellect; as in fact he does in his account of this very event, which we are now discussing: for he has called what took place, confusion; and yet, if he had only intended to speak of the origin of languages, he would have given a more felicitous name, and one of better omen, calling it division instead of confusion; for things that are divided, are not confused, but, on the contrary, are distinguished from one another, and not only is the one name contrary to the other, but the one fact is contrary to the other fact.

(192) For confusion, as I have already said, is the destruction of simple powers for the production of one concrete power; but division is the dissection of one thing into many parts, as is the case when one distinguishes a genus into its subordinate species so that, if the wise God had ordered his ministers to divide language, which was previously only one, into the divisions of several dialects, he would have used more appropriate expres-

sions, which should have given a more accurate idea of the case: calling what he did, dissection, or distribution, or division, or something of that kind, but not confusion, a name which is at variance with all of them.

(193) But his especial object here is to dissolve the company of wickedness, to put an end to their confederacy, to destroy their community of action, to put out of sight and extirpate all their powers, to overthrow the might of their dominion, which they had strengthened by fearful lawlessness. (194) Do you not see that he also who made the parts of the soul did not unite any one part to another in such a way as to enable one to discharge the duties of the other? But the eyes would never be able to hear, nor the ears to see, nor the lips of the mouth to smell, nor the nostrils to taste; nor, again, could reason ever be exposed to those influences which operate upon upon the outward senses, nor again, would the outward senses be able to develop reason. (195) For the Creator knew that it was desirable that each of these parts should not hear the voice of its neighbour, but that the parts of the soul should each exert its own peculiar faculties without confusion, for the advantage of living animals, and should, with the same object, be deprived of any power of exerting themselves in common, and that all the powers of vice should be brought to confusion and utter destruction, so that they might neither in confederacy, nor separately, be injurious to the better parts.

(196) On which account Moses tells us, "The Lord scattered them from thence;" which is equivalent to, he dispersed them, he put them to flight, he banished them, he destroyed them; for to scatter is sometimes done with a view to production, and growth, and increase of other things; but there is another kind which has for its object overthrow and destruction: but God, the planter of the world, wishes to sow in every one excellence, but to scatter and drive from the world accursed impiety; that the disposition which hates virtue may at last desist from building up a city of wickedness, and a tower of impiety; (197) for when these are put to the rout, then those who have long ago been banished by the tyranny of folly, now, at one proclamation, find themselves able to return to their own country. God having drawn up and confirmed the proclamation, as the scriptures show, in which it is expressly stated that, "Even though thy dispersion be from one end of heaven to the other end of heaven, he will bring thee together from thence."[60]

(198) So that it is proper that the harmony of the virtues should be arranged and cherished by God, and that he should dissolve and destroy wickedness; and confusion is a name most appropriate to wickedness, of which every foolish man is a visible proof, having all his words, and intentions, and actions, incapable of standing an examination and destitute of steadiness.

---

[60]Deuteronomy 30:4.

ON THE MIGRATION OF ABRAHAM

(De Migratione Abrahami)

I. (1) And the Lord said to Abraham, "Depart from thy land, and from thy kindred, and from thy father's house to a land which I will show thee; and I will make thee into a great nation. And I will bless thee, and I will magnify thy name, and thou shalt be blessed. And I will bless them that bless thee, and I will curse them that curse thee; and in thy name shall all the nations of the earth be blessed."[1]

(2) God, wishing to purify the soul of man, first of all gives it an impulse towards complete salvation, namely, a change of abode, so as to quit the three regions of the body, the outward sense and speech according to utterance; for his country is the emblem of the body, and his kindred are the symbol of the outward sense, and his father's house of speech. Why so? (3) Because the body derives its composition from the earth, and is again dissolved into earth; and Moses is a witness of this when he says, "Dust thou art, and unto dust shalt thou return."[2] For he says, that man was compounded by God fashioning a lump of clay into the form of a man; and it follows of necessity that, a composite being, when dissolved, must be dissolved into its component parts. But the outward sense in nearly connected with and akin to the mind, the irrational part to the rational, since they are both parts of one soul; but speech is the abode of the father, because our father is the mind, which implants in each of its parts its own powers, and distributes its energies among them, undertaking the care and superintendence of them all; and the abode in which it dwells is speech, a dwelling separated from the rest of the house; for as the hearth is the abode of a man, so is speech of the mind: (4) at all events, it displays itself, and all the notions which it conceives, arranging them and setting them in order in speech, as if in a house.

And you must not wonder that Moses has called speech in man the abode of the mind, for he also says, that the mind or the universe, that is to say, God, has for his abode his own word. (5) And the practiser of virtue, Jacob, seizing on this apprehension, confesses in express words that, "This is no other than the house of God,"[3] an expression equivalent to, The house of God is not this thing, or anything which can be made the subject

of ocular demonstration, or, in short, anything which comes under the province of the outward senses, but is invisible, destitute of all specific form, only to be comprehended by the soul as soul. (6) What, then, can it be except the Word, which is more ancient than all the things which were the objects of creation, and by means of which it is the Ruler of the universe, taking hold of it as a rudder, governs all things. And when he was fashioning the world, he used this as his instrument for the blameless argument of all the things which he was completing.

II. (7) That he means by Abraham's country the body, and by his kindred the outward senses, and by his father's house uttered speech, we have now shown. But the command, "Depart from them," is not like or equivalent to, Be separated from them according to your essence, since that would be the injunction of one who was pronouncing sentence of death. But it is the same as saying, Be alienated from them in your mind, allowing none of them to cling to you, standing above them all; (8) they are your subjects, use them not as your rulers; since you are a king, learn to govern and not to be governed; know yourself all your life, as Moses teaches us in many passages where he says, "Take heed to thyself."[4] For thus you will perceive what you ought to be obedient to, and what you ought to be the master of. (9) Depart therefore from the earthly parts which envelop you, O my friend, fleeing from that base and polluted prison house of the body, and from the keepers as it were of the prison, its pleasures and appetites, putting forth all your strength and all your power so as to suffer none of thy good things to come to harm, but improving all your good faculties together and unitedly. (10) Depart also from thy kindred, outward senses; for now indeed you have given yourself up to each of them to be made use of as it will, and you have become a good, the property of others who have borrowed you, having lost your own power over yourself. But you know that, even though all men are silent on the subject, your eyes lead you, and so do your ears, and all the rest of the multitude of that kindred connection, towards those objects which are pleasing to themselves. (11) But if you choose to collect again those portions of yourself which you have lent away, and to invest yourself with the posses-

---

[1]Genesis 12:1.
[2]Genesis 3:19.
[3]Genesis 28:17.

[4]Exodus 34:12.

sion of yourself, without separating off or alienating any part of it, you will have a happy life, enjoying for ever and ever the fruit of good things which belong not to strangers but to yourself.

(12) But now rise up also and quit speech according to utterance, which Moses here represents God as calling your father's house, that you may not be deceived by the specious beauty of words and names, and so be separated from that real beauty which exists in the things themselves which are intended by these names. For it is absurd for a shadow to be looked upon as of more importance than the bodies themselves, or for an imitation to carry off the palm from the model. Now the interpretation resembles a shadow and an imitation, but the nature of things signified under these expressions, thus interpreted, resemble the bodies and original models which the man who aims at being such and such rather than at appearing so must cling to, removing to a distance from the other things.

III. (13) When therefore the mind begins to become acquainted with itself, and to dwell among the speculations which come under the province of the intellect, all the inclinations of the soul for the species which is comprehensible by the intellect will be repelled, which inclination is called by the Hebrews, Lot; for which reason the wise man is represented as distinctly saying, "Depart, and separate yourself from me;"[5] for it is impossible for a man who is overwhelmed with the love of incorporeal and imperishable objects to dwell with one, whose every inclination is towards the mortal objects of the outward senses.

(14) Very beautifully therefore has the sacred interpreter of God's will entitled one entire holy volume of the giving of the law, the Exodus, having thus found out an appropriate name for the oracles contained therein. For being a man desirous of giving instruction and exceedingly ready to admonish and correct, he desires to remove the whole of the people of the soul as a multitude capable of receiving admonition and correction from the country of Egypt, that is to say, the body, and to take them out from among its inhabitants, thinking it a most terrible and grievous burden that the mind which is endowed with the faculty of sight should be oppressed by the pleasures of the flesh, and should obey whatever commands the relentless desires choose to impose upon it.

(15) Therefore, after the merciful God has instructed this people, groaning and bitterly weeping for the abundance of the things concerning the body, and the exceeding supply of external things (for it is said, "The children of Israel groaned by reason of the works")[6] when, God, I say, had instructed them about their going out, the prophet himself led them forth in safety.

(16) But there are some persons who have made a treaty with the body to last till the day of their death, and who have buried themselves in it as in a chest or coffin or whatever else you like to call it, of whom all the parts which are devoted to the slavery of the body and of the passions are consigned to oblivion and buried. But if anything well affected towards virtue has shot up by the side of it, that is preserved in the recollection, by means of which good things are naturally destined to be kept alive.

IV. (17) Accordingly, the sacred scriptures command the bones of Joseph—I mean by this the only parts of such a soul as were left behind, being species which know no corruption and which deserve to have mention made of them—to be preserved, thinking it preposterous for pure things not to be united to pure things. (18) And what is especially worthy of being mentioned is this, that he believed that God would visit the race which was capable of seeing,"[7] and would not give it up for ever and ever to ignorance, that blind mistress, but would distinguish between the immortal and the mortal parts of the soul, and leave in Egypt those parts which were conversant about the pleasures of the body and the other immoderate indulgences of the passions; but with respect to those parts which are imperishable, would make a covenant that they should be conducted onwards with those persons who were going up to the cities of virtue and would further ratify this covenant with an oath.

(19) What then are the parts which are imperishable? In the first place, a perfect alienation from pleasure which says, "Let us lie down together,"[8] and let us enjoy human enjoyments; secondly, presence of mind combined with fortitude, by means of which the soul separates and distinguishes from one another those things which by vain opinions are accounted good things, as so many dreams, confessing that "the only true and accurate explanations of things are found with God;"[9] and that all those imaginings, which exist in the unsteady, puffed up, and arrogant life of those men who are not yet purified, but who delight in those pleasures which proceed from bakers, and cooks, and wine-bearers, are uncertain and indistinct; (20) so that such a man is not a subject but a ruler of Egypt, that is to say of the whole region of the body; so that "he boasted of being of the race of the Hebrews,"[10] who were accustomed to rise up and leave the objects of the outward senses, and to go over to those of the intellect; for the

---

[5]Genesis 13:9.
[6]Exodus 2:23.

[7]Genesis 50:24.
[8]Genesis 39:7.
[9]Genesis 40:8.
[10]Genesis 40:15.

name Hebrew, being interpreted, means "one who passes over," because he boasted that "here he had done nothing."[11]

For to do nothing of those things which are thought much of among the wicked, but to hate them all and reject them, is praiseworthy in no slight degree; (21) as it is to despise immoderate indulgence of the desires and all other passions; to fear God, if a man is not yet capable of loving him, and even while in Egypt to have a desire for real life.

V. Which he who sees, marvelling at (and indeed it was enough[12] to cause astonishment), says, "It is a great thing for me if my son Joseph is still alive"[13] and has not died at the same time with vain opinions and the body which is but a lifeless carcass; (22) and he also confessed that "it was the work of God,"[14] and not of any created being, that he was recognised by his brethren, and so could put into commotion and agitation, and put to the rout by force, all the dispositions devoted to the body which flattered themselves that they could stand firmly on their own doctrines; he also said that "he had not been sent away by men, but had been appointed by God"[15] for the legitimate overseeing of the body and of all external things; (23) but there are many other things also resembling these, being of a superior and more sacred kind of order; and they do not endure to abide in Egypt, the house of the body, and are never buried in a coffin at all, but depart to a distance outside of every thing mortal, and follow the words of the lawgiver, namely, Moses, who is the guide of their path.

(24) For Moses, being the nurse as it were and tutor of good works, and good expressions, and good intentions, which, even if at times they are mingled with those of an opposite character by reason of the somewhat confused medley which exists in mortal man; are nevertheless distinguished when they have passed, so that all the seeds and plants of excellence may not be destroyed and perish for ever and ever. (25) And he exhorts men very vigorously to quit that which is called the mother of every thing that is absurd, without any delay or sluggishness, but rather using exceeding swiftness; for he says that men "must sacrifice the *pascha*, in haste,"[16] and the word *pascha*, being interpreted, means a "passing over," in order that the mind, exerting its reasonings without any doubt, and also an energetic willingness and promptness, may, without ever turning back make a passing over from the passions, to grat-

itude to God the Saviour, who has led it forth beyond all its expectations to freedom.

VI. (26) And why do we wonder if he exhorts the man who is led away by the force of unreasonable passions, neither to yield, nor to allow himself to be carried away by the impetuosity of its onward course, but to exert all his strength, to resist, and if he is unable to resist effectually, then to flee. For the second advance towards safety on the part of those who are unable to make a good resistance is flight. When the occasion does not permit the man who is a combatant by nature, and who has never been a slave of the passions, but who is always undergoing the toil of resistance to every separate one of them, to put forth all his powers of antagonism at all times, lest from continuance of his struggles against them he may gradually contract a painful infection from them; for there have before now been many instances of men having become imitators of the wickedness to which they were previously antagonists, as, on the other hand, some opposers of virtue have become copiers of that.

(27) And for this reason the following scripture has been given to men, "Return to the land of thy father and to thy family, and I will be with thee;"[17] which is equivalent to saying, you have been a perfect wrestler for me, and you have been thought worthy of the prize and crown of victory, virtue having been the establisher of the contest and prospering to give prizes of victory; and now get rid of your fondness for contention, that you may not be always labouring but that you may be able to enjoy the fruit of your labours, (28) which will never happen to you if you remain here dwelling among the objects of the external senses, and wasting your time among the distinctive qualities of the body, of which Laban is the leader (and this name means "distinctive quality;") but you must be an emigrant and must return to your native land, the land of the sacred word, and in some sense of the father of all those who practice virtue, which is wisdom, the best possible abiding place for those souls which love virtue.

(29) In this country you have a race which learns everything of itself, and is self-taught, which has no share in the infantine food of milk, but which by the divine oracle "has been forbidden to go down to Egypt,"[18] and to put itself in the way of the attractive pleasures of the flesh, surnamed Isaac; (30) and if you receive his inheritance, you will of necessity discard labour, for excessive abundance of things ready prepared, and of good things offered to your hand, will be the causes of cessation from toil. And the fountain from which good things are poured forth is the presence of the bounteous and

---

[11]Genesis 40:17.
[12]Genesis 42:18.
[13]Genesis 45:28.
[14]Genesis 50:19.
[15]Genesis 45:5.
[16]Exodus 12:12.

[17]Genesis 31:3.
[18]Genesis 26:2.

beneficent God; on which account setting the seal to his loving kindness he says, "I will be with thee."

VII. (31) How then should any good thing be wanting when the all-accomplishing God is at all times present with his graces, which are his virgin daughters, which he, the Father, who begot them, always cherishes as virgins, free from all impure contact and pollution? Then all cares, and labours, and exercises of practice, have a respite; and everything that is useful is at the same time given to everybody without the employment of art, by the prescient care of nature; (32) and the rapid influx of all these spontaneous blessings is called relaxation, since the mind is then relaxed and released from its energies as to its own peculiar objects, and is as it were emancipated from its yearly burdens,[19] by reason of the multitude of the things which are incessantly showered and rained upon it; (33) and these things are in their own nature most admirable and most beautiful; for of the things of which the soul is in travail by herself, the greater part are premature and abortive progeny; but those on which God pours his showers and which he waters, are produced in a perfect, and entire, and most excellent state.

(34) I am not ashamed to relate what has happened to me myself, which I know from having experienced it ten thousand times. Sometimes, when I have desired to come to my usual employment of writing on the doctrines of philosophy, though I have known accurately what it was proper to set down, I have found my mind barren and unproductive, and have been completely unsuccessful in my object, being indignant at my mind for the uncertainty and vanity of its then existent opinions, and filled with amazement at the power of the living God, by whom the womb of the soul is at times opened and at times closed up; (35) and sometimes when I have come to my work empty I have suddenly become full, ideas being, in an invisible manner, showered upon me, and implanted in me from on high; so that, through the influence of divine inspiration, I have become greatly excited, and have known neither the place in which I was nor those who were present, nor myself, nor what I was saying, nor what I was writing; for then I have been conscious of a richness of interpretation, an enjoyment of light, a most penetrating sight, a most manifest energy in all that was to be done, having such an effect on my mind as the clearest ocular demonstration would have on the eyes.

VIII. (36) That then which is shown is that thing so worthy of being beheld, so worthy of being contemplated, so worthy of being beloved, the perfect good, the nature of which is to change and sweeten the bitternesses of the soul, the most beautiful additional seasoning, full of all kinds of sweetnesses, by the addition of which, even those things which are not nutritious become salutary food; for it is said, that "the Lord showed him (Moses) a tree, and he cast it into the water,"[20] that is to say, into the mind dissolved, and relaxed, and full of bitterness, that it might become sweetened and serviceable. (37) But this tree promises not only food but likewise immortality; for Moses tells us, that the tree of life was planted in the midst of the paradise, being, in fact, goodness surrounded as by a body-guard by all the particular virtues, and by the actions in accordance with them; for it is virtue which received the inheritance of the most central and excellent place in the soul.

(38) And he who sees is the wise man; for the foolish are blind, or at best dim sighted. On this account I have before mentioned, that the then prophets were called seers;[21] and Jacob, the practiser of virtue, was desirous to give his ears in exchange for his eyes, if he could only see what he had previously heard described, and accordingly he receives an inheritance according to sight, having passed over that which was derived from hearing; (39) for the coin of learning and instruction, which is synonymous with Jacob, is re-coined into the seeing Israel, in consequence of which he, the faculty of seeing, beholds the divine light, which is in no respect different from knowledge, which opens the eye of the soul, and leads it on to embrace the most conspicuous and manifest comprehension of existing things:[22] for as it is through music that the principles of music are understood, and through each separate art that its principles are comprehended, so also it is owing to wisdom that what is contemplated: (40) but not only is wisdom like light, the instrument of seeing, but it does also behold itself. This, in God, is the light which is the archetypal model of the sun, and the sun itself is only its image and copy; and he who shows each thing is the only all-knowing being, God; for men are called knowing only because they appear to know; but God, who really does know, is spoken of, as to his knowledge, in a manner inferior to its real nature, for everything that is ever spoken in his praise comes short of the real power of the living God.

(41) And he recommends his wisdom, not merely by the fact that it was he who created the world, but also by that of his having established the knowledge of everything that has happened,

---

[19]Here again Mangey supposes the text to be hopelessly corrupt. The word there is *ekousiōn*, for which he proposes and translates *phortōn tōn etēsiōn*.

[20]Exodus 15:25.
[21]1 Samuel 9:9.
[22]This again is Mangey's emendation. The Greek text has *ōtion*, which is either nonsense, or at least the opposite of what must be meant.

or that has been created in the firmest manner close to himself; (42) for it is said, that "God saw all the things that he had made,"[23] which is an expression equivalent not to, He directed his sight towards each thing, but to, He conceived a knowledge, and understanding, and comprehension, of all the things that he had made. It was very proper, therefore, to teach and to instruct, and to point out to the ignorant, each separate thing, but it was unnecessary to do so to the all-knowing God, who is not like man, benefited by art, but who is himself confessed to be the beginning and source of all arts and sciences.

IX. (43) And Moses speaks very cautiously, inasmuch as he defines not the present time but the future in the promise which he records, when he says, "Not that which I *do* show you, but that which I *will* show you;"[24] as a testimony to the faith with which the soul believed in God, showing its gratitude not by what had been already done, but by its expectation of the future; (44) for being kept in a state of suspense and eagerness by good hope, and thinking that even what was not present would beyond all question be present immediately, on account of its most certain faith in him who had promised, it found a reward, the perfect good; for in another passage it is said that Abraham believed in God.

And in the same way, God, when showing Moses all the land, says that, "I have shown it to thy eyes, but thou shalt not enter therein."[25] (45) Do not then fancy that this is spoken of the death of the all-wise Moses, as some inconsiderate persons believe; for it is a piece of folly to think that slaves should have the country of virtue assigned to them in preference to the friends of God. (46) But first of all, God wishes to make it understood by you that there is one place for infants and another for full-grown men, the one being called practice and the other wisdom; and secondly, that the most beautiful of all the things in nature are rather such as can be seen as can be acquired; for how can it be possible to acquire possession of those things which are endowed in the same degree with the diviner attributes? But it is not impossible to see them, though it may not be given to all men to do so, for this may be permitted only to the purest and most acute-sighted race, to whom the father of the universe, when he displays his own works, is giving the greatest of all gifts.

(47) For what life can be better than that which is devoted to speculation, or what can be more closely connected with rational existence; for which reason it is that though the voices of mortal beings are judged of by the faculty of hearing, neverthe-less the scriptures present to us the words of God, to be actually visible to us like light; for in them it is said that, "All people saw the voice of God;[26] they do not say, "heard it," since what took place was not a beating of the air by means of the organs of the mouth and tongue, but a most exceedingly brilliant ray of virtue, not different in any respect from the source of reason, which also in another passage is spoken of in the following manner, "Ye have seen that I spake unto you from out of heaven,"[27] not "Ye have heard," for the same reason.

(48) But there are passages where he distinguishes between what is heard and what is seen, and between the sense of seeing and that of hearing, as where he says, "Ye have heard the sound of the words, but ye saw no similitude, only ye heard a voice;"[28] speaking here with excessive precision; for the discourse which was divided into nouns and verbs, and in short into all the different parts of speech, he has very appropriately spoken of as something to be heard; for in fact that is examined by the sense of hearing; but that which has nothing to do with either nouns or verbs, but is the voice of God, and seen by the eye of the soul, he very properly represents as visible; (49) and having previously reminded them, "Ye saw no similitude," he proceeds to say, " Only ye heard a voice, which ye all saw;" for this must be what is understood as implied in those words. So that the words of God have for their tribunal and judge the sense of sight, which is situated in the soul; but those which are subdivided into nouns, and verbs, and other parts of speech, have for their judge the sense of hearing.

(50) But as the writer being new in all kinds of knowledge, has also introduced this novelty both in his accounts of domestic and of foreign matters, saying that the voice is a thing to be judged of by the sight, which in point of fact is almost the only thing in us which is not an object of sight, with the single exception of the mind; for the things which are the objects of the rest of the outward senses are, every one of them, visible to the sight, such as colours, tastes, smells, things that are hot or cold, things that are smooth or rough, things that are soft or hard, inasmuch as it is a body, if indeed it is a body at all, nor inasmuch as they are substantial bodies. (51) And what is meant by this I will explain more distinctly: a flavour is appreciable by the sight, not inasmuch as it is flavour, but so far it is a mere substance, for in so far as it is flavour the sense of taste will judge of it; again a smell, in so far as it is a smell, will be decided upon by the nostrils, but inasmuch as it is a bodily

[23] Genesis 1:31.
[24] Genesis 15:5.
[25] Deuteronomy 34:4.

[26] Exodus 20:18.
[27] Exodus 20:22.
[28] Deuteronomy 4:12.

substance, it will also be judged of by the eyes: and the other objects of sense will be tested in this manner; but voice is not appreciable by the sense of sight, neither inasmuch as it can be heard; but there are these two things in us which are wholly invisible—mind and speech; (52) but the sound that proceeds from us does not the least resemble the divine organ of voice; for one organ of voice is mingled with the air, and flies to a kindred region with itself, namely to the ears; but the divine organ consists of unmixed and unalloyed speech, which outstrips the sense of hearing by reason of its fineness, and which is discerned by a pure soul, by means of its acuteness in the faculty of sight.

X. (53) Therefore, after having left all mortal things, God, as I have said before, gives, as his first gift to the soul, an exhibition and an opportunity of contemplating mortal things: and in the second place he gives it an improvement in the doctrines of virtue, in respect both of their numbers and of their importance; for he says, "And I will make thee into a mighty nation," using this expression with reference to the multitude of the nation, and with reference to the increase and improvement of what was already great; (54) and that this quantity in each kind, that is to say, both as to magnitude and as to number, was greatly increased, is pointed out by the king of Egypt, where he says, "For behold," says he, "the race of the children of Israel is a great multitude."[29]

Since both these facts bear witness to the race which had the power of beholding the living God, that it had derived increase both in manner and in magnitude, and as having done so, had met with prosperity, both in its life and in its language; (55) for he does not say here (as any one would say who paid attention to the connection of the words which he was using), a numerous multitude, but he says, "A great multitude," knowing that the word numerous by itself implies an imperfect multitude, unless in addition to its numbers it has the attributes of intelligence and knowledge; for what advantage is it to comprehend many subjects of speculation, unless each of them receives a power of growth to a suitable size; for in like manner a field is not perfect in which there are innumerable plants growing on the ground, and no plant has grown up by means of the skill of the husbandman so as to arrive at perfection, unless it is now able to produce fruit.

(56) But the beginning and the end of the greatness and numerousness of good things is the ceaseless and uninterrupted recollection of God, and an invocation of his assistance in the civil and domestic, confused and continual, warfare of life; for Moses says, "Behold, the people is wise and full of knowledge; this is a mighty nation; for what nation is there so great, that has God so near, as the Lord our God is to us in all the circumstances in which we call upon him?"[30] (57) Therefore it has been plainly shown that there is power with God, which is a suitable and useful helper and defender, and the ruler himself comes nearer to the assistance of those persons who are worthy to be assisted.

XI. But who are they who are worthy to obtain such a mercy as this? It is plain that they are all lovers of wisdom and knowledge; (58) for these are the wise people and the people of knowledge of whom he speaks, each of whom may naturally be called great, since he aims at great things, and at one great thing with excessive earnestness and eagerness, namely, at never being separated from the Almighty God, but at being able to endure his approach when he comes near steadily, and without any amazement or display.

(59) This is the definition of great, to be near to God, or at least to be near to that thing which God is near; forsooth the world and the wise citizen of the world are both full of many and great good things, but all the rest of the multitude of men is involved in numerous evils, and in but few good things; for the good is rare in the agitated and confused life of man. (60) On which account it is said in the sacred scriptures, "It is not because you are numerous beyond all the nations that the Lord has selected you above them all, and has chosen you out; for in truth you are but few in comparison of all nations, but it is because the Lord loves you;"[31] for if any one were to choose to distribute the multitude of one soul as if according to nations, he would find a great many ranks totally destitute of all order, of which pleasures, or appetites or griefs, or fears, or again follies and iniquities, and all the other vices which are connected with or akin to them, are the leaders, and he would find but one rank alone well regulated, that namely which is under the leadership of right reason.

(61) Among men, then, the unjust multitude is usually honoured more than one single just person; but in the eye of God a small company that is good is preferred to an infinite number of persons who are unjust. And, on that account, he warns men never to consent to a multitude of such a character; "For," says he, "thou shalt not join with a multitude to do evil."[32] May one, then, join a few to do so? One may never join a single bad man. But a bad man, though he be but a single individual, is a multitude of wickedness, and it is the greatest possible evil to join with him; for, on the contrary, it is becoming rather to oppose him and

[29]Exodus 1:9.

[30]Deuteronomy 4:6.
[31]Deuteronomy 7:7.
[32]Exodus 23:2.

to make war upon him with fearless energy. (62) "For if," says Moses, "you go forth to war against your enemies and see a horse," the emblem of arrogant and restive passion which scorns all control, "and a rider," the symbol of the mind devoted to the service of the passions, riding upon it, "and a great body of your people," admirers of those before-mentioned passions, and following in a solid phalanx, "you shall not be terrified so as to flee from them," for you, though only a single person, shall have a single being for your ally, "because the Lord your God is on your side;" [33] (63) for his advance to battle puts an end to war, builds up peace again, overthrows numbers of long-accustomed evils, preserves the scanty race which loves God, to whom every one who becomes subject hates and abominates the ranks of the more earthly armies.

XII. (64) "For," says Moses, "you shall not eat those animals which have a multitude of feet, being numbered among all the reptiles that are upon the earth; because they are an abomination." [34] But the soul is not deserving of being hated which goes upon the earth in one part of itself, but only that which does so with all or with the greatest proportion of its parts, and which is exceedingly greedy about the things of the body, and which, in short, is unable to penetrate into and contemplate the divine revolutions of the heaven. (65) And, moreover, as the animal with many feet is accursed among reptiles, so also is that which has no feet at all; the one for the cause already mentioned, and the other because it entirely falls upon the ground in all its parts, not being supported off the ground by anything, not even for the briefest minute.

For Moses says that, "Everything which goes upon its belly is unclean;" [35] meaning, under this figurative expression, to point out those who pursue the pleasures of the belly. (66) But some go far beyond these persons in wickedness, not only indulge in every description of desire, but also acquire that passion which is akin to desire, namely, anger, wishing to excite the whole of the irrational part of the soul and to destroy the mind. For what has been said in words, indeed, is applicable to the serpent, but in reality it is meant to apply to every man who is irrational and a slave to his passions, being truly a divine oracle, "Upon thy breast and upon thy belly shalt thou go;" [36] for anger has its abode about the breast, and the seat of desire is in the belly. (67) But the foolish man proceeds always by means of the two passions together, both

anger and desire, omitting no opportunity, and discarding reason as his pilot and judge.

But the man who is contrary to him has extirpated anger and desire from his nature, and has enlisted himself under divine reason as his guide; as also Moses, that faithful servant of God, did. Who, when he is offering the burnt offerings of the soul, "washes out the belly;" [37] that is to say, he washes out the whole seat of desires, and he takes away "the breast of the ram of the consecration;" [38] that is to say, that whole of the warlike disposition, that so the remainder, the better portion of the soul, the rational part, having no longer anything to draw it in a different direction or to counteract its natural impulses, may indulge its own free and noble inclinations towards everything that is beautiful; (68) for, in this way, it will improve both in quantity and in magnitude. For it is said, "How long shall this people exasperate me? and till what time will they refuse to believe me in all the signs which I have done among them? I will smite them with death and I will destroy them, and I will make thee and thy father's house into a mighty nation, greater and mightier than this." [39]

For when the great multitude of the passions which indulge in anger and desire in the soul is put to the rout, then immediately those affections which depend on its rational nature rise up and become brilliant; (69) for as the reptile with many feet and that with no feet at all, though they are exactly opposite to one another in the race of reptiles, are both pronounced unclean, so also the opinion which denies any God, and that which worships a multitude of Gods, though quite opposite in the soul, are both profane. And of proof of this is that the law banishes them both "from the sacred assembly," [40] forbidding the atheistical opinion, as a eunuch and mutilated person, to come into the assembly; and the polytheistic, inasmuch as it prohibits any one born of a harlot from either hearing or speaking in the assembly. For he who worships no God at all is barren, and he who worships a multitude is the son of a harlot, who is in a state of blindness as to his true father, and who on this account is figuratively spoken of as having many fathers, instead of one.

XIII. (70) There have now been two gifts of God already mentioned: the hope of a life devoted to contemplation, and an improvement in good things in respect both of quantity and of magnitude. The third gift is blessing, without which it is not possible that the graces already mentioned can be confirmed; for the scriptures say, "And I

---

[33] Deuteronomy 20:1.
[34] Leviticus 11:42.
[35] Leviticus 11:43.
[36] Genesis 3:14.

[37] Leviticus 9:14.
[38] Leviticus 8:29.
[39] Numbers 14:11.
[40] Deuteronomy 23:2.

will bless thee;" that is to say, I will give thee a word which shall be praised; for the portion *eu* (in *eulogēsō*, I will bless), is always applicable to virtue. And of speech, one kind is like a spring and another kind is like a stream; (71) that which is in the mind being like the spring, and the utterance through the medium of the mouth and tongue resembling a stream. And it is great riches for either species of speech to be improved, for the mind to be so by exerting soundness of reason in everything, whether important or unimportant, or for the utterance to be so when under the guidance of right instruction; (72) for many men think, indeed, most excellently, but are betrayed by a bad interpreter, namely, speech, because they have not thoroughly worked up the whole course of encyclical instruction. Others, again, have been exceedingly skilful in explaining their ideas, but very bad hands at forming intentions, as, for instance, those who are called sophists, for the mind of these sophists is destitute of all harmony and of all real learning; but their speeches, which are uttered by the organs of their voice, are full of music and beauty.

(73) But God gives no imperfect gifts to his subjects, but all his presents are complete and perfect. On which account he now dispenses blessing not to one section only, that of speech, but to both portions; thinking it proper that the man who has received a benefit should also conceive the most excellent notions, and should also be able to explain what he has conceived in a powerful manner; for perfection, as it seems, consists in the two points, of being able to form clear and just conceptions and intentions, and also of being able to interpret them correctly. (74) Do you not see that Abel (and the name Abel is the name of one who mourns over mortal things, and attributes happiness to immortal things), has a mind wholly free from all liability to reproach? And yet, from not being practised in discussions, he is defeated by one who is clever as an antagonist in such things, Cain being able to get the better of him more through superiority of skill than of strength; (75) for which reason, though I admire him on account of the good fortune with which he was endowed by nature, I nevertheless blame the disposition in him that, when he was challenged to a contest of discussion, he came forward to contend, when he ought to have abided by his usual tranquillity, discarding all love for contention. But if he was determined by all means to enter into such a contest, then still he ought not to have engaged in it until he had sufficiently practised himself in the exercises of the art; for men who have been long versed in political strife are usually accustomed to get the better of men of uncultivated acuteness.

XIV. (76) For this reason also the all-accomplished Moss deprecates coming to a consideration of reasonable looking and plausible arguments, from the time that God began to cause the light of truth to shine upon him; through the immortal words of his knowledge and wisdom. But he is not the less led on to the contemplation of these arguments, not for the sake of becoming skilful in many things (for the contemplation of God himself and of his most sacred powers, are quite sufficient for a man who is fond of contemplation), but with a view to get the better of the sophists in Egypt, where fabulous and plausible inventions are looked upon as entitled to higher honour than a clear statement of truth.

(77) When, therefore, the mind walks abroad among the affairs of the ruler of the universe, it requires nothing further as an object of contemplation, since the mind alone is the most piercing of all eyes as applied to the objects of the intellect; but when it is directed towards those things which are properly objects of the outward senses, or to any passion, or substance, of which the land of Egypt is the emblem, then it will have need of skill and power in argument. (78) On which account Moses is directed also to take Aaron with him as an addition, Aaron being the symbol of uttered speech, "Behold," says God, "is not Aaron thy brother?"[41] For one rational nature being the mother of them both, it follows of course that the offspring are brothers, "I know that he will speak." For it is the office of the mind to comprehend, and of utterance to speak. "He," says God, "will speak for thee." For the mind not being able to give an adequate exposition of the part which is assigned to it, uses its neighbour speech as an interpreter, for the purpose of explaining what it feels.

(79) Presently he further adds, "Behold he will come to meet thee," since in truth speech when it meets the conceptions, and embodies them in words, and names stamps what had before no impression on it, so as to make it current coin. And further on he says, "And when he seeth thee he will rejoice in himself," for speech rejoices and exults when the conception is not indistinct, because it being clear and evident employs speech as an unerring and fluent expositor of itself, having a full supply of appropriate and felicitous expressions full of abundant distinctness and intelligibility.

XV. (80) At all events when the conceptions are at all indistinct and ambiguous, speech is the treading as it were on empty air, and often stumbles and meets with a severe fall, so as never to be able to rise again. "And thou shalt speak to him, and thou shalt give my words into his mouth," which is equivalent to, Thou shalt suggest to him conceptions which are in no respect different from divine language and divine arguments. (81) For without

---

[41]Exodus 4:14.

some one to offer suggestions, speech will not speak; and the mind is what suggests to speech, as God suggests to the mind. "And he shall speak for thee to the people, and he shall be thy mouth, and thou shalt be to him as God." And there is a most emphatic meaning in the expression, "He shall speak for thee," that is to say, He shall interpret thy conceptions, and "He shall be thy mouth." For the stream of speech being borne through the tongue and mouth conveys the conceptions abroad. But speech is the interpreter of the mind to men, while again mind is by means of speech the interpreter to God; but these thoughts are those of which God alone is the overseer.

(82) Therefore it is necessary for any one who is about to enter into a contest of sophistry, to pay attention to all his words with such vigorous earnestness, that he may not only be able to escape from the manoeuvres of his adversaries, but may also in his turn attack them, and get the better of them, both in skill and in power. (83) Do you not see that conjurors and enchanters, who attempting to contend against the divine word with their sophistries, and who daring to endeavor to do other things of a similar kind, labour not so much to display their own knowledge, as to tear to pieces and turn into ridicule what was done?[42] For they even transform their rods into the nature of serpents, and change water into the complexion of blood, and by their incantations they attract the remainder of the frogs to the land, and, like miserable men as they are, they increase everything for their own destruction, and while thinking to deceive others they are deceived themselves. (84) And how was it possible for Moses to encounter such men as these unless he had prepared speech, the interpreter of his mind, namely Aaron? who now indeed is called his mouth; but in a subsequent passage we shall find that he is called a prophet, when also the mind, being under the influence of divine inspiration, is called God.

"For," says God, "I give thee as a God to Pharaoh, and Aaron thy brother shall be thy prophet."[43] O the harmonious and well-organised consequence! For that which interprets the will of God is the prophetical race, being under the influence of divine possession and frenzy. (85) Therefore "the rod of Aaron swallowed up their rods,"[44] as the holy scripture tells us. For all sophistical reasons are swallowed up and destroyed by the varied skilfulness of nature; so that they are forced to confess that what is done is "the finger of God,"[45] an expression equivalent to confessing the truth of the divine scripture which

asserts that sophistry is always subdued by wisdom. For the sacred account tells us that "the tables" on which the commandments were engraved as on a pillar, "were also written by the finger of God."[46] On which account the conjurors were not able to stand before Moses, but fell down as in a wrestling match, being overcome by the superior strength of their antagonist.

XVI. (86) What then is the fourth gift? The having a great name, for God says, "I will magnify thy name;"[47] and the meaning of this, as it appears to me, is as follows; as to be good is honourable, so also to appear to be so is advantageous. And truth is better than appearance, but perfect happiness is when the two are combined. For there are great numbers of people who apply themselves to virtue in genuine honesty and sincerity, and who admire its genuine beauty, having no regard to the reputation which they may have with the multitude, and who in consequence have been plotted against, being thought wicked though in reality they are good. (87) And indeed there is no advantage whatever in seeming, unless being has also been added long before, as in the case with respect to bodies; for if all men were to fancy that one who was labouring under a disease was in good health, or that one in good health was labouring under a disease, still their opinion would not of itself create either disease or good health. (88) But the man to whom God has given both things, namely both to be good and virtuous and also to appear so, that man is truly happy, and has a name which is really magnified. And one must have a prudent regard for a good reputation as a thing of great importance, and one which greatly benefits the life which is dependent on the body. And it falls to the lot of every one who, rejoicing with contentment, changes none of the existing laws, but zealously preserves the constitution of his native land.

(89) For there are some men, who, looking upon written laws as symbols of things appreciable by the intellect, have studied some things with superfluous accuracy, and have treated others with neglectful indifference; whom I should blame for their levity; for they ought to attend to both classes of things, applying themselves both to an accurate investigation of invisible things, and also to an irreproachable observance of those laws which are notorious. (90) But now men living solitarily by themselves as if they were in a desert, or else as if they were mere souls unconnected with the body, and as if they had no knowledge of any city, or village, or house, or in short of any company of men whatever, overlook what appears to the many to be true, and seek for plain naked truth by itself, whom the sacred scripture teaches not

[42]Exodus 7:12.
[43]Exodus 7:1.
[44]Exodus 7:12.
[45]Exodus 8:19.
[46]Exodus 32:16.
[47]Genesis 12:2.

to neglect a good reputation, and not to break through any established customs which divine men of greater wisdom than any in our time have enacted or established. (91) For although the seventh day is a lesson to teach us the power which exists in the uncreated God, and also that the creature is entitled to rest from his labours, it does not follow that on that account we may abrogate the laws which are established respecting it, so as to light a fire, or till land, or carry burdens, or bring accusations, or conduct suits at law, or demand a restoration of a deposit, or exact the repayment of a debt, or do any other of the things which are usually permitted at times which are not days of festival. (92) Nor does it follow, because the feast is the symbol of the joy of the soul and of its gratitude towards God, that we are to repudiate the assemblies ordained at the periodical seasons of the year; nor because the rite of circumcision is an emblem of the excision of pleasures and of all the passions, and of the destruction of that impious opinion, according to which the mind has imagined itself to be by itself competent to produce offspring, does it follow that we are to annul the law which has been enacted about circumcision. Since we shall neglect the laws about the due observance of the ceremonies in the temple, and numbers of others too, if we exclude all figurative interpretation and attend only to those things which are expressly ordained in plain words.

(93) But it is right to think that this class of things resembles the body, and the other class the soul; therefore, just as we take care of the body because it is the abode of the soul, so also must we take care of the laws that are enacted in plain terms: for while they are regarded, those other things also will be more clearly understood, of which these laws are the symbols, and in the same way one will escape blame and accusation from men in general. (94) Do you not see that Abraham also says, that both small and great blessings fell to the share of the wise man, and he calls the great things, "all that he had," and his possessions, which it is allowed to the legitimate son alone to receive as his inheritance; but the small things he calls gifts, of which the illegitimate children and those born of concubines, are also accounted worthy. The one, therefore, resemble those laws which are natural, and the other those which derive their origin from human enactment.

XVII. (95) I also admire Leah, that woman endued with all virtue, who, at the birth of Asher, who is the symbol of that bastard wealth, which is perceptible by the outward senses, says, "Blessed am I, because all women shall call me happy."[48] For she sees plainly that she will have a favourable reputation, thinking that she deserves

to be praised, not only by those reasonings which are really masculine and manly, which have a nature free from all spot and stain, and which honour that which is really honest and incorrupt, but also by those more feminine reasonings which are in every respect overcome by those things which are visible, and which are unable to comprehend any object of contemplation which is beyond them. (96) But it is the part of a perfect soul to set up a claim, not only to be, but to also appear to be, and, to labour earnestly not merely to have a good reputation in the houses of the men, but also in the secret chambers of the women.

(97) On which account Moses also committed the preparation of the sacred works of the tabernacle not only to men, but also to women, who were to aid in making them; for all "the woven works of hyacinthine colour, and of purple and of scarlet work, and of fine linen, and of goats' hair, do the women make;" and they also contribute their own ornaments without hesitation, "seals, and ear-rings, and finger-rings, and armlets, and tablets, all jewels of gold,"[49]—everything, in short, of which gold was the material, gladly giving up the ornaments of their person in exchange for piety; (98) and, moreover, carrying their zeal to a still higher degree, they likewise consecrated even their mirrors, that a laver might be made of them,"[50] in order that those who were about to assist at the sacrifices, washing their hands and their feet, that is to say, those works about which the mind is occupied and on which it is fixed, may have a view of themselves in a mirror according to the recollection of those mirrors of which the laver was made; for in this way they will never permit anything disgraceful to remain in any portion of the soul. And now they will dedicate the offering of fasting and patience, the most beautiful and sacred, and perfect of offerings.

(99) But these real citizens and virtuous women are really as it were the outward senses, by whom Leah, that is virtue, desires to be honoured. But they who kindle an additional fire against the miserable mind are destitute of any city. For we read in the scripture that even, "women still burnt additional fire to Moab."[51] (100) But may we not in this way say that so each of the outward senses of the foolish man when set on fire by the appropriate objects of outward sense, does also set fire to the mind, spreading over it an exceeding and interminable flame with irresistible vigour and impetuosity. At all events it is best to propitiate the array of women, that is to say, of the outward senses in the soul, just as it is desirable to do so with respect to the men, that is to say,

---

[48] Genesis 30:13.

[49] Exodus 35:22.
[50] Exodus 38:8.
[51] Numbers 21:30.

with respect to the particular reasonings. For in this manner we shall arrange a more excellent system of life in a very beautiful manner.

XVIII. (101) On this account also the self-instructed Isaac prays to the lover of wisdom, that he may be able to comprehend both those good things which are perceptible by the outward senses, and those which are appreciable only by the intellect. For he says, "May God give thee of the dew of heaven, and of the fatness of the earth,"[52] a prayer equivalent, to May he in the first place pour upon thee a continual and heavenly rain appreciable by the intellect, not violently so as to wash thee away, but mildly and gently like dew, so as to benefit thee. And in the second place, may he bestow upon thee that earthly wealth which is perceptible by the outward senses, fat and fertile, having drained off its opposite, namely poverty, from the soul and from all its parts.

(102) But if you examine the great high priest, that is to say reason, you will find him entertaining ideas in harmony with these, and having his sacred garments richly embroidered by all the powers which are comprehensible either by the outward senses or by the intellect; the other portion of which clothing would require a more prolix explanation than is practicable on the present occasion, and we must pass it by for the present. But the extreme portions, those namely at the head and at the feet, we will examine.

(103) There is then on the head "a golden leaf,"[53] pure, having on it the impression of a seal, "Holiness to the Lord." And on the feet there are, "on the fringe of the inner garment, bells and small flowerets."[54] But this seal is an idea of ideas, according to which God fashioned the world, being an incorporeal idea, comprehensible only by the intellect. And the flowerets and the bells are symbols of distinctive qualities perceptible by the outward senses; of which the faculties of hearing and of seeing are the judges. (104) And he adds, with exceeding accuracy of investigation, "The voice of him shall be heard as he enters into the holy place," in order that when the soul enters into the places appreciable by the intellect, and divine, and truly holy, the very outward senses may likewise be benefited, and may sound in unison, in accordance with virtue; and our whole system, like a melodious chorus of many men, may sing in concert one well-harmonised melody composed of different sounds well combined, the thoughts inspiring the leading notes (for the objects of intellect are the leaders of the chorus); and the objects of the external senses, singing in melodies, accord the symphonies

which follow, which are compared to individual members of the chorus.

(105) For, in short, as the law says, it was not right for the soul to be deprived of "its necessaries, and its garments, and its place of abode,"[55] these three things; but it ought rather to have had each of them allotted to it in a durable manner. Now the necessaries of the soul are those good things which are perceptible only by the intellect, which ought, and indeed are bound by the law of nature, to be attached to it; and the clothing means those things which relate to the exterior and visible ornament of human life; and the place of abode is continued diligence and care respecting each of the species before mentioned, in order that the objects of the outward senses may appear as the invisible objects of the intellect do also.

XIX. (106) There is, also, a fifth gift, which consists only in the bare fact of existence; and it is mentioned after all the previous ones, not because it is inferior to them, but rather because it overtops and excels them all; for what can be a greater blessing than to be formed by nature, and to be, without any falsehood or fictitious pretence, really good and worthy of the most perfect praise? (107) "For," says God, "thou shalt be blessed"[56] (*eulogētos*); not merely a person who is blessed (*eulogēmenos*), for this latter fact is estimated by the opinions and reports of the multitude, but the other depends on a person being, in real truth, deserving of blessings; (108) for as the being praiseworthy (*to epaineton einai*) differs from being praised, being superior to it; and as the being blameworthy differs from being blamed, in being worse; for the one depends upon a person's natural character, while the other is affirmed only with reference to his being considered such and such. And real genuine nature is a more reliable thing than opinion; so, also, to be blessed by men, that is to say, to be celebrated by their praises and benedictions, is of less value than to be formed by nature so as to be worthy of blessing, even though all men should be silent respecting one, and this last is what is meant in the scriptures by the term blessed (*eulogētos*).

XX. (109) These are the good things which are given to him who is about to be wise. But let us now examine what God, for the sake of the wise man, bestows on the rest of mankind also. He says, "I will bless those who bless thee, and curse those who curse thee."[57] (110) Now that this is said by way of doing honour to the good man, is plain to every one. And this, too, is not the only reason why it is said, but it is said also on account of the

[52]Genesis 27:28.
[53]Exodus 28:36.
[54]Exodus 28:34.

[55]Exodus 21:10.
[56]Genesis 12:2.
[57]Genesis 12:3.

harmonious consequence which exists in things; for he who praises a good man is himself worthy of encomium, and he who blames him is, on the other hand, deserving of blame. But it is not so much the power of those who utter or who write praise or blame that is trusted to, as the real character of what is due; so that those persons would not really appear to praise or to blame at all who, in either case, adopt or introduce any falsehood of their own. (111) Do you not see flatterers who, day and night, weary and annoy the ears of those to whom they address their flatteries, and who not only nod assent to every word that they say, but who also string together long sentences, and connect rhapsodies, and often pray to them with their mouths, but who are continually cursing them in their hearts? (112) What, then, would any one in his senses say? Would he not pronounce that those who speak thus are, in reality, enemies rather than friends, and do in reality blame them rather than praise them, even if they put together whole dramas full of panegyric and sing them in their honour?

(113) Therefore, the vain Balaam, although he sang hymns of exceeding sublimity to God, among which, also, is that one beginning, "God is not as a man,"[58] the most beautiful of all songs, and who uttered panegyrics on the seeing multitude, Israel, going through a countless body of particulars, is rightly judged by the wise lawgiver to have been an impious man and accursed, and to have been cursing rather than blessing; (114) for he says that he was hired for money by the enemy, and so became an evil prophet of evil things, bearing in his soul most bitter curses against the God loving nature, but being compelled to utter prophetically with his mouth and tongue the most exquisite and sublime prayers in their favour; for the things that he said, being very excellent, were, in fact, suggested by the God who loves virtue; but the curses which he conceived in his mind (for they were wicked) were the offspring of his mind, which hated virtue.

(115) And the sacred scripture bears testimony to this fact; for it says, "God did not grant to Balaam leave to curse thee, but turned his curses into blessing;"[59] though, in fact, all the words that he uttered were full of good omen. But he who looks into all that is laid up in the recesses of the heart, and who alone has the power to see those things which are invisible to created beings, from these secret things has passed a condemnatory decree, being in his own person at once the most indubitable of witnesses and the most incorruptible of judges, since even the contrary thing is praised, namely, for a man who appears

to calumniate and to accuse with his mouth, in his heart to be blessing, and praising, and speaking words of good omen. (116) This, as it would seem, is the custom of those who correct youth, and of preceptors, and of parents, and of elders and of rulers, and of laws; for they, at times, do each of them reprove and punish, and by these means render the souls of those who are under their instruction better. And of these men no one is an enemy to his pupil, but they are all of them friendly to all of them; but it is the office of friends who have a genuine and unalloyed good will to others to speak freely, without any unfriendly purpose.

(117) Therefore, as far as blessings, and praises, and prayers, or, on the other hand, reproaches and curses are concerned, one must not so much be guided by what proceeds out of the mouth by utterance, as by what is in the heart, by which, as by the original source of them all, both kinds of speeches are estimated.

XXI. (118) These, then, are the things which, he says, happen in the first instance to others on account of the good man, when they seek to load him with either praise or blame, or with blessings or curses. But that which comes next in order is the most important thing; that when they are silent, still no portion of the rational nature is left without a participation in the benefits; for God says that, "In thee shall all the nations of the world be blessed." (119) And this is a promise exceedingly full of doctrine; for if the mind is always free from disease and from injury, it then exerts all the tribes of feelings which affect it, and all its powers in a state of sound health, namely, its of seeing and of hearing, and all those which belong to the outward senses; and, moreover, all its appetites which are conversant about pleasures and desires, and all those feelings likewise which being reduced from a state of agitation to one of tranquillity, receive a better character from the change.

(120) Before now, indeed, cities, and countries, and peoples, and nations of the earth, have enjoyed the greatest happiness and prosperity in consequence of the virtue and prudence of the individual; especially so when, in addition to a good disposition and wisdom, God has also given him irresistible power, as he may have given to a musician or to any artist the proper instruments for music, or for carrying out any other art, or as wood is supplied as a material for fire; (121) for in good truth the just man is the prop of all the human race; and he, bringing all that he has into a common stock for the advantage of these who can use it, bestows his treasures ungrudgingly, and whatever he finds that he has not got in himself, he prays for to the only giver of all wealth, the all-bounteous God.

And God, opening the treasures of heaven, pours forth and showers down upon him all kinds of good things together; so that all the channels on earth are filled with them to overflowing. (122)

---

[58] Numbers 23:19.
[59] Deuteronomy 23:5.

And these blessings he at all times freely bestows, never rejecting the prayer of supplication which is addressed to him; for it is said in another passage, when Moses addresses him with supplication: "I am favourable to them according to thy word."[60] And this expression, as it seems, is equivalent to the other: "In thee all the nations of the earth shall be blessed." On which account also the wise Abraham, who had had experience of the goodness of God in all things, believes that even if all other things are destroyed, still a small fragment of virtue would be preserved, like a spark of fire, and that for the sake of this little spark, he pities those other things also, so as to raise them up when fallen, and rekindled them when extinct.

(123) For even the slightest spark of fire that is still smouldering, when it is fanned and re-kindled will set fire to a large pile: and so too the smallest spark of virtue, when it beams up, being wakened into life by good hopes, gives light to what has previously been dim-sighted and blind, and causes what has been withered to shoot up again, and whatever is barren and unproductive it transforms and brings to abundance of prolific power. Thus a good, which is but rare, is, by the kindness of God, made abundant and showered upon men, making everything else to resemble itself.

XXII. (124) Let us therefore pray that the mind may be in the soul like a pillar in a house, and, in like manner, that the just man may be firmly established in the human race for the relief of all diseases; for while he is in vigorous health, one must not abandon all hope of complete safety, as through the medium of him, I imagine God the Saviour extending his all-healing medicine, that is to say, his propitious and merciful power to his suppliants and worshippers, bids them employ it for the salvation of those who are sick; spreading it like a salve over the wounds of the soul, which folly, and injustice, and all the other multitude of vices, being sharpened up, have grievously inflicted upon it. (125) And a most visible example of this is the righteous Noah, who, when so many portions of the soul were swallowed up in the great deluge, himself vigorously overtopped the waves and floated on their surface, and so rose above all the dangers which threatened him; and when he had escaped in safety, he sent out great and beautiful roots from himself, from which, like a tree, the whole crop of wisdom sprang up, which, bearing useful fruit, put forth the three fruits of the seeing creature, Israel, the measures of time, Abraham, Isaac, and Jacob.

(126) For, virtue is, and will be, and has been in everything; which virtue perhaps is at times obscured among men by the want of opportunity,

but which opportunity the minister of God again brings to light. Since Sarah, that is to say, prudence, brings forth a male child, flourishing, not according to the periodical seasons of the year, but according to those seasons and felicitous occasions which have no connection with time; for it is said, "I will surely return and visit thee according to the time of life; and Sarah, thy wife, shall have a son."[61]

XXIII. (127) We have now, then, said enough about gifts which God is accustomed to bestow on those who are to become perfect, and through the medium of them on others also.

In the next passage it is said, that "Abraham went as the Lord commanded him."[62] (128) And this is the end which is celebrated among those who study philosophy in the best manner, namely, to live in accordance with nature. And this takes place when the mind, entering into the path of virtue, treads in the steps of right reason, and follows God, remembering his commandments, and at all times and in all places confirming them both by word and deed;" (129) for "he went as the Lord commanded him." And the meaning of this is, as God commands (and he commands in a beautiful and praiseworthy manner), in that very manner does the virtuous man act, guiding the path of his life in a blameless way, so that the actions of the wise man are in no respect different from the divine commands. (130) At all events, God is represented in another passage as saying, "Abraham has kept all my law."[63] And law is nothing else but the word of God, enjoining what is right and forbidding what is not right, as he bears witness, where he says, "He received the law from his words."[64]

If, then, the divine word is the law, and if the righteous man does the law, then by all means he also performs the word of God. So that, as I said before, the words of God are the actions of the wise man. (131) Accordingly, the end is according to the most holy Moses, to follow God; and he says also in another passage, "Thou shalt walk after the Lord thy God;"[65] not meaning that he should employ the motion of his legs; for the earth is the support of a man, but whether the whole world is sufficient to be the support of God, I do not know; but he seems here to be speaking allegorically, intending to represent the way in which the soul follows the divine doctrines, which has a direct reference to the honour due to the great cause of all things.

XXIV. (132) And he also, with a wish further to excite an irresistible desire of what is good, enjoins one to cleave to it; for he says, "Thou shalt

---

[60]Numbers 14:20.

[61]Genesis 18:10.
[62]Genesis 7:4.
[63]Genesis 26:5.
[64]Deuteronomy 33:4.
[65]Deuteronomy 13:4.

fear the Lord thy God, and him only shalt thou serve; and thou shalt cleave to him." [66] What, then, is this cleaving? What? Surely it is piety and faith; for these virtues adapt and invite the mind to incorruptible nature. For Abraham also, when he believed, is said to have "come near to God." [67] (133) If, therefore, while you are walking you are neither fatigued, so as to give way and stumble, nor are so careless as to turn to either the right hand or to the left hand, and so to stray and miss the direct road which lies between the two; but if, imitating good runners, you finish the course of life without stumbling or error, you will deservedly obtain the crown and worthy prize of victory when you have arrived at your desired end.

(134) For is not this the crown and the prize of victory not to miss the proposed end of one's labours, but to arrive at that goal of prudence which is so difficult to be reached? What, then, is the object of having right wisdom? To be able to condemn one's own folly and that of every created being. For to be aware that one knows nothing is the end of all knowledge, since there is only one wise being, who is also the only God. (135) On which account Moses very beautifully has represented the father of the universe as being also the inspector and superintendent of all that he has created, saying, "God saw all that he had made, and behold it was very good." [68] For it was not possible for any one to have an accurate view of all that had been created, except for the Creator.

(136) Come, then, ye who are full of arrogance, and ignorance, and of exceeding insolence, ye that are wise in your own conceit, and who say not only that ye know accurately what each thing is, but that you are also able to explain the causes why it is so, showing daring with great rashness, as if ye had either been present at the creation of the world, and had actually seen how and from what each separate thing was made, or had been counsellors of the Creator concerning the things which were created. (137) Come, and at once abandoning all other things, learn to know yourselves, and tell us plainly what ye yourselves are in respect of your bodies, in respect of your souls, in respect of your external senses, and in respect of your reason.

Tell us now with respect to one, and that the smallest, perhaps, of the senses, what sight is, and how it is that you see; tell us what hearing is, and how it is that you hear; tell us what taste is, what touch is, what smell is, and how it is that you exercise the energies of each of these faculties; and what the sources of them are from which they originate. (138) For do not tell me long stories about the moon and the sun, and all the other things in heaven and in the world, which are at such a distance from us and which are so different in their natures, empty-minded creatures that you are, before you examine into and become acquainted with yourselves; for when you have learnt to understand yourselves, then perhaps one may believe you when you enter into explanations respecting other things. But till you are able to tell what you yourselves are, do not expect ever to be looked upon as truth-telling judges or witnesses with respect to others.

XXV. (139) Since, then, these things are in this state, the mind, when it is rendered perfect, will pay its proper tribute to the God who causes perfection, according to that most sacred scripture, "For the law is, that tribute belongs to the Lord." [69] When does the mind pay it? When? "On the third day it comes to the place which God has told it of," [70] having passed by the greater portions of the differences of time, and being now passing over to that nature which has no connection with time; (140) for then it will sacrifice its beloved son, not a man (for the wise man is not a slayer of his children), but the male offspring of a virtuously living soul, the fruit which germinates from it, as to which it knows not how it bore it, the divine shoot, which, when it appears, the soul then having appeared to be pregnant, confesses that it does not understand the good which has happened to it saying, "Who will tell to Abraham?" [71] as if, in fact, he would refuse to believe about the rising up of the self-taught race, that "Sarah was suckling a child," not that the child was being suckled by Sarah. For the self-taught offspring is nourished by no one, but is itself the nourishment of others as being competent to teach, and having no need to learn; (141) for "I have brought forth a son," not like the Egyptian women, in the flower of my age and in the height of my bodily vigour, but like the Hebrew souls, "in my old age," [72] when all the objects of the outward senses and all mortal things are faded, and when the objects of the intellect and immortal things are in their full vigour and worthy of all estimation and honour.

(142) And I have brought forth, too, without requiring the aid of the midwife's skill; for we bring forth even before any skill or knowledge of man can come to us, without any of the ordinary means of assistance to help us, God having sown and generated an excellent offspring, which, in accordance with the law made concerning gratitude, very properly requites its creator with gratitude and honour. For, says God, "My gifts, and my offerings, and

---

[66] Deuteronomy 10:20.
[67] Genesis 18:23.
[68] Genesis 1:31.

[69] Numbers 31:40.
[70] Genesis 22:4.
[71] Genesis 21:7.
[72] Exodus 1:18.

my first fruits, you have taken care to bring to me."[73]

XXVI. (143) This is the end of the path of those who follow the arguments and injunctions contained in the law, and who walk in the way which God leads them in; but he who falls short of this, on account of his hunger after pleasure and his greediness for the indulgence of his passions, by name Amalek;[74] for the interpretation of the name Amalek is, "the people that licks up" shall be cut off. (144) And the sacred scriptures teach us that this disposition is an insidious one; for when it perceives that the most vigorous portion of the power of the soul has passed over, then, "rising up from its ambuscade, it cuts to pieces the fatigued portion like a rearguard."

And of fatigue there is one kind which easily succumbs through the weakness of its reason which is unable to support the labours, which are to be encountered in the cause of virtue, and so, like those who are surprised in the rearguard, it is easily overcome. But the other kind is willing to endure honourable toil, vigorously persevering in all good things, and not choosing to bear anything whatever that is bad, not even though it be ever so trifling, but rejecting it as though it were the heaviest of burdens.

(145) On which account, the law has also, by a very felicitous appellation, called virtue Leah, which name, being interpreted, means "wearied;" for she very naturally thought the life of the wicked heavy and burdensome, and in its own nature wearisome; and did not choose even to look upon it, turning her eyes only on what is beautiful; (146) and let the mind labour not only to follow God without any relaxation or want of vigour, but also to walk onwards by the straight path, turning to neither side, neither to the right nor yet to the left, as the earthly Edom did, seeking out of the way lurking places, at one time being full of excesses and superfluities, and at another of differences and short comings; for it is better to proceed along the middle road, which is that which is really the royal road, and which the great and only King, God, has widened to be a most suitable abode for the souls that love virtue. (147) On which account some also of those who prosecute a gentle kind of philosophy, which is conversant chiefly about the society of mankind, have pronounced the virtues to be means, placing them on confines between two extremes. Since, on the one hand, excessive pride, being full of much insolence is an evil, and to take up with a humble and self-abasing demeanour is to expose one's self to be trampled upon; but the mean, which

is compounded of both, in a gentle manner is advantageous.

XXVII. (148) We must also inquire what the meaning of the expression, "He went with Lot,"[75] is. Now, the name Lot, being interpreted, means "declination;" and the mind declines or inclines, at one time rejecting what is good, and at another time what is evil. And both these declinations are often seen in one and the same thing. For there are some hesitating and wavering people who incline to both sides in turn, like a ship which is tossed about by different winds, or like the different sides of a scale, being unable to rest firmly on one thing; people whom one cannot praise even when they turn to the better side, for they are influenced by impulse, and not by deliberate meaning. (149) Now, of these men Lot is a spectator, who Moses here says went with the lover of wisdom. But it was very well that when he began to accompany him he should unlearn ignorance, and should never again return to it. But still he goes with him, not in the hope of deriving improvement from an imitation of a better man, but with a view of persecuting him also with a counter attraction and allurements in an opposite direction, and of leading him where there was a chance of his falling.

(150) And a proof of this is, that the one, having fallen back again into his ancient disease, departs, having been taken prisoner by those enemies who are in the soul; but the other, having guarded against all his designs, concealed in ambuscade, took every imaginable care to live at a distance from him. But the separate habitation he will arrange hereafter, but not yet. For at present, his speculations, as would be likely to be the case with a man who has but lately begun to apply himself to divine contemplation, have a want of solidity and steadiness in them. But when they have become more compact, and are established on a firmer footing, then he will be able to separate from himself the alluring and flattering disposition as an irreconcileable enemy, and one difficult to subdue: (151) for this is that disposition which attaches itself to the soul in such a manner as to be difficult to shake off, hindering it from proceeding swiftly on its progress towards virtue.

This, too, when we leave Egypt, that is to say, the whole of the district connected with the body, being anxious to unlearn our subjection to the passions, in accordance with the language and precepts of the prophet Moses, follows us close, checking and impeding our zeal in the departure, and out of envy causing delay to the rapidity of setting forth; (152) for it is said, "And a great mixed multitude went up with them, and sheep,

---

[73]Numbers 28:2.
[74]Deuteronomy 25:17.

[75]Genesis 12:4.

and oxen, and very much cattle." [76] But this mixed multitude, if one is to speak the plain truth, are the cattle-like and irrational doctrines of the soul.

XXVIII. And it is with particular beauty and propriety that he calls the soul of the wicked man multitude: for it is truly a company which has been collected and brought together from all quarters, and composed of a promiscuous body of numerous and antagonist opinions, being, though only one in point of number, of infinite variety by reason of its versatility and diversity; (153) on which account, besides the word "mixed," there is also added the epithet "great;" for he who looks at one end only is truly simple, and unmixed, and plain; but he who proposes to himself many objects of life is manifold, and mixed, and rough, in real truth: on which account the sacred scriptures say, that the practiser of virtue, Jacob, was a smooth man, and that Esau, the practiser of what is shameful, was a hairy or rough man.

(154) On account, then, of this mixed and rough multitude collected together from mixed opinions collected from all imaginable quarters, the mind which was able to exert great speed when it was fleeing from the country of the body, that is, from Egypt, and which was able in those days to receive the inheritance of virtue, being assisted by a threefold light, the memory of past things, the energy of present things, and the hope of the future, passed that exceeding length of time, forty years, in going up and down, and all around, wandering in every direction by reason of the diversity of manners, when it ought rather to have proceeded by the straight and most advantageous way.

(155) This is he who not only rejoiced in a few species of desire, but who also chose to pass by none whatever entirely, so that he might obtain the whole entire genus in which every species is included; for it is said that, "the mixed multitude that was among them desired all kinds of concupiscence," [77] that is to say, the very genus of concupiscence itself, and not some one species; and sitting down they wept. For the mind is conscious that it is possessed of but slight power, and when it is not able to obtain what it desires, it weeps and groans; and yet it ought to rejoice when it fails to be able to indulge its passions, or to become infected with diseases, and it ought to think their want and absence a very great piece of good fortune. (156) But it very often happens to the followers of virtue, also, to become languid and to weep, either because they are bewailing the calamities of the foolish, on account of their participation in their common nature, and their natural love for their race, or through excess of joy.

And this excess of joy arises whenever on a sudden an abundance of all kinds of good coming together are showered down to overflowing, without having been previously expected; in reference to which kind of joy it is that the poet appears to me to have used the expression—

Smiling amid her tears. [78]

(157) For exceeding joy, the best of all feelings, falling on the soul when completely unexpected, makes it greater than it was before, so that the body can no longer contain it by reason of its bulk and magnitude; and so, being closely packed and pressed down, it distils drops which it is the fashion to call tears, concerning which it is said in the Psalms, "Thou shalt give me to eat bread steeped in tears;" [79] and again, "My tears have been my bread day and night;" [80] for the food of the mind are tears as are visible, proceeding from laughter seated internally and excited by virtuous causes, when the divine desire instilled into our hearts changes the song which was merely the lament of the creature into the hymn of the uncreated God.

XXIX. (158) Some persons then repudiate this mixed and rough multitude, and raise a wall of fortification to keep it from them, rejoicing only in the race which loves God; but some, on the other hand, form associations with it, thinking it desirable to arrange their own lives according to such a system that they can place them on the confines between human and divine virtues, in order that they may touch both those which are virtues in truth and those which are such in appearance.

(159) Now the disposition which concerns itself in the affairs of state adheres to this opinion, which disposition it is usual to call Joseph, with whom, when he is about to bring his father, there go up "all the servants of Pharaoh, and the elders of his house, and all the elders of the land of Egypt, and all the whole family of Joseph, himself, and his brothers, and all his father's house." [81] (160) You see here that this disposition which is conversant about affairs of state is placed between the house of Pharaoh and his father's house, in order that it might equally reach the affairs of the body, that is to say, of Egypt; and those of the soul, which are all laid up in his father's house as in a treasury; for when he says, "I am of God," [82] and all the other things which are akin to or connected with him abide among the established laws of his father's house; and when he mounts up into the second chariot of the mind, which appears to bear sovereign sway, namely, Pharaoh, he is again estab-

---

[76] Exodus 12:38.
[77] Numbers 11:4.
[78] Homer's Iliad 6.484.
[79] Psalm 80:5.
[80] Psalm 42:3.
[81] Genesis 50:7.
[82] Genesis 50:19.

lishing Egyptian pride. (161) And he is more miserable who is looked upon as a king of considerable renown, and who is born along in the chariot which has the precedence; for to be pre-eminent in what is not honourable is the most conspicuous disgrace, just as it is a lighter evil to come off second best in such a contest.

(162) But you may learn to perceive how wavering a disposition such a man has from the oaths which he swears, swearing at one time "by the health of Pharaoh,"[83] and then again, on the contrary, "not by the health of Pharaoh." But this latter formula of oath, which contains a negation, looks as if it were the injunction of his father's house, which is always meditating the destruction of the passions, and wishing that they should die; but the other brings us back to the discipline of Egypt, which desires that these passions should be preserved; (163) on which account, although so great a multitude went up together, he still does not call it a mixed multitude, since to a person who is endowed with a real power of seeing, and who is a lover of virtue, every thing which is not virtue nor an action of virtue, appears to be mixed and confused; but to him who still loves the things of earth, the prizes of earth do by themselves seem to be worthy of love and worthy of honour.

XXX. (164) Accordingly, as I have already said, the lovers of wisdom will raise a wall of exclusion against the man who, like a drone, has resolved to injure his profitable labours, and who follows him with this object, and he will receive those who, out of their admiration of what is honorable, follow him with a view to imitating him; assigning to each of them that portion which is suited to them; for, says he, "of the men who went with me, Eschol, Annan, and Mamre, shall receive a share."[84] And by these names of persons he means dispositions which are good by nature and fond of contemplation; (165) for Eschol is an emblem of good disposition, having a name of fire, since a good disposition is full of good daring and fervour, and adheres to what it has ever applied itself. And Annan is the symbol of a man fond of contemplation; for the name, being interpreted, means "the eyes," from the fact that the eyes of the soul also are opened by cheerfulness; and of both of these persons a life of contemplation is the inheritance, which is entitled Mamre, which name is derived from seeing; and to the contemplative man, the faculty of seeing is most appropriate and most peculiarly belonging.

(166) But when the mind, having been under the tuition of these trainers, finds nothing wanting for practice, it then proceeds onwards with and accompanies perfect wisdom, not outstripping it

or not being outstripped by it, but marching alongside of it step by step, with equal pace. And the words of scripture show this, in which it is distinctly stated that "they both of them went together, and came to the plain which God had mentioned to them;" (167) a most excellent equality of virtues, better than any rivalry, an equality of labour with a natural good condition of body, and an equality of art with self-instructed nature, so that both of them are able to carry off equal prizes of virtue; as if the arts of painting and statuary were not only able, as they are at present, to make representations devoid of motion or animation, but were able also to invest the objects which they paint or form with motion and life; for in that case the arts which were previously imitative of the works of nature would appear now to have become the natures themselves.

XXXI. (168) But whoever is raised on high to such a sublime elevation will never any more allow any of the portions of his soul to dwell below among mortal men, but will draw them all up to himself as if they were suspended by a rope; for which reason a sacred injunction of the following purport was given to the wise man, "Go thou up to the Lord, thou, and Aaron, and Nadab, and Abihu, and seventy of the elders of Israel."[85] (169) And the meaning of this injunction is as follows, "Go up, O soul, to the view of the living God, in an orderly manner, rationally, voluntarily, fearlessly, lovingly, in the holy and perfect numbers of seven multiplied tenfold." For Aaron is described in the law as the prophet of Moses, being loudly uttered speech prophesying to the mind. And Nadab is interpreted "voluntary," that is to say, the man who honours the Deity without compulsion; and the interpretation of the name Abihu is, "my father." This man is one who has not need of a master by reason of his folly, more than of a father by reason of his wisdom, namely such a father as God the ruler of the world. (170) And these powers are the body-guards of the mind which is worthy to bear sovereign sway, which ought also to attend upon the king, and conduct him on his way.

But the soul is afraid by itself to rise up to the contemplation of the living God, if it does not know the road, from being lifted up by a union of ignorance and audacity; and the falls which are caused by such a union of ignorance and great rashness are very serious; (171) on which account Moses prays that he may have God himself as his guide to the road which leads to him. For he says, "If thou wilt not thyself go with me, then do not thou lead me hence."[86] Because every motion which is without the divine approbation is mischievous, and it is better for men to remain here wandering

[83]Genesis 42:16.
[84]Genesis 14:24.

[85]Exodus 24:1.
[86]Exodus 33:5.

about in this mortal life, as the great portion of the human race does, than raising themselves up to heaven in pride and arrogance, to encounter an overthrow, as has happened to countless numbers of sophists, who have looked upon wisdom as only a discovery of plausible arguments, and not, as it is, a certain belief in and well-assured knowledge of facts. (172) And perhaps too there is some such meaning as this intended to be conveyed by these words,—do not raise me up on high, bestowing on me riches, or glory, or honours, or authority, or any other of those things which are usually ranked as good, unless you intend also to go with them and me yourself; for these things are often calculated to cause either great mischief, or great advantage to their possessors; advantage when God is the guide of their mind; injury when the contrary is the case. For to great numbers of people the things which are called good not being so in reality have been the causes of irremediable evils, (173) but the man who follows God does of necessity have for his fellow travellers all those reasons which are the attendants of God, which we are accustomed to call angels.

At all events, it is said that "Abraham went with them conducting them on their way."[87] Oh the admirable praise! according to which, he who was conducting others was himself conducted by them, giving what he was receiving; not giving one thing instead of another, but only that one single thing, which was prepared as a retributory gift, (174) for until a man is made perfect he uses divine reason as the guide of his path, for that is the sacred oracle of scripture: "Behold, I send my angel before thy face that he may keep thee in the road, so as to lead thee into the land which I have prepared for thee. Attend thou to him, and listen to him; do not disobey him; for he will not pardon your transgressions, for my name is in him."[88] (175) But when he has arrived at the height of perfect knowledge, then, running forward vigorously, he keeps up with the speed of him who was previously leading him in his way; for in this way they will both become attendants of God who is the guide of all things; no one of those who hold erroneous opinions accompanying them any longer, and even Lot himself, who turned on one side the soul, which might have been upright and inflexible, removing and living at a distance.

XXXII. (176) And "Abraham," says Moses, "was seventy-five years of age, when he departed out of Charran." Now concerning the number of seventy-five years (for this contains a calculation corresponding to what has been previously advanced,) we will enter into an accurate examination hereafter. But first of all we will examine what Charran is, and what is meant by the departure from this country to go and live in another. (177) Now it is not probable that any one of those persons who are acquainted with the law are ignorant that Abraham had previously migrated from Chaldaea when he came to live in Charran. But after his father died he then departed from this land of Chaldaea, so that he has now migrated from two different places. (178) What then shall we say?

The Chaldeans appear beyond all other men to have devoted themselves to the study of astronomy and of genealogies; adapting things on earth to things sublime, and also adapting the things of heaven to those on earth, and like people who, availing themselves of the principles of music, exhibit a most perfect symphony as existing in the universe by the common union and sympathy of the parts for one another, which though separated as to place, are not disunited in regard of kindred. (179) These men, then, imagined that this world which we behold was the only world in the existing universe, and was either God himself, or else that it contained within itself God, that is, the soul of the universe. Then, having erected fate and necessity into gods, they filled human life with excessive impiety, teaching men that with the exception of those things which are apparent there is no other cause whatever of anything, but that it is the periodical revolutions of the sun, and moon, and other stars, which distribute good and evil to all existing beings.

(180) Moses indeed appears to have in some degree subscribed to the doctrine of the common union and sympathy existing between the parts of the universe, as he has said that the world was one and created (for as it is a created thing and also one, it is reasonable to suppose that the same elementary essences are laid at the foundations of all the particular effects which arise, as happens with respect to united bodies that they reciprocally contain each other); (181) but he differs from them widely in their opinion of God, not intimating that either the world itself, or the soul of the world, is the original God, nor that the stars or their motions are the primary causes of the events which happen among men; but he teaches that this universe is held together by invisible powers, which the Creator has spread from the extreme borders of the earth to heaven, making a beautiful provision to prevent what he has joined together from being dissolved; for the indissoluble chains which bind the universe are his powers.

(182) On which account even though it may be said somewhere in the declaration of the law, "God is in the heaven above, and in the earth beneath," let no one suppose that God is here spoken of according to his essence. For the living God contains everything, and it is impiety to suppose that he is contained by any thing, but what is meant is, that his power according to which he made, and

---

[87]Genesis 18:16.
[88]Exodus 23:20.

arranged, and established the universe, is both in heaven and earth. (183) And this, to speak correctly, is goodness, which has driven away from itself envy, which hates virtue and detests what is good, and which generates those virtues by which it has brought all existing things into existence and exhibited them as they are.

Since the living God is indeed conceived of in opinion everywhere, but in real truth he is seen nowhere; so that divine scripture is most completely true in which it is said, "Here am I," speaking of him who cannot be shown as if he were being shown, of "him who is invisible as if he were visible, before thou existedst."[89] For he proceeds onward before the created universe, and outside of it, and not contained or borne onward in any of the things whose existence began after his.

XXXIII. (184) These things then having been now said for the purpose of overturning the opinion of the Chaldeans; he thinks that it is desirable to lead off and invite away those who are still Chaldaizing in their minds to the truth of his teaching, and he begins thus:—

"Why," says he, "my excellent friends do you raise yourselves up in such a sudden manner from the earth, and soar to such a height? and why do ye rise above the air, and tread the ethereal expanse, investigating accurately the motions of the sun, and the periodical revolutions of the moon, and the harmonious and much-renowned paths of the rest of the stars? for these things are too great for your comprehension, inasmuch as they have received a more blessed and divine position. (185) Descend therefore from heaven, and when you have come down, do not, on the other hand, employ yourselves in the investigation of the earth and the sea, and the rivers, and the natures of plants and animals, but rather seek to become acquainted with yourselves and your own nature, and do not prefer to dwell anywhere else, rather than in yourselves. For by contemplating the things which are to be seen in your own dwelling, that which bears the mastery therein, and that which is in subjection; that which has life, and that which is inanimate; that which is endowed with and that which is destitute of reason; that which is immortal, and that which is mortal; that which is better, and that which is worse; you will at once arrive at a correct knowledge of God and of his works. (186) For you will perceive that there is a mind in you and in the universe; and that your mind, having asserted its authority and power over all things in you, has brought each of the parts into subjection to himself. In like manner also, the mind of the universe being invested with the supremacy, governs the world by independent law and justice, having a providential regard not only for those things which are of more importance, but also for those which appear to be somewhat obscure.

XXXIV. (187) Abandoning therefore your superfluous anxiety to investigate the things of heaven, dwell, as I said just now within yourselves, forsaking the land of the Chaldeans, that is, opinion, and migrating to Charran the region of the outward sense, which is the corporeal abode of the mind. (188) For the name Charran, being interpreted, means "a hole;" and holes are the emblems of the places of the outward sense. For in some sense they are all holes and caves, the eyes being the caves in which the sight dwells, the ears those of hearing, the nostrils of those smelling, the throat the cavern of taste, and the whole frame of the body, being the abode of touch. (189) Do ye therefore, dwelling among these things, remain tranquil and quiet, and investigate with all the exactness in your power the nature of each, and when you have learnt what there is good and bad in each part, avoid the one and choose the other.

And when you have thoroughly and perfectly considered the whole of your own habitation, and have understood what relative importance each of its parts possesses, then rouse yourselves up and seek to accomplish a migration from hence, which shall announce to you, not death, but immortality; (190) the evident proofs of which you will see even while involved in the corporeal cares perceptible by the outward senses, sometimes while in deep slumber (for then the mind, roaming abroad, and straying beyond the confines of the outward senses, and of all the other affections of the body, begins to associate with itself, looking on truth as at a mirror, and discarding all the imaginations which it has contracted from the outward senses, becomes inspired by the truest divination respecting the future, through the instrumentality of dreams), and at other times in your waking moments. (191) For when, being under the influence of some philosophical speculations, you are allured onwards, then the mind follows this, and forgets all the other things which concern its corporeal abode; and if the external senses prevent it from arriving at an accurate sight of the objects of the intellect, then those who are fond of contemplation take care to diminish the impetuosity of its attack, for they close their eyes and stop up their ears, and check the rapid motion of the other organ, and choose to abide in tranquillity and darkness, that the eye of the soul, to which God has granted the power of understanding the objects of the intellect, may never be overshadowed by any of those objects appreciable only by the outward senses.

XXXV. (192) Having then in this manner learnt to accomplish the abandonment of mortal things, you shall become instructed in the proper doctrines respecting the uncreated God, unless indeed you think that our mind, when it has put off the body,

[89] Exodus 17:6.

the external senses, and reason, can, when destitute of all these things and naked, perceive existing things, and that the mind of the universe, that is to say, God, does not dwell outside of all material nature, and that he contains everything and is not contained by anything; and further, he does not penetrate beyond things by his intellect alone, like a man, but also by his essential nature, as is natural for a God to do; (193) for it is not our mind which made the body, but that it is the work of something else, on which account it is contained in the body as in a vessel; but the mind of the universe created the universe, and the Creator is better than the created, therefore it can never be contained in what is inferior to itself; besides that it is not suitable for the father to be contained in the son, but rather for the son to derive increase from the love of the father.

(194) And in this manner the mind, migrating for a short time, will come to the father of piety and holiness, removing at first to a distance from genealogical science, which originally did erroneously persuade it to fancy that the world was the primary god, and not the creature of the first God, and that the motions and agitations of the stars were the cause to men of disaster, or, on the contrary, of good fortune. (195) After that the mind, coming to a due consideration of itself, and studying philosophically the things affecting its own abode, that is the things of the body, the things of the outward sense, the things of reason, and knowing, as the line in the poet has it—

That in those halls both good and ill are planned;[90]

Then, opening the road for itself, and hoping by travelling along it to arrive at a notion of the father of the universe, so difficult to be understood by any guesses or conjectures, when it has come to understand itself accurately, it will very likely be able to comprehend the nature of God; no longer remaining in Charran, that is in the organs of outward sense, but returning to itself. For it is impossible, while it is still in a state of motion, in a manner appreciable by the outward sense rather than by the intellect, to arrive at a proper consideration of the living God.

XXXVI. (196) On which account also that disposition which is ranked in the highest class by God, by name Samuel, does not explain the just precepts of kingly power of Saul, while he is still lying among the pots, but only after he has drawn him out from thence: for he inquires whether the man is still coming hither, and the sacred oracle answers, "Behold, he is hidden among the stuff."[91] (197) What, then, ought he who hears this answer, and who is by nature inclined to receive instruction, to do, but to draw him out at once from thence? Accordingly, we are told, "He ran up and took him out from thence, because he who was abiding among the vessels of the soul, that is, the body and the outward senses, was not worthy to hear the doctrines and laws of the kingdom (and by the kingdom, we mean wisdom, since we call the wise man a king); but when he has risen up and changed his place, then the mist around him is dissipated, and he will be able to see clearly.

Very appropriately, therefore, does the companion of knowledge think it right to leave the region of the outward sense, by name Charran; (198) and he leaves it when he is seventy-five years old; and this number is on the confines of the nature discernible by the outward senses, and that intelligible by the intellect, and of the older and younger, and also of perishable and imperishable nature; (199) for the elder, the imperishable ratio, that comprehensible by the intellect, exists in the seventy; the younger ratio, discernible by the outward senses, is equal in number to the five outward senses. In this latter also the practiser of virtue is seen exercising himself when he has not yet been able to carry off the perfect prize of victory;— for it is said, that all the souls which came out of Jacob were seventy and five;"[92]—(200) for to him, while wrestling, and not shrinking at all from the truly sacred contest, for the acquisition of virtue, belong the souls which are the offspring of the body, and which have not yet acquired reason, but are still attracted by the multitude of the outward senses.

For Jacob is the name of one who is wrestling and engaged in a contest and trying to trip up his antagonist, not of one who has gained the victory. (201) But when he appeared to have gained ability to behold God, his name was changed to Israel, and then he uses only the computation of seventy, having extirpated the number five, the number of the outward senses; for it is said, that "thy fathers went down to Egypt, being seventy souls."[93] This is the number which is familiar to Moses the wise man: for it happened that those who were selected as carefully picked men out of the whole multitude, were seventy in number; and those all elders, not only in point of age, but also in wisdom and counsel, and in prudence, and in ancient integrity of manners. (202) And this number is consecrated and dedicated to God when the perfect fruits of the soul are offered up.

For, on the feast of tabernacles, besides all other sacrifices, it is ordered that the priest should offer up seventy heifers for a burnt offering. Again, it is in accordance with the computation of sev-

---

[90]Homer, *Odyssey*, 4.392.
[91]1 Samuel 10:22.
[92]Genesis 46:27.
[93]Deuteronomy 10:22.

enty that the phials of the princes are provided, for each of them is of the weight of seventy shekels; since whatever things are associated and confederate together in the soul, and dear to one another, have a power which is truly attractive, namely, the sacred computation of seventy, which Egypt, the nature which hates virtue, and loves to indulge the passions, is introduced as lamenting; for mourning among them is computed at seventy days.[94]

XXXVII. (203) This number, therefore, as I have said before, is familiar to Moses, but the number of the five outward senses is familiar to him who embraces the body and external things, which it is customary to call Joseph; for he pays such attention to those things, that he presents his own uterine brother,[95] the offspring of the outward sense, for he had no acquaintance at all with those who were only his brothers as sons of the same father, with five exceedingly beautiful garments, thinking the outward senses things of exceeding beauty, and worthy of being adorned and honoured by him. (204) Moreover, he also enacts laws for the whole of Egypt, that they should honour them, and pay taxes and tribute to them every year as to their kings; for he commands them to take a fifth[96] part of the corn, that is to say, to store up in the treasury abundant materials and nourishment for the five outward senses, in order that each of them might rejoice while filling itself unrestrainedly with suitable food, and that it might weigh down and overwhelm the mind with the multitude of things which were thus brought upon it; for during the banquet of the outer senses; the mind is labouring under a famine, as, on the contrary, when the outward senses are fasting, the mind is feasting.

(205) Do you not see that the five daughters of Salpaad, which we, using allegorical expressions, call the outward senses, were born of the tribe of Manasseh, who is the son of Joseph, the elder son in point of time, but the younger in rank and power? and very naturally, for he is so called from forgetfulness, which is a thing of equal power with an outward sense. But recollection is placed in the second rank, after memory, of which Ephraim is the namesake; and the interpretation of the name of Ephraim is, "bearing fruit;" and the most beautiful and nutritious fruit in souls is a memory which never forgets; (206) therefore the virgins speak to one another in a becoming manner, saying, "Our father is dead." Now the death of recollection is forgetfulness: "And he has died not for his own sin,"[97] speaking very righteously, for forgetfulness

is not a voluntary affection, but is one of those things which are not actually in us, but is one of those things which are not actually in us, but which come upon us from without. And they were not his sons, but his daughters; since the power of memory, as being what has its existence by its own nature, is the parent of male children; but forgetfulness, arising from the slumber of reason, is the parent of female children, for it is destitute of reason; and the outward senses are the daughters of the irrational part of the soul.

(207) But if any one has outrun him in speed, and has become a follower of Moses, though he is not yet able to keep pace with him, he will use a compound and mixed number, namely, that of five and seventy, which is the symbol of the nature which is both perceptible by the outward senses and intelligible by the intellect, the two uniting together for the production of one irreproachable species.

XXXVIII. (208) I very much admire Rebecca, who is patience, because she, at that time, recommends the man who is perfect in his soul, and who has destroyed the roughnesses of the passions and vices, to flee and return to Charran; for she says, "Now, therefore, my child, hear my voice, and rise up and depart, and flee away to Laban, my brother, to Charran, and dwell with him certain days, until the anger and rage of thy brother is turned from being against thee, and till he forgets what thou hast done to him."[98] (209) And it is with great beauty that she here calls going by the road, which leads to the outward senses, a fleeing away; for, in truth, the mind is then a fugitive, when, having left its own appropriate objects which are comprehensible to the understanding, it turns to the opposite rank of those which are perceptible by the outward senses. And there are cases in which to run away is useful, when a person adopts this line of conduct, not out of hatred to his superior, but in order to avoid the snares which are laid for him by his inferior.

(210) What, then, is the recommendation of patience? A most admirable and excellent one. If ever, she says, you see the passion of rage and anger highly provoked and excited to ferocity either in thyself or in any one else, which is nourished by irrational and unmanageable nature, do not excite it further and make it more savage, for then perhaps it will inflict incurable wounds; but cool its fervour, and pacify its too highly inflamed disposition, for if it be tamed and rendered tractable it will do you less injury.

(211) What, then, are the means by which it can be tamed and pacified? Having, as far as appearance goes, assumed another form and another character, follow it, first of all, wherever

---

[94] Genesis 50:8.
[95] Genesis 45:22.
[96] Genesis 47:24.
[97] Numbers 27:3.

[98] Genesis 27:43.

it pleases, and, opposing it in nothing, admit that you have the same objects of love and hatred with itself, for by these means it will be rendered propitious; and, when it is pacified, then you may lay aside your pretence, and, not expecting any longer to suffer any evil at its hand, you may with indifference return to the care of your own objects; (212) for it is on this account that Charran is represented as full of cattle, and as having tenders of flocks for its inhabitants. For what region could be more suitable for irrational nature, and for those who have undertaken the care and superintendence of it, than the external senses which exist in us? (213) Accordingly, when the practiser of virtue asks, "From whence come ye?" the shepherds answer him truly, that they come "from Charran."[99] For the irrational powers come from the external sense, as the rational ones come from the mind. And when he further inquires whether they know Laban, they very naturally assert that they do know him, for the outward sense is acquainted with complexion and with every distinctive quality, as it thinks; and of complexion and distinctive qualities Laban is the symbol.

(214) And he himself, when at last he is made perfect, will quit the abode of the outward senses, and will set up the abode of the soul as belonging to the soul, which, while still among labours and among the external senses, he gives a vivid description of; for he says, "When shall I make myself, also, a house."[100] When, disregarding the objects of the external senses and the external senses themselves, shall I dwell in mind and intellect, being, in name, going to and fro among and dwelling among the objects of contemplation, like those souls which are fond of investigating invisible objects, (215) which it is usual to call midwives? For they also make suitable coverings and phylacteries for souls which are devoted to virtue; but the strongest and most defensible abode was the fear of God, to those, at least, who have him for an impregnable fortress and wall. "For," says Moses, "when the midwives feared God they made themselves houses."[101]

XXXIX. (216) The mind, therefore, going forth out of the places which are in Charran, is said "to have travelled through the land until it came to the place of Sichem, to a lofty oak."[102] And let us now consider what this travelling through the land means. The disposition which is fond of learning is inquisitive and exceedingly curious by nature, going everywhere without fear or hesitation and prying into every place, and not choosing to leave anything in existence, whether person or thing,

not thoroughly investigated; for it is by nature extraordinarily greedy of everything that can be seen or heard, so as not only not to be satisfied with the things of its own country, but even to desire foreign things which are established at a great distance. (217) At all events, they say that it is an absurd thing for merchants and dealers to cross the seas for the sake of gain, and to travel all round the habitable world, not allowing any considerations of summer, or winter, or violent gales, or contrary winds, or old age, or bodily sickness, or the society of friends, or the unspeakable pleasures arising from wife, or children, or one's other relations, or love of one's country, or the enjoyment of political connections, or the safe fruition of one's money and other possessions, or, in fact, anything whatever, whether great or small, to be any hindrance to them; (218) and yet for men, for the sake of that most beautiful and desirable of all possessions, the only one which is peculiar to the human race, namely, wisdom, to be unwilling to cross over every sea and to penetrate every recess of the earth, inquiring whenever they can find anything beautiful either to see or to hear, and tracing out such things with all imaginable zeal and earnestness, until they arrive at the enjoyment of the things which are thus sought for and desired.

(219) Do thou then, O my soul, travel through the land, and through man, bringing if you think fit, each individual man to a judgment of things which concern him; as, for instance, what the body is, and under what influences, whether active or passive, it co-operates with the mind; what the external sense is, and in what manner that assists the dominant mind; what speech is, and of what it becomes the interpreter so as to contribute to virtue; what are pleasure and desire; what are pain and fear; and what art is capable of supplying a remedy for these things; by the aid of which a man when infected with these feelings may easily escape, or else perhaps may never be infected at all: what folly is, what intemperance, what commiting injustice, what the whole multitude of other discases, which it is the nature of all destructive vice to engender; and also what are the means by which they can be averted. And also, on the contrary, what justice is, what prudence is, and temperance, and manly courage, and deliberate wisdom, and in short what each virtue is, and what the mastery over the passions is, and in what way each of these virtues is usually produced.

(220) Travel also through the greatest and most perfect being, namely this world, and consider all its parts, how they are separated in respect of place and united in respect of power; and also what is this invisible chain of harmony and unity, which connects all those parts; and if while considering these matters, thou canst not easily comprehend what thou seekest to know, persevere and be not wearied; for these matters are not attainable without

[99] Genesis 29:4.
[100] Genesis 30:30.
[101] Exodus 1:21.
[102] Genesis 12:6.

a struggle, but they are only found out with difficulty and by means of great labour; (221) on which account the man fond of learning is taken up to the field of Sichem; and the name Sichem, being interpreted means, "a shoulder," and intimates labour, since it is on the shoulders that men are accustomed to bear burdens. As Moses also mentions in another passage, when speaking of a certain athlete he proceeds in this manner, "He put his shoulder to the labour and became a husbandman."[103]

(222) So that never, O my mind, do thou become effeminate and yield; but even if any thing does appear difficult to be discovered by contemplation, still opening the seeing faculties that are in thyself, look inwards and investigate existing things more accurately, and never close the eyes whether intentionally or unintentionally; for sleep is a blind thing as wakefulness is a sharp-sighted thing. And it is well to be content if by assiduity in investigation it is granted to thee to arrive at a correct conception of the objects of thy search. (223) Do you not see that the scripture says that a lofty oak was planted in Sichem? meaning under this figurative expression to represent the labour of instruction which never gives in, and never bends through weariness, but is solid, firm, and invincible, which the man who wishes to be perfect must of necessity exert, in order that the tribunal of the soul, by name Dinah, for the interpretation of the name Dinah is "judgment" may not be seized by the exertions of that man who, being a plotter against prudence, is labouring in an opposite direction.

(224) For he who bears the same name as this place, namely Sichem, the son of Hamor, that is, of irrational nature; for the name Hamor means "an ass;" giving himself up to folly and being bred up with shamelessness and audacity, infamous man that he was, attempted to pollute and to defile the judicial faculties of the mind; if the pupils and friends of wisdom, Simeon and Levi, had not speedily come up, having made the defences of their house safe, and destroyed those who were still involved in the labour devoted to pleasure and to the indulgence of the passions and uncircumcised. For though there was a sacred scripture that, "There should be no harlot among the daughters of the seer, Israel,"[104] these men, having ravished a virgin soul, hoped to escape notice; (225) for there is never a scarcity of avengers against those who violate treaties; but even though some persons fancy there may be, they will only fancy it, and will in the reality of the fact be proved to entertain a false opinion.

For justice hates the wicked, and is implacable, and a relentless avenger of all unrighteous actions, overthrowing the ranks of those who defile virtue, and when they are overthrown, then again the soul, which before appeared to be defiled, changes and returns to its virgin state. I say, which appeared to be defiled, because, in fact, it never was defiled; for of involuntary accidents that which affects the patient is not in reality his suffering, just as what is done by a person who does wrong unintentionally, the wrong is not really his action.

---

[103]Genesis 49:15.

[104]Genesis 34:1.

WHO IS THE HEIR OF DIVINE THINGS

(Quis Rerum Divinarum Heres)

I. (1) In the treatise preceding the present one, we discussed the question of rewards to the best of our ability. Our present purpose is to examine who is the heir of the things of God; for after the wise man heard the oracle, which being divinely given, said, (2) "Thy reward is exceedingly great;"[1] he inquired, saying, "What wilt thou give me, O master?" And I shall depart childless: but my son who is the child of my handmaid will inherit after me, this Eliezer of Damascus." And in another place he says, "Since thou hast not given me any seed, but one born in my house shall be my heir." (3) And yet who would not have been amazed at the dignity and greatness of him who delivered this oracle, so as to become silent and mute before him, if not out of fear, still at all events from excess of joy? For excessive griefs stop the mouth, and so also do excessive joys; (4) on which account Moses confesses that he is "a man of a slight voice and slow of speech from the time when God first began to converse with him."[2]

And this testimony of the prophet is unerring; for it is natural for the organs of speech to be checked, and for the reason which is collected in the mind to be borne onwards with unrestrained impetuosity, philosophically examining the unceasing beauty of ideas not of words, with fluent and sublime power; (5) and the most admirable virtues are boldness and freedom of speech at suitable times towards one's betters, so that the sentence in the comic poet appears to me to be uttered with truth rather than with comic humour:—

If a slave is always dumb,
He is scarcely worth a crumb:
Let him, freely told, boldly speak.

II. (6) When then has a slave freedom of speech towards his master? Is it not when he is conscious that he has not wronged him, but that he has done and said everything with a view to the advantage of his owner? (7) When therefore is it proper for the servant of God to use freedom of speech to the ruler and master of himself, and of the whole word? Is it not when he is free from all sins, and is aware in his conscience that he loves his master, feeling more joy at the fact of being a servant of God, than he would if he were sov-ereign over the whole race of mankind, and were invested without any effort on his part with the supreme authority over land and sea. (8) And he mentions the ministrations and services by which Abraham displayed his love to his master in the last sentence of the divine oracle given to his son, "I will give to thee and to thy seed all this land, and in thy seed shall all the nations of the earth be blessed, because Abraham thy father obeyed my voice, and kept all my precepts, and all my commandments, and my laws, and my judgments."[3] (9) And it is the greatest possible praise of a servant that he does not neglect a single thing of the commandments which his master lays upon him, but that he labours earnestly without any hesitation and with all his vigour, and even beyond his power to perform them all with a well affected mind.

III. (10) There are persons, then, to whom it is becoming to listen but not to speak, with respect to whom it is said, "Be silent and hear,"[4] a very admirable injunction; for ignorance is a very bad and a very audacious thing, the first remedy for which is silence, and the second, attention to those who present you with anything worthy of your listening to. (11) Let no one, however, think that this is all that is signified by those few words, "Be silent and hear;" but that there is also something greater in them which may give a lesson to any one. For these words do not recommend you only to be silent with your tongues, and to hear with your ears, but also to conduct yourself thus in both these respects in your soul; (12) for many persons when they have come to listen to some one, have nevertheless not come with their minds, but wander outside, and keep on thinking of thousands upon thousands of things within themselves, whether concerning their relations, or strangers, or themselves, which at that moment they ought not to remember at all, but which in short they, re-collecting to themselves in regular order, and thus by reason of the excessive tumult which they keep alive in themselves, they are unable to hear the speaker. For he speaks as if he were not among men, but among inanimate statues who have indeed ears, but no sense of hearing.

(13) If, therefore, the mind chooses to associate neither with things wandering about inside, nor with those which are stored up within it, but,

---

[1]Genesis 15:1.
[2]Exodus 4:10.

[3]Genesis 26:3.
[4]Deuteronomy 27:9.

remaining quiet and silent, directs its whole attention to the speaker, keeping silent in accordance with the injunction of Moses, it will be able to listen with all attention, but otherwise it would not be able to do so.

IV. (14) Silence, then, is a desirable thing for those who are ignorant, but for those who desire knowledge, and who have at the same time a love for their master, freedom of speech is a most necessary possession. Accordingly it is said, in the book of Exodus, "The Lord will fight for us, and you will be silent."[5] And, immediately afterwards, there is added a scripture in the following words: "And the Lord said unto Moses, Why dost thou cry unto me?" As it is proper for those persons to be silent who can say nothing worthy of being listened to, and for those to speak who, through love of wisdom, believe in God; and not only to speak quietly but to cry out with exceeding noise, not indeed with the noise of the mouth and tongue, by means of which they say that the air is affected with a rotatory motion, and so is rendered capable of being perceived by the hearing, but by the all-instructed and very loudly speaking organ of that voice of which no mortal man is the hearer, but only the uncreated and immortal God.

(15) For the well-arranged and carefully attuned melody of that harmony which is perceptible by the intellect, the invisible musician, perceptible by the intellect, is alone able to comprehend; but no one of those involved in the entanglements of the outward senses can appreciate it. Accordingly, when the entire organ of the mind sounds according to the symphony of the diapason and of the double diapason, the hearer, as it were, asks (for he does not ask in reality, since everything is known to God), "Why dost thou cry unto me?" Is it in supplications that evils may be averted, or in thankfulness for a participation in good things which have been already enjoyed, or for a combination of both reasons?

V. (16) But the man who appeared to be endued with a thin voice, and with slowness of speech, and to be almost dumb, is nevertheless found to be talkative, so that in one place he is represented not merely as speaking, but even as crying out; and, in another, as exerting a ceaseless and uninterrupted flow of words; (17) for, says the scripture, "Moses spoke, and God answered him with a voice."[6] He did not speak in brief periods or sentences, but in one continuously extended speech; and God also instructed him, not in brief sentences, but gave him one unbroken and continuous answer. (18) And whenever there is an answer, there then must of necessity have been, in every case, a question. But whenever any one puts a question it is respecting something which he does not know, because he is desirous to learn; inasmuch as he is aware that there is nothing so useful with regard to acquiring knowledge as to ask, to inquire, to investigate, to appear to know nothing, and not to have an idea that one comprehends anything firmly.

(19) The wise, therefore, take God for their teacher and instructor; and those who are less perfectly initiated in wisdom take the wise men for theirs. On which account they say, also, "Do thou speak with us, and let not God speak to us, lest we die."[7] And the virtuous man uses such freedom of speech as not only to speak and cry out, but even to advance positive claims with true confidence and genuine feeling; (20) for the expression, "If thou forgivest them their sin, forgive them; and if not, then wipe me out of the book which thou hast written."[8] And this sentence also, "Did I conceive all this people in my womb? Or have I brought them forth, that thou sayest unto me, Take them up into thy bosom, as a nurse takes up her sucking child."[9] And also that passage where we read, "From whence am I to get flesh to give to all this people, because they cry unto me? Shall sheep and oxen be sacrificed, or shall all the fish of the sea be collected together, to satisfy them? And again, "Lord, why hast thou afflicted this people?" And again, "Why hast thou sent me?" And, in another place, "From the time that I went forth to speak to Pharaoh in thy name, he has afflicted the people." And again, "Thou hast not delivered thy people."[10] For these, and similar things, and any one would have feared to say to any king of this earth; but to deliver such sentiments, and to speak freely to God, was an instance of what ought not to be called extreme audacity, but of good confidence; (21) because all the wise are dear to God, and especially those who are wise with the wisdom of the most sacred giving of the law.

And freedom of speech is nearly akin to friendship; since to whom would any one speak with more freedom than to his own friend? very appropriately therefore is Moses spoken of in the scriptures as dear to God, when he goes through an account of all the dangers which he had incurred by reason of his boldness, in such a way that they seem to deserve to be attributed to friendship rather than to arrogance; for audacity belongs to the character of the arrogant man; but good confidence belongs to the friend.

VI. (22) But consider again that confidence is tempered with prudent caution; for the question, "What wilt thou give me?"[11] displays confidence,

[5]Exodus 14:4.
[6]Exodus 19:19.

[7]Exodus 20:19.
[8]Exodus 32:32.
[9]Numbers 11:11.
[10]Exodus 10:22.
[11]Deuteronomy 33:1.

and the addition, "O master," exhibits prudent confidence. And being in the habit of using two causes or two appellations, with respect to the cause of all things, namely the title of Lord, and also that of God, he has in this instance used neither of them, but calls them by the name of master, speaking with caution and with exceeding propriety; and indeed the two apppellations lord and master, are said to be synonymous. (23) But even if the two names are one and the same thing, still the titles differ in respect of the meaning attached to them; for the title lord, *kyrios*, is derived from the word *kyros*, authority, which is a firm thing, in contradistinction to that which is infirm and invalid, *hakyron*. But the term master, *despotēs*, is derived from *desmos*, a chain; from which word *deos*, fear, also comes in my opinion, so that the master is the lord, and, as one may say a lord, to be feared, not only inasmuch as he is able to strike one with fear and terror; and perhaps also since he is the master of the universe; holding it together in such a manner as to be insoluble, and binding up again what portions of it are dissolved.

(24) But he who says, "Master, what wilt thou give unto me?" does, in the real meaning of his words say, this, "I am not ignorant of thy overpowering might, and I know the formidable nature of thy sovereignty: I fear and tremble, and again I feel confidence; for thou hast given me an oracular command not to fear, (25) thou hast given to me the tongue of instruction, that I might know when I ought to speak; thou hast unloosened my mouth which before was sewed up, thou hast opened it, and hast also made it articulate; thou hast appointed it to utter what ought to be spoken, confirming that sacred oracle, "I will open thy mouth, and I will tell thee what thou oughtest to speak."[12] (26) For who was I, that thou shouldest give me a portion of thy speech, that thou shouldest promise me a reward as if it were my due, namely, a more perfect blessing of thy grace and bounty? Am I not an emigrant from my country? am I not driven away from my kindred? am I not banished and alienated from my father's house? do not all men call me an outcast and a fugitive, a desolate and dishonoured man? (27) but thou, O master, art my country, thou art my kindred, thou art my paternal hearth, thou art my honour, thou art my freedom of speech, my great, and famous, and inalienable wealth, (28) why therefore shall I not have courage to say what I think? and why shall I not ask questions, when I desire to learn something more?

But nevertheless, though I say that I feel confidence, I do again confess that I am stricken with awe and amazement, and that I do not feel within myself an unmixed spirit of battle, but fear mingled with confidence, as perhaps many people will easily imagine, a closely combined conjunction of the two feelings; (29) therefore I drink insatiably of this well-mixed cup, which persuades me neither to speak freely without prudent caution; nor, on the other hand, to think so much of caution as to lose my freedom of speech. For I have learnt to appreciate my own nothingness, and to look up to the excessive and unapproachable height of thy munificence; and whenever I know that I am myself "but dust and ashes, " or even, what is still more worthless, if there is any such thing, then I feel confidence to approach thee, humbling myself, and casting myself down to the ground, so completely changed as scarcely to seem to exist.

VII. (30) Now such a disposition of the soul, Abraham, the inspector, has deeply engraved on my memory. For, says the scripture, "Abraham came near and said, Now have I begun to speak unto the Lord, I that am but dust and ashes;"[13] since then there was an opportunity given to the creature to approach the Creator, when he recognised his own nothingness. (31) But the expression, "What wilt thou give me?" is not so much the language of one who is in doubt, as of one feeling and expressing gratitude at the multitude and greatness of the blessings which he has already enjoyed. "What wilt thou give me?" for, in fact, what more is there left for me to expect? for, O bountiful God! thy graces and mercies are boundless and unlimited, and they have no boundary and no end, bursting up like fountains full of perfection, which are continually drawn upon and are never dry. (32) And it is worth while to contemplate, not merely the ever-abounding torrent of thy bounties, but also those fields of ours which are irrigated by them; for if a superfluous and too excessive stream be poured over them, then the place will become a marshy and swampy plain instead of fertile land; for our land has need of irrigation, carefully measured out with a view to cause fertility, and not unmeasured. (33) And on this account I will ask, What wilt thou give me, thou who hast already bestowed on me unspeakable mercies, and almost all things, so that mortal nature is incapable of containing them? For what remains that I wish to know, and to have, and to acquire, is this: who could be worthy of thy works, who could deserve to inherit them?

(34) "I shall depart from life childless;"[14] having received a short-lived and ephemeral blessing, which speedily passes away, when I prayed for the contrary, namely, for one who should last many days, a long time; which should be free from all mishap, which should never die, but should be able to sow seeds itself, and to stretch forth roots for

[12]Exodus 4:12.

[13]Genesis 18:27.
[14]Genesis 15:2.

the sake of giving it firmness, and which should raise its trunk upwards to heaven, and hold its head on high; (35) for it is necessary that human virtue must walk upon the earth, and must, at the same time, strive to reach heaven; that there being hospitably received by immortality, it may pass all future time in freedom from all evil, (36) for I know that thou hatest a barren and unproductive soul, thou who art thyself the supporter of things that have no existence, and the parent of all things. Since thou hast given especial grace to the race which has the faculty of seeing, so that it shall never be barren, and never be childless; and as I myself have been assigned to that race as part of it, I am justly desirous of an heir; for, perceiving that the race is inextinguishable, I think it would be a most shameful thing of me to be indifferent to the sight of my own nature, separated from all that is good.

(37) Therefore I am a suppliant to thee, and I implore thee, that those seeds and sparks being kindled and cherished, the saving light of virtue may burn up and give light, which being borne on like a torch, delivered from hand to hand in constant succession, may last as long as the world. (38) Moreover, thou hast inspired those men who practice virtue with a desire for children of the sowing and generation of the soul; and they, having received such a portion have, in their joy, spoken and said, "The children which God hath mercifully given to thy servant,"[15] of whom migration is the nurse and guardian, whose souls are simple, and tender, and well disposed, being calculated easily to receive the beautiful and most God-like impressions of virtue; (39) and teach me also this saying, "Whether the son of Meshech, my servant, born in my house, is competent to become the inheritor of thy graces," for up to this time I have not received the son whom I hoped for, and of the one whom I have received I have no hope.

VIII. (40) But who Meshech is, and who her son is, must be examined in no superficial manner. Now the interpretation of the name Meshech is, "out of a kiss;" but a kiss differs from loving; for the one exhibits usually a discovery of souls united together by good-will, but the other intimates only a bare and superficial salutation when some necessity has brought the two parties to the same place. (41) For as the meaning "to stoop" (*kyptein*) is not contained in (*anakyptein*) "to lift up the head," nor "to drink" (*pinō*) in, "to absorb" (*katapinō*), nor "a horse" (*hippos*) in the word (*marsippos*) "a bag," so also "to love" (*philein*) is not necessarily contained in "to kiss" (*kataphilein*); since men yielding to the bitter necessities of life offer this salutation to numbers of their enemies. (42) But what that salutation is which consists of a kiss, but not of sincere friendship for us, I will

explain without any reservation or concealment. It is, forsooth, that life which exists in union with the external senses, which is called Meshech, being completely secured and defended, which there is no one who does not love, which men in general look upon as their mistress, but which virtuous men consider their handmaid, not a foreign slave or one bought with a price, but born in the house, and in some sense, a fellow citizen with themselves. Well, one class of these men have learnt to kiss this, not to love it; but the other class have learnt to love it to excess, and to think it an object of desire above all things.

(43) But Laban, the hater of virtue, will neither be able to kiss the virtues which are assigned to the man who is inclined to the practice of virtue, but, making his own life to depend on hypocrisy and false pretenses, he, as if indignant, for he is not in reality affected, says, "I was not accounted worthy to kiss my children and my daughters;"[16] speaking very naturally and decorously, for we have all been taught to hate irony irreconcileably. (44) Do thou, therefore, love the virtues, and embrace them with thy soul, and then you will be not at all desirous to kiss, which is but the false money of friendship;—"For have they not yet any part or inheritance in thy house? have they not been reckoned as aliens before thee? and hast not thou sold them and devoured the money?"[17] so that you could neither at any subsequent time recover it, after having devoured the price of their safety and their ransom. Do you pretend, therefore, to wish to kiss, or else to wage endless war against all the judges? But Aaron will not kiss Moses, though he will love him with the genuine affection of his heart. "For," says the scripture, "he loved him, and they embraced one another."[18]

IX. (45) But there are three kinds of life. The first life, to God; the second, with respect to the creature; the third, is on the borders of both, being compounded of the two others. Now, the life to God has not descended to us, and has not come to the necessities of the body. Again, life with respect to the creature has not wholly ascended up to heaven, nor has it sought to ascend, but it lurks in unapproachable recesses, and rejoices in a life which is no life. (46) And the mingled kind is that one which often ascends upwards, being conducted upwards by the better part, and it gazes on divine things, and contemplates them; but still it often turns back, being dragged in the contrary direction by the worse part: and when the portion of the better life, as if placed in the balance of a scale, outweighs the whole, then the weight of the opposite kinds of life is dragged in the contrary

---

[15] Genesis 33:5.

[16] Genesis 31:28.
[17] Genesis 31:14.
[18] Exodus 18:7.

direction, so that the lightest weight appears to be in the opposite scale.

(47) But Moses having, without any contest or doubt, given the crown of victory to that kind of life which is life to God, brings that forward as the best, likening the other two kinds to two women, one of whom he calls beloved, and the other hated, giving them both most appropriate names. (48) For who is there who is not at times influenced by the pleasures and delights which he receives by means of his eyes, or by those which reach him through the medium of his ears, or of his sense of taste, or of his sense of smell and touch? And who is there who does not hate the contrary things, want and self-denial, and a life of austerity, and seeking after knowledge, which has never any share in amusement or laughter, but is full of gravity, and cares and labours, loving contemplation, an enemy to ignorance, superior to money, and glory, and pleasure, but under the dominion of temperance and true glory, and of that wealth which sees and is not blind? These, then, are at all times the eldest offspring of wisdom.

X. (49) But Moses thinks those things which, though younger in point of time are nevertheless honourable by nature, worthy of the first honours of the birth-right, giving them a double share, and taking from the others half of their share; for, says he, "If a man have two wives, the one beloved and the other hated, and if they both bear children, then when he is about to distribute his property, he shall not be able to give the portion belonging to the first-born to the son of her who is beloved," [19] namely, to the son of pleasure; for he is but young, even though in point of time he may be old; but he looks upon the son of her who is hated, namely, of wisdom, as the elder, ever since he was a child; and, accordingly, to him he has assigned a double share.

(50) But because we have, on a previous occasion, explained the figurative sense of this passage, we will now pass on to what comes next, to the passage before us; after we have first explained this point, that "God is said to have opened the womb of her who was hated," and thus to have caused to arise an offspring of virtuous practices and good actions, while the wife, who was reputed to be beloved, was from that time forth barren: (51) "For the Lord," says the scripture, "seeing that Leah was hated, opened her womb, but Rachel was barren." [20] Is it not then the case, that when the soul is pregnant, and begins to bring forth such things as are becoming to the soul, then all those objects of the outward senses are barren and unproductive, objects to which the salutation

belongs, which is given by a kiss and not by genuine affection?

XI. (52) Each individual then among us is the son of life according to the outward sense, which he calls Meshech, honouring and admiring the foster-mother and nurse of the mortal race, namely, the outward sense, whom also, when the earthly mind, by name Adam, saw after it had been created, he named her life his own death; (53) for, says the scripture, "Adam called his wife's name Eve (zoē), because she was the mother of all living," [21] that is to say, of those who are in real truth dead as to the life of the soul; but they who really live have wisdom for their mother and the outward sense for their slave, which has been created by nature for the purpose of ministering to knowledge; (54) and the name of that man who was born of life (zoē), whom we have recognized by a kiss, he calls Damascus, which name, being interpreted, means "the blood of the sack;" by this figurative language, calling the body a sack, with great power and felicity; and by blood, he means the life which depends on the blood.

(55) For since the soul is spoken of in two ways, first of all as a whole, secondly, as to the dominant part of it, which, to speak properly, is the soul of the soul, just as the eye is both the whole orb, and also the most important part of that orb, that namely by which we see; it seemed good to the law-giver that the essence of the soul should likewise be two-fold; blood being the essence of the entire soul, and the divine Spirit being the essence of the dominant part of it; accordingly he says, in express words, "The soul of all flesh is the blood thereof." [22] (56) He does well here to attribute the flow of blood to the mass of flesh, combining two things appropriate to one another; but the essence of the mind he has not made to depend on any created thing, but has represented it as breathed into man by God from above. For, says Moses, "The Creator of the universe breathed into his face the breath of life, and man became a living soul," [23] who also, it is recorded, was fashioned after the image of the Creator.

XII. (57) So that the race of mankind also is twofold, the one being the race of those who live by the divine Spirit and reason; the other of those who exist according to blood and the pleasure of the flesh. This species is formed of the earth, but that other is an accurate copy of the divine image; (58) and that description of us which is but fashioned clay, and which is kneaded up with blood, has need, in no slight degree, of assistance from God; on which account it is said, this Damascus

---

[19] Deuteronomy 21:15.
[20] Genesis 29:31.

[21] Genesis 3:20.
[22] Genesis 9:8.
[23] Genesis 2:7.

of Eleazar.[24] But the name Eleazar, being interpreted, means, "God is my helper." Since the mass of the body, which is filled with blood, being of itself easily dissolved and dead, has its existence through, and is kept alive by, the providence of God, who holds his arm and shield of defence over it, while our race cannot, by any resources of its own, exist in a state of firmness and safety for a single day.

(59) Do you not see that the second of the sons of Moses has also the same name as this man? For, "the name of the second," says the scripture, "was Eleazar."[25] And he adds the reason: "for the Lord has been my helper, and has delivered me out of the hand of Pharaoh." (60) But those who are still companions of that life which owes its existence to blood, and which is appreciable by the outward senses, are attacked by that disposition which is such a formidable disperser of piety, by name Pharaoh; from whose sovereignty, full as it is of lawlessness and cruelty, it is impossible to escape, unless Eleazar be born in the soul, and unless one puts one's hope of succour in the only Saviour.

(61) And it is with particular beauty that he speaks of Damascus with reference, not to his father, but to his mother; in order to show that the soul depending on blood, by means of which the brute animals live, is akin properly to the female race; the race of his mother, and has no share in the male race. But this is not the case with virtue, that is with Sarah; (62) for she has none but a male offspring, being borne only of God who is the father of all things, being that authority which has no mother. "For truly," says the scripture, "she is my sister by my father's side, but not by my mother's."[26]

XIII. (63) We have now explained what it was necessary for you to be apprised of as a preliminary. For the first part of the argument had a sort of enigmatical obscurity. But we must examine with more accurate particularity what the man who is fond of learning seeks. Perhaps then it is something of this sort: to know whether any one who is desirous of that life which is dependent on blood and who claims an interest in the objects of the outward sense, can become an inheritor of incorporeal and divine things? (64) for of such only he who is inspired from above is thought worthy, having received a portion of heavenly and divine inheritance, being in fact the most pure mind, disregarding not merely the body but also the other fragment of the soul, which being devoid of reason is mixed up with blood, kindling the fervid passions and excited appetites. (65) Accordingly, it

pushes its inquiries in this manner: since you have not given to me a seed which is capable of becoming its own instructor, namely, that seed which is able to be comprehended by the intellect, "Shall the slave born in my house be my heir?" the offspring of that life which is dependent upon blood. (66) Then God, making haste, anticipated the speaker, sending, as one may say, instruction on in advance of speech. "For immediately," says the scripture, "the voice of God came to him, saying, He shall not be thy heir;"[27] nor any one else of those who come to an exhibition of the outward senses. For the incorporeal natures are the inheritors of those things which can only be appreciated by the intellect.

(67) And it has been especially observed here, that the scripture does not say he spoke to him or conversed with him, but the expression is, "The voice of God came to him;" as if God uttering a loud and unceasing sound, in order that the voice being thus distributed into every soul, might leave no part destitute of proper instruction, but that all parts might every where be filled, with healthy learning.

XIV. (68) Who, then, shall be the heir? Not that reasoning which remains in the prison of the body according to its own voluntary intentions, but that which is loosened from those bonds and emancipated, and which has advanced beyond the walls, and if it be possible to say so, has itself forsaken itself. "For he," says the scripture, "who shall come out from thee, he shall be thy heir." (69) Therefore if any desire comes upon thee, O soul, to be the inheritor of the good things of God, leave not only thy country,[28] the body, and thy kindred, the outward senses, and thy father's house, that is speech; but also flee from thyself, and depart out of thyself, like the Corybantes, or those possessed with demons, being driven to frenzy, and inspired by some prophetic inspiration. (70) For while the mind is in a state of enthusiastic inspiration, and while it is no longer mistress of itself, but is agitated and drawn into frenzy by heavenly love, and drawn upwards to that object, truth removing all impediments out of its way, and making every thing before it plain, so that it may advance by a level and easy road, its destiny is to become an inheritor of the things of God.

(71) But, O mind! take confidence, and explain to us how you depart and emigrate from those former things, you who utter things perceptible only by the intellect to those who have been taught to hear rightly, always saying, I emigrated from my sojourn in the body when I learnt to despise the flesh , and I emigrated from the outward sense when I learnt to look upon the objects of outward

[24]Genesis 15:2.
[25]Exodus 18:4.
[26]Genesis 20:12.

[27]Genesis 15:3.
[28]Genesis 12:1.

sense as things which had no existence in reality—condemning its judicial faculties as spurious and corrupted, and full of false opinion, and also condemning the objects submitted to that judgment as speciously devised to allure and to deceive, and to snatch the truth from out of the middle of nature. Again, I departed from speech when I convicted it of great unreasonableness, although it talked of sublime subjects and puffed itself up; (72) for it dared a not inconsiderable deed of daring, namely, to show me bodies through the medium of shadows, and things by means of words, which was impossible; therefore it kept stumbling about over repeated obstacles, and kept on talking vainly, being unable by common expressions to give a clear representation and understanding of the peculiar properties of the subjects with which it was dealing. (73) But I, learning by experience, like an infant and untaught child, decided that it was better to depart from all these things, and to attribute the powers of each to God, who makes and consolidates the body, and who prepares the outward senses so as to feel appropriately, and who gives to speech the power of speaking at its desire; (74) and in the same manner in which you have departed from the other things, now rise up and emigrate from thyself. But what is the meaning of this expression? Do not treasure up in thyself the faculties of perceiving, and thinking, and comprehending, but offer and dedicate these things to him who is the cause of thinking accurately, and of comprehending without being deceived.

XV. (75) But it is the holier of the all-sacred places in the temple which receives this offering; for it appears that there are two; the one discernible only by the intellect, and the other perceptible by the outward senses. Now, of these creatures which are perceptible by the outward senses, this world is the receptacle; but of those things which are truly invisible, the world, which is discernible only by the intellect, is the magazine: (76) but he that goes out from us and desires to become an attendant of God, is the inheritor of the much celebrated wealth of nature; he bears witness, who says, "He brought him out, and said unto him, Look up to heaven;"[29] since that is the treasury of the good things of God. "May the Lord," says he, "open to thee the treasury of his good things,"[30]—that is, the heaven; out of which he who furnishes the supply does incessantly rain the most perfect joys.

Look up, then, so as to convict the blind race of common men, which, though it appears to see, is blind. (77) For how can it be otherwise than blind, when it sees evil instead of good, and what is unjust instead of what is just, and the indulgence of the passions, instead of a mastery over them,

and things mortal, instead of things immortal, and when it runs away from its monitors and correctors, and from conviction and instruction, and admits flatterers, and the reasonings of idleness, and ignorance, and luxury, all exerted in the cause of pleasure? (78) The good man, then, alone sees; in reference to whom the ancients also called the prophets, seers.[31]

But he who advanced further outwards, not only seeing, but seeing God, was called Israel; the meaning of which name is, "seeing God." But others, even if they ever do open their eyes, still bend them down towards the earth, pursuing only earthly things, and being bred up among material objects; (79) for the one raises his eyes to the sky, beholding the manna, the divine word, the heavenly, incorruptible food of the soul, which is food of contemplation: but the others fix the eye on garlic and onions, food which causes pain to the eyes, and troubles the sight, and makes men wink, and on other unsavoury food, of leeks, and dead fish, the appropriate provender of Egypt. (80) "For," says the scripture, "we remembered the fish which we ate in Egypt without payment, and the gourds, and the cucumbers, the leeks, the onions, and the garlic; but now our soul is dry and our eyes behold nothing but manna."[32]

XVI. (81) And the statement, "He led him out"[33] (*exēgagen auton exō*), has a bearing also on moral considerations, though some persons, through their want of instruction in moral philosophy, are accustomed to ridicule it, saying, "For is any one ever led out in (*eisō exagetai*), or led in out (*eiserchetai exō*)?" "Certainly," I would reply, "you ridiculous and very foolish man; for you have never learnt how to trace the dispositions of the soul; but by this language of yours you only seek to understand those motions of the bodies which are exerted in change of place. On which account it seems paradoxical to you to speak of any one coming out into (*exerchetai eisō*), or going in out (*eiserchetai exō*); but to those acquainted with Moses none of these things seem inconsistent."

(82) Would you not say that the perfect high priest when, being in the inmost shrine, he is performing his national sacrifices, is both within and without at the same time? within in respect of his visible body, but without in respect of his soul, which is roaming about and wandering? And again, on the other hand, would you not say that a man who was not of the family consecrated to the priesthood, but who was a lover of God and beloved by God, though standing without the holy shrine, was nevertheless in reality in its inmost parts? looking upon his whole life in the body as a sojourning in

---

[29] Genesis 15:5.
[30] Deuteronomy 28·12.

[31] 1 Samuel 9:9.
[32] Numbers 11:5.
[33] Genesis 15:5.

a foreign land; but while he is able to live only in the soul, then he thinks that he is abiding in his own country.

(83) For every fool is outside of friendship, even though he may not depart for one moment from daily association with people. But every wise man is within friendship, even if he be dwelling at a distance, not merely in a different country, but in another climate and region of the world. But, according to Moses, a friend is so near to one as to differ in no respect from one's own soul, for he says, "the friend who is like thy soul."[34] (84) And again he says, "The priest shall not be a man by himself, when he goeth into the holy of holies, until he cometh out;"[35] speaking not with reference to the motions of the body, but to those of the soul; for the mind, while it is offering holy sacrifices to God in all purity, is not a human but a divine mind; but when it is serving any human object, it then descends from heaven and becomes changed, or rather it falls to the earth and goes out, even though the mind may still remain within.

(85) Very correctly, therefore, it is said, he led him out *(exēgagen exō)* of the prison according to the body, of the caves existing in the external senses, of the sophistries displayed in deceitful speech; and beyond all this, out of himself and out of the idea that by his own self-exerted, self-implanted, and independent power he was able to conceive and comprehend.

XVII. (86) And after he has conducted him out, he says to him, "Look up to heaven, and count the stars, if thou art able to number them; thus shall be thy seed."[36] He says very beautifully, "Thus shall be thy seed," not so great shall it be, equal in number to the stars; for he does not intend here to allude to their multitude only, but also to an infinite number of other circumstances which contribute to entire and perfect happiness. (87) "Thus shall thy seed be," says God, as the ethereal firmament which thou beholdest, so heavenly, so full of unshadowed and pure brilliancy (for night is driven away from heaven, and darkness from virtue,) most thoroughly like the stars, beautifully adorned, having an arrangement which knows no deviation, but which is always the same and proceeding in the same way. (88) For he means him to speak of the soul of the wise man as a copy of heaven, or, if one may use such a hyperbolical expression, as an actual heaven upon earth, having pure appearances in the air, and well arranged motions, and harmonious progress, and periodical revolutions of divine character, star-like and brilliant rays of virtue.

But if it is impossible to find out the number

of the stars which are perceptible by the outward senses, how much more so must it be to count those which are discernible only by the intellect? (89) for in proportion, I suppose, as that which judges is better or worse than that which is judged of (for the mind is better than the outward sense, and the outward sense is duller than the intellect; in the same ratio do the subjects of the judgment differ; so that the objects of the intellect are infinitely superior to those of the outward senses; for the eyes in the body are the smallest imaginable portion of the eye of the soul; for the one is like the sun, but the others only resemble lamps, which are at one time lighted and at another extinguished.

XVIII. (90) Therefore it is a necessary addition which is subjoined, "Abraham believed in God,"[37] to the praise of him who did thus believe. And yet, perhaps, some one may say, "Do you judge this worthy of praise? who would not give his attention to God when saying or promising anything, even if he were the most wicked and impious of all men?" (91) To whom we will reply, "Do not, do not, my good man, without further inquiry, either rob the wise man of his due praise, or attribute to unworthy persons that most perfect of the virtues, faith; and do not blame our opinion on this point; (92) for if you are willing to enter upon a deeper investigation into this subject, and are not content with examining it superficially, you will then see clearly, that without the assistance or addition of something else, it is not easy to believe in God on account of that connection with mortality in which we are involved, which compels us to put some trust in money, and glory, and authority, and friends, and health, and vigour of body, and in numerous other things; (93) but to wash off all these extraneous things, to disbelieve in creation, which is, in all respects, untrustworthy as far as regards itself, and to believe in the only true and faithful God, is the work of a great and heavenly mind, which is no longer allured or influenced by any of the circumstances usually affecting human life.

XIX. (94) And it is well added in the scripture, "And it was counted to him for righteousness:" for nothing is so righteous as to have an unalloyed and entire belief in the only God.

(95) But this, although both just and consistent with reason, was considered an incredible thing on account of the incredulity of the generality of men, whom the holy scripture condemns, saying, that "to anchor firmly and unchangeably on the only living God, is a thing to be admired among men, who have no possession of true unmingled good, but is not to be wondered

---

[34] Deuteronomy 13:6.
[35] Leviticus 16:17.
[36] Genesis 15:5.

[37] Genesis 15:6.

at if truth guide the judgment; but it is the especial attribute of justice.

XX. (96) The scripture proceeds: "And he said unto him I am God, who brought thee out of the land of the Chaldaeans, so as to give thee this land to inherit it." These words exhibit not only a promise, but a confirmation of an ancient promise; (97) for the good which was previously bestowed upon him was the departure from the Chaldaean philosophy, which was occupied about the things of the air, which taught me to suppose that the world was not the work of God, but was God himself; and that good and evil is caused in the case of all existing things, by the motions and fixed periodical revolutions of the stars, and that on these motions the origin of all good and evil depends; and the equable (*homalē*) and regular motion of these bodies in heaven, persuaded those simple men to look upon these things as omens, for the name of the Chaldaeans being interpreted is synonymous with equability (*homalotēs*). (98) But the new blessing which is promised is the acquisition of that wisdom which is not taught by the outward senses, but is comprehended by the pure mind, and by which the best of all emigrations is confirmed; when the soul departs from astronomy and learns to apply itself to natural philosophy, and to exchange unsure conjecture for certain apprehension, and, to speak with real truth, to quit the creature for the Creator, and the world for its father and maker; (99) for the scriptures tell us, that the votaries of the Chaldaean philosophy believed in the heaven, but that he who abandoned that sect believed in the ruler of the heaven and the manager of the whole world, namely, in God. A very beautiful inheritance, greater perhaps than the power of him who receives it, but worthy of the greatness of the giver.

XXI. (100) But it is not sufficient for the lover of wisdom to have a hope of good things, and to expect all kinds of admirable things, because of the predictions given to him, but unless he also knows the manner in which he is to arrive at the succession of his inheritance, he thinks it very grievous, inasmuch as he thirsts after knowledge, and has an insatiable desire of attaining to it; on which account he puts a question, saying, "O Lord God, how shall I know that I shall inherit it?" (101) Perhaps some one may say that this question is at variance with perfect faith, for that to feel such a difficulty is the part of one who doubts, but that it is the part of one who believes to seek for nothing further. We must say, therefore, that he both doubts and has believed, but not about the same matter, far from it, for he has believed that he is to be an inheritor of wisdom, but he only seeks to know the manner in which this event will take place; that it really will take place he does by all means confidently comprehend, in accordance with the divine promises.

(102) Therefore the teacher having praised the desire for learning which he feels, begins his explanation with the first elementary instruction, in which this is set down as the first and most necessary thing, "Take for me."[38] The sentence is brief, but the meaning is great; for there are not a few things implied in these words. (103) In the first place you have, says God, no good thing of your own, but whatever you fancy that you have, another has bestowed it upon you. From which it is inferred that all things are the property of God who gives them, but that they do not belong to the creature which only existed after him, and which stretches forth its hands to take them. (104) In the second place, he says, even if you take them, take them not for yourself, but think what is thus given you a loan or deposit, and be ready to restore it to him who has deposited it with, or contributed it to you, requiting an older favour with a newer one, and an original kindness with one proffered instead of it, as justice and propriety require.

XXII. (105) For many men have become wicked in respect of such sacred deposits, having, through their immoderate covetousness improperly used the property of others as their own. But do thou, O good man! endeavour with all thy strength, not only to present what you have received without injury and without adulteration, but also to take even more care than that of such things, that he who has deposited them with you may have no grounds to blame the care which has been exercised by you. (106) And what the Creator of man has deposited in your custody are soul, speech, and external sense; which are symbolically named a heifer, a ram, and a goat, in the sacred scriptures. But these things some persons have at once appropriated through self-love, but others have stored them up so as to be able to return them in due season. (107) Now, of those who have appropriated them, it is impossible to tell the number; for who of us is there who does not think his soul, and his speech, and his external senses, all taken together, to be his own property, thinking that to feel, and to speak, and to comprehend, depend upon himself alone? (108) But of those who really preserve their faith holy and inviolate, the number is very small.

Such men attribute to God these three things: the soul, the external sense, and speech. For they have received all these things, not for themselves, but for him, in whose favour they naturally and appropriately confess that the energies according to each of these three things depend upon him, namely, the imaginations and apprehensions of the mind, the explanations of speech, and the perceptions of the outward senses. (109) Those, now, who attribute these things to themselves, have

---

[38] Genesis 15:9.

received an allotment worthy of their own perverseness, namely, a soul fond of plotting against others, polluted with irrational passions, and enveloped in a multitude of vices; at one time eager to indulge in violent insolence through its gluttony and lasciviousness, as though it were in a brothel; at another time held fast by the multitude of its iniquities as in a prison, with wicked (not men but) actions which deserve to be led before all the judges. Secondly, speech insolent, loquacious, sharpened against the truth, injurious to all who come in its way, and bringing disgrace upon those who possess it. Thirdly, the external sense, insatiable, always filling itself with the objects of the outward senses, but through its immoderate appetites never able to be satisfied, disregarding all its monitors and correctors, so as to refuse to look upon or listen to them, and to reject with disdain all that they say to it for its good. (110) But those who take these things not for themselves but for God, attribute each one of them to him, guarding that which they have acquired in a truly holy and religious manner, keeping their mind, so that it shall think of nothing else but the things relating to God and to his excellencies, and their speech so as to make it, with unrestrained mouth, and with ecomiums, and hymns, and announcements of happiness, honour the father of the universe, collecting together and exhibiting all its power of interpretation and utterance in this one office; and regulating the external senses, so that forming a conception of the whole of that world which is perceptible by them, they may, in a guileless, honest, and pure manner, relate to the soul all the heaven and earth, and the natures whose home is between the two, and all animals and plants, and their respective energies and faculties, and all their motions and their stationary existence.

(111) For God has implanted in the mind a power of comprehending that world, which is appreciable only by the intellect, by its own power, but the invisible world by means of the external senses. And if any one were able in all his parts to live to God rather than to himself, looking by means of the external senses into those things which are their proper objects, for the sake of finding out the truth; and through the medium of the soul, investigating in a philosophical spirit the proper objects of intelligence, and those things which have a real existence, and by means of his organs of voice, singing hymns in praise of the world and of its Creator, he will have a happy and a blessed life.

XXIII. (112) I think then that this is what was intimated in the words, "Take for me;" God, intending to send down the perfection of his divine virtue from heaven to earth, out of pity for our race, in order that it might not be left destitute of a better portion, prepared in a symbolical manner the sacred tabernacle and the things in it, a thing made after the model and in imitation of wisdom. (113) For he says that he has erected his oracle as a tabernacle in the midst of our impurity, in order that we may have something whereby we may be purified, washing off and cleansing all those things which dirt and defile our miserable life, full of all evil reputation as it is.

Let us now then see in what manner he has commanded us to bring in the different things which are to contribute to the furnishing of the tabernacle. "The Lord," says the scripture, "spake unto Moses saying, Speak unto the children of Israel, and take ye first-fruits for me of whatever it shall seem good to your heart to take my first-fruits."[39] (114) Therefore here also there is an injunction to take not for themselves but for God, examining who it is who gives these things, and doing no injury to what is given, but preserving it free from danger, and free from spot, perfect and entire. And the injunction, by which he orders the first fruits to be offered to himself, is full of doctrine; for in real truth the beginnings both of bodies and of things are investigated with reference to God alone; (115) and search if you wish to understand everything, plants and animals, and arts and sciences.

Are then the first castings of the seed of plants, the actions of husbandry or the invisible works of invisible nature? What more need I ask? What are the works of men and other animals? Have not they parents as co-operating causes, as it were, and also nature as the primary and more important and real cause? (116) And is not nature the fountain, and root, and foundation of all arts and sciences, or any other name you please to give the oldest of principles, nature, upon which all speculations are built up? And if nature be not first laid as the foundation, everything is imperfect, and on this account some one seems to me to have said with great felicity:—

The first beginning is quite half the whole.

XXIV. (117) Very appropriately therefore does the sacred scripture command the first-fruits to be offered up to the all-ruling God. And in another passage we read "The Lord spake unto Moses saying, Sanctify to me all the first-born: all that is first brought forth, all that openeth the womb among the children of Israel, whether of man or beast is mine,"[40] (118) so that it is openly asserted in these words, that all the first things, whether in point of time or of power, are the property of God, and most especially all the first-born; since the whole of that race which is imperishable shall justly be apportioned to the immortal God; and

---

[39]Exodus 25:1.
[40]Exodus 13:2.

if there is anything, in short, which openeth the womb, whether of man which here means speech and reason, or of beast which signfies the outward sense and the body; (119) for that which openeth the womb of all these things, whether of the mind, so as to enable it to comprehend the things appreciable only by the intellect, or of the speech so as to enable it to exercise the energies of voice, or of the external senses, so as to qualify them to receive the impressions which are made upon them by their appropriate subjects, or of the body to fit it for its appropriate stationary conditions or motions, is the invisible, spermatic, technical, and divine Word, which shall most properly be dedicated to the Father.

(120) And, indeed, as are the beginnings of God so likewise are the ends of God; and Moses is a witness to this, where he commands to "separate off the end, and to confess that it is due to God."[41] The things in the world do also bear witness. How so? (121) The beginning of a plant is the seed, and the end is the fruit, each of them being the work, not of husbandry, but of nature. Again, of knowledge the beginning is nature, as has been shown, but the end can never reach mankind, for no man is perfect in any branch of study whatever; but it is a plain truth, that all excellence and perfection belong to one Being alone; we therefore are borne on, for the future, on the confines of beginning and end, learning, teaching, tilling the ground, working up everything else, as if we were really effecting something, that the creature also may seem to be doing something; (122) therefore, with a more perfect knowledge, Moses has confessed that the first-fruits and the end belong to God, speaking of the creation of the world, where he says, "In the beginning God created ..."[42] And again he says, "God finished the heaven and the earth." (123) Now therefore he says, "Take for me," assigning to himself what becomes him, and admonishing his hearer not to adulterate what is given to him, but to take care of it in a manner worthy of its importance. And again, in another passage, he who has need of nothing, and who on this account takes nothing, will confess that he does take something, for the sake of giving to his worshippers the feeling of piety, and of implanting in them an eagerness after holiness, and moreover sharpening their zeal in his service, as one who favourably receives the genuine worship and service of a willing soul, (124) "For behold," says he, "I have taken the Levites instead of all the first-born that openeth the womb among the children of Israel; they shall be their ransom;"[43] therefore we take and give, but we are said to take with strict accuracy, but it is only by a metaphorical abuse of the term that we are said to give, for the reasons which I have already mentioned. And it is very felicitously that he has called the Levites a ransom, for nothing so completely conducts the mind to freedom as its fleeing for refuge to and becoming a suppliant of God; and this is what the consecrated tribe of the Levites particularly professes to be.

XXV. (125) Having now, therefore, said as much as is proper on these subjects, let us proceed onwards to what comes next; for we have postponed the consideration of many things which ought to be examined into with exactness. "Take for me," says God, "a heifer which has never been yoked and has never been ill-treated, tender and young,"[44] and exulting; that is to say, a soul adapted easily to receive government, and instruction, and superintendence. "Take for me also a ram" that is to say, speech contentious and perfect, capable of dissecting and overthrowing the sophistries of those who advance contrary opinions, and capable also of ensuring safety, and good order, and regularity to him who uses it. (126) "Take for me," also the external sense, which lives and directs all its energies to the world, which is perceptible by it, that is, "a goat," three complete years old, enjoying solid strength in a perfect number, having beginning, middle, and end. Besides all these things, "a turtle dove and a pigeon," that is to say, divine and human wisdom, both of them being winged, and being animals accustomed to soar on high, still different from one another, as much as genus differs from species or a copy from the model; (127) for divine wisdom is fond of lonely places, loving solitude, on account of the only God, whose possession she is; and this is called a turtledove, symbolically; but the other is quiet and tame, and gregarious, haunting the cities of men, and rejoicing in its abode among mortals, and so they liken her to a pigeon.

XXVI. (128) Moses appears to me to have intended figuratively to represent these virtues when he calls the midwives of the Egyptians, Shiphrah and Puah,[45] for the name Shiphrah, being interpreted, means "a little bird," and Puah means "red." Now it is the especial property of divine wisdom, like a bird, to be always soaring on high; but it is the characteristic of human wisdom to study modesty and temperance, so as to blush at all objects which are worthy to cause a blush; (129) and as a very manifest proof of this the scripture says, "He took for himself all these things."[46] This

---

[41]There is probably some corruption here. The marginal reference is to Number 21:41 and there are only thirty-five verses in the chapter. The same thing has occurred in one or two previous instances.
[42]Genesis 1:1.

[43]Numbers 3:12.
[44]Genesis 15:9.
[45]Exodus 1:15.
[46]Genesis 15:10.

is the praise of a virtuous man, who preserves the sacred deposit of those things which he has received, the soul, the outward sense, speech, divine wisdom, human knowledge, in a pure and guileless manner, not for himself, but only for him who has trusted him. (130) After this the scripture proceeds to say, "And he divided them in the middle," not explaining who did so, in order that you may understand that it was the untaught God who divided them, and that he divided all the natures of bodies and of things one after another, which appeared to be closely fitted together and united by his word, which cuts through everything; which being sharpened to the finest possible edge, never ceases dividing all the objects of the outward senses, (131) and when it has gone through them all, and arrived at the things which are called atoms and indivisible, then again this divider begins from them to divide those things which may be contemplated by the speculations of reason into unspeakable and indescribable portions, and to "beat the gold into thin plates," [47] like hairs, as Moses says, making them into one length without breadth, like unsubstantial lines. (132) Each therefore of the three victims he divided in the midst, dividing the soul into the rational and the irrational part, speech into truth and falsehood, and the outward sense into imaginations which can be and cannot be comprehended; and these divisions he immediately places exactly opposite to one another, that is, the rational part opposite to the irrational, truth to falsehood, what is comprehensible to what is incomprehensible, leaving the birds undivided; for it was impossible to divide the incorporeal and divine sciences into contrarieties at variance with one another.

XXVII. (133) But as the discussion on the subject of a division into equal portions, and on that of opposite contrarieties, is of great extent and of necessary importance, we will not wholly pass it by, nor will we dwell on it with prolixity, but, investigating it as it is, we will be content with such things as seem suitable to the occasion.

For as the Creator divided our soul and our limbs in the middle, so also, in the same manner, did he divide the essence of the universe when he made the world; (134) for, having taken it, he began to divide it thus: in the first instance, he made two divisions, the heavy and the light, separating that which was thick from that which was more subtle. After that, he again made a second division of each, dividing the subtle part into air and fire, and the denser portion into water and earth; and, first of all, he laid down those elements, which are perceptible by the outward senses, to be, as it were, the foundations of the world which is perceptible by the outward senses.

(135) Again, he subdivided heavy and light according to other ideas, for he divided the light into cold and hot; and the cold he called air, and that which was hot by nature he called fire. The heavy, again, he divided into wet and dry; and the dry he called land, and the wet he called water—(136) and each of these, again, received other further subdivisions; for the land was divided into continents and islands, and the water into sea and rivers, and all drinkable springs, and the air was divided into the solstices of summer and winter; fire, also, was divided into what is useful (but fire is a most insatiable and destructive thing), and also by a different division into what is saving; and this division was assigned for the conformation of the heaven.

(137) But as he divided the things when entire, so also did he divide the particular divisions, some of which were animated and others inanimate; and of those which were inanimate he made a division into those which always remain in the same place, the bond of which is habit, and those which move, not indeed in the way of changing their place, but so as to grow, which indescribable nature has vivified. Again of these, those which are of wild materials are productive of wild fruits, which are the food of brute beasts; but others producing good fruit, the cultivation of which has been called forth diligent superintendence and care, and these produce fruit for the tamest of all animals, namely, for man, that he may enjoy them. (138) And not only did he divide the inanimate things, and those which had received a soul and vitality in one manner—for of these he defined one species as that of irrational, and one as that of rational animals—but he also again subdivided each of these things, dividing the irrational into the wild and the tame species, and the rational into the mortal and the immortal. (139) Again, of the mortals he made two divisions, one of which he called men, and the other women; and, in the same manner, he divided the irrational animals into male and female.

And these things were also subjected to other necessary divisions, which made distinctions between them; winged animals being distinguished from terrestrial, terrestrial from aquatic creatures, and aquatic creatures, again, from both extremities. (140) Thus God, having sharpened his own word, the divider of all things, divides the essence of the universe which is destitute of form, and destitute of all distinctive qualities, and the four elements of the world which were separated from this essence, and the plants and animals which were consolidated by means of these elements.

XXVIII. (141) But since Moses not only uses the expression, "he divided," but says further, "he divided in the midst," it is necessary to say a few words on the subject of equal divisions; for that which is divided skilfully just in the middle makes two equal divisions. (142) And no man could ever possibly divide anything into two exactly equal

---

[47] Exodus 39:3.

parts; but it is inevitable that one of the divisions must fall a little short, or exceed a little, if not much, at all events by a small quantity, in every instance, which indeed escapes the perception of our outward senses which attend only to the larger and more tangible burdens of nature and custom, but which are unable to comprehend atoms and indivisible things. (143) But it is established by the incorruptible word of truth that there is nothing equal in inequality.

God alone therefore seems to be exactly just, and to be the only being able to divide in the middle bodies and things, in such a manner that none of the divisions shall be greater or less than the other by the smallest and most indivisible portion, and he alone is able to attain to sublime and perfect equality.

(144) If therefore there were but one idea of perfect equality, what has been said would be quite sufficient for the purpose. But as there are many, we must not hesitate to add some considerations which are suitable. For the word "equal" is used in one sense when speaking of numbers, as when we say that two are equal to two, and three to three; and speak of other numbers in the same manner. But in another sense when speaking of magnitude, as equal in length or breadth, or depth, which are all different proportions. For wrestler compared with wrestler, or cubit with cubit are equal in magnitude but different in power, as is the case also with measures and weights. (145) But the idea of equality is a necessary one, and so is that of equality in proportion, according to which a few things are looked upon as equal to many, and small things are equal to larger ones. And their proportionate equality, cities are accustomed to use at suitable times, when they command every citizen to contribute an equal share of his property, not equal in number, but in proportion to the value of his assessment, so that in some cases he who contributes a hundred drachmas will appear to have brought an equal sum with him who contributes a talent.

XXIX. (146) These things being thus previously sketched out, see now how God, dividing things in the middle, has divided them into equal portions according to all the ideas of equality which occur in the creation of the universe. He has divided the heavy things so as to make them equal in number to the light ones, two to two; that is to say, so that the earth and the water, being things of weight, are equal in number to those which are by nature light, air, and fire. Again, he has made one equal to one, the driest thing to the wettest thing, the earth to the water; and the coldest thing to the hottest thing, the air to the fire. So, in the same manner, he had divided light from darkness, and day from night, and summer from winter, and autumn from spring; and so on.

(147) Again, he has divided things so as to make his divisions equal in point of magnitude; such as the parallel cycles in heaven, and those which belong to the equinoxes both of spring and autumn, and those which belong to the winter and summer solstice. And on the earth he has divided the zones, two being equal to one another, which being placed close to the poles are frozen with cold, and on this account are uninhabitable. And two he has placed on the borders between these two and the torrid zone, and these two they say are the abode of a happy temperature of the air, one of them lying towards the south and the other towards the north.

(148) Now the divisions of time are equal in point of length, the longest day being equal to the longest night, and the shortest day being equal to the shortest night, and the mean length of day to the mean length of night. And the equal magnitude of other days and nights appears to be indicated chiefly by the equinoxes. (149) From the spring equinox to the summer solstice, day receives an addition to its length, and night, on the other hand, submits to a diminution; until the longest day and the shortest night are both completed. And then after the summer solstice the sun, turning back again the same road, neither more quickly nor more slowly than he advanced, but always preserving the same difference in the same manner, having a constantly equal arrangement, proceeds on till the autumnal equinox; and then, having made day and night both equal, begins to increase the length of the night, diminishing the day until the time of the winter solstice. (150) And when it has made the night the longest night, and the day the shortest day, then returning back again and adopting the same distances as before, he again comes to the spring equinox.

Thus the differences of time which appear to be unequal, do in reality possess a perfect equality in respect of magnitude, not indeed at the same seasons, but at different seasons of the year.

XXX. (151) And a very similar effect is seen in the different parts of animals and especially of men. For hand is equal to hand, and foot to foot, and nearly all the other limbs of the body are equal to their corresponding members in magnitude, those on the left hand being equal to those on the right. And there are an exceeding number of things which are equal to one another in power, both among wet things and dry things, the judgment on which is seen in measures and scales, and things of that kind. (152) And nearly all things are equal as respects proportion, even all the little and all the great things in the whole world. For those who have examined the questions of natural philosophy with some accuracy say that the four elements are all equal in proportionate equality. And it is by proportion that the whole world is compounded together, and united, and endowed with consistency so as to remain firm for ever, proportion having distributed equality to each of its parts. (153)

And they say also that the four elements which are in us, dryness, and moisture, and cold, and heat have all been mixed together and well adapted by proportionate equality, and in fact that our whole composition is nothing but a mixture of the four powers combined together by an equality of proportion.

XXXI. (154) But any one who examines all these things might add an interminable list of arguments and instances to this one present discussion. If he considered he would find the very smallest animals equal to the largest as to proportion; as for instance he would find the swallow equal to the eagle, the herring equal to the whale, and the ant equal to the elephant. For body and soul, and again pains and pleasures, and moreover affection for and dislike towards things, and all the other feelings which the nature of animals experience, are nearly all of them similar, being made equal by the rule of proportion. (155) Thus some men have felt confidence even to declare that the smallest of animals, man, is equal to the whole world, considering that each of them consists of a body and a rational soul, so that, using a figurative expression, they have called man a little world, and the world a large man. (156) And in teaching this they are not very wide of the mark, but they know that the art of God according to which he created all things, admitting neither any extraordinary intensity nor any relaxation; but always remaining the same, made every single existing thing perfection, the Creator employing all numbers and all the ideas which tend to perfection.

XXXII. (157) For, as Moses says, "He judged according to the little and according to the great,"[48] engendering and fashioning everything, and not taking anything away from the display of his art by reason of the obscurity of his materials, not adding anything because of their brilliancy; (158) since all the artists who have any reputation wish to work up whatever materials they take in an admirable manner, whether they are costly or whether they are inexpensive. And before now, some persons, having even an extraordinary love of distinction, have even spent more skill in working up materials of little value, than they have devoted to those which are costly, wishing to make up for the deficiencies of the material by the additional display of their skill. (159) But there is no material which has any value in the eyes of God, because he has given all materials an equal share of his skill. In reference to which it is said in the sacred scriptures, "God saw all that he had made, and, behold, it was very good."[49] But the things which receive an equal degree of praise, are by all means held in equal estimation by him who confers the praise;

(160) and what God praised was not the materials which he had worked up into creation, destitute of life and melody, and easily dissolved, and moreover in their own intrinsic nature perishable, and out of all proportion and full of iniquity, but rather his own skilful work, completed according to one equal and well-proportioned power and knowledge always alike and identical. In reference to which all things were also accounted equal and similar by all the rules of proportion, according to the principles of art and knowledge.

XXXIII. (161) And if there is any one in the world who is a praiser of equality, that man is Moses. In the first place composing hymns in its honour, and in every place, and calling it the especial property of justice, as in fact its very name to some degree shows, to divide[50] bodies and things into two equal parts; and in the second place blaming injustice, the worker of the most disgraceful inequality; (162) and inequality has been the parent of two wars, foreign and civil war, as on the other hand equality is the parent of peace. And he also utters the most manifest panegyric on justice, and the most undeniable reproach of injustice when he says, "You shall not commit injustice in any judgment, nor in measures, or weights, or balances: a just balance, and just weights, and a just heap, shall be yours."[51] And in Deuteronomy he says, "There shall not be a false weight in thy bag; thy weight shalt be true and just; there shall not be a little weight and a large one; that thy days may be multiplied upon the earth, which the Lord thy God giveth thee for an inheritance, because every one who committeth injustice is an abomination to the Lord."[52]

(163) Therefore God, who loveth justice, hates and abominates injustice, the begging of sedition and of evils; and in one passage the lawgiver represents equality as the muse of justice beginning with the creation of the entire heaven. For he says, "And God made a separation between the light and between the darkness, and he called the light day, and the darkness he called night."[53] (164) For it is equality which allotted night and day and light and darkness to existing things. It is equality also that divided the human race into man and woman, making two divisions, unequal in strength, but most perfectly equal for the purpose which nature had principally in view, the generation of a third human being like themselves. For, says Moses, "God made man; in the image of God created he him; male and female he created them."[54] He no longer says "him," but "them," in the plural number, adapt-

---

[50]The Greek is *dicha temnein*, as if *dikaiosynē*, "justice," were derived from *dicha*, "in two parts."
[51]Leviticus 19:35.
[52]Deuteronomy 25:13.
[53]Genesis 1:4.
[54]Genesis 1:26.

[48]Deuteronomy 1:17.
[49]Genesis 1:31.

ing the species to the genus, which have, as I have already said, been divided with perfect equality.

XXXIV. (165) And he apportioned cold and heat, and summer and spring, the different seasons of the year, divided by the same dividing Word. And the three days which passed before the creation of the sun, are equal in number to the three days of the first week which came after the creation of the sun, the number six being dissected equally in order to display the character of eternity and of time. For thus God allotted three days to eternity before the appearance of the sun, and those which came after the sun he allotted to time; the sun being an imitation of eternity, and time and eternity being the two primary powers of the living God; (166) the one his beneficent power, in accordance with which he made the world, and in respect of which he is called God; the other his chastening power, according to which he rules and governs what he has created, in respect of which he is further denominated Lord, and these two he here states to be divided in the middle by him standing above them both. "For," says he, "I will speak to you from above the mercy-seat, in the midst, between the two cherubims;"[55] that he might show that the most ancient powers of the living God are equal; that is to say, his beneficent and his chastising power, being both divided by the same dividing Word.

XXXV. (167) But what are the pillars of the ten generic laws which he calls tables? They are two; equal in number to the parts of the soul, the rational and irrational part, which must be instructed and corrected, being again divided by the Lawgiver; "for the tables were the work of God, and the writing was the writing of God engraven on the tables."[56] (168) And, indeed, of the ten commandments engraved on these tables which are properly and especially laws, there is an equal division into two numbers of five; the first of which contains the principle of justice relating to God, and the second those relating to man.

(169) Now of those principles of justice relating to God, the first law enunciated is one which opposes the polytheistic doctrine, and teaches us that the world is ruled over by one sole governor. The second is one forbidding men to make gods of things which are not the causes of anything, by means of the treacherous arts of painters and sculptors, whom Moses banished from his own constitution which he proposed to establish, condemning them to everlasting banishment, in order that the only true God might be honoured in truth and simplicity. (170) The third law is one about the name of the Lord, not about that name which has not yet reached his creatures; for that name is

unspeakable, but about the name which is constantly applied to him as displayed in his powers; for it is commanded that we shall not take his name in vain. The fourth commandment is concerning the seventh day, always virgin, and without any mother, in order that creation, taking care that it may be always free from labour, may in this way come to a recollection of him who does everything without being seen.

(171) The fifth commandment is about the honour due to parents. For this also is a sacred command; having reference not to men, but to him who is the cause of birth and existence of the universe, in accordance with whom it is that fathers and mothers appear to generate children; not generating them themselves, but only being the instruments of generation in his hands. (172) And this command is placed, as it were, on the borders between the two tables of laws relating to God and those relating to man, and so it bounds the five which concern piety, and that five also which comprehend a prevention of injury to one's fellows. Since mortal parents are the boundaries of the immortal powers, which, generating everything according to nature, have permitted this lowest and mortal race to imitate their own powers of generation, and so to propagate its own seed; for God is the beginning of all generation, and the mortal species of mankind, being the lowest and least honoured of all, is the end.

(173) The other table of five is the prohibition of adultery, of murder, of theft, of false witness, and of covetousness. These are generic rules, comprehending nearly all offences whatever, and to one of these rules each particular and special action is naturally referrible.

XXXVI. (174) But you see also that the regularly occurring daily sacrifices are divided into equal portions; one portion being the sacrifice which the priests offer in their own behalf, consisting of the finest wheat-flour, and the other being that which they offer on behalf of the whole nation; consisting of two lambs, which they are especially commanded to offer.[57] For the law commands them to offer one half of the sacrifices abovementioned early in the morning, and the other half at the time of the evening twilight, in order that God may receive his proper tribute of thanks for the blessings which are showered upon all men during the night.

(175) You see also that the loaves which are placed upon the sacred table are divided by the twelve into equal parts, so as to be distributed to each company of six in number, and are so placed as a memorial of the tribes which are of a corresponding number: one half of whom, virtue, that is Leah, received as her share, having become the

[55] Exodus 25:22.
[56] Exodus 32:16.

[57] Leviticus 6:20.

mother of six leaders of tribes; and the other half fell to the lot of Rachel's children and those of the other women.

(176) You see also that the twelve stones of an emerald upon the garment which reach down to the priests' feet are divided equally on the right and on the left side of the garment; on which, being divided into equal numbers of six, the names of the twelve patriarchs of the tribes were engraved, being divine characters engraved on pillars, memorials of divine natures. (177) What more need I say? Has he not also, taking two mountains symbolically to mean two races, and having again divided them on principles of the equality of proportion, allotted one to those who bless, and the other to those who curse; appointing leaders of tribes over each in order to give admonitions to those who have need of them, and to show them that the curses are equal in number to the blessings, and nearly, if it may be lawful to say so, of equal value? (178) For the praises of the good and the reproaches of the wicked are of equal service, since to avoid evil and to choose good are, among all persons of sound sense, looked upon as one and the same thing.

XXXVII. (179) A great impression is made upon me by the selection and division of the two goats which are brought as an offering for the purpose of atonement, and which are divided by an obscure and uncertain principle of division, namely, by lot. For of two principles, the one which is occupied about the affairs of divine virtue is consecrated and set apart to be offered to God; but that which devotes itself to the concerns of human unhappiness is appropriated to the banished creature, for the share which that has obtained the sacred scriptures call the scape-goat, since it is removed from its place, and pursued and driven away to a great distance from virtue.

(180) And, as is the case with respect to good and unadulterated money, so also, as there are many things in nature, does not the invisible divider appear to you to divide them into equal portions and to distribute the good money which has stood the test to the lover of instruction, and that which has not been properly coined, and which is bad, to the man who is ignorant? for, says Moses, "that which had no mark belonged to Laban, and that which was marked belonged to Jacob."[58] (181) For the soul, being as some ancient writer has said, a waxen tablet, while it is hard and resisting, repels and refuses the impressions which are attempted to be stamped upon it; and remains of necessity undistinguished by any figure. But when it becomes tractable and yielding in a moderate degree, it then receives deep impressions, and having taken off the stamp given by the seal, it preserves accu-

rately the appearances which are impressed upon it, so that they cannot be effaced.

XXXVIII. (182) Moreover, the equal division of the sacrifices of blood is certainly calculated to excite our admiration: which division the chief priest Moses, having nature for his teacher, made; for, says the scripture, "He, taking the half of the blood, poured it into the bowls; and the other half he poured out upon the altar."[59] In order to show that the sacred genus of wisdom is of a twofold nature, the one kind being divine, and the other human: (183) and the divine kind is unmingled and unadulterated, on which account it sacrifices to the pure, and unalloyed, and only God existing in unity; but the human kind is of a mixed and alloyed nature, and therefore dissipates the unanimity and community of our mixed, and combined, and compound race, and effects any thing rather than a proper harmony of either melodies or morals.

(184) But the unmixed and unadulterated portion of the soul is the pure mind, which, being inspired by heaven from above, when it is preserved in a state free from all disease and from all mishap is very suitably all poured forth and resolved into the elements of a sacred libation, and so restored in a fitting manner to God, who inspired it and preserved it free from any infliction of evil; but the mixed portion is entirely that of the outward senses, and for this part nature has made suitable craters. (185) Now, the craters of the sense of seeing are the eyes, those of hearing are the ears, those of smelling are the nostrils, and so on with the appropriate receptacles for each of the senses. On these craters the sacred word pours a portion of blood, thinking it right that the irrational part of us should become endowed with soul and vitality, and should in some manner become rational; following the guidance of admonition, and purifying itself from the deceitful alluring powers of the objects of the outward sense which aim to overcome it.

(186) Was it not in the same manner that the holy double-drachm was divided?[60] That we should purify the half of it, namely, a drachm, offering it as the ransom for our souls: which the only free, the only delivering God, when addressed in the voice of supplication, and sometimes even without any supplication, by force delivers from the cruel and bitter despotism of the passions and iniquities; but the other portion we may leave to the race which is never free, but which is of slavish disposition; of which class was the man who said, "I have loved my Lord;"[61] that is to say, the mind which is the master in me; "and my wife," that is to say, the outward sense which is dear to him,

---

[58] Genesis 30:42.

[59] Exodus 24:6.
[60] Exodus 30:13.
[61] Exodus 21:5.

and the housekeeper of his passions; "and my children," that is to say, the evils which are the offspring of them; "I will not depart free." (187) For it is quite inevitable that such a description of persons as this must obtain a lot which is no lot, and that the scapegoat bought with the double drachm, must be given to them, which is just the opposite of the drachm and of unity which is offered up to God. And it is the nature of unity not to be capable of either addition or subtraction, inasmuch as it is the image of the only complete God; (188) for all other things are intrinsically and by their own nature loose; and if there is any where any thing consolidated, that has been bound by the word of God, for this word is glue and a chain, filling all things with its essence. And the word, which connects together and fastens every thing, is peculiarly full itself of itself, having no need whatever of any thing beyond.

XXXIX. (189) Very naturally therefore does Moses say, "He who is rich will not add anything, and he who is poor will not diminish anything of the half of the double drachm,"[62] which is, as I have said before, a drachm, and a unit; to which every member might quote that line of the poet:

With thee I'll end, with thee I will begin.

(190) For even an infinitely infinite number, being made of a continuation of other numbers, when dissolved must end in a unit: and again it must begin with a unit, being afterwards compounded so as to make an illimitable multitude; on which account those who have made the investigation of such matters their study, have not called the unit a number, but rather an element, and the beginning of number.

(191) Again this heavenly food of the soul which Moses calls manna, the word of God divides in equal portions among all who are to use it; taking care of equality in an extraordinary degree. And Moses bears witness to this where he says, "He who had much had not too much, and he who had but little was in no want;"[63] since they all used that wonderful and most desirable of proportion. On which account it happened to the Israelites to learn that each of them was collecting not more for the men who were related to him than for the reasonings and manners which were akin to him. For as much as was sufficient for each man, that he was allotted in a prudent manner, so as neither to feel any want or any superfluity.

XL. (192) And we may find something very much resembling this equality, according to analogy in the case of the festival which is called the passover; and the passover is when the soul is anxious to unlearn its subjection to the irrational passions, and willingly submits itself to a reasonable mastery over them. (193) For it is expressly said, "If there be few that are in thy house so as not to be sufficient in number for a sheep, then thou shalt take thy nearest neighbour in addition, according to the number of souls,"[64] so that each person may receive a sufficient share in proportion to the number of his family, being such as he is found to be worthy of and to have need of.

(194) But when, as if it were some country, he wishes to divide out virtue among its inhabitants, he then allows the more numerous body to have more, and the less numerous to have less, thinking it reasonable not to allot a larger share to a smaller number, nor a smaller share to a larger number; for in such a case they would neither of them be suited to their respective portions.

XLI. (195) But the most manifest instance of equality in respect of number, is exhibited in the sacred offerings of the twelve princes, and again in the portions of those offerings which are distributed among the chiefs. For, says the scripture, "There shall be an equal share allotted to each of the sons of Aaron."[65] (196) Equality is also very beautifully displayed in respect of the composition of spices for purposes of fumigation; for we read, "Take to thyself sweet odours, stacte, onycha, galbanum, these sweet spices with pure frankincense, all of the most chosen kinds, all of equal weight and thou shalt make of it a perfume, a confection, after the art of the apothecary, a pure composition, a holy work."[66] For the Lord enjoins here that each of the separate portions shall be equal to each, with a view to the proper composition of the whole.

(197) And as I imagine these four ingredients of which the entire perfume is composed are emblems of the four elements of which the whole world is made; he likens the stacte to water, the onycha to land, the galbanum to the air, and the pure transparent frankincense to fire; for stacte, which derives its name from the drops (stagones) in which it falls is liquid, and onycha is dry and earth-like, the sweet smelling galbanum is added by way of giving a representation of the air, for there is fragrance in the air; and the transparency which there is in frankincense serves for a representation of fire. (198) On which account also, he has separated the things which have weight from those which are light, uniting the one class by a closely connecting combination, and bringing forth the other in a disunited form; as where he says, "Take to thyself sweet odours, stacte, onycha," these things being weighty he mentions unconnectedly,

---

[62] Exodus 30:15.
[63] Exodus 16:18.

[64] Exodus 12:16.
[65] Numbers 7:5.
[66] Exodus 30:34.

being the symbols of earth and water. Afterwards he begins afresh with the other class, which he mentions in combination, saying, "And the sweet spice of galbanum and the transparent frankincense," these again being in their own nature emblems of the light things, air and fire.

(199) And in the harmonious composition and mixture of these things is truly his most ancient and most perfect holy work, namely, the world; which, speaking of it under the emblem of perfume, he thinks is bound to show gratitude to its Creator. So that in name the composition which has been carefully fabricated by the art of the apothecary may be offered up, but in real fact for the whole world which was created by divine wisdom may be consecrated and dedicated, being made a burnt offering of early in the morning and also in the evening. (200) For such a life as this becomes the world, namely, continually and without ceasing to be giving thanks to its Father and Creator, so as to stop short of nothing but evaporating and reducing itself into its original element, in order to show that it stores up and conceals nothing, but dedicates itself wholly as a pious offering to God who created it.

XLII. (201) And I marvel also at that sacred word which runs on with zeal, in one continued course, without taking breath, "In order to stand in the midst between the dead and the living; and immediately," says Moses, "the plague was stayed."[67] But the evils which grind down and break to pieces and crush our souls were not likely either to be stayed or lightened, unless the reasoning, dear to God, had separated off the holy men who live in sincerity, from the unholy who in real truth are dead; (202) for, owing to the mere fact of being near those who are sick, it has often happened that those who were in perfect health have caught their disease, and have been on the point of death: and it was impossible for them any longer to be exposed to this affliction if they once separated by a strong boundary fixed in the middle between them, which will preserve the better part by keeping off the inroads and attacks of the worse.

(203) And I marvel still more, when listening to the sacred oracles I learn from them in what manner "a cloud came in the midst"[68] between the army of the Egyptians and the company of the children of Israel; for the cloud no longer permitted the race, which is temperate and beloved by God, to be persecuted by that which was devoted to the passions and a foe to God; being a covering and a protection to its friends, but a weapon of vengeance and chastisement against its enemies; (204) for it gently showers down wisdom on the minds which study virtue—wisdom which cannot be visited by any evil. But on those minds which are ill-disposed and unproductive of knowledge, it pours forth a whole body of punishments, bringing upon them the most pitiable destruction of the deluge.

(205) And the Father who created the universe has given to his archangelic and most ancient Word a pre-eminent gift, to stand on the confines of both, and separated that which had been created from the Creator. And this same Word is continually a suppliant to the immortal God on behalf of the mortal race, which is exposed to affliction and misery; and is also the ambassador, sent by the Ruler of all, to the subject race. (206) And the Word rejoices in the gift, and, exulting in it, announces it and boasts of it, saying, "And I stood in the midst, between the Lord and you;"[69] neither being uncreate as God, nor yet created as you, but being in the midst between these two extremities, like a hostage, as it were, to both parties: a hostage to the Creator, as a pledge and security that the whole race would never fly off and revolt entirely, choosing disorder rather than order; and to the creature, to lead it to entertain a confident hope that the merciful God would not overlook his own work. For I will proclaim peaceful intelligence to the creation from him who has determined to destroy wars, namely God, who is ever the guardian of peace.

XLIII. (207) Therefore the sacred Word, having given us instruction respecting the division into equal parts, leads us also to the knowledge of opposites, saying that God placed the divisions "opposite to one another;"[70] for in fact nearly all the things that exist in the world, are by nature opposite to one another. And we must begin with the first.

(208) Hot is opposite to cold, and dry to wet, and light to heavy, and darkness to light, and night to day; also in heaven that which is fixed is opposite to the wandering planetary motion, and in the air a clear sky is opposite to clouds, winter to summer, autumn to spring, for the one is blooming and the other fading. (209) Again, of things on earth, sweet water is opposite to bitter, and barren to fertile land. Again, there are other things contrary to one another, as visible bodies to incorporeal, things endowed with vitality to things inanimate, rational to irrational, mortal to immortal, things discernible by the outward sense to things perceptible only by the intellect; things comprehensible to things incomprehensible, elements to things concrete and perfected, beginning to end, generation to destruction, life to death, disease to health, white to black, the right to the left, jus-

---

[67]Numbers 16:48.
[68]Exodus 14:19.

[69]Numbers 16:48.
[70]Genesis 15:10.

tice to injustice, wisdom to folly, courage to cowardice, temperance to intemperance, virtue to vice; and all the species of one class to all the species of the other class.

(210) Again, grammatical knowledge is contrary to ignorance of the same subject, musical science to unacquaintance with music, an educated to an illiterate condition; and, in short, skill in art to want of skill. Again, in the different arts there are vocal elements and mute elements, there are sharp and flat sounds, there are straight and circular lines. (211) Once more, in animals and plants, there are some barren and some productive; some very prolific, others which yield but small increase; animals oviparous and viviparous; animals with soft skins, and others with hard shells; some wild and some tractable creatures; some fond of solitude, and others gregarious.

(212) To go on further: poverty is opposite to wealth, glory to want of reputation, baseness of birth to nobility, want to abundance, war to peace, law to lawlessness, a bad to a good disposition, inactivity to labour, youth to old age, power to want of power, weakness to strength. And why need I enumerate every class separately, when these are unlimited and indescribable by reason of their multitude? (213) Very beautifully, therefore, has the interpreter of the writings of nature, taking pity upon our idleness and want of consideration, taught every one of us in an invisible manner, as he does now, to arrange everything in such a way as to produce an exact opposition, not arranging them in wholes, but in equal divisions; for the one thing consists of the two opposite parts; and when that one thing is bisected then the opposite parts are easily known. (214) Is not this the thing which the Greeks say that Heraclitus, that great philosopher who is so celebrated among them, put forth as the leading principle of his whole philosophy, and boasted of it as if it were a new discovery? For it is in reality an ancient discovery of Moses, that out of the same thing opposite things are produced having the ratio of parts to the whole, as has here been shown.

XLVI. (215) These matters then we will examine into accurately on another occasion; but there is this other point also, which does not deserve to be passed over in silence. For the divisions into two equal parts which have been mentioned become six in number, since three animals were divided, so that the Word which divided them made up the number seven, dividing the two triads and establishing itself in the midst of them. (216) And a thing very similar to this appears to me to be very clearly shown in the matter of the sacred candlestick; for that also was made having six branches, three on each side, and the main candlestick itself in the middle made the seventh, dividing and separating the two triads; for it is made of carved work, a divine work of exquisite skill and

highly admired, being made of one solid piece of pure gold. For the unit, being one and single and pure, begot the number seven, which had no mother but is born of itself alone, without taking any additional material whatever to aid him.

(217) But those who praise gold say a great many other things by way of panegyric on it, but dwell on two especial points as most particularly important and excellent; one that it does not receive poison, the other that it can be beaten out or melted out into the thinnest possible plates, while still remaining unbroken. Therefore it is very naturally taken as an emblem of that greater nature, which, being extended and diffused every where so as to penetrate in every direction, is wholly full of everything, and also connects all other things with the most admirable arrangement.

(218) Concerning the candlestick above mentioned, the artist speaks again a second time and says, that from its different branches there are three arms projecting out on each side, equals in all respects to one another, and having on the top lamps like nuts, in the shape of flowers supporting the lights;[71] the seventh flower being fashioned on the top of the candlestick of solid gold, and having seven golden places for lights above them; (219) so that in many accounts it has been believed to be fashioned in such a manner because the number six is divided into two triads by the Word, making the seventh and being placed in the midst of them; as indeed is the case now. For the entire candlestick with its six most entire and principal parts was made so as to consist of seven lamps, and seven flowers, and seven lights; and the six lights are divided by the seventh. (220) And in like manner the flowers are divided by that which comes in the middle; and in the same manner also the lamps are divided by the seventh which comes in the middle. But the six branches, and the equal number of arms which shoot out are divided by the main trunk itself which makes up the number seven.

XLV. (221) But the long discussion which some people start with respect to each of these, must be postponed to a subsequent opportunity. This much alone we must remind our readers of at this moment, that the sacred candlestick and the seven lights upon it are an imitation of the wandering of the seven planets through the heaven. How so? some one will say. (222) Because, we will reply, in the same manner as the lights, so also does every one of the planets shed its rays. They therefore, being more brilliant, do transmit more brilliant beams to the earth, and brilliant beyond them all is he who is the centre one of the seven, the sun. (223) And I call him the centre, not merely because he has the central position, as some have

---

[71] Exodus 25:33.

thought, but also because he has on many other accounts a right to be ministered unto and attended by the others accompanying him as bodyguards on each side, by reason of his dignity and his magnitude, and the great benefits which he pours upon all earthly things.

(224) But men, being unable completely to comprehend the arrangement of the planets (and in fact what other of the heavenly bodies can they understand with certainty and clearness?) speak according to their conjectures. And these persons appear to me to form the best conjectures on such subjects, who, having assigned the central position to the sun, say that there is an equal number of planets, namely, those above him and below him. Those above him being Saturn, Jupiter, and Mars; then comes the Sun himself, and next to him Mercury, Venus, and the Moon, which last is close to the air. (225) The Creator therefore, wishing that there should be a model upon earth among us of the seven-lighted sphere as it exists in heaven, explained this exquisite work to be made, namely, this candlestick. And its likeness to the soul is often pointed out too; for the soul is divisible into three parts, and each of the parts, as has been already pointed out, is divided into two more. And thus there being six divisions, the sacred and divine Word, the divider of them all, very naturally makes up the number seven.

XLVI. (226) This other point also is too important to deserve to be passed over in silence: that, as there are three vessels among the sacred furniture, a candlestick, a bath, and an altar of incense; the altar of incense has reference to that gratitude which is exhibited for the bestowal of the elements, as has been shown before, since it does itself also receive a portion from these four, receiving wood from the earth, and the species which are burnt from the water; for, being first of all liquefied, they are dissolved into drops of moisture, and vapour from the air, and from the fire the spark which kindles the whole; and the composition of frankincense, and galbanum, and onycha, and stacte, is a symbol of the four elements; and the table is referred to the gratitude which is displayed for the mortal things which are made out of the elements, for loaves and libations are placed upon it, which the creatures who stand in need of nourishment must of necessity use. And the candlestick has reference to the gratitude exhibited for all the things existing in heaven, in order than no portion of the world may lie under the imputation of ingratitude; but that we may see that every single part of it gives thanks, the elements, the things made of them, and not those only which are made on earth, but also those in heaven.

XLVII. (227) And it is worth while to consider why, after having explained the measures of the table and of the altar of incense, he has given no such description of the candlestick; may it not be,

perhaps, for the reason that the elements and all the mortal things which are compounded of them, of which the table and the altar of incense are symbols, have been measured, inasmuch as they are terminated in heaven? For that which surrounds anything is invariably the measure of that which is surrounded; but the heaven, of which the candlestick is the symbol, is of infinite magnitude; (228) for it is indeed surrounded, but not, according to the account of Moses, by a vacuum, nor by any substance, nor by anything which is of equal magnitude with itself, nor by anything of unlimited size, in accordance with the marvellous fables which we touched upon when speaking of their building of the tower; but its boundary is God, and he also is its ruler and the director of its course.

(229) As, therefore, the living God is incomprehensible, so also that which is bounded by him is not measured by any measures which come with the range of our intellect; and, perhaps, inasmuch as it is of circular form and skilfully fashioned into a perfect sphere, it has no participation in either length or breadth.

XLVIII. (230) Therefore, after he has said what is becoming on this subject, he proceeds to add, "But the birds he did not divide;"[72] meaning, by the term birds, the two reasonings which are winged and inclined by nature to soar to the investigation of sublime subjects; one of them being the archetypal pattern and above us, and the other being the copy of the former and abiding among us. (231) And Moses calls the one which is above us the image of God, and the one which abides among us as the impression of that image, "For," says he, "God made man," not an image, "but after that image."[73] So that the mind which is in each of us, which is in reality and truth the man, is a third image proceeding from the Creator. But the intermediate one is a model of the one and a copy of the other. (232) But by nature our mind is indivisible; for the Creator, having divided the irrational part of the soul into six portions, has made six divisions of it, namely, sight, taste, hearing, smelling, touch, and voice; but the rational part, which is called the mind he has left undivided, according to the likeness of the entire heaven. (233) For in this, also, there is a report that the outermost sphere, which is destitute of motion, is preserved without being divided, but that the inner one is divided into six portions, and thus completes the seven circles of what are called the planets; for I imagine the heaven is in the world the same thing that the soul is in the human being. They say, therefore, that these two natures, full of reason and comprehension—that, I mean, which

---

[72] Genesis 15:10.
[73] Genesis 1:27.

exists in man and that which exists in the world—are both at all times entire and indivisible.

On this account, therefore, it is that the scriptures tell us, "He did not divide the birds." (234) For our own mind is here compared to a dove, since that is a creature which is tame and domesticated among us; and the turtle dove is compared to the model presented by the other, that is to say, by the mind of the world, the heaven; for the word of God is fond of retirement, and solitude, and privacy; not mixing itself up with the crowd of things which have been created and will be destroyed, but being at all times accustomed to roam on high, and being anxious to be an attendant only on the one supreme Being.

Therefore, the two natures are indivisible; the nature, I mean, of the reasoning power in us, and of the divine Word above us; but though they are indivisible themselves, they divide an innumerable multitude of other things. (235) For it is the divine Word which divided and distributed every thing in nature; and it is our own mind which divides every thing and every body which it comprehends, by the exertion of its intellect in an infinite manner, into an infinite number of parts, and which, in fact, never ceased from dividing. (236) And this happens by reason of its resemblance to the Creator and Father of the universe; for the divine nature, being unmingled, uncombined with any thing else, and most completely destitute of parts, has been to the whole world the cause of mixture, and combination, and of an infinite variety of parts: so that, very naturally, the two things which thus resemble each other, both the mind which is in us and that which is above us, being without parts and indivisible, will still be able in a powerful manner to divide and distribute all existing things.

XLIX. (237) Therefore, after Moses has mentioned the facts of birds not being cut in two pieces or divided, he proceeds to say, "And the birds came down and descended upon the bodies which were divided;"[74] using indeed expressions which are synonymous, but still representing the variance which exists in the facts in a most visible manner to those who are able to see. For it is contrary to nature that birds should come down, when they have been given wings for the purpose of soaring on high. (238) For, as the earth is the most appropriate place for land animals, and above all for reptiles, which do not endure even to crawl upon it, but seek caves and lurking places, avoiding the regions which are above, on account of their kinship with the things which are below; so, in the same manner, the air is the appropriate abode for the winged race, the element which is by nature light is the proper home for those creatures which are light by reason of their being feathered.

When, therefore, those creatures, whose nature it is to traverse the air and who ought to roam through the aether, descend and come down upon the land, they are unable to live a life according to their nature. (239) On the other hand, Moses approves, in no ordinary degree, of whatever reptiles are able to take a leap in an upward direction. At all events he says, "Ye shall eat of these winged reptiles which go upon four feet, and which have legs above their feet so as to be able by them to leap up from the ground."[75] But these reptiles are the emblems of souls, which like reptiles being rooted in the earthly body, when they are raised up, get strength to soar on high, taking the heaven in exchange for the earth, and immortality in exchange for destruction. (240) We must, therefore, think that they are full of every description of misery, which, having been brought up in the air, and in the aether which is the purest of all things, have changed their abode (not being able to bear the satiety of divine things), and have descended to that mortal and evil district, the earth.

And there are innumerable imaginations concerning an innumerable variety of things which roam about upon it also; some voluntary, and some out of ignorance, which are in no respect different from winged creatures, and which Moses compares to the birds that come down. (241) And of these imaginations those which take the upward course belong to the better class, since virtue, which conducts the mind towards heaven and the divine country, travels with them. But those which take the downward course belong to the worse class, since wickedness guides them and drags them in the contrary direction by force. And their very names do, to a great extent, show the opposite character of the places. For virtue *(aretē)* has derived its name not only from the word *(airesis)* choice, but also from the fact of its being lifted up *(para to airesthai)*, for it is lifted up *(airetai)* and borne on high because it always loves heavenly things; but wickedness *(kakia)* is so called from its tendency to go downwards *(apo tou katō kechōrēkenai)*, and also because it compels those who practise it to fall down to the bottom *(katapiptein)*.

(242) Accordingly the thoughts of the soul which are at variance with one another, flying towards and descending upon the earth, both come down themselves and also throw the mind down too, mingling with bodies in a disgraceful degree, and with things which are perceptible by the outward senses, not discernible by the intellect, imperfect not entire, perishable and not living. For they mix themselves up not only with bodies, but also with the divisions of the bodies which have

---

[74]Genesis 15:11.   [75]Leviticus 11:21.

been divided in two parts. And it is quite impossible that things which have been divided in this way should ever again admit of adaptation and union; since the nerves of the spirit, which were the strongest natural bond in them, are cut in two.

L. (243) Moreover, Moses introduces a very true opinion when he teaches us that justice and every virtue loves the soul, but that wickedness and every vice is attached to the body; and that what is friendly to the one is in every case of necessity hostile to the other, as is the case even now. For having figuratively represented the wars of the soul, he then introduces birds as eager to involve themselves with and to cling to the bodies, and to satiate themselves with the flesh, the inroads and attacks of which the virtuous man, desiring to check, is said to sit by them as if he were a sort of curator or overseer of them. (244) For when his domestic affairs were thrown into confusion by domestic sedition, and when the armies of the enemy were proceeding against him, he collected a wise council and deliberated with respect to the adversaries; in order that if he could possibly do so, using persuasion he might both put an end to the foreign war, and also remove the domestic confusion; for it was desirable to disperse those enemies who were gathering over him like a cloud, and who were full of irreconcileable enmity to him; and equally so to re-establish with the other party the relations which had previously existed.

(245) Now those who are irreconcilable and implacable enemies are set down thus; the follies and intemperances of the soul, cowardice and injustice, and all the other irrational appetites which are accustomed to be generated by luxuriant and impotent appetite, raising their heads high and becoming restiff, and preventing the mind from proceeding in its straight course; and very often throwing its whole system into confusion and beating it down.

(246) But the attacks and conflicts of those powers which are not irreconcilable resemble the frequent effect of the discussions and quarrels about doctrines which arise among the Sophists. For inasmuch as they all labour for one end, namely the contemplation of the things of nature, they may be said to be friends; but inasmuch as they do not agree in their particular investigations they may be said to be in a state of domestic sedition; as, for instance, those who affirm the universe to be uncreated are at variance with those who insist upon its creation; and again those who urge that it will be destroyed are at strife with those who affirm that it is indeed perishable by nature but that it never will be destroyed, because it is held together by a more powerful chain, the will of the Creator. And again, those who affirm that there is nothing self-existent, but that everything has been created, are at variance with those who are of a contrary opinion. Those too, who say that man

is the measure of all things, differ from those who would restrain the judicial faculties of the outward senses and of the intellect. And, in short, to sum up all these differences in a few words, those who represent everything as incomprehensible are at variance with those who say that a great number of things are properly understood.

(247) And the sun, and the moon, and the whole heaven, and the earth, and the air, and the water, and all the things that are connected with them, afford subject for strife and contention to those who are fond of examining into such subjects, and who investigate their essences, and distinctive qualities, and changes, and alterations, and moreover their origin and the method of their destruction; and making no superficial investigation into the magnitude and motion of the heavenly bodies, they adopt all sorts of different opinions, never agreeing together, until some man, who is at the same time skilful at disentangling controversies and calculated to judge, takes his seat on the tribunal, and comes to a clear perception of the progeny of each individual's soul, and discards those which do not deserve to be maintained, and preserves those which are good, and which he pronounces worthy of suitable providential care. (248) And all the controversies of philosophy are full of disagreement, since the truth escapes the intellect which is given to plausibilities and conjectures: for it is the very difficulty of discovering and seizing hold of the nature of truth that, in my opinion, has given rise to so many quarrels.

LI. (249) "And about the setting of the sun a trance fell upon Abraham, and, behold, fear with great darkness fell upon him."[76] Now there is one kind of trance which is sort of frantic delirium, causing infirmity of mind, either through old age, or melancholy, or some other similar cause. There is another kind which is excessive consternation, arising usually from things which happen suddenly and unexpectedly. Another kind is mere tranquility of the mind, arising when it is inclined by nature to be quiet: but that which is the best description of all is a divinely inspired and more vehement sort of enthusiasm, which the race of prophets is subject to.

(250) Now the first kind Moses mentions in the curses which are recorded in Deuteronomy; for he says that, "delirium and blindness, and aberration of mind shall seize on the impious,"[77] so that they shall differ in no respect from blind persons at mid-day, being like people feeling their way in deep darkness. (251) The second kind he mentions in many places; for he says, "And Isaac was astonished with a great astonishment, and said, Who, then, is it who went out to hunt for game

---

[76]Genesis 15:12.
[77]Deuteronomy 28:28.

for me, and who brought it to me? And I ate of it all before you came, and I have blessed him; yea, and he shall be blessed."[78] And, again, with reference to Jacob, who disbelieved those who told him that "Joseph is alive, and is ruler over the whole land of Egypt; for he," says the scripture, "was amazed in his mind, for he believed them not."[79] And, again, in Exodus, in the assembly of the people, we read: "For the whole of the mountain of Sinai was enveloped in smoke, because God descended upon it in fire. And the smoke went up as the vapour of a furnace, and the whole people was greatly astonished."[80] Also, in Leviticus, when speaking of the consecration of the priests on the eighth day, when fire came out from heaven and licked up what was on the altar, and the burnt-offerings and the fat, the historian proceeds immediately to tell us, "And the whole people saw it and were astonished, and fell upon their faces;"[81] for such astonishment as this causes alarm and consternation.

(252) And ought we not especially to wonder in the case of Esau, that he who was skilful in hunting was nevertheless himself continually caught and supplanted, having acquired his skill to his own injury and not to his advantage, and that he never used any great care to catch anything in his hunts? And also in the case of Jacob, that he hunts without having acquired any skill by learning, but only as he is moved by nature; and that he brings what he has caught to the examiner, who will distinguish whether it deserves to be approved; on which account he "eateth of it all."[82] (253) For everything that relates to meditation is wholesome food, whether it be investigation, or consideration, or hearing, or reading, or prayer, or self-reliance, or a contempt for things indifferent; and he ate, as I imagine, the first fruits of them all, but he did not eat the whole of all; for some appropriate food must be left for him who meditates as a reward for his pains. (254) And the words, "before you came," are added out of regard for the nature of the things; for if passion enters into the soul, we shall not enjoy temperance. And it convicts the worthless man as slow, and hesitating, and procrastinating, as to the works of instruction, but not as to those of intemperance. (255) Therefore Egypt contains inspectors of works, who devote themselves with energy to securing the enjoyment of passions. But Moses, on the other hand, commands the Israelites to eat the passover in haste, and to celebrate the migration from these passions in this way. And Judah says: "For if we had not delayed, we should by this time have

returned, and have arrived again in Egypt; aye, and a second time should we have returned safe from thence."[83]

(256) And very naturally did Jacob wonder whether the mind was still in the body; that is to say, whether Joseph was alive to virtue and ruling over the body, and not being ruled over by it. And any one who chooses to go through all the other instances, would be able to trace out the truth. But our present subject does not require any accurate discussion of these matters; on which account we had better return to the point from which we set out.

(257) With respect to the third kind of trance, he philosophises in this manner when speaking of the creation of the woman; "For the Lord God," says Moses, "cast a trance upon Adam, and he slept."[84] Here calling the quietness and tranquillity of mind a trance; for the slumber of the mind is the awaking of the outward sense: and, again, the awaking of the intellect is the reducing of the outward senses to a state of inactivity.

LII. (258) An instance of the fourth kind of trance is the one which we are now considering: "And about the setting of the sun a trance fell upon Abraham," he being thrown into a state of enthusiasm and inspired by the Deity. But this is not the only thing which shows him to have been a prophet, but also the express words which are engraven in the sacred scriptures as on a pillar. When some one endeavored to separate Sarah, that is, the virtue which is derived from nature, from him, as if she had not been the peculiar property of the wise man alone, but had also belonged to every one who made any pretence to wisdom, God said, "Give the man back his wife, because he is a prophet, and he will pray for thee, and thou shalt live;"[85] (259) and the sacred scriptures testify in the case of every good man, that he is a prophet; for a prophet says nothing of his own, but everything which he says is strange and prompted by some one else; and it is not lawful for a wicked man to be an interpreter of God, as also no wicked man can be properly said to be inspired; but this statement is only appropriate to the wise man alone, since he alone is a sounding instrument of God's voice, being struck and moved to sound in an invisible manner by him.

(260) Accordingly, all those whom Moses describes as just persons he has also represented as inspired and prophesying. Noah was a just man; was he not also by that fact a prophet? or did he, without being possessed by any divine inspiration, utter those prayers and curses which he applied to the generations which should come hereafter,

---

[78] Genesis 27:33.
[79] Genesis 45:26.
[80] Exodus 19:18.
[81] Leviticus 9:24.
[82] Genesis 27:33.

[83] Genesis 43:9.
[84] Genesis 2:21.
[85] Genesis 20:7.

and all of which were eventually confirmed by the reality of the facts? (261) Why should I speak of Isaac? Why of Jacob? For these are also manifestly found to have been prophets by many other circumstances, and especially by their addresses to their children. For the annunciation, "Assemble yourselves together, that I may tell you what shall happen to you in the last days"[86] was the expression of a man possessed by inspiration; for the knowledge of the future is not appropriate to, or natural to, man. (262) What shall we say of Moses? is he not celebrated everywhere as a prophet? For the scripture says, "If there shall be among you a prophet of the Lord, I will make myself known unto him in a vision,"[87] but to Moses God appeared in his actual appearance and not by a riddle. And again we read, "There arose not any more any prophet like unto Moses, whom the Lord knew face to face."[88] (263) Very admirably, therefore, does the historian here point out, that Abraham was under the influence of inspiration when he says that, "About the setting of the sun a trance fell upon him."

LIII. And under the symbol of the sun he intimates our mind: for what reasoning is in us, that the sun is in the world. Since each of them gives light, the one casting a light which is perceptible by the outward senses, to shine upon the universe; and the other shedding their beams, discernible only by the intellect by means of our apprehensions, upon ourselves. (264) As long therefore as our mind still shines around and hovers around, pouring as it were a noontide light into the whole soul, we, being masters of ourselves, are not possessed by any extraneous influence; but when it approaches its setting, then, as is natural, a trance, which proceeds from inspiration, takes violent hold of us, and madness seizes upon us, for when the divine light sets this other rises and shines, (265) and this very frequently happens to the race of prophets; for the mind that is in us is removed from its place at the arrival of the divine Spirit, but is again restored to its previous habitation when that Spirit departs, for it is contrary to holy law for what is mortal to dwell with what is immortal.

On this account the setting of our reason, and the darkness which surrounds it, causes a trance and a heaven-inflicted madness. (266) After that the historian connects with his preceding account what follows in consistency with it, saying, "And it was said to Abraham"—for in real truth the prophet, even when he appears to be speaking, is silent, and another being is employing his vocal organs, his mouth and tongue, for the explanation of what things he chooses; and operating on these organs by some invisible and very skilful act, he makes them utter a sweet and harmonious sound, full of every kind of melody.

LIV. (267) And it is well to hear what the things are which are thus said to have been predicted to Abraham. In the first place, that God does not grant to the man who loves virtue to dwell in the body as in his own native land, but only to sojourn in it as in a foreign country. "For knowing," says the scripture, "thou shalt know that thy seed shall be sojourners in a land which is not theirs."[89] But the district of the body is akin to every bad man, and in it he is desirous to abide as a dweller, not as a sojourner. (268) Accordingly, these words contain this as one lesson; another is, that the things which bring slavery and disaster and bitter humiliation, as the prophet himself tells us, upon the soul are the dwellings upon earth. For the affections of the body are truly spurious and foreign, being produced by the flesh, in which they are rooted. (269) And this slavery lasts four hundred years in accordance with the powers of the four passions.

For when pleasure rules, the mind is elated and puffed up, being carried away by empty vanity. Again, when the appetite gets the upper hand, a desire for absent things is engendered, which suspends the mind upon unaccomplished hopes, as if in a halter; for then the mind is always thirsting and yet is unable to drink, enduring the punishment of Tantalus. (270) Again, when under the influence of grief, the mind is tortured and contracted, like trees the leaves of which are falling off and withering; for all its flourishing and nutritious particles are dried up. Also, when fire obtains that supremacy, no one any longer chooses to remain, but betakes to flight and running away, thinking that this is the only way in which he can be saved. For appetite, having an attractive power even if the object which is desired retreats, compels one to pursue it; and fear, on the other hand, causing alienation, separates one from it, and makes one remove to a distance from what is presented to one's view.

LV. (271) But the supremacy of these different passions before mentioned inflicts terrible slavery on those who are ruled over by them, until God, the umpire and judge of all things, separates that which is ill treated from that which is inflicting ill treatment, and delivers the former and blesses it with perfect freedom, and inflicts upon the other a retribution for the wickedness which it has committed. (272) For we read in the next verse, "And the nation to which they shall be slaves I will judge and after that they shall go forth with great substance."[90] For it is inevitable that a mor-

[86] Genesis 49:2.
[87] Numbers 12:6.
[88] Deuteronomy 34:10.

[89] Genesis 15:13.
[90] Genesis 15:14.

tal man must obey the nature of the passions, and that a man who has been born must endure the fate which is allotted to him as appropriate; but it is the will of God to lighten the evils which are planted contemporaneously with our birth. (273) So that even if we at the beginning suffer such evils as are properly assigned to us, become slaves of cruel masters, and if God also performs what is his peculiar work, proclaiming emancipation and freedom to the souls which address their supplications to him, then he not only gives men a release from their bondage and a means of departure from their prison all guarded round as it is, but he also gives them the means of travelling, which he here calls substance.

(274) And what is this? When the mind having come down from above the heaven becomes entangled in the necessities of the body, then, although it is not allured by any of these, still, like a eunuch or impotent person, it embraces pleasant evils. But if it remains in its own nature, then, being truly a man, it resists and discards them instead of being overthrown by them, being initiated in all the parts of complete encyclical learning; from which it derives a desire for contemplation, and acquires temperance and patience, very vigorous virtues, leaving its former abode, and finding a means of return back to its own country, and bringing with it all the lessons of instruction, which are here called supplies for the journey.

LVI. (275) Having said this much on these subjects, the historian proceeds: "And thou shalt depart to thy fathers, having lived in peace, in a good old age."[91] Therefore we, who are imperfect, are made war upon, and we become slaves, and only with difficulty do we find any relief from the dangers which impend over us. But the perfect race, exempt from slavery and free from the perils of war, is bred up in peace and the firmest freedom. (276) And there is a particular lesson to be learnt from his representing the good man not as dying but departing, in order to show that the race of the soul, which is completely purified, cannot be extinguished and cannot die, but only departs in the way of migration from this earth to heaven, not undergoing that dissolution and destruction which death appears to bring with it. (277) And after the words, "Thou shalt depart," he adds, "to thy fathers." It is here worth while to consider what kind of fathers is meant; for God can never mean those who had passed their lives in the country of the Chaldeans, among whom alone he had lived as being his relations, because he had been commanded by a sacred oracle to depart from those who were his kinsmen by blood.

For, says the historian, "The Lord said unto Abraham, Depart from out of thy land, and from thy kindred, and from thy father's house, to a land which I will show thee; and I will make thee into a great nation."[92] (278) For how can it be reasonable for him who has once been removed from his abode by the interference of Divine Providence, to return and dwell again in the same place? And how could it be reasonable for one who was about to be the leader of a new nation and or another race to be again assigned to his ancient one? For God would never have given to him a new character, and a new nation and family, if he had not wholly and entirely separated himself from his ancient one. (279) For that man is truly a chief of a nation and ruler of a family, from whom, as from a root, sprang that branch so fond of investigating and contemplating the affairs of our nature, by name Israel, since an express command has been given "to remove the old things from before the face of those which are new."[93] For where is any longer the use of investigations into antiquity, and ancient, and long-established customs, to those in whom on a sudden, when they have no such expectation, God rains all kinds of new blessings in a mass?

LVII. (280) Therefore, when he says "fathers," he means not those whose souls have departed from them, and who are buried in the tombs of the land of Chaldea; but, as some say, the sun, and the moon, and the other stars; for some affirm that it is owing to these bodies that the nature of all the things in the world has its existence. But as some other persons think he means the archetypal ideas, those models of these thing which are perceptible by the outward senses and visible; which models, however, are only perceptible by the intellect and invisible; and that it is to these that the mind of the wise man emigrates. (281) Some, again, have fancied that by "fathers," are here meant the four principles and powers of which the world is composed—the earth, the water, the air, and the fire; for they say, that all created things are very properly dissolved into these elements. (282) For as nouns, and verbs, and all the other parts of speech, consist of the elements of grammar, and again are resolvable into these ultimate principles, so, in the same manner, each individual among us, being compounded of the four elements, and borrowing small portions from each essence, does, at certain fixed periods, repay what he has borrowed, giving what he has dry to the earth, what moisture he has to the water, what heat he has to the fire, and what cold he has to the air.

(283) These then are the things of the body; but the intellectual and heavenly race of the soul will ascend to the purest aether as to its father.

---

[91] Genesis 15:15.

[92] Genesis 12:1.
[93] Leviticus 26:10.

For the fifth essence, as the account of the ancients tells us, may be a certain one, which brings things round in a cycle, differing from the other four as being superior to them, from which the stars and the whole heavens appear to be generated, and of which, as a natural consequence, one must lay it down that the human soul is a fragment.

LVIII. (284) And the expression, "After having lived in peace," is used with much propriety; because nearly all or the greater portion of the human race lives rather in war and among all the evils of war. And of wars, one kind proceeds from external enemies, and is brought on by want of reputation, and by lowness of origin, and by other things of that kind. But another kind arises from one's domestic enemies; some about the body, such as weaknesses, stains, all kinds of mutilations, and a whole body of other unspeakable evils; and others affecting the soul, such as passions, diseases, infirmities, terrible and most grievous inflictions, and incurable calamities arising from folly and injustice, and other similar evils.

(285) Therefore he speaks of him who has lived in peace, who has enjoyed a serene and tranquil life, as a man truly happy and blessed. When then shall this happen? When all external things prosper with me, in such a way as to tend to my abundance and to my glory. When the things relating to the body are in a favourble state, so as to give me good health and strength; and when the things relating to my soul are in a similar state, so as to enable it to enjoy the virtues. (286) For each of these requires its own appropriate body-guards. Now the body is attended in that capacity by glory, and abundance, and a sufficient provision of wealth; and the soul by wholeness, and soundness, and thoroughly healthy state of the body; and the mind by those speculations which are concerned about the sciences.

Since it is plain to all those who are versed in the holy scriptures, that when peace is here mentioned, it is not that peace which cities enjoy. For Abraham bore a part in many terrible wars, out of which he appears to have come triumphantly. (287) And indeed the being forced to depart from his native country, and to leave his home, and his inability to dwell in his native city, and his being driven hither and thither, and wandering about by desolate and unfrequented roads, would have been a terrible war for one who had not put his trust in certain divine oracles and promises.

There would also be a third calamity, of a formidable nature, also to be borne by him, a famine, worse than the departure from his home, or than all the evils of war. (288) What peace then did he enjoy? For I imagine to be driven from his former home, and to have no settled abode, and to be unable to make an effectual resistance to very powerful monarchs, and to be oppressed with hunger, seem like indications, not of one war, but of many wars of various kinds. (289) But, according to those interpretations which are figurative, every one of these events is an instance and proof of unalloyed peace. For an absence of the passions, and a complete scarcity of them, and the destruction of inimical acts of iniquity, and a departure from the opinions of the Chaldeans to the doctrine which loves God, that is to say, from the created being, perceptible by the outward senses, to the great Cause and Creator of all things, who is appreciable only by the intellect, are things which supply a good system of laws and stability.

(290) And God promises the man who enjoys such a peace as this a glorious old age, not indeed one which shall last an exceeding time, but he promises him a life with wisdom. For tranquillity and happiness are better than length of years, in proportion as a short period of light is better than everlasting darkness. For well did one of the prophets say: "He had rather live one day in the company of virtue, than ten thousand years in the shadow of death;"[94] under this figurative expression of shadow, intimating the life of the wicked. (291) And Moses says the very same thing, intimating it by his actions rather than by his words. For the man who he says shall enjoy a glorious old age, he has at the same time represented as more short-lived than almost any one of those who preceded him. Speaking in a philosophical manner, and teaching us who it is who does truly enjoy a happy old age, that we may not conceive pride respecting old age from anything that affects the visible body; as such pride is full of shame and many disgraceful circumstances. But, that keeping our eyes fixed on wisdom of counsel, and steadiness of soul, we may ascribe to such men and testify in their favour that they have a glorious old age, (gēras) akin to, and bearing nearly the same name as honour (geras). (292) Listen, therefore, in such a spirit as to think his words a good lesson, to this statement of the lawgiver, that the good man alone has a happy old age, and that he is the most long-lived of men; but that the wicked man is the most short-lived of men, living only to die, or rather having already died as to the life of virtue.

LIX. (293) In the next verses it is said, "And in the fourth generation they shall return hither," not merely in order that the time may be exactly marked out to him, in which his descendants shall become inhabitants of the holy land, but also in order to represent to him the perfect and complete re-establishment of virtue; and this takes place as it were in the fourth generation, but how it does so it is worth while to consider.

(294) The child, after it is brought forth, during its age of infancy, till it has completed its first

---

[94] Psalm 84:11.

period of seven years, has a pure unmixed nature, very like a smooth waxen tablet, which has not yet been stamped with the indelible impressions of good or evil; for all the things which appear to be engraved upon it are soon confused and effaced by reason of its moisture: (295) this is as it were the first age of the soul.

The second is that which, after the age of infancy is passed, begins to live among evils, some of which it is also accustomed to generate from itself, and others it cheerfully receives from other sources, for the teachers of evil deeds are infinite in number: nurses, and tutors, and parents, and the laws in different states, whether written or unwritten, which make objects of admiration out of things which ought to be laughed at; and even without teachers nature itself is easily inclined to learn what is improper, so as to be continually weighed down by the abundance of its evils; (296) "For," says the scripture, "the mind of man is carefully devoted to evil from his youth."[95] This is that most accursed period which is figuratively called an age, but also especially the age of youth, in which the body is full of youthful vigour, and the soul is puffed up; the passions, which have hitherto lain hid, being now fanned into a flame, and burning up the threshing-floors, and crops, and fields, and whatever they meet with.

(297) This diseased generation or age must be remedied by some third age, acting towards it the part of medical philosophy, so that it shall be charmed with salutary and saving words, by means of which it will receive an evacuation of the immoderate satiety of evil actions, and a fulness of a sort of hungry emptiness, and terrible desolation of good deeds. (298) Therefore, after the application of this cure, there comes first the age, in which power and vigour grow up in the soul, in accordance with the most certain comprehension of wisdom, and the undeviating and solid character which exists in all virtues. This is the meaning of the expression, "And in the fourth generation they shall return hither." For according to the fourth number thus pointed out the soul, which has turned away from doing evil, is proclaimed as the inheritor of wisdom; (299) for the first number is that into which it is not possible to receive any idea of either good or evil, since the soul is as yet destitute of all impressions; and the second is that in which we indulge in a rapid course of the passions; and the third is that in which we are healed, repelling the infections of disease, and at last ceasing to feel the evil vigour of the passions; the fourth is that in which we acquire complete and perfect health and vigour, when rejecting what is bad we appear to endeavor to apply to what is good, which previously was not in our power.

LX. (300) But up to what time this is to be he tells us himself, when he says, "For the wickednesses of the Amorites are not yet fulfilled."[96] And such words as these give an occasion to weaker brethren to fancy, that Moses represents fate and necessity as the causes of all things that exist or take place; (301) but we must not be ignorant that he was well acquainted with the consequences, and connection, and reciprocal dependence of the causes of things, inasmuch as he was a philosophical man, accustomed to converse with God: and he does not attribute the causes of things which exist, or which take place, to these powers; for he imagined to himself some other more ancient power, mounted upon the universe, like a charioteer, or like the pilot of a ship; for this power steers the whole common vessel of the world in which all things sail, and he bridles the course of the winged chariot, the entire heaven, exerting an independent and absolute sovereign authority. (302) What then are we to say about these subjects? The name Amorites, being interpreted, means "talkers;" and numbers of those who have received that greatest of all blessings bestowed upon man by nature, namely speech, have abused and corrupted it, employing it ungratefully and treacherously, to the injury of her who has bestowed it. Such are flatterers, impostors, devisers of plausible sophistries, men who rather cultivate the skill to delude and to cheat, and who have no care to speak truly, and these men study indistinctness. Now indistinctness is equivalent to deep darkness in discourse; and darkness is the great assistant of robbers, (303) on which account Moses has adorned the chief priest with distinct demonstration and truth; thinking it proper that the discourse of the virtuous man should be clear, and perspicuous, and true; but men in general pursue that which is indistinct and false, under the banner of which the whole misguided multitude of ordinary careless men enrols itself.

(304) Therefore, as long as "the offences of the Amorites are not fulfilled," that is to say, the evils of sophistical arguments by reason of their not having been refuted, but while they still influence us, having an attractive power by reason of their plausibility, we being unable to turn away and forsake them, remain in their power from being allured by them. (305) But if once all unreal plausibilities are convicted and refuted by true proofs, and if their offences are shown to be full and running over, then we shall flee away without ever turning back, and as it were slipping our cables we shall set sail from the region of falsehoods and sophistries, hastening to cast anchor in the safe harbours and havens of truth.

(306) And in this way, I look upon it as suf-

---

ficiently proved in the spirit of my original proposition that it is impossible for a man to reject, and to hate, and to forsake plausible falsehood, unless the evils arising from it are seen to be full and complete; and they will be shown to be so, by its being refuted in no superficial way, by the establishment on the other hand, and by the complete confirmation of truth.

LXI. (307) In the next verse the historian proceeds to say, "and when the sun approached its setting, there was a flame;"[97] showing that virtue is a thing which is not born till late, and indeed which, as some persons have said, is only confirmed and established at the very setting of life. And he compares virtue to a flame; for as the flame consumes whatever materials are exposed to it, and gives light to all the air in its neighbourhood, in the same manner does virtue burn up all the offences, and fills the whole mind with light. (308) But while discourses, which are neither divided nor properly distributed, prevail over us by reason of their plausibilities, which he here calls the Amorites, we are not able to see the most brilliant and unshaded light. But we are like a furnace which has not a pure flame, but, as he himself says, emits only smoke, being gradually kindled by the sparks of knowledge, but not as yet being able to stand the hardening and test of pure fire.

(309) But we owe great gratitude to him who has scattered those sparks, in order that our mind may not become cold like a lifeless corpse, being warmed and vivified by the gentle increasing heat of virtue, may feel a glow until it receives the change to holy fire, like Nadab and Abihu. (310) But smoke exists before fire, and compels those who come near it to weep; but both fire and smoke often come together. For, being delighted at the messengers of virtue, we hope to attain perfection therein, and if we are not yet able to arrive at it, then we can scarcely through our grief forbear from tears. For when an excessive desire is implanted in our breasts, they hasten to pursue the desired object, and our faces are full of chagrin until we attain it.

(311) And how he has compared the soul of man, who loves instruction and who cherishes a hope of arriving at perfection, to a furnace, because each is a vessel in which food is cooked, the one being the vessel in which those meats which are perishable are prepared, and the other that suited to the reception of the imperishable virtues.

And the burning torches of fire which are lighted up are the judgments of God who bears the torch, being bright and radiant, which are accustomed to be always placed in the middle between the divided portions; I mean by this the portions set in opposition to one another, of which the whole world is composed. (312) For we read in the scripture, "The lamps of fire which were in the midst between the divided portions,"[98] that you may know that the divine powers which go through the middle of both bodies and things, destroy none of them; for both the divisions remain unhurt, but only divide and discriminate in a most excellent manner between the natures of each.

LXII. (313) Therefore, the wise man has now been sufficiently proved to be the inheritor of the knowledge of the subjects above mentioned. "For," says the historian, "on that day the Lord made a covenant with Abraham, saying, to thy seed will I give this land."[99] (314) But what land does he mean but that which has been already mentioned, to which he is now making reference? The fruit of which is the safe and most certain comprehension of the wisdom of God, according to which it preserves for its dividers all the good things which exist without any admixture or taint of evil, as if they had been incorruptible from their very beginning. (315) After this he proceeds to add, "from the river of Egypt to the great river, the river Euphrates." Showing that those men who are perfect have their beginnings in the body, and the outward sense, and the organic parts, without which we cannot live, for they are useful for instruction in the life which is in union with the body; but they have their end with the wisdom of God, which is truly the great river, overflowing with joy, and cheerfulness, and all other blessings. (316) For he has not described the country as reaching from the river Euphrates to the river of Egypt (for he would never have brought over virtue towards the passions of the body), but, on the contrary, he has said from the river of Egypt to the river Euphrates. For the migrations are from mortal things to incorruptible.

---

[97] Genesis 15:17.

[98] Genesis 15:17.
[99] Genesis 15:18.

ON MATING WITH THE PRELIMINARY STUDIES†

(De Congressu Quaerendae Eruditionis Gratia)

I. (1) "But Sarah the wife of Abraham had not borne him any child. And she had an Egyptian handmaiden, whose name was Hagar. And Sarah said unto Abraham, Behold, the Lord has closed me up, so that I should not bear children; go in unto my handmaiden that thou mayest have children by her."[1]

(2) The name Sarah, being interpreted, means "my princedom." And the wisdom which is in me, and the temperance which is in me, and the particular justice, and each of the other virtues which belong to me alone, are the princedom of me alone. For such virtue, being a queen from its birth, rules over and governs me who have determined on obeying it.

(3) Now this virtue, Moses (making a most paradoxical assertion) reports, as being both barren and also most prolific, since he affirms that the most populous of all nations is sprung from it. For, in real truth, virtue is barren with respect to all things which are evil, but is so exceedingly prolific of good things, that it stands in no need of the art of the midwife, for it anticipates it by bringing forth before its arrival. (4) Therefore animals and plants, after considerable intervals and interruptions, bring forth their appropriate fruits, once, or at most twice a year; according to the number of times which nature has appointed each of them, and which is properly adapted to the seasons of the year. But virtue without any interruption, without any interval or any cessation, is continually bringing forth at all times and on all occasions, not indeed children, but virtuous reasonings, and irreproachable counsels, and praiseworthy actions.

II. (5) But neither is wealth, which it is not possible to employ, of any advantage to its possessors, nor is the fertility of wisdom of any service to us, unless it also brings forth such things as are serviceable to us. For some persons it judges to be in every respect worthy of living in its company; but others appear to have not yet arrived at such an age, as to be able to support so highly praised and well regulated a charge; whom, however, it permits to enter upon the preliminaries of marriage, holding out to them a hope that they may hereafter consummate the wedlock.

(6) Sarah therefore, the virtue which rules over my soul, has brought forth, but, she has not brought forth for me (for I should never as yet have been able, since I am quite young, to receive her offspring); she has brought forth, I say, wisdom, and the doing of just actions, and piety, by reason of the multitude of illegitimate children whom the vain opinions have brought forth to me. For the education of the offspring, and the constant superintendence and incessant care which they require, have compelled me to neglect the legitimate children, who are really citizens. (7) It is well, therefore, to pray that virtue may not only bring forth, since she is prolific even without a prayer, but that she may bring for us; in order that we, receiving a share of her seed and of her offspring, may be happy. For she is accustomed to bring forth children to God alone, restoring with burning gratitude the first fruits of all the blessings which she has received, to him, who, as Moses says, "opened her womb,"[2] which was at all times virgin. (8) For he also says that the lamp, that archetypal model after which the copy is made, shines in one part, that is to say, in the part which is turned towards God.[3] For since that completes the number of seven, and stands in the middle of the six branches, which are divided into two lots of three each, acting as body-guards to it on either side, it sends its rays upwards toward that one being, namely God, thinking its light too brilliant for mortal sight to be able to stand its proximity.

III. (9) On this account he does not say that Sarah did not bring forth at all, but only that she did not bring forth for him, for Abraham. For we are not as yet capable of becoming the fathers of offspring of virtue, unless we first of all have a connection with her handmaiden; and the handmaiden of wisdom is the encyclical knowledge of music and logic, arrived at by previous instruction. (10) For as in houses there are vestibules placed in front of staircases, and as in cities there are suburbs, through which one must pass in order to enter into the cities; so also the encyclical branches of instruction are placed in front of virtue, for they are the road which conducts to her. (11) And as you must know that it is common for there to be great preludes to great propositions, and the greatest of all

---

† Yonge's title, *A Treatise on the Meeting for the Sake of Seeking Instruction.*
[1] Genesis 16:1.

[2] Genesis 29:31.
[3] Exodus 25:31.

propositions is virtue, for it is conversant about the most important of all materials, namely, about the universal life of man; very naturally, therefore, that will not employ any short preface, but rather it will use as such, grammar, geometry, astronomy, rhetoric, music, and all the other sorts of contemplation which proceed in accordance with reason; of which Hagar, the handmaid of Sarah, is an emblem, as we will proceed to show.

(12) "For Sarah," says Moses, "said unto Abraham, Behold, the Lord has closed me up, so that I may not bear children. Go in unto my handmaiden, that thou mayest have children by her." Now, we must take out of the present discussion those conjunctions and connections of body with body which have pleasure for their end. For this is the connection of the mind with virtue, which is desirous to have children by her, and which, if it cannot do so at once, is at all events taught to espouse her handmaid, namely, intermediate instruction.

IV. (13) And here it is worth while to admire wisdom, by reason of its modesty, which has not thought fit to reproach us with the slowness of our generation, or our absolute barrenness. And this, too, though the oracle says truly that she brought forth no child, not out of envy, but because of the unsuitableness of our own selves. For, says she, "The Lord has closed me up so, that I may not bear children." And she no longer adds the words, "to you," that she may not appear to mention the misfortunes of others, or to reproach them with theirs. (14) "Therefore," says she, "go thou in to my handmaiden," that is to say, to the intermediate instruction of the intermediate and encyclical branches of knowledge, "that you may first have children by her;" for hereafter you shall be able to enjoy a connection with her mistress, tending to the procreation of legitimate children. (15) For grammar, by teaching you the histories which are to be found in the works of poets and historians, will give you intelligence and abundant learning; and, moreover, will teach you to look with contempt on all the vain fables which erroneous opinions invent, on account of the ill success which history tells us that the heroes and demigods who are celebrated among those writers, meet with.

(16) And music will teach what is harmonious in the way of rhythm, and what is ill arranged in harmony, and, rejecting all that is out of tune and all that is inconsistent with melody, will guide what was previously discordant to concord. And geometry, sowing the seeds of equality and just proportion in the soul, which is fond of learning, will, by means of the beauty of continued contemplation, implant in you an admiration of justice. (17) And rhetoric, having sharpened the mind for contemplation in general, and having exercised and trained the faculties of speech in interpretations and explanations, will make man really rational, taking care of that peculiar and especial duty which nature has bestowed upon it, but upon no other animal whatever. (18) And dialectic science, which is the sister, the twin sister of rhetoric, as some persons have called it, separating true from false arguments, and refuting the plausibilities of sophistical arguments, will cure the great disease of the soul, deceit.

It is profitable, therefore, to aide among these and other sciences resembling them, and to devote one's especial attention to them. For perhaps, I say, as has happened to many, we shall become known to the queenly virtues by means of their subjects and handmaidens. (19) Do you not see that our bodies do not use solid and costly food before they have first, in their age of infancy, used such as had no variety, and consisted merely of milk? And, in the same way, think also that infantine food is prepared for the soul, namely the encyclical sciences, and the contemplations which are directed to each of them; but that the more perfect and becoming food, namely the virtues, is prepared for those who are really full-grown men.

V. (20) Now the first characteristics of the intermediate instruction are represented by two symbols, the race and the name. As to race, the handmaiden is an Egyptian, and her name is Hagar; and this name, being interpreted, means "emigration." For it follows of necessity that the man who delights in the encyclical contemplations, and who joins himself as a companion to varied learning, is as such enrolled under the banners of the earthly and Egyptian body; and that he stands in need of eyes in order to see and to read, and of ears in order to attend and to hear, and of his other external senses, in such a manner as to be able to unfold each of the objects of the external sense. (21) For it is not natural to suppose that the subject of judgment can possibly be comprehended without some power which is to judge; and the power which judges of the objects of the external sense is the external sense, so that without the external sense it would not be possible for any thing in that world which is perceptible by the external sense to be accurately known, though those are the matters which are the principal field for philosophical speculation.

But the external sense, being that portion of the soul which most resembles the body, is deeply rooted in the entire vessel of the soul; and the vessel of the soul is, by a figurative way of speaking, called Egypt. (22) And there is one characteristic derived from her race, which the handmaiden of virtue possesses. But what or what kind of characteristic that is which is derived from the name, we must now proceed to consider.

The intermediate instruction has the same rank and classification as a sojourner. For all knowledge, and wisdom, and virtue, are the only real native and original inhabitants and citizens of the universe. And all the others kinds of instruction, which obtain the second, and third, and lowest honours, are on the confines, between foreigners and citizens. For they are not connected with either race without some alloy, and yet again they are not connected with both according to a certain community and participation. (23) For they are sojourners from the fact of their passing their time among citizens; but from the fact of their not being settled inhabitants, they also resemble foreigners. In the same manner, according to my idea, as adopted children, inasmuch as they inherit the property of those who have adopted them, resemble real legitimate children; but inasmuch as they were not begotten by them, they resemble strangers. The same relation, then, that a mistress has to her handmaidens, or a wife, who is a citizen, to a concubine, that same relation has virtue, that is Sarah, to education, that is Hagar. So that very naturally, since the husband, by name Abraham, is one who has an admiration for contemplation and knowledge; virtue, that is Sarah, would be his wife, and Hagar, that is all kinds of encyclical accomplishments, would be his concubine. (24) Whoever, therefore, has acquired wisdom from his teachers, would never reject Hagar. For the acquisition of all the preliminary branches of education is wholly necessary.

VI. But if any one, having determined on perseveringly enduring labours in the cause of virtue, devotes himself to continued study, practising and meditating without intermission, that man will marry two citizens, and also an equal number of concubines, the handmaidens of the citizens. (25) And each of these has a different appearance and a different nature. For instance, of the two citizen wives, one is a most healthy and well established and peaceful motion, whom from the circumstances the historians called Leah: and the other resembles a whetstone and is called Rachel, in the pursuit of whom the mind, which is fond of labour and fond of exercises, is much sharpened and excited; and the name, being interpreted, means the "sight of profanation;" not because she sees profanely, but, on the contrary, because she thinks the things which are seen and which are the objects of the external senses, not brilliant but common and profane in comparison of the pure and untainted nature of those things which are invisible and which are only discernible by the intellect.

(26) For since our soul is composed of two parts, and since the one contains the rational faculties, and the other the irrational ones, it follows that each part must have its own peculiar virtue, Leah being the virtue of the rational part, and Rachel of the irrational. (27) For the one trains us, by means of the external senses and the parts of speech, to look contemptuously upon all things

which it is proper to disregard, such as glory, and wealth, and pleasure, which the principal and general multitude of common men look upon as things to be admired and striven for, their sense of hearing being corrupted, and the tribunal of all the other external senses being corrupted likewise. (28) But the other teaches us to turn away from that uneven and rough road which is never approached by souls that love virtue, and to go smoothly along the smooth road without any stumbling and without meeting any hindrances in the path. (29) Therefore the handmaiden of the former of the two citizen wives will necessarily be the power of interpretation as exercised by means of the organs of speech, and also the rational invention of sophisms, deceiving man by a well-imagined plausibility; and its necessary nourishment is meat and drink.

(30) The historian has recorded for us the names of the two handmaidens, calling them Zilpah and Billah.[4] The name Zilpah, being interpreted, means "a mouth going forth," a symbol of that nature which interprets and speaks. But Billah means "a swallowing," which is the first and most necessary support of all mortal animals. For it is by swallowing that our bodies are established firmly, and the cables of life are attached to this action as to a sure foundation. (31) Accordingly the practiser of virtue lives with all the aforesaid powers, with some as with free women and citizens, and with others as slaves and concubines. For he is enamoured of the motion of Leah; and a smooth (leia) motion existing in a body would be calculated to produce health, and, when existing in a soul, it would produce virtue and justice. But he loves Rachel, wrestling with his passions, and preparing himself for a struggle of temperance, arraying himself in opposition to all the objects of the external senses. (32) For there are two kinds of advantage, either that according to which we enjoy blessings, as in peace, or else that which comes from arraying one's self in opposition to and from removing evils as in war. Now Leah is the wife according to whom it happens to the husband to enjoy the elder, and more important, and dominant blessings; and Rachel the wife, according to whom he obtains what resemble the sports of war. Such then is his way, if left with his citizen wives.

(33) But the practiser of virtue also wants Billah, that is, swallowing, but as a slave and a concubine; for without food and vitality, living well could not possibly be the lot of man, since things indifferent are always the foundation of what is better; and he also wants Zilpah, that is to say, interpretation by means of utterance, in order that the rational part itself may, in a twofold manner, contribute to perfection, both from the fountain exist-

---

[4]Genesis 30:1.

ing in the intellect, and also from the stream flowing therefrom in the organ of the voice.

VII. (34) But these men were husbands of many wives and concubines, not only of such as were citizens, as the sacred scriptures tell us. But Isaac had neither many wives nor any concubine at all, but only his first and wedded wife, who lived with him all his life. (35) Why was this? Because the virtue acquired by teaching, which Abraham pursues, requires many things, both such as are legitimate according to prudence, and such also as are illegitimate according to the exegetical contemplations of preliminary instruction. And there is also a virtue which is made perfect by practice, to which Jacob appears to have been devoted; for exercises consist of many and various dogmas and doctrines, some leading and others following, some leading the way, and others arriving later, and bringing at one time more serious, and at other times lighter labours. (36) But the self-instructed race, of which Isaac was a partaker, the excellent country of the mastery over the passions, has received as its share a nature simple, and unmixed, and unalloyed, standing in no need of either practice or instruction in which there is need of the concubine sciences, and not only of the citizen wives; for when God has showered down from above that most requisite benefit of knowledge, self-taught, and having no need of a preceptor, it would be impossible any longer for a man to live with the slavish and concubine arts, having a desire for bastard doctrines as his children.

For the man who has arrived at this honour, is inscribed as the husband of the mistress and princess virtue; and she is called in the Greek language, perseverance, but among the Hebrews her name is Rebekkah. (37) For he who, by reason of the happy constitution of his own nature and by the prolific fertility of his soul, has attained to wisdom without encountering labour or enduring hardship, stands in need of no further improvement; (38) for he has at hand the perfect gifts of God, inspired by means of those most ancient graces, and he wishes and prays that they may remain lasting. In reference to which, it appears to me to be that the Author of all goodness gave him perseverance as his wife, in order that his mercies might endure for ever to the man who had her for his wife.

VIII. (39) Now recollection only comes in the second rank after memory, as inferior to it; and he who recollects is inferior to him who remembers; for the latter resembles a man in an uninterrupted state of good health, but the other is like a man recovering from a disease, for forgetfulness is a disease of the memory; (40) and it follows inevitably that the man who exerts his recollection has previously forgotten what he now recollects. Therefore the sacred scriptures call

memory Ephraim, which name, being interpreted, means "fruit-bearing." But the Hebrews call recollection, after forgetfulness, Manasseh; (41) for, in good truth, the soul of the man who remembers does bear as fruit the things which he has learned, losing nothing of them; but the soul of the man who exerts recollection, is only escaping from forgetfulness, by which it was detained before it recollected; therefore a citizen wife, memory, lives with the man who is endowed with remembrance. But the concubine recollection, a Syrian by birth, insolent and overbearing, lives with the man who forgets; for the meaning of the name Syria, is "sublimity;" (42) and the son of the concubine recollection is Machir, as the Hebrews call him; but the Greeks interpret the name to mean "of the father." For those who recollect a thing think that the mind is the father and cause of their recollecting, and do not consider that this same endowment of the mind did also before contain "forgetfulness," though it never would have received it if it had had memory in its power.

(43) For it is said in the scripture, "And the sons of Manasseh were Ashriel whom she bare, but his concubine, the Aramitess, bare Machir; and Machir was the father Gilead."[5] And Nachor, also, the brother of Abraham, had two wives, one a citizen and the other a concubine. And the name of the citizen was Milcah; and the name of the concubine was Rumah. (44) But let no one who is in his senses suspect that the wise legislator recorded this as a historical genealogy, but it is rather an explanation of things which are able to benefit the soul by means of symbols. And when we have translated the names into our own language, we shall understand the real meanings intended to be conveyed by them. Come, then, let us now investigate each of them.

IX. (45) The name Nachor, being interpreted, means "a rest from light;" and Milcah means "princess;" and Rumah means "she who sees something." Therefore, to have light in the mind is good; but cessation from light, and tranquillity, and immobility is not perfect good, for it is advantageous to have evils tranquil, but it is desirable to have blessings in motion; for what advantage is there in a man's having a tuneful voice, if he keeps silent? (46) or in his having the skill of a flute player, if he does not play the flute? or of his knowing the harp, if he does not strike it? or, in short, what good is there in any artist whatever, if he does not exercise his art? for theoretical knowledge, without putting it in practice, is of no advantage whatever to those who possess it. For a man, though skilful in the contest of the pancratium, or in boxing, or in wrestling, would

---

[5] 1 Chronicles 7:14.

derive no advantage from his athletic prowess if his hands were tied behind him; and he who was thoroughly practised in running would derive no advantage from his fleetness of foot if he were afflicted with the gout, or if he were to meet with any other injury to his feet. (47) And the light of the soul, which is the most brilliant and the most like the sun, is knowledge; for as the eyes are lightened up by beams, so is the mind made brilliant by wisdom, and becomes gradually accustomed to see more acutely from being continually anointed with new speculations.

Therefore, Nachor is interpreted "a cessation from light," very naturally; (48) for, inasmuch as he is a relation of the wise Abraham, he partakes of that light which is according to wisdom; but inasmuch as he did not join him in his emigration from the created to the uncreated being, from the world to the Creator of the world, he has acquired only a lame and imperfect knowledge, intermittent and delaying, or rather put together like a lifeless statue; (49) for he does not depart and quit his abode in the Chaldaean country, that is to say, he does not separate himself from the speculations concerning astronomy; honouring that which is created rather than him who created it, and the world in preference to God; or rather, I should say, looking on the world itself as an absolute independent God, and not as the work of an absolute God.

X. (50) And he takes Milcah for his wife, not being some queen who by the dispensations of fortune governs some nation of men, or some city, but only one who bears a common name, the same as here. For, just as a person would not be widely wrong who called the world, as being the most excellent of all created things, the king of the objects of the external sense; so, also, one may call the knowledge which is conversant about the heaven, which knowledge those who study astronomy and the Chaldaeans possess in an eminent degree, the queen of all the sciences. (51) This, therefore, is the wife who is a citizen; but the concubine is she who sees one only of all existing things at a time, even though it may be the most worthless of all. It is given, therefore, to the most excellent race to see the most excellent of things, namely, the really living God; for the name Israel, being interpreted, means "seeing God."

But to him who aims at the second prize, it is allowed to see that which is second best, namely, the heaven which is perceptible by the external senses, and the harmonious arrangement of the stars therein, and their truly musical and well-regulated motion. (52) The third class are the sceptics, who do not apply themselves to the most excellent objects, either of the intellect or of the external senses, which exist in nature, because they are always occupying themselves with petty sophistries, and small cavils, and criticisms. These have for their companions the concubine Rumah, who sees something which is very minute, because they are unable to approach the investigation of better things, by means of which they might benefit their own life. (53) For, as among physicians that which is called theoretical medical skill, is a long way from doing any good to those that are sick—for diseases are cured by medicines, and by operations, and by regimen, and not by discussions or theories; so also in philosophy, there is a set of word-traffickers and word-eaters, who have neither the will nor the skill to heal a life which is full of infirmities, but who, from their very earliest infancy to the extremity of old age, are not ashamed to cavil, and quibble, and wrangle about figurative expressions, as if happiness consisted in an interminable and profitless minuteness of accuracy in the matter of nouns and verbs, and not in the improving and ameliorating the moral character, the true fountain of the persons' disposition; and in expelling the vices, and driving them out of its boundaries, and establishing the virtues as settlers within them.

XI. (54) Now the wicked also have a desire for concubines, that is, for vain opinions and doctrines; accordingly Moses tells us that Thimna, the concubine of Eliphah the son of Esau, bore Amalek to Eliphah.[6] Alas, for the eminent ignobleness of the descendant! And you will see this ignobleness the more clearly, if you abandon the idea that this expression is used about a man, and rather consider the soul, with a kind of anatomical dissection. (55) The historian then calls the irrational and immoderate desires and impetuosity of the passions, Amalek; now the name Amalek, being interpreted, means "the people looking up." For as the power of fire consumes the materials which are offered to it, so in the same manner does passion, when boiling over lick up and destroy everything with which it meets. (56) And the father of this passion is very properly described as Eliphah; for this name, being interpreted, means "God has scattered me." But does it not follow that when God scatters, and disperses, and discards the soul, banishing it from himself, irrational passion is at once engendered? For He plants the mind which can really behold him, and which is really attached to God, the vine of a good kind, stretching out its roots so as to make them everlasting, and giving it abundance of fruit for the acquisition and enjoyment of the virtues. (57) On which account Moses prays, saying, "Bring them in and plant them in,"[7] in order that those divine shoots may not be

[6]Genesis 36:12.
[7]Exodus 15:17.

ephemeral, but long-lived and lasting for ever and ever.

And banishing the unjust and ungodly soul, he disperses it and drives it to a distance from himself to the region of the pleasures and appetites and acts of injustice; and this region is, with exceeding appropriateness, called the region of the impious, more fitly than that one which is fabled as existing in the shades below. For indeed, the real hell is the life of the wicked, which is audacious, and flagitious, and liable to all kinds of curses.

XII. (58) There is also in another place the following sentence deeply engraven: "When the Most High came down to scatter the nations, as he dispersed the sons of Adam,"[8] he drove out all earthly dispositions, which had no desire to see any good thing from heaven; depriving them of house and city, and rendering them truly wanderers on the face of the earth. For no house, nor city, nor anything else which relates to society and participation, is preserved for any one of the wicked; but they are deprived of all settled habitation, and dispersed abroad, being moved in every direction, and living a life of continued emigration, and not being able to become settled any where. (59) Therefore the wicked man has for his children, wickedness, by his wife who is a citizen, and passion by his concubine; for the whole soul, like a free citizen, is a companion of reason, but that which is open to reproach brings forth wickedness. But the nature of the body is a concubine, by means of whom the birth of the passion is beheld; and the body is the region of the pleasures and passions, and it is called Thamnah, (60) which name, being interpreted, signifies a "fluctuating abandonment." For the soul becomes faint and powerless by reason of the passions having received much tossing about and agitation from the body, on account of the violent storm which bursts forth from immoderate impetuosity.

(61) But as the head is the chief of all the aforementioned parts of an animal, so is Esau the chief of this race, whose name is at one time interpreted "an oak," and at another, "a thing made." It is interpreted an oak, in reference to his being unbending, and implacable, and obstinate, and stiffnecked by nature, and having folly for his chief fellow counsellor, and being as such of a truly oaken character. And it is interpreted "a thing made," inasmuch as a life according to folly is an invention and a fable, full of tragic pomp and vain boasting; and, on the other hand, of mockery and comic ridicule, having in it nothing sound, being full of falsehood, having utterly cast off truth, and disregarding as a thing of no value, that nature which is void of distinctive qualities, or of particular species, but

plain and sincere, which the practiser of virtue loves. (62) And Moses bears witness to this, when he says that "Jacob was a man without artifice, dwelling in a house;"[9] so that he who is contrary to him, must necessarily be destitute of a house, the companion of invention, and of things made, and of fabulous nonsense, or rather be himself a theatre and a fable.

XIII. (63) The connection therefore between the reason which is devoted to contemplation and those powers which are citizen wives, or concubines, has here been explained to the best of my power. We must now proceed to investigate what follows, and endeavour to frame a proper connection for an argument. "Abraham," says the sacred historian, "listened to the voice of Sarah."[10] For it is necessary for him who is a learner to be obedient to the injunctions of virtue: (64) but yet all men are not so obedient, but only those who are inspired with an exceedingly vehement love for knowledge. Since almost every day the places where there is anything to hear and the theatres are crowded, and those who study philosophy go on without ever stopping to take breath in one long continued discussion about virtue. (65) But still what advantage is derived from all that is said? For men, instead of attending, turn their mind in other directions, some to marine and mercantile affairs, others to rents and agriculture; some to public honours and affairs of state, some to the gains to be derived from each different profession and art, others to revenging themselves upon their enemies, others again to the enjoyments to be derived from the indulgence of the amorous appetites, and in short every body is under the influence of some distracting idea or other; so that, as far as the subjects of the discussion are concerned, they are completely deaf, and are present with their bodies only, but are at a distance as to their minds, being in no particular different from images or statues. (66) And if any persons do attend, they sit all that time only listening, and when they have departed they do not recollect a word of what has been said, but they have come in fact rather to be pleased through the medium of their hearing than with the view of deriving any solid advantage; so that their soul has not been able to comprehend anything or to become pregnant with any new idea, and even the cause which at first excited their pleasure soon ceases and their attention is extinguished.

(67) There is a third kind of persons to whom what is said is for a time attended to and remembered, as if still sounding in their ears; but still they are found to be sophists rather than philosophers: of these men the language indeed is praise-

---

[8]Deuteronomy 32:8.

[9]Genesis 25:27.
[10]Genesis 16:2.

worthy but the life is blameable; for they are powerful at speaking, but have no ability to do what is best. (68) It is therefore hardly possible to find a man who is inclined to attend and endowed with a good memory, honouring deeds rather than words; as is testified to in the praise of the man fond of hearing in the words, "He listened to the voice of Sarah." For he is not represented merely as hearing but also as listening to: and this last is a particularly felicitous expression to indicate one who approves of and is influenced by what he hears.

(69) And the expression, "to the voice," is not inconsiderately or incorrectly used in preference to saying—he listened to Sarah speaking. For it is the especial character of a learner to listen to the voice and words of his teacher; for by these alone is he taught. But he who acquires what is good by practice, and solitary meditation, and not by instruction, does not attend to what is said but rather to those who say it, imitating the lives of those men in their actions which are in each particular irreproachable. (70) For it is said, in the case of Jacob when he was sent away to form a marriage among his kinsmen, "Jacob listened to his mother and his father, and went into Mesopotamia."[11] He listened not to their voice, nor to their words, for it was fitting that he who was an imitator of their actions should be a practiser of virtue not a listener to speeches. For this is the peculiar character of one who is being taught, but the other is the mark of one who is enduring labours, in order that from this instance we may comprehend the difference between a practiser and a learner, the one being regulated with regard to him who is speaking, and the other with regard to his speech.

XIV. (71) Therefore, continues the sacred historian, Sarah, the wife of Abraham, having taken Hagar, the Egyptian woman, her own handmaiden, ten years after Abraham had begun to dwell in the land of Canaan, gave her to Abraham her "husband, to be his wife."[12] Wickedness is by nature an envious, and bitter, and evil-disposed thing, but virtue is gentle, and inclined to communion, and friendly; wishing in every possible manner to benefit those who are well disposed, either by its own power or by the means of others. (72) So now accordingly, as we are not able to become the fathers of children by prudence, she espouses us to her own handmaiden, encyclical instruction, as I have said before, and all but endures to be the bridesmaid and manager of the marriage; for it is said that Sarah herself took this woman and gave her to her own husband.

(73) And here it is worth while to raise the question why it is that now again Moses calls the wife of Abraham Sarah, when he had already repeatedly told us what her name was before; for he was not a writer who ever indulged in that worst description of prolixity, tautology. What, then, are we to say? Since she is about to betroth to him the handmaiden of wisdom, encyclical instruction, he says that she did not forget the duty which she owed to her mistress, but knew that she was, both in law and in her master's feelings, his wife, and that she herself was only such because of necessity and the force of opportunity. And this happens to every man who is fond of learning. And he who has experienced it may be looked upon as the most trustworthy witness to this fact. (74) At all events I, when I was first excited by the stimulus of philosophy to feel a desire for it, when I was very young connected myself with one of her handmaidens, namely, grammar; and all the offspring of which I became the father by her, such as writing, reading, and the acquaintance with the works of the poets and historians, I attributed to the mistress. (75) And at a subsequent time, forming connection with another of her handmaidens, geometry, and admiring her beauty (for she had beautiful symmetry and proportions in all her parts), I still appropriated none of the offspring, but carried them to the citizen wife, and bestowed them on her. (76) I was desirous also to form a similar connection with a third, and she was full of good rhythm, well arranged, and well limbed, and was called music. And by her I became the parent of diatonic, and chromatic, and harmonic, and combined and separate melodies, and all the different concords belonging to fourths and to fifths, and to the diapason. And, again, I concealed none of all these things, in order that my legitimate citizen wife might become wealthy, being ministered unto by a multitude of ten thousand servants; (77) for some men, being attracted by the charms of handmaidens, have neglected their true mistress, philosophy, and have grown old, some in poetry, and others in the study of painting, and others in the mixture of colours, and others in ten thousand other pursuits, without ever being able to return to the proper mistress; (78) for each act has its own peculiar brillliancies, certain attractive powers, by which some persons are allured and overcome, forgetting all the covenants which they have made with philosophy; but he who abides by the agreements which he has made, provides every thing from all quarters with a view to pleasing her.

Very appropriately, therefore, does the sacred scripture, admiring his good faith in respect of his legitimate wife, say that even now Sarah was his true wife, inasmuch as he only took his handmaid into his bed out of complaisance towards her; (79)

---

[11] Genesis 28:7.
[12] Genesis 16:3.

and, indeed, in the same manner as the encyclical branches of education contribute to the proper comprehension of philosophy, so also does philosophy aid in the acquisition of wisdom; for philosophy is an attentive study of wisdom, and wisdom is the knowledge of all divine and human things, and of the respective causes of them. Therefore, just as encyclical accomplishments are the handmaidens of philosophy, so also is philosophy the handmaiden of wisdom; (80) but philosophy teaches temperance with regard to the belly, and temperance with regard to the parts below the belly, and also temperance and restraint of the tongue. Now these qualities are said to be worthy of praise for their own sakes, but they would appear more respectable still if they were cultivated for the sake of doing honour to and giving pleasure to God.

We must, therefore, always remember the legitimate mistress when we are about to espouse her handmaidens; and let us be said indeed to be the husbands of the latter, but still let our legitimate mistress be our real wife, and not merely called such.

XV. (81) Again, she gives Hagar to him, not the first moment that he arrives in the country of the Canaanites, but after he has abode there ten years. And what the meaning of this statement is we must investigate in no careless manner.

Now, at the beginning of our existence, our soul dwelt among the passions alone as its foster-brethren, griefs, pains, fears, desires, and pleasures, which reach it through the medium of the external senses, before reason was as yet able to see good and evil, and to distinguish accurately the points wherein these things differ from one another, but while it was still wavering and hesitating, and as it were closing its eyes in profound sleep; (82) but as time advances, when advancing out of the age of infancy we are on the point of becoming young men, then, without any delay, the double trunk of virtue and wickedness springs forth out of one root, and we attain to a comprehension of them both, but still we by all means choose one of the two; those who are well disposed choosing virtue, and those of the contrary character choosing wickedness. (83) These things, now, being previously sketched out in this manner, we must become aware that Egypt is the symbol of the passions and the land of the Canaanites, the emblem of the wickednesses; so that it is in strict accordance with natural probability that God, after having roused his people and made them depart from Egypt, leads them into the country of the Canaanites; (84) for the man, as I have said before, at his very earliest birth had the Egyptian passions assigned to him to dwell among, being deeply rooted in pleasures and in pains; and at a subsequent time he departs as if to found a col-

ony, and migrates towards wickedness. His reason now being inclined to a more acute sight, and comprehending accurately both the opposite extremes of good and evil, but nevertheless choosing the worse part, because it has a great share in mortal nature, to which what is evil is in some degree akin, as also the contrary, namely, good, is akin to the divine nature.

XVI. (85) But these are the different countries of each respective nature; passions, that is to say, Egypt, being the country of the age of childhood; and wickedness, that is the land of Canaan, being the country of the age of youth. But the sacred scripture, although it is well acquainted with the different countries of the mortal race, suggests to us what ought to be done and what will be advantageous to us, enjoining us to hate the heathen, and their laws, and their customs, in that passage where he says, (86) "And the Lord spake unto Moses, saying, Speak unto the children of Israel, and say unto them, I am the Lord your God; ye shall not behave according to the customs of Egypt in which ye dwelt among them, and ye shall not walk in their laws. Ye shall do my judgments, and ye shall not do according to the customs of the land of Canaan, into which I am leading you to dwell there. And ye shall keep my commandments, and ye shall walk in them. I am the Lord your God. And ye shall keep all my commandments and my judgments, and ye shall do them. He that doeth them the same shall live in them. I am the Lord your God: and ye shall keep all my commandments and my judgments."[13]

(87) Therefore, real true life, above everything else, consists in the judgments and commandments of God, so that the customs and practices of the impious must be death: but there are some races which take no note of passions and wickednesses, from whom the multitudes of impious persons and wickedness are sprung.

(88) Therefore, ten years after our departure to settle in the land of the Canaanites let us marry Hagar, since from the first moment that we become rational beings, we seek for ignorance and a deficiency of knowledge which is pernicious in its own nature; but at a subsequent period, and at a perfect number, namely, the legal number of the decade, we come to feel a desire for that instruction which is able to benefit us.

XVII. (89) But the sons of the musicians have accurately and carefully investigated the question respecting the decade; and the most sacred Moses has composed a hymn, with no slight degree of skill, attributing the most excellent things to this number of the decade, such as prayers, first-fruits, the continual and unceasing offerings of the priests,

---

[13] Leviticus 18:1.

the observance of the passover, the atonement,[14] the remission of debts, and the return to the ancient allotments of property at the end of every fifty years;[15] the preparation and furnishing of the indissoluble tabernacle,[16] and ten thousand other things which it would take a long time to enumerate. However, we must not pass over the most important points.

(90) In the first place he represents Noah to us (and this man is the first who is specially entitled just, in the holy scriptures), as the tenth in succession from him who was formed out of the earth, not intending by this statement to indicate the number of years that had elapsed, but rather to show clearly that as the decade is the most perfect boundary and end of the numbers which proceed onwards from the unit, so also just in the soul is the perfection and true end of the actions of human life. (91) For the number three when multiplied by itself so as to make nine, the oracles have pronounced to be the most warlike of numbers; but when one is added to it so as to complete the number ten, then they receive it as a friendly one. (92) And as a proof of this, they allege the kingdoms of the nine kings,[17] (when the civil war was fanned into a flame, the four passions rising up against the five outward senses, and when the entire soul, like a city, was in danger of being subjected to an utter overthrow and destruction,) which the wise Abraham, appearing as the tenth king, put an end to, by joining in the warfare. (93) He then caused a calm instead of a storm, and health instead of disease, and life, if one may speak the plain truth, instead of death, showing himself as the trophy-bearer of God who giveth the victory, to whom also he consecrated the tenths as a grateful offering on account of his victory.

(94) Moreover, he also separates off the tenth of all the cattle which come "under the rod,"[18] I mean by this under instruction, and of all those which are of a tame and tractable sort, pronouncing them to be holy by an express provision of the law. In order that so, by many concurrent testimonies, we may learn the particular and especial appropriateness of the number ten to God, and of the number nine to our mortal race.

XVIII. (95) But also it is expressly ordered, that men should offer as first fruits the tenths, not only of animals, but also of all the things which grow up out of the earth; "For," says the scripture, "every tenth of the earth from the seed and from the fruit of every tree, is holy to the Lord: and every tenth of oxen and sheep, and everything

of any cattle which passes under the rod, of all these the tenth shall be holy to the Lord." (96) You see that he thinks that it is proper to make an offering, by way of first fruits from the corporeal mass that is around us, which is really earthly and wooden; for life, and durability, and increase, and good health, fall to his share through the divine grace. You see also, that again an express command is given to offer first-fruits from all the irrational animals that are around ourselves; and by these are meant the outward senses. For to see, and to hear, and to smell, and to taste, and also to touch are divine gifts, for which it is our duty to give thanks.

(97) But not only are we taught to thank the giver of all goodness for these earthly, and wooden, and corporeal things, and for the irrational animals, the outward senses, but also for the mind, which, to speak with strict propriety, is man in man, the better in the worse, the immortal in the mortal. (98) On this account I think it is, that God ordered to be consecrated the whole of the first-born, the tenth, I mean the tribe of Levi, taking them in exchange for the first-born, for the preservation and protection of holiness, and piety, and sacred ministrations, which all have reference to the honour of God. For the first and best thing in ourselves is our reason, and it is very proper to offer up the first-fruits of our cleverness, and acuteness, and comprehension, and prudence, and of all our other faculties which we have in connection with our reason as first-fruits to God, who has bestowed upon us this great abundance of power of exerting our intelligence. (99) From this consideration it was, that Jacob, the practiser of virtue, at the beginning of his prayers, says: "Of all that thou givest me, I will set apart and consecrate a tenth to thee."[19] And the sacred scripture, which was written after the prayers on occasion of victory, which Melchisedek, who had received a self-instructed and self-taught priesthood, makes, says: "For he gave him a tenth of all things,"[20] assigning to him the outward senses the faculty of feeling properly, and by the same sense of speech the faculty of speaking well, and by the senses connected with the mind the faculty of thinking well.

(100) Very beautifully, therefore, and at the same time most unavoidably, does the sacred historian tell us in the fashion of an incidental narrative, when the memorial of that heavenly and divine food was consecrated in the golden urn, that "gomer was the tenth part of three measures."[21] For in us men there appear to be three measures,

---

[14]Leviticus 23:27.
[15]Leviticus 25:9.
[16]Exodus 26:1.
[17]Genesis 14:1.
[18]Leviticus 27:32.

[19]Genesis 28:22.
[20]Genesis 14:20.
[21]Exodus 16:36.

the outward senses, and speech, and mind. The outward sense being the measure of the objects of outward sense, speech being the measure of nouns and verbs, and of whatever is said; and the mind being the measure of those things which can only be perceived by the intellect. (101) We must therefore offer first-fruits of each of these three measures as a sacred tenth, in order that our powers of speaking, and of feeling, and of comprehending, may be seen to be irreproachable and sound, in reference to and in connection with God. For this is the true and just measure, and the things that relate to ourselves are false and unjust measures.

XIX. (102) Very appropriately, therefore, in the case of sacrifices also, the tenth part of the measure of fine wheat flour will be brought upon the altar, together with the victims. But the number of nine, which is what is left of the number ten, will remain among us. (103) And the daily sacrifice of the priests corresponds also to these facts. For it is expressly commanded to them to offer every day the tenth part of an ephah[22] of fine wheat flour. For, passing over the ninth number, the god who was only discernible by the outward senses and by opinion, they learnt to worship the tenth, who is the only living and true God. (104) For the world had nine portions assigned to it, eight in heaven, namely the portion of the fixed stars and the seven planets which are all borne forward in the same arrangement, and the ninth being the earth in conjunction with the air and water. For of these things there is only one bond and connection, though they admit all kinds of various changes and alterations. (105) Therefore men in general have paid honours to these nine portions, and to the world which is compounded of them. But the perfect man honours only that being who is above the nine, and who is their creator, being the tenth portion, namely God. For having examined into the whole of his works, he has felt a love for the creator of them, and he has become anxious to be his suppliant and servant. On this account the priest offers up a tenth every day to the tenth, the only and everlasting God. (106) This is, to speak properly, the spiritual passover of the soul, the passing over of all the passions and of every object of the outward senses to the tenth, which is the proper object of the intellect, and which is divine.

For it is said in the scripture: "On the tenth day of this month let each of them take a sheep according to his house;[23] in order that from the tenth, there may be consecrated to the tenth, that is to God, the sacrifices which have been preserved in the soul, which is illuminated in two portions out of the three, until it is entirely changed in every part, and becomes a heavenly brilliancy like a full moon, at the height of its increase at the end of the second week, and so is able not only to guard, but even to sacrifice uninjured and faultless improvements, that is to say, propitiations. (107) For this propitiation also is established in the tenth day of the month, when the soul addresses its supplications to the tenth portion, namely to God, and has learnt, by its own sagacity and acuteness, the insignificance and nothingness of the creature, and also the excessive perfection and pre-eminent excellence in all good things of the uncreated God.

Therefore God becomes at once propitious, and propitious too, even without any supplications being addressed to him, to those who abase and humble themselves, and who are not puffed up with vain arrogance and self-opinion. (108) This is remission and deliverance, this is complete freedom of the soul, shaking off the wanderings in which it wandered, and fleeing for a secure anchorage to the one nature which cannot wander, and which rises up to return to the lot which it formerly received when it had brilliant aspirations, and when it vigorously toiled in labours which had virtuous ends for their object. For then admiring it for its exertions, the holy scripture honoured it, giving it a most especial honour, and immortal inheritance, a place namely in the imperishable race. (109) This is what the wise Abraham supplicates for, when that which in word indeed is the land of Sodom, but in real fact is the soul made barren of all good things and blinded as to its reason, is about to be burnt up, in order that if the memorial of justice, namely the tenth[24] part be found in it, it may obtain a sort of amnesty. Therefore he begins his supplication with a prayer for pardon, connected with the number fifty, and terminates with the number ten, the lowest number for whose deliverance he can dare to entreat.

XX. (110) From which consideration it appears to me to have been, that Moses, after the appointment of chiliarchs, or commanders of thousands, and of centurians, and of captains of fifties,[25] thought proper to appoint captains of ten over all, in order than if the mind was not able to be improved by means of the elder orders, it might at least be purified by these last in order. (111) And the son of the man who was devoted to learning, learnt a very beautiful doctrine when he went on that admirable embassy, asking in marriage for the self-taught wise man that most appropriate sister, namely, perseverance. For he takes ten

---

[22]Exodus 10:20.
[23]Exodus 12:3.

[24]Genesis 18:32.
[25]Exodus 18:25.

camels,[26] a reminder of the number ten, that is to say, of right instruction, from among many and, indeed, infinite memorials of the Lord. (112) He also takes of his good things, evidently not silver, nor any gold, nor any other of those things which consist of perishable materials; for Moses never gave the favourable apellation of good to any of these things, but those genuine good things which are the only good things of the soul; and those he appropriates for the use of his journey, and for his purposes of traffic, namely, instruction, improvement, study, desire, admiration, enthusiasm, prophecy, and the love of doing good actions; (113) to which objects, a man who devotes all his care, and who practices the actions calculated to ensure their attainment, when he is about, as it were, to anchor in a safe harbour after having been tossed in a stormy sea, will take two earrings, each of a drachm in weight, and two golden armlets of ten shekels weight of gold for the arms of her who is sought in marriage.[27] Oh the divine ornament! We may understand that the drachm means the faculty of hearing, and the unbroken unit, and the attractive nature; for it is not becoming for hearing to have leisure to attend to anything except to that speech alone which sets forth in a suitable manner the virtues of the one and only God. And the ten shekels weight of gold mean attempts at works; for the actions, in accordance with wisdom, are established in perfect numbers, and every one of them is more precious than gold.

XXI. (114) Something of this kind, now, is the contribution made by the princes, selected and appointed with reference to worth and merit, which they made when the soul being properly prepared and adorned by philosophy, was celebrating the festival of the dedication in a sacred and becoming manner, giving thanks to God its teacher and its guide; for it "offers up a censer full of frankincense, ten golden shekels in weight,"[28] in order that the wise man alone may judge of the odours which are exhaled by prudence and by every virtue. (115) But when they appear to be made propitious, then Moses will sing a sacred hymn over them, saying, "The Lord has smelt the smell of a sweet savour," using the word to smell here as equivalent to approving of; for God is not formed like a man, nor has he any need of nostrils, or of any other organ parts. (116) But as he proceeds onwards he speaks also of the divine abode, the tabernacle, and its ten curtains;"[29] for, in fact, the compound edifice of entire wisdom has been assigned the perfect number, the number ten.

And wisdom is the court and palace of the all governing and only absolute and independent king. (117) Accordingly, this is his abode, discernible only by the intellect; but the world is perceptible by the outward senses; since Moses made the curtains of such things as are symbols of the four elements, for they were made of fine flax, and of hyacinthine colour, and of purple, and of scarlet,—four numbers, as I have said before. Now the fine flax is an example of the earth, for the flax grows out of the earth; and the hyacinthine colour is a symbol of the air, for it is black by nature; purple *(porphyra)*, again, is a symbol of the water; for the cause of this dye is derived from the sea, being the shell-fish of the same name *(hē porphyra)*; and scarlet is a symbol of fire, for it most nearly resembles a flame.

(118) Again, that omnipotent overseer and ruler of the universe reproved the state of Egypt, when rebellious against the rein, when it was extolling with grandiloquent words the mind as an adversary of God, and bestowing on it all the ensigns of kingly authority, such as the throne, the sceptre, the diadem; and chastised it with ten stripes and severe punishment. (119) And in the same manner, also, he promises the wise Abraham that he will work for him the overthrow and complete destruction of ten nations[30] exactly, neither more nor less, and that he will give the country of those who are thus destroyed to his descendants; in every instance choosing to employ the number ten, both for praise and for blame, and also for honour and for punishment. And yet why do we mention these things? (120) For what is more important than this is the fact, that Moses gave laws to that sacred and divine assembly in a code of ten commandments in all. And these are the commandments which are the generic heads, and roots, and principles of the infinite multitude of particular laws; being the everlasting source of all commands, and containing every imaginable injunction and prohibition to the great advantage of those who use them.

XXXII. (121) Very naturally, therefore, is the connection of Abraham with Hagar, placed at the end of ten years after his arrival in the land of the Chaldeans. For it does not follow that the first moment that we become endowed with reason, while our intellect is still in a somewhat fluid state, we are able at once to derive encyclical instruction. But when we have attained to intelligence and acuteness of comprehension, then we no longer have a light and superficial mind, but rather a firm and solid intellect which we can exercise on every subject. (122) And it is for this reason that the expression which follows is added, in connection

[26]Genesis 24:10.
[27]Genesis 24:22.
[28]Numbers 7:14.
[29]Exodus 26:1.

[30]Deuteronomy 7:1.

with the former statement, "And he went in unto Hagar." For it was becoming for the scholar to go to his teacher, who was a man of learning, in order to learn such branches of instruction as are suited to the nature of man. For now, also, the pupil is represented as going to the place where he may obtain learning; but learning very often anticipates him and runs forward to meet him, having driven out envy from her habitation, and she attracts those towards her who are well inclined to her. (123) Accordingly, one may read that virtue, that is Leah, went forward to meet the practiser of virtue, and said unto him, "To-day you shall come in to me,"[31] when he was returning from the fields. For where was the man who had the care of the seeds and plants of knowledge found to come, except to that virtue which he himself had cultivated?

XXIII. (124) But there are times when virtue, as if making experiment of those who come to her as pupils, to see how much eagerness they have, does not come forward to meet them, but veiling her face like Tamar, sits down in the public road, giving room to those who are traveling along the road to look upon her as a harlot, in order that those who are over curious on the subject may take off her veil and disclose her features, and may behold the untouched, and unpolluted, and most exquisite, and truly virgin beauty of modesty and chastity. (125) Who then is he who is fond of investigating, and desirous of learning, and who thinks it not right to leave any of those things which are disguised or concealed unconsidered and examined? Who is he, I say, but the chief captain and king, he who abides and rejoices in the agreements which he has made with God, by name Judah? For says the scripture, "He turned aside out of his road to her, and said unto her, Suffer me to come in unto thee," (but he was not inclined to offer her any violence), and to see what is that power which is thus veiled, and for what purpose it is thus adorned; (126) and after they had come together it is written, "And she conceived;" but the name of the person is not expressly mentioned. For art conceives and carries along with it him who is learning it, persuading him to feel amorously inclined towards her; and also he who is learning carries with him her who is teaching him, whenever he is fond of learning.

(127) And it often happens that he who professes some one of the indifferent branches of knowledge, when he meets with a pupil of good natural qualifications, boasts of his success in teaching, thinking that he, by himself and alone, is the cause of his pupil's facility in learning. And then, becoming elated and puffing himself up, he holds his head high, and draws his eyebrows and becomes

full of pride, and asks very high terms from those who desire to become his pupils; but those whom he perceives to be poor but still to be eager for instruction, he rejects and repels, as if he were the only person who had found a treasure of wisdom. (128) This is the meaning of the expression, "to conceive," namely, to be full of pride, and to be puffed up with arrogance beyond all moderation, on which account some persons have appeared to dishonour the queen of all the intermediate and indifferent branches of knowledge, virtue, who deserves to be honoured, even for her own sake.

(129) All the souls, therefore, which, in connection with prudence, are pregnant of real things, do nevertheless bring forth, separating and distinguishing between things previously in confusion, like Rebekkah; for she having conceived in her womb ideas of two nations, the knowledge of virtue and the knowledge of wickedness, having a fortunate labour separated and distinguished between the nature of each; but those which have conceived without prudence either miscarry or else bring forth an offspring inclined to evil contention and sophistry, always either aiming darts and arrows at others, or having darts and arrows aimed at themselves. (130) And may we not say that this is natural? for some fancy that they are just conceiving, and others they they are actually pregnant, which is a very different thing; for those who think that they are already pregnant attribute their pregnancy and the birth of their offspring to themselves, and pride themselves upon it; but those who look upon themselves as now conceiving, admit that they have of themselves nothing which they can call peculiarly their own, but they receive the seed and the prospects of posterity which are showered upon them from without, and they admire him who bestows it, and repel the greatest of evils, namely self-love, by that perfect good, piety towards the gods.

XXIV. (131) In this manner also the seeds of the legitimate wisdom, which exists among men, were sown, "For there was," says the same historian, "a man of the tribe of Levi, named Amram, who took to wife one of the daughters of Levi, and had her, and she conceived and brought forth a male child; and seeing that he was a goodly child they concealed him for three months."[32] (132) This is Moses, the purest mind, the child that is really goodly; the child that received at the same time all legislative and prophetic skill by the means of inspired and heaven-bestowed wisdom; who, being by birth a member of the tribe of Levi, and being flourishing both in the things relating to his mother and in those affecting his father, clings to the truth;

---

[31] Genesis 30:16.

[32] Exodus 2:1.

(133) and the greatest profession ever made by the author and chief of this tribe is this, for he makes bold to say, that "the only God is alone to be honoured by me;" and nothing besides of all the things that are inferior to Him, neither earth, nor sea, nor rivers, nor the nature of the air, nor the nature of the winds, nor the changes of the atmosphere, nor the appearances of any animals or plants, nor the sun, nor the moon, nor the multitude of the stars moving in well-arranged revolutions, nor the whole heaven, nor the entire world.

(134) This is a boast of a great and magnanimous soul, to rise above all creation, and to overleap its boundaries, and to cling to the great uncreated God alone, according to his sacred commands, in which we are expressly enjoined "to cleave unto him."[33] Therefore he, in requital, bestows himself as their inheritance upon those who do cleave unto him, and who serve him without intermission; and the sacred scripture bears its testimony in behalf of this assertion, where it says, "The Lord himself is his inheritance."[34]

(135) Thus the souls which are already pregnant are naturally likely to bring forth children, rather than those which are now receiving the seed. But as the eyes of the body do oftentimes see obscurely, and often on the other hand see clearly, so in the same manner does the eye of the soul, at times, receive the particular impressions conveyed to it by things in a most confused and indistinct manner, and at other times it beholds them with the greatest purity and clearness; (136) therefore an indistinct and not clearly manifested conception resembles an embryo which has not yet received any distinct character or similitude within the womb: but that which is clear and distinctly visible, is like one which is completely formed, and which is already fashioned in an artistic manner as to both its inward and its outward parts, and which has already received its suitable character. (137) And with respect to these matters the following law has been enacted with great beauty and propriety: "If while two men are fighting one should strike a woman who is great with child, and her child should come from her before it is completely formed, he shall be muleted in a fine, according to what the husband of the woman shall impose on him, and he shall pay the fine deservedly. But if the child be fully formed, he shall pay life for life."[35]

For it was not the same thing, to destroy a perfect and an imperfect work of the mind, nor is what is only likened by a figure similar to what is really comprehended, nor is what is only hoped for similar to what really exists. (138) On this account, in one case, an uncertain penalty is affixed to an uncertain action; in another, a definite punishment is enacted by law against an act which is perfected, but which is perfected not with respect to virtue, but with reference to what is done in an irreproachable manner, according to some act. For it is not she who has just received the seed, but she who has been for some time pregnant, who brings forth this offspring, professing boasting rather than modesty. For it is impossible that she who has been pregnant some time should miscarry, since it is fitting that the plant should be conducted to perfection by him who sowed it; but it is not strange if some mishap should befall the woman who was pregnant, since she was afflicted with a disease beyond the art of the physician.

XXV. (139) And do not suppose that Hagar is represented as beholding herself as pregnant, by the words, "seeing that she had conceived," but as beholding her mistress Sarah; for afterwards she speaks of herself, and says, "Seeing that she was pregnant, she was despised before her."[36] Why so? (140) Because the intermediate and indifferent arts, and the sciences in accord with them, see indeed of what they are pregnant, but they nevertheless see in every respect but dimly; but the sciences comprehend clearly and very distinctly. For science is something beyond art, having derived from reason a certain firmness and exemption from error; (141) for this is the definition of art, a system of comprehensions well practised with reference to some desirable end, the word desirable being very properly added by reason of the abundance of evil arts. But the definition of science is a safe and firm comprehension, which, through reason, is not liable to any error. (142) Therefore we call music and grammar, and other pursuits, arts; for those also who are made perfect in them, as musicians, or grammarians, are called artists. But we call philosophy and the other virtues, sciences, and those who are possessed of the knowledge of them we call scientific; for they are prudent, and temperate, and philosophical, not one of whom is ever deceived in the doctrines of a philosophy which he himself has cultivated, any more than the artists, whom I have mentioned before, err in their speculations with respect to their indifferent arts.

(143) For as the eyes see, and still the mind sees more clearly by means of the eyes; and as the ears hear, but nevertheless the mind hears better through the medium of the ears; and as the nostrils smell, and yet the soul smells more precisely through the instrumentality of the nostrils; and in like manner, as the other external senses

---

[33] Deuteronomy 30:20.
[34] Deuteronomy 10:9.
[35] Exodus 21:22.

[36] Genesis 16:4.

comprehend their respective appropriate objects, still the mind comprehends them also more purely and distinctly by their ministration. For to speak properly, it is the mind which is the eye of eyes, the hearing of hearing, and the more pure external sense of each of the external senses, using them as ministers in a court of justice, and itself deciding on the nature of the objects submitted to it, so as to approve of some and to reject others. In the same way, those that are called the intermediate arts, resembling the faculties of the body, indulge in contemplations according to certain simple observations of them, but the sciences do so with greater accuracy and with exceedingly careful investigation.

(144) For the same relation that the mind bears to the outward sense, that same does science bear towards art; for, as has been said before, the soul is as it were the outward sense of the outward sense; therefore each of them has attracted to itself some slight things of nature, concerning which it labours and occupies itself, geometry having appropriated lines, and music sounds, and philosophy the whole nature of existing things. For this world is its subject matter, and so is the whole essence, both visible and invisible, of existing things.

(145) What then is there wonderful if the soul, which sees both the whole and the parts, sees them too better than they do, as if it were furnished with larger and more acute eyes? Very naturally, therefore, proper philosophy will behold intermediate instruction its handmaiden, and see that she is pregnant, more than the other will see that she is.

XXVI. (146) And yet even this is not unknown to any one, namely, that philosophy has bestowed upon all the particular sciences their first principles and seeds, from which speculations respecting them appear to arise. For it is geometry which invented equilateral and scalene triangles, and circles, and polygons, and all kinds of other figures. But it was no longer geometry that discovered the nature of a point, and line, and a superficies, and a solid, which are the roots and foundations of the aforementioned figures. (147) For from whence could it define and pronounce that a point is that which has no parts, that a line is length without breadth; that a superficies is that which has only length and breadth; that a solid is that which has the three properties, length, breadth, and depth? For these discoveries belong to philosophy, and the consideration of these definitions belongs wholly to the philosopher. (148) Again, to write and read is the undertaking of this more imperfect kind of grammar, which some people, perverting the name of, call grammatistica. But to the most perfect kind of grammar belongs the explanation of the great works of the poets and historians.

When, therefore, men are going through the different parts of speech, and they not in so doing trying to drag over to themselves and appropriate as a kind of accessory the discoveries of philosophy? (149) For it is the peculiar province of philosophy to inquire what a conjunction, what a noun, what a verb, what a common noun, what a particular noun, what is deficient in a speech, what is superfluous, what is an affirmative, what an interrogative, what an indirect question, what is a comprehensive expression, what is a supplicatory form of address. For this is a science which has been compounded for the purpose of the investigation of independent propositions, and axioms, and categorems. (150) But, moreover, has not the whole question of semi-vowels, or vowels, or such elements as are completely mute, and the consideration of the sense in which each of these expressions is ordinarily used, and in short every notion connected with the voice, and the elements, and the parts of speech, been thoroughly worked out and brought to an accurate system by philosophy? And those thieves, after having as it were carried off a few drops from her torrent, and having sought to impregnate their own shallow souls with what they have stolen, are not ashamed to bring forth her resources as their own.

XXVII. (151) On which account, being elated and proud, they disregard the mistress to whom in reality the authority and the complete confirmation of their contemplations belong. But she, perceiving their neglect, will convict them, and will speak freely to them, and say, "I am treated unjustly, and in utter violation of our agreement, as far as depends on you who transgress the covenants entered into between us; (152) for from the time that you first took to your bosom the elementary branches of education, you have honoured above measure the offspring of my handmaiden, and have respected her as your wife, and you have so completely repudiated me that you never by any chance came to the same place with me. And perhaps this may be only a suspicion of mine respecting you, arising from your open connection with my servant, which leads me to conjecture your alienation from myself, though it is not really manifest. But if your disposition is contrary to that which I suspect, still it is impossible for any one else to know this, but it is easy to God alone." (153) On which account she says very appropriately, "May God judge between thee and me;[37] not making haste to condemn him beforehand as having done her wrong, but intimating a

---

[37] Genesis 16:5.

doubt, that perhaps he may speedily do her right, which in point of fact is seen to be the case not long afterwards, when he, excusing himself and remedying her doubts, says to her, "Behold thy handmaiden is in thy hands, do unto her as it seemeth good to thee."

(154) For also, when he calls her her handmaiden, he confesses both facts, both that she is a slave and also that she is a child; for the name of the handmaiden *(paidiskē)* suits both these circumstances. At the same time also, he confesses the contrary things, opposing the child to the full-grown woman, and the mistress to her slave, all but crying out in plain words: I embrace indeed encyclical instruction as a younger maiden and as a handmaiden, but I honour knowledge and prudence as full-grown and a mistress.

(155) And the expression, "She is in thy hands," means, she is in thy power and subject to thee. And this is also a symbol of something else of this nature, namely, that the qualities of the handmaiden come to the hands of the body; for the encyclical branches of knowledge have need of the bodily organs and faculties; but the qualities of the mistress reach the soul; for the things which belong to prudence and knowledge come under the province of reason; (156) so that in proportion as the mind is more powerful and more efficacious than, and in short superior to, the hand, in the same proportion also do I look upon knowledge and wisdom as more admirable than encyclical accomplishment, and I honour them in a higher degree.

Do thou, therefore, O thou who both art the mistress, and who art so accounted by me, take all my encyclical instruction and use it as thy handmaid, doing to it as it shall seem good to thee; (157) for I am not unaware that whatever pleases thee is in all respects good even though it may not always be pleasant, and is useful even though it be far removed from being agreeable. But admonition and reproof are both good and profitable to those who stand in need of correction, which indeed the holy scriptures call by another name, and denominate affliction.

XXVIII. (158) On which account the historian presently adds, "And she afflicted her;" an expression equivalent to, she admonished and corrected her. For a sharp spear is very profitable for those who are corrupted by over security and indolences, just as it is of use with restive horses; since they can scarcely be subdued and made manageable by the whip and by gentle leading. (159) Do you not see how they are utterly unaffected by the prizes proposed to them?[38] They are fat, they are stout,

they are sleek, they breathe hard; then they take up the actions of impiety, miserable and wretched men that they are, seeking a melancholy reward, being proclaimed and crowned as conquerors by ungodliness. For by reason of the prosperity which was constantly flowing gently towards them, they looked upon themselves as silver or golden gods, after the fashion of adulterated money, forgetting the real and true coinage.

(160) And Moses testifies to this view of the matter when he says, "He got fat, he became stout, he became swollen, and forsook God who had created him."[39] So that if excessive relaxation begets the greatest of all evils, impiety, its contrary, affliction, in accordance with the law produces that perfect good, much praised correction; (161) and proceeding outward from this point, he also calls the unleavened bread the symbol of the first festival, "the bread of affliction."[40] And yet who is there who does not know that feasts and festivals produce cheerful joy and delectation, and not affliction? (162) But it is plain that he is here using in a perverted sense this word for the labour of him who is the corrector. For the most numerous and greatest blessings are usually acquired by laborious practice and exercise, and by vigorously excited labour. But the festival of the soul is emulation, which is labour to attain those things which are most excellent and which are brought to perfection; on which account it is expressly commanded to "eat the unleavened bread with bitter herbs;"[41] not by way of an additional dish, but because men in general look upon the fact of being prevented from swelling and boiling over with their appetites, but being forced to contract and restrain them as a grievous thing, thinking it a bitter thing to unlearn the indulgence of their passions, which is the real feast and festival of a mind which loves honourable contests.

XXIX. (163) It is for this reason that the law, as it appears to men, was given in a place which is called Bitterness; for to do wrong is pleasant, but to act justly is laborious. And this is the most unerring law; for the sacred history says, "And after they had gone out from the passions of Egypt they came to Marah: and they were not able to drink of the water at Marah, for it was bitter. On this account the name of that place was called Bitterness. And the people murmured against Moses, saying, What shall we drink? And Moses cried unto the Lord; and the Lord showed him a stick, and he cast it into the water, and the water was made sweet. And then he gave him justification and judg-

---

[38] This is scarcely sense, but the truth probably is that the passage is corrupt. Mangey proposes one or two emendations, but they are not very satisfactory.

[39] Deuteronomy 32:15.
[40] Deuteronomy 16:3.
[41] Exodus 12:8.

ment, (164) and then he tempted him."[42] For the invisible trial and proofs of the soul are in labouring and in enduring bitterness; for then it is hard to know which way it will incline; for many men are very speedily fatigued and fall away, thinking labour a terrible adversary, and they let their hands fall out of weakness, like tired wrestlers, determining to return to Egypt to the indulgence of their passions.

(165) But others, with much endurance and great vigour, supporting the fearful and terrible events of the wilderness pass through the contest of life, keeping their life safe from overthrow and from destruction, and rising up in vigorous contest against the necessities of nature, such as hunger, thirst, cold, and heat, which are in the habit of reducing other persons to slavery, and subduing them with great exuberance of strength. (166) And the cause of this is not merely labour, but also the sweetness with which it is combined; for the scripture says, "And the water was made sweet." But sweet and pleasant labour is called by another name, fondness for labour; for that which is sweet in labour is the love of, and desire for, and admiration of, and friendship for, what is honourable. (167) Let no one, therefore, reject such affliction as this, and let no one think that the table of festivity and cheerfulness is called the bread of affliction for injury rather than for advantage; for the soul which is rightly admonished is supported by the doctrines of instruction.

XXX. (168) This unleavened cake is so sacred that it is enjoined in the holy scriptures, "to place in the innermost part of the temple, on the golden table, twelve loaves of unleavened bread, corresponding in number to the twelve tribes; and those loaves shall be called the shew-bread."[43] (169) And again, it is in the law expressly "forbidden to offer any leaven or any honey upon the altar;"[44] for it is a difficult thing to consecrate as holy either the sweetnesses of the pleasures according to the body, or the light and unsubstantial elations of the soul, since they are by their own intrinsic nature profane and unholy.

(170) Does not, then, the prophetic word, by name Moses, very rightly speak in dignified language when he says, "Thou shalt remember all the road by which the Lord God led thee in the wilderness, and how he afflicted thee, and tried thee, and proved thee, that he might know what was in thy heart, and whether thou wouldest keep his commandments. Did he not afflict thee and oppress thee with hunger, and feed thee with manna which thy fathers knew not, that he might make thee know that man shall not live by bread alone, but by every word that proceedeth out of the mouth of God?"[45]

(171) Who, then, is so impious as to conceive that God is one who afflicts, and who brings that most pitiable death of hunger upon those who are not able to live without food? For God is good, and the cause of good things, bounteous, the saviour, the supporter, the giver of wealth, the giver of great gifts, driving out wickedness from the sacred boundaries; for thus did he drive out the burdens of the earth, Adam and Cain, from paradise. (172) Let us, then, not be led aside by words, but let us consider and examine what meaning is intended to be conveyed under figurative expressions, and pronounce that the words "he afflicted," are equivalent to "he instructed, and he admonished, and he corrected." And when it is said that he oppressed them with hunger, it does not mean that he caused a deficiency of meat and drink, but of pleasures, and desires, and fear, and grief, and acts of injustice, and, in short, of all things which are the works of wickedness or of the passions. (173) And what is said immediately afterwards is an evidence of this: "He fed thee with manna." Is it, then, proper to call that food which, without any exertion or hardship on his part, and without any trouble of his is given to man, not out of the earth as is usual, but from heaven, a marvellous work, afforded for the benefit of those who are to be permitted to avail themselves of it, the cause of hunger and affliction, and not rather, on the contrary, the cause of prosperity and happiness, of freedom from fear, and of a happy state of orderly living? (174) But men in general and the common herd think that those who are nourished on the word of God live in a miserable and wretched manner; for they are without the taste of the all-nourishing food of wisdom; but they are not aware that they are living in the height of happiness.

XXXI. (175) Thus, therefore, there is a certain description of affliction which is profitable, so that its very most humiliating form, even slavery, is accounted a great good. And there is a father who is recorded in the sacred writings as having prayed for this, for his son, namely, the most excellent Isaac for the foolish Esau; (176) for he says somewhere, "By thy sword shalt thou live, and thou shalt serve thy brother."[46] Judging that destiny to be the most advantageous one for a man who had chosen war rather than peace, and who was as it were constantly armed and engaged in battle, by reason of the sedition and disorder constantly existing in his soul, the destiny namely of being a subject and a servant, and of obeying all the com-

---

[42]Exodus 15:23.
[43]Exodus 25:30.
[44]Leviticus 2:11.

[45]Deuteronomy 8:2.
[46]Genesis 27:40.

mands which the lover of temperance should lay upon him.

(177) And it is from this consideration, as it appears to me that one of the disciples of Moses, by name the peaceful, who in his native language is called Solomon, says, "My son, neglect not the instruction of God, and be not grieved when thou art reproved by him; for whom the Lord loveth he chasteneth; and scourgeth every son whom he receives."[47] Thus, then, scourging and reproof are looked upon as good, so that by means of it agreement and relationship with God arise. For what can be more nearly related than a son is to his father, and a father to his son?

(178) But that we may not seem to be too prolix connecting one argument with another, we will, besides what we have already said, just add one most evident proof that a certain description of affliction is the work of virtue. For there is such a law as this, "Thou shalt not afflict any widow or orphan, but if thou dost afflict them with wickedness." ... What does this mean? Is it then possible to be afflicted by something else? For if afflictions were the work of wickedness alone, then it would be superfluous to add what would be admitted by all, and which would be understood without any such addition. (179) But, you will most certainly say, I know that men are reproved by virtue, and instructed by wisdom; on which account I do not blame every kind of affliction, but I very greatly admire that which is the work of justice and of the law; for that corrects by means of punishment, but that which proceeds from folly and wickedness and is pernicious, I do, as becomes me, detest, and pronounce real evil. (180) When, therefore, you hear that Hagar was afflicted by Sarah, you must not suppose that any of those things befell her, which arise from rivalry and quarrels among women; for the question is not here about women, but about minds; the one being practised in the branches of elementary instruction, and the other being devoted to the labours of virtue.

---

[47]Proverbs 3:11.

ON FLIGHT AND FINDING†

(De Fuga Et Inventione)

I. (1) "And Sarah afflicted her, and she fled from before her face. And the angel of the Lord found her sitting by a fountain of water in the wilderness, by a fountain which is in the way to Shur. And the angel of the Lord said unto her: 'Thou handmaiden of Sarah, whence art thou come? and whither art thou going?' And she answered and said: 'I am fleeing from the face of Sarah, my mistress.' And the angel of the Lord said unto her: 'Return unto thy mistress, and be thou humbled beneath her hands.' And the angel of the Lord said unto her: 'Behold, thou art with child, and thou shalt bring forth a son, and shall call his name Ishmael, because the Lord has heard the cry of thy humiliation. He shall be a rude man; his hand shall be against every man, and every man's hand against him."[1]

(2) Having in our former treatise spoken what was becoming respecting the preliminary branches of education, and respecting affliction, we will now proceed in regular order to discuss the topic of fugitives. Now Moses often mentions persons who flee, as here he says concerning Hagar, that being afflicted she fled from the face of her mistress. (3) I think therefore that there are three causes for flight—hatred, fear, and shame. Now women leave their husbands out of hatred, and for the same reason men desert their wives. But children flee from their parents, and servants from their masters, out of fear. And lastly, friends avoid their companions out of shame, when they have done anything which is displeasing to them. And before now I have known instances of fathers who have led a life of effeminate luxury, reverencing the austere and philosophical lives of their sons, and out of shame preferring to live in the country rather than in the city.

(4) Now of all these three causes, one may find instances revealed in the sacred scriptures. Accordingly, Jacob, the practiser of virtue, fled from his father-in-law Laban out of hatred, and from his brother Esau out of fear, as I shall show presently. (5) But Hagar flees out of shame. And a proof of this is, that the angel, that is the word of God, met her, with the intent to recommend her what she ought to do, and to guide her in her return to her mistress's house. For he encouraged her, and said unto her: "The Lord has heard the cry

of thy humiliation," which you uttered, not out of fear, nor yet out of hatred. For the one is the feeling of an ignoble soul, and the other of one which loves contention, but under the influence of that copy of temperance and modesty, shame. (6) For it was natural, if she had fled out of fear, that he would have encouraged her mistress, who was holding out threats to alarm her, to comfort her, and to restore her to tranquillity. For then it would have been safe for the fugitive to return, and not before. But no one intercedes for her to her mistress, inasmuch as she was already appeased by herself. But this angel, who is reproof, at the same time friendly and full of advice, out of his goodwill teaches her not to feel only shame, but also to entertain confidence, for that modesty is but half a virtue, when separated from proper boldness.

II. (7) Therefore the account which follows will show these characteristics more accurately. But we must return to the heads of the question which we have already set forth, and begin with those who flee under the influence of hatred. "For," says the scripture, "Jacob concealed his purpose from Laban the Syrian, so as not to tell him that he was fleeing, and he fled, he and all that he had."[2] (8) What then was the cause of his hatred? For perhaps you are desirous to hear this.

There are some persons who make themselves gods of substance destitute of all distinctive quality, and species, and shape, neither knowing the cause which puts things in motion, nor showing any anxiety to learn of those who do know, but being contented with their ignorance and want of understanding of the most important kind of learning, which was in fact the first and only thing of which it was absolutely necessary to labour for the understanding. (9) Laban now is one of this kind of persons; for the sacred scriptures attribute to him a flock devoid of all distinctive marks. And matter, without any distinctive characteristics, is without any marks in the universe, and so is in men the soul, which is destitute of learning and which has no instructors. (10) But there are others who belong to a better portion, who say that the mind has come and arranged everything, bringing the disorder which arose from an ochlocracy among all existing things, into the order established by the legitimate authority of kingly power. Of this

---

† Yonge's title, *A Treatise on Fugitives.*
[1] Genesis 16:8.

[2] Genesis 16:8.

company Jacob is a follower, who presides over the marked and party-coloured flock.

On the other hand the species in the universe is distinguished by marks and is of varied colour, and so also in men is the mind which has been well instructed and which is fond of learning. (11) And he who is marked, and who is the companion of true kingly power, having received a great deal of the social affection from nature, goes to him who has no distinguishing marks, and who, as I have said, makes himself gods of the material powers, and who thinks that besides them there is no effectual cause of anything, to teach him that his opinions are not correct. (12) For the world has been created, and has by all means derived its existence from some extraneous cause. But the word itself of the Creator is the seal by which each of existing things is invested with form. In accordance with which fact perfect species also does from the very beginning follow things when created, as being an impression and image of the perfect word. (13) For the animal when first created is imperfect as to quantity; and a proof of this is the gradual growth which takes place at each successive age. But it is perfect as to quality. For the same quality remains in it, as having been stamped upon it by the divine word which abides permanently and never charges.

III. (14) But seeing that he is dumb with respect to learning and to all desirable and legitimate authority, he very naturally thinks of flight. For he is afraid that in addition to not being able to derive any advantage, he may even be injured. For all connections with the foolish injures us, and very often the soul against its will becomes stamped with the impression of their insanity of mind. And, in truth, instruction is naturally a thing inimical to ignorance, and so is industry to indifference. (15) In reference to which fact the powers devoted to practice and meditation, when they are set free, cry out, giving a full account of the causes of their hatred: "Have we not any longer a share and an inheritance in the house of our father? Are we now accounted aliens by him? For he has sold us, and he has eaten up and devoured our money. All the wealth and all the glory which God took from our father shall belong to us and to our children."[3] (16) For those who are free both in name and also in their minds do not consider any foolish person as either rich or glorious, but look upon all such persons, so to say, as inglorious and poor, even if they exceed the fortune of wealthy kings. For they do not say that they will have the riches of their father, but the riches which have been taken away; nor do they say that they

shall possess his glory, but the glory which has been taken away from him.

(17) But the wicked man is deprived of all genuine riches and of all true and honourable glory; for these blessings are procured by wisdom, and temperance, and the kindred dispositions of the soul, and are inherited by those souls which love virtue. (18) Therefore, it is not the things which belong to the wicked man, but those of which he is destitute, that are the abundance and the glory of the good. And he is destitute of virtues which are their possession, in order that what is said in another place may be consistent with the passage already quoted: "Let us sacrifice the abominations of Egypt to the Lord our God."[4] For the virtues are perfect and blameless offerings, and so are the actions in accordance with virtue, which the Egyptian body, being devoted to the passions, abominates; (19) for, as in this passage, those things which, according to the principles of natural philosophy, are reckoned profane among the Egyptians are called sacred by the Israelites who see acutely, and are all offered as sacrifices; so, in the same manner, the man who is the companion of virtue will be the heir of those things of which every foolish man is deprived and destitute.

And these things are true glory, which in fact differs in no respect from knowledge, and wealth, not blind wealth, but that which is the most sharpsighted of all existing things, which never receives any base money, not even anything whatever devoid of life unless it be thoroughly tried and approved. (20) Very naturally, therefore, that person will flee from him who has no participation in divine blessings, who even in the matters in which he accuses another does without perceiving it accuse himself also, when he says, "If thou hadst told me I would have sent thee away."[5] For this very thing was a worthy cause for your being deserted, if you, being the servant of an infinite number of masters, pretending to have been invested with command and authority, proclaimed liberty to others.

(21) But I, says he, did not take a man as my assistant in the road which leads to virtue, but I listened to the divine oracles which enjoined me to depart from hence, and which even now continues to direct my course. (22) And how would you have sent me away? surely, as you boast, using pompous language, with a joy which to me would have been sorrowful, with music which would have been no music, with dances, and noises destitute of articulate sound and of reason, striking blows on the soul through the medium of the ears, and with the harp, and with sounds unsuited to the lyre,

---

[3]Genesis 31:14.

[4]Exodus 8:26.
[5]Genesis 31:27.

and unsuited to harmony, not being so much organs, as the actions of a whole life. But these are the things by reason of which I meditated flight; but you, as it seems, contemplated dragging me back from my flight, in order that I might return on account of the deceitful and seductive nature of the external senses, by which I was scarcely able to permit myself to be carried forward.

IV. (23) Hatred then, was the cause of the flight which I have been here describing; but fear was the cause of the one which I am about to mention. For, says the sacred historian, Rebekkah said unto Jacob, "Behold, Esau thy brother threateneth to kill thee: now therefore, my son, hear my voice, and rise up, and flee to Laban my brother, to Charran, and dwell with him certain days, until the anger of thy brother is turned away, and he forget what thou hast done unto him; and then I will send again, and fetch thee back from thence."[6]

(24) For it was worth while to fear, lest the worse portion of the soul, lying in an ambuscade, or else moving forwards openly to the attack, might overthrow and cast down the better part; and so the counsel of the right-minded perseverance, Rebekkah, was very good.

(25) But she says, when you see the bad man coming in with great impetuosity, against virtue, and making great account of those things which it is more proper to disregard, such as wealth, glory, and pleasure, and praising the performance of actions of injustice, as being the cause of all the advantages before mentioned: for we see that those who act unjustly, are, for the most part, men possessed of much silver, and of much gold, and of high reputation. Do not then, turn away to the opposite road, and devote yourself to a life of penury, and abasement, and austerity, and solitude; for, by doing so, you will irritate your adversary, and arm a more bitter enemy against yourself. (26) Consider, therefore, now by what conduct you may avoid his attacks; apply yourself to the same things, I do not mean the same pursuits, but to the same things which are the efficient causes of those things which have been mentioned; to honours, to offices of authority, to silver, to gold, to possessions, to money, to colours, to forms, to exceeding nicety; and when you meet with such things, then, like a skilful workman, impress the most beautiful appearance on the material substances: and perfect a most excellent work. (27) Do you not know, that if a man unacquainted with navigation, takes the management of a ship, which might otherwise have reached the harbour in safety, he overturns it? but that a man, skilful as a pilot, has often saved a ship which otherwise must have been lost? And also, some sick persons, owing to the unskilfulness of their medical attendants, have been severely afflicted with disease; while others, through the skill of their doctors, have escaped from dangerous sicknesses? And why need I have been prolix on this point; for always the things which are done with skill, are a conviction of those which are done unskilfully; and the true praise of the one is an unerring accusation of the other.

V. (28) If therefore, you wish to convict a wicked man, who is also possessed of great wealth, do not disdain an abundance of money; for the unhappy man will soon show himself in his true colours, either as an illiberal and slavish-minded skin-flint, and parer of people by usury, or else as a profligate and intemperate spendthrift, very ready to devour and to squander, and a most zealous companion of harlots and brothel-keepers, and pimps, and of every kind of profligate company. (29) But you will rather bestow your contributions on those who are in want of friends, and will do favours to, and bestow your liberality on, your country, and will assist to portion out the daughters of needy parents, giving them, in addition to their inheritance, a most sufficient dowry; and in fact, very nearly throwing all your own property into the common stock, you will invite to a participation in it all who are worthy of favour.

(30) And, in the same manner, when you wish to reprove any wicked man who is mad with a high opinion of himself and full of boasting, while you are able yourself to attain to distinguished honours, do not disdainfully reject the praise of the multitude: for by so doing you will trip up and supplant the miserable man who takes long strides, and who gives himself airs. For he will abuse his own renown for the purpose of behaving with insolence and contumely to others who are better than he, promoting those who are worse, so as to set them above them; while you, on the contrary, will give all worthy persons a share in your renown, giving in this manner security to those who are good, and by your admonitions improving those who are not so good. (31) And if you ever to go a drinking party or to a costly entertainment, go with a good confidence; for you will put to shame the intemperate man by your own dexterity. For he, falling on his belly, and opening his insatiable desires even before he opens his mouth, will glut himself in a most shameless and indecorous manner, and will seize the things belonging to his neighbour, and will lick up everything without thinking.

And when he is completely sated with eating, then drinking, as the poets say, with his mouth open, he will make himself an object for the laughter and ridicule of all those who behold him. (32) But do you adopt a moderate course without being compelled thereto, and if ever you are constrained to indulge yourself in things beyond moderation, still make reason the governor of the necessity, and never go so far as to change pleasure into unpleasantness, but, if we may speak in such a manner, be drunk in a sober manner.

VI. (33) And here therefore truth may not unreasonably blame those who, without any examination, abandon the business and means of regulating a civil life, and who say that they have learnt to despise glory and pleasure; for those men are behaving insolently, and do not really despise these things, making an open boast of their sordid, and melancholy, and stern appearance, and putting forth their austere and dirty way of living as a bait, as if they were lovers of orderly behaviour, and modestly, and endurance; (34) but they are not able to deceive those who look into them with greater accuracy, and who pierce within their disguise, and who are not led astray by outward show; for having removed these veils and coverings from the others, they see what is treasured up and concealed within, and learn what kind of qualities and nature are theirs: and if they are good they admire them, and if they are evil they ridicule them, and hate them because of their hypocrisy.

(35) Let us then say to such persons, "Are ye zealous admirers and imitators of a life which hates mixing with and joining in the society of others, a solitary and uncompanionable life? For what specimen of virtue have you ever exhibited while living in the society of others? Do ye disdain money? Have you, then, who have been professed money-dealers, been desirous to act justly? Professing to disregard the pleasures of the belly and of the parts beneath the belly, have you behaved with moderation when you have had abundant opportunities of indulging these appetites? Do you despise glory? Then, when you have been placed in situations of authority, have you cultivated an affable humility? Perhaps you have ridiculed a participation in the affairs of state, not considering how useful an employment that is. (36) Have you then first exercised yourselves in, and directed your attention to, the public and the private business of life? and having become skilful politicians and experienced economists by means of the kindred virtues of economical and political science, have you, in your exceeding abundance of these things, prepared for your migration to another and a better kind of life? For it is proper to go through a practical life before beginning the theoretical one: as being a sort of rehearsal of the more perfect contest and exhibition.

In this way it is possible to escape from the charge of hesitation and indolence. (37) Thus also an express injunction is given to the Levites to fulfil their works till the time that they are fifty years of age; and after they are released from all active ministrations, to consider and contemplate each particular thing, receiving as a reward for their well-

doing in active life, another life which delights only in knowledge and contemplation. (38) And at other times it is necessary that those who think themselves worthy to claim the just things of God, should first of all fulfil their human duties; for it is great folly to expect to attain to what is of greater importance, while one is unable properly to discharge what is of less consequence. First of all, therefore, be ye known for your virtue among men, that you may also become established by that which relates to God." This is the advice which perseverance gives to the man inclined to the practice of virtue; but we must now examine her several expressions with accuracy.

VII. (39) "Behold," says she, "Esau thy brother threatens thee." But is it not natural for that disposition, hard as oak and obstinate through ignorance, by name Esau, who offers the baits of mortal life to lead you to your destruction; such baits, I mean, as wealth, glory, pleasure, and other kindred temptations, to seek to kill thee? But do you, O my child! flee from this contest at present, for you have not as yet had complete strength for it given to you, but still the nerves of your soul, like those of a child, are somewhat soft and weak. (40) And it is for this reason that she calls him "my child," while it is a name of affection, and also one which indicates his tender age; for we look upon the disposition which is inclined to the practice of virtue, and which is young, as worthy of affection in comparison of the full-grown man.

But such a person is worthy to carry off the prizes which are proposed for children, but he is not yet able to win the prizes offered for the men. But the best contest for men to engage in is the service of the only God. Therefore if, even before we have been completely purified, (41) but while we appear only to have proceeded so far as to wash off the things which defile our life, we have arrived at the vestibule of God's service, we departed again more quickly than we approached, not being able to endure the austere way of living dictated by that service, nor the sleepless desire to please God, nor the continual and unwearied labour; (42) flee, therefore, at this present time from what is best and from what is worst. What is worst are the fabulous inventions, the unmetrical and inharmonious poems, the conceptions and persuasions which from ignorance are hard and stubborn, of which Esau is the namesake. What is best is the offering; for the race inclined to service is an offering meet to God, being consecrated to him alone in the great chief priesthood; (43) for to dwell with what is evil is most pernicious, and to dwell with perfect good is most dangerous. Accordingly Jacob both flees from Esau, and also dwells apart from his parents; for being fond of practising virtue and still labouring at it, he flees from wickedness, and yet is unable to live in company with perfect virtue so as to have no need of an instructor.

VIII. (44) On which account we read, "He will depart to Laban," not to him as the Syrian, but as the brother of his mother; that is to say, he will go to the brilliancies of life; for Laban, being interpreted, means "white." And when he has arrived there he will not hold his head too high, from being puffed up with the happy events of fortune; for the word Syrian, being translated, means "sublime." But now he does not recollect the Syrian Laban, but the brother of Rebekkah; (45) for the means of life being given to a bad man, inflate and raise up to great height the mind which is devoid of wisdom, which is called the Syrian; but if they are bestowed on a lover of instruction, then they make the mind inclined to abide by the steady and solid doctrines of virtue and excellence. This is the brother of Rebekkah, that is to say, of perseverance, and he dwells in Charran, which name, being interpreted, means "holes," a symbol of the external senses; for he who is still moving about in mortal life has need of the organs of the external senses. (46) "Dwell, therefore," says she, "O my child, with him," not all thy life, but "certain days;" that is to say, learn to be acquainted with the country of the external senses; know thyself and thy own parts, and what each is, and for what end it was made, and how it is by nature calculated to energise, and who it is who moves through those marvellous things, and pulls the strings, being himself invisible, in an invisible manner, whether it is the mind that is in thee, or the mind of the universe.

(47) And, when you have become thoroughly acquainted with yourself, then examine accurately also the peculiar qualities of Laban; the things which are accounted brilliant instances of the success of empty glory; but do not you be deceived by any one of them, but like a good workman adapt them all in a skilful manner to your own necessities; for if, while immersed in this political and much confused life, you display a stable and well-instructed disposition, I will send for you from thence that you may receive the same prize which also your parents received: and the prize is the unchangeable and unhesitating service of the only wise God.

IX. (48) And his father also gives him similar precepts, adding a few trifling injunctions; for he says, "Rise up and flee into Mesopotamia, to the house of Bethuel, the father of thy mother, and from thence take a wife to thyself of the daughters of Laban thy mother's brother."[7] (49) Again, he also forbears to speak of Laban as a Syrian, but he calls him Rebekkah's brother, who is about

to form a connection with the practiser of virtue by means of intermarriage.

Flee, therefore, into Mesopotamia, that is to say, into the middle of the rapid torrent of life, and take care not to be washed away and swollowed up by its whirlpools, but standing firmly, vigorously repel the violent, impetuous course of affairs which overflows and rushes upon thee from above, from both sides, and from every quarter; (50) for you will find the house of wisdom a calm and secure haven, which will gladly receive you when you are anchored within it.

But Bethuel in the sacred scriptures is called wisdom; and this name, being translated, means "the daughter of God;" and the legitimate daughter, always a virgin, having received a nature which shall never be touched or defiled, both on account of her own orderly decency, and also because of the high dignity of her Father. (51) And he calls Bethuel the father of Rebekkah. How, then, can the daughter of God, namely, wisdom, be properly called a father? is it because the name indeed of wisdom is feminine but the sex masculine? For indeed all the virtues bear the names of women, but have the powers and actions of full-grown men, since whatever is subsequent to God, even if it be the most ancient of all other things, still has only the second place when compared with that omnipotent Being, and appears not so much masculine as feminine, in accordance with its likeness to the other creatures; for as the male always has the precedence, the female falls short, and is inferior in rank.

(52) We say, therefore, without paying any attention to the difference here existing in the names, that wisdom, the daughter of good, is both male and a father, and that it is that which sows the seeds of, and which begets learning in, souls, and also education, and knowledge, and prudence, all honourable and praiseworthy things. And from this source it is that Jacob the practiser of wisdom, seeks to procure a wife for himself; for from what other quarter should he seek a partner rather than from the house of wisdom? and where else should he find an opinion free from all reproach, with which to live all his life? [...][8]

X. (53) But Moses has spoken more accurately about flights when he was establishing the law with respect to homicides, in which he goes through every species of homicide, that of intentional murder, that of unintentional slaying, that of murder by deliberate attack, or by crafty treachery. Repeat the law: "If any man strike another and he die, the striker shall die the death." And if a man do it not intentionally, but if God delivers

---

[7] Genesis 28:2.

[8] The rest of this chapter is lost.

him into his hand, then I will give thee a place to which he who has slain another shall flee. And if any one set upon his neighbour to slay him by treachery, and flee away, thou shalt drag him even from the altar to put him to death."[9] (54) Knowing very well that the law is here adding no superfluous word from any indescribable impetuosity in its description of the matter, I doubted within myself why it does not merely say that he who has slain another shall die, and why it has added, that he shall die the death; (55) for how else does any one die, who dies at all, except dying the death?

Therefore, betaking myself for instruction to a wise woman, whose name is Consideration, I was released from my difficulty, for she taught me that some persons who are living are dead, and that some who are dead are still live: she pronounced that the wicked, even if they arrive at the latest period of old age, are only dead, inasmuch as they are deprived of life according to virtue; but that the good, even if they are separated from all union with the body, live for ever, inasmuch as they have received an immortal portion.

XI. (56) Moreover, she confirmed this opinion of hers by the sacred scriptures, one of which ran in this form: "You who cleave unto the Lord your God are all alive to this day:"[10] for she saw that those who sought refuge with God and became his suppliants, were the only living persons, and that all others were dead. And Moses, it seems, testifies to the immortality of those persons, when he adds, "You are all alive to this day;" (57) and this day is interminable eternity, from which there is no departure; for the period of months, and years, and, in short, all the divisions of time, are only the inventions of men doing honour to number. But the unerring proper name of eternity is "today;" for the sun is always the same, without ever changing, going at one time beneath the earth, and at another time above the earth, and by him it is that day and night, the measures of time, are distinguished.

(58) She also confirmed her statement by another passage in scripture of the following purport: "Behold, I have set before thy face life and death, and good and evil."[11] Therefore, O all-wise man, good and virtue mean life, and evil and wickedness mean death. And in another passage we read, "This is thy life, and thy length of days, to love the Lord thy God."[12] This is the most admirable definition of immortal life, to be occupied by a love and affection for God unembarrassed by any connection with the flesh or with the body. (59)

Thus, the priests, Nadab and Abihu, die in order that they may live; taking an immortal existence in exchange for this mortal life, and departing from the creature to the uncreated God. And it is with reference to this fact that the symbols of incorruptibility are thus celebrated: "Then they died before the Lord;"[13] that is to say, they lived; for it is not lawful for any dead person to come into the sight of the Lord.

And again, this is what the Lord himself has said, "I will be sanctified in those who come nigh unto me."[14] "But the dead," as it is also said in the Psalms, "shall not praise the Lord,"[15] (60) for that is the work of the living; but Cain, that shameless man, that fratricide, is no where spoken of in the law as dying; but there is an oracle delivered respecting him in such words as these: "The Lord God put a mark upon Cain, as a sign that no one who found him should kill him."[16] Why so? (61) Because, I imagine, wickedness is an evil which can never end, but which is kindled and is never able to be extinguished; so that the lines of the poet may well be applied to wickedness—

And she is of no mortal race,
But an immortal foul disgrace.

Immortal, indeed, as to the life among us on earth, since with reference to the life with God it is lifeless and dead, and as some one has said, more worthless and odious than dung.

XII. (62) But it was by all means necessary that different regions should be assigned to different things, the heaven to good things, the earth to what is evil; for the tendency of good is to soar on high, and if it ever comes down to us, for its Father is very bounteous, it still is very justly anxious to return again to heaven. But if evil remains here, living at the greatest possible distance from the divine choir, always hovering around mortal life, and unable to die from among the human race. (63) This, too, one of the most eminent among the men who have been admired for their wisdom has asserted, speaking in a magnificent strain in the Theaetetus, where he says, "But it is impossible for evils to come to an end. For it is indispensable that there should always be something in opposition to God. And it is equally impossible that it should have a place in the divine regions; but it must of necessity hover around mortal nature and this place where we live; on which account we ought to endeavor to flee from this place as speedily as possible. And our flight will be a likening of

[9]Exodus 21:12.
[10]Deuteronomy 4:4.
[11]Deuteronomy 30:15.
[12]Deuteronomy 30:20.

[13]Leviticus 10:2.
[14]Leviticus 10:3.
[15]Psalm 113:25.
[16]Genesis 4:15.

ourselves to God, to the best of our power. And such a likening consists of being just and holy in conjunction with prudence."[17] (64) Very naturally, therefore, Cain, the symbol of wickedness, will not die, for wickedness must of necessity be always alive in the mortal race of mankind; so that the expression, "to die the death," is not incorrectly spoken of the homicide, for the reasons which have here been given.

XIII. (65) And the expression, "not intentionally, but if God deliver him into his hand," is used with exceeding propriety with reference to those who commit an unintentional homicide; for it seems to Moses here, that our intentional actions are the fruit of our own mind and will, but that our unintentional actions proceed from the will of God. I mean by this, not our sins, but, on the contrary, those things which are the punishment of our sins; (66) for it is not becoming for God himself to inflict punishment, as being the first and most excellent Lawgiver; but he punishes by the ministry of others, and not by his own act. It is very suitable to his character that he himself should bestow his graces, and his free gifts, and his great benefits, inasmuch as he is by nature good and bountiful. But it is not fitting that he should inflict his punishments further than by his mere command, inasmuch as he is a king; but he must act in this by the instrumentality of others, who are suitable for such purposes.

(67) And the practicer of virtue, Jacob, bears his testimony in support of this doctrine of mine, where he says, "The God who has nourished me from my youth up, the angel who delivered me from all my evils."[18] For the most ancient benefits, those by which the soul is nourished, he attributes to God, but the more recent ones, which are caused by the errors of the soul, he attributes to the servant of God. (68) On this account, I imagine it is, that when Moses was speaking philosophically of the creation of the world, while he described everything else as having been created by God alone, he mentions man alone as having been made by him in conjunction with other assistants; for, says Moses, "God said, Let us make man in our image."[19] The expression, "let *us* make," indicating a plurality of makers. (69) Here, therefore, the Father is conversing with his own powers, to whom he has assigned the task of making the mortal part of our soul, acting in imitation of his own skill while he was fashioning the rational part within us, thinking it right that the dominant part within the soul should be the work of the Ruler of all things, but that the part which is to be kept in sub-

jection should be made by those who are subject to him. (70) And he made us of the powers which were subordinate to him, not only for the reason which has been mentioned, but also because the soul of man alone was destined to receive notions of good and evil, and to choose one of the two, since it could not adopt both. Therefore, he thought it necessary to assign the origin of evil to other workmen than himself,—but to retain the generation of good for himself alone.

XIV. (71) On which account, after Moses had already put in God's mouth this expression, "Let us make man," as if speaking to several persons, as if he were speaking only of one, "God made man." For, in fact, the one God alone is the sole Creator of the real man, who is the purest mind; but a plurality of workmen are the makers of that which is called man, the being compounded of external senses; (72) for which reason the especial real man is spoken of with the article; for the words of Moses are, "The God made the man;" that is to say, he made that reason destitute of species and free from all admixture. But he speaks of man in general without the addition of the article; for the expression, "Let us make man," shows that he means the being compounded of irrational and rational nature.

(73) In accordance with this he has also not attributed the blessing of the virtuous and the cursing of the wicked to the same ministers, though both these offices receive praise. But since the blessing of the good has the precedence in panegyrics, and the affixing curses on the wicked is in the second rank of those who are appointed for these duties (and they are the chiefs, and leaders of the race, twelve in number, whom it is customary to call the patriarchs), he has assigned the better six, who are the best for the task of blessing, namely, Simeon, Levi, Judah, Issachar, Joseph, and Benjamin; and the others he has appointed for the curses, namely, the first and last sons of Leah, Reuben, and Zabulon, and the four bastard sons by the handmaidens; (74) for the chiefs of the royal tribe, and of the tribe consecrated to the priesthood, Judah and Levi, are reckoned in the former class.

Very naturally, therefore, does God give up those who have done deeds worthy of death to the hands of others for punishment, wishing to teach us that the nature of evil is banished to a distance from the divine choir, since even punishment, which, though a good, has in it some imitation of evil, is confirmed by others. (75) And the expression, "I will give thee a place to which he who has slain a man unintentionally shall flee," appears to me to be spoken with exceeding propriety; for what he calls a place is not a region filled by the body, but is rather, in a figure, God himself, because he, surrounding all things, is not sur-

---

[17] Plato, Theaetetus, p. 176.
[18] Genesis 48:15.
[19] Genesis 1:26.

rounded himself, and because he is that to which all things flee for refuge. (76) It is proper, therefore, for him who appears to have been involuntarily changed to say that this change has come upon him by the divine will, just as it is not proper for him to say so who has done evil of his own accord; and he says that he will give this place, not to him who ha slain the man, but to him with whom he is conversing, so that the inhabitant of it shall be one person, but he who flees to it for refuge another; for God has given his own word a country to inhabit, namely, his own knowledge, as if it were a native of it. But to the man who is under the pollution of involuntary error he has given a foreign home as to a stranger, not a country as to a citizen.

XV. (77) Having now said thus much in a philosophical spirit with respect to involuntary offences, he proceeds to legislate concerning the man who rises up to attack another, or who treacherously plots his death, saying, "But if any one attacks his neighbour so as to slay him by treachery, and he flees to God," that is to say to the place which has already been spoken of under a figure, from which life is given to all men. For he says also in another passage: "Whosoever shall flee thither shall live." (78) But is not everlasting life a fleeing for refuge to the living God? and is not a fleeing from his presence death? But if anyone sets upon another, he by all means is committing iniquity by deliberate purpose, and that which is done with treachery is liable to be accounted among voluntary actions, just as, on the other hand, that which is done without treachery is not subject to blame. (79) There is nothing therefore of the wicked actions which are done secretly, and treacherously, and of malice aforethought, which we can properly say are done through the will of God, but they are done only through our own will. For, as I have said before, the storehouses of wickedness are in us ourselves, and those of good alone are with God.

(80) Whosoever therefore flees for refuge, that is to say, whosoever accuses not himself, but God as the cause of his offence, let him be punished, being deprived of that refuge to the altar which tends to salvation and security, and which is meant for suppliants alone. And is not this proper? For the altar is full of victims, in which there is no spot, I mean of innocent and thoroughly purified souls. But to pronounce the Deity the cause of evil is a spot which it is hard to cure, or rather which is altogether incurable.

(81) Those who have cultivated such a disposition as to be lovers of themselves rather than lovers of God, may remain in a distance from the sacred places, in order that as polluted and impure persons, they may not behold, not even from a distance, the sacred flame of the evil which is unextinguishably set on fire, and purified, and dedicated to God with entire and perfect power. (82) Very beautifully, therefore, did one of the wise men of old, hastening on to this same conclusion, find confidence to say that "God is in no respect and in no place unjust, but he is the most righteous being possible. There is nothing that more nearly resembles him than the man who is as just as possible. Around him is the strength, and the real ability, and power of man, and also nothingness and unmanliness. For the knowledge of him is wisdom and true virtue; but the ignorance of him is real ignorance and manifest wickedness. And all other things which appear to be cleverness or wisdom, if they be displayed in political affairs are troublesome, and if in acts, are sordid."[20]

XVI. (83) Therefore, having further commanded the unholy man who is a speaker of evil against divine things to be removed from the most holy places and to be given up to punishment, he proceeds to say, "Whosoever hateth his father or his mother, let him die."[21] And in a similar strain he says, "He who accuseth his father or his mother, let him die." (84) He here all but cries out and shouts that there is no pardon whatever to be given to those who blaspheme the Deity. For if they who bring accusations against their mortal parents are led away to death, what punishment must he think that those men deserve who venture to blaspheme the Father and Creator of the universe? And what accusation can be more disgraceful than to say that the origin of evil is not in us but in God? (85) Drive away, therefore, drive away, O ye who have been initiated in, and who are the hierophants of, the sacred mysteries, drive away, I say, the souls which are mixed and in a confused crowd, and brought together promiscuously from all quarters, those unpurified and still polluted souls, which have their ears not closed, and their tongues unrestrained, and which bear about all the instruments of their misery ready prepared, in order that they may hear all things, even those which it is not lawful to hear. (86) But they who have been instructed in the difference between voluntary and involuntary offences, and who have received a tongue which speaketh good things instead of one which delighteth in accusation, when they do right are to be praised, and when they err contrary to their intention, they are not greatly to be blamed, for which reason cities have been set apart for them to flee unto for refuge.

XVII. (87) And it is worth while to examine with all the accuracy possible into some necessary points relating to this place. They are four in number. One, why it is that the cities which were

[20] Plato, Theaetetus, p. 176.
[21] Exodus 21:15.

set apart for the fugitives were not chosen out of those cities which the other tribes received as their portion, but only out of those which were assigned to the tribe of Levi. The second point is, why they were six in number, and neither more nor fewer. The third is, why three of them were beyond Jordan, and the other three in the land of the Canaanites. The fourth is, why the death of the high priest was appointed to the fugitives as a limit, after which they might return. (88) We must, therefore, say what is suitable on each of these heads, beginning with the first order.

It is with exceeding propriety that the command is given to flee only to those cities which have been assigned to the tribe of Levi; for the Levites themselves are in a manner fugitives, inasmuch as they, for the sake of pleasing God, have left parents, and children, and brethren, and all their mortal relations. (89) Therefore the original leader of the company is represented as saying to his father and mother, "I have not seen you, and my brethren I do not know, and my sons I disown,"[22] in order to be able to serve the living God without allowing any opposite attraction to draw him away. But real flight is a deprivation of all that is nearest and dearest to man. And it introduces one fugitive to another, so as to make them forget what they have done by reason of the similarity of their actions. (90) Either, therefore, it is for this reason alone, or perhaps for this other also, that the Levitical tribe of the persons set apart for the service of the temple ran up, and at one onset slew those who had made a god of the golden calf, the pride of Egypt, killing all who had arrived at the age of puberty, being inflamed with righteous danger, combined with enthusiasm, and a certain heaven-sent inspiration: "And every one slew his brother, and his neighbour, and him that was nearest to him."[23] The body being the brother of the soul, and the irrational part the neighbour of the rational, and the uttered speech that which is nearest to the mind.

(91) For by the following means alone can that which is most excellent within us become adapted for and inclined to the service of him who is the most excellent of all existing beings. In the first place, if a man be resolved into soul, the body, which is akin to it as a brother, being separated and cut off from it, and also all its insatiable desires; and in the second place when the soul has, as I have already said, cast off the irrational part, which is the neighbour of the rational part; for this, like a torrent, being divided into five channels, excites the impetuosity of the passions through all the external senses, as so many aqueducts. (92) Then,

in regular order, the reason removes to a distance and separates the uttered speech which appeared to be the nearest to it of all things, in order that speech, according to the intention, might alone be left, free from the body, free from the entanglements of the outward senses, and free from all uttered speech; for when it is left in this manner existing in a solitary manner, it will embrace that which alone is to be embraced with purity, and in such a way that it cannot be drawn away.

(93) In addition to what has been said above, we must also mention this point, that the tribe of Levi is the tribe of the ministers of the temple and of the priests, to whom the service and ministration of holy things is assigned; and they also perform sacred service who have committed unintentional homicide, since, according to Moses, "God gives into their hands"[24] those who have done things worthy of death, with a view to their execution. But it is the duty of the one body to know the good, and of the other body to chastise the wicked.

XVIII. (94) These then are the reasons on account of which they who have committed unintentional homicide fly only to those cities which belong to the ministers of the temple. We must now proceed to mention what these cities are, and why they are six in number. Perhaps we may say that the most ancient, and the strongest, and the most excellent metropolis, for I may not call it merely a city, is the divine word, to flee to which first is the most advantageous course of all. (95) But the other five, being as it were colonies of that one, are the powers of Him who utters the word, the chief of which is his creative power, according to which the Creator made the world with a word; the second is his kingly power, according to which he who has created rules over what is created; the third is his merciful power, in respect of which the Creator pities and shows mercy towards his own work; the fourth is his legislative power, by which he forbids what may not be done. [...]

(96) And these are the very beautiful and most excellently fenced cities, the best possible refuge for souls which are worthy to be saved for ever; and the establishment of them is merciful and humane, calculated to excite men, to aid and to encourage them in good hopes.

Who else could more greatly display the exceeding abundance of his mercy, all of the powers which are able to benefit us, towards such an exceeding variety of persons who err by unintentional misdeeds, and who have neither the same strength nor the same weakness? (97) Therefore he exhorts him who is able to run swiftly to strain onwards, without stopping to take breath, to the

---

[22]Deuteronomy 33:9.
[23]Exodus 32:26.

[24]Exodus 21:31.

highest word of God, which is the fountain of wisdom, in order that by drinking of that stream he may find everlasting life instead of death. But he urges him who is not so swift of foot to flee for refuge to the creative power which Moses calls God, since it is by that power that all things were made and arranged; for to him who comprehends that everything has been created, that comprehension alone, and the knowledge of the Creator, is a great acquisition of good, which immediately persuades the creature to love him who created it. (98) Him, again, who is still less ready he bids flee to his kingly power; for that which is in subjection is corrected by the fear of him who rules it, and by necessity which keeps it in order, even if the child is not kept in the right way by love for his father.

Again, in the case of him who is not able to reach the boundaries which have been already mentioned, in respect of their being a long way off, there are other goals appointed for them at a shorter distance, the cities namely of the necessary powers, the city of the power of mercy, the city of the power which enjoins what is right, the city of the power which forbids what is not right: (99) for he who is already persuaded that the deity is not implacable, but is merciful by reason of the gentleness of his nature, then, even if he has previously sinned, subsequently repents from a hope of pardon. And he who has adopted the notion that God is a lawgiver obeys all the injunctions which as such he imposes, and so will be happy; and he who is last of all will find the last refuge, namely, the escape from evil, even though he may not be able to arrive at a participation in the more desirable good things.

XIX. (100) These, then, are the six cities which Moses calls cities of refuge, five of which have had their figures set forth in the sacred scriptures, and their images are there likewise. The images of the cities of command and prohibition are the laws in the ark; that of the merciful power of God is the covering of the ark, and he calls it the mercy-seat. The images of the creative power and of the kingly power are the winged cherubim which are placed upon it. (101) But the divine word which is above these does not come into any visible appearance, inasmuch as it is not like to any of the things that come under the external senses, but is itself an image of God, the most ancient of all the objects of intellect in the whole world, and that which is placed in the closest proximity to the only truly existing God, without any partition or distance being interposed between them: for it is said, "I will speak unto thee from above the mercy-seat, in the midst, between the two cherubim."[25]

So that the word is, as it were, the charioteer of the powers, and he who utters it is the rider, who directs the charioteer how to proceed with a view to the proper guidance of the universe.

(102) Therefore, he who is so far removed from committing any intentional misdeeds, that he is even free from all unintentional offence, will have God himself for his inheritance, and will dwell in him alone. But those who fall into errors which proceed not from wilful purpose, but which are done without premeditation, will have the aforesaid places of refuge in all abundance and fulness.

(103) Now of the cities of refuge there are three on the other side of Jordan, which are at a great distance from our race. What cities are they? The word of the Governor of the universe, and his creative power, and his kingly power: for to these belong the heaven and the whole world. (104) But those which, as it were, participate in us, and which are near to us, and which almost touch the unfortunate race of mankind which is alone capable of sinning, are the three on this side of the river; the merciful power, the power which enjoins what is to be done, the power which prohibits what ought not to be done: for these powers touch us. (105) For what need can there be of prohibition to persons who are not likely to do wrong? And what need of injunction to people who are not by nature inclined to stumble? And what need of mercy can those persons have who will absolutely never do wrong at all? But our race of mankind has need of all these things because it is by nature inclined and liable to offences both voluntary and involuntary.

XX. (106) The fourth and last of the points which we proposed to discuss, is the appointing as a period for the return of the fugitives the death of the high priest, which, if taken in the literal sense, causes me great perplexity; for a very unequal punishment is imposed by this enactment on those who have done the very same things, since some will be in banishment for a longer time, and others for a shorter time; for some of the high priests live to a very old age, and others die very early, (107) and some are appointed while young men, and others not until they are old. And again of those who are convicted of unintentional homicide, some have been banished at the beginning of the high priest's entrance into office, and some when the high priest has been at the very point of death. So that some are deprived of their country for a very long time, and others suffer the same infliction only for a day, if it chance to be so; after which they lift up their heads, and exult, and so return among those whose nearest relations have been slain by them.

(108) This difficult and scarcely explicable perplexity we may escape if we adopt the inner and allegorical explanation in accordance with natural

---

[25] Exodus 25:22.

philosophy. For we say that the high priest is not a man, but is the word of God, who has not only no participation in intentional errors, but none even in those which are involuntary. (109) For Moses says that he cannot be defiled neither in respect of his father, that is, the mind, nor his mother, that is, the external sense;[26] because, I imagine, he has received imperishable and wholly pure parents, God being his father, who is also the father of all things, and wisdom being his mother, by means of whom the universe arrived at creation; (110) and also because he is anointed with oil, by which I mean that the principal part of him is illuminated with a light like the beams of the sun, so as to be thought worthy to be clothed with garments.

And the most ancient word of the living God is clothed with the word as with a garment, for it has put on earth, and water, and air, and fire, and the things which proceed from those elements. But the particular soul is clothed with the body, and the mind of the wise man is clothed with the virtues. (111) And it is said that he will never take the mitre off from his head, he will never lay aside the kingly diadem, the symbol of an authority which is not indeed absolute, but only that of a viceroy, but which is nevertheless an object of admiration. Nor will he "rend his clothes;" (112) for the word of the living God being the bond of every thing, as has been said before, holds all things together, and binds all the parts, and prevents them from being loosened or separated.

And the particular soul, as far as it has received power, does not permit any of the parts of the body to be separated or cut off contrary to their nature; but as far as depends upon itself, it preserves every thing entire, and conducts the different parts to a harmony and indissoluble union with one another. But the mind of the wise man being thoroughly purified, preserves the virtues in an unbroken and unimpaired condition, having adapted their natural kindred and communion with a still more solid good will.

XXI. (113) This high priest, as Moses says, "shall not enter into any soul that is dead." But the death of the soul is a life according to wickedness; so that he must never touch any pollution such as folly is fond of dealing with. (114) And to him also "a virgin of the sacred race is joined;" that is to say, an opinion for ever pure, and undefiled, and imperishable; for he "may never become the husband of a widow, or of one who has been divorced, or of one who is a profane person, or of one who is a harlot," since he is always proclaiming an endless and irreconcileable war against them. For it is a hateful thing to him to be widowed with respect to virtue, and to be divorced and driven away by her; and in like manner all persuasion of this kind is profane and unholy.

But that promiscuous evil abandoned to many husbands, and to the worship of many gods, that is, a harlot, he does not think fit even to look upon, being content with her who has chosen for herself one husband and father only, the all-governing God. (115) There is a certain extravagance of perfection visible in this disposition. He has known[27] the man who has vowed the great vow in some instances offending unintentionally, even if not of deliberate purpose; for he says, "But if any one die before him suddenly, he shall be at once polluted." For if of things without deliberation anything coming from without strikes down suddenly, such things do at once pollute the soul, but not with a pollution which remains for any length of time, inasmuch as they are unintentional actions. And about these actions the high priest (standing above them, as he also does above those which are voluntary) is indifferent.

(116) But I am not saying this at random, but for the sake of proving that the period of the death of the high priest is a most natural termination of exile to be appointed by the law, so as to allow of the return of the fugitives. (117) As long, therefore, as this most sacred word lives and survives in the soul, it is impossible for any involuntary error to enter into it; for it is by nature so framed as to have no participation in, and to be incapable of admitting any kind of error. But if it dies (not meaning by this that it is itself destroyed, but that it is separated from our soul), then a return is at once granted to intentional offences. (118) For if while the word remained and was healthy in us, error was driven to a distance, by all means, when the word departs, error will be introduced. For the undefiled high priest, conscience, has derived from nature this most especial honour, that no error of the mind can find any place within him; on which account it is worth our while to pray that the high priest may live in the soul, being at the same time both a judge and a convictor, who having received jurisdiction over the whole of our minds, is not altered in his appearance or purpose by any of those things which are brought under his judgment.

XXII. (119) Having now, therefore, said what was proper on the subject of fugitives, we will proceed with what follows in the regular order of the context. In the first place it is said, "The angel of the Lord found her in the way,"[28] pitying the

---

[26] Leviticus 21:11.

[27] There is some obscurity in the sense here. Mangey proposes instead of *hoide pou*, to read *oudepou*, but it does not seem any more intelligible than that in the text.

[28] Genesis 16:7.

soul which out of modesty had voluntarily committed the danger of wandering about, and very nearly becoming a conductor of her return to opinion void of error. (120) It is desirable also not to pass over in silence the things which are said in a philosophical strain by the lawgiver on the subject of discovery and investigation; for he represents some persons as neither investigating nor discovering anything, others as succeeding in both these paths, others as having chosen only one of them; of which last class some who seek do not find, and others find without having sought.

(121) Those, then, who have no desire for either discovery or investigation have shamefully debased their reason by ignorance and indifference, and though they had it in their power to see acutely, they have become blind. Thus he says that "Lot's wife turning backwards became a pillar of salt;"[29] not here inventing a fable, but pointing out the proper nature of the event.

(122) For whoever despises his teacher, and under the influence of an innate and habitual indolence forsakes what is in front of him, by means of which it may be in his power to see, and to hear, and to exert his other powers, so as to form a judgment in things of nature, and turns his head round so as to keep his eyes on what is behind him, that man has an admiration for blindness in the affairs of life, as well as in the parts of the body, and becomes a pillar, like a lifeless and senseless stone. (123) For, as Moses says, "such men have not hearts to understand, nor eyes to see, nor ears to hear,"[30] but make the whole of their life blind, and deaf, and senseless and mutilated in every respect, so as not to be worth living, caring for none of those matters which deserve their attention.

XXIII. (124) And the leader of this company is the king of the region of the body. "For," says Moses, "Pharaoh turned himself about and went into his house, and did not set his heart to this thing either,"[31] which statement is equivalent to, he did not take notice of anything whatever, but allowed himself to become dried up like a plant which has no care taken of it by the farmer, and to lose his fertility and become barren. (125) Those then who take counsel, and consider matters, and who investigate everything carefully, sharpen and rouse their minds: and the mind being duly exercised bears its appropriate fruit of cleverness and intelligence, by means of which the power of repelling all deceitful things is acquired. But the man who is an enemy to consideration blunts and breaks the edges of his wisdom; (126) we must therefore discard the truly senseless and lifeless company of such men as these, and choose those who exert their powers of consideration and discovery.

And presently the political disposition is introduced, which, without being at all over ambitious of glory, has a desire for that better generation, which the virtues have received as their inheritance, and which consequently seeks and finds it; (127) for, says the scripture, "A man found Joseph in the plain, and asked him saying, What seekest thou; and he said, I am seeking my brothers; tell me where they are feeding their flocks: and the man said unto him, They are departed from hence; for I heard them saying, Let us go into Dothan; and Joseph went after his brethren and found them in Dothan."[32] (128) The name Dothan is interpreted, "a sufficient abandonment," being a symbol of the soul which has in no slight degree but altogether escaped those vain opinions, which resemble the pursuits of women rather than those of men. On which account virtue, that is Sarah, is very beautifully described as having given up "the manner of women,"[33] which is the object of pursuit to those men who live an unmanly and truly feminine life. But the wise man is also "added when leaving,"[34] according to Moses, speaking most strictly in accordance with nature. For the deprivation of empty opinion must necessarily be the addition of true opinion.

(129) But if any one, passing his days in a mortal, and promiscuous, and variously formed life, and having abundant resources of wealth and riches, considers and inquires concerning that better generation which looks only to what is good, he is worthy of being received, if the dreams and visions of those things, which are fancied to be and which appear to be good, do not again overwhelm him and immerse him in luxury. (130) For if he abides in contemplation of the soul without any adulteration, proceeding and following in the track of the things which he is seeking, he will never give up his search till he has attained to the objects of his wishes; (131) but he will find none of the things which he desires among the wicked. Why not? Because they departed from hence. Having abandoned the studies of their friends they have changed their abode from the country of the pious, and settled in the desert of the wicked. But the real man, the convictor that dwells in the soul says this, who when he sees the soul in perplexity, and considering and investigating deeply, exerts a prudent care in its behalf, that it may not wander and so miss the right road.

[29] Genesis 19:26.
[30] Deuteronomy 29:4.
[31] Exodus 7:23.

[32] Genesis 37:15.
[33] Genesis 18:11.
[34] Genesis 25:17.

XXIV. (132) I very greatly wonder at those persons also, I mean at him who is fond of asking questions about what is in the middle between two extremes, and who says, "Behold the fire and the wood, but where is the lamb for the burnt offering?"[35] And also at him who answers, "My son, God will provide himself a lamb for a burnt offering," and who afterwards finds what is given as a ransom; "For behold a single ram was caught by his horns in a shrub of Sabec." (133) Let us therefore consider what it is that he who is seeking doubts about, and what he who answers reveals, and in the third place what the thing is which was found.

Now what the inquirer asks is something of this kind:—Behold the efficient cause, the fire; behold also the passive part, the material, the wood. Where is the third party, the thing to be effected? (134) As if he said,—Behold the mind, the fervid and kindled spirit; behold also the objects of intelligence, as it were so much material or fuel; where is the third thing, the act of perceiving? Or, again,—Behold the sight, behold the colour, where is the act of seeing? And, in short, generally, behold the external sense, behold the thing to be judge of; but where are the objects of the external sense, the material, the exertion of the feeling? (135) To him who puts these questions, answer is very properly made, "God will provide for himself." For the third thing is the peculiar work of God; for it is owing to his providential arrangement that the mind comprehends, and the sight sees, and that every external sense is exerted. "And a ram is found caught by his horns;" that is to say, reason is silent and withholding its assent; (136) for silence is the most excellent of offerings, and so is a withholding of assent to those matters of which there are not clear proofs; therefore this is all that ought to be said, "God will provide for himself,"—he to whom all things are known, who illuminates the universe by the most brilliant of all lights, himself. But the other things are not to be said by creatures over whom great darkness is poured; but quiet is a means of safety in darkness.

XXV. (137) Those also who have inquired what it is that nourishes the soul, for as Moses says, "They knew not what it was," learnt at last and found that it was the word of God and the divine reason, from which flows all kinds of instinctive and everlasting wisdom. This is the heavenly nourishment which the holy scripture indicates, saying, in the character of the cause of all things, "Behold I rain upon you bread from heaven;"[36] (138) for in real truth it is God who showers down heavenly wisdom from above upon all the intellects which are properly disposed for the reception of it, and which are fond of contemplation. But those who have seen and tasted it, are exceedingly delighted with it, and understand indeed what they feel, but do not know what the cause is which has affected them; and on this account they inquire, "What is this which is sweeter than honey and whiter than snow?" And they will be taught by the interpreter of the divine will, that "This is the bread which the Lord has given them to eat."[37]

(139) What then is this bread? Tell us. "This," says he, "is the word which the Lord has appointed." This divine appointment at the same time both illuminates and sweetens the soul, which is endowed with sight, shining upon it with the beams of truth, and sweetening with the sweet virtue of persuasion those who thirst and hunger after excellence. (140) And the prophet also having himself inquired what was the cause of meeting with success, finds it to be associated with the only God; for when he was doubting and asking, Who am I, and what am I, that I shall deliver the seeing race of Israel from the disposition hostile to God, which seems to be a king? (141) He is taught by the oracle that, "I will be with thee." And, indeed, inquiries into individual matters have a certain elegant and philosophical kind of meditation in them; for how can they avoid it? But the inquiry into the nature of God, the most excellent of all things, who is incomparable, and the cause of all things, at once delights those who betake themselves to its consideration, and it is not imperfect inasmuch as he, out of his own merciful nature, comes forward to meet it, displaying himself by his virgin graces, and willingly to all those who are desirous to see him. Not, indeed, such as he is, for that is impossible, since Moses also turned away his face,[38] for he feared to see God face to face; but as far as it is possible for created nature to approach by its own power those things which are only discernible to the mind. (142) And this also is written among the hortatory precepts, for, says Moses, "Ye shall turn unto the Lord your God, and shall find him, when ye seek him with all your heart, and with all your soul."[39]

XXVI. (143) Having now spoken at sufficient length on this point also, let us proceed in regular order to consider the third head of our subject, in which the seeking existed, but the finding did not follow it. At all events Laban, who examined the entire spiritual house of the practiser of virtue, "did not," as Moses says, "find the images,"[40] for it was full of real things, and not of dreams and

---

[35] Genesis 22:7.
[36] Exodus 16:4.

[37] Exodus 16:15.
[38] Exodus 3:6.
[39] Deuteronomy 4:29.
[40] Genesis 31:33.

vain fantasies. (144) Nor did the inhabitants of Sodom, blind in their minds, who were insanely eager to defile the holy and unpolluted reasonings, "find the road which led to this"[41] object; but, as the sacred scriptures tell us, they were wearied with their exertions to find the door, although they ran in a circle all around the house, and left no stone unturned for the accomplishment of their unnatural and impious desires.

(145) And before now some persons, wishing to be kings instead of doorkeepers, and to put an end to the most beautiful thing in life, namely order, having not only failed in obtaining the success which they hoped to meet with through injustice, but have even been compelled to part with that which they had in their hands; for the law tells us that the companions of Korah, who coveted the priesthood, lost both what they wished for and what they had: (146) for as children and men do not learn the same things, but there are institutions adapted to each age, so also there are by nature some souls which are always childish, even though they are in bodies which have grown old; and on the other hand, there are some which have arrived at complete perfection in bodies which are still in the prime and vigour of early youth.

But those men will deservedly incur the imputation of folly who desire objects too great for their own nature, since everything which is beyond one's power will vanish away through the intensity of its own vehemence. (147) And so Pharaoh also, when "seeking to kill Moses,"[42] the prophetic race, will never find him, although he has heard that a heavy accusation is brought against him, as if he has attempted to destroy all the supreme authority of the body by two attacks, (148) the first of which he made upon the Egyptian disposition, which was fortifying pleasure as a citadel against the soul; for "having smote him," with an accidental instrument that came to hand, "he buried him in the sand,"[43] thinking that the two doctrines, of pleasure being the first and greatest good, and of atoms being the origin of the universe, both proceed from the same source.

The second attack he made upon him who was cutting into small pieces the nature of the good, and assigning one portion to the soul, another to the body, and another to external circumstances; for he wishes the good to be entire, being assigned to the best thing in us, the intellect alone, as its inheritance, and not being adapted to anything inanimate.

XXVII. (149) Nor does he, who is sent forth to search for that virtue which is invincible and embittered against the ridiculous pursuits of men, by name Tamar, find her. And this failure of his is strictly in accordance with nature; for we read in the scripture, "And Judah sent a kid in the hands of his shepherd, the Adullamite, to receive back his pledge from the woman, and he found her not: and he asked the men of the place, Where is the harlot who was in Aenan by the wayside? and they said, There is no harlot in this place. And he returned back to Judah, and said unto him, I have not found her, and the men of the place say that there is no harlot there. And Judah said, Let her keep the things, only let me not be made a laughing-stock, I because I have sent the kid, and you because you have not found her."[44] Oh, the admirable trial! oh, the temptation becoming sacred things! (150) Who gave the pledge? Why the mind, forsooth, which was eager to purchase the most excellent possession, piety towards God, by three pledges or symbols, namely a ring, and an armlet, and a staff, signifying confidence and sure faith; the connection and union of reason with life, and of life with reason; and upright and unchanging instruction on which it is profitable to rely. (151) Therefore he examines the question as to whether he had properly given this pledge. What, then, is the examination? To throw down some bait having an attractive power, such as glory, or riches, or bodily health, or something similar, and to see to which it will incline, like the balance in a scale; for if there is any inclination to any one of these things the pledge is not sure. Therefore he sent a kid in order to recover back his pledge from the woman, not because he had determined by all means to recover it, but only in the case of her being unworthy to retain it. (152) And when will this be? when she willingly exchanges what is of importance for what is indifferent, preferring spurious to genuine good.

Now the genuine good things are faith, the connection and union of words with deeds, and the rule of right instruction, as on the other hand the evils are, faithlessness, a want of such connection between words and deeds, and ignorance. And spurious goods are those which depend upon appetite devoid of reason; (153) for "when he sought her he did not find her;" for what is good is hard to be found, or, one may even say, is utterly impossible to be found in a confused life. And if one inquires whether the soul, which is a harlot, is in every place of virtue, one will be distinctly told that it is not, and that it has not been previously; for a common, unchaste, and wanton, and utterly shameless woman, selling the flower of her beauty at a low price, and making her external parts both bright with purifications and washings, but leav-

---

[41]Genesis 19:11.
[42]Exodus 2:15.
[43]Exodus 2:12.

[44]Genesis 38:20.

ing her inward parts unclean and vile, and being like pictures painted with colours about the face because of the absence of all natural beauty; she who pursues that promiscuous evil called the vice of having many husbands, as if it were a good, coveting polygamy, and laying herself open for infinite variety, and being mocked and insulted at the same time by ten thousand bodies and things, "is not there."

(154) He, then, who sent the messenger to inquire, hearing this, having removed envy to a distance from himself, and being gentle in his nature, rejoices in no moderate degree, and says, "Perhaps, then, according to my prayer, she is truly a virtuous mind, a citizen wife, excelling in modesty, and chastity, and all other virtues, cleaving to one husband alone, being content with the administration of one household, and rejoicing in the authority of one husband; and if she is such an one, let her keep what I have given her—the instruction and the connection of reason with life and of life with reason, and, what is the most necessary of all things, surety and faith. (155) But let us not be laughed at as appearing to have given gifts which were not merited, while we think that we gave what is most suitable to the soul; for I, indeed, did what was proper for a man to do who wished to make experiment of and to test her disposition, throwing out a bait and sending a messenger; but he has showed me that her nature is not easily caught. (156) And it is not clear to me why it is not easily caught; for I have seen ten thousand persons of the extremely wicked class doing the same things as those who are extremely good, but not with the same purpose, since the one class has truth and the other only hypocrisy, and it is very hard to distinguish the one from the other, for very often reality is overpowered by appearance.

XXVIII. (157) Also the person who loves virtue seeks a goat by reason of his sins, but does not find one; for, already, as the sacred scripture tells us, "it has been burnt."[45] Now we must consider what is intimated under this figurative expression—how never to do any thing wrong is the peculiar attribute of God; and to repent is the part of a wise man. But this is very difficult and very hard to attain to. (158) Accordingly the scripture says that "Moses sought and sought again" a reason for repentance for his sins in mortal life; for he was very anxious to find a soul which was stripped of sin, and coming forward naked of all offence without shame. But nevertheless he did not find one, the flame, I mean by this the very quickly moving irrational desire, rushing inwards and devouring the whole soul.

(159) For what is smaller in numbers is usually overpowered by what is more numerous, and what is slower by what is more speedy, and what is to come hereafter by what is present. Now what is contracted in quantity, and slow, and future, is repentance; what is numerous, and swift, and continuous in human life is, iniquity. Very naturally, therefore, when any one falls into error, he says that he is unable to eat of what is offered by reason of his sins, so that his conscience will not permit him to be nourished by repentance; on which account it is said in the scripture, "Moses heard, and it pleased him."[46] (160) For the things which relate to the creature are very far removed from the things which relate to God; for to the creature only those things which are visible are known, but to God, even those things which are also invisible. And that man is crazy who, speaking falsely instead of truly, while still committing iniquity, asserts that he has repented. It is like as if one who had a disease were to pretend that he was in good health; for he, as it seems, will only get more sick, since he does not choose to apply any of the remedies which are conducive to health.

XXIX. (161) On one occasion Moses was urged on, by a desire of learning, to investigate the causes through which the most necessary of things in the world are brought to perfection; for seeing how many things come to an end, and are produced afresh in creation, being again destroyed, and again abiding, he marvelled, and was amazed, and cried out, saying, "The bush (*batos*) burns, and is not consumed."[47] (162) For he does not trouble his head about the inaccessible (*abatos*) country as being the abode of divine natures. But now that he is about to undertake a labour which will have no success and no end, he is relieved by the mercy and providence of God, the Saviour of all men, who has given warning out of his holy shrine, "Do not approach near this place," which is equivalent to, Do not approach this consideration; for it is a business requiring more labour, and more energy, and care, and fondness for investigation than can be suited to human power. But be content with admiring what is created; and do not be over-curious about the causes why each thing is created or destroyed.

(163) "For the place," says God, "on which thou standest is holy ground."[48] What kind of place is that? Is it not plain that it is that which relates to the principles of causes, which is the only one that he has adapted to the divine natures, not thinking any more competent to aim at a clear understanding of the principle of causes? (164) But he who,

---

[45]Leviticus 10:16.

[46]Leviticus 16:20.
[47]Exodus 3:2.
[48]Exodus 3:5.

out of his desire for learning, has raised his head above the whole world begins to inquire concerning the Creator of the world who this being is who is so difficult to see and whose nature it is so difficult to conjecture, whether he is a body, or an incorporeal being, or something above these things, or whether he is a simple nature like a unit, or a compound being or any ordinary existing thing. And when he sees how difficult to ascertain, and how difficult to understand this is, he then prays to be allowed to learn from God himself who God is; for he has never hoped to be able to learn this from any other of the beings that are around him. (165) But nevertheless, though inquiring into the essence of the living God he has heard nothing. For, says, God, "thou shalt see my back parts, but my face thou shalt not behold."[49] For it is sufficient for the wise man to know the consequences, and the things which are after God; but he who wishes to see the principal essence will be blinded by the exceeding brilliancy of his rays before he can see it.

XXX. (166) Having now said thus much concerning the third head of our subject, we will proceed to the fourth and last of the propositions we proposed to examine, according to which discovery sometimes comes to meet us without there having been any search. To this order belongs every self-taught and self-instructed wise man; for such an one has not been improved by consideration, and care, and labour, but from the first moment of his birth he has found wisdom ready prepared and showered upon him from above from heaven, of which he drinks an unmixed draught and on which he feasts, and continues being intoxicated with a sober intoxication with correctness of reason. (167) This is the man whom the law calls Isaac, whom the soul did not conceive at one time and bring forth at another, for says the scripture, "having conceived him she brought him forth,"[50] as if without any consideration of time.

For it was not a man who was now being thus brought forth, but a conception of the purest character, beautiful rather in its nature than in consequence of any study; for which reason also she who brings him forth is said to have given up the usual manner of women, that is to say her usual, and reasonable, and human customs. (168) For the self-taught race is something new, and beyond any description, and truly divine, existing not by any human conceptions, but by some inspired frenzy. Are you ignorant that the Hebrews stand in no need of midwives for their delivery? But they, as Moses says, "bring forth before the midwives can arrive," by which is meant that they have nature

alone for a coadjutor, without having any need of methods, or arts, or sciences.

And Moses gives very beautiful and very natural definitions of what is taught a man by himself; one being such a thing as is speedily discovered, the other what God himself has given us; (169) accordingly, that which is taught by others requires a long time, but what is taught a man by himself is quick, and in a manner independent of time. And the one again has God for its expounder, but the other has man. Now the first definition he has placed in the question, "What is this that thou has found so quickly, O my son?"[51] But the other is contained in the answer to this question, "What the Lord God gave unto me."

XXXI. (170) There is also a third definition of what is taught a man by himself, namely that which of its own accord rises upwards. For it is said in the hortatory injunctions, "Ye shall not sow, neither shall ye reap those things which arise from the earth of their own accord."[52]

For nature has not need of any art since God himself sows those things, and by his agricultural skill brings to perfection, as if they grew of themselves, things which do not grow of themselves, except inasmuch as they stand in need of no human assistance whatever. (171) But this is not so much a positive exhortation as an announcement of his opinion, for if he had been giving a positive recommendation he would have said, "Do not sow, and do not reap:" but as he is only giving his opinion, he says, "Ye shall not sow, neither shall ye reap." For as to those things with which we meet by the voluntary bounty of nature, of these we cannot find either the beginnings or the ends in ourselves as if we were the cause of them: therefore the beginning is the seed-time and the end the harvest time. (172) And it is better to understand these things thus: every beginning and every end is spontaneous, that is to say, it is the work of nature and not of ourselves. For instance; what is the beginning of learning. It is plain that it is a nature in the person who is taught which is well calculated to receive the particular subjects of meditation submitted to him. Again what is the beginning of being made perfect? If we are to speak plainly without keeping anything back, it is nature. Therefore he who teaches is also indeed to effect improvement, but it is God alone, the most excellent nature of all, who is able to conduct one to supreme perfection.

(173) He who is bred up among such doctrines as these has everlasting peace, and is released from wearisome and endless labours. And according to the lawgiver there is no difference between peace

---

[49] Exodus 33:23.
[50] Genesis 21:2.

[51] Genesis 27:20.
[52] Genesis 25:11.

and a week; for in each creation lays aside the appearance of energising and rests. (174) Very properly, therefore, is it said, "And the sabbath of the law shall be food for you," speaking figuratively. For the only thing which is really nourishing and really enjoyable is rest in God; which confers the greatest good, undisturbed peace. Peace, therefore, among cities is mixed up with civil war; but the peace of the soul has no mixture in it of any kind of difference.

(175) And the lawgiver appears to me to be recommending most manifestly that kind of discovery which is not preceded by any search, in the following words, "When the Lord thy God shall lead thee into the land which he swore to thy fathers that he would give thee, large and beautiful cities which thou buildest not, houses full of all good things which thou filledst not, cisterns hewn out of the quarries which thou hewedst not, vineyards and olive gardens which thou plantedst not."[53] (176) You see here the ungrudging abundance of all the great blessings which are ready, and poured forth for man's possession and enjoyment. And the generic virtues are here likened to cities, because they are of the most comprehensive kind; and the specific virtues are likened to houses, because they are contracted into a narrower circle; and the souls of a good disposition are likened to cisterns, which are well inclined to receive wisdom, as the cisterns are calculated to receive water; and the improvement, and growth, and production of fruit, are compared to vineyards and olive gardens; and the fruit of knowledge is a life of contemplation, which produces unmixed joy, equal to that which proceeds from wine; and a light appreciable only by the intellect, as if from a flame of which oil is the nourishment.

XXXII. (177) Having now said thus much on the subject of discovery, we will proceed in due order to what comes next in the context. Moses proceeds, "Therefore the angel of the Lord found her sitting by a fountain of water." Now a fountain is spoken of in many senses; in one manner our mind is meant by a fountain, in another the rational habit and instruction; in a third sense a bad disposition is intimated; in a fourth sense a good disposition, the contrary of the preceding; in a fifth sense, the Creator and Father of the universe is himself thus spoken of in a figure; (178) and there are passages written in the sacred scriptures which give proof of these things. What they are we must now consider. Now in the very beginning of the history of the law there is a passage to the following effect: "And a fountain went up from the earth, and watered all the face of the earth."[54] (179)

Those men, then, who are not initiated in allegory and in the nature which loves to hide itself, liken the fountain here mentioned to the river of Egypt, which every year overflows and makes all the adjacent plains a lake, almost appearing to exhibit a power imitating and equal to that of heaven; (180) for what the heaven during winter bestows on the other countries, the Nile affords to Egypt at the height of summer; for the heaven sends rain from above upon the earth, but the river, raining upward from below, which seems a most paradoxical statement, irrigates the corn-fields.

And it is starting from this point that Moses has described the Egyptian disposition as an atheistical one, because it values the earth above the heaven, and the things of the earth above the things of heaven, and the body above the soul; (181) but, however, we shall have an opportunity of speaking on these subjects hereafter when occasion permits.

But at present, for we must study not to be too prolix, we had better have recourse to an explanation which may be drawn from looking on the words as used figuratively; and we may say that the meaning of the statement that "a fountain went up and watered all the face of the earth," is something of this kind. (182) The dominant part of us, like a fountain, pours forth many powers through the veins of the earth as it were, till they reach the organs of the external senses, that is to say, the eyes, and ears, and nostrils, and other organs; and these organs in every animal are situated about the head and face. Therefore, the face, which is the dominant portion of the soul; making the spirit, which is calculated for seeing, reach to the eyes, that which has the power of hearing reach the ears, the spirit of smelling reach the nostrils, that of taste the mouth, and causing that of touch to pervade the whole surface of the body.

XXXIII. (183) There are also many various fountains of instruction, by means of which most nutritious reasonings have sprung up like the trunks of palm-trees; "for," says Moses, "they came to Aileim, and in Aileim there were twelve fountains of water and seventy trunks of palm-trees. And they pitched their tents there by the side of the water."[55] The name Aileim is interpreted to mean "vestibules," a symbol of the approach to virtue. For as vestibules are the beginning of a house, so also are the encyclical preliminary branches of instruction the beginning of virtue, (184) and twelve is the perfect number, of which the circle of the zodiac in the heaven is a witness, studded as it is with such numbers of brilliant constellations. The periodical revolution of the sun is another witness, for he accomplishes his circle in

[53] Deuteronomy 6:10.
[54] Genesis 2:6.
[55] Exodus 15:27.

twelve months, and men also reckon the hours of the day and of the night as equal in number to the months of the year, (185) and the passages are not few in which Moses celebrates this number, describing the twelve tribes of his nation, appointing by law the offering of the twelve cakes of shewbread, and ordering twelve stones, on which inscriptions are engraved, to be woven into the sacred robe of the garment, reaching down to the feet of the high-priest, on his oracular dress.

(186) He also celebrates the number seven, multiplied by the number ten; at one time speaking of the seventy palm-trees by the fountains, and in other passages he speaks of the elders, who were only seventy in number, to whom the divine and prophetical Spirit was vouchsafed. And again, it is the same number of heifers which are sacrificed at the solemn festival of the feast of tabernacles,[56] in a regular and proper division and order, for they are not all sacrificed together, but in seven days, the beginning being made with thirteen bulls; for thus, by every day subtracting one till they come to the number seven, the arranged number of seventy is properly completed.

(187) And when they have come to the gates of virtue, the preliminary liberal sciences, and have seen the fountains, and the stems of the palm-trees growing by them, they are said to pitch their tents, not by the palm-trees, but by the waters. Why is this? Because those who carry off the prizes of perfect virtue are adorned with palm-leaves and with fillets; but those who are still exercising themselves in the preliminary branches of instruction, as people thirsting for learning, settle themselves by the side of those sciences which are able to bedew and irrigate their souls.

XXXIV. (188) Such then are the fountains of intermediate instruction. Let us now consider the fountain of folly, concerning which the lawgiver speaks thus, "Whosoever shall lie with a woman who is sitting apart has uncovered her fountain, and she has uncovered the issue of blood; they shall both be destroyed."[57] Here he calls the external sense a woman, representing the mind as her husband. (189) When therefore the woman, having forsaken her legitimate husband, settles near those objects of the external sense which allures and destroys, and embraces them all in this amorous manner; then therefore, if the mind be turned to sleep when it is necessary that it should be awakened, it has uncovered the fountain of the external sense, that is itself, that is to say, it has rendered itself, without a covering and without a wall, and easy to be plotted against. (190) But nevertheless the woman also has uncovered the

fountain of her blood, for every external sense, when flowing towards the external object appreciable by it, is cheered and restrained by being under the dominion of the reason; and it is left in a solitary condition, being deprived of any proper governor. And as the most terrible misfortune for a city is to be without walls, so the most unfortunate state for a soul is to be without a guardian.

(191) When, then, is it without a guardian? Is it not when the sight is without any covering, being poured forth upon the objects of sight; and when the hearing is without a covering, being occupied in drinking in all kinds of sounds; and when the sense of smell is uncovered, and the kindred powers are left to themselves, and so are most ready to suffer whatever the invading enemy may be disposed to inflict? And that speech is uncovered and uttered which speaks ten thousand things in an unseasonable manner, without any thing to restrain its impetuosity; therefore flowing on unrestrainedly, it overturns many noble purposes and plans of life which were previously sailing on erect as though in calm weather.

(192) This is that great deluge in which "the cataracts of heaven were opened"[58]—by heaven I here mean the mind—and the fountains of the bottomless pit were revealed; that is to say, of the outward sense; for in this way alone is the soul overwhelmed, iniquities being broken up and poured over it from above, as from the heaven of the mind, and the passions irrigating it from below, as from the earth of the outward senses. (193) For which reason Moses forbids a man to uncover the nakedness of his father or of his mother,[59] well knowing how great an evil it is not to check and to conceal the offences of the mind and of the external senses, but to bring them forward and display them as though they were good actions.

XXXV. (194) These are the fountains of errors. We must now examine that of prudence. To this one it is that perseverance, that is to say, Rebecca, descends;[60] and after she has filled up the whole vessel of her soul she goes up again, the lawgiver, most strictly in accordance with natural truth, calling her return an ascent; for whoever brings his mind to descend from over-arrogant haughtiness is raised to a great height of virtue. (195) For Moses says, "And having gone down to the fountain, she filled her ewer, and went up again." This is that divine wisdom from which all the particular sciences are irrigated, and all the souls which love contemplation are filled with a love of what is most excellent; (196) and to this fountain the sacred scripture most appropriately assigns name,

---

[56] Numbers 29:13.
[57] Leviticus 20:18.

[58] Genesis 7:11.
[59] Leviticus 18:7.
[60] Genesis 24:15.

calling it "judgment" and "holy." For says the historian, "Having turned back, they came to the fountain of judgment; this is the fountain of Caddes,"[61] and the interpretation of the name Caddes is holy. It all but cries out and shouts that the wisdom of God is holy, bringing with it nothing of the earth, and that it is the judgment of the universe by which all contrarieties are separated from one another.

XXXVI. (197) We must now speak also concerning that highest and most excellent of fountains which the Father of the universe spake of by the mouths of the prophets; for he has said somewhere, "They have left me, the fountain of life, and they have digged for themselves cisterns already worn out, which will not be able to hold water;"[62] (198) therefore, God is the most ancient of all fountains. And is not this very natural? For he it is who has irrigated the whole of this world; and I am amazed when I hear that this is the fountain of life, for God alone is the cause of animation and of that life which is in union with prudence; for the matter is dead. But God is something more than life; he is, as he himself has said, the everlasting fountain of living.

(199) But the wicked having fled away, and having passed their time without ever tasting the draught of immortality, have digged, insane persons that they are, for themselves, and not first for God, having preferred their own actions to the heavenly and celestial things, and the things which proceed from care to those which are spontaneous and ready. (200) Then they dig, not as the wise men Abraham and Isaac did, making wells, but cisterns, which have no good nutritious stream belonging to and proceeding from themselves, but requiring an influx from without, which must proceed from instruction. While the teachers are always pouring into the ears of their disciples all kinds of doctrines and speculations of science altogether, admonishing them to retain them in their minds, and to preserve them when faithfully committed to memory.

(201) But now they are but worn-out cisterns, that is to say, all the channels of the ill-educated soul are broken and leaky, not being able to hold and to preserve the influx of those streams which are able to profit.

XXXVII. (202) We have now then said as much as the time will permit us to say on the subject of the fountains, and it is with great accuracy and propriety that the sacred scriptures represent Hagar as found at the fountain, and not as drawing water from it: for the soul has not as yet made such an advance as to be fit to use the unmixed draught of wisdom; but it is not forbidden from making its abode in its neighbourhood. (203) And all the road which is made by instruction is easy to travel, and most safe, and most solid, and strong, on which account the scripture tells us that she was found in the road leading to Shur; and the name Shur being interpreted means a wall or a direction. Therefore its convicter, speaking to the soul, says, "Whence comest thou, and whither goest thou?" And it says, not because it doubts, and not so much by the way of asking a question, as in a downcast and reproachful spirit, for an angel cannot be ignorant of anything that concerns us, and a proof of this is, (204) that he is well acquainted even with the things that are in the womb, and which are invisible to the creature, inasmuch as he says, "Behold thou art with child, and thou shalt bring forth a son, and shalt call his name Ishmael;" for to know that that which is conceived is a male child does not belong to human power, any more than it does to foretell the destruction of life which the child who is not yet born will adopt, namely, that it will be rude life, and not that of a citizen or of a polished man.

(205) The expression, "Whence comest thou?" is said by way of reproving the soul, which is fleeing from the better and dominant opinion, of which she is the handmaiden, not in name more than in fact, and by remaining in subjection to which she would gain great glory. And the expression, "And whither goest thou?" means, you are running after uncertain things, having discarded and thrown away confessed good. (206) It is well, therefore, to praise her for rejoicing at this admonition. And she shows a proof of her delighting in it, by not bringing any accusation against her mistress, and by attributing the cause of her running away to her own self, and by her making no reply to the second question, "Whither goest thou?" for it is a matter of uncertainty; and it is both safe and necessary to restrain one's self from speaking of what is uncertain.

XXXVIII. (207) Therefore the convicter of the soul approving of her in respect of her obedience says, Return unto thy mistress; for the government of the teacher is profitable to the disciple, and servitude in subjection to wisdom is advantageous to her who is imperfect; and when thou returnest, "be thou humbled under her hands:"— a very beautiful humiliation, comprehending the destruction of irrational pride. (208) For thus, after a gentle travail, thou wilt bring forth a male child, by name Ishmael, corrected by divine admonitions; for Ishmael, being interpreted, means "the hearing of God;" and hearing is considered as entitled to only the second prize after seeing; but seeing is the inheritance of the legitimate and first-born son, Israel; for the name Israel, being interpreted, means "seeing God."

For it is possible for a man to hear false state-

---

[61] Genesis 14:7.
[62] Jeremiah 2:13.

ments as though they were true, because hearing is a deceitful thing; but seeing is a sense which cannot be deceived, by which a man perceives existing things as they really are. (209) But the angel describes the characteristics of the disposition which is born of Hagar, by saying that he will be a rude man; as if he had said that he would be a man wise about rude matters, and not as yet thought worthy of that which is the truly divine and political portion of life: and this is virtue, by means of which it is the nature of the moral character to be humanised. And by his saying, "His hand shall be against every man, and every man's hand against him," he means to describe the design and plan of life of a sophist, who professes an overcurious scepticism, and who rejoices in disputatious arguments.

(210) Such a man shoots at all the followers of learning, and in his own person opposes all men, both publicly and privately, and is shot at by all who very naturally repel him as if they were acting in defence of their own offspring, that is to say, of the doctrines which their soul has brought forth.

(211) He also adds a third characteristic of him, saying, "He shall dwell before the face of all his brethren." In these words all but expressly declaring that he will wage an everlasting battle and war against them, face to face, for ever. Therefore the soul, which is pregnant with sophistical reasoning, says to the convicter who is addressing her, "Thou art God, who hast beheld me:" an expression equivalent to, Thou art the creator of my plans and of my offspring. (212) And may we not look upon this as a very natural reply on her part? For of these souls which are free, and, as it were truly citizens, the Creator is free, and a deliverer; but of slavish minds, slaves are the creators.

And the angels are the servants of God, and are considered actual gods by those who are in toil and slavery; on this account, says Moses, she called the well, "The well where I saw in front of me." (213) But O, thou soul! advancing in wisdom and plunging deep into the knowledge of the elementary parts of encyclical instruction, thou wast not able to see the cause of thy knowledge in instruction as in a mirror. But the most appropriate place for such a well is in the midst, between Caddes and Barad; and the name Barad, being interpreted, means "in common," and Caddes means "holy;" for the person who is in a state of imprisonment is on the confines between what is holy and what is profane, fleeing from what is wicked, and being not yet able to live in the company of what is perfectly good.

ON THE CHANGE OF NAMES†

(De Mutatione Nominum)

I. (1) "Abraham was ninety and nine years old; and the Lord appeared unto Abraham, and said unto him, I am thy God."[1] The number of nine, when added to the number ninety, is very near to a hundred; in which number the self-taught race shone forth, namely Isaac, the most excellent joy of all enjoyments; for he was born when his father was a hundred years old. (2) Moreover the first fruits of the tribe of Levi are given up to the priests;[2] for they having taken tithes, offer up other tenths from them as from their own fruits, which thus comprise the number of a hundred; for the number ten is the symbol of improvement, and the number a hundred is the symbol of perfection; and he that is in the middle is always striving to reach the extremity, exerting the inborn goodness of his nature, by which he says, that the Lord of the universe has appeared to him.

(3) But do not thou think that this appearance presented itself to the eyes of the body, for they see no things but such as are perceptible to the outward senses; but those objects of the outward senses are compounded ones, full of destruction; but the Deity is not a compound object, and is indestructible: but the eye which receives the impression of the divine appearance is the eye of the soul; (4) for besides this, those things which it is only the eyes of the body that see, are only seen by them because they take light as a coadjutor, and light is different, both from the object seen and from the things which see it.

But all these things which the soul sees of itself, and through its own power, it sees without the co-operation of any thing or any one else; for the things which the soul does thus comprehend are a light to themselves, (5) and in the same way also we learn the sciences; for the mind, applying its never-closing and never-slumbering eye to their doctrines and speculations, sees them by no spurious light, but by that genuine light which shines forth from itself. (6) When therefore you hear that God has been seen by man, you must consider that this is said without any reference to that light which is perceptible by the external senses, for it is natural that that which is appreciable only by the intellect should be presented to the intellect alone; and the fountain of the purest light is God; so that when God appears to the soul he pours forth his beams without any shade, and beaming with the most radiant brilliancy.

II. (7) Do not, however, think that the living God, he who is truly living, is ever seen so as to be comprehended by any human being; for we have no power in ourselves to see any thing, by which we may be able to conceive any adequate notion of him; we have no external sense suited to that purpose (for he is not an object which can be discerned by the outward sense), nor any strength adequate to it: therefore, Moses, the spectator of the invisible nature, the man who really saw God (for the sacred scriptures say that he entered "into the darkness,"[3] by which expression they mean figuratively to intimate the invisible essence), having investigated every part of every thing, sought to see clearly the much-desired and only God; (8) but when he found nothing, not even any appearance at all resembling what he had hoped to behold; he, then, giving up all idea of receiving instruction on that point from any other source, flies to the very being himself whom he was seeking, and entreats him, saying, "Show my thyself that I may see thee so as to know thee."[4]

But, nevertheless, he fails to obtain the end which he had proposed to himself, and which he had accounted the most all-sufficient gift for the most excellent race of creation, mankind, namely a knowledge of those bodies and things which are below the living God. (9) For it is said unto him, "Thou shalt see my back parts, but my face shall not be beheld by thee."[5] As if it were meant to answer him: Those bodies and things which are beneath the living God may come within thy comprehension, even though every thing would not be at once comprehended by thee, since that one being is not by his nature capable of being beheld by man. (10) And what wonder is there if the living God is beyond the reach of the comprehension of man, when even the mind that is in each of us is unintelligible and unknown to us? Who has ever beheld the essence of the soul? the obscure nature of which has given rise to an infinite number of contests among the sophists who have

---

†Yonge's title, *A Treatise on the Question Why Certain Names in the Holy Scripture Are Changed.*
[1]Genesis 17:1.
[2]Numbers 18:26.

[3]Exodus 20:21.
[4]Exodus 33:13.
[5]Exodus 33:23.

brought forward opposite opinions, some of which are inconsistent with any kind of nature.

(11) It was, therefore, quite consistent with reason that no proper name could with propriety be assigned to him who is in truth the living God. Do you not see that to the prophet who is really desirous of making an honest inquiry after the truth, and who asks what answer he is to give to those who question him as to the name of him who has sent him, he says, "I am that I am,"[6] which is equivalent to saying, "It is my nature to be, not to be described by name:" (12) but in order that the human race may not be wholly destitute of any appellation which they may give to the most excellent of beings, I allow you to use the word Lord as a name; the Lord God of three natures—of instruction, and of holiness, and of the practice of virtue; of which Abraham, and Isaac, and Jacob are recorded as the symbols. For this, says he, is the everlasting name, as if it has been investigated and discerned in time as it exists in reference to us, and not in that time which was before all time; and it is also a memorial not placed beyond recollection or intelligence, and again it is addressed to persons who have been born, not to uncreated natures.

(13) For these men have need of the complete use of the divine name who come to a created or mortal generation, in order that, if they cannot attain to the best thing, they may at least arrive at the best possible name, and arrange themselves in accordance with that; and the sacred oracle which is delivered as from the mouth of the Ruler of the universe, speaks of the proper name of God never having been revealed to any one, when God is represented as saying, "For I have not shown them my name;"[7] for by a slight change in the figure of speech here used, the meaning of what is said would be something of this kind: "My proper name I have not revealed to them," but only that which is commonly used, though with some misapplication, because of the reasons abovementioned.

(14) And, indeed, the living God is so completely indescribable, that even those powers which minister unto him do not announce his proper name to us. At all events, after the wrestling match in which the practicer of virtue wrestled for the sake of the acquisition of virtue, he says to the invisible Master, "Tell me thy name;"[8] but he said, "Why askest thou me my name?" And he does not tell him his peculiar and proper name, for says he, it is sufficient for thee to be taught my ordinary explanations. But as for names which are the symbols

of created things, do not seek to find them among immortal natures.

III. (15) Therefore do not doubt either whether that which is more ancient than any existing thing is indescribable, when his very word is not to be mentioned by us according to its proper name. So that we must understand that the expression, "The Lord was seen by Abraham,"[9] means not as if the Cause of all things had shone forth and become visible, (for what human mind is able to contain the greatness of his appearance?) but as if some one of the powers which surround him, that is to say, his kingly power, had presented itself to the sight, for the appellation Lord belongs to authority and sovereignty.

(16) But when our mind was occupied with the wisdom of the Chaldaeans, studying the sublime things which exist in the world, it made as it were the circuit of all the efficient powers as causes of what existed; but when it emigrated from the Chaldaean doctrines, it then knew that it was moving under the guidance and direction of a governor, of whose authority it perceived the appearance. (17) On which account it is said, "The Lord," not the living God, "was seen;" as if it had been meant to say, the king appeared, he who was from the beginning, but who was not as yet recognized by the soul, which, indeed, was late in learning, but which did not continue for ever in ignorance, but received a notion of there being an authority and governing power among existing things.

(18) And when the ruler has appeared, then he in a still greater degree benefits his disciple and beholder, saying, "I am thy God;"[10] for I should say to him, "What is there of all the things which form a part of creation of which thou art not the God?" But his word, which is his interpreter, will teach me that he is not at present speaking of the world, of which he is by all means the creator and the God, but about the souls of men, which he has thought worthy of a different kind of care; (19) for he thinks fit to be called the Lord and Master of bad men, but the God of those who are in a state of advancement and improvement; and of those which are the most excellent and the most perfect, both Lord and God at once. On which account, having made Pharaoh the very extreme instance of impiety, he has never once called himself his Lord or his God; but he calls the wise Moses so, for he says to him, "Behold I give thee as a god to Pharaoh."[11] But he has in many passages of the sacred oracles delivered by him, called himself Lord. (20) For instance, we read such as

[6]Exodus 3:14.
[7]Exodus 6:3.
[8]Genesis 32:29.

[9]Genesis 17:1.
[10]Genesis 17:2.
[11]Genesis 7:1.

passage as this: "Thus says the Lord;"[12] and at the very beginning we read, "The Lord spake unto Moses, saying, I am the Lord, say unto Pharaoh, the king of Egypt, all the things which I say unto thee."[13] (21) And Moses, in another place, says, "Behold, when I go forth out of the city I will spread out my hands unto the Lord, and the sounds shall cease, and the hail, and there shall be no more rain, that thou mayest know that the earth is the Lord's;" that is to say, every thing that is made of body or of earth, "and that thou," that is the mind which bears in itself the images of things, "and thy servants," that is the particular reasonings which act as body-guards to the mind, "for I know that ye do not yet fear the Lord;"[14] by which he means not the Lord who is spoken of commonly and in different senses, but him who is truly the Master of all things.

(22) For there is in truth no created Lord, not even a king shall have extended his authority and spread it from one end of the world even to the other end, but only the uncreated God, the real governor, whose authority he who reverences and fears receives a most beneficial reward, namely, the admonitions of God, but utterly miserable destruction awaits the man who despises him; (23) therefore he is held forth as the Lord of the foolish, striking them with a terror which is appropriate to him as ruler. But he is the God of those who are improved; as we read now, "I am thy God, I am thy God, be thou increased and multiplied."[15] And in the case of those who are perfect, he is both together, both Lord and God; as we read in the ten commandments, "I am the Lord thy God."[16] And in another passage it is written, "The Lord God of our fathers."[17]

(24) For he thinks it right for the wicked man to be governed by a master as by a lord; that, being in a state of alarm and groaning, he may have the fear of a master suspended over him; but him who is advancing in improvement he thinks deserving to receive benefits as from God in order that by means of these benefits he may arrive at perfection; and him who is complete and perfect he thinks should be both governed as by the Lord, and benefited as by God; for the last man remains for ever unchangeable, and he is, by all means and in all respects, the man of God: (25) and this is especially shown to be the fact in the case of Moses; for, says the scripture, "This is the blessing which Moses, the man of God, blessed."[18] O the man that thus thought worthy of this all-beautiful and

sacred recompense, to give himself as a requital for the divine Providence! (26) But do not thou think that he is in the same sense a man and the man of God; for he is said to be a man as being a possession of God, but the man of God as boasting in and being benefited by him. And if thou wishest to have God as the inheritance of thy mind, then do thou in the first place labour to become yourself an inheritance worthy of him, and thou wilt be such if thou avoidest all laws made by hands and voluntary.

IV. (27) But it is not right to be ignorant of this thing either, that the statement, "I am thy God,"[19] is made by a certain figurative misuse of language rather than with strict propriety; for the living God, inasmuch as he is living, does not consist in relation to anything; for he himself is full of himself, and he is sufficient for himself, and he existed before the creation of the world, and equally after the creation of the universe; (28) for he is immovable and unchangeable, having no need of any other thing or being whatever, so that all things belong to him, but, properly speaking, he does not belong to anything. And of the powers which he has extended towards creation for the advantage of the world which is thus put together, some are spoken of, as it were, in relation to these things; as for instance his kingly and his beneficent power; for he is the king of something, and the benefactor of something there being inevitably something which is ruled over and which receives the benefits.

(29) Akin to these powers is the creative power which is called God: for by means of this power the Father, who begot and created all things, did also disperse and arrange them; so that the expression, "I am thy God," is equivalent to, "I am thy maker and creator;" (30) and it is the greatest of all possible gifts to have him for one's maker, who has also been the maker of the whole world. The soul, indeed, of the wicked man he did not make, for wickedness is hateful to God; and the soul, which is between good and bad, he made not by himself alone, according to the most sacred historian Moses, since that, like wax, was about to receive the different impressions of good and evil. (31) On which account it is said in the scriptures, "Let us make man in our own image," that if it receives a bad impression it may appear to be the work of others, but if it receives a good impression it may then appear to be the work of him who is the Creator only of what is beautiful and good.

By all means, therefore, that must be a good man to whom he says, "I am thy God," as he has had him alone for his creator without the co-operation of any other being. (32) Moreover he brings up with this that doctrine which is estab-

---

[12] Exodus 7:17.
[13] Exodus 6:29.
[14] Exodus 9:29.
[15] Genesis 17:1, also 35:2.
[16] Exodus 20:2.
[17] Deuteronomy 4:1.
[18] Deuteronomy 33:1.

[19] Genesis 17:1.

lished in many other passages, showing that God is the creator only of those men who are virtuous and wise; and the whole of this company has voluntarily deprived itself of the abundant possession of external things, and has neglected those things which are dear to his flesh. (33) For the athletes of vigorous health and high spirit have erected their servile bodies as a sort of fortification against the soul, but those men who have been devoted to the pursuit of instruction, and who are pale, and weak, and emaciated, having overloaded the vigour of the body with the power of the soul, and if one must tell the plain truth, being entirely dissolved into one species of soul, have through the energy of their minds become quite disentangled from the body.

(34) Therefore that which is earthly is very naturally destroyed and overwhelmed when the entire mind resolves in every particular to make itself acceptable to God. But the race of these persons is rare and scarcely to be found, and one may almost say is unable to exist; and the following oracle, which is given with respect to Enoch, proves this: "Enoch pleased God, and he was not found;"[20] (35) for by what kind of contemplation could a man attain to this good thing? What seas must he cross over? What islands, or what continents, must he visit? Must he dwell among Greeks or among the barbarians? (36) Are there not even to the present day some of those persons who have attained to perfection in philosophy, who say that there is no such thing as wisdom in the world, since there is also no such thing as a wise man? for that from the very beginning of the creation of mankind up to the present moment, there has never been any one who could be considered entirely blameless, for that it is impossible for a man who is bound up in a mortal body to be entirely and altogether happy.

(37) Now whether these things are said correctly we will consider at the proper time: but at present let us stick to the subject before us, and follow the scripture, and say that there is such a thing as wisdom existing, and that he who loves wisdom is wise. But though the wise man has thus an actual existence he has escaped the notice of us who are wicked: for what is good will not unite with what is bad. (38) On this account it is that "the disposition which pleased God was not found;" as if in truth it has a real existence, but was concealed and had fled away to avoid any meeting in the same place with us, since it is said to have been translated; the meaning of which expression is that it emigrated and departed from its sojourn in this mortal life, to an abode in immortal life.

V. (39) These men then, being mad with this divinely inspired madness, were made more fero-

cious; but there are others who are companions of a more manageable and humanised wisdom. By those men piety is practised to a most eminent degree, and the observance due to man is not neglected. And the sacred oracles are witnesses of this in which Abraham is addressed (the words being put in the mouth of God), "Thou shalt be pleasing in my sight,"[21] that is to say, thou shalt be pleasing, not only to me but also to my works, in my eyes as judge, and overseer, and superintendant; (40) for if you honour your parents, or show mercy to the poor, or do good to your friends, or fight in defence of your country, or pay proper attention to the common principles of justice towards all men, you most certainly are pleasing to those with whom you associate, and you are also acceptable in the sight of God: for he sees all things with an eye which never slumbers, and he unites to himself with especial favour all that is good, and that he accepts and embraces.

(41) Therefore the practicer of virtue, even while praying, proves the very same thing, saying, "The God to whom my fathers were acceptable,"[22] and he adds the words "before him," for the sake of giving you to know the difference, the real practical difference between the expression, "to please God," by itself, and the same words with the addition of the sentence, "before him." For the one expression gives both meanings, and the other only one. (42) Thus also Moses, in his exhortatory admonitions, recommends his disciples such and such things, saying, "Thou shalt do what is pleasing before the Lord thy God,"[23] as if he were to say, Do such things as we shall be worthy to appear before God, and what he when he sees them will accept. And these things are wont to appear equally pure both externally and internally.[24] (43) And proceeding onwards from thence he wove the tent of the tabernacle with two boundaries of space, placing a veil between the two, in order to separate what is within from what is without. And also he gilded the sacred ark, the place wherein the laws were kept, both within and without; and he gave the great high priest two robes, the inner one made of linen, and the other one beautifully embroidered, with one robe reaching to the feet.

(44) For these and such things as these are symbols of the soul which in its inner parts shows itself pure towards God, and in its exterior parts shows itself without reproach in reference to the world which is perceptible to the outward senses and to this life: with great felicity therefore was

---

[20]Genesis 5:24.

[21]Genesis 17:3.
[22]Genesis 48:15.
[23]Deuteronomy 12:28.
[24]This passage is given up by Mangey as corrupt and quite unintelligible. Mangey corrects it and gives a Latin translation which I have followed.

this said to the victorious wrestler, when he was about to have his brows crowned with the garlands of victory: and the declaration made with respect to him was of the following tenor, "You have been mightily powerful both with God and with men;"[25] (45) for to have a good reputation with both classes, namely, with the uncreated God and with the creature, is the task of no small mind, but, if one must say the truth, it is one fit for that which is in the confines between the world and God.

In short, it is necessary that the good man should be an attendant of God, for the creature is an object of care to the Ruler and Father of the universe; (46) for who is there who does not know, that even before the creation of the world God was himself sufficient to himself, and that he remained as much a friend as before after the creation of the world, without having undergone any change? Why then did he make what did not exist before? Because he was good and bounteous. Shall we not then, we who are slaves, follow our master, admiring, in an exceeding degree, the great first Cause of all things, and not altogether despising our own nature?

VI. (47) But after he has said, "Be thou pleasing to me before me," he adds further, "and be thou blameless," using here a natural consequence and connection of the previous sentence. Do thou therefore all the more apply thyself to what is good that thou mayest be pleasing; and if thou canst not be pleasing, at all events abstain from open sins, that thou mayest not incur reproach. For he who does right is praiseworthy, and he who avoids doing wrong is not to be blamed. (48) And the most important prize is assigned to those who do right, namely, the prize of feeling that they are acceptable to God: but the second prize belongs to those who do no sin, that, namely, of avoiding blame; and, perhaps, in the case of the mortal race of mankind, the doing no sin is set down as equivalent to doing right; for who, as Job says is "pure from pollution, even if his life be but one single day long?"[26]

(49) In fact, the things which pollute the soul are infinite in number, and it is impossible completely to wash them away and to efface their stains; for there are, of necessity, left disasters which are akin to every mortal man, which it is natural indeed to weaken, but impossible wholly to eradicate. (50) Does any one therefore seek a just, or prudent, or temperate, or, in short, any perfectly good man, in this confused life? Be content if you find one who is not wholly unjust, or foolish, or intemperate, or cowardly, or who is not utterly worthless; for the avoidance of evil is a thing with which to be content, but the complete acquisition of the vir-

tues is unattainable to any man, such as is endowed with our nature.

(51) It was therefore with great reason that it was said, "and be thou blameless," the speaker thinking that it is a great addition towards a happy life to live without sin and without reproach; but the man who has deliberately chosen this way of life, promises to leave his inheritance in accordance with the covenant, such as is becoming to God to give, and to a wise man to accept, (52) for he says, "I will place my covenant between me and between thee;"[27] and covenants and testaments are written for the advantage of those who are worthy of the gift, so that a testament is a symbol of grace, which God has placed between himself who proffers it and man who receives it; (53) and this is the very extravagance of beneficence, that there is nothing between God and the soul except his own virgin grace. And I have written two commentaries on the whole discussion concerning testaments, and for that reason I now deliberately pass over that subject, for the sake of not appearing to repeat what I have said before; and also at the same time, because I do not wish here to interrupt the connected course of this discussion.

VII. (54) And immediately afterwards it is said, "And Abraham fell on his face:" was he not about, in accordance with the divine promises, to recognize himself and the nothingness of the race of mankind, and so to fall down before him who stood firm, by way of displaying the conception which he entertained of himself and of God? Forsooth that God, standing always in the same place, moves the whole composition of the world, not by means of his legs, for he has not the form of a man, but by showing his unalterable and immovable essence. (55) But man, being never settled firmly in the same place, admits of different changes at different times, and being tripped up, miserable man that he is (for, in fact, his whole life is one continued stumble), he meets with a terrible fall; (56) but he who does this against his will is ignorant, and he who does it voluntarily is docile; on which account he is said to fall on his face, that is to say, in his outward senses, in his speech, in his mind, all but crying out loudly and shouting that the outward sense has fallen, inasmuch as it was unable, by itself, to feel as it should, if it had not been aroused by the providence of the Saviour, to take hold of the bodies which lay in its way. And speech too has fallen, being unable to give a proper explanation of anything in existence, unless he who originally made and adapted the organ of the voice, having opened its mouth and enabled its tongue to articulate, should strike it so as to produce harmonious sounds. Moreover, the king of all the mind has fallen, being deprived of its comprehension,

---

[25] Genesis 32:28.
[26] Job 14:4.

[27] Genesis 17:2.

unless the Creator of all living things were again to raise it up and re-establish it, and furnishing it with the most acutely seeing eyes, to lead it to a sight of incorporeal things.

VIII. (57) Therefore admiring this same disposition when thus taking to flight, and submitting to a voluntary fall by reason of the confession which it had made respecting the living God, namely, that he stands in truth and is one only, while all other things beneath him are subject to all kinds of motions and alterations, he speaks to it, and allows it to enter into conversation with him, saying, "And I, behold my covenant is with thee."[28] (58) And this expression conceals beneath its figurative words such a meaning as this: There are very many kinds of covenants, which distribute graces and gifts to those who are worthy to receive them; but the highest kind of covenant of all is I myself: for God, having displayed himself as far as it was possible for that being to be displayed who cannot be shown by the words which he has used, adds further, "And I too, behold my covenant;" the beginning and fountain of all graces is I myself.

(59) For on some persons God is in the habit of bestowing his graces by the intervention of others; as, for instance, through the medium of earth, water, air, the sun, the moon, heaven, and other incorporeal powers. But he bestows them on others through himself alone, exhibiting himself as the inheritance of those who receive him, whom from that he thinks worthy of another appellation: (60) for it is said in the scripture, "Thy name shall not be called Abram, but Abraham shall thy name be." Some, then, of those persons who are fond of disputes, and who are always eager to affix a stain upon what is irreproachable, on things as well as bodies, and who wage an implacable war against sacred things, while they calumniate everything which does not appear to preserve strict decorum in speech, being the symbols of nature which is always fond of being concealed, perverting it all so as to give it a worse appearance after a very accurate investigation, do especially find fault with the changes of names.

(61) And it is only lately that I heard an ungodly and impious man mocking and ridiculing these things, who ventured to say, "Surely they are great and exceeding gifts which Moses says that the Ruler of the universe offers, who, by the addition of one element, the one letter alpha, a superfluous element;[29] and then again adding another element, the letter rho, appears to have bestowed upon men a most marvellous and great benefit;

for he has called the wife of Abram Sarrah instead of Sarah, doubling the Rho," and connecting a number of similar arguments without drawing breath, and joking and mocking, he went through many instances. (62) But at no distant period he suffered a suitable punishment for his insane, wickedness; for on a very slight and ordinary provocation he hanged himself, in order that so polluted and impure a person might not die by a pure and unpolluted death.

IX. But we may justly, in order to prevent any one else from falling into the same error, eradicate the erroneous notions which have been formed on the subject, arguing the matter on the principle of natural philosophy, and proving that these things which are here said are worthy of all attention. (63) God does not bestow on men mutes and vowels, or, in short, nouns and verbs; since when he created plants and animals, he summoned them before man as their governor, that he might give each of them their appropriate names by a reference to the knowledge which he had of all things; for, says the scripture, "Whatever Adam called any thing, that was the name thereof."[30]

(64) Therefore since God did not think fit to take upon himself even the active imposition of the names, but entrusted the task to a wise man, the author of the whole race of mankind, it is reasonable to suppose that he himself gave and arranged the different parts, and syllables, and letters of nouns, disposing not only the vowels, but even the mutes, and that he did this too to make a show of liberality and exceeding beneficence? It is impossible to say so. (65) But such things as these are the characteristic marks of different powers; small marks of great powers, marks perceptible by the outward senses of powers which are indistinct; and the powers themselves are discerned in most excellent doctrines, in true and pure conceptions, in the improvement of souls.

And it is easy to see a proof of this if we make a beginning with the man who is here spoken of as having his name changed; (66) for the name Abram, being interpreted, means "sublime father," but Abraham means the "elect father of sound;" and how these names differ from one another we shall know more clearly if we first of all read what is exhibited under each of them. (67) Now using allegorical language, we call that man sublime who raises himself from the earth to a height, and who devotes himself to the inspection of high things; and we also call him a haunter of high regions, and a meteorologist, inquiring what is the magnitude of the sun, what are his motions, how he influences the seasons of the year, advancing as he does and retreating back again, with revolutions of equal speed, and investigating as he does the

---

[28] Genesis 17:4.
[29] The text here is very corrupt. Mangey adopts the emendations of Markland, and I have followed his translation.

[30] Genesis 2:19.

subjects of the radiance of the moon, of its shape, of its waning, of its increase, and of the motion of the other stars, whether fixed or wandering; (68) for the inquiry into these matters belongs not to an ill-conditioned or barren soul, but to one which is eminently endowed by nature, and which is able to produce an entire and perfect offspring; on which account the scripture calls the meteorologist, "father," inasmuch as he is not unproductive of wisdom.

X. (69) Now the symbols represented by the name of Abram are thus accurately defined; those conveyed under the name of Abraham are such as we shall proceed to demonstrate. The meanings now are three, "the father," and "elect," and "of sound." Now by the word "sound" here, we mean uttered speech; for the sounding organ of the living animal is the organ of speech. Of this faculty we say that the father is the mind, for it is from the mind, as from a fountain, that the stream of speech proceeds. The word "elect" belongs to the mind of the wise man, for whatever is most excellent is found in him; (70) therefore the man devoted to learning and occupied in the contemplation of sublime subjects, was sketched out according to the former characteristic marks, but the philosopher, or I should rather say the wise man, was exhibited in accordance with those of which we have just given an outline.

Think not, then, any longer that the Deity bestows a change of names, but consider that what he gives is a correction of the moral character by means of symbols; (71) for having invited the nature of heaven, and whom some call a mathematician, to a participation in virtue, he made him wise and called him so. For having given an appropriate name to his transformed disposition, he named him, as the Hebrews would call it, "Abraham," but in the language of the Greeks, "the elect father of sound;" (72) for says he, On what account dost thou investigate the motions and periods of the stars? and why hast thou bounded up so high from the earth to the heavens? Is it merely that you may indulge your curiosity with respect to those matters? And what advantage could accrue to you from all this curiosity? What destruction of pleasure would it cause? What defeat of appetite? What dissolution of pain or fear? What eradication of the passions which disturb and agitate the soul? (73) For as there is no advantage in trees unless they are productive of fruit, so in the same way there is no use in the study of natural philosophy unless it is likely to confer upon a man the acquisition of virtue, for that is its proper fruit.

(74) On which account some of the ancients have compared the discussion and consideration of philosophy to a field, and have likened the physical portion of it to the plants, the logical part to the hedges and fences, the moral part to the fruit, (75) thinking that the walls which are built around

for the sake of protecting the fruit have been erected by the possessors of the land, and that the plants have been created for the sake of the production of fruit; thus, therefore, they said that in philosophy it is requisite for the consideration of the physical and the logical part of philosophy to be referred to the moral part, by which the moral character is improved, which as a desire at the same time for both the acquisition and the use of virtue. (76) This is the lesson which we have been taught concerning the man who in word indeed had his name changed, but who in reality changed his nature from the consideration of natural to that of moral philosophy, and who abandoned the contemplation of the world itself for the knowledge of the Being who created the world; by which knowledge he acquired piety, the most excellent of all possessions.

XI. (77) We will now speak of his wife, Sarah, for she too had her name changed to Sarrah by the addition of the one element, the letter rho. These, then, are the names, and we must now explain what they mean. Sarah, being interpreted, signifies "my authority," but Sarrah signifies "princess;" the former name, (78) therefore, is a symbol of specific virtue, but the latter of generic virtue. But in proportion as genus is superior to species in regard of quantity, in the same proportion does the latter name excel the former; for species is something small and perishable, but genus is numerous and immortal, (79) and the intention of God is to bestow great and immortal things instead of such as are small and perishable, and this is a task suited to his dignity.

Now the prudence which exists in the virtuous man is the authority of himself alone, and he who has it would not err if he were to say, my authority is the prudence which is in me; but that which has stretched out this authority is generic prudence, not any longer the authority of this or that person, but absolute intrinsic authority; therefore that which exists only in species will perish at the same time with its possessor, but that which, like a seal, has stamped it with an impression, is free from all mortality, and will remain for ever and ever imperishable. (80) Thus also those arts which exist only in species perish along with those who have acquired them, such as geometricians, grammarians, and musicians, but the generic arts remain exempt from destruction. And, again, he gives an additional sketch of his meaning when he teaches by the same name that every virtue is a princess, and a queen, and a ruler of all the affairs of life.

XII. (81) But it has also happened that Jacob had his name changed to Israel; and this, too, was a felicitous alteration. Why so? Because the name Jacob means "a supplanter," but the name Israel signifies "the man who sees God." Now it is the employment of a supplanter, who practices virtue, to move, and disturb, and upset the foundations of passion on which it is established, and whatever there is of any strength which is founded on them. But these things are not brought about without a struggle or without severe labour; but only when any one, having gone through all the labours of prudence, then proceeds to practise himself in the exercises of the soul and to wrestle against the reasonings which are hostile to it, and which seek to torment it; but it is the part of him who sees God not to depart from the sacred contest without the crown of victory, but rather to carry off the prize of triumph. (82) And what more flourishing and more suitable crown could be woven for the victorious soul than one by which it will be able acutely and clearly to behold the living God? At least a beautiful prize is thus proposed for the soul which delights in the practice of virtue, namely, the being endowed with sight adequate to the clear comprehension of the only thing which is really worth beholding.

XIII. (83) And it is worth while here to raise the question why Abraham, from the time that his name was changed, is always thought worthy of this same appellation, and is no longer called by his former name; but Jacob, who is also called Israel, is nevertheless called Jacob too, as he was before the change of his name; and, indeed, is called Jacob oftener than Israel.

We must say, then, that these facts are characters by which it is seen that the virtue which is taught differs from that which is acquired by practice; (84) for the man who is improved by instruction, having received a happy and virtuous nature, uses that virtue alone which, by means of memory co-operating with it, implants in him an absence of forgetfulness, so that he comprehends and takes firm hold of all the things which he has once learnt; but he who practices virtue, since he is continually exercising himself, stops to take breath, and relaxes his efforts for a while, collecting himself and recovering the vigour which was a little impaired by his exertions, just as those men do who have oiled their bodies for the contests in the arena. For these men, also, labouring at their training exercises, in order to prevent their powers being utterly broken down, anoint themselves with oil on account of the violent and continued nature of their exercise.

(85) Then the man who is improved by instruction, having an immortal monitor, receives from him a harmonious and imperishable advantage, without suffering any change; but the practiser of virtue is impelled to action by his own inclination alone, and he exercises himself in it, and labours at it in order to change that passion, which is akin to a created being; and even if he attains to perfection, he still, being fatigued, returns to his ancient kind of labour; (86) for he is more inclined to endure toil, but the other is more fortunate, for he has another person as a teacher. But this man,

by his own unassisted efforts, investigates, and inquires, and pushes his examination, investigating the mysteries of nature with great earnestness, and exerting continual and incessant labour.

(87) For this reason God, who never changes, altered the name of Abraham, since he was about to remain in a similar condition, in order that that which was to be firmly established might be confirmed by him who was standing firmly, and who was remaining in the same state in the same manner. But it was an angel who altered the name of Jacob, being the Word, the minister of God; in order that it might be confessed and ascertained, that there is none of the things whose existence is subsequent to that of the living God, which is the cause of unchangeable and unvarying firmness. ... but of that harmony which, as in a musical instrument, contains the intensity and relaxation of sounds so as to produce an artistical combination of melody.

XIV. (88) But, there being three leaders and authors of this race, the two at each extremity of it had their names changed, namely Abraham and Jacob: but the one in the middle, Isaac, always retained the same appellation. Why was this? Because both that virtue which is derived from teaching and that which is attained to by practice, admit of improvement and advancement: for the man who receives instruction desires a knowledge of those matters of which he is ignorant and he who applies himself to practice desires the crowns of victory, and the prizes which are proposed to his industrious and contemplation-loving soul. But the race which is self-taught and which derives all its learning from its own diligence inasmuch as it exists rather by nature than by study, was at the very beginning introduced as equal, and perfect, and even, there being no number whatever deficient of those which tend to completeness.

(89) Nor indeed does Joseph have any such need, he who is the president of the necessities of the body; for he also changes his name, being called Psonthomphanech by the king of the country. And what the meaning of these names is we must explain; the name Joseph, being interpreted, signifies "an addition." For things which are put by the side are an addition to those which exist by nature; for instance, gold, silver, possessions, revenues, the ministrations of servants, abundant treasure of heirlooms, and furniture, and other superfluities, and the infinite multitude of the different efficients of pleasure which some persons possess; (90) the provider and superintendant of which was called Joseph, or addition, by a very felicitous nomenclature: since he had undertaken the superintendence of the things which were to be brought in from without, and added to the natural things previously existing in the course of nature. And the sacred scriptures testify that this is the case, showing that he was the purveyor of

the food of all the corporeal region, Egypt, having stored it up in his treasure-houses.

XV. (91) Such a person as this, then, Joseph is recognized as being by his distinctive marks and name. Let us now see what sort of person is indicated by the name Psonthomphanech. Now this name being interpreted means, "a mouth judging in an answer;" for every foolish person thinks that the man who is very rich and overflowing with external possessions, must at once be wise and sensible, competent to give an answer to any question which any one puts to him, and competent also of his own head to deliver advantageous and sagacious opinions. And, in short, by such men prudence is supposed to be identical with good fortune, while one ought, on the contrary, to consider good fortune as consisting in being prudent; for it is fitting that what is unstable should be under the direction of that which stands firmly.

(92) And indeed his father gave to his own uterine brother the name of Benjamin:[31] but his mother called him the son of her sorrow, speaking most completely in accordance with nature. For the name Benjamin being interpreted means, "the son of days:" and the day is illuminated by the light of the sun which is perceptible by the outward senses: and to this we liken vain glory. (93) For that has a certain brilliancy appreciable by the outward senses in the praises which it receives from the multitude and from the common herd of men, in formally enrolled decrees, in the erection of statues and images, in purple robes and golden crowns, in chariots and teams of four horses, and processions of the multitude. He therefore who is an admirer and desirer of such things is very appropriately called a son of days: that is to say, of that light which is perceptible by the outward senses and of the brilliancy which attends vain glory. (94) This felicitous and appropriate name the elder word and real father imposes on him; but the soul which has suffered gives him a name suited to what she has suffered. For she calls him the son of her sorrow. Why so? Because those men who are borne about by vain glory are supposed indeed to be happy, but in real truth are unhappy. (95) For the things which oppose their happiness are numerous, envy, discontent, emulation, continual strife, irreconcileable enmities lasting till death, hostilities handed down in succession to one's children's children—a destiny not at all to be desired. (96) Very necessarily therefore did the divinely inspired prophet represent that vain glory as dying in the very act of bringing forth; for says he, "Rachel died, having had a bad delivery."[32] Since, in truth and reality, the sowing and generation of vain glory per-

ceptible by the outward senses is the death of the soul.

XVI. (97) And what shall we say of the sons of Joseph, Ephraim and Manasseh? Are they not, in strict accordance with nature, compared to the two eldest sons of Jacob, Reuben and Simeon? For the scripture says, "Thy two sons who were born in Egypt, before that I came into Egypt, belong to me; Ephraim and Manasseh shall be to me as Reuben and as Simeon."[33] Let us now then see in what manner the one pair are likened to the other pair.

(98) Reuben is the symbol of a good natural disposition, for the name being interpreted means, "A seeing son;" since every one who is endowed with tolerable acuteness of mind and a good disposition is capable of seeing; and Ephraim, as we have already frequently said in other places, is a symbol of memory, for his name being interpreted signifies, "productiveness of fruit," and the most excellent fruit of the soul is memory; and there is no one thing so nearly akin to another as remembering is to a man of good natural endowments. (99) Again, the name of Simeon is a symbol of learning and instruction; for, being interpreted, it signifies "listening," and it is the especial part of a learner to listen and attend to what is said. But Manasseh is a symbol of "recollection," for thus that art is called, from forgetfulness; (100) for it must of necessity happen to the man who has advanced out of forgetfulness to recollect, and recollecting especially belongs to learning, for very often his notions escape from the man who is learning, as out of weakness he is unable to retain them, and then again they return to him as at the beginning.

The condition therefore which arises from this escaping of his notions is denominated forgetfulness, and that which arises from their returning to him is called recollection. (101) Now is not memory very naturally spoken of as connected with good natural endowments, and recollection as akin to learning? And, indeed, the same relation which Simeon bears to Reuben, that is to say, learning to natural endowment, the same does Manasseh bear to Ephraim, and the same does recollection bear to memory. (102) For as the man of good natural endowments is better than he who is only a learner, for the one resembles the sense of seeing, the other that of hearing, and hearing is always reckoned as entitled to a lesser honour than seeing; so also, he who is endowed with a good memory is at all times superior to him who only recollects, because the one is combined with forgetfulness, but the other continues unalloyed and unadulterated from beginning to end.

---

[31] Genesis 35:18.
[32] Genesis 35:16.

[33] Genesis 48:5.

XVII. (103) And indeed the scriptures at one time call the father-in-law of the first prophets Jother, and at another time Raguel-Jother, when pride is flourishing and at its height; for the name Jother being interpreted means "superfluous," and pride is superfluous in an honest and sincere life, turning into ridicule, as it does, all that is equal and necessary to life, and honouring the unequal things of excess and covetousness. (104) This passion honours human things above divine, and customs above laws, and profane above sacred things, and mortal above immortal things, and, in short, appearances above reality; and it even ventures of its accord to pass on into the rank of counsellors, suggesting to the wise man not to teach those things which alone are worthy to be known, namely, "the commandments of God, and the law,"[34] but to study the covenants and contracts of men with one another, which are almost the causes of the society which exists among them being so little sociable.

But the great man is obedient in all things, thinking that little things are adapted to little people, and that great things are justly added to the great; (105) but very often this man who is wise in his own conceit, and who, passing over from the herds which the blind had assigned to him for him to guide, having sought out the divine herd, becomes no small portion of it; admiring the leader of nature, and marvelling at his way of leading which he employs in his care of his own flocks, for the name Raguel being interpreted, signifies the "pastoral care of God."[35]

XVIII. (106) The main part has now been explained; we will now proceed to adduce the proofs. In the first place the scripture represents him as the cultivator of judgment and of justice, for the name Midian, being interpreted, means "out of judgment." And this is said in a twofold sense, for some times it signifies both selection and rejection, such as usually happens to those who are competitors in those contests which are called sacred; for numbers as they appear not qualified, are rejected by the masters of the games. (107) These are the men who have been initiated in the unholy rites of Beelphegor,[36] and having widened all the mouths of the body to enable them to receive the streams which are poured into them from without, for the name Beelphegor is interpreted "the mouth above the skin," for they have overwhelmed the mind, the governor of the body, and have sunk it down to the lowest depth, so that it can never emerge, nor even hold up its head in ever so slight a degree.

(108) And it suffered this until Phineas, the lover of peace and manifest priest of God, came as a champion of his own accord, being by nature a hater of all that is evil, and filled with an admiration and desire for what is good; and as he took a coadjutor, that is to say, the well sharpened and sharp-edged sword, competent to investigate and examine everything, he could not be deceived, but exerting a vigorous strength, he pierced passion through her womb, that it might not hereafter bring forth any divinely caused evil. (109) Now between these men and the seeing race there is a terrible war, in which no one of the combatants differed in language,[37] but each returned home unwounded and safe, crowned with the garlands of victory.

XIX. (110) This now is one of the things which are shown by the name of Midian; another is that more excellent and judicial species which by the affinity of marriage is connected with the prophetic race. The scripture then says, "The priest of judgment and justice" (that is to say, of Midian) "has seven daughters;"[38] (111) by which seven daughters are frequently intimated the powers of the irrational part of the soul, the power of generation and the voice, and the five outward senses, tending the flocks of their father; for by means of these seven powers it is that all the progresses and increases of their father, the mind, exist in the perceptions which are produced from him. These, then, coming each to its appropriate object, the power of sight to colours and shapes, the sense of hearing to sounds, the faculty of smelling to scents, taste to flavours, and all the other faculties to those objects which are adapted for their exercise do in a manner imbibe some of the external objects of the outward senses, until they have filled all the channels of the soul, and from these channels they give drink to the sheep of their father; I mean by these sheep that most pure flock of the reason which bears safety and ornament at the same time.

(112) But the companions of envy and jealousy, the leaders of the wicked herd coming up, drive them away from that use of their powers which is in accordance with nature, for some conduct these things which are without, inwards to the mind as to a judge and a king, in order that they may do well from having the most excellent of governors; (113) but others take the opposite side, pursuing and proclaiming the exact contrary, while it is possible for the mind to be drawn towards them, and to give up the flock which was entrusted to it to feed.[39] Until the good disposition, devoted to virtue and inspired by God, which for awhile has appeared to be resting in inactivity, by name

---

[34] Exodus 18:11.
[35] Exodus 2:18.
[36] Numbers 25:3.

[37] Exodus 31:29.
[38] Exodus 2:16.
[39] This passage is very corrupt in the original. I have followed Mangey in adopting the corrections of Marsland.

Moses, holds his shield over them and defends them from those who would attack them, nourishing the flock of his father on wholesome words, (114) and they having escaped the attack of the enemies of intellect who admire only the external appendages, like people in tragedies, go no longer to Jother but to Raguel, for they have abandoned all connections with pride, and having connected themselves with lawful persuasion, choosing to become a portion of the sacred flock, of which the divine word is the leader, as his name shows, for it signifies the pastoral care of God.

XX. (115) But while he is taking care of his own flock, all kinds of good things are given all at once to those of the sheep who are obedient, and who do not resist his will; and in the Psalms we find a song in these words, "The Lord is my shepherd, therefore shall I lack nothing;"[40] (116) therefore the mind which has had the royal shepherd, the divine word, for its instructor, will very naturally ask of his seven daughters, "Why is it that you have contended with such great haste to come hither this day?"[41] for formerly, when you met with the objects of the outward sense, remaining a long time outside, you were a long time in returning again by reason of the manner in which you were allured by them, but now I do not know what it is that has happened to you, but you are speedy in your return, contrary to your usual custom.

(117) Therefore they will say that there were not the same causes why they should run back with such exceeding speed, making the double course from the objects of the outward sense and to the objects of the outward sense, without stopping to take breath, and with excessive impetuosity; but that the cause was rather the man who delivered them from the shepherds of the wild flock.

And they call Moses an Egyptian, a man who was not only a Hebrew, but even a Hebrew of the very purest race, of the only tribe which is consecrated, because they are unable to rise above their own nature; (118) for the outward senses, being on the confines between the objects of the intellect and those of the outward senses, we must be content if they aim at both of them, and are not allured by the objects of the outward sense alone. And to think that they are inclined only to attend to the things which are purely objects of the intellect is great folly; on which account they give him both these names, since when they call him a man, they indicate the things which are within the province of reason alone to contemplate, and when they call him an Egyptian, they indicate the objects of the external senses.

(119) When they had heard this, he will again inquire, "Where is the man?" In what part of you is the reasonable species dwelling? Why have you left it so easily, and have not rather after having once met with it, preserved that which was the most beautiful of possessions, and the most advantageous for yourselves? (120) But even if you have not done so before, at least call it to you now, that it may eat of and be supported by your improvement and your close connection with him; for perhaps he will even dwell with you, and will bring with him the winged, and divinely inspired, and prophetical race by name Zipporah.

XXI. (121) Thus much we have thought fit to say on this subject. But, moreover, Moses also changes the name of Hosea into that of Joshua; displaying by his new name the distinctive qualities of his character; (122) for the name Hosea is interpreted, "what sort of a person is this?" but Joshua means "the salvation of the Lord," being the name of the most excellent possible character; for the habits are better with respect to those persons who are of such and such qualities from being influenced by them: as, for instance, music is better in a musician, physic in a physician, and each art of a distinctive quality in each artist, regarded both in its perpetuity, and in its power, and in its unerring perfection with regard to the objects of its speculation. For a habit is something everlasting, energising, and perfect; but a man of such and such a quality is mortal, the object of action, and imperfect. And what is imperishable is superior to what is mortal, the efficient cause is better than that which is the object of action; and what is perfect is preferable to what is imperfect. (123) In this way the coinage of the above mentioned description was changed and received the stamp of a better kind of appearance.

And Caleb himself was changed wholly and entirely; "For," as the scripture says, "a new spirit was in him;"[42] as if the dominant part in him had been changed into complete perfection; for the name Caleb, being interpreted, means "the whole heart." (124) And a proof of this is to be gathered from the fact that the mind is changed, not by being biassed and inclining in one particular direction or the other, but wholly and entirely in the direction which is good; and that, even if there is any thing which is not very praiseworthy indeed, it makes that to depart by arguments conducive to repentance; for, having in this manner washed off all the defilements which polluted it, and having availed itself of the baths and purifications of wisdom, it must inevitably look brilliant.

XXII. (125) But it happens to the arch-prophet to have many names: for when he interprets and explains the oracles which are delivered by God, he is called Moses; and when he prays for and

---

[40]Psalm 23:1.
[41]Exodus 2:18.

[42]Numbers 14:24.

blesses the people, he is called the man of God;[43] and when Egypt is paying the penalty of its impious actions, he is then denominated the god of him who is the king of the country, namely, of Pharaoh.[44] And why is all this? (126) Because to alter a code of laws for the advantage of those who are to use them is the part of a man who is always handling divine things, and having them in his hands; and who is called a lawgiver by the all-knowing God, and who has received from him a great gift—the interpretation of the sacred laws, and the spirit of prophecy in accordance with them. For the name Moses, being translated, signifies "gain," and it also means handling, for the reasons which I have already enumerated. (127) But to pray and to bless are not the duties of any ordinary man, but they belong to one who has not admitted any connection with created things, but who has devoted himself to God, the governor and the father of all men. (128) And any one must be content to whom it has been allowed to use the privilege of blessing. And to be able also to procure good for others belongs to a greater and more perfect soul, and is the profession of one who is really inspired by God, which he who has attained to may reasonably be called God.

But also, this same person is God, inasmuch as he is wise, and as on this account he rules over every foolish person, even if such foolish person be established and strengthened by a haughty sceptre, and be ever so proud on this account; (129) for the Ruler of the universe, even though some persons are about to be punished for intolerable acts of wickedness, nevertheless is willing to admit some intercessors to mediate on their behalf, who, in imitation of the merciful power of the father, exercise their power of punishment with more moderation and humanity; but to do good is the peculiar attribute of God.

XXIII. (130) Having now discussed at sufficient length the subject of change and alteration of names, we will turn to the matters which come next in order in our proposed examination. Immediately after the events which we have just mentioned, came the birth of Isaac; for after God had given to his mother the name of Sarrah instead of Sarah, he said to Abraham, "I will give unto thee a son."[45] We must consider each of the things here indicated particularly. (131) Now he who is properly said to give any thing whatever must by all means be giving what is his own private property. And if this is true beyond controversy, then it would follow that Isaac must not have been a man, but a being synonymous with that most exquisite joy of all pleasures, namely, laughter, the adopted son

of God, who gave him as a soother and cheerer to the most peace-loving souls; (132) for it is absurd to suppose that there was one who was a man, and another of whom bastard and illegitimate offspring were descended: and, indeed, Moses calls the man of an intellect devoted to virtue a god, when he says, "The Lord, seeing that Leah was hated, opened her womb."[46] (133) For having felt compassion and pity for virtue as being hated by the race of mankind, and for the soul which loves virtue, he makes the nature which loves beauty barren, but opens the fountain of fecundity and gives it a prosperous labour.

(134) But Tamar, when she became pregnant of divine seeds, and did not know who it was who had sown them (for it is said that at that time "she had covered her face," as Moses did when he turned away, having a reverential fear of beholding God), still when she saw the tokens and the evidences and decided within herself that it was not a mortal man who gave these things, cried out, "To whomsoever these things belong, it is by him that I am with child."[47] (135) Whose was the ring, or the pledge, or the seal of the whole, or the archetypal appearance, according to which all the things, though devoid of species and of distinctive quality, were all stamped and marked? And whose again was the armlet, or the ornament; that is to say, destiny, the link and analogy of all things which have an indissoluble connection? Whose, again, was the staff, the thing of strong support, which wavers not, which is not moved; that is to say, admonition, correction, instruction? Whose is the sceptre, the kingly power? (136) does it not belong to God alone? Therefore, the disposition inclined to confession, that is to say, Judah, being pleased at her possessed and inspired condition, speaks freely, saying, "She has spoken justly, because I gave her in marriage to no mortal man;"[48] thinking it an impious thing to pollute divine with profane things.

XXIV. (137) And wisdom, which, after the fashion of a mother, has conceived and brought fourth the self-taught race, points out that it is God who is the sower of it; for, after the offspring is brought forth, she speaks magnificently, saying, "The Lord has caused me laughter;"[49] an expression equivalent to, he has fashioned, he has made, he has begotten Isaac, since Isaac is the same with laughter. (138) But it does not belong to every one to hear this sound, since the evil of superstition is very widely spread among us, and has overwhelmed many unmanly and ignoble souls; on which account she adds, "For whoever hears this will not rejoice with me." As if those persons were

---

[43]Deuteronomy 33:1.
[44]Exodus 7:1.
[45]Genesis 17:16.

[46]Genesis 29:31.
[47]Genesis 38:25.
[48]Genesis 17:26.
[49]Genesis 21:6.

very few whose ears are opened and pricked up so as to be inclined to the reception of these sacred words, which teach that it is the peculiar employment of the only God to sow and to beget what is good; to which words all other persons are deaf.

(139) And I know that this illustrious oracle was formerly delivered from the mouth of the prophet. "Thy fruit has been found from me: who is wise and will understand these things? who is prudent and will know them?"[50] But I have observed, and comprehended, and admired him who causes to resound, and who himself, invisible as he is, does in an invisible manner strike the organ of the voice; being amazed also at the same time at what was uttered. (140) For if there be any good thing among existing things, that, or I should rather say the whole heaven and the whole world, if one must tell the truth, is the fruit of God; being preserved upon his eternal and ever-flourishing nature as upon a tree. But it belongs to wise and understanding men to understand and to confess such things as these, and not to the ignorant.

XXV. (141) We have now then explained what is meant by the words, "I will give unto thee." We must now explain the words, "out of her." Some now have understood them as meaning that which exists out of her, thinking that it has been most correctly decided by right reason that the soul never displays any peculiar beauty of its own, but only such as comes to it from without, in accordance with the greatness of the good will of God who showers his graces upon it. (142) But others understand these words to mean instant rapidity; for that the words (*ex autēs*, which we have translated) "out of her," are here equivalent to, "at once, immediately, without any delay, without hesitation." And it is in this way that the gifts of God usually come to men, outstripping the differences of time.

There is a third class of persons who say, that virtue is the mother of all created good, without having received the seed of it from any mortal man; (143) and to those who ask, whether she who is barren has an offspring (for the holy scriptures, which some time ago represented Sarrah as barren, now confess that she will become a mother); this answer must be given, that a woman who is barren cannot, in the course of nature, bring forth an offspring, just as a blind man cannot see, nor a deaf man hear; but that the soul, which is barren of bad things, and which is unproductive of immoderate license of the passions and vices, is alone very nearly attaining to a happy delivery, bringing forth objects worthy of love, namely, the number seven, according to the hymn which is sung by Grace, that is, by Hannah, who says, "she who was barren hath born seven, and she who had many

children has become weak:"[51] (144) and what she means by, "She who has many children," is the mind, which being pregnant of mixed and promiscuous reasonings, from all quarters confused together, by reason of the multitudes which crowd around her, and of the disorder which they cause, brings forth incurable evils; and by "she who was barren," she means that the mind which had never received any mortal seed, as if it were productive of offspring, but has avoided and shunned all association and all connection with the wicked, and clings to the seventh, and to the most peaceful numbers in accordance with it, for it deserves to be pregnant of it, and to be called its mother.

XXVI. (145) This then is the meaning of the words, "out of her." We must now consider the third point, namely, what that is which is called her son. In the first place, then, there is this worthy of our admiration, that God does not say that he will give her many children, but that he will give her one only. And why is this? Because it is the nature of what is good to be investigated, not so much with respect to its number or magnitude, as with respect to its power; (146) for musical precepts, to take them for an instance, or rules of grammar, or of geometry, or of justice, or of wisdom, or of manly courage, or of temperance, are very numerous indeed; but the science itself of music, or grammar, or geometry, and still more the virtue of justice, or temperance, or wisdom, or manly courage, is only one thing, the loftiest perfection, in no respect differing from the archetypal model, after which all those numerous and countless precepts were formed.

(147) And this is why he only says that he will give her one son. And now he called it a son, not speaking carelessly or inconsiderately, but for the sake of showing that it is not a foreign, or a supposititious, nor an adopted, nor an illegitimate child, but a legitimate child, a proper citizen, inasmuch as a foreign child cannot be the offspring of a truly citizen soul, for the Greek word *teknon* (son), is derived from *tokos* (bringing forth), by way of showing the kindred by which children are, by nature, united to their parents.

XXVII. (148) And, says God, "I will bless her, and she shall be a mother of nations;"[52] because, not only is generic virtue divided into its proximate species, and into individuals subordinate to the species, as if into nations; but also because, as there are nations of living animals, so in a manner are there nations of things, to which virtue is a very great advantage; (149) for all things which are devoid and destitute of wisdom are mischievous, just as all places upon which the sun does not shine are of necessity dark; for it is by virtue

---

[50] Hosea 14:9.

[51] 1 Samuel 2:5.
[52] Genesis 17:16.

that a farmer is able to pay better attention to his crops, and by virtue that a charioteer drives his chariot in the horse-races so as to avoid falling; and by virtue too, that a pilot and a steersman guides his vessel in its voyage. (150) Virtue again has caused houses, and cities, and countries to be inhabited in a better manner, making men competent to manage houses and cities, and fit to associate with one another. Virtue has also introduced most excellent laws, and has sown the seeds of peace everywhere; since, from the contrary habit, things of a contrary character do naturally arise— war, lawlessness, bad constitutions, confusion, unnecessary voyages, overthrows, that which, in science, is the most grievous of all diseases, namely, cunning, from which, instead of art, all kinds of evil artifice has flowed. Very necessarily, therefore, will virtue be divided among all nations, which are large and collected systems of living beings and things taken together, for the advantage of those who receive her.

XXVIII. (151) Immediately afterwards it is said, "And kings of the nations shall be born of her." For those with whom she is pregnant and whom she brings forth are all rulers; not because they have been elected as such for a short period by lot, which is an uncertain thing, or by the show of hands of men who are for the most part bribed, but because they have been destined and appointed so for everlasting by nature herself. (152) And these are not my words only, but those of the most holy scriptures, in which certain persons are introduced as saying to Abraham, "Thou art a king from God among us;"[53] not out of consideration for his resources (for what resources could a man have who was an emigrant and who had no city to inhabit, but who was wandering over a great extent of impassable country?), but because they saw that he had a royal disposition in his mind, so that they confessed, in the words of Moses, that he was the only wise king.

(153) For in real truth the wise man is the king of those who are foolish, since he knows what he ought and what he ought not to do; and the temperate man is the king of the intemperate, as he has attained to no careless or inaccurate knowledge of what relates to choice and avoidance. Also the brave man is king over the cowardly, inasmuch as he has thoroughly learnt what he ought to endure and what he ought not. So too the just man is king of the unjust, as he is possessed of the knowledge of undeviating equality as to what is to be distributed. And the holy man is king over the unholy, as he is possessed with the most just and excellent notions of God.

XXIX. (154) It was natural then for the mind, being puffed up by these promises, to be elated and raised to an undue height in its own estimation; and accordingly, by way of producing conviction in us, who were accustomed to hold up our heads at the slightest trifles, "it falls down and immediately laughs the laughter of the soul," looking mournful as to its face, but smiling in its mind a great and unmixed joy having entered into it: (155) and both these feelings, namely, to laugh and also to fall, do at the same time occur to a wise man who inherits good things beyond his expectation; the one being his fate, as a proof that he is not over-proud because of his thorough knowledge of his mortal nothingness; and the other, by way of a confirmation of his piety on account of his looking upon God as the sole cause of all graces and of all good things.

(156) Let, then, the creature fall down and wear a melancholy countenance very naturally; for it has no stability in its own nature, and as far as that goes is easily dissolved; but let it be raised up again by God, and laugh, for he alone is the support and joy of it.

(157) And here any one may reasonably express a doubt how it is possible for any one to laugh when laughter had not as yet come among one branch of the creation; for Isaac is laughter, who, according to the account under our consideration at present, was not yet born. For just as it is impossible to see without eyes, or to hear without ears, or to smell without nostrils, or to exert any other of the external senses without the organs adapted to each respectively, or to comprehend without the reason, so also it is not likely that a person can have laughed, if laughter had not as yet been made. (158) What, then, are we to say? Nature foreshows many of the things which are hereafter to happen by certain symbols. Do you not see how the young bird, before it commits itself to the air, is fond of fluttering its wings and shaking its pinions, giving a previous happy indication of its hope that it will be able to fly? (159) And have you never seen a lamb, or a kid, or an ox, while still young, and before his horns are as yet grown and noticed, if by chance any one irritates him, how he opposes him, and moves forward to defend himself with those parts in which nature has planted his arms for defence? (160) And in the battles which take place with wild beasts, the bulls do not at once gore the adversaries who are opposed to them, but standing well apart, and relaxing their neck in a moderate degree and bending their heads on one side, and looking fierce, as it were, they then, after a truce, rush on with the determination of persevering in the contest. And this sort of conduct those who are in the habit of inventing new words call "sparring," being a sort of sham attack before the real one.

XXX. (161) And the soul is subject to many things of much the same kind. For when something good is hoped for it rejoices beforehand, so

---

[53] Genesis 23:6.

that in a manner it rejoices before its joy, and is delighted before its delight. And one may also compare this to what happens with respect to plants; for they, too, when they are about to bear fruit, bud beforehand and flower previously, and are green previously.

(162) Look at the cultivated vine, how marvellously it is furnished by nature with young shoots, and tendrils, and suckers, and leaves redolent of wine, which, though they utter no voice, do nevertheless indicate the joy of the tree at the coming fruit. And the day also laughs in anticipation of the early dawn, when the sun is about to rise; for one ray is a messenger of another, and one beam of light, as the forerunner of another though more obscure, is still a herald of that which shall be brighter.

(163) Therefore, joy accompanies a good when it is already arrived, and hope while it is expected. For we rejoice when it is come, and we hope while it is coming; just as in the case also with the contrary feelings; for the presence of evil brings us grief, and the expectation of evil generates fear, and fear is nothing more than grief before grief, as hope is joy before joy. For the same relation that, I imagine, fear bears to grief, that same does hope bear to joy. (164) And the external senses afford very manifest proofs of what has now been said; for smell, sitting as it were in front of taste, pronounces judgment beforehand on almost every thing which is eaten and drunk; from which fact some persons have very felicitously named it the foretaster, having a regard to its employment. And so hope is by nature adapted to have as it were a foretaste of the coming good: and to represent it to the soul, which is to have a firm possession of it.

(165) Moreover, when any one who is engaged in a journey is hungry or thirsty, if he on a sudden sees a fountain or all kinds of trees weighed down with eatable fruits, he is at once filled with a hope of enjoyment, not only before he has either eaten or drunk, but before he has either come near them or gathered of them. And do we then think that we are able to feast on the nourishment of the body before we receive it, but that the food of the mind is not able to render us cheerful beforehand, even when we are on the very point of feasting on it?

XXXI. (166) He laughed then very naturally, even though laughter did not as yet appear to have been scattered among the human race: and not only did he laugh but the woman also laughed; for it is said presently, "And Sarrah laughed in herself, saying, There has never up to the present time come any good unto me of its own accord without care on my part; but he who has promised is my Lord, and is older than all creation, and him I must of necessity believe." (167) And at the same time it also teaches us that virtue is naturally a thing to be rejoiced at, and that he who

possesses it is at all times rejoiced; and, on the contrary, that vice is a painful thing, and that he who possesses that is most miserable.

And do we even now marvel at those philosophers who affirm that virtue consists in apathy? (168) For, behold, Moses is found to be the leader of this wise doctrine, as he represents the good man as rejoicing and laughing. And in other passages he not only speaks of him in that way, but also of all those who come to the same place with him; for he says, "And when he seeth thee he will rejoice in himself;"[54] as if the bare sight of a good man were by itself sufficient to fill the mind with cheerfulness while the soul would cast off its most fearful burden, sorrow.

(169) But it is not allowed to every wicked man to rejoice, as it is said in the predictions of the prophet, "There is no rejoicing for the wicked, says God."[55] For this is truly a divine saying and oracle, that the life of every wicked man is melancholy, and sad, and full of unhappiness, even if with his face he pretends to feel happiness; (170) for I should not say that the Egyptians rejoiced in reality when they heard that the brethren of Joseph were come, but that they only feigned joy, putting on a false appearance like hypocrites; for no convictor, when standing by and pressing upon a foolish man is a pleasure to him, just as no physician is to an intemperate man who is sick; for labour attends on what is useful, and laziness on what is hurtful. And those who prefer laziness to labour are very naturally hated by those who advise them to a course which will be useful and laborious.

(171) When, therefore, you hear that "Pharaoh and all his servants rejoiced on account of the arrival of Joseph's brethren,"[56] do not think that they rejoiced in reality, unless perhaps in this sense, that they expected that he would become changed from the good things of the soul in which he had been brought up, and would come over to the profitless appetites of the body, having adulterated the ancient and hereditary coinage of that virtue which was akin to him.

XXXII. (172) The mind, then, which is devoted to pleasure, having entertained these hopes, does not think that it is sufficient to attract the younger men, and those who are as yet only attending the school of temperance, by its allurements; but it looks upon it as a terrible thing, if it cannot also bring over the elder reasoning, the more impetuous passions of which have now passed their prime; (173) for in a subsequent passage Joseph says to them, proposing injuries to them as though they were benefits, "Now, therefore, bringing with you your father and all your possessions, come

---

[54] Exodus 4:14.
[55] Isaiah 47:22.
[56] Genesis 45:16.

hither to me;"[57] speaking in this way of Egypt and of that terrible king who drags back all our paternal inheritance and the good things which really belong to us and which have advanced beyond the body (for by nature they are free), endeavoring by force to surrender them to a very bitter prison, having, as the holy scripture tells us, "appointed as guardian of the prison Pentaphres, the eunuch and chief cook,"[58] who was a man in great want of all that is good, and who had been deprived of the generative parts of the soul; and who was also unable to sow and to plant any of those things which bear upon instruction; but who like a cook slew the living animals, and cut them up and divided them in different portions limb by limb, and who wallowed about in dead and lifeless bodies and things equally, and who, by his superfluous preparations and refinements, excited and stirred up the appetites of the profitless passions, while it was natural to expect that those who were able to tame them should mollify. (174) And he also says, "I will give unto you all the good things of Egypt, and you shall eat of the marrow of the earth."[59]

But we will say unto him, We who keep our eyes fixed on the good things of the soul do not desire those of the body. For that most delicious desire of the former things, when once implanted in the mind, is well calculated to engender a forgetfulness of all those things which are dear to the flesh.

XXXIII. (175) Something like this, then, is the falsely named joy of the foolish. But the true joy has already been described, which is adapted only to the virtuous, "Therefore, falling down he laughed."[60] Not falling from God, but from himself; for he stood near the unchangeable God, but he fell from his own vain opinion. (176) On which account that pride which was wise in its own conceit, having been thrown down, and the feeling which is devoted to God having been raised in its place, and been established around the only unalterable being, he, immediately laughing, said in his mind, "Shall a child be born to one who is a hundred years old, and shall Sarrah, who is ninety years old, have a child?" (177) Do not fancy, my good friend, that the word, "he said" not with his mouth but "in his mind,"[61] has been added for no especial use; on the contrary, it is inserted with great accuracy and propriety. Why so? Because it seems by his saying, "Shall a child be born to him who is a hundred years old?" that he had a doubt about the birth of Isaac, in which he was previously stated to believe; as what was predicted a little before showed, speaking thus, "This child

shall not be thy heir, but he who shall come out of thee;" and immediately afterward he says, "Abraham believed in the Lord, and it was counted to him for righteousness."

(178) Since then it was not consistent for one who had already believed to doubt, he has represented the doubt as of no long continuance, extending only as far as the mouth of the tongue, and stopping there at the mind which is endowed with such celerity of motion; for, says the scripture, "he said in his mind," which nothing, and no person ever so celebrated for swiftness of foot, could ever be able to outstrip, since it outruns even all the winged natures; (179) on which account the most illustrious of all of the Greek poets appears to me to have said:—

"Swift as a winged bird or fleeter thought."[62]

Showing by these words the exceeding speed of its promptitude, placing the thought after the winged bird as a sort of climax; for the mind advances at the same moment to very many things and bodies, hurrying on with indescribable impetuosity, and without a moment's lapse of time it speeds at once to the borders of both earth and sea, bringing together and dividing infinite magnitudes by a single word; and at the same time it soars to such a height above the earth, that it penetrates through the air and reaches even the aether, and scarcely stops at the very furthest circle of the fixed stars.

(180) For the fervid and glowing heat of that region does not suffer to rest tranquil; on which account, overleaping many things, it is borne far beyond every boundary perceptible by the outward senses, to that which is compounded of ideas and appearances by the law of kindred. On which account in the good man there is a slight change, indivisible, unapportionable, not perceptible by the outward senses, but only by the intellect, and being in a manner independent of them.

XXXIV. (181) But, perhaps, some one may say, What then? is he who has once believed bound never to admit the slightest trace, or shadow, or moment of incredulity at all? But this man appears to me to have nothing else in his mind except an idea of proving the creature uncreated, and the mortal immortal, and the corruptible incorruptible, and man, if it be lawful to say so, God. (182) For he says that the belief which man has once conceived ought to be so firm as in no respect to differ from that which is entertained of the truly living God and which is complete in every part; for Moses, in his greater hymn, says, "God is faithful, and there is no unrighteousness in him."[63]

---

[57] Genesis 45:18.
[58] Genesis 39:1.
[59] Genesis 45:18.
[60] Genesis 17:17.
[61] Genesis 17:20.

[62] Homer, Odyssey 8.171.
[63] Deuteronomy 32:4.

(183) And it is great folly to fancy that the soul of man is able to contain the virtues of God, which never vary and which are established on the most solid footing; for it is sufficient, and one must be content to have been able to acquire the images of them, though they are inferior to the archetypal patterns by many and large numbers. (184) And is not this reasonable? for it follows of necessity that the virtues of God must be pure and unmixed, since God is not a compound being, inasmuch as he is a single nature; on the other hand, the virtues of men must be mixed with some alloy, since we ourselves are compounds, the divine and human nature being combined in us, and adapted together according to the principles of perfect music; and that which is composed of many separate things has a natural attraction to each of its parts. (185) But he is happy to whom it has happened that for the greater portion of his life he has inclined towards the more excellent and more divine part; for that he should have done so all his life is impossible, since at times the mortal weight which is opposed to him has preponderated in the opposite scale, and impending over his mind, has kept watch for the opportunities of coming upon his reason at an unfavourable time, so as to drag it back again.

XXXV. (186) Abraham therefore believed in God; but he believed as a man; that you may be aware of the peculiar attribute of mortals, and may learn that his fall did not happen to him in any other way than in consequence of the ordinances of nature. And if it was of short duration and only momentary, it is a thing to be thankful for: for many other men have been so overturned by the violence and impetuosity of error, and by its irresistible force, that they have been utterly destroyed for ever. (187) For know, my good man, that, according to the most holy Moses, virtue is not perfect in the human body, but it suffers something like torpor, and is often ever so little lame. For says the scripture, "The broader part of his thigh became torpid, on which he was lame."[64] (188) And perhaps some man of an over-confident disposition may come forward and say that this is not the language of one who disbelieves, but of one praying, so that if that most excellent of all the happy feelings were about to be produced, it would not be brought forth according to any other number than that of ninety years, that so the perfect good might arrive at its production according to perfect numbers.

(189) But the aforesaid numbers are perfect, and especially according to the sacred scriptures. And let us consider each of them: now first of all there is the son of the just Noah and the ancestor of the seeing race, and he is said to have been a hundred years old when he begat Arphaxad,[65] and the meaning of the name of Arphaxad is, "he disturbed sorrow." At all events it is a good thing that the offspring of the soul should confuse, and disorder, and destroy that miserable thing iniquity, so full of evils.

(190) But Abraham also planted a field,[66] using the ratio of an hundred for the measurement of the ground: and Isaac found some barley yielding a hundred fold.[67] And Moses also made the vestibule of the sacred tabernacle in a hundred arches,[68] measuring out the distance towards the east and towards the west. (191) Moreover the ratio of a hundred is the first fruit of the first fruit which the Levites assign to those who are consecrated to the priesthood;[69] for after they have taken the tenth from the nation they are enjoined to give unto the priests a sacred tenth of the whole share, as if from their own possessions. (192) And if a person were to consider, he might find many other instances to the praise of the aforesaid number brought forward in the law of Moses, but for the present what have been enumerated are sufficient. But if from the hundred you set aside the tenth part as a sacred first fruit to God who produces, and increases, and brings to perfection the fruit of the soul—for how can it be anything but perfect, inasmuch as it is on the confines between the first and the tenth, in the same manner in which the Holy of Holies is separated by the veil in the middle. [...][70] by which those things which are of the same genus are divided according to the differences in species?

XXXVI. (193) Therefore the good man was speaking and saying things which were really good in his mind. But the bad man at times interprets good things in a very excellent manner, but nevertheless does shameful things in a most shameful one, as Shechem does who is the offspring of folly. For he is the son of Hamon his father, and the name Hamon, being translated, means "an ass," but the name Shechem means "a shoulder" when interpreted, the symbol of labour. But that labour of which folly is the parent is miserable and full of suffering, as, on the other hand, that labour is useful to which prudence is related. (194) Accordingly the holy scriptures tell us that, "Shechem spake according to the mind of the virgin, having first humbled her."[71] It is not said then, with great purpose and accuracy, that he spake according to the mind of the damsel, for the purpose of showing distinctly that he acted in a contrary manner to

---

[64] Genesis 32:25.

[65] Genesis 11:10.
[66] Genesis 21:33.
[67] Genesis 26:12.
[68] Exodus 27:9.
[69] Numbers 18:28.
[70] There is an hiatus in the text here.
[71] Genesis 34:3.

that in which he spoke? For Dinah means "incorruptible judgment:" justice the attribute seated by God, the everlasting virgin; for the name Dinah, being interpreted, means either thing, "judgment" or "justice."

(195) Fools, then, laying violent hands upon and attempting to defile her, by means of their daily designs and practices, by their plausibility of speech escape conviction. Therefore they must either act in a manner consistent with the language that they hold, or else they must hold their tongues while committing iniquity. For it is said, "Silence is one half of evil:" as Moses says when rebuking the man who accounted the creature worthy of the principal honour, and the immortal God worthy only of the second place, "Thou has sinned, be silent." (196) For to use bombastic language, and to boast of one's evil deeds, is a double sin: and men in general are very prone to this; for they are constantly saying what is pleasing to the ever-virgin virtue, and such things as are just: but they never omit any opportunity of insulting and violating her when they are able.

For what city is there which is not full of those who are continually celebrating the praises of virtue?—(197) men who weary the ears of those who hear them by everlastingly dwelling on such subjects as these; wisdom is a necessary good; folly is pernicious; temperance is desirable; intemperance is hateful; courage is a thing proper to be cultivated; cowardice must be avoided; justice is advantageous; injustice is disadvantageous; holiness is honourable; unholiness is shameful; piety towards the gods is praiseworthy; impiety is blameable; that which is most akin to the nature of man is to design, and to act, and to speak virtuously; that which is most alien from his nature is to do the contrary of all these things.

(198) By continually stringing together these and similar aphorisms they deceive the courts of justice, and the council chambers, and the theatres, and every assembly and company which they meet; as men who put beautiful masks on ugly faces, with the intention of not being discovered by those who see them. (199) But it is of no use; for some persons will come endowed with great vigour, and occupied with a real zeal and admiration for virtue, and who will strip them of all their coverings, and disguises, and appendages which they had woven round themselves by the evil artifice of plausible speeches, and will display their soul naked by itself as it really is, and will make themselves acquainted with the secret things of their nature which are hidden as it were in recesses. And then having brought to light all its shame and all the reproaches to which it is liable, they will display them in broad daylight to every one, and show what sort of thing it is, how disgraceful and ridiculous, and what a spurious kind

of beauty it has disguised itself with by means of its appendages and coverings.

(200) And those who are prepared to avenge themselves on such profane and impure dispositions are Simeon and Levi, [72] two indeed in number, but only one in mind; on which account, in his blessings of his sons, their father numbers them together under one classification, on account of the harmonious character of their unanimity and of their violence in one and the same direction. But Moses does not make any mention of them afterwards as a pair, but classes the whole tribe of Simeon under that of Levi, combining together two essences, of which he made one impressed as it were with one idea and appearance, hearing to doing.

XXXVII. (201) When, therefore, the virtuous man knew that the promise was uttering things full of reverence and prudent caution, according to his own mind, he admitted both these feelings into his breast, namely, faith in God, and incredulity as to the creature. Very naturally therefore he says, using the language of entreaty, "Would that this Ishmael might live before thee," [73] using each word of those which he utters here with deliberate propriety, namely, the "this," the "might live," the "before thee." (202) For it is no small number of persons who have been deceived by the similarity of the names of different things, and we had better examine here what I am saying.

The name of Ishmael, being interpreted, means "the hearing of God," but some men listen to the divine doctrines to their benefit, and others listen to both his admonitions and to those of others only to their destruction. Do you recollect the case of the soothsayer Balaam? [74] He is represented as hearing the oracles of God, and as having received knowledge from the Most High, (203) but what advantage did he reap from such hearing, and what good accrued to him from such knowledge? In his intention he endeavored to injure the most excellent eye of the soul, which alone has received such instruction as to be able to behold God, but he was unable to do so by reason of the invincible power of the Saviour; therefore, being overthrown by his own insane wickedness, and having received many wounds, he perished amid the heaps of wounded, [75] because he had stamped beforehand the divinely inspired prophecies with the sophistry of the soothsayers.

(204) Very righteously, therefore, does the good man pray that this his only son, Ishmael, may be sound in mind and health, because of those per-

---

[72] Deuteronomy 33:6.
[73] Genesis 17:18.
[74] Numbers 24:17.
[75] Numbers 31:8.

sons who do not listen in a sincere spirit to the sacred admonitions, whom Moses has expressly forbidden to come into the assembly of the Ruler of the universe, (205) for those men are broken as to the generative parts of their minds, or are even rendered completely impotent in that respect, who magnify their own minds, and their external sense, as the only causes of all the events which take place among men; and there are others who are lovers of a system of polytheism, and who honour the company which is devoted to the service of many gods, being the sons of a harlot, having no knowledge of the one husband and father of the virtue-loving soul, namely, God; and are not all these men very properly driven away and banished from the assembly of God? (206) They appear to me very much to resemble those parents who accuse their sons of intemperance in wine, for they say, "This our son is disobedient,"[76] indicating, by the addition of the word "this," that they have other sons likewise who are temperate and self-denying, and who obey the injunctions of right reason and instruction; for these are the most genuine parents, by whom it is a most disgraceful thing to be accused, and a most glorious thing to be praised.

(207) Then as to the words, "This is Aaron and Moses, whom God directed to lead the children of Israel out of Egypt,"[77] and the expression, "These are those who conversed with Pharaoh the king." Let us not think that they are used superfluously, or that they do not convey some intimations beyond the mere open meaning of the words; (208) for since Moses is the purest mind, and Aaron is his speech, and moreover, since the mind has been taught to think of divine things in a divine manner, and since the speech has learnt to interpret holy things in holy language, the sophists imitating them, and adulterating the genuine coinage, say, that they also conceive rightly, and speak in a praiseworthy manner about what is most excellent.

In order, therefore, that we may not be deceived by a placing of the base money in juxtaposition with the good, by reason of the similitude of the impression, he has given us a test by which they may be distinguished. (209) What then is the test? To bring out of the region of the body the mind, endowed with the power of seeing, fond of contemplation and philosophical; for he who can do this is the same Moses; and he who is unable really to do so, but who is only said to be able, and who makes professions with infinite pomp and magnitude of language, is laughed at.

But he prays that Ishmael may live, not meaning to refer to the life in conjunction with the body,

but he prays that the divine voice, dwelling for evermore in his soul, may awaken and vivify it.

XXXVIII. (210) And he indeed prays that the hearing of sacred words and the learning of sacred doctrine may live, as has been already said; but Jacob, the practiser of virtue, prays that the good natural disposition may live; for he says, "May Reuben live and not die,"[78] does he then here pray for immortality for him, a thing impossible for man to attain to? (211) Surely not, we must then explain what it is which he intends to signify. All the lessons and all the admonitions of instruction are built up and established on the nature which is calculated to receive instruction, as on a foundation previously laid; but if there is no natural foundation previously in existence, everything is useless; for men, by nature destitute of sense, would not appear at all to differ from a stock or a lifeless stone; for nothing could possibly be adapted to them so as to cleave to them, but everything would rebound and spring back as from some hard body.

(212) But on the other hand, we may see the souls of those who are well endowed by nature, like a well-smooth waxen tablet, neither too solid nor too tender, moderately tempered, and easily receiving all admonitions and all lessons, and themselves giving an accurate representation of any impression which has been stamped upon them, being a sort of distinct image of memory.

(213) It was therefore indispensable to pray that a good natural disposition, free from all disease and from all mortality, should be joined to the rational race; for they are but few who partake of the life according to virtue, which is the most real and genuine life. I do not mean of the common herd of men only, for of them there is not one who partakes of real life: but even of those to whom it has been granted to shun the objects of human desire, and to live to God alone. (214) On which account the practiser of virtue, that courageous man, marvelled greatly, if any one being borne along the middle of the stream of life, was not dragged down by any violence, but was able to withstand the flow of abundant wealth coming over him, and to stem the impetuosity of immoderate pleasure, and to avoid being carried away by the whirlwind of vain opinion.

(215) At all events Jacob does not speak to Joseph more than the sacred scripture speaks to every one who is vigorous in his body, and who is seen to be immersed amid abundant treasures, and riches, and superfluities, and to be overcome by none of them, when he says, "For still thou livest," uttering a most marvellous sentiment, and one which is quite beyond the daily life of us who, if we have fallen in with ever so slight a breeze which bears us towards the good fortune, immed-

---

[76]Deuteronomy 21:20.
[77]Exodus 6:26.

[78]Deuteronomy 33:6.

iately set all sail and became greatly elated, and being full of great and high spirits, hurry forward with all our speed to the indulgence of our passions, and never will check our unbridled and immoderately excited desires until we run ashore and are wrecked as to the whole vessel of our souls.

XXXIX. (216) Very beautifully therefore, do we pray that this Ishmael may live. Therefore, Abraham adds, "May he live before God," looking upon it as the perfection of all happiness for the mind to be accounted worthy of him who is the most excellent of all beings, as its inspector and overseer; (217) for if, while the teacher is present the pupil cannot go wrong, and if a monitor being at hand is of service to the learner, and if while an elder person is present the younger man is adorned by modesty and temperance, and if the presence of his father or of his mother have often prevented a son when about to commit sin, even though they are only beheld by him in silence, then what excess of good must we imagine that man to enjoy, who believes that he is always watched and beheld by God? for while he fears and reverences and looks up to the dignity of him as being present, he will flee from committing iniquity with all his might.

(218) But when he prays that Ishmael may live, he does not despair of the birth of Isaac, as I have already said, but he believes in God; for it does not follow that what it is possible for God to give, it is also possible for man to receive, since to God it is easy to give the most numerous and important benefits, but to us it is not easy to accept of the gifts which are proffered to us; (219) for we must be content, if, by means of labour and diligence, we obtain a share of those good things which are familiar and customary to us. But there is no hope that we can attain to those which come of their own accord, and from some ever ready and previously prepared source, without any art, or in short, any human contrivance whatever; for inasmuch as these things are divine, they must of necessity be found out by more divine and unadulterated natures, such as have no connection with any mortal body. (220) And Moses has shown that every one, to the best of his power, ought to make grateful acknowledgments for benefits received; for instance, that the clever man ought to offer up as a sacrifice his acuteness and wisdom; the eloquent man should consecrate all his excellences of speech, by means of psalms and a regular enumeration of the greatness and panegyric on the living God; and to proceed with each species, he who is a natural philosopher should offer up his natural philosophy; he who is a moral philosopher should make an offering of his ethical philosophy; he who is skilful in any art or science should dedicate to God his knowledge of the arts and sciences.

(221) Thus again a sailor and a pilot should dedicate their successful voyage; the agricultural farmer, his productive crops; the stock-farmer, the prolific increase of his flocks and herds; the physician, the good health of his patients; the commander of an army, his success in war; the magistrate or the king will offer up his administration of the laws or his sovereign power. And, in short, the man who is not blinded by self-love, looks upon the only true maker of all things, God, as the cause of all the good things affecting his soul, or body, or his external circumstances. (222) Let no one therefore, of those who seem to be somewhat obscure and humble, from a despair of any better hope, hesitate to become a suppliant to God. But even if he no longer looks forward to any great advantages, still let him, to the best of his power, give God thanks for the blessings which he has already received, (223) and in effect, those which he has received are countless; his birth, his life, his soul, his food, his outward senses, his imagination, his inclinations, his reason; and reason is a very short word, but a most perfect and admirable thing, a fragment of the soul of the universe, or, as it is more pious to say for those who study philosophy according to Moses, a very faithful copy of the divine image.

XL. (224) It is right also to praise those inquirers after truth, who have endeavored to tear up and carry off the whole trunk of virtue, root and branch: but since they have not been able to do it, have at least taken either a single shoot, or a single bunch of fruit, as a specimen and portion of the whole tree, being all that they were able to bear.[79]

(225) It is a desirable thing, indeed, to associate at once with the entire company of the virtues; but if this be too great an indulgence to be granted to human nature, let us be content if it has fallen to our lot to be connected with any one of the particular virtues, as a portion of the whole band, such as temperance, or courage, or justice, or humanity; for the soul may produce and bring forth some good from even one of them, and so avoid being barren and unproductive of any.

(226) But will you impose any such injunctions as these on your own son? Unless you treat your servants with gentleness, do not treat those of the same rank as yourself socially. Unless you behave decorously to your wife, never bear yourself respectfully to your parents. If you neglect your father and your mother, be impious also towards God. If you delight in pleasure, you must not keep aloof from covetousness. Do you desire great riches? Then be also eager for vain-glory. (227) For what more need we add? Need you not desire to be moderate in some things unless you are able

---

[79] Numbers 13:25.

to be so in all? Would not your son say to you in such a case, My father, what do you mean? Do you wish your son to become either perfectly good or perfectly bad, and will you not be content if he keeps the middle path between the two extremes? (228) Was it not for this reason that Abraham also, at the time of the destruction of Sodom, began at fifty and ended at ten?[80]

Therefore, propitiating and supplicating God, entreat him that if there could be found among his creatures a complete remission so as to give them liberty, of which the sacred number of fifty is a symbol, at least the intermediate instruction which is equal in number to the decade, might be accepted for the sake of the deliverance of the soul which was about to be condemned. (229) But those who are instructed have many more opportunities of prayer than those who are destitute of teachers, and those who are well initiated in encyclical accomplishments have more opportunities than those who are unmusical and illiterate, inasmuch as they from their childhood almost have been imbued with all the lessons of virtue, and temperance, and all kinds of excellence. Wherefore, even if they have not entirely got rid of and effaced old marks of iniquity so as to wear a completely clean appearance, at least they have purified themselves in a reasonable and moderate degree.

(230) And it is something like this that Esau seems to have said to his father, "Have you not one blessing for me, O my father? Bless me, bless me, also, O my father!"[81] For different blessings have been set apart for different persons, perfect blessings for the perfect, and moderate blessings for the imperfect. As is the case also with bodies; for there are different exercises appropriate to those which are in health, and to those which are sick. And also different regimens of food, and different systems of living, and not the same. But some things are suitable to the one kind that they may not become at all diseased; and other things are good for the other sort, they they may be changed and rendered more healthy.

(231) Since, therefore, there are many good things existing in nature, give me that which appears to be best adapted to my circumstances, even if it be the most trifling thing possible; looking at this one point alone, whether I shall be able to bear what is given me with equanimity, and not, like a wretched person, sink under and be overwhelmed by it.

(232) Again, what do we imagine to be meant by the words, "Will not the hand of the Lord be sufficient?"[82] Do they not signify that the powers of the living God penetrate everywhere for the purpose of conferring benefits, not only on those who are noble, but on those also who appear to be in a more obscure condition, to whom also God gives such things as are suitable to the measure and weight of the soul of each individual, conjecturing and measuring in his own mind with perfect equality what is proportionate to the circumstances and requirements of each.

XLI. (233) But what makes an impression on me in no ordinary degree is the law which is enacted with respect to those who put off their sins and seem to be repentant. For this law commands that the first victim which such persons offer shall be a female sheep without spot. But, if it proceeds, "his hand is not strong enough to bring a sheep, then for the trespass which he has committed he shall bring two turtle doves or two young pigeons, one for his trespass and one for a burnt offering; (234) and if his hand cannot find a pair of turtle doves or two young pigeons, then he shall bring as his gift the tenth part of an ephah of fine flour for a sin offering; he shall not pour oil upon it, nor shall he place any frankincense thereon, because it is a sin offering; and he shall bring it to the priest, and the priest having taken it from him shall take a full handful of it, and place it as a memorial on the altar."[83]

(235) God therefore here is propitiated by three different kinds of repentance, by the aforesaid beasts, or by the birds, or by the white flour, according, in short, to the ability of him who is being purified and who repents. For small offences do not require great purifications, nor are small purifications fit for great crimes; but they should be equal, and similar, and in due proportion. (236) It is worth while, therefore, to examine what is meant by this purification which may be accomplished in three ways.

Now it may almost be said that both offences and good actions are perceived to exist in three things; in intention, or in words, or in actions. On which account Moses, teaching in his hortatory admonitions that the attainment of good is not impossible nor even very difficult, says, (237) "It is not necessary to soar up to heaven, nor to go to the borders of the earth and sea, for the attainment of it, but it is near, yea, and very near."[84] And then in a subsequent passage he shows it all but to the naked eye as one may say, where he says, "Every action is in thy mouth, or in thy heart, or in thy hands:"[85] meaning under this symbolical expression, in thy words, or in they designs, or in thy actions. For he means that human happiness consists in wise design, and good language, and righteous actions, just as the unhappiness

---

[80]Genesis 18:32.
[81]Genesis 27:28.
[82]Numbers 11:23.

[83]Leviticus 5:5.
[84]Deuteronomy 30:10.
[85]Deuteronomy 30:14.

arises from the contrary course. (238) For both well-doing and wrong-doing exist in the same regions, in the heart, or in the mouth, or in the hand; for some persons decide in the most righteous, and sagacious manner, some speak most excellently, some do only what ought to be done: again, of the three sources of error the most unimportant is to design to do what ought not to be done, the most grievous is to do what is iniquitous, the middle evil is to speak improperly. (239) But it often happens that even what is least important is the most difficult to be removed; for it is very hard to bring an agitated state of the soul to tranquillity; and one may more easily check the impetuosity of a torrent than the perversion of the soul which is hurrying in a wrong direction, without restraint. For innumerable notions coming one upon the other like the waves of a stormy sea, bearing everything along with them, and throwing everything into confusion, overturn the whole soul with irresistible violence.

(240) Therefore the most excellent, and most perfect kind of purification is this, not to admit into one's mind any improper notions, but to regulate it in peace and obedience to law, the ruler of which principles is justice. The next kind is, not to offend in one's language either by speaking falsely, or by swearing falsely, or by deceiving, or by practicing sophistry, or by laying false informations; or, in short, by letting loose one's mouth and tongue to the injury of any one, as it is better to put a bridle and an insuperable chain on those members.

XLII. (241) But why it is a more grievous offence to say what is wrong than only to think it, is very easy to see. For some times a person thinks without any deliberate previous intention of so thinking, but inconsiderately: for he is compelled to admit ideas in his mind which he does not wish to admit; and nothing which is involuntary is blameable: (242) but a man speaks intentionally, so that if he utters words which are not proper he is unhappy and is committing offence, since he does not even by chance choose to say anything that is proper, and it would be more for his advantage to adopt that safest expedient of silence: and, in the second place, anyone who is not silent can be silent if he pleases.

(243) But what is even a still more grievous offence than speaking wrongly, is unjust action. For the word, as it is said, is the shadow of the deed; and how can an injurious deed help being more mischievous than a shadow of the same character? On this account Moses released the mind, even when it yielded to many involuntary perversions and errors, from accusations and from penalties, thinking that it was rather acted upon by notions which forced their way into it, than was itself acting.

But whatever goes out through the mouth that he makes the utterer responsible for and brings

him before the tribunal, since the act of speaking is one which is in our own power. (244) But the investigation to which words are subject is a much more moderate one, and that with which words are united is a more vigorous one. For he imposes severe punishments on those who commit gross offences, and who carry out in action, and utter with hasty tongues what they have been designed in their unjust minds.

XLIII. (245) Therefore he has called the purifying victims which are to be offered up for the three offenders, the mind, speech, and the action, a sheep, and a pair of turtle doves or pigeons, and the tenth part of a sacred measure of fine flour; thinking it fit that the mind should be purified by a sheep, the speech by winged creatures, and the action by fine flour: Why is this? (246) Because, as the mind is the most excellent thing in us, so also is the sheep the most excellent among irrational animals, inasmuch as it is most gentle, and also as it gives forth a yearly produce in its fleece, for the use and also for the ornament of mankind. For clothes keep off all injury from both cold and heat, and also they conceal the unmentionable parts of nature, and in this way they are an ornament to those who use them: (247) therefore the sheep, as being the most excellent of animals, is a symbol of the purification of the most excellent part of man, the mind.

And birds are an emblem of the purification of speech: for speech is a light thing, and winged by nature, flying and penetrating in every direction more swiftly than an arrow. For what is once said can never be re-called;[86] but being borne abroad, and running on with great swiftness, it strikes the ears and penetrates every sense of hearing, resounding loudly: but speech is of two kinds, one true and the other false; (248) on which account it appears to me to be here compared to a pair of turtle doves or young pigeons: and of these birds one he says is to be looked upon as a sin offering, since the speech which is true is wholly and in all respects sacred and perfect, but that which is false is very wrong and requires correction.

(249) Again, as I have already said, fine flour is a symbol of the purification of activity, but it is sorted from the commoner sort by the hands of the bakers, who make the business their study. On which account the law says, "And the priest having taken an entire handful, shall place it on the altar as a memorial of them," by the word handful, indicating both the endeavor and the action.

(250) And he speaks with exceeding accuracy with respect to the sheep, when he says, "And if his hand be not strong enough to supply a sheep;" but with respect to the birds he says, "And if he

---

[86] This resembles what is said by Horace in A. P. 390 and in Epist. I. 18.71.

cannot find a bird." Why is this? Because it is a sign of very great strength and of excessive power, to get rid of the errors of the mind: but it does not require any great strength, to check the errors of words; (251) for, as I have said already, silence is a remedy for all the offences that can be committed by the voice, and every one may easily practise silence; but yet, by reason of their chattering habits and want of moderation in their language, many people cannot find out how to impose a limitation on their speech.

XLIV. (252) Since then, the virtuous man has been bred up among and practised in these and similar divisions and discriminations of things, does he not rightly appear to pray that Ishmael may live, if he is not as yet able to become the father of Isaac? (253) What then does the merciful God say? To him who asks for one thing he gives two, and on him who prays for what is less he bestows what is greater; for, says the historian, he said unto Abraham, "Yea, behold, Sarrah thy wife shall bring forth a son."[87] Very felicitous and significant is this answer, "Yea;" for what can be more suitable to and more like the character of God, than to promise good things and to ratify that promise with all speed! (254) But what God promises every foolish man repudiates; therefore the sacred scriptures represent Leah as hated, and on this account it is that she received that name; for Leah, being interpreted, means "repudiating and labouring," because we all turn away from virtue and think it a laborious thing, by reason of its very often imposing commands on us which are not pleasant. (255) But nevertheless, she is thought worthy of such an honourable reception from the prince, that her womb is opened by him, so as to receive the seed of divine generation, in order to cause the production of honourable pursuits and actions.

Learn therefore, O soul, that Sarrah, that is, virtue, will bring forth to thee a son; and that Hagar, or intermediate instruction, is not the only one who will do so; for her offspring is one which has its knowledge from teaching, but the offspring of the other is entirely self-taught. (256) And do not wonder, if God, who brings forth all good things, has also brought forth this race, which, though rare upon the earth, is very numerous in heaven. And you may learn this also from other things of which man consists: do the eyes see from having been taught to do so? And what do the nostrils do? Do they smell by reason of their having learnt? And do the hands touch, or the feet advance, in accordance with the commands or recommendations of instructors? (257) Again, do the appetites and imaginations (and these are the first moving powers and persuasions of the soul) exist in consequence of teaching? And has our mind gone

as a pupil to any sophist, in order to learn to think and to comprehend? All these things repudiate all kinds of instruction, and avail themselves only of the spontaneous gifts of nature to exert their appropriate energies.

(258) Why then do you any longer wonder if God showers upon men virtue, unaccompanied by any labour or suffering, such as stand in need of no superintending care or instruction, but is from the very beginning entire and perfect? And if you wish to receive any testimony in corroboration of this view, can you find any more trustworthy than that of Moses? And he says that the rest of mankind derive their food from earth, but that he alone who is endowed with the power of sight, derives his from heaven. (259) And men occupied in agriculture co-operate to produce the food from the earth; but God, the only cause and giver, rains down the food from heaven without the co-operation of any other being.

And, indeed, we read in the scriptures, "Behold, I rain upon you bread from heaven."[88] Now what nourishment can the scriptures properly say is rained down, except heavenly wisdom? (260) which God sends from above upon those souls which have a longing for virtue, God who possesses a great abundance and exceeding treasure of wisdom, and who irrigates the universe, and especially so on the sacred seventh day which he calls the sabbath; for then, he says, that there is an influx of spontaneous good things, not rising from any kind of art, but shooting up by their own spontaneous and self-perfecting nature, and bearing appropriate fruit.

XLV. (261) Virtue, therefore, will bring thee forth a legitimate male child, far removed from all effeminate passions; and thou shalt call the name of thy son by the name of the passion which thou feelest in regard to him; and thou wilt by all means feel joy; so that thou shalt give him a name which is an emblem of joy, namely, Laughter. (262) As grief and fear have their appropriate expressions which the passion, when more than usually violent and predominant, gives utterance to; so also, good counsels and happiness compel a man to employ a natural expression of them, for which no one could find out more appropriate and felicitous names, even if he were very skilful in the imposition of names. (263) On which account God says, "I have blessed him, I will increase him, I will multiply him, he shall beget twelve nations;"[89] that is to say, he shall beget the whole circle and ring of the sophistical preliminary branches of education; but I will make my covenant with Israel, that the race of mankind may receive each kind of virtue, the weaker part of them receiving both

[87] Genesis 17:19.

[88] Exodus 16:4.
[89] Genesis 17:20.

that which is taught by others, and that which is learnt by one's self, and the stronger part that which is ready and prepared.

XLVI. (264) "And at that time," says he, "she shall bring forth a son to thee;"[90] that is to say, wisdom shall bring forth joy. What time, O most marvellous being, are you pointing out? Is it that which cannot be indicated by the thing brought forth? For that must be the real time, the rising of the universe, the prosperity and happiness of the whole earth, and of heaven, and of all intermediate natures, and of all animals, and of all plants. (265) On which account Moses also took courage to say to those who had run away, and who did not dare to enter upon a war in the cause of virtue against those who were arrayed against it, "The Lord has departed from them, but the Lord is in us;"[91] for he here almost confesses in express words that God is time, who stands aloof and at a distance from every impious person, but walks among those souls which cultivate virtue. (266) "For," says he, "I will walk among you, and I will be your God."[92] But those who say that what is meant by time is only the seasons of the year are misapplying the names with great inaccuracy, like men who have not studied the nature of things with any care, but have gone on to a great degree at random.

XLVII. (267) But by way of amplifying the beauty of the creature to be born, he says that it shall be born the next year, indicating by the term, "the next year,"[93] not a difference of time, such as is measured by lunar or solar periods, but that which is truly marvellous, and strange, and new, being an age which is very different from those which are visible to the eyes and perceptible to the outward senses, being investigated in incorporeal things appreciable only by the intellect,

which, in fact, is the model and archetype of time. But an age is a name given to the life of the world, intelligible only by the intellect, as time is that given to the life of the world, perceptible by the outward senses.

(268) And in this year the man who had sown the graces of God so as to produce many more good things, in order that the greatest possible number of persons worthy to share them might participate in them, finds also the barley producing a hundredfold.[94] But he who has sown does usually also reap. (269) And he sowed, displaying the virtue, the enemy of envy and wickedness; he is, however, here said to find, not to reap. For he who has made the ear of his good deeds more productive and full, was a different person, having laid up an abundance of greater hopes well prepared, and he also proposed more abundant advantages to all those who sought them, encouraging them to hope to find them.

XLVIII. (270) And the words, "He finished speaking to him,"[95] are equivalent to saying, he made his hearer perfect, though he was devoid of wisdom before, and he filled him with immortal lessons. But when his disciple became perfect, the Lord went up and departed from Abraham, showing, not that he separated himself from him; for the wise man is naturally an attendant of God, not wishing to represent the spontaneous inclination of the disciple in order that as he had learnt while his teacher was no longer standing by him, and without any necessity urging him, giving of his own accord a specimen of himself, and displaying a voluntary and spontaneous eagerness to learn, he might for the future exert his energies by himself; for the teacher assigns a model to him who has learnt by voluntary study without any suggestions from other quarters, stamping on him a most durable species of indelible recollection.

---

[90] Genesis 15:10.
[91] Numbers 14:9.
[92] Leviticus 26:12.
[93] Genesis 18:10.

[94] Genesis 26:12.
[95] Genesis 17:22.

ON DREAMS, THAT THEY ARE GOD-SENT†

(*Quod A Deo Mittantur Somnia or De Somniis*)

BOOK 1

I. (1) The treatise before this one has contained our opinions on those visions sent from heaven which are classed under the first species; in reference to which subject we delivered our opinion that the Deity sent the appearances which are beheld by man in dreams in accordance with the suggestions of his own nature. But in this treatise we will, to the best of our power, describe those dreams which come under the second species.

(2) Now the second species is that in which our mind, being moved simultaneously with the mind of the universe, has appeared to be hurried away by itself and to be under the influence of divine impulses, so as to be rendered capable of comprehending beforehand, and knowing by anticipation some of the events of the future. Now the first dream which is akin to the species which I have been describing, is that which appeared on the ladder which reached up to heaven, and which was of this kind.

(3) "And Jacob dreamed, and behold a ladder was firmly planted on the earth, the head of which reached up to heaven; and the angels of God were ascending and descending on it. And behold there was a ladder firmly planted on the earth, and the Lord was standing steadily upon it; and he said, I am the God of Abraham thy father, and the God of Isaac: be not afraid. The earth on which thou art sleeping I will give unto thee and unto thy seed, and thy seed shall be as the dust of the earth, and it shall be multiplied as the sand on the seashore, and shall spread to the south, and to the north, and to the east; and in thee shall all the kindreds of the earth be blessed, and in thy seed also. And, behold, I am with thee, keeping thee in all thy ways, by whichever thou goest, and I will bring thee again into this land; because I will not leave thee until I have done everything which I have said unto thee."[1]

(4) But the previous considerations of the circumstances of this vision require that we should examine them with accuracy, and then perhaps we shall be able to comprehend what is indicated by the vision. What, then, are the previous circumstances? The scripture tells us, "And Jacob went up from the well of the oath, and came to Char-

ran, and went into a place and lay down there until the sun arose. And he took one of the stones of the place and placed it at his head, and went to sleep in that place." And immediately afterwards came the dream. (5) Therefore it is well at the outset to raise a question on these three points:— One, What was the well of the oath,[2] and why was it called by this name? Secondly, What is Charran, and why, after Jacob had departed from the well beforementioned, did he immediately go to Charran? Thirdly, What was the place, and why, when he was in it, did the sun at once set, and did he go to sleep?

II. (6) Let us then at once begin and consider the first of these points. To me, then, the well appears to be an emblem of knowledge; for its nature is not superficial, but very deep. Nor does it lie in an open place, but a well is fond of being hidden somewhere in secret. Nor is it found with ease, but only after great labour and with difficulty; and this too is seen to be the case with sciences, not only with such as have great and indescribable subjects of speculation, but even with respect to such as are the most insignificant. (7) Choose, therefore, whichever art you please; not the most excellent, but even the must obscure of all, which perhaps no one who has been bred a free man in the whole city would ever study of his own accord, and which scarcely any servant in the field would attend to, who, against his will, was a slave to some morose and ill-tempered master who compelled him to do many unpleasant things.

(8) For the matter will be found to be not a simple one, but rather one of great complications and variety, not easy to be seized upon, but difficult to discover, difficult to master, hostile to delay, and indolence and indifference, full of earnestness and contention, and sweat, and care. For which reason "those who dig in this well say that they cannot find even water in it;" because the ends of science are not only hard to discover, but are even altogether undiscoverable; (9) and it is owing to this that one man is more thoroughly skilled in grammar or in geometry than another, because of its being impossible to circumscribe, increase, and extend one within certain limits; for there is always more that is left behind than what comes to be learnt; and what is left watches for and catches the learner, so that even he who fancies

---

† Yonge's title, *A Treatise on the Doctrine that Dreams Are Sent from God.*

[1] Genesis 28:12.

[2] Genesis 26:33.

that he has comprehended and mastered the very extremities of knowledge would be considered but half perfect by another person who was his judge, and if he were before the tribunal of truth would appear to be only beginning knowledge; (10) for life is short, as some one has said, but art is long; of which that man most thoroughly comprehends the magnitude, who sincerely and honestly plunges deeply into it, and who digs it out like a well. And such a man, when he is at the point of death, being now grey-headed and exceedingly old, it is said, wept, not that he feared death as being a coward, but out of a desire for instruction, as feeling that he was now, for the first time, entering upon it when he was finally departing from life.

(11) For the soul flourishes for the pursuit of knowledge when the prime vigour of the body is withering away from the lapse of time; therefore, before one has arrived at one's prime and vigour by reason of a more accurate comprehension of things, it is not difficult to be tripped up. But this accident is common to all people who are fond of learning, to whom new subjects of contemplation are continually rising up and striving after old ones, the soul itself producing many such subjects when it is not barren and unproductive. And nature, also, unexpectedly and spontaneously displaying a great number to those who are gifted with acute and penetrating intellects. Therefore the well of knowledge is shown to be of this kind, having no boundary and no end.

(12) We must now explain why it was called the well of the oath. Those matters which are doubted about are decided by an oath, and those which are uncertain are confirmed in the same manner, and so, too, those which want certification receive it; from which facts this inference is drawn, that there is no subject respecting which any one can make an affirmation with greater certainty than he can respecting the fact that the race of wisdom is without limitation and without end. (13) It is well, therefore, to enrol one's self under the banners of one who discusses these matters without an oath; but he who is not very much inclined to assent to the assertions of another will at least assent to them when he has made oath to their correctness. But let no one refuse to take an oath of this kind, well knowing that he will have his name inscribed on pillars among those who are faithful to their oaths.

III. (14) However, enough of this. The next thing must be to consider why it is that as four wells had been dug by the servants of Abraham and Isaac, the fourth and last was called the well of the oath. (15) May it not be that sacred historian here desires to represent, in a figurative manner, that as in the universe there are four elements of which this world is composed, and as there are an equal number in ourselves, of which we have been fashioned before we were moulded

into our human shape, three of them are capable of being comprehended somehow or other, but the fourth is unintelligible to all who come forward as judges of it. (16) Accordingly, we find that the four elements in the world are the earth, and the water, and the air, and the heaven, of which, even if some are difficult to find, they are still not classed in the utterly undiscoverable portion.

(17) For that the earth, because it is a heavy, and indissoluble, and solid substance, is divided into mountains and champaign districts, and intersected by rivers and seas, so that some portion of it consists of islands, and some portions are continent. And again, some of it has a shallow and some a deep soil; and some is rough, and rugged, and strong, and altogether barren; and some is smooth and delicate, and exceedingly fertile; and besides all these facts we know a great number of others relative to the earth.

(18) And again, there is the water, which we know has many of the aforesaid qualities in common with the earth, and many also peculiar to itself; for some of it is sweet, and some brackish, and some is mixed up of various characteristics; and some is good to drink, and some is not drinkable; and, moreover, neither of these last qualities is invariable with respect to every creature, but there are some to which it is the one and not the other, and *vice versa*. Again, some water is by nature cold, and other water naturally hot; (19) for there is in all sorts of places an infinite number of springs pouring forth hot water, not on the land only but even in the sea: at all events, there have appeared before now veins pouring up warm water in the middle of the sea, which all the enormous efflux of salt water in all the sea that encircles the world, pouring over them from all eternity, has never been able to extinguish, nor even in the least degree to diminish.

(20) Again, we know that the air has an attractive nature, yielding to such bodies as surround it in an altitude of resistance, being the organ of life, and breath, and sight, and hearing, and all the rest of the external senses, admitting of rarification, and condensation, and motion, and tranquillity, and changes, and variations of every kind, by which it is altered and modified, and generating summers and winters, and the seasons of autumn and spring, by means of which the circle of the year is the last brought to a conclusion.

IV. (21) All these things, then, we feel: but the heaven has a nature which is incomprehensible, and it has never conveyed to us any distinct indication by which we can understand its nature; for what can we say? that it is solid ice, as some persons have chosen to assert? or that it is the purest fire? or that it is a fifth body, moving in a circle having no participation in any of the four elements? For what can we say? Has that most remote sphere of the fixed stars any density in an upward direction? or is it merely a superficies devoid of all depth, something like a plane figure? (22) And what are the stars? Are they masses of earth full of fire? For some persons have said that they are hills, and valleys, and thickets, men who are worthy of a prison and a treadmill, or of any place where there are instruments proper for the punishment of impious persons; or are they, as some one has defined them, a continuous and dense harmony, the closely packed, indissoluble mass of aether?

Again, are they animated and intelligent? or are they destitute alike of mind and vitality? Have they their motions in consequence of any choice of their own? or merely because they are compulsory? (23) What, again, are we to say of the moon? Does she show us a light of her own, or a borrowed and illegitimate one, only reflected from the rays of the sun? or is neither of these things true, but has she something mixed, as it were, so as to be a sort of combination of her own light and of that which belongs to some other body? For all these things, and others like them, belonging to the fourth and most excellent of the bodies in the world, namely, the heaven, are uncertain and incomprehensible, and are spoken of in accordance with conjectures and guesses, and not with the solid, certain reasoning of truth, (24) so that a person might venture to swear that no mortal man will ever be able to comprehend any one of these matters clearly. At all events, the fourth and dry well was called the well of the oath on this account, because the search after the fourth element in the world, that is to say the heaven, is without any result, and is in every respect fruitless.

V. But let us now see in what manner that fourth element in us is by nature in such an especial and singular manner incomprehensible.

(25) There are, then, four principal elements in us, the body, the external sense, the speech, and the mind. Now of these, three are not uncertain or unintelligible in every respect, but they contain some indication in themselves by which they are comprehended. (26) Now what is my meaning in this statement? We know already that the body is divisible into three parts, and that it is capable of motion in six directions, inasmuch as it has three dimensions, in length, in depth, in breadth; and twice as many motions, namely six, the upward motion, the downward motion, that to the right, that to the left, the forward, and the backward motion. But, moreover, we are not ignorant that it is the vessel of the soul; and we are also aware that it is subject to the changes of being young, of decaying, of growing old, of dying, of undergoing dissolution. (27) And with respect to the outward senses, we are not, so far as that is concerned, utterly dull and mutilated, but we are able to say that that also is divided into five divisions, and that there are appropriate organs for the development of each sense formed by nature; for instance, the eyes for seeing, the ears for hearing, the nostrils for smelling, and the other organs for the exercise of the respective senses to which they are adapted, and also that we may call these outward senses messengers of the mind which inform it of colours, and shapes and sounds, and the peculiar differences of vapours, and flavours, and, in short, which describe to it all bodies, and all the distinctive qualities which exist in them.

They also may be looked upon as body-guards of the soul, informing it of all that they see or hear; and if anything injurious attacks it from without, they foresee it, and guard against it, so that it may not enter by chance and unawares, and so become the cause of irremediable disaster to their mistress.

(28) Again, the voice does not entirely escape our comprehension; but we know that one voice is shrill and another deep; that one is tuneful and harmonious, and another dissonant and very unmusical; and again, one voice is more powerful, and another less so. And they differ also in ten thousand other particulars, in kind, in complexion, in distance, in combined and separate tension of the tones, in the symphonies of fourths, of fifths, and of the diapason. (29) Moreover, there are some things which we know also with respect to that articulate voice which has been allotted to man alone of all animals, as, for instance, we know that it is emitted by the mind, that it receives its articulate distinctness in the mouth, that it is by the striking of the tongue that articulate utterance is impressed upon the tones of the voice, and which renders the uttered sound not only a bare, naked, useless noise, void of all characteristic, and that it discharges the office of a herald or interpreter towards the mind which suggests it.

VI. (30) Now then is the fourth element which exists within us, the dominant mind, comprehensible to us in the same manner as these other divisions? Certainly not; for what do we think it to be in its essence? Do we look upon it as spirit, or as blood, or, in short, as any bodily substance! But it is not a substance, but must be pronounced incorporeal. Is it then a limit, or a species, or a number, or a continued act, or a harmony, or any existing thing whatever? (31) Is it, the very first moment that we are born, infused into us from without, or is it some warm nature in us which is cooled by the air which is diffused around us, like a piece of iron which has been heated at a forge, and then being plunged into cold water, is by that process tempered and hardened? (And perhaps it is from the cooling process [psyxis] to which it is thus submitted that the soul [hē psychē] derives its name.) What more shall we say? When we die, is it extinguished and destroyed together with our bodies? or does it continue to live a long time? or, thirdly, is it wholly incorruptible and immortal?

(32) Again, where, in what part does this mind lie hid? Has it received any settled habitation? For

some men have dedicated it to our head, as the principal citadel, around which all the outward senses have their lairs; thinking it natural that its body-guards should be stationed near it, as near the palace of a mighty king. Some again contend earnestly in favour of the position which they assign it, believing that it is enshrined like a statue in the heart.

(33) Therefore now the fourth element is incomprehensible, in the world of heaven, in comparison of the nature of the earth, of the water, and of the air; and the mind in man, in comparison of the body and the outward sense, and the speech, which is the interpreter of the mind; may it not be the case also, that for this reason the fourth year is described as holy and praiseworthy in the sacred scriptures? (34) For among created things, the heaven is holy in the world, in accordance with which body, the imperishable and indestructible natures revolve; and in man the mind is holy, being a sort of fragment of the Deity, and especially according to the statement of Moses, who says, "God breathed into his face the breath of life, and man became a living soul."[3]

(35) And it appears to me, that it is not without reason that both these things are called praiseworthy; for these two things, the heaven and the mind, are the things which are able to utter, with all becoming dignity, the praises, and hymns, and glory, and beatitude of the Father who created them: for man has received an especial honour beyond all other animals, namely, that of ministering to the living God. And the heaven is always singing melodies, perfecting an all-musical harmony, in accordance with the motions of all the bodies which exist therein; (36) of which, if the sound ever reached our ears, love, which could not be restrained, and frantic desires, and furious impetuosity, which could not be put an end to or pacified, would be engendered, and would compel us to give up even what is necessary, nourishing ourselves no longer like ordinary mortals on the meat and drink, which is received by means of our throat, but on the inspired songs of music in its highest perfection, as persons about to be made immortal through the medium of their ears: and it is said that Moses[4] was an incorporeal hearer of these melodies, when he went for forty days, and an equal number of nights, without at all touching any bread or any water.

VII. (37) Therefore the heaven, which is the archetypal organ of music, appears to have been arranged in a most perfect manner, for no other object except that the hymns sung to the honour of the Father of the universe, might be attuned in a musical manner; and we hear that virtue, that

is to say, Leah,[5] after the birth of her fourth son, was no longer able to bring forth any more, but restrained, or perhaps I should say, was restrained, as to her generative powers; for she found, I conceive, all her generative power dry and barren, after she had brought forth Judah, that is to say, "confession," the perfect fruit: (38) and the phrase, "Leah desisted from bearing children," differs in no respect from the statement, that the children of Isaac found no water in the fourth well."[6] Since it appears from both these figurative expressions, that every creature thirsts for God, by whom all their births take place, and from whom nourishment is bestowed to them when they are born.

(39) Perhaps therefore some petty cavilling critics will imagine that all this statement about the digging of the wells is a superfluous piece of prolixity on the part of the lawgiver: but those who deserve a larger classification, being citizens not of some petty state but of the wide world, being men of more perfect wisdom, will know well that the real question is not about the four wells, but about the parts of the universe that the men who are gifted with sight, and are fond of contemplation exercise their powers of investigation; namely, about the earth, the water, the air, and the heaven. (40) And examining each of these matters with the most accurately refined conception, in three of them they have found some things within the reach of their comprehension; on which account they have given these names, injustice, enmity, and latitude to what they have discovered. But in the fourth, that is to say in heaven, they have found absolutely nothing whatever, which they could comprehend; as we explained a little time ago: for the fourth is found to be a well destitute of water, and dry; and for the reason above mentioned it is called a well.

VIII. (41) We will now investigate what comes next, and inquire what Charran is, and why the man who went up from the well came to it. Charran then, as it appears to me, is a sort of metropolis of the outward senses: and it is interpreted at one time a pit dug, at another time holes; one fact being intimated by both these names; (42) for our bodies are in a manner dug out to furnish the organs of the outward senses, and each of the organs is a sort of hole for the corresponding outward sense in which it shelters itself as in a cave: when therefore any one goes up from the well which is called the well of the oath, as if he were leaving a harbour, he immediately does of necessity come to Charran: for it is a matter of necessity that the outward senses should receive one who comes on an emigration from that most excel-

---

[3]Genesis 2:7.
[4]Exodus 24:18.

[5]Genesis 29:35.
[6]Genesis 26:32.

lent country of knowledge, unbounded as it is in extent, without any guide.

(43) For our soul is very often set in motion by is own self after it has put off the whole burden of the body, and has escaped from the multitude of the outward senses; and very often too, even while it is still clothed in them.

Therefore by its own simple motion it has arrived at the comprehension of those things which are appreciable only by the intellect; and by the motion of the body, it has attained to an understanding of those things which are perceptible by the outward senses; (44) therefore, if any one is unable altogether to associate with the mind alone, he then finds for himself a second refuge, namely, the external senses; and whoever fails in attaining to a comprehension of the things which are intelligible only by the intellect is immediately drawn over to the objects of the outward senses; for the second organ is always to the outward senses, in the case of those things which are not able to make a successful one as far as the dominant mind. (45) But it is well for man not to grow old or to spend all his time in this course either, but rather, as if they were straying in a foreign country like sojourners, to be always seeking for a second migration, and for a return to their native land.

Therefore Laban, knowing absolutely nothing of either species or genus, or form, or conception, or of anything else whatever which is comprehended by the intellect alone, and depending solely on what lies externally visible, and such things as come under the notice of the eyes, and the ears, and the other hundred faculties, is thought worthy of Charran for his country, which Jacob, the lover of virtue, inhabits as a foreign land for a short time, always bearing in his recollection his return homewards; (46) therefore his mother, perseverance, that is Rebecca, says to him, "Rise up and flee to Laban, my brother, to Charran, and dwell with him certain days."[7] Do you not perceive then that the practiser of virtue will not endure to live permanently in the country of the outward senses, but only to remain there a few days and a short time, on account of the necessities of the body to which he is bound? But a longer time and an entire life is allotted to him in the city which is appreciable only by the intellect.

IX. (47) In reference to which fact, also, it appears to me to be that his grandfather also, by name Abraham, so called from his knowledge, would not endure to remain any great length of time in Charran, for it is said in the scriptures that "Abraham was seventy-five years old when he departed from Charran;"[8] although his father Terah, which name being interpreted means, "the

investigation of a smell," lived there till the day of his death.[9] (48) Therefore it is expressly stated in the sacred scriptures that "Terah died in Charran," for he was only a reconnoitrer of virtue, not a citizen. And he availed himself of smells, and not of the enjoyments of food, as he was not able as yet to fill himself with wisdom, nor indeed even to get a taste of it, but only to smell it; (49) for as it is said that those dogs which are calculated for hunting can by exerting their faculty of smell, find out the lurking places of their game at a great distance, being by nature rendered wonderfully acute as to the outward sense of smell; so in the same manner the lover of instruction tracks out the sweet breeze which is given forth by justice, and by any other virtue, and is eager to watch those qualities from which this most admirable source of delight proceeds, and while he is unable to do so he moves his head all round in a circle, smelling out nothing else, but seeking only for that most sacred scent of excellence and food, for he does not deny that he is eager for knowledge and wisdom.

(50) Blessed therefore are they to whom it has happened to enjoy the delights of wisdom, and to feast upon its speculations and doctrines, and even of the being cheered by them still to thirst for more, feeling an insatiable and increasing desire for knowledge. (51) And those will obtain the second place who are not allured indeed to enjoy the sacred table, but who nevertheless refresh their souls with its odours; for they will be excited by the fragrances of virtue like those languid invalids who, because they are not as yet able to take solid food, nevertheless feed on the smell of such viands as the sons of the physicians prepare as a sort of remedy for their impotency.

X. (52) Therefore, having left the land of the Chaldaeans, Terah is said to have migrated to Charran; bringing with him his son Abraham and the rest of his household who agreed with him in opinion, not in order that we might read in the account of the historical chronicles that some men had become emigrants, leaving their native country and becoming inhabitants of a foreign land as if it were their own country, but in order that a lesson of the greatest importance to life and full of wisdom, and adapted to man alone, might not be neglected.

(53) And what is the lesson? The Chaldaeans are great astronomers, and the inhabitants of Charran occupy themselves with the topics relating to the external senses. Therefore the sacred account says to the investigator of the things of nature, why are you inquiring about the sun, and asking whether he is a foot broad, whether he is greater than the whole earth put together, or whether he is even many times as large? And why are you

---

[7] Genesis 27:43.
[8] Genesis 12:4.

[9] Genesis 17:32.

investigating the causes of the light of the moon, and whether it has a borrowed light, or one which proceeds solely from itself? Why, again, do you seek to understand the nature of the rest of the stars, of their motion, of their sympathy with one another, and even with earthly things? (54) And why, while walking upon the earth do you soar above the clouds? And why, while rooted in the solid land, do you affirm that you can reach the things in the sky? And why do you endeavour to form conjectures about matters which cannot be ascertained by conjecture? And why do you busy yourself about sublime subjects which you ought not to meddle with? And why do you extend your desire to make discoveries in mathematical science as far as the heaven? And why do you devote yourself to astronomy, and talk about nothing but high subjects? My good man, do not trouble your head about things beyond the ocean, but attend only to what is near you; and be content rather to examine yourself without flattery.

(55) How, then, will you find out what you want, even if you are successful? Go with full exercise of your intellect to Charran, that is, to the trench which is dug, into the holes and caverns of the body, and investigate the eyes, the ears, the nostrils, and the other organs of the external senses; and if you wish to be a philosopher, study philosophically that branch which is the most indispensable and at the same time the most becoming to a man, and inquire what the faculty of sight is, what hearing is, what taste, what smell, what touch is, in a word, what is external sense; then seek to understand what it is to see, and how you see; what it is to hear, and how you hear; what it is to smell, or to taste, or to touch, and how each of these operations is ordinarily effected. (56) But it is not the very extravagance of insane folly to seek to comprehend the dwelling of the universe, before your own private dwelling is accurately known to you? But I do not as yet lay the more important and extensive injunction upon you to make yourself acquainted with your own soul and mind, of the knowledge of which you are so proud; for in reality you will never be able to comprehend it.

(57) Mount up then to heaven, and talk arrogantly about the things which exist there, before you are as yet able to comprehend, according to the words of the poet,

"All the good and all the evil
Which thy own abode contains;"

and, bringing down that messenger of yours from heaven, and dragging him down from his search into matters existing there, become acquainted with yourself, and carefully and diligently labour to arrive at such happiness as is permitted to man. (58) Now this disposition the Hebrews called

Terah, and the Greeks Socrates; for they say also that the latter grew old in the most accurate study by which he could hope to know himself, never once directing his philosophical speculations to the subjects beyond himself. But he was really a man; but Terah is the principle itself which is proposed to every one, according to which each man should know himself, like a tree full of good branches, in order that these persons who are fond of virtue might without difficulty gather the fruit of pure morality, and thus become filled with the most delightful and saving food.

(59) Such, then, are those men who reconnoitre the quarters of wisdom for us; but those who are actually her athletes, and who practise her exercises, are more perfect. For these men think fit to learn with complete accuracy the whole question connected with the external senses, and after having done so, then to proceed to another and more important speculation, leaving all consideration of the holes of the body which they call Charran. (60) Of the number of these men is Abraham, who attained to great progress and improvement in the comprehension of complete knowledge; for when he knew most, then he most completely renounced himself in order to attain to the accurate knowledge of him who was the truly living God. And, indeed, this is a very natural course of events; for he who completely understands himself does also very much, because of his thorough appreciation of it, renounce the universal nothingness of the creature; and he who renounces himself learns to comprehend the living God.

XI. (61) We have now, then, explained what Charran is, and why he who left the well of the oath came thither. We must now consider the third point which comes next in order, namely, what the place is to which this man came; for it is said, "He met him in the place."[10] (62) Now place is considered in three ways: firstly, as a situation filled by a body; secondly, as a divine word which God himself has filled wholly and entirely with incorporeal powers; for says the scripture, "I have seen the place in which the God of Israel stood,"[11] in which alone he permitted his prophet to perform sacrifice to him, forbidding him to do so in other places. For he is ordered to go up into the place which the Lord God shall choose, and there to sacrifice burnt offerings and sacrifices for salvation, and to bring other victims also without spot.

(63) According to the third signification, God himself is called a place, from the fact of his surrounding the universe, and being surrounded himself by nothing whatever, and from the fact of his being the refuge of all persons, and since he him-

---

[10] Genesis 28:11.
[11] Exodus 24:10.

self is his own district, containing himself and resembling himself alone. (64) I, indeed, am not a place, but I am in a place, and every existing being is so in a similar manner. So that which is surrounded differs from that which surrounds it; but the Deity, being surrounded by nothing, is necessarily itself its own place. And there is an evidence in support of my view of the matter in the following sacred oracle delivered with respect to Abraham: "He came unto the place of which the Lord God had told him: and having looked up with his eyes, he saw the place afar off." [12]

(65) Tell me, now, did he who had come to the place see it afar off? Or perhaps it is but an identical expression for two different things, one of which is the divine world, and the other, God, who existed before the world. (66) But he who was conducted by wisdom comes to the former place, having found that the main part and end of propitiation is the divine word, in which he who is fixed does not as yet attain to such a height as to penetrate to the essence of God, but sees him afar off; or, rather, I should say, he is not able even to behold him afar off, but he only discerns this fact, that God is at a distance from every creature, and that any comprehension of him is removed to a great distance from all human intellect. (67) Perhaps, however, the historian, by this allegorical form of expression, does not here mean by his expression, "place," the Cause of all things; but the idea which he intends to convey may be something of this sort;—he came to the place, and looking up with his eyes he saw the very place to which he had come, which was a very long way from the God who may not be named nor spoken of, and who is in every way incomprehensible.

XII. (68) These things, then, being defined as a necessary preliminary, when the practiser of virtue comes to Charran, the outward sense, he does not "meet" the place, nor that place either which is filled by a mortal body; for all those who are born of the dust, and who occupy any place whatever, and who do of necessity fill some position, partake of that; nor the third and most excellent kind of place, of which it was scarcely possible for that man to form an idea who made his abode at the well which was entitled the "well of the oath," where the self-taught race, Isaac, abides, who never abandons his faith in God and his invisible comprehension of him, but who keeps to the intermediate divine word, which affords him the best suggestions, and teaches him everything which is suitable to the times.

(69) For God, not condescending to come down to the external senses, sends his own words or angels for the sake of giving assistance to those who love virtue. But they attend like physicians to the disease of the soul, and apply themselves to heal them, offering sacred recommendations like sacred laws, and inviting men to practice the duties inculcated by them, and, like the trainers of wrestlers, implanting in their pupils strength, and power, and irresistible vigour. (70) Very properly, therefore, when he has arrived at the external sense, he is represented no longer as meeting God, but only the divine word, just as his grandfather Abraham, the model of wisdom, did; for the scripture tells us, "The Lord departed when he had finished conversing with Abraham, and Abraham returned to his place." [13]

From which expression it is inferred, that he also met with the sacred words from which God, the father of the universe, had previously departed, no longer displaying visions from himself but only those which proceed from his subordinate powers. (71) And it is with exceeding beauty and propriety that it is said, not that he came to the place, but that he met the place: for to come is voluntary, but to meet is very often involuntary; so that the divine Word appearing on a sudden, supplies an unexpected joy, greater than could have been hoped, inasmuch as it is about to travel in company with the solitary soul; for Moses also "brings forward the people to a meeting with God," [14] well knowing that he comes invisibly towards those souls who have a longing to meet with him.

XIII. (72) And he subsequently alleges a reason why he "met the place;" for, says he, "the sun was set." [15] Not meaning the sun which appears to us, but the most brilliant and radiant light of the invisible and Almighty God. When this light shines upon the mind, the inferior beams of words (that is of angels) set. And much more are all the places perceptible by the external senses overshadowed; but when he departs in a different direction, then they all rise and shine. (73) And do not wonder if, according to the rules of allegorical description, the sun is likened to the Father and Governor of the universe; for in reality nothing is like unto God; but those things which by the vain opinion of men are thought to be so, are only two things, one invisible and the other visible; the soul being the invisible thing, and the sun the visible one.

(74) Now he has shown the similitude of the soul in another passage, where he says, "God made man, in the image of God created he him." And again, in the law enacted against homicides, he says, "Whoso sheddeth man's blood, by man shall his blood be shed in requital for that blood, because in the image of God did I make him." [16] But the likeness of the sun he only indicates by symbols.

[12] Genesis 22:4.
[13] Genesis 18:33.
[14] Exodus 19:17.
[15] Genesis 28:11.
[16] Genesis 9:6.

(75) And it is easy otherwise by means of argument to perceive this, since God is the first light, "For the Lord is my light and my Saviour,"[17] is the language of the Psalms; and not only the light, but he is also the archetypal pattern of every other light, or rather he is more ancient and more sublime than even the archetypal model, though he is spoken of as the model; for the real model was his own most perfect word, the light, and he himself is like to no created thing. (76) Since, as the sun divides day and night, so also does Moses say that God divided the light from the darkness; for "God made a division between the light and between the darkness."[18]

And besides all this, as the sun, when he arises, discovers hidden things, so also does God, who created all things, not only bring them all to light, but he has even created what before had no existence, not being their only maker, but also their founder.

XIV. (77) And the sun is also spoken of in many passages of holy writ in a figurative manner. Once as the human mind, which men build up as a city[19] and furnish, who are compelled to serve the creature in preference to the uncreated God, of whom it is said that, "They built strong cities for Pharaoh and Peitho,"[20] that is, for discourse; to which persuasion *(to peithein)* is attributed, and Rameses, or the outward sense, by which the soul is devoured as if by moths; for the name Rameses, being interpreted, means, "the shaking of a moth;" and On, the mind, which they called Heliopolis, since the mind, like the sun, has the predominance over the whole mass of our body, and extends its powers like the beams of the sun, over everything.

(78) But he who appropriates to himself the regulation of corporeal things, by name Joseph, takes the priest and minister of the mind to be his father-in-law; for says the scripture, "he gave him Aseneth, the daughter of Peutephres, the priest of Heliopolis, for his wife."[21] (79) And, using symbolical language, he calls the outward sense a second sun, inasmuch as it shows all the objects of which it is able to form a judgment to the intellect, concerning which he speaks thus, "The sun rose upon him when he passed by the appearance of God."[22] For in real truth, when we are no longer able to endure to pass all our time with the most sacred appearances, and as it were with incorporeal images, but when we turn aside in another direction, and forsake them, we use another light, that, namely, in accordance with the external sense, which is real truth, is in no respect different from darkness, (80) which, after it has arisen, arouses as if from sleep the senses of seeing, and of hearing, and also of taste, and of touch, and of smell, and sends to sleep the intellectual qualities of prudence, and justice, and knowledge, and wisdom, which were all awake.

(81) And it is for this reason that the sacred scripture says, that no one can be pure before the evening,[23] as the disorderly motions of the outward senses agitate and confuse the intellect. Moreover, he establishes a law for the priests also which may not be avoided, combining with it an expression of a grave opinion when it says, "He shall not eat of the holy things unless he has washed his body in water, and unless the sun has set, and he has become pure."[24] (82) For by these words it is very clearly shown that there is no one whatever completely pure, so as to be fit to be initiated into the holy and sacred mysteries, to whose lot it has fallen to be honoured with these glories of life which are appreciable by the external senses. But if any one rejects these glories, he is deservedly made conspicuous by the light of wisdom, by means of which he will be able to wash off the stains of vain opinion and to become pure.

(83) Do you not see that even the sun itself produces opposite effects when he is setting from those which he causes when rising? For when he rises everything upon the earth shines, and the things in heaven are hidden from our view; but, on the other hand, when he sets then the stars appear and the things on earth are overshadowed. (84) In the same manner, also, in us, when the light of the outward senses rises like the sun, the celestial and heavenly sciences are really and truly hidden from view; but when this light is near setting, then the starlike radiance of the virtues appears, when the mind is pure, and concealed by no object of the outward senses.

XV. (85) But according to the third signification, when he speaks of the sun, he means the divine word, the model of that sun which moves about through the heaven, as has been said before, and with respect to which it is said, "The sun went forth upon the earth, and Lot entered into Segor, and the Lord rained upon Sodom and Gomorrah brimstone and fire." (86) For the word of God, when it reaches to our earthly constitution, assists and protects those who are akin to virtue, or whose inclinations lead them to virtue; so that it provides them with a complete refuge and salvation, but upon their enemies it sends irremediable overthrow and destruction.

(87) And in the fourth signification, what is meant by the sun is the God and ruler of the uni-

---

[17] Psalm 26:1.
[18] Genesis 1:4.
[19] Genesis 1:4.
[20] Genesis 11:4.
[21] Genesis 41:45.
[22] Genesis 32:31.

[23] Leviticus 4:31.
[24] Leviticus 22:6.

verse himself, as I have said already, by means of whom such offences as are irremediable, and which appear to be overshadowed and concealed, are revealed; for as all things are possible, so, likewise, all things are known to God.

(88) In reference to which faculty of his it is that he drags those persons who are living dissolutely as regards their souls, and who are in a debauched and intemperate manner, cohabiting with the daughters of the mind the outward senses, as prostitutes and harlots, to the light of the sun, in order to display their true characters; (89) for the scripture says, "And the people abode in Shittim;" now the meaning of the name Shittim is, "the thorns of passion;" which sting and wound the soul. "And the people was polluted, and began to commit whoredom with the daughters of Moab,"[25] and those who are called daughters are the outward senses, for the name Moab is interpreted, "of a father;" and the scripture adds, "Take all the chiefs of the people, and make an example of them unto the Lord in the face of the sun, and the anger of the Lord shall be turned from Israel."[26] (90) For he not only desires that the wicked deeds which are hidden shall be made manifest, and therefore turns upon them the beams of the sun, but he also by this symbolical language calls the father of the universe the sun, that being by whom all things are seen beforehand, and even all those things which are invisibly concealed in the recesses of the mind; and when they are made manifest, then he promises that he who is the only merciful being, will become merciful to the people. (91) Why so? Because, even if the mind, fancying that though it does wrong it can escape the notice of the Deity as not being able to see everything, should sin secretly and in dark places, and should after that, either by reason of its own notions or through the suggestions of some one else, conceive that it is impossible that anything should be otherwise than clear to God, and should disclose itself and all its actions, and should bring them forward, as it were, out of the light of the sun, and display them to the governor of the universe, saying, that it repents of the perverse conduct which it formerly exhibited when under the influence of foolish opinion (for that nothing is indistinct before God, but all things are known and clear to him, not merely such as have been done, but even such are merely hoped or designed, by reason of the boundless character of his wisdom), it then is purified and benefited, and it propitiates the chastiser who was ready to punish it, namely, conscience, who was previously filled with just anger towards it, and who now admits repentance as the younger brother of perfect innocence and freedom from sin.

XVI. (92) Moreover, it appears that Moses has in other passages also taken the sun as a symbol of the great Cause of all things, in which I see an instance in the law which is enacted with respect to those who borrow on pledges: let us recite the law, "If thou takest as a pledge the garment of thy neighbour, thou shalt give it back before the setting of the sun: for it is his covering, it is his only covering of his nakedness, in which he lies down. If he cries unto me I will hearken unto him, for I am merciful."[27] (93) Is it not natural that those who fancy that the lawgiver displays such earnestness about a garment should, if they do not reproach him, at least make a suggestion, saying, "What are ye saying, my good men? Do ye affirm that the Creator and ruler of the world calls himself merciful with respect to so trivial a matter, as that of a garment not being restored to the borrower by the lender?" (94) These are the opinions and notions of men who have never had the least conception or comprehension of the virtue of the almighty God, and who, contrary to all human and divine law, impart the triviality of human affairs to the uncreate and immortal nature, which is full of happiness, and blessedness, and perfection; (95) for in what respect do those lenders act unreasonably, who retain in their own hands the pledges which are deposited with them as security, until they receive back their own which they have lent? The debtors are poor, some one will perhaps say, and it is right to pity them: would it not have been reasonable and better to enact a law in accordance with which a contribution should be made to assist their necessities, rather than allow them to appear as debtors, or else one which should forbid the lending on pledges at all?

But the law which has permitted the lending on pledges, cannot fairly be indignant against those who will not give up the pledges which they have received before the proper time, as if they were acting unjustly.

(96) But if any one having come, so to say, to the very farthest limits of poverty, and, being clothed in rags, loads himself with new debts, neglecting the pity which he receives from the bystanders, which is freely bestowed, upon those who fall into such misfortunes, in their own houses, and in the temples, and in the market-place, and everywhere; (97) such a one brings and offers to his creditor, the only covering which he had for his shame, with which he has been wont to cover the secret parts of his nature, as a pledge for something. For what, I pray? Is it for some other and better garment? For no one is unprovided with necessary food as long as the springs of the rivers bubble up, and the torrents flow abundantly, and the earth gives forth its annual fruits.

---

[25]Numbers 25:1.
[26]Numbers 25:4.

[27]Exodus 22:26.

(98) Again, is any creditor so covetous of riches, or so very cruel, or so perverse, as not to be willing to contribute a tetradrachm, or even less, to one in distress? Or is any one so stingy as to be willing to lend it, but to refuse to give it? or as to take the only garment that the poor man has as a pledge? which indeed under another name may fairly be called running away with a man's clothes;[28] for men who do this are accustomed to put on other peoples' clothes, and steal them, and to leave the proper owners naked.

(99) And why has the law provided so carefully that the debtor may not be without his clothes by night, and that he may not lie down to sleep without them, but has not paid the same attention to the fact of his being indecorously naked by day? Are not all things concealed by night and darkness, so as to cause less shame, or rather none at all at that time, but are they not disclosed by day and by light, so as then to compel persons to blush more freely? (100) And why does the law not use the expression "to give," but "to restore?" For restoration takes place with respect to the property of other persons, but pledges belong rather to those who have lent on them than to those who have borrowed on them. Moreover, do you not perceive that the law has not enjoined the debtor, who has received back his garment that it may serve as bed-clothes, to bring it back again to his creditor at the return of daylight? (101) And, indeed, if the exact propriety of the language be considered, even the most stupid person may see that there is something additional meant beyond what is formally expressed. For the injunction rather resembles a maxim than a recommendation. For, if a person had been giving a recommendation, he would have said: "Give back to your debtor, at the approach of evening, the garment which has been pledged to you, if it be the only garment that he is possessed of, that he may have something with which to cover himself at night." But one who was laying down a maxim would speak thus; as indeed the law does here, "For it is his garment, the only covering of his nakedness, in which he will lie down to sleep."

XVII. (102) These things then, and other things of the same kind, may be urged in reply to those assertors of the literal sense of a passage; and who superciliously reject all other explanations. We will now, in accordance with the usual laws of allegorical speaking, say what is becoming with respect to these subjects.

We say, therefore, that a garment here is spoken of symbolically, to signify speech; for clothes keep off the injuries which are wont to visit the body, from cold and heat, and they also conceal the unmentionable parts of nature, and moreover, a cloak is a fitting garment for the body. (103) In much the same manner, speech has been given to man by God, as the most excellent of gifts; for in the first place, it is a defensive weapon against those who would attack him with innovations. For as nature has fortified all other animals with their own appropriate and peculiar means of defence, by which they are able to repel those who attempt to injure them, so also has it bestowed upon man that greatest defence and most impregnable protection of speech, with which, as with a panoply, every one who is completely clothed, will have a domestic and most appropriate bodyguard; and employing it as a champion, will be able to ward off all the injuries which can be brought against him by his enemies.

(104) In the second place, it is a most necessary defence against shame and reproach; for speech is very well calculated to conceal and obscure the faults of men.

In the third place, it conduces to the whole ornament of life: for this is the thing which improves every one, and which conducts every one to what is best; (105) for there are many disgraceful and mischievous men, who take conversation as a pledge, and deprive its proper owners of it, and utterly cut off what they ought to seek to increase; like men who ravage the lands of their enemies, and who attempt to destroy their corn and all the rest of their crops, which, if it were left unhurt, would be a great advantage to those who would use it.

(106) For some men carry on an irreconcilable and never-ending war against rational nature, and utterly extirpate its every shoot and beginning, and destroy all its first appearances of propagation, and render it, as one may say, utterly unproductive and barren of all good practices. (107) For sometimes, when it is borne onwards towards sacred instruction with irresistible impetuosity, and when it is smitten with a love of the speculations of true philosophy, they—out of jealousy and envy, fearing lest, when it has derived strength from its noble aspirations and has been elevated to a splendid height, it may overwhelm all their petty cavils and plausible devices against the truth, like an irresistible torrent—turn its energy in another direction by their own evil artifices, guiding it in another channel to vulgar and illiberal acts: and very often they seek to blunt it or to hedge it in, and in this way leave the nobility of its nature uncultivated, just as at times wicked guardians of orphan children have rendered a deep-soiled and fertile land barren.

And these most pitiless of all men have not been restrained by shame from stripping the man of his only garment, namely, speech; "For," says the scripture, "it is his only covering."—What is a man's

---

[28]The Greek word is *lōpodyteō*. A *lōpodytēs* was one who frequented the baths for the purpose of stealing the clothes of the bathers.

only covering, except speech? (108) For, as neighing is the peculiar attribute of a horse, and barking of a dog, and lowing of an ox, and roaring of a lion, so also is speaking, and speech itself, the peculiar property of man: for this is what man has received above all other animals as his peculiar gift, as a protection, a bulwark, and panoply, and wall of defence; he being, of all living creatures, the most beloved of God.

XVIII. (109) On which account the scripture adds, "This is the only covering of his nakedness;" for what can so becomingly overshadow and conceal the reproaches and disgraces of life, as speech? For ignorance is a disgrace akin to irrational nature, but education is the brother of speech, and an ornament properly belonging to man. (110) In what then will a man lie down to rest? That is to say, in what will a man find tranquillity and a respite from his labours, except in speech? For speech is a relief to our most miserable and afflicted race. As therefore, when men have been overwhelmed by grief, or by fear, or by any other evil, tranquillity, and constancy, and the kindness of friends have often restored them; so it happens, not often, but invariably, that speech, the only real averter of evil, wards off that most heavy burden which the necessities of that body in the which we are bound up, and the unforeseen accidents of external circumstances which attack us, impose upon us; (111) for speech is a friend, and an acquaintance, and a kinsman, and a companion bound up within us; I should rather say, fitted close and united to us by some indissoluble and invisible cement of nature.

On this account it is, that it forewarns us of what will be expedient for us, and when any unexpected event befalls us it comes forward of its own accord to assist us; not only bringing advantage of one kind only, such as that which he who is an adviser without acting, or an agent who can give no advice, may supply, but of both kinds: (112) for he does not display a half-complete power, but one which is perfect in every part. Inasmuch, as even if it were to fail in his endeavour, and in any conceptions which may have been formed, or efforts which may have been made, it still can have recourse to the third species of assistance, namely, consolation.

For speech is, as it were, a medicine for the wounds of the soul, and a saving remedy for its passions, which, "even before the setting of the sun," the lawgiver says one must restore: that is to say, before the all-brilliant beams of the almighty and all-glorious God are obscured, which he, out of pity for our race, sends down from heaven upon the human mind. (113) For while that most Godlike light abides in the soul, we shall be able to give back the speech, which was deposited as a pledge, as if it were a garment, in order that he who has received this peculiar possession of man, may by its means conceal the discreditable circum-

stances of life, and reap the benefit of the divine gift, and indulge in a respite combined with tranquillity, in consequence of the presence of so useful an adviser and defender, who will never leave the ranks in which he has been stationed.

(114) Moreover, while God pours upon you the light of his beams, do you hasten in the light of day to restore his pledge to the Lord; for when the sun has set, then you, like the whole land of Egypt,[29] will have an everlasting darkness which may be felt, and being stricken with blindness and ignorance, you will be deprived of all those things of which you thought that you had certain possession, by that sharp-sighted Israel, whose pledges you hold, having made one who was by nature exempt from slavery a slave to necessity.

XIX. (115) We have discussed this subject at this length with no other object except that of teaching that the mind, which is inclined to practice virtue, having irregular motions towards prolificness and sterility, and as one may say, being in a manner always ascending and descending, when it becomes prolific and is elevated to a height is illuminated with the archetypal and incorporeal beams of the rational spring of the all-perfecting sun; but when it descends and becomes unproductive, then it is again illuminated by those images of those beams, the immortal words which it is customary to call angels. (116) On which account we now read in the scripture, "He met the place; for the sun was set."[30]

For when those beams of God desert the soul by means of which the clearest comprehensions of affairs are engendered in it, then arises that second and weaker light of words, and the light of things is no longer seen, just as is the case in this lower world. For the moon, which occupies the second rank next to the sun, when that body has set, pours forth a somewhat weaker light than his upon the earth; (117) and to meet a place or a word is a most sufficient gift for those who cannot discern that God is superior to every place or word; because they have not a soul wholly destitute of light, but because, since that most unmixed and brilliant light has set, they have been favoured with one which is alloyed.

"For the children of Israel had light in all their dwellings,"[31] says the sacred historian in the book of Exodus, so that night and darkness were continually banished from them, though it is in night and darkness that those men live who have lost the eyes of the soul rather than those of the body, having no experience of the beams of virtue. (118) But some persons—supposing that what is meant here by the figurative expression of the sun is the

---

[29]Exodus 10:21.
[30]Genesis 28:11.
[31]Exodus 10:23.

external sense and the mind, which are looked upon as the things which have the power of judging; and that which is meant by place is the divine word—understand the allegory in this manner: the practiser of virtue met with the divine word, after the mortal and human light had set; (119) for as long as the mind thinks that it attains to a firm comprehension of the objects of the intellect, and the outward sense conceives that it has a similar understanding of its appropriate objects, and that it dwells amid sublime objects, the divine word stands aloof at a distance; but when each of these comes to confess its own weakness, and sets in a manner while availing itself of concealment, then immediately the right reason of a soul well-practised in virtue comes in a welcome manner to their assistance, when they have begun to despair of their own strength, and await the aid which is invisibly coming to them from without.

XX. (120) Therefore, the scripture says in the next verses, "That he took one of the stones of the place and placed it at his head, and slept in that place."[32] Any one may wonder not only at the interior and mystical doctrine contained in these words, but also at the distinct assertion, which gives us a lesson in labour and endurance: (121) for the historian does not think it becoming, that the man who is devoted to the study of virtue should adopt a luxurious life, and live softly, imitating the pursuits and rivalries of those who are called indeed happy, but who are in reality full of all unhappiness; whose entire life is a sleep and a dream, according to the holy lawgiver.

(122) These men, after they have during the whole day been doing all sorts of injustice to others, in courts of justice, and council halls, and theatres, and everywhere, then return home, like miserable men as they are, to overturn their own house. I mean not that house which comes under the class of buildings, but that which is akin to the soul, I mean the body. Introducing immoderate and incessant food, and irrigating it with an abundance of pure wine, until the reason is overwhelmed, and disappears; and the passions which have their seat beneath the belly, the offspring of satiety, rise up, being carried away by unrestrained frenzy, and falling upon, and vehemently attacking all that they meet with, are only at last appeased after they have worked off their excessive violence of excitement.

(123) But by night, when it is time to turn towards rest, having prepared costly couches and the most exquisite of beds, they lie down in the most exceeding softness, imitating the luxury of women, whom nature has permitted to indulge in a more relaxed system of life, inasmuch as their maker, the Creator of the universe, has made their bodies of a more delicate stamp. (124) Now no

such person as this is a pupil of the sacred word, but those only are the disciples of that who are real genuine men, lovers of temperance, and orderliness, and modesty, men who have laid down continence, and frugality, and fortitude, as a kind of base and foundation for the whole of life; and safe stations for the soul, in which it may anchor without danger and without changeableness: for being superior to money, and pleasure, and glory, they look down upon meats and drinks, and everything of that sort, beyond what is necessary to ward off hunger: being thoroughly ready to undergo hunger, and thirst, and heat, and cold, and all other things, however hard they may be to be borne, for the sake of the acquisition of virtue. And being admirers of whatever is most easily provided, so as to not be ashamed of ever such cheap or shabby clothes, think rather, on the other hand, that sumptuous apparel is a reproach and great scandal to life.

(125) To these men, the soft earth is their most costly couch; their bed is bushes, and grass, and herbage, and a thick layer of leaves; and the pillows for their head are a few stones, or any little mounds which happen to rise a little above the surface of the plain.

Such a life as this, is, by luxurious men, denominated a life of hardship, but by those who live for virtue, it is called most delightful; for it is well adapted, not for those who are called men, for those who really are such. (126) Do you not see, that even now, also, the sacred historian represents the practiser of honourable pursuits, who abounds in all royal materials and appointments, as sleeping on the ground, and using a stone for his pillow; and a little further on, he speaks of himself as asking in his prayers for bread and a cloak, the necessary wealth of nature? like one who has at all times held in contempt, the man who dwells among vain opinions, and who is inclined to revile all those who are disposed to admire him; this man is the archetypal pattern of the soul which is devoted to the practice of virtue, and an enemy of every effeminate person.

XXI. (127) Hitherto I have been uttering the praises of the man devoted to labour and to virtue, as it occurred to me naturally; but now we must examine what is symbolically signified under the expressions made use of.

Now it is well that we should know, that the divine place and the sacred region are full of incorporeal intelligences; and these intelligences are immortal souls. (128) Taking then one of these intelligences, and selecting one of them according as it appears to be the most excellent, this lover of virtue, of whom we are speaking, applies it to our own mind, to it as to the head of a united body; for, indeed, the mind is in a manner the head of the soul; and he does this, using the pretext indeed as if he were going to sleep, but, in reality, as being about to rest upon the word of God, and to

---

[32] Genesis 28:11.

place the whole of his life as the lightest possible burden upon it; (129) and it listens to him gladly, and receives the labourer in the paths of virtue at first, as if he were going to become a disciple; then when he has shown his approbation of the dexterity of his nature, he gives him his hand, like a gymnastic trainer, and invites him to the gymnasia, and standing firmly, compels him to wrestle with him, until he has rendered his strength so great as to be irresistible, changing his ears by the divine influences into eyes, and calling this newly-modelled disposition Israel, that is, the man who sees. [33]

(130) Then also he crowns him with the garland of victory. But this garland has a singular and foreign, and, perhaps, not altogether a well-omened name, for it is called by the president of the games torpor, for it is said, that the breadth became torpid [34] of all the rewards and of the proclamations of the heralds, and of all those most wonderful prizes for pre-eminent excellence which are had in honour; (131) for the soul which has received a share of irresistible power, and which has been made perfect in the contests of virtue, and which has arrived at the very furthest limit of what is honourable, will never be unduly elated or puffed up by arrogance, nor stand upon tiptoes, and boast as if it were well to make vast strides with bare feet; but the breadth which was extended wide by opinion, will become torpid and contracted, and then will voluntarily succumb and yield to tameness, so as being classed in an inferior order to that of the incorporeal natures, it may carry off the victory while appearing to be defeated; (132) for it is accounted a most honourable thing to yield the palm to those who are superior to one's self, voluntarily rather than through compulsion; for it is incredible how greatly the second prize in this contest is superior in real dignity and importance to the first prize in the others.

XXII. (133) Such then may be said, by way of preface, to the discussion of that description of visions which are sent from God. But it is time now to turn to the subject itself, and to investigate, with accuracy, every portion of it.

The scripture therefore says, "And he dreamed a dream. And behold a ladder was planted firmly on the ground, the head of which reached to heaven, and the angels of God were ascending and descending along it." [35] (134) By the ladder in this thing, which is called the world, is figuratively understood the air, the foundation of which is the earth, and the head is the heaven; for the large interior space, which being extended in every direction, reaches from the orb of the moon, which is described as the most remote of the order in heaven, but the nearest to us by those who contemplate sublime objects, down to the earth, which is the lowest of such bodies, is the air. (135) This air is the abode of incorporeal souls, since it seemed good to the Creator of the universe to fill all the parts of the world with living creatures. On this account he prepared the terrestrial animals for the earth, the aquatic animals for the sea and for the rivers, and the stars for the heaven; for every one of these bodies is not merely a living animal, but is also properly described as the very purest and most universal mind extending through the universe; so that there are living creatures in that other section of the universe, the air.

And if these things are not comprehensible by the outward senses, what of that? For the soul is also invisible. (136) And yet it is probable that the air should nourish living animals even more than the land or the water. Why so? Because it is the air which has given vitality to those animals which live on the earth and in the water. For the Creator of the universe formed the air so that it should be the habit of those bodies which are immovable, and the nature of those which are moved in an invisible manner, and the soul of such as are able to exert an impetus and visible sense of their own. (137) Is it not then absurd that that element, by means of which the other elements have been filled with vitality, should itself be destitute of living things? Therefore let no one deprive the most excellent nature of living creatures of the most excellent of those elements which surrounds the earth; that is to say, of the air. For not only is it not alone deserted by all things besides, but rather, like a populous city, it is full of imperishable and immortal citizens, souls equal in number to the stars.

(138) Now of these souls some descend upon the earth with a view to be bound up in mortal bodies, those namely which are most nearly connected with the earth, and which are lovers of the body. But some soar upwards, being again distinguished according to the definitions and times which have been appointed by nature. (139) Of these, those which are influenced by a desire for mortal life, and which have been familiarised to it, again return to it. But others, condemning the body of great folly and trifling, have pronounced it a prison and a grave, and, flying from it as from a house of correction or a tomb, have raised themselves aloft on light wings towards the aether, and have devoted their whole lives to sublime speculations.

(140) There are others, again, the purest and most excellent of all, which have received greater and more divine intellects, never by any chance desiring any earthly thing whatever, but being as it were lieutenants of the Ruler of the universe,

---

[33] The marginal note in our Bible translates Israel, "a prince of God."

[34] Genesis 32:25; where, however, the expression of the Bible is "the hollow of Jacob's thigh was out of joint."

[35] Genesis 28:12.

as though they were the eyes and ears of the great king, beholding and listening to everything. (141) Now philosophers in general are wont to call these demons, but the sacred scripture calls them angels, using a name more in accordance with nature. For indeed they do report *(diangellousi)* the injunctions of the father to his children, and the necessities of the children to the father.

(142) And it is in reference to this employment of theirs that the holy scripture has represented them as ascending and descending, not because God, who knows everything before any other being, has any need of interpreters; but because it is the lot of us miserable mortals to use speech as a mediator and intercessor; because of our standing in awe of and fearing the Ruler of the universe, and the all-powerful might of his authority; (143) having received a notion of which he once entreated one of those mediators, saying: "Do thou speak for us, and let not God speak to us, lest we die."[36] For not only are we unable to endure his chastisements, but we cannot bear even his excessive and unmodified benefits, which he himself proffers us of his own accord, without employing the ministrations of any other beings.

(144) Very admirably therefore does Moses represent the air under the figurative symbol of a ladder, as planted solidly in the earth and reaching up to heaven. For it comes to pass that the evaporations which are given forth by the earth becoming rarefied, are dissolved into air, so that the earth is the foundation and root of the air, and that the heaven is its head. (145) Accordingly it is said that the moon is not an unadulterated consolidation of pure aether, as each of the other stars is, but is rather a combination of the aether-like and air-like essence. For the black spot which appears in it, which some call a face, is nothing else but the air mingled with it, which is by nature black, and which extends as far as heaven.

XXIII. (146) The ladder therefore in the world which is here spoken of in this symbolical manner, was something of this sort. But if we carefully investigate the soul which exists in men, the foundation of which is something corporeal, and as it were earth-like, we shall find that the foundation to be the outward sense; and the head to be something heavenly, as it were the most pure mind. (147) But all the words of God move incessantly upwards and downwards through the whole of it, dragging it upwards along with them whenever they soar aloft, and separating it from whatever is mortal, and exhibiting to it a sight of those things which alone are worthy of being beheld; but yet not casting it down when they descend. For neither is God himself, nor the word of God, worthy of blame. But they join with them in their descent, by reason of their love for mankind and compassion for our race, for the sake of being their allies and rendering them assistance, in order that by breathing in a saving inspiration they may recall to life the soul which was still being tossed about in the body as in the river.

(148) Now the God and governor of the universe does by himself and alone walk about invisibly and noiselessly in the minds of those who are purified in the highest degree. For there is extant a prophecy which was delivered to the wise man, in which it is said: "I will walk among you, and I will be your God."[37] But the angels—the words of God—move about in the minds of those persons who are still in a process of being washed, but who have not yet completely washed off the life which defiles them, and which is polluted by the contact of their heavy bodies, making them look pure and brilliant to the eyes of virtue.

(149) But it is plain enough what vast numbers of evils are driven out, and what a multitude of wicked inhabitants is expelled in order that one good man may be introduced to dwell there. Do thou, therefore, O my soul, hasten to become the abode of God, his holy temple, to become strong from having been most weak, powerful from having been powerless, wise from having been foolish, and very reasonable from having been doting and childless.

(150) And perhaps too the practiser of virtue represents his own life as like to a ladder; for the practice of anything is naturally an anomalous thing, since at one time it soars up to a height, and at another it turns downwards in a contrary direction; and at one time has a fair voyage like a ship, and at another has but an unfavourable passage; for, as some one says, the life of those who practise virtue is full of vicissitudes: being at one time alive and waking, and at another dead or sleeping. (151) And perhaps this is no incorrect statement; for the wise have obtained the heavenly and celestial country as their habitation; having learnt to be continually mounting upwards, but the wicked have received as their share the dark recesses of hell, having from the beginning to the end of their existence practised dying, and having been from their infancy to their old age familiarised with destruction.

(152) But the practisers of virtue, for they are on the boundary between two extremities, are frequently going upwards and downwards as if on a ladder, being either drawn upwards by a more powerful fate, or else being dragged down by that which is worse; until the umpire of this contention and conflict, namely God, adjudges the victory to the more excellent class and utterly destroys the other.

XXIV. (153) There is also in this dream another

---

[36]Exodus 20:19.   [37]Leviticus 26:12.

sort of similitude or comparison apparent, which must not be passed over in silence; the affairs of mankind are naturally compared to a ladder, on account of their irregular motion and progress: (154) for as some one or other has said; "One day has cast one man down from on high and destroyed him, and another it has raised up, nothing that belongs to our human race being formed by nature so as to remain long in the same condition, but all such things changing with all kinds of alteration. (155) Do not men become rulers from having been private individuals, and private individuals from having been rulers, poor from having been rich, and very rich from having been very poor; glorious from being despised, and most illustrious from having been infamous?" [...] A very beautiful way of life: for it is very possible that the being whose habitation is the whole world, may dwell with you also, and take care of your house, so that it may be completely protected and free from injury for ever; (156) and there is such a way as this in which human affairs move upwards and downwards, meeting with an unstable and variable fortune, the anomalous character of which, unerring time proves by evidence which is not indistinct but manifest and legible.

XXV. (157) But the dream also represented the archangel, namely the Lord himself, firmly planted on the ladder; for we must imagine that the living God stands above all things, like the charioteer of a chariot, or the pilot of a ship; that is, above bodies, and above souls, and above all creatures, and above the earth, and above the air, and above the heaven, and above all the powers of the outward senses, and above the invisible natures, in short, above all things whether visible or invisible; for having made the whole to depend upon himself, he governs it and all the vastness of nature.

(158) But let no one who hears that he was firmly planted thus suppose that any thing at all assists God, so as to enable him to stand firmly, but let him rather consider this fact that what is here indicated is equivalent to the assertion that the firmest position, and the bulwark, and the strength, and the steadiness of everything is the immoveable God, who stamps the character of immobility on whatever he pleases; for, in consequence of his supporting and consolidating things, those which he does combine remain firm and indestructible.

(159) Therefore he who stands upon the ladder of heaven says to him who is beholding the dream, "I am the Lord God of Abraham thy father, and the God of Isaac; be not afraid."[38] This oracle and this vision were also the firmest support of the soul devoted to the practice of virtue, inasmuch as it taught it that the Lord and God of the universe is both these things also to his own race, being entitled both the Lord and God of all men, and of his grandfathers and ancestors, and being called by both names in order that the whole world and the man devoted to virtue might have the same inheritance; since it is also said, "The Lord himself is his inheritance."[39]

XXVI. (160) But do not fancy that it is an accidental thing here for him to be called in this place the God and Lord of Abraham, but only the God of Isaac; for this latter is the symbol of the knowledge which exists by nature, which hears itself, and teaches itself, and learns of itself; but Abraham is the symbol of that which is derived from the teaching of others; and the one again is an indigenous and native inhabitant of his country, but the other is only a settler and a foreigner; (161) for having forsaken the language of those who indulge in sublime conversations about astronomy, a language imitating that of the Chaldaeans, foreign and barbarous, he was brought over to that which was suited to a rational being, namely, to the service of the great Cause of all things.

(162) Now this disposition stands in need of two powers to take care of it, the power that is of authority, and that of conferring benefits, in order that in accordance with the authority of the governor, it may obey the admonitions which it receives, and also that it may be greatly benefited by his beneficence. But the other disposition stands in need of the power of beneficence only; for it has not derived any improvement from the authority which admonishes it, inasmuch as it naturally claims virtue as its own, but by reason of the bounty which is showered upon it from above, it was good and perfect from the beginning; (163) therefore God is the name of the beneficent power, and Lord is the title of the royal power.

What then can any one call a more ancient and important good, than to be thought worthy to meet with unmixed and unalloyed beneficence? And what can be less valuable than to receive a mixture of authority and liberality? And it appears to me that it was because the practiser of virtue saw that he uttered that most admirable prayer that, "the Lord might be to him as God;"[40] for he desired no longer to stand in awe of him as a governor, but to honour and love him as a benefactor. (164) Now is it not fitting that even blind men should become sharp-sighted in their minds to these and similar things, being endowed with the power of sight by the most sacred oracles, so as to be able to contemplate the glories of nature, and not to be limited to the mere understanding of the words? But even if we voluntarily close the eye of our soul and take no care to understand such mysteries, or if we are

---

[38] Genesis 28:13.

[39] Deuteronomy 10:9.
[40] Genesis 28:21.

unable to look up to them, the hierophant himself stands by and prompts us. And do not thou ever cease through weariness to anoint thy eyes until you have introduced those who are duly initiated to the secret light of the sacred scriptures, and have displayed to them the hidden things therein contained, and their reality, which is invisible to those who are uninitiated.

(165) It is becoming then for you to act thus; but as for ye, O souls, who have once tasted of divine love, as if you had even awakened from deep sleep, dissipate the mist that is before you; and hasten forward to that beautiful spectacle, putting aside slow and hesitating fear, in order to comprehend all the beautiful sounds and sights which the president of the games has prepared for your advantage.

XXVII. (166) There are then a countless number of things well worthy of being displayed and demonstrated; and among them one which was mentioned a little while ago; for the oracles calls the person who was really his grandfather, the father of the practiser of virtue, and to him who was really his father, it has not given any such title; for the scriptures says, "I am the Lord God of Abraham thy father," but in reality Abraham was his grandfather; and then proceeds, "And the God of Isaac," and in this case he does not add, "thy father:" (167) is it not then worth while to examine into the cause of this difference? Undoubtedly it is; let us then in a careful manner apply ourselves to the consideration of the cause.

Philosophers say that virtue exists among men, either by nature, or by practice, or by learning. On which account the sacred scriptures represent the three founders of the nation of the Israelites as wise men; not indeed originally endowed with the same kind of wisdom, but arriving rapidly at the same end. (168) For the eldest of them, Abraham, had instruction for his guide in the road which conducted him to virtue; as we shall show in another treatise to the best of our power. And Isaac, who is the middle one of the three, had a self-taught and self-instructed nature. And Jacob, the third, arrived at this point by industry and practice, in accordance with which were his labours of wrestling and contention.

(169) Since then there are thus three different manners by which wisdom exists among men, it happens that the two extremes are the most nearly and frequently united. For the virtue which is acquired by practice, is the offspring of that which is derived from learning. But that which is implanted by nature is indeed akin to the others, for it is set below them, as the root for them all. But it has obtained its prize without any rivalry or difficulty. (170) So that it is thus very natural for Abraham, as one who had been improved by instruction, to be called the father of Jacob, who arrived at his height of virtue by practice. By which

expression is indicated that not so much the relationship of one man to the other, but that the power which is fond of hearing is very ready for learning; the power which is devoted to practice being also well suited for wrestling. (171) If, however, this practiser of virtue runs on vigorously towards the end and learns to see clearly what he previously only dreamed of in an indistinct way, being altered and re-stamped with a better character, and being called Israel, that is, "the man who sees God," instead of Jacob, that is, "the supplanter," he then is no longer set down as the son of Abraham, as his father, of him who derived wisdom from instruction, but as the son of Isaac, who was born excellent by nature.

(172) These statements are not fables of my own invention, but are the oracle written on the sacred pillars. For, says the scripture: "Israel having departed, he and all that he had came to the well of the oath, and there he sacrificed a sacrifice to the God of his father Isaac."[41] Do you not now perceive that this present assertion has reference not to the relationship between mortal men, but, as was said before, to the nature of things? For look at what is before us. At one time, Jacob is spoken of as the son of his father Abraham, and at another time he is called Israel, the son of Isaac, on account of the reason which we have thus accurately investigated.

XVIII. (173) Having then said: "I am the Lord God of Abraham, the father and the God of Isaac," he adds: "Be not afraid," very consistently. For how can we any longer be afraid when we have thee, O God, as our armour and defender? Thee, the deliverer from fear and from every painful feeling? Thee, who hast also fashioned the archetypal forms of our instruction while they were still indistinct, so as to make them visible, teaching Abraham wisdom, and begetting Isaac, who was wise from his birth. For you condescended to be called the guide of the one and the father of the other, assigning to the one the rank of pupil, and to the other that of a son.

(174) For this reason, too, God promised that he would not give him the land. I mean by the land here, all-prolific virtue, on which the practiser rests from his contests and sleeps, from the fact of the life according to the outward sense being lulled asleep, and that of the soul being awakened. Receiving gladly peaceful repose there, which he did not obtain without war, and the afflictions which arise from war, not by means of bearing arms and slaying men; away with any such notion! but by overthrowing the array of vices and passions which are the adversaries of virtue.

(175) But the race of wisdom is likened to the sand of the sea, by reason of its boundless num-

---

[41]Genesis 46:1.

bers, and because also the sand, like a fringe, checks the incursions of the sea; as the reasonings of instruction beat back the violence of wickedness and iniquity. And these reasonings, in accordance with the divine promises, are extended to the very extremities of the universe. And they show that he who is possessed of them is the inheritor of all the parts of the world, penetrating everywhere, to the east, and to the west, to the south, and to the north. For it is said in the scripture: "He shall be extended towards the sea, and towards the south, and towards the north, and towards the east."[42] (176) But the wise and virtuous man is not only a blessing to himself, but he is also a common good to all men, diffusing advantages over all from his own ready store. For as the sun is the light of all those beings who have eyes, so also is the wise man light to all those who partake of a rational nature.

XXIX. (177) "For in thee shall all the nations of the earth be blessed." And this oracle applies to the wise man in respect of himself, and also in respect of others.[43] For if the mind which is in me is purified by perfect virtue, and if the tribes of that earthly part which is about me are purified at the same time, which tribes have fallen to the lot of the external senses, and of the greatest channel of all, namely the body; and if any one, either in his house, or in his city, or in his country, or in his nation, becomes a lover of wisdom, it is inevitable that that house, and that city, and that country, and that nation, must attain to a better life. (178) For, as those spices which are set on fire fill all persons near them with their fragrance, so in the same manner do all those persons who are neighbours of and contiguous to the wise men catch some of the exhalations which reach to a distance from him, and so become improved in their characters.

XXX. (179) And it is the greatest of all advantages to a soul engaged in labours and contests, to have for its fellow traveller, God, who penetrates everywhere. "For behold," says God, "I am with thee."[44] Of what then can we be in need while we have for our wealth Thee, who art the only true and real riches, who keepest us in the road which leads to virtue in all its different divisions? For it is not one portion only of the rational life which conducts to justice and to all other virtue, but the parts are infinite in number, from which those who desire to arrive at virtue can set out.

XXXI. (180) Very admirably therefore is it said in the scripture: "I will lead thee back to this land." For it was fitting that the reason should remain

with itself, and should not depart to the outward sense. And if it has departed, then the next best thing is for it to return back again. (181) And perhaps also a doctrine bearing on the immortality of the soul is figuratively intimated by this expression. For the soul, having left the region of heaven, as was mentioned a little while before, came to the body as a foreign country. Therefore the father who begot it promises that he will not permit it to be for ever held in bondage, but that he will have compassion on it, and will unloose its chains, and will conduct it in safety and freedom as far as the metropolis, and will not cease to assist it till the promises which he has made in words are confirmed by the truth of actions. For it is by all means the peculiar attribute of God to foretell what is to happen.

(182) And why do we say this? for his words do not differ from his actions; therefore the soul which is devoted to the practice of virtue, being set in motion, and roused up to the investigations relating to the living God, at first suspected that the living God existed in place; but after a short space it became perplexed by the difficulty of the question, and began to change its opinion. (183) "For," says the scripture, "Jacob awoke and said, Surely the Lord is in this place, and I knew it not;" and it would have been better, I should have said; not to know it, than to fancy that God existed in any place, he whom himself contains all things in a circle.

XXXII. (184) Very naturally, therefore, was Jacob afraid, and said in a spirit of admiration, "how dreadful is this place."[45] For, in truth, of all the topics or places in natural philosophy, the most formidable is that in which it is inquired where the living God is, and whether in short he is in any place at all. Since some persons affirm that everything which exists occupies some place or other, and others assign each thing a different place, either in the world or out of the world, in some space between the different bodies of the universe. Others again affirm that the uncreated God resembles no created being whatever, but that he is superior to everything, so that the very swiftest conception is outstripped by him, and confesses that it is very far inferior to the comprehension of him; (185) wherefore it speedily cries out, This is not what I expected, because the Lord is in the place; for he surrounds everything, but in truth and reason he is not surrounded by anything.

And this thing which is demonstrated and visible, this world perceptible by the outward senses, is nothing else but the house of God, the abode of one of the powers of the true God, in accordance with which he is good; (186) and he calls this world an abode, and he has also pronounced

[42]Genesis 28:14.
[43]The text is very corrupt here. I have followed Mangey's reading and translation.
[44]Genesis 28:15.

[45]Genesis 28:16.

it with great truth to be the gate of heaven. Now, what does this mean? We cannot comprehend the world which consists of various species, in that which is fashioned in accordance with the divine regulations, appreciable only by the intellect, in any other manner than by making a migration upwards from this other world perceptible by the outward senses and visible; (187) for it is not possible either to perceive any other existing being which is incorporeal, without deriving our principles of judgment from bodies. For while they are quiet, their place is perceived, and when they are in motion we judge of their time; but the points, and the lines, and the superficies, and in short the boundaries. [...][46] as of a garment wrapped externally around it.

(188) According to analogy, therefore, the knowledge of the world appreciable by the intellect is attained to by means of our knowledge of that which is perceptible by the outward senses, which is as it were a gate to the other. For as men who wish to see cities enter in through the gates, so also they who wish to comprehend the invisible world are conducted in their search by the appearance of the visible one. And the world of that essence which is only open to the intellect without any visible appearance or figure whatever, and which exists only in the archetypal idea which exists in the mind, which is fashioned according to its appearance, will be brought on without any shade; all the walls, and all the gates which could impede its progress being removed, so that it is not looked at through any other medium, but by itself, putting forth a beauty which is susceptible of no change, presenting an indescribable and exquisite spectacle.

XXXIII. (189) But enough of this. There is another dream also which belongs to the same class, that one I mean about the spotted flock, which the person who beheld it relates after he had awoke, saying, "The angel of God spake unto me in a dream, and said, Jacob; and I said, What is it? And he said unto me, Look up with thine eyes, and see the goats and the rams mounting on the flocks, and the she-goats, some white, and spotted, and ring-straked, and speckled: for I have beheld all that Laban does unto thee. I am that God who was seen by thee in the place of God, where thou anointedst the pillar, and vowedst a vow unto me. Now therefore, rise up and depart out of the land, and go into the land of thy birth, and I will be with thee."[47]

(190) You see here, that the divine word speaks of dreams as sent from God; including in this state-ment not those only which appear through the agency of the chief cause itself, but those also which are seen through the operation of his interpreters and attendant angels, who are thought by the father who created them to be worthy of a divine and blessed lot: (191) consider, however, what comes afterwards. The sacred word enjoins some persons what they ought to do by positive command, like a king; to others it suggests what will be for their advantage, as a preceptor does to his pupils; to others again, it is like a counsellor suggesting the wisest plans; and in this way too, it is of great advantage to those who do not of themselves know what is expedient; to others it is like a friend, in a mild and persuasive manner, bringing forward many secret things which no uninitiated person may lawfully hear.

(192) For at times it asks some persons, as for instance, Adam, "Where art thou?" And any one may properly answer to such a question, "No where?" Because all human affairs never remain long in the same condition, but are moved about and changed, whether we speak of their soul or their body, or of their external circumstances; for their minds are unstable, not always having the same impressions from the same things, but such as are diametrically contrary to their former ones. The body also is unstable, as all the changes of the different ages from infancy to old age show; their external circumstances also are variable, being tossed up and down by the impetus of ever-agitated fortune.

XXXIV. (193) When, however, he comes into an assembly of friends, he does not begin to speak before he has first accosted each individual among them, and addressed him by name, so that they prick up their ears, and are quiet and attentive, listening to the oracles thus delivered, so as never to forget them or let them escape their memory: since in another passage of scripture we read, "Be silent and listen."[48] (194) In this manner, too, Moses is called up to the bush. For, the scripture says, "When he saw that he was turning aside to see, God called him out of the bush, and said, Moses, Moses: and he said, What is it, Lord?"[49]

And Abraham also, on the occasion of offering up his beloved and only son as a burnt-offering, when he was beginning to sacrifice him, and when he had given proof of his piety, was forbidden to destroy the self-taught race, Isaac by name, from among men; (195) for at the beginning of his account of this transaction, Moses says that "God did tempt Abraham, and said unto him, Abraham, Abraham; and he said, Behold, here am I. And he said unto him, Take now thy beloved son Isaac, whom thou lovest, and offer him up." And when

---

[46] There is an hiatus here, which cannot be filled up satisfactorily. The whole of the rest of the chapter is pronounced by Mangey to be obscure and corrupt, and almost unintelligible.
[47] Genesis 31:11.

[48] Deuteronomy 27:9.
[49] Exodus 3:4.

he had brought the victim to the altar, then the angel of the Lord called him out of heaven, saying, "Abraham, Abraham," and he answered, "Behold, here am I. And he said, Lay not thy hand upon the child, and do nothing to him."[50]

(196) Also the practiser of virtue is also called one of this company dear to God, being deservedly accounted worthy of the same honour; for, says the scripture, "The angel of God said to me in my sleep, Jacob: and I answered, and said, What is it?"[51] (197) But after he has been called he exerts his attention, endeavouring to arrive at an accurate knowledge of the symbols which are displayed to him; and these symbols are the connection and generation of reasonings, as flocks and herds. For, says the scripture, "Jacob, looking up with his eyes, saw the goats and rams leaping upon the she-goats and upon the sheep." (198) Now the he-goat is the leader of the flock of goats, and the ram is the leader of the flock of sheep, and these two animals are symbols of perfect reasonings, one of which purifies and cleanses the soul of sins, and the other nourishes it and renders it full of good actions.

Such then are the leaders of the flocks in us, namely, reasons; and the flocks themselves, resembling the sheep and goats whose names they bear, rush forwards and hasten with zeal and earnestness towards justice.

(199) Therefore, looking up with the eye of his mind, which up to that time had been closed, he saw the perfect and thoroughly sharpened reasons analogically resembling the goats and rams, prepared for the diminution of offences and the increase of good actions. And he beheld how they leap upon the sheep and the goats, that is on those souls which are still young and tender, and in the vigour of youth, and beautiful in the flower of their age; not pursuing irrational pleasure, but indulging in the invisible sowing of the doctrines of prudence. (200) For this is a marriage which is blessed in its children; not uniting bodies, but adapting perfect virtues to well-disposed souls.

Therefore do all ye right reasons of wisdom leap up, form connections, sow seed, and pass by no soul which you see rich and fertile, and well-disposed, and virgin; but inviting it to association and connection with you, render it perfect and pregnant; for so you will become the parents of all kinds of good things, of a male offspring, white, variegated, ring-straked, and speckled.

XXXV. (201) But we must now examine what power each of these offspring has. Now those which are purely white *(dialeukoi)* are the most beautiful and the most conspicuous: the word *dia* being often prefixed in composition by way of

adding force to the word, so that the words *diadēlon* and *diasēmion* are commonly used to signify what is very conspicuous *(dēlon)* and very remarkable *(episēmon);* (202) therefore the meaning here is that the first-born offspring of the soul which has received the sacred seed, is purely white; being like light in which there is no obscurity, and like the most brilliant radiance: like the unclouded beam which might proceed from the rays of the sun in fine weather at mid-day. Again, by the statement that some are variegated, what is meant is, not that the flocks are marked by such a multiform and various spottedness as to resemble the unclean leprosy, and which is an emblem of a life unsteady and tossed about in any direction by reason of the fickleness of the mind, but only that they have marks drawn in regular lines and different characters, shaped and impressed with all kinds of well approved forms, the peculiarities of which, being multiplied together and combined properly, will produce a musical harmony.

(203) For some persons have looked upon the art of variegating as so random and obscure a matter, that they have referred it to weavers. But I admire not only the art itself, but the name likewise, and most especially so when I look upon the divisions of the earth and the spheres in heaven, and the differences between various plants and various animals, and that most variegated texture, I mean the world; (204) for I am compelled to suppose, that the maker of this universal textile fabric was also the inventor of all varied and variegating science; and I look with reverence upon the inventor, and I honour the art which he invented, and I am amazed at the work which is the result, and this too, though it is but a very small portion of it which I have been able to see, but still, from the portion of which has been unfolded to me, if indeed I may say that it has been unfolded, I hope to form a tolerably accurate judgment of the whole, guiding my conjectures by the light of analogy.

(205) Nevertheless I admire the lover of wisdom for having studied the same art, collecting and thinking fit to weave together many things, though different, and proceeding from different sources, into the same web; for taking the first two elements from the grammatical knowledge imparted to children, that is to say, reading and writing, and taking from the more perfect growth of knowledge the skill which is found among poets, and the comprehension of ancient history, and deriving certainty and freedom from deception from arithmetic and geometry, in which sciences there is need of proportions and calculations; and borrowing from music rhyme, and metre, and harmonies, and chromatics, and diatonics, and combined and disjoined melodies; and having derived from rhetoric invention, and language, and arrangement, and memory, and action; and from philosophy, whatever has been omitted in any of these

[50] Genesis 22:1.
[51] Genesis 31:10.

separate branches, and all the other things of which human life consists, he has put together in one most admirably arranged work, combining great learning of one kind with great learning of another kind.

(206) Now the sacred scripture calls the maker of this compound work Besaleel, which name, being interpreted, signifies "in the shadow of God;" for he makes all the copies, and the man by name Moses makes all the models, as the principal architect; and for this reason it is, that the one only draws outlines as it were, but the other is not content with such sketches, (207) but makes the archetypal natures themselves, and has already adorned the holy places with his variegating art; but the wise man is called the only adorner of the place of wisdom in the oracles delivered in the sacred scriptures.

XXXVI. And the most beautiful and varied work of God, this world, has been created in this its present state of perfection by all-wise knowledge; and how can it be anything but right to receive the art of variegating as a noble effort of knowledge? (208) the most sacred copy of which is the whole word of wisdom, which will bear about in its bosom the things of heaven and of earth, from which the practiser of virtue elaborates his notions of various things.

For after the white sheep he immediately beheld the variegated animals, stamped with the impression of instruction. (209) The third kind are the ring-straked and speckled; and what man in his senses would deny that these also are, as to their genus, variegated? but still he is not so very eager about the varieties of the members of the flocks, as about the road which leads to virtue and excellence; (210) for the prophet intends that he who proceeds along this road shall be besprinkled with dust and water; because it is related that the earth and water being kneaded together and fashioned into shape by the Creator of man, was formed into one body, not being made by hand, but being the work of invisible nature.

(211) Therefore it is the first principle of wisdom not to forget one's self, and always to keep before one's eyes the materials of which one has been compounded; for in this way a man will get rid of boasting and arrogance, which of all evils is the one most hated by God; for who that ever admits into his mind the recollection that the first principles of his formation are dust and water, would ever be so puffed by vanity as to be unduly elated? (212) On this account the prophet has thought it fit that those who are about to offer sacrifice shall be sprinkled with the aforesaid things; thinking no one worthy to appear at a sacrifice who has not first of all learnt to know himself, and to comprehend the nothingness of mankind, and the elements of which he is composed, conjecturing from them that he himself is utterly insignificant.

XXXVII. (213) These three signs, the white, the variegated, and the ring-straked and speckled, are as yet imperfect in the practiser of virtue, who has not himself as yet attained to perfection. But, in the case of him who is perfect, they also appear to be perfect. And in what manner they appear so we will examine. (214) The sacred scripture has appointed that the great High Priest, when he was about to perform the ministrations appointed by the law, should be besprinkled with water and ashes in the first place, that he might come to a remembrance of himself. For the wise Abraham also, when he went forth to converse with God, pronounced himself to be dust and ashes. In the second place, it enjoins him to put on a tunic reaching down to his feet, and the variously-embroidered thing which was called his breast-plate, an image and representation of the light-giving stars which appear in heaven.

(215) For there are, as it seems, two temples belonging to God; one being this world, in which the high priest is the divine word, his own first-born son. The other is the rational soul, the priest of which is the real true man, the copy of whom, perceptible to the senses, is he who performs his paternal vows and sacrifices, to whom it is enjoined to put on the aforesaid tunic, the representation of the universal heaven, in order that the world may join with the man in offering sacrifice, and that the man may likewise co-operate with the universe.

(216) He is now therefore shown to have these two things, the speckled and the variegated character. We will now proceed to explain the third and most perfect kind, which is denominated thoroughly white. When this same high priest enters into the innermost parts of the holy temple, he is clothed in the variegated garment, and he also assumes another linen robe, made of the very finest flax. (217) And this is an emblem of vigour, and incorruptibility, and the most brilliant light. For such a veil is a thing very difficult to be broken, and it is made of nothing mortal, and when it is properly and carefully purified it has a most clear and brilliant appearance. (218) And these injunctions contain this figurative meaning, that of those who in a pure and a guileless spirit serve the living God, there is no one who does not at first depend upon the firmness and obstinacy of his mind, despising all human affairs, which allure men with their specious bait, and injure them, and produce weakness in them. In the next place, he aims at immortality, laughing at the blind inventions with which mortals delude themselves. And last of all, he shines with the unclouded and most brilliant light of truth, no longer desiring any of the things which belong to false opinion, which prefer darkness rather than light.

XXXVIII. (219) The great high priest of the confession, then, may have now been sufficiently described by us, being stamped with the impressions above-mentioned, the white, the variegated, and the ring-straked and speckled. But he who is desirous of the administration of human affairs, by name Joseph, does not, as it appears, claim for himself any of the extreme characteristics, but only that variegated one which is in the middle between the others. (220) For we read that Joseph had a "coat of many colours,"[52] not being sprinkled with the sacred purifications, by means of which he might have known that he himself was only a compound of dust and water, and not being able to touch that thoroughly white and most shining raiment, virtue. But being clothed in the much-variegated web of political affairs, with which the smallest possible portion of truth is mixed up; and also many and large portions of plausible, probable, and likely falsehoods, from which all the sophists of Egypt, and all the augurs, and ventriloquists, and sorcerers spring; men skilful in juggling, and in incantations, and in tricks of all kinds, from whose treacherous arts it is very difficult to escape.

(221) And it is on this account that Moses very naturally represents this robe as stained with blood; since the whole life of the man who is mixed up in political affairs is tainted, warring on others and being warred against, and being aimed at, and attacked, and shot at by all the unexpected chances which befall him.

(222) Examine now the man who has great influence with the people, on whom the affairs of the city depend. Do not be alarmed at those who look with admiration upon him; and you will find many diseases lurking within him, and you will see that he is entangled in many disasters, and that fortune is dragging him violently in different directions, though he bends his neck the other way, and resists, although invisibly, and in fact that fortune is seeking to overthrow and destroy him; or else the people themselves are impatient at his supremacy, or he is exposed to the attacks of some more powerful rival. (223) And envy is a formidable enemy, and one hard to be shaken off, clinging also to everything that is called good fortune, and it is not easy to escape from it.

XXXIX. (224) What reason is there then for our congratulating ourselves on the administration of political affairs as if we were clothed in a garment of many colours, deceived by its external splendour, and not perceiving its ugliness, which is kept out of sight, and hidden, and full of treachery and guile? (225) Let us then put off this flowery robe, and put on that sacred one woven with the embroideries of virtue; for thus we shall escape the snares which want of skill, and ignorance, and want of knowledge, and education lay for us, of which Laban is the companion. (226) For when the sacred word has purified us with the sprink-

lings prepared beforehand for purification, and when it has adorned us with the select reasonings of true philosophy, and, having led us to that man who has stood the test, has made us genuine, and conspicuous, and shining, it blames the treacherous disposition which seeks to raise itself up to invalidate what is said.

(227) For the scripture says: "I have seen what Laban does unto thee,"[53] namely, things contrary to the benefits which I conferred on you, things impure, wicked, and altogether suited to darkness. But it is not right for the man who anchors on the hope of the alliance of God to crouch and tremble, to whom God says, "I am the God who was seen by thee in the place of God." (228) A very glorious boast for the soul, that God should think fit to appear to and to converse with it. And do not pass by what is here said, but examine it accurately, and see whether there are really two Gods. For it is said: "I am the God who was seen by thee;" not in my place, but in the place of God, as if he meant of some other God.

(229) What then ought we to say? There is one true God only: but they who are called Gods, by an abuse of language, are numerous; on which account the holy scripture on the present occasion indicates that it is the true God that is meant by the use of the article, the expression being, "I am the God (ho Theos);" but when the word is used incorrectly, it is put without the article, the expression being, "He who was seen by thee in the place," not of the God (tou Theou), but simply "of God" (Theou); (230) and what he here calls God is his most ancient word, not having any superstitious regard to the position of the names, but only proposing one end to himself, namely, to give a true account of the matter; for in other passages the sacred historian, when he considered whether there really was any name belonging to the living God, showed that he knew that there was none properly belonging to him; but that whatever appellation any one may give him, will be an abuse of terms; for the living God is not of a nature to be described, but only to be.

XL. (231) And a proof of this may be found in the oracular answer given by God to the person who asked what name he had, "I am that I am,"[54] that the questioner might know the existence of those things which it was not possible for man to conceive not being connected with God. (232) Accordingly, to the incorporeal souls which are occupied in his service, it is natural for him to appear as he is, conversing with them as a friend with his friends; but to those souls which are still in the body he must appear in the resemblance of the angels, though without changing his nature

---

[52] Genesis 37:3.

[53] Genesis 31:12.
[54] Exodus 3:14.

(for he is unchangeable), but merely implanting in those who behold him an idea of his having another form, so that they fancy that it is his image, not an imitation of him, but the very archetypal appearance itself.

(233) There is then an old story much celebrated, that the Divinity, assuming the resemblance of men of different countries, goes round the different cities of men, searching out the deeds of iniquity and lawlessness; and perhaps, though the fable is not true, it is a suitable and profitable one. (234) But the scripture, which at all times advances its conceptions with respect to the Deity, in a more reverential and holy tone, and which likewise desires to instruct the life of the foolish, has spoken of God under the likeness of a man, though not of any particular man; (235) attributing to him, with this view, the possession of a face, and hands, and feet, and of a mouth and voice, and also anger and passion, and moreover, defensive weapons, and goings in and goings out, and motions upwards and downwards, and in every direction, not indeed using all these expressions with strict truth, but having regard to the advantage of those who are to learn from it; (236) for the writers knew that some men are very dull in their natures, so as to be utterly unable to form any conception whatever of God apart from a body, whom it will be impossible to admonish if they were to speak in any other style than the existing one, of representing God as coming and departing like a man; and as descending and ascending, and as using his voice, and as being angry with sinners, and being implacable in his anger; and speaking too of his darts and swords, and whatever other instruments are suitable to be employed against the wicked, as being all previously ready.

(237) For we must be content if such men can be brought to a proper state, by the fear which is suspended over them by such descriptions; and one many almost say that these are the only two paths taken, in the whole history of the law; one leading to plain truth, owing to which we have such assertions as, "God is not as a man;"[55] the other, that which has regard to the opinions of foolish men, in reference to whom it is said, "The Lord God shall instruct you, like as if a man instructs his son."[56]

XLI. (238) Why then do we any longer wonder, if God at times assumes the likeness of the angels, as he sometimes assumes even that of men, for the sake of assisting those who address their entreaties to him? so that when he says, "I am the God who was seen by thee in the place of God;"[57] we must understand this, that he on that occasion

took the place of an angel, as far as appearance went, without changing his own real nature, for the advantage of him who was not, as yet, able to bear the sight of the true God; (239) for as those who are not able to look upon the sun itself, look upon the reflected rays of the sun as the sun itself, and upon the halo around the moon as if it were the moon itself; so also do those who are unable to bear the sight of God, look upon his image, his angel word, as himself.

(240) Do you not see that encyclical instruction, that is, Hagar, says to the angel, "Art thou God who seest me?"[58] for she was not capable of beholding the most ancient cause, inasmuch as she was by birth a native of Egypt. But now the mind begins to be improved, so as to be able to contemplate the governor of all the powers; (241) on which account he says himself, "I am the Lord God,"[59] I whose image you formerly beheld instead of me, and whose pillar you set up, engraving on it a most sacred inscription; and the inscription indicated that I stood alone, and that I established the nature of all things, bringing disorder and irregularity into order and regularity, and supporting the universe firmly, so that it might rest on a firm and solid foundation, my own ministering word.

XLII. (242) For the pillar is the symbol of three things; of standing, of dedication, and of an inscription: now the standing and the inscription have been described, but the dedication it is necessary should be explained to all men. (243) For heaven and the world are an offering dedicated to God who made them; and all the cosmopolitan and God-loving souls, which dedicate and consecrate themselves to him, not allowing any mortal thing to drag them in an opposite direction, are never weary of hallowing their own life, and adorning it with every kind of beauty as a meet offering for him. (244) And he is a foolish man who does not set up a pillar to God, but who erects one to himself instead, attributing stability to the things of creation, which is tossed about in every direction, and thinking those things worthy of inscriptions and panegyrics, which are in reality full of matter for blame and accusation, and which as such had better never have been mentioned in an inscription at all, or if they had, had better have been speedily erased again.

(245) On which account the holy scripture says distinctly, "Thou shalt not set up a pillar to thyself;"[60] for in truth there is nothing belonging to man that is stable, no, not though some persons persist even so obstinately in affirming it. (246) But they not only think that they stand firmly, but also that they are worthy of honours

---

[55] Numbers 23:19.
[56] Deuteronomy 1:31.
[57] Genesis 31:13.

[58] Genesis 16:13.
[59] Genesis 31:13.
[60] Deuteronomy 16:22.

and inscriptions, forgetting him who is alone worthy of honour, and who is alone firmly fixed; for while they are turning aside and wandering away from the path which leads to virtue, the outward sense leads them still more astray, that is to say, the woman who is akin to them, she also compels them to run ashore; (247) therefore, the whole soul, like a ship,[61] being shut in all around, is offered up as a pillar; for the sacred scriptures tell us that Lot's wife having turned back to look behind her, became a pillar of salt, (248) and this is said very naturally and fitly; for if any one does not look forwards at those things which are worthy of being seen and heard (and these things are the virtues and the actions done in accordance with virtue), but looks backwards at the things which are behind him, at deaf glory, and blind riches, and senseless vigour of body, and an empty elegance of mind, pursuing these objects only, and such as are akin to them, he will lie as a lifeless pillar melting away by itself; for salt is not a thing to preserve his firmness.

XLIII. (249) Very admirably therefore does the practiser of virtue, having learnt by continued study that creation is a thing in its own nature moveable, but that the uncreated God is unchangeable and immoveable, erect a pillar to God, and anoint it after he has erected it; for God says, "Thou hast anointed my pillar."[62] (250) But do not fancy that that stone was anointed with oil, but understand rather that that opinion, that God is the only being who stands firmly, was thoroughly hardened by exercise, and established in the soul by the science of wrestling, not that science by which bodies are made fat, but that by which the mind acquires strength and irresistible vigour; (251) for the man who is eager in the pursuit of good studies and virtuous objects is fond of labours, and fond of exercises; so that very naturally, having worked out the science of training which is the sister of the art of medicine, he anoints and brings to perfection all the reasonings of virtue and piety, and dedicates them, as a most beautiful and lasting offering to God.

(252) For this reason, after mentioning the dedication of the pillar, God adds that, "Thou vowedst a vow to me." Now a vow also is, to speak properly, a dedication, since he who makes a vow is said to offer up, as a gift to God, not only his own possessions, but himself likewise, who is the owner of them; (253) for says the scripture, "the man is holy who nourishes the locks of the hair of his head; who has vowed a vow." But if he is holy he is undoubtedly an offering to God, no longer meddling with anything unholy or profane; (254) and there is an evidence in favour of my argument, in the conduct of the prophetess, and mother of a prophet, Hannah, whose name being translated, signifies grace; for she says that she gives her son, "Samuel, as a gift to the Holy One,"[63] not dedicating him more as a human being, than as a disposition full of inspiration, and possessed by a divinely sent impulse; and the name Samuel being interpreted means, "appointed to God."

(255) Why then, O my soul, do you any longer waste yourself in vain speculations and labours? and why do you not go as a pupil to the practiser of virtue, taking up arms against the passions, and against vain opinion, to learn from him the way to wrestle with them? For as soon as you have learnt this art, you will become the leader of a flock, not of one which is destitute of marks, and of reason, and of docility, but of one which is well approved, and rational, and beautiful, (256) of which, if you become the leader, you will pity the miserable race of mankind, and will not cease to reverence the Deity; and you will never be weary of blessing God, and moreover you will engrave hymns suited to your sacred subject upon pillars, that you may not only speak fluently, but may also sing musically the virtues of the living God; for by these means you will be able to return to your father's house, being delivered from a long a profitless wandering in and foreign land.

BOOK 2

I. (1) In describing the third species of dreams which are sent from God, we very naturally call on Moses as an ally, in order that as he learnt, having previously been ignorant, so he may instruct us who are also ignorant, concerning these signs, illustrating each separate one of them.

Now this third species of dreams exists, whenever in sleep the mind being set in motion by itself, and agitating itself, is filled with frenzy and inspiration, so as to predict future events by a certain prophetic power. (2) For the first kind of dreams which we mentioned, was that which proceeded from God as the author of its motion, and, as some invisible manner prompted us what was indistinct to us, but well known to himself. The second kind was when our own intellect was set in motion simultaneously with the soul of the universe, and became filled with divine madness, by means of which it is allowed to prognosticate events which are about to happen; (3) and for this reason the interpreter of the sacred will very plainly and clearly speaks of dreams, indicating by this expression the visions which appear according to the first species, as if God, by means of dreams, gave suggestions which were equivalent to distinct and pre-

---

[61] Mangey thinks that this passage is corrupt, and proposes to alter *naus* into *apnous*, "dead," but it seems unnecessary.

[62] Genesis 31:13.

[63] 1 Samuel 1:28.

cise oracles. Of the visions according to the second species he speaks neither very clearly nor very obscurely; an instance of which is afforded by the vision which was exhibited of the ladder reaching up to heaven; for this version was an enigmatical one; nevertheless, the meaning was not hidden from those who were able to see with any great acuteness.

(4) But these visions which are afforded according to the third species of dreams, being less clear than the two former kinds by reason of their having an enigmatical meaning deeply seated and fully coloured, require the science of an interpreter of dreams. At all events all the dreams of this class, which are recorded by the lawgiver, are interpreted by men who are skilled in the aforesaid art.

(5) Whose dreams then am I here alluding to? Surely every one must see to those of Joseph, and of Pharaoh king of Egypt, and to those which the chief baker and chief butler saw themselves; (6) and it may be well at all times to begin our instruction with the first instances.

Now the first dreams are those which Joseph beheld, receiving two visions from the two parts of the world, heaven and earth. From the earth the dream about the harvest; and that is as follows, "I thought that we were all binding sheaves in the middle of the field; and my sheaf stood up."[64] (7) And the other relates to the circle of the zodiac, and is, "They worshipped me as the sun and the moon and the eleven stars." And the interpretation of the former one, which was delivered with great violence of reproof, is as follows, "Shall you be a king and reign over us? or shall you be a lord and lord it over us?" The interpretation of the second is again full of just indignation, "Shall I, and thy mother, and thy brethren come and fall down upon the ground and worship thee?"

II. (8) Let these things be laid down first by way of foundation; and on this foundation let us raise up the rest of the building, following the rules of that wise architect, allegory, and accurately investigating each particular of the dreams; but first we must mention what it is requisite should be attended to before the dreams. Some persons have extended the nature of good over many things, and others have attributed it to the most excellent Being alone; some again have mixed it with other things, while others have spoken of it as unalloyed.

(9) Those then who have called only what is honourable good, have preserved this nature free from alloy, and have attributed it only to what is most excellent, namely to the reason that is in us; but those who have mixed it have combined it with three things, the soul, the body, and external circumstances. And they who act thus are persons of a somewhat effeminate and luxurious way of life,

being bred up the greater part of their time, from their earliest infancy, in the women's apartments and among the effeminate race which is found in the women's apartments. But those who argue differently are men inclined to a harder regimen, being bred up from their boyhood among men, and being themselves men in their minds, embracing what is right in preference to what is pleasant, and devoting themselves to nourishment fit for athletes for the sake of strength and vigour, not of pleasure.

(10) Moses moreover represents two persons as leaders of these two companies. The leader of the noble and good company is the self-taught and self-instructed Isaac; for he records that he was weaned, not choosing to avail himself at all of tender, and milk-like, and childish, and infantine food, but only of such as was vigorous and perfect, inasmuch as he was formed by nature, from his very infancy, for acts of virtue, and was always in the prime and vigour of youth and energy. But the leader of the company, which yields and which is inclined to softer measures, is Joseph; (11) for he does not indeed neglect the virtues of the soul, but he likewise shows anxiety about the stability and permanence of the body, and also desires an abundance of worldly treasures; and it is in strict accordance with natural truth, that he is represented as drawn in different directions, since he proposes to himself many different objects in life; and being attracted by each of them, he is kept in a state of commotion and agitation, without being able to stand firm.

(12) And his case is not like that of cities, which having made a truce enjoy peace, and yet after a time are again attacked, so as to gain the victory and to be defeated alternately; for at times a great influx of riches and glory coming upon them, subdues all their cares for the body and the soul, but afterwards, being repelled by both these things, they are conquered by the adversary; (13) and in the same manner all the pleasures of the body coming upon the soul in a compact array overwhelm and efface all the objects of the intellect one after the other; and then, after a short time, wisdom, changing its course and blowing in the opposite direction with a fresh and violent breeze, causes the stream of the pleasures to slacken, and altogether moderates all the eagerness, and impetuosity, and rivalry of the external senses.

(14) Such a circle then of never-ending war revolves around the soul, subject as it is to so many changes; for when one enemy has been destroyed, then immediately there springs up another more powerful, after the fashion of the many-headed hydra; for they say, that in the case of this monster, instead of the head which was cut off another sprung up, by which statement they mean to intimate the multiform, and prolific, and almost invincible character of undying wickedness.

(15) Do not, therefore, answer [...] Joseph

[...] [65] but know that he is the image of multiform and mixed knowledge. For there appears in him a rational species of continence, which is of the masculine kind, being fashioned in accordance with his father Jacob; (16) and also that kind which is devoid of reason is likewise visible, that of the outward sense I mean, being made in the likeness of his maternal race, according to Rachel. There appears in him also the seed of bodily pleasures, which his association with the chief butlers, and chief bakers, and chief cooks has stamped upon him. There is, also visible the seed of vain opinion, on which he mounts as on a chariot by reason of his levity, being puffed up, and elated, and raising himself to a height to the destruction of equality.

III. (17) Now the character of Joseph is sketched out by the foregoing outlines. But each of his dreams must be investigated with accuracy; and first of all we must examine the one about the sheaves. "I thought," says he, "that we were all binding sheaves." The expression, "I thought," is clearly that of a person who is not certain, but who is hesitating and supposing with some amount of indistinctness, not of one who sees positively and clearly; (18) for it is very natural for persons just awakening out of a deep sleep, and still dozing at it were, to say, "I thought;" but not so for people who are thoroughly awake, and who can see distinctly. (19) And the practiser of virtue, Jacob, does not say, "I thought," but his language is, "Behold, a ladder firmly set, the head of which reached up to heaven." [66] And again he says, when "the sheep conceived I saw them with my eyes in my sleep, and behold the he-goats and the rams leapt upon the ewes and upon the she-goats, white, and variegated, and ring-straked, and speckled." [67] (20) For it happens of necessity that the sleeping conceptions also of those who think what is honourable and eligible for its own sake and more distinct and more pure, just as their waking actions are also more deserving of approbation.

IV. (21) But when I hear Jacob relating his dream I marvel at his having fancied that he was binding up the sheaves, and not reaping the corn; for the one is the task of the lower classes and of servants, but the other is the occupation of the employers, and of men more skilled in agriculture. (22) For to be able to distinguish what is necessary from what is mischievous, and what is nutritious from what is not so, and what is genuine from what is spurious, and useful fruit from a worthless root, not only in reference to those things which the land bears, but also in those which the intellect bears, is the work of most perfect virtue.

(23) Accordingly the holy scripture represents those who see, that is the sons of Israel, as reaping, and what is a most extraordinary thing, as reaping not barley or wheat, but the harvest itself; accordingly the language of Moses is, "When you reap your harvest, you shall not wholly reap the corners of your harvest." [68] (24) For he means here that the virtuous man is not merely the judge of things which differ from one another, and that he does not only distinguish the things from which some produce is derived from the produce itself; but that he is able also to distinguish while reaping the harvest, to remove this opinion of his ability to distinguish, and to eradicate a man's own opinion of himself; because he is firmly persuaded, and believes Moses when he affirms that "judgment belongs to God alone," [69] with whom are the comparisons and distinctions between all things; to whom it is well for a man to confess that he is inferior, a confession more glorious than the most renowned victory.

(25) Now the reaping a harvest is like cutting a second time what has been cut already; which when some persons fond of novelty applied themselves to they found a circumcision of circumcision, and a purification of purification; [70] that is to say, they found that the purification of the soul was itself purified, attributing the power of making bright to God, and never fancying that they themselves were competent, without the assistance of the divine wisdom, to wash and cleanse a life which is full of stains.

(26) Akin to this is the double cave, which is a symbol of the twofold and excellent recollections (the one existing in reference to the creature, and the other to the Creator), in which the virtuous man is bred up, contemplating the things which are in the world, and being also fond of inquiring about the father who made them; (27) and it is owing to these twofold recollections, in my opinion, that the double symphony in music, that of the double diapason, was invented. (28) For it was necessary that the work and the creator should be made happy in two most perfect melodies, and not both in the same one. For since the excellencies which were to be celebrated by them differed from one another, it followed of necessity that the melodies and symphonies should likewise differ from one another. The combined symphony being assigned to the world, which is a compound creation, composed of many different parts; and the disjoined melody being appropriated to him who, as to his essence, is separated from every creature, namely, to God.

(29) Moreover, the interpreter of the sacred

---

[65] There is an hiatus here, and there is a good deal of corruption about the beginning of this book.
[66] Genesis 28:12.
[67] Genesis 31:10.

[68] Leviticus 19:9.
[69] Deuteronomy 1:17.
[70] Numbers 6:2.

will again enunciates an opinion friendly to virtue, saying that it is not proper "to thoroughly reap every corner of the harvest field;" remembering the original proposition, according to which he agreed that "the tribute belonged to the Lord,"[71] to whom the authority and the conformation of these things also belong; (30) but he who is un-initiated in reaping boasts, so far as to say, "I thought that I was with the others binding up the sheaves which I had reaped."[72] And he does not consider that this is the occupation of servants and unskilled hands, as I have said a little while ago. (31) But this word sheaves is an allegorical expression by which affairs are really meant, such as each man takes in hand for the support of his house, in which he hopes to live and dwell for ever.

V. (32) There are, therefore, an infinite number of differences between sheaves, that is to say, between such affairs as support a house. There are also a countless host of differences between those who gather and take up the sheaves in their hand, so that it is impossible to mention or even to imagine them all. Still it is not out of place to describe a few of them by way of example, which he too mentioned, when he was recounting his dream. (33) For he says to his brethren, "I thought that we were binding up sheaves." Now, of brethren he has ten, who are sons of the same father as himself, and one who is by the same mother; and the name of each individual among them is an emblem of some most necessary thing. Reuben is an emblem of natural acuteness, for he is called "the son who sees," being in so far as he is a son not perfect, but in so far as he is endowed with the faculty of sight and sees acutely, he is naturally well qualified. (34) Simeon is an emblem of learning, for his name being interpreted means, "listening." Levi is a symbol of virtuous energies and actions, and of holy ministrations. Judas is an emblem of songs and hymns addressed to God. Issachar, of wages which are given for good work; but perhaps the works themselves are their own perfect reward. Zabulon is a symbol of light, since his name means the departure of night; and when the night departs and leaves us, then of necessity light arises. (35) Dan is a symbol of the distinction between, and division of, different things. Gad is an emblem of the invasion of pirates, and of a counter attack made upon them. Asser is a symbol of natural wealth, for his name being interpreted, signifies "a calling blessed," since wealth is accounted a blessed possession. (36) Napthali is a symbol of peace, for all things are open and extended by peace, as on the other hand they are closed by war; and his name being interpreted means, "widening," or "that which is opened." Ben-jamin is an emblem of young and old times; for being interpreted his name means "the son of days," and both young time and old time are measured by days and nights.

(37) Accordingly, every one of them takes up in his hand what belongs to himself; and having taken it up, binds all the parts together; the man well endowed by nature taking up the parts of dexterity, and perseverance, and memory, of which good natural endowments consist; the man who has learnt well takes up the parts of listening, tranquillity, and attention; the man willing to endeavour takes up courage and a happy confidence which does not shrink from danger; (38) the man inclined to gratitude takes up praises, panegyrics, hymns, and blessings, both in speaking and in singing; the man who is eager for wages takes up unhesitating industry, most enduring gratitude, and care, armed with a promptitude which is not to be despised; (39) he who pursues light rather than darkness takes up wakefulness and acuteness of sight; the man who is an admirer of the division of and distinction between things takes up well-sharpened reasons so as not to be deceived by things similar to one another as if they were identical, impartiality so as not to be led away by favour, and incorruptibility; (40) he who, in something of a piratical fashion, lays ambuscades against those who counterplot against him, takes up deceit, cajolery, trickery, sophistry, pretence, and hypocrisy, which being in their own nature blamable, are nevertheless praised when employed against the enemy; he who studies to be rich in the riches of nature takes up temperance and frugality; he who loves peace takes up obedience to law, a good reputation, freedom from pride, and equality.

VI. (41) It is of these things, then, that the sheaves of his brethren by the same father are composed and bound up; but the sheaf of his uterine brother is composed of days and of time, which are the causes of nothing, as if they were the causes of all things. (42) But the dreamer and interpreter of dreams himself, for he united both characters, makes a sheaf of empty opinion as of the greatest and most brilliant of possessions and the most useful to life. For which reason it is originally by his dreams, which are things dear to night, that he is made known to the king of the bodily country, and not by any performance of conspicuous actions, which require day for their exhibition. (43) After that, he is appointed overseer or governor of all Egypt, and is honoured with the second rank in the kingdom, and made inferior in honour only to the king. All which things are in the eye of wisdom, if that were the judge, more inglorious and more ridiculous than even defeat and dishonour. (44) After that he puts on a golden necklace, a most illustrious halter, the circlet and wheel of interminable necessity, not the consequence and regular order of things in life, nor the

---

[71] Numbers 31:28.
[72] Genesis 37:7.

connection of the affairs of nature as Thamar was; for her ornament was not a necklace, but an armlet. Moreover, he assumes a ring, a royal gift which is no gift, a pledge devoid of good faith, the very contrary gift to that which was given to the same Thamar by Judah the son of the seeing king, Israel; (45) for God gives to the soul a seal, a very beautiful gift, to show that he has invested with shape the essence of all things which was previously devoid of shape, and has stamped with a particular character that which previously had no character, and has endowed with form that which had previously no distinctive form, and having perfected the entire world, he has impressed upon it an image and appearance, namely, his own word.

(46) But Joseph also mounts the second chariot, being puffed up with elation of mind and vain arrogance. And he is regulator of the provisions, laying up and preserving the treasures for the body, and providing it with food from all quarters: and this is a very formidable fortification against the soul. (47) Moreover, his deliberate choice of life, and the life which he admires, is testified to in no slight degree by his name; for Joseph, being interpreted, means "addition;" and vain opinion is always adding what is spurious to what is genuine, and what is the property of others to what is one's own, and what is false to what is true, and what is superfluous to what is adequate, and luxury to what is sufficient to support existence, and pride to life.

VII. (48) Consider now what it is which I am here desirous to prove. We are nourished by meat and drink, even though the meat be the most ordinary corn, and the drink plain water from the stream. Moreover, besides this, vain opinion has added to it an infinite number of varieties of cakes, and cheese-cakes, and sweetmeats, and costly and various mixtures of an indescribable multitude of wines, for the enjoyment of pleasure rather than for a participation in necessary food properly prepared. (49) Again, the necessary seasonings for eating, are leeks, [73] and vegetables, and many fruits of trees, and cheese, and other things of that sort; and if you wish to include carnivorous men, we must, besides, add fish and meat to these items.

(50) Would it not, then, have been sufficient to broil these things upon the coals, or to roast them at the fire, and then eat them at once, after the fashion of those true heroes of old times? But the epicure is eager not only for such things as these, but he takes vain opinion for his ally, and excites the gluttonous passions which are within him, and seeks out and hunts all about for confectioners and pastrycooks of high reputation in their art. (51) And they, bringing forward the different baits for his miserable stomach, which have been invented after long consideration, and preparing all kinds of peculiar flavours, and arranging them in due order, tickle, and allure, and subdue the tongue.

Then, immediately they circumvent that foundation of the outward senses, the taste, by means of which the banquet-hunter in a very short time is rendered a slave instead of a free man. (52) For who is there who does not know that clothes were originally made as a defence against the injuries which might arise to the body from cold and heat? as the poets say somewhere:—

"Taming the wind in the winter."

(53) Who, therefore, thinks of costly purple garments? Who cares about transparent and thin summer robes? Who wishes for a garment delicate as a spider's web? Who is eager to have embroidered for him apparel flowered over with dyes and brocaded figures, by those who are skilful in sewing and weaving cunning embroidery, and are superior in their handwork to the imitative skill of the painter? Who, I say? Who, but vain opinion.

VIII. (54) And, indeed, it is for the same reasons that we had need of houses, requiring them also for protection against the attacks of wild beasts, or of men more savage in their nature than even wild beasts. Why is it, then, that we adorn the pavements and floors with costly stones? And why do we travel over Asia, and Africa, and all Europe, and the islands, searching for pillars and capitals, and architraves, and selecting them with reference to their superior beauty? (55) And why are we anxious for, and why do we vie with one another in specimens of Doric, and Ionic, and Corinthian sculpture, and in all the refinements which luxurious men have devised in addition to the existing customs, adorning the capitals of their pillars? And why do we furnish our chambers for men and for women with golden ornaments? Is it not all from our being influenced by vain opinion? (56) And yet, for sound sleep, the mere ground was sufficient (since, even to the present day, the accounts tell us that the gymnosophists, among the Indians, sleep on the ground in accordance with their ancient customs); and if it were not, at all events a couch made of carefully chosen stones or plain pieces of wood, would be a sufficient bed; (57) but now the poles of our ladders are ornamented with ivory feet, and workmen inlay our beds with costly mother-of-pearl and variegated tortoise-shell, at great expense of labour, and money, and time: and some beds are even made of solid silver or solid gold, and inlaid with precious stones, with all kinds of flowery work, and embossed golden ornaments strewed about them, as if for mere display and magnificence, and not for daily use. The contriver of all which is again the same vain opinion. (58) Again: why need we seek for more in the

---

[73] Numbers 11:4.

way of ointment than the juice pressed out of the fruit of the olive? For that softens the limbs, and relieves the labour of the body, and produces a good condition of the flesh; and if anything has got relaxed or flabby, it binds it again, and makes it firm and solid, and it fills us with vigour and strength of muscle, no less than any other unguent. (59) But the pleasant unguents of vain opinion, are set up in opposition to those that are merely useful, on which the perfumers work, and to which vast regions contribute, such as Syria, Babylon, the Indians, and the Scythians; in which nations the origins of all perfumes are found.

IX. (60) Again, with respect to drinking; what more could man really have need of than the cup of nature wrought with the perfection of art? Now such a cup our own hands supply, which, if any one brings together and forms into a hollow, applying them closely to his mouth, while another pours in the liquid to be drank, he gets not only a remedy for his thirst, but also a most indescribable pleasure. (61) Still, if one were absolutely in need of something else, would not the ivy cup of the agricultural labourer be sufficient? and why should it be requisite to have recourse to the arts of other eminent artists? And what can be the use of providing a countless multitude of gold and silver goblets, it if be not for the gratification of boastful and vain-glorious arrogance, and of vain opinion raising itself to an undue height?

(62) Again, when men wear crowns, they are not content with fragrant garlands of laurel, or ivy, or violets, or lilies, or roses, or of any three whatever, or of any flower, neglecting all the gifts of God, which he bestows upon us as the various seasons of the year, but they put golden crowns on their heads, which are a very grievous weight, wearing them in the middle of the crowded marketplace without any shame. And what can we think of such men, but that they are slaves of vain opinion, in spite of their asserting themselves not only to be free, but even to be rulers over many other persons? (63) The day would fail me if I were to go through all the varieties of human life; and yet, why need I dwell on the subject with prolixity? For who is there who has not heard, or who has not seen, such men as these? Who is there who does not associate with, and who is not familiar with them? So that the sacred scripture has very appropriately named "addition" the enemy of simplicity and the companion of pride; (64) for as superfluous shoots do grow on trees, which are a great injury to the genuine useful branches, and which the cultivators destroy and cut out from a prudent foreknowledge of what is necessary: so likewise the life of falsehood and arrogance often grows up by the side of the true life devoid of pride, of which, to this day, no cultivator has been found who has been able to cut away the injurious superfluous growth by the roots.

(65) Therefore the practisers of wisdom, knowing this in the first instance by the outward sense, and secondly, pursuing it by the mind, cry out loudly and say, "A wicked beast has seized and devoured Joseph."[74] (66) But does not that most ferocious beast, the various pride which springs up in the life of men living in irregularity and confusion, whose chief workmen are covetousness and unscrupulous cunning, devour every one who comes within his reach? Therefore grief will be added to them, even while they are alive, as though they were dead, since they have a life worthy of lamentation and mourning, since Jacob mourns for Joseph, even while he is alive.

(67) But Moses will not allow the sacred reasonings about Nadab to be bewailed;[75] for they have not been carried off by a savage beast, but have been taken up by unextinguishable violence and imperishable light; because, having discarded all fear and hesitation, they had duly consecrated the fervent and fiery zeal, consuming the flesh, and very easily and vehemently excited towards piety, which is unconnected with creation, but is akin to God, not going up to the altar by the regular steps, for that was forbidden by law, but proceeding rapidly onwards with a favourable gale, and being conducted up even to the threshold of heaven, becoming dissolved into ethereal beams like a whole burnt-offering.

X. (68) Therefore, O thou soul, that art obedient to thy teacher! thou must cut off thine hand and thy power when it begins to take hold of the parts of generation; that is to say, of things created, or of human pursuits; (69) for very often ... to cut off the hand which has laid hold of the privy parts,"[76] in the first place, because it has gladly received the pleasure which it ought rather to hate; and, secondly, because it has thought that the faculty of propagating seed was in our own power, and also, because it has attributed to the creature that power which belongs to the Creator. (70) Dost thou not see that the earthly mass, Adam, when it lays its hands upon the two trees, dies, because it has preferred the number two to the unit, and because it has admired the creature in preference to the Creator? But do thou go forth beyond the reach of the smoke and the tempest, and flee from the ridiculous pursuits of mortal life as a fearful whirlpool, and do not, as the proverb has it, touch them even with the tip of thy finger.

(71) And when thou hast girded thyself up for the sacred ministrations, having made broad thy whole hand and thy whole power, then take a firm hold of the speculations of instruction and wisdom; for the command is of this kind, "If a soul brings

---

[74] Genesis 37:33.
[75] Leviticus 10:6.
[76] Deuteronomy 25:12.

a gift or a sacrifice, the gift shall be of fine wheaten flour."[77] After that the lawgiver adds: "And when he has taken a full handful of the fine wheaten flour, with the oil, and with all the frankincense, he places the memorial on the altar of sacrifice." (72) Is not this a very beautiful and appropriate expression of Moses, to call that soul incorporeal which is about to offer sacrifice, but not to call the double mass which consists of mortality and immortality by any such name? For that which vows the vow—that which is full of gratitude—that which offers such sacrifices as are truly without spot, is one thing only, namely, the soul.

(73) What then is the offering of the incorporeal soul? What is the fine wheaten flour, a symbol of the mind purified by the suggestions of instruction, which is able to render the friend of education free from all disease, and life free from all reproach? (74) From which the priest taking a handful within his whole hand, that is to say, with the whole grasp of his mind, is commanded to offer up the whole soul itself, full of the most unalloyed and pure doctrines, as the most excellent of sacrifices, fat and in good condition, rejoicing in divine light, and redolent of the exhalations which are given forth by justice, and by the other virtues, so as always to enjoy a most fragrant, and delicious, and happy life; for the oil and the frankincense, of which the priest takes a handful with the white meat, contain a figurative assertion of this.

XI. (75) It is on this account that Moses set apart an especial festival for the sheaf; however, not for every sheaf, but for that which came from the sacred land. "For when," says he, "you come into the land which I give unto you, and when you reap its harvest, you shall bring sheaves as a first fruit of your harvest to the priest."[78] (76) And the meaning of this injunction is, when, O mind, you come into the country of virtue, which it is fitting should be offered up to God alone, being a land good for pasture, a land of rich soil, a land which beareth fruit, and when you reap the fruit (either that afforded by the land spontaneously or that which thou hast sown), which has been brought to perfection by the God who gives perfection; carry it not home to thy house; that is to say, do not store it up, and do not attribute to thyself the cause of the crop which has arisen to thee, before thou has offered the first fruits to the Cause of all wealth, and to him who persuaded thee to study the operations which confer riches. (77) And it is enjoined that you shall offer the "first fruits of your own harvest;" not of the harvest of the land, in order that we may reap and gather in the harvest for ourselves; dedicating to God all good and nutritious, and beneficial fruits.

XII. (78) But the man who is at the same time initiated in dreams and also an interpreter of dreams, is bold to say that his sheaf rose and stood upright; for in real truth, as spirited horses lift their necks high, so all who are companions of vain opinion place themselves above all things, above all cities, and laws, and national customs, and above all the circumstances which affect each individual of them. (79) Then proceeding onwards from being demagogues to being leaders of the people, and overthrowing the things which belong to their neighbours, and setting up and establishing on a solid footing what belongs to themselves, that is to say, all such dispositions as are free and by nature impatient of slavery, they attempt to reduce these also under their power; (80) on which account the dreamer adds, "And your sheaves turning towards my sheaf made obeisance unto it."[79]

For the lover of modesty marvels at and fears the stiffnecked, and the cautious person fears the self-willed man, and he who reverences holiness fears that which is impious both for himself and for others. (81) And is not this reasonable? For inasmuch as the good man is a spectator, not only of human life but also of all the things which exist in the world, he knows how many things are accustomed to be caused by necessity, and chance, and opportunity, and violence, and authority; and what numbers of propositions, and what great instances of prosperity proceeding onwards with rapidity towards heaven, the same causes have shaken and overthrown; (82) so that he will of necessity take up caution as a shield, as a protection to prevent his suffering any sudden and unexpected evil; for as I imagine what a wall is to a city, that caution is to an individual.

(83) Do not these men then talk foolishly, are they not mad, who desire to display their inexperience and freedom of speech to kings and tyrants, at times daring to speak and to do things in opposition to their will? Do they not perceive that they have not only put their necks under the yoke like brute beasts, but that they have also surrendered and betrayed their whole bodies and souls likewise, and their wives and their children, and their parents, and all the rest of the numerous kindred and community of their other relations?

And is it not lawful for the charioteer, and also for the passenger, with all freedom to spur, and to urge forward, and to check, and to hold back, according as he desires to arrange things, so as to make them greater or smaller. (84) Therefore, being pricked with goads, and flogged, and mutilated, and suffering all the cruelties which can be inflicted in an inhuman and pitiless manner before

---

[77] Leviticus 2:1.
[78] Leviticus 23:10.

[79] Genesis 37:7.

death, all together, they are led away to execution and put to death.

XIII. (85) These are the rewards of unseemly freedom of speech, not of that which is accounted such by right-thinking judges, but of that license which is full of folly, and insanity of mind, and of incurable distemper. What do you mean? Does anyone, when he sees a storm at its height, and a violent gale opposing him, and a hurricane raging tempestuously, and the sea full of vast waves, when he ought to anchor his ship, does anyone, I say, at such a moment weigh anchor and put to sea? (86) What pilot, or what captain of a ship, was ever so drunk and intoxicated, as, while all the dangers which I have just enumerated were threatening him, to be willing to set sail, lest, if his vessel became water-logged by the sea breaking over it from above, it might be swallowed up with all its crew? For, if he had been inclined to meet with a voyage free from danger, it was in his power to wait for calm weather and a smooth and favourable breeze. (87) What would one say, suppose anyone were to see a bear or a lion coming on with violence, and, while he might pacify and tame him, were to provoke him and make him savage, in order to give up himself as an unpitied meal and feast to those ravenous monsters? (88) Unless indeed anyone will assert that it is of no use to anyone to oppose the asps and serpents of Egypt, and all the other things which ... destructive poison ... inflict inevitable death on those who are once bitten by them; for that men must be content to use incantations, and so to tame those beasts, and by such means to avoid suffering any evil from them.

(89) Moreover, are there not certain men who are more savage and more treacherous than boars, or serpents, or asps? whose treacherous and malignant disposition it is impossible to escape otherwise than by gentleness and caresses? Therefore the wise Abraham will offer adoration to the sons of Cheth, and their name being interpreted, means "admiring," because the occasion persuades him to do so. (90) For he has not come to this action of adoration because he honours person who, by nature, and by hereditary qualities, and by their own habits, are enemies to reason, and who miserably waste the coinage of the soul, namely instruction, corrupting, and adulterating, and clipping it, but because he fears their present power and their scarcely conquerable strength, and is on his guard not to provoke them, he takes refuge in that great and powerful possession and weapon of virtue, that most excellent place of abode for wise souls, the double cave, which he could not occupy while warring and fighting, but only by acting as a champion and servant of reason.

(91) What? Do not we also, when we are spending our time in the market-place, frequently wonder at the masters, and also at the beasts of burden? But we wonder at these two classes, with different and not the same feelings. For we look upon the masters with honour, and upon the beasts of burden with fear, lest some injury should be done to us by them. (92) And when an opportunity offers, it is a good thing to attack our enemies and put down their power; but when we have no such opportunity, it is better to be quiet; but if we wish to find perfect safety as far as they are concerned, it is advantageous to caress them.

XIV. (93) On which account it is even now proper to praise those persons who do not yield to the president of vain opinion but who withstand him and say, "Shall you be a king and rule over us?"[80] For they do not see him actually in possession of kingly power, they do not see him as yet kindled like a flame, and shining and blazing in the unlimited fuel, but only smouldering like a spark, dreaming of glory, and not visibly having attained to it; (94) for they also suggest favourable hopes to themselves as if they will not be able to be overcome by him; for which reason they say, "Shall you reign over us?" Which is equivalent to saying, Do you expect to be a king over us while we are living, existing, strong, and breathing? Perhaps, indeed, you may make yourself master of such as are weak people, but with respect to us who are strong you will be looked upon us as a subject.

(95) And, indeed, this is the natural state of the case. For when right reason is powerful in the soul, vain opinion is put down; but when right reason is weak, vain opinion is strong. As long, therefore, as the soul has its own power still safe, and as long as it is not mutilated in any part of it, it may well have confidence to attack and aim its arrows at the pride which resists it, and it may indulge in freedom of speech, saying, "You shall not be a king, you shall not be a lord either over us, or during our lifetime over others; (96) but we, with our body-guards and shield-bearers, the offspring of wisdom, will overthrow your attacks and baffle your threats with one single sally of ours. In reference to which circumstances it is said, 'They began to hate him because of his dreams and because of his words.'"

(97) But are not all the images which pride sets up and worships mere words and dreams, while, on the contrary, those things alone deserve to be called actions and real energies which are referable to correct life and right reason? And the one class are worthy of hatred as being false, and the other class deserve friendship as being full of desirable and lovely truth. (98) Let no one, therefore, venture to bring accusations against the virtues of such men, as if they exhibited a specimen of an inhuman and unbrotherly disposition; but let any one who is disposed to do so, learn that it is

---

[80] Genesis 37:8.

not a man who is now being judged of, but the disposition which exists in the soul of each individual, which is mad on the subject of glory and arrogant pride; let him embrace these men who have adopted irreconcileable enmity and hatred towards this disposition, and let him never love what is hated by them. (99) Knowing thoroughly that such judges are never deceived so as to wander from a sound opinion, but that, having learnt from the beginning to understand who is the true king, namely, the Lord, they indignantly refuse to worship him who deprives God of his honour, and seeks to appropriate it to himself, and who invites his fellow servants to do him service.

XV. (100) On which account they say with confidence, "Shall you be a king and reign over us?" Are you ignorant that we are not independent, but that we are under the government of an immortal king, the only God? And why should you be a lord and lord it over us? for are we not under domination, and have we not now, and shall we not have for ever, and ever the same one Lord? in being whose servants we rejoice more than any one else can do in his liberty; for to be the servant of God is the most excellent of all things which are honoured in creation.

(101) I, therefore, should pray that I myself also might be able to abide firmly in the things which have been decided by these men; overseers of things, not of bodies, and just, and sober all their lives, so as never to be deceived by any of those things which are accustomed to deceive mankind. (102) But up to this time I am in a state of intoxication, and I am labouring under much uncertainty, and I have need of a staff and of a guide like a blind man; for if I had a staff to support me, then, perhaps, I might neither stumble nor fall.

(103) But if any persons who are conscious that they are but inconsiderate and precipitate, pay no attention to and do not care to follow those who have investigated all necessary matters with diligence and circumspection, nor, though they themselves are ignorant of the road, submit to the guidance of those who are acquainted with it, let them know that they have entered a course which is very difficult to travel through, and that they are entangled in it, and will not be able to advance further; (104) but I am so bound by treaties to these men, the moment I have a little recovered from my intoxication, that I think the same person both a friend and an enemy.

But at present I will drive from me and hate that dreamer no less than they do; for no one in his senses could blame me for this, that the majority of opinions and votes does always prevail; (105) but when he changes to a better course of life, and no longer dreams, and no longer worries himself by entangling himself in the vain imaginations of the slaves of vain opinion, and when he no longer dreams about night, and darkness, and the changes of uncertain matters which cannot be guessed at; (106) he, then, having awakened from deep sleep, continues awake and receives certainty instead of indistinctness, and truth instead of false conceptions, and day instead of night, and light instead of darkness, and rejects an Egyptian wife, that is to say, the pleasure of the body, when she invites him to come in to her, and to enjoy her conversation, out of an indescribable love of continence and admiration for piety, (107) and asserts his right to a share in those kindred and inherited blessings from which he appeared to be alienated, again desiring to recover that portion of virtue which properly belongs to him.

For proceeding by small and gradual improvements, as if he were now established on the summit and perfection of his own life, he cries out, what indeed he knows to a certainty from what has happened to him, that he "belongs to God,"[81] and that he belongs no more to any object of external sense which can affect any creature; (108) and then his brethren will come to a permanent reconciliation with him, changing their hatred into friendship, and their malignity into good will.

But I who am the follower of these men, for I have learnt to obey them as a servant obeys his master, will never cease to praise him for his change of mind. (109) Since Moses, also, that priest of sacred things, preserves his change of mind as what is worthy of love and of being preserved in men's recollection, from being forgotten, by the symbol of the bones[82] which he did not think proper to have buried in Egypt for ever, looking upon it as a hard thing, if the soul put forth any beautiful flower to suffer that to wither away, and to be overwhelmed and destroyed by the torrents which the Egyptian river of the passions, namely the body, which is incessantly flowing through all the outward senses, sends forth.

XVI. (110) The vision, therefore, which appeared proceeding from the earth, with reference to the sheaves and the interpretation thereof, has now been sufficiently discussed. It is time now to consider the other vision; and to examine how that is interpreted by the art of the explanation of dreams. (111) "He saw then," says the scripture, "a second dream, and he related it to his father, and to his brethren, and he said, I saw that the sun, and the moon, and the eleven stars worshipped me. And his father rebuked him, and said, What is this dream that thou hast dreamed? Shall I, and thy mother, and thy brethren, come forward and advance, and fall down to the earth and worship thee? And his brethren were jealous of him; but his father regarded his words."[83]

---

[81] Genesis 50:19.
[82] Exodus 13:19.
[83] Genesis 37:9.

(112) The studiers of sublime wisdom now say that the zodiac, the greatest of all circles in heaven, is studded with twelve animals *(zōdia)*, from which it has derived its name. And that the sun and the moon are always revolving around it, and go through each of the animals, not indeed with equal rapidity, but in unequal numbers and periods; the one doing so in thirty days, and the other in as near as may be a twelfth part of that time, that is in two days and a half; (113) therefore, he who saw this heaven-sent vision, thought that he was being worshipped by eleven stars, ranking himself among them as the twelfth, so as to complete the whole circle of the zodiac.

(114) And I recollect having before now heard some man who had applied himself to learning in no careless or indolent spirit, say that men were not the only beings which went mad with vain opinions, but that the stars did so too. And they also, said he, contend with one another for precedence, and those which are the greater claim to be attended by the lesser stars as their guards; (115) these matters, however, we may leave for the studiers of sublime subjects to investigate, and to settle how much truth and how much random assertion there is in them.

But we say, that the lover of indiscriminate study, and unreasonable contention, and vain opinion, being always puffed up by folly, wishes to assert a precedence, not only over men, but also above the nature of all existing things; (116) and he thinks that all things were created for his sake, and that it is necessary that everything, whether earth or heaven, or water or air, should bring him tribute; and he has gone to such an extravagant pitch of folly, that he is not able to reason upon such matters as even a young child might understand, and to see that no artist ever makes the whole for the sake of the part, but rather makes the part for the sake of the whole. Now the part of the whole is the man, so that he is properly asserted to have been made for the sake of perfecting the world in which he is rightly classed.

XVII. (117) But some persons are full of such exceeding folly, that they are indignant if the whole world does not follow their intentions: for this reason Xerxes, the king of Persia, being desirous to strike terror into his enemies, made a display of very mighty undertakings, altering the whole face of nature; (118) for he changed the nature of the elements of the earth and of the sea, giving land to the sea and sea to the land, by joining the Hellespont with a bridge, and breaking up Mount Athos into deep gulfs, which, being filled with sea, became so many new and artificially-cut seas, being entirely changed from the ancient course of nature. (119) And having worked wonders with respect to the earth, according to his wishes, he mounted up upon daring conceptions, like a miserable man as he was, contracting the guilt of impiety, and

seeking to soar up to heaven, as if he would move what cannot be moved, and would subjugate the host of heaven, and, as the proverb has it, he began with a sacred thing.

(120) For he aimed his arrows at the most excellent of the heavenly bodies, the sun, the ruler of the day, as if he had not himself been wounded by the invisible dart of insanity, not only because of his desiring things which were impossible, but such as were also most impious, either of which is a great disgrace to him who attempts them.

(121) It is related, also, that the very populous nation of the Germans, and theirs is a country where the sea is subject to the ebb and flow of the tide, ran down to the reflux which occurs in their country with great impetuosity, and drawing their naked swords charged and encountered the billowy sea as if it were a phalanx of enemies: (122) and these men deserve to be hated because they dare impiously to take up the arms of enemies against the free and invincible parts of nature; but they deserve also to be ridiculed for attempting what is impossible, as if they thought it practicable to wound the water as though it were a living animal, or to stab it and kill it. And again, one should grieve at the sight of such men, and fear, and flee out of fear at their attacks, and submit to all the affections of the soul which are conversant with pleasures and pains.

XVIII. (123) Moreover, it is only a very short time ago that I knew a man of very high rank, one who was prefect and governor of Egypt, who, after he had taken it into his head to change our national institutions and customs, and in an extraordinary manner to abrogate that most holy law guarded by such fearful penalties, which relates to the seventh day, and was compelling us to obey him, and to do other things contrary to our established custom, thinking that that would be the beginning of our departure from the other laws, and of our violation of all our national customs, if he were once able to destroy our hereditary and customary observance of the seventh day. (124) And as he saw that those to whom he offered violence did not yield to his injunctions, and that the rest of our people was not disposed to submit in tranquillity, but was indignant and furious at the business, and was mourning and dispirited as if at the enslaving, and overthrow, and utter destruction of their country; he thought fit to endeavour by a speech to persuade them to transgress, saying: (125) "If an invasion of enemies were to come upon you on a sudden, or the violence of a deluge, from the river having broken down all its barriers by an inundation, or any terrible fire, or a thunderbolt, or famine, or pestilence, or an earthquake, or any other evil, whether caused by men or inflicted by God, would you still remain quiet and unmoved at home? (126) And would you still go on in your habitual fashion, keeping your right hand back, and holding the other under your garments close to your sides, in order that you might not, even without meaning it, do anything to contribute to your own preservation? (127) And would you still sit down in your synagogues, collecting your ordinary assemblies, and reading your sacred volumes in security, and explaining whatever is not quite clear, and devoting all your time and leisure with long discussions to the philosophy of your ancestors? (128) Nay: rather shaking off all these ideas, you would gird yourselves up for the preservation of yourselves, and of your parents, and of your children, and, if one must tell the plain truth, of your possessions and treasures, to save them from being utterly destroyed. (129) And, indeed, I myself, am," said he, "all the evils which I have just enumerated: I am a whirlwind, I am war, and deluge, and thunderbolt, and the calamity of famine, and the misery of pestilence, and an earthquake which shakes and overthrows what stood firm before, not being merely the name of a necessity of fate, but actual, visible power, standing close to you."

(130) What then can we say that a man who says, or who merely thinks such things as these, is? Is he not an evil of an extraordinary nature? He surely must be some foreign calamity, brought from over the sea, or from some other world, since he, a man in every respect miserable, has dared to compare himself to the all-blessed God. (131) We must likewise add, that he is daring here to utter blasphemies against the sun, and the moon, and the rest of the stars, whenever anything which had been looked for according to the seasons of the year, either does not happen at all, or is brought about with difficulty; if, for instance, the summer causes too much heat, or the winter too excessive a cold, or if the spring or autumn were unseasonable, so that the one were to become barren and unfruitful, and the other to be prolific only in diseases.

(132) Therefore, giving all imaginable license to an unbridled mouth and abusive tongue, such a man will reproach the stars as not bringing their customary tribute, all but claiming for the things of earth the reverence and adoration of the heavenly bodies, and for himself above them all, in proportion as he, as being a man, looks upon himself as superior to the other animals.

XIX. (133) Such men then are classed by us as the very teachers of vain opinion. Let us now in turn look at their followers by themselves. These men are always laying plots against the practisers of virtue, and when they see them labouring to make their own life pure with guileless truth, and to exhibit it, as one may say, to the light of the moon, or of the sun, as able to stand inspection, they endeavor by deceit, or even by open violence, to hinder them, trying to drive them into the sunless country of impious men, which is occupied by deep night, and endless darkness, and ten thousand tribes of images, and appearances, and dreams, and then, having thrust them down thither, they compel them to fall down and worship them as masters.

(134) For we look upon the practiser of virtue as the sun, since the one gives light to our bodies, and the other to the things which belong to the soul: and the education which such a man uses we look upon as the moon, for the use of each is most pure and most useful in the night; and the brethren are those virtuous reasonings which are the offspring of instruction, and of a soul devoted to the practice of virtue, all of which make straight the right path of life, and which they, therefore, by all kinds of wary and cunning wrestlings, seek to overcome, and to trip up, and overthrow, and break the neck of, because they have determined neither to think nor to say anything sound themselves.

(135) For this reason his father rebukes this intractable youth (I do not mean Jacob, but right reason, which is older even than he), saying, (136) "What is this dream which thou hast dreamt?" but thou hast not seen any dream at all; hast thou fancied that things which are free by nature are to be of necessity slaves to human things, and that things which are rulers are to become subjects? and, what is more paradoxical still, subject, not to anything else but to the very things which they govern? and to be the slaves of no other things except those very things which are their own slaves? unless indeed a change of all the established things to their direct contraries is to take place, by the power of God, who is able to effect all things, and to move what is immovable, and to fix what is in a constant state of agitation.

(137) Since on what principle can you be angry with or reproach a man who sees a vision in his sleep? For he will say, I did not see it intentionally, why do you bring accusations against me, for errors which I have not committed from any deliberate purpose? I have related to you what fell upon me and made an impression on my mind suddenly, and without my desiring it. (138) But the present question is not about dreams, but about things which resemble dreams; which, to those whose minds are not highly purified appear great, and beautiful, and desirable things; while they are, in reality, trifling, and obscure, and deserving of ridicule, in the eyes of honest judges of the truth.

XX. (139) Shall I then, says he, I, that is to say, right reason, come to you? And shall the soul, which is both the mother and nurse of the company devoted to learning virtuous instruction, also come to thee? (140) And are the offspring of us too to come likewise? And are we all to stand in a row, laying aside all our former dignity, and holding up our hands and praying to thee? And are we then to prostrate ourselves on the ground, and endeavour to propitiate and adore thee? But may the sun never shine upon such transactions, since deep darkness is suited to evil deeds, and brilliant light to good deeds.

And what could be a greater evil than for pride, that deceiver and beguiler, to be praised and admired, instead of sincere and honest simplicity? (141) And it is with great propriety that the statement is added, "And his father took notice of his words." For it is the occupation of a soul which is not young, nor barren, nor wholly unfruitful, but rather of one which is really older and able to beget offspring, to cohabit with prudent caution, and to despise and overlook nothing whatever, but to have a reverential fear of the power of God, from which we cannot escape, and which we cannot overcome; and to look all around to see what its very end shall be.

(142) For this reason they say, that the sister of Moses also (and she is called Hope by us, when speaking in a figurative manner) was contemplated at a distance by the sacred scriptures, inasmuch as she kept her eyes fixed on the end of life, hoping that some good fortune might befall her, sent by the Giver of all good from above, from heaven; (143) for it has often happened that many persons, after having taken long voyages, and having sailed over a great expanse of sea with a fair wind, and without any danger, have suddenly been shipwrecked in the harbour itself, when they have been on the very point of casting anchor; (144) and many persons too, who have successfully come to the end of formidable wars of long duration, and have come off unwounded so as never to have received even a scratch on the surface of the skin, but to have escaped whole and entire as if they had only been at some popular assembly or national festival, having returned home with joy and cheerfulness, have been plotted against in their houses by those who, of all the world, least ought to have done so; being, as the proverb says, like oxen slain in their stall.

XXI. (145) As these unexpected events, which no one could ever have anticipated, do frequently happen in this manner and overthrow people, so also do they often drive the powers of the soul in a contrary direction to the proper one, and drag it in an opposite way, according to their power, and compel it to change its course: for what man, who has ever descended into the arena of life, has come off without a fall? (146) And who is there who has never been tripped up in that contest? He is happy who has not often been so. And for whom has not fortune laid snares, blowing upon him at intervals, and collecting its strength, that it may twine itself around him, and speedily carry him off before its adversary is ready for the contest? (147) Do we not know, that some persons have come from infancy to old age who have never been sensible of any irregularity, whether it be from the happy

condition of their nature, or from the care of those who brought them up and educated them, or owing to both circumstances? But then, being filled with profound peace in themselves, which is real peace, and the archetypal model of that which exists in cities, and being considered happy on that account, because they have never had a notion, not even in a dream, of the intestine war which arises from the violence of the passions, and which is the most piteous of all wars, have at last, at the very close of their lives, run on shore and made shipwreck, either through some intemperance of language or some insatiable gluttony, or some incontinent licentiousness of the parts below the belly. (148) For some, while—

"Still on the threshold of extreme old age,"

have admired the youthful, unhonoured, detestable, and disgraceful life of debauches; and others have given in to the cunning, and wicked, and calumnious, and desperate way of life of others, pursuing the first fruits of quarrelsome curiosity, when they ought rather to have discarded such habits now, even if they had been familiar to them.

(149) For which reason one ought to propitiate God, and to supplicate him perseveringly, that he will not pass by our miserable race, but that he will allow his saving mercy to be everlastingly shown towards us; for it is difficult for those who have tasted unalloyed peace to be prevented from glutting themselves with it.

XXII. (150) But, come now, this hunger is lighter evil than thirst, inasmuch as it has love and desire for its comforters; but when, through the desire of drinking, it is necessary to satisfy one's self with that other fountain, the water of which is dirty and unwholesome, then it is indispensable for the drinkers, being filled with a bitter-sweet pleasure, to live an unenviable life, betaking themselves to pernicious things as though they were advantageous, from ignorance of what is really desirable. (151) But the impetuous course of these evils is most grievous when the irrational powers of the soul attack the powers of the reason and get the better of them; (152) for as long as the herds of oxen obey their drivers, and the flocks obey their shepherds, and the goats obey the goatherds, the herds and all belonging to them go on well; but when the herdsmen who are appointed to look after the cattle become weaker than the beasts committed to their care, then everything goes wrong, and instead of regularity there arises irregularity, and disorder in the place of order, and confusion instead of steadiness, and disturbance in the place of good arrangement, since there is no longer any lawful superintending power properly established; for if there had been such a thing, it would have been destroyed before this time.

(153) What then? Do we not think that even

in ourselves there is a herd of irrational cattle, inasmuch as the irrational multitude of the soul is deprived of reason, and that the shepherd is the governing mind? But as long as that is vigorous and competent to act as the manager of the herd, everything goes on in a just, and prosperous, and advantageous manner; (154) but when any weakness or want of power supervenes to the king, then it follows of necessity that the subjects also labour with a like infirmity; and when they most completely seem to be in enjoyment of liberty, then they are a prize, lying most entirely ready for any one who pleases to contend for it to seize; for the natural course is for anarchy to be treacherous, and for government to be salutary, especially in a state where law and justice are honoured. And this is such a state as is consistent with reason.

XXIII. (155) We have now, then, spoken with sufficient accuracy about the dreams of vain opinion. Now, the different species of gluttony are conversant about drinking and eating. But the one has no need of any great variety, while the other requires a countless number of seasonings and sauces. These things, then, are referred to two managers. The matters relating to excessive drinking are referred to the chief butler, and those which belong to luxurious eating to the chief baker. (156) Now these men are, with excessive propriety, recorded to have seen visions of dreams one night; for they, each of them, labour to gratify the same need of their master, providing not simple food, but such as is accompanied with pleasure and extraordinary gratification; and each of them, separately, labours about half the food, but the two together are employed about the whole, and the one part draws on the other; (157) for men, when they have eaten, immediately desire drink; and men who have drunk immediately wish to eat; so that it is in no slight degree on this account that a vision is ascribed to them both at the same time. (158) Therefore the chief butler has the office of ministering to the appetite for wine, and the chief baker to the voracity.

And each of them sees in his vision what relates to his own business: the one sees wine and the plant which engenders wine, namely the vine; the other sees white bread lying on dishes, and himself serving up the dishes. [84]

(159) Now perhaps it may be proper first of all to examine the first dream. And it is as follows:— "In my sleep there was a vine before me; and on the vine were three branches, and it flourished and brought forth shoots, and there were on it ripe bunches of grapes. And Pharaoh's cup was in my hand, and I took the bunch of grapes and pressed it into the cup, and I gave the cup into Pharaoh's

hand." [85] (160) He speaks here in an admirable manner, and the expression, "in my sleep," is quite correct. For, in real truth, he who follows not so much the inebriety which arises from wine as that which proceeds from folly, being indignant at an upright and wakeful position, like people asleep, is thrown down and relaxed, and shuts the eyes of his soul, not being able either to see or to hear anything which is worthy of being seen or of being heard. (161) And being overthrown, he goes on a blind and guideless (I will not say path, but pathless) way through life, being pricked with thorns and briars; and sometimes too he falls down steep places, and tumbles down upon other people, so as to hurt both them and himself in a pitiable manner. (162) But the deep and long-enduring sleep in which every wicked man is held, removes all true conceptions, and fills the mind with all kinds of false images, and unsubstantial visions, persuading it to embrace what is shameful as praiseworthy. For at one time it dreams of grief as joy, and does not perceive that it is looking at the vine, the plant of folly and error. (163) "For," says the chief butler, "the vine was before me," the desired object was before him who desired it, wickedness was before the wicked man: which we, foolish men that we are, cultivate, without being aware that we are doing so to our own injury, the fruit of which we eat and drink, classing it under both species of food, which, as it would seem, we appropriate, not for one half the evils that affect us for the whole of our complete and entire misfortunes.

XXIV. (164) But it is desirable not to be ignorant that the intoxication which proceeds from the vine does not affect all who indulge in it in a similar manner, but very often affects different people in contrary ways, so that it makes some better and others worse than they are naturally. (165) For in the case of some men, it relaxes the sternness and moroseness of their character, and relieves them of their cares, and assuages their anger and their sorrow, and brings their dispositions into a milder mood, and makes their souls placable. But of others again, it cherishes the angry passions, and binds their pain firmly, and excites their feelings of love, and stimulates their rudeness; rendering the mouth talkative, their tongue unbridled, emancipating their external senses from all restraint, rendering their passions furious, and their whole mind violent and excited towards every object.

(166) So that the condition of the men first-mentioned appears to resemble an untroubled calm in fine weather, or a waveless tranquillity at sea, or a most peaceful and steady state of affairs in a city. But the condition of those whom I have last

---

[84] Genesis 40:16.

[85] Genesis 40:9.

described, is more like a violent and unremitting gale, or a sea tossed by a storm into vast billows, or a sedition, an evil more fearful than even interminable and irreconcileable war.

(167) Therefore, of these two banquet parties, the one is filled with laughter, with men promising amusement, and hoping for good fortune, and enjoying cheerfulness, and pleasant language, and mirth, and joy, and freedom from anxiety; (168) but the other is full of melancholy, and seriousness, and downcast looks, and offences, and reproaches, and wounds; of men gnashing their teeth, looking fiercely at one another, barking, strangling one another, contending with one another in every conceivable way, mutilating one another's ears and noses, and whatever parts of the body they can reach, displaying the intoxication of their whole life and their drunkenness in this unholy contest, with every kind of unseemly behaviour.

XXV. (169) It would therefore be naturally consistent to consider next that the vine is the symbol of two things: of folly, and of mirth. And each of these two, though it is indicated by many circumstances, we will explain in a few words, to avoid prolixity. (170) When any one leading us along the road, deserted by the passions and by acts of wickedness, the rod, that is, of philosophy, has led right reason to a height, and placed it like a scout upon a watch-tower,[86] and has commanded it to look around, and to survey the whole country of virtue, and to see whether it be blessed with a deep soil, and rich, and productive of herbage and of fruit, since deep soil is good to cause the learning which has been sown in it to increase, and to make the doctrines which have been planted in it, and which have grown to trees, to form solid trunks, or whether it be of a contrary character; and also to examine into actions, as one might into cities, and see whether they are strongly fortified, or whether they are defenceless and deprived of all the security which might be afforded by walls around them.

Also to inquire into the condition of the inhabitants, whether they are considerable in numbers and in valour, or whether their courage is weak and their numbers scanty, the two causes acting reciprocally on one another. (171) Then because we were not able to bear the weight of the whole trunk of wisdom, we cut off one branch and one bunch of grapes, and carried it with us as a most undeniable proof of our joy, and a burden very easy to be borne, wishing to display at the same time the branch and the fruit of excellence to those who are gifted with acuteness of mental sight, to show them, that is, the strongly-shooting and grape-bearing vine.

XXVI. (172) They then very fairly compare this vine of which we were only able to take a part, to happiness. And one of the ancient prophets bears his testimony in favour of my view of the matter, who speaking under divine inspiration has said, "The vineyard of the Lord Almighty is the house of Israel."[87] (173) Now Israel is the mind inclined to the contemplation of God and of the world; for the name Israel is interpreted, "seeing God," and the abode of the mind is the whole soul; and this is the most sacred vineyard, bearing as its fruit the divine shoot, virtue: (174) thus thinking well *(to eu phronein)* is the derivation of the word joy *(euphrosynē)*, being a great and brilliant thing so that, says Moses, even God himself does not disdain to exhibit it; and most especially at that time when the human race is departing from its sins, and inclining and bending its steps towards justice, following of its own accord the laws and institutions of nature.

(175) "For," says Moses, "the Lord thy God will return, that he may rejoice in thee for thy good as he rejoiced in thy fathers, if thou wilt hear his voice to keep all his commandments and his ordinances and his judgments which are written in the book of this law."[88] (176) Who could implant in man a desire for virtue and excellence, more strongly than is here done? Dost thou wish, says the scripture, O mind, that God should rejoice? Do thou rejoice in virtue thyself, and bring no costly offering, (for what need has God of anything of thine?) But, on the other hand, receive with joy all the good things which he bestows upon thee; (177) for he rejoices in giving, when they who receive are worthy of his grace; unless you think that those men who live blameably may be justly said to make God indignant and to excite his anger, but that those who live in a praiseworthy manner do not make him rejoice.

(178) But there is nothing which gives so much pleasure to fathers and mothers, our mortal parents, as the virtues of their children, even though they may be in want of numbers of necessary things; And does not the excellence of these aforesaid persons in like manner rejoice the Creator of the universe, who is in no want of anything whatever? (179) Do thou therefore, O mind, having learnt how mighty a thing the anger of God is, and how great a good the joy of God is, do not do anything worthy to excite his anger to thy own destruction, but study only such things as may be the means of your pleasing God. (180) And you will find these actions not to be the making of long and unusual journeys, nor the passing over unnavigable seas, or wandering without stopping to take breath to the furthest boundaries of earth and sea:

---

86 Numbers 13:18.

87 Isaiah 5:7.
88 Deuteronomy 30:9.

for good actions do not dwell at a distance and have not been banished beyond the confines of the habitable world, but, as Moses says, good is situated near you, and is planted along with you, being united to you in three necessary parts, in the heart, in the mouth, and in the hands: that is to say, in the mind, in the speech, and in the actions; since it is necessary to think and to say, and to do good things, which are made perfect by a union of good design, good execution, and good language.

XXVII. (181) I say therefore to him whose occupation is to gratify one description of gluttony, the fondness for drinking, namely to the chief butler, "Why are you labouring hard, O unhappy man? For you think that you are preparing pleasant things to give delight, but in reality you are kindling a flame of folly and intemperance, and contributing great and abundant quantities of fuel to it." (182) But perhaps he may reply, do not blame me precipitately before you have considered my case; I was appointed to pour out wine, not indeed for a man who was endowed with temperance, and piety, and all the other virtues, but for a violent, and intemperate, and unjust master, one who was very proud in his impiety, and who dared once to say, "I do not know the Lord;"[89] so that I very naturally studied what would afford him gratification: (183) and do not wonder that God is delighted with one thing, and the mind which is hostile to God, namely Pharaoh, with the contrary.

Who then is the chief butler of God? The priest who offers libations to him, the truly great high priest, who, having received a draught of everlasting graces, offers himself in return, pouring in an entire libation full of unmixed wine.

You see that there are differences between butlers in proportion to the differences existing between those whom they are waiting on; (184) on this account I, the butler of Pharaoh, who exerts his stiff-necked, and in all respects intemperate reason, in the direction of indulgences of his passions, am a eunuch, having had all the generative parts of my soul removed, and being compelled to migrate from the apartments of the men, and am a fugitive also from the women's chambers, inasmuch as I am neither male nor female; nor am I able to disseminate seed nor to receive it, being of an ambiguous nature, neither one thing nor the other; a mere false coin of human money, destitute of immortality, which is from time to time kept alive by the constant succession of children and offspring: being also excluded from the assembly and sacred meeting of the people, for it is expressly forbidden that any one who has suffered any injury or mutilation such as I have should enter in thereto.[90]

XXVIII. (185) But the high priest of whom we are speaking is a perfect man, the husband of a virgin (a most extraordinary statement), who has never been made a woman; but who on the contrary, has ceased to be influenced by the customs of women in regard to her connection with her husband.[91] And not only is this man competent to sow the seeds of unpolluted and virgin opinions, but he is also the father of sacred reasonings, (186) some of which are overseers and superintendents of the affairs of nature, such as Eleazar and Ithamar; others are ministers of the worship of God, earnestly occupied in kindling and burning up the flame of heaven; for, as they are always uttering discourses relating to holiness, they cause it to shine, bringing forth the most divine kind of piety like fire from a flint; (187) and the being who is at the same time the guide and father of those men is no insignificant part of the sacred assembly, but he is rather the person without whom the duly convened assembly of the parts of the soul could never be collected together at all; he is the president, the chairman, the creator of it, who, without the aid of any other being, is able by himself alone to consider and to do everything.

(188) He, when taken in conjunction with others, is insignificant in point of number, but when he is looked at by himself he becomes numerous; he is a tribunal, an entire council, the whole people, a complete multitude, the entire race of mankind, or rather, if one is to speak the real truth, he is a sort of nature bordering on God, inferior indeed to him, but superior to man; (189) "for when," the scripture say, "the high priest goes into the Holy of Holies he will not be a man."[92] What then will he be if he is not a man? Will he be a God? I would not venture to say that (for the chief prophet, Moses, did receive the inheritance of this name while he was still in Egypt, being called "the god of Pharaoh;")[93] nor again is he man, but he touches both these extremities as if he touched both the feet and the head.

XXIX. (190) So now one kind of vine, which has been assigned as the portion of cheerfulness, and the intoxication which arises from it, namely unmingled goodness of counsel, and the cup-bearer too who drew the wine from the divine goblet, which God himself has filled with virtues up to the lip, has been explained; (191) but the other kind, that of folly, and grief, and drunkenness, is also already depicted in a fashion but in another character, by other expressions which are used in the greater canticle; "for," says the scripture, "their vine is of the vine of Sodom and their tendrils are of the vine of Gomorrah; their grapes are the

---

[89] Exodus 5:2.
[90] Deuteronomy 23:1.

[91] Genesis 18:11.
[92] Leviticus 16:17.
[93] Exodus 7:1.

grapes of gall; their bunches are full of bitterness itself. Their wine is the madness of dragons and the incurable fury of asps."[94]

(192) You see here what great effects are produced by the drunkenness of folly: bitterness, an evil disposition, exceeding gall, excessive anger, implacability, a biting and treacherous disposition. The lawgiver most emphatically asserts the branch of the vine of folly to be in Sodom; and the name Sodom, being interpreted, means "blindness," or "barrenness;" since folly is a thing which is blind, and also barren of all good things; though, nevertheless, some people have been so greatly influenced by it as to measure, and weigh, and count everything with reference to themselves alone.

(193) Gomorrah, being interpreted, means "measure;" but Moses conceived that God was the standard of weight, and measure, and number, in the universe, but he had not the same opinion of the human mind. And he shows this in the following passage, where he says, "There shall not be in thy sack one weight, and another weight, a great and a small; there shall not be in thy house one measure, and another measure, a great and a small; (194) thy weight shall be a true and just one." But a true and just measure is, to conceive that it is the only just God alone who measures and weighs everything, and who has circumscribed the nature of the universe with numbers, and limitations, and boundaries. But it is unjust and false to imagine that these things are regulated in accordance with the human mind. (195) But the eunuch and chief butler of Pharaoh, having beheld the plant generative of folly, namely, the vine, adds besides to his delineation there stocks, that he may signify the three extremities of error according to the three different times; for a root is equivalent to extremity.

XXX. (196) When, therefore, folly has overshadowed and occupied the whole soul, and when it has left no portion of it unoccupied or free, it not only compels it to commit such errors as are remediable, but such also as are irremediable. (197) Now those which admit of a remedy are set down as the easiest and the first; but those which are irremediable are altogether terrible, and are the last of all, being so far analogous to roots. (198) And as, in my notions, wisdom begins to benefit a man in small matters, and ends at last in the absolute perfection of all well-doing, so, in the same manner folly, constraining the soul from above and leading it away from instruction by small degrees, establishes it at last at a long distance from right reason, and finally leads it to the extreme point, and utterly overthrows it.

(199) And the dream showed that after the roots appeared the vine flourished and put forth shoots and bore fruit; for, says the chief butler, "It was flourishing and bearing shoots, around which were bunches of grapes."[95] The foolish man is accustomed to display barrenness, and never to put forth even leaves, and, in fact, to be withered all his life; (200) for what could be a greater evil than folly flourishing and bearing fruit? But, says he, "the cup of Pharaoh," the vessel which is the receptacle of folly and drunkenness, and of the ceaseless intoxication of life, "is in my hand;" an expression equivalent to saying, depends upon my administration, and endeavours, and powers; for without my contrivances, the passion will not proceed rightly by its own efforts; (201) for as it is proper that the reins should be in the hands of the charioteer, and the rudder in the hands of the pilot—for this is the only way in which the course of the chariot and the voyage of the vessel can proceed successfully—so, also, the filling of the goblet with wine is in the hands and depends upon the power of him who by his art brings to perfection one of the two kinds of gluttony, namely, satiety of wine.

(202) But why has he endured to boast in respect of a matter which deserved rather to be denied than to be confessed? Would it not have been better not to have confessed at all that he was a teacher of intemperance, and not to admit that he increased the excitement of the passions by wine in the case of the intemperate man, as being an inventor and producer of a luxurious, and debauched, and most disgraceful way of life. (203) Such, however, is the case. Folly boasts of those things which ought to be concealed; and in this present case it prides itself, not only on holding in its hands the receptacle of the intemperate soul, that is to say, the cup of wine, and in showing it to all men, but also in pressing out the grapes into it; that is to say, in making that which satisfies the passion, and bringing what is concealed to light.

(204) For as children which require food, when they are about to receive the milk, squeeze and press out the breast of the nurse that feeds them, so likewise does the workman and cause of intemperance vigorously press the fountain from which the evil of abundance of wine pours forth, that he may derive food in a most agreeable manner from the drops which are squeezed out.

XXXI. (205) Such a description then as I have here given may be applied to the man who is made frantic by the influence of unmixed wines, that he is a drunken, and foolish, and irremediable evil. We must now, in turn, investigate the character of the glutton, who is akin to the drunkard, and who is a sworn companion of all kinds of voracity and greediness, labouring, without any restraint,

---

at the artificial gratification of his appetite. (206) And yet it does not require a great deal of care to arrive at his true character; for the dream which was seen is a representation of his likeness very closely resembling him; and when we have accurately examined him, let us look upon him as we would upon a representation in a mirror; (207) for "I thought," said the chief cook, "that I had three baskets of fine wheaten loaves upon my head." Now, using the word "head" in an allegorical manner, we mean by it the dominant part of the soul, that is, the mind, and we say that everything rests or depends upon that; for he once exclaimed concerning it, "All these things were in my charge." (208) Therefore when he had completed the preparation of these things which he had devised against the miserable belly, he displayed himself also, and, like a foolish man as he was, he was not ashamed to be weighed down with so great a burden, namely, the weight of three baskets; that is to say, with three portions of time.

(209) For those who advocate the cause of pleasure affirm that it consists of three times, of the memory of past delights, and of the enjoyment of those that are present, and of the hope of what are to come; (210) so that the three baskets are likened unto the three portions of time, and the cakes upon the baskets to those circumstances which are suitable to each of the portions; to the recollection of past joys, to the enjoyment of present pleasures, to the hope of future delights. And he who carries all these things is likened unto the lover of pleasure, who has filled his faithless table, a table destitute of all hospitable and friendly salt, not with one kind of luxury only, but with almost every description and species of intemperance; (211) and this is enjoyed by king Pharaoh alone, as if he were sitting at a public banquet, and devoting himself to a dispersion, and scattering, and defeat, and destruction of temperance; for the name Pharaoh, being interpreted, means "dispersion." And it is magnificent and royal piece of conduct in him not to exult in the specious advantages of wisdom, but to pride himself on those pursuits of profligacy which it is unseemly to mention, wrecking himself on insatiable appetite and gluttony, and effeminacy of life.

(212) Therefore the birds, that is to say, the chances which never could have been anticipated by conjecture, coming from outward quarters and hovering around him, will attack and kindle every thing like fire, and will destroy every thing with their all-devouring power, so that there is not a single fragment left to the bearer of the baskets for his enjoyment though he had hoped to proceed with his inventions and contrivances, for ever and ever carrying them on in a safe place, so that they could never be taken from him.

(213) And thanks be to God who giveth the victory and who renders the labours of the man who is a slave to his passions, though ever so carefully carried out, still unproductive and useless, sending down winged natures in an invisible manner for their destruction and overthrow. Therefore, the mind, being deprived of those things which it had made for itself, having, as it were, its neck cut through, will be found headless and lifeless, and like those who are fixed to a cross, nailed as it were to the tree of hopeless and helpless ignorance. (214) For as long as none of these things come upon one which arrive suddenly and unexpectedly, then those acts which are directed to the enjoyment of pleasure appear to be successful; but when such evils descend upon them unexpectedly, they are overthrown, and their maker is destroyed with them.

XXXII. (215) The dreams, therefore, of those men who divide those things which produce the taste according to every species of food, whether it be meat or drink, and such as is not necessary but superfluous, and sought only by the intemperate, have been sufficiently explained. But those of Pharaoh, who appears to exercise sovereignty over these men and over all the powers of the soul, must now be investigated if we would proceed in order and consistently with our plan.

(216) Pharaoh says, "In my dream I thought that I was standing by the bank of a river, and seven oxen came up as it were out of the river, of eminent plumpness in their flesh, and beautiful to the view, and fed in the green marsh; and behold, seven other oxen came up out of the river after them, evil to look at and ill-favoured, and lean in their flesh, such that I never saw any leaner in all Egypt; (217) and the lean and ill-favoured oxen devoured the seven former oxen which were beautiful, and picked out, and they entered into their stomachs, and still their appearance remained ill-favoured, as I have described it at first. (218) And when I had awoke I fell asleep again; and again I saw in my dream, and as it were seven ears of corn grew up on one stalk, full and beautiful. And seven other ears of corn also came up, lean and wind-beaten, close to them, and these last seven ears did swallow up the seven beautiful and full ears." [96]

(219) You see now the preface of the lover of self who being easily moved, and changeable, and fickle, both in his body and soul, says, "I thought that I was standing," and did not consider that unchangeableness and steadiness belong to God alone, and to him who is dear to God. (220) And the most evident proof of the unchangeable power which exists in him is this world, which is always in the same place and in the same condition. And if the world is immovable how can the Creator of it be any thing but firm?

---

[96] Genesis 41:17.

In the second place the sacred scriptures are likewise most infallible witnesses; (221) for it is said in them, where the words are put into the mouth of God, "I stand here and there, before you were dwelling upon the rock,[97] which is an expression equivalent to, Thus am I who am visible to you, and am here: and I am there and everywhere, filling all places, standing and abiding in the same condition, being unchangeable, before you or any one of the objects of creation had any existence, being beheld upon the highest and most ancient authority of power, from which the creation of all existing things was shed forth, and the stream of wisdom flowed; (222) "for I am he who brought the stream of water out of the solid rock,"[98] is said in another place. And Moses also bears witness to the immutability of the Deity, where he says, "I saw the place where the God of Israel stood;"[99] intimating enigmatically that he is not given to change by speaking here of his standing, and of his being firmly established.

XXXIII. (223) But there is in the Deity such an excessive degree of stability and firmness, that he gave even to the most excellent natures a share of his durability as his most excellent possession: and presently afterwards he, the most ancient author of all things, namely God, says that he is about to erect firmly his covenant full of grace (and that means his law and his word) in the soul of the just man as on a solid foundation, which shall be an image in the likeness of God, when he says to Noah, "I will establish my covenant with thee."[100] (224) And besides this, he also indicates two other things, one that justice is in no respect different from the covenant of God, the other that other beings bestow gifts which are different from the persons who receive them; but God gives not only those gifts, but he gives also the very persons who receive them to themselves, for he has given me to myself, and every living being has he given to himself; for the expression, "I will establish my covenant with thee," is equivalent to, I will give thee to thyself.

(225) And all those who are truly lovers of God desire eagerly to escape from the storm of multiplied affairs and business in which there is always tempestuous weather, and rough sea, and confusion, and to anchor in the calm and safe untroubled haven of virtue. (226) Do you not see what is said about the wise Abraham who "is standing before the Lord?"[101] For when was it likely that the mind would be able to stand, no longer inclining to different sides like the balance in a scale, except when it is opposite to God, beholding him and being beheld by him? (227) For perfect absence of motion comes to it in two ways, either from beholding him with whom nothing can be compared, because he is not attracted by anything resembling himself, or from being beheld by him, because ... which he considered worthy, the ruler has assigned to himself alone as the most excellent of beings. And indeed a divine admonition was given in the following terms to Moses: "Stand thou here with me,"[102] by which injunction both these things appear to be intimated, first, the fact that the good man is not moved, and secondly, the universal stability of the living God.

XXXIV. (228) For, in real truth, whatever is akin or near to God is appropriated by him, becoming steady and stationary by reason of his unchangeableness; and the mind, being at rest, well knows how great a blessing rest is, and admiring its own beauty, it conceives that either it is assigned to God alone as his, or else to that intermediate nature which is between the mortal and the immortal race; (229) at all events, it says, "And I stood in the midst between the Lord and you,"[103] not meaning by these words that he was standing on his own feet, but wishing to indicate that the mind of the wise man, being delivered from all storms and wars, and enjoying unruffled calm and profound peace, is superior indeed to man, but inferior to God.

(230) For the ordinary human mind is influenced by opinion, and is thrown into confusion by any passing circumstances; but the other is blessed and happy, and free from all participation in evil. And the good man is on the borders, so that one may appropriately say that he is neither God nor man, but that he touches the extremities of both, being connected with the mortal race by his manhood, and with the immortal race by his virtue.

(231) And there is something which closely resembles this in the passage of scripture concerning the high priest; "For when," says the scripture, "he goes into the holy of holies, he will not be a man till he has gone out again."[104] But if at that time he is not a man, it is clear that he is not God either, but a minister of God, belonging as to his mortal nature to creation, but as to his immortal nature to the uncreated God. (232) And he is placed in the middle class until he again goes forth among the things which belong to the body and to the flesh.

And this is the order of things according to nature, when the mind, being entirely occupied with divine love, bends its course towards the temple of God, and approaches it with all possible ear-

---

[97] Exodus 17:6.
[98] Deuteronomy 8:15.
[99] Exodus 24:10.
[100] Genesis 9:10.
[101] Genesis 18:22.
[102] Deuteronomy 5:31.
[103] Deuteronomy 10:10.
[104] Leviticus 16:17.

nestness and zeal, it becomes inspired, and forgets all other things, and forgets itself also. It remembers him alone, and depends on him alone, who is attended by it as by a body-guard, and who receives its ministrations, to whom it consecrates and offers up the sacred and untainted virtues. (233) But when the inspiration has ceased, and the excessive desire has relaxed, then it returns from divine things and becomes a man again, mixing with human affairs, which were awaiting him in the vestibule, that they might carry him off while gazing only on the things in them.

XXXV. (234) Moses therefore describes the perfect man as being neither God nor man, but, as I said before, something on the border between uncreated and the perishable nature. Again, he classes him who is improving and advancing towards perfection in the region between the dead and the living, meaning by the "living" those persons who dwell with wisdom, and by "the dead" those who rejoice in folly; (235) for it is said with respect to Aaron, that "He stood between the dead and the living, and the plague was stayed."[105] For he who is making progress is not reckoned among those who are dead as to the life of virtue, inasmuch as he has a desire and admiration of what is honourable, nor among those who are living in extreme and perfect prosperity, for there is still something wanting to the end, but he touches both extremes; (236) on which account the expression, "the plague was stayed," is very properly used rather than "the plague ceased;" for in those who are perfect the things which break, and crush, and destroy the soul cease; but in those who are advancing towards perfection, they are only diminished, as if they were only cut short and checked.

XXXVI. (237) Since then all steadiness, and stability, and the abiding for ever in the same place unchangeably and immovably, is first of all seen in the living God, and next in the word of the living God, which he has called his covenant; and in the third place in the wise man, and in the fourth degree in him who is advancing towards perfection, what could induce the wicked mind, which is liable to all sorts of curses, to think that it is able to stand by itself, while it is in reality borne about as in a deluge, and dragged hither and thither by the incessant eddies of things flowing in through the dead and agitated body? (238) "For I thought," says the scripture, "that I was standing on the bank of the river:"[106] and by the word river we say that speech is symbolically meant, since both these things are borne outward, and flow on with a vigourous and sustained speed. And the one is at one time filled up with a great abundance of water, and the other with a quantity of verbs and nouns,

and at another time they are both empty and relaxed, and in a state of quiescence; (239) again, they are of use inasmuch as the one irrigates the fields, and the other fertilizes the souls of those who receive it. And at times they are injurious by reason of overflowing, as then the one deluges the land on its borders, and the other troubles and confuses the reason of those who do not attend to it.

(240) Therefore speech is compared to a river, and the nature of speech is twofold, the one sort being better and the other worse; that is, the better kind which does good, and that of necessity is the worse kind which does harm; (241) and Moses has given most conspicuous examples of each kind to those who are able to see, for he says, "For a river goes out of Eden to water the Paradise, and from thence it is divided into four branches:"[107] (242) and by the name Eden he means the wisdom of the living God, and the interpretation of the name Eden is "delight," because I imagine wisdom is the delight of God, and God is the delight of wisdom, as it is said also in the Psalms, "Delight thou in the Lord."[108]

And the divine word, like a river, flows forth from wisdom as from a spring, in order to irrigate and fertilize the celestial and heavenly shoots and plants of such souls as love virtue, as if they were a paradise. (243) And this sacred word is divided into four beginnings, by which I mean it is portioned out into four virtues, each of which is a princess, for to be divided into beginnings,[109] does not resemble divisions of place, but a kingdom, in order than any one, after having shown the virtues as boundaries, may immediately proceed to show the wise man who follows them to be king, being elected as such, not by men, but by the only free nature which cannot err, and which cannot be corrupted; (244) for those who behold the excellence of Abraham say unto him, "Thou art a king, sent from God among us:"[110] proposing as a maxim, for those who study philosophy, that the wise man alone is a ruler and a king, and that virtue is the only irresponsible authority and sovereignty.

XXXVII. (245) Accordingly, one of the followers of Moses, having compared this speech to a river, has said in the Psalms, "The river of God was filled with water,"[111] and it is absurd to give such a title to any of the rivers which flow upon the earth. But as it seems the psalmist is here speaking of the divine word, which is full of streams and wisdom, and which has no part of itself empty

---

[105] Numbers 16:48.
[106] Genesis 41:17.

[107] Genesis 2:10.
[108] Psalm 36:4.
[109] There is an unavoidable obscurity in the translation here. The Greek word *archai*, which means beginnings, or principles, and also governments.
[110] Genesis 23:6.
[111] Psalm 65:10.

or desolate, or rather, as some one has said, which is diffused everywhere over the universe, and is raised up on high, on account of the continued and incessant rapidity of that ever-flowing spring.

(246) There is also another expression in the Psalms, such as this, "The course of the river makes glad the city of God."[112] What city? For the holy city, which exists at present, in which also the holy temple is established, at a great distance from any sea or river, so that it is clear, that the writer here means, figuratively, to speak of some other city than the visible city of God. (247) For, in good truth, the continual stream of the divine word, being borne on incessantly with rapidity and regularity, is diffused universally over everything, giving joy to all. (248) And in one sense he calls the world the city of God, as having received the whole cup of the divine draught, ... and being gladdened thereby, so as to have derived from it an imperishable joy, of which it cannot be deprived for ever.

But in another sense he applies this title to the soul of the wise man, in which God is said also to walk, as if in a city, "For," says God, "I will walk in you, and I will be your God in you."[113] (249) And who can pour over the happy soul which proffers its own reason as the most sacred cup, the holy goblets of true joy, except the cup-bearer of God, the master of the feast, the word? not differing from the draught itself, but being itself in an unmixed state, the pure delight and sweetness, and pouring forth, and joy, and ambrosial medicine of pleasure and happiness; if we too may, for a moment, employ the language of the poets.

XXXVIII. (250) But that which is called by the Hebrews the city of God is Jerusalem, which name being interpreted means, "the sight of peace." So they do not look for the city of the living God in the region of the earth, for it is not made of wood or of stone, but seek it in the soul which is free from war, and which proposes to those who are endowed with acuteness of sight a contemplative and peaceful life; (251) since where could any find a more venerable and holy abode for God amid all existing things, than the mind fond of contemplation, which is eager to behold every thing and which does not, even in a dream, feel a wish for sedition or disturbance? (252) And again, the invisible spirit which is accustomed to converse with me in an unseen manner prompts me with a suggestion, and says, O my friend, you seem to be ignorant of an important and most desirable matter which I will explain to you completely; for I have also in a most seasonable manner explained many other things to you also. (253) Know, then, O excellent man, that God alone is the truest, and

most real, and genuine peace, and that every created and perishable essence is continual war.

For God is something voluntary, and mortal essence is necessity. Whoever, therefore, is able to forsake war, and necessity, and creation, and destruction, and to pass over to the uncreated being, to the immortal God, to the voluntary principle, and to peace, may justly be called the abode and city of God. (254) Do not, therefore, consider it a different thing whether you speak of the sight of peace or the sight of God, as they are the same thing; because peace is not only the companion but also the chief of powers of the living God, which are distinguished by many names.

XXXIX. (255) And, moreover, he says to the wise Abraham, "that he will give him an inheritance of land from the river of Egypt to the great river, the river Euphrates,"[114] not meaning a portion of the land so much as a better portion in respect of our own selves. For our own body, and the passions which exist in it, and which are engendered by it, are likened to the river of Egypt, but the soul and the passions which are dear to that are likened to the river Euphrates. (256) And here a doctrine is laid down, at once most profitable to life and of the highest importance, that the good man has received for his inheritance the soul and the virtues of the soul: just as, on the contrary, the wicked man has received for his share the body and the vices of the body, and those which are engendered by the body.

(257) And the expression "from," has a double sense. One, that by which the starting point from which it begins is included; the other that by which it is excluded. For when we say that from morning to evening there are twelve hours, or from the new moon to the end of the month there are thirty days, we are including in our enumeration both the first hour and the day of the new moon. And when any one says that such and such a field is three or four furlongs distant from the city, he clearly means to leave the city itself out of that measurement. (258) So that now, too, we must consider that the expression, "from the river of Egypt," is to be understood so as to include that river; for the writer intends to remove us to a distance from the things of the body which are seen to exist in a constant flow and course which is being destroyed and destroying, that so we may receive the inheritance of the soul with the imperishable virtues, which are, moreover, deserving of immortality.

(259) Thus, therefore, by tracing it out diligently, we have found that praiseworthy speech is likened to a river; but speech which is deserving of blame is the very river of Egypt itself, untractable, unwilling to learn, as one may say in

---

[112] Psalm 45:5.
[113] Leviticus 26:12.

[114] Genesis 15:18.

a word, lifeless speech; for which reason it is also changed into blood,[115] as not being able to afford sustenance. For the speech of ignorance is not wholesome, and it is productive of bloodless and lifeless frogs, which utter only a novel and harsh sound, a noise painful to the ear. (260) And it is said, likewise, that all the fish in that river were destroyed. And by the fish are here figuratively meant the conceptions; for these things float about and exist in speech as in a river, resembling living things and filling the river with life. But in uninstructed speech all conceptions die; for it is not possible to find any thing intelligent in it, but only, as some one has said, some disorderly and unmusical voices of jackdaws.

XL. (261) We have now then said enough on these subjects. But since he not only confesses that he saw in his dream, a standing and a river, but also the banks of a river, as his words are, "I thought that I was standing by the bank (*cheilos*) of the river."[116] It must be desirable to say a few seasonable things also about the bank. (262) Now there appears to be two most necessary objects on account of which nature has adapted lips (*cheilē*) to all animals, and especially to men; one for the sake of tranquillity, for they are the strongest bulwark and fortification of the voice; the other for the sake of distinctness, for it is through them that the stream of words issues forth. For when they are closed speech is checked; for it is impossible that it should be borne outward if they are not parted. (263) And by these means nature prepares and trains man for both objects, speech and silence, watching the appropriate time for each employment.

As for instance, is anything said worth listening to? Then attend, raising no obstacle, in perfect quiet, according to the injunction of Moses, "Be silent and hear."[117] (264) For of those persons who mix themselves up with contentious discussions there is not one who can properly be considered as either speaking or listening; but this is only advantageous to him who is about to do so.

(265) Again, when you see, amid the wars and disasters of life, the merciful hand of God and his favourable power held over you and standing in defence of you, be silent yourself; for that champion stands in no need of any assistance. And there are proofs of this fact recorded in the sacred writings; such, for instance, as the verse, "The Lord will fight for us, and ye shall be silent."[118] (266) And if you see the genuine offspring and the firstborn of Egypt destroyed, namely desire, and pleasures, and pain, and fear, and iniquity, and mirth, and intemperance, and all the other qualities which are similar and akin to these, then marvel and be silent, dreading the terrible power of God; (267) for, say the scriptures, "Not a dog shall move his tongue, nor shall anything, man or beast, utter a sound;"[119] which is equivalent to saying, It does not become either the impudent tongue to bark and curse—nor the man that is within us, that is to say, our dominant mind; nor the cattle-like beast which is within us, that is to say, the outward sense—to boast, when all the evil that was in us has been utterly destroyed, and when an ally from without comes of his own accord to hold his shield over us.

XLI. (268) But there are many occasions which are not well suited to silence: and if we go to the language of ordinary prose, of which we may again see memorials laid up, how did there, ever an unexpected participation in good take place to any one? It is well, therefore, to give thanks and to sing hymns in honour of him who bestowed it. (269) What, then, is the good? The passion which is attacking us is dead, and is thrown out on its face without burial. Let us not delay, but standing still, let us sing that most sacred and becoming hymn, feeling that we are commanded to say to all men, "Let us sing unto the Lord, for he has triumphed gloriously; the horse and his rider hath he thrown into the sea."[120] (270) But the rout and destruction of the passions is indeed a good, but not a perfect good; but the discovery of wisdom is a surpassing good, and when that is found all the people will sing harmonies and melodies, not with one kind of music only, but with every sort; (271) for then, says the scripture, "Israel sang this song at the well;"[121] that is to say, in triumph for the fact that knowledge, which had long been hidden but which was sought for, had at length been found by all men, though lying deep by nature; the duty of which was to irrigate the rational fields existing in the souls of those men who are fond of contemplation.

(272) What, then, shall we say? When we bring home the legitimate fruit of the mind, does not the sacred scripture enjoin us to display in our reason, as in a sacred basket, the first fruits of our fertility; a specimen of the glorious flowers, and shoots, and fruits which the soul has brought forth, bidding us speak out distinctly, and to utter panegyrics on the God who brings things to perfection, and to say, "I have cleared away the things which were holy out of my house, and I have arranged them in the house of God:"[122] appointing as stewards and guardians of them, men

[115]Exodus 7:17.
[116]Genesis 41:17.
[117]Deuteronomy 27:19.
[118]Exodus 14:14.

[119]Exodus 11:7.
[120]Exodus 15:1.
[121]Numbers 21:17.
[122]Deuteronomy 26:13.

selected for their superior merit, and giving them the charge of these sacred things; (273) and these persons are Levites, proselytes, and orphans, and widows. But some are suppliants, some are emigrants and fugitives, some are persons widowed and destitute of all created things, but enrolled as belonging to God, the genuine husband and father of the soul which is inclined to worship.

XLII. (274) In this way, then, it is most proper both to speak and to be silent. But the wicked adopt an exactly contrary course; for they are admirers of a blamable kind of silence, and of an interpretation open to reproach, practising both lines of conduct to their own destruction and that of others. (275) But the greater part of their employment consists in saying what they ought not; for having opened their mouth and leaving it unbridled, like an unrestrained torrent, they allow their speech to run on indiscriminately, as the poet says, dragging on thousands of profitless sayings; (276) therefore those who have devoted themselves to the advocacy of pleasure and appetite, and every sort of excessive desire, building up irrational passion as a fortification against dominant reason, and preparing themselves for a contentious sort of discussion, have come at last to a regular dispute, hoping to be able to blind the race which is endowed with the faculty of sight, and to throw it down precipices, and into depths from which it will not be able at any future time to emerge. (277) But some have not only put themselves forward as rivals to human virtue, but have proceeded to such a pitch of folly as to oppose themselves also to divine virtue. Therefore Pharaoh, the king of the land of Egypt, is spoken of as the leader of the company which is devoted to the passions; for it is said to the prophet, "Behold, he is going forth to the river, and thou shalt stand in the way to meet him, on the bank of the river;"[123] (278) for it is the peculiar characteristic of the wise man to go forth to the rapidity and continual pouring forth of the irrational passion; and it is also characteristic of one man to go forth of the irrational passion; and it is also characteristic of the wise man to oppose with exceeding vigour the arguments on behalf of pleasure and desire, not with his feet, but with his mind, firmly and immoveably, standing on the bank of the river; that is to say, on the mouth and on the tongue, which are the organs of speech.

For standing firmly on these, he will be able to overturn and defeat the plausible specious arguments which advocate the cause of passion. (279) But the enemy of the race which is endowed with the power of seeing, is the people of Pharaoh, which never ceased attacking, and persecuting, and enslaving virtue, until ... it paid the penalty for the evils which it inflicted ... being overwhelmed in the sea of those iniquities ... which it excited ... So that that period exhibited an extraordinary sight, a victory which was in no doubt, and a joy greater than could have been hoped for.

(280) On which account it is said, "And Israel saw the Egyptians dead upon the sea-shore."[124] Great indeed was the hand which fought for them, compelling those who had sharpened these organs against the truth to fall by the mouth, and lips, and speech, so that they who had taken up these weapons against others should perish by their own arms and not by those of others. (281) And this announces three most glorious things to the soul; one, the destruction of the passions of Egypt; another, that this has taken place in no other spot than near the salt and bitter springs, as if on the shore of the sea, by which sophistical reason, that enemy of virtue, is poured forth; and, lastly, the sight of the disaster. (282) For no glorious thing can be invisible, but should be brought to the light and brilliancy of the sun. For so also the contrary, namely evil, should be thrust into deep darkness, and should be accounted deserving of night. And it may indeed by chance happen to some one to behold this: but what is really good should be always beheld by more piercing eyes. And what is so good as that what is good should live, and what is evil should die?

XLIII. (283) There were, therefore, three persons who uttered atrocious words which were to reach even to heaven; these men devoted themselves to studies against nature, or rather against their own souls, saying that this universe was the only thing which was perceptible to the outward senses, and visible, having never been created, and being never destined to be destroyed but being uncreated and imperishable, not requiring any superintendence, or care, or regulation, or management. (284) Afterwards piling up fresh attempts one upon another, they built up a doctrine which was not approved, and raised it to a height like a tower; for it is said, "And the whole earth spoke one language,"[125] an inharmonious agreement of all the portions of the soul, for the purpose of overthrowing that which is the most comprehensive of all existing principles, namely, authority.

(285) Therefore, a great and irresistible hand overthrew them when they were hoping to mount up even to heaven by their devices, for the purpose of destroying the everlasting kingdom; and it also dashed down the doctrine which they had built up; and the place is called confusion: (286) a very appropriate name for such an audacious and wicked attempt; for what can be more productive

123Exodus 7:15.

124Exodus 14:30.
125Genesis 11:1.

of confusion than anarchy? Are not houses which have no manager full of offences and disturbances? (287) And are not cities which are left unprovided with a king destroyed by the domination of the mob, the opposite evil to kingly power, and at the same time the greatest of all evils? And have not countries, and nations, and regions of the earth, the governments of which have been put down, lost all their ancient and great prosperity?

(288) And why need I speak of matters of human history? For even the other species of animals, flocks of birds, and herds of terrestrial beasts, and shoals of aquatic creatures, never exist without some leader of their company; but they always desire and always pay attention to their own leader, as being the sole cause of the advantages they receive; at whose absence they are scattered and destroyed. (289) Do we suppose then, that in the case of earthly creatures, which are the most insignificant portion of the universe, authority is the cause of good things and anarchy the cause of evils, but that the world itself is not filled with extreme happiness by reason of the administration of God its king?

(290) Therefore they have suffered punishment corresponding to their iniquities: for having polluted the sacred doctrine, they saw themselves polluted in like manner, all authority being taken away from among them; and being thrown themselves into confusion, but not having really caused any. But as long as they were left unpunished, being puffed up by insane pride, they sought to overthrow the authority of the universe by unholy speeches; and they set themselves up as rulers and kings, attributing the irresistible power of God to creatures which are perpetually coming to an end and being destroyed.

XLIV. (291) Therefore these ridiculous men giving themselves tragic airs and using inflated language, are accustomed to speak thus: we are they who are leaders; we are kings; On us all things depend. Who, except ourselves, is the cause of good and of the contrary? To whom, except to us, can be doing well or ill be truly attributed? They talk nonsense too in another manner, saying, that all things depend upon an invisible power, which they fancy presides over all human and divine affairs in the whole world.

(292) Uttering such insolent falsehoods as these, if after intoxication they have become sober, and have come to themselves again, and feel ashamed of the intoxication to which they have given way coming under the dominion of the external senses, and if they reproach themselves for the evil actions which they have been led on to commit by folly, giving ear to their new counsellor, which never flatters, and which cannot be corrupted, namely, repentance, having propitiated the merciful power of the living God by sacred hymns

of repentance instead of profane songs, they will find entire forgiveness.

(293) But if they are restive and obstinate for ever, and indulge in wanton behavior, as if they were independent, and free, and the rulers of others, then by a necessity which is deaf to all entreaties and implacable, they will learn to feel their own nothingness in all things both small and great; (294) for the driver who mounts upon them, putting a bridle, upon this world, as though it were a winged chariot, drawing back with main strength the reins which before were loose, and pressing the bits severely, will remind them by whip and spur of his authority as master, which they, like wicked servants, have forgotten by reason of the gentle and merciful temper of their manager; (295) for bad servants, looking upon the gentleness of masters as anarchy, fancy themselves entirely free from the power of any master at all, until their owner checks their great and increasing disease by applying punishment as a remedy.

(296) For which reason the expression is used of "a lawless soul, which with its lips distinguishes well-doing and evil-doing, and then will subsequently announce its own sin." [126] What sayest thou, O soul, full of insolence? For dost thou know what real good or real evil, real justice or real holiness, are? or what is suited to what? (297) The knowledge of those things and the power of regulating them belongs to God alone, and to whoever is dear to him. And witness is borne to this assertion by the scripture in which it is said, "I will kill and I will cause to live; I will smite and I will heal." [127] (298) But the mind which was wise in its own conceit had not even a superficial dreaming intimation of the things placed above it; but, wretched that it was, it was so completely carried away by the wind of vain opinion that it swore that those things which it had erroneously imagined stood firmly and solidly. (299) If, therefore, the violence and convulsion of the disease begin to relax, the sparks of returning health becoming gradually re-kindled, will compel it at first to confess its error, that is to say, to reproach itself, and afterwards to become a suppliant at the altar, entreating with prayers, and supplications, and sacrifices, that it may only obtain pardon.

XLV. (300) After this who can fairly raise the question why the historian of the scriptures has spoken of the river of Egypt only as having banks and has made no such mention of the Euphrates or of any other of the sacred rivers; for here he says, "Thou shalt stand in the way to meet him by the bank of the river." (301) And yet perhaps some persons in a spirit of ridicule will say that

---

[126] Leviticus 5:4.
[127] Deuteronomy 32:39.

it is not right to bring such matters as these forward for investigation, for that it rather displays a spirit of cavilling than does any good. But I imagine that such things, like sweetmeats, are prepared in the sacred scriptures, for the improvement of those who read them, and that we ought not to condemn the curiosity of those who investigate such matters, but that we should rather blame their indolence if they did not investigate them.

(302) For our present discussion is not about the history of rivers but about ways of life, which are compared to the streams of rivers, running in opposite directions to one another. For the life of the good man consists in actions; but that of the wicked man is seen to consist only in words. And speech [...] in the tongue, and mouth, and lips, and [...][128]

---

[128] The rest of this treatise is lost.

ON ABRAHAM†

(De Abrahamo)

I. (1) The sacred laws having been written in five books, the first is called and inscribed Genesis, deriving its title from the creation *(genesis)* of the world, which it contains at the beginning; although there are ten thousand other matters also introduced which refer to peace and to war, or to fertility and barrenness, or to hunger and plenty, or to the terrible destructions which have taken place on earth by the agency of fire and water; or, on the contrary, to the birth and rapid propagation of animals and plants in accordance with the admirable arrangement of the atmosphere, and the seasons of the year, and of men, some of whom lived in accordance with virtue, while others were associated with wickedness.

(2) But since of these things some are portions of the world, and some are accidents, and since the world is the most perfect and complete of all things, he has normally assigned the whole book to that subject.

We have then examined with all the accuracy that was in our power, in what manner the creation of the world was arranged in our previous treatises; (3) but since it is necessary, to be consistent with the regular order in which the sacred history proceeds to go on, now to investigate the laws, we will for the present postpone the particular laws which are copies as it were; and first of all examine the more general laws which are, as it were, the models of the others. (4) Now these are those men who have lived irreproachably and admirably, whose virtues are durably and permanently recorded, as on pillars in the sacred scriptures, not merely with the object of praising the men themselves, but also for the sake of exhorting those who read their history, and of leading them on to emulate their conduct; (5) for these men have been living and rational laws; and the lawgiver has magnified them for two reasons; first, because he was desirous to show that the injunctions which are thus given are not inconsistent with nature; and, secondly, that he might prove that it is not very difficult or laborious for those who wish to live according to the laws established in these books, since the earliest men easily and spontaneously obeyed the unwritten principle of legislation

before any one of the particular laws were written down at all.

So that a man may very properly say, that the written laws are nothing more than a memorial of the life of the ancients, tracing back in an antiquarian spirit, the actions and reasonings which they adopted; (6) for these first men, without ever having been followers or pupils of any one, and without ever having been taught by preceptors what they ought to do or say, but having embraced a line of conduct consistent with nature from attending to their own natural impulses, and from being prompted by an innate virtue, and looking upon nature herself to be, what in fact she is, the most ancient and duly established of laws, did in reality spend their whole lives in making laws, never of deliberate purpose doing anything open to reproach, and for their accidental errors propitiating God, and appeasing him by prayers and supplications, so as to procure for themselves the enjoyment of an entire life of virtue and prosperity, both in respect of their deliberate actions, and those which proceeded from no voluntary purpose.

II. (7) Since then the beginning of all participation in good things is hope, and since the soul devoted to virtue pioneers and opens this path as a plain and easy one, being anxious to attain to that which is really honourable, the sacred historian has named the first lover of hope, Enos, giving him the common name of the whole race as an especial favour. (8) For the Chaldaeans call man Enos; as if he were the only real man, who lived in expectation of good things, and who is established in good hopes; from which it is evident that they do not look upon the man devoid of hope as a man at all, but rather as an animal resembling a man, inasmuch as he is deprived of that most peculiar possession of the human soul, namely hope. (9) For which reason, being desirous to deliver an admirable panegyric on the hopeful man, the sacred historian tells us, first, that "he hoped in the father and creator of the universe,"[1] and adds in a subsequent passage, "This is the book of the generation of men,"[2] and of their fathers, and grandfathers who had existed previously; but he conceived that they were the ancestors of the mixed race, that is to say, of that purer and thoroughly

†Yonge's title, *A Treatise on the Life of the Wise Man Made Perfect by Instruction or, On the Unwritten Law, That Is To Say, On Abraham.*

[1]Genesis 4:26.
[2]Genesis 5:1.

sifted race which is the really rational one; (10) for, as the poet Homer, though the number of poets is beyond all calculation, is called "the poet" by way of distinction, and as the black [ink] with which we write is called "the black," though in point of fact everything which is not white is black; and as that archon at Athens is especially called "the archon," who is the archon eponymus and the chief of the nine archons, from whom the chronology is dated; so in the same manner the sacred historian calls him who indulges in hope, "a man," by way of pre-eminence, passing over in silence the rest of the multitude of human beings, as not being worthy to receive the same appellation.

(11) And he has very properly called the first volume, the Book of the Generation of the Real Man, speaking with perfect correctness; because the man who is full of good hope is worthy of being described and remembered, not with such a memory as is given by a record in papers, which are hereafter to be destroyed by bookworms, but by that which exists in immortal nature, where the virtuous actions are regularly recorded.

(12) If then any one were to reckon the generations, from the first man, who was made out of the earth, he will find him who, by the Chaldaeans is called Enos, and in the Greek language *anthrōpos* (the man), to be the fourth in succession, (13) and in numbers the number four is honoured among other philosophers, who have studied and admired the incorporeal essences, appreciable only by the intellect, and especially by the all-wise Moses, who magnifies the number four, and says that it is "holy and praiseworthy;"[3] and the reasons for which this character has been given to it are mentioned in a former treatise. (14) And the man who is full of good hope is likewise holy and praiseworthy; as, on the contrary, he who has no hope is accursed and blameable, being always associated with fear, which is an evil counsellor in any emergency; for they say, that there is no one thing so hostile to another, as hope is to fear and fear to hope, and perhaps this may be correctly said, for both fear and hope are an expectation, but the one is an expectation of good things, and the other, on the contrary, of evil things; and the natures of good and evil are irreconcileable, and such as can never come together.

III. (15) What has now been said about hope is sufficient; and nature has placed her at the gates to be a sort of doorkeeper to the royal virtues within, which no one may approach who has not previously paid homage to hope. (16) Therefore the lawgivers, and the laws in every state on earth, labour with great diligence to fill the souls of free men with good hopes; but he who, without any recommendation and without being enjoined to be

so, is nevertheless hopeful, has acquired this virtue by an unwritten, self-taught law, which nature has implanted in him.

(17) That which is placed in the next rank after hope is repentance for errors committed, and improvement; in reference to which principle Moses mentions next in order to Enos, the man who changed from a worse system of life to a better, who is called among the Hebrews Enoch, but as the Greeks would say, "gracious," of whom the following statement is made, "that Enoch pleased God, and was not found, because God transported him."[4] (18) For transportation shows a change and alteration: and such a change is for the better, because it takes place through the providence of God; for every thing that is with God is in very case honourable and advantageous, since that which is destitute of any divine superintendence is useless and unprofitable.

(19) And the expression, "he was not found,"[5] is very appropriately employed of him whose place was changed, either from the fact of his ancient blameable life being wiped out and effaced, and being no longer found, just as if it had never existed at all, or else because he whose place has been changed, and who is enrolled in a better class; is naturally difficult to be discovered. For wickedness is a very multiform and extensive thing, on which account it is known to many persons; but virtue is rare, so that it is not comprehended even by a few. (20) And besides, the bad man runs about through the market-place, and theatres, and courts of justice, and council halls, and assemblies, and every meeting and collection of men whatever, like one who lives with and for curiosity, letting loose his tongue in immoderate, and interminable, and indiscriminate conversation, confusing and disturbing every thing, mixing up what is true and what is false, what is unspeakable with what is public, private with public things, things profane with things sacred, what is ridiculous with what is excellent, from never having been instructed in what is the most excellent thing in season, namely silence. (21) And pricking up his ears, because of the abundance of his leisure, and his superfluous curiosity, and love of interference, he is eager to make himself acquainted with the business of other people, whether good or bad, so as at once to envy those who are prosperous, and to rejoice over those who are not so; for the bad man is by nature envious and a hater of all that is good, and a lover of all that is evil.

IV. (22) But the good man, on the contrary, is a lover of that mode of life which is not troubled

---

[3]Leviticus 19:24.

[4]Genesis 5:24.

[5]This is not the translation of the Bible which says "and Enoch walked with God, and he was not, for God took him."

by business, and withdraws, and loves solitude, desiring to escape the notice of the many, not out of misanthropy, for he is a lover of mankind, if any one in the world is so, but because he eschews wickedness, which the chief multitude eagerly embraces, rejoicing at what it ought to mourn over, and grieving at what it is becoming rather to rejoice. (23) On which account the good man shuts himself up, and remains for the most part at home, scarcely going over his threshold, or if he does go out, for the sake of avoiding the crowds who come to visit him, he generally goes out of the city, and makes his abode in some country place, living more pleasantly with such companions as are the most virtuous of all mankind, whose bodies, indeed, time has dissolved, but whose virtues the records which are left of them keep alive, in poems and in prose, histories by which the soul is naturally improved and led on to perfection.

(24) It is on this account that the sacred historian has said that the man whose place was changed was not found, inasmuch as he is difficult to find and hard to seek out. Therefore, such a man emigrates from ignorance to instruction, and from folly to wisdom and from cowardice to courage, and from impiety to piety; and, again, from devotion to pleasure to temperance, and from vaingloriousness to simplicity, qualities superior to all riches, and more valuable as a possession than any royal or imperial power. (25) For if one may speak the plain truth, that wealth which is not blind, but which is clear-sighted, is the abundance of virtues, which we must at once conclude to be the genuine and legitimate predominance of good in comparison of all other bastard and falsely named powers, and to be the just and lawful superior of them all. (26) But we must not be ignorant that repentance occupies the second place only, next after perfection, just as the change from sickness to convalescence is inferior to perfect uninterrupted health. Therefore, that which is continuous and perfect in virtues is very near divine power, but that condition which is improvement advancing in process of time is the peculiar blessing of a well-disposed soul, which does not continue in its childish pursuits, but by more vigorous thoughts and inclinations, such as really become a man, seeks a tranquil steadiness of soul, and which attains to it by its conception of what is good.

V. (27) For which reason the sacred historian very naturally classes the lover of God and the lover of virtue next in order to him who repents; and this man is in the language of the Hebrews called Noah, but in that of the Greeks, "rest," or "the just man," both being appellations very well suited to the wise man. That of "the just man" most evidently so, for nothing is better than justice, which is the chief among virtues, and which receives the highest honours like the most beautiful member of a company; and the appellation "rest" is like-

wise appropriate, since the opposite quality to rest is unnatural agitation, the cause of confusion, and tumults, and seditions, and wars, which the wicked pursue; while those who pay due honour to excellence cultivate a tranquil, and quiet, and stable, and peaceful life.

(28) And in strict consistency with himself, the lawgiver also calls the seventh day "rest," which the Hebrews call "the sabbath;" not as some persons fancy, because after six days the multitude was refrained from its habitual employments, but because in real truth, the number seven is both in the world and in ourselves free from seditions and from wars, and is of all the numbers that which is the most averse to contention, and the greater lover of peace. (29) And a proof of what I have here asserted may be found in the powers which exist in us; for six of those powers, namely the five outward senses and uttered speech, stir up continued and ceaseless war, both by sea and land, some of them doing so from a desire for the objects of the outward senses, which if they cannot obtain they are grieved, and the last by divulging with unbridled mouth numbers of things which ought to be buried in silence. (30) But the seventh power is that which proceeds from the dominant mind, which is more glorious than the other six powers, and which has by pre-eminent vigour obtained the mastery over them all, and when that retires, choosing solitude, and its own society, and living by itself, as one that has no need of any other, and that is all-sufficient for itself, being then emancipated from the cares and troubles that are found in the human race, embraces a calm and tranquil life.

VI. (31) And the lawgiver magnifies the lover of virtue in such a way, that even when he is given his genealogy, he does not trace himself as he usually does other persons, by giving a catalogue of his grandfathers and great grandfathers, and ancestors who are numbered as men and women, but he gives a list of certain virtues; and almost asserts in express words that there is no other house, or kindred, or country whatever to a wise man, except the virtues and the actions in accordance with virtues.

"For these," says he, "are the generations of Noah; Noah was a just man, perfect in his generation, and one who pleased God."[6] (32) But we must not be ignorant that when he says man here, he does not mean merely to use the common expressions for a rational mortal animal, but that he means to indicate in an eminent degree him who verifies the name, having driven away all the untameable and furious passions and brutal wickednesses of the soul; (33) and as a proof of this, after the word man he adds as an epithet, "the

---

[6]Genesis 6:9.

just," saying, "a just man," as if no unjust person were a man at all, but to speak more properly a beast in the likeness of a man, and as if he alone were a man who is an admirer of justice; (34) he also says that he was "perfect," intimating by this expression that he was possessed not of one virtue only but of all, and that being so possessed of them, he constantly exhibited every one of them according to his power and opportunities; (35) and finally crowning him like a wrestler who has gained a glorious victory, he honours him moreover with a most noble proclamation, saying that "he pleased God," (and what can there be in nature that is more excellent than this panegyric?) which is the most visible proof of excellence; for if they who displease God are miserable, those who please him are by all means happy.

VII. (36) It is not then without great correctness that after he has praised the man as being possessed of such great virtues he adds, "and he was perfect in his generation." Showing that he was not perfect absolutely, but that he was good in comparison with the others who lived at that time; (37) for in a little time he will also speak of other wise men who were possessed of unconquerable and incomparable virtue, not merely if contrasted with the wicked, nor because they were better than the other men of their age, and as such were considered worthy of acceptance and pre-eminence, but because having received a well disposed nature, they preserved it without any error or change for the worse; not fleeing from evil habits, but never having once fallen into them, and being by deliberate purpose practicers of all virtuous actions and speeches, by which system they had adorned their life.

(38) Those then are the most admirable of all men who have adopted free and noble inclinations, not in imitation of or by way of contrast to others, but from an inclination to genuine virtue and justice for its own sake; he also is to be admired who is superior to his own generation and his own age, and who is overcome by none of those things which the multitude follows; and he will be classed in the second rank, and nature will give to such men the best of her prizes; (39) and the second prize is of itself a great thing; for what is not a great and most desirable object which God offers to, and bestows upon men? And the greatest proof of this is to be found in the exceeding graces which this man attained to; (40) for as that time bore an abundant crop of injustice and impiety, and so every country, and nation, and city, and house, and every separate individual was full of wicked practices, all men of free will and of deliberate purpose, as if in an arena, vying with one another for the first rank in iniquity, and strove with all possible zeal and rivalry, every one seeking to surpass his neighbour in the magnitude of his wickedness, and failing in nothing which might render life blameless and accursed.

VIII. (41) At whom God, being naturally indignant, and being angry that that which appeared to be the most excellent of animals, and which had been thought worthy of being reckoned akin to himself by reason of his participation in reason, when he ought to have practised virtue, devoted himself rather to wickedness, and to every species of vice, appointed a fitting punishment for them, and determined to destroy the whole race at that time existing by a deluge; and not only those who dwelt in the champaign country and in the lower districts, (42) but those also who lived in the most lofty mountains, for the great deep,[7] being raised to a height which it had never reached before, burst through its mouths with its whole collective impetuosity into the seas existing among us, and they overflowed and inundated all the islands and continents; and incessant floods of everlasting fountains, and of native rivers and torrents combined together, mingled with one another, and rising to a vast height, so as to surmount everything. (43) Nor indeed was the air tranquil, for a deep and unbroken cloud overspread the whole heaven, and there were fearful storms of wind, and roarings of thunder, and flashes of lightning, and rapid hurlings of thunderbolts, ceaseless storms of rain being poured forth, so that one might have thought that all the parts of the universe were hastening to dissolve themselves into the one element of the nature of water, until, while the water from above kept pouring down, and that below kept bursting up, the streams were raised to a height above everything, so that they not only overwhelmed and hid from sight all the plains and all the level ground, but even the tops of the highest mountains, (44) for every part of the earth was under water, so that it was wholly buried and carried away, and the world was mutilated of huge portions, and appeared in all its wholeness and integrity, fearful as it is to say or even to imagine such a thing, to be utterly crippled and destroyed.

And likewise the air, with the exception of that small portion which is about the moon, was wholly obscured, being overcast by the violence and impetuosity of the water which overran all the region belonging to it with irresistible might. (45) Then were speedily destroyed all the crops and all the trees, for an unlimited quantity of water is as destructive to them as a scarcity, and innumerable flocks of animals, both tame and wild, perished at the same time; for it was natural when the most excellent race of all, that of man, had been destroyed, that none of the inferior races should be left, since they were only created to be slaves

---

[7]Genesis 7:11.

to his necessities, and to be in a manner subject to his authoritative commands as their master.

(46) When such numbers then of such mighty evils had burst forth which that time poured out—for all the portions of the world, except the heaven itself, were moved in an unnatural manner—as if they were stricken with a terrible and deadly disease.

And one house alone, that of the aforesaid just and God-loving man who had received the two highest of all gifts, was preserved; one gift being, as I have said already, the not being destroyed with all the rest of mankind, the other that of becoming himself, at a subsequent period, the founder of a new generation of mankind; for God thought him worthy to be both the end of our race and the beginning of it, the end of those men who lived before the deluge, and the beginning of those who lived after the deluge.

IX. (47) Such was he who was the most virtuous of all the men of his age, and such were the rewards which were allotted to him which the holy scriptures enumerate; and the arrangement and classification of the aforesaid three, whether you call them men or dispositions of the soul, is very symmetrical, for the perfect man is entire from the beginning; but he who has his place changed is but half entire, having appropriated the earlier period of his life to wickedness, and the subsequent time to virtue to which he afterwards came over, and with which at that subsequent time he lived. But he who hopes, as his very name shows, has still a defect, for though he is always wishing for what is good, he is not as yet able to attain to it, but he is like those who are on a voyage, who while they are eager to reach the harbour, are still kept at sea without being able to anchor in port.

X. (48) I have now then explained the character of the first triad of those who desire virtue. There is also another more important company of which we must now proceed to speak, for the former resembles those branches of instruction which are allotted to the age of childhood, but this resembles rather the gymnastic exercises of athletic men, who are really preparing themselves for the sacred contests, who, despising all care of getting their body into proper condition, labour to bring about a healthy state of the soul, being desirous of that victory which is to be gained over the adverse passions.

(49) The particulars then on which each individual differs from the other, though all are hastening to one and the same end, we will hereafter examine more minutely; but it is necessary not to pass over in silence what it seems desirable to premise concerning the whole three taken together.

(50) It happens then that they are all three of one household and of one family, for the last of the three is the son of the middle one, and the grandson of the first; and they are all lovers of God, and beloved by God, loving the only God, and being loved in return by him who has chosen, as the holy scriptures tell us, by reason of the excess of their virtues in which they lived, to give them also a share of the same appellation as himself; (51) for having added his own peculiar name to their names he has united them together, appropriating to himself an appellation composed of the three names: "For," says God, "this is my everlasting name: I am the God of Abraham, and the God of Isaac, and the God of Jacob,"[8] using there the relative term instead of the absolute one; and this is very natural, for God stands in no need of a name. But though he does not stand in any such need, nevertheless he bestows his own title on the human race that they may have a refuge to which to betake themselves in supplications and prayers, and so may not be destitute of a good hope.

XI. (52) This then is what appears to be said of these holy men; and it is indicative of a nature more remote from our knowledge than, and much superior to, that which exists in the objects of outward sense; for the sacred word appears thoroughly to investigate and to describe the different dispositions of the soul, being all of them good, the one aiming at what is good by means of instruction, the second by nature, the last by practice; for the first, who is named Abraham, is a symbol of that virtue which is derived from instruction; the intermediate Isaac is an emblem of natural virtue; the third, Jacob, of that virtue which is devoted to and derived from practice. (53) But we must not be ignorant that each of these men was endowed with all these powers, but that each derived his name from that one which predominated in him and mastered the others; for neither is it possible for instruction to be made perfect without natural endowments and practice, nor is nature able to arrive at the goal without instruction and practice, nor is practice unless it be founded on natural gifts and sound instruction.

(54) Very appropriately, therefore, he has represented, as united by relationship, these three, which in name indeed are men, but in reality, as I have said before, virtues, nature, instruction, and practice, which men also call by another name, and entitle them the three graces (charites), either from the fact of God having bestowed (kecharisthai) on our race those three powers, in order to produce the perfection of life, or because they themselves have bestowed themselves on the rational soul as the most glorious of gifts, so that the eternal name, as set forth in the scriptures, may not be used in conjunction with three men, but rather with the aforesaid powers; (55) for the

---

[8]Exodus 3:15.

nature of mankind is mortal, but that of virtues is immortal; and it is more reasonable that the name of the everlasting God should be conjoined with what is immortal than with what is mortal, since what is immortal is akin to what is imperishable, but death is hostile to it.

XII. (56) We must, however, not remain in ignorance that the sacred historian has represented the first man, him who was formed out of the earth as the father of all those who existed before the deluge; and him who, with his whole family, was the only person left out of so universal a destruction, because of his justice and his other excellencies and virtues, as the founder of the new race of men which was to flourish hereafter. And that venerable, and estimable, and glorious triad is comprehended by the sacred scriptures under one class, and called, "A royal priesthood, and a holy nation."[9] (57) And its name shows its power; for the nation is further called, in the language of the Hebrews, Israel, which name being interpreted means, "seeing God."

But of sight, that which is exercised by means of the eyes is the most excellent of all the outward senses, since by that alone all the most beautiful of existing things are comprehended, the sun and the moon, and the whole heaven, and the whole world; but the sight of the soul which is exercised, through the medium of its dominant part excel all other powers of the soul, as much as the powers of the soul excel all other powers; and this is prudence, which is the sight of the mind. (58) But he to whose lot it falls, not only by means of his knowledge, to comprehend all the other things which exist in nature, but also to behold the Father and Creator of the universe, has advanced to the very summit of happiness. For there is nothing above God; and if any one, directing towards him the eye of the soul, has reached up to him, let him then pray for ability to remain and to stand firm before him; (59) for the roads which lead upwards to him are laborious and slow, but the descent down the declivity, being rather like a rapid dragging down than a gradual descent, is swift and easy. And there are many things urged downwards, in which there is no use whatever, when God having made the soul to depend on his own powers, drags it up towards himself with a more vigorous attraction.

XIII. (60) Let thus much, then, be said generally about the three persons, since it was absolutely necessary; but we must now proceed in regular order, to speak of those qualities in which each separate individual surpasses the others, beginning with him who is first mentioned. Now he, being an admirer of piety, the highest and greatest of all virtues, laboured earnestly to follow God,

and to be obedient to the injunctions delivered by him, looking not only on those things as his commands which were signified to him by words and facts, but those also which were indicated by more express signs through the medium of nature, and which the truest of the outward senses comprehends before the uncertain and untrustworthy hearing can do so; (61) for if any one observes the arrangement which exists in nature, and the constitution according to which the world goes on, which is more excellent than any kind of reasoning, he learns, even though no one speaks to him, to study a course of life consistent with law and peace, looking to the example of good men. But the most manifest demonstrations of peace are those which the scriptures contain; and we must mention the first which also occurs the first in the order in which they are set down.

XIV. (62) He being impressed by an oracle by which he was commanded to leave his country, and his kindred, and his father's house, and to emigrate like a man returning from a foreign land to his own country, and not like one who was about to set out from his own land to settle in a foreign district, hastened eagerly on, thinking to do with promptness what he was commanded to do was equivalent to perfecting the matter. (63) And yet who else was it likely would be so undeviating and unchangeable as not to be won over by and as not to yield to the charms of one's relations and one's country? The love for which has in a manner—

"Grown with the growth and strengthened with the strength,"

of every individual, and even more, or at all events not less than the limbs united to the body have done.

(64) And we have witnesses of this in the lawgivers who have enacted the second punishment next to death, namely, banishment, against those who are convicted of the most atrocious crimes: a punishment which indeed is not second to any, as it appears to me, if truth be the judge, but which is, in fact, much more grievous than death, since death is the end of all misfortunes, but banishment is not the end but the beginning of new calamities, inflicting instead of our death unaccompanied by pain ten thousand deaths with acute sensation.

(65) Some men also, being engaged in traffic, do out of desire for gain sail over the sea, or being employed in some embassy, or being led by a desire to see the sights of foreign countries, or by a love for instruction, having various motives which attract them outwards and prevent their remaining where they are, some being led by a love of gain, others by the idea of being able to benefit their native city at its time of need in the most necessary and important particulars, others seeking to arrive at the knowledge of matters of which before they were ignorant, a knowledge which brings, at the

---

[9] Exodus 19:6.

same time, both delight and advantage to the soul. For men who have never travelled are to those who have, as blind men are to those who see clearly, are nevertheless anxious to behold their father's threshold and to salute it, and to embrace their acquaintances, and to enjoy the most delightful and wished-for sight of their relations and friends; and very often, seeing the affairs, for the sake of which they left their country, protracted, they have abandoned them, being influenced by that most powerful feeling of longing for a union with their kindred.

(66) But this man with a few companions, or perhaps I might say by himself, as soon as he was commanded to do so, left his home, and set out on an expedition to a foreign country in his soul even before he started with his body, his regard for mortal things being overpowered by his love for heavenly things. (67) Therefore giving no consideration to anything whatever, neither to the men of his tribe, nor to those of his borough, nor to his fellow disciples, nor to his companions, nor those of his blood as sprung from the same father or the same mother, nor to his country, nor to his ancient habits, nor to the customs in which he had been brought up, nor to his mode of life and his mates, every one of which things has a seductive and almost irresistible attraction and power, he departed as speedily as possible, yielding to a free and unrestrained impulse, and first of all he quitted the land of the Chaldaeans, a prosperous district, and one which was greatly flourishing at that period, and went into the land of Charran, and from that, after no very distant interval, he departed to another place, which we will speak of hereafter, when we have first discussed the country of Charran.

XV. (68) The aforesaid emigrations, if one is to be guided by the literal expressions of the scripture, were performed by a wise man; but if we look to the laws of allegory, by a soul devoted to virtue and busied in the search after the true God. (69) For the Chaldaeans were, above all nations, addicted to the study of astronomy, and attributed all events to the motions of the stars, by which they fancied that all the things in the world were regulated, and accordingly they magnified the visible essence by the powers which numbers and the analogies of numbers contain, taking no account of the invisible essence appreciable only by the intellect. But while they were busied in investigating the arrangement existing in them with reference to the periodical revolutions of the sun, and moon, and the other planets, and fixed-stars, and the changes of the seasons of the year, and the sympathy of the heavenly bodies with the things of the earth, they were led to imagine that the world itself was God, in their impious philosophy comparing the creature to the Creator.

(70) The man who had been bred up in this doctrine, and who for a long time had studied the philosophy of the Chaldaeans, as if suddenly awakening from a deep slumber and opening the eye of the soul, and beginning to perceive a pure ray of light instead of profound darkness, followed the light, and saw what he had never see before, a certain governor and director of the world standing above it, and guiding his own work in a salutary manner, and exerting his care and power in behalf of all those parts of it which are worthy of divine superintendence.

(71) In order, therefore, that he may the more firmly establish the sight which has thus been presented to him in his mind, the sacred word says to him, My good friend, great things are often made known by slight outlines, at which he who looks increases his imagination to an unlimited extent; therefore, having dismissed those who bend all their attention to the heavenly bodies, and discarding the Chaldaean science, rise up and depart for a short time from the greatest of cities, this world, to one which is smaller; for so you will be the better able to comprehend the nature of the Ruler of the universe.

(72) It is for this reason that Abraham is said to have made this first migration from the country of the Chaldaeans into the land of Charran.

XVI. But Charran, in the Greek language, means "holes," which is a figurative emblem of the regions of our outward senses; by means of which, as by holes, each of those senses is able to look out so as to comprehend the objects which belong to it. (73) But, some one may say, what is the use of these holes, unless the invisible mind, like the exhibition of a puppet show, does from within prompt its own powers, which at one time losing and allowing to roam, and at another time holding back and restraining by force? He gives sometimes an harmonious motion, and sometimes perfect quiet to his puppets. And having this example at home, you will easily comprehend that being, the understanding of whom you are so anxious to arrive at; (74) unless, indeed, you fancy that the world is situated in you as the dominant part of you, which the whole common powers of the body obey, and which each of the outward senses follows; but that the world, the most beautiful, and greatest, and most perfect of works, of which everything else is but a part, is destitute of any king to hold it together, and to regulate it, and govern it in accordance with justice.

And if it be invisible, wonder not at that, for neither can the mind which is in thee be perceived by the sight. (75) Any one who considers this, deriving his proofs not from a distance but close at hand, both from himself and from the circumstances around him, will clearly see that the world is not the first God, but that it is the work of the first God and Father of all things, who, being himself invisible, displays every thing, showing the nature of all things both small and great. (76) For he has not chosen to be beheld by the eyes of the body, perhaps because it was not consistent with holiness for what is mortal to touch what is everlasting, or perhaps because of the weakness of our sight; for it would never have been able to stand the rays which are poured forth from the living God, since it cannot even look straight at the rays of the sun.

XVII. (77) And the most visible proof of this migration in which the mind quitted astronomy and the doctrines of the Chaldaeans, is this. For it is said in the scriptures that the very moment that the wise man quitted his abode, "God appeared unto Abraham,"[10] to whom, therefore, it is plain that he was not visible before, when he was adhering to the studies of the Chaldaeans, and attending to the motions of the stars, not properly comprehending any nature whatever, which was well arranged and appreciable by the intellect only, apart from the world and the essence perceptible by the outward senses. (78) But after he changed his abode and went into another country he learnt of necessity that the world was subject, and not independent; not an absolute ruler, but governed by the great cause of all things who had created it, whom the mind then for the first time looked up and saw; (79) for previously a great mist was shed over it by the objects of the external senses, which she, having dissipated by fervent and vivid doctrines, was scarcely able, as if in clear fine weather, to perceive him who had previously been concealed and invisible.

But he, by reason of his love for mankind, did not reject the soul which came to him, but went forward to meet it, and showed to it his own nature as far as it was possible that he who was looking at it could see it. (80) For which reason it is said, not that the wise man saw God but that God appeared to the wise man; for it was impossible for any one to comprehend by his own unassisted power the true living God, unless he himself displayed and revealed himself to him.

XVIII. (81) And there is evidence in support of what has here been said to be derived from the change and alteration of his name: for he was anciently called Abram, but afterwards he was named Abraham: the alteration of sound being only that which proceeds from one single letter, alpha, being doubled, but the alteration revealing in effect an important fact and doctrine; (82) for the name Abram being interpreted means "sublime father;" but Abraham signifies, "the elect father of sound." The first name being expressive of the man who is called an astronomer, and one addicted to the contemplation of the sublime bodies in the sky, and who was versed in the doctrines of the Chal-

daeans, and who took care of them as a father might take care of his children. (83) But the last name intimating the really wise man; for the latter name, by the word sound, intimates the uttered speech; and by the word father, the dominant mind. For the speech which is conceived within is naturally the father of that which is uttered, inasmuch as it is older than the latter, and as it also suggests what is to be said. And by the addition of the word elect his goodness is intimated.

For the evil disposition is a random and confused one, but that which is elect is good, having been selected from all others by reason of its excellence. (84) Therefore, to him who is addicted to the contemplation of the sublime bodies of the sky there appears to be nothing whatever greater than the world; and therefore he refers the causes of all things that exist to the world. But the wise man, beholding with more accurate eyes that more perfect being that rules and governs all things, and is appreciable only by the intellect, to whom all things are subservient as to the master, and by whom every thing is directed, very often reproaches himself for his former way of life, and if he had lived the existence of a blind man, leaning upon objects perceptible by the outward senses, on things by their very nature worthless and unstable.

(85) The second migration is again undertaken by the virtuous man under the influence of a sacred oracle, but this is no longer one from one city to another, but it is to a desolate country, in which he wandered about for a long time without being discontented at his wandering and at his unsettled condition, which necessarily arose from it. (86) And yet, what other man would not have been grieved, not only at departing from his own country but also at being driven away from every city into an inaccessible and impassable district? And what other man would have not turned back and returned to his former home, paying but little attention to his former hopes, but desiring to escape from his present perplexity, thinking it folly for the sake of uncertain advantages to undergo admitted evils? (87) But this man alone appears to have behaved in the contrary manner, thinking that life which was remote from the fellowship of many companions the most pleasant of all.

And this is naturally the case; for those who seek and desire to find God, love that solitude which is dear to him, labouring for this as their dearest and primary object, to become like his blessed and happy nature. (88) Therefore, having now given both explanations, the literal one as concerning the man, and the allegorical one relating to the soul, we have shown that both the man and the mind are deserving of love; inasmuch as the one is obedient to the sacred oracles, and because of their influence submits to be torn away from things which it is hard to part; and the mind

---

[10]Genesis 12:7.

deserves to be loved because it has not submitted to be for ever deceived and to abide permanently with the essences perceptible by the outward senses, thinking the visible world the greatest and first of gods, but soaring upwards with its reason it has beheld another nature better than that which is visible, that, namely, which is appreciable only by the intellect; and also that being who is at the same time the Creator and ruler of both.

XIX. (89) These, then, are the first principles of the man who loves God, and they are followed by actions which do not deserve to be lightly esteemed. But the greatness of them is not evident to every one, but only to those who have tasted of virtue, and who are wont to look with ridicule upon the objects which are admired by the multitude, by reason of the greatness of the good things of the soul. (90) Therefore, God, having approved of his conduct which I have mentioned, presently rewarded the virtuous man with a great gift, inasmuch as he preserved sound and free from all pollution his marriage, which was in danger of being plotted against by a powerful and incontinent man.

(91) And the cause of this man's design upon it arose from this beginning; there having been a barrenness and scarcity of crops for a long time, owing to a long and immoderate period of rain which prevailed at one time, and to a great drought and heat which ensued afterwards. The cities of Syria being oppressed by a long continuance of famine, became destitute of inhabitants, all of them being dispersed in different directions for the purpose of seeking food and providing themselves with necessaries. (92) Therefore, Abraham, hearing that there was unlimited abundance and plenty in Egypt, since the river there irrigated the fields with its inundations at the proper season, and since the winds by their salutary temperature brought up and nourished rich and heavy crops of corn, rose up with all his household to quit Syria and to go thither. (93) And he had a wife of a most excellent disposition, who was also the most beautiful of all the women of her time. The Egyptian magistrates, seeing her and admiring her exquisite form, for nothing ever escapes the notice of men in authority, gave information to the king. (94) And the king, sending for the woman and beholding her extreme beauty, gave but little heed to the dictates of modesty or to the laws which had been established with respect to the honour due to strangers, but yielding to his incontinent desires, conceived the intention in name, indeed, to marry her in lawful wedlock, but, in fact, to seduce and defile her. (95) But she, being destitute of all succour, as being in a foreign land, before an incontinent and cruel-minded ruler (for her husband had no power to protect her, fearing the danger which impended over him from princes mightier than he),

at last, with him, took refuge in the only alliance remaining to her, the protection of God.

(96) And the merciful and gracious God, who takes compassion on the stranger, and who fights on behalf of those who are unjustly oppressed, inflicted in a moment painful sufferings and terrible chastisements on the king, filling his body and soul with all kinds of miseries difficult to be escaped or remedied, so that all his inclinations tending to pleasure were cut short, and, on the contrary, he was occupied with nothing but cares, seeking an alleviation from his endless and intolerable torments by which he was harrassed and tortured day and night; (97) and his whole household also received their share of his punishment, because none of them had felt any indignation at his lawless conduct, but had all consented to it, and had all but co-operated actively in his iniquity.

(98) In this manner the chastity of the woman was preserved, and God condescended to display the excellence and piety of her husband, giving him the noblest reward, namely, his marriage free from all injury, and even from all insult, so as no longer to be in danger of being violated; a marriage which however was not intended to produce any limited number of sons and daughters—the most God-loving of all nations—and one which appears to me to have received the offices of priesthood and prophecy on behalf of the whole human race.

XX. (99) I have heard men versed in natural philosophy interpreting this passage in an allegorical manner with no inconsiderable ingenuity and propriety; and their idea is, that the man here is a symbolical expression for the virtuous mind, conjecturing from the interpretation of his name that what is intended to be indicated is the virtuous disposition existing in the soul; and that by his wife is meant virtue, for the name of his wife is, in the Chaldaean language, Sarah, but in Greek "princess," because there is nothing more royal or more worthy of pre-eminence than virtue. (100) And the marriage in which pleasure unites people comprehends the connection of the bodies, but that which is brought about by wisdom is the union of reasonings which desire purification, and of the perfect virtues; and the two kinds of marriage here described are extremely opposite to one another; (101) for in the marriage of the bodies it is the male partner which sows the seed and the female which receives it, but in the union which takes place with regard to the soul it is quite the contrary, and it is virtue which appears to be there in the place of the woman, which sows good counsels, and virtuous speeches, and expositions of doctrines profitable to life; but the reason which is considered to be classed in the light of the man receives the sacred and divine seed, unless, indeed, there is any error in the names usually given; for certainly, in the grammatical view of the words, the word reason is masculine, and the word virtue has a feminine character.

(102) But if any one, discarding the considerations of the names which tend to throw darkness over the subject, chooses to look at the plain facts without any disguise, he will know that virtue is masculine by nature, inasmuch as it puts things in motion, and arranges them, and suggests good conceptions of noble actions and speeches; but reason is feminine, inasmuch as it is put in motion by another, and is instructed and benefited, and, in short, is altogether the patient, as its passive state is its own safety.

XXI. (103) All men, therefore, even the most vile, in word honour and admire virture as far as appearance goes; but it is the virtuous alone who obey its injunctions; on which account the king of Egypt, who is a figurative representation of the mind devoted to the body, as if he were acting in a theatre, assumes the character of a pretended participation in temperance though being an intemperate man, and in continence though being an incontinent man, and in justice though an unjust man, and he invites justice to himself, being eager to obtain a good report from the multitude; (104) and the governor of the universe seeing this, for God alone has power to look into the soul, hates him and rejects him, and by the most cruel tests and powers convicts him of an utterly false disposition.

But by what instruments are these tests carried out? Surely altogether by the parts of virtue which, whenever they enter, inflict great pain and severe wounds; for a torture is a deficiency of supply to that which is insatiable, and the torture of greediness is temperance; moreover, the man who is fond of glory is tortured while simplicity and humility are in the ascendent, and so is the unjust man when justice is extolled; (105) for it is impossible for two hostile natures to inhabit one soul, namely, for wickedness and virtue, for which reason, when they do come together, endless and irreconcilable seditions and wars are kindled between them; and yet this is the case though virtue is of a most peaceful disposition, and, as they say, is anxious whenever it is about to come to a contest of strength to make trial of its own powers first, so as only to contend if it has a prospect of being able to gain the victory; but if it finds its power unequal to the conflict, then it will never dare to descend into the arena at all, (106) for it is not disgraceful to wickedness to be defeated, inasmuch as ingloriousness is akin to it; but it would be a shameful thing for virtue, to which glory is the most appropriate and the most peculiarly belonging of all things, on which account it is natural for virtue either to secure the victory, or else to keep itself unconquered.

XXII. (107) It has been said then that the dis-

position of the Egyptians is inhospitable and intemperate; and the humanity of him who has been exposed to their conduct deserves admiration, for he[11] in the middle of the day beholding as it were three men travelling (and he did not perceive that they were in reality of a more divine nature), ran up and entreated them with great perseverance not to pass by his tent, but as was becoming to go in and receive the rites of hospitality: and they knowing the truth of the man not so much by what he said, as by his mind which they could look into, assented to his request without hesitation; (108) and being filled as to his soul with joy, he took every possible pain to make their extemporaneous reception worthy of them; and he said to his wife, "Hasten now, and make ready quickly three measures of fine meal," and he himself went forth among the herds of oxen, and brought forth a tender and well-fed heifer, and gave it to his servant; (109) and he having slain it, dressed it with all speed.

For no one in the house of a wise man is ever slow to perform the duties of hospitality, but both women and men, and slaves and freemen, are most eager in the performance of all those duties towards strangers; (110) therefore, after having feasted, and being delighted, not so much with what was set before them, as with the good will of their entertainer, and with his excessive and unbounded zeal to please them, they bestow on him a reward beyond his expectation, the birth of a legitimate son in a short time, making him a promise which is to be confirmed by one the most excellent of the three; for it would have been inconsistent with philosophy for them all to speak together at the same moment, but it was desirous for all the rest to assent while one spoke.

(111) Nevertheless he did not completely believe them even when they made him this promise, by reason of the incredible nature of the thing promised; for both he and his wife, through extreme old age, were so old as utterly to have abandoned all hope of offspring; (112) therefore the scriptures record that Abraham's wife, when she first heard what they were saying, laughed; and when they said afterwards, "Is anything impossible to God?" they were so ashamed that they denied that they had laughed; for Abraham knew that everything was possible to God, having almost learnt this doctrine as one may say from his cradle; (113) then for the first time he appears to me to have begun to entertain a different opinion of his guests from that which he conceived at first, and to have imagined that they were either some of the prophets or of the angels who had changed their spiritual and soul-like essence, and assumed the appearance of men.

XXIII. (114) We have now then described the

---

[11] Genesis 18:1, etc.

hospitable temper of the man, which was as it were a sort of addition to set off his greater virtue; but his virtue was piety towards God, concerning which we have spoken before, the most evident instance of which is to be found in his conduct now recorded towards the strangers; (115) but if any persons have fancied that house happy and blessed in which it has happened that wise men have stopped and abode, they should consider that they would not have done so, and would not even have looked into it at all, if they had seen any incurable disease in the souls of those who were therein, but I know not what excess of happiness and blessedness, I should say, existed in that house in which angels condescended to tarry and to receive the rites of hospitality from men, angels, those sacred and divine natures, the ministers and lieutenants of the mighty God, by means of whom, as of ambassadors, he announces whatever predictions he condescends to intimate to our race.

(116) For how could they ever have endured to enter a human habitation at all, unless they had been certain that all the inhabitants within, like the well-managed and orderly crew of a ship, obeyed one signal only, namely, that of their master, as the sailors obey the command of the captain? And how would they ever have condescended to assume the appearance of guests and men feasted hospitably, if they had not thought that their entertainer was akin to them, and a fellow servant with them, bound to the service of the same master as themselves? We must think indeed that at their entrance all the parts of the house became improved and advanced in goodness, being breathed upon with a certain breeze of most perfect virtue.

(117) And the entertainment was such as it was fitting that it should be, the persons who were being feasted displaying at the banquet their own simplicity towards that entertainer, and addressing him in a guileless manner, and all of them holding conversation suited to the occasion. (118) And it is a thing that deserves to be looked on as a prodigy, that though they did not drink they seemed to drink, and that though they did not eat they presented the appearance of persons eating. But this was all natural and consistent with what was going on. And the most miraculous circumstance of all was, that these beings who were incorporeal presented the appearance of a body in human form by reason of their favour to the virtuous man, for otherwise what need was there of all these miracles except for the purpose of giving the wise man the evidence of his external senses by means of a more distinct sight, because his character had not escaped the knowledge of the Father of the universe.

XXIV. (119) This then is sufficient to say by way of a literal explanation of this account; we must now speak of that which may be given if the story be looked at as figurative and symbolical.

The things which are expressed by the voice are the signs of those things which are conceived in the mind alone; when, therefore, the soul is shone upon by God as if at noonday, and when it is wholly and entirely filled with that light which is appreciable only by the intellect, and by being wholly surrounded with its brilliancy is free from all shade or darkness, it then perceives a threefold image of one subject, one image of the living God, and others of the other two, as if they were shadows irradiated by it. And some such thing as this happens to those who dwell in that light which is perceptible by the outward senses, for whether people are standing still or in motion, there is often a double shadow falling from them.

(120) Let not any one then fancy that the word shadow is applied to God with perfect propriety. It is merely a catachrestical abuse of the name, by way of bringing before our eyes a more vivid representation of the matter intended to be intimated. (121) Since this is not the actual truth, but in order that one may when speaking keep as close to the truth as possible, the one in the middle is the Father of the universe, who in the sacred scriptures is called by his proper name, I am that I am; and the beings on each side are those most ancient powers which are always close to the living God, one of which is called his creative power, and the other his royal power.

And the creative power is God, for it is by this that he made and arranged the universe; and the royal power is the Lord, for it is fitting that the Creator should lord it over and govern the creature. (122) Therefore, the middle person of the three, being attended by each of his powers as by body-guards, presents to the mind, which is endowed with the faculty of sight, a vision at one time of one being, and at another time of three; of one when the soul being completely purified, and having surmounted not only the multitudes of numbers, but also the number two, which is the neighbour of the unit, hastens onward to that idea which is devoid of all mixture, free from all combination, and by itself in need of nothing else whatever; and of three, when, not being as yet made perfect as to the important virtues, it is still seeking for initiation in those of less consequence, and is not able to attain to a comprehension of the living God by its own unassisted faculties without the aid of something else, but can only do so by judging of his deeds, whether as creator or as governor. (123) This then, as they say, is the second best thing; and it no less partakes in the opinion which is dear to and devoted to God. But the first-mentioned disposition has no such share, but is itself the very God-loving and God-beloved opinion itself, or rather it is truth which is older than opinion, and more valuable than any seeming.

But we must now explain what is intimated by this statement in a more perspicuous manner.

XXV. (124) There are three different classes of human dispositions, each of which has received as its portion one of the aforesaid visions. The best of them has received that vision which is in the centre, the sight of the truly living God. The one which is next best has received that which is on the right hand, the sight of the beneficent power which has the name of God. And the third has the sight of that which is on the left hand, the governing power, which is called lord. (125) Therefore, the best dispositions cultivate that being who exists of himself, without the aid of any one else, being themselves attracted by nothing else, by reason of all their entire attention being directed to the honour of that one being. But of the other dispositions, some derive their existence and owe their being recognized by the father to his beneficent power; and others, again, owe it to his governing power. (126) My meaning in this statement is this:—

Men when they perceive that, under the pretext of friendship, some persons come to them, being in reality only desirous to get what they can from them, look upon them with suspicion, and turn away from them, fearing their insincere, and flattering, and caressing behaviour, as very pernicious. (127) But God, inasmuch as he is not liable to any injury, gladly invites all men who choose, in any way whatever to honour him, to come unto him, not choosing altogether to reject any person whatever; and, in truth, he almost says in express words to those who have ears in the soul, "The most valuable prizes shall be offered to those who worship me for my own sake: (128) the second best to those who hope by their own efforts to be able to attain to good, or to find a means of escape from punishments. For even if the service of this latter class is mercenary and not wholly incorrupt, still it nevertheless revolves within the divine circumference, and does not stray beyond it. (129) But the rewards which shall be laid up for those who honour me for my own sake are rewards of affection; while those which are given to those who do so with a view to their own advantage are not given through affection, but because they are not looked upon as aliens. For I receive him who wishes to be a partaker of my beneficent power to a participation in my good things, and him who out of fear seeks to propitiate my governing and despotic power, I receive so far as to avert punishment from him. For I am not unaware that, in addition to these men not becoming worse, they will become better, by gradually arriving at a sincere and pure piety by their constant perseverance in serving me. (130) For even if the original dispositions, under the influ-

ence of which they originally endeavoured to please me, differ widely, still they must not be blamed, because they have in consequence only one aim and object, that of serving me."

(131) But that which is seen is in reality a threefold appearance of one subject is plain, not only from the contemplation of the allegory, but also from that of the express words in which the allegory is couched. (132) For when the wise man entreats those persons who are in the guise of three travellers to come and lodge in his house, he speaks to them not as three persons, but as one, and says, "My lord, if I have found favour with thee, do not thou pass by thy servant." [12] For the expressions, "my lord," and "with thee," and "do not pass by," and others of the same kind, are all such as are naturally addressed to a single individual, but not to many. And when those persons, having been entertained in his house, address their entertainer in an affectionate manner, it is again one of them who promises that he by himself will be present, and will bestow on him the seed of a child of his own, speaking in the following words: "I will return again and visit thee again, according to the time of life, and Sarah thy wife shall have a son." [13]

XXVI. (133) And what is signified by this is indicated in a most evident and careful manner by the events which ensued. The country of the Sodomites was a district of the land of Canaan, which the Syrians afterwards called Palestine, a country full of innumerable iniquities, and especially of gluttony and debauchery, and all the great and numerous pleasures of other kinds which have been built up by men as a fortress, on which account it had been already condemned by the Judge of the whole world. (134) And the cause of its excessive and immoderate intemperance was the unlimited abundance of supplies of all kinds which its inhabitants enjoyed. For the land was one with a deep soil, and well watered, and as such produced abundant crops of every kind of fruit every year. And he was a wise man and spoke truly who said—

"The greatest cause of all iniquity
Is found in overmuch prosperity."

(135) As men, being unable to bear discreetly a satiety of these things, get restive like cattle, and become stiff-necked, and discard the laws of nature, pursuing a great and intemperate indulgence of gluttony, and drinking, and unlawful connections; for not only did they go mad after women, and defile the marriage bed of others, but also those who were men lusted after one another,

---

[12] Genesis 18:3.
[13] Genesis 18:10.

doing unseemly things, and not regarding or respecting their common nature, and though eager for children, they were convicted by having only an abortive offspring; but the conviction produced no advantage, since they were overcome by violent desire; (136) and so, by degrees, the men became accustomed to be treated like women, and in this way engendered among themselves the disease of females, and intolerable evil; for they not only, as to effeminacy and delicacy, became like women in their persons, but they made also their souls most ignoble, corrupting in this way the whole race of man, as far as depended on them. At all events, if the Greeks and barbarians were to have agreed together, and to have adopted the commerce of the citizens of this city, their cities one after another would have become desolate, as if they had been emptied by a pestilence.

XXVII. (137) But God, having taken pity on mankind, as being a Saviour and full of love for mankind, increased, as far as possible, the natural desire of men and women for a connexion together, for the sake of producing children, and detesting the unnatural and unlawful commerce of the people of Sodom, he extinguished it, and destroyed those who were inclined to these things, and that not by any ordinary chastisement, but he inflicted on them an astonishing novelty, and unheard of rarity of vengeance; (138) for, on a sudden, he commanded the sky to become overclouded and to pour forth a mighty shower, not of rain but of fire; and as the flame poured down, with a resistless and unceasing violence, the fields were burnt up, and the meadows, and all the dense groves, and the thick marshes, and the impenetrable thickets; the plain too was consumed, and all the crop of wheat, and of everything else that was sown; and all the trees of the mountain district were burnt up, the trunks and the very roots being consumed.

(139) And the folds for the cattle, and the houses of the men, and the walls, and all that was in any building, whether of private or public property, were all burnt. And in one day these populous cities became the tomb of their inhabitants, and the vast edifices of stone and timber became thin dust and ashes. (140) And when the flames had consumed everything that was visible and that existed on the face of the earth, they proceeded to burn even the earth itself, penetrating into its lowest recesses, and destroying all the vivifying powers which existed within it so as to produce a complete and everlasting barrenness, so that it should never again be able to bear fruit, or to put forth any verdure; and to this very day it is scorched up. For the fire of the lightning is what is most difficult to extinguish, and creeps on pervading everything, and smouldering.

(141) And a most evident proof of this is to be found in what is seen to this day: for the smoke which is still emitted, and the sulphur which men dig up there, are a proof of the calamity which befell that country; while a most conspicuous proof of the ancient fertility of the land is left in one city, and in the land around it. For the city is very populous, and the land is fertile in grass and in corn, and in every kind of fruit, as a constant evidence of the punishment which was inflicted by the divine will on the rest of the country.

XXVIII. (142) But I have not gone through all these particulars for the sake of showing the magnitude of that vast and novel calamity, but because I desired to prove that of the three beings who appeared to the wise Abraham in the guise of men, the scriptures only represent two as having come to the country which was subsequently destroyed for the purpose of destroying its inhabitants, since the third did not think fit to come for that purpose. (143) Inasmuch as he, according to my conception, was the true and living God, who thought it fitting that he being present should bestow good gifts by his own power, but that he should effect the opposite objects by the agency and service of his subordinate powers, so that he might be looked upon as the cause of good only, and of no evil whatever antecedently.

(144) And kings too appear to me to imitate the divine nature in this particular, and to act in the same way, giving their favours in person, but inflicting their chastisements by the agency of others. (145) But since, of the two powers of God, one is a beneficent power and the other a chastising one, each of them, as is natural, is manifested to the country of the people of Sodom. Because of the five finest cities in it four were about to be destroyed by fire, and one was destined to be left unhurt and safe from every evil. For it was necessary that the calamities should be inflicted by the chastising power, and that the one which was to be saved should be saved by the beneficent power. (146) But since the portion which was saved was not endowed with entire and complete virtues, but was blessed with kindness by the power of the living God, it was deliberately accounted unworthy to have a sight of his presence afforded to it.

XXIX. (147) This, then, is the open explanation which is to be given of this account, and which is to be addressed to the multitude. But there is another esoteric explanation to be reserved for the few who choose for the subjects of their investigation the dispositions of the soul, and not the forms of bodies; and this shall now be mentioned.

The five cities of the land of Sodom are a figurative representation of the five outward senses which exist in us, the organs of the pleasures, by the instrumentality of which all the pleasures whether great or small are brought to perfection; (148) for we are pleased either when we behold the varieties of colours and forms, both in things inanimate and in those endowed with vitality, or when we hear melodious sounds, or again, we are delighted by the exercise of the faculty of taste in the things which relate to eating and drinking, or by that of the sense of smell in fragrant flavours and vapours, or in accordance with our faculty of touch when conversant with soft, or hot, or smooth things.

(149) Now of these five outward senses there are three which have the greatest resemblance to the brute beasts and to slaves, namely the senses of taste, smell, and touch: as it is with reference to these that those species of beasts and cattle which are the most greedy and the most strongly inclined to sexual connections are the most vehemently excited. For all day and all night they are either glutting themselves insatiably with food, or else in a state of eagerness for sexual connection. (150) But there are two of these outward senses which have something philosophical and preeminent in them, namely, sight and hearing. But the ears are in some degree more slow and more effeminate than the eyes, since the latter go with promptness and courage to what is to be seen, and do not wait until the objects themselves are in motion, but go forward to meet them, and desire to move themselves so as to face them.

But the sense of hearing inasmuch as that is slow and more effeminate, may be classed in the second rank, and the sense of seeing may be allowed an especial pre-eminence and privilege: for God has made this sense a sort of queen of the rest, placing it above them all, and stationing it as it were on a citadel, has made it of all the senses in the closest connection with the soul; (151) and any one may conjecture this from the common changes which take place in its essential organs; for when grief exists in the soul of man, the eyes are full of concern and melancholy; and on the other hand, when joy is in our heart the eyes smile and rejoice; and when fear gets the upper hand they are full of turbulent and disorderly confusion, and are subject to all kinds of irregular motions, and quiverings, and distortions.

(152) Again, if anger occupies us, the sight becomes more fierce and bloodshot; and when we are considerating or deliberating, the eyes are tranquil and motionless, and almost as intent as the mind itself; just as at moments of the relaxation and indifference of the mind, the eyes are relaxed and indifferent; (153) when a friend approaches the feeling of goodwill towards him is proclaimed by a calm and serene look; on the other hand, if we meet with an enemy, the eyes give an early indication of the displeasure of the soul; when our mind is inspired by boldness, our eyes bound forward and are ready to start from our heads; when we are oppressed with feelings of shame or modesty, they are gentle and repressed.

And, in short, we may say that the sight has been created to be an exact image of the soul, which is thus beautifully represented by it through the perfection of the Creator's skill, the eyes showing a visible representation of it, as in a mirror, since the soul has no visible nature in itself; (154) but it is not in this particular alone that the beauty of the eyes exceeds the rest of the outward senses, but also because the use of the other senses is interrupted during our waking moments; for we must not include in our statement the inactivity which results from sleep; for they are at rest whenever there is not some external object to put them in motion; but the energies of the eyes when they are open are continuous and uninterrupted, as the eyes are never satiated or wearied, but continue to operate in accordance with the connection which they have with the soul; (155) and the soul itself is everlastingly awake, and is in perpetual motion both night and day; but to the eyes, as being to a great degree partakers of the fleshly nature, a self sufficient gift was given, to be able to continue exercising their appropriate energies during one half of the entire period of life.

XXX. (156) But we must now proceed to speak of that which is the most necessary part of all, the advantage which we derive from the eyes. For it is to sight alone of the external senses that God has caused light to arise, which is both the most beautiful of all existing things, and is, moreover, the first thing which is pronounced in the sacred scriptures to be good. (157) Now the nature of light is twofold: for there is one light which proceeds from the fire which we use, a perishable light proceeding from a perishable material, and one which admits of being extinguished. But the other kind is inextinguishable and imperishable, descending to us from above heaven, as if every one of the stars was pouring down its beams upon us from an everlasting spring. And the sense of sight associates with each of these kinds of light, and through the medium of both of them does it approach the objects of sight so as to arrive at a most accurate comprehension of them. (158) Why now need we attempt to panegyrize the eyes further by a speech, when God has engraved their true praises on pillars erected in heaven, namely, the stars? For for what purpose were the rays of the sun, and the beams of the moon, and the light of all the other planets and fixed stars called into existence, except as fields for the energies of the eyes in their service of seeing? (159) On which account men, using the most excellent of all gifts, contemplate the things which exist in the world, the earth, the plants, the animals, the fruits of the earth, the seas, the effusion of waters springing from the earth and gushing forth in torrents and floods, and the varieties of fountains, some of which give forth cold and others hot water, and the nature of all things that exist in the air; and all the different species, of which we thus arrive at the knowledge, are innumerable and indescribable, and cannot be compromised in speech. And above all these things, the eyes can behold the heaven, which is truly a world created in another world, and it can also survey the beauties and divine images existing in heaven. Which now of the other external senses can boast that it has arrived at such a pitch of power as this?

XXXI. (160) But now, dismissing the consideration of those of the outward senses which are in the stables, as it were, fattening up an animal which is born with us, namely, appetite, let us investigate the nature of that sense which receives speech, namely, hearing; the continued and vigorous, and most perfect course of which exists in the atmosphere which surrounds the earth, when the violence of the winds and the noise of thunder sound with a great dragging noise and terrible crash. (161) But the eyes in a single moment can reach from earth to heaven, and taking in the extremest boundaries of the universe, reaching at the same moment to the east and to the west, and to the north and to the south, so as to survey them all at once, drag the mind towards what is visible. (162) And the mind, at once receiving a similar impression, does not continue quiet, but being in perpetual motion, and never slumbering, receiving from the sight the power of observing the objects appreciable by the intellect, comes to consider whether these things which are brought visibly before it are uncreated, or whether they have derived their origin from creation; also, whether they are bounded or infinite. Again, whether there are many worlds or only one; also, whether there are five elements of the whole universe, or whether heaven and the heavenly bodies have a peculiar and separate nature of their own, having received a more divine conformation, differing from that of the rest of the world.

(163) Again, by these means it considers if the world has been created, by whom it has been created, and who the creator is as to his essence or quality, and with what design he made it, and what he is doing now, and what his mode of existence or cause of life is; and all other such questions as the excellently-endowed mind when cohabiting with wisdom is accustomed to examine. (164) These, and similar subjects, belong to philosophers, from which it is plain that wisdom and philosophy have not derived their origin from anything else that exists in us except from that queen of the outward senses, the sight, which God saved alone of the region of the body when he destroyed the other four, because these last were slaves to the flesh and to the passions of the flesh; but the sight alone was able to raise its head and to look up, and to find other sources of delight far superior to those proceeding from the bodily pleasures, those, namely, that are derived from the contemplation of the world and the things in it. (165)

Therefore it was appropriate for one of the five outward senses, namely, the sight, like one city in the Pentapolis, to receive an especial reward and honour, and to remain while the others were destroyed, because it is not only conversant with mortal objects as they are, but is able to forsake such, and to depart to the imperishable natures, and to rejoice in the sight of them.

(166) On which account the holy scriptures very beautifully represent it as "a little city, and yet not a little one,"[14] describing the power of sight under this figure. For it is said to be little, inasmuch as it is but a small portion of the faculties which exist in us; and yet great, inasmuch as it desires great things, being eager to behold the entire heaven and the whole world.

XXXII. (167) We have now, then, given a full explanation concerning the vision which appeared to Abraham, and concerning his celebrated and all-glorious hospitality, in which the entertainer, who appeared to himself to be entertaining others was himself entertained; expounding every part of the passage with as much accuracy as we were able. But we must not pass over in silence the most important action of all, which is worthy of being listened to. For I was nearly saying that it is of more importance than all the actions of piety and religion put together. So we must say what seems to be reasonable concerning it.

(168) A legitimate son is borne to the wise man by his wedded wife, a beloved and only son, very beautiful in his person, and very excellent in his disposition. For he was already beginning to display the more perfect exercises of his age, so that his father felt a most strong and vehement affection for him, not only from the impulse of natural regard, but also from the influence of deliberate opinion, from being, as it were, a judge of his character. (169) To him, then, being conscious of such a disposition, an oracular command suddenly comes, which was never expected, ordering him to sacrifice this son on a certain very lofty hill, distant three days' journey from the city. (170) And he, although attached to his child by an indescribable fondness, neither changed colour, nor wavered in his soul, but remained firm in an unyielding and unalterable purpose, as he was at first. And being wholly influenced by love towards God, he forcibly repressed all the names and charms of the natural relationship: and without mentioning the oracular command to any one of his household out of all his numerous body of servants, he took with him the two eldest, who were most thoroughly attached to their master, as if he were bent upon the celebration of some ordinary divine rite, and went forth with his son, making four in all.

(171) And when, looking as it were from a

---

[14]Genesis 19:20.

watch-tower, he saw the appointed place afar off, he bade his servants remain there, and he gave his son the fire and the wood to carry, thinking it proper for the victim himself to be burdened with the materials for the sacrifice, a very light burden, for nothing is less troublesome than piety. (172) And as they proceeded onwards with equal speed, not marching more rapidly with their bodies than with their minds along that short road of which holiness is the end, they at last arrive at the appointed place. (173) And the father collected stones wherewith to build the altar; and when his son saw everything else prepared for the celebration of the sacrifice, but no animal, he looked to his father and said, "My father, behold the fire and the wood, but where is the victim for the burnt sacrifice?"[15] (174) Therefore, any other father, knowing what he was about to do, and being depressed in his soul, would have been thrown into confusion by his son's words, and being filled with tears, would, out of his excessive affliction, by his silence have betrayed what was about to be done; (175) but Abraham, betraying no alteration of voice, or countenance, or intention, looking at his son with steady eye, answered his question with a determination more steadily still, "My child," said he, "God will provide himself a victim for the burnt offering," although we are in a vast desert where perhaps you despair of such a thing as being found; but all things are possible to God, even all such things as are impossible and unintelligible to men. (176) And even while saying this, he seizes his son with all rapidity, and places him on the altar, and having taken his knife in his right hand, he raised it over him as if to slay him; but God the Saviour stopped the deed in the middle, interrupting him by a voice from heaven, by which he ordered him to stay his hand, and not to touch the child: calling the father by name twice, so as to turn him and divert him from his purpose, and forbid him to complete the sacrifice.

XXXIII. (177) And so Isaac is saved, God supplying a gift instead of him, and honouring him who was willing to make the offering in return for the piety which he had exhibited. But the action of the father, even though it was not ultimately given effect to, is nevertheless recorded and engraved as a complete and perfect sacrifice, not only in the sacred scriptures, but also in the middle of those who read them. (178) But to those who are fond of reviling and disparaging everything, and who are by their invariable habits accustomed to prefer blaming to praising the action which Abraham was enjoined to perform, it will not appear a great and admirable deed, as we imagine it to have been. (179) For such persons say that many other men, who have been very affectionate to their relations

and very fond of their children, have given up their sons; some in order that they might be sacrificed for their country to deliver it either from war, or from drought, or from much rain, or from disease and pestilence; and others to satisfy the demands of some habitual religious observances, even though there may be no real piety in them. (180) At all events they say that some of the most celebrated men of the Greeks, not merely private individuals but kings also, caring but little for the children whom they have begotten, have, by means of their destruction secured safety to might and numerous forces and armies, arrayed together in an allied body, and have voluntarily slain them as if they had been enemies. (181) And also that barbarous nations have for many ages practised the sacrifice of their children as if it were a holy work and one looked upon with favour by God, whose wickedness is mentioned by the holy Moses. For he, blaming them for this pollution, says, that, "They burn their sons and their daughters to their gods."[16] (182) And they say that to this very day the Gymnosophists among the Indians, when that long or incurable disease, old age, begins to attack them, before it has got a firm hold of them, and while they might still last for many years, kindle a fire and burn themselves. And, moreover, when their husbands are already dead, they say that their wives rush cheerfully to the same funeral pile, and whilst living endure to be burnt along with their husbands' bodies. (183) One may well admire the exceeding courage of these women, who look thus contemptuously on death, and disdain it so exceedingly that they hasten and run impetuously towards it as if they were grasping immortality.

XXXIV. But why, say they, ought one to praise Abraham as the attempter of a wholly novel kind of conduct, when it is only what private men and kings, and even whole nations do at appropriate seasons? (184) But I will make the following reply to the envy and ill-temper of these men.

Of those who sacrifice their children, some do so out of habit, as they say some of the barbarians do; others do it because they are unable by any other means to place on a good footing some desperate and important dangers threatening their cities and countries. And of these men, some have given up their children because they have been constrained by those more powerful than themselves: and others, out of a thirst for glory, and honour, and for renown at the present moment, and celebrity in all future ages. (185) Now those who sacrifice their children out of deference to custom, perform, in my opinion, no great exploit; for an inveterate custom is often as powerful as nature itself; so that it diminishes the terrible impression made by the action to be done, and makes even the most miserable and intolerable evils light to bear. (186) Again: surely, they who offer up their children out of fear deserve no praise; for praise is only given to voluntary good actions, but what is involuntary, is ascribed to other causes than the immediate actors—to the occasion, or to chance, or to compulsion from men.

(187) Again, if any one, out of a desire for glory, abandons his son or his daughter; he would justly be blamed rather than praised; seeking acquire honour by the death of his dearest relations, while, even if he had glory, he ought rather to have risked the loss of it to secure the safety of his children. (188) We must investigate, therefore, whether Abraham was under the influence of any one of the aforesaid motives, custom, or love of glory, or fear, when he was about to sacrifice his son.

Now Babylon and Mesopotamia, and the nation of the Chaldaeans, do not receive the custom of sacrificing their children; and these are the countries in which Abraham had been brought up and had lived most of his time; so that we cannot imagine that his sense of the misfortune that he was commanded to inflict upon himself was blunted by the frequency of such events. (189) Again, there was no fear from men which pressed upon him, for no one knew of this oracular command which had been given to him alone, nor was there any common calamity pressing upon the land in which he was living, such as could only be remedied by the destruction of his most excellent son.

(190) May it not have been, however, from a desire to obtain praise from the multitude that he proceeded to this action? But what praise could be obtained in the desert, when there was no one likely to be present who could possibly say anything in his favour, and when even his two servants were left at a distance on purpose that he might not seem to be hunting after praise, or to be making a display by bringing witnesses with him to see the greatness of his devotion?

XXXV. (191) Therefore putting a barrier on their unbridled and evil-speaking mouths, let them moderate that envy in themselves which hates everything that is good, and let them forbear to attack the virtues of men who have lived excellently, which they ought rather to reward and decorate with panegyric. And that this action of Abraham's was in reality one deserving of praise and of all love, it is easy to see from many circumstances. (192) In the first place, then, he laboured above all men to obey God, which is thought an excellent thing, and an especial object for all men's desire, by all right-minded persons, to such a degree, that he never omitted to perform anything which God commanded him, not even if it was full of arrogance and ingloriousness, or even of positive pain and misery; for which reason he also bore, in a most noble manner, and with the most

unshaken fortitude, the command given to him respecting his son.

(193) In the second place, though it was not the custom in the land in which he as living, as perhaps it is among some nations, to offer human sacrifices, and custom, by its frequency, often removes the horror felt at the first appearance of evils, he himself was about to be the first to set the example of a novel and most extraordinary deed, which I do not think that any human being would have brought himself to submit to, even if his soul had been made of iron or of adamant; for as some one has said,—

"'Tis a hard task with nature to contend."

(194) In the second place, after he had become the father of this his only legitimate son, he, from the moment of his birth, cherished towards him all the genuine feelings of affection, which exceeds all modest love, and all the ties of friendship which have ever been celebrated in the world. (195) There was added also, this most forcible charm of all, that he had become the father of this son not in the prime of his life, but in his old age. For parents become to a certain degree insane in their affection for their children of their old age, either from the circumstance of their having been wishing for their birth a long time, or else because they have no longer any hope that they shall have any more; nature having taken her stand there as at the extreme and furthest limit.

(196) Now there is nothing unnatural or extraordinary in devoting one child to God out of a numerous family, as a sort of first fruits of all one's children, while one still has pleasure in those who remain alive, who are no small comfort and alleviation of the grief felt for the one who is sacrificed. But the man who gives the only beloved son that he is possessed of performs an action beyond all powers of language to praise, as he is giving nothing to his own natural affection, but inclining with his whole will and heart to show his devotion to God. (197) Accordingly this is an extraordinary and almost unprecedented action which was done by Abraham.

For other men, even if they have yielded up their children to be sacrificed on behalf of the safety of their native land or of their armies, have either remained at home themselves, or have kept at a distance from the altar of sacrifice; or at least, if they have been present they have averted their eyes, and left others to strike the blow which they have not endured to witness. (198) But this man, like a priest of sacrifice himself, did himself begin to perform the sacred rite, although he was a most affectionate father of a son who was in all respects most excellent. And, perhaps, according to the usual law and custom of burnt offerings he was intending to solemnise the rite by dividing his son limb by limb. And so he did not divide his feelings and allot one part of his regard to his son and another part to piety to God: but he devoted the whole soul, entire and undivided, to holiness; thinking but little of the kindred blood which flowed in the victim.

(199) Now of all the circumstances which we have enumerated what is there which others have in common with Abraham? What is there which is not peculiar to him, and excellent beyond all power of language to praise? So that every one who is not struck by nature envious and a lover of evil must be struck with amazement and admiration for his excessive piety, even if he should not call at once to mind all the particulars on which I have been dwelling, but only some one of the whole number; for the conception of any one of these particulars is sufficient by a brief and faint outline to display the greatness and loftiness of the father's soul; though there is nothing petty in the action of the wise man.

XXXVI. (200) But the things which we have here been saying do not appear solely in the plain and explicit language of the text of the holy scriptures; but they appear, moreover, to exhibit a nature which is not so evident to the multitude, but which they who place the objects of the intellect above those perceptible by the outward senses, and who are able to appreciate them, recognise. And this nature is of the following description.

(201) The victim who was about to be sacrificed is called in the Chaldaean language, Isaac; but if this name be translated into the Grecian language, it signifies, "laughter;" and this laughter is not understood to be that laughter of the body which is frequent in child sport, but is the result of settled happiness and rejoicing of the mind. (202) This kind of laughter the wise man is appropriately said to offer as a sacrifice to God; showing thus, by a figure, that to rejoice does properly belong to God alone. For the human race is subject to sorrow and to exceeding fear, from evils which are either present or expected, so that men are either grieved at unexpected evils actually pressing upon them, or are kept in suspense, and disquietude, and fear with respect to those which are impending. But the nature of God is free from grief, and exempt from fear, and enjoys the immunity from every kind of suffering, and is the only nature which possesses complete happiness and blessedness.

(203) Now to the disposition which makes this confession in sincerity, God is merciful, and compassionate, and kind, driving envy to a distance from him; and to it he gives a gift in return, to the full extent of the power of the person benefited to receive it, and he all but gives such a person this oracular warning, saying, "I well know that the whole species of joy and rejoicing is the possession of no other being but me, who am the Father of the universe; (204) nevertheless, though it belongs to me, I have no objection to those who deserve it enjoying a share of it. But who can be deserving to do so, save he who obeys me and my will? for to this man it shall be given to feel as little grief as possible and as little fear as possible, proceeding along that road which is inaccessible to passions and vices, but which is frequented by excellence of soul and virtue." (205) And let no one fancy that that unmixed joy, which is without any alloy of sorrow, descends from heaven to the earth, but rather, that it is a combination of the two, that which is the better being predominant in the mixture; in the same manner as the light in heaven is unalloyed and free from any admixture of darkness, but in the sublunary atmosphere it is mingled with dark air.

(206) For this reason, it seems to me to have been, that Sarah,[17] the namesake of virtue, who had previously laughed, denied her laughter to the person who questioned her as to the cause of it, fearing lest she might be deprived of her rejoicing, as belonging to no created being, but to God alone; on which account the holy Word encouraged her, and said, "Be not afraid," thou hast laughed a genuine laugh, and thou hast a share in real joy; (207) for the Father has not permitted the race of mankind to be wholly devoured by griefs, and sorrows, and incurable anguish, but has mingled in their existence something of a better nature, thinking it fitting that the soul should sometimes enjoy rest and tranquillity; and he has also designed that the souls of wise men should be pleased and delighted for the greater portion of their existence with the contemplation of the soul.

XXXVII. (208) This is enough to say about the piety of the man, though there is a vast abundance of other things which might be brought forward in praise of it. We must also investigate his skill and wisdom as displayed towards his fellow men; for it belongs to the same character to be pious towards God and affectionate towards man; and both these qualities, of holiness towards God and justice towards man, are commonly seen in the same individual. Now it would take a long time to go through all the instances and actions which form this; but it is not out of place to record two or three.

(209) Abraham, being rich above most men in abundance of gold and silver, and having numerous herds of cattle and flocks of sheep, and being equal in his affluence and abundance to any of the men of the country, or of the original inhabitants, who were the most wealthy, and being, in fact, richer than any sojourner could be expected to be, was never unpopular with any of the people among whom he was dwelling, but was continually praised

---

[17]Genesis 18:15.

and beloved by all who had any acquaintance with him; (210) and if, as is often the case, any contention or quarrel arose between his servants and retinue and those of others, he always endeavored to terminate it quietly by his gentle disposition, discarding and driving to a distance from his soul all quarrelsome, and turbulent, and disorderly things. (211) And there is no wonder, if he was such towards strangers, who might have agreed together and with a heavy and powerful hand have repelled him, if he had begun acts of violence, when he behaved with moderation towards those who were nearly related to him in blood, but very far removed from him in disposition, and who were desolate and isolated, and very inferior in wealth to himself, willingly allowing himself to be inferior to them in the very things in which he might have been superior; (212) for there was his brother's son, when he departed from his country, who went forth with him, an inconstant, variable, whimsical man, inclining now to one side and now to another; and at one time caressing him with friendly salutations, and at another, being restive and obstinate, by reason of the inequality of his disposition; (213) on which account his household also was a quarrelsome and turbulent one, as it had no one to correct it, and especially his shepherds were so, because they were removed to a great distance from their master.

Accordingly, they, in their self-willed manner, behaving as if they claimed complete liberty, were always quarreling with the managers of the flocks of the wise Abraham, who yielded a great many points, because of the gentle disposition of their master; in consequence of which, the shepherds of his nephew turned to folly and to shameless audacity, and gave way to anger, cherishing ill-temper, and exciting a spirit of irreconcilable enmity in their hearts, until they compelled those whom they injured to turn to their own defence; (214) and when a somewhat violent battle had taken place, the good Abraham, hearing of the attack made by his servants on the others, though only in self-defence, and knowing as he did that his own household was superior both in numbers and in power, would not allow the contest to be protracted till victory declared for his party, in order that he might not grieve his nephew by the defeat of his men; but standing between the two bodies of combatants, he, by his pacific speeches, reconciled the contending parties, and that not only for the moment, but for all future time too; (215) for he knew that if they continued to dwell together, and to abide in the same place, they would be always differing in opinion and quarrelling with one another, and continually raising up quarrels and wars with one another. In order that this might not be the case, he thought it desirable to abandon the custom of dwelling together, and to separate his habitation from that of his nephew. So,

sending for his nephew, he gave him the choice of the better country, cheerfully agreeing himself to abandon whatever portion the other selected, as he should thus acquire the greatest of all gains, namely, peace; (216) and yet, what other man would ever have yielded in any point whatever to one weaker than himself, while he was stronger? and who that was able to gain the victory would ever have been willing to be defeated, without availing himself of his power? But this man alone placed the object of his desires, not in strength and superiority, but in a life free from dissension and blessed with tranquillity, as far as depended on himself; for which reason he appears the most admirable of all men.

XXXVIII. (217) Since then this panegyric, if taken literally, is applied to Abraham as a man, and since the disposition of the soul is here intimated, it will be well for us to investigate that also, after the fashion of those men who go from the letter to the spirit of any statement. (218) Now there is an infinite variety of dispositions which arise from different circumstances and opportunities in every kind of action and event; but in this instance, we must distinguish between two characters, one of which is the elder and the other the younger.

Now the elder of the two is that disposition which honours these things which are by nature principal and dominant; the younger is that which regards the things which are subject to others, and which are considered in the lowest rank.

(219) Now the principal and more dominant things are wisdom, and temperance, and justice, and courage, and every description of virtue, and the actions in accordance with virtue; the younger things are wealth, and authority, and glory, and nobility, not real nobility, but that which the multitude think so, and all those other things which belong to the third class, next after the things of the soul, and the things of the body; the class which is in fact the last. (220) Each then of these dispositions has, as it were, flocks and herds. The one which desires external things has for its flocks, gold and silver, and all those things which are materials and furniture of wealth; and, moreover, arms, engines, triremes, armies of infantry and cavalry, and fleets of ships, and all kinds of provisions to procure domination, by which firm authority is secured.

But the lover of excellence has for his flock the doctrines of each individual virtue, and its speculations respecting wisdom. (221) Moreover, there are overseers and superintendents of each of these flocks, just as there are shepherds to flocks of sheep. Of the flock of external things, the superintendents are those who are fond of money, those who are fond of glory, those who are eager for war, and all those who love authority over multitudes. And the managers of the flocks of things concerning the soul are all those who are lovers of virtue and of what is honourable, and who do not prefer spurious good things to genuine ones, but genuine to spurious good. (222) There is therefore a certain natural contest between them, inasmuch as they have no opinions in common with one another, but are always at variance and difference respecting the matter which has of all others the greatest influence in the maintenance of life as it should be, that is to say, the judgment of what things are truly good.

(223) Now, for some time the soul was warred against by some enemy, and was full of this quarrelsome principle, inasmuch as it had not yet been completely pacified, but was still troubled by some passions and diseases which prevailed over sound reason. But from the time when it began to be more powerful, and with its superior force, to destroy the fortification of the opposite opinions, becoming elated and puffed up with pride, it in a most marvellous manner began to separate and detach the disposition in itself, which admires the external materials, and as if conversing with man, says to him, Thou art unable to dwell with— (224) it is impossible that thou shouldest be connected by alliance with—a lover, of wisdom and virtue. Come, then, and migrating from thy present abode, depart to a distance, since you have no communion with me, and, indeed, cannot possibly have any. For all the things which you conceive to be on the right he imagines to be on the left; and on the contrary, whatever you think is on the left, is looked upon by him as on the right.

XXXIX. (225) Therefore the virtuous man was not only peaceful and a lover of justice, but also a man of courage and of a warlike disposition; not for the sake of making war, for he was not of a contentious and quarrelsome character, but for the sake of a lasting peace for the future, which hitherto his adversaries had destroyed. (226) And the most convincing proof of this is to be found in what he did. Four great kings had received for their inheritance the eastern portion of the inhabited world; and they were obeyed by all the eastern nations, both on this and on the other side of the Euphrates. Now all the other parts remained unharassed by contentions, obeying the commands of these kings, and contributing their yearly taxes and tribute without seeking for any excuses; but the land of the inhabitants of Sodom alone before it was destroyed by the fire began to break the peace, having been designing to revolt for a long time.

(227) For as it was a very rich country it was ruled by five kings, who had divided the cities and the land among them, though the district was not an extensive one, but fertile in corn and trees, and abounding in all kinds of fruit. What then their size gives to other cities, that the excellence of its soil gives to Sodom; on which account it had many princes for lovers who admire its beauty. (228)

These, on all other occasions, had paid the appointed revenues to the collector of the taxes, honouring and at the same time fearing those more powerful sovereigns of whom they were the viceroys.

But when they were completely sated with good things, and when, as is ordinarily the case, satiety had begotten insolence, they, cherishing a pride beyond their power! began at first to lift up their heads and to become restive. Then, like wicked servants, they set upon their masters, trusting more to their factious spirit than to their strength. (229) But their sovereigns, remembering their own nobleness and being fortified with superior power, went against them with great disdain, as if they would be able to defeat them by the mere cry of battle. And having engaged them in battle, they in a moment put some of them to flight, and others they slew in the flight, and so they destroyed their army to a man. And also they led away a vast multitude captive, which they distributed among themselves with much other booty. Moreover, they led away captive the brother's son of a wise Abraham, who had a little while before emigrated into one of the cities of the Pentapolis.

XL. (230) This was communicated to Abraham by some one of those who escaped from the defeat of his countrymen, and it grieved him exceedingly, and he would not be quiet any longer, being much concerned at what had happened, and mourning more for him alive and in captivity than if he had heard that he had been killed. For he knew that death (*teleutē*) as its very name imports, was the end (*telos*) of all living beings, and especially of the wicked, and that there are innumerable unexpected evils which lie, as it were, in ambush for the living. (231) But when he was preparing to pursue them for the purpose of delivering his brother's son, he found himself in want of allies, inasmuch as he himself was a stranger and a sojourner and as no one could dare to oppose the irresistible power of such mighty monarchs flushed with recent victory. (232) And he devised for himself a most novel alliance. For necessity is the mother of invention, and expedients are found in the most difficult circumstances when a man has set his heart on just and humane objects. For having collected together all his servants, and ordering the slaves whom he had purchased to remain at home (for he was afraid of desertion on their part), he assembled all his domestic servants, and divided them into centuries, and marched forward in their battalions; not, indeed, trusting to them, for his was still a most insignificant force, in comparison with that of the kings, but placing his confidence in the champion and defender of the just, namely in God.

(233) Therefore putting forth all his exertions he hastened on, in nowise relaxing his speed, until, watching his opportunity, he fell upon the enemy

by night, after they had supped, and when they were just on the point of betaking themselves to sleep. And some he slew in their beds, and those who were arrayed against him he utterly destroyed, and with great vigour he defeated them all, more by the courage of his soul than by the adequacy of his means. (234) And he did not cease from attacking them until he had utterly destroyed the hostile army with their kings, and slain them all to a man in front of their camp, and had brought back his brother's son after this splendid and most glorious victory, bringing back also as fair booty all their cavalry, and all the multitude of their beasts of burden, and a most enormous quantity of spoil.

(235) And when the great high priest of the most high God beheld him returning and coming back loaded with trophies, in safety himself, with all his own force uninjured, for he had not lost one single man of all those who went out with him; marvelling at the greatness of the exploit, and, as was very natural, considering that he had never met with this success but through the favour of the divine wisdom and alliance, he raised his hands to heaven, and honoured him with prayers in his behalf, and offered up sacrifices of thanksgiving for his victory, and splendidly feasted all those who had had a share in the expedition; rejoicing and sympathising with him as if the success had been his own, and in reality it did greatly concern him. For as the proverb says:—

"All that befalls from friends we common call."

And much more are all instances of good fortune common to those whose main object it is to please God.

XLI. (236) These things, then, are what are contained in the plain words of the scriptures. But as many as are able to contemplate the facts related in them in their incorporeal and naked state, living rather in the soul than in the body, will say that of the nine kings the four are the powers of the four passions which exist within us, the passion of pleasure, of desire, of fear, and of grief; and that the other five kings are the outward senses, being equal in number, the sense of sight, of hearing, of smell, of taste, and of touch. (237) For these in some degree are sovereigns and rulers, having acquired a certain power over us, but not all to an equal extent; for the five are subordinate to the four, and are compelled to pay them taxes and tribute, such as are appointed by nature. (238) For it is from the things which we see, or hear, or smell, or taste, or touch, that pleasures, and pains, and fears, and desires arise; as there is no one of the passions which has any power to exist of itself, if it were not supplied by the materials furnished by the outward senses.

(239) For it is in these things that their powers consist, either in figures and in colours, or in the faculty of speaking or hearing which depends on the voice, or in the flavours, or in odours, or by the subjects of touch, whether they are soft or hard, or rough, or smooth, or hot, or cold. For all these things are supplied to each of the passions by means of the outward senses. (240) And as long as the taxes beforementioned are paid, the alliance among the kings remains; but when they are no longer contributed, as they were before, then immediately do quarrels and wars arise. And this appears to happen when painful old age supervenes, in which none of the passions becomes weaker, but rather perhaps stronger than their ancient power; but the sight becomes dim, and the ears hard of hearing, and every one of the other outward senses more blunt, being no longer equally able as before to judge and decide accurately of every subject submitted to them, nor any longer to pay a tribute which will be equal to the number of the passions.

So that it happened very naturally that they being thoroughly exhausted and laid prostrate by them were easily put to flight by the adverse passions; (241) and the statement that follows is in strict consistency with what might be naturally expected, namely, that of the five kings two fell into wells, and three took to flight. For touch and taste reach to the very deepest portions of the body, sending down into the entrails those things which are suitable for digestion; but the eyes and ears, and the smell, roaming abroad for the most part, escape the slavery of the body.

(242) The good man—threatening to attack all of these, when he saw that those who had lately been friends and confederates were now in a state of disease, and that there was war instead of peace arising among the nine kingdoms, as the four kings were contending with the five for sovereignty and dominion—on a sudden, having watched his opportunity, attacked them; being desirous of the establishment of democracy in the soul, the most excellent of constitutions instead of tyrannies and absolute sovereignties, and wishing also to introduce law and justice instead of lawlessness and injustice, which had prevailed up to that time. (243) And what is here said is not a cunningly devised fable, but is rather one of the most completely true facts, which may be seen to be true in our own selves. For it very often happens that the outward senses observe a sort of confederacy which they have formed with the passions, supplying them with objects perceptible by the outward senses; and very often also, they raise contentions, no longer choosing to pay the tribute fairly due from them, or else being unable to do so, by reason of the presence of corrective reason; which when it has taken up its complete armour, namely, the virtues, and their doctrines and contemplations, which form an irresistible power, conquers all things in the most vigorous manner. For it is

not lawful for perishable things to dwell with what is immortal. (244) Therefore the nine sovereignties of the four passions and the five outward senses are both perishable themselves and also the causes of mortality. But the truly sacred and divine word, which uses the virtues as a starting place, being placed in the number ten, that perfect number, when it descends into the contest and exerts that more vigorous power which it has in accordance with God, subdues by main force all the aforesaid powers.

XLII. (245) And at a subsequent period his wife dies, she who was most dear to his mind and most excellent in all respects, having given innumerable proofs of her affection towards her husband in leaving all her relations together with him; and in her unhesitating migration from her own country, and in her continued and uninterrupted wanderings in a foreign land, and in her endurance of want and scarcity, and in her accompanying him in his warlike expeditions. (246) For she was always with him at all times, and in all places, never being absent from any spot, or failing to share any of his fortune, being truly the partner of his life, and of all the circumstances of his life; judging it right equally to share all his good and evil fortune together with him. For she did not, as some persons do, shun any participation in his misfortunes, but lie in wait only for his prosperity, but with all cheerfulness took her share in both, as was fitting and becoming to a wedded wife.

XLIII. (247) And though I might have many topics for panegyric on this woman, still I will only mention one, which shall be the most manifest possible proof of all the others. For she, being barren and childless, and fearing lest her husband's God-loving house might be left entirely destitute of offspring, came to her husband and spoke as follows:—(248) "We have now lived together a long time mutually pleasing each; but we have no children, which is the cause for which we ourselves came together, and for which also nature designed the original connection between husband and wife; nor indeed can there be any hope of your having any offspring by me, since I am now beyond the age of childbearing; (249) do not you then suffer for my barrenness, and do not, out of your affection for me, while you are yourself able to still become a father, be hindered from being so. For I shall not feel any jealousy towards another woman whom you may marry, not for the gratification of irrational appetite, but in order to satisfy a necessary law of nature. (250) For which reason I will not delay to deck a new bride for you, that she may fulfil what is wanting on my part. And if the prayers which we will offer up for the birth of children be blessed with success, then the children which are born shall be your own legitimate children, but by adoption they shall be by all means mine.

(251) "And that you may have no suspicion of any jealousy on my part, take, if you will, my own handmaid to wife; who is a slave indeed as to her body, but free and noble as to her mind; whose good qualities I have for a long time proved and experienced from the day when she was first introduced into my house, being an Egyptian by blood, and a Hebrew by deliberate choice. (252) We have great substance and abundant wealth, not like people who are sojourners. For even already we surpass the natives themselves in the brilliancy of our prosperity, but still we have no heir or successor, and that, too, though there might be one, if you would be guided by my advice."

(253) But Abraham, marvelling more and more at the love of his wife for her husband thus continually being renewed and gaining fresh strength, and also at her spirit of forecast so desirous to provide for the future, takes to himself the handmaid who had been approved by her to the extent of having a son by her; though as those who give the most clear and probable account say he cohabited with her only till she became pregnant; and when she conceived, which she did after no long interval, he then desisted from all connection with her, by reason of his natural continence, and also of the honour in which he held his wife. (254) So then he speedily had a son by this handmaid, but at a very distant period after this he had also a legitimate son, after he and his wife had both despaired of any offspring from one another. The bounteous God having thus bestowed on them a reward for their excellence more perfect than their highest hopes.

XLIV. (255) It is sufficient to mention this as a proof of the virtue of Abraham's wife. But the topics of praise of the wise man himself are more numerous, some of which I have lately enumerated. Moreover I will mention also one circumstance connected with the death of the wife, which ought not to be buried in silence. (256) For when Abraham had lost such a partner of his whole life, as our account has shown her to have been, and as the scriptures testify that she was, he still like a wrestler prevailed over the grief which attacked him and threatened to overwhelm his soul; strengthening and encouraging with great virtue and resolution, reason, the natural adversary of the passions, which indeed he had always taken as a counsellor during the whole of his life; but at this time above all others, he thought fit to be guided by it, when it was giving him the best and most expedient advice. (257) And the advice was this; not to afflict himself beyond all measure, as if he were stricken down with a novel and unprecedented calamity; nor, on the other hand, to give way to indifference, as if nothing had happened calculated to give him sorrow. But rather to choose the middle way in preference to either extreme; and to endeavour to grieve in a moderate degree;

not being indignant at nature for having reclaimed what belonged to her as her due; and bearing what had befallen him with a mild and gentle spirit.

(258) And there are evidences of these assertions to be seen in the holy scriptures; which it is impossible should be convicted of false witness, and they tell us that Abraham, having wept a short time over his wife's body, soon rose up from the corpse; thinking, as it should seem, that to mourn any longer would be inconsistent with that wisdom by which he had been taught that he was not to look upon death as the extinction of the soul, but rather as a separation and disjunction of it from the body, returning back to the region from whence it came; and it came, as is fully shown in the history of the creation of the world, from God.

(259) But just as no man of moderation or sense would be indignant at having to repay a debt to a lender or to return a deposit to the man who had deposited it; so, in the same manner, he did not think it becoming to show impatience when nature reclaimed what belonged to her, but preferred to bear what was inevitable with cheerfulness. (260) And when the magistrates of that country came to sympathise with him in his sorrow, seeing none of the customary signs of woe which were usually exhibited in their land by mourners, no loud wailing or howling, no beating of the breast, no loud cries of men or women, but a steady, sober depression of spirits on the part of the whole household, they marvelled exceedingly, even though they had been previously full of astonishment and admiration at all the rest of the man's way of life. (261) And then, not concealing in their own minds their ideas of the greatness and beauty of his virtue, he was all admirable, they approached him and addressed him thus:— "Thou art a king from God among us."[18] Speaking most truly, for all other kingdoms are established by man by means of wars, and military expeditions, and indescribable evils, which those persons who aim at power inflict mutually on one another, slaying one another, and raising up vast forces of infantry, and cavalry, and fleets. But the kingdom of the wise man is bestowed upon him by God; and the virtuous man receiving it is not the cause of evil to any one, but is rather the author to all his subjects of the acquisition and also of the use of good things, proclaiming to them peace and obedience to the law.

XLV. (262) There is also another praise of him recorded in his honour and testified to in the holy scriptures, which Moses has written, in which it is related of him that he believed in God; which is a statement brief indeed in words, but of great magnitude and importance to be confirmed in fact. (263) For on whom else can we believe? Are we to trust in authorities, or in glory and honour, or in abundance of wealth and noble birth, or in good health and a good condition of the senses and the mind, or in vigour of body and beauty of person? But in truth every kind of authority is unstable, as it has innumerable enemies lying it wait to attack it. And if in any instance it is firmly established, it is only so confirmed by innumerable evils and calamities which those who are in authority both inflict and suffer. (264) Again, honours and glory are most unstable, being tossed about among the indiscriminate inclinations and feeble language of careless and imprudent men; and even if they endure, their nature is not such as to produce any genuine good. (265) And as for riches and illustrious birth, those things sometimes fall to the lot of the most worthless men. And even if they should belong only to the virtuous, still they are but the praises of their ancestors and of fortune, and not of those who now possess them.

(266) Nor, again, is it right for a man to pride himself on his personal advantages, in which other animals are superior to him. For what man is stronger or more vigorous than a bull among domestic animals, or than a lion among wild beasts? And what man is more sharp-sighted than a falcon or an eagle? And what man is so richly endowed with the sense of hearing as that stupidest of all animals, the ass? Also what man is more accurate in his sense of smell than a hound, who huntsmen say can trace out by means of his nose animals who are lying at a distance, and can run up to them with perfect correctness, and course, though he has not seen them; for what sight is to other animals that is the sense of smell to hounds and to all the dogs which pursue game.

(267) Moreover, the greater part of the irrational animals enjoy excellent health, and are as far as possible entirely exempt from disease. And also in any competition in respect of beauty, some things which are even destitute of vitality, appear to me to surpass the elegance of either men or women ; as, for instance, images, and statues, and pictures, and in a word all the works of either the pictorial or plastic art which arrive at excellence in either branch, and which are the objects of study and desire both to Greeks and barbarians, who erect them in the most conspicuous places for the ornament of their cities.

XLVI. (268) Therefore, the only real, and true, and lasting good is trust in God, the comfort of life, the fulfillment of all good hopes, the absence of all evils, and the attendant source of blessings, the repudiation of all unhappiness, the recognition of piety, the inheritance of all happiness, the improvement of the soul in every respect, as it thus relies for support on the cause of all things, who is able to do everything but who wills only to do what is best. (269) For as men who are going along a slippery road stumble and fall, but they who pro-

---

[18]Genesis 23:6.

ceed by a dry, and level, and plain path, journey on without stumbling; so also those men who are conducting their soul through the road of bodily and external good things are only accustoming it to fall; for these things are full of stumbling and the most insecure of all. But they who by those speculations which are in accordance with virtue, hasten towards God, are guiding their souls in a safe and untroubled path. So that we may say with the most absolute truth, that the man who trusts in the good things of the body disbelieves in God, and that he who distributes them believes in him.

(270) But not only do the holy scriptures bear witness to the faith of Abraham in the living God, which faith is the queen of all the virtues, but moreover he is the first man whom they speak of as an elder; though they were men who had preceded him who had lived three times as many years (or even more still) as he had, not one of whom is handed down to us as worthy of the appellation. And may we not say that this is in strict accordance with natural truth? For he who is really an elder is looked upon as such, not with reference to his length of time, but to the praiseworthiness of his life. (271) Those men, therefore, who have spent a long life in that existence which is in accordance with the body, apart from all virtue, we must call only long-lived children, having never been instructed in those branches of education which befit grey hairs. But the man who has been a lover of prudence, and wisdom, and faith in God, one may justly denominate an elder, forming his name by a slight change from the first. (272) For in real truth the wise man is the first man in the human race, being what a pilot is in a ship, a governor in a city, a general of war, the soul in the body,

or the mind in the soul; or again, what the heaven is in the world, and what God is in the heaven. (273) And God, admiring this man for his faith *(pistis)* in him, giving him a pledge *(pistis)* in return, namely, a confirmation by an oath of the gifts which he had promised him; no longer conversing with him as God might with man, but as one friend with another.

For he says, "By myself have I sworn,"[19] by him that is whose word is an oath, in order that Abraham's mind may be established still more firmly and immoveably than before. (274) Let the virtuous man both be and be called the younger and the last, since he only pursues such objects as may produce revolution and as are placed in the lowest rank.

(275) Thus much is sufficient to say on this subject. But God, adding to the multitude and magnitude of the praises of the wise man one single thing as a crowning point, says that "this man fulfilled the divine law, and all the commandments of God,"[20] not having been taught to do so by written books, but in accordance with the unwritten law of his nature, being anxious to obey all healthful and salutary impulses. And what is the duty of man except most firmly to believe those things which God asserts?

(276) Such is the life of the first author and founder of our nation; a man according to the law, as some persons think, but, as my argument has shown, one who is himself the unwritten law and justice of God.

---

[19] Genesis 15:6.
[20] Genesis 26:5.

ON JOSEPH†

(De Iosepho)

I. (1) There are three different modes by which we proceed towards the most excellent end, namely, instruction, nature, and practice. There are also three persons, the oldest of the wise men who in the account given to us by Moses derive three names from these modes, whose lives I have now discussed, having examined the man who arrived at excellence in consequence of instruction, and him who was self-taught, and him who attained to the proposed end by practice. Accordingly, proceeding in regular order, I will now describe the life of the man occupied in civil affairs. And again, Moses has given us one of the patriarchs as deriving his name from this kind of life, in which he had been immersed from his earliest youth.

(2) Now, this man began from the time he was seventeen years of age to be occupied with the consideration of the business of a shepherd, which corresponds to political business. On which account I think it is that the race of poets has been accustomed to call kings the shepherds of the people; for he who is skilful in the business of a shepherd will probably be also a most excellent king, having derived instruction in those matters which are deserving of inferior attention here to superintend a flock of those most excellent of all animals, namely, of men. (3) And just as attention to matters of hunting is indispensable to the man who is about to conduct a war or to govern an army, so in the same manner those who hope to have the government of a city will find the business of a shepherd very closely connected with them, since that is as it were a sort of prelude to any kind of government. (4) Therefore, as this man's father perceived in his son a very noble ability, and too great to be left in the obscurity of a private station, he admired him, and cultivated his talent, and loved him more than his other sons; because, too, he was the son of his old age, which last cause is one of the strongest incentives to affection possible. And like a man fond of virtue, he cherished and kindled the natural good disposition of his son by excessive and most diligent care and attention, in order that it might not only not be smothered, but might shine forth more brilliantly.

II. (5) But envy is at all times an adversary to great good fortune, and at this time it attacked a house which was prospering in all its parts, and divided it, setting all the brothers in enmity against one, who displayed an ill feeling on their own parts, sufficient to counterbalance the affection of his father, hating their brother as much as their father loved him; but they did not divulge their hatred by words, but kept it in their own bosoms, on which account it very naturally became more grievous and bitter; for passions which are repressed, and which are not allowed to evaporate in language, are more difficult to bear. (6) This man, therefore, indulging a disposition free from all guile and malice, and having no suspicion of the ill will which was secretly cherished against him by his brethren, having seen a dream of favourable import, related it to them, as if they were well affected towards him.

"For," said he, "I thought that the time of harvest was arrived, and that we had all gone down to the plain to gather the crops, and had taken sickles in our hands to reap the harvest, and on a sudden my sheaf appeared to stand up, right, and to be raised up, and to erect itself; and I thought that your sheaves, as if at an appointed signal, ran up and fell down before it, and worshipped it with great earnestness."[1] (7) But they being men of acute intelligence, and shrewd in divining the nature of a matter thus intimated to them by means of a figure, with very felicitous conjectures, replied, "Dost thou think that thou shalt be king and lord over us? for this is what you are now intimating by this lying vision of yours." So their hatred was kindled against him more exceedingly than before, as it was continually receiving some fresh pretext for its increase. (8) And he, suspecting nothing, a few days afterwards saw another dream, still more astonishing than the former one, and again he related it to his brethren; for he thought that the sun, and the moon, and the eleven stars, all came and worshipped him, so that his father marvelling at what had thus happened, laid these events up in his mind, cherishing them, and considering within himself what was to happen. (9) But he reproved his son gravely, from a fear that he might be doing wrong in some respect, and said to him, "Shall I, and thy mother, and thy brethren, be able to fall down and worship thee? for by the sun you appear to indicate your father, and by the moon your mother, and by the eleven stars your eleven brethren? Let no such an idea

---

† Yonge's title, *A Treatise of the Life of a Man Occupied with Affairs of State, or On Joseph.*

[1] Genesis 37:7.

ever come into your mind, O my son. But rather let all recollection of these visions which have appeared to you be forgotten, and let them pass from your mind; for to hope and expect a superiority over those of your family and kindred, is a detestable thing in my opinion, and I think, indeed, in that of every one else, who has an regard for equality and the principles of justice that subsist among kinsman."

(10) But his father, being afraid lest from his meeting with his brothers there might arise some quarrel and disturbance with them, inasmuch as they bore ill will against him on account of the dreams which he had seen, sent them away to keep their flocks at a distance, but retained him at home till a fitting season, knowing that time is said to be a powerful physician for all the passions and diseases of the soul, and a remover of grief, and an extinguisher of anger, and a healer of fear; for it softens and mitigates everything, even such things as are, according to their own nature, hard to be cured. (11) But when he conjectured that no hatred was any longer abiding in their hearts he sent this his son forth to salute his brethren, and also to bring him word how they and their flocks of sheep were.

III. (12) This expedition of his was the origin both of great evils and also of great good, each of them being excessive beyond all expectation; for he, obeying the commands of his parents, went to visit his brethren; but they, seeing him coming towards them while at a great distance, conversed one with another, saying nothing of good omen, inasmuch as they did not choose even to call him by his name, but called him a dreamer, and a seer of visions, and such appellations as these. (13) And to such a height did they carry their rage that (I will not say all of them, but) the greater portion of them plotted his death; and designed, after having slain him, for the sake of not being detected, to throw him into a deep pit dug in the earth, for there are a great many such places in that district dug as receptacles for the rain water. (14) And they were very near incurring that most excessive pollution of fratricide, as they would have done if they had not been, though with difficulty, persuaded by the advice of their eldest brother, who counselled them not to meddle with such a pollution but merely to cast him into one of these pits, thinking then to contrive some means of saving him, so that when they had all departed he might send him back again to his father without having suffered any harm. And after they had agreed to this he came forward and saluted them; and they took him as though he had been an enemy, and stripped him of all his garments, and let him down into a vast pit, and then, having stained his cloak with the blood of a kid, they sent it to his father on the pretence that he had been slain by a wild beast.

IV. (15) But on that day it happened by some chance that certain merchants who were accustomed to convey their merchandise from Arabia to Egypt were travelling that way, and so the eleven brethren drew Joseph up out of the pit and sold him to them; the one of them who was the fourth in respect of age instigating this contrivance; for in my opinion, he was afraid lest his brother might be treacherously slain by the others, who had conceived an irreconcilable hatred against him, and therefore he proposed that he should be sold, substituting slavery for death, the lighter evil for the greater. (16) But the eldest, for he was not present when he was sold, looking down into the pit, and not seeing him whom he had left there a short time before, cried out and lamented loudly, and rent his clothes, and tossed his hands up and down like a madman, and beat his breast and tore his hair, saying, (17) "What has become of him? Tell me, is he alive, or is he dead? If he is dead, show me his corpse that I may weep over his body, and so alleviate my grief. When I see him lying dead I shall be comforted; for why should we bear ill will to the dead? There is no envy excited against those who are out of sight. And if he is alive, to what country has he departed? (18) Where is he kept? for I am not, as he was, an object of suspicion, so as to be distrusted by you." And when they replied that he had been sold, and when they showed him the money which they had received for him, he said, "A fine trade, indeed, you have been driving? Let us divide the gain: let us wear crowns of victory after thus rivalling the slavedealers, and bearing off from them the prizes of iniquity; (19) we may well pride ourselves now that we have surpassed them in barbarity, for they indeed traffic in the liberty of strangers, but we in that of those who are most nearly related to and most dear to us. Surely here is newly contrived a great disgrace and a shame which will be known far and wide. Our fathers left behind them in every part of the world memorials of their virtue and excellence; we shall leave behind us the guilt of a charge of faithlessness and treacherous inhumanity which can never be effaced; for the reputation of extraordinary actions penetrates everywhere; those which are praiseworthy being admired, and those which are blameable meeting with blame and accusation. (20) In what manner now will our father receive the news of what has happened? You will now, as far as depends upon us, have made the life of him who has hitherto been wonderfully happy and fortunate, not worth living; which will he pity, the child who has been sold, for his slavery? or those who have sold him, for their inhumanity? I am sure he will pity us much the more; since to do wrong is a more terrible evil than to suffer wrong, for the one has for an alleviation two consolations of the greatest influence, hope and pity; but the other is destitute of both these mitigations, and is more unfortunate in the judgment of every one. (21) But why do I mourn and bewail in this manner? It is better for me to be silent, lest I too should be treated in some terrible manner; for ye are most merciless men in your dispositions, and implacable; and the rage which was kindled in each of you is still furious and vehement."

V. (22) But when their father heard, not the truth indeed, that his son had been sold, but a falsehood that he was dead, and that he had been slain by wild beasts, he was smitten in his ears by the news that was reported to him, and in his eyes by what was shown to him (for they brought to him his son's coat rent and torn and defiled with quantities of blood); and being wholly bewildered by the exceeding greatness of the calamity, he lay for a long time without speaking, not being able even to lift up his head, the calamity overwhelming and completely prostrating him; (23) then suddenly pouring forth as it were a stream of tears with bitter lamentations, he bedewed his cheeks, and his chin, and his breast, and all the garments on his chest, saying at the same time such words as these, "It is not thy death that grieves me, O my son, but such a tomb as has fallen to your lot; for if you had been buried in your own land I should have been comforted; I would have cherished you, I would have tended you in sickness if you had died before me, I would have given you my last embrace, I would have closed your eyes, I would have wept over your dead body lying before me, I would have buried you sumptuously, I would have omitted none of the customary observances.

(24) "Again, even if you had died in a foreign land, I should have said, nature has claimed what was due to, and what belonged to her; and therefore, O my mind, be not cast down; for living men have indeed their separate countries, but the whole earth is the grave of the dead; and all men are destined to a speedy death; for even the longest lived man is but short lived if compared with eternity; (25) but if it was necessary that he should die violently and by treachery, it would have been a lighter evil to me for him to have been slain by men, who would have laid out his corpse, and have pitied him so far as to scatter dust over him, and at least to have concealed his body; and even if they had been the most merciless of all people, what more could they have done than have thrown him out unburied, and so got rid of him? And then, perhaps, some one of the passers by on the road, standing by, and beholding him, and conceiving pity for our common nature, would have thought him worthy of some care, and of burial; but now, as the saying is, O my son, thou has become a feast, and a banquet for savage and carnivorous wild beasts, who will eat and devour thy bowels; (26) I am compelled to endure distresses which I never had imagined, I am without any cause practised in enduring many miseries; I am a wanderer, a stranger, a slave, living under compulsion, having even my very life plotted against by those whom it least became to do so. And I have seen many things, and I have heard many things, and I have suffered many things, all of which have been incurable evils, which however I have learnt to bear with moderation, so as not to yield to them.

"But nothing has ever happened more intolerable than this misfortune which has now befallen me; which has consumed and destroyed all the vigour of my soul; (27) for what can be a greater or more pitiable calamity? The garment of my child has been brought to me, who am his father; but of him himself there is no portion brought, not a limb, not a small fragment, but he has been wholly and entirely destroyed and devoured, not being able even to receive burial; and it seems to me that even his garment would never have been sent to me at all if it had not been by the way of a reminder of my grief, and as a refreshment of my memory as to the sufferings which he endured, so as to afflict me with a never to be forgotten and never ending sorrow."

He indeed bewailed his son in these terms; but the merchants sold his son in Egypt to one of the king's eunuchs who was his chief cook.

VI. (28) It is worth while, however, after having thus explained the literal account given to us of these events, to proceed to explain also the figurative meaning concealed under that account; for we say that nearly all, or that at all events, the greater part of the history of the giving of the law is full of allegories; now the disposition which we have at present under consideration, is called by the Hebrews Joseph; but the name being interpreted in the Greek language means, "the addition of the Lord," a name most felicitously given, and most appropriate to the account given of the person so called; for the democratic constitution in vogue among states is an addition of nature which has sovereign authority over everything; (29) for this world is a sort of large state, and has one constitution, and one law, and the word of nature enjoins what one ought to do, and forbids what one ought not to do: but the cities themselves in their several situations are unlimited in number, and enjoy different constitutions, and laws which are not all the same; for there are different customs and established regulations found out and established in different nations; (30) and the cause of this the want of union, and participation existing not merely between the Greeks and the barbarians, or between the barbarians and the Greeks, but also between the different tribes of each of these respective nations.

Then they, as it would seem, blaming those things which do not deserve blame, such as unexpected occurrences or opportunities, deficiency of crops, badness of soil, their own situation either as being by the sea-side, or inland, or insular, or on the continent, or anything of that sort, are silent as to the real truth. The real truth is their covetousness, their want of good faith towards and confidence in one another, on which account they have not been satisfied with the laws of nature, but have called those regulations, which have appeared to be for the common advantage of the agreeing and unanimous multitudes, laws, so that the individual constitutions do naturally appear rather in the light of additions to the one great general constitution of nature; (31) for the laws of individual cities are additions to the one right reason of nature; and so also the man who is occupied with political affairs is an addition to the man who lives in accordance with nature.

VII. (32) And it is not without a particular and correct meaning that Joseph is said to have had a coat of many colours. For a political constitution is a many-coloured and multiform thing, admitting of an infinite variety of changes in its general appearance, in its affairs, in its moving causes, in the peculiar laws respecting strangers, in numberless differences respecting times and places. (33) For as the master of a ship collects together all the means which may tend to ensure him a favourable voyage with reference to and in dependency on the changes of the wind, not always guiding his vessel in one and the same way; and as a physician does not apply one and the same means of cure to every sick person, nor even to one person if his disease varies in its character, but watches the periods of its abatement, and of its intensity, and of its becoming full or empty, and the alterations of the causes of the sickness, and so varies his remedies as much as possible to secure the safety of his patient, applying one remedy at one time and another at another; (34) in the same manner I conceive that the man immersed in political affairs is of necessity a multiform man, assuming many different appearances, one in time of peace and another in time of war; and a different character according as those who are opposed to him are numerous or few in number, withstanding a small number with vigorous resolution, but using persuasion and gentle means towards a large body. And in some cases where there is much danger, still for the sake of the common advantage he will take the place of every one, and manage the business in hand by himself; in other cases, where it is merely a question of labour he will let others minister to him as his assistants.

(35) It was appropriately said that the man was sold. For the haranguer of the people and the demagogue, mounting the tribunal, like slaves who are being sold and exposed to view, is a slave instead of a free man, by reason of the honours which he seems to be receiving, being led away by ten thousand masters? (36) The same person is also represented as having been torn by wild beasts; and vainglory, which lies in wait for a man, is an untameable wild beast, tearing and destroying all who give into it. And they who have been purchasers are likewise sellers; for there is one master only to the citizens who live in any city; but there is a multitude of masters, one succeeding another in a certain succession and regular order. But those who have been sold three times change their masters like bad slaves, not remaining with their original ones, by reason of the speedily satisfied irregularity of their dispositions, always thirsting after novelty.

VIII. (37) This is enough to say on this part of the subject. Accordingly, the young man, having been conducted into Egypt, and there, as has already been stated, having become the slave of a eunuch, gave in a few days such proofs of virtue and excellence of disposition, that he had authority over his fellow servants given to him, and the management of the whole household committed to his charge; for already his master had learnt by many circumstances to perceive that his servant in all his words and in all his actions was under the immediate direction of divine providence. (38) Accordingly, in consequence of this opinion of his purchaser, he was appointed superintendent of his house, apparently indeed by his master, but, in fact and reality, by nature herself, which procured for him the government of a mighty city, and nation, and country. For it was necessary that one who was destined to be a statesman should be previously practised and trained in the management of a single household; for a household is a city on a small and contracted scale, and the management of a household is a contracted kind of polity; so that a city may be called a large house, and the government of a city a widely spread economy. (39) And from these considerations we may see that the manager of a household and the governor of a state are identical, though the multitude and magnitude of the things committed to their charge may be different, as in the case too with the arts of painting and statuary; for the good statuary or painter, whether he is making many and colossal figures, or only few and those of a small size, is still the same person, and the art which he is practising is the same art.

IX. (40) But while he is earning a very high reputation in the matters connected with the management of his master's house, he is plotted against by the wife of his master, because of the incontinent love which she had conceived for him; for she, being maddened by the beauty of the young man, and being unable to restrain the violence of her frenzy and passion, addressed a proposal of illicit intercourse to him; but he resisted it vigorously, and would not at all endure to approach her, by reason of the orderly and temperate disposition implanted in him by nature and habit. (41) But when she, inflaming and exciting her lawless desire, kept continually tempting him, and continually throwing herself in his way, and continually failing in her object, she at last, in the violence of her passion, had recourse to force, and seizing hold of his cloak dragged him vigorously toward the bed, her passion endowing her strength with greater vigour, as it often does strengthen even the weak. (42) But he, proving more powerful than even the alluring opportunity, uttered a cry becoming a free man, and worthy of his race, saying, What are you forcing me to? We, the descendants of the Hebrews, are guided by special customs and laws of our own; (43) in other nations the youths are permitted, after they are fourteen years of age, to use concubines and prostitutes, and women who make gain by their persons, without restraint. But among us a harlot is not allowed even to live, but death is appointed as a punishment for any one who adopts such a way of life. Therefore, before our lawful marriage we know nothing of any connection with any other woman, but, without ever having experienced any similar cohabitation, we approach our virgin brides as pure as themselves, proposing as the end of our marriage not pleasure but the offspring of legitimate children.

(44) I, therefore, having kept myself pure to this day, will not begin now to transgress the law by adultery which is the greatest of all sins, when I ought rather, even if in past time I had lived in an irregular manner, and had been led away by the impulses of youth, and had imitated the licentiousness of the natives, still not to seek to pollute the marriage of another man, an offence which who is there would not avenge with blood? For though different nations differ in other points, still all agree in this alone, that all men think him worthy of ten thousand deaths who does so, and give up the man who is detected in adultery without trial to the husband who has detected him. (45) But you, pressing me thus to load myself with guilt, would add even a third pollution in my case, since you bid me not merely commit adultery, but also to violate my mistress and my master's wife, unless, indeed, this is to be looked upon as the reason for which I entered your house, that I might neglect the duties which a servant ought to perform, and get drunk, and become intoxicated with hopes fit for my master who has bought me, polluting his marriage, and his house and his family.

(46) Nevertheless I am induced to honour him not merely as my master, but also as one who has before now been my benefactor. He has committed to my care the whole management of his household; there is nothing whatever, be it great or small, which is withdrawn from my superintendence, except you who are his wife. In return for these kindnesses is it fitting for me to requite him with such an action as you recommend to me? I will rather, as becomes me, endeavour with honourable service to requite the kindness of which he

has set me the example, and which is due him. (47) He, being my master, has made me, who was a captive and a slave, a free man and a citizen by his great goodness, as far at least as depended on him; and shall I, who am a slave, compare myself to my master as if he were a stranger and a captive? And with what disposition can I commit this unholy action? and with what face can I be impudent enough to look upon him? The consciousness of guilt which I shall have contracted will not suffer me to look him in the face, even if I should be able to be undiscovered, but in fact I shall never escape detection, for there are innumerable witnesses of all the things which are done privily who may not be silent.

(48) I forbear to say that, even if no one else should know it, or being privy to it should not divulge it, still I nevertheless shall be a witness against myself by my complexion, by my look, by my voice, as I said a little while ago, being convicted by my own conscience; and if no one else informs against me, shall I not fear nor respect, justice the assessor of God, and the overlooker of all human actions?

X. (49) He put all these arguments together and philosophised in this way till she ceased to importune him; for the desires are powerful, to cast in the shade even the most powerful of the outward senses, which he, being aware of, fled from them, leaving his garment in her hands, as she had seized hold of him. (50) This circumstance gave her an opportunity to contrive a story, and to invent a plausible tale against the young man, by means of which she might revenge herself on him; for when her husband came from the public assembly, she, pretending to play the part of a modest and orderly woman, even among the intemperate habits by which she was surrounded, said to him, with excessive indignation, "You brought a servant into us, a slave of the Hebrews, who had not only corrupted his soul, since you, in a simple manner without due inquiry, committed your household to him, but has even dared to assault my body. (51) For he was not contented with seducing only his fellow servants, inasmuch as he has become a most lascivious and debauched man, but he has attempted to defile even me, his mistress, and to use force to me; and the proofs of his insane lust are visible and clear; for when, having been very ill-treated by him, I cried out, calling to my aid assistants from within; he fled, from fear of being apprehended."

(52) And showing his garment, she appeared to give a proof of the truth of what she said; and his master thinking that it was true, ordered his officers to conduct the man to prison, erring in two most important points: first, that without giving him any time to defend himself, he, without a trial, condemned one who had done no wrong, as if he had committed the greatest crimes;

secondly, because the garment which the woman displayed as having been left behind by the young man, was indeed a proof of violence, but not of that which he had committed, but rather of that which had been offered to him, and of the fortitude with which he endured it from the woman; for if he had been offering violence, it was probable that he might have laid hold of the garment of his mistress; but it was owing to his having had violence offered to him that he was deprived of his own. (53) But perhaps he should be pardoned for his excessive ignorance, inasmuch as he lived chiefly in the cook's house, being filled with blood, and smoke, and ashes, his reasoning having no opportunity to become tranquillised and to enjoy leisure in itself, because it was confused still more, or, at all events, not less than the body.

XI. (54) I have already sketched out three characters of the man immersed in civil business; that of him who is occupied as a shepherd, that of the regulator of a house, and that of the man possessed of fortitude: and we have now discussed the two first of these sufficiently.

But the temperate man is no less connected with the regulation of political affairs than those two are; (55) for temperance is a beneficial and saving thing for all the affairs of life; and in affairs of state it is most especially so, as those who wish to understand the matter may learn from numerous and easily obtained proofs. (56) For who is there who does not know that great calamities have befallen nations, and districts, and whole countries all over the world, both by land and sea, in consequence of intemperance; for the most numerous and most serious wars have been kindled on account of love, and adultery, and the wiles of women; by which the most numerous and most excellent portion of both of the Grecian and barbarian race has been destroyed, and the youth of the cities has perished. (57) And of the consequences of intemperance, are domestic seditions, and wars, and evils upon evils in unutterable number. It is plain that the consequences of temperance, are stability, and peace, and the acquisition and enjoyment of perfect blessing.

XII. (58) It is worth while, however, to proceed in regular order, and by this course to exhibit what is intended to be intimated by this figurative history. The man who brought this servant of whom we are speaking is said to have been a eunuch; very naturally, for the multitude which purchases the services of a man skilful in affairs of state is truly a eunuch, having in appearance, indeed, the organs of generation, but being deprived of all the power requisite for generating; just as those persons who have a confused sight though they have eyes, are nevertheless deprived of the active use of them, inasmuch as they are not able to see clearly. (59) What, then, is the resemblance of eunuchs to the multitude? That the

multitude too is unable to generate wisdom, but that it studies virtue; for when a multitude of men, brought promiscuously together from all quarters and of different races, meets in the same place, what is said indeed may be proper and becoming, but what is intended and what is done is quite contrary; since the multitude embraces what is spurious in preference to what is genuine, because it is carried away by false opinion, and has not studied what is truly honourable.

(60) On which account (though it seems a most unnatural thing), a wife is represented as cohabiting with this eunuch; for the multitudes court desire, as a man courts a woman; for the sake of which it says and does everything, making it its counsellor in everything which should and should not be spoken, trifling or important, being not at all accustomed to attend to considerations of calm wisdom; (61) therefore the sacred historian very appropriately calls him the chief cook. For a cook studies nothing beyond the insatiable and immoderate pleasures of the belly, in the same manner the multitude, which is occupied with public affairs, studies only those pleasures and allurements which are conveyed by means of the hearing, by which the energies of the mind are relaxed, as one may say the nerves of the soul are in a manner loosened.

(62) And who is there who is not aware of the great quarrel which exists between physicians and cooks; since the first exert all their diligence and ingenuity in preparing things which are salutary, even if they are not pleasant; but the others, on the contrary, prepare only what is pleasant, disregarding what is advantageous? (63) Therefore, the laws which exist among a people and those who govern in accordance with the laws resemble physicians, and so also do those counsellors and judges who have a regard to the common safety and security of the state, and who use no flattery to the people. But the chief body of the younger men resembles cooks; for their object is not to supply what will be beneficial to the people, but only to contrive for the present moment to reap gratification.

XIII. (64) And the desire of the multitude, like an incontinent woman, loves the man who is experienced in state affairs, and says to him: Go forth, my good man, unto the multitude among which you are dwelling, and forget all your own individual disposition, and the pursuits, and discourses, and actions in which you have been brought up. And be guided by me, and attend to me, and do every thing which is agreeable to me; (65) for I cannot endure any thing that is austere and obstinate, and foolishly fond of truth, and pertinaciously adhering to justice, which puts on an air of importance and dignity on all occasions, which yields in no point, and never proposes to itself any object but plain expediency, without any thought of gratifying the hearers. (66) And do you not know the innumerable calumnies which some persons load you with, uttering them to my husband and your master, the multitude; for up to this time you appear to me to have been behaving like a free man, and you seem not at all to know that you are the slave of a very tyrannical master.

But if you had understood that independence of action belongs to a free man, but obedience to the orders of others to a slave, you would then, laying aside your self-willed obstinacy, have learnt to look upon me who am his wife, being desire, and to do every thing with a reference to my gratification, by which means you yourself also will receive the greatest pleasure.

XIV. (67) But the statesman is not in reality ignorant that the people has the authority of a master, but still he will not admit that he himself is its slave, but looks upon himself as free, and as entitled to consider mainly the gratification of the soul. And he will say in plain words: I have not learnt to be slave to the will of the populace, nor will I ever study such a practice, but being desirous to attain to the government and administration of the city like a good steward or well-intentioned father, I will save it in a guileless and honourable manner, without any hostile character. (68) And while I cherish these sentiments I shall be open to examination, concealing nothing, and not hiding any thing like a thief, but keeping my conscience clear as in the light of the sun and of day; for the truth is the light.

And I shall fear none of the evils with which they menace me, not even if they threaten me with death; for hypocrisy is in my eyes a more grievous evil than death. (69) And why should I encounter what I look upon in such a light? For even if the populace be a despot, am I therefore a slave, I who am born of as noble ancestors as any one in the world, entitled to be enrolled as a free citizen in the greatest and most admirable state in the whole world? (70) For as I am not influenced by gifts, nor by exhortations, nor by a love of honours, nor by a desire of power, nor by insolence, nor by a desire of seeming different from what I am, nor by intemperance, nor by cowardice, nor by injustice, nor by any other motive partaking of either passion or wickedness; what can, then, be the dominion of what I have need to fear? (71) Surely it can only be the dominion of men. But they claim authority, indeed, over my body, but none at all over me; for I estimate myself by the more excellent part of myself, namely, by the mind in accordance with which I have determined to live, thinking but little of my mortal body, which sticks to me like a limpet, and even if it is injured by something or other, I shall not be grieved at having got rid of cruel masters and mistresses who are settled within, inasmuch as I shall have escaped the most formidable necessity.

(72) If, therefore, it shall be necessary for me to act as a judge, I will decide, neither adhering to any rich man for the sake of his riches, nor gratifying a poor man by reason of my compassion for his misfortunes, but putting out of sight the rank and outward circumstances of those respecting whom I am to judge, I will honestly pronounce in favour of what shall appear to me to be just. (73) And if I am called to counsel I will bring forward such opinions as shall appear to me to be for the common advantage, even though they may not be palatable. And if I am a member of the assembly, leaving flattering speeches to others, I will adopt only such as are advantageous and salutary, reproving, admonishing, correcting, and studying not a frantic and insane license of speech, but a sober freedom.

(74) And if any one dislikes improvement, let such a one find fault with parents, and guardians, and teachers, and with all who have the care of youth, because they reprove their own children, or their orphan wards, or their pupils, and sometimes even beat them; and yet they are not to be accused of evil speaking, nor of insolent violence, but on the contrary, they must be looked upon as friends and real well-wishers; (75) for it would be utterly unworthy for me who am experienced in affairs of state, and who have all the interests of the people entrusted to me in discussions respecting what is for the advantage of the commonwealth to behave worse than a man would who has studied the art of a physician; (76) for he would not in the least regard the brilliant position or the accredited good fortune of his patient, nor whether he is of noble birth or of large fortune, nor whether he is the most renowned monarch or tyrant of all his contemporaries, but would attend to one object alone, that, namely, of preserving his health to the best of his power. And if it should be necessary to use excision or cautery, he, though a subject, or as some might say a slave, would cut or burn his governor or his master.

(77) But I, who have got for my patient not one man but a whole city sick with those more grievous diseases which the kindred desires have brought upon it, what ought I to do? Shall I, abandoning all idea of what will be of general advantage to the whole state seek to please the ears of this or that man with an ungentleman-like and thoroughly slavish flattery? I would rather choose to die than to speak merely with the object of gratifying the ear, and to conceal the truth, disregarding all thought of what is really advantageous. (78) "Now then," as the tragedian says:—

"Now then let fire, let biting steel come on;
Burn, scorch my flesh, and glut your appetite
Drinking my dark, warm blood; for here I swear
Sooner shall those bright stars which deck the heaven
Descend beneath the earth, the earth itself

Soar upwards to the sky, than servile words
Of flattery creep from out my mouth to thee."

(79) But the people, when it is the master, cannot endure a statesman of so masculine a spirit, and one who keeps so completely aloof from the passions, from pleasure, from fear, from grief, from desire; but it arrests its well-wisher and friend, and punishes him as an enemy, in doing which it first of all inflicts upon itself the most grievous of all punishments, namely, ignorance; in consequence of which state it does not itself learn that lesson which is the most beautiful and profitable of all, namely, obedience to its governor, from which the knowledge how to govern subsequently springs.

XV. (80) Having now discussed this matter at sufficient length, let us see what follows next.

The young man, having been calumniated to his master by his master's wife, who was in love with him, and who had invented against him the accusation to which she herself was liable, is not allowed to make any defence, but is led away to prison. And while he was in prison he displayed such exceeding virtue that even the most abandoned persons there marvelled and were amazed, and looked upon it as an alleviation of their calamities to have found such a man as the averter of evil from them. (81) And of the cruelty and inhumanity of which gaolers are full there is no one who is ignorant. For they are both by nature pitiless, and also by constant practice they are made more and more brutal, and increase in ferocity day by day, never seeing, or saying, or doing any good thing, but committing only acts of violence and barbarity. (82) For as men who have very strongly knit bodies, when besides their natural strength they add to it the practice of wrestlers, become stronger still, and acquire an irresistible power and a surpassing perfection of body, so in the same manner when an untameable and implacable nature adds habit to its natural ferocity, it becomes inaccessible to, and immovable by any kind of pity or any single respectable or humane feeling.

(83) And as those who associate with good men are improved in their disposition by such association, rejoicing in the pleasant and good persons with whom they are living; so also do they who are living with the wicked take the impression of their wicked ways; for habit is a very powerful thing to put a force upon nature, and to make it resemble itself. (84) now keepers of prisons live among thieves and robbers, and housebreakers, and men of insolence and violence, and murderers, and adulterers, and plunderers of temples, from every one of whom they contract some wickedness, and collect a sort of contribution: and from their manifold mixture, make up one thoroughly confused and wholly polluted iniquity.

XVI. (85) Nevertheless, even such a man as

this was propitiated by the virtue of this young man, and not only gave him liberty and security, but even entrusted to him a share of authority over all the prisoners; so that in word, indeed, and as far as the title went, he continued to be the gaoler; but in reality he has made over all the active part of the work to the young man, in consequence of which conduct of his the prisoners were benefited in no slight degree. (86) Accordingly they no longer thought fit to call the place a prison, but a house of correction: for instead of tortures and punishments which they had previously undergone night and day, being beaten and bound with chains, and suffering every imaginable kind of ill-treatment; they were now admonished with the language and doctrines of philosophy, and also by the life and conduct of their teacher, which was more effective than any discourse in the world; (87) for he, by placing his own life full of temperance and every kind of virtue before them, as a picture and well-constructed model of virtue, changed even those who had appeared to be utterly incurable, so that the long diseases of their souls now got a respite, since they were afflicting themselves for what they had hitherto done, and were repenting of it, and uttering such expressions as these, "Where was there all this good formerly which we originally failed to find? For behold! now it shines forth to such a degree that we are ashamed to face it, seeing our deformity in it as in a looking-glass."

XVII. (88) While they then were being improved in this manner two of the king's eunuchs are brought into the prison; the one being his chief butler, and the other his chief baker, having been accused and condemned for malversation in the offices committed to their charge. And Joseph took the same care of them that he took of the others, praying that he might be able to make all those who were entrusted to his care in no respect inferior to irreproachable persons. (89) And when no long period had elapsed, he went to visit his prisoners on one occasion, when he saw these eunuchs more full of perplexity, and more downcast than they had been before; and conjecturing from their excessive grief that some strange event had befallen them, he inquired the reason of their sorrow. (90) And when they answered him, that they were full of distress and perplexity because they had seen dreams, and because there was no one who could interpret them to them, he said "Be of good cheer, and relate them to me; for so, if God will, you shall be led to understand them; for he is willing to reveal, to those who are desirous of the truth, those things which are concealed in darkness."

(91) Then the chief butler spoke first, and said, "I thought that a great vine grew up, having three roots, and one very vigorous trunk, and flourishing, and bearing bunches of grapes as if in the height of autumn, and when the grapes became

dark and ripe I picked the bunches, and squeezed the grapes into the king's cup, in order to convey to my sovereign a sufficient quantity of unmixed wine." (92) And Joseph, pausing for awhile, said, "Thy vision announces good fortune to thee, and a recovery of thy former situation; for the three roots of the vine signify figuratively three days, after which the king will remember thee, and will send for thee from hence, and will pardon thee, and will permit thee to resume the former rank, and shalt again pour him out wine for confirmation of thy authority, and shalt give the cup into thy master's hand." And the chief butler rejoiced when he heard these things.

XVIII. (93) And the chief baker, gladly receiving this interpretation, and rejoicing in the idea that he too had seen a favourable dream (though his dream was of a very contrary character), being deceived by the fair hopes which were held out to the other, spoke as follows:—"And I, too, fancied that I was carrying a basket, and that I was holding three baskets full of cakes upon my head. And the upper basket was full of all sorts of cakes which the king was accustomed to eat; and there were in it confections and delicacies of all kinds imaginable for the king's food: and the birds flew down and took them from off my head, and devoured them insatiably till they had eaten them all up; and none of the things which I had so skilfully prepared were left." (94) But Joseph replied, "I wish that the vision had not appeared to you, or that, if any one would speak of it, he had done so at a distance, so that I might not have heard him, and that his account had been given out of the reach of my ears, for I disliked to be a messenger of evil: for I sympathise with those who are in distress, being greatly grieved at what befalls them by reason of my own humanity. (95) But since interpreters of dreams are bound to speak the truth, since they are interpreters of the divine oracles, and prophets of the divine will, I will explain your dream to you, and conceal nothing; for to speak truly is in every case the best thing, and is, moreover, the most holy of all holy speeches.

(96) "The three baskets are a symbol of three days: and after three days the king will command you to be crucified, and your head to be cut off, and the birds will fly down and feast upon your flesh, until you are wholly devoured." (97) And the chief baker, as was natural, was confused at this, and cast down greatly, expecting the fate which was thus denounced against him, and being full of misery in his mind. But when the three days had passed, the king's birth-day came, on which all the natives of the country made an assembly and a feast, and especially those in the king's palace. (98) Therefore, while the magistrates were feasting, and while all the household and all the servants were revelling as in a public banquet, the king,

remembering his eunuchs who were in prison, commanded them to be brought; and when he had seen them he confirmed the interpretation of their dreams which Joseph had given, ordering one of them to be crucified, and to have his head cut off, and restoring to the other the office which he had formerly enjoyed.

XIX. (99) But the chief butler, after he was released, forgot him who had foretold his release to him, and who had alleviated all the misfortunes which had befallen him, perhaps, indeed, because every ungrateful man is forgetful of benefits, and perhaps, too, because of the providence of God, who designed that the prosperity of the young man should not be owing to man, but rather to himself; (100) for after two years he, by means of a dream, and by two visions, predicted to the king the good and evil which was about to happen to his land, each of the visions indicating the same thing, so as to produce a firmer belief in them.

(101) For he thought that seven oxen were coming slowly up out of the river, fat and very well fleshed, beautiful to look upon, and that they began to feed by the river; after which seven others, equal in number, destitute of flesh in a strange degree, and very lean, came up, exceedingly ill-favoured, and they too fed alongside of the others. Then, on a sudden, the better oxen were devoured by the inferior ones, and yet those who ate them were in none, not even in the very slightest degree, increased in bulk in their bodies, but were still leaner than before, or at all events, not less lean; (102) and when he had awakened and gone to sleep a second time, he had a second vision appear to him; for he thought that seven ears of wheat sprang up from one root, equal in magnitude, and that they grew and flourished, and rose up to a height with great vigour; and then that seven other ears, thin and weak, grew up near them, and the root with good ears was devoured by the weak ears when they too had grown up. (103) Seeing this sight he remained sleepless all the rest of the night, for cares stinging and wounding him kept him awake, and at dawn he sent for the sophists and related his dream; (104) and as none of them was able, by any probable conjectures, to trace out the truth, the chief butler came forward and said, "O master, there is a hope that you may find the man whom you are seeking; for when I and the chief baker had done evil against you you ordered us to be committed to prison; and in that prison there was a servant of the chief cook, a Hebrew, to whom both the chief baker and I related some dreams which had appeared to us, and he answered them with such felicity and accuracy of interpretation, that all that he foretold to either of us came to pass, the punishment to the chief baker, which was appointed to him, and I found you favourable and merciful to me."

XX. (105) Therefore the king hearing these

things, orders men to go in haste and summon the young man before him; but they having cut his hair, for the hair, both of his head and of his beard, had grown very long while he was kept in prison, and having given him a splendid garment instead of a sordid one, and having adorned him in other ways, led him before the king; (106) who, perceiving from his appearance that he was a free-born and noble man (for there are certain outward characteristics which are stamped upon the persons of some people whom one sees, which are not visible to all, but only to such as have very clear-sighted eyes in their mind), said, "My soul forebodes that my dreams will not be altogether permanently hidden in uncertainty; for this young man exhibits an appearance of wisdom, by which he will be able to reveal the truth, and, as it were, dissipate the darkness by light, and the ignorance of the sophists at our court by his knowledge," And then he related to him his dream.

(107) But Joseph, without being at all dismayed at the rank and majesty of the speaker, conversed with him rather as a king with a subject than like a subject with a king, using freedom of speech, though mingled with respect, and he said: "God has shown you before what he is about to do in your country. Do not imagine that the two visions which have appeared to thee are two different dreams; they are but one and the reduplication of them is not superfluous, but is intended to produce the conviction of a firmer belief; (108) for the seven fat oxen, and the seven flourishing and vigorous ears of corn, show seven years of great fertility and plenty; and the seven lean and ill-favoured oxen which came up after the fat ones, and the seven withered and shrivelled ears of corn, denote seven other years of famine; (109) therefore the first period of seven years thus denoted will arrive first, having great and abundant fertility of crops, in which the river will every year overflow all the land of Egypt with inundations, and all the plains, as if they had never been irrigated or fertilised before.

"And after these years there will come a period of seven years entirely contrary to them bringing with it a terrible want and scarcity of necessary things, during which time the river will not overflow, nor will the earth be fertilised, so that it will forget its former prosperity, and so that all that was left from the former abundance of the crops will be consumed.

(110) "This then is the interpretation of the dreams which have appeared to you. But there is something divine which prompts me and communicates some suggestions to me which may be salutary in this disease; and the most terrible disease of all cities and countries is famine, which must be checked or mitigated to some degree that it may not be so exceedingly strong as to devour the inhabitants; (111) how then can it be mitigated? That which shall be more than sufficient of the crop

in the seven years, during which the plenty lasts, after having taken so much as is adequate to the nourishment of the people, and that will be perhaps a fifth part, must be stored up in granaries in the cities and villages, not removing the crops to any great distance, but storing them in the countries to which they belong, and keeping them there for the relief of the people who dwell in each district; (112) and it will be well to bring together the crop with the sheaves, not thrashing it out, nor winnowing, nor sifting it at all, for four reasons.

"First of all, because if it is thus protected by the straw it will remain uninjured a longer time; secondly, in order that every year the people may be reminded of the former period of plenty while they are threshing and winnowing; for the imitation of the former real blessings is calculated to produce a second pleasure; (113) thirdly, in order to prevent any exact calculation of the quantity stored up, as, while the crop is in the ear and in the sheaf, it is of uncertain amount and not easily to be described; that so the hearts of the people of the land may not faint beforehand at the consumption of what has been treasured up, but may use with cheerfulness the nourishment of the corn which is thus provided for them, (for hope is of all things the most strengthening), and so many to a certain extent feel relief in the bitter disease of scarcity; fourthly, because in this way fodder may also be provided for the cattle, as the straw and the chaff derived from the threshing of the wheat will be of use to them in this way.

(114) And you must appoint a man to superintend all these measures, of great prudence, and great acuteness, and well approved in all matters, who may be able without incurring hatred or envy to do all that I have here described in a proper manner, without giving to the multitude any reason to suspect the impending famine; for it would be a sad thing for them to anticipate their distress, and so to faint in their souls through despair; (115) and if any one should inquire the reason of all this being done, the superintendent may say that, as in peace it is right to provide things that may be necessary in war, so also it is desirable in years of plenty to provide against want; and that wars and famine are in their nature uncertain, and in short so are all the different events which befell men unexpectedly at different times; for which therefore it is necessary to be prepared; and not when such things have befallen one, then to seek a remedy when it is no longer of any avail."

XXI. (116) And when the king had heard these words, and had seen that the interpretation of the dreams did thus with felicity and accuracy of conjecture arrive at the truth, and that the advice which the young man gave appeared to be of exceeding use in the way of providing against the uncertainty of the future, he ordered those who were about him to approach nearer so that they might hear what he said; and then he spoke as follows: Can we, O men, find any man equal to this man who has the spirit of God resting on him? (117) And when they all praised his words, and raised their voices in accordance with them, he looked upon Joseph as he was standing before him and said: The man whom you advise me to seek out is near at hand; the wise and intelligent man whom we have need of is at no great distance; you yourself are he whom, in accordance with our recommendation, we ought to seek for, for you do not appear to me to have been inspired by anything short of God himself, when you said what you have now said to me. Go then, and take the superintendence of my household and the government of all Egypt; (118) and no one will blame my indifference or easiness, as if I were yielding to indolence and selfish love of ease, under this calamity so difficult to be remedied; for great natures are often tested without requiring a long time for their examination, compelling men by their intrinsic weight and power to be rapid, and to discard all delay in receiving them, and some affairs do not admit to any delay or procrastination when the occasions compel us to necessary promptness of action.

(119) After speaking thus, Pharaoh appointed Joseph his lieutenant in the kingdom, or rather, if one is to speak the exact truth, actual king, leaving to himself only the name of kingly power; but in reality yielding up the whole sovereignty to him, and behaving in every respect so as to confer honour on the young man. (120) Therefore he gave him a royal seal, and a sacred robe, and a golden circlet to go round his neck, and he made him to ride in the second chariot which he had, and commanded him in that state to go round the city, a herald also going round with him, and announcing his appointment to those who were ignorant of it. (121) Moreover, he changed his name with reference to his interpretation of dreams, giving him an appellation according to the language of the country, and he gave him for his wife the most beautiful and noble of all the women of Egypt, the daughter of the priest of the sun.

These things happened when Joseph was about thirty years of age. (122) And such is the end of pious persons; for, even if they stumble they do not wholly fall, but rise again after an interval, and are re-established in a firm and solid manner, so as not to be completed prostrated. (123) For who would ever have expected that in one day the same man would become a master from having been a slave, and from having been a prisoner would rise up the most illustrious of men, and that the under turnkey of the keeper of the prison would become the king's lieutenant, and that he would dwell in the king's palace instead of in the gaol, having the highest honour in the whole land instead of being held in the greatest disrepute? (124) Neverthe-

less these things really did come to pass, and similar things often will come to pass when it seems good to God. Only let there be one single spark of excellence and virtue implanted in the soul, and that must some day or other be fanned into a flame and shine forth.

XXII. (125) But since we have prospered to ourselves to give not only an explanation of the literal account given to us, but also of its more figurative meaning, we must say what is necessary to be said concerning that also. Perhaps now some persons of rash and inconsiderate dispositions will laugh; nevertheless, I will speak without concealing anything. And I will say that the statesman is at all times an interpreter of dreams, not classing him by this statement among the charlatans and vain chatterers, and men who put forth sophistical pretences by way of making money, or among those who profess the explanation of visions which have appeared to persons in their sleep in the hope of acquiring gain; but I mean that the statesman is accustomed to interpret accurately the great, and common, and universal general dreams, not only of sleeping but also of waking persons.

(126) And this dream, to speak the truth, is the life of man; for as in the visions which appear to us in sleep, which seeing we do not see, and hearing we do not hear, and tasting and touching we do not either taste or touch, and speaking we do not speak, and walking we do not walk, and while appearing to exert other motions or to win other positions we are not in reality in any such motions or positions; but they are mere empty fancies without any truth in them of the mind which fancies to itself a sketch, and makes to itself a representation of things which are not, as if they were; and in like manner the fancies which occur to waking people resemble the dreams of sleepers. They have come, they have departed; they have appeared, they have disappeared; before they could be scarcely comprehended they have flown away. (127) And let every one who dreams in this way inquire within himself and he will find a proof of these things within, and without any proofs from me he will know the truth of what I say, especially if he happens to be at all an old man. He was at one time an infant, and after that a child, and then a boy, and then a youth, and subsequently a young man, and then a man, and last of all an old man, (128) but he was not all these things at the same time. Did not the infant disappear before the child, and the child before the boy, and the boy before the youth, and the youth before the young man, and the young man before the full-grown man, and the man in the prime of life before the old man? and did not old age disappear in death? (129) Perhaps, also, every one of the different ages of life yields in vigour to the one which comes next to it, and so dies before its time, nature by these means teaching us not to fear the death which

comes upon all men, inasmuch as we have found it easy to bear the previous deaths, the death that is of the infant, and that of the child, and that of the boy, and that of the youth, and that of the young man, and that of the full grown man, not one of whom exist any longer when old age has arrived.

XXIII. (130) And are not all the other things, relating to the body, dreams? Is not beauty an ephemeral thing, wasting away almost before it comes to its prime? And is not health an unsure thing by reason of the wickednesses which lie in wait to upset it? Again, is not strength a thing easily destroyed by diseases arising from innumerable causes? and is not the accuracy of all our outward senses easily overturned by the entrance of any vicious humour? (131) As to external things, who is there who is ignorant of the uncertainty of them? In one day vast riches have often come absolutely to nothing. Numbers of persons who have been of the highest consideration, and who have enjoyed the highest honours that the earth affords, have come into disrepute from causes which they neglected or despised. The most mighty powers and authority of kings have been overthrown, and have disappeared in a very brief moment of time.

(132) There is an example to testify to the truth of my argument in Dionysius, who lived at Corinth, who had been tyrant of Sicily, and who, after he was expelled from his dominions, took refuge in Corinth; and though he had been so mighty a sovereign, became a schoolmaster. (133) There is another witness to the same point in Croesus, the king of Lydia, the wealthiest of all monarchs, who, having conceived the hope of destroying the kingdom of the Persians, not only lost all his men, but was taken prisoner, and was at the point of being burnt alive. (134) And there are witnesses of dreams not only among men, but also among cities, and nations, and countries; Greece is such, and the region of the barbarians, and inhabitants of continents, and islanders, and Europe and Asia, and the west, and the east; for absolutely nothing whatever has ever remained in its original condition; but everything has in every particular been subject to change. (135) Egypt had once the supreme authority over many nations, but now it is a slave. The Macedonians at one time were so flourishing and powerful that they had obtained the supreme dominion over the whole world; but now they pay yearly tribute, which is levied on them by their masters, to the collectors of the revenue.

(136) Where is the house of the Ptolemies, and the glory of all the individual successors of Alexander which at one time shone over all the bounds both of earth and sea? Where is the liberty of so many independent nations and cities? On the other hand, where is the slavery of those which were subject to them? Did not the Persians at one time reign over the Parthians? and do not

the Parthians now, through the changes of human affairs, and through the extraordinary and total alterations which are continually taking place, rule over the Persians? (137) Some persons flatter themselves with ideas of long and interminable prosperity; but they find that their good fortune is only the beginning of great calamities; and hastening forward as if to an inheritance of good things, they find instead, terrible reverses; and on the contrary it has often happened, that when they have expected evil fortune they have met with good.

(138) Athletes, who have prided themselves on their personal good condition, and power, and vigour of body, and who have hoped to obtain an indisputable victory, have often been either refused permission to contend for the prize at all, not having been approved of, or else, after they have descended into the arena, they have been defeated; while others who have despaired of arriving even at the second honours, have been crowned with the garland of victory, and have carried off the first prize.

(139) Again, some persons setting sail in the summer (for that is the season for fair voyages) have been shipwrecked; while others, who have expected to be overwhelmed by reason of being forced to put to sea, have reached their harbour uninjured, without having even incurred any danger. As some merchants hasten forward as if to confessed gain, being ignorant of the losses which are awaiting them; while others who have anticipated losses, have in effect met with great profits—(140) so very uncertain is fortune on either side, whether for good or evil; and human affairs are as it were, weighed in a scale, being lightened or depressed according as the weights in each scale are unequal. And a terrible indistinctness and dense darkness is spread over human affairs. And we wander about as if in a deep sleep, without being able to arrive at anything with perfect accuracy of reasoning, or to seize hold of anything with a firm and retentive grasp; for all things are like shadows and phantoms.

(141) And as in processions, what comes first passes by quickly and escapes the sight; and as in torrents, the stream which is hurried by outruns, by its swiftness and rapidity, the comprehension of man, so likewise do the affairs of life, being rapidly borne onwards, and passing by swiftly, appear indeed to be stationary, but in fact, do not stand still a moment, but are continually being dragged onwards. (142) And men awake too, who, as far as the uncertain character of their comprehensions goes, are in no respect different from people asleep, deceiving themselves, think themselves competent to contemplate the nature of things with reasoning powers which cannot err; in whose case every one of their external senses is a hindrance to knowledge, being hurried by spectacles, and by

peculiarities of flavours or odours, to which they incline, and by which they are perverted, and in consequence of which they prevent any part of the soul from being in a sound state, and from advancing without stumbling as if along a level road. And humble pride, and great littleness, and all other similar states which are made up of inequality and anomaly, compel men to walk in a sort of giddiness, and create great dizziness and perplexity.

XXIV. (143) Since, then, life is full of all this irregularity, and confusion, and indistinctness, it is necessary that the statesman as well as the philosopher should approach the science of the interpretation of dreams, so as to understand the dreams and visions which appear by day to people who believe themselves to be awake, being guided by probable conjectures and rational probabilities, and in this way he must explain each separate one, and show that such and such a thing is honourable, another disgraceful, that this is good or that is bad; that this thing is just, that thing is on the contrary unjust; and so on in the same way with respect to prudence, and courage, and piety, and holiness, and expediency, and usefulness; and in like manner of the opposite things, with respect to what was not useful nor reasonable, what was ignoble, impious, unholy, inexpedient, pernicious, and selfish.

(144) Moreover, he warns you in this way: is this something belonging to another? do not covet it. Is it your own? use it as not using it. Have you great abundance? share it with others; for the beauty of riches is not in the purse, but in the power it gives one to succour those who are in need. Have you but little? do not envy those who have much; no one will pity a poor man who is always envious. Are you in high reputation, and are you held in much honour? be not insolent on that account. Are you lowly in your fortunes? still let not your spirit be depressed. Does everything succeed with you according to your wish? fear a change. Do you often stumble? hope for good fortune hereafter; for the change of human affairs are apt to be in a direction opposite to the course they have formerly taken.

(145) The moon and the sun, indeed, and the whole of the heaven have clearness bright and distinct, inasmuch as all things are alike which exist permanently in the heaven; and as they are all measured by the rules of truth itself, in harmonious order and in the most admirable agreement. But as for earthly things, which are full of great disorder and confusion, they are inharmonious and discordant, to speak with perfect correctness, so that dense darkness has overtaken some of them, while others resemble the most brilliant light, or rather they are themselves the clearest and purest of light.

(146) If, therefore, any one should wish to look closely into the nature of things, he will find that heaven is everlasting day, free from all participation in night or in any kind of shade, inasmuch as it is surrounded uninterruptedly by a brilliant display of inextinguishable and unadulterated light. (147) And in the same proportion as among us those who are awake are superior to those who are asleep, so also in the universal world the things of heaven are superior to the things of earth; since the one enjoys an everlasting wakefulness which knows no sleep, on account of its energies which never stray, and never stumble, and which proceed rightly and successfully in every thing; while the others are oppressed by sleep, and if they wake up for a short time they are again pulled down and buried in slumber; because they are unable to look steadfastly and correctly at any thing with their souls, but are always straying and stumbling. For they are overshadowed by false opinions, by which they are compelled to submit to dreams, and are always behind the real truth, and are unable to comprehend any thing with a firm and tenacious grasp.

XXV. (148) Moreover, Joseph is figuratively said to have been mounted upon the second best chariot which the king had, for the following reason. The statesman stands in the second rank next to the king; for he is not a private individual nor a king, but some one on the confines between the two. Being indeed superior to a private individual, and inferior in respect of authority to an absolute and independent king, having the people for his king; on behalf of whom he had determined to do every thing with a pure and perfectly guileless good faith; (149) and he is borne as it were on high in a well-built chariot, being lifted on high both by the things committed to his charge and by the people, and especially so when he contains in his mind every thing, whether small or great, without any one ever opposing or resisting him, but all being cheerfully governed by him under God to their own safety like sailors enjoying a fair voyage.

And the ring which the king gives him is the most manifest proof of confidence which the people, his king, places in the statesman, and also of that trust with which the statesman relies on the people which is as powerful as a king. (150) And the golden circlet round his neck appears to indicate figuratively both high reputation and punishment at the same moment. For as long as all the affairs which concern the administration of the state proceed prosperously as far as he is concerned, he is proud, and is looked upon with veneration, and is honoured by the multitudes. But the moment that any unforeseen mishap occurs to him, not indeed intended, for such error deserves reproach, but arising from pure chance, which always deserves pardon, he is not the less dragged downwards by the ornament around his neck, and is humbled, his master all but saying to him in plain words, "I, indeed, gave you this circlet to be around thy neck, to be both an ornament while my affairs were going on well, and a halter when they were proceeding unfavourably."

XXVI. (151) Moreover, I have also heard people discussing this passage with great apparent accuracy in a more figurative manner and according to quite a different interpretation. And their notion of it is this.

They say that the king of Egypt means our mind: the governor of the region of the body in every individual in us, and who like a king claims the supreme power. (152) And by him when he has become devoted to the service of the body three objects are especially laboured at as being accounted worthy of exceeding care, namely, meat, and sweetmeats, and drinkables. With reference to which fact he also employs three persons to superintend the objects aforesaid, his chief baker, and his chief butler, and his chief cook. The one of whom presides over those things which relating to eating, the second over those things which belong to drinking, and the last to those sweetenings and sauces which belong to the confections. (153) And they are all eunuchs; because the man who is devoted to pleasure is barren and unproductive of every thing which is most necessary, such as modesty, temperance, continence, justice, and every kind of virtue. For there is no one thing so hostile to another as pleasure is to virtue, for the sake of which most people neglect all those matters which alone it is worth while to attend to, gratifying their unrestrained appetites, and submitting to all the commands which they impose upon them.

(154) Therefore, the chief cook is not committed to prison at all, nor does he fall into any misfortune, because his sauces and sweetenings are not among the things which are very necessary, not being pleasures but only provocations to pleasure, such as are easily extinguished. But of the two who are occupied in the employment of the miserable belly, the chief baker and the chief butler, since eating and drinking are of all the things which are useful to life those which have the greatest power to keep the being together, and those who have the management of those things, if they bestow great care upon them, do very justly obtain praise; while, if they neglect them, they are thought worthy of anger or punishment.

(155) But there is a difference in their punishments, because the need of the two things is different; that of food being the most indispensable, but that of wine not being very useful; for men can live without any wine, using only the pure drink of spring water. (156) On which account there is a reconciliation made with, and pardon bestowed upon, the chief butler, as upon one who has erred in the least important particular. But the offences of the chief baker admit of no reconciliation and of no forgiveness, but incur an anger which leads

to death, as he has been guilty of wrong in the most necessary matters; for want of food is followed by death. On which account he who has erred on these points very appropriately is put to death by hanging, suffering an evil similar to that which he has inflicted; for he also has hanged, and suffocated, and stretched out the famishing man by means of hunger.

XXVII. (157) This is enough to say on this subject. Accordingly Joseph, being appointed the king's lieutenant, and having undertaken the government and superintendence of the whole of Egypt, went forth in order to become acquainted with all the natives, and investigated all the laws that were established in the different cities, and caused a great affection for himself to arise in the breasts of those who saw him, not only because of the services which he conferred upon every one of them, but also by the unspeakable and unrivalled graces of his appearance and by the courtesy with which he associated with them. (158) But when, in accordance with the interpretation of the dreams, the first seven years of fertility arrived, he collected one-fifth of the produce every year by means of his subordinate officers and others who were employed under him in the public offices, and by this means he collected such a vast quantity of sheaves of corn as no one recollected as having ever existed at any previous time. And the most evident proof of this is that they could not possibly be counted, even although thousands and thousands of persons were occupied in the task, whose sole business it was to devote all their energies to count them.

(159) And when these seven years had passed, during which the plain of Egypt was fertile, the famine began, which, as it proceeded and increased, was not confined to Egypt; for as it became diffused, and from time to time extended, so as to be always comprehending fresh cities and countries in succession, it reached to the farthest borders of the land, both in the eastern and western direction, so as to reach at last over the whole world all around. (160) Accordingly, it is said that no general pestilence ever extended so widely, not even that which the sons of the physicians call "the creeping pestilence;" for that also attacks all parts at once, and proceeding onwards rapidly like fire, utterly and completely devours the whole mass of the ulcerated body. (161) Accordingly, they selected the men of the highest reputation in every district, and sent them into Egypt to procure corn; for already the prudence of the young man was celebrated in all quarters, who had thus provided abundant food against a time of necessity. (162) And he at first commanded all the treasure-houses to be opened, calculating that he should make the people more cheerful when they had beheld the store that was provided, and that in some degree he should be feeding their souls rather than their

bodies on good hopes. After that, by means of those to whom the office of regulating the distribution of corn was committed, he sold it to all who wished to buy, keeping a constant eye on the future, and seeing that what was impending even more clearly than the present.

XXVIII. (163) And at this crisis, his father also,[2] since his necessary food had by this time become scarce, not being aware of the good fortune of his son, sent ten of his sons to buy food, keeping the youngest at home, who was the uterine and own brother of the king's lieutenant. (164) And they, when they had arrived in Egypt, met their brother as if he were a stranger, and being amazed at the dignity with which they beheld him surrounded, they addressed him with prostration according to the ancient fashion, the dreams now receiving confirmation and fulfilment. (165) And he, when he beheld those who had sold him, immediately recognised them all, though he was not in the least recognised by any one of them himself, since God was not yet willing to reveal the truth on account of some necessary causes which at that time it was better should be buried in silence; and therefore he either altered the countenance of their brother who governed the country, so as to give him a more dignified appearance, or else he perverted the accurate judgment of the mind of those who beheld him.

(166) But he acted not like a young man who, being the lieutenant and magistrate invested with such extensive powers, and having attained to the authority next to that of the king himself, to whom the east and west looked up, and elated with the pride of manhood and the vastness of his authority, might now that the opportunity of revenge had presented itself, have shown his remembrance of the ill-treatment which he had received; but he bore what happened with self-restraint, and governed his own soul, and with great prudence feigned a perfect ignorance of and strangeness to them, and both by his looks, and by his voice, and by all the rest of his behaviour he pretended to be displeased at them. He said to them, "My men, you say nothing peaceful; but some one of the king's enemies has sent you forth as spies, and you, performing a base service for him, have expected to escape detection. But nothing that is done treacherously does escape detection, even if it be enveloped in profound darkness."

(167) And when they endeavoured to make excuses for themselves, they argued that he was accusing them of what had never taken place, for that they had not come from a hostile people, and that they were not themselves imbued with any unfriendly feelings toward the people of the country, and that they could never have been induced to undertake such an office as that of spies, for that they were by nature men of peace, and that they had learnt, almost from their childhood, from a most holy, and pious, and religious father, to honour stability and tranquillity; and that their father was a man who had had twelve sons, the youngest of whom, as he was not yet of an age to bear a long journey, was remaining at home, while we, whom you see here are ten more, and the remaining is not.

XXIX. When he heard this, and heard those who had sold him all speak of him as dead, what think you did Joseph feel in his soul? (168) for even if he did not utter the feelings which then encompassed him, still they unquestionably were burning within his breast, and exciting, and kindling strange emotions within him; nevertheless, with deep wisdom and humanity does he address them, saying, "If, in good truth, you have not come hither to spy the land, then, in order to prove your good faith to me, remain here some short period, and write a letter and send for your youngest brother, and let him come to you; (169) or if, for your father's sake, you are anxious to depart, lest he perchance may be alarmed at your protracted absence, in that case depart all the rest of you, but let one of you remain behind as a hostage, until you return again with your youngest brother; and if you do not obey, then the most terrible death shall be your punishment."

(170) He then threatened them in this manner, looking sternly at them, and giving them every sign of violent anger, as far as appearances could go, and so he left them. But they, being full of consciousness and depression, afflicted themselves for their former treachery towards their brother, saying, "That wickedness which we committed is the cause of all our present evils, since justice, which takes the regulation of all human affairs, is now contriving some punishment for us; for having been quiet for a short time it is now awakened, displaying its nature, which is at all times relentless and implacable towards those who are deserving of punishment, and how can we deny that we are deserving of it? (171) We in a merciless manner disregarded our brother when he besought us and supplicated us, though he had done no wrong, but had only, in the fulness of his natural affection, related to us, as to his nearest relations, the visions which had appeared to him in sleep; for which cause we, the most brutal and savage of men, became enraged, and committed (for we must not now deny the truth) most impious actions; (172) therefore let us now expect to suffer these things and even worse, we who, though we are almost the only men in the whole world who are called noble by birth, by reason of the exceeding virtues of our fathers, and grandfathers, and ancestors, have nevertheless disgraced our kin-

---

[2]Genesis 42:1.

dred, hastening to cover ourselves with notorious infamy."

(173) But the eldest of the brethren, who also at the very beginning had opposed them when they were originally concocting their treachery, said to them, "Repentance is useless after the thing has been done; I exhorted you, I entreated you, pointing out to you how enormous the impiety you were meditating was, I begged you not to indulge your passion; but though you ought to have assented to me, you yielded to your own inconsiderate folly; (174) therefore, we now are reaping the fruit of your self-will and impiety, and now the treachery which we exercised towards him is required at our hands; and he who requires it is not man, but either God, or reason, or the law of God."

XXX. (175) The brother whom they had sold heard them conversing in this manner without saying anything himself, as he had hitherto spoken to them by an interpreter. And being overcome by his feelings, he was unable to restrain his tears, and turned away that he might not be seen by them, and pouring forth hot and incessant tears, and so, having relieved himself for a short time, he wiped his eyes and returned to them, and commanded the second in age of the brothers to be bound in the sight of them all, since he, as it were, corresponded to himself, who was the youngest but one; for in a large number the second corresponds to the last but one, as the first does to the last. (176) Perhaps, too, he bound him because the greatest share of the guilt belonged to him, as he was almost the original author of the plot against him, and as it was he who excited the others to the enmity which they displayed against him; for if he had arrayed himself on the side of the eldest when he gave his merciful and humane counsel, being younger than he, but older than all the rest, perhaps, and indeed most probably, the iniquity would have been checked, in consequence of those who had the highest rank and honour agreeing and co-operating together in the matter, which fact would have carried great weight with it; (177) but now, he, departing from the merciful and more excellent side of the question, went over to the unmerciful and cruel one, and putting himself forward as the leader of it, he in this way encouraged those who were inclined to join him in his audacious action, so that they unshrinkingly carried out their nefarious purpose.

This is the reason why he appears to me to have been selected from the whole body for the purpose of being bound. (178) But the others now prepared for their return home, since the governor of the country had given charge to the officers to whom the sale of the wheat was entrusted to fill all the bags of his brothers, as though they had been strangers, and privily to replace in the mouths of their sacks the money which they had brought, without mentioning to any one that they had so restored it; and in the third place, to give them also abundant food which might be sufficient, and more than sufficient for them, on the way, in order that the corn which they had bought might be conveyed undiminished to their father.

(179) But while they were on their way, and expressing, as was natural, their compassion for their brother who was in prison, and being equally grieved also for their father's sake at this second calamity which he was to hear of, his flourishing family of children being thus diminished and curtailed at every journey, and saying that he would never believe that he was kept in prison, because those who had been once stricken with misfortune are always dreading a repetition of the same calamity, evening overtook them, and having relieved their beasts of their burdens, they lightened them, but received themselves heavier anxiety than ever in their minds; for in times of rest to the body, the mind receives the impression made by unexpected events more readily, so as to be very severely weighed down and oppressed by them.

XXXI. (180) For one of them, having opened one of the sacks, saw in the mouth of it his purse full of money; and when he had counted it, he found the whole price which he had paid down for the corn restored to him; and being amazed, he brought it to his brothers; and they, not imagining that it was meant as a favour to them, but rather, suspecting that it was a plot against them, were in great despondency (181) and wishing to examine all their sacks, set off again for fear of being pursued, and made all imaginable speed, almost, as one may say, running without stopping to take breath, and so they completed a journey which should have taken many days, in a short time. (182) Then, one after another embracing their father, with copious tears, they all clung to him, and kissed him; and while he returned their embraces, although his soul speedily began to forebode some new calamity, for while they were thus approaching and saluting him he perceived the absence of the son who was left behind, and in his own mind blamed him for his slowness in being behind the others; for he was looking at them as they came in, being anxious to behold the number of his children complete.

(183) But when no one from without came in besides, they, seeing that he was in a state of agitated suspense, said, "O my father! doubt is worse than even the certain knowledge of unexpected calamities; for when one is certainly apprised of such, one may discover a road to safety: but ignorance and doubt are the cause of error and perplexity; listen then, to the sad story which we have to tell, but which still must be told.

(184) "The brother whom you sent along with us to buy corn, and who has not returned with us, is alive; for we must release you from the more

terrible apprehension that he may be dead; but he is alive, and is remaining in Egypt with the governor of the country, who, whether it be from any false accusation which has been laid against us, or from any suspicion which he has himself conceived, charged us with being spies. (185) And when we said all that the time would allow us to say in our defence, and mentioned you as being our father, and the brothers who were not of our company, one of them being dead, and the other remaining with you, who we said tarried behind at home on account of his age, inasmuch as he was still a child, making known and revealing to him all the circumstances of our family by reason of our absence of all suspicion, we availed nothing; but he said, that the only proof that could be given him of our truth and honesty would be the coming of our youngest brother to see him; for which reason he also detained the second of us, as a pledge and surety for his coming. (186) Therefore his command is most grievous to us. But the occasion is also more imperious than even his command, which we must necessarily submit to from our want of necessaries, since Egypt is the only country which can supply us, who are thus oppressed by famine, with necessary food."

XXXII. (187) But he, groaning most bitterly, said, "Whom shall I lament first? the youngest but one, who was not the last, but the first to encounter the series of disasters which has befallen our family? or the second, on whom the second evil has fallen, namely, captivity, which is only inferior in misery to death? or the youngest, who is now to undertake that most detestable journey, since go he must, without being warned by the calamities which have befallen his brethren? and I, torn to pieces as to all my limbs and all my parts (for children are the limbs of their parents), am in danger of becoming utterly childless who was so short a time ago accounted happy in the number and excellence of my children."

(188) But the eldest replied, "I gave you my two sons as hostages, the only children that I have, slay them if I bring not back again to you, safe and sound, the brother whom you entrust to my hand, and who, by his visit to Egypt, will effect two things of the greatest importance for us; first, he will give a most evident proof that we are not spies and enemies; and, secondly, he will enable us to recover our brother, whom we have left in captivity."

(189) But as his father was much grieved and said that he did not know what to do, because while he had but two sons of one mother, one of them was now dead, and the other was left desolate and almost alone, so that he dreaded the journey, and though alive would die from fear before he could accomplish it, from a recollection of those fearful events which his elder brother had encountered; while he was speaking thus, the brethren put forward as their spokesman him who was the bold-

est among them, and by nature inclined to take the lead, and who was eloquent in speech, and he said what seemed good to them all; (190) for they agreed, as their necessary food was falling short, for the corn which they had previously bought was now exhausted, and as the famine was again pressing upon and overwhelming them, to go for more in one united body, but not to go at all if the youngest still remained behind; because the governor of the country had forbidden them to appear before him without him.

(191) And their father, calculating like a wise man that it was better to expose one son to the uncertain and doubtful danger of the future, than to encounter the certain loss of so large a family, which the whole house must endure if they continued to be overwhelmed by the present scarcity, that most incurable of diseases, says to them, (192) "But if the necessity which presses upon us is more powerful than my wishes, we must yield: for perhaps, perhaps I say, nature may be devising something better which she does not choose as yet to reveal to our minds. (193) Depart, therefore, taking with you your youngest brother as you have determined; but do not go in the same manner as ye went before. For formerly you had only need of money to buy corn, since no one knew you, and since you had not at that time suffered any intolerable calamity. But now you require presents also; for three reasons. First of all, to propitiate the governor and dispenser of corn, to whom you say that you are known. Secondly, in order that so you may the more speedily recover him who is held in captivity, by thus paying down a large ransom for him. And thirdly, for the sake of as far as possible removing any idea of your being spies. (194) Therefore, taking presents of all that our land supplies, offer them to the man as a kind of first fruits, and take double money, both that which you paid before, for perhaps it was restored to you through the oversight of some one, and also another sum sufficient to buy corn; (195) and take with you also my prayer, which we offer to God our Saviour, that you who are strangers may go acceptably to the natives of the country, and that you may return in safety, giving back to your father those necessary pledges, his children, and bringing back the brother whom you have left in bondage, and also the youngest, as yet unacquainted with trouble, whom you are now taking with you." And so they took their departure and hastened towards Egypt.

XXXIII. (196) Then a few days afterwards they arrived in Egypt, and when the governor of the country saw them he was greatly pleased, and ordered the steward of his house to prepare a sumptuous dinner, and to bring the men in that they might partake of his salt and of his table. (197) And when they were brought in to dinner they were in a state of great suspense, as not knowing what would be done with them, and were in confusion, suspecting that they might perhaps have a false accusation of theft brought against them on the ground of their having taken away the price of the corn that they had bought and which they had found in their sacks, as if they had done so wilfully. So then they came up to the steward of the house, and made a defence on a subject on which no one ventured to accuse them, purging their consciences, and, at the same time, displaying the money which they had brought back and offering to return it. (198) But he cheered them with favourable and humane language, saying, "There is no one so impious as to found a false accusation on the graces of God, who is all-merciful. He it is who has rained treasures into your sacks, giving you not only food but also riches out of his abundant store." (199) So they being comforted, then arranged in order the presents which they had brought from home to display them to the governor. And when the master of the house came in they offered them to him. (200) And when he had inquired of them how they were, and whether their father, of whom they had previously spoken, was still alive, they answered nothing concerning themselves, but concerning their father they replied that he was alive and well. And when he had prayed for him, and addressed them in the most favourable and God-fearing manner, looking upon his brother by the same mother, when he saw him he could not restrain his tears, but being now overcome by his feelings, he turned himself about before he made himself known to them, and going out on a pretext as if some urgent cause compelled him (for it was not a favourable opportunity for him to tell them the truth), he wept in a secret chamber of his house and poured forth abundance of tears.

XXXIV. (201) Then when he had washed his hands he restrained his sorrow by the power of reason, and coming back again he feasted the strangers, returning to them the brother who had come with them before, and who had been kept as a hostage for the appearance of the youngest. And with them there also feasted others of the nobles of the Egyptians. (202) And the manner of their entertainment was to each party in accordance with their national customs, since Joseph thought it wrong to overturn ancient laws, and especially at a banquet where the pleasures should be more numerous than the annoyances. (203) And as he commanded them all to sit down in order according to their age, as the men had not yet learnt the fashion of lying down on occasions of banqueting, they marvelled to see whether the Egyptians would adopt the same habits as the Hebrews, having a regard to regular order, and knowing how to distinguish between the honours due to the eldest and the youngest. (204) Perhaps, too, they thought this man who manages all

the common business of the house, because the country has hitherto been less refined in matters relating to eating, has now not only introduced regularity and good order into great matters, by which the affairs of peace and war are accustomed to be brought to a successful issue, but also into those things which are usually accounted of less importance, most of which, indeed, refer mainly to amusement. For the object of banquets is cheerfulness, and they do not at all allow the guests to be too solemn and austere-looking.

(205) While they were praising the arrangements of the feast in this quiet way, tables are brought indeed, of no great costliness or luxury, as, by reason of the famine, their host did not think it proper to revel too much amid the distresses of others; and they, like men of sense and understanding, praised this part of his conduct also, because he had thus avoided an unseemly magnificence, which is a thing calculated to provoke envy, saying that he was maintaining the character at the same time of one who sympathised with the needy, and also of a liberal entertainer, placing himself between the two, and avoiding all cause for blaming him in either particular. (206) Therefore his preparations for the entertainment escaped all ill-will being suited to the time, and what was wanting was made up by continual cheerfulness, and by pledging one another in wine, and by good wishes, and by exhortations to eat what there was, which to persons of gentlemen-like and accomplished minds was more pleasant than all the sumptuous dishes and liquors which men fond of eating and of epicurism provide for eating and drinking, which are in reality deserving of no serious care, but by which they do in truth display their little-mindedness with great pomp.

XXXV. (207) And on the next day he sent, the first thing in the morning, for the steward of his household, and commanded him to fill all the sacks of the men which they had brought with them with corn, and a second time to put back in the mouths of their sacks the price which they had brought with them, and to put in the sack of the youngest the most beautiful of his silver cups out of which he himself was accustomed to drink; (208) and he cheerfully did as he was commanded, taking care that no one was a witness of his actions. And they, not knowing any of the things which had been done thus secretly, departed, rejoicing in all the good fortune which had befallen them beyond all their expectations; (209) for what they had expected was this, to have a false accusation laid against them, as if they had stolen the money which has been restored to them, and never to recover their brother whom they had left as a hostage, and perhaps also, besides that, to lose their youngest brother who would be seized upon by force by the man who had been so determined that he should be brought.

(210) But what has happened to them was better than their most sanguine prayers, since, in addition to having no false accusations laid against them, they had also been admitted to the bread and salt of the governor, which among all men is a token of genuine friendship, and had also recovered their brother without having received any injury, without having had recourse to the intercession and entreaty of any mediator, and were also taking back their youngest brother in safety to their father, having escaped all suspicion of being spies, and bearing with them an abundant quantity of food, and having good and well-founded hopes for the future, for they thought that even if necessary food was repeatedly to fail them, they should never again themselves be in exceeding want as before, but might return joyfully to the governor of the country as to a friend and not a stranger.

XXXVI. (211) But while they were feeling disposed in this way, and revolving such thoughts in their souls, a sudden and unexpected confusion came upon them, for the steward of the household, being commanded to do so, ran after them as if to attack them, bringing with him a vast multitude of servants, waving his hands, and making signs to them to stop, (212) and then coming up to them out of breath he said, "You have now set the seal to all the accusations that have been brought against you; you have returned evil for good, and turned back upon the same road of iniquity as before; you have not only stolen and carried off the price of the corn, but you have committed even a greater offence than that, for wickedness which has obtained forgiveness gets more shameless; (213) you, you very grateful and very peaceful men, have stolen the most beautiful and most valuable drinking cup belonging to my master, the very cup in which he pledged you; you who did not even know what was meant by the name of spy, and who brought back double money to restore that which you had previously paid and professed to have found in your sacks,—a trick, as it should seem, and a bait to enable you to catch and snare a more valuable prize; but wickedness does not always prosper, but though always endeavoring to escape notice it is detected."

(214) While he was running on in this way against them they stood motionless and speechless, those most grievous of all evils, sorrow and fear, falling upon them thus suddenly, so that they were unable even to open their mouths, for the advent of unexpected evils makes even those who are eloquent actually speechless; (215) but at length they recovered themselves, and lest they should seem to be silent, because they were self-convicted by their own consciences, they spoke and said, "How shall we reply and defend ourselves, and to whom? for you who are our accuser are going to be our judge also; you, who even if others had accused us ought to have been our advocate from the experience that you have already had of us. The money which on the former occasion we found replaced in our sacks, we brought back again in order to restore it, though no one had convicted us of having received it again, and do you suppose that after that we became so completely changed as to requite our entertainer with injury and theft? This was not so; and never let it enter your mind that we have done any such thing; (216) but whichever of us brethren is found to have the cup let him die the death; for if any such wicked deed has been done there are many reasons why we should suffer death in atonement of it; in the first place, because covetousness and a desire for the property of others is a most wicked thing; secondly, because to attempt to injure those who have done one good is a most impious action; thirdly, because for men who are proud of the nobility of their birth to dare to destroy the reputation of their ancestors by scandalous actions of their own is a most shameful disgrace; and since if any one of us has stolen the cup of the governor he is liable to all these reproaches, let him die as one who has performed actions worthy of ten thousand deaths."

XXXVII. (217) And while speaking thus they unloose the burdens from off their beasts and take them down, and encourage the steward with all diligence to search them, and to look for the cup, and he, not being unaware that it was lying in the sack of the youngest, inasmuch as he himself had secretly placed it there, behaved cunningly, and began with the eldest, and so went on in regular order, taking them according to their ages, and searching, while each willingly brought forward his sack and displayed its contents, till he came to the last, in whose possession the sought-for cup was found, so that they all when they saw it lifted up their voices, and lamented, and rent their clothes, groaning heavily, and shedding tears, and before his execution bewailing their brother while he was still alive, and bewailing also their father no less than him, because he had foretold the calamities which would happen to his son, on which account he was unwilling to permit their brother to travel with them when they wished him to do so.

(218) And being downcast and confused they returned back by the same road to the city, being quite overwhelmed at what had happened, and looking at what had taken place as a plot, and not suspecting their brother of covetousness.

Then when they were brought before the governor of the country they displayed their real affection and brotherly love with genuine feeling, (219) for falling altogether at his knees as if they were all liable to be punished for the theft, a wickedness too great to be mentioned, they all wept over him, and besought him, and gave themselves up to him, and offered to submit to voluntary slavery, and called him their master, speaking of themselves as foreign captives, as slaves, as bought with a price, and omitting no name whatever indicative of the most complete slavery; (220) but he, wishing to try them still more, addressed them in a most angry manner, and with the greatest possible severity, and said to them, "May I never be guilty of such an action as to condemn such a number to captivity for the sin of one, for how can it be right to summon those persons to share in a punishment who have had no share in the commission of the offence? Let him alone be punished, since he alone has committed the crime. (221) I know therefore that by your laws you condemn the man who has been found guilty of theft to be put to death in front of the city; but I, wishing to act in all respects in a gentle and most merciful manner, will mitigate the punishment, and adjudge him to slavery instead of to death."

XXXVIII. (222) And when they were grieved at his threat, and wholly overwhelmed at the false accusations brought against them, the fourth in age, and he was one of a daring character, combined with modesty, and full of true courage, inasmuch as he had studied freedom of speech without impudence, came forward and said, "I entreat you, O master! not to give way to your passion; nor, because you are placed in the rank next to the king, to be in a hurry to condemn us before you have heard our defence. (223) When on our former journey hither, you inquired of us concerning our brother and our father, we answered you: Our father was an old man, aged, not more because of the power of time, than because of his uninterrupted misfortunes, by which he had been constantly exercised like a wrestler, and has passed his whole life amid labours and calamities hard to be borne.

"And our brother is very young, a mere child, loved beyond all measure by his father, since he is the son of his old age, and because also he had but him and one other child by the same mother, and this one alone is left, since the elder died a violent death. (224) And when you commanded us to bring our brother hither, and threatened us that, if he did not come, you would not permit us to come into your sight, we departed in great depression of spirits; and with difficulty, when we had arrived at home, did we declare the commands which we had received from you to our father. (225) And he at first wholly refused, being greatly alarmed for the child; but as necessary food was becoming scarce, and as not one of us dared to come hither to buy food without our youngest brother, by reason of your vehement commands; he was at last, with difficulty, persuaded to send him with us, blaming us bitterly for having confessed that we had another brother, and pitying himself very much for being about to be separated from him; for he is but a child and wholly ignorant of business, and not only of business in a foreign land, but even of such as is transacted in his own city.

(226) "How, then, shall we approach our father who is under the influence of such feelings? And with what eyes shall we be able to behold him without this his youngest son? He will die most miserably if he only hears that his son has not returned; and then all those who delight in hatred and in evil-speaking, and who rejoice in such misfortunes of their neighbours, will call us murderers and parricides, (227) and the greater part of the accusation will fall upon me; for I promised my father to give him up many things, confessing that I received my brother as a pledge, which I was to restore whenever he was re-claimed from me. And how shall I be able to restore him unless you are prevailed upon to show us mercy? I entreat you, then, to have pity on the old man, and to give a thought to the evils by which he will be grieved, if he does not receive back again him whom he has unwisely entrusted to my hands.

(228) "Nevertheless, do you exact punishment for the injuries which you imagine to have been done to you; and that punishment I will volunteer to submit to. Set me down as your slave from this day forth. I will cheerfully undergo the fate of those who have been just bought, if you will only be willing to let the child go free; (229) and not only shall you, if you will give him his liberty, receive thanks from him and me, but also from him who is not present, but who will then be relieved from his anxiety, the father of these men here, and of all the family; for we are all your suppliants, having fled for succour to your right hand, and may we never fail to obtain it.

(230) "Let, then, compassion for the age of the old man seize your heart, who during his whole life has constantly devoted himself to the labours of virtue. He has brought all the cities of Syria to receive him, and to submit to his authority, and to do him honour; even though he guides himself by foreign customs and laws very different from them, and although he is in all respects very unlike the natives of the land. But the excellence of his life, and the consistency and uniformity of his actions with his words, and of his words with his actions, have prevailed, so that he has been able to win over those who, out of regard for their national customs, were not at first well-disposed towards him. (231) You will do him such a favour that it will not be possible for him to receive a greater. For what can be a more valuable gift to a father, than to allow him to receive back a son of whose safety he has despaired?"

XXXIX. (232) But all this conduct was but an experiment, just as the former circumstances had been too, because the governor of the country was desirous to see what kind of good-will they had towards him who was his brother by the same mother. For he had been afraid that they felt some kind of natural dislike towards him, as children of a stepmother often do to the family of a previous wife of their father, who may have been held in equal honours by him. (233) It was with this view that he both reproached them as spies and inquired about their family, for the sake of knowing whether his brother was still alive, or whether he had been put out of the way by treachery. And he retained one while he allowed the rest to depart, after they had agreed to bring back their youngest brother with them, whom he desired to see above all things, and so to be relieved of his bitter and grievous sorrow on his account. (234) And when he arrived, and when he beheld his brother, he was then in a slight degree relieved from his anxiety, and he invited them to an entertainment, and while he was feasting them he regaled his own brother by the same mother with more costly viands and luxuries than the rest, looking carefully at every one of them, and judging from their countenances whether there was any envy secretly cherished in their hearts. (235) And when he saw them all cheerful, and all eager, and earnest for the honour of the youngest, conjecturing now by two strong proofs that there was no hatred smouldering beneath, he devised a third mode of trial likewise, bringing a charge against their youngest brother, that he appeared to have committed a theft; for this was likely to be the clearest possible proof of the disposition of each of them and of the affection which they bore to their brother, who was thus falsely accused.

(236) From all which circumstances he now clearly saw that his mother's offspring was not looked upon with hostile feelings and was not plotted against, and he also received a very probable impression respecting the events which had befallen himself, and learnt to think that he had suffered what he had, not so much because of the treachery of his brethren, as through the direction of the providence of God who sees things afar off, and who beholds the future no less than the present.

XL. (237) After this he had recourse to a reconciliation and agreement with his brethren, being influenced by his own affectionate disposition, and from his desire to cause no shame to his brethren, and to give no cause of reproach against them because of their conduct towards him, he did not choose that any of the Egyptians should be present on the occasion of his first making himself known to them. (238) But he ordered all the servants to leave the apartment, and suddenly pouring forth a stream of tears, and signing to them with his right hand to approach nearer to him, that no one else might be able by chance even to hear any thing that passed, he said unto them, "I, being about to reveal a matter which had long been kept in the shade, and which has appeared to be hidden by the long lapse of time, do now by myself disclose it to you by yourselves. I myself am that brother whom you sold to go into Egypt, I whom you now behold standing here."

(239) And when they were all amazed at seeing him beyond all their expectation, and were greatly agitated, and, as if under the influence of some violent attraction, cast their eyes down to the ground, and stood motionless, mute, and speechless, he said, "Be not cast down; I give you complete forgiveness for all the things which you have done to me. Do not think that you want any one else as a mediator. (240) I, of my own absolute power and of my own voluntary inclination, come of my own accord to an agreement with you; being guided by two especial signs, first, by my piety towards my father, to whom I owe a great deal of gratitude, and also, secondly, by my own natural humanity, which I feel towards all men, and especially towards those of my own blood.

(241) "And I think that it was not you, but God, who was the author of the events which happened to me, because he desired that I should be the servant and minister of his grace and gifts which he thought fit to bestow on the human race in the time of their greatest necessity. (242) And in the very outset you may receive a proof of what I say in the things which you see. I am the governor of all the land of Egypt, and the honours which I enjoy are next to those of the king himself, and the aged monarch honours me, though I am only a young man, as if I were his father; and I am honoured and obeyed not only by the people of the country but also by numerous other nations, whether they are subject to Egypt or independent; for they all have need of me, the governor of the land, by reason of their present scarcity. (243) For silver and gold, and what is still more necessary than either of these things, namely, food, is all stored up in my treasure-houses alone, and it is I who distribute and dispense what they want for their unavoidable necessities to each individual, so that nothing is wanting either for food or for the satisfying of their natural wants.

(244) "And I have not detailed all this to you from a wish to exalt myself or to give myself airs, but that you may know that it is no one of you or any man whatsoever that has been the cause of my being first a slave and afterwards a prisoner. For on one occasion a false accusation was brought against me, and I was thrown into prison. But he who changed that extremity of calamity and misfortune into the highest and most complete good fortune was God, with whom all things are possible.

(245) "Since these then, are my opinions, do not fear any longer, but discard all your sorrow and anxiety, and change to a joyful cheerfulness; and it will be well for you to hasten to your father, and to be the first to take him the good news of my being found, for reports are quick in penetrating everywhere."

XLI. (246) So they one after another began to pour forth praises of him without ceasing, and panegyrized him with unmodified encomium, each relating some different circumstance to his credit, one extolling his forgiving spirit, another his affection towards his family, and another his acuteness; and the whole company of them extolled his piety, and attributed to God the happy end to which everything had been brought, and being no longer melancholy or out of humour at the unexpected events which befell them, on their first arrival or at their original difficulties; (247) they also praised his excessive patience and fortitude, combined with modesty, when he, who had experienced such vicissitudes of fortune, neither when he was a slave, allowed himself to say a single word to the injury of his brothers, as having sold him, nor, when he was led away to prison, did he in his despondency say a single word that he should not have said, nor, though he remained there a long time, as prisoners usually do, did he, as is so much the custom, compare his misfortunes with those of his fellow prisoners so as to reveal anything, (248) but kept silence as if he had no knowledge of the cause of the events that had happened to him.

Nor again, when he was interpreting the dreams either to the eunuch or to the king, which was a favourable occasion for relating his own story, did he ever say a word about his own nobility of birth, nor yet when he was appointed lieutenant of the king, and received the superintendence and government of the whole of Egypt, even with the view of not being thought an ignoble and obscure person, but one who was really descended of noble ancestors, not a slave by nature, but one who had been exposed to intolerable treachery, and calamities at the hands of persons from whom he was least entitled to expect it.

(249) Moreover in addition to all this, great praise was bestowed on his affability and courtesy; for being acquainted with the insolence and rudeness of other governors, they marvelled at the absence of pretence and display which they saw in him, and they admired his kindness too, who, though the moment that he beheld them after their first journey he might have put them to death, or on the last occasion either, merely by refusing to supply them with food when oppressed with hunger, was not content with not punishing them, but even gave them necessary food gratuitously as though they had been persons worthy of favour, ordering the price they had paid to be restored to them: (250) and all the circumstances of their treachery towards him, and of their selling him, were so wholly concealed from, and unknown to any one, that the magistrates of the Egyptians sympathised with him in his joy, as if this was the first occasion of the brothers of the governor having arrived; moreover they invited them to hospitality, and made haste to relate their arrival to the king, and everything everywhere was full of joy, no less than would have been the case if the plain had suddenly become fertile, and the famine had changed into abundance.

XLII. (251) But the king, when he heard that Joseph had a father and a numerous family, advised him to press his father to remove into Egypt with all his house, promising to give them the most fertile district in Egypt on their arrival. Therefore Joseph gave his brothers chariots, and waggons, and a great multitude of beasts of burden, loaded with all necessary things, and a number of servants, that they might conduct his father into Egypt in safety.

(252) But when they arrived at home, and told their father their story about their brother, which was so apparently incredible and beyond all his hopes, he did not believe them; for even though those who brought the account were trustworthy, still the greatness and extraordinary character of the circumstances which they reported, did not allow him to believe them easily: (253) but when the old man saw the vast preparation, and the supplies of all necessary things, at such a time, in such abundance, corresponding to the good fortune of his son which they were reporting to him, he praised God that he had made complete that part of his house which seemed to be deficient; (254) but his joy immediately begat fear again in his soul, respecting his departure from his natural laws and customs; for he knew that youth is by nature prone to fall, and that in foreign nations there is great indulgence given to error; and especially in the country of Egypt, a land in a state of utter blindness respecting the true God, in consequence of their making created and mortal things into gods.

Moreover, the addition of riches and glory is a snare to weak minds, and he also recollected that he had been left to himself, as no one had gone forth out of his father's house with him to keep him in the right way, but he had been left solitary and destitute of all good instructions, and might therefore be supposed to be ready to change and adopt their foreign customs. (255) Therefore, when that Being who alone is able to behold the invisible soul, saw him in this frame of mind, he took pity on him and appearing unto him by night while he was lying asleep, said unto him, "Fear nothing about your departure into Egypt; I myself will guide you on your way, and will give you a safe and pleasant journey; and I will restore you your long lamented son, who was once many years ago believed by you to have died, but who is not only alive, but is even governor of all that mighty country."

So Jacob, being filled with good hopes, rose up in the morning with joy, and hastened on his way; (256) and when his son heard that he was near, for scouts and watchers who were placed along the road gave him notice of everything, he went with speed to meet his father when he was at no great distance from the borders of the land; and they met one another near the city, which is called the city of heroes, and they fell into one another's arms placing their heads on each other's necks, and soaking their garments with tears, and satisfying themselves abundantly with long enduring embraces, and unwillingly at last loosing one another, they proceeded to the palace. (257) And when the king beheld them he was amazed at the dignity of Jacob's appearance, and he received and saluted him not as the father of his lieutenant but as his own, with all possible respect and honour; and after showing him not only all the ordinary but also many extraordinary marks of respect, he gave him a most excellent district of land of the greatest fertility; and hearing that his sons were skilful breeders of cattle, having great substance in flocks and herds, he appointed them overseers of all his own flocks and herds, and committed to their charge his goats, and his oxen, and his sheep, and all his innumerable animals of every kind.

XLIII. (258) And the young man, Joseph, displayed such excessive good faith and honesty in all his dealings, that though the time and the circumstances of the time gave him innumerable opportunities of making money, so that he might, in a short period, have become the richest man of that age or kingdom, he still so truly honoured genuine riches before illegitimate wealth, and the treasure which sees rather than that which is blind, that he stored up all the silver and gold which he collected as the price of the corn in the king's treasury, not appropriating a single drachm of it to his own use, but being satisfied with nothing beyond the gifts which the king bestowed on him voluntarily, in acknowledgment of his services.

(259) And in this manner he governed Egypt, and other countries also with it, and other nations, while oppressed with the famine, in a manner too admirable for any description to do it justice, distributing food to all in a proper manner, and looking, not only at the present advantage, but also at what would be of future benefit: (260) therefore, when the seventh year of the scarcity arrived, he sent for the farmers (for there was now a prospect of fertility and abundance), and gave them barley and wheat for seed, taking care that no one should appropriate what he gave for other purposes, but should sow what he received in the fields, to which end he selected men of honesty and virtue as overseers and superintendents, who were to take care that the sowing was properly performed.

(261) And when a long time after the famine his father died, his brothers were filled with secret misgivings, and feared lest now he should remember the evil that they had done to him, and should retaliate upon them and afflict them, and so they came to him and besought him earnestly, bringing with them their wives and children. (262) And he

wept and said, "The occasion indeed is a natural one, to fill with secret apprehension those who have done intolerable things, and who are convicted more by their own consciences than by anything else; for the death of our father has revived in you the ancient fear which you entertained before our reconciliation, that I had merely bestowed pardon on you for the sake of not grieving our father; but I do not change my disposition with the changes of time, nor, after I have agreed to a reconciliation and forgiveness, will I ever do anything inconsistent with such agreement; (263) for I have not been postponing revenge and watching for opportunities to wreak it, but I once for all gave you immunity from all punishment, being influenced partly by feelings of respect for my father, for I must speak in plain truth, and partly by natural necessary affection for you.

(264) "But if I did every thing that was merciful and humane for my father's sake while he was alive, I will also adhere to it now that he is dead. But in my real opinion no good man ever dies, but such will live for ever and ever, without growing old, in an immortal nature which is no longer bound up in the necessities of the body. (265) And why should I remember only that father who was created and born? We have also the uncreated, immortal, everlasting God for our father, who sees all things and hears all people, even when silent, and who always sees even those things which lie hidden in the recesses of the mind, and whom I look upon and invoke as a witness of my sincere reconciliation; (266) for 'I am (and do not you be astonished at my words), I am in the place of God,'[3] who has changed your evil designs against me so as to bring forth from them an abundance of good things. Be ye therefore fearless, and know that for the future you shall enjoy still better fortune than hitherto you have while our father was still alive."

XLIV. (267) Having encouraged his brethren with these words he confirmed his promises still more by actions, leaving out nothing which could show his care for his brethren.

And after the famine, when the inhabitants were now full of joy at the fertility and prosperity of the country he was honoured by all men, who thus recompensed him for the benefits which they had received from him in the season of their despair. (268) And the report of him became noised abroad, and filled all the cities with his glory and reputation.

And he lived a hundred and ten years, and then died at a good old age, having enjoyed the greatest perfection of beauty, and wisdom, and eloquence of speech. (269) The beauty of his person is testified to by the violent love with which

---

[3] Genesis 50:19.

he inflamed the wife of the eunuch; his wisdom by the evenness of his conduct in the indescribable variety of circumstances that attended the whole of his life, by which he wrought regularity among things that were irregular, and harmony among things that were discordant. His eloquence of speech is displayed in his interpretation of the dreams, in his affability in ordinary conversation, and by the persuasion which followed his words; in consequence of which his subjects all obeyed him cheerfully and voluntarily, rather than from any compulsion.

(270) Of these hundred and ten years he spent seventeen, till the expiration of his boyhood, in his father's house; and thirteen he passed amid unforeseen events, being plotted against, and sold, and becoming a slave, and having false accusations brought against him, and being thrown into prison; and the remaining eighty years he spent in authority and in all manner of prosperity, being the most excellent manager and administrator both of scarcity and plenty, and the most competent of all men to manage affairs under either complexion of circumstances.

ON THE LIFE OF MOSES, I†

(De Vita Mosis, I)

I. (1) I have conceived the idea of writing the life of Moses, who, according to the account of some persons, was the lawgiver of the Jews, but according to others only an interpreter of the sacred laws, the greatest and most perfect man that ever lived, having a desire to make his character fully known to those who ought not to remain in ignorance respecting him, (2) for the glory of the laws which he left behind him has reached over the whole world, and has penetrated to the very furthest limits of the universe; and those who do really and truly understand him are not many, perhaps partly out of envy, or else from the disposition so common to many persons of resisting the commands which are delivered by lawgivers in different states, since the historians who have flourished among the Greeks have not chosen to think him worthy of mention, (3) the greater part of whom have both in their poems and also in their prose writings, disparaged or defaced the powers which they have received through education, composing comedies and works full of Sybaritish profligacy and licentiousness to their everlasting shame, while they ought rather to have employed their natural endowments and abilities in preserving a record of virtuous men and praiseworthy lives, so that honourable actions, whether ancient or modern, might not be buried in silence, and thus have all recollection of them lost, while they might shine gloriously if duly celebrated; and that they might not themselves have seemed to pass by more appropriate subjects, and to prefer such as were unworthy of being mentioned at all, while they were eager to give a specious appearance to infamous actions, so as to secure notoriety for disgraceful deeds.

(4) But I disregard the envious disposition of these men, and shall proceed to narrate the events which befell him, having learnt them both from those sacred scriptures which he has left as marvellous memorials of his wisdom, and having also heard many things from the elders of my nation, for I have continually connected together what I have heard with what I have read, and in this way I look upon it that I am acquainted with the history of his life more accurately than other people.

II. (5) And I will begin first with that with which it is necessary to begin.

Moses was by birth a Hebrew, but he was born, and brought up, and educated in Egypt, his ancestors having migrated into Egypt with all their families on account of the long famine which oppressed Babylon and all the adjacent countries; for they were in search of food, and Egypt was a champaign country blessed with a rich soil, and very productive of every thing which the nature of man requires, and especially of corn and wheat, (6) for the river of that country at the height of summer, when they say that all other rivers which are derived from winter torrents and from springs in the ground are smaller, rises and increases, and overflows so as to irrigate all the lands, and make them one vast lake. And so the land, without having any need of rain, supplies every year an unlimited abundance of every kind of good food, unless sometimes the anger of God interrupts this abundance by reason of the excessive impiety of the inhabitants.

(7) And his father and mother were among the most excellent persons of their time, and though they were of the same time, still they were induced to unite themselves together more from an unanimity of feeling than because they were related in blood; and Moses is the seventh generation in succession from the original settler in the country who was the founder of the whole race of the Jews.

III. (8) And he was thought worthy of being bred up in the royal palace, the cause of which circumstance was as follows. The king of the country, inasmuch as the nation of the Hebrews kept continually increasing in numbers, fearing lest gradually the settlers should become more numerous than the original inhabitants, and being more powerful should set upon them and subdue them by force, and make themselves their masters, conceived the idea of destroying their strength by impious devices, and ordered that of all the children that were born the females only should be brought up (since a woman, by reason of the weakness of her nature, is disinclined to and unfitted for war), and that all the male children should be destroyed, that the population of their cities might not be increased, since a power which consists of a number of men is a fortress difficult to take and dif-

---

†Yonge's full title, *A Treatise on the Life of Moses, that is to say, On the Theology and Prophetic Office of Moses, Book I.*

ficult to destroy.[1]

(9) Accordingly as the child Moses, as soon as he was born, displayed a more beautiful and noble form than usual, his parents resolved, as far as was in their power, to disregard the proclamations of the tyrant. Accordingly they say that for three months continuously they kept him at home, feeding him on milk, without its coming to the knowledge of the multitude; (10) but when, as is commonly the case in monarchies, some persons discovered what was kept secret and in darkness, of those persons who are always eager to bring any new report to the king, his parents being afraid lest while seeking to secure the safety of one individual, they who were many might become involved in his destruction, with many tears exposed their child on the banks of the river, and departed groaning and lamenting, pitying themselves for the necessity which had fallen upon them, and calling themselves the slayers and murderers of their child, and commiserating the infant too for his destruction, which they had hoped to avert.

(11) Then, as was natural for people involved in a miserable misfortune, they accused themselves as having brought a heavier affliction on themselves than they need have done. "For why," said they, "did we not expose him at the first moment of his birth?" For people in general do not look upon one who has not lived long enough to partake of salutary food as a human being at all. "But we, in our superfluous affection, have nourished him these three entire months, causing ourselves by such conduct more abundant grief, and inflicting upon him a heavier punishment, in order that he, having at last attained to a great capacity for feeling pleasures and pains, should at last perish in the perception of the most grievous evils."

IV. (12) And so they departed in ignorance of the future, being wholly overwhelmed with sad misery; but the sister of the infant who was thus exposed, being still a maiden, out of the vehemence of her fraternal affection, stood a little way off watching to see what would happen, and all the events which concerned him appear to me to have taken place in accordance with the providence of God, who watched over the infant. (13) Now the king of the country had an only daughter, whom he tenderly loved, and they say that she, although she had been married a long time, had never had any children, and therefore, as was natural, was very desirous of children, and especially of male offspring, which should succeed to the noble inheritance of her father's prosperity and imperial

authority, which was otherwise in danger of being lost, since the king had no other grandsons.

(14) And as she was always desponding and lamenting, so especially on that particular day was she overcome by the weight of her anxiety, that, though it was her ordinary custom to stay in doors and never to pass over the threshold of her house, yet now she went forth with her handmaidens down to the river, where the infant was lying. And there, as she was about to indulge in a bath and purification in the thickest part of the marsh, she beheld the child, and commanded her handmaidens to bring him to her. (15) Then, after she had surveyed him from head to foot, and admired his elegant form and healthy vigorous appearance, and saw that he was crying, she had compassion on him, her soul being already moved within her by maternal feelings of affection as if he had been her own child.

And when she knew that the infant belonged to one of the Hebrews who was afraid because of the commandment of the king, she herself conceived the idea of rearing him up, and took counsel with herself on the subject, thinking that it was not safe to bring him at once into the palace; (16) and while she was still hesitating, the sister of the infant, who was still looking out, conjecturing her hesitation from what she beheld, ran up and asked her whether she would like that the child should be brought up at the breast by some one of the Hebrew women who had been lately delivered; (17) and as she said that she wished that she would do so, the maiden went and fetched her own mother and that of the infant, as if she had been a stranger, who with great readiness and willingness cheerfully promised to take the child and bring him up, pretending to be tempted by the reward to be paid, the providence of God thus making the original bringing up of the child to accord with the genuine course of nature. Then she gave him a name, calling him Moses with great propriety, because she had received him out of the water, for the Egyptians call water "mos."

V. (18) But when the child began to grow and increase, he was weaned, not in accordance with the time of his age, but earlier than usual; and then his mother, who was also his nurse, came to bring him back to the princess who had given him to her, inasmuch as he no longer required to be fed on milk, and as he was now a fine and noble child to look upon. (19) And when the king's daughter saw that he was more perfect than could have been expected at his age, and when from his appearance she conceived greater good will than ever towards him, she adopted him as her son, having first put in practice all sorts of contrivances to increase the apparent bulk of her belly, so that he might be looked upon as her own genuine child,

---

[1] The similitude of this passage to Sir William Jones' Ode is very remarkable: "What constitutes a state."

and not as a supposititious one; but God easily brings to pass whatever he is inclined to effect, however difficult it may be to bring to a successful issue.

(20) Therefore the child being now thought worthy of a royal education and a royal attendance, was not, like a mere child, long delighted with toys and objects of laughter and amusement, even though those who had undertaken the care of him allowed him holidays and times for relaxation, and never behaved in any stern or morose way to him; but he himself exhibited a modest and dignified deportment in all his words and gestures, attending diligently to every lesson of every kind which could tend to the improvement of his mind. (21) And immediately he had all kinds of masters, one after another, some coming of their own accord from the neighbouring countries and the different districts of Egypt, and some being even procured from Greece by the temptation of large presents. But in a short time he surpassed all their knowledge, anticipating all their lessons by the excellent natural endowments of his own genius; so that everything in his case appeared to be a recollecting rather than a learning, while he himself also, without any teacher, comprehended by his instinctive genius many difficult subjects; (22) for great abilities cut out for themselves many new roads to knowledge.

And just as vigorous and healthy bodies which are active and quick in motion in all their parts, release their trainers from much care, giving them little or no trouble and anxiety, and as trees which are of a good sort, and which have a natural good growth, give no trouble to their cultivators, but grow finely and improve of themselves, so in the same manner the well disposed soul, going forward to meet the lessons which are imparted to it, is improved in reality by itself rather than by its teachers, and taking hold of some beginning or principle of knowledge, bounds, as the proverb has it, like a horse over the plain.

(23) Accordingly he speedily learnt arithmetic, and geometry, and the whole science of rhythm and harmony and metre, and the whole of music, by means of the use of musical instruments, and by lectures on the different arts, and by explanations of each topic; and lessons on these subjects were given him by Egyptian philosophers, who also taught him the philosophy which is contained in symbols, which they exhibit in those sacred characters of hieroglyphics, as they are called, and also that philosophy which is conversant about that respect which they pay to animals which they invest with the honours due to God.

And all the other branches of the encyclical education he learnt from Greeks; and the philosophers from the adjacent countries taught him Assyrian literature and the knowledge of the heavenly bodies so much studied by the Chaldaeans. (24) And this knowledge he derived also from the Egyptians, who study mathematics above all things, and he learnt with great accuracy the state of that art among both the Chaldaeans and Egyptians, making himself acquainted with the points in which they agree with and differ from each other—making himself master of all their disputes without encouraging any disputatious disposition in himself—but seeking the plain truth, since his mind was unable to admit any falsehood, as those are accustomed to do who contend violently for one particular side of a question; and who advocate any doctrine which is set before them, whatever it may be, not inquiring whether it deserves to be supported, but acting in the same manner as those lawyers who defend a cause for pay, and are wholly indifferent to the justice of their cause.

VI. (25) And when he had passed the boundaries of the age of infancy he began to exercise his intellect; not, as some people do, letting his youthful passions roam at large without restraint, although in him they had ten thousand incentives by reason of the abundant means for the gratification of them which royal places supply; but he behaved with temperance and fortitude, as though he had bound them with reins, and thus he restrained their onward impetuosity by force. (26) And he tamed, and appeased, and brought under due command every one of the other passions which are naturally and as far as they are themselves concerned frantic, and violent, and unmanageable. And if any one of them at all excited itself and endeavoured to get free from restraint he administered severe punishment to it, reproving it with severity of language; and, in short, he repressed all the principal impulses and most violent affections of the soul, and kept guard over them as over a restive horse, fearing lest they might break all bounds and get beyond the power of reason which ought to be their guide to restrain them, and so throw everything everywhere into confusion.

For these passions are the causes of all good and of all evil; of good when they submit to the authority of dominant reason, and of evil when they break out of bounds and scorn all government and restraint.

(27) Very naturally, therefore, those who associated with him and every one who was acquainted with him marvelled at him, being astonished as at a novel spectacle, and inquiring what kind of mind it was that had its abode in his body, and that was set up in it like an image in a shrine; whether it was a human mind or a divine intellect, or something combined of the two; because he had nothing in him resembling the many, but had gone beyond them all and was elevated to a more sublime height. (28) For he never provided his

stomach with any luxuries beyond those necessary tributes which nature has appointed to be paid to it, and as to the pleasures of the organs below the stomach he paid no attention to them at all, except as far as the object of having legitimate children was concerned.

(29) And being in a most eminent degree a practiser of abstinence and self-denial, and being above all men inclined to ridicule a life of effeminacy and luxury (for he desired to live for his soul alone, and not for his body), he exhibited the doctrines of philosophy in all his daily actions, saying precisely what he thought, and performing such actions only as were consistent with his words, so as to exhibit a perfect harmony between his language and his life, so that as his words were such also was his life, and as his life was such likewise was his language, like people who are playing together in tune on a musical instrument.

(30) Therefore men in general, even if the slightest breeze of prosperity does only blow their way for a moment, become puffed up and give themselves great airs, becoming insolent to all those who are in a lower condition than themselves, and calling them dregs of the earth, and annoyances, and sources of trouble, and burdens of the earth, and all sorts of names of that kind, as if they had been thoroughly able to establish the undeviating character of their prosperity on a solid foundation, though, very likely, they will not remain in the same condition even till tomorrow, (31) for there is nothing more inconstant than fortune, which tosses human affairs up and down like dice. Often has a single day thrown down the man who was previously placed on an eminence, and raised the lowly man on high. And while men see these events continually taking place, and though they are well assured of the fact, still they overlook their relations and friends, and transgress the laws according to which they were born and brought up; and they overturn their national hereditary customs to which no just blame whatever is attached, dwelling in a foreign land, and by reason of their cordial reception of the customs among which they are living, no longer remembering a single one of their ancient usages.

VII. (32) But Moses, having now reached the very highest point of human good fortune, and being looked upon as the grandson of this mighty king, and being almost considered in the expectations of all men as the future inheritor of his grandfather's kingdom, and being always addressed as the young prince, still felt a desire for and admiration of the education of his kinsmen and ancestors, considering all the things which were thought good among those who had adopted him as spurious, even though they might, in consequence of the present state of affairs, have a brilliant appearance; and those things which were thought good

by his natural parents, even though they might be for a short time somewhat obscure, at all events akin to himself and genuine good things.

(33) Accordingly, like an uncorrupt judge both of his real parents and of those who had adopted him, he cherished towards the one a good will and an ardent affection, and he displayed gratitude towards the others in requital of the kindness which he had received at their hands, and he would have displayed the same throughout his whole life if he had not beheld a great and novel iniquity wrought in the country by the king; (34) for, as I have said before, the Jews were strangers in Egypt, the founders of their race having migrated from Babylon and the upper satrapies in the time of the famine, by reason of their want of food, and come and settled in Egypt, and having in a manner taken refuge like suppliants in the country as in a sacred asylum, fleeing for protection to the good faith of the king and the compassion of the inhabitants; (35) for strangers, in my opinion, should be looked upon as refugees, and as the suppliants of those who receive them in their country; and, besides, being suppliants, these men were likewise sojourners in the land, and friends desiring to be admitted to equal honours with the citizens, and neighbours differing but little in their character from original natives.

(36) The men, therefore, who had left their homes and come into Egypt, as if they were to dwell in that land as in a second country in perfect security, the king of the country reduced to slavery, and, as if he had taken them prisoners in the laws of war, or had bought them from masters in whose house they had been bred, he oppressed them and treated them as slaves, though they were not only free men, but also strangers, and suppliants, and sojourners, having no respect for nor any awe of God, who presides over the rights of free men, and of strangers, and of suppliants, and of hospitality, and who beholds all such actions as his. (37) Then he laid commands on them beyond their power to fulfil, imposing on them labour after labour; and, when they fainted from weakness, the sword came upon them.

He appointed overseers over their works, the most pitiless and inhuman of men, who pardoned and made allowance for no one, and whom they from the circumstances and from their behaviour called persecutors of work. (38) And they wrought with clay, some of them fashioning it into bricks, and others collecting straw from all quarters, for straw is the bond which binds bricks together; while others, again, had the task allotted to them of building up houses, and walls, and gates, and cutting trenches, bearing wood themselves day and night without interruption, having no rest or respite, and not even being allowed time so much as to sleep, but being compelled to perform all the works not only of workmen but also of journeymen, so that in a short time their bodies failed them, their souls having already fainted beneath their afflictions.

(39) And so they died, one after another, as if smitten by a pestilential destruction, and then their taskmasters threw their bodies away unburied beyond the borders of the land, not suffering their kinsmen or their friends to sprinkle even a little dust on their corpses, nor to weep over those who had thus miserably perished; but, like impious men as they were, they threatened to extend their despotism over the passions of the soul (that cannot be enslaved, and which are nearly the only things which nature has made completely free), oppressing them with the intolerable weight of a necessity beyond their powers.

VIII. (40) At all these events Moses was greatly grieved and indignant, not being able either to chastise the unjust oppressors of his people nor to assist those who were oppressed, but he gave them all the assistance that was in his power, by words, recommending their overseers to treat them with moderation, and to relax and abate somewhat of the oppressive nature of their commands, and exhorting the oppressed who were labouring thus to bear their present distresses with a noble spirit and to be men in their minds, and not to let their souls faint as well as their bodies, but to hope for good fortune after their present adversity; (41) for that all things in this world have a tendency to change to the opposite, cloudy weather to fine, violent gales to calm and absence of wind, storms and heavy billows at sea to fair weather and an unruffled surface of the water; and much more are human affairs likely to change, inasmuch as they are more unstable than anything.

(42) By using these charms, as it were, like a good physician, he thought he should be able to alleviate their afflictions, although they were most grievous. But whenever their distress abated, then again their taskmasters returned and oppressed them with increased severity, always after the respite adding some new evil which should be even more intolerable than their previous sufferings; (43) for some of their overseers were very savage and furious men, being, as to their cruelty, not at all different from poisonous serpents or carnivorous beasts—wild beasts in human form—being clothed with the form of a human body so as to give an appearance of gentleness in order to deceive and catch their victim, but in reality being harder than iron or adamant.

(44) One of these men, then, the most violent of them, when, in addition to yielding nothing of his purpose, he was even exasperated at the exhortations of Moses and rendered more savage by them, beating those who did not labour with energy and unremittingly at the work which was imposed upon them, and insulting them and subjecting them to every kind of ill-treatment, so as even to be the death of many, Moses slew, thinking the deed a pious action; and, indeed, it was a pious action to destroy one who only lived for the destruction of others.

(45) When the king heard of this action he was very indignant, thinking it an intolerable thing, not for one man to be dead, or for another to have killed him, whether justly or unjustly, but for his grandson not to agree with him, and not to look upon his friends or his enemies as his own, but to hate persons whom the king loved, and to love persons whom the king looked upon as outcasts, and to pity those whom he regarded with unchangeable and implacable aversion.

IX. (46) But when the Egyptian authorities had once got an opportunity of attacking the young man, having already reason for looking upon him with suspicion (for they well knew that he would hereafter bear them ill-will for their evil practices, and would revenge himself on them when he had an opportunity) they poured in, at all times and from all quarters, thousands and thousands of calumnies into the willing ears of his grandfather, so that they even implanted in his mind an apprehension that Moses was plotting to deprive him of his kingdom, saying to him: "He will strip you of your crown. He has no humble designs or notions. He is continually seeking to busy himself in what does not concern him, and to acquire some additional power. He is eager for the kingdom before his time. He caresses some people; he threatens others; he kills others without a trial; he hates all those who are the best affected towards you. Why do you delay? Why do you not cut short all his designs and machinations? Delay on the part of those against whom they are plotting is of the greatest advantage to those who wish to attack them."

(47) As they urged these arguments to the king he retreated to the contiguous country of Arabia, where it was safe to abide, entreating God that he would deliver his countrymen from inextricable calamities, and would worthily chastise their oppressors who omitted no circumstance of insolence and tyranny, and would double his joy by allowing him to behold the accomplishment of both these prayers. And God heard his prayers, looking favourably on his disposition, so devoted to what is good, and so hostile to what is evil, and not long after he pronounced his decision upon the affairs of that land as became a God. (48) But while he was preparing to display the decision which he was about to pronounce, Moses was devoting himself to all the labours of virtue, having a teacher within himself, virtuous reason, by whom he had been trained to the most virtuous pursuits of life, and had learnt to apply himself to the contemplation

and practice of virtue and to the continual study of the doctrines of philosophy, which he easily and thoroughly comprehended in his soul, and committed to memory in such a manner as never to forget them; and, moreover, he made all his own actions, which were intrinsically praiseworthy, to harmonise with them, desiring not to seem wise and good, but in truth and reality to be so, because he made the right reason of nature his only aim; which is, in fact, the only first principle and fountain of all the virtues.

(49) Any one else, perhaps, fleeing from the implacable fury of the king, and coming now for the first time into a foreign land, when he had not as yet associated with or learnt the customs of the natives, and not knowing with any accuracy of the objects in which they delighted or which they regarded with aversion, would have been desirous to enjoy tranquillity and to live in obscurity, escaping the notice of men in general; or else, if he had wished to come forward in public, he would have endeavoured by all means to propitiate the powerful men and those in the highest authority in the country by persevering attentions, as men from whom some advantage or assistance might be expected, if any pursuers should come after him and endeavour to drag him away by force. (50) But this man proceeded by the path which was the exact opposite of that which was the probable one for him to take, following the healthy impulses of his soul, and not allowing any one of them to be impeded in its progress. On which account, at times, with the fervour of youth, he attempted things beyond his existing strength; looking upon justice as an irresistible power, by which he was encouraged so as to go spontaneously to the assistance of the weaker side.

X. (51) I will also mention one action which was done by him at that time, even although it may be but a trifling one in appearance, but still it proceeded from a lofty spirit. The Arabs are great breeders of cattle, and they all feed their flocks together, not merely men, but also women, and youths, and maidens with them, and this, too, not merely in the obscurer classes and lower ranks of life, but also among the most eminent persons of the nation.

(52) Now there were seven damsels, whose father was the priest, and they all came to a certain fountain leading their flocks, and having loosened their vessels and let them down by thongs they succeeded one another in drawing up the water, so as for them all to have an equal share in the work; and in this way they cheerfully and rapidly filled the troughs which were at hand. (53) And when other shepherds came up they disregarded the weakness of the damsels and endeavoured to drive them away with their flocks, and then brought their own herds to the drink that was

prepared, desiring to reap the fruits of the labour of others. (54) But Moses, seeing what was done, for he was at no great distance, hastened and ran up; and, when he had come near to them, he said: "Will not you desist from behaving thus unjustly, thinking this solitary place a fitting field for the exercise of your covetousness? Are you not ashamed to have such cowardly arms and hands? You are long-haired people, female flesh, and not men. The damsels behave like vigorous youths, hesitating about nothing that they ought to do; but you, young men, are now behaving lazily, like girls. (55) Will you not depart? Will you not be off and give place to those who arrived first, to whom the water belongs, and who are entitled to it; when you ought rather to have drawn water for them, that so they might have had it in greater abundance? And are you, on the contrary, endeavouring to take away from them what they themselves have got ready?

"But I swear, by the celestial eye of justice, which sees what is done even in the most solitary places, that you shall not take it from them. (56) And at all events, now justice has sent me and appointed me to bring them assistance who never expected such an officer; for I am an ally to these damsels who are thus injured by violence, and I come with a might which you evil-doers and covetous people cannot face, but you shall feel it wounding you in an invisible manner, if you do not change your ways." (57) He said this; and they, being alarmed at his words, since while he was speaking he appeared inspired, and his appearance became changed, so that he looked like a prophet, and fearing lest he might be uttering divine oracles and predictions, they obeyed and became submissive, and brought back the flock of the maidens to the troughs, first of all removing their own cattle.

XI. (58) So the damsels went home exceedingly delighted, and they related all that had happened to them beyond their hopes, so that they wished their father with an earnest desire to see the stranger. At all events he blamed them for their ingratitude, speaking as follows: "What were ye about, that ye let him go, when you ought at once to have brought him hither, and to have entreated him to come if he declined? Or when did you see any inhospitality in me? Or do you expect never again to fall into difficulties? Those who are forgetful of services must needs lack defenders, but nevertheless hasten after him, for as yet the error which you have committed may be repaired; and go with haste and invite him first of all to a hospitable reception, and then endeavour to requite his service, for great thanks are due to him."

(59) So they made haste, and went after him, and overtook him at no great distance from the fountain; and when they had delivered their father's

message to him, they persuaded him to return home with them. And their father was at once greatly struck by his appearance, and soon afterwards he learnt to admire his wisdom, for great natures are very easily discovered, and do not require a length of time to be appreciated, and so he gave him the most beautiful of his daughters to be his wife, conjecturing by that one action of his how completely good and excellent he was, and testifying that what is good is the only thing which deserves to be loved, and that it does not require any external recommendation, but bears in itself proofs by which it may be known and understood.

(60) And after his marriage, Moses took his father-in-law's herds and tended them, being thus instructed in the lessons proper to qualify him for becoming the leader of a people, for the business of a shepherd is a preparation for the office of a king to any one who is destined to preside over that most manageable of all flocks, mankind, just as hunting is a good training-school for men of warlike dispositions; for they who are practising with a view to learning the management of an army, previously study the science of hunting, brute animals being as some raw material exposed to their attacks in order for them to practise the art of commanding on each occasion of war or of peace, (61) for the pursuit of wild beasts is a training-school of strategy to be developed against enemies, and the care and management of tame animals is a royal training for the government of subjects; for which reason kings are called shepherds of their people, not by way of reproach, but as a most especial and pre-eminent honour.

(62) And it appears to me, who have examined the matter not with any reference to the opinions of the many, but solely with regard to truth (and he may laugh who pleases), that that man alone can be a perfect king who is well skilled in the art of the shepherd, being thus instructed as to more important matters by experience of the inferior animals; for it is impossible for great things to be brought to perfection before small ones.

XII. (63) Therefore Moses, having become the most skilful herdsman of his time, and the most prudent provider of all the necessary things for his flock, and of all things which tended to their advantage, because he never delayed or hesitated, but exerted a voluntary and spontaneous cheerfulness in all things necessary for the animals under his charge, (64) saw his flocks increase with great joy and guileless good faith, so that he soon incurred the envy of the other herdsmen, who saw nothing in their own flocks resembling the condition of his; but they thought themselves well off if they continued as before, while the flock of Moses would have been thought to be falling off if it had not improved, every day, by reason of the vast augmentations that it was in the habit of receiv-

ing in beauty from its high condition and fatness, and in number from the prolific character of the females, and the wholesome way in which it was fed and managed.

(65) And when Moses was leading his flock into a situation full of good water and good grass, where there was also a great deal of herbage especially suitable for sheep, he came upon a certain grove in a valley, where he saw a most marvellous sight. There was a bush or briar, a very thorny plant, and very weak and supple. This bush was on a sudden set in a blaze without any one applying any fire to it, and being entirely enveloped from the root to the topmost branch by the abundant flame, as though it had proceeded from some fountain showering fire over it, it nevertheless remained whole without being consumed, like some impassible essence, and not as if it were itself the natural fuel for fire, but rather as if it were taking the fire for its own fuel. (66) And in the middle of the flame there was seen a certain very beautiful form, not resembling any visible thing, a most Godlike image, emitting a light more brilliant than fire, which any one might have imagined to be the image of the living God. But let it be called an angel, because it merely related (*diēngelleto*) the events which were about to happen in a silence more distinct than any voice by reason of the marvellous sight which was thus exhibited.

(67) For the burning bush was a symbol of the oppressed people, and the burning fire was a symbol of the oppressors; and the circumstance of the burning bush not being consumed was an emblem of the fact that the people thus oppressed would not be destroyed by those who were attacking them, but that their hostility would be unsuccessful and fruitless to the one party, and the fact of their being plotted against would fail to be injurious to the others. The angel, again, was the emblem of the providence of God, who mitigates circumstances which appear very formidable, so as to produce from them great tranquillity beyond the hopes or expectation of any one.

XIII. (68) But we must now accurately investigate the comparison here made. The briar, as has been already said, is a most weak and supple plant, yet it is not without thorns, so that it wounds one if one only touches it. Nor was it consumed by fire, which is naturally destructive, but on the contrary it was preserved by it, and in addition to not being consumed, it continued just as it was before, and without undergoing any change whatever itself, acquired additional brilliancy.

(69) All these circumstances are an allegory to intimate the suggestions given by the other notions which at that time prevailed, almost crying out in plain words to persons in affliction, "Do not faint; your weakness is your strength, which shall pierce and wound innumerable hosts. You shall

be saved rather than destroyed, by those who are desirous to destroy your whole race against their will, so that you shall not be overwhelmed by the evils with which they will afflict you, but when your enemies think most surely that they are destroying you, then you shall most brilliantly shine out in glory."

(70) Again, the fire, which is a destructive essence, convicting the men of cruel dispositions, says, Be not elated so as to rely on your own strength; be admonished rather when you see irresistible powers destroyed. The consuming power of flame is itself consumed like firewood, and the wood, which is by its intrinsic nature capable of being burnt, burns other things visibly like fire.

XIV. (71) God, having shown this prodigious and miraculous sight to Moses, gave him, in this way, a most visible lesson as to the events which are about to be accomplished; and he begins to exhort him, by divine admonitions and predictions, to apply himself to the government of his nation, as one who was to be not only the author of its freedom, but also its leader in its migration from Egypt, which should take place at no distant period; promising to be present with him as his coadjutor in every thing. (72) For says God, "I myself have had compassion for a long time on them while ill-treated and subjected to insolence hard to be borne, while there was no man to lighten their sufferings, nor to pity their calamities; for I have seen them all, each individual privately and the whole nation, with one accord turning to address supplications and prayer to me, and hoping for assistance from me. And I am by nature merciful, and propitious to all sincere suppliants. (73) But go thou to the king of the country, without fearing any thing whatever; for the former king is dead from whom you fled for fear of his plotting against thee. And another king now governs the land, who has no ill-will against thee on account of any thing, and who has taken the elders of the nation into his council; tell him that the whole nation is called forth by me, by my divine oracle, that in accordance with the customs of their ancestors they may depart three days' journey out of the country, and there may sacrifice unto me."

(74) But Moses, not being ignorant that even his own countrymen would distrust his word, and also that every one else would do so, said, "If then they ask what is the name of him who sent thee, and if I know not what to reply to them, shall I not seem to be deceiving them?" (75) And God said, "At first say unto them, I am that I am, that when they have learnt that there is a difference between him that is and him that is not, they may be further taught that there is no name whatever that can properly be assigned to me, who am the only being to whom existence belongs. (76) And if, inasmuch as they are weak in their natural abil-

ities, they shall inquire further about my appellation, tell them not only this one fact that I am God, but also that I am the God of those men who have derived their names from virtue, that I am the God of Abraham, and the God of Isaac, and the God of Jacob, one of whom is the rule of that wisdom which is derived from teaching, another of natural wisdom, and the third of that which is derived from practice. And if they are still distrustful they shall be taught by these tokens, and then they shall change their dispositions, seeing such signs as no man has hitherto either seen or heard."

(77) Now the tokens were as follows. The rod which Moses held in his hand God ordered him to throw down on the ground; and immediately it received life, and crawled along, and speedily became the most powerful of all the animals which want feet, namely, an immense serpent, complete in all its parts. And when Moses retreated from the beast, and out of fear was on the point of taking to flight, he was called back again; and when God laid his commands upon him, and inspired him with courage, he laid hold of it by the tail; (78) and the serpent, though still crawling onwards, stopped at his touch, and being stretched out at its full length again returned to its original elements and because the same rod as before, so that Moses marvelled at both the changes, not knowing which was the most wonderful; as he was unable to decide between them, his soul being overwhelmed with these appearances of equal strangeness.

(79) This now was the first sign.

The second miraculous token was afforded to him at no great distance of time. God commanded him to put one of his hands in his bosom and hide it there, and a moment afterwards to draw it out again. And when he had done what he was commanded, his hand in a moment appeared whiter than snow. Again, when he had put his hand a second time into his bosom, and had a second time drawn it forth, it returned to its original complexion, and resumed its proper appearance. (80) These two lessons he was taught in solitude, when he was alone with God, like a pupil alone with his master, and having about him the instruments with which these wonders were worked, namely, his hand and his rod, with which indeed he walked along the road.

(81) But the third he could not carry about with him, nor could he be instructed as to that beforehand; but it was destined to astonish him not less than the others, deriving the origin of its existence from Egypt. And this was its character. God said, "The water of the river, as much as you can take up in your hand and pour upon the ground shall be dark blood, being both in colour and in power transformed with a complete transformation." (82) And, as was natural, this also appeared credible

to Moses, not merely by reason of the truth-telling nature of the speaker but also because of the marvels that had already been shown to him, with respect to his hand and to his rod.

(83) But though he believed the words of God, nevertheless he tried to avoid the office to which God was appointing him, urging that he was a man of a weak voice, and slow of speech, and not eloquent, and especially so ever since he had heard God himself speaking. For judging the greatest human eloquence to be mere speechlessness in comparison with the truth, and being also prudent and cautious by nature, he shrunk from the undertaking, thinking such great matters proper for proud and bold men and not for him. And he entreated God to choose some one else who would be able easily to accomplish all the commands which he thus laid upon him. (84) But he approved of his modesty, and said, "Art thou ignorant who it is that giveth to man a mouth, and who has formed his windpipe and his tongue, and all the apparatus of the articulate voice? I am he. Therefore, fear thou nothing. For when I approve, everything will become articulate and clear, and will change for the better, and improve; so that no one shall hinder thee, but the stream of thy words shall flow forth in a rapid and smooth current as if from a pure fountain. And if there is any need of an interpreter, thou shalt have thy brother, who will be a subordinate mouthpiece for thee, that he may utter to the multitude the words which he receives from thee, while thou utterest to him the words that thou receivest from God."

XV. (85) Having heard these things (for it is not at all safe or free from danger to oppose the commands of God), he departed and proceeded with his wife and children by the road leading to Egypt, on which he met with his brother and persuaded him to accompany him, announcing to him the oracular commands which he had received from God. And his brother's soul was already wrought up to obedience by divine providence, so that he, without hesitation, agreed to his proposal and readily followed him. (86) And when they thus arrived in Egypt with one mind and soul, they first of all collected together the elders of the nation in a secret place, and there they laid the commands of God before them, and told them how God had conceived pity and compassion for them, promised them freedom and a departure from thence to a better country, promising also that he himself would be their guide on their road.

(87) And after these events, they take courage now to converse with the king with respect to sending forth their people from his territories that they might sacrifice to God; for they said, "That it was necessary that their national sacrifices should be accomplished in the wilderness, inasmuch as they were not performed in the same manner as the sacred rites of other nations, but according to a system and law removed from the ordinary course, on account of the special peculiarities of their habits." (88) But the monarch, who from his cradle had had his soul filled with all the arrogance of his ancestors, and who had no notion in the world of any God appreciable only by the intellect apart from those objects which are visible to the sight, answered them with insolence, saying, "Who is it whom I am to obey? I know not this new Lord of whom you are speaking. I will not let the nation go to be disobedient and headstrong under pretence of fasts and sacrifices."

(89) And then, like a man of cruel and passionate disposition and implacable in his anger, he commanded the overseers of the works to oppress them still more, because they had previously given them some relaxation and leisure, saying that, it was from this relaxation and leisure, that their forming designs of feasting and sacrifice had arisen; for that men who were in great straits did not think of these things, but only those whose life had been spent in much east and luxury.

(90) Therefore the Jews had now to endure more terrible afflictions than before, and were indignant at Moses and his brother as deceivers, and accused them, sometimes secretly and sometimes openly, and charged them with impiety in appearing to have spoken falsely against God; and accordingly Moses began to exhibit the marvellous wonders which he had been previously taught, thinking that thus he should be able to bring over those who saw them from their former incredulity to believe all that he said. (91) And this exhibition of prodigies was carefully displayed before the king and magistrates of the Egyptians.

XVI. Therefore, when all the powerful men of the state were assembled round the king, the brother of Moses taking his rod, and shaking it in a very remarkable and demonstrative manner, threw it on the ground, and it immediately became a serpent. And all those who were standing around saw it, and marvelled and, in alarm and terror, withdrew, and fled. (92) But all the sophists and magicians who were present said, "Why are you thus alarmed? we also are not unpractised in such tricks as these, and we are skilled in an art which can produce similar effects." And then each of them threw down the rod which he held in his hand, and so there was a multitude of serpents which went crawling about that rod which had first been changed. (93) And that serpent, with the excess of his power, raised himself up on high, and dilated his chest, and opened his mouth, and with the violent impulse of an attractive drawing in of his breath, drew them all towards him as if he had surrounded a large cast of fishes in a net cast around them, and then, when he had swallowed them all, he returned to his original nature of a stick.

(94) So now the marvellous sight thus exhibited to them wrought a fear in the soul of every one of these wicked and malicious men, so that they no longer fancied that what was done was the trick or artifice of men, devised merely for deceit; but they saw that it was a more divine power which was the cause of these things, to which all things are easy. (95) But when by the evident might of what was done they were compelled to confess this, they still were not the less audacious, clinging to their original inhumanity and impiety as to some inalienable virtue, and not pitying those who were unjustly enslaved, nor doing any such things as they were commanded by the word of God. And though God himself had declared his will to them by demonstrations clearer than any verbal commands, namely, by signs and wonders, still they required a yet more severe impression to be made upon them, and it was necessary for him to rise up against them with still greater power; and accordingly, those foolish men, whom reason and command could not influence, are corrected by a series of afflictions: and ten punishments were inflicted on the land; (96) so that the number of the chastisements might be complete which was inflicted upon those who had completed their sins; and the punishment far transcended all ordinary visitations.

XVII. For the elements of the universe, earth, water, air, and fire, of which the world was made, were all by the command of God, brought into a state of hostility against them, so that the country of those impious men was destroyed, in order to exhibit the height of the authority which God wielded, who had also fashioned those same elements at the creation of the universe, so as to secure its safety, and who could change them all whenever he pleased, to effect the destruction of impious men.

(97) And he divided his punishments, entrusting three, those which proceeded from those elements which are composed of more solid parts, namely, earth and water, from which all the corporeal distinctive realities are perfected, to the brother of Moses. An equal number, those which proceeded from the elements which are the most prolific of life, namely, air and fire, he committed to Moses himself alone. One, the seventh, he entrusted to both in common; the other three, to make up the whole number of ten, he reserved for himself.

(98) And first of all he began to bring on the plagues derived from water; for as the Egyptians used to honour the water in an especial degree, thinking that it was the first principle of the creation of the universe, he thought it fitting to summon that first to the affliction and correction of those who thus honoured it. (99) What then happened no long time after the events I have already mentioned? The brother of Moses, by the divine command, smote with his rod upon the river, and immediately, throughout its whole course, from Ethiopia down to the sea, it is changed into blood and simultaneously with its change, all the lakes, and ditches, and fountains, and wells, and spring, and every particle of water in all Egypt, was changed into blood, so that, for want of drink, they digged round about the banks of the river, but the streams that came up were like veins of the body in a hoemorrhage, and spirted up channels of blood like springs, no transparent water being seen anywhere. (100) And all the different kinds of fish died, inasmuch as all the vivifying power of the river was changed to a destructive power, so that everything was everywhere filled with foetid odours, from such vast number of bodies putrifying all together. Moreover, a great number of men perished from thirst, and their bodies lay in heaps in the roads, since their relations had not strength to convey those who had died to the tombs; (101) for this evil lasted seven days, until the Egyptians entreated Moses, and Moses entreated God, to show pity on those who were thus perishing. And God, being merciful in his nature, changed the blood back again to wholesome water, restoring to the river its pristine clear and vivifying streams.

XVIII. (102) But again, after a brief respite, the Egyptians returned to the same cruelty and carelessness as before, as if either justice had been utterly banished from among men, or as if those who had endured one punishment were not wont to be chastised a second time; but when they suffered they were taught like young children, not to despise those who corrected them; for the punishment which followed, on the track of the last, was slow indeed to come, while they were also slow, but when they hastened to do wrong, it ran after them and overtook them.

(103) For again, the brother of Moses, being ordered to do so, stretched out his hand and held his rod over all the canals, and lakes, and marches; and at the holding forth of his rod, so immense a multitude of frogs came up, that not only the market-place, and all the spots open to the air, were filled with them, but likewise all the stables for cattle, the houses, and all the temples, and every building, public or private, as if nature had designed to send forth one race of aquatic animals into the opposite region of earth, to form a colony there, for the opposite region to water is earth. (104) Inasmuch then as they could not go out of doors, because all the passages were blocked up, and could not remain in-doors, for the frogs had already occupied all the recesses, and had crawled up to the very highest parts of the houses, they were now in the very greatest distress, and in complete despair of safety. (105) Again, therefore, they have recourse to the same means of escape by entreat-

ing Moses, and the king now promised to permit the Hebrews to depart, and they propitiated God with prayers. And when God consented, some of the frogs at once returned into the river, and there were also heaps of those which died in the roads, and the people also brought loads of them out of their houses, on account of the intolerable stench which proceeded from them, and the smell from their dead carcases, in such numbers, went up to heaven, especially as frogs, even while alive, cause great annoyance to the outward senses.

XIX. (106) And when they had a little recovered from this punishment, then, like wrestlers at the games, who have recovered fresh strength after a struggle, that so they may contend again with renewed vigour, they again returned to their original wickedness, forgetting the evils which they had already experienced.

(107) And when God had put an end to the punishments which were to proceed out of the water, he brought up others out of the land, still employing the same minister of punishment; and he now, in obedience to the command which he received, smote the ground with his rod, and an abundance of lice was poured out everywhere, and it extended like a cloud, and covered the whole of Egypt. (108) And that little animal, even though it is very small, is exceedingly annoying; for not only does it spoil the appearance, creating unseemly and injurious itchings, but it also penetrates into the inmost parts, entering in at the nostrils and ears. And it flies into the eyes and injures the pupils, unless one takes great care; and what care could be taken against so extensive a plague, especially when it was God who was inflicting the punishment? (109) And perhaps some one may here ask why God punished the land with such insignificant and generally despised animals, omitting bears, and lions, and leopards, and the other races of wild beasts who devour human flesh; and if he did not send these, at least, he might have sent Egyptian asps, the bites of which have naturally the power to cause death instantly.

(110) But if such a man really does not know, let him learn, first of all, that God was desirous rather to admonish the Egyptians than to destroy them: for if he had designed to destroy them utterly once for all, he would not have employed animals to be, as it were, his coadjutors in the work of destruction, but rather such heaven-sent afflictions as famine and pestilence; (111) and in the second place, let him also learn a lesson which is necessary to be learnt, and applicable to every condition and age of life; and what is the lesson? This; that men, when they make war, seek out the most mighty powers to gain them over to their alliance, such as shall make amends for their own want of power: but God, who is the supreme and mightiest of all powers, having need of no assistant, if

ever he desires to use any instruments as it were for the punishments which he desires to inflict, does not choose the most mighty or the greatest things as his ministers, since he takes but little heed of their capacity, but he uses insignificant and small agents, which he renders irresistible and invincible powers, and by their means he chastises those who do wrong, as he does in this instance, (112) for what can be more insignificant than a louse? And yet it was so powerful that all Egypt fainted under the host of them, and was compelled to cry out, that "this is the anger of God." For all the earth put together, from one end to the other, could not withstand the hand of God, no nor all the universe.

XX. (113) Such then were the chastisements which were inflicted by the agency of the brother of Moses.

But those in which Moses himself was the minister, and from what parts of nature they were derived, must be next considered. Now next after the earth and the water, the air and the heaven, which are the purest portions of the essences of the universe, succeeded them as the medium of the correction of the Egyptians: and of this correction Moses was the minister; (114) and first of all he began to operate upon the air.

For Egypt almost alone, if you except those countries which lie to the south of the equator, never is subject to that one of the seasons of the year which is called winter, perhaps, as some say, from the fact of its not being at any great distance from the torrid zone, since the essence of fire flows from that quarter in an invisible manner, and scorches everything all around, or perhaps it is because the river overflows at the time of the summer solstice, and so consumes all the clouds before they can collect for winter; (115) for the river begins to rise at the beginning of the summer, and to fall towards the end of summer; during which period the etesian gales increase in violence blowing from a direction opposite to the mouths of the Nile, and by which it is prevented from flowing freely into the sea, and by the violence of which winds, the sea itself is also raised to a considerable height, and erects vast waves like a long wall, and so the river is agitated within the country.

And then when the two streams meet together, the river descending from its sources above, and the waters which ought to escape abroad being turned back by the beating of the sea, and not being able to extend their breadth, for the banks on each side of the river confine its streams, the river, as is natural, rises to a height, and breaks its bounds; (116) perhaps also it does so because it was superfluous for winter to occur in Egypt; for the object for which showers of rain are usually serviceable, is in this instance provided for by the river which overflows the fields, and turns them into one vast lake, to make them productive of the annual crops; (117) but nature does not expend her powers to no purpose when they are not wanted, so as to provide rain for a land which does not require it, but it rejoices in the variety and diversity of scientific operations, and arranges the harmony of the universe from a number of opposite qualities.

And for this reason it supplies the benefits which are derivable from water, to some countries, by bestowing it on them from above, namely from heaven, and to others it gives it from below by means of springs and rivers; (118) though then the land was thus arranged, and enjoyed spring during the winter solstice, and since it is only the parts along the seacoasts that are ever moistened with a few drops of rain, and since the country beyond Memphis, where the palace of the king of Egypt is, does never even see snow at all; now, on the contrary, the air suddenly assumed a new appearance, so that all the things which are seen in the most stormy and wintry countries, come upon it all together; abundance of rain, and torrents of dense and ceaseless hail, and heavy winds met together and beat against one another with violence; and the clouds burst, and there were incessant lightnings, and thunders, and continued roarings, and flashes which made a most wonderful and fearful appearance.

For though the lightning and the thunderbolts penetrated and descended through the hail, being quite a contrary substance, still they did not melt it, nor were the flashes extinguished by it, but they remained as they were before, and ran up and down in long lines, and even preserved the hail. (119) And not only did the excessive violence of the storm drive all the inhabitants to excessive despair, but the unprecedented character of the visitation tended likewise to the same point. For they believed, as was indeed the case, that all these novel and fearful calamities were caused by the divine anger, the air having assumed a novel appearance, such as it had never worn before, to the destruction and overthrow of all trees and fruits, by which also great numbers of animals were destroyed, some in consequence of the exceeding cold, others though the weight of the hail which fell upon them, as if they had been stoned, while some again were destroyed by the fire of the lightning. And some remained half consumed, bearing the marks of the wounds caused by the thunderbolts, for the admonition and warning of all who saw them.

XXI. (120) And when this evil had abated, and when the king and his court had again resumed their confidence, Moses stretched forth his rod into the air, at the command of God. And then a south wind of an uncommon violence set in, which increased in intensity and vehemence the whole of that day and night, being of itself a very great

affliction; for it is a drying wind, causing headaches, and terrible to bear, calculated to cause grief, and terror, and perplexity in Egypt above all countries, inasmuch as it lies to the south, in which part of the heaven the revolutions of the light-giving stars take place, so that whenever that wind is set in motion, the light of the sun and its fire is driven in that direction and scorches up every thing. (121) And with this wind a countless number of animals was brought over the land, animals destroying all plants, locusts, which devoured every thing incessantly like a stream, consuming all that the thunderstorms and the hail had left, so that there was not a green shoot seen any longer in all that vast country.

(122) And then at length the men in authority came, though late, to an accurate perception of the evils that had come upon them, and came and said to the king, "How long wilt thou refuse to permit the men to depart? Dost thou not understand, from what has already taken place, that Egypt is destroyed?" And he agreed to all they said, yielding as far as appearances went at least; but again, when the evil was abated at the prayer of Moses, the wind came from the sea side, and took up the locusts and scattered them. (123) And when they had been completely dispersed, and when the king was again obstinate respecting the allowing the nation to depart, a greater evil than the former ones was descended upon him.

For while it was bright daylight, on a sudden, a thick darkness overspread the land, as if an eclipse of the sun more complete than any common one had taken place. And it continued with a long series of clouds and impenetrable density, all the course of the sun's rays being cut off by the massive thickness of the veil which was interposed, so that day did not at all differ from night. For what indeed did it resemble, but one very long night equal in length to three days and an equal number of nights? (124) And at this time they say that some persons threw themselves on their beds, and did not venture to rise up, and that some, when any of the necessities of nature overtook them, could only move with difficulty by feeling their way along the walls or whatever else they could lay hold of, like so many blind men; for even the light of the fire lit for necessary uses was either extinguished by the violence of the storm, or else it was made invisible and overwhelmed by the density of the darkness, so that most indispensable of all the external senses, namely, sight, though unimpaired, was deprived of its office, not being able to discern any thing, and all the other senses were overthrown like subjects, the leader having fallen down. (125) For neither was any one able to speak or to hear, nor could any one venture to take food, but they lay themselves down in quiet and hunger, not exercising any of the outward senses, but being wholly overwhelmed by the affliction, till Moses again had compassion on them, and besought God in their behalf. And he restored fine weather, and produced light instead of darkness, and day instead of night.

XXII. (126) Such, they say, were the punishments inflicted by the agency of Moses alone, the plague, namely, of hail and thunderstorms, the plague of locusts, and the plague of darkness, which rejected every imaginable description of light.

Then he himself and his brother brought on one together, which I shall proceed to relate.

(127) At the command of God they both took up ashes from the furnace in their hands, which Moses on his part sprinkled in the air. Then a dust arose on a sudden, and produced a terrible, and most painful, and incurable ulceration over the whole skin both of man and of the brute beasts; and immediately their bodies became swollen with the pustules, having blisters all over them full of matter which any one might have supposed were burning underneath and ready to burst; (128) and the men were, as was natural, oppressed with pain and excessive agony from the ulceration and inflammation, and they suffered in their souls even more than in their bodies, being wholly exhausted with anguish. For there was one vast uninterrupted sore to be seen from head to foot, those which covered any particular part of any separate limb spreading so as to become confused into one huge ulcer; until again, at the supplication of the lawgiver, which he made on behalf of the sufferers, the disease became more tolerable.

(129) Therefore, in this instance the two brothers afforded the Egyptians this warning in unison, and very properly; the brother of Moses acting by means of the dust which rose up, since to him had been committed the superintendence of the things which proceeded from the earth; and Moses, by means of the air which was thus changed for the affliction of the inhabitants, and his ministrations were assigned to the afflictions to be cause by the air and by the heaven.

XXIII. (130) The remaining punishments are three in number, and they were inflicted by God himself without any agency or ministration of man, each of which I will now proceed to relate as well I can.

The first is that which was inflicted by means of that animal which is the boldest in all nature, namely, the dog-fly *(kynomuia)* which those person who invent names have named with great propriety (for they were wise men); combining the name of the appellation of the most impudent of all animals, a fly and a dog, the one being the boldest of all terrestrial, and the other the boldest of all flying, animals. For they approach and run up fearlessly, and if any one drives them away, they

still resist and renew their attack, so as never to yield until they are sated with blood and flesh.

(131) And so the dog-fly, having derived boldness from both these animals, is a biting and treacherous creature; for it shoots in from a distance with a whizzing sound like an arrow; and when it has reached its mark it sticks very closely with great force. (132) But at this time its attack was prompted by God, so that its treachery and hostility were redoubled, since it not only displayed all its own natural covetousness, but also all that eagerness which it derived from the divine providence which went it forth, and armed it and excited it to acts of valour against the natives.

(133) And after the dog-fly there followed another punishment unconnected with any human agency, namely, the mortality among the cattle; for all the herds of oxen, and flocks of goats, and vast flocks of sheep, and all the beasts of burden, and all other domestic animals of every kind died in one day in a body, as if by some agreement or at some given signal; foreshowing the destruction of human beings which was about to take place a short time afterwards as in a pestilential disease; for the sudden destruction of irrational animals is said to be an ordinary prelude to pestilential diseases.

XXIV. (134) After which the tenth and last punishment came, exceeding in terror all that had gone before, namely, the death of the Egyptians themselves. Not of them all, for God had not decreed to make the whole country desolate, but only to correct it. Nor even of the greatest number of the men and women of every age all together, but he permitted the rest to live, and only passed sentence of death on all the first-born, beginning with the eldest of the king's sons, and ceasing with the first-born son of the most obscure grinder at the mill; (135) for, about midnight, all those children who had been the first to address their fathers and their mothers, and who had also been the first to be addressed by them as their sons, though they were in good health and in full vigour of body, all, without any apparent cause, were suddenly slain in the flower of their youth; and they say that there was not a single house in the whole land which was exempt from the visitation.

(136) But at dawn of day, as was natural, when every one beheld his nearest and dearest relatives unexpectedly dead, with whom up to the evening before they had lived in one home and at one table, being overwhelmed with the most bitter grief, filled every place with lamentation. So that it came to pass, on account of the universality of the calamity, as all men were weeping altogether with one accord, that there was but one universal sound of wailing heard over the whole land from one end

to the other. (137) And, for a while, they remained in their houses, no one being aware of the misfortune which had befallen his neighbour, but lamenting only for his individual loss. But when any one went out of doors and learnt the misfortunes of others also, he at once felt a double sorrow, grieving for the common calamity, in addition to his own private misfortune, a greater and more grievous sorrow being thus added to the lesser and lighter one, so that every one felt deprived of all hope of consolation.

For who was likely to comfort another when he himself stood in need of the same consolation? (138) But, as is usual in such circumstances, men thinking that the present evils were the beginning of greater ones, and being filled with fear lest those who were still living should also be destroyed, ran weeping to the king's palace, and rent their clothes, and cried out against the sovereign, as the cause of all the terrible evils that had befallen them. (139) "For if," said they, "immediately when Moses at the beginning first came to him he had allowed his nation to depart, we should never have experienced any one of the miseries that have befallen us at all. But he yielded to his natural obstinacy and haughtiness, and so we have reaped the ready reward of his unreasonable contentiousness." Then one man encouraged another to drive the Jewish people with all speed out of the whole country, and not to allow them to remain one day, or rather one single hour, looking upon every moment that they abode among them as an irremediable calamity.

XXV. (140) So they, being now driven out of the land and pursued, coming at last to a proper notion of their own nobility and worth, ventured upon a deed of daring such as became the free to dare, as men who were not forgetful of the iniquitous plots that had been laid against them; (141) for they carried off abundant booty, which they themselves collected, by means of the hatred in which they were held, and some of it they carried themselves, submitting to heavy burdens, and some they placed upon their beasts of burden, not in order to gratify any love of money, or, as any usurer might say, because they coveted their neighbours' goods. (How should they do so?) But, first of all, because they were thus receiving the necessary wages from those whom they had served for so long a time; and, secondly, because they had a right to afflict those at whose hands they had suffered wrong with afflictions slighter than, and by no means equal to, what they endured.

For how can the deprivation of money and treasures be equivalent to the loss of liberty? on behalf of which those who are in possession of their senses dare not only to cast away all their property, but even to venture their lives? (142) So they now prospered in both particulars: whether in that

they received wages as it in price, which they now exacted from unwilling paymasters, who for a long period had not paid them at all; and, also, as if they were at war, they looked upon it as fitting to carry off the treasures of the enemy, according to the laws of conquerors; for it was the Egyptians who had set the example of acts of injustice, having, as I said before, enslaved foreigners and suppliants, as if they had been prisoners taken in war. And so they now, when an opportunity offered, avenged themselves without any preparation of arms, justice itself holding a shield over them, and stretching forth its hand to help them.

XXVI. (143) Such, then, were the afflictions and punishments by which Egypt was corrected; not one of which ever touched the Hebrews, although they were dwelling in the same cities and villages, and even houses, as the Egyptians, and touching the same earth and water, and air and fire, which are all component parts of nature, and which it is impossible to escape from. And this is the most extraordinary and almost incredible thing, that, by the very same events happening in the same place and at the same time, one people was destroyed and the other people was preserved. (144) The river was changed into blood, but not to the Hebrews; for when these latter went to draw water from it, it underwent another change and became drinkable.

Frogs went up from the water upon the land, and filled all the market-places, and stables, and dwelling-houses; but they retreated from before the Hebrews alone, as if they had been able to distinguish between the two nations, and to know which people it was proper should be punished and which should be treated in the opposite manner.

(145) No lice, no dog-flies, no locusts, which greatly injured the plants, and the fruits, and the animals, and the human beings, ever descended upon the Hebrews. Those unceasing storms of rain and hail, and thunder and lightning, which continued so uninterruptedly, never reached them; they never felt, no not even in their dreams, that most terrible ulceration which caused the Egyptians so much suffering; when that most dense darkness descended upon the others, they were living in bright daylight, a brilliancy as of noon-day shining all around them; when, among the Egyptians, all the first-born were slain, not one of the Hebrews died; for it was not likely, since even that destruction of such countless flocks and herds of cattle never carried off or injured a single flock or a single beast belonging to the Hebrews.

(146) And it seems to me that if any one had been present to see all that happened at that time, he would not have conceived any other idea than that the Hebrews were there as spectators of the miseries which the other nation was enduring; and, not only that, but that they were also there for

the purpose of being taught that most beautiful and beneficial of all lessons, namely, piety. For a distinction could otherwise have never been made so decidedly between the good and the bad, giving destruction to the one and salvation to the other.

XXVII. (147) And of those who now went forth out of Egypt and left their abodes in that country, the men of age to bear arms were more than six hundred thousand men, and the other multitude of elders, and children, and women were so great that it was not easy to calculate it. Moreover, there also went forth with them a mixed multitude of promiscuous persons collected from all quarters, and servants, like an illegitimate crowd with a body of genuine citizens. Among these were those who had been born to Hebrew fathers by Egyptian women, and who were enrolled as members of their father's race. And, also, all those who had admired the decent piety of the men, and therefore joined them; and some, also, who had come over to them, having learnt the right way, by reason of the magnitude and multitude of the incessant punishments which had been inflicted on their own countrymen.

(148) Of all these men, Moses was elected the leader; receiving the authority and sovereignty over them, not having gained it like some men who have forced their way to power and supremacy by force of arms and intrigue, and by armies of cavalry and infantry, and by powerful fleets, but having been appointed for the sake of his virtue and excellence and that benevolence towards all men which he was always feeling and exhibiting; and, also, because God, who loves virtue, and piety, and excellence, gave him his authority as a well-deserved reward. (149) For, as he had abandoned the chief authority in Egypt, which he might have had as the grandson of the reigning king, on account of the iniquities which were being perpetrated in that country, and by reason of his nobleness of soul and of the greatness of his spirit, and the natural detestation of wickedness, scorning and rejecting all the hopes which he might have conceived from those who had adopted him, it seemed good to the Ruler and Governor of the universe to recompense him with the sovereign authority over a more populous and more powerful nation, which he was about to take to himself out of all other nations and to consecrate to the priesthood, that it might for ever offer up prayers for the whole universal race of mankind, for the sake of averting evil from them and procuring them a participation in blessings.

(150) And when he had received this authority, he did not show anxiety, as some persons do, to increase the power of his own family, and promote his sons (for he had two) to any great dignity, so as to make them at the present time partakers in, and subsequently successors to, his sovereignty; for as he always cherished a pure and guileless disposition in all things both small and great, he now subdued his natural love and affection for his children, like an honest judge, making these feelings subordinate to his own incorruptible reason; (151) for he kept one most invariable object always steadily before him, namely, that of benefiting those who were subjected to his authority, and of doing everything both in word and deed, with a view to their advantage, never omitting any opportunity of doing anything that might tend to their prosperity.

(152) Therefore he alone of all the persons who have ever enjoyed supreme authority, neither accumulated treasures of silver and gold, nor levied taxes, nor acquired possession of houses, or property, or cattle, or servants of his household, or revenues, or anything else which has reference to magnificence and superfluity, although he might have acquired an unlimited abundance of them all. (153) But as he thought it a token of poverty of soul to be anxious about material wealth, he despised it as a blind thing, but he honoured the far-sighted wealth of nature, and was as great an admirer as any one in the world of that kind of riches, as he showed himself to be in his clothes, and in his food, and in his whole system and manner of life, not indulging in any theatrical affectation of pomp and magnificence, but cultivating the simplicity and unpretending affable plainness of a private individual, but a sumptuousness which was truly royal, in those things which it is becoming for a ruler to desire and to abound in; (154) and these things are, temperance, and fortitude, and continence, and presence of mind, and acuteness, and knowledge, and industry, and patience under evil, and contempt of pleasure, and justice, and exhortations to virtue and blame, and lawful punishment of offenders, and, on the contrary, praise and honour to those who did well in accordance with law.

XXVIII. (155) Therefore, as he had utterly discarded all desire of gain and of those riches which are held in the highest repute among men, God honoured him, and gave him instead the greatest and most perfect wealth; and this is the wealth[2] of all the earth and sea, and of all the rivers, and of all the other elements, and all combinations whatever; for having judged him deserving of being made a partaker with himself in the portion which he had reserved for himself, he gave him the whole world as a possession suitable for his heir: (156) therefore, every one of the elements obeyed him as its master, changing the power which it had by nature and submitting to his commands. And perhaps there was nothing wonderful in this; for if it be true according to the proverb,—

---

[2] The text here is very corrupt.

"That all the property of friends is common;"

and if the prophet was truly called the friend of God, then it follows that he would naturally partake of God himself and of all his possessions as far as he had need; (157) for God possesses everything and is in need of nothing; but the good man has nothing which is properly his own, no, not even himself, but he has a share granted to him of the treasures of God as far as he is able to partake of them. And this is natural enough; for he is a citizen of the world; on which account he is not spoken of as to be enrolled as a citizen of any particular city in the habitable world, since he very appropriately has for his inheritance not a portion of a district, but the whole world.

(158) What more shall I say? Has he not also enjoyed an even greater communion with the Father and Creator of the universe, being thought unworthy of being called by the same appellation? For he also was called the god and king of the whole nation, and he is said to have entered into the darkness where God was; that is to say, into the invisible, and shapeless, and incorporeal world, the essence, which is the model of all existing things, where he beheld things invisible to mortal nature; for, having brought himself and his own life into the middle, as an excellently wrought picture, he established himself as a most beautiful and Godlike work, to be a model for all those who were inclined to imitate him.

(159) And happy are they who have been able to take, or have even diligently laboured to take, a faithful copy of this excellence in their own souls; for let the mind, above all other parts, take the perfect appearance of virtue, and if that cannot be, at all events let it feel an unhesitating and unvarying desire to acquire that appearance; (160) for, indeed, there is no one who does not know that men in a lowly condition are imitators of men of high reputation, and that what they see, these last chiefly desire, towards that do they also direct their own inclinations and endeavours.

Therefore, when the chief of a nation begins to indulge in luxury and to turn aside to a delicate and effeminate life, then the whole of his subjects, or very nearly the whole, carry their desire for indulging the appetites of the belly and the parts below the belly beyond all reasonable bounds, except that there may be some persons who, through the natural goodness of their disposition, have a soul far removed from treachery, being rather merciful and kind.

(161) If, on the other hand, the chief of a people adopts a more austere and dignified course of life, then even those of his subjects, who are inclined to be very incontinent, change and become temperate, hastening, either out of fear or out of shame, to give him an idea that they are devoted to the same pursuits and inclinations that he is; and, in fact, the lower orders will never, no, nor will mad men even, reject the customs and habits of their superiors: (162) but, perhaps, since Moses was also destined to be the lawgiver of his nation, he was himself long previously, through the providence of God, a living and reasonable law, since that providence appointed him to the lawgiver, when as yet he knew nothing of his appointment.

XXIX. (163) When then he received the supreme authority, with the good will of all his subjects, God himself being the regulator and approver of all his actions, he conducted his people as a colony into Phoenicia, and into the hollow Syria (Coele-syria), and Palestine, which was at that time called the land of the Canaanites, the borders of which country were three days' journey distant from Egypt. (164) Then he led them forward, not by the shortest road, partly because he was afraid lest the inhabitants should come out to meet and to resist him in his march, from fear of being overthrown and enslaved by such a multitude, and so, if a war arose, they might be again driven back into Egypt, falling from one enemy to another, and being driven by their new foes upon their ancient tyrants, and so become a sport and a laughing-stock to the Egyptians, and have to endure greater and more grievous hardships than before.

He was also desirous, by leading them through a desolate and extensive country, to prove them, and see how obedient they would be when they were not surrounded by any abundance of necessaries, but were but scantily provided and nearly in actual want.

(165) Therefore, turning aside from the direct road he found an oblique path, and thinking that it must extend as far as the Red Sea, he began to march by that road, and, they say, that a most portentous miracle happened at that time, a prodigy of nature, which no one anywhere recollects to have ever happened before; (166) for a cloud, fashioned into the form of a vast pillar, went before the multitude by day, giving forth a light like that of the sun, but by night it displayed a fiery blaze, in order that the Hebrews might not wander on their journey, but might follow the guidance of their leader along the road, without any deviation. Perhaps, indeed, this was one of the ministers of the mighty King, an unseen messenger, a guide of the way enveloped in this cloud, whom it was not lawful for men to behold with the eyes of the body.

XXX. (167) But when the king of Egypt saw them proceeding along a pathless track, as he fancied, and marching through a rough and untrodden wilderness, he was delighted with the blunder they were making respecting their line of march, thinking that now they were hemmed in, having no way of escape whatever. And, as he repented of having let them go, he determined to pursue them, thinking that he should either subdue the multitude by fear, and so reduce them a second time to slavery, or else that if they resisted he should slay them all from the children upwards. (168) Accordingly, he took all his force of cavalry, and his darters, and his slingers, and his equestrian archers, and all the rest of his light-armed troops, and he gave his commanders six hundred of the finest of his scythe-bearing chariots, that with all becoming dignity and display they might pursue these men, and join in the expedition and so suing all possible speed, he sallied forth after them and hastened and pressed on the march, wishing to come upon them suddenly before they had any expectation of him.

For an unexpected evil is at all times more grievous than one which has been looked for, in proportion as that which has been despised finds it easier to make a formidable attack than that which has been regarded with care.

(169) The king, therefore, with these ideas, pursued after the Hebrews, thinking that he should subdue them by the mere shout of battle. And, when he overtook them, they were already encamped along the shore of the Red Sea. And they were just about to go to breakfast, when, at first, a mighty sound reached them, as was natural from such a host of men and beasts of burden all proceeding on with great haste, so that they all ran out of their tents to look round, and stood on tip-toes to see and hear what was the matter. Then, a short time afterwards, the army of the enemy came in sight as it rose over a hill, all in arms, and ready arranged in line of battle.

XXXI. (170) And the Hebrews, being terrified at this extraordinary and unexpected danger, and not being well prepared for defence, because of a scarcity of defensive armour and of weapons (for they had not marched out for war, but to found a colony), and not being able to escape, for behind was the sea, and in front was the enemy, and on each side a vast and pathless wilderness, reviled against Moses, and, being dismayed at the magnitude of the evils that threatened them, began, as is very common in such calamities, to blame their governors, and said: (171) "Because there were no graves in Egypt in which we could be buried after we were dead, have you brought us out hither to kill and bury us here? Or, is not even slavery a lighter evil than death? Having allured the multitude with the hope of liberty, you have caused them to incur a still more grievous danger than slavery, namely, the risk of the loss of life. (172) Did you not know our simplicity, and the bitterness and cruel anger of the Egyptians? Do you not see the magnitude of the evils which surround us, and from which we cannot escape? What are we to do? Are we, unarmed, to fight against men in complete armour? or shall we flee now that we are hemmed in as by nets cast all around us by our pitiless enemies—hemmed in by pathless deserts and impassable seas? Or, even, if the sea was navigable, how are we to get any vessels to cross over it?"

(173) Moses, when he heard these complaints, pardoned his people, but remembered the oracles of God. And, at the same time, he so divided and distributed his mind and his speech, that with the one he associated invisibly with God, in order that God might deliver him from otherwise inextricable calamities; and, with the other, he encouraged and comforted those who cried out to him, saying: "Do not faint and despair. God does not deliver in the same way that man does. (174) Why do you only trust such means of deliverance as seem probable and likely? God, when he comes as an assistant, stands in need of no adventitious preparations. It is his peculiar attribute to find a path amid inextricable perplexities. What is impossible to every created being is possible and easy to him above."

(175) Thus he spoke to them while yet standing still. But after a short time he became inspired by God, and being full of the divine spirit and under the influence of that spirit which was accustomed to enter into him, he prophesied and animated them thus: "This army which you behold so splendidly equipped with arms, you shall no more see arrayed against you; for it shall fall, utterly and completely overthrown, so that not a relic shall be seen any more upon the earth, and that not at any distance of time, but this very next night."

XXXII. (176) He then spoke thus. But when the sun had set, immediately a most violent south wind set in and began to blow, under the influence of which the sea retreated; for, as it was accustomed to ebb and flow, on this occasion it was driven back much further towards the shore, and drawn up in a heap as if into a ravine or a whirlpool. And no stars were visible, but a dense and black cloud covered the whole of the heaven, so that the night became totally dark, to the consternation of the pursuers. (177) And Moses, at the command of God, smote the sea with his staff. And it was broken and divided into two parts, and one of the divisions at the part where it was broken off, was raised to a height and mounted up, and being thus consolidated like a strong wall, stood quiet and unshaken; and the portion behind the Hebrews was also contracted and raised in, and prevented from proceeding forwards, as if it were held back by invisible reins. And the intermediate space, where the fracture had taken place, was dried up and became a broad, and level, and easy road.

When Moses beheld this he marvelled and rejoiced; and, being filled with joy, he encouraged his followers and exhorted them to march forward with all possible speed. (178) And when they were about to pass over, a most extraordinary prodigy was seen; for the cloud, which had been their guide, and which during all the rest of the period of their march had gone in front of them, now turned back and placed itself at the back of the multitude to guard their rear; and, being situated between the pursuers and the pursued, it guided the one party so as to keep them with safety and perfect freedom from danger, and it checked and embarrassed the others, who were hastening on to pursue them. And, when the Egyptians saw this, they were entirely filled with disorder and confusion, and through their consternation they threw all their ranks into disorder, falling upon one another and endeavouring to flee, when there was no advantage to be derived from flight.

(179) For, at the first appearance of morning, the Hebrews passed over by a dry path, with their wives, and families, and infant children. But the portions of the sea which were rolled up and consolidated on each side overwhelmed the Egyptians with their horses and chariots, the tide being brought back by a strong north wind and poured over them, and coming upon them with vast waves and overpowering billows, so that there was not even a torchbearer left to carry the news of this sudden disaster back to Egypt.

(180) Then the Hebrews, being amazed at this great and wonderful event, gained a victory which they had never hoped for without bloodshed or loss; and, seeing the instantaneous and complete destruction of the enemy, formed two choruses, one of men and the other of women, on the sea shore, and sang hymns of gratitude to God, Moses leading the song of the men, and his sister that of the women; for these two persons were the leaders of the choruses.

XXXIII. (181) And when they had departed from the sea they went on for some time travelling, and no longer feeling any apprehension of their enemies. But when water failed them, so that for three days they had nothing to drink, they were again reduced to despondency by thirst, and again began to blame their fate as if they had not enjoyed any good fortune previously; for it always happens that the presence of an existing and present evil takes away the recollection of the pleasure which was caused by former good. (182) At last, when they beheld some fountains, they ran up full of joy with the idea that they were going to drink, being deceived by ignorance of the truth; for the springs were bitter.

Then when they had tasted them they were bowed down by the unexpected disappointment, and fainted, and yielded both in body and soul, lamenting not so much for themselves as for their helpless children, whom they could not endure without tears to behold imploring drink; (183) and some of those who were of more careless dispositions, and of no settled notions of piety, blamed all that had gone before, as if it had turned out not so as to do them any good, but rather so as to lead them to a suffering of more grievous calamities than ever; saying that it was better for them to die, not only once but three times over, by the hands of their enemies, than to perish with thirst; for they affirmed that a quick and painless departure from life did in no respect differ from freedom from death in the opinion of wise men, but that that was real death which was slow and accompanied by pain; that what was fearful was not to be dead but only to be dying.

(184) When they were lamenting and bewailing themselves in this manner, Moses again besought God, who knew the weakness of all creatures, and especially of men, and the necessary wants of the body which depends for its existence on food, and which is enslaved by those severe task-mistresses, eating and drinking, to pardon his desponding people, and to relieve their want of everything, and that too not after a long interval of time, but by a prompt and undeferred liberality, since by reason of the natural impotency of their mortal nature, they required a very speedy measure of assistance and deliverance.

(185) But he, by his bountiful and merciful power, anticipated their wishes, sending forth and opening the watchful, anxious eye of the soul of his suppliant, and showed him a piece of wood which he bade him take up and throw into the water, which indeed had been made by nature with such a power for that purpose, and which perhaps had a quality which was previously unknown, or perhaps was then first endowed with it, for the purpose of effecting the service which it was then about to perform: (186) and when he had done that which he was commanded to do, the fountains became changed and sweet and drinkable, so that no one was able to recognise the fact of their having been bitter previously, because there was not the slightest trace or spark of their ancient bitterness left to excite the recollection.

XXXIV. (187) And so having appeased their thirst with double pleasure, since the blessing of enjoyment when it comes beyond one's hopes delights one still more, and having also replenished their ewers, they departed as from a feast, as if they had been entertained at a luxurious banquet, and as if they were intoxicated not with the drunkenness which proceeds from wine, but with a sober joy which they had imbibed purely, while pledging and being pledged by the piety of the ruler who was leading them; (188) and so they arrive at a second halting place, well supplied with water, and well shaded with trees, called Aileem, irrigated with twelve fountains, near which were young and vigorous trunks of palm trees to the number of seventy, a visible indication and token of good to the whole nation, to all who were gifted with a clear-sighted intellect.

(189) For the nation itself was divided into twelve tribes, each of which, if pious and religious, would be looked upon in the light of a fountain, since piety is continually pouring forth everlasting and unceasing springs of virtuous actions. And the elders and chiefs of the whole nation were seventy in number, being therefore very naturally likened to palm trees which are the most excellent of all trees, being both most beautiful to behold, and bearing the most exquisite fruit, which has also its vitality and power of existence, not buried in the roots like other trees, but situated high up like the heart of a man, and lodged in the centre of its highest branches, by which it is attended and guarded like a queen as it really is, they being spread all round it. (190) And the intellect too of those persons who have tasted of holiness has a similar nature; for it has learned to look upwards and to soar on high, and is continually keeping its eye fixed on sublime objects, and investigating divine things, and ridiculing, and scorning all earthly beauty, thinking the last only toys, and divine things the only real and proper objects worthy of its attention.

XXXV. (191) But after these events only a short time elapsed, when they became oppressed by famine through the scarcity of provisions, as if one necessary thing after another was to foil them in succession: for thirst and hunger are very cruel and terrible mistresses, and having portioned out the afflictions between them, attacked them by turns; and it so fell out that when the first calamity was relaxed the second came on, which was most intolerable to those who had to bear it, inasmuch as having only just fancied that they were delivered from thirst, they now found another evil, namely famine, lying in ambush to attack them; (192) and not only was their present scarcity terrible, but they were also in despair as to the supply of necessary food for the future; for when they saw the vast and extensive desert around them, so utterly unproductive of any kind of crop, their hearts sank within them.

For all around were rugged and precipitous rocks, or else a salt and brackish plain, and stony mountains, or deep sands reaching up and forming mountains of inaccessible height; and moreover there was no river, neither winter torrent nor ever-flowing stream; there were no springs, no plant growing from seed, no tree whether for fruit or timber, no animal whether flying or terrestrial, except some few poisonous reptiles born for the destruction of mankind, and serpents, and scorpions. (193) So then the Hebrews, remembering the plenty and luxury which they had enjoyed in Egypt, and the abundance of all things which was bestowed upon them there, and contrasting it with the universal want of all things which they were now experiencing, were grieved and indignant, and talked the matter over with one another, saying:—

"We left our former abodes and emigrated, from a hope of freedom, happy only in the promises of our leader; as far as his actions go, we are of all men the most miserable. (194) What will be the end of this long and interminable journey? Everyone else, whether sailing over the sea or marching on foot, has some limit before him at which he will eventually arrive; some being bound for marts and harbours, others for some city or country; but we alone have nothing to look forward to but a pathless desert, and a difficult journey, and terrible hopelessness, and despair; for as we advance, the desert lies before us like an ever open, vast, and pathless sea which widens and increases every day. (195) But Moses having raised our expectations, and puffed us up with fine speeches, and filled our ears with vain hopes, racks our bodies with hunger and does not give us even necessary food. He has deceived this vast multitude with the name of a settlement in a colony; having first of all led us out of an inhabited country into an uninhabitable district, and now sending us down to the shades below, which is the last journey of life."

XXXVI. (196) Moses, being reviled in this way, was nevertheless not so much grieved at their accusations which they brought against himself, as at the inconstancy of their own resolutions and minds. For though they had already experienced an infinite number of blessings which had befallen them unexpectedly and out of the ordinary course of affairs, they ought, in his opinion, not to have allowed themselves to be led away by any specious or plausible complaints, but to have trusted in him, as they had already received the clearest possible proofs that he spoke truly about everything.

(197) But again, when he came to take into consideration the want of food, than which there is no more terrible evil which can afflict mankind, he pardoned them, knowing that the multitude is by nature inconstant and always moved by present circumstances, which cause it to forget what has gone before, and despair of the future. (198) Therefore, as they were all in the extremity of suffering, and expecting the most fearful misery which they fancied was lying in ambush for them and close at hand, God, partly by reason of his natural love and compassion for man, and partly because he desired to honour the commander whom he had appointed to govern them, and still more to show his great piety and holiness in all matters whether visible or invisible, pitied them and relieved their distress.

(199) Therefore he now devised an entirely

new kind of benefit, that they, being taught by manifest signs and displays of his power, might feel reverence for him, and learn for the future not to be impatient if anything turned out contrary to their wishes, but to endure present evils with fortitude, in the expectation of future blessings.

(200) What then happened? The very next day, about sun-rise, a dense and abundant dew fell in a circle all round about the camp, which rained down upon it gently and quietly in an unusual and unprecedented shower; not water, nor hail, nor snow, nor ice, for these are the things which the changes of the clouds produce in the winter season; but what was now rained down upon them was a very small and light grain, like millet, which, by reason of its incessant fall, rested in heaps before the camp, a most extraordinary sight. And the Hebrews marvelled at it, and inquired of the commander what this rain was, which no man had ever seen before, and for what it was sent.

(201) And he was inspired, and full of the spirit of prophecy, and spoke to them as follows: "A fertile plain has been granted to mortal men, which they cut up into furrows, and plough, and sow, and do everything else which relates to agriculture, providing the yearly fruits so as to enjoy abundance of necessary food. But it is not one portion only of the universe, but the whole world that belongs to God, and all its parts obey their master, supplying everything which he desires that they should supply. (202) Now therefore, it has seemed good to him that the air should produce food instead of water, since the earth has often brought forth rain; for when the river in Egypt every year overflows with inundations and irrigates all the fields, what else is that but a rain which is showered up from below?" (203) That other would have been indeed a most surprising fact if it had stopped there; but now he wrought wonders with still more surprising circumstances; for all the population bringing vessels one after another, collected what fell, some putting them upon beasts of burden, others loading themselves and taking them on their shoulders, being prudently eager to provide themselves with necessary food for a longer time. (204) But it was something that would bear to be stored up and dispensed gradually, since God is accustomed always to give his gifts fresh.

Accordingly, they now prepared enough for their immediate necessities and present use, and ate it with pleasure. But of what was left till the next day they found not a morsel unhurt, but it was all changed and fetid, and full of little animals of the kind which usually cause putrefaction. So this they naturally threw away, but they found fresh quantities of it ready for food, so that it fell out that this food was carried down every day with the dew. (205) But the holy seventh day had an especial honour; for, as it is not permitted to do any-thing whatever on that day (and it is expressly commanded that men are then to abstain from every work, great or little), so that they were not able to collect food that day, instead of food for one day, God rained upon them a double quantity, and ordered them to collect what shall be food enough for two days. And what was then collected remained sound, no portion of it becoming spoiled as it had before.

XXXVII. (206) I will also relate a circumstance which is more marvellous than even this one; for, though they were travelling for forty years, yet during all this long period of time they had an abundant supply of all necessary things in their appointed order, as is the case in clubs and messes which are regularly measured out with a view to the distribution of what is required by each individual. And, at the same time, they learnt the value of that long-wished for day; (207) for, having inquired for a long time what the day of the creation of the world as, the day on which the universe was completely finished, and, having received this question from their fathers and their ancestors undecided, they at last, though with great difficulty, did ascertain it, not being taught only by the sacred scriptures, but also by a certain proof which was very distinct; for, as that portion of the manna (as has been already said) which was more than was wanted on the other days of the week was spoiled, still that portion which was rained down on the day before the seventh not only did not change its nature, but was dispensed in a twofold quantity. (208) And the use was as follows.

At dawn they collected what had been showered down, and then they ground or pounded it; and then they roasted it and made every sweet food of it, like honey cheesecake, and so they ate it, without requiring any exceeding skill on the part of the preparers of the food. (209) But they also had no scarcity of, nor any great distance to go for, the means of making life even luxurious, as if they had been in a populous and productive land, since God had determined out of his great abundance to supply them with plenty of all things which they required even in the wilderness; for, in the evenings, there was an uninterrupted cloud of quails borne to them from the sea, which overshadowed the whole camp, flying very near the ground so as to be easily caught. Therefore, the Hebrews, taking them and preparing them as each individual liked, enjoyed the most exquisite meat, pleasing themselves and varying their food with this necessary and delicious addition.

XXXVIII. (210) Accordingly, they had a great abundance of these birds, as they never failed. But, a second time, a terrible scarcity of water came upon them and afflicted them; and, as they again speedily began to despair of their safety, Moses, taking his sacred rod with which he had wrought the signs in Egypt, being inspired by God, smote the precipitous rock. (211) And the rock being struck this seasonable blow, whether it was that there was a spring previously concealed beneath it, or whether water was then for the first time conveyed into it by invisible channels pouring in all together and being forced out with violence, at all events the rock, I say, was cleft open by the force of the blow and poured forth water in a stream, so that it not only then furnished a relief from thirst, but also supplied for a long time an abundance of drink for so many myriads of people.

For they filled all their water vessels, as they had done before, from the fountains which were bitter by nature, but which, by divine providence, were changed to sweet water. (212) And, if any one disbelieves these facts, he neither knows God nor has he ever sought to know him; for, if he had, he would have instantly known, he would have known and surely comprehended, that all these unexpected and extraordinary things are the amusement of God; looking at the things which are really great and deserving of serious attention, namely, the creation of the heaven, and the revolutions of the planets and fixed stars, and the shining of light—of the light of the sun by day and that of the moon by night—and the position of the earth in the most centre spot of the universe, and the vast dominions of the different continents and islands, and the innumerable varieties of animals and plants, and the effusion of the sea, and the rapid courses of the ever-flowing rivers and winter mountain torrents, and the streams of everlasting springs, some of which pour forth cold and others hot water, and the various changes and alterations of the air and climate, and the different seasons of the year, and an infinite number of other beautiful objects.

(213) And the whole of a man's life would be too short if he wished to enumerate all the separate instances of such things, or even to detail fully all that is to be seen in one complete portion of the world; aye, if he were to be the most long-lived man that has ever been seen. But all these things, though they are in truth really wonderful, are despised by us by reason of our familiarity with them. But the things to which we are not accustomed, even though they may be unimportant, still make an impression upon us from our love of novelty, while we yield to strange ideas concerning them.

XXXIX. (214) And now, as they had gone over a vast tract of land previously untravelled, there appeared some boundaries of habitable country and some suburbs, as it were, of the land to which they were proceeding, and the Phoenicians inhabited it. But they, hoping that a tranquil and peaceable life would now be permitted to them, were deceived in their expectation; (215) for the king of the country, being afraid lest he might be destroyed, roused up all the youth of his cities, and collected an army, and went forth to meet them to keep them from his borders. And if they attempted to force their way, he showed that he would proceed to repel them with all his forces, his army being fresh, and now for the first time levied and marshalled for battle, while the Hebrews were wearied and worn out with their long travelling and with the scarcity of meat and drink which had in turns oppressed them.

(216) But when Moses had learnt from his scouts that the army of the enemy was marshalled at no great distance, he chose out those men who were in the flower of their youth, and appointed one of his subordinate officers, named Joshua, to be their general, while he himself went to procure a more powerful alliance; for, having purified himself with the customary purification, he rode up with speed to a neighbouring hill, and there he besought God to hold his shield over the Hebrews and to give them the victory and the mastery, as he had delivered them before from more formidable dangers and from other evils, not only dissipating the calamities with which they were threatened at the hands of men, but also all those which the transformation of the elements so wonderfully caused in the land of Egypt, and from those which the long scarcity inflicted upon them in their travels.

(217) And just as the two armies were about to engage in battle, a most marvellous miracle took place with respect to his hands; for they became by turns lighter and heavier. Then, whenever they were lighter, so that he could hold them up on high, the alliance between God and his people was strengthened, and waxed mighty, and became more glorious. But whenever his hands sank down the enemy prevailed, God showing thus by a figure that the earth and all the extremities of it were the appropriate inheritance of the one party, and the most sacred air the inheritance of the other. And as the heaven is in every respect supreme to and superior over the earth, so also shall the nation which has heaven for its inheritance be superior to their enemies.

(218) For some time, then, his hands, like the balances in a scale, were by turns light, and by turns descended as being heavy; and, during this period, the battle was undecided. But, on a sudden, they became quite devoid of weight, using their fingers as if they were wings, and so they were raised to a lofty height, like winged birds who traverse the heaven, and they continued at this height until the Hebrews had gained an unquestionable victory, their enemies being slain to a man from the youth upward, and suffering with justice what they had endeavoured to inflict on others, contrary to what was befitting.

(219) Then Moses erected an altar, which from the circumstances that had taken place he named the refuge of God, on which he offered sacrifices in honour of his victory, and poured forth prayers of gratitude to God.

XL. (220) After this battle he considered that it was proper to reconnoitre the country into which the nation was being led as a colony (and it was now the second year that they had been travelling), not wishing that his followers should (as is often the case) change their designs out of ignorance, but that they should learn by accurate report, what the nature of the country really was, availing themselves of the positive knowledge of the inhabitants, and should then consider what was best to be done; (221) and accordingly he chose out twelve men, to correspond in number to the twelve tribes, one out of each tribe to be the leader of it, selecting the most approved men, with reference to their excellence, in order that no quarrels might arise from any one party being better or worse off than another, but that they might all, by the agency of those to whom the matter was entrusted, be equally instructed as to the state of affairs among the inhabitants, if only the spies who were sent out brought a true report.

(222) And when he had selected the men he spoke to them as follows: "The inheritance which is before us is the prize of those labours and dangers which we have endured hitherto, and are still enduring, and let us not lose the hope of these things, we who are thus conducting a most populous nation to a new settlement. But the knowledge of the places, and of the men, and of the circumstances, is most useful, just as ignorance of these particulars is most injurious. (223) We have therefore appointed you as spies, that we, by your eyes and by your intellects, may see the state of things there; ye, therefore, must be the ears and eyes of all these myriads of people, that thus they may arrive at an accurate comprehension of what is indispensable to be known.

(224) "Now what we wish to know consists of three points; the number of the inhabitants, and the strength of their cities, whether they are planted in favourable situations, whether they are strongly built and fortified, or the contrary. As to the country, we wish to know whether it has a deep and rich soil, whether it is good to bear all kinds of fruits, both of such plants as are raised from seed and of fruit-trees; or whether, on the contrary, it has a shallow soil; that so we may be prepared against the power and numbers of the inhabitants with equal forces, and against the fortified state of buildings and cities by means of engines and machines, for the destruction of cities.

"And it is indispensable to understand the nature of the country, and whether it is a good land or not; for to encounter voluntary dangers for a poor and bad land is an act of folly; (225) and our weapons, and our engines, and all our power, consist solely in our trust and confidence in God. Having this preparation we will yield to no danger or fear, for this is sufficient with great superfluity of power to subdue otherwise invincible strength, which relies only on bodily vigour and on armies, and on courage, and skill, and numbers; since to that too we owe it, that even in a vast wilderness we have full supplies of everything, as if we were in well-stocked cities; (226) and the time in which it is most easy to come to a proper understanding of the good qualities of the land is the spring, the season which is now present; for in the season of spring what has been sown is coming to perfection, and the natures of the trees are beginning to propagate themselves further. It will be better, therefore, for you to enter the land now, and to remain till the middle of the summer, and to bring back with you fruits, as samples of what is to be procured from a prosperous and fertile country."

XLI. (227) When they had received these orders, they went forth to spy out the land, being conducted on their way by the whole multitude who feared lest they might be taken prisoners and so be put to death, and lest in that way two great evils might happen to them, namely, the slaughter of the men who were the eye of each tribe, and also ignorance of what was being done by their enemies who were plotting against them, the knowledge of which was most desirable. (228) So, taking with them scouts to examine the road and guides to show them the way, they accompanied them at their first setting out. And when they approached the borders of the country they ran up to the highest mountain of all those in that district, and from thence they surveyed the land, part of which was an extensive champaign district, fertile in barley, and wheat, and herbage; and the mountain region was not less productive of vines, and all kinds of other trees, and rich in every kind of timber, full of dense thickets, and girdled by rivers and fountains so as to be abundantly well watered, so that even from the foot of the mountain district to the highest summit of the hills themselves, the whole region was covered closely with a net-work of shady trees, and more especially the lower ridges, and the deep valleys and glens.

(229) They also surveyed all the strongest cities, looking upon them in two points of view; first, with reference to their advantages of situation, and also to the strength of their fortification; also, when they inquired respecting the inhabitants, they saw that they were very numerous indeed, and giants of exceeding tallness with absolutely gigantic bodies, both as to their magnitude and their strength. (230) When they had seen thus much they waited to get a more accurate knowl-

edge of everything: for first impressions are not trustworthy, but require the slow confirmation of time.

They also took great care to gather specimens of the productions of the land, though they were not as yet ripe and solid, but only just beginning to be properly coloured, that they might show them to all the multitude, for which reason they selected such as would not be easily spoiled; (231) but what above all things astonished them was the fruit of the vines, for the branches were of unrivalled sizes, stretching along all the young shoots and branches in a way that seemed almost incredible. Therefore, having cut off one branch, and having suspended it on a stick by the middle, the ends of which they gave to two young men, placing one on one side and one on the other, and others succeeding them as bearers of it as the former bearers got tired, for the weight was very great, they carried it so, the whole body of the spies not at all agreeing with respect to some points of necessary importance.

XLII. (232) Accordingly, there were a great many contest between them even before they returned to the camp, but not very serious ones, in order that there might not be seditions between them from any of them adhering very contentiously to his own opinion, or from different persons giving different accounts, but they became more violent after their return; (233) for some of them brought back formidable stories of the strength of the different cities, and the great populousness and opulence of each of them, exaggerating and making the most of everything in their description so as to cause excessive consternation among their hearers; while others, on the contrary, disparaged and made light of all that they saw, and exhorted their fellow countrymen not to faint but to persevere in their design of colonising that country, as they would subdue the natives with a mere shout; for that no city whatever would be able to resist the onset of so mighty a power attacking it with its united force, but would be overwhelmed with its might and submit at once.

Moreover, each of the spies infused into the souls of his hearers some portion of his own spirit, the cowardly spreading cowardice, and the indomitable and bold diffusing confidence united with sanguine hope. (234) But these last made but a fifth part of those who were frightened out of their senses, while they, on the other hand, were five times as numerous as the high-spirited; and the small number of those who displayed any courage, is often beaten down by the vast number of those who behaved in a cowardly manner, as they say was the case at this time also; for they who maintained the better side of the question were only two, while those who made the contrary report were ten; and these last so entirely prevailed over the two former, that they led away the whole multitude after them, alienating them from the two, and binding them wholly to themselves.

(235) But about the country itself they all brought back the same report with perfect unanimity, praising the beauty both of the champaign and of the mountainous district. But then they further cried out, "But what is the advantage to us of those good things which belong to others, when they are guarded by a mighty force, so that they can never be taken from their owners?" And so, attacking the two who brought the opposite report, they were very near stoning them, preferring to hear pleasant rather than useful things, and also preferring deceit to truth. (236) At which their leader was indignant, and he was also at the same time afraid lest some heaven-inflicted evil might descend upon them, since they so obstinately persisted in despairing and in disbelieving the word of God, which indeed took place. For of the spies, the ten who brought back cowardly tiding all perished by a pestilential disease, with those of the multitude who united in their feelings of despondency, and only the two who had agreed and counselled the people not to fear but to persevere in the plan of the colony were saved, because they were obedient to the word of God, on which account they received the especial honour of not being involved in the destruction of the others.

XLIII. (237) This was the reason why they did not arrive sooner in the land which they went forth to colonize; for though they might, in the second year after their departure from Egypt, have conquered all the cities in Syria, and divided the inheritance amongst themselves, still they turned aside from the direct and short road, and wandered about, using one long, and difficult, and pathless line of march after another, so as to be incessantly toiling both in soul and body, and enduring the necessary and deserved punishment of their excessive impiety: (238) accordingly, for eight and thirty years more, after the two years which I have already mentioned as having elapsed, the life of a complete generation of mankind did they wander up and down, traversing the pathless wilderness; and at last in the fortieth year, they with difficulty came to the borders of the country which they had reached so many years before.

(239) And at the entrance to this country there dwelt other tribes akin to themselves, who they thought would cheerfully join them in the war against their neighbours, and would co-operate in everything necessary for the establishment of the colony; and if they hesitated to do that, they thought that at all events they would range themselves on neither side, but would preserve a strict neutrality, holding up their hands; (240) for in fact the ancestors of both nations, both of the Hebrews and of those who dwelt on the skirts of the coun-

try, were brethren descended from the same father and the same mother, and moreover were twins; for it was from two brothers, who had thus increased with numerous descendants, and had enjoyed a great productiveness of offspring, that each of their families had grown into a vast and numerous nation.[3]

But one of these nations had clung to its original abodes; but the other, as has been already mentioned, having migrated to Egypt by reason of the famine, at this subsequent period was now returning, (241) and one of the two preserved its respect for its kindred though it had been for such a length of time separated from it, still having a regard for those who no longer preserved any one of their ancestral customs, but who had in every respect departed from their ancient habits and constitutions, thinking that it became those who claimed to be of civilised natures, to give and yield something to the name of relationship.

(242) But the other utterly overturned all notions of friendship and affection, giving in to fierce, and unfriendly, and irreconcilable dispositions, and language, and counsels, and actions; and thus keeping alive the ill-will of their original ancestor to his brother; for the first founder of their race, though he had himself given up his birthright to his brother, yet a short time afterwards endeavoured to assert his claim to what he had abandoned voluntarily, violating his agreement, and he sought to slay his brother, threatening him with death if he did not surrender what he had purchased. And now the whole nation after the interval of so many generations, renewed the ancient enmity between one individual and another.

(243) Therefore Moses, the leader of the Hebrews, although he might with one single effort, aye with the mere shout of his army, have subdued the whole nation, still, by reason of the aforesaid relationship did not think fit to do so; but desired only to use the road through their country, promising that he would in every respect observe the treaties between them, and not despoil them of territory, or cattle, or of any booty, that he would even pay a price for water if there should be a scarcity of drink, and for anything else that they might require to buy, as not being supplied with it; but they violently rejected their peaceful invitations, threatening them with war, if they heard of their crossing over their borders or even of their setting foot upon them.

XLIV. (244) But as the Hebrews received their answer with great indignation, and prepared at once to oppose them, Moses stood in a place from whence he would be well heard, and said, "O men,

your indignation is reasonable and just; for though we, in a peaceable disposition, have made them good and friendly offers, they have made us an evil reply out of their evil and perverse disposition. (245) But it does not follow that because they deserve to pay the penalty for their cruelty, therefore it is desirable for us to proceed to take vengeance upon them, by reason of the honour due to our own nation, that we may show that in this particular we are good and different from wicked men, inasmuch as we consider not only whether such and such persons deserve to be punished, but whether also it is proper that they should receive their punishment from us."

(246) On this he turned aside and led his army by another road, since he knew that all the roads in that district were surrounded with garrisons, by those who were not in danger of receiving any injury, but who out of envy and jealousy would not allow them to proceed by the shortest road; (247) and this was the most manifest proof of their sorrow, which they felt in consequence of the nation having obtained their liberty, namely when they rejoiced when they were enduring that bitter slavery of theirs in Egypt; for it follows of necessity that those men to whom the good fortune of their neighbours causes grief, do also rejoice at their evil fortune, even if they do not admit that they do so; (248) for they had already related to their neighbours, as to persons in accordance with themselves, and cherishing the same thoughts, all the misfortunes and also all the agreeable pieces of good fortune which had happened to them, not knowing that they had proceeded to a great degree of iniquity, and that they were full of unfriendly, and hostile, and malicious thoughts towards them, so that they were like to grieve at their good fortune, but to rejoice at any thing of a contrary tendency.

(249) But when their malevolence was fully revealed, the Hebrews were nevertheless restrained from coming to open war with them by their ruler, who thus displayed two most excellent qualities at the same time; namely prudence and a compassionate disposition; for to take care that no evil should happen to any one is the part of wisdom, and not to be willing even to repel one's own kinsmen is a proof of a humane disposition.

XLV. (250) Therefore he passed by the cities of these nations; but a certain king of the neighbouring country, Canaan by name, when his spies reported to him that the army of the Hebrews, which was making in his direction was at no great distance, thinking that it was in a state of confusion and disorder, and that he should be able easily to conquer it if he were to attack it at once, proceeded forth with the youth of his nation well armed and equipped, and marched with all speed, and put the van of their host to flight as soon as

---

[3]The brothers are Jacob and Esau, Jacob being the father of the Israelites and Esau of the Edomites.

he encountered them, inasmuch as they were not arrayed or prepared for battle; and having taken many prisoners, and being elated at the prosperity beyond his hopes which he had met with, he marched on thinking that he should defeat all the others also.

(251) But the Hebrews, for they were not dismayed at the defeat of their advanced guard, but had rather derived even more confidence than they had felt before, being eager also to make amends by their eagerness for battle for the loss of those of their number who had been taken prisoners, exhorted one another not to faint nor to yield. "Let us rise up," said they; "let us at once invade their land. Let us show that we are in no wise alarmed or depressed, by our vigour in action and our confidence. The end is very often judged of by the beginning. Let us seize the keys of the country and strike terror into the inhabitants as deriving prosperity from cities, and inflicting upon them in return the want of necessary things which we bring with us out of the wilderness." (252) And they, at the same time, exhorted one another often with these words, and likewise began to dedicate to God, as the first fruits of the land, the cities of the king and all the citizens of each city. And he accepted their views and inspired the Hebrews with courage, and prepared the army of the enemy to be defeated.

(253) Accordingly, the Hebrews defeated them with mighty power, and fulfilled the agreement of gratitude which they had made, not appropriating to themselves the slightest portion of the booty. And they dedicated to God the cities with all the men and treasures that were in them, and, from what had thus taken place, they called the whole country an offering to God; (254) for, as every pious man offers unto God the first fruits of the fruits of the year, which he collects from his own possessions, so in the same manner did the Hebrews dedicate the whole nation of this mighty country into which they had come as settlers, and that great spoil, the kingdom which they had so speedily subdued, as a sort of first-fruit of their colony; for they did not think it consistent with piety to distribute the land among themselves, or to inherit the cities, before they had offered up to God the first fruits of that country and of those cities.

XLVI. (255) A short time afterwards, having found a copious spring of water which supplied drink to all the multitude, and the spring was in a well and on the borders of the country, drawing it up and drinking it as though it had been not water but pure wine, they were refreshed in their souls, and those among the people who loved God established choruses and dances in a circle around the well, out of their cheerfulness and joy, and sang a new song to God, the possessor and giver of their inheritance and the real leader of their colony, because now at the first moment of their coming forth from the direction in which they had so long been dwelling in to the inhabited land which they were ordained to possess, they had found abundant drink, and therefore they thought it right not to pass this spring by without due honour.

(256) For this well had been originally cut not by the hands of private individuals, but of kings, who had laboured in rivalry of one another, as the tale went, not only in the discovery of the water, but likewise in the digging of the well, in order that by its magnificence it might be seen to be a royal work, and that the power and magnanimity of those who built it might appear from the beginning. (257) And Moses, rejoicing at the unexpected blessings which from time to time were presenting themselves to him, advanced further, dividing the youth of his people into the vanguard and the rearguard, and placing the old men, and the women, and the children in the centre, that they might be protected by those who were thus at each extremity, in the case of their having to encounter any force of the enemy either in front or behind.

XLVII. (258) A few days afterwards he entered the country of the Amorites, and sent ambassadors to the king, whose name was Sihon, exhorting him to the same measures to which he had previously invited his kinsman. But he not only replied to these ambassadors when they came with great insolence, but he very nearly put them to death, and would have done so if the law with respect to ambassadors had not hindered him; but he did collect an army and made against them, thinking that he should immediately be able to subdue them in war. (259) But when he encountered them he then found that he had to fight not men who had no experience or practice in the art of war, but men skilful in all warfare and truly invincible, who only a short time before had done many and important valiant achievements, displaying great personal valour, and great wisdom, and excellence of sense and virtue.

Owing to which qualities they subdued these their enemies with great ease and defeated them with great loss, but they took no part of the spoil, desiring to dedicate to God the first booty which they gained; (260) and, on this occasion, they guarded their own camp vigorously, and then, with one accord and with equally concerted preparation, rushed forward in opposition to the enemy as he advanced and charged them, availing themselves of the invincible alliance of the just God, in consequence of which they had the greatest boldness, and became cheerful and sanguine combatants.

(261) And the proof of this was clear; there was no need of any second battle, but the first was also the only one, and in it the whole power of

the enemy was frustrated for ever. And it was utterly overthrown, and immediately it disappeared for ever. (262) And about the same time the cities were both empty and full; empty of their ancient inhabitants, and full of those who now succeeded to their dominions over them. In the same manner, also, the stables of cattle in the fields, being made desolate, received instead men who were in all respects better than their former masters.

XLVIII. (263) This war struck all the Asiatic nations with terrible consternation, and especially all those who were near the borders of the Amorites, inasmuch as they looked upon the dangers as being nearer to themselves. Accordingly, one of the neighbouring kings, by name Balak, who ruled over a large and thickly inhabited country of the east, before he met them in battle, feeling great distrust of his own power, did not think fit to meet them in close combat, being desirous to avoid carrying on a war of extermination by open arms; but he had recourse to inquiries and divination, thinking that by some kind of ruse or other he might be able to overthrow the irresistible power of the Hebrews.

(264) Now there was a man at that time very celebrated for his skill in divination, dwelling in Mesopotamia, who was initiated in every branch of the soothsayers' art. And he was celebrated and renowned above all men for his experience as a diviner and prophet, as he had in many instances foretold to many people incredible and most important events; (265) for, on one occasion, he had predicted heavy rain to one nation at the height of summer; to another he had foretold a drought and burning heat in the middle of winter. Others he had forewarned of a dearth which should follow a season of abundance; and, on the other hand, plenty after famine. In some instances he had predicted the inundations of rivers; or, on the contrary, their falling greatly and becoming dried up; and the departure of pestilential diseases, and ten thousand other things. From all which he had obtained a name of wide celebrity, as he was believed to have foreseen them all, and so he had attained to great renown and his glory had spread everywhere and was continually increasing.

(266) So this man, Balak, now sent some of his companions, entreating him to come to him, and he gave him some presents at once, and he promised to give him others also, explaining to him the necessity which he was in, on account of which he had sent for him. But he did not treat the messengers with any noble or consistent disposition, but with great courtesy and civility evaded their request, as if he were one of the most celebrated prophets, and as such was accustomed to do nothing whatever without first consulting the oracle, and so he declined, saying that the Deity would not permit him to go with them. (267) So the messengers returned back to the king, without having succeeded in their errand. And immediately other messengers of the highest rank in the whole land were sent on the same business, bringing with them more abundant presents of money, and promising still more ample rewards than the former ambassadors had promised. (268) And Balaam, being allured by the gifts which were already proffered to him, and also by the hopes for the future which they held out to him, and being influenced also by the rank of those who invited him, began to yield, again alleging the commands of the Deity as his excuse, but no longer with sincerity. Accordingly, on the next day he prepared for his departure, relating some dreams by which he said he had been influenced, affirming that he had been compelled by their manifest visions not to remain, but to follow the ambassadors.

XLVI. (269) But when he was on his road a very manifest sign met him in the way, showing him plainly that the purpose for which he was travelling was displeasing to God, and ill-omened; for the beast on which he was riding, while proceeding onwards in the straight road, at first stopped suddenly, (270) then, as if some one was forcibly resisting it, or standing in front and driving it back by force, it retreated, moving first to the right and then to the left, and could not stand still, but kept moving, first to one side and then to the other, as if it had been under the influence of wine and intoxication; and though it was repeatedly beaten, it disregarded the blows, so that it very nearly threw its rider, and though he stuck on did still hurt him considerably; (271) for close on each side of the path there were walls and strong fences; therefore, when the beast in its violent motions struck heavily against the walls, the owner had his knee, and leg, and foot pressed and crushed, and was a good deal lacerated.

(272) The truth is, that there was, as it seems, a divine vision, which, as the beast, on which the diviner was seeking, saw at a great distance as it was coming towards him, and it was frightened at it; but the man did not see it, which was a proof of his insensibility, for he was thus shown to be inferior to a brute beast in the power of sight, at a time when he was boasting that he could see, not only the whole world, but also the Creator of the world.

(273) Accordingly, having after some time seen the angel opposing him, not because he was desiring to see so astonishing a spectacle, but that he might become acquainted with his own insignificance and nothingness, he betook himself to supplications and prayers, entreating to be pardoned, on the ground that he had acted as he had done out of ignorance, and had not sinned of deliberate purpose.

(274) Then, as he said that he ought to return

back again, he asked of the vision which appeared to him, whether he should go back again to his own house; but the angel beholding his insincerity, and being indignant at it (for what need was there for him to ask questions in a matter which was so evident, which had its answer plain in itself, and which did not require any more positive information by means of words, unless a person's ears are more to be trusted than his eyes, and words than things), said, "Go on in the journey in which you have set out, for you shall do no good to those who have sent for you, and you must say what I prompt you, without any thoughts of your own, finding utterance, as I will guide the organs of your speech in the way that shall be just and expedient, for I will direct your words, predicting all that shall happen through the agency of your tongue, though you yourself understand nothing of it.

L. (275) But when the king heard that he was now near at hand, he went forth with his guards to meet him; and when they met at first there were, as was natural, greetings and salutations, and then a brief reproof of his tardiness and of his not having come more readily. After this there were feastings and costly entertainments, and all those other things which are usually prepared on the occasion of the reception of strangers, everything with royal magnificence being prepared, so as to give an exaggerated idea of the power and glory of the king.

(276) The next day at the rising of the sun, Balak took the prophet and led him up to a high hill, where it also happened that a pillar had been erected to some deity which the natives of the country had been accustomed to worship; and from thence there was seen a portion of the camp of the Hebrews, which was shown to the magician from this point, as if from a watch tower. (277) And he when he beheld it said: "Do thou, O king, build here seven altars, and offer upon every one of them a bullock and a ram. And I will turn aside and inquire of God what I am to say."

So, having gone forth, immediately he became inspired, the prophetic spirit having entered into him, which drove all his artificial system of divination and cunning out of his soul; for it was not possible that holy inspiration should dwell in the same abode with magic. Then, returning back to the king, and beholding the sacrifices and the altars flaming, he became like the interpreter of some other being who was prompting his words, (278) and spoke in prophetic strain as follows: "Balak has sent for me from Mesopotamia, having caused me to take a long journey from the east, that he might chastise the Hebrews by means of curses. But in what manner shall I be able to curse those who have not been cursed by God? For I shall behold them with my eyes from the loftiest mountains, and I shall see them with my mind; and I shall never be able to injure the people which shall

dwell alone, not being numbered among the other nations, not in accordance with the inheritance of any particular places, or any apportionment of lands, but by reason of the peculiar nature of their remarkable customs, as they will never mingle with any other nation so as to depart from their national and ancestral ways. (279) Who has ever discovered with accuracy the first origin of the birth of these people? Their bodies, indeed, may have been fashioned according to human means of propagation; but their souls have been brought forth by divine agency, wherefore they are nearly related to God. May my soul die as to the death of the body, that it may be remembered among the souls of the righteous, such as the souls of these men are."

LI. (280) When Balak heard these words he was grieved within himself; and after he had stopped speaking, not being able to contain his sorrow, he said: "You were invited hither to curse my enemies, and are you not ashamed to offer up prayers for their good? I must, without knowing it, have been deceiving myself, thinking you a friend; who were, on the contrary, without my being aware of it, enrolled among the ranks of the enemy, as is now plain. Perhaps, too, you made all the delay in coming to me by reason of the regard for them, which you were secretly cherishing in your soul, and your secret dislike to me and to my people; for, as the old proverb says, what is apparent affords the best means of judging of what is not visible."

(281) But Balaam, his moment of inspiration being now past, replied: "I am exposed in this to a most unjust charge, and am undeservedly accused; for I am saying nothing of my own, but whatever the Deity prompts me to say. And this is not the first time that I have said and that you have heard this, but I declared it on the former occasion when you sent the ambassadors, to whom I made the same answer." (282) But as the king thought either that the prophet was deceiving him, or that the Deity might change his mind, and the consequence of a change of place might alter the firmness of his decision, he led him off to another spot, where, from an exceedingly long, and high, and distant hill, he might be able to show him a part of the army of his enemies.

Then, again, he built seven altars and sacrificed the same number of victims that he had sacrificed at first, and sent the prophet to look for favourable omens and predictions. (283) And he, as soon as he was by himself, was again suddenly filled by divine inspiration, and, without at all understanding the words which he uttered, spoke everything that was put into his mouth, prophesying in the following manner:—

"Rise up and listen, O king! prick up thy ears and hear. God is not able to speak falsely as if he were a man, nor does he change his purpose like the son of man. When he has once spoken, does he not abide by his word? For he will say nothing at all which shall not be completely brought to pass, since his word is also his deed. I, indeed, have been brought hither to bless this nation, and not to curse it. (284) There shall be no labour or distress among the Hebrews. God visibly holds his shield over them, who also dissipated the violence of the Egyptian attacks, leading forth all these myriads of people as one man. Therefore they disregarded auguries and every other part of the prophetic art, trusting to the one sole Governor of the world alone. And I see the people rising up like a young lion, and exulting as a lion. He shall feast on the prey, and for drink he shall drink the blood of the wounded; and, when he is satisfied, he shall not turn to sleep, but he shall be awake and sing the song of victory."

LII. (285) But Balak, being very indignant at finding that all the assistance which he expected to derive from divination was turning out contrary to his hopes, said: "O man, neither curse them at all, nor bless them at all; for silence, which is free from danger, is better than unpleasant speeches." And when he had said this, as if he had forgotten what he had said, owing to the inconstancy of his mind, he led the prophet to another place, from which he could show him a part of the Hebrew army; and again he invited him to curse them. (286) But the prophet, as being even more wicked than the king, although he had always replied to the accusations which were brought against him with one true excuse, namely, that he was saying nothing out of his own head, but was only interpreting the words of another, being himself carried away and inspired, when he ought no longer to have accompanied him but to have gone away home, ran forward even more eagerly than his conductor, although in his secret thoughts he was oppressed by a heavy feeling of evil, yet still desired in his mind to curse this people, though he was forbidden to do so with his mouth.

(287) So, coming to a mountain greater than any of those on which he had stood before, and which reached a very long way, he bade the king perform the same sacrifices as before, again building seven altars, and again offering up fourteen victims, on each altar two, a bullock and a ram. And he himself did no longer, according to his usual custom, go to seek for divination and auguries, since he much loathed his art, looking upon it as a picture which had become defaced through age, and had been obscured, and lost its felicity of conjecture. But he now, though with difficulty, understood the fact that the designs of the king, who had hired him, did not correspond with the will of God.

(288) Therefore, turning to the wilderness, he saw the Hebrews encamped in their tribes, and he saw their numbers and their array, and admired it as being like the order of a city rather than of a camp, and, becoming inspired, he again spoke. (289) What, then, said the man who saw truly, who in his sleep saw a clear vision of God with the ever open and sleepless eyes of his soul?

"How goodly are thy abodes, O army of Hebrews; they tents are shady as groves, as a paradise on the bank of a river, as a cedar by the waters. (290) A man shall hereafter come forth out of thee who shall rule over many nations, and his kingdom shall increase every day and be raised up to heaven. This people hath God for its guide all the way from Egypt, who leads on their multitude in one line. (291) Therefore they shall devour many nations of their enemies, and they shall take all their fat as far as their very marrow, and shall destroy their enemies with their far-shooting arrows. He shall lie down to rest like a lion, and like a lion's whelp, fearing no one, but showing great contempt for every one, and causing fear to all other nations. Miserable is he who shall stir up and rouse him to anger. Blessed are they that bless thee, and cursed are they that curse thee."

LIII. (292) And the king, being very indignant at these words, said: "Having been invited hither to curse my enemies, you have now prayed for and blessed them these three times. Fly, therefore, quickly, passion is a hasty affection, lest I be compelled to do something more violent than usual. (293) Of what a vast amount of money, O most foolish of men, of how many presents, and of how much renown, and celebrity, and glory, hast thou deprived thyself in thy madness! Now you will return to thy home from a foreign land, bearing with thee no good thing, but only reproaches and (as it seems likely) great disgrace, being ridiculed and despised for that knowledge on which you formerly so greatly prided yourself."

(294) And Balaam replied: "All that I have hitherto uttered have been oracles and words of God; but what I am going to say are merely the suggestions of my own mind: and taking him by the right hand, he, while they two were alone, gave him advice, by the adoption of which he might, as far as possible, guard against the power of his enemies, accusing himself of the most enormous crimes. For why, some one may perhaps say, do you thus retire into solitude and give counsel suggesting things contrary to the oracles of God, unless indeed that your counsels are more powerful than his decrees?"

LIV. (295) Come, then, let us examine into his fine recommendations, and see how cunningly they were contrived with reference to the most certain defeat of those who had hitherto always been able to conquer. As he knew that the only way by which the Hebrews could be subdued was by leading them to violate the law, he endeavoured to seduce them by means of debauchery and intemperance, that mighty evil, to the still greater crime of impiety, putting pleasure before them as a bait; (296) for, said he, "O king! the women of the country surpass all other women in beauty, and there are no means by which a man is more easily subdued than by the beauty of a woman; therefore, if you enjoin the most beautiful of them to grant their favours to them and to prostitute themselves to them, they will allure and overcome the youth of your enemies. (297) But you must warn them not to surrender their beauty to those who desire them with too great facility and too speedily, for resistance and coyness will stimulate the passions and excite them more, and will kindle a more impetuous desire; and so, being wholly subdued by their appetites, they will endure to do and to suffer anything.

(298) "And let any damsel who is thus prepared for the sport resist, and say, wantonly, to a lover who is thus influenced, "It is not fitting for you to enjoy my society till you have first abandoned your native habits, and have changed, and learnt to honour the same practices that I do. And I must have a conspicuous proof of your real change, which I can only have by your consenting to join me in the same sacrifices and libations which I use, and which we may then offer together at the same images and statues, and other erections in honour of my gods. (299) And the lover being, as it were, taken in the net of her manifold and multiform snares, not being able to resist her beauty and seductive conversation, will become wholly subdued in his reason, and, like a miserable man, will obey all the commands which she lays upon him, and will be enrolled as the slave of passion."

LV. (300) This, then, was the advice which Balaam gave to Balak. And he, thinking that what he said to him did not want sense, repealed the law against adulteries, and having abrogated all the enactments which had been established against seduction and harlotry, as if they had never been enacted at all, exhorted the women to admit to their favours, without any restraint, every man whom they chose. (301) Accordingly, when licence was thus given, they brought over a multitude of young men, having already long before this seduced their minds, and having by their tricks and allurements perverted them to impiety; until Phinehas, the son of the chief priest, being exceedingly indignant at all that was taking place (for it appeared to him to be a most scandalous thing for his countrymen to give up at one time both their bodies and souls—their bodies to pleasure, and their souls to transgression of the law, and to works of wickedness), undertook a bold and impetuous action, such as was becoming to a young, and grave, and virtuous man.

(302) For when he saw a man of his nation sacrificing with and then entering into the tent of a harlot, and that too without casting his eyes down on the ground and seeking to avoid the notice of the multitude, but making a display of his licentiousness with shameless boldness, and giving himself airs as if he were about to engage in a creditable action, and one deserving of smiles—Phinehas, I say, being very indignant and being filled with a just anger, ran in, and while they were still lying on the bed, slew both the lover and the harlot, cutting them in two pieces in the middle, because they thus indulged in illicit connections.

(303) When some persons of those who admired temperance, and chastity, and piety, saw this example, they, at the command of Moses, imitated it, and slew all their own relations and friends, even to a man, who had sacrificed to idols made with hands, and thus they effaced the stain which was defiling the nation by this implacable revenge which they thus wreaked on those who had set the example of wrong doing, and so saved the rest, who made a clear defence of themselves, demonstrating their own piety, showing no compassion on any one of those who were justly condemned to death, and not passing over their offences out of pity, but looking upon those who slew them as pure from all sin.

Therefore they did not allow any escape whatever to those who sinned in this way, and such conduct is the truest praise; (304) and they say that twenty-four thousand men were slain in one day, the common pollution, which was defiling the whole army, being thus at once got rid of. And when the works of purification were thus accomplished, Moses began to seek how he might give an honour worthy of him who had displayed such permanent excellence to the son of the chief priest, who was the first who hastened to inflict chastisement on the offenders. But God was beforehand with him ,giving to Phinehas, by means of his holy word, the greatest of all good things, namely, peace, which no man is able to bestow; and also, in addition to this peace, he gave him the perpetual possession of the priesthood, an inheritance to his family, which could not be taken from it.

LVI. (305) But when none of the civil and intestine evils remained any longer, but when all the men who were suspected of having either forsaken the ways of their ancestors or of treachery had perished, it appeared to be a most favourable opportunity for making an expedition against Balak, a man who had both planned to do, and had also executed an innumerable host of evil deeds, since he had planned them through the agency of the prophet, who he hoped would be able, by means of his curses, to destroy the power of the Hebrews, and who had executed his purpose by the agency of the licentiousness and incontinence of the women, who destroyed the bodies of those who associated with them by debauchery, and their souls by impiety.

(306) Therefore Moses did not think fit to carry on war against him with his whole army, knowing that superfluous numbers are apt to meet with disaster in consequence of those very numbers; and also, at the same time, thinking it useful to have stations of reserve, to be assistants to those of their allies who appeared likely to fail; but he selected a thousand picked men of the youth of the nation, selected man by man, out of each tribe, twelve thousand in all, for that was the number of the tribes, and he appointed Phinehas to be the commander in the war, as he had already given proof of the happy daring which becomes a general; and after he had offered up sacrifices of good omen, he sent forth his warriors, and encouraged them in the following words:—

(307) "The present contest is not one for dominion or sovereignty, nor is it waged for the sake of acquiring the property of others, though these are the objects for which alone, or almost invariably, wars take place; but this war is undertaken in the cause of piety and holiness, from which the enemy has alienated our relations and friends, being the causes of bitter destruction to those who have been brought under their yoke. (308) It is therefore absurd for us to be the slayers of our own countrymen, for having offended against the law, and to spare our enemies, who have violated it in a much worse degree, and to slay, with every circumstance of violence, those who were only learning and beginning to sin, but to leave those who taught them to do so unpunished, who are, in reality, the guilty causes of all that has taken place, and of all the evils which our countrymen have either done or suffered."

LVII. (309) Therefore being nerved by these exhortations, and being kindled and filled with noble courage which was indeed in their souls already, they went forth to that contest with invincible spirit as to a certain victory; and when they engaged with the enemy, they displayed such incredible vigour and courage that they slew all their enemies, and returned themselves unhurt, every one of them, not one of their number having been slain or even wounded.

(310) Any one who did not know what had taken place, might have supposed, when he saw them returning, that they were coming in, not from war and from a pitched battle, but rather from a display and field-day of exercise under arms, such as often take place in time of peace; and these field-days are days of exercise and practice, while the men train themselves among friends to attack their enemies.

(311) Therefore they destroyed all their cities, razing them to the ground or else burning them, so that no one could tell that any cities had ever been inhabited in that land.

And they led away a perfectly incalculable number of prisoners, of whom they chose to slay all the full-grown men and women, the men because they had set the example of wicked counsels and actions, and the women because they had beguiled the youth of the Hebrews, becoming the causes to them of incontinence and impiety, and at the last of death; but they pardoned all the young male children and all the virgins, their tender age procuring them forgiveness; (312) and as they had taken a vast booty from the king's palace, and from private houses, and also from the dwellings of all kinds in the open country (for there was not less booty in the country places than in the cities), they came to the camp, laden with all the wealth which they had taken from the enemy.

(313) And Moses praised Phinehas their general, and those who had served under him for their good success, and also because they had not been covetous of their own advantage, running after booty and thinking of nothing, but appropriating the spoil to themselves, but because they had brought it all into the common stock, so that they who had staid behind in the tents might share in the booty; and he ordered those men to remain outside the camp for some days, and the high priest he commanded to purify both the men themselves, and those of their allies who had returned from fighting by their side, of bloodshed; (314) for even though the slaughter of the enemies of one's country is according to law, still he who kills a man, even though justly and in self-defence, and because he has been attacked, still appears to be guilty of blood by reason of his supreme and common relationship to a common father; on which account those who had slain enemies were in need of rites of purification, to cleanse them from what was looked upon as a pollution.

LVIII. (315) However, after no long lapse of time he divided the booty among those who had taken a part in the expedition, and they were but a small number, giving one half among those who had remained inactive at home, and the other half to those who were still in the camp; for he looked upon it as just and equitable to give the share of the advantages gained, to those who had shared in the contest, if not with their souls, at all events with their bodies; for as the spectators were not inferior to the actual combatants in their zeal, they were inferior only in point of time and in respect of their being anticipated.

(316) And as the smaller body had received each a larger share of the booty, by reason of their having been the foremost in encountering danger, and the larger body had received each a smaller share, by reason of their having remained at home;

it appeared indispensable that they should consecrate the first fruits of the whole of the booty; those therefore who had remained at home brought a fiftieth, and those who had been actually engaged in the war, brought and contributed a five hundredth part; and of ten first fruits Moses commanded that portion which came from those who had borne a part in the expedition, to be given to the high priest, and that portion which came from those who had remained in the camp, to the keepers of the temple whose name were the Levites.

(317) And the captains of thousands, and centurions, and all the rest of the multitude of commanders of battalions and companies willingly contributed special first fruits, as an offering for their own safety, and that of those who had gone out to war, and for the victory which had been gained in a manner beyond all hope, giving up all the golden ornaments which had fallen to the lot of each individual, in the apportionment of the booty, and the most costly vessels, of which the material was gold.

All which things Moses took, and, admiring the piety of those who contributed them, dedicated them in the consecrated tabernacle as a memorial of the gratitude of the men; and the division of the first fruits was very beautiful; (318) those which had been given by the men who had borne their share in the war, he distributed among the keepers of the temple as among men who had only displayed one half of virtue, namely eagerness without action; but the first fruits of those who had warred and fought, who had encountered danger with their bodies and lives, and thus had displayed perfect and complete excellence, he allotted to him who presided over the keepers of the temple, namely to the high priest; and the first fruits of the captains, as being the offerings of chiefs and rulers, he allotted to the great ruler of all, namely to God.

LIX. (319) All these wars were carried on and brought to an end before the Hebrews had crossed Jordan, the river of the country, being wars against the inhabitants of the country on the other side of Jordan, which was a rich and fertile land, in which there was a large champaign fertile in corn, and also very productive of herbage and fodder for cattle; (320) and when the two tribes who were occupied in feeding cattle saw this country, the two tribes being a sixth part of the whole Hebrew host, they besought Moses to permit them to take their inheritance in that district, where in fact they were already settled; for they said that the place was very suitable for cattle to be kept, and fed, and bred in, inasmuch as it was well watered and full of good herbage, and as it produced spontaneously abundant grass for the feeding of sheep.

(321) But as he thought that they claimed a sort of right, by some kind of pre-eminence, to

receive their share and the honours due to them before their time, or else that they preferred this petition by reason of their being unwilling to encounter the wars which were impending, as there were still many kings who were making ready to attack them, and who were the possessors of all the country inside the river, he was very indignant at their request, and answered them in anger, and said, (322) "Shall you then sit here and enjoy leisure, and yield to indolence at so improper a time? and shall the wars which still threaten us, afflict all your countrymen, and your relations, and your friends, and shall the prizes be given to you alone, as if you had all contributed to the success? And shall battles and wars, and distresses, and the most extreme dangers await others? (323) But it is not just that you should enjoy peace, and the blessings that flow from peace, and that the rest should endure wars and all the other indescribable evils which they bring with them, and that the whole should only be looked upon as an adjunct of a part; while, on the contrary, it is for the sake of the whole that the parts are thought worthy of any inheritance at all. (324) Ye are all entitled to equal honour, ye are one race, ye have the same fathers, one house, ye have the same customs, a community of laws, and an infinite number of other things, every one of which binds your kindred closer together, and cements your mutual good will; why then when you are thought worthy of equal shares of the most important and most necessary things, do you show a covetous spirit in the division of the lands, as if you were rulers despising your subjects as masters looking disdainfully on your slaves?"

(325) You ought to have derived instruction from the afflictions of others; for it is the part of wise men not to wait till misfortunes come upon themselves. But now, though you have domestic examples in your own fathers, who went and spied out this land, and in the calamities which befell them, and all who participated in their despondency (for they all perished except two), and when, therefore, you ought to take care and avoid resembling them in any respect whatever, still, foolish-minded men that ye are, ye are imitating their cowardice, as if by such conduct you would be more strongly fortified against capture; and you check and damp the eagerness of those who are desirous to display their manhood and valour, relaxing and depressing their spirits; (326) therefore, while you are hastening to do wrong, you are also hastening to incur punishment.

For justice is always a long time before it can be put in motion, but when it is once put in motion it makes great haste and speedily overtakes those who flee from it. (327) When, therefore, all our enemies are destroyed, and when there is no other war which can be expected or feared as impending, and when all those in our present alliance have been, on examination, found to be without reproach nor liable to any charge of desertion or treachery, or of any misconduct which could possibly tend to our defeat, but shall be seen to have endured steadfastly from the beginning to the end, with their bodily exertion and with all eagerness of mind, and when the whole country is cleared of those who have previously inherited it, then rewards and prizes for valour shall be given to all the tribes with perfect fairness.

LX. (328) So they, bearing this rebuke with moderation, as being genuine sons of a very kindly-disposed father (for they knew that Moses was not a man to behave insolently because of his power and authority, but one who cared for all of them, and honoured justice and equality, and who hated wickedness, not so as to reproach or insult the wicked, but so as to be constantly endeavouring by admonition and correction to improve those who were susceptible of improvement), said to him, "Very naturally you are indignant, if you imagine that we now are anxious to desert the alliance and to obtain our allotments before the proper time; (329) but you must know that we are not alarmed at any undertaking that calls for valorous and virtuous exertion, even though it may be most laborious. And we judge that the task of virtue is to obey you who are such a brave and wise ruler, and not to fear to encounter dangers, and to be willing to bear our share in all future expeditions until all our business is brought to a fortunate conclusion.

(330) "We, therefore, as we have agreed before, will remain in our ranks and cross over Jordan in complete armour, giving no soldier any excuse for lagging behind. But our infant children, and our daughters, and wives, and mothers, and the bulk of our cattle, shall, if you have no objection, be left behind, after we have made houses for our children and wives, and stables for our cattle that they may not be exposed to any incursion of the enemy, and so suffer injury from being taken in unwalled and unprotected dwellings."

(331) And Moses answered with a mild look and even still gentler voice, "If you speak the truth and behave honestly, the allotments which you have asked for shall remain assured to you. Leave behind you now, as you desire, your wives and children, and flocks and herds, and go yourselves across Jordan in your ranks with the rest of the soldiers in full armour, arrayed for battle, as if you were prepared to fight at once, if it should be needful. (332) And hereafter when all our enemies are destroyed, and when, peace being established, we have made ourselves masters of the whole country, and have begun to divide it among ourselves, then you also shall return to your families to enjoy the good things which belong to you, and to possess the region which you have selected."

(333) When Moses had said this, and given them this promise, they were filled with cheerfulness and joy, and established their families in safety as well as their flocks and herds in well-fortified and impregnable strongholds, the greater part of which were artificial. And taking their arms they marched forth more cheerfully than any of the rest of the allied forces, as if they alone had been going to fight, or at all events to fight in the first ranks as the champions of the whole army, for he who has received any gift beforehand is more eager in the cause in which he is engaged, since he thinks that he is repaying a necessary debt, and not giving a free gift.

(334) I have now, then, given an account of what was done by Moses while invested with kingly power. I must now proceed to relate in order all the actions which he performed in accordance with virtue, and also successfully as a chief priest, and also in his character as a lawgiver; for he also exercised these two powers as very closely connected with his kingly authority.

ON THE LIFE OF MOSES, II†

(De Vita Mosis, II)

I. (1) The first volume of this treatise relates to the subject of the birth and bringing up of Moses, and also of his education and of his government of his people, which he governed not merely irreproachably, but in so exceedingly praiseworthy a manner; and also of all the affairs, which took place in Egypt, and in the travels and journeyings of the nation, and of the events which happened with respect to their crossing the Red Sea and in the desert, which surpass all power of description; and, moreover, of all the labours which he conducted to a successful issue, and of the inheritances which he distributed in portions to his soldiers.

But the book which we are now about to compose relates to the affairs which follow those others in due order, and bear a certain correspondence and connection with them.

(2) For some persons say, and not without some reason and propriety, that this is the only way by which cities can be expected to advance in improvement, if either the kings cultivate philosophy, or if philosophers exercise the kingly power. But Moses will be seen not only to have displayed all these powers—I mean the genius of the philosopher and of the king—in an extraordinary degree at the same time, but three other powers likewise, one of which is conversant about legislation, the second about the way of discharging the duties of high priest, and the last about the prophetic office; (3) and it is on these subjects that I have now been constrained to choose to enlarge; for I conceive that all these things have fitly been united in him, inasmuch as in accordance with the providential will of God he was both a king and a lawgiver, and a high priest and a prophet, and because in each office he displayed the most eminent wisdom and virtue.

We must now show how it is that every thing is fitly united in him. (4) It becomes a king to command what ought to be done, and to forbid what ought not to be done; but the commanding what ought to be done, and the prohibition of what ought not to be done, belongs especially to the law, so that the king is at once a living law, and the law is a just king. (5) But a king and a lawgiver ought to pay attention not only to human things, but also to divine ones, for the affairs of neither kings nor subjects go on well except by the intervention of divine providence; on which account it was necessary that such a man as Moses should enjoy the first priesthood, in order that he might with perfectly conducted sacrifices, and with a perfect knowledge of the proper way to serve God, entreat for a deliverance from evil and for a participation in good, both for himself and for the people whom he was governing, from the merciful God who listens favourably to prayers.

(6) But since there is an infinite variety of both human and divine circumstances which are unknown both to king, and lawgiver, and chief priest, for a man is no less a created and mortal being from having all these offices, or because he is clothed with such a vast and boundless inheritance of honour and happiness, he was also of necessity invested with the gift of prophecy, in order that he might through the providence of God learn all those things which he was unable to comprehend by his own reason; for what the mind is unable to attain to, that prophecy masters. (7) Therefore the connection of these four powers is beautiful and harmonious, for being all connected together and united one to another, they unite in concert, receiving and imparting a reciprocity of benefits from and to one another, imitating the virgin graces with whom it is an immutable law of their nature that they cannot be disunited, with respect to whom one might fairly say, what is habitually said of the virtues, that he who has one has them all.

II. (8) And first of all we must speak of the matters which relate to his character and conduct as a lawgiver.

I am not ignorant that the man who desires to be an excellent and perfect lawgiver ought to exercise all the virtues in their complete integrity and perfection, since in the houses of his nation some are near relations and some distant, but still they are all related to one another. And in like manner we must look upon some of the virtues as connected more closely with some matters, and on others as being more removed from them. (9) Now these four qualities are closely connected with and related to the legislative power, namely, humility, the love of justice, the love of virtue, and the hatred of iniquity; for every individual who has any desire for exercising his talents as a lawgiver is under the

† Yonge's full title, *A Treatise on the Life of Moses, that is to say, On the Theology and Prophetic Office of Moses, Book II.*

influence of each of these feelings. It is the province of humanity to prepare for adoption such opinions as will benefit the common weal, and to teach the advantages which will proceed from them. It is the part of justice to point out how we ought to honour equality, and to assign to every man his due according to his deserts. It is the part of the love of virtue to embrace those things which are by nature good, and to give to every one who deserves them facilities without limit for the most unrestrained enjoyment of happiness. It is also the province of the hatred of iniquity to reject all those who dishonour virtue, and to look upon them as common enemies of the human race.

(10) Therefore it is a very great thing if it has fallen to the lot of any one to arrive at any one of the qualities before mentioned, and it is a marvellous thing, as it should seem, for any one man to have been able to grasp them all, which in fact Moses appears to have been the only person who has ever done, having given a very clear description of the aforesaid virtues in the commandments which he established. (11) And those who are well versed in the sacred scriptures know this, for if he had not had these principles innate within him he would never have compiled those scriptures at the promptings of God. And he gave to those who were worthy to use them the most admirable of all possessions, namely, faithful copies and imitations of the original examples which were consecrated and enshrined in the soul, which became the laws which he revealed and established, displaying in the clearest manner the virtues which I have enumerated and described above.

III. (12) But that he himself is the most admirable of all the lawgivers who have ever lived in any country either among the Greeks or among the barbarians, and that his are the most admirable of all laws, and truly divine, omitting no one particular which they ought to comprehend, there is the clearest proof possible in this fact, the laws of other lawgivers, (13) if any one examines them by his reason, he will find to be put in motion in an innumerable multitude of pretexts, either because of wars, or of tyrannies, or of some other unexpected events which come upon nations through the various alterations and innovations of fortune; and very often luxury, abounding in all kind of superfluity and unbounded extravagance, has overturned laws, from the multitude not being able to bear unlimited prosperity, but having a tendency to become insolent through satiety, and insolence is in opposition to law.

(14) But the enactments of this lawgiver are firm, not shaken by commotions, not liable to alteration, but stamped as it were with the seal of nature herself, and they remain firm and lasting from the day on which they were first promulgated to the present one, and there may well be a hope

that they will remain to all future time, as being immortal, as long as the sun and the moon, and the whole heaven and the whole world shall endure. (15) At all events, though the nation of the Hebrews experienced so many changes both in the direction of prosperity and of the opposite destiny, no one, no not even the very smallest and most unimportant of all his commandments was changed, since every one, as it seems, honoured their venerable and godlike character; (16) and what neither famine, nor pestilence, nor war, nor sovereign, nor tyrant, nor the rise of any passions or evil feelings against either soul or body, nor any other evil, whether inflicted by God or deriving its rise from men, ever dissolved, can surely never be looked upon by us in any other light than as objects of all admiration, and beyond all powers of description in respect of their excellence.

IV. (17) But this is not so entirely wonderful, although it may fairly by itself be considered a thing of great intrinsic importance, that his laws were kept securely and immutably from all time; but this is more wonderful by far, as it seems, that not only the Jews, but that also almost every other nation, and especially those who make the greatest account of virtue, have dedicated themselves to embrace and honour them, for they have received this especial honour above all other codes of laws, which is not given to any other code. (18) And a proof of this is to be found in the fact that of all the cities in Greece and in the territory of the barbarians, if one may so say, speaking generally, there is not one single city which pays any respect to the laws of another state. In fact, a city scarcely adheres to its own laws with any constancy for ever, but continually modifies them, and adapts them to the changes of times and circumstances.

(19) The Athenians rejected the customs and laws of the Lacedaemonians, and so did the Lacedaemonians repudiate the laws of the Athenians. Nor, again, in the countries of the barbarians do the Egyptians keep the laws of the Scythians, nor do the Scythians keep the laws of the Egyptians; nor, in short, do those who live in Asia attend to the laws which obtain in Europe, nor do the inhabitants of Europe respect the laws of the Asiatic nations.

And, in short, it is very nearly an universal rule, from the rising of the sun to its extreme west, that every country, and nation, and city, is alienated from the laws and customs of foreign nations and states, and that they think that they are adding to the estimation in which they hold their own laws by despising those in use among other nations. (20) But this is not the case with our laws which Moses has given to us; for they lead after them and influence all nations, barbarians, and Greeks, the inhabitants of continents and islands, the eastern nations and the western, Europe and Asia; in short, the whole habitable world from one extremity to the other.

(21) For what man is there who does not honour that sacred seventh day, granting in consequence a relief and relaxation from labour, for himself and for all those who are near to him, and that not to free men only, but also to slaves, and even to beasts of burden; (22) for the holiday extends even to every description of animal, and to every beast whatever which performs service to man, like slaves obeying their natural master, and it affects even every species of plant and tree; for there is no shoot, and no branch, and no leaf even which it is allowed to cut or to pluck on that day, nor any fruit which it is lawful to gather; but everything is at liberty and in safety on that day, and enjoys, as it were, perfect freedom, no one ever touching them, in obedience to a universal proclamation.

(23) Again, who is there who does not pay all due respect and honour to that which is called "the fast," and especially to that great yearly one which is of a more austere and venerable character than the ordinary solemnity at the full moon? on which, indeed, much pure wine is drunk, and costly entertainments are provided, and everything which relates to eating and drinking is supplied in the most unlimited profusion, by which the insatiable pleasures of the belly are inflamed and increased. (24) But on this fast it is not lawful to take any food or any drink, in order that no bodily passion may at all disturb or hinder the pure operations of the mind; but these passions are wont to be generated by fulness and satiety, so that at this time men feast, propitiating the Father of the universe with holy prayers, by which they are accustomed to solicit pardon for their former sins, and the acquisition and enjoyment of new blessings.

V. (25) And that beauty and dignity of the legislation of Moses is honoured not among the Jews only, but also by all other nations, is plain, both from what has been already said and from what I am about to state. (26) In olden time the laws were written in the Chaldaean language, and for a long time they remained in the same condition as at first, not changing their language as long as their beauty had not made them known to other nations; (27) but when, from the daily and uninterrupted respect shown to them by those to whom they had been given, and from their ceaseless observance of their ordinances, other nations also obtained an understanding of them, their reputation spread over all lands; for what was really good, even though it may through envy be overshadowed for a short time, still in time shines again through the intrinsic excellence of its nature.

Some persons, thinking it a scandalous thing that these laws should only be known among one half portion of the human race, namely, among the barbarians, and that the Greek nation should be wholly and entirely ignorant of them, turned their attention to their translation.

(28) And since this undertaking was an important one, tending to the general advantage, not only of private persons, but also of rulers, of whom the number was not great, it was entrusted to kings and to the most illustrious of all kings. (29) Ptolemy, surnamed Philadelphus, was the third in succession after Alexander, the monarch who subdued Egypt; and he was, in all virtues which can be displayed in government, the most excellent sovereign, not only of all those of his time, but of all that ever lived; so that even now, after the lapse of so many generations, his fame is still celebrated, as having left many instances and monuments of his magnanimity in the cities and districts of his kingdom, so that even now it is come to be a sort of proverbial expression to call excessive magnificence, and zeal, for honour and splendour in preparation, Philadelphian, from his name; (30) and, in a word, the whole family of the Ptolemies was exceedingly eminent and conspicuous above all other royal families, and among the Ptolemies, Philadelphus was the most illustrious; for all the rest put together scarcely did as many glorious and praiseworthy actions as this one king did by himself, being, as it were, the leader of the herd, and in a manner the head of all the kings.

VI. (31) He, then, being a sovereign of this character, and having conceived a great admiration for and love of the legislation of Moses, conceived the idea of having our laws translated into the Greek language; and immediately he sent out ambassadors to the high-priest and king of Judea, for they were the same person. (32) And having explained his wishes, and having requested him to pick him out a number of men, of perfect fitness for the task, who should translate the law, the high-priest, as was natural, being greatly pleased, and thinking that the king had only felt the inclination to undertake a work of such a character from having been influenced by the providence of God, considered, and with great care selected the most respectable of the Hebrews whom he had about him, who in addition to their knowledge of their national scriptures, had also been well instructed in Grecian literature, and cheerfully sent them.

(33) And when they arrived at the king's court they were hospitably received by the king; and while they feasted, they in return feasted their entertainer with witty and virtuous conversation; for he made experiment of the wisdom of each individual among them, putting to them a succession of new and extraordinary questions; and they, since the time did not allow of their being prolix in their answers, replied with great propriety and fidelity as if they were delivering apophthegms which they

had already prepared. (34) So when they had won his approval, they immediately began to fulfil the objects for which that honourable embassy had been sent; and considering among themselves how important the affair was, to translate laws which had been divinely given by direct inspiration, since they were not able either to take away anything, or to add anything, or to alter anything, but were bound to preserve the original form and character of the whole composition, they looked out for the most completely purified place of all the spots on the outside of the city.

For the places within the walls, as being filled with all kinds of animals, were held in suspicion by them by reason of the diseases and deaths of some, and the accursed actions of those who were in health. (35) The island of Pharos lies in front of Alexandria, the neck of which runs out like a sort of tongue towards the city, being surrounded with water of no great depth, but chiefly with shoals and shallow water, so that the great noise and roaring from the beating of the waves is kept at a considerable distance, and so mitigated. (36) They judged this place to be the most suitable of all the spots in the neighbourhood for them to enjoy quiet and tranquillity in, so that they might associate with the laws alone in their minds; and there they remained, and having taken the sacred scriptures, they lifted up them and their hands also to heaven, entreating of God that they might not fail in their object. And he assented to their prayers, that the greater part, or indeed the universal race of mankind might be benefited, by using these philosophical and entirely beautiful commandments for the correction of their lives.

VII. (37) Therefore, being settled in a secret place, and nothing even being present with them except the elements of nature, the earth, the water, the air, and the heaven, concerning the creation of which they were going in the first place to explain the sacred account; for the account of the creation of the world is the beginning of the law; they, like men inspired, prophesied, not one saying one thing and another another, but every one of them employed the self-same nouns and verbs, as if some unseen prompter had suggested all their language to them. (38) And yet who is there who does not know that every language, and the Greek language above all others, is rich in a variety of words, and that it is possible to vary a sentence and to paraphrase the same idea, so as to set it forth in a great variety of manners, adapting many different forms of expression to it at different times.

But this, they say, did not happen at all in the case of this translation of the law, but that, in every case, exactly corresponding Greek words were employed to translate literally the appropriate Chaldaic words, being adapted with exceeding propriety to the matters which were to be explained; (39) for just as I suppose the things which are proved in geometry and logic do not admit any variety of explanation, but the proposition which was set forth from the beginning remains unaltered, in like manner I conceive did these men find words precisely and literally corresponding to the things, which words were alone, or in the greatest possible degree, destined to explain with clearness and force the matters which it was desired to reveal. (40) And there is a very evident proof of this; for if Chaldaeans were to learn the Greek language, and if Greeks were to learn Chaldaean, and if each were to meet with those scriptures in both languages, namely, the Chaldaic and the translated version, they would admire and reverence them both as sisters, or rather as one and the same both in their facts and in their language; considering these translators not mere interpreters but hierophants and prophets to whom it had been granted it their honest and guileless minds to go along with the most pure spirit of Moses.

(41) On which account, even to this very day, there is every year a solemn assembly held and a festival celebrated in the island of Pharos, to which not only the Jews but a great number of persons of other nations sail across, reverencing the place in which the first light of interpretation shone forth, and thanking God for that ancient piece of beneficence which was always young and fresh.

(42) And after the prayers and the giving of thanks some of them pitched their tents on the shore, and some of them lay down without any tents in the open air on the sand of the shore, and feasted with their relations and friends, thinking the shore at that time a more beautiful abode than the furniture of the king's palace.

(43) In this way those admirable, and incomparable, and most desirable laws were made known to all people, whether private individuals or kings, and this too at a period when the nation had not been prosperous for a long time. And it is generally the case that a cloud is thrown over the affairs of those who are not flourishing, so that but little is known of them; (44) and then, if they make any fresh start and begin to improve, how great is the increase of their renown and glory? I think that in that case every nation, abandoning all their own individual customs, and utterly disregarding their national laws, would change and come over to the honour of such a people only; for their laws shining in connection with, and simultaneously with, the prosperity of the nation, will obscure all others, just as the rising sun obscures the stars.

VIII. (45) Now what has been here said is quite sufficient for the abundant praise of Moses as a lawgiver. But there is another more extensive praise which his own holy writings themselves contain, and it is to them that we must now turn for the purpose of exhibiting the virtue of him who compiled them.

(46) Now these writings of Moses may be divided into several parts; one of which is the historical part, another is occupied with commands and prohibitions, respecting which part we will speak at some other time when we have first of all accurately examined that part which comes first in the order of our division. (47) Again, the historical part may be subdivided into the account of the creation of the world, and the genealogical part. And the genealogical part, or the history of the different families, may be divided into the accounts of the punishment of the wicked, and of the honours bestowed on the just; we must also explain on what account it was that he began his history of the giving of the law with these particulars, and placed the commandments and prohibitions in the second order; (48) for he was not like any ordinary compiler of history, studying to leave behind him records of ancient transactions as memorials to future ages for the mere sake of affording pleasure without any advantage; but he traced back the most ancient events from the beginning of the world, commencing with the creation of the universe, in order to make known two most necessary principles. First, that the same being was the father and creator of the world, and likewise the lawgiver of truth; secondly, that the man who adhered to these laws, and clung closely to a connection with and obedience to nature, would live in a manner corresponding to the arrangement of the universe with a perfect harmony and union, between his words and his actions and between his actions and his words.

IX. (49) Now of all other lawgivers, some the moment that they have promulgated positive commands as to what it is right to do and what it is right not to do, proceed to appoint punishments for those who transgress those laws; but others, who appear to have proceeded on a better plan, have not begun in this manner, but, having first of all built and established their city in accordance with reason, have then adapted to this city which they have built, that constitution which they have considered the best adapted and most akin to it, and have confirmed this constitution by the giving of laws. (50) But he, thinking the first of the two courses above mentioned to be tyrannical and despotic, as indeed it is, namely, that of laying positive commands on persons as if they were not free men but slaves, without offering them any alleviation; and that the second course was better indeed, but was not entirely to be commended, must appear to all judges to be superior in each of the above considerations.

(51) For both in his commandments and also in his prohibitions he suggests and recommends rather than commands, endeavouring with many prefaces and perorations to suggest the greater part of the precepts that he desires to enforce, desiring rather to allure men to virtue than to drive them to it, and looking upon the foundation and beginning of a city made with hands, which he has made the commencement of his work a commencement beneath the dignity of his laws, looking rather with the most accurate eye of his mind at the importance and beauty of his whole legislative system, and thinking it too excellent and too divine to be limited as it were by any circle of things on earth; and therefore he has related the creation of that great metropolis, the world, thinking his laws the most fruitful image and likeness of the constitution of the whole world.

X. (52) At all events if any one were inclined to examine with accuracy the powers of each individual and particular law, he will find them all aiming at the harmony of the universe, and corresponding to the law of eternal nature: (53) on which account those men who have had unbounded prosperity bestowed upon them, and all things tending to the production of health of body, and riches, and glory, and all other external parts of good fortune, but who have rejected virtue, and have chosen crafty wickedness, and all others kinds of vice, not through compulsion, but of their own spontaneous free will, looking upon that which is the greatest of all evils as the greatest possible advantage, he looks upon as enemies not of mankind only, but of the entire heaven and world, and says that they are awaiting, not any ordinary punishments, but new and extraordinary ones, which that constant assessor of God, justice, who detests wickedness, invents and inflicts terribly upon them, turning against them the most powerful elements of the universe, water and fire, so that at appointed times some are destroyed by deluges, others are burnt with fire, and perish in that manner.

(54) The seas were raised up, and the rivers both such as flow everlastingly, and the winter torrents were swollen and washed away, and carried off all the cities in the plain; and those in the mountain country were destroyed by incessant and irresistible impetuosity of rain, ceasing neither by day nor by night, (55) and when at a subsequent period the race of mankind had again increased from those who had been spared, and had become very numerous, since the succeeding generations did not take the calamities which had befallen their ancestors as a lesson to teach themselves wisdom and moderation, but turned to acts of intemperance and became studiers of evil practices, God determined to destroy them with fire. (56) Therefore on this occasion, as the holy scriptures tell us, thunderbolts fell from heaven, and burnt up those wicked men and their cities; and even to this day there are seen in Syria monuments of the unprecedented destruction that fell upon them, in

the ruins, and ashes, and sulphur, and smoke, and dusky flame which still is sent up from the ground as of a fire smouldering beneath; (57) and in this way it came to pass that those wicked men were punished with the aforesaid chastisements, while those who were eminent for virtue and piety were well off, receiving rewards worthy of their virtue.

(58) But when the whole of that district was thus burnt, inhabitants and all, by the impetuous rush of the heavenly fire, one single man in the country, a sojourner, was preserved by the providence of God because he had never shared in the transgressions of the natives, though sojourners in general were in the habit of adopting the customs of the foreign nations, among which they might be settled, for the sake of their own safety, since, if they despised them, they might be in danger from the inhabitants of the land. And yet this man had not attained to any perfection of wisdom, so as to be thought worthy of such an honour by reason of the perfect excellence of his nature; but he was spared only because he did not join the multitude who were inclined to luxury and effeminacy, and who pursued every kind of pleasure and indulged every kind of appetite, gratifying them abundantly, and inflaming them as one might inflame fire by heaping upon it plenty of rough fuel.

XI. (59) But in the great deluge I may almost say that the whole of the human race was destroyed, while the history tells us that the house of Noah alone was preserved free from all evil, inasmuch as the father and governor of the house was a man who had never committed any intentional or voluntary wickedness. And it is worth while to relate the manner of his preservation as the sacred scriptures deliver it to us, both on account of the extraordinary character of it, and also that it may lead to an improvement in our own dispositions and lives.

(60) For he, being considered a fit man, not only to be exempted from the common calamity which was to overwhelm the world, but also to be himself the beginning of a second generation of men, in obedience to the divine commands which were conveyed to him by the word of God, built a most enormous fabric of wood, three hundred cubits in length, and fifty in width, and thirty in height, and having prepared a number of connected chambers within it, both on the ground floor and in the upper story, the whole building consisting of three, and in some parts of four stories, and having prepared food, brought into it some of every description of animals, beasts and also birds, both male and female, in order to preserve a means of propagating the different species in the times that should come hereafter; (61) for he knew that the nature of God was merciful, and that even if the subordinate species were destroyed, still there would be a germ in the entire genus which should be safe from destruction, for the sake of preserving a similitude to those animals which had hitherto existed, and of preventing anything that had been deliberately called into existence from being utterly destroyed.

XII. On which account everything was now made obedient to Noah; and even beasts, which up to that time had been savage, became gentle, and being tamed, followed him as their shepherd and superintendent; (62) and after they had all entered into the ark, if any one had beheld the entire collection, he would not have been wrong if he had said that it was a representation of the whole earth, containing, as it did, every kind of animal, of which the whole earth had previously produced innumerable species, and will hereafter produce such again.

(63) And what was expected happened at no long period after; for the evil abated, and the destruction caused by the deluge was diminished every day, the rain being checked, and the water which had been spread over the whole earth, being partly dried up by the flame of the sun, and partly returning into the chasms and rivers, and other channels and receptacles in the earth; for, as if God had issued a command to that effect, every nature received back, as a necessary repayment of a loan, what it had lent, that is, every sea, and fountain, and river, received back their waters; and every stream returned into its appropriate channel.

(64) But after the purification, in this way, of all the things beneath the moon, the earth being thus washed and appearing new again, and such as it appeared to be when it was at first created, along with the entire universe, Noah came forth out of his wooden edifice, himself and his wife, and his sons and their wives, and with his family there came forth likewise, in one company, all the races of animals which had gone in with them, for the generation and propagation of similar creatures in future.

(65) These are the rewards and honours for pre-eminent excellence given to good men, by means of which, not only did they themselves and their families obtain safety, having escaped from the greatest dangers which were thus aimed against all men all over the earth, by the change in the character of the elements; but they became also the founders of a new generation, and the chiefs of a second period of the world, being left behind as sparks of the most excellent kind of creatures, namely, of men, man having received the supremacy over all earthly creatures whatsoever, being a kind of copy of the powers of God, a visible image of his invisible nature, a created image of an uncreated and immortal original.[1]

---

[1] Yonge's translation includes a separate treatise title

XIII. (66) We have already, then, gone through two parts of the life of Moses, discussing his character in his capacity of a king and of a lawgiver. We must now consider him in a third light, as fulfilling the office of the priesthood.

Now this man, Moses, practised beyond all other men that which is the most important and most indispensable virtue in a chief priest, namely, piety, partly because he was endowed with most admirable natural qualities; and philosophy, receiving his nature like a fertile field, cultivated and improved it by the contemplation of excellent and beautiful doctrines, and did not dismiss it until all the fruits of virtue were brought to perfection in him, in respect of words and actions. (67) Therefore he, with a few other men, was dear to God and devoted to God, being inspired by heavenly love, and honouring the Father of the universe above all things, and being in return honoured by him in a particular manner. And it was an honour well adapted to the wise man to be allowed to serve the true and living God. Now the priesthood has for its duty the service of God. Of this honour, then, Moses was thought worthy, than which there is no greater honour in the whole world, being instructed by the sacred oracles of God in everything that related to the sacred offices and ministrations.

XIV. (68) But, in the first place, before assuming that office, it was necessary for him to purify not only his soul but also his body, so that it should be connected with and defiled by no passion, but should be pure from everything which is of a mortal nature, from all meat and drink, and from all connection with women. (69) And this last thing, indeed, he had despised for a long time, and almost from the first moment that he began to prophesy and to feel a divine inspiration, thinking that it was proper that he should at all times be ready to give his whole attention to the commands of God. And how he neglected all meat and drink for forty days together, evidently because he had more excellent food than that in those contemplations with which he was inspired from above from heaven, by which also he was improved in the first instance in his mind, and, secondly, in his body, through his soul, increasing in strength and health both of body and soul, so that those who saw him afterwards could not believe that he was the same person.

(70) For, having gone up into the loftiest and most sacred mountain in that district in accordance with the divine commands, a mountain which was very difficult of access and very hard to ascend, he is said to have remained there all that time without eating any of that food even which is necessary for life; and, as I said before, he descended again forty days afterwards, being much more beautiful in his face than when he went up, so that those who saw him wondered and were amazed, and could no longer endure to look upon him with their eyes, inasmuch as his countenance shone like the light of the sun.

XV. (71) And while he was still abiding in the mountain he was initiated in the sacred will of God, being instructed in all the most important matters which relate to his priesthood, those which come first in order being the commands of God respecting the building of a temple and all its furniture. (72) If, then, they had already occupied the country into which they were migrating, it would have been necessary for them to have erected a most magnificent temple of the most costly stone in some place unincumbered with wood, and to have built vast walls around it, and abundant and well-furnished houses for the keepers of the temple, calling the place itself the holy city. (73) But, as they were still wandering in the wilderness, it was more suitable for people who had as yet no settled habitation to have a moveable temple, that so, in all their journeyings, and military expeditions, and encampments, they might be able to offer up sacrifices, and might not feel the want of any of the things which related to their holy ministrations, and which those who dwell in cities require to have.

(74) Therefore Moses now determined to build a tabernacle, a most holy edifice, the furniture of which he was instructed how to supply by precise commands from God, given to him while he was on the mount, contemplating with his soul the incorporeal patterns of bodies which were about to be made perfect, in due similitude to which he was bound to make the furniture, that it might be an imitation perceptible by the outward senses of an archetypal sketch and pattern, appreciable only by the intellect; (75) for it was suitable and consistent for the task of preparing and furnishing the temple to be entrusted to the real high priest, that he might with all due perfection and propriety make all his ministrations in the performance of his sacred duties correspond to the works which he was now to make.

XVI. (76) Therefore the general form of the model was stamped upon the mind of the prophet, being accurately painted and fashioned beforehand invisibly without any materials, in species which were not apparent to the eye; and the completion of the work was made in the similitude of the model, the maker giving an accurate representation of the impression in material substances cor-

---

at this point: *On the Life of Moses, That Is to Say, On the Theology and Prophetic Office of Moses, Book III.* Accordingly, his next paragraph begins with roman numeral I (=XIII in the Loeb). Yonge's "treatise" concludes with number XXXIX (=LI in the Loeb). The publisher has elected to follow the Loeb numbering.

responding to each part of the model, (77) and the fashion of the building was as follows.

There were eight and forty pillars of cedar, which is the most incorruptible of all woods, cut out of solid trunks of great beauty, and they were all veneered with gold of great thickness. Then under each pillar there were placed two silver pedestals to support it, and on the top of each was placed one golden capital; (78) and of these pillars the architect arranged forty along the length of the tabernacle, one half of them, or twenty, on each side, placing nothing between them, but arranging them and uniting them all in regular order, and close together, so that they might present the appearance of one solid wall; and he ranged the other eight along the inner breadth, placing six in the middle space, and two at the extreme corners, one on each side at the right and left of the centre. Again, at the entrance he placed four others, like the first in all other respects except that they had only one pedestal instead of two, as those opposite to them had, and behind them he placed five more on the outside differing only in the pedestals, for the pedestals of these last were made of brass.

(79) So that all the pillars of the tabernacle taken together, besides the two at the corners which could not be seen, were fifty-five in number, all conspicuous, being the number made by the addition of all the numbers from the unit to the complete and perfect decade.

(80) And if any were inclined to count those five pillars of the outer vestibule in the open air separately, as being in the outer court as it was called, there will then be left that most holy number of fifty, being the power of a rectangular triangle, which is the foundation of the creation of the universe, and is here entirely completed by the pillars inside the tabernacle; there being first of all forty, twenty on either side, and those in the middle being six, without counting those which were out of sight and concealed at the corners, and those opposite to the entrance, from which the veil was suspended, being four; (81) and the reason for which I reckon the other five with the first fifty, and again why I separate them from the fifty, I will now explain.

The number five is the number of the external senses, and the external sense in man at one time inclines towards external things, and at another time comes back again upon the mind, being as it were a kind of handmaid of the laws of its nature; on which account it is that the architect has here allotted a central position to the five pillars, for those which are inside of them leant towards the innermost shrine of the tabernacle, which under a symbol is appreciable only by the intellect; and the outermost pillars, which are in the open air, and in the outer courtyard, and which are also per-

ceptible by the external senses, (82) in reference to which fact it is that they are said to have differed from the others only in the pedestals, for they were made of brass. But since the mind is the principal thing in us, having an authority over the external senses, and since that which is an object of the external senses is the extremity, and as it were the pedestal or foundation of it, the architect has likened the mind to gold, and the object of the external sense to brass.

(83) And these are the measures of the pillars, they are ten cubits in length, and five cubits and a half in width, in order that the tabernacle may be seen to be of equal dimensions in all its parts.

XVII. (84) Moreover the architect surrounded the tabernacle with very beautiful woven work of all kinds, employing work of hyacinth colour, and purple, and scarlet, and fine linen for the tapestry; for he caused to be wrought ten cloths, which in the sacred scriptures he has called curtains, of the kinds which I have just mentioned, every one of them being eight and twenty cubits in length, and extending four cubits in width, in order that the complete number of the decade, and also the number four, which is the essence of the decade, and also the number twenty-eight, which is likewise a perfect number, being equal to its parts; and also the number forty, the most prolific and productive of all numbers, in which number they say that man was fashioned in the workshop of nature.

(85) Therefore the eight and twenty cubits of the curtains have this distribution: there are ten along the roof, for that is the width of the tabernacle, and the rest are placed along the sides, on each side nine, which are extended so as to cover and conceal the pillars, one cubit from the floor being left uncovered in order that the beautiful and holy looking embroidery might not be dragged. (86) And of the forty which are included in the calculation and made up of the width of the ten curtains, the length takes thirty, for such is the length of the tabernacle, and the chamber behind takes nine. And the remaining one is in the outer vestibule, that it may be the bond to unite the whole circumference.

(87) And the outer vestibule is overshadowed by the veil; and the curtains themselves are nearly the same as veils, not only because they cover the roof and the walls, but also because they are woven and embroidered by the same figures, and with hyacinth colour, and purple, and scarlet, and fine linen. And the veil, and that thing, too, which was called the covering, was made of the same things. That which was within was placed along the five pillars, that the innermost shrine might be concealed; and that which was outside being placed along the five pillars, that no one of those who were

not holy men might be able from any secret or distant place to behold the holy rites and ceremonies.

XVIII. (88) Moreover, he chose the materials of this embroidery, selecting with great care what was most excellent out of an infinite quantity, choosing materials equal in number to the elements of which the world was made, and having a direct relation to them; the elements being the earth and the water, and the air and the fire. For the fine flax is produced from the earth, and the purple from the water, and the hyacinth colour is compared to the air (for, by nature, it is black), and the scarlet is likened to fire, because each is of a red colour; for it followed of necessity that those who were preparing a temple made by hands for the Father and Ruler of the universe must take essences similar to those of which he made the universe itself.

(89) Therefore the tabernacle was built in the manner that has been here described, like a holy temple. And all around it a sacred precinct extended a hundred cubits in length and fifty cubits in width, having pillars all placed at an equal distance of five cubits from one another, so that there were in all sixty pillars; and they were divided so that forty were placed along the length and twenty along the breadth of the tabernacle, one half on each side.

(90) And the material of which the pillars were composed was cedar within, and on the surface without silver; and the pedestals of all of them were made of brass, and the height was equal to five cubits. For it seemed to the architect to be proper to make the height of what was called the hall equal to one half of the entire length, that so the tabernacle might appear to be elevated to double its real height. And there were thin curtains fitted to the pillars along their entire length and breadth, resembling so many sails, in order that no one might be able to enter in who was not pure.

XIX. (91) And the situation was as follows. In the middle was placed a tent, being in length thirty cubits and in width ten cubits, including the depth of the pillars. And it was distant from the centre space by three intervals of equal distance, two being at the sides and one along the back chamber. And the interval between was by measurement twenty cubits. But along the vestibule, as was natural, by reason of the number of those who entered, the distance between them was increased and extended to fifty cubits and more; for in this way the hundred pillars of the hall were intended to be made up, twenty being along the chamber behind, and those which the tent contained, thirty in number, being included in the same calculation with the fifty at the entrances; (92) for the outer vestibule of the tabernacle was placed as a sort of boundary in the middle of the two fifties, the one, I mean, towards the east where the entrance

was, and the other being on the west, in which direction the length of the tabernacle and the surrounding wall behind was.

(93) Moreover, another outer vestibule, of great size and exceeding beauty, was made at the beginning of the entrance into the hall, by means of four pillars, along which was stretched the embroidered curtain in the same manner as the inner curtains were stretched along the tabernacle, and wrought also of similar materials; (94) and with this there were also many sacred vessels made, an ark, and a candlestick, and a table, and an altar of incense, and an altar of sacrifice. Now, the altar of sacrifice was placed in the open air, right opposite to the entrances of the tabernacle, being distant from it just so far as was necessary to give the ministering officers room to perform the sacrifices that were offered up every day.

XX. (95) But the ark was in the innermost shrine, in the inaccessible holy of holies, behind curtains; being gilded in a most costly and magnificent manner within and without, the covering of which was like to that which is called in the sacred scriptures the mercy-seat. (96) Its length and width are accurately described, but its depth is not mentioned, being chiefly compared to and resembling a geometrical superficies; so that it appears to be an emblem, if looked at physically, of the merciful power of God; and, if regarded in a moral point of view, of a certain intellect spontaneously propitious to itself, which is especially desirous to contract and destroy, by means of the love of simplicity united with knowledge, that vain opinion which raises itself up to an unreasonable height and puffs itself up without any grounds.

(97) But the ark is the depository of the laws, for in that are placed the holy oracles of God, which were given to Moses; and the covering of the ark, which is called the mercy-seat, is a foundation for two winged creatures to rest upon, which are called, in the native language of the Hebrews, cherubim, but as the Greeks would translate the word, vast knowledge and science. (98) Now some persons say, that these cherubim are the symbols of the two hemispheres, placed opposite to and fronting one another, the one beneath the earth and the other above the earth, for the whole heaven is endowed with wings.

(99) But I myself should say, that what is here represented under a figure are the two most ancient and supreme powers of the divine God, namely, his creative and his kingly power; and his creative power is called God; according to which he arranged, and created, and adorned this universe, and his kingly power is called Lord, by which he rules over the beings whom he has created, and governs them with justice and firmness; (100) for he, being the only true living God, is also really the Creator of the world; since he brought things

which had no existence into being; and he is also a king by nature, because no one can rule over beings that have been created more justly than he who created them.

XXI. (101) And in the space between the five pillars and the four pillars, is that space which is, properly speaking, the space before the temple, being cut off by two curtains of woven work, the inner one of which is called the veil, and the outer one is called the covering: and the remaining three vessels, of those which I have enumerated, were placed as follows:—The altar of incense was placed in the middle, between earth and water, as a symbol of gratitude, which it was fitting should be offered up, on account of the things that had been done for the Hebrews on both these elements, for these elements have had the central situation of the world allotted to them. (102) The candlestick was placed on the southern side of the tabernacle, since by it the maker intimates, in a figurative manner, the motions of the stars which give light; for the sun, and the moon, and the rest of the stars, being all at a great distance from the northern parts of the universe, make all their revolutions in the south. And from this candlestick there proceeded six branches, three on each side, projecting from the candlestick in the centre, so as altogether to complete the number of seven; (103) and in all the seven there were seven candles and seven lights, being symbols of those seven stars which are called planets by those men who are versed in natural philosophy; for the sun, like the candlestick, being placed in the middle of the other six, in the fourth rank, gives light to the three planets which are above him, and to those of equal number which are below him, adapting to circumstances the musical and truly divine instrument.

XXII. (104) And the table, on which bread and salt are laid, was placed on the northern side, since it is the north which is the most productive of winds, and because too all nourishment proceeds from heaven and earth, the one giving rain, and the other bringing to perfection all seeds by means of the irrigation of water; (105) for the symbols of heaven and earth are placed side by side, as the holy scripture shows, the candlestick being the symbol of heaven, and that which is truly called the altar of incense, on which all the fumigatory offerings are made, being the emblem of the things of earth.

(106) But it became usual to call the altar which was in the open air the altar of sacrifice, as being that which preserved and took care of the sacrifices; intimating, figuratively, the consuming power of these things, and not the lambs and different parts of the victims which were offered, and which were naturally calculated to be destroyed by fire, but the intention of him who offered them; (107) for if the man who made the offerings was foolish and ignorant, the sacrifices were no sacrifices, the victims were not sacred or hallowed, the prayers were ill-omened, and liable to be answered by utter destruction, for even when they appear to be received, they produce no remission of sins but only a reminding of them.

(108) But if the man who offers the sacrifice be bold and just, then the sacrifice remains firm, even if the flesh of the victim be consumed, or rather, I might say, even if no victim be offered up at all; for what can be a real and true sacrifice but the piety of a soul which loves God? The gratitude of which is blessed with immortality, and without being recorded in writing is engraved on a pillar in the mind of God, being made equally everlasting with the sun, and moon, and the universal world.

XXIII. (109) After these things the architect of the tabernacle next prepared a sacred dress for him who was to be appointed high priest, having in its embroidery a most exceedingly beautiful and admirable work; and the robe was two-fold; one part of which was called the under-robe, and the other the robe over the shoulders. (110) Now the under-robe was of a more simple form and character, for it was entirely of hyacinthine colours, except the lowest and exterior portions, and these were ornamented with golden pomegranates, and bells, and wreaths of flowers; (111) but the robe over the shoulders or mantle was a most beautiful and skilful work, and was made with most perfect skill of all the aforesaid kinds of material, of hyacinth colour, and purple, and fine linen, and scarlet, gold thread being entwined and embroidered in it.

For the leaves were divided into fine hairs, and woven in with every thread, (112) and on the collar stones were fitted in, two being costly emeralds of exceeding value, on which the names of the patriarchs of the tribes were engraved, six on each, making twelve in all; and on the breast were twelve other precious stones, differing in colour like seals, in four rows of three stones each, and these were fitted in what was called the logeum (113) and the logeum was made square and double, as a sort of foundation, that it mighty bear on it, as an image, two virtues, manifestation and truth; and the whole was fastened to the mantle by fine golden chains, and fastened to it so that it might never get loose; (114) and a golden leaf was wrought like a crown, having four names engraved on it which may only be mentioned or heard by holy men having their ears and their tongues purified by wisdom, and by no one else at all in any place whatever.

(115) And this holy prophet Moses calls the name, a name of four letters, making them perhaps symbols of the primary numbers, the unit, the number two, the number three, the number four: since all things are comprised in the number

four, namely, a point, and a line, and a superficies, and a solid, and the measures of all things, and the most excellent symphonies of music, and the diatessaron in the sesquitertial proportion, and the chord in fifths, in the ratio of one and a half to one, and the diapason in the double ratio, and the double diapason in the fourfold ratio. Moreover, the number four has an innumerable list of other virtues likewise, the greater part of which we have discussed with accuracy in our dissertation on numbers.

(116) And in it there was a mitre, in order that the leaf might not touch the head; and there was also a cidaris made, for the kings of the eastern countries are accustomed to use a cidaris, instead of a diadem.

XXIV. (117) Such, then, is the dress of the high priest. But we must not omit to mention the signification which it conceals beneath both in its whole and in its parts. In its whole it is a copy and representation of the world; and the parts are a representation of the separate parts of the world.

(118) And we must begin with the long robe reaching down to the feet of the wearer. This tunic is wholly of the colour of a hyacinth, so as to be a representation of the air; for by nature the air is black, and in a measure it reaches down from the highest parts to the feet, being stretched from the parts about the moon, as far as the extremities of the earth, and being diffused everywhere. On which account also, the tunic reaches from the chest to the feet, and is spread over the whole body, (119) and unto it there is attached a fringe of pomegranates round the ankles, and flowers, and bells. Now the flowers are an emblem of the earth; for it is from the earth that all flowers spring and bloom; but the pomegranates *(rhoiskoi)* are a symbol of water, since, indeed, they derive their name from the flowing *(rhysis)* of water, being very appropriately named; and the bells are the emblem of the concord and harmony that exist between these things; for neither is the earth without the water, nor the water without the earthly substance, sufficient for the production of anything; but that can only be effected by the meeting and combination of both.

(120) And the place itself is the most distinct possible evidence of what is here meant to be expressed; for as the pomegranates, and the flowers, and the bells, are placed in the hem of the garment which reaches to the feet, so likewise the things of which they are the symbols, namely, the earth and water, have had the lowest position in the world assigned to them, and being in strict accord with the harmony of the universe, they display their own particular powers in definite periods of time and suitable seasons.

(121) Now of the three elements, out of which and in which all the different kinds of things which are perceptible by the outward senses and perishable are formed, namely, the air, the water and the earth, the garment which reached down to the feet in conjunction with the ornaments which were attached to that part of it which was about the ankles have been plainly shown to be appropriate symbols; for as the tunic is one, and as the aforesaid three elements are all of one species, since they all have all their revolutions and changes beneath the moon, and as to the garment are attached the pomegranates, and the flowers; so also in certain manner the earth and the water may be said to be attached to and suspended from the air, for the air is their chariot.

(122) And our argument will be able to bring forth twenty probable reasons that the mantle over the shoulders is an emblem of heaven. For in the first place, the two emeralds on the shoulder-blades, which are two round stones, are, in the opinion of some persons who have studied the subject, emblems of those stars which are the rulers of night and day, namely, the sun and moon; or rather, as one might argue with more correctness and a nearer approach to truth, they are the emblems of the two hemispheres; for, like those two stones, the portion below the earth and that over the earth are both equal, and neither of them is by nature adapted to be either increased or diminished like the moon. (123) And the colour of the stars is an additional evidence in favour of my view; for to the glance of the eye the appearance of the heaven does resemble an emerald; and it follows necessarily that six names are engraved on each of the stones, because each of the hemispheres cuts the zodiac in two parts, and in this way comprehends within itself six animals.

(124) Then the twelve stones on the breast, which are not like one another in colour, and which are divided into four rows of three stones in each, what else can they be emblems of, except of the circle of the zodiac? For that also is divided into four parts, each consisting of three animals, by which divisions it makes up the seasons of the year, spring, summer, autumn, and winter, distinguishing the four changes, the two solstices, and the two equinoxes, each of which has its limit of three signs of this zodiac, by the revolutions of the sun, according to that unchangeable, and most lasting, and really divine ratio which exists in numbers; (125) on which account they attached it to that which is with great propriety called the logeum. For all the changes of the year and the seasons are arranged by well-defined, and stated, and firm reason; and, though this seems a most extraordinary and incredible thing, by their seasonable changes they display their undeviating and everlasting permanence and durability.

(126) And it is said with great correctness, and exceeding beauty also, that the twelve stones all

differ in their colour, and that no one of them resembles the other; for also in the zodiac each animal produces that colour which is akin to and belongs to itself, both in the air, and in the earth, and in the water; and it produces it likewise in all the affections which move them, and in all kinds of animals and of plants.

XXV. (127) And this logeum is described as double with great correctness; for reason is double, both in the universe and also in the nature of mankind, in the universe there is that reason which is conversant about incorporeal species which are like patterns as it were, from which that world which is perceptible only by the intellect was made, and also that which is concerned with the visible objects of sight, which are copies and imitations of those species above mentioned, of which the world which is perceptible by the outward senses was made.

Again, in man there is one reason which is kept back, and another which finds vent in utterance: and the one is, as it were a spring, and the other (that which is uttered) flows from it; and the place of the one is the dominant part, that is, the mind; but the place of the one which finds vent in utterance is the tongue, and the mouth, and all the rest of the organs of the voice.

(128) And the architect assigned a quadrangular form to the logeum, intimating under an exceedingly beautiful figure, that both the reason of nature, and also that of man, ought to penetrate everywhere, and ought never to waver in any case; in reference to which, it is that he has also assigned to it the two virtues that have been already enumerated, manifestation and truth; for the reason of nature is true, and calculated to make manifest, and to explain everything; and the reason of the wise man, imitating that other reason, ought naturally, and appropriately to be completely sincere, honouring truth, and not obscuring anything through envy, the knowledge of which can benefit those to whom it would be explained; (129) not but what he has also assigned their two appropriate virtues to those two kinds of reason which exist in each of us, namely, that which is uttered and that which is kept concealed, attributing clearness of manifestation to the uttered one, and truth to that which is concealed in the mind; for it is suitable to the mind that it should admit of no error or falsehood, and to explanation that it should not hinder anything that can conduce to the most accurate manifestation.

(130) Therefore there is no advantage in reason which expends itself in dignified and pompous language, about things which are good and desirable, unless it is followed by consistent practice of suitable actions; on which account the architect has affixed the logeum to the robe which is worn over the shoulder, in order that it may never get loose, as he does not approve of the language being separated from the actions; for he puts forth the shoulder as the emblem of energy and action.

XXVI. (131) Such then are the figurative meanings which he desires to indicate by the sacred vestments of the high priest; and instead of a diadem he represents a cidaris on the head, because he thinks it right that the man who is consecrated to God, as his high priest, should, during the time of his exercising his office be superior to all men, not only to all private individuals, but even to all kings; (132) and above this cidaris is a golden leaf, on which an engraving of four letters was impressed; by which letters they say that the name of the living God is indicated, since it is not possible that anything that it in existence, should exist without God being invoked; for it is his goodness and his power combined with mercy that is the harmony and uniter of all things.

(133) The high priest, then, being equipped in this way, is properly prepared for the performance of all sacred ceremonies, that, whenever he enters the temple to offer up the prayers and sacrifices in use among his nation, all the world may likewise enter in with him, by means of the imitations of it which he bears about him, the garment reaching to his feet, being the imitation of the air, the pomegranate of the water, the flowery hem of the earth, and the scarlet dye of his robe being the emblem of fire; also, the mantle over his shoulders being a representation of heaven itself; the two hemispheres being further indicated by the round emeralds on the shoulder-blades, on each of which were engraved six characters equivalent to six signs of the zodiac; the twelve stones arranged on the breast in four rows of three stones each, namely the logeum, being also an emblem of that reason which holds together and regulates the universe.

(134) For it was indispensable that the man who was consecrated to the Father of the world, should have as a paraclete, his son, the being most perfect in all virtue, to procure forgiveness of sins, and a supply of unlimited blessings; (135) perhaps, also, he is thus giving a previous warning to the servant of God, even if he is unable to make himself worthy of the Creator, of the world, at least to labour incessantly to make himself worthy of the world itself; the image of which he is clothed in, in a manner that binds him from the time that he puts it on, to bear about the pattern of it in his mind, so that he shall be in a manner changed from the nature of a man into the nature of the world, and, if one may say so (and one may by all means and at all times speak the plain truth in sincerity), become a little world himself.

XXVII. (136) Again, outside the outer vestibule, at the entrance, is a brazen laver; the architect having not taken any mere raw material for the manufacture of it, as is very common, but having employed on its formation vessels which had been constructed with great care for other purposes; and which the women contributed with all imaginable zeal and eagerness, in rivalry of one another, competing with the men themselves in piety, having determined to enter upon a glorious contest, and to the utmost extent of their power to exert themselves so as not to fall short of their holiness.

(137) For though no one enjoined them to do so, they, of their own spontaneous zeal and earnestness, contributed the mirrors with which they had been accustomed to deck and set off their beauty, as the most becoming first fruits of their modesty, and of the purity of their married life, and as one may say of the beauty of their souls. (138) The maker then thought it well to accept these offerings, and to melt them down, and to make nothing except the laver, in order that the priests who were about to enter the temple might be supplied from it, with water of purification for the purpose of performing the sacred ministrations which were appointed for them; washing their feet most especially, and their hands, as a symbol of their irreproachable life, and of a course of conduct which makes itself pure in all kinds of praiseworthy actions, proceeding not along the rough road of wickedness which one may more properly call no road at all, but keeping straight along the level and direct path of virtue.

(139) Let him remember, says he, let him who is about to be sprinkled with the water of purification from this laver, remember that the materials of which this vessel was composed were mirrors, that he himself may look into his own mind as into a mirror; and if there is perceptible in it any deformity arising from some agitation unconnected with reason or from any pleasure which would excite us, and raise us up in hostility to reason, or from any pain which might mislead us and turn us from our purpose of proceeding by the straight road, or from any desire alluring us and even dragging us by force to the pursuit of present pleasures, he seeks to relieve and cure that, desiring only that beauty which is genuine and unadulterated.

(140) For the beauty of the body consists in symmetry of parts, and in a good complexion, and a healthy firmness of flesh, having also but a short period during which it is in its prime; but the beauty of the mind consists in a harmony of doctrines and a perfect accord of virtues, which do not fade away or become impaired by lapse of time, but as long as they endure at all are constantly acquiring fresh vigour and renewed youth, being set off by the preeminent complexion of truth, and the agreement of its words with its actions, and of its actions with its words, and also of its designs with both.

XXVIII. (141) And when he had been taught the patterns of the sacred tabernacle, and had in turn himself taught those who were gifted with acute comprehension, and well-qualified by nature for the comprehension and execution of those works, which it was indispensably necessary should be made; then, as was natural, when the temple had been built and finished, it was fitting also, that most suitable persons should be appointed as priests, and should be instructed in what manner it was proper for them to offer up their sacrifices, and perform their sacred ministrations.

(142) Accordingly, Moses selected his brother, choosing him out of all men, because of his superior virtue, to be high priest, and his sons he appointed priests, not giving precedence to his own family, but to the piety and holiness which he perceived to exist in those men; and what is the clearest proof of this is, that he did not think either of his sons worthy of this honour (and he had two); while he must inevitably have appointed both of them, if he had attached any importance to love for his family; (143) and he appointed them with the unanimous consent of the whole nation, as the sacred scriptures have recorded, which was a most novel mode of proceeding, and one especially worthy of being mentioned; and, in the first place, he washed them all over with the most pure and vivifying water of the fountain; and then he gave them their sacred vestments, giving to his brother the robe which reached down to his feet, and the mantle which covered the shoulders, as a sort of breast-plate, being an embroidered robe, adorned with all kinds of figures, and a representation of the universe. And to all his nephews he gave linen tunics, and girdles, and trowsers; (144) the girdles, in order that the wearers might be unimpeded and ready for all their sacred ministrations, were fastened up tight round the loose waists of the tunics; and the breeches, that nothing which ought to be hidden might be visible, especially when they were going up to the altar, or coming down from the high place, and doing everything with earnestness and celerity.

(145) For if their equipment had not been so accurately attended to for the sake of guarding against the uncertain future, and for the sake of providing for an energetic promptness in the sacred ministrations, the men would have appeared naked, not being able to preserve the becoming order necessary to holy men dedicated to the service of God.

XXIX. (146) And when he had thus furnished them with proper vestments, he took very fragrant ointment, which had been made by the skill of the perfumer, and first of all he anointed the altar in the open air, and the laver, sprinkling it with the perfume seven times; after that he anointed the tabernacle and every one of the sacred vessels, the ark, and the candlestick, and the altar of incense, and the table, and the censers, and the vials, and all the other things which were either necessary or useful for the sacrifices; and last of all bringing the high priest close to himself, he anointed his head with abundant quantities of oil.

(147) When he had done all this, he then, in strict accordance with what was holy, commanded a heifer and two rams to be brought; the one that he might sacrifice it for the remission of sins, intimating by a figure that to sin is congenital with every created being, however good it may be, inasmuch as it is created, and that therefore it is indispensable that God should be propitiated in its behalf by means of prayers and sacrifices, that he may not be provoked to chastise it. (148) And of the rams, one he required for a whole burnt-offering of gratitude for the successful arrangement of all those things, of which every individual has such a share as is suited to him, deriving benefit from all the elements, enjoying the earth for his abode and in respect of the nourishment which is derived from it; the water for drinking, and washing, and sailing on; the air for breathing and for the comprehension of those things which are the objects of our outward senses (since the air is the medium in which they all are exerted), and for the seasons of the year; enjoying fire both of that kind which is used for cooking food and for warming one's self, and also that heavenly kind which is serviceable for light and for all the objects of sight. (149) The other ram he employed for the complete accomplishment of the purification of the priests, which he appropriately called the ram of perfection, since the priests were intended to exercise their office in teaching proper and convenient rites and ceremonies to the servants and ministers of God. (150) And he took the blood, and with some of it he poured a libation all round the altar, and part he took, holding a vial under it to catch it, and with it he anointed three parts of the body of the initiated priests, the tip of the ear, the extremity of the hand, and the extremity of the foot, all on the right side, signifying by this action that the perfect man must be pure in every word and action, and in his whole life, for it is the hearing which judges of his words, and the hand is the symbol of action, and the foot of the way in which a man walks in life; (151) and since each of these members is an extremity of the body, and is likewise on the right side, we must imagine that it is here indicated by a figure that improvement in every thing is to be arrived at by a certain dexterity, being a portion of supreme felicity, and being the true aim in life, which a man must necessarily labour to attain, and to which he ought to refer all his actions, aiming at them in his life, as in the practice of archery men aim at a target.

XXX. (152) Accordingly, he first of all anointed the three parts before mentioned of the bodies of the priests with the unmixed blood of one of the victims, that, namely, which was called the ram of perfection; and afterwards, taking some of the blood which was upon the altar, being the blood of all the victims mingled together, and some also of the unguent which has already been mentioned, which the ointment makers had prepared, and mixing some of the oil with the mingled blood of the different victims, he sprinkled some upon the priests and upon their garments, with the intention that they should have a share not only in that purity which was external and in the open air, but also of that which was in the inmost shrine, since they were about to minister within the temple. And all the things within the temple were anointed with oil.

(153) And when they had brought forward other sacrifices in addition to the former ones, partly the priests sacrificing for themselves, and partly the elders sacrificing on behalf of the whole nation, then Moses entered into the tabernacle, leading his brother by the hand (and it was the eighth and last day of the festival, for the seven previous days had been devoted to the initiation of the hierophants), he now initiated both him and his nephews. And when he had entered in he taught him as a learned teacher might instruct an ignorant pupil, in what way the high priest ought to perform the ministrations which are performed inside the temple.

(154) Then, when they had both come out and held up their hands in front of their head, they, with a pure and holy mind, offered up such prayers as were suitable and becoming for the nation. And while they were still praying a most marvellous prodigy happened; for from out of the inmost shrine, whether it was a portion of the purest possible aether, or whether the air, according to some natural change of the elements, had become dissolved with fire, on a sudden a body of flame shone forth, and with impetuous violence descended on the altar and consumed all that was thereon, with the view, as I imagine, of showing in the clearest manner that none of the things which had been done had been done without the especial providence of God.

(155) For it was natural that an especial honour should be assigned to the holy place, not only by means of those things in which men are the workmen employed, but also by that purest of all essences, fire, in order that the ordinary fire which is used by men might not touch the altar; perhaps by reason of its being defiled by ten thousand impurities. (156) For it is concerned not only with irrational animals when they are roasted or boiled for the unjust appeasing of our miserable bellies, but also in the case of men who are slain by hostile attack, not merely in a small body of three or four, but in numerous hosts.

(157) At all events, before now, arrows charged with fire have been aimed at vast naval fleets and have burnt them; and fire has destroyed whole cities, which have blazed away till they have been consumed down to their very foundations and reduced to ashes, so that no trace whatever has remained of their former situation.

(158) It appears to me that this was the reason for which God rejected from his sacred altar the fire which is applied to common uses, as being defiled; and that, instead of it, he rained down celestial flame from heaven, in order to make a distinction between holy and profane things, and to separate the things belonging to man from the things belonging to God; for it was fitting that a more incorruptible essence of fire than that which served the common purposes of life should be set apart for sacrifices.

XXXI. (159) And as many sacrifices were of necessity offered up every day, and especially on all days of solemn assembly and festival, both on behalf of each individual separately and in common for the whole nation, for innumerable and various reasons, inasmuch as the nation was very populous and very pious, there was a need also of a multitude of keepers of the temple for the sacred and subordinate ministrations. (160) And, again, the election of these officers was conducted in a novel and not in the ordinary manner. God chose out one of the twelve tribes, having selected it for its superior excellence, and appointed that to furnish the keepers of the temple, giving it rewards and peculiar honours in return for its pious acting. And the action which it had to perform was of this kind.

(161) When Moses had gone up into the neighbouring mountain and had remained several days alone with God, the fickle-minded among the people, thinking that his absence was a favourable opportunity, as if they had no longer any ruler at all, rushed unrestrainedly to impiety, and, forgetting the holiness of the living God, became eager imitators of the Egyptian inventions. (162) Then, having made a golden calf in imitation of that which appeared to be the most sacred animal in that district, they offered up unholy sacrifices, and instituted blasphemous dances, and sang hymns which differed in no respect from dirges, and, being filled with strong wine, gave themselves up to a twofold intoxication, the intoxication of wine and that of folly, revelling and devoting the night to feasting, and, having no foresight as to the future, they spent their time in pleasant sins, though justice had her eye upon them, who saw them while they would not see, and decided what punishments they deserved.

(163) But when the continued outcries in the camp, from men collected in numerous and dense crowds, reached over a great distance, so that the sound penetrated even to the summit of the mountain, Moses, hearing the uproar, was in great perplexity, as being at the same time a devout worshipper of God and a friend to mankind, not being able to bring his mind to quit the society of God with whom he was conversing, and in which he, being alone with him, was conferring with him by himself, nor, on the other hand, could he be indifferent to the multitude thus full of anarchy and wickedness; (164) for he recognised the tumult, since he was a very shrewd man at conjecturing, from inarticulate sounds of no distinct meaning, the passions of the soul which were inaccessible to and out of the reach of the conjectures of others, because he perceived at once that the noise proceeded partly from intoxication, since intemperance had produced satiety and a disposition to insult the law.

(165) And being drawn both ways, and under strong attraction in both directions, he fluctuated this way and that way, and did not know what he ought to do; and while he was considering the matter the following command was given to him. "Go down quickly; descend from this place, the people have turned with haste to lawlessness, having fashioned a god made with hands in the form of a bull, they are falling down before that which is no god, and sacrificing unto him, forgetting all the things that they have seen, and all that they have heard, which might lead them to piety." (166) So Moses, being amazed, and being also constrained by this command, believes those incredible events, and springs down to be a mediator and reconciler; not however, in a moment, for first of all he addressed supplications and prayers on behalf of his nation to God, entreating God that he would pardon these their sins; then, this governor of and intercessor for his people, having appeased the Ruler of the universe, went down at the same time rejoicing and feeling sorrowful; he rejoiced indeed that God had admitted his supplication, but he was full of anxiety and depression, being greatly indignant at the lawless transgression of the multitude.

XXXII. (167) And when he came into the middle of the camp, and marvelled at the sudden way in which the multitude had forsaken all their ancient habits, and at the vast amount of falsehood which they had embraced instead of truth, he, seeing that the disease had not extended among them all, but that some were still sound, and still cherished a disposition which loathed wickedness; wishing to distinguish those who were incurable from those who felt indignation at what had taken place, and to know also whether any of those who had offended repented them of their sin, caused a proclamation to be made; and it was indeed a shrewd test of the inclination of each individual, to see how he was disposed to holiness, or to the contrary.

(168) "Whoever," said he, "is on the side of

the Lord, let him come to me." It was but a brief sentence which he thus uttered, but the meaning concealed under it was important; for what was intimated by his words was the following sense: "If any one does not think anything whatever that is made by hands, or anything that is created, a god, but believes that there is one ruler of the universe only, let him come to me."

(169) Now of the others, some resisted by reason of the admiration which they had conceived for the Egyptian pride, and they did not attend to what he said; others wanted courage to come nearer to him, perhaps out of fear of punishment; or else perhaps they dreaded punishment at the hand of Moses, or a rising up against them on the part of the people; for the multitude invariably attack those who do not share in their frenzy.

(170) But that single tribe of the whole number which was called the tribe of Levi, when they heard the proclamation, as if by one preconcerted agreement, ran with great haste, displaying their earnestness by their promptness and rapidity, and proving the keenness of the desire of their soul for piety; (171) and, when Moses saw them rushing forward as if starting from the goal in a race, he said, "Surely it is not with your bodies alone that you are hastening to come unto me, but you shall soon bear witness with your minds to your eagerness; let every one of you take a sword, and slay those men who have done things worthy of ten thousand deaths, who have forsaken the true God, and made for themselves false gods, of perishable and created substances, calling them by the name which belongs only to the uncreated and everlasting God; let every one, I say, slay those men, whether it be his own kinsmen or his friends, looking upon nothing to be either friendship or kindred but the holy fellowship of good men."

(172) And the tribe of Levi, outrunning his command with the most eager readiness, since they were already alienated from those men in their minds, almost from the first moment that they beheld the beginning of their lawless iniquity, killed them all to a man, to the number of three thousand, though they had been but a short time before their dearest friends; and as the corpses were lying in the middle of the place of the assembly of the people, the multitude beholding them pitied them, and fearing the still fervid, and angry, and indignant disposition of those who had slain them, reproved them out of fear; (173) but Moses, gladly approving of their exceeding virtue, devised in their favour and confirmed to them an honour which was appropriate to their exploit, for it was fitting that those who had undertaken a voluntary war for the sake of the honour of God, and who had carried it out successfully in a short time, should be thought worthy to receive the priesthood and charge of officiating in his service.

XXXIII. (174) But, since there is not one order only of consecrated priests, but since to some of them the charge is committed of attending to all the prayers, and sacrifices, and other most sacred ceremonies, being allowed to enter into the inmost and most holy shrine; while others are not permitted to do any of these things, but have the duty of taking care of and guarding the temple and all that is therein, both day and night, whom some call keepers of the temple; a sedition arose respecting the precedency in honour, which was to many persons in many ways the cause of infinite evils, and it broke out now from the keepers of the temple attacking the priests, and endeavouring to deprive them of the honour which belonged to them; and they thought that they should be able easily to succeed in their object, since they were many times more numerous than the others.

(175) But for the sake of not appearing to be planning any innovations of their own heads, they persuaded also the eldest of the twelve tribes to embrace their opinions, which last tribe was followed by many of the more fickle of the populace, as thinking it entitled to the precedence and to the principal share of authority over the whole host.

(176) Moses now knew that a great plot was in agitation against him; for he had appointed his brother high priest in accordance with the will of God, which had been declared to him. And now false accusations were brought against him, as if he had falsified the oracles of God, and as if he had done so and made the appointment by reason of his family affection and goodwill towards his brother. (177) And he, being very naturally grieved at this, inasmuch as he was not only distrusted by such accusations while exhibiting his own good faith in a most genuine manner, but he was also grieved at those actions of his being calumniated which had for their object the honour of God, and which were of such a nature as to deserve by themselves that even such a man who had in other respects shown an insincere disposition should be looked upon as behaving in this case with truth; for truth is the invariable attendant of God.

But he did not think fit to give any explanation by words respecting his appointment of his brother, knowing that it was difficult to endeavour to persuade those who were previously possessed by contrary opinions to change their minds; but he besought God to give the people a visible demonstration that he had in no respect behaved with dishonesty respecting the appointment to the priesthood. (178) And he, therefore, commanded that twelve rods should be taken, so as to be equal in number to the tribes of the nation; and he commanded further that the names of the other patriarchs of the tribes should be written on eleven of the rods, but on the remaining one the name of his brother, the high priest, and then that they should all be carried into the temple as far as the inmost shrine; and the officer who did what he had been commanded waited in expectation to see the result.

(179) And on the next day, in obedience to a command from God, he went into the temple, while all the people were standing around, and brought out the rods, the others differing in no respect from the state in which they were when they were put in; but the one on which the name of his brother was written had undergone a miraculous change; for like a fine plant it suddenly put forth shoots all over, and was weighed down with the abundance of its crop of fruit.

XXXIV. (180) And the fruit were almonds, which is a fruit of a different character from any other. For in most fruit, such as grapes, olives, and apples, the seed and the eatable part differ from one another, and being different are separated as to their position, for the eatable part is outside, and the seed is shut up within; but in the case of this fruit the seed and the eatable part are the same, both of them being comprised in one species, and their position is one and the same, being without strongly protected and fortified with a twofold fence, consisting partly of a very thick bark, and partly of what appears in no respect short of a wooden case, (181) by which perfect virtue is figuratively indicated.

For as in the almond the beginning and the end are the same, the beginning as far as it is seed, and the end as far as it is fruit; so also is it the case with the virtues; for each one of them is at the same time both beginning and end, a beginning, because it proceeds not from any other power, but from itself; and an end, because the life in accordance with nature hastens towards it. (182) This is one reason; and another is also mentioned, more clear and emphatic than the former; for the part of the almond which looks like bark is bitter, but that which lies inside the bark, like a wooden case, is very hard and impenetrable, so that the fruit, being enclosed in these two coverings, is not very easily to be got at.

(183) This is an emblem of the soul which is inclined to the practice of meditation, from which he thinks it is proper to turn it to virtue by showing it that it is necessary first of all to encounter danger. But labour is a bitter, and distasteful, and harsh thing, from which good is produced, for the sake of which one must not yield to effeminate indolence; (184) for he who seeks to avoid labour is also avoiding good. And he, again, who encounters what is disagreeable to be borne with fortitude and manly perseverance, is taking the best road to happiness; for it is not the nature of virtue to abide with those who are given up to delicacy and luxury, and who have become effeminate in their souls, and whose bodies are enervated by

the incessant luxury which they practise every day; but it is subdued by such conduct, and determined to change its abode, having first of all arranged its departure so as to depart to, and abide with, the ruler of right reason.

(185) But, if I must tell the truth, the most sacred company of prudence, and temperance, and courage, and justice seeks the society of those who practise virtue, and of those who admire a life of austerity and rigid duty, devoting themselves to fortitude and self-denial, with wise economy and abstinence; by means of which virtues the most powerful of all the principles within us, namely, reason, improves and attains to a state of perfect health and vigour, overthrowing the violent attacks of the body, which the moderate use of wine, and epicurism, and licentiousness, and other insatiable appetites excite against it, engendering a fulness of flesh which is the direct enemy of shrewdness and wisdom.

(186) Moreover, it is said, that of all the trees that are accustomed to blossom in the spring, the almond is the first to flourish, bringing as it were good tidings of abundance of fruit; and that afterwards it is the last to lose its leaves, extending the yearly old age of its verdure to the longest period; in each of which particulars it is an emblem of the tribe of the priesthood, as Moses intimates under the figure of this tree that this tribe shall be the first of the whole human race to flourish, and likewise the last; as long as it shall please God to liken our life to the revolutions of the spring, destroying covetousness that most treacherous of passions, and the fountain of all unhappiness.

XXXV. (187) Since, therefore, I have now stated that in the absolutely perfect governor there ought to be four things, royal power, the legislative disposition, and the priesthood, and the prophetic office (in order that by his legislative disposition he may command such things as are right to be done, and forbid such things as are not proper to be done, and that by his priesthood he may arrange not only all human but likewise all divine things; and that by his prophetic office he may predict those things which cannot be comprehended by reason): having fully discussed the first three, and having shown that Moses as a most excellent king, and lawgiver, and high priest, I come in the last place to show that he was also the most illustrious of prophets.

(188) I am not unaware then that all the things which are written in the sacred books are oracles delivered by him; and I will set forth what more peculiarly concerns him, when I have first mentioned this one point, namely, that of the sacred oracles some are represented as delivered in the person of God by his interpreter, the divine prophet, while others are put in the form of question and answer, and others are delivered by Moses

in his own character as a divinely-prompted lawgiver possessed by divine inspiration. (189) Therefore, all the earliest oracles are manifestations of the whole of the divine virtues, and especially of that merciful and bounteous character by means of which he trains all men to virtue, and especially the race which is devoted to his service, to which he lays open the road leading to happiness.

(190) The second class have a sort of admixture and communication in them, the prophet asking information on the subjects as to which he is in difficulty, and God answering him and instructing him. The third sort are attributed to the lawgiver, God having given him a share of his prescient power, by means of which he will be able to foretell the future.

(191) Therefore, we must for the present pass by the first; for they are too great to be adequately praised by any man, as, indeed, they could scarcely be panegyrised worthily by the heaven itself and the nature of the universe; and they are also uttered by the mouth, as it were, of an interpreter. But interpretation and prophecy differ from one another. And concerning the second kind I will at once endeavour to explain the truth, connecting with them the third species also, in which the inspired character of the speaker is shown, according to which it is that he is most especially and appropriately looked upon as a prophet.

XXXVI. (192) And we must here begin with the promise. There are four places where the oracles are given by way of question and answer, being contained in the exposition of the law, and having a mixed character. For, first, the prophet feels inspiration and asks questions, and then the father prophesies to him, giving him a share of his discourse and replies. And the first case where this occurs is one which would have irritated, not only Moses, who was the most holy and pious man that ever lived, but even any one who had only had a slight taste of piety.

(193) A certain man, illegitimately born of two unequal parents, namely, an Egyptian father and a Jewish mother, and who disregarded the national and hereditary customs which he had learnt from her, as it is reported, inclined to the Egyptian impiety, being seized with admiration for the ungodly practices of the men of that nation; (194) for the Egyptians, almost alone of all men, set up the earth as a rival of the heaven considering the former as entitled to honours equal with those of the gods, and giving the latter no especial honour, just as if it were proper to pay respect to the extremities of a country rather than to the king's palace. For in the world the heaven is the most holy temple, and the further extremity is the earth; though this too is in itself worthy of being regarded with honour; but if it is brought into comparison with the air, is as far inferior to it as light is to dark-

ness, or night to day, or corruption to immortality, or a mortal to God. (195) For, since that country is not irrigated by rain as all other lands are, but by the inundations of the river which is accustomed every year to overflow its banks; the Egyptians, in their impious reason, make a god of the Nile, as if it were a copy and a rival of heaven, and use pompous language about the virtue of their country.

XXXVII. (196) Accordingly, this man of mixed race, having had a quarrel with some one of the consecrated and well-instructed house of Israel, becoming carried away by his anger, and unable to restrain himself, and being also an admirer and follower of the impiety of the Egyptians, extended his impiety from earth to heaven, cursing it with his accursed, and polluted, and defiled soul, and with his wicked tongue, and with the whole power of all his vocal organs in the superfluity of his ungodliness; though it ought to be blessed and praised, not by all men, indeed, but only by those who are most virtuous and pious, as having received perfect purification. (197) Wherefore Moses, marvelling at his insanity and at the extravagance of his audacity, although he was filled with a noble impetuosity and indignation, and desired to slay the man with his own hand, nevertheless feared lest he should be inflicting on him too light a punishment; for he conceived that no man could possibly devise any punishment adequate to such enormous impiety.

(198) And since it followed of necessity that a man who did not worship God could not honour his father either, or his mother, or his country, or his benefactors, this man, in addition to not reverencing them, dared to speak ill of them. And then what extravagance of wickedness did he fall short of? And yet evil-speaking, if compared with cursing, is the lighter evil of the two. But when intemperate language and an unbridled tongue are subservient to lawless folly, then inevitably and invariably some iniquitous conduct must follow.

(199) O man! does any one curse God? What other god can he invoke to ratify and confirm his curse? Is it not plain that he must invoke God to give effect to his curses against himself? Away with such profane and impious ideas!

It would be well to cleanse that miserable soul which has been insulted by the voice, and which has sued the ears for ministers, keeping the external senses blind. (200) And was not either the tongue of the man who uttered such impiety loosened, or the ears of him who was destined to hear such things closed up? unless, indeed, that was done in consequence of some providential arrangement of justice, which does not think that either any extraordinary good or that any enormous evil ought to be kept in darkness, but that such should be revealed in order to the most complete manifestation of virtue or vice, so that it may adjudge the one to be worthy of acceptance and the other of punishment. (201) On this account Moses ordered the man to be thrown into prison and bound with chains; and then he addressed propitiatory prayers to God, begging him to be merciful to the necessities of the external senses (by means of which we both see what it is not proper to see, and hear what it is not lawful to hear), and to point out what the author of such a strange and unprecedented blasphemy and impiety ought to suffer.

(202) And God commanded him to be stoned, considering, as I imagine, the punishment of stoning to be a suitable and appropriate one for a man who had a stony and hardened heart, and wishing at the same time that all his fellow countrymen should have a share in inflicting punishment on him, as he knew that they were very indignant and eager to slay him; and the only punishment which so many myriads of men could possibly join in was that which was inflicted by throwing stones.

(203) But after the punishment of this impious murderer, a new commandment was enacted, which had never before been thought worthy of being reduced to writing; but unexpected innovations cause new laws to be devised for the repression of their evils. At all events, the following law was immediately introduced: "Whoever curses God shall be guilty of sin, and whoever names the name of the Lord shall die."[2] (204) Well done, O all-wise man! You alone have drunk of the cup of unalloyed wisdom. You have seen that it was worse to name God than even to curse him; for you would never have treated lightly a man who had committed the heaviest of all impieties, and inflicted the heaviest punishment possible on those who committed the slightest faults; but you fixed death, which is the very greatest punishment imaginable, as the penalty for the man who appeared to have committed the heaviest crime.

XXXVIII. (205) But, as it seems, he is not now speaking of that God who was the first being who had any existence, and the Father of the universe, but of those who are accounted gods in the different cities; and they are falsely called gods, being only made by the arts of painters and sculptors, for the whole inhabited world is full of statues and images, and erections of that kind, of whom it is necessary however to abstain from speaking ill, in order that no one of the disciples of Moses may ever become accustomed at all to treat the appellation of God with disrespect; for that name is always most deserving to obtain the victory, and is especially worthy of love.

(206) But if any one were, I will not say to blas-

pheme against the Lord of gods and men, but were even to dare to utter his name unseasonably, he must endure the punishment of death; (207) for those persons who have a proper respect for their parents do not lightly bring forward the names of their parents, though they are but mortal, but they avoid using their proper names by reason of the reverence which they bear them, and call them rather by the titles indicating their natural relationship, that is, father and mother, by which names they at once intimate the unsurpassable benefits which they have received at their hands, and their own grateful disposition. (208) Therefore these men must not be thought worthy of pardon who out of volubility of tongue have spoken unseasonably, and being too free of their words have repeated carelessly the most holy and divine name of God.

XXXIX. (209) Moreover, in accordance with the honour due to the Creator of the universe, the prophet hallowed the sacred seventh day, beholding with eyes of more acute sight than those of mortals its pre-eminent beauty, which had already been deeply impressed on the heaven and the whole universal world, and had been borne about as an image by nature itself in her own bosom; (210) for first of all Moses found that day destitute of any mother, and devoid of all participation in the female generation, being born of the Father alone without any propagation by means of seed, and being born without any conception on the part of any mother. And then he beheld not only this, that it was very beautiful and destitute of any mother, neither being born of corruption nor liable to corruption; and then, in the third place, he by further inquiry discovered that it was the birthday of the world, which the heaven keeps as a festival, and the earth and all the things in and on the earth keep as a festival, rejoicing and delighting in the all-harmonious number of seven, and in the sabbath day.

(211) For this reason the all-great Moses thought fit that all who were enrolled in his sacred polity should follow the laws of nature and meet in a solemn assembly, passing the time in cheerful joy and relaxation, abstaining from all work, and from all arts which have a tendency to the production of anything; and from all business which is connected with the seeking of the means of living, and that they should keep a complete truce, abstaining from all laborious and fatiguing thought and care, and devoting their leisure, not as some persons scoffingly assert, to sports, or exhibitions of actors and dancers, for the sake of which those who run madly after theatrical amusements suffer disasters and even encounter miserable deaths, and for the sake of these the most dominant and influential of the outward senses, sight and hearing, make the soul, which should be the heavenly

---

[2]Leviticus 24:15.

nature, the slave of these senses. (212) But, giving up their time wholly to the study of philosophy, not of that sort of philosophy which word-catchers and sophists, seek to reduce to a system, selling doctrines and reasonings as they would any other vendible thing in the market. Men who (O you earth and sun!) employ philosophy against philosophy, and yet never wear a blush on their countenance; but who, applying themselves to the kindred philosophy, which they make up of these component parts, namely, of intention, and words, and actions, all united into one species, in order to the acquisition and enjoyment of happiness.

(213) Now some one disregarding this injunction, even while he yet had the sacred words of God respecting the holy seventh day still ringing in his ears, which God had uttered without the intervention of the prophet, and, what is the most wonderful thing of all, by a visible voice which affected the eyes of those who were present even more than their ears, went forth through the middle of the camp to pick up sticks, well knowing that all the people in the camp were perfectly quiet and doing nothing, and even while he was committing the iniquity was seen and detected, all disguise being impossible; (214) for some persons, having gone forth out of the gates to some quiet spot, that they might pray in some retired and peaceful place, seeing a most unholy spectacle, namely this man carrying a faggot of sticks, and being very indignant, were about to put him to death; but reasoning with themselves they restrained the violence of their wrath, that they might not appear, as they were only private persons, to chastise any one rather than the magistrates, and that too uncondemned; though indeed in other respects the transgression was manifest and undeniable, wishing also that no pollution arising from an execution, even though most righteously inflicted, should defile the sacred day.

But they apprehended him, and led him away to the magistrate, with whom the priests were sitting as assessors; and the whole multitude collected together to hear the trial; (215) for it was invariably the custom, as it was desirable on other days also, but especially on the seventh day, as I have already explained, to discuss matters of philosophy; the ruler of the people beginning the explanation, and teaching the multitude what they ought to do and to say, and the populace listening so as to improve in virtue, and being made better both in their moral character and in their conduct through life; (216) in accordance with which custom, even to this day, the Jews hold philosophical discussions on the seventh day, disputing about their national philosophy, and devoting that day to the knowledge and consideration of the subjects of natural philosophy; for as for their houses of prayer in the different cities, what are they, but

schools of wisdom, and courage, and temperance, and justice, and piety, and holiness, and every virtue, by which human and divine things are appreciated, and placed upon a proper footing?

XL. (217) On this day, then, the man who had done this deed of impiety was led away to prison; and Moses being at a loss what ought to be done to the man (for he knew that he had committed a crime worthy of death, but did not know what was the most suitable manner for the punishment to be inflicted upon him), came with his invisible soul to the invisible judgment seat, and asked of that Judge who heareth everything before it is related to him what his sentence was. (218) And that Judge delivered his sentence that the man ought to die, and in no other way than being stoned, since in his case, as in that of the criminal mentioned above, his mind had been changed to a dumb stone, and he had committed the most complete of offences, in which nearly every other sin is comprised which can be committed against the laws enacted respecting the reverence due to the seventh day.

(219) Why so? Because, not ŏnly mere handicraft trades, but also nearly all other acts and businesses, and especially all such as have reference to any providing of or seeking for the means of life, are either carried on by means of fire themselves, or, at all events, not without those instruments which are made by fire. On which account Moses, in many places, forbids any one to handle a fire on the sabbath day, inasmuch as that is the most primary and efficient source of things and the most ancient and important work; and if that is reduced to a state of tranquillity, he thought that it would be probable that all particular works would be at a stand-still likewise. (220) And wood is the material of fire, so that a man who is picking up wood is committing a crime which is akin to and nearly connected with that of burning fire, doubling his transgression, in fact, partly in that he was collecting what it was commanded should remain unmoved, and partly that what he was collecting was that which is the material of fire, the beginning of all arts.

XLI. (221) Therefore both those instances which I have mentioned comprise the punishments of wicked men, appointed and confirmed by question and answer. And there are two other instances, not of the same, but of a different character; the one of which has reference to the succession of an inheritance; the other, as far at least as it appears to me, to a sacrifice which was performed at an unseemly time. And we must first discuss the latter of the two.

(222) Moses puts down the beginning of the vernal equinox as the first month of the year, attributing the chief honour, not as some persons do to the periodical revolutions of the year in regard

of time, but rather to the graces and beauties of nature which it has caused to shine upon men; for it is through the bounty of nature that the seeds which are sown to produce the necessary food of mankind are brought to perfection. And the fruit of trees in their prime, which is second in importance only to the necessary crops, is engendered by the same power, and as being second in importance it also ripens late; for we always find in nature that those things which are not very necessary are second to those which are indispensable. (223) Now wheat and barley are among the things which are very necessary; as, likewise, are all the other species of food, without which it is impossible to live. But oil, and wine, and almonds are not among necessaries, since men often live without them to the very extremity of old age, extending their life over a number of years.

(224) Accordingly, in this month, about the fourteenth day of the month, when the orb of the moon is usually about to become full, the public universal feast of the passover is celebrated, which in the Chaldaic language is called pascha; at which festival not only do private individuals bring victims to the altar and the priests sacrifice them, but also, by a particular ordinance of this law, the whole nation is consecrated and officiates in offering sacrifice; every separate individual on this occasion bringing forward and offering up with his own hands the sacrifice due on his own behalf. (225) Therefore all the rest of the people rejoiced and was of joyful countenance, every one thinking that he himself was honoured by this participation in the priesthood.

But the others passed the time of the festival amid tears and groans, their own relations having lately died, whom they were now mourning for, and were overwhelmed with a two fold sorrow, having, in addition to their grief for their relations who were slain, the pain also which arose from being deprived of the pleasure and honour which accrue from the offering up of sacrifice, as they were not purified or cleansed on that day, inasmuch as their mourning had not yet lasted beyond the appointed and legitimate period of lamentation. (226) These men coming, after the assembly was over, to the ruler of the people, being full of melancholy and depression, related to him what had happened, namely, "that the recent death of their relations was an unavoidable affliction to which they could not help yielding, and that it was a further grief that, on that account, they were unable to bear their share in the sacrifice of the passover. (227) And then they besought him that they too might make their offerings no less than the others, and that the misfortune which had befallen them in the death of their kinsmen might not be reckoned against them as an iniquity of theirs, so as to produce them punishment instead of compassion; for

that they thought that they were worse off than even the people who were dead, since these last had, indeed, no sense of the grievous privation, but they who continued live would appear to die the death perceptible to the outward sense."

XLII. (228) When he heard this he saw that the justification which they alleged was not inconsistent with reason and truth, and that the excuse which they alleged for not having previously offered their sacrifice was founded in necessity, and that they were entitled to merciful consideration. And while he as wavering in his opinion, and inclining this way and that way as if in the balance of a scale, for compassion and justice inclined him one way, and on the other side the law of the sacrifice of the passover weighed him down, in which the first month and the fourteenth day of the month are appointed for the offering of the sacrifice; accordingly, Moses, being perplexed and balancing between consent and refusal, besought God to decide the question and to announce his decision to him by an oracular command. (229) And God listened to his entreaty and gave him an oracle bearing not only on the circumstances which had taken place, but on all such as should hereafter happen with reference to the same subject, if people should ever again find themselves in a similar case.

He likewise, out of the abundance of his providence, gave further and general directions with respect to other individuals who at any time, for one reason or other, should be unable to offer up their sacrifice with the whole of the rest of the nation. (230) We must now, therefore, proceed to relate the oracular commands which were thus given by God with reference to these cases.[3]

He says, "The mourning for a relation is a necessary sorrow to those who are related by blood, and it is not set down as a piece of guilty indifference. (231) As long, therefore, as it lasts, until the time that is appointed by law for it to cease, let the man be repelled from the sacred precincts, which must be kept pure, not only from all intentional pollution, but likewise from all such as is involuntary. But when the legal time for mourning is expired, then let the mourners be no longer deprived of an equal share in the performance of the sacrifices, that those who are alive may not become an adjunct to those who are dead. And let them, as if they were in a second class, come again in the second month, on the fourteenth day of the month, and let them sacrifice in the same manner as the former sacrificers, and let them adopt the sacrifice in the same way as they did, in a similar manner and under similar rules."

(232) Also, let the same regulations be observed with respect to those who are hindered,

---

[3]Numbers 9:10.

not by mourning, but by a distant journey, from offering up their sacrifice in common with and at the same time with the whole nation. "For those who are travelling in a foreign land, or dwelling in some other country, do no wrong, so as to deserve to be deprived of equal honour with the rest, especially since one country will not contain the entire nation by reason of its great numbers, but has sent out colonies in every direction."

XLIII. (233) Having now, then, given this account of those who were too late to sacrifice the festival of the passover with the rest of the nation by reason of some unexpected circumstances, but who were desirous to fulfil the duty which had thus been omitted, even though late, still in the necessary manner, I now proceed to the last injunction relating to the succession to inheritances; that being, in like manner, of a mixed character, and consisting of question and answer.

(234) There was a certain man, named Shalpaath, a man of high character and of a distinguished tribe. He had four daughters, but not a single son. And after the death of their father the daughters, being afraid that they should be deprived of their father's inheritance, because the allotments of such inheritances were given to the male heirs, came to the ruler of the people with the modesty befitting maidens, not because they were eager for riches, but because they desired to preserve the name and reputation of their father. (235) And they said to Moses, "Our father is dead; and he died without having been mixed up in any of those seditions in which it has happened that so many thousands have been slain; but he was a cultivator of a life free from trouble and notoriety; unless, indeed, it is to be considered as a crime that he was without male offspring. And we are now here orphans in appearance, but in real fact desiring to find a father in you; for a lawful ruler is as closely connected with his subjects as a father."[4]

(236) And Moses marvelled at the wisdom of the maidens, and at their affection for their father, nevertheless he hesitated, being biased in some degree by other thoughts in accordance with which it seemed proper for men to divide the inheritances among themselves, that so they might receive the due reward of their military services and of the wars which they had gone through. But nature, which has given to woman protection from all such contests, does likewise by so doing plainly deprive them of their right to a share in what is put forward as a reward for encountering them.

(237) On which account the mind of Moses was very naturally in a state of indecision, and was dragged different ways, so that Moses laid his perplexities before God, whom he knew to be the only being who could with true and unerring judgment decide such delicate differences with a complete display of truth and justice. (238) But the Creator of the universe, the Father of the world, who holds together earth and heaven, and the water and the air, and everything which is composed of any one of these things, and who rules the whole world, the King of gods and men, did not think it unbecoming for him to take upon himself the part of arbitrator respecting these orphan maidens. And, as arbitrator, he, in my opinion, did more for them than if he had been merely a judge of the law, inasmuch as he is merciful and beneficent, and has filled all things everywhere with his beneficent power for he gave great praise to the maidens.

(239) O! Master how can any one sing your praises adequately, with what mouth, with what tongue, with what organisation of voice? Can the stars become a chorus and pour forth any melody which shall be worthy of the subject? Even if the whole of the heaven were to be dissolved into voice, would it be able to recount even a portion of your virtues? "Very rightly," says God, "have the daughters of Shalpaath spoken." (240) Who is there who can fail to perceive how great a praise this is when God bears witness in their favour? Come, now, ye who are violent; ye, who give yourselves airs because of your virtuous actions; ye, who hold up your hands higher than nature justifies, and who raise your eyebrows; ye, among whom the widowhood of woman is a cause for laughter, though it is a most pitiable evil; and in whose thoughts the desolation of orphan children is ridiculed even more shamefully than the distress before mentioned.

(241) So now, seeing that those who appeared in such a low and unfortunate condition were not marked by God among the neglected and obscure, though all the kingdoms of the whole habitable world are the most insignificant portion of his dominion, because the whole circumference and space of the world is but the extremity of his works, learn a necessary lesson from this fact.

(242) But Moses, having praised the conversation of the maidens, did not either leave them without their due honour and reward, nor yet, on the other hand, did he raise them to an equal degree of honour with the men on whom the brunt of the war falls; but to the latter he allotted the inheritances as the prizes which belonged to them as a reward for the gallant exploits which they had performed. But the former he thought worthy of grace and kindness, not of reward; as he showed most plainly by the expressions which he used, speaking of "gifts" and "presents," but not of "requital" or "recompense." For the one form of language is suited to those who receive what they have a right to, and the other belongs to those who are treated with gratuitous favour.

---

[4] Numbers 27:4.

XLIV. (243) And having given his divine directions respecting the petitions which the orphan maidens had preferred, he proceeds to lay down a more general law concerning the succession to inheritances, summoning the sons in the first instance to the sharing of the paternal property; and, if there should be no sons, then the daughters in the second place, to whom he says that it is proper to attach the inheritance as an external and adventitious ornament, but not as a possession belonging to and rightly connected with them; for that which is attached to anything has no actual relationship to that which is adorned by it, inasmuch as it is devoid of all harmony and union with it. (244) And, after the daughters, then he invites the brothers to share it in the third place; and, in the fourth place, he assigns the property to the uncles on the father's side, showing under this figure that the fathers might, if alive be the heirs of their sons.

For it is a very foolish idea to imagine that when he allots the inheritance of the nephew to his father's brother, out of a regard to his relationship to his father, he has excluded the father himself from the succession. (245) But since the law permits the property of parents to be inherited by the children, but does not allow the parents themselves to inherit, he has abstained from any express mention of the subject as one to be deprecated and of evil omen, in order that the father and mother might not seem to receive any gain from the inconsolable affliction of the loss of children dying prematurely; but he indirectly intimated their right to be invited to such an inheritance when he conceded it to the uncles, in order that in this way he might attain the best objects of cultivating propriety and of avoiding the improper alienation of the estate. And, after the uncles, the fifth class of inheritors was to be composed of the nearest relations, to the first of whom he invariably assigns the inheritance.

XLV. (246) Having now, as I was forced to do, gone through the entire account of those sacred commands referring to a mixed possession of an inheritance, I shall now proceed to show the oracles which were divinely given by the inspiration of the prophet; for this was a subject which I promised to explain.

Now the beginning of his divine inspiration, which was also the commencement of prosperity to his nation, arose when he was sent out of Egypt to dwell as a settler in the cities of Syria, with many thousands of his countrymen; (247) for both men and women, having accomplished together a long and desolate journey through the wilderness, destitute of any beaten road, at last arrived at the sea which is called the Red Sea. Then, as was natural, they were in great perplexity, neither being

able to cross over by reason of their want of vessels, nor thinking it safe to return back by the way by which they had come. (248) And while they were all in this state of mind, a still greater evil was impending over them; for the king of the Egyptians, having collected a power which was far from contemptible, a vast army of cavalry and infantry, sallied forth in pursuit of them, and made haste to overtake them, that he might avenge himself on them for the departure which he had been compelled by undeniable communications from God to permit them to take.

But, as it should seem, the disposition of wicked men is unstable, so that, like any thing in a lightly-balanced scale, it inclines on very slight causes to different directions at different times. (249) So now, the Hebrews being intercepted between their enemies and the sea, despaired of their safety, some looking on the most miserable death as a blessing to be prayed for; and others thinking it better to perish by the agency of the parts of nature than to become a laughing-stock to their enemies, were inclined to throw themselves into the sea; and now, being laden with heavy burdens, they sat down on the sea shore, that when they saw the enemy near they might more readily leap into the sea. (250) For now, by reason of the necessity which environed them, and from which they saw no means of extricating themselves, they were in great agitation, being full of expectation of a miserable death.

XLVI. But when the prophet saw that the whole nation was now enclosed like a shoal of fish, and in great consternation, he no longer remained master of himself, but became inspired, and prophesied as follows:—

(251) "The fear is necessary, and the terror is inevitable, and the danger is great; in front of us is the widely open sea, there is no retreat to which we can flee, we have no vessels, behind are the phalanxes of the enemy ready to attack us, which march on and pursue us, never stopping to take breath. Where shall any one turn? Which way can any one look to escape? Every thing from every quarter has unexpectedly become hostile to us, the sea, the land, men, and the elements of nature. (252) But be ye of good cheer; do not faint; stand still without wavering in your minds; await the invincible assistance of God; it will be present immediately of its own accord; it will fight in our behalf without being seen. Before now you have often had experience of it, defending you in an invisible manner. I see it now preparing to take part in the contest; casting halters round the necks of the enemy, who are now, as if violently dragged onward, going down into the depths of the sea like lead. You now see them while still alive; but I conceive the idea of them as dead. And this very day

you yourselves shall also behold them dead."[5]

(253) He then now said these things to them, things greater than any hopes that could have been formed. And they very speedily experienced in the real facts the truth of his divine words; for what he thus predicted by means of the power divinely given to him, came to pass in a manner more marvellous than can be well expressed. The sea was broken asunder, each portion retired back, there was a consolidation of the waves along each broken-off fragment throughout the whole breadth and depth, so that the waves stood up like the strongest walls; and there was a straight line cut of a road thus miraculously made, which was a path for the Hebrews between the congealed waters, (254) so that the whole nation without any danger passed on foot through the sea, as if on a dry road and on a stony soil; for the sand was dried up, and its usually fine grains were now united into one compact substance.

Then, also, there was a rush onwards of their enemies pursuing them, without stopped to take breath, hastening to their own destruction, and a driving forward of the cloud that guarded the rear of the Hebrews, on which there was a certain divine appearance of fire emitting a brilliant blaze, and a reflux of the sea, which up to that moment had been cut in two parts and stood asunder, and a sudden returning of the part which had been cut off and dried up into its original channel, (255) and an utter destruction of the enemy, whom the walls the sea, which had been congealed and which now turned back again, overwhelmed, and the sea pouring down and hurrying into what had just been a road, as if into some deep ravine, washed away every thing, and there was evidence of the completeness of the destruction in the bodies which floated on the waters, and which strewed the surface of the sea; and a great agitation of the waves, by which all the dead were cast up into a heap on the opposite shore, becoming a necessary spectacle to those who had been delivered, and to whom it had been granted not merely to escape from their dangers, but also to behold their enemies punished, in a manner too marvellous for description, by no human but by a divine power.

(256) For this mercy Moses very naturally honoured his Benefactor with hymns of gratitude. For having divided the host into two choruses, one of men and one of women, he himself became the leader of that of the men, and appointed his sister to be the chief of that of the women, that they might sing hymns to their father and Creator, joining in harmonies responsive to one another, by a combination of dispositions and melody, the former

being eager to offer the same requital for the mercies which they had received, and the latter consisting of a symphony of the deep male with the high female voices, for the tones of men are deep and those of women are high; and when there is a perfect and harmonious combination of the two a most delightful and thoroughly harmonious melody is effected. (257) And he persuaded all those myriads of men and women to be of one mind, and to sing in concert the same hymn at the same time in praise of those marvellous and mighty works which they had beheld, and which I have been just now relating. At which the prophet rejoicing, and seeing also the exceeding joy of his nation, and being himself too unable to contain his delight, began the song. And they who heard him being divided into two choruses, sang with him, taking the words which he uttered.

XLVII. (258) This is the beginning and preface of the prophecies of Moses under the influence of inspiration. After this he prophesied about the first and most necessary of all things, namely, food, which the earth did not produce, for it was barren and unfruitful; and the heaven rained down not once only, but every day for forty years, before the dawn of day, an ethereal fruit under the form of a dew very like millet seed. (259) And Moses, when he saw it, commanded them to collect it; and being full of inspiration, said: "You must believe in God, inasmuch as you have already had experience of his mercies and benefits in matters beyond all your hopes. This food may not be treasured up or laid up in garners. Let no one leave any portion of it till the morning."

(260) When they heard this, some of those who had no firm piety, thinking perhaps that what was now said to them was not an oracle from God, but merely the advice of their leader, left some till the next day. And it putrified, and at first filled all the camp around with its foul smell, and then it turned to worms, the origin of which always is from corruption. (261) And Moses, when he saw this, was naturally indignant with those who were thus disobedient; for how could he help being so, when those who had beheld such numerous and great actions which could not possibly be perverted into mere fictitious and well contrived appearances, but which had been easily accomplished by the divine providence, did not only doubt, but even absolutely disbelieved, and were the hardest of all man to be convinced? (262) But the Father established the oracle of his prophet by two most conspicuous manifestations, the one of which he gave immediately by the destruction of what had been left, and by the evil stench which arose, and by the change of it into worms, the vilest of animals; and the other demonstration he afforded subsequently, for that which was over and above after that which had been collected by the multitude,

---

was always melted away by the beams of the sun, and consumed, and destroyed in that manner.

XLVIII. (263) He gave a second instance of his prophetical inspiration not long afterwards in the oracle which he delivered about the sacred seventh day. For though it had had a natural precedence over all other days, not only from the time that the world was created, but even before the origination of the heaven and all the objects perceptible to the outward senses, men still knew it not, perhaps because, by reason of the continued and uninterrupted destructions which had taken place by water and fire, succeeding generations had not been able to receive from former ones any traditions of the arrangement and order which had been established in the connection of preceding times, which, as it was not known, Moses, now being inspired, declared to his people in an oracle which was borne testimony to by a visible sign from heaven. (264) And the sign was this.

A small portion of food descended from the air on the previous days, but a double portion on the day before the seventh day. And on the previous days, if any portion was left it became liquefied and melted away, until it was entirely changed into dew, and so consumed; but on this day it endured no alteration, but remained in the same state as before, and when this was reported to him, and beheld by him, Moses did not so much conjecture as receive the impulse of divine inspiration under which he prophesied of the seventh day.

(265) I omit to mention that all such conjectures are akin to prophecy; for the mind could never make such correct and felicitous conjectures, unless it were a divine spirit which guided their feet into the way of truth; (266) and the miraculous nature of the sign was shown, not merely in the fact of the food being double in quantity, nor in that of its remaining unimpaired, contrary to the usual customs, but in both these circumstances taking place on the sixth day, from the day on which this food first began to be supplied from heaven, from which day the most sacred number of seven begun to be counted, so that if any one reckons he will find that this heavenly food was given in exact correspondence with the arrangement instituted at the creation of the world.

For God began to create the world on the first day of a week of six days: and he began to rain down the food which has just been mentioned on the same first day; (267) and the two images are alike; for as he produced that most perfect work, the world, bringing it out of non-existence into existence, so in the same manner did he produce plenty in the wilderness, changing the elements with reference to the pressing necessity, that, instead of the earth, the air might bestow food without labour, and without trouble, to those who had no opportunity of providing themselves with food at their leisure.

(268) After this he delivered to the people a third oracle of the most marvellous nature, namely that on the seventh day the air would not afford the accustomed food, and that not the very slightest portion would fall upon the earth, as it did on other days; (269) and this turned out to be the case in point of fact; for he delivered this prediction on the day before; but some of those who were unstable in their dispositions, went forth to collect it, and being deceived in their expectations, returned unsuccessful, reproaching themselves for their unbelief, and calling the prophet the only true prophet, the only one who knew the will of God, and the only one who had any foreknowledge of what was uncertain and future.

XLIX. (270) Such then are the predictions which he delivered, under the influence of inspiration, respecting the food which came down from heaven; but he also delivered others in succession of great necessity, though they appeared to resemble recommendations rather than actual oracles; one of which is that prediction, which he delivered respecting their greatest abandonment of their national customs, of which I have already spoken, when they made a golden calf in imitation of the Egyptian worship and folly, and established dances and prepared an altar, and offered up sacrifices, forgetful of the true God and discarding the noble disposition of their ancestors, which had been increased by piety and holiness, (271) at which Moses as very indignant, first of all, at all the people having thus suddenly become blind, which but a short time before had been the most sharp-sighted of all nations; and secondly, at a vain invention of fable being able to extinguish such exceeding brilliancy of truth, which even the sun in its eclipse or the whole company of the stars could never darken; for it is comprehended by its own light, appreciable by the intellect and incorporeal, in comparison of which the light, which is perceptible by the external senses, is like night if compared to day.

(272) And, moved by this cause, he no longer continued as before, but leaped as it were out of his former appearance and disposition, and became inspired, and said, "Who is there who has not consented to this error, and who has not given sanction to what ought not to be sanctioned? Let all such come over to me."[6] (273) And when one tribe had come over to him, and not less with their minds than with their bodies, who indeed had some time before been eager for the slaughter of the impious and wicked doers, and who had sought for a

---

[6]Exodus 32:26.

leader and chief of their host who would justly point out to them the opportunity and proper manner of repressing their wickedness; then he, seeing that they were enraged and full of good confidence and courage, was inspired still more than before, and said, "Let every one of you take a sword, and go swiftly through the whole army, and slay not only strangers, but also those who are nearest and dearest to him of his own friends and relations, attacking them all, judging his action to be a most holy one, as being in the defence of truth and of the honour due to God, to fight for which, and to be the champion of which objects, is the lightest of labours."

(274) So they rushed forth with a shout, and slew three thousand, especially those who were the leaders of this impiety, and not only were excused themselves from having had any participation in the wicked boldness of the others, but were also enrolled among the most noble of valiant men, and were thought worthy of an honour and reward most appropriate to their action, to wit the priesthood.

For it was inevitable that those men should be ministers of holiness, who had shown themselves valiant in defence of it, and had warred bravely as its champions.

L. (275) I have also another still more marvellous and prodigy-like oracle to report, which indeed I have mentioned before, when I was relating the circumstances of the high priesthood of the prophet, one which he himself uttered when fully inspired by the divine spirit, and which received its accomplishment at no long period afterwards, but at the very moment that it was delivered.

(276) There were two classes of ministrations concerning the temple; the higher one belonging to the priests, and the lower one to the keepers of the temple; and there were at this time three priests, but many thousand keepers of the temple. (277) These men, being puffed up at the exceeding greatness of their own numbers, despised the scanty numbers of the priests; and so they concerted two impious attempts at the same time, the one of which was the destruction of those who were superior to them, and the other was the promotion of the inferior body, the subjects as it were attacking the leaders, to the confusion and overthrow of that most excellent and most beneficial thing for the people, namely order.

(278) Then, joining together and assembling in one place, they cried out upon the prophet as if he had given the priesthood to his brother, and to his nephews, out of consideration for their relationship to him, and had given a false account of their appointment, as if it had not taken place under the direction of divine providence, as we have represented. (279) And Moses, being vexed and grieved beyond measure at these things, although

he was the meekest and mildest of men, was not so excited to a just anger by his disposition, which hated iniquity, that he besought God to reject their sacrifice. Not because there was any chance of that most righteous Judge receiving the unholy offerings of wicked men, but because the soul of the man who loved God could not be silent for his part, so eager was it that the wicked should not prosper, but should always fail in their purpose; (280) and while he was still boiling over and inflamed with anger by this lawful indignation he became inspired, and changed into a prophet, and uttered the following oracles.

"Apostasy is an evil thing, but these faithless men shall be taught, not only by words but also by actions; they shall, by personal suffering, learn my truth and good faith, since they would not learn it by ordinary instruction; (281) and this shall be discerned in the end of their life: for it they receive the ordinary death according to nature, then I have invented these oracles; but if they experience a new and unprecedented destruction, then my truth will be testified to; for I see chasms of the earth opening against them, and widened to the greatest extent, and numbers of men perishing in them, dragged down into the gulf with all their kindred, and their very houses swallowed up, and the men going down alive into hell." (282) And when he ceased speaking the earth was cloven asunder, being shaken by an earthquake, and it was burst open, especially where the tents of those wicked men were so that they were all swallowed up together, and so hidden from sight.

For the parts which were rent asunder came together again as soon as the purpose for which they had been divided was accomplished.

(283) And a little after this thunderbolts fell on a sudden from heaven, and slew two hundred men, the leaders of this sedition, and destroyed them all together, not leaving any portion of their bodies to receive burial. (284) And the rapid and unintermittent character of the punishment, and the magnitude of each infliction, rendered the piety of the prophet conspicuous and universally celebrated, as he thus brought God forward as a witness of the truth of his oracular denunciations.

(285) We must also not overlook this circumstance, that both earth and heaven, which are the first principles of the universe, bore their share in the punishment of these wicked men, for they had rooted their wickedness in the earth, and extended it up to the sky, raising it to that vast height, (286) on which account each of the elements contributed its part to their chastisement, the earth, so as to drag down and swallow up those who were at that time weighing it down, bursting asunder and dividing; and the heaven, by tearing up and destroying them, raining down a mighty storm of much fire, a most novel kind of rain, and

the end was the same, (287) both to those who were swallowed up by the earth and to those who were destroyed by the thunderbolts, for neither of them were seen any more; the one body being concealed by the earth, the chasm being united again and meeting as before, so as to make solid ground; and the other people being consumed entirely by the fire of the thunderbolts.

LI. (288) And some time afterwards, when he was about to depart from hence to heaven, to take up his abode there, and leaving this mortal life to become immortal, having been summoned by the Father, who now changed him, having previously been a double being, composed of soul and body, into the nature of a single body, transforming him wholly and entirely into a most sun-like mind; he then, being wholly possessed by inspiration, does not seem any longer to have prophesied comprehensively to the whole nation altogether, but to have predicted to each tribe separately what would happen to each of them, and to their future generations, some of which things have already come to pass, and some are still expected, because the accomplishment of those predictions which have been fulfilled is the clearest testimony to the future.

(289) For it was very appropriate that those who were different in the circumstances of their birth and in the mothers, from whom they were descended, should differ also in the variety of their designs and counsels, and also in the excessive diversity of their pursuits in life, and should there-fore have for their inheritance, as it were, a different distribution of oracles and predictions. (290) These things, therefore, are wonderful; and most wonderful of all is the end of his sacred writings, which is to the whole book of the law what the head is to an animal.

(291) For when he was now on the point of being taken away, and was standing at the very starting-place, as it were, that he might fly away and complete his journey to heaven, he was once more inspired and filled with the Holy Spirit, and while still alive, he prophesied admirably what should happen to himself after his death, relating, that is, how he had died when he was not as yet dead, and how he was buried without any one being present so as to know of his tomb, because in fact he was entombed not by mortal hands, but by immortal powers, so that he was not placed in the tomb of his forefathers, having met with particular grace which no man ever saw; and mentioning further how the whole nation mourned for him with tears a whole month, displaying the individual and general sorrow on account of his unspeakable benevolence towards each individual and towards the whole collective host, and of the wisdom with which he had ruled them.

(292) Such was the life and such was the death of the king, and lawgiver, and high priest, and prophet, Moses, as it is recorded in the sacred scriptures.

THE DECALOGUE†

(De Decalogo)

I. (1) I have in my former treatises set forth the lives of Moses and the other wise men down to his time, whom the sacred scriptures point out as the founders and leaders of our nation, and as its unwritten laws; I will now, as seems pointed out by the natural order of my subject, proceed to describe accurately the character of those laws which are recorded in writing, not omitting any allegorical meaning which may perchance be concealed beneath the plain language, from that natural love of more recondite and laborious knowledge which is accustomed to seek for what is obscure before, and in preference to, what is evident.

(2) And to those who raise the question why the lawgiver gave his laws not in cities but in the deep desert, we must say, in the first place, that the generality of cities are full of unspeakable evils, and of acts of audacious impiety towards the Deity, and of injustice on the part of the citizens to one another; (3) for there is nothing which is wholly free from alloy, what is spurious getting the better of what is genuine, and what is plausible of what is true; which things in their nature are false, but which suggest plausible imaginations to the engendering of deceit in cities; (4) from whence also that most designing of all things, namely pride, is implanted, which some persons admire and worship, dignifying and making much of vain opinions, with golden crowns and purple robes, and numbers of servants and chariots, on which those men who are looked upon as fortunate and happy are borne aloft, sometimes harnessing mules or horses to their chariots, and sometimes even men, who bear their burdens on their necks, through the excess of the insolence of their masters, weighed down in soul even before they faint in body.

II. (5) Pride is also the cause of many other evils, such as insolence, arrogance, and impiety. And these are the beginnings of foreign and civil wars, allowing nothing whatever to rest in peace in any part, whether it be public or private, by sea or by land. (6) And why need I mention the offences of such men against one another? For even divine things are neglected by pride, even though they are generally thought to be entitled to the highest honour. And what honour can there be where there is not truth also which has an honour-able name and reality, since falsehood, on the other hand, is by nature devoid of honour; (7) and the neglect of divine things is evident to those who see clearly; for they, having fashioned an infinite variety of appearances by the arts of painting and sculpture, have surrounded them with temples and shrines, and have erected altars, and adorned them with images and statues, and erections of that kind, giving celestial honours to all sorts of inanimate things, (8) and these men the sacred scriptures very felicitously liken to men born of a harlot.

For as these men are inscribed as the children of all the lovers whom their mothers have had and call their fathers, from ignorance of the one who is by nature their real father, so also these men in cities, not knowing the truly and really existing and true God, have made deities of an innumerable host of false gods. (9) Then, as different beings were treated with divine honours by different nations, the diversity of opinions respecting the Supreme Being, begot also disputes about all kinds of other subjects; and it was from having a regard to these facts in the first place that Moses decided on giving his laws outside of the city.

(10) He also considered this point, in the second place, that it is indispensable that the soul of the man who is about to receive sacred laws should be thoroughly cleansed and purified from all stains, however difficult to be washed out, which the promiscuous multitude of mixed men from all quarters has impregnated cities with; (11) and this is impossible to be effected unless the man dwells apart; and even then it cannot be done in a moment, but only at a much later period, when the impressions of ancient transgressions, originally deeply imprinted, have become by little and little fainter, and gradually become more and more dim, and at last totally effaced; (12) in this manner those who are skilful in the art of medicine, save their patients; for they do not think it advisable to give food before they have removed the causes of their diseases; for while the diseases remain, food is useless, being the pernicious materials of their sufferings.

III. (13) Very naturally therefore, having led his people from the injurious associations prevailing in the cities, into the desert, that he might purify their souls from their offences he begun to bring them food for their minds; and what could this food be but divine laws and reasonings? (14) The third cause is this; as men who set out on a long voyage do not when they have embarked on board ship,

†Yonge's title, *A Treatise Concerning the Ten Commandments, Which Are the Heads of the Law.*

and started from the harbour, then begin for the first time to prepare their masts, and cables, and rudders, but, while still remaining on the land, they make ready everything which can conduce to the success of their voyage; so in the same manner Moses did not think it fit that his people, after they had received their inheritances, and settled as inhabitants of their cities, should then seek laws in accordance with which they were to regulate their cities, but that, having previously prepared laws and constitutions, and being trained in those regulations, by which nations can be governed with safety, they should then be settled in their cities, being prepared at once to use the just regulations which were already prepared for them, in unanimity and a complete participation in and proper distribution of those things which were fitting for each person.

IV. (15) And some persons say that there is also a fourth cause which is not inconsistent with, but as near as possible to the truth; for that, as it was necessary that a conviction should be implanted in the minds of men that these laws were not the inventions of men, but the most indubitable oracles of God, he on that account, led the people as far as possible from the cities into the deep wilderness, which was barren not only of all fruits that admitted of cultivation, (16) but even of wholesome water, in order that, when after having found themselves in want of necessary food, and expecting to be destroyed by hunger and thirst, they should on a sudden find themselves amid abundance of all necessary things, spontaneously springing up around them; the heaven itself raining down upon them food called manna, and as a seasoning delicacy to that meat an abundance of quails from the air; and the bitter water being sweetened so as to become drinkable, and the precipitous rock pouring forth springs of sweet water; then they might no longer look back upon the Nile with wonder, nor be in doubt as to whether those laws were the laws of God, having received a most manifest proof of the fact from the supplies by which they now found their scarcity relieved beyond all their previous expectations; (17) for they would see that he, who had given them a sufficiency of the means of life was now also giving them a means which should contribute to their living well; accordingly, to live at all required meat and drink which they found, though they had never prepared them; and towards living well, and in accordance with nature and decorum, they required laws and enactments, by which they were likely to be improved in their minds.

V. (18) These are the causes which may be advanced by probable conjecture, to explain the question which is raised on this point; for the true causes God alone knows. But having said what is fitting concerning these matters, I shall now proceed in regular order to discuss the laws themselves with accuracy and precision: first of all of necessity, mentioning this point, that of his laws God himself, without having need of any one else, thought fit to promulgate some by himself alone, and some he promulgated by the agency of his prophet Moses, whom he selected, by reason of his pre-eminent excellence, out of all men, as the most suitable man to be the interpreter of his will.

(19) Now those which he delivered in his own person by himself alone, are both laws in general, and also the heads of particular laws; and those which he promulgated by the agency of his prophet are all referred to those others; (20) and I will explain each kind as well as I can.

VI. And first of all, I will speak of those which rather resemble heads of laws, of which in the first place one must at once admire the number, inasmuch as they are completed in the perfect number of the decade, which contains every variety of number, both those which are even, and those which are odd, and those which are even-odd;[1] the even numbers being such as two, the odd numbers such as three, the even-odd such as five, it also comprehends all the varieties of the multiplication of numbers, and of those numbers which contain a whole number and a fraction, and of those which contain several fractional parts; (21) it comprehends likewise all the proportions; the arithmetical, which exceeds and is exceeded by an equal number: as in the case of the numbers one, and two, and three; and the geometrical, according to which, as the proportion of the first number is to the second, the same is the ratio of the second to the third, as is the case in the numbers one, two and four; and also in multiplication, which double, or treble, or in short multiply figures to any extent; also in those which are half as much again as the numbers first spoken of, or one third greater, and so on.

It also contains the harmonic proportion, in accordance with which that number which is in the middle between two extremities, is exceeded by the one, and exceeds the other by an equal part; as is the case with the numbers three, four, and six.

(22) The decade also contains the visible peculiar properties of the triangles, and squares, and other polygonal figures; also the peculiar properties of symphonic ratios, that of the diatessaron in proportion exceeding by one fourth, as is the ratio of four to three; that of fifths exceeding in the ratio of half as much again, as is the case with the proportion of three to two. Also, that of the diapason, where the proportion is precisely twofold, as is the ratio of two to one, or that of the double diapason, where the proportion is fourfold, as in the ratio of eight to two. (23) And it is in

---

[1] Liddell and Scott explain this as meaning such even numbers as become odd when divided, as 2, 6, 10, 14, etc.

reference to this fact that the first philosophers appear to me to have affixed the names to things which they have given them. For they were wise men, and therefore they very speciously called the number ten the decade *(tēn dekada)*, as being that which received every thing *(hōsanei dechada ousan)*, from receiving *(tou dechesthai)* and containing every kind of number, and ratio connected with number, and every proportion, and harmony, and symphony.

VII. (24) Moreover, at all events, in addition to what has been already said, any one may reasonably admire the decade for the following reason, that it contains within itself a nature which is at the same time devoid of intervals and capable of containing them. Now that nature which has no connection with intervals is beheld in a point alone; but that which is capable of containing intervals is beheld under three appearances, a line, and a superficies, and a solid. (25) For that which is bounded by two points is a line; and that which has two dimensions or intervals is a superficies, the line being extended by the addition of breadth; and that which has three intervals is a solid, length and breadth having taken to themselves the addition of depth. And with these three nature is content; for she has not engendered more intervals or dimensions than these three. (26) And the archetypal numbers, which are the models of these three are, of the point the limit, of the line the number two, and of the superficies the number three, and of the solid the number four; the combination of which, that is to say of one, and two, and three, and four completes the decade, which displays other beauties also in addition to those which are visible.

(27) For one may almost say that the whole infinity of numbers is measured by this one, because the boundaries which make it up are four, namely, one, two, three, and four; and an equal number of boundaries, corresponding to them in equal proportions, make up the number of a hundred out of decades; for ten, and twenty, and thirty, and forty produce a hundred. And in the same way one may produce the number of a thousand from hundreds, and that of a myriad from thousands. (28) And the unit, and the decade, and the century, and the thousand, are the four boundaries which generate the decade, which last number, besides what has been already said, displays also other differences of numbers, both the first, which is measured by the unit alone, of which an instance is found in the numbers three, or five, or seven; and the square which is the fourth power, which is an equally equal number. Also the cube, which is the eighth power, which is equally equal equally, and also the perfect number, the number six, which is made equal to its component parts, three, and two, and one.

VIII. (29) But what is the use now of enum-

erating the excellencies of the decade, which are infinite in number; treating our most important task as one of no importance, which is, indeed, of itself most all-sufficient, and worthy material for the study of those who devote themselves to mathematics?

The other points we must pass over for the present; but perhaps it may not be out of place to mention one by way of example; (30) for those who have devoted themselves to the doctrines of philosophy say that what are called the categories in nature are ten only in number,—quality, essence, quantity, relation, action, passion, possession, condition, and those two without which nothing can exist, time and place. (31) For there is nothing which is devoid of participation in these things; as, for instance, I partake of essence, borrowing of each one of the elements of which the whole world was made, that is to say, of earth and water, and air and fire, what is sufficient for my own existence.

I also partake of quality, inasmuch as I am a man; and of quantity, inasmuch as I am a man of such and such a size. I also partake of relation, when any one is on my right hand or on my left. Again, I am in action when I rub or burn any thing. I am in passion when I am cut or rubbed by any one else. I am discerned as a possessor, when I am clothed or equipped with anything. And I am seen in condition, when sitting still or lying down. And I am altogether in time and place, since not one of all the categories just mentioned can exist without both these things.

IX. (32) This, then, may be enough to say on these subjects; but it is necessary now to connect with these things what I am about to say, namely, that it was the Father of the universe who delivered these ten maxims, or oracles, or laws and enactments, as they truly are, to the whole assembled nation of men and women altogether. Did he then do so, uttering himself some kind of voice? Away! let not such an idea ever enter your mind; for God is not like a man, in need of a mouth, and of a tongue, and of a windpipe, (33) but as it seems to me, he at that time wrought a most conspicuous and evidently holy miracle, commanding an invisible sound to be created in the air, more marvellous than all the instruments that ever existed, attuned to perfect harmonies; and that not an inanimate one, nor yet, on the other hand, one that at all resembled any nature composed of soul and body; but rather it was a rational soul filled with clearness and distinctness, which fashioned the air and stretched it out and changed it into a kind of flaming fire, and so sounded forth so loud and articulate a voice like a breath passing through a trumpet, so that those who were at a great distance appeared to hear equally with those who were nearest to it.

(34) For the voices of men, when they are spread over a very long distance, do naturally

become weaker and weaker, so that those who are at a distance from them cannot arrive at a clear comprehension of them, but their understanding is gradually dimmed by the extension of the sound over a larger space, since the organs also by which it is extended are perishable. (35) But the power of God, breathing forth vigorously, aroused and excited a new kind of miraculous voice, and diffusing its sound in every direction, made the end more conspicuous at a distance than the beginning, implanting in the soul of each individual another hearing much superior to that which exists through the medium of the ears. For the one, being in some degree a slower kind of external sense, remains in a state of inactivity until it is struck by the air, and so put in motion. But the sense of the inspired mind outstrips that, going forth with the most rapid motion to meet what is said.

X. (36) This, then, may be enough to say about the divine voice. But a person may very reasonably raise the question on what account it happened, when there were so vast a number of myriads of men collected into one place that Moses chose to deliver each of the ten commandments in such a form as if they had been addressed not to many persons but to one, saying:—

Thou shalt not commit adultery.
Thou shalt not steal.
Thou shalt not kill. [2]

And giving the other commandments in the same form.

(37) We must say, therefore that he is desirous here to teach that most excellent lesson to those who read the sacred scriptures, that each separate individual by himself when he is an observer of the law and obedient to God, is of equal estimation with a whole nation, be it ever so populous, or I might rather say, with all the nations upon earth. And if I were to think fit I might proceed further and say, with all the world; (38) because in another passage of the scriptures God, praising a certain just man, says, "I am thy God." [3]

But the same being was also the God of the world; so that all those who are subject to him are arranged according to the same classification, and, if they be equally pleasing to the supreme Governor of them all, they partake of an equal acceptance and honour.

(39) And, secondly, we must say that any one addressing himself to an assembly in common as to a multitude is not bound to speak as if he were conversing with a single individual, but sometimes he commands or forbids a thing in a particular manner in such a way that whatever he commands does at once appear requisite to be done by every one who hears him, and does also seem to be commanded to the whole collective multitude together; for the man who receives an admonition as if addressed to himself personally is more inclined to obey it; but he who hears it as if it were only directed to him in common with others is, to a certain degree, rendered deaf to it, making the multitude a kind of veil and excuse for his obstinacy.

(40) A third view of the question is, that no king or tyrant may ever despise an obscure private individual, from being full of insolence and haughty pride; but that such an one, coming as a pupil to the school of the sacred laws, may relax his eyebrows, unlearning his self-opinionativeness, and yielding rather to true reason. (41) For if the uncreated, and immortal, and everlasting God, who is in need of nothing and who is the maker of the universe, and the benefactor and King of kings, and God of gods, cannot endure to overlook even the meanest of human beings, but has thought even such worthy of being banqueted in sacred oracles and laws, as if he were about to give him a love-feast, and to prepare for him alone a banquet for the refreshing and expanding of his soul instructed in the divine will and in the manner in which the great ceremonies ought to be performed, how can it be right for me, who am a mere mortal, to hold my head up high and to allow myself to be puffed up, behaving with insolence to my equals whose fortunes may, perhaps, not be equal to mine, but whose relationship to me is equal and complete, inasmuch as they are set down as the children of one mother, the common nature of all men?

(42) I will, therefore, behave myself in an affable, and courteous, and conciliatory manner to all men, even if I should obtain the dominion over the whole earth and the whole sea, and especially to those who are in the greatest difficulties and of the least reputation, and who are destitute of all assistance from kindred of their own, to those who are orphaned of either or of both their parents, to women who have experienced widowhood, and to old men who have either never had any children at all, or who have lost at an early age those who have been born to them; (43) for, inasmuch as I myself am a man, I will not think it right to cherish a pompous and tragedian-like dignity of manner, but I will keep myself within my nature, not transgressing its boundaries, but accustoming my mind to bear human events with complacency and equanimity. Not only because of the unforeseen changes by which things of one character assume a different appearance, both in the case of those in prosperity and of those who are in adversity, but also because it is becoming, even if prosperity were to remain unaltered and unshaken that a man should not forget himself.

For these reasons it appears to me to have been that God expressed his oracular commandments

[2] Exodus 20:13.
[3] Genesis 17:1.

in the singular number, as if they were directed to a single individual.

XI. (44) And, moreover, as was natural, he filled the whole place with miraculous signs and works, with noises of thunder too great for the hearing to support, and with the most radiant brilliancy of flashes of lightning, and with the sound of an invisible trumpet extending to a great distance, and with the march of a cloud, which, like a pillar, had its foundation fixed firmly on the earth, but raised the rest of its body even to the height of heaven; and, last of all, by the impetuosity of a heavenly fire, which overshadowed everything around with a dense smoke. For it was fitting that, when the power of God came among them, none of the parts of the world should be quiet, but that everything should be put in motion to minister to his service.

(45) And the people stood by, having kept themselves clean from all connection with women, and having abstained from all pleasures, except those which arise from a participation in necessary food, having been purifying themselves with baths and ablutions for three days, and having washed their garments and being all clothed in the purest white robes, and standing on tiptoe and pricking up their ears, in compliance with the exhortations of Moses, who had forewarned them to prepare for the solemn assembly; for he knew that such would take place, when he, having been summoned up alone, gave forth the prophetic commands of God.

(46) And a voice sounded forth from out of the midst of the fire which had flowed from heaven, a most marvellous and awful voice, the flame being endowed with articulate speech in a language familiar to the hearers, which expressed its words with such clearness and distinctness that the people seemed rather to be seeing than hearing it. (47) And the law testifies to the accuracy of my statement, where it is written, "And all the people beheld the voice most evidently." For the truth is that the voice of men is calculated to be heard; but that of God to be really and truly seen. Why is this? Because all that God says are not words, but actions which the eyes determine on before the ears.

(48) It is, therefore, with great beauty, and also with a proper sense of what is consistent with the dignity of God, that the voice is said to have come forth out of the fire; for the oracles of God are accurately understood and tested like gold by the fire. (49) And God also intimates to us something of this kind by a figure. Since the property of fire is partly to give light, and partly to burn, those who think fit to show themselves obedient to the sacred commands shall live for ever and ever as in a light which is never darkened, having his laws themselves as stars giving light in their soul. But all those who are stubborn and disobedient are for ever inflamed, and burnt, and consumed by their internal appetites, which, like flame, will destroy all the life of those who possess them.

XII. (50) These, then, were the things which it was necessary to explain beforehand.

But now we must turn to the commands themselves, and investigate everything which is marked by especial importance or difference in them.

Now God divided them, being ten, as they are, into two tables of five each, which he engraved on two pillars. And the first five have the precedence and pre-eminence in honour; but the second five have an inferior place assigned to them. But both the tables are beautiful and advantageous to life, opening to men wrought and level roads kept within limits by one end, so as to secure the unwavering and secure progress of that soul which is continually desiring what is most excellent.

(51) Now the most excellent five were of this character, they related to the monarchial principle on which the world is governed; to images and statues, and in short to all erections of any kind made by hand; to the duty of not taking the name of God in vain; to that of keeping the holy seventh day in a manner worthy of its holiness; to paying honour to parents both separately to each, and commonly to both. So that of the one table the beginning is the God and Father and Creator of the universe; and the end are one's parents, who imitate his nature, and so generate the particular individuals.

And the other table of five contains all the prohibitions against adulteries, and murder, and theft, and false witness, and covetousness. (52) But we must consider, with all the accuracy possible, each of these oracles separately, not looking upon any one of them as superfluous. Now the best beginning of all living beings is God, and of all virtues, piety. And we must, therefore, speak of these two principles in the first place.

There is an error of no small importance which has taken possession of the greater portion of mankind concerning a subject which was likely by itself, or, at least, above all other subjects, to have been fixed with the greatest correctness and truth in the mind of every one; (53) for some nations have made divinities of the four elements, earth and water, and air and fire. Others, of the sun and moon, and of the other planets and fixed stars. Others, again, of the whole world. And they have all invented different appellations, all of them false, for these false gods put out of sight that most supreme and most ancient of all, the Creator, the ruler of the great city, the general of the invincible army, the pilot who always guides everything to its preservation, (54) for they call the earth Proserpine, and Ceres, and Pluto. And the sea they call Neptune, inventing besides a number of marine deities as subservient to him, and vast companies of attendants, both male and female. The air they call Juno; fire, Vulcan; and the sun, Apollo; the moon, Diana; and the evening star, Venus; Lucifer, they call Mercury; (55) and to every one of the stars they have affixed names and given them to the inventors of fables, who have woven together cleverly-contrived imaginations to deceive the ear, and have appeared to have been themselves the ingenious inventors of these names thus given.

(56) Again, in their descriptions, they divided the heaven into two parts, each one hemisphere, the one being above the earth and the other under the earth, which they called the Dioscuri;[4] inventing, besides, a marvellous story concerning their living on alternate days. (57) For, as the heaven is everlasting revolving, in a circle without any cessation or interruption, it follows of necessity that each of the hemispheres must every day be in a different position from that which it was in the day before, everything being turned upside down as far as appearance goes, at least; for, in point of fact, there is no such thing as any uppermost or undermost in a spherical figure. And this expression is only used with reference to our own formation and position; that which is over our head being called uppermost, and that which is in the opposite direction being called undermost.

(58) Accordingly, to one who understands how to apply himself to philosophy in a genuine, honest spirit, and who lays claim to a guiltless and pure piety, God gives that most beautiful and holy commandment, that he shall not believe that any one of the parts of the world is its own master, for it has been created; and the fact of having been created implies a liability to destruction, even though the thing created may be made immortal by the providence of the Creator; and there was a time once when it had no existence, but it is impiety to say that there was a previous time when God did not exist, and that he was born at some time, and that he does not endure for ever.

XIII. (59) But some persons indulge in such foolish notions respecting their judgments on these points, that they not only look upon the things which have been mentioned above as gods, but as each separate one of them as the greatest and first of gods, either because they are really ignorant of the true living God, from their nature being uninstructed, or else because they have no desire to learn, because they believe that there is no cause of things invisible, and appreciable only by the intellect, apart from the objects of the external senses, and this too, though the most distinct possible proof is close at hand; (60) for though, as it is owing

to the soul that they live, and form designs, and do everything which is done in human life, they nevertheless have never been able to behold their soul with their eyes, nor would they be able if they were to strive with all imaginable eagerness, wishing to see it as the most beautiful possible of all images or appearances, from a sight of which they might, by a sort of comparison, derive a notion of the uncreated and everlasting God, who rules and guides the whole world in such a way as to secure its preservation, being himself invisible.

(61) As, therefore, if any one were to assign the honours of the great king to his satraps and viceroys, he would appear to be not only the most ignorant and senseless of men, but also the most fool-hardy, giving to slaves what belongs to the master; in the same manner, let the man who honours the Creator, with the same honours as those with which he regards the creature, know that he is of all men the most foolish and the most unjust, in giving equal things to unequal persons, and that too not in such a way as to do honour to the inferior, but only to take it from the superior.

(62) There are again some who exceed in impiety, not giving the Creator and the creature even equal honour, but assigning to the latter all honour, and respect, and reverence, and to the former nothing at all, not thinking him worthy of even the common respect of being recollected; for they forget him whom alone they should recollect, aiming, like demented and miserable men as they are, at attaining to an intentional forgetfulness. (63) Some men again are so possessed with an insolent and free-spoken madness, that they make an open display of the impiety which dwells in their hearts, and venture to blaspheme the Deity, whetting an evil-speaking tongue, and desiring, at the same time, to vex the pious, who immediately feel an indescribable and irreconcilable affliction, which enters in at their ears and pervades the whole soul; for this is the great engine of impious men, by which alone they bridle those who love God, as they think it better at the moment to preserve silence, for the sake of not provoking their wickedness further.

XIV. (64) Let us, therefore, reject all such impious dishonesty, and not worship those who are our brothers by nature, even though they may have received a purer and more immortal essence than ourselves (for all created things are brothers to one another, inasmuch as they are created; since the Father of them all is one, the Creator of the universe); but let us rather, with our mind and reason, and with all our strength, gird ourselves up vigorously and energetically to the service of that Being who is uncreated and everlasting, and the maker of the universe, never shrinking or turning aside from it, nor yielding to a desire of pleasing the multitude, by which even those who might be saved are often destroyed.

---

[4] *Dios kouroi.* Sons of Jupiter, i.e., Castor and Pollux. The Gemini or Twins of the Zodiac. The story of their living and dying on alternate days is alluded to by Virgil, Aen. 6.121, where Aeneas says (as it is translated by Dryden)—"If Pollux, off'ring his alternate life, / Could free his brother; and can daily go / By turns aloft, by turns descend below."

(65) Let us, therefore, fix deeply in ourselves this first commandment as the most sacred of all commandments, to think that there is but one God, the most highest, and to honour him alone; and let not the polytheistical doctrine ever even touch the ears of any man who is accustomed to seek for the truth, with purity and sincerity of heart; (66) for those who are ministers and servants of the sun, and of the moon, and of all the host of heaven, or of it in all its integrity or of its principal parts, are in grievous error; (how can they fail to be, when they honour the subjects instead of the prince?) but still they sin less grievously than the others, who have fashioned stocks, and stones, and silver, and gold, and similar materials according to their own pleasure, making images, and statues, and all kinds of other things wrought by the hand; the workmanship in which, whether by statuary, or painter, or artisan, has done great injury to the life of man, having filled the whole habitable world.

(67) For they have cut away the most beautiful support of the soul, namely the proper conception of the ever-living God; and therefore, like ships without ballast, they are tossed about in every direction for ever, being borne in every direction, so as never once to reach the haven, and never to be able to anchor firmly in truth, being blind respecting that which is worth seeing, and the only object as to which it is absolutely necessary to be sharp-sighted; (68) and such men appear to me to have a more miserable life than those who are deprived of their bodily sight; for these latter have either been injured without their own consent, or else have endured some terrible disease of the eyes, or else have been plotted against by their enemies; but those others by their own deliberate intention, have not only dimmed the eye of their soul, but have even chosen utterly to discard it; (69) on which account pity is bestowed on the one class as unfortunate, but the other class are justly punished as being wicked, who in conjunction with others have not chosen to recognize that fact which even an infant child would understand, namely, that the Creator is better than the creature; for he is both more ancient in point of time, and is also in a manner the father of that which he has made.

He is also superior in power, for the agent is more glorious than the patient.

(70) And though it would be proper, if they had not committed sins, to deify the painters and statuaries themselves with exceeding honours, they have left them in obscurity, giving them no advantage, but have looked upon the figures which have been made, or the pictures which have been painted by them, as gods; (71) and these artists have often grown old in poverty and obscurity, dying, worn out by incessant misfortunes, while the things which they have fabricated, are made splendid with purple, and gold, and all sorts of costly splendour which wealth can furnish, and are worshipped not only by freemen but even by men of noble birth, and of the greatest personal strength and beauty.

For the race of priests is scrutinised with the greatest rigour and minuteness, to see whether they are without blemish, and to see whether the whole combination of the parts of their bodies is entire and perfect; (72) and these are not the worst points of all, bad as they are: but this is entirely intolerable, for I have known before now, some of the very men who have made the things, praying and sacrificing to the very things which have been made by them, when it would have been more to their purpose to worship either of their own hands, or, if they feared the reproach of self-conceit, and therefore did not choose to do that, at all events to worship their anvils, and hammers, and graving tools, and compasses, and other instruments, by means of which the materials have been fashioned into shape.

XV. (73) And yet it is well for us, speaking with all proper freedom, to say to those who have shown themselves so devoid of sense; "My good men, the best of all prayers, and the end, and proper object of happiness, is to attain to a likeness to God. (74) Do you therefore pray to become like those erections of yours, that so you may reap the most supreme happiness, neither seeing with your eyes, nor hearing with your ears, nor respiring, nor smelling with your nostrils, nor speaking, nor tasting with your mouth, nor taking, nor giving, nor doing anything with your hands, nor walking with your feet, nor doing anything at all with any one of your members, but being as it were confined and guarded in the temple, as if in a prison, and day and night continually imbibing the steam from the sacrifices offered up; for this is the only one good thing which can be attributed to any kind of building or erection." (75) But I think that when they hear these things, they will be indignant, as if they were listening not to prayers, but to curses, and that they will take refuge in such defence as chance may furnish them with, bringing retaliatory accusations; which may be the greatest proof of the manifest and undesirable impiety of those men, who look upon those beings as gods, to whom they themselves would never wish to have their own natures assimilated.

XVI. (76) Let no one therefore of those beings who are endowed with souls, worship any thing that is devoid of a soul; for it would be one of the most absurd things possible for the works of nature to be diverted to the service of those things which are made by hand; and against Egypt, not only is that common accusation brought, to which the whole country is liable, but another charge also, which is of a more special character, and with great fitness; for besides falling down to statues, and images they have also introduced irrational animals, to the honours due to the gods, such as bulls, and rams, and goats, inventing some prodigious fiction with regard to each of them; (77) and as to these particular animals, they have indeed some reason for what they do, for they are the most domestic, and the most useful to life.

The bull, as a plougher, draws furrows for the reception of the seed, and is again the most powerful of all animals to thresh the corn out when it is necessary to purify it of the chaff; the ram gives us the most beautiful garments for the coverings of our persons; for if our bodies were naked, they would easily be destroyed either through heat, or though intense cold, caused at one time by the blaze of the sun, and at another by the cooling of the air. (78) But as it is they go beyond these animals, and select the most fierce, and untameable of all wild animals, honouring lions, and crocodiles, and of reptiles the poisonous asp, with temples, and sacred precincts, and sacrifices, and assemblies in their honour, and solemn processions, and things of that kind.

For if they were to seek out in both elements, among all the things given to man for his use by God, searching through earth and water, they would never find any animal on the land more savage than the lion, or any aquatic animal more fierce than the crocodile, both which creatures they honour and worship; (79) they have also deified many other animals, dogs, ichneumons, wolves, birds, ibises, and hawks, and even fish, taking sometimes the whole, and sometimes only a part; and what can be more ridiculous than this conduct?[5] (80) And, accordingly, the first foreigners who arrived in Egypt were quite worn out with laughing at and ridiculing these superstitions, till their minds had become impregnated with the conceit of the natives; but all those who have tasted of right instruction, are amazed and struck with consternation, at their system of ennobling things which are not noble, and pity those who give into it, thinking the men, as is very natural, more miserable than even the objects which they honour, since they in their souls are changed into those very animals, so as to appear to be merely brutes in human form, now returning to their original nature.

(81) Therefore, God, removing out of his

sacred legislation all such impious deification of undeserving objects, has invited men to the honour of the one true and living God; not indeed that he has any need himself to be honoured; for being all-sufficient for himself, he has no need of any one else; but he has done so, because he wished to lead the race of mankind, hitherto wandering about in trackless deserts, into a road from which they should not stray, that so by following nature it might find the best end of all things, namely, the knowledge of the true and living God, who is the first and most perfect of all good things; from whom, as from a fountain, all particular blessings are showered upon the world, and upon the things are people in it.

XVII. (82) Having now spoken of the second commandment to the best of our ability, let us proceed to investigate the one which follows with accuracy, as is pointed out by the order in which they come.

The next commandment is, "not to take the name of God in vain."

Now the principle on which this order or arrangement proceeds is very plain to those who are gifted with acute mental vision; for the name is always subsequent in order to the subject of which it is the name; being like the shadow which follows the body. (83) Having, therefore, previously spoken of the existence of God, and also of the honour to be paid to the everlasting God; he then, following the natural order of connection proceeds to command what is becoming in respect of his name; for the errors of men with respect to this point are manifold and various, and assume many different characters.

(84) That being which is the most beautiful, and the most beneficial to human life, and suitable to rational nature, swears not itself, because truth on every point is so innate within him that his bare word is accounted an oath. Next to not swearing at all, the second best thing is to keep one's oath; for by the mere fact of swearing at all, the swearer shows that there is some suspicion of his not being trustworthy. (85) Let a man, therefore, be dilatory, and slow if there is any chance that by delay he may be able to avoid the necessity of taking an oath at all; but if necessity compels him to swear, then he must consider with no superficial attention, every one of the subjects, or parts of the subject, before him; for it is not a matter of slight importance, though from its frequency it is not regarded as it ought to be. (86) For an oath is the calling of God to give his testimony concerning the matters which are in doubt; and it is a most impious thing to invoke God to be witness to a lie.

Come now, if you please, and with your reason look into the mind of the man who is about to swear to a falsehood; and you will see that it is not tranquil, but full of disorder and confusion, accusing itself, and enduring all kinds of insolence

---

[5] This was one of the things which especially excited the ridicule of the Romans. Juvenal says, Sat. 15.1, (as it is translated by Gifford)—"Who knows not to what monstrous gods, my friend, / The mad inhabitants of Egypt bend? / The snake devouring ibis, these enshrine / Those think the crocodile alone divine; / Others, where Thebes' vast ruins strew the ground / And shattered Memnon yields a magic sound, / Set up a glittering brute of uncouth shape, / And bow before the image of an ape! / Thousands regard the hound with holy fear, / Not one Diana."

and evil speaking; (87) for the conscience which dwells in, and never leaves the soul of each individual, not being accustomed to admit into itself any wicked thing, preserves its own nature always such as to hate evil, and to love virtue, being itself at the same time an accuser and a judge; being roused as an accuser it blames, impeaches, and is hostile; and again as a judge it teaches, admonishes, and recommends the accused to change his ways, and if he be able to persuade him, he is with joy reconciled to him, but if he be not able to do so, then he wages an endless and implacable war against him, never quitting him neither by day, nor by night, but pricking him, and inflicting incurable wounds on him, until he destroys his miserable and accursed life.

XVIII. (88) "What sayest thou?" I should say to the perjured man, "will you dare to go to any one of your own acquaintances and say, My friend, come and bear witness for me that you have seen and heard, and been present at a whole catalogue of things which you have neither seen, nor heard? I think not; for that would be an act of incurable insanity; (89) with what face can you while sober, and while appearing to be master of yourself look upon your friend, and say, By reason of our acquaintance and companionship, act unjustly, violate the law, commit impiety for my sake; for it is plain that if he heard such a request, he would quickly renounce that companionship which you now believe to exist, reproaching himself for having ever had any friendship at all with a man of such a character as you, and would flee from you, as from a savage, and maddened, wild beast.

(90) "Will you then, without shame call upon God, the father and sovereign of the world, to give his testimony in favour of those things, to witness which you will not venture even to bring your friend? And if you do so, will you do it knowing that he sees everything and hears everything, or not knowing this fact? (91) If you know it not you are an atheist, and atheism is the beginning of all iniquity, and, in addition to your atheism, you are also adding the wickedness of an oath, by swearing by him who in your opinion is not attending to you, nor paying any regard to human affairs.

But if you are well assured that he does exert his providence in respect of such matters, still you are not free from the charge of excessive impiety, saying to God, if not with your mouth and tongue, still at all events with your conscience: Bear false witness for me, aid me in my wickedness, assist me in my impiety. I have but one hope of preserving a fair reputation among men, namely by concealing the truth; be thou wicked for another's sake, you who are the better, for the sake of one who is worse; you who are God, the most excellent of all beings, for the sake of a man, and that too a wicked one.

XIX. (92) But there are also some people who,

without any idea of acquiring gain, do from a bad habit incessantly and inconsiderately swear upon every occasion, even when there is nothing at all about which any doubt is raised, as if they were desirous to fill up the deficiency of their argument with oaths, as if it would not be better to cut their conversation short, or I might rather say to utter nothing at all, but to preserve entire silence, for from a frequency of oaths arises a habit of perjury and impiety. (93) On which account the man who is going to take an oath ought to investigate everything with care and exceeding accuracy, considering whether the subject is of serious importance, and whether it has really taken place, and whether, if it has, he has comprehended it properly; and considering himself, also, whether he is pure in soul, and body, and tongue, having the first free from all violation of the law, the second from all defilement, and the last from all blasphemy.

For it is an impiety for any disgraceful words to be uttered by that mouth by which the most sacred name is also mentioned. (94) Let him also consider whether the place and the time are suitable; for before now I have known some persons, in profane and impure places (in which it is not fitting that mention should be made of either their father or their mother, or of even any old man among their kindred who may have lived a virtuous life), swearing, and stringing together whole sentences full of oaths, using the name of God with all the variety of titles which belong to him, when they should not, out of sheer impiety.

(95) And let him who pays but little heed to what has been said here know, in the first place, that he is impure and defiled; and, in the second place, that the most terrible punishments are constantly lying in wait for him; that justice who keeps her eye upon all human affairs, being implacable and inflexible towards all enormities of such a character; and, when she does not think fit to inflict her punishments at once, still exacting satisfaction with abundant usury whenever the opportunity seems to offer in combination with the general advantage.

XX. (96) The fourth commandment has reference to the sacred seventh day, that it may be passed in a sacred and holy manner. Now some states keep the holy festival only once in the month, counting from the new moon, as a day sacred to God; but the nation of the Jews keep every seventh day regularly, after each interval of six days; (97) and there is an account of events recorded in the history of the creation of the world, comprising a sufficient relation of the cause of this ordinance; for the sacred historian says, that the world was created in six days, and that on the seventh day God desisted from his works, and began to contemplate what he had so beautifully created; (98) therefore, he commanded the beings also who were destined to live in this state, to imitate God in this particular also, as well as in all others, applying themselves to their works for six days, but desisting from them and philosophising on the seventh day, and devoting their leisure to the contemplation of the things of nature, and considering whether in the preceding six days they have done anything which has not been holy, bringing their conduct before the judgment-seat of the soul, and subjecting it to a scrutiny, and making themselves give an account of all the things which they have said or done; the laws sitting by as assessors and joint inquirers, in order to the correcting of such errors as have been committed through carelessness, and to the guarding against any similar offences being hereafter repeated.

(99) But God, on one occasion, employed the six days for the completion of the world, though he had no need of any length of time for such a purpose; but each man, as partaking of a mortal nature, and as being in need of ten thousand things for the unavoidable necessities of life, ought not to hesitate, even to the end of his life, to provide himself with all requisites, always allowing himself an interval of rest on the sacred seventh day. (100) Is it not a most beautiful recommendation, and one most admirably adapted to the perfecting of, and leading man to, every virtue, and above all to piety? The commandment, in effect says: Always imitate God; let that one period of seven days in which God created the world, be to you a complete example of the way in which you are to obey the law, and an all-sufficient model for your actions.

Moreover, the seventh day is also an example from which you may learn the propriety of studying philosophy; as on that day, it is said, God beheld the works which he had made; so that you also may yourself contemplate the works of nature, and all the separate circumstances which contribute towards happiness.

(101) Let us not pass by such a model of the most excellent ways of life, the practical and the contemplative; but let us always keep our eyes fixed upon it, and stamp a visible image and representation of it on our own minds, making our mortal nature resemble, as far as possible, his immortal one, in respect of saying and doing what is proper. And in what sense it is said that the world was made by God in six days, who never wants time at all to make anything, has been already explained in other passages where we have treated of allegories.

XXI. (102) Now, those who have applied themselves to mathematical studies, fully explain the precedence and pre-eminence to which the number seven is entitled among all existing things, tracing it out with great care and exceeding minuteness and accuracy; for among numbers seven is the virgin number, the nature which has no mother, that which is most nearly related to the unit, the foundation of all numbers; the idea of the planets,

just as the unit is of the immovable sphere; for of the unit and the number seven consists the incorporeal heaven, the model of the visible heaven, and the heaven is made up of indivisible and divisible nature. (103) Now, indivisible nature has assigned to it the first, and highest, and immovable circumference, which the unit inspects and overlooks; but the divisible nature has received that circumference which is inferior both in power and in arrangement, which the number seven inspects, which, being divided into six parts, has produced what are called the seven planets; (104) not indeed that any of the heavenly bodies do really wander *(peplanētai)*, inasmuch as they all enjoy a divine, and happy, and blessed nature, to all of which characteristics a freedom from wandering is most closely akin: at all events, they always preserve a kind of identity in a constantly similar motion, and pass a long eternity without ever admitting any change or variation whatever. But because they revolve in a manner contrary to the indivisible and outermost sphere, they have been named planets *(planētes)*, though without any strict propriety, by men speaking at random, who have by such language attributed their own propensity to wander to the heavenly bodies, which, in fact, never quit that position in the divine lamp in which they have been originally placed. (105) For all these reasons, and more besides, the number seven is honoured. But there is no one cause on account of which it has received its precedence so completely, as because it is by its means that the Creator and Father of the universe is most especially made manifest; for the mind beholds God in this as in a mirror, acting, and creating the world, and managing the whole universe.

XXII. (106) And after this commandment relating to the seventh day he gives the fifth, which concerns the honour to be paid to parents, giving it a position on the confines of the two tables of five commandments each; for being the concluding one of the first table, in which the most sacred duties to the Deity are enjoined, it has also some connection with the second table which comprehends the obligations towards our fellow creatures; (107) and the cause of this, I imagine, is as follows:

The nature of one's parents appears to be something on the confines between immortal and mortal essences. Of mortal essence, on account of their relationship to men and also to other animals, and likewise of the perishable nature of the body. And of immortal essence, by reason of the similarity of the act of generation to God the Father of the universe. (108) But it has often happened that men have attached themselves to one of these divisions, and have seemed to neglect the other; for being filled with a sincere love for piety, they have renounced all other occupations and considerations, and have devoted the whole of their lives to the service of God.

(109) But they who have thought that beyond their duties to their fellow men there was no such thing as goodness, have clung solely to their fellowship with and to the society of men, and, being wholly occupied by a love of the society of men, have invited all men to an equal participation in all their good things, labouring at the same time to the best of their power to alleviate all their disasters. (110) Now, one may properly call both these latter, these philanthropic men, and also the former class, the lovers of God, but half perfect in virtue; for those only are perfect who have a good reputation in both points: but those who do not attend to their duties towards men so as to rejoice with them at their common blessings, or to grieve with them at events of a contrary character, and who yet do not devote themselves to piety and holiness towards God, may be thought to have changed into the nature of wild beasts, the very pre-eminence among whom, in point of ferocity, those are entitled to who neglect their parents, being hostile to both the divisions of virtue above mentioned, namely, piety towards God, and their duty towards men.

XXIII. (111) Let them, then, not be ignorant that they are convicted before the two tribunals which are the only ones which exist in nature, of impiety as regards their duty towards God, as not worshipping those who have introduced beings who do not exist into existence, and who, in this respect, have imitated God; and as regards their duty towards men, of misanthropy and cruelty. (112) For to whom else will those men do good who neglect their nearest relations and those who have bestowed the greatest gifts upon them, some of which are of so great a character that they do not admit of any requital? For how can he who has been begotten by a parent, in requital again beget his parents, since nature has bestowed on parents this especial endowment in respect of their children, which can never be requited or recompensed? On which account it is becoming to a man to feel exceeding indignation when people, because they are unable to make a full return for the benefits which they have received, do not choose to make the very slightest; (113) to whom I might say, with perfect propriety, that wild beasts even must be made tame towards men; and, indeed, I have frequently known instances of lions being domesticated, and bears and leopards, and made gentle, not only to those who feed them, by reason of their gratitude for necessaries, but also to others, on account, in my opinion, of their resemblance to their feeders.

For it is always well that what is worse should follow what is better, from a hope of deriving improvement; (114) but in this case I shall be constrained to use an entirely opposite language. You who are men, are imitators of some wild beasts. Even the beasts have learnt and know how to requite with service those who have done them service. Dogs who keep the house will defend their masters, and encounter death for their sakes when any danger suddenly overtakes them. And they say that the dogs employed among flocks of sheep will fight on behalf of the flocks, and endure till they either obtain the victory or meet with death, for the sake of protecting the shepherds themselves from injury.

(115) Is it not then the most shameful of all shameful things for a man, in respect of the requital of favours, to be left behind by a dog, for that being, which of all others is the most gentle, to be outrun by the most audacious of beasts? But if we will not be taught by the land animals, let us go across to the nature of the winged birds which traverse the air, and learn what we have need of from them.

(116) In the case of storks the old birds remain in their nests because they are unable to fly; but their children, I had very nearly said, traverse the whole of earth and sea, and from all quarters provide their parents with what is necessary for them. (117) And so they, living in a tranquillity worthy of their time of life, enjoy all abundance, and pass their old age in luxury; while their children make light of all the hardships they undergo to furnish them with the means of support, under the influence both of piety and also of the expectation that they also in their old age will receive the same treatment from their descendants; and so they now discharge the indispensable debt which they owe their parents, knowing that in proper time, they will themselves receive what they are now bestowing. And there are also others who are unable to support themselves, for children are no more able to do so at the commencement of their existence, than their parents are at the end of their lives. On which account the children, having while young been fed in accordance with the spontaneous promptings of nature, now with joy do in return support the old age of their parents.

(118) Is it not right, then, after these examples, that men who neglect their parents should cover their faces from shame, and reproach themselves for disregarding those things which they ought to have cared for alone, or in preference to any thing else whatever? And this too, when they would not have been so much conferring benefits as requiting them? For the children have nothing of their own which does not belong to the parents, who have either bestowed it upon them from their own substance, or have enabled them to acquire it by supplying them with the means.

(119) And have then these men within the borders of their souls piety and holiness, the chiefs of all the virtues? No; rather they have driven them beyond their borders, and forced them into exile; for parents are the servants of God for the propagation of children, and he who dishonours the

servant dishonours also the master. (120) But some persons, who are rather audacious, magnify the title of parents, saying that the father and mother are evident gods, inasmuch as they imitate the uncreated God in their production of living animals, limiting, however, their assertion in this way, that the one is the God of the whole world, but the others only of those children whom they have begotten. And it is impossible that the invisible God can be piously worshipped by those people who behave with impiety towards those who are visible and near to them.

XXIV. (121) Having then now philosophized in this manner about the honour to be paid to parents, he closes the one and more divine table of the first five commandments.

And being about to promulgate the second which contains the prohibitions of those offences which are committed against men, he begins with adultery, looking upon this as the greatest of all violations of the law; (122) for, in the first place, it has for its source the love of pleasure, which enervates the bodies of those who indulge in it, and relaxes the tone of the soul, and destroys the essences of it, consuming every thing that it touches, like unquenchable fire, and leaving nothing which affects human life uninjured, (123) inasmuch as it not only persuades the adulterer to commit iniquity, but also teaches him to join others in wickedness, making an association in things in which there ought to be no such participation. For when this violent passion seizes on a man it is impossible for the appetites to arrive at the accomplishment of their object by one person alone, but it is indispensable that two should share in the action, the one taking the place of the teacher, and the other that of the pupil, for the complete confirmation of those most disgraceful evils, intemperance and licentiousness.

(124) Nor can one allege as an excuse that it is only the body of the woman who is committing adultery that is corrupted, but, if one must tell the truth, even before the corruption of the body the soul is accustomed to alienation from virtue, being taught in every way to repudiate and to hate its husband. (125) And it would be a less grievous evil if this hatred were displayed without disguise; for it is easiest to guard against what is plainly seen. But at present it is with difficulty suspected, and difficult of detection, being concealed by cunning and wicked arts, and at times it assumes the contrary appearance of love and affection, by means of its trickery and deceit.

(126) Accordingly, adultery exhibits the destruction of three houses by its means; that of the house of the man who sustains the violation of all the vows which were made to him at his marriage, and the loss of all the hopes of legitimate children, of which he is now deprived; and two others, namely, the house of the adulterer, and that of his wife. For each of these is filled with insolence, and dishonour, and the most excessive disgrace. (127) And if their connections and families are very numerous, then by reason of their intermarriages and the mutual connections formed with different houses the iniquity and injury will proceed and infect the whole city all around. (128) Moreover, the doubt as to the legitimacy of the children is a most terrible evil.

For if the wife be not chaste, it is quite a matter of doubt and uncertainty to what father the children belong. And then, if the matter remain undiscovered, the children of adultery enter unjustly into the classification of legitimate children, and make a race spurious to which they have no pretensions to belong, and receive an inheritance which in appearance indeed is their own patrimony, but which in reality has no connection with them. (129) And then the adulterer, behaving with insolence and pluming himself upon his iniquity in having propagated an offspring full of reproach, when he has satiated his appetites will depart, leaving the object behind him, and turning into ridicule the ignorance that exists of the unholy wickedness which he has committed, on the part of the man against whom he has sinned.

And the husband, like a blind man, knowing nothing of what has been going on in his own house, will be compelled to nourish and to cherish as his own the offspring sprung from his greatest enemies. (130) And it is plain that if such a wickedness takes place, the most miserable of all persons must be the wretched children, who have done no wrong themselves, and who cannot be assigned to either family, neither to that of the husband of the adulteress, nor to that of the adulterer. (131) Since, then, illicit cohabitation produces such great calamities, adultery is very naturally a detestable thing hated by God, and has been set down as the first of all transgressions.

XXV. (132) The second commandment of this second table is to do no murder. For nature, having produced man as a gregarious and sociable creature, and the most easily domesticated of all animals, has invited it to a fellowship of opinion and partnership, giving him reason, as a means to lead to a harmony and admixture of dispositions. And he who slays any man must not be ignorant that he is overturning the laws and ordinances of nature, which have been beautifully established for the common advantage of all men. (133) Moreover, let him be aware that he is liable to the charge of sacrilege as having plundered the most sacred of all the possessions of God; for what is a more venerable or more sublime offering to God than man? For gold, and silver, and precious stones, and all such other valuable materials, are only an inanimate ornament of inanimate erections; (134) but man, who is the most excellent of all animals, in respect of that predominant part that is in him, namely, his soul, is also most closely related to the heaven, which is the purest of all things in its essence, and as the common language of the multitude affirms, to the Father of the world, inasmuch as he has received mind, which is of all the things that are upon the earth the closest copy and most faithful representation of the everlasting and blessed idea.

XXVI. (135) The third commandment of the second table of five is not to steal. For he who keeps continually gaping after the property of others is the common enemy of the city, since, as far as his inclination goes, he would deprive all men of their property; and in respect of his power he actually does deprive some, because his covetousness is extended to the greatest imaginable length, and because his impotence, coming too late after it, is contracted into a small space, and can scarcely extend so as to overtake more than a few.

(136) Therefore as many robbers as have the strength to do so plunder whole cities, paying no attention to the punishments with which they are threatened, because they appear to themselves to be superior to the laws. These are those men who are oligarchical in their natures, who have set their hearts on tyrannies and absolute power, who commit enormous thefts, concealing their robbery, as it is in reality, under the specious and imposing names of authority and supremacy.

(137) Let every one then learn from his earliest infancy, never privily to steal anything that belongs to any one else, not even though it may be the merest trifle, because the habit, when it becomes inveterate, is more powerful than nature; and small things, if they are not checked, increase and grow, becoming gradually greater and greater till they reach a formidable magnitude.

XXVII. (138) And after he has forbidden stealing he proceeds in regular order to prohibit bearing false witness, knowing that those who bear false witness are liable to many great accusations, and in short to every kind of terrible charge; for in the first place they are corrupting that holy thing, truth, than which there is no more sacred possession among men, which like the sun sheds a light upon all things, so that not one of them may be kept in darkness; (139) and in the second place, in addition to speaking falsely, they also as it were envelop facts in night and dense darkness, and they co-operate with those who offend, and they join in attacking those who are injured by others, affirming that they positively know and have completely comprehended what they in reality have not seen nor heard, and of which they know nothing.

(140) Moreover, they also commit a third violation of the law, which is more grievous than either of those which have been mentioned before; for, when there is a scarcity of demonstrations, either by reasons or by letters, then those who have questions in dispute betake themselves to witnesses, whose words are rules to the judges concerning those matters on which they are to deliver their opinion; for it is necessary for the judges to attend to them alone, when there is nothing else existing which can contribute to proof in the matter in question; from which it arises that those who are borne down by evidence in this way meet with injustice when they might have won their cause, and that those who attend to the false witnesses are recorded as unjust and illegal judges, instead of just and legal ones.

(141) Moreover, this kind of crafty wickedness outstrips all other offences in its impiety; for it is not customary for judges to decide without being sworn, but rather after having taken the most fearful oaths, which those men transgress who deceive others, more than they do who are deceived by them, since the error of the one is not intentional, but the others do deliberately plot against them, and do of malice aforethought sin, persuading those in whose power it is to give the decisive vote to err, not knowing what they do, so that things which deserve no chastisement meet with punishment and loss.

XXVIII. (142) Last of all, the divine legislator prohibits covetousness, knowing that desire is a thing fond of revolution and of plotting against others; for all the passions of the soul are formidable, exciting and agitating it contrary to nature, and not permitting it to remain in a healthy state, but of all such passions the worst is desire. On which account each of the other passions, coming in from without and attacking the soul from external points, appears to be involuntary; but this desire alone derives its origin from ourselves, and is wholly voluntary. (143) But what is it that I am saying? The appearance and idea of a present good, or of one that is accounted such, rouses up and excites the soul which was previously in a state of tranquillity, and raises it to a high degree of elation, like a light suddenly flashing before the eyes; and this passion of the soul is called pleasure.

(144) But the contrary to good is evil, which, when it forces its way in, and inflicts a mortal wound, immediately fills the soul against its will with depression and despondency; and the name of the passion is sorrow. (145) But when the evil presses upon the soul, when it has not as yet taken up its habitation in it, but when it is only impending, being about to come and to agitate it, it sends before it agitation and suspense, as express messengers, to fill the soul with alarm; and this passion is denominated fear. (146) And when any one, having conceived an idea of some good which is not present, hastens to lay hold of it, he then drives his soul forward to a great distance, and extending it in the greatest possible degree, from his anxiety to attain the object of his desires, he is stretched as it were upon the rack, being anxious to lay hold of the thing, but being unable to reach

it, and being in the same condition with those who are pursuing people who are running away, following with an inferior speed, but with unrivalled eagerness.

(147) And something of the same kind appears to happen, also, with respect to the external senses; for very frequently the eyes, hastening to come to the comprehension of something which is removed to a great distance, strain themselves, exerting themselves to the very fullest extent of and even beyond their power, are unsuccessful, and grow dim in the empty space between themselves and their object, wholly failing in attaining to an accurate knowledge of the subject before them, and moreover impairing and injuring their sight by the exceeding intensity of their efforts and steady gaze.

(148) And, again, sometimes when an indistinct noise is borne towards us from a long distance, the ears are excited, and feeling as it were a fair breeze, are eager and hasten to approach nearer to it if possible, from a desire that the sound should be distinctly apprehended by the sense of hearing. (149) But the noise, for it is still obscure as it seems, strikes the ear but faintly, not giving forth any more distinct tone by which it may be understood, so that the desire of comprehending it, being unsuccessful and unsatisfied, is excited more and more, the desire causing a Tantalus-like kind of punishment.

For Tantalus, whenever he seemed about to lay his hands on any of the objects which he desired, was invariably disappointed, and the man who is overcome by desire, being always thirsting for what is not present, is never satisfied, wallowing about among vain appetites, (150) like those diseases which would creep over the whole body, if they were not checked by excision or cautery, and which would overrun and seize upon the whole composition of the body, not leaving a single part in a sound state; in like manner, unless discourse in accordance with philosophy did not, like a good physician, check the influx of appetite, all the affairs of life would of necessity be set in motion in a manner contrary to nature; for there is nothing exempt from such an affliction, nothing which can escape the dominion of passion, but, when once it has obtained immunity and license, it devours everything and becomes by itself everything in every part.

(151) Perhaps it is a piece of folly to make a long speech upon matters which are so manifest, as to which there is no individual and no city that is ignorant, that they are not only every day, but even every hour, as one may say, supplying a visible proof of the truth of my assertion. Is the love of money, or of women, or of glory, or of any one of the other efficient causes of pleasure, the origin of slight and ordinary evils? (152) Is it not owing to this passion that relationships are broken asunder, and change the good will which originates in nature into an irreconcilable enmity? And are not great countries and populous kingdoms made desolate by domestic seditions, through such causes? And are not earth and sea continually filled with novel and terrible calamities by naval battles and military expeditions for the same reason? (153) For, both among the Greeks and barbarians, the wars between one another, and between their own different tribes, which have been so celebrated by tragedians, have all flowed from one source, namely, desire of money, or glory, or pleasure; for it is on such subjects as these that the race of mankind goes mad.

XXIX. (154) However, enough of these matters. Still we must not be ignorant of this fact either, that the ten commandments are the heads of all the particular and special laws which are recorded throughout all the history of the giving of the law related in the sacred scriptures. (155) The first law is the fountain of all those concerning the government of one supreme Ruler, and they show that there is one first cause of the world, one Ruler and King, who guides and governs the universe in such a way as conduces to its preservation, having banished from the pure essence of heaven all oligarchy and aristocracy, those treacherous forms of government which arise among wicked men, as the offspring of disorder and covetousness.

(156) And the second commandment is the summary of all those laws which can possibly be enacted, about all the things made by hands, such as images and statues, and, in short, erections of any kind, of which the painters' and statuaries' arts are pernicious creators, for that commandment forbids such images to be made, and prohibits the cleaving to any of the fabulous inventions about the marriage of gods and the birth of gods, and the number of indescribable and painful calamities which are represented to have ensued from both such circumstances.

(157) By the third commandment he restrains people from taking oaths, and limits the objects for which one may swear, defining when and where it may be lawful, and who may swear, and how the swearer ought to be disposed, both in his soul and body, and many other minute particulars, concerning those who keep their oaths, and the contrary.

XXX. (158) And the fourth commandment, the one about the seventh day, we must not look upon in any other light than as a summary of all the laws relating to festivals, and of all the purificatory rites enjoined to be observed on each of them. But the service appointed for them was one of holy ablutions, and prayers deserving to be heard, and perfect sacrifices. (159) And in speaking of the seventh here, I mean both that which is combined with the number six, the most generative of all numbers, and also that which, without being combined with the number six, is added to it, being made to resemble the unit, each of which numbers is reckoned among the festivals; for the lawgiver refers to the term, the sacred festival of the new moon, which the people give notice of with trumpets, and the day of fasting, on which abstinence from all meats and drinks is enjoined, which the Hebrews call, in their native language, pascha, on which the whole nation sacrifices, each individual among them, not waiting for the priests, since on this occasion the law has given, for one especial day in every year, a priesthood to the whole nation, so that each private individual slays his own victim on this day.

(160) And also the day on which is offered the sheaf of corn, as an offering of gratitude for the fertility and productiveness of the plain, as exhibited in the fulness of the ears of corn. And the day of pentecost, which is numbered from this day by seven portions of seven days, in which it is the custom to offer up loaves, which are truly called the loaves of the first fruits, since, in fact, they are the first fruits of the productions and crops of eatable grain, which God has given to mankind, as the most tractable of all his creatures.

(161) But to the seventh day of the week he has assigned the greatest festivals, those of the longest duration, at the periods of the equinox both vernal and autumnal in each year; appointing two festivals for these two epochs, each lasting seven days; the one which takes place in the spring being for the perfection of what is being sown, and the one which falls in autumn being a feast of thanksgiving for the bringing home of all the fruits which the trees have produced.

And seven days have very appropriately been appointed to the seventh month of each equinox, so that each month might receive an especial honour of one sacred day of festival, for the purpose of refreshing and cheering the mind with its holiday.

(162) There are also other laws brought forward, enacted with great wisdom and excellence, conducing to the production of gentleness and fellowship among men, and inviting them to simplicity and equality; of these some have reference to that which is called the sabbatical year, in which it is expressly commanded that the people shall leave the whole land uncultivated, neither sowing, nor ploughing, nor preserving the trees, nor doing any other of the works which relate to agriculture; (163) for God thought the land, both the champaign and the mountainous country, after it had been labouring for six years in the production of crops, and the yearly yielding of its expected fruits, worthy of some relaxation, for the sake of recovering its breath as it were, and that, becoming free again, if one may say so, it might exert the spontaneous riches of its own nature.

(164) There are also other laws about the fiftieth year, in which what has been enumerated above is performed in the most complete manner; and, what is the most important thing of all, the restitution is made of the different portions of land to those families which originally received them, a transaction full of humanity and equity.

XXXI. (165) And the fifth commandment, that about the honour due to parents, conceals under its brief expression, many very important and necessary laws, some enacted as applicable to old and young men, some as bearing on the relations existing between rulers and subjects, others concerning benefactors and those who have received benefits, others affecting slaves and masters; (166) for parents belong to the superior class of all these divisions just mentioned, the class, I mean, of elders, of rulers, of benefactors, and of masters; and children are in the inferior class, in which are ranked the younger people, the subjects, those who have received benefits, and slaves.

(167) There are also many other commandments given, some to the young, admonishing them to receive gladly the admonitions of old age; others to the old, bidding them take care of the young; some to subjects, enjoining them to show obedience to their rulers; others to the rulers, commanding them to consult for the advantage of those who are under their authority; some to those who have received benefits, recommending them a requital of the favours which have been conferred on them; others to those who have set the example of beneficence, bidding them not to exact a strict restitution as if they were usurers; some to servants, encouraging them to show an affectionate service towards their masters, others to the masters recommending them to practise that gentleness and mildness towards their slaves, by which the inequality of their respective conditions is in some degree equalised.

XXXII. (168) The first table of five, then, is completed in these commandments, exhibiting a comprehensive character; but of the special and particular laws the number is very great.

Of the second table, the first commandment is that against adulterers, under which many other commands are conveyed by implication, such as that against seducers, that against practisers of unnatural crimes, that against all who live in debauchery, that against all men who indulge in illicit and incontinent connections; (169) but the lawgiver has set down all the different species of such intemperance, not for the sake of exhibiting its manifold, and diverse, and ever-changing varieties, but in order to cause those who live in an unseemly manner to show most evident signs of depression and shame, drinking in with their ears all the reproaches heaped together which they incur, and which may well make them blush.

(170) The second brief commandment, the prohibition of slaying men, is that under which are implied all those necessary and most universally

advantageous laws, relating to acts of violence, to insults, to assaults, to wounds, to mutilation.

(171) The third, that which forbids stealing, is the one under cover of which are enacted all the regulations which have been laid down, respecting the repudiation of debts, and those who deny what has been deposited with them, and who form unhallowed partnerships, and indulge in shameless acts of rapine, and, in short, in any kind of covetousness by which some person are induced, either openly or secretly to appropriate the possessions of others.

(172) The fourth, that which is concerning the duty of not bearing false witness, is one under which many other prohibitions are conveyed, such as that of not deceiving, of not bringing false accusations, of not co-operating with those who are committing sin, of not making a pretence of good faith a cloak for faithlessness; for all which objects suitable laws have been enacted.

(173) The fifth is that which cuts off desire, the fountain of all iniquity, from which flow all the most unlawful actions, whether of individuals or of states, whether important or trivial, whether sacred or profane, whether they relate to one's life and soul, or to what are called external things; for, as I have said before, nothing ever escapes desire, but, like a fire in a wood, it proceeds onward, consuming and destroying everything; (174) and there are a great many subordinate sins, which are prohibited likewise under this commandment, for the sake of correcting those persons who cheerfully receive admonitions, and of chastising those stubborn people who devote their whole lives to the indulgence of passion.

XXXIII. (175) I have now spoken in this manner, at sufficient length, concerning the second table of five commandments, which make up the whole number of ten, which God himself promulgated with the dignity befitting their holy character; for it was suitable to his own nature to promulgate in his own person the heads and principles of all particular laws, but to send forth the particular and special laws by the most perfect of the prophets, whom he selected for his pre-eminent excellence, and filled with his divine spirit, and then appointed to be the interpreter of his holy oracles.

(176) After having explained these matters, let us now proceed to relate the cause for which God, having pronounced these ten commandments or laws, in simple injunctions and prohibitions, appointed no punishment for those who should violate them, as lawgivers usually do. The reason is this: he was God, and being so he was at once the good Lord, the cause of good alone, and of no evil; (177) therefore, thinking it most appropriate to his own nature to deliver saving commands unalloyed, and partaking of no punishment, so that no one yielding to a foolish counsellor might accidentally choose what is best, but might do so from wise consideration and of his own deliberate purpose, he did not think fit to give his oracles to mankind in connection with any denunciation of punishment; not because he meant to give immunity to transgressors, but because he knew that justice was sitting by him, and surveying all human affairs, and that she would never rest, as being by nature a hater of evil and looking upon the chastisement of sinners as her own most appropriate task.

(178) For it is proper for all the ministers and lieutenants of God, just as for generals in war, to put in practice severe punishments against those deserters, who forsake the ranks of the just one; but it becomes the great King, that general safety should be ascribed to him, as preserving the universe in peace, and giving at all times, to all people, in all riches and abundance, all the blessings of peace: for, in truth, God is the president of peace, but his subordinate ministers are the chiefs of war.

THE SPECIAL LAWS, I[†]

(De Specialibus Legibus, I)

I. (1) The genera and heads of all special laws, which are called "the ten commandments," have been discussed with accuracy in the former treatise. We must now proceed to consider the particular commands as we read them in the subsequent passages of the holy scriptures; and we will begin with that which is turned into ridicule by people in general. (2) The ordinance of circumcision of the parts of generation is ridiculed, though it is an act which is practised to no slight degree among other nations also, and most especially by the Egyptians, who appear to me to be the most populous of all nations, and the most abounding in all kinds of wisdom. (3) In consequence of which it would be most fitting for men to discard childish ridicule, and to investigate the real causes of the ordinance with more prudence and dignity, considering the reasons why the custom has prevailed, and not being precipitate, so as without examination to condemn the folly of mighty nations, recollecting that it is not probable that so many myriads should be circumcised in every generation, mutilating the bodies of themselves and of their nearest relations, in a manner which is accompanied with severe pain, without adequate cause; but that there are many reasons which might encourage men to persevere and continue a custom which has been introduced by previous generations, and that these are from reasons of the greatest weight and importance.

(4) First of all, that it is a preventive of a painful disease, and of an affliction difficult to be cured, which they call a carbuncle;[1] because, I imagine, when it becomes inflamed it burns; from which fact it has derived that appellation. And this disease is very apt to be engendered among those who have not undergone the rite of circumcision. (5) Secondly, it secures the cleanliness of the whole body in a way that is suited to the people consecrated to God; with which object the Egyptian priests, being extravagant in their case, shave the whole of their bodies; for some of these evils which ought to be got rid of are collected in and lodge under the hair and the prepuce. (6) Thirdly, there is the resemblance of the part that is circumcised to the heart; for both parts are prepared for the sake of generation; for the breath contained within the heart is generative of thoughts, and the generative organ itself is productive of living beings.

Therefore, the men of old thought it right to make the evident and visible organ, by which the objects of the outward senses are generated, resemble that invisible and superior part, by means of which ideas are formed. (7) The fourth, and most important, is that which relates to the provision thus made for prolificness; for it is said that the seminal fluid proceeds in its path easily, neither being at all scattered, nor flowing on its passage into what may be called the bags of the prepuce. On which account those nations which practise circumcision are the most prolific and the most populous.

II. (8) These considerations have come to our ears, having been discussed of old among men of divine spirit and wisdom, who have interpreted the writings of Moses in no superficial or careless manner. But, besides what has been already said, I also look upon circumcision to be a symbol of two things of the most indispensable importance. (9) First of all, it is a symbol of the excision of the pleasures which delude the mind; for since, of all the delights which pleasure can afford, the association of man with woman is the most exquisite, it seemed good to the lawgivers to mutilate the organ which ministers to such connections; by which rite they signified figuratively the excision of all superfluous and excessive pleasure, not, indeed, of one only, but of all others whatever, though that one which is the most imperious of all.

(10) The second thing is, that it is a symbol of a man's knowing himself, and discarding that terrible disease, the vain opinion of the soul; for some men, like good statuaries, have boasted that they can make that most beautiful animal, man; and, being puffed up with arrogance, have deified themselves, hiding from sight the true cause of the creation of all things namely, God, although they might have corrected that error from a consideration of other persons among whom they live; (11) there are among them many men who have no children, and many barren women whose connections lead to nothing, so that they grow old in childlessness.

We must therefore eradicate evil opinions from the mind, and all other ideas which are not devoted to God.

This, then, is enough to say on these subjects.

[†] Yonge's title, *A Treatise on Circumcision.*
[1] The Greek word is *anthrax,* which also signifies a coal. The Latin, from which our carbuncle is derived, *carbunculus,* a diminutive of *carbo,* which also means a coal.

(12) But we must now turn to the special and particular laws; and first of all to those which relate to those people by whom it is well to be governed, those which have been enacted concerning monarchy.[2]

III. (13) Some persons have conceived that the sun, and the moon, and the other stars are independent gods, to whom they have attributed the causes of all things that exist. But Moses was well aware that the world was created, and was like a very large city, having rulers and subjects in it; the rulers being all the bodies which are in heaven, such as planets and fixed stars; (14) and the subjects being all the natures beneath the moon, hovering in the air and adjacent to the earth. But that the rulers aforesaid are not independent and absolute, but are the viceroys of one supreme Being, the Father of all, in imitation of whom they administer with propriety and success the charge committed to their care, as he also presides over all created things in strict accordance with justice and with law.

Others, on the contrary, who have not discovered the supreme Governor, who thus rules everything, have attributed the causes of the different things which exist in the world to the subordinate powers, as if they had brought them to pass by their own independent act. (15) But the most sacred lawgiver changes their ignorance into knowledge, speaking in the following manner: "Thou shalt not, when thou seest the sun, and the moon, and the stars, and all the host of heaven, be led astray and fall down and worship them."[3] With great felicity and propriety has he here called the reception of these bodies as gods, an error; (16) for they who see that the different seasons of the year owe their existence to the advances and retreats of the sun, in which periods also the generation of animals, and plants, and fruits, are perfected according to well-defined times, and who see also that the moon is the servant and successor of the sun, taking that care and superintendence of the world by night which the sun takes by day; and also that the other stars, in accordance with their sympathy with things on earth, labour continually and do ten thousand things which contribute to the duration of the existing state of things, have been led into an inextricable error, imagining that these bodies are the only gods.

(17) But if they had taken pains to travel along the straight and true road, they would soon have known that just as the outward sense is the sub-ordinate minister of the mind, so in the same manner all the objects of the outward senses are servants of that which is appreciable only by intellect, being well contented if they can attain to the second place in honour. (18) But it is altogether ridiculous to imagine that the mind, which is the smallest thing in us, being in fact invisible, is the ruler of those organs which belong to the external senses, but that the greatest and most perfect ruler of the whole universe is not the King of kings; that the being who sees, is not the ruler of those who do not see.

(19) We must, therefore, look on all those bodies in the heaven, which the outward sense regards as gods, not as independent rulers, since they are assigned the work of lieutenants, being by their intrinsic nature responsible to a higher power, but by reason of their virtue not actually called to render in an account of their doings. (20) So that, transcending all visible essence by means of our reason, let us press forward to the honour of that everlasting and invisible Being who can be comprehended and appreciated by the mind alone; who is not only the God of all gods, whether appreciable only by the intellect or visible to the outward senses, but is also the creator of them all. And if any one gives up the service due to the everlasting and uncreated God, transferring it to any more modern and created being, let him be set down as mad and as liable to the charge of the greatest impiety.

IV. (21) But there are some persons who have given gold and silver to sculptors and statuaries, as people able to fashion gods for them. And they, taking the lifeless materials and using a mortal model, have (which is a most extraordinary thing) made gods, as far as appearance went, and have built temples and erected altars, and dedicated them to them, honouring them with excessive pains and diligence, with sacrifices and processions, and all kinds of other sacred ceremonies and purifications; the priests and priestesses exciting themselves to the very extremity of their power to extend this kind of pride and vanity. (22) To whom the Father of the universe thus speaks, saying: "You shall not make to yourselves gods of silver and gold;"[4] all but teaching them in express words, "You shall not make to yourselves any gods whatever of this or of any other material, nor shall you worship anything made with hands," being forbidden expressly with respect to the two most excellent materials; for silver and gold are esteemed the most honourable of all materials.

(23) And, besides this distinct prohibition, there is another meaning which appears to me to be intended to be figuratively conveyed under these words, which is one of very great influence as con-

---

[2] Yonge's translation includes a separate treatise title at this point: *On Monarchy, Book I*. Accordingly, his next paragraph begins with roman numeral I (=III in Loeb). Yonge's "treatise" concludes with number IX (=XI in the Loeb). The publisher has elected to follow the Loeb numbering.

[3] Deuteronomy 4:19.

[4] Exodus 20:20.

tributing to the formation of the moral character, and which convicts in no slight degree those who are covetous of money and who seek to procure silver and gold from all quarters, and when they have acquired it treasure it up, as though it were some divine image, in their inmost shrines, looking upon it as the cause of all good things and of all happiness. (24) And all the poor men that are possessed of that terrible disease, the love of money, but who, from not having any riches of their own which they can think worthy of their attention, fix their admiration on the wealth of their neighbours, and, for the purpose of offering adoration to it, come the first thing in the morning to the houses of those who have abundance, as if they were noble temples at which they were going to offer prayers, and to entreat blessings from their owners as if from the gods.

(25) And to these men, Moses says, in another passage, "You shall not follow images, and you shall not make to yourselves molten gods."[5] Teaching them, by figurative language, that it is not right to pay such honours to wealth as one would pay to the gods; for those celebrated materials of wealth, silver and gold, are made to be used, which, however, the multitude follows, looking upon them as the only causes of wealth which is proverbially called blind, and the especial sources of happiness. (26) These are the things which Moses calls idols, resembling shadows and phantoms, and having about them nothing strong, or trustworthy, or lasting; for they are tossed about like the unstable wind, and are subject to all kinds of variations and changes. And the greatest possible proof of this is that, when people have not at all expected it, it suddenly has descended upon them; and, again, when they fancied that they had taken firm hold of it, it has flown away.

And when, indeed, it is present, then images appear as in a mirror, deceiving the outward senses and imposing upon them with traps, and appearing as if they would last for a long time, while in reality they do not endure. (27) And why need I explain how unstable the wealth and pride of men are, which vain opinions decorate with showy colours? For, before now, some men have existed who have affirmed that all other animals and plants, of which there is any birth or any decay, are in one continual and incessant state of transition, and that the external sense of this transition is somewhat indistinct, inasmuch as the swiftness of nature surpasses the very quickest and most precise glance of the vision.

V. (28) But not only are wealth, and glory, and all other such things, mere phantoms and unsubstantial images, but also all the other deceits which the inventors of fables have devised, puffing themselves up by reason of their ingenuity, while they have been raising a fortification of false opinion in opposition to the truth, bringing in God as if by some theatrical machine, in order to prevent the everlasting and only true existing God from being consigned to oblivion, are so likewise. But such men have adapted their falsehood to melodies, and rhythm, and metres, with a reference to what is persuasive, thinking that by these means they should easily cajole all who read their works.

(29) Not but what they have also joined to themselves the arts of statuary and painting as co-partners in their system of deceit, in order that, bringing over the spectators by well-fabricated appearances of colours, and forms, and distinctive qualities, and having won over by their allurements those principal outward senses of sight and hearing, the one by the exquisite beauty of lifeless forms, and the other by a poetical harmony of numbers—they may ravish the unstable soul and render it feeble, and deprive it of any settled foundation.

(30) On this account, Moses, being well aware that pride had by that time advanced to a very high pitch of power, and that it was well guarded by the greater part of mankind, and that too not from compulsion but of their own accord, and fearing lest those men who are admirers of uncorrupted and genuine piety may be carried away as by a torrent, stamped a deep impression on the minds of men, engraving piety on them, in order that the impression he thus made might not become confused or weakened, so as at last to become wholly effaced by time. And he is constantly prophesying and telling his people that there is one God, the creator and maker of the universe; and at other time he teaches them that he is the Lord of all created things, since all that is firm, and solid, and really stable and sure, is by nature so framed as to be connected with him alone. (31) And it is said in the scriptures that, "Those that are attached to the living God do all live."[6]

Is not this, then, a thrice happy life, a thrice blessed existence, to be contented with performing due service to the most venerable Cause of all things, and not to think fit to serve his subordinate ministers and door-keepers in preference to the King himself? And this life is an immortal one, and is recorded as one of great duration in the pillars of nature. And it is inevitably necessary that these writings should last to all eternity with the world itself.

VI. (32) But the Father and Ruler of the universe is a being whose character it is difficult to arrive at by conjecture and hard to comprehend; but still we must not on that account shrink from an investigation of it. Now, in the investigations

---

[5] Leviticus 19:4.

[6] Deuteronomy 4:4.

which are made into the nature of God, there are two things of the greatest importance, about which the intellect of the man who devotes himself to philosophy in a genuine spirit is perplexed. One is, whether there is any Deity at all? this question arises from the atheism (which is the greatest of all vices) of those men who study philosophy. The other question is, supposing there to be a God, what he is as to his essence?

Now the former question it is not very difficult to determine; but the second is not only difficult, but perhaps impossible. We must, however, consider both these matters.

(33) It has invariably happened that the works which they have made have been, in some degree, the proofs of the character of the workmen; for who is there who, when he looks upon statues or pictures, does not at once form an idea of the statuary or painter himself? And who, when he beholds a garment, or a ship, or a house, does not in a moment conceive a notion of the weaver, or shipbuilder, or architect, who has made them?

And if any one comes into a well-ordered city, in which all parts of the constitution are exceedingly well arranged and regulated, what other idea will he entertain but that this city is governed by wise and virtuous rulers? (34) He, therefore, who comes into that which is truly the greatest of cities, namely, this world, and who beholds all the land, both the mountain and the champaign district full of animals, and plants, and the streams of rivers, both overflowing and depending on the wintry floods, and the steady flow of the sea, and the admirable temperature of the air, and the varieties and regular revolutions of the seasons of the year; and then too the sun and moon, the rulers of day and night, and the revolutions and regular motions of all the other planets and fixed stars, and of the whole heaven; would he not naturally, or I should rather say, of necessity, conceive a notion of the Father, and creator, and governor of all this system; (35) for there is no artificial work whatever which exists of its own accord? And the world is the most artificial and skilfully made of all works, as if it had been put together by some one who was altogether accomplished and most perfect in knowledge.

It is in this way that we have received an idea of the existence of God.

VII. (36) Again, even if it is very difficult to ascertain and very hard properly to comprehend, we must still, as far as it is possible, investigate the nature of his essence; for there is no employment more excellent than that of searching out the nature of the true God, even though the discovery may transcend all human ability, since the very desire and endeavour to comprehend it is able by itself to furnish indescribable pleasures and delights. (37) And the witnesses of this fact are those who have not merely tasted philosophy with

their outermost lips, but who have abundantly feasted on its reasonings and its doctrines; for the reasoning of these men, being raised on high far above the earth, roams in the air, and soaring aloft with the sun, and moon, and all the firmament of heaven, being eager to behold all the things that exist therein, finds its power of vision somewhat indistinct from a vast quantity of unalloyed light being poured over it, so that the eye of his soul becomes dazzled and confused by the splendour.

(38) But he does not on that account faint and renounce the task which he has undertaken, but goes on with invincible determination towards the sight which he considers attainable, as if he were a competitor at the games, and were striving for the second prize, though he has missed the first. And guess and conjecture are inferior to true perception, as are all those notions which are classed under the description of reasonable and plausible opinions.

(39) Though, therefore, we do not know and cannot accurately ascertain what each of the stars is as to its pure and real essence, still we are eager to investigate the subject, delighting in probable reasonings, because of the fondness for learning which is implanted in our nature. (40) And so in the same way, though we cannot attain to a distinct conception of the truly living God, we still ought not to renounce the task of investigating his character, because even if we fail to make the discovery, the very search itself is intrinsically useful and an object of deserved ambition; since no one ever blames the eyes of the body because they are unable to look upon the sun itself, and therefore shrink from the brilliancy which is poured upon them from its beams, and therefore look down upon the earth, shrinking from the extreme brilliancy of the rays of the sun.

VIII. (41) Which that interpreter of the divine word, Moses, the man most beloved by God, having a regard to, besought God and said, "Show me thyself"—all but urging him, and crying out in loud and distinct words—"that thou hast a real being and existence the whole world is my teacher, assuring me of the fact and instructing me as a son might of the existence of his father, or the work of the existence of the workman. But, though I am very desirous to know what thou art as to thy essence, I can find no one who is able to explain to me anything relating to this branch of learning in any part of the universe whatever. (42) On which account, I beg and entreat of thee to receive the supplication of a man who is thy suppliant and devoted to God's service, and desirous to serve thee alone; for as the light is not known by the agency of anything else, but is itself its own manifestation, so also thou must alone be able to manifest thyself. For which reason I hope to receive pardon, if, from want of any one to teach me, I am so bold as to flee to thee, desiring to receive instruction from thyself."

(43) But God replied, "I receive, indeed, your eagerness, inasmuch as it is praiseworthy; but the request which you make is not fitting to be granted to any created being. And I only bestow such gifts as are appropriate to him who receives them; for it is not possible for a man to receive all that it is easy for me to give. On which account I give to him who is deserving of my favour all the gifts which he is able to receive. (44) But not only is the nature of mankind, but even the whole heaven and the whole world is unable to attain to an adequate comprehension of me. So know yourself, and be not carried away with impulses and desires beyond your power; and let not a desire of unattainable objects carry you away and keep you in suspense. For you shall not lack anything which may be possessed by you."

(45) When Moses heard this he betook himself to a second supplication, and said, "I am persuaded by thy explanations that I should not have been able to receive the visible appearance of thy form. But I beseech thee that I may, at all events, behold the glory that is around thee. And I look upon thy glory to be the powers which attend thee as thy guards, the comprehension of which having escaped me up to the present time, worketh in me no slight desire of a thorough understanding of it."

(46) But God replied and said, "The powers which you seek to behold are altogether invisible, and appreciable only by the intellect; since I myself am invisible and only appreciable by the intellect. And what I call appreciable only by the intellect are not those which are already comprehended by the mind, but those which, even if they could be so comprehended, are still such that the outward senses could not at all attain to them, but only the very purest intellect. (47) And though they are by nature incomprehensible in their essence, still they show a kind of impression or copy of their energy and operation; as seals among you, when any wax or similar kind of material is applied to them, make an innumerable quantity of figures and impressions, without being impaired as to any portion of themselves, but still remaining unaltered and as they were before; so also you must conceive that the powers which are around me invest those things which have no distinctive qualities with such qualities, and those which have no forms with precise forms, and that without having any portion of their own everlasting nature dismembered or weakened. (48) And some of your race, speaking with sufficient correctness, call them ideas (ideai), since they give a peculiar character (idiopoiousi) to every existing thing, arranging what had previously no order, and limiting, and defining, and fashioning what was before destitute of all limitation, and defination, and fashion; and,

in short, in all respects changing what was bad into a better condition.

(49) "Do not, then, ever expect to be able to comprehend me nor any one of my powers, in respect of our essence. But, as I have said, I willingly and cheerfully grant unto you such things as you may receive. And this gift is to call you to the beholding of the world and all the things that are in it, which must be comprehended, not indeed by the eyes of the body, but by the sleepless vision of the soul. (50) The desire of wisdom alone is continual and incessant, and it fills all its pupils and disciples with famous and most beautiful doctrines."

When Moses heard this he did not cease from his desire, but he still burned with a longing for the understanding of invisible things. [...][7]

IX. (51) And he receives all persons of a similar character and disposition, whether they were originally born so, or whether they have become so through any change of conduct, having become better people, and as such entitled to be ranked in a superior class; approving of the one body because they have not defaced their nobility of birth, and of the other because they have thought fit to alter their lives so as to come over to nobleness of conduct. And these last he calls proselytes (proselytous), from the fact of their having come over (proselelythenai) to a new and God-fearing constitution, learning to disregard the fabulous inventions of other nations, and clinging to unalloyed truth.

(52) Accordingly, having given equal rank and honour to all those who come over, and having granted to them the same favours that were bestowed on the native Jews, he recommends those who are ennobled by truth not only to treat them with respect, but even with especial friendship and excessive benevolence. And is not this a reasonable recommendation? What he says is this.

"Those men, who have left their country, and their friends, and their relations for the sake of virtue and holiness, ought not to be left destitute of some other cities, and houses, and friends, but there ought to be places of refuge always ready for those who come over to religion; for the most effectual allurement and the most indissoluble bond of affectionate good will is the mutual honouring of the one God." (53) Moreover, he also enjoins his people that, after they have given the proselytes an equal share in all their laws, and privileges, and immunities, on their forsaking the pride of their fathers and forefathers, they must not give a license to their jealous language and unbridled tongues, blaspheming those beings whom the other body

---

[7] Mangey thinks that there is a considerable hiatus here. What follows relates to the regulations respecting proselytes, which as the text stands is in no way connected with what has gone before about the worship of God.

looks upon as gods, lest the proselytes should be exasperated at such treatment, and in return utter impious language against the true and holy God; for from ignorance of the difference between them, and by reason of their having from their infancy learnt to look upon what was false as if it had been true, and having been bred up with it, they would be likely to err.

(54) And there are some of the Gentiles, who, not attending to the honour due to the one God alone, deserve to be punished with extreme severity of punishment, as having forsaken the most important classification of piety and holiness, and as having chosen darkness in preference to the most brilliant light, and having rendered their own intellect blind when it might have seen clearly. (55) And it is well that a charge should be given to all those who have any admiration for virtue to inflict all such punishment out of hand without any delay, not bringing them before either any judgment seat, or any council, or any bench of magistrates, but giving vent to their own disposition which hates evil and loves God, so as to chastise the impious with implacable rigour, looking upon themselves as everything for the time being, counsellors, and judges, and generals, and members of the assembly, and accusers, and witnesses, and laws, and the people; that so, since there is no conceivable hindrance, they may with all their company put themselves forward fearlessly to fight as the champions of holiness.

X. (56) There is, in the history of the law, a record of one man who ventured on this exploit of noble daring, for when he saw some men connecting themselves with foreign women, and by reason of their allurements neglecting all their national customs and laws, and practising fabulous ceremonies, he was seized with a sudden enthusiasm in the presence of the whole multitude; and driving away all those on each side who were collected to see the sight, he slew one man who was so daring as to put himself forward as the leader and chief of this transgression of the law (for the impious deed had been already displayed and made a public exhibition of), and while he was openly performing sacrifices to images and unholy idols, he, I say, without being influenced by any fear, slew him, together with the woman who was with him; the one on account of his inclination to learn those things which it would have been more advantageous for him not to have learnt, and the woman because she was his preceptress in evil.

(57) This action being done of a sudden, in the warm impetuosity of the moment, admonished a vast multitude of those who were prepared to commit similar follies; therefore God, having praised this virtuous exploit done in this manner, out of a voluntary and spontaneous zeal, recompensed the doer with two rewards, namely, peace and the priesthood. With the one, because he judged him

who had thus voluntarily encountered a contest for the sake of the honour of his God worthy to enjoy a life safe from war; and with the other, because the priesthood is the most fitting honour for a pious man, who professes an eagerness for the service of the Father of all, to serve whom is not only better than all freedom, but even than royal authority.

(58) But some men have gone to such a pitch of extravagant madness, that they have left themselves no retreat or way to repentance, but hasten onwards to the slavery and service of images made by hands, confessing it in distinct characters, not written on paper, as is the custom in the case of slaves, but branding the characters deep on their persons with a burning iron, in order that they may remain ineffacebly, for these things are not dimmed or weakened by time.

XI. (59) And the most sacred Moses appears to have preserved the same object and intention in all other cases whatever, being a lover and also a teacher of truth, which he desires to stamp and to impress upon all his disciples, expelling all false opinions, and compelling them to settle far from their minds. (60) At all events, knowing that the act of divination co-operates in no slight degree with the errors of the lives of the multitude, so as to lead them out of the right way, he did not suffer his disciples to use any species of it whatever, but drove all who paid it any observance far from his everlasting constitution, and banished all sacrificers and purifiers, and augurs, and soothsayers, and enchanters, and men who applied themselves to the art of prophesying from sounds; (61) for all these men are but guessers at what is probable and likely, at different times adopting different notions from the same appearances, because the subjects of their art have no stable and constant character, and because the intellect has never devised any accurate test by which those opinions which are approved may be examined.

(62) And all these things are but the furniture of impiety. How so? Because he who attends to them, and who allows himself to be influenced by them, disregards the cause of all things, looking upon those things alone as the causes of all things, whether good or evil; and he does not perceive that he is making all the cares of life to depend upon the most unstable supports, upon the motion of birds and feathers in the air, in this and that direction; and upon the paths of reptiles, crawling along the ground, which creep forth out of their holes in quest of food; and even upon entrails, and blood, and dead corpses, which, the moment that they are deprived of life, fall to pieces and become confused; and being deprived of their original nature which belonged to them, are changed, and subjected to a transformation for the worse.

(63) For he thinks it right, that the man who is legally enrolled as a citizen of his constitution

must be perfect, not indeed in those things in which the multitude is educated, such as divination, and augury, and plausible conjectures, but in the observances due to God, which have nothing doubtful or uncertain about them, but only indubitable and naked truth.

(64) And since there is implanted in all men a desire of the knowledge of future events, and as, on account of this desire, they have recourse to sacrifices and to other species of divination, as if by these means they would be able to search out and discover the truth (but these things are, in reality, full of indistinctness and uncertainty, and are continually being convicted by themselves). He, with great energy, forbids his disciples to apply themselves to such sources of knowledge; and he says, that if they are truly pious they shall not be deprived of a proper knowledge of the future; (65) but that some other prophet[8] will appear to them on a sudden, inspired like himself, who will preach and prophesy among them, saying nothing of his own (for he who is truly possessed and inspired, even when he speaks, is unable to comprehend what he is himself saying), but that all the words that he should utter would proceed from him as if another was prompting him; for the prophets are interpreters of God, who is only using their voices as instruments, in order to explain what he chooses.

Having now then said this, and other things like this, concerning the proper idea to be entertained of the one real, and true, and living God; he proceeds to express in what manner one ought to pay him the honours that are his due.[9]

XII. (66) We ought to look upon the universal world as the highest and truest temple of God, having for its most holy place that most sacred part of the essence of all existing things, namely, the heaven; and for ornaments, the stars; and for priests, the subordinate ministers of his power, namely, the angels, incorporeal souls, not beings compounded of irrational and rational natures, such as our bodies are, but such as have the irrational parts wholly cut out, being absolutely and wholly intellectual, pure reasonings, resembling the unit.

(67) But the other temple is made with hands; for it was desirable not to cut short the impulses of men who were eager to bring in contributions for the objects of piety, and desirous either to show their gratitude by sacrifices for such good fortune

as had befallen them, or else to implore pardon and forgiveness for whatever errors they might have committed. He moreover foresaw that there could not be any great number of temples built either in many different places, or in the same place, thinking it fitting that as God is one, his temple also should be one.

(68) In the next place, he does not permit those who desire to perform sacrifices in their own houses to do so, but he orders all men to rise up, even from the furthest boundaries of the earth, and to come to this temple, by which command he is at the same time testing their dispositions most severely; for he who was not about to offer sacrifice in a pure and holy spirit would never endure to quit his country, and his friends, and relations, and emigrate into a distant land, but would be likely, being under the influence of a more powerful attraction than that towards piety, to continue attached to the society of his most intimate friends and relations as portions of himself, to which he was most closely attached. (69) And the most evident proof of this may be found in the events which actually took place.

For innumerable companies of men from a countless variety of cities, some by land and some by sea, from east and from west, from the north and from the south, came to the temple at every festival, as if to some common refuge and safe asylum from the troubles of this most busy and painful life, seeking to find tranquillity, and to procure a remission of and respite from those cares by which from their earliest infancy they had been hampered and weighed down, (70) and so, by getting breath as it were, to pass a brief time in cheerful festivities, being filled with good hopes and enjoying the leisure of that most important and necessary vacation which consists in forming a friendship with those hitherto unknown, but now initiated by boldness and a desire to honour God, and forming a combination of actions and a union of dispositions so as to join in sacrifices and libations to the most complete confirmation of mutual good will.

XIII. (71) Of this temple the outer circuit, being the most extensive both in length and width, was fortified by fortifications adorned in a most costly manner. And each of them is a double portico, built and adorned with the finest materials of wood and stone, and with abundant supplies of all kinds, and with the greatest skill of the workmen, and the most diligent care on the part of the superintendants. But the inner circuits were less extensive, and the fashion of their building and adorning was more simple. (72) And in the centre was the temple itself, beautiful beyond all possible description, as one may conjecture from what is now seen around on the outside; for what is innermost is invisible to every human creature except the high

---

[8] This prophecy, Deuteronomy 18:18, is always looked upon as one of the most remarkable of the early prophecies of our Saviour.

[9] Yonge's translation includes a separate treatise title at this point: *On the Monarchy, Book II.* Accordingly, his next paragraph begins with roman numeral I (=XII in the Loeb). Yonge's "treatise" concludes with number XV (=XXVI in the Loeb). The publisher has elected to follow the Loeb numbering.

priest alone, and even he is enjoined only to enter that holy place once in each year.

Everything then is invisible. For he carries in a brasier full of coals and frankincense; and then, when a great smoke proceeds from it, as is natural, and when everything all around is enveloped in it, then the sight of men is clouded, and checked, and prevented from penetrating in, being wholly unable to pierce the cloud. (73) But, being very large and very lofty, although built in a very low situation, it is not inferior to any of the greatest mountains around. The buildings of it are of most exceeding beauty and magnificence, so as to be universal objects of admiration to all who behold them, and especially to all foreigners who travel to those parts, and who, comparing them with their own public edifices, marvel both at the beauty and sumptuousness of this one.

(74) But there is no grove of plantation in the space which surrounds it, in accordance with the prohibitions of the law, which for many reasons forbid this. In the first place, because a building which is truly a temple does not aim at pleasure and seductive allurements, but at a rigid and austere sanctity. Secondly, because it is not proper that those things which conduce to the verdure of trees should be introduced, such as the dung of irrational animals and of men. Thirdly, because those trees which do not admit of cultivation are of no use, but are as the poets say, the burden of the earth; while those which do admit of cultivation, and which are productive of wholesome fruit, draw off the attention of the fickle-minded from the thoughts of the respect due to the holy place itself, and to the ceremonies in which they are engaged. (75) And besides these reasons, shady places and dense thickets are places of refuge for evil doers, since by their enveloping them in darkness they give them safety and enable them, as from an ambuscade, suddenly to fall upon any whom they choose to attack. But wide spaces, open and uncovered in every direction, where there is nothing which can hinder the sight, are the most suitable for the distinct sight of all those who enter and remain in the temple.

XIV. (76) But the temple has for its revenues not only portions of land, but also other possessions of much greater extent and importance, which will never be destroyed or diminished; for as long as the race of mankind shall last, the revenues likewise of the temple will always be preserved, being coeval in their duration with the universal world. (77) For it is commanded that all men shall every year bring their first fruits to the temple, from twenty years old and upwards; and this contribution is called their ransom. On which account they bring in the first fruits with exceeding cheerfulness, being joyful and delighted, inasmuch as simultaneously with their making the offering they are sure to find either a relaxation

from slavery, or a relief from disease, and to receive in all respects a most sure freedom and safety for the future.

(78) And since the nation is the most numerous of all peoples, it follows naturally that the first fruits contributed by them must also be most abundant. Accordingly there is in almost every city a storehouse for the sacred things to which it is customary for the people to come and there to deposit their first fruits, and at certain seasons there are sacred ambassadors selected on account of their virtue, who convey the offerings to the temple. And the most eminent men of each tribe are elected to this office, that they may conduct the hopes of each individual safe to their destination; for in the lawful offering of the first fruits are the hopes of the pious.

XV. (79) Now there are twelve tribes of the nation, and one of them having been selected from the others for its excellence has received the priesthood, receiving this honour as a reward for its virtue, and fidelity, and its devout soul, which it displayed when the multitude appeared to be running into sin, following the foolish choices of some persons who persuaded their countrymen to imitate the vanity of the Egyptians, and the pride of the nations of the land, who had invented fables about irrational animals, and especially about bulls, making gods of them. For this tribe did of its own accord go forth and slay all the leaders of this apostacy from the youth upwards, in which they appeared to have done a holy action, encountering thus a contest and a labour for the sake of piety.

XVI. (80) Now these are the laws which relate to the priests. It is enjoined that the priest shall be entire and unmutilated, having no blemish on his body, no part being deficient, either naturally or through mutilation; and on the other hand, nothing having been superfluous either from his birth or having grown out subsequently from disease; his skin, also, must never have changed from leprosy, or wild lichen, or scab, or any other eruption or breaking out; all which things appear to me to be designed to be symbols of the purity of his soul. (81) For if it was necessary to examine the mortal body of the priest that it ought not be imperfect through any misfortune, much more was it necessary to look into his immortal soul, which they say is fashioned in the form of the living God.

Now the image of God is the Word, by which all the world was made. (82) And after enjoining that the priest is to be of pure blood, and sprung from fathers of noble birth, and that he must be perfect in body and soul, laws are enacted also respecting the garments which the priest must wear when he is about to offer the sacred sacrifices and to perform the sacred ceremonies. (83) And this dress is a linen tunic and a girdle, the latter to cover those parts which must not be displayed in their nakedness near the altar of sacrifice. And the tunic is for the sake of promptness in performing the requisite ministrations; for they are but lightly clad, only in their tunics, when they bring their victims, and the libations, and the other requisite offerings for sacrifice, being apparelled so as to admit of unhesitating celerity.

(84) But the high priest is commanded to wear a similar dress when he goes into the holy of holies to offer incense, because linen is not made of any animal that dies, as woollen garments are. He is also commanded to wear another robe also, having very beautiful embroidery and ornament upon it, so that it may seem to be a copy and representation of the world. And the description of the ornament is a clear proof of this; (85) for in the first place the whole of the round robe is of hyacinthine colour, a tunic reaching to the feet, being an emblem of the air, since the air also is by nature black, and in a manner may be said to be reaching to the feet, as it is extended from above from the regions about the moon, to the lowest places of the earth. (86) Next there was a woven garment in the form of a breastplate upon it, and this was a symbol of the heaven; for on the points of the shoulders are two emerald stones of most exceeding value, one on one side and one on the other, each perfectly round and single on each side, as emblems of the hemispheres, one of which is above the earth and the other under the earth. (87) Then on his chest there are twelve precious stones of different colours, arranged in four rows of three stones in each row, being fashioned so as an emblem of the zodiac. For the zodiac also consists of twelve animals, and so divides the four seasons of the year, allotting three animals to each season.

(88) And the whole place is very correctly called the logeum *(logeion)*, since every thing in heaven has been created and arranged in accordance with right reason *(logois)* and proportion; for there is absolutely nothing there which is devoid of reason. And on the logeum he embroiders two woven pieces of cloth, calling the one manifestation and the other truth. (89) And by the one which he calls truth he expresses figuratively that it is absolutely impossible for falsehood to enter any part of heaven, but that it is entirely banished to the parts around the earth, dwelling among the souls of impious men. And by that which he calls manifestation he implies that the natures in heaven make manifest every thing that takes place among us, which of themselves would be perfectly and universally unknown.

(90) And the clearest proof of this is that if there were no light, and if the sun did not shine, it would be impossible for the indescribable variety of qualities of bodies to be seen, and for all the manifold differences of colours and forms to be distinguished from one another. And what else could exhibit to us the days and the nights, and

the months and the years, and in short the divisions of time, but the harmonious and inconceivable revolutions of the sun, and moon, and other stars? (91) And what could exhibit the true nature of number, except those same bodies just mentioned in accordance with the observation of the combination of the parts of time? And what else could have cut the paths through the ocean and through such numerous and vast seas, and shown them to navigators, except the changes and periodical appearances of the stars? And wise men have observed, (92) also, an innumerable quantity of other circumstances, and have recorded them, conjecturing from the heavenly bodies the advent of calm weather and of violent storms, and the fertility or barrenness of crops, and the mild or violently hot summers, and whether the winters will be severe or spring-like, whether there will be droughts or abundance of rain, whether the flocks and trees will be fruitful, or on the contrary barren, and all such matters as these. For the signs of every thing on earth are engraved and firmly fixed in heaven.

XVII. (93) And besides this, golden pomegranates are attached to the lower parts of the tunic, reaching to the feet, and bells and borders embroidered with flowers.

And these things are the emblems of earth and of water; the flowers are the emblems of the earth, inasmuch as it is out of it that they all rise and derive strength to bloom. And the pomegranates[10] as above mentioned are the emblems of water, being so named from the flowing of the stream. And the harmony, and concord, and unison of sound of the different parts of the world is betokened by the bells. (94) And the arrangement is a very excellent one; for the upper garment, on which the stones are placed, which is called the breast-plate, is a representation of heaven, because the heaven also is the highest of all things.

And the tunic that reaches to the feet is in every part of a hyacinthine colour, since the air also is black, and is placed in the second classification next in honour to the heaven. And the embroidered flowers and pomegranates are on the hem, because the earth and water have been assigned the lowest situation in the universe.

(95) This is the arrangement of the sacred dress of the high priest, being a representation of the universe, a marvellous work to be beheld or to be contemplated. For it has an appearance thoroughly calculated to excite astonishment, such as no embroidered work conceived by man ever was for variety and costly magnificence; (96) and it also attracts the intellect of philosophers to ex-

---

[10]The Greek for a pomegranate is *rhoia*, or *rhoiskos*, which Philo imagines to be derived from *rheō*, "to flow."

amine its different parts. For God intends that the high priest should in the first place have a visible representation of the universe about him, in order that from the continual sight of it he may be reminded to make his own life worthy of the nature of the universe, and secondly, in order that the whole world may co-operate with him in the performance of his sacred rites.

And it is exceedingly becoming that the man who is consecrated to the service of the Father of the world should also bring his son to the service of him who has begotten him.

(97) There is also a third symbol contained in this sacred dress, which it is important not to pass over in silence. For the priests of other deities are accustomed to offer up prayers and sacrifices solely for their own relations, and friends, and fellow citizens. But the high priest of the Jews offers them up not only on behalf of the whole race of mankind, but also on behalf of the different parts of nature, of the earth, of water, of air, and of fire; and pours forth his prayers and thanksgivings for them all, looking upon the world (as indeed it really is) as his country, for which, therefore, he is accustomed to implore and propitiate its governor by supplications and prayers, beseeching him to give a portion of his own merciful and humane nature to the things which he has created.

XVIII. (98) After he has given these precepts, he issues additional commandments, and orders him, whenever he approaches the altar and touches the sacrifices, at the time when it is appointed for him to perform his sacred ministrations, not to drink wine or any other strong drink, on account of four most important reasons, hesitation, and forgetfulness, and sleep, and folly. (99) For the intemperate man relaxes the powers of his body, and renders his limbs more slow of motion, and makes his whole body more inclined to hesitation, and compels it by force to become drowsy. And he also relaxes the energies of his soul, and so becomes the cause to it of forgetfulness and folly. But in the case of abstemious men all the parts of the body are lighter, and as such more active and moveable, and the outer senses are more pure and unalloyed, and the mind is gifted with a more acute sight, so that it is able to see things beforehand, and never forgets what it has previously seen; (100) in short, therefore, we must look upon the use of wine to be a most unprofitable thing for all the purposes of life, inasmuch as by it the soul is weighed down, the outward senses are dimmed, and the body is enervated.

For it does not leave any one of our faculties free and unembarrassed, but is a hindrance to every one of them, so as to impede its attaining that object to which it is by nature fitted. But in sacred ceremonies and holy rites the mischief is most grievous of all, in proportion as it is worse and more intolerable to sin with respect to God

than with respect to man. On which account it probably is that it is commanded to the priest to offer up sacrifices without wine, in order to make a difference and distinction between sacred and profane things, and pure and impure things, and lawful and unlawful things.

XIX. (101) But since the priest was a man before he was a priest, and since he is of necessity desirous to indulge the appetites which prompt him to seek for the connections of love, he procures for him a marriage with a pure virgin, and one who is born of pure parents, and grandfathers, and great-grandfathers, selected for their excellency with reference both to their virtue and to their noble birth. (102) For God does not allow him even to look upon a harlot, or a profane body or soul, or upon any one who, having put away her pursuit of gain, now wears an elegant and modest appearance, because such a one is unholy in respect of her former profession and way of life; though in other respects she may be looked upon as honourable, by reason of her having purified herself of her former evil courses. For repentance for past sins is a thing to be praised; and no one else need be forbidden to marry her, only let her not come near a priest. For the especial property of the priesthood is justice and purity, which from the first beginning of its creation to the end, seeks a concord utterly irreproachable.

(103) For it would be mere folly that some men should be excluded from the priesthood by reason of the scars which exist on their bodies from ancient wounds, which are the emblem of misfortune indeed, but not of wickedness; but that those persons who, not at all out of necessity but from their own deliberate choice, have made a market of their beauty, when at last they slowly repent, should at once after leaving their lovers become united to priests, and should come from brothels and be admitted into the sacred precincts. For the scars and impressions of their old offences remain not the less in the souls of those who repent. (104) On which account it is wisely and truly said in another passage, that "One may not bring the hire of a harlot into the temple."[11] And yet the money is not in itself liable to any reproach, except by reason of the woman who received it, and the action for which it was given to her. How then could one possibly admit those women to consort with priests whose very money is looked upon as profane and base, even though as to its material and stamp it may be good and lawful money?

XX. (105) The regulations, therefore, are laid down with precision in this manner for the high priest, so that he is not allowed either to marry a widow, nor one who is left desolate after the death of the man to whom she has been espoused,

---

[11] Deuteronomy 23:18.

nor one who has been divorced from a husband who is still alive, in order that the sacred seed may be sown for the first time in a field which is hitherto untrodden and pure, and that his offspring may have no admixture of the blood of any other house. And in the second place, in order that the pair coming together with souls which have as yet known no defilement or perversion, may easily form their dispositions and characters in a virtuous manner. For the minds of virgins are easily attracted and drawn over to virtue, being exceedingly ready to be taught.

(106) But the woman who has had experience of another husband is very naturally less inclined to obedience and to instruction, inasmuch as she has not a soul perfectly pure, like thoroughly smooth wax, so as to receive distinctly the doctrines which are to be impressed upon it, but one which is to a certain degree rough from the impressions which have been already stamped upon it, which are difficult to be effaced, and so remain, and do not easily receive any other impression, or if they do they render it confused by the irregularity of their own surface. (107) Let the high priest, therefore, take a pure virgin to be his wife; I say a virgin, meaning not only one with whom no other man has even been connected, but one in connection with whom no other man has ever been named in reference to the agreement of marriage, even though her body may be pure.

XXI. (108) But besides this, injunctions are given to the particular and inferior priests concerning their marriages, which are the very same in most points, which are given to those who have the supreme priesthood. But they are permitted with impunity to marry not only maidens but widows also; not, indeed, all widows, but those whose husbands are dead. For the law thinks it fitting to remove all quarrels and disputes from the life of the priests. And if they had husbands living there very likely might be disputes from the jealousy which is caused by the love of men for women. But when the first husband is dead, then with him the hostility which could be felt towards the second husband dies also. (109) And even on other accounts he might have thought that the high priest ought to be of superior purity and holiness, as in other matters so also in the connection of marriage, and on this account it may have been that God only allowed the high priest to marry a virgin.

But to the priests of the second rank he remitted something of the rigour of his regulations concerning the connection with women, permitting them to marry women who have made trials of other husbands.

XXII. (110) And besides these commands, he also defined precisely the family of the women who might be married by the high priest, commanding him to marry not merely a woman who was a virgin, but also one who was a priestess, the daughter of a priest, that so both bridegroom and bride might be of one house, and in a manner of one blood, so as to display a most lasting harmony and union of disposition during the whole of their lives. (111) The others also were permitted to marry women who were not the daughters of priests, partly because their purificatory sacrifices are of but small importance, and partly because he was not willing entirely to disunite and separate the whole nation from the order of the priesthood; for which reason he did not prevent the other priests from making intermarriages with any of their countrywomen, as that is relationship in the second degree; for sons-in-law are in the place of sons to their fathers-in-law, and fathers-in-law instead of fathers to their sons-in-law.

XXIII. (112) These, then, are the ordinances which were established respecting marriage, and respecting what greatly resembles marriage, the procreation of children. But since destruction follows creation, Moses also gave the priests laws relating to death,[12] commanding them not to permit themselves to be defiled in respect of all people whatsoever, who might happen to die, and who might be connected with them through some bond of friendship, or distant relationship: but allowing them to mourn for six classes only, their fathers or their mothers, their sons of their daughters, their brothers or their sisters, provided that these last were virgins; (113) but the high priest he absolutely forbade to mourn in any case whatever; and may we not say that this was rightly done? For as to the ministrations which belong to the other priests, one individual can perform them instead of another, so that, even if some be in mourning, still none of the usual observances need be omitted; but there is no one besides the high priest himself, who is permitted to perform his duties instead of him; for which reason, he must always be kept free from all defilement, never touching any dead body, in order that, being always ready to offer up prayers and sacrifices on behalf of the whole world at suitable seasons, he may continue to fulfil the duties of his office without hindrance.

(114) And otherwise too, besides this consideration, the man who has been assigned to God, and who has become the leader of his sacred band of worshippers, ought to be disconnected with, and alienated from, all things of creation, not being so much the slave of the love of either parents, or children, or brothers, as either to omit or to delay any one of those holy actions, which it is by all means better should be done at once; (115) and God commands the high priest neither to rend his clothes over his very nearest relations when they die, nor to take from his head the ensign of the priesthood, nor in short to depart from the holy

---

[12] Leviticus 23:1.

place on any plea of mourning, that, showing proper respect to the place, and to the sacred ornaments with which he himself is crowned, he may show himself superior to pity, and pass the whole of his life exempt from all sorrow.

(116) For the law designs that he should be the partaker of a nature superior to that of man; inasmuch as he approaches more nearly to that of the Deity; being, if one must say the plain truth, on the borders between the two, in order that men may propitiate God by some mediator, and that God may have some subordinate minister by whom he may offer and give his mercies and kindnesses to mankind.

XXIV. (117) After he has said this, he immediately proceeds to lay down laws, concerning those who are to use the first fruits, "If therefore, any one,"[13] says he, "should mutilate the priests as to their eyes, or their feet, or any part of their bodies, or if he should have received any blemish, let him not partake of the sacred ministrations by reason of the defects which exist in him, but still let him enjoy those honours which are common to all the priests, because of his irreproachable nobility of birth." (118) "Moreover, if any leprosies break out and attack him or if any one of the priests be afflicted with any flux, let him not touch the sacred table, nor any of the duties which are set apart for his race, until the flux stop, or the leprosy change, so that he become again resembling the complexion of sound flesh."[14]

(119) And, if any priest do by any chance whatever touch anything that is unclean, or if he should have impure dreams by night, as is very often apt to be the case, let him during all that day touch nothing that has been consecrated, but let him wash himself and the ensuing evening, and after that let him not be hindered from touching them. (120) And let the sojourner in the priest's house, and the hireling, be prevented from approaching the first fruits; the sojourner, because it is not every one who is a neighbour who shares a man's hearth and eats at his table;[15] for there is reason to fear that some such person may cast away what is hallowed, using as a cloak for his impiety the pretence of some unseasonable humanity; for one might not give all men a share of all things, but only of such as are adapted to those who are to receive them; otherwise, that which is the most beautiful and most beneficial of all the things in this life, namely order, will be wasted away and destroyed by that which is the most mischievous of all things, namely, confusion.

(121) For if in merchant vessels the sailors were to receive an equal share with the pilot of the ship, and if in ships of war the rowers and the mariners were to receive an equal share with the captain, and if in military camps the cavalry of the line were to receive an equal share with their officers, the heavy armed infantry with their colonels, and the colonels with the generals; again, if in cities the parties before the court were to be placed on the same footing with the judges, the committeemen with the ministers, and in short private individuals with the magistrates, there would be incessant troubles and seditions, and the equality in words would produce inequality in fact; for it is an unequal measure to give equal honour to persons who are unequal in rank or desert; and inequality is the root of all evil. (122) On which account one must not give the honours of the priests to sojourners, just as one must not give them to any one else, who in that case, because of their proximity, would be meddling with what they have no business; for the honour does not belong to the house, but to the race.

XXV. (123) In like manner, no one must give this sacred honour to a hireling, as his wages, or as a recompense for his service; for sometimes he who receives it being unholy will employ it for illegitimate purposes, making the honours due to purity of birth common, and profaning all the sacred ceremonies and observances relating to the temple; (124) on which account the law altogether forbids any foreigner to partake in any degree of the holy things, even if he be a man of the noblest birth among the natives of the land, and irreproachable as respects both men and women, in order that the sacred honours may not be adulterated, but may remain carefully guarded in the family of the priests; (125) for it would be absurd that the sacrifices and holy ordinances, and all the other sacred observances pertaining to the altar, should be entrusted not to all men but to the priests alone; but that the rewards for the performance of those things should be common and liable to fall to the share of any chance persons, as if it were reasonable that the priests should be worn out with labours and toils, and nightly and daily cares, but that the rewards for such pains should be common and open to those who do nothing.

(126) But, he proceeds, let the priest who is his master give to the slave who is born in his house, and to him who has been purchased with money, a share of meat and drink from the first fruits. In the first place, because the master is the only source of supply to the servant, and the inheritance of the master are the sacred offices of humanity, by which the slave must necessarily be supported. (127) In the second place, because it is by all means necessary that they should not do what is to be done unwillingly; and servants, even though we may not like it, since they are always about us and living with us, preparing meat, and drink, and delicacies for their masters beforehand,

---

[13]Leviticus 21:17.
[14]Leviticus 22:4.
[15]Leviticus 22:10.

and standing at their tables, and carrying away the fragments that are left, even though they may not take any openly, will at all events secretly appropriate some of the victuals, being compelled by necessity to steal, so that instead of one injury (if indeed it is an injury to their masters that they should be supported at their expense), they are compelled to add a second to it, namely, theft; in order that, like thieves, they may enjoy what has been consecrated by their masters who live irreproachably themselves; which is the most unreasonable thing possible.

(128) Thirdly, one ought to take this also into consideration, that share of the first fruits will not be neglected merely because they are distributed to the servants, through their fear of their masters; for this is sufficient to stop their mouths, preventing the arrogance of such persons from showing itself.

XXVI. (129) Having said thus much he proceeds next to put forth a law full of humanity. If, says he, the daughter of a priest, having married a man who is not a priest, becomes a widow by the death of her husband, or if she be left childless while he is still alive, let her return again to her father's house, to receive her share of the first fruits which she enjoyed when she was a virgin;[16] for in some degree and in effect she is now also a virgin, since she has neither husband nor children, and has no other refuge but her father; (130) but if she has sons or daughters, then the mother must of necessity be classed with the children; and the sons and daughters, being ranked as of the family of their father, draw their mother also with them into his house.[17]

XXVII. (131) The law did not allot any share of the land to the priests, in order that they like others might derive revenues from the land, and so possess a sufficiency of necessary things; but admitting them to an excessive degree of honour, he said that God was their inheritance, having a reference to the things offered to God; for the sake of two objects, both that of doing them the highest honour, since they are thus made partners in those things which are offered up by pious men, out of gratitude to God; and also in order that they might have no business about which to trouble themselves except the offices of religion, as they would have had, if they were forced to take care of their inheritance.

And the following are the rewards and pre-

eminent honours which he assigns to them; (132) in the first place, that the necessary food for their support shall at all times be provided for them without any labour or toil of their own; for God commands those who are making bread, to take of all the fat and of all the dough, a loaf as first fruits for the use of the priests, making thus, by this legitimate instruction, a provision for those men who put aside these first fruits, proceeding in the way that leads to piety; (133) for being accustomed at all times to offer first fruits of the necessary food, they will thus have an everlasting recollection of God, than which it is impossible to imagine a greater blessing; and it follows of necessity, that the first fruits offered by the most populous of nations must be very plentiful, so that even the very poorest of the priests, must, in respect of his abundance of all necessary food, appear to be very wealthy.

(134) In the second place, he commands the nation also to give them the first fruits of their other possessions; a portion of wine out of each winepress; and of wheat and barley from each threshing floor.

And in like manner they were to have a share of oil from all; the olive trees, and of eatable fruit from all the fruit trees, in order that they might not pass a squalid existence, having only barely enough of necessary food to support life, but that they might have sufficient for a certain degree of comfort and luxury, and so live cheerfully on abundant means, with all becoming ornament and refinement.

(135) The third honour allotted to them is an assignment of all the first-born males, of all kinds of land animals which are born for the service and use of mankind; for these are the things which God commands to be given to the men consecrated to the priesthood; the offspring of oxen, and sheep, and goats, namely calves, and lambs, and kids, inasmuch as they both are and are considered clean, both for the purposes of eating and of sacrifice, but he orders that money shall be given as a ransom for the young of other animals, such as horses, and asses and camels, and similar beasts, without disparaging their real value; (136) and the supplies thus afforded them are very great; for the people of this nation breed sheep, and cattle, and flocks of all kinds above all other peoples, separating them with great care into flocks of goats, and herds of oxen, and flocks of sheep, and a vast quantity of other troops of animals of all kinds.

(137) Moreover the law, going beyond all these enactments in their favour, commands the people to bring them the first fruits, not only of all their possessions of every description, but also of their own lives and bodies; for the children are separable portions of their parents as one may say; but if one must tell the plain truth, they are insep-

---

[16] Leviticus 22:12.

[17] Yonge's translation includes a separate treatise title at this point: *On the Question: What the Rewards and Honours Are Which Belong to the Priests.* Accordingly, his next paragraph begins with roman numeral I (=XVII in the Loeb). Yonge's "treatise" concludes with number VI (=XXXII in the Loeb). The publisher has elected to follow the Loeb numbering.

arable as being of kindred blood, [...] [18] and being bound to them by the allurements of united good will, and by the indissoluble bonds of nature.

(138) But nevertheless, he consecrates also their own first-born male children after the fashion of other first fruits, as a sort of thanks-offering for fertility, and a number of children both existing and hoped for, and wishing at the same time that their marriages should be not only free from all blame, but even very deserving of praise, the first fruit arising from which is consecrated to God; and keeping this in their minds, both husbands and wives ought to cling to modesty, and to attend to their household concerns, and to cherish unanimity, agreeing with one another, so that what is called a communion and partnership may be so in solid truth, not only in word, but likewise in deed.

(139) And with reference to the dedication of the first-born male children, in order that the parents may not be separated from their children, nor the children from their parents, he values the first fruits of them himself at a fixed price in money ordering everyone both poor and rich to contribute an equal sum, not having any reference to the ability of the contributors, nor to the vigour or beauty of the children who were born; but considering how much even a very poor man might be able to give; (140) for since the birth of children happens equally to the most noble and to the most obscure persons of the race, he thought it just to enact that their contribution should also be equal, aiming, as I have already said, particularly to fix a sum which should be in the power of everyone to give.

XXVIII. (141) After this he also appointed another source of revenue of no insignificant importance for the priests, bidding them to take the first fruits of every one of the revenues of the nation namely, the first fruits of the corn, and wine, and oil, and even of the produce of all the cattle, of the flocks of sheep, and herds of oxen, and flocks of goats, and of all other animals of all kinds; and how great an abundance of these animals there must be, any one may conjecture from the vast populousness of the nation; (142) from all which circumstances it is plain that the law invests the priests with the dignity and honour that belongs to kings; since he commands contributions from every description of possession to be given to them as to rulers; (143) and they are accordingly given to them in a manner quite contrary to that in which cities usually furnish them to their rulers; for cities usually furnish them under compulsion, and with great unwillingness and lamentation, looking upon the collectors of the taxes as common enemies and destroyers, and making all kinds of different excuses at different times, and neglecting all laws and ordinances, and with all this jumbling and evasion do they contribute the taxes and payments which are levied on them.

(144) But the men of this nation contribute their payments to the priests with joy and cheerfulness, anticipating the collectors, and cutting short the time allowed for making the contributions, and thinking that they are themselves receiving rather than giving; and so with words of blessing and thankfulness, they all, both men and women, bring their offerings at each of the seasons of the year, with a spontaneous cheerfulness, and readiness, and zeal, beyond all description.

XXIX. (145) And these things are assigned to the priests from the possessions of each individual, but there are also often especial revenues set apart for them exceedingly suitable for the priests, which are derived from the sacrifices which are offered up; for it is commanded that two portions from two limbs of every victim shall be given to the priests, the arm from the limb on the right side, and the fat from the chest; for the one is a symbol of strength and manly vigour, and of every lawful action in giving, and taking, and acting: and the other is an emblem of human gentleness as far as the angry passions are concerned; (146) for it is said that these passions have their abode in the chest, since nature has assigned them the breast for their home as the most suitable place; around which as around a garrison she has thrown, in order more effectually to secure them from being taken, a very strong fence which is called the chest, which she has made of many continuous and very strong bones, binding it firmly with nerves which cannot be broken.

(147) But from the victims which are sacrificed away from the altar, in order to be eaten, it is commanded that three portions should be given to the priest, an arm, and a jaw-bone, and that which is called the paunch; the arm for the reason which has been mentioned a short time ago; the jaw-bone as a first fruit of that most important of all the members of the body, namely the head, and also of uttered speech, for the stream of speech could not flow out without the motion of these jaws; for they being agitated [19] (and it is very likely from this, that they have derived their name), when they are struck by the tongue, all the organisation of the voice sounds simultaneously; (148) and the paunch is a kind of excrescence of the belly.

And the belly is a kind of stable of that irrational animal the appetite, which, being irrigated by much wine-bibbing and gluttony, is continually washed with incessant provision of meat and drink,

---

[18] The above passage is quite unintelligible in the Greek, and is given up by Mangey as irremediably corrupt.

[19] The Greek word here used is *seiō*, and the word used for jawbone is *siagōn*, which Philo appears to think may be derived from *seiō*.

and like a swine is delighted while wallowing in the mire; in reference to which fact, a very suitable place indeed has been assigned to that intemperate and most unseemly beast, namely, the place to which all the superfluities are conveyed. (149) And the opposite to desire is temperance, which one must endeavour, and labour, and take pains by every contrivance imaginable to acquire, as the very greatest blessing and most perfect benefit both to an individual and to the state.

(150) Appetite therefore, being a profane, and impure, and unholy thing, is driven beyond the territories of virtue, and is banished as it ought to be; but temperance, being a pure and unblemished virtue, neglecting everything which relates to eating and drinking, and boasting itself as superior to the pleasures of the belly, may be allowed to approach the sacred altars, bringing forward as it does the excrescence of the body, as a memorial that it may be reminded to despise all insatiability and gluttony, and all those things which excite the appetites to this pitch.

XXX. (151) And beyond all these things he also orders that the priests who minister the offering of the sacrifices, shall receive the skins of the whole burnt offerings (and they amount to an unspeakable number, this being no slight gift, but one of the most exceeding value and importance), from which circumstances it is plain, that although he has not given to the priesthood a portion of land as its inheritance, in the same manner that he has to others, he has yet assigned to them a more honourable and more untroubled share than any other tribe, granting them the first fruits of every description of sacrifice and offering. (152) And to prevent anyone of those who give the offerings, from reproaching those who receive them, he commands that the first fruits should first of all be carried into the temple, and then orders that the priests shall take them out of the temple; for it was suitable to the nature of God, that those who had received kindness in all the circumstances of life, should bring the first fruits as thank-offering, and then that he, as a being who was in want of nothing, should with all dignity and honour bestow them on the servants and ministers who attend on the service of the temple; for to appear to receive these things not from men, but from the great Benefactor of all men, appears to be receiving a gift which has in it no alloy of sadness.

XXXI. (153) Since, then, these honours are put forth for them, if any of the priests are in any difficulty while living virtuously and irreproachably, they are at once accusers of us as disregarding the law, even though they may not utter a word. For if we were to obey the commands which we have received, and if we were to take care to give the first fruits as we are commanded, they would not only have abundance of all necessary things, but would also be filled with all kinds of supplies cal-

culated for enabling them to live in refinement and luxury. (154) And if ever at any subsequent time the tribe of the priests is found to be blessed with a great abundance of all the necessaries and luxuries of life, this will be a great proof of their common holiness, and of their accurate observance of the laws and ordinances in every particular.

But the neglect of some persons (for it is not safe to blame every one) is the cause of poverty to those who have been dedicated to God, and, if one must tell the truth, to the men themselves also. (155) For to violate the law is injurious to those who offend, even though it may be an attractive course for a short time; but to obey the ordinances of nature is most beneficial, even if at the time it may wear a painful appearance and may show no pleasant character.

XXXII. (156) Having given all these supplies and revenues to the priests, he did not neglect those either who were in the second rank of the priesthood; and these are the keepers of the temple, of whom some are placed at the doors, at the very entrance of the temple, as door-keepers; and others are within, in the vestibule of the temple, in order that no one who ought not to do so might enter it, either deliberately or by accident. Others, again, stand all around, having had the times of their watches assigned to them by lot, so as to watch by turns night and day, some being day watchmen and others night watchmen. Others, again, had charge of the porticoes and of the courts in the open air, and carried out all the rubbish, taking care of the cleanliness of the temple, and the tenths were assigned as the wages of all these men; for these tenths are the share of the keepers of the temple.

(157) At all events the law did not permit those who received them to make use of them, until they had again offered up as first fruits other tenths as if from their own private property, and before they had given these to the priests of the superior rank, for then it permitted them to enjoy them, but before that time it would not allow it.

(158) Moreover, the law allotted to them forty-eight cities, and in every city, suburbs, extending two hundred cubits all round, for the pasture of their cattle, and for the other necessary purposes of which cities have need. But of these cities, six were set apart, some on the near side, and some on the further side of Jordan, three on each side, as cities of refuge for those who had committed unintentional murder. (159) For as it was not consistent with holiness for one who had by any means whatever become the cause of death to any human being to come within the sacred precincts, using the temple as a place of refuge and as an asylum, Moses gave a sort of inferior sanctity to the cities above mentioned, allowing them to give great security, by reason of the privileges and honours conferred upon the inhabitants, who were

to be justified in protecting their suppliants if any superior power endeavoured to bring force against them, not by warlike preparations, but by rank, and dignity, and honour, which they had from the laws by reason of the venerable character of the priesthood.

(160) But the fugitive, when he has once got within the borders of the city to which he has fled for refuge, must be kept close within it, because of the avengers waiting for him on the outside, being the relations by blood of the man who has been slain, and who, out of regret for their kinsman, even if he has been slain by one who did not intend to do so, are still eager for the blood of him who slew him, their individual and private grief overpowering their accurate notions of what is right. And should he go forth from the city, let him know that he is going forth to undoubted destruction; for he will not escape the notice of any one of the slain man's relations, by whom he will at once be taken in nets and toils, and so he will perish. (161) And the limit of his banishment shall be the life of the high priest; and when he is dead, he shall be pardoned and return to his own city.

Moses, having promulgated these and similar laws about the priests, proceeds to enact others concerning animals, as to what beasts are suitable for sacrifice.[20]

XXXIII. (162) Or the creatures which are fit to be offered as sacrifices, some are land animals, and some are such as fly through the air. Passing over, therefore, the infinite varieties of birds, God chose only two classes out of them all, the turtledove and the pigeon; because the pigeon is by nature the most gentle of all those birds which are domesticated and gregarious, and the turtle-dove the most gentle of those which love solitude. (163) Also, passing over the innumerable troops of land animals, whose very numbers it is not easy to ascertain, he selected these especially as the best—the oxen, and sheep, and goats; for these are the most gentle and the most manageable of all animals. At all events, great herds of oxen, and numerous flocks of goats and sheep, are easily driven by any one, not merely by any man, but by any little child, when they go forth to pasture, and in the same way they are brought back to their folds in good order when the time comes. (164) And of this gentleness, there are many other proofs, and the most evident are these: that they all feed on herbage, and that no one of them is carnivorous, and that they have neither crooked talons, nor any projecting tusks or teeth whatever;

for the back parts of the upper jaw do not hold teeth, but all the incisor teeth are deficient in them: (165) and, besides these facts, they are of all animals the most useful to man. Rams are the most useful for the necessary covering of the body; oxen, for ploughing the ground and preparing the arable land for seed, and for the growth of the crops that shall hereafter come to be threshed out, in order that men may partake of and enjoy food; and the hair and fleeces of goats, where one is woven, or the other sewn together, make movable tents for travellers, and especially for men engaged in military expeditions, whom their necessities constantly compel to abide outside of the city in the open air.

XXXIV. (166) And the victims must be whole and entire, without any blemish on any part of their bodies, unmutilated, perfect in every part, and without spot or defect of any kind. At all events, so great is the caution used with respect not only to those who offer the sacrifices, but also to the victims which are offered, that the most eminent of the priests are carefully selected to examine whether they have any blemishes or not, and scrutinise them from head to foot, inspecting not only those parts which are easily visible, but all those which are more out of sight, such as the belly and the thighs, lest any slight imperfection should escape notice. (167) And the accuracy and minuteness of the investigation is directed not so much on account of the victims themselves, as in order that those who offer them should be irreproachable; for God designed to teach the Jews by these figures, whenever they went up to the altars, when there to pray or to give thanks, never to bring with them any weakness or evil passion in their soul, but to endeavour to make it wholly and entirely bright and clean, without any blemish, so that God might not turn away with aversion from the sight of it.

XXXV. (168) And since, of the sacrifices to be offered, some are on behalf of the whole nation, and indeed, if one should tell the real truth, in behalf of all mankind, while others are only in behalf of each individual who has chosen to offer them; we must speak first of all of those which are for the common welfare of the whole nation, and the regulations with respect to this kind of sacrifice are of a marvellous nature.

(169) For some of them are offered up every day, and some on the days of the new moon, and at the festivals of the full moon; others on days of fasting; and others at three different occasions of festival. Accordingly, it is commanded that every day the priests should offer up two lambs, one at the dawn of day, and the other in the evening; each of them being a sacrifice of thanksgiving; the one for the kindnesses which have been bestowed during the day, and the other for the mercies which have been vouchsafed in the night, which God is

---

[20]Yonge's translation includes a separate treatise title at this point: *On Animals Fit for Sacrifice, or On Victims*. Accordingly, his next paragraph begins with roman numeral I (=XXXIII in the Loeb). Yonge's "treatise" concludes with number XV (=XLVII in the Loeb). The publisher has elected to follow the Loeb numbering.

incessantly and uninterruptedly pouring upon the race of men. (170) And on the seventh day he doubles the number of victims to be offered, giving equal honour to equal things, inasmuch as he looks upon the seventh day as equal in dignity to eternity, since he has recorded it as being the birthday of the whole world. On which account he has thought fit to make the sacrifice to be offered on the seventh day, equal to the continuation of what is usually sacrificed in one day.

(171) Moreover, the most fragrant of all incenses are offered up twice every day in the fire, being burnt within the veil, both when the sun rises and sets, before the morning and after the evening sacrifice, so that the sacrifices of blood display our gratitude for ourselves as being composed of blood, but the offerings of incense show our thankfulness for the dominant part within us, our rational spirit, which was fashioned after the archetypal model of the divine image. (172) And loaves are placed on the seventh day on the sacred table, being equal in number to the months of the year, twelve loaves, arranged in two rows of six each, in accordance with the arrangement of the equinoxes; for there are two equinoxes every year, the vernal and the autumnal, which are each reckoned by periods of six months.

At the vernal equinox all the seeds sown in the ground begin to ripen; about which time, also, the trees begin to put forth their fruit. And by the autumnal one the fruit of the trees has arrived at a perfect ripeness; and at this period, again, is the beginning of seed time. Thus nature, going through a long course of time, showers gifts after gifts upon the race of man, the symbols of which are the two sixes of loaves thus placed on the table. (173) And these loaves, also, do figuratively intimate that most useful of all virtues, temperance; which is attended by frugality, and economy, and moderation as so many bodyguards, on account of the pernicious attacks which intemperance and covetousness prepare to make upon it. For, to a lover of wisdom, a loaf is a sufficient nourishment, keeping the bodies free from disease, and the intellect sound, and healthy, and sober. (174) But high seasonings, and cheesecakes, and sweetmeats, and all the other delicacies which the superfluous skill of confectioners and cooks concoct to cajole the illiterate, and unphilosophical, and most slavish of all the outward senses, namely, taste, which is never influenced by any noble sight, or by any perceptible lesson, but only by desire to indulge the appetites of the miserable belly, constantly engenders incurable diseases both in the body and the mind.

(175) And with the loaves there is also placed on the table frankincense and salt. The one as a symbol that there is no sweetmeat more fragrant and wholesome than economy and temperance, if wisdom is to be the judge; while salt is an emblem of the duration of all things (for salt preserves everything over which it is sprinkled), and also of sufficient seasoning.

(176) I know that those men who devote themselves wholly to drinking parties and banquets, and who care only for costly entertainments, will make a mock at these things and turn them into ridicule, miserable slaves as they are of birds, and fishes, and meat, and all such nonsense as that, and not being able to taste of true freedom, not even in a dream. And all such men are to be disregarded and despised by those who seek to live in accordance with the will of God, in a manner pleasing to the true and living God; who, having learnt to despise the pleasures of the flesh, pursue the delights and luxuries of the mind, having exercised themselves in the contemplation of the objects of nature.[21]

(177) After he had ordered these things concerning the seventh day, he said that for the new moons it is necessary to offer ten whole burntofferings in all: two young bulls, one ram, seven lambs. For since the month is perfect in which the moon makes its way through its cycle, he thought that a perfect number of animals should be sacrificed.[22] (178) The number ten is the completely perfect number which he most appropriately assigned to the animals which have been mentioned: the two young bulls since there are two motions of the moon as it continually runs its double-course—the motion of waxing until full moon and the motion of waning until its conjunction with the sun; one ram since there is one principle of reason by which the moon waxes and wanes in equal intervals, both as it increases and diminishes in illumination; the seven lambs because it receives the perfect shapes in periods of seven days—the half-moon in the first seven day period after its conjunction with the sun, full moon in the second; and when it makes its return again, the first is to half-moon, then it ceases at its conjunction with the sun. (179) With the sacrificial victims he ordered that the finest wheaten flour mixed with oil be offered and wine in stipulated amounts for drink-offerings. The reason is that even these are brought to maturity by the orbits of the moon in the annual seasons, especially as the moon helps to ripen fruits; wheat and wine and oil—the most helpful substances for life and the most essential

---

[21]Sections 177–193 were omitted in Yonge's translation because the edition on which Yonge based his translation, Mangey, lacked this material. These sections have been newly translated for this edition.

[22]An alternative would be to understand *teleion* as a predicate adjective and supply an *einai* which would mean "that the number of animals to be sacrificed should be perfect." The absence of a definite article before "perfect number" suggests the translation in the text is preferable.

for use by humans—are suitably dedicated together with all sacrifices.

(180) For the feast which begins the sacred month[23] double sacrifices are fitly offered since the reason for it is double: one, since it is the new moon; the other, since it is the feast which begins the sacred month. Regarding the fact that it is the new moon it is distinctly stated that sacrifices equal to the other new moons are to be sacrificed. Regarding the fact that it is the feast which begins the sacred month, the gifts are doubled apart from the young bulls. For one rather than two is offered since the judge has thought it correct to use the indivisible nature of the number one instead of the divisible number two at the beginning of the year.

(181) In the first season—he calls springtime and its equinox the first season—he ordered that a feast which is called "the feast of unleavened bread" be celebrated for seven days and declared that every day was equal in honor in religious services. For he commanded that each day ten whole burnt offerings should be sacrificed just as they are for the new moons, making the total number of whole burnt offerings apart from those dealing with the trespass offerings seventy. (182) For he thought that the same reason governed the relation of the new moon to the month which governed the relation of the seven days of the feast to the equinox that took place in the seventh month. As a result he declared sacred both the beginning of each month and the beginning, consisting of the same number of days as the new moons, of the aggregate seven months.

(183) In the middle of spring the harvest takes place during which season thank offerings are offered to God from the field because it has produced fruit in abundance and the crops are being harvested. This feast is the most publicly celebrated feast and is called "the feast of the first produce," named etymologically from the circumstance that the first of the produce, the first fruits, are dedicated at that time. (184) We are ordered to offer two young bulls as sacrifices, one ram, and seven lambs—these ten are sacred whole burnt offerings—and in addition, two lambs as meat for the priests which he calls "lambs of preservation" since food is preserved for humans out of multiple and varied circumstances. For destructive forces frequently occur: some by heavy rains, some by droughts, some by other unspeakably great

changes in nature; and again, some are humanly produced through the invasion of enemies who attempt to lay waste their neighbors' land. (185) Suitably then, the preservation offerings are offered to the one who has dispersed all plots as thank offerings. They are offered with loaves which, after the people have brought them to the altar and lifted them up to heaven, they give to the priests along with the meat of the sacrifice of preservation for a most appropriate sacred feast.

(186) When the third season takes place in the seventh month at the autumnal equinox, at the beginning of the month, the feast which begins the sacred month named "the feast of trumpets" and which was discussed earlier is celebrated. On the tenth day the fast takes place which they take seriously—not only those who are zealous about piety and holiness, but even those who do nothing religious the rest of the time. For all are astounded, overcome with the sacredness of it; in fact, at that time the worse compete with the better in self-control and virtue. (187) The reputation of the day is due to two reasons: one that it is a feast and the other that it is purification and escape from sins for which amnesty has been given by the favors of the gracious God who has assigned the same honor to repentance that he has to not committing a single sin.[24] (188) Therefore he declared that since it was a feast the sacrifices should be the same number as those of the feast which begins the sacred month: a young bull, a ram, and seven lambs. In this way he mixed the number one with the number seven and lined the end up with the beginning, for the number seven has been appointed the end of things and the number one the beginning. He added three sacrifices since it was for purification. For he ordered that two he-goats and a ram be offered. Then he said that it was necessary to offer the ram as a whole burnt offering, but to cast lots for the he-goats. The he-goat selected by lot for God must be sacrificed, but the other was to be sent out into a pathless and inaccessible desolate place carrying on himself the curses of those who had committed offenses, but who were purified by changes for the better and who have washed themselves from their old lawlessness with a new sense of loyalty to the law.

(189) On the fifteenth day, at full moon, the feast which is called "the feast of booths" is celebrated for which the supplies of the sacrifices are more numerous. For during seven days, seventy young bulls, fourteen rams and ninety-eight lambs are sacrificed—all animals as whole burnt offerings.

---

[23] The exact meaning of *ieromēnia* is unclear. The best explanation of the term was suggested by a scholiast on Pindar *Nem.* 3.2 who explained that the beginnings of months were sacred (A. B. Drachmann, *Scholia Vetera in Pindari Carmina* [3 vols., Leipzig: B. G. Teubner, 1903–27] 3:42). Thus understood to be Philo's designation for the feast day which opens the sacred month, it is here consistently translated "the feast which begins the sacred month."

[24] L. Cohn emended *mēden* to *mēde* in order to avoid the notion of sinlessness in the text. The translation follows the MSS since they offer the more difficult reading and this is a rhetorical statement designed to commend repentance, not make an observation on human perfection.

We are ordered to consider the eighth day sacred, a day which I must deal with carefully when the entire account of the feasts is thoroughly examined. On this day as many sacrifices are offered as on the feast which begins the sacred month.

(190) The sacrifices which are whole burnt offerings and are joint offerings on behalf of the nation or—to speak more accurately—on behalf of the entire race of humanity have been addressed to the best of my ability. However, a he-goat accompanies the whole burnt offerings on each day of the feast. He is called "concerning sins" and is sacrificed for the forgiveness of sins. His meat is distributed[25] to the priests for food. (191) What is the reason for this? Is it because a feast is a time of good cheer, and undeceiving and true good cheer is good sense firmly established in the soul, and this unwavering good sense is impossible to receive without a cure from sins and cutting off of the passions? For it would be out of place if each of the animals of the whole burnt offerings is sacrificed only when it is found undamaged and unhurt, but the mind of the sacrificer has not been purified in every way and cleansed by making use of washings and lustrations which the right reason of nature pours into God-loving souls through healthy and uncorrupt ears. (192) In addition the following ought to be said. These festal and holiday rests have in the past often opened up countless avenues to sins. For unmixed beverage and luxurious diets with excessive drinking arouse the insatiable desires of the stomach and also kindle the desires of the parts beneath the stomach. As these desires both flow and stream out in every way, they produce a surge of unspeakable evils using the fearless stimulant of the feast as a refuge to avoid suffering anything. (193) Knowing these things, he did not allow them to celebrate a feast in the same way as other peoples, but at the very time of good cheer he first commanded that they purify themselves by bridling the impulses of pleasure. Then he summoned them into the temple for participation in hymns and prayers and sacrifices so that both from the place and from the things seen and said through the most powerful of senses, sight and hearing, they might come to love self-control and piety. Last of all, he reminded them not to sin through the sacrifice for sin. For the one who is asking for anmesty for the sins he has committed is not so dominated by evil that at the very time he is asking for release from old wrongs he should begin other new ones.

XXXVI. (194) After the lawgiver has given these commands with reference to these subjects,

he begins to distinguish between the different kinds of sacrifices, and he divides the victims into three classes. The most important of which he makes a whole burnt offering; the next an offering for preservation; the last, a sin-offering. And then he adapts suitable ceremonies and rites to each, aiming, in no inadequate manner, at what is at the same time decorous and holy. (195) And the distinction which he makes is one of great beauty and propriety, having a close connection and a sort of natural kindred with the things themselves; for if any one were to wish to examine minutely the causes for which it seemed good to the first men to betake themselves at the same time to sacrifices to show their gratitude, and also to supplications, he will find two most especial reasons for this conduct. Firstly, that it conduces to the honour of God, which ought to be aimed at not for the sake of any other reason, but for itself alone, as being both honourable and necessary; and, secondly, for the benefits which have been poured upon the sacrificers themselves, as has been said before. And the benefit they derive is also twofold, being both an admission to a share of good things and a deliverance from evils.

(196) Therefore the law has assigned the whole burnt offering as a sacrifice adequate to that honour which is suited to God, and which belongs to God alone, enjoining that what is offered to the all-perfect and absolute God must be itself entire and perfect, having no taint of mortal selfishness in it. But that sacrifice which is offered for the sake of men, since its appearance admits of distinction, the law has distinguished also, appointing it to be a sacrifice for the participation in blessings which mankind has enjoined, and calling it a thank-offering for their preservation. And for the deliverance from evils it has allotted the sacrifice called a sin-offering, so that these are very appropriately their sacrifices for these causes; (197) the whole burnt-offering being sacrificed for God himself alone, who must be honoured for his own sake, and not for that of any other being or thing; and the others for our sake; the thank-offering for our preservation, for the safety and amelioration of human affairs; and the sin-offering for the cure of those offences which the soul has committed.

XXXVII. (198) And we must now enumerate the laws which have been enacted respecting each sacrifice, making our commencement with that which is the most excellent. Now, the most excellent sacrifice is the whole burnt-offering. The law says, "In the first place the victim shall be a male, carefully selected for its excellence from all the animals which are fit for sacrifice, a calf, or a lamb, or a kid. And then let him who brings it wash his hands, and lay his hands on the head of the victim. (199) And after this let some one of the priests take the victim and sacrifice it, and let another hold a bowl under it, and, having caught some of the

---

[25] Although S. Daniel included a negative in her edition (PAPM 24)—[ouk] *aponemetai* ("is not distributed")—in order to harmonize this statement with 1.232 and 1.244, this translation has followed the more difficult reading.

blood, let him go all around the altar and sprinkle it with the blood, and let him flay the victim and divide it into large pieces, having washed its entrails and its feet. And then let the whole victim be given to the fire of the altar of God,[26] having become many things instead of one, and one instead of many."

(200) These things, then, are comprehended in express words of command. But there is another meaning figuratively concealed under the enigmatical expressions. And the words employed are visible symbols of what is invisible and uncertain. Now the victim which is to be sacrificed as a whole burnt offering must be a male, because a male is both more akin to domination than a female and more nearly related to the efficient cause; for the female is imperfect, subject, seen more as the passive than as the active partner. (201) And since the elements of which our soul consists are two in number, the rational and the irrational part, the rational part belongs to the male sex, being the inheritance of intellect and reason; but the irrational part belongs to the sex of woman, which is the lot also of the outward senses. And the mind is in every respect superior to the outward sense, as the man is to the woman; who, when he is without blemish and purified with the proper purifications, namely, the perfect virtues, is himself the most holy sacrifice, being wholly and in all respects pleasing to God.

(202) Again, the hands which are laid upon the head of the victim are a most manifest symbol of irreproachable actions, and of a life which does nothing which is open to accusation, but which in all respects is passed in a manner consistent with the laws and ordinances of nature; (203) for the law, in the first place, desires that the mind of the man who is offering the sacrifice shall be made holy by being exercised in good and advantageous doctrines; and, in the second place, that his life shall consist of most virtuous actions, so that, in conjunction with the imposition of hands, the man may speak freely out of his cleanly conscience, and may say, (204) "These hands have never received any gift as a bribe to commit an unjust action, nor any division of what has been obtained by rapine or by covetousness, nor have they shed innocent blood, nor have they wrought mutilation, nor works of insolence, nor acts of violence, nor have they inflicted any wounds; nor, in fact, have they performed any action whatever which is liable to accusation or to reproach, but have been ministers in everything which is honourable and advantageous, and which is honoured by wisdom, or by the laws, or by honourable and virtuous men."

XXXVIII. (205) And the blood is poured out in a circle all round the altar, because a circle is the most complete of all figures, and also in order that no part whatever may be left empty and unoccupied by the libation of life; for, to speak properly, the blood is the libation of the life. Therefore the law here symbolically teaches us that the mind, which is always performing its dances in a circle, is by every description of words, and intentions, and actions which it adopts, always showing its desire to please God.

(206) And it is commanded that the belly and the feet shall be washed, which command is a figurative and very expressive one; for, by the belly it is figuratively meant to be signified that it is desirable that the appetites shall be purified, which are full of stains, and intoxication, and drunkenness, being thus a most pernicious evil, existing, and concocted, and exercised to the great injury of the life of mankind. (207) And by the command that the feet of the victim should be washed, it is figuratively shown that we must no longer walk upon the earth, but soar aloft and traverse the air.

For the soul of the man who is devoted to God, being eager for truth, springs upward and mounts from earth to heaven; and, being borne on wings, traverses the expanse of the air, being eager to be classed with and to move in concert with the sun, and moon, and all the rest of the most sacred and most harmonious company of the stars, under the immediate command and government of God, who has a kingly authority without any rival, and of which he can never be deprived, in accordance with which he justly governs the universe.

(208) And the division of the animal into limbs shows plainly that all things are but one, or that they are derived from one, and dissolved into one; which some persons have called satiety and also want, while others have called it combustion and arrangement: combustion, in accordance with the supreme power of God, who rules all other things in the world; and arrangement, according to the equality of the four elements which they all mutually allow to one another.

(209) And when I have been investigating these matters, this has appeared to me to be a probable conjecture; the soul which honours the living God, ought for that very reason to honour him not inconsiderately nor ignorantly, but with knowledge and reason; and the reasoning which we indulge in respecting God admits of division and partition, according to each of the divine faculties and excellencies; for God is both all good, and is also the maker and creator of the universe; and he also created it having a foreknowledge of what would take place, and being its preserver and most blessed benefactor, full of every kind of happiness; all which circumstances have in themselves a most dignified and praiseworthy character, both separately and when looked at in conjunction with their kindred qualities; (210) and we must speak in the same way of other matters.

---

[26] Leviticus 1:3.

When you wish to give thanks to God with your mind, and to assert your gratitude for the creation of the world, give him thanks for the creation of it as a whole, and of all its separate parts in their integrity, as if for the limbs of a most perfect animal; and by the parts I mean, for instance, the heaven, and the sun, and the moon, and the fixed stars; and secondly the earth, and the animals, and plants which spring from it; and next the seas and rivers, whether naturally springing from the ground or swollen by rain as winter torrents, and all the things in them: and lastly, the air and all the changes that take place in it; for winter, and summer, and spring, and autumn, being the seasons of the year, and being all of great service to mankind, are what we may call affections of the air for the preservation of all these things that are beneath the moon.

(211) And if ever you give thanks for men and their fortunes, do not do so only for the race taken generally, but you shall give thanks also for the species and most important parts of the race, such as men and women, Greeks and barbarians, men on the continent, and those who have their habitation in the islands; and if you are giving thanks for one individual, do not divide your thankfulness in expression into gratitude for minute trifles and inconsiderable matters, but take in your view the most comprehensive circumstances, first of all ,his body and his soul, of which he consists, and then his speech, and his mind, and his outward senses; for such gratitude cannot of itself be unworthy of being listened to by God, when uttered, for each of these particulars.

XXXIX. (212) These things are enough for us to say respecting the sacrifice of the whole burnt-offering. We must now proceed in due order to consider that offering which is called the sacrifice for preservation; for with respect to this one it is a matter of consequence whether the victim be male or female; and when it is slain, these three parts are especially selected for the altar, the fat, and the lobe of the liver, and the two kidneys; and all the other parts are left to make a feast for the sacrificer; (213) and we must consider with great accuracy the reason why these portions of the entrails are in this case looked upon as sacred, and not pass this point by carelessly.

Often when I have been considering this matter in my own mind, and investigating all these commandments, I have doubted why the law selected the lobe of the liver, and the kidneys, and the fat, as the first fruits of the animals thus sacrificed; and did not choose the heart or the brain, though the dominant part of the man resides in one of these parts; (214) and I think also that many other persons who read the sacred scriptures with their mind, rather than merely with their eyes, will ask the same question. If therefore they, when they have considered the matter, can find any more

probable reason, they will be benefiting both themselves and us; but if they cannot, let them consider the cause which has been discovered by us, and see whether it will stand the test; and this is it.

The dominant power alone of all those that exist in us is able to restrain our natural folly, and injustice, and cowardice, and our other vices, and does restrain them; and the abode of this dominant power is one or other of the aforesaid portions of us, that is, it is either the brain or the heart; (215) therefore the sacred commandment has thought fit that one should not bring to the altar of God, by means of which a remission and complete pardon of all sins and transgressions is procured, that vessel from which the mind having at one time been abiding in it, has gone forth on the trackless road of injustice and impiety, having turned out of the way which leads to virtue and excellence; for it would be folly to suppose that sacrifices were not to procure a forgetfulness of offences, but were to act as a reminder of them.

This it is which appears to me to be the reason why neither of those two parts, which are of supreme importance, namely, the brain or the heart, is brought to the altar; (216) and the parts which are commanded to be brought have a very suitable reason why they should be; the fat is brought because it is the richest part, and that which guards the entrails; for it envelops them and makes them to flourish, and benefits them by the softness of its touch.

And the kidneys are commanded to be selected on account of the adjacent parts and the organs of generation, which they, as they dwell near them, do, like good neighbours, assist and co-operate with, in order that the seed of nature may prosper without anything in its vicinity being any obstacle to it; for they are channels resembling blood, by which that part of the purification of the superfluities of the body which is moist is separated from the body; and the testicles are near by which the seed is irrigated.

And the lobe of the liver is the first fruit of the most important of the entrails, by means of which the food is digested, and being conveyed into the stomach is diffused through all the veins, and so conduces to the durability of the whole body; (217) for the stomach, lying close to the gullet which swallows the food, receives it as soon after it has first been chewed by the teeth and been made smooth, and so digests it; and the body again receives it from the stomach and performs the second part of the service required, to which indeed it has been destined by nature, giving forth a juice to aid in liquefying the food; and there are tow pipes like channels in the belly, which pour forth chyle into the liver, through the two channels which are originally placed in it.

(218) And the liver has a twofold power, a secretive one, and also a power of making blood.

Now the secretive power secretes everything which is hard and difficult to be digested, and removes it into the adjacent vessels of gall; and the other power turns all that portion of the food which is pure and properly strained, by the means of its own innate flame, into life-like vivifying blood; and presses it into the heart, from which, as has been already said, it is conveyed through the veins and by these channels is diffused through the whole body to which it becomes the nourishment.

(219) We must also add to what has been here said, that the nature of the liver being a lofty character and very smooth, by reason of its smoothness is looked upon as a very transparent mirror, so that when the mind, retreating from the cares of the day (while the body is lying relaxed in sleep, and while no one of the outward senses is any hindrance or impediment), begins to roll itself about, and to consider the objects of its thought by itself without any interruption, looking into the liver as into a mirror, it then sees, very clearly and without any alloy, every one of the proper objects of the intellect, and looking round upon all vain idols, and seeing that no disgrace can accrue to it, but taking care to avoid that and to choose the contrary, and being contented and pleased with all that it sees, it by dreams obtains a prophetic sight of the future.

XL. (220) And there are two days only during which God permits the nation to make use of the sacrifice for preservation, enjoining them to carve nothing of it till the third day, on many accounts, first of all, because all the things which are ever placed on the sacred table, ought to be made use of in due season, while the users take care that they shall suffer no deterioration from the lapse of time; but the nature of meat that has been kept is very apt to become putrid, even though it may have been seasoned in the cooking; (221) secondly, because it is fitting that the sacrifices should not be stored up for food, but should be openly exposed, so as to afford a meal to all who are in need of it, for the sacrifice when once placed on the altar, is no longer the property of the person who has offered it, but belongs to that Being to whom the victim is sacrificed, who, being a beneficent and bounteous God, makes the whole company of those who offer the sacrifice, partakers at the altar and messmates, only admonishing them not to look upon it as their own feast, for they are but stewards of the feast, and not the entertainers; and the entertainer is the man to whom all the preparation belongs, which it is not lawful to conceal while preferring parsimony and illiberal meanness to humanity which is a noble virtue.

(222) Lastly, this command was given because it so happens that the sacrifice for preservation is offered up for two things, the soul and the body, to each of which the lawgiver has assigned one day for feasting on the meats, for it was becoming that

a number of days should be allotted for this purpose equal to the number of those parts in us which were designed to be sacred; so that in the first day we should, together with our eating of the food, receive a recollection of the salvation of our souls; and on the second day be reminded of the sound health of our bodies. (223) And since there is no third object which is naturally appointed as one that should receive preservation, he has, with all possible strictness, forbidden the use of those meats being reserved to the third day, commanding that if it should so happen that, out of ignorance or forgetfulness, any portion was left, it should be consumed with fire; and he declares that the man who has merely tasted of it is blameable, saying to him, "Though thinking that you were sacrificing, O foolish man, you have not sacrificed; I have not accepted the unholy, unconsecrated, profane, unclean meats which you have roasted, O gluttonous man; never, even in a dream, having a proper idea of sacrifice."

XLI. (224) To this species of sacrifice for preservation that other sacrifice also belongs, which is called the sacrifice of praise, and which rests on the following principle.[27] The man who has never fallen into any unexpected disaster whatever, neither as to his body nor as to his external circumstances, but who has passed a tranquil and peaceful life, living in happiness and prosperity, being free from all calamity and all mishap, steering through the long voyage of life in calmness and serenity of circumstances, good fortune always blowing upon the stern of his vessel, is, of necessity, bound to requite God, who has been the pilot of his voyage, who has bestowed upon him untroubled salvation and unalloyed benefits, and, in short, all sorts of blessings unmingled with any evil, with hymns, and songs, an prayers, and also with sacrifices, and all other imaginable tokens of gratitude in a holy manner; all which things taken together have received the one comprehensive name of praise.

(225) This sacrifice the lawgiver has not commanded to be spread like the one before mentioned over two days,[28] but he has confined it to one only, in order that these men, who meet with ready benefits freely poured upon them, may offer up their requital freely and without any delay.

XLII. (226) This is sufficient to say on these subjects. We must now proceed, in due order, to consider the third sacrifice, which is called the sin-offering. This is varied in many ways, both in respect to the persons and to the description of victims offered; in respect of persons, that is, of the high priest, and of the whole nation, and of the ruler in his turn, and of the private individual;

27 Leviticus 19:1.
28 Leviticus 7:5.

in respect of the victim offered, whether it be a calf, or a kid, or a she-goat, or a lamb. (227) Also there is a distinction made, which is very necessary, as to whether they are voluntary or involuntary, with reference to those who, after they have erred, change for the better, confessing that they have sinned, and reproaching themselves for the offences that they have committed, and turning, for the future, to an irreproachable way of life.

(228) The sins therefore of the high priest, and of the whole nation, are atoned for by animals of equal value, for the priest is commanded to offer up a calf for each. The sins of the ruler are atoned for by an inferior animal, but still a male, for a kid is the appointed victim. The sins of the private individual by a victim of an inferior species, for it is a female, not a male, a she-goat, that is sacrificed; (229) for it was fitting that a ruler should be ranked above a private individual, even in his performance of sacred ceremonies also: but the nation is superior to the ruler, since the whole must, at all times, be superior to the part. But the high priest is accounted worthy of the same honour as the whole nation, in respect of purification and of entreating a forgiveness of his sins from the merciful power of God.

And he receives an equality of honour, not so much as it appears for his own sake, as because he is a servant of the nation, offering up a common thank-offering for them all in his most sacred prayers and most holy sacrifices. (230) And the commandment given respecting these matters is one of great dignity and admirable solemnity. "If," says the law, "the high priest have sinned unintentionally," and then it adds, "so that the people has sinned too," all but affirming in express words that the true high priest, not the one incorrectly called so, has no participation in sin; and if ever he stumble, this will happen to him, not for his own sake, but for the common errors of the nation, and this error is not incurable, but is one which easily admits of a remedy. (231) When, therefore, the calf has been sacrificed, the lawgiver commands the sacrificer to sprinkle some of the blood with his finger seven times in front of the veil which is before the holy of holies, within the former veil, in which place the sacred vessels are placed; and after that to smear and anoint the four horns of the altar, for it is square; and to pour out the rest of the blood at the foot of the altar, which is in the open air. (232) And to this altar they are commanded to bring three things, the fat, and the lobe of the liver, and the two kidneys, in accordance with the commandment given with reference to the sacrifice for preservation; but the skin and the flesh, and all the rest of the body of the calf, from the head to the feet, with the entrails, they are commanded to carry out and to burn in an open place, to which the sacred ashes from the altar have been conveyed.

The lawgiver also gives the same command with respect to the whole nation when it has sinned. (233) But if any ruler has sinned he makes his purification with a kid,[29] as I have said before; and if a private individual has sinned, he must offer a she-goat or a lamb; and for the ruler he appoints a male victim, but to the private individual a female, making all his other injunctions the same in both cases, to anoint the horns of the altar in the open air with blood, to bring the fat and the lobe of the liver, and the two kidneys, and to give the rest of the victim to the priests to eat.

XLIII. (234) But since, of offences some are committed against men, and some against holy and sacred things; he has hitherto been speaking with reference to those which are unintentionally committed against men; but for the purification of such as have been committed against sacred things he commands a ram to be offered up, after the offender has first paid the value of the thing to which the offence related, adding one fifth to the exact value.

(235) And after having put forth these and similar enactments with reference to sins committed unintentionally, he proceeds to lay down rules respecting intentional offences. "If any one," says the law, "shall speak falsely concerning a partnership, or about a deposit, or about a theft, or about the finding of something which another has lost, and being suspected and having had an oath proposed to him, shall swear, and when he appears to have escaped all conviction at the hands of this accusers, shall himself become his own accuser, being convicted by his own conscience residing within, and shall reproach himself for the things which he has denied, and as to which he has sworn falsely, and shall come and openly confess the sin which he has committed, and implore pardon; (236) then pardon shall be given to such a man, who shows the truth of his repentance, not by promises but by works, by restoring the deposit which he has received, and by giving up the things which he has stolen or found, or of which in short he has in any way deprived his neighbour, paying also in addition one fifth of the value, as an atonement for the evil which he had done."[30]

(237) And then, after he has appeased the man who had been injured, the law proceeds to say, "After this let him go also into the temple, to implore remission of the sins which he has committed, taking with him an irreproachable mediator, namely, that conviction of the soul which has delivered him from his incurable calamity, curing him of the disease which would cause death, and wholly changing and bringing him to good health." And it orders that he should sacrifice a ram, and

---

[29] Leviticus 4:22.
[30] Leviticus 5:20.

this victim is expressly mentioned, as it is in the case of the man who has offended in respect of the holy things; (238) for the law speaks of an unintentional offence in the matter of holy things as of equal importance with an intentional sin in respect of men; if we may not indeed say that this also is holy, since an oath is added to it, which, as having been taken for an unjust cause, it has corrected by an alteration for the better.

(239) And we must take notice that the parts of the victim slain as a sin-offering which are placed upon the altar, are the same as those which are taken from the sacrifice for preservation, namely the lobe of the liver, and the fat, and the kidneys; for in a manner we may speak also of the man who repents as being preserved, since he is cured of a disease of the soul, which is worse than the diseases of the body; (240) but the other parts of the animal are assigned to be eaten in a different manner; and the difference consists in three things; in the place, and time, and in those who receive it.[31] Now the place is the temple; the time is one day instead of two; and the persons who partake of it are the priests, and the male servants of the priests, but not the men who offer the sacrifice. (241) Therefore the law does not permit the sacrifice to be brought out of the temple, with the intent that, if the man who repents has committed any previous offence also, he may not now be overwhelmed by envious and malicious men, with foolish dispositions and unbridled tongues, always lying in wait for reproach and false accusation; but it must be eaten in the sacred precincts, within which the purification has taken place.

XLIV. (242) And the law orders the priests to feast on what is offered in the sacrifice for many reasons; first of all, that by this command it may do honour to him who has offered the sacrifice, for the dignity of those who eat of the feast is an honour to those who furnish it; secondly, that they may believe the more firmly that those men who feel repentance for their sins do really have God propitious to them, for he would never have invited his servants and ministers to a participation in such a banquet, if his forgiveness of those who provided it had not been complete; and thirdly, because it is not lawful for any one of the priests to bear a part in the sacred ceremonies who is not perfect, for they are rejected for the slightest blemish.

(243) And God comforts those who have ceased to travel by the road of wickedness, as if they now, by means of the race of the priesthood, had received a pure purpose of life for the future, and had been sent forth so as to obtain an equal share of honour with the priests. And it is for this reason that the victim sacrificed as a sin-offering is consumed in one day, because men ought to

delay to sin, being always slow and reluctant to approach it, but to exert all possible haste and promptness in doing well.

(244) But the sacrifices offered up for the sins of the high priest, or for those of the whole nation, are not prepared to be eaten at all, but are burnt to ashes, and the ashes are sacred as has been said; for there is no one who is superior to the high priest or to the whole nation, or who can as such be an intercessor for them, as to the sins which they have committed.

(245) Very naturally, therefore, is the meat of this sacrifice ordered to be consumed by fire, in imitation of the whole burnt offerings, and this to the honour of those who offer it; not because the sacred judgments of God are given with reference to the rank of those who come before his tribunal, but because the offences committed by men of pre-eminent virtue and real holiness are accounted of a character nearly akin to the good actions of others; (246) for as a deep and fertile soil, even if it at times yields a bad crop, still bears more and better fruit than one which is naturally unproductive, so in the same manner it happens that the barrenness of virtuous and God-fearing men is more full of excellence than the best actions which ordinary people perform by chance; for these men cannot intentionally endure to do anything blameable.

XLV. (247) Having given these commandments about every description of sacrifice in its turn, namely, about the burnt offering, and the sacrifice for preservation, and the sin-offering, he adds another kind of offering common to all the three, in order to show that they are friendly and connected with one another; and this combination of them all is called the great vow; (248) and why it received this appellation we must now proceed to say.

When any persons offer first fruits from any portion of their possessions, wheat, or barley, or oil, or wine, or the best of their fruits, or the first-born males of their flocks and herds, they do so actually dedicating those first fruits which proceed from what is clean, but paying a price as the value of what is unclean; and when they have no longer any materials left in which they can display their piety, they then consecrate and offer up themselves, displaying an unspeakable holiness, and a most superabundant excess of a God-loving disposition, on which account such a dedication is fitly called the great vow; for every man is his own greatest and most valuable possession, and this even he now gives up and abandons.

(249) And when a man has vowed this vow the law gives him the following command; first of all, to touch no unmixed wine, nor any wine that is made of the grape, nor to drink any other strong drink whatever, to the destruction of his reason, considering that during this period his reason also

[31] Leviticus 6:9.

is dedicated to God; for all which could tend to drunkenness is forbidden to those of the priests who are employed in the sacred ministrations, they being commanded to quench their thirst with water; (250) in the second place they are commanded not to show their heads, giving thus a visible sign to all who see them that they are not debasing the pure coinage of their vow; thirdly, they are commanded to keep their body pure and undefiled, so as not even to approach their parents if they are dead, nor their brothers; piety overcoming the natural good will and affection towards their relations and dearest friends, and it is both honourable and expedient that piety should at all times prevail.

XLVI. (251) But when the appointed time for their being released[32] from this vow has arrived, the law then commands the man who has dedicated himself to bring three animals to procure his release from his vow, a male lamb, and a female lamb, and a ram; the one for a burnt offering, the second for a sin-offering, and the ram as a sacrifice for preservation; (252) for in some sense the man who has made such a vow resembles all these things. He resembles the sacrifice of the entire burnt offering, because he is dedicating to his preserver not only a portion of the first fruits of other things, but also of his own self. And he resembles the sin-offering, inasmuch as he is a man; for there is no one born, however perfect he may be, who can wholly avoid the commission of sin. He resembles also the offering for preservation, inasmuch as he has recorded that God the saviour is the cause of his preservation, and does not ascribe it to any physician or to any power of his; for those who have been born themselves, and who are liable to infirmity, are not competent to bestow health even on themselves.

Medicine does not benefit all persons, nor does it always benefit the same persons; but there are times even when it does them great injury, since its power depends on different things, both on the thing itself and also on those persons who use it. (253) And a great impression is made on me by the fact that of three animals offered up in these different sacrifices, there is no one of a different species from the others, but they are every one of the same kind, a ram, and a male lamb, and a female lamb; for God wishes, as I said a little while ago, by this commandment to point out that the three kinds of sacrifice are nearly connected with and akin to one another; because, both the man who repents is saved, and the man who is saved from the diseases of the soul repents, and because both of them hasten with eagerness to attain to an entire and perfect disposition, of which the sacrifice of the whole burnt-offering is a symbol.

(254) But since the man has begun to offer himself as his first fruits, and since it is not lawful for the sacred altar to be polluted with human blood, but yet it was by all means necessary that a portion should be consecrated, he has taken care to take a portion, which, being taken, should cause neither pain nor defilement; for he has cut off[33] the hair of the head, the superfluities of the natural body, as if they were the superfluous branches of a tree, and he has committed them to the fire on which the meat of the sacrifice offered for preservation will be suitably prepared,[34] in order that some portion of the man who has made the vow, which it is not lawful to place upon the altar, may still at all events be combined with the sacrifice, burning the fuel of the sacred flame.

XLVII. (255) These sacred fires are common to all the rest of the people. But it was fitting that the priests also should offer up something on the altar as first fruits, not thinking that the services and sacred ministrations to which they have been appointed have secured them an exemption from such duties. And the first fruits suitable for the priests to offer do not come from anything containing blood, but from the purest portion of human food; (256) for the fine wheaten flour is their continual offering; a tenth part of a sacred measure every day; one half of which is offered up in the morning, and one half in the evening, having been soaked in oil, so that no portion of it can be left for food; for the command of God is, that all the sacrifices of the priests shall be wholly burnt, and that no portion of them shall be allotted for food.

Having now, then, to the best of our ability, discussed the matters relating to the sacrifices, we will proceed in due order to speak concerning those who offer them.[35]

XLVIII. (257) The law chooses that a person who brings a sacrifice shall be pure, both in body and soul;—pure in soul from all passions, and diseases, and vices, which can be displayed either in word or deed; and pure in body from all such things as a body is usually defiled by. (258) And it has appointed a burning purification for both these things; for the soul, by means of the animals which are duly fit for sacrifices; and for the body, by ablutions and sprinklings; concerning which we will speak presently; for it is fit to assign the pre-eminence in honour in every point to the superior and dominant part of the qualities exist-

---

33 Numbers 6:18.
34 Leviticus 6:13.
35 Yonge's translation includes a separate treatise title at this point: *On Those Who Offer Sacrifice*. Accordingly, his next paragraph begins with roman numeral I (=XLVIII in the Loeb). Yonge's "treatise" concludes with number XVI (=LXIII in the Loeb). The publisher has elected to follow the Loeb numbering.

ing in us, namely, to the soul. (259) What, then, is the mode of purifying the soul?

"Look," says the law, "take care that the victim which thou bringest to the altar is perfect, wholly without participation in any kind of blemish, selected from many on account of its excellence, by the uncorrupted judgments of the priests, and by their most acute sight, and by their continual practice derived from being exercised in the examination of faultless victims. For if you do not see this with your eyes more than with your reason, you will not wash off all the imperfections and stains which you have imprinted on your whole life, partly in consequence of unexpected events, and partly by deliberate purpose; (260) for you will find that this exceeding accuracy of investigation into the animals, figuratively signifies the amelioration of your own disposition and conduct; for the law was not established for the sake of irrational animals, but for that of those who have intellect and reason." So that the real object taken care of is not the condition of the victims sacrificed in order that they may have no blemish, but that of the sacrificers that they may not be defiled by any unlawful passion.

(261) The body then, as I have already said, he purifies with ablutions and bespringklings, and does not allow a person after he has once washed and sprinkled himself, at once to enter within the sacred precincts, but bids him wait outside for seven days, and to be besprinkled twice, on the third day and on the seventh day; and after this it commands him to wash himself once more, and then it admits him to enter the sacred precincts and to share in the sacred ministrations.

XLIX. (262) We must consider what great prudence and philosophical wisdom is displayed in this law; for nearly all other persons are besprinkled with pure water, generally in the sea, some in rivers, and others again in vessels of water which they draw from fountains. But Moses, having previously prepared ashes which had been left from the sacred fire (and in what manner shall be explained hereafter), appointed that it should be right to take some of them and to put them in a vessel, and then to pour water upon them, and then, dipping some branches of hyssop in the mixture of ashes and water, to sprinkle it over those who were to be purified. (263) And the cause of this proceeding may very probably be said to be this:—

The lawgiver's intention is that those who approach the service of the living God should first of all know themselves and their own essence. For how can the man who does not know himself ever comprehend the supreme and all-excelling power of God? (264) Therefore, our bodily essence is earth and water, of which he reminds us by this purification, conceiving that this result—namely, to know one's self, and to know also of what one is composed, of what utterly valueless substances

mere ashes and water are—is of itself the most beneficial purification. (265) For when a man is aware of this he will at once reject all vain and treacherous conceit, and, discarding haughtiness and pride, he will seek to become pleasing to God, and to conciliate the merciful power of that Being who hates arrogance.

For it is said somewhere with great beauty, "He that exhibits over proud words or actions offends not men alone but God also, the maker of equality and of every thing else that is most excellent." (266) Therefore, to us who are amazed and excited by this sprinkling the very elements themselves, earth and water, may almost be said to utter distinct words, and to say plainly, we are the essence of your bodies; nature having mixed us together, divine art has fashioned us into the figure of a man. Being made of us when you were born, you will again be dissolved into us when you come to die; for it is not the nature of any thing to be destroyed so as to become non-existent; but the end brings it back to those elements from which its beginnings come.

L. (267) But now it is necessary to fulfil our promise and to explain the peculiar propriety involved in this use of ashes. For they are not merely the ashes of wood which has been consumed by fire, but also of an animal particularly suited for this kind of purification. (268) For the law orders [36] that a red heifer, which has never been brought under the yoke, shall be sacrificed outside of the city, and that the high priest, taking some of the blood, shall seven times sprinkle with it all the things in front of the temple, and then shall burn the whole animal, with its hide and flesh, and with the belly full of all the entrails. And when the flame begins to pour down, then it commands that these three things shall be thrown into the middle of it, a stick of cedar, a stick of hyssop, and a bunch of saffron; and then, when the fire is wholly extinguished, it commands that some man who is clean shall collect the ashes, and shall again place them outside of the city in some open place.

(269) And what figurative meanings he conceals under these orders as symbols, we have accurately explained in another treatise, in which we have discussed the allegories.

It is necessary, therefore, for those who are about to go into the temple to partake of the sacrifice, to be cleansed as to their bodies and as to their souls before their bodies. For the soul is the mistress and the queen, and is superior in every thing, as having received a more divine nature. And the things which cleanse the mind are wisdom and the doctrines of wisdom, which lead to the contemplation of the world and the things in it; and the sacred chorus of the rest of the virtues, and

---

[36] Numbers 19:1.

honourable and very praiseworthy actions in accordance with the virtues. (270) Let the man, therefore, who is adorned with these qualities go forth in cheerful confidence to the temple which most nearly belongs to him, the most excellent of all abodes to offer himself as a sacrifice. But let him in whom covetousness and a desire of unjust things dwell and display themselves, cover his head and be silent, checking his shameless folly and his excessive impudence, in those matters in which caution is profitable; for the temple of the truly living God may not be approached by unholy sacrifices.

(271) I should say to such a man: My good man, God is not pleased even though a man bring hecatombs to his altar; for he possesses all things as his own, and stands in need of nothing. But he delights in minds which love God, and in men who practise holiness, from whom he gladly receives cakes and barley, and the very cheapest things, as if they were the most valuable in preference to such as are most costly. (272) And even if they bring nothing else, still when they bring themselves, the most perfect completeness of virtue and excellence, they are offering the most excellent of all sacrifices, honouring God, their Benefactor and Saviour, with hymns and thanksgivings; the former uttered by the organs of the voice, and the latter without the agency of the tongue or mouth, the worshippers making their exclamations and invocations with their soul alone, and only appreciable by the intellect, and there is but one ear, namely, that of the Deity which hears them. For the hearing of men does not extend so far as to be sensible of them.

LI. (273) And that this statement is true, and not mine but that of nature, is testified to a certain degree by the evident nature of the thing itself, which affords a manifest proof which none can deny who do not cleave to credulity out of a contentious disposition. It is testified also by the law which commands two altars to be prepared, differing both as to the materials of which they are made, as to the places in which they are erected, and as to the purposes to which they are applied; (274) for one is made of stones, carefully selected so to fit one another, and unhewn, and it is erected in the open air, near the steps of the temple, and it is for the purpose of sacrificing victims which contain blood in them. And the other is made of gold, and is erected in the inner part of the temple, within the first veil, and may not be seen by any other human being except those of the priests who keep themselves pure, and it is for the purpose of offering incense upon; (275) from which it is plain that God looks upon even the smallest offering of frankincense by a holy man as more valuable than ten thousand beasts which may be sacrificed by one who is not thoroughly virtuous. For in proportion, I imagine, as gold is more valuable than stones, and as the things within the inner temple are more holy than those without, in the same proportion is the gratitude displayed by offerings of incense superior to that displayed by the sacrifice of victims full of blood, (276) on which account the altar of incense is honoured not only in the costliness of its materials, and in the manner of its erection, and in its situation, but also in the fact that it ministers every day before any thing else to the thanksgivings to be paid to God. For the law does not permit the priest to offer the sacrifice of the whole burnt offering outside before he has offered incense within at the earliest dawn.[37]

(277) And this command is a symbol of nothing else but of the fact that in the eyes of God it is not the number of things sacrificed that is accounted valuable, but the purity of the rational spirit of the sacrificer. Unless, indeed, one can suppose that a judge who is anxious to pronounce a holy judgment will never receive gifts from any of those whose conduct comes before his tribunal, or that, if he does receive such presents, he will be liable to an accusation of corruption; and that a good man will not receive gifts from a wicked person, not even though he may be poor and the other rich, and he himself perhaps in actual want of what he would so receive; and yet that God can be corrupted by bribes, who is most all-sufficient for himself and who has no need of any thing created; who, being himself the first and most perfect good thing, the everlasting fountain of wisdom, and justice, and of every virtue, rejects the gifts of the wicked. (278) And is not the man who would offer such gifts the most shameless of all men, if he offers a portion of the things which he has acquired by doing injury, or by rapine, or by false denial, or by robbery, to God as if he were a partner in his wickedness? O most miserable of all men!

I should say to such a man, "You must be expecting one of two things. Either that you will be able to pass undetected, or that you will be discovered. (279) Therefore, if you expect to be able to pass undetected, you are ignorant of the power of God, by which he at the same time sees everything and hears everything. And if you think that you will be discovered, you are most audacious in (when you ought rather to endeavour to conceal the wicked actions which you have committed) bringing forward to light specimens of all your iniquitous deeds, and giving yourself airs, and dividing the fruits of them with God, bringing him unholy first fruits. And have you not considered this, that the law does not admit of lawlessness, nor does the light of the sun admit of darkness; but God is the archetypal model of all laws, and the sun,

---

[37] Exodus 30:8.

which can be appreciated only by the intellect, is the archetypal model of that which is visible to the senses, bringing forth from its invisible fountains visible light to afford to him who sees."

Moreover, there are other commandments relating to the altar.[38] (280) This injunction also is very admirably and properly set down in the sacred tablets of the law, that the wages of a harlot are not to be received into the temple, and inasmuch as she has earned them by selling her beauty, having chosen a most infamous life for the sake of shameful gain; (281) but if the gifts which proceed from a woman who has lived as a concubine are unholy, how can those be different which proceed from a soul which is defiled in the same manner, which has voluntarily abandoned itself to shame and to the lowest infamy, to drunkenness and gluttony, and covetousness and ambition, and love of pleasure, and to innumerable other kinds of passions, and diseases, and wickednesses? For what time can be long enough to efface those defilements, I indeed do not know.

(282) Very often in truth time has put an end to the occupation of a harlot, since, when women have outlived their beauty, no one any longer approaches them, their prime having withered away like that of some flowers; and what length of time can ever transform the harlotry of the soul which from its youth has been trained in early and habitual incontinence, so as to bring it over to good order? No time could do this, but God alone, to whom all things are possible, even those which among us are impossible.

(283) Accordingly, the man who is about to offer a sacrifice ought to examine and see, not whether the victim is without blemish, but whether his mind is sound, and entire, and perfect. Let him likewise investigate the causes for which he is about to offer the sacrifice; for it must be as an expression of thankfulness for kindnesses which have been shown to him, or else of supplication for the permanence of his present blessings, or for the acquisition of some future good, or else to avert some evil either present or expected; for all which objects he should labour to bring his reason into a state of good health and sanity; (284) for if he is giving thanks for benefits conferred upon him, he must take care not to behave like an ungrateful man, becoming wicked, for the benefits are conferred on a virtuous man; or if his object be to secure the permanence of his present prosperity and happiness, and to be enabled to look forward to such for the future, he must still show himself

worthy of his good fortune, and behave virtuously; or if he is asking to escape from evils, let him not commit actions deserving of correction and punishment.

LII. (285) The law says, "A fire shall be kept burning on the altar which shall never be extinguished, but shall be kept burning for ever."[39] I think with great reason and propriety; for, since the graces of God are everlasting, and unceasing, and uninterrupted, which we now enjoy day and night, and since the symbol of gratitude is the sacred flame, it is fitting that it should be kindled, and that it should remain unextinguished for ever. (286) And, perhaps, the lawgiver designed by this command to connect the old with the new sacrifices, and to unite the two by the duration and presence of the same fire by which all such sacrifices are consecrated, in order to demonstrate the fact that all perfect sacrifices consisted in thanksgiving, although, according to the diversity of the occasions on which they are offered, more victims are offered at one time and fewer at another. (287) But some are verbal symbols of things appreciable only by the intellect, and the mystical meaning which is concealed beneath them must be investigated by those who are eager for truth in accordance with the rules of allegory.

The altar of God is the grateful soul of the wise man, being compounded of perfect numbers undivided and indivisible; for no part of virtue is useless. (288) On this soul the sacred fire is continually kept burning, preserved with care and unextinguishable. But the light of the mind is wisdom; as, on the contrary, the darkness of the soul is folly. For what the light discernible by the outward senses is to the eyes, that is knowledge to reason with a view to the contemplation of incorporeal things discernible only by the intellect, the light of which is continually shining and never extinguished.

LIII. (289) After this the law says, "On every offering you shall add salt."[40] By which injunction, as I have said before, he figuratively implies a duration for ever; for salt is calculated to preserve bodies, being placed in the second rank as inferior only to the soul; for as the soul is the cause of bodies not being destroyed, so likewise is salt, which keeps them together in the greatest degree, and to some extent makes them immortal. (290) On which account the law calls the altar *thysiasterion*, giving it a peculiar name of especial honour, from its preserving (*diatereo*) the sacrifices (*tas thysias*) in a proper manner, and this too though the flesh is consumed by fire; so as to afford the most evident proof possible that God looks not upon the victims as forming the real sacrifice, but

---

[38] Yonge's translation places sections 280–284 after what is section 345 in the Loeb and makes them part of a new treatise entitled *On the Commandment that the Wages of a Harlot Are Not To Be Received in the Sacred Treasury.* The sections are included here in their proper place.

[39] Leviticus 6:9.
[40] Leviticus 2:13.

on the mind and willingness of him who offers them, that so the durability and firmness of the altar may be ensured by virtue.

(291) Moreover, it also ordains that every sacrifice shall be offered up without any leaven or honey, not thinking it fit that either of these things should be brought to the altar. The honey, perhaps, because the bee which collects it is not a clean animal, inasmuch as it derives its birth, as the story goes, from the putrefaction and corruption of dead oxen,[41] just as wasps spring from the bodies of horses. (292) Or else this may be forbidden as a figurative declaration that all superfluous pleasure is unholy, making, indeed, the things which are eaten sweet to the taste, but inflicting bitter pains difficult to be cured at a subsequent period, by which the soul must of necessity be agitated and thrown into confusion, not being able to settle on any sure resting place.

(293) And leaven is forbidden on account of the rising which it causes; this prohibition again having a figurative meaning, intimating that no one who comes to the altar ought at all to allow himself to be elated, being puffed up by insolence; but that such persons may keep their eyes fixed on the greatness of God, and so obtain a proper conception of the weakness of all created beings, even if they be very prosperous; and that so cherishing correct notions they may correct the arrogant loftiness of their minds, and discard all treacherous self-conceit.

(294) But if the Creator and maker of the universe, who has no need of anything which he has created, not looking at the exceeding greatness of his own power and at his own authority, but at your weakness, gives you a share of his own merciful power, supplying the deficiencies with which you are overwhelmed, how do you think it fitting that you should behave towards men who are akin to you by nature, and who are springing from the same elements with yourself, when you have brought nothing into the world, not even yourself? (295) For, my fine fellow, you came naked into the world, and you shall leave it again naked, having received the interval between your birth and death

as a loan from God; during which what ought you to do rather than take care to live in communion and harmony with your fellow creatures, studying equality, and humanity, and virtue, repudiating unequal, and unjust, and irreconcilable unsociable wickedness, which makes that animal which is by nature the most gentle of all, namely, man, a cruel and untractable monster?

LIV. (296) Again, the law commands that candles shall be kept burning from evening until morning[42] on the sacred candlesticks within the veil, on many accounts. One of which is that the holy places may be kept illuminated without any interruption after the cessation of the light of day, being always kept free from any participation in darkness, just as the stars themselves are, for they too, when the sun sets, exhibit their own light, never forsaking the place which was originally appointed for them in the world. (297) Secondly, in order that by night, also, a rite akin to and closely resembling the sacrifices by day may be performed so as to give pleasures to God, and that no time or occasion fit for offering thanksgiving may ever be left out, which is a duty most suitable and natural for night; for it is not improper to call the blaze of the most sacred light in the innermost shrine itself a sacrifice.

(298) The third, which is a reason of the very greatest importance, is this. Since we are not only well treated while we are awake, but also when we are asleep, inasmuch as the mighty God gives sleep as a great assistance to the human race, for the benefit of both their bodies and souls, of their bodies as being by it relieved of the labours of the day, and of their souls as being lightened by it of all their cares, and being restored to themselves after all the disorder and confusion caused by the outward senses, and as being then enabled to retire within and commune with themselves, the law has very properly thought fit to make a distinction of the actions of thanksgiving, so that sacrifices may be made on behalf of those who are awake by means of the victims which are offered, and on behalf of those who are asleep, and of those who are benefited by sleep, by the lighting of the sacred candles.

LV. (299) These, then, and other commandments like them, are those which are established for the purpose of promoting piety, by express injunctions and prohibitions. But those which are in accordance with philosophical suggestions and recommendations must be explained in this manner; for the lawgiver, in effect, says, "God, O mind of man! demands nothing of you which is either oppressive, or uncertain, or difficult, but only such things as are very simple and easy. (300) And these are, to love him as your benefactor; and if

---

[41]This refers to the same idea so beautifully expressed by Virgil, Georgie 4.548 (as it is translated by Dryden)—"His mother's precepts he performs with care; / The temple visits and adores with prayer; / Four altars raises; from his herd he culls, / For slaughter, four the fairest of his bulls; / Four heifers from his female store he took, / All fair and all unknowing of the yoke, / Nine mornings thence with sacrifice and prayers, / The powers atoned, he to the grove repairs. / Behold a prodigy! for from within / The broken vowels and the bloated skin, / A buzzing noise of bees his ears alarms: / Straight issue through the sides assembling swarms, / Dark as a cloud they make a wheeling flight, / Then on a neighbouring tree, descending light: / Like a large cluster of black grapes they show, / And make a large dependance from the bough."

you fail to do so, at all events, to fear him as your Governor and Lord, and to enter zealously upon all the paths which may please him, and to serve him in no careless or superficial manner, but with one's whole soul thoroughly filled as it ought to be with God-loving sentiments, and to cleave to his commandments, and to honour justice, by all which means the world itself continues constantly in the same nature without ever changing, and all other things which are contained in the world have a tendency towards improvement, such as the sun and the moon, and the whole multitude of the rest of the stars, and the entire heaven.

But the mountains of the earth are elevated to the greatest possible height, and the champaign country, like other fusible essences, is spread over a body of wide extent, and the sea also changes so as to become united with sweet waters, and the rains also become in their turn similar to the sea. Therefore every one of those things is still fixed within the same boundaries as those within which it was originally created, when it was first disposed of in regular order. But you shall be better, living quite irreproachably. (301) And what of all these things is either grievous or laborious? You are not compelled to pass over unnavigable seas; or, when tossed about by the billows of the middle of winter and the force of contrary winds, to wander about the sea in every direction; or to travel on foot over rough and pathless byeways, always being in dread of the haunts of robbers, or of the attacks of wild beasts; or to watch all night to protect your walls in the open air, while the enemy are lying in ambush for you, and threatening you with the very extremity of danger.

Come, now, let no unpleasant topics be brought up in pleasant circumstances. We must use words of good omen with reference to such advantageous matters. (302) It is only necessary for the mind to consent and everything will be ready. Are you not aware that both that heaven which is invisible to the outward senses, and that likewise which is appreciable only by the intellect, belongs to God: the heaven of heavens as we may call it; and again, that the earth and all that is in it, and the whole world, both that which is visible and that which is invisible and incorporeal, being a model of the real heaven?

LVI. (303) But, nevertheless, he selected out of the whole race of mankind those who were really men for their superior excellence; and he elected them and thought them worthy of the highest possible honour, calling them to the service of himself, to that everlasting fountain of all that is good; from which he has showered forth other virtues, drawing forth, at the same time, for our enjoyment, combined with the greatest possible advantage, a drink contributing more than ever nectar, or at all events not less, to make those who drink of it immortal.

(304) But those men are to be pitied, and are altogether miserable, who have never banquetted on the labours of virtue; and they have remained to the end the most miserable of all men who have been always ignorant of the taste of moral excellence, when it was in their power to have feasted on and luxuriated among justice and equality. But these men are uncircumcised in their hearts, as the law expresses it, and by reason of the hardness of their hearts they are stubborn, resisting and breaking their traces in a restive manner; (305) whom the Lord reproves, saying, "Be ye circumcised as to your hard-heartedness;"[43] that means, "do ye eradicate the overbearing character of your dominant part, which the immoderate impulses of the passing hour have sown and caused to grow within you, and which the wicked husbandman of the soul, folly, planted.

(306) Again, it says, "Let not your necks be stiff,"[44] that is to say, let not your mind be unbending and self-willed, and let it not admit into itself that most blameable ignorance of excessive perverseness. But discarding obstinacy and moroseness of nature as an enemy, let it change so as to become gentle, and inclined to obey the laws of nature. (307) Do you not see that the most important and greatest of all the powers of the living God are his beneficent and his punishing power? And his beneficent power is called God, since it is by means of this that he made and arranged the universe. And the other, or punishing power, is called Lord, on which his sovereignty over the universe depends. And God is God, not only of men, but also of gods; and he is mighty, being truly strong and truly powerful.[45]

LVII. (308) But, nevertheless, though he is so great in excellence and in power, he feels pity and compassion for all those who are most completely sunk in want and distress, not considering it beneath his dignity to be the judge in the causes of proselytes, and orphans, and widows, and disregarding kings and tyrants, and men in high commands, and honouring the humility of those men above mentioned, I mean the proselytes, with precedence, on this account. (309) These men, having forsaken their country and their national customs in which they were bred up, which, however, were full of the inventions of falsehood and pride, becoming genuine lovers of truth, have come over to piety; and becoming in all worthiness suppliants and servants of the true and living God, they very properly receive a precedence which they have deserved, having found the reward of their fleeing to God in the assistance which they now receive from him. (310) And in the case of

---

[43]Deuteronomy 10:16.
[44]Deuteronomy 10:18.
[45]Deuteronomy 10:17.

orphans and widows, since they have been deprived of their natural protectors, the one class having lost their parents, and the others their husbands, they have no refuge whatever to which they can flee, no aid which they can hope for from man, being utterly destitute; on which account they are not deprived of the greatest hope of all, the hope of relief from God, who, because of his merciful character, does not refuse to provide and to care for persons so wholly desolate.

(311) "Let then," says the law, "God alone be thy boast, and thy greater glory,"[46] And do not pride thyself either on thy wealth, or on thy glory, or on the beauty of thy person, or on thy strength, or on anything of the same kind as the objects at which foolish empty-headed persons are apt to be elated; considering that, in the first place, these things have no connection at all with the nature of good, and secondly, that they are liable to rapid changes, fading away in a manner before they have time to flourish permanently. (312) And let us cling to the custom of addressing our supplications to him, and let us not, after we have subdued our enemies, imitate their impiety in those matters of conduct in which they fancy that they are acting piously, burning their sons and their daughters to their gods, not, indeed, that it is the custom of all the barbarians to burn their children. (313) For they are not become so perfectly savage in their natures as to endure in time of peace to treat their nearest and dearest relatives as they would scarcely treat their irreconcilable enemies in time of war.

But that they do in reality inflame and corrupt the souls of the children of whom they are the parents from the very moment that they are out of their swaddling clothes; not imprinting on their minds, while they are still tender, any true opinions respecting the one only and truly living God. Let us not then be overcome by, and fall down before, and yield to their good fortune as if they had prevailed by reason of their piety. (314) For present prosperity is given to many persons for a snare, being only a bait to be followed by excessive and incurable evils. And it is very likely that even men who are unworthy may be allowed to be successful, not for their own sakes, but in order that we who act impiously may be more vehemently grieved and pained, who having been born in a God-fearing city, and having been bred up in laws which would imbue men with every virtue, and having been instructed from our earliest youth in all such pursuits as are most honourable to men, neglect them all, and cling only to such practices as deserve to be neglected, considering all good things as subjects for amusement, and looking upon things fit only for sport as seriously good.

LVIII. (315) And if, indeed, any one assuming the name and appearance of a prophet,[47] appearing to be inspired and possessed by the Holy Spirit, were to seek to lead the people to the worship of those who are accounted gods in the different cities, it would not be fitting for the people to attend to him being deceived by the name of a prophet. For such an one is an impostor and not a prophet, since he has been inventing speeches and oracles full of falsehood, (316) even though a brother, or a son, or a daughter, or a wife, or a steward, or a firm friend, or any one else who seems to be well-intentioned towards one should seek to lead one in a similar course; exhorting one to be cheerful among the multitude, and to approach the same temples and to adopt the same sacrifices; but such an one should be punished as a public and common enemy, and we should think but little of any relationship, and one should relate his recommendations to all the lovers of piety, who with all speed and without any delay would hasten to inflict punishment on the impious man, judging it a virtuous action to be zealous for his execution.

(317) For we should acknowledge only one relationship, and one bond of friendship, namely, a mutual zeal for the service of God, and a desire to say and do everything that is consistent with piety. And these bonds which are called relationships of blood, being derived from one's ancestors, and those connections which are derived from intermarriages and from other similar causes, must all be renounced, if they do not all hasten to the same end, namely, the honour of God which is the one indissoluble bond of all united good will. For such men will lay claim to a more venerable and sacred kind of relationship; (318) and the law confirms my assertion, where it says that those who do what is pleasing to nature and virtuous are the sons of God, for it says, "Ye are the sons of the Lord your God,"[48] inasmuch as you will be thought worthy of his providence and care in your behalf as though he were your father. And that care is as much superior to that which is shown by a man's own parents, as I imagine the being who takes it is superior to them.

LIX. (319) In addition to this the lawgiver also entirely removes out of his sacred code of laws all ordinances respecting initiations, and mysteries, and all such trickery and buffoonery; not choosing that men who are brought up in such a constitution as that which he was giving should be busied about such matters, and, placing their dependence on mystic enchantments, should be led to neglect the truth, and to pursue those objects which have very naturally received night and darkness for their portion, passing over the

---

[46]Deuteronomy 10:21.

[47]Deuteronomy 13:1.
[48]Deuteronomy 14:1.

things which are worthy of light and of day. Let no one, therefore, of the disciples or followers of Moses either be initiated himself into any mysterious rites of worship, or initiate any one else; for both the act of learning and that of teaching such initiations is an impiety of no slight order.

(320) For if these things are virtuous, and honourable, and profitable, why do ye, O ye men who are initiated, shut yourselves up in dense darkness, and limit your benefits to just three or four men, when you might bring down the advantages which you have to bestow into the middle of the market place, and benefit all men; so that every one might without hindrance partake of a better and more fortunate life? (321) for envy is never found in conjunction with virtue. Let men who do injurious things be put to shame, and seeking hiding places and recesses in the earth, and deep darkness, hide themselves, concealing their lawless iniquity from sight, so that no one may behold it. But to those who do such things as are for the common advantage, let there be freedom of speech, and let them go by day through the middle of the market place where they will meet with the most numerous crowds, to display their own manner of life in the pure sun, and to do good to the assembled multitudes by means of the principal of the outward senses, giving them to see those things the sight of which is most delightful and most impressive, and hearing and feasting upon salutary speeches which are accustomed to delight the minds even of those men who are not utterly illiterate.

(322) Do you not see that nature has concealed none of those works which are deservedly celebrated and honourable, but has exhibited openly the stars and the whole of heaven, so as to cause the sight pleasure, and to excite a desire for philosophy, and she also displays her seas, and fountains, and rivers, and the excellencies of the atmosphere, and the beautiful adaptation of the winds to the various seasons of the year, and of plants, and of animals, and, moreover, the innumerable species of fruits, for the use and enjoyment of men? (323) Would it not have been right, then, for you, following her example and design, to give to those who are worthy of it all things that are necessary for their advantage? But now it very often happens that no good men at all are initiated by them, but that sometimes robbers, and wreckers, and companies of debauched and polluted women are, when they have given money enough to those who initiate them, and who reveal to them the mysteries which they call sacred. But let all such men be driven away and expelled from that city, and denied all share in that constitution, in which honour and truth are reverenced for their own sake. And this is enough to say on this subject.

LX. (324) But the law, being most especially an interpreter of equal communion, and of courteous humanity among men, has preserved the honour and dignity of each virtue; not permitting any one who is incurably sunk in vice to flee to them, but rejecting all such persons and repelling them to a distance. (325) Therefore, as it was aware that no inconsiderable number of wicked men are often mingled in these assemblies, and escape notice by reason of the crowds collected there, in order to prevent that from being the case in this instance, he previously excludes all who are unworthy from the sacred assembly, beginning in the first instance with those who are afflicted with the disease of effeminacy, men-women, who, having adulterated the coinage of nature, are willingly driven into the appearance and treatment of licentious women. He also banishes all those who have suffered any injury or mutilation in their most important members, and those who, seeking to preserve the flower of their beauty so that it may not speedily wither away, have altered the impression of their natural manly appearance into the resemblance of a woman.

(326) The law also excludes not only all harlots, but also those who being born of a harlot bear about them the disgrace of their mother, because their original birth and origin have been adulterated. (327) For this passage (if there is any passage at all in the whole scripture which does so) admits of an allegorical interpretation; for there is not one description only of impious and unholy men, but there are many and different. For some persons affirm that the incorporeal ideas are only an empty name, having no participation in any real fact, removing the most important of all essences from the list of existing things, though it is in fact the archetypal model of all things which are the distinctive qualities of essence, in accordance with which each thing is assigned to its proper species and limited to its proper dimensions.

(328) The sacred pillars of the law call all these men broken; for such an injury as is implied by that term leaves a man destitute of all distinctive quality and species, and what is so broken is nothing else, to speak the strict truth, than mere shapeless material.

Thus, the doctrine which takes away species throws every thing into confusion, and moreover brings back that want of proper form which existed before the elements were reduced into proper order. (329) And what can be more absurd than this? For it is out of that essence that God created every thing, without indeed touching it himself, for it was not lawful for the all-wise and all-blessed God to touch materials which were all misshapen and confused, but he created them by the agency of his incorporeal powers, of which the proper name is "ideas," which he so exerted that every genus received its proper form.

But this opinion has created great irregularity and confusion. For when it takes away the things by means of which the distinctive qualities exist, it at the same time takes away the distinctive qualities themselves. (330) But other persons, as if they were engaged in a contest of wickedness, being anxious to carry off the prizes of victory, go beyond all others in impiety, joining to their denial of the ideas a negative also of the being of God, as if he had no real existence but were only spoken of for the sake of what is beneficial to men.

Others, again, out of fear of that Being who appears to be present everywhere and to see everything, are barren of wisdom, but devoted to the maintenance of that which is the greatest of all wickednesses, namely impiety. (331) There is also a third class, who have entered on the contrary path, guiding a multitude of men and women, of old and young, filling the world with arguments in favour of a multiplicity of rulers, in order by such means to eradicate all notions of the one and truly living God from the minds of men. (332) These are they who are symbolically called by the law the sons of a harlot. For as mothers who are harlots do not know who is the real father of their children, and cannot register him accurately, but have many, or I might almost say all men, their lovers and associates, the same is the case with those who are ignorant of the one true God. For, inventing a great number whom they falsely call gods, they are blinded as to the most important of all existing things which they ought to have thoroughly learnt, if not alone, at all events as the first and greatest of all things from their earliest childhood; for what can be a more honourable thing to learn than the knowledge of the true and living God?

LXI. (333) The law also excludes a fourth class, and a fifth, both hastening to the same end, but not with the same intention; for, as they are both followers of the same great evil, self-will, they have divided between them the whole soul as a kind of common inheritance, consisting of a rational and an irrational part; and the one class has appropriate the rational part, which is the mind, and the other the irrational part which is again subdivided into the outward senses; (334) therefore, the champions of the mind attribute to it the predominance in and supreme authority over all human affairs, and affirm that it is able to preserve all past things in its recollection, and to comprehend all present things with great vigour, and to divine the future by probable conjecture; (335) for this is the faculty which sowed and planted all the fertile soil in both the mountainous and champaign districts of the earth, and which invented agriculture, the most useful of all sciences for human life. This also is the faculty which surveyed the heaven, and by a proper contemplation of it made the earth accessible to ships by an ingenuity beyond all powers of description; (336) this, also invented letters, and music, and the whole range of encyc-

lical instruction, and brought them to perfection. This also, is the parent of that greatest of all good things, philosophy, and by means of its different parts it has benefited human life, proceeding by the logical portion of it to an infallible interpretation of difficulties, and by its moral part to a correction of the manners and dispositions of men; and by its physical division to the knowledge of the heaven and the world.

And they have also collected and assembled many other praises of the mind on which they dwell, having a continual reference to the species already mentioned, about which we have not at the present time leisure to occupy ourselves.

LXII. (337) But the champions of the outward senses extol their praises, also, with great energy and magnificence; enumerating in their discourse all the wants which are supplied by their means, and they say that two of them are the causes of living; smell and taste; and two of living well, seeing and hearing; (338) therefore, by means of taste the nourishment derived from food is conveyed into the system, and by means of the nostrils the air on which every living thing depends; for this also is a continual food, which nourishes and preserves men, not only while they are awake, but also while they are asleep. And the proof of this is clear; for if the passage of the breath be obstructed for even the shortest period, to such a degree as wholly to cut off the air which is intended by nature to be conveyed into the system from without, inevitable death will of necessity ensue.

(339) Again, of the more philosophical of the outward senses by means of which the living well is produced, the power of sight beholds the light which is the most beautiful of all essences, and by means of the light it beholds all other things, the sun, the moon, the stars, the heaven, the earth, the sea, the innumerable varieties of plants and animals, and in short all bodies, and shapes, and odours, and magnitudes whatever, the sight of which has given birth to excessive wisdom, and has begotten a great desire for knowledge.

(340) And even without reckoning the advantage derived from these things; sight also affords us the greatest benefits in respect of the power of distinguishing one's relatives and strangers, and friends, and avoiding what is injurious and choosing what is beneficial.

Now each of the other parts of the body has been created with reference to appropriate uses, which are of great importance, as, for instance, the feet were made for walking, and for all the other uses to which the legs can be applied; again, the hands were created for the purpose of doing, or giving, or taking anything; and the eyes, as a sort of universal good, afford both to the hands and feet, and to all the other parts of the body the cause of being able to act or move rightly; (341) and that this is the case is most unerringly demonstrated by the evidence of those who have suffered any mutilation in these members, who cannot in real truth be said to have either feet or hands, and who by the reality of their condition prove the correctness of their name, which they say that men of old gave them not so much by way of reproach as out of compassion, calling them impotent, out of surprise at what they see.

(342) Again, hearing is the thing by which melodies and rhythm, and all parts and divisions of music are distinguished; for song and speech are salutary and wholesome medicines, the one charming the passions and the inharmonious qualities within us by its rhythm, and our unmelodious qualities by its melodies, and bridling our immoderate vehemence by its fixed measures; (343) and each of those parts of it are various and multiform, as the musicians and poets do testify, whom we must believe; and speech, checking and cutting short all the impulses which lead to wickedness, and healing those who are under the dominion of folly and misery, and strengthening those who are inclined to yield in a cowardly manner, and subduing those who resist more obstinately, becomes thus the cause of the greatest advantages.

LXIII. (344) The advocates of the mind and of the outward senses, having put these arguments together, make gods of both of them, the one deifying the first, and the other the last; both classes out of their self-will and self-conceit forgetting the truly living God. On which account the lawgiver very naturally excludes them all from the sacred assembly, calling those who would take away the ideas, broken in the stones, and those too who are utterly atheistical, to whom he has given the appropriate name of eunuchs; and those who are the teachers of an opposite system of theogony, whom he calls the sons of a harlot; and besides all these classes he excludes also the self-willed and self-conceited, some of whom have deified reason, and others have called each separate one of the outward senses gods.

For all these men are hastening to the same end, even though they are not all influenced by the same intentions.

(345) But we who are the followers and disciples of the prophet Moses, will never abandon our investigation into the nature of the true God; looking upon the knowledge of him as the true end of happiness; and thinking that the true everlasting life, as the law says, [49] is to live in obedience to and worship of God; in which precept it gives us a most important and philosophical lesson; for in real truth those who are atheists are dead as to their souls, but those who are marshalled in the ranks of the true living God, as his servants, enjoy an everlasting life. [50]

---

[49] Deuteronomy 4:4.

[50] Yonge's translation includes a separate treatise title at this point: *On the Commandment that the Wages of a Harlot Are Not To Be Received in the Sacred Treasury.* The first three paragraphs of this "treatise" are actually sections 280–284 of *The Special Laws, I* which have been relocated to their proper positon. The remainder of the "treatise" more correctly belongs to *On the Sacrifices of Abel and Cain* 1.21–33 and have been relocated accordingly.

THE SPECIAL LAWS, II†
(De Specialibus Legibus, II)

I. (1) In the treatise preceding this one we have discussed with accuracy two articles of the ten commandments, that which relates to not thinking that any other beings are absolute gods, except God himself; and the other which enjoins us not to worship as God any object made with hands. And we also spoke of the laws which relate specially to each of these points. But we will now proceed to discuss the three which come next in the regular order, again adapting suitable special laws to each.

(2) And the first of these other commandments is not to take the name of God in vain; for the word of the virtuous man, says the law, shall be his oath, firm, unchangeable, which cannot lie, founded steadfastly on truth. And even if particular necessities shall compel him to swear, then he should make the witness to his oath the health or happy old age of his father or mother, if they are alive; or their memory, if they are dead. And, indeed, a man's parents are the copies and imitations of divine power, since they have brought people who had no existence into existence.

(3) One person is recorded in the law, one of the patriarchs of the race, and one of those most especially admired for his wisdom, "as swearing by the face of his father," for the benefit, I imagine, of all those who might live afterwards, and with the object of giving necessary instruction, so that posterity might honour their parents in the proper manner, loving them as benefactors and respecting them as rulers appointed by nature, and might therefore not rashly invoke the name of God. (4) And these men also deserve to be praised who, when they are compelled to swear, by their slowness, and delay, and evasion, cause fear not only to those who see them, but to those also who invite them to take an oath; for when they do pronounce the oath they are accustomed to say only thus much, "By the—;" or, "No, by the—;" without any further addition, giving an emphasis to these words by the mutilation of the usual form, but without uttering the express oath. (5) However, if a man must swear and is so inclined, let him add, if he pleases, not indeed the highest name of all, and

the most important cause of all things, but the earth, the sun, the stars, the heaven, the universal world; for these things are all most worthy of being named, and are more ancient than our own birth, and, moreover, they never grow old, lasting for ever and ever, in accordance with the will of their Creator.

II. (6) And some men display such easiness and indifference on the subject, that, passing over all created things, they dare in their ordinary conversation to rise up to the Creator and Father of the universe, without stopping to consider the place in which they are, whether it be profane or sacred; or the time, whether it be suitable; or themselves, whether they are pure in body and soul; or the business, whether it be important; or the occasion, whether it is necessary; but (as the proverb says), they pollute everything with unwashed feet, as if it were decent, since nature has bestowed a tongue upon them, for them to let it loose unrestrained and unbridled to approach objects which it is impious to approach.

(7) When they ought rather to employ that most excellent of all the organs by which voice and speech (the most useful things in human life, and the causes of all communion among men) are made distinct and articulate, in a manner to contribute to the honour, and dignity, and blessing of the great Cause of all things. (8) But now, out of their excessive impiety, they use the most awful names in speaking of the most unimportant matters, and heaping one appellation upon another in a perfect crowd they feel no shame, thinking that by the frequency and number of their uninterrupted oaths they will attain to the object which they desire, being very foolish to think so; for a great number of oaths is no proof of credibility, but rather of a man's not deserving to be believed in the opinion of men of sense and wisdom.

III. (9) But if any one being compelled to swear, swears by anything whatever in a manner which the law does not forbid, let him exert himself with all his strength and by every means in his power to give effect to his oath, interposing no hindrance to prevent the accomplishment of the matter thus ratified, especially if neither implacable anger or frenzied love, or unrestrained appetites agitate the mind, so that it does not know what is said or done, but if the oath has been taken with sober reason and deliberate purpose. (10) For what is better than to speak with perfect truth throughout one's

---

† Yonge's title, *A Treatise on the Special Laws, Which Are Referred to Three Articles of the Decalogue, Namely the Third, Fourth, and Fifth; About Oaths, and the Reverence Due to Them; About the Holy Sabbath; About the Honour To Be Paid to Parents.*

whole life, and to prove this by the evidence of God himself? For an oath is nothing else but the testimony of God invoked in a matter which is a subject of doubt, and to invoke God to witness a statement which is not true is the most impious of all things.

(11) For a man who does this, is all but saying in plain words (even though he hold his peace), "I am using thee as a veil for my iniquity; do thou co-operate with me, who am ashamed to appear openly to be behaving unjustly. For though I am doing wrong, I am anxious not to be accounted wicked, but thou canst be indifferent to thy reputation with the multitude, having no regard to being well spoken of." But to say or imagine such things as these is most impious, for not only would God, who is free from all participation in wickedness, but even any father or any stranger, provided he were not utterly devoid of all virtue, would be indignant if he were addressed in such a way as this.

(12) A man, therefore, as I have said, must be sure and give effect to all oaths which are taken for honourable and desirable objects, for the due establishment of private or public objects of importance, under the guidance of wisdom, and justice, and holiness.

IV. And in this description of oaths those most lawful vows are included which are offered up in consequence of an abundance of blessings, either present or expected; but if any vows are made for contrary objects, it is not holy to ratify them, (13) for there are some men who swear, if chance so prompts them, to commit theft, or sacrilege, or adultery, or rape, or to inflict wounds or slaughter, or any similar acts of wickedness, and who perform them without any delay, making an excuse that they must keep their oaths, as if it were not better and more acceptable to God to do no iniquity, than to perform such a vow and oath as that. The national laws and ancient ordinances of every people are established for the sake of justice and of every virtue, and what else are laws and ordinances but the sacred words of nature having an authority and power in themselves, so that they differ in no respect from oaths?

(14) And let every man who commits wicked actions because he is so bound by an oath, beware that he is not keeping his oath, but that he is rather violating one which is worthy of great care and attention to preserve it, which sets a seal as it were to what is honourable and just, for he is adding wickedness to wickedness, adding lawless actions to oaths taken on improper occasions, which had better have been buried in silence. (15) Let such a man, therefore, abstain from committing iniquity, and seek to propitiate God, that he may grant to him the mercy of that humane power which is innate in him, so as to pardon him for the oaths which he took in his folly. For it is incurable madness and insanity to take upon himself two-fold evils, when he might put off one half of the burden of them.

(16) But there are some men who, out of the excess of their wicked hatred of their species, being naturally unsociable and inhuman, or else being constrained by anger as by a hard mistress, think to confirm the savageness of their natural disposition by an oath, swearing that they will not admit this man or that man to sit at the same table with them, or to come under the same roof; or, again, that they will not give any assistance to such a one, or that they will not receive any from him as long as he lives. And sometimes even after the death of their enemy, they keep up their irreconcileable enmity, not allowing their friends to give the customary honours even to their dead bodies when in the grave. (17) I would recommend to such men, as to those I have mentioned before, to seek to propitiate the mercy of God by prayers and sacrifices, that so they may find some cure for the diseases of their souls which no man is competent to heal.

V. (18) But there are other persons, also, boastful, puffed up with pride and arrogance, who, being insatiably greedy of glory, are determined to obey none of the precepts which point to that most beneficial virtue, frugality; but even if any one exhorts them to it, in order to induce them to shake off the obstinate impetuosity of the appetites, they look upon all their admonitions as insults, and drive their course on headlong to every kind of effeminate luxury, despising those who seek to correct them, and making a joke of and turning into ridicule all the honourable and advantageous recommendations of wisdom. (19) And if such men happen to be in such circumstances as to have any abundance and superfluity of the means of living, they declare with positive oaths that they will indulge in all imaginable expense for the use and enjoyment of costly luxury. For instance, a man who has lately come into the enjoyment of considerable riches, embraces a prodigal and extravagant course of life; and when some old man, some relation perhaps, or some friend of his father, comes and admonishes him, exhorting him to alter his ways and to come over to a more honourable and strict behaviour, he is indignant beyond all measure at the advice, and being obstinate in his contentious disposition, swears that as long as he has the means and resources necessary for supplying his wants he will not practise any single way which leads to economy or moderation, neither in the city nor in the country, neither when travelling by sea nor by land, but that he will at all times and in all places show how rich and liberal he is; but as it seems to me such conduct as this is not so much a display of riches as of insolence and intemperance.

(20) And yet many men who have before now been placed in situations of great authority, and even many who now are so, though they have most abundant resources of all kinds, and enormous riches, wealth continually and uninterruptedly flowing upon them as if from some unceasing spring, do nevertheless at times turn to the same things which we poor men use, to earthenware cups, and small cheap loaves, and olives, or cheese, or vegetables, for a seasoning to their dinners; and in the summer put on a girdle and a linen garment, and in winter any whole and stout cloak, and for sleep use a bed made on the ground, discarding gladly couches made of ivory or wrought in tortoiseshell and gold, and coverlets of various embroidery, and rich clothes and purple dyes, and the luxury of sweet and elaborate confectionery, and costly viands; (21) and the reason of this conduct is not merely that they have a virtuous and abstemious disposition by nature, but also that they have enjoyed a good education from their earliest youth, which has taught them to honour what belongs to man rather than what belongs to authority, which also taking up its settled abode in the soul, I may almost say reminds it every day of its humanity, drawing it down from lofty and arrogant thoughts, and reducing it within due bounds, and correcting whatever is unequal by the introduction of equality.

(22) Therefore such men fill their cities with vigour and abundance, and with good laws and peace, depriving them of no good thing whatever, but providing them with all requisite blessings in the most unlimited and unsparing manner; for this conduct and actions of this sort are the achievements of men of real nobility, and of men who may truly be called governors. (23) But the actions of men newly become rich, of men who by some blunder of fortune have arrived at great wealth, who have no notion, not even in their dreams, of wealth which is genuine and truly endowed with sight, which consists of the perfect virtues, and of actions in accordance with such virtues, but who stumble against that wealth which is blind, leaning upon which, and therefore of necessity missing the right road, they turn into one which is no road at all, admiring objects which deserve no honour at all, and ridiculing things that are honourable by nature; men whom the word of God reproves and reproaches in no moderate degree for introducing oaths on unfitting occasions; for such men are difficult to purify and difficult to cure, so as not to be thought deserving pardon even by God, who is all-merciful by nature.

VI. (24) But the law takes away from virgins and from married women the power of making vows independently, pronouncing the parents of the one class, and the husbands of the other, their lords; and with reference to any confirmation or disavowal of their oaths, declaring that that power belongs in the one case to the father, and in the other to the husband. And very reasonably, for the one class by reason of their youth are not aware of the importance of oaths, so that they stand in need of the advice of others to judge for them; while the other class do often out of easiness of disposition take oaths which are not for the interest of their husbands, on which account the law invests the husbands and fathers with authority either to ratify their oaths or to declare them void.

(25) And let not widows swear inconsiderately, for they have no one who can beg them off from the effect of their oaths; neither husbands, from whom they are now separated, nor fathers, whose houses they have quitted when they departed from home on the occasion of their marriage, since it is unavoidable that their oaths must stand as being confirmed through the absence of any one to take care of the interests of the swearers.

(26) But if any one knows that any one else is violating his oath, and does not inform against him, or convict him, being influenced by friendship, or respect, or fear, rather than by piety, he shall be liable to the same punishment as the perjured person;[1] for assenting to one who does wrong differs in no respect from doing wrong one's self. (27) And punishment is inflicted on perjured persons in some cases by God and in others by men; but those punishments which proceed from God are the most fearful and the most severe, for God shows no mercy to men who commit such impiety as that, but allows them to remain for ever unpurified, and in my opinion with great justice and propriety, for the man who despises such important matters cannot complain if he is despised in his turn, receiving a fate equal to his actions. (28) But the punishments which are inflicted by men are of various characters, being death, or scourging;[2] those men who are more excellent and more strict in their piety inflicting death on such offenders, but those who are of milder dispositions scourging them with rods publicly in the sight of all men; and to men who are not of abject and slavish dispositions scourging is a punishment not inferior in terror to death.

VII. (29) These then are the ordinances contained in the express language of these commandments; but there is also an allegorical meaning concealed beneath, which we must extract by a careful consideration of the figurative expressions used. We must be aware, therefore, that the correct principles of nature recognise the power both of the father and of the husband as equal, but still in dif-

---

[1]Leviticus 5:21.
[2]Deuteronomy 19:16.

ferent respects. The power of the husband exists because of his sowing the seed of the virtues in the soul, as in a fertile field; that of the father arises from its being his natural office to implant good counsels in the minds of his children, and to stimulate them to honourable and virtuous actions; and because, when he has done so, he cherishes them with salutary doctrines, which education and wisdom supply; (30) and the mind is compared at one time to a virgin, and at another to a woman who is a widow, and again to one who is still united to a husband.

It is compared to a virgin, when it preserves itself pure, and undefiled, free from the influence of pleasures and appetites, and likewise of pains and fears, treacherous passions, and then the father who begot it retains the regulation of it; and her principle, as in the case of a virtuous woman, she now being united to pure reason, in accordance with virtue, will exert a proper care to defend her, implanting in her, like a husband, the most excellent conceptions. (31) But the soul which is deprived of the wisdom and guardianship of a parent, and of the union of right reason, being widowed of her most excellent defences, and abandoned by wisdom, if it has chosen a life open to reproach, must be bound by its own conduct, not having reason in accordance with wisdom to act as intercessor, to relieve her of the consequences of her sins, neither has a husband living with her, nor as a father who has begotten her.

VIII. (32) But in the case of those persons who have vowed not merely their own property or some part of it, but also their own selves, the law has affixed a price to their vows, not having a regard to their beauty, or their importance, or to any thing of that kind, but with reference to the number of the individuals separating the men from the women, and the infants from those who are full grown. (33) For the law ordains[3] that from twenty years of age to sixty the price of a man shall be two hundred drachmas of solid silver money, and of a woman a hundred and twenty drachmas. And from five years of age to twenty, the price of a male child is eighty, and of a female child forty drachmas. And from infancy to five years old, the price of a male is twenty; of a female child, twelve drachmas.[4] And in the case of men who have lived beyond sixty years of age, the ransom of the old men is sixty, and of the old women forty drachmas. (34) And the law has regulated this ransom with reference to the same age both in men and women on account of three most important considerations. First of all, because the importance of their vow is equal and similar, whether it be made by a person of great or of little importance. Secondly, because it is fitting that those who have made a vow should not be exposed to the treatment of slaves; for they are valued at a high or at a low price, according to the good condition and beauty of their bodies, or the contrary. Thirdly, which, indeed, is the most important consideration of all, because inequality is valued among men, but equality is honoured by God.

IX. (35) These are the ordinances established in respect of men, but about animals the following commands are given. If any one shall set apart any beast; if it be a clean beast of any one of the three classes which are appropriate to sacrifice, such as an ox, or a sheep, or a goat, he shall surely sacrifice it, not substituting either a worse animal for a better, or a better for a worse. For God does not take delight in the fleshiness of fatness of animals, but in the blameless disposition of the man who has vowed it. But if he should make a substitution, then he must sacrifice two instead of one; both the one which he had originally vowed, and the one which he wished to substitute for it.

(36) But if any one vows one of the unclean animals, let him bring it to the most venerable of the priests; and let him value it, not exaggerating its price, but adding to its exact value one-fifth, in order that if it should be necessary to sacrifice an animal that is clean instead of it, the sacrifice may not fall short of its proper value. And this is ordained also for the sake of causing the man who has vowed it to feel grieved at having made an inconsiderate vow, having vowed an animal which is not clean, looking upon it, in my opinion, for the moment as clean, being led away by error of mind through some passion.

(37) And if the thing which he has vowed be his house, again he must have the priest for a valuer. But those who may chance to buy it shall not pay an equal ransom for it; but if the man who has vowed it chooses to ransom it, he shall pay its price and a fifth besides, punishing his own rashness and impetuous desire for his two faults, his rashness for making the vow, and his impetuous desire for wishing for things back again which he had before abandoned. But if any one else brings it he shall not pay more than its value. (38) And let not the man who has made the vow make any long delay either in the accomplishment of his vow or in procuring a proper valuation to be made of it. For it is absurd to attempt to make strict covenants with men, but to look upon agreements made with God who has no need of any thing, and who has no deficiency of any thing as unnecessary to be observed, while those who do so are by their delays and slowness convicting themselves of the greatest of offences, namely, of a neglect of him whose service they ought to look upon as the beginning and end of all happiness.

---

[3]Leviticus 27:3.
[4]Leviticus 10:3.

This is enough to say of oaths and vows.[5]

X. (39) The next commandment is that concerning the sacred seventh day, in which are comprehended an infinite number of most important festivals. For instance, there is the release of those men who by nature were free, but who, through some unforeseen necessity of the times, have become slaves, which release takes place every seventh year. Again, there is the humanity of creditors towards their debtors, as they forgive their countrymen their debts every seventh year. Also there is the rest given to the fertile ground, whether it be in the champaign or in the mountainous country, which also takes place every seventh year. Moreover, there are those ordinances which are established respecting the fiftieth year.

And of all these things the bare narration (without looking to any inner and figurative signification) is sufficient to lead those who are well disposed to perfect virtue, and to make even those who are obstinate and stubborn in their dispositions more docile and tractable.

(40) Now we have already spoken at some length about the virtue of the number seven, explaining what a nature it has in reference to the number ten; and also what a connection it has to the decade itself, and also to the number four, which is the foundation and the source of the decade. And now, having been compounded in regular order from the unit, it in regular order produces the perfect number twenty-eight; being multiplied according to a regular proportion equal in all its parts, it makes at last both a cube and a square. I also showed how there is an infinite number of beauties which may be extracted from a careful contemplation of it, on which we have not at present time to dilate. But we must examine every one of the special matters which are before us as comprehended in this one, beginning with the first.

The first matter to be considered is that of the festivals.[6]

XI. (41) Now there are ten festivals in number, as the law sets them down. The first is that which any one will perhaps be astonished to hear called a festival. This festival is every day.

The second festival is the seventh day, which

the Hebrews in their native language call the sabbath.

The third is that which comes after the conjunction, which happens on the day of the new moon in each month.

The fourth is that of the passover which is called the passover.

The fifth is the first fruits of the corn—the sacred sheaf.

The sixth is the feast of unleavened bread, after which that festival is celebrated, which is really the seventh day of seven days.

The eighth is the festival of the sacred moon, or the feast of trumpets.

The ninth is the fast.

The tenth is the feast of tabernacles, which is the last of all the annual festivals, ending so as to make the perfect number of ten. We must now begin with the first festival.

THE FIRST FESTIVAL

XII. (42) The law sets down every day as a festival, adapting itself to an irreproachable life, as if men continually obeyed nature and her injunctions. And if wickedness did not prosper, subduing by their predominant influence all those reasonings about what things might be expedient, which they have driven out of the soul of each individual, but if all the powers of the virtues remained in all respects unsubdued, then the whole time from a man's birth to his death would be one uninterrupted festival, and all houses and every city would pass their time in continual fearlessness and peace, being full of every imaginable blessing, enjoying perfect tranquillity. (43) But, as it is at present, covetousness and the system of mutual hostility and retaliation with which both men and women are continually forming designs against one another, and even against themselves, have destroyed the continuity of cheerfulness and happiness.

And the proof of what I have just asserted is visible to all men; (44) for all those men, whether among the Greeks or among the barbarians, who are practisers of wisdom, living in a blameless and irreproachable manner, determining not to do any injustice, nor even to retaliate it when done to them, shunning all association with busy-bodies, in all the cities which they inhabit, avoid all courts of justice, and council halls, and market-places, and places of assembly, and, in short, every spot where any band or company of precipitate headstrong men is collected, (45) admiring, as it were, a life of peace and tranquillity, being the most devoted contemplators of nature and of all the things in it. Investigating earth and sea, and the air, and the heaven, and all the different natures in each of them; dwelling, if one may so say, in their minds, at least,

---

[5] Yonge's translation includes a separate treatise title at this point: *On the Number Seven*. His next division begins and ends with roman numeral I (=X in the Loeb). The publisher has elected to follow the Loeb numbering.

[6] Yonge's translation includes a separate treatise title at this point: *To Show That the Festivals Are Ten in Number*. This "treatise" begins with roman numeral I (=XI in the Loeb), enumerates each of the ten festivals individually, and extends through Loeb number 214. The publisher has elected to follow the Loeb numbering.

with the moon, and the sun, and the whole company of the rest of the stars, both planets and fixed stars. Having their bodies, indeed, firmly planted on the earth, but having their souls furnished with wings, in order that thus hovering in the air they may closely survey all the powers above, looking upon them as in reality the most excellent of cosmopolites, who consider the whole world as their native city, and all the devotees of wisdom as their fellow citizens, virtue herself having enrolled them as such, to whom it has been entrusted to frame a constitution for their common city.

XIII. (46) Being, therefore, full of all kinds of excellence, and being accustomed to disregard all those good things which affect the body and external circumstances, and being inured to look upon things indifferent as really indifferent, and being armed by study against the pleasures and appetites, and, in short, being always labouring to raise themselves above the passions, and being instructed to exert all their power to pull down the fortification which those appetites have built up, and being insensible to any impression which the attacks of fortune might make upon them, because they have previously estimated the power of its attacks in their anticipations (for anticipation makes even those things light which would be most terrible if unexpected), their minds in this manner calculating that nothing that happens is wholly strange, but having a kind of faint perception of everything as old and in some degree blunted. These men, being very naturally rendered cheerful by their virtues, pass the whole of their lives as a festival.

(47) These men, however, are therefore but a small number, kindling in their different cities a sort of spark of wisdom, in order that virtue may not become utterly extinguished, and so be entirely extirpated from our race. (48) But if men everywhere agreed with this small number, and became, as nature originally designed that they should, all blameless and irreproachable, lovers of wisdom, delighting in all that is virtuous and honourable, and thinking that and that alone good, and looking on everything else as subordinate and slaves, as if they themselves were the masters of them, then all the cities would be full of happiness, being wholly free from all the things which are the causes of pain or fear, and full of all those which produce joy and cheerfulness. So that no time would ever cease to be the time of a happy life, but that the whole circle of the year would be one festival.

XIV. (49) Wherefore, if truth were to be the judge, no wicked or worthless man can pass a time of festival, no not even for the briefest period, inasmuch as he must be continually pained by the consciousness of his own iniquities, even though, with his soul, and his voice, and his countenance, he may pretend to smile; for how can a man who is full of the most evil counsels, and who lives with folly, have any period of genuine joy? A man who is in every respect unfortunate and miserable, in his tongue, and his belly, and all his other members, (50) since he uses the first for the utterance of things which ought to be secret and buried in silence, and the second he fills full of abundance of strong wine and immoderate quantities of food out of gluttony, and the rest of his members he uses for the indulgence of unlawful desires and illicit connections, not only seeking to violate the marriage bed of others, but lusting unnaturally, and seeking to deface the manly character of the nature of man, and to change it into a womanlike appearance, for the sake of the gratification of his own polluted and accursed passions.

(51) On which account the all-great Moses, seeing the pre-eminence of the beauty of that which is the real festival, looked upon it as too perfect for human nature and dedicated it to God himself, speaking thus, in these very words: "The feast of the Lord."[7] (52) In considering the melancholy and fearful condition of the human race, and how full it is of innumerable evils, which the covetousness of the soul begets, which the defects of the body produce, and which all the inequalities of the soul inflict upon us, and which the retaliations of those among whom we live, both doing and suffering innumerable evils, are continually causing us, he then wondered whether any one being tossed about in such a sea of troubles, some brought on deliberately and others unintentionally, and never being able to rest in peace nor to cast anchor in the safe haven of a life free from danger, could by any possibility really keep a feast, not one in name, but one which should really be so, enjoying himself and being happy in the contemplation of the world and all the things in it, and in obedience to nature, and in a perfect harmony between his words and his actions, between his actions and his words.

(53) On which account he necessarily said that the feasts belonged to God alone; for he alone is happy and blessed, having no participation in any evil whatever, but being full of all perfect blessings. Or rather, if one is to say the exact truth, being himself the good, who has showered all particular good things over the heaven and earth. (54) In reference to which fact, a certain pre-eminently virtuous mind among the people of old,[8] when all its passions were tranquil, smiled, being full of and completely penetrated with joy, and reasoning with itself whether perhaps to rejoice was not a peculiar attribute of God, and whether it might not itself miss this joy by pursuing what are thought

---

[7] Leviticus 23:2.
[8] Genesis 18:10.

delights by men, was timorous, and denied the laughter of her soul until she was comforted.

(55) For the merciful God lightened her fear, bidding her by his holy word confess that she did laugh, in order to teach us that the creature is not wholly and entirely deprived of joy; but that joy is unmingled and the purest of all which can receive nothing of an opposite nature, the chosen peculiar joy of God. But the joy which flows from that is a mingled one, being alloyed, being that of a man who is already wise, and who has received as the most valuable gift possible such a mixture as that in which the pleasant are far more numerous than the unpleasant ingredients. And this is enough to say on this subject.

THE SECOND FESTIVAL

XV. (56) But after this continued and uninterrupted festival which thus lasts through all time, there is another celebrated, namely, that of the sacred seventh day after each recurring interval of six days, which some have denominated the virgin, looking at its exceeding sanctity and purity. And others have called the motherless, as being produced by the Father of the universe alone, as a specimen of the male kind unconnected with the sex of women; for the number seven is a most brave and valiant number, well adapted by nature for government and authority. Some, again, have called it the occasion, forming their conjectures of that part of its essence which is appreciable only by the intellect, from the objects intelligible to their outward senses. (57) For whatever is best among the objects of the external senses, the things by means of which the seasons of the year and the revolutions of time are brought to perfection in their appointed order, partake of the number seven. I mean that there are seven planets; that the stars of the Bear are seven, that the Pleiads are seven, and the revolutions of the moon when increasing and waning, and the orderly well-regulated circuits of the other bodies, the beauty of which exceeds all description.

(58) But Moses, from a most honourable cause, called it consummation and perfection; attributing to the number six the origination of all the parts of the world, and to the number seven their perfection; for the number six is an odd-even number, being composed of twice three, having the odd number for the male and the even number for the female, from the union of which, production takes place in accordance with the unalterable laws of nature. (59) But the number seven is free from all such commixture, and is, if one must speak plainly, the light of the number six; for what the number six engendered, that the number seven displayed when brought to perfection. In reference to which fact it may properly

be called the birthday of the world, as the day in which the work of the Father, being exhibited as perfect with all its parts perfect, was commanded to rest and abstain from all works.

(60) Not that the law is the adviser of idleness, for it is always accustoming its followers to submit to hardships, and training them to labour, and it hates those who desire to be indolent and idle; at all events, it expressly commands us to labour diligently for six days,[9] but in order to give some remission from uninterrupted and incessant toil, it refreshes the body with seasons of moderate relaxation exactly measured out, so as to renew it again for fresh works. For those who take breath in this way, I am speaking not merely about private individuals but even about athletes, collect fresh strength, and with more vigorous power, without any shrinking and with great endurance, encounter everything that must be done. (61) And the works meant are those enjoined by precepts and doctrines in accordance with virtue.

And in the day he exhorts us to apply ourselves to philosophy, improving our souls and the dominant part of us, our mind. (62) Accordingly, on the seventh day there are spread before the people in every city innumerable lessons of prudence, and temperance, and courage, and justice, and all other virtues; during the giving of which the common people sit down, keeping silence and pricking up their ears, with all possible attention, from their thirst for wholesome instruction; but some of those who are very learned explain to them what is of great importance and use, lessons by which the whole of their lives may be improved.

(63) And there are, as we may say, two most especially important heads of all the innumerable particular lessons and doctrines; the regulating of one's conduct towards God by the rules of piety and holiness, and of one's conduct towards men by the rules of humanity and justice; each of which is subdivided into a great number of subordinate ideas, all praiseworthy. (64) From which considerations it is plain that Moses does not leave those persons at any time idle who submit to be guided by his sacred admonitions; but since we are composed of both soul and body, he has allotted to the body such work as is suited to it, and to the soul also such tasks as are good for that. And he has taken care that the one shall succeed the other, so that while the body is labouring the soul may be at rest, and when the body is enjoying relaxation the soul may be labouring; and so the best lives with the contemplative and the active life, succeed to one another in regular alternations. The active life having received the number six, according to the service appointed for the body; and the

---

[9]Exodus 20:9.

contemplative life the number seven, as tending to knowledge and to the perfecting of the intellect.

XVI. (65) It is forbidden also on this day to kindle a fire, as being the beginning and seed of all the business of life; since without fire it is not possible to make any of the things which are indispensably necessary for life, so that men in the absence of one single element, the highest and most ancient of all, are cut off from all works and employments of arts, especially from all handicraft trades, and also from all particular services. (66) But it seems likely that it was on account of those who were less obedient, and who were the least inclined to attend to what was done, that Moses gave additional laws, besides, thinking it right, not only that those who were free should abstain from all works on the seventh day, but also that their servants and handmaids should have a respite from their tasks, proclaiming a day of freedom to them also after every space of six days, in order to teach both classes this most admirable lesson; (67) so that the masters should be accustomed to do some things with their own hands, not waiting for the services and ministrations of their servants, in order that if any unforeseen necessities came upon them, according to the changes which take place in human affairs, they might not, from being wholly unaccustomed to do anything for themselves, faint at what they had to do; but, finding the different parts of the body active and handy, might work with ease and cheerfulness; and teaching the servants not to despair of better prospects, but having a relaxation every six days as a kind of spark and kindling of freedom, to look forward to a complete relaxation hereafter, if they continued faithful and attached to their masters.

(68) And from the occurrence of the free men at times submitting to the tasks of servants, and of the servants enjoying a respite and holiday, it will arise that the life of mankind advances in improvement towards perfect virtue, from their being thus reminded of the principles of equality, and repaying each other with necessary services, both those of high and those of obscure rank.

(69) But the law has given a relaxation, not to servants only on the seventh day, but also to the cattle. And yet by nature the servants are born free; for no man is by nature a slave. But other animals are expressly made for the use and service of man, and are therefore ranked as slaves; but, nevertheless, those that ought to bear burdens, and to endure toil and labour on behalf of their owners, do all find a respite on the seventh day. (70) And why need I mention other particulars? The ox, the animal who is born for the most important and most useful of all the purposes of life, namely, for the plough, when the earth is already prepared for seed; and again, when the sheaves are brought into the barn, for threshing in order

to the purification of the crop, is on this day unharnessed, keeping as a festival that day which is the birthday of the year. And thus its holiness pervades every thing and affects every creature.

XVII. (71) And Moses thinks the number seven worthy of such reverence that even all other things which at all partake of it are honoured by him; at all events, on every seventh year he ordains a remission of debts, assisting the poor, and inviting the rich to humanity;[10] that so they, from their abundance, giving to those that are in want, may also look forward to receiving services from them in the case of any disaster happening to them. For the accidents of human life are numerous, and life is not always anchored on the same bottom, but is apt to change like the fickle wind which blows in different directions at different times. (72) It is well, therefore, that the kindness shown by the creditors should extend to all the debtors. But since all men are not naturally inclined to magnanimity, but some men are the slaves of money, or perhaps not very rich, the law has appointed that they should contribute what will not inconvenience them when parted with.

(73) For while it does not permit them to lend on usury to their fellow countrymen, it has allowed them to receive interest from foreigners; calling the former, with great felicity of expression, their brothers, in order to prevent any one's grudging to give of his possessions to those who are as if by nature joint inheritors with themselves; but those who are not their fellow countrymen are called strangers, as is very natural. For the being a stranger shows that a person has no right to a participation in any thing, unless, indeed, any one out of an excess of virtue should treat even those in the conditions of strangers as kindred and related, from having been bred up under a virtuous state of things, and under virtuous laws which look upon what is virtuous alone as good.

(74) But the action of lending on usury is blameable; for a man who borrows on usury has not abundant means of living, but is clearly in some want; and he does so as being compelled to add the interest to his principal in order to subsist, and so he at last becomes of necessity very poor; and while he thinks that he is deriving advantage he is in reality injured, just as foolish animals are when they are deceived by a present bait. (75) But I should say to such persons, "O you who lend on usury, why do you seek to disguise your unsociable disposition by an apparent pretence of good fellowship? And why do you in words, indeed, pretend to be a humane and considerate person, while in your actions you exhibit a want of humanity and a terrible hardness of heart, exacting more than

---

[10]Deuteronomy 15:1.

you gave, and sometimes even doubling your original loan, so as to make the poor man an absolute beggar? (76) Therefore no one sympathises with you in your distress, when, having endeavoured to obtain more, you fail to do so, and besides lose even what you had before. But, on the contrary, all men are glad of your misfortunes, calling you a usurer, and a skinflint, and all kinds of names like those, looking on you as one who lies in wait for human misfortunes, and who esteems the misfortunes of others his own prosperity."

(77) But, as some have said, wickedness is a most laborious thing; and he who lends on usury is blind, not seeing the time of repayment, in which he will scarcely, or perhaps not at all, receive the things which in his covetousness he had hoped to gain. (78) Let such a man pay the penalty of his avaricious disposition, not recovering back what he has expended, so as to make a gain of the misfortunes of men, deriving a revenue from unbecoming sources. But let the debtors be thought worthy of a humanity enjoined by the law, not paying back their loans and usurious interest upon them, but paying back merely the original sum lent. For again, at a proper season, they will give the same assistance to those who have aided them, requiting those who set the example of kindness with equal services.

XVIII. (79) After having given these commandments, Moses proceeds in regular order to establish a law full of all gentleness and humanity. "If," says this law, "one of thy brethren be sold to thee, let him serve thee for six years; and in the seventh year let him be set free without any payment,"[11] (80) Here again Moses calls their fellow countrymen their brothers, implanting in the soul of the owner by this appellation an idea of relationship to his servant, that he may not neglect him as a stranger, towards whom he has no bond of goodwill. But that, yielding to a feeling of affection for him as a relation, in consequence of the lesson which the holy scripture thus suggests, he may not feel indignant when his servant is about to recover his freedom. (81) For it has come to pass that such men are called slaves *(douloi)*, but they are in reality only servants *(thētes)*, serving their masters for the sake of their necessities. And even though they had a thousand times over given their masters absolute power and authority over them, (82) still their masters ought to be gentle to them, considering these beautiful injunctions of the law. O man, he is a hireling who is called a slave, and he also is a man, having a most sublime relationship to you, inasmuch as he is of the same nation as yourself; and perhaps he is even of the same tribe and the same borough as your-

self, and is now reduced to this condition through want. (83) Do you, therefore, casting out of your soul that treacherous evil, insolence, behave to him as if he were a hireling, giving some things and receiving others. And so he will, with all energy and cheerfulness perform the services due to you, at all times and in all places, never delaying, but by his speed and willingness anticipating your commands. And do you, in return, provide him with food and raiment, and take all other necessary care of him; not yoking him to the plough like a brute beast, and not oppressing him with heavy burdens beyond his power to bear, nor treating him with insolence, nor reducing him to painful despondency by threats and infliction of punishment; but giving him proper relaxation and well-regulated periods of rest; for the precept, "Let nothing be too much," applies to every case, and especially to the conduct of masters to their servants.

(84) Therefore, when he has served you for a very sufficient time, for six years, then, when the most sacred number, the seventh year is about to arrive, let him who is free by nature depart in freedom; and grant him this kindness without hesitating as to your part, my good man, but joyfully, because you have now an opportunity of doing a service to that most excellent of all animals, man, in the most important of all matters; for there is no blessing to a slave greater than freedom. (85) Do you, therefore, set him free joyfully; and, moreover, make him a present from your own property, from each portion of your possessions, giving to him who has served you faithfully means to support himself on his journey. For it will tend to your credit if he does not leave your house in poverty but having a plentiful supply for all his necessities, so that he may not again, through want, fall into his previous calamity, namely, slavery, being compelled through want of his daily food to sell himself, and so your kindness will be lost. This, then, is enough to say about the poor.

XIX. (86) In the next place Moses commands the people to leave the land fallow and untilled every seventh year, for many reasons;[12] first of all, that they may honour the number seven, or each period of days, and months, and years; for every seventh day is sacred, which is called by the Hebrews the sabbath; and the seventh month in every year has the greatest of the festivals allotted to it, so that very naturally the seventh year also has a share of the veneration paid to this number, and receives especial honour.

(87) And the second reason is this, "Be not," says the lawgiver, "wholly devoted to gain, but even willingly submit to some loss," that so you may bear with the more indifference involuntary calamity if

---

[11] Deuteronomy 15:12.

[12] Leviticus 25:4.

it should ever fall upon you, and not grieve and despond, as if at some new and strange occurrence; for there are some rich men so unfortunate in their dispositions, as, when want comes upon them, to groan and despond no less than they might do if they were deprived of all their substance. (88) But of the followers of Moses, all who are true disciples, being practised in good laws, are accustomed, from their earliest age, to bear want with patience, by the custom of leaving their fertile land fallow; and being also taught magnanimity, and one may almost say, to let slip out of their hands, from deliberate intention, revenues of admitted certainty.

(89) The third reason appears to me to be thus, which is intimated in a somewhat figurative manner, namely, to show that it does not become any one whatever to weigh down and oppress men with burdens; for if one is to allow a period of rest to the portions of the earth which cannot by nature have any share in the feelings of pleasure or of pain, how much the more must men be entitled to a similar relaxation, who have not only these outward senses, which are common to the brute beasts, but also the especial gift of reason, by which the painful feelings which arise from toil and fatigue, are more vividly imprinted on their imaginations?

(90) Cease, therefore, ye who are called masters, from imposing harsh and intolerable commands on your slaves, which break the strength of the body by their compulsion, and compel the soul to faint even before the bodies; (91) for there is no objection to your exerting a moderate degree of authority, giving orders by which you will receive the services to which you are entitled, and in consequence of which your servants will cheerfully do what they are desired; and then they will discharge their duties but for a short period, as if early exhausted, and, if one must say the truth, brought by their labours to old age before their time; but like athletes, preserving their youthful vigour for a long time, who do not become fat and corpulent, but who are accustomed, by exertion and sweat, to train themselves, so as to be able to acquire the things which are necessary and useful for life.

(92) Moreover let the governors of cities cease to oppress them with continual and excessive taxes and tributes, filling their own stores with money, and in preserving as a treasure the illiberal vices which defile their whole lives; (93) for they do, on purpose, select as collectors of their revenues the most pitiless of men, persons full of all kinds of inhumanity, giving them abundant opportunity for the exercise of their covetousness; and they, in addition to their own innate severity of temper, receiving free license from the commands of their masters, and having determined to do everything so as to please them, practise all the harshest measures which they can imagine, having no notion of gentleness or humanity, not even in their dreams; (94) therefore they throw everything into disorder and confusion, levying their exactions, not only on the possessions of the citizens, but also on their persons, with insults and violence, and the invention of new and unprecedented torture.

And before now I have heard of some persons who, in their ferocity and unequalled fury, have not spared even the dead; but have been so brutal as even to venture to beat the dead corpses with goads; (95) and when some one blamed their brutality, in that not even death, that relief and real end of all miseries, could prevent their victims from being insulted by them, but that, instead of a grave and the customary funeral rites, they were exposed to continued insult, they made a defence worse even than the accusation brought against them, saying that they were insulting the dead, not for the sake of abusing the dumb and senseless dust, for there was no advantage in that, but for the sake of making those who through ties of blood or of friendship were nearly connected with them feel compassion for them, and so inducing them to pay a ransom for their bodies, thus doing them the last service in their power.

XX. (96) Then, O you most worthless of all men! I would say to them, have you not first learnt what you are now teaching? or do you know how to invite other people to compassion even by the most inhuman actions, and yet have you eradicated all merciful and humane feelings from your own souls? And do you act in this way in spite of not being in want of good advisers, and especially of our laws, which have released even the earth from its yearly burdens, giving it a relaxation and a respite? (97) and it, although it seems to be inanimate, is nevertheless fully prepared to make a requital and to recompence favours, hastening to pay back any gift which it has received; for as it receives an exemption every seventh year, and is not forced to exert itself that year, but is set wholly free for the whole circle of the year, in the subsequent year produces double, or sometimes, many times, larger crops than usual from its great productiveness.

(98) And in like manner you may see the trainers acting in the same way towards the athletes; for when they are exercising them with continual and uninterrupted practice, before they are wholly knocked up, they refresh them, giving a respite not only from their exertions in training, but also from their strict regimen of eating and drinking, relaxing the severity of their diet so as to produce a cheerfulness of soul and good condition of body. (99) And yet they are not to be looked upon as teachers of indolence and luxury, inasmuch as their professed business is to train men to the endurance of labours, but by a certain method and artificial system they add to their

natural strength a strength more powerful still, and to their innate vigour a more energetic vigour still, increasing their previous powers by reciprocal remission and exertion, as by a well-regulated harmony.

(100) And I have learnt all this from all-wise nature, which, knowing the industrious and laborious condition of our race, has distributed them into day and night, giving to us the one for wakefulness, and the other for sleep; (101) for she felt a natural anxiety, like a careful mother, that her offspring should not be worn out with toil; for by day she excites our bodies, and rouses them up to all the necessities and duties belonging to life, compelling those to work who would gladly be accustomed to cultivate the leisure of idleness, and an effeminate and luxurious life. But by night, as if she were sounding a retreat in time of war, she invites us to rest, and to take care of our bodies. (102) And those men who have laid aside a heavy weight of business, which has lasted from morning till evening, do now lay their burdens aside and return home and devote themselves to ease, and indulging in profound sleep, refresh themselves after the labours of the day. (103) This long interval between sleeping and waking nature has allotted to men, that they may by turns labour diligently and by turns rest, so as to have all the parts of their bodies more ready for action, and more active and powerful.

XXI. (104) And the lawgiver, who is a prophetic spirit, gave us our laws, having a regard to these things, and proclaimed a holiday to the whole country, restraining the farmers from cultivating the land after each six years' incessant industry. But it was not only on account of the motives which I have mentioned that he gave these injunctions, but also because of his innate humanity, which he thinks fit to weave in with every part of his legislation, stamping on all who study the holy scriptures a sociable and humane disposition.

(105) For he commands his people every seventh year to forbear to enclose any piece of land, but to let all the olive gardens and vineyards remain open, and all their other possessions, whether they be seed-land or trees, that so the poor may be able to enjoy the spontaneously growing crops without fear, in a greater, or at all events not in a less degree than the owners themselves. (106) On which account he does not allow the masters to cultivate the land, having in view the object of not causing them any annoyance from the feeling that they are at all the expense, but that they do not receive any revenue from their lands to make up for the expense, while the poor enjoy all the crops as their own; and he permits those who appear to be strangers to enjoy all these things, raising them from their apparent lowly condition, and from the reproach of being beggars.

(107) Is it not then fit to love these laws which are full of such abundant humanity? by which the rich men are taught to share the blessings which they have with and to communicate them to others: and the poor are comforted, not being for ever compelled to frequent the houses of the indigent to supply the deficiencies by which they themselves are oppressed; (108) but there are times when the widows and orphan children, as if they had been deriving a revenue from their own properties, namely the spontaneously growing crops, as I have said before, and all other classes of person who are disregarded from not being wealthy do at last find themselves in the possession of plenty, being on a sudden enriched by the gift of God, who has called them to share with the possessors themselves in the number of the sacred seven.

(109) And all those who breed flocks and herds lend their own cattle with fearlessness and impunity to graze on the land of others, choosing the most fertile plains, and the lands most suitable for the feeding of their cattle, availing themselves of the license of the jubilee; and they are not met by any ill-will or illiberality on the part of the masters, as having the property in these lands by old custom, which having prevailed for a very long time, so as to become familiar, has now prevailed even over nature.

XXII. (110) Having laid down these principles as a kind of foundation of gentleness and humanity, he then puts together seven sevens of years, and so makes the fiftieth year an entirely sacred year, enacting with reference to it some ordinances of especial honour beyond those which relate to the ordinary years of communication of property.

(111) In the first place he gives this commandment. He thinks it fitting that all property that has been alienated should now be restored to its original masters in order that the inheritances originally apportioned to the different tribes may be preserved, and that no one who originally received an allotment may be wholly deprived of his possessions. (112) Since it often happens that unforeseen circumstances come upon men by which they are compelled to sell what belongs to them. And so he provided in a suitable manner for their necessities, and prevented those who purchased the lands from being deceived, allowing the one to sell their lands, and teaching the others very plainly the conditions on which they are going to purchase. (113) For the law says Do not give a price as if for an everlasting possession, but only for a definite number of years, which must be less than fifty; for the sale effected ought not to be a sale of the lands owned, but a sale of the crops, for two most weighty reasons; one, that the whole country is called the possession of God, and it is impious for any one else to be recorded as the

masters of the possessions of God; and secondly, because a separate allotment has been assigned to each land-owner, of which the law does not choose the man who originally received the allotment to be deprived. (114) Therefore, the law invites the man who is able to recover his original property within the period of fifty years, or any one of his nearest relations, to use every exertion to repay the price which he received, and not to be the cause of loss to the man who purchased it, and who served him at a time when he was in need of assistance. (115) And at the same time it sympathises with the man who is in too great a state of indigence to do so, and bestows its compassion on him, giving him back his former property with the exception of any fields which have been consecrated by a vow, and are so placed in the class of offerings to God. And it is contrary to divine law that any thing which has been offered to God should ever by lapse of time become profane. On which account it is commanded that the accurate value of those fields shall be fully exacted, without showing any favour to the man who dedicated the offering.

XXIII. (116) These are the commandments which are given with respect to the divisions of the land and the inheritances so portioned out. There are others also enacted with respect to houses. And since of houses some are in cities, being within walls; while others are open abodes in the country, and not within any walls; the law has directed that those in the country shall always be redeemed with money, and that those which are not redeemed before the fiftieth year shall be restored without any payment to their original owners, just as their other possessions;[13] for the houses are a portion of the man's possessions. (117) But those which are within walls shall be liable to be redeemed by those who have sold them for a full year;[14] but if they be not redeemed within that year, then after that year they shall be confirmed to those who had bought them, the jubilee of the fiftieth year not injuring the claim of the purchasers.

(118) And the reason of these enactments is that God wills to give even to strangers an opportunity of becoming firmly established in the land. For since they have no participation in the land, inasmuch as they are not numbered among those to whom the inheritances have been apportioned, the law has allotted to them a property in houses, being desirous that they who have come as suppliants to the laws, and who have taken refuge under their protection, should not be homeless wanderers in the land. (119) For the cities, when

the land was originally portioned out in inheritances, were not divided among the tribes, nor indeed were they originally built together in streets, but the inhabitants of the land preferred to make their abode in their open houses in the fields. But afterwards they quitted these houses and came together, the feeling of a love of fellowship and communication, as was natural, becoming stronger after a lapse of time, and so they built houses in the same place, and cities, of which they allowed a share also to the strangers, that they might not be destitute of every thing both in the country and in the cities.

XXIV. (120) And concerning the tribe which was set apart as consecrated for the priesthood, the following laws are established. The law did not bestow upon the keepers of the temple any portion of the land, considering the first fruits of it a sufficient revenue for them. But it allotted them eight and forty cities to dwell in, and a suburb of two thousand cubits around each city.[15] (121) Therefore, it did not confirm the houses in these cities in the same manner that it did those in the other cities which are built within walls, to the purchasers, if those who had sold them were not able to redeem them within the year, but it permitted them to be redeemed at any time, like the open houses in the country taken from the gentiles, to which they corresponded. Since the Levites had received only houses in this district, of which the lawgiver did not think it fit that those who received them should be deprived any more than those to whom the allotments of the open houses in the country had fallen. And this is enough to say about the houses.

XXV. (122) But the laws established with respect to those who owed money to usurers, and to those who had become servants to masters, resemble those already mentioned; that the usurers shall not exact usurers' interest from their fellow countrymen, but shall be contented to receive back only what they lent; and that the masters shall behave to those whom they have bought with their money not as if they were by nature slaves, but only hirelings, giving them immunity and liberty, at once, indeed, to those who can pay down a ransom for themselves, and at a subsequent period to the indigent, either when the seventh year from the beginning of their slavery arrives, or when the fiftieth year comes, even if a man happen to have fallen into slavery only the day before. For this year both is and is looked upon as a year of remission; every one retracing his steps and turning back again to his previous state of prosperity.

(123) But the law permits the people to acquire

---

[13] Leviticus 25:31.
[14] Leviticus 25:19.

[15] Leviticus 35:5.

a property in slaves who are not of their own countrymen, but who are of different nations; intending in the first place that there should be a difference between one's own countrymen and strangers, and secondly, not desiring completely to exclude from the constitution that most entirely indispensable property of slaves; for there are an innumerable host of circumstances in life which require the ministrations of servants.[16]

(124) Sons shall inherit their parents' property, but if there should be no sons, then the daughters would inherit. For just as in their nature men take precedence over women, so also in families they shall have the first share, inheriting property and filling the station of those who have died, being held by a law of necessity that lets no earthborn mortal live forever. (125) But if virgins are left behind unmarried, with no dowry having been set apart by the parents while they were still living, they shall receive a share equal to that of the males. But the presiding power must take care to watch over those who are left behind and of their growth and of the expenses for sustenance and the training that is appropriate for girls, and, whenever the time should come, for appropriate marriage, husbands approved in all things having been selected by merit. (126) Preferably they should be relatives, but if not, they should at least be of the same deme and tribe, so that the lots assigned as dowries will not be alienated through marriages but remain in the tribal allotments as ordered from the beginning.

(127) But if someone should have no offspring, then let the brothers of the deceased succeed to the inheritance. For the place in the family after sons and daughters belongs to brothers. And if someone who has no brothers should die, the uncles on the father's side should succeed to the property, and if there are no uncles, then the aunts, the closest of the remaining household members and other relatives. (128) But if scarcity should seize the family, so that no blood relations are left, then let the tribe be the heir. For the tribe is also a kind of family, if we draw a larger and more complete circle.

(129) The perplexity raised by some, however, should be laid to rest: Seeing that the law mentions all members of the family, the deme, and the tribe in the order of succession to inheritances, why did it remain silent only about parents, who, it would seem, should be just as eligible to inherit their children's property as the children are to inherit theirs? Here is the answer, my good fel-

low! Since the law is divine, and since it always aims at following the logic of nature, it did not wish to introduce any ill-omened provisions; for parents pray to leave behind living offspring who will have succeeded to their name, their lineage, and their property, while their worst enemies call down the opposite on them as a curse, namely, that the sons and daughters should die before their parents. (130) Therefore in order to avoid making explicit provisions for a situation that would be ill-fitting and discordant with the harmony and concord that characterize the administration of the whole cosmos—namely, the case where children die and parents survive—the law both necessarily and fittingly omitted ordering that mothers and fathers should inherit the property of sons and daughters, knowing that this outcome was out of accord with life and nature. (131) So then, the law was careful not to say in so many words that parents inherit when their children die, in order not to seem to reproach grieving parents by allotting to them a benefit that no one would want, and in order not to call misfortunes to mind; but it allotted the property to them in another way, as a small consolation for a great evil. (132) How, then, does it do this? It puts down the father's brother as the heir of his nephews, no doubt rewarding the uncle for the father's sake—unless anyone is so silly as to suppose that one who honors someone for the sake of someone else thereby chooses to dishonor the latter. Those who pay attention to their friends' acquaintances do not thereby neglect their friends, do they? Do not those who show the most solicitous care for those whom they honor also welcome their friends? In precisely the same way, when when the law names the father's brother to share in the inheritance on account of the father, how much more does it name the father! It does not do this explicitly, for the reasons cited, but it makes clear the will of the lawgiver with surer force than an explicit mention.

(133) The eldest son does not share equally with those who came after him but is considered worthy of a double portion, since two people who were previously husband and wife became father and mother on account of the first offspring, and once he came along he was the first to call those who engendered him by these names. Furthermore—and this is the most essential point—the household that was previously childless became one blessed with a son for the continuance of the human race. The seed of this continuance is marriage, and its fruit is the begetting of children, of whom the eldest is the head. (134) I suppose that it is for this reason that the first-born sons of the enemies who had given no quarter, as the holy scriptures reveal, were all cut off in their youth in one night, while the firstborn of the people of the nation were dedicated to God

---

[16] Sections 124–139 were omitted in Yonge's translation because the edition on which Yonge based his translation, Mangey, lacked this material. These lines have been newly translated for this edition.

as a thank-offering and were thus consecrated. For it was necessary to weigh down the former with a heavy and inconsolable grief, the destruction of those who held first place, but to reward the savior God with the firstfruits, whose lot was the pre-eminence among the children.

(135) But there are some men who after getting married and having children have at length unlearned prudence and drifted into incontinence. Lusting after other women, these men have wronged their first wives and behaved toward their children from them no longer as fathers but as uncles, imitating the impious behavior of step-mothers toward previously born children. They have given themselves and their property over entirely to their new wives and to their sons, having been overcome by pleasure, the most shameful passion. The law would not have hesitated to bridle these lusts somehow if it had been possible, lest they kick up their heels even more; (136) but since it was difficult, or rather impossible, to cure this wild frenzy, the law abandoned the man as being in the grip of an incurable disease. It did not, however, overlook the son of the woman wronged on account of the new love but commanded that he should receive a double share of the distribution left for the brothers. (137) There are many reasons for this. For in the first place it punishes the guilty man by compelling him to do something good for the son whom he has chosen to treat badly; and it makes clear the invalidity of his inconsiderate judgment in that it profits the one who was in danger of suffering loss at his hands by putting itself in the role of the parent—the role abandoned by the natural father with regard to the firstborn son. (138) Secondly, it shows mercy and compassion on those who have been treated unjustly, whose burden of distress it lightens by giving them a share in grace and gift; for the double portion of the inheriting son was no less likely to please the mother, who will be encouraged by the kindness of the law, which did not permit her and her off-spring to be totally overcome by their enemies. (139) In the third place, being a good referee of justice, it considered in itself that the father had freely lavished provisions upon the sons of the beloved wife due to his affection for her, while he considered the sons of the hated wife to deserve nothing due to his hatred for their mother. Thus the former had inherited more than their equal share during his lifetime, while the latter were in danger even upon his death of being deprived of the whole patrimony. So then, in order to equal-ize the distribution to the sons of both wives, it set aside a double portion as the rightful inheri-tance of the eldest, the son of the wife who had been put away. This is enough regarding these things.

THE THIRD FESTIVAL

XXVI. (140) Following the order which we have adopted, we proceed to speak of the third festi-val, that of the new moon. First of all, because it is the beginning of the month, and the begin-ning, whether of number or of time, is honour-able. Secondly, because at this time there is nothing in the whole of heaven destitute of light. (141) Thirdly, because at that period the more pow-erful and important body gives a portion of nec-essary assistance to the less important and weaker body; for, at the time of the new moon, the sun begins to illuminate the moon with a light which is visible to the outward senses, and then she dis-plays her own beauty to the beholders. And this is, as it seems, an evident lesson of kindness and humanity to men, to teach them that they should never grudge to impart their own good things to others, but, imitating the heavenly bodies, should drive envy away and banish it from the soul. [17]

(142) The fourth reason is that of all the bodies in the heaven, the moon traverses the zodiac in the least appointed time: it accomplishes its orbit in a monthly interval. For this reason the law has honored the end of its orbit, the point when the moon has finished at the beginning point from which it began to travel, by having called that day a feast so that it might again teach us an excellent lesson that in the affairs of life we should make the ends harmonious with the beginnings. This will happen if we hold the reins on our first impulses with the power of reason and do not permit them to refuse the reins and to run free like animals with-out anyone in charge of the herd. (143) With regard to the benefits which the moon provides to all on earth, why is it necessary to run through and detail them? Their proofs are obvious. Or isn't it by its waxings that rivers and springs overflow, and again by its wanings that they diminish; that seas some-times retreat and are drawn down through their ebb and flow, and at other times suddenly run full through the tide; that the air experiences all sorts of shifts in the form of clear weather, cloudy weather, and other changes? Don't the fruits of cultivated crops and trees grow and come to matur-ity through the orbits of the moon which nurses and ripens each of the growing crops through dew-laden and very gentle breezes? (144) But this is not the appropriate occasion, as I said, to speak at length about the praise of the moon by running through and enumerating the benefits which it pro-vides to animals and to all on the earth. For these reasons and others similar to them, the new moon

[17] Sections 142–144 were omitted in Yonge's transla-tion because the edition on which Yonge based his trans-lation, Mangey, lacked this material. These lines have been newly translated for this volume.

has been honored and taken its place among the feasts.

THE FOURTH FESTIVAL

XXVII. (145) And after the feast of the new moon comes the fourth festival, that of the passover, which the Hebrews call pascha, on which the whole people offer sacrifice, beginning at noonday and continuing till evening. (146) And this festival is instituted in remembrance of, and as giving thanks for, their great migration which they made from Egypt, with many myriads of people, in accordance with the commands of God given to them; leaving then, as it seems, a country full of all inhumanity and practising every kind of inhospitality, and (what was worst of all) giving the honour due to God to brute beasts; and, therefore, they sacrificed at that time themselves out of their exceeding joy, without waiting for priests. And what was then done the law enjoined to be repeated once every year, as a memorial of the gratitude due for their deliverance.

These things are thus related in accordance with the ancient historic accounts. (147) But those who are in the habit of turning plain stories into allegory, argue that the passover figuratively represents the purification of the soul; for they say that the lover of wisdom is never practising anything else except a passing over from the body and the passions. (148) And each house is at that time invested with the character and dignity of a temple, the victim being sacrificed so as to make a suitable feast for the man who has provided it and of those who are collected to share in the feast, being all duly purified with holy ablutions.

And those who are to share in the feast come together not as they do to other entertainments, to gratify their bellies with wine and meat, but to fulfil their hereditary custom with prayer and songs of praise. (149) And this universal sacrifice of the whole people is celebrated on the fourteenth day of the month, which consists of two periods of seven, in order that nothing which is accounted worthy of honour may be separated from the number seven. But this number is the beginning of brilliancy and dignity to everything.

THE FIFTH FESTIVAL

XXVIII. (150) And there is another festival combined with the feast of the passover, having a use of food different from the usual one, and not customary; the use, namely, of unleavened bread, from which it derives its name. And there are two accounts given of this festival, the one peculiar to the nation, on account of the migration already described; the other a common one, in accordance with conformity to nature and with the harmony of the whole world. And we must consider how accurate the hypothesis is.

This month, being the seventh both in number and order, according to the revolutions of the sun, is the first in power; (151) on which account it is also called the first in the sacred scriptures. And the reason, as I imagine, is as follows. The vernal equinox is an imitation and representation of that beginning in accordance with which this world was created. Accordingly, every year, God reminds men of the creation of the world, and with this view puts forward the spring, in which season all plants flourish and bloom; (152) for which reason this is very correctly set down in the law as the first month, since, in a manner, it may be said to be an impression of the first beginning of all, being stamped by it as by an archetypal seal.[18]

(153) Although the month in which the autumnal equinox occurs is first in sequence according to solar orbits, it is not considered first in the law. The reason is that at that time, after all the crops have been harvested, the trees lose their leaves and everything that springtime produced in the height of its glory is withering under dry winds after it has been made dry by the flaming heat of the sun. (154) Therefore he thought that to apply the name "first" to the month in which the hill country and the plain become barren and infertile, was incongruous and unfitting. For it is necessary that the most beautiful and desirable phenomena belong to those things which are first and have received the position of leadership, those phenomena through which the reproduction and growth of animals and fruit and crops take place, but not the ominous destructive forces. (155) And this feast is begun on the fifteenth day of the month, in the middle of the month, on the day on which the moon is full of light, in consequence of the providence of God taking care that there shall be no darkness on that day.

(156) And, again, the feast is celebrated for seven days, on account of the honour due to that number, in order that nothing which tends to cheerfulness and to the giving of thanks to God may be separated from the holy number seven. (157) And of the seven days, Moses pronounces two, the first and the last, holy; giving, as is natural, a preeminence to the beginning and to the end; and wishing, as if in the case of a musical instrument, to unite the two extremities in harmony.

(158) And the unleavened bread is ordained because their ancestors took unleavened bread with them when they went forth out of Egypt, under the guidance of the Deity; or else, because at that time (I mean at the spring season, during

---

[18] Sections 153–154 were omitted in Yonge's translation because the edition on which Yonge based his translation, Mangey, lacked this material. These lines have been newly translated for this volume.

which this festival is celebrated) the crop of wheat is not yet ripe, the plains being still loaded with the corn, and it not being as yet the harvest time, and therefore lawgiver has ordained the use of unleavened food with a view to assimilating it to the state of the crops. For unleavened food is also imperfect or unripe, as a memorial of the good hope which is entertained; since nature is by this time preparing her annual gifts for the race of mankind, with an abundance and plenteous pouring forth of necessaries.

(159) The interpreters of the holy scriptures do also say that the unleavened food is a gift of nature, but that barmed bread is a work of art. (160) Since, therefore, the vernal festival is a commemoration of the creation of the world, and since that it was inevitable that the most ancient persons, those formed out of the earth, must have used the gifts of the world without alteration, pleasure not having as yet obtained the dominion, the lawgiver ordained that food which was the most suitable to the occasion, wishing to kindle every year a desire to walk in the paths of a holy and rigid way of life.[19] (161) The setting out of twelve loaves—the same number as the tribes—on the sacred table especially guarantees the things which have been said. For they are all unleavened, the clearest example of an unmixed food which has been prepared not by human skill for pleasure but by nature for the most essential use. These things are sufficient for this topic.

THE SIXTH FESTIVAL

XXIX. (162) There is also a festival on the day of the paschal feast, which succeeds the first day, and this is named the sheaf, from what takes place on it; for the sheaf is brought to the altar as a first fruit both of the country which the nation has received for its own, and also of the whole land; so as to be an offering both for the nation separately, and also a common one for the whole race of mankind; and so that the people by it worship the living God, both for themselves and for all the rest of mankind, because they have received the fertile earth for their inheritance; for in the country there is no barren soil but even all those parts which appear to be stony and rugged are surrounded with soft veins of great depth, which, by reason of their richness, are very well suited for the production of living things.[20]

(163) The reason is that a priest has the same relation to a city that the nation of the Jews has to the entire inhabited world. For it serves as a priest—to state the truth—through the use of all purificatory offerings and the guidance both for body and soul of divine laws which have checked the pleasures of the stomach and those under the stomach and [tamed] the mob [of the senses][21] by having appointed reason as charioteer over the irrational senses; they also have driven back and overturned the undiscriminating and excessive urges of the soul, some by rather gentle instructions and philosophical exhortations, others by rather weighty and forcible rebukes and by fear of punishment, the fear which they brandish threateningly. (164) Apart from the fact that the legislation is in a certain way teaching about the priesthood and that the one who lives by the laws is at once considered a priest, or rather a high priest, in the judgment of truth, the following point is also remarkable. The multitude of gods, both male and female, honored in individual cities happens to be undetermined and indefinite. The poetic clan and the great company of humans have spoken fabulously about them, people for whom the search for truth is impractical and beyond their capability of investigation. Yet all do not reverence and honor the same gods, but different people different gods. The reason is that they do not consider as gods those belonging to another land but make the acceptance of them the occasion for laughter and a joke. They charge those who honor them with great foolishness since they completely violate sound sense. (165) But if he is, whom all Greeks together with all barbarians acknowledge with one judgment, the highest Father of both gods and humans and the Maker of the entire cosmos, whose nature—although it is invisible and unfathomable not only to sight but also to perception—all who spend their time with mathematics and other philosophy long to discover, leaving aside none of the things which contribute to the discovery and service of him, then it was necessary for all people to cling to him and not as if through some mechanical device to introduce other gods into participation of equal honors. (166) Since they slipped in the most essential matter, the nation of the Jews—to speak most accurately—set aright the false step of others by having looked beyond everything which has come into existence through creation since it is generate and corruptible in nature, and chose only the service of the ungenerate and eternal. The first reason for this is because it is excellent; the second is because it is profitable to be dedicated and associated with the Older rather

---

[19]Section 161 was omitted in Yonge's translation because the edition on which Yonge based his translation, Mangey, lacked this material. These lines have been newly translated for this volume.

[20]Sections 163–174 were omitted in Yonge's translation because the edition on which Yonge based his translation, Mangey, lacked this material. These lines have been newly translated for this volume.

[21]There is a clear problem with the text here, i.e., the noun *ochlon* lacks a verb.

than those who are younger and with the Ruler rather than those who are ruled and with the Maker rather those things which come into existence. (167) For this reason it amazes me that some dare to charge the nation with an anti-social stance, a nation which has made such an extensive use of fellowship and goodwill toward all people everywhere that they offer up prayers and feasts and first fruits on behalf of the common race of human beings and serve the really self-existent God both on behalf of themselves and of others who have run from the services which they should have rendered. (168) These are the things they do for the entire race of human beings. On the other hand they give thanks for themselves for many things. The first is that they are not perpetually wandering here and there among islands and continents and like foreigners and those without a permanent abode who have settled the lands of others and occupy others' wealth are reproached since they have acquired no portion of land from lack of means, but have acquired a land and cities and for a long time have been in possession of their own inheritance, for which reason it has been a sacred duty for them to offer the first fruits. (169) The second is that they did not receive a worthless and common land, but a good and fertile land both for the breeding of domestic animals and the abundance of unspeakably great crops. For there is no poor soil in it, and even the parts that seem to be stony and hardened are broken up with soft and especially deep veins which because of their richness are good for crop production. (170) In addition to these things, they did not receive a desolate land, but one in which there was a populous nation and great cities abounding in men. Yet the cities were emptied of their inhabitants and the entire race disappeared except for a small part: some as a result of wars and others as a result of divinely sent attacks because of their new and strange practices of wrongs and all of the impieties they used to commit through their great efforts to demolish the laws of nature. These things happened so that those who replaced them might be sobered by the calamities of others, and learn from their deeds that those who become devotees of evil deeds will suffer the same fate but those who have honored a life of virtue will possess their assigned portion, numbered not among emigrants but among the native residents. (171) That the first fruit is a handful for their own land and for all lands, offered in thanksgiving for prosperity and a good season which the nation and the entire race of human beings were hoping to enjoy, has been demonstrated. We should not be unaware that many benefits have come by means of the first fruit: first, memory of God—it is not possible to find a more perfect good than this; then, the most just recompense to the real Cause of the fruitfulness. (172)

For the things which occur as a result of agricultural skill are few or none at all: to build up furrows, to dig and spade all around a plant, to deepen a trench, to cut off excessive growths, or to perform any similar task. But the things which come from nature are all essential and useful: the most fertile ground, a land well-watered by springs and both spring-fed and seasonal rivers and sprinkled with annual rains, mild temperatures of air moved by breezes which are most conducive for life, countless types of crops and plants. For which of these has a human either discovered or engendered? (173) Nature which has engendered these things has not begrudged a man its own goods, but considered him to be the governing part of mortal animals because he has a share in reason and good sense. She therefore chose him on the basis of his merit and summoned him to participate in her own goods. For these things it is right that the host, God, be praised and admired since he sees to it that the truely hospitable earth, all of it, is always full of not only the necessities but even of the things which make for a luxurious life. (174) In addition to these things, we should not fail to pay our regard to benefactors. For the person who is thankful to God who needs nothing and is self-sufficient, will also make it a habit to be thankful to humans who are in need of how many countless things.

And there are many meanings intended by this offering of the first fruits. In the first place they are a memorial of God; secondly, they are a most just requital to be offered to him who is the real cause of all fertility; (175) and the sheaf of the first fruits is barley, calculated for the innocent and blameless use of the inferior animals; for since it is not consistent with holiness to offer first fruits of everything, since most things are made rather for pleasure than for any actually indispensable use, it is also not consistent with holiness to enjoy and partake of any thing which is given for food, without first giving thanks to that being to whom it is becoming and pious to offer them.

That portion of the food which was honoured with the second place, namely, barley, was ordered by the law to be offered as first fruits; for the first honours were assigned to wheat, of which it has deferred the offering of the first fruits, as being more honourable, to a more suitable season.

XXX. (176) The solemn assembly on the occasion of the festival of the sheaf having such great privileges, is the prelude to another festival of still greater importance; for from this day the fiftieth day is reckoned, making up the sacred number of seven sevens, with the addition of a unit as a seal to the whole; and this festival, being that of the first fruits of the corn, has derived its name of pentecost from the number of fifty, *(pentēkostos)*. And on it it is the custom to offer up two leavened loaves made of wheat, as a first fruit of the best kind of food made of corn; either because, before the fruit of the year is converted to the use of man, the first produce of the new crop, the first gathered corn that appears is offered as a first fruit, in order that by an insignificant emblem the people may display their grateful disposition;[22] (177) We must disclose another reason. Its nature is wondrous and highly prized for numerous reasons including the fact that it consists of the most elemental and oldest of the things which are encased in substances, as the mathematicians tell us, the right-angled triangle. For its sides, which exist in lengths of three and four and five, combine to make up the sum twelve, the pattern of the zodiac cycle, the doubling of the most fecund number six which is the beginning of perfection since it is the sum of the same numbers of which it is also the product.[23] To the second power, it seems, they produce fifty, through the addition of 3 x 3 and 4 x 4 and 5 x 5. The result is that it is necessary to say that to the same degree that fifty is better than twelve, the second power is better than the first power. (178) If the image of the lesser is the most beautiful sphere of those which are in heaven, the zodiac, then of what would the better, the number fifty, be a pattern than a completely better nature? This is not the occasion to speak about this. It is sufficient for the present that the difference has been noted so that a principal point is not considered to be subordinate.

(179) The feast which takes place on the basis of the number fifty has received the name "the feast of the first produce" since during the feast it is customary to offer two leavened loaves made from wheat as the first fruit of grain, the best food. It is named "the feast of the first produce" either[24] because before the annual crop has proceeded to human use, the first produce of the new grain and the first fruit which has appeared are offered as first fruit. (180) For it is just and religiously correct that those who have received the greatest gift from God, the abundance of the most necessary as well as most beneficial and even the sweetest food, should not enjoy it or have any use of it at all before they offer the first fruits to the Supplier. They are giving him nothing since all things and possessions and gifts are his, but through a small

symbol demonstrate a thankful and God-loving character to the one who needs no favors but showers continuous and ever-flowing favors. (181) Or else because the fruit of wheat is most especially the first and most excellent of all productions.

(182) And the bread is leavened because the law forbids any one to offer unleavened bread upon the altar; not in order that there should be any contradiction in the injunctions given, but that in a manner the giving and receiving may be of one sort; the receiving being gratitude from those who offer it, and the giving an unhesitating bestowal of the customary blessings on those who offer. [...][25] Not indeed to that [...][26]

(183) For those for whom it is lawful and permissible will use what has once been consecrated; and it is lawful for those who are consecrated to the priesthood, who have received the right given by the humaneness of the law to share in the things offered on the altar which are not consumed by the unquenchable fire, either as a wage for their services or as a prize for contests in which they compete on behalf of piety or as a sacred allotment in view of the fact that with regard to the land they have not acquired their appropriate part in the same way as the other tribes. (184) And it is permitted to the priests; and the leaven is also an emblem of two others things; first of all of that most perfect and entire food, than which one cannot, among all the things of daily use, find any which is better and more advantageous; and the fruit of wheat is the best of all the things that are sown; so that it is fitting, that that should be offered as the most excellent of first fruits, for the most excellent gift. (185) The second is a more figurative meaning, implying that every thing which is leavened is apt to inflate and elate; and joy is an irrational elation of the soul.

Now man is not by nature disposed to rejoice at anything that exists more than at an abundant and sufficient supply of necessaries; for which it is very proper to give thanks joyfully, making a display of gratitude, for the invisible happiness affecting the mind, which shall be perceptible to the outward senses through the medium of the leavened loaves; (186) and these first fruits are loaves, not corn, because when there is corn there is no longer anything wanting for the enjoyment of food, for it is said that the wheat is the last of all the grains which are sown to ripen and to come to harvest.

---

[22] Sections 177–180 were omitted in Yonge's translation because the edition on which Yonge based his translation, Mangey, lacked this material. These lines have been newly translated for this volume.

[23] Literally, "being the sum of its own parts to which it is equal." In mathematical notation: $1 + 2 + 3 = 6 = 1 \times 2 \times 3$.

[24] The "or" is in section 181.

[25] The whole of this passage appears corrupt and unintelligible. Mangey especially points out that what was forbidden was not to offer unleavened bread, but leavened bread upon the altar. See Exodus 23:18.

[26] Part of section 183 was omitted in Yonge's translation because the edition on which Yonge based his translation, Mangey, lacked this material. These lines have been newly translated for this volume.

(187) And there are thus two most excellent acts of thanksgiving having a reference to two distinct times; to the past, in which we have been saved from experiencing the evils of scarcity and hunger while living in happiness and plenty; and to the future, because we have provided ourselves with supplies and abundant preparations for it.

THE EIGHTH FESTIVAL

XXXI. (188) Immediately after comes the festival of the sacred moon; in which it is the custom to play the trumpet in the temple at the same moment that the sacrifices are offered. From which practice this is called the true feast of trumpets, and there are two reasons for it, one peculiar to the nation, and the other common to all mankind. Peculiar to the nation, as being a commemoration of that most marvellous, wonderful, and miraculous event that took place when the holy oracles of the law were given; (189) for then the voice of a trumpet sounded from heaven, which it is natural to suppose reached to the very extremities of the universe, so that so wondrous a sound attracted all who were present, making them consider, as it is probable, that such mighty events were signs betokening some great things to be accomplished. (190) And what more great or more beneficial thing could come to men than laws affecting the whole race?

And what was common to all mankind was this: the trumpet is the instrument of war, sounding both when commanding the charge and the retreat. ...

There is also another kind of war, ordained of God, when nature is at variance with itself, its different parts attacking one another. (191) And by both these kinds of war the things on earth are injured. They are injured by the enemies, by the cutting down of trees, and by conflagrations; and also by natural injuries, such as droughts, heavy rains, lightning from heaven, snow and cold; the usual harmony of the seasons of the year being transformed into a want of all concord.

(192) On this account it is that the law has given this festival the name of a warlike instrument, in order to show the proper gratitude to God as the giver of peace, who has abolished all seditions in cities, and in all parts of the universe, and has produced plenty and prosperity, not allowing a single spark that could tend to the destruction of the crops to be kindled into flame.

THE NINTH FESTIVAL

XXXII. (193) And after the feast of trumpets the solemnity of the fast is celebrated,[27] Perhaps some of those who are perversely minded and are not ashamed to censure excellent things will say, "What sort of a feast is this where there is no eating and drinking, no troupe of entertainers or audience, no copious supply of strong drink nor the generous display of a public banquet, nor moreover the merriment and revelry of dancing to the sound of flute and harp, and timbrels and cymbals, and the other instruments of music which awaken the unruly lusts through the channel of the ears? (194) For it is in these and through these, it seems, that they think good cheer consists. They do this in ignorance of the true good cheer which the all-wise Moses saw with the most sharp-sighted eyes and so proclaimed the fast a feast and named it the greatest of feasts in our ancestral language, "a Sabbath of Sabbaths," or as the Greeks would say, a seven of sevens and a holier than things holy. He did this for many reasons.

(195) The first reason is the temperance which the lawgiver is continually exhorting men to display at all times, both in their language and in their appetites, both in and below the belly. And he most especially enjoins them to display it now, when he devotes a day to the particular observances of it. For when a person has once learnt to be indifferent to meat and drink, those very necessary things, what can there be of things which are superfluous that he would find any difficulty in disregarding?

(196) The second reason is, that every one is at this time occupied in prayers and supplications, and since they all devote their entire leisure to nothing else from morning till evening, except to most acceptable prayers by which they endeavour to gain the favour of God, entreating pardon for their sins and hoping for his mercy, not for their own merits but through the compassionate nature of that Being who will have forgiveness rather than punishment.

(197) The third is an account of the time at which this fast is fixed to take place; for by this season all the fruits which the earth has produced during the whole year are gathered in. And therefore to proceed at once to devour what has been produced Moses looked upon as an act of greediness; but to fast, and to abstain from touching food, he considered a mark of perfect piety which teaches the mind not to trust to the food which it may have prepared as the cause of health or life. (198) Therefore those who, after the gathering in of the harvest, abstain from the food, do almost declare in express words, "We have with joy received, and we shall cheerfully store up the bounteous gifts of nature; but we do not ascribe

---

[27] Part of sections 193–194 was omitted in Yonge's translation because the edition on which Yonge based his translation, Mangey, lacked this material. These lines have been newly translated for this volume.

to any corruptible thing the cause of our own durable existence, but we attribute that to the Saviour, to the God who rules in the world, and who is able, either by means of these things or without them, to nourish and to preserve us.[28] (199) At all events, behold, he nourished our forefathers even in the desert for forty years.[29] How he opened fountains to give them abundant drink; and how he rained food from heaven sufficient for each day so that they might consume what they needed, and rather than hording or bartering or taking thought of the bounties received, they might rather reverence and worship the bountiful Giver and honour him with hymns and benedictions such as are due him."

(200) The day of the fast is always celebrated on the tenth day of the month by order of the law. Why is it on the tenth? As we have specified in our treatments of it,[30] it is named complete perfection by wise men[31] and encompasses all the proportions, the arithmetical and the harmonic and the geometric, and in addition the harmonies: the 4:3 ratio through four notes, the 3:2 ratio through five notes, the 2:1 ratio through the octave, the 4:1 ratio through the double octave, and it also has the 9:8 ratio so that it is the most perfect summation of musical theories. From this fact it is named complete perfection.[32] (201) Therefore God has ordained that abstinence from food should take place in accordance with the perfect number, for the sake of affording the best nourishment to the best thing which is in us; that no one may suppose that the interpreter of God's word is enjoining hunger, the most intolerable of all evils, but only a brief cutting off of the stream which flows into the channels of the body. (202) For thus the clear stream which proceeds from the fountain of reason was likely to be borne smoothly and evenly to the soul, since the uninterrupted use of food inundating the body contributes also to confuse the reason. But if the supply of food be checked, then the reason getting a firm footing as in a dry road, will be able to proceed in safety without stumbling; (203) and besides it was fitting that when the supply of all things had turned out according to the wishes of the people and become completed, they should, amid the abundance of their harvest, preserve a commemoration of their previous want by abstinence from food, and should offer up prayers, in order that they might never come to a real experience of a want of necessary food.

THE TENTH FESTIVAL

XXXIII. (204) The last of all the annual festivals is that which is called the feast of tabernacles, which is fixed for the season of the autumnal equinox. And by this festival the lawgiver teaches two lessons, both that it is necessary to honour equality, the first principle and beginning of justice, the principle akin to unshadowed light; and that it is becoming also, after witnessing the perfection of all the fruits of the year, to give thanks to that Being who has made them perfect. (205) For the autumn *(metopōron)*, as its very name shows is the season which comes after *(meta)* the fruits of the year *(tēn opōran)* are now gathered into the granaries, on account of the providence of nature which loves the living creatures upon the earth.

(206) And, indeed, the people are commanded to pass the whole period of the feast under tents, either because there is no longer any necessity for remaining in the open air labouring at the cultivation of the land, since there is nothing left in the land, but all ... is stored up in the barns, on account of the injuries which otherwise might be likely to visit it from the burning of the sun or the violence of the rains.[33]

(207) For when the crops which provide nourishment are in the fields, you act as a manager and guard of those necessities not by having cooped yourself up like a woman who belongs at home, but by having gone out to the fields. If severe cold or summer heat befalls you as you live in the open air, the overgrowths of the trees are handy shelters. If you get under their protection, you will be able to escape easily the harm from each. But when all the crops are in, go in with them to look for a more substantial abode for rest in place of the toils which you endured as you worked the land. Or again, it may be a reminder of the long journey of our ancestors which they made through a wide desert, living in tents for many years at each station. (208) And it is proper in the time of riches to remember one's poverty, and in an hour of glory to recollect the days of one's disgrace, and at a sea-

---

[28]Part of sections 199-200 was omitted in Yonge's translation because the edition on which Yonge based his translation, Mangey, lacked this material. These lines have been newly translated for this volume.

[29]Deuteronomy 8:2.

[30]This is probably a reference to the tractate *Concerning Numbers* mentioned in *QG* 4.110 and *Mos.* 2.115.

[31]*Panteleia* is a Pythagorean name for the number ten.

[32]The text literally says: "the 1⅓ through four, the 1½ through five, the doubled through the octave, the quadrupled through the double octave, and it also has the 1⅛ ratio ..." Philo has a fuller statement in *Opif.* 48. In each instance he is following the Pythagoreans who applied number theory to music. For similar treatments see Plutarch, *Moralia* 1139D (*Mus.* 23) and Sextus Empiricus *Adv. Math.* 7.94–95.

[33]Portions of sections 207, 209, 212, 213 were omitted in Yonge's translation because the edition on which Yonge based his translation, Mangey, lacked this material. These lines have been newly translated for this volume.

son of peace to think upon the dangers that are past. (209) In addition to the pleasure it provides, a not inconsiderable advantage for the practice of virtue comes from this. For people who have had prosperity and adversity before their eyes and have pushed the latter away and are enjoying the free use of the better, of necessity become thankful in disposition and are being urged on to piety by fear of a change of state to the contrary condition. As a result they honor God in songs and words for their present wealth and persistently entreat and conciliate him with supplications that they will no longer be tested with calamities.

(210) Again, the beginning of this festival is appointed for the fifteenth day of the month, on account of the reason which has already been mentioned respecting the spring season, also that the world may be full, not by day only but also by night, of the most beautiful light, the sun and moon on their rising opposite to one another with uninterrupted light, without any darkness interposing itself between so as to divide them. (211) And after the festival has lasted seven days, he adds an eighth as a seal, calling it a kind of crowning feast, not only as it would seem to this festival, but also to all the feasts of the year which we have enumerated; for it is the last feast of the year, and is a very stable and holy sort of conclusion, befitting men who have now received all the produce from the land, and who are no longer in perplexity and apprehension respecting any barrenness or scarcity. (212) Perhaps, however, the first cubic number, the number eight, was assigned to the feast for the following reason. It is in its capacity[34] the beginning of solid substance at the transition from the incorporeal, the end of the intelligible. The intelligible [make the transition][35] to a solid nature through the scale of ascending powers. (213) And in fact, the autumnal feast, just as I said, as a kind of summation and end of all the feasts in the year seems to be more stable and steadier since people have already received the revenue from the land and are no longer in a state of fear and baffled by doubts about productivity or dearth. For the anxious thoughts of farmers are not settled until the crops are in because of the losses just waiting to happen from so many people and animals.

(214) I have spoken in this way about the sacred week and the sacred number seven at more than usual length, wishing to show that all the feasts of the year are, as it were, the offspring of the num-

ber seven, which stands in the relation of a mother. […][36] Follies and joys; and because in such assemblies and in a cheerful course of life there are thus established seasons of delight unconnected with any sorrow or depression supporting both the body and the soul; the one by the pleasure and the other by the opportunities for philosophical study which they afford.[37]

XXXIV. (215) There is, besides all these, another festival[38] sacred to God, and a solemn assembly on the day of the festival which they call castallus,[39] from the event that takes place in it, as we shall show presently. Now that this festival is not in the same rank, nor of the same importance with the other festivals, is plain from many considerations. For, first of all, it is not one to be observed by the whole population of the nation as each of the others is. Secondly, none of the things that are brought or offered are laid upon the altar as holy, or committed to the unextinguishable and holy fire. Thirdly, the very number of days which are to be observed in the festival are not expressly stated.

XXXV. (216) Nevertheless, any one may easily see that it has about it some of the characteristics of a sacred festival, and that it comes very near to having the privileges of a solemn assembly. For every one of those men who had lands and possessions, having filled vessels with every different species of fruit borne by fruit-bearing trees; which vessels, as I have said before, are called castalli, brings with great joy the first fruits of his abundant crop into the temple, and standing in front of the altar gives the basket to the priest, uttering at the same time the very beautiful and admirable hymn prescribed for the occasion; and if he does not happen to remember it, he listens to it with all attention while the priest recites it. (217) And the hymn is as follows:—"The leaders of our nation renounced Syria, and migrated to Egypt. Being but few in number, they increased till they became a populous nation. Their descendants being oppressed in innumerable ways by the natives of the land, when no assistance did any longer appear to be expected from men, became the suppliants of God, having fled for refuge to entreat his assistance. (218) Therefore he, who is mer-

---

[34]The term *dynamei* is problematic here. It normally means "squared"—as Colson recognized—but is here understood more generally.

[35]There is no verb in the text. The translation follows one of Cohn's conjectures [*metabainei*] which matches *metabasin* nicely.

[36]I have translated this as it is printed in Schwichest's edition. Mangey makes the treatise end at "mother."

[37]Yonge's translation includes a separate treatise title at this point: *On the Festival of the Basket of First-Fruits* and notes that it is not given in Mangey's edition. Accordingly, his next paragraph begins with roman numeral I (=XXXIV in the Loeb). Yonge's "treatise" concludes with number IV (=Loeb XXXVII). The publisher has elected to follow the Loeb numbering.

[38]Deuteronomy 26:1.

[39]Castallus is interpreted "a basket with a pointed bottom."

ciful to all who are unjustly treated, having received their supplication, smote those who oppressed them with signs and wonders, and prodigies, and with all the marvellous works which he wrought at that time. And he delivered those who were being insulted and enduring every kind of perfidious oppression, not only leading them forth to freedom, but even giving them in addition a most fertile land; (219) for it is from the fruits of this land, O bounteous God! that we now bring you the first fruits; if indeed it is a proper expression to say that he who receives them from you brings them to you. For, O Master! they are all your favours and your gifts, of which you have thought us worthy, and so enabled us to live comfortably and to rejoice in unexpected blessings which thou hast given to us, who did not expect them."

XXXVI. (220) This hymn is sung from the beginning of summer to the end of autumn, by two choruses replying to one another uninterruptedly, on two separate occasions, each at the end of one complete half of ten years; because men cannot all at once bring the fruits of the seasons to God in accordance with his express command, but different men bring them at different seasons; and sometimes even the same persons bring first fruits from the same lands at different times; (221) for since some fruits become ripe more speedily, and others more slowly, either on account of the differences of the situations in which they are grown, as being hotter or colder, or from innumerable other reasons, it follows that the time for offering the first fruits of such productions is undefined and uncertain, being extended over a great space. (222) And the use of these first fruits is permitted to the priests, since they had no portion of the land themselves, and had no possessions from which they could derive revenue; but their inheritance is the first fruits from all the nation as the wages of their holy ministrations, which they perform day and night.

XXXVII. (223) I have now said thus much respecting the number seven, and the things referring to it among the days, and the months, and the years; and about the festivals which are connected with this number seven, following the regular connection of the heads of the subject, which I proposed to myself according to the order in which they are mentioned in the sacred history. And I shall now proceed in regular order to consider the commandment which comes next, which is entitled the one about the honour due to parents.[40]

XXXVIII. (224) Having already spoken of four commandments which, both as to the order in which they are placed and as to their importance, are truly the first; namely, the commandment about the lenity of that sovereign authority by which the world is governed, and that which commands that man should not look upon any representation or figure of anything as God, and that which forbids the swearing falsely, or indeed the swearing carelessly and vainly at all, and that concerning the sacred seventh day—all which commandments tend to piety and holiness. I now proceed to the fifth commandment, relating to the honour due to parents; which is, as I showed in the mention I made of it separately before, on the borders between those which relate to the affairs of men and those which relate to God.

(225) For parents themselves are something between divine and human nature, partaking of both; of human nature, inasmuch as it is plain that they have been born and that they will die; and of divine nature, because they have engendered other beings, and have brought what did not exist into existence: for, in my opinion, what God is to the world, that parents are to their children; since, just as God gave existence to that which had no existence, they also, in imitation of his power, as far at least as they were able, make the race of mankind everlasting.

XXXIX. (226) And this is not the only reason why a man's father and mother are deserving of honour, but here are also several other reasons. For among all those nations who have any regard for virtue, the older men are esteemed above the younger, and teachers above their pupils, and benefactors above those who have received kindnesses from them, and rulers above their subjects, and masters above their slaves. (227) Accordingly, parents are placed in the higher and superior class; for they are the elders, and the teachers, and the benefactors, and the rulers, and the masters. And sons and daughters are placed in the inferior class; for they are the younger, and the pupils, and the persons who have received kindnesses, and subjects, and slaves. And that every one of these assertions is correct is plain from the circumstances that take place, and proofs derived from reason will establish the truth of them yet more undeniably.

XL. (228) I affirm, therefore, that that which produces is always older than that which is produced, and that that which causes anything is older than that of which it is the cause; but those who beget or bring forth a child are in some sense the causes and producers of the child which is begot-

---

[40] Yonge's translation includes a separate treatise title at this point: *On the Honour Commanded To Be Paid to Parents*. Accordingly, his next paragraph begins with roman numeral I (=XXXVIII in the Loeb). Yonge's "treatise" concludes with number XI (=XLVIII in the Loeb). The publisher has elected to follow the Loeb numbering.

ten or brought forth, and they stand in the light of teachers, inasmuch as all that they know themselves they teach to their children from their earliest infancy, and they not only exercise and train them in the supernumerary accomplishments, impressing reasonings on the minds of their children when they come to their prime, but they also teach them those most necessary lessons which refer to choice and avoidance, the choice, that is to say, of virtues, and the avoidance of vices, and of all the energies in accordance with them. (229) For who can be more completely the benefactors of their children than parents, who have not only caused them to exist, but have afterwards thought them worthy of food, and after that again of education both in body and soul, and have enabled them not only to live, but also to live well; (230) training their body by gymnastic and athletic rules so as to bring it into a vigorous and healthy state, and giving it an easy way of standing and moving not without elegance and becoming grace, and educating the soul by letters, and numbers, and geometry, and music, and every kind of philosophy which may elevate the mind which is lodged in the mortal body and conduct it up to heaven, and can display to advantage the blessed and happy qualities that are in it, producing an admiration of and a desire for an unchangeable and harmonious system, which they will afterwards never leave if they preserve their obedience to their captain.

(231) And in addition to the benefits which they heap upon them, they have likewise authority over the children of whom they are the parents, not as is the case in cities, in consequence of some drawing of lots or election, so that any one can find fault with his governor as having become so either by some blunder of fortune and not by reason, or it may be by the impetuosity of the multitude, the most inconsiderate and foolish of all things, but being established in this post by the most excellent and perfect wisdom of the sublime nature, which regulates all divine and human affairs in accordance with justice.

XLI. (232) For these reasons it is allowable for parents even to accuse their children, and to reprove them with considerable severity, and even, if they do not submit to the threats which are uttered to them by word of mouth, to beat them, and inflict personal punishment on them, and to imprison them; and if they behave with obstinacy and resist this treatment, becoming stiff-necked through the greatness of their incurable wickedness, the law permits them to chastise them even to the extent of putting them to death.[41] But still this permission is not given to either the father by himself, or to the mother by herself, by reason

of the greatness of the punishment, which it is not fitting should be determined by one, but by both together, for it is not probable that both the parents will agree about putting their child to death unless his iniquities are very grievous, and weigh down by a certain undoubted preponderance that firm affection which is firmly implanted in the parents by nature.

(233) But parents have received not only the power of a ruler and governor over their children, but also that of a master, according to both the very highest characteristics of the possession of servants, namely, possessing them as born in the house, and also as purchased with money, for they expend a price many times greater than their real value on their children and for the sake of their children, in wages to nurses, and instructors, and teachers, besides all the expenses which they incur for their dress and their food, and their other care of them when well and when sick, from their earliest infancy till the time that they are full grown. And not only are those looked upon as servants born in the house who have actually been brought forth within the walls, but those also are so regarded who by the laws of nature receive from the masters of the house a sufficient support to maintain them in life after they are born.

XLII. (234) Since this, then, is the case, those who do honour their parents are not doing anything worthy of praise, since even any single one of the commandments already mentioned is sufficient to invite them to regard their parents with reverence. But are not those men worthy of blame, and accusation, and the very extremity of punishment, who neither respect them as older than themselves, nor listen to them as their teachers, nor think them worthy of any requital as their benefactors, nor obey them as their rulers, nor fear them as their masters? (235) Therefore the law says, "Honour thy father and thy mother next after God;"[42] assigning to them the second place in honour, on the same principle as nature herself has ranked them in her decision of their proper place and duties.

And you will not honour them more by any line of conduct than by endeavouring and appearing to be virtuous persons. As the being such is a seeking of virtue without pride and without guile, and appearing such aims at virtue in connection with a good reputation and praise from one's associates; (236) for parents, thinking but little of their own advantage, think the virtue and excellence of their children the perfection of their own happiness, for which reason it is that they are anxious that they should obey the injunctions which are laid upon them, and that they should be obedient

[41]Deuteronomy 21:18.   [42]Deuteronomy 5:16.

to all just and beneficial commands; for a father will never teach his child anything which is inconsistent with virtue or with truth.

XLIII. (237) And any one may conjecture that pious respect is due to parents, not only from what has been said above, but also from the manner in which persons behave to those who are of the same age with their parents; for the man who shows respect to an old man, or to an old woman, who is no relation to him, must appear in some degree to be remembering his own father and mother, and, out of this consideration, to be looking upon them as the images of his parents, who are the real models. (238) On which account, in the sacred scriptures, it is not only commanded that young men should rise up and give the best seats to their elders, but also that they should rise up before them when they pass by;[43] showing honour to the grey hairs of old age, to which there is a hope that they may come themselves if they now yield precedence to them.

(239) And this commandment also seems to me to have been enacted with exceeding beauty and propriety; for the law says, "Let each man fear his father and his mother,"[44] enjoining fear rather than affection, not as being more advantageous and profitable with reference to the present occasion, for the first of these feelings affects foolish persons when they are being instructed or reproved, and folly cannot be cured by any other means than fear. But the second feeling, namely, affection towards their parents, it is not fitting should be inculcated on children by the injunctions of a lawgiver, for nature requires that that should be spontaneous. For it has implanted it so deeply from very infancy in the souls of those who are so completely united by blood, and by the services done by the parents to the children, that it is always self-taught and spontaneous, and has no need of commandments to enforce it.

(240) But the law has enjoined fear, because children are accustomed to feel an easy indifference. For though parents attend to their children with an exceeding violence of affection, providing them with necessary things from all quarters, and bestowing all good things upon them, and shrinking from no labour and from no danger, being bound to them by love stronger than any oaths, still some persons do not receive their affection as if it aimed solely at their good, being full of luxury and arrogance; and coveting a luxurious life, and becoming effeminate both in body and soul, permitting them in no respect to entertain proper dispositions as through the native powers of their minds, which they are not ashamed to overthrow, and to ener-

vate, and to deprive of each separate energy, and so they come not to fear their natural correctors, their fathers and mothers yielding to and indulging their own private passions and desires. (241) But we must also urge on the parents of such persons that they employ more weighty and severe admonitions in order to cure this impetuous obstinacy of their children, and we must warn the children to reverence their parents, fearing them as their rulers and natural masters; for it is with difficulty even by these considerations that they will be brought to hesitate to act unjustly.

XLIV. (242) I have now then gone through all the five heads of laws in the first table, and have noticed also all the particular points which had any reference to any individual. I must also now point out the punishments affixed to the transgression of these laws.

(243) Now there is one common penalty affixed to them all, namely, death, through which all such offences have a kind of relationship to one another. But the causes of this sentence being pronounced in such cases are different, and we must begin with the last, the one that relates to parents, since it is in reference to this one that the words are still ringing in our ears, "If any one shall beat his father or his mother, let him be stoned."[45]

And very justly, for it is not fit that that man should live who insults those who are the causes of his living; (244) but some of the men of high rank, and some of the lawgivers, looking rather at the vain opinions of men than at the truth, have softened this commandment, and instituted as a penalty, for those who beat their fathers, that their hands should be cut off; and for the sake of bearing a good reputation in the eyes of hasty and inconsiderate persons, they profess to them that it is becoming, that the parts with which such men have struck their parents should be cut off; (245) but it is a piece of folly to be angry with the servants rather than with those who are the causes of such folly; for it is not the hands that behave with such insolence, but insolent men perform their actions with their hands, and it is the men who must be punished, unless indeed it can be called fitting to let men go who have committed murder with the sword, and to content one's self with throwing away the sword; and unless, on the contrary, one ought not to give honour to those who have shown pre-eminent valour in war, but to the inanimate coats of armour, by means of which they have behaved themselves valiantly; (246) and unless again it is reasonable, in the case of those who have gained the victory in the gymnastic games, in the stadium, or the double race, or the long straight course, or in the contest of boxing, or in the pancratium,

[43] Leviticus 19:32.
[44] Leviticus 19:3.
[45] Exodus 21:15.

to attempt to crown only the legs and arms of the conquerors, and to let the whole of their bodies remain unhonoured.

Surely it would be a ridiculous thing to lay down such principles as these, and to abstain in consequence from punishing or honouring those who were the real causes of the results in question; for we do not pass over a man who has given a splendid exhibition of musical skill, playing exquisitely on the flute or the lyre, and think the instruments themselves worthy of proclamations and honours. (247) Why, then, should we deprive of their hands men who beat their fathers, O you most noble lawgivers? Is it that they may for the future be wholly useless for any purpose whatever, and that they may exact as a tribute, not once a year but every day, from those whom they have treated with iniquity, compelling them to supply them with necessary food, as being unable to provide for themselves? For their father is not so wholly hard-hearted as to endure to see even a son who has so grievously offended against him dying of hunger, after his anger has been blunted by time. (248) And even if he has not laid hands upon his parents, but has only spoken ill of those whom he was bound to praise and bless, or if he has in any other manner done anything which can tend to bring his parents into disrepute, still let him die.[46] For since he is a common enemy, and if one may tell the plain truth, he is a public enemy of all men, to whom else can he be kind and favourable when he is not so to the authors of his being, by whose means he came into this world, and of whom he is a sort of supplement?

XLV. (249) Again, let the man who has profaned the sacred seventh day as far as it may have lain in his power, be liable to the punishment of death. For, on the contrary, it is proper rather to provide whatever is profane, be it a thing or be it a person, with means of purification, in order to induce a change for the better, since "envy," as some one has said, "goes forth out of the divine company." But to dare to adulterate or to deface the holy coinage is an act which displays an extraordinary degree of impiety.

(250) In that ancient migration which took place when the people of Israel left Egypt, and when the whole multitude was travelling through the pathless wilderness, when the seventh day came all those myriads of men which I have described before rested in their tents in perfect tranquillity; but one man, and he not one of the most despised or lowest class of the people, disregarding the commands which were laid upon the nation, and ridiculing those who attended to them, went forth to pick up sticks, but in reality to show his con-

tempt for and violation of the law. (251) And he indeed came back bearing with him a faggot in his arm, but the men who remained in their tents although inflamed with anger and exasperated by his conduct, nevertheless did not at once proceed to very harsh measures against him that day by reason of the holy reverence due to the day, but they led him before the ruler of the people, and made known his impious action, and he having committed him to prison, after a command had been given to put him to death, gave the man up to those who had originally seen him to execute. As therefore, in my opinion, it was not permitted to kindle a fire on the seventh day for the reason which I have already mentioned, so likewise it was not lawful to collect any fuel for a fire.

XLVI. (252) Against those who call God as a witness in favour of assertions which are not true, the punishment of death is ordained in the law;[47] and very properly, for even a man of moderate respectability will never endure to be cited as a witness, and to have his name registered in support of a lie. But it seems to me that he would look upon any one who proposed such a thing to him as a thoroughly faithless enemy; (253) on which account we must say this, that him, who swears rashly and falsely, calling God to witness an unjust oath, God, although he is merciful by nature, will yet never release, inasmuch as he is thoroughly defiled and infamous from guilt, even though he may escape punishment at the hands of men. And such a man will never entirely escape, for there are innumerable beings looking on, zealots for and keepers of the national laws, of rigid justice, prompt to stone such a criminal, and visiting without pity all such as work wickedness, unless, indeed, we are prepared to say that a man who acts in such a way as to dishonour his father or his mother is worthy of death, but that he who behaves with impiety towards a name more glorious than even the respect due to one's parents, is to be borne with as but a moderate offender.

(254) But the lawgiver of our nation is not so foolish as, after putting to death men who are guilty of minor offences, then to treat those who are guilty of heavier crimes with mildness, since surely it is a greater iniquity than even to speak disparagingly or to insult one's parents, to show a contempt for the sacred name of God by means of perjury. (255) And if even he who swears in an unbecoming manner is guilty and blameable, of what punishment is that man worthy who denies the one only true and living God and now honours the creature above the Creator, and chooses to honour not only the earth and the water, or the air, or the fire, the elements of the universe, or

---

[46] Exodus 21:16.

[47] Deuteronomy 19:19.

again the sun and moon, and the planets and fixed stars, and the whole of heaven, and the universal world, but even stocks and stones, which mortal workmen have fashioned, and which by them have been shaped into human figures?

(256) Therefore, let such a man be himself likened to images carved by the hand; for it ought not to be that that man should have any soul himself who honours things destitute of soul or life, and especially after he has been a disciple of Moses, whom he has often heard announcing to him and under the influence of divine inspiration declaring those most sacred and holy admonitions, "Take not the name of any other gods into thy soul for a remembrance of them, and utter not their names with thy voice, but keep both thy mind and thy speech far from all other interpositions, and turn them wholly to the Father and Creator of the universe, that thus thou mayest cherish the most virtuous and godly thoughts about his single government, and mayest speak words that are becoming and most profitable both to thyself and to those that hear thee."[48]

XLVII. (257) We have now then mentioned the punishments which are ordained against those who neglect the five commandments. But the rewards which are offered to those who keep them, even though the law has not set them forth in express words of injunction, are nevertheless figuratively intimated. (258) Therefore the fact of not thinking that there are any other gods but the true God, nor imagining that things made by the hand of man are gods, and the fact of not committing perjury, are things which have no need of any other reward, for the mere fact, in my opinion, of practising these virtues is itself a most excellent and most perfect reward. For at what circumstance can a lover of truth feel more really delighted than at the devotion of himself to one God, and attending in a guileless and pure manner to his service? (259) And when I speak of witnesses, I mean not such persons as are slaves to pride, but such as are devoted to an admiration of goodness free from all error, by whom the truth is honoured.

For wisdom itself is the reward of wisdom; and justice, and each of the other virtues, is its own reward. And truth, as being the most beautiful in the whole company, and as being the chief of all the holy virtues, is in much greater degree its own recompense and reward, affording as it does happiness to all who practise it, and blessings of which they cannot be deprived to their children and descendants.

XLVIII. (260) Again, those who properly keep the sacred sabbath are benefited in two most important particulars, both body and soul; as to their body, by a rest from their continual and incessant labours; and as to their soul, by forming most excellent conceptions respecting God as the Creator of the universe and the careful protector of all the things and beings which and whom he has made. And he made the whole universe in one week. It is plain, therefore, from these things that the man who honours the seventh day will himself find honour.

(261) In the same way let not him who honours his parents dutifully seek for any further advantage, for if he considers the matter he will find his reward in his own conduct. Not but what, since this commandment is inferior in importance to the first five commandments, which have a more divine character, inasmuch as this is concerned with mortal subjects, God has given an inducement to obey this one, saying, "Honour thy father and thy mother, that it may be well with thee, and that thy days may be long in the land;"[49] (262) affixing thus two rewards to this injunction, one being in fact the participation in virtue, for "well" means virtue, or at least cannot subsist without virtue; while the other is, if one is to say the truth, immortality by length of days, and a life of long duration, which thou wilt preserve even in the body living with thy soul, purified with a perfect purification.

These things have now been discussed at sufficient length. Let us after this, since the opportunity offers, consider the commandments in the second table.

---

[48] Exodus 23:13.

[49] Exodus 20:12.

THE SPECIAL LAWS, III†

(De Specialibus Legibus, III)

I. (1) There was once a time when, devoting my leisure to philosophy and to the contemplation of the world and the things in it, I reaped the fruit of excellent, and desirable, and blessed intellectual feelings, being always living among the divine oracles and doctrines, on which I fed incessantly and insatiably, to my great delight, never entertaining any low or grovelling thoughts, nor ever wallowing in the pursuit of glory or wealth, or the delights of the body, but I appeared to be raised on high and borne aloft by a certain inspiration of the soul, and to dwell in the regions of the sun and moon, and to associate with the whole heaven, and the whole universal world.

(2) At that time, therefore, looking down from above, from the air, and straining the eye of my mind as from a watch-tower, I surveyed the unspeakable contemplation of all the things on the earth, and looked upon myself as happy as having forcibly escaped from all the evil fates that can attack human life. (3) Nevertheless, the most grievous of all evils was lying in wait for me, namely, envy, that hates every thing that is good, and which, suddenly attacking me, did not cease from dragging me after it by force till it had taken me and thrown me into the vast sea of the cares of public politics, in which I was and still am tossed about without being able to keep myself swimming at the top. (4) But though I groan at my fate, I still hold out and resist, retaining in my soul that desire of instruction which has been implanted in it from my earliest youth, and this desire taking pity and compassion on me continually raises me up and alleviates my sorrow. And it is through this fondness for learning that I at times lift up my head, and with the eyes of my soul, which are indeed dim (for the mist of affairs, wholly inconsistent with their proper objects, has overshadowed their acute clear-sightedness), still, as well as I may, I survey all the things around me, being eager to imbibe something of a life which shall be pure and unalloyed by evils.

(5) And if at any time unexpectedly there shall arise a brief period of tranquillity, and a short calm and respite from the troubles which arise from state affairs, I then rise aloft and float above the troubled waves, soaring as it were in the air, and being, I may almost say, blown forward by the breezes of knowledge, which often persuades me to flee away, and to pass all my days with her, escaping as it were from my pitiless masters, not men only, but also affairs which pour upon me from all quarters and at all times like a torrent. (6) But even in these circumstances I ought to give thanks to God, that though I am so overwhelmed by this flood, I am not wholly sunk and swallowed up in the depths. But I open the eyes of my soul, which from an utter despair of any good hope had been believed to have been before now wholly darkened, and I am irradiated with the light of wisdom, since I am not given up for the whole of my life to darkness.

Behold, therefore, I venture not only to study the sacred commands of Moses, but also with an ardent love of knowledge to investigate each separate one of them, and to endeavour to reveal and to explain to those who wish to understand them, things concerning them which are not known to the multitude.

II. (7) And since of the ten commandments which God himself gave to his people without employing the agency of any prophet or interpreter, five which are engraved in the first tablet have been already discussed and explained, as have also all the particular injunctions which were comprehended under them; and since it is now proper to examine and expound to the best of our power and ability the rest of the commandments which are found in the second table, I will attempt as before to adapt the particular ordinances which are implied in them to each of the general laws.

(8) Now on the second table this is the first commandment, "Thou shalt not commit adultery," because, I imagine, in every part of the world pleasure is of great power, and no portion of the world has escaped its dominion, neither of the things on earth, nor of the things in the sea, nor even of those in the air, for all animals, whether walking on the earth, or flying in the air, or swimming in the water, do at all times rejoice in pleasure, and cultivate it, and obey its behests, and look to its eye and to its nod, obeying it with cheerfulness, however arrogant and proud they may be, and all but anticipating its commands, by the promptness and unhesitating rapidity of their service.

(9) Therefore, even that pleasure which is in

---

† Yonge's title, *A Treatise on Those Special Laws Which Are Referrible to Two Commandments in the Decalogue, the Sixth and Seventh, Against Adulterers and All Lewd Persons, and Against Murderers and All Violence.*

accordance with nature is often open to blame, when any one indulges in it immoderately and insatiably, as men who are unappeasably voracious in respect of eating, even if they take no kind of forbidden or unwholesome food; and as men who are madly devoted to association with women, and who commit themselves to an immoderate degree not with other men's wives, but with their own. (10) Still this sort of reproach, as affecting most men, is one rather of the body than of the soul, since the body has a vehement flame within, which consumes the food which is offered to it, and seeks other food at no great distance, by reason of the abundant moisture, the stream of which is conveyed into the most secret parts of the body, creating an itching, and stinging, and incessant tickling. (11) But those men who are frantic in their desires for the wives of others, and at times even for those of their nearest relations or dearest friends, and who live to the injury of their neighbours, attempting to vitiate whole families, however numerous, and violating all kinds of marriage vows, and making vain the hopes which men conceive of having legitimate children, being afflicted with an incurable disease of the soul, must be punished with death as common enemies to the whole race of mankind, in order that they may no longer live in perfect fearlessness, so as to be at leisure to corrupt other houses, nor become teachers of others, who may learn by their example to practise evil habits.

III. (12) Moreover the law has laid down other admirable regulations with regard to carnal conversation; for it commands men not only to abstain from the wives of others, but also from certain relations, with whom it is not lawful to cohabit; (13) therefore Moses, detesting and loathing the customs of the Persians, repudiates them as the greatest possible impiety, for the magistrates of the Persians marry even their own mothers, and consider the offspring of such marriages the most noble of all men, and as it is said, they think them worthy of the highest sovereign authority. (14) And yet what can be a more flagitious act of impiety than to defile the bed of one's father after he is dead, which it would be right rather to preserve untouched, as sacred; and to feel no respect either for old age or for one's mother, and for the same man to be both the son and the husband of the same woman; and again for the same woman to be both the mother and wife of the same man, and for the children of the two to be the brothers of their father and the grandsons of their mother, and for that same woman to be both the mother and grandmother of those children whom she has brought forth, and for the man to be at the same time both the father and the uterine brother of those whom he has begotten?

(15) These enormities formerly took place among the Greeks in the case of Oedipus, the son of Laius,[1] and the actions were committed out of ignorance and not voluntarily, and yet that marriage brought on such a host of evils that nothing was wanting to make up the amount of the most complete wretchedness and misery, (16) for there ensued from it a continual succession of wars, both domestic and foreign, which were bequeathed like an inheritance from their fathers and ancestors to their children and descendants; and there were destructions of cities which were the greatest in Greece, and destructions of embattled armies, and slaughter of nations and of allies which had come to the assistance of either side, and mutual slaughter of the most gallant leaders in each army, and unreconcileable enmities about sovereignty and authority, and fratricides, by which not only the families and countries of the persons immediately concerned were utterly extinguished and destroyed, but the greater portion of the whole Greek nation also, for cities which were previously populous now became desolate and void of their inhabitants, and were left as a memorial of the calamities of Greece, and a miserable sight for all beholders.

(17) Nor, indeed, do the Persians, among whom such practices are frequent, avoid similar evils, for they are continually involved in military expeditions and battles, killing and being killed, and at one time invading their neighbours and at others repelling those who rise up against them. And many enemies rise up against them from many quarters, since it is not the nature of the barbarians to rest in tranquillity; therefore, before the existing sedition is appeased, another springs up, so that no season of the year is ever indulged in peace and quietness, but they are compelled to live under arms night and day, bearing for the greater portion of their lives hardships in the open air while serving in the camps, or else living in cities from the complete absence of all peace. (18) I forbear to mention the great and intolerable violence and pride of success exhibited by the kings, whose first contests begin at the very first assumption of their sovereign power with the greatest of all iniquities, fratricide, as thus alone do they imagine that they will be safe from all attacks and treachery on the part of their brothers if they appear to have put them to death with reason and justice.

(19) And it seems to me that all these things arise from the unhallowed connections of sons with their own mothers, because justice, who surveys all human affairs, revenges herself thus on those

---

[1] This is the subject, in fact, of the Oedipus Tyrannus of Sophocles. Philo alludes afterwards to the wars which are the subject of the *Ept' epi Tēbas* of Aeschylus.

who act improperly for their wickedness; for not only do those who act thus commit impiety, but those also who voluntarily signify their assent to the arbitrary conduct of those who do such actions.

(20) But our law guards so carefully against such actions as these that it does not permit even a step-son, when his father is dead, to marry his step-mother, on account of the respect which he owes to his father, and because the titles mother and step-mother are kindred names, even though the affections of the souls may not be identical; (21) for the man who is thought to abstain from her who has been the wife of another man, because she is called his step-mother, will much more abstain from his own natural mother. And if any one, on account of his recollection of his father, shows a respectful awe of her who has formerly been his wife, it is quite evident that he, because of the respect which he feels towards both his parents, is not likely to meditate any improper conduct to his mother; since it would be downright folly for a man who studies to please one half of his family, to appear to neglect it in its wholeness and integrity.

IV. (22) There follows after this a command not to espouse one's sister: which is an injunction of great excellence, and one which contributes very greatly to temperance and good order. Therefore the Athenian lawgiver, Solon, when he permitted men to marry their sisters by the same father, forbade them to marry those by the same mother. But the lawgiver of the Lacedaemonians, on the other hand, allowed of marriages between brothers and sisters by the same mothers, but forbade those between brothers and sisters by the same father. (23) While the lawgiver of the Egyptians, ridiculing the cautious timidity of the others as if they had established imperfect ordinances, gave the reins to lasciviousness, supplying in great abundance that most incurable evil of intemperance both to body and soul, and permitting men fearlessly and with impunity to marry all their sisters, whether by both parents or by one, or by either, whether father or mother, and that too not only if younger than, but even when older than, or of the same age as themselves; for twins are very often born, which nature, indeed, at their very birth has dissevered and separated, but which incontinence and love of pleasure has invited to an association which ought never to be entered into, and to a most inharmonious agreement.

(24) But the most sacred Moses, rejecting all those ordinances with detestation, as being quite inconsistent with and at variance with any praiseworthy kind of constitution, and as laws which encouraged and trained people to the most disgraceful of all habits, almost peremptorily prohibited any connection with a man's sister, whether by both parents, or whether only by one of the

two; (25) for why should any one seek to deface the beauty of modesty? And why make virgins destitute of all modesty, to whom it is becoming to blush? And, moreover, why should one be willing to limit the associations and connections with other men, and to confine a most honourable thing within the narrow space of the walls of a single house, which ought rather to be extended and diffused over all continents, and islands, and the whole inhabited world? For the intermarriages with strangers produce new relationships, which are in no respect inferior to those which proceed from ties of blood.

V. (26) On which account our lawgiver has also forbidden other matrimonial connections, commanding that no man shall marry his granddaughter, whether she be his son's or his daughter's child; nor his niece; nor his aunt; nor his grandmother, by either father or mother; nor any woman who has been the wife of his uncle, or of his son, or of his brother; nor, again, any step-daughter, whether virgin or widow, whether his own wife be alive or even after her death. For, in principle, a step-father is the same as a father, and therefore he ought to look upon his wife's daughter in the same light as his own.

(27) Again. He does not permit the same man to marry two sisters, neither at the same time nor at different periods, even if he have put away the one whom he previously married; for while she is living, whether she be cohabiting with him or whether she be put away, or if she be living as a widow, or if she be married to another man, still he did not consider it holy for her sister to enter upon the portion of her who had been unfortunate; by this injunction teaching sisters not to violate the requirements of justice towards their relations, nor to make a stepping stone of the disasters of one so united to themselves by blood, nor to acquiesce in or to pride themselves in receiving attentions from those who have shown themselves enemies to their relations, or to reciprocate any kind offices received from them.

(28) For from such things as these arise bitter jealousies and quarrels, and enmities which scarcely admit of reconciliation, but which bring on indescribable hosts of misfortunes; for that would be just as if the different members of the body were to abandon the harmony and fellowship in which they are put together by nature, and to quarrel with one another, which circumstance must necessarily cause incurable diseases and mischiefs. And sisters are like limbs, which, although they are separated from one another, are nevertheless all adapted to one another by nature and natural relationship. And jealousy, which is the most grievous of all passions, is continually producing new, and terrible, and incurable mischiefs.

(29) Again. Moses commands, do not either

form a connection of marriage with one of another nation, and do not be seduced into complying with customs inconsistent with your own, and do not stray from the right way and forget the path which leads to piety, turning into a road which is no road. And, perhaps, you will yourself resist, if you have been from your earliest youth trained in the best possible instruction, which your parents have instilled into you, continually filling your mind with the sacred laws. And the anxiety and fear which parents feel for their sons and daughters is not slight; for, perchance, they may be allured by mischievous customs instead of genuine good ones, and so they may be in danger of learning to forget the honour belonging to the one God, which is the beginning and end of extreme unhappiness.

(30) But if, proceeds the lawgiver, a woman having been divorced from her husband under any pretence whatever, and having married another, has again become a widow, whether her second husband is alive or dead, still she must not return to her former husband, but may be united to any man in the world rather than to him, having violated her former ties which she forgot, and having chosen new allurements in the place of the old ones. (31) But if any man should choose to form an alliance with such a woman, he must be content to bear the reputation of effeminacy and a complete want of manly courage and vigour, as if he had been castrated and deprived of the most useful portion of the soul, namely, that disposition which hates iniquity, by which the affairs both of houses and cities are placed on a good footing, and as having stamped deeply on his character two of the greatest of all iniquities, adultery and the employment of a pander; for the reconciliations which take place subsequently are indications of the death of each. Let him, therefore, suffer the punishment appointed, together with his wife.

VI. (32) And there are particular periods affecting the health of the woman when a man may not touch her, but during that time he must abstain from all connection with her, respecting the laws of nature. And, at the same time, he must learn not to waste his vigour in the pursuit of an unseemly and barbarous pleasure; for such conduct would be like that of a husbandman who, out of drunkenness or sudden insanity, should sow wheat or barley in lakes or flooded torrents, instead of over the fertile plains; for it is proper to cast seed upon fields when they are dry, in order that it may bear abundant fruit. (33) But nature each month cleanses the womb, as if it were some field of marvellous fertility, the proper season for fertilising which must be watched for by the husband as if he were a skilful husbandman, in order to withhold his seed and abstain from sowing it at a time when it is inundated; for, if he do not do so, the seed, without his perceiving it, will be swept away

by the moisture, not only having all its spiritual energies relaxed, but having them, in fact, utterly dissolved.

These are the persons who form animals in that workshop of nature, the womb, and who perfect with the most consummate skill each separate one of the parts of the body and soul. But when the periods of illness which I have spoken of are interrupted, then he may with confidence shower his seed into the ground ready to receive it, no longer fearing that there will be any loss of the seed thus sown. (34) But those people deserve to be reproached who are ploughing a hard and stony soil. And who can these be but they who have connected themselves with barren women? For such men are only hunters after intemperate pleasure, and in the excess of their licentious passions they waste their seed of their own deliberate purpose. Since for what other reason can they espouse such women? It cannot be for a hope of children, which they are aware must, of necessity, be disappointed, but rather to gratify their excess in lust and incurable incontinence.

(35) As many men, therefore, as marry virgins in ignorance of how well they will turn out as regards their prolificness, or the contrary, when after a long time they perceive, by their never having any children, that they are barren, and do not then put them away, are still worthy of pardon, being influenced by habit and familiarity, which are motives of great weight, and being also unable to break through the power of those ancient charms which by long habituation are stamped upon their souls. (36) But those who marry women who have been previously tested by other men and ascertained to be barren, do merely covet the carnal enjoyment like so many boars or goats, and deserve to be inscribed among the lists of impious men as enemies to God; for God, as being friendly to all the animals that exist, and especially to man, takes all imaginable care to secure preservation and duration to every kind of creature. But those who seek to waste all their power at the very moment of putting it forth are confessedly enemies of nature.

VII. (37) Moreover, another evil, much greater than that which we have already mentioned, has made its way among and been let loose upon cities, namely, the love of boys, which formerly was accounted a great infamy even to be spoken of, but which sin is a subject of boasting not only to those who practise it, but even to those who suffer it, and who, being accustomed to bearing the affliction of being treated like women, waste away as to both their souls and bodies, not bearing about them a single spark of a manly character to be kindled into a flame, but having even the hair of their heads conspicuously curled and adorned, and having their faces smeared with vermilion, and paint, and things of that kind, and having their eyes pencilled beneath, and having their skins anointed with fragrant perfumes (for in such persons as these a sweet smell is a most seductive quality), and being well appointed in everything that tends to beauty or elegance, are not ashamed to devote their constant study and endeavours to the task of changing their manly character into an effeminate one. (38) And it is natural for those who obey the law to consider such persons worthy of death, since the law commands that the man-woman who adulterates the precious coinage of his nature shall die without redemption, not allowing him to live a single day, or even a single hour, as he is a disgrace to himself, and to his family, and to his country, and to the whole race of mankind.

(39) And let the man who is devoted to the love of boys submit to the same punishment, since he pursues that pleasure which is contrary to nature, and since, as far as depends upon him, he would make the cities desolate, and void, and empty of all inhabitants, wasting his power of propagating his species, and moreover, being a guide and teacher of those greatest of all evils, unmanliness and effeminate lust, stripping young men of the flower of their beauty, and wasting their prime of life in effeminacy, which he ought rather on the other hand to train to vigour and acts of courage; and last of all, because, like a worthless husbandman, he allows fertile and productive lands to lie fallow, contriving that they shall continue barren, and labours night and day at cultivating that soil from which he never expects any produce at all.

(40) And I imagine that the cause of this is that among many nations there are actually rewards given for intemperance and effeminacy. At all events one may see men-women continually strutting through the market place at midday, and leading the processions in festivals; and, impious men as they are, having received by lot the charge of the temple, and beginning the sacred and initiating rites, and concerned even in the holy mysteries of Ceres.

(41) And some of these persons have even carried their admiration of these delicate pleasures of youth so far that they have desired wholly to change their condition for that of women, and have castrated themselves and have clothed themselves in purple robes, like those who, having been the cause of great blessings to their native land, walk about attended by body-guards, pushing down every one whom they meet.

(42) But if there was a general indignation against those who venture to do such things, such as was felt by our lawgiver, and if such men were destroyed without any chance of escape as the common curse and pollution of their country, then many other persons would be warned and corrected by their example. For the punishments of those persons who have been already con-

demned cannot be averted by entreaty, and therefore cause no slight check to those persons who are ambitious of distinguishing themselves by the same pursuits.

VIII. (43) But some persons, imitating the sensual indulgences of the Sybarites and of other nations more licentious still, have in the first place devoted themselves to gluttony and wine-bibbing, and other pleasures affecting the belly and the parts adjacent to the belly, and then when fully sated have behaved with such extraordinary insolence (and it is natural for satiety to produce insolence) that in their insanity of passion they have gone frantic and been so maddened as to desire to longer human beings, whether male or female, but even brute beasts, as they say that in ancient times in Crete, the wife of Minos the king, by name Pasiphaë, fell in love with a bull, (44) and became very violent in her passion from her despair of being able to gratify it (for love which fails in its object is usually increased in no ordinary degree), so that at last she reported to Daedalus the affliction by which she was overwhelmed, and he was the most skilful of all workmen of his time.[2]

And he, being very ingenious, so as by his contrivances to discover things undiscoverable to any one else, made a cow of wood, and put Pasiphaë into it at one of the sides, and the bull rushed at the wooden cow as if it had been an animal of its own kind. And Pasiphaë, becoming pregnant at a certain period, brought forth an animal half man and half beast, called the minotaur.[3]

(45) And it is very likely that there may be other Pasiphaës also, with passions equally unbridled, and that not women only, but men likewise may fall madly in love with animals, from whom, perhaps, indescribable monsters may be born, being memorials of the excessive pollution of men; owing to which, perhaps, those unnatural creations of unprecedented and fabulous monsters will exist, such as hippocentaurs and chimaeras, and other similar animals. (46) But so great are the precautions which are taken against them in the holy laws of God, that in order to prevent the possibility of men ever desiring any unlawful connection, it is expressly commanded that even animals of different kinds shall not be put together. And no Jewish shepherd will endeavour to cross a sheep with a he-goat, or a ram with a she-goat,

---

[2]This story is alluded to by many poets, and especially by Virgil, Aeneid 6.24 (as it is translated by Dryden)— "There too, in living sculpture, might be seen / The mad affection of the Cretan queen: / Then how she cheats her bellowing lover's eye: / The rushing leap; the doubtful progeny: / The lower part a beast, a man above; / The monument of their polluted love."
[3]Ovid describes this animal more than once (A.A. 2.24; Her. 10.101).

or a cow with a horse; and if he does, he must pay the penalty as breaking a solemn law of nature who is desirous to keep the original kinds of animals free from all spurious admixture. (47) And some persons prefer mules to every other kind of animal for the yoke, since their bodies are very compact, and are very strong and powerful; and accordingly, in the pastures and stalls where they keep their horses, they also keep asses of an extraordinary size, which they call celones, in order that they may breed with the mares; and then the mares produce a mixed animal, half horse and half ass, which, since Moses knew that its production was wholly contrary to nature, he forbade the existence of with all his might by a general injunction, that that no union or combination between different kinds of animals should on any account be permitted.

(48) Therefore he provided thus against those evils in a manner suited to and consistent with nature; and from a long distance off, as from a watchtower, he admonished men and kept them in the straight path, in order that both men and women, learning from these percepts of his, might abstain from unlawful connections. (49) If, therefore, a man seek to indulge himself with a quadruped, or if a woman surrender herself to a quadruped, they shall all die, both the man or woman and the quadruped. The human beings, because they have gone beyond even the bounds of intemperance itself, becoming discoverers of unprecedented appetites, and because with their new inventions they have introduced most detestable pleasures, the very mention of which is infamous; and the beasts shall die, because they have been subservient to such iniquities, and also to prevent their bringing forth or begetting any thing intolerable, as would naturally be the result of such pollutions.

(50) Moreover, those who have even a slight care for what is becoming would never use such animals as those for any purpose of life, but would reject and abominate them, loathing their very sight, and thinking that whatever they touched would at once become impure and polluted. And it is not well that those things which are of no use for life should live at all, since they are only a superfluous burden on the earth, as some one has called them.

IX. (51) Again, according to the injunctions of the sacred scriptures the constitution of the law does not recognise a harlot; as being a person alienated from good order, and modesty, and chastity, and all other virtues, who has filled the souls both of men and women with intemperance, polluting the immortal beauty of the mind, and honouring above it the short-lived perishable beauty of the body prostituting herself to every chance comer, and selling her beauty as if it were some vendible thing in the market, doing and saying every thing with a view to catch the young men. And she excites her lovers to contests with one another, proposing herself as the most disgraceful prize for those who gain the victory. Let her, therefore, be stoned as an injury and mischief to, and a common pollution of, the whole state, having corrupted the graces of nature, which she ought to have adorned further by her own excellence.

X. (52) The law has pronounced all acts of adultery, if detected in the fact, or if proved by undeniable evidence, liable to the punishment of death; but cases in which guilt is only suspected, it does not choose should be investigated by men, but it brings them before the tribunal of nature; since men are able to judge of what is visible, but God can judge also of what is unseen, since he alone is able to behold the soul distinctly, (53) therefore he says to the man who suspects such a thing, "Write an accusation, and go up to the holy city with thy wife, and standing before the judges, lay bare the passion of suspicion which affects you, not like a false accuser or treacherous enemy, seeking to gain the victory by any means whatever, but as a man may do who wishes accurately to ascertain the truth without any sophistry. (54) And the woman, having incurred two dangers, one of her life, and the other of her reputation, the loss of which last is more grievous than any kind of death, shall judge the matter with herself; and if she be pure, let her make her defence with confidence; but if she be convicted by her own conscience, let her cover her face, making her modesty the veil for her iniquities, for to persist in her impudence is the very extravagance of wickedness. (55) But if the charge which is made against her be contested, and if the evidence be doubtful, so as not to incline to either side, then let the two parties go up to the temple, and let the man stand in front of the altar, in the presence of the priest for the day, and then let him state his suspicions and his grounds for them, and let him produce and offer some barley flour, as a species of oblation on behalf of his wife, to prove that he accuses her, not out of insult, but with an honest intention, because he has a reasonable doubt. (56) And the priest shall take the barley and offer it to the woman, and shall take away from her the head-dress on her head, that she may be judged with her head bare, and deprived of the symbol of modesty, which all those women are accustomed to wear who are completely blameless; and there shall not be any oil used, nor any frankincense, as in the case of other sacrifices, because the sacrifice now offered is to be accomplished on no joyful occasion, but on one which is very grievous. (57) And the reason why the flour is to be made of barley is, perhaps, because the food which is made of barley is of a somewhat ambiguous character, and is suited for the use both of irrational animals and of needy men; and is therefore a sign that a woman who has committed adultery differs in no respect from the beasts, whose connections with one another are promiscuous and incessant; but she who is pure from all such accusations is devoted to that manner of life which befits human beings.

(58) Then the law proceeds to say, the priest, having taken an earthen vessel, shall pour forth pure water, having drawn it from a fountain, and shall also bring a lump of clay from the ground of the temple, which also I think has in it a symbolical reference to the search after truth; for the earthenware vessel is appropriate to the commission of adultery because it is easily broken, and death is the punishment appointed for adulterers; but the earth and the water are appropriate to the purging of the accusation, since the origin, and increase, and perfection of all things, take place by them: (59) on which account it was very proper for the law-giver to set them both off by epithets, saying, that the water which the priest was to take must be pure and living water, since blameless woman is pure as to her life, and deserves to live; and the earth too is to be taken, not from any chance spot, but from the soil of the ground of the temple, which must, of necessity, be most excellent, just as a modest woman is.

(60) And when all these things are previously prepared, the woman with her head uncovered, bearing the barley flour in her hand, as has been already specified, shall come forward; and the priest standing opposite to her and holding the earthenware vessel in which are the water and the earth, shall speak thus: (61) "If you have not transgressed the laws of your marriage, and if no other man has been associated with you, so that you have not violated the rights of him who is joined to you by the law, you are blameless and innocent; but if you have neglected your husband and have followed empty appetites, either loving some one yourself or yielding to some lover, betraying your nearest and dearest connections, and adulterating them by a spurious mixture, then learn that you are deservedly liable to every kind of curse, the proofs of which you will exhibit on your body. Come then and drink the draught of conviction, which shall uncover and lay bare all thy hidden and secret actions."

(62) Then the priest shall write these words on a paper and dip it in the water which is in the earthenware vessel, and give it to the woman. And she shall drink it and depart, awaiting the reward of her modesty or the extreme penalty of her incontinence; for if she has been falsely accused she may hope for seed and children, disregarding all apprehensions and anxieties on the subject of barrenness and childlessness. But if she is guilty

then a great weight and bulk, from her belly swelling and becoming full, will come upon her, and a terribly evil condition of her womb will afflict her, since she did not choose to keep it pure for her husband, who had married her according to the laws of her nation. (63) And the law takes such exceeding pains to prevent any irregularity taking place with respect to marriages, that even in the case of husbands and wives who have come together for legitimate embraces, in strict accordance with the laws of marriage, after they have arisen from their beds it does not allow them to touch anything before they have had recourse to washings and ablutions; keeping them very far from adultery and from all accusations referring to adultery.

XI. (64) But if any one should offer violence to a widow after her husband is dead, or after she has been otherwise divorced from him, and defile her, committing a lighter offence than adultery, and one that may perhaps be about half as serious, he shall not indeed be liable to the punishment of death, but he shall be impeached for violence, and insolence, and intemperance, having thus adopted the most infamous conduct as if it had been the most creditable; and the tribunal of the judge shall decide and condemn him to the penalty that he deserves to suffer.

(65) Again, seduction is an offence which is similar and nearly related to adultery, as they are both sprung from one common mother, incontinence. But some of those persons who are accustomed to dignify shameful actions by specious names, call this love, blushing to confess the real truth concerning its character. But, nevertheless, though it may be akin to it, it is not in every respect similar to it, because it is an offence that does not spread so as to affect many families, as is the case with adultery, but it is limited to one house alone, that of the virgin who has been seduced.

(66) Therefore we must say to a man who desires to enjoy a virgin who is a free-born citizen, "My good man, rejecting your shameless rashness and audacity, the sources of treachery and faithlessness, and all such feelings, do not allow yourself to be discovered to be wicked, either openly or secretly, (67) but if, indeed, you have any legitimate feeling of love for the maiden in your soul, go to her parents, if they are alive, and if they are not, then go to her brother or to her guardians, or to any other persons who chance to be her protectors, and having discovered to them your feelings towards her, as a free-born man should do, ask her in marriage, and implore them not to account you unworthy.

(68) "For no one of those who have the guardianship of the maiden entrusted them could be so base as to oppose an earnest and persevering entreaty, and especially as to refuse you since you,

would be found, by strict examination, not to have falsely pretended a passion which you do not feel, or to have conceived only a superficial love for her, but one which is genuine and thoroughly established."[4]

(69) But if any one, being insane and frantic, repudiating and discarding all the suggestions of reason, were to submit himself wholly to passion and desire as his masters, and looking, as people say, on might as stronger than right, were to ravish and seduce women, treating free-born women as slaves, and doing acts of war in time of peace, let such a man be led before the judges. (70) And if the damsel who has been forced has a father, let him take counsel and deal with the ravisher about espousing her; then if he refuse to do so, he shall give the damsel a dowry for another husband, being fined in a sum of money sufficient for this purpose. But if he consents and registers her as his wife, let him marry her at once without any delay, confessing a second time that he owes her the same dowry, and let him have no permission to delay or evade the fulfilment of this marriage; both because of his own conduct, in order that the mishap which took place respecting her first connection with a man may be comforted by a firm marriage, which nothing shall ever separate but death. (71) But if the damsel be an orphan and have no father, then let her be asked by the judges whether she is willing to take this man for her husband or not; and whether she agrees to do so or whether she refuses, still let her have the same dowry that the man would have agreed to give her while her father was yet alive.

XII. (72) Some people think that a licensed concubinage is an offence something between seduction and adultery, when the two parties come together, and agree to live as man and wife by a certain agreement, but before the marriage ceremony is completed, some other man meeting with the woman, or forcing her has connection with her; but in my opinion this also is a kind of adultery; for such an agreement as is here mentioned is equivalent to a marriage, for in it the names of the woman and of the man are both registered, and all other things which were to lead to their union; (73) on which account, the law orders both the parties to be stoned if with one and the same mind they agree together to commit adultery; for it is impossible that, unless they both set out with the same intention, they should be looked upon as equal in iniquity, if they had not both sinned in an equal degree; (74) at all events it often happens that the offence is enhanced or diminished, with reference to the difference of place in which it is committed.

For, as it seems, such an offence is greater if it be committed in a city, and less it if be committed outside the walls of any city, in a wilderness; for in such a place there is not one to assist the maiden, even though she may have said and done everything, which could conduce to the preservation of her virginity, unattacked and undefiled; but in a city there are halls of council, and courts of justice, and great assemblies of generals, and aediles, and rulers of the markets, and other magistrates; and besides all these there is the people; (75) for there is in the soul of every man, even though he may be a private individual, a feeling which is hostile to iniquity, which, when it is excited, makes the man who cherishes it a champion for the time being, and a spontaneous and voluntary defender of the person who appears to be unjustly treated.

XIII. (76) Therefore justice in every case pursues the man who has committed violence, nor is his iniquity excused by the difference of the place, so that cannot be any plea to defend him from the consequence of his violence and lawlessness; but as I have said before, there will be compassion and pardon for the damsel in the one case, and in the other inexecrable punishment will visit her.

(77) And concerning her the judge must examine the matter very carefully, not referring everything to or making everything depend upon the place; for it is possible that a woman may be ravished against her will even in the middle of the city; and on the other hand even if outside the city, she may have voluntarily given herself up to an illicit connection. Wherefore the law, making a very careful and very admirably conceived defence, on behalf of a damsel ravished in the wilderness, says, "for the damsel cried out, and there was no one to help her;"[5] so that if she neither cried out nor resisted, but willingly consented to her ravisher, she must be looked upon as guilty, having only put forward the fact of the place, as a sophistical excuse to make it appear that she had been ravished.

(78) And yet in the city what advantage can her efforts be to a damsel, who is willing to do everything for the sake of preserving her own reputation, but who is unable to succeed by reason of the strength of the man who is assaulting her? for what advantage could she derive from those who live in the same house if he were to bind her with ropes, or to gag her mouth, so that she could not utter even a word; for in some sense she then, although dwelling in a city, is in reality in a wilderness, inasmuch as she is destitute of all protection; but if she be in a wilderness, and yet willingly gives herself up to her ravisher, she is in no different condition from a woman in a city.

---

[4]Deuteronomy 22:13.

[5]Deuteronomy 22:27.

XIV. (79) There are also some persons easily sated with their connection with the same woman, being at once both mad for women and women haters, full of promiscuous and irregular dispositions, who at once give themselves up to their first impulses whatever they may be; letting those passions proceed without restraint which they ought to curb, and like blind men, without any consideration, without any prudence, stumbling upon any bodies or any things, upsetting, and overturning, and confusing everything in their violent impetuosity and haste, and suffering evils as great as those which they inflict; (80) and concerning these men we have this law enacted.

When those men who marry virgins in accordance with the law,[6] and who have sacrificed on the occasion and celebrated their marriage feast, and who yet afterwards preserve no natural affection for their wives but treat them with insolence, and behave to freeborn citizens as if they were courtesans, if they seek to procure a divorce, and to being able to find any pretext for such a separation, then betake themselves to bringing forward false accusations, and from an absence of any clear grounds of impeachment direct all their charges at things which cannot be made certain, and come forward and accuse them, saying that though they fancied that they had been marrying virgins, they found on the first occasion of their having intercourse together, that they were not so. When, I say, these men make such charges let all the elders be assembled to decide on the case, and let the parents of the woman who is accused also appear, to make their defence in this their common danger.

(81) For in such a case, not only are their daughters themselves in danger, as to their reputation as having preserved the chastity of their bodies, but their guardians are likewise imperilled, not only because they have not kept them safe till the important period of their marriageable age, but because they have given in marriage as virgins those who have been defiled by others, deceiving and imposing upon those who have taken them to wife.

(82) Then if they appear to have justice on their side, let the judges impose a pecuniary fine on those who have invented these false accusations, and let them also sentence those who have assaulted them to corporeal punishment, and let them also pronounce, what to those men will be the most unpleasant of all things, a confirmation of their marriage, if their wives will still endure to cohabit with them; for the law permits them at their own choice to remain with them or to abandon them, and will not allow the husbands any option either way, on account of the false accusations which they have brought.

THE LAW CONCERNING MURDERERS

XV. (83) The name of homicide is that affixed to him who has slain a man; but in real truth it is a sacrilege, and the very greatest of all sacrileges, because, of all the possessions and sacred treasures in the whole world, there is nothing more holy in appearance, nor more godlike than man, the all-beautiful copy of an all-beautiful model, a representation admirably made after an archetypal rational idea.

(84) We must therefore, without hesitation, pronounce the homicide or murderer an impious and atrociously wicked person, committing as he does the greatest of all atrocities and impieties, and he ought to be put to death as having done things which can never be pardoned, since, being worthy of ten thousand deaths, he escapes by one only, because the way to death being easy, does not permit his existence to be protracted, so as to endure a multitude of punishments; but there can be nothing wrong in his suffering the same treatment as that which he has inflicted on others, (85) and yet how can it be the same, if it be different as to its time, as to its mode of infliction, as to the intention, and as to the persons? Does not the beginning of acts of violence come first, and the repelling or retaliating them come subsequently? And is not murder the most lawless of all things, but the punishment of murderers the most lawful action possible?

Again, he who has slain a man has satisfied his desire which he entertained when he slew him; but he who has been slain, inasmuch as he is now put out of the way, can neither attack him in retaliation, nor can he gratify himself by taking revenge. Moreover, the one was able by his own hands to carry out the designs which he conceived by himself; but the other can never succeed in procuring his punishment, unless his relations and friends become his champions, taking compassion on him for the calamity which has befallen him. (86) If now any one aims a blow with a sword at any one, with the intention of killing him, and does not kill him, he will still be guilty of murder, since he was a murderer in his intention, even though the end did not keep pace with his wish.

Again, let that man be liable to the same punishment who, by previous contrivance and machinations (not daring to behave bravely, and to stand face to face with his enemy and attack him openly), treacherously plots and compasses his slaughter; for such a man is equally liable to the curse denounced against murderers, and even though he may not be one with his hands he is so in his soul; (87) for, as, in my opinion, one must not only look upon those people as enemies who fight against

---

[6]Deuteronomy 22:13.

us by sea or by land, but also those who are prepared for either kind of warfare, and who are erecting battering rams and engines against our harbours and our walls; and as we do in fact judge thus of them, even though they come to no actual conflict, so also we must consider murderers, not only those who perform the mere act of killing, but those who do anything which tends to slaying, whether openly or secretly, even if they do not eventually perpetrate the action.

(88) And if out of fear or out of audacity, two very contrary feelings, but both blameable, they venture to flee to the temple as if they would there find an asylum, we must prevent their doing so, if we can: but if they are beforehand with us, and do effect their entrance, then we must take them out and give them up for execution, affirming the principle that the temple does not give an asylum to impious men; for every one who commits actions of incurable guilt is an enemy to God; and murderers do commit such actions, since those who are murdered have suffered disasters which are incurable. (89) Or shall we say that to those who have done no wrong the temple is still inaccessible until they have washed themselves, and sprinkled themselves, and purified themselves with the accustomed purifications; but that those who are guilty of indelible crimes, the pollution of which no length of time will ever efface, may approach and dwell among those holy seats; though no decent person, who has any regard for holy things would even receive them in his house?

XVI. (90) Therefore, since they have heaped iniquity upon iniquity, adding lawlessness and impiety to murder, they must be dragged out of the temple to undergo their punishment, since, as I have said before, they have committed actions worthy of ten thousand deaths instead of one; as otherwise, the temple would be shut against the relations and friends of the man who has been so treacherously murdered, if the murderer were to be dwelling in it, since they could never endure to come into the same place with him. But it would be absurd that, for the sake of one man, and him the most lawless of men, a great number of persons, and those too the very persons who have been injured by him, should be excluded from the temple—men who, besides that they have done no wrong themselves, have even sustained an unseasonable affliction through his actions.

(91) And perhaps, indeed, the lawgiver seeing far into futurity by the acuteness of his reasoning powers, was, by such commandments, providing against any bloodshed ever taking place in the temple by the entrance of any of the friends of the murdered man into it, whom natural affection, a very ungovernable feeling, would urge, full of enthusiasm and violent rage as they would be, almost to slay the murderer with their own hands,

while if such an event were to take place it would be most impious sacrilege; for then the blood of the sacrifices would be mingled with the blood of murderers; that which has been consecrated to God with that which is wholly impure.

It is on this account that Moses commands that the murderer shall be given up, even from the altar itself.

XVII. (92) But some persons who have slain others with swords, or spears, or darts, or clubs, or stones, or something of that kind, may possibly have done so without any previous design, and without having for some time before planned this deed in their hearts, but may have been excited at the moment, yielding to passion more powerful than their reason, to commit the homicide; so that it is but half a crime, inasmuch as the mind was not for some long time before occupied by the pollution.

(93) But there are others also of the greatest wickedness, men polluted both in hands and mind, who, being sorcerers and poisoners, devoting all their leisure and all their solitude to planning seasonable attacks upon others, who invent all kinds of contrivances and devices to bring about calamities on their neighbours. (94) On which account, Moses commands that poisoners and sorceresses shall not be allowed to live one day or even one hour, but that they shall be put to death the moment that they are taken, no pretext being for a moment allowed them for putting off or delaying their punishment. For those who attack one openly and to one's face, any body may guard against; but of those who plot against one secretly, and who disguise their attacks by the concealed approaches of poison, it is not easy to see the cunning beforehand. (95) It is necessary, therefore, to anticipate them, inflicting upon them that death which other persons would else have suffered by their means.

And again, besides this, he who openly slays a man with a sword, or with any similar weapon, can only kill a few persons at one time; but one who mixes and compounds poisonous drugs with food, may destroy innumerable companies at once who have no suspicion of his treachery. (96) Accordingly, it has happened before now that very numerous parties of men who have come together in good fellowship to eat of the same salt and to sit at the same table, have suffered at such a time of harmony things wholly incompatible with it, being suddenly killed, and have thus met with death instead of feasting. On which account it is fitting that even the most merciful, and gentle, and moderate of men should approve of such persons being put to death, who are all but the same as murderers who slay with their own hand; and that they should think it consistent with holiness, not to commit their punishment to others, but to execute it themselves. (97) For how can it be anything but a most terrible evil for any one to contrive the death of another by that food which is given as the cause of life, and to work such a change in that which is nutritious by nature as to render it destructive; so that those who, in obedience to the necessities of nature, have recourse to eating and drinking, having no previous idea of any treachery, take destructive food as though it were salutary?

(98) Again, let those persons meet with the same punishment who, though they do not compound drugs which are actually deadly, nevertheless administer such as long diseases are caused by; for death is often a lesser evil than diseases; and especially than such as extend over a long time and have no fortunate or favourable end. For the illnesses which arise from poisons are difficult to be cured, and are often completely incurable. (99) Moreover, in the case of men who have been exposed to machinations of this kind, it often happens that diseases of the mind ensue which are worse even than the afflictions of the body; for they are often attacked by delirium and insanity, and intolerable frenzy, by means of which the mind, the greatest blessing which God has bestowed upon mankind, is impaired in every possible manner, despairing of any safety or cure, and so is utterly removed from its seat, and expelled, as it were, leaving in the body only the inferior portion of the soul, namely, its irrational part, of which even beasts partake, since every person who is deprived of reason, which is the better part of the soul, is changed into the nature of a beast, even though the characteristics of the human form remain.

XVIII. (100) Now the true magical art, being a science of discernment, which contemplates and beholds the books of nature with a more acute and distinct perception than usual, and appearing as such to be a dignified and desirable branch of knowledge, is studied not merely by private individuals, but even by kings, and the very greatest of kings, and especially by the Persian monarchs, to such a degree, that they say that among that people no one can possibly succeed to the kingdom if he has not previously been initiated into the mysteries of the magi. (101) But there is a certain adulterated species of this science, which may more properly be called wicked imposture, which quacks, and cheats, and buffoons pursue, and the vilest of women and slaves, professing to understand all kinds of incantations and purifications, and promising to change the dispositions of those on whom they operate so as to turn those who love to unalterable enmity, and those who hate to the most excessive affection by certain charms and incantations; and thus they deceive and gain influence over men of unsuspicious and innocent dispositions, until they fall into the greatest calamities, by means of which great numbers of friends and relations have wasted away by degrees, and so have been rapidly destroyed without any noise being made. (102) And I imagine that the lawgiver, having a regard to all these circumstances, would on that account not permit the punishments due to poisoners to be postponed to any subsequent occasion, but ordained that the executioners should at once proceed to inflict the due penalty on them; for delay rather excites the guilty to make use of the time that is allowed them to carry out their iniquities, inasmuch as they are already condemned to death, while it fills those who are already suspicious and apprehensive of misfortune with a more urgent fear, as they look upon the life of their enemies to be their own death.

(103) Therefore, as if we only see snakes, and serpents, and any other venomous animals, we at once, without a moment's delay, kill them before they can bite, or wound, or attack us at all, taking care not to expose ourselves to any injury from them by reason of our knowledge of the mischief which is inherent in them; in the same manner it is right promptly to punish those men who, though they have had a gentle nature assigned to them by means of that fountain of reason which is the cause and source of all society, do nevertheless of deliberate purpose change it themselves to the ferocity of untameable beasts, looking upon the doing injury to as many people as they can to be their greatest pleasure and advantage.

XIX. (104) This may be sufficient to say on the present occasion concerning poisoners and magicians. Moreover, we ought also not to be ignorant of this, that very often unexpected occasions arise in which a person slays a man without having ever prepared himself for this action, but because he has been suddenly transported with anger, which is an intolerable and terrible feeling, and which injures beyond all other feelings both the man who entertains and the man who has excited it; (105) for sometimes a man having come into the market-place on some important business, meeting with some one who is inclined precipitately to accuse him, or who attempts to assault him, or who begins to pick a quarrel with him and engages him in a conflict, for the sake of separating from him and more speedily escaping him, either strikes his opponent with his fist or takes up a stone and throws it at him and knocks him down.

(106) And if the wound which the man has received is mortal, so that he at once dies, then let the man who has struck him also die, suffering the same fate himself which he inflicted on the other. But if the man does not die immediately after receiving the blow, but is afflicted by illness in consequence and takes to his bed, and having been properly attended to rises up again, even though

he may not be able to walk well without support, but may require some one to support him or a stick to lean upon, in that case the man who struck him shall pay a double penalty, one as an atonement for the injury done, and one for the expenses of the cure. (107) And when he has paid this he shall be acquitted as to the punishment of death, even if the man who has received the blow should subsequently die; for perhaps he did not die of the blow, since he got better after that and recovered so far as to walk, but perhaps he died from some other causes, such as often suddenly attack those who are of the most vigorous bodily health, and kill them.

(108) But if any one has a contest with a woman who is pregnant, and strike her a blow on her belly, and she miscarry, if the child which was conceived within her is still unfashioned and unformed, he shall be punished by a fine, both for the assault which he committed and also because he has prevented nature, who was fashioning and preparing that most excellent of all creatures, a human being, from bringing him into existence. But if the child which was conceived had assumed a distinct shape[7] in all its parts, having received all its proper connective and distinctive qualities, he shall die; (109) for such a creature as that is a man, whom he has slain while still in the workshop of nature, who had not thought it as yet a proper time to produce him to the light, but had kept him like a statue lying in a sculptor's workshop, requiring nothing more than to be released and sent out into the world.

XX. (110) On account of this commandment he also adds another proposition of greater importance, in which the exposure of infants is forbidden, which has become a very ordinary piece of wickedness among other nations by reason of their natural inhumanity; (111) for if it is proper to provide for that which is not yet brought forth by reason of the definite periods of time requisite for such a process, so that even that may not suffer any injury by being plotted against, how can it be otherwise than more necessary to take similar care of the child when brought to perfection and born, and sent forth, as it were, into that colony which has been assigned to the human race, for the purpose of having a share of the bounties of nature which she sends forth from the land, and from the water, and from the air, and from the heaven? bestowing on men the sight of the heavenly bodies, and the power and supreme authority over all the things on earth, and supplying all the external senses with abundant supplies of all things, and presenting to the mind as the great king, by means of those outward senses as its body-guards, all the

things which are visible to them, and, without employing their agency, all those things which are appreciable only by reason.

(112) Accordingly, let those parents who deprive their children of all these blessings, giving them no share of any one of them from the moment of their birth, know that they are violating the laws of nature, and accusing themselves of the very greatest enormities, of a devotion to pleasure, and a hatred of their species, and murder, and the very worst kind of murder, infanticide; (113) for those men are devoted to pleasure who are not influenced by the wish of propagating children, and of perpetuating their race, when they have connection with women, but who are only like boars or he-goats seeking the enjoyment that arises from such a connection. Again, who can be greater haters of their species than those who are the implacable and ferocious enemies of their own children? Unless, indeed, any one is so foolish as to imagine that these men can be humane to strangers who act in a barbarous manner to those who are united to them by ties of blood. (114) And as for their murders and infanticides they are established by the most undeniable proofs, since some of them slay them with their own hands, and stifle the first breath of their children, and smother it altogether, out of a terribly cruel and unfeeling disposition; others throw them into the depths of a river, or of a sea, after they have attached a weight to them, in order that they may sink to the bottom more speedily because of it.

(115) Others, again, carry them out into a desert place to expose them there, as they themselves say, in the hope that they may be saved by some one, but in real truth to load them with still more painful suffering; for there all the beasts which devour human flesh, since there is no one to keep them off, attack them and feast on the delicate banquet of the children, while those who were their only guardians, and who were bound above all other people to protect and save them, their own father and other, have exposed them. And carnivorous birds fly down and lick up the remainder of their bodies, when they are not themselves the first to discover them; for when they discover them themselves they do battle with the beasts of the earth for the whole carcass.

(116) And even suppose that some one passing by on his road is moved by a feeling of gentle compassion to take pity on and show mercy to the exposed infants, so as to take them up and give them food, and to show them other portions of the attention that is requisite, what do we think of such a humane action? Do we not look upon it as an express condemnation of the real parents, when those who are in nowise related to them show the tender foresight of parents, but the parents do not display even the kindness of strangers?

---

[7]Exodus 21:22.

(117) Therefore, Moses has utterly prohibited the exposure of children, by a tacit prohibition, when he condemns to death, as I have said before, those who are the causes of a miscarriage to a woman whose child conceived within her is already formed.

And yet those persons who have investigated the secrets of natural philosophy say that those children which are still within the belly, and while they are still contained in the womb, are a part of their mothers; and the most highly esteemed of the physicians who have examined into the formation of man, scrutinising both what is easily seen and what is kept concealed with great care, by means of anatomy, in order that, if there should be any need of their attention to any case, nothing may be disregarded through ignorance and so become the cause of serious mischief, agree with them and say the same thing. (118) But when the children are brought forth and are separated from that which is produced with them, and are set free and placed by themselves, they then become real living creatures, deficient in nothing which can contribute to the perfection of human nature, so that then, beyond all question, he who slays an infant is a homicide, and the law shows its indignation at such an action; not being guided by the age but by the species of the creature in whom its ordinances are violated.

(119) If, indeed, it seemed reasonable to be at all influenced by the age, then I think that a person might very reasonably be even more indignant at those who slay infants. For when full-grown people are killed, there may be ten thousand plausible excuses for assaults upon or quarrels with them; but in the case of mere infants only just launched into human life and shown to the light of day, it is impossible for the greatest liar to invent an accusation against them, as they are wholly void of offence. On which account those ought to be looked upon as the most inhuman and pitiless of all men who entertain plots for the destruction of those infants, and justly does the sacred law detest such criminals and pronounce them worthy of death.

XXI. (120) The sacred law says that the man, who has been killed without any intention that he should be so on the part of him who killed him, has been given up by God into the hands of his slayers;[8] in this way designing to make an excuse for the man who appears to have slain him as if he had slain a guilty person. (121) For the merciful and forgiving God can never be supposed to have given up any innocent person to be put to death; but whoever ingeniously escapes the judgment of a human tribunal by means of his own cunning and wariness, he is convicted when brought before the invisible tribunal of nature, by which alone the uncorrupted truth is discerned without being kept in the dark by the artifices of sophistical arguments.

For such an investigation does not admit of arguments at all, laying bare all devices and intentions, and bringing the most secret counsels to light; and, in one sense, it does not look upon a man who has slain another as liable to justice, inasmuch as he has only sinned to be the minister of a divine judgment, but still he will have incurred an obscure and slight kind of defilement, which, however, may obtain allowance and pardon. (122) For God employs those who commit slight and remedial errors against those who have perpetrated enormous and unpardonable crimes as ministers of punishment; not, indeed, that he approves of them, but that he avails himself of them as suitable instruments of punishment, so that no one who is himself pure in his whole life and descended from virtuous parents may have homicide imputed to him, even if he be the greatest man in the world.

(123) Therefore, the law has pronounced the sentence of banishment upon him who has slain a man, yet not of banishment any where, nor for ever; for it has assigned six cities,[9] one fourth portion of what the whole sacred tribe received as its inheritance, for those who were convicted of homicide; which, from the circumstances connected with them, it has named cities of refuge. And it fixed the time of this banishment as the length of the life of the high priest, permitting the exiles to return home after his death.

XXII. (124) And the cause of the first of these injunctions was this. The tribe which has been mentioned received these cities as a reward for a justifiable and holy slaughter, which we must look upon as the most illustrious and important of all the gallant actions that were ever performed. (125) For when the prophet, after having been called up to the loftiest and most sacred of all the mountains in that district, was divinely instructed in the generic outlines of all the special laws,[10] and was out of sight of his people for many days; those of the people who were not of a peaceable disposition filled every place with the evils which arise from anarchy, and crowned all their iniquity with open impiety, turning into ridicule all those excellent and beautiful lessons concerning the honour due to the one true and living God, and having made a golden bull, an imitation of the Egyptian Typhos, and brought to it unholy sacrifices, and festivals unhallowed, and instituted profane and impious dances, with songs and hymns instead of

---

[8]Exodus 21:13.

[9]Numbers 35:1.
[10]Exodus 32:1.

lamentations; (126) then the tribe aforesaid, being very terribly indignant at their sudden departure from their previous customs, and being enflamed with zeal by reason of their natural disposition which hated iniquity, all became full of rage and of divine enthusiasm, and arming themselves, as at one signal, and with great contempt and one unanimous attack, came upon the people, drunk thus with a twofold intoxication of impiety and of wine, beginning with their nearest and dearest friends and relations, thinking those who loved God to be their only relations and friends. And in a very small portion of the day, four-and-twenty thousand men were slain; the calamities of whom were a warning to those who would otherwise have joined themselves to their iniquity, but who now were alarmed lest they should suffer a similar fate.

(127) Since then these men had undertaken this expedition of their own accord and spontaneously, in the cause of piety and holy reverence for the one true and living God, not without great danger to those who had entered in the contest, the Father of the universe received them with approbation, and at once pronounced those who had slain those men to be pure from all curse and pollution, and in requital for their courage he bestowed the priesthood on them.

XXIII. (128) Therefore the lawgiver enjoins that the man who has committed an unintentional murder should flee to some one of the cities which this tribe has received as its inheritance, in order to comfort him and to teach him not to despair of any sort of safety; but to make him, while safe through the privilege of the place, remember and consider that not only on certain occasions is forgiveness allowed to those who have designedly slain any person, but that even great and preeminent honours and excessive happiness is bestowed on them.

And if such honours can ever be allowed to those who have slain a man voluntarily, how much more must there be allowance made for those who have done so not with any design, so that, even if no honour be bestowed on them, they may at least not be condemned to be put to death in retaliation.

By which injunctions the lawgiver intimates that every kind of homicide is not blameable, but only that which is combined with injustice; and that of other kinds some are even praiseworthy which are committed out of a desire and zeal for virtue; and that which is unintentional is not greatly to be blamed.

(129) This, then, may be enough to say about the first cause; and we must now explain the second.

The law thinks fit to preserve the man who, without intending it, has slain another, knowing that in his intention he was not guilty, but that with his hands he has been ministering to that justice which presides over all human affairs. For the nearest relations of the dead man are lying in wait for him in a hostile manner seeking his death, while others, out of their excessive compassion and inconsolable grief for the dead, are eager for their revenge; in their unreasoning impetuosity not regarding either the truth or the justice of nature. (130) Therefore, the law directs a man who has committed a homicide under these circumstances not to flee to the temple, inasmuch as he is not yet purified, nor yet into any place which is neglected and obscure, lest, being despised, he should be without resistance given up to his enemies; but to flee to the sacred city, which lies on the borders between the holy and profane ground, being in a manner a second temple; for the cities of those who are consecrated to the priesthood are more entitled to respect than the others, in the same proportion, I think, as the inhabitants are more venerable than the inhabitants of other cities; for the lawgiver's intention is by means of the privilege belonging to the city which has received them to give more complete security to the fugitives. (131) Moreover, I said before, he has appointed a time for their return, the death of the high priest, for the following reason.[11]

As the relations of each individual who has been slain treacherously lie in wait to secure themselves revenge and justice upon those who treacherously slew him; in like manner the high priest is the relation and nearest of kin to the whole nation; inasmuch as he presides over and dispenses justice to all who dispute in accordance with the laws, and offers up prayers and sacrifices every day on behalf of the whole nation, and prays for blessings for the people as for his own brethren, and parents, and children, that every age and every portion of the nation, as if it were one body, may be united into one and the same society and union, devoted to peace and obedience to the law.

(132) Therefore, let every one who has slain a man unintentionally fear him, as the champion and espouser of the cause of those who have been slain, and let him keep himself close within the city to which he has fled for refuge, no longer venturing to advance outside of the walls, if he has any regard for his own safety, and for keeping his life out of the reach of danger.

(133) When, therefore, the law says, let not the fugitive return till the high priest is dead, it says something equivalent to this: Until the high priest is dead, who is the common relation of all the people, to whom alone it is committed to decide the affairs of those who are living and those who are dead.

[11] Numbers 35:25.

XXIV. (134) Such, then, is the reason which it is fitting should be communicated to the ears of the younger men. But there is another which may be well set before those who are elder and settled in their characters, which is this.

It is granted to private individuals alone to be pure from voluntary offences, or if any one chooses, he may add the other priests also to this list; but it can only be given as an especial honour to the high priest to be pure from both kinds, that is from both voluntary and involuntary offences; (135) for it is altogether unlawful for him to touch any pollution whatever, whether intentionally or out of some unforeseen perversion of soul, in order that he, as being the declarer of the will of God may be adorned in both respects, having a disposition free from reproach, and prosperity of life, and being a man to whom no disgrace ever attaches. (136) Now it will be consistent with the character of such a man to look with suspicion on those who have even unintentionally slain a man, not indeed regarding them as under a curse, but also not as pure and wholly free from offence, even though they may have appeared most completely to obey the intention of nature, who used them as her instruments to avenge herself on those whom they have slain, whom she had privately judged by herself and condemned to death.

XXV. This is enough to say concerning free men and citizens.

The lawgiver proceeds in due order to establish laws concerning slaves who are killed by violence.

(137) Now servants are, indeed, in an inferior condition of life, but still the same nature belongs to them and to their masters. And it is not the condition of fortune, but the harmony of nature, which, in accordance with the divine law is the rule of justice. On which account it is proper for masters not to use their power over their slaves in an insolent manner, displaying by such conduct their insolence and overbearing disposition and terrible cruelty; for such conduct is not a proof of a peaceful soul, but of one which, out of an inability to regulate itself, covets the irresponsibility of a tyrannical power. (138) For the man who fortifies his own house like a citadel, and does not allow a single person within it to speak freely, but who behaves savagely to every one, by reason of his innate misanthropy and barbarity, which has perhaps even been increased by exercise, is a tyrant in miniature; and by his conduct now it is plainly shown that he will not stop even there if he should acquire greater power. (139) For then he will at once go forth to attack other cities and countries, and nations, after having previously enslaved his own native land, so as to prove that he is not inclined to behave mercifully to any one who shall ever become subject to

him. (140) Let, then, such a man be well assured that he will not always escape punishment for his continual ill-treatment of many persons; for justice, which hates iniquity, will be his enemy, she who is the assistant and champion of those who are treated with injustice, and she will exact of him a strict account of, and reckoning for, those who have fallen into calamity through his means, (141) even if he should say that he had only inflicted blows on them to correct them, not designing to kill them. For he will not at once get off with a cheerful countenance, but he will be brought before the tribunal and examined by accurate investigators of the truth, who will inquire whether he slew him intentionally or unintentionally. And if he be found to have plotted against him with a wicked disposition, let him die; not having any excuse made for him on the ground of his being the servants' master, so as to procure his deliverance.

(142) But if the servants who have been beaten do not die at once after receiving the blows, but live one day or two, then the master shall no longer be liable to be accused of murder, having this strong ground of defence that he did not kill them on the spot by beating, nor afterwards when he had them in his house, but that he suffered them to live as long as they could, even though that may not have been very long. Besides that, no one is so silly as to attempt to distress another by conduct by which he himself also will be a loser. (143) But any one who kills his servant injures himself much more, since he deprives himself of the services which he received from him while alive, and, moreover, loses the price which he paid for him which, perhaps, was large. If, however, the servant turn out to have done any thing worthy of death, let him bring him before the judges and prove his offence, making the laws the arbiters of his punishment and not himself.

CONCERNING THOSE BRUTE BEASTS WHICH
ARE THE CAUSES OF A MAN'S DEATH

XXVI. (144) If a bull gore a man and kill him, let him be stoned. [12] For his flesh may not be either offered in sacrifice by the priests, nor eaten by men. Why not? Because it is not consistent with the law of God that man should take for food or for a seasoning to his food the flesh of an animal which has slain a man. (145) But if the owner of the beast knew that he was a savage and ferocious animal, and did not confine him, nor shut him up and take care of him, or if he had heard from others that he was not quiet, and still allowed him to feed at liberty, he shall be liable to a prosecution as guilty of the man's death. And then the animal which gored the man shall die, and his master

_____

[12] Exodus 21:28.

shall be put to death also, or else shall pay a ransom and a price for his safety, and the court of justice shall devise what punishment he ought to suffer, what penalty he ought to pay.

(146) And if it be a slave who has been killed then he shall pay his full value to his master; but if the bull have gored not a man but another animal, then the owner of the beast which killed him shall take the dead animal and give his master another like him instead of him, because he was aware beforehand of the fierceness of his own beast, and did not guard against it. And if the bull has killed a sheep which belonged to some one else, he shall again restore this man one like it instead of it, and be thankful to him for not exacting a greater penalty of him, since it was he who was the first to do any injury.

CONCERNING PITS

XXVII. (147) Some persons are accustomed to dig very deep pits, either in order to open springs which may bubble up, or else to receive rain water, and then they widen drains under ground; in which case they ought either to build round the mouths of them, or else to put a cover on them; but still they often, out of shameful carelessness or folly, have left such places open, by which means some persons have met with destruction. (148) If, therefore, any traveller passing along the road, not knowing beforehand that there is any such pit, shall step on the hole, and fall in, and be killed, any one of the relations of the dead man who chooses may bring an accusation against those who made the pit, and the tribunal shall decide what punishment they ought to suffer, or what penalty they ought to pay.[13]

But if a beast fall in and perish, then they who dug the pit shall pay its value to its owner as if it were still alive, and they shall have the dead body for themselves.

(149) Again, those men also are committing an injury akin to and resembling that which has just been mentioned, who when building houses leave the roof level with the ground though they ought to protect them with a parapet, in order that no one may fall down into the hole made without perceiving it. For such men, if one is to tell the plain truth, are committing murder, as far as they themselves are concerned, even though no one fall in and perish; accordingly let them be punished equally with those who have the mouths of pits open.

XXVIII. (150) The law expressly enjoins that it shall not be lawful to take any ransom from murderers who ought to be put to death, for the purpose of lessening their punishment, or substituting banishment for death. For blood must be atoned for by blood, the blood of him who has been treacherously slain by that of him who has slain him. (151) Since men of wicked dispositions are never wearied of offending, but are always committing atrocious actions in the excess of their wickedness, and increasing their iniquities, and extending them beyond all bounds or limits.

For the lawgiver would, if it had been in his power, have condemned those men to ten thousand deaths. But since this was not possible, he prescribed another punishment for them, commanding those who had slain a man to be hanged upon a tree. (152) And after having established this ordinance he returned again to his natural humanity, treating with mercy even those who had behaved unmercifully towards others, and he pronounced, "Let not the sun set upon persons hanging on a tree;"[14] but let them be buried under the earth and be concealed from sight before sunset. For it was necessary to raise up on high all those who were enemies to every part of the world, so as to show most evidently to the sun, and to the heaven, and to the air, and to the water, and to the earth, that they had been chastised; and after that it was proper to remove them into the region of the dead, and to bury them, in order to prevent their polluting the things upon the earth.

XXIX. (153) Moreover, there is this further commandment given with great propriety, that the fathers are not to die in behalf of their sons, nor the sons in behalf of their parents, but that every one who has done things worthy of death is to be put to death by himself alone. And this commandment is established because of those persons who set might above right, and also for the sake of those who are too affectionate; (154) for these last, out of their extraordinary and extravagant good will, will be often willing cheerfully to die for others, the innocent thus giving themselves up for the guilty, and thinking it a great gain not to see them punished; or else sons giving themselves up for their fathers in the idea that, if deprived of them they would for the future live a miserable life, more grievous than any kind of death.

(155) But to such persons one must say, "This your good-will is out of season." And all things which are out of season are very properly blamed, just as things that are done seasonably are praised on that account. Moreover, it is right to love those who do actions worthy to attract love. But no wicked man can be really a friend to any one. And wickedness alienates relations, and even those who are the most attached of relations, when men violate all the principles of justice. For the agreement as to principles of injustice and as to the other

---

[13]Exodus 21:33.   [14]Deuteronomy 21:23.

virtues, is a closer tie than relationship by blood; and if any one violates such an agreement, he is set down not only as a stranger and a foreigner, but even as an irreconcilable enemy.

(156) "Why then do you pervert and misapply the name of good-will which is a most excellent and humane one, and conceal the truth, exhibiting as a veil an effeminate and womanly disposition? For are not those persons womanly in whose minds reason is overcome by compassion? And you do this in order to effect a double iniquity, delivering the guilty from punishment, and thinking it fair to punish yourselves, who are blameable in no respect whatever, instead of them."

XXX. (157) But these men have this to say in excuse of themselves, that they are not pursuing any private advantage for themselves, and also that they are influenced by excessive affection for their nearest relations, for the sake of the preservation of whom they will cheerfully submit to die. (158) But who, I will not say of moderate men, but even of those who are very inhuman indeed in their dispositions, would not reject such barbarous and actually brutally disposed persons as those who, either by secret contrivance or by open audacity, inflict the greatest calamities on one person as a punishment for the faults of another, putting forward as a pretext the plea of friendship, or of relationship, or of fellowship, or something of that kind, as a justification for the destruction of those who have done no wrong? And at times they even do these things without having suffered any injury at all out of mere covetousness and a love of rapine.

(159) Not long ago a certain man who had been appointed a collector of taxes in our country, when some of those who appeared to owe such tribute fled out of poverty, from a fear of intolerable punishment if they remained without paying, carried off their wives, and their children, and their parents, and their whole families by force, beating and insulting them, and heaping every kind of contumely and ill treatment upon them, to make them either give information as to where the fugitives had concealed themselves, or pay the money instead of them, though they could not do either the one thing or the other; in the first place, because they did not know where they were, and secondly, because they were in still greater poverty than the men who had fled. (160) But this tax-collector did not let them go till he had tortured their bodies with racks and wheels, so as to kill them with newly invented kinds of death, fastening a basket full of sand to their necks with cords, and suspending it there as a very heavy weight, and then placing them in the open air in the middle of the market place, that some of them, being tortured and being overwhelmed by all these afflictions at once, the wind, and the sun, and the mockery of the passers by, and the

shame, and the heavy burden attached to them, might faint miserably; and that the rest, being spectators, might be grieved and take warning by their punishment, (161) some of whom, having a more acute sense of such miseries in their minds than that which they could receive though their eyes, since they sympathised with these unfortunates as if they were themselves suffering in the persons of others, put an end to their own lives by swords, or poison, or halters, thinking it a great piece of good luck for persons, liable to such misery, to be able to meet with death without torture.

(162) But those who did not make haste to kill themselves, but who were seized before they could do so, were led away in a row, as in the case of actions for inheritance, according to their nearness of kindred, the nearest relations first, then those next to them in succession, in the second or third place, till they came to the last; and then, when there were no relations left, the cruelty proceeded on to the friends and neighbours of the fugitives; and sometimes it was extended even into the cities and villages, which soon became desolate, being emptied of all their inhabitants, who all quitted their homes, and dispersed to places where they hoped that they might escape detection.

(163) But perhaps it is not wonderful if men, barbarians by nature, utterly ignorant of all gentleness, and under the command of despotic authority, which compelled them to give an account of the yearly revenue, should, in order to enforce the payment of the taxes, extend their severities, not merely to properties but also to the persons, and even to the lives, of those from whom they thought they could exact a vicarious payment. (164) But now, even those persons who are the very standard and rule of justice, the lawgivers themselves, having a regard to appearance rather than to truth, have endured to become, instead, standards of injustice, commanding the children of a traitor to be put to death with the traitor himself, and in the case of tyrants the five families most nearly related to them.

(165) Why is this I should say? For if indeed they have shared in their wickedness, then let them likewise share in their punishment; but if they have not participated in that, and if they have not been imitators of such actions, and if they have not been elated by the prosperity of their kinsmen, so as to exult in it, why should they be put to death? Is it for this reason alone, that they are their relations? Are the punishments then inflicted for the relationship, or for the lawless conduct? (166) Perhaps you yourselves, O you venerable lawgivers, have had virtuous relations; but suppose they had been wicked, then it seems to me that you not only would never yourselves have devised any such commandments as this, but would have been furious with any one else who proposed such a law,

because [...] [15] taking care to avoid all liability to terrible calamity, and desiring to live in security, is now in great danger, and is exposed to an equal degree of misfortune.

For the one condition is liable to fear, which, though a person may guard against for himself, he will still not despise the safety of another, but the other state is free from all apprehension, and by it men have often been persuaded to neglect the safety of innocent men.

(167) Therefore our lawgiver, considering these things and perceiving the errors of others, rejects them and hates them as destructive of the most excellent constitution, and consigns to punishment all those who give way to such, whether it be out of indifference, or out of inhumanity and wickedness, and never permits any of their countrymen or friends to be substituted for them, making themselves an addition to the crimes which the others have already committed; (168) on which account he has expressly forbidden sons to be put to death instead of their parents, or parents instead of their sons, thinking it right that they who have committed the crimes should also bear the punishment, whether it be a pecuniary fine, or stripes, and more severe personal chastisement, or even wounds and mutilation, and dishonour, and exile, or any other judicial sentence; for though he only names one kind of punishment, forbidding one person to be put to death for another, he also comprises other kinds, which he does not expressly mention.

ABOUT WOMEN NOT BEHAVING IMMODESTLY

XXXI. (169) Market places, and council chambers, and courts of justice, and large companies and assemblies of numerous crowds, and a life in the open air full of arguments and actions relating to war and peace, are suited to men; but taking care of the house and remaining at home are the proper duties of women; the virgins having their apartments in the centre of the house within the innermost doors, and the full-grown women not going beyond the vestibule and outer courts; (170) for there are two kinds of states, the greater and the smaller. And the larger ones are called really cities; but the smaller ones are called houses.

And the superintendence and management of these is allotted to the two sexes separately; the men having the government of the greater, which government is called a polity; and the women that of the smaller, which is called oeconomy. (171) Therefore let no woman busy herself about those

things which are beyond the province of oeconomy, but let her cultivate solitude, and not be seen to be going about like a woman who walks the streets in the sight of other men, except when it is necessary for her to go to the temple, if she has any proper regard for herself; and even then let her not go at noon when the market is full, but after the greater part of the people have returned home; like a well-born woman, a real and true citizen, performing her vows and her sacrifices in tranquillity, so as to avert evils and to receive blessings.

(172) But when men are abusing one another or fighting, for women to venture to run out under pretence of assisting or defending them, is a blameable action and one of no slight shamelessness, since even, in the times of war and of military expeditions, and of dangers to their whole native land, the law does not choose that they should be enrolled as its defenders; looking at what is becoming, which it thinks desirable to preserve unchangeable at all times and in all places, thinking that this very thing is of itself better than victory, or then freedom, or than any kind of success and prosperity. (173) Moreover, if any woman, hearing that her husband is being assaulted, being out of her affection for him carried away by love for her husband, should yield to the feelings which overpower her and rush forth to aid him, still let her not be so audacious as to behave like a man, outrunning the nature of a woman; [16] but even while aiding him let her continue a woman.

For it would be a very terrible thing if a woman, being desirous to deliver her husband from an insult, should expose herself to insult, by exhibiting human life as full of shamelessness and liable to great reproaches for her incurable boldness; (174) for shall a woman utter abuse in the marketplace and give vent to unlawful language? and if another man uses foul language, will not she stop her ears and run away? But as it is now, some women are advanced to such a pitch of shamelessness as not only, though they are women, to give vent to intemperate language and abuse among a crowd of men, but even to strike men and insult them, with hands practised rather in works of the loom and spinning than in blows and assaults, like competitors in the pancratium or wrestlers. And other things, indeed, may be tolerable, and what any one might easily bear, but that is a shocking thing if a woman were to proceed to such a degree of boldness as to seize hold of the genitals of one of the men quarrelling.

(175) For let not such a woman be let go on the ground that she appears to have done this action in order to assist her own husband; but let her be impeached and suffer the punishment due

---

[15]There appears to be an hiatus in the text here. There is clearly a want of connection and coherence in the rest of the sentence as it stands now.

[16]Deuteronomy 25:11.

to her excessive audacity, so that if she should ever be inclined to commit the same offence again she may not have an opportunity of doing so; and other women, also, who might be inclined to be precipitate, may be taught by fear to be moderate and to restrain themselves.

And let the punishment be the cutting off of the hand which has touched what it ought not to have touched.

(176) And it is fitting to praise those who have been the judges and managers of the gymnastic games, who have kept women from the spectacle, in order that they might not be thrown among naked men and so mar the approved coinage of their modesty, neglecting the ordinances of nature, which she has appointed for each section of our race; for neither is it right for men to mix with women when they have laid aside their garments, but each of the sexes ought to avoid the sight of the other when they are naked, in accordance with the promptings of nature. (177) Well, then, of those things of which we are to abstain from the sight, are not the hands much more to be blamed for the touch? For the eyes, being wholly at freedom, are nevertheless often constrained so as to see things which they do not wish to see; but the hands are ranked among those parts which are completely under subjection, and obey our commands, and are subservient to us.

XXXII. (178) And this is the cause which is often mentioned by many people. But I have heard another also, alleged by persons of high character, who look upon the greater part of the injunctions contained in the law as plain symbols of obscure meanings, and expressed intimations of what may not be expressed. And this other reason alleged is as follows.

There are two kinds of soul, much as there are two sexes among human relations; the one a masculine soul, belonging to men; the other a female soul, as found in women. The masculine soul is that which devotes itself to God alone, as the Father and Creator of the universe and the cause of all things that exist; but the female soul is that which depends upon all the things which are created, and as such are liable to destruction, and which puts forth, as it were, the hand of its power in order that in a blind sort of way it may lay hold of whatever comes across it, clinging to a generation which admits of an innumerable quantity of changes and variations, when it ought rather to cleave to the unchangeable, blessed, and thrice happy divine nature.

(179) Very naturally, therefore, the law commands[17] that the executioner should cut off the hand of the woman which has laid hold of what it

should not, speaking figuratively, and intimating not that the body shall be mutilated, being deprived of its most important part, but rather that it is proper to extirpate all the ungodly reasonings of the soul, using all things which are created as a stepping-stone; for the things which the woman is forbidden to take hold of are the symbols of procreation and generation. (180) And, moreover, keeping up a consistent regard to nature, I will also say this, that the unit is the image of the first cause, and the number two of the divisible matter that is worked upon. Whoever, therefore, receives the number two, honouring it above the unit, must be taught to know that he is, in so doing, approving of the matter more than of God. On which account the law has thought fit to cut off this apprehension of the soul as if it were a hand; for there can be no greater impiety than to ascribe the power of the agent to that which is passive.

XXXIII. (181) And any one may here fitly blame those who appoint that punishments, in nowise corresponding to the offences, are to be inflicted on the offenders, imposing pecuniary penalties for assaults, or stigma and infamy for wounds and mutilations, or a banishment beyond the borders of the land for intentional murders, and everlasting exile or imprisonment for thefts; for irregularity and inequality are enemies to a constitution which is eager for the truth. (182) And our law, being the interpreter and teacher of equality, commands that offenders should undergo a punishment similar to the offence which they have committed; that, for instance, they should suffer punishment in their property if they have injured their neighbour in his property; in their persons, if they have injured him in his body, or in his limbs, or the organs of his outward senses; and, if their evil designs have extended to his life, then the law commands that the punishment should affect the life of the malefactor.

For to exact a different and wholly unequal punishment which has no connection with or resemblance to the offence, but which is wholly at variance with it in all its characteristics, is the conduct of those who violate the laws rather than of those who would establish them. (183) And when we say this, we mean provided no circumstances occur to give a different complexion to the affair; for it is not the same thing to inflict blows on one's father and on a stranger, nor to speak ill of a ruler and of a private person, nor to do anything which is forbidden on common ground or in holy places, or at the time of a festival, or of a solemn assembly, or of a public sacrifice; or, again, on the days on which there is no holiday or sacred observance, or on those which are completely common and profane. And all other things of this kind one must examine with a view to judge of

---

[17] Deuteronomy 25:12.

the propriety of increasing or diminishing the punishment.

(184) Again. "If," says the law, "any one strike out the eye of a servant or of a handmaiden, he shall let them depart free."[18] Because, as nature has assigned the chief position in the body to the head, having bestowed upon it a situation the most suitable to that pre-eminence, as it might give a citadel to a king (for having sent it forth to govern the body it has established it on a height, putting the whole composition of the body from the neck to the feet under it, as a pedestal might be placed under a statue), so also it has given the pre-eminence among the organs of the external senses to the eyes. At all events, it has assigned them a position above all the others, as if they were the chiefs, wishing to honour them not only by other things, but also by this most evident and conspicuous of all signs.

XXXIV. (185) Now it would take a long time to enumerate all the necessities which the eyes supply to, and all the services which they perform for, the human race. But one, the most excellent of all, we may mention. It is the heaven which has showered philosophy upon us, it is the human mind which has received and which contains it, but it is sight which has entertained and been its host; for that is the faculty which was the first to see the level roads through the air.

(186) And philosophy is the fountain of all blessings, of all things which are really good. And he who draws from this fountain, so as thus to acquire and make use of virtue is praiseworthy; but he who does it with the object of accomplishing wicked purposes and of condemning others is blameable. For the one is like a man at an entertainment, who is delighting both himself and all who are feasting in his company; but the other is like one who is swallowing down strong wine, in order to make himself and his neighbour drunk.

(187) Now in what way it is that the sight may be said to have entertained philosophy as its host we must now proceed to explain. Having looked up to heaven it beheld the sun, and the moon, and the planets, and the fixed stars, the most beautiful host of heaven, the ornament of the world. (188) After that it arrived at a perception of the rising and setting of these bodies, and their harmonious motions, and the fixed seasons of their periodical revolutions, and their meetings, and eclipses, and re-appearances. After that it proceeded onwards to a comprehension of the increase and decrease of the moon; of the motions of the sun along the breadth of heaven, as he comes from the south towards the north, and again recedes from the north towards the south, in order to the

generation of the fruits of the year, so that they may all be brought to perfection, and ten thousand other wonderful things besides these. And having looked round and surveyed the things in the earth, and in the sea, and in the air, with great diligence displayed all the things in each of these elements to the mind.

(189) But as the mind was unable by itself to comprehend all these things from merely beholding them by the faculty of sight, it did not stop merely at what was seen by it, but being devoted to learning, and fond of what is honourable and excellent, as it admired what it did see, it adopted this probable opinion, that these things are not moved spontaneously and at random by any irrational impulse of their own, but that they are set in motion and guided by the will of God, whom it is proper to look upon as the Father and Creator of the world. Moreover, that these things are not unrestrained by any bounds, but that they are limited by the circumference of one world, as they might be by the walls of a city, the world itself being circumscribed within the outermost sphere of the fixed stars.

Moreover it considered also that the Father who created the world does by the law of nature take care of that which he has created, exerting his providence in behalf of the whole universe and of its parts. (190) In the next place it also considered what was the essence of the visible world, and whether all the things in the world had the same essence, or whether different things had different essences, and also of what substances everything was made, and for what reasons it was made, and by what powers the world was held together, and whether these powers were corporeal or incorporeal. (191) For what can the investigation into these and similar subjects be called but philosophy? And what more fitting name could one give to the man who devoted himself to the investigation of these topics than that of a philosopher? For by his examination of the nature of God, and of the world, and of all the things in it, whether plants or animals, and of those models which are only appreciable by the intellect, and again of the perfected representations of those models which are visible to the outward senses, and of the virtues and vices which exist in all created things, he shows that his disposition is one truly devoted to learning, and contemplation, and philosophy; and this greatest of blessings to mortal man is bestowed upon him by the faculty of sight.

(192) And this faculty seems to me to deserve this pre-eminence, since it is more nearly related to the soul than any one of the other outward senses, for they all of them have some kind of connection with the intellect; but this one obtains the first and principal rank as the nearest relation does in a private house. (193) And any one may con-

---

[18] Exodus 21:26.

jecture this from many circumstances, for who is there who does not know that when persons are delighted their eyes betray their pleasure, and sparkle, but that when they are grieved their eyes are full of depression and heaviness; and if any heavy burden of grief oppresses, and crushes, and overwhelms the mind, they weep; and if anger obtains and preponderance, the eyes swell, and become bloodshot and fiery; (194) and again change so as to be gentle and soft when the anger is relaxed. Again, when the man is immersed in deep thought and contemplation, the eyes seem fixed as if they in a manner joined in his gravity; but in the case of those who are of no great wisdom the sight wanders, because of their vacancy of intellect, and is restless, and in short the eyes sympathise with the affections of the soul, and are wont to change along with it in innumerable alternations, on account of the closeness of their connection with it; for it seems to me that there is no one visible thing which God has made so complete a representation of that which is invisible as the sight is of the mind.

XXXV. (195) If therefore any one has ever plotted against this most excellent and most dominant of all the outward senses, namely sight, so as ever to have struck out the eye of a free man, let him suffer the same infliction himself, but not so if he have only struck out the eye of a slave; not because he is entitled to pardon, or because the injury which he has done is less, but because the man who has been injured will have a still worse master if he has been mutilated in retaliation, since he will for ever bear a grudge against him for the calamity which has fallen upon him, and will revenge himself on him every day as an irreconcileable enemy by harsh commands beyond his power to perform, by which the slave will be so oppressed that he will be ready to die.

(196) Therefore the law has provided that the man who has thus done injury to his slave shall not be allowed to escape free, and yet has not commanded that the man who has already suffered the loss of his eye shall be ill-treated still further, enjoining that if any one strikes out the eye of his servant he shall without hesitation grant him his freedom; (197) for thus he will suffer a double punishment for the actions which he has committed, in being deprived of the value of his servant and also of his services, and thirdly, which is worse than either of the things already mentioned, in being compelled to do good to his enemy in the most important matters, whom very likely he wished to be able to ill-treat for ever. And the slave has a double consolation for the evils which he has been subjected to in being not only emancipated, but also in having escaped a cruel and inhuman master.

XXXVI. (198) The law also commands that if any one strike out the tooth of a slave he shall bestow his freedom on the slave; why is this? because life is a thing of great value, and because nature has made the teeth the instruments of life, as being those by which the food is eaten. And of the teeth some are fitted for eating meat and all other eatable food, and on that account are called incisors, or cutting teeth; others are called molar teeth from their still further grinding and smoothing what has been cut by the incisors; (199) on which account the Creator and Father of the universe, who is not accustomed to make anything which is not appointed for some particular use, did not do with the teeth as he did with every other part of the body, and make them at once, at the first creation of the man, considering that as while an infant he was only intended to be fed upon milk they would be a superfluous burden in his way, and would be a severe injury to the breasts, filled as they are at that time with springs of milk, from which moist food is derived, as they would in that case be bitten by the child while sucking the milk. (200) Therefore, having waited for a suitable season (and that is when the child is weaned), he then causes the infant to put forth the teeth which he had prepared for it before, as the most perfect food now supplied to it requires the organs above-mentioned now that the child rejects the food of milk.

(201) If therefore any one, yielding to an insolent disposition, strikes out the tooth of his servant, that organ which is the minister and provider of those most necessary things, food and life, he shall emancipate him whom he has injured, because by the evil which he inflicted on him he has deprived him of the service and use of his tooth.

"Is then," some one will say, "a tooth of equal value with an eye?" (202) "Each," I would reply, "is of equal value for the purposes for which they were given, the eye with reference to the objects of sight, the teeth with reference to those which are eatable." But if any one were to desire to institute a comparison, he would find that the eye is entitled to the highest respect among all the parts of the body, inasmuch as being occupied in the contemplation of the most glorious thing in the whole world, namely the heaven; and that the tooth is useful as being the masticator of food, which is the most useful thing as contributing to life. And he who strikes out a man's eye does not hinder him from living, but a most miserable death awaits the man who has all his teeth knocked out.

(203) And if any one meditates inflicting injury in these parts on his servants, let him know that he is causing them an artificial famine in the midst of plenty and abundance; for what advantage is it to a man that there should be an abundance of food, if the instruments by which he may be enabled to make use of it are taken from him and lost, through the agency of his cruel, and pitiless, and inhuman

master? (204) It is for this reason that in another passage the lawgiver forbids creditors to exact from their debtors a molar tooth or a grinder as a pledge, giving as a reason that the person who does so is taking a man's life in pledge; for he who deprives a man of the instruments of living is proceeding towards murder, entertaining the idea of plotting even against life.

(205) And the law has taken such exceeding care that no one shall ever be the cause of death to another, that it does not look upon those who have even touched a dead body, which has met with a natural death, as pure and clean, until they have washed and purified themselves with sprinklings and ablutions; and even after they are perfectly clean it does not permit them to go into the temple within seven days, enjoining them to use purifying ceremonies on the third and seventh day. (206) And again, in the case of persons who have gone into the house in which any one has died, the law enjoins that no one shall touch them until they have both washed their bodies and also the garments in which they were clothed, and, in a word, it looks upon all the furniture and all the vessels, and everything which is in the house, as unclean and polluted; (207) for the soul of a man is a valuable thing, and when that has quitted its habitation, and passed to another place, everything that is left behind by it is polluted as being deprived of the divine image, since the human mind is made as a copy of the mind of God, having been created after the archetypal model, the most sublime reasoning.

(208) And the law says, "Let everything which a man that is unclean has touched be also unclean as being polluted by a participation in that which is unclean." And this sacred injunction appears to have a wide operation, not being limited to the body alone, but proceeding as it would seem also to investigate the dispositions of the soul, (209) for the unjust and impious man is peculiarly unclean, being one who has no respect for either human or divine things, but who throws everything into disorder and confusion by the immoderate vehemence of his passions, and by the extravagance of his wickedness, so that everything which he touches becomes faulty, having its nature changed by the wickedness of him who has taken them in hand. For in like manner the actions of the good are, on the contrary, all praiseworthy, being made better by the energies of those who apply themselves to them, since in some degree what is done resembles in its character the person who does it.

THE SPECIAL LAWS, IV†

(De Specialibus Legibus, IV)

I. (1) I have in my previous treatises spoken of the laws relating to adultery and murder, and to all the subordinate offences which come under those head, with, as I persuade myself, all the accuracy which the case admits of, and now, proceeding in the regular order, I must consider what is the third commandment in the second table, but the eighth in all, if the two tables are taken together, namely, the commandment, "Thou shalt not steal."[1]

(2) Whoever carries off or leads away the property of another when he has no right to do so, if he does it openly and by main force, shall be set down as a common enemy, and shall be prosecuted as having with lawless wickedness contrived a shameless act of audacity. But if he has done it secretly, endeavouring to escape notice like a thief, exhibiting some modesty, and making the darkness the veil of his iniquity, let him then be punished privately as only liable to condemnation in respect of the one individual whom he endeavoured to injure; and let him restore double the value of the thing stolen, making amends by his own most righteous suffering for the unrighteous advantage he has endeavoured to gain.

(3) But if he is a poor man, and consequently unable to pay the penalty, let him be sold (for it is fitting that that man should be deprived of his freedom who for the sake of his most iniquitous gain has endured to become a slave to guilt), that he who has been ill-treated may not be allowed to depart without consolation, as if he appeared to have his claims disregarded by reason of the poverty of the man who has robbed him. (4) And let no one accuse this ordinance of inhumanity; for the man who is sold is not left as a slave for ever and ever, but within the space of seven years he is released by a common proclamation as I have shown in my treatise on the number seven.

(5) And let him be content to pay the double penalty, or even to be sold, since he has committed no slight offence; sinning in the first place in that, not being content with what he had, he has desired more, encouraging a feeling of covetousness, a treacherous and incurable wickedness. Secondly, because he has cast his eyes on the property of others and longed for it, and has laid plots to deprive his neighbour of his own, depriving the owner of what belongs to him. Thirdly, because through his desire to escape detection, he very often keeps to himself all the advantage that can be derived from the thing he appropriates, and diverts the accusation so as to cause it to fall upon the innocent, thus making the investigation of the truth blind. (6) And such a man appears in some degree to be himself his own accuser, being convicted by his own conscience of the theft of those things which he has secretly stolen, being filled either with shame or fear, one of which feelings is a proof of his considering his action a disgraceful one, for it is only disgraceful actions which cause shame, and the other is a sign of his thinking it deserving of punishment, for punishment causes fear.

CONCERNING HOUSEBREAKERS

II. (7) If any one being insanely carried away by a desire for the property of others attempts to steal it, and not being able easily to carry it off breaks into a house at night, using the darkness as a veil to conceal his wicked action, if he be caught in the fact before the sun has risen, he may be slain by the master of the house in the breaches, having accomplished the lesser object which he had proposed to himself, namely, theft, but having been hindered by some one from accomplishing the greater crime which might have followed it, namely, murder; since he was prepared with iron house-breaking tools which he bore, and other arms, to defend himself from any attack.

But if the sun has risen, then let him no longer be slain by the hand of the master of the house, but let him be led away and brought before the magistrates and judges, to suffer whatever punishment they condemn him to. (8) For while men are remaining in their houses at night, and when they have betaken themselves to rest, whether they be rulers or private individuals, in either case there is no refuge or assistance for the offender; on which account the inmate of the house has the power of punishment in his own hands, being appointed magistrate and judge by the very time itself.

(9) But in the day time the courts of justice and the council chambers are open, and the city is full of persons who will help to arrest the criminal; some of whom have been formally appointed guardians of the laws; and others, without any such

---

†Yonge's title, *A Treatise on Those Special Laws Which Are Contained Under and Have Reference to the Eighth and Ninth, and Tenth Commandments.*
[1]Exodus 20:13.

appointment, by their natural disposition which hates iniquity, take up the cause of those who are injured; and before these men the thief must be brought; for thus the man who seeks revenge will escape the charge of arrogance or rashness, and appear to be acting in the spirit of the democracy.

(10) But if, when the sun has risen and is shining upon the earth, any one slays a robber with his own hand before bringing him to trial, he shall be held guilty, as having been guided by passion rather than by reason, and as having made the laws second to his own impulses. I should say to such a man, "My, friend, do not, because you have been injured by night by a thief, on this account in the daylight yourself commit a worse theft, not indeed affecting money, but affecting the principles of justice, in accordance with which the constitution of the state is established."

ABOUT THE THEFT OF A SHEEP OR AN OX

III. (11) Now other thefts are to be atoned for by a payment of double the value of the thing stolen; but if any one steals an ox or a sheep, the law thinks such a man worthy of a greater punishment, giving a particular honour and precedence to those animals which are the most excellent among all tame flocks and herds, not only by reason of the beauty of their bodies, but also because of the service they are of to the life of man. And on this account the lawgiver has not affixed a fine of equal amount to the theft of each animal, but having calculated the use of both and the purposes for which both are available, he has appraised their value in this way.

(12) For he commands that the thief shall restore four sheep and five oxen in the place of the one which he has stolen; since a sheep gives four kinds of tribute, milk, and cheese, and its fleece, and a lamb, every year: but an ox furnishes five; three of which are the same as those of the sheep—the milk, the cheese, and the offspring; but two are peculiar to itself, the ploughing of the earth, and the threshing of the corn; the first of which actions is the first step towards the sowing of the crops, and the other is the end, being for the purification of the crop after it is gathered in, in order to the more easy use of it for food.

CONCERNING KIDNAPPERS

IV. (13) A kidnapper also is a thief; but he is, moreover, a thief who steals the very most excellent thing that exists upon the earth. Now, in the case of inanimate things, and of those animals which are of no very great use indeed in life, he has commanded twice the value of them to be paid to their owners by those who steal them, as has been said before. And again, in the case of those tame and very useful flocks and herds of sheep and oxen, he has ordered the payment to be four-fold or fivefold; (14) but man, as it seems, has been assigned the most pre-eminent position among the animals, being, as it were, a near relation of God himself, and akin to him in respect of his participation in reason; which makes him immortal, although he is liable to death. On which account every one who feels any admiration of virtue is full of exceeding anger, and is utterly implacable against kidnappers, who for the sake of most iniquitous gain dare to inflict slavery on those who are free by birth, and who partake of the same nature as themselves.

(15) For if masters perform a praiseworthy action when they emancipate servants born in their house or purchased with money, even though they have often not done them any great service, from the slavery in which they are held, because of their own humanity by which they are influenced, how heavy ought to be the accusation which is brought against those who deprive of that most excellent of all possessions, freedom, those who are at present in possession of it; when it is an object for which man, who has been well born and properly brought up, would think it glorious to die? (16) And before now, some men, increasing their own innate wickedness, and directing the natural treachery of their characters to a violation of all rights, have studied to bring slavery not only upon strangers and foreigners, but even upon those of the same nation as themselves; and sometimes, even upon men of the same borough and of the same tribe, disregarding the community of laws and customs, in which they have been bred up with them from their earliest infancy, which nature stamps upon their souls as the firmest bond of good will in the case of all those who are not very intractable and greatly addicted to cruelty; (17) who, for the sake of lawless gain sell slaves to slave-dealers, and enslave them to any chance persons, transporting them to a foreign land, so that they shall never any more salute their native land, not even in a dream, nor taste of any hope of happiness.

For these kidnappers would be committing a lighter iniquity if they themselves retained the services of those whom they have enslaved, but as the case stands at present they commit a double wrong, in selling them again, and thus making them two masters instead of one, and raising up two slaveries as enemies to their condition. (18) For they, being aware of the former prosperous condition of those whom they have carried off, might perhaps repent, feeling a tardy and late compassion for those who are thus fallen, having a proper awe of the uncertainty of fortune eluding all conjectures. But those who buy persons in this condition, out of ignorance of their families, will neglect them as if they were sprung from successive generations of slaves, having no inducement in their souls to display that gentleness and humanity towards them which it would be natural for them to preserve in the case of slaves who had become so after having been originally and naturally free-born.

(19) And let whatever punishment the court of justice shall sentence them to be inflicted upon those who kidnap and enslave those of another nation; but upon those who kidnap those of their own country and of their own blood, and who sell them for slaves, shall be passed the unalterable sentence of death. For, in fact, one's own countrymen are not far from blood relations, and they must very nearly come under the same definition with them.

CONCERNING DAMAGE

V. (20) "In the field also," as some one of the old writers has said, "lawsuits arise;" since covetousness and a desire for the possessions of others does not exist only in the city, but is found also outside the walls, inasmuch as it has its abode not only in various places, but also in the minds of insatiable and contentious men. (21) On which account those cities which enjoy the best codes of laws elect double superintendents, and rulers, and providers of a common regularity and safety; one class to manage within the walls, whom they call curators of the city; the others without the walls, to whom also they give an appropriate name, for they call them agrarian magistrates.

But what need could there be of agrarian magistrates if there were not some persons in the fields living only for the injury of their neighbours? (22) If, therefore, any shepherd or goatherd, or oxherd, or in short any manager of any kind of cattle, drives his herds to feed and pasture upon another man's land, sparing neither crops nor trees, he shall pay a fine equal to the value of those crops and trees. (23) And he may be very well content to escape with this punishment, having met with a very merciful and exceedingly indulgent law, which, though he has adopted the conduct of implacable foreign enemies, who are accustomed to lay waste the lands and to destroy the cultivated trees of the inhabitants, has, nevertheless, not chastised him as a common enemy, inflicting upon him death, or exile, or of, lastly, a confiscation of all his property; but has merely sentenced him to make good the damage done to the owner.

(24) For as the lawgiver was always seeking pretexts by which to lighten whatever misfortunes have been suffered by reason of the excessive gentleness and humanity which he derived from nature and from habit, he found an excuse for the shepherd on the ground that the nature of cattle was inconsiderate and disobedient, and especially so when in pursuit of food. (25) Let the shepherd, then, be guilty, as having originally driven his herd into an unsuitable place, but still let him not bear the blame of every thing that has ensued from his doing so. For it is natural to suppose that, as soon as he perceived the mischief that had taken place he endeavoured to drive them out again, but that his beasts resisted him, luxuriating in the green pasture, and the tender crops, and shoots which they were devouring.

CONCERNING NOT SETTING FIRE TO BRAMBLES INCONSIDERATELY

VI. (26) And not only do those men do damage who devour the property of others with their flocks and herds, but so also do those who inconsiderately and carelessly kindle a fire; for if the power of fire catches hold of any appropriate fuel, it spreads in every direction, and extends and devours all around. And when it has once got ahead it defies all the means of extinguishing it which any one seeks to apply, taking the very things employed for that purpose as food for its increase, until having consumed every thing it is at last exhausted by itself. (27) It is right, therefore, never to leave any fire either in a house or in any stables in the fields unguarded, since we well know that a single spark has often smouldered long, and at last has been fanned into a flame, and so has consumed great cities, especially when the flame has been borne onwards by a favourable wind.

(28) Accordingly, in savage wars the first, the middle, and the last power which is excited is that of fire, to which the enemies trust more than they do to their squadrons of infantry, or cavalry, or to their fleets, or to their unlimited supplies of arms and naval stores. For if any one with good aim shoots a fiery arrow among a numerous squadron of ships he may burn it with all the crews, or he may thus destroy vast camps with all their baggage, and furniture, and equipments, on which the army rested its hopes of victory.

(29) If, then, any one scatters fire among a heap of brambles or thorns, and the fire kindles and burns a threshing floor full of wheat, or barley, or vetches, or sheaves of corn which have been gathered together, or any fertile plain full of pasture, then the man who scattered the fire shall pay the amount of the damage done, in order that by his suffering he may learn to take good care and to guard against the beginnings[2] of things, and may not awaken and stir up an invincible power which might otherwise have remained quiet.

CONCERNING DEPOSITS

VII. (30) A deposit is the most sacred of all those things which relate to the associations of men with regard to property, inasmuch as it depends upon the good faith alone of the man who has received it. For loans are proved by contracts and

---

[2] This resembles Ovid, which may be translated—"Check the first rise: all remedy's too late / When long delay has made the mischief great."

writings, and things which, independent of loans, are openly used, have all the persons who see them for witnesses. (31) But this is not the case with deposits, but the owner by himself gives them privily to the man who receives them by himself, looking carefully round the place, and not even taking a slave with him for the purpose of carrying the thing to be deposited, even though he be ever so affectionate to his master; for each of the two parties appears to be anxious to avoid discovery; the one depositing the thing in order to receive it again, and the other being desirous not to be known to have received it.

But we ought by all means to look upon the invisible God as an unseen third party to every concealed action, whom it is natural to make as a witness for both parties; the receiver calling him to witness that he will restore the deposit when it is demanded back from him, and the other making him to see that he receives it back at the proper time.

(32) Let, then, the man who commits this great wickedness and denies his deposit not be ignorant that he has deceived him who committed it to him of his hope, and that he is concealing a wicked disposition under specious language, and that he is hypocritically pretending a bastard sort of faith while in reality faithless, showing that all his pledges are worthless and all his oaths disregarded, so that he neglects all human and all divine obligations; and that he is denying two deposits at once; firstly, the deposit of him who entrusted his property to his care; and secondly, that of that most unerring and infallible witness who sees all the actions of all men, and hears all the words of all men, whether they are willing that he should do so or not.

(33) But if the man who has received a deposit as a sacred thing thinks that he ought to keep it without fraud, duly honouring truth and good faith, but yet others who are always plotting against their neighbours' property, such as cutpurses or housebreakers, break in treacherously and steal the deposit so entrusted, then he shall pay as a penalty double the value of what has been stolen by the thieves. (34) And if they are not taken, then the man who received the deposit shall go of his own accord before the divine tribunal, and stretching out his hands to heaven shall swear by his own life that he himself had no hand in the theft from any desire to appropriate what had been deposited with him, and that he did not voluntarily give it up to any one else; and that, moreover, he is not making a false statement of a robbery which has never taken place.[3]

For it would be absurd to punish a man who has done no wrong, or for a man who had taken refuge in the assistance of a friend when he was being injured by others, now to become the cause of injury to that friend.

(35) And deposits consist not only of inanimate things but also of animals: the danger of which last is twofold; first, that while they share in common with inanimate things in being liable to be stolen, and also one which is distinct and peculiar to themselves, that they are liable to die. We have hitherto been speaking only of the first kind of deposit, but we must now also explain the law about the second.

(36) If now any cattle which have been entrusted as a deposit die, then he who has received the deposit shall send for him who committed it to him, and show him the matter, protecting himself from any evil suspicion; but if the depositor be absent, then it is not proper to send for any one else, whose notice perhaps the depositor might have been desirous to escape; but when the depositor returns home, his friend shall swear to him that he has not been concealing any unjust appropriation of the animals by a false statement of their death. (37) And if any one receives anything not as a deposit, but because he has borrowed it to use, whether it is a vessel or an animal; then if he be robbed of it, whichever it may be, or if the animal die, while the man who lent it is living with the borrower, the borrower shall not be liable, as the owner himself can be brought as a witness that there is no false pretence in the business; but if the lender be not with him at the time, he shall pay the value. (38) Why so? because it is possible that the man who used the animal when the owner was not present may have either worn him out by continual labour so as to kill him, or may have worn out the vessel, from not taking any care of the property of another of which he ought to have been careful, and to have put it away, and not to have given thieves an easy opportunity of stealing it.

(39) But as our lawgiver was acute beyond all other men at discerning the consequences of actions, he proceeds to enact a series of prohibitions, one after another, preserving a due connection between them, and taking care that his later commandments shall be consistent with his earlier cones. And with this harmonious connection of what was to be said by him, he tells us that he was divinely inspired by the person of God speaking to him in this manner:—

"Ye shall not steal.

"Ye shall not speak falsely, and bring false accusations against your neighbour.

"And ye shall not swear by my name to compass an unjust end, and ye shall not profane my name."[4]

---

[3]Exodus 22:7.

[4]Leviticus 19:11.

(40) These injunctions are given with great beauty and very instructively; for the thief being convicted by his own conscience denies and speaks falsely, fearing the punishment which would ensue upon his confession. And he who denies an action seeks to attach the imputation to some one else, bringing a false accusation against him, and imagines devices to make his false accusation appear probable; and every false accuser is at once a perjured man, thinking but little of piety, since he has not just proofs; on which account he has recourse to what is called the inartificial mode of proof, that by oaths, thinking that by the invocation of God he shall produce belief among those who hear him.

But let such an one know that he is ungodly and impious, inasmuch as he is defiling that which by nature is undefiled, the good and holy name of God.

THOU SHALT NOT BEAR FALSE WITNESS[5]

VIII. (41) This is the ninth of the ten commandments, being the fourth in number of those in the second table; but one which is calculated to bestow ten thousand benefits on human life if it be kept, as, on the other hand, it may injure men in innumerable ways if it is neglected; (42) for the false accuser is to be blamed, but he who bears witness to what is false is more guilty still; for the one acts only from a desire to protect himself, but the other is wicked from his wish to co-operate with another in iniquity. And in the comparison of wicked men he who does wrong for his own sake is less unrighteous than he who does so for another. (43) And every judge looks with suspicion on an accuser, as likely to pay but little attention to truth for the sake of coming off in safety himself, on which account the accuser stands in need of a preface to beg the attention of the hearer while he is speaking; but if the judge has no prejudice against a witness on any personal grounds he receives his evidence with a willing mind and open ears, while he is covering over those most excellent things, truth and good faith, with specious language. And the false witnesses use seductive words as a sportsman uses bait for the purpose of attaining the objects which he desires and aims at.

(44) For which reasons, in many parts of his enactment of the law, he commands that we should not approve of any wicked man or action.[6] For any approbation of what is not virtuous is likely to lead to giving false evidence; since every one to whom iniquity is a disagreeable and hateful thing is a friend of truth. (45) Now there is no great wonder in a man's having connected himself with one wicked person, who has incited him to an action resembling his own character; but it is a sign of a noble soul, and of a disposition practised in manly resolutions not to follow a multitude to do evil, like a man borne down over a precipice by the collective force of a torrent. (46) For some people, among the multitude, think some things lawful and just, even though they be most flagitious, not judging correctly; for it is well to follow nature, but this impulse of the multitude is wholly at variance with the following of nature.

(47) If, then, some persons, being assembled together in companies and numerous multitudes, attempt to make any innovations, one must not consent to them, since they are adulterating the ancient and approved coinage of the state; for one wise counsel is superior to many attempts, but ignorance, in conjunction with numbers, is a great evil; (48) but some persons practise such an excess of wickedness that they not only accuse mortal men, but adhere and cling to their unrighteousness, so as even to raise their lies as high as heaven, and to bear their testimony against the blessed and happy nature of God.

And by these men I mean soothsayers, and diviners, and augurs, and all other persons who practise what they call divination studying, an art without any art, if one must tell the plain truth, a mere bare imitation of the real inspiration and prophetic gift; (49) for a prophet does not utter anything whatever of his own, but is only an interpreter, another Being suggesting to him all that he utters, while he is speaking under inspiration, being in ignorance that his own reasoning powers are departed, and have quitted the citadel of his soul; while the divine spirit has entered in and taken up its abode there, and is operating upon all the organization of his voice, and making it sound to the distinct manifestation of all the prophecies which he is delivering.

(50) But all those persons who pursue the spurious and pretended kind of prophecy are inverting the order of truth by conjectures and guesses, perverting sincerity, and easily influencing those who are of unstable dispositions, as a violent wind, when blowing in a contrary direction, tosses about and overturns vessels without ballast, preventing them from anchoring in the safe havens of truth. For such persons think proper to say whatever they conjecture, not as if they were things which they themselves had found out, but as if they were divine oracles revealed to themselves alone, for the more complete inducement of great and numerous crowds to believe a deceit.

(51) Such persons our lawgiver very appropriately calls false prophets, who adulterate the true prophecy, and overshadow what is genuine by their spurious devices; but in a very short time all their manoeuvres are detected, since nature does not choose to be always hidden, but, when a suitable opportunity offers, displays her own power with irresistible strength. (52) For as in the

[5]Exodus 20:16.
[6]Exodus 23:1.

case of eclipses of the sun the rays which have, for a brief moment, been obscured, a short time afterwards shine forth again, exhibiting an unclouded and far-seen brilliancy without anything whatever coming over the sun at all, but one unalloyed blaze beaming forth from him in a serene sky; so also, even though some persons may deliver predictions, practising a lying art of prophecy, and disguising themselves under the specious name of prophetic inspiration, falsely taking the name of God in vain, they will be easily convicted. For, again, the truth will come forth and will beam forth, shedding around a most conspicuous light, so that the falsehood which has previously overshadowed it will disappear.

(53) Moreover there also was an excellent[7] commandment that Moses gave when he ordained that the judge should "not receive the testimony of one witness."[8] First of all, because it is possible that one person may without designing it have a false impression of a thing, or may be careless about it and therefore be deceived. For there are innumerable false opinions, which frequently arise from an innumerable variety of grounds; (54) and secondly, because it is most unjust to trust to one witness against many persons, or indeed against only one individual; in the first place, because many are more entitled to belief than one, since the one is not superior in number to many, and equality of number is inconsistent with any preponderance; for why should the judge trust a single witness, bearing testimony against another, rather than the defendant pleading in his own behalf? But, as it should seem, it is best to suspend one's opinion, where there is no deficiency and no excess to guide the judgment.

ON THE OFFICE AND CHARACTER OF A JUDGE

IX. (55) The law thinks that all those who adhere to the sacred constitution, established by Moses, ought to be free from all unreasonable passions, and from all wickedness; and most especially ought all men to be so, who are either appointed by lot or elected to judge between others; for it is an absurdity for these men to be themselves liable to the imputation of error, who undertake to dispense justice to others, whom it becomes to give a faithful copy of the works of nature, presenting an accurate representation of a model picture; (56) for as the power of fire which disperses warmth to all other things which it reaches, was, long before doing so, warm as far as it was itself concerned, and as, on the contrary, the power of snow cools other things, by the fact of its being itself cooled previously, so also ought

the judge to be full of pure unalloyed justice, if he is to irrigate all who come before him with justice, in order that from him, as from a sweet fountain, a wholesome spring may be afforded to all who thirst for a dispensation of good law.

(57) And this will be the case if any one who undertakes the office of a judge looks upon it as if he were at the same time judging and being judged himself, and when he takes up the pebble with which he is to give his vote, were at the same time to take up wisdom so as not to be deceived, and justice so as to dispense to each party what they deserve, and courage so as never to yield to supplications or to feelings of compassion, so as to diminish the punishment due to convicted offenders; (58) for the man who studies these virtues may reasonably be looked upon as a common benefactor, like a good pilot tranquillising the storms of affairs in such a manner as to secure the preservation and safety of those who have committed their interests to him.

X. (59) In the first place the law enjoins the judge not to listen to vain reports.[9] Why is this? The law says, "My good man, let thy ears be purified." And they will be purified if they are continually washed out with a stream of virtuous language, never admitting the long, and false, and vain, and hackneyed protestations, so deserving to be ridiculed, of fabulists or vain babblers, or hyperbolical exaggerations, who make a great deal of things of no importance; (60) and this is what is meant by the injunction not to listen to vain reports, and also by another precept in some degree consistent with the former.

For, says the lawgiver, he who attends to those who give evidence on hearsay is attending to vanity and not to sound reason because the eyes do indeed dwell with the very things which are done, taking hold of them as one may say, and comprehending and seizing upon them in all their parts, the light co-operating with them, by means of which all things are illuminated and clearly proved; but the ears, as one of the philosophers of old has very truly said, are less trustworthy than the eyes, inasmuch as they are not themselves present at the transactions, but are attracted by words as the interpreter of facts, which are not always disposed to tell the truth; (61) for which reasons some of the lawgivers among the Greeks, having transcribed some of the laws from the two tables of Moses, appear to have established very wise regulations, forbidding any one to mention in his testimony anything that he has heard, on the ground that it is right to look upon what a man has seen as trustworthy, but on what he has heard as not in all respects certain.

XI. (62) The second commandment given to

---

[7]Numbers 35:30.
[8]Deuteronomy 17:6; 19:15.

[9]Exodus 23:1.

a judge is not to receive gifts;[10] for gifts, says the law, blind the eyes that see, and pervert justice, and do not permit the mind to travel along the level road which leads to righteousness; (63) and to receive bribes to aid in unjust actions is the action of very wicked men indeed; and even to do so for the purpose of furthering good objects is the conduct of persons who are half wicked; for there are some judges speciously disguised, half wicked, something between just and unjust, armed indeed in the cause of those who are injured, as their champions against those who injure them, but still not desirous to cause them to prevail, without deriving any advantage to themselves from their victory, though they ought to prevail; but making their decision corrupt and mercenary.

(64) Then, when any one blames them, they affirm that they have not perverted justice; for that those have been defeated who ought to have been defeated, and that those have gained their cause who ought to have got the better; alleging a most unworthy and false defence; for a righteous judge ought to exhibit two things, a judgment in strict accordance with the law, and incorruptibility; but he who is a judge for bribes, even though he decides justly, does without perceiving it defile a thing which is beautiful by nature.

(65) Moreover, he also offends in two other points; in the first place, because he is accustoming himself to be covetous of money; which is the beginning of the very greatest iniquities; and secondly, because he is injuring the man whom he ought to benefit; by making him pay a price for justice; (66) on which account Moses has very instructively commanded, that the judge shall pursue what is righteous in a righteous manner;[11] intimating under this figurative expression, that it is possible to do so in an unrighteous manner, because of those men who sell just and legal decisions for money, and not only in the courts of justice, but everywhere in every part of land and sea, and I had almost said in all the transactions of life.

(67) For instance, it has happened before now, that a man who has received a deposit of small value, has given it back again when demanded, more by way of laying a snare for him who receives it back, than with any idea of serving him, in order that by showing good faith in things of small value as a bait he may cover over the look of his faithlessness in greater things, and such conduct is nothing else than pursuing justice in an unrighteous manner; for the restitution of what did not belong to him was just, but it was done in an unrighteous manner, inasmuch as it was only done as a bait to attract more.

(68) And the cause of all such offences is principally the inclination to and the familiar habit of falsehood, which, from their very birth and swaddling clothes, their nurses and mothers, and all the whole multitude in the house, whether free-born persons or slaves, habituate them to and familiarise them with both by words and actions, adapting it to and uniting it with their souls, as a necessary part of them by nature, though, if it had in truth been implanted in them by nature, it would have been necessary to eradicate it by instilling good habits into them instead.

(69) And what in life is there equally beautiful with truth, which the all-wise legislator erected in the most sacred place, in that part of the dress of the chief priest, where the dominant part of the soul lies, wishing to adorn it with the most beautiful and glorious of all ornaments? And next to truth he has placed power as akin to it, which he has in this case called manifestation, being the two images of the two kinds of speech which exist in us, the secret speech and the lettered speech, for the lettered speech requires manifestation, by which the secret thoughts in all our hearts are made known to our neighbour, but the secret speech has need of truth for the perfection of life and actions, by means of which the road to happiness is found out.

XII. (70) The third commandment given to a judge is to investigate the transactions themselves, in preference to showing any regard to the parties to the suit; and to attempt, in every imaginable manner, to separate himself from all respect of persons; constraining himself to an ignorance and forgetfulness of all those things of which he has any knowledge or recollection; such as relations, friends, countrymen or foreigners, enemies or hereditary connections, so that neither affection nor hatred may overshadow his knowledge of justice; for he must stumble like a blind man, who is advancing without a staff, and who has no one to guide him in whom he can rely firmly.

(71) For which reason it is fitting that a righteous judge should have it even concealed from him who the parties to the suit are, and that he should look at the undisguised, simple nature of the transactions themselves; so as not to be liable to judge in accordance with random opinion, but according to real truth, and to be guided by such an opinion as this, that judgment is of God;[12] and that the judge is the minister and steward of his judgment; and a steward is not allowed to give away the things of his master, as he has received as a pledge the most excellent of all the things which exist in human life, from the most excellent of all beings.

XIII. (72) And in addition to what has already been said, there is another most admirable pre-

---

[10]Exodus 23:8.
[11]Deuteronomy 16:19.

[12]Deuteronomy 1:17.

cept given which enjoins the judge "not to show pity upon the poor man in his judgment."[13]

While in other precepts the lawgiver has filled nearly the whole of the law with precepts of mercy and humanity, and has uttered great threats against arrogant and insolent men, and has proposed great rewards for those who endeavour to make amends for the misfortunes of their neighbours, and who look upon their superfluities not as their own exclusive possessions, but as the common property of every one in want; (73) for it was a felicitous and true saying of one of the wise men of old, that men never act in a manner more resembling the gods than when they are bestowing benefits; and what can be a greater good than for mortal men to imitate the everlasting God?

(74) Let not then the rich man collect in his house vast quantities of silver and gold, and store them up, but let him bring them forward freely in order by his cheerful bounty to soften the hard condition of the poor; nor let any man be puffed up with vain glory, and raise himself and boast himself in pride and arrogance, but let a man rather honour equality, and allow freedom of speech to those of low estate. And let the man who enjoys vigour of body be the prop of those who are weaker, and let him not like the men at the gymnastic contests strive by every means to overthrow those who are inferior in strength, but let him be willing and eager to assist with his own power those who, as far as they themselves are concerned, are ready to faint. (75) For all those who have drunk deep of the fountains of wisdom, having banished envy entirely out of their minds, are of their own accord, and without any prompting, ready to undertake the assistance of their neighbours, pouring the streams of their words into their souls through their ears, so as to impart to them a participation in similar knowledge with themselves. And when they see young men of good dispositions springing up like flourishing and vigorous shoots of a vine, they rejoice, thinking that they have found proper inheritors for this wealth of their souls, which is the only real riches, and having taken them they cultivate their souls with doctrines and good meditations, until they arrive at full strength and maturity, so as to bring forth the fruit of excellence.

(76) Many such ornaments as these are woven into and inserted among the laws, in order to enrich the poor on whom it is always proper to have compassion except at the time of giving judgment, for compassion is due to misfortunes; but he who behaves wickedly with deliberate purpose is not unfortunate but unrighteous, (77) and punishment is due to the unrighteous just as honours should be confirmed to the just, so that no wicked man who is in difficulties, and who conceals the truth,

ought to escape punishment through the pity excited by his poverty, since he has done what deserves not pity (how should it?) but great anger.

And let the man who undertakes the duty of a judge, like a skilful money-changer, divide and distinguish between the natures of things, in order that confusion may not be caused by the mixing together of what is good with what is spurious. (78) And there are many other things which may be said with respect to false witnesses and judges; but for the sake of avoiding prolixity we must proceed now to the last of the ten commandments, which is delivered also in a concise and summary form as each of the others is: and this commandment is, "Thou shalt not covet."

ON COVETING

XIV. (79) Every passion is open to and deserving of blame, inasmuch as every immoderate and violent impulse, and every irrational and unnatural emotion of the soul is also faulty and blameable, for what is either of these things but an ancient passion spread over a wider extent? If any one, therefore, does not set limits to these feelings, nor put a bridle on them as on restive horses, he will be afflicted by an evil difficult to remedy, and then, without being aware of it, he will, because of their unrestrainable character, be carried away by them, as a charioteer sometimes is by a chariot, and hurried into ravines and pits from which it is difficult to rise up, and very hard to escape with safety.

(80) But of all the passions there is not one so grievous as a covetous desire of what one has not got, of things which are in appearance good, but not in reality; a desire which produces grievous anxieties which are hard to satisfy; for such a passion puts the reason to flight, and banishes it to a great distance, involving the soul in great difficulties, while the object which is desired flies away contemptuously, retreating not with its back but with its face to one; (81) for when a person perceives this passion of covetousness after having started up rapidly, then resting for a short time, either with a view to spread out its alluring toils, or because it has learnt to entertain a hope of succeeding in its object, he then retires to a longer distance uttering reproaches against it; but the passion itself, being left behind and coming too late to succeed, struggles, bearing a Tantalus-like punishment in its miserable future; for it is said that Tantalus, when he desired to obtain any liquor to drink, was not able to do so, as the water retreated from his lips,[14] and if he wished to gather

---

[14]The story of Tantalus is told in Homer, Od. 11.581 (as it is translated by Pope)— "There Tantalus along the Stygian bounds, / Pours out deep groans (with groans all hell resounds); / Ev'n in the circling floods refreshment craves, / And pines with thirst among a sea of waves;

any fruit, it all disappeared, the productiveness of the trees becoming suddenly barren; (82) for as those implacable and inexorable mistresses of the body, thirst and hunger, do very often strain it more, or at all events not less, than those unhappy persons are strained who are racked by the torture even to death, unless when they have become violent some one appeases them with meat and drink; in like manner, covetous desire, having first rendered the soul empty through its forgetfulness of what is present and its recollection of what is removed to a great distance, fills it with impetuosity and madness, and introduces into it masters worse than even its former tyrants, but having the same names with them, namely, hunger and thirst, not, however, now of those things which conduce to the enjoyment of the belly, but of money, and glory, and authority, and beauty, and of innumerable other things which appear to be objects of desire and contention in human life.

(83) And as the disease which the physicians call the herpes,[15] does not stop in one part of the body, but moves about and overruns the skin, and, as its name shows, creeps about *(dierpei)*, and becomes diffused in every direction, and spreading widely seizes hold of and infects with its contact the whole combination of the different parts of the body from the head to the feet, so in the same manner does covetous desire spread over the whole soul, and leave not even the smallest portion of it free from its inroads, imitating the power of fire when supplied with abundant fuel, for that spreads and burns away till it has devoured and destroyed everything with which it meets.

XV. (84) So great and so excessive an evil is covetous desire; or rather, if I am to speak the plain truth concerning it, it is the source of all evils. For from what other source do all the thefts, and acts of rapine, and repudiation of debt, and all false accusations, and acts of insolence, and, moreover, all ravishments, and adulteries, and murders, and, in short, all mischiefs, whether private or public, or sacred or profane, take their rise? (85) For most truly may covetous desire be said to be the original passion which is at the bottom of all these mischiefs, of which love is one and the most significant offspring, which has not once but many times filled the whole world with indescribable evils; which even the whole circumference of the world has not been large enough to contain, but out of

their vast number they, as if carried on by the impetuosity of a torrent, have fallen into the sea, and all seas in every region have been filled with hostile fleets. It is owing to this passion that all the terrible evils which are caused by naval wars have happened; and, coming upon all continents and all islands together, have thrown them into confusion, spreading everywhere and returning in their own steps like the warriors in the diaulos,[16] or like the ebb and flow of the tides of the sea, returning to the point from which they originally set out.

(86) And by looking at it in this manner we shall more clearly perceive the power of this passion. Everything which covetous desire lays hold of is by it changed for the worse, like poisonous serpents or deadly poisons. Now what is it that I mean when I say this?

(87) If this passion is directed towards money, it makes thieves, and cut-purses, and clothes-stealers, and house-breakers, and taints men with the guilt of the repudiation of debts, of the denial of deposits, of bribery and sacrilege, and all such iniquities as those. (88) If it is directed towards glory, it makes men insolent, overbearing, fickle, and unstable in their dispositions, depending wholly on what is said to them and on what they hear, at the same time humbled and elated by reason of the variety and inconstancy of the multitudes who praise and blame them with inconsiderate impetuosity, inconsiderate in their enmity and in their friendship, so as easily to change from one to the other, and fills them with all sorts of humours akin to and resembling these.

(89) Again, if the desire takes the direction of wishing for authority and power, it renders men's natures seditious, unequal, and tyrannical, it makes them cruel and inhuman enemies of their native countries, implacable masters unable to restrain themselves, irreconcileable forces to all who are equal to themselves in might, flatterers of those who are more powerful than themselves, in order to be able to attack them treacherously.

If what is desired is beauty of person, it makes men seducers, ravishers, adulterers, paederasts, practisers of licentiousness and incontinence, it teaches them to regard the greatest evils as the most fortunate of blessings. This passion, also, when it extends to the tongue, often causes innumerable evils; (90) for some persons desire either to be silent about what ought to be mentioned, or to mention what ought to be buried in silence, and avenging justice pursues them if they reveal things improperly, or, on the contrary, if they are unseasonably silent.

(91) When it affects the parts about the belly it makes men gluttonous, insatiable, intemperate,

---

/ When to the water he his lip applies, / Back from his lip the treacherous water flies. / Above, beneath, around his hapless head, / Trees of all kinds delicious fruitage spread; / There figs, sky-dyed, a purple hue disclose, / Green looks the olive, the pomegranate glows; / There dangling pears exalting scents unfold, / And yellow apples ripen into gold. / The first he strives to seize; but blasts arise, / Toss it on high, and whirl it to the skies."
[15] So called from *herpō*, "to creep."

---

[16] The diaulos was the race in which the runners ran to the goal and back to the starting post.

debauched, admirers of a profligate life, delighting in drunkenness, and epicurism, slaves to strong wine, and fish, and meat, pursuers of feasts and tables, wallowing like greedy dogs; owing to all which things their lives are rendered miserable and accursed, and they are reduced to an existence more grievous than any death. (92) For this reason those who have tasted deeply of philosophy, not merely with their lips, but feasting thoroughly on its profound doctrines, investigating the nature of the soul, and comprehending its threefold character, and how it is divided into reason, and anger, and appetite, have attributed the chief post to reason as the principal authority, assigning to it the head as its most appropriate abode, where also the company of the outward senses, who are always present as the body-guards of the mind as their king, are stationed; (93) and assigning the breast as the abode of anger, partly in order that the man, being, like a soldier, armed with this as with a breastplate, so that, even if it be not utterly free from all injury, it may, at least, be difficult to subdue, and partly in order that, dwelling near the mind, it may be benefited by its neighbour, who charms it by its wisdom, and who renders the passions gentle and manageable; and to appetite they assign the place around the navel, and to that part which is called the diaphragm. (94) For it was proper that that, as having the smallest participation in reason, should be removed as far as possible from the palace of the mind and located almost at the very extremities; and that which is the most insatiable and the most intemperate of all, the passions, should be confined to the pastures of cattle, where they can find food and opportunities for the propagation of their species.

XVI. (95) And the most holy Moses appears to me to have had a regard to all these circumstances, and on that account to have commanded that men should discard this passion, detesting it as the most disgraceful thing and the cause of most disgraceful actions; and, therefore, to have prohibited it above all other feelings as an engine for the destruction of the soul; but if that engine is destroyed and the soul brought back to its obedience, to the guidance of reason, the man will become entirely filled with peace and obedience to law and all sorts of perfect good things, so as to produce complete happiness.

(96) But as he was fond of brevity and accustomed to cut short things which were inclined to be countless in point of number, by a mode of teaching which was confined to general instances, he begins to admonish and to correct one appetite, that which is concerned about the belly; conceiving that the other appetites will not be equally restive, but will be brought to order by learning that the most important and authoritative of the whole has become obedient to the laws of moderation.

(97) What, then, is the lesson which he gives us about this origin of all vices? There are two things of a most comprehensive nature, meat and drink. He, then, has not left either of them unrestrained, but has bridled them with especial commands most calculated to lead them to temperance and to humanity, and to the greatest of all virtues, piety; (98) for he commanded men to offer first fruits of corn, and wine, and oil, and cattle, and other things;[17] and to distribute the first fruits among the sacrificers and the priests; among the sacrificers because of the gratitude due to God for the abundance and fertility of all things, and to the priests because of their sacred ministrations about the temple, and therefore they were worthy to receive wages for their services in respect of the sacred ceremonies.[18] (99) And he utterly forbids any one to taste of anything, or to take any portion of anything, before separating off the first fruits, wishing also by this injunction to inculcate the practice of most useful temperance; for he who has learnt not to throw himself greedily on all the abundance which the seasons of the year have brought, but to wait till the first fruits are consecrated, is likely to be able to restrain the restive obstinacy of the passions, making them gentle and manageable.

CONCERNING ANIMALS

XVII. (100) Moreover, Moses has not granted an unlimited possession and use of all other animals to those who partake in his sacred constitution, but he has forbidden with all his might all animals, whether of the land, or of the water, or that fly through the air, which are most fleshy and fat, and calculated to excite treacherous pleasure, well knowing that such, attracting as with a bait that most slavish of all the outward senses, namely, taste, produce insatiability, an incurable evil to both souls and bodies, for insatiability produces indigestion, which is the origin and source of all diseases and weaknesses.

(101) Now of land animals, the swine is confessed to be the nicest of all meats by those who eat it, and of all aquatic animals the most delicate are the fish which have no scales; and Moses is above all other men skilful in training and inuring persons of a good natural disposition to the practice of virtue by frugality and abstinence, endeavouring to remove costly luxury from their characters, (102) at the same time not approving of unnecessary rigour, like the lawgiver of Lacedaemon, nor undue effeminacy, like the man who taught the Ionians and the Sybarites lessons of luxury and license, but keeping a middle path between the two courses, so that he has relaxed what was

---

[17] Numbers 18:12.
[18] Numbers 18:31.

over strict, and tightened what was too loose, mingling the excesses which are found at each extremity with moderation, which lies between the two, so as to produce an irreproachable harmony and consistency of life, on which account he has laid down not carelessly, but with minute particularity, what we are to use and what to avoid.

(103) One might very likely suppose it to be just that those beasts which feed upon human flesh should receive at the hands of men similar treatment to that which they inflict on men, but Moses has ordained that we should abstain from the enjoyment of all such things, and with a due consideration of what is becoming to the gentle soul, he proposes a most gentle and most pleasant banquet; for though it is proper that those who inflict evils should suffer similar calamities themselves, yet it may not be becoming to those whom they ill treated to retaliate, lest without being aware of it they become brutalized by anger, which is a savage passion; (104) and he takes such care to guard against this, that being desirous to banish as far as possible all desire for those animals abovementioned, he forbids with all his energy the eating of any carnivorous animal at all, selecting the herbivorous animals out of those kinds which are domesticated, since they are tame by nature, feeding on that gentle food which is supplied by the earth, and having no disposition to plot evil against anything.

WHAT QUADRUPEDS ARE CLEAN
XVIII. (105) The animals which are clean and lawful to be used as food are ten in number; the heifer, the lamb, the goat, the stag, the antelope, the buffalo, the roebuck, the pygarga, the wild-ox, and the chamois,[19] for he always adheres to that arithmetical subtilty which, as he originally devised it with the minutest accuracy possible, he extends to all existing things, so that he establishes no ordinances, whether important or unimportant, without taking and as it were adapting this number to it as closely connected with the regulations which he is ordaining.

Now of all the numbers beginning from the unit, the most perfect is the number ten, and as Moses says, it is the most sacred of all and a holy number, and by it he now limits the races of animals that are clean, wishing to assign the use of them to all those who partake of the constitution which he is establishing. (106) And he gives two tests and criteria of the ten animals thus enumerated[20] by two signs, first, that they must part the hoof, secondly, that they must chew the cud; for those which do neither, or only one of these things, are unclean.

And these signs are both of them symbols of instruction and of the most scientific learning, by which the better is separated from the worse, so that all confusion between them is prevented; (107) for as the animal which chews the cud, while it is masticating its food draws it down its throat, and then by slow degrees kneads and softens it, and then after this process again sends it down into the belly, in the same manner the man who is being instructed, having received the doctrines and speculations of wisdom in at his ears from his instructor, derives a considerable amount of learning from him, but still is not able to hold it firmly and to embrace it all at once, until he has resolved over in his mind everything which he has heard by the continued exercise of his memory (and this exercise of memory is the cement which connects ideas), and then he impresses the image of it all firmly on his soul. (108) But as it seems the firm conception of such ideas is of no advantage to him unless he is able to discriminate between and to distinguish which of contrary things it is right to choose and which to avoid, of which the parting of the hoof is the symbol; since the course of life is twofold, the one road leading to wickedness and the other to virtue, and since we ought to renounce the one and never to forsake the other.

WHAT BEASTS ARE NOT CLEAN
XIX. (109) For this reason all animals with solid hoofs, and all with many toes are spoken of by implication as unclean; the one because, being so, they imply that the nature of good and evil is one and the same; which is just as if one were to say that the nature of a concave and a convex surface, or of a road up hill and down hill, was the same. And the other, because it shows that there are many roads, though, indeed, they have no right to be called roads at all, which lead the life of man to deceit; for it is not easy among a variety of paths to choose that which is the most desirable and the most excellent.

WHAT AQUATIC ANIMALS ARE CLEAN
XX. (110) Having laid down these definitions with respect to land animals, he proceeds to describe what aquatic creatures are clean and lawful to be used for food; distinguishing them also by two characteristics as having fins or scales.[21] For those which have neither one nor the other, and those which have only one of the two, he rejects and prohibits.[22] And he must state the cause, which is not destitute of sense and propriety; (111) for all those creatures which are destitute of both, or even of one of the two, are sucked down by the current, not being able to resist the

---

[19] Deuteronomy 14:4.
[20] Leviticus 11:3.

[21] Leviticus 11:9.
[22] Deuteronomy 14:10.

force of the stream; but those which have both these characteristics can stem the water, and oppose it in front, and strive against it as against an adversary, and struggle with invincible good will and courage, so that if they are pushed they push in their turn; and if they are pursued they turn upon their foe and pursue it in their turn, making themselves broad roads in a pathless district, so as to have an easy passage to and fro.

(112) Now both these things are symbols; the former of a soul devoted to pleasure, and the latter of one which loves perseverance and temperance. For the road which leads to pleasure is a down-hill one and very easy, being rather an absorbing gulf than a path. But the path which leads to temperance is up hill and laborious, but above all other roads advantageous. And the one leads men downwards, and prevents those who travel by it from retracing their steps until they have arrived at the very lowest bottom, but the other leads to heaven; making those who do not weary before they reach it immortal, if they are only able to endure its rugged and difficult ascent.

ABOUT REPTILES[23]

XXI. (113) And adhering to the same general idea the lawgiver asserts that those reptiles which have no feet, and which crawl onwards, dragging themselves along the ground on their bellies, or those which have four legs, or many feet, are all unclean as far as regards their being eaten.

And here, again, when he mentions reptiles he intimates under a figurative form of expression those who are devoted to their bellies, gorging themselves like cormorants, and who are continually offering up tribute to their miserable belly, tribute, that is, of strong wine, and confections, and fish, and, in short, all the superfluous delicacies which the skill and labour of bakers and confectioners are able to devise, inventing all sorts of rare viands, to stimulate and set on fire the insatiable and unappeasable appetites of man.

And when he speaks of animals with four legs and many feet, he intends to designate the miserable slaves not of one single passion, appetite, but of all the passions; the genera of which were four in number; but in their subordinate species they are innumerable. Therefore, the despotism of one is very grievous, but that of many is most terrible, and as it seems intolerable.

(114) Again, in the case of those reptiles who have legs above their feet, so that they are able to take leaps from the ground, those Moses speaks of as clean; as, for instance, the different kinds of locusts, and that animal called the serpent-fighter, here again intimating by figurative expressions the manners and habits of the rational soul.

For the weight of the body being naturally heavy, drags down with it those who are but of small wisdom, strangling it and pressing it down by the weight of the flesh.

(115) But blessed are they to whose lot it has fallen, inasmuch as they have been well and solidly instructed in the rules of sound education, to resist successfully the power of mere strength, so as to be able, by reason of what they have learnt, to spring up from the earth and all low things, to the air and the periodical revolutions of the heaven, the very sight of which is to be admired and earnestly striven for by those who come to it of their own accord with no indolence or indifference.

CONCERNING FLYING CREATURES[24]

XXII. (116) Having, therefore, in his ordinances already gone through all the different kinds of land animals and of those who live in the water, and having distinguished them in his code of laws as accurately as it was possible, Moses begins to investigate the remaining class of animals in the air; the innumerable kinds of flying creatures, rejecting all those which prey upon one another or upon man, all carnivorous birds, in short, all animals which are venomous, and all which have any power of plotting against others. (117) But doves, and pigeons, and turtle-doves, and all the flocks of cranes, and geese, and birds of that kind, he numbers in the class of domestic, and tame, and eatable creatures, allowing every one who chooses to partake of them with impunity.

(118) Thus, in each of the parts of the universe, earth, water, and air, he refuses some kinds of each description of animal, whether terrestrial, or aquatic, or aërial, to our use; and thus, taking as it were fuel from the fire, he causes the extinction of appetite.

CONCERNING CARCASSES AND BODIES WHICH HAVE BEEN TORN BY WILD BEASTS

XXIII. (119) Moreover, Moses commands[25] that no man shall take of any dead carcass, or of any body which has been torn by wild beasts; partly because it is not fitting that man should share a feast with untameable beasts, so as to become almost a fellow reveller in their carnivorous festivals; and partly because perhaps it is injurious and likely to cause disease if the juice of the dead body becomes mingled with the blood, and perhaps, also, because it is proper to preserve that which has been pre-occupied and seized beforehand by death untouched, having a respect to the necessities of nature by which it has been seized.

(120) Now many of the lawgivers both among the Greeks and barbarians, praise those who are

---

[23] Leviticus 11:20.

[24] Leviticus 11:10.
[25] Leviticus 5:2.

skilful in hunting, and who seldom fail in their pursuit or miss their aim, and who pride themselves on their successful hunts, especially when they divide the limbs of the animals which they have caught with the huntsmen and the hounds, as being not only brave hunters but men of very sociable dispositions. But any one who was a sound interpreter of the sacred constitution and code of laws would very naturally blame them, since the lawgiver of that code has expressly forbidden any enjoyment of carcasses or of bodies torn by beasts for the reasons before mentioned.

(121) But if any one of those persons who devote themselves wholly to meditations on and to the practice of virtue were suddenly to become fond of gymnastic exercises and of hunting, looking upon hunting as a sort of prelude to and representation of the wars and dangers that have to be encountered against the enemy, then, whenever such a man is successful in his sport, he ought to give the beasts which he has slain to his dogs as a feast for them, and as a reward or wages for their successful boldness and their irreproachable alliance. But he ought not himself to touch them, inasmuch as he has been previously taught in the case of irrational animals, what sentiments he ought to entertain, respecting his enemies.

For he ought to carry on war against them, not for the sake of unrighteous gain like those who make a dishonest traffic of all their actions, but either in revenge for some calamities which he has previously suffered at their hands, or with a view toward some which he expects to suffer.

(122) But some men, with open mouths, carry even the excessive luxury and boundless intemperance of Sardanapalus to such an indefinite and unlimited extent, being wholly absorbed in the invention of senseless pleasures, that they prepare sacrifices which ought never be offered, strangling their victims, and stifling the essence of life, [26] which they ought to let depart free and unrestrained, burying the blood, as it were, in the body. For it ought to have been sufficient for them to enjoy the flesh by itself, without touching any of those parts which have an connection with the soul or life.

(123) On which account Moses, in another passage, establishes a law concerning blood, that one may not eat the blood nor the fat. [27] The blood, for the reason which I have already mentioned, that it is the essence of the life; not of the mental and rational life, but of that which exists in accordance with the outward senses, to which it is owing that both we and irrational animals also have a common existence.

CONCERNING THE SOUL OR LIFE OF MAN

XXIV. For the essence of the soul of man is the breath of God, especially if we follow the account of Moses, who, in his history of the creation of the world, says that God breathed into the first man, the founder of our race, the breath of life; breathing it into the principal part of his body, namely the face, where the outward senses are established, the body-guards of the mind, as if it were the great king. And that which was thus breathed into his face was manifestly the breath of the air, or whatever else there may be which is even more excellent than the breath of the air, as being a ray emitted from the blessed and thrice-happy nature of God.

(124) But Moses commanded men to abstain from eating fat, because it is gross.

And again, he gave us this injunction, in order to inculcate temperance and a zeal for an austere life: for some things we easily abandon, and without any hesitation; though we do not willingly encounter any anxieties or labours for the sake of the acquisition of virtue. (125) For which reason these two parts are to be taken out of every victim and burnt with fire, as a kind of first fruits, namely, the fat and the blood; the one being poured upon the altar as a libation; and the other as a fuel to the flame, being applied instead of oil, by reason of its fatness, to the consecrated and holy flame.

(126) The lawgiver blames some persons of his time as gluttons, and as believing that the mere indulgence of luxury is the happiest of all possible conditions, not being content to live in this manner only in cities in which there were abundant supplies and stores of all kinds of necessary things, but carrying their effeminacy even into pathless and untrodden deserts, and choosing in them also to have markets for fish and meat, and all things which can contribute to an easy life: (127) then, when a scarcity arose, they assembled together and raised an outcry, and looked miserable, and with shameless audacity impeached their ruler, and did not desist from creating disturbances till they obtained what they desired; and they obtained it to their destruction, for two reasons: first of all, that it might be shown that all things are possible to God, who can find a way in the most difficult and apparently hopeless circumstances; and secondly, that punishment might fall on those who were intemperate in their gluttonous appetites, and obstinate resisters of holiness.

(128) For a vast cloud being raised [28] out of the sea showered down quails about the time of sunrise, and the camp and all the district around it for a day's journey for a well-girt active man was

---

[26] Leviticus 17:11.
[27] Leviticus 3:17.

[28] Exodus 16:13.

overshadowed all about with the birds.[29] And the height of the flight of the birds was distant from the ground a height of about two cubits, in order that they might be easily caught. (129) It would have been natural therefore for them, being amazed at the marvellous nature of the prodigy which they beheld, to be satisfied with the sight, and being filled with piety to nourish their souls on that, and to abstain from eating flesh; but these men, on the contrary, stirred up their desires even more than before, and pursued these birds as the greatest good imaginable, and catching hold of them with both their hands filled their bosoms; then, having stored them up in their tents, they sallied forth to catch others, for immoderate covetousness has no limit. And when they had collected every description of food they devoured it insatiably, being about, vain-minded generation that they were, to perish by their own fulness; (130) and indeed at no distant time they did perish by the purging of their bile,[30] so that the place itself derived its name from the calamity which fell upon them, for it was called the graves of their lust,[31] than which there is not in the soul, as the scripture teaches us, any greater evil.

(131) For which reason Moses says with great beauty in his recommendations, "Let not every man do that which seemeth good to his own eyes,"[32] which is equivalent to saying, let not any one gratify his own desire, but let each person seek to please God, and the world, and nature, and wise men, repudiating self-love, if he would become a good and virtuous man.

XXV. (132) This may be sufficient to say, being in fact all that I am able to advance, about the laws which bear on appetite and desire by way of filling up the whole body of the ten commandments, and of the subordinate injunctions contained in them; for if we are to look upon the brief heads which were oracularly delivered by the voice of God, as the generic laws, and all the particular ordinances which Moses subsequently interpreted and added as the special laws; then there is need of great care and skill in order to preserve the arrangement unconfused in order to an accurate comprehension of it, and I therefore have taken great care, and have assigned and apportioned to each of these generic laws of the whole code all that properly belonged to it.

(133) But enough of this. We must however not remain ignorant that as separately there are some particular injunctions related to each one of the ten generic commandments, which have

nothing in common with any one of the others; so also there are some things to be observed which are common to the whole, being adapted not to one or two, as people say, but to the whole ten commandments.

(134) And I mean by this those virtues which are of common utility, for each one of these ten laws separately, and all of them together, train men and encourage them to prudence, and justice, and piety, towards God and all the rest of the company of virtues, connecting sound words with good intentions, and virtuous actions with wise language, that so the organ of the soul may be wholly and entirely held together in a good and harmonious manner so as to produce a well-regulated and faultless innocence and consistency of life.

(135) We have spoken before of that queen of all the virtues, piety and holiness, and also of prudence and moderation; we must now proceed to speak of justice which is conversant about subjects which are akin and nearly related to them.[33]

XXVI. (136) One portion of justice, and that not an unimportant one, relates to courts of justice and to the judge, which indeed I have mentioned before, when I was going through the subject of testimony, and dwelling on it at some length, in order that nothing which belonged to the subject should be omitted; and as I am not fond of repetitions, unless indeed some necessity arising from the imperious character of the occasion compels me to it, I will pass that part of the subject over now, and will turn my attention to the other portions, having just said thus much as a preface.

(137) The law says, it is proper to lay up justice in one's heart, and to fasten it as a sign upon one's head, and as frontlets before one's eyes, figuratively intimating by the former expression that one ought to commit the precepts of justice, not to one's ears, which are not trustworthy, for there is no credit due to the ears, but to that most important and dominant part, stamping and impressing them on the most excellent of all offerings, a well approved seal; (138) and by the second expression, that it is necessary not only to form proper conceptions of what is right, but also to do what one has decided upon as proper without delay. For the hand is the symbol of actions, to which Moses here commands the people to attach and fasten justice, saying, that it shall be a sign, of what indeed he has not expressly stated, because it is not a sign as I conceive of one particular thing, but of many, and, I may almost say, of everything with which the life of man is concerned. (139) And by the third expression, he implies that justice is discerned everywhere as being close to the eyes.

[29] Numbers 11:31.
[30] Numbers 11:20.
[31] See Numbers 11:34: "And he called the name of that place Kibroth-hattaavah, because there they buried the people that lusted."
[32] Deuteronomy 11:8.

[33] Yonge's translation includes a separate treatise title at this point: On Justice. The publisher has elected to follow the Loeb numbering.

Moreover he says that, these things must have a certain motion; not one that shall be light and unsteady, but such as by its agitation may rouse the sight to the spectacle manifest before it; for motion is calculated to attract the sight, inasmuch as it excites and rouses it; of, I might rather say, inasmuch as it renders the eyes awake and sleepless.

(140) But the man to whom it happens to represent to the eyes of his mind things which are not quiet but which are in motion, and exerting energies in accordance with nature, is entitled to be set down as a perfect man, and no longer to be reckoned among learners and pupils, but among teachers and instructors; and he ought to allow all the young men who are desirous to do so, to drink of his wisdom as of an abundant stream flowing from a living fountain of lessons and doctrines.[34]

And if there is any one who, out of modesty, is wanting of courage, and therefore delays, and is slow to approach him for the purpose of learning, let him go to him of his own accord, and pour into his ears a collection of admonitions, until the channels of his soul are filled with them. (141) And let him instruct in the principles of justice all his relatives and friends, and all young men, at home and on the road, and when they are going to bed, and when they rise up; that in all their positions, and in all their motions, and in all places whether private or public, not only waking, but also while asleep, they may be delighted with the image and conception of justice.

For there is no delight more exquisite than that which proceeds from the whole soul being entirely filled with justice, while devoted to the study of its everlasting doctrines and meditations, so that it has no vacant place at which injustice can effect an entrance.

(142) Moreover, he ordains that those who have written out these things should afterwards affix them to every house belonging to a friend, and to the gates which are in their walls; that all people, whether coming in or going out, whether citizens or strangers, reading the writing thus fixed on pillars before the gates, may have an unceasing recollection of all that ought to be said or that ought to be done; and that every one may take care neither to do nor to suffer injury; and that all persons, whether going into their houses or going out of them, men and women, children and servants, may do all that is proper and becoming to one another and to themselves.

THAT IT IS NOT LAWFUL TO ADD ANYTHING
TO OR TO TAKE ANYTHING FROM THE LAW
XXVII. (143) The lawgiver also gives this most admirable injunction, that one must not add any-

thing to, or take anything away from the law, but that it is a duty to keep all the ordinances as originally established in an equal and similar state to that in which they were at first delivered without alteration; for, as it seems, there might otherwise be an addition of what is injust; for there is nothing which has been omitted by the wise lawgiver which can enable a man to partake of entire and perfect justice.

(144) Moreover, by this command Moses intimates the perfection of all other virtue; for each separate virtue is free from all deficiency, and is complete, deriving its perfection from itself; so that if there were any addition thereto, or anything taken away therefrom, it would be utterly and entirely changed and altered, so as to assume a contrary character. (145) What I meant to say is this, all who are profoundly ignorant and uninstructed, all who have the very slightest smattering of education, know that courage is a virtue which is conversant about terrible objects; is a science teaching one what he ought to endure and dare. (146) But if any one, under the influence of that ignorance which proceeds from insolence, should be so superfluous as to fancy himself capable of correcting that which requires no correction, and should consequently venture to add anything or take away anything, he, by so doing, is altering the whole appearance of the thing, changing that which had a good character into unseemliness; for by any addition to courage he will produce audacity, but if he takes anything away from it he will produce cowardice, not leaving even the name of courage, that most useful of all virtues to life.

(147) In the same manner, if any one makes an addition, be it ever so small, or ever so great, to that queen of the virtues, piety, or if he takes anything away from it, he will change and metamorphose its whole appearance, and make it something quite different; for any addition will engender superstition, and any diminution will produce impiety, real piety itself wholly disappearing under the operation, which every one should pray for, that it may be continually conspicuous and brilliant, since it is the cause of the greatest of all blessings, inasmuch as it produces a knowledge of the service of God, which one ought to look upon as more important and more precious than any dominion or authority. (148) And we may give instances of every other virtue resembling what we have said about these just mentioned; but since I am in the habit of avoiding prolixity, I will be satisfied with what has been stated, which may be a sufficient guide to what might be said respecting these virtues which we omit to mention.

ABOUT NOT MOVING LAND-MARKS
XXVIII. (149) There is also this commandment ordained which is of great common utility, that, "Thou shalt not move thy neighbours' land-

---

[34]Deuteronomy 6:7.

marks which the former men have set up."[35] And this injunction is given, as it seems, not only with respect to inheritances, and to the boundaries of the land, in order to prohibit covetousness respecting them, but also as a guard to ancient customs; for customs are unwritten laws, being the doctrines of men of old, not engraved on pillars or written on paper which may be eaten by moths, but impressed in the souls of those living under the same constitution.

(150) For the children ought to inherit from the father of their being the national customs in which they have been brought up, and in which they have lived from their cradle, and not to despise them merely because they are handed down without being written. For the man who obeys the written laws is not justly entitled to any praise, inasmuch as he is influenced by compulsion and the fear of punishment. But he who abides by the unwritten laws is worthy of praise, as exhibiting a spontaneous and unconstrained virtue.[36]

XXIX. (151) Some persons have contended that all magistracies ought to have the officers appointed to them by lot; which however is a mode of proceeding not advantageous for the multitude, for the casting of lots shows good fortune, but not virtue; at all events many unworthy persons have often obtained office by such means, men whom, if a good man had the supreme authority, he would not permit to be reckoned even among his subjects: (152) for even those who are called lesser rulers by some persons, those whom men entitled masters, do not admit every one whom they can possibly find to be their servants, whether born in the house or bought with money; but they will only take those who are obedient, and at times they sell all those of incurably bad dispositions in a lot, as not being worthy to be the slaves of good men.

(153) Therefore it is not right to make men masters and rulers of entire cities and nations, who obtain those places by lot, which is a sort of blunder on the part of fortune, which is an unstable and fickle thing. Beyond all question, casting of lots can have no connection with ability to attend upon the sick; for physicians do not obtain their employments by lot, but because their experience is approved of; (154) again, with reference to the successful voyage and safety of men at sea, it is not any man who may obtain the office of pilot by lot, who is sent at once to the stern to steer the vessel, and who then by his ignorance may cause a needless wreck in calm and tranquil weather, but that person has that charge given to him who, from his earliest youth, appears to have learnt and carefully studied the business of a pilot; this is a man who has made many voyages, and who has traversed every sea, or at all events most seas, and who has carefully ascertained the character of all the marts, and harbours, and anchorages, and places of refuge in the different islands and continents, and who is still better, or at all events not worse acquainted with the tracks over the sea, than he is with the roads on land, through his accurate observation of the heavenly bodies; (155) for having remarked the various motions of the stars, and having followed and being guided by their regular revolutions, he has learnt to be able to make out for himself an unerring and easy path through the pathless waste of waters, so that (what seems the most incredible of all things), beings whose nature it is to live on the land are able to traverse the sea which can only be crossed by sailing.

(156) And if any one should be about to undertake the government or regulation of large and populous cities, full of inhabitants, and should attempt to settle the constitution of such, and should undertake the superintendence of private, and public, and sacred affairs, a task which any one may rightly call the art of arts, and the science of sciences, he would not trust to the uncertain chances of time, passing over the accurate and trustworthy test of truth; and the test of truth is proof combined with reason.

XXX. (157) The all-wise Moses seeing this by the power of his own soul, makes no mention of any authority being assigned by lot, but he has chosen to direct that all offices shall be elected to; therefore he says, "Thou shalt not appoint a stranger to be a ruler over thee, but one of thine own brethren,"[37] implying that the appointment is to be a voluntary choice, and an irreproachable selection of a ruler, whom the whole multitude with one accord shall choose; and God himself will add his vote on favour of, and set his seal to ratify such an election, that being who is the confirmer of all advantageous things, looking upon the man so chosen as the flower of his race, just as the sight is the best thing in the body.

XXXI. (158) And Moses gives also two reasons, on account of which it is not proper for strangers to be elected to situations of authority; in the first place, that they may not amass a quantity of silver, and gold, and flocks, and raise great and iniquitously earned riches for themselves, out of the poverty of those who are subjected to them; and secondly, that they may not make the nation quit their ancient abodes to gratify their own covetous desires, and so compel them to emigrate, and

---

[35]Deuteronomy 19:14.

[36]Yonge's translation includes a separate treatise title at this point: *On the Creation of Magistrates.* Accordingly, his next paragraph begins with roman numeral I (=XXIX in the Loeb). Yonge's "treatise" concludes with number XIV (=XLII in the Loeb). The publisher has elected to follow the Loeb numbering.

[37]Deuteronomy 17:15.

to wander about to and fro in interminable wanderings, suggesting to them hopes of the acquisition of greater blessings, which shall never be fulfilled, by which they come to lose those advantages of which they were in the secure enjoyment. (159) For our lawgiver was aware beforehand, as was natural that one who was a countryman and a relation, and who had also an especial share in the sublimest relationship of all, (and that sublimest of relationships is one constitution and the same law, and one God whose chosen nation is a peculiar people); so that he would never offend in any manner similar to those which I have been mentioning, but, on the other hand, instead of causing the inhabitants to quit their abodes, he would be likely even to afford a safe return to such of his countrymen as were dispersed in a foreign land; and instead of taking away the property of others, he would even give his own property to those who were in need of it, making his own wealth common.

XXXII. (160) And from the first day on which any one enters upon his office, he orders that he shall write out a copy of the book of the law[38] with his own hand, which shall supply him with a summary and concise image of all the laws, because he wishes that all the ordinances which are laid down in it shall be firmly fixed in his soul; for while a man is reading the notions of what he is reading fleet away, being carried off by the rapidity of his utterance; but if he is writing they are stamped upon his heart at leisure, and they take up their abode in the heart of each individual as his mind dwells upon each particular, and settles itself to the contemplation of it, and does not depart to any other object, till it has taken a firm hold of that which was previously submitted to it. (161) When therefore he is writing, let him take care, every day, to read and study what he has written, both in order that he may thus attain to a continual and unchangeable recollection of these commands which are virtuous and expedient for all men to observe, and also that a firm love of and desire for them may be implanted in him, by reason of his soul being continually taught and accustomed to apply itself to the study and observance of the sacred laws.

For familiarity, which has been engendered by long acquaintance, engenders a sincere and pure friendship, not only towards men, but even also towards such branches of learning as are worthy to be loved; (162) and this will take place if the ruler studies not the writings and memorials of some one else but those which he himself has written out; for his own works are, in a certain degree, more easily to be understood by each individual, and they are also more easily to be comprehended; (163) and besides that a man, while he is reading

them, will have such considerations in his mind as these: "I wrote all this; I who am a ruler of such great power, without employing any one else as my scribe, though I had innumerable servants. Did I do all this, in order to fill up a volume, like those who copy out books for hire, or like men who practise their eyes and their hands, training the one to acuteness of sight, and the others to rapidity of writing? Why should I have done this? That was not the case; I did it in order that after I had recorded these things in a book, I might at once proceed to impress them on my heart, and that I might stamp upon my intellect their divine and indelible characters: (164) other kings bear sceptres in their hands, and sit upon thrones in royal state, but my sceptre shall be the book of the copy of the law; that shall be my boast and my incontestible glory, the signal of my irreproachable sovereignty, created after the image and model of the archetypal royal power of God.

(165) "And by always relying upon and supporting myself in the sacred laws, I shall acquire the most excellent things. In the first place equality, than which it is not possible to discern any greater blessing, for insolence and excessive haughtiness are the signs of a narrow-minded soul, which does not foresee the future.

(166) "Equality, therefore, will win me good will from all who are subject to my power, and safety inasmuch as they will bestow on me a just requital for my kindness; but inequality will bring upon me terrible dangers, and these I shall escape by hating inequality, the purveyor of darkness and wars; and my life will be in no danger of being plotted against, because I honour equality, which has no connection with seditions, but which is the parent of light and stability. (167) Moreover, I shall gain another advantage, namely, that I shall not sway this way and that way, like the dishes in a scale, in consequence of perverting and distorting the commandments laid down for my guidance. But I shall endeavour to keep them, going through the middle of the plain road, keeping my own steps straight and upright, in order that I may attain to a life free from error or misfortune."

(168) And Moses was accustomed to call the middle road the royal one, inasmuch as it lay between excess and deficiency; and besides, more especially, because in the number three the centre occupies the most important place, uniting the extremities on either side by an indissoluble chain, it being attended by these extremities as its bodyguards as though it were a king.

(169) Moreover, Moses says that a long-enduring sovereignty is the reward of a lawful magistrate or ruler who honours equality, and who without any corruption gives just decisions in a just manner, always studying to observe the laws; not for the sake of granting him a life extending over many years, combined with the administration of

---

[38] Deuteronomy 17:18.

the commonwealth, but in order to teach those who do not understand that a governor who rules in accordance with the laws, even though he die, does nevertheless live a long life by means of his actions which he leaves behind him as immortal, the indestructible monuments of his piety and virtue.

XXXIII. (170) And it becomes a man who has been thought worthy of the supreme and greatest authority to appoint successors who may govern with him and judge with him, and, in concert with him, may ordain everything which is for the common advantage; for one person would not be sufficient, even if he were ever so willing, and if he were the most powerful man in the world, both in body and soul, to support the weight and number of affairs which would come upon him, as he would faint under the pressure and rapidity of all kinds of business coming in upon him continually every day from all quarters, unless he had a number of persons selected with reference to their excellence who might co-operate with him by their prudence, and power, and justice, and godly piety, men who not only avoid arrogance, but even detest it as an enemy and as the very greatest of evils.

(171) For these men would stand by, and assist, and co-operate with a virtuous and holy man, one who hated evils equally with themselves, and would be the most suitable persons to lighten and relieve his labours. And, besides, since of the matters which would force themselves upon his attention, some are of greater importance and others of less, the chief will very reasonably commit those which are more unimportant to his lieutenants, while he himself would of necessity become the most accurate judge of the weightier matters. (172) But the affairs which we ought to look upon as the most weighty are not, as some persons think, those in which persons of reputation are at variance with other persons of reputation, or rich men with rich men, or princes with princes; for, on the contrary, are rather where there are powerful men on one side, and private individuals, men of no wealth, or dignity, or reputation, on the other, men whose sole hope of escaping intolerable evils lies in the judge himself.

(173) And we can find clear instances of both kinds in the sacred laws, which it is well for us to imitate; for there was once a time in which Moses, alone by himself, decided all causes and all matters of legal controversy, labouring from morning till night. But after a time his father-in-law came to him, and seeing with what a weight of business he was overwhelmed, as all those who had any disputes were everlastingly coming upon him, he gave him most excellent advice, counselling him to choose subordinate magistrates, that they might decide the less important affairs, and that he might have only the more serious causes

to occupy him, and by this means provide himself with time for rest.[39] (174) And Moses, being convinced by the arguments of Jethro (for, indeed, they were for his good), having chosen the men of the highest reputation in the whole nation, he appointed them his lieutenants and judges, bidding them refer the more important cases to him.

(175) And the history of the sacred laws contains this arrangement duly recorded, for the instruction of the rulers in all succeeding generations, that, in the first place, they may not despise the assistance of fellow counsellors, as if they were able to themselves to superintend everything, since that all-wise and godly man, Moses, did not reject them; and, secondly, that they may learn to choose subordinates of the second class and of the third class, so as to provide for themselves not being driven to neglect matters of greater importance, through being wholly occupied by affairs of a more trifling nature; for it is impossible for human nature to attend to everything at once.

XXXIV. (176) We have here mentioned one example of what we before alluded to. We must now add an instance of the second kind. I said that the causes of men of humble condition were important; for the widow, and the orphan, and the stranger are powerless and humble. And it is right that the supreme King should be the judge in their case, the Ruler who has the supreme authority over the whole nation; since, according to Moses, even God, the Ruler of the universe, did not exclude them from the provisions of his laws; (177) for when Moses, that holy interpreter of the will of God, is raising a hymn in praise of the virtues of the living God in these terms, "God is great and mighty, one who is no respecter of persons, and who does not take gifts to guide him in his judgment."[40] he adds, in whose case it is that he gives judgment, not in the case of satraps, and tyrants, and men who have the power by land and sea, but he gives judgment respecting the stranger, and the orphan, and the widow.

(178) In the case of the first, because he has made his own kinsmen, whom alone it was natural for him to have as allies and champions, his irreconcileable enemies, by quitting their camp and taking up his abode with the truth, and with the honour of the one Being who is entitled to honour, abandoning all the fabulous inventions and polytheistic notions which his fathers, and grandfathers, and ancestors, and all his kindred, who cleave to the beautiful settlement which he has forsaken, were wont to honour.

In the case of the second, because he is deprived of his father and mother, his natural defenders and protectors, and by consequence of

---

[39] Exodus 18:14.
[40] Deuteronomy 10:17.

the only power which was bound to show itself as his ally.

And lastly, in the case of the woman who is a widow because she has been deprived of her husband, who succeeded her parents as her guardian and protector; for a husband is to his wife in point of relationship what her parents are to a virgin. (179) And one may almost say that the whole nation of the Jews may be looked upon in the light of orphans, if they are compared with all other nations in other lands; for other nations, as often as they are afflicted by any calamities which are not of divine infliction, are in no want of assistance by reason of their frequent intercourse with other nations, from their habitual dealings in common. But this nation of the Jews has no such allies by reason of the peculiarity of its laws and customs. And their laws are of necessity strict and rigorous, as they are intended to train them to the greatest height of virtue; and what is strict and rigorous is austere. And such laws and customs the generality of men avoid, because of their inclination for and their adoption of pleasure.

(180) But, nevertheless, Moses says that the great Ruler of the universe, whose inheritance they are, does always feel compassion and pity for the orphan and desolate of this his people, because they have been dedicated to him, the Creator and Father of all, as a sort of first-fruits of the whole human race. (181) And the cause of this dedication to God was the excessive and admirable righteousness and virtue of the founders of the nation, which remain like undying plants, bearing a fruit which shall ever flourish to the salvation of their descendants, and to the benefit of all persons and all things, provided only that the sins which they commit are such as are remediable and not wholly unpardonable.

(182) Let not any one then think that nobility of birth is a perfect good, and therefore neglect virtuous actions, considering that that man deserves greater anger who, after he has been born of virtuous parents, brings disgrace on his parents by reason of the wickedness of his disposition and conduct; for if he has domestic examples of goodness which he may imitate, and yet never copies them, so as to correct his own life, and to render it healthy and virtuous, he deserves reproach.

XXXV. (183) The law also forbids, by a most just and reasonable prohibition, the man who has undertaken the care and government of the common interests of the state, to behave with treachery among the people;[41] for a treacherous disposition is the mark of an illiberal and very slavish soul, which seeks to overshadow its real nature by hypocrisy; (184) for, in reality, a ruler ought

to stand up in defence of his subjects as a father would in defence of his children, that he may be honoured by them as if they were his own real children; on which account good rulers are the common parents of their cities and nations, if one may say the plain truth, displaying equal, and sometimes even superior, good will to them; (185) but those men who acquire great power and authority to the injury and damage of their subjects, ought to be entitled, not rulers, but enemies, inasmuch as they are acting the part of implacable foes.

Not but what those who injure one treacherously are even more wicked than those who oppose one openly, since it is possible to repel the one without difficulty, as they display their hostility without disguise; but the evil-mindedness of the others is difficult to detect and hard to unveil, being like the conduct of men on the stage, who are clothed in a dress which does not belong to them, in order to conceal their real appearance.

(186) But there is a kind of pre-eminence and superior authority, which I had almost said pervades every part of life, varying only in respect of magnitude and quantity; for what the king of a city is, that also is the first man in a village, and the master of a house, and a physician among the sick, and a general in his camp, and an admiral with respect to his crew and to his passengers, and a captain of a ship in regard to merchant vessels and transports, and a pilot among common sailors, every one of whom has power to make things either better or worse. But they ought to wish to conduct themselves in everything for the best, and the best is to use all their energies to assist people and not to injure them; (187) for this is to act in imitation of God, since he also has the power to do either good or evil, but his inclination causes him only to do good. And the creation and arrangement of the world shows this, for he has summoned what had previously no being into existence, creating order out of disorder, and distinctive qualities out of things which had no such qualities, and similarities out of things dissimilar, and identity out of things which were different, and intercommunion and harmony out of things which had previously no communication nor agreement, and equality out of inequality, and light out of darkness; for he is always anxious to exert his beneficent powers in order to change whatever is disorderly from its present evil condition, and to transform it so as to bring it into a better state.

XXXVI. (188) Therefore it is right for good rulers of a nation to imitate him in these points, if they have any anxiety to attain to a similitude to God; but since innumerable circumstances are continually escaping from and eluding the human mind, inasmuch as it is entangled among and embarrassed by so great a multitude of the external senses, as is very well calculated to seduce and deceive it by false opinions, since in fact it is,

---

as I may say, buried in the mortal body, which may very properly be called its tomb, let no one who is a judge be ashamed to confess that he is ignorant of that of which he is ignorant, (189) for in the first place the man who is deceived becomes worse than he was before, because he has expelled truth from the confines of his soul; in the second place, he will do exceeding mischief to those on whose causes he is deciding by delivering a blind decision in consequence of his not seeing what is just.

(190) When, therefore, he does not clearly comprehend a case by reason of the perplexed and unintelligible character of the circumstances which throw uncertainty and darkness around it, he ought to decline giving a decision, and to send the matter before judges who will understand it more accurately. And who can these judges be but the priests, and the ruler and governor of the priests? (191) For the genuine, sincere worshippers of God are by care and diligence rendered acute in their intellects, inasmuch as they are not indifferent even to slight errors, because of the exceeding excellence of the Monarch whom they serve in every point.

On which account it is commanded that the priests shall go soberly [42] to offer sacrifice, in order that no medicine such as causes men to err, or to speak and act foolishly may enter into the mind and obscure its vision, (192) and perhaps because the real genuine priest is at once also a prophet, having attained to the honour of being allowed to see the only true and living God, not more by reason of his birth than by reason of his virtue. And to a prophet there is nothing unknown, since he has within himself the sun of intelligence, and rays which are never overshadowed, in order to a most accurate comprehension of those things which are invisible to the outward senses, but intelligible to the intellect.

XXXVII. (193) Again, merchants and pedlars, and people in the market, and all those who deal in things necessary for life, [43] and who in consequence are conversant with measures, and weights, and balances, since they sell things both dry and wet, are put in subjection to the superintendants of the market, and these superintendants are bound to govern them if they act with moderation, doing what is right, not out of fear, but voluntarily, for spontaneous good conduct is in every case more honourable than that which proceeds from compulsion.

(194) On which account the law orders these merchants and dealers, and all other persons who have adopted this way of life, to take care to provide themselves with just balances, and measures, and weights, not practising any wicked manoeuvres to the injury of those who purchase of them, but to do and say everything with a free and guileless soul, considering this, that unjust gains are injurious, but that that wealth which is acquired in accordance with justice a man cannot be deprived of; (195) and since wages are offered to artisans as a reward for their work, and since it is people in want who are artisans, and not men who have an abundance of wealth, the law commands that the payment of their wages shall not be delayed, but that their employers shall pay them the wages agreed upon the same day that they are earned; [44] for it is absurd for the rich to avail themselves of the services of the poor, and yet for those who live in plenty and affluence not at once to give the poor the proper remuneration for those services. (196) Are not these things very conspicuous instances to teach us to guard against greater offences? For he who will not allow a payment which is sure to be eventually repaid to be delayed beyond the proper time, fixing the evening of the day for the time on which the artisan, at his return home, is to carry his wages home with him, does not he much more by such a commandment prohibit rapine and theft, and the repudiation of debts, and all things of that sort, fashioning and moulding the soul according to the approved characteristics of virtue and piety?

XXXVIII. (197) Also this commandment is given with exceeding propriety, [45] which forbids anyone from blaspheming and speaking ill, especially of a deaf man, and of one who is unable to perceive by the aid of his outward senses the injuries which are done to him, nor to retaliate in an equal manner under similar circumstances; for that is the most iniquitous conflict of all, in which the one side is considered only in acting, and the other only in suffering; (198) and those who speak ill of the dumb, or of people whose sense of hearing is defective, are committing the same offences as those who put stumbling blocks in the way of the blind, or who offer other obstacles to their progress; for in this case also it is impossible for the blind to step over the obstacles, as they are not aware of their existence, so they stumble over them, and both are hindered in their progress and hurt their feet. (199) Accordingly, with great propriety and fitness, does the law threaten those who devise and execute wickedness of this kind with punishment at the hand of God; since he alone holds his protecting hand over and defends those who are unable to protect themselves, and all but says in plain words to those who injure the innocent, (200) "O foolish minded men, do you expect to escape detection while turning the misfortunes

---

[42] Leviticus 10:9.
[43] Leviticus 19:36.

[44] Deuteronomy 24:15.
[45] Leviticus 19:14.

of those men into ridicule, and committing offences against those very parts in respect of which they are unfortunate, attacking their ears by false accusations, and their eyes by putting stumbling blocks in their path? But you will never escape the notice of God, who sees everything and governs everything, while you insult in this manner the calamities of miserable men, so as to avoid meeting with similar distresses yourselves, inasmuch as your bodies are also liable to all kinds of diseases, and your outward senses are susceptible of injury and mutilation, being such as, by a very slight and ordinary cause, they are often not only impaired, but crippled by incurable mutilations.

(201) Why then should those who forget themselves, and who in their arrogance fancy that they themselves are superior to the ordinary natural weakness of mankind, and that they are out of the reach of the invisible and unexpected attacks of fortune, which often aims sudden blows at all people, and which has often wrecked men, who up to that moment had enjoyed a prosperous voyage through life, when they had almost arrived in the very harbour of ultimate happiness, why, I say, should such men triumph in and insult the misfortunes of others, having no respect for justice, the ruler of human life, who sits by the side of the great Ruler of the universe, who surveys all things with sleepless and most piercing eyes, and sees what is in recesses as clearly as if it was in the pure sunlight?

(202) It seems to me that these men would not spare even the dead, in the extravagance of their cruelty, but, according to the proverb so commonly quoted, would even slay the slain over again, since they in a manner think fit to insult and ill treat those members of them which are already dead; for eyes which do not see are dead, and ears which are devoid of the power of hearing are devoid of life; so that if the man himself to whom these members belong, were to be extinct, they would then show their merciless and implacable nature, doing no humane or compassionate action, such as is shown to the dead, even by their enemies in irreconcileable wars. And this may be enough to say on this subject.

XXXIX. (203) After this the lawgiver proceeds to connect with these commandments a somewhat similar harmony or series of injunctions; commanding breeders not to breed from animals of different species; not to sow a vineyard so as to make it bear two crops at once; and not to wear garments woven of two different substances, which are a mixed and base work. Now the first of these injunctions we have already mentioned in our treatise on adulterers, in order to make it more evident, that our people ought not to be anxious for marriages with foreigners, corrupting the dispositions of the women, and destroying also the good hopes which might be conceived of the propaga-

tion of legitimate children. For the lawgiver, who has forbidden all copulation between irrational animals of different species, appears to have utterly driven away all adulterers to a great distance. (204) And we must now speak again of this rule in this our treatise on justice.

For we must take care not to pass over the opportunity of adapting it to as many particulars as possible. It is just then to bring together those things which are capable of union; now animals of the same species are by nature capable of union, as, on the other hand, all animals of different species are incapable of any admixture or union, and the man who brings unlawful connections to pass between such animals is an injust man, transgressing the ordinances of nature; (205) but that which is the really sacred law takes such exceeding care to provide for the maintenance of justice, that it will not permit even the ploughing of the land to be carried on by animals of unequal strength, and forbids a husbandman to plough with an ass and a heifer yoked to the same plough, lest the weaker animals, being compelled to exert itself to keep up with the superior power of the stronger animal, should become exhausted, and sink under the effort; (206) and the bull is looked upon as the stronger animal, and is enrolled in the class of clean beasts and animals, while the ass is a weaker animal and of the class of unclean beasts; but nevertheless he has not grudged those animals which appear to be weaker, the assistance which they can derive from justice, in order, as I imagine, to teach the judges most forcibly, that they are never in their decisions to give the worse fate to the humbly born, in matters the investigation of which depends not on birth but on virtue and vice.

(207) And resembling these injunctions is the last commandment concerning things yoked in pairs, namely, that it is unlawful to wear together substances of a different character, such as wool and linen; for in the case of these substances, not only does the difference prevent any union, but also the superior strength of the one substance is calculated rather to tear the other than to unite with it, when it is wanted to be used.

XL. (208) The commandment which came in the middle of the three injunctions about pairs, was that one was not to sow a vineyard so as to make it bear two crops at the same time; the object of this law being, in the first place, that those things which are of different species might not be confused by being mixed together; for crops grown from seed have no connection with trees, nor trees with crops grown from seed; on which account nature has not appointed to them both the same time for the production of their fruits, but has assigned to the one the spring as the season of their harvest, while to the others it has appointed the end of summer, as the season for the gathering of their fruits; (209) accordingly, it happens that at the same period of the year the one are become withered having been in bloom at an earlier time, while the others are just budding having been dried up before; for the crops which are produced from seed begin to flourish in the winter, when the trees are losing their leaves; and in the spring, on the contrary, when all the crops which are produced from seed are drying up, the wood of all trees, whether wild or improved by cultivation, are shooting; and one may almost say, that the period in which the crops which are produced from seed come to perfection is the same as that in which those of the trees derive the beginning of their productiveness.

(210) Very naturally therefore, has God separated things so wholly different from one another, both in their natures and in the period of their flowering, and in the seasons of their producing their appropriate fruits, and has appointed different situations for them, producing order out of disorder; for order is closely connected with arrangement, and disorder with a want of arrangement.

(211) And in the second place, in order that the two different species may not go through a reciprocal system of inflicting and suffering injury, because of one kind drawing away the nourishment from the other kind, while if that nourishment is divided into small portions, as happens in times of famine and of scarcity of necessaries, all plants of every kind will in every place become weak, and will be either afflicted with barrenness, becoming utterly unproductive, or at all events will never bear tolerably fine fruit, inasmuch as they have been previously weakened by want of nourishment.

(212) And in the third place, in order that the naturally fertile land may not be oppressed with burdens beyond its strength, partly by the continued and uninterrupted thickness of the crops which are sown, and of the trees which are planted in the same place, and partly by the doubling of the crops, which are exacted from the ground; for it ought to be quite sufficient for the owner to draw one yearly tribute from one spot, just as it is sufficient for a king to receive his tribute from a city once a year; and to endeavour to extract larger revenues is the act of exceeding covetousness, by which all the laws of nature are attempted to be overturned.

(213) For which reason the law might well say to those who have determined to sow their vineyards with seed out of pure covetousness; "Do not you be worse than those kings who have subdued cities with arms and warlike expeditions, for even they, from a prudent regard for the future and from a proper wish to spare their subjects, are content to receive one payment of tribute each year, as they are desirous not to reduce them utterly to the very extremity of want and distress in a short time; (214) but if you in the spring exact from the same piece of ground crops of barley and of wheat, and in the summer the crops from the fruit-bearing trees, you will be exhausting it by a double contribution; for then it will very naturally grow faint and fail, like an athlete, who is never abroad any time to take breath and to collect his strength for the beginning of another contest.

(215) "But you seem rashly to forget those precepts of general advantage which I enjoined you to observe. For, at all events, if you had recollected the commandment concerning the seventh year, in which I commanded you to allow the land to remain fallow and sacred, without being exhausted by any agricultural operation of any kind, by reason of the labours which it has been going through for the six preceding years, and which is has undergone, producing its crops at the appointed seasons of the year in accordance with the ordinances of nature; you would not now be introducing innovations, and giving vent to all your covetous desires, be seeking for unprecedented crops, sowing a land fit for the growth of trees, and especially one planted with vines, in order by two crops every year, both being founded in iniquity, to increase your substance out of undue avarice, amassing money by lawless desires."

(216) For the same man would never endure to let his land lie fallow every seventh year without exacting any revenue from it, for the sake of not having his land exhausted by over-production, but of allowing it to recover itself by rest, and yet at the same time to oppress and overwhelm it by double burdens; (217) therefore I have judged it necessary to pronounce all acquisition or exaction of wealth in this way unholy and impious; I mean the production of the fruit of trees, and of such crops as are derived from seed, because such fertility does in a manner exhaust and destroy the vivifying principle in the good soil, and, because too, by requiring so much, the owner of the land is insulting and abusing the bounty and liberality of God, giving full reins to his unrighteous desires, and not restraining them by any limits.

(218) Ought we not, then, to feel an attachment to such commandments as these, which tend to restrain us from and to remove us to a great distance from the acts of covetousness, which are common among men, blunting the edge of the passion itself? For if the private individual, who, in the matter of his plants, has learnt to renounce all unrighteous gain, if he should acquire power in weightier matters and become a king, would adopt the same practice towards men and women, not exacting twofold tributes from them, not exhausting his subjects with taxes and contributions; for the habits in which he has been brought up would be sufficient for him, and would be able to soften the harshness of his disposition, and in a manner to educate him, and to re-mould him to

a better character. And that is a better character which justice impresses upon the soul.

XLI. (219) These, then, are the laws which he appoints to be observed by each individual. But there are other commandments of a more general nature of which he enjoins the observance to the whole nation in common, recommending them to attend to them, not only with regard to their own friends and allies, but also to those who are unconnected with their alliance. (220) For if, says Moses,[46] they shut themselves up within their walls and make their necks stiff, then let your young men arm themselves well, and being provided with all the preparations necessary for war, go forth and fortify their camp all around, and watch in expectancy, not indulging their anger so as to neglect reason, but taking care to apply themselves to what must be done firmly and strenuously. (221) Let them, therefore, at once send out heralds to invite the enemy to an agreement, and at the same time let them display the power and considerable character of the force which is encamped; and if the enemy, repenting of the evil designs which they had conceived, submit and turn to peace in any manner, then let the people gladly receive them and make a truce with them; for peace, even though it be very unfavourable, is more advantageous than war.

(222) But if they persevere in their folly, and push it further, acting with audacity, then let our people, display vigorous confidence, relying also on the invincible alliance of justice, and so let them advance, placing their destructive engines against the walls, and when they have made a breach in some part of them let them all enter in together; and shooting with their spears with correct aim, and brandishing their swords, and slaying the enemies all around, let them repel them unshrinkingly, inflicting upon them what they were intended to suffer themselves, (223) until they have overthrown the whole army arrayed against them, every man of them, and taken their silver, and their gold, and all the booty. And let them bring fire against their city, and burn it so that it may never, after an interval of rest, again raise its head and excite wars and tumults, with the view also of terrifying and warning the neighbouring states, since it is by the calamities of others that men are taught to act with moderation.

But let them suffer the maidens and the women to go free, inasmuch as they did not expect to suffer any of the evils which war brings upon men at their hands, as they are exempt from all military service through their natural weakness. (224) From all which it is plain that the nation of the Jews is allied with and friendly to all those who are of the same sentiments, and all who are

peaceful in their intentions; and that it is not to be despised as one that submits to those who begin to treat it with injustice out of cowardice; but when it goes forth to defend itself, it distinguishes between those who are habitually plotting against it and those who are not; (225) for to be eager to slay all men, and even those who have committed but slight offences, or no offences at all against one, I should call the conduct of an inhuman and pitiless soul, as it would be also to treat women as if they were an addition to the men who carry on war, when their way of life is naturally peaceful and domestic.

(226) But our lawgiver implants such a love of justice in all men who live under the institution which he has established, that he does not permit them to injure the fertile land of even an hostile city by ravaging it, or by cutting down the trees, so as to destroy the crops. (227) "For why," says he, "do you bear a grudge against inanimate things, which are in their nature quiet, and which produce wholesome fruits? Does the tree, my friend, display the hostile spirit of a man that is an enemy, so that you are to tear it up by the roots in retaliation for the evils which it has inflicted, or which it has designed to inflict upon you? (228) On the contrary, it assists you, bestowing on you, when you are victorious, an abundance of necessary food, and of supplies which conduce to rendering life happy and luxurious; for it is not men alone who contribute revenues to their lords, but plants offer even more useful tribute at the fixed seasons of the year, a tribute without which men cannot live." (229) But there is no prohibition against their cutting down those trees which are barren and unproductive, and which are not cultivated for food, for the purpose of making staves, or poles, or posts, or fences; and, when occasion requires, ladders, and engines, and wooden towers; for the chief use of these kinds of trees is for such and other similar purposes.

XLII. (230) We have now enumerated the matters which belong to justice; but as for justice itself, what poet or orator could celebrate it, in worthy terms, since it is beyond all panegyric and all praise? At all events, there is one most important good thing belonging to it,[47] which, even if one were to pass over and be silent about all its other parts, would be an all-sufficient panegyric on it; (231) for this is the principle of equality, which is, as those who have accurately investigated the secrets of nature have handed down to us, the mother of justice; and equality is a light which is never shaded; the sun (if one must speak the plain truth) appreciable by the intellect alone, since inequality, on the contrary, in which that which is

---

[46]Deuteronomy 20:1.

[47]The text has *eumeneia*, which Mangey pronounces corrupt.

superior and that which is inferior are both found, is the beginning and source of darkness; (232) it is equality which, by its unchangeable laws and ordinances, has arranged, in their present beautiful order, all the things in heaven and earth; for who is there who does not know this fact, that the days are measured in due proportion to the nights, and the nights in due proportion to the days, by the sun, according to the equality of proportionate distances?

(233) Nature, therefore, has marked out those periods in every year, which are called the equinoxes, from the state of things which exists at that time, namely, the spring and the autumnal equinox, with such distinctness, that even the most illiterate persons are aware of the equality which then exists between the extent of the days and of the nights. (234) Again, are not the periods of the moon, as she advances and retraces her course, from a crescent to a full circle, and again, from a complete orb to a crescent, also measured by an equality of distances? For as great and as long as the period and amount of her increase is, so also is her diminution, in both respects, as to magnitude and duration, as to the number of days and the size of her orb.

(235) And as, in that purest of all essences, heaven, equality is honoured with especial honours, so also is she in the neighbour of heaven, the air. For as the year is portioned out into four divisions, the air is formed by nature to endure changes and alterations at what are called the seasons of the year, and it displays an indescribable regularity in its irregularity; for as the atmosphere is divided by an equal number of months into winter, and spring, and summer, and autumn, it completes the whole year by allotting three months to each season; as, in fact, the very name of the year *(eniautos)* intimates. For it in itself *(autos en autō)* contains everything, being complete in itself, though otherwise it would not be able to effect this, if it were not aided by the regular revolutions of the seasons of the year.

(236) Again, this same equality extends from the heavenly bodies, and from those which are raised on high, to the things upon earth, raising on high its own pure nature, which is akin to the air, and sending downwards its beams like the sun, as a sort of secondary light, (237) for all the things which are inharmonious or irregular among us are caused by inequality, and all those which have in them that regularity which becomes them are the work of equality, which, in the universal essence of the universe, one may fairly call the world, and in cities one may entitle it that best regulated and most excellent of all constitutions, democracy, and in bodies health, and in souls virtue.

(238) For, on the contrary, inequality is the cause of diseases and wickednesses; and the existence of the longest lived man of the human race would fail, if he were to attempt to enumerate all the praiseworthy qualities of equality, and of its offspring, justice. In consequence of which it seems to me to be best to be satisfied with what has already been said, which may be sufficient to rouse up the recollection of those persons who are fond of learning, and to leave the remaining circumstances unwritten in their souls, as divine images in a most sacred place.

ON THE VIRTUES[†]
(De Virtutibus)

ON COURAGE

I. (1) Having previously said all that appeared to be necessary about justice, and those precepts which are closely connected with it, I now proceed in regular order to speak of courage, not meaning by courage that warlike and frantic delirium, under the influence of passion as its counsellor, which the generality of men take for it, but knowledge;[1] (2) for some persons, being elated by boldness when they have bodily strength to assist them, array themselves in the ranks of war, in complete armour, and slay innumerable hosts of the enemy to a man, gaining by their exploits the unseemly but fine sounding name of preeminent valour, being accounted by the multitude which judges of such matters exceedingly glorious in their victory, though in fact they have been savage and brutal both in nature and practice, having thirsted for human blood.

(3) But then as some men who, always remaining in their own houses, while their bodies have been worn away either by long sickness or by painful old age, still being healthy and vigorous in the better part of their soul, and being full of high thoughts, and inspired with a braver and happier fortitude, never, not even in their dreams, meddling with warlike weapons, nevertheless by their exposition and advocacy of wise counsels for the common advantage, have often re-established both the private affairs of individuals, and the common prosperity of their country when it was in danger, putting forth unyielding and inflexible reasonings concerning what has been really expedient.

(4) These men, then, are they who practise real courage, being studiers and practisers of wisdom; but those other men have only what does not deserve to be so called though it assumes the name, as they live in that incurable disease, ignorance, which one may very fitly and properly call audacity, just as people say that in coins base metal often bears the same impression as the real stamp and money.

II. (5) Moreover, there is also no small number of other things in human life which are confessed to be very difficult to endure, such as poverty, and want of reputation, and mutilation, and various kinds of diseases, by which weak spirited men are broken down, not being able to raise themselves at all through their want of courage; but those men who are full of high thoughts and noble spirits, rise up to struggle against these things, and contend against them with fortitude and exceeding vigour, ridiculing and greatly despising their threats and attacks against their poverty; arraying wealth, not that wealth which is blind, but that which sees acutely, whose images and treasures the soul is naturally proud to treasure up; (6) for poverty has overthrown innumerable multitudes of men, who, like wearied athletes, have fainted and fallen, being reduced to a state of prostration by their want of real courage.

And if truth is to be the judge, then no one whatever is really poor, who has the indestructible and inalienable riches of nature for his purveyor, the air, that first and most necessary and incessant support of life, being continually inhaled night and day, and besides that the numberless fountains, and the inexhaustible supply not only of winter torrents but of regular rivers, furnishing everlasting streams for drink, and besides this the abundance of all kinds of food to eat, and all descriptions of trees which are continually bearing their yearly fruits; for these are treasures of which no one is destitute, but all men in every quarter of the globe enjoy them in the greatest abundance.

(7) But if any persons, utterly disregarding the true wealth of nature, pursue instead the riches of vain opinions, relying on those riches which are blind instead of on those which are gifted with acute sight, and taking a guide for their road who is himself crippled, such men must of necessity fall down.

III. (8) We have then before now described that wealth which is the guard of the body, being the thing discovered by and bestowed on men by nature; but that more dignified and respectable kind, which belongs not to all men but to those who are themselves truly respectable and glorious, must now be spoken of; this kind of wealth wisdom furnishes by means of rational, and moral, and natural doctrines, and meditations from which the virtues are derived, which eradicate luxury from the soul, engendering in it a desire for temperance and frugality, in accordance with the resemblance to God at which it aims; (9) for God is a being who is in need of nothing, as there is

---

[†]Yonge's title, *A Treatise on Three Virtues, That Is To Say, On Courage, Humanity, and Repentance.*
[1]This seems to be an imitation of what Plato says in the Protagoras. "We must not look upon all bold *(tharraleous)* men as courageous *(andreious)*, for boldness is derived from human skill, or from anger, or from madness; but courage arises only from nature, and from a good disposition of the soul."—P. 350.

nothing of which he is destitute, but as he is himself all-sufficient for himself.

But the bad man is one of extravagant tastes, being always thirsting for what he has not got, because of his insatiable and unappeasable appetites which he fans and excites like fire, and kindles into a flame, directing them towards every kind of gain, whether great or small; but the virtuous man wants but little, being placed as it were on the borders between the immortal and the mortal nature, having wants indeed by reason of his body being mortal, and his freedom from extravagance because his soul is continually longing for immortality: (10) and so they array wealth against poverty, and glory against a want of reputation; for praise, having excellence and virtue as a starting point, and flowing forth from it as from an everlasting fountain, does not mix with the multitude of inconsiderate men, who are in the habit of laying bare the inconsistency of the soul, with unstable declarations, which sometimes they are not ashamed to sell cheaply in their desire of base gains, uttering them in reproach of men selected for their excellence.

But the number of such men is small, for virtue is not a thing frequently met with in the race of men: (11) but since no perfect antidote or remedy can be found for the mutilation of the outward senses, by which thousands and thousands of persons have died prematurely while still living, prudence, that best of all qualities within us, sets itself against it to prevent it, implanting eyes in our intellect, which, by reason of its sagacious capacity, are altogether and entirely superior in acuteness of vision to the eyes of the body: (12) for these last see only the surfaces of the things presented to them, and require light from without to enable them to do that, but the intellect penetrates into the inmost recesses of bodies, closely surveying and investigating the whole of them, and each separate part, and also the natures of those incorporeal things, which the external senses are unable to contemplate at all.

For the mind may almost be said to possess all the acuteness of vision of the eye, without being in need of any spurious light, but being in itself a star, and as it were a sort of representation or copy of the heavenly bodies: (13) accordingly, the diseases of the body inflict very little injury on us, while our souls are in a sound state; and the sound health of the soul consists in a good admixture of the powers conversant with hunger, and appetite, and reason, the reasoning power having the predominance, and guiding the other two, as a charioteer guides and restrains restive horses; (14) the proper name of this healthy state of the soul is moderation,[2] which produces salvation to the

thinking part of the faculties in us; for as it is constantly in danger of being overwhelmed by the impetuosity of the passions, moderation suffers it not to be sunk in the depths, but lifts it up and raises it on high, endowing it with soul and vitality, and in some sense with immortality.

(15) But in all the subjects which I have here mentioned, there are admonitions and lessons engraved lastingly in many passages of the law, persuading the obedient with great gentleness, and the disobedient with some severity, to despise all the things which affect the body and all external circumstances, looking upon a life in accordance with virtue to be the one proper end and object, and desiring everything else which appears conducive to this end; (16) and if I had not in my former treatises dwelt upon all points connected with simplicity and humility, I would on this present occasion endeavour to explain the matter at some length, connecting and adapting together all the precepts which appear to lie scattered about in different places but as I have already said all that the occasion required on these topics, it is not necessary to recapitulate my arguments; (17) those, however, who are not indifferent to the subject, but who have applied themselves with diligence to the study of the preceding treatises, ought to be aware that nearly all the things which I have said about simplicity and humility apply likewise to courage, since that also is the attribute of a vigorous, and noble, and very well regulated soul, to despise all the things which pride is in the habit of dignifying and extolling, to the utter destruction of life in accordance with truth.

IV. (18) But such great anxiety and energy is displayed by the law in attaining the object of training and exercising the soul so as to fill it with courage, that it has even descended to particulars in the matter of raiment, enjoining what men ought to wear, and prohibiting with all its might a man from wearing the garments of a woman, in order that no trace of shadow of the female may be attached to the male part of mankind, to its discredit; for the law, being at all times in perfect consistency and accordance with nature, desires to establish laws which shall be akin to and in perfect harmony with one another from beginning to end, even in those minute points which, by reason of their insignificance, appear to be beneath the notice of ordinary legislators.

(19) For as it perceived that the figures of men and women, looking at them as if they had been sculptured or painted forms, were very dissimilar, and, moreover, that the same kind of life was not assigned to both the sexes (for to the woman is assigned a domestic life, while a political one is

---

[2] The Greek word is *sōphrosynē*, from *sōzō*, "to pre-

serve," and *phēn*, "the mind," or as Philo says, from *sōtēria*, "salvation," *tō phronounti*, "to our thinking part."

more suited to the man), so also in respect of other matters which were not actually the works of nature, but still were in strict accordance with nature, it judged it expedient to deliver injunctions which were the result of sound sense and wisdom. And these related to the mode of living, and to apparel, and to other things of that kind; (20) for it thought it desirable that he who is truly a man should show himself a man in these particulars also, and especially in the matter of dress, since, as he wears that both day and night, he ought to take care that there is no indication in it of any want of manly courage.

(21) And, in the same manner, having also equipped the woman in the ornaments suited to her, the law prohibits her from assuming the dress of a man, keeping at a distance men-women just as much as it does women-men; for the lawgiver was well aware that when only one single thing in the proper economy of the house was removed, nothing else would remain in the same position as it ought and as it was in before.

V. (22) Moreover, as the affairs of men are usually looked at with reference to two different times, that of peace and that of war, one can see that there are particular virtues which are visible at each period. Now, of the other virtues we have spoken previously, and we shall speak again if any necessity shall arise; but, at the present moment, we had better examine courage, not in a superficial manner, the works of which, even in time of peace, the lawgiver has celebrated in many passages of his delivery of the law, always having a due regard to the time, as we mentioned in the proper place.

Therefore, now we will begin to speak of its effects as relating to war, having first premised thus much by way of preface, (23) that when he makes out the roll of all the soldiers of the army he does not think it expedient to summon forth all the youth of the nation, but some he excuses, stating very reasonable causes for their exemption from military service. And, above all, he exempts all those who are alarmed or cowardly, as they would be likely to be taken prisoners by reason of their innate effeminacy, and to cause fear to the rest who were fighting alongside of them; (24) for a man's neighbour is very apt to take the impression of any one of his faults, and especially this is the case since men's reason is confused at that time by reason of the disorder of the contest, and is unable to attain to an accurate notion of the real picture of affairs; for, at such a time, they are wont to call prudent caution timidity, and to look upon fear as a prudent knowledge of the future, and upon a desire for safety as unmanly cowardice, investing most shameful conduct with specious and dignified appellations.

(25) In order, therefore, that the affairs of his own people may not be injured by the cowardice of those who go forth to battle, while the enemy obtains success and glory, slaying those cowardly foes with great contempt, and being also aware that an inactive irresolute coward was of no use at all, but was rather a hindrance to success, the lawgiver removed from the army all those who were devoid of boldness, and those who were inclined to faint or shrink out of cowardice, just as I imagine no general would compel men afflicted with any bodily infirmity to go forth to war, but would allow their weak health to plead their excuse. (26) And cowardice is a disease, and a worse one, too, than any of those which affect the body, inasmuch as it destroys the faculties of the soul; for diseases of the body, indeed, are at their height but for a short period, but cowardice is an evil which grows with the man in a greater degree, or, at all events, not less than the parts of the body which are united to it, cleaving to the soul from its earliest infancy to the very extremity of old age, unless God himself interpose to cure it; for all things are possible to God.

(27) And, moreover, the lawgiver does not summon even all the men of impetuous courage, not even although they are full of strength and energy, both in soul and body, and eager to be the foremost in the conflict and in the encountering of danger; but, having praised them for their good will, because they display a disposition willing to share in the dangers of their countrymen, and eager, and void of fear, he proceeds to inquire whether they are entangled in any important circumstances which have a strong influential power of attraction. (28) For, says he, "If any one has lately built a house, and has not as yet entered it to dwell in it; or if any one has planted a newly-arranged vineyard, having himself planted the cuttings in the ground, but which has not yet arrived at the season of its bearing fruit; or if any one has espoused a virgin and not consummated his marriage; he shall be excused from all military service." Humanity here finding an excuse for such exemption for two causes; (29) first of all, in order that, since the events of war are uncertain, others who have never laboured in the work may not reap the fruits of these men's toil; for it appeared to be a hard thing for a man to be unable even to enjoy what really belonged to him, but for one man to build a house and another to dwell in it; and for one man to plant a vineyard and for another, who never planted it, to enjoy the fruit thereof; and for one man to espouse a wife, but for one who has not espoused her to complete the marriage; as it was not expedient that those who had entertained good hopes respecting life to find them all baffled and vain. (30) And, secondly, that men might not be warring with their bodies while their souls were far from the battle; for it is impossible but that the minds of men in such a condition as has been described above must be held back and kept on the stretch, from a desire to enjoy the

things from which they have been torn away. For as men who are hungry or thirsty, if they only get a sight of anything to eat or to drink, pursue it and run after it without ever turning aside in their eagerness to reach it, so also men who have laboured to obtain a legitimate wife, or a house, or the possession of a farm, and who in their hopes believe that the time for their enjoyment of each of these objects is all but arrived, if they are then deprived of that enjoyment, resist, so that though they may be present in body elsewhere, they are not present with the better part of their soul, by which it is that men succeed or fail.

VI. (31) Therefore our lawgiver does not think it proper to include those men, or any in a similar condition, in the roll of his soldiers, but only such as have no domestic circumstances of such a nature to detain them, in order that with free and unembarrassed inclinations they may engage in the pursuit of danger without shrinking; for as a weak or crippled body derives no advantage from a panoply of armour, which it will rather discard as being unable to bear it, so, in the same manner, a vigorous body causes affliction to a diseased soul by not being in conformity with its existing circumstances. (32) And our lawgiver, having a regard to these facts, selects not only the captains, and the generals, and the other leaders of the army, but also picks out separately each individual soldier, examines in what state he is in respect of good condition of body and firmness of mind, examining his body to see if it is uninjured in all its parts, and in sound health, and in all its joints and limbs well adapted for the positions and actions which may be required of it; examining the soul also, to see whether it is full of confidence and proper courage, whether it is intrepid, fearless, and inspired with a noble spirit, whether it is eager for honour and inclined to prefer death with glory to an inglorious life; (33) for each one of these qualities and circumstances is individually a separate power, if one is to say the plain truth. And if they are all united together in one individual, then they do most abundantly exhibit a certain invincible and irresistible might, subduing all their enemies without loss.

VII. (34) And the sacred volumes contain the most undeniable proofs of what has been here stated. The most numerous of all nations is that of the Arabians, whose ancient name was the Madienaeans. These people being inimicably disposed towards the Hebrews, for no other cause more than because they honour and worship the highest and mightiest Cause of all things, as being dedicated to the Creator and Father of the universe as his peculiar people, and having tried every imaginable device and exhausted every contrivance to cause them to abandon the worship of the one only true and living God, and to forsake holiness and adopt impiety, thought that if they could do so they should be easily able to get the better of

them. But when, in spite of having both done and said innumerable things, they had failed in everything, like dying people who now despair of their safety, they contrived a device of the following nature. (35) Having sent for the most beautiful of their women, they said to them, You see how invincible the multitude of the Hebrews is; and a defence to them more formidable than even their number is their unanimity and agreement; and the greatest and most powerful cause of this unanimity is the idea which they entertain of the one God, from which, as from a fountain, they derive a united and indissoluble affection for one another. (36) But man may be caught by pleasure, and especially by such pleasure as proceeds from connections with women. And ye are very beautiful, and beauty is by nature a seductive thing; and youth is a season of life very apt to fall into intemperance. (37) And do not be afraid of the names of concubinage or adultery, as if they would bring shame upon you, but set against the names the advantages which will ensue from the facts, by which you will change your evil reputation, which will endure only for a day, into a glory which will never grow old or die; abandoning your bodies, indeed, as far as appearance goes, which, however, is only a desire and manoeuvre to defeat the enemy, and preserving still the virginity of your souls, on which you will for the future set the everlasting seal of purity. (38) And this war will have a novel glory as having been brought to a successful issue by means of women, and not by means of men.

For we confess that our sex is in danger of being defeated, because our enemies are better provided with all the appliances of war and necessaries for battle; but your sex is more completely armed, and you will gain the greatest of all advantages, namely the victory; carrying off the prize without having to encounter any danger; for without any loss or bloodshed, or indeed, I may rather say, without even a struggle, you will overpower the enemy at the first sight of you, merely by being beheld by him.

(39) When they heard this, they ceased to think of or to pay the very slightest regard to their character for purity of life, being quite devoid of all proper education, and accordingly they consented, though during all the rest of their lives they had put on a hypocritical appearance of modesty, and so now they adorned themselves with costly garments, and necklaces, and all those other appendages with which women are accustomed to set themselves off, and they devoted all their attention to enhancing their natural beauty, and making it more brilliant (for the object of their pursuit was not an unimportant one, being the alluring of the young men who were well inclined to be seduced), and so they went forth into public. (40) And when they came near to them they put forth

immodest wanton looks, and sought to entice them with caressing words, and dances, and lascivious movements; and in this way they enticed the shallow-minded company of the young men, youths whose dispositions had no ballast nor steadiness in them.

And by the shame of their own bodies they captivated the souls of those who came to them, bringing them over to unholy sacrifices which ought not to have been sacrificed, and to libations which should never have been offered in honour of deities made with hands, and thus they alienated them from the worship of the one only and truly divine God. And when they had accomplished their purpose, they sent the glad tidings to the men of their nation; (41) and they would have been likely to draw over others also of the firmer and stronger-minded sort, if the bountiful and merciful God had not taken compassion upon their unhappy state, and by the prompt punishment of those who had gone astray and wrought folly (and they were twenty-four thousand men), by which he admonished and checked by terror those others who were in danger of being carried away by the torrent.

(42) But the ruler of the whole nation, infusing into the ears of his people doctrines of piety, and charming the souls of his subjects with them, selected and picked out a thousand men of each tribe, choosing them with regard to their excellence, and he bade them to inflict upon the enemy punishment for the treachery which they had contrived by means of the women, when they hoped to destroy the whole multitude by casting them down from the heights of their pure and sublime piety, though, in effect, they were only able to delude those whom I have enumerated.

VIII. (43) These men, then, being arrayed against them, a small number against many myriads of men, and availing themselves of their skill, and exerting all their courage, as if each individual were himself a host, rushed upon the dense phalanxes in a contemptuous manner, and slaying all whom they met, they mowed down the thickly-packed battalions, and all the forces which were in reserve as a reinforcement to fill up the ranks where men were slain, so that they overthrew many myriads with their mere single shout, till not one of all the youth in the opposing army was left. And they slew also all the women who had assented to the unholy devices of the men, taking the maidens alive, because of their compassion for their innocent age, (44) and though they brought this terrible war to a successful termination, they lost not a single one of their own men; but every man who went forth unto battle returned back again unwounded and unhurt, just as he entered the conflict, or rather, if one is to say the real truth, with redoubled vigour; for their joy at this victory made their strength not inferior to what it had been at first; (45) and the cause of this, was simply that they even courted danger in their anxiety to engage in the contest in the cause of piety, in which God, that invincible ally, fights in front of them as their champion, inspiring their minds with wise counsels, and implanting the mightiest vigour in their bodies.

(46) And there is evident proof that God was their ally, in the fact that many myriads of men were defeated by a few, and that not one man of the enemy escaped, and that not one of their own troops was slain, and that the army was not diminished in either number or power; (47) on which account Moses says in his exhortations to his people:[3] "If you practise justice, and holiness, and the other virtues, you shall enjoy a life untroubled by wars and invariably peaceful; or if any war comes upon you, you shall with ease subdue your enemies, God being the leader of your host, although invisibly, who takes care to put forth his might to save the good. (48) Therefore, if thy enemies come upon thee with many myriads of men, a host both of infantry, and of cavalry, trusting in the beauty of their armour; and if they pre-occupy all the strong and defensible places, and become masters of the country, and if they rejoice in unbounded supplies, still do not you be alarmed and fear, even if you are destitute of the things of which they have plenty, such as allies, and arms, and situations, and good opportunities, and the supplies of war."

(49) For very often a violent wind, falling upon them as upon a merchant vessel laden with all kinds of good things, has at once overthrown and destroyed these things; while upon those who have been imperfectly supplied, and who have been sorrowful, hanging down their heads like ears of corn withering under drought and disease, God has suddenly showered down and poured forth his saving powers, and has caused them to rise up and become prosperous and perfect. (50) From which it is plain that he cleaves to what is holy and righteous; for those whose ally is God are consummately happy, but those to whom he is an enemy are sunk in the lowest depths of misery.

This appears sufficient to say on the present occasion on the subject of courage.

ON HUMANITY

IX. (51) We must now proceed in due order to consider that virtue which is more nearly related to piety, being as it were a sister, a twin sister, namely, humanity, which the father of our laws loved so much that I know not if any human being was ever more attached to it. For he knew that this was as it were a plain and level road conducting to holiness; and, therefore, he trained and instructed all the people who were in subjection to himself in precepts of fellowship, the most excel-

---

[3]Deuteronomy 28:15.

lent of all lessons, exhibiting to them his own life as an archetypal model for them to copy.

(52) Every thing, then, that was ever done by him from his earliest infancy to old age in the way of taking care and providing for each separate individual and for all men in general, has been already explained in the three books of the treatise which I have set forth about the life of Moses. But it is necessary also to make mention of one or two points which he set in order when at the point of death; for they are indicative of that continual and uninterrupted virtue which he stamped upon his own soul, which was thus fashioned after the divine model, in such a way that it should be free from all indistinctness and confusion. (53) For when the appointed limit of human existence was on the point of being reached by him, and when by distinct intimation from God he became aware that he was about to depart from the world, he did not act like any other person, whether king or private individual, whose only anxiety and prayer is to leave their inheritance to their children; but although he had become the father of two sons, he was not so much under the influence of the natural affection and love for his offspring which he undoubtedly felt as to bequeath his authority to either of them. And yet, even he had some suspicion of the worth of his children; at all events, he had no lack of virtuous and pious nephews, who were, indeed, already invested with the high priesthood, as a reward of their virtue.

(54) But, perhaps, he did not think fit to draw them away from the divine ministrations which belonged to their office, or, as was very likely, he considered that it would be impossible for them to attend to both matters, the priesthood and the royal authority, the one of which employments professes to be devoted to the worship of God, the other to the government of and to the care of providing for men. Perhaps, also, he did not think fit to become himself the judge in so important a matter, especially as it is an attribute of almost divine power to see thoroughly who is by nature well adapted for such authority, as it is the Deity alone to whom it is easy to see into the dispositions of men.

X. (55) And the clearest proof of what I have said may be afforded by the following consideration. He had a friend and pupil, one who had been so almost from his very earliest youth, Joshua by name, whose friendship he had won, not by any of the arts which are commonly in use among other men, but by that heavenly and unmixed love from which all virtue is derived. This man lived under the same roof, and shared the same table with him, except when solitude was enjoined to him on occasions when he was inspired and instructed in divine oracles. He also performed other services for him in which he was distinguished from the multitude, being almost his lieutenant, and regulating in con-junction with him the matters relating to his supreme authority.

(56) But yet, though Moses had thus an accurate knowledge of him from his experience of him for a long time, and though he knew his excellence both in word and deed, and the greatness of his good will towards his nation, yet he did not think fit to leave him as his successor himself, fearing lest he might perchance be deceived in looking on that man as good who in reality was not so, since the tests by which one can judge of human nature are in a great degree indistinct and unstable. (57) On which account he did not trust to his own knowledge, but he supplicated and entreated God, who alone can behold the invisible soul, who sees accurately the mind of man, to choose and select the most suitable man for the supreme authority, one who would care for the people who were to be his subjects like a father. And stretching his pure, and, as one may say in a somewhat metaphorical manner, his virgin hands towards heaven, he said, (58) "Let the Lord God of spirits and of all flesh look out for himself a man to be over this multitude, to undertake the care and superintendence of a shepherd, who shall lead them in a blameless manner, in order that this nation may not become corrupt like a flock which is scattered abroad, as having no shepherd."[4]

(59) And yet who was there of all the men of that time who would not have been amazed if he had heard this prayer? Who was there who would not have said, "What art thou saying, master? hast not thou legitimate children? hast thou not nephews? Above all men, leave thy authority to thy children first, for they are thy natural heirs; but if thou disapprovest of them, at all events bequeath it to thy nephews; (60) and if thou lookest upon them also as unfit, having a greater regard for the whole nation than for thy nearest and dearest relations, still thou hast an irreproachable friend who has given a proof of his perfect virtue to you who art all-wise and capable to judge of it. Why, then, do thou not think fit to show your approbation of him, if thy object is not to select one on account of his family but on account of his virtue?"

(61) But Moses would reply: "It is proper to make God the judge in every thing, and most especially in those things in which the acting well or ill brings innumerable multitudes to happiness, or on the contrary to misery. And there is nothing of greater importance than sovereign authority, to which all the affairs of cities, in war or peace, are committed. For as in order to make a successful voyage one has need of a pilot who is both virtuous and skilful, in the same manner there is need of a very wise governor, in order to secure the good government of the subjects in every quarter.

---

[4]Numbers 27:16.

(62) Moreover, wisdom is a thing not only more ancient than my own birth, but even than the creation of the universal world; nor is it lawful nor possible for any one to decide in such a matter but God alone, and those who love wisdom with guilelessness, and sincerity and truth; (63) and I have learnt by myself not to approve of, as fit for dominion, any one of those men who appear to be suitable.

"I, indeed, myself, did neither undertake the charge of caring for and providing for the common prosperity of my own accord, nor because I was appointed to the office by any human being; but I undertook to govern this people because God manifestly declared his will by visible oracles and distinct commandments, and commanded me to rule them; and I, after having besought and supplicated him to excuse me, because I had a respect unto the greatness of the business, at last, after he had repeated his commandments many times, I with fear obeyed. (64) How, then, can it be any thing but absurd for me not now to follow in the same steps, and, after I myself, when about to assume the supreme authority, had had God for my elector and approver, not now in my turn to refer to him alone the appointment of my successor, without calling in the assistance of any human wisdom which is likely to be akin in some degree to folly, especially as the government to be undertaken is not one over any ordinary nation, but one which is the most populous of all nations everywhere, and one which puts forth the most important of all professions, the worship of the one true and living God, who is the Creator and the father of the universe? (65) For whatever advantages are derived from the most approved philosophy to its students, full as great are derived by the Jews from their laws and customs, inasmuch as through them they have rejected all errors about gods who have been created themselves; for there is no created being who is truly God, but such a one is so only in appearance and opinion, being destitute of that most indispensable quality in God, namely, eternity."

XI. (66) This, now, is the first and most conspicuous proof of his great humanity and good faith towards and affection for all those of his own people, and there is also another which is not inferior to that which I have already mentioned. For when Joshua, being his most excellent pupil and the imitator of his amiable and excellent disposition, had been approved of as the ruler of the people by the judgment of God, Moses was in no respect downcast as some other men might have been at the fact of its not having been his own sons or nephews who were appointed; (67) but he was filled with unrestrained joy because there was secured to the nation a governor who was in all respects excellent (for he was sure that the man who was pleasing to God must be virtuous and pious); and accordingly, taking him by the right hand, he led him forth to the assembled multitude, not being at all alarmed at the idea of his own impending death, but feeling that he had received a new cause of joy in addition to his former reasons for cheerfulness, not only from the recollection of his former happiness, in which he had passed his life abundantly in every species of virtue, but from the hope also that he was now about to become immortal, changing from this corruptible to an incorruptible life; and accordingly, with a cheerful look proceeding from the joy which he felt in his soul, he spoke to them with joy and exultation in the following manner, and said:

(68) "It is time for me now to be released from the life in the body; and my successor in the government of your nation is this man, having been appointed thereto by God." And then he proceeded to detail to them the oracular words of God which he had received as the proofs of this his successor's appointment by God; and the people believed them. (69) And then, looking upon Joshua, he exhorted him to approve himself a valiant man, and to be very strong in good and wise counsel, and to show himself the interpreter of his counsels, and to accomplish all his purposes with unyielding and vigorous decision. And he said thus much to him though he was not perhaps in need of any recommendation, but because he would not conceal their mutual affection for one another and for the whole people, by which he was spurred on as it were to lay bare before him what he thought would be advantageous.

(70) He had also received an oracular command to call his successor and to render him full of confidence and good courage to undertake the care of the nation, without being apprehensive of the great burden of the authority committed to him, in order that he might be a standard and rule for all governors who should come hereafter, and who should look upon Moses as their model; so that none of them should ever grudge good advice to their successors, but should train, and exercise, and instruct their souls with their suggestions and counsels.

(71) For the advice of a good man is often able to raise up again those men whose minds are prostrate, and to elevate them again to a height, implanting in them a noble and intrepid spirit, which shall thus be established firmly above all circumstances and exigencies of time.

(72) Accordingly, after having held a discourse in which he uttered sentiments suited both to the people who had been committed to his care, and to those who were to be the inheritors of his authority, he begins to hymn the praises of God in a song, uttering the last psalm of thanksgiving in this life while still in the body, for all the kindnesses and mercies of extraordinary and unprecedented kinds, which he had received from his birth

to this his old age; (73) and having collected a most divine assembly to hear these praises, namely, the elements of the universe, and the most comprehensive parts of the whole world, the earth and the heaven, one of which is the dwelling of mortals, and the other the home of the immortals, he sang his hymn of praise in the middle of them all, with every description of harmony and symphony which men and ministering angels hear; (74) the one, as being pupils, in order to learn to display their own grateful dispositions in a similar manner, and the others as presiding over them, and as by their own experience being able to take care that no part of this hymn shall be out of tune, and also as feeling some doubt whether any human being bound up in a mortal body could be able to attune his soul to music in the same manner as the sun, and the moon, and the rest of the company of the stars, having properly conformed himself to that divine instrument, the heaven, and to the universal world. (75) And the declarer of the will of God being thus placed amid the beings who form the host of heaven, mingled with his grateful hymns of praise to God proofs of his own genuine affection and good will towards his nation, while he reproved them for their previous sins, and gave them admonitions, and advice, and precepts for the present occasion, and exhortations for the future, inspiring them with favourable hopes, which it was inevitable that favourable events would of necessity follow.

XII. (76) And when he had finished his hymn of melodious praise, which was thus in a manner woven together and made up of piety and humanity, he began to be changed and to depart from mortal existence to immortal life, and gradually to feel a separation of the different parts of which he was composed, namely of his body, which was now removed from him like a shell from a fish, from his soul which was thus laid bare and naked, and which desired its natural departure from hence.

(77) Then, having prepared all things for his departure, he did not approach the actual termination of his existence until he had shown respect to all the tribes of his nation by harmonious and consistent prayers in their behalf, honouring them all to the number of twelve by the recapitulation of the name of the patriarch of each tribe, all which prayers we must believe will certainly be accomplished, for the man who offered up the prayers was a devout servant of God, and God is merciful, and the persons on whose behalf the supplications were uttered were men of pure and noble birth, classed in the highest rank possible by the supreme leader of the people, the Creator and Father of the universe.

(78) And the things which were entreated for in the petitions were real blessings, not only that such things might fall to their share in this mortal life, but still more so when the soul should be released from the bondage of the flesh; (79) for Moses alone, looking upon it as it should seem that his whole nation had from the very beginning the closest of all possible relationships to God, one much more genuine than that which consists of ties of blood, made it the inheritor of all the good things which the nature of mankind is capable of receiving, giving from his own store things which he had himself, and entreating God to supply what he himself was not possessed of, knowing that the fountains of his graces are everlasting, but yet that they are not dispensed to all men, but only to such as are suppliants for them; and suppliants are those persons who love virtue and piety, and it is lawful for them to drink up those most sacred springs, inasmuch as they are continually thirsting for wisdom.

XIII. (80) We have now, then, spoken of the proofs of the humanity of the lawgiver, which he displayed by the admirable disposition of his own excellent nature, and also partly by the expositions which he has given in the sacred volumes. We must now proceed to speak of the precepts which he left behind him, commanding that they should be observed by future ages, and we must enumerate, if not all (for that would not be easy), at all events the principal topics which are most closely connected with and most nearly resembling his counsels; (81) for, according to him, gentleness and humanity have not their habitation only in the communion of society which takes place among men, but also of his great liberality and bounty he diffuses it exceedingly, and extends it even to the irrational animals, and to the different species of wholesome trees. And what ordinances he established with respect to each of these things we must proceed to enumerate separately, making our beginning with men.

XIV. (82) Therefore Moses forbids a man to lend on usury to his brother, [5] meaning by the term brother not only him who is born of the same parents as one's self, but every one who is a fellow citizen or a fellow countryman, since it is not just to exact offspring from money, as a farmer does from his cattle. (83) And he enjoins his subjects not to hang back on that account, and to be more slow to contribute to the necessities of others, but rather with open hands and willing minds very cheerfully to give to those who have need, considering that gratitude may in some degree be looked upon as interest repaid at a more favourable season for what was lent in an hour of necessity, being repaid by the voluntary inclination of the receiver of the kindness. And if a person be not willing wholly to give, still at all events let him lend, so as to give the temporary use of what is wanted freely and cheerfully, without expecting to

---

[5] Deuteronomy 23:19.

receive anything beyond the principal. (84) For in this way the poor will not become poorer, by being compelled to restore more than they received; nor will they who lent be doing iniquity if they only receive back what they lent. And yet they will not receive nothing more, for with the principal, instead of the interest which they have not demanded to receive, they will gain the best and most honourable of all human things, as they will have displayed kindness and magnanimity, and will have earned a fair reputation and goodwill. And what acquisition is there which is equal to this? (85) for indeed the mightiest monarch appears poor and helpless if he is put in comparison with one single virtue, for he has only inanimate riches buried in his treasuries or in the recesses of the earth, but the wealth of virtue is stored up in the dominant part of the soul; and that purest of all essences, heaven, claims itself a share in that, as likewise does the Creator and Father of the universe, God.

Therefore we must look upon and denominate the opulence of money-changers and usurers as poverty, though they appear to themselves to be mighty kings, while they have never beheld that wealth which is really endowed with sight, no not even in their dreams. (86) And these men run into such extravagances of wickedness, that if they have not money, they make usurious advances even of food, lending it on condition of receiving back again more than they lent. Accordingly, such men will speedily afford a contribution to those who ask for one, preparing famine and scarcity against a time of plenty and abundance, and making a revenue of the hunger of the bellies of miserable men, weighing out the food as it were in a scale, and taking care not to give overweight. (87) Therefore he necessarily commands those who live under his sacred constitution to avoid every description of revenues of this kind, for all such pursuits were the sign of a thoroughly slavish and illiberal mind, which must be changed into savageness and into the resemblance of brute beasts, before it could adopt them.

XV. (88) Again, among the different commands which conduce to the extension of humanity, there is this one also established,[6] that every employer is to pay the wages of the poor man the same day that they are earned, not only because, since he has fulfilled the purpose for which he was hired, it is just that he should without any delay receive the reward of his service, but also because, as some persons have said, since the handicrafts-man or burden-carrier is only a daily servant and short lived, suffering hardships with his whole body like any common beast of burden, he fixes all his hopes upon his wages, which if he receives at once,

he is rejoiced, being both glad now, and ready to work twice as hard to-morrow with all cheerfulness; but if he does not get his wages, then, besides being exceedingly disappointed, he is weakened in his nerves and sinews through sorrow, and becomes faint, so that he is unable to move himself to the performance of his ordinary tasks.

XVI. (89) Again, the lawgiver says, let no one who lends on usury enter the house of his debtors to take by force any security or pledge for his debt,[7] but let him stand without in the outer court, and wait there entreating his debtor quietly to bring him a pledge; and if he have a pledge to give, let him not evade giving it, since it is fitting that the creditor should not by reason of his power behave in an arrogant manner, so as to insult those who have borrowed of him; and that the debtor also should out of his recollection of the loan of another person's property which he has received, not refuse to give an adequate security.

XVII. (90) And who is there who can avoid admiring the proclamation or commandment about reapers and gatherers of the fruit of the vineyard?[8] For Moses commands that at the time of harvest the farmer shall not gather up the corn which falls from the sheaves, and that he shall not cut down all the crop, but that he shall leave a portion of the field unreaped, by this law rendering the rich magnanimous and communicative of their wealth, from being compelled thus to neglect some portion of their own lawful property, and not to be eager to save it all, nor to collect it all together, not to bring it all home and lay it up in store, and making the poor at the same time more cheerful and contented. For as the poor have no property of their own, he allows them to go into the fields of their fellow countrymen, and to reap of what they have left as if it were their own. (91) And at the season of autumn he again enjoins the possessors of the land, when they are gathering their fruits, not to pick up those fruits which fall to the ground, nor to glean the vineyards a second time.

And he also gives the same command to those who are gathering olives.[9] Like a most affectionate father, whose children are not all in the enjoyment of equal good fortune, since some of them live in abundance, while others are reduced to the very extremity of poverty; but he, commiserating and pitying them, summons them to partake of the possessions of their brethren, using what thus belongs to others as if it were their own, not in so doing inviting them to any action of shameless wrong, but supplying their real necessities, allowing them a participation, not in the crops alone,

[6]Leviticus 19:13.

[7]Deuteronomy 24:10.
[8]Deuteronomy 24:19.
[9]Deuteronomy 24:20.

but even in the land themselves likewise, as far as appearance is concerned.

(92) But there are men who are so sordid in their minds, being wholly devoted to the acquisition of money and labouring to the death for every description of gain, without paying any attention to the source from which it is derived, that they glean their vineyards again after they have gathered the fruit, and beat their olive branches a second time, and reap the whole of the land which bears barley and the whole of the land which bears wheat, convicting themselves of an illiberal and slavish littleness of soul, and also displaying their impiety; (93) for they themselves have contributed but a small part of what was necessary for the cultivation of their lands, but the greater number and the most important of the means to render the land fertile and productive have been supplied by nature, such as seasonable rains, a proper temperature of the atmosphere, those nurses of the seeds sown and springing up—heavy and continual dews, vivifying breezes, the beneficial bestowal of the seasons of the year, so that the summer shall not scorch the crops nor the frost chill them, nor the revolutions of spring and autumn deteriorate or diminish what is produced.

(94) And though these men know and actually see that nature is continually perfecting her work by these means, and is enriching them with her abundant bounties, nevertheless they endeavour to appropriate the whole of her liberality to themselves, and, as if they themselves were the causes of everything, they give no share of any of their wealth to any one, showing at one and the same time their inhumanity and their impiety.

These men accordingly, since they have not laboured in the cause of virtue of their own free will, he reproves and chastises against their will by his sacred laws, which the virtuous man obeys voluntarily, and the wicked man unwillingly.

XVIII. (95) The laws command[10] that the people should offer to the priests first fruits of corn, and wine, and oil, and of their domestic flocks, and of wools. But that of the crops which are produced in the fields, and of the fruits of the trees, they should bring in full baskets in proportion to the extent of their lands; with hymns made in praise of God, which the sacred volumes preserve recorded in writing. And, moreover, they were not to reckon the first-born of the oxen, and sheep, and goats in their herds and flocks as if they were their own, but were to look upon these also as first-fruits, in order that, being thus trained partly to honour God, and partly also not to seek for every possible gain, they might be adorned with those chief virtues, piety and humanity.

(96) Again. The law says,[11] if you see the beast of any one of your relations or friends, or, in short, of any man whatever whom you know, wandering in the wilderness, bring him back and restore him to him; and, if the master be a long way off, then keep the animal with your own until he returns, and then he shall receive back the deposit which he has not entrusted to you, but which you, having found, spontaneously restore to him from your own natural feelings of fellowship.

XIX. (97) Again. Are not all the enactments about the seventh year so formally established, enjoining the people to leave all the land that year fallow and uncultivated, and allowing the poor to go with impunity over the fields of the rich to gather the fruits which that year grow spontaneously as the gift of nature, most merciful and humane ordinances? (98) The law says,[12] "Six years let the inhabitants of the land enjoy the fruits as a reward for the acquisitions which they have made and for the labours which they have undergone in cultivating the land; but for one year, namely, the seventh, let the poor and needy enjoy it, as no work pertaining to agriculture has been done in that year." For, if any work had been done, it would have been absurd for one man to labour and for another to reap the fruit of his labours.

But this ordinance was given in order that, the lands being left this year in some manner without any owners, no cultivation of the land contributing to its fertility, the produce, although full and complete, might be seen to proceed wholly from the bounty of God, coming forth as it were to meet and relieve the necessitous.

(99) Again. What are we to say of the commandments given relating to the fiftieth year?[13] Do not they go to the very furthest extent of humanity? And, indeed, who would deny it, unless he had only tasted of this sacred code of laws with anything more than the edges of his lips, and had not feasted and revelled in its most sweet and beautiful doctrines? (100) For, in this fiftieth year, all the ordinances which are given relating to the seventh year are repeated, and some of greater magnitude are likewise added, for instance, a resumption of a man's own possessions which he may have yielded up to others through unexpected necessity; for the law does not permit any one permanently to retain possession of the property of others, but blockades and stops up the roads to covetousness for the sake of checking desire, that treacherous passion, that cause of all evils; and, therefore, it has not permitted that the owners should be for ever deprived of their original property, as that would be punishing them for their pov-

[10] Deuteronomy 24:4.

[11] Exodus 23:4.
[12] Exodus 23:10.
[13] Leviticus 25:8.

erty, for which we ought not to be punished, but undoubtedly to be pitied.

(101) There is also an innumerable host of other special ordinances relating to one's fellow countrymen of great humanity and beauty; but, as I have mentioned them at sufficient length in my former treatises, I shall be satisfied with what I have said on those subjects, which I then put forth seasonably as a kind of specimen of the whole.

XX. (102) Moreover, after the lawgiver has established commandments respecting one's fellow countrymen, he proceeds to show that he looks upon strangers also as worthy of having their interests attended to by his laws, since they have forsaken their natural relations by blood, and their native land and their national customs, and the sacred temples of their gods, and the worship and honour which they had been wont to pay to them, and have migrated with a holy migration, changing their abode of fabulous inventions for that of the certainty and clearness of truth, and of the worship of the one true and living God. (103) Accordingly, he commands the men of his nation to love the strangers, not only as they love their friends and relations, but even as they love themselves, doing them all the good possible both in body and soul; and, as to their feelings, sympathising with them both in sorrow and in joy, so as to appear all one creature, though the parts are divided; mutual fellowship uniting the whole and rendering it compact and coherent.

(104) There is no need of my saying anything about meats, and drinks, and garments, and all the other matters which relate to the usual way of living and to the necessary requirements of life, which the law enjoins that the foreigners shall receive from the natives of the land; for all these things follow the one general law of benevolence, which enjoins every man to love and cherish a stranger in the same degree with himself.

XXI. (105) Moreover, extending and carrying further that humanity which is naturally so attractive, he also gives commandments respecting sojourners, thinking it fitting that those persons who, through any temporary distresses, have been driven from their homes should requite those who have received them with a certain degree of honour, with all imaginable respect, if they have done good to them and have treated them with friendliness and hospitality, and with a moderate degree of respect of they have done nothing more than merely receiving them into the land; for to be allowed to abide in a city with which one is wholly unconnected, or, I might even say, to be allowed only to tread on the soil which belongs to another, is in itself a bounty of sufficient magnitude for those persons who are unable to dwell in their own land.

(106) But the lawgiver here, going beyond all the ordinary boundaries of humanity, thinks it fitting and ordains that such sojourners shall bear no ill-will even to those men who, after having received them in the land, may have ill-treated them, since, though their actions may not have been kind, their name at least resembles the characteristics of humanity. Therefore he says, in express terms, "Thou shalt not curse the Egyptian, because thou wast a sojourner in the land of Egypt."[14] (107) And yet what evil did the Egyptians ever omit to inflict upon this nation, being continually adding new devices of cruelty to the old ones, and proceeding by all sorts of fresh contrivances to heap inhumanity on inhumanity?

But, nevertheless, because originally they received them in the land, not shutting their cities against them, and not making their country inaccessible to them when they first came, the lawgiver says, "Let them, as a reward for their friendly reception of you, have a treaty of peace with you. (108) And if any of them should be willing to forsake their old ways and to come over to the customs and constitutions of the Jews, they are not to be rejected and treated with hostility as the children of enemies, but to be received in such a manner that in the third generation they may be admitted into the assembly, and may have a share of the divine words read to them, being instructed in the will of God equally with the natives of the land, the descendants of God's chosen people.

XXII. (109) These, then, are the ordinances which he enacts for the sojourners in respect of those who have received them into their land, and he also establishes other merciful laws, full of gentleness and humanity, on behalf even of enemies;"[15] for he thinks it right with respect to them, even if they are at the gates, and standing under the very walls ready to attack them in their complete armour, and raising their warlike engines against them, that they shall, nevertheless, not be accounted enemies until the citizens have sent heralds to them and invited them to peace, that so, if they will yield, they may find that greatest of all blessings, namely, friendship; but if they are uncomplying and refuse, then the citizens, having also gained the alliance and co-operation of justice, might go to repel them with a good hope of victory.

(110) Moreover, if, after having taken prisoners in a sally, you should entertain a desire for a beautiful woman amongst them,[16] do not satiate your passion, treating her as a captive, but act with gentleness, and pity her change of fortune, and alleviate her calamity, regulating everything for the best; (111) and you will alleviate her sufferings if you cut the hair of her head, and trim her nails,

---

[14] Deuteronomy 27:3.
[15] Deuteronomy 20:10.
[16] Deuteronomy 21:10.

and take off from her the garment which she wore when she was taken prisoner, and leave her alone for thirty days, during which period you shall permit her with impunity to mourn and bewail her father and her mother, and her other relations, from whom she has been separated by their death, or by their being subjected to the calamity of slavery which is worse than death. (112) And, after that period, you shall cohabit with her as with a legitimate wedded wife; for it is right that one who is about to ascend the bed of her husband, not for hire, like a harlot who makes a traffic of the flower of her beauty, but either out of love for him who has espoused her, or for the sake of the procreation of children, should be thought worthy of the ordinances which belong to a legitimate marriage. (113) On which account the lawgiver has given all his laws with great beauty.

For, in the first place, he had not permitted appetite to proceed onwards in its unbridled course, with stiff-necked obstinacy, but he has checked its vehement impetuosity, compelling it to rest for thirty days. And in the second place he has tested love, trying whether it is a frantic passion, easily satisfied, and, in fact, wholly originating in desire, or whether it has any share in that most pure essence of well-tempered reason, for reason will bridle the desire, not allowing it to proceed to any acts of insolence, but compelling it to abide the appointed period of a month of probation. (114) And, in the third place, he shows his compassion for the captive, if she is a virgin, because it is not her parents who are now giving her in marriage, arranging for her a most desirable connection; and if she is a widow, because she, being deprived of her first husband, is about how to make experiment of another, and this too while he still holds over her the power of a master, even though he studies to exhibit equality; for that which is subject to a master must always be apprehensive of his power, even though he may be very merciful.

(115) But if any one, being filled with desire, and being afterwards sated with enjoyment, no longer chooses to continue his cohabitation with his captive, then the lawgiver does not so much punish him as admonish him and correct him, with a view to the improvement of his disposition, for he commands him in such a case not to sell her,[17] nor to retain her any longer as a slave, but to give her liberty freely, and to allow her to depart from his house with impunity, in order that she may not be exposed to some intolerable suffering when any other woman is introduced into the house, by their both quarrelling, as is often the case, out of jealousy, the master being at the same time brought into subjection to more recent charms, and despising those by which he was previously allured.

XXIII. (116) And thus the lawgiver pouring precept after precept into ready and obedient ears, enjoins humanity.[18]

Moreover, even if any beasts of burden belonging to the enemy while bearing burdens are oppressed by the weight, and fall down beneath them, he commands that the people should not pass them by, but that they should lighten their burdens and raise them up, teaching them thus by remote examples not to be delighted at the unexpected misfortunes even of those who hate them, knowing that to rejoice in the disasters of others is a malignant and odious passion, both akin to and contrary to envy; akin to it, because each of these feelings proceeds from passion, and because they approach near to, and one may almost say reciprocate, one another; but contrary, because the one feeling causes grief at the good fortune of another, and the other excites joy at the misfortunes of one's neighbour.

(117) Also the law proceeds to say, If you see the beast of one who is thy enemy[19] wandering about, leave the excitements to quarrelling to more perverse dispositions, and lead the animal back and restore him to his owner; for so you will not be benefiting him more than yourself; since he will by this means save only an irrational beast which is perhaps of no value, but you will get the greatest and most valuable of all things in nature, namely, excellence. (118) And there will follow of necessity, as sure as shadow follows a body, the dissolution of your enmity; for the man who has received a benefit is willingly induced to make peace for the future as being enslaved by the kindness shown to him; and he who has conferred the benefit, having his own good action for a counsellor, is already almost prepared in his mind for a complete reconciliation. (119) And this is an object which the most holy prophet is endeavouring to bring to pass throughout the whole of his code of laws, studying to create unanimity, and fellowship, and agreement, and that due admixture of different dispositions by which houses, and cities, and altars, and nations, and countries, and the whole human race may be conducted to the very highest happiness.

(120) But up to the present time these are only wishes; but they will be hereafter, as I at least persuade myself, most real facts, since God will give a plentiful harvest of virtue, as he does give the harvest of the fruits of the seasons; which we shall never fail to attain to if we cherish a desire for them from our earliest infancy.

XXIV. (121) The ordinances, then, which he laid down for the observance of free-born men are these and others like them. And as it seems he

---

[17]Deuteronomy 21:14.

[18]Exodus 23:5.
[19]Exodus 23:4.

also has established other regulations consistent with them respecting slaves; all of which tend to engender gentleness and humanity, of which he gives a share even to salves. (122) Accordingly[20] he thinks it fit that those who, because of their need of necessary sustenance, have devoted themselves to the service of others, ought not to be compelled to endure any thing unworthy of a liberal freedom of birth; advising those who have the advantage of their ministrations to have a regard to the unexpected misfortunes which have befallen their servants, and to feel respect for their change of condition.

And he does not allow those who become debtors for daily loans, and who, by a parabolical and metaphorical expression, have received both the name and unhappy condition of ephemeral animals, or those who through some even still more urgent necessity have become slaves from having been free men, to suffer misery for ever, but he gives them entire deliverance in the seventh year. (123) For, says he, a period of six years for servitude is sufficient for those debtors who cannot repay the loans to the lender, or who for any other reason have become slaves after having been free. And those who were not naturally slaves are not to be deprived of all happiness and liberty for ever, but are again to return to their former state of freedom, of which they were deprived through some unforeseen calamities.

(124) "And if," the lawgiver proceeds to say, "one who has been a slave of another for three generations, from fear of the threats of his master, or from a consciousness of having committed some offence, or, if he has committed no offence at all but has a savage and inhuman master, flees for refuge to some one else, in the hope to obtain assistance from him, do not reject him; for it is not consistent with holiness to abandon a suppliant, and even a slave is a suppliant, inasmuch as he has taken refuge on thy hearth, where it is fitting that he should find an asylum, especially if without any guile he has come to offer honest service. And if he cannot obtain this protection, at all events let him be sold to some one else; for it is uncertain what may be the effect of his change of masters, and an uncertain evil is easier to bear than a confessed one."

XXV. (125) These, then, are the ordinances which he appoints to be observed concerning one's own relations, and strangers, and friends, and enemies, and slaves, and free men, and in short respecting the whole of the human race. And moreover, he extends his principles of humanity and compassion even to the race of irrational animals, allowing them always to share of these benefits as of a pleasant fountain; (126) for in the case of

domestic animals, with reference to flocks of sheep, and of goats, and herds of oxen, he commands the people to abstain from using of those animals which are just born, or from taking them either for food or under pretence of sacrificing them. For he looked upon it as a proof of a cruel disposition to plot against such creatures the moment they are born, so as to cause and immediate separation between the offspring and the mother, for the sake of the pleasures of the belly, or rather on account of some absurd and preposterous unpleasantness which the soul fancies.

(127) Therefore, he says to the man who is about to live in accordance with his most sacred constitution, "My good man, there is a great abundance of things of which you are permitted the enjoyment, to which there is no blame attached; for, perhaps, it would have been pardonable if it were not so, since want and scarcity compel men to do many things which otherwise they would not intend. But you ought to be pre-eminent in temperance and the practice of all virtues; being reckoned in the most admirable of all classifications and enrolled in obedience to a most excellent captain, the right reason of nature, by all which considerations you ought to be rendered humane, avoiding receiving in your mind any thing which is wrong. (128) And why in addition to the pains which the animal bears in parturition, should you also inflict other pains from external causes, by the immediate separation of the mother from her offspring? For it is inevitable that she will resist and be indignant when they are thus parted, by reason of the affection implanted by nature in every mother towards her offspring, and especially at the time of their birth; since at this time the breasts are full of milk-like springs, and then if through want of the child which is to suck them the flow of milk receives a check, they become hardened by being distended by the weight of the milk, and the women themselves are overwhelmed with pain.

(129) Therefore, says the law, give her offspring to the mother, if not for the whole time, still at all events for the first seven days, to rear on her milk, and render not unprofitable those fountains of milk which nature has bestowed upon her breasts, destroying that second bounty of hers which she has prepared with great prudence, perceiving from a distance by her everlasting and perfect wisdom what will hereafter happen. (130) For her first bounty was the birth by means of which that which had no existence was brought into being; the second bounteous gift was the flow of milk, the most tender and seasonable food for a tender creature, which, though it is only one thing, is at the same time both meat and drink. For inasmuch as part of the milk is of a watery nature, it is drink; and inasmuch as part of it is of a somewhat solid nature, it is meat; and it is endowed with these characteristics from a prudent foresight to prevent

the lately born offspring from suffering disaster, through want lying in wait for it at different times, taking care thus that, by the one and the same application of each kind of food, it may escape those cruel mistresses, hunger and thirst.

(131) Do you then, you excellent and most admirable parents, read this law and hide your faces, you who are continually plotting the deaths of your children, you who entertain cruel designs against your offspring, so as to expose them the moment that they are born, you irreconcileable enemies of the whole race of mankind; (132) for who is there to whom you ever entertain good will, when you are the murderers of your own children? You who, as far as lies in your power, make cities desolate, beginning with the destruction of your nearest relations; you who overturn all the laws of nature, and pull down all that she builds up; you who are savage and untameable in the barbarity of your souls, raising up destruction against birth, and death against life? (133) Do not you see, that it has been a care to that all-wise and all-good lawgiver, that not even in the case of brute beasts shall the offspring be separated from the mother until it has been nourished by her milk? And this is ordained principally for your sake, you noble persons, that if you have it not by nature, you may at least learn proper affection for your kindred by instruction, and having regard to the examples of lambs and kids, who are not hindered from revelling in the most abundant possible supply of necessary food, which nature itself prepares for them in the most convenient places, by which easy enjoyment of food is granted to those that stand in need of it the lawgiver providing, with great zeal and care, that no one shall intercept the bountiful and saving gifts of God.

XXVI. (134) And being desirous to implant the seeds of gentleness and humanity in the minds of men, by every kind of expedient imaginable, he adds also another injunction akin to the preceding one, forbidding any one to sacrifice the mother and the offspring on the same day, for even if they are both to be sacrificed, still it must be at different times, for it is the greatest extravagance of barbarity to slay in one day the animal which has been born and her who is the cause of its birth. (135) And for what object is this done? one is slain on pretence of sacrifice, the other for the gratification of the belly.

If then it is on pretence of offering them in sacrifice, then the very name is given with falsehood; for animals taken for such purpose are victims, not sacrifices.[21] And what altar of God would ever receive such unholy sacrifices? And as for the fire, would it not of its own accord divide itself in two parts and stand asunder, avoiding all the contamin-

ation which might arise from any contact with such a profane thing? I imagine that it would not have remained, no, not for even the briefest time, but would have been immediately extinguished, out of a watchful care that the air, and the most holy nature of the Spirit, should not be polluted by the ascending flames.

(136) And if they are not taken to be offered in sacrifice, but with a view to feast on them, then who can there be who would not loathe and reject all these new and unprecedented kinds of preposterous gluttony? for such men are, indeed, pursuing pleasures which are out of all reason. And what pleasure can it be to men who are eating meat, to devour, on the same occasion, the flesh of the others and of their offspring? And if any one were to desire to mangle the limbs of the two animals together, and to run them in a spit and to roast them, and so to devour them, I do believe that the very limbs themselves would not remain quiet, but would be filled with indignation and would utter speech, through their fury at the extraordinary character if the unprecedented injury done to them, and would revile, with innumerable reproaches for their gluttony, those men who had thus prepared this unmentionable banquet.

(137) But the law banishes to a distance from the sacred precincts all animals which are pregnant, not permitting them to be sacrificed until they have brought forth, looking on the animals which are still in the womb as equal to what has just been born; not because those which have never yet come to light are really looked upon as of equal importance with living creatures, but this ordinance is given to banish to a distance the rashness of those persons who are in the habit of confounding everything; (138) for if animals, which grow and increase like plants, and which are considered to be as it were parts of the mothers which have conceived them, being still united to them, and being destined hereafter, after an appointed period of months, to be separated from the close connection to which they are at present attached, are, because of the hope that at some future time they may become living creatures, preserved at present by the safety thus guaranteed to their mothers, in order that the aforesaid pollution may not come to pass; how can it be that the animals, when brought forth, shall not be preserved in a still greater degree, which in their own proper persons have received the gift of life and body? for it is the most impious of all customs, to slay both offspring and mother at one time and on one day.

(139) And it appears to me that some lawgivers, having started from this point, have also promulgated the law about condemned women, which commands that pregnant women, if they have committed any offence worthy of death, shall nevertheless not be executed until they have brought forth, in order that the creature in their

---

womb may not be slain with them when they are put to death. (140) But these men have established these enactments with reference to human beings, but this lawgiver of ours, going beyond them all, extends his humanity even to brute beasts, in order that ... we being accustomed to practise all the things ordained in his laws, may display an excessive degree of humanity, abstaining from pursuing any one, or even from annoying them in retaliation for any annoyance which we have received at their hands, and that we may not store up in secret our own good things, so as to keep them to ourselves, but may bring them into the middle, and offer them freely to all men everywhere, as if they were our kinsmen and our natural brothers.

(141) Moreover, let wicked sycophants calumniate the whole nation as one given to inhumanity, and our laws as enjoining unsociable and inhuman observances, while the laws do thus openly show compassion on even the herds of cattle, and while the whole nation from its earliest youth is, as far as the disobedient nature of their souls will admit of, brought over by the honest admonitions of the law to a peaceable disposition. (142) And our lawgiver endeavours to surpass even himself, being a man of every kind of resource which can tend to virtue, and having a certain natural aptitude for virtuous recommendations; for he commands that one shall not take an animal from the mother, whether it be a lamb, or a kid, or any other creature belonging to the flocks or herds, before it is weaned. And having also given a command that no one shall sacrifice the mother and the offspring on the same day, he goes further, and is quite prodigal on the particularity of his injunctions, adding this also, "Thou shalt not seethe a lamb in his mother's milk." [22]

(143) For he looked upon it as a very terrible thing for the nourishment of the living to be the seasoning and sauce of the dead animal, and when provident nature had, as it were, showered forth milk to support the living creature, which it had ordained to be conveyed through the breasts of the mother, as if through a regular channel, that the unbridled licentiousness of men should go to such a height that they should slay both the author of the existence of the other, and make use of it in order to consume the body of the other.

(144) And if any one should desire to dress flesh with milk, let him do so without incurring the double reproach of inhumanity and impiety. There are innumerable herds of cattle in every direction, and some are every day milked by the cowherds, or goatherds, or shepherds, since, indeed, the milk is the greatest source of profit to all breeders of stock, being partly used in a liquid state and partly allowed to coagulate and solidify,

so as to make cheese. So that, as there is the greatest abundance of lambs, and kids, and all other kinds of animals, the man who seethes the flesh of any one of them in the milk of its own mother is exhibiting a terrible perversity of disposition, and exhibits himself as wholly destitute of that feeling which, of all others, is the most indispensable to, and most nearly akin to, a rational soul, namely, compassion.

XXVII. (145) I also greatly admire that law which, like a singer in a well-trained chorus, is perfectly in accord with those which have gone before it, and which forbids a man to "muzzle the ox which treadeth out the corn." [23] For it is he who, before the sowing was performed, cut the furrows through the deep-soiled plain, and prepared the field for the operations of heaven and for the labours of the husbandman; for the latter, so that he might sow it at a seasonable time, and for the other, that the deep bosom of the earth might receive its bounty displayed in gentle showers, and in consequence might treasure up rich nutriment for the seed and dispense it to it gradually until it should swell into the full ear and bring its annual fruit to perfection.

And, after the corn is brought to perfection, then again the ox is necessary for another service, namely, for the purification of the sheaves, and the separation of the chaff from the genuine useful grain.

(146) And since I have explained this distinct and humane command respecting the oxen which tread out the corn, I will now proceed to speak of that one which relates to the animals which plough, which is also of the same family; for the lawgiver also forbids the husbandman to yoke the ox and the ass together in the same plough for ploughing, [24] considering in this not only the difference of nature between the two animals, because the one is clean, while the ass is one of the unclean beasts, and it is not becoming to bring together animals which are so utterly alienated, but also because they are unequal in point of strength, he takes care of that which is the weaker, in order that it may not be oppressed and worn out by the greater power of the other. And, indeed, the ass, which is the weaker animal, is driven outside of the sacred precincts; but the more vigorous beast, namely, the ox, is offered up as a victim in the most perfect sacrifices. (147) But, nevertheless, the lawgiver neither neglected the safety of the unclean animals, nor did he permit those which were clean to use their strength in disregard of justice, crying out and declaring loudly in express words, if one may say so, to those persons who have ears in their soul, not to injure any one of a different nation, unless they have some

---

[22] Exodus 23:19.

[23] Deuteronomy 25:4.
[24] Deuteronomy 22:10.

grounds for bringing accusations against them beyond the fact of their being of another nation, which is not ground of blame; for those things which are not wickedness, and which do not proceed from wickedness, are free from all reproach.

XXVIII. (148) And, being full of mercy in every part, he again displays it in an abundant and exceeding degree, crossing over from the beings endowed with reason to the brute beasts, and from the brute beasts to plants, concerning which we must now proceed immediately to speak, since we have spoken sufficiently already about men, and about all animals which are endowed with life.

(149) He has forbidden in express words[25] to cut down for timber any trees which bear eatable fruit, and to ravage a plain bearing corn before its proper season for the purpose of destroying it, and, in short, to destroy any kind of crop in any manner, in order that the race of mankind may enjoy an abundance of nourishment without any limitation, and may have a sufficiency not only of necessary food, but also of such as conduce to making life luxurious. For the crop of wheat and corn is necessary, as being set apart for the actual daily food of man; but the innumerable varieties of the fruits which grow on trees are given to make his life luxurious; and very often, in times of scarcity, even these become a secondary food.

XXIX. (150) And, going beyond all other lawgivers in humanity, he does not allow his people even to ravage the country of their enemies, but he commands them to abstain from cutting down the trees, thinking it unjust that the anger which is excited against men should wreak itself on things which are innocent of all evil. (151) And, besides this, by this commandment he points out that it is right not to look only at the present, but also by the acuteness of the reasoning powers to survey the future afar off as from a watch-tower, since nothing remains long in the same condition, but everything is subject to alternations and variations; so that it is natural that those who have for a while been enemies, when they have sent heralds and made overtures towards reconciliation, should again become friends in the bonds of peace. (152) And it would be a wicked thing to deprive one's friends of necessary food, who have probably stored up nothing which can be of use to them because of the uncertainty of the future.

For this was an admirable saying[26] which was in vogue among the ancients, that one must enter into friendships without at the same time being blind to the possibility that it may be turned into enmity, and that one must repel an enemy as if he may hereafter become a friend, in order that each man might, through this consideration, lay up something in his own soul which might conduce to his safety, and might not, being laid completely bare and defenceless, in word and in deed repent of his too great facility of temper, blaming himself when there is no need of any such thing.

(153) And cities also should act upon this principle, providing in peace the things which will be necessary in time of war, and in time of war the things which will be desirable in peace, and abstaining from placing such implicit, boundless confidence in their allies, as if they could never possibly change so as to become their enemies; nor, on the other hand, exhibiting such distance towards their enemies as if they would never be able to bring them over to reconciliation and peace. (154) Moreover, if nothing is to be done in favour of one's enemies because of any hope of reconciliation, still, at all events, no plant is an enemy, but all plants are at peace with and useful to one. And those which produce eatable fruit are exceedingly necessary, as their fruit is either actual food or equivalent to food. And why should men be excited to enmity against things which are not hostile, cutting them down, or burning them, or tearing them up by the roots; things which nature herself has brought to perfection by streams of water, and by the admirable temperature of the summer, so that they contribute annual revenues to mankind as subjects to their kings?

(155) Moses, therefore, as a good superintendant, exerted all care to implant, not only in animals, but also in plants, invincible strength and vigour, and especially in such as produce eatable fruit, since they are worthy of more care, and are not of equal size and vigour with the wild trees of the forest, since they stand in need of the skill of the husbandman to endow them with greater vigour; (156) for he commands the young plants to be nursed carefully for the space of three years, while the husbandman prunes away the superfluous off-shoots, in order that the trees may not be weighed down and exhausted by them, in which case the fruit borne by them would become small and weak through insufficiency of nourishment, and he must also dig round it and clear the ground, in order that no injurious plant may grow near it,

---

[25] Deuteronomy 20:19.
[26] This idea is deservedly reprobated by Cicero, De Amic. 16. "We shall be able to arrive at another definition of true friendship when we have first mentioned what Scipio was accustomed to blame with great indignation. He used to say that no sentence more hostile to friendship, or more at variance with every correct notion of it, could possibly be found, than that one of the man who said that it became a man always to form a friendship with the idea that he might some day or other hate his friend. And he said that he could never be induced to believe that this, as some people fancied, had been said by Bias, who was accounted one of the seven wise men, but he looked upon it as the saying of some profligate or ambitious man, or of some one who referred everything to the preservation of his own powers."

so as to hinder its growth. And he does not allow the fruit to be gathered out of season at any one's pleasure, not only because, if that were done, it would be imperfect and produced from imperfect trees (for so also animals which are not perfect themselves cannot produce a perfect offspring), but also because the young plants themselves would be injured, and would in a manner be bowed down and kept as creepers on the earth, by being prevented from shooting up into straight and stout trunks.

(157) Accordingly, many husbandmen at the commencement of the spring watch their young trees, in order at once to destroy whatever fruit they show before it gets to any growth or comes to any size, from fear lest, if it be suffered to remain on, it may bring weakness to the parent tree. For it might happen, if some one did not take care beforehand, when the tree ought to bring fruit to perfection, that it will either bear none at all, or not be able to ripen any, being completely weakened by having been allowed to satiate itself with bearing before its proper time, just as old vine-stems when weighed down, are exhausted both in root and trunk.

(158) But after three years, when the roots have got some depth and have taken a firmer hold of the soil, and when the trunk, being supported as it were on a firm unbending foundation, brows up with vigour, it is then in the fourth year able to bear fruit in perfection and in proper quantity: (159) and in the fourth year he permits the fruit to be gathered, not for the enjoyment and use of man, but that the whole crop may be dedicated to God as the first-fruits, partly as a thank-offering for mercies already received, and partly from hope of good crops for the future, and of a revenue to be derived from the tree hereafter.

(160) You see, therefore, what great humanity and compassion our lawgiver displays, and how he diffuses his kindness over every species of man, even if they are foreigners, or even enemies; and secondly, how he extends it also to brute beasts, even though they be not clean, and in fact to every thing, to sown crops, and to trees. For the man who has learnt the principles of humanity with respect to those natures which are devoid of sense, is never likely to err with respect to those which are endowed with life; and he who never attempts to act with severity towards creatures which have only life, is taught a long way off to take great care of those which are also blessed with reason.

XXX. (161) Having, then, by such precepts as these, civilised and made gentle the minds of those who live under the constitution of his laws, he has separated them from haughtiness and arrogance, those most grievous and burdensome of evils, which men in general cling to as the greatest of goods, and especially when riches, or glory, or authority supply them with unlimited abundance; (162) for arrogance is very often engendered in men of no reputation or character, just as any other of the passions, or diseases, or infirmities of the soul, but it does not receive any growth or increase in such men, but, like fire, it is extinguished for want of fuel. But in great men it is very conspicuous, since they, as I said before, have food for this evil in riches, and glory, and authority, with which the men are entirely filled, and like those who have drunk great quantities of strong wine become intoxicated, and in their drunkenness they attack slaves and free men all alike, and at times even whole cities; for satiety produces insolence, as the proverb of the ancients tells us.[27] (163) On which account Moses, when declaring the will of God, enjoins men to abstain from every description of offence, and, above all, from arrogance. And afterwards he reminds them of the things which are wont to kindle passion, such as abundance of immoderate eating, and extravagant wealth in houses, and lands, and cattle; for when they possess these things, they presently become unable to restrain themselves, being distended with pride and puffed up; and the only hope that remains of such men being cured, consists in preventing them from forgetting God.

(164) For as when the sun arises, the darkness disappears and all places are filled with light, so in the same manner when God, that sun appreciable only by the intellect, arises and illuminates the soul, the whole darkness of vices and passions is dissipated, and the pure and lovely appearance of bright and radiant virtue is displayed to the world.

XXXI. (165) And still more does he seek to check and eradicate haughtiness, choosing to collect together the causes on account of which he enjoins men to erect in their souls an undying recollection of God; "For God," says Moses, "gives strength to get power,"[28] speaking in this very instructively; for the man who has been accurately and thoroughly taught that he has received an endowment of great strength and vigour from God, will take into consideration the weakness which belonged to him before he received this great gift, and will consequently repel all haughty, and arrogant, and overbearing thoughts, and will give thanks to him who has been the cause of this change for the better. And arrogance is inconsistent with a grateful soul, as on the contrary ingratitude is nearly akin to haughtiness.

(166) Are your affairs prosperous and flourishing? then, receiving and increasing that strength of body which perhaps you did not expect, get power; and what is meant by this expression must

---

[27]The expression occurs in Theognis, 16.7.
[28]Deuteronomy 8:18.

be accurately investigated by those who do not very clearly see what is implied in it.

Many persons endeavour to bring upon others, what is exactly contrary to the benefits which they have themselves received; for either, having themselves become rich, they prepare poverty for others, or having arrived at a high degree of honour and reputation, they become to others the causes of dishonour and infamy: (167) but it is right rather that the wise and prudent man should, to the best of his power, endeavour to bring his neighbours also into the same condition; and that the temperate man should seek to make others temperate, the brave man to make others courageous, the righteous man to make others just, and in short every good man ought to try to make everyone else good; for these qualities are, as it seems, powers, which the virtuous man will cling to as his own; but infirmity and weakness, on the contrary, are inconsistent with a virtuous character.

(168) And in another place also the lawgiver gives this precept, which is most becoming and suitable to a rational nature, that men should imitate God to the best of their power, omitting nothing which can possibly contribute to such a similarity as the case admits of.

XXXII. Since then you have received strength from a being who is more powerful than you, give others a share of that strength, distributing among them the benefits which you have received yourself, in order that you may imitate God by bestowing gifts like his; (169) for all the gifts of the supreme Ruler are of common advantage to all men; and he gives them to some individuals, not in order that they when they have received them may hide them out of sight, or employ them to the injury of others, but in order that they may bring them into the common stock, and invite all those whom they can find to use and enjoy them with them.

(170) We say therefore, that the men possessed of great riches, and of high renown, and of great strength of body, and of great learning, ought to endeavour to make everyone with whom they meet, rich, and strong, and learned, and in short good, and that they ought not to prefer envy and jealousy to virtue, so as to oppose those who might otherwise attain to prosperity; (171) and the law has very beautifully brought those who are inflated by arrogance, and are altogether possessed by incurable pride, not before the tribunal of men, but before the judgment seat of God, to which alone it has assigned the office of judging them; for it says, "Whosoever attempts to do anything in a haughty arrogant manner, makes God angry." [29]

(172) Why so, because in the first place, haughty

arrogance is a vice of the soul; but the soul is invisible to any one but God.

And anyone who punishes, if he does so blindly, is blameable, as ignorance is his accuser: but if he does so with his eyes open, he is to be praised as doing everything with knowledge; and secondly, because every haughty arrogant man is full of vain groundless pride, looks upon himself as neither man nor demigod, but rather as an actual deity, as Pindar says, [30] thinking himself worthy to overstep all the boundaries of human nature.

(173) And as the soul of such a man is blameable, so also is his body in all its positions and motions, for he walks on tip-toes, and lifts his head on high, strutting and giving himself airs, and he is elated and puffed up beyond his nature, and though he does see yet it is only with distorted optics, and though he hears he hears amiss; and he treats his servants as though they were cattle, and free men as though they were his slaves, and his kinsmen as strangers, and his friends as flatterers, and citizens as foreigners; (174) and he looks upon himself as the most wealthy, the most distinguished, the most beautiful, the strongest, the wisest, the most prudent, the most righteous, the most rational, and the most learned of all men; and then he looks upon all the rest of mankind as poor, of no reputation, dishonoured, foolish, unjust, ignorant, mere dregs of mankind, entitled to no consideration.

Very naturally then such a man will be likely to meet, as the interpreter of the will of God tells us, with God himself as his adversary and chastiser.

ON REPENTANCE

XXXIII. (175) The most holy Moses, being a lover of virtue, and of honour, and, above all things, of the human race, expects all men everywhere to show themselves admirers of piety and of justice, proposing to them, as to conquerors, great rewards if they repent, namely, a participation in the best of all constitutions, and an enjoyment of all things, whether great or small, which are to be found in it.

(176) Now those blessings which are of the greatest importance in the body are good health, without disease; and in a matter of navigation, a successful voyage, without danger; and in the soul, an undying recollection of all things worthy to be remembered.

And the blessings of the second class are those which consist of re-establishment, such as a recovery from diseases; a long wished for escape from and safety after great dangers encountered in a

---

[29] Numbers 15:30.

[30] Pindar says nothing of the sort. The passage which Philo appears to allude to is the beginning of the second Olympic Ode which Horace has translated, Od. I. 12.1.

voyage, and a recollection which ensues after forgetfulness; the brother and closest relation of which is repentance, which is not indeed ranked in the first and highest class of blessings, but which has the principal in the class next to the first. (177) For absolutely never to do anything wrong at all is a peculiar attribute of God, and perhaps one may also say of a God-like man. But when one has erred, then to change so as to adopt a blameless course of life for the future is the part of a wise man, and of one who is not altogether ignorant of what is expedient.

(178) On which account he calls to him all persons of such a disposition as this, and initiates them in his laws, holding out to them admonitions full of reconciliation and friendship, which exhort men to practise sincerity and to reject pride, and to cling to truth and simplicity, those most necessary virtues which, above all others, contribute to happiness; forsaking all the fabulous inventions of foolish men, which their parents, and nurses, and instructors, and innumerable other persons with whom they have been associated, have from their earliest infancy impressed upon their tender souls, implanting in them inextricable errors concerning the knowledge of the most excellent of all things.

(179) And what can this best of all things be except God? whose honours those men have attributed to beings which are not gods, honouring them beyond all reason and moderation, and, like empty minded people that they are, wholly forgetting him. All those men therefore who, although they did not originally choose to honour the Creator and Father of the universe, have yet changed and done so afterwards, having learnt to prefer to honour a single monarch rather than a number of rulers, we must look upon as our friends and kinsmen, since they display that greatest of all bonds with which to cement friendship and kindred, namely, a pious and God-loving disposition, and we ought to sympathise in joy with and to congratulate them, since even if they were blind previously they have now received their sight, beholding the most brilliant of all lights instead of the most profound darkness.

XXXIV. (180) We have now then described the first and most important of the considerations which belong to repentance. And let a man repent, not only of the errors by which he was for a long time deceived, when he honoured the creature in preference to that uncreated being who was himself the Creator of all things, but also in respect of the other necessary and ordinary pursuits and affairs of life, forsaking as it were that very worst of all evil constitutions, the sovereignty of the mob, and adopting that best of all constitutions, a well-ordered democracy; that is to say, crossing over from ignorance to a knowledge of those things to be ignorant of which is shameful; from folly to wisdom, from intemperance to temperance, from

injustice to righteousness, from cowardice to confident courage. (181) For it is a very excellent and expedient thing to go over to virtue without ever looking back again, forsaking that treacherous mistress, vice.

And at the same time it is necessary that, as in the sun shadow follows the body, so also a participation in all other virtues must inevitably follow the giving due honour to the living God; (182) for those who come over to this worship become at once prudent, and temperate, and modest, and gentle, and merciful, and humane, and venerable, and just, and magnanimous, and lovers of truth, and superior to all considerations of money or pleasure; just as, on the contrary, one may see that those who forsake the holy laws of God are intemperate, shameless, unjust, disreputable, weak-minded, quarrelsome, companions of falsehood and perjury, willing to sell their liberty for luxurious eating, for strong wine, for sweetmeats, and for beauty, for pleasures of the belly and of the parts below the belly; the miserable end of all which enjoyment is ruin to both body and soul.

(183) Moreover, Moses delivers to us very beautiful exhortations to repentance, by which he teaches us to alter our way of life, changing from an irregular and disorderly course into a better line of conduct; for he says that this task is not one of any excessive difficulty, nor one removed far out of our reach, being neither above us in the air nor on the extreme borders of the sea, so that we are unable to take hold of it; but it is near us, abiding, in fact, in three portions of us, namely, in our mouths, and our hearts, and our hands;[31] by symbols, that is to say, in our words, and counsels, and actions; for the mouth is the symbol of speech, and the heart of counsels, and the hands of actions, and in these happiness consists. (184) For when such as the words are, such also is the mind; and when such as the counsels are, such likewise are the actions; then life is praiseworthy and perfect. But when these things are all at variance with one another life is imperfect and blameable, unless some one who is at the same time a lover of God and beloved by God takes it in hand and produces this harmony.

For which reason this oracular declaration was given with great propriety, and in perfect accordance with what has been said above,[32] "Thou hast this day chosen the Lord to be thy God, and the Lord has this day chosen thee to be his people." (185) It is a very beautiful exchange and recompense for this choice on the part of man thus displaying anxiety to serve God, when God thus without any delay takes the suppliant to himself as his own, and goes forth to meet the intentions of the

---

[31] Deuteronomy 30:11.
[32] Leviticus 26:12.

man who, in a genuine and sincere spirit of piety and truth, hastens to do him service.

But the true servant and suppliant of God, even if by himself he be reckoned and classed as a man, still in power, as has been said in another place, is the whole people, inasmuch as he is equal in value to a whole people. And this is naturally the case in other matters also; (186) for, as in a ship, the pilot is of as much importance as all the rest of the crew put together; and, as in an army, the general is of as much value as the whole of the army, since, if he is slain, the whole army is defeated as much as if it had been slain to a man and utterly destroyed; so in the same manner the wise man is, as to importance, on a par with the whole nation, being defended by that indestructible impregnable fortress, piety towards God.[33]

ON NOBILITY

XXXV. (187) We ought to rebuke in no measured language those who celebrate nobility of birth as the greatest of all blessings, and the cause also of great blessings, if in the first place they think those men nobly born who are sprung from persons who were rich and glorious in the days of old, when those very ancestors themselves, from whom they boast to be descended, were not made happy by their unlimited abundance; since, in truth, that which is really good does not naturally or necessarily lodge in any external thing, nor in any of the things which belong to the body, and indeed I may even say not in every part of the soul, but only in the dominant and most important portion of it.

(188) For when God determined to establish this in us out of his own exceeding mercy and love for the human race, he would not find any temple upon earth more beautiful or more suited for its abode than reason: for the mind makes, as it were, an image of the good and consecrates it within itself, and if any persons disbelieve in it of those who have either never tasted wisdom at all, or else have done so only with the edges of their lips (for silver and gold, and honours, and offices, and vigour and beauty of body, resemble those men who are appointed to situations of authority and power, in order to serve virtue as if she were their queen), never having obtained a sight of the most brilliant of all lights.

(189) Since, then, nobility of mind, perfectly purified by complete purifications, is the proper inheritance, we ought to call those men alone noble who are temperate and just, even though they may be of the class of domestic slaves, or may have

been bought with money. But to those persons who, being sprung from virtuous parents, do themselves turn out wicked, the region of nobleness is wholly inaccessible; (190) for every bad man is destitute of a house, and destitute of a city, having been driven from his proper country, namely, virtue; which is the real, genuine country of all wise men: and ignobleness does of necessity attach itself to such a man, even though he be descended from grandfathers and great grandfathers whose lives were wholly irreproachable, since he studies to alienate himself from them and detaches himself from and removes to the greatest possible distance from real nobility in all his words and actions. (191) But moreover, besides that wicked men cannot possibly be noble, I also see that they are all of them irreconcileable enemies to nobility, inasmuch as they have destroyed the reputation which accrued to them from their ancestors, and have dimmed and extinguished all the brilliancy which did exist in their race.

XXXVI. (192) And it is for this reason, as it appears to me, that some most affectionate fathers disown and disinherit their sons, cutting them off from their homes and from their kindred, when the wickedness which is displayed in them has over-mastered the exceeding and all-pervading love which is implanted by nature in parents. (193) And the truth of this assertion of mine is easy to be seen from other circumstances also. What good could it ever be to any man that his ancestors had been endowed with ever such great acuteness of vision if he himself were deprived of his eyes? How could that fact assist him to see? Or again, supposing a person to have an impediment in his speech, how would his utterance be assisted by the fact that his parents or his grandfathers had had fine voices? And how will a man who has been emaciated and exhausted by a long and wasting disease, be assisted to recover his former strength, if the original founders of his race are, on account of their strength as athletes, enrolled among the Olympic conquerors, or the victors at any other periodical games? For their bodily infirmities will equally remain in the same condition as before, not receiving any amelioration from the successes of their relations.

(194) In the same manner, just parents are of no advantage to unjust men, nor temperate parents to intemperate children, nor, in short, are ancestors of any kind of excellence of any advantage to wicked descendants; for even the laws themselves are of no advantage to those who transgress them, as they are meant to punish them, and what is it that we ought to look upon as unwritten laws, except the lives of those persons who have imitated virtue? (195) On which account, I imagine, that nobility herself, if God were to invest her with the form and organs of a man, would stand before those obstinate and unworthy descendants

---

[33] Sections 187–227 appear out of sequence in Yonge's edition under a separate treatise title: *On Nobility*. The publisher has elected to include them here to conform to the Cohn-Wendland (Loeb) sequence and numbering.

and speak thus: "Relationship is not measured by blood alone, where truth is the judge, but by a similarity of actions, and by a careful imitation of the conduct of your ancestors. But you have pursued an opposite line of conduct, thinking hateful such actions as are dear to me, and loving such deeds as are hateful to me; for in my eyes modesty, and truth, and moderation, and a due government of the passions, and simplicity, and innocence, are honourable, but in your opinion they are dishonourable; and to me all shameless behaviour is hateful, and all falsehood, and all immoderate indulgence of the passions, and all pride, and all wickedness. But you look upon these things as near and dear to you. (196) Why, then, do you, when by your actions you show all possible eagerness to alienate yourselves from them, sheltering yourselves under a plausible name, hypocritically pretend in words to a relationship? For I cannot endure seductive insinuations falsely put on, or any deceit; because it is easy for any persons to find out specious arguments, but it is not easy to change an evil disposition into a good one.

(197) "And I, looking therefore at these facts, both now consider and shall always think those persons who have kindled sparks of enmity my enemies, and I shall look upon them with more suspicion than upon those who have been reproached openly for want of nobility; for they, indeed, have this to allege in their defence, that they have no connection at all with excellence. But you are justly liable to punishment who act thus after having been born of noble houses, and being fond of making your boast of your noble descent, and of looking upon it as your glory; for, though archetypal models of virtue have been established in close connection with, and in a manner implanted in you, you have determined to give no good impression of them yourselves. (198) But that nobility is placed only in the acquisition of virtue, and that you ought to imagine that he who has that is the only man really noble, and not the man who is born of noble and virtuous parents, is plain from many circumstances."

XXXVII. (199) Again, who is there who would deny that those men who were born of him who was made out of the earth were noble themselves, and the founders of noble families? persons who have received a birth more excellent than that of any succeeding generation, in being sprung from the first wedded pair, from the first man and woman, who then for the first time came together for the propagation of offspring resembling themselves. But, nevertheless, when there were two persons so born, the elder of them endured to slay the younger;[34] and, having committed the great and most accursed crime of fratricide, he first defiled the ground with human blood. (200) Now, what good did the nobility of his birth do to a man who had displayed this want of nobleness in his soul? which God, who surveys all human things and actions, detested when he saw it; and, casting it forth, affixed a punishment to it, not slaying him at once, so that he should arrive at an immediate insensibility to misfortunes, but suspending over him ten thousand deaths in his external senses, by means of incessant griefs and fears, so as to inflict upon him the sense of the most grievous calamities.

(201) Now there was, in the subsequent generations, a man very greatly approved of, a most holy man, whose piety the sacred historian, who has written the books called the law, has thought worthy of being recorded in the sacred volumes. Accordingly, in the great deluge when all the cities of the world were utterly destroyed (for even the highest mountains were overwhelmed by the increase and continual rising of the rapid flood), he alone was saved, with all his kindred, having received such a reward for his virtue that it is not possible to imagine a greater one.[35]

(202) This man, again, had three sons; and, though they had had their share in the blessing thus bestowed upon their father, one of them dared to turn his father, the cause of his safety, into ridicule, laughing at him, and mocking and reviling him, because of an error which he committed unintentionally, and displaying to those who did not see it what he ought to have, concealed, so as to bring disgrace on him who had begotten him.[36] Therefore, having now fallen from his brilliant nobility of birth and having become accursed, and having also become the beginning of misery to all his posterity, he suffered all those evils which it was fitting for a man to suffer who had disregarded all the honour due to his parents.

(203) But why should I speak of these men, and pass over the first man who was created out of the earth? who, in respect of the nobleness of his birth can be compared to no mortal whatever, inasmuch as he was fashioned by the hand of God, and invested with a form in the likeness of a human body by the very perfection of all plastic art. And he was also thought worthy of a soul, which was derived from no being who had as yet come into existence by being created, but God breathed into him as much of his own power as mortal nature was capable of receiving. Was it not, then a perfect excess of all nobleness, which could not possibly come into comparison with any other which is ever spoken of as favours? (204) for all persons who lay claim to that kind of eminence rest their claims on the nobility of their ancestors.

---

[34] Genesis 4:1.

[35] Genesis 7:1.
[36] Genesis 9:22.

But even those men who have been their ancestors were only animals, subject to disease and to corruption, and their prosperity was, for the most part, very unstable. But the father of this man was not mortal at all, and the sole author of his being was God. And he, being in a manner his image and likeness according to the dominant mind in the soul, (205) though it was his duty to preserve that image free from all spot of blemish, following and imitating as far as was in his power the virtues of him who had created him, since the two opposite qualities of good and evil (what is honourable and what is disgraceful, what is true and what is false) were set before him for his choice and avoidance, deliberately chose what was false, and disgraceful, and evil, and despised what was good, and honourable, and true; for which conduct he was very fairly condemned to change an immortal for a mortal existence, being deprived of blessedness and happiness, and therefore he naturally was changed so as to descend into a laborious and miserable life.[37]

XXXVIII. (206) But, however, let these men be set down as common rules and limits for all men, in order to prevent them from priding themselves on their noble birth, and so departing from and losing the rewards of excellence. But there are also other especial rules given to the Jews besides the common ones which are applicable to all mankind; for they are derived from the original founders of the nation, to whom the virtues of their ancestors were absolutely of no benefit at all, inasmuch as they were detected in blameable and guilty actions, and were convicted, if not by any other human being, at all events by their own consciences, which is the sole tribunal in the world which is never led away by any artifices of speech.

(207) The first man of them had a numerous family, inasmuch as he had children by three wives, not forming these connections for the sake of pleasure, but because of his hope of multiplying his race. But, of all his children, one alone was appointed to be the inheritor of his father's possessions; and all the rest, being disappointed of their reasonable hopes, and having failed to obtain any portion whatever of their father's wealth, departed to live in different countries, having been completely alienated from that celebrated nobility of birth.

(208) Again, to the one who was approved of as the heir, there were born two sons, twins, resembling one another in no particular except in the hands, and even in them only by some especial providence of God, inasmuch as they were alike neither in their bodies nor in their minds, for the younger one was obedient to both his parents, and was really amiable and pleasing, so that he obtained the praises even of God; while the elder was disobedient, being intemperate in respect of the pleasures of the belly and of the parts beneath the belly, by a regard for which he was induced even to part with his birth-right, as far as he himself was concerned, though he repented immediately afterwards of the conditions on which he had forfeited it, and sought to slay his brother, and, in fact, to do everything imaginable by which he could be likely to pain his parents; (209) therefore they, in the first place, offered up prayers for his brother to the supreme God, who accepted them, and who did not choose to leave any one of them unaccomplished; while to the others they gave, out of compassion, a subordinate rank, appointing that he should serve his brother, thinking, as indeed is the truth, that the fact of not being his own master, is good for a wicked man.

(210) And if the elder brother had cheerfully submitted to the servitude, he would have been thought worthy of a secondary reward, as having come off second in a contest of virtue; but as the case stands, having behaved in a self-willed manner, and having refused to submit to servitude, he became the cause of great reproach, both to himself and to his descendants, so that his miserable life has been indelibly recorded for a most manifest proof that nobility of birth is of no service whatever to those who do not deserve to have it.

XXXIX. (211) These men therefore are both of that class which is open to reproach; men whom, as they showed themselves wicked men, though descended from virtuous fathers, the virtues of their fathers failed to profit in the least, while the vices which existed in their souls did them infinite mischief; and I can also speak of others, who, on the contrary, ranged themselves in a better class, after having been born in a worse, since their forefathers were guilty, while their own life was to be admired and was full of praise and virtue.

(212) The most ancient person of the Jewish nation was a Chaldaean by birth, born of a father who was very skilful in astronomy, and famous among those men who pass their lives in the study of mathematics, who look upon the stars as gods, and worship the whole heaven and the whole world; thinking, that from them do all good and all evil proceed, to every individual among men; as they do not conceive that there is any cause whatever, except such as are included among the objects of the outward senses. (213) Now what can be more horrible than this? What can more clearly show the innate ignobleness of the soul, which, by consequence of its knowledge of the generality of things, of secondary causes, and of things created, proceeds onwards to ignorance of the one most ancient uncreated Being, the Creator of the universe, and who is most excellent on this account, and for many other reasons also, which the human

---

[37]Genesis 3:19.

reason is unable to comprehend by reason of their magnitude?

(214) But this man, having formed a proper conception of this in his mind, and being under the influence of inspiration, left his country, and his family, and his father's house, well knowing that, if he remained among them, the deceitful fancies of the polytheistic doctrine abiding there likewise, must render his mind incapable of arriving at the proper discovery of the true God, who is the only everlasting God and the Father of all other things, whether appreciable only by the intellect or perceptible by the outward senses; while, on the other hand, he saw, that if he rose up and quitted his native land, deceit would also depart from his mind. changing his false opinions into true belief.

(215) At the same time, also, the divine oracles of God which were imparted to him excited still further that desire which longed to attain to a knowledge of the living God, by which he was guided, and thus went forth with most unhesitating earnestness to the investigation of the one God. And he never desisted from this investigation till he arrived at a more distinct perception, not indeed of his essence, for that is impossible, but of his existence, and of his over-ruling providence as far as it can be allowed to man to attain to such; (216) for which reason he is the first person who is said to have believed in God,[38] since he was the first who had an unswerving and firm comprehension of him, apprehending that there is one supreme cause, and that he it is which governs the world by his providence, and all the things that are therein. And having attained to a most firm comprehension of the virtues, he acquired at the same time all the other virtues and excellencies also, so that he was looked upon as a king by those who received him,[39] not indeed in respect of his appointments, for he was only a private individual, but in his magnanimity and greatness of soul, inasmuch as he was of a royal spirit.

(217) For, indeed, his servants at all times steadfastly observed him, as subjects observe a ruler, looking with admiration at the universal greatness of his nature and disposition, which was more perfect than is customary to meet with in a man; for he did not use the same conversation as ordinary men, but, like one inspired, spoke in general in more dignified language.

Whenever, therefore, he was possessed by the Holy Spirit he at once changed everything for the better, his eyes and his complexion, and his size and his appearance while standing, and his motions, and his voice; the Holy Spirit, which, being breathed into him from above, took up its lodging in his soul, clothing his body with extraordinary beauty, and investing his words with persuasiveness at the same time that it endowed his hearers with understanding.

(218) Would not any one, then, be quite correct to say that this man who thus left his native land, who thus forsook all his relations and all his friends, was the most nobly related of all men, as aiming at making himself a kinsman of God, and labouring by every means in his power to become his disciple and friend? And that he was deservedly ranked in the very highest class among the prophets, because he trusted in no created being in preference to the uncreated God, the Father of all? And being honoured as king, as I have said before, by those who received him among them, not as having obtained his authority by warlike arms, or by armed hosts, as some persons have done, but having received his appointment from the all-righteous God, who honours the lovers of piety with independent authority, to the great advantage of all who are associated with them.

(219) This man is the standard of nobleness to all who come to settle in a foreign land, leaving that ignobleness which attaches to them from foreign laws and unbecoming customs, which give honours, such as are due only to God, to stocks, and to stones, and, in short, to all kinds of inanimate things; and who have thus come over to a constitution really full of vitality and life, the president and governor of which is truth.

XL. (220) This nobleness has been an object of desire not only to God-loving men, but likewise to women, who have discarded the ignorance in which they have been bred up, which taught them to honour, as deities, creatures made with hands, and have learnt instead that knowledge of there being only one supreme Ruler of the universe, by whom the whole world is governed and regulated; (221) for Tamar was a woman from Syria Palestina, who had been bred up in her own native city, which was devoted to the worship of many gods, being full of statues, and images, and, in short, of idols of every kind and description. But when she, emerging, as it were, out of profound darkness, was able to see a slight beam of truth, she then, at the risk of her life, exerted all her energies to arrive at piety, caring little for life if she could not live virtuously; and living virtuously was exactly identical with living for the service of and in constant supplication to the one true God.

(222) And yet she, having married two wicked brothers in turn, one after the other, first of all the one who was the husband of her virginity, and lastly him who succeeded to her by the law which enjoined such a marriage, in the case of the first husband not having left any family, but nevertheless, having preserved her own life free from all stain, was able to attain to that fair reputation which falls to the lot of the good, and to be the beginning of nobleness to all those who came after her.

---

[38] Genesis 15:6.
[39] Genesis 23:6.

But even though she was a foreigner still she was nevertheless a freeborn woman, and born also of freeborn parents of no insignificant importance; (223) but her handmaidens were born of parents who lived on the other side of the Euphrates on the extremities of the country of Babylon, such as were given as part of their dowry to maidens of high rank when they were married, but still were often thought worthy to be taken to the bed of a wise man; and so they first of all were raised from the title of concubines to the name and dignity of wives, and in a short time, I may almost say, instead of being looked upon as handmaidens they were raised to an equality in point of dignity and consideration with their mistresses, and, which is the most extraordinary circumstance of all, were even invited by their mistresses to this position and dignity.

For envy does not dwell in the souls of the wise, and whenever that is not present they all have all things in common.

(224) And the illegitimate sons borne by those handmaidens differed in no respect from the legitimate children of the real wives, not only in the eyes of the father who begot them, for it is not at all surprising if he who was the father of them all displayed an equal degree of good-will to them all, since they were all equally his children; but they also were equally esteemed by their stepmothers. For they, laying aside all that dislike which women so commonly feel towards their stepsons, changed it into an unceasing affection with which they united themselves to them. (225) And the stepsons, showing a reciprocal good will to them, honoured their stepmothers as if they had been their natural mothers. And their brothers, being separated from them only by the mixture in their blood, nevertheless did not think them worthy of only a half degree of affection, but even increased their feelings so that they entertained a twofold degree of love for them, being equally beloved by them in return; and thus more than filled up what might else have appeared likely to be deficient, showing an eagerness to exhibit the same harmony and union of disposition with them that they did with their brethren by both parents.

XLI. (226) We must not, therefore, give in to those persons who seek to creep stealthily into the possession of a property belonging to others, namely, nobility of birth, as though it were of right their own, and who, with the exception of those whom I have mentioned, might justly be looked upon as enemies not only of the race of the Jews but of all the human race in every quarter. Of the one because they give a truce to those of the same nation, allowing them to despise sound and stable virtue, through trusting implicitly in the virtue of their ancestors; and of the others because, even if they could attain to the highest and most absolute perfection of all excellence, they would still derive no advantage themselves, because of their not having irreproachable fathers and grandfathers.

(227) Than which I do not know that there can possibly be a more mischievous doctrine, if there is no avenging punishment to follow those who being descended of virtuous parents have made themselves, and if on the contrary no honour is to be assigned to those who have become good though born of wicked parents, though the law judges each man by himself, and does not praise or blame any one with reference to the virtues or vices of his ancestors.

ON REWARDS AND PUNISHMENTS
(De Praemiis et Poenis)

I. (1) We find, then, that in the sacred oracles delivered by the prophet Moses, there are three separate characters; for a portion of them relates to the creation of the world, a portion is historical, and the third portion is legislative. Now the creation of the world is related throughout with exceeding beauty and in a manner admirably suited to the dignity of God, taking its beginning in the account of the creation of the heaven, and ending with that of the formation of man; the first of which things is the most perfect of all imperishable things, and the other of all corruptible and perishable things. And the Creator, connecting together immortal and mortal things at the creation, made the world, making what he had already created the dominant parts, and what he was about to create the subject parts.

(2) The historical part is a record of the lives of different wicked and virtuous men, and of the rewards, and honours, and punishments set apart for each class in each generation.

The legislative part is sub-divided into two sections, one of which has a more general object proposed to it, laying down accordingly a few general comprehensive laws; the other part consists of special and particular ordinances. And the general heads of these special ordinances are ten, which are said not to have been delivered to the people by an interpreter, but to have been fashioned in the lofty region of the air, and to have been connected by a rational distinctness and utterance. While the others, I mean the particular and minute laws, were delivered by the prophet.

(3) And as, in my former treatises, I have dwelt upon each of these to as great an extent as the time permitted me, and as I have also enlarged upon all the different virtues which the lawgiver has assigned to peace and war, I will now proceed in regular order to mention the rewards which have been proposed for virtuous men, and the punishments threatened to the wicked; (4) for, after he had trained all those who are living under his constitution and laws by gentle precepts, and admonitions, and expectations, and subsequently by more severe threats and warning, he summoned them all to hear the promulgation of the law; and they all, coming as to a sacred meeting, displayed their own eager choice and approbation of those laws in such a way as to give a most convincing proof of their truth. (5) And then some of them were found to be diligent labourers in the practice of virtue, not disappointing the good hopes which were formed of them, nor dishonouring the laws which were their instructors. Others were found to be unmanly, and effeminate, and cowardly, out of the innate weakness and imbecility of their souls, who, fainting before any real danger or trouble came upon them, disgraced themselves and became the ridicule of the spectators. (6) On which account the one class received decisions in their favour, and proclamations in their honour, and all such rewards as are usually given to conquerors; while the others departed not only without the garlands of victory, but even after having sustained a most disgraceful defeat, more grievous than any which befalls a man in the gymnastic contests. For there the bodies, indeed, of the athletes are overthrown, but so that they can be easily raised again; but in this case it is the whole life which falls, which, when once it is overthrown, it is scarcely possible to raise again.

(7) And our lawgiver announces a very suitable arrangement and appointment of privileges and honours for the one; and, on the contrary, of punishments for the others, as affecting individuals, and houses, and cities, and countries, and nations, and vast regions of the earth.

II. And, first of all, we must investigate the subject of honours, since that is both more profitable and more pleasant to hear of, taking our commencement from the particular instances of individuals.

(8) The Greeks say that in ancient times the famous Triptolemus was raised aloft and borne on winged dragons, and that while flying along in this manner he sowed the grains of wheat over the whole of the earth, in order that, instead of eating acorns, the human race might for the future have wholesome, and advantageous, and most pleasant food. This story, then, like many other tales, being, as it were, a fabulous fiction, may well be left to those who are accustomed to study sophistry rather than wisdom, and juggling tricks in preference to the truth; (9) for originally and simultaneously with the first creation of the universe, God supplied all living creatures with necessary food, producing it out of the earth, and, above all things, providing the race of mankind with all that was requisite, to whom also he gave the supremacy over every animal born of the earth. For, among the works of the Deity, there is nothing posthumous, but all those things which appear to

be brought to perfection at a subsequent time by the care, and diligence, and skill of men are in all cases previously produced in a half-finished state by the provident care of nature, so that it is not a wholly absurd statement that all learning is only recollection.

(10) However, these questions may be postponed for subsequent discussion. But we must now consider that most necessary of all things, the sowing of seed, which the Creator has sown in a very excellent soil, namely, in the rational soul. (11) Now, of this the most important seed is hope, the fountain of all men's lives; for it is by the hope of gain that the money-changer applies himself to many kinds of traffic; and it is through hope of a favourable voyage that the sailor passes over long seas; and it is from hope of glory that the ambitious man applies himself to public affairs, and to the superintendence of the commonwealth and matters of state. It is through hope of decisions in their favour and of crowns, that those who exercise their bodies in athletic labours enter the gymnastic contests. Hope is the source of all happiness; hope excites those persons who are filled with an admiration of virtue to study philosophy, under the idea that by her means they will be able to obtain a clear sight of the nature of all existing things, and to do things which are in accordance with and consistent with the perfection of those who most excellent modes of life—and contemplative and the practical, which he who attains to is at once truly happy.

(12) Now some persons have either, like enemies, stifled and destroyed all the seeds of hope by kindling all the vices in the soul, or else, like persons ignorant of and indifferent to the skill of the husbandman, they have allowed them to perish through neglect. There are also some persons who, appearing to be diligent husbandmen, but who yet, esteeming self-love above piety, have attributed the causes of their successes to themselves. (13) And all these men are very blameable, and he alone is worthy of being accepted who attributes his hope to God, both as being the author of his birth and as being alone able to keep him free from injury and free from utter destruction.

What reward, then, is assigned to the man who is crowned as conqueror in this contest? Man is a compound animal, made up of a mortal and immortal nature, not being the same with nor yet entirely different from the one who has obtained the prize. (14) This man the Chaldaeans name Enos, but this name, when translated into the Grecian language, means "a man," he having received the common name of the whole race for his own name, as an especial honour; as if it was not right for any one to be considered as a man at all who does not hope in God.

III. (15) And after the victory of hope there is another contest in which repentance contends for the prize; having, indeed, no share in that nature which is invincible, and which never changes its purpose, and which is always of the same character, entertaining the same disposition, but which is on a sudden seized with an admiration for and love of the better part, and which is anxious to leave the covetousness and injustice in which it has been bred up, and to go over to moderation and justice, and the other virtues; (16) for these are twofold prizes, which are proposed for twofold successes, first of all for the abandonment of what is disgraceful, and, secondly, for the choice of what is excellent; and the prizes are a departure from home, and solitude.

For Moses says, with reference to one who fled from the audacious innovations of the body, and who came over to the interest of the soul, "He was not found because God changed his place;"[1] (17) and by this enigmatical expression the two things are clearly intimated, the migration by the change of place, and the solitude by his not being found. And very appropriately is this stated; for if in real truth man had resolved at all times to show himself really superior to the passions, despising all pleasures and all appetites, then he would require to prepare himself diligently, fleeing without ever turning his head round, and forsaking his home, and his country, and his relations, and his friends; (18) for familiar custom is an attractive thing, so that there is reason to fear that if a man remains behind he may be taken prisoner, being caught by such powerful charms all round, the appearances of which will again rouse up the disgraceful though at present dormant appetites for evil pursuits, and will restore to vitality those recollections which it was creditable to have forgotten.

(19) Accordingly, many persons have become corrected and improved by migrations from their native land, having been cured by such means of their frenzied and wicked desires, by reason of the sight no longer being able to furnish to the passion the images of pleasure. For in consequence of the separation which has taken place, this passion has only a vacuum through which to rove, since there is no longer any object present by which it can be inflamed. (20) And if it does rise up and quit its former abode, still let it avoid the assemblies of the multitude, embracing solitude; for there are snares in a foreign land resembling those, which are found in a man's own country into which those men must fall who are careless and do not look before them, and who rejoice in the society of the multitude; for the multitude is a very concentration of every thing that is irregular, disorderly, improper, and blameable, with which it is a most

---

[1]Genesis 5:24.

mischievous thing for the man who is now for the first time passing over to the ranks of virtue to proceed. (21) For as the bodies of those men who are only just beginning to recover from a long attack of sickness are very subject to a relapse; so the soul which is just recovering its health finds its intellectual vigour weak and wavering, so that there is room to apprehend that the evil passions may return which were wont to be excited in it by a habit of living in the society of inconsiderate men.

IV. (22) Then, after these contests in which repentance is concerned, he proposes a third class of prizes, relating to justice, which every one who practises obtains a twofold reward; in the first place, that of preservation at the time of general destruction; and secondly, that of being the steward and guardian of every description of animal which is coupled in pairs for the purpose of raising a second stock instead of that which from time to time perishes; (23) for the Creator provided that the same being should be both the end of the generation which is condemned and the beginning of that which is irreproachable, teaching those who say that the world is destitute of all providence by works and not by words, that in accordance with the law which he promulgated and established in the nature of things, all the innumerable multitudes of men which live in obedience to injustice are not to be compared to one single individual who lives as a follower of justice.

Now this man the Greeks call Deucalion, but the Chaldaeans name him Noah; and it was in his time that the great deluge took place. (24) And after this triad there was a second triad still more holy and more pious, of one family. For father, and son, and grandson all directed all their views to the same end of life, namely, to please the Creator and Father of the universe, despising all those objects which the generality of men admire; glory, and riches, and pleasure, and laughing at that pride which is continually being put together and set forth with all kinds of fictitious ornaments in order to deceive the spectators. (25) This is that which makes gods of inanimate things, a great and almost impregnable fortification by the sophistries and manoeuvres of whom every city is allured, and since it takes especial hold on the souls of the young. For having entered into them it establishes itself and dwells in them from the earliest infancy to old age, subduing all those on whom God has not poured the beams of his truth. But pride is the adversary of truth, and is hard to be removed, though when it is subdued by a stronger power than itself then it does depart.

(26) And this class of men is small, indeed, in number; but in power it is very numerous and very great, so that even the whole circle of the earth cannot contain it. And it reaches even to heaven; for as it is possessed of an indescribable

love of contemplation and of being always among divine objects, when it has thoroughly investigated and explained all that nature which is perceptible to the sight, it immediately proceeds onwards to that which is incorporeal and appreciable only by the intellect, without requiring the assistance of any one of the outward senses, indeed discarding even the irrational parts of the soul, and employing those parts only which are called mind and reason.

(27) Therefore, the first establisher of the sentiments devoted to God, namely, Abraham, the first person who passed over from pride to truth, employing that virtue which proceeds from instruction as a means towards perfection, chooses as his reward faith in God. And because he, by the innate goodness of his natural dispositions, had acquired a spontaneous, self-taught, and self-implanted virtue, joy was given to him as a prize. Again, to his grandson, the meditator on and practiser of virtue, who attained to what was good by indefatigable and incessant labours, the crown which was given was the sight of God. And what can any one conceive to be either more useful or more respectable than to believe in God and throughout one's whole life to be continually rejoicing and beholding the living God?

V. (28) And let us now perceive each of these things more accurately, without allowing ourselves to be led away by names, but investigating them in their inmost parts, and going deep into them with our minds. Therefore, he who has in all sincerity believed God has by so doing received a disbelief in all other things which are created and perishable, beginning with those things in himself which exalt themselves very highly, namely, reason and the outward sense. For each of these things has a private consistory and tribunal of its own, which is erected in the one in order to ensure the proper consideration of the objects appreciable only by the intellect, the end of which is truth; and in the other for the perception of visible things, the end of which is opinion. (29) Therefore, the unstable, and erroneous, and untrustworthy character of opinion is plain from this circumstance; for it anchors upon images and probabilities. And every image is deceitful, exhibiting itself by a certain attractive similarity in lieu of the original thing itself.

But reason, which is the leader of the outward sense, thinking that the decision about all things which are perceptible only by the intellect, and which are always the same and in the same condition, belongs to itself, is convicted of being in error on many points. For when it directs its view to particular instances which are innumerable, it finds itself powerless, and unequal to the task, and faints under it, like a wrestler who is tripped up by some more mighty power; (30) but the man to whom it has been granted to see and thoroughly examine all corporeal and all incorporeal things, and to lean upon and to found himself upon God alone, with firm and steadfast reason and unalterable and sure confidence, is truly happy and blessed.

(31) After faith the next prize which is offered as destined for the man who acquires virtue by the gift of nature, as being victorious without a struggle, is joy. For this man is named as the Greeks would call him, Laughter, but as the Chaldaeans would entitle him, Isaac. And laughter is an emblem in the body of that unseen joy which exists in the mind. And joy is the most excellent and the most beautiful of all the pleasant affections of the mind, (32) by means of which the whole soul is in every part entirely filled with cheerfulness, rejoicing in the Father and Creator of all men and things, namely, in God, and rejoicing also in those things which are done without wickedness, even though they may not be pleasant, as being done virtuously, and as contributing to the duration of the universe.

(33) For as in great and dangerous sicknesses a physician sometimes actually takes away parts of the body, aiming at ensuring the sound health of the rest, and as when storms arise the pilot often throws overboard the cargo, out of a prudent regard to the safety of the men sailing in the ship; and yet the physician is not blamed for the mutilation of the body, nor the pilot for the loss of the cargo, but on the contrary both of them are praised as having seen and ensured what was advantageous in preference to what was pleasant; (34) so in the same manner we must always look with proper admiration at the nature of the entire universe, and we must be pleased with all things which are done in the world without intentional wickedness, inquiring not whether any thing has been done which is not altogether pleasant, but whether the world, like a city enjoying good laws, is guided and governed in a manner calculated to ensure its safety. (35) This man, therefore, is happy in no less a degree than the one whom I mentioned before, inasmuch as he is free from all depression or melancholy, and as he enjoys a life exempt from sorrow and exempt from fear, having no connection, not even in a dream, with any painful or austere plans of life, because every part of his soul is wholly occupied by joy.

VI. (36) And next to the man who has acquired self-taught virtue, and who has availed himself of the riches of nature, the third person who is made perfect is the meditator on and practiser of virtue, who receives as his especial reward the sight of God; for as he has had experience of all the things which can occur in human life, and as he has attained to a most intimate understanding of them, and has shrunk from no labour and from no

danger which might enable him to track out and overtake that most desirable thing, truth, he has found in connection with human life and with the human race a great deal of darkness both by land and sea, and in the air, and in the atmosphere. For the atmosphere and the whole of heaven has presented to him the appearance of night, since every nature which is discernible by the outward senses is indefinite; and what is indefinite is akin to and closely resembling darkness.

(37) Accordingly, he who had during the preceding periods of his life had the eyes of his soul closed, now began, though with difficulty, to open them for the continual labours which were before him, and to pierce through and dissipate the mist which had overshadowed him. For an incorporeal ray of light, purer than the atmosphere, suddenly beaming upon him, displayed to him the fact of the world appreciable only by the intellect being guided by a regular governor. (38) But that governor or guider, being surrounded on all sides by unalloyed light, was difficult to be perceived and difficult to be understood by conjecture, since the power of sight was obscured by the brilliancy of those beams. But nevertheless the sight, although a great violence of fire was poured upon it, held out against it out of an immense desire of seeing what was before it. (39) And the Father pitied its sincere desire and eagerness to see, and gave it power, and did not grudge the acuteness of the sight thus directed a perception of himself, as far at least as a created and mortal nature could attain to such a thing, not indeed such a perception as should show him what God is, but merely such as should prove to him that he exists; (40) for even this, which is better than good, and more ancient than the unit, and more simple than one, cannot possibly be contemplated by any other being; because, in fact, it is not possible for God to be comprehended by any being but himself.

VII. But the fact that he does exist, though it is comprehensible from the mere name of existence, is nevertheless not understood by every one, or at all events not in the best way by every one; but some men have expressly and wholly denied that there is any deity at all; while others have doubted and hesitated, as if they were unable to affirm with certainty whether he has any existence or not. Others again, who have more through habit than from any exertion of their reason, received ideas about the existence of God from those who have brought them up, have seemed to be pious by a sort of felicity of conjecture, if they have stamped their piety with an impression of superstition. (41) But if any men, by a great depth of real knowledge, have been able to represent to themselves the Creator and Governor of this universe, they, according to the common phrase, have advanced upwards from below;

for having entered into this world as into a city regulated by admirable laws, and having beheld the earth consisting of mountains, and of plains, and full of seed-crops, and of trees, and of fruits, and also of all kinds of animals; and beholding also seas, and ports, and lakes, and rivers of all sorts, whether proceeding from winter floods, or from everlasting springs, diffused over the surface of it, and the admirable temperature of the breezes and of the atmosphere, and the harmonious changes and well-ordered revolutions of the seasons of the year, and beyond all these things, the sun and moon, the planets and fixed stars, and the whole heaven, and all the host of heaven in its proper arrangement, and, in fact, the whole real world revolving in admirable order and regularity: (42) admiring, and being struck with awe and amazement at these things, they are come to form notions consistent with what they behold, that all these beautiful things, excessive as they are, and of such admirable arrangement and contrivance, were not produced spontaneously but were the work of some maker, the Creator of the whole world, and therefore that there must of necessity be a superintending providence.

For it is a law of nature, that the Creator must take care of what he has created. (43) But these admirable men, so superior to all others, have, as I said, raised themselves upwards from below, ascending as if by some ladder reaching to heaven, so as, through the contemplation of his works, to form a conjectural conception of the Creator by a probable train of reasoning. And if any persons have been able to comprehend him by himself, without employing any other reasonings as assistants towards their perception of him, they deserve to be recorded as holy and genuine servants of his, and sincere worshippers of God. (44) In this company is the man who in the Chaldaean language is denominated Israel, but in the Greek "seeing God;" not meaning by this expression seeing what kind of being God is, for that is impossible, as I have said before, but seeing that he really does exist; not having learnt this fact from any one else, nor from anything on earth, nor from anything in heaven, nor from any one of the elements, nor from anything compounded of them, whether mortal or immortal, but being instructed in the fact by God himself, who is willing to reveal his own existence to his suppliant.

(45) And how this impression was made, it is worth while to see by the observation of some similitude. Take this sun, which is perceptible by our outward senses, do we see it by any other means than by the aid of the sun? And do we see the stars by any other light than that of the stars? And, in short, is not all light seen in consequence of light? And in the same manner God, being his own light, is perceived by himself alone, nothing and no other being co-operating with or assisting him, or being at all able to contribute to the pure comprehension of his existence; (46) therefore those persons are mere guessers who are anxious to contemplate the uncreated God through the medium of the things which he created, acting like those persons who seek to ascertain the nature of the unit through the number two, when they ought, on the other hand, to employ the investigation of the unit itself to ascertain the nature of the number two; for the unit is the first principle.

But these men have arrived at the real truth, who form their ideas of God from God, of light from light.

VIII. (47) We have now described the greatest prize of all: but in addition to these prizes, the meditator on virtue receives another prize, not well-sounding indeed as to name, but very excellent to be conceived of; and this prize is called "the torpor of breadth," speaking figuratively. Now by breadth haughtiness and arrogance are typified; the soul, in those conditions, pouring forth an immoderate effusion over objects which are not desirable: and by torpor is typified the contraction of conceit, an elated and puffed-up thing. (48) But nothing is so expedient, as that unrestrained and unlimited impulses should be repressed and reduced to torpor, through the spirit of the mind being extinguished: so that the immoderate violence of the passions having become enfeebled, it may give breadth to the better part of the soul. (49) And we must also consider how exceedingly suitable a prize has thus been assigned to each of the three individuals; for to him who has been made perfect by education, faith is given as his reward; since it is necessary that he who learns must trust the man who teaches him in the matters concerning which he is instructing him; for it is difficult, or rather I might say impossible, for a man to be instructed who distrusts his teacher.

(50) Again: to him who arrives at virtue by his own good natural disposition, joy is given; for a good natural disposition is a thing to be rejoiced at, and so are the gifts of nature; since the mind derives enjoyment from all displays of acuteness and felicitous inventions, by which it finds the object which it is seeking without trouble; as if there was some prompter within enriching it with inventions; for the prompt discovery of matters previously, not certainly understood, is a subject of joy.

(51) Again: to him who has acquired wisdom by meditation and practice, sight is given. For after the practical life of youth comes the contemplative life of old age, which is the most excellent and the most sacred, which God has sent down from above to take its place in the stern like a pilot, and has given the helm into his hand as being able to guide the course of all earthly things; for with-

out contemplation based on knowledge, there is nothing whatever that is good done.

IX. (52) Having thus mentioned one man of each class, since I am anxious not to be prolix, I will proceed to what comes next in the order of discussion. Now, this man was proclaimed as conqueror, and crowned as such in the sacred contests. And when I speak of sacred contests, I do not mean those which are accounted such by other nations, for they are in reality unholy, affixing, as they do, rewards and honours to acts of violence, and insolence, and injustice, instead of the very extremity of punishment, which of right belongs to them: but I mean rather such as the soul is by nature formed to go through, which, by means of prudence, drives away folly and wicked cunning, and by temperance drives away prodigality and stinginess, and by courage drives away both rashness and cowardice, and the other vices which are in direct opposition to the respective virtues, and which are of no use either to themselves or to any one else; (53) therefore all the virtues are presented as virgins.

And the most excellent of all, having taken the post of leader as if in a chorus, is piety and righteousness, which Moses, the interpreter of the will of God, possessed in a most eminent degree. On which account, besides an innumerable host of other circumstances which are recorded of him in the accounts which have come down to us of his life, he has received also four most especial prizes, in being invested with sovereign power, with the office of lawgiver, with the power of prophecy, and with the office of high priest. (54) For he was a king, not indeed according to the usual fashion with soldiers and arms, and forces of fleets, and infantry, and cavalry, but as having been appointed by God, with the free consent of the people who were to be governed by him, and who wrought in his subjects a willingness to make such a voluntary choice.

For he is the only king of whom we have any mention as being neither a speaker nor one frequently heard, nor possessed of wealth or riches, since he was anxious rather about the wealth which sees than about that which is blind, and, if one is to speak the truth without any concealment, one who looked upon the inheritance of God as his peculiar property. (55) And this same man was likewise a lawgiver; for a king must of necessity both command and forbid, and law is nothing else but a discourse which enjoins what is right and forbids what is not right; but since it is uncertain what is expedient in each separate case (for we often out of ignorance command what is not right to be done, and forbid what is right), it was very natural for him also to receive the gift of prophecy, in order to ensure him against stumbling; for a prophet is an interpreter, God from within prompting him what he ought to say; and with God nothing is blameable.

(56) In the fourth place he received the high priesthood, by means of which he, prophesying in accordance with knowledge, worships the living God, and by which also he will bring before him in a propitiating manner, the thanksgivings of his subjects when they do well, and their prayers and supplications if at any time they are unfortunate; now since all these things belong to one class, they ought to be held together and united by mutual bonds, and to be perceived in the same man, since he who is deficient in any one of the four is imperfect in his authority, as he is consequently invested with but a crippled authority over the common interests.

X. (57) We have now thus spoken at sufficient length concerning the rewards proposed for each individual man: but rewards are also offered to whole houses, and to very numerous families.

When the nation was originally divided into twelve tribes, there were at once appointed patriarchs equal in number to the tribes, being not merely of one house or family, but connected by a still more genuine relationship: for they were all brothers having one and the same father; and the father and grandfather of these men were, with their father, the original founders of the whole nation.

(58) Therefore the first man who forsook pride and came over to truth, and who despised the jugglery of the Chaldaic branches of learning, because of that more perfect vision which had been granted to him, after having seen which he was so captivated that he followed the vision, just as they say that wire is attracted by the magnet, becoming instead of a sophist which he had been before a wise man in consequence of instruction—he had many children: but they were not all virtuous, though there was one who was utterly blameless, to whom he bound the cables of his whole race, and thus brought them to a safe anchorage.

(59) Again his son who had acquired spontaneous and self-taught wisdom had two sons, one a wild and untameable man, full of anger and desire, and one in short who raised up the irrational part of his soul as a fortification against the rational part; but the other a mild and gentle follower and worker of virtue, placed in the more excellent class of equality and simplicity, the very champion of reason and declared enemy of folly: (60) he is the third of the founders of his race, a man with many sons, and the only one truly happy in this children, being free from all injury in every part of his family, and like a fortunate husbandman seeing all his seed in a state of safety, and well cultivated, and bearing fruit.

XI. (61) And every one of these three individuals has in the account which we have received of him a figurative meaning concealed below it, which we must now consider. Now the moment that any one is taught anything, it happens to him to forsake ignorance and to come over the knowledge; and ignorance is a thing of a multiform character: on this account the first of the three is said to have had many children, but not to have thought any one of them worthy for him to call his son, except one: for in a manner he who learns discards the offspring of ignorance, and repudiates them as inimical and hostile to him.

(62) Now by nature all we who are men, before the reason that is in us is brought to perfection, live on the borders between virtue and vice, without ever inclining as yet to either side: but when the mind, beginning to put forth its wings, sees an appearance of the good with its whole soul, impressing it in all its parts, it immediately bursts through all restraint, and being borne on wings rushes towards it, leaving behind the kindred evil which was born with it, which it flees from, proceeding in the other direction without ever turning back: (63) this is what he intends to imply by an enigmatical expression when he says that the man who was endowed by nature with a good disposition had two sons, twins: for every man has at the beginning simultaneously with his birth, a soul which is pregnant with twins, namely, good and evil, bearing the impression of both of them: but when it receives the blessed and happy part, then by the force of one single attraction it inclines to the good, never once leaning towards the other side, and never even wavering so as to appear to be balancing between the two.

(64) But that soul which besides having a good natural disposition has also received a good education, and has been trained by the third mentioned person in the meditations of virtue, so that none of them float at random on the surface, but that they are all firmly glued and fixed in their places, as if united by some compact sinews, acquires health and acquires power, which are followed by a good complexion, owing to modesty, and also good health and beauty.

(65) And thus the soul becoming a perfect company of virtues, by means of these three most excellent patronesses, nature, instruction, and meditation, and not having left one single spot in itself empty, so as to allow of the entrance of anything else, engenders perfect number, namely, two lots of sons, of six in each, being a representation and imitation of the circle of the zodiac, in order to the improvement of everything in them: this is the family exempt from all injury, being continually devoted to the study of the holy scriptures, both in their literal sense and also in the allegories figuratively contained in them: which received as a prize, as I have said before, the supreme authority over each of the tribes of the nation. (66)

Of this house therefore, as it increased and became very populous in process of time, well regulated cities were founded, being schools of wisdom, and justice, and holiness, in which also the means of acquiring all other virtue was investigated in a grave manner suited to the importance of the subject.

XII. (67) Therefore those rewards which were thus long since assigned to the good, both publicly and privately, have now been described though somewhat in outline, but sufficiently to enable anyone to comprehend with tolerable ease what has been omitted. We must now proceed in regular order to consider in turn the punishments appointed for the wicked, speaking of them in a somewhat general way since the time does not allow of my enumerating all the particular instances.

(68) Now there was at the very beginning of the world when the race of men had not as yet multiplied, a fratricide: this is the first man who ever was under a curse; the first man who imprinted on the pure earth the unprecedented pollution of human blood; the first man who checked the fertility of the earth which was previously blooming, and producing all kinds of animals, and plants, and flourishing with every kind of productiveness; the first man who introduced destruction as a rival against creation, death against life, sorrow against joy, and evil against good. (69) What then could possibly have been inflicted upon him, which would have been an adequate punishment for him, who thus in one single action left no description of violence and impiety unperformed? Perhaps some one will say he should have been put to death at once; this is a human mode of reasoning, fit for one who does not consider the great tribunal of all for men look upon death as the extreme limit of all punishments, but in the view of the divine tribunal it is scarcely the beginning of them.

(70) Since then the action of this man was a novel one, it was necessary that a novel punishment should be devised for him; and what was it? That he should live continually dying, and that he should in a manner endure an undying and never ending death; for there are two kinds of death; the one that of being dead, which is either good or else a matter of indifference; the other that of dying, which is in every respect an evil; and the more protracted the dying the more intolerable the evil. (71) Consider now then how it is that death can be said to be never ending in this man's case; since there are four different affections to which the soul is liable, two of them being conversant with good either present or future, namely, pleasure and desire; and two with evil either present or expected, namely, sorrow and fear; it cuts up the pair of those which are conversant with good by the roots, in order that the man may never receive pleasure from any accident of fortune, nor

ever feel a desire even for anything pleasant; and it leaves him only those affections conversant about evil, sorrow without any mixture of cheerfulness, and unmingled fear, (72) for the scripture says[2] that God laid a curse upon the fratricide, so that he should be continually groaning and trembling.

Moreover he put a mark upon him, that he might never be pitied by any one, so that he might not die once, but might, as I have said before, pass all his time in dying, amid griefs, and pains, and incessant calamities; and what is most grievous of all, might have a feeling of his own miseries, and be afflicted both with the evils which were before him, and also from a foresight of the number of misfortunes which were constantly impending over him, which nevertheless he was unable to guard against, since hope was wholly taken from him, which God has implanted in the race of mankind, in order that thus, having an innate comfort in themselves, they might feel their sorrows relieved, provided they had not committed any inexpiable crimes.

(73) Therefore, as a man who is being carried away by a torrent shudders at the nearest waves by which he is being hurried away, and still more at those coming upon him from above, since the one is continually and incessantly propelling him forward with violence, but the other being raised above him threatens to overwhelm him utterly, so in the same manner those evils which are present are grievous, but those which proceed from fear of the future are more grievous still; for fear continually supplies sorrowful feelings as from an ever-lasting spring.

XIII. (74) These punishments, then, are those which were decided on to be inflicted on the first slayer of his brother. But others were also appointed for households which had entered into any conspiracy to unite in crime.

And there were some men appointed to be keepers of the temple and ministers in the sacred offices, classed as a kind of door-keepers. These men, being wholly filled with unreasonable pride, rose up in rebellion against the priests, desiring to appropriate their honours and privileges to themselves.

(75) And, having elected as chief of their conspiracy the eldest of their body, who also, with a few of those who joined in this audacious folly, was the leader of the whole enterprise, they left the outer courts and precincts of the tabernacle and entered into the most holy places, expelling those who, by the oracular commands of God, had been thought worthy of the priesthood.

(76) Therefore, as was natural, a great confusion spread among the whole multitude, in consequence of things being disturbed which never ought to have been moved, and of the laws being openly violated and all the ordinances for the regular service of the temple being thrown into confusion by wicked disobedience, (77) at which the governor and president of the nation was indignant. And, at first, displaying a stern disposition, though without any anger (for he was the meekest of men and by nature incapable of anger), he endeavoured by arguments to persuade them to alter their conduct, and not to transgress the bounds laid down for them, nor to seek to overturn the ordinances established with respect to holy and consecrated things on which the hopes of the whole nation depended. (78) But when he would not succeed in the least, but found that the people were deaf to all his entreaties, since they looked upon him as wholly under the influence of domestic affection and thought that it was on that account that he had made his brother high priest, and had given the inferior priesthood to his nephews, he still was not so much indignant at that, though it was a shocking thing, as at this other all terrible idea that they were imputing to him a contempt for the sacred oracles, in accordance with which the election of priests had taken place.[3] [...] [4]

XIV. (79) And there is a distinct evidence in confirmation of what I have now said recorded in the sacred scriptures; because, in the first place, the sacred historian records the prayers which he commonly calls blessings. "If,"[5] says he, "you keep the commandments of God and are obedient to his injunctions, and receive what is said to you, not merely so far as to listen to them, but also to fulfil them by the actions of your lives, you shall have as a first reward victory over your enemies; (80) for the commandments are not burdensome or too weighty for the ability of you who are to live by them to obey, nor is the good which is promised to you removed to any distance, either beyond the sea, or at the furthest extremities of the country, so as to require a long and painful journey to avail yourselves of it." Nor did the lawgiver at once set out on his departure from earth to heaven, so that no one else being raised on high and borne aloft on wings could attain to the obedience which he enjoined; but the obedience remained near and very close to men, being fixed separately in three parts of us, in the mouth, and heart, and hands; that is to say, in the speech, and designs, and actions of every one.

(81) For if such as the designs are, such also

---

[2]Genesis 4:14.

[3]Numbers 16:1.
[4]There appears to be a considerable hiatus in the text here.
[5]Deuteronomy 30:10.

are the speeches; and such as the words spoken, such also are the actions; and if these things are bound up with each other, reciprocally preceding and following one another through the indissoluble bonds of harmony; then happiness prevails, and this is the truest wisdom and prudence. For wisdom has reference to the service of God, and prudence to the regulation of human life.

(82) Therefore, as long as the commandments conveyed in the laws are only spoken, they meet with but little or no acceptance; but when words in proper consistency and conformity with them are added to them in all the pursuits of life, then those commandments, being brought forth as it were from deep darkness to light, will shine forth in all respectability and glory; (83) for who, even of those who are naturally envious, would hesitate to say that this is the only wise and truly learned race of men, which has the sense not to leave the divine commands destitute of and unattended by corresponding actions, but which takes care to fulfil the words with praiseworthy actions? (84) This class of men lives not far from God, keeping always before its eyes the beautiful things of heaven, and being guided in all its ways by heavenly love; so that if any one were to inquire of what character a great nation is, one might very properly answer—it is a nation whose most sacred prayers God hears, and to whose invocations, proceeding as they do from a pure conscience, he gladly draws near.

XV. (85) But since there are also two classes of enemies—the one being men, who are so deliberately, out of covetousness; the other being beasts, who are not so out of any deliberate purpose, or through study, but as being endowed with a nature utterly alien to ours—we must proceed to speak of them both in turn, and we will take, in the first place, the beasts which are our natural enemies; for these are hostile not to one city, or to one nation, but to the whole race of mankind, and that too not for any definite or limited period of time, but for an indefinite and illimitable eternity.

(86) Of these some fear man as their master, and crouch beneath him with an angry fear; others, again, being bold and fearless, watch their opportunity and are the first to begin the warfare and attack him; if they are weaker than he, by an ambush; and if they are stronger, openly. (87) For this war is one which admits of no truce and of no termination, but is like that existing between the wolves and the sheep, and between all wild beasts, whether living in the water or on the land, and men; and no mortal can terminate it, but only the one uncreated God, when he selects some persons as worthy to be the saviours of their race; men who are peaceful, indeed, in disposition, fond of unanimity and fellowship with others, with whom envy has either absolutely never had any connec-

tion at all, or else it has speedily departed from them; and these men have determined to throw all their own private good things into the common stock for the use and enjoyment of all.

(88) For if this good should ever at any future time shine upon the world, so that we may be able to see the time in which the savage animals shall become manageable, long before that the wild passions in the soul will be tamed, and it is not possible to imagine a greater blessing than that; for is it not a piece of absolute folly to imagine that we can ever avoid injuries from wild beasts which are outside, while we are continually training up the passions within ourselves to a terrible degree of savageness? On which account we must not despair that when the passions of our mind are tamed and subdued, then the wild beasts also will be broken in. (89) Then it seems to me that bears, and lions, and leopards, and those beasts which are found only in India, elephants and tigers, and all other animals whose courage and strength are invincible, will change from their solitary and unsociable habits, and adopt a more gregarious life, and, by a gradual imitation of those animals which live in troops, will become softened and accustomed to the sight of men, being no longer in a constant state of excitement and fury against him, but rather feeling awe of him as their ruler and natural master, and will behave with proper respect to him; and some of them, with an exceeding greatness of tameness and affection for their master, like Maltese dogs, will even fawn upon them and wag their tails with a cheerful motion. (90) Then the species of scorpions, and serpents, and other reptiles will keep their venom inoperative; and the Egyptian river will produce those animals, which are at present carnivorous and which feed on man, called crocodiles and hippopotami, in a tame and gentle condition; and the sea too will produce innumerable kinds of animals, among all of which the virtuous man will be sacred and unhurt, since God honours virtue and has given it immunity from all designs against it as a proper reward.

XVI. (91) Thus, then, the most ancient war, both in point of time and in nature, will be put an end to, when all the wild beasts will be tamed and will have altered their dispositions so as to become manageable. But the more modern war, which has arisen out of the deliberate purposes of men from their covetousness, will be likewise easily put an end to, as it appears to me, since men will be ashamed to be seen to be more savage than even the brute beasts, after they have escaped all injury and damage from them; (92) for it will naturally appear a most shameful thing for venomous, carnivorous, man-devouring, unsociable, ferocious animals to have become friendly to man, changing to a peaceful disposition, and for man, who is by nature a gentle animal, with a natural inclination to sociality and unanimity, to renounce peace and seek the destruction of his fellows.

(93) Therefore, says the lawgiver, peace shall never come at all into the country of the pious, but shall fall to pieces of itself, and shall be dashed to pieces against itself, when the enemies perceive against what fierce and invincible enemies the contest is, and employ against them the irresistible alliance of justice; for virtue is a great, and dignified, and very venerable thing, and is by itself, when in tranquillity, able to alleviate the attacks of great evils. (94) And even if some men are in their frenzy driven to quarrel, indulging their spontaneous and implacable desire for war, until indeed they are actually engaged, they will, being full of confidence, behave with great insolence, but after they have once come to a regular contest they will then find that they have made an empty boast, and that they are unable to gain the victory; for as they will be repelled by force equal to their own,[6] or even more powerful still, they will flee in great confusion, a hundred fleeing before five, and a host of ten thousand before a hundred men, and those who had come by one road fleeing by a great number.

(95) Some will even flee when no one pursues at all except fear, turning their backs towards the enemy, so as to afford a full mark for shooting, so that it will be very easy for the whole army to fall, being slain to a man; for a man will come forth,[7] says the word of God, leading a host and warring furiously, who will subdue great and populous nations, God sending that assistance which is suitable for pious men; and this assistance is an intrepid hardihood of soul, and an irresistible strength of body, either of which things is formidable to the enemy, and if both qualities are united they are completely invincible. (96) Moreover he says, "That some of the enemy will be unworthy of being defeated and of perishing by the hands of men, to which he will oppose swarms of wasps,[8] who shall fight for the pious, so as to overwhelm their enemies with shameful destruction; (97) and he predicts, that he will not only always firmly retain the bloodless victory thus gained, but that he will also have an irresistible power of dominion, so as to be able to benefit the people subject to him, who may become so, whether out of good will, or out of fear, or out of shame; for he will have in him three things of the greatest importance, all contributing greatly to rendering his authority indestructible, namely, dignity, and terror, and beneficence, by means of which

qualities the ends above-mentioned will be gained; for dignity causes respect, and terror causes fear, and beneficence causes good will; which, when they are mixed together, and adapted, and united in the soul, render subjects obedient to their rulers.

XVII. (98) These, then, are the first things which he says will happen to those who obey God, and who at all times and in all places observe his commandments, and who adapt them to every part of their lives, so that no one going astray under the influence of disease may wander from them. The second thing is wealth, which must of necessity follow peace and authority; (99) but the simple wealth of nature is food and shelter, and food is bread and water from the spring, which are both diffused over every part of the habitable world; but of shelter there are two kinds, first of all clothes, and secondly a house, on account of the injuries which result from exposure to cold and heat; each of which protections, if any one chooses to discard superfluous and excessive extravagance, is very easily provided.

(100) But those who admire what has been described above, having rather a desire for the gifts of nature than for those of vain opinion, devoting themselves to frugality, and simplicity, and temperance, will have a great abundance and means for all kinds of delicate living without any labour or study; for wealth will come to those who know how to use it in a befitting manner, as to those who are at the same time the most proper, and, in fact, the most nearly related to it and thoroughly worthy of it, gladly fleeing from all association with intemperate and insolent men, that it may not pass by those persons whose existence is a common benefit to mankind, and supply those who live to the injury of their neighbours; (101) for there is a passage in the word of God,[9] that, "on those who observe the sacred commands of God, the heaven will shower down seasonable rains, and the earth will bring forth for them abundance of all kinds of fruits, the champaign country producing crops from seed, and the mountainous country fruit from trees;" and that no period will ever be left entirely destitute of benefits for them, but that they shall without interruption, incessantly receive the favours of God, the time of harvest succeeding the season of gathering the grapes, and the season of gathering the grapes following the seed time, (102) so that men, without any cessation or any interruption, are continually carrying home one crop and hoping for another, while one as it were lies in wait for the next; so that the beginnings of those which come on after are connected with the ends of those which have preceded them, and

---

[6]Leviticus 26:8.
[7]Numbers 24:7.
[8]Exodus 23:28.

[9]Leviticus 26:3.

thus make a kind of circle and revolving body, which is endowed with every imaginable good.

(103) For the great multitude of things which are thus produced will be sufficient both for present use and enjoyment, and also for an unlimited abundance of supply in the time to come, the grain constantly coming up and flourishing, as the successors of the old, and filling up the void, which would otherwise be cursed by their decay and disappearance. There are also cases in which, by reason of the ineffable plenty, no one will think at all of those stores which have been collected long ago, but leaves them without any care or any attempt to store them, permitting every one who pleases to use them without restraint and with perfect impunity.

(104) For as to those men for whom that true wisdom is stored up, which has been derived from constant meditation and practice in wisdom and holiness, on them the wrath which consists of money upon earth is abundantly poured, since the treasure-houses, by the providence and care of God, are kept continually full; because the impulses of the mind, and the endeavours of the hands, are not hindered in any way, so as to prevent the successful attainment of these objects, which are constantly pursued with anxiety. (105) But those persons who, by reason of their impiety or unrighteousness, have not a heavenly inheritance, have also no abundant possession or share of the good things upon the earth; and even if any such thing should come to them, it quickly departs again, as if it had originally happened to them, not for the advantage of the immediate recipients, but in order that a more vehement sorrow may overwhelm them, such as must, of necessity, follow the being deprived of an important blessing.

XVIII. (106) And at that time, says the law, you, by reason of the abundant fertility, shall do what you now suffer. For now, indeed, you pay no respect either to the laws or to the customs of your country and of your forefathers, but neglecting them altogether equally, you fail to obtain what is necessary, and keep counting the houses of the usurers and money-changers, being continually wishing to borrow at heavy interest; (107) and then, as I said a minute ago, you shall do the contrary. For, by reason of your own unlimited abundance, you yourself shall lend to others, and that not lending little things, nor lending to few persons, but you shall lend large sums, and to many people, indeed to whole nations, all your affairs prospering and turning out well, both in the country and in the city; all things in the city, as respects offices of authority, and honour, and glory, and reputation, by means of wise conjectures, and prudent counsels, and conduct tending both in word and deed to the general advantage; and all the things in the country in consequence of the abundant production of all necessary things, such as corn, and wine, and oil, and all other productions which conduce to a comfortable and easy life, and these are the innumerable kinds of fruit from different trees, and the prolific increase of herds of oxen, and flocks of goats, and other kinds of cattle.

(108) But some one may say, What is the use of all these things to one who is not likely to leave heirs and successors behind him? The law, setting as it were the seal to its acts of beneficence, replies: No one shall be without offspring, nor shall there be a barren woman; but all the genuine and sincere servants of God shall fulfil the law of nature as respects the propagation of their species; (109) for the men shall become fathers, and the fathers shall be happy in their offspring, and the women shall be happy mothers of children, so that every house shall be a full company of a numerous family, no part and no name being omitted of all those which are appropriated to relations, whether referring to relations upwards, such as uncles and grandfathers, or to descending relations on the other hand of a similar kindred, such as brothers, nephews, grandsons by the sons' side, grandsons by the daughters' side, cousins, counsins' children, and every kind of blood relations. (110) But no man shall die prematurely or without having fulfilled the legitimate end of his being among those men who observe the laws, nor shall such fail to reach the age which God has allotted to the race of man. But the human being proceeding upwards from childhood, as it were by the different stages of a ladder, and at the appointed periods of time fulfilling the regularly determined boundaries of each age, will eventually arrive at the last of all, that which is near to death, or rather to immortality; being really and truly happy in his old age, leaving behind him a house happy in numerous and virtuous children in his own place.

XIX. (111) This is what the lawgiver in one passage says, while declaring the will of God, that, "thou shalt complete the number of thy days," prophesying thus with great beauty and using great propriety and naturalness of language. For the man who is destitute of all learning, and who disregards the law, does not speak either in reason nor in number, as the old proverb says; but he who has a fair share of instruction and who adheres to the holy laws, receives as his first reward, since he is proved to be a respectable and reputable man, a share in number and arrangement. (112) And very admirable is this fulness and completeness, not of months or years, but of days, so that no day whatever in the life of a virtuous man ever leaves an empty and open door for the entrance of sins, but is filled in all its parts and all its intervals with absolute virtue and excellence.

For virtue and goodness are judged of not by quantity but by quality, for which reason I look upon it that even one day spent with perfect correctness is of equal value with the entire good life of a wise man. (113) This is what is enigmatically implied in other expressions, where the holy writer says that such a man "shall deserve blessings both at his coming in and going out;" because the virtuous man is praiseworthy in all his positions and in all his actions, both indoors and out of doors, whether engaged in affairs of state or in the regulation of his household, regulating all his affairs inside his house with economy, and all the business out of doors with a due regard to principles of state government in the way in which it is most expedient for them to be regulated.

(114) If, then, any one proves himself a man of such a character in the city he will appear superior to the whole city, and if a city show itself of such a character it will be the chief of all the country around; and if a nation do so it will be the lord of all the other nations, as the head is to the body occupying the pre-eminence of situation, not more for the sake of glory than for that of advancing the interests of those that see. For continual appearances of good models stamp impressions closely resembling themselves on all souls which are not utterly obdurate and intractable; (115) and I say this with reference to those who wish to imitate models of excellent and admirable beauty, that they may not despair of a change for the better, nor of an alteration and improvement from that dispersion, as it were, of the soul which vice engenders, so that they may be able to effect a return to virtue and wisdom.

(116) For when God is favourable every thing is made easy. And he is favourable to those who display modesty and due reverence, and who seek to pass over from intemperance to temperance, and who reproach themselves for all the blameable actions of their life, and for all the base images which they have stamped upon their polluted souls, and who aim at a tranquil state of the passions, and who keep constantly in view, as the proper object of their pursuit, a calmness and serenity of life.

(117) As therefore God, by one single word of command, could easily collect together men living on the very confines of the earth, bringing them from the extremities of the world to any place which he may choose, so also the merciful Saviour can bring back the soul after its long wandering, after it has been straying about in every direction, and been ill-treated by pleasure and desire, most imperious mistresses, and guide it easily from a trackless waste into a regular road when it has once determined to flee from evil without ever looking back, a flight not liable to reproach, but the cause of its preservation, which no one will do wrong to pronounce more desirable than any return.

XX. (118) These, then, of which we have already spoken, are what are called external goods, victory over one's enemies, superiority in war, confirmation of peace, and abundance of those good things which belong to peace, riches, and honours, and authorities, and the praises which always follow those who are successful, as they are extolled by every mouth both of friends and enemies, by the one through fear, and by the others out of good will.

We must now proceed to speak of what is more nearly connected with us than these things, namely, about those things which affect the body. (119) The lawgiver says, then, that a perfect freedom from disease in every respect, both privately and generally, shall be allotted to those persons who labour in the service of virtue and who make the sacred laws the guides of all their speeches and actions in life; and if there should any infirmity affect them it will not be for the sake of injuring them, but with a view to remind a mortal that he is mortal, so as to eradicate overbearing pride and improve his disposition. And sound health will follow, and a good condition of the outward senses, and a perfectness and completeness in all the parts, conducive to the unimpeded performance of those duties for which each man has been born. (120) For God has thought fit to give as a reward to the virtuous a house thoroughly well built and well put together from the foundations to the roof; and the most natural house for the soul is the body, inasmuch as it does many things necessary and useful for life, and especially on account of the mind which has been purified by perfect purifications; (121) and which, having been initiated in the divine mysteries, and having learnt to dwell only among the motions and periodical revolutions of the heavenly bodies, God has honoured with tranquillity, wishing it to be completely undisturbed and exempt from any contact of those passions which the necessities of the body engender, adding, out of covetousness, a desire for sovereignty over the passions.

For either the heaven has caused a chill to something, or has scorched something, or has made something dry, or else, on the contrary, has melted and liquefied it; from all which causes the mind is unable to keep its path through life quite straight and independent. (122) But if it has its abode in a healthy body, then it will with great care and tranquillity dwell among and devote all its leisure to the meditations of wisdom, having obtained a happy and fortunate existence. (123) This is the mind which has drunk strong draughts of the beneficent power of God, and has feasted on his sacred words and doctrines. This is the mind in which the prophet says that God walks as in his palace; for the mind of the wise man is in truth the palace and the house of God.

And he who is the God of all things is peculiarly called the God of this mind; and again this mind is by a peculiar form called his people, not the people of any particular rulers, but of the one only and true ruler, the Holy One of holies.

(124) This is the mind which a little while ago was enslaved to many pleasures and many desires, and to innumerable necessities arising from weaknesses and desires; but its evils God crushed in slavery, having elected to bring it to freedom. This is the mind which has received a favour not to be suppressed in silence, but rather to be proclaimed abroad and announced in every quarter, on account of the authority and power of its champion and defender, by which it was not thrust down to the tail, but was raised upwards to the head.

(125) But all these statements are uttered in a metaphorical form, and contain an allegorical meaning. For as in an animal the head is the first and best part, and the tail the last and worst part, or rather no part at all, inasmuch as it does not complete the number of the limbs, being only a broom to sweep away what flies against it; so in the same manner what is said here is that the virtuous man shall be the head of the human race whether he be a single man or a whole people. And that all others, being as it were parts of the body, are only vivified by the powers existing in the head and superior portions of the body.

(126) These are the prayers on behalf of good men who fulfil the laws by their actions which it is said will be accomplished by the grace of the bounteous and beneficent God, who honours and rewards all that is good for the sake of its similarity to himself.

We must now consider the curses appointed against those who transgress the commandments and the laws. [10]

XXI. (127) The lawgiver of our nation denounces the first curse as the lightest of evils, namely, poverty and indigence, and a want of all necessary things, and a participation in every kind of destitution; for, says he, "The enemy shall lay waste the corn-fields before they are ripe, and when the corn is ripened they shall suddenly come and reap it." [11] Thus causing a twofold calamity, famine to their friends and abundance to their enemies; for the prosperity of one's enemies is more, or, at all events, not less painful than one's own misfortunes.

(128) And even if one's enemies are quiet, still those evils which proceed from nature and which are even more grievous, are not quiet; for you, indeed, sow the deep and fertile soil of the plain, but suddenly a cloud of locusts shall fly down and reap your crop, and what is left behind for you to carry home to your barns will bear but a very small proportion to what is sown.

And, again, you shall plant a vineyard with unsparing expense, and incessant industry, and labour, such as it is natural for husbandmen to undergo; but when the vines are come to perfection, and are flourishing and weighed down with their own productiveness, the worms shall come and gather the grapes. (129) And when you see your oliveyards flourishing, and an unbounded exuberance of fruit on the trees, you will very naturally be delighted from the hope of a successful harvest which you will be led to entertain, but when you begin to carry home the fruit, then you will be filled rather with sorrow than with joy; for the oil and all the fatness of the fruit will all flow away and disappear imperceptibly, and what is outside will be only a vain burden, empty, left only to deceive the empty soul. And, in short, all the seed crops and all the trees will be destroyed, fruit and all, by blight of one kind or another.

XXII. (130) And there are other misfortunes also lying in wait for the men besides those which have been mentioned, all equally contributing to produce want and scarcity; for those things, by means of which nature used to provide men with good things, namely, the earth and the heaven, will both be rendered barren, the one being full of abortions and unable to bring any fruit to perfection, and the other changing its nature so as to produce an unproductive state of the seasons of the year, so that neither winter, nor summer, nor spring, nor autumn return in their appointed order, but are all violently wrenched from it, and thrown into a confusion destitute of all distinctive quality and completely disturbed, by the command of the supreme authority. (131) For then there will be no rain, no showers, no gentle springs, no soft drops of moisture, no dew, nor anything else which can contribute to the growth of plants; but, on the contrary, all things which are calculated to dry them up when beginning to grow, all things destructive of the fruit when beginning to ripen, and adapted to prevent it from ever coming to perfection.

For, says God, "I will make the heaven of brass for you, and the earth iron." [12] Implying by this enigmatical expression that neither of them shall accomplish the tasks which naturally belong to them and for which they were created; (132) for how could iron ever bear ears of corn, or how could brass produce rain, of which all animals stand in

---

[10] Yonge's translation includes a separate treatise title at this point: *On Curses*. Accordingly, his next paragraph begins with roman numeral I (=XXI in the Loeb). Yonge's "treatise" concludes with number IX (=XXIV in the Loeb). The publisher has elected to follow the Loeb numbering.

[11] Deuteronomy 28:33.

[12] Deuteronomy 28:23.

need, and especially that animal so liable to misfortune and in need of so many things, man?

And God intimates here not only barrenness and the destruction of the seasons of the year, but also the beginnings of wars, and of all the intolerable and ineffable evils which arise in wars; for brass and iron are the materials for warlike arms. (133) And the earth, indeed, shall produce dust, and masses of dirt shall be brought down from above, from heaven, weighing down the fruit and destroying it by choking, in order that nothing may be omitted which can tend to complete destruction; for numerous families will be made desolate, and cities will suddenly become empty of their inhabitants, remaining as monuments of their former prosperity and records of subsequent disaster, for the warning of those who are capable of receiving correction.

XXIII. (134) And such a complete scarcity of all necessary things will seize the people that, being wholly destitute of and indifferent to them, they will turn even to devouring one another, eating not only the gentiles and those who are no relations to them, but even their nearest and dearest kinsfolk; for the father will take the flesh of his son, and the mother will eat of the life-blood of her daughter, brothers will eat their brothers, and children will devour their parents; and, in fact, the weaker will be continually the prey of the more powerful; and that wicked and accursed food, that of Thyestes, will seem to them like a joke when compared with the excessive and intolerable evils which their necessities bring upon them; (135) for, as in the case of other persons, while they are in prosperity they desire length of life to be able to enjoy all good things, so also even those men overwhelmed with misery will have a vehement desire for life established in them, though it can only lead them to a participation in immoderate and interminable evils, all of which are likewise irremediable.

For it would have been better for such men to have escaped misery by cutting off their griefs through death, which persons who are not utterly out of their senses are accustomed to do. But these men are arrived at such a degree of folly that they would be willing to live even to the longest possible time of life, being eager for and insatiably desirous of the greatest extremities of misery.

(136) Such evils, that which appears at first to be the lightest of all misfortunes, namely, poverty, is naturally calculated to produce, when it is the result of the vengeance of God; for even though cold, and thirst, and want of food may be terrible, still they might at times be objects worth being prayed for, if they only produced instantaneous death without any delay. But when they last a long time and waste away both body and soul, then they are calculated to reproduce the very greatest of

the calamities recorded by the tragic poets, which appear to me to be described in a spirit of fabulous exaggeration.

XXIV. (137) Again. To free-born people slavery is a most intolerable evil, to avoid which wise men are willing even to die, resisting in a gallant spirit which despises all danger the attacks of those who seek to inflict upon them the domination of a master.

Also, an invincible enemy is an intolerable evil. And if the same person be both things at once, namely, a master and an enemy, who can endure such a complication of calamities? For such a person will be possessed of the power of inflicting injury through his authority as a master, and he will be disinclined to pardon any one by reason of his irreconcileable enmity. (138) Therefore the lawgiver pronounces that those persons who neglect the sacred laws shall have their enemies for their masters, who will treat them unmercifully, not only as having been reduced under their power by invincible attacks, but also as having voluntarily submitted to them through unforeseen calamities which famine and the want of necessaries has caused; for some persons think it well to choose lesser evils, if by so doing they can avoid greater ones; if, indeed, any one of the misfortunes above mentioned can be called a slight evil. (139) Such men, becoming slaves, endure the services imposed on them by stern commands with their bodies, but when they are oppressed as to their souls with the anguish of still more bitter spectacles, they will sink under them; for they will see their enemies becoming the inheritors of houses which they have built, or of vineyards which they have planted, or of possessions which they have acquired, enjoying the good things and stores which have been prepared by others.

And they will see their enemies feasting on the fattest of their cattle, and sacrificing them, and preparing them for the sweetest enjoyment, without being able to deprive those persons of anything who have thus robbed them. They will also see their wives, whom they married in holy wedlock for the purpose of propagating legitimate children, their modest, domestic, affectionate wives, insulted like so many courtesans. (140) And they will rush forward to defend and to avenge them, but beyond resisting they will not be able to effect anything, being deprived of all their strength and utterly disabled; for they will be exposed as a mark for their enemies, an object for plunder, and ravage, and violence, and insult, and wounds, and injuries, and contumely, and utter destruction, so that nothing belong to them can escape, but no one dart of the enemy shall miss its blow, but every one of them shall be well aimed and successful.

(141) They shall be cursed in their cities and in their villages, and cursed in their town-houses

and in their dwellings in the fields. Cursed will be their plains and all the seed which is sown in them; cursed will be the fertile soil of the mountain district, and all the kinds of trees which produce eatable fruit; cursed will be their herds of cattle, for they will be rendered barren and unproductive; cursed will be all their fruits and all their crops, for at the most critical period of their ripening they will be found to be all full of wind and destroyed. (142) The storehouses full of food and money shall be made empty; no source of revenue shall be productive any more; all the arts, all the various businesses and employments, and all the innumerable varieties of life, shall be of no use to those who adopt them; for the hopes of those who are anxious shall fail to be fulfilled; and, in short, whatever they touch, in consequence of their wicked pursuits and wicked actions, the head, and front, and end of which is the abandonment of the service of God, shall all be vain and unprofitable.

XXV. (143) For these things are the rewards of impiety and lawless iniquity. And, in addition to these things, there are diseases of the body which separately afflict and devour each limb and each part, and which also rack and torture it all over with fevers, and chills, and wasting consumptions, and terrible rashes, and scrofulous diseases, and spasmodic convulsions of the eyes, and putrefying sores and abscesses, and cutaneous disorders extending over the whole of the skin, and disorders of the bowels and inward parts, and convulsions of the stomach, and obstructions in the passages of the lungs preventing the patient from breathing easily, and paralysis of the tongue, and deafness of the ears, and imperfections of the eyes, and a general dimness and confusion of all the other senses, things which, though terrible, will yet hardly appear so when compared with other things more grievous still; (144) when, for instance, all the vivifying qualities which existed in the blood contained in the veins have escaped from it, and when the breath which is contained in the lungs and windpipe is no longer capable of receiving a salutary admixture of the outward air so nearly connected with it; (145) and when the veins are all relaxed and dissolved, which state is followed by a complete prostration of the harmony and due arrangement of the limbs, which were indeed previously distressed by the violent rush of a briny and very bitter stream stealthily pervading them; which, when it was shut up in a narrow passage having no easy outlet, being then pressed close and pressing other parts, conduces to the production of bitter and almost intolerable pains, from which are engendered the diseases of gout and arthritic pains and diseases, for which no salutary remedy has ever been discovered, but which are incurable by any human means.

(146) Some persons, when they behold these things, will be alarmed, marvelling to see how those who a little while ago were fat and full of good flesh, and flourishing exceedingly in health and vigour, have so on a sudden wasted away and become merely withered muscles and a thin skin; and how the women, formerly luxurious, and tender, and delicate by reason of the luxury to which they have been accustomed from their earliest infancy, now, from the terrible afflictions to which they have been subjected, have become wild in their souls, and wild-looking in their bodies.

(147) Then, then indeed, their enemies shall pursue them, and the sword shall exact its penalty; and they, fleeing to the cities, where they think that they have obtained a place of safety, being deluded by treacherous hopes, shall perish to a man being caught and destroyed by the ambuscades of their enemies.

XXVI. (148) And if, after all these calamities, they are not chastened, but still proceed by crooked paths, and turn off from the straight roads which lead to truth, then cowardice and fear shall be established in their souls, [13] and they shall flee when no one pursues, and shall be routed and destroyed by false reports, as does often happen. The lightest sound of leaves falling through the air shall cause as great an agony of fear and apprehension as the most formidable war waged by the most powerful of enemies ought to produce, so that children shall be indifferent to the fate of their parents, and parents to that of their children, and brothers to that of their brethren, looking upon it that if they go to their assistance they may themselves incur the danger of captivity, while their best chance of safety consists in escaping by themselves.

(149) But the hopes of wicked men do never obtain their accomplishment, and those who hope to escape thus will be still more, or at all events not less, taken prisoners than those who were previously laid hold of. And even if some such persons do escape notice, they will still be exposed to insidious attacks from their natural enemies; and these are those most furious wild beasts who are well armed by the endowments of nature, and which God, simultaneously with the original creation of the universe, made for the purpose of striking terror into those men who were incapable of taking warning, and for executing implacable justice on those whose wickedness was incurable; (150) and those who behold their cities razed to the very foundations will hardly believe that they were ever inhabited, and they will turn the sudden misfortunes which befall men after brilliant instances of prosperity into a proverb, recording

[13] Leviticus 26:36.

all the instances which are mentioned or passed over in history.[14]

(151) There shall also come upon them asthmas, and consumptions affecting the internal organs, producing heaviness and despondency, with great afflictions, and making all life unstable, and hanging, as one may say, from a halter. And fears incessantly succeeding one another will toss the mind up and down, agitating it night and day, so that in the morning they shall pray for the evening, and in the evening they shall pray for the morning, on account of the visible horrors which surround them when awake, and the detestable images which present themselves to them in their dreams when sleeping. (152) And the proselyte who has come over being lifted up on high by good fortune, will be a conspicuous object, being admired and pronounced happy in two most important particulars, in the first place because he has come over to God of his own accord, and also because he has received as a most appropriate reward a firm and sure habitation in heaven, such as one cannot describe. But the man of noble descent, who has adulterated the coinage of his noble birth, will be dragged down to the lowest depths, being hurled down to Tartarus and profound darkness, in order that all men who behold this example may be corrected by it, learning that God receives gladly virtue which grows out of hostility to him, utterly disregarding its original roots, but looking favourably on the whole trunk from its lowest foundation, because it has become useful and has changed its nature so as to become fruitful.

XXVII. (153) The cities being thus destroyed as if by fire, and the country being rendered desolate, the land will at last begin to obtain a respite, and, as one may say, to recover breath, and to look up again, after having been much exercised and harassed by the intolerable violence of its inhabitants, who drive away all the virgin periods of seven years out of the country, and discarded them from their minds; for nature taught men the only, or to speak more securely, the first festivals, namely, the recurring periods of seven days and seven years, making them times of rest, the seventh day being the period of rest for men, and the seventh year for the land. (154) But these men, utterly disregarding the whole of this law, and violating all the obligations implied in salt, or treaties, or the altar of mercy, or the common hearth, considerations by which friendship and unanimity is usually cemented, for all such things are either the

number seven itself, or exist in consequence of that number, oppressed (at least the more powerful of them did so) those men who were weaker with constant and uninterrupted commands, and they oppressed the land also, continually in their covetousness pursuing unrighteous gains, and inflaming their desires so as to excite their unbridled and unjust passions to an insatiable degree.

(155) For instead of granting to men who are in the truest point of view their brothers, as having one common mother, namely, nature, instead, I say, of giving them the appointed holiday after each period of six days, and instead of giving the land a respite after each space of six years without oppressing it either with sowing of seed or planting of trees, (156) in order that it may not be exhausted by incessant labours: instead of acting thus, these men, neglecting all these admirable commandments, have oppressed both the bodies and souls of all men over whom they have had any power, with incessant severities, and have torn to pieces the strength of the deep-soiled earth, exacting revenues from it in an insatiable spirit beyond its power to contribute, and crushing it out altogether and in every part with exactions not only yearly, but even daily.

(157) For all which conduct, these men shall incur the penalties and curses mentioned above: and the country being thoroughly exhausted, and having been forced to submit to innumerable afflictions, shall at last be relieved by being delivered from the burden of its impious inhabitants, and when looking around it, shall see no one left of those who destroyed its grandeur and beauty, but shall behold the market-places all free from their tumults, and wars, and acts of iniquity, and full of tranquillity, and peace, and justice; then it shall recover its youth and former vigour, and shall enjoy tranquillity, and shall have rest at the festive seasons recurring at the sacred numbers of seven, recovering its strength again like an athlete who has been fatigued by his exertions.

(158) Then, like an affectionate mother, it shall pity the sons and the daughters whom it has lost, who now that they are dead are, and still more were, when alive, a grief and sorrow to their parents; and becoming young a second time, it will again be fertile as before, and will produce an irreproachable offspring, an improvement on its former progeny; for she that was desolate, as the prophet says,[15] is now become happy in her children and the mother of a large family. Which prophetic saying has also an allegorical meaning, having reference to the soul; (159) for when the family is very large, and the soul is full, all kinds of passions and vices, surrounding it like so many children, such

---

[14]This contrast of present misery with former splendour is one of the circumstances mentioned by Thucydides as enhancing the terrors of the disasters the Athenians met with in Sicily. 7.75.

[15]Isaiah 54:1.

for instance as pleasures, appetites, folly, intemperance, injustice, it is sad and diseased; and being exceedingly prostrate through illness, it is near to death, but when it is barren and has no such offspring, or when it has lost them, then it becomes changed in all its parts and becomes a pure virgin, (160) and having received the divine seed, it fashions and brings to life a new family, very admirable in their nature, and of great beauty and perfection, such as prudence, courage, temperance, justice, holiness, piety, and all other virtues and good dispositions, of which not only is their birth a blessing accompanied by happiness in its children, but the mere expectation of such a birth is a blessing, since it cheers its weakness by the anticipations of hope; (161) and hope is joy before joy, even though it may be somewhat defective in comparison with perfect joy. But still, it is in both these respects better than that which comes after; first, because it relaxes and softens the dry rigidity of care; and secondly, because by its anticipations it gives a forewarning of the impending perfect good.

XXVIII. (162) I have now, then, without making any concealment of softening the truth in any degree, explained the curses and the punishments which it is fit for those persons to endure who have despised the sacred laws of justice and piety, and who have submitted themselves to the adoption of polytheistic opinions, the end of which is impiety through forgetfulness of the instruction originally imparted to them by their forefathers, which they learnt in their earliest infancy, when they were taught to look upon the nature of the One as the only supreme God, to whom alone those persons may properly be assigned as his inheritance who pursue the genuine truth instead of cunningly invented fables.

(163) If, however, they receive these exertions of power not as aiming at their destruction, but rather at their admonition and improvement, and if they feel shame throughout their whole soul, and change their ways, reproaching themselves for their errors, and openly avowing and confessing all the sins that they have committed against themselves with purified souls and minds, so as in the first place to exhibit a sincerity of conscience utterly alien from falsehood and concealing nothing evil beneath; and secondly, having their tongues also purified so as to produce improvement in their hearers, they will then meet with a favourable acceptance from their merciful saviour, God, who bestows on the race of mankind his especial and exceedingly great gift, namely, relationship to his own word; after which, as its archetypal model, the human mind was formed.

(164) For even though they may be at the very extremities of the earth, acting as slaves to those enemies who have led them away in captivity, still they shall all be restored to freedom in one day, as at a given signal; their sudden and universal change to virtue causing a panic among their masters; for they will let them go, because they are ashamed to govern those who are better than themselves.

IX. (165) But when they have received this unexpected liberty, those who but a short time before were scattered about in Greece, and in the countries of the barbarians, in the islands, and over the continents, rising up with one impulse, and coming from all the different quarters imaginable, all hasten to one place pointed out to them, being guided on their way by some vision, more divine than is compatible with its being of the nature of man, invisible indeed to every one else, but apparent only to those who were saved, having their separate inducements and intercessions, (166) by whose intervention they might obtain a reconciliation with the Father. First of all, the merciful, and gentle, and compassionate nature of him who is invoked, who would always rather have mercy than punishment. In the second place, the holiness of all the founders of the nation, because they, with souls emancipated from the body, exhibiting a genuine and sincere obedience to the Ruler of all things, are not accustomed to offer up ineffectual prayers on behalf of their sons and daughters, since the Father has given to them, as a reward, that they shall be heard in their prayers. (167) And, thirdly, that quality, on account of which above all others, the good will of the beings above-mentioned is conciliated, and that is the improvement and amelioration of those persons who are brought to treaties and agreements, who have, with great difficulty, been able to come from a pathless wilderness into a beaten road, the end of which is no other than that of pleasing God as sons please a father.

(168) And when they come cities will be rebuilt which but a short time ago were in complete ruins, and the desert will be filled with inhabitants, and the barren land will change and become fertile, and the good fortune of their fathers and ancestors will be looked upon as a matter of but small importance, on account of the abundance of wealth of all kinds which they will have at the present moment, flowing forth from the graces of God as from ever-running fountains, which will thus confer vast wealth separately on each individual, and also on all the citizens in common, to an amount beyond the reach even of envy.

(169) And the change in everything will be immediate, for God will nourish the virtues against the enemies of those who have repented, who have delighted in the ruined fortunes of the nation, reviling them, and making a mockery of them, as if they themselves were destined to have a season of good fortune, which could never be put an end

to, which they hope to leave, in regular succession, to their children and to their posterity; thinking, at the same time, that they will for ever behold their adversaries in lasting and unchangeable misfortunes, laid up for even remote future generations; (170) not perceiving, in their insanity, that they enjoyed that brilliant fortune which fell to their share a little while before, not for their own merits, but for the sake of giving a warning and admonition to others, for whom, as they had forsaken their national and hereditary customs, the only salutary remedy which could be found was the grief which they felt to excess when their enemies carried off their property.

Therefore, weeping for and bewailing their own defeat, they will turn back again to the ancient prosperity of their ancestors, retracing all their steps with great exactness, and without its even happening to them to stray from the proper course and to be wrecked; (171) but they who have turned their lamentations into ridicule, and have decided on celebrating, as public festivals, the days which they consider unlucky, and of feasting in memorial of matters for which they mourn, and who, in short, make themselves happy at all the unhappiness of others, when they begin to receive the due reward of their inhumanity, will learn that they have sinned, not against obscure and neglected persons, but against men of noble birth, having fuel to kindle their nobleness to a proper warmth, which, when it is properly fanned into a flame, then their glory, which a little while ago appeared to be extinguished, blazes out again.

(172) For as, when the trunk of a tree is cut down, if the roots are not taken away, new shoots spring up, by which the old trunk is again restored to life as it were; in the very same manner, if there be only left in the soul ever so small a seed of virtue, when everything else is destroyed, still, nevertheless, from that little seed there spring up the most honourable and beautiful qualities among men; by means of which, cities, which were formerly populous and flourishing, are again inhabited, and nations are led to become wealthy and powerful. [16]

---

[16] Yonge's translation includes several sections at this point under a separate treatise title: *On Nobility*. The publisher has elected to relocate the material as sections 187–227 of *On the Virtues* to conform to the Cohn-Wendland (Loeb) sequence and numbering.

EVERY GOOD MAN IS FREE†

(Quod Omnis Probus Liber Sit)

I. (1) My former treatise, O Theodotus, was intended to prove that every wicked man was a slave, and that proposition I fully established by many natural and unquestionable arguments; and this other treatise is akin to that one, being its full brother both by the father's and the mother's side, and being even, in some sort, a twin with it, since in it we will proceed to show that every virtuous man is free.

(2) Now it is said, that the most sacred sect of the Pythagoreans, among many other excellent doctrines, taught this one also, that it was not well to proceed by the plain ordinary roads, not meaning to urge us to walk among precipices (for it was not their object to weary our feet with labour), but intimating, by a figurative mode of speech, that we ought not, either in respect of our words or actions, to use only such as are ordinary and unchanged; (3) and all men who have studied philosophy in a genuine spirit, showing themselves obedient to this injunction, have looked upon it as a sentence, or rather as a law of equal weight with a divine oracle; and, departing from the common opinions of men, they have cut out for themselves a new and hitherto untravelled path, inaccessible to such as have no experience of wise maxims and doctrines, building up systems of ideas, which no one who is not pure either may or can handle.

(4) Now when I speak of men not being pure, I mean those who have either been utterly destitute of education, or else who have tasted of it obliquely, and not in a straight-forward manner, changing the stamp of the beauty of wisdom so as to give an impression of the unsightliness of sophistry. (5) These men, not being able to discern that light which is appreciable only by the intellect, by reason of the weakness of the eyes of their soul, which are by nature easily dazzled by too much brightness, like men living in night and darkness, do not believe those who live in the light of day, and regard everything which they speak of as having been them most distinctly through the beams of the sun shining powerfully upon them, as prodigious pictures, like so many visions or dreams, in no respect different from the exhibitions of jugglers; (6) for how can it be anything but a complete marvel and absurdity to call those men exiles, who do not only live in the middle of the city, but who even take a part in the councils, and courts of justice, and public assemblies, and who, at times, fulfil the duties of clerks of the market, and of superintendants of gymnastic games, and of other offices of different kinds; (7) and, on the other hand, to call those men citizens who have either never been enrolled as such at all, or else have had sentences of infamy or of banishment pronounced against them; men who have been driven beyond the boundaries of the land, and who are unable, not only to set foot upon the country, but even to behold their native soil from a distance, unless they are urged on by some insane frenzy to rush upon certain death; for there are innumerable persons to detect and to punish all those who return from banishment, being both sharpened by their own feelings, and acting in obedience to the commands of the laws.

II. (8) Again, how can it be anything but a most unreasonable assertion, one full of complete shamelessness of insanity, (or I really know not what to call it, for the preposterousness of such a saying is so great that it is not easy to find a proper name for it), to call those men rich who are in a state of complete indigence, and destitute of even necessaries, living hardly and miserably, scarcely procuring enough for their daily subsistence, exposed to famine, as their own peculiar lot among the general plenty and abundance of others, feeding only on the breath of virtue, as they say that grasshoppers feed on air; (9) and then, on the other hand, to call those men poor who are surrounded on all sides by silver and gold, and abundance of possessions and revenues, and an inexhaustible supply of endless good things of every sort, the wealth of which has not only advantaged all their relations and friends, but has even proceeded beyond the family, and been of benefit to great crowds of persons of the same borough, or of the same tribe as the owners; aye, and going further still, it even supplies the city itself with everything which is needful in either peace or war.

(10) Moreover, those who speak thus have, in obedience to the same dream, ventured to speak of slavery as the real condition of men of the greatest importance and genuine nobility of birth, men who can refer not only to their immediate parents, but to their grandfathers and remote ancestors up to the very first founders of their race, as having been in the highest esteem both among men and women; while, on the other hand, they speak of men, whose last three generations have been

---

† Yonge's title, *A Treatise To Prove That Every Man Who is Virtuous is Also Free.*

branded as slaves, born of slaves, who have never been anything but slaves, as free.

(11) But all these things are, as I have said before, the inventions of men whose intellects are obscured, and who are slaves to opinions utterly under the influence of the outward senses, whose judgment is continually corrupted by those who are brought before its tribunal, and as such is unstable. (12) But they ought, if they had really been at all anxious for the truth, not to show themselves, in respect of their minds, inferior to those who have been diseased in their bodies; for such invalids, out of their desire for good health, commit themselves to the physicians. But these other men hesitate to get rid of that disease of the soul, ignorance, by becoming the associates of wise men; from whom they might not only learn to escape ignorance, but they might also acquire that peculiar possession of man, namely, knowledge.

(13) And since, as that sweetest of all writers, Plato, says, envy is removed far from the divine company, but wisdom, that most divine and communicative of all things, never closes its school, but is continually open to receive all who thirst for salutary doctrines, to whom she pours forth the inexhaustible stream of unalloyed instruction and wisdom, and persuades them to yield to the intoxication of the soberest of all drunkenness. (14) And her disciples, like persons who have been initiated into the sacred and holy mysteries, when they are at last entirely filled with the knowledge proffered to them, reproach themselves bitterly for their previous neglect, as not having taken proper care of their time, but having lived a life which was hardly deserving to be called life, in which they have been utterly destitute of wisdom.

(15) Those men, therefore, act worthily who, in every case and everywhere, have resolved to dedicate the whole of their youth as the first fruits of their earliest vigour to nothing in preference to education, in which it is well for a man to spend both his youth and his age; for as they say that vessels even when empty do nevertheless retain the odour of whatever was originally poured into them,[1] so also are the souls of the young deeply impressed with the indelible character of those conceptions which were the first to be offered to their minds, which cannot be at all washed away by the torrent of any ideas which flow over the mind afterwards, but they to the last show the character originally given to them.

III. However, we have said enough of these matters. (16) We must now examine with accuracy that which we have taken as the subject of our investigation, that we may not be led astray through

being deceived by the indistinctness of words and expressions; but that, understanding accurately what it is of which we are speaking, we may frame our determinations felicitously.

(17) Slavery, then, is of two kinds; slavery of the soul and slavery of the body.

Now, of our bodies, men are masters; but over our souls, wickedness and the passions have the dominion. And we may speak of freedom in the same manner. For one kind of freedom gives fearlessness of body in respect of any dangers which can come upon it from men of still more powerful body; while the other produces peace to the mind, by putting a check upon the authority of the passions. (18) Now, about the former kind, scarcely any one ever raises any question; for the chances of fortune which happen to men are infinite in number, and it often happens that men of the highest virtue have fallen into unexpected misfortunes, and so have lost the freedom which belonged to them through their birth. But there is room for inquiry about those manners which neither desires, nor fears, nor pleasures, nor pains, have ever brought under the yoke, as if they had come forth out of confinement, and as if the chains by which they had been bound were now loosened.

(19) Therefore, discarding all mention of those kinds of freedom which are only a pretence, and of all those names also which are quite unconnected with nature, but which owe their existence only to opinion, such as slaves born in the house, slaves purchased with money, slaves taken in war, let us now investigate the character of the man who is truly free, who is alone possessed of independence, even if ten thousand men set themselves down as his masters; for he will quote that line of Sophocles, which differs in no respect from the doctrines of the Pythagoreans—

"God is my ruler, and no mortal man."[2]

(20) For, in real truth, that man alone is free who has God for his leader; indeed, in my opinion, that man is even the ruler of all others, and has all the affairs of the earth committed to him, being, as it were, the viceroy of a great king, the mortal lieutenant of an immortal sovereign. However, this assertion of the actual authority of the wise man may be postponed to a more suitable opportunity.

We must at present examine minutely the question of his perfect freedom. (21) If now any one advancing deeply into the matter should choose to investigate it closely, he will see clearly that there is no one thing so nearly related to another as independence of action. On which account there

---

[1] Compare Moore—"You may break, you may shatter the vase if you will, / But the scent of the roses will hang round it still."

[2] It is not known from what play this line comes; it is placed among the Incerta Fragments, No. 89, by Brunck.

are a great many things which stand in the way of the liberty of a wicked man; covetousness of money, the desire of glory, the love of pleasure, and so on. But the virtuous man has absolutely no obstacle at all since he rises up against, and resists, and overthrows, and tramples on love, and fear, and cowardice, and pain, and all things of that kind, as if they were rivals defeated by him in the public games. (22) For he has learnt to disregard all the commands which those most unlawful masters of the soul seek to impose upon him, out of his admiration and desire for freedom, of which independence and spontaneousness of action are the most especial and inalienable inheritance; and by some persons the poet is praised who composed this iambic—

"No man's a slave who does not fear to die,"[3]

as having had an accurate idea of the consequences of such courage; for he conceived that nothing is so calculated to enslave the mind as a fear of death, arising from an excessive desire of living.

IV. (23) But we must consider that not only is the man who feels no anxiety to avoid death incapable of being made a slave, but the same privilege belongs to those who are indifferent to poverty, and want of reputation, and pain, and all those other things which the generality of men look upon as evils, being themselves but evil judges of things, since they pronounce a man a slave from a computation of what things he has need of, looking at the duties which he is compelled to perform, when they ought to look rather at his free and indomitable disposition; (24) for the man who out of a lowly and slavish spirit submits himself to lowly and slavish actions in spite of his deliberate judgment, is really and truly a slave; but he who adapts his circumstances and actions to the present occasion, and who voluntarily and in an enduring spirit bears up against the events of fortune, not looking at any thing of human affairs as extraordinary, but having by diligent consideration fully assured himself that all divine things are honoured by eternal order and happiness; and that all mortal things are tossed about in an everlasting storm and fluctuation of affairs so as to be subject to the greatest variety of changes and vicissitudes, and who, from those considerations, bears all that can befall him with a noble courage, is at once both a philosopher and a free man. (25) On which account he will neither obey every one who imposes a command upon him, not even if he threatens him with insults, and tortures, and even still more formidable evils; but he will bear a gallant spirit, and will cry out in reply to such menaces—

"Yes, burn and scorch my flesh, and glut your hate,
Drinking my life-warm blood; for heaven's stars
Shall quit their place, and darken 'neath the earth,
And earth rise up and take the place of heaven,
Before you wring from me a word of flattery."[4]

V. (26) I have before now seen among the competitors in the pancratium, at the public games, one man inflicting all kinds of blows both with his hands and feet, all of them with great accuracy of aim and omitting nothing which could conduce to victory, and yet after at time fainting and desponding, and at last quitting the arena without the crown of victory; and the other who has received all his blows, being thoroughly hardened with great firmness of flesh, and being tough and unyielding, and filled with the true spirit of an athlete, and invigorated throughout his whole body, being like so much iron or stone, not at all yielding to the blows inflicted by the other, at last, by the endurance and resolution of his spirit, defeating the power of his adversary so as to obtain a complete victory. (27) And the condition of the virtuous man appears to me very much to resemble that of this person. For having thoroughly fortified his soul with strong and powerful reasoning, he so compels the man who is offering him violence to desist from weariness, before he himself can be compelled to do any thing contrary to his opinion of propriety. But perhaps this is incredible to those who do not know by experience that virtue is of the character that I have mentioned, just as that other case would be to those who have never seen the combatants in the pancratium; but nevertheless it is strictly true. (28) And it was from a regard to this fact that Antisthenes said that "the virtuous man was a burden hard to be borne."

For as folly is a light thing easily tossed about in every direction, so, on the contrary, wisdom is a well established and immovable thing of a weight which is not easily agitated. (29) Accordingly the lawgiver of the Jews[5] represents the hands of the wise man as a heavy, intimating by this figurative expression the gravity of his actions, which are supported in no superficial but in a solid manner by his inflexible mind. (30) Therefore, he is not under the compulsion of any thing, as being one who despises pains, and who looks with contempt on death, and who, by the law of nature, has all foolish men for his subjects. For in the same manner as goatherds, and cowherds, and shepherds lead their respective flocks of goats, and cattle, and sheep, but shepherds cannot manage a drove of oxen, so in the same manner the generality of men,

---

[3] This line is from an unknown tragedy by Euripides. Fragmenta Incerta, 348.

[4] This is a fragment of Euripides from the Syleus. Fr. 2.

[5] Genesis 16:9.

being like so many cattle, stand in need of a guide and governor. And their proper governors are virtuous men, being placed in the position of shepherds to the multitude; (31) for Homer is constantly in the habit of calling kings shepherds of their people.[6] But nature has appropriated this appellation as more peculiarly belonging to the good, since the wicked are rather tended by others than occupied in serving them; for they are led captive by strong wine, and by beauty, and by delicate eating, and sweetmeats, and by the arts of cooks and confectioners, to say nothing of the thirst of gold, and silver, and other things of a higher character. But men of the other class are not allured or led astray by any thing, but are rather inclined to admonish those whom they perceive to be caught in the toils of pleasure.

VI. (32) And of the assertion that the being compelled to perform services to others is not of itself an indication of slavery, there is a most clear proof in what occurs in war; for one can behold men engaged in military expeditions, all acting by their own means, and not only carrying complete armour, but being also loaded like beasts of burden with everything required for their necessary wants, and going out to fetch water, and fuel, and fodder for the cattle. (33) And why need I dwell at length on what is done against the enemy in such expeditions, in respect of their labours in cutting ditches, or erecting walls, or building ships, and doing with their hands and their whole bodies everything which relates to every kind of necessary employment or art.

(34) Moreover, there is in peace also another kind of war not wholly dissimilar from that which is carried on under arms, which want or reputation, and poverty, and terrible want of necessary things excites, by which men are compelled and constrained to put their hands to the most ignominious and slavish tasks, digging and cultivating the ground and labouring at the employments of handicrafts-men, and serving without hesitation for the sake of procuring food to support life; very often even bearing burdens through the middle of the market-place, in the sight of those who are of their own age, and have grown up with them, and been their school-fellows and companions through life.

(35) There are others also who are slaves by birth, and who have nevertheless been raised by the bounty of fortune to the condition of freemen; for they have become stewards of houses, and properties, and large possessions, and sometimes they are even appointed rulers of their fellow slaves. And many such have had committed to them the guardianship of the wives and orphan children of their masters, being preferred to the confidential offices which belong properly to friends and relations, but, nevertheless they are slaves, though employed in borrowing, in buying, in collecting revenues, and though they are themselves attended by other servants. What is there wonderful then if, on the contrary also, some persons, originally nobly born, by a sudden failure of good fortune, are subjected to such necessities as properly belong to slaves, (36) and by being compelled to obey others are deprived of their own freedom?

Moreover, in some degree, children are forced to submit to the commands of their father or their mother; and pupils, also, submit to whatever their teachers enjoin; for no one is willingly a slave. Now, parents will never display such an extravagant and unnatural dislike to their children as to compel their own offspring to submit to such menial offices as are only a symbol of slavery.

(37) And if any one beholding some persons who may have been bought and sold by traffickers in men, looks upon them at once as slaves, he is widely removed from the truth; for an act of selling does not make him who purchases the master, nor him who is sold the slave, since fathers at times have paid a price for their sons, and sons have often laid down a ransom for their fathers, in cases where they have been carried away as prisoners by some piratical sally, or have been taken captive in regular warfare, though still the laws of nature, which are more stable than those of men, describe them as free. (38) And, before now, some persons in the excess of their confidence have brought matters into so completely altered a condition that they have actually become masters instead of slaves, in spite of having been bought. At all events, I have often seen some young persons of great beauty, and of great wit in conversation, getting the complete mastery over those who had purchased them, by two great incentives, the exquisiteness of their beauty and the elegance of their language; for these are engines able to overthrow any soul which wants stability and a solid foundation, being the most powerful of all the contrivances which were ever invented for the overthrow of cities.

(39) And a proof of this may easily be given; for we may see that those who have become the masters of such persons serve them, and address entreaties to them, and eagerly entreat their favour as they would that of fortune or of the good genius; and if they are neglected by them they are vexed, and if they only obtain a gentle or favourable look from them they dance for joy. (40) Unless, indeed, any one would say that a man who has bought a lion has become the master of the lion, when if he merely look with a threatening glance at him he will soon learn to his cost what kind of a master, what a savage and ferocious tyrant he has purchased. What shall we say then? Shall we not look upon a wise man as more difficult to enslave than a lion, when he in his free-

dom and invincible soul has much more courage than any creature can have which consists of a body which is by nature a slave, however great his strength may be by which he resists his masters.

VII. (41) And every one may learn to appreciate the true freedom of which the virtuous man is in the enjoyment from other circumstances.

"No slave can e'er true happiness enjoy."[7]

For what can be more miserable than to have no power over anything, not even over one's self? But then a man is happy, inasmuch as he bears within himself the foundation and complement of virtue and excellence, in which consists the supreme power over all things, [...][8] so that beyond all controversy and of necessity the virtuous man is free.

(42) Besides all this, would not any one affirm that the friends of God are free? unless indeed one can think it consistent to attribute to the companions of kings, not only freedom but even at times a great degree of authority, when they commit magistracies to them, and when they, in consequence, fulfil the offices of subordinate rulers; and yet, at the same time, to speak of slavery in connection with the gods of heaven, when those men, on account of the love which they have shown to God, have also at once become beloved by God, being requited by him with good will equal to their own, truth being the judge, so that they as the poets say, are universal princes and kings of kings.

(43) But the lawgiver of the Jews ventures upon a more bold assertion even than this, inasmuch as he was, as it is reported, a student and practiser of plain philosophy; and so he teaches that the man who is wholly possessed with the love of God and who serves the living God alone, is no longer man, but actually God, being indeed the God of men, but not of the parts of nature, in order to leave to the Father of the universe the attributes of being both King and God of gods. (44) Is it right, then, to think a man who is invested with such privileges as these a slave, or rather as the only one who is free? Who, even though he may not be thought worthy by himself of being classed as God, one nevertheless ought by all means to pronounce happy, by reason of his having God for his friend; for God is not a weak champion, nor regardless of the rights and claims of friendship, inasmuch as he is the God of companionship, and as he presides over everything that belongs to companions.

(45) Moreover, as among cities, some being governed by an oligarchy or by tyrants, endure slav-

ery, having those who have subdued them and made themselves masters of them for severe and cruel tyrants; while others, existing under the superintending care of the laws and under those good protectors, are free and happy. So also in the case of men; those who are under the dominion of anger, or appetite, or any other passion, or of treacherous wickedness, are in every respect slaves; and those who live in accordance with the law are free.

(46) But the unerring law is right reason; not an ordinance made by this or that mortal, a corruptible and perishable law, a lifeless law written on lifeless parchment or engraved on lifeless columns; but one imperishable, and stamped by immortal nature on the immortal mind. (47) On which account any one may reasonably marvel at the dim-sightedness of those who do not see the particular characters of things which are so clear, and who say that for those mighty nations of the Athenians and Lacedaemonians, the laws of Solon and Lycurgus are quite sufficient to ensure the liberty of the people if they only have the mastery and dominion, and if the people who live in those cities do dutifully obey them, and who yet affirm that right reason, which is the fountain from which all other laws do spring, is not sufficient for wise men to enable them to arrive at a participation in freedom, even though they obey it in all the particulars as to what it commands and what it prohibits.

(48) Moreover, in addition to what has been already said, there is one most undeniable proof of freedom, equality of speech, which all virtuous men use to one another; on which account they say that the following iambics are inspired with the true spirit of genuine philosophy:—

"For slaves no freedom have, not e'en in speech."

And again:—

"You're but a slave, and may not dare to speak."

(49) As, therefore, musical science gives to all those who have studied music an equal right to speak on matters connected with their art; and as a man who is learned in grammar or in geometry has a right to speak among grammarians and mathematicians, so also the law in life allows the same privilege to those who are learned in the way in which men ought to live. (50) But all virtuous men are skilful in all the affairs which belong to life, inasmuch as they also are so with respect to the things which belong to universal nature; and some of them are free; and so therefore are they who have the freedom of speaking to them on equal terms; therefore no virtuous man is a slave, but all are free.

VIII. (51) And from the same principle as a starting-point it will also be clearly shown that the

---

[7]Some editions print this as a quotation, but Mangey does not. It is not known where it comes from if it is one.

[8]There is a considerable hiatus in the text here.

foolish man is a slave; for as the laws which prevail with respect to music do not give those who are ignorant of it a right of speaking about it in terms of equality with those who are well versed in it; nor do the laws respecting grammar give those ignorant of that knowledge a right of speaking about it on terms of equality with those who are well skilled in it; nor, in short, does the law with respect to any art confer such a right on those who are ignorant of it towards those who are learned in it; so also the law which relates to the establishing proper principles of life does not give those who are strangers to any such true principles a right of speaking really on such topics to those who have studied and learnt them. (52) But to all free men, perfect equality of speech on all subjects is given by the law; and some virtuous men are free; and of the proper principles of life, the foolish are utterly ignorant, but the wise are most profoundly versed in them: therefore it is not the case that ever any foolish or wicked men are free, but they are all slaves.

(53) And Zeno, as much as any one else, being under the influence of virtue, ventures boldly to assert that the wicked have not a right to any equality of speech towards the virtuous; for he says, "Shall not the wicked man suffer if he contradicts the virtuous man?" Therefore the wicked man has not a right to freedom of speech as respects the virtuous man. (54) I know that many persons will rail at this assertion as one which is dictated rather by self-conceit than by real wisdom. But if, after they have desisted from mocking and ridiculing it, they will condescend to investigate the matter and to examine clearly into what is really said, then, recognising and admiring its perfect truth, they will become aware that there is nothing for which a man will suffer more than for disregarding the words of a wise man. (55) For loss of money, and the brand of dishonour, and banishment, and insults by means of beating, and all other things of that sort, injure a man but little, or rather not at all, when compared with acts of wickedness and the things which are the results of acts of wickedness. But it happens that the generality of men, not being able to perceive the injuries of the soul by reason of the mutilated state of their reason, are grieved only at external calamities, being wholly deprived of the faculty of judging correctly, which is the only one by which they can comprehend the injury received by the intellect. (56) But if they were able to look up and see clearly, then, beholding the deceits which arise out of folly, and the perplexities which proceed from covetousness, and all the intoxicated folly to which intemperance gives rise, and all the transgressions of the law in which injustice indulges, they would be filled with interminable grief at the injuries sustained by the best portion of themselves, and would be incapable of receiving comfort by reason of the excessive greatness of the evil.

(57) But Zeno appears to have drawn this maxim of his as it were from the fountain of the legislation of the Jews,[9] in the history of which it is recorded that in a case where there were two brothers, the one temperate and the other intemperate, the common father of them both, taking pity on the intemperate one who did not walk in the path of virtue, prays that he may serve his brother, conceiving that service which appears in general to be the greatest of evils is the most perfect good to a foolish man, in order that thus he may be deprived of his independence of action, so as to be prevented from misconducting himself with impunity, and that he may be improved in his disposition by the superintending management of him who is appointed to be his master.

IX. (58) What has now then been said with the view of establishing the truth in the matter inquired into is, in my opinion, sufficient. But since physicians are accustomed to cure various diseases with still more various remedies, it is necessary that we should bring a series of proofs, keeping close to the subject, in order to establish those propositions which appear paradoxical by reason of their unusual character. For some people, even if they are convicted by ever so close a series of proofs, can hardly be brought to see their error. (59) Therefore, it is not an incorrect assertion that the man who does everything wisely does everything well; and he who does everything well does everything correctly; and he who does everything correctly does everything also in an unerring, and blameless, and irreproachable, and faultless, and beneficial manner: so that he will have free permission to do everything, and to live as he pleases. And he who has this liberty must be free.

But the virtuous man does do everything wisely; therefore he alone is free. (60) And indeed the man whom it is not possible either to compel to do anything, or to prevent from doing anything, cannot possibly be a slave; and one cannot compel or prevent the virtuous man. Therefore the virtuous man cannot be a slave; and that he is never under compulsion or under any restraint is quite plain; for that man is under restraint who does not obtain what he desires. But the wise man only desires such things as proceed from virtue, in which it is impossible for him to be disappointed. And again, if he is under compulsion, then it is plain that he does something against his will; but in all cases where there are actions, they are either good ones proceeding from virtue, or evil ones proceeding from wickedness, or else they are of an intermediate and indifferent character. (61) Now

---

[9]Genesis 28:1.

the actions which proceed from virtue, the creature man performs, not through compulsion but voluntarily, for everything which he does is the result of his deliberate choice; and the actions which proceed from wickedness, inasmuch as they ought to be avoided, he does not do even in dreams; nor again, is it likely that he would perform those actions which are of an indifferent character, between which the mind, as if in a scale, is equally balanced, not being induced to yield to them, as having any attractive power, nor, on the other hand, to regard them with any particular aversion as worthy of hatred; from all which it is plain, that the virtuous man does nothing against his will, and nothing under compulsion; and if he were a slave he would be acting under compulsion: so that the virtuous man must be free.

X. (62) But since some persons, who have paid but very little attention to literary pursuits, not understanding demonstrative arguments, which establish only general principles of action, are accustomed to ask us, "Who then are the men, whether previously existing or now alive, whom you thus represent to us?" it is well to make answer, that in former times there were some persons who surpassed all their contemporaries in virtue, taking God alone for their guide, and living in strict accordance with the law, that is to say, with the right reason of nature, and who were not only free themselves, but who also filled all who came near to them with a spirit of freedom. And now also, in our own time, there are some who are, as it were, images of them, bearing on themselves the stamp of the virtue of those wise men as their archetypal model; (63) for it does not follow, that although the souls of such as contradict those virtuous men are deprived of all liberty for having been completely led away and enslaved by folly and other vices, that on this account the whole human race is so too.

But it is no wonder if we do not see numerous companies of those men advancing as it were in a solid body. In the first place, because whatever is exceedingly beautiful is rare; secondly, because men who are removed from the main crowd of inconsiderately judging persons, have abundant leisure for the contemplation of the things of nature, endeavouring, as far as it may be in their power, to correct life in general (for virtue is a thing of great benefit to the whole community); but when they are unable to succeed in their object, by reason of the numbers of absurdities which are continually impeding them in the different cities, which the different passions and vices of the soul have given strength to, they then retire into solitude, in order not to be carried away by the violence and rush of these absurdities, as by a wintry torrent.

(64) But if there were any real anxiety for improvement in us, we ought carefully to trace out the hiding-places of these men, and to sit down before them as suppliants, and to entreat them to come forward to impart a tincture of civilization to life which was previously savage, by announcing, instead of inward slavery and innumerable evils, peace and an abundance of all other good things to flow over it continually.

(65) But as things are, we do investigate all retreats only for the sake of money, and with this object we open the hard and rugged beings of the earth; and a great deal of the champaign country is opened in mines, and no small part of the mountainous district also, while we are seeking for gold, and silver, and brass, and iron, and all kinds of materials. (66) But vain opinion, setting up pride as a god, has descended down to the very lowest depths of the sea in its researches to see whether there is any beautiful thing which might become an object of the outward senses lying covered anywhere; and finding many species of precious stones, some adhering closely to the rocks, and others lying concealed in oyster-shells, which are more valuable still, has thus shown a great desire to deceive the sight; (67) and for the sake of the requirements of wisdom, or temperance, or courage, or justice, even that portion of the earth which is naturally inaccessible is travelled over, and seas which are dangerous to navigate are sailed over at any season of the year by sailors. (68) And yet, what need is there, either of long journeys over the land, or of long voyages, for the sake of investigating the seeking out virtue, the roots of which the Creator has laid not at any great distance, but so near, as the wise lawgiver of the Jews says, [10] "They are in thy mouth, and in thy heart, and in thy hands:" intimating by these figurative expressions the words, and actions, and designs of men; all of which stand in need of careful cultivation.

(69) These men, therefore, who prefer idleness to industry, have not only hindered the shoots of virtue from thriving, but have even dried up all the roots, and withered and destroyed them; while those on the contrary, who look upon idleness as pernicious and who are willing to labour, cultivate it as husbandmen would cultivate flourishing shoots of good kinds of plants, with incessant care, and thus they raise the virtues to the height of heaven itself in ever-flourishing and undying branches, bearing a fruit of happiness which never ceases, or rather, as some say, not bearing happiness, but rather actually being happiness, which Moses was in the habit of calling by one compound name, *holokarpōmata* (whole offerings of entire fruit). (70) For in respect of those things which grow out of the ground, the fruit is not trees, nor are the trees fruit. But with respect to those which grew in the soul, these their whole branches do

---

[10] Deuteronomy 30:14.

entirely change into the nature of the fruit; for instance, into wisdom, and justice, and courage, and temperance.

XI. (71) Since, then, we have such great assistance towards arriving at virtue, must we not blush to assert that there is any necessary deficiency of wisdom in the human race, when we might, by following it up, like a spark smouldering among wood, kindle it into a flame? But the fact is, that we do display great hesitation and incessant slackness in the pursuit of those objects towards which we ought to hasten eagerly as most closely connected with and nearly akin to us, and by this hesitation and indolence the seeds of virtue are destroyed; while, on the contrary, those things which we ought to neglect we show an insatiable desire and longing for.

(72) It is owing to this that the whole earth and sea are full of men who are rich and of high reputation, and who indulge in all kinds of pleasure; but that the number of those who are prudent, and just, and virtuous, is very small; but that of which the numbers are small, though it may be rare, is nevertheless not non-existent. (73) And all Greece and all the land of the barbarians is a witness of this; for in the one country flourished those who are truly called "the seven wise men," though others had flourished before them, and have also in all probability lived since their time. But their memory, though they are now very ancient, has nevertheless not been effaced by the lapse of ages, while of others who are more modern, the names have been lost through the neglect of their contemporaries. (74) And in the land of the barbarians, in which the same men are authorities both as to words and actions, there are very numerous companies of virtuous and honourable men celebrated. Among the Persians there is the body of the Magi, who, investigating the works of nature for the purpose of becoming acquainted with the truth, do at their leisure become initiated themselves and initiate others in the divine virtues by very clear explanations. And among the Indians there is the class of the gymnosophists, who, in addition to natural philosophy, take great pains in the study of moral science likewise, and thus make their whole existence a sort of lesson in virtue.

XII. (75) Moreover Palestine and Syria too are not barren of exemplary wisdom and virtue, which countries no slight portion of that most populous nation of the Jews inhabits. There is a portion of those people called Essenes, in number something more than four thousand in my opinion, who derive their name from their piety, though not according to any accurate form of the Grecian dialect, because they are above all men devoted to the service of God, not sacrificing living animals, but studying rather to preserve their own minds in a state of holiness and purity. (76) These men, in the first place, live in villages, avoiding all cities on account

of the habitual lawlessness of those who inhabit them, well knowing that such a moral disease is contracted from associations with wicked men, just as a real disease might be from an impure atmosphere, and that this would stamp an incurable evil on their souls. Of these men, some cultivating the earth, and others devoting themselves to those arts which are the result of peace, benefit both themselves and all those who come in contact with them, not storing up treasures of silver and of gold, nor acquiring vast sections of the earth out of a desire for ample revenues, but providing all things which are requisite for the natural purposes of life; (77) for they alone of almost all men having been originally poor and destitute, and that too rather from their own habits and ways of life than from any real deficiency of good fortune, are nevertheless accounted very rich, judging contentment and frugality to be great abundance, as in truth they are.

(78) Among those men you will find no makers of arrows, or javelins, or swords, or helmets, or breastplates, or shields; no makers of arms or of military engines; no one, in short, attending to any employment whatever connected with war, or even to any of those occupations even in peace which are easily perverted to wicked purposes; for they are utterly ignorant of all traffic, and of all commercial dealings, and of all navigation, but they repudiate and keep aloof from everything which can possibly afford any inducement to covetousness; (79) and there is not a single slave among them, but they are all free, aiding one another with a reciprocal interchange of good offices; and they condemn masters, not only as unjust, inasmuch as they corrupt the very principle of equality, but likewise as impious, because they destroy the ordinances of nature, which generated them all equally, and brought them up like a mother, as if they were all legitimate brethren, not in name only, but in reality and truth.

But in their view this natural relationship of all men to one another has been thrown into disorder by designing covetousness, continually wishing to surpass others in good fortune, and which has therefore engendered alienation instead of affection, and hatred instead of friendship; (80) and leaving the logical part of philosophy, as in no respect necessary for the acquisition of virtue, to the word-catchers, and the natural part, as being too sublime for human nature to master, to those who love to converse about high objects (except indeed so far as such a study takes in the contemplation of the existence of God and of the creation of the universe), they devote all their attention to the moral part of philosophy, using as instructors the laws of their country which it would have been impossible for the human mind to devise without divine inspiration.

(81) Now these laws they are taught at other times, indeed, but most especially on the seventh

day, for the seventh day is accounted sacred, on which they abstain from all other employments, and frequent the sacred places which are called synagogues, and there they sit according to their age in classes, the younger sitting under the elder, and listening with eager attention in becoming order. (82) Then one, indeed, takes up the holy volume and reads it, and another of the men of the greatest experience comes forward and explains what is not very intelligible, for a great many precepts are delivered in enigmatical modes of expression, and allegorically, as the old fashion was; (83) and thus the people are taught piety, and holiness, and justice, and economy, and the science of regulating the state, and the knowledge of such things as are naturally good, or bad, or indifferent, and to choose what is right and to avoid what is wrong, using a threefold variety of definitions, and rules, and criteria, namely, the love of God, and the love of virtue, and the love of mankind.

(84) Accordingly, the sacred volumes present an infinite number of instances of the disposition devoted to the love of God, and of a continued and uninterrupted purity throughout the whole of life, of a careful avoidance of oaths and of falsehood, and of a strict adherence to the principle of looking on the Deity as the cause of everything which is good and of nothing which is evil. They also furnish us with many proofs of a love of virtue, such as abstinence from all covetousness of money, from ambition, from indulgence in pleasures, temperance, endurance, and also moderation, simplicity, good temper, the absence of pride, obedience to the laws, steadiness, and everything of that kind; and, lastly, they bring forward as proofs of the love of mankind, goodwill, equality beyond all power of description, and fellowship, about which it is not unreasonable to say a few words.

(85) In the first place, then, there is no one who has a house so absolutely his own private property, that it does not in some sense also belong to every one: for besides that they all dwell together in companies, the house is open to all those of the same notions, who come to them from other quarters; (86) then there is one magazine among them all; their expenses are all in common; their garments belong to them all in common; their food is common, since they all eat in messes; for there is no other people among which you can find a common use of the same house, a common adoption of one mode of living, and a common use of the same table more thoroughly established in fact than among this tribe: and is not this very natural? For whatever they, after having been working during the day, receive for their wages, that they do not retain as their own, but bring it into the common stock, and give any advantage that is to be derived from it to all who desire to avail themselves of it; (87) and those who

are sick are not neglected because they are unable to contribute to the common stock, inasmuch as the tribe have in their public stock a means of supplying their necessities and aiding their weakness, so that from their ample means they support them liberally and abundantly; and they cherish respect for their elders, and honour them and care for them, just as parents are honoured and cared for by their lawful children: being supported by them in all abundance both by their personal exertions, and by innumerable contrivances.

XIII. (88) Such diligent practisers of virtue does philosophy, unconnected with any superfluous care of examining into Greek names render men, proposing to them as necessary exercises to train them towards its attainment, all praiseworthy actions by which a freedom, which can never be enslaved, is firmly established.

(89) And a proof of this is that, though at different times a great number of chiefs of every variety of disposition and character, have occupied their country, some of whom have endeavoured to surpass even ferocious wild beasts in cruelty, leaving no sort of inhumanity unpractised, and have never ceased to murder their subjects in whole troops, and have even torn them to pieces while living, like cooks cutting them limb from limb, till they themselves, being overtaken by the vengeance of divine justice, have at last experienced the same miseries in their turn: (90) others again having converted their barbarous frenzy into another kind of wickedness, practising an ineffable degree of savageness, talking with the people quietly, but through the hypocrisy of a more gentle voice, betraying the ferocity of their real disposition, fawning upon their victims like treacherous dogs, and becoming the causes of irremediable miseries to them, have left in all their cities monuments of their impiety, and hatred of all mankind, in the never to be forgotten miseries endured by those whom they oppressed: (91) and yet no one, not even of those immoderately cruel tyrants, nor of the more treacherous and hypocritical oppressors was ever able to bring any real accusation against the multitude of those called Essenes or Holy.[11] But everyone being subdued by the virtue of these men, looked up to them as free by nature, and not subject to the frown of any human being, and have celebrated their manner of messing together, and their fellowship with one another beyond all description in respect of its mutual good faith, which is an ample proof of a perfect and very happy life.

XIV. (92) But it is necessary for us (since some persons do not believe that there is any perfect virtue in the multitude, but that whatever in

---

11The Greek is *essaiōn ē hosiōn*, as if *essaiōn* was only a variety of the word *hosiōn*, "holy."

such persons appears like virtue only reaches a certain point of increase and growth), to bring forward as corroborative testimonies the lives of some particular good men who are the most undeniable evidences of freedom.

(93) Calanus was an Indian by birth, one of the gymnosophists; he, being looked upon as the man who was possessed of the greatest fortitude of all his contemporaries, and that too, not only by his own countrymen, but also by foreigners, which is the rarest of all things, was greatly admired by some kings of hostile countries, because he had combined virtuous actions with praiseworthy language; (94) accordingly, Alexander, the king of the Macedonians, wishing to exhibit to Greece the wisdom that was to be found in the territories of the barbarians, as being a sort of faithful copy and representation of an archetypal model, in the first instance invited Calanus to quit his home, and come and take up his abode with him, by which means he said he would acquire the greatest imaginable glory throughout all Asia and all Europe; (95) and when he could not persuade him by fair means, he said to him, "You shall be compelled to follow me." And he replied with great felicity of expression and in a noble spirit; "What then shall I be worth, O Alexander, when you exhibit me to the Greeks, after I have been compelled to do what I do not like?" Now is not this speech, or rather is not this idea, full of real freedom? And moreover in his writings also, which are more durable than his expressions, he has erected, as if on a pillar, indelible signs of his indomitably free disposition; (96) and this is proved by the letter which he sent to the king.

CALANUS TO ALEXANDER, GREETING

"Your friends are endeavouring to persuade you to apply force and compulsion to the philosophers of the Indians, though not even in their sleep have they beheld our actions; for you will be able indeed to transport our bodies from place to place, but you will not be able to compel our souls to do what they do not like, any more than you would be able to make bricks or timber utter words; we can cause the greatest troubles and the greatest destruction to living bodies; now we are superior to this power; we are burnt even while living, there is no king nor ruler who will ever succeed in compelling us to do what we do not choose to do; and we are in no respect like unto the philosophers of the Greeks, who study speeches to deliver to a public assembly; but our actions do always correspond to our words, and our speeches which are short have a power different from that of our actions, and secure for us freedom and happiness."

(97) At such positive refusals then, and at such brave sentiments, is it not natural for any one to quote that saying of Zeno that, "It would be easier to sink a bladder which was full of wind, than to compel any virtuous man whatever, against his will, to commit any action which he had never intended." For the soul of such a man will never submit, and can never be defeated, since it has been fortified by right reason with solid doctrines.

XV. (98) Moreover, both poets and historians are witnesses to the real freedom of virtuous men, in whose doctrines both Greeks and barbarians are equally bred up almost from their very cradles, and by which they are improved in their dispositions, changing everything in their souls which is adulterated by a blameable way of bringing up and of living, into good coinage; (99) accordingly just see what Hercules says in Euripides. [12]

"Yes, burn and scorch my flesh, and glut your hate,
Drinking my life-warm blood; for heaven's stars
Shall quit their place, and darken 'neath the earth,
And earth rise up and take the place of heaven,
Before you wring from me a word of flattery."

For in real truth flattery, and adulation, and hypocrisy, in which what is uttered is at variance with the sentiments which are really felt, are the most slavish of things. But without any disguise, and in a genuine honest spirit of truth to speak with freedom what is dictated by a clear conscience, is a line of conduct suited to those who are nobly born. (100) Again, do not you see this same virtuous man himself, that even when he is sold he does not appear to be a servant, but he strikes all who behold him with awe, as not being merely free, but as even being about to prove the master of him who has purchased him? (101) At all events, Mercury replies to a man who inquires whether he is worthless—

"By no means worthless, on the contrary,
In every part most venerable: never
Low, nor of no account, as though a slave.
But as to raiment brilliant to behold,
And with the club he bears most energetic.
But no one willingly becomes the buyer
Of one who soon the master will become
Of him and all his house. And every one
Who sees thee, fears thee, for your eye is fire
Like that of any bull prepared for war
Gainst Afric lions." [13]

Then, again, he speaks in conclusion of his disposition—

"I now do blame you for your stubborn silence,
As if you were not subject to a master,
But sought to govern rather than be governed."

---

[12]See 100:4.
[13]Euripides Frag. Incert. 495.

(102) But when, after Syleus had bought him, he was sent into the fields, he showed by his actions the indomitable freedom of his nature; for having sacrificed the choicest of the bulls which were there to Jupiter, he made a pretence of a feast, and having drunk a vast quantity of wine at one meal, he lay down very contentedly to digest it; (103) and when Syleus came, and got angry both at the loss and also at the easy indifference of his servant, and at his preposterous contempt for his master, he never changed colour, nor made any difference in his conduct, but said with the most perfect confidence—

"Sit down and drink, and thus you shall
At once appreciate my character,
And learn to be my master in reality."

(104) Shall we then say that he is the slave, or rather the master of his master, when he dares in this manner not only to accost him with such freedom, but even to impose injunctions on him who has purchased him, as if he would beat and insult him if he were to be stubborn and disobedient, and, if he introduced any one to assist him, as if he would destroy them all to a man?

Therefore the writings which were delivered respecting this purchase must have been an utter absurdity and a mere joke, since they would be trampled upon by the more effectual power of the slave bought under them, being of less value than unwritten covenants, and being likely to be utterly destroyed by moths, or time, or mould and rust.

XVI. (105) But it is not right, some one will say, to bring forward the actions of heroes as proofs of the correctness of an argument, for that they were greater than the common run of human nature, and were more on a par with the heavenly beings themselves, as having been born of a sort of mixed generation, and having sprung from mortal and immortal seed at the same time, being correctly entitled demigods, the mortal part of their composition being tempered by the incorruptible part, so that there is nothing extraordinary in the fact of their having despised those mortals who designed to bring slavery upon them.

(106) However, let it be so. Are then Anaxagoras and Zeno the Eleatic heroes, or descended from gods? And nevertheless they, when tortured with the most unprecedented devices of cruelty by savage tyrants, wholly pitiless by nature, and even more than usually exasperated against them, looking on their bodies as if they belonged to strangers, or even to enemies, disregarded and utterly disdained the formidable evils with which they were afflicted; (107) for through the love of knowledge having accustomed their souls from the very beginning to keep aloof from all participation with the passions, and to cling to education and wisdom, they easily endured the prospect of its emigrating

from the body, and made it a dweller with prudence and courage, and other virtues. (108) Therefore, the one being hung up and violently stretched for the sake of making him divulge some secret, showed himself mightier than fire or iron, though they are the strongest things in nature, and biting off his tongue with his teeth, spit it at his torturer, that he might not involuntarily utter what he ought to bury in silence, under the influence of agony; (109) and the other said with great fortitude, "Beat Aristarchus's skin, for you cannot beat Aristarchus himself." These instances of brave fortitude, wholly full of daring, exceed in no slight degree the nobleness of those heroes, because the one class have a glory handed down to them by their ancestors without any actions of their own, while the fame of the others is founded on deeds of virtue deliberately performed, which very naturally make immortal those who practise them in a guileless spirit.

XVII. (110) I know also that combatants in the pancratium very often, out of the excess of their spirit of rivalry, and of their eagerness for victory, when their bodies are exhausted do you keep up their spirits, and strive with their soul alone, which they have accustomed to look contemptuously on danger, and thus they endure toil and pain to the very end of their life. (111) Shall we then fancy that those men who have practised themselves so as to arrive at vigour of body, have been able to trample on the fear of death, either through hope of victory or from the desire of escaping the sight of their own defeat; but those who train up in themselves the invisible mind, which is really and truly the man himself, bearing about him the appearance perceptible by the outward senses as his house, and who educate it by the principles and maxims of philosophy and the rules of virtue, will not be willing to die for the sake of freedom, in order to perform the journey appointed for them by fate with an indomitable and free spirit?

(112) They say that on one occasion, at one of the sacred games, two athletes who were contending with one another with equally matched strength and courage, doing the same things to one another, and suffering the same things, did not desist from the contest till they both fell dead.

"My too brave son, thy courage will destroy thee,"[14]

some one may say with reference to such persons. (113) However is the death of such combatants glorious when it is encountered for the sake of some wild olives and parsley-leaves, and must it not be much more so when endured for the sake of freedom, the love of which, if one must tell the plain truth, is firmly established in the soul alone,

---

[14] Hom. Il. 6:409.

as if it were some extraordinary portion of it firmly united with it, which if it were cut off the whole composition of the man must necessarily be destroyed?

(114) The indomitable spirit of a Lacedaemonian boy, whether derived from his birth or from nature, is celebrated, in which nation they are accustomed to hunt carefully for the virtues; for when he had been carried off as a prisoner by some one of the soldiers of Antigonus, he submitted to whatever was put upon him which became a free man, but refused to submit to menial offices, saying that he was not going to be a slave; and yet by reason of his age he could not as yet have been thoroughly educated in the laws of Lycurgus, because he had only tasted them, but he judged a violent death preferable to the life which was before him, and, despairing of any deliverance, he cheerfully slew himself.

(115) It is also related that some Dardanian women who had been taken prisoners by the Macedonians, looking upon slavery as the most disgraceful of all evils, threw their children, whom they were carrying in their bosoms, into the deepest part of the river, saying at the same time, "At all events you shall not be slaves, but, before you can begin to experience such a miserable life, you shall cut off all such necessity, and travel in freedom the inevitable and last road of human existence."

(116) Again, the tragedian, Euripides, introduces Polyxena disregarding death, and thinking only of freedom, on which account she speaks in the following manner:

"Willingly now I die; and let no foe
Seize me with violent hands; for I myself
With cheerful courage will put forth my neck.
For God's sake touch me not; but leave me free,
That having lived in freedom, I may die
Unviolated by a master's hand."[15]

XVIII. (117) Do we then imagine that there can be such a profound love of freedom firmly fixed in women and children, one of which classes is by nature light-minded, and the other is of an age which is easily perverted and liable to stumble, so that they, for the sake of not being deprived of it, cheerfully proceed from death to immortality, but that those men who have tasted of unalloyed wisdom are not at once thoroughly free, bearing about in themselves, as they do, a sort of perpetual fountain of happiness, namely virtue, which no designing or hostile power has ever been able to dissolve, since it has the everlasting inheritance of authority and sovereign power?

(118) But in truth we hear of whole nations also, who, for the sake of freedom and of good faith towards their deceased benefactors, have voluntarily encountered utter destruction, as they say that the Xanthians did no long time ago; for when Brutus, one of those men who attacked Julius Caesar, invaded their territory and made war upon them, they, fearing not so much the destruction of their city as slavery at the mercy of a murderer who had killed his king and his benefactor (for Caesar was both to him), resisted at first with great vigour to the very utmost extent of their power, (119) and though they were being gradually destroyed, they still held out; and when at last they had exhausted all their strength, they all collected their wives, and parents, and children into their houses, and there slew them separately, and then collecting the slaughtered bodies in a heap, they set fire to them, and slew themselves on the top of all, and so with a noble and free spirit encountered the fated end of all men.

(120) But these men, wishing to escape the pitiless inhumanity of tyrannical enemies, preferred death with glory to an inglorious life; but those to whom the chances of fortune gave a longer life, have endured their dangers and afflictions with fortitude, imitating the courage and endurance of Hercules, for he also showed himself superior to the commands of Eurystheus.

(121) Accordingly the Cynic philosopher, Diogenes, exhibited such a loftiness and greatness of spirit, that when he was taken prisoner by some robbers, and when they fed him very sparingly, and scarcely gave him even necessary food, he was not weighed down by the circumstances which surrounded him, and did not fear the inhumanity of the masters into whose power he had fallen, but said "that it was a most absurd thing for pigs or sheep, when they were going to be sold, to be carefully provided with abundant food, so as to be rendered fat and fleshy; but for the most excellent of all animals, man, to be reduced to a skeleton by bad food and continual scarcity, and so to be rendered of less value than before." (122) And then, when he had obtained sufficient food, and when he was about to be sold with the rest of the captives, he sat down first, and breakfasted with great cheerfulness and courage, giving some of his breakfast to his neighbours. And seeing one of them not merely sorrowful, but in a state of extreme despondency, he said, "Will you not give up being miserable? take what you can get."

"For the golden haired Niobe asked for her food,
Though her twelve noble children lay welt'ring in blood;
Six daughters, fair emblems of virtue and truth,
And six sons, the chief flower of the Lydian youth."

(123) And then, speaking boldly to some one who seemed inclined to become a purchaser, and who asked him the question, "What do you know?" he

---

[15] Euripides, Hecuba, 548.

replied, "I know how to govern men:" his soul from within, as it appears, prompting his free, and noble, and naturally royal spirit. And then he at once, with his natural indifference and serenity, turned to facetious discourse, at which all the rest, who were all full of despondency were annoyed. (124) Accordingly it is said that, seeing one of the intended purchasers afflicted with the female disease, as he did not even look like a man, he went up to him, and said, "Do you buy me, for you appear to me to be in want of a husband;" so that he, being grieved and downcast by reason of the infirmities of which he was conscious, slunk away, while all the rest admired the ready wit and happy courage of the philosopher.

Shall we then say that such a man as this was in a state of slavery, and not rather in a state of freedom, only without any irresponsible authority?

(125) And there was also a man of the name of Choereas, a man of considerable education, who was a zealous imitator of Diogenes's freedom of speech; for he, being an inhabitant of Alexandria in Egypt, on one occasion, when Ptolemy was offended with him, and was uttering no slight threats against him, thinking that the freedom which was implanted in his nature was in no respect inferior to the royal authority of the other, replied—

"Rule your Egyptian slaves; but as for me,
I neither care for you, nor fear your wrath
And angry threats." [16]

(126) For noble souls have something authoritative within them, and do not allow their brilliancy to be obscured by the injustice of fortune, but their spirit encourages them to contend on equal terms with those who are very high in rank and very proud, pitting their freedom of spirit against the insolence of the others.

(127) It is said that Theodorus, who was surnamed the Atheist, when he was banished from Athens, and had come to the court of Lysimachus, when one of those in power there reproached him with his banishment, mentioning the cause of it too, namely, that he had been expelled because he had been condemned for atheism and for corrupting the youth, replied, "I have not been banished, but the same thing has befallen me which befell Hercules, the son of Jupiter; (128) for he also was put ashore by the Argonauts, without having done anything wrong, but only because as he himself was both crew and ballast enough for a vessel, so that he burdened the ship, and caused fear to his fellow voyagers lest the vessel should become water-logged; and I too have been driven from my country because the bulk of the citizens at Athens were unable to keep pace with the loftiness and greatness of my mind, and therefore I was envied by them." (129) And when, after this reply, Lysimachus asked him, "Were you also banished from your native land through envy?" he replied a second time, "Not indeed through envy, but because of the exceedingly high qualities of my nature, which my country could not contain; (130) for as when Semele, at the time that she was pregnant with Bacchus, was unable to bear her offspring until the appointed time for her delivery, Jupiter pitied her, and saved from the flames the offspring which she bore in her womb, being as yet imperfect, and granted it equal honours with the heavenly deities, so also some deity, or some god, has made me leave my country by reason of its being too narrow to contain the ample burden of a philosophic mind, and decided on transporting me to a place more fortunate than Athens, and settling me there."

XIX. (131) And moreover any one who considers the matter may find even among the brute beasts examples of the freedom which exists among men, as he may of all other human blessings. At all events, cocks are accustomed to contend with one another, and to display such an actual affection for danger, that in order to save themselves from yielding or submitting, even if they are inferior in power to their adversary they will not bear to be inferior in courage, for they endure even to death. (132) And Miltiades, the famous general of the Athenians, seeing this, when the king of the Persians having roused up all the might of Asia, was invading Europe with many myriads of soldiers, as if he were going to destroy all Greece with the mere shout of his army, having collected all the allies at the festival called the panathenaea, showed them a battle between these birds, thinking that the encouragement which they would derive from such a sight would be more powerful than any argument. (133) And he was not deceived, for when they had seen the patient enduring and honourable feeling of these irrational animals, which could not be subdued by any means short of death itself, they snatched up their arms and rushed eagerly to war, as resolving to fight against their enemies with their bodies, and being utterly indifferent to wounds and death, being willing to die for their freedom, so that at all events they might be buried in the still free soil of their native country; for there is nothing which acts so forcibly in the way of exhortation so as to improve the character, as an unhoped for success in the case of those whom men look upon as inferior to themselves.

(134) Moreover the tragic writer, Ion, mentions the contentious spirit of those birds in the following lines:

---

[16]This is a parody on Hom. Il. 1.180, where Agamemnon speaks to Achilles.

"Nor though wounded in each limb,
Nor though his eyes with blows are dim,
Will he forget his might;
But still, though much fatigued, will crow,
Preferring death to undergo
Than slavery, or slight."

(135) And why, then, should we think that wise men will not cheerfully encounter death in preference to slavery? And is it not absurd to imagine that the souls of young and nobly born men will turn out inferior to those of game-cocks in the contest of virtue, and will be barely fit to stand in the second place? (136) And yet who is there who has even the least tincture of education who does not know this fact, that freedom is a noble thing and slavery a disgraceful one, and that what is honourable belongs to virtuous men, and what is disgraceful to worthless ones? From which it is seen most undeniably, that no virtuous man can ever be a slave, not if ten thousand persons, with all imaginable deeds to prove themselves masters, threaten them; and that no foolish or worthless man can ever be free, not even if he were Croesus, or Midas, or the great king of Persia himself.

(137) But the beauty of freedom, which is much celebrated, and the deformity of slavery, which is accursed, are continually borne witness to as having that character by the more ancient cities and nations whose existence has been of long duration, being as it were immortal among mortal things, and their testimony cannot err; (138) for, for what other object are councils and assemblies convened nearly every day, rather than about freedom, with a view to the confirmation of it if it is present, and to the acquisition of it if it is absent? And what other object have Greece and the nations of the barbarians ever had in all the continual seditions and wars which have taken place among or between those peoples, except to avoid slavery, and to obtain liberty? (139) On which account in all battles the chief exhortation of all captains, and commanders, and generals is this, "O soldiers and allies, let us now repel that greatest of all evils, slavery, which the enemy is attempting to bring upon us; let us never endure the loss of that greatest of all human blessings, liberty. This is the beginning and fountain of all happiness, from which all particular blessings flow."

(140) And it is for this reason that the most sharp-sighted of all the Greek nations, namely, the Athenians (for what the pupil is to the eye, or reasoning to the soul, that also is Athens to Greece), when they send out a solemn procession to the venerable goddesses, [17] never allow any slave whatever to take any part in it, but perform everything concerning it by the agency of free men and women

who are accustomed to such duties, even then not taking any chance persons, but only such as have cultivated a blameless innocence of life; since the most excellent of the youths prepare the cakes for the feast, looking upon that office as conducing (which indeed it does) to their credit and honour.

(141) And it happened not long ago, when some actors were representing a tragedy, and repeating those iambics of Euripides: [18]

"For e'en the name of freedom is a jewel
Of mighty value; and the man who has it
E'en in a small degree, has noble wealth;"

I myself saw all the spectators standing on tip-toe with excitement and delight, and with loud outcries and continual shouts combining their praise of the sentiments, and with praise also of the poet, as having not only honoured freedom by his actions, but having extolled its very name.

(142) I also admire the Argonauts, who made the whole crew of their vessel to consist of the freemen, not allowing a single slave to embark even for the purpose of performing the most indispensable services, but at that period they chose to do everything for themselves, looking upon independent action as the brother of freedom; (143) and if it may be allowed me at all to attend to what is said by the poets (and why should we not do so, for they are the instructors of the lives of all mankind, and just as individual parents are the instructors of their children, so too do they become so to the whole body of a city, correcting the entire population?), then I say that the Argo herself, when Jason was her captain, as if she were at that time endowed with a soul and with reasoning powers, did not permit any slaves to embark on board of her, since her nature was that of one devoted to freedom, on which account Aeschylus, with reference to her, says—

"And tell me where's the sacred beam
That dared the dangerous Euxine stream?" [19]

(144) And we must not pay the slightest attention to threats and menaces which some persons hold out over even wise men, but we must say as Antigonides the flute-player did; for it is related that he, when one of his rivals in art being angry with him, said to him, "I will buy you for a slave," said with very profound wit, "Then I will teach you to play the flute;" (145) and in the same way it would become the virtuous man to say to any one who appeared inclined to purchase him, "Therefore you will be able to learn wisdom." And if any one were to threaten him with banishment

---

[17] The Furies.

[18] Fragmenta Incerta, 495.
[19] Aesch. Fragm. 648.

beyond the borders of the country, it would become him to reply, "Every land is my country;" (146) and if any one were to threaten him with loss of money, he might make answer, "A moderate means of subsistence are sufficient for me:" while if any one were to menace him with stripes or death, he would reply, "These things have no terrors for me, for am I inferior to a boxer or to a wrestler in the pancratium, who, seeing merely some indistinct images of virtue, because they have laboured merely at the one object of producing a good condition of body, endure both blows and death with fortitude; for in me the mind, which is the ruler of the body, has been invigorated by courage, and so completely fortified, that it is able to show itself superior to any kind of pain."

XXI. (147) We must take care, therefore, never to catch a beast of that character which, being formidable not only in respect of its strength but also in its appearance, displays an almost invincible power, which is far from deserving to be despised. (148) It often happens that places which serve as asylums for fugitives and slaves give them complete freedom from fear and perfect security, as if they were in possession of equal honours and privileges with their masters, and sometimes one may see those who are slaves of old standing, as descended from grandfathers, and even more remote ancestors still, who have all been slaves by a kind of hereditary succession, yet, when once they have taken refuge in temples as suppliants, speaking freely and fearlessly in perfect security.

(149) There are some too, who even argue about their own rights and just claims with those who are their owners, not merely on equal terms, but actually as if they were far superior to them, replying to them with great energy and even contemptuously; for the one party is enslaved by the conviction which their consciences force upon them, however nobly born they may be; while the others feel in perfect security as to their persons, from the general recognition of the place in which they are as an asylum, and therefore they display the free and noble disposition of soul, which God has made of such a nature as never to be subdued by any external circumstances, (150) unless indeed any one is so utterly destitute of reason as to fancy that it is the place itself which is the cause of their confidence and freedom of speech, and that that most god-like of all things, virtue, has nothing to do with it, though it is owing to virtue alone that sanctity attaches either to the places or to anything which is endowed with sense.

(151) And, indeed, in the case of those who take refuge in places which are looked upon as asylums, seeking security only in the places themselves, it constantly happens to such persons to be much influenced by a great variety of other circumstances, by the corruption of their wives, the loss of reputation by their children, and the deceit-

fulness of love, while those who take refuge in virtue, as in a strong and indestructible and invincible fortification, disregard all attacks which the treachery of the passions aims and directs against them. (152) Now any one who is defended by this power may naturally say with all freedom, that other persons indeed are taken captive by all kinds of accidental things, but, as the tragic poet has it,

"I am well skilled both to obey myself
And rule myself: well weighing all events
By virtue's standard."[20]

(153) Accordingly also Bias, of Priene, is said, when Croesus threatened him, to have threatened him in return, in a most contemptuous manner, bidding him eat onions, by which figurative expression he meant that he should weep, since the eating of onions excites tears.

(154) Thus wise men, looking upon nothing as more royal than virtue, which is the regulator of the whole of their lives, do not fear the authority of other men, whom they look upon rather as subject to themselves; in reference to which idea, they are all accustomed to consider double-minded and treacherous people illiberal and slavish; (155) on which account also there is a good deal of propriety in the expression—

"Never was heard of slave uprightly held,
But stooping always with a downbent neck."[21]

For a crooked, and wily, and deceitful disposition, is a most ignoble thing; just as an upright, and straightforward, and undisguised, and unsuspicious soul, betokens a most noble character, its words harmonising with its intentions, and its intentions with its words.

(156) We may fairly enough laugh at those men who, when once they have got released from the actual possession of an owner, think themselves free from that moment; for these men, when emancipated, are perhaps no longer servants, just as before, but they are all slaves, deeply branded slaves, obeying not indeed men (for this would not be so terrible), but even the most dishonoured of even inanimate things, strong wine, vegetables, cheesecakes, and all the other things which the superfluous labours of bakers and confectioners invent, as enemies of the miserable belly. (157) Accordingly Diogenes, when he on one occasion saw one of those who are called illiberal and slavish persons giving himself airs, and a great many others sympathising in his pleasures, marvelling at their want of reason and judgment said, "It is just as if any one were to proclaim, that some one

---

[20] This again is from the Syleus of Euripides.
[21] From Theognis Carm. 41.

of his servants was, from this day forth, to be accounted a good grammarian, or geometrician, or musician, without his having the very slightest idea of the art; for just as the proclamation would not make men learned, so also it would not make them free (for then it would be a blessed thing), but all that it could do would be to make them no longer slaves.

XXII. (158) Therefore having put an end to empty opinion, on which the chief multitude of men depends, and being devoted to that most sacred possession, truth, let us not use incorrect terms so as to attribute to those who thus call themselves citizens any real share in a free constitution, or any real liberty; nor, on the other hand, let us reproach those who have been born in the house of a master, or who have been bought with money as slaves, but let us rather pass over all ideas of birth, all writings implying mastership, and, in short, everything relating to the body, and let us confine ourselves to investigating the nature of the soul.

(159) For if it is driven to and fro by appetite, or if it is attracted by pleasure, or turned out of the way by fear, or contracted by grief, or tortured by want, it then makes itself a slave, and makes him who possesses such a soul the slave of ten thousand masters. But if it has resisted and subdued ignorance by prudence, and intemperance by temperance, and cowardice by bravery, and covetousness by justice; it then adds to its indomitable free spirit, power and authority.

(160) And all the souls which are not as yet partakers of either of these two classes, neither of that which is enslaved, nor of that by which prudence is confirmed, but which are still naked like those of completely infant children; those we must nurse and cherish carefully, prescribing for them at first tender food instead of milk, namely, instruction in the encyclical sciences, and after that stronger food, such as is prepared by philosophy, by which they will be strengthened so as to become manly, and in good condition, and conducted on to a favourable end, not more that are recommended by you than enjoined by the oracle, "To live in conformity to nature."

ON THE CONTEMPLATIVE LIFE
OR SUPPLIANTS
(De Vita Contemplativa)

I. (1) Having mentioned the Essenes, who in all respects selected for their admiration and for their especial adoption the practical course of life, and who excel in all, or what perhaps may be a less unpopular and invidious thing to say, in most of its parts, I will now proceed, in the regular order of my subject, to speak of those who have embraced the speculative life, and I will say what appears to me to be desirable to be said on the subject, not drawing any fictitious statements from my own head for the sake of improving the appearance of that side of the question which nearly all poets and essayists are much accustomed to do in the scarcity of good actions to extol, but with the greatest simplicity adhering strictly to the truth itself, to which I know well that even the most eloquent men do not keep close in their speeches.

Nevertheless we must make the endeavour and labour to attain to this virtue; for it is not right that the greatness of the virtue of the men should be a cause of silence to those who do not think it right that anything which is creditable should be suppressed in silence; (2) but the deliberate intention of the philosopher is at once displayed from the appellation given to them; for with strict regard to etymology, they are called therapeutae and therapeutrides,[1] either because they profess an art of medicine more excellent than that in general use in cities (for that only heals bodies, but the other heals souls which are under the mastery of terrible and almost incurable diseases, which pleasures and appetites, fears and griefs, and covetousness, and follies, and injustice, and all the rest of the innumerable multitude of other passions and vices, have inflicted upon them), or else because they have been instructed by nature and the sacred laws to serve the living God, who is superior to the good, and more simple than the one, and more ancient than the unit; (3) with whom, however, who is there of those who profess piety that we can possibly compare? Can we compare those who honour the elements, earth, water, air, and fire? to whom different nations have given different names, calling fire Hephaestus, I imagine because of its kindling,[2] and the air Hera, I imagine because

of its being raised up,[3] and raised aloft to a great height, and water Poseidon, probably because of its being drinkable,[4] and the earth Demeter, because it appears to be the mother[5] of all plants and of all animals.

(4) But these names are the inventions of sophists: but the elements are inanimate matter, and immovable by any power of their own, being subjected to the operator on them to receive from him every kind of shape or distinctive quality which he chooses to give them. (5) But what shall we say of those men who worship the perfect things made of them, the sun, the moon, and the other stars, planets, or fixed-stars, or the whole heaven, or the universal world? And yet even they do not owe their existence to themselves, but to some creator whose knowledge has been most perfect, both in mind and degree. (6) What, again, shall we say of the demi-gods? This is a matter which is perfectly ridiculous: for how can the same man be both mortal and immortal, even if we leave out of the question the fact that the origin of the birth of all these beings is liable to reproach, as being full of youthful intemperance, which its authors endeavour with great profanity to impute to blessed and divine natures, as if they, being madly in love with mortal women, had connected themselves with them; while we know gods to be free from all participation in and from all influence of passion, and completely happy.

(7) Again, what shall we say of those who worship carved works and images? the substances of which, stone and wood, were only a little while before perfectly destitute of shape, before the stone-cutters or wood-cutters hewed them out of the kindred stuff around them, while the remainder of the material, their near relation and brother as it were, is made into ewers, or foot-pans, and other common and dishonoured vessels, which are employed rather for uses of darkness than for such as will bear the light; (8) for as for the customs of the Egyptians, it is not creditable even to mention them, for they have introduced irrational

---

[1] From therapeuō, "to heal."
[2] The Greek is exapsis, as if ēphaistos were also derived from aptomai, being akin to aphē.

[3] The Greek word is hairesthai, to which Hēra has some similarity in sound.
[4] The Greek word is poton, derived from 3rd sing. perf. pass. of pinō pepotai, from the 2nd sing. of which Peposai, poseidōn may probably be derived.
[5] The Greek word is mētēr, evidently the root of Dēmētēr.

beasts, and those not merely such as are domestic and tame, but even the most ferocious of wild beasts to share the honours of the gods, taking some out of each of the elements beneath the moon, as the lion from among the animals which live on the earth, the crocodile from among those which live in the water, the kite from such as traverse the air, and the Egyptian ibis. (9) And though they actually see that these animals are born, and that they are in need of food, and that they are insatiable in voracity and full of all sorts of filth, and moreover poisonous and devourers of men, and liable to be destroyed by all kinds of diseases, and that in fact they are often destroyed not only by natural deaths, but also by violence, still they, civilised men, worship these untameable and ferocious beasts; though rational men, they worship irrational beasts; though they have a near relationship to the Deity, they worship creatures unworthy of being compared even to some of the beasts; though appointed as rulers and masters, they worship creatures which are by nature subjects and slaves.

II. (10) But since these men infect not only their fellow countrymen, but also all that come near them with folly, let them remain uncovered, being mutilated in that most indispensable of all the outward senses, namely, sight. I am speaking here not of the sight of the body, but of that of the soul, by which alone truth and falsehood are distinguished from one another. (11) But the therapeutic sect of mankind, being continually taught to see without interruption, may well aim at obtaining a sight of the living God, and may pass by the sun, which is visible to the outward sense, and never leave this order which conducts to perfect happiness. (12) But they who apply themselves to this kind of worship, not because they are influenced to do so by custom, nor by the advice or recommendation of any particular persons, but because they are carried away by a certain heavenly love, give way to enthusiasm, behaving like so many revellers in bacchanalian or corybantian mysteries, until they see the object which they have been earnestly desiring.

(13) Then, because of their anxious desire for an immortal and blessed existence, thinking that their mortal life has already come to an end, they leave their possessions to their sons or daughters, or perhaps to other relations, giving them up their inheritance with willing cheerfulness; and those who know no relations give their property to their companions or friends, for it followed of necessity that those who have acquired the wealth which sees, as if ready prepared for them, should be willing to surrender that wealth which is blind to those who themselves also are still blind in their minds.

(14) The Greeks celebrate Anaxagoras and Democritus, because they, being smitten with a desire for philosophy, allowed all their estates to be devoured by cattle. I myself admire the men who thus showed themselves superior to the attractions of money; but how much better were those who have not permitted cattle to devour their possessions, but have supplied the necessities of mankind, of their own relations and friends, and have made them rich though they were poor before? For surely that was inconsiderate conduct (that I may avoid saying that any action of men whom Greece has agreed to admire was a piece of insanity); but this is the act of sober men, and one which has been carefully elaborated by exceeding prudence.

(15) For what more can enemies do than ravage, and destroy, and cut down all the trees in the country of their antagonists, that they may be forced to submit by reason of the extent to which they are oppressed by want of necessaries? And yet Democritus did this to his own blood relations, inflicting artificial want and penury upon them, not perhaps from any hostile intention towards them, but because he did not foresee and provide for what was advantageous to others. (16) How much better and more admirable are they who, without having any inferior eagerness for the attainment of philosophy, have nevertheless preferred magnanimity to carelessness, and, giving presents from their possessions instead of destroying them, so as to be able to benefit others and themselves also, have made others happy by imparting to them of the abundance of their wealth, and themselves by the study of philosophy? For an undue care for money and wealth causes great waste of time, and it is proper to economise time, since, according to the saying of the celebrated physician Hippocrates, life is short but art long. (17) And this is what Homer appears to me to imply figuratively in the Iliad, at the beginning of the thirteenth book, by the following lines,—

"The Mysian close-fighting bands,
And dwellers on the Scythian lands,
Content to seek their humble fare
From milk of cow and milk of mare,
The justest of mankind."[6]

As if great anxiety concerning the means of subsistence and the acquisition of money engendered injustice by reason of the inequality which it produced, while the contrary disposition and pursuit produced justice by reason of its equality, according to which it is that the wealth of nature is defined, and is superior to that which exists only in vain opinion.

(18) When, therefore, men abandon their property without being influenced by any predominant

---

[6] Il. 13.5.

attraction, they flee without even turning their heads back again, deserting their brethren, their children, their wives, their parents, their numerous families, their affectionate bands of companions, their native lands in which they have been born and brought up, though long familiarity is a most attractive bond, and one very well able to allure any one. (19) And they depart, not to another city as those do who entreat to be purchased from those who at present possess them, being either unfortunate or else worthless servants, and as such seeking a change of masters rather than endeavouring to procure freedom (for every city, even that which is under the happiest laws, is full of indescribable tumults, and disorders, and calamities, which no one would submit to who had been even for a moment under the influence of wisdom), (20) but they take up their abode outside of walls, or gardens, or solitary lands, seeking for a desert place, not because of any ill-natured misanthropy to which they have learnt to devote themselves, but because of the associations with people of wholly dissimilar dispositions to which they would otherwise be compelled, and which they know to be unprofitable and mischievous.

III. (21) Now this class of persons may be met with in many places, for it was fitting that both Greece and the country of the barbarians should partake of whatever is perfectly good; and there is the greatest number of such men in Egypt, in every one of the districts, or nomi as they are called, and especially around Alexandria; (22) and from all quarters those who are the best of these therapeutae proceed on their pilgrimage to some most suitable place as if it were their country, which is beyond the Mareotic lake, lying in a somewhat level plain a little raised above the rest, being suitable for their purpose by reason of its safety and also of the fine temperature of the air.

(23) For the houses built in the fields and the villages which surround it on all sides give it safety; and the admirable temperature of the air proceeds from the continual breezes which come from the lake which falls into the sea, and also from the sea itself in the neighbourhood, the breezes from the sea being light, and those which proceed from the lake which falls into the sea being heavy, the mixture of which produces a most healthy atmosphere.

(24) But the houses of these men thus congregated together are very plain, just giving shelter in respect of the two things most important to be provided against, the heat of the sun, and the cold from the open air; and they did not live near to one another as men do in cities, for immediate neighbourhood to others would be a troublesome and unpleasant thing to men who have conceived an admiration for, and have determined to devote themselves to, solitude; and, on the other hand, they did not live very far from one another on account of the fellowship which they desire to cultivate, and because of the desirableness of being able to assist one another if they should be attacked by robbers.

(25) And in every house there is a sacred shrine which is called the holy place, and the monastery in which they retire by themselves and perform all the mysteries of a holy life, bringing in nothing, neither meat, nor drink, nor anything else which is indispensable towards supplying the necessities of the body, but studying in that place the laws and the sacred oracles of God enunciated by the holy prophets, and hymns, and psalms, and all kinds of other things by reason of which knowledge and piety are increased and brought to perfection.

(26) Therefore they always retain an imperishable recollection of God, so that not even in their dreams is any other object ever presented to their eyes except the beauty of the divine virtues and of the divine powers. Therefore many persons speak in their sleep, divulging and publishing the celebrated doctrines of the sacred philosophy. (27) And they are accustomed to pray twice every day, at morning and at evening; when the sun is rising entreating God that the happiness of the coming day may be real happiness, so that their minds may be filled with heavenly light, and when the sun is setting they pray that their soul, being entirely lightened and relieved of the burden of the outward senses, and of the appropriate object of these outward senses, may be able to trace out truth existing in its own consistory and council chamber. (28) And the interval between morning and evening is by them devoted wholly to meditation on and to practice of virtue, for they take up the sacred scriptures and philosophise concerning them, investigating the allegories of their national philosophy, since they look upon their literal expressions as symbols of some secret meaning of nature, intended to be conveyed in those figurative expressions.

(29) They have also writings of ancient men, who having been the founders of one sect or another have left behind them many memorials of the allegorical system of writing and explanation, whom they take as a kind of model, and imitate the general fashion of their sect; so that they do not occupy themselves solely in contemplation, but they likewise compose psalms and hymns to God in every kind of metre and melody imaginable, which they of necessity arrange in more dignified rhythm. (30) Therefore, during six days, each of these individuals, retiring into solitude by himself, philosophises by himself in one of the places called monasteries, never going outside the threshold of the outer court, and indeed never even looking out.

But on the seventh day they all come together as if to meet in a sacred assembly, and they sit down in order according to their ages with all becoming gravity, keeping their hands inside their garments, having their right hand between their chest and their dress, and the left hand down by their side, close to their flank; (31) and then the eldest of them who has the most profound learning in their doctrines, comes forward and speaks with steadfast look and with steadfast voice, with great powers of reasoning, and great prudence, not making an exhibition of his oratorical powers like the rhetoricians of old, or the sophists of the present day, but investigating with great pains, and explaining with minute accuracy the precise meaning of the laws, which sits, not indeed at the tips of their ears, but penetrates through their hearing into the soul, and remains there lastingly; and all the rest listen in silence to the praises which he bestows upon the law, showing their assent only by nods of the head, or the eager look of the eyes.

(32) And this common holy place to which they all come together on the seventh day is a twofold circuit, being separated partly into the apartment of the men, and partly into a chamber for the women, for women also, in accordance with the usual fashion there, form a part of the audience, having the same feelings of admiration as the men, and having adopted the same sect with equal deliberation and decision; (33) and the wall which is between the houses rises from the ground three or four cubits upwards, like a battlement, and the upper portion rises upwards to the roof without any opening, on two accounts; first of all, in order that the modesty which is so becoming to the female sex may be preserved, and secondly, that the women may be easily able to comprehend what is said being seated within earshot, since there is then nothing which can possibly intercept the voice of him who is speaking.

IV. (34) And these expounders of the law, having first of all laid down temperance as a sort of foundation for the soul to rest upon, proceed to build up other virtues on this foundation, and no one of them may take any meat or drink before the setting of the sun, since they judge that the work of philosophising is one which is worthy of the light, but that the care for the necessities of the body is suitable only to darkness, on which account they appropriate the day to the one occupation, and a brief portion of the night to the other; (35) and some men, in whom there is implanted a more fervent desire of knowledge, can endure to cherish a recollection of their food for three days without even tasting it, and some men are so delighted, and enjoy themselves so exceedingly when regaled by wisdom which supplies them with her doctrines in all possible wealth and abundance, that they can even hold out twice as great a length of time, and will scarcely at the end of six days taste even necessary food, being accustomed, as they say that grasshoppers are, to feed on air, their song, as I imagine, making their scarcity tolerable to them.

(36) And they, looking upon the seventh day as one of perfect holiness and a most complete festival, have thought it worthy of a most especial honour, and on it, after taking due care of their soul, they tend their bodies also, giving them, just as they do to their cattle, a complete rest from their continual labours; (37) and they eat nothing of a costly character, but plain bread and a seasoning of salt, which the more luxurious of them do further season with hyssop; and their drink is water from the spring; for they oppose those feelings which nature has made mistresses of the human race, namely, hunger and thirst, giving them nothing to flatter or humour them, but only such useful things as it is not possible to exist without. On this account they eat only so far as not to be hungry, and they drink just enough to escape from thirst, avoiding all satiety, as an enemy of and a plotter against both soul and body.

(38) And there are two kinds of covering, one raiment and the other a house: we have already spoken of their houses, that they are not decorated with any ornaments, but run up in a hurry, being only made to answer such purposes as are absolutely necessary; and in like manner their raiment is of the most ordinary description, just stout enough to ward off cold and heat, being a cloak of some shaggy hide for winter, and a thin mantle or linen shawl in the summer; (39) for in short they practise entire simplicity, looking upon falsehood as the foundation of pride, but truth as the origin of simplicity, and upon truth and falsehood as standing in the light of fountains, for from falsehood proceeds every variety of evil and wickedness, and from truth there flows every imaginable abundance of good things both human and divine.

V. (40) I wish also to speak of their common assemblies, and their very cheerful meetings at convivial parties, setting them in opposition and contrast to the banquets of others, for others, when they drink strong wine, as if they had been drinking not wine but some agitating and maddening kind of liquor, or even the most formidable thing which can be imagined for driving a man out of his natural reason, rage about and tear things to pieces like so many ferocious dogs, and rise up and attack one another, biting and gnawing each other's noses, and ears, and fingers, and other parts of their body, so as to give an accurate representation of the story related about the Cyclops and the companions of Ulysses, who ate, as the poet says, fragments of human flesh,[7] and that more savagely than even he himself; (41) for he was only avenging himself on those whom he conceived to be his enemies,

---

[7] Odyssey 9:355.

but they were ill-treating their companions and friends, and sometimes even their actual relations, while having the salt and dinner-table before them, at a time of peace perpetrating actions inconsistent with peace, like those which are done by men in gymnastic contests, debasing the proper exercises of the body as coiners debase good money, and instead of athletes *(athlētai)* becoming miserable men *(athlioi)*, for that is the name which properly belongs to them.

(42) For that which those men who gain victories in the Olympic games, when perfectly sober in the arena, and having all the Greeks for spectators do by day, exerting all their skill for the purpose of gaining victory and the crown, these men with base designs do at convivial entertainments, getting drunk by night, in the hour of darkness, when soaked in wine, acting without either knowledge, or art, or skill, to the insult, and injury, and great disgrace of those who are subjected to their violence.

(43) And if no one were to come like an umpire into the middle of them, and part the combatants, and reconcile them, they would continue the contest with unlimited licence, striving to kill and murder one another, and being killed and murdered on the spot; for they do not suffer less than they inflict, though out of the delirious state into which they have worked themselves they do not feel what is done to them, since they have filled themselves with wine, not, as the comic poet says, to the injury of their neighbour, but to their own. (44) Therefore those persons who a little while before came safe and sound to the banquet, and in friendship for one another, do presently afterwards depart in hostility and mutilated in their bodies.

And some of these men stand in need of advocates and judges, and others require surgeons and physicians, and the help which may be received from them. (45) Others again who seem to be a more moderate kind of feasters when they have drunk unmixed wine as if it were mandragora, boil over as it were, and lean on their left elbow, and turn their heads on one side with their breath redolent of their wine, till at last they sink into profound slumber, neither seeing nor hearing anything, as if they had but one single sense, and that the most slavish of all, namely, taste. (46) And I know some persons who, when they are completely filled with wine, before they are wholly overpowered by it, begin to prepare a drinking party for the next day by a kind of subscription and picnic contribution, conceiving a great part of their present delight to consist in the hope of future drunkenness; (47) and in this manner they exist to the very end of their lives, without a house and without a home, the enemies of their parents, and of their wives, and of their children, and the enemies of their country, and the worst enemies of

all to themselves. For a debauched and profligate life is apt to lay snares for every one.

VI. (48) And perhaps some people may be inclined to approve of the arrangement of such entertainments which at present prevails everywhere, from an admiration of, and a desire of imitating, the luxury and extravagance of the Italians which both Greeks and barbarians emulate, making all their preparations with a view to show rather than to real enjoyment, (49) for they use couches called triclinia, and sofas all round the table made of tortoiseshell, and ivory, and other costly materials, most of which are inlaid with precious stones; and coverlets of purple embroidered with gold and silver thread; and others brocaded in flowers of every kind of hue and colour imaginable to allure the sight, and a vast array of drinking cups arrayed according to each separate description; for there are bowls, and vases, and beakers, and goblets, and all kinds of other vessels wrought with the most exquisite skill, their clean cups and others finished with the most elaborate refinement of skilful and ingenious men; (50) and well-shaped slaves of the most exquisite beauty, ministering, as if they had come not more for the purpose of serving the guests than of delighting the eyes of the spectators by their mere appearance.

Of these slaves, some, being still boys, pour out the wine; and others more fully grown pour water, being carefully washed and rubbed down, with their faces anointed and pencilled, and the hair of their heads admirably plaited and curled and wreathed in delicate knots; (51) for they have very long hair, being either completely unshorn, or else having only the hair on their foreheads cut at the end so as to make them of an equal length all round, being accurately sloped away so as to represent a circular line, and being clothed in tunics of the most delicate texture, and of the purest white, reaching in front down to the lower part of the knee, and behind to a little below the calf of the leg, and drawing up each side with a gentle doubling of the fringe at the joinings of the tunics, raising undulations of the garment as it were at the sides, and widening them at the hollow part of the side.

(52) Others, again, are young men just beginning to show a beard on their youthful chins, having been, for a short time, the sport of the profligate debauchees, and being prepared with exceeding care and diligence for more painful services; being a kind of exhibition of the excessive opulence of the giver of the feast, or rather, to say the truth, of their thorough ignorance of all propriety, as those who are acquainted with them well know.

(53) Besides all these things, there is an infinite variety of sweetmeats, and delicacies, and confections, about which bakers and cooks and confectioners labour, considering not the taste, which is the point of real importance, so as to make the

food palatable to that, but also the sight, so as to allure that by the delicacy of the look of their viands,[8] they turn their heads round in every direction, scanning everything with their eyes and with their nostrils, examining the richness and the number of the dishes with the first, and the steam which is sent up by them with the second.

Then, when they are thoroughly sated both with the sight and with the scent, these senses again prompt their owners to eat, praising in no moderate terms both the entertainment itself and the giver of it, for its costliness and magnificence. (54) Accordingly, seven tables, and often more, are brought in, full of every kind of delicacy which earth, and sea, and rivers, and air produce, all procured with great pains, and in high condition, composed of terrestrial, and acquatic, and flying creatures, every one of which is different both in its mode of dressing and in its seasoning.

And that no description of thing existing in nature may be omitted, at the last dishes are brought in full of fruits, besides those which are kept back for the more luxurious portion of the entertainment, and for what is called the dessert; (55) and afterwards some of the dishes are carried away empty from the insatiable greediness of those at table, who, gorging themselves like cormorants, devour all the delicacies so completely that they gnaw even the bones, which some left half devoured after all that they contained has been torn to pieces and spoiled. And when they are completely tired with eating, having their bellies filled up to their very throats, but their desires still unsatisfied, being fatigued with eating.

(56) However, why need I dwell with prolixity on these matters, which are already condemned by the generality of more moderate men as inflaming the passions, the diminution of which is desirable? For any one in his senses would pray for the most unfortunate of all states, hunger and thirst, rather than for a most unlimited abundance of meat and drink at such banquets as these.

VII. (57) Now of the banquets among the Greeks the two most celebrated and most remarkable are those at which Socrates also was present, the one in the house of Callias, when, after Autolycus had gained the crown of victory, he gave a feast in honour of the event, and the other in the house of Agathon, which was thought worthy of being commemorated by men who were imbued with the true spirit of philosophy both in their dispositions and in their discourses, Plato and Xenophon, for they recorded them as events worthy to be had in perpetual recollection, looking upon it that future generations would take them as models for a well managed arrangement of future banquets; (58) but nevertheless even these, if compared with the banquets of the men of our time who have embraced the contemplative system of life, will appear ridiculous. Each description, indeed, has its own pleasures, but the recorded by Xenophon is the one the delights of which are most in accordance with human nature, for female harp-players, and dancers, and conjurors, and jugglers, and men who do ridiculous things, who pride themselves much on their powers of jesting and of amusing others, and many other species of more cheerful relaxation, are brought forward at it. (59) But the entertainment recorded by Plato is almost entirely connected with love; not that of men madly desirous or fond of women, or of women furiously in love with men, for these desires are accomplished in accordance with a law of nature, but with that love which is felt by men for one another, differing only in respect of age; for if there is anything in the account of that banquet elegantly said in praise of genuine love and heavenly Venus, it is introduced merely for the sake of making a neat speech; (60) for the greater part of the book is occupied by common, vulgar, promiscuous love, which takes away from the soul courage, that which is the most serviceable of all virtues both in war and in peace, and which engenders in it instead the female disease, and renders men men-women, though they ought rather to be carefully trained in all the practices likely to give men valour.

(61) And having corrupted the age of boys, and having metamorphosed them and removed them into the classification and character of women, it has injured their lovers also in the most important particulars, their bodies, their souls, and their properties; for it follows of necessity that the mind of a lover of boys must be kept on the stretch towards the objects of his affection, and must have no acuteness of vision for any other object, but must be blinded by its desire as to all other objects private or common, and must so be wasted away, more especially if it fails in its objects. Moreover, the man's property must be diminished on two accounts, both from the owner's neglect and from his expenses for the beloved object.

(62) There is also another greater evil which affects the whole people, and which grows up alongside of the other, for men who give into such passions produce solitude in cities, and a scarcity of the best kind of men, and barrenness, and unproductiveness, inasmuch as they are imitating those farmers who are unskilful in agriculture, and who, instead of the deep-soiled champaign country, sow briny marshes, or stony and rugged districts, which are not calculated to produce crops of any kind, and which only destroy the seed which is put into them. (63) I pass over in silence the different fabulous fictions, and the stories of persons with two bodies, who having originally been stuck to one

---

[8] The remainder of this section originally appeared in section 55. The material has been reordered to reflect the Loeb sequence.

another by amatory influences, are subsequently separated like portions which have been brought together and are disjoined again, the harmony having been dissolved by which they were held together; for all these things are very attractive, being able by novelty of their imagination to allure the ears, but they are despised by the disciples of Moses, who in the abundance of their wisdom have learnt from their earliest infancy to love truth, and also continue to the end of their lives impossible to be deceived.

VIII. (64) But since the entertainments of the greatest celebrity are full of such trifling and folly, bearing conviction in themselves, if any one should think fit not to regard vague opinion and the character which has been commonly handed down concerning them as feasts which have gone off with the most eminent success, I will oppose to them the entertainments of those persons who have devoted their whole life and themselves to the knowledge and contemplation of the affairs of nature in accordance with the most sacred admonitions and precepts of the prophet Moses.

(65) In the first place, these men assemble at the end of seven weeks, venerating not only the simple week of seven days, but also its multiplied power, for they know it to be pure and always virgin; and it is a prelude and a kind of forefeast of the greatest feast, which is assigned to the number fifty, the most holy and natural of numbers, being compounded of the power of the right-angled triangle, which is the principle of the origination and condition of the whole.

(66) Therefore when they come together clothed in white garments, and joyful with the most exceeding gravity, when some one of the ephemereutae (for that is the appellation which they are accustomed to give to those who are employed in such ministrations), before they sit down to meat standing in order in a row, and raising their eyes and their hands to heaven, the one because they have learnt to fix their attention on what is worthy looking at, and the other because they are free from the reproach of all impure gain, being never polluted under any pretence whatever by any description of criminality which can arise from any means taken to procure advantage, they pray to God that the entertainment may be acceptable, and welcome, and pleasing; (67) and after having offered up these prayers the elders sit down to meat, still observing the order in which they were previously arranged, for they do not look on those as elders who are advanced in years and very ancient, but in some cases they esteem those as very young men, if they have attached themselves to this sect only lately, but those whom they call elders are those who from their earliest infancy have grown up and arrived at maturity in the speculative portion of philosophy, which is the most beautiful and most divine part of it.

(68) And the women also share in this feast, the greater part of whom, though old, are virgins in respect of their purity (not indeed through necessity, as some of the priestesses among the Greeks are, who have been compelled to preserve their chastity more than they would have done of their own accord), but out of an admiration for and love of wisdom, with which they are desirous to pass their lives, on account of which they are indifferent to the pleasures of the body, desiring not a mortal but an immortal offspring, which the soul that is attached to God is alone able to produce by itself and from itself, the Father having sown in it rays of light appreciable only by the intellect, by means of which it will be able to perceive the doctrines of wisdom.

IX. (69) And the order in which they sit down to meat is a divided one, the men sitting on the right hand and the women apart from them on the left; and in case any one by chance suspects that cushions, if not very costly ones, still at all events of a tolerably soft substance, are prepared for men who are well born and well bred, and contemplators of philosophy, he must know that they have nothing but rugs of the coarsest materials, cheap mats of the most ordinary kind of the papyrus of the land, piled up on the ground and projecting a little near the elbow, so that the feasters may lean upon them, for they relax in a slight degree the Lacedaemonian rigour of life, and at all times and in all places they practise a liberal, gentlemanlike kind of frugality, hating the allurements of pleasure with all their might.

(70) And they do not use the ministrations of slaves, looking upon the possession of servants of slaves to be a thing absolutely and wholly contrary to nature, for nature has created all men free, but the injustice and covetousness of some men who prefer inequality, that cause of all evil, having subdued some, has given to the more powerful authority over those who are weaker.

(71) Accordingly in this sacred entertainment there is, as I have said, no slave, but free men minister to the guests, performing the offices of servants, not under compulsion, nor in obedience to any imperious commands, but of their own voluntary free will, with all eagerness and promptitude anticipating all orders, (72) for they are not any chance free men who are appointed to perform these duties, but young men who are selected from their order with all possible care on account of their excellence, acting as virtuous and wellborn youths ought to act who are eager to attain to the perfection of virtue, and who, like legitimate sons, with affectionate rivalry minister to their fathers and mothers, thinking their common parents more closely connected with them than those who are related by blood, since in truth to men of right principles there is nothing more nearly akin than virtue; and they come in to perform their

service ungirdled, and with their tunics let down, in order that nothing which bears any resemblance to a slavish appearance may be introduced into this festival.

(73) I know well that some persons will laugh when they hear this, but they who laugh will be those who do things worthy of weeping and lamentation. And in those days wine is not introduced, but only the clearest water; cold water for the generality, and hot water for those old men who are accustomed to a luxurious life. And the table, too, bears nothing which has blood, but there is placed upon it bread for food and salt for seasoning, to which also hyssop is sometimes added as an extra sauce for the sake of those who are delicate in their eating, for just as right reason commands the priest to offer up sober sacrifices, (74) so also these men are commanded to live sober lives, for wine is the medicine of folly, and costly seasonings and sauces excite desire, which is the most insatiable of all beasts.

X. (75) These, then, are the first circumstances of the feast; but after the guests have sat down to the table in the order which I have been describing, and when those who minister to them are all standing around in order, ready to wait upon them, and when there is nothing to drink, some one will say ... but even more so than before, so that no one ventures to mutter, or even to breathe at all hard, and then some one looks out some passage in the sacred scriptures, or explains some difficulty which is proposed by some one else, without any thoughts of display on his own part, for he is not aiming at reputation for cleverness and eloquence, but is only desirous to see some points more accurately, and is content when he has thus seen them himself not to bear ill will to others, who, even if they did not perceive the truth with equal acuteness, have at all events an equal desire of learning. (76) And he, indeed, follows a slower method of instruction, dwelling on and lingering over his explanations with repetitions, in order to imprint his conceptions deep in the minds of his hearers, for as the understanding of his hearers is not able to keep up with the interpretation of one who goes on fluently, without stopping to take breath, it gets behind-hand, and fails to comprehend what is said; (77) but the hearers, fixing their eyes and attention upon the speaker, remain in one and the same position listening attentively, indicating their attention and comprehension by their nods and looks, and the praise which they are inclined to bestow on the speaker by the cheerfulness and gentle manner in which they follow him with their eyes and with the fore-finger of the right hand.

And the young men who are standing around attend to this explanation no less than the guests themselves who are sitting at meat. (78) And these explanations of the sacred scriptures are delivered by mystic expressions in allegories, for the whole of the law appears to these men to resemble a living animal, and its express commandments seem to be the body, and the invisible meaning concealed under and lying beneath the plain words resembles the soul, in which the rational soul begins most excellently to contemplate what belongs to itself, as in a mirror, beholding in these very words the exceeding beauty of the sentiments, and unfolding and explaining the symbols, and bringing the secret meaning naked to the light to all who are able by the light of a slight intimation to perceive what is unseen by what is visible.

(79) When, therefore, the president appears to have spoken at sufficient length, and to have carried out his intentions adequately, so that his explanation has gone on felicitously and fluently through his own acuteness, and the hearing of the others has been profitable, applause arises from them all as of men rejoicing together at what they have seen and heard; (80) and then some one rising up sings a hymn which has been made in honour of God, either such as he has composed himself, or some ancient one of some old poet, for they have left behind them many poems and songs in trimetre iambics, and in psalms of thanksgiving and in hymns, and songs at the time of libation, and at the altar, and in regular order, and in choruses, admirably measured out in various and well diversified strophes.

And after him then others also arise in their ranks, in becoming order, while every one else listens in decent silence, except when it is proper for them to take up the burden of the song, and to join in at the end; for then they all, both men and women, join in the hymn. (81) And when each individual has finished his psalm, then the young men bring in the table which was mentioned a little while ago, on which was placed that most holy food, the leavened bread, with a seasoning of salt, with which hyssop is mingled, out of reverence for the sacred table, which lies thus in the holy outer temple; for on this table are placed loaves and salt without seasoning, and the bread is unleavened, and the salt unmixed with anything else, (82) for it was becoming that the simplest and purest things should be allotted to the most excellent portion of the priests, as a reward for their ministrations, and that the others should admire similar things, but should abstain from the loaves, in order that those who are the more excellent person may have the precedence.

XI. (83) And after the feast they celebrate the sacred festival during the whole night; and this nocturnal festival is celebrated in the following manner: they all stand up together, and in the middle of the entertainment two choruses are formed at first, the one of men and the other of women, and for each chorus there is a leader and chief selected, who is the most honourable and most excellent of the band. (84) Then they sing hymns which have been composed in honour of God in many metres and tunes, at one time all singing together, and at another moving their hands and dancing in corresponding harmony, and uttering in an inspired manner songs of thanksgiving, and at another time regular odes, and performing all necessary strophes and antistrophes.

(85) Then, when each chorus of the men and each chorus of the women has feasted separately by itself, like persons in the bacchanalian revels, drinking the pure wine of the love of God, they join together, and the two become one chorus, an imitation of that one which, in old time, was established by the Red Sea, on account of the wondrous works which were displayed there; (86) for, by the commandment of God, the sea became to one party the cause of safety, and to the other that of utter destruction; for it being burst asunder, and dragged back by a violent reflux, and being built up on each side as if there were a solid wall, the space in the midst was widened, and cut into a level and dry road, along which the people passed over to the opposite land, being conducted onwards to higher ground; then, when the sea returned and ran back to its former channel, and was poured out from both sides, on what had just before been dry ground, those of the enemy who pursued were overwhelmed and perished.

(87) When the Israelites saw and experienced this great miracle, which was an event beyond all description, beyond all imagination, and beyond all hope, both men and women together, under the influence of divine inspiration, becoming all one chorus, sang hymns of thanksgiving to God the Saviour, Moses the prophet leading the men, and Miriam the prophetess leading the women.

(88) Now the chorus of male and female worshippers being formed, as far as possible on this model, makes a most humorous concert, and a truly musical symphony, the shrill voices of the women mingling with the deep-toned voices of the men. The ideas were beautiful, the expressions beautiful, and the chorus-singers were beautiful; and the end of ideas, and expressions, and chorus-singers, was piety; (89) therefore, being intoxicated all night till the morning with this beautiful intoxication, without feeling their heads heavy or closing their eyes for sleep, but being even more awake than when they came to the feast, as to their eyes and their whole bodies, and standing there till morning, when they saw the sun rising they raised their hands to heaven, imploring tranquillity and truth, and acuteness of understanding.

And after their prayers they each retired to their own separate abodes, with the intention of again practising the usual philosophy to which they had been wont to devote themselves.

(90) This then is what I have to say of those who are called therapeutae, who have devoted themselves to the contemplation of nature, and who have lived in it and in the soul alone, being citizens of heaven and of the world, and very acceptable to the Father and Creator of the universe because of their virtue, which has procured them his love as their most appropriate reward, which far surpasses all the gifts of fortune, and conducts them to the very summit and perfection of happiness.

ON THE ETERNITY OF THE WORLD[†]
(De Aeternitate Mundi)

I. (1) In every uncertain and important business it is proper to invoke God, because he is the good Creator of the world, and because nothing is uncertain with him who is possessed of the most accurate knowledge of all things. But of all times it is most necessary to invoke him when one is preparing to discuss the incorruptibility of the world; for neither among the things which are visible to the outward senses is there anything more admirably complete than the world, nor among things appreciable by the intellect is there anything more perfect than God. But the mind is at all times the governor of the outward sense, and that which is appreciable by the intellect is at all times superior to that which is visible to the outward senses, but those persons in whom there is implanted a vigorous and earnest love of truth willingly undergo the trouble of making inquiries relative to the subordinate things, from that which is superior to and the ruler over them.

(2) If then, we, who have been practised and trained in all the doctrines of prudence, and temperance, and virtue, have discarded all the stains of the passions and diseases, perhaps God would not disdain to give to souls completely purified and cleansed, so as to appear in his image, a knowledge of heavenly things either by means of dreams, or of oracles, or of signs, or of wonders. But since we have on us the marks of folly, and injustice, and of all other vices strongly stamped upon us and difficult to be effaced, we must be content even if we are only able by them to discover some faint copy and imitation of the truth. (3) It is right, therefore, for those who are investigating the question whether the world if perishable, since the two words, "corruption," and "the world," will be in continual use, first of all to investigate the precise meaning of both expressions, in order that we may know what is now signified, and what has been ordained. And we must enumerate, not indeed everything which is signified by those words, but so much as is useful for the purpose of our present instruction.

II. (4) The world, therefore, is spoken of in its primary sense as a single system, consisting of the heaven and the stars in the circumference of the earth, and all the animals and plants which are upon it; and in another sense it is spoken of merely as the heaven. And Anaxagoras, having a regard to this fact, once made answer to a certain person who asked of him what the reason was why he generally endeavoured to pass the night in the open air, that he did so for the sake of beholding the world, by which expression he meant the motions and revolutions of the stars.

And in its third meaning, as the Stoics affirm, it is a certain admirably-arranged essence, extending to the period of conflagration, either beautifully adorned or unadorned, the periods of the motion of which are called time.

But at present the subject of our consideration is the world, taken in the first sense of the word, which being one only, consists of the heaven, and of the earth, and of all that is therein. (5) And the term corruption is used to signify a change for the worse; it is also used to signify the utter destruction of that which exists, a destruction so complete as to have no existence at all; for as nothing is generated out of nothing, so neither can anything which exists be destroyed so as to become non-existence.[1] For it is impossible that anything should be generated of that which has no existence anywhere, as equally so that what does exist should be so utterly destroyed as never to be mentioned or heard of again. And indeed in this spirit the tragedian says:—

> "Nought that e'er has been
> Completely dies, but things combined
> Before another union find;
> Quitting their former company,
> And so again in other forms are seen."[2]

(6) Nor is it so very silly a thing to doubt whether the world is destroyed so as to pass into a state of non-existence, but rather whether it is subjected to a change from a new arrangement, being dissolved as to all the manifold forms of its elements and combinations so as to assume one and the same appearance, or whether, like a thing broken and dashed to pieces, it is subjected to a complete confusion of its different fragments.

III. (7) And there are three different opinions on the subject which we are at present discussing. Since some persons affirm that the world is

[†] Yonge's title, *A Treatise on the Incorruptibility of the World.*

[1] This is similar to Lucretius's doctrine—Nil igitur fieri de nihilo posse putandum est.

[2] From the Chrysippus of Euripides.

eternal, and uncreated, and not liable to any destruction; while others, on the contrary, say that it has been created and is destructible. There are also others who take a portion of each of these two opinions, agreeing with the last-mentioned sect that it has been created, but with the former class that it is indestructible; and thus they have left behind them a mixed opinion, thinking that it is at the same time created and imperishable.

(8) However, Democritus and Epicurus, and the principal number of the Stoic philosophers, affirm both the creation and the destructibility of the world, though they do not all speak in similar senses; for some give a sketch of many worlds, the generation of which they attribute to the concourse and combination of atoms, and their destruction they impute to the dissolution and breaking up of the combined particles.

But the Stoics speak of one world only, and affirm that God is the cause of its creation, but that the cause of its corruption is no longer God, but the power of invincible, unwearied fire, which pervades all existing things, in the long periods of time dissolving everything into itself, while from it again a regeneration of the world takes place through the providence of the Creator. (9) And according to these men there may be one world spoken of as eternal and another as destructible, destructible in reference to its present arrangement, and eternal as to the conflagration which takes place, since it is rendered immortal by regenerations and periodical revolutions which never cease.

(10) But Aristotle, with a knowledge as to which I know not to what degree I may call it holy and pious, affirmed that the world was uncreated and indestructible, and he accused those who maintained a contrary opinion of terrible impiety, for thinking that so great a visible God was in no respect different from things made with hands, though he contains within himself the sun, and the moon, and all the rest of the planets and fixed stars, and, in fact, the whole of the divine nature; (11) and he said in a cavilling and reproachful tone, that formerly he had feared for his house lest it should be overthrown by violent gales, or extraordinary storms, or by lapse of time, or through the want of the proper care requisite to preserve it, but that now he had a much greater fear hanging over him in consequence of those men who by their reasonings want to destroy the whole world. (12) But some say that it was not Aristotle who invented this doctrine, but some of the Pythagoreans; but I have met with a work of Ocellus, a Lucanian by birth, entitled, "A Treatise on the Nature of the Universe," in which he has not only asserted that the world is indestructible, but he has even endeavoured to prove it so by demonstrative proofs.

IV. (13) But some say that the world has been proved by Plato in the Timaeus to be both uncreated and indestructible, in the account of that divine assembly in which the younger gods are addressed by the eldest and the governor of them all in the following terms;[3] "O ye gods of gods, those works of which I am the father and the creator are indissoluble as long as I choose that they shall be so. Now everything which has been bound together is capable of being dissolved, but it is the part of an evil ruler to dissolve that which has been well combined and arranged, and which is in good condition. Wherefore, since you also have been created, you are not of necessity immortal or utterly indissoluble; nevertheless you shall not be dissolved, nor shall you be exposed to the fate of death, inasmuch as you have my will to keep you united, which is a still greater and more powerful bond than those by which you were bound together when you were first created."

(14) But some persons interpret Plato's words sophistically, and think that he affirms that the world was created, not inasmuch as it has had a beginning of creation, but inasmuch as if it had been created it could not possibly have existed in any other manner than that in which it actually does exist as has been described, or else because it is in its creation and change that the parts are seen. (15) But the forementioned opinion is better and truer, not only because throughout the whole treatise he affirms that the Creator of the gods is also the father and creator and maker of everything, and that the world is a most beautiful work of his and his offspring, being an imitation visible to the outward senses of an archetypal model appreciable only by the intellect, comprehending in itself as many objects of the outward senses as the model does objects of the intellect, since it is a most perfect impression of a most perfect model, and is addressed to the outward sense as the other is to the intellect.[4]

(16) But also because Aristotle bears witness to this fact in the case of Plato, who, from his great reverence for philosophy, would never have spoken falsely, and also because no one can possibly be more to be credited in the case of a teacher than his pupil, especially when the pupil is such a man as this who did not apply himself to instruction lightly with an indifference easily satisfied, but who even endeavoured to surpass all the discoveries of former men, and did actually devise some novelties and enrich every part of philosophy with some most important discoveries.

V. (17) But some persons think that the father of the Platonic theory was the poet Hesiod, as they conceive that the world is spoken of by him as created and indestructible; as created, when he says,—

---

[3] Timaeus, p. 40.
[4] There is probably some corruption in the text here.

"First did Chaos rule
Then the broad-chested earth was brought to light,
Foundation firm and lasting for whatever
Exists among mankind;"[5]

and as indestructible, because he has given no hint of its dissolution or destruction.

(18) Now Chaos was conceived by Aristotle to be a place, because it is absolutely necessary that a place to receive them must be in existence before bodies. But some of the Stoics think that it is water, imagining that its name has been derived from effusion.[6] But however that may be, it is exceedingly plain that the world is spoken of by Hesiod as having been created: (19) and a very long time before him Moses, the lawgiver of the Jews, had said in his sacred volumes that the world was both created and indestructible, and the number of the books is five. The first of which he entitled Genesis, in which he begins in the following manner: "in the beginning God created the heaven and the earth; and the earth was invisible and without form." Then proceeding onwards he relates in the following verses, that days and nights, and seasons, and years, and the sun and moon, which showed the nature of the measurement of time, were created, which, having received an immortal portion in common with the whole heaven, continue for ever indestructible.

(20) But we must place those arguments first which make out the world to be uncreated and indestructible, because of our respect for that which is visible, employing an appropriate commencement. To all things which are liable to destruction there are two causes of that destruction, one being internal and the other external; therefore you may find iron, and brass, and all other substances of that kind destroyed by themselves when rust, like a creeping disease, overruns and devours them; and by external causes when, if a house or a city is burnt, they also are consumed in the conflagration, being melted by the violent impetuosity of the fire.

A similar end also befalls animals, partly when they are sick of diseases arising internally, and partly when they are destroyed by external causes, being sacrificed, or stoned, or burnt, or when they endure an unclean death by hanging.

(21) And if the world also is destroyed, then it must of necessity be so either by some external cause, or else by some one of the powers which exist within itself; and both these alternatives are impossible, for there is nothing whatever outside of the world, since all things are brought together in order to make it complete and full, for it is in this way that it will be one, and whole, and free from old age; it will be one, because if anything were left outside of it, then another world might be created resembling that which exists now; and whole, because the whole of its essence is expended on itself; and exempt from old age and from all disease, since those bodies which are liable to be destroyed by disease or old age are violently overthrown by external causes, such as heat, and cold, and other contrary qualities, no power of which is able to escape so as to surround and attack the world, all those being entirely enclosed within, without any part whatever being separated from the rest.

But if indeed there is any external thing it must by all means be a vacuum, or else a nature absolutely impassive, which it would be impossible should either suffer or do anything. (22) And again, it will also not be dissolved by any cause existing within itself; first of all because, if it were, then the part would be greater and more powerful than the whole, which is the greatest possible absurdity, for the world, enjoying an unsurpassable power, influences all its parts, and is not itself influenced or moved by any one of them; in the second place because, since there are two causes of corruption, the one being internal and the other external, those things which are competent to admit the one must also by all means be liable to the other; (23) and a proof of this may be found in oxen, and horses, and men, and other animals of similar kinds, because it is their nature to be destroyed by the sword, or to be liable to die by disease; for it is difficult, or I might rather say impossible, to find anything which, being by nature at the mercy of some external cause perceptible by the intellect, will still not be liable to corruption … by itself when the world was not.[7]

(24) Since, therefore, the arrangement of the world is such as I have endeavoured to describe it, so that there is no part whatever left out, so as for any force to be applied, it has now been proved that the world will not be destroyed by any external thing, because in fact nothing whatever external has been left at all; nor will it be destroyed by anything in itself on account of the proof which has already been considered and stated, according to which that which was obnoxious to the power of one of those causes was also naturally susceptible of the influence of the other.

VI. (25) And there are testimonies also in the Timaeus to the fact of the world being exempt from disease and not liable to destruction, such as these: "Accordingly, of the four elements the constitution of the world receives each in all its integrity;

---

[5] Hesiod, Theogon, 116.
[6] *Chysis*, as if chaos were derived from *cheō*, "to pour."

[7] Yonge's MS. sequence for sections 24–77 differs from the Cohn-Wendland text (Loeb). The material has been reordered to reflect the Loeb sequence.

for he who compounded it made it to consist of the whole of fire, and the whole of water, and the whole of air, and the whole of earth, not leaving any portion or any power of any one of them outside, from the following intentions:—(26) in the first place, in order that the whole might be as far as possible a perfect animal made up of perfect parts. And besides all these things, he ordained that it should be one, inasmuch as there is nothing left out of which another similar world could be composed. Moreover, he willed that it should be exempt from old age, and free from all disease, considering that those things which in the body are hot or cold, or which have mighty powers, if standing all around and falling upon it unseasonably, would be likely to dissolve it, and, by introducing diseases and old age, cause it to decay and perish. For this cause, and because of this reason, God made the whole universe to consist of entire and perfect elements, and exempt from old age and free from disease."

(27) Let this be taken as a testimony delivered by Plato to the imperishable nature of the world. Its uncreated character follows from the truth of natural philosophy; for dissolution must of necessity attend everything which is born, and incorruptibility must inevitably belong to everything which is unborn; since the poet who wrote the following iambic verse,

"All that is born must surely die,"[8]

appears to have spoken very correctly when he asserted this connection of destructibility with birth.

(28) The argument may be stated in a different way as follows. All compound things which are destroyed are dissolved into the elements of which they were compounded; accordingly, dissolution is nothing else but a return of everything to its original constituent parts; just as, on the contrary, composition is that which compels the things combined to come together in a manner contrary to their nature; and indeed, this appears to be the most exact truth; (29) for men are composed of the four elements which together make up the whole of the universe, the heaven, the earth, the air, and fire, borrowing a few parts of each in a manner at first sight hardly consistent with nature. But the things which are thus combined together are necessarily deprived of a motion in accordance with nature; for instance, warmth is deprived of its upward motion, and coldness of its downward tendency, the earthy and somewhat weighty substance being lightened and assuming the higher place, which the most earth-like of our own parts, the head, has obtained in us. (30) But of all bonds,

that is the worst which is forged by violence, and which, being violent, is also short-lived; for it is speedily broken by those who are bound in it, since they become restive from their desire for a motion in accordance with nature, to which they hasten; for as the tragic poet says,—

"And for things sprung from earth, they must
Return unto their parent dust,
While those from heavenly seed which rise
Are borne uplifted to the skies.
Nought that has once existed dies,
Though often what has been combined
Before, we separated find,
Invested with another form."[9]

(31) And this law and ordinance is established with reference to everything which is destroyed, that wherever composite things are existing in combination they are thrown into disorder instead of into the order in accordance with nature, which they previously enjoyed, and they are removed to situations opposite to those in which they were previously placed, so that they seem in a manner to be sojourners; and when they are dissolved again, then they return to the appropriate parts allotted to them by nature.

VII. (32) But since the world has no participation in that irregularity which exists in the things which I have just been mentioning, let us stop awhile and consider this point.

If the world were liable to corruption and destruction, it follows of necessity that all its parts would at present be arranged in a position not in accordance with nature: but it is impious even to imagine such a thing as this; for all the parts of the world have received the most excellent position possible, and an arrangement of the purest symmetry and harmony; so that each individual part, being content with its place as a native country to it, does not seek any change for the better. (33) On this account it is that the most central position of all has been assigned to the earth, to which all things belonging to it adhere, and to which they descend again even if you throw them into the air: and this is a proof that their place is in accordance with nature; for wherever anything is borne without any violence, and where it then remains firm and stationary, that is clearly its natural place. And then, in the second place, water was poured over the earth, and air and fire had gone from the central to the upper part, air having received for its portion the region which is on the borders between air and fire, and fire having received the highest place of all: on which account, if you light a torch and press it down towards the ground, nevertheless the flame will still turn in a

---

[8]Timaeus, p. 32.

[9]A fragment from the Chryssipus of Euripides.

contrary direction, and lightening itself in accordance with the natural motion of fire, will rise upwards: (34) if, then, motion contrary to nature is the cause of corruptibility and destruction in the case of other animals, but if in the case of the world every one of its parts is arranged in complete accordance with nature, having had appropriate positions allotted to each of them, then surely the world must most justly be pronounced incorruptible and imperishable.

(35) Moreover this point is manifest to every one, that every nature is desirous to keep and preserve, and if it were possible to make immortal, everything of which it is the nature; the nature of trees, for instance, desires to preserve trees, and the nature of animals desires to preserve each individual animal. (36) But particular nature is of necessity unable to conduct what it belongs to to eternity; for want, or heat, or cold, or innumerable other ordinary circumstances, when they affect particular things, shake them and dissolve the bond which previously held them together, and at last break them to pieces; but if nothing resembling any of these things were lying in wait outside, then in that case nature itself, as far as it is possible, would preserve everything both great and small free from old age.

(37) It follows therefore of necessity, that the nature of the world must desire the durability of the universe; for it is not worse than particular natures, so that it should run away and desert its proper duties, and attempt to produce disease instead of health, and corruption and destruction instead of complete safety, since,—

"High over all she lifts her beauteous face,
And towers above her nymphs with heavenly grace,
Fair as they all appear."[10]

But if this be true, then the world cannot be capable of destruction. Why so? Because the nature which holds it together is itself invincible by reason of its exceeding strength and power, by which it gets the mastery over every thing else which might be likely to injure it; (38) wherefore Plato has well said:[11]—"For nothing ever departed from it, nor did anything ever come to it from any quarter; for that was not possible; for there was nothing in existence which could come; for since it supplies itself with nutriment out of its own consumption, it also does everything and suffers everything in itself and by itself, and is compounded with the most consummate art. For he who created it thought that it would be better if wholly self-

sufficient, than if in continual need of accessories from other quarters."

VIII. (39) However, this argument also is a most demonstrative one, on which I know that vast numbers of philosophers pride themselves as one most accurately worked out, and altogether irresistible; for they inquire what reason there is for God's destroying the world. For if he destroys it at all he must do so either with the intention of never making a world again, or with the object of creating a second fresh one; (40) now the former idea is inconsistent with the character of God; for it is proper to change disorder into order, and not order into disorder; in the second place, it is so because it would give rise to repentance, which is an affliction and a disease of the soul.

For he ought either never to have created a world at all, or else, if he judged that it was a fitting employment for him, he ought to have been pleased with it after it was made. (41) But the second reason deserves no superficial examination; for if he were intending to make another world instead of that which exists at present, then of necessity this second world that would be made, in that case, would be either worse than, or similar to, or better than the first; everyone of which ideas is inadmissible; for if the new world is to be worse than the former, then the maker must be also worse: but all the works of God are without blemish, beyond all reproach and wholly faultless, inasmuch as they are wrought with the most consummate skill and knowledge; for as the proverb says;—

"For e'en a woman's wisdom's not so coarse
As to despise the good and choose the worse."

But it is consistent with the character of, and becoming to God to give form to what is shapeless, and to invest what is most ugly with admirable beauty.

(42) Again, if the new world is to be exactly like the old one, then the maker is only wasting his labour, and differs in no respect from infant children who, very often while playing on the sea shore raise up little mounds of sand, and then pull them down again with their hands and destroy them; for it would have been much better than making another world exactly like the former, neither to take anything from, nor to add anything to, nor to change either for the better or for the worse, what existed originally, but to let it remain just as it was.

(43) If, on the other hand, he is about to make a world better than the former one, then the maker too must be better than the maker of the former world, so that when he made the former world he was inferior both in his skill and in his intellect, which it is impious even to imagine, for God is at all times equal and similar to himself, being neither

---

[10]Homer, Odyssey 6.107, where the lines quoted are applied to Latona among her nymphs.
[11]Timaeus, p. 33.

capable of any relaxation which can make him worse, nor of any extension which can make him better. Men, indeed, do admit of such inequalities in either direction, being naturally liable to alter either for the better or for the worse, and continually admitting of increase, and advance, and improvement, and everything contrary to these states; (44) and besides this, the works of us who are but mortal men may very appropriately be perishable, but the works of the immortal must in all consistency and reason be likewise imperishable, for it is natural that what is made should resemble the nature of the maker.

IX. (45) And, indeed, this I imagine is evident to every one, that if the earth were to be destroyed, then all land animals of every kind must also perish with it; and if the water were destroyed, all aquatic animals must perish; and in like manner if the air and fire were to be destroyed, all the animals which traverse the air or which are born in the fire must come to an end at the same time. (46) Therefore, on the same principle, if the heaven is destroyed, the sun and moon will also be destroyed, and all the other planets likewise will be destroyed, and all the fixed stars, and all that host of gods visible to the outward senses which was formerly considered so happy; and to imagine this is nothing else than to fancy the gods themselves in a process of destruction, for this is equivalent to considering men immortal. And yet in a comparison between different objects devoid of honour, if you were to consider the matter, you would find it more consistent with probability to look on men as immortal than to believe that the gods are perishable, since it might happen through the grace of God, for it is not improbable that a mortal might receive immortality, but it is impossible for gods to lose their immortality even if the sophistries of mankind should run on to ever such a degree of wicked insanity.

(47) And, moreover, those persons who allege conflagrations and regenerations of the world, think and confess that the stars are gods, which nevertheless they are not ashamed to destroy as far as their arguments go; for they are bound to prove them to be either red hot pieces of iron, as some do affirm, who argue about the whole of the heaven as if it were a prison, talking utter nonsense, or else to look upon them as divine and godlike natures, and then to attribute to them that immortality which belongs to gods.

But as it is, they have wandered so far from true doctrine, that without being aware of it they have attributed corruptibility and perishableness to providence (and that is the soul of the world) by the inconsistent principles which they advocate. (48) Therefore Chrysippus, the most celebrated philosopher of that sect, in his treatise about Increase, utters some such prodigious assertions as these, and after he has prefaced his doctrines

with the assertion that it is impossible for two makers of a species to exist in the same substance, he proceeds, "Let it be granted for the sake of argument and speculation that there is one person entire and sound, and another wanting one foot from his birth, and that the sound man is called Dion and the cripple Theon, and afterwards that Dion also loses one of his feet, then if the question were asked which had been spoiled, it would be more natural to say this of Theon;" but this is the assertion of one who delights in paradox rather than in truth, (49) for how could it be said that he who had suffered no mutilation whatever, namely Theon, was taken off, and that Dion, who had lost a foot, was not injured? Very appropriately, he will reply, for Dion, who had had his foot cut off, falls back upon the original imperfection of Theon, and there cannot be two specific differences in the same subject, therefore it follows of necessity that Dion must remain, and that Theon must be taken off—

"So are we slain by arrows winged
With our own feathers," [12]

as the tragic poet says. For any one, copying the form of this argument and adapting it to the entire world, may prove in the clearest manner that providence itself is liable to corruption. (50) Consider the matter thus: let the world be the subject of our argument, as Dion was just now, for it is perfect, and let the soul of the world take the place of Theon, who was imperfect, since a part is less than the whole; and as the foot was cut off from Dion, so also let everything which resembles a body be cut off from the world; (51) therefore it is necessary to say that the world has not been destroyed though its body has been taken away, just as Dion was not destroyed by having his foot cut off, but the soul of the world it is that has perished, like Theon, who suffered no artificial mutilation, for the world also receded to a lesser substance when all of it that resembled a body was taken away. And the soul was destroyed because there could not be two specific differences affecting the same and since it is imperishable it follows of necessity that the world also must be imperishable.

X. (52) However, time also affords a very great argument in favour of the eternity of the world, for if time is uncreated, then it follows of necessity that the world also must be uncreated. Why so? Because, as the great Plato says, it is days, and nights, and months, and the periods of years

---

[12] From the Myrmidons of Aeschylus. The passage is evidently the original of the stanza in Waller's Ode to a Lady Singing— "That eagle's fate and mine are one, / Who on the shaft that made him die, / Espied a feather of his own, / Wherewith he wont to soar so high."

which have shown time, and it is surely impossible that time can exist without the motion of the sun, and the rotary progress of the whole heaven. So that it has been defined very felicitously by those who are in the habit of giving definitions of things, that time is the interval of the motion of the world, and since this is a sound definition, then the world must be co-eval with time and also the cause of its existence.

(53) And it is the most absurd of all ideas to fancy that there ever was a time when the world did not exist, for its nature is without any beginning and without any end, since these very expressions, "there was," "when," "formerly," all indicate time; and keeping to this view, then, according to the theory of the conflagration [...] [13] he at a late period of his life entertained doubts and withheld any positive opinion; for it does not belong to youth, but to old age, to see clearly things of solemn importance which it is desirable to understand, and especially as to matters which it is not the outer sense, which is irrational and deceitful, that determines, but the pure and unalloyed intellect.

For that which has no existence is not put in motion, but it has been shown already that time is an interval of the motion of the world. It follows, therefore, of necessity, that each of these things must have subsisted from all eternity, without receiving any beginning of generation, and being in consequence not liable to any corruption. (54) Perhaps some quibbling Stoic will say that time is admitted to be an interval of the motion of the world, but not of that world only which is arranged and adorned by itself, but also of that one which is conceived of in connection with the conflagration which has been spoken of; to whom we must reply,—"My good man, you, misapplying words, call what is disorderliness and a want of arrangement order (kosmos), for if this thing which we see is correctly and appropriately called the world (kosmos), [14] being arranged and adorned (kekosmēmenos) as we see it by man, by the perfection of his skill, then any one would be surely correct in calling the change which is wrought in it by fire a want of order."

XI. (55) But Critolaus, a man who devoted himself very much to literature, and a lover of the Peripatetic philosophy, agreeing with the doctrine of the eternity of the world, used the following arguments to prove it: "If the word was created, then it follows of necessity that the earth was created also; and if the earth was created, then beyond all question the human race was so too. But man was not created, since he subsists of an everlasting race, as shall be proved, therefore the world is eternal."

(56) But I must now proceed to examine the argument which I postponed just now, if indeed things that are so evident stand in need of any demonstration; but, indeed, proofs are necessary on account of the inventors of fables who, filling all life with their falsehoods, have utterly driven truth out of the land, and have not merely banished it from cities and houses, but have even deprived each separate individual of that most valuable possession, and, for the purpose of alluring his sight, have invented metres and rhythm as a bait and a snare, by which they cajole the ears of fools, just as ugly and shapeless courtesans allure the eyes by necklaces and spurious ornaments in the absence of all genuine beauty, (57) for they say that the generation of mankind by means of one another is a more recent work of nature, but that the more original and ancient mode of their birth is out of the earth, since she both is and is considered the mother of all men. And they say that those men who are celebrated among the Greeks as having sprung from seed were produced and grew up as trees do now, being perfect and completely armed sons of the earth. (58) But that this is a mere fiction of fable it is easy to see from many circumstances.

For the very moment that the first man was born there was a necessity for his receiving growth in accordance with the previously defined measures and numbers of time, for nature has arranged the different ages as certain steps along which man in a manner ascends and descends; he ascends while he is growing, and he descends at the period when he is lessening; and the boundary of the uppermost steps is the prime of life at which when a man has arrived he no longer makes any further advance; but as runners who run the diaulos turn back again upon the same path which they have already travelled, so too does man retrace his steps, giving back in the weakness of old age what he has received from vigorous youth; (59) but to fancy that any one has ever been born absolutely perfect is the part of those who are ignorant of the laws of nature, which are unchangeable ordinances.

For our minds, being vitiated by the contagion of the mortal body which is united to them, are very naturally liable to changes and alterations, but the works of the nature of the universe are unalterable, since she has dominion over all things, and by means of the stability of whatever desires she has once established she preserves the definitions which have been originally fixed in an unchangeable state. (60) If then she had originally thought it proper that men should be born perfect, now also man would still be born in a perfect state, without ever being an infant, or a boy, or a youth, but

---

[13] There is supposed to be a very large hiatus here.
[14] Philo is playing here on the two meanings of the word kosmos, which signified both "order" and "the world."

he would at once be a man, and perhaps he would be altogether exempt from all diminution, for up to the prime of a man's life all his changes tend towards increase, but from that period up to old age and death they exist with a gradual diminution; and it is natural to suppose that he who has no share in the former must also be free from the subsequent changes.

(61) And what is there that can hinder men from shooting up now out of the ground like plants, as they say that they did in former times? For the earth has not yet grown old so as to appear to have become barren by reason of the lapse of time, but it remains in the same condition as before, being always young, because it is a fourth part of the universe, and for the sake of ensuring the duration of the universe it is bound not to decay, because its kindred elements, water, air, and fire, all remain for ever exempt from old age. (62) And there is a visible proof of the uninterrupted and everlasting vigour of the earth in the plants which spring from it, for being purified, either by the overflowing of rivers, as they say that Egypt is, or by annual rains, by such irrigation it refreshes and recruits its exhausted powers, and then, having rested for a while, it recovers its natural powers to the full extent of its original vigour, and then it begins again with a repetition of the production of similar things to those which it produced before to supply abundant food to every description of animal.

XII. (63) In reference to which fact it appears to me that the poets were very felicitous in the appellation which they gave to the earth when they called it Pandora, inasmuch as it gives all things,[15] both such as are required for use and such as serve to pleasure and to enjoyment, and that not to some only but to all animals which enjoy life. Accordingly, if any one, when the spring was in its prime, should be borne on wings and raised aloft, and look down from his height upon the mountain and champaign country, and see the one abounding in rich grass, and verdant, producing herbage, and fodder, and barley, and wheat, and innumerable other kinds of crops such as are grown from seed which the husbandmen have strewn, and which the season of the year affords of its own accord, and the other overshadowed with branches and leaves by which the trees are adorned, and very full of fruits (not only such as are suitable for food, but also of such as are able to heal suffering, for the fruit of the olive relieves the fatigue of the body, and that of the vine, when drunk in moderation, relaxes the excessive pains of the soul), (64) and rich also in the fragrant airs which are borne around from flowers, and the indescribable peculiarities of the various flowers which are diversified by divine skill.

And then, if he turns aside his eyes from those trees which admit of cultivation, and beholds in their turn poplars, and cedars, and pines, and ashes, and the lofty oaks, and the dense and unceasing masses of all the other wild trees which overshadow the most numerous and the greatest of the mountains, and the greater part of the border country wherever there is any deep soil, he will then know that the vigour of the earth, which is always young, is unremitting, unsubdued, and unwearied.

(65) So that since it is in no degree deprived of any portion of its former strength, if it had ever done so before, it would be bringing forth men now also, for two most forcible reasons, one in order that it might not quit the classification belonging to it, especially in the sowing and production of that most excellent of all the creatures which dwell upon the earth, the ruler of all, man, and secondly for the sake of divine assistance to women, who after they have conceived are for about ten months weighed down with the most severe pains, and when they are about to bring forth do very often die in the very pains of labour.

(66) Is it not then altogether a terrible piece of stupidity to imagine that the earth contains any womb calculated for the production of men? for the womb is the place which vivifies the animal, being as some one has called it the workshop of nature, in which it fashions nothing but animals; but it is not a portion of the earth, but of a female animal, carefully fashioned so as to be adapted for the production of living creatures, since otherwise it would be necessary for us to attribute breasts to the earth as to a woman, when it produces men and they are born, so that when first born they may have appropriate food.

But there is no river nor fountain in the whole habitable world which is said ever to have produced milk instead of water; (67) and in addition to this, as it is necessary that a child just born must be fed on milk, so also must he avail himself of the protection of clothing on account of the injury which ensues from cold or heat to children while they are being reared, on which account nurses and mothers, to whom the care of infants when just born is of necessity committed, wrap them up in swaddling clothes; but if they were produced out of the earth, how would it be possible that, being left completely naked, they would not be at once destroyed either by the coldness of the air on the one hand, or the burning heat of the sun on the other? for when great cold or great heat gets the mastery, it produces diseases and corruptions.

(68) But after the inventors of fables once began to neglect the truth they then ventured to add to their monstrous stories the fiction that those men who sprung from seed were born also to complete armour; for what smith, or what new Vulcan, was there under the earth so skilful as in a

---

[15] *Panta dōroumenēn.*

moment to prepare so many suits of armour? and what experience had creatures just born to enable them to use their weapons? for man is a very peaceful animal, nature having given to him reason as his especial honour, by means of which he charms and tames the savage passions. It would have been much better instead of arms to give him a herald's wand, a symbol of agreement and peace suitable to a reasonable nature, in order the he might so proclaim peace instead of war to all men everywhere.

XIII. (69) We have now then discussed at sufficient length the nonsense in opposition to truth which is uttered by those who build up falsehood and fables. But we must be well assured that men have from all eternity sprung from other men in constant succession, the man implanting the seed in the woman as in a field, and the woman receiving the seed so as to preserve it, and nature by her unseen operations fashioning everything, and each separate part of the body and of the soul, and giving to the whole race of mankind that which each individual separately is unable to receive, namely, the principle of immortality; for though the individual members are continually perishing, yet the race remains undying as a truly divine work. But if man, who is but a small portion of the universe, is eternal, then certainly the world itself must have been uncreated so as to be imperishable.

XIV. (70) But Critolaus, in arguing in support of his opinion, brought forward an argument of this kind,—"That which is the cause to man of his being in health is itself free from disease, and, in like manner, the cause of his keeping awake must itself be sleepless; and if this is the case, that which is the cause of his existing for ever must itself also be everlasting." Now the cause of man's existing for ever is the world, since it is so to all other things whatever; therefore the world also is immortal. (71) Nevertheless, this point also is worthy of one consideration: that everything which is born must by all means at the beginning be imperfect, but as time advances he must increase till he arrives at complete perfection, so that if the world was born it was at one time (that I may use the expressions appropriate to the ages of men) a mere infant, and subsequently increasing in periods of years and lapse of time, it at last and with great difficulty arrived at perfection, for of necessity the period at which that which of all things has the longest existence must be late. (72) But if any one fancies that the world has ever really been subjected to such changes as these, it is time that he should learn that he has been under the influence of incurable madness, for it is plain that if that is the case not only will its bodily appearance be increased, but its mind also will receive growth, since they who attribute liability to perish to it conceive it to be a rational creature. (73) Therefore, just like a man, it will

be devoid of reason at the commencement of its existence, but endowed with reason at the age when it is in its prime, which it is impious not only to say, but even to think, for how can we imagine the most perfect visible circumference which surrounds us, and which contains within itself so many individual inhabitants, is not always perfect both in soul and body, being exempt from all those evils in which everything which has been born and which is perishable is implicated?

XV. (74) And in addition to this he says, that there are three causes of death to living animals, besides the external causes which may affect them, namely, disease, old age, and want, by no one of which is the world liable to be attacked or subdued, for that it is composed of entire elements, since there is no part of them which is left out or which remains at liberty, so that any violence can be offered to it, and it also is superior to those powers from which diseases arise; and they yielding keep the world free from all disease, and free from old age, and in a state of the most perfect self-sufficiency as to all its requirements, and without need of anything, since there is nothing wanting to it which can possibly contribute to its durability, and wholly exempt from all successions and alternations of fulness and emptiness, which animals being subject to by reason of their unregulated insatiability, bring upon themselves death instead of life, or, to speak more accurately, a life which is more pitiable than any destruction.

(75) Moreover, if we saw that there was no such thing as any eternal nature to be seen, those who assert the liability of the world to destruction would not appear to be so guilty of disparaging the world without any excuse, since they would have no example whatever of anything being everlasting; but since fate, according to the doctrine of those who have investigated the principles of natural philosophy most accurately, is a thing without any beginning and without any end, connecting all the causes of everything, as to leave no break and no interruption, why may we not in like manner also affirm of the nature of the world that it subsists for a great length of time, being, as it were, an arrangement of what is otherwise in no order, a harmony of what is otherwise wholly destitute of such harmony, an agreement of what is otherwise without agreement, a union of things previously separated, a condition of stocks and stones, a nature of things growing from seed and of trees, a life of all animals, the mind and reason of men, and the most perfect virtue of virtuous men?

But if the nature of the world is uncreated and indestructible, then it is plain that the world is held together and powerfully preserved by an everlasting indissoluble chain. (76) But some of those who used to hold a different opinion, being overpowered by truth, have changed their doctrine; for beauty has a power which is very attractive, and the truth is beyond all things beautiful, as false-hood on the contrary is enormously ugly; there-fore Boethus, and Posidonius, and Panaetius, men of great learning in the Stoic doctrines, as if seized with a sudden inspiration, abandoning all the sto-ries about conflagrations and regeneration, have come over to the more divine doctrine of the incor-ruptibility of the world; (77) and it is said also that Diogenes, when he was very young, agreed entirely with those authors ...

XVI. (78) But Boethus adduces the most con-vincing arguments, which we shall proceed to men-tion immediately; for if, says he, the world was created and is liable to destruction, then some-thing will be made out of nothing, which appears to be most absurd even to the Stoics. Why so? Because it is not possible to discover any cause of destruction either within or without, which will destroy the world. For on the outside there is nothing except perhaps a vacuum, inasmuch as all the elements in their integrity are collected and contained within it, and within there is no imper-fection so great as to be the cause of dissolution to so great a thing.

Again, if it is destroyed without any cause, then it is plain that from something which has no ex-istence will arise the engendering of destruction, which is an idea quite inadmissible by reason; (79) and, indeed, they say that there are altogether three generic manners of corruption, one which arises from division, another which proceeds from a destruction of the distinctive quality which holds the thing together, and the third from confusion; therefore the things which consist of a union of separate members, such as flocks of goats, herds of oxen, choruses, armies; or, again, bodies which are compounded of limbs joined together, are dis-solved by disjunction and separation. But wax, when stamped with a new impression, or softened before being remodelled so as to present a new and different appearance, is corrupted by a destruc-tion of the distinctive quality which previously held it together. Other things are corrupted by confu-sion, as the medicine which the physicians call tetrapharmacon, for the powers of the drugs brought together and combined were destroyed in such a manner as to produce one perfect medi-cine of especial virtue.

(80) By which, then, of these modes of cor-ruption is it becoming to say that the world is destroyed? By that which is caused by separation? No, for it is not compounded of separate mem-bers so that its different parts can be dispersed, nor of portions joined together so that they can be dissolved; nor is it united together in a similar manner to our own bodies, for they have the seeds of decay in themselves, and they are subject to influence of a great variety of things by which they are at times injured; but the power of the world

is invincible, since by its great superiority to other things it has dominion over everything.

(81) Is it then destroyed by a complete destruc-tion of its distinctive qualities? This again is impos-sible, for there remains, as the adversaries affirm, a quality of arrangement which by the process of conflagration is only diminished to a lesser sub-stance ... Is it destroyed then by confusion? Away with such an idea, (82) for in that case it would be necessary to confess that the corruption of a body can be reduced to a state of non-existence. Why so? Because if each of the particular ele-ments were destroyed separately, it would be pos-sible for it to become changed into another; but if they are altogether destroyed at one and the same moment by confusion, then it would be nec-essary to imagine what is absolutely impossible.

(83) Again, besides these arguments, if all things, say they, were destroyed by fire, then what will God have to do during all that time, except absolutely nothing? And is it not reasonable to say so? For at present, he overlooks and presides over everything, and regulates everything like a gen-uine father, and if one is to say the truth, he guides and directs everything, sitting as it were by the side of the sun, and moon, and the other planets, and fixed stars, and also by the air, and the other parts of the world, and he co-operates with them in everything which can conduce to the durability of the universe and to its blameless management, in accordance with right reason. (84) But if every-thing is destroyed, then he will have an existence which will be rendered absolutely miserable, by inactivity and irremediable want of employment; than which what idea can be more absurd? I hes-itate to add, what it would be impious to say, that death will ensue to God if absolute inactivity falls to his lot; for if you take away the perpetual motion of the soul, then you will beyond all question also destroy the soul itself. And the soul of the world, in the opinion of those who maintain the opposite doctrine, is God.

XVII. (85) Is it not however worth while to examine this question, in what manner there can be a regeneration of all those things which have been destroyed by fire, and resolved into fire? for when their substance has been wholly destroyed by the fire, it follows of necessity that the fire itself must also be extinguished as no longer having any nourishment. Therefore, as long as it remained the seminal principle of arrangement was likewise preserved, but when it is destroyed that principle is destroyed with it. But it would be impious, and an impiety of double dye, not only to attribute destruction to the world, but also to take away the possibility of its regeneration; as if God delighted in disorder, and irregularity, and all kinds of evil things. (86) But we must examine this question more accurately, in the following manner.

There are three species in fire; the coal, and the flame, and the light. Now coal is the fire in its earthy substance, which, like a sort of spiritual habit, couches and lies hid in a sort of cavern, pervading it all to its very extremities. And the flame is that part which, being raised on high, is lifted up from its fuel. And the light is that which is emitted from the flame, so as to co-operate with the eyes, in order to enable them to comprehend what is seen. And the flame occupies the middle position between the coal and the light; for when it is extinguished it ends in coal, and when it is kindled it excites the light, which, being deprived of its burning power, blazes. (87) If therefore, we affirm that the world is dissolved by conflagration, it would not be coal, because, in that case there will be a great deal of the earthy substance left behind, in which also fire must necessarily be contained. But we must agree, that none of the other bodies subsist any longer, but that earth, and water, and air, are all dissolved into unmixed fire. (88) Nor, again, would it become flame; for that can only exist in connexion with nourishment; and, if nothing is left behind, being deprived of all nourishment it will immediately be extinguished. It follows from all this, that it cannot become light either; for light by itself has no substance at all, but flows from the things before mentioned, coal and flame, not in a great degree from the coal, but very much from the flame; for it is diffused over a very great space indeed. But if, as has been already proved, those things had no existence from the conflagration of all things, then there could not be any light either. For the abundant, and vast, and extensive brilliancy of mid-day, when the sun proceeds under the earth, is at once caused to disappear by night, especially if it be a moonless night. Therefore the world is not destroyed by fire, but is indestructible. And if it should be destroyed by fire, there could not be another created.

XVIII. (89) On which account some of the Stoics also, being gifted with a more acute discernment, and perceiving that they would infallibly be convicted, thought it well to be beforehand in preparing assistance as it were for a defunct proposition. But what they prepared was of no use; for, since fire is the cause of all motion, and since motion is the beginning of generation, for it is impossible that anything whatever should be generated without motion, they said that before the new world began to be formed, when it was beginning to be fashioned, the whole fire would not be extinguished in that conflagration; that they affirmed that some would still remain, but yet only a small portion. For they were exceedingly cautious, lest if it should be wholly extinguished, the consequence would be that everything would remain motionless and devoid of ornament, inasmuch as the cause of motion would no longer be in any existence. (90) But all these ideas are the

invention of quibblers, who employ all their artifices in opposition to the truth. Why so? Because it is impossible, as has been proved already, that the world, after it has been destroyed by conflagration, should become similar to coal, inasmuch as there is a vast quantity of earthy substance left in which the fire must of necessity lie in ambush. And perhaps too the conflagration could not prevail in every quarter, if the heaviest and most invincible of the elements, namely the earth, still remains, without being dissolved; but it must of necessity change, either into flame or into light: into flame, as Cleanthes thought; into light, as Chryssipus conceived. (91) But if it becomes flame, then, when it approaches extinction, it will be extinguished all at once, and not partially or gradually. For the nutriment exists along with it; on which account, while there is a great deal of it, it increases and is diffused; but when it is stunted it becomes less.

And any one might conjecture the truth of what takes place from what he sees happen among us. A lamp, when any one pours oil upon it, gives forth a most brilliant flame; but when any one ceases to supply it with that nutriment, and leaves only a small portion in the lamp, then the lamp is at once extinguished, and does not give out the smallest portion of flame.

(92) If again this is not the case, but if the world becomes light, then again it changes altogether. Why so? Because it has no substance or character of its own, but is generated from flame, and when this is wholly and completely extinguished in all its parts, it follows of necessity that the light also must be extinguished, and that not partially, but altogether. For what flame is to nourishment, that also is light to flame. (93) As therefore the flame is extinguished concurrently with the want of nourishment, so also is the light simultaneously with the flame, so that it is actually impossible for the world to be capable of regeneration, if there is no seminal principle lurking and kindled within it, but if all things are expended and destroyed, some by fire, and some by want. From all which arguments it is plain that the world is for ever uncreated and imperishable.

XIX. (94) Nevertheless, as Chryssipus says, some suppose that fire resolves all the arrangement of the universe when the elements are separated into itself, so that it becomes the seed of the world which is about to be made; and suppose in consequence that, of all the ideas which he and his sect have entertained on the subject, none are falsified. Granting, in the first place, that generation proceeds from seed, and that all dissolution is a resolving back into seed; in the second place, because it is argued by natural philosophers that the world is a rational nature, inasmuch as it is not only possessed of life, but is also endowed with intellect, and moreover even with wisdom; by these arguments he establishes that contrary proposition to that which he intends, namely, that it will never be destroyed. (95) But the proofs are ready at hand to those who do not fear to join in the investigation.

Therefore the world resembles either a plant or an animal. But whether it is a plant or whether it is an animal, still, if it be destroyed by conflagration, it will never be itself its own seed. And the circumstances which take place among ourselves bear witness that nothing, whether great or less, when destroyed, has ever been separated in such a manner as to engender seed. (96) Do you not see how many materials of plants susceptible of cultivation there are, and how many kinds of wild plants too are diffused over every portion of the earth? Every one of these trees, as long as the trunk is in good health, together with its fruit, produces also a seed to propagate its species; but becoming destroyed after a lapse of time, and being wholly withered, roots and all, it never becomes resolved into a ripened seed. (97) And so too in the same manner the different kinds of animals, which it is not easy even to enumerate by reason of their multitude, as long as they survive and flourish vigorously, produce a seed, which is calculated to propagate their species; but when they are dead there is no longer any seed.

For it would be absurd for a man when he is alive to employ only the eighth part of his soul, which is called the generative power, for the propagation of a being like himself, but after he is dead to exert the whole of himself for the same purpose; for death can never be more energetic or efficacious than life. (98) And besides, there is no single existing thing which is brought to perfection by seed alone without its appropriate nourishment. For seed resembles the beginning, and the beginning by itself does not make perfect; for beware of imagining that the ear of corn blossoms and ripens solely from the seed, which is cast by the husbandman on the ploughed field; for in truth, dryness and moisture, the twofold moisture which is derived from the earth, co-operate in the greatest degree towards its growth. And so the creature which is fashioned in the womb is not permitted by nature to be brought to life and perfection by the seed alone, but also by the nourishment shed upon it from without, which the woman who has conceived supplies.

(99) Why then do I say this? Because in the case of such a conflagration as that of which I have been speaking, the seed alone will be left, there being no nutriment remaining, since everything which was to have supplied nutriment will have been resolved into fire; so that the world, which would be to be formed, according to the principle of regeneration, will have a lame and imperfect form and character, since that which is chiefly required to co-operate towards its perfection, on which, as

on a staff, the seminal origin ought to, and naturally does, lean, is destroyed; but this would be absurd, as is shown, and made manifest from the clearest evidence.

(100) Again, all those things which derive their origin from seed are of a greater magnitude than the seed which gives them their existence, and are seen to fill a more extended space; for very often trees, whose tops reach to heaven itself, shoot up out of a very small grain of seed; and the fattest and tallest animals grow from a very small quantity of moisture, which is laid as their foundation; but there happens that which was mentioned a little while ago, that these, at the time nearest to their birth are very little, but that subsequently they keep on increasing in size till they arrive at complete perfection.

(101) But in the case of the universe the exact contrary will take place, for here the seed will both be greater and will also fill a larger space; and the ultimate perfection at which the thing formed arrives will be smaller, and will appear in a smaller space; and the world, originally derived from a seed, will not progress from a very small thing towards increase, but, on the other hand, will be diminished from a greater magnitude to a smaller; (102) and it is easy to see the truth of what is here said.

Every body, when it is resolved into fire, is dissolved, and melted, and diffused; and when the flame which is in it is extinguished, it is then contracted and shrunk up to nothing; but there is no need of arguments to prove a thing which is so clear, as if it were obscure; and, indeed, the world, if consumed by fire, will become greater, inasmuch as all its essence will then be dissolved into the thinnest air; and it appears to me that the Stoics have foreseen this, and on that account have, in their arguments, assumed that a vacuum of infinite extent will be left abandoned on the outside of the world; that so, since it is fated to be subjected to a certain diffusion of boundless extent, it may not be in want of a place which may be capable of receiving that diffusion. (103) When therefore it has been extended and increased to such a degree, as to be very nearly equal to the infinite extent of the vacuum by the boundless and illimitable extension of its own diffusion, it then, according to them, is itself the principle of seed to itself; but when, according to a perfect regeneration of the parts, its entire substance [...] [16] being contracted in the extinction of the fire into dense air; but when the air again is contracted, and when it settles down into water, then again the water is still further condensed, so as to be changed into earth, which is the best of all the elements. But all these arguments are beyond the ordinary ideas

---

[16] There seems a line or two lost here.

of those who are able to consider and argue upon the consequences of these things.

XX. (104) However, besides what has been here said, any one may use this argument also in corroboration of his opinion, which will certainly convince all those who are not determined to be obstinate beyond all bounds; of those things which in pairs are exactly contrary to one another it is impossible that one thing should be, and that the other should not be; for since there is white it follows as a matter of absolute necessity that there must also be black, and since there is a great there must likewise be a little; since there is an odd there must inevitably be an even; since there is a sweet there must be a bitter; since there is day there must be night; and so on in an infinite number of similar cases; but if a conflagration should take place, then something would ensue which is impossible; for then, of things in a pair, the one will happen and the other will not.

(105) Come, now, let us consider the matter thus: if everything is resolved into fire, there is then something light, and rare, and warm; for all these are the especial properties of fire; but there can be nothing heavy, or cold, or thick, which are the opposites of the qualities which I have just enumerated. How then can any one more completely overturn the idea of the universal disorder which would be involved in such a conflagration than by showing that those things which by a law of nature must exist together, are by this process separated from their natural conjunction? And the separation has extended to such a degree, that those who maintain this doctrine attribute eternal durability to the one and deny any existence at all to the other.

(106) Again, there is this assertion made by some of those who diligently employ themselves in investigating truth which appears to me to be a sufficiently felicitous one; if the world is destroyed it will either be destroyed by some other efficient cause, or by God; now there is certainly nothing else whatever from which it can receive its destruction, for there is nothing whatever which it does not surround and contain; but that which is surrounded and confined within something else is manifestly inferior in power to that which surrounds and confines it, by which it is therefore mastered; on the other hand, to say that it is destroyed by God is the most impious of all possible assertions; for God is the cause not of disorder, and irregularity, and destruction, but of order, and beautiful regularity, and life, and of every good thing, as is confessed by all those whose opinions are based on truth.

XXI. (107) But a person may very likely wonder at those who talk about conflagrations and regenerations, not only on account of the arguments which I have just been adducing, by which they are convicted of maintaining erroneous opinions, but also above all other reasons for this one; for since there are four elements of which the world consists, namely, earth, water, air, and fire, why is it that they are to separate fire from all the others, and to affirm that all the others are dissolved into that one? For some one may say, if it is necessary that they should all be resolved into one, why should they not be resolved into air, or water, or earth? For these elements also contain powers of great magnitude; but yet no one has ever said that the world was to pass away into air, or into water, or into earth; so that it would be equally natural to deny that it is resolved into fire.

(108) Moreover, it would have become them, perceiving the beautiful equality which exists in the world, to fear and to feel too great awe to venture to condemn so divine a thing to death; for there is a most admirable system of compensation existing in the four elements which arrange and dispense their vicissitudes by the rulers of equality, and the definitions of justice; (109) for as the seasons of the year, in their proper alternations of revolutions, go through their regular cycle, completing their periodical changes without any cessation; in the same manner suppose that the elements of the world in the course of their continual interchanges with one another (though it is a most paradoxical assertion), when they appear to be perishing are in reality being made immortal, passing over the same course again and again, so as to have their existence infinitely protracted.

(110) Therefore the steep road begins with the earth; for when it is wasted away it endures a change to water, and the water when it has evaporated is changed into air, and the air when rarefied is changed into fire; but the downward road descends from the head, when the fire in consequence of the conflagration which ensues settles down into air, and again when the air being closely pressed settles down into water, and when the water by its copious effusion is condensed so as to be changed into earth.

(111) Heraclitus therefore spoke very correctly when he said that, "Water was the death of the soul, and earth the death of water." For thinking that the breath was the soul, he indicates, by this figurative and enigmatical expression, that the end of air is the production of water, and again that the end of water is the production of earth; and when he speaks of death he does not mean utter destruction, but a change into some other element; (112) that equalised proportion of the elements which is attempered by itself being thus preserved eternal and uninjured, as is not only probable but absolutely inevitable; since what is unequal is essentially unjust, and injustice is the offspring of wickedness, and wickedness is banished from the abode of immortality. But the world is of a divine magnitude, and has been shown to be the abode of those gods which are visible to the outward

senses; and to affirm that this world is destroyed is the part of those who do not see the connection of nature and the united consequence and coherence of things.

XXII. (113) But some of those persons who have fancied that the world is everlasting, inventing a variety of new arguments, employ also such a system of reasoning as this to establish their point: they affirm that there are four principal manners in which corruption is brought about, addition, taking away, transposition, and alteration; accordingly, the number two is by the addition of the unit corrupted so as to become the number three, and no longer remains the number two; and the number four by the taking away of the unit is corrupted so as to become the number three; again, by transposition the letter Z becomes the letter H when the parallel lines which were previously horizontal (⊐) are placed perpendicularly (| |), and when the line which did before pass upwards, so as to connect the two is now made horizontal, and still extended between them so as to join them. And by alteration the word *oinos, wine,* becomes *oxos, vinegar.*

(114) But of the manner of corruption thus mentioned there is not one which is in the least degree whatever applicable to the world, since otherwise what could we say? Could we affirm that anything is added to the world so as to cause its destruction? But there is nothing whatever outside of the world which is not a portion of it as the whole, for everything is surrounded, and contained, and mastered by it. Again, can we say that anything is taken from the world so as to have that effect? In the first place that which would be taken away would again be a world of smaller dimensions than the existing one, and in the second place it is impossible that any body could be separated from the composite fabric of the whole world so as to be completely dispersed. (115) Again, are we to say that the constituent parts of the world are transposed? But at all events they remain in their original positions without any change of place, for never at any time shall the whole earth be raised up above the water, nor the water above the air, nor the air above the fire. But those things which are by nature heavy, namely the earth and the water, will have the middle place, the earth supporting everything like a solid foundation, and the water being above it; and the air and the fire, which are by nature light, will have the higher position, but not equally, for the air is the vehicle of the fire; and that which is carried by anything is of necessity above that which carries it.

(116) Once more: we must not imagine that the world is destroyed by alteration, for the change of any elements is equipollent, and that which is equipollent is the cause of unvarying steadiness, and of untroubled durability, inasmuch as it neither seeks any advantage itself, and is not subject to the inroads of other things which seek advantages at its expense; so that this retribution and compensation of these powers is equalized by the rules of proportion, being the produce of health and endless preservation, by all which considerations the world is demonstrated to be eternal.

XXIII. (117) Theophrastus, moreover, says that those men who attribute a beginning and destructibility to the world are deceived by four particulars of the greatest importance, the inequalities of the earth, the retreat of the sea, and dissolution of each of the parts of the universe, and the destruction of different terrestrial animals in their kinds; (118) and he proceeds to establish the first point thus: if the earth had never had any beginning of its creation, then there would have been no portion of it rising above the rest so as to be conspicuous, but all the mountains would have been level, and all the pieces of rising ground would have been even with the plain.

For as there are such vast showers falling from heaven throughout all ages, it would be natural that of any places which were originally raised on high some would be broken down and washed away by torrents, and others would subside of their own accord and so become lowered, and that every place everywhere would be smoothed; (119) but now, as things are, the constant inequalities which exist, and the vast heights of many mountains, reaching up even to the sky, are so many proofs that the earth is not eternal.

For otherwise, as I have said before, all the earth would long since have been rendered level from one extremity to the other by the vast rains which would have fallen from the eternal commencement of time; for it is the character of the nature of water, and especially of such as descends in a heavy fall from lofty places, to push some things away by force, and to cut out and hollow other places by its continual dropping, and in this manner to operate on the hard, rugged, stony ground not less than men digging. (120) And again, the sea, as they affirm, is already somewhat diminished, and for proof of this fact we can appeal to the most celebrated islands, Rhodes and Delos, for these were in ancient times invisible, being overwhelmed by and sunk under the sea, but by lapse of time, as the sea gradually diminished, they by slow degrees rose above it and came into sight, as the histories which are written concerning them record. (121) And they used to call Delos Anaphe, confirming the account here given by both names, since when it appeared above the waters[17] it became evident,[18] having been formerly invisible

---

[17]The Greek word is *anaphaneisa*, from which *Anaphē* is derived.
[18]*Dēlē*, from which *Dēlos* is derived.

and unseen.[19] On which account Pindar says respecting Delos—

"Hail, island raised by God,
Chosen abode
Of fair Latona's son with golden hair.
Hail, ocean's youngest child,
The last immoveable domain
That o'er his bosom smiled.
Upraised from beneath the billowy main
Mortals may call you Delos, but the choir
That dwells upon Olympus' height,
Their chosen bards inspire
To praise thee as earth's brightest, holiest light."[20]

For Pindar has here called Delos the daughter of the ocean, intending by this enigmatical expression to convey the idea which I have mentioned.

(122) And in addition to these arguments they adduce the facts that many great and deep bays and gulfs of vast seas have been dried up, and have become land, and have so turned out no insignificant addition to the adjacent country when sown and planted, and on that soil there is still left plenty of proof of such spots having formerly been sea, in the pebbles, and shells, and other things which are commonly washed up on the sea-shore being found in them.

(123) But if the sea is gradually being diminished then the earth also will be diminished; and in long revolutions of years every one of the elements will be entirely consumed and destroyed; and the whole air will be consumed, being diminished by little and little; and all things will be absorbed and dissolved into the one substance of fire.

XXIV. (124) And for the purpose of establishing the third alternative of this question they use the following argument: beyond all question that thing is destroyed all the parts of which are liable to destruction; but all the parts of the world are liable to destruction, therefore the world also is liable to destruction.

(125) But we must now proceed to consider the question which we postponed till the present time. What sort of a part of the earth is that, that we may begin from this, whether it is greater or less, that is not dissolved by time? Do not the very hardest and strongest stones become hard and decayed through the weakness of their conformation (and this conformation is a sort of course of a highly strained spirit, a bond not indissoluble, but only very difficult to unloose), in consequence of which they are broken up and made fluid, so

that they are dissolved first of all into a thin dust, and afterwards are wholly wasted away and destroyed? Again, if the water were never agitated by the winds, but were left immoveable for ever, would it not from inaction and tranquillity become dead? at all events it is changed by such stagnation, and becomes very foetid and foul-smelling, like an animal deprived of life. (126) And so also the corruptions of the air are plain to everyone, for it is the nature of the atmosphere to become sick and to decay, and, as one may say, in a manner to die; since what else is it which a man, who is not aiming at selecting plausible language, but only at truth, would call a plague except a death of the atmosphere, which diffuses its own disease and suffering to the destruction of everything which is endowed with life?

(127) And why need I speak at great length concerning fire? for if it is deprived of nourishment it is immediately extinguished, becoming, as the poets say, tame by its own natural qualities, on which account it depends upon, and is raised up by the duration of the fuel which is supplied and kindled, but when that is expended the fire also disappears. (128) And they say that the dragons in India are exposed to the same kind of fate, for that they crawl upon the greatest of all beasts, namely elephants, and creep over their backs and the whole of their bellies, and then, if they can find a vein, they divide that and drink the blood, sucking it insatiably, with a strong breath and a vigorous noise. Meantime the elephants, though greatly drained, and though becoming gradually exhausted, hold out for some time, leaping about in their perplexity, and lashing their sides with their trunks in the hope of being able to shake off the dragons. After a time, as the vital principle is continually becoming more and more exhausted, they are no longer able to leap about, but stand trembling and quivering, and after a little more time their legs become too weak to support them, and they are thrown down and die for want of blood. And when they are fallen down those animals which were the causes of their death die with them in the following manner: (129) since the dragons have no longer any nourishment, they attempt to loosen the bonds with which they twined themselves round the elephants, wishing now to get released from them, but they are pressed down by the weight of the elephants and crushed, and much more so when the animal has become a lifeless, hard, and stone-like substance; for though they wriggle about and try every expedient in order to effect their release from the power of the animal which weighs them down, and by which they are entangled, though they have long practised themselves in every variety of wile, amid all kinds of difficulties and distresses, they at last become too weak to resist, like men who have been starved to death, or who have been caught by a wall which

---

[19]Yonge's translation places the following excerpt after section 122. Present arrangement reflects the Loeb sequence.
[20]This is part of an ode now lost.

has suddenly fallen down upon them, and not being able even to lift up their heads they die of suffocation.

If then, each of the separate parts of the world awaits utter destruction, it is plain that the world which is compounded of these can not be itself exempt from destruction.

(130) We must now consider with accuracy the fourth and remaining argument. Thus they argue: if the world were eternal then the animals also would be eternal, and much more the human race, in proportion as that is more excellent than the other animals; but, on the contrary, those who take delight in investigating the mysteries of nature consider that man has only been created in the late ages of the world; for it is likely, or I should rather say it is inevitably true, that the arts co-exist with man, so as to be exactly co-eval with him, not only because methodical proceedings are appropriate to a rational nature, but also because it is not possible to live without them; (131) let us therefore examine the dates of each of these, disregarding the fables invented by the tragedians about the gods; but if man is not eternal then neither is any other animal, so that then neither are the places which receive them, the earth, or the water, or the air; from all which considerations it is plain that this world is liable to destruction.

XXV. (132) But it is necessary to encounter such quibbling arguments as these, lest some persons of too little experience should yield to and be led away by them; and we must begin our refutation of them from the same point from which the Sophists begin their deceit. They say, "There could no longer be any inequalities existing on the earth, if the world were eternal." Why not, my most excellent friends? For other persons will come up and say that the natures of trees are in no respect different from mountains; but just as they at certain seasons lose their leaves, and again at certain seasons recover their verdure again; (on which account there is admirable truth in those lines of the poet:—

"Like leaves on trees the race of man is found,
Now green in youth, now withering on the ground;
Another race the following spring supplies;
They fall successive and successive rise."[21]

And so in like manner some portions of the mountains are broken off, and others grow in their stead: (133) but after a long lapse of time the additional growth becomes conspicuous because the trees having a more rapid nature, display their increase with great rapidity; but mountains have a slower character, on which account it happens that the additions which take place in their case are not perceptible by the outward senses except after a long time.

(134) And these men appear to be ignorant of the manner in which they are produced, since if they had not been, perhaps they would have been silent out of shame; but still there is no reason why we should not teach them; but there is nothing new in what is now said, neither are they our words but the ancient sayings of wise men, by whom nothing which was necessary for knowledge has been left uninvestigated; (135) when the fiery principle which is contained beneath, in the earth, is thrust upwards by the natural power of fire, it proceeds to its own appropriate place; and if it meets with any respite or relaxation, though ever so slight, it draws up with it a large portion of the earthy substance, as much as it can; and when it has emerged from the earth it proceeds more slowly; but the earthy substance being compelled to follow it for a long time, being at last raised to an immense height, is contracted at the top, and at last comes to end on a sharp point imitating the general appearance of the flame of fire; (136) for there arises then a most violent contention between two things which are natural adversaries, the lightest and the heaviest of things, each of them pressing onwards to reach its own place, and each striving against the violent efforts of the other; accordingly the fire, which is drawing up the earth with it, is compelled to sink down by its descending power; and the earth naturally inclining to the lowest point is nevertheless to a certain degree made light, and lifted up by the upward tendencies of fire, and so is raised on high, and being at last overpowered by the more influential power which lightens it is thrust upwards towards the natural seat of fire, and established on high.

(137) Why then need we wonder if the mountains are not entirely washed away by the impetuosity of the rains, when so great a power, which keeps them together, and by which they are raised up, is very firmly and steadfastly connected with them? For if they were released from the bond which holds them together, it would be natural for them to be entirely dissolved and to be dispersed by the water; but since they are bound together by this power of fire, they resist the impetuosity of the rains more surely.

XXVI. These things, then, may be said by us with respect to the argument that the inequalities of the surface of the earth are no proof of the world having been created and being liable to destruction; (138) but with respect to that argument which was endeavoured to be established by the diminution of the sea, we may reasonably adduce this statement in opposition to it: "Do not look only at the islands which have risen up out of the sea, nor at any portions of land which, having been formerly buried by the waters, have in subsequent times become dry land; for obstinate contention

---

[21]Homer, Il. 6.147.

is very unfavourable to the consideration of natural philosophy, which considers the search after truth to be the chief object of rational desire; but look rather at the contrary effects: consider how many districts on the main-land, not only such as were near the coast, but even such as were completely in-land, have been swallowed up by the waters; and consider how great a portion of land has become sea and is now sailed over by innumerable ships." (139) Are you ignorant of the celebrated account which is given of that most sacred Sicilian strait, which in old times joined Sicily to the continent of Italy?[22] and where vast seas on each side being excited by violent storms met together, coming from opposite directions, the land between them was overwhelmed and broken away; from which circumstance the city built in the neighbourhood was called Rhegium,[23] and the result was quite different from what any one would have expected; for the seas which had formerly been separated now flowed together and were united in one expanse; and the land which had previously united was now separated into two portions by the strait which intersected it, in consequence of which Sicily, which had previously formed a part of the mainland, was now compelled to be an island.

(140) And it is said that many other cities also have disappeared, having been swallowed up by the sea which overwhelmed them; since they speak of three in Peloponnesus—

"Aegira and fair Bura's walls,
And Helica's lofty halls,
And many a once renowned town,
With wreck and seaweed overgrown,"

as having been formerly prosperous, but now overwhelmed by the violent influx of the sea. (141) And the island of Atalantes which was greater than Africa and Asia, as Plato says in the Timaeus, in one day and night was overwhelmed beneath the sea in consequence of an extraordinary earthquake and inundation and suddenly disappeared, becoming sea, not indeed navigable, but full of gulfs and eddies. (142) Therefore that imaginary and fictitious diminution of the sea has no connection with the destruction or durability of the world; for in fact it appears to recede indeed from some parts, but to rise higher in others; and it would have been

proper rather not to look at only one of these results but at both together, and so to form one's opinion, since in all the disputed questions which arise in human life, a wise and honest judge will not deliver his opinion before he has heard the arguments of the advocates on both sides.

XVII. (143) And as for the third argument, it is convicted by itself, as being derived only from an unsound system of questioning proceeding from the assertions originally made; for in truth it does not necessarily follow that a thing, all the parts of which are liable to corruption, is likewise perishable itself; but this is only inevitably true of that thing of which all the parts are perishable when taken collectively and together in the same place and at the same time, since in the case of a person who has the tip of his finger cut off, he is not disabled from living, but if he had the whole collection of all his parts and limbs cut off at once, he would die immediately. (144) Therefore in the same manner, if all the elements of the world together were all to disappear at one and the same moment, then it would be necessary to admit that the world was liable to corruption and destruction; but if each of these elements separately only changes its nature so as to assimilate to that of its nature, it is then rendered immortal rather than destroyed, according to the philosophical statement of the tragic poet—

"Nought that has once existed dies,
Though often what has been combined
Before, we separated find,
Invested with another form."

(145) For it is the greatest folly imaginable to estimate the antiquity of the human race from the state of art; for if any one were to follow the absurdity of such a system of reasoning as this, he will prove the world to be very young indeed, and to have been made scarcely a thousand years, since all those men whom we have heard of traditionally as the discoverers in different branches of science do not to back to a greater number of years than that which I have mentioned.

(146) But if we must speak of the arts as coeval with the race of mankind, then we must speak, drawing our arguments from natural history, and not inconsiderately or carelessly. And what is this history? The destruction of the things on the earth, not all together, but of the greatest number of them, is attributed to two principal causes, the indescribable violence and power of fire and water. And they say that each of these elements attacks them in its turn, after very long periods of revolving years. (147) When, therefore, a conflagration seizes upon things, a stream of ethereal fire being poured down from above is frequently diffused over them, overrunning many districts of the habitable world; and when a deluge draws down the whole

---

[22]This is alluded to by Virgil, Aen. 3.419 (as it is translated by Dryden)—"The Italian shore / And fair Sicilia's coast were one before / An earthquake caused the flaw; the roaring tides / The passage broke that land from land divides, / And where the lands retired the rushing ocean rides / Distinguished by the straits on either hand / Now rising cities in long order stand, / And fruitful fields; so much can time invade / The mouldering work that beauteous nature made."

[23]*Rhēgion*, from *rhēgnymi*, "to break."

of the rainy nature of water, the regular rivers and torrents overflowing, and not only that, but even far exceeding the ordinary measure of a common flood, and breaking down their banks with their violence, or else overleaping them, and rising to an enormous height, from which they swell and are diffused over all the adjacent champaign country, and the land is in the first instance divided into huge lakes, as the water is continually settling down into the more hollow parts, and afterwards flows still higher, and inundates the isthmuses which separate the lakes, till at last everything presents the appearing of one vast sea from the union of so many waters.

(148) And then it happens that, through the violence of these powers contending against one another in turn, the inhabitants of the places exposed to it are destroyed; those who dwell on the mountains and higher ground, and in ill-watered districts, being destroyed by fire, as not having a sufficiency of water, which is the natural weapon with which to repel fire, and those, on the other hand, being destroyed by water who live on the banks of rivers or lakes, or on the shores of the sea,

for evils like to attack those who are nearest first, or indeed solely.

(149) Accordingly, when the greater part of mankind is destroyed in the manners above mentioned, besides an infinity of other ways of less power and importance, it follows of necessity that the arts also must fail, for it cannot be possible to discuss science by itself without some one to reduce it to method and practice. But when those common pestilences relax their fury, and when the human race begins again to recover vigour and to flourish, descending from those who have not been previously destroyed by the evils which pressed upon them, then the arts also begin again to exist, not indeed as they were at fist, but in thinner numbers from the diminution of the numbers of those who practise them.

(150) I have now then set forth to the best of my ability what I have been able to learn or to understand concerning the indestructibility of the world, and in the subsequent treatises I shall proceed to show what may be said against each of the arguments here stated.

FLACCUS

(In Flaccum)

I. (1) Flaccus Avillius succeeded Sejanus in his hatred of and hostile designs against the Jewish nation. He was not, indeed, able to injure the whole people by open and direct means as he had been, inasmuch as he had less power for such a purpose, but he inflicted the most intolerable evils on all who came within his reach.

Moreover, though in appearance he only attacked a portion of the nation, in point of fact he directed his aims against all whom he could find anywhere, proceeding more by art than by force; for those men who, though of tyrannical natures and dispositions, have not strength enough to accomplish their designs openly, seek to compass them by manoeuvres.

(2) This Flaccus being chosen by Tiberius Caesar as one of his intimate companions, after the death of Severus, who had been lieutenant-governor in Egypt, was appointed viceroy of Alexandria and the country round about, being a man who at the beginning, as far as appearance went, had given innumerable instances of his excellence, for he was a man of prudence and diligence, and great acuteness of perception, very energetic in executing what he had determined on, very eloquent as a speaker, and skilful too at discerning what was suppressed as well as at understanding what was said. (3) Accordingly in a short time he became perfectly acquainted with the affairs of Egypt, and they are of a very various and diversified character, so that they are not easily comprehended even by those who from their earliest infancy have made them their study.

The scribes were a superfluous body when he had made such advances towards the knowledge of all things, whether important or trivial, by his extended experience, that he not only surpassed them, but from his great accuracy was qualified instead of a pupil to become the instructor of those who had hitherto been the teachers of all other persons. (4) However, all those things in which he displayed an admirable system and great wisdom concerning the accounts and the general arrangement of the revenues of the land, though they were serious matters and of the last importance, were nevertheless not such as gave any proofs of a soul fit for the task of governing; but those things which exhibited a more brilliant and royal disposition he also displayed with great freedom. For instance, he bore himself with considerable dignity, and pride and pomp are advantageous things for a ruler; and he decided all suits of importance in conjunction with the magistrates, he pulled down the overproud, he forbade promiscuous mobs of men from all quarters to assemble together, and prohibited all associations and meetings which were continually feasting together under pretence of sacrifices, making a drunken mockery of public business, treating with great vigour and severity all who resisted his commands.

(5) Then when he had filled the whole city and country with his wise legislation, he proceeded in turn to regulate the military affairs of the land, issuing commands, arranging matters, training the troops of every kind, infantry, cavalry, and light-armed, teaching the commanders not to deprive the soldiers of their pay, and so drive them to acts of piracy and rapine, and teaching each individual soldier not to proceed to any actions unauthorised by his military service, remembering that he was appointed with the especial object of preserving peace.

II. (6) Perhaps some one may say here: "Do you then, my good man, you who have determined to accuse this man, bring no accusation whatever against him, but on the contrary, weave long panegyrics in his honour? Are you not doting and mad?"

"I am not mad, my friend, nor am I a downright fool, so as to be unable to see the consequences of connexion of things. (7) I praise Flaccus, not because it is right to praise an enemy, but in order to make his wickedness more conspicuous; for pardon is given to a man who does wrong from ignorance of what is right; but he who does wrong knowingly has no excuse, being already condemned by the tribunal of his own conscience."

III. (8) For having received a government which was intended to last six years, for the first five years, while Tiberius Caesar was alive, he both preserved peace and also governed the country generally with such vigour and energy that he was superior to all the governors who had gone before him. (9) But in the last year, after Tiberius was dead, and when Gaius had succeeded him as emperor, he began to relax in and to be indifferent about everything, whether it was that he was overwhelmed with most heavy grief because of Tiberius (for it was evident to everyone that he grieved exceedingly as if for a near relation, both by his continued depression of spirits and his incessant weeping, pouring forth tears without end as if from an inexhaustible fountain), or whether it was because he was disaffected to his successor, because he preferred devoting himself to the party of the real rather than to that of the adopted children, or whether it was because he had been one of those who had joined in the conspiracy against the mother of Gaius, having joined against her at the time when the accusations were brought against her, on account of which she was put to death, and having escaped through fear of the consequence of proceeding against him.

(10) However, for a time he still paid some attention to the affairs of the state, not wholly abandoning the administration of his government; but when he heard that the grandson of Tiberius and his partner in the government had been put to death at the command of Gaius, he was smitten with intolerable anguish, and threw himself on the ground, and lay there speechless, being utterly deprived of his senses, for indeed his mind had long since been enervated by grief.

(11) For as long as that child lived he did not despair of some sparks still remaining of his own safety, but now that he was dead, he considered that all his own hopes had likewise died with him, even if a slight breeze of assistance might still be left, such as his friendship with Macro, who had unbounded influence with Gaius in his authority; and who, as it is said, had very greatly contributed to his obtaining the supreme power, and in a still higher degree to his personal safety, (12) since Tiberius had frequently thought of putting Gaius out of the way, as a wicked man and one who was in no respects calculated by nature for the exercise of authority, being influenced also partly by his apprehensions for his grandson; for he feared lest, when he himself was dead, his death too would be added to the funerals of his family.

But Macro had constantly bade him discard these apprehensions from his mind, and had praised Gaius, as a man of a simple, and honest, and sociable character; and as one who was very much attached to his cousin, so that he would willingly yield the supreme authority to him alone, and the first rank in everything. (13) And Tiberius, being deceived by all these representations, without being aware of what he was doing, left behind him a most irreconcileable enemy, to himself, and his grandson, and his whole family, and to Macro, who was his chief adviser and comforter, and to all mankind; (14) for when Macro saw the Gaius was forsaking the way of virtue and yielding to his unbridled passions, following them wherever they led him and against whatever objects they led him, he admonished and reproved him, looking upon him as the same Gaius who, while Tiberius was alive, was mild-tempered and docile; but to his misery he suffered most terrible punishment for his exceeding good-will, being put to death with his wife, and children, and all his family, as a grievous and troublesome object to his new sovereign. (15) For whenever he saw him at a distance coming towards him, he used to speak in this manner to those who were with him: "Let us not smile; let us look sad: here comes the censor and monitor; the all-wise man, he who is beginning now to be the schoolmaster of a full-grown man, and of an emperor, after time itself has separated him from and discarded the tutors of his earliest infancy."

IV. (16) When, therefore, Flaccus learnt that he too was put to death, he utterly abandoned all other hope for the future, and was no longer able to apply himself to public affairs as he had done before, being enervated and wholly broken down in spirit. (17) But when a magistrate begins to despair of his power of exerting authority, it follows inevitably, that his subjects must quickly become disobedient, especially those who are naturally, at every trivial or common occurrence, inclined to show insubordination, and, among people of such a disposition, the Egyptian nation is pre-eminent, being constantly in the habit of exciting great seditions from very small sparks.

(18) And being placed in a situation of great and perplexing difficulty he began to rage, and simultaneously, with the change of his disposition for the worse, he also altered everything which had existed before, beginning with his nearest friends and his most habitual customs; for he began to suspect and to drive from him those who were well affected to him, and who were most sincerely his friends, and he reconciled himself to those who were originally his declared enemies, and he used them as advisers under all circumstances; (19) but they, for they persisted in their ill-will, being reconciled with him only in words and in appearance, but in their actions and in their hearts they bore him incurable enmity, and though only pretending a genuine friendship towards him, like actors in a theatre, they drew him over wholly to their side; and so the governor became a subject, and the subjects became the governor, advancing the most unprofitable opinions, and immediately confirming and insisting upon them; (20) for they became executors of all the plans which they had devised, treating him like a mute person on the stage, as one who was only, by way of making up the show, inscribed with the title of authority, being themselves a lot of Dionysiuses, demagogues, and of Lampos, a pack of cavillers and word-splitters; and of Isidoruses, sowers of sedition, busy-bodies, devisers of evil, troublers of the state; for this is the name which has, at last, been given to them.

(21) All these men, having devised a most grievous design against the Jews, proceeded to put it in execution, and coming privately to Flaccus said to him, (22) "All your hope from the child of Tiberius Nero has now perished, and that which was your second best prospect, your companion Macro, is gone too, and you have no chance of favour with the emperor, therefore we must find

another advocate, by whom Gaius may be made propitious to us, (23) and that advocate is the city of Alexandria, which all the family of Augustus has honoured from the very beginning, and our present master above all the rest; and it will be a sufficient mediator in our behalf, if it can obtain one boon from you, and you cannot confer a greater benefit upon it than by abandoning and denouncing all the Jews."

(24) Now though upon this he ought to have rejected and driven away the speakers as workers of revolution and common enemies, he agrees on the contrary to what they say, and at first he made his designs against the Jews less evident, only abstaining from listening to causes brought before his tribunal with impartiality and equity, and inclining more to one side than to the other, and not allowing to both sides an equal freedom of speech; but whenever any Jew came before him he showed his aversion to him, and departed from his habitual affability in their case; but afterwards he exhibited his hostility to them in a more conspicuous manner.

V. (25) Moreover, some occurrences of the following description increased that folly and insolence of his which was derived from instruction rather than from nature. Gaius Caesar gave Agrippa, the grandson of Herod the king, the third part of his paternal inheritance as a sovereignty, which Philip the tetrarch, who was his uncle on his father's side, had previously enjoyed. (26) And when he was about to set out to take possession of his kingdom, Gaius advised him to avoid the voyage from Brundusium to Syria, which was a long and troublesome one, and rather to take the shorter one by Alexandria, and to wait for the periodical winds; for he said that the merchant vessels which set forth from that harbour were fast sailers, and that the pilots were most experienced men, who guided their ships like skilful coachmen guide their horses, keeping them straight in the proper course. And he took his advice, looking upon him both as his master and also as a giver of good counsel.

(27) Accordingly, going down to Dicaearchia, and seeing some Alexandrian vessels in the harbour, looking all ready and fit to put to sea, he embarked with his followers, and had a fair voyage, and so a few days afterwards he arrived at his journey's end, unforeseen and unexpected, having commanded the captains of his vessels (for he came in sight of Pharos about twilight in the evening) to furl their sails, and to keep a short distance out of sight in the open sea, until it became late in the evening and dark, and then at night he entered the port, that when he disembarked he might find all the citizens buried in sleep, and so, without any one seeing him, he might arrive at the house of the man who was to be his entertainer. (28) With so much modesty then did this man arrive, wishing if it were possible to enter without being perceived by any one in the city.

For he had not come to see Alexandria, since he had sojourned in it before, when he was preparing to take his voyage to Rome to see Tiberius, but he desired at this time to take the quickest road, so as to arrive at his destination with the smallest possible delay. (29) But the men of Alexandria being ready to burst with envy and ill-will (for the Egyptian disposition is by nature a most jealous and envious one and inclined to look on the good fortune of others as adversity to itself), and being at the same time filled with an ancient and what I may in a manner call an innate enmity towards the Jews, were indignant at any one's becoming a king of the Jews, no less than if each individual among them had been deprived of an ancestral kingdom of his own inheritance.

(30) And then again his friends and companions came and stirred up the miserable Flaccus, inviting, and exciting, and stimulating him to feel the same envy with themselves; saying, "The arrival of this man to take upon him his government is equivalent to a deposition of yourself. He is invested with a greater dignity of honour and glory than you. He attracts all eyes towards himself when they see the array of sentinels and bodyguards around him adorned with silvered and gilded arms. (31) For ought he to have come into the presence of another governor, when it was in his power to have sailed over the sea, and so to have arrived in safety at his own government? For, indeed, if Gaius did advise or rather command him to do so, he ought rather with earnest solicitations to have deprecated any visit to this country, in order that the real governor of it might not be brought into disrepute and appear to have his authority lessened by being apparently disregarded."

(32) When he heard this he was more indignant than before, and in public indeed he pretended to be his companion and his friend, because of his fear of the man who directed his course, but secretly he bore him much ill-will, and told every one how he hated him, and abused him behind his back, and insulted him indirectly, since he did not dare to do so openly; (33) for he encouraged the idle and lazy mob of the city (and the mob of Alexandria is one accustomed to great license of speech, and one which delights above measure in calumny and evil-speaking), to abuse the king, either beginning to revile him in his own person, or else exhorting and exciting others to do so by the agency of persons who were accustomed to serve him in business of this kind. (34) And they, having had the cue given them, spent all their days reviling the king in the public schools, and stringing together all sorts of gibes to turn him into ridicule.

And at times they employed poets who compose farces, and managers of puppet shows, displaying their natural aptitude for every kind of disgraceful employment, though they were very slow at learning anything that was creditable, but very acute, and quick, and ready at learning anything of an opposite nature. (35) For why did he not show his indignation, why did he not commit them to prison, why did he not chastise them for their insolent and disloyal evil speaking? And even if he had not been a king but only one of the household of Caesar, ought he not to have had some privileges and especial honours? The fact is that all these circumstances are an undeniable evidence that Flaccus was a participator in all this abuse; for he who might have punished it with the most extreme severity, and entirely checked it, and who yet took no steps to restrain it, was clearly convicted of having permitted and encouraged it; but whenever an ungoverned multitude begins a course of evil doing it never desists, but proceeds from one wickedness to another, continually doing some monstrous thing.

VI. (36) There was a certain madman named Carabbas, afflicted not with a wild, savage, and dangerous madness (for that comes on in fits without being expected either by the patient or by bystanders), but with an intermittent and more gentle kind; this man spent all this days and nights naked in the roads, minding neither cold nor heat, the sport of idle children and wanton youths; (37) and they, driving the poor wretch as far as the public gymnasium, and setting him up there on high that he might be seen by everybody, flattened out a leaf of papyrus and put it on his head instead of a diadem, and clothed the rest of his body with a common door mat instead of a cloak and instead of a sceptre they put in his hand a small stick of the native papyrus which they found lying by the way side and gave to him; (38) and when, like actors in theatrical spectacles, he had received all the insignia of royal authority, and had been dressed and adorned like a king, the young men bearing sticks on their shoulders stood on each side of him instead of spear-bearers, in imitation of the bodyguards of the king, and then others came up, some as if to salute him, and others making as though they wished to plead their causes before him, and others pretending to wish to consult with him about the affairs of the state.

(39) Then from the multitude of those who were standing around there arose a wonderful shout of men calling out Maris; and this is the name by which it is said that they call the kings among the Syrians; for they knew that Agrippa was by birth a Syrian, and also that he was possessed of a great district of Syria of which he was the sovereign; (40) when Flaccus heard, or rather when he saw this, he would have done right if he had apprehended the maniac and put him in prison, that he might not give to those who reviled him any opportunity or excuse for insulting their super-

iors, and if he had chastised those who dressed him up for having dared both openly and disguisedly, both with words and actions, to insult a king and a friend of Caesar, and one who had been honoured by the Roman senate with imperial authority; but he not only did not punish them, but he did not think fit even to check them, but gave complete license and impunity to all those who designed ill, and who were disposed to show their enmity and spite to the king, pretending not to see what he did see, and not to hear what he did hear.

(41) And when the multitude perceived this, I do not mean the ordinary and well-regulated population of the city, but the mob which, out of its restlessness and love of an unquiet and disorderly life, was always filling every place with tumult and confusion, and who, because of their habitual idleness and laziness, were full of treachery and revolutionary plans, they, flocking to the theatre the first thing in the morning, having already purchased Flaccus for a miserable price, which he with his mad desire for glory and with his slavish disposition, condescended to take to the injury not only of himself, but also of the safety of the commonwealth, all cried out, as if at a signal given, to erect images in the synagogues, (42) proposing a most novel and unprecedented violation of the law.

And though they knew this (for they are very shrewd in their wickedness), they adopted a deep design, putting forth the name of Caesar as a screen, to whom it would be impiety to attribute the deeds of the guilty; (43) what then did the governor of the country do? Knowing that the city had two classes of inhabitants, our own nation and the people of the country, and that the whole of Egypt was inhabited in the same manner, and that Jews who inhabited Alexandria and the rest of the country from the Catabathmos on the side of Libya to the boundaries of Ethiopia were not less than a million of men; and that the attempts which were being made were directed against the whole nation, and that it was a most mischievous thing to distress the ancient hereditary customs of the land; he, disregarding all these considerations, permitted the mob to proceed with the erection of the statues, though he might have given them a vast number of admonitory precepts instead of any such permission, either commanding them as their governor, or advising them as their friend.

VII. (44) But he, for he was eagerly cooperating in all that was being done amiss, thought fit to use his superior power to face the seditious tumult with fresh additions of evil, and as far as it depended on him, one may almost say that he filled the whole of the inhabited world with civil wars; (45) for it was sufficiently evident that the report about the destruction of the synagogues, which took its rise in Alexandria would be immediately spread over all the districts of Egypt, and would extend from that country to the east and to the oriental nations, and from the borders of the land in the other direction, and from the Mareotic district which is the frontier of Libya, towards the setting of the sun and the western nations. For no one country can contain the whole Jewish nation, by reason of its populousness; (46) on which account they frequent all the most prosperous and fertile countries of Europe and Asia, whether islands or continents, looking indeed upon the holy city as their metropolis in which is erected the sacred temple of the most high God, but accounting those regions which have been occupied by their fathers, and grandfathers, and great grandfathers, and still more remote ancestors, in which they have been born and brought up, as their country; and there are even some regions to which they came the very moment that they were originally settled, sending a colony of their people to do a pleasure to the founders of the colony.

(47) And there was reason to fear lest all the populace in every country, taking what was done in Egypt as a model and as an excuse, might insult those Jews who were their fellow citizens, by introducing new regulations with respect to their synagogues and their national customs; (48) but the Jews, for they were not inclined to remain quiet under everything, although naturally entirely disposed towards peace, not only because contests for natural customs do among all men appear more important than those which are only for the sake of life, but also because they alone of all the people under the sun, if they were deprived of their houses of prayer, would at the same time be deprived of all means of showing their piety towards their benefactors, which they would have looked upon as worse than ten thousand deaths, inasmuch as if their synagogues were destroyed they would no longer have any sacred places in which they could declare their gratitude, might have reasonably said to those who opposed them: (49) You, without being aware of it, are taking away honour from your lords instead of conferring any on them. Our houses of prayer are manifestly incitements to all the Jews in every part of the habitable world to display their piety and loyalty towards the house of Augustus; and if they are destroyed from among us, what other place, or what other manner of showing that honour, will be left to us? (50) For if we were to neglect the opportunity of adhering to our national customs when it is afforded to us, we should deserve to meet with the severest punishment, as not giving any proper or adequate return for the benefits which we have received; but if, while it is in our power to do so, we, in conformity with our own laws which Augustus himself is in the habit of confirming, obey in everything, then I do not see what great, or even what small offence can be laid to our charge; unless any one were to impute to us

that we do not transgress the laws of deliberate purpose, and that we do not intentionally take care to depart from our national customs, which practices, even if they at first attack others, do often in the end visit those who are guilty of them.

(51) But Flaccus, saying nothing that he ought to have said, and everything which he ought not to have said, has sinned against us in this manner; but those men whom he has studied to gratify, what has been their design? Have they had the feelings of men wishing to do honour to Caesar? Was there then a scarcity of temples in the city, the greatest and most important parts of which are all allotted to one or other of the gods, in which they might have erected any statues they pleased? (52) We have been describing the evidence of hostile and unfriendly men, who seek to injure us with such artifice, that even when injuring us they may not appear to have been acting iniquitously, and yet that we who are injured by them cannot resist with safety to ourselves; for, my good men, it does not contribute to the honour of the emperor to abrogate the laws, to disturb the national customs of a people, to insult those who live in the same country, and to teach those who dwell in other cities to disregard unanimity and tranquillity.

VIII. (53) Since, therefore, the attempt which was being made to violate the law appeared to him to be prospering, while he was destroying the synagogues, and not leaving even their name, he proceeded onwards to another exploit, namely, the utter destruction of our constitution, that when all those things to which alone our life was anchored were cut away, namely, our national customs and our lawful political rights and social privileges, we might be exposed to the very extremity of calamity, without having any stay left to which we could cling for safety, (54) for a few days afterwards he issued a notice in which he called us all foreigners and aliens, without giving us an opportunity of being heard in our own defence, but condemning us without a trial; and what command can be more full of tyranny than this?

He himself being everything—accuser, enemy, witness, judge, and executioner, added then to the two former appellations a third also, allowing any one who was inclined to proceed to exterminate the Jews as prisoners of war. (55) So when the people had received this license, what did they do? There are five districts in the city, named after the first five letters of the written alphabet, of these two are called the quarters of the Jews, because the chief portion of the Jews lives in them. There are also a few scattered Jews, but only a very few, living in some of the other districts. What then did they do? They drove the Jews entirely out of four quarters, and crammed them all into a very small portion of one; (56) and by reason of their numbers they were dispersed over the sea-shore, and desert places, and among the tombs, being deprived of all their property; while the populace, overrunning their desolate houses, turned to plunder, and divided the booty among themselves as if they had obtained it in war. And as no one hindered them, they broke open even the workshops of the Jews, which were all shut up because of their mourning for Drusilla,[1] and carried off all that they found there, and bore it openly through the middle of the market-place as if they had only been making use of their own property.

(57) And the cessation of business to which they were compelled to submit was even a worse evil than the plunder to which they were exposed, as the consequence was that those who had lent money lost what they had lent, and as no one was permitted, neither farmer, nor captain of a ship, nor merchant, nor artisan, to employ himself in his usual manner, so that poverty was brought on them from two sides at once, both from rapine, as when license was thus given to plunder them they were stripped of everything in one day, and also from the circumstance of their no longer being able to earn money by their customary occupations.

IX. (58) And though these were evils sufficiently intolerable, yet nevertheless they appear actually trifling when compared with those which were subsequently inflicted on them, for poverty indeed is a bitter evil, especially when it is caused by the machinations of one's enemies, still it is less than insult and personal ill treatment even of the slightest character. (59) But now the evils which were heaped upon our people were so excessive and inordinate, that if a person were desirous to use appropriate language, he would never call them insults of assaults, but, as it appears to me, he would actually be wholly at a loss for suitable expressions, on account of the enormity of the cruelties now newly invented against them, so that if the treatment which men experience from enemies who have subdued them in war, however implacable they may be by nature, were to be compared with that to which the Jews were subjected, it would appear most merciful. (60) Enemies, indeed, plunder their conquered foes of their money, and lead away multitudes in captivity, having incurred the same risk of losing all that they had if they themselves had been defeated. Not but that in all such cases there are very many persons for whom their relations and friends put down a ransom, and who are thus emancipated from captivity, inasmuch as though their enemies could not be worked upon by compassion, they could by love of money.

But what is the use of going on in this way,

some one will say, for as long as men escape from danger it signifies but little in what way their preservation is brought to pass? (61) Moreover, it has often happened that enemies have granted to those who have fallen in battle the honour of funeral rites, those who were gentle and humane burying them at their own expense, and those who have carried on their enmity even against the dead giving up their bodies to their friends under a truce, in order that they might not be deprived of the last honour of all, the customary ceremonies of sepulture.

(62) This, then, is the conduct of enemies in time of war; let us now see what was done by those who a little while before had been friends in time of peace.

For after plundering them of everything, and driving them from their homes, and expelling them by main force from most of the quarters of the city, our people, as if they were blockaded and hemmed in by a circle of besieging enemies, being oppressed by a terrible scarcity and want of necessary things, and seeing their wives and their children dying before their eyes by an unnatural famine (63) (for every other place was full of prosperity and abundance, as the river had irrigated the corn lands plentifully with its inundations, and as all the champaign country, which is devoted to the purposes of bearing wheat, was this year supplying a most abundant over-crop of corn with very unusual fertility), (64) being no longer able to support their want, some, though they had never been used to do so before, came to the houses of their friends and relations to beg them to contribute such food as was absolutely necessary as a charity; others, who from their high and free-born spirit could not endure the condition of beggars, as being a slavish state unbecoming the dignity of a freeman, came down into the market with no other object than, miserable men that they were, to buy food for their families and for themselves.

(65) And then, being immediately seized by those who had excited the seditious multitude against them, they were treacherously put to death, and then were dragged along and trampled under foot by the whole city, and completely destroyed, without the least portion of them being left which could possibly receive burial; (66) and in this way their enemies, who in their savage madness had become transformed into the nature of wild beasts, slew them and thousands of others with all kinds of agony and tortures, and newly invented cruelties, for wherever they met with or caught sight of a Jew, they stoned him, or beat him with sticks, not at once delivering their blows upon mortal parts, lest they should die speedily, and so speedily escape from the sufferings which it was their design to inflict upon them.

(67) Some persons even, going still great and greater lengths in the iniquity and license of their barbarity, disdained all blunter weapons, and took

---

[1]She was the sister of the emperor, and at her death her brother ordered that divine honours should be paid to her.

up the most efficacious arms of all, fire and iron, and slew many with the sword, and destroyed not a few with flames. (68) And the most merciless of all their persecutors in some instances burnt whole families, husbands with their wives, and infant children with their parents, in the middle of the city, sparing neither age nor youth, nor the innocent helplessness of infants. And when they had a scarcity of fuel, they collected faggots of green wood, and slew them by the smoke rather than by fire, contriving a still more miserable and protracted death for those unhappy people, so that their bodies lay about promiscuously in every direction half burnt, a grievous and most miserable sight.

(69) And if some of those who were employed in the collection of sticks were too slow, they took their own furniture, of which they had plundered them, to burn their persons, robbing them of their most costly articles, and burning with them things of the greatest use and value, which they used as fuel instead of ordinary timber. (70) Many men too, who were alive, they bound by one foot, fastening them round the ankle, and thus they dragged them along and bruised them, leaping on them, designing to inflict the most barbarous of deaths upon them, (71) and then when they were dead they raged no less against them with interminable hostility, and inflicted still heavier insults on their persons, dragging them, I had almost said, though all the alleys and lanes of the city, until the corpse, being lacerated in all its skin, and flesh, and muscles from the inequality and roughness of the ground, all the previously united portions of his composition being torn asunder and separated from one another, was actually torn to pieces.

(72) And those who did these things, mimicked the sufferers, like people employed in the representation of theatrical farces; but the relations and friends of those who were the real victims, merely because they sympathized with the misery of their relations, were led away to prison, were scourged, were tortured, and after all the ill treatment which their living bodies could endure, found the cross the end of all, and the punishment from which they could not escape.

X. (73) But after Flaccus had broken through every right, and trampled upon every principle of justice, and had left no portion of the Jews free from the extreme severity of his designing malice, in the boundlessness of his wickedness he contrived a monstrous and unprecedented attack upon them, being ever an inventor of new acts of iniquity, (74) for he arrested thirty-eight members of our council of elders, which our saviour and benefactor, Augustus, elected to manage the affairs of the Jewish nation after the death of the king of our own nation, having sent written commands to that effect to Manius Maximus when he was about to take upon himself for the second time the gov-

ernment of Egypt and of the country, he arrested them, I say, in their own houses, and commanded them to be thrown into prison, and arranged a splendid procession to send through the middle of the market-place a body of old men prisoners, with their hands bound, some with thongs and others with iron chains, whom he led in this plight into the theatre, a most miserable spectacle, and one wholly unsuited to the times. (75) And then he commanded them all to stand in front of their enemies, who were sitting down, to make their disgrace the more conspicuous, and ordered them all to be stripped of their clothes and scourged with stripes, in a way that only the most wicked of malefactors are usually treated, and they were flogged with such severity that some of them the moment they were carried out died of their wounds, while others were rendered so ill for a long time that their recovery was despaired of.

(76) And the enormity of this cruelty is proved by many other circumstances, and it will be further proved most evidently and undeniably by the circumstance which I am about to mention. Three of the members of this council of elders, Euodius, and Trypho, and Audro, had been stripped of all their property, being plundered of everything that was in their houses at one onset, and he was well aware that they had been exposed to this treatment, for it had been related to him when he had in the first instance sent for our rulers, under pretence of wishing to promote a reconciliation between them and the rest of the city; (77) but nevertheless, though he well knew that they had been deprived of all their property, he scourged them in the very sight of those who had plundered them, that thus they might endure the twofold misery of poverty and personal ill treatment, and that their persecutors might reap the double pleasure of enjoying riches which did in no respect belong to them, and also of feasting their eyes to satiety on the disgrace of those whom they had plundered.

(78) Now, though I desire to mention a circumstance which took place at that time, I am in doubt whether to do so or not, lest if it should be looked upon as unimportant, it may appear to take off from the enormity of these great iniquities; but even if it is unimportant in itself, it is nevertheless an indication of no trifling wickedness of disposition. There are different kinds of scourges used in the city, distinguished with reference to the deserts or crimes of those who are about to be scourged. Accordingly, it is usual for the Egyptians of the country themselves to be scourged with a different kind of scourge, and by a different class of executioners, but for the Alexandrians in the city to be scourged with rods by the Alexandrian lictors, (79) and this custom had been preserved, in the case also of our own people, by all the predecessors of Flaccus, and by Flaccus him-

self in the earlier periods of his government; for it is possible, it really is possible, even in ignominy, to find some slight circumstance of honour, and even in ill treatment to find something which is, to some extent, a relaxation, when any one allows the nature of things to be examined into by itself, and to be confined to its own indispensable requirements, without adding from his own ingenuity any additional cruelty or treachery, to separate and take from it all that is mingled with it of a milder character.

(80) How then can it be looked upon as anything but most infamous, that when Alexandrian Jews, of the lowest rank, had always been previously beaten with the rods, suited to freemen and citizens, if ever they were convicted of having done anything worthy of stripes, yet now the very rulers of the nation, the council of the elders, who derived their very titles from the honour in which they were held and the offices which they filled, should, in this respect, be treated with more indignity than their own servants, like the lowest of the Egyptian rustics, even when found guilty of the very worst of crimes? (81) I omit to mention, that even if they had committed the most countless iniquities, nevertheless the governor ought, out of respect for the season, to have delayed their punishment; for with all rulers, who govern any state on constitutional principles, and who do not seek to acquire a character for audacity, but who do really honour their benefactors, it is the custom to punish no one, even of those who have been lawfully condemned, until the famous festival and assembly, in honour of the birth-day of the illustrious emperor, has passed. (82) But he committed this violation of the laws at the very season of this festival, and punished men who had done no wrong; though certainly, if he ever determined to punish them, he ought to have done so at a subsequent time; but he hastened, and would admit of no delay, by reason of his eagerness to please the multitude who was opposed to them, thinking that in this way he should be able, more easily, to gain them over to the objects which he had in view.

(83) I have known instances before now of men who had been crucified when this festival and holiday was at hand, being taken down and given up to their relations, in order to receive the honours of sepulture, and to enjoy such observances as are due to the dead; for it used to be considered, that even the dead ought to derive some enjoyment from the natal festival of a good emperor, and also that the sacred character of the festival ought to be regarded. (84) But this man did not order men who had already perished on crosses to be taken down, but he commanded living men to be crucified, men to whom the very time itself gave, if not entire forgiveness, still, at all events, a brief and temporary respite from punishment; and he did

this after they had been beaten by scourgings in the middle of the theatre; and after he had tortured them with fire and sword; (85) and the spectacle of their sufferings was divided; for the first part of the exhibition lasted from the morning to the third or fourth hour, in which the Jews were scourged, were hung up, were tortured on the wheel, were condemned, and were dragged to execution through the middle of the orchestra; and after this beautiful exhibition came the dancers, and the buffoons, and the flute-players, and all the other diversions of the theatrical contests.

XI. (86) And why do I dwell on these things? for a second mode of barbarity was afterwards devised against us, because the governor wished to excite the whole multitude of the army against us, in accordance with the contrivance of some foreign informer. Now the information which was laid against the nation was, that the Jews had entire suits of armour in their houses; therefore, having sent for a centurion, in whom he placed the greatest confidence, by name Castor, he ordered him to take with him the boldest soldier of his own band, to go with haste, and, without saying a word to any one, to enter the houses of the Jews, and to search them, and see whether there was any store of arms laid up in them; (87) and he ran with great speed to perform the commands which had been given him. But they, having no suspicion of his intentions, stood at first speechless with astonishment, their wives and their children clinging to them, and shedding abundance of tears, because of their fear of being carried into captivity, for they were in continual expectation of that, looking upon it as all that was wanting to complete their total misery. (88) But when they heard from some of those who were sent to make the search an inquiry as to where they had laid up their arms, they breathed awhile, and opening all their secret recesses displayed everything which they had, (89) being partly delighted and partly grieving; delighted at the opportunity of repelling the false accusation which was thus brought against them by its own character, but indignant, in the first place, because calumnies of such a nature, when concocted and urged against them by their enemies, were believed beforehand; and, secondly, because their wives, who were shut up, and who did not actually come forth out of their inner chambers, and their virgins, who were kept in the strictest privacy, shunning the eyes of men, even of those who were their nearest relations, out of modesty, were now alarmed by being displayed to the public gaze, not only of persons who were no relations to them, but even of common soldiers.

(90) Nevertheless, though a most rigorous examination took place, how great a quantity of defensive and offensive armour do you think was found? Helmets, and breast-plates, and shields, and daggers, and javelins, and weapons of every

description, were brought out and piled up in heaps; and also how great a variety of missile weapons, javelins, slings, bows, and darts? Absolutely not a single thing of the kind; scarcely even knives sufficient for the daily use of the cooks to prepare and dress the food. (91) From which circumstance, the simplicity of their daily manner of life was plainly seen: as they made no pretence to magnificence or delicate luxury; the nature of which things is to engender satiety, and satiety is apt to engender insolence, which is the beginning of all evils.

(92) And indeed it was not a long time before that, that the arms had been taken away from the Egyptians throughout the whole country by a man of the name of Bassus, to whom Flaccus had committed this employment. But at that time one might have beheld a great fleet of ships sailing down and anchoring in the harbours afforded by the mouths of the river, full of arms of every possible description, and numerous beasts of burden loaded with bags made of skins sewn together and hanging like panniers on each side so as to balance better, and also almost all the waggons belonging to the camp filled with weapons of every sort, which were brought in rows so as to be all seen at once, and arranged together in order. And the distance between the harbour and the armoury in the king's palace in which the arms were commanded to be deposited was about ten stadia; (93) it was then very proper to investigate the houses of the men who had amassed such quantities of arms; for as they had often actually revolted, they were naturally liable to be suspected of designing revolutionary measures, and it was quite fitting that, in imitation of the sacred games, those who had superintended the collection of the arms should keep a new triennial festival in Egypt, in order that they might not again be collected without any one being aware of it, or else that at all events only a few might be collected instead of a great number, from the people not having time enough to assemble any great number.

(94) But why were we to be exposed to any treatment of the sort? For when were we ever suspected of any tendency to revolt? And when did we bear any other than a most peaceful character among all men? And the habits in which we daily and habitually indulge, are they not irreproachable, tending to the lawful tranquillity and stability of the state? In fact, if the Jews had had arms in their houses, would they have submitted to be stripped of above four hundred dwellings, out of which they were turned and forcibly expelled by those who plundered them of all their properties? Why then was not this search made in the houses of those people who had arms, if not of their own private property, at all events such as they had carried off from others?

(95) The truth is, as I have said already, the whole business was a deliberate contrivance designed by the cruelty of Flaccus and of the multitude, in which even women were included; for they were dragged away as captives, not only in the market-place, but even in the middle of the theatre, and dragged upon the stage on any false accusation that might be brought against them with the most painful and intolerable insults; (96) and then, when it was found that they were of another race, they were dismissed; for they apprehended many women as Jewesses who were not so, from want of making any careful or accurate investigation. And if they appeared to belong to our nation, then those who, instead of spectators, became tyrants and masters, laid cruel commands on them, bringing them swine's flesh, and enjoining them to eat it. Accordingly, all who were wrought on by fear of punishment to eat it were released without suffering any ill treatment; but those who were more obstinate were given up to the tormentors to suffer intolerable tortures, which is the clearest of all possible proofs that they had committed no offence whatever beyond what I have mentioned.

XII. (97) But it was not out of his own head alone, but also because of the commands and in consequence of the situation of the emperor that he sought and devised means to injure and oppress us; for after we had decreed by our votes and carried out by our actions all the honours to the emperor Gaius, which were either within our power or allowable by our laws, we brought the decree to him, entreating him that, as it was not permitted to us to send an embassy ourselves to bear it to the emperor, he would vouchsafe to forward it himself. (98) And, after he had read all the articles contained in the decree, and having often nodded his head in token of his approbation of them, smiling, and being very much delighted, or else pretending to be pleased, he said: "I approve of you very greatly in all things, for your piety and loyalty, and I will forward it as you request, or else I myself will act the part of your ambassador, that Gaius may be aware of your gratitude. (99) And I myself will bear witness in your favour to all that I know of the orderly disposition and obedient character of your nation, without exaggerating anything; for truth is the most sufficient of all panegyrics."

(100) At these promises we were greatly delighted, and we gave him thanks, hoping that the decree would be thoroughly read and appreciated by Gaius. And indeed it was natural enough, since all the things that are promptly and carefully sent by the lieutenant-governors are read and examined without delay by you; (101) but Flaccus, wholly neglecting all our hopes, and all his own words, and all his own promises, retained the decree, in order that we, above all the men under the sun, might be looked upon as enemies to the emperor. Was not this the conduct of one who had been

vigilant afar off, and who had long been contriving his design against us, and who was not now yielding to some momentary impulse, and attacking us on a sudden without any previous contrivance with unreasonable impetuosity, being led away by some fresh motive? (102) But God, as it seems, he who has a care for all human affairs, scattered his flattering speeches cunningly devised to mislead the emperor, and baffled the counsels of his lawless disposition and the manoeuvres which he was employing, taking pity on us, and very soon he brought matters into such a train that Flaccus was disappointed of his hopes.

(103) For when Agrippa, the king, came into the country, we set before him all the designs which Flaccus had entertained against us; and he set himself to rectify the business, and, having promised to forward the decree to the emperor, he taking it, as we hear, did send it, accompanied with a defence relating to the time at which it was passed, showing that it was not lately only that we had learnt to venerate the family of our benefactors, but that we had from the very first beginning shown our zeal towards them, though we had been deprived of the opportunity of making any seasonable demonstration of it by the insolence of our governor. (104) And after these events justice, the constant champion and ally of those who are injured, and the punisher of everything impious, whether it be action or man, began to labour to work his overthrow. For at first they endured the most unexampled insults and miseries, such as had never happened under any other of our governors, ever since the house of Augustus first acquired the dominion over earth and sea; (105) for some men of those who, in the time of Tiberius, and of Caesar his father, had the government, seeking to convert their governorship and viceroyalty into a sovereignty and tyranny, filled all the country with intolerable evils, with corruption, and rapine, and condemnation of persons who had done no wrong, and with banishment and exile of such innocent men, and with the slaughter of the nobles without a trial; and then, after the appointed period of their government had expired, when they returned to Rome, the emperors exacted of them an account and relation of all that they had done, especially if by chance the cities which they had been oppressing sent any embassy to complain; (106) for then the emperors, behaving like impartial judges, listening both to the accusers and to the defendant on equal terms, not thinking it right to pre-judge and pre-condemn anyone before his trial, decided without being influenced either by enmity or favour, but according to the nature of truth, and pronouncing such a judgment as seemed to be just. (107) But in the case of Flaccus, that justice which hates iniquity did not wait till the term of his government had expired, but went forward to meet him before the usual time, being indignant at the immoderate extravagance of his lawless iniquity.

XIII. (108) And the manner in which he was cut short in his tyranny was as follows. He imagined that Gaius was already made favourable to him in respect of those matters, about which suspicion was sought to be raised against him, partly by his letters which were full of flattery, and partly by the harangues which he was continually addressing to the people, in which he courted the emperor by stringing together flattering sentences and long series of cunningly imagined panegyrics, and partly too because he was very highly thought of by the greater part of the city. (109) But he was deceiving himself without knowing it; for the hopes of wicked men are unstable, as they guess what is more favourable to them while they suffer what is quite contrary to it, as in fact they deserve.

For Bassus, the centurion, was sent from Italy by the appointment of Gaius with the company of soldiers which he commanded. (110) And having embarked on board one of the fastest sailing vessels, he arrived in a few days at the harbour of Alexandria, off the island of Pharos, about evening; and he ordered the captain of the ship to keep out in the open sea till sunset, intending to enter the city unexpectedly, in order that Flaccus might not be aware of his coming beforehand, and so be led to adopt any violent measures, and render the service which he was commanded to perform fruitless.

(111) And when the evening came, the ship entered the harbour, and Bassus, disembarking with his own soldiers, advanced, neither recognizing nor being recognized by any one; and on his road finding a soldier who was one of the quaternions of the guard, he ordered him to show him the house of his captain; for he wished to communicate his secret errand to him, that, if he required additional force, he might have an assistant ready.

(112) And when he heard that he was supping at some persons' house in company with Flaccus, he did not relax in his speed, but hastened onward to the dwelling of his entertainer; for the man with whom they were feasting was Stephanion, one of the freedmen of Tiberius Caesar; and withdrawing to a short distance, he sends forward one of his own followers to reconnoitre, disguising him like a servant in order that no one might notice him or perceive what was going forward. So he, entering in to the banqueting-room, as if he were the servant of one of the guests, examined everything accurately, and then returned and gave information to Bassus. (113) And he, when he had learnt the unguarded condition of the entrances, and the small number of the people who were with Flaccus (for he was attended by not more than ten or fifteen slaves to wait upon him), gave the signal to his soldiers whom he had with him, and

hastened forward, and entered suddenly into the supperroom, he and the soldiers with him, who stood by with their swords girded on, and surrounded Flaccus before he was aware of it, for at the moment of their entrance he was drinking health with some one, and making merry with those who were present.

(114) But when Bassus had made his way into the midst, the moment that he saw him he became dumb with amazement and consternation, and wishing to rise up he saw the guards all round him, and then he perceived his fate, even before he heard what Gaius wanted with him, and what commands had been given to those who had come, and what he was about to endure, for the mind of man is very prompt at perceiving at once all those particulars which take a long time to happen, and at hearing them all together. (115) Accordingly, every one of those who were of this supper party rose up, being through fear unnerved, and shuddering lest some punishment might be affixed to the mere fact of having been supping with the culprit, for it was not safe to flee, nor indeed was it possible to do so, since all the entrances were already occupied. So Flaccus was led away by the soldiers at the command of Bassus, this being the manner in which he returned from the banquet, for it was fitting that justice should begin to visit him at a feast, because he had deprived the houses of innumerable innocent men of all festivity.

XIV. (116) This was the unexampled misfortune which befell Flaccus in the country of which he was governor, being taken prisoner like an enemy on account of the Jews, as it appears to me, whom he had determined to destroy utterly in his desire for glory. And a manifest proof of this is to be found in the time of his arrest, for it was the general festival of the Jews at the time of the autumnal equinox, during which it is the custom of the Jews to live in tents; (117) but none of the usual customs at this festival were carried out at all, since all the rulers of the people were still oppressed by irremediable and intolerable injuries and insults, and since the common people looked upon the miseries of their chiefs as the common calamity of the whole nation, and were also depressed beyond measure at the individual afflictions to which they were each of them separately exposed, (118) for griefs are redoubled when they happen at the times of festival, when those who are afflicted are unable to keep the feast, both by reason of the deprivation of their mirthful cheerfulness, which a general assembly requires, and also from the presence of sorrow by which they were now overcome, without being able to find any remedy for such terrible disasters.

(119) And while they were yielding to excessive sorrow, and feeling overwhelmed by most severe anguish, and they were all collected in their houses at the approach of night, some persons came in to inform them of the apprehension of the governor which had then taken place. And they thought that this was to try them, and was not the truth, and were grieved all the more from thinking themselves mobbed, and that a snare was thus laid for them; (120) but when a tumult arose through the city, and the guards of the night began to run about to and fro, and when some of the cavalry were heard to be galloping with the utmost speed and with all energy to the camp and from the camp, some of them, being excited by the strangeness of the event, went forth from their houses to inquire what had happened, for it was plain that something strange had occurred. (121) And when they heard of the arrest that had taken place, and that Flaccus was now within the toils, stretching up their hands to heaven, they sang a hymn, and began a song of praise to God, who presides over all the affairs of men, saying, "We are not delighted, O Master, at the punishment of our enemy, being taught by the sacred laws to submit to all the vicissitudes of human life, but we justly give thanks to thee, who hast had mercy and compassion upon us, and who hast thus relieved our continual and incessant oppressions."

(122) And when they had spent the whole night in hymns and songs, they poured out through the gates at the earliest dawn, and hastened to the nearest point of the shore, for they had been deprived of their usual places for prayer, and standing in a clear and open space, they cried out, (123) "O most mighty King of all mortal and immortal beings, we have come to offer thanks unto thee, to invoke earth and sea, and the air and the heaven, and all the parts of the universe, and the whole world in which alone we dwell, being driven out by men and robbed of everything else in the world, and being deprived of our city, and of all the buildings both private and public within the city, and being made houseless and homeless by the treachery of our governor, the only men in the world who are so treated. (124) You suggest to us favourable hopes of the setting straight of what is left to us, beginning to consent to our prayers, inasmuch as you have on a sudden thrown down the common enemy of our nation, the author and cause of all our calamities, exulting in pride, and trusting that he would gain credit by such means, before he was removed to a distance from us, in order that those who were evilly afflicted might not feel their joy impaired by learning it only by report, but you have chastised him while he was so near, almost as we may say before the eyes of those whom he oppressed, in order to give us a more distinct perception of the end which has fallen upon him in a short time beyond our hopes."

XV. (125) And besides what I have spoken of there is also a third thing, which appears to me to have taken place by the interposition of divine providence; for after he had set sail at the beginning of winter, for it was rightly ordained that he should have his fill of the dangers of the sea, inasmuch as he had filled all the elements of the universe with his impieties, after suffering innumerable hardships he with difficulty got safety to Italy, and the moment that he had arrived there he was pursued by accusations which were brought against him, and which were brought before two of his greatest enemies, Isidorus and Lampo, (126) who a little while before were in the position of subjects to him, calling him their master, and benefactor, and saviour, and names of that sort, but who now were his adversaries, and that too displaying a power not only equal to but far superior to his own, not merely from the confidence which men feel in the justice of their cause, but, what was a matter of great moment, because they saw that the Judge of all human affairs was his irreconcileable enemy, being about now to take upon himself the form of a judge from a prudent determination not to appear to condemn any one beforehand unheard, and not to act the part of an enemy, who before hearing either accusation or defence, has already condemned the defendant in his mind, and has sentenced him to the most severe punishments. (127) But nothing is so terrible as for men who have been the more powerful to be accused by their inferiors, and for those who have been rulers to be impeached by their former subjects, which is as if masters were being prosecuted by their natural or purchased slaves.

XVI. (128) And yet even this in my opinion was a lighter evil when compared with another which was greater still; for it was not people who were merely in the simple rank of subjects who now, discarding that position and conspiring together, on a sudden attacked him with their accusations; but those who did so were men who during the chief part of the time that he had had the government of the country had been in a position of the greatest enmity and hatred to him, Lampo having been under a prosecution for impiety against Tiberius Caesar, and having been almost worn out by the matter which had been thus impending over his head fore two years; (129) for the judge who had a grudge against him caused all sorts of delays and every possible protraction of the cause on various pretexts, wishing even if he escaped from the accusation, at all events to keep the terror of the future as uncertain hanging over his head for the longest possible period, so as to make his life more miserable even than death. (130) And then again when he seemed to have come off victorious, saying that he was insulted and injured in his property (for he was compelled to become a gymnasiarch), either by being economical and illiberal in his expenses, pretending that he had not sufficient wealth for such unlimited expenditure, or perhaps really not having enough; but before he came to the trial, making a parade of being very rich, but when he did come to the proof then appearing not to be a man of exceeding wealth, having acquired nearly all the riches which he had by unjust actions.

(131) For standing by the rulers when they gave judgment, he took notes of all that took place on the trial as if he were a clerk; and then he designedly passed over or omitted such and such points, and interpolated other things which were not said. And at times, too, he made alterations, changing and altering, and perverting matters, and turning things up-side down, aiming to get money by every syllable, or, I might rather say, by every letter, like a hunter after musty records, (132) whom the whole people with one accord did often with great felicity and propriety of expression call a pen-murderer, as slaying numbers of persons by the things which he wrote, and rendering the living more miserable than even the dead, as, though they might have got the victory and been in comfort, they were subjected to miserable defeat and poverty, their enemies having bought victory, and triumph, and wealth, of a man who sold and made his market of the properties of others.

(133) For it was impossible for rulers who had the charge of so vast a country entrusted to them, when affairs of every sort, both private and public, were coming in upon them fresh every day, to remember everything which they had heard, especially as they had not only to fill the part of judges, but also to take accounts of all the revenues and taxes, the investigation into which occupied the greater portion of the year. (134) And the man to whom it was entrusted to take charge of that most important of all deposits, namely, justice, and of those most holy sentiments which had been delivered and urged before them, caused forgetfulness to the judges, registering those who ought to have had sentence in their favour as defeated, and those who ought to have been defeated as victorious, after the receipt of his accursed pay, or, to speak more properly, wages of iniquity.

XVII. (135) Such, then, was the character of Lampo, who was now one of the accusers of Flaccus.

And Isidorus was in no respect inferior to him in wickedness, being a man of the populace, a low demagogue, one who had continually studied to throw everything into disorder and confusion, an enemy to all peace and stability, very clever at exciting seditions and tumults which had no existence before, and at inflaming and exaggerating such as were already excited, taking care always to keep about him a disorderly and promiscuous mob of all the refuse of the people, ready for every kind of atrocity, which he had divided into regular sections as so many companies of soldiers.

(136) There are a vast number of parties in the city whose association is founded in no one

good principle, but who are united by wine, and drunkenness, and revelry, and the offspring of those indulgencies, insolence; and their meetings are called synods and couches by the natives. (137) In all these parties or the greater number of them Isidorus is said to have borne the bell, the leader of the feast, the chief of the supper, the disturber of the city. Then, whenever it was determined to do some mischief, at one signal they all went forth in a body, and did and said whatever they were told. (138) And on one occasion, being indignant with Flaccus because, after he had appeared originally to be a person of some weight with him, he afterwards was no longer courted in an equal degree, having hired a gang of fellows from the training schools and men accustomed to vociferate loudly, who well their outcries as if in regular market to those who are inclined to buy them, he ordered them all to assemble at the gymnasium; (139) and they, having filled it, began to heap accusations on Flaccus without any particular grounds, inventing all kinds of monstrous accusations and all sorts of falsehoods in ridiculous language, stringing long sentences together, so that not only was Flaccus himself alarmed but all the others who were there at this unexpected attack, and especially, as it may be conjectured, from the idea that there must certainly have been some one behind the scenes whom they were studying to gratify, since they themselves had suffered no evil, and since they were well aware that the rest of the city had not been ill-treated by him.

(140) Then, after they had deliberated awhile, they determined to apprehend certain persons of them and to inquire into the cause of this indiscriminate and sudden rage and madness. And the men who were arrested, without being put to the torture, confessed the truth and added proofs to their words by what had been done, detailing the pay which had been already given and that which, in accordance with his promises, was subsequently to be paid, and the men who were appointed to distribute it as the leaders of the sedition, and the place where it was to break out, and the time when the giving of the bribes was to take place.

(141) And when every one, as was very natural, was indignant at this, and when the city was mightily offended, that the folly of some individuals should attach to it so as to dim its reputation, Flaccus determined to send for some of the most honourable men of the people, and, on the next day to bring forward before them those who had distributed the bribes, that he might investigate the truth about Isidorus, and also that he might make a defence of his own system of government, and prove that he had been unjustly calumniated; and when they heard the proclamation there came not only the magistrates but also the whole city, except that portion which was about to be convicted of having been the agents of corruption or the corrupted.

And they who had been employed in this honourable service, being raised up on the platform, (142) that they might be elevated and conspicuous and be recognised by all men, accused Isidorus as having been the cause of all the tumults and of the accusations which had been brought against Flaccus, and as having given money and bribes to no small number of them by himself. "Since else," said they, "where could we have got such great abundance? (143) We are poor men, and are scarcely able to provide our daily expenses for absolute necessaries: and what evil did we ever suffer from the governor, so as to be forced to bear him ill will? Nay, but it is he who was the cause of all these things, the author of them all, he who is always envious of those who are in prosperity, and an adversary of all stability and wholesome law."

And when those who were present came to the knowledge of these things, (144) for what was thus said was a very evident proof and evidence of the intentions of the person accused, they all raised an outcry, some calling out that he should be degraded, others that he should be banished, others that he should be put to death, and these last were the most numerous; and the others changed their tone and joined them, so that at last they all cried out, with one accord and with one voice, to slay the common pest of the land, the man to whom it was owing that, ever since he had arrived in the country and taken any part in public affairs, no part of the city or of the common interests had ever been left in a sound or healthy condition; (145) and he, indeed, being convicted by his conscience, fled away in-doors, fearing lest he should be seized; but Flaccus did nothing against him, thinking that now that he had voluntarily removed himself, everything in the city would soon be free from sedition and contention.

XVIII. (146) I have related these events at some length, not for the sake of keeping old injuries in remembrance, but because I admire that power who presides over all freemen's affairs, namely, justice, seeing that those men who were so generally hostile to Flaccus, those by whom of all men he was most hated, were the men who now brought their accusations against him, to fill up the measure of his grief, for it is not so bitter merely to be accused as to be accused by one's confessed enemies; (147) but this man was not merely accused, though a governor, by his subjects, and that by men who had always been his enemies, when he had only a short time before been the lord of the life of every individual among them, but he was also apprehended by force, being thus subjected to a twofold evil, namely, to be defeated and ridiculed by exulting enemies, which is worse than death to all right-minded and sensible people.

(148) And then see what an abundance of disasters came upon him, for he was immediately stripped of all his possessions, both of those which he inherited from his parents and of all that he had acquired himself, having been a man who took especial delight in luxury and ornament; for he was not like some rich men, to whom wealth is an inactive material, but he was continually acquiring things of every useful kind in all imaginable abundance; cups, garments, couches, miniatures, and everything else which was any ornament to a house; (149) and besides that, he collected a vast number of servants, carefully selected for their excellencies and accomplishments, and with reference to their beauty, and health, and vigour of body, and to their unerring skill in all kinds of necessary and useful service; for every one of them was excellent in that employment to which he was appointed, so that he was looked upon as either the most excellent of all servants in that place, or, at all events, as inferior to no one.

(150) And there is a very clear proof of this in the fact that, though there were a vast number of properties confiscated and sold for the public benefit, which belonged to persons who had been condemned, that of Flaccus alone was assigned to the emperor, with perhaps one or two more, in order that the law which had been established with respect to persons convicted of such crimes as his might not be violated.

(151) And after he had been deprived of all his property, he was condemned to banishment, and was exiled from the whole continent, and that is the greatest and most excellent portion of the inhabited world, and from every island that has any character for fertility or richness; for he was commanded to be sent into that most miserable of all the islands in the Aegaean Sea,[2] called Gyara, and he would have been left there if he had not availed himself of the intercession of Lepidus, by whose means he obtained leave to exchange Gyara for Andros, which was very near it. (152) Then he was sent back again on the road from Rome to Brundusium, a journey which he had taken a few years before, at the time when he was appointed governor of Egypt and the adjacent country of Libya, in order that the cities which had then seen him exulting and behaving with great insolence in the hour of his prosperity, might now again behold him full of dishonour. (153) And thus he being now become a conspicuous mark by reason of this total change of fortune, was overwhelmed with more bitter grief, his calamities being constantly rekindled and inflamed by the addition of fresh miseries, which, like relapses in sickness, compel the recollection of all former disasters to return, which up to that time appeared to be buried in obscurity.

XIX. (154) And after he had crossed the Ionian Gulf he sailed up the sea which leads to Corinth, being a spectacle to all the cities in Peloponnesus which lie on the coast, when they heard of his sudden reverse of fortune; for when he disembarked from the vessel all the evil disposed men who bore him ill will ran up to see him, and others also came to sympathize with him—men who are accustomed to learn moderation from the misfortunes of others. (155) And at Lechaeum, crossing over the isthmus into the opposite gulf, and having arrived at Cenchreae, the dockyard of the Corinthians, he was compelled by the guards, who would not permit him the slightest respite, to embark immediately on board a small transport and to set sail, and as a foul wind was blowing with great violence, after great sufferings he with difficulty arrived safe at the Piraeus.

(156) And when the storm had ceased, having coasted along Attica as far as the promontory of Sunium,[3] he passed by all the islands in order, namely, Helena, and Ceanus, and Cythnos, and all the rest which lie in a regular row one after another, until at last he came to the point of his ultimate destination, the island of Andros, (157) which the miserable man beholding afar off poured forth abundance of tears down his cheeks, as if from a regular fountain, and beating his breast, and lamenting most bitterly, he said, "Men, ye who are my guards and attendants in this my journey, I now receive in exchange for the glorious Italy this beautiful country of Andros, which is an unfortunate island for me. (158) I, Flaccus, who was born, and brought up, and educated in Rome, the heaven of the world, and who have been the schoolfellow and companion of the granddaughters of Augustus, and who was afterwards selected by Tiberius Caesar as one of his most intimate friends, and who have had entrusted to me for six years the greatest of all his possessions, namely, Egypt. (159) What a change is this! In the middle of the day, as if an eclipse had come upon me, night has overshadowed my life. What shall I say of this little islet? Shall I call it my place of banishment, or my new country, or harbour and refuge of misery? A tomb would be the most proper name for it; for I, miserable that I am, am now in a manner conducted to my grave, attending my own funeral, for either I shall destroy my miserable life through my sorrow, or if I am able to cling to life among my miseries, I shall in that case find a distant death, which will be felt all the time of my life."

(160) These, then, were the lamentations which he poured forth, and when the vessel came

---

[2]This was a common place of banishment for criminals, Juvenal 1.72.

[3]Now Cape Colonna.

near the harbour he landed, stooping down to the very ground like men heavily oppressed, being weighed down by his calamities as if the heaviest of burdens was placed upon his neck, without being able to look up, or else not daring to do so because of the people whom he might meet, and of those who came out to see him and who stood on each side of the road. (161) And those men who had conducted him hither, bringing the populace of the Andrians, exhibited him to them all, making them all witnesses of the arrival of the exile in their island.

(162) And they, when they had discharged their office, departed; and then the misery of Flaccus was renewed, as he no longer beheld any sight to which he was accustomed, but only saw sad misery presented to him by the most conspicuous evidence, while he looked around upon what to him was perfect desolation, in the middle of which he was placed; so that it seemed to him that a violent execution in his native land would have been a lighter evil, or rather, by comparison with his present circumstances, a most desirable good; and he gave himself up to such violence of grief, that he was in no respect different from a maniac, and leaped about, and ran to and fro, and clapped his hands, and smote his thighs, and threw himself upon the ground, and kept continually crying out, (163) "I am Flaccus! who but a little while ago was the governor of the mighty city, of the populous city of Alexandria! the governor of that most fertile of all countries, Egypt! I am he on whom all those myriads of inhabitants turned their eyes! who had countless forces of infantry, and cavalry, and ships, formidable, not merely by their number, but consisting of all the most eminent and illustrious of all my subjects! I am he who was every day accompanied when I went out by countless companies of clients! (164) But now, was not all this a vision rather than reality? and was I asleep, and was this prosperity which I then beheld a dream—phantoms marching through empty space, fictions of the soul, which perhaps registered non-existent things as though they had a being? Doubtless, I have been deceived. (165) These things were but a shadow and no real things, imitations of reality and not a real truth, which makes falsehood evident; for as after we have awakened we find none of those things which appeared to us in our dreams, but all such things have fled in a body and disappeared, so too, all that brilliant prosperity which I formerly enjoyed has now been extinguished in the briefest moment of time."

XX. (166) With such discourses as these, he was continually being cast down, and in a manner, as I may say, prostrated; and avoiding all places where he might be likely to meet with many persons on account of the shame which clung to him, he never went down to the harbour, nor could he endure to visit the marketplace, but shut himself up in his house, where he kept himself close, never venturing to go beyond the outer court. (167) But sometimes indeed, in the deepest twilight of the dawn, when every one else was still in bed, so that he could be seen by no one whatever, he would go forth out of the city and spend the entire day in the desolate part of the island, turning away if any one seemed likely to meet him; and being torn as to his soul with the memorials of his misfortunes which he saw about him in his house, and being devoured with anguish, he went back home in the darkness of the night, praying, by reason of his immoderate and never-ending misery, that the evening would become morning, dreading the darkness and the strange appearances which represented themselves to him when he went to sleep, and again in the morning he prayed that it might be evening;[4] for the darkness which surrounded him was opposed to everything light or cheerful.

(168) And a few months afterwards, having purchased a small piece of land, he spent a great deal of his time there living by himself, and bewailing and weeping over his fate. (169) It is said too, that often at midnight he became possessed like those who celebrate the rites of the Corybantes, and at such times he would go forth out of his farm-house and raise his eyes to heaven and to the stars, and beholding all the beauty really existing in the world, he would cry out, (170) "O King of gods and men! you are not, then, indifferent to the Jewish nation, nor are the assertions which they relate with respect to your providence false; but those men who say that that people has not you for their champion and defender, are far from a correct opinion. And I am an evident proof of this; for all the frantic designs which I conceived against the Jews, I now suffer myself. (171) I consented when they were stripped of their possessions, giving immunity to those who were plundering them; and on this account I have myself been deprived of all my paternal and maternal inheritance, and of all that I have ever acquired by gift or favour, and of everything else that ever became mine in any other manner. (172) In times past I reproached them with ignominy as being foreigners, though they were in truth sojourners in the land entitled to full privileges, in order to give pleasure to their enemies who were a promiscuous and disorderly multitude, by whom I, miserable man that I was, was flattered and deceived; and for this I have been myself branded with infamy, and have been driven as an exile from the whole of the habitable world, and

---

[4]This is evidently taken from Deuteronomy 28:66, "And thy life shall hang in doubt before thee; and thou shalt fear day and night, and shalt have none assurance of thy life: in the morning thou shalt say, Would God it were even! and at even thou shalt say, Would God it were morning! for the fear of thine heart wherewith thou shalt fear, and for the sight of thine eyes which thou shalt see."

am shut up in this place. (173) Again, I led some of them into the theatre, and commanded them to be shamelessly and unjustly insulted in the sight of their greatest enemies; and therefore I justly have been myself led not into a theatre or into one city, but into many cities, to endure the utmost extremity of insult, being ill-treated in my miserable soul instead of my body; for I was led in procession through the whole of Italy as far as Brundusium, and through all Peloponnesus as far as Corinth, and through Attica, and all the islands as far as Andros, which is this prison of mine; (174) and I am thoroughly assured that even this is not the limit of my misfortunes, but that others are still in store for me, to fill up the measures as a requital for all the evils which I have done. I put many persons to death, and when some of them were put to death by others, I did not chastise their murderers. Some were stoned; some were burnt alive; others were dragged through the middle of the market-place till the whole of their bodies were torn to pieces. (175) And for all this I know now that retribution awaits me, and that the avengers are already standing as it were at the goal, and are pressing close to me, eager to slay me, and every day, or I may rather say, every hour, I die before my time, enduring many deaths instead of one, the last of all." [5]

(176) And he was continually giving way to dread and to apprehension, and shaking with fear in every limb and every portion of his body, and his whole soul was trembling with terror and quivering with palpitation and agitation, as if nothing in the world could possibly be a comfort to the man now that he was deprived of all favourable hopes; (177) no good omen ever appeared to him, everything bore a hostile appearance, every report was ill-omened, his waking was painful, his sleep fearful, his solitude resembling that of wild beasts, nevertheless the solitude of his herds was what was most pleasant to him, any dwelling in the city was his greatest affliction; his safe reproach was a solitary abiding in the fields, a dangerous, and painful, and unseemly way of life; every one who approached him, however justly, was an object of suspicion to him. (178) "This man," he would say, "who is coming quickly hither, is planning something against me, he does not look as if he were hastening for any other object, but he is pursuing me; this pleasant looking man is laying a snare for me; this free-spoken man is despising me; this man is giving me meat and drink as they feed cattle before killing them. (179) How long shall I, hard-hearted that I am, bear up against such terrible calamities? I well know that I am afraid of death,

since out of cruelty the Deity will not punish me violently, to cut short my miserable life, in order to load me to excess with irremediable miseries, which he treasures up against me, to do a pleasure to those whom I treacherously put to death."

XXI. (180) While repeating these things over and over again and writhing with his agony, he awaited the end of his destiny, and his uninterrupted sorrow agitated, and disturbed, and overturned his soul. But Gaius, being a man of an inhuman nature and insatiable in his revenge, did not, as some persons do, let go those who had been once punished, but raged against them without end, and was continually contriving some new and terrible suffering for them; and, above all men, he hated Flaccus to such a degree, that he suspected all who bore the same name, from his detestation of the very appellation; (181) and he often repented that he had condemned him to banishment and not to death, and though he had a great respect for Lepidus who had interceded for him, he blamed him, so that he was kept in a state of great alarm from fear of punishment impending over him, for he feared lest, as was very likely, he, because he had been the cause of another person having been visited by a lighter punishment, might himself have a more severe one inflicted upon him.

(182) Therefore, as no one any longer ventured to say a word by way of deprecating the anger of the emperor, he gave loose to his fury, which was now implacable and unrestrained, and which, though it ought to have been mitigated by time, was rather increased by it, just as recurring diseases are in the body when a relapse takes place, for all such relapses are more grievous than the original attacks.

(183) They say that on one occasion Gaius, being awake at night, began to turn his mind to the magistrates and officers who were in banishment, and who in name indeed were looked upon as unfortunate, but who in reality had now thus acquired a life free from trouble, and truly tranquil and free. (184) And he gave a new name to this banishment, calling it an emigration, "For," said he, "it is only a kind of emigration the banishment of these men, inasmuch as they have all the necessaries of life in abundance, and are able to live in tranquillity, and stability, and peace. But it is an absurdity for them to be living in luxury, enjoying peace, and indulging in all the pleasures of a philosophical life."

(185) Then he commanded the most eminent of these men, and those who were of the highest rank and reputation, to be put to death, giving a regular list of their names, at the head of which list was Flaccus. And when the men arrived at Andros, who had been commanded to put him to death, Flaccus happened, just at that moment, to be coming from his farm into the city, and they, on their way up from the port, met him, (186) and

---

[5]This is like the passage in Shakespeare—"Cowards die many times before their deaths; / The brave men only taste of death but once."

while yet at a distance they perceived and recognised one another; at which he, perceiving in a moment the object for which they were come (for every man's soul is very prophetic, especially of such as are in misfortune), turning out of the road, fled and ran away over the rough ground, forgetting, perhaps, that Andros was an island and not the continent. And what is the use of speed in an island which the sea washes all round? for one of two things must of necessity happen, either that if the fugitive advances further he must be carried into the sea, or else arrested when he has reached the farthest boundary. (187) Therefore, in a comparison of evils, destruction by land must be preferable to destruction by sea, since nature has made the land more closely akin to man, and to all terrestrial animals, not only while they are alive, but even after they are dead, in order that the same element may receive both their primary generation and their last dissolution.

(188) The officers therefore pursued him without stopping to take breath and arrested him; and then immediately some of them dug a ditch, and the others dragged him on by force in spite of all his resistance and crying out and struggling, by which means his whole body was wounded like that of beasts that are despatched with a number of wounds; (189) for he, turning round them and clinging to his executioners, who were hindered in their aims which they took at him with their swords, and who thus struck him with oblique blows, was the cause of his own sufferings being more severe; for he was in consequence mutilated and cut about the hands, and feet, and head, and breast, and sides, so that he was mangled like a victim, and thus he fell, justice righteously inflicting on his own body wounds equal in number to the murders of the Jews whom he had unlawfully put to death.

(190) And the whole place flowed with blood which was shed from his numerous veins, which were cut in every part of his body, and which poured forth blood as from a fountain. And when the corpse was dragged into the trench which had been dug, the greater part of the limbs separated from the body, the sinews by which the whole of the body is kept together being all cut through.

(191) Such was the end of Flaccus, who suffered thus, being made the most manifest evidence that the nation of the Jews is not left destitute of the providential assistance of God.

HYPOTHETICA†
APOLOGY FOR THE JEWS
(Apologia Pro Iudaeis)

From Eusebius, P.E. 8.5.11 ff.

(5.11) And first of all I will adduce what Philo says respecting the journey of the Jews into Egypt, of which he has given an account, following that which is given by Moses in the first book of the Pentateuch, to which he has affixed the superscription, "hypothetically;" where, arguing in behalf of the Jews as if he were addressing himself to their accusers, he speaks in the following manner, affirming,—

(6.1) That their ancient ancestor, the original founder of their race, was a Chaldaean; and that this people emigrated from Egypt, after having in former times left its abode in Syria, being very numerous and consisting of countless myriads of people; and that when the land was no longer able to contain them, and moreover when a high spirit began to show itself in the dispositions of their young men, and when, besides this, God himself by visions and dreams began to show them that he willed that they should depart, and when, as the Deity brought it about, nothing was less an object of desire to them than their ancient native land; on that account this ancestor of theirs departed and journeyed into Egypt, whether in consequence of some express determination of God, or whether it was in consequence of some prophetic instinct of his own; so that from that time to the present the nation has had an existence and a durability, and has become so exceedingly populous, as it is at this moment.

(6.2) And then, after a few more sentences, he says,—

And they were led in this journey and emigration of theirs by a man who, if you will have it so, was in no respect superior to the generality of his fellow countrymen, so incessantly did they reproach him as a trickster and one who deceived them with words. An admirable amount and kind of trickery and deceit no doubt it was, by which

he not only completely saved the whole people which was oppressed by want of water and hunger, and by ignorance of the way, and in a complete state of destitution of all things, and led them forward as if in all prosperity, and conducted them through all the nations lying around, and kept them without any quarrelling with one another, and in a state of complete subordination and obedience to himself. (6.3) And this too, not for a short time, but for a period of such length, that it is not likely that even a single family would continue in perfect unanimity and prosperity for such a time; for no thirst, no hunger, no decay of body, nor fear of the future, no ignorance of what was to befall them, ever excited that deceived people, who were being led, as some will have it, to their destruction, to rise against him who was deceiving them. Yet what would you have us say? (6.4) That he had such excessive art, or such great eloquence of speech, or such shrewdness, that he could triumph over so many difficulties of such a nature, which seemed likely to lead to the destruction of them all? Surely you must confess, either that the natures of the men under him were not utterly ignorant or obstinate, but were obedient and not inclined to neglect a prudent care of the future; or else that they were as wicked and perverse as possible, but that God softened their obstinacy, and was, as it were, a leader to them in respect both of the present and of the future.

For that of these alternatives which appears to you to be the truest of the two, appears equally to contribute to the praise, and honour, and admiration of the whole nation.

(6.5) These things, then, are what I have to say about this exodus. But when they came into this land, how they were settled here, and how they got possession of the country, they show in their sacred records. And I moreover do not think it necessary to describe it as by way of history, but rather to enter into some speculations concerning them as to what was their natural and likely course. (6.6) For which of these two alternatives will you embrace? That while they were still very numerous, although at last they were evilly afflicted, still, while they were powerful and had arms in their hands, they took the country by force, fighting with and defeating both the Syrians and Phoenicians who met them in that their land? Or shall we suppose that they were unwarlike, and destitute of manly courage, and altogether defi-

---

† Yonge has a section titled *Fragments of Lost Works,* which includes what is recognized as Philo's *Hypothetica* and *On Providence (Fragments I and II).* These fragments appear in Eusebius' *Preparation of the Gospel (P.E.). Hypothetica* and *On Providence (Fragments I and II)* appear out of sequence in Yonge's edition and have been reordered to conform to the Cohn-Wendland (Loeb) sequence. Yonge also includes some of Eusebius' prefatory material for *On Providence (Fragments I and II)* not included in Loeb.

cient in point of numbers, and destitute of any supplies for war; but that they met with respectful treatment from those nations, and obtained their land from them, who willingly surrendered it to them? and that then immediately, or at no distant period, they built a temple, and did everything else which has any bearing on religion and piety?

(6.7) For these circumstances, as it seems, would prove them to have been a God-loving people, and beloved by God, and confessed to be such even by their enemies; for those people into whose territories they had suddenly come, as if to deprive them of them, were of necessity their enemies. (6.8) And if they met with respectful treatment and honour from them, how can we deny that they surpassed all other men in good fortune?

And what shall we say after this in the second place, or in the third place? Shall we speak of their admirable code of laws, of their obedience, or of their devotion, and justice, and holiness, and piety? But in truth they looked upon that man, whoever he was, who gave them these laws, with such excessive admiration and veneration, that whatever he approved of they immediately thought best also. (6.9) Therefore, whether he spoke, being influenced by his own reason, or because he was inspired by the Deity, they referred every word of his to God. And though many years have passed, I cannot tell the exact number, but more than two thousand, still they have never altered one word of what was written by him, but would rather endure to die ten thousand times than to do any thing in opposition to his laws and to the customs which he established.

(6.10) After Philo has said this, he proceeds to give an abridgment of the constitution established in the nation of the Jews by the laws of Moses, speaking thus:—

(7.1) Now, is there anything among that people resembling these circumstances, anything which appears to be of a mild and gentle character, and which admits of invocations of justice, and pleas, and delays, and of assessments of damages, and on the other hand of counter assessments? Not a word, but every thing is simple, plain, and straightforward. If you indulge in illicit connexions, if you commit adultery, if you do violence to a child (for do not speak of doing so to a boy, but even to a female child); and in like manner, if you prostitute yourself, if you suffer any thing disgraceful contrary to what becomes your age, or appear to do so, or are about to do so, death is the penalty for such wickedness.

(7.2) Again, if you behave with insult towards a slave, or towards a free person, if you confine such an one in bonds, if you lead him away and sell him, if you steal any thing, whether common or sacred, if you commit acts of impiety, not only by your deeds but even by any chance word, I will not venture to say against God himself (may God

be merciful to us, and of the same opinion about these matters), but against your father, or your mother, or your benefactor, death is equally the penalty. And that too, not a common, or ordinary, or natural death; but he who has merely uttered a single impious word must be stoned, as having committed no inferior impiety.

(7.3) He also gives many other injunctions, such as these, that wives shall serve their husbands, not indeed in any particular so as to be insulted by them, but in the spirit of reasonable obedience in all things; that parents shall govern their children for their preservation and benefit; that every one shall be the lord of his own possessions, provided he has not dedicated them to God, nor spoken of God as their owner; but if he has vowed them only by a single word, then it is not lawful for him to lay hands upon or to touch them, but he must at once separate himself from them all. (7.4) May I never be guilty of plundering the things which belong to God, or of stealing what has been offered and dedicated to him by others. And even, as I have said before, if a single word to that effect has unintentionally fallen from a man, he must, instead of taking away from what is already dedicated, add some offering of his own; for if he has said the word, he, by so speaking, deprives himself of every thing. But if he repents, or wishes to recall and amend what he has said, he shall be deprived also of his very life. (7.5) And the same principle extends to other things, of which he is the owner.

If a man by any words dedicates that which is requisite to support a wife, she shall be sacred and entitled to receive the support. If a father makes such a promise to his son, or a master to his servant, the rule is the same. And the way in which a man may be released from any promise or vow which he has made in such a manner can only be in the most perfect and complete way, when the high priest discharges him from it; for he is the person entitled to receive it in due subordination to God. And the next way is that which consists in propitiating the mercy of God in behalf of those who are the more immediate owners of the thing vowed, so that he may not accept of what is thus dedicated, since it is necessary to them. (7.6) There are, besides these rules, ten thousand other precepts, which refer to the unwritten customs and ordinances of the nation.

Moreover, it is ordained in the laws themselves that no one shall do to his neighbour what he would be unwilling to have done to himself.

That a man shall not take up what he has not put down, neither out of a garden, nor out of a wine-press, nor out of a threshing-floor; and that absolutely no one shall take anything, whether it be great or small, out of a heap. That no one shall refuse fire to one who begs it of him.

That no one shall cut off a stream of water, but

that everyone shall contribute food to beggars and cripples, and that such shall have favour with God. (7.7) That no one shall keep any one from performing funeral honours to the dead, but shall even throw upon them so much earth as if sufficient to protect them from impiety: that no one shall violate or move, in any manner or degree whatever, the graves, or tombs, or memorials of those who are dead. That no one shall add bonds, or any evil, or heap any additional suffering on him who is in trouble. That no one shall eradicate the generative powers of a man. That no one shall cause the offspring of women to be abortive by means of miscarriage, or by any other contrivance. That no one shall treat animals, in any respect, in a manner contrary to the injunctions imposed, whether by God or by a lawgiver.

That no one shall cause his seed to disappear. That no one shall enslave his offspring. (7.8) That no one shall apply a false balance, or an inadequate measure, or bad money. That no one shall tell the secrets of his friends in a foreign land. Where, in God's name, are these yokes of oxen of ours gone? And look also at other commandments besides these. It is ordained, that no one shall fix the residence of the parents apart from that of the children, not even if they are prisoners of war; nor that of a wife from that of her husband, even though a man may be her master, having purchased her lawfully.

(7.9) These commandments now are of a more solemn and important character, but there are others of apparently a trivial and ordinary kind. It is not lawful, says the lawgiver, to strip a nest wholly of its young; it is not lawful to reject the supplication of animals of any kind whatever, which flee to you for refuge, not even if any of them are very insignificant. You may say, perhaps, that these things are of no consequence whatever, but still, at least, the law which speaks of these particulars is of importance, and deserving of all imaginable care and attention; and the declarations are important, and so are the curses which threaten those who violate these laws with destruction; and God looks over all such matters, and is an avenger and punisher on every occasion and in every place.

(7.10) And then after a few more sentences he adds,—

And if it should happen that during a whole day, or I should rather say, not one day only but many, and those too not coming immediately one after another, but with intervals between them, even intervals of a week at a time, the custom, as is always natural, which is drawn from ordinary days prevails. Do you not wonder, that not a single one of all these commandments has been violated? (7.11) Is not this a mark of great temperance and self-restraint, derived to them from practice alone, so that they act towards one another with perfect equality, and are able to derive strength from those

actions if it be necessary? Surely not so; but the lawgiver thought that it ought to be derived from some great and admirable circumstance, that they should not only be competent to do other things in the same manner, but should also be imbued with a thorough knowledge of their national laws and customs.

(7.12) What then did he do on this sabbath day? he commanded all the people to assemble together in the same place, and sitting down with one another, to listen to the laws with order and reverence, in order that no one should be ignorant of anything that is contained in them; (7.13) and, in fact, they do constantly assemble together, and they do sit down one with another, the multitude in general in silence, except when it is customary to say any words of good omen, by way of assent to what is being read. And then some priest who is present, or some one of the elders, reads the sacred laws to them, and interprets each of them separately till eventide; and then when separate they depart, having gained some skill in the sacred laws, and having made great advances towards piety.

(7.14) Do not these objects appear to you to be of greater importance than any other pursuit can possibly be? Therefore they do not go to interpreters of laws to learn what they ought to do; and even without asking, they are in no ignorance respecting the laws, so as to be likely, through following their own inclinations, to do wrong; but if you violate or alter any one of the laws, or if you ask any one of them about their national laws or customs, they can all tell you at once, without any difficulty; and the husband appears to be a master, endowed with sufficient authority to explain these laws to his wife, a father to teach them to his children, and a master to his servants.

(7.15) And again, it is easy to speak in the same manner with respect to the seventh year, though, perhaps, one is not to say exactly the same things, for they do not abstain from all work as they do on the sabbath days, only they leave their land fallow till the next year, in order that so it may become productive; for they think that thus it becomes much better after having had this rest, and then that it may be cultivated again, and not be dried up and exhausted by the uninterrupted continuance of cultivation; (7.16) and you may see that a similar practice conduces to strength of body, for not only do intervals of relaxation contribute to health, but you may see too that physicians also enjoin a degree of rest at times from work; for what is incessant, and uninterrupted, and always the same, is likely to be injurious, especially in the case of hard work, the cultivation of the land.

(7.17) And a proof of this is, that if any one were to recommend the people to cultivate the land itself much more, and to add this seventh year also, and should promise them that the usual crops of fruit should reward their labours, they still would not adopt his advice, for they think that they are not alone entitled to rest from their labours, and yet even if they were to do so, it would be nothing strange; but they think that their land also deserves a certain degree of rest and exemption, in order again to receive a fresh beginning of care and cultivation; (7.18) since, in God's name, what could hinder them from letting it out during the year of jubilee thus proposed, and then receiving its annual produce once a year from those who rented and cultivated it? But as I said before, they will not admit of any such expedient in any manner or degree whatever, out of care, as it seems to me, for the welfare of the land; (7.19) and this is truly a very great proof of their humanity and moderation.

For, since they themselves rest from their labours during that year, they think that it is not right either to collect the fruits or crops which are produced, nor to lay up any thing which has not accrued to them from their own labours; but, as if God provided for them while the land is thus enjoying rest and regulating itself according to its will, they think that any one who chooses or who is in want, any traveller or stranger, may gather the fruit that year with impunity.

(7.20) However, this is enough to say to you on these matters; for, as to the fact of this law existing among them with regard to the seventh day and seventh year, you will not inquire of me, as you have perhaps heard it often from many persons, both physicians, and investigators of natural history, and philosophers, who discuss this law about the seventh year, as to the effect which it has on the nature of the universe, and especially on the nature of man.

This is what he says about the seventh day ... I shall be contented with the testimony of Philo on the present occasion, which he has given about the matter which I am here explaining in many passages of his treatises. And now do you take that work which he has written in defence of the Jewish nation, and read the following sentences in it.

(11.1) But our lawgiver trained an innumerable body of his pupils to partake in those things, who are called Essenes, being, as I imagine, honoured with this appellation because of their exceeding holiness.

And they dwell in many cities of Judaea, and in many villages, and in great and populous communities. (11.2) And this sect of them is not an hereditary of family connexion; for family ties are not spoken of with reference to acts voluntarily performed; but it is adopted because of their admiration for virtue and love of gentleness and humanity. (11.3) At all events, there are no children among the Essenes, no, nor any youths or persons only just entering upon manhood; since the dispositions of all such persons are unstable and liable to change, from the imperfections incident to their age, but they are all full-grown men, and even already declining towards old age, such as are no longer carried away by the impetuosity of their bodily passions, and are not under the influence of the appetites, but such as enjoy a genuine freedom, the only true and real liberty. (11.4) And a proof of this is to be found in their life of perfect freedom; no one among them ventures at all to acquire any property whatever of his own, neither house, nor slave, nor farm, nor flocks and herds, nor any thing of any sort which can be looked upon as the fountain or provision of riches; but they bring them together into the middle as a common stock, and enjoy one common general benefit from it all.

(11.5) And they all dwell in the same place, making clubs, and societies, and combinations, and unions with one another, and doing every thing throughout their whole lives with reference to the general advantage; (11.6) but the different members of this body have different employments in which they occupy themselves, and labour without hesitation and without cessation, making no mention of either cold, or heat, or any changes of weather or temperature as an excuse for desisting from their tasks. But before the sun rises they betake themselves to their daily work, and they do not quit it till some time after it has set, when they return home rejoicing no less than those who have been exercising themselves in gymnastic contests; (11.7) for they imagine that whatever they devote themselves to as a practice is a sort of gymnastic exercise of more advantage to life, and more pleasant both to soul and body, and of more enduring benefit and equability, than mere athletic labours, inasmuch as such toil does not cease to be practised with delight when the age of vigour of body is passed; (11.8) for there are some of them who are devoted to the practice of agriculture, being skilful in such things as pertain to the sowing and cultivation of lands; others again are shepherds, or cowherds, and experienced in the management of every kind of animal; some are cunning in what relates to swarms of bees; (11.9) others again are artisans and handicraftsmen, in order to guard against suffering from the want of any thing of which there is at times an actual need; and these men omit and delay nothing, which is requisite for the innocent supply of the necessaries of life.

(11.10) Accordingly, each of these men, who differ so widely in their respective employments, when they have received their wages give them up to one person who is appointed as the universal steward and general manager; and he, when he has received the money, immediately goes and purchases what is necessary and furnishes them with food in abundance, and all other things of which the life of mankind stands in need. (11.11)

And those who live together and eat at the same table are day after day contented with the same things, being lovers of frugality and moderation, and averse to all sumptuousness and extravagance as a disease of both mind and body. (11.12) And not only are their tables in common but also their dress; for in the winter there are thick cloaks found, and in the summer light cheap mantles, so that whoever wants one is at liberty without restraint to go and take whichever kind he chooses; since what belongs to one belongs to all, and on the other hand whatever belongs to the whole body belongs to each individual.

(11.13) And again, if any one of them is sick he is cured from the common resources, being attended to by the general care and anxiety of the whole body. Accordingly the old men, even if they happen to be childless, as if they were not only the fathers of many children but were even also particularly happy in an affectionate offspring, are accustomed to end their lives in a most happy and prosperous and carefully attended old age, being looked upon by such a number of people as worthy of so much honour and provident regard that they think themselves bound to care for them even more from inclination than from any tie of natural affection.

(11.14) Again, perceiving with more than ordinary acuteness and accuracy, what is alone or at least above all other things calculated to dissolve such associations, they repudiate marriage; and at the same time they practise continence in an eminent degree; for no one of the Essenes ever marries a wife, because woman is a selfish creature and one addicted to jealousy in an immoderate degree, and terribly calculated to agitate and overturn the natural inclinations of a man, and to mislead him by her continual tricks; (11.15) for as she is always studying deceitful speeches and all other kinds of hypocrisy, like an actress on the stage, when she is alluring the eyes and ears of her husband, she proceeds to cajole his predominant mind after the servants have been deceived.

(11.16) And again, if there are children she becomes full of pride and all kinds of license in her speech, and all the obscure sayings which she previously meditated in irony in a disguised manner she now begins to utter with audacious confidence; and becoming utterly shameless she proceeds to acts of violence, and does numbers of actions of which every one is hostile to such associations; (11.17) for the man who is bound under the influence of the charms of a woman, or of children, by the necessary ties of nature, being overwhelmed by the impulses of affection, is no longer the same person towards others, but is entirely changed, having, without being aware of it, become a slave instead of a free man.

(11.18) This now is the enviable system of life of these Essenes, so that not only private individuals but even mighty kings, admiring the men, venerate their sect, and increase their dignity and majesty in a still higher degree by their approbation and by the honours which they confer on them.

ON PROVIDENCE (Fragment I)

(De Providentia, I)

From Eusebius P.E. 7.21.336b–337a

But that you may not think that I am here arguing in a sophistical manner, I will produce a man who is a Hebrew as the interpreter for you of the meaning of the scripture; a man who inherited from his father a most accurate knowledge of his national customs and laws, and who had learnt the doctrines contained in them from learned teachers; for such a man was Philo. Listen then, to him, and hear how he interprets the words of God.

Why, then, does he use the expression, "In the image of God I made man,"[1] as if he were speaking of that of some other God, and not of having made him in the likeness of himself? This expression is used with great beauty and wisdom. For it was impossible that anything mortal should be made in the likeness of the most high God the Father of the universe; but it could only be made in the likeness of the second God, who is the Word of the other; for it was fitting that the rational type in the soul of man should receive the impression of the Word of God, since the God below the Word is superior to all and every rational nature; and it is not lawful for any created thing to be made like the God who is above reason, and who is endowed with a most excellent and special form appropriated to himself alone.

This is what I wish to quote from the first book of the questions and answers of Philo.

And the Hebrew Philo, in his treatise on Providence, speaks in this way concerning matter.

But concerning the quantity of the essence, if indeed it really has any existence, we must also speak. God took care at the creation of the world that there should be an ample and most sufficient supply of matter, so exact that nothing might be wanting and nothing superfluous. For it would have been absurd in the case of particular artisans, for them, when they are occupied in making anything, and especially anything of much value, to calculate the exact quantity of materials which they require; but for that being who is the original inventor of numbers and measures, and the qualities which exist and are found in them, to omit to take care to have just what was proper. I will speak now with all freedom, and say that the world had need for its fabrication of some precise quantity of materials, neither more nor less; since otherwise it would not have been perfect, nor complete in all its parts, being thoroughly well made, nor would it have been made perfect of a perfect essence.

For it is an indispensable part of a workman who is thoroughly well skilled in his art, before he begins making any thing, to see that his materials are exactly sufficient; therefore a man, even if he were most eminently skilled in the knowledge of other things, still if he were not able altogether to avoid error, which is so natural to mortals, would be very likely to be deceived in respect of the quantity of materials which he required when he was about to proceed to the exercise of art; sometimes adding to it as too little, and sometimes taking away from it as too much. But that Being who is, as it were, a kind of fountain of all knowledge, was not likely to supply anything in deficient or in superfluous quantities, inasmuch as he employs measures elaborated in a most wonderful manner, so as to display perfect accuracy, and all of the most praiseworthy character. But he who is inclined to talk nonsense, at random, will easily do it, looking upon the different works of all artisans as causes, and as having been made in a more excellent manner, either by the addition or by the subtraction of some material or other. But it is the peculiar occupation of sophistry to quibble and cavil; while it is the task of wisdom to investigate accurately everything that exists in nature.

---

[1] Genesis 1:27.

ON PROVIDENCE (Fragment II)

(De Providentia, II)

From Eusebius, P.E. 8.14.386–399

These things then are what may be said on the subject of the world having been created. And the same man also says a great number of very novel and bold things in his treatise on Providence, on the subject of the universe being governed by prudence; first of all putting forward the propositions of the atheists, and then proceeding to reply to each of them in regular order. And I will now proceed to extract some of the arguments which he adduces, even though they may appear somewhat prolix, because they are nevertheless necessary and important, abridging indeed the greater portion of them. (1) Now he conducts his argument in this way; these are his words.

Do you say then that there is providence in such a vast confusion and disorder of affairs? For, in fact, which of the circumstances and occurrences of human life is regulated by any principle or order? which of them is not full of all kinds of irregularity and destruction? Are you the only person who is ignorant that blessings in complete abundance are heaped upon the most wicked and worthless of mankind? such, for instance, as wealth, a high reputation, honour in the eyes of the multitude, authority? moreover, health, a good condition of the outward senses, beauty, strength, and unimpeded enjoyment of all good things, by means of an abundance of supplies and resources and preparations of every kind, and in consequence of the peaceful good fortune and good condition of the body? But all the lovers and practisers of wisdom and prudence, and every kind of virtue, everyone of them I may almost say, are poor, unknown, inglorious, and in a mean condition.

(2) Having said thus much with respect to the outward circumstances of, and a vast number of other things affecting, these men, he then immediately proceeds to refute the objections of his adversaries by the following arguments.

God is not a tyrant who practises cruelty and violence and all the other acts of insolent authority like an inexorable master, but he is rather a sovereign invested with a humane and lawful authority, and as such he governs all the heaven and the whole world in accordance with justice. (3) And there is no form of address with which a king can more appropriately be saluted than the name of father; for what, in human relationships, parents are to their children, that also sovereigns are to their states, and God towards the world, having adapted these two most beautiful things by the unchangeable laws of nature, by an indissoluble union, namely the authority of the leader with the anxious care of a relation; (4) for as parents are not wholly indifferent to even ill-behaved children, but, having compassion on their unfortunate dispositions, they are careful and anxious for their welfare, looking upon it as an act of relentless and irreconcileable enemies to insult and increase their misfortunes, but as the part of friends and relations to lighten their disasters: (5) and indeed in the excess of their liberality they even give more to such children than to those who have always been well conducted, knowing well that to these last their own moderation is at all times an abundant resource and means of riches, but that the others have no other hope except in their parents, and that if they are disappointed in that they will be destitute of even the necessaries of life.

(6) So in the same manner, God, how is the father of all rational understanding, takes care of all those beings who are endowed with reason, and exercises a providential power for the protection even of those who are living in a blameable manner, giving them at the same time opportunity of correcting their errors, and nevertheless not violating the dictates of his own merciful nature, of which virtue and humanity are the regular attendants, being willing to have their dwelling in the God-created world; (7) this one argument now, do thou, O my soul, take to thyself, and store up within thyself as a sacred deposit, and this other also as consistent with and in perfect harmony with it. Do not ever be so deceived and wander from the truth to such a degree as to think any wicked man happy, even though he may be richer than Croesus, and more sharp-sighted than Lyceus, and more powerful than Milo of Crotena, and more beautiful than Ganymede,—

"Whom the immortal gods, for beauty's sake,
Did raise up from the vile earth to heaven,
To be the cup-bearer of mighty Jove."[1]

(8) Accordingly, such a man, having shown his own daemon, I mean to say his own mind, to be the slave of ten thousand thousand different masters, such as love, appetite, pleasure, fear, pain,

---

[1] Homer's Iliad 20.234.

folly, intemperance, cowardice, injustice, he can never possibly be happy, even if the multitude, being utterly misled and deprived of their judgment, were to think him so, being corrupted by a double evil, pride and vain opinion, by which souls without ballast must infallibly be tossed about and driven out of their course; for these evils, above all others, injure the chief multitude of mankind.

(9) If, then, fixing the eyes of the mind steadily upon the truth, you should be inclined to contemplate the providence of God as far as the powers of human reason are capable of doing it, then, when you have attained to a closer conception of the true and only good, you will laugh at those things which belong to men which you for some time admired; for what is worse is always honoured in the absence of what is better, as it then usurps its place; but when that which is better appears, then that which is worse retires, and is contented with the second prize. (10) Therefore, admiring that godlike excellence and beauty, you will by all means perceive that none of the things previously mentioned were by themselves thought worthy of the better portion by God. On which account the mines of silver and gold are the most worthless portion of the earth, which is altogether and wholly unfit for the production of fruits and food; (11) for abundance of riches is not like food, a thing without which one cannot live. And the one great and manifest test of all these things is hunger, by which it is seen what is in truth really necessary and useful; for a person when oppressed by hunger would gladly give all the treasures in the whole world in exchange for a little food; (12) but when there is an abundance of necessary things poured out in a plentiful and unlimited supply, and flowing over all the cities of the land, then we, the citizens, indulging luxuriously in the good things provided by nature, are not contented to stop at them alone, but set up satiated insolence as the guide of our lives, and devoting ourselves to the acquisition of silver and gold, and of everything else by which we hope to acquire gain, proceed in everything like blind men, no longer exciting the eyes of our intellect by reason of our covetousness, so far as to see that riches are but the burden of the earth, and are the cause of continual and uninterrupted war instead of peace.

(13) Our garments are indeed, as some one of the poets says somewhere, "the flower of the sheep;" but with reference to the art displayed in their manufacture, they are the praise of the weavers. And if any one is proud of any glory which he may have acquired, being greatly delighted at his popularity among worthless people, he should know that he also is worthless, for he delights in them. (14) And let such a man pray to receive purification so as to have the disease of his ears healed, as it is through his ears that his soul is affected with great diseases. Again: let those men who are proud of their personal strength and activity learn not to be high-minded on such an account, looking at countless kinds of both domesticated and wild beasts, which are also endowed with great strength and power; for it is the most absurd thing imaginable for one who is a man to pride himself on the good qualities of beasts, and that too when the beasts themselves are thought of no importance whatever by him.

(15) Again: why should any man in his senses rejoice at beauty of person, which a short period must extinguish before it has flourished for any great length of time, since time always obscures its deceitful prime? and this too, when he sees that even in lifeless things there are objects of surpassing beauty, such as the works of painters, and sculptors, and other artists, displayed in paintings, and statues, and all kinds of embroidery, and weaving, which are held in the greatest honour in Greece and in the countries of the barbarians in every city. (16) Of these things, then, as I have said, not one is accounted by God worthy of the better portion.

And why should we wonder if they are not highly esteemed by God? for they are not even by those men who are very religious and devout, among whom those things which are really good and virtuous are held in honour, inasmuch as they have a good and well-disposed nature, and have improved their natural good qualities by study and practice, of which a genuine true philosophy is the maker. (17) But those who have devoted themselves to a bastard kind of philosophy have not even imitated physicians who give their attention to the body, the slave of the soul, though nevertheless they affirm that they are healing the mistress, that is to say, the soul itself; for then, when any such man is sick, even if he be the great king himself, passing over all the colonnades, and the men's chambers, and the women's chambers, and the pictures, and the silver and the gold, whether in money or in bullion, and the vast treasures of cups and works of embroidery, and all the rest of the celebrated ornaments of kings, and the multitude of his servants, and of his friends, or relatives, and subjects, and the chief officers who are about his person, and his body-guards, they come up to his bedside, paying no attention even to the decorations of his person, and not stopping to notice with admiration that his bed is inlaid with precious stones, or that his coverlet is of the finest workmanship and the most exquisite embroidery, nor that the fashion of his garments is of superlative beauty, but they even pull off the clothes in which he is wrapped, and lay hold of his hands, and press his veins, and feel his pulse, and note its beating accurately to see if it is in a healthy condition; very often too, they pull up his tunic and feel whether his stomach is too full, whether his chest is feverish, whether his heart beats irregularly. And then, when they have ascertained the symptoms, they apply the appropriate remedies.

(18) And in like manner, it would become philosophers who profess to be versed in the healing science as applicable to the soul, which is by nature the dominant part of the man, to despise all the things which erroneous opinion raises up as objects of pride, and to penetrate within, and to lay their hands upon the intellect itself, to see whether through passion its pulses are of an uneven rapidity and moving in an irregular and unnatural manner, and to touch the tongue, and see whether it is rough and devoted to evil-speaking, whether it is prostituted to evil purposes and unmanageable; also to touch the belly, and see whether it is swollen with the insatiable characteristics of desire, and, in short, of any other passions, and diseases, and infirmities, and to examine every one of those feelings, if they appear to be in a state of confusion, so that they may not be ignorant of what is proper to be applied to the soul with a reference to its cure.

(19) But now being lightened up all round by the brilliancy of external things, as being unable to see that light which is perceptible only by the intellect, they have passed their whole existence in a state of error, not being able to penetrate as far as royal thought, but being with difficulty able to reach the outer courts, and admiring those servants who stand at the gates of virtue, wealth, and glory, and health, and other kindred circumstances, they fall down in adoration before them. (20) But as it would be an extravagance of insanity to take blind men for judges of colour, or deaf men as judges of the sounds of music, so it is a most preposterous act to take wicked men as judges of real good. For these men are mutilated in the most important parts of themselves, namely, their intellect, over which folly has shed a deep darkness. (21) Do we then now wonder if Socrates, and such and such a virtuous man, has lived in purity? men who have never once studied any of the means of providing themselves with pecuniary resources, and who have never, even when it was in their power, condescended to accept great gifts which have been tendered to their acceptance by wealthy friends or mighty kings, because they looked upon the acquisition of virtue as the only good, the only beautiful thing, and have therefore laboured at that, and disregarded all other good things.

(22) And who is there who would not disregard spurious good things in comparison of genuine ones? But if while they received a mortal body, and were full of liability to all kinds of human disasters, and lived among such a number of unjust actions and unrighteous men, of which the very number is not easy to compute accurately, they

were plotted against by their enemies, why do we blame nature when we ought rather to accuse the barbarity of those who thus set upon them? (23) For so in like manner, if they had been placed in a pestilential climate, they would inevitably have become sick; and wickedness is even more, or at all events not less, destructive than a pestilential state of the atmosphere. But as when there is rain the wise man, if he is in the open air, must inevitably get wet through, and if the cold north wind blows he must be oppressed by cold and shivering, and when summer is at its height he must feel the heat, for it is a law of nature that the bodies of men should be simultaneously affected by the changes of the seasons; so also in the same way a man who lives in such places,

"Where slaughters dire and famines might prevail,
And all the ills which thus mankind assail,"

must inevitably pay the penalty which such evils inflict upon him.

(24) Since in the case of Polycrates at least, in retaliation for the terrible acts of injustice and impiety which he committed, there fell upon him great misery in his subsequent life as a terrible requital for his previous good fortune. Add to this that he was chastised by a mighty sovereign, and was crucified by him, fulfilling the prediction of the oracle: "I knew," said he, "long before I took it into my head to go to consult the oracle, that I was anointed by the sun and washed by Jupiter," for these enigmatical assertions, expressed in symbolical language having been originally couched in unintelligible language, afterwards receive a most manifest confirmation by the events which followed them. (25) But it was not only at the end of his existence, but indeed during the whole period of his life from its earliest commencement that he was, though without being aware of it, making his soul to depend wholly on his body; for as he was always in a state of alarm and trepidation, he feared the multitude of enemies who might possibly attack him, being well assured that no one in the world was really well affected towards him, but that every one was hostile to him, and would turn out implacable enemies if he should be unfortunate.

(26) Again, if unsuccessful and yet of neverending precautions those writers who have written the history of Sicily are witnesses, for they say that the tyrant of Sicily suspected even his most affectionately loved wife; and a proof of this is that he ordered the entrance of his chamber by which she was about to have access to him to be strewed with planks, in order that she might never come upon him without being observed, but that the noise and tumult made by her stepping on these boards might indicate her approach beforehand; and besides this he compelled her to come not

only without her robe, but even naked in every part, and even in those which ought not to be seen by men. And in addition to this he ordered the whole of the flooring along the road to be cut in width and depth like a trench made by farmers, out of fear lest anything should be secretly concealed so as to plot against him, which would inevitably be detected by the leaps and long steps which a person coming along this path would be compelled to take.

(27) Of how many miseries, then, was that man full who took all these precautions and practised all these contrivances against his own wife, whom he ought to have trusted above all other human beings? But he was like those men who scale precipices and climb over abrupt and steep mountains for the purpose of attaining to a more accurate comprehension of the natures of things in heaven, who at last after they have with great difficulty ascended to some overhanging ridge, find themselves unable to advance any further as they are too much exhausted to think of attempting the remaining portion of the mountain, and also want courage to descend, being giddy at the sight of the chasms and ravines below them; (28) for he, being in love with sovereign power as a godlike thing to be desired above all other objects, looked upon it as unsafe either to remain where he was or to retreat, for he considered that if he remained where he was innumerable other evils would come upon him in rapid and uninterrupted succession, while if he decided on retracing his steps his very life would be in danger, as there were enemies around, if not as to their bodies at all events in their minds, against him.

(29) And he also showed the truth of all this by the treatment to which he exposed a friend of his who spoke of the life of a tyrant as one of complete and absolute happiness; for, having invited him to a banquet which had been prepared in a most brilliant and costly manner, he ordered a sharp sword to be suspended over his head by a very fine thread, and when he, after he had sat down to the banquet, on a sudden perceived it, not daring to rise up and quit his place for fear of the tyrant, and not being able to enjoy any of the things which were prepared out of fear, he disregarded all the abundant and superb luxuries by which he was surrounded, and keeping his neck and his eyes turned upwards, sat in the expectation of instant death.[2]

(30) And when Dionysius perceived the state in which he was, he said to him, "Do you then at last begin to understand the true character of that illustrious and enviable life of ours, for this is what it really is if a man chooses to speak of it without flattery or disguise, since it contains indeed a great abundance of resources and supplies, but no enjoyment of any real blessing; and it causes its possessor incessant fears and irremediable and unavoidable dangers, and a disease worse than the most contagious or most fatal sickness, which is continually threatening inevitable death. (31) But the inconsiderate multitude, being deceived by the outward brilliancy and splendour of the position, are like people who are attracted by showy looking courtesans, who, concealing their real deformity under fine clothes and golden ornaments, and pencilling their eyes from want of any real beauty, manufacture a spurious beauty in order to lie in wait for and catch the beholders.

(32) Now men who are placed in situations of great prosperity are full of such unhappiness as this, of the greatness of which they themselves are fully aware, and they do not at all keep it to themselves, but like men who under compulsion divulge secret things, they often utter the truest possible expressions, which are extorted from them by suffering, living in the continual company of punishment both present and expected, just like cattle who are being fattened up for sacrifice, for they too are treated with the greatest possible attention in order to be fit to be sacrificed by reason of their fleshiness and good condition. (33) There are also some men who have suffered punishment, and that not concealed, but visible, and notorious for the impiety of the means by which they have acquired riches, the names and numbers of whom it would be superfluous to enumerate, but it will be sufficient to bring forward one instance as a specimen of the whole.

It is said, then, by those who have written the History of the Sacred War in Phocis that as there was a law established that any one who was guilty of sacrilege should be either thrown down a precipice, or drowned in the sea, or burnt alive, that those men who had pillaged the temple at Delphi, by name Philomelus, and Onomarchus, and Phayllus, divided these punishments among them, for that the first fell down a rugged and precipitous rock and was dashed to pieces on the stones, and that the second, when the horse which he was riding grew restive and plunged down towards the sea, was overwhelmed by the waves, and so fell alive into a devouring gulf; and Phayllus was wasted

---

[2] Horace alludes to the story of Damocles, Od. III. 1.16 (which may be translated)—"Care murders sleep; the man who's learnt to dread / The sword unsafely trembling o'er his head, / In vain to court his sad distracted taste / The table groans beneath the varied feast. / Sad Philomel's untutored song is vain, / And vain the swelling

---

flute's more laboured strain, / To close his eyes in sleep, the envied lot / Of weary peasant in his humbler cot."

away by a consumptive disease (for the way in which the story is told about him is twofold), or else perished in the temple at Abae, being burnt in it when it was destroyed by fire. (34) For it must be the mere spirit of obstinacy and arguing to say that all these events took place by mere chance, for if indeed one or two of them had been punished at different periods or by some other mode of punishment, then it would have been reasonable to impute their fate to the uncertainty of fortune, but when they all died together and at one time, and by no other punishment but by that precise end which is appointed in the laws for the punishment of such crimes as those of which they had been guilty, it is surely fair to say that they perished by the direct condemnation of God.

(35) But if any of the violent men who are unmentioned, and who have at different times risen up against the people in their several states, and have enslaved not only other nations, but their own countries too, have still died without meeting with punishment, it is not to be wondered at, for in the first place man does not judge as God judges, because we investigate what is visible to ourselves, but he descends into the secret recesses of the soul without making any noise, and there contemplates the mind in the clear light, as if in the sun; for stripping off from it all the ornaments in which it is enveloped, and seeing its devices and intentions naked, he immediately distinguishes between the bad and the good.

(36) Let not us then, preferring our own judgment to that of God, assert that it is more unerring or more full of wisdom than his, for that is not consistent with holiness; for in the one there are many things which deceive it, such as the treacherous outward senses, the insidious character of the passions, the most terrible attacks of vice, but in the other there is nothing which can at all conduce to deceit or error, but justice and truth, by which each separate action is determined on, and in this way is naturally rectified in the most praiseworthy manner.

(37) Do not thou, then, my good friend, consider tyrannical power, that most unprofitable of all things, to be a seasonable possession; for neither is punishment disadvantageous, but it is either more beneficial, or at all events not injurious to the good to suffer due punishment, on which account it is expressly comprehended in all laws which are wisely enacted, and those who have established such laws are praised by every one; for what a tyrant is in a people, that is punishment in a law.

(38) When therefore a want and terrible scarcity of virtue seizes upon cities, and when a great abundance of folly overwhelms everything, then God, like the stream of an overflowing torrent, being desirous to wash away all the power and impetuosity of wickedness, in order to purify our race, gives vigour and power to those men who by their natures are fitted to exercise dominion, (39) for without a stern soul wickedness cannot be got rid of. And just as cities keep executioners for the punishment of murderers, and traitors, and sacrilegious persons, not because they approve of the dispositions of the men, but because they have need of the serviceable part of their ministrations; in the same manner the Ruler of this mighty city, the world, appoints tyrants, like ordinary executioners, to be over those cities in which he sees that violence, and injustice, and impiety prevail, and all other kinds of evils in abundance, that he may by these means put an end to their existence. (40) And then he thinks it right to pursue the guilty, as men who have been serving these vices from the impulses of an impure and pitiless soul, with every punishment imaginable, as the ringleaders; for as the power of fire when it has consumed the fuel which was given to it, at last consumes itself also, so also do those who have received supreme power over nations, when they have exhausted the cities and rendered them destitute of inhabitants, at last perish themselves among them, suffering due punishment for all that they have done.

(41) And why should we wonder if God employs the agency of tyrants to get rid of wickedness when widely diffused over cities, and countries, and nations? For he very often uses other ministers, and himself brings about the same end by his own resources, inflicting upon the nation famine, or pestilence, or earthquakes, or any other heaven-sent calamity, by which great and numerous multitudes perish every day, and by which a great portion of the habitable world is made desolate, on account of his care for the preservation of virtue.

(42) Therefore I have now, as I conceive, spoken at sufficient length on the present subject, namely, that no wicked man is happy, by which fact above all others it may be established that there is such a thing as providence; but if you are not thoroughly convinced, then tell me boldly what is the doubt which is still lurking in your mind, for then both of us by labouring together shall be able to see clearly what the real truth is.

(43) And after some more arguments, he proceeds thus:—

God causes the violent storms of wind and rain which we see, not for the injury of those who traverse the sea, as you fancied, or of those who till the earth, but for the general benefit of the whole of the human race, for with his water he cleanses the earth, and with his breezes he purifies all the regions beneath the moon, and by the united influence of both he nourishes and promotes the growth and brings to perfection both animals and plants. (44) And if at times these things do injure those who put to sea or who till the land at unseasonable moments, it is not to be wondered at, for these men are but a small portion of the human race, and the care of God is exerted for the benefit of all mankind.

As, therefore, in a gymnastic school oil is placed there for the common benefit of every one, but still it often happens that the master of the school, by reason of some political necessity changes the arrangement of the usual hours of exercise, by which means some of those who wish to anoint themselves come too late; in like manner God, who takes care of the whole world as if it were a city committed to his charge, does sometimes cause the summer to resemble winter, and winter to assume the characteristics of spring, for the common benefit of the universe, even though some captains of ships, or some cultivators of the ground, may very likely be injured by this irregularity of the seasons. (45) Therefore He, being aware that the occasional interchanges of the elements with one another, out of which the world was made, and of which it consists, are a work of the greatest importance and necessity, supplies them without allowing anything to be an obstacle to them; and frost and snow-storms, and other things of that kind, follow the cooling of the air. And, again, lightnings and thunders arise from the collision and repercussion of the clouds, none of which things are perhaps effected by any immediate exertion of providence, but the rains and winds are the causes of existence, and nourishment, and growth to all things which are upon the earth, and these phenomena are the natural consequences of those others.

(46) For just as it often happens, when the master of a gymnastic school, out of rivalry, has gone to extravagant expense, then some of those who are ignorant of all that is becoming, having been bespattered with oil instead of water, let all the drops from them fall upon the boards, and then a most slippery mud is the result: nevertheless a man, whose appreciations were just would not say that the hard and the slippery state of the ground was caused by the intention of the master of the school, but that these things had resulted accidentally, in consequence of the abundant quantity of the things supplied. (47) Again, the rainbow, and the halo, and all other things of that kind, are natural consequences of those things becoming mingled with the clouds, not being occurrences which lead and influence nature, but being the results and consequences of the operations of nature.

Not but what these very things themselves do also afford some signs of great importance to wise men, for, guiding their conjectures by them, they predict calms and storms of wind, and fine weather, and tempests. (48) Do you not see that porticoes

which embellish the cities? the greater part of these look towards the south, in order that those who walk under them may be warm in the winter, and may be cool in the summer.

There is also another thing which does not happen through the intention of Him who made it, and what is this? the shadows which fall from the feet indicate the hours to our experience. (49) And again, fire is a most important work of nature, but the consequence of fire is smoke, and nevertheless even this too at times is of some service. At all events in the heat, in the middle of the day, when the fire is rendered invisible by the brilliancy of the beams of the sun, the approach of enemies is indicated by the smoke, (50) and the principle which causes the rainbow is also the same which, in some degree, regulates eclipses.

For eclipses are a natural consequence of the rules which regulate the divine natures of the sun and moon; and they are indications either of the impending death of some king, or of the destruction of some city, as Pindar also has told us in enigmatical terms, alluding to such events as the consequences of the omens which I have now been mentioning.[3]

---

[3] This theory of the eclipses of the sun and other natural prodigies being prophetic of events on earth, is expressed by Virgil in a passage of the most exquisite beauty in reference to Caesar's death, Georg. 1.462 (as it is translated by Dryden)—"The unerring sun by certain signs declares / What the late eve or early morn prepares, / And when the south projects a stormy day, / And when the clearing north will puff the clouds away. / The sun reveals the secrets of the sky, / And who dares give the source of light the lie? / The change of empires often he declares, / Fierce tumults, hidden treasons, open wars. / He first the fate of Caesar did foretell, / And pitied Rome, when Rome in Caesar fell, / In iron clouds concealed the public light, / And impious mortals feared eternal night. / Nor was the fact foretold by him alone, / Nature herself stood forth and seconded the sun. / Earth, air, and seas with prodigies were signed, / And birds obscene and howling dogs divined; / What rocks did Aetna's bellowing mouth expire / From her torn entrails! and what floods of fire. / What clanks were heard in German skies afar / Of arms and armies rushing to the war. / Dire earthquakes rent the solid Alps below, / And from their summits shook the eternal snow. / Pale spectres in the close of night were seen, / And voices heard of more than mortal men. / In silent groves dumb sheep and oxen spoke, / And streams ran backward and their beds forsook; / The yawning earth disclosed the abyss of hell, / The weeping statues did the wars foretell, / And holy sweat from brazen idols fell. / Then rising in his might, the king of floods / Rushed through the forests, tore the lofty woods, / And rolling onwards, with a sweepy sway / Bore houses, lands, and labouring hinds away. / Blood sprang from wells, wolves howled in turns by night, / And boding victims did the priests affright. / Such peals of thunder never poured from high, / Nor forky lightnings flashed from such a sullen sky; / Red meteors ran across the ethereal space, / Stars disappeared and comets took their place. / *For this* the Emathian plains once more were strewed / With

(51) And the circle of the Milky Way partakes of the same natural essences with the other stars; but merely the fact that it is hard to account for, is no reason that those who are accustomed to investigate the principles of nature should shrink from examining into it; for the discovery of those things is most beneficial, and the investigation of them is intrinsically most delightful for its own sake, to those who are fond of learning.

(52) For as the sun and moon exist in consequence of Providence, so also do all things in heaven, even though we are unable to trace out accurately the respective natures and powers of each, and are, therefore, reduced to silence about them; (53) and earthquakes, and pestilences, and the fall of thunderbolts, and things of that kind, are said indeed to be sent by God, but, in reality, they are not so, for God is absolutely not the cause of any evil whatever of any kind, but the natural changes of the elements produce these effects, not as circumstances which guide nature, but as those which are followed by necessary results, and which do themselves follow naturally upon their antecedent causes. (54) And if some people, who think themselves entitled to immunity meet with some injury from these things, they are still not to find fault with their management and dispensation; for, in the first place, it does not follow, that if some persons are reckoned virtuous among men, they are so in real truth; since the criteria by which God judges are far more accurate than any of the tests by which the human mind is guided. And, in the second place, prophetic wisdom loves to contemplate those things in the world which are of the most comprehensive nature, as in the case of monarchies, and in the governments of armies, we see that it is not any obscure, ignoble, or chance person who is appointed to govern the cities or the armies.

(55) And some persons say that as on occasion of the slaying of tyrants, it is lawful that their relations also should be put to death, in order that transgressions may be checked by the terrible magnitude of the punishment inflicted: in like manner in pestilential diseases, it is necessary that some of those who are not guilty should be involved in the destruction, in order that others who are at a distance may learn moderation. Besides that, it is inevitable that those who are exposed to a pestilential atmosphere must become diseased just as all persons who are exposed to a storm on board a ship must be all exposed to equal danger. (56) But those wild beasts which are courageous have been created; for we must not suppress the truth (as if one were to anticipate the defence likely to

be made by a man of powerful eloquence and tear it to pieces beforehand), in order that men may, by practising against them, acquire hardihood for the contests of war; for gymnastic exercises and continued hunting train men and inure their souls in a greater degree even than their bodies to rely upon their own courage, and energy, and strength, so as to disregard the sudden attacks of their enemies.

(57) But those men who are of peaceable character are at liberty to keep themselves not only within their walls, but also even within tents, and there to live in privacy, safe from the designs of any enemies, having vast and countless herds of domestic animals to help their enjoyment; since boars and lions, and animals of that kind, are by their own instinct driven to a distance from cities, not being inclined to expose themselves to danger in consequence of the devices of men. (58) And if any men, being influenced by a spirit of laziness and indolence, living without arms and without preparation, dwell fearlessly among the haunts of wild beasts, then if anything happens to them they must blame not nature but themselves, because when they might have guarded against any such disasters, they have neglected them. Accordingly, before now, I have seen at the horse-races some persons acting in a most careless manner, who, when they ought to have sat still and to have beheld the races in an orderly manner, standing in the middle have been knocked down by the horses' feet and by the wheels, and have met with a proper reward for their folly.

(59) We have now, then, said enough on this subject.

But of reptiles, those which are venomous have not been called into existence by an immediate providence, but by the natural consequences of events, as I said before; for they are brought into life when the moisture which is in them changes to a more violent heat; and some are vivified by putrefaction, as, for instance, the putrefaction of meat produces maggots, and that which is caused by perspiration produces lice; but all those which are produced out of a kindred substance, and which have their generation in accordance with the usual spermatic principles which I have mentioned before, are very naturally ascribed to an immediate providence. (60) And I have also heard two accounts given of them as having been created for the advantage of mankind, which I should not think it well to conceal. Now one of them is the following.

Some persons have said that venomous animals contribute greatly to many of the objects of physicians, and that those who reduce that science to a regular system use them in a proper manner, and, acting with great wisdom and prudence, have discovered antidotes, so as to be able to contribute to the unexpected safety of those who were

---

Roman bodies, and just heaven thought good / To fatten twice those fields with Roman blood."

in the greatest possible danger; and even at the present time one may see those persons who apply themselves to the study of medicine, in a careful and diligent manner, using all these animals and plants in a most skilful manner in the composition of drugs.

(61) The other account has no reference to the practice of physicians, but only as it would seem to the studies of philosophers. For it says that all these things have been prepared by God as engines of punishment against offenders, just as generals and rulers prepare halters and chains. On which account, though they are quiet at other times, they are brought out with great power in the case of people who have been condemned, and whom nature in her incorruptible tribunal has sentenced to death; (62) for that they lurk in secret holes and in houses, is a falsehood; for it is seen that these creatures flee out of the cities into the fields and into desert places, to avoid man as their master. Not but what, if this is true, there is a certain sense and principle in it; for rubbish is heaped up in recesses: and quantities of sweepings, and refuse, and such things, are what venomous reptiles love to lurk in, besides the fact that their smell has an attractive power over them.

(63) Again, if swallows live among us, it is not at all strange, for we abstain from hunting them; and a desire of safety is implanted not only in the souls of rational creatures, but also in those of irrational animals.

But of those animals which tend to our enjoyment, there is not one which lives with us by reason of the designs which we form against them, except that some do live with those nations to whom the use of them is forbidden by the law. (64) There is a city of Syria, on the sea shore, Ascalon by name: when I was there, at the time when I was on my journey towards the temple of my native land for the purpose of offering up prayers and sacrifices therein, I saw a most incalculable number of pigeons on the roads and about every house; and when I inquired the cause of their being there in such numbers, they said that it was not lawful to catch them, for that the use of them had been prohibited to the inhabitants from the earliest ages; and so the bird had become so thoroughly tame through fearlessness, that it not only hovered about the roofs and came into the houses, but approached their tables also, and grew luxurious in the alliance which it had thus formed.

(65) And in Egypt we may see a still more marvellous thing; for the crocodile is the most odious of all animals, and one addicted to devour man; and it is born and brought up in the most sacred way, and although residing in the depths, it feels the benefits which it receives from mankind; for in those tribes, among which it is honoured, it multiplies in the greatest degree, but among those who injure it it never appears at all: so that there are places where even the most timid persons when sailing by leap out of their ships and swim about with their children.

(66) And in the country of the Cyclops, since the race of these men is a fabulous invention, there is no eatable fruit whatever produced except such as is raised from seed and cultivated by husbandmen, just as nothing is produced from that which does not exist; but we must not accuse Greece as being sterile and unproductive, for there is a great deal of deep and rich soil in it; and if the land of the barbarians is superior in fruitfulness, though it is superior in the food which it produces, it is inferior in the men who are nourished by the food, and for whose sake the food is produced.

For Greece is the only country which really produces man, that heavenly plant, that divine offshoot, producing that most accurately refined reason which is appropriated by and akin to knowledge; and the cause is this, it is the nature of the intellect to be rendered acute by the lightness of the air; (67) on which account Heraclitus said with great propriety, "Where the soil is dry, there the soul is most wise and most excellent;" and any one may conjecture this from the fact, that men who are sober and contented with a little are wise, and that those who are continually filling themselves with meat and drink are the least sensible, as if their reasoning faculties were drowned by the quantity which they swallow.

(68) And on this account we see, in the countries of the barbarians, trees and plants grow to the greatest possible size, by reason of the abundance of nourishment which they receive; and we see too, that the irrational animals which are found in these regions are the most prolific of any, but the mind is not so, or, at all events, it is so in a very slight degree, because it is elevated and raised out of the aether itself, while the incessant and uninterrupted evaporations of earth and water have freely boiled over it. (69) Again, the different kinds of fish, and birds, and terrestrial animals, are not grounds for accusing nature, which invites us to pleasure by those means, but are a terrible reproach to us for our intemperate use of them, for it was necessary, for the due completion of the universe, in order that there should be order and regularity in every portion of it, that there should be produced every possible species of animal. But it was not necessary that that animal, which of all others is most akin to wisdom, namely, man, should rush with such eagerness to the enjoyment of it, as to change his nature into something resembling the ferocity of wild beasts; (70) on which account, even up to the present time, those who have any regard for temperance entirely abstain from such things, eating only vegetables,

and herbs, and the fruits of trees, as the most delicious and wholesome food.

And these men are instructors for those who look upon the practice of eating such animals to be in accordance with nature, and correct them, and are lawgivers to their respective cities, being men who take care to check the immoderate vehemence of the appetites, and who do not permit the unrestrained use of everything to everybody.

(71) Again, if roses, and crocuses, and all the other beautiful variety of flowers which we see, contribute to health, it would not follow that they all contribute to pleasure; for the indescribable variety of them makes the powers of some of them more conspicuous than those of others, just as there is a commingling of male and female, contributing to the generation of an animal; neither of them being calculated, by itself, to produce the effect which the two produce in combination.

(72) These things are said, in a most convincing manner, with reference to the rest of the questions raised by you, being quite sufficient to produce conviction in the minds of all who are not obstinately contentious on the subject of God taking great care of human affairs.[4]

---

[4]Yonge's edition includes numerous miscellaneous fragments including *From the Parallels of John of Damascus* (which includes Greek fragments from *Quaestiones in Genesis et Exodum*, whose translation is generally based on Armenian), from *An Anonymous Collection in the Bodleian Library at Oxford*, and from *An Unpublished Manuscript in the Library of the French King*. These have been relocated to an appendix in this volume.

ON THE EMBASSY TO GAIUS†
THE FIRST PART OF THE TREATISE ON VIRTUES
(De Virtutibus Prima Pars, Quod Est De Legatione Ad Gaium)

I. (1) How long shall we, who are aged men, still be like children, being indeed as to our bodies gray-headed through the length of time that we have lived, but as to our souls utterly infantine through our want of sense and sensibility, looking upon that which is the most unstable of all things, namely, fortune, as most invariable, and that which is of all things in the world the most steadfast, namely, nature, as utterly untrustworthy? For, like people playing at draughts, we make changes, altering the position of actions, and considering the things which are the result of fortune as more durable than those which result from nature, and the things which proceed in accordance with nature as less stable than those which are the result of chance. (2) And the reason of all this is, that we form our judgment of present events without paying any prudential attention to the future, being influenced by the erroneous guidance of our outward senses instead of the secret operations of the intellect; for the things which are openly conspicuous and before our hands so as to be taken up by them, are comprehended by our eyes, but our reasoning power outstrips them, hastening onwards to what is invisible and future; but nevertheless, we obscure the vision of our reason, though it is far more acute than those bodily powers of sight which are exercised by the eyes, some of us confusing it by indulgence in wine and satiety, and others by that greatest of all evils, namely, ignorance.

(3) Nevertheless, the existing opportunity and the many and important proportions which arise to be decided on at the present time, even if some people should be incredulous that the Deity exercises a providential foresight with regard to human affairs, and especially on behalf of a nation which addresses its supplications to him, which belongs especially to the father and sovereign of the universe, and the great cause of all things; and these propositions are sufficient to persuade them of this truth.[1]

(4) And this nation of suppliants is in the Chaldaic language called Israel, but when the name is translated into the Greek language it is called, "the seeing nation;" which appellation appears to me to be the most honourable of all things in the world, whether private or public; (5) for if the sight of elders, or instructors, or rulers, or parents, excites those who behold them to reverence and orderly conduct, and to an admiration of and desire for a life of moderation and temperance, how great a bulwark of virtue and excellence must we not expect to find in those souls which, after having investigated the nature of every created thing, have learnt to contemplate the uncreated and Divine Being, the first good of all, the one beautiful, and happy, and glorious, and blessed being; better, if one is to tell the plain truth, than the good itself; more beautiful than the beautiful itself; more happy than happiness itself; more blessed than blessedness itself; and, in short, if anything else in the world is so, more perfect than any one of the above-mentioned things.

(6) For reason cannot make such advances as to attain to a thorough comprehension of God, who can neither be touched nor handled; but it withdraws from and falls short of such a height, being unable to employ appropriate language as a step towards the manifestation (I will not say of the living God, for even if the whole heaven were to become endowed with articulate voice, it would not be furnished with felicitous and appropriate expressions to do justice to such a subject); but even of his subordinate powers, those, for instance, by which he created the world and by which he reigns over it as its king, and by which he foresees the future, and all his other beneficent, and chastising, and corrective powers. (7) Unless, indeed, we ought to class his correction among his beneficent powers, not only because such a display is a portion of his laws and ordinances (for law is made up of two things, the honour of the good, and the chastisement of the wicked), but also because punishment reproves, and very often even corrects, and ameliorates those who have done wrong; and if it fails to do so with respect to them, at all events it does so to those who are near the offenders thus punished; for the punishment of others makes most men better, for fear lest they themselves should suffer the same things.

II. (8) For who—when he saw Gaius, after the death of Tiberius Caesar, assuming the sovereignty of the whole world in a condition free from all sedi-

---

†Yonge's title, *A Treatise on the Virtues and on the Office of Ambassadors. Addressed to Caius.* The publisher has chosen to use 'Gaius' rather than Yonge's variant spelling of the name.

[1]There seems some corruption in the text here.

tion, and regulated by and obedient to admirable laws, and adapted to unanimity and harmony in all its parts, east and west, south and north; the barbarian nations being in harmony with the Greeks, and the Greeks with the barbarians, and the soldiers with the body of private citizens, and the citizens with the military; so that they all partook of and enjoyed one common universal peace—could fail to marvel at and be amazed at his extraordinary and unspeakable good fortune, (9) since he had thus succeeded to a ready-made inheritance of all good things, collected together as it were in one heap, namely, to numerous and vast treasures of money, and silver and gold, some in bullion, and some in coined money, and some again being devoted to articles of luxury, in drinking cups and other vessels, which are made for display and magnificence; and also countless hosts of troops, infantry, and cavalry, and naval forces, and revenues which were supplied in a never-ending stream as from a fountain; (10) and the sovereignty of the most numerous, and most valuable, and important portions of the habitable world, which is fact one may fairly call the whole world, being not only all that is bounded by the two rivers, the Euphrates and the Rhine; the one of which confines Germany and all the more uncivilised nations; and the Euphrates, on the other hand, bridles Parthia and the nations of the Sarmatians and Scythians, which are not less barbarous and uncivilised than the Germanic tribes; but, even as I said before, all the world, from the rising to the setting sun, all the land in short on this side of the Ocean and beyond the Ocean, at which all the Roman people and all Italy rejoiced, and even all the Asiatic and European nations.

(11) For as they had never yet all together admired any emperor who had ever existed at that time, not expecting to have in future the possession, and use, and enjoyment of all private and public good things, but thinking that they actually had them already as a sort of superfluity of prosperity which happiness was waiting to fill to the brim: (12) accordingly now there was nothing else to be seen in any city, but altars, and victims, and sacrifices, and men clothed in white garments, and crowned with garlands, and wearing cheerful countenances, and displaying their joy by the brightness of their looks, and festivals, and assemblies, and musical contests, and horse-races, and revels, and feasts lasting the whole night long, with the music of the flute and of the lyre, and rejoicings, and holidays, and truces, and every kind of pleasure addressed to every one of the senses.

(13) On this occasion the rich were not better off than the poor, nor the men of high rank than the lowly, nor the creditors than the debtors, nor the masters than the slaves, since the occasion gave equal privileges and communities to all men, so that the age of Saturn, which is so celebrated by the poets was no longer looked upon as a fiction and a fable,[2] on account of the universal prosperity and happiness which reigned every where, and the absence of all grief and fear, and the daily and nightly exhibitions of joy and festivity throughout every house and throughout the whole people, which lasted continually without any interruption during the first seven months of his reign.

(14) But in the eighth month a severe disease attacked Gaius who had changed the manner of his living which was a little while before, while Tiberius was alive, very simple and on that account more wholesome than one of great sumptuousness and luxury; for he began to indulge in abundance of strong wine and eating of rich dishes, and in the abundant license of insatiable desires and great insolence, and in the unseasonable use of hot baths, and emetics, and then again in winebibbing and drunkenness, and returning gluttony, and in lust after boys and women, and in everything else which tends to destroy both soul and body, and all the bonds which unite and strengthen the two; for the rewards of temperance are health and strength, and the wages of intemperance are weakness and disease which bring a man near to death.

III. (15) Accordingly, when the news was spread abroad that he was sick while the weather was still suitable for navigation (for it was the beginning of the autumn, which is the last season during which nautical men can safely take voyages, and during which in consequence they all return from the foreign marts in every quarter to their own native ports and harbours of refuge, especially all who exercise a prudent care not to be compelled to pass the winter in a foreign country); they, forsaking their former life of delicateness and luxury, now wore mournful faces, and every house and every city became full of depression and melancholy, their grief being now equal to and counterbalancing the joy which they experienced a short time before. (16) For every portion of the habitable world was diseased in his sickness, feeling affected with a more terrible disease than that which was oppressing Gaius; for his sickness was that of the body alone, but the universal malady which was oppressing all men every where was one which attacked the vigour of their souls, their peace, their hopes, their participation in and enjoyment of all good things; (17) for men began to remember how numerous and how great are the evils which spring from anarchy, famine, and war, and the destruction of trees, and devastations, and deprivation of lands, and plundering of money, and

---

[2] The golden age was said to have existed during the reign of Saturn upon earth. So Tibullus and Virgil.

the intolerable fear of slavery and death, which no one can relieve, all which evils appeared to admit of but one remedy, namely the recovery of Gaius.

(18) Accordingly when his disease began to abate, in a very short time even the men who were living on the very confines of the empire heard of it and rejoiced, for nothing is swifter than report,[3] and immediately every city was full of suspense and expectation, being continually eager for better news, until at length his perfect recovery was announced by fresh arrivals, at which news they again returned to their original cheerfulness, each thinking the health of Gaius to be his own salvation; (19) and this feeling pervaded every continent and every island, for no one can recollect so great and general a joy affecting any one country or any one nation, at the good health or prosperity of their governor, as now pervaded the whole of the habitable world at the recovery of Gaius, and at his being able to resume the exercise of his power and having completely got rid of his sickness.

(20) For they all rejoiced, from ignorance of the truth, like men who are now for the first time beginning to exchange a wandering and uncivilised mode of life for a social and civilised system, and instead of dwelling in desert places, and the open air, and the mountain districts, to live in walled cities, and instead of living without any governor, or protector, or lawgiver, to be now established under the care of a governor to be a sort of shepherd and leader of a more domesticated flock; (21) for the human mind is apt to be blind towards the perception of what is really expedient and beneficial for it, being influenced rather by conjecture and notions of probability than by real knowledge.

IV. (22) At all events it was not long before Gaius—who was now looked upon as a saviour and benefactor, and who was expected to shower down some fresh and everlasting springs of benefits upon all Asia and Europe, so as to endow the inhabitants with inalienable happiness and prosperity, both separately to each individual and generally to the whole state—began, as the proverb has it, at home, and changed into a ferocity of disposition, or, I should rather say, displayed the savageness which he had previously overshadowed by pretence and hypocrisy; (23) for he put to death his cousin who had been left as the partner of his kingdom, and who was in fact a more natural successor to it than he himself; for he himself was only Tiberius's grandson by adoption, but the other was so by blood; arguing as a pretext that he had detected him in plotting against him, though his very age was a sufficient refutation of any such accusation; for the unhappy victim was only just emerging from boyhood, and beginning to rank

among the youths. (24) And, as some persons say, if Tiberius had lived a short time longer, Gaius would have been made away with, as he began to be looked upon by him with unalterable suspicion, and the genuine grandson of Tiberius would have been named the future emperor, and the inheritor of his paternal kingdom.

(25) But Tiberius was carried off by fate, before he could bring his designs to their completion; and Gaius thought that he should be able to escape all evil report which might arise from his transgressing the principles of justice with respect to his partner by outwitting him. (26) And the contrivance which he adopted was of the following character. Having assembled all the chief magistrates, he said: "I am desirous that he who is my cousin by birth and my brother in affection, in accordance with the instruction of Tiberius who is now dead, shall be a partner with me in my absolute authority. But you yourselves perceive that he is as yet a mere child, and that he is in need of masters, and teachers, and guardians; (27) since what can be a more desirable blessing for me than that my one mind and one body shall not be loaded with so great a weight of the cares of government, but for me to have some one who may be able to lighten and alleviate them by sharing them? I, therefore," said he: "passing over and being superior to all tutors, and masters, and guardians, register myself as his father, and him as my son."

V. (28) With these words he deceived both those who were present and the youth himself; for his proposal was a mere bait, his intention being not to invest him with the power which he expected, but to deprive him of even that which he already had, according to the law affecting coheirs and partners; and accordingly now he plotted against him with absolute fearlessness, having no regard for nor fear of any one; for by the laws of the Romans the most complete and absolute authority over the son belongs to the father, besides the fact of Gaius having the imperial authority which was wholly irresponsible, since no one could either venture or had any power to demand an account from him of any thing whatever that he might do.

(29) Accordingly, looking upon this youth to be like a thirds-man in the games, he proceeded to overthrow him, feeling no compassion, either for the fact of his having been brought up with him, or his being so nearly related to him, or for his age, but having no idea of sparing this miserable youth, doomed to an early death; his own partner in the government, his co-heir, who had formerly been expected to be all but the absolute emperor, by reason of his being the nearest relation to Tiberius; for when their fathers are dead, the grandsons are usually looked upon by their grandfathers as standing in the position of sons.

---

[3] So Virgil says, Aen. 4.174.

(30) It is said moreover, that this youth, being ordered to slay himself with his own hands, while a centurion and a captain of a thousand were standing by (who had been expressly commanded to take no part in the horrid deed, since it was not lawful for the descendants of the emperors to be put to death by any one else; for Gaius remembered the laws amid his lawless acts, and had some regard for piety in all his impious deeds, imitating as well as he could the nature of truth); he, not knowing how to kill himself, for he had never seen any one else put to death, and had never had any practice in fighting with weapons, which is the usual exercise and course of instruction for children who are being educated with a view to become leaders and rulers, on account of the wars which they may have to conduct, at first exhorted those officers who had come to him to put him to death themselves, stretching out his neck; (31) but when they did not dare to do so, he himself taking the sword inquired in his ignorance and want of experience what was the most mortal place, in order that by a well-directed blow he might cut short his miserable life; and they, like instructors in misery, led him on his way, and pointed out to him the part into which he was to thrust his sword; and he, having thus learnt his first and last lesson, became himself, miserable that he was, his own murderer under compulsion.

VI. (32) But when this first and greatest undertaking had been accomplished by Gaius, there being no longer left any one who had any connexion with the supreme authority, to whom any one who bore him ill-will, and who was suspected by him, could possibly turn his eyes; he now, in the second place, proceeded to compass the death of Macro, a man who had co-operated with him in every thing relating to the empire, not only after he had been appointed emperor, for it is a characteristic of flattery to court those who are in a state of prosperity, but who had previously assisted him in his measures for securing that authority.

(33) For Tiberius, who was a man of very profound prudence, and the most able to all the men of his court at perceiving the hidden intentions of any man, and who was as pre-eminent in intelligence and acuteness as he was in good fortune, did very often look with suspicion upon Gaius as being evil disposed towards all the house of Claudius, and as being related to him only on the mother's side,[4] and he feared for his grandson, lest he, being left a mere child, should be put to death by him. (34) And he judged him, moreover, very little fitted for an authority of such magnitude, both on account of the unsociableness and ferocity of his nature, and the inequality of his temper; for he was continually giving way to the most frantic and most inconsistent moods, not preserving any consistency either in his words or in his actions; (35) all which Macro studied with all his strength at every opportunity, pacifying the suspicions of Tiberius and all the prejudices with which he perceived that his mind was inflamed against Gaius by reason of his ceaseless fear and anxiety for his grandson.

(36) For he represented to him, that Gaius was a person of a good and obedient disposition, and one who entertained the greatest affection for his cousin, so that out of his exceeding regard for him he would be willing even to abandon the government and to yield it up to him by himself, but that excessive modesty was anything but advantageous to many persons, in consequence of which Gaius, who was of a most guileless and single-minded disposition, was looked upon by many as crafty and designing.

(37) And when he could not persuade him, by all the arguments drawn from probabilities which he advanced, he brought forward that which rested upon specific agreements, adding, "I myself will be his security, I who deserve to have confidence placed in me, inasmuch as I have given sufficient proof that I myself am individually a friend to Caesar, and a friend to Tiberius, since it was I who carried into execution, your intentions respecting the downfall of Sejanus.

(38) And, in short, he was very assiduous, and energetic, and comprehensive in his praises of Gaius, if, indeed, one may speak of speeches in defence of a man as equivalent to panegyrics on him, which were rather addressed to the doing away with the unfavourable impressions and suspicion, excited by obscure and indistinct hints and accusations. In short, all the things which any one could say on behalf of any brother or legitimate child, such and more too did Macro say to Tiberius in behalf of Gaius. (39) And the cause of this was according to the report which obtained among the generality of people, not only that Macro had, on the other hand, been greatly courted by him, as one who had the greatest, or, indeed, all the power under the empire; but also that Macro's wife was favourable to him, for a reason which ought not to be mentioned, and she every day urged on, and encouraged, and entreated her husband to omit no exertion of his zeal and energy on behalf of the young man. And a wife is a very powerful engine to divert or to persuade the mind of her husband, especially if she be one of an amorous temperament, for because of her own consciousness she becomes more given to flattery.

(40) And Macro, being ignorant of the dishonour done to his marriage-bed and to his family, and looking upon her flattery as a proof of her sincere good will and affection for him, was deceived, and

---

[4] Caligula was the son of Germanicus and Agrippina.

without being aware of it was led, by her intrigues, to embrace his bitterest enemies as his best friends.

VII. (41) Therefore, as he knew that he had preserved him ten thousand times, when he was in the most imminent danger of being put to death, he used to offer him undisguised, sincere, and honest admonitions and advice, with perfect freedom of speech; for, like a good workman, he was desirous that what he looked upon as his own work should remain uninjured and indestructible, without being put an end to, either by himself or by any one else; (42) therefore, whenever he saw him sleeping at any entertainment he would go round and awaken him, having, at the same time, a regard for what was becoming and also for his safety, for a man who is asleep is a good object for treachery; and whenever he beheld him looking with an excited eye at any dancers, or even sometimes dancing with them, or not smiling with dignity upon actors of farcical and laughable spectacles, but rather grinning like a boy, or wholly carried away by the tunes of some harp-player or chorus, so as on some occasions even to join in their song, he would, if he was sitting or going near him, give him a nudge, and endeavour to check him.

(43) And very often, when he was reclining near him, he would whisper in his ear, and admonish him gently and quietly, so that no one else might hear what was said, saying, "You ought not only not to be like any one else here, but like no one else whatever, neither at any spectacle, or at anything that is to be heard, or in anything else that ever affects the outward senses, but you ought rather to surpass all other men in every action of your life, as much as you surpass them in your good fortune, (44) for it is unreasonable for the ruler of all the earth and of all the sea to be subdued by a song or by an exhibition of dancing, or by any ridiculous jest or piece of acting, or by anything else of that kind; and not on every occasion, and in every place, to remember his position as emperor, like a shepherd and protector of the flock, availing himself of everything that can tend to any kind of amelioration, from every word, and from every action, of every description whatever."

(45) Then again he would add, "When you are present at any theatrical contest, or at any gymnastic games, or at any of the contests in the hippodrome, do not consider the pursuits themselves so much as the behaving correctly in all such pursuits, and entertain thoughts of this nature: (46) if some men labour in this manner to bring to perfection things that can in no respect benefit human life, but which only afford pleasure and amusement to the spectators, in such a way as to be praised and admired, and to receive rewards, and honours, and crowns, and to have their names proclaimed as conquerors; what ought that man to do who is skilful in the most sublime and most important of all arts? (47) Now the greatest and most excellent of all sciences is the science of government, by means of which every country which is good and fertile, whether it be champaign or mountainous, is cultivated, and every sea is navigated without danger by heavily-laden merchant-vessels, to communicate to the different countries the useful productions of each, out of a natural desire for participation and association, so that each land receives what it stands in need of, and sends abroad in requital those good things of which it has a superfluity; (48) for envy has never obtained a dominion over the whole of the habitable world, nor even over those great divisions of it, the whole of Europe or the whole of Asia, but it lurks in holes like a venomous reptile, creeping out in small districts to attack an individual man, or a single family, or, if it is very violent and powerful, perhaps one city; but it never attacks a larger circle of a whole nation or a whole country, especially ever since your august family has really begun to rule over all men in every part of the world.

(49) "For your house has discovered and brought to light everything that is good, even in the midst of evils, and has banished all evils to the extremities of the earth, and beyond its borders to the very depths of Tartarus, and has brought back, from the most distant borders of the earth and sea, those profitable and beneficial things which were in a manner banished into the habitable world around us; and now all these things are entrusted to your power, to be governed by your authority.

(50) "Accordingly you, having been conducted by nature to the supreme helm of the world, and having the government of everything placed in your hand, must guide the universal ship of all mankind in a safe and salutary manner, rejoicing and delighting in nothing more than in doing good to your subjects; (51) for different people have different contributions to bestow, which individuals necessarily offer in their several cities. But the most suitable gift for a ruler to give is to adopt wise counsels with respect to those who are subject to his authority, and to execute intentions which have been rightly formed, and to bestow on them good things without any limitation, with a liberal hand and mind, except such as it may be better to keep in reserve from a prudent foreknowledge of the uncertainty of the future."

VIII. (52) The unhappy man kept dinning suggestions of this kind into his ears in the hope of improving Gaius; but he, being a contentious and quarrelsome person, turned his mind in the directly opposite direction, as if he were exhorted to do exactly the contrary, and he conceived a most determined disgust for his monitor, so as never to behold him with a cheerful countenance; and sometimes when he saw him at a distance he would speak as follows to those near him: (53) "Here comes the teacher of one who has no longer any right to be looked upon as a pupil;—here comes the pedagogue of one who is no longer a child, the monitor of one who is wiser than himself, the man who thinks it proper that the emperor should obey his subject, who sets himself up as a man deeply versed by experience in the science of government, and as a teacher of it, though from whom he has learnt the principles of sovereign government I know not; (54) for from the moment that I left my cradle, I have had ten thousand instructors, fathers, brothers, uncles, cousins, and grandfathers, up to the very founders of my family, in fact every one related to me either on my father's or my mother's side, who had acquired absolute power for themselves, even without taking into consideration the fact that, by their being the authors of my being, they had implanted in me some degree of royal power and some natural aptitude for government. (55) For as similitudes of both body and soul exist both in the form, and position, and motions of men, and also as the inclinations, and dispositions, and actions of men are preserved in some degree of similitude through the principles of descent, so also is it probable that the very same principles should convey an outline of similitude in respect of one's aptitude for government. (56) Shall any one, then, who is ignorant dare to instruct me who am the reverse of ignorant? me who, even before my birth, while I was yet in my mother's womb, was fashioned as an emperor in the workshop of nature? For how can it be possible for persons, who but a short time before were private individuals, to contemplate as they should the intentions of an imperial soul? But some persons in their shameless audacity dare to put themselves forward as interpreters and perfecters of the principles of government, when in reality they scarcely ought to be enrolled among those who have any understanding whatever of the matter."

(57) And as he thus diligently laboured to alienate himself from Macro, he began also to invent false but plausible and specious grounds for blaming and accusing him; for passionate and irritable natures, especially when belonging to powerful men, are very ingenious at weaving plausibilities. Now, the pretexts which he made use of against him were of the following natures. (58) He said Macro thought thus: "Gaius is my work; the work of Macro. I am more truly, or at all events not less truly, his father than his own parents. He would have been destroyed, over and over again, by Tiberius, who thirsted for his blood, if it had not been for me and for my powers of persuasion. And moreover, when Tiberius was dead, I, who had under my command the whole force of the army, immed-

iately placed him in the position which Tiberius had occupied, teaching him that the state had indeed sustained a loss of one man, but that the imperial authority continued unaltered, as entire as ever."

(59) And many people have given credit to these assertions of his as if they were true, not being acquainted with the false and crafty disposition of the speakers; for hitherto the dishonest and designing character of his disposition was not made manifest. But a few days afterwards the miserable man was put to death, with his wife, receiving the extremity of punishment as a reward for his exceeding good will towards his slayer. (60) This is the consequence of doing kindnesses to ungrateful people; for in return for the benefits which they have received, they inflict the greatest of injuries on those from whom they have received them. Accordingly, Macro, who had done everything in sincerity with the most earnest eagerness and zeal for the good of Gaius, in the first place in order to save him from death, and afterwards in order that he by himself might succeed to the imperial authority, received for his reward the fate which I have mentioned.

(61) For it is said that the wretched man was compelled to kill himself with his own hand; and his wife, too, experienced the same misery, even though she indeed had at one time been believed to be on the most intimate terms of familiarity with Gaius; but they say that none of the allurements of love are stable and trustworthy because it is a passion which quickly breeds satiety.

IX. (62) But after Macro and all his house had been sacrificed, Gaius then began to design a third more grievous piece of treachery still. His father-in-law had been Marcus Silanus, a man full of wisdom, and very illustrious by birth. He, after his daughter had died by an early death, still was very attentive and affectionate to Gaius, showing all imaginable regard for him, not so much like a father-in-law as like an actual father, and he hoped that he should find that Gaius also entertained equal good will towards him, transforming himself according to the principles of equality from a son-in-law into a son; but he was, without knowing it, cherishing mistaken opinions, and deluding himself, (63) for he was continually uttering affectionate speeches, keeping back nothing which could tend to the amelioration and improvement of Gaius's disposition and way of life and mode of government, speaking with all freedom, and looking upon his own surpassing nobility of birth and nearness of connexion by marriage as circumstances which gave him grounds for great familiarity and openness, for his daughter had been dead only a very short time, so that the laws and bonds which bind such kinsmen were scarcely destroyed, and one may almost say were still quivering with life, some relics of the breath of vitality being still left, as it were, and remaining warm in the body. (64) But Gaius, looking upon every admonition as an insult, because he fancied that he himself was the wisest and most virtuous of all men, and moreover the most valorous and the most just, hated all who ventured to offer him instruction more than even his avowed enemies.

(65) Therefore, looking on Silanus as a bore, who only wished to check the impetuosity and indulgence of his appetites, and discarding all recollection of and regard for his deceased wife, he treacherously put her father to death, who was also his own father-in-law.

X. (66) And by this time the matter began to be widely talked about in consequence of the continual deaths of so many eminent men, so that now these things began to be spoken of in every mouth as intolerable infamy and wickedness; not indeed openly, from fear, but gently and under the breath, in whispers; (67) and then again, by a sudden change (for the multitude is very unstable in everything, in intentions, and words, and actions), men, disbelieving that one who but a little while before was merciful and humane could have become altered so entirely, for Gaius had been looked upon as affable, and sociable, and friendly, began to seek for excuses for him, and after some search they found such, saying with regard to his cousin and co-heir in the kingdom things such as these: (68) "The unchangeable law of nature has ordained that there should be no partnership in the sovereign power, and it has established by its own unalterable principles what this man must inevitably have suffered at the hands of his more powerful co-heir. The one who was the more powerful has chastised the other. This is not murder. Perhaps, indeed, the putting that youth to death was done providentially for the advantage of the whole human race, since if one portion had been assigned as subjects to the one, and another portion to the other, there would have arisen troubles and confusion, and civil and foreign war. And what is better than peace? and peace is caused by good government on sound principles. And no government can be good but that which is free from all contentions and from all disputes, and then everything else is made right by it."

(69) And in reference to the case of Macro, they said, "The man was puffed up with pride in an immoderate degree; he had no idea of that great lesson which came from Delphi, 'know thyself.' And they say that knowledge is the cause of happiness, and that ignorance is the parent of unhappiness. What could have possessed him to make such an alteration and change in their relative positions as to thrust himself, who was a subject, into the rank of a governor, and to depress Gaius, who was the emperor, into the place of a subject? For it is the part of a ruler to command, and that was what Macro did; but it is the duty of a subject to obey, and that was what he considered that Gaius was to submit to."

(70) For these inconsiderate men, without giving themselves the trouble of inquiring into the truth, called the recommendations of Macro commands, and called him who gave advice a governor, out of ignorance and insensibility, or else out of flattery suppressing the truth and giving a false colouring to the nature of both names and things.

(71) And in reference to Silanus they said, "Silanus was a most ridiculous person when he took it into his head that a father-in-law would have as much influence with his son-in-law as a real father has with a son. And yet even real fathers who are in a private station submit to their sons when they are in great offices and in places of high authority, being quite content with the second place; but this foolish man, even when he was no longer his father-in-law, kept on claiming privileges which did not belong to him, without perceiving that with the death of his daughter the connexion which had originated in the marriage of Gaius with her had also died, (72) for intermarriages are the bonds which unite families between which there is no kindred, changing alienation into near connexion; but when that bond is dissolved, then the union is dissolved likewise, especially when it is dissolved by a circumstance which cannot be altered or remedied, namely, by the death of the woman who was given in marriage into another family."

(73) Such conversations as these were held in every company, the speakers being wholly influenced by their wish that the emperor should not appear to be cruel; for as they had hoped that such humanity and gentleness was seated in the soul of Gaius as had not existed in either of the previous emperors, they thought it would be a most strange thing if he now made so great and so sudden a change to an entirely contrary disposition.

XI. (74) Having now, then, entirely accomplished the three undertakings above-mentioned, with reference to three most important divisions, two of them belonging to the country, one to the class of counsellors and the other to the knights, and the third affecting his own relations, and considering that now that he had thus put down the mightiest and most powerful of his foes, he must have struck all the rest with the utmost terror, alarming the counsellors by the death of Silanus (75) (for he was inferior to no one in the senate), and the knights by the execution of Macro (for he, like the leader of a chorus, had long been considered the very first man of the knights for reputation and glory), and all his blood relations by the slaughter of his cousin and joint inheritor of the kingdom, he no longer chose to remain fettered by the ordinary limits of human nature, but aspired to raise himself above them, and desired to be looked upon as a god.

(76) And at the beginning of this insane desire they say that he was influenced by such a train of reasoning as the following: for as the curators of the herds of other animals, namely cowherds, and goatherds, and shepherds, are neither oxen nor goats, nor sheep, but men who have received a more excellent portion, and a more admirable formation of mind and body; so in the same manner, said he, is it fitting that I who am the leader of the most excellent of all herds, namely, the race of mankind, should be considered as a being of a superior nature, and not merely human, but as one who has received a greater and more holy portion. (77) Accordingly, having impressed this idea on his mind, like a vain and foolish man as he was, he bore about in himself a fallacious fable and invention as if it had been a most undeniable truth; and after he had once carried his boldness and audacity to such a pitch as to compel the multitude to admit of his most impious deification, he attempted to do other things consistent with and conformable to it, and in this way he advanced up to the highest point by slow degrees as if he were ascending up steps.

(78) For he began at first to liken himself to those beings who are called demigods, such as Bacchus, and Hercules, and the twins of Lacedaemon; turning into utter ridicule Trophonius, and Amphiaraus, and Amphilochus, and others of the same kind, with all their oracles and secret ceremonies, in comparison of his own power. (79) In the next place, like an actor in a theatre, he was continually wearing different dresses at different times, taking at one time a lion's skin and a club, both gilded over; being then dressed in the character of Hercules; at another time he would wear a felt hat upon his head, when he was disguised in imitation of the Spartan twins, Castor and Pollux; sometimes he also adorned himself with ivy, and a thyrsus, and skins of fawns, so as to appear in the guise of Bacchus.

(80) And he looked upon himself as being in this respect superior to all of these beings, because each of them while he had his own peculiar honours had no claim to those which belonged to the others, but he in his envious ambition appropriated all the honours of the whole body of demigods at once, or I should rather say, appropriated the demigods themselves; transforming himself not into the triple-bodied Geryon, so as to attract all beholders by the multitude of his bodies; but, what was the most extraordinary thing of all, changing and transforming the essence of one body into every variety of form and figure, like the Egyptian Proteus, whom Homer has represented as being susceptible of every variety of transformation, into all the elements, and into the animals, and plants, which belong to the different elements.[5]

(81) And yet why, O Gaius! did you think yourself in need of spurious honours, such as the temples and statues of the beings above-mentioned are often filled with? You ought rather to have imitated their virtues. Hercules purified both the earth and the sea, performing labours of the greatest possible importance and of the highest benefit to all mankind, in order to eradicate all that was mischievous and calculated to injure the nature of each of the elements. (82) Bacchus rendered the vine susceptible of cultivation, and extracted a most delicious drink from it, which is at the same time most beneficial to the souls and bodies of men, leading the first to cheerfulness, working in them a forgetfulness of evils and a hope of blessings, and making the latter more healthy, and vigorous, and active, and supple. (83) And individually it renders each man better, and alters populous families and households, leading them from a squalid and laborious life of vexation to a course of relaxation and cheerful happiness, and causing to every city on earth, both Grecian and barbarian, incessant festivity, and mirth, and entertainment, and revelry; for of all these things is good wine the cause.

(84) Again, it is said that the twin sons of Jupiter, Castor and Pollux, are partakers of immortality. For since the one was mortal and the other immortal, the one who had had the more excellent portion assigned to him did not choose to behave in a selfish manner, but rather to display his good will and affection towards his brother; (85) for having acquired the idea that eternity was never-ending, and considering that he was to live for ever, and that his brother was to be dead for ever, and that in conjunction with his own immortality he should likewise be enduring an undying sorrow on account of his brother, he conceived and carried out a most marvellous system of counterbalancing, mingling mortality with himself and immortality with his brother, and thus he modified inequality, which is the beginning of all injustice, by equality, which is the fountain of justice.

---

[5] The passage in Homer is to be found at Odyssey 4.363. It is imitated more concisely by Virgil, Georg. 4.410, who makes Cyrene tell Aristaeus (which is thus translated by Pope)—"Instant he wears, elusive of the rape, / The mimic force of every savage shape: / Or glides with liquid lapse a murm'ring stream, / Or wrapt in flame, he glows at every limb. / Yet still retentive, with redoubled might / Thro' each vain passive form constrains his flight. / But when, his native shape resumed, he stands / Patient of conquest, and your cause demands; / The cause that urg'd the bold attempt declare, / And soothe the vanquish'd with a victor's prayer. / The bands relaxed, implore the seer to say / What godhead interdicts the wat'ry way."

XII. (86) All these beings, O Gaius! were admired on account of the benefits which they had conferred on mankind, and they are admired for them even up to the present time, and they were deservedly thought worthy of veneration and of the very highest honours. But come now, and tell us yourself in what achievement of yours do you pride yourself and boast yourself as being in the least similar to their actions? (87) Have you imitated the twin sons of Jupiter in their brotherly affection, that I may begin with that point? Did you not rather, O hard-hearted and most pitiless of men! inhumanly slaughter your brother, the joint inheritor of the kingdom with you, even before he had arrived at the full vigour of manhood, when he was still in early youth. Did you not afterwards banish your sisters, lest they also should cause you any reasonable apprehension of the deprivation and loss of your imperial power?

(88) Have you imitated Bacchus in any respect? Have you been an inventor of any new blessings to mankind? Have you filled the whole of the habitable world with joy as he did? Are all Asia and Europe inadequate to contain the gifts which have been showered upon mankind by you? (89) No doubt you have invented new arts and sciences, like a common pest and murderer of your kind, by which you have changed all pleasant and acceptable things into vexation and sorrow, and have made life miserable and intolerable to all men everywhere, appropriating to yourself in your intolerable and insatiable greediness all the good and beautiful things which belonged to every one else, whether from the east or from any other country of the universe, carrying off everything from the south, everything from the north, and in requital giving to and pouring down upon those whom you had plundered every sort of mischievous and injurious things from your own bitter spirit, everything which is ever engendered in cruel, and destructive, and envenomed dispositions; these are the reasons why you appeared to us as a new Bacchus.

(90) But I suppose you imitated Hercules in your unwearied labours and your incessant displays of valour and virtue; you, O most wretched of men! having filled every continent and every island with good laws, and principles of justice, and wealth, and comfort, and prosperity, and abundance of other blessings, you, wretched man, full of all cowardice and iniquity, who have emptied every city of all the things which can conduce to stability and prosperity, and have made them full of everything which leads to trouble and confusion, and the most utter misery and desolation.

(91) Tell me then, O Gaius! do you, after having made all these contributions to universal destruction, do you, I say, seek to acquire immortality in order to make the calamities which you have heaped upon mankind, not of brief duration and short-lived, but imperishable and everlasting? But I think, on the contrary, that even if you had previously appeared to be a god, you would beyond all question have been changed on account of your evil practices into an ordinary nature, resembling that of common perishable mortals; for if virtues can make their possessors immortal, then beyond all doubt vices can make them mortal. (92) Do not, therefore, inscribe your name by the side of that of the twin sons of Jupiter, those most affectionate of deities, you who have been the murderer and destruction of your brethren, nor claim a share in the honours of Hercules or Bacchus, who have benefited human life. You have been the undoer and destroyer of those good effects which they produced.

XIII. (93) But the madness and frenzy to which he gave way were so preposterous, and so utterly insane, that he went even beyond the demigods, and mounted up to and invaded the veneration and worship paid to those who are looked upon as greater than they, as the supreme deities of the world, Mercury, and Apollo, and Mars.

(94) And first of all he dressed himself up with the caduceus, and sandals, and mantle of Mercury, exhibiting a regularity in his disorder, a consistency in his confusion, and a ratiocination in his insanity.

(95) Afterwards, when he thought fit to do so, he laid aside these ornaments, and metamorphosed and transformed himself into Apollo, crowning his head with garlands, in the form of rays, and holding a bow and arrows in his left hand, and holding forth graces in his right, as if it became him to proffer blessings to all men from his ready store, and to display the best arrangement possible on his right hand, but to contract the punishments which he had it in his power to inflict, and to allot to them a more confined space on his left. (96) And immediately there were established choruses, who had been carefully trained, singing paeans to him, the same who had, a little while before, called him Bacchus, and Evius, and Lyaeus, and sang Bacchic hymns in his honour when he assumed the disguise of Bacchus.

(97) Very often, also, he would clothe himself with a breastplate, and march forth sword in hand, with a helmet on his head and a shield on his left arm, calling himself Mars, and on each side of him there marched with him the attendants of this new and unknown Mars, a troop of murderers and executioners who had already performed him all kinds of wicked services when he was raging and thirsting for human blood; (98) and then when men saw this they were amazed and terrified at the marvellous sight, and they wondered how a man who did exactly the contrary to what was done by those beings to whom he claimed to be equal in honour, did not choose to imitate their virtues, but assumed the outward character of each with the most abom-

inable conduct. And yet all those ornaments and decorations which belonged to them were attached to his statues and images, which indicated by symbols the benefits which the beings who are thus honoured confer upon the race of mankind. (99) Mercury, for instance, requires wings attached to his ankles. Why so? Is it not because it behoves him to be the interpreter and declarer of the will of the gods (from which employment, in fact, he derives his Greek name of Hermes[6]), announcing good news to mankind (for not only no god but no sensible man ever will become the messenger of evil), and therefore it is necessary for him to be exceedingly swift-footed, and all but winged, from the unhesitating rapidity with which he requires the proceed. Since it is right that beneficial news should be announced with great promptness, just as bad news ought to be brought slowly, unless indeed any one should prefer saying that such ought to be entirely suppressed in silence.

(100) Again, he takes with him his caduceus or herald's wand, as a token of reconciliation and peace, for wars receive their respites and terminations by means of heralds, who restore peace; and wars which have no heralds to terminate them cause endless calamities to both parties, both to those who invade their neighbours and to those who are endeavouring to repel the invasion. (101) But for what purpose did Gaius assume the winged sandals of Mercury? Was it because he wished to spread with power, and rapidity, and loudness that miserable and ill-omened intelligence which ought rather to be buried in silence altogether, conveying his voice everywhere with unceasing celerity? And yet what need had he of such rapid motion? for even while standing still he poured forth unspeakable evils upon evils as if from an unceasing fountain, showering them down upon every portion of the habitable world. (102) And of what use was the herald's wand to him, who never either said or did anything bearing upon peace, but who rather filled every house and every city within Greece and in the countries of the barbarians with civil wars? Let him, therefore, imposter that he is, lay aside the name of Mercury, since by assuming it he is only profaning an appellation which does not belong to him.

XIV. (103) Again, of all the attributes of Apollo, what is there which in the least degree resembles his characteristics? He wears a crown emitting rays all around, the artist who made it having given a most admirable representation of the beams of the sun; but how can the sun, or in fact any light at all, be a welcome object to him, and not rather night, or anything else, if there be such more com-

pletely enveloped darkness, or even anything darker than darkness itself, for the performance of his lawless actions? Since good actions do require the brilliancy of noonday for their proper display, but shameful actions, as they say, are suited to the extreme depths of Tartarus, into which they ought to be thrust in order to be concealed from sight, as is becoming. (104) Let him also transpose the things which he bears in each of his hands, and not pollute the proper arrangement, for let him bear his arrows and his bow in his right hand, for he knows how with good aim to shoot at and to pierce men and women, and whole families, and populous cities, to their complete destruction. (105) And let him either at once throw away his graces altogether, or else let him keep them in the shade in his left hand, for he has defaced their beauty, directing all his eyes and exciting all his desires against vast properties, so as to plunder them in an iniquitous manner, in consequence of which their owners were murdered, finding themselves unfortunate through their good fortune.

(106) But no doubt he with great felicity gave a new representation of the medical skill of Apollo, for this god was the inventor of healing medicines,[7] so as to cause health to men, thinking fit himself to heal the diseases which were inflicted by others, by reason of the excessive mildness and gentleness of his own nature and habits, (107) but this man, on the contrary, loads those who are in good health with disease, and inflicts mutilations on those who are sound, and in short visits the living with most cruel death, caused by the hand of man before the time of their natural death, preparing every imaginable engine of destruction in abundant plenteousness, by means of which, if he had not himself been previously put to death in accordance with justice, everything glorious or respectable in every city would long ago have been destroyed.

(108) For his designs were prepared against all those in authority and all those possessed of riches, and especially against those in Rome and those in the rest of Italy, by whom such quantities of gold and silver had been treasured up that even if all the riches of all the rest of the habitable world had been collected together from its most distant borders, it would have been found to be very inferior in amount.

On this account he began, he, this hater of the

---

[6] *i.e.* from *hermēneuō*, "to interpret."

[7] This is one of the attributes of Apollo of which he boasts to Daphne, Met. l. 461 (as it is translated by Dryden)—"Medicine is mine; what herbs and simples grow / In fields and forests, all their powers I know, / And am the great physician called below. / Alas, that fields and forests can afford / No remedies to heal their lovesick lord. / To cure the pains of love no plant avails, / And his own physic the physician fails."

citizens, this devourer of the people, this pestilence, this destructive evil, began to banish all the seeds of peace from his country, as if he were expelling evil from holy ground; (109) for Apollo is said to have been not only a physician but also an excellent prophet, by his oracular predictions announcing what was likely to conduce to the advantage of mankind, in order that no one, being overshadowed by uncertainty, going on without seeing his way before him like a blind man, might hastily fall into unexpected evils as if they were the greatest benefits; but that men having previously acquired a knowledge of the future as if it were really present, and looking at it with the eye of their mind, might guard against future evils just as they can see evils actually before them with the bodily eye, and in this way secure themselves against any irremediable disaster.

(110) Is it fitting now to compare with these oracles of Apollo the ill-omened warning of Gaius, by means of which poverty, and dishonour, and banishment, and death were given premature notice of to all those who were in power and authority in any part of the world? What connexion or resemblance was there between him and Apollo, when he never paid any attention to any ties of kindred or friendship? Let him cease, then, this pretended Apollo, from imitating that real healer of mankind, for the form of God is not a thing which is capable of being imitated by an inferior one, as good money is imitated by bad.

XV. (111) A man, indeed, may expect anything rather than that a man endowed with such a body and such a soul, when both of them are effeminate and broken down, could ever possibly be made like to the vigour of Mars in either particular; but this man, like a mummer transforming himself on the stage, putting on all sorts of masks one after another, sought to deceive the spectators by a series of fictitious appearances. (112) Come, then, let him be subjected to an examination in respect of all the particulars of his soul and body, by reason of his utter unlikeness to the aforesaid deity in every position and in every motion. Was he not utterly unlike Mars, not in respect only of his appearance as celebrated in fable, but as to his natural qualities? Mars, who is endued with pre-eminent valour, which we know to be a power calculated to avert evil, to be the assistant and ally of all who are unjustly oppressed, as indeed his very name shows, (113) for he appears to me to be called Mars from his helping,[8] which is the same as assisting, being as such the god who is able to put down wars and to cause peace, of which this representation of his was the enemy, being the comrade of wars, and the man who changed peace and stability into disorder and confusion.

XVI. (114) Have we not, then, learned from all these instances, that Gaius ought not to be likened to any god, and not even to any demi-god, inasmuch as he has neither the same nature, nor the same essence, nor even the same wishes and intentions as any one of them; but appetite as it seems is a blind thing, and especially so when it takes to itself vain-gloriousness and ambition in conjunction with the greatest power, by which we who were previously unfortunate are utterly destroyed, (115) for he regarded the Jews with most especial suspicion, as if they were the only persons who cherished wishes opposed to his, and who had been taught in a manner from their very swaddling-clothes by their parents, and teachers, and instructors, and even before that by their holy laws, and also by their unwritten maxims and customs, to believe that there was but one God, their Father and the Creator of the world; (116) for all others, all men, all women, all cities, all nations, every country and region of the earth, I had almost said the whole of the inhabited world, although groaning over what was taking place, did nevertheless flatter him, dignifying him above measure, and helping to increase his pride and arrogance; and some of them even introduced the barbaric custom into Italy of falling down in adoration before him, adulterating their native feelings of Roman liberty.

(117) But the single nation of the Jews, being excepted from these actions, was suspected by him of wishing to counteract his desires, since it was accustomed to embrace voluntary death as an entrance to immortality, for the sake of not permitting any of their national or hereditary customs to be destroyed, even if it were of the most trivial character, because, as is the case in a house, it often happens that by the removal of one small part, even those parts which appeared to be solidly established fall down, being relaxed and brought to decay by the removal of that one thing, (118) but in this case what was put in motion was not a trifle, but a thing of the very greatest importance, namely, the erecting the created and perishable nature of a man, as far at least as appearance went, into the uncreated and imperishable nature of God, which the nation correctly judged to be the most terrible of all impieties (for it would have been easier to change a god into man, than a man into God), besides the fact of such an action letting in other most enormous wickedness, infidelity and ingratitude towards the Benefactor of the whole world, who by his own power givers abundant supplies of all kinds of blessings to every part of the universe.

XVII. (119) Therefore a most terrible and irreconcileable war was prepared against our nation,

---

[8]The Greek word is *arēgein*, from which Philo supposes *Arēs*, the Greek name of Mars, to be derived.

for what could be a more terrible evil to a slave than a master who was an enemy? And his subjects are the slaves of the emperor, even if they were not so to any one of the former emperors, because they governed with gentleness and in accordance with the laws, but now that Gaius had eradicated all feelings of humanity from his soul, and had admired lawlessness (for looking upon himself as the law, he abrogated all the enactments of other lawgivers in every state and country as so many vain sentences), we were properly to be looked upon not only as slaves, but as the very lowest and most dishonoured of slaves, now that our ruler was changed into our master.

XVIII. (120) And the mixed and promiscuous multitude of the Alexandrians perceiving this, attacked us, looking upon it as a most favourable opportunity for doing so, and displayed all the arrogance which had been smouldering for a long period, disturbing everything, and causing universal confusion, (121) for they began to crush our people as if they had been surrendered by the emperor for the most extreme and undeniable miseries, or as if they had been subdued in war, with their frantic and most brutal passion, forcing their way into their houses, and driving out the owners, with their wives and children, which they rendered desolate and void of inhabitants. (122) And no longer watching for night and darkness, like ordinary robbers out of fear of being detected, they openly plundered them of all their furniture and treasures, carrying them off in broad daylight, and displaying their booty to every one whom they met, as if they had inherited it or fairly purchased it from the owners.

And if a multitude joined together to share any particular piece of plunder, they divided it in the middle of the market-place, reviling it and turning it all into ridicule before the eyes of its real owners. (123) These things were of themselves terrible and grievous; how could they be otherwise? Surely it was most miserable for men to become beggars from having been wealthy, and to be reduced on a sudden from a state of abundance to one of utter indigence, without having done any wrong, and to be rendered houseless and homeless, being driven out and expelled from their own houses, that thus, being compelled to dwell in the open air day and night, they might be destroyed by the burning heat of the sun or by the cold of the night.

(124) Yet even these evils were lighter than those which I am about to mention; for when the populace had driven together these countless myriads of men, and women, and children, like so many herds of sheep and oxen, from every quarter of the city, into a very narrow space as if into a pen, they expected that in a few days they should find a heap of corpses all huddled together, as they would either have perished by hunger through the

want of necessary food, as they had not prepared themselves with any thing requisite, through a foreknowledge of the evils which thus suddenly came upon them; (125) or else through being crushed and suffocated from want of any adequate space to breathe in, all the air around them becoming tainted, and all that there was of vivifying power in their respiration being cut off, or, if one is to say the truth, utterly expelled, by the breath of those who were expiring among them. By which, each individual being inflamed, and in a manner oppressed by a descent of fever upon him, inhaled a hot and unwholesome breath through his nostrils and mouth, heaping, as the proverb has it, fire on fire; (126) for the power which resides in the inmost parts changed its nature, and became most excessively fiery; upon which, when the external breezes, being moderately cool, blow, all the organs of the respiratory powers flourish, and are in a good and healthy condition; but when these breezes change and become hot, then those organs must of necessity be in a bad state, fire being added to fire.

XIX. (127) As they then were no longer able to endure the misery of the place within which they were enclosed, they poured forth into desolate parts of the wilderness, and to the shore, and among the tombs, in their eagerness to find any pure and untainted air. And if any of them had previously been left in the other parts of the city, or if any had come in thither from the fields out of ignorance of the evils which had visited their companions, they fell into every variety of misfortune, being stoned, or else wounded with sharp tiles, or beaten on the most mortal parts of the body, and especially on the head, with branches of maple and of oak, in such a way as to cause death.

(128) And some of those persons who are accustomed to pass their time in idleness and inaction, sitting around, occupied themselves in watching those who, as I have said before, were thus driven together and crammed into a very small space, as if they were a force which they were blockading; lest any one should secretly escape without their perceiving it. And a great many were designing to effect their escape from want of necessaries, disregarding their own safety from a fear that, if they remained, the whole body might perish with famine. So those men, expecting that they would endeavour to escape, kept a continual watch, and the moment that they caught any one, they immediately put him to death with every circumstance of insult and cruelty.

(129) And there was another company lying in wait for them on the quays of the river, to catch any Jews who arrived at those spots, and to plunder them of every thing which they brought for the purposes of traffic; for, forcing their way into their ships they took out the cargo before the eyes of

its lawful owners, and then, binding the hands of the merchants behind them, they burnt them alive, taking the rudders, and helms, and punt-poles, and the benches for the rowers to sit upon, for fuel. (130) And thus these men perished by a most miserable death being burnt alive in the middle of the city; for sometimes, for want of other timber they brought piles of faggots together, and tying them up, they threw them on the miserable victims; and they, being already half burnt, were killed, more by the smoke of the green wood than by the flames, as the new faggots gave forth only an unsubstantial and smoky sort of flame, and were soon extinguished, not being able to be reduced to ashes by reason of their lightness.

(131) And many who were still alive they took and bound, and fastened their ankles together with thongs and ropes, and then dragged them through the middle of the market-place, leaping on them, and not sparing their corpses even after they were dead; for, tearing them to pieces limb from limb, and trampling on them, behaving with greater brutality and ferocity than even the most savage beasts, they destroyed every semblance of humanity about them, so that not even a fragment of them was left to which the rites of burial could be afforded.

XX. (132) But as the governor of the country, who by himself could, if he had chosen to do so, have put down the violence of the multitude in a single hour, pretended not to see what he did see, and not to hear what he did hear, but allowed the mob to carry on the war against our people without any restraint, and threw our former state of tranquillity into confusion, the populace being excited still more, proceeded onwards to still more shameless and more audacious designs and treachery, and, arraying very numerous companies, cut down some of the synagogues (and there are a great many in every section of the city), and some they razed to the very foundations, and into some they threw fire and burnt them, in their insane madness and frenzy, without caring for the neighbouring houses; for there is nothing more rapid than fire, when it lays hold of fuel.

(133) I omit to mention the ornaments in honour of the emperor, which were destroyed and burnt with these synagogues, such as gilded shields, and gilded crowns, and pillars, and inscriptions, for the sake of which they ought even to have abstained from and spared the other things; but they were full of confidence, inasmuch as they did not fear any chastisement at the hand of Gaius, as they well knew that he cherished an indescribable hatred against the Jews, so that their opinion was that no one could do him a more acceptable service than by inflicting every description of injury on the nation which he hated; (134) and, as they wished to curry favour with him by a novel kind of flattery, so as to allow, and for the future to give the rein to, every sort of ill treatment of us without ever being called to account, what did they proceed to do? All the synagogues that they were unable to destroy by burning and razing them to the ground, because a great number of Jews lived in a dense mass in the neighbourhood, they injured and defaced in another manner, simultaneously with a total overthrow of their laws and customs; for they set up in every one of them images of Gaius, and in the greatest, and most conspicuous, and most celebrated of them they erected a brazen statue of him borne on a four-horse chariot. (135) And so excessive and impetuous was the rapidity of their zeal, that, as they had not a new chariot for four horses ready, they got a very old one out of the gymnasium, full of poison, mutilated in its ears, and in the hinder part, and in its pedestal, and in many other points, and as some say, one which had already been dedicated in honour of a woman, the eminent Cleopatra, who was the great grandmother of the last.

(136) Now what amount of accusation he brought against those who had dedicated this chariot on this very account is notorious to every one; for what did it signify if it was a new one and belonging to a woman? Or what if it was an old one and belonging to a man? And what, in short, if it was wholly dedicated to the name of some one else? Was it not natural that those who were offering up a chariot of this sort on behalf of the emperor should be full of cautious fear, lest some one might lay an information against them before our emperor, who took such especial care that every thing which at all affected or related to himself should be done in the most dignified manner possible?

(137) But these men expected to be most extravagantly praised, and to receive greater and more conspicuous advantages as rewards for their conduct, in thus dedicating the synagogues to Gaius as new pieces of consecrated ground, not because of the honour which was done to him by this proceeding, but because in this way they exhausted every possible means of insulting and injuring our nation. (138) And one may find undeniable and notorious proofs of this having been the case.

For, in the first place, one may derive them from about ten kings or more who reigned in order, one after another, for three hundred years, and who never once had any images or statues of themselves erected in our synagogues, though there were many of their relations and kinsmen whom they considered, and registered as, and spoke of as gods. (139) And what would they not have done in the case of those whom they looked upon as men? a people who look upon dogs, and wolves, and lions, and crocodiles, and numerous other beasts, both terrestrial and aquatic, and numerous birds, as gods, and erect in their honour altars, and temples, and shrines, and consecrated precincts, throughout the whole of Egypt?

XXI. (140) Perhaps some people who would not have opened their mouths then will say now: "They were accustomed to pay respect to the good deeds done by their governors rather than to their governors themselves, because the emperors are greater than the Ptolemies, both in their dignities and in their fortunes, and are justly entitled to receive higher honours. (141) Then, O ye most foolish of all mankind! that I may not be compelled to utter any thing disrespectful or blasphemous, why did you never think Tiberius, who was emperor before Gaius, who indeed was the cause that Gaius ever became emperor, who himself enjoyed the supreme power by land and sea for three and twenty years, and who never allowed any seed of war to smoulder or to raise its head, either in Greece or in the territory of the barbarians, and who bestowed peace and the blessings of peace up to the end of his life with a rich and most bounteous hand and mind upon the whole empire and the whole world; why, I say, did you not consider him worthy of similar honour? (142) Was he inferior in birth? No; he was of the most noble blood by both parents. Was he inferior in his education? Who, of all the men who flourished in his time, was either more prudent or more eloquent? Or in his age? What king or emperor ever lived to more prosperous old age than he? Moreover, he, even while he was still a young man, was called the old man as a mark of respect because of his exceeding wisdom. This man, though he was so wise, and so good, and so great, was passed over and disregarded by you.

(143) Again, why did you not pay similar honour to him who exceeded the common race of human nature in every virtue, who, by reason of the greatness of his absolute power and his own excellence, was the first man to be called Augustus, not receiving the title after another by a succession of blood as a part of his inheritance, but who was himself the origin of his successors, having that title and honour? He who first became emperor, when all the affairs of the state were in disorder and confusion; (144) for the islands were in a state of war against the continents, and the continents were contending with the islands for the pre-eminence in honour, each having for their leaders and champions the most powerful and eminent of the Romans who were in office. And then again, great sections of Asia were contending against Europe, and Europe against Asia, for the chief power and dominion;[9] the European and Asiatic nations rising up from the extremities of the earth, and waging terrible wars against one another over all the earth, and over every sea, with enormous armaments, so that very nearly the whole race of mankind would have been destroyed by mutual slaughter and made utterly to disappear, if it had not been for one man and leader, Augustus, by whose means they were brought to a better state, and therefore we may justly call him the averter of evil.

(145) This is Caesar, who calmed the storms which were raging in every direction, who healed the common diseases which were afflicting both Greeks and barbarians, who descended from the south and from the east, and ran on and penetrated as far as the north and the west, in such a way as to fill all the neighbouring districts and waters with unexpected miseries. (146) This is he who did not only loosen but utterly abolish the bonds in which the whole of the habitable world was previously bound and weighed down. This is he who destroyed both the evident and the unseen wars which arose from the attacks of robbers. This is he who rendered the sea free from the vessels of pirates, and filled it with merchantmen.[10] (147) This is he who gave freedom to every city, who brought disorder into order, who civilized and made obedient and harmonious, nations which before his time were unsociable, hostile, and brutal. This is he who increased Greece by many Greeces, and who Greecised the regions of the barbarians in their most important divisions: the guardian of peace, the distributor to every man of what was suited to him, the man who proffered to all the citizens favours with the most ungrudging liberality, who never once in his whole life concealed or reserved for himself any thing that was good or excellent.

XXII. (148) Now this man who was so great a benefactor to them for the space of three and forty years, during which he reigned over Egypt, they passed over in silence and neglect, never erecting any thing in their synagogues to do him honour; no image, no statue, no inscription.

(149) And yet if ever there was a man to whom it was proper that new and unprecedented honours should be voted, it was certainly fitting that such

---

[9] He alludes here to the war between Caesar and Pompey. Pompey had been governor of Syria, and Virgil speaks of him as relying on his eastern forces, Aen. 6.832 (as it is translated by Dryden)—"The pair you see in equal armour shine, / Now, friends below, in close embraces join; / But when they leave the shady realms of night, / And clothed in bodies breathe your upper light, / With mortal hate each other shall pursue, / What wars, what wounds, what slaughter shall ensue. / From Alpine heights the father first descends, / His daughter's husband in the plain attends, / His daughter's husband arms his eastern friends."

[10] He is attributing an honour to Augustus which does not belong to him. It was Pompey who cleared the sea of pirates.

should be decreed to him, not only because he was as it were the origin and fountain of the family of Augustus, not because he was the first, and greatest, and universal benefactor, having, instead of the multitude of governors who existed before, entrusted the common vessel of the state to himself as one pilot of admirable skill in the science of government to steer and govern; for the verse,

"The government of many is not good,"[11]

is very properly expressed, since a multitude of votes is the cause of every variety of evil; but also because the whole of the rest of the habitable world had decreed him honours equal to those of the Olympian gods. (150) And we have evidence of this in the temples, and porticoes, and sacred precincts, and groves, and colonnades which have been erected, so that all the cities put together, ancient and modern, which exhibit magnificent works, are surpassed, by the beauty and magnitude of the buildings erected in honour of Caesar, and especially by those raised in our city of Alexandria.

(151) For there is no sacred precinct of such magnitude as that which is called the Grove of Augustus, and the temple erected in honour of the disembarkation of Caesar, which is raised to a great height, of great size, and of the most conspicuous beauty, opposite the best harbour; being such an one as is not to be seen in any other city, and full of offerings, in pictures, and statues; and decorated all around with silver and gold; being a very extensive space, ornamented in the most magnificent and sumptuous manner with porticoes, and libraries, and men's chambers, and groves, and propylaea, and wide, open terraces, and court-yards in the open air, and with everything that could contribute to use or beauty; being a hope and beacon of safety to all who set sail, or who came into harbour.

XXIII. (152) Therefore, though they had such admirable pretexts for such conduct, and all the nations in every part of the world inclined to agree with them, they nevertheless neither made any innovations in their synagogues, but kept the law in every particular; and refused any marks of respect and veneration which might have been looked upon as due to Caesar. Perhaps some cautious and sensible person may ask: "Why were all these honours denied to him?" I will tell the reason, without suppressing any thing.

(153) They were aware of the attention which he paid to every thing, and of the very exceeding care which he took that the national laws and customs prevailing in each nation should be confirmed and preserved, being equally anxious for the preservation of the rights of foreign nations in this respect, as for those of the Romans; and that he received his honours, not for the destruction of the laws existing in any people, filling himself with pride and arrogance, but in a spirit of proper conformity with the magnitude of so vast an empire, which is dignified and honoured by such marks of respect being paid to the emperor.

(154) And there is most undeniable proof that he was never influenced or puffed up by the excessive honours paid to him, in the fact that he did not approve of any one's addressing him as master or god, but if any one used such expressions he was angry; and we may see it too in his approbation of the Jews, who he well knew most religiously avoided all such language.

(155) How then did he look upon the great division of Rome which is on the other side of the river Tiber, which he was well aware was occupied and inhabited by the Jews? And they were mostly Roman citizens, having been emancipated; for, having been brought as captives into Italy, they were manumitted by those who had bought them for slaves, without ever having been compelled to alter any of their hereditary or national observances. (156) Therefore, he knew that they had synagogues, and that they were in the habit of visiting them, and most especially on the sacred sabbath days, when they publicly cultivate their national philosophy. He knew also that they were in the habit of contributing sacred sums of money from their first fruits and sending them to Jerusalem by the hands of those who were to conduct the sacrifices. (157) But he never removed them from Rome, nor did he ever deprive them of their rights as Roman citizens, because he had a regard for Judaea, nor did he never meditate any new steps of innovation or rigour with respect to their synagogues, nor did he forbid their assembling for the interpretation of the law, nor did he make any opposition to their offerings of first fruits; but he behaved with such piety towards our countrymen, and with respect to all our customs, that he, I may almost say, with all his house, adorned our temple with many costly and magnificent offerings, commanding that continued sacrifices of whole burnt offerings should be offered up for ever and ever every day from his own revenues, as a first fruit of his own to the most high God, which sacrifices are performed to this very day, and will be performed for ever, as a proof and specimen of a truly imperial disposition.

(158) Moreover, in the monthly divisions of the country, when the whole people receives money or corn in turn, he never allowed the Jews to fall short in their reception of this favour, but even if it happened that this distribution fell on the day of their sacred sabbath, on which day it is not lawful for them to receive any thing, or to give any

---

[11] Hom. Il. 2:204.

thing, or in short to perform any of the ordinary duties of life, he charged the dispenser of these gifts, and gave him the most careful and special injunctions to make the distribution to the Jews on the day following, that they might not lose the effects of his common kindness.

XXIV. (159) Therefore, all people in every country, even if they were not naturally well inclined towards the Jewish nation, took great care not to violate or attack any of the Jewish customs of laws. And in the reign of Tiberius things went on in the same manner, although at that time things in Italy were thrown into a great deal of confusion when Sejanus was preparing to make his attempt against our nation; (160) for he knew immediately after his death that the accusations which had been brought against the Jews who were dwelling in Rome were false calumnies, inventions of Sejanus, who was desirous to destroy our nation, which he knew alone, or above all others, was likely to oppose his unholy counsels and actions in defence of the emperor, who was in great danger of being attacked, in violation of all treaties and of all honesty.

(161) And he sent commands to all the governors of provinces in every country to comfort those of our nation in their respective cities, as the punishment intended to be inflicted was not meant to be inflicted upon all, but only on the guilty; and they were but few. And he ordered them to change none of the existing customs, but to look upon them as pledges, since the men were peaceful in their dispositions and natural characters, and their laws trained them and disposed them to quiet and stability.

XXV. (162) But Gaius puffed himself up with pride, not only saying, but actually thinking that he was a god. And then he found no people, whether among the Greeks or among the barbarians, more suitable than the Alexandrians to confirm him in his immoderate and unnatural ambition; for they are in an extraordinary degree inclined to flattery, and trick, and hypocrisy, being thoroughly furnished with all kinds of cajoling words, and prone to confuse every thing with their unbridled and licentious talk. (163) And the name of God is held in so little veneration among them, that they have given it to ibises, and to the poisonous asps which are found in their country, and to many other savage beasts which exist in it. So that they, very naturally, giving in to all kinds of addresses and invocations to him, addressed him as God, deceiving men of shallow comprehension, who were wholly inexperienced in the impiety prevailing in Egypt, though they are detected by those who are acquainted with their excessive folly, or, I should rather say, with their preposterous impiety.

(164) Of which, Gaius, having no experience, imagined that he was really believed by the Alexandrians to be God, since they, without any disguise, openly and plainly used all the appellations without any limitation, with which they were accustomed to invoke the other gods. (165) In the next place, he believed that the innovations which they made with respect to their synagogues, were all made with a pure conscience, and from a sincere honour and respect for him, partly being influenced by the ephemerides in the way of memorial, which some persons sent him from Alexandria; for these things were what he very much delighted to read, to such a degree that the writings of all other authors, whether in prose or in poetry, were looked upon by him as absolutely odious in comparison with the delight which these documents afforded him, and partly by the language of some of his domestics, who were continually jesting with him and ridiculing all serious things.

XXVI. (166) The greater portion of these men were Egyptians, wicked, worthless men, who had imprinted the venom and evil disposition of their native asps and crocodiles on their own souls, and gave a faithful representation of them there. And the leader of the whole Egyptian troops, like the coryphaeus of a chorus, was a man of the name of Helicon, an accursed and infamous slave, who had been introduced into the imperial household to its ruin; for he had acquired a slight smattering of the encyclical sciences, by imitation of and rivalry with his former master, who gave him to Tiberius Caesar. (167) And at that time he had no especial privilege, since Tiberius had a perfect hatred of all youthful sallies of wit for the mere purposes of amusement, as he, from almost his earliest youth, was of a solemn and austere disposition.

(168) But when Tiberius was dead, and Gaius succeeded to the empire, he then, following a new master, who invited him to every description of relaxation and luxury, such as could delight every one of his outward senses, said to himself: "Rise up, O Helicon! now is your opportunity. You have now an auditor, and a spectator, who is of all men in the world the best calculated to receive the exhibition of your talents favourably. You are a man of very attractive natural talents. You are able to joke graceful, and to say witty, things beyond any one else. You are skilful in all kinds of amusements, and trifling, and fashionable sports. And you are equally accomplished in those branches of the encyclical education which are not so ordinarily met with. Moreover, you have a readiness of speech and repartee which is far from unpleasing. (169) If therefore you mingle with your jestings any little stimulus which is in the least unwelcome or painful, so as to excite not only laughter but any feelings of bitterness, on the part of one who is always ready to suspect evil, you will be deliberately alienating from yourself a master who is the very well

inclined by nature to listen to any accusations which are brought before him in a joking manner; for his ears, as you well know, are always open, and are constantly on the watch to listen to all those who are in the habit of interweaving accusations of others with their sycophancy. (170) And do not seek for any more abundant causes; for you have a sufficient foundation with respect to the customs of the Jews and the national laws of that people, in which you yourself were bred up, and in which you have been instructed from your very earliest childhood, not by one man only, but by that most chattering and vexatious portion of the city of Alexandria. So now, make an exhibition of your learning."

XXVII. (171) By these preposterous and accursed arguments he excited his own expectations, and trained himself, and inflamed his own wishes; and then he attended upon and courted Gaius, day and night, never leaving him for a moment, but being with him at all times and on all occasions, and employing every moment when he was by himself, or when he was resting, to pour forth accusations against our nation, like a most infamous man as he was, exciting pleasure in the mind of the emperor by ridiculing the Jews and their laws and customs, that thus his calumnies might wound us the more effectually; for he never openly confessed himself to be our accuser, nor could he in fact make such a confession; but he went by all kinds of crooked paths, and practised every sort of manoeuvre, and thus was a more dangerous and formidable enemy than even those men who openly recorded their hatred of and hostility towards us.

(172) They say also that some of the ambassadors of the Alexandrians, being completely aware of this, had secretly hired him by considerable bribes, and not only by money but by hopes of future honours, which they led him to expect he might attain to at no distant period, when Gaius should come to Alexandria. (173) And he, being continually declaiming of that time in which, while his master was present, and in conjunction with him, he should be almost supreme in his power over a large portion of the world (for it was notorious enough that by his assiduous courting of Gaius, he would be able to acquire power over the most illustrious portion of the citizens, and over all those who are held in especial honour by the most magnificent and glorious city,[12] promised every thing).

(174) We, therefore, being for a long time unsuspicious of this natural enemy, who as plotting against us from his concealment, took precautions only against our external foes; but when we perceived that he too was to be guarded against, we searched into the matter carefully, considering every expedient to see if we could, by any means, propitiate and conciliate the man who was thus aiming and shooting at us, by every means and from every place, with great accuracy of aim and power of injuring us; (175) for he was in the habit of playing at ball with him, and of exercising himself in gymnastic sports with him, and of bathing with him, and breakfasting with him, and he was with Gaius when he was wont to go to rest, filling the part of chamberlain and chief body-guard to him, an office which was not entrusted to any one else, so that he alone had all kinds of favourable opportunities for being listened to at leisure by the emperor, when he was removed from any external tumults and distractions, and able quietly to hear what he principally desired.

(176) And he mingled numbers of satirical and quizzing observations with his more formal and serious accusations, in order to excite pleasure in his hearers by that means, and to do us the greatest possible amount of injury; for the quizzing and ridiculing appeared, as he used it, to be the principal object at which he aimed, though it was in reality only his indirect one; and the accusations which he launched against us appeared to be mere casual observations, dropped accidentally, though in reality they were his primary and sole object, while he was trying every expedient possible, (177) and so, like sailors who have a fair wind blowing on their stern, he was borne onwards with a full sail before a favourable gale, heaping upon us and stringing together one accusation after another, while the mind of his hearer was fashioned in a more solid and retentive mould, so that the recollection of the accusations was not easily eradicated.

XXVIII. (178) Accordingly, we being in a great strait and in most difficult circumstances, we, though we had availed ourselves of every expedient which we could possibly think of in order to propitiate and conciliate Helicon, could find no means of doing so and no access to him, since no one dared either to accost or to approach him, by reason of his exceeding insolence and cruelty with which he behaved to every one; and also because we were not aware, whether there was any especial reason for his alienation from the Jewish nation; since he was also exciting and exasperating his master against our people, and, accordingly, we left off labouring at this point, and turned our attention to what was of greater importance.

For it appeared good to present to Gaius a memorial, containing a summary of what we had suffered, and of the way in which we considered that we deserved to be treated; (179) and this memorial was nearly an abridgment of a longer petition which we had sent to him a short time before, by the hand of king Agrippa; for he, by chance, was staying for a short time in the city, while on his way into Syria to take possession of

---

[12] There seems some corruption in the text here.

the kingdom which had been given to him; (180) but we, without being aware of it, were deceiving ourselves, for before also we had done the same, when we originally began to set sail, thinking that as we were going before a judge we should meet with justice; but he was in reality an irreconcilable enemy to us, attracting us, as far as appearance went, with favourable looks and cheerful address; (181) for, receiving us favourably at first, in the plains on the banks of the Tiber (for he happened to be walking about in his mother's garden), he conversed with us formally, and waved his right hand to us in a protecting manner, giving us significant tokens of his good will, and having sent to us the secretary, whose duty it was to attend to the embassies that arrived, Obulus by name, he said, "I myself will listen to what you have to say at the first favourable opportunity."

So that all those who stood around congratulated us as if we had already carried our point, and so did all those of our own people, who are influenced by superficial appearances. (182) But I myself, who was accounted to be possessed of superior prudence, both on account of my age and my education, and general information, was less sanguine in respect of the matters at which the others were so greatly delighted. "For why," said I, after pondering the matter deeply in my own heart, "why, when there have been such numbers of ambassadors, who have come, one may almost say, from every corner of the globe, did he say on that occasion that he would hear what we had to say, and no one else? What could have been his meaning? for he was not ignorant that we were Jews, who would have been quite content at not being treated worse than the others; (183) but to expect to be looked upon as worthy to receive especial privileges and precedence, by a master who was of a different nation and a young man and an absolute monarch, would have seemed like insanity. But it would seem that he was showing civility to the whole district of the Alexandrians, to which he was thus giving a privilege, when promising to give his decision speedily; unless, indeed, disregarding the character of a fair and impartial hearer, he was intending to be a fellow suitor with our adversaries and an enemy of ours, instead of behaving like a judge."

XXIX. (184) Having these ideas in my mind, I resisted the sanguine hopes of the others, and had no rest in my mind day or night. But while I was thus giving way to despondency and lamenting over my ignorance of the future (for it was not safe to postpone matters), on a sudden another most grievous and unexpected calamity fell upon us, bringing danger not on one section of the Jews only, but on all the nation together. (185) For we had come from Rome to Dicaearchia attending upon Gaius; and he had gone down to the sea-side and was remaining near the gulf, having left for a while his own palaces, which were numerous and superbly furnished. (186) And while we were anxiously considering his intentions, for we were continually expecting to be summoned, a man arrived, with blood-shot eyes, and looking very much troubled, out of breath and palpitating, and leading us away to a little distance from the rest (for there were several persons near), he said, "Have you heard the news?" And then when he was about to tell us what it was he stopped, because of the abundance of tears that rose up to choke his utterance. (187) And beginning again, he was a second and a third time stopped in the same manner. And we, seeing this, were much alarmed and agitated by suspense, and entreated him to tell us what the circumstance was on account of which he said that he had come; for he could not have come merely to weep before so many witnesses. "If, then," said we, "you have any real cause for tears, do not keep your grief to yourself; we have been long ago well accustomed to misfortune."

(188) And he with difficulty, sobbing aloud, and in a broken voice, spoke as follows: "Our temple is destroyed! Gaius has ordered a colossal statue of himself to be erected in the holy of holies, having his own name inscribed upon it with the title of Jupiter!" (189) And while we were all struck dumb with astonishment and terror at what he had told us, and stood still deprived of all motion (for we stood there mute and in despair, ready to fall to the ground with fear and sorrow, the very muscles of our bodies being deprived of all strength by the news which we had heard); others arrived bearing the same sad tale. (190) And then we all retired and shut ourselves up together and bewailed our individual and common miseries, and went through every circumstance that our minds could conceive, for a man in misfortune is a most loquacious animal, wrestling as we might with our misery. And we said to one another, "We have sailed hither in the middle of winter, in order that we might not be all involved in violation of the law and in misfortunes proceeding from it, without being aware what a winter of misery was awaiting us on shore, far more grievous than any storm at sea. For of the one nature is the cause, which has divided the seasons of the year and arranged them in due order, but nature is a thing which exerts a saving power; but the other storm is caused by a man who cherishes no ideas such as become a man, but is a young man, and a promoter of all kinds of innovation, being invested with irresponsible power over all the world.

"And youth, when combined with absolute power and yielding to irresistible and unrestrained passion, is an invincible evil. (191) And will it be allowed to us to approach him or to open our mouth on the subject of the synagogues before this insulter of our holy and glorious temple? For it is quite evident that he will pay no regard whatever to things of less importance and which are held in inferior estimation, when he behaves with insolence and contempt towards our most beautiful and renowned temple, which is respected by all the east and by all the west, and regarded like the sun which shines everywhere. (192) And even if we were allowed free access to him, what else could we expect but an inexorable sentence of death? But be it so; we will perish. For, indeed, a glorious death in defence of and for the sake of the preservation of our laws, is a kind of life.

"But, indeed, if no advantage is derived from our death, would it not be insanity to perish in addition to what we now have to endure, and this too, while we appear to be ambassadors, so that the calamity appears rather to affect those who have sent us than those who remain? (193) Not but what those of our fellow countrymen who are by nature most inclined to detest all wickedness, will accuse us of impiety, as if we, in the extremity of dangers, when our whole country was tossed about and threatened, were remembering some private interests of our own out of selfishness. For it is necessary that small things must yield to great ones, and that private objects must yield to the general interests; since, when they are destroyed, there is an end of the constitution and of the nation. (194) For how can it be holy or lawful for us to struggle in any other manner, pointing out that we are citizens of Alexandria, over whom a danger is now impending, that namely, of the utter destruction of the general constitution of the Jewish nation; for in the destruction of the temple there is reason to fear that this man, so fond of innovation and willing to dare the most audacious actions, will also order the general name of our whole nation to be abolished.

(195) "If, therefore, both the objects on account of which we were sent are overthrown, perhaps some one will say, What then, did they not know that they had to negotiate for a safe return? But I would reply to such a man, You either have not the genuine feelings of a nobly born man, or else you were not educated like one, and have never been trained in the knowledge of the sacred scriptures; for men who are truly noble are full of hope, and the laws too implant good hopes in all those who do not study them superficially but with all their hearts. (196) Perhaps these things are meant as a trial of the existing generation to see how they are inclined towards virtue, and whether they have been taught to bear evils with resolute and firm minds, without yielding at the first moment; all human considerations then are discarded, and let them be discarded, but let an imperishable hope and trust in God the Saviour

remain in our souls, as he has often preserved our nation amid inextricable difficulties and distresses."

XXX. (197) These were the sort of things which we said, bewailing at the same time our unexpected calamities, and yet also encouraging one another with the hope of a change to a more tranquil and peaceful state of things. And after a little consideration and delay, we said to those who had brought us this doleful news, "Why sit ye here quietly, having just kindled sparks of eagerness in our ears by which we are set on fire and rendered all in a blaze, when you ought rather to add to what you have told us an account of the causes which have operated on Gaius."

(198) And they replied, "You know the principal and primary cause of all; for that indeed is universally known to all men. He desires to be considered a god; and he conceives that the Jews alone are likely to be disobedient; and that therefore he cannot possibly inflict a greater evil or injury upon them than by defacing and insulting the holy dignity of their temple; for report prevails that it is the most beautiful of all the temples in the world, inasmuch as it is continually receiving fresh accessions of ornament and has been for an infinite period of time, a never-ending and boundless expense being lavished on it. And as he is a very contentious and quarrelsome man, he thinks of appropriating this edifice wholly to himself. (199) And he is excited now on this subject to a much greater degree than before by a letter which Capito has sent to him.

"Capito is the collector of the imperial revenues in Judaea, and on some account or other he is very hostile to the nations of the country; for having come thither a poor man, and having amassed enormous riches of every imaginable description by plunder and extortion, he has now become afraid lest some accusation may be brought against him, and on this account he has contrived a design by which he may repel any such impeachment, namely, by calumniating those whom he has injured; (200) and a circumstance which we will now mention, has given him some pretext for carrying out his design.

"There is a city called Jamnia; one of the most populous cities in all Judaea, which is inhabited by a promiscuous multitude, the greatest number of whom are Jews; but there are also some persons of other tribes from the neighbouring nations who have settled there to their own destruction, who are in a manner sojourners among the original native citizens, and who cause them a great deal of trouble, and who do them a great deal of injury, as they are continually violating some of the ancestral national customs of the Jews. (201) These men hearing from travellers who visit the city how exceedingly eager and earnest Gaius is about his own deification, and how disposed he is to look unfavourably upon the whole race of Judaea, thinking that they have now an admirable opportunity for attacking them themselves, have erected an extemporaneous altar of the most contemptible materials, having made clay into bricks for the sole purpose of plotting against their fellow citizens; for they knew well that they would never endure to see their customs transgressed; as was indeed the case.

(202) "For when the Jews saw what they had done, and were very indignant at the holiness and sanctity and beauty of the sacred place being thus obscured and defaced, they collected together and destroyed the altar; so the sojourners immediately went to Capito who was in reality the contriver of the whole affair; and he, thinking that he had made a most lucky hit, which he had been seeking for a long time, writes to Gaius dilating on the matter and exaggerating it enormously; (203) and he, when he had read the letter, ordered a colossal statue gilt all over, much more costly and much more magnificent than the rich altar which had been erected in Jamnia, by way of insult to be set up in the temple of the metropolis, having for his most excellent and sagacious counsellors Helicon, that man of noble birth, a chattering slave, a perfect scum of the earth, and a fellow of the name of Apelles, a tragic actor, who when in the first bloom of youth, as they say, made a market of his beauty, and when he was past the freshness of youth went on the stage; (204) and in fact all those who go on the stage selling themselves to the spectators, and to the theatres, are not lovers of temperance and modesty, but rather of the most extreme shamelessness and indecency.

"On this account Apelles was taken into the rank of a fellow counsellor of the emperor, that Gaius might have an adviser with whom he might indulge in mocking jests, and with whom he might sing, passing over all considerations of the general welfare of the state, as if everything in every quarter of the globe was enjoying profound peace and tranquillity under the laws.

(205) "Therefore Helicon, this scorpion-like slave, discharged all his Egyptian venom against the Jews; and Apelles his Ascalonite poison, for he was a native of Ascalon; and between the people of Ascalon and the inhabitants of the holy land, the Jews, there is an irreconcileable and never-ending hostility although they are bordering nations."

(206) When we heard this we were wounded in our souls at every word he said and at every name he mentioned; but those admirable advisers of admirable actions a little while afterwards met with the fit reward of their impiety, the one being bound by Gaius with iron chains for other causes, and being put to the torture and to the rack after

periods of relief, as is the case with people affected with intermittent diseases; and Helicon was put to death by Claudius Germanicus Caesar, for other wicked actions, that, like a madman as he was, he had committed; but there occurrences took place at a later date.

XXXI. (207) And the letter respecting the erection of the statue was written not in plain terms, but with as much caution and prudence as possible, taking every measure which could tend to security; for he commands Petronius, the lieutenant and governor of all Syria, to whom indeed he wrote the letter, to lead half the army which was on the Euphrates, to guard against any passage of that river by any of the eastern kings or nations, into Judaea as an escort to the statue; not in order to honour its erection with any especial pomp, but to chastise with death any attempt that might be made to hinder it.

(208) What sayest thou, O master? Are you making war upon us, because you anticipate that we will not endure such indignity, but that we will fight on behalf of our laws, and die in defence of our national customs? For you cannot possibly have been ignorant of what was likely to result from your attempt to introduce these innovations respecting our temple; but having previously learnt with perfect accuracy what was likely to happen as well as if it had already taken place, and knowing the future as thoroughly as if it were actually present, you commanded your general to bring up an army in order that the statue when erected might be consecrated by the first sacrifice offered to it, being of a most polluted kind, stained with the blood of miserable men and women.

(209) Accordingly Petronius, when he had read what he was commanded to do in this letter, was in great perplexity, not being able to resist the orders sent to him out of fear, for he heard that the emperor's wrath was implacable not only against those who did not do what they were commanded to do, but who did not do it in a moment; and on the other hand, he did not see how it was easy to perform them, for he knew that the Jews would willingly, if it were possible, endure ten thousand deaths instead of one, rather than submit to see any forbidden thing perpetrated with respect to their religion; (210) for all men are eager to preserve their own customs and laws, and the Jewish nation above all others; for looking upon their laws as oracles directly given to them by God himself, and having been instructed in this doctrine from their very earliest infancy they bear in their souls the images of the commandments contained in these laws as sacred; (211) and secondly, as they continually behold the visible shapes and forms of them, they admire and venerate them in their minds and they admit such foreigners as are dis-

posed to honour and worship them, to do so no less than their own native fellow citizens.

But all who attempt to violate their laws, or to turn them into ridicule, they detest as their bitterest enemies, and they look upon each separate one of the commandments with such awe and reverence that, whether one ought to call it the invariable good fortune or the happiness of the nation, they have never been guilty of the violation of even the most insignificant of them; (212) but above all other observances their zeal for their holy temple is the most predominant, and vehement, and universal feeling throughout the whole nation; and the greatest proof of this is that death is inexorably pronounced against all those who enter into the inner circuit of the sacred precincts (for they admit all men from every country into the exterior circuit), unless he be one of their own nation by blood.

(213) Petronius, having regard to these considerations, was very reluctant to attempt what he was commanded to do, considering what a great and wicked piece of daring he should be committing, and invoking all the deliberative powers of his soul as to a council, he inquired into the opinion of each of them, and he found every faculty of his mind agreeing that he should change nothing of these observances and customs which had been hallowed from the beginning of the world; in the first place because of the natural principles of justice and piety by which they were dictated, and secondly because of the danger which threatened any attempt at innovation upon them, not only from God, but also from the people who would be insulted by such conduct. (214) He also gave a thought to the circumstances of the nation itself, to its exceeding populousness, so that it was not contained as every other nation was by the circuit of the one region which was allotted to it for itself, but so that, I may almost say, it had spread over the whole face of the earth; for it is diffused throughout every continent, and over every island, so that everywhere it appears but little inferior in number to the original native population of the country.

(215) Was it not, then, a most perilous undertaking to draw upon himself such innumerable multitudes of enemies? And was there not danger of allies and friends from all quarters arriving to their assistance? It would be a result of very formidable danger and difficulty, besides the fact that the inhabitants of Judaea are infinite in numbers, and a nation of great stature and personal strength, and of great courage and spirit, and men who are willing to die in defence of their national customs and laws with unshrinking bravery, so that some of those who calumniate them say that their courage (as indeed is perfectly true) is beyond that of any barbarian nation, being the spirit of free and nobly born men.

(216) And the state of all the nations which lie beyond the Euphrates added to his alarm; for he was aware that Babylon and many others of the satrapies of the east were occupied by the Jews, knowing this not merely by report but likewise by personal experience; for every year sacred messengers are sent to convey large amounts of gold and silver to the temple, which has been collected from all the subordinate governments, travelling over rugged, and difficult, and almost impassable roads, which they look upon as level and easy inasmuch as they serve to conduct them to piety.

(217) Therefore, being exceedingly alarmed, as was very natural, lest if they heard of the unprecedented design of erecting this colossal statue in the temple, they might on a sudden direct their march that way and surround him, some on one side and some on the other, so as to hem him in completely, and co-operating with and joining one another might treat the enemy who would be thus enclosed in the midst of them with terrible severity, he hesitated long, attaching great weight to all these considerations.

(218) Then again he was drawn in the opposite direction by considerations of a contrary character, saying to himself, "This is the command of one who is my master and a young man, and of one who judges everything which he wishes to have done to be expedient and becoming, and who is resolved that everything which he has once decided on shall be at once performed even though it may be the most injurious measure possible and full of all contention and insolence; and now having passed beyond all human nature he has actually recorded himself to be God; and great danger of my life impends over me whether I oppose him or whether I comply with his commands; if I comply with them the result will very probably be war, and one that perhaps may be attended with doubtful success and which will be far from turning out as it is expected to do; and if I oppose him I shall then be exposed to the open and implacable hatred of Gaius."

(219) And with this opinion of his, many of those Romans who were joined with him in the administration of the affairs of Syria coincided, knowing that the anger of Gaius and the punishments which he would inflict would come upon them first as being accomplices in the disobedience to the injunctions which he had sent; (220) but at last when it arrived the fashion of the statue afforded them a pretext for delay during which they might have time for a more deliberate consideration of the matter; for they did not send any man from Rome (as it appears to me because the providence of God overruled the matter in this way,

who thus invisibly stayed the hand of these wicked doers), nor did he command the most skilful man or him who was accounted so in Syria to manage the matter, since while he was pressing on this lawless action with all speed a war was suddenly kindled.

(221) Therefore having now opportunity to consider what course would be most advantageous (for when great events suddenly come altogether, they break down and perplex the mind), he commanded the statue to be made in some one of the bordering regions. (222) Therefore Petronius, sending for the most skilful and renowned artists in Phoenicia, gave them the materials requisite for the making of the statue; and they took them to Sidon, and there proceeded to make it.

He also sent for the magistrates of the Jews and the priests and rulers of the people, both to announce to them the commands which he had received from Gaius and also to counsel them to submit cheerfully to the commands which had been imposed by their master, and to give due consideration to the dangers before their eyes; for that the most warlike of the military powers in Syria were all ready, and would soon cover all the country with dead bodies; (223) for he thought that if he could previously weaken their resolution he would be able by their means to work upon all the rest of the multitude and to persuade them not to oppose the will of the emperor; but, as was natural, he was wholly disappointed in his expectations; for it is said indeed that they were amazed at his first words, and that at first they were utterly overwhelmed by his announcement of their real danger and misery, and that they stood speechless and poured forth a ceaseless abundance of tears as if from a fountain, tearing their beards and the hair of their head, and saying, (224) "We who were formerly very fortunate, have now advanced through many events to an exceeding old age that we might at last behold what no one of our ancestors ever saw. With what eyes can we endure to look upon these things? Let them rather be torn out, and let our miserable lives and our afflicted existence be put an end to, before we behold such an evil as this, such an intolerable spectacle which it is impious to hear of or to conceive."

XXXII. (225) In this way did they bewail their fate; but when the inhabitants of the holy city and of all the region round about heard of the design which was in agitation, they all arrayed themselves together as if at a concerted signal, their common misery having given them the word, and went forth in a body, and leaving their cities and their villages and their houses empty, they hastened with one accord into Phoenicia, for Petronius happened to be in that country at the moment. (226) And when some of the guards of Petronius saw a countless multitude hastening towards them they ran to their general to bring him the news, and to warn him to take precautions, as they expected war; and while they were relating to him what they had seen, he was still without any guards; and the multitude of the Jews suddenly coming upon him like a cloud, occupied the whole of Phoenicia, and caused great consternation among the Phoenicians who thus beheld the enormous population of the nation; (227) and at first so great an outcry was raised, accompanied with weeping and beating of the breast, that the very ears of those present could not endure the vastness of the noise; for it did not cease when they ceased, but continued to vibrate even after they were quiet: then there were approaches to the governor, and supplications addressed to him such as the occasion suggested; for calamities are themselves teachers of what should be done in an existing emergency.

And the multitude was divided into six companies, one of old men, one of young men, one of boys; and again in their turn one band of aged matrons, one of women in the prime of life, and one of virgins; (228) and when Petronius appeared at a distance all the ranks, as they had been appointed, fell to the ground, uttering a most doleful; howling and lamentation, mingled with supplications. But when he commanded them to rise up, and to come nearer to him, they would for a long time hardly consent to rise, and scattering abundance of dust upon their heads, and shedding abundance of tears, they put both their hands behind them like captives who are fettered in this way, and thus they approached him.

(229) Then the body of the old men, standing before him, addressed him in the following terms: "We are, as you see, without any arms, but yet as we passed along some persons have accused us as being enemies, but even the very weapons of defence with which nature has provided each individual, namely our hands, we have averted from you, and placed in a position where they can do nothing, offering our bodies freely an easy aim to any one who desires to put us to death. (230) We have brought unto you our wives, and our children, and our whole families, and in your person we will prostrate ourselves before Gaius, having left not one single person at home, that you may either preserve us all, or destroy us all together by one general and complete destruction. Petronius, we are a peaceful nation, both by our natural disposition and by our determined intentions, and the education which has been industriously and carefully instilled into us has taught us this lesson from our very earliest infancy. (231) When Gaius assumed the imperial power we were the first people in all Syria to congratulate him, Vitellius at that time being in our city, from whom you received the government as his successor, to whom writings concerning these matters were sent, and the

happy news proceeding onwards from our city, where it had been received with joy, reached the other cities with similar acceptance. (232) Ours was the first temple which received sacrifices for the happy reign of Gaius. Did it do so that it might be the first or the only temple to be deprived of its customary modes of worship?

"We have now left our cities, we have abandoned our houses and our possessions, we will cheerfully contribute to you all our furniture, all our cattle, and all our treasures, everything in short which belongs to us, as a willing booty. We shall think that we are receiving them, not giving them up. We only ask one thing instead of and to counterbalance all of them, namely, that no innovations may take place in respect of our temple, but that it may be kept such as we have received it from our fathers and our forefathers. (233) And if we cannot prevail with you in this, then we offer up ourselves for destruction, that we may not live to behold a calamity more terrible and grievous than death. We hear that great forces of infantry and cavalry are being prepared by you against us, if we oppose the erection and dedication of this statue. No one is so mad as, when he is a slave, to oppose his master. We willingly and readily submit ourselves to be put to death; let your troops slay us, let them sacrifice us, let them cut us to pieces unresisting and uncontending, let them treat us with every species of cruelty that conquerers can possibly practise, (234) but what need is there of any army? We ourselves, admirable priests for the purpose, will begin the sacrifice, bringing to the temple our wives and slaying our wives, bringing our brothers and sisters and becoming fratricides, bringing our sons and our daughters, that innocent and guiltless age, and becoming infanticides. Those who endure tragic calamities must needs make use of tragic language. (235) Then standing in the middle of our victims, having bathed ourselves deeply in the blood of our kinsfolk (for such blood will be the only bath which we shall have wherewith to cleanse ourselves for the journey to the shades below), we will mingle our own blood with it, slaughtering ourselves upon their bodies. (236) And when we are dead, let this commandment be inscribed over us as an epitaph, 'Let not even God blame us, who have had a due regard to both considerations, pious loyalty towards the emperor and the reverential preservation of our established holy laws.'

"And this will be what will be deservedly said of us if we give up our miserable life, holding it in proper contempt. (237) We have heard of a most ancient tradition, which has been handed down throughout Greece by their historians, who have affirmed that the head of the Gorgon had such mighty power, that those who beheld it immediately became stones and rocks. But this appears only to be a fiction and fable, the truth being that great, and unexpected, and wonderful events do often bring after them great disaster; for instance, the anger of a master causes death, or calamities equivalent to death.

(238) "Do you suppose (may God forbid that any such event should ever take place) that if any of our countrymen were to see this statue being brought into our temple, it would not change them into stones? Their limbs being all congealed, and their eyes becoming fixed so as not to be capable of motion, and their whole body losing all its natural motions in every one of its united parts and limbs! (239) We will, however, now, O Petronius, address to you one last and most righteous and just request; we say that you ought not to do what you are commanded, but we entreat you to grant us a respite, and we most earnestly supplicate you to delay a little while till we appoint an embassy, and send it to approach your master, and to convey our entreaties to him. (240) Perhaps in our embassy we may find some argument or other to persuade him, either by bringing before him all the considerations respecting the honour of God, or the preservation of our indestructible and unalterable laws, or by urging upon him that we ought not to be subjected to a worse fate than all the nations even in the very most remote extremities of the earth, who have been allowed to preserve their national customs; with reference to which his grandfather and great-grandfather came to a righteous decision when they confirmed and set the seal to our customs with all care. (241) Perhaps when he hears these arguments he will be more merciful to us. The intentions of the great do not always continue the same, and those which are adopted in anger are the quickest to change. We have been grievously calumniated. Suffer us to refute the false accusations which have been brought against us. It is hard to be condemned without being heard in our own defence.

(242) "And if we fail to convince him, what will after that prevent him from doing the things which he at present intends to do? Until, then, we have sent this embassy, do not cut off all the hopes of so many myriads of men, since our zeal and earnestness is displayed not in the cause of gain, but in that of religion; though indeed we speak foolishly in using such an expression as that, for what can be a more real and beneficial gain to them than holiness?"

XXXIII. (243) They uttered these complaints and entreaties with great agony and misery of soul, with exceeding sobbing and difficulty of speech, for all their limbs sweated with apprehension, and their ceaseless tears flowed in torrents, so that all who heard them, and Petronius himself, sympathised with their sorrow, for he was by nature a man very kind and gentle in his natural disposition, so that he was easily influenced by what was now said or heard; and what was said appeared to be entirely just, and the misery of those whom he now beheld appeared most pitiable; (244) and rising up, and retiring with his fellow counsellors, he took counsel as to what he ought to do, and he saw that those who a short time before opposed the wishes of the Jews with all their might were now wavering and perplexed, and that those who had previously been hesitating were now for the most part inclined to compassion, at which he was pleased.

Nevertheless, though he was well acquainted with the disposition of the emperor, and how implacable and inexorable he was in his anger, (245) he still had himself some sparks of the Jewish philosophy and piety, since he had long ago learnt something of it by reason of his eagerness for learning, and had studied it still more ever since he had come as governor of the countries in which there are vast numbers of Jews scattered over every city of Asia and Syria; or partly because he was so disposed in his mind from his spontaneous, and natural, and innate inclination for all things which are worthy of care and study.

Moreover, God himself appears often to suggest virtuous ideas to virtuous men, by which, while benefiting others, they will likewise be benefited themselves, which now was the case with Petronius. What then was his resolution? (246) Not to hurry on the artists, but to persuade them to continue to finish the statue which they had in hand, taking pains and labouring as far as might be possible not to be inferior to the most renowned models, but to take plenty of time, so as to make their work perfect, since things which are done in a hurry are very often inferior, but things which are done with great pains and skill require a length of time. (247) But the embassy which they entreated leave to send he determined not to permit, for he considered that it would not be safe for him to allow it; still he determined not to oppose those who wished to refer the whole matter to the supreme sovereign and master, but neither to agree with nor to contradict the multitude, for he considered that either line of conduct was fraught with danger.

(248) Moreover, he determined to write a letter to Gaius, not in any respect accusing the Jews, and on the other hand not giving any accurate account of their entreaties and supplications, and to explain the delay which was taking place in the erection of the statue, partly because the preparation of it required a certain space of time for its completion, and partly, he reminded him, that the season of the year was in some degree the cause of unavoidable delay, in which there was no question but that Gaius must of necessity acquiesce, (249) for it was just at that moment the very height

of the wheat harvest and of all the other cereal crops; and he said that he was afraid lest out of despair of the preservation of their national and hereditary laws and customs, the men might conceive such a contempt for life as either themselves to lay waste their lands, or to burn all the corn-bearing district, whether mountainous or champaign country, and, therefore, that he might require a guard to secure a careful gathering in of the crops, and that not only of such as were borne on the arable land but of those produced by fruit-bearing trees; (250) for he himself was intending, as is said, to sail to Alexandria in Egypt, but so great a general did not choose to cross the open sea both by reason of the danger and also of the numerous fleet which would be required as his escort, and also from his regard for his own person, as everything requisite for his comfort would be more easily provided if he took the circuitous route through Asia and Syria; (251) for he would, if he coasted along, be able to sail every day and land every night, especially if he took with him a sufficient number of ships of war, and not transports, in which a coasting voyage is more successful, just as one across the open sea is better for merchantmen. (252) Therefore it was necessary that abundant quantities of forage and food should be prepared for his cattle in every one of the Syrian cities, and especially in all such as were on the coast, for a numerous multitude would be proceeding both by land and sea, collected not only from Rome itself and from Italy, but that which had also followed him from all the other provinces of the empire as far as Syria, being partly the regular guard of the magistrates, and partly the regular army of infantry and cavalry, and the naval force, and also a troops of servants but little inferior in number to the army. (253) Moreover, there was need not only of such an abundance of supplies as might be sufficient for all necessary purposes, but also for all the superfluous prodigality of which Gaius was fond. If he reads these writings perhaps he will not only not be angry, but will be even pleased with our prudential caution, as having caused this delay not from any regard for the Jews, but for the sake of providing for the collection of the harvest.

XXXIV. (254) And when his assessors had delivered their opinions, he commanded letters to be written, and appointed active men, who were accustomed to make rapid journey, to convey them. And they, when they had arrived at their journey's end, delivered the letters; but the emperor, before he had finished reading them, became swollen with anger, and went on making marks at every page, in fury and indignation; (255) and when he had come to the end of the letter, he clapped his hands together, saying, "Of a truth, Petronius, you seem but little to comprehend that you are the subject of the emperor; the uninterrupted series of governments to which you have been preferred have filled you with guile. Up to the present time it seems to me that you have no notion of acknowledging that you know, even by hearsay, that Gaius is emperor, but you shall very speedily find it out by your own experience, (256) for you are careful about the laws of the Jews, a nation which I hate above every other, and you are indifferent about the imperial commands of your sovereign. You fear the multitude. Had you not with you then the military forces which all the eastern nations, and the chief of them all, the Parthians, fear? (257) But you pitied them, you paid more attention to feelings of compassion than to the express commands of Gaius.

"Make your pretext of the harvest, but you yourself shall soon find that you have brought on your own head a punishment which cannot be averted by any pretexts of excuses. Blame the necessity for collecting the crops, and for making adequate provision for my armies, for even if a complete scarcity were to oppress Judaea, still are there not vast regions on its borders of great fertility and productiveness, sufficient and able to supply all necessary food, and to make up for the deficiency of one district? (258) But why do I speak in this way before acting? And why is there no one who anticipates my intentions? He who delays shall first find out that he is receiving the wages of his delay by suffering in his own person. I will say no more, but I shall not forget the matter."

(259) And after a brief interval, he dictated to one of his secretaries an answer to Petronius, praising him in appearance for his prudence, and for his careful and accurate consideration of the future, for he was very careful with respect to the governors of the provinces, seeing that they had at all times great facilities for making innovations or revolutions, especially if they happened to be in districts of importance, and in command of powerful armies such as was on the Euphrates for the protection of Syria. (260) Therefore, being very civil to him in words and in his letters, he concealed his anger till a favourable opportunity, though he was very much exasperated; but at the end of the letter, after having mentioned every other subject, he desired him not to be so anxious about anything as about the speedy erection and dedication of the statue, for that by this time the harvest must have been able to be got in, whether the excuse was originally an honest and true or only a plausible one.

XXXV. (261) However a short time afterwards King Agrippa arrived in Rome, according to custom, to pay his respects to Gaius, and he knew absolutely nothing either of what Petronius had written in his letter, or of what Gaius had written in his first or second epistle, but by his irregular motions and agitations, and by the excitement which shone in his eyes, he conjectured that he had some anger smouldering beneath, and he considered, and pondered, and turned over every matter in every direction, racking his brain for every reason, whether great or small, to see whether he had said or done anything unbecoming, (262) and when he felt sure that he had done absolutely nothing, he conjectured, as was natural, that it was some one else with whom he was offended. But again, when he saw that he looked morosely at him, and that he kept his eyes continually fixed on him, and on no one else who was ever present, he began to be alarmed, and though he often thought of putting the question to him, he restrained himself, reflecting in this manner: "Perhaps by doing so I may draw down on myself the threats which as it is are destined for others, by bringing upon myself a suspicion of being a busybody, and a rash and audacious man."

(263) Therefore, when Gaius saw that he was in a state of great alarm and perplexity, for he was very acute at comprehending a man's inmost designs and feelings from his outward appearance and expression of countenance, he said, "You are embarrassed, O Agrippa. I will relieve you from your perplexity. (264) Though you have lived with me for such a length of time, are you yet ignorant that I speak not only with my voice, but also with my eyes, intimating everything, to say the least of it, as much in one way as in the other? (265) Your loyal and excellent fellow citizens, the only nation of men upon the whole face of the earth by whom Gaius is not esteemed to be a god, appear now to be even desiring to plot my death in their obstinate disobedience, for when I commanded my statue in the character of Jupiter to be erected in their temple, they raised the whole of their people, and quitted the city and the whole country in a body, under pretence of addressing a petition to me, but in reality being determined to act in a manner contrary to the commands which I had imposed upon them."

(266) And when he was about to add other charges against them Agrippa fell into such a state of grief that he changed into all sorts of colours, becoming at the same moment bloodshot, and pale, and livid, (267) for he was all over agitation and trembling from the top of his head down to his feet, and a quivering and shaking seized upon and disordered all his limbs and every member of his body, all his sinews, and muscles, and nerves being relaxed and enfeebled, so that he fainted away, and would have fallen down if some of the bystanders had not supported him.

And they being commanded to carry him home, bore him to his palace, where he lay for some time in a state of torpor without any one understanding what sudden misfortune had brought him into this state. (268) Therefore Gaius was exasperated still more against our nation, and cherished a more furious anger against us than before, "For," said he, "if Agrippa, who is my most intimate and dearest friend, and one bound to me by so many benefits, is so completely under the influence of his national customs that he cannot bear even to hear a word against them, but faints away to such a degree as to be near dying, what must one expect will be the feelings of others who have no motive or influence to draw them the other way?"

(269) Agrippa, then, during all that day and the greater portion of the next day, lay in a state of profound stupor, being completely unconscious of everything that passed; but about evening he raised his head a little, and for a short time opened, though with difficulty, his languid eyes, and with dim and indistinct vision looked upon the people who surrounded him, though he was not as yet able to distinguish clearly between their several forms and features; (270) and then again relapsing into sleep, he became tranquil, getting into a better condition than at first, as those about him could conjecture from his breathing and from the state of his body.

(271) And afterwards, when he awoke again, and rose up, by asked, "Where now am I? Am I with Gaius? Is my lord himself here?" And they replied, "Be of good cheer; you are by yourself in your own palace. (272) Gaius is not here. You have now had a sufficient tranquil sleep, but now turn and raise yourself, and rest upon your elbow, and recognise those who are about you; they are all your own people, those of your friends, and freedmen, and domestics, who honour you above all others, and who are honoured by you in return."

(273) And he, for he was now beginning to recover from his state of stupefaction, saw feelings of sympathy in every one's face, and when his physicians ordered most of them to leave the room, that they might refresh his body with anointing and seasonable food, (274) "Go," said he, "for you must by all means take care that I may have a more carefully regulated way of life, for it is not sufficient for me, unfortunate man that I am, to ward off hunger by a bare, and scanty, and economical, and precise use of necessary food; nor should I have attended to any such matters if it had not been my object to provide my miserable nation with the last resource which my mind suggests to me by way of assisting it." (275) Accordingly, he, shedding abundance of tears, and eating just what was necessary without any sauce or seasoning, and drinking no mixed wine but only tasting water, soon left off eating. "My miserable stomach," said he, "recoils from the things which it demanded; and now what ought I do but address myself to Gaius with respect to existing circumstances?"

XXXVI. (276) And having taken tablets, he writes to him in the following manner: "O master, fear and shame have taken from me all courage to come into your presence to address you; since fear teaches me to dread your threats; and shame, out of respect for the greatness of your power and dignity, keeps me silent. But a writing will show my request, which I now here offer to you as my earnest petition. (277) In all men, O emperor! a love of their country is innate, and an eagerness for their national customs and laws. And concerning these matters there is no need that I should give you information, since you have a heart-felt love of your own country ,and a deeply-seated respect for your national customs. And what belongs to themselves appears beautiful to every one, even if it is not so in reality; for they judge of these things not more by reason than by the feelings of affection. (278) And I am, as you know, a Jew; and Jerusalem is my country, in which there is erected the holy temple of the most high God. And I have kings for my grandfathers and for my ancestors, the greater part of whom have been called high priests, looking upon their royal power as inferior to their office as priests; and thinking that the high priesthood is as much superior to the power of a king, as God is superior to man; for that the one is occupied in rendering service to God, and the other has only the care of governing them. (279) Accordingly I, being one of this nation, and being attached to this country and to such a temple, address to you this petition on behalf of them all; on behalf of the nation, that it may not be looked upon by you in a light contrary to the true one; since it is a most pious and holy nation, and one from the beginning most loyally disposed to your family.

(280) "For in all the particulars in which men are enjoined by the laws, and in which they have it in their power to show their piety and loyalty, my nation is inferior to none whatever in Asia or in Europe, whether it be in respect of prayers, or of the supply of sacred offerings, or in the abundance of its sacrifices, not merely of such as are offered on occasions of the public festivals, but in those which are continually offered day after day; by which means they show their loyalty and fidelity more surely than by their mouth and tongue, proving it by the designs of their honest hearts, not indeed saying that they are friends to Caesar, but being so in reality.

(281) "Concerning the holy city I must now say what is necessary. It, as I have already stated, is my native country, and the metropolis, not only of the one country of Judaea, but also of many, by reason of the colonies which it has sent out from time to time into the bordering districts of Egypt, Phoenicia, Syria in general, and especially that part of it which is called Coelo-Syria, and also with those more distant regions of Pamphylia, Cilicia,

the greater part of Asia Minor as far as Bithynia, and the furthermost corners of Pontus. And in the same manner into Europe, into Thessaly, and Boeotia, and Macedonia, and Aetolia, and Attica, and Argos, and Corinth and all the most fertile and wealthiest districts of Peloponnesus. (282) And not only are the continents full of Jewish colonies, but also all the most celebrated islands are so too; such as Euboea, and Cyprus, and Crete.

"I say nothing of the countries beyond the Euphrates, for all of them except a very small portion, and Babylon, and all the satrapies around, which have any advantages whatever of soil or climate, have Jews settled in them. (283) So that if my native land is, as it reasonably may be, looked upon as entitled to a share in your favour, it is not one city only that would then be benefited by you, but ten thousand of them in every region of the habitable world, in Europe, in Asia, and in Africa, on the continent, in the islands, on the coasts, and in the inland parts. (284) And it corresponds well to the greatness of your good fortune, that, by conferring benefits on one city, you should also benefit ten thousand others, so that your renown may be celebrated in every part of the habitable world, and many praises of you may be combined with thanksgiving.

(285) "You have thought the native countries of some of your friends worthy of being admitted to share all the privileges of the Roman constitution; and those who but a little while ago were slaves, became the masters of others who also enjoyed your favour in a higher, or at all events not in a lower degree, and they were delighted too at the causes of your beneficence. (286) And I indeed am perfectly aware that I belong to the class which is in subjection to a lord and master, and also that I am admitted to the honour of being one of your companions, being inferior to you in respect of my birthright and natural rank, and inferior to no one whomsoever, not to say the most eminent of all men, in good will and loyalty towards you, (287) both because that is my natural disposition, and also in consequence of the number of benefits with which you have enriched me; so that if I in consequence had felt confidence to implore you myself on behalf of my country, if not to grant to it the Roman constitution, at least to confer freedom and a remission of taxes on it, I should not have thought that I had any reason to fear your displeasure for preferring such a petition to you, and for requesting that most desirable of all things, your favour, which it can do you no harm to grant, and which is the most advantageous of all things for my country to receive.

(288) "For what can possibly be a more desirable blessing for a subject nation than the good will of its sovereign? It was at Jerusalem, O emperor! that your most desirable succession to the empire was first announced; and the news of your advancement spread from the holy city all over the continent on each side, and was received with great gladness. And on this account that city deserves to meet with favour at your hands; (289) for, as in families the eldest children receive the highest honours as their birthright, because they were the first to give the name of father and mother to their parents, so, in like manner, since this is first of all the cities in the east to salute you as emperor, it ought to receive greater benefit from you than any other; or if not greater, at all events as great as any other city.

(290) "Having now advanced these pleas on the ground of justice, and made these petitions on behalf of my native country, I now come at last to my supplication on behalf of the temple. O my lord and master, Gaius! this temple has never, from the time of its original foundation until now, admitted any form made by hands, because it has been the abode of God. Now, pictures and images are only imitations of those gods who are perceptible to the outward senses; but it was not considered by our ancestors to be consistent with the reverence due to God to make any image or representation of the invisible God. (291) Agrippa, when he came to the temple, did honour to it, and he was thy grandfather; and so did Augustus, when by his letters he commanded all first fruits from all quarters to be sent thither; and by the continual sacrifice. And thy great grandmother ...

(292) "On which account, no one, whether Greek or barbarian, satrap, or king, or implacable enemy; no sedition, no war, no capture, no destruction, no occurrence that has ever taken place, has ever threatened this temple with such innovation as to place in it any image, or statue, or any work of any kind made with hands; (293) for, though enemies have displayed their hostility to the inhabitants of the country, still, either reverence or fear has possessed them sufficiently to prevent them from abrogating any of the laws which were established at the beginning, as tending to the honour of the Creator and Father of the universe; for they knew that it is these and similar actions which bring after them the irremediable calamities of heaven-sent afflictions. On which account they have been careful not to sow an impious seed, fearing lest they should be compelled to reap its natural harvest, in a fruit bearing utter destruction.

XXXVII. (294) "But why need I invoke the assistance of foreign witnesses when I have plenty with whom I can furnish you from among your own countrymen and friends? Marcus Agrippa, your own grandfather on the mother's side, the moment that he arrived in Judaea, when Herod, my grandfather, was king of the country, thought fit to go up from the sea-coast to the metropolis, which was inland. (295) And when he had beheld the temple, and the decorations of the priests, and the piety and holiness of the people of the country, he marvelled, looking upon the whole matter as one of great solemnity and entitled to great respect, and thinking that he had beheld what was too magnificent to be described. And he could talk of nothing else to his companions but the magnificence of the temple and every thing connected with it.

(296) "Therefore, every day that he remained in the city, by reason of his friendship for Herod, he went to that sacred place, being delighted with the spectacle of the building, and of the sacrifices, and all the ceremonies connected with the worship of God, and the regularity which was observed, and the dignity and honour paid to the high priest, and his grandeur when arrayed in his sacred vestments and when about to begin the sacrifices. (297) And after he had adorned the temple with all the offerings in his power to contribute, and had conferred many benefits on the inhabitants, doing them many important services, and having said to Herod many friendly things, and having been replied to in corresponding terms, he was conducted back again to the sea coast, and to the harbour, and that not by one city only but by the whole country, having branches strewed in his road, and being greatly admired and respected for his piety.

(298) "What again did your other grandfather, Tiberius Caesar, do? does not he appear to have adopted an exactly similar line of conduct? At all events, during the three and twenty years that he was emperor, he preserved the form of worship in the temple as it had been handed down from the earliest times, without abrogating or altering the slightest particular of it.

XXXVIII. (299) "Moreover, I have it in my power to relate one act of ambition on his part, though I suffered an infinite number of evils when he was alive; but nevertheless the truth is considered dear, and much to be honoured by you. Pilate was one of the emperor's lieutenants, having been appointed governor of Judaea. He, not more with the object of doing honour to Tiberius than with that of vexing the multitude, dedicated some gilt shields in the palace of Herod, in the holy city; which had no form nor any other forbidden thing represented on them except some necessary inscription, which mentioned these two facts, the name of the person who had placed them there, and the person in whose honour they were so placed there. (300) But when the multitude heard what had been done, and when the circumstance became notorious, then the people, putting forward the four sons of the king, who were in no respect inferior to the kings themselves, in fortune or in rank, and his other descendants, and those magistrates who were among them at the time, entreated him to alter and to rectify the innovation which he had committed in respect of the shields; and not to make any alteration in their national customs, which had hitherto been preserved without any interruption, without being in the least degree changed by any king of emperor.

(301) "But when he steadfastly refused this petition (for he was a man of a very inflexible disposition, and very merciless as well as very obstinate), they cried out: 'Do not cause a sedition; do not make war upon us; do not destroy the peace which exists. The honour of the emperor is not identical with dishonour to the ancient laws; let it not be to you a pretence for heaping insult on our nation. Tiberius is not desirous that any of our laws or customs shall be destroyed. And if you yourself say that he is, show us either some command from him, or some letter, or something of the kind, that we, who have been sent to you as ambassadors, may cease to trouble you, and may address our supplications to your master.'

(302) "But this last sentence exasperated him in the greatest possible degree, as he feared least they might in reality go on an embassy to the emperor, and might impeach him with respect to other particulars of his government, in respect of his corruption, and his acts of insolence, and his rapine, and his habit of insulting people, and his cruelty, and his continual murders of people untried and uncondemned, and his never ending, and gratuitous, and most grievous inhumanity. (303) Therefore, being exceedingly angry, and being at all times a man of most ferocious passions, he was in great perplexity, neither venturing to take down what he had once set up, nor wishing to do any thing which could be acceptable to his subjects, and at the same time being sufficiently acquainted with the firmness of Tiberius on these points. And those who were in power in our nation, seeing this, and perceiving that he was inclined to change his mind as to what he had done, but that he was not willing to be thought to do so, wrote a most supplicatory letter to Tiberius. (304) And he, when he had read it, what did he say of Pilate, and what threats did he utter against him! But it is beside our purpose at present to relate to you how very angry he was, although he was not very liable to sudden anger; since the facts speak for themselves; (305) for immediately, without putting any thing off till the next day, he wrote a letter, reproaching and reviling him in the most bitter manner for his act of unprecedented audacity and wickedness, and commanding him immediately to take down the shields and to convey them away from the metropolis of Judaea to Caesarea, on the sea which had been named Caesarea Augusta, after his grandfather, in order that they might be set up in the temple of Augustus. And accordingly, they were set up in that edifice. And in this way he pro-

vided for two matters: both for the honour due to the emperor, and for the preservation of the ancient customs of the city.

XXXIX. (306) "Now the things set up on that occasion were shields, on which there was no representation of any living thing whatever engraved. But now the thing proposed to be erected is a colossal statue. Moreover, then the erection was in the dwelling-house of the governor; but they say, that which is now contemplated is to be in the inmost part of the temple, in the very holy of holies itself, into which, once in the year, the high priest enters, on the day called the great fast, to offer incense, and on no other day, being then about in accordance with our national law also to offer up prayers for a fertile and ample supply of blessings, and for peace of all mankind. (307) And if any one else, I will not say of the Jews, but even of the priests, and those not of the lowest order, but even those who are in the rank next to the first, should go in there, either with him or after him, or even if the very high priest himself should enter in thither on two days in the year, or three or four times on the same day, he is subjected to inevitable death for his impiety, (308) so great are the precautions taken by our lawgiver with respect to the holy of holies, as he determined to preserve it alone inaccessible to and untouched by any human being.

"How many deaths then do you not suppose that the people, who have been taught to regard this place with such holy reverence, would willingly endure rather than see a statue introduced into it? I verily believe that they would rather slay all their whole families, with their wives and children, and themselves last of all, in the ruins of their houses and families, and Tiberius knew this well. (309) And what did your great-grandfather, the most excellent of all emperors that ever lived upon the earth, he who was the first to have the appellation of Augustus given him, on account of his virtue and good fortune; he who diffused peace in every direction over earth and sea, to the very furthest extremities of the world? (310) Did not he, when he had heard a report of the peculiar characteristics of our temple, and that there is in it no image or representation made by hands, no visible likeness of Him who is invisible, no attempt at any imitation of his nature, did not he, I say, marvel at and honour it? for as he was imbued with something more than a mere smattering of philosophy, inasmuch as he had deeply feasted on it, and continued to feast on it every day, he partly retraced in his recollection all the precepts of philosophy which his mind had previously learnt, and partly also he kept his learning alive by the conversation of the literary men who were always about him; for at his banquets and entertainments, the greatest part of the time was devoted to learned

conversation, in order that not only his friends' bodies but their minds also might be nourished.

XL. (311) "And though I might be able to establish this fact, and demonstrate to you the feelings of Augustus, your great grandfather, by an abundance of proofs, I will be content with two; for, in the first place, he sent commandments to all the governors of the different provinces throughout Asia, because he heard that the sacred first fruits were neglected, enjoining them to permit the Jews alone to assemble together in the synagogues, (312) for that these assemblies were not revels, which from drunkenness and intoxication proceeded to violence, so as to disturb the peaceful condition of the country, but were rather schools of temperance and justice, as the men who met in them were studiers of virtue, and contributed the first fruits every year, sending commissioners to convey the holy things to the temple in Jerusalem.

(313) "And, in the next place, he commanded that no one should hinder the Jews, either on their way to the synagogues, or when bringing their contributions, or when proceeding in obedience to their national laws to Jerusalem, for these things were expressly enjoined, if not in so many words, at all events in effect; (314) and I subjoin one letter, in order to bring conviction to you who are our mater, what Gaius Norbanus Flaccus wrote, in which he details what had been written to him by Caesar, and the superscription of the letter is as follows: (315)—

CAIUS NORBANUS FLACCUS, PROCONSUL, TO THE GOVERNORS OF THE EPHESIANS, GREETING.

"'Caesar has written word to me, that the Jews, wherever they are, are accustomed to assemble together, in compliance with a peculiar ancient custom of their nation, to contribute money which they send to Jerusalem; and he does not choose that they should have any hindrance offered to them, to prevent them from doing this; therefore I have written to you, that you may know that I command that they shall be allowed to do these things.'

(316) "Is not this a most convincing proof, O emperor, of the intention of Caesar respecting the honours paid to our temple which he had adopted, not considering it right that because of some general rule, with respect to meetings, the assemblies of the Jews, in one place should be put down, which they held for the sake of offering the first fruits, and for other pious objects?

(317) "There is also another piece of evidence, in no respect inferior to this one, and which is the most undeniable proof of the will of Augustus, for he commanded perfect sacrifices of whole burnt offerings to be offered up to the most high God every day, out of his own revenues, which are performed up to the present time, and the victims

are two sheep and a bull, with which Caesar honoured the altar of God, well knowing that there is in the temple no image erected, either in open sight or in any secret part of it. (318) But that great ruler, who was inferior to no one in philosophy, considered within himself, that it is necessary in terrestrial things, that an especial holy place should be set apart for the invisible God, who will not permit any visible representation of himself to be made, by which to arrive at a participation in favourable hopes and the enjoyment of perfect blessings.

(319) "And your grandmother, Julia Augusta, following the example of so great a guide in the paths of piety, did also adorn the temple with some golden vials and censers, and with a great number of other offerings, of the most costly and magnificent description; and what was her object in doing this, when there is no statue erected within the temple? for the minds of women are, in some degree, weaker than those of men, and are not so well able to comprehend a thing which is appreciable only by the intellect, without any aid of objects addressed to the outward senses; (320) but she, as she surpassed all her sex in other particulars, so also was she superior to them in this, by reason of the pure learning and wisdom which had been implanted in her, both by nature and by study; so that, having a masculine intellect, she was so sharpsighted and profound, that she comprehended what is appreciable only by the intellect, even more than those things which are perceptible by the outward senses, and looked upon the latter as only shadows of the former.

XLI. (321) "Therefore, O master, having all these examples most nearly connected with yourself and your family, of our purposes and customs, derived from those from whom you are sprung, of whom you are born, and by whom you have been brought up, I implore you to preserve those principles which each of those persons whom I have mentioned did preserve; (322) they who were themselves possessed of imperial power do, by their laws, exhort you, the emperor; they who were august, speak to you who are also Augustus; your grandfathers and ancestors speak to their descendant; numbers of authorities address one individual, all but saying, in express words: Do not you destroy those things in our councils which remain, and which have been preserved as permanent laws to this very day; for even if no mischief were to ensue from the abrogation of them, still, at all events, the result would be a feeling of uncertainty respecting the future, and such uncertainty is full of fear, even to the most sanguine and confident, if they are not despisers of divine things.

(323) "If I were to enumerate the benefits which I myself have received at your hands, the day would be too short for me; besides the fact that it is not proper for one who has undertaken to speak on one subject to branch off to a digression about some other matter. And even if I should be silent, the facts themselves speak and utter a distinct voice. (324) You released me when I was bound in chains and iron. Who is there who is ignorant of this? But do not, after having done so, O emperor! bind me in bonds of still greater bitterness: for the chains from which you released me surrounded a part of my body, but those which I am now anticipating are the chains of the soul, which are likely to oppress it wholly and in every part; (325) you abated from me a fear of death, continually suspended over my head; you received me when I was almost dead through fear; you raised me up as it were from the dead. Continue your favour, O master, that your Agrippa may not be driven wholly to forsake life; for I shall appear (if you do not do so) to have been released from bondage, not for the purpose of being saved, but for that of being made to perish in a more conspicuous manner.

(326) "You have given me the greatest and most glorious inheritance among mankind, the rank and power of a king, at first over one district, then over another and a more important one, adding to my kingdom the district called Trachonitis and Galilee. Do not then, O master! after having loaded me with means of superfluity, deprive me of what is actually necessary. Do not, after you have raised me up to the most brilliant light, cast me down again from my eminence to the most profound darkness. (327) I am willing to descend from this splendid position in which you have placed me; I do not deprecate a return to the condition in which I was a short time ago; I will give up everything; I look upon everything as of less importance than the one point of preserving the ancient customs and laws of my nation unaltered; for if they are violated, what could I say, either to my fellow countrymen or to any other men? It would follow of necessity that I must be looked upon as one of two things, either as a betrayer of my people, or as one who is no longer accounted a friend by you. And what could be a greater misery than either of these two things? (328) For if I am still reckoned among the company of your friends, I shall then receive the imputation of treason against my own nation, if neither my country is preserved free from all misfortune, nor even the temple left inviolate. For you, great men, preserve the property of your companions and of those who take refuge in your protection by your imperial splendour and magnificence. (329) And if you have any secret grief or vexation in your mind, do not throw me into prison, like Tiberius, but deliver me from any anticipation of being thrown into prison at any future time; command me at once to be put out of the way. For what advantage would it be to me to live, who place

my whole hopes of safety and happiness in your friendship and favour?"

XLII. (330) Having written this letter and sealed it, he sent it to Gaius, and then shutting himself up he remained in his own house, full of agony, confusion, and disorder, and anxiety, as to what was the best way of approaching and addressing the emperor; for he and his people had incurred no slight danger, but they had reason to apprehend expulsion from their country, and slavery, and utter destruction, as impending not only over those who were dwelling in the holy land, but over all the Jews in every part of the world.

(331) But the emperor, having taken the letter and read it, and having considered every suggestion which was contained in it, was very angry, because his intentions had not been executed: and yet, at the same time, he was moved by the appeals to his justice and by the supplications which were thus addressed to him, and in some respects he was pleased with Agrippa, and in some he blamed him. (332) He blamed him for his excessive desire to please his fellow countrymen, who were the only men who had resisted his orders and shown any unwillingness to submit to his deification; but he praised him for concealing and disguising none of his feelings, which conduct he said was a proof of a liberal and noble disposition. (333) Therefore being somewhat appeased, at least as far as appearance went, he condescended to return a somewhat favourable answer, granting to Agrippa that highest and greatest of all favours, the consent that this erection of his statue should not take place; and he commanded letters to be written to Publius Petronius the governor of Syria, enjoining him not to allow any alterations or innovations to be made with respect to the temple of the Jews. (334) Nevertheless, though he did grant him the favour, he did not grant it without any alloy, but he mingled with it a grievous terror; for he added to the letter,—

"If any people in the bordering countries, with the exception of the metropolis itself, wishing to erect altars or temples, nay, images of statues, in honour of me and of my family are hindered from doing so, I charge you at once to punish those who attempt to hinder them, or else to bring them before the tribunal." (335) Now this was nothing else but a beginning of seditions and civil wars, and an indirect way of annulling the gift which he appeared to be granting. For some men, more out of a desire of mortifying the Jews than from any feelings of loyalty towards Gaius, were inclined to fill the whole country with erections of one kind or another. But they who beheld the violation of their national customs practised before their eyes were resolved above all things not to endure such an injury unresistingly. But Gaius, judging those who were thus excited to disobedience to be worthy of the most severe punishment possible, a second time orders his statue to be erected in the temple. (336) But by the providence and care of God, who beholds all things and governs all things in accordance with justice, not one of the neighbouring nations made any movement at all; so that there was no occasion for these commands being carried into effect, and these inexorably appointed calamities all terminated in only a moderate degree of blame.

(337) What advantage, then, was gained? some one will say; for even when they were quiet, Gaius was not quiet; but he had already repented of the favour which he had showed to Agrippa, and had re-kindled the desires which he had entertained a little while before; for he commanded another statue to be made, of colossal size, of brass gilt over, in Rome, no longer moving the one which had been made in Sidon, in order that the people might not be excited by its being moved, but that while they remained in a state of tranquillity and felt released from their suspicions, it might in a period of peace be suddenly brought to the country in a ship, and be suddenly erected without the multitude being aware of what was going on.

XLIII. (338) And he was intending to do this while on his voyage along the coast during the period which he had allotted for his sojourn in Egypt. For an indescribable desire occupied his mind to see Alexandria, to which he was eager to go with all imaginable haste, and when he had arrived there he intended to remain a considerable time, urging that the deification about which he was so anxious, might easily be originated and carried to a great height in that city above all others, and then that it would be a model to all other cities of the adoration to which he was entitled, inasmuch as it was the greatest of all the cities of the east, and built in the finest situation in the world. For all inferior men and nations are eager to imitate great men and great states.

(339) Moreover, Gaius was in other respects a man in whose nature there was nothing stable or trustworthy so that, even if he did anything good or kind, he speedily repented of it, and in such a manner that he soon attempted to annul what he had done in such a way as to cause even greater affliction and injury to those whom he had favoured. (340) For instance, he released some prisoners, and then for no reason whatever he threw them into prison a second time, inflicting upon them a second calamity more grievous than the first, namely, that which was caused by unexpected misfortune. (341) Again, he condemned some persons to banishment who had expected sentence of death; not because they were conscious of having committed crimes deserving of death, or indeed of any punishment at all, even the lightest, but because of the extravagant inhumanity of their

master they did not expect to escape. Now to these men, banishment was a downright gain, and equivalent almost to a restoration, since they looked upon it that they had escaped the greatest of all evils, the danger of death. (342) But no long period elapsed before he sent some soldiers after them, though no new circumstances had arisen, and put to death simultaneously the most excellent and nobly-born of the exiles who were living in the different islands as their own countries, and who were bearing their misfortunes in the most contented manner, inflicting in this way the greatest and most pitiable and unexpected misery on many of the noblest families in Rome.

(343) And if he ever gave any one a sum of money as a gift, he demanded it back again at some future time, not a simple loan but he also required interest and compound interest, and often treating the persons themselves who had received it from him as thieves, and punishing them with the severest penalties for having stolen it; for he was not contented that those miserable men should return what had been given to them, but he compelled them also to give up all their property which they had inherited from their parents, or relations, or from any friends, or which, having selected a life of industry and profit, they had acquired by their own resources.

(344) And those who appeared to be in the greatest credit with him, and who lived with him in a round of pleasure, as one may say, with great appearances of friendship and good will, were greatly injured by him, being compelled to expend large sums in irregular, and illegal, and sudden journeys, and in entertainments; for they lavished whole properties in the preparation of a single banquet, so that they were compelled to have recourse to usurers, so vast was his prodigality; (345) therefore many men deprecated the receiving of any favours from him, thinking not only that it was of no advantage, but even that they were only a bait and a snare to lead them into intolerable suffering.

(346) So great therefore was his inequality of temper towards every one, and most especially towards the nation of the Jews to which he was most bitterly hostile, and accordingly beginning in Alexandria he took from them all their synagogues there, and in the other cities, and filled them all with images and statues of his own form; for not caring about any other erection of any kind, he set up his own statue every where by main force; and the great temple in the holy city, which was left untouched to the last, having been thought worthy of all possible respect and preservation, he altered and transformed into a temple of his own, that he might call it the temple of the new Jupiter, the illustrious Gaius.

(347) What is this that you say? Do you, who are a man, seek to take to yourself the air and the

heaven, not being content with the vast multitude of continents, and islands, and nations, and countries of which you enjoy the sovereignty? And do you not think any one of the gods who are worshipped in that city or by our people worthy of any country or city or even of any small precinct which may have been consecrated to them in old time, and dedicated to them with oracles and sacred hymns, and are you intending to deprive them of that, that in all the vast circumference of the world there may be no visible trace or memorial to be found of any honour or pious worship paid to the true real living God? (348) Truly you are suggesting fine hopes to the race of mankind; are you ignorant that you are opening the fountains of evils of every kind, making innovations, and committing acts of audacious impiety such as it is wicked to do and even to think of?

XLIV. (349) It is worth while to make mention of what we both saw and heard, when we were sent for to encounter a contest on behalf of our national constitution; for the moment that we entered into the presence of the emperor we perceived, from his looks and from the state of agitation in which he was, that we had come not before a judge but before an accuser, or rather I should say before the open enemy of those whom he looked upon as opposed to his will; (350) for it would have been the part of a judge to sit with assessors selected because of their virtue and learning, when a question of the greatest importance was being investigated which had lain dormant for four hundred years, and which was now raised for the first time among many myriads of Alexandrian Jews; and it would have been proper for the contending parties with their advocates to stand on each side of him, and for him to listen to them both in turn; first to the accusation and then in turn to the defence, according to a period measured by water,[13] and then retiring the judge should deliberate with his assessors as to what he ought publicly to deliver as his sentence on the justice of the case; but what was actually done resembled rather the conduct of an implacable tyrant, exhibiting uncontrolled authority and displeasure and pride.

(351) For besides that he in no particular behaved in the manner which I have just been describing as proper, having sent for the managers of two gardens, the Maecenatian and the Lamian garden, and they are near one another and close to the city, in which he had spent three or four days, for that was the place in which this theatrical spectacle, aimed at the happiness of a

---

[13] The time allotted to the speeches of advocates in the Athenian courts of justice was measured by a water-clock, *klepsydra*, something like our hour-glass of sand.

whole nation, was intended to be enacted in our presence, he commanded all the outer buildings to be opened for him, for that he wished to examine them all minutely; (352) but we, as soon as we were introduced into his presence, the moment that we saw him, bent to the ground with all imaginable respect and adoration, and saluted him calling him the emperor Augustus; and he replied to us in such a *gentle and courteous and humane* manner that we not only despaired of attaining our object, but even of preserving our lives; (353) for, said he, "You are haters of God, inasmuch as you do not think that I am a god, I who am already confessed to be a god by every other nation, but who am refused that appellation by you." And then, stretching up his hands to heaven, he uttered an ejaculation which it was impious to hear, much more would it be so to repeat it literally.

(354) And immediately all the ambassadors of the opposite portion were filled with all imaginable joy, thinking that their embassy was already successful, on account of the first words uttered by Gaius, and so they clapped their hands and danced for joy, and called him by every title which is applicable to any one of the gods.

XLV. (355) And while he was triumphing in these super-human appellations, the sycophant Isidorus, seeing the temper in which he was, said, "O master, you will hate with still juster vehemence these men whom you see before you and their fellow countrymen, if you are made acquainted with their disaffection and disloyalty towards yourself; for when all other men were offering up sacrifices of thanksgiving for your safety, these men alone refused to offer any sacrifice at all; and when I say, 'these men,' I comprehend all the rest of the Jews." (356) And when we all cried out with one accord, "O Lord Gaius, we are falsely accused; for we did sacrifice, and we offered up entire hecatombs, the blood of which we poured in a libation upon the altar, and the flesh we did not carry to our homes to make a feast and banquet upon it, as it is the custom of some people to do, but we committed the victims entire to the sacred flame as a burnt offering: and we have done this three times already, and not once only; on the first occasion when you succeeded to the empire, and the second time when you recovered from that terrible disease with which all the habitable world was afflicted at the same time, and the third time we sacrificed in hope of your victory over the Germans."

(357) "Grant," said he, "that all this is true, and that you did sacrifice; nevertheless you sacrificed to another god and not for my sake; and then what good did you do me? Moreover you did not sacrifice to me." Immediately a profound shuddering came upon us the first moment that we heard this expression, similar to that which overwhelmed us when we first came into his presence. (358) And while he was saying this he entered into the outer buildings, examining the chambers of the men and the chambers of the women, and the rooms on the ground floor, and all the apartments in the upper story, and blaming some points of their preparation as defective, and planning alterations and suggesting designs, and giving orders himself to make them more costly (359) and then we being driven about in this way followed him up and down through the whole place, being mocked and ridiculed by our adversaries like people at a play in the theatre; for indeed the whole matter was a kind of farce: the judge assumed the part of an accuser, and the accusers the part of an unjust judge, who look upon the defendants with an eye of hostility, and act in accordance with the nature of truth. (360) And when a judge invested with such mighty power begins to reproach the person who is on his trial before him it is necessary to be silent; for it is possible even to defend one's self in silence, and especially for people who are able to make no reply on any of the subjects which he was not investigating and desiring to understand, inasmuch as our laws and our customs restrained our tongues, and shut and sewed up our mouths.

(361) But when he had given some of his orders about the buildings, he then asked a very important and solemn question; "why is it that you abstain from eating pig's flesh?" And then again at this question such a violent laughter was raised by our adversaries, partly because they were really delighted, and partly as they wished to court the emperor out of flattery, and therefore wished to make it appear that this question was dictated by wit and uttered with grace, that some of the servants who were following him were indignant at their appearing to treat the emperor with so little respect, since it was not safe for his most intimate friends to do so much as smile at his words. (362) And when we made answer that, "different nations have different laws, and there are some things of which the use is forbidden both to us and to our adversaries;" and when some one said, "there are also many people who do not eat lamb's flesh which is the most tender of all meat," he laughed and said, "they are quite right, for it is not nice." (363) Being joked with and trifled with and ridiculed in this manner, we were in great perplexity; and at last he said in a rapid and peremptory manner, "I desire to know what principles of justice you recognise with regard to your constitution."

(364) And when we began to reply to him and to explain it, he, as soon as he had a taste of our pleading on the principles of justice, and as soon as he perceived that our arguments were not contemptible, before we could bring forward the more

important things which we had to say, cut us short and ran forward and burst into the principal building, and as soon as he had entered he commanded the windows which were around it to be filled up with the transparent pebbles very much resembling white crystal which do not hinder the light, but which keep out the wind and the heat of the sun. (365) Then proceeding on deliberately he asked in a more moderate tone, "What are you saying?" And when we began to connect our reply with what we had said before, he again ran on and went into another house, in which he had commanded some ancient and admirable pictures to be placed.

(366) But when our pleadings on behalf of justice were thus broken up, and cut short, and interrupted, and crushed as one may almost say, we, being wearied and exhausted, and having no strength left in us, but being in continual expectation of nothing else than death, could not longer keep our hearts as they had been, but in our agony we took refuge in supplications to the one true God, praying him to check the wrath of this falsely called god. (367) And he took compassion on us, and turned his mind to pity. And he becoming pacified merely said, "These men do not appear to me to be wicked so much as unfortunate and foolish, in not believing that I have been endowed with the nature of God;" and so he dismissed us, and commanded us to depart.

XLVI. (368) Having then escaped from what was rather a theatre and a prison than a court of justice (for as in a theatre, there was a great noise of people hissing, and groaning, and ridiculing us in an extravagant manner, and as in a prison, there were many blows inflicted on our bodies, and tortures, and things to agitate our whole souls by the blasphemies which those around us uttered against the Deity, and the threats which they breathed forth against ourselves, and which the emperor himself poured forth with such vehemence, being indignant with us not in behalf of any one else, for in that case he would soon have been appeased, but because of himself and his great desire to be declared a god, in which desire he considered that the Jews were the only people who did not acquiesce, and who were unable to subscribe to it), (369) we at last recovered our breath, not because we had been afraid of death from a base hankering after life, since we would have cheerfully embraced death as immortality if our laws and customs could have been established by such

means, but because we knew that we should be destroyed with great ignominy, without any desirable object being secured by such means, for whatever insults ambassadors are subjected to are at all times referred to those who sent them.

(370) It was owing to these considerations that we were able to hold up our heads for a while, but there were other circumstances which terrified us, and kept us in great perplexity and distress to hear what the emperor would decide, and what he would pronounce, and what kind of sentence he would ultimately deliver; for he heard the general tenor of our arguments, though he disdained to attend to some of our facts. But would it not be a terrible thing for the interests of all the Jews throughout the whole world to be thrown into confusion by the treatment to which we, its five ambassadors, were exposed? (371) For if he were to give us up to our enemies, what other city could enjoy tranquillity? What city would there be in which the citizens would not attack the Jews living in it? What synagogue would be left uninjured? What state would not overturn every principle of justice in respect of those of their countrymen who arrayed themselves in opposition to the national laws and customs of the Jews? They will be overthrown, they will be shipwrecked, they will be sent to the bottom, with all the particular laws of the nation, and those too which are common to all and in accordance with the principles of justice recognized in every city.

(372) We, then, being overwhelmed with affliction, in our misery perplexed ourselves with such reasonings as these; for even those who up to this time had seemed to co-operate with us were now wearied of taking our part. Therefore, when we called them forth, they being within, did not remain, but came forth privily in fear, knowing well the desire which the emperor had to be looked upon as God.

(373) We have now related in a concise and summary manner the cause of the hatred of Gaius to the whole nation of the Jews; we must now proceed to make our palinode to Gaius.[14]

---

[14] Yonge's edition inserts a separate treatise not found in Cohn-Wendland (Loeb), entitled *Concerning the World*. In a note, Yonge asserts that it is virtually identical to the Loeb treatise, *On the Eternity of the World* (which Yonge titled, *On the Incorruptibility of the World*). This treatise has been relegated to an appendix in this volume.

QUESTIONS AND ANSWERS ON GENESIS, I†

(Quaestiones et Solutiones in Genesin, I)

(1) Why does Moses, revolving and considering the creation of the world, say: "This is the book of the generation of heaven and earth, when they were created?" (Genesis 2:4).

The expression, "when they were created," indicates as it seems an indeterminate time not accurately described. But this argument will confute those authors who calculate a certain number of years reduced to one, from the time when it is possible that the world may have been created.

And again, the expression: "This is the book of the generation," is as it were indicative of the book as it follows, which contains an account of the creation of the world; in which it is intimated that what has been related about the creation of the world is consistent with strict truth.

(2) What is the object of saying, "And God made every green herb of the field, before it was upon the earth, and every grass before it had sprung up?" (Genesis 2:5).

He here by these expressions intimates in enigmatical language the incorporeal species; since the expression, "before it was upon the earth," indicates the arriving at perfection of every herb, and of all seeds and trees. But as to what he says, that "before it had sprung up upon the earth," he had made every green herb, and grass, et caetera, it is plain that the incorporeal species, as being indicative of the others, were created first, in accordance with intellectual nature, which those things which are upon the earth perceptible to the outward senses were to imitate.

(3) What is the meaning of saying: "A fountain went up from the earth, and watered all the face of the earth?" (Genesis 2:6).

But here the question is how it could be that the whole earth was watered by one fountain, not only on account of its size, but also because of the inequality of the mountainous and champaign situations? Unless, indeed, just as the whole force of the king's cavalry is called "the horse," so the whole multitude of the veins of the earth which supply drinkable water, may perhaps be called the fountain, inasmuch as they all bubble up like a fountain.

And that expression is peculiarly appropriate which says that the fountain watered, not the whole earth, but its face; as in the living being it waters the chief and predominant part (the mind or the countenance). Since that is the most important part of the earth which can be good and fertile and productive, and that is the part which stands in need of the nourishment of fountains.

(4) What is the man who was created? And how is that man distinguished who was made after the image of God? (Genesis 2:7).

This man was created as perceptible to the senses, and in the similitude of a Being appreciable only by the intellect; but he who in respect of his form is intellectual and incorporeal, is the similitude of the archetypal model as to appearance, and he is the form of the principal character; but this is the word of God, the first beginning of all things, the original species or the archetypal idea, the first measure of the universe.

Moreover, that man who was to be created as a vessel is formed by a potter, was formed out of dust and clay as far as his body was concerned; but he received his soul by God breathing the breath of life into his face, so that the temperament of his nature was combined of what was corruptible and of what was incorruptible. But the other man, he who is only so in form, is found to be unalloyed without any mixture proceeding from an invisible, simple, and transparent nature.

(5) Why is it said that God breathed into his face the breath of life? (Genesis 2:7).

In the first place because life is the principal part of the body; for the rest was only made as a sort of foundation or pedestal, and then life was put upon it as a statue. Besides, the sense is the fountain of the animal form, and sense resides in the face.

Secondly, man is created to be a partaker not

† Yonge's title, *A Volume of Questions, and Solutions to Those Questions, Which Arise in Genesis*. Yonge had access only to Aucher's Latin translation of Aucher's Armenian version (J. B. Aucher's *Philonis Judaei paralipomena Armena: libri videlicet quatuor in Genesin, libri duo in Exodum*, Venice, 1826). Apparently Yonge does not have access to *Questions and Answers on Exodus* in either Latin or Armenian, although fragments of *Questions and Answers on Exodus* appear in Yonge's edition in "Fragments, Extracted from the Parallels of John of Damascus."

only of a soul but also of a rational soul; and the head is the temple of the reason, as some writers have called it.

(6) Why is God said to have planted a Paradise? And for whom? And what is meant by a paradise? (Genesis 2:8).

The word paradise, if taken literally, has no need of any particular explanation; for it means a place thickly crowded with every kind of tree; but symbolically taken, it means wisdom, intelligence both divine and human, and the proper comprehension of the causes of things; since it was proper, after the creation of the world, to establish a contemplative system of life, in order that man, by the sight of the world and of the things which are contained in it, might be able to attain to a correct notion of the praise due to the Father.

And since it was not possible for him to behold nature herself, nor properly to praise the Creator of the universe without wisdom, therefore the Creator planted the outlines of it in the rational soul of the principal guide of man, namely the mind, as he planted trees in the paradise. And when we are told that in the middle was the tree of life, that means the knowledge not only of the creature, but also of the greater and supreme cause of the universe; for if any one is able to arrive at a certain comprehension of that, he will be fortunate and truly happy and immortal.

Moreover, after the creation of the world human wisdom was created, as also after the creation of the world the Paradise was planted; and so the poets say that the chorus of musicians was established in order to praise the Creator and his works; as Plato says, that the Creator was the first and greatest of causes, and that the world was the most beautiful of all creatures.

(7) Why in Adin, or Eden, is God said to have planted the Paradise towards the east? (Genesis 2:8).

This is said in the first place because the motion of the world proceeds from the rising of the sun to its setting. And it first exists in that quarter from which it is moved; secondly, because that part of the world which is in the region of the east is called the right side; and that which is in the region of the west is called the left side of the world.

Moreover the poet bears witness to this, calling the birds from the east *dexteras* or right, and those on the west *sinistras* or left;[1] when he says, whether they go to the right to the day and to the sun, or whether they go to the left towards the dusky evening.

But the name Eden, when rightly understood, is an indication of all kinds of delights, and joys, and pleasures; since all good things and all blessings derive their beginning from the place of the Lord. Thirdly, because wisdom itself is splendour and light.

(8) Why did God place man whom he had created in the Paradise, but not that man who is after his own image? (Genesis 2:15).

Some persons have said, when they fancied that the Paradise was a garden, that because the man who was created was endowed with senses, therefore he naturally and properly proceeded into a sensible place; but the other man, who is made after God's own image, being appreciable only by the intellect, and invisible, had all the incorporeal species for his share; but I should rather say that the paradise was a symbol of wisdom, for that created man is a kind of mixture, as having been compounded of soul and body, having work to do by learning and discipline; desiring according to the law of philosophy that he may become happy; but he who is according to God's own image is in need of nothing, being by himself a hearer, and being taught by himself, and being found to be his own master by reason of his natural endowments.

(9) Why does Moses say that every tree in the Paradise was beautiful to look upon and good to eat? (Genesis 2:9).

He says this because the virtue of trees is of a twofold nature, consisting in bearing leaves and fruit, one of which qualities is referred to the pleasing of the sight, the other to the gratification of the taste; but the word beautiful was not employed inappropriately. Indeed it is very proper that the plants should be always green and flourishing perpetually, as belonging to a divine Paradise, which as such must be everlasting; and it is fit too that they should never degenerate so as to lose their leaves.

But of the fruit he says, not that it was beautiful, but that it was good, speaking in a very philosophical spirit; since men take food, not only because of the pleasure which it affords, but also because of its use; and use is the flowing forth and imparting of some good.

(10) What is meant by the tree of life, and why it was placed in the middle of the Paradise? (Genesis 2:9).

Some people have believed that, if there were really plants of a corporeal and deadly nature, there are also some which are causes of life and immortality, because, they say, life and death are opposed to one another, and because some plants are ascertained to be unwholesome, therefore of necessity there must be others from which health may be derived. But what these are which are wholesome they know not; for generation, as the opinion of the wise has it, is the beginning of corruption.

---

[1] He is referring here to Homer (as Pope translates it)—"Ye vagrants of the sky! your wings extend, / Or where the suns arise, or where descend; / To right, to left, unheeded take your way, / While I the dictates of high Heaven obey."

But perhaps we ought to look on these things as spoken in an allegorical sense; for some say the tree of life belongs to the earth, inasmuch as it is the earth which produces everything which is of use for life, whether it be the life of mankind or of any other animal; since God has appointed the situation in the centre for this plant, and the centre of the universe is the earth. There are others who assert that what is meant by the tree of life is the centre between the seven circles of heaven; but some affirm that it is the sun which is meant, as that is nearly in the centre, between the different planets, and is likewise the cause of the four seasons, and since it is owing to him that every thing which exists is called into existence.

Others again understand by the tree of life the direction of the soul, for this it is which renders the sense nervous and solid, so as to produce actions corresponding to its nature, and to the community of the parts of the body. But whatever is in the middle is in a manner the primary cause and beginning of things, like the leader of a chorus. But still, the best and wisest authorities have considered that by the tree of life is indicated the best of all the virtues of man, piety, by which alone the mind attains to immortality.

(11) What is meant by the tree of the knowledge of good and evil? (Genesis 2:9).

This indeed exhibits that meaning which is sought for in the letter of the Scriptures more clearly to the sight, as it bears a manifest allegory on the face of it. What is meant then under this figure is prudence, which is the comprehension of science, by which all things are known and distinguished from one another, whether they be good and beautiful, or bad and unseemly, or in short every sort of contrariety is discerned; since some things belong to the better class, and some to the worse.

Therefore the wisdom which exists in this world is not in truth God himself, but the work of God; that it is which sees and thoroughly investigates every thing. But the wisdom which exists in man sees in an incorrect and mixed manner with somewhat darkened eyes; for it is found to be incompetent to see and comprehend clearly and without alloy each particular thing separately. Moreover, there is a kind of deception mingled with human wisdom; since very often there are some shadows found which hinder the eyes from contemplating a brilliant light; since what the eye is in the body, such also is the mind and wisdom in the soul.

(12) What the river is which proceeded out of Adin by which the Paradise is watered, and from which the four rivers proceed, the Phison, and the Gihon, and the Tigris, and the Euphrates? (Genesis 2:10).

The sources of the Deglath and of the Ara-

zania, that is to say of the Tigris and Euphrates, are said to arise in the mountains of Armenia; but there is no paradise there at this day, nor do both the sources of both these rivers remain there. Perhaps, therefore, we ought to consider that the real situation of the Paradise is in a place at a distance from this part of the world which we inhabit, and that it has a river running beneath the earth. which pours forth many veins of the largest size; so that they, rising up together, pour themselves forth into other veins, which receive them on account of their great size, and then those have been suppressed by the gulfs of the waves; on which account, through the impulse given to them by the violence which is implanted in them, they burst out on the face of the earth in other places, and also among others in the mountains of Armenia. Therefore, those things which have been accounted the sources of the rivers, are rather their flowing course; or again, they may be said to be correctly looked upon as sources, because by all means we must consider the holy scriptures infallible, which point out the fact of four rivers; for the river is the beginning, and not the spring.

But perhaps this passage also contains an allegorical meaning; for the four rivers are the signs of four virtues: Phison being the sign of prudence, as deriving its name from parsimony;[2] and Gihon being the sign of sobriety, as having its employment in the regulation of meat and drink, and as restraining the appetites of the belly, and of those parts which are below the belly, as being earthly; the Tigris again is the sign of fortitude, for this it is which regulates the raging commotion of anger within us; and the Euphrates is the sign of justice, since there is nothing in which the thoughts of men exult more than in justice.

(13) Why is that he not only describes the situation of the Euphrates, but also says that the Phison goes round all the land of Evilat, and that the Gihon goes round all the land of Ethiopia, and that the Tigris goes toward Assyria? (Genesis 2:14).

The Tigris is a very cruel and mischievous river, as the citizens of Babylon bear witness, and so do the magi, who have found it to be of a character quite different from the nature of other rivers; however they might also have another reason for looking on it with aversion.

But the Euphrates is a gentler, and more salubrious, and more nourishing stream. On which account, the wise men of the Hebrews and Assyrians speak of it as one which increases and extends itself; and on this account it is not here characterised by its connection with other things, as the other three rivers are, but by itself.

---

[2] From *pheidō*, "parsimony."

My own opinion is, that these expressions are all symbolical, for prudence is the virtue of the rational part of man; and it is in this that wickedness is sometimes found. And fortitude is that portion of the human character which is liable to degenerate into anger. And sobriety, again, may be impaired by the desires, but anger and concupiscence are the characteristics of beasts; therefore the sacred historian has here described those three rivers by the places which they flow round. But he has not described the Euphrates in that manner, as being the symbol of justice, for there is no certain and limited portion of it allotted to the soul, but a perfect harmony of the three parts of the soul and of the three virtues is possessed by it.

(14) Why God placed man in the Paradise with a twofold object, namely, that he might both till it and keep it, when the Paradise was in reality in need of no cultivation, because it was perfect in everything, as having been planted by God; nor, again, did it require a keeper, for who was there to ravage it? (Genesis 2:15).

These are the two objects which a cultivation of the land must attain to and take care of, the cultivation of the land and the safe keeping of the things which are in it, otherwise it will be spoiled by laziness or else by devastation. But although the Paradise did not stand in need of these exertions, nevertheless it was proper that he who had the regulation and care of it committed to him, namely, the first man, should be as it were a sort of pattern and law to all workmen in future of everything which ought to be done by them.

Moreover it was suitable that, though all the Paradise was full of everything, it should still leave the cultivator some grounds for care, and some means of displaying his industry; for instance, by digging around it, and tending it, and softening it, and digging trenches, and irrigating it by water; and it was needful to attend to its safety, although there was no one to lay it waste, because of the wild beasts, also more especially in respect of the air and water; as, for instance, when a drought prevailed, to irrigate it with a plenteous supply of water, and in moister weather to check the superabundance of moisture by directing the course of the streams in other directions.

(15) Why, when God commanded the man to eat of every tree within the Paradise, he speaks in the singular number, and says, "Thou shalt eat;" but when he commands that he shall abstain from the tree which would give him the knowledge of good and evil, he speaks in the plural number, and says, "Ye shall not eat of it, for in the day in which ye eat of it ye shall surely die?" (Genesis 2:16).

In the first place he uses this language because one good was derived from many; and that also is not unimportant in these principles, since he who

has done anything which is of utility is one, and he who attains to anything useful is also one; but when I say one, I am speaking not of that which in point of number comes before duality, but of that one creative virtue by which many beings rightly coalesce, and by their concord imitate singularity, as a flock, a herd, a troop, a chorus, an army, a nation, a tribe, a family, a state; for all these things being many members form one community, being united by affection as by a kiss; when things which are not combined, and which have no principle of union by reason of their duality and multitude, fall into different divisions, for duality is the beginning of discord.

But two men living as if they were one, by the same philosophy, practise an unalloyed and brilliant virtue, which is free from all taint of wickedness; but where good and evil are mingled together the combination contains the principle of death.

(16) What is the meaning of the expression, "Ye shall surely die?" (Genesis 2:17).

The death of the good is the beginning of another life; for life is a twofold thing, one life being in the body, corruptible; the other without the body, incorruptible. Therefore one wicked man surely dies the death, who while still breathing and among the living is in reality long since buried, so as to retain in himself no single spark of real life, which is perfect virtue. But a good man, who deserves so high a title, does not surely die, but has his life prolonged, and so attains to an eternal end.

(17) Why God says, "It is not good for man to be alone; let us make him a help meet for him?" (Genesis 2:18).

By these words God intimates that there is to be a communion, not with all men, but with those who are willing to be assisted and in their turn to assist others, even though they may scarcely have any power to do so; since love consists not more in utility than in the harmonious concord of trustworthy and steadfast manners; so that every one who joins in a communion of love may be entitled to utter the expression of Pythagoras, "A friend is another I."

(18) Why, when God had already said, "Let us make a help for man," he creates beasts and cattle? (Genesis 2:19).

Perhaps some gluttons and insatiably greedy persons may say that God did this because beasts and flying things were, as it were, necessary food for man, and his meetest helper; for that the eating of meat assists the belly so as to conduce to the health and vigour of the body. But I should think that by reason of the evil implanted in them by nature animals of all kinds, whether terrestrial or flying in the air, were in this age hostile to and contrary to man; but that in the case of the first man, as one adorned with every imaginable virtue, they were, as it were, allies, and a reinforcement in war, and familiar friends, as being tame and domestic by nature, and this was the sole principle of their familiarity with man, for thus it was fit that servants should dwell with their lord.

(19) Why the creation of animals and flying creatures is mentioned a second time, when the account of their creation had already been given in the history of the six days? (Genesis 2:19).

Perhaps those things which were created in the six days were incorporeal angels, indicated under these symbolical expressions, being the appearances of terrestrial and flying animals, but now they were produced in reality, being the copies of what had been created before, images perceptible by the outward senses of invisible models.

(20) Why did God bring every animal to man, that he might give them their names? (Genesis 2:19).

He has here explained a great source of perplexity to the students of philosophy, admonishing them that names proceed from having been given, and not from nature; for a natural nomenclature is with peculiar fitness assigned to each creature when a man of wisdom and pre-eminent knowledge appears; and, in fact, the office of assigning the names to animals is one which particularly belongs to the mind of the wise man alone, and indeed to the first man born out of the earth, since it was fitting that the first of the human race, and the sovereign of all the animals born out of the earth, should have the dignity assigned to him.

For inasmuch as he was the first person to see the animals, and as he was the first person who deserved to govern them all as their chief, so also it was fitting that he should be their first namer and the inventor of their names, since it would have been inconsistent and mad to leave them without any names, or to allow them to receive names from any one born at a later period, which would have been an insult to and a derogation from the honour and glory due to the first born.

But we may also adopt this idea, that the giving of names to the different animals was so easily arranged that the very moment that Adam gave the name the animal itself also heard it; being influenced by the name thus given to it as by a familiar indication closely connected with it.

(21) Why does Moses say, "He brought the animals to Adam, that he might see what he would call them," when God can never entertain a doubt? (Genesis 2:19).

It is in truth inconsistent with the nature of God to doubt; therefore it does not appear that he was in doubt on this occasion, but that since he had given intellect to man as being the first man born out of the earth and endowed with a great desire for virtue, by which he was made thoroughly wise as if he had been endowed with wisdom by nature,

so as to consider all things like the proper Ruler and Lord of all, God now caused him to be influenced to display the proper performance of his task, and saw what was really the most excellent point of his mind.

Besides this, by this statement he evidently indicates the perfect free-will existing in us, refuting those who affirm that everything exists by a certain necessity.

Or else because it belonged to man to employ the animals, therefore he also gave him authority to give them names.

(22) What is the meaning of the expression, "And whatever he called each living thing, that was the name thereof?" (Genesis 2:19).

We must consider that Adam gave names not only to all living creatures, but also to plants, and to everything else which is inanimate, beginning with the more excellent class; for the living creature is superior to that which has not life. Therefore the scripture considers the mention of the better part sufficient, indicating by this mention to all who are not utterly devoid of sense, that he in fact gave names to everything, since it was easy to fix names to things without life, which were never likely to change their place, and which had no passions of the soul to exercise, but the giving of proper appellations to living creatures was a more difficult task on account of the motions of their bodies and the various impulses of their souls, in accordance with the imagination and the variety of the outward senses, and the different agitations of the mind from which the effects of their works proceed. Therefore the mind could give names to the more difficult classes of living creatures. And on this account it was a very proper expression to employ, that he gave them names as being easy to name, because they were near.

(23) What is the meaning of the expression: "But for Adam there was not found a helper like to him?" (Genesis 2:20).

Every thing was helping and assisting the prince of the human race: the earth, the rivers, the sea, the air, the light, the heaven. Moreover, every species of fruit and plant co-operated with him, and every herd of cattle, and every beast which was not savage. Nevertheless, of all these things which were assisting him, there was nothing like himself, inasmuch as they were none of them human beings. Therefore, God gave a certain indication that he might show that man ought to be an assistant to and co-operator with man, being endowed with perfect similarity to one another in both body and soul.

(24) What is the meaning of the statement, "And God sent a trance upon Adam, and caused him to sleep?" (Genesis 2:21).

How it is that man sleeps is a question which has caused an extraordinary amount of perplexity to philosophers. But yet our prophet has distinctly explained this question; for sleep is in itself properly a trance, not of that kind which is more nearly allied to insanity, but of that which is in accordance with the dissolution of the senses and the absence of counsel; for then the senses withdraw from those things which are their proper object, and the intellect withdraws from the senses, not strengthening their nerves, nor giving any motion to those parts which have received the power of action, inasmuch as they are withdrawn from the objects perceptible by the outward senses.

(25) What the rib is which God took from the man whom he had formed out of the earth, and which he made into a woman? (Genesis 2:21-22).

The letter of this statement is plain enough; for it is expressed according to a symbol of the part, a half of the whole, each party, the man and the woman, being as sections of nature co-equal for the production of that genus which is called man. But with respect to the mind, man is understood in a symbolical manner, and his one rib is virtue, proceeding from the senses; but woman, who is the sensation of counsel, will be more variable.

But some think that the rib means valour and vigour, on which account men call a boxer who has strong loins eminently strong.

Therefore, the lawgiver relates that the woman was formed out of the rib of the man, indicating by that expression, that one half of the body of the man is woman. And this is testified to by the formation of the body, by the way in which it is put together, by its motions and vigour, by the force of the soul, and its strength; for all things are regarded as in a twofold light; since, as the formation of the man is more perfect, and, if one may so say, more double than the formation of the woman, so also it required half the time, that is to say forty days; when, for the imperfect, and, if I may so call it, half section of the man, that is to say the woman, there was need of a double allowance, that is to say, of eighty days, so that the doubling of the time required for the nature of the man might be changed, in order to the formation of the peculiar properties of the woman; for that body, and that soul, the nature of which is in a twofold ratio, the body and soul, that is, of the man, require but half of the delineation and formation: but that body of which the nature and construction is in the ratio of one half, namely, that of the woman, her formation and delineation is in a twofold ratio.

(26) Why Moses calls the form of the woman a building? (Genesis 2:22).[3]

The union and plentitude of concord formed by the man and woman is symbolically called a house; but every thing is altogether imperfect and destitute of a home, which is deserted by a woman; for to the man the public affairs of the state are committed, but the particular affairs of the house belong to the woman; and a want of the woman will be the destruction of the house; but the actual presence of the woman shows the regulation of the house.

(27) Why, as other animals and as man also was made, the woman was not also made out of the earth, but out of the rib of the man? (Genesis 2:21).

This was so ordained in the first place, in order that the woman might not be of equal dignity with the man. In the second place, that she might not be of equal age with him, but younger; since those who marry wives more advanced in years than themselves deserve blame, as having overturned the law of nature. Thirdly, the design of God was, that the husband should take care of his wife, as of a necessary part of himself; but that the woman should requite him in turn with service, as a portion of the universe. In the fourth place, he admonishes man by this enigmatical intimation, that he should take care of his wife as of his daughter; and he admonishes the woman that she should honour her husband as her father. And very rightly, since the woman changes her habitation, passing from her own offspring to her husband. On which account, it is altogether right and proper that he who has received should take upon himself the liability in respect of what has been given; and that she who has been removed should worthily give the same honour to her husband which she has previously given to her parents; for the husband receives his wife from her parents, as a deposit which is entrusted to him; and the woman receives her husband from the law.

(28) Why, when the man saw the woman who had been formed in this manner, he proceeded to say: "She" (for "this," *touto*) "is now bone of my bone and flesh of my flesh: she shall be called woman, because she has been taken out of man?" (Genesis 2:23).[4]

He might have been amazed at what he had seen, and have said in a negative manner: How can this exquisite and desirable beauty have been derived from bones and from flesh which are endowed with neither beauty nor elegance, being of a form so far more beautiful, and endowed with such excessive life and grace? The matter is incredible because she is like; and yet it is credible,

---

[3] The margin of our bible points out that the Hebrew word translated "made," means strictly "builded."

[4] Woman, *virgo*, or *virago*, is here looked upon as derived from *vir*, "man;" he also derives *gynē* from *gennaō*.

because God himself has been her creator and painter.

Again, he might have said affirmatively: Truly she is a living being, my bone and my flesh, for she exists by having been taken from that bone and flesh of mine. But he makes mention of his bone and flesh in a very natural manner; for the human or corporeal tabernacle is the combination of bones, and flesh, and entrails, and veins, and nerves, and ligaments, and blood-vessels, and breathing tubes, and blood. And she is called woman (in Greek *gynē*) with great correctness, as the power of producing with fertility, either because she becomes pregnant through the reception of the seed, and so brings forth; or, as the prophet says, because she was made out of man, not out of the earth, as he was; nor from seed, as all mankind after them; but of a certain intermediate nature; and like a branch, brought out of one vine to produce another vine.

(29) Why he says, "Therefore shall a man leave his father and his mother, and cleave to his wife, and they shall be two in one flesh?" (Genesis 2:24).

He here orders man to behave himself towards his wife with such excess of affection in their intercourse, that he is willing to leave his parents, not in order that by that means it may be more suitable, but as they would scarcely be a motive for his fidelity to his wife. And we must remark, that it is very excellent and prudently done, that he has avoided saying that the woman is to leave her parents and cleave to her husband, since the character of the man is bolder than the nature of the woman; but he says that the man ought to do this for the sake of the woman; for he is borne on by a cheerful and willing impulse to the concord of knowledge, to which, becoming wholly devoted, he restrains and regulates his desires, and clings to his wife alone like bird-lime. Especially because he himself, delighting in his master-like authority, is to be respected for his pride: but the woman, being in the rank of a servant, is praised, for assenting to a life of communion.

And when it is said that the two are one flesh, that indicates that the flesh is very tangible and fully endowed with outward senses, on which it depends to be afflicted with pain and delighted with pleasure, so that both the man and woman may derive pleasure and pain from the same sources, and may feel the same; aye, and may still more think the same.

(30) Why both of them, the man and the woman, are said to have been naked, and not to have been ashamed? (Genesis 2:25).

They were not ashamed, in the first place, because they were in the neighbourhood of the world, and the different parts of the world are all naked, each of them indicating some peculiar qualities, and having peculiar coverings of their own.

In the second place, on account of the sincerity and simplicity of their manners and of their natural disposition, which had not taint of pride about it. For ambition had as yet no existence. Thirdly, because the climate and the mildness of the atmosphere was a sufficient covering for them, so as to prevent either cold or heat from hurting them. In the fourth place, because they, by reason of the relationship existing between themselves and the world, could not receive injury from any part of it whatever, as being related to them.

(31) Why does Moses say that the serpent was more cunning than all the beasts of the field? (Genesis 3:1).

One may probably affirm with truth that the serpent in reality is more cunning than any beast whatever. But the reason why he appears to me to be spoken of in these terms here is on account of the natural proneness of mankind to vice, of which he is the symbol. And by vice I mean concupiscence, inasmuch as those who are devoted to pleasure are more cunning, and are the inventors of stratagems and means by which to indulge their passions. Being, forsooth, very crafty in devising plans, both such as favour pleasure and also such as procure means of enjoying it. But it appears to me that since that animal, so superior in wisdom, was about to seduce man, it is not the whole race that is here meant to be spoken of as so exceedingly wise, but only that single serpent, for the reason above mentioned.

(32) Did the serpent speak with a human voice? (Genesis 3:2).

In the first place, it may be the fact that at the beginning of the world even the other animals besides man were not entirely destitute of the power of articulate speech, but only that man excelled them in a greater fluency and perspicuity of speech and language. In the second place, when anything very marvellous requires to be done, God changes the subject natures by which he means to operate. Thirdly, because our soul is entirely filled with many errors, and rendered deaf to all words except in one or two languages to which it is accustomed; but the souls of those who were first created were rendered acute to thoroughly understand every voice of every kind, in order that they might be pure from evil and wholly unpolluted. Since we indeed are not endowed with senses in such perfection, for those which we have received are in some degree depraved, just as the construction of our bodies too is small; but the first created men, as they received bodies of vast size reaching to a gigantic height, must also of necessity have received more accurate senses, and, what is more excellent still, a power of examining into and hearing things in a philosophical manner. For some people think, and perhaps with some reason, that they were endowed with such eyes as enabled them to behold even those natures, and essences, and operations, which exist in heaven, as also ears by which they could comprehend every kind of voice and language.

(33) Why did the serpent accost the woman, and not the man? (Genesis 3:2).

The serpent, having formed his estimate of virtue, devised a treacherous stratagem against them, for the sake of bringing mortality on them. But the woman was more accustomed to be deceived than the man. For his counsels as well as his body are of a masculine sort, and competent to disentangle the notions of seduction; but the mind of the woman is more effeminate, so that through her softness she easily yields and is easily caught by the persuasions of falsehood, which imitate the resemblance of truth.

Since therefore, in his old age, the serpent[5] strips himself of his scales from the top of his head to his tail, he, by his nakedness, reproaches man because he has exchanged death for immortality. His nature is renewed by the beast, and made to resemble every time. The woman, when she sees this, is deceived; when she ought rather to have looked upon him as an example, who, while showing his ingenuity towards her, was full of devices, but she was led to desire to acquire a life which should be free from old age, and from all decay.

(34) Why the serpent tells the woman lies, saying, "God has said, Ye shall not eat of every tree in the Paradise," when, on the contrary, what God really had said was, "Ye shall eat of every tree in the Paradise, except one?" (Genesis 3:4).

It is the custom for contending arguers to speak falsely in an artful manner, in order to produce ignorance of the real facts, as was done in this case, since the man and woman had been commanded to eat of all the trees but one. But this insidious prompter of wickedness coming in, says that the order which they had received was that they should not eat of them all. He brought forward an ambiguous statement as a slippery stumbling-block to cause the soul to trip. For this expression, "Ye shall not eat of every tree," means in the first place either, not even of one, which is false; or, secondly, not of every one, as if he intended to say, there are some of which you may not eat, which is true. Therefore he asserts such a falsehood more explicitly.

(35) Why, when it was commanded them to avoid eating of one plant alone, the woman made also a further addition to this injunction, saying, "He said, Ye shall not eat of it, neither shall ye touch it?" (Genesis 3:3).

In the first place she says this, because taste and every other sense after its kind consists in the touch appropriate to it. In the second place she says it that it may seem to condemn them themselves, who did what they had been forbidden. For if even the mere act of touching it was prohibited, how could they who, besides touching the tree, presumed to eat of the fruit, and so added a greater transgression to the lesser one, be anything but condemners and punishers of themselves?

(36) What is the meaning of the expression, "Ye shall be as gods, knowing good and evil?" (Genesis 3:5).

Whence was it that the serpent found the plural word "gods," when there is only one true God, and when this is the first time that he names him? But perhaps this arises from there having been in him a certain prescient wisdom, by which he now declared the notion of the multitude of gods which was at a future time to prevail amongst men; and, perhaps, history now relates this correctly at its first being advanced not by any rational being, nor by any creature of the higher class, but as having derived its origin from the most virulent and vile of beasts and serpents, since other similar creatures lie hid under the earth, and their lurking places are in the holes and fissures of the earth.

Moreover, it is the inseparable sign of a being endowed with reason to look upon God as essentially one being, but it is the mark of a beast to imagine that there are many gods, and these too devoid of reason, and who can scarcely be said with propriety to have any existence at all.

Moreover, the devil proceeds with great art, speaking by the mouth of the serpent. For not only is there in the Divinity the knowledge of good and evil, but there is also an approval of what is good and a repudiation of what is evil; but he does not speak of either of these feelings because they were useful, but only suggested the mere knowledge of the two contrary things, namely, of good and evil. In the second place, the expression, "as gods," in the plural number, is in this place not used inconsiderately, but in order to give the idea of there being both a bad and a good God. And these are of a twofold quality. Therefore it is suitable to the notion of particular gods to have a knowledge of contrary things; but the Supreme Cause is above all others.

(37) Why the woman first touched the tree and ate of its fruit, and the man afterwards, receiving it from her? (Genesis 3:6).

The words used first of all, by their own intrinsic force, assert that it was suitable that immortality and every good thing should be represented as under the power of the man, and death and every evil under that of the woman. But with reference to the mind, the woman, when understood

---

[5]The ancients believed that the serpent became young again by casting his skin. Ovid says—Anguibus exuitur tenui cum pelle vetustas.

symbolically, is sense, and the man is intellect. Moreover, the outward senses do of necessity touch those things which are perceptible by them; but it is through the medium of the outward senses that things are transmitted to the mind. For the outward senses are influenced by the objects which are presented to them; and the intellect by the outward senses.

(38) What is the meaning of the expression, "And she gave it to her husband to eat with her?" (Genesis 3:6).

What has been just said bears on this point also, since the time is nearly one and the same in which the outward senses are influenced by the object which is presented to them, and the intellect has an impression made on it by the outward senses.

(39) What is the meaning of the expression, "And the eyes of both of them were opened?" (Genesis 3:7).

That they were not created blind is manifest even from this fact that as all other things, both animals and plants, were created in perfection, so also man must have been adorned with the things which are his most excellent parts, namely, eyes. And we may especially prove this, because a little while before the earth-born Adam was giving names to all the animals on the earth. Therefore it is perfectly plain that he saw them before doing so. Unless, indeed, Moses used the expression "eyes" in a figurative sense for the vision of the soul, by which alone the perception of good and evil, of what is elegant or unsightly, and, in fact, of all contrary natures, arise. But, if the eye is to be taken separately as counsel, which is called the warning of the understanding, then again there is a separate eye, which is a certain something devoid of sound reason, which is called opinion.

(40) What is the meaning of the expression, "Because they knew that they were naked?" (Genesis 3:7).

They first arrived at the knowledge of this fact, that is to say, of their nakedness, after they had eaten of the forbidden fruit. Therefore, opinion was like the beginning of wickedness, when they perceived that they had not as yet used any covering, inasmuch as all parts of the universe are immortal and incorruptible; but they themselves immediately found themselves in need of some corruptible coverings made with hands. But this knowledge was in the nakedness itself, not as having been in itself the cause of any change, but because their mind now conceived a novelty unlike the rest of the universal world.

(41) Why they sewed fig-leaves into girdles? (Genesis 3:8).

They did this in the first place, because the fruit of the fig is very pleasant and agreeable to the taste. Therefore the sacred historian here, by a symbolical expression, indicates those who sew together and join pleasures to pleasures by every means and contrivance imaginable. Therefore they bind them around the place where the parts of generation are seated, as that is the instrument of important transactions.

And they do this, secondly, because although the fruit of the fig-tree is, as I have already said, sweeter than any other, yet its leaves are harder. And, therefore, Moses here wishes by this symbol to intimate that the motions of pleasure are slippery and smooth in appearance, but that they, nevertheless, are in reality hard, so that it is impossible that he who feels them should be delighted, unless he was previously sorrowful, and he will again become sorrowful. For to be always sorrowing is a melancholy thing between a double grief, the one being at its beginning, and the other coming before the first is ended.

(42) What is meant by the statement that the sound was heard of God walking in the Paradise? was it the sound of his voice, or of his feet? and can God be said to talk? (Genesis 3:8).

Those gods who are in heaven, perceptible to our outward senses, walk in a ring, proceeding onwards by a circuitous track; but the Supreme Cause is steadfast and immoveable, as the ancients have decided. But the true God gives some indication also, as if he wished to give a sense of motion. For in truth even without his uttering any words, the prophets hear him, by a certain virtue of some diviner voice sounding in their ears, or perhaps being even articulately uttered.

As therefore God is heard without uttering any sound, so also he gives an idea of walking when he is not walking, nay, though he is altogether immoveable. But do you not see that before they had tasted of wickedness, as they were stable and constant, and immoveable and tranquil, and uniform, so also in an equal manner must they have looked upon the Deity as immoveable, as in fact he is. But they once had become endued with cunning, they, by judging from themselves, began to strip him of his attributes of immobility and unchangeableness, and conjectured that he too was subject to variation and change.

(43) Why while they are hiding themselves from the face of God, the woman is not mentioned first, since she was the first to eat of the forbidden fruit: but why the man is spoken of in the first place; for the sacred historian's words are, "And Adam and his wife hid themselves?" (Genesis 3:9).

The woman, being imperfect and depraved by nature, made the beginning of sinning and prevaricating; but the man, as being the more excellent and perfect creature, was the first to set the example of blushing and of being ashamed, and indeed, of every good feeling and action.

(44) Why they did not hide themselves in some

other place, but in the middle of the trees of the Paradise? (Genesis 3:9).

Every thing is not done by sinners with wisdom and sagacity, but it often happens that while thieves are watching for an opportunity of plunder, having no thoughts of the Deity who presides over the world, the booty which is close to them and lying at their feet is by some admirable management wrested from them without delay: and something of this kind took place on the present occasion. For when they ought rather to have fled to a distance from the garden in which their offence had taken place, they still were arrested in the middle of the Paradise itself, in order that they might be convicted of their sin too clearly to find any refuge even in flight itself. And this statement indicates in a figurative manner that every wicked man takes refuge in wickedness, and that every man who is wholly devoted to his passions flies to those passions as to an asylum.

(45) Why God asks Adam, "Where art thou?" when he knows everything: and why he does not also put the same question to the woman? (Genesis 3:10).

The expression, "Where art thou?" does not here seem to be a mere interrogatory, but rather a threat and a conviction: "Where art thou now, O man? from how many good things art thou changed? having forsaken immortality and a life of the most perfect happiness, you have become changed to death and misery in which you are buried."

But God did not condescend to put any question to the woman at all, looking upon her as the cause of the evil which had occurred, and as the guide to her husband to a life of shame.

But there is an allegorical meaning in this passage, because the principal part is the man, his guide, the mind, having in itself the masculine principle, when it gives ear to any one introduces also the defect of the female part, namely that of the outward sense.

(46) Why the man says, "The woman gave me of the tree, and I did eat;" but the woman does not say, "The serpent gave to me," but, "The serpent beguiled me and I did eat?" (Genesis 3:12–13).

The literal expression here affords grounds for that probable opinion that woman is accustomed rather to be deceived than to devise anything of importance out of her own head; but with the man the case is just the contrary. But as regards the intellect, everything which is the object of the outward senses beguiles and seduces each particular sense of every imperfect being to which it is adapted. And the sense then, being vitiated by the object, infects the dominant and principal part, the mind, with its own taint. Therefore the mind receives the impression from the outward sense,

giving it that which it has received itself. For the outward sense is deceived and beguiled by the sensible object submitted to it, but the senses of the wise man are infallible, as are also the cogitations of his mind.

(47) Why God curses the serpent first, then the woman, and the man last of all? (Genesis 3:14).

The reason is that the order of the verses followed the order in which the offences were committed. The first offence was the deceit practised by the serpent; the second was the sin of the woman which was owing to him when she abandoned herself to his seduction; the third thing was the guilt of the man in yielding rather to the inclination of the woman than to the commandment of God. But this order is very admirable, containing within itself a perfect allegory; inasmuch as the serpent is the emblem of desire, as is proved, and the woman of the outward sense; but the man is the symbol of intellect. Therefore the infamous author of the sin is desire; and that first deceives the outward sense, and then the outward sense captivates the mind.

(48) Why the curse is pronounced on the serpent in this manner, that he shall go on his breast and on his belly, and eat dust, and be at enmity with the woman? (Genesis 3:16).

The words in themselves are plain enough, and we have evidence of them in what we have seen. But the real meaning contains an allegory concealed beneath it; since the serpent is the emblem of desire, representing under a figure a man devoted to pleasure. For he creeps upon his breast and upon his belly, being filled with meat and drink like cormorants, being inflamed by an insatiable cupidity, and being incontinent in their voracity and devouring of flesh, so that whatever relates to food is in every article something earthly, on which account he is said to eat the dust.

But desire has naturally a quarrel with the outward sense, which Moses here symbolically calls the woman; but where the passions appear to be as it were guardians and champions in behalf of the senses, nevertheless they are beyond all question still more clearly flatterers forming devices against them like so many enemies; and it is the custom of those who are contending with one another to perpetrate greater evils by means of those things which they concede. Forsooth they turn the eyes to the ruin of the sight, the ears to hearing what is unwelcome; and the rest of the outward senses to insensibility. Moreover they cause dissolution and paralysis to the entire body, taking away from it all soundness, and foolishly building up instead a great number of most mischievous diseases.

(49) Why the curse pronounced against the woman is the multiplication of her sadness and

groans, that she shall bring forth children in sorrow, and that her desire shall be to her husband, and that she shall be ruled over by him? (Genesis 3:16).

Every woman who is the companion for life of a husband suffers all those things, not indeed as a curse but as necessary evils. But speaking figuratively, the human sense is wholly subjected to severe labour and pain, being stricken and wounded by domestic agitations. Now the following are the children in the service of the outward senses: the sight is the servant of the eyes, hearing of the ears, smelling of the nostrils, taste of the mouth, feeling of the touch.

Since the life of the worthless and wicked man is full of pain and want, it arises of necessity from these facts that every thing which is done in accordance with the outward sense must be mingled with pain and fear. In respect of the mind a conversion of the outward sense takes place towards the man not as to a companion, for it, like the woman, is subject to authority as being depraved, but as to a master, because it has chosen violence rather than justice.

(50) Why God, as he had pronounced a curse on the serpent and on the woman which bore a relation to themselves and to one another, he did not pronounce a similar one upon the man, but connected the earth with him, saying, "Cursed is the earth for thy sake; in sorrow shalt thou eat of it, thorns and thistles shall it bring forth unto thee, and thou shalt eat the grass of the field: in the sweat of thy brow shalt thou eat thy bread?" (Genesis 3:17).

Since all intellect is a divine inspiration, God did not judge it right to curse him in the manner deserved by his offence; but converted his curse so as to fall upon the earth and his cultivation of it. But man, as a body of co-equal nature and similar character to that of the earth and understanding, is its cultivator. When the cultivator is endowed with virtue and diligence, then the body produces its proper fruit, namely sanity, an excellent state of the outward senses, strength, and beauty. But if the cultivator be a savage, then every thing is different. For the body becomes liable to a curse, since it has for its husbandman an intellect unchastised and unsound. And its fruit is nothing useful, but only thorns and thistles, sorrow and fear, and other vices which every thought strikes down, and as it were pierces the intellect with its darts.

But grass here is symbolically used for food; since man has changed himself from a rational animal into a brute beast, having neglected all divine food, which is given by philosophy, by means of distinct words and laws to regulate the will.

(51) What is the meaning of the expression, "Until thou returnest to the earth from which thou wast taken;" for man was not created out of the earth alone, but also of the divine Spirit? (Genesis 3:18).

In the first place it is clear, that the first man who was formed out of the earth was made up both of earth and heaven; but because he did not continue uncorrupt, but despised the commandment of God, fleeing from the most excellent part, namely, from heaven, he gave himself up wholly as a slave to the earth, the denser and heavier element.

In the second place, if any one burns with a desire of virtue, which makes the soul immortal, he, beyond all question, attains to a heavenly inheritance; but because he was covetous of pleasure, by which spiritual death is engendered, he again gives himself over a second time to the earth, on which account it is said to him, "Dust thou art, and unto dust shalt thou return;" therefore the earth, as it is the beginning of a wicked and depraved man, so also it is his end; but heaven is the beginning and end of him who is endowed with virtue.

(52) Why Adam called his wife Life, and affirmed to her, "Thou art the mother of all living?" (Genesis 3:20).

In the first place, Adam gave to the first created woman that familiar name of Life, inasmuch as she was destined to be the fountain of all the generations which should ever arise upon the earth after their time.

In the second place, he called her by this name because she did not derive the existence of her substance out of the earth, but out of a living creature, namely, out of one part of the man, that is to say, out of his rib, which was formed into a woman, and on that account she was called "life," because she was first made out of a living creature, and because the first beings who were endowed with reason were to be generated from her. Nevertheless, it is possible that this may have been a metaphorical expression; for is not the outward sense, which is a figurative emblem of the woman, called with peculiar propriety "life?" because it is by the possession of these senses that the living being is above all other means distinguished from that which is not alive, as it is by that that the imaginations and impulses of the soul are set in motion, for the senses are the causes of each; and, in real truth the outward sense is the mother of all living creatures, for as there could be no generation without a mother, so also there could be no living creature without sense.

(53) Why God made garments of skins for Adam and his wife, and clothed them? (Genesis 3:21).

Perhaps some one may laugh at the expressions here used, considering the small value of the garments thus made, as if they were not at all worthy of the labour of a Creator of such dignity and greatness; but a man who has a proper appreciation of wisdom and virtue will rightly and deservedly look upon this work as one very suitable for a God, that, namely, of teaching wisdom to those who were before labouring to no purpose; and who, having but little anxiety about procuring useful things, being seized with an insane desire for miserable honours, have given themselves up as slaves to convenience, looking upon the study of wisdom and virtue with detestation, and being in love with splendour of life and skill in mean and handicraft arts, which is in no way connected with a virtuous man.

And these unhappy men do not know that a frugality, which is in need of nothing, becomes, as it were, a relation and neighbour to man, but that luxurious splendour is banished to a distance as an enemy; therefore the garment made of skins, if one should come to a correct judgment, deserves to be looked upon as a more noble possession than a purple robe embroidered with various colours.

Therefore this is the literal meaning of the text; but if we look to the real meaning, then the garment of skins is a figurative expression for the natural skin, that is to say, our body; for God, when first of all he made the intellect, called it Adam; after that he created the outward sense, to which he gave the name of Life. In the third place, he of necessity also made a body, calling that by a figurative expression, a garment of skins; for it was fitting that the intellect and the outward sense should be clothed in a body as in a garment of skins; that the creature itself might first of all appear worthy of divine virtue; since by what power can the formation of the human body be put together more excellently, and in a more becoming manner, than by God? on which account he did put it together, and at the same time he clothed it; when some prepare articles of human clothing and others put them on; but this natural clothing, contemporary with the man himself, namely, the body, belonged to the same Being both to make and to clothe the man in after it was made.

(54) Who those beings are to whom God says, "Behold, Adam has become as one of us, to know good and evil?" (Genesis 3:22).

The expression, "one of us," indicates a plurality of beings; unless indeed we are to suppose, that God is conversing with his own virtues, which he employed as instruments, as it were, to create the universe and all that is in it; but that expression "as," resembles an enigma, and a similitude, and a comparison, but is not declaratory of any dissimilarity; for that which is intelligible and sensibly good, and likewise that which is of a contrary character, is known to God in a different manner from that in which it is known to man; since, in the same way in which the natures of those who inquire and those who comprehend, and the things

themselves too which are inquired into, and perceived, and comprehended, are distinguished, virtue itself is also capable of comprehending them. But all these things are similitudes, and forms, and images, among men; but among the gods they are prototypes, models, indications, and more manifest examples of things which are somewhat obscure; but the unborn and uncreated Father joins himself to no one, except with the intention of extending the honour of his virtues.

(55) What is the meaning of the words, "Lest perchance he put forth his hand and take of the tree of life, and eat and live for ever;" for there is no uncertainty and no envy in God? (Genesis 3:23).

It is quite true that God never feels either uncertainty or envy; nevertheless he often employs ambiguous things and expressions, assenting to them as a man might do; for, as I have said before, the supreme providence is of a twofold nature, sometimes being God, and not acting in any respect as a man; but, on some occasions, as a man instructs his son, so likewise should the Lord God give warning to you.

Therefore the first of these circumstances belongs to his sovereign power, and the second to his disciplinary, and to the first introduction to instruction, so as to insinuate into man's heart a voluntary inclination, since that expression, "lest perchance," is not to be taken as a proof of any hesitation on the part of God, but in relation to man, who, by his nature, is prone to hesitation, and is a denunciation of the inclinations which exist in him.

For when any appearance of anything whatever occurs to any man, immediately there arises within him an impulse towards that which appears, being caused by that very thing which appears. And from this arises the second hesitating kind of uncertainty, distracting the mind in various directions, as to whether the thing is fit to be accepted, or acquired, or not. And very likely present circumstances have a respect to that second feeling; for, in truth, the Divinity is incapable of any cunning, or malevolence, or wickedness: it is absolutely impossible that God should either envy the immortality or any other good fortune belonging to any being. And we can bring the most undeniable proof of this; for it was not in consequence of any one's entreaties that he created the world; but, being a merciful benefactor, rendering an essence previously untamed and unregulated, and liable to suffering, gentle and pleasant, he did so by a vast harmony of blessings, and a regulated arrangement of them, like a chorus; and he being himself the only sure being, planted the tree of life by his own luminous character.

Moreover, he was not influenced by the mediation or exhortation of any other being in communicating incorruptibility to man. But while man existed as the purest intellect, displaying no appearance either of work or of any evil discourse, he was certain to have a fitting guide, to lead him in the paths of piety, which is undoubted and genuine immortality. But from the time when he began to be converted to depravity, wishing for the things which belong to mortal life, he wandered from immortality; for it is not fitting that craft and wickedness should be rendered immortal, and moreover it would be useless to the subject; since the longer the life is which is granted to the wicked and depraved man, the more miserable is he than others, so that his immortality becomes a grave misfortune to him.

(56) Why now he calls the Paradise "pleasure," when he is sending man forth out of it to till the ground from which he was taken. (Genesis 3:23).

The distinction of agriculture is conspicuous, when man in the state of paradise, practising the cultivation of wisdom as if he were employed in the cultivation of trees, and enjoying the food of imperishable and most useful fruits, was himself endowed with immortality likewise. After that, being expelled from the place of wisdom, he experienced the opposite effects of ignorance, by which the body is polluted, and at the same time the intellect is blinded, and, being exposed to a want of proper food, he wastes away, and yields to a miserable death.

On which account, now, in contempt of the foolish man, God calls the Paradise "pleasure," in order to put it in opposition to a life of pain, and misery, and savageness. In truth, the life which is passed in wisdom is a pleasure, full of liberal joy, and is the constant enjoyment of a rational soul; but that life which is destitute of wisdom is found to be both savage and miserable, although it is excessively deceived by the appetites, which pain both precedes and follows.

(57) Why God places a cherubim in front of the Paradise, and a flaming sword, which turned every way, to keep the way of the tree of life? (Genesis 3:24).

The name cherubim designates the two original virtues which belong to the Deity, namely, his creative and his royal virtues. The one of which has the title of God, the other, or the royal virtue, that of Lord. Now the form of the creative power is a peaceable, and gentle, and beneficent virtue; but the royal power is a legislative, and chastising, and correcting virtue. Moreover, by the flaming sword he here symbolically intimates the heaven: for the air is of a flaming colour, and turns itself round, revolving about the universe.

Therefore, all these things assumed to themselves the guardianship of the Paradise, because they are the presidents over wisdom, like a mirror; since, to illustrate my meaning by an example, the wisdom of the world is a sort of mirror of the divine virtues, in the similitude of which it was perfected, and by which the universe and all the things in it are regulated and arranged. But the way to wisdom is called philosophy (a word which means the love or the pursuit of wisdom). And since the creative virtue is endued with philosophy, being both philosophical and royal, so also the world itself is philosophical.

Some persons however have fancied that it is the sun which is indicated by the flaming sword; because, by its constant revolutions and turnings every way, it marks out the seasons of the year, as being the guardian of human life and of every thing which serves to the life of all men.

(58) Whether it was properly said with respect to Cain: "I have gotten a man from the Lord?" (Genesis 4:1).

Here there is a distinction made, as to—from some one, and out of some one, and by some thing. Out of some one, as out of materials; from some one, as from a cause; and by some thing, as by an instrument. But the Father and Creator of all the world is not an instrument, but a cause. Therefore he wanders from right wisdom who says, "That what has been made has been made, not from God, but by God."

(59) Why the sacred historian first describes the employment of the younger brother, Abel, saying: "He was a keeper of sheep; but Cain was a cultivator of the earth?" (Genesis 4:2).

Since, although the virtuous son was in point of time younger than the wicked son, yet in point of virtue he was older. On which account, on the present occasion, when their actions are to be compared together, he is placed first. Therefore one of them exercises a business, and takes care of living creatures, although they are devoid of reason, gladly taking upon himself the employment of a shepherd, which is a princely office, and as it were a sort of rehearsal of royal power; but the other devotes his attention to earthly and inanimate objects.

(60) Why Cain after some days offers up the first-fruits of his fruits, but when it is said that "Abel offered up first-fruits of the first-born of his flock and of the fat," "after some days" is not added? (Genesis 4:3–4).

Moses here intimates the difference between a lover of himself, and one who is thoroughly devoted to God; for the one took to himself the first-fruits of his fruits, and very impiously looked upon God as worthy only of the secondary and inferior offerings; for the expression, "after some days," implies that he did not do so immediately; and when it is said that he offered of the fruits, that intimates that he did not offer of the best fruits which he had, and herein displays his iniquity.

But the other, without any delay, offered

up the first-born and eldest of all his flocks, in order that in this the Father might not be treated unworthily.

(61) Why, when he had begun with Cain, he still mentions him here in the second place, when he says: "And God had respect unto Abel and unto his offerings; but unto Cain and unto his sacrifices he paid no attention?" (Genesis 4:5).

In the first place, because the good man, who is by nature first, is not at first perceived by the outward senses of any man except in his own turn, and by people of virtuous conduct. Secondly, because the good and the wicked man are two distinct characters; he accepts the good man, seeing that he is a lover of what is good, and an eager student of virtue; but he rejects and regards with aversion the wicked man, presuming that he will be prone to that side by the order of nature. Therefore he says here with exceeding fitness, that God had regard, not to the offerings, but to those who offered them, rather than to the gifts themselves; for men have regard to and regulate their approbation by the abundance and richness of offerings, but God looks at the sincerity of the soul, having no regard to ambition or illusion of any kind.

(62) What is the meaning of the distinction here made between a gift and a sacrifice? (Genesis 4:4).

The man who slays a sacrifice, after having made a division, pours the blood around the altar and takes the flesh home; but he who offers it as a gift, offers as it should seem the whole to him who accepts it. Therefore, the man who is a lover of self is a distributor, like Cain; but he who is a lover of God is the giver of a free gift, as was Abel.

(63) How it was that Cain became aware that his offering had not pleased God? (Genesis 4:5).

Perhaps he resolved his doubts, an additional cause being added, for sorrow seized upon him and his countenance fell. Therefore, he took the sorrow which he felt as an indication that he had been sacrificing what was not pleasing or approved of, when joy and happiness would have been suited to one who was sacrificing with purity of heart and spirit.

(64) Why is it that the expression used is not, because you do not offer rightly; but, because (or unless) you do not divide rightly? (Genesis 4:7).

In the first place, we must understand that right division and improper division are nothing else but order and the want of it. And it is by order that the universal world and its parts were made; since the Creator of the world, when he began to arrange and regulate the previously untamed and unarranged power which was liable to suffering, employed section and division. For he placed the heavy elements which were prone to descend downwards by their own nature, namely, the earth and the water, in the centre of the universe; but he placed the air and the fire at a greater altitude,

as they were raised on high by reason of their lightness.

But separating and dividing the pure nature, namely heaven, he carried it round and diffused it over the universe, so that it should be completely invisible to all men; containing within itself the whole universe in all its parts.

Again, the statement that animals and plants are produced out of seeds, some moist and some dry, what else does it mean but the inevitable dissection and separation of distinction? Therefore it follows inevitably, that this order and arrangement of the universe must be imitated in all things, especially in feeling and acknowledging gratitude; by which we are invited to requite in some degree and manner the kindnesses of those who have showered greater benefits liberally on us. Moreover, to pay one's thanks to God is an action which is intrinsically right in itself: and it is not to be disapproved of that he should receive the offerings due to him at the earliest moment, and fresh gifts from the first-fruits of every thing, not being dishonoured by any negligence on our part. Since it is not fitting that man should reserve for himself the first and most excellent things which are created, and should offer what is only second best to the all-wise God and Creator; for that division would be faulty and blameworthy, showing a most preposterous and unnatural arrangement.

(65) What is the meaning of the expression: "You have done wrongly; now rest?" (Genesis 4:8).

He is here giving very useful advice; since, to do no wrong at all is the greatest of all good things: but he who sins, and who thus blushes and is overwhelmed with shame, is near akin to him, being, if I may use such a phrase, as the younger brother to the elder; for those persons who pride themselves on their errors as if they had not done wrong, are afflicted with a disease which is difficult to cure, or rather which is altogether incurable.

(66) Why he seems to be giving what is good into the hand of a wicked man, when he says, "And unto thee shall be his desire?" (Genesis 4:8).

He does not deliver good into his hand; but the expression is heard with different feelings; since he is speaking, not of a pious man, but after the action is accomplished, saying of him: The desire and respect of the impiety of this man's wickedness will be towards you. Do not therefore talk about necessity, but about your own habits, in order that thus he may represent the voluntary action.

And again, the sentence, "And you shall be his ruler over him," has a reference to the operation. In the first place, you begin to act with wickedness; and now behold, another iniquity follows that great and injurious iniquity. Therefore, he both thinks and affirms that this is the principal part of all voluntary injury.

(67) Why he slew his brother in the field? (Genesis 4:9).

That as all in fecundity and sterility arises from a neglect of sowing and planting land a second time, he may be kept continually in mind of his wicked murder, and self-blamed for it; since the ground was not to be the same for the future, after it was compelled, contrary to its nature, to drink of human blood, to bring forth food to that man who imbued it with the polluted stain of blood.

(68) Why he who knows all things asks the fratricide: "Where is thy brother Abel?" (Genesis 4:10).

He puts this question to him because he wishes the man to confess voluntarily and spontaneously, of his own accord, so that he may not imagine that every thing is done out of necessity; for he who had slain another through necessity, would have confessed unwillingly, as having done the deed unwillingly; since that which does not depend upon ourselves does not deserve accusation; but the man who has done wrong intentionally denies it; for those who do wrong are liable to repentance. Therefore, he has interwoven this principle in all parts of his legislation, because the Deity himself is never the cause of evil.

(69) Why he who had slain his brother makes answer as if he were replying to a man; and says, "I do not know: am I my brother's keeper?" (Genesis 4:9).

It is the opinion of an atheist to think that the eye of God does not penetrate through every thing, and behold all things at the same time; piercing not only through what is visible, but also through every thing which lurks in the deepest and bottomless unfathomable abysses.

Suppose a person said to him, "How can you be ignorant where your brother is, and how is it that you do not know that, when as yet he is one out of the only four human beings which exist in the world? He being one with both his parents, and you his only brother." To this question the reply made is: "I am not my brother's keeper." O what a beautiful apology! And whose keeper and protector ought you to have been, rather than your brother's? But if you have excited your diligence to give effect to violence, and injury, and fraud, and homicide, which are the foulest and most abominable of actions, why did you consider the safety of your brother a secondary object?"

(70) What is the meaning of the expression, "The voice of thy brother's blood cries to me out of the earth?" (Genesis 4:10).

This is especially an example by which to take warning; for the Deity listens to those who are worthy, although they be dead, knowing that they are alive as to an incorporeal life. But he averts his countenance from the prayers of the wicked, although they are living a flourishing life, inasmuch as he looks upon them as dead to any real life, carrying about their bodies like a sepulchre; and having buried their miserable souls in it.

(71) Why he is said to be cursed upon the earth? (Genesis 4:11).

The earth is the last portion of the world, therefore if that utters curses, we must consider that the other elements do likewise pour forth adequate maledictions; for instance, the fountains, and rivers, and sea, and the air, and the land, and the fire, and the light, and the sun, and moon, and stars, and in short the whole heaven. For if inanimate and earthly nature, throwing off the yoke, wars against injury, why may not still rather those natures do so which are of a purer character? But as for him, against whom the parts of the world carry on war, what hope of safety he can have for the future, I know not.

(72) What is the meaning of the curse, "You shall be groaning and trembling upon the earth?" (Genesis 4:13).[6]

This also is a general principle; for in all evils there are some things which are perceived immediately, and some which are felt at a later period; for those which are future cause fear, and those which are felt at once bring sorrow.

(73) What is the meaning of Cain saying, "My punishment is too great for you to dismiss me? (Genesis 4:12).

In truth there is not misery greater than to be deserted and despised by God; for the anarchy of fools is cruel and very intolerable; but to be despised by the great King, and to fall down as an abject person cast down from the government of the Supreme Power is an indescribable affliction.

(74) What is the meaning of Cain, when he says, "Everyone who shall find me will kill me:" when there was scarcely another human being in the world except his parents? (Genesis 4:14).

In the first place he might have received injury from the parts of the world which indeed were made for the advantage of the good and that they might partake of them, but which nevertheless, derived from the wicked no slight degree of revenge. In the second place it may be that he said this, because he was apprehensive of injury from beasts, and reptiles; for nature has brought forth these animals with the express object of their being instruments of vengeance on the wicked.

In the third place, some people may imagine that he is speaking with reference to his parents, on whom he had inflicted an unprecedented sorrow, and the first evil which had happened to them, before they knew what death was.

(75) Why whoever should slay Cain should be

---

[6]Our translation is, "My punishment is greater than I can bear."

liable to bear a sevenfold punishment? (Genesis 4:15).

As our soul consists of eight portions, being accustomed to be divided in its rational and irrational individuality into seven subordinate parts, namely into the five outward senses, and the instrument of vice, and the faculty of generation; those seven parts exist among the causes of wickedness and evil, on which account they likewise fall under judgment; but the death of the principal and dominant portion of man, namely of the mind, is principally the wickedness which exists in it. Whoever therefore slays the mind, mingling in it folly, and insensibility, instead of sense, will cause dissolution also of the seven irrational parts; since, just as the principal and leading part had a portion from virtue, in the same manner likewise are its subject divisions composed.

(76) Why a sign is put on him who had slain his brother, that no one should kill him who found him; when it would have been natural to do the contrary, namely, to give him over to the hands of an executioner to be put to death? (Genesis 4:16).

This is said because, in the first place, the change of the nature of living is one kind of death; but continual sorrow and unmixed fear are destitute of joy and devoid of all good hope, and so they bring on many terrible and various evils which are so many sensible deaths.

In the second place, the sacred historian designs at the very beginning of his work to enunciate the law about the incorruptibility of the soul, and to confute as deceitful those who look upon the life which is contained in this body as the only happy life; for behold one of the two brothers is guilty of those enormous crimes which have already been mentioned, namely, impiety and fratricide; and he is still alive, and begetting offspring, and building cities. But the other who was praised in respect of his piety is treacherously put to death; while the voice of the Lord not only clearly cries out that that existence which is perceptible by the outward senses is not good, and that such a death is not evil, but also that that life which is in the flesh is not life, but that there is another give to man free from old age, and more immortal, which the incorporeal souls have received; for that expression of the poet about Scylla,

"That is not mortal but an endless woe,"[7]

is asserted in the same familiarity about a person who lives ill and passes a long life for many years in the practice of wickedness.

In the third place, since Cain had perpetrated

this fratricide of enormous guilt above all other crimes, he presents himself to him, quite forgetful of the injury that he has done, imposing on all judges a most peaceful law for the first crime; not that they are not to destroy malefactors, but that resting for a while with great patience and long suffering, they shall study compassion rather than severity.

But God himself, with the most perfect wisdom, has laid down the rule of familiarity and intelligence with reference to the first sinner: not slaying the homicide, but destroying him in another manner; since he scarcely permitted him to be enumerated among the generations of his father, but shows him proscribed not only by his parents but by the whole race of mankind, allotting him a state separate from that of others, and secluded from the class of rational animals, as one who had been expelled, and banished, and turned into the nature of beasts.

(77) Why Lamech, after the fifth generation, blames himself for the fratricide of his elder Cain; saying, as the scripture reports, to his wives, Adah and Zillah; "I have slain a man to my injury and a young man to my hurt; since if vengeance is taken upon Cain sevenfold, it shall certainly be taken on Lamech seventy and sevenfold?" (Genesis 4:23).

In numerals one is before ten, both in order and in virtue, for it is the first beginning and element and measure of all things. But the number ten is subsequent, and is measured by the other, being inferior to it, both in order and virtue; therefore, also, the number seven is antecedent in its origin to and more ancient than the number seventy, but the number seventy is younger than the number seven, and contains the calculation of generations.

These premises being laid down, he who first committed sin, as if he had been really always ignorant of evil, like the first odd number, namely, the unit, is chastised more simply; but the second offender, because he had the first for an example, so that there cannot possibly be any excuse made for him, is guilty of a voluntary crime, and because he did not receive honourable wisdom from that more simple punishment, the consequence will be that he will both suffer all that first punishment, and will, moreover, receive this second one, which is contained in the number ten.

For as in the horse-races they pay the groom who has trained the horse twice as great a reward as they give to the driver, so some wicked men, inclined to acts of injustice, gain the miserable triumph of victory and then are punished with a double punishment, both by the first one which is contained in the unit, and also by the second which is contained in the number ten; besides, Cain being the author of a homicide, when he was ignorant of the greatness of the pollution which he was

---

[7]The line occurs in Homer, Odyss. 12.118.

incurring, because no death had hitherto taken place in the world, suffered a more simple punishment, namely, only a sevenfold penalty in the order of the unit; but as his imitator could not take refuge in the same plea of ignorance, he ought to be subjected to a twofold punishment, not only to one equal and similar to that which had been inflicted on the first offender, but also another, which should be the seventh among the decades. In truth, according to the law, the trial which is before the tribunal is a sevenfold one; first of all, the eyes are put on their trial, because they beheld what was not lawful; secondly, the ears are impeached, because they heard what they ought not to have heard; thirdly, the smell is brought into question, as having been reduced by smoke and vapour; fourthly, the taste is accused, as being subservient to the pleasures of the belly; fifthly, a charge is brought against touch, by means of which, besides the operations of the senses abovementioned, in respect of those things which prevail over the spirit, other things, also, are superadded separately, such as the takings of cities, the captivities of men, the destructions of those citadels of cities in which wisdom dwells; sixthly, an accusation is urged against the tongue and other instruments of speech, for being silent as to what should be spoken of, and speaking of what should be buried in silence; and, in the seventh place, the lower part of the belly is impeached for inflaming and exciting the passions by immoderate lust.

This is the meaning of that expression, according to which a sevenfold vengeance was taken upon Cain, but a seventy and sevenfold vengeance upon Lamech for the causes above mentioned, because he was the second offender, not having been taught by the punishment of the first delinquent, and therefore he is altogether worthy to receive his punishment, which is the more simple one, like the unit in numerals, and, also, a manifold punishment too equal to the number ten.

(78) Why Adam, when he begat Seth, introduces him saying, "God has raised up for me another seed in the place of Abel whom Cain slew?" (Genesis 4:25).

In real truth Seth is another seed and the beginning of a second nativity of Abel, in accordance with a certain natural principle; for Abel is like to one who comes down below from above, on which account it was that he perished injuriously; but Seth resembles one who is proceeding upwards from below, on which account he also increases. And in proof of this argument Abel is explained as having been brought back and offered upwards to God. But it is not proper that everything should be raised and borne upwards, but only that which is good, for God is in no respect whatever the cause of evil.

Therefore, whatever is indistinct and uncertain, and mingled, and in confusion and disorder, has also, very properly, blame and praise mingled together: praise, because it honours the cause, and blame, since as the occurrence happened fortuitously, so it is without any plans having been formed or any gratitude expressed. Moreover, nature also separated the two sons from him; it rendered the good one worthy of immortality, resolving him into a voice interceding with God; but the wicked one it gave over to corruption.

But the name Seth is interpreted "watered," according to the variation of plants which grow by being watered, and put forth shoots and bear fruit. But these things are the symbols of the soul, so that it is not lawful to assert that the Divinity is the cause of all things equally, of the bad as well as of the good, but only of the good, and that alone ought to be planted alive.

(79) Why Enos, the son of Seth, hoped to call upon the name of the Lord God? (Genesis 4:26).

The name Enos is interpreted "man;" and it is received as meaning, not the whole of the combined man, but as the rational part of the soul, namely, the intellect, to which it is peculiarly becoming to hope, for irrational animals are devoid of hope; but hope is a sort of presage of joy, and before joy there is an expectation of good things.

(80) Why, after the mention of hope, Moses says, "This is the book of the generations of men?" (Genesis 5:1).

It is by this that he made what has been said before worthy of belief. What is man? Man is a being which, beyond all other races of animals, has received a copious and wonderful portion of hope; and this is as it were inscribed on his very nature, and celebrated there; for the human intellect hopes by its own nature.

(81) Why, in the genealogy of Adam, Moses no longer mentions Cain, but only Seth, who, he says, was according to his appearance and form; on which account he proceeds to retain the generations which descend from him in his genealogy? (Genesis 5:3).

It can neither be lawful to enumerate a wicked and sinful murderer either in the list of reason or in that of number; for he must be cast out like dung, as some one said, looking upon him as one of such a character; and on this account the sacred historian neither points him out as the successor of his father who had been formed out of the dust, nor as the head of succeeding generations; but he distributes both these characteristics to him who was without pollution, and names Seth, who is a drinker of water, as having been watered by his father, and as begetting hope in his own increase and progress; on which account it is not inconsiderately and foolishly that he says that he was born according to the form and appearance of his father, to the reproof of his elder brother, who, on account of the foulness of the murder which he had committed, has nothing in him resembling his father, either in body or soul.

And on this account Moses has separated him from the family, and has given his share to his brother, being the noble privilege of the birthright of the first-born.

(82) What is the meaning of the verse, Enoch pleased God after he begat Methuselah, two hundred years? (Genesis 5:22).

God appointed by the law the fountains of all good things to be under the principles of generation itself. And what I mean is something of this sort. A little while before he appointed mercy and pardon to exist, now again he decrees that penitence shall exist, not in any degree mocking or reproaching these men, who are believed to have offended, and at the same time giving the soul an opportunity to mount up from wickedness to virtue, like the conversion of those who are proceeding towards a snare. For behold, the man being made a husband and a father together with his birth, makes a beginning of honesty.

And he is said to please God, for although he does not persevere in piety from the moment that he is born, nevertheless, all that remaining period is counted to him as having been spent in a praiseworthy mode of life, because he pleased God for so many years. And these things are said, not because it perhaps was, but it might perhaps have seemed different; but he approves of the order of things, for indulgence having been exemplified, in this case of Cain, after no long interval of time, he introduces this statement, that Enoch practised repentance, warning us by it that repentance alone can procure indulgence.

(83) Why Enoch, who cultivated repentance, is said to have lived before his repentance a hundred and sixty-five years, but two hundred after his repentance? (Genesis 5:22).[8]

This number of a hundred and sixty-five is combined of the singular addition of ten numbers from the unit to ten; as one, two, three, four, five, six, seven, eight, nine, ten, the total of which is fifty-five. And again, from that by the addition of ten numbers, which, removing the unit proceed upwards by twos, and two, four, six, eight, ten, twelve, fourteen, sixteen, eighteen, twenty, which make a hundred and ten; the combination of which, with the numbers first mentioned, produces a hundred and sixty-five; and in this addition the even numbers amount to twice as much as the odd numbers; for the woman is more violent than the man, in the preposterous manner in which the wicked man rules over the virtuous man, the out-

ward sense over the mind, the body over the outward sense, and matter over its cause.

But the number two hundred, in which repentance was practised, is combined of two numbers of one hundred, the first hundred of which intimates a purification from injustice, but the other indicates the plenitude of perfect virtue. In truth, before anything else is done, the first thing is to cut off from a sick body every diseased part, and after that means of cure are to be applied to it, for this is the first step, and the other the second. Moreover, the number two hundred consists of fours, for it is produced as from seed, from four triangular numbers, and from four tetragons, and from four pentagons, and from four hexagons, and from four heptagons; and, as one may say, it fixes its step on the number seven. Now the four triangles are these, one, three, six, ten, which make twenty; the four tetragons are one, four, nine, sixteen, which make thirty; from the four pentagons, one, five, twelve, twenty-two, is made the number forty. Moreover, the four hexagons, one, six, fifteen, twenty-eight, make fifty; and the four heptagons, one, seven, eighteen, thirty-four, make sixty; and all these numbers put together make two hundred.

(84) Why the man who lives a life of repentance is said to have lived three hundred and sixty-five years? (Genesis 5:23).

In the first place, the year contains three hundred and sixty-five days; therefore, by the symbol of the solar orbit, the sacred historian here indicates the life of the repentant man.

In the second place, as the sun is the cause of day and night, performing his revolutions by day above the hemisphere of the earth, and his course by night under the earth, so also the life of the man of repentance consists of alternations of light and darkness; of darkness, that is, of times of agitation and circumstances of injury; and of light, when the light of virtue and its radiant brilliancy arises.

In the third place, he has assigned to him a complete number, as the sun is ordained to be the chief of the stars of heaven, under an appointed number, in the time which came before the period of his repentance, to lead to the oblivion of the sins previously committed; since, as God is good, he bestows the greatest favours most abundantly, and, at the same time, he effaces the former offences of those who devote themselves to him, and which might deserve chastisement, by a recollection of their virtues.

(85) Why, when Enoch died, the sacred historian adds the assertion, "He pleased God?" (Genesis 5:24).

In the first place, he says this because, by such a statement, he implies that the soul is immortal,

---

[8]This is at variance with the statement in the Bible, which says he lived sixty-five years before the birth of Methuselah, and walked with God three hundred years.

inasmuch as after it is stripped of the body, it still pleases a second time.

In the second place, he honours the repentant man with praise, because he has persevered in the same alteration of manners, and has never receded till he has arrived at complete perfection of life; for behold, some men appear to be readily sated after they have only tasted of excellence; and after a hope of recovery has been given to them, they relapse again into the same disease.

(86) What is the meaning of the expression, "He was not found because God translated him?" (Genesis 5:24).

In the first place, the end of virtuous and holy men is not death but a translation and migration, and an approach to some other place of abode.

In the second place, in this instance something marvellous did take place; for he was supposed to be carried off in such a way as to be invisible, for then he was not found: and a proof of this is, that he was sought for as being invisible, not only as having been carried away from their sight, since translation into another place is nothing else than a placing of a person in another situation; but it is here suggested, that he was translated from a visible place, perceptible by the outward senses, into an incorporeal idea, appreciable only to the intellect. This mercy also was bestowed on the great prophet, for his sepulchre also was known to no one.

And besides these two there was another, Elijah, who ascended from the things of earth into heaven, according to the divine appearance which was then presented to him, and who thus followed higher things, or, to speak with more exact propriety, was raised up to heaven.

(87) How it was that immediately upon the nativity of Noah his father says, "He will make us rest from labours and sorrows, and from the earth, which the Lord God has cursed?" (Genesis 5:29).

The fathers of the saints did not prophesy except for grave reasons and on important occasions; for although those who were rendered worthy of prophetical panegyric did not prophesy at all times or on all subjects, they did so at all events on one occasion and on one subject, with which they were acquainted. Nor is this of no importance, but it is an emblem and an example, since Noah is a kind of surname of righteousness, of which, when the intellect is made a partaker, it causes us to rest from all wicked works, and releases us from sorrows and from fears, and renders us secure and joyful.

It also causes us to rest from that earthly nature which has been previously laid under a curse, which this body, when affected by pain, is connected with, especially in those persons who give cause for it, and who wear out their lives with pleasure. Nevertheless, if we examine attentively

the events and circumstances, and compare them with the letter of the scriptures, the prophecy which has been already produced is deceived, because, in the time of this man, there did not arise any putting down of evils, but a more vehement obstinacy in sin and great afflictions, and the unprecedented event of the deluge. But you must note carefully, that Noah is the tenth in generation from the earth-born Adam.

(88) What is meant by the three sons of Noah being named Shem, Ham, and Japhet? (Genesis 5:32).

These names are the symbols of three human things, what is good, what is bad, and what is indifferent; Shem is the symbol of what is good, Ham of what is bad, and Japhet of what is indifferent.

(89) Why from the time that the deluge drew near, the human race is said to have increased so as to become a multitude? (Genesis 6:1).

Divine mercies do always precede judgment; since the first work of God is to do good, and to destroy follows afterwards; but he himself (when terrible evils are about to happen) loves to provide and is accustomed to provide that previously an abundance of many and great blessings shall be produced. On this principle also Egypt, when there was about to be a barrenness and famine for seven years as the prophet himself says,[9] was for an equal number of years continuously made exceedingly fertile by the beneficent and saving power of the Creator of the universe.

And in the same way in which he showers benefits upon men, he also teaches them to depart and to abstain from sin; that these blessings may not be turned into the contrary. And on this account now, by the freedom of their institutions, the cities of the world have increased in generous virtue, so that if any corruption supervenes subsequently they may disapprove of their own acts of wickedness as extraordinary and irremediable; not at all looking upon the divinity as the cause of them, for that has no connection with wickedness or misery, for the task of the Deity is only to bestow blessings.

(90) What is the meaning of the expression, "My spirit shall not always strive with man, because he is but flesh?" (Genesis 6:3).

An oracle is here promulgated as if it were a law; for the divine spirit is not a motion of the air, but intellect and wisdom; just as it also flows over the man who with great skill constructed the tabernacle of the Lord, namely upon Bezaleel, when the scripture says, "And he filled him with the divine spirit of wisdom and understanding." Therefore that spirit comes upon men, but does not abide or persevere in them; and the Lord himself adds

---

[9] Genesis 41:28.

the reason, when he says, "Because they are flesh." For the disposition of the flesh is inconsistent with wisdom, inasmuch as it makes a bond of alliance with desire; on which account it is evident that nothing important can be in the way of incorporeal and light souls, or can be any hindrance to their discerning and comprehending the condition of nature, because a pure disposition is acquired together with constancy.

(91) Why it is said that the days of man shall be a hundred and twenty years? (Genesis 6:4).

God appears here to fix the limit of human life by this number, indicating by it the manifold prerogative of honour; for in the first place this number proceeds from the units, according to combination, from the number fifteen; but the principle of the number fifteen is that of a more transparent appearance, since it is on the fifteenth day that the moon is rendered full of light, borrowing its light of the sun at the approach of evening, and restoring it to him again in the morning; so that during the night of the full moon the darkness is scarcely visible, but it is all light.

In the second place, the number a hundred and twenty is a triangular number, and is the fifteenth number consisting of triangles.

Thirdly, it is so because it consists of a combination of odd and even numbers, being contained by the power of the faculty of the concurring numbers, sixty-four and fifty-six; for the equal number of sixty-four is compounded of the uniting of these eight odd numbers, one, three, five, seven, nine, eleven, thirteen, fifteen; the reduction of which, by their parts into squares, makes a sum total of sixty-four, and that is a cube, and at the same time a square number.

But again from the seven double units there arises the unequal number of fifty-six, being compounded of seven double pairs, which generate other productions of them, two, four, six, eight, ten, twelve, fourteen; the sum total of which is fifty-six.

In the fourth place, it is compounded of four numbers, of one triangle, namely fifteen; and of another square, namely twenty-five; and of a third quinquangular figure, thirty-five; and of a fourth a sexangular figure forty-five, by the same analogy: for the fifth is always received according to each appearance; for from the unity of the triangles the fifth number becomes fifteen; again the fifth of the quadrangular number from the unit makes twenty-five; and the fifth of the quinquangular number from the unit makes thirty-five; and the fifth of the sexangular number from the unit makes forty-five.

But every one of these numbers is a divine and sacred number, consisting of fifteens as has been already shown; and the number twenty-five belongs to the tribe of Levi. [10] And the number thirty-five comes from the double diagram of arithmetic, geometry, and harmony; but sixteen, and eighteen, and nineteen, and twenty-one, the combination of which numbers amounts to seventy-four, is that according to which seven months' children are born. And forty-five consists of a triple diagram; but to this number, sixteen, nineteen, twenty-two, and twenty-eight, belong: the combination of which makes eighty-five, according to which nine months' children are produced.

Fifthly, this diagram has fifteen parts, and a twofold composition, peculiarly belonging to itself; forsooth when divided by two it gives sixty, the measure of the age of all mankind; when divided by three it gives forty, the idea of prophecy; when divided by four it gives thirty, a nation; when divided by five, it makes twenty-four, the measure of day and night; when divided by six, it gives twenty, a beginning; when divided by eight, we have fifteen, the moon in the fulness of brilliancy; when divided by ten, it makes twelve, the zodiac embellished with living animals; when divided by twelve, it makes ten, holy; when divided by fifteen, it gives eight, the first ark; when divided by twenty, it leaves six, the number of creation; when divided by twenty-four, it makes five, the emblem of the outward sense; when divided by thirty it makes four, the beginning of solid measure; when divided by forty, it gives three, the symbol of fulness, the beginning, the middle, and the end; when divided by sixty, it makes two, which is woman; and when divided by the whole number of a hundred and twenty, the product is one, or man.

And every one of all these numbers is more natural, as is proved in each of them, but the composition of them is twofold, for the product is two hundred and forty, which is a sign that it is worthy of a twofold life; for as the number of years is doubled, so also we may imagine that the life is doubled too; one being in connection with the body, the other being detached from the body, according to which every holy and perfect man may receive the gift of prophecy.

Sixthly, because the fifth and sixth figures arise, the three numbers being multiplied together, three times four times five, since three times four times five make sixty; so in like manner the next following numbers four times five times six make a hundred and twenty, for four times five times six make a hundred and twenty.

Seventhly, when the number twenty has been taken in, which is the beginning of the reduction of mankind, I mean twenty, and being added to itself two or three times, so as to make twenty, forty, and sixty, these added together make a hun-

---

[10]See Numbers 8:24.

dred and twenty. But perhaps the number a hundred and twenty is not the general term of human life, but only of the life of those men who existed at that time, and who were to perish by the deluge after an interval of so many years, which their kind Benefactor prolonged, giving them space for repentance; when, after the aforesaid term, they lived a longer time in the subsequent ages.

(92) On what principle it was that giants were born of angels and women? (Genesis 6:4).

The poets call those men who were born out of the earth giants, that is to say, sons of the earth.[11] But Moses here uses this appellation improperly, and he uses it too very often merely to denote the vast personal size of the principal men, equal to that of Hajk[12] or Hercules.

But he relates that these giants were sprung from a combined procreation of two natures, namely, from angels and mortal women; for the substance of angels is spiritual; but it occurs every now and then that on emergencies occurring they have imitated the appearance of men, and transformed themselves so as to assume the human shape; as they did on this occasion, when forming connexions with women for the production of giants. But if the children turn out imitators of the wickedness of their mothers, departing from the virtue of their fathers, let them depart, according to the determination of the will of a depraved race, and because of their proud contempt for the supreme Deity, and so be condemned as guilty of voluntary and deliberate wickedness.

But sometimes Moses styles the angels the sons of God, inasmuch as they were not produced by any mortal, but are incorporeal, as being spirits destitute of any body; or rather that exhorter and teacher of virtue, namely Moses, calls those men who are very excellent and endowed with great virtue the sons of God; and the wicked and depraved men he calls bodies, or flesh.

(93) What is the meaning of the expression: "God considered anxiously, because he had made man upon the earth; and he resolved the matter in his mind?" (Genesis 6:6).[13]

Some persons imagine that it is intimated by these words that the Deity repented; but they are very wrong to entertain such an idea, since the Deity is unchangeable. Nor are the facts of his caring and thinking about the matter, and of his agitating it in his mind, any proofs that he is repenting, but only indications of a kind and determinate counsel, according to which he displays care,

revolving in his mind the cause why he had made man upon the earth.

But since this earth is a place of misery, even that heavenly being, man, who is a mixture compounded of soul and body, from the very hour of his birth to that of his death, is nothing else but the slave of the body. That the Deity therefore should meditate and deliberate on these matters is nothing surprising; since most men take to themselves wickedness rather than virtue, being influenced by the twofold impulse mentioned above; namely, that of a body by its nature corruptible, and placed in the terrible situation of earth, which is the lowest of all places.

(94) Why God, after having threatened to destroy mankind, says that he will also destroy all the beasts likewise; using the expression, "from man to beast, and from creeping things to flying creatures;" for how could irrational animals have committed sin? (Genesis 6:7).

This is the literal statement of the holy scripture, and it informs us that animals were not necessarily and in their primary cause created for their own sake, but for the sake of mankind and to act as the servants of men; and when the men were destroyed, it followed necessarily and naturally that they also should be destroyed with them, as soon as the men, for whose sake they had been made, had ceased to exist.

But as to the hidden meaning conveyed by the statement, since man is a symbol for the intellect which exists in us, and animals for the outward sense, when the chief creature has first been depraved and corrupted by wickedness, all the outward sense also perishes with him, because he had no relics whatever of virtue, which is the cause of salvation.

(95) Why God says, I am indignant that I made them? (Genesis 6:7).

In the first place, Moses is here again relating what took place, as if he were speaking of some illustrious action of man, but, properly speaking, God does not feel anger, but is exempt from, and superior to, all such perturbations of spirit. Therefore Moses wishes here to point out, by an extravagant form of expression, that the iniquities of man had grown to such a height, that they stirred up and provoked to anger even that very Being who by his nature was incapable of anger.

In the second place he warns us, by a figure, that foolish actions are liable to punishment, but that those which proceed from wise and deliberate counsel are praiseworthy.

(96) Why it is afterwards said, that Noah found grace in the sight of the Lord? (Genesis 6:8).

In the first place, the time calls for a comparison; since all the rest of mankind has been rejected for their ingratitude, he places the just man in the place of them all, asserting that he had found favour

---

[11] The Greek name *Gigas* is said to be derived from *gē* and *gennaō*, "to bring forth."

[12] Hajk is an addition of the Armenian translator; it is the name of a fabulous patriarch of the Armenian nation.

[13] The translation of our Bible is, "It repented God that he had made man upon the earth."

with God, not because he alone was deserving of favour, when the whole universal body of the human race had had benefits and mercies heaped on them, but because he alone had seemed to be mindful of the kindnesses which he had received.

In the second place, when the whole generation had been given over to destruction, with the exception of one single family, it followed inevitably that that remaining household should be asserted to have shown itself worthy of the divine grace, that it might be, as it were, a seed and a spark of a new race of mankind. And what could be a greater grace and mercy than that the man, of whom this is said, should be at the same time the end and beginning of the family of mankind?

(97) Why does Moses enumerate the generations of Noah with reference not to his ancestors but to his virtues? (Genesis 6:9).

He does this in the first place, because all the men of that age were wicked: secondly, he is here imposing a law upon the will, because, to an anxious follower of virtue, virtue itself stands in the place of a real generation, if indeed men are the means of the generation of men, but the virtues of minds. And on this account it is that he says, he was a just man, perfect, and one who pleased God; but justice, and perfection, and grace before God, are the greatest of virtues.

(98) What was the meaning of Moses when he says, "And all the earth was corrupt in the sight of God, and the earth was filled with iniquity?" (Genesis 6:11).

Moses himself has given us the reason why he speaks thus, in the sentence in which he asserts that iniquity had arisen by reason of the corruption of the earth; for deliverance from iniquity is righteousness, both in all the parts of the world, in heaven, that is, and earth, and among men.

(99) What is the meaning of his saying, "All flesh had corrupted his way upon the earth?" (Genesis 6:12).

In the first place, the sacred historian calls the man who is devoted to the love of himself, flesh; therefore, when he had already said he was flesh, he introduces not the same flesh, but the flesh of the same being, namely, of man, or perhaps he is speaking even of man abstractedly considered; for every one who passes a life destitute of all civilisation, and bewildered by intemperance, is flesh.

In the second place, he supposes here the cause of spiritual corruption to be, as in truth it is, the flesh, because that is the seat of desire; and from it, as from a living spring, arise all the peculiar appetites, and passions, and other affections.

In the third place, he very naturally says, that all flesh had corrupted his way; for "his" is a partial case, declined from the nominative case of the pronoun "he, she, or it;" for as for the being to whom we refer honour, we scarcely dare to speak of him by his own name, but we call him He. And it is from this that the principle of the Pythagorean philosophers was derived, who said, "He said it," speaking of their master in a glorious manner, since they feared to speak of him by name. And the same custom has obtained in cities and in private houses; for the servants, when speaking of the arrival of their master, say, "Here he comes;" and so when the prince of any individual city arrives, they use the same form of speech, "He comes," when they speak of him.

But what is the purpose of this prolix enumeration of all these instances on my part? The truth is, that I wished to show that it is the Father of the universe who is spoken of here; since, indeed, all his good qualities, and all his marvellous names, are widely celebrated by the praise bestowed upon the virtues; and, therefore, out of reverence he has used that name more cautiously, because he was about to bring on the world the destruction of the flood; but the case of the pronoun "He" is used by way of honour in these phrases. "All flesh had corrupted *His* ways," inasmuch as it is truly convicted of having corrupted the way of the Father, in accordance with the lusts, and desires, and pleasures of the body; for these are the enemies and opposers of the laws of continence, and parsimony, and chastity, and fortitude, and justice; by which the road which leads to God is found out and widened, so that it should everywhere be a beaten and plain road.

(100) What is the meaning of the statement, "All the time of man has come against me, because the earth is filled with iniquity?" (Genesis 6:13). [14]

Those who resist the order of fate proceed upon these and many other arguments, especially in that of sudden death, which oftentimes produces great slaughter in a short period of time; as, for instance, in the overthrow of houses, in conflagrations, in shipwrecks, in civil tumults, in battles of cavalry, in wars by land and in wars by sea, and in pestilences. To all those who advance arguments of this kind we repeat the same assertions which are here made by the prophet, on the principle which is derived from himself. If indeed that expression, "All the time of man has come against me," has a meaning of this kind, the term which has been determined as the period of living for all mankind, behold it is now brought to one point and terminated at once by the deluge; and since this is the case, they will not live any longer according to the principle of fate which has been fixed; so that the time of each separate individual is now

---

[14] The version given here does not in the least resemble that in our Bible.

reduced to one, and has received its destined termination at the same time, by I know not what harmony and periodical revolution of the stars, by which bodies the whole race of mankind is continually preserved or destroyed. Let those, therefore, all receive these things in any manner in which they choose who study these things, and those too who argue against them.

Nevertheless we must first of all make this statement, that nothing can be found so contrary to, so opposite to, so wholly repugnant to, the wonderful virtue of the Deity as iniquity; therefore, after he said, "All the time of all mankind has come up against me," he adds also the reason of its contrariety to him, that the earth is filled with iniquity.

In the second place, Time, under the name of Chronos or Saturn, is looked upon as a god by the wickedest of men, who are desirous to lose sight of the one essential Being, on which account he says, "The time of all mankind has come up against me," because in fact the heathen make human time into a god, and oppose him to the real true God. But, however, it is now insinuated, in other passages also of scripture, which run thus, "Time has departed to a distance from them, but the Lord is in us:"[15] just as if he were to say, time is looked upon by wicked men as the cause of the world, but by wise men and virtuous men time is not looked upon in this light, but God only, from whom all times and seasons do proceed.

Again, God is the cause, not of all things, but only of good things and good men, and of those men and things which are in accordance with virtue; for as he is free from all wickedness, so likewise he cannot be the cause of it.

In the third place, by that expression which he uses in this manner, he indicates the excess of impiety, saying, "that the time of all mankind has arrived," that is to say, that all men, in every part of the world, have agreed together, with one mind, to work wickedness; but the other assertion which is here made, that the whole earth is filled with iniquity, amounts to this, that there is no part of it whatever free from wickedness, and which is also to receive and to bear righteousness. And the expression, "against me," establishes the proof of what has been said, inasmuch as it is only the judgment of divine election which is altogether firm and lasting.

---

[15] Numbers 14:9. Compare with this Isaiah 8, Jeremiah 46:21–28, Psalm 80:16.

QUESTIONS AND ANSWERS ON GENESIS, II

(Quaestiones et Solutiones in Genesin, II)

(1) What is the preparation of Noah? (Genesis 6:14).

If any one should wish to make an examination of the question of that ark of Noah's on more natural principles, he will find it to have been the preparation of the human body, as we shall see by the examination of each particular respecting it separately.

(2) Why does he make the ark of squared pieces of wood? (Genesis 6:16).

He does this in the first place, because the figure of a square, wherever it may be placed, is steady and firm, consisting as it does of right angles, and it is confirmed in a purer and clearer manner by the nature of the human body.

In the second place, he does this because, although our body is an instrument, and although every portion of it is rounded off, nevertheless the limbs which are compounded of all these portions do, by some manner or other, evidently reduce that circular orb to the figure of a quadrangle or square. For example, take the breast which is rather square than circular; in the same manner take the belly, after it is swollen with food or by any natural excess, for there are some men excepted from our present argument. But if any one looks upon the arms and hands, and back and thighs, and feet of a man, he will find all these limbs compounded of a mixture of the square, with the circular figure at the same time.

In the third place, a quadrangular piece of wood shows in its extension nearly every sort imaginable of uneven distinction, inasmuch as its length is greater than its breadth, and its breadth greater than its depth. And such also is the formation of our bodies, which are compounded of one extension which is great, of another which is of moderate size, of another which is small, great in its length and small in its depth.

(3) Why does God say, you shall make the ark in nests? (Genesis 6:14).[1]

He gives this order very naturally, for the human body is formed of holes like nests; every one of which is nourished and grows like a young bird, a certain spiritual force which exists in it from its earliest origin penetrating through it, as, for instance, some of the holes and nests are the eyes, in which the faculty of sight has its abode; other nests are the ears, which are the place where hearing is situated. A third class of nests are the nostrils, in which the sense of smell is lodged. The fourth nest, which is of larger dimensions than those already mentioned, is the mouth, which is the seat of the taste; and it has been made of large size, since, besides taste, there is also another still more important instrument, which is that of articulate speech, reposing in it, namely, the tongue, which, as Socrates was wont to say, by beating in every direction in various manners, and by touching different parts, composes and forms a word, being, in truth, an instrument under the immediate guidance of reason.

And the nest is placed under the skull, and that which is called the membrane of the brain is a certain nest, as it were, of the genius of each man: as also the chest is a nest, in which abide the lungs and the heart, and both these things are receptacles of other internal organs; the lungs being the place in which the power of breathing is lodged, and the heart being the abode of both the blood and the breath, for it has two ventricles, which are, as it were, a certain kind of nests or receptacles in the breast; blood, from which the veins, as if they could perceive its operations, are irrigated; and a breathing-hole, which again is extended over and irrigates the perceptive channels of respiration.

And both the harder as well as the softer parts do, like nests prepared for the purpose, nourish the bones as real nests nourish young birds; the harder portion of which, namely, the marrow, is the nest, and the softer flesh is the nest of pleasure and pain; and if any one should wish to investigate the other parts, he will find that, in every respect, the nature of man has much the same foundation as the ark.

(4) Why does God command the ark to be smeared with pitch, both on the inside and on the outside? (Genesis 6:14).

Pitch is so called by reason of its bird-lime like tenacity, because it glues together whatever was disunited before, so as to form one indissoluble and indivisible joint. For everything which is held together by bird-lime is immediately held to a nat-

---

[1] The word in our Bible is *rooms*, not nests.

ural union; but our body being composed of many parts is united on the outside, and is held together by its own proper habit, but the previous habit of connection which binds those things together is the soul, which, being situated in the middle, penetrates through every part till it reaches the surface, and then is turned back again from the surface to the centre, so that our spiritual nature is rolled up compactly in a double fold, being united in a firm solidity and union.

Therefore this ark is smeared with pitch, both on the inside and the outside, for the reason here given.

But that ark which is placed in the holy of holies, and as covered over with gold, is the similitude of the world appreciable only by the intellect, as is declared in the account given of it: since just as there is a world appreciable by the intellect incarnate in incorporeal figures existing at the same time, consisting of a union of all figures by a certain invisible harmony; for, in proportion as gold is a more noble material than pitch, in the same ratio is that ark, which is in the holy of holies, superior to this one of which we are now speaking.

And again, God ordained that its measure should be quadrangular, from a regard to usefulness; but his object in the other ark was not so much that it should be useful as that it should be exempt from all possibility of decay; for the nature of incorporeal things, appreciable only by the intellect, is to be exempt from decay, being incorruptible and permanent. The one ark is tossed to and fro by the winds and the waters, but the other has its station constantly in the holy of holies; and being stable it is akin to divine nature, as the other, which is tossed about in every direction, and moved from one place to another, is akin to and the emblem of created nature. Besides this, that ark of the flood being, as it were, an example of corruption, is raised on high, but the other, which is in the holy of holies, imitates the incorruptible condition of eternity.

(5) Why did God give the measures of the ark in the following manner; the length to be of three hundred cubits, and the breadth thereof to be fifty cubits, and the height to be thirty cubits: and above it was to be raised to a point in one cubit, being brought together gradually like an obelisk? (Genesis 6:15).

It was necessary that so vast a work should be constructed in conformity with literal directions, in order that so many animals, some of them of vast size, should be received into it, as individuals of each class were introduced with the food necessary for them; but if the matter is considered properly with reference to its symbolical meaning, then, for the comprehension of the formation of our body, we shall require to make use not of the quantity of cubits, but of the certain principles and proportions which are observed in them.

But the proportions which are contained in them are of sixfold, and double, and other portions are added. For three hundred is six times as many as fifty, and ten times as many as thirty; and again fifty is by two thirds a larger number than thirty. Such then are also the proportions of the body; for if any one should choose to investigate the matter and inquire into it carefully in all its points, he will find that man is made in an exact proportion of measurement, neither being too long or too little; and if a string be let down from his head to his feet, he will find that to reach that distance it requires a string six times as long as the width of his chest, and ten times as long as the depth of his ribs and their breadth as a second part of depth added thereto. Such is the certain proportion, received in accordance with nature, of the human body formed on exact measurement of the most excellently made men, who are incorrect neither in the way of excess nor of defect.

But again, it was with great wisdom and propriety that God ordained the summit to be completed in one cubit; for the upper part of the ark imitates the unity of the body; the head being forsooth as the citadel of the king, having for its inhabitant the chief of all, the intellect.

But those parts which are below the head are divided into separate portions, as for instance into the hands, and in an especial degree into the lower parts, since the thighs, and legs, and feet are all kept distinct from one another, therefore whoever should wish to understand these matters, on the principle which I have pointed out, will easily comprehend the analogy of the cubits as I have related it.

But above all things he must not be ignorant that each of these different numbers of cubits has separately a certain necessary proportion and principle, beginning with the first, those in the length of the ark. Therefore in its length it is composed of three hundred units, placed next to one another in continuation, according to the augmentation of units, from these twenty-four numbers, one, two, three, four, five, six, seven, eight, nine, ten, eleven, twelve, thirteen, fourteen, fifteen, sixteen, seventeen, eighteen, nineteen, twenty, twenty-one, twenty-two, twenty-three, twenty-four. But the twenty-fourth number is above all others a natural number, being distributed among the hours of day and night, and also among the characters of language,[2] and literal speech; and it is also compounded of three cubes, being complete, full, and compacted in equality.

For the number three constantly exhibits, as belonging to itself, the first equality of all, having a beginning, and a middle, and an end, all of which

---

[2] He is referring to the Greek alphabet, which consists of twenty-four letters.

are equal to one another; and eight is the first cube, because it again has declared its first equality with the rest.

But the number twenty-four has likewise a great number of other virtues, since it is the substance of the number three hundred, as has been already pointed out; this then is its first virtue; and it has another, since it is compounded of twelve quadrangular figures, joined to one another by a continuous unity; and besides of two long figures, and twelve double figures, being forsooth compounded of twos separately increased by two and two.

Therefore the angular numbers which make up together the twelve quadrangular figures are these; one, three, five, seven, nine, eleven, thirteen, fifteen, seventeen, nineteen, twenty-one, and twenty-three; but the quadrangular figure combines the following numbers, one, four, nine, sixteen, twenty-five, thirty-six, forty-nine, sixty-four, eighty-one, a hundred, a hundred and twenty-one, and a hundred and twenty-four.

But those angular numbers which compose the other long figures are these; one, four, six, eight, ten twelve, fourteen, sixteen, eighteen, twenty, twenty-two, twenty-four, being twelve in all; and after these come the compound numbers, two, six, twelve, twenty, thirty, forty-two, fifty-six, seventy-two, ninety, a hundred and ten, a hundred and thirty-two, and a hundred and fifty-six; being also twelve. And if you put together the twelve quadrangular figures, you will find a hundred and forty-four, and if you add the other twelve long figures, you will find a hundred and fifty-six; and from the combination of the two you will get the number three hundred, and the concord of full, and complete, and perfect nature rising up to the equal and infinite harmony; for a complete and perfect nature is the maker of equality, according to the nature of a triangle; but the equal and the infinite are the factors of inequality, according to the composition of the other long figure.

But the universe consists of a combination of equality and inequality, on which account the Creator himself, even amid the destruction of all earthly things, placed a sort of fixed pattern of stability in the ark.

This then is enough to say about the number three hundred. We must now proceed to speak of the fifty cubits, on the following principle; for in the first place it is composed of the right angle of the quadrangular figures; for a right angle is compounded of three, four, and five; and the square of these is nine, sixteen, and twenty-five, the sum total of which when added together is fifty; in the second place, the perfect number fifty is composed of these four triangles linked together, one, three, six, ten; and again of these four equal quadrangles also united together, one, four, nine, sixteen; therefore these triangles when collected together make

twenty; and the quadrangles make thirty; and twenty and thirty added together make fifty.

But if the triangle and the quadrangle are added together, they make a heptangular figure: so that it is contained by its virtue in the number of fifty, that divine and holy number; to which the prophet had regard when he proclaimed the jubilee festival; and the whole of the jubilee year is free and a deliverer.

The third theorem is three triangles beginning with the unit, connected together in a continuous series, and three cubes beginning also with the unit, and connected together in a similar manner, which together make fifty; the examples of the first are one, four, and nine, which make fourteen; the examples of the second are, one, eight, and twenty-seven, which together make thirty-six; and the sum total of the two when added together is fifty.

Again, thirty is in an especial manner a natural number, for as in the series of units the number three is, so is the number thirty in the series of decimals; and that makes up the cycle of the moon, being the collection of separate months in full delineation; secondly, it is composed of four numbers, which are united in the continual series of these quadrangular figures, one, four, nine, and sixteen, which together make up thirty; on which account it was not without some foundation and sufficient reason that Heraclitus called that number "generation," when he said: a man in thirty years from the time of his birth can become a grandfather, inasmuch as he arrives at the age of puberty in his fourteenth year, at which age he is capable of becoming a father; and at the end of the year his offspring arrives at the birth, and again in fifteen years more begets another offspring like himself; and out of these names of grandfathers, fathers, and sons, as also out of the names of grandmothers, mothers, and daughters, a generation complete in its offspring is produced.

(6) What is the meaning of a door in the side: for he says, "Thou shalt make a door in the side?" (Genesis 6:16).

That door in the side very plainly betokens a human building, which he has becomingly indicated by calling it, "in the side," by which door all the excrements of dung are cast out. In truth, as Socrates says, whether because he learnt it from Moses or because he was influenced by the facts themselves, the Creator, having due regard to the decency of our body, has placed the exit and passage of the different ducts of the body back out of the reach of the sense, in order that while getting rid of the fetid portions of bile, we might not be disgusted by beholding the full appearance of our excrements. Therefore he has surrounded that passage by the back and posteriors, which project out like hills, as also the buttocks are made soft for other objects.

(7) Why has he said that the lower part of the

ark was to be made with two and with three stories? (Genesis 6:16).

He has here admirably indicated the receptacles of food, calling them the inner parts of the house; since food is corruptible, and what is corruptible belongs to the inward part, because it is borne downwards, since some small portions of meat and drink which we take are borne upwards, but the greater part is secreted and cast out into dung; and the intestines have been made in two and in three stories, because of the providence of the Creator in order to supply abundant support to his creatures; for if he had made the receptacles of food and its passage having a direct communication between the bowels and the buttocks, some awkward circumstances must have taken place; in the first place there would have been a frequent deficiency, and want and hunger, and sudden evacuations also arising from divers unseasonable events; in the second place there would have been an immense hunger, for when the receptacles are emptied, it is inevitable that hunger and thirst must immediately supervene, like absolute mistresses in difficulty from pregnancy, and then it follows also that the pleasant appetite for food must be perverted into greediness and into an unphilosophical state; for nothing is so very inconvenient as for the belly to be empty.

And in the third place, there will be death waiting at the door; since those persons must speedily be overtaken by death who the very moment that they have done eating begin again to be hungry, and the moment that they have drunk are again thirsty, and who before they are thoroughly filled are again evacuated and oppressed by hunger; but owing to the long coils and windings of the bowels we are delivered from all feelings of hunger, from all greediness, and from being prematurely overtaken by death; for while the food which has been taken remains within us, not for such a time only as the distance to be passed requires, but for so long as was necessary for us, a change in it is effected; since by the pressure to which it is subjected, the strength of the food is extracted in the first instance in the belly; then it is armed in the liver, and drawn out; after that whatever predominant flavour there was is emitted upwards to the separate parts, in the case of boys in order to contribute to their growth, and in the case of fullgrown men to add to their strength; and then nature, collecting the remaining portions into dung and excrement, casts them out.

Therefore a great deal of time is necessarily required for the arrangement of so many and such important affairs, nature effecting its operations without difficulty by perseverance.

Moreover the ark itself appears to me to be very fitly compared to the human body; for as nature is exceedingly prolific of living creatures, for that very reason it has prepared an opposite receptacle similar to the earth for the creatures corrupted and destroyed by the flood; for whatever was alive and supported on the earth, the ark now bore within itself in a more general manner, and on that account God ordained it, being borne upon the waters as it was, to be as it were like the earth, a mother and a nurse, and to exhibit the fathers of the subsequent race as if pregnant with it, together with the sun and moon, and the remaining multitude of the stars, and all the host of heaven; because men beholding by means of that which was made by art, a comparison and analogy to the human body, might in that manner be more manifestly taught, for this was the cause of the various disputes among mankind; since there is nothing which has so much contributed to keep man in a servile condition as the essential humours of the body, and the defects which arise in consequence of them, and most especially the vicious pleasures and desires.

(8) Why does he say that the deluge will be to the corrupting of all flesh in which there is the breath of life beneath the heaven? (Genesis 6:17).

One may almost say that what he had previously spoken in riddles he has now made plain; for there was no other cause for the corruption of mankind, except that, being slaves to pleasure and to desire, they did everything, and were anxious about everything for that reason only; moreover they passed a life of extreme misery.

But he added also, in a very natural manner, the place where the breath of life is, using the expression, "under heaven," because forsooth there are living beings also in heaven; for a happy body has not been made out of a heavenly substance, as if in truth it had received some peculiar and admirable condition, superior to that of other living creatures, but heaven appears to have been made especially worthy of and for the sake of these admirable and divine living beings, all of which are intellectual spirits; so that they give a share and participation in themselves and in the essence of vitality even to the creatures which exist upon the earth, and give life to all those which are capable of receiving it.

(9) Why does he say, all things which existed upon the earth shall be consumed; for what sin can the beasts commit? (Genesis 6:13).

In the first place, as, when a sovereign is slain in battle the military valour of the kingdom is also crushed, so also he now has thought it reasonable that when the whole human race, bearing analogy to a sovereign, is destroyed, he should also destroy simultaneously with it the species of beasts likewise, on which account also in pestilences the beasts die first, and especially those which are bred up with and associate with men, such as dogs and similar animals, and afterwards the men die too.

In the second place, as, when the head is cut off, no one blames nature if the other portions of the body also, numerous and important as they are, are destroyed along with it, so too now no one can find fault with anything, since man is as it were the head and chief of all animals, and when he is destroyed it is not at all strange if all the rest of the beasts are destroyed also along with him.

In the third place, animals were originally made, not for their own sakes, as has been said by the philosophers, but in order to do service to mankind, and for their use and glory; therefore it is very reasonable that when those beings are destroyed for the sake of whom they had their existence, they also should be deprived of life, and this is the reason of this assertion in its literal sense; but with respect to its hidden meaning we may say, when the soul is exposed to a deluge from the overflow of vices, and is in a manner stifled by them, those portions also which are on the earth, the earthly parts I mean of the body, must of necessity likewise perish along with it; for life passed in wickedness is death; the eyes though they see perish, inasmuch as they see wrongly; the ears also though they hear perish, inasmuch as they hear wrongly; and the whole body of the senses perishes, inasmuch as they are all exercised wrongly.

(10) What is the meaning of the expression, I will set up my treaty with you? (Genesis 6:9).

In the first place, he here warns us that no man is the inheritor of the divine substance, except him who is endowed with virtue; since the inheritance of men is possessed when they themselves are no longer in existence, but when they are dead; but as God is everlasting he grants a participation in his inheritance to wise men, rejoicing at their entering into possession of it; for he who has entered into possession of everything is in want of nothing, but they who are in distress from a want of all things are in the possession of no portion of truth.

And on this account God, showing himself favourable to the virtuous, benefits them, bestowing on the those things of which they have need.

In the second place, he bestows on the wise man a certain and more ample inheritance; for he does not say, I will set up my treaty for you, but with you; that is to say, you are yourself a just and true treaty, which I will set up for the race endued with reason, who have need of virtue, for a possession and a glory to them.

(11) Why does he say: "Enter thou and all thy house into the ark, because I have seen that thou art a just man before me in that generation?" (Genesis 7:1).

In the first place, certain faith receives approbation, inasmuch as for the sake of one man who is just and worthy many men are saved by reason of their relationship to him; as is the case too with sailors and armies, when the one have a good captain and the others an excellent and skilful general.

In the second place, he extols the just man with praise, who thus acquires virtues, not for himself alone, but also for his whole family, which in this way deserves safety. And it is with peculiar propriety that this expression is added, namely, "I have seen that thou art a just man before me;" for men approve of the life of any one upon one principle, and God on quite a different one; for they judge by what is visible, but he derives his tests from the invisible designs of the soul.

Moreover, that is a very remarkable expression which is added as an insertion, namely, the one which says, "I have seen that thou art a just man in this generation;" that he might not appear to condemn those who had gone before, nor cut off the future hope of coming generations. This is the sense of the passage taken according to the letter.

But if we look at its inward meaning, when God will save the intellect of the soul, which is the principal part of the man, that is to say, the head of the family, then also he will save the whole family along with him; I mean all the parts, and all those who bear an analogy to the parts, and to the word which is uttered, and to the circumstances of the body; for what the intellect is in the soul, that also is the soul in the body. All the parts of the soul are in good condition, owing to the result of counsels, and all its family derives the benefit along with it. But when the whole soul is in a good condition, then also its habitation is again found to be benefited by purity of morals and sobriety, those overstrained desires which are the causes of diseases being cut off.

(12) Why does he order seven of each of the clean animals, male and female, to be taken into the ark, but of the unclean animals only two, male and female, in order to preserve seed upon all the earth? (Genesis 7:2).

By divine ordinance he has asserted the number seven to be clean, and the number two to be unclean; since the number seven is clean by nature, inasmuch as that is a virgin number, free from all admixture, and without any parent. Nor does it generate any thing, nor is it generated, as each of those numbers which are below the number ten, on account of their similitude to the unit, because it is uncreated and unbegotten, and nothing is generated by it, although it is itself the cause of creation and generation; because it rouses the virtues of all things which are well-arranged, for the generation of created beings.

But the number two is not clean. In the first place, because it is empty, not solid; and because it is not full, therefore neither is it clean; because it is likewise the beginning of infinite immensity by reason of its materiality. It also labours under inequality on account of the other long numbers; for all the other numbers after two which are increased in a twofold proportion are long numbers. But that which is unequal is not clean, as neither is that which is material; but that which proceeds from such is fallible and inelegant, being destitute of the purity of reason to conduct it to completeness and perfection; and it conducts it to such by its own intrinsic power, and by songs of harmony and equality.

This is enough to say on the physical part of the subject; it remains for us to speak of its moral bearings.

The irrational parts of our soul which are destitute of intellect are divided into seven; that is to say, into the five senses, and the vocal organ, and the seminal organ. Now these in a man endued with virtue are all clean, and by nature feminine, inasmuch as they belong to the irrational species; but to a man who has come into full possession of his inheritance they are masculine; for men endued with virtue are also the parents of the virtue of counsel to themselves, the best part of them not permitting them to come to the external senses in a precipitate and unbridled manner, but repressing them and leading them back to right reason.

But in the wicked man there exists a twofold wickedness; since the unjust man is full of doubts and perplexities, as a hesitating person, mingling things which ought not to be mixed, and connecting them with one another, confounding those things which may very easily be kept separate. Such are those passions which imbue the soul with some particular colour, like a man spotted and leprous in body, the originally sound counsel being infected and contaminated by that which is destructive and fatal. But the principle of the entrance and of the custody of animals is added in a natural manner; for he says, "for the sake of nourishing seed." If we take the expression according to the letter, inasmuch as, although particular individuals may be destroyed, still at least a race is preserved to be the seed of future generations; forsooth that the intention of God, conceived at the formation of the world, might remain for ever and ever unextinguishable, the different races of creatures being preserved.

But if we regard the inward meaning of the words, it is necessary that in the irrational parts of the soul, likewise, there should be motions which are clean, as certain seminal principles, although the animals themselves are not clean; since the nature of mankind is capable of admitting contrarieties, for instance, virtue and wickedness; each of which he delineated at the creation of the world, by the tree bearing the name of the tree of knowledge of good and evil. Forsooth our intellect, in which there is both knowledge and intelligence, comprehends both good and evil; but good is akin to the number seven, and evil is the brother of duality.

Moreover, the law of wisdom, which abounds in beauty, says expressly and carefully, that seed is to be nourished, not in one place only, but in all the earth, both naturally, in the first instance, and also morally, in its peculiar sense; because it is very natural, and suitable to the character of God, to cause that which in all parts and divisions of the world is said again to be the seed of living beings, to fill places which have been evacuated a second time with similar creatures, by a repeated generation; and not altogether to desert our body, inasmuch as it is an earthly substance, as if it were a thing deserted by and void of all principle of life.

Since, if we practise the drinking of wines and the eating of meats, and indulge in the ardent desire of the female, and in short practise in all things a delicate and luxurious life, we are then only the bearers of a corpse in the body; but if God, taking compassion on us, turns away the overflow of vices and renders the soul dry, he will then begin to make the body living, and to animate it with a purer soul, the governing principle of which is wisdom.

(13) Why, after the entrance of Noah into the ark, did seven days elapse, after which the deluge came? (Genesis 7:10).

The kind Saviour of the world allows a space for the repentance of sinners, in order that when they see the ark placed in front of them as a sort of type, made with respect to the then present time, and when they see all the different kinds of living creatures shut up in it which the earth used to bear on its surface, according to its parts adapted to the different species, they might believe the predictions of the deluge which had been made to them, so that, fearing total destruction above all things, they might be speedily converted, destroying and eradicating all their iniquity and wickedness.

In the second place, this language is a most manifest representation of the exceeding great abundance of the kind mercy of the beneficent Saviour, by destroying the wickedness of many years, which from the time of their birth to old age has extended itself over their conduct in those persons who practise penitence for a few days, for the divine nature forgets all evil and is a lover of virtue. When therefore it beholds faithful virtue in the soul, it gives it honour in a wonderful degree, in order, in the first place, to take away all kinds of evil which impend over it from its sins.

In the third place, the number of seven days after the entrance of Noah into the ark, during which the command of God kept off the flood, is a recollection of the creation of the world, the birthday festival of which is kept on the seventh day, showing manifestly the authority of the Father; just as if he were to say, "I am the Creator of the world, commanding things to exist which have no existence; and at the same time I am he who am now about to destroy the world with a great flood. But the original cause of the creation of the world was the goodness which is in me, and my kindness; and the cause of its impending destruction is the ingratitude and impiety of those persons who have been loaded with benefits by me."

Therefore he causes an interval of seven days, in order that the unbelieving may remember, and that those who have abandoned their faith in the Parent of the world may in a suppliant spirit return to the Creator of all things, and so may entreat him again that his works may be everlasting; and that they may offer their entreaty, not with mouth and tongue, but rather with the heart of amendment and penitence.

(14) Why did the rain of the deluge last forty days and an equal number of nights? (Genesis 7:4).

In the first place, the word day is used in a double sense. The one meaning that time which is from morning to evening, that is to say, from the first rising of the sun in the east to his sinking in the west. Therefore they who make definitions, say, "That is day, as long as the sun shines on the earth."

In another sense, the word day is used of the day and night together. And in this sense we say that a month consists of thirty days, combining together and computing the period of night in the same calculation.

These premises having been first laid down thus, I say that the word now spoken of has not been incorrectly employed, inasmuch as it implies forty days and forty nights; but is also so used in order to suggest a double number determined for the generation of mankind, namely, forty and eighty, as many men skilled in medicine, and indeed also in physical science, have suggested; but it is especially described in the sacred law, which was to them also the first principle of natural science.

Since therefore destruction was on the point of overwhelming all men and women every where on account of the excessive combination of iniquities and quarrels, the Judge of all considered it becoming to allot an equal time to their destruction to that which he had consumed in the original creation of nature and to the work of giving life to the world; for the principle of procreation is the perseverance of seed in the different parts; but it was necessary to honour the male creature with pure light, which knows not the shade; but the woman had a mixture in her body of night and darkness.

Therefore, in the creation of the whole world, the excess of the male or the unequal number, being composed of unity, becomes the parent of square numbers; but the woman who is an unequal number, being compounded of duality, becomes the parent of other long numbers. Moreover, the square is splendour and light combining together by the equality of the sides; but the other numbers being long necessarily exhibit night and darkness by reason of their inequality, since that which is in excess throws a shade over that which lies beneath the excess.

In the second place, the number forty is the produce of many virtues, as has been suggested in another place. It is also often used for the judgment of legislation, both with reference to those persons who have done any thing rightly deserving of praise and honour, and also with reference to those who on account of their sins meet with reproaches and punishments; so that it is superfluous to adduce proofs to demonstrate what is evident.

(15) What is the meaning of the expression, "I will destroy every living substance that I have made from off the face of the earth?" (Genesis 7:4).

Do you not all shrink back in astonishment when you hear these words, by reason of the beauty of the sentence? for he has not said, "destroy from the earth," but "from the face of the earth," that is to say from its surface; in order, that is, that in the lowest depth of the earth the vital efficacy of all seeds might be preserved unhurt, and free from all injury which could possibly bring damage to it; since the Creator was not forgetful of his original design, but destroys those only who come in his way, and who move only on the surface of the earth, but leaves the roots in the depth, in order to produce the generation of other causes.

Moreover, that expression, "I will destroy," was also written by divine inspiration; for it happens that if we remove the letters which require to be removed, the whole table for the reception of letters remains the same. By which he proves that he will destroy the fickle generation on account of their impiety, but the conversation and essence of the human race he will preserve for ever and ever to be the seed of future generations. And what follows agrees with this, since to the expression, "I will destroy," this other is also added, all natural existence, every thing which exists, or rises upon the earth; but existence is the destruction of the opposite characteristics; and that which is dissolved loses quality, but retains body and materiality. This is the letter of what is said.

But in the inward meaning, the flood is symbolically representative of spiritual dissolution. When therefore by the grace of the Father we desire to throw away and to wash off all sensible and corporeal qualities by which the intellect was infected as by swelling sores, then the muddy slime is got rid of as by a deluge, sweet waters and wholesome fountains supervening.

(16) Why does he say: "Noah did every thing which the Lord commanded (or ordered) him?" (Genesis 7:5).

A noble panegyric for the just man. In the first place, because with an ingenuous mind and a purpose full of affection towards God he performed, not a part of what he had been commanded, but the whole of God's commands. But the second is the more true expression, because he does not choose so much to command as to order him; for masters command their slaves, but friends order friends, and especially elder friends order younger ones. Therefore it is a marvellous gift to be found even in the rank of servants, and in the list of ministers of God; and it is a superabundant excess of kindness for any one to be a beloved friend to the most glorious Uncreated Essence.

Moreover, the sacred writer has here carefully employed both names, the Lord God, as declaratory of his superior powers of destroying and benefiting, using the word Lord first, and placing the name God, giving the idea of beneficence, second; since it was a time of judgment let the name which is the indication of his destroying power come first. But still, as he is a kind and merciful king, he leaves as relics the seminal elements by which the vacant places may be replenished, for which reason, at the first beginning of the account of the creation, the expression, "Let there be," was not an exterminating act of power, but a beneficent one.

Therefore, at the creation, he changed the appellations and use of names; but as the name God is an indication of his beneficent power, the sacred writer has more frequently employed that in his account of the creation of the universe, but after everything was perfected then he called him Lord, in reference to the creation itself, for this name betokens royal power and the ability to destroy; since, where the act of generation is God is used first in order, but when punishment is spoken of the name Lord is placed before the name God.

(17) Why did the deluge take place in the six hundredth year of the life of Noah, and in the seventh month, and on the twenty-seventh day of the month? (Genesis 7:11).

Perhaps it happened that the just man was born at the beginning of the month, at the first beginning of the commencement of that very year which they are accustomed to call the sacred year, out of honour, otherwise the sacred historian would not have been so carefully accurate in fixing the day and month when the deluge began to the seventh month and the twenty-seventh day of the month.

But, perhaps, by this minuteness he intended manifestly to indicate the precise time of the vernal equinox, for that always occurs on the twenty-seventy day of the seventh month.

But why was it that the deluge fell on the day of the vernal equinox? Because about that time the birth and increase of everything take place, whether living creatures or plants; therefore the vengeance and punishment inflicted brings with it the more terrible and dreadful threats, as happening at the period of plenty and fertility of the sheaves of corn, and indeed, in the very midst of that productiveness, and bringing the evil of utter destruc-

tion as a reproof of the impiety of those who are exposed to the punishment.

For behold, says he, all nature contains its own productions within itself in the greatest abundance, namely, wheat and barley, and everything else which is produced from seed, brought on to complete generation, as, also, it begins to generate the fruits of trees; but you, like mortals, corrupt its mercies, perverting the divine gifts, and purposes, and mysteries.

But if the deluge had taken place at the autumnal equinox, when there was nothing growing on the earth, but when all the crops were collected into their proper storehouses, it would not have, in any degree, been looked upon as a punishment, but rather as a benefit, as the water would have cleansed the plains and the mountains. But as the first man who was produced out of the earth was also created at the same season of the year, he whom the divine writer calls Adam, because in fact it was on every account proper that the grandfather, or original parent, or father of the human race, or by whatever name we may choose to designate that original founder of our kind, should be created at the season of the vernal equinox, when all earthly productions were full of their fruit; but the vernal equinox takes place in the seventh month, which is also called the first in other passages, with reference to a different idea.

Since, therefore, the first beginning of the generation of our race, after the destruction caused by the deluge, commenced with Noah, men being again sown and procreated, therefore he also is recognised as resembling the first man born of the earth, as far as such resemblance or recognition is possible. And the six hundredth year has for its origin the number six; and the world was created under the number six, therefore, by this same number does he reprove the wicked, putting them to shame because he would, unquestionably, never, after he had created the universe by means of the number six, have destroyed all the men who lived on the earth under the form of six, if it had not been for the preposterous excess of their iniquities. For the third power of six and the minor power is the number six hundred, and the mean between both is sixty, since the number ten more evidently represents the likeness of unity, and the number a hundred represents the minor power.

(18) What is the meaning of the expression, "And the fountains of the deep were broken, and the springs of heaven were opened?" (Genesis 7:11).

The literal meaning is plain enough, for it suggests the two extremities of the universe, the heaven and the earth, to have met together for the destruction of mortals deserving of condemnation, the waters running forth to meet one another from all quarters, for part of them bubbled up from out of the earth, and part descended downwards from heaven; and in truth, that expression is very explicit, "The fountains were broken up," for when a rupture is effected then the thing confined rushes forth without any hindrance.

But with reference to the interior meaning of the expression we may as well say this: the heaven is symbolically the human intellect, and the earth is the sense and body, therefore there is great distress and calamity when neither remains, but when each threatens a secret attack. But what is the exact meaning of my words?

It often happens that acuteness of intellect exhibits cunning and wickedness, and bears itself with bitterness in every respect when the lusts of the body are restrained and bridled; but the contrary fact often prevails, and the lusts rejoice in their opportunities and proceed onward, gaining strength from luxury and abundance of means; therefore, the gate of these lusts is the outward sense combined with the body; but when the intellect, neglecting outward circumstances, is consistent with itself, then the senses lie harmless, as if completely abandoned; but when both are united, the intellect in exerting all cunning and wickedness, and the body irrigated with all the senses and gorged with every kind of vice to satiety, then we are exposed to a deluge; and this is in fact a great deluge, when the streams of the intellect are opened by iniquity, and folly, and greedy desire, and injustice, and arrogance, and impiety, and when the fountains of the body are opened by lust, and desire, and intemperance, and obscenity, and gluttony, and lasciviousness, with relations and sisters, and all irremediable diseases.

(19) What is the meaning of the expression, "And the Lord shut him in, closing the doors of the ark?" (Genesis 7:16).

Since we have said that the structure of the human body is symbolically indicated by the ark, we must take notice, also, that on the outside this body is enclosed by a hard and dense skin, to be a covering to all its parts; for nature has made this as a sort of coat, to prevent either cold or heat from being able to do man injury.

The literal meaning of the expression is plain enough, for the door of the ark is carefully shut by divine virtue for the sake of security, lest the water should enter in at any part, as it was to be tossed about by the waves for an entire year.

(20) What is the meaning of the expression, "And the water was greatly increased, and bore up the ark which floated upon the water?" (Genesis 7:17).

The literal meaning is plain enough, but it contains an allegorical reference to our bodies, which ought to be borne up as if on the water, and by fluctuating with our necessities to subdue hunger and thirst, cold and heat, by which it is agitated, disturbed, and kept in motion.

(21) Why did the water overflow fifteen cubits above all the highest mountains? (Genesis 7:19).

With respect to the literal statement we must remark that the excess was not merely one of fifteen cubits above all high mountains but above those which were a great deal more lofty and high than some others; therefore it was a great deal more than that height above the lower ones.

But we must interpret this statement allegorically; for the loftier mountains shadow forth the senses in our body, because it has been permitted to them to occupy the abode of stability in the lofty region of our head. And there are five numbers of these, each to be considered separately, so that they amount in all to fifteen.

As, there is the faculty of sight, the thing which is visible, the act of seeing.

The faculty of hearing, the thing which is audible, and the act of hearing.

The faculty of smelling, the thing which can be smelled, and the act of smelling.

The faculty of taste, the thing which can be tasted, and the act of tasting.

The faculty of touch, the thing which can be touched, and the act of touching.

These are the fifteen cubits in excess; for they also are overwhelmed by the overflow, being destroyed by the unseasonable influx of infinite vices and evils.

(22) What is the meaning of the expression, "And all flesh capable of motion perished?" (Genesis 7:21).

It is with especial propriety, and strictly in accordance with natural truth, that the sacred historian has here pronounced all flesh capable of motion devoted to destruction; for flesh excites pleasures, and is excited by pleasures; and such affections are the causes of the destruction of souls, as on the other hand sobriety and patience are the causes of safety.

(23) What is the meaning of the expression, "And everything which was on the dry land died?" (Genesis 7:22).

The literal meaning is notorious, because in that great deluge everything which was upon the earth was destroyed and perished; but with respect to the secret meaning, as, since the material of timber, when it is parched and dry, is readily consumed by fire, so, likewise, when the soul is not mingled with wisdom, and justice, and piety, and the other enduring virtues, which alone are able to impart real joy to the thoughts, then it, being parched up and dried like a plant which is deprived of any power of budding or producing seed, or like a withered trunk, dies, being handed over to the mercy of the overwhelming overflow of the body.

(24) What is the meaning of the words, "It destroyed every living substance which was on the face of the earth?" (Genesis 7:23).

The literal meaning of these words only

announces a plain statement of a fact, but it may be turned into an allegory in this manner. It is not without reason that the sacred historian has used the words "a living substance," for that is characteristic of ambition and pride, which lead men to despise both divine and human laws; but ambition and arrogance do rather appear on the face of our earthly and corporeal nature with an elated countenance and contracted brows.

Since there are some persons who come nearer to one with their feet, but with their chests, and necks, and heads lean back, and are actually borne backwards and bend away like a balance, so that with one half of their body, in consequence of the position of their feet, they project forward, but backward with the upper portion of their chests, drawing themselves back like those persons whose muscles and nerves are in pain, by which they are prevented from stooping in a natural manner. But men of this kind it was determined to put an end to, as one may see from the records of the Lord and the divine history of the scriptures.

(25) What is the meaning of the words, "Noah remained alone, and they who were with him in the ark?" (Genesis 7:24).

The literal meaning of this is evident; but with respect to its concealed sense we may advance an opinion, that the intellect which is desirous of studying justice and wisdom does, like a tree, discard all noxious shoots which bud forth about it, and rejects all extravagant humours of superfluous vigour, I mean immoderate excess of the affections, and wickedness, and all the effects of such.

Therefore he is here said to have been left alone with those of his own kindred, and his kindred are properly all those designs and thoughts of each individual, which are regulated in accordance with virtue, on which account the statement is added "And he remained alone, and they who were with him," in order to reveal a more genuine joy; but he remained in the ark, that is to say, in the body, because it was purified from every vice and spiritual disease, as the intellect was not yet put in such a condition as to be wholly incorporeal.

And on this account also, we must render thanks to the merciful Father, because he received his consort and colleague no longer as one endowed with superior power, but to be subordinate to his own power, on which account also the body is not submerged in the deluge, but rising above the flood is not at all destroyed by the eddies of the cataracts, which a crapulous, libidinous, vanity-loving will, overflowing all things, raises to an eminence.

(26) Why is it that the sacred writer says, "And God was mindful of Noah, and of the beasts, and of the cattle," but does not add that he remembered his wife and children? (Genesis 8:1).

As the husband agrees with and is equal to his wife, and as the father is equal to his sons, there is no need of mentioning more names than one, but one, the first, is sufficient; therefore, by naming Noah he, in effect, names all those who were with him of his family; for when husband, and wife, and children, and relations are all agitated by discord, then it is no longer possible for such to be called one family, but instead of being one they are many; but when harmony exists then one family is exhibited by one superior of the house, and all are seen to depend upon that one, like the branches of a tree which shoot out from it, or the fruit upon a vine branch which does not fall off from it.

And in another part, also, the prophet has said, "Have a regard to Abraham your father, and to Sarah who brought you forth," where, because in fact it was one family, he displays the agreement by mentioning the woman.

(27) Why is it that the sacred writer made mention first of the beasts and afterwards of the cattle, saying that God remembered Noah, and the beasts, and the cattle? (Genesis 8:1).

In the first place, that poetical rule has not been expressed in vain, that he led the bad into the middle; therefore he places the beasts in the middle, between the domestic animals, that is to say the men and the cattle, in order that they might be tamed and civilized by having an intimate association with both.

In the second place, he thought it scarcely reasonable to bestow a provident benefit on the beasts by themselves, because he was about immediately to add a statement of the beginning of the diminution of the deluge. This is the explanation of the statement taken literally.

But with respect to the inner meaning, that just intellect, dwelling in the body as if in the ark, possesses both beasts and living animals, not those particular ones which bite and hurt, but, that I may use such an expression, those general kinds which contain in themselves the principles of seed and origination; since without these the soul cannot be manifest in the body. Moreover, the soul of the foolish man employs all poisonous and deadly animals, but that of the wise man those only which have changed the nature of wild beasts into that of domestic creatures.

(28) What is the meaning of the expression, "He brought a breath over the earth, and the water ceased?" (Genesis 8:2).

Some people say that what is here meant by "a breath" is the wind, at which the deluge ceased. But I am not aware that water is diminished by wind, but only that it is disturbed and agitated into waves, for if it were otherwise the vast extent of the sea would have been wholly dried up long ago.

Therefore it appears to me that the sacred writer here means the breath of the Deity, by which the whole universe obtains security at the same time with the calamities of the world, and with those things which exist in the air, and in every mixture of plants and animals. Since the deluge of that time was no trifling infliction of water, but an immense and boundless overflow, extending almost beyond the pillars of Hercules and the great Mediterranean Sea, since the whole earth and all the spaces of the mountains were covered with water; and it is scarcely likely that such a vast space could have been cleared by a wind, but rather, as I have said, it must have been done by some invisible and divine virtue.

(29) What is the meaning of the expression, "The fountains of the deep were closed, and the cataracts of heaven?" (Genesis 8:2).

In the first place, it is agreed upon by all that in the first period of forty days the waters of punishment fell uninterruptedly, the lowest fountains of the earth being burst asunder; and from above, the cataracts of heaven being opened, and pouring down until all places, both level and mountainous, were covered with the inundation; and for another period of a hundred and fifty entire days the waters did not cease to fall, nor did the streams cease to flow, nor the springs to burst up, though still in milder quantities, not so as to increase the existing flood, but only so as to secure the duration of the existence of the deluge, which was also assisted from on high; and this is what is indicated in the meantime by the statement that after a hundred and fifty days the fountains and the cataracts were closed up; therefore, while as yet they were not closed up it is plain that they were in action.

In the second place, it was necessary that that which afforded the excessive supply of waters for the deluge, namely, the double reservoir of water, the one from the fountains of the earth, and the other from the pourings forth of heaven, should be both closed, for the more the stores from which any material is supplied fail, the more it is consumed by itself, especially when divine virtue has given the command.

This is the literal meaning of the expression. But with respect to the inner sense of the passage, since the deluge of the mind arises from two things, for it arises partly from counsel, as if from heaven, and in another degree also from the body and from sense, as if from earth, the vices being reciprocally introduced by the passions and the passions by the vices, it was inevitably necessary that the word of the divine physician entering in as a salutary visitation for the purpose of healing the disease, should prevent both kinds of overflow for the future; for it is the first principle of the medical art to drive away the cause of the infirmity and to leave no longer any materials for disease; and the scripture teaches this, also, in the case of the leper, for when the leprosy is checked and is prevented from extending further, it then fixes the station and abode of the leprous man in the same place by a law, because the character of being sta-

tionary implies cleanliness, for that which is moved contrary to nature is unclean.

(30) What is the meaning of the statement that after a hundred and fifty days the water began to abate? (Genesis 8:3).

We must here inquire whether those hundred and fifty days, during which the water was abating, are to be distinguished from the four months, or whether they have a reference to the days previously mentioned, during which the deluge went on unceasingly, as still increasing.

(31) Why does he say, "The ark settled in the seventh month on the seven and twentieth day of the month?" (Genesis 8:4).

It is reasonable here to consider how the beginning of the deluge commences in the seventh month, on the twenty-seventh day of the month, and how the diminution, when the ark rested on the top of the mountains, again took place in the seventh month and on the twenty-seventh day of the month; therefore we must say, that there is here an homonymy of months and days, for the beginning of the flood took place in the seventh month, beginning at the birthday of the just man, near the time of the vernal equinox, and its diminution took place in the seventh month, beginning from the highest point of the flood at the autumnal equinox, since the two equinoxes are separated from one another by seven months, having an interval of five months between them.

For the seventh month of the equinox is also by its virtue the first month, because the creation of the world took place in it, on account of the abundance of all things at that season. And, in like manner, the seventh month of the autumnal equinox, which, according to time, is the first in dignity, having its principle of that number seven derived from the air; therefore, the deluge took place in the seventh month, not according to time but according to nature, having for its principle and commencement the spring season.

(32) Why does he say, "In the tenth month, on the first day of the month, the heads of the mountains appeared?" (Genesis 8:4).

As in numerals the number ten is the extreme bound of the units, being a definitive and perfect number, so too it is the cycle and end of the units, and also the beginning and cycle of the decades, and of infinity of numbers; thus the Creator, on the cessation of the deluge, condescended that the tops of the mountains should appear in the number of the decade, being a definitive and perfect number.

(33) Why was it after forty days that the just man opened the window of the ark? (Genesis 8:5).

We must observe carefully that the divine historian uses the same number in speaking of the influx of the deluge and in mentioning the cessation and complete removal of the evil; forsooth on the twenty-seventh day of the seventh month in the six hundredth year of the life of Noah, that is to say in the six hundredth year after his nativity, the deluge began at the spring season; but on the twenty-seventh day of the seventh month, the ark rested on the top of the mountains at the vernal equinox.

But it is plain from these circumstances that the deluge became invisible in the six hundred and first year of Noah's life, again on the seventh month and the twenty-seventh day of it, so that after the lapse of an entire year, it again settled and established the earth as it was at the moment of its destruction, in the spring season, budding forth and covered with verdure and full of all kinds of fruits.

But again in a similar manner the overflow of the deluge took place for forty days, the cataracts of heaven being opened and fountains bursting upwards from the lowest depths of the earth; and again a hope of renewal took place at intervals of forty days after a sufficient cessation of the rains, when he opened the window; and again the duration of the permanent deluge lasted for a period of a hundred and fifty days, as also its gradual diminution occupied a period of a hundred and fifty days; so that we may well admire the equality of the arrangement, for the evil increased and ceased according to the same number, like the moon, which from its first rise proceeds in its increase according to an equal number, going onward to its perfect fulness of light, and then again with an equal number in its decrease, returning back to its original state, after having been previously full; and in like manner in the case of divine chastisements, the Creator preserves a regular order, banishing all irregularity from the divine borders.

(34) What is the window of the ark, which the just man opens? (Genesis 8:6).

The literal statement scarcely admits of any difficulty or doubt, inasmuch as it is plain; but with reference to the inner meaning we have this to say: each separate part of the senses has imitated the windows of the body, since it is through them as through windows that the comprehension of sensible objects enters into the intellect, and again it is through them that the intellect stretches forth as if escaping; but a portion of these windows, the senses, the more noble portion too, I say, is the sight; inasmuch as that above all the rest is akin to the soul, and it is intimately acquainted with light, the most beautiful of the essences, and it is the minister of sacred things; moreover that is the one which first laid open the road to philosophy.

For beholding the regular motion of the sun, and of the moon, and the erratic course of the other planets, and the unerring circular motion of the whole heaven, and the order and harmony there existing beyond all calculation, as if it were the one real creator of the whole world, it by itself related to its one chief counsellor and director all that it

saw: and then intellect, seeing those things with its acute eye, and by those things discerning superior demonstrative ideas, and the cause of all those things, immediately perceived that there was a God at the same moment that it arrived at the conception of generation and providence, because forsooth it was plain that this visible nature was not created by itself: for it was impossible that such a harmony, and order, and reason, and most consistent analogy, and that a concord of such a character and extent, and that such true and perfect felicity should exist by its own power: but it was necessary that there must be some Creator and parent of it acting like a governor and director, who generated these things, and then having generated them preserves them safe and sound.

(35) Why did he send out a raven first? (Genesis 8:6).

If we look to the literal statement, the raven is said to be an animal particularly set apart for being sent on messages and employed in offices; for to this very day many people watch its mode of flight and its chattering, judging that it gives some intimation of unknown facts; but with respect to the hidden meaning, as a raven is a black, and arrogant, and speedy animal, it is a sign of wickedness, which brings night and darkness over the soul, and it is also swift to meet all the things of the world in its flight.

And also that it is very bold, so as at times to cause the destruction of those who seek to catch it, since pride produces also rash impudence, the opposite of which is virtue, which is consistent with the brilliancy of light, and is by nature decorated with a modest bashfulness; therefore it is quite natural that if there was any darkness remaining behind in the intellect, darkness which exists in accordance with folly, he should expel that and send it out beyond his borders.

(36) Why did the raven after it had gone forth not return, when there was not yet any part of the earth dried? (Genesis 8:7).

This passage admits of an allegorical interpretation since injustice is contrary to the light of justice; so that in comparison of the admirable actions of the man endued with virtue, it thinks it more desirable to rejoice with its kinsman the deluge; for injustice is a lover of confusion and corruption.

(37) Why does he speak here in an incorrect manner, "Till the water was dried up from the earth;" when it was not the water which was dried up from the earth, but the earth which was dried from the water? (Genesis 8:7).

He uses this expression in an allegorical sense, indicating by the fall of the waters the immensity of vices, by which when saturated and vigorous the soul is corrupted, but when they are dried up and withered, it is preserved; for then they cannot inflict any mischief upon it, since they are become impotent and dead.

(38) Why does he in the second place send forth the dove, and why does he send it forth from himself to see whether the water had ceased, when he uses no such expressions about the raven? (Genesis 8:8).

In the first place, the dove is a clean animal, and in the second place it is tame, civilised, and one which associates with mankind, on which account also the honour has been allotted to it of being offered up upon the altar in sacrifices; and on this account the sacred writer, sanctioning this honour and adding the weight of his assertion, has said, he sent it forth from himself, declaring by this expression that it was to see whether the water was abated, he displays the common anxiety felt by both.

But those birds, the raven and the dove, are symbols of wickedness and virtue: for the one, whether it is wickedness or the raven, has no house, nor habitation, nor city, being an insolent unsociable bird; but the other, namely virtue, has a regard to humanity, and to the public good: and so the man endowed with virtue sends that bird forth as his ambassador for desirable and salutary objects, wishing to receive from it desirable information; and she, like an ambassador, brings us back genuine pleasure, so that what is hurtful may be guarded against, and what is useful may be diligently and carefully admitted.

(39) Why did the dove, when it found no rest for its feet, return to Noah? (Genesis 8:9).

Is not the reason of this evident, and is it not a plain proof that wickedness and virtue are symbolically indicated by the raven and the dove? For behold the dove, which is the last sent out, finds no rest. How, then, could the raven, who departed previously, while the calamity of the deluge was still prevailing, find any place, and make a settlement? For the raven was neither a swan nor an ibis, nor did he belong to the class of aquatic birds.

But the sacred writer here points out in an enigmatical manner, that wickedness, when it has gone forth out of doors, to the swelling whirlpools of the vices and passions which overflow and corrupt the soul and life, joyfully admits them, and dwells with and takes up its abode with them, as with its nearest friends and relations; but virtue, turning away with loathing from even the first sight of them, at once springs back, and does not return, scarcely finding rest for its feet; finding, in fact, no standing ground anywhere, and no place worthy of itself. For what other greater evil can there be than this, that virtue should not be able to find in the soul any place ever so small for rest and for abiding in?

(40) What is the meaning of the statement, "Putting forth his hand, he received her, and brought her in to himself?" (Genesis 8:9).

The literal meaning is plain, but with respect to the hidden sense we must elicit the truth care-

fully. The wise man employs truth as an overseer of and ambassador in important affairs, which, when it perceives that those natures are worthy of it, abides among and dwells with them, correcting them, and making them better, since wisdom is a very common, and equal, and useful thing. But when, with reference to the opposite natures, it sees that in some points they are preposterously redundant and in others altogether deficient, it returns to its proper place; and the man endowed with virtue admits it in word, putting forth his hand to take it, and in fact opening all his intellect for its reception, and unfolding it by the perfect number, full and equal, with all imaginable promptitude.

Nor even then, when he had sent her forth from himself to examine the natures of other things, had he separated it from himself, but had only acted like the sun, which sends forth his beams to give light to all things, because it is not at all consistent with the character of his boundless light to be separated at all.

(41) Why did he, after waiting yet seven other days, send forth the dove a second time? (Genesis 8:10).

This is an excellent example for life, since although it will behold natures obstinate at first, still the hope of changing them into better natures is scarcely allowed to drop; and as a prudent physician does not in a moment apply a perfect cure to a disease, or effect a complete restoration to health, but employs salutary medicines after he has given nature an opportunity of first opening the way to recovery, so too the man endowed with virtue behaves with respect to the employment of the word which is in accordance with the law of wisdom.

But the number seven is the sacred and dominical number, according to which the Father of the universe, when he made the world, is said to have looked upon his work. And the contemplation of the world, and of all the things contained in it, is nothing else but philosophy, and that excellent and select portion of it which wisdom contains, comprehending within itself also a work still more necessary to be seen.

(42) What is the meaning of the expression, "The dove returned a second time to him about evening, having in her mouth a leaf and a thin branch of olive?" (Genesis 8:11).

All these separate points are selected and approved signs—the returning, the returning about evening, the having an olive-leaf and a thin branch of that tree, and oil, and the having it in her mouth; but yet every one of these signs can be examined with a certainty beyond certainty, for the return is distinct from its previous return, for that one bore with it an announcement of nature being wholly corrupted and rebellious, and being wholly destroyed by the deluge, that is to say, by great ignorance and insolence; but this second return brings the news of the world beginning to repent, but to find repentance is not an easy task, but is a difficult and laborious business.

And it is on this account that the dove arrived in the evening, having passed the whole day from morning to evening in its visitations; in word, indeed, examining places, but in fact investigating the different parts of nature itself by continual visitation, and seeing them all clearly from beginning to end, for the evening is the indication of the end.

The third sign, again, is its bringing a leaf; but a leaf is a small part of a tree, still it does not exist without a tree. And the beginning of displaying repentance is somewhat corresponding to this, since the beginning of correction has some slight indications about it, which we may call a leaf, by which it appears to receive guardianship, but can easily be shaken off; so that the hope shall in that case not be great of attaining the desired improvement, which is typified by the leaf of no other tree but of the olive alone, and oil is the material of light. For wickedness, as I have said before, is profound darkness, but virtue is luminous brilliancy, and repentance is the beginning of light. But you must not yet suppose that the beginning of repentance is only visible in branches just germinating and beginning to look green, but that it exists too while they are still dry, and while the seminal principle is dry and quiescent.

And it is on this account that the fifth sign is shown, that, namely, of the dove when it comes bearing a slender branch.

And the sixth sign is that this slender branch was in its mouth, for the number six is the first perfect number, since virtue bears in its mouth, that is to say in its conversation, the seeds of wisdom and justice, or, in one word, of honesty of the soul; and not only bears this, but gives some portion of participation in it even to the foolish, by drawing up water for their souls, and irrigating them with the desire of repentance for their sins.

(43) Why is it said, "And Noah knew that the waters had ceased from off the earth?" (Genesis 8:11).

The literal statement is plain, since if the leaf had been taken up from off the water it would have been wet and soaked, but now he says that it was dry and slender, as if it had become dry by being on the earth which was dried. But with reference to its inward meaning, the wise man takes it as a symbol of repentance, and wishes to check the calamities of excessive obstinacy by taking the leaf, since it was not yet green, but slender, for the reason which has been already mentioned.

At the same time we may admire the Father on account of his exceeding kindness, for although corruption had prevailed over all the men who lived on the earth from the excess of their iniquities, still there remained some relics of antiquity and

of that which was from the beginning, and a slight seed of previous virtues; by which it is intimated nevertheless that the memory of all the good deeds that have been done from the beginning is not wholly destroyed. On which account a certain prophet, the kinsman and friend of Moses, uttered an oracle of this kind, "If the omnipotent Lord had not left us a seed, we should have been like blind and barren people,"[3] able neither to know the truth nor to generate it. And the Chaldaeans in their native language call blindness and sterility Sodom and Gomorrah.

(44) Why, in the third place, after seven other days, did he again send forth the dove, which did not again return to him? (Genesis 8:12).

According to the word, the dove made no more return to him; but what in fact is meant is virtue, which, however, is not an indication of alienation, since, as I have said before, she was not separated from him at that time, but sent forth like a sun-beam to pay a visit of examination to the natures of others, but then, not finding any one to listen to her precepts of correction, she returns, and properly comes to him alone. But this time she is no longer the possession of one single individual, but is rather a common good to all those who have been willing to receive the emanations of wisdom as if coming up from the earth, those persons, that is, who from the very beginning have laboured under a great thirst of perfect wisdom.

(45) Why in the six hundred and first year of the life of Noah, and on the first day of the first month, did the waters of the deluge cease from off the earth? (Genesis 8:13).

The word first, according to the defect of time, is spoken of with reference either to the month or the man, and each interpretation has reason to support it; for if we are bound to maintain that the water began to abate in the first month, we are equally obliged to consider that the sacred historian intended also to speak of the seventh month, that is, of that month which is the second equinox, since the same month is both the first and the seventh; that is to say, the first as respects nature and virtue, and the seventh in point of time.

Therefore in another place he says,[4] "This month is unto you the beginning of months, the first among the months of the year;" calling that the first which is so in respect of nature and virtue, and which as to number is in time the seventh month, since the equinox has its appointed order in regular series, and in point of time is assigned the better season of the year. But if you take that word first to have reference to the man, then it will be used with more truth, and with strict propriety, for the just man was truly and properly

3 Isaiah 1:9.
4 Exodus 12:2.

the first, as in a vessel the captain is the first man, and in a state the prince. But he is first not only in virtue, but also in order, inasmuch as in the very circumstances of the regeneration of the second sowing of the human race he was the beginning and the first.

Moreover, it is very admirably considered with reference to this passage, that the deluge took place during the life of the first man, and that again, when it abated, things returned to their former steadiness, since after the deluge took place he had to live by himself with his whole family, and after that evil was removed he alone was found upon the earth during the latter period of his life until the regeneration of mankind began.

But it is not to no purpose that this testimony is given both of the preceding portion of his life, and also of the later period, for he alone burnt with a desire for that genuine life which is in accordance with virtue, while all the rest of the world were hastening on to death by reason of their fatal wickednesses. Therefore of necessity the evil ceased on the six hundred and first year of his life, since in truth the destruction came with reference to the sixth number, and safety was restored in unity since unity is more a generativeness of the soul, and is the best for giving life, wherefore also a deficiency of water in the sea takes place at the new moon, in order that the units may be preferred in dignity both among months and years, when God saves those things which are upon the earth; since the man who cultivates just habits is called by the Hebrews in their native language Noah, but by the Greeks he is named *Dikaios*; however, he is not exempted from the laws affecting the body.

For although he is not subordinate to the power of others, but is a prince, yet still, because he is nevertheless devoted to death, as he is dead, the principle of that number six is connected with unity; since it was not in one year taken separately that the deluge ceased, but together with the number six (as contained in the number six hundred), which is connected with it according to corporeality and inequality; since the other being a long number is in the first place six (that is to say, six hundred); on which account it is said, in the six hundred and first year. But the just man is so in his generation, not in that which is general, nor again in that in which he is just by comparison with the general corruption, but according to some especial generation; for his generation bears with it a certain comparison. But that man also is deserving of praise whom God selected beyond all other generations as being considered worthy of life, placing a limit to that life, and to him as being about to be both the end and the beginning of each generation and of each age; the end of that which is corruptible, the beginning of that which is to follow.

And truly it is much more proper to praise him who, bending upwards with his whole body, looked up by reason of his friendship with God.

(46) What is the meaning of the expression, "And Noah opened the roof of the ark?" (Genesis 8:13).

The text stands in need of no explanation. But with reference to its meaning, because the ark is symbolically our body, we must consider that that is spoken of as the roof of our body, which covers it and for a long time preserves its strength; such is concupiscence, by which the body is preserved and made to last, in a moderate degree, that is, and in accordance with the law of nature; as also it is dissolved by pain.

When therefore the intellect is attracted by a desire for heavenly things it wishes to spring upwards, and in that way it bursts asunder every appearance of concupiscence; so that that thing being as it were removed which threw a veil of shade over it and obscured it, it might be able to apply its senses to undisguised and incorporeal natures.

(47) Why is it that the earth was dried up in the seventh month, and on the twenty-seventh day? (Genesis 8:14).

Do you not see that he here calls that month the seventh, which a little while before he styles the first? for the seventh, as far as related to time, is the same, as I have said before, as that which is the first in nature, being the beginning of the equinox. But it is with great propriety that the beginning of the deluge is fixed to the seventh month, and the twenty-seventh day of the month; and again, the end and cessation of the deluge is fixed to the same seventh month and the same day; for, both the deluge and the removal of life took place at the equinox; the principle of which we have indicated a little time ago; for the seventh month is found to be synonymous with months and days of this time, and then again, the twenty-seventh day occurs with the same meaning, when the ark rested on the mountains.

This is the month which by nature is the seventh, but in point of time the first, which in fact is the month of the equinox. Therefore, at the equinoxes a power of selection is given for seven months and twenty-seven days; for the deluge took place in the seventh month, on which the vernal equinox takes place; so that it is in time the seventh, but in nature the first.

And the cessation of the deluge and the display of mercy belong to the same measure, when the ark rested on the tops of the mountains; again in truth in the seventh month, but not the same month, but in that in which the autumnal equinox occurs; that is to say, the seventh by nature, but the first in point of time.

But the most perfect cure, the fact of the evil being wholly dried up, is again fixed to the seventh month and the twenty-seventh day of the vernal season; in order that both the beginning and the end of the deluge might find its boundary at the same season; and that the middle season when human life is repaired, is fixed to the intermediate season.

In the meantime that expression is more certainly to be observed, namely, that the whole year, by a strict computation of days, made the deluge equal to the exact time of the remedy; for it began in the six hundredth year of Noah's age, in the seventh month, and on the twenty-seventh day; so that the whole space of the intermediate time completed a perfect year, the beginning being placed at the vernal equinox, and the flood also ending equally at the same epoch of the vernal equinox. And in this manner, after all things on earth, things full of fruit, had undergone destruction, as I have said before, now that the persons who used the fruits were also destroyed, the earth being wholly relieved of all evil was again found full of seeds and fruit-bearing trees, according to the production of spring; for he thought it reasonable that, as the earth after it had suffered the deluge was in a similar condition when dried again to that in which it was before, so it should now show itself, and pay the debt which it owed to nature.

Nor ought any one to wonder that in one day the earth when left to itself produced every thing by divine virtue, both seeds and trees, all complete, entirely and suddenly, with perfect and excellent herbs, and grain, and plants, and fruits; since in the creation of the world on one day of the six he finished and brought to perfection the whole generation of plants. But the present fruits were already perfect in themselves, and produced all kinds of fruits in a manner suitable and corresponding to the season of spring; for all things are possible to God, who scarcely requires time to effect any thing.

(48) Why was it that after the earth was dried, Noah did not depart out of the ark, before he had received a fresh command from God, for God said to Noah: "Go forth, thou, and thy wife, and thy sons, and thy sons' wives, together with all the rest of the living creatures?" (Genesis 8:16).

Justice is commonly inspired with fear, as on the other hand injustice is rash and self-confident. But the proof of a fear of God is the not giving up more to, or guiding one's self more by one's own reason than by God. And above all other men it was natural for that man who had seen the whole earth suddenly become an immense sea, to suspect that it might be possible that the same misfortune would again return.

Besides this, he also gave a thought to the corresponding consequence, namely, that as he had entered into the ark at the command of God, so it was fitting that he should also leave it at the command of the same being; for let no one believe that

he can ever do any thing perfectly unless God himself guides him by his preventing precepts.

(49) Why, when they entered into the ark was the order as follows: first himself and his sons, and after them his wife and his sons' wives, but when they went forth the order was changed, for the sacred historian says, "Noah and his wife went forth, and after them his sons and his sons' wives?" (Genesis 8:18).

By the literal statement the sacred writer gives an obscure intimation, in the order in which they entered, that the propagation of seed was taken away, but by the order of their egress he implies the continuance of the process of generation; since, while they are entering, the sons are mentioned together which their father, and the daughters-in-law with their mother-in-law, but when they are going forth the wives are all mated again, the father being accompanied by his wife, and each of his sons also by his wife, since he chose to show by fact rather than by words everything which it is fitting for his friends to do.

Moreover he had in express words, and not by any vague intimations, commanded the men, as they were about to enter into the ark, that they while there were to keep themselves from connection with women; but now that they were about to depart from it, he plainly intimates to them that offspring is to be begotten in accordance with nature, by the order in which he appoints their going forth; nor did he employ words only, in order to make his proclamation about the state of the ark, saying, "After a destruction of all things on earth, of such a character and of such extent, do not indulge in pleasures, for that is not decorous. It is sufficient, however, for you to have received your lives; but while you are actually in the ark, to ascend up into the marriage bed with your wives would be a proof of your being devoted to lasciviousness."

And, indeed, it was natural for them, as being relations to those who were being destroyed, to be moved with compassion for the perishing human race, especially because they themselves also were still in doubt whether, from some quarter or other, calamity might not fall also upon themselves; and besides these considerations it was absurd, while those who were alive were perishing, for those in the ark to be contriving that others who did not exist should be born, being warm at an unreasonable time, and burning with an inopportune desire. But after the anger of God ceased, then he commanded those who had been delivered from the calamity, when they had again gone forth out of the ark in order, to apply themselves to the procreation of a succeeding generation, when he tells us, that the men did not go forth with the men, nor the women with the women, but the wives with their husbands.

But with respect to the inner meaning of this fact, we must say this, that when the mind is about to wash off and cleanse away its sins, then it is fit for male to live with male, that is to say, for the intellect, the chief part of the man, to be as a father, united to each separate thought, as a father to his sons, without any admixture of the female race, which is in accordance with the outward sense; since it is a time of battle, in which it is necessary to keep the order of the cohort distinct, and to preserve it strictly in order, that the soldiers may not be mingled in confusion, and so, instead of gaining a victory over the enemy, be conquered themselves; but when the purification is completed, and when the soul is dried up from all ignorance, and when a complete deliverance from everything pernicious has taken place, then it becomes the man to collect his scattered forces together, not in order that masculine counsels may be rendered effeminate by softness, but that the female race, that is to say, the outward senses, may clothe themselves with the vigour of the male, attaining to masculine counsels, and from their receiving seed for the production of a generation; so that, from this time forth they may cherish, in all things, sentiments of wisdom, and honour, and justice, and courage, and, in one word, of virtue. But, besides this, it will be reasonable also to take notice, that when once a confusion, in the similitude of a deluge, has overwhelmed the intellect, and when the different senses, being perplexed by the affairs of this world, like so many bulwarks erected against them, begin to quarrel, it is utterly impossible that any one should be able, either to sow, or to conceive, or to generate any good thing. But when all the hostile attacks of various agitations and passions are checked, and when the ceaseless invasions of lawless counsels are repressed, then the soul produces virtue and excellent works, as the most fertile portion of the earth, when dried, produces fruits.

(50) Why did Noah build an altar without having been commanded to do so? (Genesis 8:20).

The requital of gratitude which is due to God ought to be offered to him without command, and without any delay or hesitation, showing the mind to be free from vices; for it becomes that man, who has been endued with blessings by God, to offer him his thanks with a grateful and willing mind; but he who delays to do so, waiting for an express command, is ungrateful, being as it were compelled by necessity to honour his benefactor.

(51) Why is he said to have built an altar to God, and not to the Lord? (Genesis 8:20).

In passages of beneficence and regeneration, as at the creation of the world, the sacred writer only refers to the beneficent virtue of the Creator, by which he makes everything in its integrity, and he implies this by concealing the royal name of Lord, as one which bears with it supreme author-

ity; therefore now also, since what he is describing is the beginning of the renewed generation of mankind, he borrows for his description the beneficent virtue, which bears the name of God; for he used the kingly attribute, which declares his imperial power, by which he is called Lord, when he was describing the punishment inflicted by the flood.

(52) What is the meaning of the statement, "He took of the cattle and of the flying animals, and he offered whole burnt offerings on the altar?" (Genesis 8:20).

All this is said with reference to an inward meaning, both because he received everything from God as a favour and gift; and also because he took of the clean sorts of animals, and burnt those which were unpolluted and clean, as entire and pure first fruits; for they are proper victims for good men to offer, and are themselves entire, being full of integrity; and they may be classed as fruits, for fruit is the end, for the sake of which the plant exists.

This indeed is the literal statement; but with respect to the inner meaning, the clean cattle and the clean birds are the outward senses and intellect of the wise man, with the thoughts which are received in his mind; all which things it is reasonable to offer in their integrity as entire and perfect fruit, in the way of a display of gratitude to the Father, and to offer them to him as an unpolluted and clean oblation of a victim.

(53) Why does he offer his sacrifice to the beneficent virtue of God, but the acceptance of it takes place by means of both the qualities of the Lord and God, for Moses says, "And the Lord God smelled a savour of sweetness?" (Genesis 8:20).

He says this since, when unexpectedly, after all hope is gone, we are preserved from dangers which are coming over us, we then, looking solely at the beneficence of him who has preserved us, do, on account of our joy, display ingratitude, and prefer the benefits which we have received rather to the beneficent power than to the Lord. But the beneficent preserver himself, by means of both his attributes, looks down upon and honourably accepts grateful minds, that he may not appear to halt in rewarding them; but he declares that such a display of gratitude is pleasing to both attributes of the one God.[5]

(54) What is the meaning of the words, "And the Lord God said, repenting him, I will not again proceed to curse the earth for the works of man, for the thoughts of the mind of man are toward, and are diligently and ceaselessly exercised in, wickedness from his youth up; therefore I will not now proceed to smite all living flesh as I have done at other times?" (Genesis 8:21).

---

[5] Or, "But the one God very much likes to act by means of both his attributes."—*Note to the Latin version.*

The reasons alleged appear to indicate a change of purpose, which is an affection not usual nor akin to the divine virtue; for the dispositions of mankind are variable and inconstant, so that all affairs among them are altogether uncertain; but with God nothing is uncertain, nothing incomprehensible, for he is a being of mighty and consistent determination; how then, when reasons of the same kind are present to him, because he was forsooth aware from the very beginning that the mind of man was deliberately inclined to wallow in wickedness from his youth on, could he have originally intended to destroy the human race by a flood; and yet afterwards say, that he did not intend to destroy it any more, when the same evils still exist in the mind? But we must think that every kind of expression of this sort is, by law, connected with learning and the utility of instruction rather than with the nature of truth, since there are, as it were, two kinds which occur in the whole course of the law; in the first place, as it is said, "Not as a man;" and in the second place, as it is said, "As a man," the one God is believed to instruct his son.

That first expression relates to the actual truth; for, in real fact, God is not as a man, nor again, as the sun, nor as the heaven, nor as the world, which is perceptible by the outward senses, but as God, if it is justifiable to assert that also; since that most happy and blessed being will not endure similitude, or comparison, or enigmatical description; nay, rather he surpasses even blessedness and felicity itself, and whatever can be imagined as better than and preferable to them.

But the second expression relates to instruction and direction, I mean the express words, "As a man," in order that it may be observed, that he is willing to impress us beings, born of the earth, lest perchance we should unceasingly incur his anger and his chastisement by our implacable hostility to him, without any peace; for it is sufficient for him to be roused and embittered against us once, and once to exact vengeance against sinners; but to inflict punishment over and over again for the same thing is the conduct of a savage and ferocious disposition: since, says he, "when I shall inflict deserved retribution, as is possible, on every one, I will cause a burning recollection of my design to be preserved."

Therefore behold, the sacred historian has excellently expressed himself, saying, "That God observed in his mind," for his mind and disposition rejoice in a superior degree of constancy; but our wills are found to be inconsistent and vacillating, on which account we cannot be properly said to observe and think with our minds, since it is by the thoughts that the passage of the mind is allowed to take place,[6] but the human intellect is unable to be extended over everything, since it is incapable of penetrating all things in a perfect and suitable manner.

But that expression, "I will not proceed any more to curse the earth," is used with great propriety, for it is not becoming to add more curses to what has already been done, because the evils that have been inflicted are already complete; because, although they are in some sense imperfect, inasmuch as the Father is kind and merciful, and most humane, still he is rather inclined to alleviate the evil than to add to men's misery. But that is as it were the same thing, according to a common proverb, to wash a brick, or to draw water properly, and wholly to eradicate wickedness, with all its deeply imprinted tokens from the mind of man; for if it is implanted in it at first, it does not exist accidentally, but is engraven deeply on it and clings to it.

But since the mind is a potential and principal part of the soul, he introduces that word "diligently;" but that which has been weighed with diligence and care is exquisite thought, examined more certainly than certainty itself. But this diligence does not tend to any one evil, but as is plain, to mischief, and to all mischief; nor does it exist in a perfunctory manner; but man is devoted to it from his youth, not only in a manner, but from his very cradle, as if he were in some degree united to, and nourished, and bred up with sin.

But yet God says, "I will not any more smite all flesh;" giving notice that he will not, at any future time, destroy every portion of mankind altogether, but only single individuals, in ever such great numbers, who perpetrate unspeakable wickednesses; for he does not leave wickedness unpunished, nor does he grant it liberty or impunity, but indulging his care for the human race on account of his original design, he of necessity fixes destruction as a punishment for sinners.

(55) What is the meaning of the expression, "Sowing-time and harvest, cold and heat, summer and spring, shall not cease day nor night?" (Genesis 8:22).

If taken literally this expression signifies the continuation of the duration of the annual seasons, and that the earthly temperature adapted to animals and plants is not again to be destroyed; since indeed, if the weather is corrupted it would corrupt them likewise, and if it is preserved in its existing state it would preserve them also safe and sound; for it is according to the weather and temperature that all animals and plants are preserved safe and sound, without any infirmity, being accustomed, in some measure, to be produced sepa-

---

[6] "If you connect the Armenian words in a different manner, the sense will be 'meditation is the purification of the course of the mind,' and this is perhaps better."— *Note by the Latin Translator.*

rately, in an admirable way, and to grow up together. But nature is like a harmony, composed of opposite sounds, both flat and sharp; for thus, also, the world is compounded of opposite qualities, for when, in the first place, the mortal commixtures of cold and heat, of moisture and dryness, preserve their natural order, without any confusion, they are themselves a cause which prevents destruction from overwhelming everything upon the earth.

But if we regard the inward sense of the passage, the seed time is the beginning and the harvest time is the end, and both the beginning and the end are concurrent causes of safety, for either thing alone is by itself imperfect, because the beginning requires an end, and the end has a natural inclination for the beginning; but cold and heat bring round winter and autumn; for the autumn is fiery, but only in such a degree as succeeding in its annual revolution to cool the fiery summer.

And, symbolically, with reference to the mind, cold indicates fear, since it causes terror and trepidation; but heat indicates anger, because an angry disposition bears in itself a resemblance to flame and fire; for it is necessary that those things should always exist and always remain among created and corruptible beings; since summer and spring have been instituted for the production of fruits; spring for the perfection of the seeds, and summer for the perfecting of fruits and the buds of trees.

These things indeed are discerned symbolically in addition to the inward sense of the words, producing a double fruit; what is necessary being computed in the season of spring, and what is superfluous in the summer. Therefore necessary food is for the most part for the body, being whatever is produced freely from seeds; as virtues are necessary for the soul. But as many fruits as come by way of excess from trees in summer, besides the advantage which they are to the body, do also bring corporeal goods to the mind, as external advantages: for these external advantages are subservient to the body, and the body is subservient to the mind, and the mind to God. But day and night are the measures of times and numbers; and time and number exist without interruption. Day indicates lucid wisdom, and night betokens obscure folly.

(56) Why was it that God, blessing Noah and his sons, said, "Increase, and multiply, and replenish the earth, and rule over it; and let your fear and the dread of you be upon all beasts, and upon flying fowls, and upon reptiles, and upon the fishes which I have placed under your hand?" (Genesis 9:1).

This devotion of the inferior animals to man, God also at the beginning of the creation bestowed on the sixth day upon man, after he had created him in his own image; for the scripture saith, "And God made man; in the image of God created he

him; male and female created he them. And God blessed them, and said, Be fruitful, and multiply, and replenish the earth; and be ye lords over it, and be ye rulers of the fishes, and of the flying fowls, and of every creeping thing that creepeth upon the earth."

And did he not by these words evidently intimate that Noah, at the beginning of what we may call the second creation of mankind, was found equal in honour to that creature who in the first instance was made as to his form in the likeness of himself? Therefore he equally assigned both to the one and to the other the principality and power over all the creatures that live upon the earth.

But do thou diligently take notice that he showed this man, who at the time of the deluge was the only just man and the king of all the creatures which live upon the earth, to be equal in honour, not to the identical man who was first created and formed out of the earth, but to that one who was made according to the likeness and form of the true incorporeal entity, to whom also he gives power, making him a king, not the very created man (or the man formed out of the earth), but him who is according to his form and similitude, that is to say, incorporeal.

Wherefore also the creation of that man, who as to his form is incorporeal, was marked to have taken place on the sixth day, in accordance with the perfect number six; but the creation of that man who was created after the completion of the world and subsequent to the generation of all animals on the seventh day, because it is after that that the manly figure was fashioned out of clay. Therefore after the days of generation he says, "on the seventh day of the world;" for God had not yet rained upon the earth, and no man did exist who could cultivate the earth. And then he proceeds to say, "But God formed a man out of the clay of the earth, and breathed into his face the breath of life, and man became a living soul."

Therefore how he can be made worthy of the same kingly power according to the image of the man thus formed, he, I mean, who is the beginning of the second creation of mankind, is indicated by the letter of the history that relates these events.

But with reference to the inward sense of the passage we must give an explanation in the following manner. God wills that the souls of wise men should increase in the magnitude and multitude of the beauty of their virtues, and should fill the mind as if it were the earth with those beauties, leaving no portion empty and void so as to become occupied by folly. And he wills also that they should rule over, and strike terror into, and inflict alarm upon all beasts; that is to say, he wills that all wickedness should be subdued by their will, since wickedness is of an untamed and savage nature. Also he willed that they should be lords over all flying fowls, which by reason of their lightness are raised on high, being armed with courage and empty pride, and which thus cause the greatest mischief, being scarcely controlled at all by fear. Moreover, he made them rulers over all creeping things, which are the symbols of destructive vices, for they creep through the whole soul, namely, concupiscence, desire, sadness, and cowardice, striking and goading; as also they are indicated by the fishes, which eagerly cultivate a moist and delicate life, but one which is far from being sober, wise, or lasting.

(57) Why does God say, "Every creeping thing which lives shall be to you for food?" (Genesis 9:3).

Creeping things are of a twofold nature; some being venomous, and others domestic. The venomous ones are serpents, which, instead of feet, use their bellies and breasts, creeping upon the earth; but the domestic ones are those which have legs above their feet. This is the literal meaning of the statement.

But if we look to the inward sense of it, then the creeping things represent the foul vices, but the clean ones represent joy; for in connexion with the passion of concupiscence there will exist joy and pleasure; and in connexion with desire there will be will and counsel, and in connexion with sorrow goading and compunction, and in connexion with avidity there will be fear.

Therefore such disordered perturbations of the passions threaten souls with death and destruction; but the joys do really live, as he himself has warned us in an allegory; and they also give life to those who possess them.

(58) What is the meaning of the expression, "As the green herb I have given you all things?" (Genesis 9:3).

Some persons say that by this expression, "As the green herb I have given you all things," the eating of flesh was permitted. But I say that even though God had intended to give that permission, still that before all things he must have intended to establish by law the necessary use of herbs, that is to say of vegetables. And under the general name of herb he includes all the other additional descriptions of green food, without mentioning them expressly in the law. But now the power of this command is adapted not to one nation alone among all the select nations of the earth which are desirous of wisdom, among which religious continence is honoured, but to all mankind, who cannot possibly be universally prohibited from eating flesh.

Nevertheless, perhaps the present expression has no reference to eating food, but rather to the possession of the power to do so; for in fact every herb is not necessarily good to eat, nor again is it the uniform and invariable food of all uniform living animals; since God said that some herbs were poisonous and deadly, and yet they are included in the number all. Perhaps therefore, I say, he means to express this, that all brute beasts are subjected to the power of man, as we sow herbs and take care of them by the cultivation of the land.

(59) What is the meaning of the expression, "You shall not eat flesh in the blood of its life?" (Genesis 9:4).

God appears by this command to indicate that the blood is the substance of the soul; I mean of that soul which exists by the external senses and by vitality, not of that which is spoken of with a certain especial pre-eminence, being the rational and intellectual soul; for there are three parts of the human soul; one the nutritive part, another that which is connected with the external senses, and the third that which exists in reason. Therefore the rational part is the substance of the divine spirit according to the sacred writer Moses: for in his account of the creation of the world, he says, "God breathed into his face the breath of life," as being what was to constitute his life. But of that part of the soul which is connected with the external senses and with vitality, blood is the substance; for he says in another place, "The blood exists in every breath of flesh."

It is with great propriety in fact that he has called the blood the breath of all flesh, because there are in the flesh senses and passions, but not intellect nor thoughts. But again by the expression "the spirit of blood," he intimates that the spirit is one thing and the blood another; so that the essence of the soul is truly and beyond all possible question spirit. But that spirit has a place not by itself separately, apart from the blood in the body; but it is interwoven and mingled with the blood.

As also the veins which exhibit a pulse, as if they were vessels to convey breathing, bear with them most unmixed and pure air, but blood likewise, though perhaps in a less degree; for there are two vessels, the veins and the breathing channels; but the veins have more blood than breath, and the breathing channels have more breath than blood. Therefore the proper admixture in each vessel is distinct, as the greater and the lesser proportion.

This is the meaning of these words when taken literally; but if we look to their inner meaning, he calls the blood of the soul that warm and fiery virtue belonging to it which we name courage. And he who is full of this wisdom despises all food, and every pleasure of the belly, and of those parts which are below the belly. But if any one adopts a profligate life, and becomes a wanderer like the wind, and gradually inactive from laziness and a luxurious life, he in fact does nothing else but fall upon his belly, as a reptile creeping upon the earth, and greedily licking up earthly things, closing his life without ever tasting of that heavenly food which the souls which are desirous of wisdom receive.

(60) What is the meaning of the expression,

"The blood of your souls will I require from every beast, and from the hand of man's brother will I require the life of man?" (Genesis 9:5).

The multitude of creatures which do injury is twofold; some being beasts, and others men. But beasts are rather the least injurious of the two, because they have no actual familiarity with those whom they wish to injure, principally because they do not fall under their power, but destroy those who have properly power over them. But when he speaks of brothers, he means men who are murderers, intimating these three things. First of all, that all we men are akin to one another, and are brothers, being connected with one another according to the relation of the highest kind of kindred; for we have received a lot, as being the children of one and the same mother, rational nature.

In the second place, he intimates that very commonly numerous and terrible quarrels arise, and acts of treachery take place, between relations, and rather between brothers, on account of the division of their inheritance, or on account of some superiority of dignity in the household; since a quarrel between those of the same family is worse and altogether unseemly, because brothers who are really so by the ties of nature meet in contest with a great knowledge of one another's internal circumstances; being therefore well aware what kind of attack they must employ in their present warfare.

But, in the third place, as it appears to me, he employs the appellation of brothers in order to warn men of the implacable and severe punishment which is reserved for murderers; that they, without meeting any compassion, shall suffer what they have inflicted; for they have not slain strangers, but their own brothers in blood.

It is with exceeding great propriety that he calls God the protector and overseer of those who are slain by man; for although men despise the revenge, yet let them not behave negligently, but although impure men of savage disposition escape for the moment from danger, still let them know that they are already caught and brought before the greater tribunal of justice, namely, before the divine judgment-seat, which rises up to inflict vengeance on the wicked for the defence of those who have received shameful and unworthy treatment.

This is the literal meaning of the words; but if we look to the inward sense of them they have a regard to the merit of the purity of the soul, to which it is suitable to avoid unceasing destruction brought in from outward parts; which merit, that propitious and beneficent being, the most merciful and only Saviour, does not despise; but he expels and destroys all its enemies who stand around it, calling them beasts, and men brothers; for beasts are a symbolical expression for furious men threatening calamitous death; but men and

brothers are both separate individual thoughts, and words uttered by mouth and tongue, because they are akin to them, and, by consequence, they bring on great and destructive evils, leaving no stone unturned, no work or word omitted to do injury.

(61) What is the meaning of the expression, "Whoso sheddeth man's blood by man shall his blood be shed?" (Genesis 9:6).

There is no excess in this declaration, but rather an indication of a still more formidable denunciation, because he says, "He himself shall be poured out like blood who pours out blood." For that which is poured out flows forth and is lost, so that it has no longer any power or substance. And by this he shadows forth the fact that the souls of those who perpetrate unworthy actions imitate the mortal body in its corruption, as far as corruption is accustomed to come upon individuals; for the body is then dissolved into those parts of which it was composed, returning into its proper elements. But the miserable soul, labouring under distresses, is borne hither and thither by the overflow of a lascivious life; and the very evils which have grown up along with it are accustomed to suffer the same overflow, in the manner of the parts of the limbs.

(62) Why is it that he speaks as if of some other god, saying that he made man after the image of God, and not that he made him after his own image? (Genesis 9:6).

Very appropriately and without any falsehood was this oracular sentence uttered by God, for no mortal thing could have been formed on the similitude of the supreme Father of the universe, but only after the pattern of the second deity, who is the Word of the supreme Being; since it is fitting that the rational soul of man should bear the type of the divine Word; since in his first Word God is superior to the most rational possible nature. But he who is superior to the Word holds his rank in a better and most singular pre-eminence, and how could the creature possibly exhibit a likeness of him in himself? Nevertheless he also wished to intimate this fact, that God does rightly and correctly require vengeance, in order to the defence of virtuous and consistent men, because such bear in themselves a familiar acquaintance with his Word, of which the human mind is the similitude and form.

(63) What is the meaning of the words, "There shall not again be a deluge to destroy all the earth?" (Genesis 9:11).

By his last saying he declares sufficiently that there may be various inundations, but that there shall never be one of such a character as to be able to change the whole earth into a lake or sea.

This is the literal meaning of this saying.

But if we look to its inward sense, there a divine kindness is intimated, according to which, although it is not every part of the soul which is allowed to make proficiency in every virtue, still some are adorned in a considerable degree. So that, supposing any one is not able to display excellence in his whole body, he still may labour with all diligence to acquire all the means in his power to display excellence; and that exertion is within his reach. And it does not follow that if any one is less highly endowed, or is unable to make every portion of his life altogether perfect, that he is on that account to despair of those things which he is able to do and to attain to.

Since as there is power in every individual, he who does not exert himself in accordance with it is both idle and ungrateful; idle because of his laziness, and ungrateful because, though he has received most excellent means, he still sets himself in opposition to the essential qualities of things.

(64) Why does God say that, as a sign that he will never again bring a deluge over the whole earth, he will place his bow in the clouds? (Genesis 9:13).

Some persons imagine that by the bow he means that thing which by some is called Jupiter's belt, from its figure, dwelling on its continual similitude to the rainbow; but I do not perceive that that has been positively asserted. In the first place, because the bow aforesaid ought to have a peculiar and essential nature of its own, because it is called the bow of God; for he says, "I will set *my* bow in the clouds." But that which belongs to God and is said to have been set in any place as his, indicates plainly that it is not devoid of essence or of substance.

But the belt of Jupiter has not, properly speaking, any separate nature of its own, but is merely an appearance of the solar rays on a wet cloud, all the phaenomena of which are non-existent and incorporeal. And moreover, this is a further proof of that, that it is never seen at night, though clouds exist by night as well as by day.

In the second place, we must also say that even in the day-time, when clouds obscure the whole face of heaven, the belt of Jupiter is never at all seen in them. But what remains may also be affirmed without any falsehood, when the Maker of the law says, "I will set my bow in the clouds;" for, behold, while clouds are present there is no appearance of the belt of Jupiter visible. But he said, "Where there is a collection of clouds let there be a bow seen in the clouds." Still it often happens, when the clouds are collected and when the air is obscured and thickened, that no appearance of a rainbow is seen anywhere.

We must consider, therefore, whether haply the sacred historian indicates something else by this mention of the bow, namely, that in the very exercise of the mercy of God, and also in the moment of his bitterness towards men on earth, there still shall not be any ultimate destruction of them, in the fashion of a bow, which is too soft and unfit for such a purpose, nor shall there be

any violence added, so as to cause a rapid destruction, but there shall be a moderate determination, each attribute being carefully measured; for the great deluge took place with a breaking asunder and disruption of the clouds and of all things; as he himself asserts, when he says, "The fountains of the deep were broken up." And yet it was not an unmeasured vehemence.

Moreover, a bow is not itself a weapon, but only an instrument for the use of weapons, namely, for the arrow which strikes; and the arrow being sent forth by means of the bow strikes a part which is at a distance, while the parts which are nearest to it remain unhurt. And this is given as a proof that the whole earth shall never for the future suffer any deluge, since no one arrow ever hits all places, but only those which are at a distance.

Therefore the divine virtue, being invisible, is symbolically indicated by the bow in the cloud; being in truth dissolved according to the figure of tranquillity, and condensed in accordance with a cloud; so that it does not permit all the clouds to be altogether dissolved into water, so that the earth may not be made a lake by an inundation, which it carefully forbids, and arranges the condensation of air, checking it as by a bridle, though it is at that time the more accustomed to exhibit itself as rebellious by reason of its excessive fulness. For by reason of the clouds it also shows itself to be replenished, dripping, and saturated.

(65) Why is it that after the sons of the just man have been named Shem, Ham, and Japhet, he relates only the generations of the middle one, saying, "And Ham was the Father of Canaan;" and afterwards he adds, "These are the three sons of Noah?" (Genesis 9:18).

Mentioning four men, Noah and his sons, he says that these were obedient. Because the grandson Canaan was in his habits like his Father who begat him, on that account, instead of mentioning only one, he includes both in his enumeration, so that they are four in number, three in virtue. But in the meantime in the scripture he mentions only the generations of the middle one, on account of the just man whom he is going to speak of subsequently, because although he was his father, since Ham is the Father of Canaan, still he does not mention the father with blame, but with respect to the man with whom he thought it fair that the son should be a partaker, he yet did not give the father a participation with him.

In the second place, perhaps he thus gives a premonitory warning also to those persons who by the acuteness of their mental vision can see a long way off what is at a distance, namely, that he designs to take away the land of the Canaanites from them after the lapse of many ages, and to give it to his chosen people who are thoroughly devoted to God. Therefore he chooses to designate the chief inhabitant of that region, namely

Canaan, and to show that he both practised singular and peculiar wickedness of his own, and also all the wickedness of his father, so that in every part he might be convicted of an ignoble slavery and submission.

This is the literal meaning of these words. But if we have a regard to the inward sense, he does not say that Ham had a son named Canaan, but he predicates offspring of him alone, saying, "Ham was the Father of Canaan." Since such a disposition as that of Ham is always the Father of such designs as those of Canaan, and that the very names themselves intimate this. For if we translate them into another language, Ham means heat or hot; and Canaan means merchants, or buyers, or causes, or recipients.

Accordingly, he is not now speaking manifestly of generations, nor is he saying that one man is the Father or the son of another man, but he is evidently demonstrating the connection between one counsel and another, by reason of its alienation from all familiarity with virtue.

ABOUT THE CULTIVATION OF
THE EARTH

(66) What is the meaning of the statement, "Noah began to be a cultivator of the earth?" (Genesis 9:20).

He is here comparing Noah to the first created man who was formed out of the earth; for in that manner also does he speak of him when he came forth out of the ark; since both then and now there took place a first beginning of the cultivation of the land, each being after a deluge. For also, at the time of the original creation of the world the earth was, as it were, a lake, being covered by an inundation of water, for the sacred historian could not tell us that God said, "Let the waters be gathered together into one body, and let the dry land appear," unless it had previously been inundated with waters which now returned into certain depths of the earth.

Nor again is the expression a purposeless one, "He began to be a tiller of the earth," for in the second generation he was himself the beginning of men, and also of seed, and of the cultivation of the land, and of the life of all other things. This is the literal meaning of the words.

But if we look to their inner sense, a distinction is made between being a cultivator of the earth and a tiller of it; as the murderer of his brother is represented as tilling the earth, but not as cultivating it. For by the earth our body is symbolically represented, which is by its nature earthly, and which the unjust and wicked man tills like a lazy hireling, but which the man endued with virtue cultivates like a skilful manager of plants and an agriculturist of good works appointed to superintend it. Because the workman of the body, the mind, as being carnal, procures carnal pleasures;

but the cultivator of the earth is careful to produce useful fruits, those, namely, which are to be obtained by the study of continence, and modesty, and sound wisdom; and he prunes away all superfluous excesses and bad habits which spring up around, like the thin and misplaced branches of trees.

(67) Why does the just man first plant a vineyard? (Genesis 9:20).

It was very natural for it to be a subject of anxiety and doubt to him in what quarter he was to find any plants after the deluge, when everything upon the earth was destroyed. Therefore it appeared natural, as was said a little while ago, that the earth was made dry in the spring season; therefore when the spring produced the buds of trees, the roots and stems of the vine could easily be found by the just man still alive, and might thus be collected by him.

But we have to consider why the first thing he did was to plant a vineyard, and why he did not rather sow wheat and barley, since the latter are necessary productions of the earth, without which life cannot be supported, but the former is only a material for superfluous pleasure. The answer is that Noah, adopting a salutary design, consecrated and offered up to God those things which are necessary to support life and which require no co-operation for the production of the fruit; but the superfluous plants he devoted to men; for the use of wine is superfluous and not necessary. As therefore God ordered fountains of water fit to drink to burst up from the earth without the co-operation of man, so he also of his own accord granted to man in a similar manner wheat and barley, in order that he himself might be the sole giver of each kind of food which serves for necessary eating and drinking. But he did not take away the power nor grudge them providing for themselves by their own industry those things which contribute to pleasure.

(68) What is the meaning of the statement, "He drank of the wine and was drunken?" (Genesis 9:21).

In the first place, the just man did not drink the wine, but a portion of the wine, not the whole of it; in which case an incontinent and debauched man does not quit his means of debauchery, till he has first swallowed all the wine that there is before him; but by the religious and sober man everything necessary for food is used in a moderate degree. And the expression, "he was drunken," is here to be taken simply as equivalent to "he used the wine."

But there are two modes of getting drunk, the one is that of an intemperate sottishness which misuses wine, and this offence is peculiar to the depraved and wicked man; the other is the use of wine, and this belongs to the wise. It is therefore in the second of these meanings that the consistent and wise Noah is here called drunken, not as having misused but as having used wine.

(69) What is the meaning of the statement, "He was naked in his house?" (Genesis 9:21).

This is a praise of the wise man both in the literal sense of the words, and also in their hidden meaning, that his exhibition of nakedness took place not out of doors but in his house, being concealed by the roof and walls of his house; for the nakedness of the body is concealed by a house which is made of stones and beams of wood: but the covering and clothing of the soul is the discipline of wisdom.

Therefore there are two kinds of nakedness, one which takes place by accident, which is the result of an involuntary offence, because the just man, using, if I may say so, his honesty as if it were a garment with which he is clothed, stumbles out of his own accord like men who are intoxicated, or who are afflicted with insanity; for in such men their offences are not deliberately committed: but it is his task and pleasing duty to clothe himself, as with a garment, with the discipline and study of honesty.

There is also another kind of nakedness of the soul which is caused by perfect virtue, which expels from itself the whole carnal weight of the body, as if it were flying from a tomb, as indeed it has long been buried in it as in a tomb; as also it avoids pleasures, and also a great number of miseries arising from the different passions and many anxieties arising from misfortunes, and indeed all the evil effects of these different circumstances. He therefore, who has been able with distinction to pass through such various and great dangers, and to escape such injuries, and to emancipate himself from such evils, has attained to the destiny of happiness, without any stain or disgrace; for I should pronounce this to be the ornament and badge of beauty in those individuals who have been rendered worthy to pass their existence in an incorporeal manner.

(70) Why is it that the sacred writer has not simply said, Ham saw his nakedness, but Ham the father of Canaan saw the nakedness of his father? (Genesis 9:22).

By stating the fact thus, he both blames the son in the father and the father in the son, as performing together in common the deed of folly, and iniquity, and impiety, and every other kind of wickedness. This is the literal meaning of the statement; and as to the inner sense, we must look at that in the same manner in which we have hitherto treated these subjects.

(71) What is the meaning of the statement, "He told it to his two brothers out of doors?" (Genesis 9:22).

The sacred historian is here adding to the gravity of the transaction. In the first place, because he did not report the involuntary evil of his father

to one brother only, but to both of them; and no doubt if he had had any more he would have told it to them all, as he did in fact to every one he could; and he did so with ridicule in his very words, making a jest of what ought not to have been treated with laughter and derision, but rather with shame and fear mingled with reverence.

In the second place, when the historian says he told it them, not in the house but out of the house, he evidently points out that he displayed his father when naked, not only to his brothers, but also to the bystanders with whom they were, both men and women.

This is the literal information conveyed by the words. But if we look to their inward meaning, then we shall see that a depraved and malignant habit of life is full of derision and contempt: and it is a bad thing to judge of the miseries of others even by one's self like a chastising judge. But in this case what has happened is worse than this, for any man with a joyful mind to ridicule the involuntary misfortune of a devoted disciple of wisdom, and to make a song of and proclaim abroad his misery, is the part of a thoroughly hostile accuser, who ought rather to have pardoned such an occurrence than to have added accusation or vituperation to it.

Moreover, because these three things are, as I have said before, as it were brothers together; namely, good, bad, and indifferent, being all the offspring of one parent thought: in accordance with each of these principles, they have been found to be overseers, some celebrating virtues with praise, others upholding acts of malignity, and others supporting riches and honours and other good things which, however, are not attached to and which are external to the body.

The overseers who emulate wickedness rejoice at the fall of the wise man, and ridicule and disparage him, as if he had done no good by the part which he adopts and to which he applies himself as better for the mind, or for his body, or for his external circumstances, to his internal virtues or to any of the good things which are around and exterior to his body. Unless indeed that man alone is eminently able to attain his object, who applies himself to iniquity, as that alone is accustomed to confer advantages on human life.

Pronouncing these and similar precepts, those who are overseers of iniquity ridicule those who devote themselves to virtue, and to those things by which virtue is produced and consolidated: as some look upon those things to be which are around the body, and outside it, and which may be regarded in the light of instruments serving to that end.

(72) What is the meaning of the statement, "Shem and Japhet, taking a garment, laid it upon both their shoulders and went backwards, and covered the nakedness of their father, and they themselves did not see it?" (Genesis 9:23).

The literal meaning of the statement is evident; but with respect to the inner sense contained in it, we must say that the light man who is in too great haste only sees those things which are before his eyes and exposed to his sight: but that the evil man also sees those things which are at his back, that is to say, the future.

And since what is posterior is postponed to what is anterior, so is what is future to what is present, the sight of which is peculiar to the virtuous and wise man, who in truth is a second Lynceus, being according to the fables gifted with eyes in every part.

Therefore every wise man, who is not so much man as actual intellect, walks backward, that is to say, he sees what is behind him or future, as if it were placed in brilliant light; and seeing every thing on all sides of him with a perfect sight, and looking all around him, he is found to be armed, and protected, and fortified, so that no part of his soul is ever found naked or in an unseemly plight, on account of any accidents which occur unfortunately.

(73) What is the meaning of the statement, "And Noah became sober after the wine?" (Genesis 9:24).

The literal meaning is too notorious. Therefore we need only here speak of what concerns the inner sense of the words. When the intellect is strengthened, it is able by its soberness to discern with a certain accuracy all things, both before and behind it, both present, I mean, and future; but the man who can see neither what is present nor what is future with accuracy, is afflicted by blindness; but he who sees the present, but who cannot also foresee the future, and is not at all cautious, such a man is overcome by drunkenness and intoxication; and he, lastly, who is found to be able to look all around him, and to see, and discern, and comprehend the different natures of things, both present and future, the watchfulness of sobriety is in that man.

(74) Why is it that after the sacred historian has enumerated Ham in the middle of the offspring of Noah, or has placed him in the middle between his brethren, he nevertheless points out that he was the younger, saying, "Noah saw what his younger son had done to him?" (Genesis 9:25).

This is a manifest allegory, because he here takes as the younger, not him who was so in age and in point of time, but him who was younger in mind; since wickedness is unable to attain to a perception of the learning which is proper to the elder; but the elder thoughts belong to a will which is truly growing old, not indeed in body, but in mind.

(75) Why did Noah when praying for Shem speak thus: "Blessed is the Lord God, the God of Shem: and Canaan shall be his servant?" (Genesis 9:23).

The names Lord and God are here used together on account of his principal attributes, both of benevolence and of kingly power by which the world was created; for as king he created the world according to his beneficence; but after he had completed it then the world was arranged and set in order by his attribute of kingly power. Therefore he at that time rendered the wise man worthy of a common honour, which the whole world also received, all the parts of the world being formed in an admirable manner with the attributes of the Lord and God, doing so by his especial prerogative, munificently pouring forth the favour and liberality of his beneficent power.

And it is on this account that the beneficent power of God is mentioned twice. Once, as has been already stated, being placed in apposition to his kingly power; and a second time without any such connexion, in order, forsooth, that the wise man having been rendered worthy of his gifts, both such as are common to him with others and such as are peculiar to himself, he might also be rendered acceptable both to the world and to God; to the world on account of the excellence imparted to him in common with it, and to God for such as was peculiar to himself.

(76) Why, when Noah prayed for Japhet, did he say, "God shall enlarge Japhet, and bid him to dwell in the house of Shem: and Canaan shall be their servant?" (Genesis 9:27).

Without examining the literal statement, for the meaning of that is plain, we had better approach the inner sense contained in it, and examine that, in which the second and third blessings mentioned are capable of an enlarged and ample extension. As, for instance, good health, and a vigorous state of the outward senses, and beauty, and strength, and opulence, and nobleness of birth, and friends, and the power of a prince, and numbers of other things. And on this account he said, "God shall enlarge," etc.

Because taken separately, the abundant possession of such numerous and great blessings has of itself been injurious to many persons who have scarcely dwelt with justice, or wisdom, or any other virtues, the complete possession of which dispenses to man in an admirable manner the advantages which are external to and which surround the body; but the deprivation or absence of them leaves him without the enjoyment or use of them; and man, if deprived of all good protectors, and of the use of these enjoyments, is exposed to as much suffering as he is capable of. Therefore he prays on behalf of he man who has those things which are around and exterior to the body, that he may dwell in the house of the wise man; so that attending to the rules of all good men he may see and regulate his own course by their example.

(77) Why because Ham had sinned did God

pronounce that his son Canaan should be the servant of Ham and Japhet? (Genesis 9:27).

In the first place, God pronounced this sentence because both father and son had displayed the same wickedness, being both united together and not separated, and both indulging in the same disposition.

But in the second place, he did so because the father would be exceedingly afflicted at the curse thus laid upon the son, being sufficiently conscious that he was punished not so much for his own sake as for that of his father. And so the leader and master of the two suffered the punishment of his wicked counsels, and words, and actions.

This is the literal meaning of the statement. But if we look to its inward meaning, then in reality they are no more two different men than two different dispositions. And this is made plain by the names given to them, which manifestly denote the nature of the facts; for Ham being interpreted means heat or hot; and Canaan means merchants of causes.

(78) Why was it that Noah lived after the deluge three hundred and fifty years? (Genesis 9:28).

It is now declared that in two periods of seven years the form of the world was originally created and now renewed under Noah. But the wise man lives for a period of fourteen quarters of a century; and fourteen times twenty-five is equal to seven times fifty, or fifty times seven. And it is the principle of the seventh year and also of the fiftieth, which has an especial order of its own explained and ordained in Leviticus.

(79) Why among the three sons of Noah does Ham appear always to occupy the middle place, but the two extremities are varied; for when their birth is mentioned, Shem is placed in the first rank, in this manner, Shem, Ham, and Japhet; but when they are spoken of as fathers, then Japhet is mentioned first, and the beginning of the enumeration of the nations is derived from Japhet himself? (Genesis 10:1).

Those who inquire into the literal nature of the divine writings think thus of the order in which these men are mentioned, looking upon him who is the first named, that is Shem, as the younger; and upon him who is named the last, that is Japhet, as the elder. However they may choose to think of this let them, being guided by the principle of mere opinion. But we who look to the real meaning of these statements think that there is here a reference to the three things, good, bad, and indifferent; which last are called secondary goods; and we must therefore think that the sacred writer always puts the bad in the middle, so that being confined at either extremity it may be subdued on one side by the one, and on the other side by the other; so that, being confined, it may be kept in and subdued.

But the good and the indifferent, or secondary good, change the order with one another; for when there is such great evil present, and yet not wholly and altogether, the good rejoices in the first place, having the position of the dispenser and chief of the whole. But when it is placed in the position of the will in a state of conspiracy, and injustice remains not only in the intellect but is also conducted to its end by unjust works, then that first good is changed from its original order into another place, together with all the good habits which depend upon it, rejecting all education and all arrangement, as being wholly unable to attain its proposed end, just as a physician does when he sees an incurable disease.

But the elder good manages that virtue which is around the body and exterior to it; therefore, by observing the extremities with greater caution, and closing in the beast within its toils, it is sufficiently demonstrated that it does not dare to bite or injure any more. But while it feels that it has done no injury, it is transferred into a more secure and more permanent position, and then, a higher and better fortified place being assigned to it, it easily retains the lower position too as one easy to be preserved; for, in consequence of the superior power of its guardian, it is always practicable to watch it closely, since nothing is more mighty than virtue.

(80) Why do the people of Ceos, and of Rhodes, and the isles of the Gentiles, spring from Japhet? (Genesis 16:4–5).

Since he has the name denoting breadth (namely Japhet), being expanded in his growth and increase, that part of the things of the world which have been assigned by nature for the use of mankind, that is to say, the earth, can no longer hold him, therefore he passes over into the other part, that is to say, the sea and the islands belonging to it.

This is the literal meaning of the statement.

But if we look to its inner sense, all the external blessings which are bestowed by nature, such as riches, and honour, and principalities, are lavished and poured forth in every direction on those men into whose hands they come, and are also extended widely to others who are not so much within reach; so that in a greater, or at all events, in no less a degree do they surround and hem the man in, in accordance with the greediness of the lovers of riches and glory, since they are eager for principalities, and are never satisfied because of their insatiable desires.

(81) Why the eldest son of Ham is Chus. (Genesis 10:6).

The sacred historian has here produced a word most completely in accordance with nature, saying that Chus was the elder son of evil, Chus being the dissolved and loose nature of the earth, for the earth, when dense and fertile, and moist, is full of herbs, and hills, and trees, and is well arranged for the production of different fruits; but when dissolved and reduced to dust and dry, it is unfruitful and barren; and besides it is tossed about in the air, when it is raised from the ground by the wind, by its dust making the air all alive.

Such as this is the first origin and the first shoots of evil being destitute of the generation of good pursuits, and the cause of barrenness to the soul and to all its parts.

(82) Why was Chus the father of Nimrod, who began to be a giant and a hunter before the Lord: on which account they said, "Like Nimrod the mighty hunter before the Lord?" (Genesis 10:8).

The father in this case, having a nature truly dissolute, does not at all keep fast the spiritual bond of the soul, nor of nature, nor of consistency of manners, but rather like a giant born of the earth, prefers earthly to heavenly things, and thus appears to verify the ancient fable of the giants and Titans; for in truth he who is an emulator of earthly and corruptible things is always engaged in a conflict with heavenly and admirable natures, raising up earth as a bulwark against heaven; and those things which are below are adverse to those which are above.

On which account there is much propriety in the expression, he was a giant against God, which thus declares the opposition of such beings to the deity; for a wicked man is nothing else than an enemy, contending against God: on which account it has become a proverb that every one who sins greatly ought to be referred to him as the original and chief of sinners, being spoken of "as a second Nimrod."

Therefore his very name is an indication of his character, for it is interpreted Aethiopian, and his art is that of hunting, both of which things are detestable: an Aethiopian because unmitigated wickedness has no participation in light, but imitates night and darkness: and the practice of the huntsman is as much as possible at variance with rational nature, for he who lives among wild beasts wishes to live the life of a beast, and to be equal to the brutes in the vices of wickedness.

QUESTIONS AND ANSWERS ON GENESIS, III

(Quaestiones et Solutiones in Genesin, III)

(1) What is the meaning of the expression, "I am the Lord thy God who brought thee out of the land of the Chaldaeans to give thee this land for an inheritance?" (Genesis 15:7).

As the literal statement is plain enough, we need only consider the inner meaning, which was meant to be interpreted in this manner.

The law of the Chaldaeans taken symbolically is mathematical speculation, one part of which is recognised to be astronomy, which the Chaldaeans study with great industry and with great success. Therefore God is here honouring the wise man with a gift; in the first place, by taking men out of the sect of the astrologers, that is to say, away from the hallucinations of the Chaldaeans, which, as they are difficult to detect and refute, are found to be the cause of great evils and wickedness, since they ascribe the attributes of the Creator to created things, and persuade men to worship and to venerate the works of the world as God.

In the second place, God honours him by granting to him the wisdom which bears fruit, which he has here symbolically called the earth; but the Father of the universe shows that wisdom and virtue are invariable and immutable, since it is not consistent with his character that God should show to any one that which can undergo any variation or change, for that which is shown by the being who is immutable and consistent must be so too; but that which is liable to change, as being incessantly in the habit of suffering variation, admits of no proper or divine demonstration.

(2) Why does he say, "Lord, by what shall I know that I shall inherit it?" (Genesis 15:8).

He here is seeking a sign for a ratification of the promise; but two things only are described deserving of study; one that which is an affection of the mind, namely, the belief in God according to his literal word; the other a being borne on with the most exceeding desire not to be left in want of some signs, by which the hearer may feel, to the conviction of his outer senses, a confirmation of the promise: and to him who has given the promise he offers worthy veneration by the appellation, "Lord."

For by this title he says, I know thee to be the Lord and prince of all things, who art also able to do all things, and there is no disability with thee. But in truth, if I have already given credence to thy promise, still I nevertheless wish to obtain speedily if not a completion of it, yet at all events some evident signs by which its consummation may be indicated; in truth I am thy creature, and even if I were to arrive at the highest degree of excellence, I am not always able to restrain the violence of my desire, so as not, when I have seen or heard anything good, to be contented with obtaining it slowly and not immediately; therefore I entreat that thou wilt give me some means of knowledge, by which I may comprehend those future events.

(3) Why is it that he says, "Take for me a heifer of three years old, and a goat of three years old, and a raven of three years old, and a turtle dove and a pigeon?" (Genesis 15:9).

He here mentions five animals, which are offered on the sacred altar; for these are divided into classes of victims, three kinds of terrestrial animals, the ox, the goat, and the sheep; and two kinds of birds, the turtle dove and the pigeon; for the sacred writer constantly tells us that the everlasting reverence of victims derived its origin from the patriarch, who was also the origin of the race: but instead of the expression, "Bring to me," he has very admirably used the words, "Take for me;" since there is nothing especially and peculiarly belonging to the creature, but everything is the gift of and blessing bestowed by God, who is altogether willing that when any one has received anything he should offer thanks for it with all his heart.

But he orders him to take every animal at the age of three years; since three is a full and perfect number, consisting of a beginning, a middle, and an end; but still we may raise the question, why of these three animals, he takes two females, the heifer, and the she-goat, and one male, the ram; may it not be perhaps because the heifer and the she-goat are offered as an atonement for sin; but the sheep is not, as sin arises from frailty, and the female is frail?

This much I have thought fit to say with especial appositeness to this question; but I am not however ignorant that all things of this kind offer a handle to those who wish to cavil, to disparage the sacred scriptures; therefore in this instance they say that there is nothing here described and indicated but a command to sacrifice, by the division of the animals and an examination of their entrails; and what is visible in them they affirm to be an indication of what is convenient, and of the similitude which arises from things visible.

But those men, as it appears to me, are of that class which forms a part alone from a judgment of the whole, but which on the contrary does not from a judgment of a part from the whole, which last is the better way of coming to an opinion, as being that by which both the name and the fact are altogether established.

Therefore the giving of the law, that is to say the sacred scriptures, that I may so express myself, is a sort of living unity, the whole of which one ought to examine carefully with all one's eyes, and so discern with truth, and certainty, and clearness, the universal intention of the whole of the scripture without dissecting or lacerating its harmony, or disuniting its unity; by any other mode everything would appear utterly inconsistent and absurd, being dissociated from all community or equity.

What then is the intention of the delivery of the law as exhibited to us? It is scientific, and so is everything which describes scientific species; since the offering of sacrifice and all science admits of a consistent usage, and of expression well adapted to them, and of various opinions, by which not only the footsteps of truth are occupied, but sometimes are even darkened, as affection is by flattery; but in such way that the very things which are genuine and established by experiment are perverted by things which are both inconsistent and unproved.

And the natures of the animals above mentioned have an intimate connection with the parts of the universe; the ox is connected with the earth, as being an animal employed in drawing the plough and in tilling the earth; the goat again is connected with the water (it is called in Greek and Armenian *aix*, or ajx), being an animal deriving its name from driving and rushing on (from *agō* or *aissō*); since water is an impetuous thing, and the course of rivers, and the extent of the breadth of the sea, and the sea itself agitated as it is by its ebb and flow, are witnesses of the propriety of the name and of the closeness of the connection.

And the ram *(aries)* is connected with the air, as being a very violent and vivacious animal, on which account too the ram is more useful to mankind than any other animal as affording them raiment.

Therefore, on account of these reasons, as I think, God orders him first to take these two female animals, the cow and the she-goat; since both these elements, earth and water, are material, and for the most part feminine. But the third he will have a male, namely the ram; because the air or wind has been explained as masculine; since the natures of all things are divided into bodies or into earth and water, and female animals exist by nature. But that which exhibits a similitude to the soul is arranged under the head of air and the breath of life. And this, as I have said, is masculine. If therefore we are to call that masculine which is the moving and active cause we must call that feminine which is moved and passive.

But the whole heaven is found to be familiarly connected with flying birds such as the pigeon and turtle dove, being distributed as it is into the rotatory path of the planets and fixed stars.

Therefore he dedicates the pigeon to the planets, for that is a tame and domestic animal, as also the planets are more familiarly connected with us as being nearer to the earth, and as having sympathies with us; but he consecrates the turtle dove to the fixed stars, for that animal is a lover of solitude, and flees from the conversation of the multitude, and from all connection of every kind. And so also the globe itself is remote, and a thing which wanders into the furthest extremities of the world.

Therefore both the species of these two birds are assimilated to the divine attributes, since as Plato, the disciple of Socrates, says it is fitting that the heaven should have a swift chariot by reason of its very swift rotatory motion, which in fact surpasses even the birds themselves in the velocity of their course. But the birds above mentioned are singers; the prophet indicating by an enigmatical expression that perfect music which exists in heaven harmoniously adapted from the motion of the stars, since it is a proof of human art when the corresponding music of the voices of animals and of living instruments is adapted together by the industry of genius. But this heavenly music has been abundantly extended over the earth by the Creator, as he has also extended the rays of the sun, being always prompt to exercise his beneficent care for the human race.

For such music excites frenzy in the ears, and brings unrestrained pleasure to the mind; and so causes men to forget even their meat and drink, and even when hunger brings death to the door to be willing even to die out of a desire to hear music.

And if the song of the Sirens,[1] as Homer tells

---

[1] He alludes here to the description in Homer, Od. 12.39–47 (as translated by Pope)—"Next, where the Sirens dwell, you plough the seas; / Their song is death, and makes destruction please. / Unblest the man, whom music wins to stay / Nigh the curst shore, and listen to the lay; / No more that wretch shall view the joys of life, / His blooming offspring, or his beauteous wife! / In verdant meads they sport, and wide around / Lie human bones that whiten all the ground; / The ground polluted floats with human gore, / And human carnage taints the dreadful shore." And further on in the same book, the poet describes the effect of these songs upon Ulysses,

us, invites the heathen so forcibly, that they forget while listening to it, their country, their houses, their friends, and necessary food; how much more must that most perfect and consummate music, so truly heavenly and endowed with the highest degree of harmony, when it touches the organs of the ear, compel men to go mad and to yield to rapture.

But the reason on account of which every one of the animals to be offered is to be three years of age has already been explained; and we must now discuss it under another form of mystery, since it has been seen that every one of those things which were called into existence and subsequently to the moon, such as the earth, water, and air, rejoice in an order connected with the number three.

In the divisions of earth there is a vast quantity of dry continent, islands and peninsulas. Water is divided into sea, rivers, and lakes; and the air into the two equinoxes, the vernal and the autumnal; and they may be taken as one, for they have an equal proportion of day and night, and accordingly the equinoxes are neither hot nor cold. Add to these the changes of summer and winter, for the sun is borne through those three circles into the seasons of summer, winter, and the equinoxes. Therefore, in the first place, the natural arrangement will be of this kind; and the moral arrangement is properly thus.

In every one of us there are three things: flesh, the outward sense, and reason; therefore the calf exhibits a familiarity with the corporeal substance, since our flesh is subdued by, and kept in subservience to, and in connection with the ministrations of life; also their nature is female according to matter, being calculated rather to be passive and to be subject rather than the be active.

But the similitude of the she-goat is connected with the communion of the outward senses, either because all the objects of those outward senses are each borne towards their appropriate sensation, or because each impulse and motion of the soul takes place in consequence of an imagination formed of the objects received through the medium of the external senses. And this is followed, in the first place, by a certain inflexion or alienation, which by some is called an occasion, that is to say, an impulse affecting each kind of sense. But

since the female is the outward sense, as being passive on consequence of what is subjected to the outward senses, therefore God has adapted to it a female animal, the she-goat.

But the ram is akin to the word, or to reason. In the first place, because it is a male animal; secondly, because it is a working animal; and thirdly, because it is the cause of the world, and of the firmament; that is to say, the ram is so by means of the clothing which it supplies; and reason, or the word, is so in the arrangement of life; for whatever is not irregular and absurd immediately exhibits reason. And there are two species of reason; the one derived from that nature by which the affairs of the world subjected to the outward senses are finished; the other from that of those things which are called incorporeal species, by which the affairs of that world which is the object of the intellect are brought to their accomplishment. Therefore the pigeon and the turtle dove are found to resemble these.

The pigeon, forsooth, resembles speculation in natural philosophy; for it is a more familiar bird, as the objects of the outward sense are exceedingly familiar to the sight: and the soul of the inquirer into natural science flies upward as if it were furnished with wings; and being borne aloft is carried round the heaven, discerning every part of every thing, and the principles of every separate thing; for the turtle dove imitates that species which is the subject of intellect and incorporeal; for as that animal is fond of solitude, so it is superior to the violent species which come under the outward sense, associating itself as it does with the invisible species by its essence.

(4) Why does he say, "And he took unto him all these things?" (Genesis 15:10).

He has added also that expression, "And he took unto him," with especial propriety; for it is the sign of a soul thoroughly imbued with the love of God to ascribe whatever good and noble theories and feelings it receives, not unto itself, but wholly to God who is the giver of all benefits.

(5) What is the meaning of, "He divided them in the middle and laid the pieces opposite to one another?" (Genesis 15:10).

Also the whole structure of the body, as of flesh, is to be looked at in such a light as this according to its whole creation; for the parts are brothers; not as they are divided and placed opposite to one another; but, being naturally inclined to one another, and having a mutual regard to one another, on account of their natural co-operation; the original Creator who gave them life making this division for the sake of usefulness, so that one part should be opposed to the other part, and again that both should reciprocally seek one another in all necessary ministrations.

In this way he has directly separated the sense

Od. 12.183–194 (as translated by Pope)—"O stay, O pride of Greece! Ulysses, stay! / O cease thy course and listen our to lay! / Blest is the man ordained our voice to hear, / The song instructs the soul, and charms the ear. / Approach! thy soul shall into raptures rise! / Approach! and learn new wisdom from the wise! / We know whate'er the kings of mighty name / Achieved at Ilion in the field of Fame; / Whate'er beneath the sun's bright journey lies. / O stay and learn new wisdom from the wise!"

of sight, distributing it equally to two eyes by placing the nose between them and thus turning each eye to the other; for the pupils, if I may so say, lean both in one direction so as mutually to behold the same thing, scarcely ever straying beyond the position in which they are placed, but only looking towards one another, especially when anything comes across their sight.

And in similar manner the faculty of hearing is distributed between the two ears, which are both reciprocally turned to one another, both tending to one and the same operation. And the sense of smell is divided between the two nostrils, being turned towards the two tubes of the nostrils, which are not revolving around or inclined towards the cheeks, so as being drawn in two different directions to look the one towards the right and the other towards the left, but being both collected together and turned inwards they await all smells with a common action.

So also the hands are not made of an appearance contrary to that of one another, but being like brothers and like divisible parts, looking to one another mutually, and being prepared by nature for an operation and employment suitable to them, they thus act in the operations of receiving, giving, and working. And the feet are not constituted differently from the hands; as each of them behaves in such a manner that they both yield the one to the other, and progress is effected by the motion of both together, so that nothing can be accomplished by one alone. Nor is it only the feet and shins, but also the legs and knee-pans, and hips, and the breasts, and in fact every part on the right or left of the body, being divided in a similar manner, indicate one general harmony and correspondence and union as it were of connatural parts; that is to say, of all of those different members enumerated according to their separate species.

And generally, whoever considers together and in an equal manner all the above mentioned parts thus subdivided, in reference to their joint operation, will find one nature combined of the two parts. As the hands, united and connected together with the fingers, are seen when in union with them to exhibit a harmony; and the feet, when re-united in operation, are seen to tend to union; and the ears, when similarly combined in the figure of an amphitheatre, are seen to unite themselves, in effect extending across the space which separates them.

Therefore our nature, continually making in this manner a division of those parts which exist in us according to each separate species, has first of all separated and arranged the different sections, placing them as it were opposite to one another in the same way in which it has arranged the world; and it has also arranged them with reference to the easy discharge of their several duties. And again

it has combined each of these members according to each species into one action, and into the same operation, collecting together all of them when considered generally.

Nor is it only the parts of the body which any one may see thus united and in pairs, separated in their union, and again united in their division, but the parts of the soul are so too. But since the two superior sections of this are so many separate classes, namely the rational and the irrational, so also the separate parts of each section have their own appropriate division; as for instance, the rational part is divided into the intention and into the uttered word; and that part which exists in accordance with the outward senses is divided into the four senses; for the fifth sense, touch, is common to the other four, two of which, those with which we see and hear, are philosophical senses, so that it is by means of them that the power of living well is acquired for us; the others are nonphilosophical, namely smell and taste, but are servile, being created only for living; for the sense of smell, by means of its exercise, contains many things which awaken it, and receives a continual breathing which is as it were the continual food of living creatures; therefore smell and taste support this mortal body, but sight and hearing afford service to the immortal soul.

Therefore these divisions of our members, according to our body and soul, were made and separated by the Creator; however, we must know that the parts of the world also are arranged in two divisions and are placed opposite to one another; the earth being divided into mountainous and champaign districts; the water into sweet and salt, sweet being that which is supplied by springs and rivers, and salt being that which comes from the sea; as also the atmosphere is divided into summer and winter, and also into spring and autumn.

And it is on this account that Heraclitus wrote his books about nature, having borrowed his theory of contraries from our sacred historian, with the addition of an infinite number of laborious arguments.

(6) Why is it said, "But he did not divide the birds?" (Genesis 15:10).

He is shadowing forth a fifth and periodical nature, from which the ancients say that the heaven was made; for the four elements are mixtures rather than elements: by which he subdivides those things which are already divided into those materials of which they were originally composed, as the earth includes within itself a portion of the elements of water, and also of air, and also of fire, which however obtains the appellation not so much in accordance with our apprehension of it, as with our sight; and again the water is not so clear or pure, as not to have some participation in wind and earth; and so also in each of the other elements there is a certain tempering and combination; but the fifth substance is the only one which has been made unmixed and pure, on which account it was not accustomed to be mentioned at all.

Therefore it is well said, he did not divide the birds; since the heavenly nature, both of the planets and also of the fixed stars, is raised on high like that of birds, in the similitude of both kinds, that is to say, of clean birds, the turtle dove and the pigeon, which scarcely admit of being divided or cut up; for the indivisible nature is of a fifth essence, more unmixed and pure than the others, and therefore it more closely resembles unity.

(7) What is the meaning of, "And the birds descended on the bodies which were divided?" (Genesis 15:11).

Since the three animals, the heifer, and the she-goat, and the ram, were divided in a symbolical manner, they are signs, as we have already said, of the earth, and water, and air; still it is necessary to give now a reason for this, examining the truth carefully under the mystery of a similitude.

Perhaps therefore he designs and intimates by the descent of the birds on the cut pieces an invasion of enemies; for all the nature of the world beneath the moon is full of battles and ill will, both domestic and external; and the birds in truth appear to fly down on the divided bodies for the sake of meat and drink; naturally indeed it is the stronger which descend upon the weaker animals, as upon dead bodies, attacking them in general unexpectedly, but they do not fly down on the turtle dove and pigeon, since the heavenly bodies are free from desires and unconscious of suffering wrong.

(8) Why is it that he says, "Abraham passed over and sat upon them?" (Genesis 15:11).

Those who think that sacrifice is indicated by the matters about which we are at present speaking will say that the virtuous man, sitting as it were in a synagogue, has examined into the entrails of the divided animals, as if that were looked upon as an unerring symbol for the declaration of the truth; but we, who adhere to Moses and who are thoroughly acquainted with the views of that teacher, one who, turning away his face from every sophistical appearance and prognostic, trusted in God alone, will rather say, that he has here introduced the just man who is endued with virtue with the birds themselves, who were congregated together and flying about over him, intending to denote nothing else by this parabolical presentation, but that he is desirous of hindering injustice and covetousness, and is most hostile to quarrels and wars, and a lover of consistency and peace; for he himself is truly a guardian of peace.

Since no one state has ever rested in tranquillity owing to the conduct of the wicked, but kingdoms have become fixed steadily when one or two men endued with virtue have arisen, whose vir-

tue has put an end to civil disturbances, God granting to those who are earnest in the pursuit of virtue good habits calculated to procure them honour; and not to them only, but to those also who approach near to the production of general advantage.

(9) What is the meaning of the words, "About the time of the setting of the sun a trance fell upon Abraham; and lo, a great horror of darkness came over him?" (Genesis 15:12).

A certain divine excess was suddenly rendered calm to the man endued with virtue; for the trance, or ecstacy as the word itself evidently points out, is nothing else than a departure of the mind wandering beyond itself. [2]

But the class of prophets loves to be subject to such influences; for when it is divining, and when the intellect is inspired with divine things, it no longer exists in itself, since it receives the divine spirit within and permits it to dwell with itself; or rather, as he himself has expressed it, as spirit falls upon him; since it does not come slowly over him, but rushes down upon him suddenly.

Moreover, that which he has added afterwards applies admirably, that a great horror of darkness fell upon him. For all these things are ecstacies of the mind; for he also who is in a state of alarm is not in himself; but darkness is a hindrance to his sight; and in proportion as the horror is greater, so also do his powers of seeing and understanding become more obscured.

And this is not said without reason: but as an indication of the evident knowledge of prophecy by which oracles and laws are given from God.

(10) Why was it said to him, "Thou shalt know to a certainty that thy seed shall be a stranger in a land that is not theirs, and shall be reduced to slavery, and shall be grievously afflicted for four hundred years?" (Genesis 15:13).

That expression is admirably used, "It was said to him," since a prophet is supposed to utter something, but yet he is not pronouncing any command of his own, but is only the interpreter of another who sends something into his mind; and moreover whatever he does utter and deliver in words is all true and divine. And in the first place, he declares that a family of the human race is to dwell in a land belonging to another; for all things which are beneath the heaven are the possession of God, and those living creatures which exist on the earth may more properly and truly be said to be sojourners in a foreign land than to be dwelling in a country of their own which by nature they have not got.

In the second place, he thus declares to us that every mortal is a slave after his kind. But no man

---

[2] *ekstasis,* derived from *existamai,* in 2nd aor. act. *exestēn,* "I was beside myself."

is found to be free, but every one has many masters who vex and afflict him both within and without; for instance, without there are the winter which affects him with the cold, the summer which scorches him with heat, and hunger, and thirst, and many other calamities; and within there are pleasures and concupiscences, and sorrows, and fears. But his servitude is limited to a period of four hundred years, during which the aforesaid pleasures shall rise up against him. On which account it has been said above, that Abraham passed over and sat upon them, hindering and repelling them; as far as the literal words go, repelling those carnivorous birds which were hovering over the divided animals, but in fact repelling the afflictions which come upon men. Since a man who is in his own proper nature a lover of, and also by diligent practice a studier of virtue, is a most humane physician of our race, and a true protector of it, and guardian of it from evil. For all these things have an allegorical reference to the soul.

For while the soul of the wise man, descending from above from the sky, comes down upon and enters a mortal and is sown in the field of the body, it is truly sojourning in a land which is not his own. Since the earthly nature of the body is wholly alien from pure intellect, and tends to subdue it and to drag it downwards into slavery, bringing every kind of affliction upon it, until the sorrow, bringing the attractive multitude of vices to judgment, condemns them; and thus at last the soul is restored to freedom. And it is on this account that he subsequently adds the sentence, "Nevertheless the nation which they shall send I will judge: and afterwards they shall go forth with great substance;" namely, with the same measure, and still better. Because then the mind is released from its mischievous colleague, departing out of the body and being transferred not only with freedom but also with much substance; so as to leave nothing good or useful behind to its enemies.

Since every rational soul is productive, but he who thinks himself loaded and endued with virtue in his own counsel, is unable to preserve his fruit unto the end. For it becomes a virtuous man to attain to the objects which he has intended of his own accord, as also the counsels of wisdom correspond to those objects. Since, as some trees, although they appear productive at the first season of the budding of their fruits, are yet unable to bring them to maturity, so that the whole fruit before it becomes ripe is shaken off by every trifling cause; in the same manner the souls of inconstant men feel many influences which contribute to their productiveness, but nevertheless are unable to keep them sound till they arrive at perfection, as a man studious of virtue ought to do in order eventually to gather them as his own possessions.

(11) What is the meaning of, "But thou shalt go to thy fathers in peace, being nourished in a fair old age?" (Genesis 15:15).

He here clearly indicates the incorruptibility of the soul: when it transfers itself out of the abode of the mortal body and returns as it were to the metropolis of its native country, from which it originally emigrated into the body. Since to say to a dead man, "Thou shalt go to thy fathers," what else is this but to propose to him and set before him a second existence apart from the body as far as it is proper for the soul of the wise man to dwell by itself?

But when he says this he does not mean by the fathers of Abraham his father, and his grandfather, and his great-grandfathers after the flesh, for they were not all deserving of praise so as to be by any possibility any honour to him who arrived at the succession of the same order, but he appears by this expression to be assigning to him for his fathers, according to the opinion of many commentators, all the elements into which the mortal man when deceased is resolved.

But to me he appears to intend to indicate the incorporeal substances and inhabiters of the divine world, whom in other passages he is accustomed to call angels. Moreover the words which follow are not by any means without an object, that he is nourished in peace and in a fair old age. For the wicked and depraved man is nourished in battle, and lives and departs in a very bad old age. But the good man, in both phases of existence, both in that which is in connection with the body and in that which is apart from the body, cultivates peace, and is alone completely virtuous, such as no foolish person is found to be, even though he should live longer than an elephant; on which account he here carefully said, "Thou shalt go to thy fathers, being nourished—not in an advanced old age, but—in a fair old age." For many foolish persons also have their lives extended to a greatly lengthened period, but it is only the man who is desirous of virtue who enjoys a good old age and one endued with virtue.

(12) Why is it that he says, "And in the fourth generation they shall return again hither?" (Genesis 15:16).

The number four is more fit than any other number, for this reason, that as it is more perfect, and is the root and foundation of the perfect number ten; and it is according to the principle of the number four that all collected are to return hither, as he himself has said. But as he by himself is perfect, so also those of whom he is the father are evidently perfect.

But what is it that I am saying? In the generation of animals the sowing of the seed has the first place; in the second place, comes the fact of each instrument being, in some manner, impressed by something akin to nature; thirdly, there is the growth after the first formation of the creature; fourthly, after everything else comes the perfection, that is to say, the birth. And the same principle and order prevail in plants; the seed is cast into the earth, then it pushes its way both upwards and downwards, partly in roots and partly in branches; after that it increases; and fourthly, it produces fruit; and in the same manner again the trees, when made, first of all produce fruit, which subsequently grows; then, as it becomes ripe, it changes colour; and, fourthly, and this is the last operation, it completes and perfects its work, the consequence of which is the use and enjoyment of it by men.

(13) What is the meaning of, "For the sins of the Amorites were not as yet completed?" (Genesis 15:16).

Some persons have said, that by this expression of the principle of Moses fate is expressly introduced, as if, in truth, everything was to be accomplished according to some particular hour and appointed period of time.

(14) What is the meaning of, "And when the sun was in the west a flame arose?" (Genesis 15:17).

It means either that the sun himself appeared in the west in the similitude of a flame, or that some other flame appeared at eventide, not lightning, but some fire like it, which descended from above. The manifest interpretation of the oracle is this; but we must now discuss that which regards the inner sense.

(15) What is the meaning of the expression, "Behold there was a smoking furnace and torches of fires, which passed through the middle of those divisions?" (Genesis 15:18).

The literal expression of the statement is plain, for the fountain or root of the divine word will have the victims consumed, not by that fire which is given for our use, but by that which descends from above, out of heaven, in order that the purity of the essence of heaven may bear witness to the sanctity of the victims.

But if we regard the inward meaning of the words, all things which are done beneath the moon are here compared to a smoking furnace, on account of the vapour which rises up out of the earth and water. As also the divisions of nature are, as has been already shown, every portion of the world being divided into two parts; and by these there are kindled, as it were, torches of fire, being powers which are more rapid in motion and more efficacious, being burning, in truth, like divine fiery discourses, at one time keeping the whole universe in a state of integrity reciprocally with themselves, and at another cleansing away the superfluous darkness.

But the following interpretation may also be

given with propriety in a more familiar manner. Human life is like unto a smoking furnace, because it has not a pure fire and an unalloyed brilliancy, but a great deal of smoke, smoking darkly through the flame, which causes mist and darkness, and an obscuration, not of the body but of the soul, so that this last cannot discern things clearly, until God the redeemer commands the heavenly lamps to arise, I mean those more pure and more holy radiations which unite those parts previously divided in two, on the right hand and on the left, and, at the same time, illuminate them, being the causes of harmony and of lucid clearness.

(16) Why did he say, "On that day, God made a covenant with Abraham, saying, To thy seed will I give this land, from the river of Egypt to the great river Euphrates?" (Genesis 15:19).

The literal expression describes the boundaries of the space which lies in the middle, between the two rivers Egyptus and Euphrates, for anciently the river was also called by the same name as the district, Egypt, as the poet also testifies when he says—

"And in the river Egypt did I fix
My double-oared ships."[3]

But if we look to the inner meaning of the expression, it intimates happiness, which is the perfect fulness of three good things, namely, of spiritual, and corporeal, and external blessings, as some of those men describe it in their panegyrics, who were afterwards called philosophers, such as Aristotle and the Peripatetics; nevertheless, such a giving of the law as this is called Pythagorean.

Therefore the Egypt is a symbol of corporeal and external blessings, and the Euphrates of spiritual advantages, in which alone, it is plain, their real joy consists, which has wisdom and all the other virtues for its foundation; and the boundaries of this happiness are very rightly described as beginning with the Egyptus and ending with the Euphrates; for the things affecting the soul come at the end, which we usually approach with difficulty after we have passed through corporeal and external things, in such a manner that, by this progress, we have felt our unity, the integrity of our outward senses, and the beauty and strength which existed in our youth, advance, increase, and come to maturity. And in a similar manner, those things which relate to acquiring gain and to trafficking, as the management of ships, and agriculture, and commerce; for it is well said, that all things, especially those above-mentioned, become a young man.

(17) Who are the Kenites, the Kenezites, and

---

[3] The line is in Odyssey 14.258.

the Kadmonites, and the Hittites, and the Periz-zites, and the Rephaims, and the Amorites, the Canaanites, the Girgashites, and the Jebusites? (Genesis 15:20).

Ten nations of wickedness are here enumer-ated, which he here destroys because of their neighbourhood, since the number ten, when false and improperly stamped, is very near to that which is good and an object of affection; but the com-plete perfection of the number ten is exceedingly fit, as being the measure of infinite numbers, since the world is arranged in accordance with it, and so likewise is the mind of the wise man, the sub-stance of which, nevertheless, wickedness per-verts and overthrows, despising all very neces-sary powers, so that that alone remains which the sacred writer has said, namely, that the pursuit of virtue is a blessing, for the wicked man is such that he embraces vague opinions rather than truth, and of such is Ishmael, though the seed of the prophets.

(18) Why it was that Sarah, the wife of Abra-ham, bore him no children? (Genesis 16:1).

The mother of opinion is here spoken of as bar-ren. In the first place in order that the son of gen-eration might appear more wonderful, as being born by a miracle. In the second place in order that his conception and nativity might appear to be owing not more to the marriage of the man than to divine providence. For it is not owing to the faculty of conception that a barren woman should bear a son, but rather to the operation of divine power. This is the literal meaning of the statement.

But if we look to its inward sense, then we shall say, in the first place, that to bring forth is pecu-liar to the female sex, as to beget is the office of the male: therefore God wills in the first place to render the mind, which is filled with virtue, like to the male sex rather than to the female, think-ing it suited to its character to be active, not pas-sive. In the second place both do generate, both the virtuous mind and the wicked one: but they generate in a different manner, and they produce contrary offspring, the virtuous mind producing good and useful things, but the depraved or wicked mind producing base and useless things.

In the third place he who is still advancing and making progress is to be incited to the summit itself, and is near to the light which by some per-sons is said to be delivered to oblivion, and to be made unknown. He therefore, as he is making progress, does not generate bad things, nor yet good things, because he is not yet perfect; but he resembles that man who is neither sick nor yet thoroughly well, but who, after a long sickness, is at last proceeding to convalescence.

(19) What is the meaning of the statement, she had an Egyptian handmaid whose name was Hagar? (Genesis 16:1).

Hagar is interpreted travelling, and she is the servant of a more perfect nature, being by nature an Egyptian less naturally; for the study of encyc-lical learning loves an abundance of knowledge, and abundant knowledge is, as it were, the handmaid of virtue, since the whole course and connection of sciences and arts is subservient to his use who is able to profit by their acquisition so as to attain to virtue, for virtue has the soul for its abode; but the course of arts and sciences stands in need of bodily instruments.

But the body is symbolically Egypt; therefore the sacred writer here properly asserts the like-ness of encyclical knowledge to Egypt. Neverthe-less he has also given it a name by reason of its travelling abroad, since sophistry is a foreign thing, unconnected with the acquisition of that wisdom which alone is native, and which alone is neces-sary, which is the mistress of intermediate wis-dom, and which conducts itself in a beautiful course through the guidance of encyclical studies.

(20) Why did Sarah say to Abraham, Behold the Lord has shut me up so that I shall not bring forth: go in now unto my handmaid so as to beget a son by her? (Genesis 16:2).

In the actual letter of this statement it is the same thing to feel no envy, and also to provide for the welfare of the wise man who is her husband and her genuine brother; so that she, wishing to find a remedy for her own barrenness by means of her handmaid of whom she was mistress, gives her as a concubine to her husband. But there is a still greater abundance of her affection towards her husband indicated by this; for as she herself was accounted barren, she did not think it rea-sonable that the family of her husband should be left entirely without offspring, but preferred his advantage to her own dignity. This is what is indi-cated by this statement taken literally.

But if we look to the inner sense of the pas-sage it bears such an interpretation as this: it becomes those persons who are unable in respect of their virtue to bring forth beautiful works deserving of praise, to apply themselves to the intermediate kind of study, and, if I may so express myself, to procure themselves children from the encyclical branches of knowledge; for an abundance of knowledge is as it were the whetstone of the mind and of the intellect.

And it is with great propriety that she says, The Lord has shut me up; for that which is shut up is generally opened again at a seasonable time. Therefore she was not destitute of hope, nor was her wisdom fixed in the belief that she should be for ever without offspring, but she knew that some day or other she should bring forth. Nevertheless she will not bring forth at present, but when the soul displays the purity of its perfection. But inas-much as it is at present imperfect it is satisfied with using a milder kind of learning, such as is attainable by encyclical studies. On which account it is not without a purpose that in the sacred contests at Olympia also, those who are unable to attain to the first prize of victory are contented to be thought worthy of the second; for there is offered to the competitors a first, and a second, and a third prize by the presidents of the games, who are representatives of nature. So now to her the sacred writer attributes the first prize of virtues, and the second prize of encyclical study.

(21) Why has he called Abraham's wife Sarah, for he says, Sarah the wife of Abraham, taking her handmaid Hagar the Egyptian, gave her into his hand? (Genesis 16:2).

The sacred writer here sums up with his approbation the marriage of the good on account of those who are incontinent and lascivious; for those persons despise their wise wives for the sake of concubines, whom they love with a frantic passion: on which account he here introduces the man endued with virtue, the constant husband of one wife, at that time in which it was lawful for him to make use of her handmaid; and his wife in fact indicates that he is wise, that is to say temperate, when he enters into the bed of another woman, since his connection with his concubine was only a connection of the body for the sake of propagating children; but his union with his wife was that of two souls joined together in harmony by heavenly affection. This is the literal effect of the statement.

But if we look to the inner meaning of it, then he who has truly entrusted all his secret wishes to wisdom, and justice, and the other virtues, when once he has received the counsel of wisdom, and has tasted the joys of a matrimonial connection with it, remains constant to it as the partner and companion of his life; although encyclical education would lead him in a beautiful course, since when the man eminent in virtue has become master of the sciences of geometry, and arithmetic, and grammar, and rhetoric, and the other exercises of the mind, he is not the less on that account mindful of the pursuit of honesty, but is borne on towards the one as to a necessary aim, to the other as an accessory.

But it is altogether fair that that fact also should meet with our approbation,—the fact I mean of his calling his handmaid also by the name of wife, because he went up to her bed out of complacency to and at the exhortation of his real wife, and not of his own genuine inclination; on which account he no longer calls her his handmaid, that even if it were not wholly deserved still his handmaid having been given to him to wife might at least obtain the same title.

But those who study allegory may be allowed to say that the exercise of the middle disciplines also stands in the place of a concubine, having nevertheless the shape and ornaments of a wife, for all encyclical learning re-produces in itself and imitates genuine virtue.

(22) What is the meaning of, "When she saw that she had conceived her mistress was despised before her?" (Genesis 16:4).

The sacred writer now carefully calls Sarah the mistress when it might else have been thought that her dignity was diminished, and that she was surpassed by her handmaid, that she, that is, who had no children, was surpassed by her who was gifted with offspring.

But this kind of language is extended to nearly all the necessary affairs of human life: for a poor man who is wise is more approved of and is superior in authority to a rich man who is destitute of wisdom and reputation, or than a boasting man; and even a sick man who is wise is better than a foolish man who is well; for whatever is united with wisdom is genuine, and is endued with an authority of its own, but whatever is combined with folly is found to be slavish and inconstant.

But it has been excellently said not that she despised her mistress, but that her mistress was despised; for the one statement would imply an accusation of the person, but the other contains only a declaration of an event. The scripture forsooth does not intend here to impute blame to any one while praising another, but only to hand down in an intelligible manner the pure truth of the facts.

This is what is indicated by the literal statement. But if we seek the inner meaning of the words, whoever honours and embraces rank before genius and wisdom, and whoever esteems and considers the external senses of more importance than prudence and counsel, is departing from the real character of things, thinking that they have brought forth much offspring, and that having produced a great generation of visible things they are great and perfect goods, and in a singular degree noble, but that barrenness in this respect is evil, and deserving of disapprobation, because they do not see that invisible seed and that offspring which is appreciable only by the intellect, which the mind is accustomed to generate in itself and by itself.

(23) Why does Sarah as it were repent of what she has done, saying to Abraham, I am receiving injury from you: I gave my handmaid into your bosom, and now, because she sees that she has conceived, I am despised before her? (Genesis 16:5).

This language indicates her anxiety and hesitation; displaying them first in the expression, "since," that is to say from the time that I gave my handmaiden, and in the second place it betokens a regard to the person of whom complaint is made, for she says, "I am receiving injury from you," a statement which in fact is a reproof, since she thinks that her husband ought always to be preserved without any stain, or any liability to blame, always virtuous and true, and in no respect forgetful of her, for she always introduces him, honouring him with all possible veneration, and calling him lord.

Nevertheless, the first fact stated by her is true; for from the time that she gave her handmaiden to him to be his concubine, she herself was looked upon as despised. This is the literal meaning of her words.

But if we look to their inner sense, when any one bestows on another the handmaid of wisdom, she being influenced by the counsels of sophistry, will, because she is ignorant of propriety, despise her mistress; for as she herself possesses encyclical knowledge, and is delighted with its brilliancy, where every one of the separate branches of education is by itself very attractive to the soul, as if it possesses the power of drawing it by force to itself, then she, the handmaiden, can no longer agree with her mistress, that is to say, with the image of wisdom and its glorious and admirable beauty, until that acute judge of all things, the word of God, coming in, separates and distinguishes what is probable from what is true, and the middle from the extremities, and what is second from what is placed in the first rank. On which account Sarah says, at the end of her remonstrance, "Let God judge between me and thee."

(24) Why does Abraham say, "Behold thy handmaid is in thy hand, do unto her what seems good to thee?" (Genesis 16:6).

The literal expression used by the wise man contains a panegyric; for he does not call the woman who had conceived by himself, his wife, or his concubine, but the handmaiden of his wife. But since he saw that she also was a mother, he did not indulge in anger and embitter the feelings of her mind, but rather tranquillised her, and made her prudent.

But the passage contains an allegory in the expression, "In thy hand:" as if, if I may so say, sophistry lives under the dominion of wisdom, which indeed does spring forth from the same fountain, but only in one part, and not directly; nor does it preserve the whole of its emanations pure, but draws up with its waters many fetid things, and many others of a similar character. Since, therefore, it is in thy hand and in thy power (for to whomsoever wisdom belongs, he is possessed also of all the branches of encyclical learning), do with it whatsoever pleases thee, for I am quite persuaded that you will judge with not more severity than justice; because that very thing is especially agreeable to you: I mean the distributing to every one according to his deserts, and giving to no one more than is just, either in the way of honouring or despising him.

(25) Why does he say, Sarah afflicted her? (Genesis 16:6).

The literal meaning of the words is plain: but if we look to the inner sense of them, they contain a principle of this kind. It is not every affliction that is injurious, but there are even some occasions when they are salutary; and this is experienced by sick men at the hands of physicians, and by boys under their tutors, and by foolish people from those who correct them so as to bring them to wisdom. And this I can by no means consent to call affliction, but rather the salvation and benefit of both soul and body.

Now a part of such benefit wisdom affords to the circle of encyclical knowledge; rightly admonishing the soul which is devoted to an abundance of discipline, and which is pregnant with sophism, not to rebel as if it had acquired some great and excellent good, but to acquiesce and venerate that superior and more excellent nature as its genuine mistress, in whose power is constancy itself, and authority over all things.

(26) Why did Hagar flee from her face? (Genesis 16:6).

It is not every soul which is capable of proper respect and of submitting to salutary discipline, but the mind which is gentle, and good-tempered, and consistent loves reproof, and becomes more and more attached to those who correct it. But the stubborn soul becomes malignant and hates them, and turns from them, and flees away from them, preferring those discourses which are agreeable rather than those which tend to his advantage, and looking upon them as more excellent.

(27) What is the meaning of the statement, "The angel of the Lord found her sitting by a fountain of water in the desert in the way to Sur?" (Genesis 16:7).

All these statements are as it were symbols by which the sacred writer indicates that the well-instructed soul, which is the possession of virtue, is nevertheless not yet able to discern the beauty of her mistress. They are, I say, symbols; I mean the statements that she was found, and that she was found by an angel in the desert, and in no other way than that leading to Sur. However we must begin with what is plain.

Now the too subtle sophist and the real lover of disputations is commonly unable to be detected by reason of his artifices and sophistical persuasions, with which he is accustomed to deceive and perplex men. But he who, being free from bad habits, has only an eager desire for obtaining instruction by the course of encyclical training, although he is difficult to be detected, is yet not altogether incapable of being so; for perdition is near at hand to him who cannot be detected, but safety to him who can be discovered, especially when he is sought for and found by a more holy and more excellent spirit. And who is more holy and more excellent than the angel of the Lord? For it is to him that it has been entrusted to seek out the erring soul, the soul which, on account of its presumed erudition, is continually ignorant of her whom it ought to respect, but still she could be susceptible of correction and amendment; for which object she was sought out. Nor was she found imperfect, but ready to the hand, since the soul was found which had fled from perfect virtue, not being able to submit to discipline.

But the third symbol takes place after she is found and after the discovery has been made by an angel, namely, in the fact of her being found by a fountain, that is to say, by nature; for it is nature which bestows on clever people abilities in proportion to the industry of each individual, effacing unseasonable learning, which is no learning at all: and praise is implied in the very place in which the soul is found, which is thirsting after genius and after its placid law, wishing to draw water while in the society of those who drink wine; for thus it associates with those who feed upon and are delighted with the exercise of proper training, where nature itself affords sufficient nourishment, namely, education and instruction as if from a fountain.

The fourth symbol is contained in the fact that the discovery took place in the desert; since difficulty coming over each of the outward senses, together with an influx of each separate desire, represses the mind, and does not permit it to drink pure water: but when it cannot avoid these things as in the desert, it acquiesces, and, abandoning the thoughts which agitated and perplexed it, it becomes convalescent, so as to receive a hope not only of life, but even of eternal life.

The fifth symbol is contained in the fact that she was found in the way; for dispositions which are incorrigible are led by devious paths; but that one which can be changed for the better, lo! it proceeds along the road which leads to virtue, and that road is like a fortified wall and guardian to the souls which are capable of being saved, for Sur means a fortified wall.

Do you not see, then, that the whole is a symbolical, or indeed a legitimate, figure of an improving soul? And, in fact, the soul which is improving does not perish as one which is wholly foolish does; for if the divine word be found by it, then again it seeks it; and he who is not pure and clean in his habits and disposition, flees from the divine word; but yet he has a fountain of water in which he washes away his vices and wickednesses, drawing from thence the fertility of the law.

Besides this, it loves the desert, to which it has fled from its vices and wickednesses, and when it has once beheld the way of virtue it returns from the devious paths of wickedness. And all these things are fortified walls and bulwarks to it, so as to protect it from being ever injured by any words of circumstances which attack it, and from suffering any damage.

(28) Why did the angel say to her, "Hagar, the handmaid of Sarah, whence comest thou, and whither goest thou?" (Genesis 16:8).

The plain letter of the question requires no explanation, for it is exceedingly clear; but with reference to the inner meaning contained in it, there is come asperity expressed; since the divine word is full of instruction, and is a physician of the infirmity of the soul. Therefore the angel says to her, "Whence comest thou?" knowest thou not what good thou has abandoned? Art thou not altogether lame and blind? For thou dost not see at all; and though endowed with the outward senses, dost not feel, and dost not appear to me to have any portion whatever of intellect, as if thou wert quite senseless.

But "whither goest thou?" From what excellence to what misery? Why have you so erred as to cast away the blessings which you had in your power, and to pursue good things which are more remote?

Do not, do not, I say, act thus; but, quitting your insane impetuosity, go back again, and return into the same way as before, looking upon wisdom as thy mistress, her whom you had before as your governess and directress in all the things which you did.

(29) What is the meaning of the answer, "I am fleeing from the face of Sarah, my mistress?" (Genesis 16:8).

It is reasonable to praise a sincere disposition, and to think it friendly to truth. And moreover it is reasonable now to admit the veracity of a mind which confesses what it has suffered; for she says, "I am fleeing from the face," that is to say, I have recoiled at the outward appearance of wisdom and virtue; since, beholding its royal and imperial presence, she trembled, not being able to endure to look upon its majesty and sublimity, but rather thinking it an object of avoidance; for there are some people who do not turn from virtue from any hatred of it, but from a reverential modesty, looking upon themselves as unworthy to live with such a mistress.

(30) Why did the angel say to her, "Return to thy mistress and be humbled beneath her hands?" (Genesis 16:8).

As the letter is plain, we must rather investigate its inner meaning. The word of God corrects that soul which is able to be lured, and instructs it, and converts it, leading it to wisdom as its mistress, that it may not, through being abandoned by its mistress, rush at once into absurd folly. But it warns it, not only to return to virtue, but also to be humbled beneath its hands, that is to say, beneath its several excellencies.

But there are two kinds of humiliation; one, in accordance with defect, which arises from spiritual infirmity, which it is easy to overcome, seize upon, and reprove. But there is another kind which the word of the Lord enjoins, proceeding from reverence and modesty; such as that humility which children exhibit to their fathers, pupils to their masters, and young men to the aged; since it is very advantageous to be obedient, and to be subject to those who are better than one's self; for he who has learnt to be under authority is in a moment imbued with a power which he alone may exercise; for, although any one were to be clothed with the authority of all the earth and sea, yet he would not be able to possess the royal supremacy of virtue, unless he had first been instructed and taught to obey.

(31) Why did the angel say to her, "I will multiply thy seed, and it shall not be numbered for multitude?" (Genesis 16:9).

It is the honour of the docile mind not to be presumptuous or rebellious on account of its progress in knowledge, or because of the very useful seed which it has received from various kinds of erudition; for it does not any more, as word-catchers and cavillers do, employ all the arguments of encyclical learning to establish any whimsical object, but to prove the truth which is contained in them. And when it has begun to prosecute that by diligent investigation, it is then rendered worthy to behold the sight of its mistress, free from all acceptance of persons, and from all reproof.

(32) What is the meaning of the statement, "The angel said to her, Behold, thou hast conceived, and thou shalt bring forth a son, and shalt call his name Ishmael, because the Lord has heard the voice of thy affliction?" (Genesis 16:11).

The literal sense of the words admits of no question except this allegorical explanation. Erudition, which is acquired and trained by the dispensation of virtue as a mistress, is found not to be barren, but it has conceived the seed of wisdom; and when it has conceived it brings forth; but it brings forth a work which is not perfect but imperfect, like an infant which has need of care, and ailment, and nourishment; for in truth, it is quite plain that the offspring of a perfect soul is perfect, that is to say, its words and works; but that of the soul of the second class, which is still lying in servitude and subordination, is more imperfect. On which account it has a certain name given to it, Ishmael, which is interpreted "the hearing of God." But hearing is honoured with the second dignity among the outward senses, being next to sight; for nature has arranged a succession of ranks in the contests of the senses, giving the first place to the eyes, the second to the ears, the third to the nostrils, and the fourth to that sense by which we taste.

(33) What is the meaning of the statement, "He shall be a wild man; his hand shall be upon every one, and every one's hand shall be upon him, and he shall dwell over against all his brethren?" (Genesis 16:12).

If we look to the letter of the statement, up to this time Ishmael has not any brothers, for he was the first child of his parents. But the sacred writer is here figuring a certain nature, too secret to be thoroughly investigated; for he has set forth the figure of his future character. And such a figure evidently represents the sophist whose mother is erudition or wisdom. But the sophist himself is a man of wild opinions; since the wise man as being civilized is fitted for living in cities, and for urbanity, or for statesmanlike and political companionship; but he who is wild and a man of wild opinions is immediately also quarrelsome.

And it is on this account that the sacred writer makes an addition, saying, "His hand shall be upon every one, and every one's hand shall be upon him;" for the abundance of science and the use of erudition is able to contradict all men. As those men of the present day who are called academicians and inquirers, consistently setting no bounds to the determinations of their will and resolution, and among the different opinions which they investigate preferring neither this nor that one, admit those men to be philosophers who attack the opinions of every sect; and those whom it has been usual to call opposers of will, as if they called them *thelēmachoi* or *thelēmamachoi*, because they in the first place raise contentions and declare themselves the champions of their national sect, not to be convinced or put down by those who oppose them. But they are all kinsmen, and as it were brothers of the same womb, being the offspring of one mother, namely, of philosophy.

And it is on this account that he says, "And he shall dwell over against all his brethren;" for in good truth the academician and the inquirer are diametrically opposed to sects, finding fault in each of them with their certain limitation of the resolution.

(34) Why does he say, "But Hagar called on the name of the Lord, who spoke to her, saying, 'Thou God who hast had regard unto me.' Because he said, 'In truth I have beheld thee appearing before me.'" (Genesis 16:13).

In the first place, take notice carefully that the angel, after the manner of the handmaiden of wisdom, was a minister to her on the part of God. But still why is he here called Lord or God who ought only to have been styled his angel? It was in order to adapt the fact to the proper person; for it was right that the Lord and chief of all the universe should appear to wisdom as God, and that his word should appear as a minister to the hand-maid and servant of wisdom.

But we may not suppose that she mistakenly looked upon the angel as God; for those who are unable to behold the first cause may easily be deceived and look upon the second as the first; in the same manner as he who has but weak sight, not being able to behold the sun which is in heaven in its real appearance, thinks that the ray which falls upon the earth is the sun itself; and those who have never seen the king attribute frequently the dignity of the supreme sovereign to his ministers.

And in truth mild and rustic men who never have beheld a city, not even from the summits of the hills where they live, think every country house or farm-yard a mighty city, and look upon the people who dwell there as citizens of a great city, out of ignorance of what a city really is.

(35) What is the meaning of, "On this account she called that well the well of him whom I have seen face to face?" (Genesis 16:14).

The well has both a spring and depth. But the learning of the students of encyclical science is neither all on the surface, nor is it destitute of first principles; for it has for its source corrective discipline. Therefore it is with perfect correctness that she says that the angel appeared before the well as God; since the erudition of the encyclical training possessing the second rank is supposed to rejoice in the first authority, though it is in reality separated from that first wisdom which it is permitted to wise men to behold, but not to sophists.

(36) Why is the well said to have been between Cadesh and Pharan? (Genesis 16:14).

Cadesh is interpreted holy, but Pharan is translated hail, or corn.

(37) What is the meaning of the statement, "Hagar brought forth a son to Abraham?" (Genesis 16:15).

It is made in perfect accordance with nature; for no habit of possession brings forth for itself, but for him who possesses it; as grammar does for the grammarian, and music for the musician, and mathematical science for the mathematician; because it is a part of him, and stands in need of him. And the habit is not received as a thing in need of something, just as fire has no need of heat, for it is heat to itself; and it gives a portion of the participation in it to those who approach it.

(38) Why is Abraham said to have been eighty and six years old when Hagar bore Ishmael to him? (Genesis 16:16).

Because the number which follows eighty, that is to say six, is the first perfect number, being equal to its parts, and being the first number which is composed of the multiplication of an odd and an even number; receiving also something from its efficient cause according to the odd or redundant number, and from its material and effective cause according to the even number. On which account, among the most ancient of our ancestors, some persons have called it matrimony, and others harmony; and our sacred historian too has divided the creation of the world into six days.

But among numbers, eighty rejoices in perfect harmony, since it is composed of two generous diameters in a double and treble proportion, according to the figure of a square of four sides. And it contains within itself all the four inferences; the arithmetical, and the geometrical, and the harmonious one.

Being in the first place composed of double numbers, as of six, eight, nine, twelve, the union of which makes thirty-five; in the second place of triple number, six, nine, twelve, eighteen, the sum of which amounts to forty-five. And from these two numbers thirty-five and forty-five, the whole number eighty is completed.

Again, when the sacred historian Moses himself began by divine inspiration to utter the oracular precepts which he was commissioned to deliver, he was eighty years old. And the first man who existed of our nation according to the law of circumcision, being circumcised on the eighth day, being eminent for virtue, bears that name of joy, being called Isaac in the Chaldaic tongue, and Isaac means laughter; being naturally called so because nature rejoices or laughs at everything, being never vexed at any thing which is done in the world, but rather looking with complacency on every thing which occurs as being done well and profitably.

(39) Why when he was ninety and nine years old does the sacred writer say, "The Lord God appeared to him and said, I am the Lord thy God?" (Genesis 17:1).

He here makes use of both the titles of each superior virtue, applying them in the case of his address to the wise man, because it was by them that all things were created, and by them that the world is regulated after it had been created. By one of them therefore the wise man, just in the same manner as the world itself, was fashioned and made according to the likeness of God; and God is the name of creative virtue; and by the other of them that he was made according to the Lord, as falling under his authority and supreme power.

Therefore he designs here to show that the man who is conspicuous in virtue is both a citizen of the world, and also equal in dignity to the whole world, declaring that both the virtues of the world, the divine and the royal attributes, are in a singular manner appointed to and set over him as protectors. And it was with great correctness and propriety that this appearance took place when he was about ninety and nine years old, because that number is very near the hundred. And the number a hundred is composed of the number ten multiplied by itself, which the sacred historian calls the holy of holies.

Since the first court, the first ten, is simply called holy, and that is permitted to be entered by the sweepers of the temple; but the ten of tens, which he again enjoins the sweepers of the temple to pay above all things to the existing high priest, is the number ten computed along with the number a hundred, for what else is the tenth of the tenths but the hundredth?

However the number ninety and nine has been set forth and adorned not only by its affinity to the number a hundred, but it has also received a particular participation in a wonderful nature, since it consists of the number fifty, and of seven times seven. For the fiftieth year, as the year of Pentecost or the Jubilee, is called remission in the giving forth of the law, as then all things are given their liberty, whether living or inanimate.

And the mystery of the seventh year is one of quiet and profound peace to both body and soul. For the seventh is the recollection of all the good things which come of their own accord without industry or labour, which at the first creation of the world nature produced of herself; but the number forty-nine, consisting as it does of seven times seven, indicates no trifling blessings, but rather those which have virtue and wisdom, in such a degree as to contribute to invincible and mighty constancy.

(40) What is the meaning of, "Do thou please me, and keep thyself from stain, and I will make my treaty between me and thee, and I will multiply thee exceedingly? (Genesis 17:1).

God here lays down a law for the human race in a somewhat familiar manner; for he who has no participation in wickedness and is free from evil, will be perfectly good, which is peculiar to incorporeal natures. But those who are in the body are called good in proportion to the measure in which wickedness and the practice of sin are removed from them. Therefore the life of those men has appeared honourable, not that of those who have been free from sickness from the beginning to the end, but that of those who from a state of infirmity have advanced to sanity; on which account he says directly and plainly, "Keep thyself free from stain," for it is sufficient to conduct a mortal nature to felicity not to be blamed, and neither to do nor say anything deserving of reproof; and such conduct is at once pleasing to the Father.

Therefore it is that he said, "Do thou please me, and keep thyself free from stain." Where the form of expression implies a mutual conversion; since the habits which please God do not deserve reproof, and he who keeps himself free from stain and avoids reproof in all things is altogether pleasing to God. Therefore he promises to bestow a double blessing on him who keeps himself free

from all reproof; in the first place, to make him the guardian of the deposits of the divine covenant: and in the second place to cause him to increase to a multitude without any limit.

For that expression, "I will make my treaty, or covenant, between me and thee," shows the office of guardianship of the truth which is entrusted to an honest man; for the whole treaty of God is the incorporeal word; which is the form and measure of the universe according to which this world was made. And then repeating the expression, "I will multiply thee exceedingly," twice manifestly shows the immense numbers to which the multitude promised shall grow, I mean the increase which shall take place in the people, not in human virtue.

(41) What is the meaning of, "Abraham fell on his face?" (Genesis 17:3).

The present expression is the interpretation of what has already been promised; for God had said, "Keep thyself free from stain," but there is not other cause of a man leading a life which is disapproved but the outward sense, because that is the origin and source of the passions; on which account he rightly and properly falls on his face, that is to say, the offences caused by the outward senses fall to the bottom, showing that the man is now devoted to all good works.

This is enough to say in the first place, But in the second place we must say that he was so struck by the manifest appearance of the living God that he was scarcely able to behold him through fear, but fell to the ground and offered adoration, being overwhelmed with awe at the appearance which presented itself to him.

In the third place, he fell to the ground on account of the revelation thus made to him, at the form of his appearance by the living God who exists alone, whom he knew and regarded as truth opposed to created nature; since the one exists in unvarying constancy and the other vacillates and falls into its proper place, that is to say, to the earth.

(42) What is the meaning of, "And God conversed with him, saying, And I, behold, my covenant is with thee, and thou shalt be the father of a multitude of nations?" (Genesis 17:4).

Since he had previously used the expression, "treaty," he now proceeds to say, do not seek that treaty in letters, since I myself, in accordance with what has been said before, am myself the genuine and true covenant.

For after he has shown himself and said, "I," he makes an addition, saying, "Behold, my covenant," which is nothing but I myself; for I am myself my covenant, according to which my treaty and agreement are made and agreed to, and according to which again all things are properly distributed and arranged. Now the form of this prototypal treaty is put together from the ideas and incorporeal measures and forms in accordance with which this world was made. Is it not therefore a climax to the benefits which the Father bestowed on the wise man, to raise him up and conduct him not only from earth to heaven, nor only from heaven to the incorporeal world appreciable only by the intellect, but also to draw him up from this world to himself, showing himself to him, not as he is in himself, for that is not possible but as far as the visual organs of the beholder who beholds virtue herself as appreciable by the intellect are able to attain to.

And it is on this account that he says, "Be no more a son but a father; and the father, not of one individual but of a multitude; and of a multitude, not according to a part, but of all nations;" therefore of the revealed promises two admit of a literal interpretation, but the third of one which is rather spiritual. One of those which admit of a literal interpretation is to be construed in this way: in truth thou shalt be the father of nations, and shalt beget nations, that is to say, each individual among thy sons shall be the founder of a nation.

But the second is of this kind; like a father you shall be clothed with power over, and authority to rule, many nations; for a lover of God is necessarily and at once also a lover of men; so that he will diligently devote his attention, not only to his relations but also to all mankind, and especially to those who are able to go through the discipline of strict attention, and who are of a disposition the reverse of anything cruel or hard, but of one which easily submits to virtue, and willingly gives obedience to right reason.

But the third we may explain under this allegory: the multitude of nations spoken of indicates as it were the multifarious inclination of the will in each of our minds, both those inclinations which it is accustomed to form with reference to itself, and also those others which it admits by the agency of the senses, as they enter clandestinely through the intervention of the imagination, and if the mind possesses the supreme authority over all these, it, like a common father, turns them to better objects, cherishing their infant opinions, as it were, with milk, exhorting those which are older and more mature, though still imperfect, to improvement, and honouring with commendation those which perform their duty aright; and again, putting a bridle, by means of discipline and reproof, on those which rebel and act rashly; since, wishing to imitate the Deity, it receives a twofold influx from the virtues of that same being, one from his beneficent attributes and another from his avenging might, as if from two sources; therefore the docile receive his kindness, and towards the rebellious he uses reproof; so that some are led to improvement by praise and others by chastisement: in truth, he who is eminent for virtue is able to be of great, and extensive, and just service to all, according to his power.

(43) What is the meaning of, "Thy name shall not be called Abram, but Abraham shall thy name be?" (Genesis 17:5).

Some of those who are destitute of all knowledge of music and dancing, some indeed being wholly foolish and keeping aloof from the divine company, mock the one existing or only wise Being, immaculate by nature, saying, in a tone of vituperation, "Oh the great gift, the governor and Lord of the whole universe has given one letter, by which the name of the patriarch was to be increased and become of great importance, so as to be made a trisyllable instead of a dissyllable!" Oh the great misery, and wickedness, and impiety, of such men! If some persons dare, in any respect, to endeavour to detract from God, being deceived by the outward appearance of a name, when they ought rather to thrust their minds down into the depths, and inquire into the things themselves more closely, on account of the real magnitude and importance of the possession.

Besides this, why do ye not think the concession of one letter, although a small and easy gift, nevertheless an act of providence? and why do ye not weigh its value? since, above all things, the very first element of language, as expressed in letters, is A, both in order and in virtue. In the second place, it is also a vowel, and the very first of vowels, being placed above them as their head. In the third place, because it does not belong to long properties, nor to short properties, but it is of the number of those which comprise each characteristic, for it is extended into greater length, and then again it is recalled into shortness, by reason of its softness, resembling wax, and being figured into many shapes, and afterwards figuring words, according to infinite numbers; besides all this it is a cause, for it is the brother of unity, from which all things begin and in which all things terminate.

Therefore, when any one sees such great beauty, and a letter set forth with such great importance and necessity, how can he accuse it as if he had not seen this? for if he has seen it, he then shows himself to be a person of insulting disposition and a hater of what is good; and if he has not seen a fact, which is so easy to comprehend, how does he presume to ridicule and despise that which he does not understand as if he did understand it? But however these things may be said by the way, as I stated before. But we must now examine into its necessary and most important task.

The addition of the letter A, by one single element, changed and reformed the whole character of the mind, causing it, instead of the sublime knowledge and learning of sublime things, that is to say, instead of astronomy, to acquire a comprehension of wisdom, since it is by the knowledge of things above that the faculty is acquired of mounting up to one portion of the world, that is to say, to heaven, and to the periodical revolutions and motions of the stars; but wisdom has reference to the nature of all things, both such as are visible to the outward senses, and such as are appreciable only by the intellect, for the intellect is the wisdom which gives a knowledge of divine and human things and of their principles.

Therefore, in divine things there is something which is visible, and something else which is invisible, and a demonstrative idea. And in human affairs there are some things which are corporeal and some which are incorporeal; to attain to the right comprehension of which is a great task, and a real employment for the abilities and courage of man. But to be able, not only to behold the substances and natures of the universe, but also the principles which regulate each separate fact, indicates a virtue more perfect than that which is allotted to mankind; for it is necessary for the mind, which perceives so many and such great things, to be altogether and wholly eye, and to dispense with sleep, passing its whole existence in the world in a state of incessant wakefulness, and being surrounded by a light which knows no darkness, and which exhibits the appearance of light itself, as by an ever-flashing lightning, taking God for its leader and guide, to the comprehension of the knowledge of those things which are, and to the faculty of explaining their principles.

Therefore the dissyllabic name Abram is explained as meaning "excellent father," on account of his affinity to the knowledge of sublime wisdom, that is, astronomy and mathematics. But the trisyllabic name Abraham is interpreted "the father of elect sound," being the name of a really wise man; for what else is sound in us, except the utterance of a pronounced word? for which object we have an instrument constructed by nature, passing through the thick tube of the throat, and united with the mouth and tongue; and the father of such a sound is our intellect, and elect intellect is endued with virtue.

But if we are to keep to exact propriety, then it is plain that the mind is the familiar and natural father of the uttered word, because it is the especial property of the father to beget, and the word is born from the mind; and it will be a certain proof of this if we recollect that when it is set in motion by counsels it sounds, and when they are absent it ceases to sound: and the evidences of this are the rhetoricians and philosophers who demonstrate its habit by objects; for whenever the mind publishes abroad different heads of designs, and in the manner of a mother about to bring forth produces each individual means previously stored up in itself, then also the word, flowing forth like a fountain,

is borne to the ears of the bystander as to its appropriate receptacles: but when those are wanting, then it also is unable to publish itself further, and rests, and the sound is inactive as being struck by no one.

Now therefore, O ye men, full and crammed with superfluous loquacity, ye men devoid of wisdom, does not the gift of one single element appear to you to have been such that by the intervention of a single letter the wise man is rendered worthy of the divine attribute of wisdom, than which there is nothing more excellent in our nature? because instead of the sublime erudition of astronomy he gave him intellect, that is to say, instead of a small part of wisdom, he gave him the whole and perfect blessing of entire wisdom, since a knowledge of things above is included and comprehended in wisdom, as a part is included in the whole; for mathematics are only a part.

But it becomes you, O men, to consider this point also, that the man who is well instructed and skilful in the investigation of the nature of things above may by possibility be a man of depraved and wicked habits; but the wise man is altogether approved as virtuous. Shall we then now any longer ridicule this gift, than which nothing more excellent can be found? For what is more shameful than wickedness or more excellent than virtue? Can anything be found here not good, and is it not wholly opposed to evil? Or can this gift be compared to riches, or honour, or liberty, or health, or to any other superfluous possession of any kind around or exterior to the body?

For the whole of philosophy is thus added to our life as a sort of college of medicine to the soul, in order from thence to dispense to it freedom from suffering and immunity from disease; but in truth it is noble to be a philosopher, and that wonderful knowledge is truly noble; and the end is even more admirable, on account of which the act is called into existence.

Here therefore is wisdom, and that the best kind of wisdom, which God called in the Chaldaic dialect Abraham, namely the father of elect sound, giving as it were a definition of a wise man; for as the definition of man is a mortal animal endowed with reason, so also the mysterious definition of a wise man is the father of elect sound.

(44) What is the meaning of, "I will greatly increase thee, and set thee among the nations, and kings shall proceed from thee?" (Genesis 17:6).

That expression, "I will greatly increase thee," was used to the wise man with exceeding propriety; since every wicked or bad man does increase and advance, not to improvement but towards deficiency; as withering flowers advance not towards life but towards death; but the man whose life is extended long and is greatly increased is like a passing cloud, or like the continually flowing stream of a river, because as it increases it is extended more and more out of doors, as its wisdom also is divine.

And that expression, "I will set thee among the nations," was used in order that God might the more evidently demonstrate that he was making him worthy to be as a foundation and firm support to the nations through his wisdom, not only to his own nation, but also to all other peoples who in various manners are in want in respect of their minds, as has been said before; since the wise man is the redeemer of nations and intercessor for them before God, and since it is he who implores pardon for the sins of his relations.

Last of all, the promise, "Kings shall come forth from thee," is again used with especial propriety; for everything which relates to wisdom is a royal seed; the offspring of the chief and master according to nature: but the wise man has no seed or fruit of his own, but is fertile and abundant in the seed which proceeds from the great cause himself.

(45) What is the meaning of, "I will give this land to thee and to thy seed after thee, in which thou hast sojourned, namely all the land of Canaan, for an everlasting possession?" (Genesis 17:8).

The letter of the promise is so clear that the language does not stand in need of any explanation whatever; but with respect to the inward meaning of it we must have recourse to an allegory of this kind.

The mind which is endowed with virtue is rather a sojourner in the corporeal space allotted to it, than a regular inhabitant of it; for its real country is the air and the heaven; and the earth, and the earthly body in which it is said to sojourn, is only a colony; therefore the Father, conferring a benefit upon it, gives to it the sovereign authority over all the things of the earth for ever and ever, as he says himself, for an everlasting possession; so that it for the future shall not be governed by the body, but shall always be its master and ruler, having the body for its servant and attendant.

(46) What is the meaning of, "And every male of you shall be circumcised, and you shall circumcise, or you shall be circumcised, in, the flesh of your foreskin?" (Genesis 17:10).

I see here a twofold circumcision, one of the male creature, and the other of the flesh; that which is of the flesh takes place in the genitals, but that which is of the male creature takes place, as it seems to me, in respect of his thoughts.

Since that which is, properly speaking, masculine in us is the intellect, the superfluous shoots of which it is necessary to prune away and to cast off, so that it, becoming clean and pure from all wickedness and vile, may worship God as his priest.

This therefore is what is designated by the second circumcision, where God says by an express law, "Circumcise the hardness of your hearts," that is to say, your hard and rebellious thoughts and ambition, which when they are cut away and removed from you, your most important part will be rendered free.

(47) Why orders he the males only to be circumcised? (Genesis 17:11).

For in the first place, the Egyptians, in accordance with the national customs of their country, in the fourteenth year of their age, when the male begins to have the power of propagating his species, and when the female arrives at the age of puberty, circumcise both bride and bridegroom.

But the divine legislator appoints circumcision to take place in the case of the male alone for many reasons: the first of which is, that the male creature feels venereal pleasures and desires matrimonial connexions more than the female, on which account the female is properly omitted here, while he checks the superfluous impetuosity of the male by the sign of circumcision.

But the second reason is, that the material of the female is supplied to the son from what remains over of the eruption of blood, while the immediate maker and cause of the son is the male. Because therefore the male supplies the most indispensable part in the fact of generation, God deservedly represses his pride by the figure of circumcision, but the material or feminine cause, as being inactive, does not display ambition in the same degree. And this is enough to say on this head.

But afterwards we must note this likewise, that the intellect in us is endued with the power of sight, therefore it is necessary to cut away its superfluous shoots. And these superfluous shoots are empty opinions, and all the actions which are done in accordance with them. So that the intellect after circumcision may only bear about with itself what is necessary and useful; and that whatever causes pride to increase may be cut away; with which also the eyes are circumcised as if they did not see.

(48) Why did he say, "And let the child, every male child, be circumcised at eight days old?" (Genesis 17:12).

He orders the freeborn to be circumcised, which, in the first place, was permitted on account of diseases that might arise; for it is more difficult to heal a disease in the genitals, and it is commonly done by burning by fire those parts over which a membrane grows, but this rarely affects those who have been circumcised.

And in truth, if it were possible that other infirmities also could be avoided by amputating any member or any part of the body, so that though it was amputated still the operation of each necessary part would not be hindered, then without the knowledge of mortal man he would be transmitted into immortality.

But that here it was thought fit that man should be circumcised out of a provident care for his mind without any previous infirmity is plain, since not the Jews alone, but also the Egyptians, and Arabians, and Ethiopians, and nearly all the nations who live in the southern parts of the world, down to the torrid zone are circumcised.

What then is the chief reason of this fact? except that in those districts, and especially in the summer, when the genitals are protected with a skin, it burns and is injured by inflammation, but when that covering is laid bare by circumcision it is cooled, and the disease is repelled; and on this account the northern nations and others, to whom the cooler portion of the habitable earth has been allotted, are not circumcised, for not only is the solar heat moderate in those regions, but so is also all inflammatory disease which affects the membranes of the members. Let every one take a firm judgment, and from that time when the disease comes in more vigorously; for it never comes at all in the winter, but in the summer it shows itself and flourishes and ripens; for it loves, if I may so say, like fire to burn in those parts.

In the second place, it was not only from a regard to sound health that our ancestors diligently employed this method of cure, but also from a regard to the multiplication of the human race, seeing that nature was very vivacious and too eager to propagate the human species.

Therefore they knew, like wise men, how the seed when poured over the folds of the membrane is often accustomed to be wasted and so to become unfruitful; but if no impediment arises then it would easily be able to arrive at the situation suited to receive it. On which account also those nations which adopt the practice of circumcision have grown into an exceedingly numerous population: and our legislator, weighing the consequences also, commanded the circumcision of infants to be performed at an earlier age, keeping in view the same effect of circumcision with regard to the population.

Therefore it is in truth, as it seems to me, that the Egyptians also in the fourteenth year of their children's age, in which the desire to propagate the species usually begins, have said that it is suitable to circumcise them, with the view of increasing the population; but it was better and more carefully done in our nation, where the circumcision of infants was ordained, since perhaps the man when grown up would delay the operation out of fear, because he then has a will of his own.

In the third place, he says this with a view to cleanliness in the sacred oblations; for in truth those who enter into the courts of the temples are made clean by sprinkling and ablutions. Moreover the Egyptians scrape the whole body, removing all the hairs which cover and envelop the body, so as to appear white all over; but the circumcision of the skin is no small assistance towards cleanliness, otherwise everyone would abhor it when he beheld it as it is in itself.

In the fourth place, there are in us two generative principles, one in the soul and one in the body; the generative principle of the soul is the intellect, and that of the body is the corporeal organ; therefore the ancients chose to refer the generative principle of the body to an imitation of the intellect which is rather the generative principle of the heart. And in truth there is nothing to which it is found more like than the circumcision of the heart; these therefore are real facts like the celebrated reasons for things which have been investigated. But we must now speak of those which have greater symbols belonging to them and which exhibit a certain principle.

Therefore the circumcision of the skin is said to be a symbol, but as one indicating that it is proper to cut away all superfluous and extravagant desires, by studying continence and religion; for as the skin of the prepuce is quite superfluous for generation, and is moreover especially injurious by reason of the disease of inflammation which burns within it, so also an over abundance of desire is as superfluous as it is pernicious, superfluous because it is not necessary, and pernicious because it is the cause of diseases to both body and soul; and by the greater desire he also warns us that all the other desires are likewise to be cut off. And that is called the greater desire which has a regard to the matrimonial connexion of the male and the female; since it is the beginning of a great thing, namely, of generation; and since it creates a great affection on the part of the father towards her who is to bring forth; for it is natural for them both to be influenced by love and affection for their offspring. Therefore, he here warns us to cut away not only all the superfluous desires, but also pride, as being a great wickedness and an associate of wickedness.

For pride, as the language of the ancients tells us, is what keeps men back and hinders them in their improvement; since it will not exhibit that honesty which it really possesses, thinking that it is itself an adequate cause for anything. Moreover it naturally influences those who think themselves the causes of generation; so that they scarcely ever turn their minds at all to behold the true Father of the universe. For he is in truth the one real and genuine Father of all; and we, who are called fathers, are only instruments of his, serving to generation; since, as in a wonderful resemblance, all things which are represented in appearance are yet in reality inanimate, but that which strengthens the nerves is invisible, and yet is itself the cause of virtue, and of motion, and of sight. So, in like manner, from everlasting and invisible space there extends the Creator of the universe, and we, like so many puppets, are strengthened by him with nerves for the purpose which belongs to us, namely, sowing seed and raising a generation; unless we choose to fancy that a flute is blown by itself, and is not made by an artist in a way adapted for the production of harmony, by whom it was constructed as an instrument for service and for its own necessary end.

(49) Why does he order circumcision to be performed on the eighth day? (Genesis 17:12).

The number eight has many beauties in it; for it is, in the first place, a cubic number. Secondly, it has beauties, because it everywhere contains in itself the form of equality, because longitude, and breadth, and depth, which are all equal to one another, are indicated by the first number eight.

In the third place, the composition of the number eight produces agreement, namely, the number thirty-six, which the Pythagoreans call agreement, since that is the first number in which odd numbers being added together agree with even numbers. If, indeed, four odd numbers from the unit are separately taken and added together and four even numbers beginning with two, they united make thirty-six. Now the odd numbers are these: one, three, five, seven, which make sixteen. And the even numbers are these: two, four, six, eight, which make twenty. And the addition of the two together makes thirty-six, which is in truth a more fertile number.

Since it is a square, having each side composed of the number six; the first of which is both odd and even; which some persons most correctly call harmony or matrimony; and it was by the employment of this number that the Creator of the universe made the world, as the holy and admirable book of Moses relates.

In the fourth place, the idea of eight produces sixty-four, which is the first number, which is a cube and also a square, being the type of incorporeal substance appreciable only by the intellect and invisible, and also of corporeal substance. Of incorporeal substance, inasmuch as it produces superficies according to the square; and of corporeal substance, as producing a solid according to the cube.

In the fifth place, it is always a kindred number to the virgin number seven, for seven makes up the parts of eight; because four is the half of it, two is the fourth part of it, one the eighth of it, and four, two, and one, added together, make seven.

In the sixth place, the power of eight is sixty-four, which we call the first number, being both a cube and a square.

In the seventh place, taken separately from the units by these doubled numbers, one, two, four, eight, sixteen, thirty-two, the sum makes sixty-four.

And the number eight has also other more distinguished virtues still, which we have enumerated in another place; but now it seems better to explain the principle which corresponds to the present question, and which depends on the grounds now laid down.

But in the first place we must premise this: that nation to whom it is enjoined, having the commandments give to it, that it should be circumcised on the eighth day, is called in the Chaldaic language Israel, that is to say, "he that seeth by day." Therefore God wills, in the first place, that he should be a partaker both of his own just rights, and also of those which exist according to election, and according to the principle of Genesis (or creation), by that first number six, which immediately followed the creation. This number, in fact, the Father and Creator of all things evidently exhibited to the world as the festival of generation, completing the world on the sixth day. And the other number, that which is according to election, he exhibited by the number eight, which is the beginning of the second seven; as eight is seven and one, so the race which has been honoured is always a race receiving that number also in addition, so that it should be elect, both by nature and in accordance with the decree of the Father.

In the second place, the number eight exhibits equality everywhere, showing that all its separations are equal, as has been already said, I mean its length, and breadth, and depth. And equality it is which is the parent of equity and justice, by which he shows that the nation which loves God is adorned with equity or justice, and has advanced to complete possession.

In the third place, eight is not only a measure of complete equity in all its dimensions, but is the very first number that is so, for it is the first cube; since the number eight indicates equality, and so it has the second and not the first rank: therefore it demonstrates in a symbolical manner that that nature was the first which was ever completely furnished with consummate and perfect equity and justice, and that it is the first nature of the human race, not in point of creation or of time, but in the dignity of virtue, as if justice united with equality were a connatural part of it.

In the fourth place, since there are four elements, the appearances of earth, water, air, and fire; fire has received for its figure a shape becoming a similar name, a pyramid;[4] and air has received for its figure an eight-sided one; water, a twenty-sided one; and the earth, a cube. Therefore he thought it necessary that the earth, which was to be the allotment of the race of man, who were endowed with virtue, should participate in

---

[4] *pyramis*, resembling the word *pyr*, "fire."

the cubic number, as the whole earth has been formed in its figure. And a part of it receives the parts of that which should bring forth, because by nature the earth is very fertile, producing all the various and distinct species of every kind of animal and plant.

(50) Why does he order all slaves to be circumcised, those born in the family and also those who are bought? (Genesis 17:12).

The literal meaning is plain; for it is fitting that servants should imitate their masters on account of their necessary employment, and the services to which they are bound in life. But with respect to the inner object of the command, those dispositions are what may be called born in the family which are influenced by nature itself, and those are bought which can be changed for the better by teaching and instruction. Each of these has its appropriate employment, and requires like a plant to be cleared and pruned in order that the good and fruitful parts may acquire constancy; for fertile plants produce many superfluous things by reason of their fecundity, and those superfluities must be cut away; but those who are taught by instructors cut away their ignorance.

(51) What is the meaning of, "And it shall be my covenant (or agreement) in your flesh?" (Genesis 17:13).

God is willing to do good, not only to the man who is endued with virtue, but he wishes that the divine word should regulate not only his soul but his body also, as if it had become its physician. And it must be its care to prune away all excesses of seeing, and hearing, and taste, and smell, and touch, and also those of the instrument of voice and articulation, and also all the redundant and pernicious impulses of the genitals, as also of the whole body, the effect of which is, that at times we are delighted by our passions and at times pained by them.

(52) Why is it that he pronounces a sentence of death on an infant, saying, "Every male child who is not circumcised, who has not been circumcised (or, as the Greek has it, who shall not be circumcised) in the flesh of his foreskin on the eighth day, that soul shall be cut off from his generation?" (Genesis 17:14).

The law never declares a man guilty for any unintentional offence; since even those who have committed an unintentional homicide are pardoned by it, cities being set apart into which such men may flee and there find security; for whoever escapes to them is rendered secure and free from danger; and no one has the power to drag him forth, or to cite him before the tribunal of the judge for the deed.

Therefore, if a boy is not circumcised on the eighth day after his birth, what offence will he have

committed that he is to be held guilty, and suffer the penalty of death?

Some persons may perhaps say that the form of the command points to the parents themselves, for they look upon them as despisers of the command of the law. But others say that it has here exerted excessive severity against infants, as it seems, imposing this heavy penalty in order that grown up persons who break the law may thus be irrevocably subjected to most severe punishment. This is the literal effect of the words.

But if we look to their inward meaning, then what is male in us is most especially the intellect, and that God here commands to be circumcised on the eighth day, for the reason previously stated, not in any other part, but in the flesh of the foreskin, by this expression symbolically indicating those parts which in the flesh do subsequently become the organs of pleasure and impulse. And on this account it is that he introduces a legitimate reason, warning men that the intellect, which is not circumcised and cleared away from the flesh and the vices of the flesh, is corrupt and cannot be saved.

But that this language is not to be applied to the man, but to the intellect, which is thus put in a sound condition, he tells us in the subsequent words, saying, "that soul shall be cut off," not that human body, or that man, but that soul and mind. Cut off from what? From its generation; for the whole generation is incorrupt. Therefore the wicked man is removed from incorruption to corruption.

(53) Why does God say, "Sara thy wife shall not be called Sara, but Sarra shall be her name?" (Genesis 17:15).

Here again some foolish persons may laugh at the addition of one single letter, that is to say, of a hundred, for in Greek characters the letter r means a hundred; but if they jest in this way they are foolish, as being unwilling to behold the inward merits of things and to cleave to the footsteps of truth; for that element, r, which is here thought of merely as the addition of one letter, is the parent of all harmony, making things great instead of small, general instead of particular, and mortal instead of immortal; since Sara, when called Sara with one r, is interpreted "thy princedom," but with two r's, Sarra, "princess." Let us then be careful, and see how these two names are distinguished from one another. In me wisdom (or prudence), integrity (or temperance), justice, and fortitude have only a prince-like power and are mortal; moreover, when I die they die too.

But this wisdom is herself a princess, and justice is a prince too, and each separate one of these virtues is not the principal or princely part in me, but is itself a mistress and a queen, an everlasting monarchy and sovereignty. Do you not now see the magnitude of the gift? By this slight change, God changes the part into the whole, the species into the genus, the corruptible into the incorruptible. And all these things are previously dispensed on account of the impending birth of a more perfect joy than all joys, whose name is Isaac.

(54) Why does he say, "And from her I will give thee children, and I will bless him, and he shall be over the nations, and kings of the nations shall come forth from him?" (Genesis 17:16).

It is scarcely proper to inquire why he has said children in the plural number, when he meant their only and beloved son; for the intention of God's words applies to his offspring, from which nations and kings should arise.

This is the literal meaning of the words. But if we look to their more inward sense, when the soul possesses that virtue, small and mortal as it is, which is only particular, she is still barren. But from the time that it acquires a share of the divine and incorruptible virtue, it begins to conceive and to bring forth varieties of nations, namely, of all other holy and sacred persons; for every one of the everlasting virtues is subject to an immense number of voluntary laws, which bear in themselves a similarity to nations and kingdoms; for virtue and the generations of virtue are royal things, being previously instructed by nature what it is which rejoices in princely power, and has no knowledge of a servile condition.

(55) Why did Abraham fall on his face and laugh? (Genesis 17:17).

Two things are indicated by his falling on his face. One an act of adoration on account of the excess of his divine ecstacy; the other that it corresponds to and is suitable to the aforesaid harmony, by which the intellect has confessed that God alone exists in a continual and unvarying existence. But those creatures which owe their existence to creation and generation, all are subject to changes in time; for they fall to a certain extent, inasmuch as they are accustomed to rise up, and to be corrected in accordance with their original appearance.

And it was very natural for Abraham to laugh at the promise, as he was then filled with the great hope that the things which he expected should be accomplished, especially because he had received a manifest revelation from that appearance, by which he became more thoroughly acquainted with him who exists for everlasting without variation, and with him also who is continually stooping and falling.

(56) Why did Abraham appear to hesitate about the promise, for the sacred writer says, He said in his mind, shall there be a son to one who is a hundred years old; and shall Sarra, who is ninety years old, bring forth a child? (Genesis 22:18).

This expression, "he said in his mind," is not added without an object or gratuitously, for words which are articulated in the tongue and the mouth incur guilt, and become liable to punishment, but those which are restrained within the mind are not liable to punishment, because the mind without any intention on its part is led away by irregularities, all kinds of passions being introduced from different quarters, which it for a while resists, being indignant at them, and wishing to keep aloof from their representations.

But perhaps we should not say that he hesitated, but rather that he was struck by wonderment at the amazing nature of the gift, and so said, "Behold my body is advanced in years, and has passed the age of generation; nevertheless all things are possible to God, so that he may transmute old age into youth, and lead those who have no seed nor fruit to fertility and generation: and if a man who is a hundred years and a woman who is ninety years old become parents, all common- place occurrences and all regularity of nature will be done away, and it will be clearly seen that it is only the power and the grace of God."

But what virtue the number one hundred has must now be explained.

In the first place, a hundred is the power of the number ten.

In the second place, the number ten thousand is the power of this number a hundred, and ten thousand is the brother of the unit, for as one times one is one, so ten thousand times one is ten thousand.

In the third place, every part of the number a hundred is honourable.

In the fourth place, this number consists of thirty-six and sixty-four, which is a cube, and at the same time a triangle.

In the fifth place, it is composed of all these separate odd numbers: one, three, five, seven, nine, eleven, thirteen, fifteen, seventeen, nineteen, which added together make a hundred.

In the sixth place, it is composed of these four numbers: one and its double, and four and its double; as one, two, four, eight, which make fifteen, and of these four numbers also added together, one, four, fifteen, sixty-four, which make eighty-five. And the principle of doubling pervades all these numbers, containing that principle which is by fours and by fives: and the principle of four times and twice pervades them all.

In the seventh place, it is composed of five numbers taken simply, one, two, three, four, which make ten; and of five triangular numbers, one, three, six ten, which make twenty; and of five quadrangular numbers, one, four, nine, sixteen, which make thirty; and of five quinquangular numbers, one, five, twelve, twenty-two, which make forty: and all these added together make a hundred.

In the eighth place, it is composed of four cubes taken simply beginning with the unit, for after giving one, two, three, four, their cubes one, eight, twenty-seven, sixty-four, make a hundred.

In the ninth place, it is divided into forty and sixty, each of which is a very natural number; and in accordance with the first order of decimals up to ten thousand in a quinquangular figure the number a hundred holds the middle place; for instance: one, ten, a hundred, one thousand, ten thousand, where a hundred is the middle number of one, ten, a hundred, one thousand, and ten thousand.

But we ought also not to pass over in silence the number ninety as far as it concerns the visible characters.

As it seems to me the number ninety is second only to the number a hundred, inasmuch as the tenth part of it, that is to say ten, is taken away, since I see that in the law two-tenths of the first-fruits were set apart, first a tenth of the whole, secondly a tenth of the remainder, for when a tenth of the fruits of the earth, of corn, or wine, or oil, is taken, another tenth is also taken from the remainder; therefore of these two that which is the first and principal one is honoured with the greater share; and in the second place that which follows it, since the number a hundred of the years of the wise man comprises both the first-fruits with which it is consecrated, both the first and the second kind; but the number ninety of the years of the female parent, comprehends the second and lesser first-fruits, namely, the remainder of the first, which is the great one among the sacred numbers.

This therefore may be called the first vision in the sacred law which is familiar; and the other has a general character, for the number ninety is fertile; on which account also it happens that the woman begins to bring forth in the ninth month; but the tenth is the sacred and perfect number; and when the two numbers nine and ten are multiplied together ninety is made, as being the virtue of the sacred birth, receiving a fertile generation according to the number nine, and a holy one according to ten.

(57) Why did Abraham say to God, O may this my son Ishmael live before thee? (Genesis 17:18).

In the first place, I do not despair, says he, O Lord, of a better generation, but I believe thy promise: nevertheless, it would be a sufficient blessing for me for this son to live who in the meantime is a living son, standing visibly, even though he be not so according to the legitimate blood, but is only born of a concubine.

In the second place, that blessing which he is now asking for is an additional one; for he does not entreat for life alone for his sons, but for an especial life in God; and we must suppose that there is nothing more perfect than the rejoicing in the presence of God with a salutary soundness of mind, which is equal to immortality.

In the third place, he by a conjecture intimates that the divine law, when heard, ought not to be considered enough if merely heard, but that it ought also to enter more deeply into the inward man, and to form his principal part; for that life is worthy of being beheld by the Deity which is formed in accordance with his word.

(58) Why does the divine oracle, in the way of intimation, say to Abraham, Yes, be it so: behold Sarah thy wife shall also bring forth a son unto thee? (Genesis 17:19).

The meaning of this sentence is as follows: that confession and admission, says God, is on my part an admission of thy wish, being manifestly full of unadulterated joy; and your faith is not doubtful, but without any hesitation it has a share of modest awe and reverence; therefore that which thou hast received before, as to be done unto thee on account of thy faith in me, shall certainly be done; for this is what is meant by yes.

(59) Why does he say, But behold I will also listen to thee concerning Ishmael, and I will bless him, and he shall become the father of twelve nations? (Genesis 17:20).

God says, I will grant to thee both the first and the second blessing, that is to say, both the blessings of nature and the blessings of instruction; by nature that which is according to the legitimate course of nature, that is Isaac, and by instruction that which is according to Ishmael, who is not legitimate: for hearing, when compared with sight, is like the illegitimate compared with the legitimate, and what is brought about by instruction is not of the same class with that which owes its existence to nature; and the man who is desirous of encyclical wisdom becomes the father of nations, for the encyclical number is a period of twelve days and years.

(60) Why does he say, But I will set up my covenant with Isaac, whom Sarah shall bring forth about this time in the succeeding year? (Genesis 17:21).

As in men's wills some persons are set down as heirs, and some are entered as worthy of gifts which they are to receive from the heirs, so also in the divine testament that man is set down as the heir who is by nature a worthy disciple of God being adorned with all perfect virtues; but he who is introduced by learning, and is made subject to the law of wisdom, and partakes in encyclical instruction, is not at all an heir, but only a receiver of gifts gratuitously given.

But it is said with great wisdom and propriety that his mother shall bring forth Isaac in the succeeding year, since this birth unto life does not belong to the present time, but to another great and holy time; and that which is divine rejoices in excessive abundance, and is by no means like the nations of this world.

(61) Why does he say, Abraham was ninety and nine years old when he was circumcised, and Ishmael his son was thirteen years old? (Genesis 17:24).

The number of ninety and nine years is arranged here as approximating to the number a hundred. And it is in accordance with this number that it is arranged that the seed of the perfect man becomes the beginning of generation, which appears more evidently in the number a hundred; but the number thirteen is composed of the first square numbers of four and nine, the odd and even numbers; so that the even number has for its sides a twofold material form; and the odd number has an operative form, from all which a triple number is made, which is the greatest and most perfect of the festival victims which the examinations of the sacred scriptures contain.

This is one reason. A second also it may be allowed to us to mention, that the age namely of thirteen years is very near to and a partaker with the fourteenth year, in which the motions of seed towards generation begin to have life. In order, therefore, that no foreign seed should be sown, he arranged that the first generations should be kept pure, figuring the instrument of generating under the figure of generation.

In the third place, he teaches that he who is about to go through the operations of matrimony ought by all means first of all to cut away concupiscence, reproving all lascivious and effeminate persons as those who bring together superfluous mixtures which were not for the sake of the generation of children but to gratify incontinent desires.

(62) Why did Abraham also circumcise strangers? (Genesis 17:27).

The wise man is as useful as the humane man, who saves and invites to himself not only his relations and neighbours, but also strangers and men of another family, giving them a share of his own habit of patient and religious continence; for these are the foundations of constancy, which is the object of all virtue, and the point at which it rests.

APPENDICES

A TREATISE CONCERNING THE WORLD†

I. There is no existing thing equal in honour to God, but he is the one Ruler, and Governor, and King, to whom alone it is lawful to govern and regulate everything; for the verse—

"A multitude of masters is not good,
Let there one sovereign be, one king of all,"[1]

is not more appropriate to be said with respect to cities and men than to the world and God, for it follows inevitably that there must be one Creator and Master of one world; and this position having been laid down and conceded as a preliminary, it is only consistent with sense to connect with it what follows from it of necessity. Let us now, therefore, consider what inferences these are.

God being one being, has two supreme powers of the greatest importance. By means of these powers the incorporeal world, appreciable only by the intellect, was put together, which is the archetypal model of this world which is visible to us, being formed in such a manner as to be perceptible to our invisible conceptions just as the other is to our eyes. Therefore some persons, marvelling at the nature of both these worlds, have not only worshipped them in their entirety as gods, but have also deified the most beautiful parts of them, I mean for instance the sun, and the moon, and the whole heaven, which, without any fear or reverence, they called gods. And Moses, perceiving the ideas which they entertained, says, "O Lord, King of all gods,"[2] in order to point out the great superiority of the Ruler to his subjects.

And the original founder of the Jewish nation was a Chaldaean by birth, being the son of a father who was much devoted to the study of astronomy, and being among people who were great studiers of mathematical science, who think the stars, and the whole heaven, and the whole world gods; and they say that both good and evil result from their speculations and belief, since they do not believe in anything as a cause which is apart from those things which are visible to the outward senses.

But what can be worse than this, or more cal-culated to display the want of true nobility existing in the soul, than the notion of causes in general being secondary and created causes, combined with an ignorance of the one first cause, the uncreated God, the Creator of the universe, who for these and innumerable other reasons is most excellent, reasons which because of their magnitude human intellect is unable to apprehend? but this founder of the Jewish nation having conceived an idea of him in his mind, and looking upon him as the true God, forsook his native country and his family, and his father's house, knowing that if he remained, the deceits of the polytheistic doctrine also remaining in his soul would render his intellect incapable of discovering the nature of the one God, who is alone everlasting, and the father of everything else, whether appreciable only by the intellect or perceptible to the outward senses; but if he departed and emigrated, then he saw that deceit would also depart from his mind, which would then change its erroneous opinions into truth. And at the same time the oracular commands of God, which had been given to him, did further excite the desire which he felt to become acquainted with the living God. And he went forth like a man under the immediate guidance of others, with the most unhesitating promptness, to search after the knowledge of the one God; and he did not relax in his search till he had arrived at a more accurate and correct perception, not indeed of his essences (for that is impossible), but of his existence and of his providence; on which account he is the first man of whom it is said that he believed in God, since he was the first who had an accurate and positive notion of him, believing that there is one supreme cause of all things, which by his providence takes care of the world and of all things that are therein.

Since the Creator of the world bringing an essence previously without any order and in complete confusion, into distinct order and regularity, began to arrange and adorn the earth and the water, and established them in the middle of the world, and the trees, and air, and fire he drew up from the middle to the higher regions, and he fixed the regions of the aether all around, placing it as a boundary to and a preserver of the things which were inside, from which also it derived its name of heaven.[3] And these things, then, were the per-

---

†Yonge's edition includes this treatise not found in Cohn-Wendland (Loeb). In a note, Yonge asserts that it is virtually identical to the Loeb treatise, *On the Eternity of the World* (which Yonge titled, *On the Incorruptibility of the World*).

[1] Hom. II. 2.204.
[2] Deuteronomy 10:17.

[3] *Horos* is the Greek word for boundary, from which Philo thinks that *ouranos*, "heaven," is derived.

fect seeds of the whole universe, but the great and all productive tree raised from this seed is this world, of which the aforesaid branches are the offshoots.

II. Where, then, God placed the roots, and what foundation it has upon which it is so firmly fixed like a statue, we must now consider. It is not natural that any body which is left behind should wander out of its limits, since God has made and arranged in its proper place, the materials of the whole universe. For it was fitting that the greatest of all works, being also the most perfect, should be created by the greatest of all workmen. And it would not have been completely perfect if it had not been completed in perfect parts. So that if this world consists of every kind of material, nothing being beyond, and not even the most insignificant thing being omitted, it follows of necessity that whatever is outside the world must either be vacuum or nothing at all. If it be a vacuum, then how can it be found to balance the world, which is full and closely packed, and the heaviest of all things, when there is nothing solid to support it? from which consideration it would appear to resemble a vision. Since the mind is always looking for a corporeal basis, it is natural to suppose that one whole should have such a thing if it happens to be put in motion, and the world above all things, inasmuch as it is the greatest of bodies, and as it embraces in its bosom a multitude of other bodies as its own appropriate parts. Therefore, if any one wishes to escape the perplexities which arise in treating of doubtful matters, let him speak his mind freely, and affirm that there is no material so strong as to be able to support the weight of the world. But the eternal law of the everlasting God is the strong and lasting support of the universe. This law being extended from the centre of the world to its furthest extremities, and again back from its extremities to the centre, moves on in the unwearied irresistible course of nature, uniting and binding together all the parts of the universe. For the Father who established it made it to be the indissoluble bond of the universe.

Therefore we are naturally led to conclude that the whole earth will not be dissolved by water, which its bosoms contain; nor again will fire be extinguished by the air, nor again will the air be burnt up and consumed by fire, since the divine law has placed itself as a boundary to keep all these elements distinct from one another. As yet the all-productive plant was not rooted, and had not the power which was to be derived from being rooted. But of the subordinate, particular, and less important plants, some were moveable in such a way as easily to change their places, and some, without being liable to any change of places, were made as if they were to stand for ever in the same position. Those therefore which are exposed to a motion which involves a change of place, which we

call animals, were added to the most entire and perfect parts of the universe. The earth receiving the terrestrial animals, the water the aquatic animals; the air those creatures which fly; and the stars being assigned to the heaven.

III. But the Creator created two different kinds both in the earth, and in the water, and in the air. In the air he placed those animals which fly, and other powers also which cannot by any means, or on any occasion, be comprehended by the outward senses. Thus the company of incorporeal souls is arranged in regular order according to their nature. For it is said that some of them are separated off and assigned to mortal bodies, and that, at certain definite and predetermined periods, they again depart from them. But that others of a more divine nature are utterly regardless of any situation in earth, but are raised to a great height, and placed in the aether itself, being of the purest possible character, which those among the Greeks who have studied philosophy call heroes and daemones, and which Moses, giving them a most felicitous appellation, calls angels, acting as they do the part of ambassadors and messengers, announcing to the subjects all kinds of blessings from their rulers, and acting as servants to the king to whom they are subject; and they, descending into the body as into a river, at one time are carried away by the violence of a most irresistible current and swallowed up, and at other times, being wholly unable to resist the powers of destruction, at first, indeed, raise their heads above the flood, and afterwards sink down again to the place from whence they have started.

These, then, are the souls of those who devote themselves to the vigorous study of philosophy respecting divine subjects, from the beginning to the end of their existence studying things which may concern them after the life has left the body, that thus they may enjoy an incorporeal and endless life in the presence of the uncreated and immortal God. But those souls of other men which I have spoken of as being overwhelmed, being such as have disregarded wisdom, giving themselves up to uncertain circumstances, such as depend wholly on chance, of which none have any reference to the soul or to the intellect, but all to the body, which is but a corpse to which we are joined, or to other things even more inanimate and insensible than that; I mean such things as glory, and riches, and power, and honour, and all such other things as through the deceitfulness of false opinions are looked upon as real and living objects by people who do not see what is really beautiful.

Therefore, if you look upon souls, and daemones, and angels, as things differing indeed in name, but as meaning in reality one and the same thing, you will thus get rid of the heaviest of all evils, superstition. For as people in general speak of good daemones and bad daemones, in the same manner also do they speak of good and bad souls; and so they speak of some angels as being by their title worthy ambassadors from men to God, and from God to men, being sacred and inviolable guardians on account of their blameless and most excellent service which they have allotted to them. And, again, if you look upon others as unholy and unworthy of any such appellation, you will not err. And the Psalmist himself is a witness in favour of what I have here asserted, where he speaks as follows: "He sent among them the anger of his wrath, by the operation of evil angels."[4]

Again, all animals that swim and zoophytes are allotted to the water, and all terrestrial animals and plants to the land. And the plants he placed with their heads downwards, fixing their heads in the deepest parts of the earth; but the heads of the irrational animals he dragged up from the earth and placed upon a lofty neck, placing the fore-feet beneath them as a kind of pedestal. But man has had a separate formation of a higher character; for in the case of other animals, God has placed their eyes in the side of their heads and bent them down to the ground, on which account they are all inclined downwards to the earth. But the eyes of man, on the other hand, he has raised up, that he might behold the heavens, being not a terrestrial but a celestial plant, as the old saying is.[5]

But the other class, who affirm that our intellect is a portion of ethereal nature, connect man in a relationship with the air. Accordingly, the great Moses has not spoken of the rational soul as it resembled in its species any created thing, but he has called it the image of the divine and invisible God, looking upon it to be a glorious and carefully wrought image, the seal of God, the character of which is the everlasting Word; for, says he, "God breathed into his face the breath of life."[6] So that it follows inevitably that he who received it must be made in the image and likeness of him who sent it. On which account he also says that man was created in the image of God, and not in the likeness of any created thing.

IV. But, taking up our discourse again at the beginning for the sake of clearness, let us say that of bodies some have put on habit, and others nature, and others soul, and others a rational soul. Therefore those stocks and stones which are torn from any intimate connection, have made for themselves that strongest of all forms, namely habit, and that is a breath returning constantly to itself;

for it begins at the centre and extends to the furthest extremities, and when it has touched the outermost circumference it turns back again until it arrives at the same place from which it originally started. This is the continued course of habit over which it runs and returns. And he has allotted a nature of their own to plants, having combined it of many powers, especially the nutritious and the generative power. And the Creator has made the soul different from nature in three particulars—the outward sense, and fancy, and impulse. Now plants have no participation in any of these things, but every living animal has a share in all of them. Therefore the outward sense, as its very name in my opinion shows, is a certain imposition which represents to the intellect the things which have appeared to it. And it represents to the fancy a sort of outline in the soul, being, as it were, a kind of representation of light; for those things which each of the outward senses has introduced, like a ring as it were or a seal, it impresses on them its own character, or else it preserves the impression which has been made until the rival of memory, forgetfulness, having softened the impression, at least makes it very dim, or else entirely effaces it; and what has appeared to have been impressed upon it disposes the soul at one time as if it belonged to it, and at another time as if it belonged to some other: and this feeling is called impulse, which those who have attempted to give accurate definitions have called the primary motion of the soul.

V. In such important particulars are animals superior to plants. Let us now therefore see in what man is superior to the other animals. He now has received as an especial and pre-eminent honour, the gift of intellect, by which he is accustomed to comprehend the natures of all things, whether they be bodies or things; for as the predominant part in the body is the sight, and as the nature of light is the most important part of the universe, so in the same manner the most important and influential of all the parts in us is the mind; for this is the light of the soul, being irradiated and enlightened by its own beams, by which that dense and profound darkness, ignorance of facts which was shed around it, is dissipated.

And this portion of the soul is not composed of the same elements as those of which the other parts are made, but it has a pure and more excellent essence, from which the divine natures were made; on which account the intellect alone, of all the parts within us, appears very reasonably and naturally to be imperishable, for that is the only portion which the Father who generated it has thought worthy of freedom, and loosing the bands of necessity, he has allowed it to roam at large without restraint, having endowed it with a share of his own most glorious and becoming attribute, free-will, the highest present which it was able to

---

[4] Psalm 77:49.

[5] This is in accordance with the idea of Ovid, who says (as may be translated)—"And while all other creatures from their birth, / With downcast eyes gaze on their kindred earth, / Man walks erect, and proudly scans the heaven / From which he sprung, to which his hopes are given."

[6] Genesis 2:7.

receive. For the other animals in whose souls there does not exist that intellect which is thus especially appropriated to freedom, have been given up to them to submit to their yoke and to receive their bridle in their mouths, so as to serve them as servants obey their masters.

But man having a spontaneous will, subject to no promptings but those of his own nature, and exerting his energies in accordance with his own deliberate purpose, is very properly subject to blame for whatever unjust actions he commits from deliberate intention, and to praise for all the good deeds which he intentionally performs; for as he has received from God a power of voluntary motion, and as he is in this respect like unto God himself, being delivered from all subservience to that most severe and grievous mistress, necessity, he very properly is open to accusation when he does not pay worship to that being who has thus delivered him. Therefore he will most justly in such a case suffer the punishment which has been inexorably pronounced against ungrateful people who do not deserve freedom. On which account also, the body being raised up towards the purest portion of the universe, the heaven, raises its eyes upwards, that so by an observation of what is visible, it may arrive at an adequate comprehension of what is invisible.

Since, therefore, it would be impossible to behold the attraction of the intellect towards the living God, excepting as far as those who are attracted towards him can themselves perceive it, for each man in an individual and especial degree knows what happens to himself, he has made a visible image of the invisible eye, namely, the eyes of the body which are thus able to look towards the sky. For when the eyes, which are made of perishable materials, have gone to such heights as even to soar upwards to the heaven which is removed to such an immense distance from the regions of the earth, and to touch its borders, to how great a distance must we not suppose that the eyes of the soul can reach? which, being excited by a vehement desire to see the one Being clearly and distinctly, stretch forward not only to the furthest extremity of the sky, but, leaving beneath them the boundaries of the universal world, hasten onwards to the uncreated.

VI. Having now, therefore, gone through the whole question of the more important plants in the world, let us see in what manner also the all-wise God has fashioned the trees which exist in man, that lesser world. Therefore immediately having taken our body as a region of fertile soil, he has made in it the outward senses as so many channels; and then he has carefully trained each of those outward senses as a plant susceptible of cultivation and of the greatest use, implanting the sense of hearing in the ears, and that of seeing in the eyes, and that of smell in the nostrils, and all the other senses in the places akin to and appropriate to them. And I have a witness in favour of this my argument in that god-like man who speaks thus in the Psalms: "He that planted the ear, shall he not hear? and he that fashioned the eye, must not he see?"[7]

Moreover, those other faculties which reside apart from the main body, being situated in the legs and hands and the other parts of the body, whether within or without, all these faculties, I say, are noble and excellent offshoots. And the more excellent and more perfect parts he very appropriately stationed near the dominant portion of the whole, as being in the centre, and able preeminently to bring forth fruit, as being the lord of the whole. And these faculties are perception and comprehension, and felicity of conjecture, and study, and recollection, and habit, and disposition, and every variety of art, and certainty of knowledge, and an ever-mindful apprehension of the speculations of every kind of virtue. Now, no one can properly or sufficiently cultivate any one of these within, but the one uncreated Maker of them, and who has not merely created them, but who also makes all these plants to correspond to everything which takes place; he alone can manage them and perfect them as they should be perfected.

VII. And the way in which Paradise was planted is in strict conformity with what has been here said; for we read that "God planted a Paradise in Eden, towards the east, and there he placed the man whom he had made."[8] Now, to think that this means that God planted vines and olives, and trees of apples and pomegranates, and things of that kind, is great and incurable folly. But in order that no one might imagine that the Creator had need of anything that he had created, Moses has made a most important declaration when he says, "The Lord, the King of ages, for ever and ever."[9] Accordingly, God is both the Father, and the Creator, and the Governor, in reality and truth, of all the things that are in heaven and in the whole world. And, indeed, the future is concealed and separated from the present moment at one time by a brief, and at another time by a long interval. But God is also the Creator of time, for he is the Father of that which is the father of time; and the father of time is the world, which proves that its own birth is the motion of time. But nothing is future to God, because he is in possession of and the author of the boundaries of time; for it is not time, but rather the archetype and model of time. But in eternity nothing is passed, nothing is future, but everything is at the present moment.

VIII. Having now, then, discussed these mat-

---

[7] Psalm 93:9.
[8] Genesis 2:8.
[9] Exodus 15:18.

ters at sufficient length, we must proceed to investigate its imperishableness. Now, there are three opinions in vogue among the philosophers on this subject: some affirming it is everlasting, and uncreated, and free from all liability to destruction; others, on the contrary, that it is created and perishable. There is also a sect which has adopted some portions of the doctrine of each of the beforementioned parties, taking from the latter sect the doctrine that it is created, and from the former the idea that it is imperishable; and thus they have left a mixed opinion, looking upon it as at the same time created and yet imperishable.

Therefore Democritus, and Epicurus, and the chief body of the philosophers of the Stoic school, believe the generation and also the destructibility of the world; but they do not all do so in the same manner. For some give a sketch of many worlds, the creation of which they attribute to the concourse and conflicting combination of atoms, and their destruction they attribute to the repercussion and shattering of what has been thus formed. But the Stoics affirm that there is one world, and that God is the cause of its creation, but that God is not the cause of its destruction; but that the power which is contained in existing things, in the long periods of never-ending time, attracts everything to itself, from which again a regeneration of the world is caused by the prudence of the Creator.

But Aristotle pronounced the world to be both uncreated and imperishable, and he affirmed that those who maintained a contrary doctrine were guilty of terrible impiety, as they considered that so great a work of God was in no respect superior to things made by the hand of men. And they say too that it has been proved to be both uncreated and imperishable by Plato in his Timaeus.

But some persons interpret Plato's words sophistically, and think that he affirms that the world was created, not inasmuch as it has had a beginning of creation, but inasmuch as if it had been created it could not possibly have existed in any other manner than that in which it actually does exist as has been described, or else because it is in its creation and change that the parts are seen. But the forementioned opinion is better and truer, not only because throughout the whole treatise he affirms that the Creator of the gods is also the father and creator and maker of everything, and that the world is a most beautiful work of his and his offspring, being an imitation visible to the outward senses of an archetypal model appreciable only by the intellect, comprehending in itself as many objects of the outward senses as the model does objects of the intellect, since it is a most perfect impression of a most perfect model, and is addressed to the outward sense as the other is to the intellect.

But also because Aristotle bears witness to this fact in the case of Plato, who, from his great reverence for philosophy, would never have spoken falsely.

But some persons think that the father of the Platonic theory was the poet Hesiod, as they conceive that the world is spoken of by him as created and indestructible; as created, when he says,—

"First did Chaos rule;
Then the broad-chested earth was brought to light,
Foundation firm and lasting for whatever
Exists among mankind;"[10]

and as indestructible, because he has given no hint of its dissolution or destruction.

Now Chaos was conceived by Aristotle to be a place, because it is absolutely necessary that a place to receive them must be in existence before bodies. But some of the Stoics think that it is water, imagining that its name has been derived from effusion.[11] But however that may be, it is exceedingly plain that the world is spoken of by Hesiod as having been created: and a very long time before him Moses, the lawgiver of the Jews, had said in his sacred volumes that the world was both created and indestructible, and the number of the books is five. The first of which he entitled Genesis, in which he begins in the following manner: "In the beginning God created the heaven and the earth; and the earth was invisible and without form."

IX. But we must place those arguments first which make out the world to be uncreated and indestructible, because of our respect for that which is visible, employing an appropriate commencement. To all things which are liable to destruction there are two causes of that destruction, one being internal and the other external; therefore you may find iron, and brass, and all other substances of that kind destroyed by themselves when rust, like a creeping disease, overruns and devours them; and by external causes when, if a house or a city is burnt, they also are consumed in the conflagration, being melted by the violent impetuosity of the fire.

A similar end also befalls animals, partly when they are sick of diseases arising internally, and partly when they are destroyed by external causes, being sacrificed, or stoned, or burnt, or when they endure an unclean death by hanging.

And if the world also is destroyed, then it must of necessity be so either by some external cause, or else by some one of the powers which exist within itself; and both these alternatives are impossible, for there is nothing whatever outside of the world, since all things are brought together in order to make it complete and full, for it is in this way that it will be one, and whole, and free from old

---

[10] Hesiod, Theogon. 116.
[11] *Chysis*, as if chaos were derived from *cheō*, "to pour."

age; it will be one, because if anything were left outside of it, then another world might be created resembling that which exists now; and whole, because the whole of its essence is expended on itself; and exempt from old age and from all disease, since those bodies which are liable to be destroyed by disease or old age are violently overthrown by external causes, such as heat, and cold, and other contrary qualities, no power of which is able to escape so as to surround and attack the world, all those being entirely enclosed within, without any part whatever being separated from the rest.

But if indeed there is any external thing it must by all means be a vacuum, or else a nature absolutely impossible, which it would be impossible should either suffer or do anything. And again, it will also not be dissolved by any cause existing within itself; first of all because, if it were, then the part would be greater and more powerful than the whole, which is the greatest possible absurdity, for the world, enjoying an unsurpassable power, influences all its parts, and is not itself influenced or moved by any one of them; in the second place because, since there are two causes of corruption, the one being internal and the other external, those things which are competent to admit the one must also by all means be liable to the other; and a proof of this may be found in oxen, and horses, and men, and other animals of similar kinds, because it is their nature to be destroyed by the sword, or to be liable to die by disease.

X. Since, therefore, the arrangement of the world is such as I have endeavoured to describe it, so that there is no part whatever left out, so as for any force to be applied, it has now been proved that the world will not be destroyed by any external thing, because in fact nothing whatever external has been left at all; nor will it be destroyed by anything in itself on account of the proof which has already been considered and stated, according to which that which was obnoxious to the power of one of those causes was also naturally susceptible of the influence of the other.

And there are testimonies also in the Timaeus to the fact of the world being exempt from disease and not liable to destruction, such as these: "Accordingly, of the four elements the constitution of the world receives each in all its integrity; for he who compounded it made it to consist of the whole of fire, and the whole of water, and the whole of air, and the whole of earth, not leaving any portion or any power of any one of them outside, from the following intentions:—in the first place, in order that the whole might be as far as possible a perfect animal made up of perfect parts. And besides all these things, he ordained that it should be one, inasmuch as there is nothing left out of which another similar world could be composed. Moreover, he willed that it should be

exempt from old age, and free from all disease, considering that those things which in the body are hot or cold, or which have mighty powers, if standing all around and falling upon it unseasonably, would be likely to dissolve it, and, by introducing diseases and old age, cause it to decay and perish. For this cause, and because of this reason, God made the whole universe to consist of entire and perfect elements, and exempt from old age and free from disease."

XI. Let this be taken as a testimony delivered by Plato to the imperishable nature of the world. Its uncreated character follows from the truth of natural philosophy; for dissolution must of necessity attend everything which is born, and incorruptibility must inevitably belong to everything which is unborn; since the poet who wrote the following iambic verse,

"All that is born must surely die," [12]

appears to have spoken very correctly when he asserted this connection of destructibility with birth.

The argument may be stated in a different way as follows. All compound things which are destroyed are dissolved into the elements of which they were compounded; accordingly, dissolution is nothing else but a return of everything to its original constituent parts; just as, on the contrary, composition is that which compels the things combined to come together in a manner contrary to their nature; and indeed, this appears to be the most exact truth; for men are composed of the four elements which together make up the whole of the universe, the heaven, the earth, the air, and fire, borrowing a few parts of each in a manner at first sight hardly consistent with nature. But the things which are thus combined together are necessarily deprived of a motion in accordance with nature; for instance, warmth is deprived of its upward motion, and coldness of its downward tendency, the earthy and somewhat weighty substance being lightened and assuming the higher place, which the most earth-like of our own parts, the head, has obtained in us. But of all bonds, that is the worst which is forged by violence, and which, being violent, is also short-lived; for it is speedily broken by those who are bound in it, since they become restive from their desire for a motion in accordance with nature, to which they hasten; for as the tragic poet says,—

"And for things sprung from earth, they must
Return unto their parent dust,
While those from heavenly seed which rise
Are borne uplifted to the skies.

---

[12] Timaeus, p. 32.

Nought that has once existed dies,
Though often what has been combined
Before, we separated find,
Invested with another form." [13]

And this law and ordinance is established with reference to everything which is destroyed, that wherever composite things are existing in combination they are thrown into disorder instead of into the order in accordance with nature, which they previously enjoyed, and they are removed to situations opposite to those in which they were previously placed, so that they seem in a manner to be sojourners; and when they are dissolved again, then they return to the appropriate parts allotted to them by nature.

But since the world has no participation in that irregularity which exists in the things which I have just been mentioning, let us stop awhile and consider this point.

If the world were liable to corruption and destruction, it follows of necessity that all its parts would at present be arranged in a position not in accordance with nature: but it is impious even to imagine such a thing as this; for all the parts of the world have received the most excellent position possible, and an arrangement of the purest symmetry and harmony; so that each individual part, being content with its place as a native country to it, does not seek any change for the better. On this account it is that the most central position of all has been assigned to the earth, to which all things belonging to it adhere, and to which they descend again even if you throw them into the air: and this is a proof that their place is in accordance with nature; for wherever anything is borne without any violence, and where it then remains firm and stationary, that is clearly its natural place. And then, in the second place, water was poured over the earth, and air and fire have gone from the central to the upper part, air having received for its portion the region which is on the borders between air and fire, and fire having received the highest place of all: on which account, if you light a torch and press it down towards the ground, nevertheless the flame will still turn in a contrary direction, and lightening itself in accordance with the natural motion of fire, will rise upwards: if, then, motion contrary to nature is the cause of corruptibility and destruction in the case of other animals, but if in the case of the world every one of its parts is arranged in complete accordance with nature, having had appropriate positions allotted to each of them, then surely the world must most justly be pronounced incorruptible and imperishable.

XII. Moreover this point is manifest to every one, that every nature is desirous to keep and pre-serve, and if it were possible to make immortal, everything of which it is the nature; the nature of trees, for instance, desires to preserve trees, and the nature of animals desires to preserve each individual animal. But particular nature is of necessity unable to conduct what it belongs to to eternity; for want, or heat, or cold, or innumerable other ordinary circumstances, when they affect particular things, shake them and dissolve the bond which previously held them together, and at last break them to pieces; but if nothing resembling any of these things were lying in wait outside, then in that case nature itself, as far as it is possible, would preserve everything both great and small free from old age.

It follows therefore of necessity, that the nature of the world must desire the durability of the universe; for it is not worse than particular natures, so that it should run away and desert its proper duties, and attempt to produce disease instead of health, and corruption and destruction instead of complete safety, since,

"High over all she lifts her beauteous face,
And towers above her nymphs with heavenly grace,
Fair as they all appear." [14]

But if this be true, then the world cannot be capable of destruction. Why so? Because the nature which holds it together is itself invincible by reason of its exceeding strength and power, by which it gets the mastery over every thing else which might be likely to injure it; wherefore Plato has well said: [15] "For nothing ever departed from it, nor did anything ever come to it from any quarter; for that was not possible; for there was nothing in existence which could come; for since it supplies itself with nutriment out of its own consumption, it also does everything and suffers everything in itself and by itself, and is compounded with the most consummate art. For he who created it thought that it would be better if wholly self-sufficient, than if in continual need of accessories from other quarters."

XIII. However, this argument also is a most demonstrative one, on which I know that vast numbers of philosophers pride themselves as one most accurately worked out, and altogether irresistible; for they inquire what reason there is for God's destroying the world. For if he destroys it at all he must do so either with the intention of never making a world again, or with the object of creating a second fresh one; now the former idea is inconsistent with the character of God; for it is proper to change disorder into order, and not

---

[13] A fragment from the Chrysippus of Euripides.

[14] Homer, Odyssey 6.107, where the lines quoted are applied to Latona among her nymphs.
[15] Timaeus, p. 33.

order into disorder: in the second place, it is so because it would give rise to repentance, which is an affliction and a disease of the soul.

For he ought either never to have created a world at all, or else, if he judged that it was a fitting employment for him, he ought to have been pleased with it after it was made. But the second reason deserves no superficial examination; for if he were intending to make another world instead of that which exists at present, then of necessity this second world that would be made, in that case, would be either worse than, or similar to, or better than the first; every one of which ideas is inadmissible; for if the new world is to be worse than the former, then the maker must be also worse: but all the works of God are without blemish, beyond all reproach and wholly faultless, inasmuch as they are wrought with the most consummate skill and knowledge; for as the proverb says;—

"For e'en a woman's wisdom's not so coarse
As to despise the good and choose the worse."

But it is consistent with the character of, and becoming to God to give form to what is shapeless, and to invest what is most ugly with admirable beauty.

Again, if the new world is to be exactly like the old one, then the maker is only wasting his labour, and differs in no respect from infant children who, very often while playing on the sea shore raise up little mounds of sand, and then pull them down again with their hands and destroy them; for it would have been much better than making another world exactly like the former, neither to take anything from, nor to add anything to, nor to change either for the better or for the worse, what existed originally, but to let it remain just as it was.

If, on the other hand, he is about to make a world better than the former one, then the maker too must be better than the maker of the former world, so that when he made the former world he was inferior both in his skill and in his intellect, which is impious even to imagine, for God is at all times equal and similar to himself, being neither capable of any relaxation which can make him worse, nor of any extension which can make him better. Men, indeed, do admit of such inequalities in either direction, being naturally liable to alter either for the better or for the worse, and continually admitting of increase, and advance, and improvement, and everything contrary to these states; and besides this, the works of us who are but mortal men may very appropriately be perishable, but the works of the immortal must in all consistency and reason be likewise imperishable, for it is natural that what is made should resemble the nature of the maker.

XIV. But Boethus adduces the most convincing arguments, which we shall proceed to mention immediately; for if, says he, the world was created and is liable to destruction, then something will be made out of nothing, which appears to be most absurd even to the Stoics. Why so? Because it is not possible to discover any cause of destruction either within or without, which will destroy the world. For on the outside there is nothing except perhaps a vacuum, inasmuch as all the elements in their integrity are collected and contained within it, and within there is no imperfection so great as to be the cause of dissolution to so great a thing.

Again, if it is destroyed without any cause, then it is plain that from something which has no existence will arise the engendering of destruction, which is an idea quite inadmissible by reason; and, indeed, they say that there are altogether three generic manners of corruption, one which arises from division, another which proceeds from a destruction of the distinctive quality which holds the thing together, and the third from confusion; therefore the things which consist of a union of separate members, such as flocks of goats, herds of oxen, choruses, armies; or, again, bodies which are compounded of limbs joined together, are dissolved by disjunction and separation. But wax, when stamped with a new impression, or softened before being remodelled so as to present a new and different appearance, is corrupted by a destruction of the distinctive quality which previously held it together. Other things are corrupted by confusion, as the medicine which the physicians call tetrapharmacon, for the powers of the drugs brought together and combined were destroyed in such a manner as to produce one perfect medicine of especial virtue.

By which, then, of these modes of corruption is it becoming to say that the world is destroyed? By that which is caused by separation? No, for it is not compounded of separate members so that its different parts can be dispersed, nor of portions joined together so that they can be dissolved; nor is it united together in a similar manner to our own bodies, for they have the seeds of decay in themselves, and they are subject to influence of a great variety of things by which they are at times injured; but the power of the world is invincible, since by its great superiority to other things it has dominion over everything.

Is it then destroyed by a complete destruction of its distinctive qualities? This again is impossible, for there remains, as the adversaries affirm, a quality of arrangement which by the process of conflagration is only diminished to a lesser substance ... Is it destroyed then by confusion? Away with such an idea, for in that case it would be necessary to confess that the corruption of a body can be reduced to a state of non-existence. Why so? Because if each of the particular elements were destroyed separately, it would be possible for it to become changed into another; but if they are altogether destroyed at one and the same moment by confusion, then it would be necessary to imagine what is absolutely impossible.

XV. Is it not however worth while to examine this question, in what manner there can be a regeneration of all those things which have been destroyed by fire, and resolved into fire? for when their substance has been wholly destroyed by the fire, it follows of necessity that the fire itself must also be extinguished as no longer having any nourishment. Therefore, as long as it remained the seminal principle of arrangement was likewise preserved, but when it is destroyed that principle is destroyed with it. But it would be impious, and an impiety of double dye, not only to attribute destruction to the world, but also to take away the possibility of its regeneration; as if God delighted in disorder, and irregularity, and all kinds of evil things. But we must examine this question more accurately, in the following manner.

There are three species in fire; the coal, and the flame, and the light. Now coal is the fire in its earthy substance, which, like a sort of spiritual habit, couches and lies hid in a sort of cavern, pervading it all to its very extremities. And the flame is that part which, being raised on high, is lifted up from its fuel. And the light is that which is emitted from the flame, so as to co-operate with the eyes, in order to enable them to comprehend what is seen. And the flame occupies the middle position between the coal and the light; for when it is extinguished it ends in coal, and when it is kindled it excites the light, which, being deprived of its burning power, blazes. If therefore, we affirm that the world is dissolved by conflagration, it would not be coal, because, in that case there will be a great deal of the earthy substance left behind, in which also fire must necessarily be contained. But we must agree, that none of the other bodies subsist any longer, but that earth, and water, and air, are all dissolved into unmixed fire. Nor, again, would it become flame; for that can only exist in connexion with nourishment; and, if nothing is left behind, being deprived of all nourishment it will immediately be extinguished. It follows from all this, that it cannot become light either; for light by itself has no substance at all, but flows from the things before mentioned, coal and flame, not in a great degree from the coal, but very much from the flame; for it is diffused over a very great space indeed. But if, as has been already proved, those things had no existence from the conflagration of all things, then there could not be any light either. So that it is impossible for the world to be susceptible of any regeneration, inasmuch as there is no spermatic principle smouldering beneath; from which consideration it is plain that it is uncreated, and that it will be for ever imperishable.

XVI. However, besides what has been here said, any one may use this argument also in corroboration of his opinion, which will certainly convince all those who are not determined to be obstinate beyond all bounds; of those things which in pairs are exactly contrary to one another it is impossible that one thing should be, and that the other should not be; for since there is white it follows as a matter of absolute necessity that there must also be black, and since there is a great there must likewise be a little; since there is an odd there must inevitably be an even; since there is a sweet there must be a bitter; since there is day there must be night; and so on in an infinite number of similar cases; but if a conflagration should take place, then something would ensue which is impossible; for then, of things in a pair, the one will happen and the other will not.

Come, now, let us consider the matter thus: if everything is resolved into fire, there is then something light, and rare, and warm; for all these are the especial properties of fire; but there can be nothing heavy, or cold, or thick, which are the opposites of the qualities which I have just enumerated. How then can any one more completely overturn the idea of the universal disorder which would be involved in such a conflagration than by showing that those things which by a law of nature must exist together, are by this process separated from their natural conjunction? And the separation has extended to such a degree, that those who maintain this doctrine attribute eternal durability to the one and deny any existence at all to the other.

Again, there is this assertion made by some of those who diligently employ themselves in investigating truth which appears to me to be a sufficiently felicitous one; if the world is destroyed it will either be destroyed by some other efficient cause, or by God; now there is certainly nothing else whatever from which it can receive its destruction, for there is nothing whatever which it does not surround and contain; but that which is surrounded and confined within something else is manifestly inferior in power to that which surrounds and confines it, by which it is therefore mastered; on the other hand, to say that it is destroyed by God is the most impious of all possible assertions; for God is the cause not of disorder, and irregularity, and destruction, but of order, and beautiful regularity, and life, and of every good thing, as is confessed by all those whose opinions are based on truth.

XVII. But some of those persons who have fancied that the world is everlasting, inventing a variety of new arguments, employ also such a system of reasoning as this to establish their point: they affirm that there are four principal manners in which corruption is brought about, addition, taking away, transposition, and alteration; accordingly, the number two is by the addition of the unit corrupted so as to become the number three, and no longer remains the number two; and the number four by the taking away of the unit is corrupted so as to become the number three; again, by transposition the letter Z becomes the letter H when the parallel lines which were previously horizontal ($\equiv$) are placed perpendicularly ($| \ |$), and when the line which did before pass upwards, so as to connect the two is now made horizontal, and still extended between them so as to join them. And by alteration the word *oinos, wine,* becomes *oxos, vinegar.*

But of the manner of corruption thus mentioned there is not one which is in the least degree whatever applicable to the world, since otherwise what could we say? Could we affirm that anything is added to the world so as to cause its destruction? But there is nothing whatever outside of the world which is not a portion of it as the whole, for everything is surrounded, and contained, and mastered by it. Again, can we say that anything is taken from the world so as to have that effect? In the first place that which would be taken away would again be a world of smaller dimensions than the existing one, and in the second place it is impossible that any body could be separated from the composite fabric of the whole world so as to be completely dispersed. Again, are we to say that the constituent parts of the world are transposed? But at all events they remain in their original positions without any change of place, for never at any time shall the whole earth be raised up above the water, nor the water above the air, nor the air above the fire. But those things which are by nature heavy, namely the earth and the water, will have the middle place, the earth supporting everything like a solid foundation, and the water being above it; and the air and the fire, which are by nature light, will have the higher position, but not equally, for the air is the vehicle of the fire; and that which is carried by anything is of necessity above that which carries it.

Once more: we must not imagine that the world is destroyed by alteration, for the change of any elements is equipollent, and that which is equipollent is the cause of unvarying steadiness, and of untroubled durability, inasmuch as it neither seeks any advantage itself, and is not subject to the inroads of other things which seek advantages at its expense; so that this retribution and compensation of these powers is equalized by the rules of proportion, being the produce of health and endless preservation, by all which considerations the world is demonstrated to be eternal.

XVIII. Theophrastus, moreover, says that those men who attribute a beginning and destructibility to the world are deceived by four particulars of the greatest importance, the inequalities of the earth, the retreat of the sea, the dissolution of each of the parts of the universe, and the destruction of different terrestrial animals in their kinds; and he proceeds to establish the first point

thus: if the earth had never had any beginning of its creation, then there would have been no portion of it rising above the rest so as to be conspicuous, but all the mountains would have been level, and all the pieces of rising ground would have been even with the plain.

For as there are such vast showers falling from heaven throughout all ages, it would be natural that of any places which were originally raised on high some would be broken down and washed away by torrents, and others would subside of their own accord and so become lowered, and that every place everywhere would be smoothed; but now, as things are, the constant inequalities which exist, and the vast heights of many mountains, reaching up even to the sky, are so many proofs that the earth is not eternal.

For otherwise, as I have said before, all the earth would long since have been rendered level from one extremity to the other by the vast rains which would have fallen from the eternal commencement of time; for it is the character of the nature of water, and especially of such as descends in a heavy fall from lofty places, to push some things away by force, and to cut out hollow others places by its continual dropping, and in this manner to operate on the hard, rugged, stony ground not less than men digging. And again, the sea, as they affirm, is already somewhat diminished, and for proof of this fact we can appeal to the most celebrated islands, Rhodes and Delos, for these were in ancient times invisible, being overwhelmed by and sunk under the sea, but by lapse of time, as the sea gradually diminished, they by slow degrees rose above it and came into sight, as the histories which are written concerning them record. And they used to call Delos Anaphe, confirming the account here given by both names, since when it appeared above the waters [16] it became evident, [17] having been formerly invisible and unseen.

And in addition to these arguments they adduce the facts that many great and deep bays and gulfs of vast seas have been dried up, and have become land, and have so turned out no insignificant addition to the adjacent country when sown and planted, and on that soil there is still left plenty of proof of such spots having formerly been sea, in the pebbles, and shells, and other things which are commonly washed up on the sea-shore being found in them.

But if the sea is gradually being diminished then the earth also will be diminished; and in long revolutions of years every one of the elements will be entirely consumed and destroyed; and the whole air will be consumed, being diminished by little and

---

[16] The Greek word is *anaphaneisa,* from which *Anaphē* is derived.
[17] *Dēlē,* from which *Dēlos* is derived.

little; and all things will be absorbed and dissolved into the one substance of fire.

And for the purpose of establishing the third alternative of this question they use the following argument: beyond all question that thing is destroyed all the parts of which are liable to destruction; but all the parts of the world are liable to destruction, therefore the world also is liable to destruction.

But we must now proceed to consider the question which we postponed till the present time. What sort of a part of the earth is that, that we may begin from this, whether it is greater or less, that is not dissolved by time? Do not the very hardest and strongest stones become hard and decayed through the weakness of their conformation (and this conformation is a sort of course of a highly strained spirit, a bond not indissoluble, but only very difficult to unloose), in consequence of which they are broken up and made fluid, so that they are dissolved first of all into a thin dust, and afterwards are wholly wasted away and destroyed? Again, if the water were never agitated by the winds, but were left immoveable for ever, would it not from inaction and tranquillity become dead? at all events it is changed by such stagnation, and becomes very foetid and foul-smelling, like an animal deprived of life. And so also the corruptions of the air are plain to everyone, for it is the nature of the atmosphere to become sick and to decay, and, as one may say, in a manner to die; since what else is it which a man, who is not aiming at selecting plausible language, but only at truth, would call a plague except a death of the atmosphere, which diffuses its own disease and suffering to the destruction of everything which is endowed with life?

And why need I speak at great length concerning fire? for if it is deprived of nourishment it is immediately extinguished.

If then, each of the separate parts of the world awaits utter destruction, it is plain that the world which is compounded of these can not be itself exempt from destruction.

We must now consider with accuracy the fourth and remaining argument. Thus they argue: if the world were eternal then the animals also would be eternal, and much more the human race, in proportion as that is more excellent than the other animals; but, on the contrary, those who take delight in investigating the mysteries of nature consider that man has only been created in the late ages of the world; for it is likely, or I should rather say it is inevitably true, that the arts co-exist with man, so as to be exactly co-eval with him, not only because methodical proceedings are appropriate to a rational nature, but also because it is not possible to live without them; let us therefore examine the dates of each of these, disregarding the fables invented by the tragedians about the gods;

but if man is not eternal then neither is any other animal, so that then neither are the places which receive them, the earth, or the water, or the air; from all which considerations it is plain that this world is liable to destruction.

XIX. But it is necessary to encounter such quibbling arguments as these, lest some persons of too little experience should yield to and be led away by them; and we must begin our refutation of them from the same point from which the Sophists begin their deceit. They say, "There could no longer be any inequalities existing on the earth, if the world were eternal." Why not, my most excellent friends? For other persons will come up and say that the natures of trees are in no respect different from mountains; but just as they at certain seasons lose their leaves, and again at certain seasons recover their verdure again; (on which account there is admirable truth in those lines of the poet:—

"Like leaves on trees the race of man is found,
Now green in youth, now withering on the ground;
Another race the following spring supplies;
They fall successive and successive rise.") [18]

And so in like manner some portions of the mountains are broken off, and others grow in their stead: but after a long lapse of time the additional growth becomes conspicuous, because the trees having a more rapid nature display their increase with great rapidity; but mountains have a slower character, on which account it happens that the additions which take place in their case are not perceptible by the outward senses except after a long time.

And these men appear to be ignorant of the manner in which they are produced, since if they had not been, perhaps they would have been silent out of shame; but still there is no reason why we should not teach them; but there is nothing new in what is now said, neither are they our words but the ancient sayings of wise men, by whom nothing which was necessary for knowledge has been left uninvestigated; when the fiery principle which is contained beneath, in the earth, is thrust upwards by the natural power of fire, it proceeds to its own appropriate place; and if it meets with any respite or relaxation, though ever so slight, it draws up with it a large portion of the earthy substance, as much as it can; and when it has emerged from the earth it proceeds more slowly; but the earthy substance being compelled to follow it for a long time, being at last raised to an immense height, is contracted at the top, and at last comes to end on a sharp point imitating the general appearance of the flame of fire; for there

---

[18] Homer, Il. 6.147.

arises then a most violent contention between two things which are natural adversaries, the lightest and the heaviest of things, each of them pressing onwards to reach its own place, and each striving against the violent efforts of the other; accordingly the fire, which is drawing up the earth with it, is compelled to sink down by its descending power; and the earth naturally inclining to the lowest point is nevertheless to a certain degree made light, and lifted up by the upward tendencies of fire, and so is raised on high, and being at last overpowered by the more influential power which lightens it is thrust upwards towards the natural seat of fire, and established on high.

Why then need we wonder if the mountains are not entirely washed away by the impetuosity of the rains, when so great a power, which keeps them together, and by which they are raised up, is very firmly and steadfastly connected with them? For if they were released from the bond which holds them together, it would be natural for them to be entirely dissolved and to be dispersed by the water; but since they are bound together by this power of fire, they resist the impetuosity of the rains more surely.

XX. These things, then, may be said by us with respect to the argument that the inequalities of the surface of the earth are no proof of the world having been created and being liable to destruction; but with respect to that argument which was endeavoured to be established by the diminution of the sea, we may reasonably adduce this statement in opposition to it: "Do not look only at the islands which have risen up out of the sea, nor at any portions of land which, having been formerly buried by the waters, have in subsequent times become dry land; for obstinate contention is very unfavourable to the consideration of natural philosophy, which considers the search after truth to be the chief object of rational desire; but look rather at the contrary effects: consider how many districts on the main-land, not only such as were near the coast, but even such as were completely inland, have been swallowed up by the waters; and consider how great a portion of land has become sea and is now sailed over by innumerable ships." Are you ignorant of the celebrated account which is given of that most sacred Sicilian strait, which in old times joined Sicily to the continent of Italy? and where vast seas on each side being excited by violent storms met together, coming from opposite directions, the land between them was overwhelmed and broken away; from which circumstance the city built in the neighbourhood was called Rhegium,[19] and the result was quite different from what any one would have expected; for

the seas which had formerly been separated now flowed together and were united in one expanse; and the land which had previously united was now separated into two portions by the strait which intersected it, in consequence of which Sicily, which had previously formed a part of the mainland, was now compelled to be an island.

XXI. And it is said that many other cities also have disappeared, having been swallowed up by the sea which overwhelmed them; since they speak of three in Peloponnesus—

"Aegira and fair Bura's walls,
And Helica's lofty halls,
And many a once renowned town,
With wreck and seaweed overgrown,"

as having been formerly prosperous, but now overwhelmed by the violent influx of the sea. And the island of Atalantes which was greater than Africa and Asia, as Plato says in the Timaeus, in one day and night was overwhelmed beneath the sea in consequence of an extraordinary earthquake and inundation and suddenly disappeared, becoming sea, not indeed navigable, but full of gulfs and eddies. Therefore that imaginary and fictitious diminution of the sea has no connection with the destruction or durability of the world; for in fact it appears to recede indeed from some parts, but to rise higher in others; and it would have been proper rather not to look at only one of these results but at both together, and so to form one's opinion, since in all the disputed questions which arise in human life, a wise and honest judge will not deliver his opinion before he has heard the arguments of the advocates on both sides.

XXII. And as for the third argument, it is convicted by itself, as being derived only from an unsound system of questioning proceeding from the assertions originally made; for in truth it does not necessarily follow that a thing, all the parts of which are liable to corruption, is likewise perishable itself; but this is only inevitably true of that thing of which all the parts are perishable when taken collectively and together in the same place and at the same time, since in the case of a person who has the tip of his finger cut off, he is not disabled from living, but if he had the whole collection of all his parts and limbs cut off at once, he would die immediately. Therefore in the same manner, if all the elements of the world together were all to disappear at one and the same moment, then it would be necessary to admit that the world was liable to corruption and destruction; but if each of these elements separately only changes its nature so as to assimilate to that of its nature, it is then rendered immortal rather than destroyed, according to the philosophical statement of the tragic poet—

---

[19]*Rhēgion*, from *rhōgnymi*, "to break."

"Nought that has once existed dies,
Though often what has been combined
Before, we separated find,
Invested with another form."

For it is the greatest folly imaginable to estimate the antiquity of the human race from the state of art; for if any one were to follow the absurdity of such a system of reasoning as this, he will prove the world to be very young indeed, and to have been made scarcely a thousand years, since all those men whom we have heard of traditionally as the discoverers in different branches of science do not go back to a greater number of years than that which I have mentioned.

But if we must speak of the arts as co-eval with the race of mankind, then we must speak, drawing our arguments from natural history, and not inconsiderately or carelessly. And what is this history? The destruction of the things on the earth, not all together, but of the greatest number of them, is attributed to two principal causes, the indescribable violence and power of fire and water. And they say that each of these elements attacks them in its turn, after very long periods of revolving years. When, therefore, a conflagration seizes upon things, a stream of ethereal fire being poured down from above is frequently diffused over them, overrunning many districts of the habitable world; and when a deluge draws down the whole of the rainy nature of water, the regular rivers and torrents overflowing, and not only that, but even far exceeding the ordinary measure of a common flood.

Accordingly, when the greater part of mankind is destroyed in the manners above mentioned, besides an infinity of other ways of less power and importance, it follows of necessity that the arts also must fail, for it cannot be possible to discuss science by itself without some one to reduce it to method and practice. But when those common pestilences relax their fury, and when the human race begins again to recover vigour and to flourish, descending from those who have not been previously destroyed by the evils which pressed upon them, then the arts also begin again to exist, not indeed as they were at first, but in thinner numbers from the diminution of the numbers of those who practise them.

I have now then set forth to the best of my ability what I have been able to learn or to understand concerning the indestructibility of the world.

FRAGMENTS

*About the unstable and changeable condition
of human affairs.*

Page 326. C. — If one is to tell the plain truth, man is without real power in anything, never taking a firm hold of anything. I do not mean merely of common things, but not even of those which concern himself; neither of health, nor of a good condition of the outward senses, nor of soundness in respect of the other parts of his body, nor of his voice, nor of his presence of mind; for as to wealth, or glory, or friends, or power, or all the other things which depend on fortune, who is there who does not know how thoroughly unstable they are? So that we must of necessity confess that the supreme power over everything belongs to one being alone, the true Lord of all existing things.

About impious men, sinners, etc.

Page 341. D. — If you wish to be governed under God as your king, take care not to sin; but if you commit sin, how can you be under the government of God as your king?

*About those people who have renounced
such and such a line of conduct, and then
turning back again, have adopted that very line
which they had renounced.*

Page 343. D. — Some men, making improvement, have returned back to virtue before coming to the end, the ancient principle of oligarchy having destroyed the principle of aristocracy lately engendered in the soul, which having been quiet for a little while, has subsequently come up over again with greater power than before.

Page 343. D. — When a man rightly establishes himself in a virtuous life, with meditation, and practice, and good government, and when having been known by all men as a pious man and one who fears God, he falls into sin, that is a great fall, for he has ascended up to the height of heaven, and fallen down into the abyss of hell.

About resurrection and judgment.

Page 349. A. — It is not possible with God that a wicked man should lose his good reward for a single good thing which he may have done among a great number of evil actions; nor, on the other hand, that a good man should escape punishment, and not suffer it, if among many good actions he

has done wickedly in anything, for it is infallibly certain that God distributes everything according to a just weight and balance.

Page 349. B. — The mind is the witness to each individual of the things which they have planned in secret, and conscience is an incorruptible judge, and the most unerring of all judges.

About those who are ruled.

Page 359. A. — He who has learnt how to submit to be ruled, immediately learns how to rule others; for even if a man were invested with the supreme power over all the earth and all the sea, he would not be a true ruler unless he had also learnt and been previously taught to submit to the rule of others.

About anarchy.

Page 359. D. — Alas, how many and great evils are produced by anarchy! Famine, war, the devastation of lands, the deprivation of money, abductions, fears of slavery, and death.

About the foolish and senseless man, etc.

Page 362. E. — No wicked man is rich, not even though he should be the owner of all the mines in the whole world; but all foolish men are poor. Every foolish man is straitened, being oppressed by covetousness, and ambition, and a love of pleasure, and things of that sort, which do not permit the mind to dwell at ease or to enjoy plenty of room.

Page 363. A. — There is no greater evil to a man than folly, and the being deprived of the proper use of his reasoning powers and intellect.

Page 363. A. — Ignorance is the cause of disease and destruction.

*About deceit affecting the management of
a household.*

Page 367. D. — Every stratagem is not blameable, since guardians of the night appear to act properly when they lie in wait for robbers, and generals when they form ambuscades against the enemy, whom they cannot catch without a stratagem; and the same principle is applicable to what are called manoeuvres, and to the artifices practised in the contests of wrestlers, for in such cases deceit is accounted honourable.

About impossible things.

Page 370. B. — It is as impossible that the love of the world can co-exist with the love of God, as for light and darkness to co-exist at the same time with one another.

About holy men.

Page 372. E. — The happy nature is that which rejoices on every occasion, and which is not discontented with anything whatever which exists in the world, but is pleased with whatever happens, as being good, and beautiful, and expedient.

About leisure and quiet.

Page 376. A. — The wise man endeavours to secure quiet and leisure, and periods of rest from work, that he may devote himself peacefully to the meditations on divine matters.

About evil-speaking.

Page 369. D. — Foul speakers and random accusers, who seek to make a display of their art with vain words, being slow to learn what is good, are very quick and ready at learning what is of the opposite character.

About counsel.

Page 397. D. — Everything which is not done with reason is discreditable, just as what is done with reason is beautiful.

About old men.

Page 404. C. — Old age is an unruffled harbour.

Page 404. C. — Old age is the time when the vigour of the body is passed by; the period when the passions can be checked.

About gymnasia.

Page 405. D. — Continued practice makes knowledge firm, just as want of practice engenders ignorance. And, again, practice in any matter increases experience.

Page 405. D. — Study is the nurse of knowledge.

About calumny.

Page 436. D. — Calumniators and men discarded from the divine grace, who are afflicted with the same evil disposition of calumny with him, are in all respects hated and detested by God, and removed to a distance from all happiness.

Page 436. D. — What can be worse than calumny? for it seduces the ears and perplexes the minds of those who listen to it, and it makes them brutal and always on a watch for evil, like men engaged in hunting; but those who are well ballasted and restrained by prudent reason, hate the man who utters calumnies more than him against whom they are uttered, reproving and seeking to check all desire of blaming others until it be either proved by evidence or demonstrated by undeniable proof.

About justice and virtue.

Page 438. D. — If any one embraces all the virtues with earnestness and sobriety, he is a king, even though he may be in a private station.

About voluntary and involuntary sins.

Page 526. B. — As to sin intentionally is unjust, so to sin unintentionally and out of ignorance is not at once justifiable, but perhaps it is something between the two, that is between righteousness and unrighteousness, and is of what some persons call an indifferent character, for no sin can be an act of righteousness.

About initiation into divine mysteries.

Page 533. C. — It is not lawful to speak of the sacred mysteries to the uninitiated.

About the sea.

Page 551. D. — It is proper to marvel at the sea, by means of which countries requite one another for the good things which they receive from each other, and by which they receive what they are in need of, and export what they have a superfluity of.

About equality.

Page 556. D. — To give equal things to unequal people is an action of the greatest injustice.

About physicians and medical science.

A good physician would not be inclined to apply every kind of salutary medicine at once and on the same day to a patient, as he would know that by such a course he would be doing him more harm than good, but he would measure out the proper opportunities, and then give saving medicines in a seasonable manner; and he would apply different remedies at different times, and so he would bring about the patient's restoration to health by gentle degrees.

About opportunity.

Page 563. C. — Say what is right, and at the time when it is right, and you will not hear what is not right.

Page 563. C. — It is well to economise time.

About mysteries.

Page 576. D. — Chatterers divulging what ought to be kept buried in silence, do in a manner from a disease of the tongue pour forth into people's ears things which are not worthy of being heard.

About people who are in a state of pupillage.

Page 613. D. — To inquire and put questions is the most useful of habits with a view to acquiring instruction.

Page 613. D. — He who hungers and thirsts after knowledge, and who is eager to learn what he does not know, abandoning all other objects of care, is eager to become a disciple, and day and night watches at the doors of the houses of wise men.

Page 613. D. — For any one to know that he is ignorant is a piece of wisdom, just as to know that one has done wrong is a piece of righteousness.

About reproach.

Page 630. C. — Never reproach any one with misfortune, for nature is impartial, and the future is uncertain; lest if you yourself should fall into similar misfortunes, you should be found to be convicted and condemned by your own conscience.

About a proper constitution.

Page 657. C. — It is advantageous to submit to one's betters.

About a blameable constitution.

From the fifth book of the Essays on Genesis.

Page 658. E. — A shameless look, and a high head, and a continual rolling of the eyes, and a pompous strut in walking, and a habit of blushing at nothing, however discreditable, are signs of a most infamous soul, which stamps the obscure topics of the reproaches which belong to itself upon the visible body.

About familiarity and habituation.

Page 681. D. — A change of all kinds of circumstances at once to the opposite direction is very harsh, especially when the existing powers are established by the length of time that they have lasted.

About correction.

Page 683. D. — It is useful to be warned by the misfortunes of others.

Page 683. D. — Punishment very often warns and corrects those who do wrong; but if it fails to do so to them, at all events it corrects the bystanders, for the punishments of others improve most people, from fear lest they should suffer similar evils.

About associating with wicked men.

Page 692. A. — Associations with wicked men are mischievous, and very often the soul against its will receives the impression of the insane wickedness of one's associates.

About wisdom.

Page 693. E. — Every wise man is a friend of God.

About haughty men.

Page 693. E. — Self-conceit, as the proverb of the ancients has it, is the eradication of all improvement, for the man who is full of self-conceit is incapable of improvement.

Self-conceit is by nature an unclean thing.

About natural things.

Page 711. C. — As it is difficult to inoculate anything in a manner contrary to nature, and to introduce anything into nature which does not belong to it, so likewise is it hard to change things which are of such and such a nature from that nature, and to restrain them; for it has been well said by some one, everything is vain if nature sets herself against it.

About man.

From the Questions arising in Genesis.

Page 748. A. — What is the meaning of the expression, "until"[1] thou return to the dust from which thou wast taken? For man was not formed of the dust alone, but also of the divine Spirit; but since he did not continue in an unchanged condition, he neglected the divine command, and cutting off that constitution which imitated the heaven from his better part, he made himself over wholly to the earth; for if he had been a lover of virtue, which is immortal, he would beyond all question have received heaven for his inheritance, but since what he sought was pleasure, by means of which the death of the soul is brought upon mankind, he became appropriated to the earth.

About Adam.

From the Questions arising in Genesis.

Page 748. B. — "And God brought all the animals to Adam, to see what he would call them;"[2] for God does not doubt, but since he has given mind to man, the first born and most excellent of his creatures, according to which he, being endowed with knowledge, is by nature enabled to reason; he excites him, as an instructor excites his pupil, to a display of his powers, and he contemplates the most excellent offspring of his soul. And, again, he visibly by the example of this man gives an outline of all that is voluntary in us, looking with disfavour on those who affirm that everything happens through necessity, by which some men must be influenced, he on that account commanded man to take upon himself the regulation of these things. And this is an employment peculiarly fitting for

---

[1] Genesis 3:19.
[2] Genesis 2:19.

man, as being endowed with a very high degree of knowledge and most surpassing prudence, the giving of names to the animals being suited to him not only as being wise, but also as being the first nobly born creature.

For it was fitting that he should be the founder of the human race, and also the king of everything that is born of the earth, and that he should have this as an especial honour of his own, that, as he was the first who had any acquaintance with the animals, he might also be the first inventor and pronouncer of their names; for it would have been absurd for them to be left without names, and subsequently to have names given to them by some younger man, to the honour and glory of the elder.

And when Adam saw the figure of his wife, as the prophet says, and that it had been produced not by any connexion, nor out of a woman, as human beings in after times were produced, but that she was as it were a nature on the borders between these two kinds, like a graft from a shoot of another vine taken off and grafted into a second one, on which account he says, "For this cause a man shall leave his father and his mother, and shall cleave to his wife, and they two shall become one flesh;"[3] in saying which he used a most gentle expression, which was at the same time most perfectly true, meaning that they would be united by sympathy in their griefs and joys.

From the same book, or else from the last book of
the Questions arising in Exodus.

Truly the divine place is inaccessible, and one which is hard to be approached, nor is it given even to the purest intellect to be able to ascend to such a height as to touch it. It is impossible for human nature to behold the face of the living God; but the word "face" is not used here in its literal meaning, but it is a metaphorical expression, here intended to manifest the purest and simplest form of the living God, since man is not recognized more by anything than by his face, according to his peculiar distinctive qualities and form. For God does not say, "I am not visible in my nature." But who, in fact, is more visible than he who is the Father of all visible things? And being such with regard to being seen, I am, says he, seen by no mortal man; and the reason of this is the inability of the created man to behold him.

And that I may not become prolix while weaving in all kinds of arguments, it is inevitable that God must first be created (which is not possible), in order for any one to be able to comprehend God. But if any one dies as to this mortal life, but still lives, having received in exchange a life of immortality, perhaps he will see what he never saw before.

All the different philosophical sects which have flourished in Greece, and in the countries of the barbarians, when investigating the secrets of nature, have never been able to arrive at a clear perception of even the most trivial circumstances; and a clear proof of this assertion may be found in the disagreements, and dissensions, and contentions of those of each sect who are seeking to establish their own opinions, and to overthrow those of their adversaries. And the households of those who have been contending for the predominance of this and that sect, have been the causes of universal wars, blinding the human mind by their contradictory quarrels, which might otherwise have been able to see the truth, and fighting hard about what doctrines ought to be abandoned and what ought to be preserved.

Now he who desires to form to himself a conception of the most excellent of all beings, ought in the first place to stand firm in his mind, being steadfastly fixed in one opinion, and not varying or wandering in different directions. And in the next place, he ought to take his stand upon nature, and upon solid grounds, and to abandon all barren and corruptible things, for if anything of a somewhat effeminate character approach him, he will be disappointed of his object, and he will be unable, even if he exert the most acute faculties of sight imaginable, to behold the uncreated God; so that he will become blind before he sees him, on account of the brilliancy of his beams and the flood of light which distils therefrom. Do you not see that the power of fire in the case of those who stand at a measured distance from it affords light to them, but it burns those who approach too near? Take care that you do not suffer such an injury as this in your mind, and lest an extravagant desire of an impossible object destroy you.

About those who are governed.
Out of the first book of the Questions in Genesis.

Page 749. E. — As pillars support whole houses, so also the power of God supports the whole world, and the best and most God-loving section of the human race.

Out of the Questions in Genesis.

Page 750. C. — If any one is either in any house, or village, or city, or nation, who is a lover of wisdom, it is absolutely inevitable that that house or city should be the better for his existence in it, for a virtuous man is a common good to all men, bestowing on them advantages proceeding from himself as from a prepared store.

About people who carry news, and act as
intermediate bearers of answers.
From the Questions arising in Exodus.

Page 751. B. — The influx of evils agitates and disturbs the soul, enveloping it in a giddiness which

---

[3]Genesis 2:24.

darkens its perceptions, and compels it to suffer that power of sight which by nature was preeminent, but which by habit has become blinded, to be obscured.

Page 751. B. — There is nothing so opposite to and inconsistent with the most holy powers of God as injustice.

About the sinner and offender.
From the Questions arising in Genesis.

Page 751. C. — Never to err in any point whatever is the greatest blessing; but when one has erred, to repent is next akin to it, as a younger good, if one may say so, by the side of an elder, for there are some persons who exult in the offences which they have committed as if they had done good actions, though they are in reality afflicted with a disease difficult to be cured, or I should rather say incurable.

About its being impossible to escape from God.
From the last book of Questions arising in Exodus.

Page 752. A. — He contains all things, while yet he is himself contained by nothing; for as place is that which contains bodies, and that to which they flee for refuge, so also the divine reason contains the universe and is that which has completed it.

About truth and faithful evidence.
From the second book of the Questions in Exodus.

Page 754. C. — By some lawgivers the practice of giving hearsay evidence has been forbidden, on the ground that the truth is established by the eyesight, but falsehood by hearing.

About quiet and ease.
From the fourth book of the Questions in Genesis.

The wise man is desirous of peace and leisure, that he may have time for meditation on heavenly things.

From the fifth book.

Page 754. E. — For thus the lover of wisdom never unites with any rash person, even though he may be closely united to him by blood; nor does he ever consent to dwell with a wicked man, being separated from the multitude by his reasoning powers, on account of which he is said not to be a fellow voyager, or a fellow citizen, or a companion of such men.

Page 754. E. — The wise man is a sojourner and a settler, having come as an emigrant from a life of confusion and disorder to one suitable to peaceful and happy men.

About the fearful expulsion.
From the first book of the Questions in Genesis.

Page 772. B. — But the essence of the angels is spiritual, but they are very often made to resemble the appearance of men, being transformed on any emergencies which arise.

From the second book of the same Questions.

Page 772. B. — All the powers of God are winged, being always eager and striving for the higher path which leads to the Father.

About heretics.
From the first book of the Questions in Exodus.

Page 774. B. — All those who have stumbled, being unable to proceed with upright feet, go on slowly, being fatigued a long time before they come to their journey's end; so also the soul is hindered from proceeding successfully on the path which leads to piety if it has previously fallen in with any of the byroads of wickedness, for they are great hindrances to it, and the causes of its stumbling, by means of which the mind becoming lame, proceeds too slowly on the road, according to nature; and this road, according to nature, is that which ends at the Father of the universe.

From the same book.

The contentious investigations which men enter into about the virtues of God, improve the intellect and train it in most pleasant labours, which are also most beneficial to it, and especially when men do not (as those of the present day do) disguise themselves under a false appellation, and contend for the doctrines in appearance only, but do, in an honest and true heart, seek out truth in connection with knowledge.

From the second book of the same treatise.

... not being more anxious to display melody and harmony in their voices than in their minds; the eloquence of the wise man does not display its beauty in words only, but in the matters which it proves by its words.

From the last book of the Questions in Exodus.

Those men who apply themselves to the study of the holy scriptures ought not to cavil and quibble at syllables, but ought first to look at the spirit and meaning of the nouns and verbs used, and at the occasions on which and the manners in which each expression is used; for it often happens that the same expressions are applied to different things at different times; and, on the contrary, opposite expressions are at different times applied to the same thing with perfect consistency.

From the Questions in Genesis.

Those men act absurdly who judge of the whole from a part, instead of, on the contrary, forming their estimate of a part from their knowledge of the whole; for this is the more proper way to form one's opinion of anything, whether it be a body or a doctrine; therefore the divine code of laws is, in a manner, a united creature, which one must regard in all its parts and members at once with all one's eyes, and one must contemplate the meaning and sense of the whole scripture with accuracy and clearness, not disturbing its harmony nor dissevering its unity; for the parts will have a very different appearance and character if they are once deprived of their union.

From the fourth book of the same treatise.
Let there then be a law against all those who profess to look on what is venerable and divine, in any other than a respectful and holy spirit, inflicting punishment on their blindness.

From the second book of the Questions in Exodus.
Page 775. — There is nothing either more pleasant or more deserving of respect than to serve God, whose power is superior to that of the mightiest sovereign; and it appears to me that the greatest kings have also been chief priests, showing, by their actions, that it is right for those who are the masters of other men nevertheless to serve as servants of God.

About a king not being greatly respected.
From the first book of the Questions in Genesis.
Page 775. E. — No foolish man is a king even though he be invested with supreme power by sea and land, but he only is a king who is a virtuous and God-loving man, even though he may be deprived of those supplies and revenues, by means of which kings in general are strengthened in their sovereignty; for as a rudder, or a collection of drugs, or a flute, or a harp, are all superfluities to a man who has no knowledge of the art of steering, or medicine, or music, because he is not able to employ any one of them to the purpose for which it is made, while they may be said to be excellently adapted to and to be very seasonable for a pilot, or a physician, or a musician; so also, since kingcraft is an art, and the best of arts, we must look upon him who does not know how to exert it as a private individual; and as the man who does know how to exert it well as the only king.

About the stable and unstable man.
From the Questions in Genesis.
Page 776. E. — A facility of change must of necessity belong to man, by reason of the unsteadiness of external circumstances. Accordingly we thus oftentimes, after we have chosen friends, and have associated with them for some time, though we have nothing to accuse them of, turn away from them with aversion as enemies.

About those who change their minds and blame themselves.
Page 776. E. — These are the words of Philo:—
Cain, as he was ignorant of the greatness of the cause, that he should never fall into death, suffered a more simple punishment; but his imitator, not being able to take refuge in the plea of ignorance, is subjected to a double punishment; on which account Lamech shall be avenged seventy and seven fold, for the reason above mentioned, according to which he was the second offender who had not thought fit to take warning from the punishment of him who had offended before, and he clearly receives his punishment, being a more simple one; as in numbers the units have a highly multiplied power, resembling that of the decades, such as now Lamech, changing his mind, denounces against himself.

From the same book of the same author.
Page 777. — To be aware of what one has done amiss, and to blame one's self, is the part of a righteous man; but to be insensible to such things causes still more grievous evils to the soul, and the conduct of wicked men.

About the courage of a woman.
From Philo, from the Questions arising in Exodus.
Page 777. B. — It is said by men who have applied themselves to the study of natural philosophy, that the female is nothing else but an imperfect male.

About the oracles of God.
The words of Philo, out of the second book of his Questions arising in Genesis.
Page 782. A. — It is not lawful to divulge the sacred mysteries to the uninitiated until they are purified by a perfect purification; for the man who is not initiated, or who is of moderate capacity, being unable either to hear or to see that nature which is incorporeal and appreciable only by the intellect, being deceived by the visible sight, will blame what ought not to be blamed. Now, to divulge sacred mysteries to uninitiated people, is the act of a person who violates the laws of the privileges belonging to the priesthood.

From the same author.
Page 782. B. — It is absurd that there should be a law in cities that it is not lawful to divulge sacred mysteries to the uninitiated, but that one may speak of the true rites and ceremonies which lead to piety and holiness to ears full of folly. All men must not partake of all things, nor of all discourses, above all, of such as are sacred; for those that desire to be admitted to a participation in such things, ought to have many qualifications beforehand. In the first place, what is the greatest and

most important, they ought to have deep feelings of piety towards the only true and living God, and correct notions of holiness, avoiding all inextricable errors which perplex so many about images and statues, and in fact about any erections whatever, and about unlawful ceremonies, or illicit mysteries.

In the second place, they must be purified with all holy purifications, both in soul and body, as far as it is allowed by their national laws and customs. In the third place, they must give credible evidence of their entering into the common joy, so that they may not, after having partaken of the sacred food, like intemperate youths, be changed by satiety and overabundance, becoming like drunken men; which is not lawful.

About evil-doers.
The words of Philo, out of the Questions arising in Exodus.

Page 782. D. — The man who lives in wickedness, bears about destruction within him, since he has living with him that which is both treacherous, designing, and hostile to him. For the conscience of the wicked man is alone a sufficient punishment to him, inflicting cowardice on his soul from its own inmost feelings, as it feared blows.

From the same author.

Page 782. D. — The life of the wicked man is subject to pain and sorrow, and full of fear; and in everything which it does according to the outward senses, it is mingled with fear and grief.

About monks who break their vows.
The words of Philo, from the Questions arising in Exodus.

Page 784. C. — The reasoning of some persons is very rapidly satiated, who, though they have been borne upwards on wings for a little while, yet do presently return back again; not so much flying upwards, says Philo, as being dragged down again to the lowest depths of hell. But happy are they who do not draw back.

From the same author.

Page 784. C. — Before now, some persons who have tasted happiness, being very speedily satiated, after they have given hopes of their being in health, have fallen back into the same disease as before.

From the same author, out of the Questions arising in Genesis.

Page 784. D. — To commit perjury is impious and mischievous.

About good friends.
The words of Philo, out of the first book of the Questions arising in Exodus.

Page 788. I. — We ought to look upon those men as our friends who are inclined to assist us, and to requite our kindnesses with kindness, even if they are destitute of power; for friendship is a thing which is seen more in moments of necessity, than in a steady conjunction or union of dispositions. So that in the case of each person who unites with another in an association of friendship, one may apply the expression of Pythagoras to him, and say, "A friend is a second I."

About the mercies of God.
The words of Philo, out of the first book of the Questions arising in Exodus.

Page 789. A. — When the fruits of these crops which are raised from seed are in a state of perfection, they receive the beginnings of the generation of trees in order that the mercies of God may last for ever, and then that one continually succeeding the other, and connecting ends with beginnings and beginnings with ends, they may be in reality never ending.

From the second book of the same treatise.

Page 789. A. — The mercies of God give us not only what is necessary, but also all such things as conduce to a more excessive and liberal enjoyment of life.

FRAGMENTS FROM A MONKISH MANUSCRIPT

About man: to show that God when he made him endowed him with free will.

It is said to you, O noble man, who live in obedience to the divine precepts, endeavour with all thy might not only to preserve the gifts which you have received unimpaired and unalloyed, but also think them worthy of all imaginable honour and regard, as being endowed with free will and independent power, so that he who has committed them to your charge may have no reason to find fault with you for having neglected to take proper care of them; and the Creator of the world has entrusted to your care to employ them according to your own deliberative purpose, a soul, and speech, and the outward senses. Therefore, those men who receive these gifts in a proper spirit, and who preserve them for him who has bestowed them on them, have kept their intellect carefully in such a way that it shall never think of anything else than of God and his virtues; and their speech in such a manner that with unwearied mouth it shall honour the Father of the universe with praises and hymns; and their outward senses in such a way that after they have represented to themselves the whole of the world which is perceptible to those senses, namely, the heaven and the earth, and the natures which are between those two, they may relate what they have been in a pure and guileless manner to the soul.

About people who are governed.

The words of Philo, from the fourth book of his Allegorical Interpretation of the Sacred Laws.

If you take away their resources of wealth from politicians, you will find nothing left but empty arrogance devoid of sense, for as long as there is an abundant supply of external good things, wisdom and presence of mind appear also to attend them, but when that plenty is taken away all appearance of wisdom is taken away at the same time.

About the best men.

From the same author, in his Treatise on Drunkenness.

Good men, to speak somewhat metaphorically, are of more value than whole nations, since they support cities and constitutions as buttresses support large houses.

From the same author.

If it depended on wicked men, no city would ever enjoy tranquillity; but states continue free from seditious troubles on account of the righteousness of one or two men who live in them, whose virtue is a remedy for the diseases of war, because God, who loves mankind, grants this effect as a reward to those who are virtuous and honourable, so that they should not only benefit themselves, but all who are near them.

From the same author.

There is no place upon earth more sacred than the mind of a wise man, while all the virtues hover around like so many stars.

About things which are uncertain and unknown to us.

The words of Philo.

The comprehension of the future does not belong to the nature of man.

From the same author.

All things are not known to the mortal race.

From the same author.

God alone is acquainted with the ultimate results of things.

About evil report.

Quiet, which is free from danger, is better than words, the object of which is only to give pleasure.

About self-satisfied people, etc.

The words of Philo.

The lawgiver says, "You shall not do all the things which we will do here this day,[4] every one doing

that which is pleasant in his own sight," by which words he declares as loudly as possible that there is no evil which may not be produced by selfishness and self-sufficiency, which must be eradicated from the mind as unholy feelings. Let no one embrace that which is pleasing to himself rather than that which is agreeable to nature, for the one is found to be the cause of mischief and the other the cause of benefit.

From the same author.

Those who do everything for their own sake alone practise selfishness, which is the greatest of evils, which produces unsociability, want of fellowship, unfriendliness, injustice, impiety, for nature has made man not like those beasts which love solitude, but like the gregarious beasts which live together like the most sociable of all creatures, that he may live not to himself alone, but also to his father, and to his mother, and to his brethren, and to his wife, and to his children, and to all his other relations and friends, and to those of the same borough as himself, and to those of the same tribe, and to his native country, and to his fellow countrymen, and to all mankind, and moreover to the different parts of the universe, and to the whole world, and much more to the Father and Creator of the world, for he must be (if at least he is really endowed with reason) sociable, loving the world, and loving God, that he may also be beloved by God.

About God being incomprehensible.

From the first book of the Questions arising in Exodus.

There are thousands and thousands, I do not say only of important matters, but also of those which appear to be most trivial, which escape the human intellect.

From the same author.

No one may so far yield to unreasonable folly as to boast that he has seen the invisible God.

About the doctrine that God has made angels to be guardians of us.

The words of Philo, from the first book of the Questions arising in Genesis.

As pillars support whole houses, so also do the divine powers support the whole world, and that most excellent and God-loving race of mankind.

About avoiding sin.

From the treatise on the Giants.

I think it absolutely impossible that no part of the soul should become tainted, not even the outer-

---

most and lowest parts of it, even if the man appears to be perfect among men.

About slowness of counsel.

Slow counsel is profitless, and change of purpose in extremities is mischievous.

About heretical teachers, etc.
From the same book.

A teacher of a good and virtuous disposition, even if he sees his pupils at first stiff-necked by nature, does not despair of producing in them a change for the better; but, like a good physician, he does not apply a remedy at once at the first moment of the disease attacking the patient, but he gives nature time that it may recede a little, so that he may first make ready the path to safety, and then apply healthful and salutary remedies. And in the same manner does the virtuous man apply the arguments and doctrines of philosophy.

If, when a pupil is first introduced to you, and first comes to learn of you, you hasten to eradicate all his ignorance at once, and attempt to introduce every kind of knowledge in a lump, you will produce the contrary effect to that which you desire, for it will not be likely that such an eradication, having taken place all in a moment, will continue effectual, nor that the pupil will be able at once to contain such an abundant influx and overflow of instruction; but being exceedingly perplexed and troubled, he will resist both these operations, that of eradicating one thing and that of introducing another; but the system of taking away his ignorance with gentleness and moderation, and of, in the same manner, gently instilling wisdom into the mind, will be the causes of admitted advantage.

About people who meditate and design mischief.
The words of Philo, from his treatise on Things Improperly Named.

The ordinary production of wickedness enslaves the mind, even if it has not as yet produced any perfect fruit; for it is, as the proverb says, washing a brick, or taking up water in a net, to try and eradicate wickedness out of the soul of man. For "behold," says Moses, "with what designs the minds of all men are impressed."[5] And he speaks truly, for he does not say, what designs are attached to and adapted to it, but that which has been considered with care and deliberation is also explained with accuracy, and this too not slowly and with difficulty, but from man's earliest youth, or as one may almost say, from his very cradle, as if it were a part of him, kept in continual exercise.

About cowardly and wavering people.

Those who are unmanly from an innate effem-

inacy, falling down of their own accord before they meet with any opposition, are a disgrace and ridicule to themselves.

From the same author.

Wickedness in a foolish man has a twin offspring, for the foolish man is wavering and hesitating, mingling considerations together which ought not to be mingled, and humbling and confusing what ought to be kept distinct, having as many colours in his soul as a viper has in his body, and polluting even his sound thoughts with those which cause trouble and death.

From the same author.

The thoughts of a bad man are one thing, and his words another, and his actions indeed are many, but they are all inconsistent and at variance one with another, for he does not say what he thinks, and he has decided on the contrary of what he affirms, and he does things which are not consistent with his original designs, so that, to speak truly, one may say that the life of the wicked man is a life of enmity.

About distinctness.
The words of Philo.

That which is not distinct is unsuited to a free man, being the most shameful product of folly and haughtiness; for as distinctness in everything that is to be done is a mark of acuteness and wisdom, and deserves honour and praise, so also an absence of shame is a sign of folly and infamy, on which account the other definition which you disregard, classifies a man who is afflicted with this disease thus, saying, he is impious who does not know how to respect the face of an honourable man, nor to rise up in the presence of an elder,[6] nor to guide his own steps in the right way.

About those who serve God.

The servants of virtuous men submit to voluntary obedience to God, for they are not servants to human caprices, but to wise men; and he who is the servant of wisdom may justly be said to be also the servant of God.

About just men.
The words of Philo.

An irreconcileable and endless war is carried on by the atheists against the godly, so that they threaten them even with slavery.

About justice.
The words of Philo.

Justice, above all things, conduces to the safety

---

[5] Genesis 8:21.

[6] Juvenal speaks of this as a custom of the ancient Romans.

both of mankind and of the parts of the world, earth and heaven.

About the judgments of God.
From the same author.

It is good to begin every day with divine and holy employments, and after that to proceed to the necessary duties of life. On this account God has commanded us[7] to take care to obey his commandments, and especially at the first moment of the dawn, as soon as we are risen, to pay our adoration to Him, that their offerings to God may precede every human occupation, having the recollection of God for their prompter and leader.

From the same author.

Every soul which piety fertilises with its own mysteries is necessarily awake for all holy services, and eager for the contemplation of those things which are worth being seen, for this is the feeling of the soul at the great festival, and this is the true season of joy.

About the difference between God and man.
The words of Philo.

The things of creation are far removed from the uncreated God, even though they are brought into close proximity following the attractive mercies of the Saviour.

About bold and brave men.
The words of Philo, from his treatise about the Giants.

It is a sign of courage not to be easily alarmed by the terrors of death, and to be full of cheerful confidence in dangers, and to be of valiant hardiness amid disasters, and to prefer dying with honour to being saved disgracefully, and to wish to be the cause of victory; and a happy boldness, and a cheerfulness of soul, and fortitude, are the attendants of a manly spirit.

About equality.
The words of Philo.

As an equality of measurement is the cause of the most perfect blessings, so also a want of measure is the cause of the greatest evils, as it dissolves that most useful bond of equality.

About drunkenness.
From the same author.

Inequality is a grievous thing and the cause of differences, just as equality is free from all annoyances and contributes to unite men for advantageous ends.

---

[7]Deuteronomy 6:7.

From the same author.

Obedience to the law and equality are the seeds of peace, and the causes of safety and continued durability; but inequality and covetousness are excitements to war, and dissolvers of all existing things.

About evil-doers.
The words of Philo.

Those things which chastise the first, are, if men are wise, preventatives of the second.

About the eye and sight.
The words of Philo, from the treatise about the Creation of the World.

The outward senses resemble windows; for through them, as through windows, the comprehension of the objects of the outward senses enters into the mind, and again through them the mind goes out to investigate such objects. But the sight is a part of these windows, that is to say, of the outward senses, since above all others it is akin to the soul, because it is nearly connected with the most beautiful of all things, namely light, and is a servant of divine things; and, indeed, that is the sense which first opened the way to philosophy. For when the eye had beheld the motions of the sun and moon, and the periodical revolutions of the stars, and the unvarying motions of the whole host of heaven, and the indescribable order and harmony of the whole universe, and the one unerring Creator of the world, it then related what it had seen to reason, as having the supreme authority; and reason, having beheld with a still more acutely piercing eye both these things, and things of a still more sublime character in their appearance and species, and the great cause of all things, it then immediately arrived at a due conception of God, and of creation, and of providence; considering that the whole nature of all things was not brought into existence of its own accord, but that of necessity it had a creator, and a father, and a guide, and a governor, who also created it, and who also preserves everything which he has created.

About contentment.
The words of the same author.

If you have a great deal of wealth, take care and do not be carried away by its overflow; but endeavour to take hold of some dry ground, in order to establish your mind with proper firmness; and this will be the proper exertion of justice and fairness. And if you should have abundant supplies of all the things requisite for the indulgence of those passions which lie beneath the belly, be not carried away by such plenty, but oppose to them a saving degree of contentedness, taking in this way dry ground to stand upon instead of an absorbing quicksand.

By the same author.
One should practise being contented with a little, for this is being near God; but the contrary habit is being very far from him.

About faith in and piety towards God.
The words of Philo.
What can be a real sacrifice except the piety of a soul devoted to the love of God? whose grateful feelings are made immortal by God, having conferred on them an immortal duration like that of the sun and the moon, and the whole world.

About wicked and impious men.
From the same author.
The hopes of wicked men are unstable, as they expect a good fate, but suffer a contrary destiny of which they are worthy.

About a bad conscience.
The words of Philo, from his treatise on Men and Things which are Improperly Named.
Who is there who does wrong who is not convicted by his own conscience as if he were in a court of justice, even though no man correct him?

About advisers.
The words of Philo, from the Questions in Genesis.
Since the mind of those who have not studied philosophy is blind with respect to many of the circumstances of life, one must take those who do see the character of affairs for one's guides.

About hasty talkers.
The words of Philo.
He who has not shame or fear for his companions, has an unbridled mouth and a licentious tongue.

About perfection.
The words of Philo.
Perfection and an absence of deficiency are found in God alone. But deficiency and imperfection exist in every man. For man is taught, even if he be the wisest of his race, by some other man, and he knows nothing without being taught by his own nature. And if one man has more knowledge than another, still he has it not naturally, but because of instruction which he has received.

About those who think lowlily of themselves.
The words of Philo.
These things are proved to be most completely natural, that the descent of the soul is its elation by means of self-conceit, and that its ascent and elevation is its return from arrogance.

From the same author.
It is desirable to eradicate self-conceit, which is the friend of endurance, and prudence, and justice, [8] and also to destroy overbearing pride; for it is no small proof and exercise of folly to study virtue in an illegitimate manner.

From the same author.
If you are puffed up by glory and authority so as to desire great things, then remember, like the skilful pilot of a ship, to take in your sails, that you may not be carried away into absurd conduct.

About sleep.
The words of Philo.
Sleep, according to the prophet, is a trance, not indeed in accordance with insanity, but proceeding from a relaxation of the outward senses and the retreat of reason; for at that time the outward senses cease from attaching themselves to their proper objects, and the mind is quiet, neither being any longer under the influence nor affording any motion to them, and they, being in consequence cut off from any energy because they are separated from the objects which are perceptible to them, are dissolved in a state of motionless inactivity.

From the same author.
Very naturally some who have been wise enough to arrive at correct notions of the truth, have described sleep as a thing to teach us to meditate upon death, and a shadow and outline of the resurrection which is hereafter to follow, for it bears in itself visible images of both conditions, for it removes the same man from his state of perfection and brings him back to it.

About promises, etc.
The words of Philo.
It is better absolutely never to make any promise at all than not to assist another willingly, for no blame attaches to the one, but great dislike on the part of those who are less powerful, and intense hatred and long enduring punishment from those who are more powerful, is the result of the other line of conduct.

About haughty men, etc.
From the first book of the Sacred Allegory of the Holy Laws.
Some persons say that the last thing which the wise man puts off is the tunic of vain glory, for even if a man gets the mastery over his other pas-

---

[8] It is evident that there is great corruption in this and the next sentence.

sions, still he is inclined by nature to be influenced by glory and the praises of the multitude.

From the same author.
Self-conceit is an impure thing by nature.

About promises, etc.
The words of Philo.
To give thanks to God is intrinsically right, but not to do so to him in the first place, and not to begin with the first reasons for gratitude, is blameable, for it is not right to give the chief honour to the creation, and the inferior honour to God, who is the giver of all things in the creation; and indeed that is a most culpable division, inasmuch as it is laying down a certain disorder of order.

About envy.
The words of Philo.
Envy naturally attaches itself to whatever is great.

About industrious people.
The words of the same author.
The most perfect and greatest of all good things are usually the result of laborious exercise and energetic vigorous labour.

From the same author.
It is absurd for a man who is in the pursuit of honours to flee from labours by which honours are acquired.

About the soul and the mind.
From the same author.
What is the meaning of the expression, "You shall not eat the flesh in the blood of the soul?"[9] God appears by this expression to intend to show that the blood is the essence of the soul, that is to say, of the soul endowed with the outward senses, not the soul spoken of in the most excellent sense of the word, that is to say, as far as it is endued with reason and intellect; for there are three divisions of the soul, one part being nutritious, a second being endued with the outward senses, and the third being endued with reason. Accordingly the divine Spirit is the essence of the rational portion, according to the sacred historian of the creation of the world, for he says that "God breathed into his face the breath of life."[10] But of that part which is endued with the outward senses, and which has the revivifying power, blood is the essence, for he says in another place that "the soul of all flesh is the blood;"[11] but what is connected with the flesh is the outward sense and the passions, and not

the mind and the intellect; not but what that expression, "in the blood of the soul," also indicates that the soul is one thing and the body another. So that in real truth the breath is the essence of the soul, but it has not any place of itself independently of the blood, but it resembles and is combined with blood.

About the assistance of God.
The words of Philo, from the fourth book of
his treatise on the Allegories contained
in the Sacred Laws.
The extremity of happiness is the assistance of God, for there can be no such thing as want when God gives his aid.

About the creation of the world.
From the same author, from the first book of the
Questions arising in Genesis.
It is impossible that the harmony, and arrangement, and reason, and analogy, and that all the great accord and real happiness which we see existing in the world can have been originated by themselves, for it follows inevitably that these things must have had a creator, and a father, and a regulator and governor, who generated them in the first place, and who now preserves what he has generated.

About the church of God.
From the same author.
God wishing to send down from heaven to the earth an image of his divine virtue, out of his compassion for our race, that it might not be destitute of a more excellent portion, and that he might thus wash off the pollutions which defile our miserable existence, so full of all dishonour, established his church among us.

About seeking God.
From the same author, from the last book of the
Questions arising in Exodus.
The one most powerful relaxation of the soul leads to the sacred love of the one living God, teaching mankind to take God as its guide in all their plans, and words, and actions.

From the same author.
The extremity of happiness is to rest unchangeably and immovably on God alone.

About the last day.
The words of Philo, from the second book of the Questions arising in Exodus.
The stars are turned round and revolve in a regular circle, some proceeding on in the same manner through the whole heaven, and others have special eccentric motions of their own.

---

[9] Genesis 9:4.
[10] Genesis 2:9.
[11] Deuteronomy 12:23.

About the detestation of wickedness felt by God.

The words of Philo, from the second book of the Questions arising in Exodus.

Some men think that repentance appears at times to take possession of God on account of the oaths which he has sworn, but they do not form correct notions; for apart from the fact that the Deity does not change, neither the expression, "God repented," nor that, "And it grieved him at the heart,"[12] is indicative of repentance, for the Deity is unchangeable; but they only show the character of the pure intellect which is now deeply meditating on the cause for which he created man upon the earth.

By the same author, from the same book.

There is no hesitation and no envy in God; but he often uses expressions indicative of hesitation or of uncertainty from a reference to man, who is susceptible of such feelings; for as I have often said, there are altogether two supreme sources; in the one case God does not speak as man speaks, in the other he instructs man as a man instructs his son, the former being a sign of his power, the second of the way in which he teaches and guides man.

About promises.

The words of Philo, from the last book of the Questions arising in Exodus.

He who does not offer to God first fruits of his own free will does not really offer first fruits at all, even if he brings everything which is great, with a most royal abundance of treasure; for the real first fruits consist not in the things offered, but in the pious disposition of him who offers them.

About the mildness of God and his love for mankind.

The words of Philo, from the Questions arising in Exodus.

The mercies of God do always outstrip justice, for the work which he has chosen for himself is that of doing good, and the task of punishing follows that; and it is common, when great evils are about to arise, for an abundance of great and numerous blessings to happen first.

FRAGMENTS PRESERVED BY ANTONIUS

SER. I.

The virtues alone know how to regulate the affairs of men.

The contemplation of virtue is exceedingly beautiful, and actions according to it, and the exercise of it, are desirable above all things.

SER. II.

If you wish to have a good reputation in a twofold manner, then honour exceedingly those who are doing well, and reprove those who are doing ill.

SER. VIII.

When you are entreated to pardon offences, pardon willingly those who have offended against you, because indulgence given in requital for indulgence, and reconciliation with our fellow servants, is a means of averting the divine anger.

SER. IX.

The virtuous man is a lover of his race, and he is merciful and inclined to pardon, and never bears ill will towards any man whatever, but thinks it right to surpass in doing good rather than in injuring.

What is beautiful is then beautiful, when a man has no need of the assistance of another, but when he contains in himself all the signs of excellence as his own.

SER. X.

It is well that the worse should always follow the better, on account of the hope of improvement.

SER. XI.

One ought to call a city, and a country, and a house, happy, when they contain a virtuous man; and one ought to call those miserable, when they have no such man within them.

SER. XVI.

Those who are tyrannical in their natures, but without power, make their designs succeed by treachery.

SER. XX.

The friendships of the wicked are mischievous, and very often the soul of such men, being influenced by such associations, takes the impressions of downright insanity.

It is not the country which makes men bad, or the city which makes them good, but the habits of living with such and such men.

SER. XXVIII.

One need not dread the blow of a weak man, nor the threat of a fool.

Light-minded men, like empty vessels, may easily be taken and moved by their ears.

SER. XXX.

Nothing that is done can be beautiful without scientific contemplation, for knowledge is the offspring of counsel, but folly is the source of all evils.

Every argument on behalf of justice is superfluous, when those who listen are unanimous in a bad object.

---

[12] Genesis 6:6.

SER. XXXVIII.

The wicked man disturbs the city, and is eager for the confusion and the disorder of all men and all things within the city; for a desire of interference, and covetousness, and the acts of a demagogue, and the influence with the populace, are looked upon as honours by such a man, and quiet he looks upon with disdain.

Excellence is a thing difficult to find, or rather is absolutely undiscoverable in a troubled life.

SER. XLIII.

There is nothing so calculated to cause good will as kind words, on account of good actions.

SER. XLVII.

It is sufficient not to bear witness one's self, but that which stands in need of the advocacy of another is inadequate to bring conciliation to the mind.

SER. LII.

Reject with aversion the deceitful words of flatterers, for they, obscuring reason, do not contribute to the truth of things; for either they praise actions which are deserving of blame, or else they often blame things beyond all praise.

SER. LVI.

Peace is the greatest blessing which no man is able to afford, since this is a divine action.

SER. LVII.

Behave to your servants in the same manner in which you desire that God should behave to you; for as we hear them we shall be heard by him, and as we regard them we shall be regarded by him. Let us therefore let our compassion outrun compassion, that we may receive a like requital from him for our mercy to them.

SER. LXIX.

How great a relief of nature is sleep, it is the image of death, and the rest of the outward senses.

Sleep is one thing only, but the desire of it has many reasons and causes; I mean from nature, from food, from fate, and perhaps also from excessive and intense fasting, by means of which the flesh, becoming unnerved and deprived of strength, wishes to recover itself for subsequent actions by means of sleep.

As much drinking is called a habit, so is much sleep, and it is difficult to get rid of an inveterate habit.

SER. LXXIV.

Pardon is apt to engender repentance.

SER. LXXIX.

Shamelessness is the characteristic of a worthless man, and modesty of a virtuous man, but never to feel either ashamed or bold is a mark of one who is slow of comprehension, and who is without the power of giving assent.

SER. LXXXII.

Since God penetrates invisibly in the region of the soul, let us prepare that region in the best manner that we are able to, or rather that it may be a habitation fit for God, otherwise, without our being aware of it, God will depart and remove to some other abode.

The mind of a wise man is the house of God, and he is called, in an especial manner, the God of all mankind, as the prophet says when speaking of the mind of a wise man, he calls it "that in which God walks,"[13] as in a palace.

What is visible and actually before us is comprehended by the eyes, but the pure faculty of reason extends even to what is unseen and future.

SER. LXXXVII.

God who is merciful by nature will never exonerate from guilt the man who swears falsely for an unrighteous object, as such a man is impure and defiled, even though he may escape the punishments inflicted by men.

SER. XCIX.

Those things which are kept in the dark for a while by envy, are at last released and brought to light.

SER. CIV.

In his essential character a king is equal to every man, but in the power of his authority and rank he is equal to God who ruleth over all things; for there is nothing on earth that is higher than he. Therefore it becomes him as being a mortal not to be too much elated, and as being a kind of God not to yield too much to passion; for if he is honoured as being of the likeness of God, nevertheless he is in some degree entangled in terrestrial and vile dust, by means of which he should learn simplicity and meekness towards all men.

SER. CXVI.

A severe master is best for untractable and foolish servants; for they, fearing his threats and punishments, though against their will, are made to do right by fear.

SER. CXVIII.

It is the greatest praise of a servant to neglect nothing which his master commands, but to attempt with an honest heart to perform in a proper and successful manner, even if it be beyond his

---

[13] Leviticus 26:12.

power, all that is commanded him with energy and without hesitation.

SER. CXXIII.

When once the wife of Philo was asked in an assembly of many women why she alone of all her sex did not wear any golden ornaments, she replied: "The virtue of a husband is a sufficient ornament for his wife."

SER. CXXX.

The virtues of children are the glory of their fathers.

Those who are well acquainted with what is honourable and virtuous, are happy in their children.

SER. CXXXV.

To drink poison out of a golden goblet, and to take advice from a foolish friend, is the same thing.

New vessels are better than old ones, but old friendship is better than new.

The fruits produced by the earth come once a year; but those which we derive from friendship are to be gathered on every occasion. Many men select for their friends not those who are the most virtuous, but those who are rich.

Many who appear to be friends are not so, and many who do not appear to be such are so in reality; but it is the part of a wise man to discern both these classes.

SER. CLII.

Youth which is not willing to work is laying up misfortunes for old age.

SER. CLVI.

What is bad is, not being punished here, but being worthy of punishment hereafter.

SER. CXXXV.

God has implanted hope in the human race that, having a comfort innate in them, those who have committed errors which are not irremediable may feel their sorrows lightened.

SER. CLXXXII.

Pleasure appears to be an equable kind of motion, but in reality it both is and is found to be rough.

THE FOLLOWING FRAGMENTS ARE FROM AN ANONYMOUS COLLECTION IN THE BODLEIAN LIBRARY AT OXFORD

EXTRACTS FROM PHILO
About friends.

A steadiness towards one's friends is a sign of a general stability of disposition, on which account one ought not to form friendship till one has carefully tested the characters of those with whom he proposes to form it; for not only is the forming of such friendship pleasant, but so also is the feeling that one has not to bear by one's self burdens which oppress the soul, and not to depart from the association; for he who is the cause of differences in friendship is not known to the generality of men, but he is accustomed to bring common blame upon both parties, and very commonly on the innocent party more than on the guilty one.

Of secret things, you may share with mean persons those which increase your virtue; but as to those which deteriorate your mind, you must not pursue them yourself, nor impute them to your friends.

The life of man is like a sea, it is liable to every description of agitation and change, even in the height of prosperity; for nothing earth-born is firmly established, but all such things are carried about to and fro, like a vessel which is driven about in the sea by contrary winds.

About sin.

Let us fear not the diseases which come upon us from without, but those offences on which account diseases come, diseases of the soul rather than of the body.

About pain.

Every foolish man is in a strait, being oppressed by covetousness, and love of glory, and desire of pleasure, and things of that sort, which do not allow the mind freedom of motion.

About gluttony.

The sons of the physicians have laid it down as a maxim that regularity is the parent of a healthy condition of the body, paying but little attention to the health of the soul; but we lay it down that regularity is not only destructive of all diseases of the body, but much more do we recognise the fact that the truest health is that which destroys the passions which injure the soul.

About custom and familiarity.

An inveterate habit is more powerful than nature, and little things, if they are not hindered, grow up and increase and become of a large size.

THE FOLLOWING FRAGMENTS ARE FROM AN UNPUBLISHED MANUSCRIPT IN THE LIBRARY OF THE FRENCH KING

From the works of the Hebrew Philo, on Genesis 6:7.

Why is it that God, when he threatens to extirpate mankind, does also destroy the irrational animals? Because the irrational animals were not originally created designedly for their own sakes, but for the sake of man, and to perform services of which he might be in need; and when man was destroyed it followed naturally that they should also be destroyed at the same time, when the beings for whose sake they had been created were no longer in existence.

From the same author, on Genesis 17:14.

The law does not treat any action done involuntarily as guilty, since it even pardons a man who has committed murder unintentionally; but if a child is not circumcised eight days after its birth, what evil has it done so as to be subjected to the punishment of death? Therefore some persons say that the manner of the punishment is to be referred to its parents, and think that they ought to be punished severely as having neglected the commandments of the law; and others think that it is by an excess of indignation that God is here represented as inflicting punishment, as far as appearance goes, on the child, in order that this inevitable punishment may be inflicted on those people of mature age who have violated the law.

Not because the action of circumcision is important in itself, but because if that is neglected the covenant itself is treated with contempt when the seal by which it is recognised and ratified is not made perfect.

From the same author, on Genesis 19:23.

Why did the sun go forth upon the land when Lot entered into Segor? And he says the very same place is a safety for those who are making progress, and a punishment to those who are inwardly wicked. And again the moment that the sun rises in the beginning of the day it brings with it justice; wishing to show that the sun, and the day, and the light, and everything else in the world which is beautiful and honourable, are given only to the virtuous and to no worthless man who embraces incurable wickedness.

From the same author, on Genesis 27:24–27.

Having been spies rather than friends under truce, and being prepared for either alternative; for war if they saw that the other was weak, and for peace if they found him stronger than themselves.

From the same author, on Genesis 26:28, etc.

These are the covenants which they made, not to be destroyed as the other nations had been, and the Philistines were at a subsequent period by the Israelites; whom the holy scriptures call sometimes Canaanites, and sometimes Cappadocians; but afterwards the Cappadocians emigrated.

From the same author, on Genesis 26:30.

Not on account of praise, for the wise man is not attracted by flattery or by any other kind of subserviency, but because he has accepted their repentance.

From the same author, on Genesis 27:6, etc.

When he had two sons, the one good and the other guilty, he says that he will bless the guilty one, not because he preferred him to the good one, but because he knew that the other one could do right by himself, but that the other was convicted by his own disposition, and had no hope whatever of salvation except in the prayers of his father; and if he did not obtain them, then he would be the most miserable of all men.

From the same author, on Genesis 27:11, etc.

It is proper here to admire also the good will of his mother, who confessed herself willing to take upon herself the cause for his sake, in order that her son might have the honour to which the two were entitled, for she is carried away by her affection for both of them; for she had feared his father, lest she should be looked upon as imposing on him, and to be filching away the honour to which the other was entitled; and his mother, lest he should be considered by her as disobedient to her when she urged him vehemently; on which account he says, with great prudence and propriety, Will not my father curse me? and I shall be bringing a curse on myself. He had confidence because of the promise of God, which said, "The elder shall serve the younger." But, on the other hand, he feared as a man, lest the blessing of his father, as a just man, should overturn the assertion of God.

From the same author, on Genesis 27:30.

He is not so indignant at his disappointment in not obtaining the blessings, as at the fact of his brother having been thought worthy of them; for being of an envious disposition, he regarded his want of success as more desirable than even his own advantage, and he shows this by his great and bitter lamentations, and by his subsequent exclamation, "Bless me now also, O my father."

From the same author.

But if he obtained it by fraud, a man will be inclined to say, he was not to be praised. What then does his father say? "And he shall be blessed." But he appears by what he here says to intimate, in an enigmatical and obscure manner, that it does not follow that every stratagem is blameable, since guardians of the night when they lie in wait for robbers, and generals when they form ambuscades for enemies whom they would not be able to subdue by open force, appear to act rightly: and what are called stratagems proceed on the same principle as the contests of wrestlers, for in these cases too tricks are accounted honourable; and those who by trickery get the better of their antagonists are thought worthy of the prize, and of the crown of victory; so that it is not a charge against a man to say, he has done a thing by trick, but it is rather a panegyric, being equivalent to saying, he has done it skilfully, for the virtuous man does not do anything unskilfully.

From the same author, on Exodus 20:25.

What is the meaning of "thy dagger," and what comes next? Those who by their nature venture to make improper attempts, and who by their own private endeavours metamorphose the works of nature, defile what ought not to be defiled, for all the things of nature are perfect and complete, and stand in need of no addition.

From the same author, on Exodus 22:19.

He shows most evidently that he is a proselyte, inasmuch as he is not circumcised in the flesh of his foreskin, but in the pleasures and appetites, and all the other passions of the soul; for the Hebrew race was not circumcised in Egypt, but being ill-treated with every imaginable circumstance of ill-treatment by the natural cruelty of the natives of the country to strangers, it nevertheless lived among them with fortitude and patience, and that no more from compulsion than voluntarily, because of the refuge which it possessed in God the saviour, who, sending down his beneficent power, delivered his suppliants from their difficult and apparently inextricable troubles.

On this account Moses adds, "For you know the soul of a proselyte."[14] Now what is the mind of a proselyte? a forsaking of the opinions of the worshippers of many gods, and a union with those who honour the one God, the Father of the universe. In the second place, some persons call foreigners also proselytes, and those are strangers who have come over to the truth in the same manner with those who have been sojourners in Egypt; for the one are strangers newly arrived in the country, but the last are strangers also to the customs and laws, but the common name of proselytes is given to both.

From the same author, on Exodus 22:22.

It is forbidden to injure a widow and orphan, for these are under the protection of the especial providence of God, since they are deprived of their natural protectors and guardians, for God wills that those who enjoy natural associations should make amends to the others from their own abundance of resources.

From the same author, on Exodus 23:1.

He says that we must not approach folly or falsehood, either with the ears or with any other of the outward senses, for great injuries are the result of being deceived; on which account some lawgivers have forbidden any one to give hearsay evidence, since the truth is confirmed by eyesight, but falsehood by hearing.

From the same author, on Exodus 23:6.

Poverty by itself claims compassion, in order to correct its deficiencies, but when it comes to judgment, it then has for the arbitrator the law of equity, for justice is a divine and incorruptible thing, on which account it is expressly affirmed in another passage that the judgment of God is just.[15]

From the same author, on Exodus 23:18.

Instead of saying leavened bread must not come among the things which are offered, but all things which are brought as a sacrifice or an offering must be unleavened, he intimates two most necessary things by an obscure and symbolical expression; one being to despise pleasure, for leaven is the seasoning of food and not food itself; and the other being that it is not right for men to be elated, because of being puffed up by vain self-conceit; for each is a wicked state, and pleasure and self-conceit are both the offspring of one mother, deceit.

The blood of the sacrifices is a proof of a soul making its offerings to God; and it is not in accordance with the divine law that things which will not unite should be mingled together.

From the same author, on Exodus 23:20.

One must suppose that the angel mentioned a little before indicated the voice of God; for the prophet is the messenger of the Lord, who is the real speaker; for it is inevitable that he who hears with his ears, that is to say who firmly receives what is said, must also accomplish what is said to him by his actions; for an action is the proof of what is said; and he who is obedient to what is said, and who performs actions corresponding to his orders, must of necessity have him who has commanded him for his ally and champion, who in appearance indeed brings assistance to his pupil, but in reality to his own doctrines and commandments, ... which his enemies and adversaries seek to overthrow.

From the same author, on Exodus 23:24.

Pillars symbolically mean the doctrines which appear to stand and to be firmly established. Now of the doctrines established in this firm way, some are good, which ought to be stored up and to be fixed in a most lasting manner; but others are open to blame, and such it is desirable should be overthrown. But the expression, "overthrowing you will overthrow, and destroying you will destroy," has such a meaning as the following.

---

[14] Exodus 23:9.

[15] Deuteronomy 32:4.

Some men pull down some things as if they meant to raise them again, and destroy some things as if they meant at a future time to re-establish them. But God wills that what has been once destroyed and pulled down shall never be raised or re-established again, but shall be utterly destroyed and for ever, as being contrary to what is good or beautiful.

From the same author, on Exodus 23:28.

And we ought to consider that the wasps are a sign of unexpected power coming by the divine mission; which, bringing down its blows from high places so as to reach the extremity of the ear, takes a good aim with all its strokes, and regulating them well will meet with no failure whatever itself.

From the same author, on Exodus 23:31.

These things God announced to them, if they obeyed him and kept his commandments. But when they were found to be transgressing and disobedient to the divine law, he then contracted his promise from Dan to Beersheba.

From the same author, on Exodus 24:9, 10.

The express command as uttered has a subsequent proposition evident, as all were preserved in safety. But the real meaning is that they all were of one mind in respect of piety and differed in no good thing.

From the same author, on Exodus 24:10.

When he speaks of the seventy men he means those with Moses, and Aaron, and Nadab, and Abihu. And the statement that they did not differ, rather shows that they all equally saw the place where God had stood, than that nothing was left.

From the same author, on Exodus 24:13.

He is most manifestly offended with those who being near thought, out of their impiety or folly, that the motions of the Deity were those of peace, and belonging to the act of changing his abode; for behold he says expressly, not that the God who exists in essence, and who is duly thought of in respect of his existence, came down, but that his glory came down. And the acceptation of the word glory may be twofold; for in one sense it may signify the presence of his powers, since the power of his army is spoken of as the glory of a king; and in another sense it may refer to the appearance of him alone, and to the apprehension of his divine glory; so that an idea of the actual arrival of God may have been created in the minds of those who were present, as if he had come in order to give a most undeniable information to the laws which were about to be given.

From the same author, on Exodus 24:17.

But he says that the appearance of the glory of the Lord is very like unto flame, or rather not that it is so, but that it appears like it to the beholders; since God shows what he chose to appear to be, in order to strike the beholders with amazement without in reality being what he appeared. Accordingly he brings him before the face of the children of Israel, affirming in the plainest language that it was an appearance as of flame, but not a real flame. But as flame consumes every material which is exposed to it, so also when the true conception of God once enters into the soul, it destroys all the heterodox reasonings of impiety, and purifies and sanctifies the whole mind.

From the same author, on Exodus 24:18.

Because the generation which had thus quitted its former abode was about to be condemned, and to wander in a state of desolation for forty years, having received innumerable benefits, but having displayed its ingratitude in still more countless instances.

INDICES

SUBJECT INDEX

SCRIPTURE INDEX

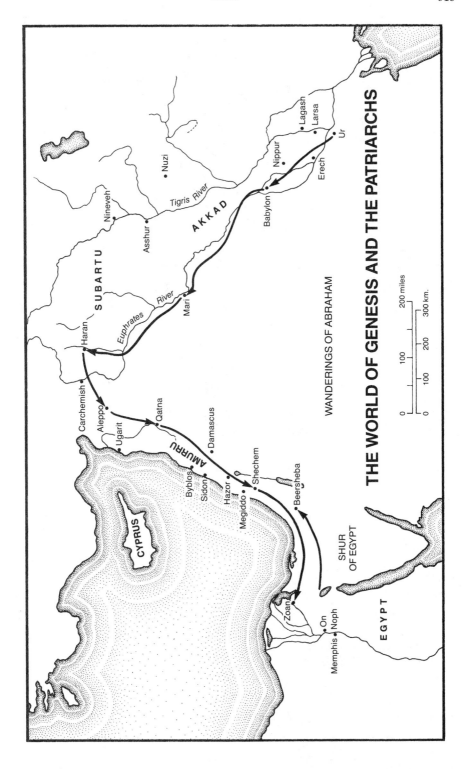

THE WORLD OF GENESIS AND THE PATRIARCHS

WANDERINGS OF ABRAHAM

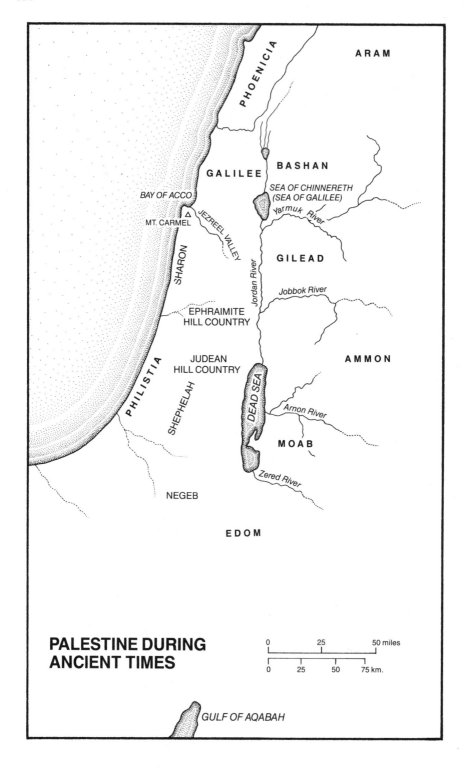

PALESTINE DURING ANCIENT TIMES

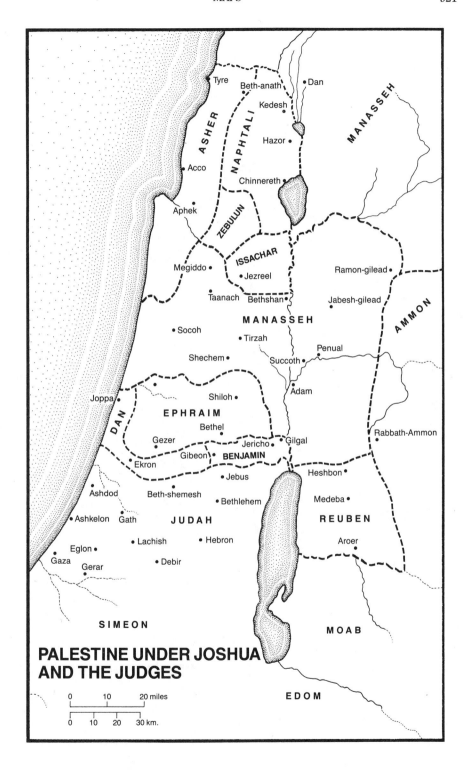

PALESTINE UNDER JOSHUA AND THE JUDGES

ASHER

NAPHTALI

MANASSEH

Tyre

Beth-anath

Dan

Kedesh

Hazor

Acco

Chinnereth

ZEBULUN

Aphek

ISSACHAR

Megiddo

Jezreel

Ramon-gilead

Taanach   Bethshan

Jabesh-gilead

AMMON

MANASSEH

Socoh

Tirzah

Penual

Shechem

Succoth

Adam

Joppa

DAN

EPHRAIM

Shiloh

Bethel

Rabbath-Ammon

Gezer

Jericho   Gilgal

Gibeon   **BENJAMIN**

Ekron

Jebus

Heshbon

Ashdod

Beth-shemesh

Bethlehem

Medeba

Ashkelon   Gath

JUDAH

REUBEN

Eglon

Lachish   Hebron

Aroer

Gaza

Gerar   Debir

SIMEON

MOAB

EDOM

| 0 | 10 | 20 miles |
| 0 | 10 | 20 | 30 km. |

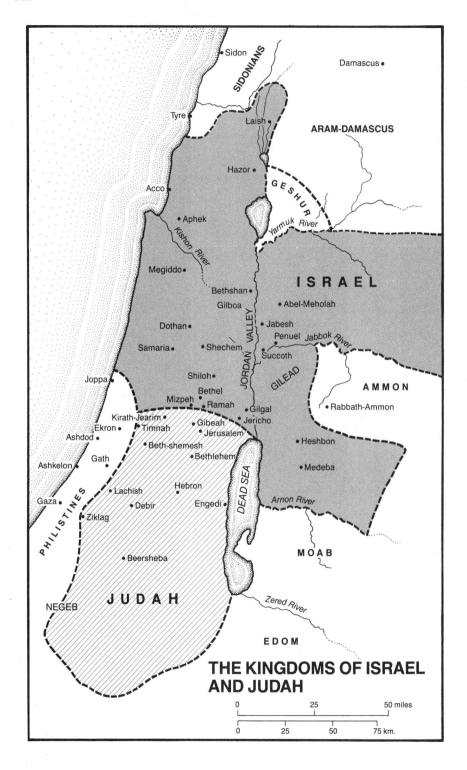

THE KINGDOMS OF ISRAEL AND JUDAH